EU[...]
ON A SHOESTRING

Vivek Wagle
Susie Ashworth
David Atkinson
Carolyn Bain
Chris Baty
Neal Bedford
Andrew Bender
Geert Cole
Graeme Cornwallis
Jan Dodd
Steve Fallon
Kate Galbraith
Duncan Garwood
Paul Greenway
Susie Grimshaw
Kathryn Hanks
Des Hannigan
Paul Harding
Paul Hellander
Debra Herrmann
Patrick Horton
Sarah Johnstone
Cathryn Kemp
Alex Landragin
Matt Lane
Cathy Lanigan
Alex Leviton
Leanne Logan
Lisa Mitchell
Sally O'Brien
Jeanne Oliver
Tom Parkinson
Josephine Quintero
Simon Richmond
Kalya Ryan
Andrew Stone
Rachel Suddart
Dani Valent
Mara Vorhees
Kim Wildman
David Willett
Nicola Williams
Neil Wilson
Pat Yale

LONELY PLANET PUBLICATIONS
Melbourne | Oakland | London | Paris

Ísafjörður
GREENLAND SEA
Faxaflói
Akureyri
Reykjavík
ICELAND
Egilsstaðir
Heimaey
Þórsmörk
Seyðisfjörður
Vestmannaeyjar
Vík
Arctic
NORWEGIAN SEA
FAROE ISLANDS
Tórshavn
0 250 500km
0 150 300mi
Ålesund
Shetland Islands
Orkney Islands
Bergen
NORWAY
Outer Hebrides
Stavanger
Inverness
ATLANTIC OCEAN
Scotland
Aberdeen
Oban
Dundee
Kristiansand
Skagerrak
Glasgow
Edinburgh
Derry
NI
Belfast
NORTH SEA
Aalborg
Newcastle-upon-Tyne
DENMARK
Isle of Man
Galway
IRELAND
Århus
Middlesborough
Irish Sea
Dublin
York
Odense
Killarney
Cork
Liverpool
Manchester
Rosslare
BRITAIN
Frisian Islands
Lübeck
Wales
Birmingham
St George's Channel
Swansea
England
NETHERLANDS
Hamburg
Cardiff
Oxford
The Hague
Amsterdam
Bristol
London
Rotterdam
Hanover
Plymouth
Portsmouth
Düsseldorf
Channel Islands
English Channel
Brussels
Cologne
Le Havre
BELGIUM
GERMANY
Brest
St Malo
Rouen
Frankfurt/Main
Quimper
Caen
Rheims
Luxembourg
Paris
Rennes
LUXEMBOURG
St Nazaire
Nantes
Blois
Nancy
Stuttgart
Tours
Dijon
Strasbourg
Munich
Freiburg
La Rochelle
FRANCE
LIECHTENSTEIN
Bern
Bay of Biscay
Lausanne
Zürich
Vaduz
Limoges
Geneva
SWITZERLAND
La Coruña
Bordeaux
Lyon
Mt Blanc 4807m
Gijón
Santander
Milan
Venice
Vigo
Santiago de Compostela
Clermont-Ferrand
ALPS
Bilbao
Bayonne
SAN MARINO
León
San Sebastián
Turin
Toulouse
Genoa
Porto
PYRENEES
Avignon
Nîmes
Bologna
Pamplona
Nice
PORTUGAL
Marseille
MONACO
Salamanca
Andorra la Vella
Golfe du Lion
Coimbra
Pisa
Florence
Zaragoza
ANDORRA
Lisbon
Madrid
Tarragona
Barcelona
Corsica
Elba
Évora
Badajoz
Ajaccio
Rome
Toledo
SPAIN
Valencia
Mallorca
Menorca
Faro
Seville
Córdoba
Sassari
Ibiza
Palma
Granada
Cádiz
Alicante
Balearic Islands
Sardinia
Málaga
Murcia
Strait of Gibraltar
Cagliari
Gibraltar Br
Almería
Tangier
Ceuta Sp
MEDITERRANEAN SEA
TYRRHENIAN SEA
Tetouan
Melilla Sp
Palermo
Rabat
Oran
Algiers
Bizerte
Casablanca
Fès
Annaba
Pantelleria
Meknès
Oujda
Tunis
Constantine
Italy
CANARY ISLANDS
Marrakesh
Sousse
Isole Pelagie
MOROCCO
TUNISIA
Las Palmas
Agadir
ATLAS
ALGERIA
El Aaiun
Tripoli
LIBYA

EUROPE
BARENTS SEA
White Sea
FINLAND
SWEDEN
Gulf of Bothnia
ESTONIA
LATVIA
LITHUANIA
RUSSIA
BALTIC SEA
POLAND
BELARUS
KAZAKHSTAN
UKRAINE
CZECH REPUBLIC
SLOVAKIA
AUSTRIA
HUNGARY
MOLDOVA
ROMANIA
SLOVENIA
CROATIA
BOSNIA HERCEGOVINA
YUGOSLAVIA
BULGARIA
MACEDONIA
ALBANIA
ITALY
GREECE
TURKEY
GEORGIA
AZERBAIJAN
ARMENIA
IRAN
SYRIA
IRAQ
LEBANON
CYPRUS
ISRAEL & the Palestinian Territories
JORDAN
SAUDI ARABIA
EGYPT
LIBYA
MALTA
BLACK SEA
CASPIAN SEA
Sea of Azov
MEDITERRANEAN SEA
Nordkapp
Murmansk
Tromsø
Ivalo
Narvik
Kiruna
Bodø
Mo i Rana
Arkhangelsk
Kemi
Luleå
Oulu
Trondheim
Umeå
Vaasa
Yekaterinburg
Petrozavodsk
Jyväskylä
Tampere
Lillehammer
Bollnäs
Turku
Helsinki
Vyborg
St Petersburg
Oslo
Uppsala
Stockholm
Tallinn
Örebro
Yaroslavl
Kazan
Novgorod
Nizhny Novgorod
Norrköping
Linköping
Tartu
Pskov
Jönköping
Gothenburg
Ventspils
Riga
Moscow
Samara
Helsingborg
Copenhagen
Malmö
Liepāja
Daugavpils
Klaipėda
Kaunas
Vitsebsk
Smolensk
Tula
Kaliningrad
Vilnius
Gdańsk
Stralsund
Minsk
Mahileu
Schwerin
Szczecin
Hrodna
Białystok
Voronezh
Homel
Berlin
Poznań
Warsaw
Brest
Łódź
Lublin
Leipzig
Dresden
Wrocław
Katowice
Kraków
Kharkiv
Volgograd
Zhytomyr
Kyiv
Prague
Plzeň
Ostrava
Lviv
Dnipropetrovsk
Donetsk
Rostov-on-Don
Brno
Košice
Vienna
Linz
Salzburg
Bratislava
Győr
Budapest
Chişinău
Odesa
Cluj-Napoca
Szeged
Krasnodar
Grozny
Ljubljana
Zagreb
Timişoara
Simferopol
Trieste
Sevastopol
Sukhumi
Tbilisi
Belgrade
Bucharest
Constanta
Craiova
Zadar
Ancona
Sarajevo
Split
Yerevan
Varna
Pescara
Dubrovnik
Prishtina
Sofia
Burgas
Podgorica
Plovdiv
Samsun
Trabzon
Erzurum
Skopje
Zonguldak
Tirana
İstanbul
Sivas
Van
Naples
Bari
Ankara
Salerno
Taranto
Thessaloniki
Bursa
Kayseri
Diyarbakır
Vlore
Larisa
Corfu
Izmir
Mosul
Reggio di Calabria
Ionian Islands
Patras
Athens
Piraeus
Kuşadası
Adana
Catania
Aleppo
Antalya
Kalamata
Rhodes
Kaş
Lefkosia (Nicosia)
Valletta
Homs
Baghdad
Hania
Iraklio
Lemessos
Beirut
Damascus
Amman
Jerusalem
Benghazi
Alexandria
Cairo

Europe
3rd edition – February 2003
First published – March 1999

Published by
Lonely Planet Publications Pty Ltd ABN 36 005 607 983
90 Maribyrnong St, Footscray, Victoria 3011, Australia

Lonely Planet Offices
Australia Locked Bag 1, Footscray, Victoria 3011
USA 150 Linden St, Oakland, CA 94607
UK 10a Spring Place, London NW5 3BH
France 1 rue du Dahomey, 75011 Paris

Photographs
Many of the images in this guide are available for licensing from Lonely Planet Images.
www.lonelyplanetimages.com

Front cover photographs
Top to Bottom: Short black coffee and eau de vie, Nice, France (Greg Elms, LPI). Golden Tuscan landscape near La Foce, Italy (Diana Mayfield, LPI). Rock towers and sun lovers, Sicily, Italy (Dallas Stribley, LPI). Couple riding scooter, Paris, France (David Hanover, Getty).

European Expeditions title page photograph
On the Grand Canal, Venice, Italy (Jon Davison, LPI)

ISBN 1 74059 314 6

Printed by SNP SPrint (M) Sdn Bhd
Printed in Malaysia

Contents – Text

Contents – Maps

GERMANY

GREECE

HUNGARY

ICELAND

IRELAND

ITALY

LATVIA

LIECHTENSTEIN

LITHUANIA

LUXEMBOURG

MACEDONIA

MALTA

MOROCCO

MOSCOW & ST PETERSBURG

THE NETHERLANDS

NORWAY

POLAND

PORTUGAL

ROMANIA

SLOVAKIA

SLOVENIA

SPAIN

SWEDEN

SWITZERLAND

TURKEY

YUGOSLAVIA

The Authors

Vivek Wagle

Vivek Wagle compiled *Europe on a shoestring* based on chapters researched for the Europe series, updated the Spain chapter, wrote the Festival Fever special section and contributed to the 'European Expeditions' special section (his sticky paws are all over this edition).

Vivek began his globetrotting at an early age, moving (well, being moved) from India to Pakistan and thence to the USA, all before the age of four. Since then, he has lived in Indonesia, worked in Australia and played in countries throughout the Americas, Europe, Asia, Africa and Oceania. Antarctica will come. After finishing a degree in philosophy from Harvard University he headed cross-country for the misty San Francisco Bay Area. He has worked as an editor in Lonely Planet's Oakland and Melbourne offices and has authored Lonely Planet guides to Mexico and Western Europe. He's dreading the day when he's no longer eligible for youth discounts.

From Vivek

Extreme thanks to the army of authors that made this the best guide to Europe ever. Props to the publishing and production teams in Oakland and Melbourne, who made everything possible. Special thanks to Mary Neighbour and Tony Davidson for getting the project rolling, to Robert Reid and Celia Wood for keeping me in line, and to Karen Fry for providing a roof for this vagrant. A big-league shout out to Nina Rousseau and Yvonne Bischofberger, whose tireless efforts kept everything on track and up to speed. Thanks to Janet Brunckhorst for sustained technical and moral support. Great appreciation to partners-in-crime Tammy Fortin, who researched the festivals special section and Facts for the Visitor chapter, and Alex Hershey, who sculpted the Finland chapter. A tip o' the hat to Ryan Ver Berkmoes, who let me hit the road. Much love to the family: Mom, Dad, Nani and Ayesha. And thanks to all Europeans – you rock. Stylishly.

Susie Ashworth

Susie updated the Switzerland and Liechtenstein chapters. She caught her first glimpse of the stunning Swiss Alps during her obligatory year-long backpacking trip in the late 1980s, where she gained an addiction for Lindt chocolate that still remains a problem. She's done odd jobs in London, written headlines and corrected spelling for magazines in Sydney and travelled rural Oz with her life packed into a camper trailer. These days, she works as an editor at Lonely Planet and lives in Melbourne with her partner and two cats.

David Atkinson

David updated the France chapter. He is a London-based freelance writer, specialising in travel, and has previously both lived and worked in Vietnam and Japan. During this time, he was mistaken for a gun runner, ate freshly killed snake and learned to do a mean karaoke Elvis medley. His stories have been published in the *Guardian*, *The Weekend FT*, the *South China Morning Post* and *Time Magazine Asia*. He is a member of the British Guild of Travel Writers. More from his website at w www.travelwriters.com/davidatkinson.

Carolyn Bain

Carolyn updated the Sweden chapter. Melbourne-born Carolyn was raised on Abba music and first travelled around Scandinavia as a teenager, while living and studying in Denmark. That experience left her with a love of all the best that Scandinavia has to offer – open, egalitarian societies populated by unfairly attractive people, long summer nights and cosy winters, wonderful art and design, pickled fish (or perhaps not...) – and she jumped at the chance to return to Sweden for this project. She has covered other great destinations for Lonely Planet, including the Greek Islands, New Zealand and Texas.

Chris Baty

Chris worked on the Germany chapter – his first authoring assignment for Lonely Planet. His deep admiration for the German people began in 1992, when a study abroad programme took him deep into the maw of a northern European winter. Heeding the example of the savvy natives, Chris soon discovered that beer and chocolate, in sufficient quantities, can sate the body's need for actual sunlight. He hasn't been the same since. Chris lives in Oakland, California where he supplements his vast travel-writing fortune with other equally questionable part-time occupations: music journalism and novel writing.

Neal Bedford

Neal updated the Danube Bend, Transdanubia, Lake Balaton, and Great Plains sections of the Hungary chapter. Born in Papakura, New Zealand, Neal gave up an exciting career in accounting for the mundane life of a traveller. Travel led him through a number of countries and jobs, ranging from an au pair in Vienna to a fruit picker in Israel. Deciding to give his life some direction, he landed the lucrative job of packing books in Lonely Planet's London office. One thing led to another and he managed to cross over into the mystic world of authoring. He now resides in Vienna.

Andrew Bender

Andrew updated the Germany chapter. Yet another LP author with an MBA, Andy worked with companies in Japan and the US but leapt to write full time after selling his first travel article. His writing has since appeared in *Travel & Leisure*, *Fortune*, *In Style* and the *Los Angeles Times*. He also reviews restaurants and edits the *Kyoto Diary*. Other LP titles include *Germany* (2002) and *Norway* (2002). At home in Los Angeles, he rollerblades at the beach, eats Asian food and schemes over ways to spoil his nephews, Ethan and Matthew.

Graeme Cornwallis

Graeme wrote and updated the Iceland and Norway chapters in this book. Born and raised in Edinburgh, Graeme later wandered around Scotland before coming to rest in Glasgow. While studying astronomy at Glasgow University, he developed a passion for peaks – particularly the Scottish Munros – and bagged all 284 summits over 3000ft in Scotland at least once. Graeme has travelled extensively throughout Scandinavia, Asia, North and South America and the Pacific. Mountaineering successes include trips to the Bolivian Andes, Arctic Greenland and Norway. When he's not hiking, climbing or travelling, Graeme teaches mathematics and physics at home in Glasgow.

Jan Dodd

Jan updated the Marrakesh section of the Morocco chapter. Seemingly incompatible with careers and pension plans, Jan Dodd opted instead for travelling. She later found herself writing guidebooks and somewhere along the way tumbled head over heels for Marrakesh. Unable to kick the mint-tea habit, Jan jumped at the opportunity to work on the new edition of *Morocco*. She's now the proud possessor of razor-sharp bargaining skills and a house full of carpets. When not admiring her *babouche* collection, Jan also writes for several other guidebook publishers, magazines, newspapers and websites.

Steve Fallon

Steve updated the introductory Budapest and Northern Hungary sections of the Hungary chapter. A native of Boston, he graduated from Georgetown University with a degree in languages. After working for several years for an American daily newspaper and earning a masters degree in journalism, he travelled to Hong Kong, where he lived for over a dozen years, worked for a variety of publications and ran a travel bookshop. Steve has written or contributed to more than two dozen Lonely Planet titles, including the Lonely Planet Journeys title *Home with Alice: A Journey in Gaelic Ireland*.

Kate Galbraith

Kate updated the Bosnia-Hercegovina chapter. Kate fell in love with Bosnia in 1996 when she worked for a local news agency in Sarajevo. She has been astounded by the changes the city has undergone since then, from the development of inter-entity bus lines to the introduction of a Versace gallery in Sarajevo centre. Before settling back into Bosnia for Lonely Planet, she made a grand tour of Eastern Europe as a freelance writer. She suspects that she may forever be a wanderer.

Duncan Garwood

Duncan worked on the Italy chapter. His writing career has so far taken him from the vaporous depths of London's largest sewage farm to the more traditional attractions of northern and central Italy. His first taste of travelling came with a four-month trip to India prior to a history degree at York University and a spell in corporate journalism. In 1997, however, he gave up leafy Berkshire for life in the Italian sun. He currently lives in the wine-rich hills overlooking Rome, dividing his time between writing, dreaming and teaching English to, among others, Italian Miss World contenders.

Paul Greenway

Paul updated the Poland and Bulgaria chapters. Gratefully plucked from the blandness and security of the Australian Public Service, Paul has now worked on over 20 Lonely Planet titles, including *Jordan*, *Bulgaria* and *Botswana*, as well as various guides for India, Indonesia, Africa and the Middle East. During the rare times that he's not travelling – or writing, reading and dreaming about it – Paul relaxes to (and pretends he can play) heavy rock, eats and breathes Australian Rules Football, and will go to any lengths to avoid settling down.

Susie Grimshaw

Susie updated the Portugal chapter. Born in Cheshire, she was itching to travel from an early age and read American Studies at University in the hopes of securing an exchange placement on the other side of the pond. The economic climate at the time did not permit such frivolous behaviour, so she went off her own bat and has never looked back, chalking up the miles in the USA, Asia and Europe. Susie was delighted to return to Portugal so she could resume her comparative study of custard tarts. Previously, she nobly volunteered to review restaurants for *Out to Eat London*.

Kathryn Hanks

Kathryn worked on the Britain chapter. She graduated with a degree in English and before taking up predictable career route number one (journalism) she followed the English graduate's second predictable career path (teaching) but in the altogether more exciting realms of Tanzania. Before this, she'd only really ever travelled around Europe and gleefully seized the opportunity to cram her passport full of stamps from various East African countries. She had to be dragged back to her native UK to spend two years editing a business magazine, and was fortunate enough to be rescued by Lonely Planet and shown what Britain's really like.

Des Hannigan

Des updated the Denmark chapter. Many years ago, Des set out from his native Scotland to look for unbroken sunshine in some exotic locale. He got lost on the way and ended up at sea, spending fifteen years as a fisherman on the often unsunny waters of Britain's Atlantic approaches. Then he took up news reporting in the mistaken hope that it might make for an easier life. From hack work he moved into guidebook work and has written guides to Andalucía, Rhodes, Corfu, southern Spain, North Pakistan and most of northern Europe, including Denmark, as well as several walking and rock-climbing guides. He lives in sunny Cornwall, England.

Paul Harding

Paul researched and updated the Finland chapter. Melbourne-born, Paul spent his formative years as a newspaper reporter in country Victoria before being sucked into the backpacker vortex. After travelling extensively in Europe and Southeast Asia, he worked as editor of a London travel magazine before landing at Lonely Planet's Melbourne home for wayward travellers. Paul is the author of Lonely Planet's *Read this First: Europe* and *İstanbul to Kathmandu* guides, and has contributed to *Australia, New Zealand, New South Wales, India, South India, Middle East* and *South-East Asia*.

Paul Hellander

Paul worked on the Albania and Cyprus chapters. He has never really stopped travelling since he first looked at a map in his native England. He graduated with a degree in Greek before heading for Australia where he trained interpreters and translators in Modern Greek. Paul has contributed to many LP titles including the following guides: *Greece, France, Cyprus, Israel & the Palestinian Territories, Singapore, Central America* and *South America*. His photos have also appeared in many LP guides. When not travelling, he lives in Adelaide, South Australia. He was last spotted setting his compass for the Dodecanese Islands in Greece.

Debra Herrmann

Debra, who updated the Estonia chapter, started out from the Wimmera region of southeastern Australia. After subsisting as a junior in the design and advertising business, copywriting anything from seedy nightclubs to Swedish cars, she soon realised the value of a passport. Over 30 countries proved irresistible in the years that followed and, after a visa-friendly foray into publishing in London, led to the one employer who would regard this as a logical career path – Lonely Planet. Her other contributions to the Lonely Planet list include *Estonia, Latvia & Lithuania, Europe on a shoestring* and *Lonely Planet Unpacked Again*.

Patrick Horton

Patrick Horton explored Serbia and Montenegro for the Yugoslavia chapter and, if that wasn't enough, went straight on to research an 'interesting' part of Russia for a different title. Patrick, writer and photographer, was born with restless feet. He travelled extensively in his native Britain before hitting the around-the-world trail in 1985. He prefers the more arcane areas of the world, such as North Korea, Eritrea, East Timor or Tonga, or riding a motorcycle over the Himalayas.

Patrick has had photographs published in many Lonely Planet guides and has worked on the *Australia, Eastern Europe, Ireland* and *Delhi* guides.

Sarah Johnstone

Sarah updated the Austria chapter. She's not really keen on author biographies, but the publishers insist. A freelance journalist raised in Queensland but based in London, she has previously worked for Reuters, Virgin Atlantic's in-flight magazine, *Hot Air*, and *Business Traveller*, among others. Her writing has also appeared in the *Times*, the *Independent on Sunday* and the *Face*. A great big coward, somehow Sarah still occasionally finds herself in places like Soweto or Libya (before the UN embargo was lifted – oops). A serial hugger of central heating systems the world over, she managed to find the Austrian outdoors a bit chilly, too.

Cathryn Kemp

Cathryn swapped tabloids for travel to update the Lithuania chapter. Cathryn started travelling in 1990 when she studied art at the Moscow Institute of Architecture and had several trips through Russia and Ukraine. After a masters degree in fine art and photography in Barcelona and graduating from Winchester School of Art in 1995, with camera in hand, she backpacked across Asia, Europe, Australia, New Zealand and South America – interspersed with a budding career in journalism. For five years Cathryn has written for British national and regional newspapers with some freelance photography thrown in – but travel just keeps getting in the way.

Alex Landragin

Alex updated the France and Andorra chapters. He was born in France's Champagne region before his family moved to Australia. He worked as a writer/editor at Lonely Planet's Melbourne HQ before opting for a life on the road. For this guide, Alex and his father drove the backroads of western France and Andorra at breakneck speed, racing from one restaurant to the next with bottomless appetites. Alex has also updated sections of the *Australia* and *Victoria* guides and between assignments is writing a novel in wine country near Melbourne.

Matt Lane

Matt worked on the Germany chapter. Born in England, he grew up in country Australia where he started what was to be a checkered non-career in journalism. Three newspaper jobs, a stint in television, some freelancing and travel, and one-third of a graphic design degree later, he wound up at Lonely Planet. This is his third LP job, having also worked on the most recent editions of *Australia* and *Queensland*. He lives in northeast Victoria, Australia, with his wife.

Cathy Lanigan

Cathy updated The Netherlands chapter. She worked as a journalist, turkey-egg collector, newspaper editor and politician between stints travelling in Europe, Asia, the Middle East and North Africa. She now works for Lonely Planet recruiting authors and occasionally being one. When not traipsing around the world with her partner and two-year-old in tow, she hangs out in country Victoria, Australia. Cathy has contributed to Lonely Planet's *Middle East* guide and updated *Travel with Children*.

Alex 'Pooky' Leviton

Alex updated the Slovenia chapter. Possibly Lonely Planet's shortest author ever at 4'9", Alex felt right at home in tiny Slovenia. She was raised in Los Angeles, but quickly escaped to the far reaches of Humboldt County. After college, she got a job at an alternative science/conspiracy theory magazine. This experience led her to leave the country, repeatedly. Alex has visited 46 countries on six continents. She worked on *Slovenia* while in her last semester at UC Berkeley's Graduate School of Journalism, and is currently a freelance writer and editor based in San Francisco.

Leanne Logan & Geert Cole

Leanne and Geert updated the Britain, Belgium and Luxembourg chapters. Leanne, a journalist from Australia, and Geert, a stained-glass artist from Belgium, met over a decade ago and have been writing and updating Lonely Planet guides ever since. This time round they were aided, and occasionally distracted, by their six-month-old daughter, Eleonor. Good at finding dead cockroaches under hotel beds and testing the breaking point of restaurant staff, Eleonor made life on the road more fun than ever. When not travelling, the trio can be found tending vegies, planting trees and watching wallabies at their rural retreat in northern New South Wales, Australia.

Lisa Mitchell

Lisa updated the Greece chapter. She discovered the world was big on a spree across Europe, the UK, Southeast Asia and Australia in the '80s. She returned to earn her byline deciphering 'techno goss' in the computer press, spat the CPU and became a writer and editor of lifestyle sections for a city newspaper. She sashayed momentarily into TV drama, later joining a women's magazine in dot com land. As deadlines and pocket money allow, Lisa pants up small mountains in high places. Her playgrounds include Alaska, Colorado, British Columbia, Patagonia and New Zealand. She works as a freelance writer in Melbourne.

Sally O'Brien

Sally worked on the Italy chapter. Born in Melbourne, and raised in Seoul and Sydney, Sally edited various Lonely Planet titles before deciding to try her luck as an author. She's written for *Sydney*,

Australia and *Sicily*, and covered Rome and Southern Italy for this book, where she amused one and all with her imaginative Italian and her version of driving on the right-hand side of the road. She's happy to keep getting sent there, despite predictably strange occurrences at train, bus and ferry stations and the aforementioned driving fiascos. When not authoring, she likes tea drinking and procrastinating.

Jeanne Oliver

Jeanne updated the Croatia chapter. Born in New Jersey, she spent her childhood dreaming of future voyages. After a BA in English and a stint at the *Village Voice* newspaper, Jeanne got a law degree. Her legal practice was interrupted by ever-more frequent trips to far-flung destinations and she set off on an around-the-world trip landing in Paris. She wrote freelance assignments for magazines and guidebooks before joining Lonely Planet in 1996. She has written first editions of Lonely Planet's *Croatia, Normandy, Crete* and *Crete Condensed* and has updated chapters in *Greece, Germany, Mediterranean Europe* and *France*.

Tom Parkinson

Tom updated the Morocco chapter. A modern languages graduate, Tom's other travel experiences have taken him round Europe from Amsterdam to Zagreb, including a year in Berlin, as well as luring him further afield to Tanzania and Bali. After five years editing dictionaries on vacations, he was well aware of how annoying freelance authors can be, so jumped at the chance to become one, contributing to the Music section of LP *Britain* and visiting Morocco as his first full assignment. Currently straddling the difficult transition from feckless youth to irresponsible adult, Tom hopes to continue writing until he is utterly unemployable.

Josephine Quintero

Josephine updated the Spain chapter. Born in England she started travelling with a backpack and guitar in the late '60s (didn't everyone?). She eventually landed in Kuwait where she edited the *Kuwaiti Digest*, and made several side trips that included Yemen and India. She was briefly held hostage during the Iraqi invasion of Kuwait, and moved to the more relaxed shores of Andalucía shortly thereafter. She has worked as a ghostwriter on several books, as well as contributed to more than 15 travel guides, and numerous in-flight magazines, including *Highlife* (British Airways).

Simon Richmond

Simon updated the St Petersburg & Around St Petersburg sections of the Moscow & St Petersburg chapter. After his first visit to St Petersburg in 1994, Simon knew it would not be his last encounter with this magical city. The award-winning writer travelled from St Petersburg to Vladivostok for Lonely Planet's *Trans-Siberian Railway* guide in 2001, then returned in 2002 to research the *Russia & Belarus* guide and contributed to the *Eastern Europe* guide. Co-author of other Lonely Planet titles including *İstanbul to Kathmandu, South Africa, Cape Town, Central Asia* and *Walking in Australia*, Simon also writes for several other guidebook publishers, magazines and newspapers.

Kalya Ryan

Kalya updated the Britain and Getting There & Away chapter. She grew up in Sydney and northern New South Wales, spent some time educating herself in Canberra, shacked up in Edinburgh for a year, but now calls Melbourne home (mainly because Lonely Planet agrees to pay her to edit guidebooks there). She likes Piña Coladas and getting caught in the rain...no, that's a lie, she prefers beer and avoids rain whenever she can.

Andrew Stone

Andrew worked on the Ireland chapter. He began travelling early, living in Africa and Iran before he was nine. Many years later he launched his journalistic career writing for a business weekly.

Sadly, the excitement of the supply chain logistics sector put a strain on his heart and he resigned on doctors' advice. Deciding to travel in Asia, he based himself in Hong Kong where he got up late, played too much Tetris and watched Korean sitcoms, while his family thought he was writing guidebooks. After a lengthy stint exploring Australia and New Zealand he took on this, his first assignment with Lonely Planet.

Rachel Suddart

Rachel updated the Getting Around chapter. Originally from the Lake District and a graduate of Manchester University, she spent several years trying to work out how to combine her love for writing with her incurable wanderlust. In 2000 she had her first taste of authorship when she took part in a BBC documentary. After getting her foot stuck firmly in the door she took on a full-time role in Lonely Planet's London office. She has contributed to several LP titles.

Dani Valent

Dani worked on the France chapter. In eight years of travel writing for Lonely Planet, she has worked on over a dozen guides to destinations on four continents. She still loves coming home to Melbourne, Australia where she dreams about making the perfect crème brûlée and playing Aussie Rules football for Carlton. (She'd probably get a game, too.)

Mara Vorhees

Mara updated the Moscow and Around Moscow sections of the Moscow & St Petersburg chapter. Born in St Clair Shores, Michigan, Mara's fascination with world cultures and a penchant for good deeds led her into international development. She set out to assist Russia in its economic transition. After two years spent mainly fighting with the tax police (and losing), she resorted to seeing and saving the world by other means. The pen-wielding traveller has since worked on Lonely Planet guides *Trans-Siberian Railway, Russia & Belarus* and *Moscow*. When she's not traipsing around the former Soviet bloc, she resides in Somerville, Massachusetts, with her husband and her cat.

Kim Wildman

Kim, who updated the Romania chapter, grew up in Toowoomba Queensland, with parents who unwittingly instilled in her the desire to travel at a young age by extending the immediate family to include 11 exchange students. After graduating from Queensland College of Art, having studied photography, Kim headed to the USA and Bermuda. Her next adventure to southern Africa was the inspiration to combine her three loves: photography, writing and travel. Kim also has a BA in journalism and has worked on Lonely Planet's *Europe on a shoestring, Romania & Moldova, South Africa, Lesotho & Swaziland* and *West Africa*, and co-authored *Athens*.

David Willett

David worked on the Greece chapter. David is a freelance journalist based near Bellingen on the north coast of New South Wales, Australia. He grew up in Hampshire, England, and wound up in Australia in 1980 after stints working on newspapers in Iran (1975–78) and Bahrain. He is a regular visitor to Greece as coordinator of Lonely Planet's guide to *Greece*, and has contributed to various other guides, including *Africa*, *Australia*, *Indonesia*, *South-East Asia*, *Mediterranean Europe* and *Western Europe*.

Nicola Williams

Nicola worked on the Latvia chapter of this book – prompting a much-welcome return to a country she bussed the length and breadth of as features editor of the *Baltic Times* in 1995–96. After 12 more months exploring the Baltics as Vilnius-based editor-in-chief of the *In Your Pocket* city-guide series, she swapped Lithuanian *cepelinai* for Lyonnaise *andouillette*. Nicola has written several Lonely Planet titles including first editions of *Estonia, Latvia & Lithuania, Romania & Moldova, Provence & the Côte d'Azur, The Loire* and *Milan, Turin & Genoa*.

Neil Wilson

Neil updated the Slovakia and Czech Republic chapters. After working as a petroleum geologist in Australia and the North Sea and doing geological research at Oxford University, Neil gave up the rock business for the precarious life of a freelance writer and photographer. Since 1988 he has travelled in five continents and written around 35 travel and walking guidebooks. He has worked on Lonely Planet's *Georgia, Armenia & Azerbaijan, Czech & Slovak Republics, Slovenia, Scotland* and *Edinburgh* guides. Although he was born in Glasgow, Neil defected to the east at the age of 18 and has lived in Edinburgh ever since.

Pat Yale

Pat updated the Turkey chapter. She first visited Turkey in 1974 in an old van that didn't look as if it would make it past Dover. Since throwing in sensible careerdom (ie, teaching), she has co-authored several editions of Lonely Planet's *Turkey* as well as worked on other Lonely Planet titles. At the time of writing she was living in a restored cave house with all mod cons and many cats in Göreme, Cappadocia.

This Book

Europe on a shoestring is part of Lonely Planet's Europe series, which includes *Western Europe*, *Eastern Europe*, *Mediterranean Europe*, *Central Europe* and *Scandinavian Europe*.

The first edition of this book was compiled and edited by Scott McNeely, based on chapters that were originally researched for the other books in the series.

The second edition of *Europe on a shoestring* was updated by a small army of authors and coordinated by Kalya Ryan and Mark Germanchis.

This edition was compiled by Vivek Wagle, based on chapters researched for the Europe series by authors whose names are listed on the previous pages. Vivek also wrote the Festival Fever special section. The European Expeditions special section was conceived by Robert Reid and created by Yvonne Bischofberger, Nina Rousseau, Vivek Wagle and Maria Vallianos.

From the Publisher

This edition of *Europe on a shoestring* was coordinated by crack team Nina Rousseau and Yvonne Bischofberger, together with super-organised project manager Celia Wood. Editors and proofers extraordinaire were Pete Cruttenden, Helen Yeates, Will Gourlay, Darren O'Connell, Melanie Dankel, Elizabeth Swan, Kyla Gillzan, Nancy Ianni, Bridget Blair, Tegan Murray, Cherry Prior, Simon Sellars, Evan Jones, Yvonne Byron, Tony Davidson, Isabelle Young, Sally O'Brien, Michelle Ramage, Greg Alford, Lucas McKenna, Victoria Harrison, Rebecca Hobbs, Susannah Farfor and Marg Toohey. Cartographic and layout assistance came in the form of Valentina Kremenchutskaya, James Ellis, Anneka Imkamp, Jarrad Needham, Natasha Velleley, Tessa Rottiers, Sally Morgan, Adrian Persoglia , Csanád Csutoros, Chris Thomas, Nick Stebbing, Steven Cann, Vicki Beale, Indra Kilfoyle, Sonya Brooke, Jacqui Saunders, Lachlan Ross and Larisa Baird. Thanks also to Heather Dickson, Robert Reid, Bruce Evans, Kate McDonald, Mark Griffiths, Adriana Mammarella, Maria Vallianos, Emma Koch, Quentin Frayne, Mark Germanchis, Simon Bracken (cover design) and Lonely Planet Images. And to Vivek, it's been a pleasure. Many, many thanks from Nina and Yvonne to every single person who helped with the production of this book – you all totally rock!

THANKS
Many thanks to the travellers who used the last edition and wrote to us with helpful hints, advice and interesting anecdotes. Your names appear in the back of this book.

Grateful acknowledgment is made for reproduction permission: Penguin Books Ltd: Excerpt from *The Italians*, Luigi Barzini (1964).

Thanks also to Mountain High Maps ® Copyright © 1993 Digital Wisdom, Inc.

Foreword

ABOUT LONELY PLANET GUIDEBOOKS

The story begins with a classic travel adventure: Tony and Maureen Wheeler's 1972 journey across Europe and Asia to Australia. There was no useful information about the overland trail then, so Tony and Maureen published the first Lonely Planet guidebook to meet a growing need.

From a kitchen table, Lonely Planet has grown to become the largest independent travel publisher in the world, with offices in Melbourne (Australia), Oakland (USA), London (UK) and Paris (France).

Today Lonely Planet guidebooks cover the globe. There is an ever-growing list of books and information in a variety of media. Some things haven't changed. The main aim is still to make it possible for adventurous travellers to get out there – to explore and better understand the world.

At Lonely Planet we believe travellers can make a positive contribution to the countries they visit – if they respect their host communities and spend their money wisely. Since 1986 a percentage of the income from each book has been donated to aid projects and human rights campaigns, and, more recently, to wildlife conservation.

Although inclusion in a guidebook usually implies a recommendation we cannot list every good place. Exclusion does not necessarily imply criticism. In fact there are a number of reasons why we might exclude a place – sometimes it is simply inappropriate to encourage an influx of travellers.

UPDATES & READER FEEDBACK

Things change – prices go up, schedules change, good places go bad and bad places go bankrupt. Nothing stays the same. So, if you find things better or worse, recently opened or long-since closed, please tell us and help make the next edition even more accurate and useful.

Lonely Planet thoroughly updates each guidebook as often as possible – usually every two years, although for some destinations the gap can be longer. Between editions, up-to-date information is available in our free, monthly email bulletin *Comet*. The *Scoop* section of our website covers news and current affairs relevant to travellers. Lastly, the *Thorn Tree* bulletin board and *Postcards* section carry unverified, but fascinating, reports from travellers.

Tell us about it! We genuinely value your feedback. A well-travelled team at Lonely Planet reads and acknowledges every email and letter we receive and ensures that every morsel of information finds its way to the relevant authors, editors and cartographers.

Everyone who writes to us will find their name listed in the next edition of the appropriate guidebook, and will receive the latest issue of *Comet* or *Planet Talk*. The very best contributions will be rewarded with a free guidebook.

We may edit, reproduce and incorporate your comments in Lonely Planet products such as guidebooks, websites and digital products, so let us know if you don't want your comments reproduced or your name acknowledged.

How to contact Lonely Planet:
Online: e talk2us@lonelyplanet.com.au, w www.lonelyplanet.com
Australia: Locked Bag 1, Footscray, Victoria 3011
UK: 10a Spring Place, London NW5 3BH
USA: 150 Linden St, Oakland, CA 94607

Introduction

Your head jerks up and your eyes snap open as the awkward thud of the landing gear hitting earth jars you from the unrestful half-doze in which you've spent the last few hours. Furiously blinking in a vain attempt to clear the stinging redness from your vision, you moan softly as your head resumes its throbbing and your throat begins to itch again. Dazedly, you stumble down the aisle with your fellow passengers, sniffing for that taste of free air, desperate for a drink, and aching in all your joints. And you couldn't be more thrilled.

Welcome to Europe. This is it – the big time, the grand show, the Trip of Your Lifetime. You have good cause to be excited. Whether you're new to this whole travelling gig or a hardened veteran of decades of globe-trotting, your trip to Europe will be the one that you'll never forget. There's a reason that this destination is always in vogue, consistently attracting millions of visitors per year and burning itself in the memories and imaginations of every single one.

Europe exudes a powerful energy grounded in its legendary history and sharpened by its key position at the cutting edge of the modern world. Forming the basis of much of global culture today, European traditions and ways have been shaped by a seemingly endless procession of innovations, conflicts and reawakenings. When you step onto European soil, you are almost certainly touching ground that has been stained by the blood of countless battles. These clashes – partially the product of an almost unimaginable diversity of races and cultures tightly packed into a petite parcel of land – have created and destroyed vast empires, allowed for the spreading and cultivation (and, occasionally, the destruction) of myriad cultures, and in the process shaped the history of the world.

But now, perhaps more so than ever in their shared history, Europeans are turning from the chaos of war and adopting a communal future. The worlds of Western and Eastern Europe are converging, as common currencies and laws, the dismantling of barriers, and the gradual disappearing of international violence from the continent strip away so many of the causes for strife. It's an exciting time to visit, as travelling has never been easier, yet individual nations and regions are still clinging firmly to independent identities, steadfastly maintaining their traditions, languages and beliefs while accepting that the future lies in commonality. Meanwhile, forward-looking nations are moving quickly to protect their lands from overdevelopment and misuse, providing the visitor with enchanting, majestic escapes from the style and substance of modern European life.

It all smacks of epic adventure – and, as any good storyteller knows, such adventures are best undertaken with trustworthy companions. And the book you're currently holding is one such companion. It is our intent to serve you not as a tour guide, but rather as a friend who's been there and has learned a couple of tricks. We're not going to prescribe what to do, but we'll certainly offer suggestions. When it comes to finding you a comfortable place to rest or making sure that you don't miss the last bus out of town, we're there for you. Of course, sometimes we won't be able to contain our excitement and will nudge you to say, 'Hey, check this out – it's really unbelievable!' But most of the time we'll try to point you in the right direction and let you play the explorer yourself. You are going to have a marvellous time no matter what, but the way to make the most out of your trip is to let your interests and intuition be your guide.

If this is all new to you, don't worry. We'll take you aside right at the beginning and bring you up to speed before letting you play with the others. In no time, you'll be cultivating your own storylines and amassing experience and knowledge that you, in turn, can pass on to fellow travellers.

Hey look – isn't that your backpack coming 'round the luggage carousel? Time to snatch it up, grab that last drink of water, and sprint to the bus stop so you don't miss that last connection to the hostel.

Enjoy the ride.

Facts for the First-Time Visitor

OK, so you've just graduated and you're rarin' for The Big Trip. Or maybe your new job has doubled your vacation time, giving you several weeks to make the voyage that you've always dreamt of. Or perhaps you've just retired and are ready to teach those ungrateful kids a lesson by spending their inheritance in the Old World. Whatever your situation, if this is your first major trip abroad, then this is the chapter for you.

Planning your own journey for the first time can be daunting. There are the big questions: 'Where and when do I go? Will it be safe? How much will it cost?' – as well as those nagging details, such as 'How many socks should I pack?' The issues and initial hassles can seem daunting, but you should never feel overwhelmed. Remember: gazillions of people visit Europe each year, and many of them are far, far more inept than you. The very fact that you're reading this book gives you a head start on the lion's share of travellers.

In this chapter, we'll take you through the basics of planning and packing for a trip and then help you to create a budget and stick to it. Next, we'll provide tips on staying safe by staying smart during your journey, and we'll round off with some useful hints on being a responsible, courteous traveller. When you're done, you'll be ready for the nuts 'n' bolts information that follows in the Facts for the Visitor, Getting There & Away and Getting Around chapters.

CAREFUL OR CAREFREE: THE GOLDEN MEAN

If you want advice about travelling in Europe, go back to the source. Heralded Hellenic philosopher Aristotle theorised that virtue lies between extremes, claiming that finding the 'happy medium' is the formula for success. If you're tempted to plan out every single minute of your trip, you'll inevitably be frustrated by unexpected hassles, delays and costs. On the other hand, if you just pack up and go with hardly any planning, you'll probably find yourself paying much more than you have to and missing out on some fantastic opportunities.

The happiest travellers are those who have found the balance, doing enough planning to ensure a rewarding trip, while being flexible enough to take the unforeseen in their stride. You'll soon discover what mix of adventurousness and meticulousness is right for you.

THE ESSENTIALS

If George Orwell had written a travel guide, he might have noted that all items are essential, but some are more essential than others. Your mother would never allow you to forget the importance of clean underwear, but before even that come the absolute-must-have, can't-live-without items below.

Passport

A passport is your most important travel document. It contains a photo, an ID number (which is required on all sorts of travel documents) and blank pages for foreign officials to stamp when you enter (and sometimes leave) their country. In countries that require a pre-arranged travel visa (see later), a visa will be stapled or stamped into your passport and later validated when you arrive at that country's borders. For more information, see Passports in the Facts for the Visitor chapter.

Visas

Citizens of the USA, Canada and the UK need only a valid passport to enter many European countries (Australians and New Zealanders are not so lucky). See Visas in the Facts for the Visitor chapter for which countries, if any, require pre-arranged travel visas. The Internet is another good place to search for up-to-date visa requirements.

Insurance

A travel insurance policy that covers theft, medical treatment, emergency evacuation and personal liability is must. See Visas & Documents and Health in the Facts for the Visitor chapter.

Money

The first step is to calculate a realistic budget that suits your bank account and desired style of travel. We'll help you with that later in this chapter. Next, it's important to establish safe, dependable methods of accessing your cash while abroad (bank card, credit card, travellers cheques etc). Lastly, have a secure method of transporting your money and valuables (for example, in a money belt, neck pouch or belt pouch). Detailed information is in the following Costs & Money and Safety & Security sections, as well as Money in the Facts for the Visitor chapter.

Other Useful Documents

The following passes and ID cards may not be 'essential', but in many cases they will save you heaps of money. Deciding which you need is an important pretrip exercise, as they're mostly cheaper (and often easier) to purchase before leaving home.

Rail Passes These offer a flexible, low-cost way of getting around Europe. If you plan to visit more than a few countries on a single trip, you will definitely save money with a rail pass. The most common passes are Inter-Rail (for European citizens) and Eurail (for non-Europeans), both of which offer unlimited travel within a set number of days in many (but not all) European countries. For a complete rundown, see International Rail Passes in the Getting Around chapter.

Hostelling & Camping Cards A hostelling card is useful, if not always mandatory, for staying at Europe's 'official' hostels – ie, ones that belong to an international network such as Hostelling International (HI). Since many hostels give discounts to cardholders, a hostelling card will soon pay for itself. There are similar benefits with a Camping Card International, which gives discounts at many camping grounds. For additonal information, see under Accommodation in the Facts for the Visitor chapter.

Student Cards Registered students can save a pile of money with an International Student Identification Card (ISIC). Discounts vary from country to country – at best you'll save up to 50% on museum entry fees and 10% to 30% on some buses, trains and ferries. For details, see Student & Youth Cards in the Facts for the Visitor chapter.

WHEN & WHERE TO GO

This section outlines options for timing your trip optimally and planning it out. More specific information on when to go is in the Facts for the Visitor chapter and the individual country chapters.

Timing

Most first-time travellers visit Europe in summer (roughly mid-June to late August). On the plus side, summer is packed with cultural events, the weather is warm and the days are long. Most public transport networks are in full operation, a definite plus in places like Scotland, Ireland, Greece and the Scandinavian countries.

The bad news is that you will battle heavy crowds in major cities, prices will be higher and the weather can be sweltering, especially in southern Europe. The worst month of all is August, when millions of European families and holiday-makers hit the road, packing beach towns, ferries and trains like sardines. When it comes to crowds and high prices, the general rule of thumb is that June is better than July, and July is better than August. Depending on your itinerary the best times to visit Europe are late May/early June and September, when the crowds thin, prices drop and the weather is still good.

And don't forget about winter. Except at Christmas and New Year, winter crowds are much thinner (a big plus in places like Prague and Paris) and prices are dramatically lower. Winter is also a time for skiing some of the world's finest slopes such as Switzerland, France, Austria, Italy etc, and some of the world's cheapest slopes, including Romania, Poland, Slovakia etc.

Travelling Companions

If you're hitting the road with others, keep in mind that travel can put relationships to the test like few other experiences. Many a long-term friendship has collapsed under the strains of constant negotiations about where to stay and eat, what to see and where to go next. But many friendships have also become closer than ever before. You won't find out until you try, but make sure you agree on itineraries and routines beforehand and try to remain flexible about everything – even in the heat of an August afternoon in Paris or Berlin. Travelling with someone else also has financial benefits, as single rooms are more expensive per person than a double in most countries.

If travel is a good way of testing established friendships, it's a magnificent way of making new ones. Hostels and camping grounds are good places to meet fellow travellers, so even if you're travelling alone you need never be lonely.

If It's Tuesday, It Must Be...Slovenia?

Though often ridiculed, the mad dash that crams eight or nine countries into a month does have its merits. If you think this might be your only chance to see Europe's great sights, a quick scouting tour will let you canvass the options. Rail passes that offer unlimited travel within a set period of time provide the best way to do this.

On the other hand, if you have the luxury of spending time in one place, it's often delightful (and cheaper) to stay put for a while, discover some of the lesser-known sights, make a few local friends and settle in.

Planning an Itinerary

Many first-time travellers make the mistake of trying to see too much in too little time. With a Eurail or Inter-Rail train pass it's easy to hop from city to city at a dizzying pace, which may lead to travel burnout. It's often best to pick a handful of countries to explore in depth and leave the rest for a second, third or fourth trip.

If you have a rail pass, make sure your itinerary meshes with its restrictions and requirements. For example, if you visit 12 countries on a 10-day Eurail pass, you may have to cover some additional travel costs. It's much the same with an Inter-Rail pass, which is divided into zones and may not cover all the countries you intend to visit.

Sample Itineraries

When you're ready to plot an actual itinerary, consider the following simple strategies for a month-long trip to Europe – but don't forget that flexibility is the key to a less stressful, more enjoyable trip. So once you've crafted the perfect itinerary, don't be afraid to stuff it in your backpack and ignore it. Dozens (if not hundreds) of fellow travellers will proffer tips and suggestions during your travels, and there is no substitute for their first-hand knowledge and advice. Also, be sure to check out the 'European Expeditions' special section in this guide for some itinerary ideas.

The Great Cities Pick a few major cities that you absolutely must visit – for example, London, Barcelona, Paris, Munich, Prague, Vienna and Venice. Budget at least 2½ days in each city, and add a day each for travelling between them. So far that's 17 days. Now spend a few hours researching day trips from your chosen cities. If you budget one day-trip per city, you're at 24 days. Now add three days for impromptu side trips and/or sleeping late and relaxing, and three days for travel-related delays (slow trains, bus strikes and random acts of road congestion), for a total of 30 days. With two months, you could double the amount of cities you visit, spend more time in each city, or use the extra time to get to know the smaller towns in the regions.

The main disadvantage of a city itinerary is that you will spend large chunks of time on trains and buses, especially if you include far-flung cities (eg, İstanbul and Helsinki). Also, you'll miss out on small towns and villages, which can be both charming and cheap.

Divide & Conquer Pick four to six countries and budget a week or so each for the larger countries, four to five days for the smaller countries. Within each country, budget two or three days in the capital city, the remaining days for lesser-known towns, villages and regions. A sample trip might include Britain (five days), the Netherlands (three days), Germany (six days), Czech Republic (three days), Hungary (two days), Turkey (five days), Greece (four days), Italy (six days) and France (six days), plus a day or two back to Britain, for a total of 42 days. If you can, budget a few days en route between your chosen countries – for example, between the Czech Republic and Italy you could add two days each in Vienna and Ljubljana (Slovenia's capital).

With this approach, you can cover the aspects of each country you enjoy (eg, beaches on Greek islands, hiking in the Alps, partying in Amsterdam). In addition, you can identify several regions and hit each of them, splitting up Europe at will. However, you might not have enough time to explore each region fully, leaving you wanting more at the end of your trip.

Planning Aids

Congratulations! You're already holding one of the very best pretrip planning aids. Get your money's worth by reading as much as possible before leaving home, especially this book's Facts for the Visitor, Getting There & Away and Getting Around chapters.

In addition to Lonely Planet's numerous European titles, there are hundreds of other useful guidebooks to Europe. Many cater to specific interests and special needs, such as vegetarians, hard-core hikers, architecture enthusiasts, gays and lesbians, history buffs, nudists and more. The best starting point is your local bookstore's travel section.

On the Internet, there's no better place to start than Lonely Planet's comprehensive website (W www.lonelyplanet.com). The Scoop feature gives you the skinny on the latest happenings around the world, while you can get advice and swap anecdotes with other travellers on the free Thorn Tree bulletin board.

There are other sites dedicated to each and every country in Europe. Ignore the overtly commercial sites (the ones selling high-end hotel packages etc) and focus on those that offer photos, travel tips, up-to-date political news, and notes or comments from fellow travellers. See Digital Resources in the Facts for the Visitor chapter, and the Digital Resources section of each country chapter, for more information.

WHAT TO PACK

Experienced travellers the world over agree on one basic tenet: Pack light! Almost all first-time travellers overpack, and virtually no-one ever comes home saying, 'I packed too little'! If you're really concerned about underpacking, take a little extra money. Whatever you think you're missing will almost certainly be available. If it isn't, then you might consider living without it – after all, obviously everyone else around you does.

A backpack is still the budget traveller's friend and constant companion. No other device offers such convenience and accessibility. For most travellers, a sturdy backpack with adjustable and padded straps, lower-back support and plenty of zipper compartments is an essential pretrip purchase. On the downside, a backpack doesn't offer much protection for your valuables, the straps tend to get caught on things and some airlines may refuse to accept responsibility if the pack is damaged or tampered with.

Travelpacks, a combination backpack and shoulder bag, are very popular. The backpack straps zip away inside the pack when they are not needed, so you almost have the best of both worlds. Some packs have sophisticated shoulder-strap adjustment systems and can be used comfortably even on long hikes. Backpacks or travelpacks can be made reasonably theft-proof with small padlocks. Do not skimp on a backpack, because having a strap or harness break when you're 100km from the nearest city is truly miserable. Moreover, replacement packs are not always easy to find on the road – can you say 'high-quality backpack with adjustable straps' in Croatian?

It's best to bring two pairs of shoes. For day-to-day walking bring a sturdy pair of lightweight shoes. Sneakers (tennis shoes) are comfortable but will instantly brand you as a tourist. Also bring a pair of waterproof sandals for showers, beaches and sightseeing. Hiking boots are essential for serious trekkers. Avoid blisters by wearing new shoes and sandals at least two hours a day for two weeks before leaving home.

Even if you spend most of your trip on a Greek beach, bring at least one pair of long pants. Some churches and mosques require visitors to wear long pants or a full-length skirt and refuse entry to people in shorts. Lightweight cotton pants are best. Blue jeans are bulky, get dirty quickly and take forever to dry.

Sleeping bags make handy blankets on trains and buses (though they are bulky to carry in your pack). If you stay in hostels you will need a sleeping bag or a sleep sheet with a built-in pillow case (cover). Otherwise you must rent one each night for €1 to €2.50. There's nothing worse than being a 'backpacker' who brought a suitcase, especially if that suitcase contains seven pairs of shoes, five sweaters and the complete works of William Shakespeare. Bearing in mind that you can buy virtually anything on the spot, a packing list could include the following:

- underwear, socks
- lightweight towel and swimming gear
- a pair (or two) of lightweight cotton pants (jeans are bulky and hard to launder)
- a pair of shorts or a skirt
- a few T-shirts and shirts
- a warm sweater
- a solid pair of walking shoes
- sturdy sandals for showers and beaches
- a coat or jacket
- a raincoat or waterproof jacket
- a medical kit and sewing kit
- a small padlock

- a Swiss Army knife
- a small flashlight (torch)
- sunglasses
- toothpaste, toothbrush, soap and other toiletries
- a few plastic bags (to store wet/dirty clothes)

COSTS & MONEY

Europe can be monstrously expensive or dirt-cheap, depending on how and where you travel. The best advice is to calculate a budget before leaving home and try to stick to it. Do some pretrip research and weigh the costs and benefits of the countries you most want to visit. For example, beer drinkers will enjoy the Czech republic and most of Eastern Europe, where beer averages less than €1.50 for 500mL. In Scandinavia the same beer could cost a whopping €6.

All travellers should budget for emergencies. A credit card is useful for unexpected expenses. We also recommend setting aside €130 to €170 in cash for the 'worst-case scenario', which goes something like this: taxi to embassy (€10) to replace lost passport (€30 to €50), taxi to airport (€15) to replace lost airline ticket (€10 to €30) and to catch flight back home, taxi back to town (€15) because you missed the flight, dinner and much-needed drink (€15), fleabag hotel for one night (€25), and taxi back to the airport (€10).

For a comprehensive run-down on travellers cheques, wire transfers, bank cards, ATMs and more, see under Money in the Facts for the Visitor chapter.

Sample Costs

See the 'Average Daily Costs (€)' boxed text for a rough estimate of per-person daily expenses in euros. Even with a rail pass you must pay for some private trains, buses, ferries and local transport – we've given a rough average in the 'local transport' category.

The cost of a return airfare is your first major expense and will vary greatly depending on where you are flying from, what time of year it is and what special deals, if any, are available. Fares from the USA range from around US$250 to US$800 (€256 to €818). See the Getting There & Away chapter for more information.

Be sure to add a bit of padding when calculating the grand total for a 30-day trip, as you will probably sleep in both hostels and hotels, eat some meals at restaurants and cook some meals for yourself etc. In general, you'll need €35 to €40 for an absolutely bare-bones trip with few luxuries. Add in airfare and a rail pass for a total of €2500 or so. A more realistic – and comfortable – budget is €50 a day, which brings the total up to €2800.

Daily budgets will be around €5 to €10 less if you spend more time in Eastern Europe, Turkey and Morocco. Add €10 to €15 per day in Scandinavian countries.

10 Tips to Stay on Budget

If you're serious about staying on budget, for every splurge there must be an equal and opposite money-saver. There are many free things to do in Europe, from hiking to beach bumming to loitering on a piazza. The following tips can also save you money:

Alcohol Buy alcohol at supermarkets and drink with the locals on main squares, gardens and beaches (where it's legal and acceptable to do so).

Clothes Wash your clothes in hotel and hostel sinks.

Doubles and triples Spread lodging costs among a few trustworthy travelling companions. At many hotels and hostels, quads (four-person rooms) are cheaper than triples and triples are cheaper than doubles.

Free concerts Enjoy free concerts and cultural events – ask at tourist offices and check around town for fliers and posters.

Average Daily Costs (€)

Expenses	Western	Mediterranean	Scandinavian	Eastern
Camping	10-15	5-10	8-20	3-8
Hostel	15-30	10-15	15-30	5-10
Budget hotel (double)	35-80	25-50	60-90	15-50
Cheap restaurant meal	7-10	5-10	10-15	3-8
Local transport	3-6	2-5	5-10	1-5
Museum fees	5-12	3-5	5-10	2-5
One beer (500mL)	2-5	2-6	3-5	0.50-3
15-day rail pass	450-500 (Eurail, all areas)			

Free days Take advantage of many museums' free days. Also ask about joint-entry tickets and discount passes for tourists.

Markets Buy food at open-air markets and supermarkets. Remember that a tube of mustard or garlic spread can transform dull bread and cheese into a tasty meal.

Overnight trains Take overnight trains on long trips to save the cost of a night in a hostel or hotel.

Phonecard Use a phonecard (instead of coins or tokens) to make phone calls within Europe. If dialling home, you may save money with a 'Home Direct' service offered by your local telephone company.

Restaurants Always ask to see a menu with prices at restaurants and cafés. Also ask if there's a surcharge for sitting inside, on the patio, at a table etc.

Towns and villages Don't spend all your time in big cities. Prices are generally lower in towns and villages.

Smart Ways to Blow your Budget

Successful budgets strike a balance between low cost and high reward. Europe on a budget of €10 a day is a low cost, low reward strategy – you may save a heap of money, but you will see absolutely nothing. Aim instead to get the maximum value for your money, even if that means occasionally going over budget.

Car rental Renting a car can be good value in the right circumstances, especially if you're travelling in a small group and do not already have a rail pass. In remote or rural regions that are poorly served by buses and trains, a rental car will save you time and trouble. It may also enable you to sleep at a far-flung (but cheap) camping ground instead of a (more expensive) hostel or hotel.

Cheap hostels Don't assume that the cheapest hostel or hotel is also the best value. A hostel may charge only €20 for a double, but factor in the incidentals: you and a friend arrive by bus (50c each), pay extra for showers (€1 each), rent sheets (€1), take a bus back to town (50c) and then catch an early bus back (50c) in order to make the 11pm curfew. Grand total: €13.50 per person. If you stay at a central hotel with €35 doubles and free showers, the cost is €17.50 per person. That extra €4 per person saves you three bus rides and an early evening staring at a hostel TV.

Local food If you don't make an effort to sample local cuisines, you are denying yourself one of travelling's great pleasures. Self-service and budget restaurants are OK, but every now and again try a pricier, acclaimed local option. Many restaurants offer set-priced meals and lunch specials that are good values.

Splashing out You spent 12 hours on an overnight train to reach a small town in the Swiss Alps/Moroccan desert/French wine country. You booked into a cheap hostel for two nights and saved a bundle shopping at the local supermarket. You've done a good job keeping costs down, so don't baulk at splashing out on a skiing/trekking/chateau tour, even if the cost exceeds your daily budget.

SAFETY & SECURITY

Travelling in Europe is generally quite safe. Violent crime is rare and the threat from terrorists and religious fanatics is low. The main threats facing travellers are pickpockets and scam artists. Specific perils are covered in the Dangers & Annoyances section in this book's individual country chapters. The following outline a range of general guidelines that all travellers should keep in mind.

General Security

You can deter most thieves by wearing a money belt and never letting your bags out of sight. Small zipper locks are handy (but not fool-proof) for securing backpacks and daypacks. On trains and buses it's wise to lock your bags to a luggage rack, preferably with a sturdy combination cable.

Sadly, some travellers finance their wanderlust by taking advantage of fellow travellers. Never leave bags unattended in a hostel or hotel, not even for five seconds. No kidding.

If you are concerned, store your luggage in a locker (found at many train and bus stations). You should always carry passports, money and airline tickets on your person – never leave them in a hotel room, even if it seems safe. Some hotels offer safe-deposit boxes in which your possessions are guaranteed security. Luggage-storage rooms are OK, but there's no guarantee that hotel or hostel staff, even fellow travellers, won't help themselves to your belongings.

Flaunting cameras, portable CD players and other expensive electronic goods is only asking for trouble. Remember that a €500 camera represents months of wages in some countries. Keep all valuables in a daypack or backpack when they're not being used. Never leave them sitting in the open on trains or buses.

Last but not least, don't be cavalier anywhere. Crime is a worldwide phenomenon.

Carrying Cash Would you walk around in your hometown with huge wads of cash?

They're Just Helping You Travel Light

One traveller tells of the time when he arrived in a major Western European airport and made his way to the information desk. He put his backpack down – *between his legs* – and proceeded to talk to the clerk at the counter. When he was done, he reached down and found...nothing.

If your pack's not locked up, *always* maintain physical contact with it, lest you are involuntarily turned from a backpacker into a daypacker.

(Manhattanites, put your hands down.) You probably wouldn't, and there's no reason to do so on the streets of Europe. Carry no more than 10% to 15% of your total trip money in cash. The remainder could be in travellers cheques, which can be replaced in case of loss or theft. More useful are ATM cards that are linked to a cheque or savings account back home. Bank-issued ATM cards linked to the Visa/Plus, Eurocard and MasterCard/Cirrus networks are widely accepted in European countries, and they allow you to draw small amounts of local currency every few days. Some credit cards also allow you to draw cash at foreign ATMs and banks for a fee (plus interest if you don't pay the balance quickly).

Photocopies Make two sets of photocopies of your passport, airline ticket, travellers cheques, insurance papers and credit cards. It's a good idea to keep one set safely separated from the original documents and leave the other set at home.

Money Belts Carrying a wallet or purse is like wearing a flashing neon billboard that says 'there is money here, please take some'. It is much safer to keep travellers cheques, passports, airline tickets etc close to your skin in a money belt that is worn under your clothes. You can carry a small amount of money for quick transactions in an easily accessible wallet or purse (preferably kept in a front pocket rather than a back pocket), but keep the bulk of your cash and all important documents in a money belt. These are sold at luggage stores, travel shops and even some bookshops. Neck pouches are OK, but not if you wear them (as many travellers inexplicably do) on the outside of your clothes.

Have at least one contingency plan in the unlikely event that your money belt is stolen. Some travellers walk around with €100 in their shoe (risky); others stash €50 in their aspirin bottle. We recommend sewing €50 in cash into hard-to-reach corners of your backpack (preferably) or daypack.

Daypacks Small daypacks are useful for carrying guidebooks, cameras, portable stereos and the like. This makes them a favourite target for thieves – it only takes a few seconds for a practised hand to unzip your bag and rifle through its contents. Small zipper locks may deter a novice thief, but they will not stop an expert pickpocket from slashing your bag in the blink of an eye. The best advice is to keep your daypack in front of you when in crowded areas and keep a close eye on it at all times.

Scams & Swindles

Each year Lonely Planet receives hundreds of letters from travellers who have been duped by predatory scam-artists. As new swindles constantly appear, there is no single way to protect yourself. The best advice is to keep your wits about you, and to approach all situations with a healthy dose of scepticism.

We try to list specific scams in individual country chapters. The following is a general list of deceits common throughout Europe.

Druggings Your mother was right: it is unwise to accept food and drinks from strangers. Travellers are especially vulnerable on trains and buses. The typical ploy involves someone you've just met offering to buy or share a drink or snack. Your new 'friend' may seem offended if you do not accept their small token of friendship; if you acquiesce, you may wake 10 hours later with a throbbing headache and a missing backpack.

Gassings have also been reported on a handful of overnight international trains. The usual scenario involves the release of a sleep-inducing gas into a sleeping compartment in the middle of the night. Once the gas takes effect, the perpetrator searches the victims for money belts and whatever valuables are lurking in their luggage. The best protection is to lock the door of your sleeping compartment (use your own lock if there isn't one) and to lock your bags to luggage racks. Never sleep alone in a train compartment.

Black Markets The black market is a thing of the past in most European countries. With the passing of communism most countries have begun the transition to free-market economics. In the process currencies have been freed from government controls (the main reason that black markets exist) and are now fully convertible.

Where black markets do exist, the rates are only marginally better than bank rates. Moreover, many black-market money changers will not hesitate to dupe foreign travellers. Each year Lonely Planet warns travellers not to change money on the black market, and each year we receive letters from travellers who wish they had heeded our warnings.

Phony Cops 'Can I see some ID?' In some countries, especially Eastern European ones, you may encounter people claiming to be from the tourist police, the special police, the super-secret police, whatever. Unless they're wearing a uniform and have good reason for accosting you (eg, you're robbing a bank), treat their claims with suspicion.

One common scam runs like this: a random person asks you to change money. You say no, and seconds later an 'undercover' police officer 'arrests' the money changer. The undercover agent then asks to check your passport and money, in case it's counterfeit.

Needless to say, never show your passport or cash to anyone on the street. Simply walk away. If they flash a badge, politely offer to accompany them to the nearest police station.

CULTURAL SENSITIVITY

This section is about 'ugly' tourists. You know the type. They tend to shout at people, always loudly, about how things are so much better/more efficient/cheaper in their home country. Whether the ugly tourist is drunk, ignorant or simply rude, witnessing such an outburst is very embarrassing. It's even worse if the ugly tourist is from your own country.

Embarrassing situations can arise from simple misunderstandings, for example, Bulgarians and Albanians tend to shake their head side to side to say 'yes', up and down to say 'no'. We discuss such issues in the Culture & Conduct section in individual country chapters. Also keep in mind the following general guidelines.

Not everyone speaks English Do not assume that everyone in Europe speaks English. If you ask a question in English and are met with blank stares, don't just repeat the question slowly and loudly in English. This is extremely rude and patronising.

Hello My Friend!

After a few weeks in Europe you will recognise the type – a nice man (rarely a woman) who speaks good English, is very friendly and goes out of his way to be helpful. The actual scam varies from country to country, but all share one common feature – lulling you into a false sense of trust. At some point your new friend will gently suggest something that, under normal circumstances, you would not do. Perhaps your new friend will kindly offer to watch your bags, inexplicably disappearing (along with your possessions) by the time you return. Maybe he'll help carry your stuff, while an accomplice grabs a camera or a daypack.

In some cases your new friend is less a thief and more a hustler. It's late and you don't have a hostel or hotel reservation. Coincidentally, your new friend knows this great hotel just across town. This ploy could involve an exorbitant taxi fare and an inflated hotel price, with your new friend scoring hefty commissions from the taxi driver and hotel owner.

There is no limit to the number of scams out there. Don't be paranoid, and don't cut yourself off from the people you meet on the road, the vast majority of whom are honestly interested in striking up a friendship. Yet it pays to be suspicious of overly friendly people, especially on long-distance trains and buses (after all, most people are less than friendly after 10 hours on a train). Never allow strangers to watch your bags and never allow a situation to evolve in ways that make you feel uncomfortable. If your new friend is genuine, they will certainly understand if you say 'no' to taking a taxi at 1am in a strange town to an unfamiliar hotel.

Local language Learn a few phrases in the local language, such as 'please', 'thank you', 'excuse me' and 'do you speak English?' We include language guides at the back of this book to help with the basics.

Blend in It's always best to blend in. For example, aggressive queue-jumping is a way of life in some European countries. If you're involved in a queue skirmish, don't make a scene, don't get into a huff and don't lecture an old lady on the etiquette of queuing as it's practised in your home country. When in Finland, do as the Finnish do.

There are countless other examples. The best advice is to keep an open mind, observe your surroundings and learn from the locals themselves what is appropriate and inappropriate behaviour. Don't impose your views on a foreign culture.

A FINAL WORD

After reading all the information presented in this chapter, you may be feeling a bit intimidated and worried. Don't be. Keep in mind that by virtue of reading this chapter alone, you are much better prepared for a trip to Europe than most people. Also remember that the vast, vast majority of people who travel to Europe have a wonderful time and never experience major trauma. Don't let paranoia get the better of you. You have a wonderful time ahead of you – now read on to get the most out of your trip!

European Expeditions

European Expeditions – Western Europe

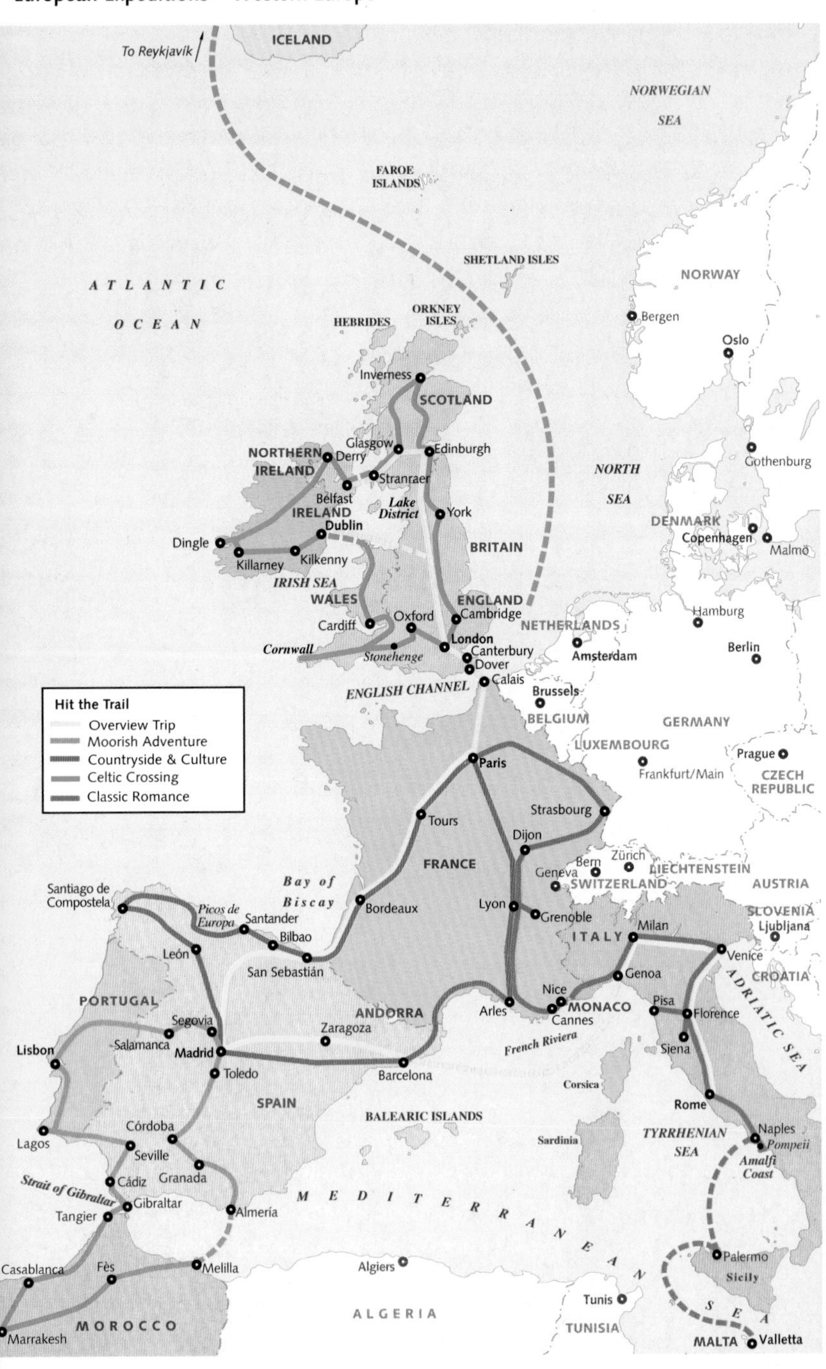

Moorish Adventure Party till dawn in Madrid before high-tailing it to historic Toledo. In Córdoba visit the 8th-century mosque, then marvel at the spectacular Alhambra of Granada and sunbake on an Almerían beach.

Escape (albeit slowly) on a ferry to Morocco. Fuel up on tasty tapas in Melilla and travel to traditional Fès, Morocco's symbolic heart. See the sun set on the red-earth walls of Marrakesh's *medina* before heading north to the modern metropolis of Casablanca. Return to Europe via vibrant Tangier and the great limestone lump of Gibraltar.

Sample sherry in Cádiz, click castanets and watch flamenco in Seville, then recover with a snorkelling spree at Lagos. Keep the action pumping with Lisbon's thriving nightlife before returning to Madrid via glorious Salamanca and venerable Segovia.

BILL WASSMAN

Puerta de Alcalá, Madrid

Countryside & Culture Immerse yourself in culture and experience both big-city verve and countryside tranquillity with a jaunt through France and Spain.

Make like Hemingway and scribe your thoughts from Paris to San Sebastián, via cosmopolitan Tours and grandiose Bordeaux. Hug the Basque coast to Bilbao, and admire the contemporary architecture of the Museo Guggenheim, before heading to bustling Santander. Walk the limestone massifs of Picos de Europa then follow the pilgrim route to lively Santiago de Compostela. Wind south through León, before challenging your senses with chaotic Madrid. Be captivated by Barcelona, then retrace Van Gogh's brushstrokes in Arles. Seek inspiration along the French Riviera before returning to gay Paree where you can dab your own impressions onto canvas.

NICOLA WILLIAMS

Fields of poppies, France

Celtic Crossing Crash the club scene in Old London Town, then turn north before your bank account heads south. At Cambridge, hear the majestic King's College choir, then nip up to medieval York, where you can visit the Lake District, and go on to romantic Edinburgh. At Inverness, spot bottlenose dolphins and hunt for the Loch Ness monster. Prime up with the 'weejies' at Glasgow before heading to Belfast. When you've had your fill of Guinness at Derry, fish for your dinner at Dingle Peninsula. Explore Killarney National Park, visit attractive Kilkenny and blether over a pint in an authentic Dublin boozer.

Ogle castles in Wales, visit the vibrant university capital Cardiff, catch some rays at Cornwall and check out Oxford, Cambridge's scholarly rival. Return to frenetic London via mystical Stonehenge and, for those seeking the Northern Lights, catch a cheap flight to Reykjavík.

RICHARD CUMMINS

Time for a pint? Dublin

Classic Romance In Paris, dunk croissants in a bowl of *café au lait*, reflect on past loves at Pont Neuf. Before Eiffel-saturation sets in, head to Strasbourg, then spice it up with a trek to Dijon. Spend a night in grand Lyon and gain some altitude at Grenoble in the stunning French Alps. Self-bronze and people-watch in Cannes and the cultured Riviera capital, Nice.

Notch another conquest in your passport by entering Italy via Monaco (where everyone's a princess), buy a sock in Milan (you can only afford one), then make a beeline for the gondolas of Venice. Back on land, soak up the passion and history of Florence – day trips to Pisa and Siena are a must! Be overawed by monumental Rome, then wend your way to energetic Naples and ancient Pompeii. Explore the spectacular Amalfi Coast, before island-hopping to Sicily – enjoy leisurely Palermo – and Malta, where architectural excellence beckons.

JULIET COOMBE

Carnevale, Venice

European Expeditions – Central Europe

Hellenic Odyssey Planning a journey of Homeric proportions is simple: city slickers will love Athens, home of the Acropolis and 2004 Olympic Games host. Travel overland via Trikala and Delphi (don't forget to pay your respects to the Oracle). Ruins of Apollo's temple stand near Corinth, but history doesn't get much older than at Mycenae. Amid olive groves, wander ancient ruins at Sparta before visiting Olympia, the original Olympic Games' venue.

Ferry from Patras to Ios, the bad boy of the Greek Isles, renowned for sun, sand and sex. Island-hop to Paros – famous for the pure white marble used to carve the *Venus de Milo* – before pumping up the pace at Mykonos. Bask on Naxos, a classic isle with sandy beaches and whitewashed houses. From volcanic Santorini, encircled by dramatic cliffs, visit Iraklio and charming Hania on Crete.

JOHN ELK III

Mighty ruins, Greece

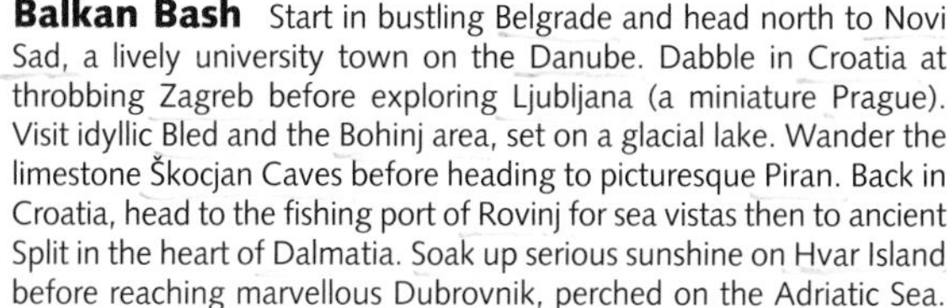

Balkan Bash Start in bustling Belgrade and head north to Novi Sad, a lively university town on the Danube. Dabble in Croatia at throbbing Zagreb before exploring Ljubljana (a miniature Prague). Visit idyllic Bled and the Bohinj area, set on a glacial lake. Wander the limestone Škocjan Caves before heading to picturesque Piran. Back in Croatia, head to the fishing port of Rovinj for sea vistas then to ancient Split in the heart of Dalmatia. Soak up serious sunshine on Hvar Island before reaching marvellous Dubrovnik, perched on the Adriatic Sea.

For a Bosnia-Hercegovina taster, visit medieval Mostar and dynamic Sarajevo. In Albania, listen to opera at Tirana (or visit the ubiquitous Irish pub), and discover Roman and Byzantine ruins at Durrës and the ancient city of Appollonia. Detour to Macedonia and see the Balkan's deepest lake at Ohrid or visit the museum-town Gjirokastra.

JON DAVISON

Get crispy in Croatia

Romantic Germanic-Slavic Tour Quaff beer and feast on sausage in Munich before receiving your culture injections at Zürich and Bern. Eat fondue in Geneva, windsurf at Lausanne, chill out at Interlaken, traverse the mighty peaks of the Jungfrau region and wander through scenic Lucerne From the tiny capital of Vaduz, head to Innsbruck, nestled in the valley of the River Inn. Catch Mozart mania in Salzburg, then relax at the beautiful Salzkammergut Lakes before waltzing your way to arts-soaked Vienna.

Escape the tourist trail with a visit to medieval Ceský Krumlov, and České Budějovice, the original home of Budvar (Budweiser). After a visit to historic Kutna Hora, revel in the fairy-tale romance of magical Prague. Day trip to the 14th-century Karlštejn Castle and Konopiště Chateau before the smell of bratwurst lures you back to Munich.

JONATHAN SMITH

Town Hall, Prague

Passport Puncher From cosmopolitan Frankfurt/Main, head to the swingin' university town of Göttingen. Be inspired by Bach at Leipzig and relive history at Dresden before catching a smoky cabaret in thriving Berlin. Follow brisk sea breezes to wonderful, wonderful Copenhagen. Explore Helsingør Castle, rock out at Roskilde and be barbaric at medieval Trelleborg's Viking rings. Cycle Odense, Hans Christian Andersen's hometown, and day trip to the renaissance Esgekov Castle. From Bagenkop via Kiel, pipe your way to Bremen via picturesque Lübeck and bridge-obsessed Hamburg. Relax in a canalside Amsterdam café, then hit the cobbled streets of The Hague, bustling Utrecht, edgy Rotterdam and old-world Maastricht.

Set world affairs straight at Brussels' EU headquarters, visit baroque Antwerp and experience the 'real' Belgium in Ghent. Day trip to medieval Bruges and see panoramic views from Luxembourg city.

MARTIN MOOS

Queen for a day, Holland

European Expeditions – Eastern & Scandinavian Europe

Ottoman Sweep From bustling Sofia tour the amazing striped Rila Monastery before heading to must-see Plovdiv. Admire picturesque Veliko Târnovo and the beach town of Varna on the Black Sea coast. Cruise the coastline to colourful İstanbul before joining the Aussies and Kiwis on their pilgrimage to Gallipoli.

Stay at Selçuk, amble the Roman ruins of Ephesus, and marvel at the monumental tomb of King Mausolus at Bodrum, before chilling out at superb beach towns Patara and Kaş. From the bustling harbour town of Antalya, set sail to Cyprus, the birthplace of the legendary goddess Aphrodite. Stop over in Side before heading to Konya, home of the whirling dervishes. At amazing Göreme explore its spectacular underground cities, 'fairy chimneys' and medieval frescoes, before passing through Ankara on the way back to İstanbul.

DIANA MAYFIELD

Underground Göreme

Glasnost & the Baltics Tread the historic Kremlin precinct at Moscow, navigate the canals that snake through St Petersburg and discover the glorious Hermitage museum. See classical Stalinist architecture at Tallinn and experience the chilling former-KGB cells at Tartu.

Ski the slopes at Valmiera and upgrade your athletic skills with a bobsled down the Olympic run at Sigulda. At Rīga, form your own boy band and try out for the Eurovision Song Contest. For something more sobering you can day trip to the concentration camp at Salaspils.

In Lithuania, head south to sea-port Klaipėda and discover the lush natural beauty of the Curonian Split. At Šiauliai see the Hill of Crosses, a forest of thousands of crosses planted in memory of those who were deported to Siberia. Finish up by passing through Kaunas (with its reputation for post-Soviet mafioso) to proud Vilnius.

DONALD C & PRISCILLA ALEXANDER EASTMAN

Onion domes, Tallinn

Arctic Adventure Put a dent in your pocket with some icy adventures: start at friendly Malmö, then swing by quiet Lund before visiting the beautiful capital of Stockholm and its gorgeous Gamla Stan (Old Town). Head from time-worn Turku to the intimate capital of Helsinki, power north to charming Kuopio and cycle the bike paths of Oulu.

Santa Claus can be real at Rovaniemi with some reindeer-sledding safaris; unwind at Sodankylä's Midnight Sun International Film Festival. Catch the boat from Narvik, and fish at the Lofoten Islands, spectacular peaks of glacier-carved mountains shooting from the sea. From Bodø head to medieval Trondheim, visit the hill-country of Balestrand, cultural Bergen and scenic Flåm. After receiving the Nobel Peace Prize in Oslo hit the sunny coast of Göthenburg.

CHRISTIAN ASLUND

Midnight skiing, Narvik

Buffer Against the West Tour the major Warsaw Pact areas that provided Russia with a 'shield' against Western democracy. From cosmopolitan Warsaw, head south to historical Kraków, then witness the eerie stillness of Auschwitz.

Proceed into Slovakia and check out the medieval walled town of Levoča and the canyons of Slovenský Raj National Park. Traverse the rugged Tatra Mountains (on foot or skis), be awe-inspired by the gentler natural beauty of the Malá Fatra hills before returning to the historic cityscape of lively Bratislava.

In Hungary, see medieval Sopron before journeying to unforgettable Budapest via the spectacular Danube Bend. Stop in at relaxed Cluj-Napoca, amble the cobbled streets of Sighişoara, marvel at the baroque facades in Braşov, and castle-spot at Râşnov. Sharpen your fangs at 'Dracula's' castle in Bran before heading south to Bucharest.

MARTIN MOOS

Thermal baths, Budapest

PAUL BERNHARDT

Set the pace in Portugal

MARTIN MOOS

Ice-skating outside the Hôtel de Ville in Paris

CHRISTOPHER GROENHOUT

Illuminating London

MARTIN MOOS

So, which country am I in again?

DAVID WALL

Thousand-year-old village of Eze on the stunning French Riviera

CHRISTOPHER WOOD

Magnificent fjord, Flåm

STEPHEN SAKS

Travelling in style!

ROCCO FASANO

Easy riders earn a well-deserved rest

Facts for the Visitor

Compared with several other destinations around the world, Europe is a well-developed and organised region. Indeed, it would certainly be possible to just chuck a few clothes in a suitcase and head overseas without a care in your heart, leaving all the planning for when you arrive. It's not worth extensive planning – anything you think of beforehand will sort itself out on the road, right?

Well, no. You can eschew most planning if you have a massive bank account just waiting to be depleted, but for most mortals this is not an option. For humbler folks, a bit of prior knowledge and careful preparation can make your travel budget stretch further than you ever thought possible. Furthermore, you'll be assured that the things you want to see and do will be open or available during the time that you visit, and you will avoid some nasty surprises. Sure, Europe is built-up and very accommodating of tourists – but when you're short on supplies and desperately looking for a place to crash, you might be shocked at how closely a rural Scottish town, for example, can resemble its Laotian counterparts.

Travellers who have not been to Europe before should cleanse their palate with a visit to the preceding Facts for the First-Time Visitor chapter, then head back here for some meat-and-potatoes information.

PLANNING

When to Go

Any time can be the best time to visit Europe, depending on your interests. Summer lasts roughly from June to September and offers the best weather for most outdoor pursuits in the northern half of Europe. In the southern half (Mediterranean coast, Iberian Peninsula, Morocco, southern Italy, Greece and Turkey), where the summers tend to be hotter, you can extend that period by one or perhaps even two months either way.

You'll be far from the only tourist in Europe during summer. All of France and Italy, for instance, goes on holiday in August. Prices can be high, accommodation fully booked and attractions packed. August is a difficult month for European travel – avoid beach resorts if possible, and branch out into Eastern Europe or Turkey until early Septmeber when the crowds in Western and southern Europe start to thin out .

Much better deals – and far fewer crowds – provide the allure of the shoulder seasons on either side of summer. In April and May, for instance, flowers are in bloom and the weather can be surprisingly mild. 'Indian summers' (prolonged periods of gorgeous weather) are common in September and October.

For those keen on winter sports, resorts in the Alps and the Pyrenees begin operating in late November and move into full swing after the New Year, closing down when the snows begin to melt in March, or even April.

The Climate and Planning sections in the individual country chapters explain what to expect and when to expect it.

As a rule, spring and autumn tend to be wetter and windier than summer and winter. The temperate maritime climate along the Atlantic is relatively wet all year, with moderate extremes in temperature. The Mediterranean coast is hotter and drier, with most rainfall occurring during the mild winter. The continental climate in central and Eastern Europe and the Alps tends to show much stronger extremes in weather between summer and winter.

Books & Maps

Lonely Planet produces a wide range of travel guides and other books to complement and expand on the information provided in this book. The guide you're holding right now is tailored for travellers who wish to see a great deal of Europe without spending an incredible amount of money. Other books provide more in-depth information on specific areas and cater to a wider range of budgets.

As well as more detailed regional titles to Western, Mediterranean, Eastern, Central and Scandinavian Europe, Lonely Planet publishes individual guides to most of the countries in this book, as well as to regions within some countries. That's how dedicated we are.

Lonely Planet also publishes city guides to some of Europe's great capitals (London, Paris, Rome, Berlin, Amsterdam, Dublin, etc) and walking guides to Britain, Italy, Turkey, Switzerland and more. For cyclists we have created cycling guides to Britain and France, and for foodies the Lonely Planet World Food series covers Ireland, Italy, Morocco, Spain and Turkey. Budding photographers can improve their technique with a copy of Lonely Planet's *Travel Photography: A Guide to Taking Better Pictures*.

Good maps are easy to come by once you're in Europe, but you might want to buy a few beforehand to plan your route. The maps in this book will help you get an idea of where you might want to go and will be a useful reference when you arrive in a city. Lonely Planet also publishes plastic-coated full-colour maps to some of Europe's greatest cities – Amsterdam, Barcelona, Berlin, Brussels, Budapest, Dublin, Istanbul, London, Paris, Prague and Rome – with a full index of streets and sights plus transit routes and walking tours.

Proper road maps are essential if you're driving or cycling. You can't go wrong with Michelin maps. Some people prefer the maps meticulously produced by Freytag & Berndt, Kümmerly & Frey and Hallwag. As a rule, maps published by European automobile associations (the AA in Britain, the ADAC and AvD in Germany etc) are excellent and sometimes free if membership of your local association gives you reciprocal rights. Tourist offices are often another good source for (usually free and fairly basic) maps.

What to Bring

It's very easy to find almost anything you need in most European countries and, since you'll probably buy things as you go along, it's better to start with too little rather than too much. Check out the packing list in the Facts for the First-Time Visitor chapter.

As for clothing, remember that insulation works on the principle of trapped air, so several layers of thin clothing are warmer than a single thick one (and will be easier to dry). You'll also be much more flexible if the weather suddenly turns warm. Just be prepared for rain at any time of year.

A padlock is useful to lock your bag to a luggage rack in a bus or train; it may also be needed to secure your hostel locker. During city sightseeing, a small daypack is better than a shoulder bag at deterring thieves.

A Swiss Army knife comes in handy for all sorts of things. Any pocketknife is fine, but make sure it includes such essentials as a bottle opener and strong corkscrew! Just remember that on flights from the USA, and most airports, you'll probably have to pack your knife in checked luggage.

Toiletries are readily available almost anywhere, but you will need your own supply of paper in many public toilets and those at camping grounds. Tampons are available at pharmacies and supermarkets in all but the most remote places. Condoms, both locally made and imported, are widely available throughout Europe. That said, it's easier to find quality condoms and the like in France than it is in, say, Turkey or Albania.

A tent and sleeping bag are vital if you want to save money by camping. Even if you're not camping, a sleeping bag is still very useful. A sleeping sheet with pillow cover (case) is necessary if you plan to stay in hostels; otherwise, you may have to hire or purchase one.

Other optional items to consider include a compass, a flashlight (torch), a calculator for currency conversions, an adapter plug for electrical appliances, a universal bath/sink plug (an empty film canister will sometimes work), a few clothes pegs and a large cotton handker-chief that you can soak in water fountains and use to cool yourself off, while touring cities during the hot European summer months.

RESPONSIBLE TOURISM

We don't want to get too preachy here, but it's essential to remember that as a visitor, you have a responsibility to the local people and to the environment. For guidelines on how to avoid offending the people you meet, read the following Appearances & Conduct section. When it comes to the environment, the key rules are to preserve natural resources and to leave the countryside as you find it. Those Alpine flowers look much better on the mountainside than squashed in your pocket (many species are protected anyway).

Littering is irresponsible and offensive. Mountain areas have fragile ecosystems; stick to prepared paths wherever possible and always carry your rubbish away with you. Don't use detergents or toothpaste in or near watercourses, even if they are biodegradable. If you just gotta go when you're out in the wilderness, bury human waste in holes at least 15cm deep and at least 100m from any watercourse.

Recycling is a way of life in countries such as Austria, Germany and Switzerland, and you will be encouraged to follow suit. Traffic congestion on the roads is a major problem, and visitors will do themselves and residents a favour if they forgo driving and use public transport.

Appearances & Conduct

Although dress standards are fairly informal in northern Europe, your clothes may have significant bearing on how you're treated in southern Europe (especially in Spain, Portugal, Italy and Greece, as well as Turkey and Morocco).

Dress casually, but keep your clothes clean, and ensure sufficient body cover (trousers or a knee-length dress) if your sightseeing includes churches, monasteries, synagogues or mosques. In most Muslim countries, including Morocco and Turkey, women or men in shorts or sleeveless shirts are virtually in their underwear in the eyes of more conservative locals. Even in non-Muslim countries, wearing shorts away from the beach or camping ground is not very common among men. Some nightclubs and fancy restaurants may refuse entry to people wearing jeans, a tracksuit or sneakers (trainers).

While nude bathing is usually restricted to certain beaches, topless bathing is very common in many parts of Europe. Nevertheless, women should be wary of taking their tops off as a matter of course. The rule is that if nobody else seems to be doing it, you shouldn't either.

Most border guards and immigration officials are too professional to judge people entirely on their appearance, but first impressions do count. You may find life easier if you are well presented when dealing with officialdom. Most Europeans have a 'been there, done that' opinion of hair length. Nevertheless, the 'long hair = despicable hippie' syndrome still survives in some places (Morocco, for example).

You'll soon notice that Europeans are heavily into shaking hands and even kissing when they greet one another. Don't worry about the latter with those you don't know too well, but get into the habit of shaking hands with virtually everyone you meet. In many parts of Europe, it's also customary to greet the proprietor when entering a shop, café or quiet bar, and to say goodbye when you leave.

Going Against the Grain

In general, carefully observing the actions of the nontravellers around you, respecting their behaviour and emulating it to a degree provide good rules for responsible travel. However, there are occasionally times when local denizens provide a poor act to follow. Often in less-developed areas, residents will demonstrate no qualms about littering freely, harassing strangers (especially women) and exhibit utter disdain for their surroundings or the comfort of others. In such situations, it's easy to despair – after all, what difference can one well-behaved traveller make?

While we certainly don't advocate lecturing citizens on how to live their lives and treat their land, you can avoid being part of the problem by refusing to join in with the destructive behaviour. Remember: as a foreigner, you will be viewed as something of an ambassador of your people. Keep this in mind when you decide how to present yourself – and represent others.

VISAS & DOCUMENTS

Passport

Your most important travel document is your passport. Many countries require that your passport remain valid for at least six month after you *leave*. If your passport is just about to expire, renew it before you go. This may not be easy to do overseas.

Applying for or renewing a passport can take anything from an hour to several months, so don't leave it till the last minute. Bureaucratic wheels usually turn faster if you do everything in person rather than relying on the post or agents, but check first what you need to take with you (photos of a certain size, birth certificate, population register extract, signed statements, exact payment in cash etc).

US citizens must apply in person (but may usually renew by mail) at a US Passport Agency office or at some courthouses and post offices. Australian citizens can apply at a post office or the passport office in their state capital; Britons can pick up application forms from major post offices, and the passport is issued by the regional passport office; Canadians can apply at regional passport offices; New Zealanders can apply at any district office of the Department of Internal Affairs.

Once you start travelling, carry your passport on your person at all times and be sure to guard it carefully. Camping grounds and hotels sometimes inconveniently insist that you hand over your passport for the duration of your stay, but a driving licence or Camping Card International usually solves the problem.

Citizens of the European Union (EU) and those from certain other European countries (eg, Switzerland) don't need a valid passport to travel to another EU country or even some non-EU countries; a national identity card is sufficient. If you want to exercise this option, check with your travel agent or the embassies of the countries you plan to visit.

Visas

A visa is a stamp in your passport or on a separate piece of paper permitting you to enter the country in question and stay for a specified period of time. Often you can get the visa at the border or at the airport on arrival, but not always. Check first with the embassies or consulates of the countries you plan to visit. This option is seldom available on train travel.

There's a wide variety of visas, including tourist, transit and business ones. Transit visas are usually cheaper than tourist or business visas, but they only allow a very short stay (one or two days) and can be difficult to extend. Fortunately for citizens of the USA, Canada, Australia and the UK, most European countries require no visas for folks from those nations. With a valid passport they'll be able to visit most European countries for up to three (sometimes even six) months, provided they have some sort of onward or return ticket and/or 'sufficient means of support' (money).

In line with the Schengen Agreement there are no passport controls at the borders between Austria, Belgium, Denmark, Finland, France, Germany, Iceland, Italy, Greece, Luxembourg, the Netherlands, Norway, Portugal, Spain and Sweden, Portugal; an identity card should suffice, but it's always safest to carry your passport. The other EU countries (Britain, and Ireland) are not yet full members of Schengen and still maintain low-key border controls over traffic from other EU countries.

Border procedures between EU and non-EU countries can still be fairly thorough, though citizens of Australia, Canada, Israel, Japan, New Zealand, Norway, Switzerland and the USA do not need visas for tourist visits to any Schengen country.

All non-EU citizens visiting a Schengen country and intending to stay for longer than three days or to visit another Schengen country are supposed to obtain an official entry stamp in their passport either at the point of entry or from the local police within 72 hours. This is very loosely enforced, however, and in general registering at a hotel will be sufficient.

For those who do require visas, it's important to remember that these will have a 'use-by' date, and you'll be refused entry after that period has elapsed. It may not be checked when entering these countries overland, but major problems can arise if it is requested during your stay or on departure and you can't produce it.

Visa requirements can change, and you should always check with the individual embassies or a reputable travel agent before travelling. In some cases it's easier to get your visas as you go along, rather than arranging them all beforehand. Notable exceptions include Russia (for St Petersburg or Moscow) and the Baltic states. Carry spare passport photos (you may need from one to four every time you apply for a visa).

Eastern Europe Visas are usually issued immediately by consulates in Eastern Europe, although some may levy a 50% to 100% surcharge for 'express service'. Nationals requiring visas (everyone needs one for Russia) are strongly advised to get them at a consulate beforehand and not to rely on it being available at every border crossing. They're often cheaper in your home country anyway.

Consulates are generally open weekday mornings (if there's both an embassy and a consulate, you want the consulate). Consulates in countries not neighbouring the one you want to visit are far less crowded (for example, get your Polish visa in Bucharest, your Hungarian visa in Sofia or Warsaw, your Slovakian visa in Zagreb etc). Take your own pen and be sure to have a good supply of passport photos that actually look like you (if such a thing exists).

Travel Insurance

A travel-insurance policy to cover theft, loss and medical problems is a good idea. The policies handled by STA Travel and other student travel organisations are usually good value. Some policies offer lower and higher medical-expense options; the higher ones are chiefly for countries such as the USA that have extremely high medical costs. There is a wide variety of policies available, so check the small print.

Some policies specifically exclude 'dangerous activities', which can include scuba diving, motorcycling and even trekking. A locally acquired motorcycle licence is not valid under some policies.

You may prefer a policy that pays doctors or hospitals directly rather than having you pay on the spot and claim later. If you have to claim later, make sure you keep all documentation. Some policies ask you to call back (reverse charges) to a centre in your home country, where an immediate assessment of your problem is made. Check that the policy covers ambulances or an emergency flight home.

International Driving Permit

Many non-European driving licences are valid in Europe, but it's still a good idea to get an International Driving Permit (IDP) if you intend to drive. This little document (basically a translation of the vehicle class and personal details noted on your own licence) can make life much simpler when hiring cars and motorcycles. An IDP is not valid unless accompanied by your original licence. One can be obtained for a small fee from your local automobile association – bring along a passport photo and a valid licence.

Hostel Cards

A hostelling card is useful – if not always mandatory – for those staying at hostels (particularly HI hostels). Some hostels in Europe don't require that you be a hostelling association member, but they will often charge less if you have a hostelling card. Many hostels will issue one on the spot or after a few stays, though this might cost a bit more than getting it in your home country. See Hostels under Accommodation later in this chapter for more information.

Camping Card International

The Camping Card International (CCI; formerly the Camping Carnet) is a camping ground ID that can be used instead of a passport when checking into a camp site and includes third-party insurance. As a result, many camping grounds offer a small discount if you sign in with one. CCIs are issued by automobile associations, camping federations and, sometimes, on the spot at camping grounds. In the UK, the AA issues them to its members for UK£4.50.

Student & Youth Cards

The most useful of these is the International Student Identity Card (ISIC), a plastic ID-style card with your photograph, which provides substantial discounts on many forms of transport (including airlines and local public transport), cheap or free admission to museums and sights, and inexpensive meals in some student cafeterias and restaurants.

If you're under 26 but not a student, you can apply for a GO25 card issued by the Federation of International Youth Travel Organisations (FIYTO) or the Euro26 card, both of which go under different names in various countries. Both give much the same discounts and benefits as an ISIC. All these cards are issued by student unions, hostelling organisations or youth-oriented travel agencies such as STA and Council Travel. You can also get information on the Web (W www.istc.org).

Seniors Cards

Museums and other sights, public swimming pools and spas and transport companies frequently offer discounts to retired people, old age pensioners and those over 60 (slightly younger for women). Make sure you bring proof of age – that suave signore in Italy or that polite Parisian mademoiselle is not going to believe you're a day over 39.

European nationals aged over 60 can get a Railplus (formerly Rail Europe Senior) Card. For more information see Rail Passes & Cheap Train Tickets in the Getting Around chapter.

International Health Certificate

You'll need this yellow booklet only if you're arriving in Europe from certain parts of Asia, Africa and South America, where diseases such as yellow fever are prevalent. Otherwise, don't sweat it.

CUSTOMS

Duty-free goods are no longer sold to those travelling from one EU country to another. For goods purchased at airports or on ferries outside the EU, the usual allowances apply for tobacco (200 cigarettes, 50 cigars or 250g of loose tobacco), alcohol (1L of spirits or 2L of liquor with less than 22% alcohol by volume;

2L of wine) and perfume (50g of perfume and 0.25L of toilet water).

Do not confuse these with duty-paid items (including alcohol and tobacco) bought at normal shops and supermarkets in another EU country, where certain goods might be more expensive. (Cigarettes in France, for example, are half the price they are in the UK.) Then the allowances are more than generous: 800 cigarettes, 200 cigars or 1kg of loose tobacco; 10L of spirits (more than 22% alcohol by volume), 20L of fortified wine or aperitif, 90L of wine or 110L of beer; unlimited quantities of perfume.

MONEY

Exchanging Money

As of 1 January 2002, most EU countries use the single currency called the euro. While many folks bemoan the loss of their beloved francs, marks, pesetas and drachmas, the euro makes life a lot easier for the traveller – especially since its value hovers close to that of the US dollar.

Exchange rates at the time of writing were:

country	unit		euro
America	US$1	=	€1
Australia	AUS$1	=	€0.57
Japan	¥100	=	€0.82
New Zealand	NZ$1	=	€0.50
United Kingdom	UK£1	=	€1.60

In general, US dollars and euros are the most easily exchanged currencies in Europe. You lose out through commissions and customer exchange rates every time that you change money, so if you only visit Norway, for example, you may be better off buying kroner straight away if kroner are available from your bank at home.

Nearly all European currencies are fully convertible, but you may have trouble exchanging some of the lesser-known ones at small banks. The importation and exportation of certain currencies (eg, Moroccan dirham) is restricted or banned entirely, so try to get rid of any local currency before you leave the country. Get rid of Scottish and Northern Irish pounds before leaving the UK; nobody outside Britain will touch them.

Most airports, central train stations, big hotels and many border posts have banking facilities outside normal office hours, sometimes on a 24-hour basis. You'll often find automatic exchange machines outside banks or tourist offices that accept the currencies of up to two dozen countries. Post offices in Europe often perform banking tasks, tend to be open longer hours, and outnumber banks in remote places. Be aware, though, that while they always exchange cash, they might balk at handling travellers cheques unless they're denominated in the local currency.

The best exchange rates are usually at banks. Bureaux de change usually – but not always – offer worse rates or charge higher commissions. Hotels are almost always the worst places to change money. American Express (AmEx) and Thomas Cook offices usually do not charge commission for changing their own cheques, but may offer a less favourable exchange rate than banks.

Cash Nothing beats cash for convenience …or risk. If you lose it, it's gone forever and very few travel insurers will come to your rescue. Those that do will limit the amount to somewhere around US$300/UK£200. For tips on carrying your money safely, see Theft in the Dangers & Annoyances section, later in this chapter.

It's still a good idea, though, to bring some local currency in cash, if only to tide you over until you get to an exchange facility or find an automatic teller machine (ATM). The equivalent of, say, US$50 or US$100 should usually be enough. Some extra cash in an easily exchanged currency (eg, US dollars or German marks) is also a good idea, especially in Eastern Europe.

Many travellers stash a small amount of emergency funds in their sock or into a special, difficult-to-access pocket. This may be a lifesaver in drastic situations; figure out whether it's worth it for you.

Travellers Cheques The exchange rate for travellers cheques, in most European countries these days, is slightly better than the exchange rate for cash.

The main idea of carrying travellers cheques rather than cash is the protection they offer from theft, though they are losing their popularity as more travellers – including those on tight budgets – deposit their money in their bank at home and withdraw it as they go along using ATMs.

AmEx, Visa and Thomas Cook travellers cheques are widely accepted and have efficient replacement policies. If you're going to remote places, it's worth sticking to AmEx, since small local banks may not always accept other brands.

When you change cheques, don't look at just the exchange rate; ask about fees and commissions as well. There may be a service fee per cheque, a flat transaction fee or a percentage of the total amount irrespective of the number of cheques. Some banks charge fees (often exorbitant) to cash cheques and not cash; others do the reverse.

Cheques are available in various currencies, but ones denominated in US dollars, British pounds and euros are the easiest to cash. Still, you may not be comfortable using a currency you're not familiar with and watching it converted into still another (eg, an Australian cashing pound sterling cheques into Finnish markka).

Keeping a record of the cheque numbers and those you have used is vital when it comes to replacing lost travellers cheques. You should keep this separate from the cheques themselves.

Credit Cards & ATMs If you are not familiar with the many options available, ask your bank to explain the workings, and the relative merits of credit, credit/debit, debit, charge and cash cards.

A major advantage of credit cards is that they allow you to pay for expensive items (eg, airline tickets) without your having to carry great wads of cash around. They also allow you to withdraw cash at selected banks or from the many ATMs that are linked up internationally. However, if an ATM in Europe swallows a card that was issued outside Europe, it can be a major headache. Also, some credit cards aren't hooked up to ATM networks unless you specifically ask your bank to do this.

Cash cards, which you use at home to withdraw money directly from your bank account or savings account, can be used throughout Europe at ATMs linked to international networks like Cirrus and Maestro.

Credit and credit/debit cards such as Visa and MasterCard are widely accepted. MasterCard is linked to Europe's extensive Eurocard system, and Visa (sometimes called Carte Bleue) is particularly strong in France and Spain. However, these cards often have a credit limit that is too low to cover major expenses like long-term car rental or airline tickets and can be difficult to replace if lost abroad. Also, when you get a cash advance against your Visa or MasterCard credit card account, your issuer charges a transaction fee and/or finance charge. With some issuers, the fees can reach as high as US$10 plus interest per transaction, so it's best to check with your card issuer before leaving home and it's useful to the compare rates.

Charge cards such as AmEx and Diners Club have offices in the major cities of most countries that will replace a lost card within 24 hours. However, charge cards are not widely accepted off the beaten track.

The best advice is not to put all your eggs in one basket. If you want to rely heavily on bits of plastic, go for two different cards, an AmEx or Diners Club, for instance, along with a Visa or MasterCard. Better still is a combination of credit or cash card and travellers cheques so you have something to fall back on if an ATM swallows your card or the banks in the area are closed.

A word of warning: fraudulent shopkeepers have been known to quickly make several charge slip imprints with your credit card when you're not looking, and then simply copy your signature from the one that you authorise. Don't let your card out of sight, and always check your statements upon your return.

International Transfers Telegraphic transfers can occasionally be ridiculously expensive. Despite their name, they can also be quite slow. Be sure to specify the name of the bank and the name and address of the branch where you'd like to pick it up.

It's quicker and easier to have money wired via an AmEx office (US$60 for US$1000). Western Union's Money Transfer system (available at post offices in some countries) and Thomas Cook's MoneyGram service are also popular.

Black Market A 'black market' exists whenever a government puts restrictions on free currency trading through regulations that prohibit banks and licensed foreign-exchange dealers from changing the national currency into 'hard' currency. A black market is eliminated overnight when a currency is made internally convertible, the way that most

Eastern European currencies have gone. Therefore, the days when you could get five times the official rate for cash on the streets of Warsaw and Bucharest are gone for good.

Changing money on the street is extremely risky, not only because it is illegal, but because many of the people offering to change are professional thieves with years of experience in cheating tourists. We absolutely do not recommend that you use the black market – these days it is simply too risky, and the rates on offer are usually no better than those on offer at the bank.

Guaranteed Cheques Another way of carrying money or obtaining cash is by guaranteed personal cheque. Eurocheques, available if you have a European bank account, are guaranteed up to a certain limit. When cashing them (eg, at post offices), you will be asked to show your Eurocheque card bearing your signature and registration number, and perhaps a passport or ID card. Your Eurocheque card should be kept separately from the cheques. Many hotels and merchants refuse to accept Eurocheques because of the relatively large commissions.

Costs

The secret to budget travel in Europe is cheap accommodation. Europe has a highly developed network of camping grounds and hostels, some of them quite luxurious, and they're great places to meet people.

Other money-saving strategies include preparing your own meals and avoiding alcohol, using a student card and buying any of the various rail and public transport passes (see the Getting Around chapter). Also remember that the more time you spend in any one place, the lower your daily expenses are likely to be as you get to know your way around.

Including transport (but not private motorised transport), your daily expenses could work out to around €35 to €40 a day if you are operating on a rock-bottom budget. This means camping or staying in hostels, eating economically and using a transport pass. Travelling on a moderate budget, you would be able to manage on €60 to €80 a day. This would allow you to stay at cheap hotels, guesthouses or B&Bs, eat at cheap restaurants and savour the occasional beer.

Be warned that these budgets are rough estimates. Daily expenses will be much higher (€10 to €15 extra per day) if you spend all your time in Paris and London, or travel exclusively in Scandinavian countries. Conversely, you will spend less per day in Eastern Europe (though not in Prague or Budapest), Greece, Portugal, Turkey and Morocco.

For more information on budgeting, see under Costs & Money in the Facts for the First-Time Visitor chapter.

A general warning about the prices we list in this book: they're likely to change, usually moving upward, but if last season was particularly slow they may remain the same or even come down a bit. Nevertheless, relative price levels should stay fairly constant. If hotel A costs twice as much as hotel B, it's likely to stay that way.

Tipping & Bargaining

In many European countries it's usually common for a service charge to be added onto restaurant bills, in which case no tipping is necessary. In other countries, simply rounding up the bill is often sufficient. For more details about tipping, see the individual country chapters.

Taxes & Refunds

A kind of sales tax called value-added tax (VAT) applies to most goods and services in many European countries. In most countries, visitors can claim back the VAT on purchases that are being taken out of the country. Those actually residing in one EU country are not entitled to a refund on VAT paid on goods bought in another EU country. Thus, an American citizen living in London is not entitled to a VAT rebate on items bought in Paris, while an EU passport holder residing in New York is.

The procedure for making the claim is fairly straightforward, though it may vary somewhat from country to country, and there are minimum-purchase amounts imposed. First of all, make sure the shop offers duty-free sales (often identified with a sign reading 'Tax-Free for Tourists').

When making your purchase, ask the shop attendant for a VAT-refund voucher (sometimes called a Tax-Free Shopping Cheque) filled in with the correct amount and the date. This can either be refunded directly at international airports on departure or stamped at ferry ports or border crossings and mailed back for refund.

POST & COMMUNICATIONS

Post

From major European centres, air mail typically takes about five days to North America and about a week to Australasian destinations though mail from the UK can be much faster and from Greece much slower. Postage costs vary from country to country, as does post office efficiency.

You can collect mail from poste restante sections at major post offices. Ask people writing to you to print your name clearly and capitalise and underline your surname. When collecting mail, your passport may be required for identification and you may have to pay a small fee. If an expected letter is not awaiting you, ask to check under your given name; letters commonly get misfiled. Post offices usually hold mail for about a month, but sometimes less (in Germany, for instance, they hold mail for two weeks only). Unless the sender specifies otherwise, mail will always be sent to the city's main post office.

You can also have mail (but not parcels) sent to you at AmEx offices as long as you have an AmEx card or are carrying AmEx travellers cheques. When you buy the cheques, ask for a booklet listing all the AmEx offices worldwide.

Telephone

You can ring abroad from almost any phone box in Europe. Public telephones accepting stored-value phonecards (available from post offices, telephone centres, newsstands or retail outlets) are virtually the norm now; in some countries, France for example, coin-operated phones are almost impossible to find.

Lonely Planet's eKno global communication service provides low-cost international calls, a range of innovative messaging services, an online travel vault where you can securely store all your important documents, free email and travel information, all in one easy service. You can join online at W www.ekno.lonelyplanet.com, where you can also find the best local access numbers to connect to the 24-hour customer service centre. Once you have joined, check the eKno website for the latest access numbers for each country and updates on new features. For local calls, you're usually better off with a local card.

Without a phonecard, you can ring from a telephone booth inside a post office or telephone centre and settle your bill at the counter.

> **Fax for the Visitor**
>
> Apart from any urgent business-related correspondence you might be sending to the home office, you probably won't be using fax machines a whole lot while in Europe. If, by some chance, you do need access to fax services, the central post office will usually take good care of you.

Reverse-charge (collect) calls are often possible, but not always. From many countries, however, the Country Direct system lets you phone home by billing the long-distance carrier you use at home. These numbers can often be dialled from public phones without even inserting a phonecard.

Email & Internet Access

The vast majority of shoestring travellers in Europe rely on Internet 'cafés' (more and more a misnomer these days) to keep in cyber-touch. If this is the route you're going, you'll need to carry three pieces of information with you so you can access your Internet mail account: your incoming (POP or IMAP) mail server name, your account name and your password. Your Internet Service Provider (ISP) or network supervisor will give you these. Armed with this information, you should be able to access your Internet mail account from any Internet-connected machine in the world, provided it runs some kind of email software. It pays to become familiar with the process for doing this before you leave home.

A far more popular option to collect mail through Internet cafés is to open a free Web-based email account on-line (you can do this at W www.ekno.lonelyplanet.com, W www.yahoo.com, W www.hotmail.com or a number of other sites). You can then access your mail from anywhere in the world from any Net-connected machine running a standard Web browser.

You'll find Internet cafés throughout Europe. Check out the country chapters in this book, and see W www.netcafeguide.com for an up-to-date list. You may also find public Internet access in post offices, libraries, hostels, hotels, universities and so on.

To find out more information about travelling with a portable computer, see W www.teleadapt.com and also W www.warrior.com. Major ISPs such as **AOL** (W *www.aol.com*), **CompuServe** (W *www.compuserve.com*) and

IBM Net *(W www.ibm.com)* have dial-in nodes throughout Europe; it's best to download a list of the dial-in numbers before you leave home.

DIGITAL RESOURCES

The World Wide Web is a rich resource for travellers. You can research your trip, hunt for bargain air fares, book hotels, check on weather conditions or chat with locals and other travellers about the best places to visit (or avoid!).

The following websites offer useful information about Europe, its cities, transport systems, currencies etc. Country-specific websites are listed in the relevant country chapters.

Lonely Planet There's no better place to start your Web explorations than the Lonely Planet website. Here you'll find succinct summaries on travelling to most places on earth, postcards from other travellers and the Thorn Tree bulletin board, where you can link up with a community of thousands of fellow travellers to ask questions before you go or dispense advice when you get back. You can also find travel news and updates to many of our most popular guidebooks, while the subWWWay section links you to the most useful travel resources elsewhere on the Web at W www.lonelyplanet.com

Tourist Offices This site lists tourist offices at home and around the world for most countries. W www.towd.com/

Rail Information Here you can check on train fares and schedules on the most popular routes in Europe, including information on rail and youth passes. W www.raileurope.com

Airline Information This popular site lists what airlines fly where, when and for how much. W www.travelocity.com

Airline Tickets At this site, you can name the price you're willing to pay for an airline seat and if an airline has an empty seat (for which it would rather get something than nothing) you could be lucky. W www.priceline.com

Currency Conversions A quick stop at this site will give you up-to-the-second exchange rates of hundreds of currencies worldwide. W www.xe.net/ucc

NEWSPAPERS & MAGAZINES

Keeping up with the news in English is obviously no problem in the UK or Ireland. In larger European towns you can buy the excellent *International Herald Tribune* on the day of publication, as well as the colourful but superficial *USA Today*. Among other English-language newspapers widely available are the *Guardian*, the *Financial Times* and the *Times*. *The European* weekly newspaper is also readily available, as are *Newsweek*, *Time* and the *Economist*.

VIDEO SYSTEMS

If you want to record or buy video tapes to play back home, you won't get a picture if the image registration systems are different. Europe generally uses PAL (France uses SECAM), which is incompatible with the North American and Japanese NTSC system. Australia also uses PAL.

PHOTOGRAPHY

Both where you'll be travelling and the weather will dictate what film to take or buy locally. In places like Ireland and Britain, where the sky is often overcast, photographers should bring high-speed film (eg, 200 to 400 ASA). For southern Europe (or northern Europe under a blanket of snow and sunny skies) slower film is the answer (eg, 100 to 200 ASA).

Film and camera equipment is available everywhere in Europe, but obviously shops in the larger cities and towns have a wider selection. Avoid purchasing film at major tourist centres (eg, at kiosks below the Eiffel Tower in Paris or at the Tower of London). Canisters may have been stored badly or have long passed their sell-by dates. They will certainly be ludicrously expensive.

TIME

The standard international time measurements, GMT and UTC, are identical, and both are calibrated to the prime meridian, which passes through Greenwich in England. For the sake of comparison, if it's noon in Britain (GMT/UTC) it's 4am on the US west coast (GMT/UTC minus eight hours), 7am on the US east coast (GMT/UTC minus five hours), 1pm in Paris (GMT/UTC plus one hour; also called Central European Time), 2pm in Greece (GMT/UTC plus two hours) and 10pm in Sydney (GMT/UTC plus 10 hours).

In most European countries, clocks are turned one hour ahead for daylight-saving time on the last Sunday in March, and turned back again on the last Sunday in October. During daylight-saving time, Britain and Ireland are GMT/UTC plus one hour, Central European Time is GMT/UTC plus two hours and Greece is GMT/UTC plus three hours.

ELECTRICITY

Voltage & Cycle

Most of Europe runs on 220V, 50Hz AC. The exceptions are the UK, which uses 240V, and Spain, which runs at 220V and sometimes at 125V, depending on the network (some houses can have both). Some old buildings and hotels in Italy (including Rome) might also have 125V. All EU countries were supposed to have been standardised at 230V by now, but like everything else in the EU, this is taking longer than anticipated.

Check the voltage and cycle (usually 50Hz) used in your home country. Most appliances that are set up for 220V will handle 240V without modifications (and vice versa); the same goes for 110V and 125V combinations. Just don't mix 110/125V with 220/240V without a transformer.

Several countries outside Europe (such as the USA and Canada) have 60Hz AC, which will affect the speed of electric motors even after the voltage has been adjusted to European values, so CD and tape players (where motor speed is all-important) will be useless. But things like electric razors, hair dryers, irons and radios will be fine.

Plugs & Sockets

The UK and Ireland use a design with three flat pins, two for current and one for earthing/grounding. Most of Continental Europe uses the 'europlug', which has two round pins. Many europlugs and some sockets don't have provision for grounding since most local home appliances are double-insulated; when provided, grounding usually consists of two contact points along the edge, although Italy, Greece and Switzerland use a third round pin in such a way that the standard two-pin plug still fits the sockets…most of the time.

If your plugs are of a different design, you'll need an adapter. Get one before you leave, since the adapters available in Europe usually go the other way. If you find yourself without one, however, a specialist electrical-supply shop should be able to help.

HEALTH

Travel health depends on your predeparture preparations, your day-to-day health care while travelling and how you handle any medical problem that does develop. Fortunately Europe is a fairly healthy place in which to travel. Your main risks are sunburn, insect bites, foot blisters and an upset stomach from overeating or drinking.

Predeparture Planning

Shots are not really necessary for Europe, but they may be an entry requirement if you're coming from an infected area. Yellow fever is the most likely requirement. If you're going to Europe with stopovers in Asia, Africa or South America, check with your travel agent or with the embassies of the countries you plan to visit.

There are, however, a few routine vaccinations that are recommended whether you're travelling or not, and this Health section assumes that you've had them: polio (usually administered during childhood), tetanus and diphtheria (usually administered together during childhood, with a booster shot every 10 years) and measles. See your physician or nearest health agency about these. You might also consider having an immunoglobulin or hepatitis A (Havrix) vaccine before extensive travels in southern Europe; a tetanus booster; an immunisation against hepatitis B before travelling to Malta; or a rabies (pre-exposure) vaccination.

All vaccinations should be recorded on an International Health Certificate (see that entry in the Visas & Documents section). Don't leave this till the last minute, as the vaccinations may have to be staggered over a period of time.

Make sure you're healthy before you start travelling. If you are going on a long trip, make sure your teeth are OK. If you wear glasses take a spare pair and your prescription.

If you require a particular medication, take an adequate supply as it may not be available locally. Take part of the packaging showing the generic name, rather than the brand, which will make getting replacements easier. It's a good idea to have a legible prescription or letter from your doctor to show that you legally use the medication.

Basic Rules

Food Salads and fruit should be safe throughout Europe, though care should be taken in Morocco, the more remote parts of Turkey and southern Europe. If you're at all unsure, wash fruits and vegies with purified water and peel foods where possible.

Ice cream is usually OK, but not if it has melted and been refrozen. Take great care with fish or shellfish (cooked mussels that haven't opened properly can be dangerous, for instance), and avoid undercooked meat.

If a place looks clean and well run and if the vendor also looks clean and healthy, then the food is probably safe. In general, places that are packed with travellers or locals will be fine. Be careful with food that has been cooked and left to go cold.

Picking mushrooms is a favourite pastime in some parts of Europe as autumn approaches, but make sure you don't eat any that haven't first been positively identified as safe. Many cities and towns have set up inspection tables at markets or at entrances to national parks to separate the good from the deadly.

Oh – and for those worried about mad cow disease and the ol' foot-and-mouth sickness, lay your anxieties to rest. The Europeans have successfully eliminated the threats posed by these illnesses and now maintain some of the highest standards for meat of any region worldwide.

Water Tap water is safe to drink in most parts of Europe. In countries where it is unsafe (noted in the relevant country chapters), bottled water is usually widely available and reasonably priced. Where tap water is unsafe to drink, don't use it to brush your teeth or wash your face. Try not to splash your mouth in showers, and avoid foods that may have been washed in tainted water (eg, salad, peeled fruits and vegetables). Also avoid ice cubes and the like.

Throughout Europe be wary of natural water unless you can be sure that there are no people or cattle upstream; run-off from fertilised fields is also a concern. If you are planning extended hikes where you have to rely on natural water, it may be useful to know about water purification.

The simplest way of purifying water is to boil it thoroughly. Technically this means boiling for 10 minutes, something that happens very rarely. Remember that at high altitude water boils at a lower temperature, so germs are less likely to be killed.

Simple filtering will not remove all dangerous organisms, so if you cannot boil water it should be treated chemically. Chlorine tablets (Puritabs, Steritabs or other brand names) will kill many – but not all – pathogens. Iodine is very effective in purifying water and is available in tablet form (such as Potable Aqua), but follow the directions carefully and remember that too much iodine can be harmful.

Medical Problems & Treatment

Local pharmacies or neighbourhood medical centres are good places to visit if you have a small medical problem and can explain what the problem is. Hospital casualty wards will help if it's more serious. US natives in particular might be astounded at the relatively low cost of health care in Europe.

Major hospitals and emergency numbers are mentioned in the various individual country chapters of this book. Tourist offices and hotels can put you on to a doctor or dentist, and your embassy or consulate will probably know one who speaks your language.

Environmental Hazards

Altitude Sickness Lack of oxygen at high altitudes (over 2500m) affects most people to some extent. Effects occur because less oxygen reaches the muscles and the brain, requiring the heart and lungs to compensate by working harder. Symptoms of Acute Mountain Sickness (AMS) usually develop during the first24 hours at high altitude but may be delayed up to three weeks. Mild symptoms include headache, lethargy, dizziness, difficulty sleeping and loss of appetite. AMS may become more severe without warning and can prove fatal. Severe symptoms include breathlessness, a dry, irritating cough (which may progress to the production of pink, frothy sputum), severe headache, lack of coordination and balance, confusion, irrational behaviour, vomiting, drowsiness and unconsciousness. There is no hard-and-fast rule as to what is too high: AMS has been fatal at 3000m, although 3500m to 4500m is the usual range.

Treat mild symptoms by resting at the same altitude until recovery, usually a day or two. Paracetamol or aspirin can be taken for headaches. If symptoms persist or become worse, however, immediate descent is necessary; even 500m can help. Drug treatments should never be used to avoid descent or to enable further ascent.

Heat Exhaustion & Heat Stroke Dehydration and salt deficiency can cause heat exhaustion. Take time to acclimatise to high temperatures, drink sufficient liquids and do not do anything too physically demanding.

Salt deficiency is characterised by fatigue, lethargy, headaches, giddiness and muscle cramps; salt tablets may help, but adding extra salt to your food is better.

Heat stroke is a serious, occasionally fatal condition that can occur if the body's heat-regulating mechanism breaks down and the body temperature rises to dangerous levels. Long, continuous periods of exposure to high temperatures and insufficient fluids can leave you vulnerable to heat stroke.

The symptoms are feeling unwell, not sweating very much (or at all) and a high body temperature (39°C to 41°C or 102°F to 106°F). Where sweating has ceased the skin becomes flushed and red. Severe, throbbing headaches and lack of coordination will also occur, and the sufferer may be confused or aggressive. Eventually the victim will become delirious or convulse. Hospitalisation is essential, but in the interim get victims out of the sun, remove their clothing, cover them with a wet sheet or towel and then fan continually. Give fluids if they are conscious.

Hypothermia Too much cold can be just as dangerous as too much heat. Be prepared for cold, wet or windy conditions even if you're just out walking.

Hypothermia occurs when the body loses heat faster than it can produce it and the core temperature of the body falls. It is surprisingly easy to progress from very cold to dangerously cold due to a combination of wind, wet clothing, fatigue and hunger, even if the air temperature is above freezing. It is best to dress in layers; silk, wool and some of the new artificial fibres are all good insulating materials. A hat is important, as a lot of heat is lost through the head. A strong, waterproof outer layer (and a 'space' blanket for emergencies) are essential. Carry basic supplies, including food containing simple sugars to generate heat quickly and fluid to drink.

Symptoms of hypothermia are exhaustion, numb skin (particularly toes and fingers), shivering, slurred speech, irrational or violent behaviour, lethargy, stumbling, dizzy spells, muscle cramps and violent bursts of energy. Sufferers may claim that they are warm and attempt to take off their clothes.

To treat mild hypothermia, first get the person out of the wind and/or rain, remove their clothing if it's wet and replace it with dry, warm clothing. Give them hot liquids – *not* alcohol – and some high-kilojoule (calorie), easily digestible food. Do not rub victims, instead allow them to warm themselves slowly. This should be enough to treat the early stages of hypothermia. The early recognition and treatment of mild hypothermia is the only way to prevent severe hypothermia, which is a critical condition.

Jet Lag A person experiences jet lag when travelling by air across more than three time zones (each time zone usually represents a one-hour time difference. It occurs because many of the functions of the human body (such as temperature, pulse rate and emptying of the bladder and bowels) are regulated by internal 24-hour cycles. When we travel long distances rapidly, our bodies take time to adjust to the 'new time' of our destination, and we may experience fatigue, disorientation, insomnia, anxiety, impaired concentration and loss of appetite. These effects will usually be gone within a few days of arrival, but to minimise the impact of jet lag:

- Rest for a few days prior to departure
- Try to select flight schedules that minimise sleep deprivation; arriving late in the day means you can go to sleep soon after you arrive. For very long flights, try to organise a stopover.
- Avoid excessive eating (which bloats the stomach) and alcohol (which causes dehydration) during the flight. Instead, drink plenty of noncarbonated, nonalcoholic drinks such as fruit juice or water.
- Avoid smoking
- Make yourself comfortable by wearing loose-fitting clothes and perhaps bringing an eye mask and earplugs to help you sleep
- Try to sleep at the appropriate time for the time zone you are travelling to

Motion Sickness Eating lightly before and during a trip will reduce the chances of motion sickness. If you are prone to motion sickness try to find a place that minimises movement – near the wing on aircrafts, close to midships on boats, near the centre on buses. Fresh air usually helps; reading and cigarette smoke do not. Commercial motion-sickness preparations, which can cause drowsiness, have to be taken before the trip commences. Ginger (available in capsule form) and peppermint (including mint-flavoured sweets) are natural preventatives.

Infectious Diseases

Stomach Problems Simple things like a change of water, food or climate can all cause a mild bout of diarrhoea, but a few rushed toilet trips with no other symptoms is not indicative of a major problem.

Dehydration is the main danger with any diarrhoea, particularly in children or the elderly, as dehydration can occur quite quickly. Under all circumstances fluid replacement (at least equal to the volume being lost) is the most important thing to remember. Weak black tea with a little sugar, soda water, or soft drinks allowed to go flat and diluted 50% with clean water are all good. With severe diarrhoea a rehydrating solution is preferable to replace minerals and salts lost. Lomotil or Imodium can be used to bring relief from the symptoms, but they do not actually cure the problem.

Viral gastroenteritis is caused not by bacteria but, as the name suggests, by a virus. It is characterised by stomach cramps, diarrhoea, and sometimes by vomiting and/or a slight fever. The only real way to treat it is to rest and drink lots of fluids.

Fungal Infections Fungal infections occur more commonly in hot weather and are usually found on the scalp, between the toes or fingers, in the groin (jock itch) and on the body (ringworm). You get ringworm (which is a fungal infection, not a worm) from infected animals or other people. Moisture encourages these infections.

To prevent fungal infections wear loose, comfortable clothes, avoid artificial fibres, wash frequently and dry carefully. If you do get an infection, wash the infected area at least daily with a disinfectant or medicated soap and water, and rinse and dry well. Apply an antifungal cream or powder like tolnifate (Tinaderm). Try to expose the infected area to air or sunlight as much as possible and wash all towels and underwear in hot water, change them often and let them dry in the sun.

Hepatitis This is a general term for inflammation of the liver. It is a common disease worldwide. The symptoms are fever, chills, headache, fatigue, feelings of weakness and aches and pains, followed by loss of appetite, nausea, vomiting, abdominal pain, dark urine, light-coloured faeces, jaundiced (yellow) skin and the whites of the eyes may turn yellow. Hepatitis A is transmitted by contaminated food and drinking water. You should seek medical advice, but there is not much you can do apart from resting, drinking lots of fluids, eating lightly and avoiding fatty foods. People who have had hepatitis should avoid alcohol for some time after the illness, as the liver needs time to recover.

There are almost 300 million chronic carriers of hepatitis B in the world. It is spread through contact with infected blood, blood products or body fluids, for example through sexual contact, unsterilised needles and blood transfusions, or contact with blood via small breaks in the skin. Other risk situations include having a shave, tattoo, or having your body pierced with contaminated equipment. The symptoms of type B may be more severe and may lead to long-term problems.

HIV & AIDS HIV, the Human Immunodeficiency Virus, invariably develops into AIDS (Acquired Immune Deficiency Syndrome), which is a fatal disease. HIV is a major problem in many European countries, especially France. Any exposure to blood, blood products or body fluids may put the individual at risk. The disease is often transmitted through sexual contact or dirty needles; vaccinations, acupuncture, tattooing and body piercing can be potentially as dangerous as intravenous drug use. HIV/AIDS can also be spread through infected blood transfusions; some developing countries do not screen blood used for transfusions. Fear of HIV infection should never preclude treatment for serious medical conditions.

Sexually Transmitted Diseases Gonorrhoea, herpes and syphilis are among these diseases; sores, blisters or rashes around the genitals, discharges or pain when urinating are common symptoms. With some STDs, such as wart virus or chlamydia, symptoms may be less marked or not observed at all – especially in women. Syphilis symptoms eventually disappear completely, but the disease continues and can cause severe problems in later years. While abstinence from sexual contact is the only 100% effective method of prevention, using condoms is also effective. The treatment of gonorrhoea and syphilis is with antibiotics. The different sexually transmitted diseases each require specific antibiotics. There is no cure for herpes or AIDS.

Cuts, Bites & Stings

Bedbugs & Lice Bedbugs live in various places, but particularly in dirty mattresses and bedding, evidenced by spots of blood on bedclothes or on the wall. Bedbugs leave itchy bites in neat rows. Calamine lotion or a sting relief spray may help.

All lice cause itching and discomfort. They will live in your hair (head lice), your clothing (body lice) or in your pubic hair (crabs). You catch lice through direct contact with infected people or by sharing combs, clothing and the like. Powder or shampoo treatment will kill the lice, and infected clothing should then be washed in very hot, soapy water and left in the sun to dry.

Bites & Stings Bee and wasp stings are often more painful than they are dangerous. However, in people who are allergic to them severe breathing difficulties may occur and require urgent medical care. Calamine lotion or a sting relief spray will give relief and ice packs will reduce the pain and swelling.

Mosquitoes can be a nuisance in southern and Eastern Europe, but can almost drive you insane during the summer months in northern Europe, particularly around lakes and rivers. They can also cause sleepless nights in a swampy country like the Netherlands. Fortunately, mosquito-borne diseases like malaria are for the most part unknown in Western Europe. Most people get used to mosquito bites after a few days as their bodies adjust, and the itching and swelling will become less severe. An antihistamine cream may help alleviate the symptoms. For some people, a daily dose of vitamin B will keep mosquitoes at bay.

Midges – small, blood-sucking flies related to mosquitoes – are a major problem in some parts of Europe (eg, Scotland and parts of England) during summer.

Ticks You should always check all over your body if you have been walking through a potentially tick-infested area, as ticks can cause skin infections and other more serious diseases. If a tick is found attached, press down around the tick's head with tweezers, grab the head and gently pull upwards. Avoid pulling the rear of the body as this may squeeze the tick's gut contents through the attached mouth parts into the skin, increasing the risk of infection and disease. Smearing chemicals on the tick will not make it let go and is not recommended.

Lyme disease is a tick-transmitted infection that may be acquired in parts of southern Europe. The illness usually begins with a spreading rash at the site of the tick bite and is accompanied by fever, headache, extreme fatigue, aching joints and muscles and mild neck stiffness. If untreated, these symptoms usually resolve over several weeks but over subsequent weeks or months disorders of the nervous system, heart and joints may develop. Treatment works best early in the illness. Medical help should be sought.

Another tick that can bring on more than just an itch is the forest tick, which burrows under the skin, causing inflammation and even encephalitis. It has become a common problem in parts of central and Eastern Europe, especially eastern Austria, Germany, Hungary and the Czech Republic. You might consider getting an FSME (meningo-encephalitis) vaccination if you plan to do extensive hiking and camping between May and September.

Rabies Although rare in most countries in Western Europe, rabies is a fatal viral infection. It is nonexistent in the UK, Ireland, Portugal, Monaco and Malta. Many animals can be infected (such as dogs, cats, foxes and bats), and it is their saliva which is infectious. Any bite, scratch or even lick from a warm-blooded, furry animal should be cleaned immediately and thoroughly. Scrub with soap and running water, and then apply alcohol or iodine solution. Medical help should be sought promptly to receive a course of injections to prevent the onset of symptoms and death.

Snakes To minimise your chances of being bitten always wear boots, socks and long trousers when walking through undergrowth where snakes may be present. Don't put your hands into holes and crevices, and be careful when collecting firewood.

Snake bites do not cause instantaneous death, and antivenenes are usually available. Immediately wrap the bitten limb tightly, as you would for a sprained ankle, then attach a splint to immobilise it. Keep the victim still and seek medical help, if possible with the dead snake for identification. Don't attempt to catch the snake if there is a possibility of being bitten again. Tourniquets and sucking out the poison have now been comprehensively discredited.

Women's Health

Antibiotic use, synthetic underwear, sweating and contraceptive pills can lead to fungal vaginal infections when travelling in hot climates. Maintaining good personal hygiene and wearing loose-fitting clothes and cotton underwear will help to prevent these infections. Fungal infections, characterised by a rash, itch and discharge, can be treated with a vinegar or lemon-juice douche, or with yogurt. Nystatin, miconazole or clotrimazole pessaries or vaginal cream are the usual treatment.

Sexually transmitted diseases are a major cause of vaginal problems. Symptoms include a smelly discharge, painful intercourse and sometimes a burning sensation when urinating. Male sexual partners must also be treated. Medical attention should be sought and remember, in addition to these diseases, HIV or hepatitis B may also be acquired during exposure. Besides abstinence, the best thing is to practise safer sex using condoms.

WOMEN TRAVELLERS

Women are more likely to attract unwanted attention in rural Spain and southern Italy, particularly Sicily, where many men still think that staring suavely at or calling out to a passing woman is paying her a flattering compliment. This behaviour is not confined to these areas, however, and the potential is, sadly, everywhere. Slightly conservative dress can help to deter lascivious gazes and wolf whistles, dark sunglasses help avoid unwanted eye contact. Marriage is highly respected in southern Europe, and a wedding ring (on the left ring finger) sometimes helps, along with talk about 'my husband'. Hitchhiking alone in these areas is asking for trouble.

GAY & LESBIAN TRAVELLERS

The *Spartacus International Gay Guide* (Bruno Gmünder, Berlin; US$39.95) is a good male-only international directory of gay entertainment venues in Europe and elsewhere. It's best when used in conjunction with listings in local gay papers, usually distributed for free at gay bars and clubs. For lesbians, *Women's Travel in Your Pocket* (Ferrari Publications, London; UK£8.99) is a good international guide.

See the following individual country chapters for contact addresses of useful organisations, as well as gay and lesbian venues.

DISABLED TRAVELLERS

If you have a physical disability, contact your national support organisation (preferably the 'travel officer' if there is one) and ask about the countries you plan to visit. They often have complete libraries devoted to travel, and can put you in touch with travel agents who specialise in tours for the disabled.

The British-based **Royal Association for Disability & Rehabilitation** *(Radar; ☎ 020-7250 3222, fax 020-7250 0212; 12 City Forum, 250 City Rd, London EC1V 8AF)* publishes a useful guide entitled *European Holidays & Travel Abroad: A Guide for Disabled People* (UK£5), which gives a good overview of facilities available to disabled travellers in Western Europe and one to places farther afield called *Long-Haul Holidays* (in odd-numbered years). *Accessible Holidays in the British Isles* (£7.50) includes Ireland.

SENIOR TRAVELLERS

Senior citizens are entitled to many discounts in Europe on things like public transport, museum admission fees etc, provided they show proof of age. In some cases seniors might need a special pass. The minimum qualifying age is generally 60 or 65 for men and slightly younger for women.

In your home country, a lower age may already entitle you to all sorts of interesting travel packages and discounts (on car hire, for instance) through organisations and travel agents that cater for senior travellers. Start hunting at your local senior citizens advice bureau.

DANGERS & ANNOYANCES

On the whole, you should experience few problems travelling in most European countries, even alone, as the region is well developed and relatively safe. But do exercise common sense. Whatever you do, don't leave friends and relatives back home worrying about how to get in touch with you in case of emergency. Work out a list of places where they can contact you or, best of all, phone or email home now and then.

For more information on dangers, scams and travel precautions see Safety & Security in the Facts for the First-Time Visitor chapter.

Precautions

Hassles created by losing your passport can be considerably reduced if you have a record of its number and issue date; even better are photocopies of the relevant data pages. A copy of your birth certificate is also useful.

Also add the serial numbers of your travellers cheques (cross them off as you cash them) and photocopies of your credit cards, airline ticket and other travel documents. Keep all this emergency material separate from your passport, cheques and cash, and leave extra copies with someone you can rely on back home. If you do lose your passport, notify the police immediately to get a statement, and contact your nearest consulate.

Theft

Theft is definitely a problem in Europe, and nowadays you also have to be wary of other travellers. The most important things to guard are your passport, papers, tickets and money (in that order). It's always best to carry these next to your skin in a sturdy money belt or pouch hooked to your belt.

Train station lockers or luggage storage counters are useful places to store your bags (but never valuables) while you wander around and get your bearings in a new town. Be very suspicious about people who offer to help you operate your locker. Carry your own padlock for hostel lockers.

You can lessen the risks further by being careful of snatch thieves. Cameras or shoulder bags are an open invitation for these people, who sometimes operate from motorcycles or scooters and expertly slash the strap before you have a chance to react. A small daypack is better, but watch your back. Be very careful at cafés and bars; loop the strap around your leg while seated.

Pickpockets are most active in dense crowds, especially in busy train stations and on public transport during peak hours. A common ploy is for one person to distract you while another zips through your pockets. Beware of gangs of kids waving newspapers and demanding attention. In the blink of an eye, a wallet or camera can go missing.

Be careful even in hotels; don't leave valuables lying around in your room. Parked cars containing luggage and other bags are prime targets for petty criminals in most cities.

Drugs

Always treat drugs with a great deal of caution. There are a lot of drugs available in Europe, sometimes quite openly (eg, in the Netherlands), but that doesn't mean it's legal. Even a little 'harmless' hashish can cause a great deal of trouble in some places.

Don't even think about bringing drugs home with you either. With what they may consider 'suspect' stamps in your passport (eg, Amsterdam's Schiphol airport), energetic customs officials could well decide to take a closer look.

ACTIVITIES

Europe offers countless opportunities to indulge in more active pursuits than sightseeing. The varied geography and climate supports the full range of outdoor pursuits: windsurfing, skiing, fishing, trekking, cycling and mountaineering. For local information see the individual country chapters.

Cycling

Much of Europe is ideally suited to cycling. In the northwest, the flat terrain ensures that bicycles are a popular form of everyday transport, though rampant headwinds often spoil the fun. In the rest of the region, hills and mountains can make for heavy going, but this is offset by the dense concentration of things to see. Cycling is a great way to explore many of the Mediterranean islands, though the heat can get to you after a while (make sure you drink enough fluids).

Popular cycling areas among holidaymakers include the Belgian Ardennes, the west of Ireland, the upper reaches of the Danube in southern Germany, anywhere in the Alps (for those fit enough) and the south of France.

If you are arriving from outside Europe, you can often bring your own bicycle along on the plane (see Bicycle in the Getting Around chapter). Alternatively, look in this book for places where you can hire one (make sure it has plenty of gears if you plan anything serious), though except in Ireland they might take a dim view of rentals lasting more than a week.

Skiing

In winter, Europeans flock to the hundreds of resorts in the Alps and Pyrenees for downhill skiing and snowboarding. Cross-country skiing is also very popular in some areas.

A skiing holiday can be an expensive one due to the costs of ski lifts, accommodation and the inevitable après-ski drinking sessions. Equipment hire (or even purchase), on the other hand, can be relatively cheap if you follow the tips in this book, and the hassle of bringing your own skis may not be worth it. As a rule, a skiing holiday in Europe will work out twice as expensive as a summer holiday of the same length; the exceptions are Romania, Slovakia, Czech Republic and Poland, where skiing is still cheap compared with Western Europe. Cross-country skiing costs less than downhill, since you don't rely as much on ski lifts.

The skiing season generally lasts from early December to late March, though at higher altitudes it may extend an extra month either way. Snow conditions can vary greatly from one year to the next and from region to region, but January and February tend to be the best (and busiest) months. During the snow season, the Thursday and Friday editions of the *International Herald Tribune* have a weekend ski report on snow conditions at every major ski resort in Europe.

Ski resorts in the French and Swiss Alps offer great skiing and facilities, but they're also the most expensive. Expect high prices, too, in the German Alps, though Germany has cheaper (but far less spectacular) options in the Black Forest and Harz Mountains. Austria is generally slightly cheaper than France and Switzerland. Prices in the Italian Alps are similar to Austria (with some upmarket exceptions like Cortina d'Ampezzo), and can work out relatively cheaply with the right package.

Possibly the cheapest skiing in Western Europe is found in the Pyrenees in Spain and Andorra, and in the Sierra Nevada range in the south of Spain.

Hiking

Keen hikers can spend a lifetime exploring Europe's many exciting trails. Probably the most spectacular are in the Alps and Italian Dolomites, which are crisscrossed with well-marked trails In season, food and accommodation are available along the way. The equally sensational Pyrenees are less developed, which can add to the experience as you often rely on remote mountain villages for rest and sustenance. Hiking areas that are less well known, but nothing short of stunning, are Sardinia, northern Portugal, Turkey, Morocco, Slovakia, Poland, Romania and Bulgaria. The Picos de Europa range in Spain is also outrageously rewarding.

The **Ramblers' Association** (☎ *020-7339 8500*) is a London charity that promotes long-distance walking in the UK and can help with maps and information. The British-based **Ramblers Holidays** (☎ *01707-331133*) offers hiking-oriented trips in Europe and elsewhere.

Windsurfing & Surfing

After swimming and fishing, windsurfing could well be the most popular of the many water sports on offer in Europe. It's easy to rent sailboards in many tourist centres, and courses are usually available for beginners.

Believe it or not, you can also go surfing in Europe. Forget the shallow North Sea and Mediterranean and the calm Baltic, but there can be excellent surf, and an accompanying surfer scene, in southwest England and west Scotland (wetsuit advisable!), along Ireland's northwest coast, on the Atlantic coast of France and Portugal, and along the north and southwest coasts of Spain.

COURSES

If your interests are more cerebral, you can enrol in courses in Europe on anything from language to alternative medicine. Of course, the best way to learn a language is to immerse yourself in its home culture. Language courses are available to foreigners through universities or private schools, and are justifiably popular. But you can also take courses in art, literature, architecture, drama, music, cooking, alternative energy, photography and organic farming, among other subjects.

The best sources of information are the cultural institutes maintained by many European countries around the world; failing that, try their national tourist offices or embassies. Student exchange organisations, student travel agencies such as STA and Council Travel, and organisations like YMCA/YWCA and Hostelling International (HI) can also put you on the right track. Ask about special holiday packages that include a course.

WORK

Unfortunately for those dreaming of financing their trip by working along the way, European countries aren't keen on handing out jobs to foreigners (especially with unemployment rates what they are in some areas). Officially, an EU citizen is allowed to work in any other EU country, but the paperwork isn't always straightforward for long-term employment. Other country/nationality combinations require special work permits that can be almost impossible to arrange, especially for temporary work. However, that doesn't prevent enterprising travellers from topping up their funds occasionally by working in the hotel or restaurant trades at beach or ski resorts or teaching a little English – and they don't always have to do this illegally.

The UK, for example, issues special 'working holiday' visas to Commonwealth citizens who are aged between 17 and 27, valid for two years. Your national student exchange organisation may be able to arrange temporary work permits to several countries through special programmes.

If you have a parent or grandparent who was born in an EU country, you may have certain rights you never knew about. Get in touch with that country's embassy and ask about dual citizenship and work permits (if you go for citizenship, also ask about any obligations, such as military service and residency). Ireland is particularly easy-going about granting citizenship to people with an Irish parent or grandparent, and with an Irish passport, the EU is your oyster. Be aware that your home country may not recognise dual citizenship.

If you do find a temporary job, the pay may be less than that offered to locals. The one big exception is teaching English, but these jobs are hard to come by – at least officially. Other typical tourist jobs (picking grapes in France, washing dishes in Alpine resorts, working at a bar in Greece) often come with board and lodging, and the pay is little more than pocket money, but you'll have a good time partying with other travellers.

✓*Work Your Way Around the World* by Susan Griffith gives good, practical advice on a wide range of issues. Its publisher, Vacation Work, has many other useful titles, including *Summer Jobs Abroad*, edited by David Woodworth. *Working Holidays*, published by the Central Bureau for Educational Visits & Exchanges in London, is another good source.

If you play an instrument or have other artistic talents, you could try working the streets. As every Peruvian pipe player (an his fifth cousin) knows, busking is fairly common in major European cities like Amsterdam and Paris. However, it's illegal in some parts of Switzerland and Austria; in Belgium and Germany, where it has been more or less tolerated in the past, crackdowns are not unknown. Most other countries require municipal permits that can be hard to obtain. Talk to other buskers first.

Selling goods on the street is generally frowned upon and can be tantamount to vagrancy, apart from at flea markets. It's also a hard way to make money if you're not selling something special. Most countries require permits for this sort of thing. It's fairly common, though officially illegal, in the UK, Germany and Spain.

ACCOMMODATION

The cheapest places to stay in Europe are camping grounds, followed by hostels and then accommodation in student dormitories. Cheap hotels are virtually unknown in the northern half of Europe, but guesthouses, pensions, private rooms and B&Bs often offer good value. Self-catering flats and cottages are worth considering with a group, especially if you plan to stay somewhere for a while.

See the Facts for the Visitor sections in the individual country chapters for an overview of the local accommodation options. During peak holiday periods, accommodation can be hard to find and it's advisable to book ahead. Even camping grounds can fill up, especially in or around big cities.

Reservations

Cheap hotels in popular destinations (eg, Paris, London, Rome), especially the well-run ones in desirable or central neighbourhoods, fill up quickly. It's a good idea to make your reservations as far ahead as possible. A three-minute international phone call to reserve a room (followed, if necessary, by written confirmation and/or deposit) is a lot cheaper than wasting your first day in a city looking for a place to stay.

For those who arrive in a country by air and without a reservation, there is often an airport accommodation-booking desk, although it rarely covers the cheaper strata of hotels. Tourist offices often have extensive accommodation lists, and the more helpful ones will go out of their way to find you something suitable. In most countries the fee for this service is very low, and if accommodation is tight, it can save you a lot of running around. This is also an easy way to get around any language problems. Agencies offering private rooms can be also good value. Staying with a local family doesn't always mean that you'll lack privacy, but you'll probably have less freedom than in a hotel.

Sometimes people will come up to you on the street offering a private room or a hostel bed. This can be good or bad. There's no hard-and-fast rule – but always check on a map to ensure that it's not way out in a dingy suburb, and negotiate a clear price. As always, be careful when someone offers to carry your luggage: they might carry it away altogether.

Camping

Camping is immensely popular in Europe (especially among Germans, Dutch, Czechs and Poles) and provides the cheapest accommodation available. There's usually a charge per tent or site, per person and per vehicle. National tourist offices should have booklets or brochures listing camping grounds all over their country. See the under Visas & Documents earlier for information on the Camping Card International.

In large cities, most camping grounds will be some distance from the centre. Hence, camping is most popular with people who have their own transportation. If you're on foot, the money you save by camping can quickly be eaten up by the bus or train fares spent on commuting to/from a town centre. You may also need a tent, sleeping bag and cooking equipment (though not always).

For these reasons, camping is ironically often not an option for many shoestring travellers. Therefore, this book lists camping grounds only in areas where camping is easily accessible from the interesting parts of a city, or where it's common for travellers to bed down en masse under the stars (for example, on some Greek islands). Lists of camping grounds are always available from tourist offices.

Camping other than on designated camping grounds is difficult because the population density of Western Europe makes it hard to find a suitable spot to pitch a tent away from prying eyes. It is also illegal without permission from the local authorities (the police or local council office) or from the owner of the land (don't be shy about asking – you may be pleasantly surprised by the response).

In some countries, such as Austria, the UK, France and Germany, free camping is illegal on all but private land, and in Greece it's illegal altogether. This doesn't prevent hikers from occasionally pitching their tent, and they'll usually get away with it if they have only a small tent, are discreet, stay only one or two nights, take the tent down during the day and do not light a campfire or leave rubbish. At worst, they'll be woken up by the police and asked to move on.

Hostels

Hostels offer the cheapest (secure) roof over your head in Europe, and you don't have to be a youngster to use them. Bavaria (Germany) is one of the few places with a strict age limit (27 years old) for hostelling members. Most hostels are part of the national youth hostel association (YHA), which is affiliated with Hostelling International (HI – formerly the International Youth Hosts Federation). Many European countries will take a few years to change their logos, so don't be distressed if you see the initials IYHF instead of HI.

Technically, you're supposed to be a YHA or HI member to use affiliated hostels, but you can often stay by paying an extra charge (this will usually be set against future membership). Stay enough nights and you're automatically a member. Seriously.

To join the HI, ask at any hostel or contact your local or national hostelling office. There's a useful website at **w** www.iyhf.org with links to most HI sites. There are many hostel guides with listings available, including the *HI Europe* (UK£7.50) and the *England & Wales YHA Accommodation Guide* (UK£2.99). The offices for English-speaking countries appear below. Otherwise, check the individual country chapters for addresses.

Australia Australian Youth Hostels Association (☎ 02-9565 1699, fax 9565 1325, **e** yha@yha.org.ay) Level 3, 10 Mallett St, Camperdown, NSW 2050

Canada Hostelling International Canada (☎ 613 237 7884, fax 237 7868, **e** info@hostellingintl.ca) Suite 400, 205 Catherine St, Ottawa, Ontario K2P 1C3

England & Wales Youth Hostels Association (☎ 01629-592600, fax 592702, **e** customerservices@yha.org.uk) Trevelyan House, Dimple Rd, Matlock, Derbyshire DE4 3YH

Ireland An Óige (Irish Youth Hostel Association; ☎ 01-830 4555, fax 830 5808, **e** mailbox@anoige.ie) 61 Mountjoy St, Dublin 7

New Zealand Youth Hostels Association of New Zealand (☎ 03-379 9970, fax 365 4476, **e** info@yha.org.nz) 3rd floor, 193 Cashel St, Union House, Christchurch

Northern Ireland Hostelling International Northern Ireland (☎ 028-9031 5435, fax 9043 9699, **w** www.hini.org.uk) 22–32 Donegall Rd, Belfast BT12 5JN

Scotland Scottish Youth Hostels Association (☎ 01786-891400, fax 891333, ⓔ info@syha.org.uk) 7 Glebe Crescent, Stirling FK8 2JA

South Africa Hostelling International South Africa (☎ 021-424 2511, fax 424 4119, ⓔ info@hisa.org.za) PO Box 4402, Cape Town 8000

USA Hostelling International/American Youth Hostels (☎ 202-783 6161, fax 783 6171, ⓔ members@hiayh.org) Suite 840, 733 15th St NW, Washington DC 20005

Private Hostels There are some privately run hostelling organisations in Europe, not to mention hundreds of unaffiliated hostels. Unlike HI hostels, private hostels have fewer rules (eg, no curfew, no daytime lockout) and are often booked by small groups of independent travellers rather than large and noisy groups of European school children. The main drawback of private hostels is that the facilities will often vary greatly (unlike HI hostels, which must meet minimum safety and cleanliness standards).

University Accommodation

Some university towns rent out their student accommodation during the holiday periods. This is a very popular practice in France, the UK and in many Eastern European countries (see those individual country chapters for more details), as universities become more accountable financially.

University accommodation will sometimes be in single rooms (although it's more commonly in doubles or triples) and may have cooking facilities. For details inquire at the college or university itself, at the student information services or at the local tourist offices.

B&Bs, Guesthouses & Hotels

There's a huge range of accommodation above the hostel level. In the UK and Ireland, the myriad B&Bs are the real bargains in this field, where you get a room (a bed) and breakfast in a private home. In some areas every other house will have a B&B sign out front. In other countries, similar private accommodation (though often without breakfast) may go under various names: pension, guesthouse, *Gasthaus*, *Zimmer frei* ('rooms available'), *chambre d'hôte* and so on. Although the majority of guesthouses are simple affairs, there are more expensive ones, where you'll find en suite bathrooms and other luxuries.

Above this level are hotels, which at the bottom of the bracket may be no more expensive than B&Bs or guesthouses, while at the other extreme extend to luxury five-star properties with price tags to match. Although categorisation depends on the country, the hotels recommended in this book will generally range from no stars to one or two stars. You'll often find inexpensive hotels clustered around the bus and train station areas. These are generally good places to start hunting, but try avoid establishments that...well, say they're likely to charge by the hour. If you get our drift.

Check your hotel room and the bathroom before you agree to pay for a room, and make sure you know the price. Discounts are often available for groups or for longer stays. Ask about breakfast: sometimes it's included, but other times it may be obligatory and you'll have to pay extra. If the sheets don't look clean, ask to have them changed right away. Also check the location of fire exits.

If you think a hotel room is too expensive, ask if there's anything cheaper. Often hotel owners may try to steer you into more expensive rooms. In southern Europe in particular, hotel owners may be open to a little bargaining if times are slack. In France and the UK it is common practice for business hotels (usually more than two stars) to slash their rates by up to 40% on Friday and Saturday nights when business is dead. Save your big hotel splurge for the weekend.

FOOD

Few regions in the world offer such a variety of cuisines in such a small area as Europe. The Facts for the Visitor sections in the individual country chapters contain details of local cuisines, and the Places to Eat sections list suggestions.

Restaurant prices vary enormously. The cheapest places for a decent meal are often the self-service restaurants in department stores or street-side food stalls. University restaurants are dirt cheap, but the food tends to be bland and you may not be allowed in if you're not a local student. Kiosks often sell cheap snacks that can be as much a part of the national cuisine as the fancy dishes.

Self-catering – buying ingredients at a shop or market and preparing them yourself – can be a cheap and wholesome way of eating. Even if you don't cook, a picnic lunch on a park bench with a half a loaf of fresh bread, some local cheese, salami and a tomato or two, washed down with a bottle of local wine, can be one of the recurring highlights of your trip. It also makes a nice change from restaurant food.

If you have dietary restrictions (you're a vegetarian or you keep kosher or halal, for example) tourist organisations may be able to advise you about suitable restaurants. We list several vegetarian restaurants in this book.

In general, vegetarians needn't worry about going hungry in Europe; many restaurants have at least one vegetarian dish, and southern European menus in particular tend to contain many vegetable dishes and salads. Some restaurants will prepare dishes on request, but you should ask about this in advance. Vegetarians will have a harder time in Eastern Europe and meat-heavy countries such as Spain, where even so-called 'vegetable soup' is often made with meat stock.

ENTERTAINMENT

Nowhere in the world does the nightlife buzz the way it does in parts of Europe. Spain and the Greek islands in particular are notorious for their round-the-clock party scenes, while France and Germany offer chic, classy clubs and excellent live-music options. Throughout Western Europe, including Britain and Ireland, big cities and even larger towns will offer an array of night-time pursuits. While the possibilities may not be as manifold in Eastern Europe, there's usually at least one huge club in cities, and cover charges and drinks are generally a lot more reasonable.

There are fewer clubs and bars in Turkey and Morocco but you will be more likely to find some in resort areas.

Café culture was an integral part of European life long before it came to Seattle or Melbourne. Of course, Paris is famous for its streetside scene, but you may be surprised at how pervasive coffee and tea shops are throughout Eastern Europe as well. Almost anywhere on the continent, if the weather's willing you can sit outside and enjoy people-watching and pleasant conversation while sipping on some potent brews.

Finally, and perhaps most importantly, what is considered 'elite culture' in much of the world often ranks as everyman's entertainment in Europe. Sure, some opera houses and theatres maintain a reputation for stuffiness, but owing to lavish public spending on the arts and a commitment to arts education in schools, Europeans enjoy unparalleled opportunities to immerse themselves in 'high' culture. You should not miss out on chances to buy rush or standing-room tickets to concerts and plays that might be outrageously expensive in your home country. Eastern Europe in particular offers performances of outstanding calibre at proletarian prices.

Indeed, taking full advantage of the cultural and entertainment options Europe provides is the work of many lifetimes. But that's not to say that you can't get a fantastic start on one trip. Go crazy.

Getting There & Away

Step one of your trip can be the most daunting: ponying up enough cash just to reach Europe. Never fear – in these days of competition, there are plenty of cheap tickets out there for those who do their homework. If you've been entertaining visions of roughing it on a ship bound for a sunny Mediterranean port, though, you might want to think again. Transatlantic ships are both infrequent and relatively expensive, and the journey won't leave much time to see Europe itself.

Some travellers still arrive or leave overland from Africa and the Middle East (see the Overland Trails section later in this chapter). A particularly romantic method of ingress is from Asia via the Trans-Siberian Railway; see Lonely Planet's *Trans-Siberian Railway* for the scoop on this adventure.

> **Warning**
>
> The information in this chapter is particularly vulnerable to change: prices for international travel are volatile, routes are introduced and cancelled, schedules change, special deals come and go, and rules and visa requirements are amended. You should check directly with the airline or a travel agent to make sure you understand how a fare (and ticket you may buy) works and be aware of the security requirements for international travel.
>
> The upshot of this is that you should get opinions, quotes and advice from as many airlines and travel agents as possible before you part with your hard-earned cash. The details given in this chapter should be regarded as pointers and are not a substitute for your own careful, up-to-date research.

AIR

Your air ticket will take the single biggest bite out of your budget, but discounted fares can dull the pain. With any type of ticket, it's a good idea to reconfirm onward or return bookings 72 hours before departure on international flights.

Buying Tickets

If you're paying full fare, then you should be flying in 1st or business class. However, even 'discount' economy tickets can vary widely in price. Shrewd planning and careful research will put you in a seat for perhaps half or a third of what the passengers next to you paid.

Long-term travellers can choose from plenty of discount tickets that are valid for 12 months, allowing multiple stopovers with open dates. For short-term travel, cheaper fares are available by travelling mid-week, staying away at least one Saturday night and taking advantage of promotional offers.

When looking for bargain airfares, try travel agents rather than the airlines. Even when airlines feature promotional fares and special offers, they generally sell fares only at the official listed price. One exception to this rule is the expanding number of 'no-frills' carriers operating in the USA and northwestern Europe, which mostly sell direct to travellers. Unlike the 'full-service' airlines, these carriers often make one-way tickets available at around half the return fare, rendering it easy to put together a return ticket when you fly to one place but leave from another.

The other exception is Internet booking. Many airlines offer excellent Web-only fares. They may sell seats by auction or simply cut prices to reflect the reduced cost of electronic selling. Many travel agencies worldwide have websites, which can make the Internet a quick and easy way to compare prices, a good start for when you're ready to begin negotiating with your favourite travel agency. Online ticket sales work well if you are doing a simple one-way or return trip on specified dates. However, superswift fare generators are no substitute for a travel agent who knows all about special deals, can suggest strategies for avoiding lay-overs and can offer advice on everything from which airline has the best vegetarian food to the best travel insurance to bundle with your ticket.

The days when travel agencies routinely fleeced travellers by running off with their money are a thing of the past. Still, it's generally unadvisable to send money (even cheques) via post unless the agency is well established. Paying by credit card generally offers protection, as most card issuers provide refunds if you can prove you didn't get what you paid for. Similar protection can be obtained by buying a ticket from a bonded agent, such as one covered by the Air Transport Operators' Licensing (ATOL) scheme in the UK. Agencies that accept only cash should be treated warily. At the very least, get your ticket right away, and *never* 'come back tomorrow'. After you've booked or paid your deposit, call the airline and confirm the reservation.

Better-known agencies offer slightly higher fares and much more security. Firms such as STA Travel, which has offices worldwide, are not going to disappear overnight and they do offer good prices to most destinations. See later in this chapter for details on these agencies.

If you purchase a ticket and later want to make changes to your route or get a refund, you need to contact the original travel agency. Airlines issue refunds only to ticket purchasers – usually the travel agency that bought the ticket for you. Many travellers change routes halfway through their trips, so think carefully before you buy a ticket that is not easily refunded.

Student & Youth Fares Full-time students and youths under 26 have access to better deals than other travellers. These deals may not always be cheaper fares but can include more flexibility to change flights and/or routes. You have to show a document proving your date of birth or a valid International Student Identity Card (ISIC) when buying your ticket and boarding the plane. It's not unknown for non-students to get fake student cards, but if you get caught using a falsified card you could have your ticket confiscated and be subjected to other penalties.

Frequent Fliers Most airlines offer frequent-flier deals that can earn you a free air ticket or other goodies. To qualify, you have to accumulate sufficient mileage with the same airline or airline alliance. Many airlines have 'blackout periods' – times when you cannot fly free on your frequent-flier points (eg, Christmas and Chinese New Year). The worst thing about frequent-flier programmes is that they tend to lock you into one airline, and that airline may not always have the cheapest fares or most convenient flight schedule.

Courier Flights These flights are a great bargain if you're lucky enough to find one. In essence, you give up your baggage allowance in exchange for a cheap ticket. You can bring along a carry-on bag, but that's all. In addition, your stay in Europe might be limited to one or two weeks unless you opt to fly one way. Transatlantic return fares start at US$150 from the US east coast; from Australia, you may be able to get to Europe for as little as A$800.

You can find out more about courier flights from the **International Association of Air Travel Couriers** *(IAATC; ☎ 352-475 1584, fax 475 5326; Ⓦ www.courier.org)*, **Now Voyager Travel** *(☎ 212-216 0644, fax 335 5243; Ⓦ www.nowvoyagertravel.com)* and **As You Like It Travel** *(☎ 212-216 0644, fax 947 6117; Ⓦ www.asulikeit.com)*, all based in the USA.

Round-the-World Tickets 'RTW' tickets can work out to be no more expensive or even cheaper than an ordinary return ticket. Official RTW tickets are usually put together by a combination of two or more airlines and permit you to fly anywhere you want on their route systems as long as you don't backtrack. Other restrictions are that you (usually) must book the first sector in advance and cancellation penalties apply. There may be restrictions on how many stops (or kilometres) you are permitted. Prices start at about UK£800, A$1900 or US$1100, depending on the season and length of ticket validity. An alternative type of RTW ticket is one put together by a travel agent using a combination of discounted tickets. These can be much cheaper than the official ones, but usually carry a lot of restrictions. For more details contact a travel agency or airline.

Travellers with Special Needs

Most international airlines can cater to people with special needs – travellers with disabilities, people with young children and even children travelling alone. Travellers with special dietary preferences (vegetarian, kosher etc) can request appropriate meals with advance notice. If you are travelling in a wheelchair, most international airports can provide an escort from the check-in desk to plane where needed, and ramps, lifts, toilets and phones are generally available.

Airlines usually allow babies up to two years of age to fly for 10% of the adult fare, although a few may allow them free of charge. Reputable international airlines usually provide nappies (diapers), tissues, talcum and various other happiness-facilitating products. For children between the ages of two and 12, the fare on international flights is usually 50% of the regular fare or 67% of a discounted fare.

The USA

Discount travel agencies in the USA are known as 'consolidators'. San Francisco is America's ticket consolidator capital, although some good deals can be found in Los Angeles, New York and other big cities. Look for consolidators in the yellow pages or major daily newspapers.

The *New York Times, LA Times, Chicago Tribune* and *San Francisco Chronicle* all feature weekly travel sections in which you'll find any number of travel agency ads. **STA Travel** *(☎ 800-781-4040; w www.sta.com)* has offices in major cities. Call either agency or visit the websites for office locations.

You should be able to fly from New York to London or Paris and back for US$250 to US$500 in the low season and US$400 to US$800 in the high season. For equivalent fares from the west coast you can add US$100 to US$300 higher.

If you fly stand-by, one-way fares can work out remarkably cheap. New York-based **Airhitch** *(☎ 212-864 2000; w www.airhitch .org)* can get you to/from Europe for US$195 to US$265, depending on your departure region. Another option is a courier flight; see that section earlier in this chapter.

To/from Eastern Europe Long-haul airfares to/from Eastern Europe are not the continent's biggest bargains. Your best bet is to buy the cheapest possible ticket to somewhere in Western or Central Europe and then proceed by bus or train from there. Look for a ticket to London, Amsterdam, Athens, İstanbul or anywhere in Germany. Vienna is a convenient gateway to the Czech Republic, Slovakia, Hungary and Slovenia.

Scandinavia You should be able to fly return from New York or Boston to Copenhagen, Oslo or Stockholm for around US$500 in the low season and US$800 in the high season.

Icelandair *(☎ 800-223-5500; w www.icelandair.com)* flies from New York, Boston, Baltimore/Washington, Minneapolis-St Paul and Orlando via Reykjavík to Oslo, Stockholm and Copenhagen. On all of its transatlantic flights it allows a free stopover in Reykjavík – a great excuse to spend a few days in Iceland. On the other hand, for those planning on flying within Scandinavian and Baltic Europe, **Scandinavian Airlines** *(☎ 800-221-2350; w www.scandinavian.net)* has regional air passes available to passengers who fly on their transatlantic flights.

Canada

Canadian discount air-ticket sellers are called 'consolidators'; their air fares tend to be about 10% higher than those sold in the USA. The *Globe & Mail, Toronto Star, Montreal Gazette* and *Vancouver Sun* carry travel agency ads and are a good place to find cheap fares.

Travel CUTS *(☎ 800-667-2887; w www.travelcuts.com)* is Canada's national student travel agency and has offices in all major cities. **Airhitch** (see the USA section) has stand-by fares to/from Toronto, Montreal and Vancouver.

For travel to Scandinavia or Baltic Europe, **Icelandair** (see The USA section) has low-cost seasonal flights from Halifax, Nova Scotia, to Oslo, Stockholm and Copenhagen via Reykjavík.

Australia & New Zealand

Cheap flights from Australia and New Zealand to Europe generally go via South-East Asian capitals, involving stopovers in Kuala Lumpur, Bangkok or Singapore. If a long stopover between connections is necessary, transit accommodation is sometimes included in the ticket price. If the airline doesn't pay for the stopover, you may want to consider a more expensive ticket that does.

Quite a few travel offices specialise in discount air tickets. Some travel agencies, particularly smaller ones, advertise cheap airfares in the travel sections of weekend newspapers, such as the *Age* in Melbourne and the *Sydney Morning Herald*. And with Australia's large and well-organised minority populations, it pays to check special deals in the press targeted towards these groups.

In Australia, two well-known agencies for cheap fares are **STA Travel** *(☎ 1300-733 035; w www.statravel.com.au)*, with offices in all major cities and on many university campuses, and **Flight Centre** *(☎ 133 133; w www.flightcentre.com.au)*, with dozens of offices throughout Australia. Flights from Australia to a European destination on Thai, Malaysian, Qantas and Singapore Airlines range from about A$1700 to A$2500. All have frequent promotional fares, so it pays to check daily newspapers. Further Web-only savings can often unearthed at the websites.

Flying from Perth, flights are often a couple of hundred dollars cheaper than those that originate in other Australian cities. Another option for travellers wanting to go to Britain between November and February is to hook up with a charter flight returning to the UK. These low-season, one-way fares do have restrictions but may work out to be considerably cheaper. Ask your travel agent for details.

In New Zealand, **STA Travel** (☎ *0508-782 872;* 🅦 *www.statravel.co.nz)* and **Flight Centre** *(☎ 800 243 544;* 🅦 *www.flightcentre.co.nz)* are popular. The cheapest fares to Europe are routed through Asia. A discounted return flight to London from Auckland costs around NZ$1800. A RTW ticket with Air New Zealand or Lufthansa via the USA is around NZ$2400 in the low season.

The UK

For information on travelling between the UK and the rest of Europe, see the Getting Around chapter.

Africa

Nairobi, Kenya, and Johannesburg, South Africa, are probably the best places on the continent to buy tickets to Europe, thanks to myriad discount shops and lively competition. **Africa Travel Centre** *(☎ 021-423 4530;* 🅦 *www.backpackers.co.za)* in Cape Town is worth trying for cheap tickets. Once again, **STA** *(*🅦 *www.statravel.co.za)* is a reliable option. Fares from Johannesburg or Cape Town start at about R2900 to London or Paris, R3000 to Rome and R3200 to Prague.

Several West African countries, such as Senegal and The Gambia, offer cheap charter flights to France and Britain. Charter fares to Morocco and Tunisia can be quite cheap if you're lucky enough to find a seat, but a boat is likely to be the best option for travel from these countries.

Asia

Singapore and Bangkok are the discount airfare capitals of Asia. Shop around and ask the advice of other travellers before handing over any money. Guess who has branches in cities as far-flung as Hong Kong, Tokyo, Singapore, Bangkok, Manila, Jakarta and Kuala Lumpur? Yup, it's **STA** *(*🅦 *www.sta.com)*. Return fares to Europe can start as low as US$500.

In India, tickets may be even cheaper from the discount shops around Delhi's Connaught Place. Check with other travellers about their current trustworthiness.

LAND

The UK

There are a number of possibilities for getting between the UK and the rest of Europe by bus or train. For details on these services, see the Getting Around chapter and the individual country chapters.

Africa & Asia

Morocco and most of Turkey lie outside Europe, but the rail systems of both countries are still covered by Inter-Rail (Zone F and Zone G, respectively). The price of a cheap return train ticket from London to Morocco compares favourably with equivalent bus fares.

It is possible to get to Western Europe by rail from Central and Eastern Asia, though count on spending at least eight days doing it. You can choose from four different routes to Moscow: the Trans-Siberian (9297km from Vladivostok), the Trans-Mongolian (7860km from Beijing) and the Trans-Manchurian (9001km from Beijing), which all use the same tracks across Siberia but have different routes east of Lake Baikal; and the Trans-Kazakhstan, which runs between Moscow and Urumqi in northwest China. Prices vary enormously, depending on where you buy the ticket and what is included – advertised 2nd-class fares start at around US$500 from Beijing to Moscow.

Websites worth consulting for trans-Siberian packages include 🅦 www.monkey shrine.com, 🅦 www.finnsov.fi, 🅦 www.trans-siberian.co.uk, 🅦 www.regent-holidays. co.uk and 🅦 www. russia-travel.com/train.htm. Lonely Planet's Trans-Siberian Railway is a comprehensive guide to the route with details of costs, travel agencies who specialise in the trip and highlights. The Big Red Train Ride by Eric Newby is a good choice as reading material to take along for the ride.

There are countless travel options between Moscow and the rest of Europe. Most people will opt for the train, usually to/from Berlin, Helsinki, Munich, Budapest or Vienna.

Overland Trails

In the early 1980s, the trail from East and South Asia began losing popularity, as the regime in Iran and the war in Afghanistan made life difficult for independent travellers. Although Iran is a bit more lenient these days,

Afghanistan is as bad as ever, and only the most hardy (or foolhardy) would want to wend their way through this route. However, travel from Central Asia, especially the former Soviet republics, remains feasible. For details on this route (think plenty of paperwork and mounds of dust), see Lonely Planet's *Central Asia*.

Getting to Europe from Africa involves a Mediterranean ferry crossing (see the following Sea section), as the most feasible overland routes through the continent and Middle East have all but closed down.

SEA

There are numerous ferry routes between different regions of Europe. Several different companies serve the English Channel and the Baltic and North Seas. For details of these services, see the Getting Around chapter, as well as the individual country chapters.

Mediterranean Ferries

There are many ferries across the Mediterranean between Africa and Europe. The ferry you take will depend on where you plan to travel in Africa, but options include Spain–Morocco, Italy–Tunisia, France–Morocco and France–Tunisia. There are also ferries between Greece and Israel via Cyprus. Ferries are often filled to capacity in summer, especially to and from Tunisia, so book well in advance if you're taking a vehicle across. See the relevant country chapters for details.

Passenger Ships & Freighters

Regular long-distance passenger ships disappeared with the advent of cheap air travel and were replaced by a small number of luxury cruise ships. An alternative to these floating five-stars is freighters, which are far more numerous than cruise ships and offer the traveller many more routes from which to choose. The *OAG Cruise & Ferry Guide*, available at **W** www2.oag.com/tt/catalog/travagent.html, is the most comprehensive source of information, though *Travel by Cargo Ship*, by Hugo Verlomme et al, is also a good source. Passenger freighters typically carry from six to 12 passengers (more than 12 would require a doctor on board) and, though less luxurious than dedicated cruise ships, give you a real taste of life at sea. Schedules tend to be flexible and costs vary, but they seem to hover around a not-too-cheap US$200 a day. Vehicles can often be included for an additional fee.

DEPARTURE TAX

Some countries charge you a fee for the honour of leaving from their airports or seaports. Such fees are usually included in the price of your ticket, but it pays to check this when purchasing it. If not, you'll have to have the fee ready when leaving. Details of departure taxes are given at the end of the Getting There & Away sections of individual country chapters.

Getting Around

Travel within the EU, whether by air, rail or car, was made easier by the Schengen Agreement, which abolished border controls between most member states. Britain and Ireland are the only EU countries currently outside the agreement.

AIR

Air travel is a good way to get you to Europe, but within the continent it's generally expensive and inflexible compared with ground transport. While using aeroplanes for short hops can be prohibitively expensive, for longer trips it might actually be cheaper than buses or trains.

Air travel within the EU was deregulated in 1997. The current 'open skies' policy allows flexibility in routing, wide competition and relatively low prices. Although the skies are still dominated by larger carriers, there are several small, no-frills airlines that sell budget tickets directly to the customer. They operate routes from the UK to most European countries, though they sometimes use smaller, less convenient airports.

London is a good centre for picking up cheap, restricted-validity tickets through discount-ticket shops. Some airlines, such as the UK-based **easyJet** *(W www.easyjet.com)*, give discounts for tickets purchased via the Internet; easyJet's one-way fares from the UK to Barcelona, Madrid or Nice start at UK£55. Amsterdam and Athens are other good places for cheap tickets in Europe.

So-called 'open-jaw' returns, wherein you travel into a country via one city and exit from another, are worth considering, though they often work out more expensive than simple returns. In the UK, **Trailfinders** *(☎ 020-7937 1234; W www.trail finders.co.uk)* and **STA Travel** *(☎ 0870 160 0599; W www.statravel .co.uk)* can do you tailor-made versions of these tickets. Your chosen cities don't necessarily have to be in the same country. STA sells Young Europe Special (YES) passes, which allow travel around Europe at UK£39, UK£59 or UK£79 per flight (minimum four flights, maximum 10). The offer is open to all students under 31 years and anybody under 26. While STA sells tickets to all travellers it caters especially to young people and students.

Charter flights can work out as a cheaper alternative to scheduled flights, especially if you are over 26 and not a student. Other travel agencies include **Bridge the World** *(☎ 0870-444 7474; 4 Regent Place, London W1R 5FB)*; and **Flightbookers** *(☎ 0870 010 7000; W www.ebookers.com; 177-178 Tottenham Court Rd, London W1P 9LF)*.

BUS

International Buses

International bus travel tends to take second place to train travel in Europe. Buses are often cheaper – sometimes substantially so – but also generally slower and less comfortable.

Eurolines Europe's biggest network of international buses is provided by a group of companies operating under the name **Eurolines** *(W www.eurolines.co.uk)*. Representatives of Eurolines include:

Deutsche-Touring (☎ 069-790 350) Am Römerhof 17, Frankfurt
Eurolines Austria (☎ 01-712 04 53) Autobusbahnhof Wien-Mitte, Landstrasser Hauptstrasse, 1030 Vienna
Eurolines Czech Republic (☎ 02-2421 3420) Opletalova 37, Prague 1
Eurolines France (☎ 08 36 69 52 52) Gare Routière Internationale, 28 ave du Général de Gaulle, 75020 Paris
Eurolines Italy (☎ 055-35 71 10) Via Mercadante 2b, 50144 Florence
Eurolines Nederland (☎ 020-560 87 88) Rokin 10, 1012 KR Amsterdam
Eurolines Peninsular (☎ 93-490 4000) Estació d'Autobuses de Sants, Calle Viriato, Barcelona, Spain
Eurolines UK (☎ 0870-514 3219) 52 Grosvenor Gardens, London SW1, Britain
Volánbusz (☎ 1-117 2562) Erzsébet tér, V Budapest, Hungary

These branches may be able to advise you on other bus companies and deals.

Eurolines has six circular explorer routes, always starting and ending in London (no discounts). The popular London–Amsterdam–Brussels–Paris route costs UK£62, while London–Dublin–Galway–Limerick–Kilarney–Cork–London costs UK£59. Eurolines also offers passes that are cheaper than, but not as extensive or flexible as, rail passes. They cover

31 European cities as far afield as Edinburgh, Stockholm, Bucharest, Rome and Madrid. The cost is UK£229 for 30 days (UK£186 for youths and senior citizens) or UK£267 for 60 days (UK£205). Passes are cheaper in the low season (mid-September to the end of March).

On ordinary return trips, youths under 26 and seniors over 60 pay less; eg, a London–Munich return ticket costs UK£90 for adults, UK£82 for youths/seniors. Explorer or return tickets are valid for six months.

Busabout A popular option is **Busabout** *(☎ 020-7950 1661; Ⓦ www.busabout.com; 258 Vauxhall Bridge Rd, Victoria, London SW1)*, whose buses do complete circuits around Europe, stopping at major cities. You get unlimited travel per sector and can 'hop off' at any scheduled stop, then 'hop on' a later bus. Buses are often oversubscribed, so book each sector to avoid being stranded. It departs every two days from April to the end of October (May to September for Spain and Portugal). The circuits cover all countries in continental Western Europe, and you pay extra to add on Greece, Scandinavia or a London–Paris link.

Busabout's Consecutive Pass allows unlimited travel within the given time period. For a one-month pass the cost is UK£329 for adults, UK£289 for students and those under 26. Passes are also available for two or three weeks, two or three months, or for the whole season. The Flexipass allows you to select travel days within the given period. Six days in a month cost UK£169/149 adult/youth; 25 days in four months run to UK£549/499.

National Buses

Domestic buses provide a viable alternative to trains in most countries. Again, they are usually slightly cheaper and somewhat slower. Buses are generally best for shorter hops such as getting around cities and reaching remote villages. They are often the only option in mountainous regions. Reservations are rarely necessary. On many city buses you usually buy your ticket in advance from a kiosk or machine and cancel it on entering the bus. See the individual country chapters for more details on local buses.

TRAIN

Comfortable, frequent and reliable, trains are a popular way of getting around Europe. The Channel Tunnel makes it possible to get from Britain to continental Europe using the **Eurostar** *(Ⓦ www.eurostar.co.uk)* service. In some countries, such as Italy, Spain and Portugal, fares are subsidised; in others, European rail passes make travel more affordable.

If you plan to travel extensively by train, it might be worth getting hold of the Thomas Cook *European Timetable,* which gives a complete listing of train schedules and indicates where supplements apply or where reservations are necessary. It is updated monthly and is available from Thomas Cook outlets in the UK and from **Forsyth Travel Library** *(☎ 800-367 7984)* in the USA. In Australia, contact **Mercury Travel Books** *(☎ 02-9341 8700; Ⓔ mercurytravel@optushome.com.au).*

If you are planning travel in just a few countries it might be worth obtaining the national timetables published by the state railways. The *European Planning & Rail Guide* is an informative annual magazine. To get a copy, contact the US-based **Budget Europe Travel Service** *(☎ 877-441 2387; Ⓦ www.budgeteuropetravel.com).* It's free within the USA; send US$3 if you want to have it posted elsewhere.

Paris, Milan and Vienna are important hubs for international rail connections. See the relevant city sections for details and discount-ticket agencies. Note that European trains sometimes split en route to service two destinations, so even if you're on the right train, make sure you're also in the correct carriage.

Express Trains

Fast trains or those that make few stops are identified by the symbols 'EC' (EuroCity) or 'IC' (InterCity). The French TGV, Spanish AVE and German ICE trains are even faster. Supplemental fares can apply on fast trains, and it is a good idea (sometimes obligatory) to reserve seats at peak times and on certain lines.

Overnight Trains

Overnight trains usually offer a choice of couchette or sleeper. Again, reservations are advisable, as sleeping options are allocated on a first-come, first-served basis.

Couchette bunks are comfortable enough, if lacking in privacy. There are four per compartment in 1st class, six in 2nd class. A bunk costs a fixed price of around US$15 for most international trains, irrespective of the length of the journey.

Sleepers are the most comfortable option, offering beds for one or two passengers in 1st class, two or three passengers in 2nd class. Charges vary depending upon the journey, but they are significantly more expensive than couchettes. Most long-distance trains have a dining (buffet) car or an attendant who wheels a snack trolley through carriages. Prices tend to be steep.

Security

Stories sometimes surface about passengers being gassed or drugged and then robbed, but bag-snatching is more of a worry. Sensible security measures include always keeping your bags in sight (especially at stations), chaining them to the luggage rack, and locking compartment doors overnight. For more information see Safety & Security in the Facts for the First-Time Visitor chapter.

International Rail Passes

European rail passes are worth buying only if you plan to do a reasonable amount of intercountry travelling within a short space of time. If you decide to purchase a rail pass, shop around for the best price, as they can vary between outlets. Take care of your pass, as it cannot be replaced or refunded if lost or stolen.

Note that supplemental charges (eg, for some express and overnights trains) and seat reservation fees (mandatory on some trains, a good idea on others) are not covered by rail passes – always ask. European passes get reductions on Eurostar through the Channel Tunnel and on certain ferries. Pass-holders must always carry their passport with them for identification purposes.

Eurail These passes can be bought only by residents of non-European countries, and they're supposed to be purchased before arriving in Europe. They can be purchased within Europe if your passport proves you've been there for less than six months, but the outlets where you can do this are limited, and the passes will be more expensive. If you've lived in Europe for more than six months, you are eligible for a cheaper Inter-Rail pass (see later).

Eurail passes are valid for unlimited travel on national railways and some private lines within Austria, Belgium, Denmark, Finland, France (including Monaco), Germany, Greece, Hungary, Ireland, Italy, Luxembourg, the Netherlands, Norway, Portugal, Spain, Sweden and Switzerland (including Liechtenstein). The UK is not covered. Eurail is also valid on some Italy–Greece and Sweden–Finland ferries. Reductions are given on some other ferry routes and on river/lake steamer services in various countries. For more information on prices in your local currency and where to buy the passes check out **W** www.eurail.com.

Eurail passes offer reasonable value for those under 26. A Youth pass gives unlimited 2nd-class travel within a choice of five validity periods: 15/21 days (US$401/518) or one/two/three months (US$644/910/1126). The Youth Flexi pass, also for 2nd class, is valid for freely chosen days within a two-month period: 10 days for US$473 or 15 days for US$622. Overnight journeys commencing after 7pm count as the following day's travel. The traveller must fill out (in ink) the relevant box in the calendar before starting a day's travel.

For those aged 26 or over, the equivalent passes provide 1st-class travel. Prices are about 50% higher than the youth equivalents. Two people travelling together can get a 'saver' version of either pass for a 15% discount. Eurail passes for children are also available.

Europass Also for non-Europeans, the Europass gives unlimited travel on freely chosen days within a two-month period. Youth (under 26) and adult (solo, or two sharing) versions are available, and purchasing requirements and sales outlets are as for Eurail passes. Europasses are cheaper than Eurail passes as they cover only France, Germany, Italy, Spain and Switzerland. Youth/adult prices range from US$253/360 for five travel days to US$497/710 for a maximum 15 days. 'Associate countries' (really regions) can be added on to the basic pass for an additional fee. The four 'associate countries' are Austria/Hungary, Belgium/Luxembourg/Netherlands, Greece (including ferries from Italy) and Portugal.

Regional Passes Eurail also offers the Selectpass where travellers can choose up to 10 days' travel in two months in three of 17 European countries. Youth/adult prices start at US$243/346 for five days' travel in two months.

Other Eurail passes include the Benelux Tour Rail Pass (for travel in Belgium, the

Netherlands and Luxembourg), which costs US$110/225 youth/adult and is valid for 2nd-class travel over any five days in a one-month period. There are similar deals with the Balkan Rail Pass (Bulgaria, Greece, Macedonia, Romania, Turkey and Yugoslavia), Iberic Rail Pass (Spain and Portugal), European East Pass (Austria, Czech Republic, Hungary, Poland and Slovakia) and ScanRail Pass (Denmark, Finland, Norway and Sweden).

Inter-Rail & Euro Domino Inter-Rail passes are available to European residents of at least six months standing (passport identification required). Terms and conditions vary slightly between countries, but in the country of origin there is a discount of around 50% on normal fares. For more information check out W www.interrailnet.com.

The Inter-Rail pass is split into zones. Zone A is Ireland and Britain (though if you buy your Zone A pass in Britain, you get no discount with the adult version and only 34% off with the youth one); B is Sweden, Norway and Finland; C is Denmark, Germany, Switzerland and Austria; D is the Czech Republic, Slovakia, Poland, Hungary and Croatia; E is France, Belgium, the Netherlands and Luxembourg; F is Spain, Portugal and Morocco; G is Italy, Greece, Turkey, Slovenia and Italy-Greece ferries; and H is Bulgaria, Romania, Yugoslavia and Macedonia.

The normal Inter-Rail pass is for people under 26, though other travellers can get the Inter-Rail 26+ version. The standard/26+ price for any one zone is UK£139/209 for 22 days. Multizone passes are valid for one month: two zones cost UK£189/265, three zones UK£209/299 and the all-zone global pass is UK£249/355.

There is a Euro Domino pass for each of the countries covered in the Inter-Rail pass, and they're worth considering if you're homing in on a particular region. Adults (travelling 1st or 2nd class) and youths under 26 can opt for three to eight days' travel within one month. Examples of youth/adult prices for eight days in 2nd class are UK£59/115 for Greece and UK£130/168 for Spain.

National Rail Passes

If you intend to travel extensively within one country, national rail passes can sometimes save you a lot of money. Look for details in the Getting Around sections of the country chapters. Plan ahead if you intend to take this option, as some passes can only be purchased prior to arrival in the country.

Cheap Tickets

When weighing up options, consider alternatives to rail passes, such as cheap ticket deals that include advance-purchase reductions, one-off promotions or special circular-route tickets. Normal international tickets are valid for two months, and you can make as many stops as you like en route; make your intentions known when purchasing, and inform train conductors how far you're going before they punch your ticket.

For a small fee, European residents can buy a Railplus Card, entitling the holder to a 25% discount on international train journeys. In most countries, it's sold only to those aged 60 and over. However, some national rail networks may make the Railplus Card available to young people or other travellers.

TAXI

Taxis in Europe are metered and rates are usually high. There might also be supplements for things like luggage, time of day, location of pick-up and extra passengers. Good bus, rail and underground railway networks often render taxis unnecessary, but if you need one in a hurry they can be found idling near train stations or outside big hotels. Lower fares make taxis more viable in some countries, such as Spain, Greece, Portugal and Turkey.

CAR & MOTORCYCLE

Travelling with your own vehicle is both flexible and the best way to get to remote places. Unfortunately, the independence does tend to isolate you from the local people. Also, cars are usually inconvenient in city centres, where it's worth ditching your vehicle and relying on public transport. Various car-carrying trains can help you avoid long, tiring drives. **Eurotunnel** (W *www.eurotunnel.com*) transports cars through the Channel Tunnel. Costs vary according to type of car, time of day or year, length of stay etc, so check the website for prices and any special deals.

Paperwork & Preparations

Always carry proof of ownership of your vehicle (Vehicle Registration Document for British-registered cars) when touring Europe. An EU driving licence is acceptable for those driving throughout Europe. Old-style green UK licences are no good for Spain or Italy and should be backed up by a German translation in Austria. If you have any other type of licence, you should obtain an International Driving Permit (IDP) from your motoring organisation (see Visas & Documents in the Facts for the Visitor chapter). Check what type of licence is required in your destination prior to departure.

Third-party motor insurance is compulsory. Most UK policies automatically provide this for EU countries. Get your insurer to issue a Green Card (which may cost extra), an internationally recognised proof of insurance, and check that it lists all the countries you intend to visit. You'll need this in the event of an accident outside the country where the vehicle is insured. Also ask your insurer for a European Accident Statement form, which can simplify things if worst comes to worst. Never sign statements that you can't read or understand – insist on a translation and sign that only if it's acceptable. For non-EU countries, check the requirements with your insurer. Travellers from the UK can obtain additional advice and information from the **Association of British Insurers** *(☎ 020-7600 3333; Ⓦ www.abi.org.uk)*.

Taking out a European motoring assistance policy – such as AA Five Star Service or RAC Eurocover Motoring Assistance – is a good investment. Expect to pay about UK£50 for 14 days' coverage, with a 10% discount for association members. Non-Europeans might find it cheaper to arrange international coverage with their national motoring organisation before leaving home. Ask your motoring organisation for details about the free services offered by affiliated organisations around Europe.

Every vehicle that travells across an international border should display a sticker showing its country of registration. A warning triangle, to be used in the event of breakdown, is compulsory almost everywhere. Some recommended accessories include a first-aid kit (compulsory in Austria, Slovenia, Croatia, Yugoslavia and Greece), a spare bulb kit (compulsory in Spain), and a fire extinguisher (compulsory in Greece and Turkey). Bail bonds are no longer required for Spain. Residents in the UK should contact the **RAC** *(☎ 0800-550 055; Ⓦ www.rac.co.uk)* or **AA** *(☎ 08705-500 600)* for more information. In the USA, contact **AAA** *(Ⓦ www.aaa.com)*.

Road Rules

Except in Britain and Ireland, drive on the right. Vehicles brought over from either of these countries should have their headlights adjusted to avoid blinding oncoming traffic (a simple solution on older headlight lenses is to cover up a triangular section of the lens with tape). Priority is usually given to traffic approaching from the right in countries that drive on the right-hand side.

Speed limits vary from country to country. You may be surprised at the apparent disregard for traffic regulations in some places (particularly in Italy and Greece), but as a visitor it is always best to be cautious. Many driving infringements are subject to an on-the-spot fine. Always ask for a receipt.

European drink-driving laws are particularly strict. The blood-alcohol concentration (BAC) limit when driving is between 0.05% and 0.08%, but in certain areas (such as Gibraltar and some Eastern European countries) it can be 0%.

Roads

Conditions and types of roads vary across Europe. The fastest routes are generally four- or six-lane dual carriageways/highways (two or three lanes either side) called 'autoroutes', *autostrade* etc. These tend to skirt cities and plough through the countryside in straight lines, often avoiding the most scenic bits. Some incur tolls, which are often quite hefty (eg, in Italy, France and Spain), but there will always be an alternative route. Motorways and other primary routes are generally in good condition.

Road surfaces on minor routes are unreliable in some countries (eg, Romania, Ireland, Morocco and Greece) although normally they will be more than adequate. These roads are narrower and progress is generally much slower. However, to compensate this, you can expect much better scenery and plenty of interesting villages along the way.

Rental

Big international rental firms will give you reliable service and good vehicles. Usually you will have the option of returning the car to a different outlet at the end of the rental period. Prebook for the lowest rates; if you walk into an office and ask for a car on the spot, you will pay through the nose, even allowing for special deals. Fly-drive combinations and other programmes are worth looking into.

Check the following sites, from which you can make reservations online.

Alamo (w) www.alamo.com
Avis (w) www.avis.com
Budget (w) www.budget.com
Europcar (w) www.europcar.com
Hertz (w) www.hertz.com

Brokers can cut costs. In the UK, **Holiday Autos** *(☎ 0870 400 0099; (w) www.holidayautos.com)* has low rates and either offices or representatives in over 20 countries. In the USA call **Kemwel Holiday Autos** *(☎ 877 820 0668; (w) www.kemwel.com)*. In the UK, a competitor that has even lower prices is **Autos Abroad** *(☎ 08700 667 788; (w) www.autosabroad.co.uk)*.

If you want to rent a car and haven't pre-booked, look for national or local firms, which can often undercut the big companies by up to 40%. Nevertheless, you need to be wary of dodgy operations that take your money and point you towards some clapped-out wreck, or where the rental agreement is bad news if you have an accident or the car is stolen. Read what you sign.

No matter where you rent, make sure you understand what is included in the price (unlimited or paid kilometres, tax, injury insurance, collision damage waiver etc) and what your liabilities are. We recommend taking the collision damage waiver, though you can probably skip the injury insurance if you and your passengers have decent travel insurance. Ask in advance if you can drive a rented car across borders from a country where hire prices are low to another where they're high.

The minimum rental age is usually 21 or even 23, and you'll probably need a credit card. Note that prices at airport rental offices are usually higher than at branches in the city centre.

Motorcycle and moped rental is common in some countries, such as Italy, Spain, Greece and southern France. Sadly, it's also common for inexperienced riders leap on rented bikes and very quickly fall off them again, leaving a layer or two of skin on the road in the process.

Purchase

The purchase of vehicles in some European countries is illegal for non-nationals or non-EU residents. Britain is probably the best place to buy; second-hand prices are good and, whether buying privately or from a dealer, the absence of language difficulties will help you establish exactly what you are getting and what guarantees you can expect if you break down.

Bear in mind that British cars have steering wheels on the right. If you want left-hand drive and can afford to buy new, car prices are usually reasonable in Greece, France, Germany, Belgium, Luxembourg and the Netherlands. Paperwork can be tricky wherever you buy, and many countries have compulsory road-worthiness checks on older vehicles.

Leasing

Leasing a vehicle involves fewer hassles than purchasing and can work out considerably cheaper than hiring over longer periods. The Renault Eurodrive scheme provides new cars for non-EU residents for a period of between 17 and 170 days. Under this arrangement, a Renault Clio 1.2 for 24 days would cost €545 (if picked up/dropped off in France), including insurance and roadside assistance. Check out the options before leaving home. In the USA, Kemwel Holiday Autos (see Rental, earlier) arranges European leasing deals.

Camper Van

One popular way to tour Europe is for a group of three or four people to band together and buy or rent a camper van. London is the usual embarkation point. Look at the advertisements in London's free magazine *TNT* if you wish to form or join a group. *TNT* is also a good source for purchasing a van, as is the *Loot* newspaper.

Some second-hand dealers offer a 'buy-back' scheme for when you return from the Continent, but we've received warnings that some dealers don't fully honour their refund commitments. Anyway, buying and reselling privately should be more advantageous if you have the time. **Down Under Insurance** *(☎ 020-7402 9211; (w) www.downunderinsurance.co.uk)* offers a Camper Van policy.

Camper vans usually feature a fixed high-top or elevating roof and two to five bunk beds. Apart from the essential camping gas cooker, you may get a sink, fridge and built-in cupboards. Prices vary considerably, and it's worth getting advice from a mechanic to determine whether you're being offered a fair price. Getting a mechanical check (from UK£35) is a good idea before you buy. Once on the road you should be able to keep budgets lower than backpackers using trains, but don't forget to set money aside for emergency repairs.

The main advantage of going by camper van is flexibility; with transport, eating and sleeping requirements all taken care of in one unit, you are tied to nobody's timetable but your own. It's also easier to set up at night than if you rely on a car and tent.

A disadvantage of camper vans is that you are in a confined space for much of the time. Four adults in a small van can soon get on each other's nerves, particularly if the group has been formed at short notice. You might also miss out on experiences in the world outside your van. Other negatives are that vans are not very manoeuvrable around town, and you'll often have to leave your gear unattended inside (many people bolt extra locks onto the van). They're also expensive to buy in spring and hard to sell in autumn.

Motorcycle Touring

Europe is made for motorcycle touring, with good-quality winding roads, stunning scenery, and an active motorcycling scene. Just make sure your wet-weather gear is up to scratch.

Rider and passenger crash helmets are compulsory everywhere in Europe. Austria, Belgium, France, Germany, Luxembourg, Portugal and Spain also require that motorcyclists use headlights during the day; in other countries it is recommended.

On ferries, motorcyclists rarely have to book ahead as they can generally be squeezed in. Take note of the local custom about parking motorcycles on pavements (sidewalks). Though this is illegal in some countries, the police usually turn a blind eye provided the vehicle doesn't obstruct pedestrians. Don't try this in Britain, however.

Fuel

Fuel prices can vary enormously (though it's always more expensive than in North America or Australia). Refuelling in Luxembourg or Andorra is about 30% cheaper than in neighbouring countries. The Netherlands, France and Italy have Europe's most expensive petrol; Gibraltar and Andorra are by far the cheapest in Western Europe. Greece, Spain and Switzerland are also reasonably cheap. Motoring organisations such as the RAC can supply more details.

Unleaded petrol is widely available throughout Europe (though not always in Romania, Albania, Slovakia or Yugoslavia) and is usually slightly cheaper than super (premium grade, the only 'leaded' choice in some countries). Diesel is usually significantly cheaper, though the difference is marginal in Britain, Ireland and Switzerland.

BICYCLE

Touring Europe by bike may seem daunting, but a UK organisation can help. The **Cyclists' Touring Club** *(CTC; ☎ 0870-873 0060; W www.ctc.org.uk; Cotterell House, 69 Meadrow, Godalming, Surrey GU7 3HS)* can supply information to members on cycling conditions in Europe as well as detailed routes, itineraries and maps. Membership includes specialised insurance and costs UK£27/16.50/10 annually for adults/seniors/youths under 26.

A primary consideration on a cycling tour is to travel light, but you should take a few tools and spare parts, including a puncture-repair kit and an extra inner tube. Panniers are essential to balance your possessions on either side of the bike frame. A bike helmet is also a very good idea. Take a good lock and *always* use it when you leave your bike unattended.

Michelin maps indicate scenic routes, which can help you plan good cycling itineraries. Seasoned cyclists can average 80km a day, but there's no point in overdoing it. The slower you travel, the more locals you are likely to meet. If you get tired of pedalling or simply want to skip a boring section, you can put your feet up on the train. On slower trains, bikes can usually be transported as luggage, subject to a small supplementary fee. Fast trains can rarely accommodate bikes; they might need to be sent as registered luggage and may end up on a different train from the one you take. This is often the case in France and Spain. Eurostar (the train service through the Channel Tunnel) charges UK£20 to send a bike as registered luggage on its routes. You can also transport your bicycle with you on Eurotunnel through the Channel Tunnel. With a bit of tinkering and dismantling (eg, removing wheels), you might be able to get your bike into a bag or sack and take it on a train as hand luggage.

The **European Bike Express** *(☎ 01642-251 440; W www.bike-express.co.uk)* is a coach service based in the UK where cyclists can travel with their bicycles. It runs in the summer from northeastern England to France, Italy and Spain, with pick-up/drop-off points en route. The maximum return fare is UK£179 (UK£10 off for CTC members).

Rental & Purchase

It is easy to hire bikes throughout most of Europe on an hourly, half-day, daily or weekly basis. Many train stations have bike-rental counters. See the country chapters for more details. It is sometimes possible to return the bike at a different outlet so you don't have to retrace your route.

There are plenty of places to buy in Europe (shops sell new and second-hand bicycles, or you can check local papers for private vendors), but you'll need a specialist bicycle shop for a bike capable of withstanding a European tour. CTC can provide a leaflet on purchasing. Cycling is very popular in the Netherlands and Germany, and those countries are good places to pick up a well-equipped touring bicycle. European prices are quite high (certainly higher than in North America), however non-Europeans should be able to claim back VAT on the purchase.

Transporting a Bicycle

For major cycling tours, it's best to have a bike you're familiar with, so consider bringing your own rather than buying on arrival. You should be able to take it along with you on the plane relatively easily. You can either take it apart and pack everything in a bike bag or box, or simply wheel it to the check-in desk, where it should be treated as a piece of luggage. You may have to remove the pedals and turn the handlebars sideways so that it takes up less space in the aircraft's hold; check all this with the airline well in advance, preferably before you pay for your ticket. If your bicycle and other luggage exceed your weight allowance, ask about alternatives or you may suddenly find yourself being charged a fortune (US$75 or more) for excess baggage.

HITCHING

Hitching is never entirely safe in any country in the world, and we cannot recommend it. Travellers who decide to hitch should understand that they are taking a small but potentially serious risk. People who do choose to hitch will be safer if they travel in pairs and let someone know where they plan to go.

Hitching can be the most rewarding and frustrating way of getting around. You get to meet and interact with local people and can be forced into unplanned detours that may yield unexpected highlights off the beaten track. But you might get stuck on the side of the road to nowhere with nowhere (or nowhere cheap) to stay. Then it begins to rain.

That said, hitchers can end up making good time, but obviously your plans need to be flexible in case you're invisible to passing motorists. A man and woman travelling together is probably the best combination. Two or more men should expect some delays; two women together will make good time and be relatively safe. A woman hitching on her own is taking a big risk, particularly in parts of southern Europe.

Don't try to hitch from city centres; take public transport to the suburban exit routes. Hitching is usually illegal on motorways (freeways) – stand on the slip roads, or approach drivers at petrol stations and truck stops. Look presentable and cheerful, and make a cardboard sign indicating your intended destination in the local language. Never hitch where drivers can't stop in good time or without causing an obstruction. At dusk, give up and find somewhere to stay. If your itinerary includes a ferry crossing (for instance, across the Channel), it might be worth trying to score a ride before the ferry rather than after, since vehicle tickets sometimes include a number of passengers free of charge. This applies to Eurotunnel via the Channel Tunnel.

It is sometimes possible to arrange a lift in advance. Scan student notice boards in colleges, or contact ride-sharing agencies. Such agencies are particularly popular in France and Germany *(Mitfahrzentralen)*. See Hitching in the relevant country chapters.

If you're considering hitching around Europe, check out **W** www.bugeurope.com and **W** www.hitchhikers.org.

BOAT

Several different ferry companies compete on the main ferry routes, resulting in a comprehensive but complicated service. The same ferry company can have a host of different prices for the same route, depending on the time of day or year, validity of the ticket, and length of your vehicle. Vehicle tickets include the driver and often up to five passengers free of charge. It's worth planning (and booking) ahead where possible as there may be special reductions on off-peak crossings and advance-purchase tickets. On English Channel routes, apart from one-day or short-term excursion returns, there is little price advantage in buying a return ticket versus two singles.

Stena Line (Ⓦ *www.stenaline.com*) is one of the world's largest ferry companies. It serves Britain Ireland, Scandinavia and the Netherlands. **P&O Ferries** (Ⓦ *www.poferries.com*) and **Brittany Ferries** (Ⓦ *www.britanny-ferries.com*) sail direct from England and Ireland to the Netherlands, Belgium, France and northern Spain. The shortest of the cross-Channel routes (Dover–Calais or Folkestone–Boulogne) are also the busiest, though there is now great competition from the Channel Tunnel. Stena and P&O recently combined forces on the Newhaven–Dieppe and Dover–Calais routes. Italy (Brindisi or Bari) to Greece (Corfu, Igoumenitsa and Patras) is also a popular route. The Greek islands are connected to the mainland and each other by a spider web of routings; see Lonely Planet's *Greek Islands* for details.

Rail-pass holders are entitled to discounts or free travel on some lines (see the earlier Train section), and most ferry companies give discounts to disabled drivers. Food on ferries is often expensive (and lousy), so it is worth bringing your own. Also be aware that if you take your vehicle on board, you are usually denied access to it during the voyage.

Central Europe can be reached from the north, west and east by ferry via the North or Baltic Seas. There are direct links from Newcastle and Harwich in the UK to Hamburg a couple of times a week, and a slew of other sea craft transport cars and people between Germany and Scandinavia. Regularly scheduled services include a 2½-hour crossing from Kiel to Bagenkop (on the Danish island of Langeland), to Gothenburg in Sweden (14 hours) and all the way to Oslo (19½ hours). There are also ferries going to Denmark, Sweden and/or Finland from the eastern German ports of Travemünde and, on Rügen Island, Sassnitz.

Poland also has a ferry service (year-round, for the most part) to Scandinavia. Routes include Gdynia–Karlskrona and Gdańsk–Nynäshamn in Sweden; and Świnoujście to Copenhagen in Denmark.

See Getting There & Away in the Germany and Poland chapters for more details.

ORGANISED TOURS

Package tours cater for all tastes, interests and ages. See your travel agent or look in the small ads in newspaper travel pages. A bit of Internet surfing can yield excellent results for those seeking unusual tours. Specialists include **Ramblers Holidays** (☎ *01707-331 133;* Ⓦ *www.ramblersholidays.co.uk*) in Britain and **CBT Tours** (☎ *800 736 2453;* Ⓦ *www.cbttours.com*) in the USA for bicycle trips.

Young revellers can party on Europe-wide bus tours. **Contiki** (☎ *020-8290 6777;* Ⓦ *www.contiki.com*) and **Top Deck** (☎ *020-7370 4555;* Ⓦ *www.topdecktravel.co.uk*) offer camping or hotel-based bus tours for the 18-to-35 age group. Contiki's tours last from five to 46 days. Both companies have London offices plus offices or company representatives in Europe, North America, Australasia and South Africa.

New Millennium Holidays (☎ *0870 240 3217;* Ⓦ *www.newmillennium-holidays.com; Icon House, 209 Yardley Road, Birmingham B27 6LZ, England*) runs inexpensive bus and air tours year-round from the UK to Central and Eastern Europe, including Russia. Packages vary from 10 to 17 days, some combining two or three countries, with half-board or B&B accommodation. Another British company highly experienced in booking travel to Eastern Europe is **Regent Holidays** (☎ *0117-921 1711, fax 925 4866;* Ⓦ *www.regent-holidays.co.uk; 15 John St, Bristol BS1 2HR*).

In Australia you can obtain a detailed brochure outlining dozens of upmarket tours (including to Russia) from the **Eastern Europe Travel Bureau** (☎ *02-9262 1144;* Ⓦ *www.eetbtravel.com; Level 5, 75 King St, Sydney, NSW 2000*).

For people aged over 50, **Saga Holidays** (*UK* ☎ *0800-300 500; Saga Building, Middelburg Square, Folkestone, Kent CT20 1AZ • USA* ☎ *800-343 0273; 222 Berkeley St, Boston, MA 02116*) offers holidays ranging from cheap coach tours to luxury cruises (and has cheap travel insurance).

National tourist offices in most countries offer organised trips to points of interest. These may range from one-hour city tours to several-day excursions. They often work out more expensive than going it alone but are sometimes worth it if you are really pressed for time.

Festival Fever

Looking to party down in the Old World? Europe boasts more festivals than you can shake a tambourine at. Some countries, such as Spain, are renowned for their year-round fiesta schedule, while other countries wait until special times of the year to go nuts. Here are some of our favourite festivals from across the continent.

Air Guitar World Championships (Finland)

Unleash the Hendrix inside you! You're entitled to enter this 'globally significant competition' only if you've registered beforehand at the website, but anyone can (and everyone *should*) watch. During the first round, the contestant must play a tune selected by the judges; in the second round, the contestant picks his or her own tune. No actual guitars are involved.
Late August, Oulu; **W** *www.omvf.net*

Bastille Day (France)

Vive la revolution! The national holiday of France commemorates the beginning of the end for the French monarchy. Back on this date in 1789, the people got together and stormed the Bastille. Fireworks at the Eiffel Tower, parties, dances and a military parade on the Champs Élysée are the order of the day.
14 July, Paris; **W** *www.paris.org*

Castle Party (Poland)

If white face paint, black clothing and industrial metal are your bag, then hightail it to Poland for this dark celebration – it's the biggest Gothic festival the world has to offer. Don't be surprised if you meet folks with names like 'Lord Shadow Krypt'. And watch your neck.
Late July, Bolkow; **W** *www.castleparty.imagina.pl*

Edinburgh International Festival (Britain)

This fancy-pants fling features classical music (mostly Western orchestral pieces), dance and theatre. Started in 1947, it's Europe's major arts festival. Those looking for a more chaotic scene should check out the concurrent Fringe Festival, where anyone can play.
Mid- to late August, Edinburgh, Scotland; **W** *www.eif.co.uk*

Feria de Abril (Spain)

Seville's April fair started out as a cattle fair in 1846. It has since evolved into a week-long fiesta featuring a festive *caseta* (tent) city filled with dancing women wearing flamenco outfits. The most important bullfight in Seville takes place the same week. It's a nonstop party atmosphere.
Mid-April, Seville, Andalucía; **W** *www.sol.com*

Fès Festival of Sacred Music (Morocco)

At the beginning of the hot Moroccan summer, travellers cleanse their souls with moving performances of spiritual and religious music from around the world. Works from a wide range of traditions are presented over a period of 10 uplifting days.
Late May to mid-June, Fès; **W** *www.fezfestival.org*

Gay Pride Parade (the Netherlands)

Europe's gay capital hosts its largest annual pride parade, also known as the 'canal parade': participants literally float down the canals on, well,

Cover Image: Burn, baby, burn! Gay Pride Parade, the Netherlands (Photo by Paul Beinssen)

Inset: Jazz muso blows his horn, Prague Festival (Photo by Jonathan Smith)

floats – and boats. Celebrations come complete with a film festival and nonstop partying (the leather-fetish party is among the more tame events).
Early August, Amsterdam; **W** *www.amsterdampride.nl*

Glastonbury Festival (Britain)

King Arthur and his childhood chums probably played Kick the Tankard on these very same green fields. Packed with artists and up-and-coming rock bands, this summer festival appeals to a broad range of audiences.
Late June, Pilton, England; **W** *www.glastonburyfestivals.co.uk*

High Times Cannabis Cup (the Netherlands)

This is a kind of hemp expo fair, when hempologists taste-test the counterculture's favourite, and most readily available, herb in Amsterdam's plethora of coffee shops and seed banks. We'd love to know how they judge this one.
Late November, Amsterdam; **W** *www.hightimes.com*

Il Palio (Italy)

It seems folk in the Sienese districts of old used to fight a lot. One fine day in 1147, however, they decided to replace the bloodshed with a pony race; since then they've raced around Siena's Piazza del Campo twice a year, to the delight of multitudes. A parade introduces the race and a huge feast celebrates it afterwards.
2 July & 16 August, Siena, Tuscany; **W** *www.ilpaliodisiena.com*

International Ankara Music Festival (Turkey)

This is Turkey's huge Western classical music festival. Orchestral and chamber-music performances are the highlights, although jazz, ballet and modern dance are also on display.
Late April to mid-May, Ankara; **W** *www.ankarafestival.com*

International Festival of Fantasy, Thriller & Science Fiction Film (Belgium)

Although the website notes that this film fair is targeted towards a 'wide range of audiences', you're more likely to find the Comic Book Store Guy from *The Simpsons* than J-Lo at this one. It's *the* event for fans of the fantasy, thriller and science-fiction genres, celebrating 20 years of bringing together those who can't stay away from the shelves at the back of the bookshop.
Mid- to late March, Brussels; **W** *www.bifff.org*

DAVID PEEVERS

Right: Sultry sounds at Berlin's Jazzfest

Jazzfest Berlin (Germany)

If you're a jazz addict, this is the festival for you. It's touted as one of Europe's most important events for modern jazz artists.
Late October to early November, Berlin; **W** *www.berlinerfestspiele.de*

Oktoberfest (Germany)

The first beer fest began as a celebration of the marriage of King Ludwig I to Princess Therese of Saxon-Hildburghausen on 12 October 1810. According to the official website, the 1999 Oktoberfest saw 6.5 million visitors drink 5.8 million litres of beer and devour 84 oxen, 320,000 sausages and 589,000 roast chickens. Enjoy.
Late September to early October, Bavaria; **W** *www.oktoberfest.de*

Original Marathon (Greece)

The original marathon was run by Phidippides, an Athenian messenger who covered 24 (some say 26) miles delivering to Athens the news of a Greek victory over Persian invaders in the town of Marathon in 490 BC. The current marathon route is supposedly the exact route that Phidippides took, with the finish line in the Olympic Stadium (where the original Olympics were held). This is an open international marathon.
Early November, Marathon to Athens; **W** *www.athensmarathon.com*

Prague Spring International Music Festival (Czech Republic)

Possibly the best-value big-ticket festival in all of Europe, the Prague Spring International Musical Festival is dedicated to the world's great orchestral works. Performances by internationally renowned companies are supplemented by workshops and concerts by youth orchestras.
Late May to mid-June, Prague; **W** *www.festival.cz*

Roskilde Festival (Denmark)

Billed as 'Europe's biggest four-day rock festival', the Roskilde event brings mainstream, chart-topping bands to town. Backpackers camp out in the town of Roskilde and hang around as the festivities unfold.
Late June, Roskilde; **W** *www.roskilde-festival.dk*

Sanfermines (Spain)

This is the big one, the one you see on TV; Hemingway describes its famous running of the bulls in his novel *The Sun Also Rises*. Folk music, vespers and bullfighting add to this celebration of the patron saint of fools. Be sure to book accommodation well in advance.
Early July, Pamplona (Iruña), Navarre; **W** *www.sanfermin.com*

Spirit of Speyside Whisky Festival (Britain)

Don yer kilt, tour the distilleries, drink the malt whisky and shoot the clay pigeons. This festival is an alcoholic's delight, complete with barrel-making contests, highland dancing, traditional Scottish music and golf. Bring your own aspirin.
Early May, Speyside, Scotland; **W** *www.spiritofspeyside.com*

St Patrick's Festival (Ireland)

The feast for St Patrick's 'falling asleep' (or death) is the Irish national holiday (St Paddy drove the 'snakes' – pagans – from Ireland and brought Christianity to the Emerald Isle). Events include outdoor theatre performances, music (traditional Irish concerts, marching bands etc) Irish dancing and, of course, the famous St Patrick's Day parade.
15 to 17 March, Dublin; **W** *www.stpatricksday.ie*

Albania

Until 1990 a closed communist country, Albania caught world attention as the last domino to tumble in Eastern Europe's sudden series of democratic revolutions. Albania had chosen a curious form of isolation, submitting to Stalinist-type dictatorship and relative dissociation from neighbouring nations. Emerging from this shell proved troublesome, as the country spiralled into violence and anarchy in the late 1990s. Since then, however, the situation has improved enormously, and Albania is cautiously opening its doors once more.

The Republika e Shqipërisë (Land of the Eagle) is Europe's last unknown. Here travellers can find enchanting classical ruins, the charming 'museum town' of Gjirokastra, colourful folklore, and majestic landscapes of mountains, forests, lakes and sea.

Albania: the Basics

Local name Shqipëria

Capital Tirana

Population 3.5 million

Languages Albanian, Greek

Currency 1 lekë = 100 quintars

Avoid at all costs Tripping on rubbish in the streets

Express some scepticism by saying *Ti i bën petullat me ujë!* (You make pancakes from water!)

Facts about Albania

HISTORY

In the 2nd millennium BC, the Illyrians occupied the western Balkans. The Greeks arrived as peaceful traders, then the Romans came to conquer. Under the Romans, Illyria enjoyed peace and prosperity. After Rome fell, invasions by migrating peoples forced ethnic Illyrians south.

In 1344 Albania was annexed by Serbia, then threatened by the Ottoman Turks and Venetians. From 1443 to 1468 the national hero Skënderbeg (George Kastrioti) led Albanian resistance to the Turks, winning 25 battles that he fought against them. Eventually, though, the land fell to the Ottomans.

The late 19th and early 20th centuries saw Albanians in Kosovo struggling unsuccessfully for independence. With the outbreak of WWI, Albania was occupied by various armies. In 1920 Ahmet Zogu became the ruler of Albania and declared himself King Zogu I, but his collaboration with Italy backfired in April 1939 when Mussolini invaded Albania. On 8 November 1941 the Albanian Communist Party was founded with Enver Hoxha (pronounced 'hodja') as first secretary (pronounced 'dictator').

In January 1946 the People's Republic of Albania was proclaimed, with Enver Hoxha as president. Albania initially allied itself with Stalin's USSR, but in 1961 broke off relations and reoriented itself towards China. From 1966 to 1967 Albania experienced a Chinese-style cultural revolution. Administrative workers were transferred to remote areas and younger cadres were placed in leading positions. Agriculture was collectivised and organised religion banned.

Following Hoxha's death in 1985, Albania embarked on a programme of liberalisation and, after student demonstrations in December 1990, the government agreed to allow opposition parties. The government also announced a reform programme, and party hardliners were purged.

The March 1992 elections ended 47 years of communist rule. But a severe crisis developed in late 1996, when private pyramid investment schemes collapsed spectacularly. Around 70% of Albanians lost their savings, and nationwide disturbances and violence resulted. In spring 1999 Albania faced a crisis of a different sort – the influx of 465,000 war refugees from neighbouring Kosovo. While this put a tremendous strain on resources, the net effect has been positive. A substantial amount of international aid money has poured in, the service sector has grown and inflation has dropped.

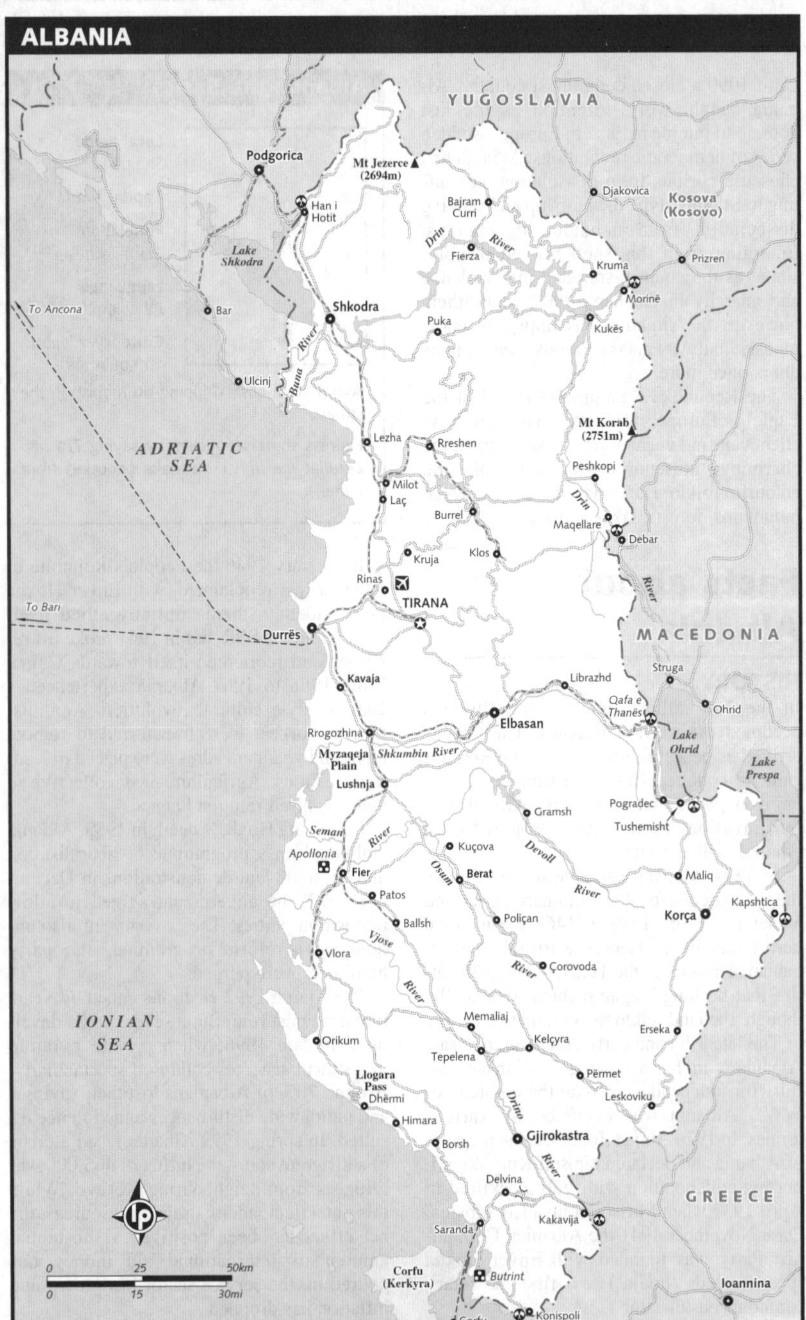

ALBANIA
YUGOSLAVIA
Podgorica
Mt Jezerce
(2694m)
Han i Hotit
Bajram Curri
Djakovica
Kosova (Kosovo)
Lake Shkodra
Drin River
Fierza
Prizren
Kruma
Morinë
To Ancona
Bar
Shkodra
Puka
Kukës
Buna River
Ulcinj
ADRIATIC SEA
Mt Korab
(2751m)
Lezha
Rreshen
Peshkopi
Milot
Laç
Drin
Burrel
Maqellare
Debar
Kruja
Klos
Rinas
TIRANA
River
To Bari
Durrës
MACEDONIA
Kavaja
Librazhd
Struga
Qafa e Thanës
Ohrid
Elbasan
Rrogozhina
Lake Ohrid
Myzaqeja Plain
Shkumbin River
Lake Prespa
Lushnja
Gramsh
Pogradec
Tushemisht
Seman River
Apollonia
Kuçova
Devoll River
Osum
Fier
Berat
Maliq
Patos
Ballsh
Poliçan
Korça
Kapshtica
Vjose River
Vlora
River
Çorovoda
IONIAN SEA
Memaliaj
Orikum
Kelçyra
Tepelena
Erseka
Llogara Pass
Përmet
Dhërmi
Leskoviku
Drino River
Himara
Gjirokastra
Borsh
Delvina
GREECE
Kakavija
Saranda
Corfu (Kerkyra)
Butrint
Ioannina
Konispoli
Corfu
0 25 50km
0 15 30mi

By 2002 the country found itself in a kind of miniboom, with money being poured into construction projects and infrastructure.

GEOGRAPHY

Over three-quarters of this 28,748-sq-km country consists of mountains and hills. The coastal plain extends over 200km from north to south and up to 50km inland. The 2000m-high forested mountain spine that stretches along the entire length of Albania culminates at Mt Jezerce (2694m) in the north.

CLIMATE

Summers are hot, clear and dry, and winters, when 40% of the rain falls, are cool, cloudy and moist. The high interior plateau can get very cold as continental air masses move in. July is the warmest month, but even April and October are quite pleasant.

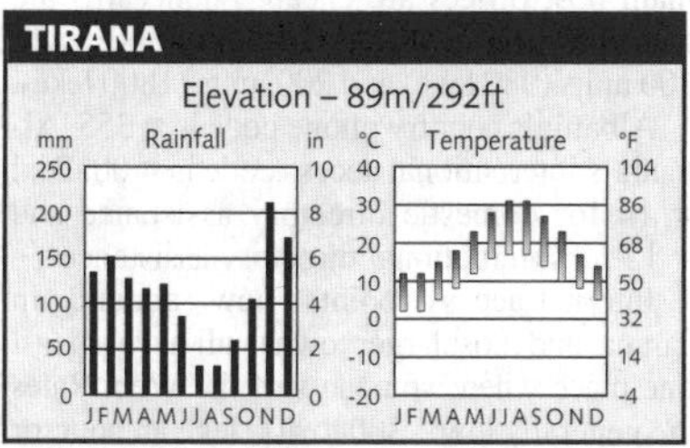

GOVERNMENT & POLITICS

Albania is a parliamentary democracy with a president as head of state.

POPULATION & PEOPLE

The Albanians are a Mediterranean people physically different from the more Nordic Slavs. The Shkumbin River forms a boundary between the Gheg cultural region of the north and the Tosk region in the south. The people in these regions still vary in dialect, musical culture and traditional dress.

SOCIETY & CONDUCT

The *Kanun* is an ancient social law outlining most aspects of social behaviour, including the treatment of guests. Albanians can be very hospitable and will often offer travellers free lodging and food. While payment may be acceptable sometimes, a small gift of a book or a memento from home will often suffice.

Albanians, like Bulgarians, shake their heads to say yes and usually nod to say no.

Be respectful when visiting mosques – remove your shoes and avoid visits during prayer times.

LANGUAGE

Albanian (Shqipja) is an Indo-European dialect of ancient Illyrian. Italian is the most useful foreign language, English a strong second. Greek is useful in the south. See the Language chapter at the back of the book for pronunciation guidelines and useful words and phrases.

Facts for the Visitor

HIGHLIGHTS

The beauty and mystique of Albania's mountains and coastal region makes the country itself a highlight. The striking fortress town of Gjirokastra in the south is worth a visit, as are the stunning and well-preserved Roman ruins at Butrint, also in the far south.

TOURIST OFFICES

There are no tourist information offices in Albania, but hotel receptionists or travel agents will sometimes give you directions.

VISAS & DOCUMENTS

No visa is required from citizens of Australia, EU countries, New Zealand or the US. Citizens of most countries are required to pay an 'entry tax' at the border. The entry tax for most visitors is US$10. Israeli citizens pay US$30.

Upon arrival you will fill in an arrival and departure card. Keep the departure card, which will be stamped, with your passport and present it when you leave.

EMBASSIES & CONSULATES

Albanian Embassies & Consulates

Below are some of the main addresses for Albanian embassies:

France (☎ 01 45 53 51 32) 13 rue de la Pompe, Paris 75016
Germany (☎ 0302-593 0550, fax 593 0599) Friedrichstrasse 231, D-10969 Berlin
Greece (☎ 21 0723 4412, fax 0723 1972) Karahristou 1, GR-114 21 Athens
UK (☎ 020-7730 5709, fax 7828 8869) 24 Buckingham Gate, 2nd Floor, London SW1 E6LB
USA (☎ 202-223 4942, fax 628 7342) 2100 S St NW, Washington DC 20008

Embassies & Consulates in Albania

The following embassies are in Tirana (area code ☎ 042):

Bulgaria (☎ 233 155, fax 232 272) Rruga Skënderbeg 12
Germany (☎ 232 048, fax 233 497) Rruga Skënderbeg 8
Greece (☎ 223 959, fax 234 443) Rruga Frederik Shiroka 3
Macedonia (☎ 233 036, fax 232 514) Rruga Lekë Dukagjini 2
Turkey (☎ 233 399, fax 232 719) Rruga E Kavajës 31
UK (☎ 234 973, fax 247 697) Rruga Skënderbeg 12
USA (☎ 247 285, fax 232 222) Rruga Elbasanit 103
Yugoslavia (☎ 232 089, fax 223 042) Rruga e Durresit 192/196

MONEY

Currency & Exchange Rates

Albanian banknotes come in denominations of 100, 200, 500 and 1000 lekë. There are 5, 10, 20 and 50 lekë coins. Notes issued after 1997 are smaller.

Everything can be paid for with lekë; however, most hotel and transport prices in this chapter are quoted in US dollars or euros, both of which are readily accepted as alternative currencies.

country	unit		lekë
Australia	A$1	=	73.20 lekë
Canada	C$1	=	88.60 lekë
Eurozone	€1	=	118 lekë
Japan	¥100	=	107.20 lekë
NZ	NZ$1	=	60 lekë
UK	UK£1	=	199.20 lekë
US	US$1	=	140 lekë

Exchanging Money

Some banks will change US-dollar travellers cheques into US cash without commission. Travellers cheques may be used at major hotels, but cash is preferred everywhere. Credit cards are accepted only in larger hotels and travel agencies, and a few places in Tirana and Durrës will offer credit-card advances (usually for MasterCard). At the time of research, one ATM had just opened in Tirana.

Every town has its free currency market, which usually operates on the street in front of the main post office or state bank. Be careful and make sure you count the money twice before tendering yours. The advantages are that you get a good rate and avoid the 1% bank commission.

In Albania US dollars are the favourite foreign currency, although euros are also acceptable. However, you will not be able to exchange Albanian currency outside of the country.

Tipping

Round up the bill in restaurants. You will normally agree on a fare beforehand with taxi drivers, so an extra tip will not be necessary.

POST & COMMUNICATIONS

There are few public mailboxes outside of main towns, but an increasing number of modern post offices.

Long-distance telephone calls made from main post offices are cheap. Phonecards are available in versions of 50 units (560 lekë), 100 units (980 lekë) and 200 units (1800 lekë).

Albania's country phone code is ☎ 355. Albania's international access code is ☎ 00. Dial ☎ 14 for domestic directory assistance and ☎ 12 for international directory assistance.

Internet-access points now abound in Tirana, and most larger towns will have at least one place where you can surf the Web. Rates are generally low – 300 to 400 lekë an hour, or part thereof. Some Internet centres also offer cheap international phone connections.

DIGITAL RESOURCES

Useful websites are W www.albanian.com (the Albanian WWW Home Page) and W www.albania.co.uk (a good information source on current events).

BOOKS

See Lonely Planet's *Eastern Europe Phrasebook* for a helpful list of translated Albanian words and phrases.

WOMEN TRAVELLERS

It is recommended that you travel in pairs or with male companions in order to avoid unwanted attention – particularly outside Tirana. Dress should be conservative.

GAY & LESBIAN TRAVELLERS

Homosexuality became legal in Albania early in 1995; however, attitudes are still highly conservative.

DISABLED TRAVELLERS

Few special facilities exist for travellers in wheelchairs.

DANGERS & ANNOYANCES

You are advised to avoid travelling in the far north of the country around Bajram Curri and along the road corridor from Shkodra to Kukës, as banditry may still occur. There may still be land mines near the northern border with Kosovo around Bajram Curri.

Beware of pickpockets on crowded city buses, and don't flash money around. Take special care if accosted by Roma (Gypsy) women and children begging; avoid eye contact and head to the nearest hotel.

As Albania was closed for so long, black travellers may encounter some curious stares. At worst, proprietors of small hotels may try to refuse service.

Corrupt police may attempt to extort money from you. Strongly resist paying them anything without getting an official receipt. Always keep at least a copy of your passport with you.

BUSINESS HOURS

Most businesses open at 8.30am, and some close for a siesta from noon to 4pm, opening again from 4pm to 7pm. Banking hours are shorter (generally 8.30am to 2pm).

PUBLIC HOLIDAYS & SPECIAL EVENTS

Public holidays in Albania include New Year's Day (1 January), Easter Monday (March/April), Labour Day (1 May), Independence Day (28 November), Liberation Day (29 November) and Christmas Day (25 December).

Muslim Ramadan is practised and Bajram is celebrated at variable times of the year.

ACCOMMODATION

Accommodation has undergone a rapid transformation in Albania, with the opening of new, custom-built, private hotels to replace the dismal state hotels. Priced at about US$35 to US$50 and upwards per person per night (usually including breakfast), these are modern, well-appointed establishments.

Another positive development is the conversion of homes or villas into so-called private hotels. For budget travellers, these are without doubt the best way to go. You can often find unofficial accommodation in private homes by asking around. For security reasons, camping is inadvisable.

Emergencies

For urgent service you should call the following country-wide numbers: ambulance ☎ 17, fire ☎ 18 and police ☎ 23 322.

FOOD & DRINKS

Albanian cuisine has been strongly influenced by Turkey. Grilled meats such as *shishqebap* (shish kebab), *romstek* (minced meat patties) and *qofte* (meat balls) are served all across the Balkan countries. Some local dishes include *çomlek* (meat and onion stew), *fërges* (a rich beef stew), *rosto me salcë kosi* (roast beef with sour cream) and *tavë kosi* (mutton with yoghurt). Lake Shkodra carp and Lake Ohrid trout are the most common fish dishes. For dessert, try the *akullore* (ice cream), which is very popular everywhere.

Albanians take their coffee as *kafe turke* (Turkish coffee) and *kafe ekspres* (espresso). Avoid tap water and unbottled drinks.

Albanian white wine is better than the vinegary red. However, the red *Shesi e Zi* from either Librazhd or Berat is an excellent drop. *Raki* (a clear brandy distilled from grapes) is taken as an aperitif – always ask for homemade if possible *(raki ë bërë në shtëpi)*. There's also *konjak* (cognac), *uzo* (a colourless aniseed-flavoured liqueur like Greek ouzo) and various fruit liqueurs. *Fërnet* is a medicinal aperitif containing herbal essences, made at Korça.

ENTERTAINMENT

Check the local theatre for performances. There's usually a disco or two to complement the zillions of cafés in a given town; ask around for what's hot.

Getting There & Away

AIR

Several airlines serve Tirana. It's usually cheaper, though, to fly into Greece. See Getting There & Away in the Tirana section for phone numbers of main airlines.

LAND

Buses to Thessaloniki (€35, 10 hours) leave at 6am daily from in front of **Albanian Interlines** (☎ *222 272; Bulevardi Zogu I*). Buses to Athens (€50, 24 hours) also leave from here three times a week. Buses to Prishtina, Kosovo, leave daily from beside the Tirana International Hotel at 6pm (€30, 12 hours). For Macedonia, take the daily bus to Tetovo (also from here), and from Tetovo take a frequent local bus to Skopje.

Buses for İstanbul and Sofia leave from **Albtransport** (☎ *223 026; Rruga Mine Peza; open 8am-4pm Mon-Fri*). The Sofia bus (€35, 15 hours) leaves at 10am on Wednesday. Two buses for İstanbul (€55, 24 hours) depart at 10am and 1pm on Monday, and go via Sofia.

Bringing a car or motorcycle to Albania is a risky business as theft and bad roads can be a problem. Additionally, your insurance Green Card may not cover Albania.

SEA

The Italian company Adriatica di Navigazione offers ferry services to Durrës from Bari (US$60, 8½ hours) daily and from Ancona (US$85, 19 hours) four times a week. Cars cost US$90/100 respectively. Bicycles are carried free.

In Bari, ferry tickets are available at **Agestea** (☎ *080-553 1555;* ⓔ *agestea.bari02@interbusiness.it; Via Liside 4*) and in Ancona it's **Maritime Agency Srl** (☎ *071-204 915;* ⓔ *tickets.adn@maritime.it; Via XXIX Settembre 10*). In Albania tickets are sold by any number of travel agencies in Durrës or Tirana.

The fastest ferry connection between Bari and Durrës is via the passenger catamarans operated by **Quality Lines** (€60, 3½ hours). These high-speed vessels leave Durrës daily at 10am and 4.30pm. The Durrës agent can be contacted on ☎ 052-24 571.

See Getting There & Away under Saranda later for information on travel to and from Corfu and the port of Saranda.

DEPARTURE TAX

The airport departure tax is US$10, payable in dollars or lekë. A US$4 tariff is imposed on people leaving Albania by ferry, and there's a US$1 daily tariff on vehicles, payable upon crossing the border out of the country.

Getting Around

BUS & MINIBUS

Most Albanians travel around in private *furgon* (minibuses) or larger buses. These run fairly frequently throughout the day between Tirana and Durrës (38km) and other towns north and south. Buses to Tirana depart from towns all around Albania at the crack of dawn. Fares are low (eg, Tirana-Durrës is 100 lekë). Tickets are rarely issued. Shared *furgon* run between cities when they are full or almost full. They usually cost about twice the bus fare, but they're still cheap. Pay the driver or assistant once you leave the minibus.

City buses operate in Tirana, Durrës and Shkodra. Watch your possessions on crowded city buses.

TRAIN

Nobody who can afford other types of transport takes the train. The reason is obvious as you board – the decrepit carriages typically have broken windows and no toilets.

Daily passenger trains leave Tirana for Shkodra (3½ hours, 98km), Fier (4¼ hours), Ballsh (five hours) and Vlora (5½ hours). Seven trains a day also make the 1½-hour trip between Tirana and Durrës.

CAR & MOTORCYCLE

Based in Tirana's Hotel Europapark, **Avis** (☎ *04-235 011, fax 235 042;* ⓔ *gazi@albaniaonline.net*) is the only car-rental company in the country. Driving is fraught with peril and not recommended.

HITCHING

With buses so cheap, hitching will probably only be an emergency means of transport. Most will take you if they possibly can.

Tirana (Tiranë)

☎ 042 • pop 440,000

It wasn't too long ago that Albania's capital was a dusty, languid town virtually unknown to the outside world. Few cars ran along its wide boulevards, and there was no building more than four stories tall. Today it's a bustling, busy metropolis, with more cars than its streets can cope with. Restaurants and cafés have mushroomed, and buildings creep skywards where once only a minaret had been the city's most distinguishing feature.

Orientation

The city revolves around central Skënderbeg Square (Sheshi Skënderbeg). Running south is Bulevardi Dëshmorët e Kombit, which leads to the university building. Running north, Bulevardi Zogu I leads to the train station. Most major services and hotels are within a few minutes' walk of Skënderbeg Square.

Information

Tourist Offices Tirana has no official tourist office, but travel agencies can help you out (see later). One helpful publication is *Tirana In Your Pocket,* available at bookshops and some of the larger kiosks for 300 lekë.

Money While there are plenty of banks in Tirana, a free currency market operates directly in front of the main post office. Just one ATM, at the Greek-owned **Alpha Bank** *(Bulevardi Zogu I)*, is in operation. The Hotel Europapark Tirana has a **currency exchange booth** *(open 10.30am-5pm Mon-Fri)* that offers MasterCard advances, cashes travellers cheques for a 1% commission and exchanges cash. **World Travel** *(☎ 227 998; Mine Peza 2)*, the American Express representative, cashes travellers cheques for a 2% commission.

Post & Communications The **main post office** *(open 8am-8pm Mon-Fri)* and telephone centre are adjacent on a street jutting west from Skënderbeg Square. Another telephone centre is on Bulevardi Zogu I, 400m past Skënderbeg Square on the right.

There are several places to access the Internet. The best is **Net 1** *(☎ 257 433; Rruga Nikolla Tupe 1/b; open 9am-11pm)*, which charges 300 lekë per hour or part thereof.

Travel Agencies A good place to arrange ferry tickets from Durrës, or to book private rooms, is **Albania Travel & Tours** *(☎ 329 83, fax 339 81; Rruga Durrësit 102; open daily)*. Other travel agencies abound, but not all operators speak English.

Medical & Emergency Services Most foreigners use the **ABS Health Foundation** *(☎ 234 105; ⓔ ABS@maf.org; 360 Rruga Qemal Stafa; open Mon-Fri)*, across the street from the 'New School'.

The emergency phone number for an ambulance is ☎ 127 and for the police ☎ 129.

Things to See & Do

Most visits to Tirana begin at **Skënderbeg Square**, a great, open space in the heart of the city. On the northern side is the **National Museum of History** *(admission 300 lekë; open 8am-1pm Mon-Sat)*, Albania's largest and finest museum. To the east is another massive building, the **Palace of Culture**. Construction began as a gift from the Soviet people in 1960. The entrance to the **National Library** is on the south side of the building. Opposite this is the cupola and minaret of the **Et'hem Bey mosque** (1789–1823), one of the most distinctive buildings in the city. Enter to see the beautifully painted dome. Tirana's **clock tower** *(☎ 243 292; open 9am-1pm & 4pm-6pm Mon, Wed & Sat)*, built in 1830, stands beside the mosque.

On the south side of the square is the **Skënderbeg equestrian statue** (1968) looking straight up Bulevardi Zogu I. Behind Skënderbeg's statue the boulevard leads to the three arches of **Tirana University** (1957). As you stroll down this tree-lined boulevard you'll see Tirana's **art gallery** *(open Tues-Sun)*, a onetime stronghold of socialist realism.

Stalinist Tirana The wide Bulevardi Dëshmorët e Kombit was once stomping ground of Albania's Stalinist *Nomenklatura* (political elite). Along here and to the west you can see the sights of Tirana's not-too-distant Stalinist past.

Start your walk down Bulevardi Dëshmorët e Kombit at the now brightly painted **government buildings**, housing various ministries. Just behind the last building on the left were the headquarters of the once much-feared *Sigurimi*, communist Albania's dreaded secret police.

Continue along Bulevardi Dëshmorët e Kombit to the bridge over the Lana River. On the right across the river is the dour-looking former **Central Committee building** (1955) of the Party of Labour. Opposite is the **Prime Minister's Residence**.

Follow Rruga Ismail Qemali, the street on the south side of the Central Committee building, and enter the once totally forbidden **Block** – the former exclusive and strictly off-limits residential district of the Communist Party faithful.

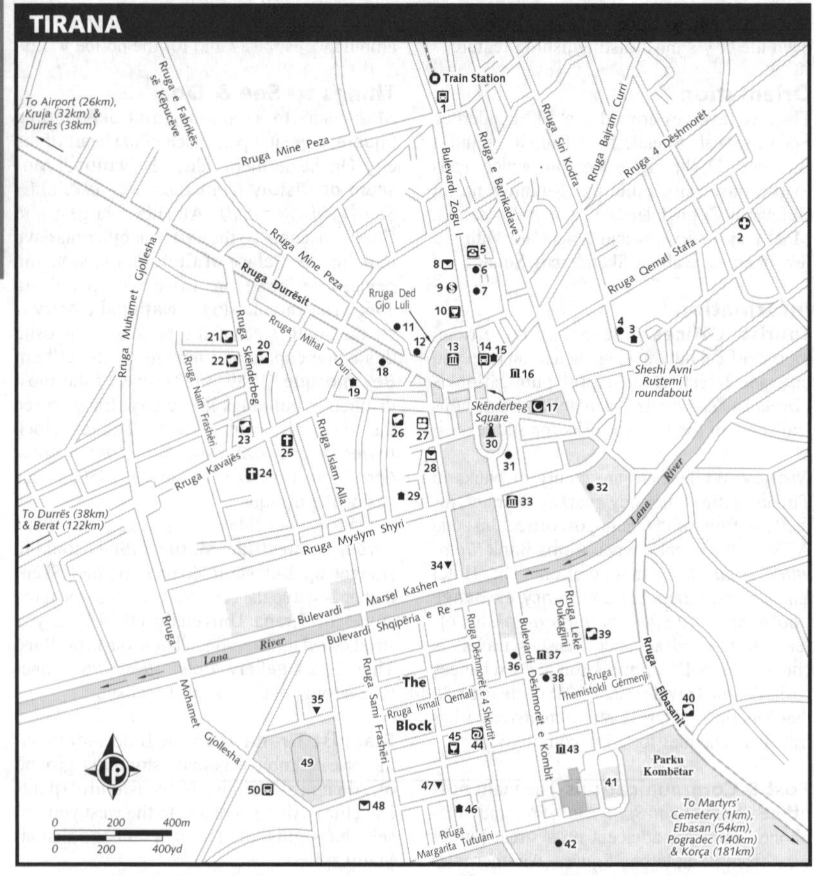

The **Varrezat e Dëshmorëve** (Martyrs' Cemetery) is the resting place of some 900 partisans who died during WWII. The hill-top setting, with a beautiful view over the city and mountains, is subdued, and a great white figure of Mother Albania (1972) stands watch.

Places to Stay

Staying in apartments or with local families is the best budget option, but they can be hard to find. Newer private hotels are pleasant but expensive.

Albania Travel & Tours (see Travel Agencies, earlier) has private rooms for around 2600 lekë per person. Other travel agencies may also find you a private room.

Tiny **Hotel Endri** *(☎ 244 168, 229 334; Pall 27, Sh. 3 Ap. 30, Rruga Vaso Pasha 27; rooms US$20)* is a decent deal. The 'hotel', which essentially consists of two rooms adjacent to manager Petrit Alikaj's apartment, is sparkling-clean and new, and has very nice bathrooms with excellent showers. Handily, Petrit is also a taxi driver.

Qëndra Stefan *(Stephen Center; ☎/fax 253 924; e stephenc@icc.al.eu.org; Rruga Hoxha Tasim 1; singles/doubles US$30/50 including breakfast)* is probably a better option and certainly much easier to find. Rooms are modern, bright and breezy, and for nonsmokers and nondrinkers only.

Just off Rruga Durrësit is nifty **Hotel California** *(☎/fax 232 228; Rruga Mihal Duri 21; singles/doubles US$50/70 including breakfast)*, which has clean rooms with minibar and TV.

TIRANA

PLACES TO STAY
3 Qëndra Stefan
15 Tirana International Hotel; Turkish Airlines
19 Hotel California
29 Europa International Hotel
46 Hotel Endri

PLACES TO EAT
34 La Voglia
35 Ujevara
47 Il Passatore

OTHER
1 Bus & Minibus Station to Durrës & North
2 ABS Health Foundation
4 Public Market
5 Telephone Centre
6 Albania Interlines
7 Olympic Airways
8 Post Office Sub Branch
9 Alpha Bank ATM
10 London Bar
11 Albtransport
12 Albania Travel & Tours
13 National Museum of History; Alitalia
14 Bus Departure Point for Prishtina
16 Palace of Culture; International Bookshop
17 Et'hem Bey Mosque; Clock Tower
18 World Travel
20 Bulgarian Embassy
21 German Embassy
22 UK Embassy
23 Greek Embassy
24 Orthodox Church of Holy Evangelist
25 Catholic Church of St Anthony
26 Turkish Embassy
27 Kinema Millennium
28 Main Post Office; Telephone Centre
30 Skënderbeg Equestrian Statue
31 Government Buildings; Former Sigurimi HQ
32 Parliament
33 Art Gallery
36 Former Central Committee Building
37 Prime Minister's Residence
38 Avis Car Rentals, Hotel Europapark Tirana; Currency Exchange; Swiss; Austrian Airlines
39 Macedonian Embassy
40 US Embassy
41 Qemal Stafa Stadium
42 Tirana University
43 Palace of Congresses
44 Net 1
45 Murphy's
48 Post Office Sub Branch
49 Selman Stërmasi (Dinamo) Stadium
50 Southern Bus Station

A pleasant private hotel is **Europa International Hotel** *(☎/fax 227 403; Rruga Myslym Shyri 44/2; singles/doubles US$60/70 including breakfast)*, which has modern rooms and parking out front. It can be hard to find, as it is actually off Rruga Myslym Shyri in the back streets. Ask for directions.

Places to Eat

There is no shortage of small restaurants, cafés and snack bars on and around Skënderbeg Square and Bulevardi Dëshmorët e Kombit.

If you fancy breakfast, a cuppa or a sandwich, call at **Qëndra Stefan** (see Places to Stay), a friendly, nonsmoking place run by Americans.

Among Tirana's innumerable pizza places, the two-floor **La Voglia** *(☎ 228 678; Rruga Dëshmorët e 4 Shkurtit; pizza 350-400 lekë)*, near the river, serves a very good pizza.

One of Tirana's more popular restaurants is **Il Passatore** *(Antonella's; ☎ 233 420; Rruga Vaso Pasha 22/1; mains 1200 lekë per person)*. Food and service here are excellent, with delicious specials of fish or pasta and a diverse salad bar.

A little out of the way is **Ujevara** *(☎ 243 702; Rruga Gjin Bue Shpata; pasta dishes 600-700 lekë)*. Italian pasta and fresh salads are the key ingredients at this pleasant eatery near the southern bus station.

Entertainment

For the lowdown on events and exhibitions, check the leaflet *ARTirana*. Also check the posters outside the **Palace of Culture** *(performances from 7pm, 6pm winter)* for opera or ballet.

Tirana's Irish pub, **Murphy's** *(☎ 038-203 7854; Rruga Abdyl Frashëri)* serves up Guinness and many other brews, making it a darling of the expat community. **London Bar** *(☎ 228 851; Bulevardi Zogu I 51)*, near Tirana International Hotel, is also popular.

Pop concerts and other musical events often take place in the **Qemal Stafa Stadium** next to the university.

Getting There & Away

Air Many of the airline offices are on Rruga Durrësit, just off Skënderbeg Square. **Alitalia** *(☎ 230 023; Skënderbeg Square)* has an office behind the National Museum of History, and **Swiss International Airlines** *(☎/fax 232 011)* and **Austrian Airlines** *(☎/fax 374 355)* are at Hotel Europapark Tirana. **Olympic Airways** *(☎ 228 960; Ve-Ve Business Centre, Bulevardi Zogu I)* is behind the Tirana International Hotel, and **Turkish Airlines** *(☎ 234 185)* is in Tirana International Hotel.

Bus There are two main bus/minibus departure points: the Selman Stërmasi (Dinamo)

Stadium, for buses to the south; and the lot in front of the train station, for buses to Durrës and the north.

The following table will give you an idea of distances and average costs involved for departures from Tirana. Minibuses are usually 40% to 50% more expensive than buses.

destination	distance (km)	duration (hrs)	cost (lekë)
Berat	122	3½	250
Durrës	38	1	100
Fier	113	3	260
Gjirokastra	232	8	1000
Kukës	208	8	1000
Saranda	284	8	800
Shkodra	116	2½	300
Vlora	147	4	300

Both buses and minibuses normally leave when full.

Train Eight trains a day go to Durrës (55 lekë, one hour, 36km). Trains also depart for Shkodra (150 lekë, 3½ hours, twice daily) and Vlora (210 lekë, 5½ hours, twice daily).

Getting Around

A taxi to/from the airport should cost about €30 or US$20. Taxi stands dot the city and charge 400 lekë for a ride inside Tirana (600 lekë at night). Make sure you reach an agreement with the driver before setting off. **Radio Taxi** *(☎ 377 777)*, with 24-hour service, is particularly reliable.

Around Tirana

DURRËS

☎ 052 • pop 85,000

Once the grim, workaday main port of Albania, Durrës is now a relaxed, more laid-back alternative to the capital. Moreover, it retains the time-honoured tradition of the *xhiro* – the evening street promenade, when all the town comes out to walk and talk, to see and to be seen.

Unlike Tirana, Durrës is an ancient city, founded by the Greeks in 627 BC. Roman ruins and Byzantine fortifications embellish the town. On a bay southeast of the city are long, sandy beaches where tourist hotels and restaurants have sprung up.

The **Savings Bank of Albania** *(open 8am-2pm Mon-Fri)*, across from the train station, changes travellers cheques and offers MasterCard advances for a 1% commission. The post office and phone centre are one block west of the stations. Among several Internet cafés is **Interalb Internet** *(Rruga N Frashëri)*, charging 240 lekë per hour.

The **Archaeological Museum**, which faces the waterfront promenade near the port, is worth a visit. Look for the Belle of Durrës mosaic, which gives a view of ancient Dyrrachium. Beyond the museum are the 6th-century **Byzantine city walls**. As you're exploring the city centre, stop to see the **Roman baths** directly behind Aleksandër Moisiu Theatre, on the central square.

The impressive but unrestored **Roman amphitheatre**, built between the 1st and 2nd centuries AD, is on the hillside just inside the walls. You can see a small, built-in 10th-century Byzantine church decorated with wall mosaics.

Walk up to the former **palace of King Ahmet Zogu**, on the hill top west of the amphitheatre, and enjoy the views (there's no admission to the palace).

Places to Stay

Durrës has a handful of pleasant, mid-priced hotels in the centre, and a string of new resort-style hotels on the beaches south of town. **Albania Travel & Tours** *(☎ 24 276, ☎/fax 25 450; Rruga Durrah; open daily)*, near the port, may be able to help arrange a private room with advance notice.

The best budget choice is **B&B Tedeschini** *(☎ 24 343, 038 224 6303; ⓔ ipmcrsp@icc.al.eu.org; Dom Nikoll Kaçorri 5; B&B US$15)* in a gracious, 19th-century house. From the square fronting the mosque, walk towards the restaurant Il Castello. Take the first right, then a quick left, then a quick right.

The 13-room **Hotel Lido** *(☎/fax 27 941; Rruga Aleksandër Goga; singles/doubles US$35/46)*, in the centre of town, has clean, pleasant rooms with phone, fridge, heating TV, and air-conditioning.

Cheery **Hotel Pepeto** *(☎ 24 190, ☎/fax 26 346; singles/doubles US$40/60)*, just to the east of the square fronting the mosque, is another good choice, with rates that include breakfast and laundry. The owner speaks English.

Places to Eat

By far the best place to eat in town is **Il Castello** *(☎ 268 87; Rruga H Troplini 3)*, which has outstanding pastas (try the seafood pasta at 450 lekë) and a good selection of fish. **Mondial Pizzeria** *(☎ 27 946; Rruga Taulantia)*, on the waterfront on the way to Arragosta, is a busy little pizzeria serving good-sized pizzas and pasta dishes. Along the beach strip, numerous restaurants offer seaside dining. The niftiest place for a coffee or beer is the **Bar Torra**, in the tower beside the port entrance.

Getting There & Away

Albania's railway network centres on Durrës. Eight trains a day run to Tirana (55 lekë, one hour), two to Shkodra (150 lekë, 3½ hours) and two to Vlora (210 lekë, five hours) via Fier. Minibuses to Tirana (150 lekë, one hour) and buses (100 lekë, one hour) leave from beside the train station whenever they're full.

Numerous travel agencies along Rruga Durrah handle ferry bookings.

Southern Albania

The south of the country is rich in historical and natural beauty. Southeast of the vast Myzaqeja plain, the land becomes extremely mountainous, with lovely valleys. The 124km of Ionian coast from Saranda to Vlora is stunning, with 2000m mountains falling directly to the sea.

GJIROKASTRA (GJIROKASTËR)

☎ 0762 • pop 24,500

Travellers from Greece may well find this strikingly picturesque town an ideal spot for the first night's stay in Albania. Gjirokastra is like an Albanian eagle perched on the mountainside with a mighty citadel for its head. The **castle** *(admission 500 lekë; open 8am-8pm daily)* is its main feature. The bizarre sight of a disintegrating **US military jet** on the ramparts adds an unreal air to the scene.

The best place to stay is **Guest House Haxhi Kotoni** *(☎ 35 26; Lagja Palorto 8, Rruga Bashkim Kokona; singles/doubles 1500/2000 lekë)*. This neat but tiny B&B offers clean and comfy double rooms with bathroom, TV and heating.

Eating options are thin. **Bar Fantazia** *(☎ 69 91)* commands the best view in the Old Town. Walk downhill to the new town for a wider variety of choices.

Buses to Gjirokastra depart from or stop on the main highway, 1½km from the Old Town. Taxis can take you into town for about 200 lekë. Buses to Tirana (1000 lekë, eight hours) are fairly frequent; there are four a day to Saranda (300 lekë, 1½ hours). You'll need to take a taxi to get to the Greek border at Kakavija (1500 lekë, 30 minutes).

SARANDA (SARANDË)

☎ 0732 • pop 12,000

Saranda is a small town on the Gulf of Saranda, between the mountains and the Ionian Sea. This southernmost harbour was once the ancient port of Onchesmos. For foreigners, it's a useful point for getting to/from Corfu in Greece. The town's beaches are slowly being re-landscaped, and the long promenade makes for some relaxed evening strolls.

Change money at **Exchange Mario** *(☎ 23 61; Rruga Vangeli Gramoza)* or with the crowds of moneychangers near the central square. Check email at **Ecom Internet** *(☎ 39 95; Rruga Adem Shema)*, close to the centre.

The ancient ruins of **Butrint** *(☎ 46 00; admission 700 lekë; open 8am-7.30pm)*, 18km south of Saranda, are surprisingly extensive and interesting. The poet Virgil (70–19 BC) claimed that the Trojans founded Buthroton (Butrint), but no evidence of this has been found. A cab to Butrint will cost around 2000 lekë.

The **Blue Eye spring**, about 15km east of Saranda, signposted *Syri i Kalter* to the left off the Gjirokastra road and before the ascent over the pass to the Drino valley, is definitely worth seeing. Its iridescent blue water gushes from the depths of the earth and feeds the Bistrica River. The spring's actual depth is still unknown.

An excellent budget accommodation choice is **Hotel Lili** *(☎ 37 64; Lagja No 3; singles/doubles 3000/5000 lekë)*. All rooms have fridges, fans, TV and use of a washing machine. Superb wood-oven pizzas are served up at **Pizzeri Evangjelos** *(☎ 54 29; ne Shetitore; pizzas 350-600 lekë)*.

A daily ferry and hydrofoil service plies between Saranda and Corfu (€14 one way). Call **Finikas Lines** *(☎ +30-9-4485 3228)* in Corfu for schedules. The hydrofoil normally leaves Saranda at 10am.

Buses to Tirana (1000 lekë, eight hours) and Gjirokastra (300 lekë, 1½ hours) leave from Saranda's bus station four times daily.

FIER & APOLLONIA

☎ 0623 • pop 48,500

Fier is a large oil town by the Gjanica River, 89km south of Durrës. By far the most interesting sight is the ruins of ancient **Apollonia** (Pojan), 12km west. Apollonia was founded by Corinthian Greeks in 588 BC and quickly grew into an important city-state, minting its own currency. Under the Romans the city became a great cultural centre with a famous school of philosophy.

Julius Caesar rewarded Apollonia with the title 'free city' for supporting him against Pompey the Great during a civil war in the 1st century BC, and sent his nephew Octavius, the future Emperor Augustus, to complete his studies there. Only a small part of ancient Apollonia has so far been uncovered, but look out for the picturesque 3rd century BC **House of Mosaics**, which is one of the site's highlights.

Northern Albania

Visits to northern Albania still involve an element of risk due to continuing instability in security. The main road corridor from Tirana to the Yugoslav border is generally fine, but travellers are advised to avoid independent travel west of Shkodra, between that town and Kukës, and further north around Bajram Curri.

Shkodra, the historic old Gheg capital near the lake of the same name, is a pleasant introduction to Albania for those arriving from Yugoslavia. South of here is **Lezha** and **Skënderbeg's tomb**.

Andorra

Tiny Andorra, nestled in the Pyrenees mountains between France and Spain, is something of an anomaly. Rather than wonder why this ludicrously diminutive land exists independently, most travellers – over eight million yearly – breeze through its innumerable duty-free shops and enjoy its budget skiing. These activities, together with great summer walking and dramatic scenery, bring both wealth and unsightly development.

True to logic-defying form, Andorrans are a minority in their own country, forming only about a quarter of the total population of 66,000, the majority of whom are Spaniards. From the Middle Ages until as recently as 1993, Andorra's sovereignty was invested in two princes: the Catholic bishop of the Spanish town of La Seu d'Urgell and the French king or president. Nowadays, democratic Andorra is a parliamentary co-princedom, with the bishop and president remaining nominal heads of state.

Andorra: the Basics

Capital
Andorra la Vella

Population
66,000

Language
Catalan

Currency
euro (€) = 100 centimes

Avoid at all costs Andorra la Vella's horrendous traffic jams.

Facts for the Visitor

VISAS & DOCUMENTS

You don't need a visa to enter Andorra – the authorities appear to think that if Spain or France will let you in, that's good enough for them – but bring your passport or national ID card with you.

MONEY

Although it's not a full member of the EU, Andorra has purloined the euro from its neighbours (see under Money in the Facts for the Visitor chapter earlier in this book for information about currency-exchange rates). There are many ATMs and banks throughout the country, especially in Andorra la Vella.

POST & COMMUNICATIONS

France and Spain operate separate systems with their own Andorran stamps, which are needed only for international mail (letters within the country are delivered free). Regular French and Spanish stamps cannot be used.

Andorra's country code is ☎ 376. You are not able make a reverse-charge (collect) call from Andorra.

ACTIVITIES

Above the main valleys, you'll find attractive lake-dotted mountain country, good for skiing in winter and walking in summer. The largest and best ski resorts are Soldeu-El Tarter and Pas de la Casa/Grau Roig. The others – Ordino-Arcalís, Arinsal and Pal – are cheaper but often colder and windier. Ski passes cost €19 to €30 a day, depending on location and season; downhill ski gear costs €8 to €10 a day to hire, and snowboards are €15 to €18 a day.

Tourist offices can supply a useful English-language booklet, *Sport Activities*, describing numerous hiking and mountain-bike routes. In summer, mountain bikes can be rented for around €18 a day.

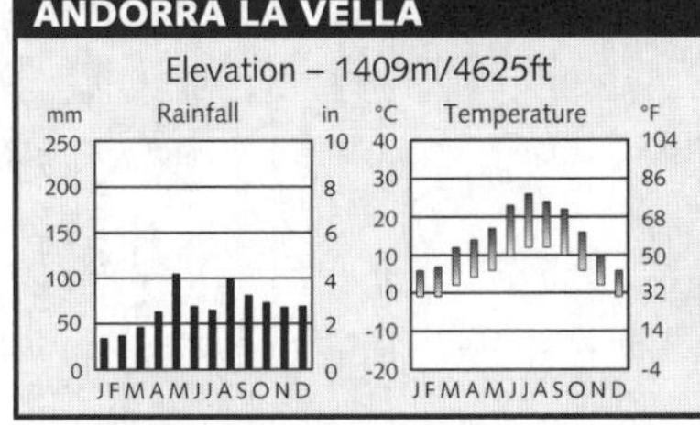

ACCOMMODATION

Tourist offices stock a comprehensive free brochure, *Hotels, Restaurants, Apartaments i Cámpings*. The prices it quotes are merely indicative of what each place costs. There are no youth hostels and, outside Andorra la Vella,

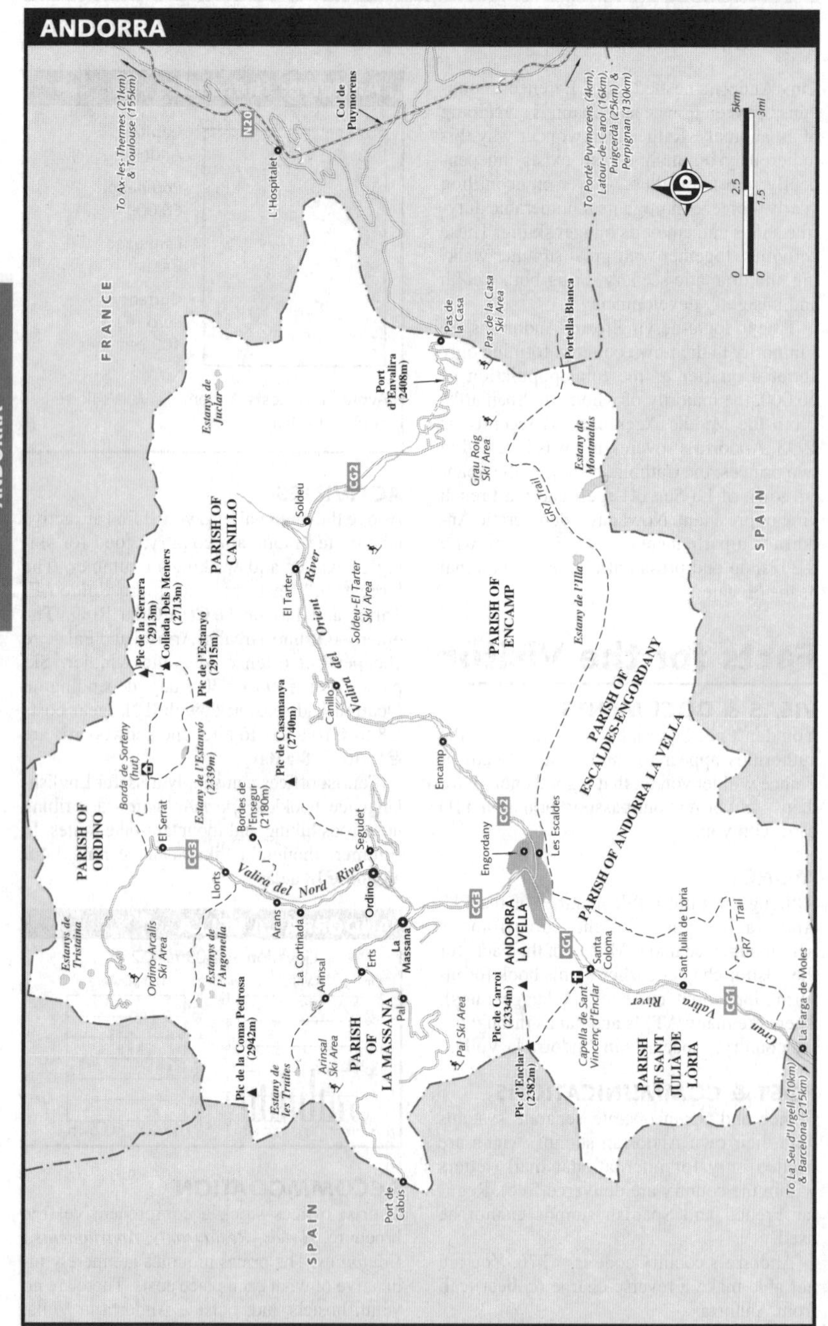
ANDORRA
FRANCE
SPAIN
SPAIN
To Ax-les-Thermes (21km) & Toulouse (155km)
N20
L'Hospitalet
Col de Puymorens
To Porté Puymorens (4km), Latour-de-Carol (16km), Puigcerdà (25km) & Perpignan (130km)
0
2.5
5km
0
1.5
3mi
Pas de la Casa
Pas de la Casa Ski Area
Portella Blanca
Port d'Envalira (2408m)
Estanys de Juclar
Grau Roig Ski Area
Estany de Montmalús
GR7 Trail
CG2
Soldeu
PARISH OF CANILLO
Pic de la Serrera (2913m)
Collada Dels Meners (2713m)
Pic de l'Estanyó (2915m)
El Tarter
Soldeu-El Tarter Ski Area
Valira del Orient River
PARISH OF ENCAMP
Estany de l'Illa
Canillo
Pic de Casamanya (2740m)
Borda de Sorteny (hut)
Estany de l'Estanyó (2339m)
Bordes de l'Ensegur (2180m)
Encamp
PARISH OF ESCALDES-ENGORDANY
PARISH OF ANDORRA LA VELLA
PARISH OF ORDINO
El Serrat
CG3
Segudet
Llorts
Valira del Nord River
Ordino
Engordany
Les Escaldes
Arans
La Cortinada
CG3
ANDORRA LA VELLA
Estanys de Tristaina
Ordino-Arcalís Ski Area
Estanys de l'Angonella
La Massana
Erts
Arinsal
CG1
Santa Coloma
Sant Julià de Lòria
GR7 Trail
Pic de la Coma Pedrosa (2942m)
Arinsal Ski Area
PARISH OF LA MASSANA
Pal
Pal Ski Area
Pic de Carroi (2334m)
Capella de Sant Vincenç d'Enclar
Gran Valira River
CG1
La Farga de Moles
Estany de les Truites
Pic d'Enclar (2382m)
PARISH OF SANT JULIÀ DE LÒRIA
Port de Cabús
To La Seu d'Urgell (10km) & Barcelona (215km)

Emergencies

The Europe-wide telephone number ☎ 112 can be used for emergency police, fire brigade and ambulance services.

few budget options for independent travellers. In compensation, there are plenty of camping grounds, many beautifully situated. In the high season (December to March and July and August), some hotels put prices up substantially and others don't take in independent travellers.

For walkers, Andorra has 26 off-the-beaten-track *refugis* (mountain refuges); all except one are unstaffed and free. Ask for the free *Mapa de Refugis i Grans Recorreguts*, which pinpoints and describes all the refuges.

Getting There & Around

The only way to reach Andorra, unless you trek across the mountains, is by road.

LAND

France

Autocars Nadal (☎ *821138*) has two buses a day (€20, four hours; Monday, Wednesday, Friday and Sunday), linking Toulouse's *gare routière* (bus station) and Andorra la Vella.

By rail, take a train from Toulouse to either L'Hospitalet (2¼ to 2¾ hours, four daily) or Latour-de-Carol (2½ to 3¼ hours). Two daily connecting buses link Andorra la Vella with both L'Hospitalet (€6.80) and Latour-de-Carol (€8.20). On Saturday, up to five buses run from L'Hospitalet to Pas de la Casa, just inside Andorra.

Spain

Alsina Graells (☎ *827379*) runs up to seven buses daily between Barcelona's Estació del Nord and Andorra la Vella's Avinguda de Tarragona bus station (€18, four hours). **Eurolines** (☎ *860010*) operates four services daily (€17.88) between Andorra (from the Hotel Diplomátic car park, opposite the bus station) and Barcelona's Sants bus station.

Samar/Andor-Inter (☎ *826289*) operates three times weekly between Andorra and Madrid (€27, nine hours), via Zaragoza (€13).

La Hispano Andorrana (☎ *821372*) has five to eight buses each day between La Seu d'Urgell, across the border, and Carrer Doctor Nequi in Andorra la Vella (€2.05, hourly until 9pm).

LOCAL TRANSPORT

Ask at a tourist office for a timetable of the eight bus routes, run by **Cooperativa Interurbana** (☎ *820412*), which follow Andorra's three main highways. Destinations from the Avinguda Príncep Benlloch bus stop in Andorra la Vella include Ordino (€0.84, every half an hour), Arinsal (€1.38, three daily), Soldeu (€2.16, hourly) and Pas de la Casa (€4.36, up to four daily).

Andorra la Vella

pop 23,300 • elevation 1029m

Andorra la Vella is squeezed into the Riu Gran Valira Valley and is mainly engaged in retailing electronic and luxury goods. With the constant din of jackhammers ringing in your ears, and the shopping-mall architecture, you might think you're in Hong Kong but for the snowcapped peaks and an absence of noodle shops.

The main drag's name changes from Avinguda del Príncep Benlloch to Avinguda de Meritxell and then to Avinguda de Carlemany. The tiny historic quarter of Barri Antic is split by this heavily trafficked artery.

Wherefore Andorra?

Right, here's the lowdown on Andorra. By tradition, Andorra's independence is credited to Charlemagne, who captured the region from Muslims in AD 803. In 843, Charlemagne's grandson, Charles II, granted the Valls d'Andorra (Valleys of Andorra) to Sunifred, Count of Urgell, whose base was in Catalunya. From the counts, Andorra later passed to the bishops of La Seu d'Urgell.

In the 13th century, after a successional dispute between the bishops and the French counts of Foix, Andorra's first constitutional documents – the Pareatges – established a system of shared sovereignty between the two rivals. This feudal setup created a peculiar political equilibrium that saved Andorra from being swallowed by its powerful neighbours.

Information

The **municipal tourist office** *(☎ 827117; Plaça de la Rotonda; open daily)* sells stamps and telephone cards. The **national tourist office** *(☎ 820214; open daily)* is off Plaça de Rebés. ATMs and banks are all over this mercantile city. **Crèdit Andorrà** *(Avinguda de Meritxell 80)* has a 24-hour exchange machine that accepts banknotes of 15 currencies. The AmEx representative is **Viatges Relax** *(☎ 822044; Carrer de Mossén Tremosa 2)*.

La Poste *(Carrer de Pere d'Urg 1)* is the French post office and **Correus i Telègrafs** *(Carrer de Joan Maragall 10)* is the Spanish one. You can make international calls from pay phones or from the **Servei de Telecomunicacions d'Andorra** *(STA; Carretera de l'Obac; open 9am-9pm daily)*.

E-Café *(☎ 865677; Carrer de l'Alzinaret 5; open 10am-9pm Mon-Fri Oct-July, plus 4pm-8pm Sat Aug & Sept)*, just off Plaça de Guillemo, is a cheerful place to log on and charges €3.60 per hour.

Things to See & Do

The small Barri Antic is the heart of Andorra la Vella. Narrow cobblestone streets around the **Casa de la Vall** are flanked by attractive stone houses. Built in 1580 as a private home, the Casa de la Vall has served as Andorra's parliament building since 1702. Downstairs is **El Tribunal de Corts** *(☎ 829129)*, the only courtroom in the country. Free guided tours (available in English) are given from 9.30am to 1pm and 3pm to 7pm Monday to Saturday and from 10am to 2pm Sunday except during August, when tours are the same time every day of the week. In summer, book at least a week ahead to insure a spot, though individuals can often be squeezed in at the last minute.

The **Plaça del Poble**, a large public square just south of Plaça de Rebés, occupies the roof of a modern government office building. Giving good views, it's a popular local gathering place, especially in the evening.

If you've enough left in the kitty for some shopping, you can make savings on things like sports gear, photographic equipment, shoes and clothing; prices are around 25% lower than in Spain or France.

Places to Stay

Camping Valira *(Avinguda de Salou; sites 2 people & tent €12; open year-round)* has a

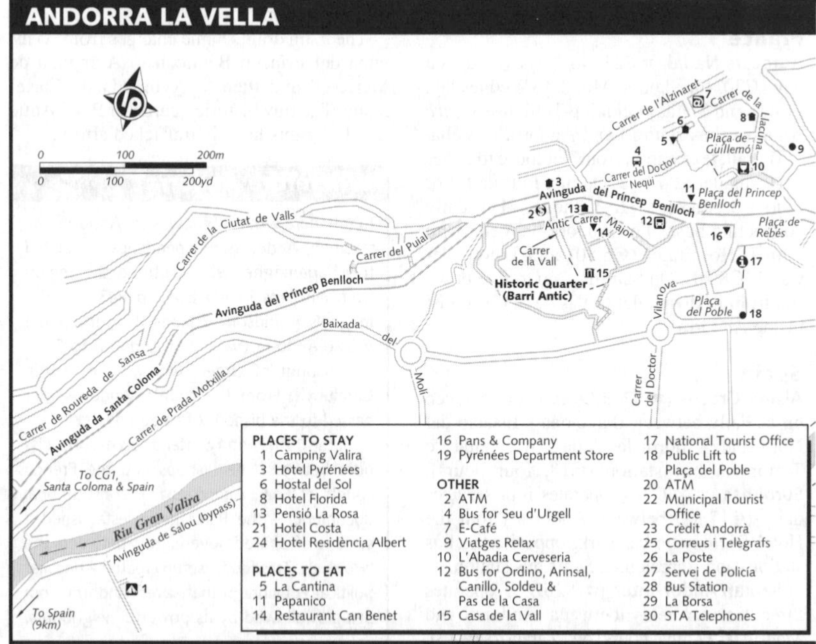

small indoor swimming pool. The friendly **Hostal del Sol** *(☎ 823701; Plaça de Guillemó; singles/doubles with shower €12/24)* has spruce rooms. Also in the Barri Antic, **Pensió La Rosa** *(☎ 821810; Antic Carrer Major 18; dorm beds €13, singles/doubles €19/22)* has plain single and double rooms, as well as triples, quads and a dormitory sleeping six.

Hotel Costa *(☎ 821439; 3rd floor, Avinguda de Meritxell 44; singles/doubles €11/20)* has clean, no-frills rooms; the entrance is in the shopping arcade. **Hotel Residència Albert** *(☎ 820156; Avinguda del Doctor Mitjavla 16; singles/doubles/triples €20/35/42)* is also very basic but clean and good value. Most rooms have a bathroom.

More upmarket, the delightful **Hotel Florida** *(☎ 820105, fax 861925; ⓔ hotelflorida@andorra.ad; Carrer de la Llacuna 15; singles/doubles low season €28/36, high season €40/68)*, one block from Plaça de Guillemó, has well-equipped rooms, and the rates include breakfast.

Although rooms are good value at **Hotel Pyrénées** *(☎ 860006, fax 820265, ⓔ ph@mypic.ad; Avinguda del Princep Benlloch 20; singles/doubles €33/52.30)*, you must take half-board during peak periods, which could cut into your budget.

Places to Eat

Pans & Company *(Plaça de Rebés 2; baguettes €2.50-3.30)* is good for baguettes with a wide range of fillings. **La Cantina** *(Plaça de Guillemó; salads €4.50-6.60, set menu €7.20)* is a friendly family-run place offering good salads and pizzas. In the Barri Antic, **Papanico** *(Avinguda del Príncep Benlloch; tapas €2-5)* is fun for morning coffee or late-night snacks. It has tasty tapas and does a range of sandwiches and hunky *platos combinados* (a combined plate of food). **Restaurant Can Benet** *(Antic Carrer Major 9; mains €8.50-15)* is a delightful place.

There are **fast-food outlets** opposite the bus station and at Avinguda de Meritxell 105.

For self-caterers, the **Pyrénées department store** *(Avinguda de Meritxell 21)* has a well-stocked supermarket on the 2nd floor.

Entertainment

L'Abadia Cerveseria *(☎ 820825; Cap del Carrer 2; open 6pm-3am Mon-Sat)* is a great place to sample an amber liquid in the wee

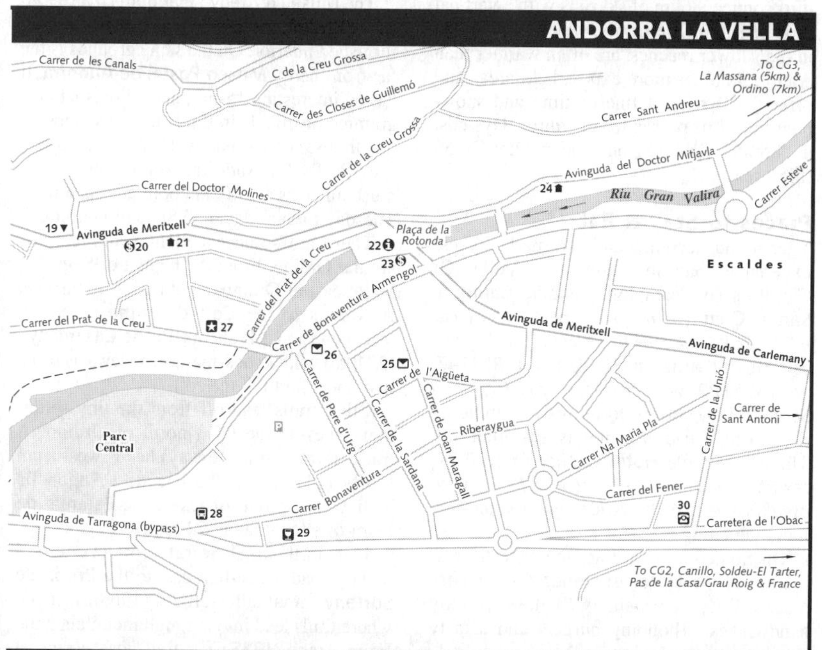

hours. **La Borsa** *(Avinguda de Tarragona; open Thur-Sat)* is an old favourite among the city's several nightclubs.

Getting There & Away

For details of bus services from Andorra la Vella to points around the country, see the individual destinations later in the chapter.

Around Andorra

CANILLO & SOLDEU

Canillo, 11km east of Andorra la Vella, and Soldeu, a further 7km up the valley along the CG2, are as complementary as summer and winter.

In summer, Canillo offers canyon clambering, a *vía ferrata* climbing gully and climbing wall, the year-round Palau de Gel with ice rink and swimming pool, guided walks and endless possibilities for hiking. The helpful **tourist office** *(☎ 851002)* is on the main road at the east end of the village.

During winter, Soldeu and its smaller neighbour **El Tarter** come into their own, as 23 lifts (including a cabin lift up from Canillo) connect 86km of ski runs with a vertical drop of 850m. The slopes, which are wooded in their lower reaches, are often warmer than Andorra's other more exposed ski areas and offer the Pyrenees' finest skiing and snowboarding. Lift passes for one/three days cost €24.50/63 (low season) and €27.50/70.50 (high season).

Places to Stay & Eat

Year-round, accommodation is markedly less expensive than in Andorra la Vella. Of Canillo's five camping grounds, **Camping Santa Creu** *(☎ 851462; person/tent/car €2.85/2.85/2.85)* is the greenest and quietest. **Hostal Aina** *(☎ 851434, fax 851747; beds €10.22, with breakfast €12.02; open Sept–15 June)* offers dormitory accommodation – ring ahead in winter as it is often full. The comfortable **Hotel Canigó** *(☎ 851024, fax 851824; rooms per person €18.25, with breakfast €21.85)* provides good value-for-money lodging.

On Soldeu's main drag, the cheerful restaurant at the **Hotel Bruxelles** *(sandwiches €2.70-3.50, set menu €8)* does yummy sandwiches, whopping burgers and a tasty lunch menu.

Entertainment

The music pounds on winter nights in Soldeu. Pussy Cat and its neighbour, Fat Albert, both one block from the main drag, rock until far too late for impressive skiing next day.

Getting There & Around

Buses run from Andorra la Vella to El Tarter and Soldeu (€2.16, 40 minutes, hourly) between 9am and 8pm. In winter there are free shuttle buses (just flash your ski pass) between Canillo and the two upper villages. These run approximately hourly (with a break from noon to 3pm) until 11pm.

All three villages are also on the bus route between Andorra la Vella and the French railheads of Latour-de-Carol and L'Hospitalet.

ORDINO & AROUND

Despite recent development, Ordino (population 1000), situated 8km north of Andorra la Vella on highway CG3, retains a traditional Andorran character, with most buildings still in local stone. At 1000m it's a good starting point for summer activity holidays. The **tourist office** *(☎ 737080; open daily)* is located on the CG3.

The **Museu d'Areny i Plandolit** *(☎ 836908)* is a 17th-century manor house with a richly furnished interior. On the same grounds is the far-from-nerdy **Museo Postal de Andorra**. It has an interesting 15-minute audiovisual programme (available in English) and stamps by the thousand, issued by France and Spain specifically for Andorra. Admission to each museum costs €2.40 and both are open from Tuesday to Saturday, and Sunday morning.

There are some excellent walking trails around Ordino. From the hamlet of **Segudet**, 500m east of Ordino, a path goes up through fir woods to the **Coll d'Ordino** (1980m), reached in about 1½ hours. **Pic de Casamanya** (2740m), with knock-me-down views, is some two hours north of the coll.

Other trails lead off from the tiny settlements beside the CG3 north of Ordino. A track (three hours one way) heads west from **Llorts** (1413m) up the Riu de l'Angonella Valley to a group of lakes, the **Estanys de l'Angonella**, at about 2300m.

Just north of **El Serrat** (1600m), a secondary road leads 4km east to the **Borda de Sorteny** mountain refuge (1969m), from where trails lead into the high mountain area. From **Arans** (1385m), a trail goes northeast towards **Bordes de l'Ensegur** (2180m), where there's an old shepherd's hut.

The cheapest accommodation option in Ordino is the cavernous **Hotel Casamanya** *(☎ 835011; singles/doubles €28/32)*. **Bar Restaurant Quim** *(Plaça Major; set menu €8.50)* has a basic lunch menu. Next door, **Restaurant Armengol** *(set menu €10)* has a good range of meat dishes.

Up the valley about 200m north of Llorts is **Camping Mitxéu** *(☎ 850022; 2 people & tent €7.20; open mid-June–mid-Sept)*, one of Andorra's most beautiful camping grounds. The **Hotel Vilaró** *(☎ 850225; singles/doubles €15/27.65)* is 200m south of Ordino.

Buses between Andorra la Vella and Ordino (€0.84) run about every half-hour from 7am to 9pm daily. Buses to El Serrat (€1.45), via Ordino, leave Andorra la Vella at 1pm and 8.30pm. The valley is also served by four buses daily (10 in the ski season) linking Ordino and Arcalís.

ARINSAL

In winter, Arinsal, about 10km northwest of Andorra la Vella, has good skiing and snowboarding, and a lively après-ski scene. There are 13 lifts (including a smart cabin lift to hurtle you up from the village), 28km of pistes and a vertical drop of 1010m.

In summer, Arinsal is a good departure point for medium-grade mountain walks. From Aparthotel Crest at Arinsal's northern extremity, a trail leads northwest, then west to **Estany de las Truites** (2260m), a natural lake. The steepish walk up takes around 1½ hours. From here, it's another 1½ to two hours to **Pic de la Coma Pedrosa** (2964m), Andorra's highest point.

Places to Stay & Eat

Just above Estany de les Truites is **Refugi de Coma Pedrosa** *(☎ 327955; beds €7; open June-late Sept)*. It also offers snacks and meals (dinner €11). The large, well-equipped **Camping Xixerella** *(☎ 836613; sites per adult/tent/car €4.50/4.50/4.50; open year-round)*, between Arinsal and Pal, has an outdoor swimming pool.

In Arinsal, **Hostal Pobladó** *(☎ 835122, fax 836879; e hospoblado@andornet.ad; singles/doubles €15/29, with shower €20/39)*, beside the cabin lift, is friendliness itself. It has a lively bar (which offers Internet access on the side) and breakfast is an extra €3.

As a change from the plentiful snack and sandwich joints, try **Refugi de la Fondue**, which does cheese or meat fondue dishes. **Restaurant el Moli** *(pasta & pizza €5.50-7.50)* bills itself as Italian, but also has more exotic fare. **Rocky Mountain** has a gringo menu with dishes such as T-bone steak and 'New York style cheesecake'.

During winter, Arinsal fairly throbs after the sun sets. In summer, it can be almost mournful. When the snow's around, call by **Surf** *(mains €7.50-13.50)*, near the base of the cabin lift. A pub and dance venue as well as a restaurant, it specialises in juicy Argentinian meat dishes. **Quo Vadis** occasionally has live music.

Getting There & Away

Buses leave Andorra la Vella for Arinsal (€1.38) via La Massana at 9.30am, 1pm and 6.15pm. There are also more than 10 buses daily between La Massana and Arinsal. In winter, Skibus (€2) runs five times daily between La Massana and Arinsal.

Austria

What a difference a century makes. Under the mighty Habsburgs, Austria began the 1900s as Central Europe's dominant political force. Today, after one of the biggest downsizings in history, the modern state has reconciled itself to being a minor player in European affairs.

Nevertheless, Austria remains a tourism superpower, attracting sports nuts and culture vultures year-round. Its Schwarzenegger-sized Alps beckon skiers, snowboarders and hikers, while its baroque architecture and Art Deco masterpieces are unparalleled. Home-grown strains of Mozart and Strauss serenade visitors, gently winning them over.

Austria: the Basics

Local name Österreich

Capital Vienna

Population 8.1 million

Language German

Currency 1 euro (€) = 100 centimes

Avoid at all costs Discussions about Jörg Haider, the county's most controversial right-wing politician. (It almost always ends in an argument.)

Complain by saying *Wie weit ist es noch zum Gipfel?* (How much further to the top of this mountain?)

Facts about Austria

HISTORY

In 803 Charlemagne established the Ostmark in the Danube basin. Interrupted periods of growth and prosperity under the Holy Roman Emperors and Babenbergs resulted in duchy status for the territory by 1156. After the last Babenberg died heirless, the Habsburgs took over and ruled Austria until WWI.

The Habsburgs expanded Austria mainly through purchase and marriage. In 1477 Emperor Maximilian I gained control of Burgundy and the Netherlands, and his son Philip married the Infanta of Spain in 1496. Philip's son, Holy Roman Emperor Charles V, handed over Austria, Hungary and Bohemia to his brother Ferdinand in 1521.

Following decades saw the devastating Thirty Years' War between Catholics and Protestants and invasion by the Turks, after which Austria was ready for some enlightened rule. In 1740 Maria Theresa ascended the throne, despite being ineligible to do so as a woman. During her 40-year rule, Austria developed as a modern state. Maria Theresa centralised control, established a civil service, reformed the army and the economy, and introduced a public education system.

In 1867 Emperor Franz Josef came to power as ruler of Austria-Hungary. The dual monarchy established a common defence, foreign policy and economic structure, ushering in a period of prosperity. The situation changed abruptly in 1914 when the emperor's nephew, Archduke Franz Ferdinand, was assassinated in Sarajevo on 28 June. Austria-Hungary declared war on Serbia and WWI began.

At the end of the war, Austria became a republic and lost Czechoslovakia, Poland, Hungary and Yugoslavia, causing severe economic difficulties, political turmoil and social unrest. Hitler and the Nazis fomented war and invaded the country, manipulating the Austrians into meek acceptance of the *Anschluss* (annexation). In 1945 the Allies restored the heavily bombed country to its 1937 frontiers. Allied troops did not fully withdraw from Austria until 1955.

Since WWII, Austria has worked hard to overcome economic difficulties. Although it's now a full EU member, Austrians have always been ambivalent about the union. Relations worsened in 1999 and 2000 when sanctions were imposed on Austria after members of the far-right Freedom Party entered a new coalition government. The Freedom Party was led by Jörg Haider who was notorious for making several pro-Nazi statements during his political career.

The country again made world headlines in November 2000 when the Gletscherbahn railway in Kaprun caught fire, killing 155 people in Europe's worst Alpine disaster.

Blowing in the Wind

Folk wisdom attributes many evils to the *Föhn*, a hot, dry wind that sweeps down from the mountains in early spring and autumn. It has been held responsible for a variety of things ranging from restless farm animals and poor exam performances to increased car accidents or suicides. Some travellers have learnt to use the phenomenon to their advantage: *Ne' nicht das Bier hat mich gestern abend dumm im Kopf gemacht, sondern der Föhn.* ('It wasn't the beer that had me acting silly last night – it was the *Föhn*'.)

GEOGRAPHY

Two-thirds of Austria's 83,855 sq km are mountainous, with three chains running west to east: the Northern Limestone Alps, the Central (High) Alps and the Southern Limestone Alps. The Grossglockner at 3797m is Austria's highest peak. The most fertile land is in the Danube Valley. Cultivation is intensive and roughly 90% of Austria's food is home-grown.

CLIMATE

Average rainfall is 71cm per year. Maximum temperatures in Vienna are January 1°C, April 15°C, July 25°C and October 14°C. Minimum temperatures are lower by about 10°C (summer) to 4°C (winter). Salzburg and Innsbruck can be as hot as Vienna but are colder on winter nights.

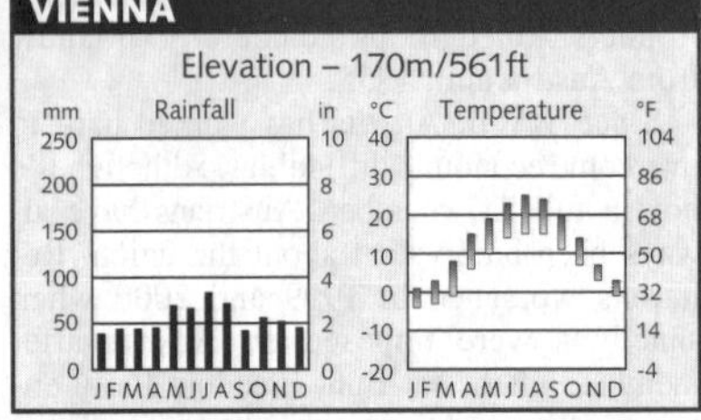

GOVERNMENT & POLITICS

Austria is a federal republic with a bicameral parliament. The chancellor is head of the federal government. Austria's love-hate relationship with the far-right Freedom Party and Jörg Haider reveals that at least some pro-Nazi sentiment persists.

ARTS

Austria is renowned for its musical heritage. The Habsburgs' generous patronage led to the perfection of various classical music forms – symphony, concerto, sonata, opera and operetta – by the era's most eminent exponents. Haydn, Mozart, Beethoven, Brahms and Schubert all made Vienna their home during this period. The waltz also originated in the city.

Architecture is another important tradition. The Gothic style was popular, before architect Fischer von Erlach developed a distinct Austrian baroque style from the Italian model in the 17th century. In the late 19th century, the Austrian Secessionist movement embraced Art Nouveau, while architects Otto Wagner and Adolf Loos moved progressively away from ornamentation to functionalism.

LANGUAGE

About 98% of Austrians speak German, although there are Croatian- and Slovenian-speaking pockets in the southeastern provinces of Burgenland and Carinthia respectively. English is widely understood, but knowledge of some German is useful (see the Language chapter at the back of this book).

Facts for the Visitor

HIGHLIGHTS

Spectacular Vienna is at the top of most travellers' lists, followed by picture-book Salzburg. Innsbruck and Graz are vibrant provincial capitals. To ski or snowboard, head to one of the many resorts concentrated in Tirol.

PLANNING

When to Go

Summer sightseeing and winter sports make Austria a year-round destination, though alpine resorts are pretty dead in May, June and November. High seasons are July to August and Christmas to late February.

Maps

Freytag & Berndt (☎ *533 85 85; 01, Kohlmarkt 9)* stocks a vast selection of good maps in varying scales. Its 1:100,000 series and 1:50,000 blue series are popular with hikers. Extremely detailed maps are produced by the Austrian Alpine Club. Bikeline maps are useful for cyclists.

TOURIST OFFICES

Efficient, helpful tourist offices (usually called *Kurverein*, *Verkehrsamt* or *Tourismusverband*) inhabit all towns and villages of touristic interest. At least one staff member will speak English. Most offices offer free maps and room-finding services.

Austrian National Tourist Office (ANTO) branches abroad include the following:

Australia (☎ 02-9299 3621, fax 9299 3808, ⓔ info@antosyd.org.au) 1st floor, 36 Carrington St, Sydney, NSW 2000
UK (☎ 020-7629 0461, fax 7499 6038, ⓔ info@anto.co.uk) 14 Cork St, London W1S 3NS
USA (☎ 212-944 6880, fax 730 4568, ⓔ info@oewnyc.com) PO Box 1142, New York, NY 10108-1142

EMBASSIES & CONSULATES

Austrian Embassies & Consulates

Australia (☎ 02-6295 1533, fax 6239 6751, ⓦ www.austriaemb.org.au) 12 Talbot St, Forrest, Canberra, ACT 2603
Canada (☎ 613-789 1444, fax 789 3431, ⓔ embassy@austro.org) 445 Wilbrod St, Ottawa, Ont KIN 6M7
New Zealand (☎ 04-499 6393, fax 499 6392) Austrian Consulate, Level 2, Willbank House, 587 Willis St, Wellington – does not issue visas or passports; contact the Australian office for these services
UK (☎ 020-7235 3731, fax 7235 8025, ⓦ www.austria.org.uk) 18 Belgrave Mews West, London SW1X 8HU
USA (☎ 202-895 6700, fax 895 6750, ⓔ obwascon@sysnet.net) 3524 International Court NW, Washington, DC 20008

Embassies & Consulates in Austria

The following foreign embassies are in Vienna.

Australia (☎ 01-506 74 04) Mattiellistrasse 2–4
Canada (☎ 01-531 38-3000) 01, Laurenzerberg 2
Czech Republic (☎ 01-894 37 41) 14, Penzingerstrasse 11-13
Germany (☎ 01-711 54-0) 03, Metternichgasse 3
Hungary (☎ 01-537 80-300) 01, Bankgasse 4–6
Italy (☎ 01-712 51 21-0) 03, Rennweg 27
New Zealand *Honorary consul in Vienna:* (☎ 01-318 85 05)
Embassy in Berlin, Germany: (☎ 030 20 62 10)
Slovakia (☎ 01-318 90 55) 19, Armbrustergasse 24
Switzerland (☎ 01-795 05-0) 03, Prinz Eugen Strasse 7
UK (☎ 01-716 13-0) 03, Jaurèsgasse 12
USA *Embassy:* (☎ 01-313 39-0) 09, Boltzmanngasse 16
Consular: Gartenbaupromenade 2/4)

MONEY

Austria uses the euro. Changing cash usually attracts the lowest commission rates, but always check first. Some private offices charge as much as 10% commission on transactions. The most efficient way to manage your money is with the ATM card with a Cirrus or Plus sign on it that you use at home to access your bank account. You can often change money at post offices.

Expenses are average for Western Europe, and prices are highest in big cities and ski resorts. Budget travellers can get by on €40 a day, after rail-card costs; double this if you want to avoid self-catering or staying in hostels. The *minimum* you can expect to pay per person is €10 for a hostel and €3.50/5.80 for a lunch/dinner, excluding drinks.

In restaurants, round off the bill so that it includes an approximate 10% tip and pay it directly to the waiters (surly though they may be). Taxi drivers will expect tips of 10%.

POST & COMMUNICATIONS

Post

A few main post offices in big cities are open late, or even 24 hours. Stamps are available in *Tabak* (tobacco) shops. *Postlagernde Sendungen* (poste restante) can be sent care of any post office and is held for a month (address it to 'Postamt' followed by the postcode); a passport must be shown to collect mail. AmEx will also hold mail for 30 days for customers who have its charge card.

Telephone & Fax

It costs €0.12 a minute to call anywhere in Austria, be it next door or across the country. The minimum tariff in phone boxes is €0.20, but as some call boxes now take only *Telefon-Wertkarte* (phonecards) it's often more convenient to buy one of those.

International direct dialling is nearly always possible. To call collect, you have to dial a free phone number; ask directory assistance on ☎ 118200. The national and international rate is cheapest from 6pm to 8am, and on weekends; rates drop greatly for national calls, but only marginally for

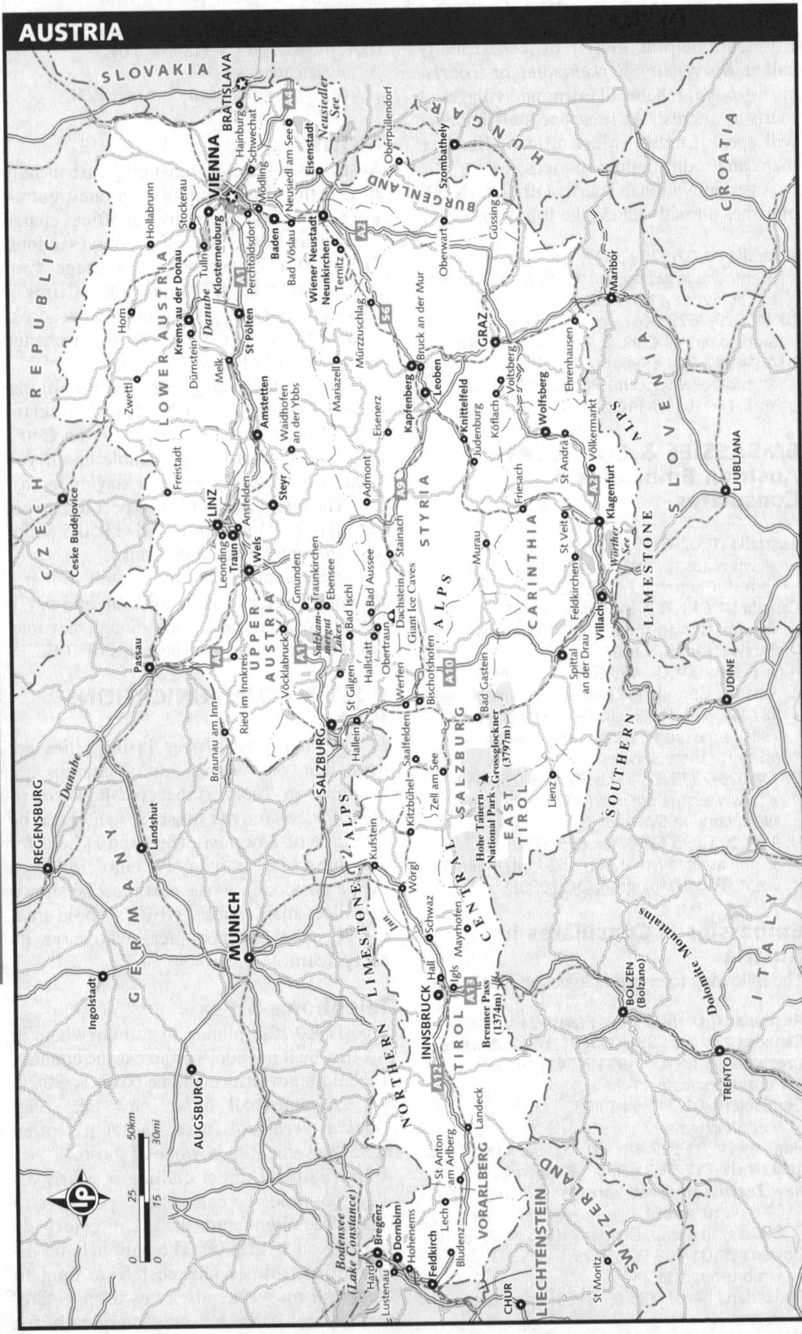

AUSTRIA

international calls. Cut-price telephone call centres in cities offer the best rates.

Email & Internet Access

Terminals in coffeehouses and bars tend to be more expensive than in dedicated Internet cafés, and cheaper online facilities lurk in public libraries. The **Bignet chain** *(W www.bignet.at)* has reliable well-equipped outlets in Vienna, Salzburg and Linz. Many post offices now also offer Internet access, although you need to buy a pre-paid card before using these 'Surf points'. The same card works at Bignet outlets.

DIGITAL RESOURCES

The Austrian National Tourist Office website at W www.austria-tourism.at is a good starting point, while the Austrian Press & Information Service at W www.austria.org offers weekly news and visa details. Another useful website is the Austrian Railways (Österreiche Bundesbahnen or ÖBB) at W www.oebb.at, which has train times and fares. For cheap eats, check out the listing of university canteens, or mensas, at W www.mensen.at.

BOOKS

Lonely Planet has guides to *Austria* and *Vienna*, and Western/Central Europe phrasebooks. Also worthy of note is *The Xenophobe's Guide to the Austrians* by Louis James, which is informative and amusing.

GAY & LESBIAN TRAVELLERS

Public attitudes to homosexuality are less tolerant than in most other Western European countries, except perhaps in Vienna. A good information centre in Vienna is **Rosa Lila** *(☎ 01-586 8150; 06, Linke Wienziele 102)*. The age of consent for gay men is 18; for everyone else it's 14. Vienna has a Pride march, the Rainbow Parade, on the last Saturday in June.

DISABLED TRAVELLERS

Local tourist offices usually have good information on facilities for the disabled; the Vienna office, for example, has a free 90-page booklet.

SENIOR TRAVELLERS

Senior travellers are entitled to many transport and sightseeing discounts. The official qualifying age in Austria is 65 for men and 60 for women, but some attractions do offer discounts for those aged 62 and over. The Vienna-based **Seniorenbüro der Stadt Wien** *(☎ 01-4000-8580; 08, Schlesingerplatz 2; open 8am-3.30pm Mon-Fri)* can give advice.

Phone Quirks

Don't worry if a telephone number you're given has only four digits, as many as nine or somewhere in between. The Austrian system often adds direct-dial (DW) extensions to the main number – after a hyphen. Thus, say ☎ 12 345 is a main number, ☎ 12 345-67 will be an extension, which could be a phone or fax. Mostly, a -0 gives you the switchboard operator. In this chapter, where an organisation's phone and fax numbers are based on the same main number the fax is only marked by a hyphen and extension number. In these cases, you send a fax by dialling the main number, dropping the phone extension (if there is one, ie, any digits following a hyphen) and adding the fax extension.

DANGERS & ANNOYANCES

Pickpockets generally work in Vienna's two main train stations and pedestrian centre, and there has been some trouble with unlicensed people offering rooms at Westbahnhof in Vienna.

Anti-foreigner feeling seems to be directed at Eastern European, Turkish and African immigrants. If you look like you are from those places, you could be in for some unnecessary questioning by police.

Physical and verbal harassment are less common than in many other countries.

EMERGENCIES

For urgent service you should call the following country-wide numbers:

Alpine rescue	☎ 140
Ambulance	☎ 144
Doctor (after hours)	☎ 141
Fire	☎ 122
Police	☎ 133
Vehicle breakdown assistance	☎ 120 or 123
Rape Crisis Hotline	☎ 01-717 19 (Vienna only)

BUSINESS HOURS

Shops are usually open 8am to 6pm or 7.30pm weekdays, to 1pm or 5pm Saturday. They sometimes close for up to two hours at noon, except in big cities. Some shops in train stations have extended hours. Banking hours are commonly 9am to 12.30pm and 1.30pm to 3pm Monday to Friday, with late closing on Thursday to 5.30pm.

PUBLIC HOLIDAYS & SPECIAL EVENTS

Public holidays are 1 and 6 January, Easter Monday, 1 May, Ascension Day, Whit Monday, Corpus Christi, 15 August, 26 October, 1 November, and 8, 25 and 26 December.

Numerous local events take place throughout the year, so check with the tourist office. ANTO compiles an updated list of events. Vienna and Salzburg have almost continuous music festivals. Linz has the Bruckner Festival in September.

Look out for *Fasching* (Shrovetide carnival) in early February, maypoles on 1 May, midsummer night's celebrations on 21 June, the autumn cattle roundup at the end of October, much flag-waving on national day on 26 October and St Nicholas Day parades on 5 and 6 December.

ACTIVITIES

Austria has world-renowned skiing and snowboarding areas, particularly in Vorarlberg and Tirol. There are plenty of winter sports in Salzburg province, Upper Austria and Carinthia, where prices can be lower. Equipment can always be hired at resorts. Generally, you need a complete or partial day pass to ride on ski lifts. For one day, count on spending €20 to €38 for a ski pass. Rental generally starts at €15 for downhill equipment and €11 for cross-country rental; rates drop for multiple days. The skiing season starts in December and lasts well into April at higher-altitude resorts. Year-round skiing is possible at the Stubai Glacier near Innsbruck.

Walking and climbing are popular with visitors and Austrians alike. There are 10 long-distance national hiking routes (Weitwanderwege), and six European routes (E-paths) that pass through Austria. National options include the northern alpine route from Lake Constance to Vienna, via Dachstein, or the central route from Feldkirch to Hainburger Pforte, via Hohe Tauern National Park.

Mountaineering should not be undertaken without the proper equipment or experience. Tirol province has numerous mountain guides and mountaineering schools; these are listed in the *Walking Guide Tirol*, which is free from the ANTO and the Tirol regional tourist office (see Information under Innsbruck later in this chapter). The **Austrian Alpine Club** *(Österreichischer Alpenverein, ÖAV; ☎ 0512-58 78 28, fax 58 88 42; w www.alpenverein-ibk.at; Wilhelm Greil Strasse 15, A-6010 Innsbruck)* has touring programmes and maintains a current list of alpine huts.

ACCOMMODATION

Reservations are recommended in July and August and at Christmas and Easter. Reservations are binding on either side and compensation may be claimed if you do not take a reserved room or if a reserved room is unavailable. An excellent cheap option is to take a room in a private house (€12 to €22 per person). Look for the ubiquitous *Zimmer frei* signs. Tourist offices can supply lists of accommodation and often make reservations. Breakfast is almost always included.

Camping

There are more than 400 camping grounds, but most close in winter. They charge around €2.60 to €5.80 per person, plus about €3 for a tent and €3 for a car. Free camping in camper vans is OK (in tents it's illegal), except in urban and protected rural areas. Contact the **Austrian Camping Club** *(Österreichischer Camping Club; ☎ 01-711 99-1272; Schubertring 1-3, A-1010 Vienna)*.

Hostels

Austria has an excellent network of HI *Jugendherbergen* (hostels). Membership cards are always required, except in a few private hostels. Non-members pay a surcharge of about €3 per night for a guest card; after six nights, the guest card counts as a full membership card. Some hostels will accept reservations by telephone, and some are part of the worldwide computer reservations system. Hostel prices are around €10 to €18.

Austria has two hostel associations: the **Österreichischer Jugendherbergsverband** *(☎ 01-533 53 53, fax 535 08 61; w www.oejhv.or.at; 01, Schottenring 28, A-1010*

Vienna) and the **Österreichischer Jugendherbergswerk** *(☎ 01-533 18 33, fax -85; W www.oejhw.or.at; 01, Helferstorferstrasse 4, Vienna).*

Hotels & Pensions

With very few exceptions, rooms are clean and adequately appointed. Expect to pay from €25/45 for a single/double. In budget accommodation, a room with a private shower may mean a room with a shower cubicle rather than a proper en suite bathroom. Prices in major cities (particularly Vienna) are significantly higher than in the untouristed rural areas. A small country inn *Gasthaus* or *Gasthof* or a guesthouse *Pension* tends to be more intimate than a hotel. Self-catering chalets or apartments are common in ski resorts.

FOOD & DRINKS

The main meal is at midday. Most restaurants have a *Tagesteller* or *Tagesmenu* (set meal), which provides the best value for money. The cheapest deal is in university *mensas*. Wine taverns are fairly cheap eateries, and Asian restaurants and pizzerias are plentiful. For a stand-up snack, head for a *Würstel Stand* (sausage stall).

Hearty soups often include *Knödel* (dumplings) or pasta. *Wiener Schnitzel* (a veal or pork cutlet coated in breadcrumbs) is Austria's best-known dish, but *Huhn* (chicken) is also popular. Paprika is used to flavour several dishes, including *Gulasch* (beef stew). Look out for regional dishes such as *Tiroler Bauernschmaus*, a selection of meats served with sauerkraut, potatoes and dumplings. Austrians eat lots of meat, although it's increasingly easier for vegetarians to survive.

Famous desserts include the *Strudel* (baked dough filled with a variety of fruits) and *Salzburger Nockerl* (egg, flour and sugar pudding). Pancakes are also popular.

Eastern Austria specialises in producing white wines. Austria is famous for its lager beer; also try *Weizenbier* (wheat beer). Beer is usually served by the 0.5L or 0.3L.

Historian Simon Schama wryly observed that Austria managed to 'resist the Turkish siege but (was) defenceless against the coffee bean'. Locals love to linger over a cup of coffee in *Kaffeehäuse* or *Café Konditoreien* (coffeehouses).

ENTERTAINMENT

Entertainment venues are legion in many parts of Austria. There are numerous late-night bars, clubs and music venues in Vienna, Graz, Innsbruck and Salzburg and there are plenty of convivial (and sometimes rowdy) apres ski in winter resorts.

In cinemas (cheaper on Monday) some films are dubbed, but look for *OF*, meaning *Original Fassung* (original-language production), or *OmU*, meaning *Original mit Untertiteln* (original language with subtitles).

The main season for opera, theatre and concerts is September to June. Cheap, standing-room tickets are often available shortly before performances begin.

Getting There & Away

AIR

The airports at Vienna, Linz, Graz, Salzburg, Innsbruck and Klagenfurt all receive international flights. Vienna is the busiest, with several daily, nonstop flights to major transport hubs such as Amsterdam, Berlin, Frankfurt, London, Paris and Zürich.

LAND

Buses depart from London's Victoria Station five days a week (daily in summer), arriving in Vienna 22 hours later (adult/student one way/return UK£65/99, senior UK£59/89). For services to Eastern Europe see Getting There & Away under Vienna later in this chapter. The website for Eurolines in Austria is W www.eurolines.at.

Austria has excellent rail connections. Vienna is its main hub (see Getting There & Away under Vienna later in this chapter); Salzburg has at least hourly trains to Munich with onward connections north. Express services to Italy go via Innsbruck or Villach; trains to Slovenia are routed through Graz. Reserving 2nd-class train seats in Austria costs €3.60; in 1st class it's free. Supplements sometimes apply on international trains.

There are many automobile entry points from the Czech Republic, Hungary, Slovakia, Slovenia and Switzerland. There are no border controls to/from Germany and Italy. Austria levies fees for its entire motorway network (see W www.vignette.at).

Getting Around

BUS

Public yellow or orange/red buses are called **Bundesbus** *(☎ 01-711 01)*. Sometimes buses duplicate rail routes, but generally they operate in the more inaccessible mountainous regions. They're clean, efficient and on time. Advance reservations are possible, but sometimes you can only buy tickets from the drivers. Fares are comparable to train fares.

TRAIN

Trains are efficient and frequent. Eurail and Inter-Rail passes are valid on the vast state rail network, but generally not on the private rail lines. Austrian Railways does *not* charge a supplement for national travel on faster EC (Eurocity) and IC (Intercity) trains. Conductors have been known to reassure travellers, 'We're not in Germany here, you know'. Tickets can be purchased on the train, but they cost about €3 extra. In this chapter, fares quoted are for 2nd class.

If you're under 26 or a senior, the VORTEILScard (under 26/over 26/senior €18.10/93.70/25.40; valid one year) is great value. Even without one, reduced fares are sometimes available for people under 26; wave your passport and ask.

Stations are called *Bahnhof* (train station) or *Hauptbahnhof* (main train station). Single/return tickets for journeys over 100km are valid for three days/one month and you can break your journey, but tell the conductor first. Some provinces have zonal day passes, (valid for trains and buses), which may save money compared with buying ordinary tickets. Nationwide train information can be obtained by dialling ☎ 05-1717.

AUSTRIA

CAR & MOTORCYCLE

Visitors require an international driver's licence. There's a steep fine for drink-driving (over 0.05% blood alcohol content) and your licence may be confiscated. Usual speed limits are 50km/h in towns, 130km/h on motorways and 100km/h on other roads.

Contact the **Austrian Automobile Club** *(Österreichischer Automobil, Motorrad und Touring Club, ÖAMTC; ☎ 01-711 99-0; Schubertring 1-3, A-1010 Vienna)* for more information.

Hertz, Avis, Budget and Europcar have offices in major cities. Prices are between €30 and €60 a day, but local rental agencies may have cheaper prices. Many contracts forbid customers to take cars outside Austria.

BICYCLE

Bicycles can no longer be hired from train stations, and at the time of writing private operators were only beginning to step into the breach. Some hostels rent bikes, but if you get stuck ask the tourist office. You can expect to pay anything from €6 a day in smaller cities to a hefty €30 in Vienna. You can always take your bike on slow trains (daily/weekly/ monthly ticket for €2.95/6.55/ 19.65); on fast trains you might have to send your bike as registered luggage (€10.20).

HITCHING

Lonely Planet doesn't recommend hitching, as it's never entirely safe. It's illegal for minors under 16 to hitch in Burgenland, Upper Austria, Styria and Vorarlberg, or for anyone to hitch on motorways. Otherwise, trucks are your best bet, particularly when stopped at border posts *Autohof* (parking stops). Show your destination on a sign and stay clear of the route from Salzburg to Munich; it's been named one of Europe's most difficult spots to get a lift. Austria has only one *Mitfahrzentrale* (hitching agency). See Car & Motorcyle under Getting There & Away in the Vienna section.

LOCAL TRANSPORT

Buses, trams and underground railways are efficient and reliable. Most towns have an integrated system and offer good-value daily or 24-hour tickets (€2.90 to €4.30), which are available in advance from dispensers or Tabak shops. Even single tickets can sometimes only be purchased prior to boarding buses/trams.

Taxis are metered. If you need one, look around train stations and large hotels.

Vienna (Wien)

☎ 01 • pop 1.6 million

Austria's capital is so like an eccentric grandmother that it's hard not to feel affection for her. Her home is full of colourful treasures, from Habsburg riches to the outpourings of Art Nouveau artists. She shares memories of companions such as Johann Strauss and Sigmund Freud – all of which make her a great storyteller. And although she's a tad stuffy and conservative, she's lightened up a bit these days.

Orientation

Many historic sights are in the Innere Stadt (Old City). This is encircled by the Danube Canal to the northeast and a series of broad boulevards called the Ring or Ringstrasse. Most central attractions are within walking distance of each other. Stephansdom, right in the heart of the city, is the principal landmark.

When reading addresses, remember the number of a building *follows* the street name. Any number *before* the street name denotes the district, of which there are 23. District 1 (the Innere Stadt) is the central region, mostly within the Ring. Generally, the higher the district number, the farther from the centre.

The main train stations are Franz Josefs Bahnhof to the north, Westbahnhof to the west and Südbahnhof to the south; transferring between them is easy. Most hotels and pensions are in the centre and to the west.

Information

Tourist Offices The **main tourist office** *(☎ 24 555, fax -666; w www.info.wien.at; 01, Am Albertinaplatz; open 9am-7pm daily)* provides an excellent city map and same-day hotel bookings (€2.90). Postal inquiries should be addressed to the Vienna Tourist Board, A-1025 Wien.

Information and room reservations (€3.50 to €4 commission) are also available in Westbahnhof and Südbahnhof (6.30am, 7am to 9pm, or 10pm daily). There is also an **information and hotel reservation counter** *(open 8am-11pm Mon-Fri, 9am-7pm Sat & Sun)* in the airport arrival hall.

The **Austria Information Office** *(☎ 587 20 00, fax 588 66-20; e oeinfo@oewwien.via.at; 04, Margaretenstrasse 1; open 10am-5pm Mon-Fri, till 6pm Thur)* also provides information. **Jugend-Info Wien** *(☎ 17 99; 01, Babenbergerstrasse 1; open noon-7pm Mon-Sat)*, a youth information centre, can get tickets for varied events at reduced rates for those aged between 14 and 26.

Money Banks are open 8am or 9am to 3pm Monday to Friday, until 5.30pm on Thursday; smaller branches close from 12.30pm to 1.30pm. Numerous Bankomat ATMs allow cash withdrawals. Train stations have extended hours for exchanging money.

Post & Communications The **main post office** *(Hauptpost 1010; 01, Fleischmarkt 19; open 24 hrs)* is close to the Danube Canal. There are also post offices at Südbahnhof, Franz Josefs Bahnhof and Westbahnhof.

For a listing of public Internet centres, go to Jugend-Info Wien (see Tourist Offices earlier). Some places are free, like **Haus Wien Energie** *(☎ 58 20 00; 06, Mariahilfer Strasse 63)*. The most central Internet cafés are a branch of **Bignet** *(Kärntner Strasse 61; open daily)* at €1.45 for 10 minutes; and **Surfland Internetcafe** *(Krugerstrasse 10; open daily)* for an initial charge of €1.40, and €0.08 per minute afterwards. Most hostels have Internet access.

Travel Agencies **American Express** *(☎ 515 40, fax -777; 01, Kärntner Strasse 21-23; open 9am-5.30pm Mon-Fri, 9am-noon Sat)* is handily located in the middle of Kärtner Strasse. The **Österreichisches Komitee für Internationalen Studienaustausch** *(ÖKISTA; ☎ 401 48-0, fax -2290; e info@oekista.co.at; 09, Garnisongasse 7; open 9am-5.30pm Mon-Fri)* is a specialist in student and budget fares, linked to STA Travel.

Medical Services For medical attention, try the **Allgemeines Krankenhaus** *(general hospital; ☎ 404 00; 09, Währinger Gürtel 18-20)*.

Things to See & Do

Architectural riches provide constant testimony to the power and wealth of the Habsburg dynasty. Don't miss the ostentatious public buildings and statues lining the Ring. Stand-out buildings include the neo-Gothic ***Rathaus*** (city hall), Greek Revival–style *Parlament* (check out the Athena statue), 19th-century Burgtheater and baroque Karlskirche.

The plush pedestrian thoroughfare Kärntner Strasse leads directly to Stephansplatz and the prime landmark of **Stephansdom** (St Stephen's Cathedral). The latticework spire of this 13th-century Gothic masterpiece rises high above the city. Take the lift up the **north tower** *(admission €3.50)* or the stairs up the higher **south tower** *(admission €2.50)*.

Some of the Habsburgs' internal organs reside in the **Katakomben** *(€3; open daily)*. Others are in the **Augustinerkirche** *(01, Augustinerstrasse 3)*. Additionally you'll find the flower-strewn coffin of the celebrated Empress Elisabeth ('Sissi'), alongside that of her husband, Franz Josef, in the morbidly

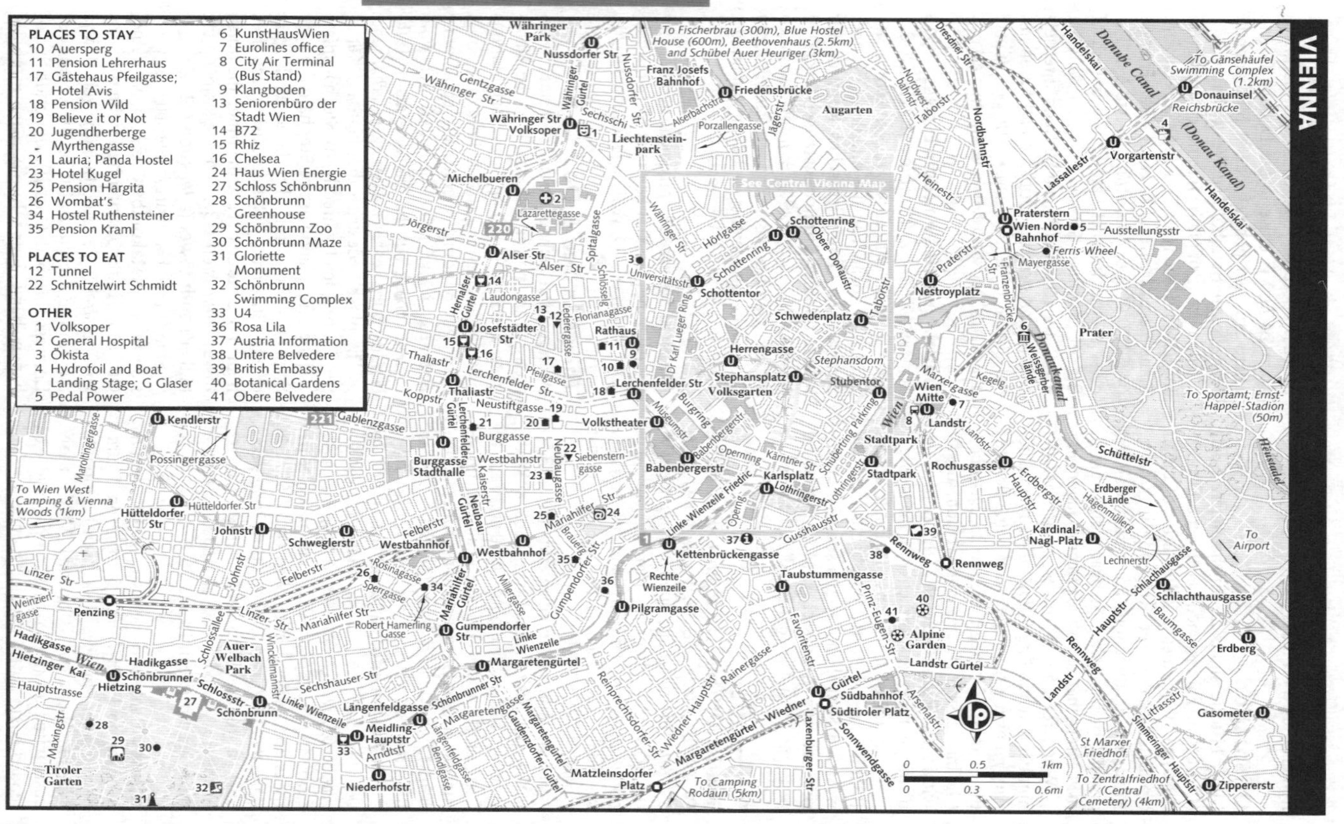
VIENNA
PLACES TO STAY
10 Auersperg
11 Pension Lehrerhaus
17 Gästehaus Pfeilgasse; Hotel Avis
18 Pension Wild
19 Believe it or Not
20 Jugendherberge Myrthengasse
21 Lauria; Panda Hostel
23 Hotel Kugel
25 Pension Hargita
26 Wombat's
34 Hostel Ruthensteiner
35 Pension Kraml
PLACES TO EAT
12 Tunnel
22 Schnitzelwirt Schmidt
OTHER
1 Volksoper
2 General Hospital
3 Ökista
4 Hydrofoil and Boat Landing Stage; G Glaser
5 Pedal Power
6 KunstHausWien
7 Eurolines office
8 City Air Terminal (Bus Stand)
9 Klangboden
13 Seniorenbüro der Stadt Wien
14 B72
15 Rhiz
16 Chelsea
24 Haus Wien Energie
27 Schloss Schönbrunn
28 Schönbrunn Greenhouse
29 Schönbrunn Zoo
30 Schönbrunn Maze
31 Gloriette Monument
32 Schönbrunn Swimming Complex
33 U4
36 Rosa Lila
37 Austria Information
38 Untere Belvedere
39 British Embassy
40 Botanical Gardens
41 Obere Belvedere
See Central Vienna Map

compelling **Kaisergruft** *(01, Neuer Markt; admission €3.60)*.

Starting at Stephansplatz, if you turn left from Graben into Kohlmarkt, you'll reach the St Michael's Gateway of the **Hofburg** (Imperial Palace). The Hofburg has been periodically enlarged since the 13th century, resulting in a mix of architectural styles. In the small Swiss Courtyard are the **Burgkapelle**, home to the Vienna Boys' Choir, and **Schatzkammer** *(Imperial Treasury; adult/senior & student under 27 €7/5; open Wed-Mon)*.

Schloss Schönbrunn & Schloss Belvedere The Habsburgs' summer palace was the sumptuous 1440-room **Schloss Schönbrunn** *(☎ 811 13-0; 13, Schönbrunner Schlossstrasse 47; self-guided 22/40-room tour adult €7.50/9.80, student €6.90/7.99; open 8.30am-5pm daily Apr-Oct, 8.30am-4.30pm daily Nov-Mar; U-Bahn No 4)*. Crowds make it tough to appreciate in summer, but it's still an impressive mini-Versailles. Mozart played his first royal concert in the Mirror Room at the ripe age of six. Ancillary attractions include gardens, a maze, a greenhouse, a zoo and swimming complex. The **Gloriette Monument** *(adult/concession €2.10/1.45)*, offers a wonderful view over the palace grounds and beyond from its roof. Two different ticket combinations (€14/17.20) provide good value in the summer.

Schloss Belvedere is a baroque palace, which houses the **Österreichische Galerie** *(Austrian Gallery; ☎ 795 57-261; adult/student €7.50/5; open 10am-6pm Tues-Sun)* in the two buildings that flank the spacious gardens. You'll find instantly recognisable works such as Gustav Klimt's *The Kiss*, accompanied by other late-19th/early-20th-century Austrian works, and a baroque museum.

Museums A huge range of art amassed by the Habsburgs is showcased at the **Kunsthistorisches Museum** *(Museum of Fine Arts; ☎ 525 24-0; W www.khm.at; 01, Maria Theresien-Platz; adult/concession €8.70/6.50; open 10am-6pm Tues-Sun, till 10pm Thur)*. The collection includes works by Rubens, van Dyck, Holbein, Caravaggio and Peter Brueghel the Elder.

The extremely popular Art Nouveau **Secession Building** *(☎ 587 53 07; Friedrichstrasse 12; adult/student €5/3; open 10am-6pm Tues-Sun, till 10pm Thur)* was built in 1898 and bears an intricate golden dome that the Viennese say looks like a 'golden cabbage'. It does. Inside, the highlight is Klimt's 34m-long *Beethoven Frieze*.

Hey, where did the floor go? The fairytale **KunstHausWien** *(☎ 712 04 91-0; 03, Untere Weissgerberstrasse 13; adult/concession €8/6, temporary exhibitions €14/11, half-price Mon; open 10am-7pm daily)* sweeps you off your feet with its uneven surfaces, irregular corners and coloured ceramics. Designed by Friedensreich Hundertwasser, it's reminiscent of Anton Gaudí's buildings in Barcelona.

The **Leopold Museum** *(☎ 525 70-0; 07, Museumsplatz 1; adult/concession €9/5.50; open Wed-Mon 11am-7pm, to 9pm Fri)* is the highest-profile spot in Vienna's new *Museumsquartier*, containing the world's largest collection of Egon Schiele paintings. The complex also includes the new main home of the **Museum of Modern Art**, the **City Art Gallery** and the **Zoom Children's museum**. A combined ticket to all (€25) can be bought from the ticket office in the complex.

The amazing **Haus der Musik** *(House of Music; ☎ 516 48-51; Seilerstätte 30; W www.haus-der-musik.at; adult/student & senior €8.50/6.50; open 10am-10pm daily)* tickles your eardrums and blows your mind, allowing you to create 'brain operas' through your movement and touch. Next stop is the **Sigmund Freud Museum** *(☎ 319 1596; 09, Berggasse 19; admission €4.36; open 9am-6pm July-Sept, till 5pm Oct-June)*, a memorial to the father of psychoanalysis.

The **Albertina** *(☎ 534 83; W www.albertina.at)* is reopening in mid-March 2003 after a lengthy refurbishment, which means Albrecht Dürer's *Hare* will be on display again.

Cemeteries Beethoven, Schubert, Brahms and Schönberg have memorial tombs in the **Zentralfriedhof** *(Central Cemetery; 11, Simmeringer Hauptstrasse 232-244)*. Mozart also has a monument, but he's actually buried in the **St Marxer Friedhof** *(Cemetery of St Mark; 03, Leberstrasse 6-8)*. Initially unmarked, his grave now has a poignant memorial.

Organised Tours

Several companies offer tours of the city and surrounding areas, either by coach, on foot (try the Third Man Tour, which visits spots featured in the film, including the underground sewers)

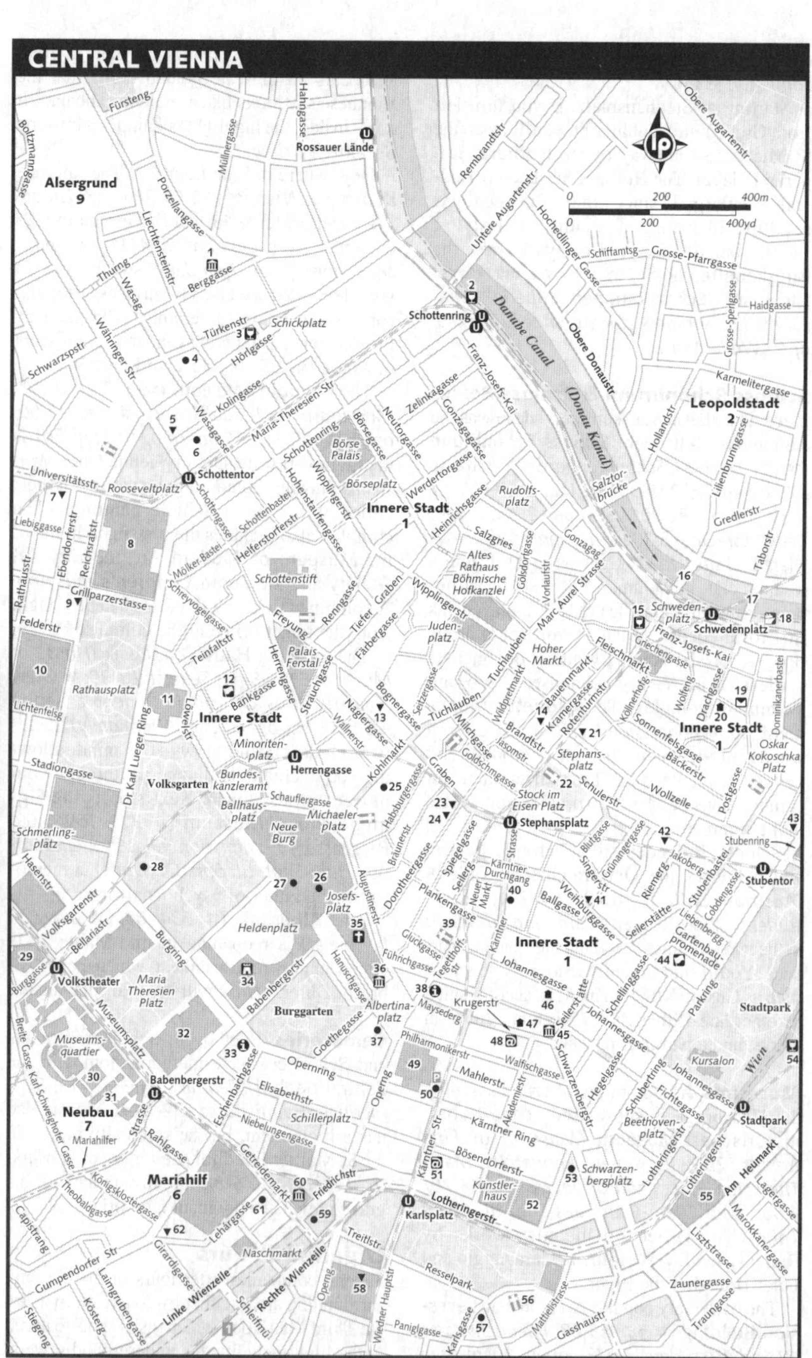
CENTRAL VIENNA
Alsergrund
9
Rossauer Lände
Schottenring
Danube Canal
(Donau Kanal)
Leopoldstadt
2
Schottentor
Innere Stadt
1
Börse Palais
Börseplatz
Rudolfsplatz
Salztorbrücke
Schottenstift
Altes Rathaus Böhmische Hofkanzlei
Judenplatz
Hoher Markt
Schwedenplatz
Rathausplatz
Palais Ferstal
Minoritenplatz
Herrengasse
Bundeskanzleramt
Volksgarten
Ballhausplatz
Michaelerplatz
Neue Burg
Stephansplatz
Stock im Eisen Platz
Stephansplatz
Oskar Kokoschka Platz
Schmerlingplatz
Josefsplatz
Heldenplatz
Stubentor
Volkstheater
Maria Theresien Platz
Burggarten
Albertinaplatz
Museumsquartier
Babenbergerstr
Neubau
7
Mariahilfer
Mariahilf
6
Schillerplatz
Karlsplatz
Künstlerhaus
Schwarzenbergplatz
Beethovenplatz
Kursalon
Stadtpark
Wien
Naschmarkt
Resselpark
AUSTRIA

CENTRAL VIENNA

PLACES TO STAY
20 Hotel Post
46 Music Academy & Mensa
47 Hotel zur Wiener Staatsoper

PLACES TO EAT
5 Café Stein
7 University Mensa & Café
9 Café Einstein
13 Esterházykeller
14 Wrenkh
21 Pizza Bizi
23 Trzesniewski
24 Café Hawelka
41 Immervoll
42 Gulaschmuseum
43 Café Prückl
58 Technical University Mensa
62 Café Sperl

OTHER
1 Sigmund Freud Museum
2 Flex
3 Billy's Bones
4 Ökista
6 Reisebuchladen (Bookshop & Tourguide)
8 University
10 Rathaus (City Hall)
11 Burgtheater (National Theatre)
12 Hungarian Embassy
15 Krah Krah
16 Marienbrücke
17 Schwedenbrücke
18 Danube Canal Tour Landing Stage
19 Main Post Office
22 Stephansdom (St Stephen's Cathedral)
25 Freytag & Berndt
26 Schatzkammer
27 Burgkapelle
28 Volksgarten
29 Volksoper (People's Opera)
30 Leopold Museum
31 Kindermuseum (ZOOM Children's Museum)
32 Musuem of Fine Arts
33 Jugend-Info Wien
34 Hofburg
35 Augustinerkirche
36 Albertina
37 Bundestheaterverkassen (State Theatre Ticket Office)
38 Main Tourist Office
39 Kaisergruft
40 American Express
44 US Embassy
45 Haus der Musik
48 Surfland Internetcafe
49 Staatsoper (State Opera)
50 Wien Ticket
51 Bignet
52 Musikverein
53 Austrian Airlines
54 Meierei im Stadtpark
55 Konzerthaus; Akademietheater
56 Karlskirche
57 Ökista
59 DDSG Blue Danube
60 Secession Building
61 Wiener Festwochen

or bicycle: contact **Pedal Power** *(☎ 729 72 34; 02, Ausstellungsstrasse 3)*. **Reisebuchladen** *(☎ 317 33 84; 09, Kolingasse 6)* gives an interesting 'alternative Vienna' tour (€24). Boat operators conduct Danube Canal tours; the tourist office has details.

Special Events

The Vienna Festival, from mid-May to mid-June, has a wide-ranging arts programme. Contact **Wiener Festwochen** *(☎ 589 22-22, fax -49; W www.festwochen.or.at; Lehárgasse 11, A-1060 Vienna)*, for details.

Vienna's Summer of Music runs from mid-July to mid-September; contact **Klang-Boden** *(☎ 4000-8410; 01, Stadiongasse 9)*. Reduced student tickets go on sale at the venue 10 minutes before the performance.

At the end of June, look out for free rock, jazz and folk concerts in the Donauinselfest. The free open-air **Opera Film Festival** on Rathausplatz runs throughout July and August.

Vienna's traditional **Christmas market** *(Christkindlmarkt)* takes place in front of the city hall between mid-November and 24 December. Other seasonal events include New Year concerts and gala balls (January and February), the **Vienna Spring Marathon** (April/May) and the **Schubert Festival** (November). The tourist office has details.

Places to Stay

Vienna can be a budget traveller's nightmare. Cheaper places are often full, especially in summer. Reserve beforehand. Tourist offices list private rooms and offer a useful *Camping* pamphlet. They will also book rooms.

Camping To get to the **Wien West** *(☎ 914 23 14; 14, Hüttelbergstrasse 80; site per adult/tent/car €5/3/2; open year-round)*, take U4 or the S-Bahn to Hütteldorf, then bus No 148 or 152. **Camping Rodaun** *(☎ 888 41 54; 23, An der Au 2; site per adult/tent/car €5.45/4.36/1 open late Mar–mid-Nov)* is another option. Take S1 or S2 to Liesing then bus No 60A.

Hostels & Student Residences The savvy backpacker heads to **Wombat's** *(☎ 897 23 36, fax 897 25 77; e wombats@chello.at; 15, Grangasse 6; dorm beds/doubles €14/18)*. This hostel's clean, modern rooms have won it favourable reviews from all quarters. Nearby is **Hostel Ruthensteiner** *(☎ 893 42 02, fax 893 27 96; e info@hostel.ruthensteiner.com; 15, Rod Hamerling Gasse 24; dorm beds from €11.50)*. It's an older building, but it has a nice garden and is still very lively. There are small charges for sheets, credit card payments & breakfast and (€10 key deposit).

Moving towards the centre, in an area of cheap restaurants and second-hand clothes shops you'll find **Jugendherberge Myrthengasse** *(☎ 523 63 16, fax 523 58 49; ⓔ hostel@chello.at; 07, Myrthengasse 7; dorm beds/doubles €15/17; check-in 11am-4pm)*.

The dorms can feel a bit claustrophobic in **Believe It or Not** *(☎ 526 46 58; 07, Apartment 14, Myrthengasse 10; dorm beds €12.50)* and **Panda Hostel** *(☎ 522 53 53; 07, 3rd floor, Kaiserstrasse 77; dorm beds €12)*. However, both offer kitchen facilities, if no breakfast, and are friendly places.

If you're still stuck, there are two large HI hostels out in the suburbs: **Brigittenau** *(☎ 332 82 94, fax 330 83 79; ⓔ jgh1200wien@chello.at; 20, Friedrich Engels Platz 24; dorm beds from €15)* and **Hütteldorf-Hacking** *(☎ 877 02 63, fax -2; ⓔ jgh@wigast.com; 13, Schlossberggasse 8; dorm beds from €13.90)*.

Student residences are available to tourists from July to September while students are on holiday. The cheapest, and one of the nicest, is **Blue Hostel House** *(☎ 369 55 85-0, fax -12; 19, Peter Jordan Strasse 29; singles/doubles €16/26.20)*. It's not that near to the centre, though. Other *Studentenheime* include **Gästehaus Pfeilgasse & Hotel Avis** *(☎ 401 74, fax 401 76-20; 08, Pfeilgasse 4-6; singles/doubles/triples from €21/38/51)*; and **Music Academy** *(☎ 514 84-7700, fax -7799; ⓔ jagersberger@mdw.ac.at; 01, Johannesgasse 8; singles/doubles from €35/56)*.

Several residences can be booked through **Albertina Hotels** *(☎ 512 74 93, fax 512 1968; ⓦ www.albertina-hotels.at)*.

AUSTRIA

Hotels & Pensions The **Lauria** *(☎ 522 25 55; ⓔ lauria.apartments@chello.at; 07, 3rd floor, Kaiserstrasse 77; twins/doubles/triples/quads from €35/40/45/70)* is a great place for young couples or small groups. Its rooms are comfortable and personable, and there's a kitchen.

Pension Lehrerhaus *(☎ 404 23 58-100, fax -69; 08; Lange Gasse 20; singles/doubles from €27/49)* was designed to accommodate visiting teachers but now offers excellent value to all with its basic but clean rooms. Breakfast is not included.

Pension Hargita *(☎ 526 19 28, fax 526 04 92; ⓔ pension@hargita.at; 07, Andreasgasse 1; singles/doubles from €31/45; breakfast on request)* surely must be the cleanest and most charming pension in Vienna for the price. The owner's warm manner, pastel-coloured rooms and spruced-up entrance hall will make you forgive the absence of a lift. Book ahead. Family run and traditionally decorated **Pension Kraml** *(☎ 587 85 88, fax 586 75 73; ⓔ pension.kraml@chello.at; 06, Brauergasse 5; singles/doubles from €26/48)* is another sound choice.

Friendly **Hotel Kugel** *(☎ 523 33 55, fax -5; 07, Siebensterngasse 43; singles/doubles from €33/45)* is near tram tracks, but you don't hear much noise inside. The four-poster beds in some of its more upmarket rooms make it popular with American tourists, but it offers good bargains as well.

Proud to call itself 'gay-friendly, everyone-friendly', **Pension Wild** *(☎ 406 51 74, fax 402 21 68; 08, Langegasse 10; singles/doubles from €37/45)* has luxury rooms, as well as its traditionally cheaper accommodation, with showers and toilets outside the rooms. 'Wild' is the family name, not a description.

Hotel Post *(☎ 515 83-0, fax -808; 01, Fleischmarkt 24; singles/doubles from €42/68)* is in the heart of things. With its parquet flooring in the rooms, long carpeted hallways and decorative cast-iron lift, it feels like a grand old 19th-century boarding house. The rooms without bathrooms are a fantastic bargain.

Hotel zur Wiener Staatsoper *(☎ 513 12 74, fax -15; ⓔ office@zurwienerstaatsoper.at; 01, Krugerstrasse 11; singles/doubles from €76/109)* is famous for its appealing facade. Its rooms are small, but its prices are great for such a central location.

Places to Eat

You can buy groceries outside normal shopping hours at the train stations. *Würstel* stands are scattered around the city and provide a quick snack of sausage and bread for around €2.50. *Wiener Schnitzel* is available everywhere; goulash is also common. Vienna is renowned for its excellent pastries and desserts, which are very effective at transferring the bulk from your moneybelt to your waistline.

Restaurants The best deals are in the various *mensas*, usually open for weekday lunches between 11am and 2pm. Meals are €3 to €5, often with a reduction for students. Good options are at **University Mensa** *(01, Universitätsstrasse 7; open 8am-6pm Mon-Fri)*, **Technical University Mensa** *(04, Resselgasse 7-9)*, and **Music Academy Mensa**

(01, Johannesgasse 8) – the only one inside the Ring. **Tunnel** *(08, Florianigasse 39; breakfast €2.50, lunch specials €4; pizzas €5-7; other mains €4-10; open daily)* is also a satisfying student haunt.

There are several cheap places in the centre to fuel up. **Trzesniewski** *(01, Dorotheergasse 1; open sandwiches €0.73 each; open Mon-Sat)* is the most traditional, albeit not for those with an egg, onion or fish phobia. **Pizza Bizi** *(01, Rotenturmstrasse 4; pizzas €5.70; open daily)* is rather less quaint – a fact that hardly registers with the multilingual crowd who flock here for the cheap meals and convenience.

Gulaschmuseum *(01, Schulerstrasse 20; veg & meat dishes from €6)* serves every type of goulash you can imagine, and quite a few you can't, including the rather celebrated chocolate goulash for dessert.

Visiting **Café Einstein** *(01, Rathausplatz 4; mains from €4)* is a smart move. By the university, it has some of the cheapest *Wiener Schnitzels* in town. For somewhere that exudes more authentic Viennese atmosphere, venture into **Schnitzelwirt Schmidt** *(07, Neubaugasse 52; schnitzels from €5; open Mon-Sat)*. Maybe it's carrying such huge portions to people's tables that makes the waiters so temperamental.

Its name means 'always full', and **Immervoll** *(☎ 513 522 88; 01 Weihburggasse 17; mains from €7)* pretty well always is. Customers can't resist its pleasant environment and dishes such as gnocchi and *Wiener Schnitzel*. **Wrenkh** *(☎ 533 15 26; 01, Bauernmarkt 10; lunch mains €11)* is a classy vegetarian restaurant, with lip-smacking Mediterranean, Austrian and Asian dishes – from risottos to tofu dishes.

Coffeehouses 'Vienna's coffeehouses are full of people who want to be alone...without feeling lonely', wrote local 19th-century author Alfred Polgar. Today, a good Viennese café provides somewhere to relax, people-watch and catch up on international newspapers. In the slightly worn, 1950s-style **Café Prückl** *(01, Stubenring 24)*, you get the feeling that you're surrounded by locals.

One of the most charmingly unspoilt of Vienna's coffeehouses is **Café Sperl** *(06, Gumpendorfer Strasse 11)*. Original architectural features, a dishevelled pile of papers, billiard tables and a cast of interesting characters can make you reluctant to finish up your coffee. **Café Hawelka** *(01, Dorotheergasse 6; open Wed-Mon)* is smoky, crowded and noisy, with nicotine-stained walls, which is precisely why its many regulars love it.

Heurigen Wine taverns, known as *Heurigen*, usually have a relaxed atmosphere, which becomes increasingly lively as the evening progresses. The more touristy taverns feature traditional live music; native Viennese tend to prefer a music-free environment. Opening times are approximately 4pm to 11pm, and wine costs around €2.50 per *Viertel* (0.25L).

Heurigen are concentrated in the wine-growing suburbs to the north, south and west of the city. Taverns are so close together that it is best to pick a region and just explore.

The *Heurigen* areas of Nussdorf and Heiligenstadt are near each other at the terminus of tram D. In 1817, Beethoven lived in the **Beethovenhaus** *(19, Pfarrplatz 3, Heiligenstadt)*. Down the road (bus No 38A from Heiligenstadt or tram 38 from the Ring) is Grinzing. There are several *Heurigen* in a row where Cobenzlgasse and Sandgasse meet. Alternatively, catch bus 38A east to Ambrüstergasse and follow Kahlenberger Strasse to **Schübel Auer** *(19 Kahlenberger Strasse; open Mon-Sat)*, which has a great food buffet and atmosphere.

Stammersdorf (tram No 31) and Strebersdorf (tram No 32) are cheaper, quieter regions. At **Esterházykeller** *(01, Haarhof 1; open daily from 11am, closed Sat & Sun evenings)*, you can get an approximate taste of the *Heurigen* experience without leaving the centre.

Entertainment

From the sweet strains of Mozart to the smoky dub lounge of DJ-duos Kruder & Dorfmeister or Pulsinger & Tunakan, Vienna prefers to take its entertainment sitting down. (It's no coincidence this city spawned a band called the Sofa Surfers.) If you'd prefer to drink and dance the night away, flip through *City* (€1) and *Falter* (€2.05) magazines. The tourist office has copies of *Vienna Scene* and produces monthly events listings.

The state ticket office, **Bundestheaterverkassen** *(☎ 514 44-7880; 01, Goethegasse 1)* sells tickets for the Staatsoper, Volksoper, Burgtheater and Akademietheater. For other places, try **Wien Ticket** *(☎ 588 85)* in the hut by the Oper, which also charges little or no commission.

Cheap *Stehplatz* (standing-room) tickets are often the best deal. Tickets touted on the streets by numerous be-wigged Mozart wannabes are truly overpriced.

Nightclubs & Bars The Innere Stadt area around Ruprechtsplatz, Seitenstettengasse and Rabensteig has been dubbed the *Bermudadreieck* (Bermuda Triangle) for the way drinkers disappear into its numerous pubs and clubs. **Krah Krah** *(01, Rabensteig 8)* has 50 different brands of beer and is open 11am until late. Other good places for a beer are the shady garden at **Fischerbräu** *(Billrothstrasse 17)* or smoky Irish pub **Billy's Bones** *(Schickplatz 4)*.

If you head for the U-Bahn arches near the Gürtel you'll find a good choice of bars. **Chelsea** *(08, Lechenfelder Gürtel 29-31)* has DJs, occasional indie bands, and English football via satellite. **Rhiz** *(08, Lechenfelder Gürtel No 37-38)* is a comfy hang-out, favouring modern electronic music, while **B72** *(08, Lechenfelder Gürtel No 72)*, is slightly more posey. It features various bands and DJs.

More serious clubbing goes on in the young and lively **Flex** *(Schottenring & Donaukanal)* by the water, and in **Volksgarten** *(01, Burgring 1)*, which is three linked venues: a café with DJs and garden, disco with theme evenings, and the more formal 'Walzer Dancing' place. **Meierei im Stadtpark** *(Heumarkt 3)* is another favourite for catching up on Vienna's DJ scene.

U4 *(12, Schönbrunner Strasse 222)* is one of Vienna's longest-standing discos. Each night has a different theme. Sunday is 1960s and 1970s music; Thursday is gay night.

AUSTRIA

Classical Music In a city that Beethoven, Brahms, Haydn, Mozart and Schubert once called home, it's a pity not to visit the opera or orchestra. Performances at the **Staatsoper** *(State Opera; ☎ 514 44-2960; 01, Opernring 2; seats from €5, standing room €3.65)*, are lavish, formal affairs. The **Volksoper** *(People's Opera; ☎ 514 44-3670; 09 Währinger Strasse 78; seats from €4, standing room €1.50-21)* puts on more modern, or niche performances, and is a little more relaxed. At both these venues, standing-room tickets go on sale an hour before each performance, and you may need to queue three hours before that for major productions. An hour before the curtain goes up, unsold tickets also go on sale at cheap prices (from €3.65) to students under 27 (home-university ID plus ISIC card necessary).

The **Musikverein** *(☎ 505 18 90; 01, Bösendorferstrasse 12; seats €15-110, standing room €5-7)* is the opulent and acoustically perfect (unofficial) home of the world-class Vienna Philharmonic Orchestra. Here, standing tickets can be bought three weeks in advance at the box office.

There are no opera performances in July and August. Ask the tourist office for details of free concerts at the Rathaus or in churches.

Never mind NSync – the **Vienna Boys' Choir** is the original boy band. They sing in the Hofburg's **Burgkapelle** *(☎ 533 99 27; e hofmusikkapelle@asn-wien.ac.at; seats €5.10-27.65, standing room free; 9.15am Sun, except July–mid-Sept)*. Tickets are sold Fridays and an hour before the show. Concerts are routinely sold out and there's often a crush of fans to meet them afterwards. The choir also regularly performs in the **Konzerthaus** *(03, Lothringstrasse 20; 3.30pm Fri May, June, Sept & Oct)*.

Getting There & Away

Air There are daily nonstop flights to all major European destinations. Check with **Austrian Airlines** *(☎ 1789; city office 01, Kärntner Ring 18)*.

Bus Since the central bus station at Wien Mitte was closed in 2000, departures are split between different locations. Buses to Budapest (€28, 3½ hours) leave opposite the offices of **Eurolines** *(☎ 7102 0453; w www.eurolines.at; 03, Invalidenstrasse 5-7; open daily)*. Eurolines buses to Prague depart twice daily from 01, Rathausplatz 5 (€23, five hours). Meanwhile, ÖBB services to Bratislava (€11, 1½ hours) leave from Südtirolerplatz near Südbahnhof. Call ☎ 93000-34305 for details.

Train Schedules are often subject to change, and not all destinations are exclusively serviced by one station, so check with train information centres that are in stations or call ☎ 05-1717.

International trains leave from either Westbahnhof or Südbahnhof. Westbahnhof has trains to Western and northern Europe and western Austria. Services head to Salzburg roughly every hour; some continue to Munich and terminate in Paris (14½ hours total). To Zürich, there are two day trains (€78, nine hours) and one night train. Eight trains a day go to Budapest (€33, 3½ hours).

Südbahnhof has trains to Italy, Slovakia, the Czech Republic, Hungary, Poland and southern Austria. Five trains a day go to Bratislava (€14, 1½ hours) and four to Prague (€36, five hours), with two of those continuing to Berlin (10 hours total).

Wien-Mitte Bahnhof handles local trains only, Franz Josefs Bahnhof handles local and regional trains.

Car & Motorcycle The Gürtel is an outer ring road that joins up with the A22 on the northern bank of the Danube and the A23 southeast of town. All the main road routes intersect with this system. **Rot-Weiss-Rot Mitfahrzentrale** (☎ *408 22 10;* ⓔ *office@mfz.at)* links hitchhikers and drivers. Examples of fares for hitchhikers are Salzburg €18.20, Innsbruck €25.45, Frankfurt €36.35 and Munich €25.45.

Boat Fast hydrofoils travel eastwards in the summer to Bratislava and Budapest, once per day. Hydrofoils travel to Bratislava (one way/return €19/29, 1½ hours) once daily on Wednesday and Sunday; to Budapest (€65/89, 5½ hours), at least daily. Bookings can be made through **DDSG Blue Danube** (☎ *588 80-0, fax -440;* ⓦ *www.ddsg-blue-danube.at; 01, Friedrichstrasse 7)* or **G Glaser** (☎*/fax 726 08 20;* ⓦ *www.members.aon.at/danube; 02, Handelskai 265).*

Getting Around

To/From the Airport **Wien Schwechat airport** (☎ *7007-2233)* is 19km east of the city centre. There are buses every 20 or 30 minutes, 24 hours a day, between the airport and the city air terminal at the Hotel Hilton (€5.80). Buses also run every 30 or 60 minutes from Westbahnhof and Südbahnhof (not from midnight to 3.30am). By 2003, the reconstructed S-Bahn (S7 line) to the airport might be running again from Wien Mitte, instead of Sudbahnhof. Taxis should cost €25 to €30. CK Airport Service (☎ 1731) does the trip for €21.

Local Transport Taxis are metered for city journeys: €2 or €2.10 flag fall, plus €1.09 or €1.38 per kilometre – the higher rate is on Sunday and at night. There is a €2 surcharge for phoning a radio taxi.

Vienna has a comprehensive and unified public transport network. Flat-fare tickets are valid for trains, trams, buses, the underground (U-Bahn) and suburban (S-Bahn) trains. All advance-purchase tickets must be validated in the machines before use. Single tickets cost €1.60 via machines on buses/trams. Otherwise they cost €1.30 each from ticket machines in U-Bahn stations. *Stunden-Netzkarte* (passes for 24 hours) cost €4.30.

Danube Valley

The strategic importance of the Danube (Donau) Valley meant that control of the area was hotly contested throughout history. As a result, there are hundreds of castles and fortified abbeys in the region. The 36km Wachau section of the Danube, between Krems and Melk, is the river's most picturesque stretch, with wine-growing villages, forested slopes and vineyards at every bend.

Several companies operate boats along the Danube, generally from early April to late October. **DDSG Blue Danube** (☎ *01-588 80-0, fax -440;* ⓦ *www.ddsg-blue-danube.at; 01, Friedrichstrasse 7, Vienna)* has three departures daily (from May to September) and one daily departure (in April and October) passing through the Wachau. From Melk to Krems (1¾ hours) or from Krems to Melk (three hours) costs €15.50/20.50 one way/return; shorter journeys between Melk and Spitz cost €9/12. **Brandner** (☎ *07433-25 90-21;* ⓔ *schiffahrt@brander.at)* offers the same trips at the same prices.

Ardagger (☎ *07479-64 64-0,* ⓔ *dsa@pgv.at)* connects Linz and Krems three times a week in each direction in summer. **Donauschiffahrt Wurm ģ Köck** (☎ *0732-78 36 07;* ⓦ *www.donauschiffahrt.com; Untere Donaulände 1, Linz)* has twice-daily services between Linz and Passau in Germany (six hours), which stop in the Wachau. **G Glaser** (☎*/fax 01-726 08 20;* ⓦ *www.members.aon.at/danube; 02, Handelskai 265, Vienna)* sails between Passau and Budapest, stopping at Krems and Melk en route.

KREMS AN DER DONAU

☎ 02732 • pop 23,000

Historic Krems sits on the Danube's northern bank, surrounded by terraced vineyards. It consists of three linked areas: Krems, the smaller town of Stein and the connecting suburb of Und. To appreciate the surroundings, stroll in and around the cobblestone, pedestrian-only main thoroughfare of Landstrasse, noting the baroque houses and adjoining courtyards, Gothic churches and ancient city walls.

You'll find the **tourist office** *(☎ 826 76; e austropa.krems@netway.at; Undstrasse 6)* in the Kloster Und. **Net-Café** *(Untere Landstrasse 35)* offers Internet access, while bicycle rental is available from **Hentschl** *(☎ 822 83; Wienerstrasse 129)*.

A highlight is the **Weinstadt Museum** *(☎ 80 15 67; Körnermarkt 14; adult/concession €3.60/2.50; open 10am-6pm Tues-Sun Mar-Nov)*, which presents ancient sculpture in a former medieval Dominican monastery.

Accommodation options include **ÖAMTC Camping Krems** *(☎ 844 55; Wiedengasse 7; person/tent/car €3.65/4.36/3.65)*, near the boat station, and the HI **Jugendherberge** *(☎ 834 52; Ringstrasse 77; dorm beds from €12)*. Both are open April to October. **Gästehaus Einzinger** *(☎ 823 16, fax -6; Steiner Landstrasser 82; singles/doubles €36/48)* has atmospheric, individually designed rooms around a leafy courtyard.

The **boat station** *(Schiffsstation)* is a 20-minute walk west from the train station along Donaulände. Between three and five buses leave daily from outside the train station to Melk (€5.80, 65 minutes). Trains to Vienna (€10.40, one hour) arrive at Franz Josefs Bahnhof.

MELK

☎ 02752 • pop 6500

Melk has received international attention for its impressive Benedictine monastery, which was featured in the epic medieval German poem *Nibelungenlied* and Umberto Eco's bestselling novel *The Name of the Rose*.

The train station is 300m from the town centre. Get the skinny at the **tourist office** *(☎ 523 07-410, fax -490; e melk@smaragd.at; Babenbergerstrasse 1; open 9am-noon & 2pm-6pm Mon-Fri, 10am-2pm Sat, daily summer, closed Nov-Mar)*. Internet access is available at **Teletechnik Wepper** *(Wienerstrasse 3)*.

On a hill overlooking the town is the ornate golden abbey **Stift Melk** *(☎ 555-232; w www.stiftmelk.at; adult/senior/student under 27 yrs from €5/4.72/2.54; guided tours €1.45 extra; open 9am-5pm daily Apr-Nov, to 6pm May-Sept, guided tours only Nov-Mar)*. Once a noble abode, then home to monks since the 11th century, the abbey is now housed in a building that was erected in the 18th century after a devastating fire. Consequently, it's an elaborate example of baroque architecture, lauded for its imposing marble hall, beautiful library and curved terrace.

Camping Melk *(adult/tent/car €2.60/2.60/1.90; open Mar-Oct)* is on the western bank of the canal that joins the Danube. Reception is in the restaurant **Melker Fährhaus** *(☎ 532 91; Kolomaniau 3)*.

At the HI **Jugendherberge** *(☎ 526 81, fax 542 57; Abt Karl Strasse 42; dorm beds €12, under 19 yrs €10; reception open 7am-10am, 5pm-10pm)*, you can reserve a bed and leave your bags during the day. The hostel is open from April to November. **Gasthof Weisses Lamm** *(☎ 540 85; Linzer Strasse 7; from €20 per person)* has basic but reasonably pleasant rooms.

Restaurant **Pasta e Pizza** *(Jakob Prandtauerstrasse 4; pizzas from €6)* is tucked away from the main tourist trail. There is a **Spar supermarket** *(Rathausplatz 9)* for self-caterers.

Boats leave from the canal by Pionierstrasse, 400m behind the monastery. Trains to Vienna Westbahnhof (€12, 60 to 70 minutes) are direct or go via St Pölten.

LINZ

☎ 0732 • pop 208,000

Poor Linz. Its small Old Town centre just can't compete with Vienna or Salzburg. Its biggest claims to 'fame' had been being Adolf Hitler's favourite town and having a type of cake – Linzer Torte – named after it. So the city decided to carve out a niche for itself in contemporary culture and technology.

Most of the town is on the southern bank of the Danube. The **tourist office** *(☎ 7070-1777, fax 700 11; Hauptplatz 1; open daily)*, on the main square, has a free room-finding service and sells discount cards for museums.

The **Ars Electronica Center** *(☎ 72 72-0; Hauptstrasse 2; adult/student €6/3; open 10am-6pm Wed-Sun)*, an art and technology centre on the Danube's northern bank, offers several simulated experiences – including the world's only public 'cave', a virtual environment where you can travel through space and time; free Internet access is included. The **Neue Galerie** *(☎ 7070 3600; Blütenstrasse*

15; adult/student from €5/3; open 10am-6pm Mon-Fri, to 10pm Thurs, 10am-1pm Sat) continues the shock-of-the-new theme, with temporary exhibitions ranging from Keith Haring to modern local artists.

For more traditional sightseeing, stroll around the large, baroque **Hauptplatz** or head to the **Schlossmuseum** *(castle museum; ☎ 77 44 19; Tummelplatz 10; adults/concession €4/2.20; open Tues-Sun)*.

Tickets for classical music performances during autumn's **Bruckner Festival** *(☎ 77 52 30; Brucknerhaus Kasse, Untere Donaulände, A-4010 Linz)* should be booked early. The ***Pflasterspektakel*** performing-arts street festival is held in summer.

Places to Stay & Eat

Camping is southeast of town at **Pichlinger See** *(☎ 30 53 14; Wiener Bundesstrasse 937; adult/tent & car €4/9.08; open Apr-Oct)*.

The pick of Linz's three HI hostels is the **Jugendgästehaus** *(☎ 66 44 34, fax -75; Stanglhofweg 3; dorm beds/singles/doubles €14/20/27)*, on bus routes 17, 19 and 27. The other two are the **Jugendherberge** *(☎ 78 27 20, fax 78 17 894; e zentral@jutel.at; Kapuzinerstrasse 14; dorm beds from €12; open around Apr-Oct)* and the **Landesjugendherberge** *(☎ 73 70 78, fax -15; Blütenstrasse 19-23; dorm beds from €9)*. Each closes its reception at intermittent times, so phone ahead.

Recently renovated **Wilder Mann** *(☎/fax 65 60 78; e wilder-mann@aon.at; Goethestrasse 14; singles/doubles from €26.20/46.60, with bathroom €31.30/53.80)* offers good value in a city that is otherwise pretty short of budget accommodation.

Würstel stands abound. **Mangolds** *(Hauptplatz 3; salads from €1.13 per 100g; open Mon-Sat)* offers self-serve vegetarian food. **Josef Stadtbräu** *(Landstrasse 49; lunches from €7)* is a popular evening haunt for its beer garden, but it also attract midday diners.

Getting There & Around

Linz is on the main rail and road route, approximately halfway between Vienna and Salzburg. Trains to Salzburg (€16.50) and Vienna (€21.80) both take between 1¼ to two hours and leave roughly every hour. City transport tickets are bought before boarding: €0.70 per journey or €2.90 for a day card. Some bus services stop early evening.

The South

The two main southern states, Styria (Steiermark) and Carinthia (Kärnten) retain elements of Italian, Slovenian and Hungarian culture, with which they have historical connections.

GRAZ

☎ 0316 • pop 245,0000

Underrated Graz hopes its reign as European City of Culture in 2003 will bring it the same lasting success as previous incumbents such as Helsinki, Reykjavik and, er, Bergen in Norway. Austria's second-largest city is dominated by its Schlossberg, or castle hill, which looms over the medieval town centre. The River Mur cuts a north-south path west of the hill, dividing the old centre from the main train station. Tram Nos 3, 6 and 14 run from the station to the central Hauptplatz.

At the train station is a basic **tourist information desk** *(open 8.30am-5.30pm Mon-Fri)*. More detailed information is available from the **main tourist office** *(☎ 80 75-0, fax -15; e info@graztourismus.at; Herrengasse 16; open 9am-6pm Mon-Fri, 9am-3pm Sat, 10am-3pm Sun, later in June-Sept)*. Send mail at the **main post office** *(Hauptpostamt 8010; Neutorgasse 46; open 7.30am-8pm Mon-Fri, 8am-noon Sat)*. **Bicycle** *(☎ 82 13 57-0; Kaiser-Franz-Josef Kai 56)* can rent you a set of two wheels. **Café Zentral** *(Andreas Hofer Platz)* has Internet access.

Things to See & Do

Most visitors head straight for the **Schlossberg** to enjoy the views and see the fortress remnants. These include a bell tower, bastion and garrison museum, and the charming clock tower – with its minute and hour hands reversed – which is the emblem of Graz. There are three main ways to ascend: the glass Schlossberglift hewn through the hill, the Schlossbergbahn funicular railway, or the 260 steps near the lift. Gates are sometimes locked at the top of other paths up to the castle.

The Old Town's highlights include the **cathedral** *(cnr Hofgasse & Bürgergasse)* and, across Hofgasse, the **Burg** complex of the Styrian parliament. Left of the door marked 'Stiege III' is a double-winding staircase as good as any MC Escher drawing.

The **Landeszeughaus** *(Armoury; ☎ 82 87 96; Herrengasse 16; admission €4.30; open 9am-5pm Tues-Sun Mar-Oct, 10am-3pm*

Tues-Sun Nov & Dec) depicts Graz's successes in resisting Ottoman invasions. Being in the company of 32,000 weapons and armour pieces is a rather chilling experience.

Graz sports many funky street sculptures. Several temporary installations, including an artificial island in the River Mur, will join them for the City of Culture celebrations. Contact **Graz 2003** *(☎ 2003; w www.graz03.at)* for information.

Places to Stay

Graz is the nearest city to the Austrian Grand Prix circuit at Spielberg; book in advance around May.

Camping Central *(☎ 378 51 02, fax 69 78 24; Martinhofstrasse 3; bus No 32 from Jakominiplatz; 1/2-persons with tent €13/20; open Apr-Nov)* is 5.5km southwest of the centre.

Closer in is the HI **Jugendgästehaus** *(☎ 71 48 76, fax -88; Idlhofgasse 74; dorm beds/doubles from €14/21.50; reception open 7am-10pm daily, closed 10am-5pm Sat, Sun & holidays)*. Cartoon motifs set a friendly tone.

Hotel Strasser *(☎ 71 39 77, fax 71 68 56; e hotel@clicking.at; Eggenberger Gürtel 11; singles/doubles from €25.50/42)* has spacious, well-kept rooms that make it a pleasant surprise for a cheap hotel close to the train station. The same applies for nearby **Pension Jos** *(☎ 71 05 05, fax 71 04 06; Friedhofgasse 14; singles/doubles with bath from €29/51)*.

Places to Eat

If you're self-catering don't miss the farmers' markets at Kaiser-Franz-Josef Platz (Monday to Saturday) and Lendplatz (Saturday). They sell local produce, including many varieties of apples, fresh fruit juices and schnapps. There is a **Billa** supermarket in the Annenpassage shopping centre, opposite the train station.

Cheap eats are available all around the university, especially at **Mensa Markt** *(Schubertstrasse 2-4; menus around €4)* and the cellar bar **Girardikeller** *(Leonhardstrasse 28; mains €4; open 5pm-2am Tues-Fri, 6pm-2am Sat, plus 4am-9am 'breakfast club' Fri-Sun)*.

Vegetarian lunches are served at **Salateria** *(Leonhardstrasse 18; mains from €3.30; open 11am-2pm Mon-Fri)*, and at other times at **Mangolds Vollwert Restaurant** *(Griesgasse 11; salad from €1 per 100g; open Mon-Sat)*.

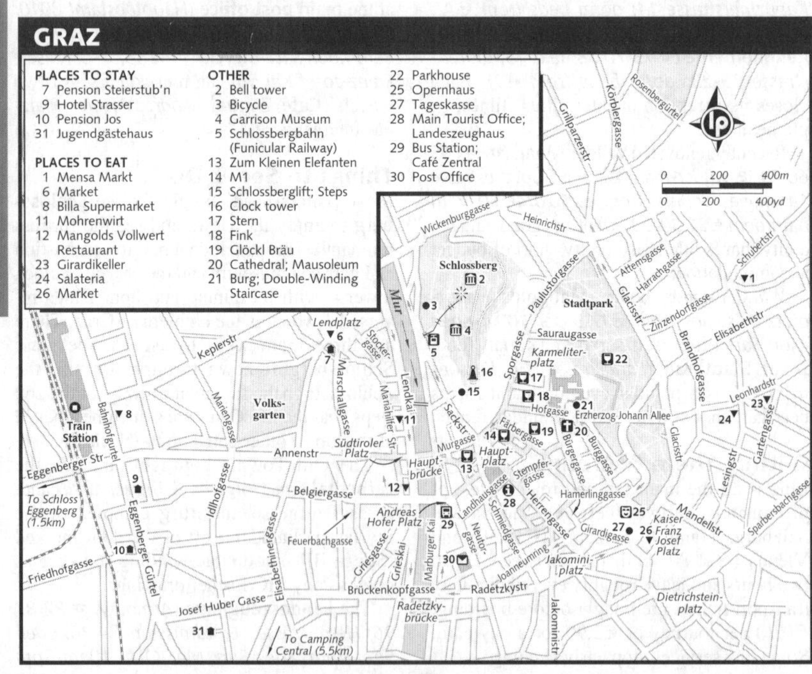

AUSTRIA

Thanks to its salads in pumpkin-seed oil, fish specialities and *Pfand'l* (pan-grilled dishes), Styrian cuisine feels healthier than other Austrian cooking. A good place to sample it is low-key **Mohrenwirt** *(Mariahilfer Strasse 16; mains from €5; open Sat-Wed).*

Entertainment

Many favourite nightspots double as restaurants – among them **Stern** *(Sporgasse 38)*, which draws a varied crowd, and the more exclusive **Fink** *(Freheitsplatz 2)*. **Zum Kleinen Elefanten** *(Neu Weltgasse 3)* is a relaxed café that also hosts a wide range of live bands.

Graz, like Vienna, has an area of bars known as the Bermudadreieck. It's between Sporgasse, Färbergasse and Stempfergasse, where you'll find venues ranging from the humble **Glöckl Bräu** *(Glockenspielplatz 2-3)* to the third-floor **M1** *(Färbergasse 1)*, favoured by the beautiful people. If the weather's warm, you also want to head for **Parkhouse** *(Stadtpark 2)*. This island of bonhomie in the park is a great place to meet locals. At night, with music pumping out at the trees, there's a special vibe.

Graz hosts classical and other musical events throughout the year. The **Tageskasse** *(☎ 8000; Kaiser Josef Platz 10)* sells tickets for the Opernhaus (opera). Cheap student deals, last-minute returns and standing-room tickets are all available.

Getting There & Around

Direct IC trains to Vienna's Südbahnhof depart every two hours (€25, 2¾ hours). Trains depart every two hours to Salzburg (€33, 4¼ hours), either direct or changing at Bischofshofen. Two daily direct trains depart for Ljubljana (€33, four hours), and every hour or two to Budapest via Szentgotthard and Szombathely (€41, 6½ hours). Trains to Klagenfurt (€26, three hours) go via Bruck an der Mur. The bus station is at Andreas Hofer Platz.

Public transport tickets cover the Schlossbergbahn, which runs from Sackstrasse up the Schlossberg, and bus No 631 to/from the airport. Tickets cost €1.45 each (€11.63 for a strip of 10). The 24-hour pass costs €3.

KLAGENFURT

☎ 0463 • pop 87,000

The capital of Carinthia (Kärnten), Klagenfurt seems rather unassuming to be the seat of power of Austria's most controversial politician, Jörg Haider. The tourist industry revolves around the nearby lake and theme park filled with models of famous buildings.

The heart of the city is Neuer Platz (New Square), 1km north of the main train station. Across the square, in the Rathaus, you'll find the **tourist office** *(☎ 53 72 23, fax 53 72 95; e tourismus@klagenfurt.at; open 8am-6.30pm Mon-Fri, 10am-3pm Sat & Sun, longer in summer)*. The **main post office** *(Postamt 9010; Dr Hermann Gasse)* is one block west of Neuer Platz. Internet access is available at **Gates Cafebar** *(Waagplatz 7)*.

The **Neuer Platz** is dominated by the town emblem, the Dragon Fountain. At the western end of the pedestrianised **Alter Platz** (Old Square) is the 16th-century Landhaus, with a striking **Wappensall** *(Hall of Arms; adult/student €2/1; open Sat & Sun Apr-Sept)*. Paintings of 655 coats-of-arms cover the walls, while the trompe l'oeil ceiling creates the illusion of a balcony above them.

Wörther See, 4km west of the centre, is one of the region's warmer lakes, thanks to subterranean thermal springs. You can swim or go boating in summer.

Places to Stay & Eat

At **Camping Strandbad** *(☎ 211 69, fax -93)*, in Europa Park, you'll be close to many major attractions in summer. The modern HI **Jugendherberge** *(☎ 23 00 20, fax -20; Neckheimgasse 6; dorm beds/doubles €16.30/20)*, also near the university and Europa Park, offers Internet access. Bus No 12 is the closest stop. Back in town, try **Pension Klepp** *(☎ 322 78; Platzgasse 4; singles/doubles €22/37)* for a cheap option.

The **University Mensa** *(Universitätsstrasse 90; open 11am-2.30pm Mon-Fri, mains from €4)* is by Europa Park. Back in the centre, the stalls in **Benediktinerplatz market** serve hot meals for about €4.

Gasthaus Pirker *(cnr Adlergasse & Lidmanskygasse; mains from €6)* has cheap Austrian food, while **Zum Augustin** *(Pfarrhofgasse 2; mains from €7)* impresses with tasty regional food and a range of beers. The hip café **Pankraz** *(8 de Mai Strasse 16; sandwiches €3.50)* attracts a wide range of people from students and Goths to yuppies.

Getting There & Around

Trains to Graz depart every one to two hours (€33, three hours). Trains to western Austria, Italy and Germany go via Villach, 40 minutes away.

Bus drivers sell single tickets for €1.60, while a strip of 10 costs €12. Passes for 24 hours cost €3.30. For the Europa Park vicinity, take bus Nos 10, 11, 12, 20, 21 or 22 from Heiligengeistplatz in the centre.

Salzburg

☎ 0662 • pop 145,000

Salzburg certainly has chocolate-box appeal (literally, in fact, when it comes to the rows of Mozartkugeln confectionery, named after its most famous son). From its quaint Old Town nestled below the medieval Hohensalzburg Fortress to its baroque palace and manicured gardens, the city presents one picture-postcard vista after another.

If all this isn't enough to explain its tourist appeal, there's also the Von Trapp family story, which was partly filmed here. Yup, those hills sure are alive to *The Sound of Music*.

Orientation & Information

The city centre is split by the River Salzach. The old part of town (mostly pedestrianised) is on the southern bank, with the Hohensalzburg Fortress on the hill above. Most attractions are this side of the river, as is the fashionable shopping street of Getreidegasse. On the northern bank is the new town and business centre, with most of the cheaper hotels.

The **main tourist office** *(☎ 889 87-330; Mozartplatz 5; open 9am-6pm Mon-Sat, daily May-Oct & Dec; hotel reservations ☎ 889 87-314, fax -32)* will book rooms for €2 to €4. Other tourist offices are scattered about town.

Banks are open 8am to noon and 2pm to 4.30pm Monday to Friday. The **main post office** *(Hauptpostamt 5010; Residenzplatz 9; open 7am-7pm Mon-Fri, 8am-10am Sat)* is within sight of the tourist office. **International Telephone Discount** *(Kaiserschützenstrasse 8; open 9am-11pm daily)* is across the large plaza from the train station. For Internet access, try **Bignet** *(Judengasse 5-7; open 9am-10pm daily)* at €1.45 for 10 minutes or **Piterfun** *(Ferdinand-Porsche-Strasse 7)* at €1.80 for 10 minutes.

Things to See & Do

Start at the **Dom** (Cathedral) on Domplatz, which has three bronze doors symbolising faith, hope and charity. Head west along Franziskanergasse, and turn left into a courtyard for **St Peter's Abbey**, dating from AD 847. Among the lovingly tended graves you'll find the entrance to the **catacombs** *(adult/student €1/0.70; open 10.30am-5pm summer, 10.30am-3.30pm winter)*. The western end of Franziskanergasse opens out into Max Reinhardt Platz, where you'll see the back of Fisher von Erlach's **Collegiate Church** *(Universitätsplatz)* – an outstanding example of baroque architecture.

Towering above Salzburg is the **Festung Hohensalzburg** *(Mönchsberg 34; ☎ 84 24 30-11; admission €3.55, with interior pass & audio guide €7.10; open 9am-6pm 15 Mar-14 June, 8.30am-8pm 15 June-14 Sept, 9am-5pm 15 Sept-14 Mar)*, home to the archbishop-princes who ruled Salzburg from 798. Inside are ornate state rooms, torture chambers and two museums. The opulence is impressive, but perhaps not as compelling as the grotesque torture masks and scary-looking chastity belt in one of the museums. If you don't want to walk 15 minutes up the hill, catch the **Festungsbahn** *(Festungsgasse 4; €2.80)*.

Schloss Mirabell was built by worldly prince-archbishop Wolf Dietrich for his mistress in 1606. Its attractive gardens featured in *The Sound of Music*, and white-clad brides and their grooms flock here during summer to have their pictures taken. 'Musical Spring' concerts (among others) are held in the palace. Dietrich's not-so-humble monument to himself lies in the graveyard of 16th-century St Sebastian's Church, on Linzer Gasse.

It's supremely ironic that although Mozart found Salzburg stifling and couldn't wait to leave, his life here is one of the city's major drawcards. People flock to his **Geburtshaus** *(Birthplace; ☎ 84 43 13; Getreidegasse 9; adult/student & seniors €5.50/4.50; open 9am-6pm daily, to 7pm July & Aug)* and **Wohnhaus** *(Residence; ☎ 87 42 27-40; Makartplatz 8; admission & opening hours as for the Geburtshaus)* to see musical instruments, sheet music, letters, family paintings and other memorabilia of the composer's early years. A combined ticket to both houses for students/seniors costs €9/7.

In the **Residenz** *(Residenzplatz 1; ☎ 80 42-2690; adult/student €7.25/5.50)*, you can visit the archbishops' baroque state rooms and a gallery housing 16th- and 17th-century Dutch and Flemish paintings. The **Rupertinum** *(☎ 80 42 23 36; Wiener Philharmoniker Gasse 9; adult/student €7/4.36;*

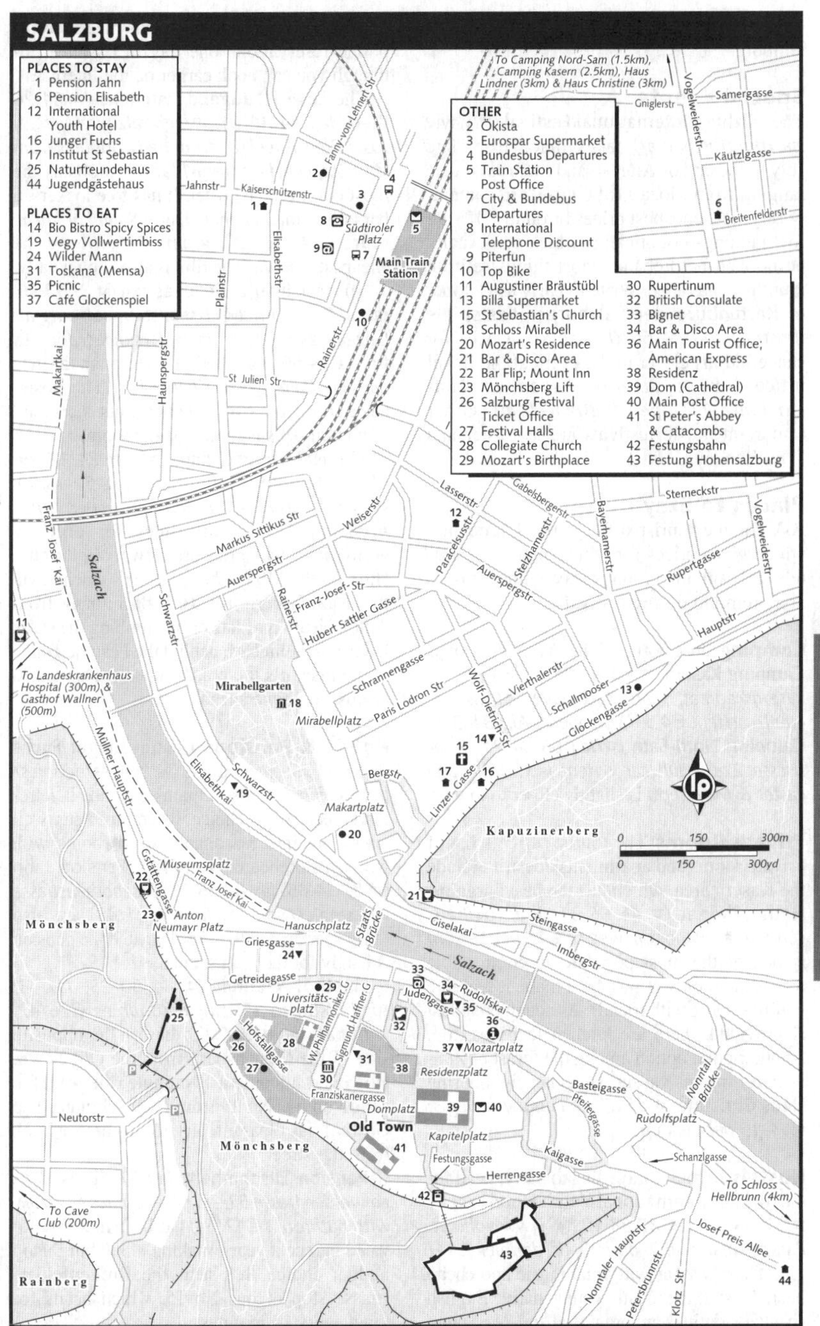
SALZBURG
PLACES TO STAY
1 Pension Jahn
6 Pension Elisabeth
12 International Youth Hotel
16 Junger Fuchs
17 Institut St Sebastian
25 Naturfreundehaus
44 Jugendgästehaus
PLACES TO EAT
14 Bio Bistro Spicy Spices
19 Vegy Vollwertimbiss
24 Wilder Mann
31 Toskana (Mensa)
35 Picnic
37 Café Glockenspiel
OTHER
2 Ökista
3 Eurospar Supermarket
4 Bundesbus Departures
5 Train Station Post Office
7 City & Bundebus Departures
8 International Telephone Discount
9 Piterfun
10 Top Bike
11 Augustiner Bräustübl
13 Billa Supermarket
15 St Sebastian's Church
18 Schloss Mirabell
20 Mozart's Residence
21 Bar & Disco Area
22 Bar Flip; Mount Inn
23 Mönchsberg Lift
26 Salzburg Festival Ticket Office
27 Festival Halls
28 Collegiate Church
29 Mozart's Birthplace
30 Rupertinum
32 British Consulate
33 Bignet
34 Bar & Disco Area
36 Main Tourist Office; American Express
38 Residenz
39 Dom (Cathedral)
40 Main Post Office
41 St Peter's Abbey & Catacombs
42 Festungsbahn
43 Festung Hohensalzburg
To Camping Nord-Sam (1.5km), Camping Kasern (2.5km), Haus Lindner (3km) & Haus Christine (3km)
To Landeskrankenhaus Hospital (300m) & Gasthof Wallner (500m)
To Cave Club (200m)
To Schloss Hellbrunn (4km)
Main Train Station
Südtiroler Platz
Mirabellgarten
Mirabellplatz
Makartplatz
Kapuzinerberg
Mönchsberg
Rainberg
Old Town
Salzach
Museumsplatz
Anton Neumayr Platz
Hanuschplatz
Universitätsplatz
Residenzplatz
Mozartplatz
Domplatz
Kapitelplatz
Rudolfsplatz
0 150 300m
0 150 300yd
AUSTRIA

open 10am-5pm Tues-Sun) contains contemporary art.

Special Events

The **Salzburg International Festival** *(w www.salzburgfestival.at)* takes place from late July to the end of August, and includes music ranging from Mozart (of course!) to contemporary. The cheapest prices (around €12) are for standing-room tickets, which can usually be booked beforehand. Most things sell out months in advance. Write as early as October to **Kartenbüro der Salzburger Festspiele** *(Postfach 140, A-5010 Salzburg)*. Check for cancellations closer to the event at the **ticket office** *(☎ 80 45, fax-401; Herbert von Karajan Platz 11; open 9.30am-7pm)*. Other important music festivals are at Easter and Whit Sunday.

Places to Stay

Ask for the tourist office's hotel brochure, which gives prices for hotels, pensions, hostels and camping grounds. Accommodation is at a premium during festivals.

Camping Just north of the A1 Nord exit is **Camping Kasern** *(☎/fax 45 05 76; e camping kasern@aon.at; Carl Zuckmayer Strasse 4; adult/car/tent €4.50/3/3; open 1 Apr-31 Oct)*. **Camping Nord-Sam** *(☎/fax 66 04 94; Samstrasse 22a; adult/car & tent €5.50/8; open Easter & May-Sept)* is slightly closer to town.

Private Rooms The tourist office's list of private rooms and apartments doesn't include the Kasern area, which has the best bargains. **Haus Lindner** *(☎ 45 66 81; e info@haus-lindner.at; Panoramaweg 5; €15 per person)* is one of the most popular. Its comfortable rooms and homy atmosphere make it feel like you're staying with friends. Although breakfast is provided, there are kitchen facilities, too. Another good option among the forest of *Zimmer frei* (rooms vacant) signs is neighbouring **Haus Christine** *(☎ 45 67 73; Panoramaweg 3; €14-15 per person)*.

Hostels If you're travelling to party, head for the sociable **International Youth Hotel** *(YoHo; ☎ 87 96 49, fax 87 88 10; w www.yoho.at; Paracelsusstrasse 9; dorm beds/doubles €14/19)*. There's a bar with loud music and cheap beer, the staff are mostly young, native English speakers, outings are organised and *The Sound of Music* is screened daily. This place accepts phone reservations one day in advance, although you can book earlier on the Internet.

The large HI **Jugendgästehaus** *(☎ 84 26 70-0, fax 84 11 01; e jgh.salzburg@jgh.at; Josef Preis Allee 18; dorm beds/doubles from €13/22; check-in from 11am)* is probably the most comfortable hostel. It has free lockers, a bar and a small kitchen. Daily *Sound of Music* **tours** *(8.45am & 1.30pm, €25.45)* are the cheapest in town. The film is also shown daily.

To reach **Institut St Sebastian** *(☎ 87 13 86, fax -85; e office@st-sebastian-salzburg.at; Linzer Gasse 41; dorm beds/singles/doubles from €14.50/26/38.50)*, turn through the gate marked *Feuerwache Bruderhof*. The hostel has a roof terrace and kitchens, but the sound of church bells is loud in some rooms.

The **Naturfreundehaus** *(☎/fax 84 17 29; Mönchsberg 19; dorm beds €12.50-13.50; showers €0.80; 1am curfew, open mid-April–mid-Oct)* compensates for ordinary dorm rooms with priceless views over the city. High on the Mönchsberg hill, it's reached via the Mönchsberg lift (€2.40 return) from Anton Neumayr Platz or by climbing the stairs from Toscanini Hof, behind the Festival Halls. Sometimes it's too cold to open the unheated rooms, so phone ahead.

Hotels & Pensions Central **Junger Fuchs** *(☎ 87 54 96; Linzer Gasse 54; singles/doubles/triples €26/34/44)* remains a solid, if unremarkable, budget choice. Its cramped stairwell opens out into reasonably sized rooms with wooden floorboards. Rooms at **Pension Jahn** *(☎ 87 14 05, fax 87 55 35; Elisabethenstrasse 31; singles/doubles from €31/43)* are also fairly spartan, but they're clean and the pension is handy for the train station.

Gasthof Wallner *(☎ 84 50 23, fax -3; Aiglhofstrasse 15; singles/doubles €26/42, with bathroom €40/60)* lies on the opposite side of the Mönchsberg from the Old Town. However, it's only a 10-minute ride from the centre on bus No 29 from Hanuschplatz. The Gasthof has pleasant, airy rooms are set back from the street.

Pension Elisabeth *(☎/fax 87 16 64; Vogelweiderstrasse 52; singles/doubles €33/39, with bathroom €42/64)* has been nicely renovated in recent years, making it Salzburg's top budget choice. It's near the Breitenfelderstrasse stop of bus No 15, which heads for town every 15 minutes.

AUSTRIA

Places to Eat

There's a **fruit and vegetable market** at Mirabellplatz Thursday morning. On Universitätsplatz and Kapitelplatz there are **market stalls** and **fast-food stands**. There's a **Billa supermarket** *(Schallmooser Hauptstrasse)* and a **Eurospar** supermarket by the train station.

The most convenient university mensa is **Toskana** *(Sigmund Haffner Gasse 11; lunch €3.50; open 11.30am-2pm Mon-Fri)*. For vegetarian nourishment, try **Vegy Vollwertimbiss** *(Schwarzstrasse 21; lunch menu €7.20; open 11am-5pm Mon-Fri)* or the holistic **Bio Bistro Spicy Spices** *(☎ 87 07 12; Wolf-Dietrich-Strasse 1; mains €5)*.

Picnic *(Judengasse 15; sandwiches from €4.72, pasta from €5.67; open daily May-Sept, closed Tues Oct-Apr)* seems an enduringly popular joint. It serves cheap snacks, including 'big sandwiches' that are so big you can't get your mouth around them.

Wilder Mann *(off Getreidegasse 20; mains €5-7.90; open Mon-Fri)* serves traditional Austrian food in a friendly, bustling environment. Tables, both inside and out, are often so packed it's almost impossible not to get to chatting with fellow diners. **Stadtalm** *(Mönchsberg 19c; mains from €7; open daily mid-April–mid-October)* is a great place to tuck into a well-priced meal while you admire the view.

Entertainment

When you enter **Augustiner Bräustübl** *(Augustinergasse 4-6; open 3pm-11pm Mon-Fri, 2.30pm-11pm Sat & Sun)* you hear the contented hum of the crowd well before you descend the steps into the beer halls or garden. The brew produced by local monks – served by the litre (€5) or half-litre (€2.50) in ceramic mugs – does a good job as a social lubricant.

There's a lively stretch of bars, clubs and discos near Hotel Altstadt on Rudolfskai, including Irish pubs with live music. Directly across the river, there's also a little scene along Steingasse. Both these strips quieten down soon after midnight. Real night owls need to head to **Bar Flip** *(Gstättengasse 17)* or **Mount Inn** *(Gstättengasse 21)*, which both keep humming until 4am. The legendary **Cave Club** *(☎ 84 00 26; W www.cave-club.at; Leopoldskronstrasse 26)* is still pumping out hard-core techno.

Getting There & Away

The **airport** *(☎ 85 80)* handles flights to Amsterdam, Brussels, Frankfurt, London, Paris and Zürich. Contact **Austrian Airlines** *(☎ 85 45 11-0)* or no-frills **Ryanair** *(W www.ryanair.com)*, which has flights from London.

Bundesbuses to Kitzbühel (one way €12, 2¼ hours) and other ski resorts depart at least three times a day from Südtiroler Platz, across from the train-station post office. Those going to the Salzkammergut region leave from just to the left of the main station exit. Destinations include Bad Ischl (€7.40, 1¾ hours), Mondsee (€4.50, 50 minutes), St Gilgen (€4.50, 50 minutes) and St Wolfgang (€6.70, 1½ hours). There are timetable boards at each departure point and a bus information office in the train station. Alternatively, call ☎ 4660-333 for information.

Fast trains leave for Vienna (€33.40, 3¼ hours) via Linz every hour. The express service to Klagenfurt (€26.10, three hours) goes via Villach. The quickest way to Innsbruck (€28, two hours) is by the 'corridor' train through Germany via Kufstein, which leaves at least every two hours. There are trains every 30 to 60 minutes to Munich (€22, two hours).

Three autobahns converge on Salzburg: the A1 from Linz, Vienna and the east; A8/E52 from Munich and the west; and A10/E55 from Villach and the south. The A10 goes south to Carinthia.

Getting Around

Bus drivers sell single tickets for €1.60. Day passes (€2.90) must be bought from the automatic machines at major stops, Tabak shops or tourist offices.

Flag fall in a taxi is €2.40 (€3.20 at night), plus about €1.10 per kilometre inside the city, €1.60 per kilometre outside the city. To book a taxi, call ☎ 87 44 00. **Top Bike** *(☎ 0676 476 72 59)* rents bikes from the Intertreff Café outside the train station and from the main city bridge.

AROUND SALZBURG

Hellbrunn

Four kilometres south of Salzburg's Old Town is the popular **Schloss Hellbrunn** *(☎ 82 03 72-0; Fürstenweg 37; adult/student €7.50/5.50; open 9am-4.30pm Apr-Oct, later in summer)*. Built in the 17th century by bishop Markus Sittikus, Wolf Dietrich's nephew, this castle is mainly known for its ingenious trick fountains and water-powered figures. Expect to get wet! Admission includes a tour of the baroque palace. Other parts of the garden (without fountains) are open year-round and are free to visit.

The **Hellbrunn Zoo** *(adult/student €6.50/4.70; open 8.30am-6.60pm daily in summer, 8.30am-4.30pm daily in winter)* is as naturalistic and as open-plan as possible.

City bus No 55 runs to the palace every half-hour from Salzburg Hauptbahnhof, via Rudolfskai in the Old Town (Salzburg tickets are valid).

Werfen

☎ 06468 • pop 3000

Werfen is a rewarding day trip from Salzburg. The **tourist office** *(☎ 5388; e info@werfen.at; Markt 24; open 9am-7pm Mon-Fri, 5pm-7pm Sat mid-July–mid-Aug; 9am-5pm Mon-Fri rest of year)* is in the village main street.

The **Hohenwerfen Fortress** *(adult/student €9/7.50; open daily Apr-Nov)* stands on the hill above the village. Originally built in 1077, it now occupies a building dating from the 16th century. Admission includes an exhibition, a guided tour of the interior and a dramatic falconry show. The walk up from the village takes 20 minutes.

The **Eisriesenwelt Höhle** *(Giant Ice Caves; ☎ 5646; adult/student & senior €7.20/6.50; open May-Oct)* are the largest accessible ice caves in the world. The vast, natural ice formations are elaborate and beautiful. The tour lasts an arduous 75 minutes – take warm clothes. Both attractions can be visited in one day if you start early.

Get to Werfen from Salzburg by highway 10 or train (€6, 50 minutes). A minibus service (return €5.50) from the station leads to the cave car park, from where you can walk to the cable car (adult/concession return €8.80/8). The whole route can be hiked, but it's a very hard four-hour ascent, rising 1100m above the village.

Salzkammergut

Salzkammergut is a picturesque holiday region of mountains and lakes east of Salzburg. The main season is summer, when hiking and water sports – or simply relaxing – are popular pursuits. In winter, some hiking paths stay open and there's downhill or cross-country skiing.

A central point for information is the resort town of Bad Ischl, smack-dab in the middle of Salzkammergut. Staff are helpful at the private **Salzkammergut Touristik** *(☎ 06132-240 00-0; e office@salzkammergut.co.at; Götzstrasse 12; open 9am-8pm daily)*. The area is dotted with hostels and affordable hotels. Rooms in private homes are usually the best deals. Tourist offices can supply accommodation lists and make bookings.

Major rail routes bypass the heart of Salzkammergut, but regional trains cross the area in a north-south direction. You get on this route from Attnang Puchheim on the Salzburg–Linz line. Regular Bundesbuses connect the region's towns and villages, though less frequently on weekends, and passenger boats ply the waters of the Attersee, Traunsee, Mondsee, Hallstätter See and Wolfgangsee.

HALLSTATT

☎ 06134 • pop 1150

There's evidence of human settlement at Hallstatt as long as 4500 years ago – and who wouldn't want to move into such a breathtaking location as early as possible? The village perches on a steep mountainside, beside a placid lake. Mining salt in the peak was the main activity for thousands of years, but today tourism is the major money-spinner.

Seestrasse is the main street. To reach the **tourist office** *(☎ 8208, fax 83 52; e hallstatt-info@eunet.at; Seestrasse 169; open 9am-noon, 1pm-5pm Mon-Fri, also 10am-2pm Sat & Sun summer)* turn left from the ferry. The **post office** *(Postamt 4830)* is around the corner.

Above the village are the **Salzbergwerk** *(Saltworks; ☎ 8400; admission €14, with funicular €20; open 9am-4pm daily, later Apr-Oct)*. There are two scenic hiking trails you could take instead. Near the mine, 2000 graves were discovered, dating from 1000 to 500 BC. Don't miss the macabre **Beinhaus** *(Bone House; admission €1)* near the village parish church, which contains rows of decorated skulls from the 15th century and later. Around the lake at Obertraun are the **Dachstein Rieseneishöhle** *(Giant Ice Caves; admission €8; open early May–mid-Oct)*. A cable car provides easy access.

Places to Stay & Eat

Some private rooms are only available during the busiest months of July and August; others require a minimum three-night stay. Ask at the tourist office.

For camping there's **Campingplatz Höll** *(☎ 8322, Lahn 201; adult/tent/car €5.80/3.70/2.90; open Apr-Oct)*. Tax is extra. There are two hostels: the HI **Jugendherberge**

(☎ 8212; Salzbergstrasse 50; dorm beds €9.30, sheets €3.30; breakfast €2.50; check-in 5pm-6pm; open around May-Oct), which is usually full in July and August, and the **TVN Naturfreunde Herberge** *(☎/fax 8318; Kirchenweg 36; dorm beds €10, sheets €2.50; breakfast €2.50)*.

Hallstatt's steep footpaths help you work up an appetite. Good restaurants include **Bräu Gasthof** *(Seestrasse 120; meals from €7.40; open daily for meals 1 May-26 Oct)* for typical Austrian food in an old-fashioned atmosphere and **Gasthof Weisses Lamm** *(Mortonweg 166; mains from €7.50)* for some healthier options.

Getting There & Away

About six buses a day run to/from Obertraun and Bad Ischl. Beware: services finish very early and the last guaranteed departure from Bad Ischl is 4.10pm. There are at least nine train services a day from Bad Ischl (€2.80, 50 minutes). The station is across the lake (ferry crossing €1.80). The last ferry departs the train station at 6.44pm (leaving Hallstatt at 6.10pm).

WOLFGANGSEE

You can swim or go boating on this lake, climb the mountain above it or just sit on the shore, gazing at the scenery. The lake is dominated by the Schafberg (1783m) on the northern shore. Next to it is the resort of St Wolfgang. On the main street by the entrance to the road tunnel is the **tourist office** *(☎ 06138-2239-0; e info@stwolfgang.at; open Mon-Sat)*. St Gilgen, on the western shore, provides easy access to Salzburg, 29km away. Its **tourist office** *(☎ 06227-2348; e info@stgilgen.co.at; Mozartplatz 1; open Mon-Fri, daily in summer)* is in the Rathaus.

St Wolfgang's 14th-century **Pilgrimage Church** *(open 9am-6pm daily)* sports a winged high altar created by Michael Pacher between 1471 and 1481. Another major drawcard is the **Schafberg**. Some people like to climb mountains because they're there; these lunatics will love the four-hour **hike** to the peak. Others prefer the less strenuous **train ride** *(€21 return; open May-Oct)* to the top.

Camping Appesbach *(☎ 06138-2206; Au 99; adult €5, tent & car €6; open Easter-Oct)* is on the lakefront, 1km from St Wolfgang heading towards Strobl. St Gilgen has a good HI **Jugendgästehaus** *(☎ 06227-2365; Mondseestrasse 7; dorm beds/twins/doubles €12.35/14.53/18.16; check-in 5pm-7pm)*, where some rooms have a lake view. Both St Wolfgang and St Gilgen have numerous pensions, private rooms and holiday apartments, mostly starting at about €18 per person.

A ferry (€4.30, 50 minutes) operates from Strobl to St Gilgen, stopping at various points en route, including St Wolfgang. Services are from late April to 26 October. Buses from St Wolfgang to St Gilgen and Salzburg go via Strobl, on the eastern side of the lake. You can reach St Gilgen from Salzburg by bus (€4.50, 50 minutes).

Tirol

Tirol's wonderful mountain scenery renders it an ideal playground for hikers and mountaineers, and its glitzy ski resorts add glamour. The province is divided in two: East Tirol has been isolated from the main part of the state ever since prosperous South Tirol was ceded to Italy at the end of WWI.

Train and bus journeys within Tirol are cheaper using VVT tickets, which can be bought only within Tirol (from train stations etc). The **IVB Kundenbüro** *(☎ 0512-53 07-103; Stainerstrasse 2, Innsbruck)* can give more information.

INNSBRUCK

☎ 0512 • pop 111,000

As a two-time host to the Winter Olympics Games – in 1964 and 1976 – Innsbruck could be easily mistaken for a sports-mad destination with little else to offer than skiing, snowboarding and a landmark ski-jump. How wrong that would be. An important trading post since the 12th century, the city was home to one branch of the Habsburgs. Emperor Maximilian erected the golden roof in the Old Town.

Innsbruck lies in the valley of the River Inn, scenically squeezed between the northern chain of the Alps and the Tuxer mountain range to the south. The town centre is very compact, with the main train station (Hauptbahnhof) only a 10-minute walk from the pedestrian-only Old Town centre (Altstadt).

Information

The **main tourist office** *(☎ 53 56-36, fax -41; e info@innsbruck.tvb.co.at; Burggraben 3; open 9am-6pm Mon-Sun)* books hotel rooms (€3 commission) and sells tickets. Ask for the free tear-off map. There are hotel reservation centres in the **main train station** *(open 9am-9pm daily, to 10pm in summer)* and at motorway exits near the city. Two additional information sources are the **Jugendwarteraum** *(open mid-Sept–mid-July)*, in the train station, and the **Tirol Information office** *(☎ 72 72, fax -7; ⓔ tirol.info@tirolwerbung.at; Maria Theresien Strasse 55; open 8am-6pm Mon-Fri)*.

You can change cash at the **main post office** *(Hauptpostamt 6010; Maximilianstrasse 2; open 7am-11pm Mon-Fri, 7am-9pm Sat, 8am-9pm Sun)*. Apparently owned by someone who's seen the film *My Beautiful Laundrette* a few times, the fabulous, neon-coloured **Bubble Point Wasch Salon** *(Brixner Strasse 1)* allows you to read your email cheaply (10 minutes' Internet access for €1) while doing your laundry.

Things to See & Do

For an overview of the city, climb the 14th-century **Stadtturm** *(City Tower; ☎ 56 15 00; Herzog Friedrich Strasse; adult/student €2.50/2.00; open 10am-5pm daily, to 8pm summer)*. Across the square is the famous **Goldenes Dachl** (Golden Roof), comprising 2657 gilded copper tiles dating from the 16th century. Emperor Maximilian used to observe street performers from the balcony beneath. A minute or so north of the Golden Roof is the baroque cathedral. After visiting the cathedral, turn back southwards and note the elegant 15th- and 16th-century buildings as you stroll down Maria Theresien Strasse to the 1767 **Triumphal Arch**.

AUSTRIA

The **Hofburg** *(Imperial Palace; ☎ 58 71 86; Rennweg 1; adult/senior/student €5.45/4/3.65; open 9am-4.30pm daily)* has been rebuilt and restyled several times since 1397, particularly by Empress Maria Theresa. The baroque Giant's Hall is a highlight. Diagonally across Universitätsstrasse is the **Hofkirche** *(Imperial Church; ☎ 58 43 02; Universitätsstrasse 2; adult/student under 27 €2.20/1.45; Sun free; open daily)*, housing Maximilian I's empty sarcophagus and 28 giant Habsburg statues.

In a spacious park on a hill east of the centre, **Schloss Ambras** *(☎ 34 84 46; Schlossstrasse 20; adult/concession Apr-Oct €7.50/5.50, Nov-Mar €4.30/2.90; open 10am-5pm daily Apr-Oct, 2pm-5pm Wed-Mon Nov-Mar)* is an impressive medieval castle. It features a Renaissance Spanish Hall, an armoury and a portrait of Vlad IV Tzespech Dracul – the model for Dracula.

The **Swarovski Kristallwelten** *(Crystal Worlds; ☎ 05224 51080; ⓔ scs.visitors-centre@swarovski.com; Kristallweltenstrasse 1; admission €5.45; open 9am-6pm daily)* are a series of caverns featuring the famous Swarovski crystals. Greats like Salvador Dalí, Andy Warhol and Keith Haring designed some of the sparkly displays.

The ski region around Innsbruck has been totally refurbished. A one-day pass is €20 to €26. Downhill equipment rental starts at €15. You can ski or snowboard all year at the popular **Stubai Glacier**. A one-day pass costs €35. Catch the white IVB Stubaltalbahn bus or ask the tourist office about the free ski bus in winter. The last bus back is usually at 5.30pm. Several places offer complete packages to the glacier, which compare favourably with going it alone.

Places to Stay

Camping West of the town centre, **Camping Innsbruck Kranebitten** *(☎/fax 28 41 80; Kranebitter Allee 214; sites per adult/tent/car €5.55/3/3; open year-round)* has a restaurant is on site.

Hostels & Private Rooms None of Innsbruck's hostels are particularly convenient, but **Jugendherberge St Nikolaus** *(☎ 28 65 15, fax -14; ⓔ innsbruck@hostelnikolaus.at; Innstrasse 95; dorm beds/doubles from €13/18; check-in 5pm-10pm)* is probably the most central. The staff can be a trifle patronising, but they mean well. It has a bar and restaurant and is a sociable place.

More privacy can be found in the hostel's sister at **Glockenhaus pension** *(Weiherburggasse 3; singles/doubles €29/43.60)*, up the hill.

The **Jugendherberge Innsbruck** *(☎ 34 61 79, fax -12; Reichenauerstrasse 147; dorm beds first night €12.05, additional nights €9.50; open 7am-10am, 3pm-11pm, 5pm winter)* is a huge, Soviet-style concrete monstrosity that's nicer inside than out. It has a kitchen and washing machines and an 11pm curfew. Take bus O from Museumstrasse.

Two extra hostels to try in summer are **St Paulus Hostel** *(☎ 34 42 91; Reichenauerstrasse 72; open mid-June–early Sept)* and **Jugendwohnheim Fritz Prior** *(☎ 58 58 14, fax -4; Rennweg 17b; open July, Aug & New Year)*. Both have similar prices to the above hostels, with check-in from 5pm.

The tourist office has lists of private rooms in Innsbruck and Igls (south of town) from €15 per person.

Hotels & Pensions Already pleasant before, **Pension Paula** *(☎ 29 22 62, fax 29 30 17; ⓔ office@pensionpaula.at; Weiherburggasse 15; singles/doubles from €26/44)* has upped the ante by renovating its bathrooms. Book ahead.

Two other cheapish options sit on the northern bank of the Inn River: **Gasthof Innbrücke** *(☎ 28 19 34, fax 27 84 10; ⓔ innbruecke@magnet.at; Innstrasse 1; singles/doubles from €25.50/43.60)* and **Gasthof Weisses Lamm** *(☎ 831 56; Mariahilfstrasse 12; singles/doubles €33/55)*.

Eat breakfast elsewhere if staying at **Pension Stoi** *(☎ 58 54 34, fax 872 82; Salurner Strasse 7; singles/doubles from €29/47)*, a small price to pay for such decent, centrally located rooms. Coming from the train station, turn left after the Neuner Sport shop.

Binders *(☎ 334 36-0, fax 334 39-99; Dr. Glatz Strasse 20; singles/doubles from €36/49)* is for those whose taste for modern comfort and style exceeds their budget. Enjoy the feeling of luxury.

Two hotels in the Old Town stand out. **Weisses Kreuz** *(☎ 594 79, fax -90; ⓔ hotel.weisses.kreuz@eunet.at; Herzog Friedrich Strasse 31; singles/doubles from €35/89)* once played host to Mozart and resonates with history. Across the street, **Weinhaus Happ** *(☎ 58 29 80, fax -11; ⓔ office@weinhaus-happ.at; Herzog Friedrich Strasse 14; singles/doubles from €51/88)* has rooms with views of the Golden Roof.

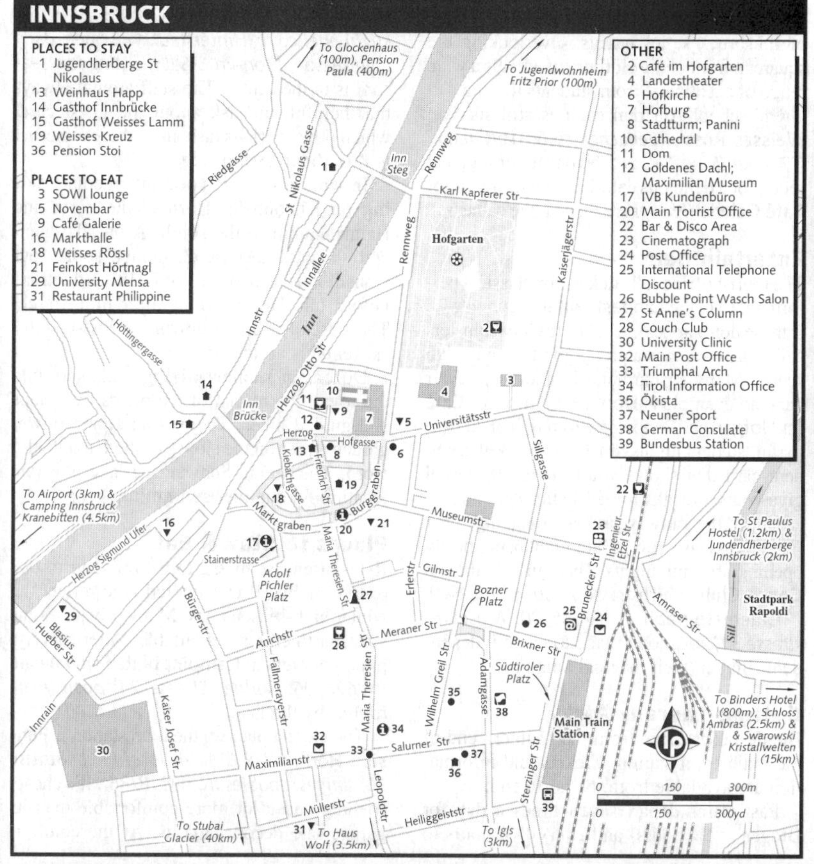

Places to Eat

For groceries and fresh produce, there is the supermarket **Feinkost Hörtnagl** *(Burggasse)* or a large indoor food market by the river in **Markthalle** *(Herzog Siegmund Ufer; open Mon-Fri & Sat morn)*.

Enjoy great views of the Alps at **University Mensa** *(Herzog Siegmund Ufer 15; open 11am-1.30pm Mon-Sat; mains from €4.60)*. Another mensa is the **SOWI lounge** *(Universitätsstrasse 15; open 8am-5pm Mon-Thur, 10am-3pm Fri; mains from €3)*.

The first floor of self-service **Panini** *(cnr Hofgasse & Herzog Friedrich Strasse; meals from €3.60)* overlooks the Golden Roof. Non-meat-eaters will find solace at veg **Restaurant Philippine** *(☎ 58 91 57; Müllerstrasse 9; meals €7-8; open 11.30am-2pm & 6.30pm-8pm Mon-Sat)*.

Novembar *(Universitätstrasse 1; small meals from €6.60, mains from €12.40)* is one of Innsbruck's 'in' haunts. Overlooking the square in front of the Hofburg, it attracts a wide range of customers, from students to suits.

Old-school Austrian eateries still survive. **Weisses Rössl** *(Kiebachgasse 8; daily menu €7; open Mon-Sat)* is a favourite for regional food. For a delicious café-latte, make tracks for **Café Galerie** *(Pfarrgasse 6)*, near the cathedral.

Entertainment

The tourist office sells tickets for classical performances in the **Landestheater** *(Rennweg 2)*. If these don't appeal, 'eyebk' (as local hipsters call Innsbruck) has a pretty good bar and club scene. Many restaurants double as popular bars; an example is **Dom** *(Pfarrgasse 3)*. **Café im Hofgarten** *(Rennweg 6A)* has been known to run 'student nights' on Tuesday. With a student card that shows you're over 20, they'll give you six drinks for €10 after 8pm.

Under the railway arches along Ingenieur Etzel Strasse is a row of late-night bars (mostly opening after midnight). Then, there's the hip **Couch Club** *(Anichstrasse 7; open Thur-Sat)*.

Cinematograph *(☎ 57 85 00; Museumstrasse 31)* is a good place to catch independent films in their original language.

Getting There & Away

Bundesbuses leave from the southern end of the main train station. Tickets and information are available from the north end.

Fast trains depart seven times a day for Bregenz (2¾ hours) and every two hours to Salzburg (two hours). Regular express trains head north to Munich via Kufstein (two hours) and south to Verona (3½ hours). There are hourly connections to Kitzbühel (€13.30, 1¼ hours). On many trains to Lienz, people travelling with Austrian passes may have to pay a surcharge for going through Italy.

The A12 and highway 171 are the main roads to the west and east. Highway 177 heads north to Germany and Munich. The A13 toll motorway and toll-free highway 182 go south to Italy.

Tickets for local transport cost €1.60. Bike rental is available from **Neuner Sport** *(☎ 56 15 01; Salurner Strasse 5)*.

KITZBÜHEL

☎ 05356 • pop 8200

Kitzbühel is a fashionable, prosperous winter resort, offering excellent skiing. The **tourist office** *(☎ 62155-0, fax 62307; ⓔ info@kitzbuehel.com; Hinterstadt 18; open daily high season, Mon-Fri & Sat morning low season)* is in the centre. The staff are not always that helpful, but ask about the guest card, which offers various discounts. Access the Net at **Kitz Video** *(Schlossergasse 10)*.

In winter, there is good intermediate **skiing** on Kitzbüheler Horn to the north and Hahnenkamm to the south. A one-day general ski pass costs €32, though some pensions/hotels can offer 'Ski Hit' reductions before mid-December or after mid-March. The cost of a day's downhill/cross-country ski rental is around €11/9.

Dozens of summer **hiking** trails surround the town; the tourist office offers free maps and guided hikes. There is an alpine flower garden (free) on the slopes of the Kitzbüheler Horn. The scenic Schwarzsee lake is a fine location for summer **swimming**.

Places to Stay & Eat

Rates often rise by €2 to €4 for stays of one or two nights. Prices quoted here reflect the winter high-season peak. Many private rooms and apartments are available. Alternatively, pitch your tent at **Campingplatz Schwarzsee** *(☎ 628 06; Reither Strasse 24; open year-round)* by the lake.

The closest place to the train station is **Pension Hörl** *(☎/fax 631 44; Josef Pirchl Strasse 60; singles/doubles from €18/36)*. It's cheap, friendly and a lot more comfortable than its garage-sale decor suggests. At the comfortable and convenient **Pension Mühlbergerhof** *(☎ 62835, fax 644 88; Schwarzseestrasse 6; from €33 per person)*, the owners serve breakfast with produce from their farm.

On Bichlstrasse there's a **Billa** supermarket. **Asia Markt** *(Josef Pirchl Strasse 16; meals from €4.50; open Mon-Sat)* serves light, weekday lunches and early evening meals.

A trip to Kitzbühel isn't complete without visiting **Huberbräu Stüberl** *(Vorderstadt 18; meals from €6.45; open daily)*, where diners and drinkers congregate around the Austrian food and beers.

Getting There & Away

Direct trains to Innsbruck (€13.30, one to two hours) leave Kitzbühel every two hours or so, but there are hourly services to Wörgl, where you can change for Innsbruck. Trains to Salzburg (€19.60, two hours) leave roughly hourly. Getting to Lienz by public transport is awkward. The train is slow and the bus is infrequent (€10, two hours).

LIENZ

☎ 04852 • pop 13,000

Many travellers view the capital of East Tirol principally as a handy stopover on the way to Italy, but it's also a good base for skiing or hiking. That's thanks to the jagged Dolomite mountain range, which crowds the southern skyline.

Staff at the **tourist office** *(☎ 652 65, fax -2; e lienz@netway.at; Europaplatz 1; open 8am-6pm Mon-Fri, 9am-noon Sat, also Sun summer & winter high seasons)* will find rooms free of charge, or you can use the hotel board (free telephone) outside. To get on the Internet visit **Net-Planet/Odin's** *(Schweizergasse 3)*.

There is downhill **skiing** on the Zettersfeld and Hochstein peaks (one-day pass €26). However, the area around Lienz is more renowned for its cross-country skiing; the town fills up for the annual *Dolomitenlauf* cross-country race in mid-January.

Just south of town, **Camping Falken** *(☎ 640 22; Eichholz 7; open mid-Dec–Oct)* is the best place in Austria to wash your clothes (at least according to the newspaper article on its laundromat wall). It's the view, baby. Most of the private rooms around the town don't have quite the same close-up of the Dolomite range but are great value nonetheless. **Haus Egger** *(☎ 720 98; Alleestrasse 33; rooms €14 per person)* or **Gästehaus Masnata** *(☎ 655 36; Drahtzuggasse 4; apartments around €19-20 per person)* both allow single-night stays.

There are **ADEG** supermarkets on Hauptplatz and Tiroler Platz. **Imbissstube** *(Albin Egger Strasse 5; half a chicken with roll €3)* has mouth-watering spiced rotisserie chicken. There are lots of places to try regional dishes, such as **Adlerstüberl** *(Andrä Kranz Gasse 5; meals from €8)*.

Except for the 'corridor' route to Innsbruck, trains to the rest of Austria connect via Spittal Millstättersee to the east. Trains to Salzburg (€25) take at least three hours. Villach, between Spittal and Klagenfurt, is a main junction for rail routes to the south.

Hitting the Hay

Rural Austria provides plenty of tranquillity for the traveller – but, as is often the case, a peaceful rest stop for visitors often translates into boredom for residents. To combat the monotony of country life, Austrians have developed a number of indigenous pastimes. One popular autumn activity is *Heuhupfen* (hay-jumping), in which participants leap from barn roofs into bales of freshly harvested hay. Though foreigners might consider this ultra-toned-down version of skydiving primarily a children's activity, they may be surprised at the number of adults who throw themselves into the endeavour with gusto.

Where there is autumn, spring and love soon follow. As far as Austrians are concerned, this means that what goes down eventually comes back up. Rather than leaping to the ground, they celebrate this season with the art of *Fensterln* (literally, 'windowing'), wherein men en masse drag ladders to women's windows and ascend to rendezvous with the lady of their choice. Prizes for winning remain unclear.

HOHE TAUERN NATIONAL PARK

Flora and fauna are protected in this 1786-sq-km hiking paradise, which straddles Tirol, Salzburg and Carinthia.

It contains **Grossglockner** (3797m), Austria's highest mountain, which towers over the 10km-long Pasterze Glacier. The best viewing point is **Franz Josefs Höhe**, reached from Lienz by Bundesbus (mid-June to late September). The route north (Highway 107, the Grossglockner Hochalpenstrasse) is breathtakingly scenic.

Vorarlberg

The small state of Vorarlberg trickles down from the Alps to the shores of Lake Constance (Bodensee) and provides a convenient gateway to Germany, Liechtenstein, and Switzerland. To travel the province, buy VVV tickets (see Tirol, earlier in this chapter).

The Arlberg region, shared by Vorarlberg and neighbouring Tirol, has some of Austria's best skiing. **St Anton am Arlberg** is the largest resort, where you're as likely to hear an Antipodean 'G'day' or Scandinavian *God dag* as an Austrian *Grüss' Di*. The **tourist office** (*☎ 05446-226 90; e st.anton@netway.at*), on the main street, has details about runs.

Accommodation is mainly in a bewildering number of small B&Bs. Many budget places (from €26 per person in winter high season) are booked months or even years in advance.

St Anton is on the main railway route between Bregenz and Innsbruck, less than 1½ hours from either. It's close to the eastern entrance of the Arlberg Tunnel, the toll road connecting Vorarlberg and Tirol. In winter, several buses a day run to Lech (€3.42, 40 minutes) from St Anton.

Belgium

Think of Belgium (België in Flemish, Belgique in French) and it's 'Bruges, beer and chocolate' that generally spring to mind. While Brits might add 'boring' to that list and businesspeople would arrive at the 'European Union', few other word associations are likely to pop up. Belgium, you see, has an identity problem. A little country surrounded by Europe's big guys, it's been fought over by bossy neighbours for most of its history. Nationhood only came about less than 200 years ago, and since then rivalry between the two main language communities – the Flemish and the Walloon – has kept nationalism at bay.

This much-embattled country spawned Western Europe's first great towns, and it was here that medieval artists are credited with inventing oil painting. When you add in fabulous restaurants, thousands of bars and cafés, great beer and chocolate, avant-garde fashion and rich Art Nouveau architecture, you'll discover that Belgium's not boring – it just hasn't learnt to boast.

Belgium: the Basics

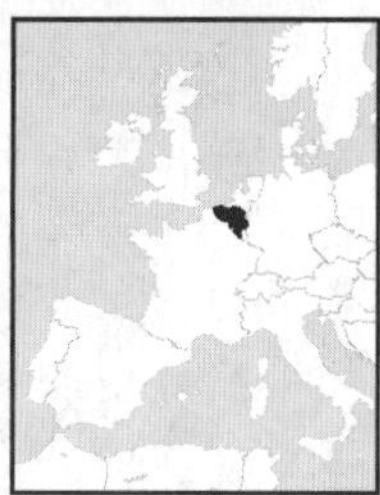

Local names Belgique, België

Capital Brussels

Population 10.2 million

Languages Flemish, French, German

Currency euro (€) = 100 centimes

Avoid at all costs The Manneken Pis

Converse on a favourite topic by saying *Wat een geluk dat die Trappist monniken voor bier hebben gekozen en niet voor botermelk./Quelle chance que les moines Trappistes ont choisi la bié're et pas le babeurre.* (Thank goodness those Trappist monks chose beer and not buttermilk.)

Facts about Belgium

HISTORY

Belgium's position between France, Germany, the Netherlands, Luxembourg and, across the North Sea, England, has long made it one of Europe's main battlegrounds. Prosperous throughout both the 13th and 14th centuries, Ypres, Bruges and Ghent were the first major cities, booming from the manufacture and trade of cloth. The Flemish weavers were ruined, however, by competition from England and subsequently the towns faded. Trade moved east to Antwerp, which soon became the greatest port in Europe.

When Protestantism swept Europe in the 16th century, the Low Countries (present-day Belgium, the Netherlands and Luxembourg) embraced it, much to the chagrin of their ruler, the fanatically Catholic Philip II of Spain. Responding to his unleashing of the cruel Inquisition, Protestants rioted during the Iconoclastic Fury, ransacking the churches. The Revolt of the Netherlands lasted 80 years, and in the end roughly laid the region's present-day borders – Holland and its allied provinces victoriously expelling the Spaniards while Belgium and Luxembourg stayed under their rule.

In 1814 the United Kingdom of the Netherlands incorporated Belgium and Luxembourg. Sixteen years later, the Catholic Belgians revolted, subsequently winning independence from the Netherlands.

The Germans invaded in 1914, and Ypres was wiped off the map. In WWII the country was taken by a surprise German attack in May 1940. Postwar Belgium was characterised by an economic boom, later accentuated by Brussels' appointment as the headquarters of the EU and NATO.

Throughout the 1990s, a number of political and judicial scandals have left Belgium with the nickname of the 'Italy of the north'. Reform has been slow and that, combined with the continuing friction between the Flemish and Walloon communities, has left many Belgians questioning the future of their country.

GEOGRAPHY

Occupying 30,520 sq km, Belgium is one of Europe's smallest nations. The north is flat,

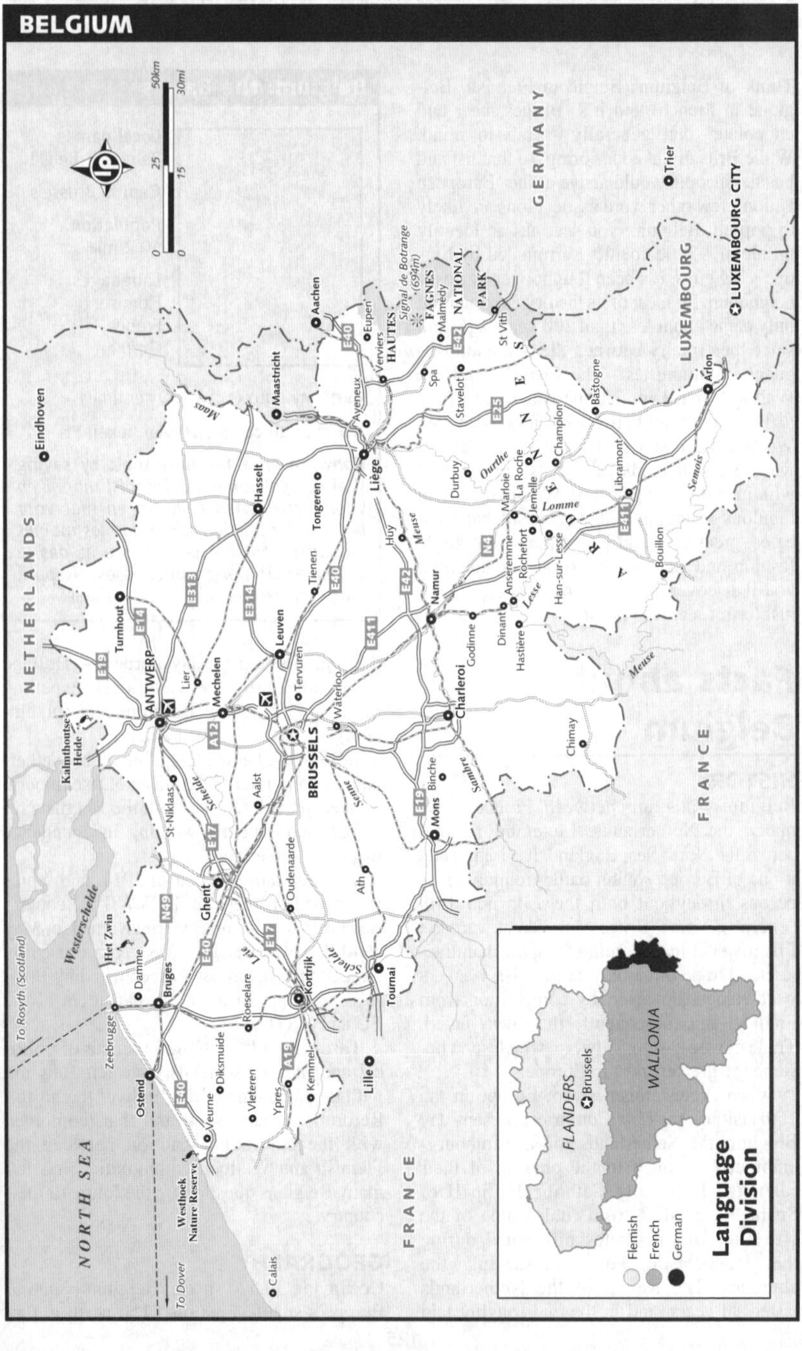
BELGIUM
NETHERLANDS
GERMANY
LUXEMBOURG
FRANCE
NORTH SEA
ARDENNES
HAUTES FAGNES NATIONAL PARK
Signal de Botrange (694m)
0 25 50km
0 15 30mi
To Rosyth (Scotland)
To Dover
Westerschelde
Maas
Meuse
Ourthe
Lomme
Lesse
Semois
Sambre
Senne
Schelde
Leie
Eindhoven
Maastricht
Aachen
Eupen
Verviers
Malmédy
Spa
Stavelot
St Vith
Bastogne
Champlon
Libramont
Arlon
Trier
LUXEMBOURG CITY
Durbuy
La Roche
Marloie
Jemelle
Rochefort
Han-sur-Lesse
Anseremme
Dinant
Hastière
Bouillon
Godinne
Namur
Huy
Liège
Ayeneux
Tongeren
Hasselt
Tienen
Leuven
Tervuren
Waterloo
BRUSSELS
Mechelen
Lier
Turnhout
ANTWERP
Kalmthoutse Heide
St-Niklaas
Aalst
Ghent
Oudenaarde
Ath
Mons
Binche
Charleroi
Chimay
Tournai
Kortrijk
Roeselare
Bruges
Damme
Het Zwin
Zeebrugge
Ostend
Diksmuide
Vleteren
Ypres
Kemmel
Veurne
Westhoek Nature Reserve
Lille
Calais
E19
E14
E313
E314
E40
E411
E42
E25
N4
A12
E17
N49
A19
Language Division
FLANDERS
WALLONIA
Brussels
Flemish
French
German

the south dominated by the hilly, forested Ardennes, and the 66km North Sea coastline monopolised by resorts.

CLIMATE

The country has a generally mild, maritime climate. July and August are the warmest months. They are also the wettest, although precipitation is spread pretty evenly over the year. The Ardennes is often a few degrees colder than the rest of the country, with occasional snow from November to March.

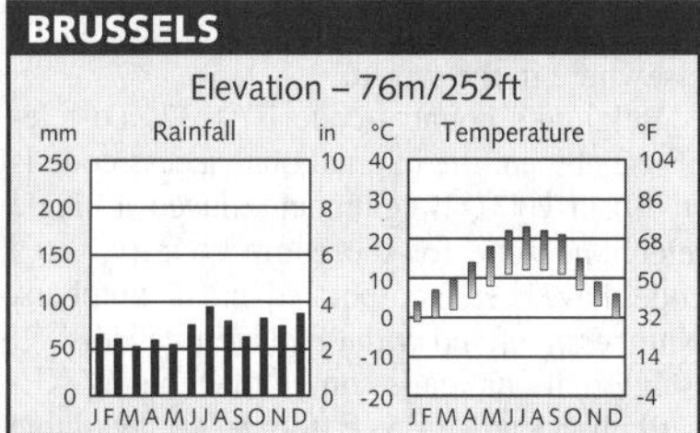

GOVERNMENT & POLITICS

Belgium is a constitutional hereditary monarchy, led by the king and a parliament. In 1993 the government was decentralised through the creation of three regional governments, which represented the Flemish and Walloon communities (Flanders and Wallonia respectively), as well as the Brussels region.

POPULATION & PEOPLE

Belgium's population is basically split in two: the Flemish and the Walloons. Language is the dividing factor, made official in 1962 when the Linguistic Divide was drawn across the country. To the north lies Flemish-speaking Flanders (Vlaanderen); to the south is Francophone Wallonia (La Wallonie).

SOCIETY & CONDUCT

It is customary to greet shopkeepers and café/pub owners when entering their premises. In 2001, Belgium decriminalised the possession of cannabis for personal use.

LANGUAGE

See Population & People for information about the Linguistic Divide. For a run-down of the Flemish (Dutch), French and German languages, see the Language chapter at the back of this book. English is widely spoken, although less frequently in Wallonia.

Facts for the Visitor

HIGHLIGHTS

For plazas and museums, Brussels is the place (its nightlife ain't bad, either). Bruges' canals are always popular, while Antwerp's old buildings draw crowds. The In Flanders Fields Museum, Ypres, is a moving sight.

Walkers will really appreciate the La Roche, Rochefort or Hautes Fagnes areas of the Ardennes.

PLANNING

Spring is the best time to go, as there's less chance of rain, many flowers (including daffodils and tulips) are in bloom and tourist crowds are minimal.

TOURIST OFFICES

Local Tourist Offices

The Flemish tourist authority (Toerisme Vlaanderen) and the Walloon tourist authority (Office de Promotion du Tourisme) have a joint **tourist office** *(☎ 02-504 03 90, fax 02- 504 02 70; ⓔ info@toerismevlaanderen.be; Rue du Marché aux Herbes 63, B-1000 Brussels)*.

Tourist Offices Abroad

Belgian tourist offices abroad include:

Canada (☎ 514-484 3594, fax 489 8965) PO Box 760, Succursale NDG, Montreal, QC, H4A 3S2

France (☎ 01 47 42 41 18, fax 01 47 42 71 83) Blvd des Capucines 21, 75002 Paris

Germany (☎ 0221-27 75 90, fax 27 75 91) Cäcilienstrasse 46, 50667 Cologne

The Netherlands *Flanders:* Toerisme Vlaanderen-Brussel (☎ 070-416 81 10, ⓔ verkeersbureau@toerisme-vlaanderen.nl) Koninginnegracht 86, NL-2514 AJ The Hague *Wallonia:* Belgisch Verkeersbureau voor de Ardennen en Brussel (☎ 023-534 44 34; ⓔ belgisch.verkeersbureau@wxs.nl) PO 2324 NL-2002 CH Haarlem

UK *Flanders:* Tourism Flanders-Brussels (☎ 020-7458 0044, 0800-954 5245, fax 7458 0045, ⓔ info@flanders-tourism.org) 31 Pepper St, London E14 9RW *Wallonia:* Belgian Tourist Office Brussels-Ardennes (☎ 0800-954 5245, fax 7531 0393, ⓔ info@belgiumtheplaceto.be) 217 Marsh Wall, London E14 9FJ

USA (☎ 212-758 8130, fax 355 7675, ⓔ info@visitbelgium.com) 780 Third Ave, Suite 1501, New York, NY 10017

VISAS & DOCUMENTS

Visitors from many countries need only a valid passport for three-month visits. Regulations are basically the same as for entering the Netherlands (see that chapter for details).

EMBASSIES

Belgian Embassies

Belgian embassies abroad include:

Australia (☎ 02-6273 2501, fax 6273 3392) 19 Arkana St, Yarralumla, Canberra, ACT 2600
Canada (☎ 613-236 7267/69, fax 236 7882) 80 Elgin St, 4th floor, Ottawa, ON, K1P 1B7
New Zealand (Honorary Consulate ☎ 09-379 6690, fax 09-309 9570) 18 Waterloo Quadrant, Auckland
UK (☎ 020-7470 3700, fax 7259 6213) 103–105 Eaton Square, London SW1 9AB
USA (☎ 202-333 6900, fax 333 3079) 3330 Garfield St NW, Washington DC 20008

Embassies in Belgium

The following embassies are in Brussels:

Australia (☎ 02 231 05 00, fax 02 230 68 02) Rue Guimard 6, B-1040
Canada (☎ 02 741 06 11, fax 02 741 06 43) Ave de Tervueren 2, B-1040
France (☎ 02 548 87 11, fax 02 513 68 71) Rue Ducale 65, B-1000
Germany (☎ 02 774 19 11, fax 02 772 36 92) Ave de Tervueren 190, B-1150
Ireland (☎ 02 230 53 37, fax 02 230 53 12) Rue Froissart 89, B-1040
Luxembourg (☎ 02 737 57 00, fax 02 737 57 10) Ave de Cortenbergh 75, B-1000
The Netherlands (☎ 02 679 17 11, fax 02 679 17 75) Ave Herrmann-Debroux 48, B-1160
New Zealand (☎ 02 512 10 40, fax 02 513 48 56) Square de Meeus 1, 7th floor, B-1000
UK (☎ 02 287 62 11, fax 02 287 63 55) Rue d'Arlon 85, B-1040
USA (☎ 02 508 21 11, fax 02 511 27 25) Blvd du Régent 27, B-1000

MONEY

Belgium uses the euro. Banks are the best place to change money. Out of hours (see Business Hours later) there are exchange bureaus with poorer rates. All the major credit cards are widely accepted. You'll find ATMs in major cities and at Zaventem (Brussels) airport.

If you stay at hostels and eat very cheaply, you can get by on between €35 to €40 per day. Most museums offer a concession price for students and seniors. Tipping is not obligatory and bargaining not customary.

Value-added tax, or VAT (BTW in Flemish, TVA in French), is 6% for food, hotels and camping, and either 17% or 21% for everything else. To get a rebate, you must get your purchase invoice stamped by customs as you leave.

POST & COMMUNICATIONS

Post offices are generally open 8am or 9am to 5pm or 6pm Monday to Friday and on Saturday mornings. Poste restante can attract a €0.35 fee (often waived). Letters under 20g cost €0.42 within Belgium, €0.52 in the EU, €0.74 in the rest of Europe and €0.84 for elsewhere in the world.

Belgium's country code is ☎ 32. To telephone abroad, the international access code is ☎ 00. In 2000, Belgium introduced a single telephone zone for the entire country. Area codes have been incorporated into all numbers. Numbers prefixed with 0800 are free calls.

International calls can be made using XL-Call phonecards (€5, €10 or €20), available from post offices.

Internet cafés are plentiful; expect to pay €3 to €4.50 per hour.

DIGITAL RESOURCES

A couple of excellent websites offering heaps of information on transport, accommodation and tourism, plus links to other Belgium-related sites, are W www.visitbelgium.com and W www.trabel.com.

BOOKS

Lonely Planet's *Belgium & Luxembourg* guide has comprehensive coverage of these neighbouring countries. For an affectionate look at Belgium's many idiosyncrasies, pick up *A Tall Man in a Low Land*, by Englishman Harry Pearson; it's full of witty insight and observations.

WOMEN TRAVELLERS

Belgium is relatively safe for women. In the event of rape or attack, contact **SOS Viol** *(☎ 02 534 36 36)* or **Helpline** *(☎ 02 648 40 14)*.

GAY & LESBIAN TRAVELLERS

Attitudes to homosexuality are becoming less conservative and same-sex marriages are now legal. The age of consent is 16.

The biggest gay and lesbian organisation in Flanders, Ghent, is **Federatie Werkgroepen Homoseksualiteit** *(FWH; W www.fwh.be;*

Kammerstraat 22). It also operates an information and help hotline called **Holebifoon** *(☎ 09 238 26 26; open 6pm-10pm daily)*.

The main French-speaking gay and lesbian group is **Tels Quels** *(☎ 02 512 45 87, fax 02 511 31 48; Rue du Marché au Charbon 81)* in Brussels. It also runs a helpline, **Télégal** *(☎ 02 502 79 38; open 8pm-midnight daily)*.

DISABLED TRAVELLERS

Belgium is not terribly user-friendly for travellers with a mobility problem. For information, contact **Mobility International** *(☎ 03 236 51 19, fax 03 272 27 93; Koorstraat 1, B-3510 Kermt)*.

SENIOR TRAVELLERS

Most museums and other attractions offer reductions to seniors over 65. Travellers aged over 65 pay only €2.50 for a return day trip by train (2nd class) to anywhere in Belgium.

DANGERS & ANNOYANCES

As in some other parts of Western Europe, racism has increased in the last decade. Hostility here is primarily directed at the nation's immigrant populations, particularly Turks and Moroccans.

BUSINESS HOURS

In general, shops are open 8.30am or 9am to noon and 2pm to 6pm Monday to Saturday. Shops in some cities also open on Sunday. Banks are open 9am to noon or 1pm, and 2pm to 4pm or 5pm weekdays, and Saturday mornings. In large cities, shops and banks often don't close for lunch.

PUBLIC HOLIDAYS & SPECIAL EVENTS

Public holidays include New Year's Day, Easter Monday, Labour Day (1 May), Ascension Day, Whit Monday, Festival of the Flemish Community (11 July; Flanders only), Belgium National Day (21 July), Assumption (15 August), Festival of the Walloon Community (27 September; Wallonia only), All Saints' Day (1 November), Armistice Day (11 November) and Christmas Day.

The religious festival of Carnival is celebrated throughout Belgium, but is at its most colourful in the villages of Binche and Stavelot. There's a swarm of local and national, artistic or religious festivals – pick up the tourist office's free brochure.

EMERGENCIES

The national emergency numbers are police ☎ 101 and fire/ambulance ☎ 100. The Europe-wide emergency number, ☎ 112, can also be used. In the event of a breakdown, the Touring Club de Belgique offers 24-hour roadside assistance through **Touring Secours** *(☎ 070 34 47 77)*.

ACTIVITIES

The Ardennes is Belgium's outdoor playground. The hilly, forested terrain here favours kayaking, hiking or mountain biking and, in winter, cross-country skiing. Cycling is also a hit in flat Flanders.

ACCOMMODATION

In summer, all forms of accommodation are heavily booked. The national tourist office will reserve accommodation for free and has camping and hotel brochures, as well as booklets on B&Bs and rural houses available for weekly rental. Once you're in Belgium, local tourist offices offer free accommodation booking services.

Camping rates vary widely, but on average you will be looking to pay between €6.50 to €13 for two adults, a tent and vehicle.

There are private hostels in some cities. Otherwise, Belgium has two HI hostelling groups. The **Vlaamse Jeugdherbergcentrale** *(☎ 03 232 72 18, fax 03 231 81 26; ⓔ info@vjh.be; Van Stralenstraat 40, B-2060 Antwerp)* runs hostels in Flanders. The HI hostelling counterpart for Walloon is **Les Auberges de Jeunesse** *(☎ 02 219 56 76, fax 02 219 14 51; ⓔ info@laj.be; Rue de la Sablonnière 28, B-1000 Brussels)*. Rates for members range from €12.50 to €14.50 per night for dormitory accommodation. Some hostels provide singles/doubles for €22.50/17.50 per person.

B&Bs/guesthouses (*gastenkamers* in Flemish, *chambres d'hôtes* in French) are rapidly gaining ground in Belgium – prices range from €30 to €60 for singles and €45 to €80 for doubles. Unfortunately many B&Bs will not accept stays of one night.

Budget hotels roughly charge around €35 to €50 for a single room and from €50 to €70 for double rooms. Breakfast is usually included and the cheaper rooms have communal bathroom facilities.

FOOD & DRINKS

Belgian cuisine is highly regarded throughout Europe – some say it's second only to French, while in others' eyes it's equal. It combines French style with German portions. Meat and seafood are abundantly consumed, and then of course there are *frites* (chips or fries), which the Belgians swear they invented.

Meat, poultry and hearty vegetable soups figure prominently on menus, but it's the *mosselen/moules* (mussels) cooked in white wine and served with a mountain of *frites* that's regarded as the national dish. Game, including pheasant and boar, is an autumn speciality from the Ardennes, which is also famed for its ham. Horse, rabbit and guinea fowl are also typical offerings. Many cafés and brasseries these days cater to vegetarian tastes (but not to vegans).

Beer rules – and deservedly so. The quality is excellent and the variety incomparable. The most noted are the abbey-brewed Trappist beers, dark in colour, grainy in taste and dangerously strong (from 6% to 12% alcohol by volume). Then there's *lambiek/lambic*, a spontaneously fermented beer, which is available sweet or sour depending on what's added during fermentation.

Sweet Emotion

Somewhat of a superstar in his native Belgium, actor/writer Noel Godin achieved international notoriety in 1998 when he and his cohorts ambushed an unsuspecting Bill Gates and proceeded to cream the billionaire – literally. According to news reports, Godin and his groupies flung dozens of cream pies at the software magnate, scoring at least four direct hits.

This was far from the first time Godin – or 'Le Gloupier', as he styles himself – had caked a celebrity. His longtime goal, to take self-important people who lack a sense of humour down a notch, was first realised in 1969, when he 'entarted' a French novelist. Since then, Godin has struck scores of public figures (but has never harmed any; even when attacked, his followers respond pacifically). His charismatic nature combined with a contempt for egoists has struck a chord with his compatriots, while his gleefully mischievous actions has gained him fans around the world.

So let this be a warning to those with great plans: Never feel that you are so high that a cream pie can't knock you off your pedestal.

ENTERTAINMENT

Nightlife centres around the ubiquitous bars and cafés; other options include opera, theatre, dance, music festivals and puppet theatres.

Getting There & Away

AIR

SN Brussels Airlines (☎ *070 35 11 11*) flies to many European destinations as well as to some countries in sub-Saharan Africa.

The country's main international airport is Zaventem (also known as Brussels National), 14km northeast of Brussels.

LAND

Bus

Eurolines operates international bus services to and from Belgium. Tickets can be bought from its offices in Antwerp, Brussels or Liège, or from travel agencies. Reduced fares for people aged under 26 or over 60 are offered.

Eurolines has regular buses to many western, eastern, Mediterranean and central European destinations, as well as to Scandinavia and North Africa. Depending on the destination and the time of year, its buses stop in Brussels, Antwerp and Bruges. Services from Brussels include Amsterdam (€15, four hours, seven per day), Cologne (€19, four hours, one per day), London (€46, 8½ hours, four per day) and Paris (€17, 3¾ hours, eight per day).

Train

Belgium built continental Europe's first railway line (Brussels–Mechelen) in the 1830s. The national network is run by the Belgische Spoorwegen/Société National des Chemins de Fer Belges. For all international inquiries (including Eurostar and Thalys trains) call ☎ 02 528 28 28.

Brussels is the international hub and has three main train stations – Gare du Nord, Gare Centrale and Gare du Midi. Gare du Midi is the main station for international connections; the Eurostar and Thalys fast trains stop here only.

Eurostar (W *www.eurostar.com*) trains between Brussels and London (2¾ hours, nine trains per day) operate through the Channel

Tunnel. Standard 2nd-class one-way/return fares are €223/352, but there are cheaper weekend and mid-week fares are available (conditions apply).

Thalys *(W www.thalys.com)* fast trains connect Brussels with Paris (€61.20, 1½ hours, hourly), Cologne (€33.90, 2½ hours, seven trains per day) and Amsterdam (€36.90, 2½ hours, 10 per day). Cheaper Thalys fares are available on weekends and for trips booked well in advance. Those aged under 26 get a 50% discount.

Examples of one-way, 2nd-class adult fares to some neighbouring countries include Amsterdam (€30, 2½ hours, hourly), Cologne (€29.50, three hours, every two hours), and Luxembourg city (€23.80, 2¾ hours, hourly). On Saturday and Sunday, the return fares are reduced by 40%.

Car & Motorcycle

The main motorways into Belgium are the E19 from the Netherlands, the E40 from Germany, the E411 from Luxembourg and the E17 and E19 from France.

SEA

Hoverspeed *(W www.hoverspeed.com)* runs a high-speed Seacat, which sails from Ostend to Dover (England) in two hours (two services per day). One-way fares for cars plus one adult cost around €225. Passengers are charged €37.

Superfast Ferries *(W www.superfast.com)* is a new service operating between Zeebrugge and Rosyth near Edinburgh in Scotland. The overnight voyage takes 17½ hours. One-way fares for cars range from €92 to €228, depending on the season. Passenger fares start at €70 in a nine-bed cabin.

Getting Around

BUS

Buses connect towns and villages in more remote areas, particularly throughout the Ardennes. Local tourist offices will generally have details.

TRAIN

Belgium's public transport system is dominated by its efficient rail network. There are four levels of service: InterCity (IC) trains (the fastest), InterRegional (IR), local (L) and peak-hour (P) commuter trains. Depending on the line, there will be an IC and an IR train every half-hour or hour. Most train stations have either luggage lockers or luggage rooms. For all national train information, call ☎ 02 555 25 55.

On weekends, return tickets within Belgium are reduced by 40% for a single passenger or the first in a group (to a maximum of six people), and 60% for the rest of the group. Another option to consider if you're travelling in a small group (three to five people) is a Multi Pass. A pass for three/four/five people (of whom one must be over 26 years) costs €35/40/44 and is valid for one journey anywhere in the country.

Many rail passes are available. The Benelux Tourrail, which gives five days travel in one month in Belgium, the Netherlands and Luxembourg, costs €174/116 (1st/2nd class) for those aged 26 and over and €87 (2nd class only) for under 26s.

CAR & MOTORCYCLE

Motoring information can be obtained from the **Touring Club de Belgique** *(☎ 02 233 22 11; Rue de la Loi 44, B-1040 Brussels)*.

Car rental (including insurance, VAT and unlimited kilometres) ranges from around €45 to €70 a day or €180 to €240 a week. The following rental firms are available: **Avis** *(☎ 02 537 12 80; Rue Américaine 145)*, **Budget** *(☎ 02 646 51 30; Ave Louise 327b)*, **Hertz** *(☎ 02 513 28 86; Blvd Maurice Lemonnier 8)* and **National/Alamo** *(☎ 02 753 20 60; Zaventem airport)*.

BICYCLE

Getting around by bike is very feasible in Flanders, where many roads have separate cycle lanes. Bikes can be hired from private operators in some cities. A more expensive option is to hire one from a train station – prices are €6.50/8.90 per half/full-day (plus a €12.50 deposit) and the bike must be returned to the same station. Bikes can be taken on trains (only from stations in cities and major towns) for €4.10.

HITCHING

Hitching is illegal on motorways, and you'll find few Belgians hitching these days. TaxiStop agencies (see Travel Agencies in the Brussels section) match drivers with travellers on the road for a reasonable fee.

LOCAL TRANSPORT

Buses and trams (and small metro systems in Brussels and Antwerp) are efficient and reliable. Single tickets cost €1, or you can buy a multistrip ticket – 10 strips for €7.50 – or a one-day card for €2.90. Services generally run until about 11pm or midnight.

Taxis are metered and expensive (€1.60 per kilometre).

Brussels (Brussel, Bruxelles)

pop 970,500

Brussels is an unpretentious mix of grand edifices and modern skyscrapers. Its character largely follows that of the nation it governs: modest and confident, but rarely striving to overtly impress. Having grown from a 6th-century marshy village on the banks of the Senne River (filled in long ago for sanitary reasons), this bilingual city is now headquarters of the EU and NATO and home to Europe's most impressive central square.

Orientation

The Grand Place, Brussels' imposing 15th-century market square, sits dead centre in the Petit Ring, a pentagon of boulevards enclosing central Brussels. Gare Centrale, Brussels' most central train station, is about five minutes' walk from the Grand Place; Gare du Midi, where most international trains arrive, is 1.5km from the famous square.

Information

Tourist Offices There are two offices: one for Brussels, while the other is for national information.

Tourist Information Brussels *(TIB; ☎ 02 513 89 40, fax 02 513 83 20; e info@brusselstourism.be; open Mon-Sat, daily Easter-Dec)* is in the city hall at Grand Place. It sells two discount passes – the Must of Brussels (€15.60), which gives access to most of the top attractions, and the Brussels Passport (€7.50), a booklet containing discounts to museums/restaurants and two public transport one-day cards.

The **national tourist office** *(☎ 02 504 03 90, fax 02 504 02 70; Rue du Marché aux Herbes 63; open daily)* is another source of information.

BELGIUM

Money Outside banking hours (see Business Hours earlier), there are exchange bureaus at the airport (open until 10pm), at Gare Centrale and Gare du Nord (both open until 8.30pm) and at Gare du Midi (until 10pm). ATMs are at the airport and on the Grand Place. A good central exchange agency is **Baslé** *(Rue au Beurre 23)*. You can also try **Thomas Cook** *(☎ 02 513 28 45; Grand Place 4)*.

Post & Communications The **main post office** *(1st floor, Centre Monnaie, Blvd Anspach; open 8am-6pm Mon-Fri, 9.30am-3pm Sat)* is near Place de Brouckère.

To get online there's **easyEverything** *(☎ 02 211 08 20; Place de Brouckère 9; open 8am-11.30pm)*. It charges €1 for 30 to 60 minutes, depending on the time of day.

Travel Agencies A good general travel agency is **Connections** *(☎ 02 550 01 00; Rue du Midi 19)*. **AirStop/TaxiStop** *(AirStop ☎ 070 23 31 88, TaxiStop ☎ 070 22 22 92; Rue du Fossé aux Loups 28)* offers cheap charter flights and paid rides (€3.30 per 100km) in cars going to other European cities.

Medical & Emergency Services For 24-hour medical emergencies, dial ☎ 100. **Helpline** *(☎ 02 648 40 14)* is a Brussels-based, 24-hour English-speaking crisis line and information service.

Things to See & Do

Grand Place is the obvious starting point. It was formerly home to the craft guilds, whose rich halls – topped by golden figures that glisten by day and are illuminated by night – line the square.

Off Grand Place to the south on Rue Charles Buls is an example of the city's once-famous Art Nouveau cult – an 1899 **gilded plaque** dedicated to the city by its appreciative artists. It's beside a reclining **statue of Everard 't Serclaes**, a 14th-century hero.

Manneken Pis, the statue of a small boy peeing, is a couple of blocks to the southwest on the corner of Rue du Chêne and Rue de l'Étuve. So famous is this little fellow that he now has his own museum, the **House of Manneken Pis** *(Rue du Chêne 19; open 9am-5pm Mon-Fri)*. The whole thing is magically disappointing – what a feeble tourist attraction!

One block northeast of the Grand Place is the **Galeries St Hubert**, Europe's oldest glass-covered shopping arcade (and home to Neuhaus, one of the oldest chocolate shops). Alternatively, head east up the hill past the Gare Centrale to Rue Royale and the refined upper town. Here you'll find the **Palais Royal** and, nearby, Paul Saintenoy's Art Nouveau showpiece, the Old England Building **Old England Building** (home to a superb museum of musical instruments).

Museums The Grand Place is home to several museums, such as the **Musée de la Ville de Bruxelles** *(adult/concession €2.50/2; open 10am-5pm Tues-Fri, 10am-1pm Sat & Sun)*, offering a historical run-down on the city.

The **Musées Royaux des Beaux-Arts** *(w www.fine-arts-museum.be; Rue de la Régence 3; adult/concession €5/3.50; open 10am-5pm Tues-Sun)* houses Belgium's premier collections of ancient and modern art. The Flemish Primitives, Brueghel and Rubens are all well represented.

The **Musée des Instruments de Musique** *(w www.mim.fgov.be; Rue Montagne de la Cour 2; adult/concession €3.75/2.50; open 9.30am-5pm Mon-Fri, 10am-5pm Sat & Sun)* boasts the world's biggest collection of musical instruments. It's housed in the stunning Old England building, a must-see Art Nouveau example.

Tintin fans should not miss the **Centre Belge de la Bande Dessinée** *(Rue des Sables 20; admission €6.20; open 10am-6pm Tues-Sun)*. It has the nation's best ensemble of comic-strip art, and occupies an airy Art Nouveau building designed by Horta.

About 500m northwest of Gare du Midi is the **Musée Bruxellois de la Gueuze** *(Rue Gheude 56; admission €3; open 9am-5pm Mon-Fri, 10am-5pm Sat)*, in Anderlecht, a working brewery still using traditional methods. It's here that you can sample Brussels' unique *gueuze* beer.

The **Musée Magritte** *(Rue Esseghem 135; metro Belgica then tram No 18; admission €6; 10am-6pm Wed-Sun)*, in Jette, opens up the home and world of surrealist artist René Magritte.

Special Events

Ommegang is the most prestigious annual event in Belgium. The 16th-century-style procession is staged within the illuminated Grand Place in early July. Just as popular is the biennial flower carpet that colours the square in mid-August (even-numbered years). Immerse yourself in music at the annual Brussels Jazz Marathon (last weekend in May). The Grand Place, together with the Sablon and Place Ste Catherine, also host free open-air concerts throughout summer.

Places to Stay

Hostels & Guesthouses Three HI-affiliated hostels are dotted around Brussels, all with the same prices – singles/doubles per person for €22.50/17.50 and dorm beds from €12.50 to €14.50. The most central is **Bruegel** *(☎ 02 511 04 36, fax 02 512 07 11; e brussel@vjh.be; Rue du St Esprit 2)*. About 15 minutes' walk from the centre is **Jacques Brel** *(☎ 02 218 01 87, fax 02 217 20 05; e brussels.brel@laj.be; Rue de la Sablonnière 30)*. **Génération Europe** *(☎ 02 410 38 58, fax 02 410 39 05; e brussels.europe@laj.be; Rue de l'Éléphant 4)* is a 20-minute walk northwest of the Grand Place.

A central option is **Sleep Well** *(☎ 02 218 50 50, fax 02 218 13 13; e info@ sleepwell.be; Rue du Damier 23; 6/8-bed dorms €14.55/12.80, singles/doubles per person €24.45/18.75, triples/quads €18.75/16.15)*, which is a modern and popular.

The newly renovated **Centre Vincent van Gogh** *(☎ 02 217 01 58, fax 02 219 79 95; e chab@ping.be; Rue Traversière 8; dorm beds in 6/10-bed dorm €11.50/9, singles/doubles €21/15.50)* is hip – the age limit is 35. It's 1.25km north, uphill from Gare Centrale or take the metro to Botanique.

For B&B accommodation, contact **Bed & Brussels** *(☎ 02 646 07 37, fax 02 644 01 14; w www.bnb-brussels.be)*.

Hotels In the appealing Ste Catherine quarter, 10 minutes' walk northwest of the Grand Place, you'll find **Résidence Les Écrins** *(☎ 02 219 36 57, fax 02 223 57 40; e les.ecrins@skynet.be; Rue du Rouleau 15; rooms without/with bath €50/70)*. Just off Ave Louise is the homy **Hôtel Rembrandt** *(☎ 02 512 71 39, fax 02 511 71 36; e rembrandt@ brutele.be; Rue de la Concorde 42; singles/doubles €37/54, with bath €60/75)*.

One of the best mid-range choices is **Hôtel Noga** *(☎ 02 218 67 63, fax 02 218 16 03; e info@nogahotel.com; Rue du Béguinage 38; singles/doubles Fri & Sat €60/75, Sun-Thur from €75/95)*. It's well positioned in the Ste Catherine quarter.

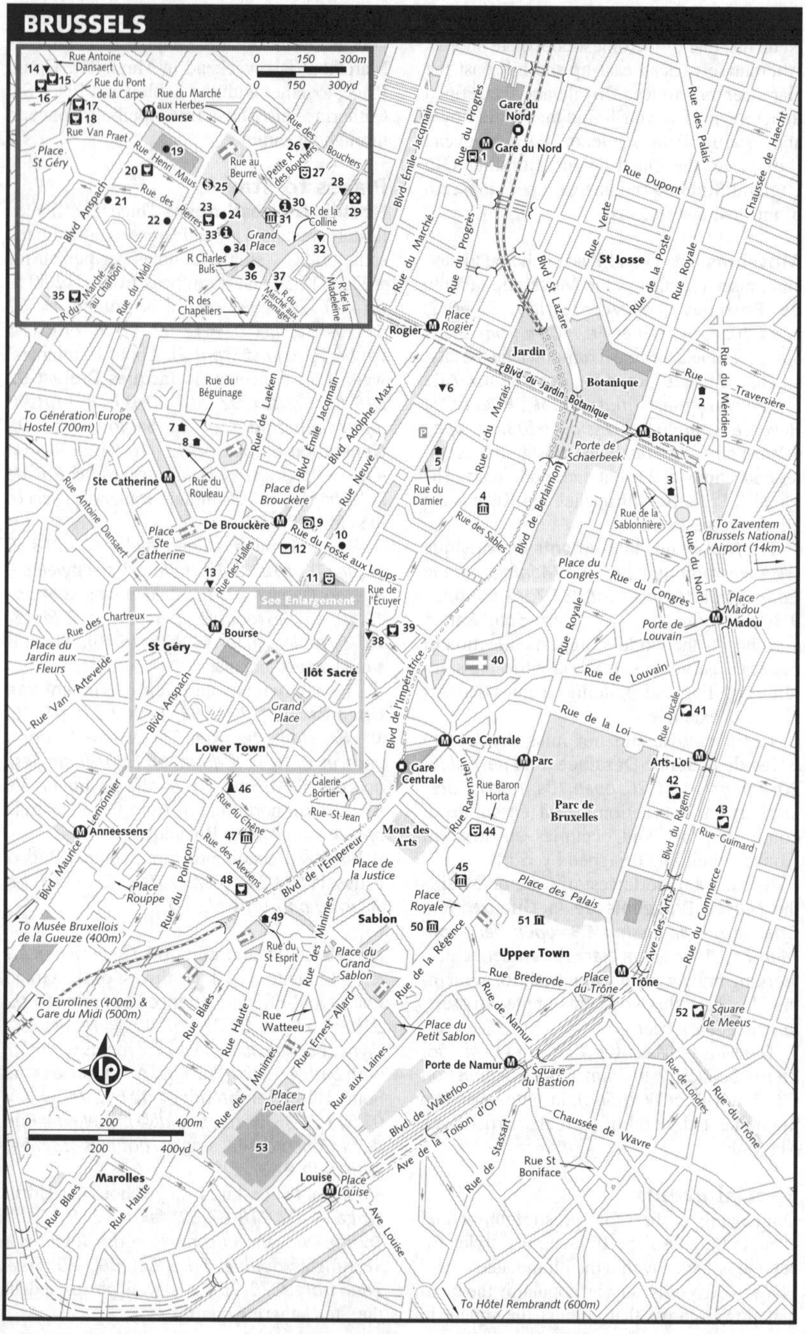

BRUSSELS

Rue Antoine Dansaert
14
15
16
Rue du Pont de la Carpe
17
18
Rue du Marché aux Herbes
Bourse
0 150 300m
0 150 300yd
Rue Van Praet
Place St Géry
19
Rue Henri Maus
20
Rue au Beurre
Rue des Bouchers
26
Petite R des Bouchers
27
28
29
25
Rue des Pierres
21
22
23
24
30
31
R de la Colline
Blvd Anspach
33
Grand Place
32
34
R Charles Buls
36
37
35
R du Marché au Charbon
Rue du Midi
R des Chapeliers
R du Marché aux Fromages
R de la Madeleine

Gare du Nord
Rue du Progrès
1
Blvd Émile Jacqmain
Rue des Palais
Chaussée de Haecht
Rue Dupont
Rue Verte
Rue du Marché
St Josse
Rue de la Poste
Rue Royale
Blvd St Lazare
Place Rogier
Rogier
Jardin
Botanique
Blvd du Jardin Botanique
Rue Traversière
Rue du Méridien
2
Rue du Béguinage
6
Rue de Laeken
Blvd Émile Jacqmain
Blvd Adolphe Max
Rue du Marais
To Génération Europe Hostel (700m)
7
8
Porte de Schaerbeek
Botanique
5
Rue du Rouleau
Ste Catherine
Place de Brouckère
Rue Neuve
Rue du Damier
Blvd de Berlaimont
3
Rue de la Sablonnière
Rue Antoine Dansaert
4
To Zaventem (Brussels National) Airport (14km)
De Brouckère
9
Rue des Sables
Place Ste Catherine
10
Rue du Fossé aux Loups
12
Place du Congrès
Rue du Congrès
Rue du Nord
13
Rue des Halles
11
Place Madou
Madou
Rue de l'Écuyer
See Enlargement
Rue des Chartreux
Bourse
39
Porte de Louvain
38
Place du Jardin aux Fleurs
St Géry
Rue Van Artevelde
Îlot Sacré
40
Rue Royale
Rue de Louvain
Blvd Anspach
Grand Place
Blvd de l'Impératrice
Rue de la Loi
Rue Ducale
41
Lower Town
Gare Centrale
Gare Centrale
Parc
Arts-Loi
46
Galerie Bortier
Rue Baron Horta
42
Rue du Chêne
Rue St Jean
Rue Ravenstein
Parc de Bruxelles
43
Anneessens
Blvd Maurice Lemonnier
47
Mont des Arts
44
Rue Guimard
Rue des Alexiens
Blvd de l'Empereur
Place de la Justice
45
Blvd du Régent
Place Rouppe
Rue du Poinçon
48
Place des Palais
Place Royale
Rue du Commerce
To Musée Bruxellois de la Gueuze (400m)
49
Rue des Minimes
Sablon
50
51
Rue du St Esprit
Rue de la Régence
Upper Town
Ave des Arts
Place du Grand Sablon
Rue Brederode
Place du Trône
Trône
To Eurolines (400m) & Gare du Midi (500m)
Rue Blaes
Rue Haute
Rue de Namur
52
Square de Meeus
Rue Watteeu
Rue Ernest Allard
Place du Petit Sablon
Porte de Namur
Square du Bastion
Rue aux Laines
Rue de Londres
Rue des Minimes
Place Poélaert
Blvd de Waterloo
Rue du Trône
Chaussée de Wavre
0 200 400m
0 200 400yd
Ave de la Toison d'Or
53
Rue de Stassart
Rue St Boniface
Marolles
Louise
Place Louise
Rue Blaes
Rue Haute
Ave Louise
To Hôtel Rembrandt (600m)

BELGIUM

BRUSSELS

PLACES TO STAY
2 Centre Vincent van Gogh
3 Jacques Brel Hostel/ Les Auberges de Jeunesse
5 Sleep Well Hostel
7 Hôtel Noga
8 Résidence Les Écrins
49 Bruegel Hostel

PLACES TO EAT
6 Super GB Supermarket (City 2 Shopping Centre)
13 Super GB Supermarket
14 Le Pain Quotidien
26 Aux Armes de Bruxelles
28 Taverne du Passage
32 Panos
37 Frites/Pitta-Bread Places
38 Hémisphères

BARS
15 L'Archiduc
16 Le Greenwich
17 Bizon
18 Roi des Belges
20 Falstaff
23 The Music Village
35 Tels Quels
39 À la Mort Subite
48 La Fleur en Papier Doré

OTHER
1 Eurolines Bus Station/ Main Office
4 Centre Belge de la Bande Dessinée
9 easyEverything
10 AirStop/TaxiStop
11 Théâtre Royal de la Monnaie
12 Main Post Office
19 Bourse (Stock Exchange)
21 Ancienne Belgique
22 Usit/Connections
24 Thomas Cook
25 Baslé
27 Théâtre Royal de Toone
29 Galeries St Hubert
30 National Tourist Office
31 Musée de la Ville de Bruxelles
33 Tourist Information Brussels (TIB)
34 Hôtel de Ville (City Hall)
36 Art Nouveau Plaque; Everard 't Serclaes Statue
40 Saints Michel & Gudule Cathedral
41 French Embassy
42 US Embassy
43 Australian Embassy
44 Palais des Beaux-Arts
45 Old England Building; Musée des Instruments de Musique
46 Manneken Pis
47 House of Manneken Pis
50 Musées Royaux des Beaux-Arts
51 Palais Royal
52 NZ Embassy
53 Palais de Justice

Places to Eat

Rue Marché aux Fromages, just near the Grand Place, is packed with a range of *frites* and pitta-bread places. For a half-baguette sandwich (€2.50), head to **Panos** *(Rue du Marché aux Herbes 85)*.

Brussels' dining heart is Rue des Bouchers (Butcher's Street), near the Grand Place. Here you'll find lobster, crab, mussels and fish awaiting conspicuous consumption in one terrace restaurant after another. Most are tourist traps, but **Aux Armes de Bruxelles** *(☎ 02 511 55 98; Rue des Bouchers 13; mains around €20; open Tues-Sun)* is a notable exception. Expect efficient service and Belgian classics.

Taverne du Passage *(☎ 02 512 37 31; Galerie de la Reine 30; dishes €12-21)*, in the Galeries St Hubert, has been serving no-nonsense Belgian cuisine since 1928, dished up by the friendliest waiters you'll find.

For wholesome savoury pies and filled sandwiches in a nonsmoking environment there's **Le Pain Quotidien** *(☎ 02 502 23 61; Rue Antoine Dansaert 16)*, a country-style bakery/tearoom.

Hémisphères *(☎ 02 513 93 70; Rue de l'Écuyer 65; mains €8-10)* does Middle Eastern food in silky surroundings.

For those wishing to self-cater there are two handy **Super GB supermarkets** *(City 2 shopping centre, Rue Neuve • Rue des Halles; both open 9am-8pm Mon-Sat)*.

Entertainment

The *Bulletin* magazine's 'What's On' guide lists live contemporary and classical music, opera, dance and the cinema scene. Otherwise, there are enough bars and cafés for a very long crawl.

Le Greenwich *(Rue des Chartreux 7)*, **À la Mort Subite** *(Rue Mont aux Herbes Potagères 7)*, **La Fleur en Papier Doré** *(Rue des Alexiens 53)* and **Falstaff** *(Rue Henri Maus 17)* are wonderful old cafés each with a unique ambience. Try them all.

Roi des Belges *(Rue Van Praet 35)* is where the young and trendy flock, while nearby **Bizon** *(Rue du Pont de la Carpe 7)* is a happening grunge bar with occasional live bands.

Those into Art Deco and live jazz shouldn't go past the **L'Archiduc** *(Rue Antoine Dansaert 6)*. For more jazz there's **The Music Village** *(Rue des Pierres 50)*.

Fuse *(Rue Blaes 208; metro Port de Hal; open from 10pm Thur-Sat)* is the city's biggest club.

For gay and lesbian venues, ask at the bar of **Tels Quels** *(☎ 02 512 45 87, fax 02 511 31 48; Rue du Marché au Charbon 81)*.

A range of local and international bands play at **Ancienne Belgique** *(☎ 02 548 24 24; Blvd Anspach 110)*.

The main performing-arts venues are the **Palais des Beaux-Arts** *(☎ 02 507 82 00; Rue Ravenstein 23)* and the **Théâtre Royal**

de la Monnaie *(☎ 02 229 12 11; Place de la Monnaie)*.

For something different there's **Théâtre Royal de Toone** *(☎ 02 511 71 37; Petite Rue des Bouchers 21)*, a marionette theatre where the cast speak the local Brussels' dialect.

Getting There & Away

Air See under Getting There & Away earlier in this chapter and the introductory Getting There & Away chapter earlier in this book.

Bus The main office of **Eurolines** *(☎ 02 274 13 50; Rue du Progrès 80)* is next to Gare du Nord, and most of its buses depart from here. There's a smaller **Eurolines office** *(☎ 02 538 20 49; Ave Fonsny 9)* near Gare du Midi.

Train There are **train information offices** *(open 6.30am-9pm)* at all three stations. For all national inquiries, call ☎ 02 555 25 55.

Getting Around

Public transport maps are handed out from the tourist offices or metro information kiosks. The national airport, Zaventem, is connected to all three central stations by four trains per hour (€2.35, 30 minutes). Taxis generally charge about €25 to €30.

Brussels' efficient bus, tram and metro network is operated by the Société des Transports Intercommunaux de Bruxelles (MIVB in Flemish, STIB in French). Single-journey tickets cost €1.40, five/10-journey cards €6/9 and a one-day card (valid for two people on Saturdays and Sundays) is €3.60. Valid on all public transport, tickets can be bought from metro stations or bus drivers; the one-day card is also available from the TIB. Public transport runs until about midnight.

For a taxi, hail one at a rank or phone **Taxis Bleus** *(☎ 02 268 00 00)* or **Taxis Verts** *(☎ 02 349 49 49)*.

AROUND BRUSSELS

Waterloo, the battleground where Napoleon was defeated and European history changed course in 1815, is 18km south of Brussels. The sites are not terribly interesting and are spread over several kilometres, making it tedious to get around with public transport.

The **Musée Royal de l'Afrique Centrale** *(☎ 02 769 52 11; Leuvensesteenweg 13; metro Montgomery then tram No 44; adult/concession €4/1.50; open Tues-Sun)*, at Tervuren, is 14km to the east. It contains artefacts from the Democratic Republic of Congo, collected during the scandalous reign of Léopold II.

Flanders

ANTWERP (ANTWERPEN, ANVERS)

pop 456,706

Worldly and seedy, historic and hedonistic – that's Antwerp. Second in size to the capital and often more likable, the city is Belgium's most underrated drawcard. Once Western Europe's greatest economic centre, Antwerp was dealt blow after blow by Catholic-Protestant feuding and Dutch blockades. It wasn't until Napoleon arrived and the French rebuilt the docks that Antwerp got back on its feet.

Today compact Antwerp brims with self-confidence. As a world port, its atmosphere is international, though at times down-at-heel. Don't let the occasional dodginess get to you – enjoy the contrasts.

Information

The **tourist office** *(☎ 03 232 01 03, fax 03 231 19 37; ⓔ visit@antwerpen.be; Grote Markt 13; open daily)* dispenses information.

Good exchange rates (for cash or US-dollar travellers cheques only) are offered by **Leo Stevens exchange bureau** *(☎ 03 232 18 43; De Keyserlei 64; open 9am-5pm Mon-Fri)*. **Travelex** *(☎ 03 226 29 53; Koningin Astridplein 33; open 8.30am-9pm Mon-Fri, 9am-9pm Sat, 10am-7pm Sun)* is another handy option. There's a **KBC Bank** *(☎ 03 206 82 10; Eiermarkt 20)* in the base of the Torengebouw (Europe's first skyscraper).

The **main post office** *(Groenplaats 43)* is in the old centre and has handy branch offices that are located opposite Centraal Station and on Jezusstraat. The **Belgacom Teleboetiek** *(Jezusstraat 1)* sells phonecards and handles faxes. For Internet access, try **2Zones** *(☎ 03 232 24 00; Wolstraat 15; open 11am-midnight daily)*, which charges €4.50 per hour. No-frills **Internet Café** *(☎ 03 234 38 13; Korte Koepoortstraat 9)*, costs €1.50/3 for 30/60 minutes and is cheaper option.

Things to See & Do

Start exploring at the **Grote Markt**, with its impressive Stadhuis (City Hall), imposing guildhalls and voluptuous Brabo Fountain.

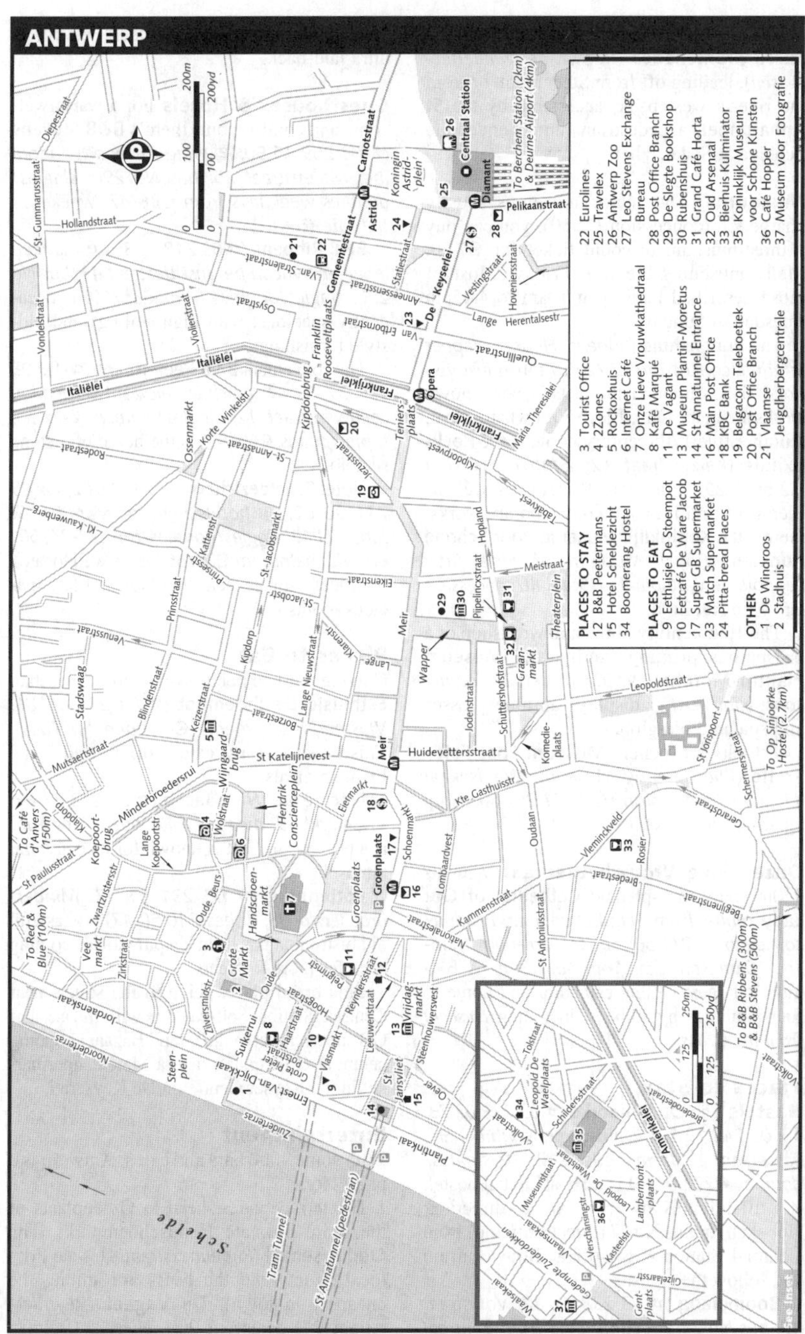
ANTWERP
PLACES TO STAY
12 B&B Peetermans
15 Hotel Scheldezicht
34 Boomerang Hostel
PLACES TO EAT
9 Eethuisje De Stoempot
10 Eetcafé De Ware Jacob
17 Super GB Supermarket
23 Match Supermarket
24 Pitta-bread Places
OTHER
1 De Windroos
2 Stadhuis
3 Tourist Office
4 2Zones
5 Rockoxhuis
6 Internet Café
7 Onze Lieve Vrouwkathedraal
8 Kafé Marqué
11 De Vagant
13 Museum Plantin-Moretus
14 St Annatunnel Entrance
16 Main Post Office
18 KBC Bank
19 Belgacom Teleboetiek
20 Post Office Branch
21 Vlaamse Jeugdherbergcentrale
22 Eurolines
25 Travelex
26 Antwerp Zoo
27 Leo Stevens Exchange Bureau
28 Post Office Branch
29 De Slegte Bookshop
30 Rubenshuis
31 Grand Café Horta
32 Oud Arsenaal
33 Bierhuis Kulminator
35 Koninklijk Museum voor Schone Kunsten
36 Café Hopper
37 Museum voor Fotografie
Centraal Station
To Berchem Station (2km) & Deurne Airport (4km)
To Op Sinjoorke Hostel (2.7km)
To B&B Ribbens (300m) & B&B Stevens (500m)
To Red & Blue (100m)
To Café d'Anvers (150m)
Schelde
St Annatunnel (pedestrian)
Tram Tunnel
Grote Markt
Groenplaats
Meir
Italiëlei
Frankrijklei
De Keyserlei
Gemeentestraat
Astrid
Opera
Diamant
Pelikaanstraat
Theaterplein
Leopoldstraat
Nationalestraat
Amerikalei
Volkstraat
See Inset
0 100 200m
0 100 200yd
0 125 250m
0 125 250yd

The city's skyline is best viewed from the raised **promenades** (known as *wandelterrassen*), leading off from Steenplein, or from the river's west bank, accessible by the **St Annatunnel**, a pedestrian tunnel under the Schelde at St Jansvliet.

Museums The major museums mostly charge €5 (concession €2.50); you can buy a three-museum discount ticket for €7.50. Many museums are free Friday. Most of those described here open 10am to 4.45pm Tuesday to Sunday.

The **Rubenshuis** *(Rubens' House; Wapper 9; adult/concession €5/2.50)* tops most visitors' lists, although the artist's best-known works are in the Onze Lieve Vrouwkathedraal. Another fine 17th-century home is the **Rockoxhuis** *(Keizerstraat 12; adult/concession €2.50/1.25)*. For more Rubens, as well as Flemish Primitives and contemporary works, there's the **Koninklijk Museum voor Schone Kunsten** *(Royal Museum of Fine Arts; Leopold de Waelplaats 1-9; adult/concession €5/4)* in Het Zuid.

The 16th-century home and workshop of a prosperous printing family, the **Museum Plantin-Moretus** *(Vrijdagmarkt 22; adult/concession €4/2)* displays antique presses and splendid old globes.

The city's excellent **Museum voor Fotografie** *(Photography Museum; Waalsekaai 47; adult/concession €2.50/1.25)* opens up again in spring 2003.

Onze Lieve Vrouwkathedraal With its 120m spire, the splendid **Cathedral of Our Lady** *(entry from Handschoenmarkt; adult/concession €2/1.50; open 10am-5pm Mon-Fri, 10am-3pm Sat, 1pm-4pm Sun)* is Belgium's largest Gothic cathedral and home to four paintings by Rubens, including *Descent from the Cross*.

Places to Stay

Hostels The **Op Sinjoorke** *(☎ 03 238 02 73, fax 03 248 19 32; ⓔ antwerpen@vjh.be; Eric Sasselaan 2; dorm beds €12.50, singles/doubles €22.50/35)* is a HI-affiliated hostel. It's 10 minutes by tram No 2 (direction: Hoboken) or bus No 27 (direction: Zuid) from Centraal Station – get off at Bouwcentrum and follow the signs.

Boomerang *(☎ 03 238 47 82; Volkstraat 49; bus No 23 direction: Zuid from Centraal Station; dorm beds €12, sheets €2.50)* is ultra laid-back.

Guesthouses & Hotels For a warm welcome and comfy rooms there's **B&B Stevens** *(☎ 03 259 15 90; ⓔ greta.stevens@pandora.be; Molenstraat 35; bus No 290; singles/doubles weekdays from €36/47, weekends flat rate €60)*.

B&B Ribbens *(☎ 03 248 15 39; ⓔ marleen.engelen@yucon.be; Justitiestraat 43; bus No 290; singles/doubles from €35/60)* is decadently spacious, with high ceilings and old-style furnishings.

The convenient **B&B Peetermans** *(☎/fax 03 231 37 92; ⓔ enich.anders@antwerpen.be; Leeuwenstraat 12; singles/doubles €45/50, triples/quads €65/80)* is the home of a stone sculptor.

Hotel Scheldezicht *(☎ 03 231 66 02, fax 03 231 90 02; ⓔ hotelscheldezicht@pi.be; St Jansvliet 12; singles/doubles/triples €35/50/60, with bathroom €38/55/65)* is well located on a leafy square near the river and has spacious rooms.

Places to Eat

Craving mashed potatoes? Go no further than **Eethuisje De Stoempot** *(☎ 03 231 36 86; Vlasmarkt 12; mains €8; open Fri-Tues)*. This down-to-earth eatery offers traditional Flemish meals.

Eetcafé De Ware Jacob *(☎ 03 213 37 89; Vlasmarkt 19; meals €7-12; open Tues-Sun)* is a brown café that is known for its convivial atmosphere.

Pottenbrug *(☎ 03 231 51 47; Minderbroedersrui 38; dishes €10.50-17)* is a tasteful old bistro that has been keeping locals coming back for more for years.

Pitta-bread places reign in the streets near Centraal Station. Self-caterers will find a Super GB supermarket in the Grand Bazaar shopping centre at Groenplaats, and a Match supermarket in the Keyser Centre on De Keyserlei.

Entertainment

With some 4000 bars and cafés, Antwerp is a party city.

For terrace cafés, head to Groenplaats or the more intimate Handschoenmarkt. The **Oud Arsenaal** *(Pijpelincxstraat 4)* is a quirky local haunt (and the beers are among the cheapest in town). **De Vagant** *(Reyndersstraat 21)* deals out 200 *jenevers* (Belgian gins). **Bierhuis Kulminator** *(Vleminckveld 32)* is *the* place to sink a host of Belgian brews – there's more than 600 on the menu. Go glamorous at **Grand Café Horta** *(Hopland 2)*.

For live jazz, head to **Café Hopper** *(Leopold De Waelstraat 2)* in Het Zuid.

Kafé Marqué *(Grote Pieter Potstraat 3; open from 11pm Fri & Sat)* is a central club doing rock and Britpop. A hipper-than-thou club crowd heads to **Café d'Anvers** *(Verversrui 15; open Fri-Sun)* in the sailor's quarter. **Red & Blue** *(Lange Schipperskapelstraat 11)* bills itself as the country's biggest gay disco.

Getting There & Away

Bus For information about buses, see under Getting There & Away at the beginning of this chapter. **Eurolines** *(☎ 03 233 86 62)* buses depart from Van Stralenstraat 8.

Train Antwerp has two main train stations: Centraal Station, about 1.5km from the old city centre, and Berchem station, 2km southeast of Centraal Station. The magnificent Centraal Station is undergoing extensive underground expansion, expected to be finished in 2005 (until then you may find train services into Centraal Station disrupted).

National connections that leave from Antwerp include IC trains to Brussels (€5.30, 35 minutes), Bruges (€10.80, 70 minutes) and Ghent (€6.80, 45 minutes). There are also frequent trains to Amsterdam (€25.20 to €31, two hours).

Getting Around

A good network of buses, trams and a pre-metro (a tram that runs underground for part of its journey) is run by De Lijn. Public transport information kiosks are at pre-metro stations Diamant (in front of Centraal Station) and Groenplaats. The main bus hubs are Koningin Astridplein next to Centraal Station and Franklin Rooseveltplaats a few blocks west. You can hire bikes for €2.50/12.50 per hour/day from **De Windroos** *(☎ 03 480 93 88, Steenplein 1a)*.

GHENT (GENT, GAND)

pop 230,000

Medieval Europe's largest city outside Paris is Ghent. Its glory lies in its industrious and rebellious past. Sitting at the junction of the Leie and Schelde Rivers, by the mid-14th century it was Europe's biggest cloth producer, importing wool from England and employing thousands of people. Home to many students, Ghent may not be as picturesque as Bruges, but ultimately it's more *real*.

Orientation & Information

The Korenmarkt is the westernmost square, and is technically the city's centre. It's a 25-minute walk from the main train station, St Pietersstation, and is regularly connected to the station by tram Nos 1, 10 and 11. Halfway between the two is the university quarter, based along St Pietersnieuwstraat.

The **tourist office** *(☎ 09 266 52 32, fax 09 225 62 88; ⓔ toerisme@gent.be; Botermarkt 17a; open daily)* is able to help with general inquiries. The **Europabank** *(St Pietersstation)* and the **Goffin Change** *(Mageleinstraat 36)* are both open daily. You can send mail at the **post office** *(Lange Kruisstraat 55)*.

Things to See & Do

Ghent's most noted sight is the Van Eyck brothers' *Adoration of the Mystic Lamb*. It is housed in the **crypt** *(admission €2.50; open 9.30am-4.45pm Mon-Sat, 1pm-4.30pm Sun Easter-Nov; 10.30am-3.45pm Mon-Sat, 1pm-3.30pm Sun Nov-Easter)* of **St Baafskathedraal** *(entry on St Baafsplein; admission free; open 8.30am-6pm daily)*. This 15th-century painting is a lavish representation of medieval religious thinking and one of the earliest-known oil paintings. Ticket sales stop 45 minutes before closing time.

Rising from the old Cloth Hall, the 14th-century **belfort** *(belfry; Botermarkt; adult/concession €3/1.75; open 10am-1pm & 2pm-6pm daily)* affords spectacular views that look out over the city.

With moat, turrets and arrow slits, the fearsome 12th-century **Gravensteen** *(St Veerleplein 11; adult/concession €6.20/1.20; open 9am-6pm daily, 9am-5pm Nov-Mar)* is the quintessential castle. It was built to protect the townsfolk as well as to intimidate them into law-abiding submission.

The **Museum voor Schone Kunsten** *(Citadelpark; adult/concession €2.50/1.20; open 10am-6pm Tues-Sat)* is home to some Flemish Primitives and a couple of typically nightmarish works by Hieronymus Bosch.

Places to Stay

Ghent's attractive hostel, **De Draecke** *(☎ 09 233 70 50, fax 09 233 80 01; ⓔ gent@vjh.be;*

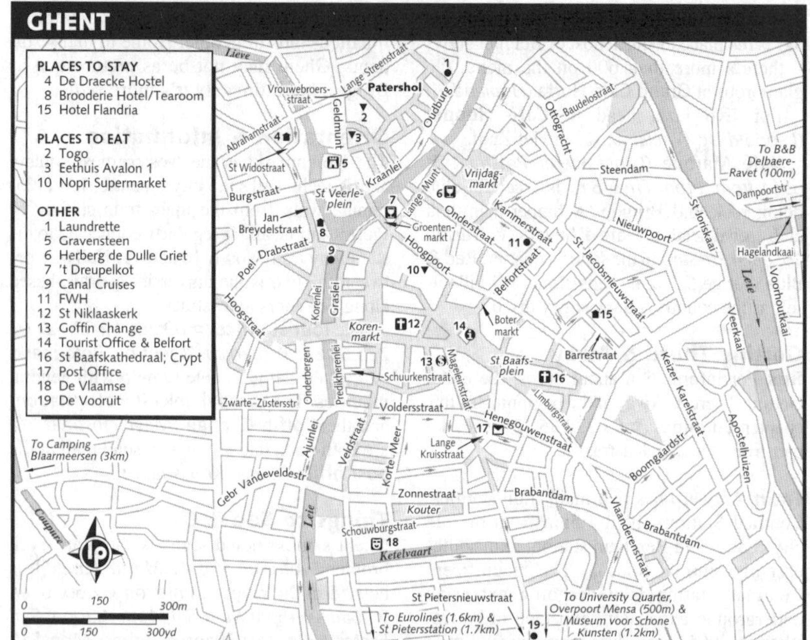

St Widostraat 11; tram No 1, 10 or 11 from train station to St Veerleplein; beds in 6-bed dorm with bath €14.50, doubles €35) occupies a renovated warehouse that is right in the heart of town.

Gilde der Gentse Gastenkamers *(GGG; ☎ 09 233 30 99; W www.bedandbreakfast.gent-be; Tentoonstellingslaan 69, 9000 Ghent)* organises the city's B&Bs. One excellent option is **B&B Delbaere-Ravet** *(☎/fax 09 233 43 52; e s.deravet@worldonline.be; Hagelandkaai 38; bus No 70 or 71 from St Pietersstation to bus stop Dampoortstation; singles/doubles €35/50)*.

Hotel Flandria *(☎ 09 223 06 26, fax 09 233 77 89; e gent@flandria-centrum.be, Barrestraat 3; singles/doubles €33/38)* is a warren of cheap but decent rooms. More atmospheric is **Brooderie** *(☎ 09 225 06 23; Jan Breydelstraat 8; singles/doubles €38/58)*. This bakery-cum-tearoom has four lovely rooms upstairs.

Places to Eat

The student ghetto around Pietersnieuwstraat, about 10 minutes' walk southeast of the Korenmarkt, is the best area for cheap eats. Here too you will find the **Overpoort mensa** *(☎ 09 264 71 10; Overpoortstraat 49; open lunch & dinner Mon-Fri; meals from €5)*, a self-service student cafeteria.

Eethuis Avalon 1 *(☎ 09 224 37 24; Geldmunt 32; mains €8-10; open lunch only Mon-Sat)* is a quaint vegetarian restaurant. Another wholesome place is **Brooderie** (see Places to Stay), a rustic, nonsmoking tearoom.

Restaurants are dotted around the Patershol quarter, a thicket of cobbled lanes with an old-world ambience. **Togo** *(☎ 09 223 65 51; Vrouwebroersstraat 21; mains from €13)* has been around for years and is consistently good. It specialises in African cuisine.

Self-caterers should try the **Nopri supermarket** *(Hoogpoort 42)*.

Entertainment

Herberg De Dulle Griet *(Vrijdagmarkt 50)* is one of the city's best-known beer pubs, while tiny **'t Dreupelkot** *(Groentenmarkt 12)* specialises in *jenevers* and has a pleasant waterfront terrace.

De Vooruit *(☎ 09 267 28 28; St Pietersnieuwstraat 23)* is the venue for dance and theatre. Opera is most commonly performed at **De Vlaamse Opera** *(☎ 09 225 24 25; Schouwburgstraat 3)*.

Getting There & Away

Buses leave from the **Eurolines office** *(☎ 09 220 90 24; Koningin Elisabethlaan 73)*, 100m from the train station.

The **train station information office** *(☎ 09 222 44 44; open 7am-9pm daily)* can help with rail queries. There are IC trains to Antwerp (€6.80, 45 minutes), Bruges (€4.70, 20 minutes), Brussels (€6.40, 45 minutes) and Ypres (€8.30, one hour).

BRUGES (BRUGGE)

pop 120,000

Bruges could be described as the 'perfect' tourist attraction. Suspended in time centuries ago when its lifeline – the Zwin estuary – silted up, it is now one of Europe's best-preserved medieval cities and it's also Belgium's most-visited town.

Bruges was a prosperous cloth manufacturing town and the centre of Flemish Primitive art between the 12th and 15th centuries. Today, more than two million tourists inundate this compact city each year and, at the height of summer, it seethes. Stay out late on a midsummer evening, or time your visit for spring when daffodils carpet the tranquil Begijnhof, and Bruges will reveal its age-old beauty.

Orientation

Central Bruges fits neatly into an oval-shaped series of canals. It's great for amblers, with sights sprinkled within leisurely walking distance of its compact centre. There are two central squares, the Markt and the Burg. The train station is about 1.5km south of the Markt.

Information

The main **tourist office** *(☎ 050 44 86 86, fax 050 44 86 00; e toerisme@brugge.be; Burg 11; open Mon-Sat daily Apr-Sept)* handles inquiries and also has a handful of luggage lockers in the foyer.

Reasonable rates are offered at **Weghsteen & Driege Exchange** *(☎ 050 33 33 61; Oude Burg 6; open 9am-noon & 2pm-4.30pm Mon-Fri)*; it handles cash only. The **BBL Bank** *(Markt 19)* is convenintly central, or, alternatively, there's the tourist office's **exchange bureau** *(open daily)*.

Send mail at the **post office** *(Markt 5)*. Get online cheaply at **Happyrom** *(Ezelstraat 8)* for €3 per hour; there's neither staff nor atmosphere. For conversation and conviviality try **The Coffee Link** *(☎ 050 34 99 73; w www.thecoffeelink.com; Mariastraat 38)* for €5 per hour.

Things to See & Do

Bruges is the sort of place you get to know quickly. You can start a walking tour at the **Markt**, the city's medieval core, from which rises the mighty **belfort** *(adult/concession €5/3; open 9.30am-5pm daily)*. Climb 366 steps to reach the top of this 83m-high belfry. The nearby **Burg**, connected to the Markt by an alley lined with lace shops, features Belgium's oldest **Stadhuis** (town hall), as well as the **Heiligbloed-Basiliek** (Basilica of the Holy Blood), where a few coagulated drops of Christ's blood are said to be kept. From the Burg, go through the archway marking Blinde Ezelstraat (Blind Donkey St) to the **Vismarkt** (fish market). From here, Steenhouwersdijk leads into **Groenerei**, a short but delightful promenade along a pretty part of the canal.

Immediately west of Vismarkt is **Huidenvettersplein**, a dinky little square lined with popular restaurants. This is the start of the **Dijver**, along which you'll find departure points for **canal cruises**, as well as the town's premier museums. Nearby is the **Onze Lieve Vrouwekerk**, which houses Michelangelo's *Madonna and Child*, a delicate statue and his only sculpture to leave Italy in his lifetime.

Museums There is a €15 discount ticket (valid for five museums of your choice), which is worthwhile if you plan to visit the following museums (all open 9.30am to 5pm Tuesday to Sunday).

The **Groeningemuseum** *(Dijver 12; admission €7)* is home to the city's prized collection of art from the 14th to the 20th century. Most notable is the impressive section on Flemish Primitives. The **Arentshuis** *(Dijver 16; admission €2.50)* contains two collections: lace, and the artwork of Frank Brangwyn, a Bruges-born artist of British parentage. An excellent collection of applied and decorative arts is displayed in the recently reorganised **Gruuthuse-museum** *(Dijver 17; admission €5)*. The prestigious **Memlingmuseum** *(Mariastraat 38; admission €7)* occupies the recently restored, 12th-century St Janshospitaal complex (a former hospital) and houses works by Hans Memling, one of the early Flemish Primitives.

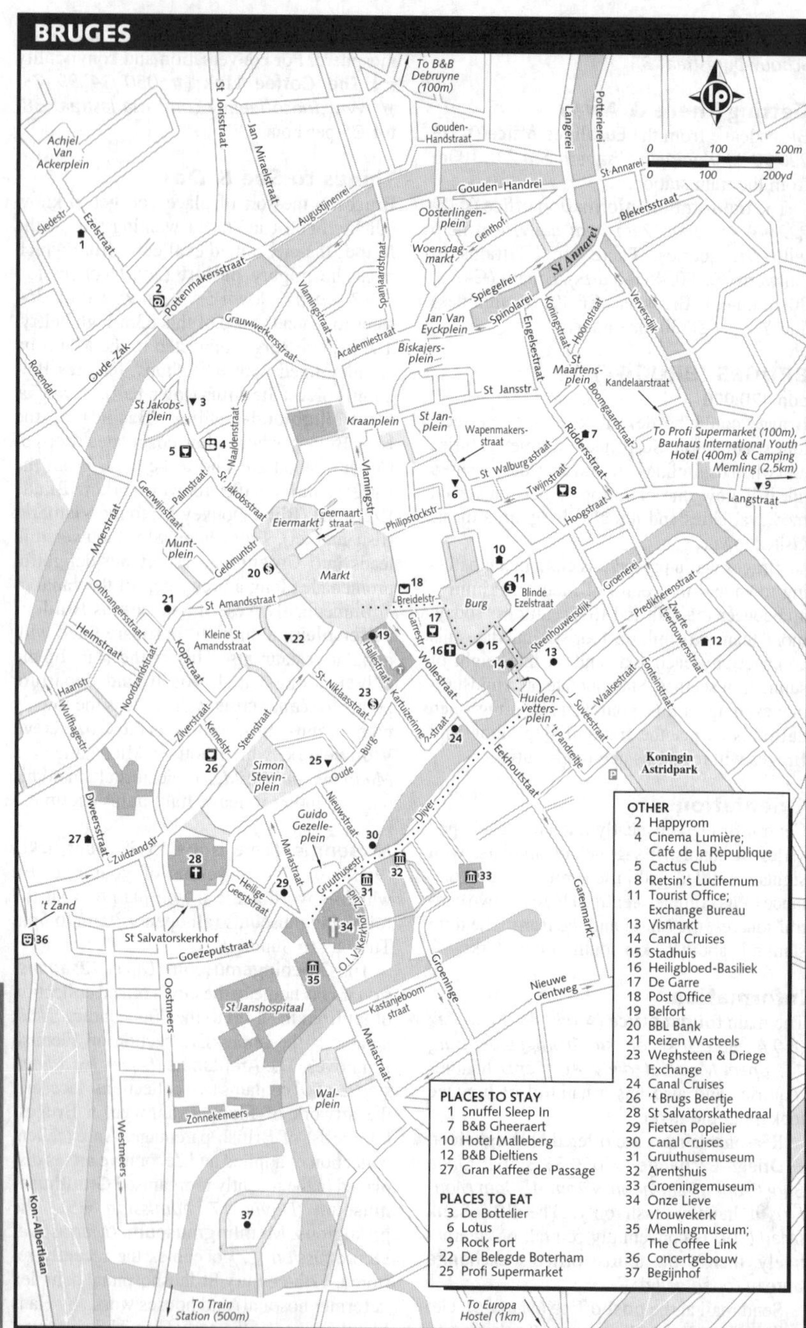
BRUGES
To B&B Debruyne (100m)
0 100 200m
0 100 200yd
OTHER
2 Happyrom
4 Cinema Lumière; Café de la Rèpublique
5 Cactus Club
8 Retsin's Lucifernum
11 Tourist Office; Exchange Bureau
13 Vismarkt
14 Canal Cruises
15 Stadhuis
16 Heiligbloed-Basiliek
17 De Garre
18 Post Office
19 Belfort
20 BBL Bank
21 Reizen Wasteels
23 Weghsteen & Driege Exchange
24 Canal Cruises
26 't Brugs Beertje
28 St Salvatorskathedraal
29 Fietsen Popelier
30 Canal Cruises
31 Gruuthusemuseum
32 Arentshuis
33 Groeningemuseum
34 Onze Lieve Vrouwekerk
35 Memlingmuseum; The Coffee Link
36 Concertgebouw
37 Begijnhof
PLACES TO STAY
1 Snuffel Sleep In
7 B&B Gheeraert
10 Hotel Malleberg
12 B&B Dieltiens
27 Gran Kaffee de Passage
PLACES TO EAT
3 De Bottelier
6 Lotus
9 Rock Fort
22 De Belegde Boterham
25 Profi Supermarket
To Profi Supermarket (100m), Bauhaus International Youth Hotel (400m) & Camping Memling (2.5km)
To Train Station (500m)
To Europa Hostel (1km)
Markt
Burg
Koningin Astridpark
St Janshospitaal
't Zand
Eiermarkt
Kraanplein
Simon Stevin-plein
Guido Gezelle-plein
Huidenvetters-plein
Wal-plein
St Jakobs-plein
Munt-plein
Jan Van Eyckplein
Oosterlingen-plein
Woensdag-markt
Biskajers-plein
St Jan-plein
St Maartens-plein
Achjel Van Ackerplein
St Annarei
Langestraat
Vlamingstraat
Wollestraat
Steenstraat
Dijver
Mariastraat
Oude Burg
Breidelstr
Blinde Ezelstraat
Nieuwe Gentweg
Gatenmarkt
Kon. Albertlaan
Oostmeers
Westmeers
Zonnekemeers
Goezeputstraat
St Salvatorskerkhof
Potterierei
Langerei
Gouden-Handrei
Gouden-Handstraat
Augustijnenrei
Pottenmakersstraat
Ezelstraat
Sledestr
Oude Zak
Rozendal
Moerstraat
Geldmuntstr
St Amandsstraat
Kleine St Amandsstraat
Noordzandstraat
Zuidzandstr
Dweersstraat
Helmstraat
Ontvangersstraat
Kopstraat
Zilverstraat
Kemelstr
Hallestraat
St-Niklaasstraat
Kartuizerinnen-straat
Eekhoutstraat
Groeninge
Kastanjeboom straat
Nieuwstraat
Manastraat
Gruuthusestr
O.L.V. Kerkhof Zuid
Heilige Geeststraat
Philipstockstr
Geernaart-straat
St Walburgastraat
Wapenmakers-straat
St Jansstr
Ridderstraat
Hoogstraat
Twijnstraat
Boomgaardstraat
Kandelaarstraat
Engelsestraat
Koningstraat
Hoornstraat
Spinolarei
Spiegelrei
Genthof
Academiestraat
Grauwwerkersstraat
Spanjaardstraat
Vlamingstraat
Jan Miraelstraat
St Jorisstraat
Blekersstraat
Verversdijk
Groenerei
Predikherenstraat
Zwarte-Leertouwersstraat
Fonteinstraat
Waalsestraat
J. Suveestraat
't Pandreitje
Steenhouwersdijk
Garrestr
Naaldenstraat
St Jakobsstraat
Palmstraat
Geerwijnstraat
Haanstr
Wulfhagestr
BELGIUM

Begijnhof The Begijnhof was home to a 13th-century religious community of unmarried or widowed women who were known as *begijnen* (Beguines). It's lined with modest, whitewashed houses, which these days are inhabited by single women of all ages. The large convent at the rear of the square is home to Benedictine nuns. The Begijnhof is about 10 minutes' walk south of the Markt.

Places to Stay

Hostels There are a number of hostels that compete for Bruges' backpacker market.

The newly renovated hostel, **Snuffel Sleep In** (*☎ 050 33 31 33, fax 050 33 32 50; ⓔ info@snuffel.be; Ezelstraat 47-49; bus No 3 or 13 from train station; dorm beds €11-13, double rooms €15*) includes breakfast for €2 and has funky rooms, friendly staff and a kitchen at the disposal of guests.

Gran Kaffee de Passage (*☎ 050 34 02 32, fax 050 34 01 40; Dweersstraat 26-28; bus 'Centrum' from train station; dorm beds €12.50, doubles with breakfast from €35*) has modern dorms as well as a hotel section next door. The restaurant here is enticing and breakfast costs €2.

Bauhaus International Youth Hotel (*☎ 050 34 10 93, fax 050 33 41 80; ⓔ bauhaus@bauhaus.be; Langestraat 135; bus No 6 or 16 from train station; dorm beds €11, singles without/with shower €15.50/24, doubles without/with shower €29/36*) is big place that is constantly expanding. Facilities include a bar, restaurant and Internet café, but it's all a bit soulless.

The HI-affiliated **Europa** (*☎ 050 35 26 79, fax 050 35 37 32; ⓔ brugge@vjh.be; Baron Ruzettelaan 143; dorm beds €12.50, beds in 4-bed room €14.50*) is 500m south of the city walls but seriously lacks atmosphere.

Guesthouses & Hotels There's a swarm of B&Bs and many represent excellent value.

There are three lofty rooms at **B&B Gheeraert** (*☎ 050 33 56 27, fax 050 34 52 01; ⓔ paul.gheeraert@skynet.be; Riddersstraat 9; singles/doubles/triples €45/50/70*), all of which are simply gorgeous.

B&B Dieltiens (*☎ 050 33 42 94, fax 050 33 52 30; ⓔ koen.dieltiens@skynet.be; Waalsestraat 40; singles/doubles €45/50, 3/4-person rooms €70/90, 1-night supplement €7.50*) has been welcoming visitors for years, and the hospitality still shines.

Those averse to stairs should head to **B&B Debruyne** (*☎ 050 34 76 07, fax 050 34 02 85; ⓔ marie.debruyne@advalvas.be; Lange Raamstraat 18; singles/doubles €45/50, 3/4-person rooms €70/90*), a highly original home.

The Hotel Malleberg (*☎ 050 34 41 11, fax 050 34 67 69; Hoogstraat 7; singles/doubles €60/72, 3/4-person rooms €100/117*) is an immaculate two-star hotel that has eight lovely rooms.

Places to Eat

For a sandwich, try rustic little **De Belegde Boterham** (*☎ 050 34 91 31; Kleine St Amandsstraat*). Pleasant **Lotus** (*☎ 050 33 10 78; Wapenmakerstraat 5; small/large meals €7.90/8.45; open lunch only Mon-Sat*) is a stylish vegetarian restaurant.

Forget time at **De Bottelier** (*☎ 050 33 18 60; St Jakobsstraat 50; mains €10-14*); the menu here will suit most. **Rock Fort** (*☎ 050 33 41 13; Langstraat 15; dishes €13-19*) does fusion cuisine in intimate surroundings.

Self-caterers should head to the **Profi supermarkets** (*Oude Burg 22 • Langestraat 55*).

Entertainment

If you're absolutely fanging for a beer, or better still, 300 different types of them, go directly to **'t Brugs Beertje** (*Kemelstraat 5*). Another great bar is **De Garre** (*Garre 1*).

Retsin's Lucifernum (*Twijnstraat 8; open Fri & Sat*) is one of Belgium's weirdest places to drink – a huge mansion strewn with moody paintings.

Live contemporary and world music generally happens at the **Cactus Club** (*☎ 050 33 20 14; St Jakobsstraat 33*). **Cinema Lumière** (*☎ 050 34 34 65; St Jakobsstraat 36a*) screens foreign and mainstream films. Find out what's happening around town at **Café de la République** (*St Jakobsstraat 36*) next door. For performing arts there's the new **Concertgebouw** (*'t Zand*).

Getting There & Away

From mid-May to mid-September, there's a daily Eurolines bus from Bruges to London (€46, six hours). **Reizen Wasteels** (*☎ 050 33 65 31; Geldmuntstraat 30a*) sells tickets.

The **station information office** (*☎ 050 38 23 82; open 7am-8.30pm daily*) can help with rail queries. There are IC trains to Brussels (€10.30, one hour), Antwerp (€10.80, 70 minutes), Ghent (€4.70, 20 minutes) and

Kortrijk (€5.60, 40 minutes). From Kortijk there are hourly connections to Ypres (€8.45, 1½ hours).

Getting Around

There's a small network of buses, most leaving from the Markt, and many pass by the train station. For route and timetable information ring ☎ 059 56 53 53.

You can rent bikes from **Fietsen Popelier** *(☎ 050 34 32 62; Mariastraat 26)*, which will cost €6/9 per half/full day.

YPRES (IEPER)

pop 35,000

Stories have long been told about the WWI battlefields of Flanders. There were the tall red poppies that rose over the flat, flat fields; the soldiers who disappeared forever in the quagmire of battle; and the little town of Ypres, which was wiped off the map.

Sitting in the country's southwest corner, Ypres and its surrounding land constituted the last bastion of Belgian territory unoccupied by the Germans in WWI. As such, the Ypres Salient was a barrier to a German advance towards the French coastal ports around Calais. More than 300,000 Allied soldiers were killed here during four years of fighting, which left the medieval town flattened. Convincingly rebuilt, its outlying farmlands are today dotted with cemeteries and memorials, and in early summer, the poppies still flower.

Orientation & Information

The town's hub is the Grote Markt. It's a 10 minute walk from the train station; you head straight up Stationsstraat and, at the end, turn left onto Tempelstraat and then right onto Boterstraat. Three blocks on is the Renaissance-style Lakenhalle (cloth hall) with its 70m-high belfry.

The **Ypres Visitors Centre** *(☎ 057 22 85 84, fax 057 22 85 89; Grote Markt; open daily)* is in the Lakenhalle.

Things to See

Ypres ranked alongside Bruges and Ghent as an important cloth town in medieval times, and its postwar reconstruction holds true to its former prosperity.

The excellent **In Flanders Fields Museum** *(Grote Markt 34; Ⓦ www.inflandersfields.be; adult/child €7.50/3.50; open 10am-5pm or 6pm daily Apr-Sept, closed Monday Oct-Mar)* is a moving testament to the wartime horrors experienced by ordinary people.

One of the saddest reminders of the Great War is Ypres' **Meensepoort** (Menin Gate), inscribed with the names of 55,000 British and Commonwealth troops who were lost in the quagmire of the trenches and who have no graves. A bugler sounds the last post here at 8pm every evening. It's about 300m from the tourist office.

Around Ypres, in outlying fields and hamlets, are 170 **cemeteries** and many **memorials** to those who died on the Ypres Salient. These wartime reminders are scattered over a large area – if you've limited time it's best to go with an organised tour. **Salient Tours** *(☎ 057 91 02 23)* has been around for years and runs 2½- to four-hour tours for €15/22. **Flanders Battlefield Tours** *(☎ 057 36 04 60)* is a newcomer and charges €10/14.

Places to Stay & Eat

For camping, there's **Jeugdstadion** *(☎ 057 21 72 82; Ⓔ info@jeudstadion.be; Leopold III laan 16; camping per person €3, tent sites €1.50)*, 900m southeast of the town centre. The closest private hostel is **De Iep** *(☎/fax 057 20 88 11; Poperingseweg 34; dorm beds €14.10)*, 2km west of town.

The new **B&B Hortensia** *(☎ 057 21 24 06; Rijselsestraat 196; singles/doubles/triples €42/54/69)* is modern, spacious and a treat.

The old-fashioned **Old Tom** *(☎ 057 20 15 41, fax 057 21 91 20; Ⓔ oldtom@pandora.be; singles/doubles €49/58)*.

Cafés and restaurants line the Grote Markt – a consistently good choice is **In het Klein Stadhuis** *(☎ 057 21 55 42; mains €10.60-15.50)*, a simple brasserie right next to the town hall.

Eethuis De Ecurie *(☎ 057 21 73 78; Rijselsestraat 49; dishes €13-17)* offers innovative cuisine and an enticing atmosphere (despite once being a horse stable).

If it's picnic supplies that you're after any picnic supplies, there's the **Super GB supermarket** *(Vandepeereboomplein 15)*.

Getting There & Around

There are direct hourly trains go to Kortrijk (€3.20, 30 minutes) and Ghent (€8.30, one hour). To Brussels (€12.70, 1½ hours), Antwerp (€14.20, two hours), Bruges (€8.45, 1½ hours) and Tournai (€6.80, one hour), change trains in Kortrijk.

Regional buses leave from outside the train station. Rent bicycles from the Jeugdstadion (see Places to Stay & Eat earlier in this chapter) for €5 per day.

Central Wallonia

TOURNAI (DOORNIK)

pop 68,365

The Walloon town of Tournai is, together with Tongeren in Flanders, classified as one of the oldest cities in Belgium. Just 10km from the French border and 80km southwest of Brussels, it was once a Roman trading settlement known as Tornacum. The town's focal point, the five-towered cathedral, is one of the country's finest.

The train station is a 10-minute walk from the centre of town – head straight up Rue Royale until you reach the cathedral. To the left up the hill is the **tourist office** *(☎ 069 22 20 45, fax 069 21 62 21; e tourisme@tournai.be; Vieux Marché aux Poteries 14; open daily)*, near the base of the belfry.

Things to See & Do

Tournai's austere 12th-century **cathedral** is undergoing extensive repairs after tornado damage in 1999 and will probably be closed for another decade. The treasury (entry via Rue des Chapeliers) has remained open.

After a decade-long facelift, the 13th-century **belfry** *(Vieux Marché aux Poteries; admission €2)* has reopened. Climb the 257 steps for a great view.

The town's most prestigious museum is the **Musée des Beaux-Arts** *(Enclos St Martin; admission €3)*, in a building designed by Victor Horta. The **Musée de la Tapisserie et des Arts du Tissu** *(Museum of Tapestry and Cloth Arts; Place Reine Astrid; admission €2.50)* is testament to the revival of the city's historically important tapestry industry. Both museums are open 10am to noon and 2pm to 5.30pm daily (closed Tuesday).

Places to Stay & Eat

The **Auberge de Jeunesse** *(☎ 069 21 61 36, fax 069 21 61 40; Rue St Martin 64; dorm beds €12.50, singles/doubles €22.50/35)* is a pleasant, HI-affiliated hostel that's a 20-minute walk from the station.

The **Hôtel d'Alcantara** *(☎ 069 21 26 48, fax 069 21 28 24; Rue des Bouchers St Jacques 2; singles/doubles from €73/83)* is a charmingly discreet hotel with modern rooms.

L'Écurie d'Ennetières *(☎ 069 21 56 89; Ruelle d'Ennetières; mains €7.50-12.50)* is a lovely mid-range French restaurant. **Pita Pyramide** *(☎ 069 84 35 83; Rue Tête d'Or 7)* sells stuffed pitta breads for €3.80. Picnic supplies can be bought from the **Super GB supermarket** across the road.

Getting There & Away

There are regular trains to Kortrijk (€3.80, 40 minutes), Brussels (€9.30, one hour) and Ypres via Kortrijk (€6.80, one hour).

LIÈGE (LUIK)

pop 189,903

Liège is one of those cities people tend to love or loath. Sprawled along the Meuse River in the eastern part of Wallonia, it's busy and gritty and is the sort of place that takes time to get to know. If you're passing en route to the Ardennes, stop off to see its evocative museums.

Orientation & Information

The central district is strewn along the western bank of the Meuse River, which splits in two creating the island of Outremeuse. The main train station, Gare Guillemins, is 2km south of Place St Lambert, the city's heart.

The main **Office du Tourisme** *(☎ 04 221 92 21, fax 04 221 92 22; e office.tourisme@liege.be; Féronstrée 92; open daily)* can help with information. For regional information, head to the **provincial tourist office** *(Fédération du Tourisme de la Province de Liège; ☎ 04 232 65 10; Blvd de la Sauvenière 77)*. At Gare Guillemins there's a small bureau dispensing both city and provincial information.

Things to See & Do

Excellent views of the city can be had from the top of the **Montagne de Bueren** – an impressive flight of 373 stairs that lead up from Hors Château. On Sunday mornings there's **La Batte**, a street market that stretches along 1.5km of riverfront quays.

The old, picturesque area around the tourist office is home to the city's best museums. The **Musée d'Art Religieux et d'Art Mosan** *(Museum of Religious Art & Meuse Valley Art; Rue Mêre Dieu; admission €2.50; open 11am-6pm Tues-Sat, 11am-4pm Sun)* is stuffed with relics and paintings from the region. The nearby **Musée de la Vie Wallonne** *(Walloon*

Life Museum; Cour des Mineurs; admission €2; open 10am-5pm Tues-Sat, 10am-4pm Sun) presents local customs from days gone by. Life as it was for some in the 18th century is depicted in the **Musée d'Ansembourg** *(Féronstrée 114; admission €1.50; open 1pm-6pm Tues-Sun)*, a Regency-style mansion. Don't miss the six-faced clock.

Places to Stay

The big HI-affiliated **Auberge de Jeunesse** *(☎ 04 344 56 89, fax 04 344 56 87; ⓔ liege@laj.be; Rue Georges Simenon 2; bus No 4 from Gare Guillemins; dorm beds €12.80, singles/doubles €20.50/30)* is in Outremeuse.

Newly renovated **Hôtel Les Acteurs** *(☎ 04 223 00 80, fax 04 221 19 48; ⓔ lesacteurs@skynet.be; Rue des Urbanistes 10; bus No 1 or 4 from station; singles/doubles from €50/60)* is a breath of fresh air, with modern, comfy rooms.

The **Hôtel Simenon** *(☎ 04 342 86 90, fax 04 344 26 69; ⓔ simenon@swing.be; Blvd de l'Est 16; rooms from €62; breakfast €6.20)* occupies a 1908 Art Nouveau house in Outremeuse. The gaily decorated rooms reflect the writings of local author Georges Simenon.

Places to Eat

For serene surroundings, cross the river to Outremeuse, where there's an old cobbled street, **En Roture**, lined with little restaurants. In the city centre, Rue St-Jean-en-Isle is also filled with restaurants and brasseries. Nearby, **La Feuille de Vigne** *(☎ 04 222 20 10; Rue Sœurs de Hasque 12; meals €7.50-9; open noon-3pm Mon-Sat)* is a health-food shop and vegetarian eatery. One of the best brasseries is **As Ouhès** *(☎ 04 223 32 25; Place du Marché 21; dishes €10-17)*. This place specialises in rich Walloon cuisine – the servings are extra generous and the prices reasonable.

Self-caterers should try the **Delhaize supermarket** *(Place de la Cathédrale)*.

Getting There & Away

Bus The office of **Eurolines** *(☎ 04 222 36 18; Rue des Guillemins 94)* is near the main train station. Buses depart 50m away on the corner of Rue des Guillemins and Rue d'Artois.

Train The main station, Gare Guillemins, is 2km from Place St Lambert, connected by bus No 1 or 4. There's a **train information office** *(☎ 04 224 26 10; open 7am-9.30pm daily)*.

The Thalys fast train connects Liège with Cologne (€23.30, 1¼ hours, seven trains per day) but there are also cheaper, normal trains (€18.80, 1½ hours, eight per day). Other regular connections include Brussels (€10.80, 1¼ hours, two per hour), Maastricht (€7, 30 minutes, hourly) and Luxembourg city (€24.30, 2½ hours, seven per day). Locally, there are hourly trains to Namur (€6.40, 50 minutes), Spa (€3.20, 50 minutes) and Tongeren (€3.30, 30 minutes).

Getting Around

Inner-city buses leave from the right as you leave Gare Guillemins. Bus No 1 or 4 plies between here and the centre.

AROUND LIÈGE

Tongeren

pop 30,000

The Flemish town of Tongeren is about 20km north of Liège. It has the honour (together with Tournai) of being one of Belgium's oldest cities. The original locals put up considerable resistance under the leadership of Ambiorix when the area was conquered by Roman troops in 15 BC; impressive findings from this period are on display in the impressive **Gallo-Roman Museum** *(☎ 012 67 03 30; Kielenstraat 15; admission €5; open noon-5pm Mon, 9am-5pm Tues-Fri, 10am-6pm Sat & Sun)*, in the heart of town. Tongeren is also well known for its Sunday **antique market**.

For more information, visit the **tourist office** *(☎ 012 39 02 55, fax 012 39 11 43; Stadhuisplein 9; open daily)*.

Overnighters will find a pleasant HI hostel, **Begijnhof** *(☎ 012 39 13 70, fax 012 39 13 48; ⓔ tongeren@vjh.be; St Ursulastraat 1; dorm beds €12.50)* or you could try the mid-range **Hotel Lido** *(☎ 012 23 19 48, fax 012 39 27 27; Grote Markt 19; singles/doubles €60/70)*.

Spa

pop 11,000

Spa was for centuries the luxurious retreat for royalty and the wealthy, who came to drink, bathe and cure themselves in the mineral-rich waters that bubble forth here. Today it is a rather run-down reminder of what was, but is nevertheless pleasant enough for a day or overnight.

The town, about 35km southeast of Liège, is connected by regular trains (see Getting There

& Away under Liège). The local **Office du Tourisme** *(☎ 087 79 53 53, fax 087 79 53 54; officetourismespa@skynet.be; Place Royale 41; open daily)* can help with inquiries.

Hautes Fagnes National Park

Bordering the Eifel Hills in Germany, with which it forms one geographical entity, the Hautes Fagnes park is a region of swampy heath and woods. In the park is the **Botrange Nature Centre** *(☎ 080 44 03 00, fax 080 44 44 29; e botrange.centrenature@ skynet.be; adult/concession €3/1.50; Route de Botrange 131; open 10am-6pm daily)*, close to the highest point in Belgium – the Signal de Botrange (694m). This area is a popular base for walkers, cyclists and cross-country skiers. Those wanting just a short walk (1½ hours) through this bleak but interesting landscape should head to the boardwalk at Fagne de Polleur, nearby at Mt Rigi.

The Botrange Nature Centre is about 50km east of Liège. It takes at least 1¼ hours to get to on public transport from Liège – take the train to Verviers and then bus No 390 in the direction of Elsenborn.

The Ardennes

Home to deep river valleys and high forests, Belgium's southeastern corner is often overlooked by travellers who are hopping between the old art towns and the capital. However here, in the provinces of Namur, Liège and Luxembourg, you will find tranquil villages nestled into the grooves of the Meuse, Lesse and Ourthe Valleys or sitting atop the verdant hills. This is where the Battle of the Bulge raged.

The town of Namur is the best base for exploration – it's well positioned on the railway line to Luxembourg and has rail and bus connections to some of the region's less-accessible spots. Without your own transport, getting around this region can take time.

NAMUR (NAMEN)

pop 105,000

Just 50km southeast of Brussels, alluring Namur is the capital of Wallonia. The small city is slightly overwhelmed by its 15th-century citadel. The **tourist office** *(☎ 081 24 64 49; Square Léopold; open daily)* is 200m to the left of the station, as you leave. There's also a small tourist kiosk at Place du Grognon at the base of the citadel.

Things to See & Do

Perched dramatically above the town, the **citadel** *(☎ 081 22 68 29; admission free)* can be reached on foot, by car along the Route Merveilleuse, or by a shuttle bus (€1), which departs half-hourly from the tourist office. Guided visits for adults/children cost €6/3.

Of the handful of museums, the two most intriguing are the **Félicien Rops** *(☎ 081 22 01 10; Rue Fumal 12; adult/concession €2.50/1.25)*, which has works by the 19th-century Namur-born artist who fondly illustrated erotic lifestyles, and the tiny **Trésor du Prieuré d'Oignies** *(☎ 081 23 03 42; Rue Julie Billiart 17; adult/concession €1.25/0.50)*, a one-roomed hoard of exquisite Gothic treasures in a modern convent.

Places to Stay & Eat

The riverfront **Auberge de Jeunesse** *(☎ 081 22 36 88, fax 081 22 44 12; e namur@laj.be; Ave F Rops 8; bus No 3 or 4 from station; dorm beds €14.50)* is 3km from the train station.

Grand Hôtel de Flandre *(☎ 081 23 18 68, fax 081 22 80 60; Place de la Station 14; singles/doubles from €56/73)* is a place that has no-nonsense rooms.

Tea Time Café *(☎ 0496 52 44 22; Rue St Jean 35)* provides excellent filled baguettes (€3.25), as well as crepes and waffles. Snacks plus French-style meals are served at **Brasserie Henry** *(☎ 081 22 02 04; Place St Aubain 3; mains €8.50-15, 3-course menus €21.50; open noon-midnight)*.

Getting There & Away

From Namur's **train station** *(☎ 081 25 22 22)* there are trains to Brussels (€6.40, one hour, half-hourly), Luxembourg city (€21.50, 1¾ hours, hourly) and Liège (€6.40, 50 minutes, hourly). For information regarding regional trains see the individual Getting There & Away sections for Dinant, Han-sur-Lesse, Rochefort, La Roche-en-Ardenne and Bastogne later in this chapter.

Local and regional buses are operated by **TEC** *(☎ 081 25 35 55; office open 7am-7pm daily)*, which has an office opposite the train station. Regional buses leave from the bus station near the C&A department store (to the left of the train station as you leave).

DINANT

pop 12,500

This heavy, distinctive town, 28km south of Namur, is one of the Ardennes' real touristy hot spots. Its bulbous cathedral competes for attention with the cliff-front citadel, while below, a hive of boat operators competes for the Meuse River day-trippers or the Lesse Valley kayakers. The **tourist office** *(☎ 082 22 28 70; ⓔ info@dinant-tourisme.be; Ave Cadoux 8; open daily)* can assist visitors.

Things to See & Do

The **citadel**, open year-round, is accessible by cable car – a combined ticket for an adult/child costs €5/3.75.

For **kayaking**, several companies have trips leaving in the morning from Houyet, 21km upriver, and ending at Anseremme next to Dinant five hours later. Try **Kayaks Ansiaux** *(☎ 082 22 23 25; Rue du Vélodrome 15)* in Anseremme.

The **boat cruises** down the Meuse are far more sedate. The **Bateaux Bayard** *(☎ 082 22 30 42; Quai No 10, Blvd Churchill)*, company runs a 45-minute return trip to Anseremme, which costs €4.80/3.50 for an adult/child, and a 3½-hour return cruise to Hastière which costs €11/9 for an adult/child.

Places to Stay

Hotels are not plentiful, and there's no hostel. **Hôtel de la Couronne** *(☎ 082 22 24 41; info@hotellacouronne.com; Rue Sax 1; singles/doubles from €50/62)* is pleasant and central. The new riverfront **Hôtel Ibis** *(☎ 082 21 15 00; ⓔ hotelibis.dinant@belgacom.net; Rempart d'Albeau 16; singles/doubles from €75/84)* is architecturally bland but does boost the meagre accommodation scene.

Getting There & Away

Trains from Namur to Dinant (€3.40, 30 minutes) run hourly and bus No 34 (50 minutes, every two hours) also connects the two.

HAN-SUR-LESSE & ROCHEFORT

pop 23,500

The millennia-old limestone grottoes are the drawcard of these two villages, which sit just 8km apart on the Lesse and Lomme Rivers, respectively. The most impressive **Han caves** *(adult/child €10.30/5.90; open 10am-noon & 1.30pm-4.30pm Apr-Oct; tours at 11.30am, 1pm, 2.30pm and 4pm only Nov & Dec, Feb & Mar)* are impressive and a little way out of town – a tram takes you to the entrance and a boat brings you back. Rochefort's cave, which is also known as the **Grotte de Lorette** *(adult/child €5.95/3.95; open Easter–early-Nov)*, is much smaller and less impressive.

The **Han tourist office** *(☎ 084 37 75 96; ⓔ han.tourisme@euronet.be; Place Théo Lannoy)* and the **Rochefort tourist office** *(☎ 084 34 51 72; ⓔ valdelesse@tiscalinet.be; Rue de Behogne 5)* are the local tourist offices and can provide information.

Places to Stay

Both villages have private hostels with dormitory-style accommodation costing €12.50 for people aged 26 years and over, or €10 for under 26s. Contact the **Han Gîte d'Étape hostel** *(☎ 084 37 74 41; ⓔ g.han@skynet.be; Rue du Gîte d'Étape 10; open year-round)* or the **Rochefort Gîte d'Étape hostel** *(☎ 084 21 46 04; ⓔ giterochefort@skynet.be; Rue du Hableau 25)*.

The grey-stone **Hôtel des Ardennes** *(☎ 084 37 72 20, fax 084 37 80 62; Rue des Grottes 2; singles/doubles from €48/60)* in Han has local charm and a good restaurant. Rochefort has a better range of hotels including the bright **Hotel La Fayette** *(☎ 084 21 42 73; ⓔ hotel.lafayette@swing.be; Rue Jacquet 87; singles/ doubles from €37/42)* or the atmospheric **Le Vieux Logis** *(☎ 084 21 10 24, fax 084 22 12 30; Rue Jacquet 71; singles/doubles €48/58)*.

Getting There & Away

Take the Namur-Luxembourg train to Jemelle (40 minutes, hourly) and transfer to the hourly bus No 29 (seven minutes to Rochefort, 14 minutes to Han).

LA ROCHE-EN-ARDENNE

pop 4100

Hugging a bend in the Ourthe River, La Roche is a vibrant little town, hidden in a deep valley, crowned by a ruined **castle** and surrounded by verdant hills much enjoyed by walkers. If you want to get into kayaking or mountain biking, this is your playground. The **tourist office** *(☎ 084 36 77 36; ⓔ infolr@skynet.be; Place du Marché 15)* dispenses information. **Ardenne Aventures** *(☎ 084 41 19 00; Rue du Hadja 1)* hires mountain bikes and kayaks, and organises white-water rafting (October to March only).

Places to Stay

Camping Le Vieux Moulin *(☎ 084 41 13 80; Petite Strument 62; camping per adult/tent €2.50/7.50; open Easter-31 Oct)* is beautifully positioned.

Villa Les Olivettes *(☎ 084 41 16 52, fax 084 41 21 69; e info@lesolivettes; Chemin de Soeret 12; dorm beds €15, singles/doubles from €54/74)* is popular with horse-riding enthusiasts. In addition to hotel rooms, it has a separate *auberge* with dormitory-style accommodation (four to eight beds); breakfast is not included.

For a quaint B&B, head to **Le Vieux La Roche** *(☎ 084 41 25 86; e levieuxlaroche@online.be; Rue du Chalet 45; rooms €38)*, with five homy rooms.

Captivating **Moulin de la Strument** *(☎ 084 41 15 07, fax 084 41 10 80; e strument@skynet.be; Petite Strument 62; singles/doubles €60/66)* is a hotel/restaurant with eight rooms beside a babbling stream.

Places to Eat

Succulent crepes are the house speciality of **Le Clos René** *(☎ 084 41 26 17; Rue Châmont 30; meals €4-5)*. It's in the heart of town and prices are reasonable. Note the glass floor.

For classic French cuisine and extremely attentive service, head to **La Clairefontaine** *(☎ 084 41 24 70; Route de Hotton 64; 3/6-course meals €19/52)*, an old-fashioned hotel/restaurant 1.5km from town.

The **Spar supermarket** *(Quai du Gravier 1)* has picnic supplies for self-catered lunches.

Getting There & Away

From Namur, take a Luxembourg-bound train to Marloie, then bus No 15 (eight per day) to La Roche (35 minutes).

BASTOGNE

pop 12,500

It was here, north of Arlon and close to the Luxembourg border, that thousands of soldiers and civilians died during the Battle of the Bulge in the winter of 1944–45. Testament to these events is a huge, star-shaped **American memorial**, known also as Mardasson, on a hill 2km from Bastogne. The neighbouring **Bastogne Historical Centre**, *(☎ 061 21 14 13; adult/child €7.50/5; open 10am-4.30pm Feb-June & Sept-Dec, 9.30am-6pm July-Aug)* is an unimpressive glorification of war. The new **tourist office** *(☎ 061 21 27 11; Place McAuliffe)* is in the heart of town.

Places to Stay

Camping de Renval *(☎ 061 21 29 85; Route de Marche 148; closed 1-15 Jan)* is 1km from the tourist office. **Hôtel du Sud** *(☎ 061 21 11 14; e info@hotel-du-sud.be; Rue de Marche 39; singles/doubles from €45/54)* has OK rooms. More upmarket is **Hôtel Collin** *(☎ 061 21 43 58; e infos@hotel-collin.com; Place McAuliffe 8; singles/doubles from €67/80)*.

Getting There & Away

From Namur, take a Luxembourg-bound train to the rail junction of Libramont, from where bus No 163b departs every two hours for Bastogne's defunct train station (35 minutes).

Bosnia-Hercegovina

Sandwiched between Croatia and Yugoslavia, the extremely mountainous country of Bosnia-Hercegovina has been a meeting point of East and West for nearly two millennia. From the mingling of Orthodox Byzantium and Catholic Rome to today's heterogeneous population of Croats, Serbs and Slavic Muslims, the country has developed one of Europe's most fascinating cultures.

This diversity has come at a price. Torn by the pan-Balkan war of the early 1990s, Bosnia-Hercegovina entered the 21st century physically devastated and ethnically divided. But peace is currently enforced by NATO, and a large international civilian presence is working to reintegrate and rebuild the country. Even though much of its heritage has been destroyed, Bosnia-Hercegovina shows proud resilience through its scars.

Bosnia-Hercegovina: the Basics

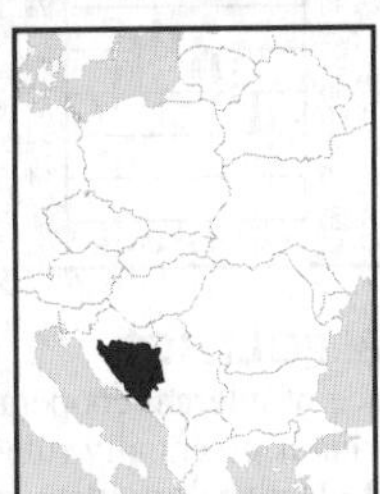

Capital Sarajevo

Population 3.8 million

Language Bosnian

Currency 1 convertible mark (KM) = 100 convertible pfennigs

Avoid at all costs Landmines

Make friends by saying *Hocemo li na kafu?* (Shall we have coffee?)

Facts about Bosnia-Hercegovina

HISTORY

The region's ancient inhabitants were Illyrians, followed by Romans. Slavs arrived in the late-6th and early 7th centuries. Numerous invasions followed, and by 1463 Bosnia-Hercegovina was a Turkish province. During 400 years of Turkish rule, Bosnia-Hercegovina became the boundary between the Islamic and Christian worlds.

After Turkey's 1878 defeat by Russia, Habsburg Austria occupied the land. In 1914, a Bosnian Serb assassinated the Habsburg heir in Sarajevo, and WWI commenced. Following the war, Bosnia-Hercegovina was taken into the Kingdom of the Serbs, Croats and Slovenes. The country was renamed Yugoslavia in 1929.

In the republic's first free elections in November 1990, the communists were easily defeated by nationalists. Croats and Muslims united to declare independence in 1991. Bosnian-Serb nationalists began to seize territory, commencing a period of 'ethnic cleansing' to expel Muslims from the north and east. By 1992 a three-way war among Serbs, Croats and Muslims seemed to portend the complete breakup of the nation. Despite pressure from the West, the conflict mounted. Croatia began attacking Croatian Serbs, while Bosnian Serbs chained UN peacekeepers to potential air targets. In July 1995 Bosnian-Serbs attacked the safe area of Srebrenica, slaughtering an estimated 6000 Muslims who were fleeing the area.

At last, battered by NATO air strikes, the Serbs agreed to peace talks. The resulting Dayton Agreement of 1995 maintained Bosnia-Hercegovina's prewar boundaries but divided it into two 'entities'. The Federation of Bosnia-Hercegovina (the Muslim and Croat portion) would administer 51% of the country, including Sarajevo, and the Serb Republic of Bosnia-Hercegovina (Republika Srpska, or RS) would rule 49%.

Although Bosnia-Hercegovina remains divided, tensions have ebbed. Bosnians are returning home – 90,000 people returned in 2001. Pan-Balkan war crimes are now being tried at the Hague, but the two most-wanted Bosnian Serb war criminals – leader Radovan Karadžić and his military henchman Ratko Mladić – remain at large.

GEOGRAPHY & CLIMATE

Bosnia-Hercegovina is a mountainous country of 51,129 sq km on the west side of the Balkan Peninsula, almost cut off from the sea by Croatia. Owing to its altitude, it gets hot in summer but quite chilly in winter; snowfall can last until April.

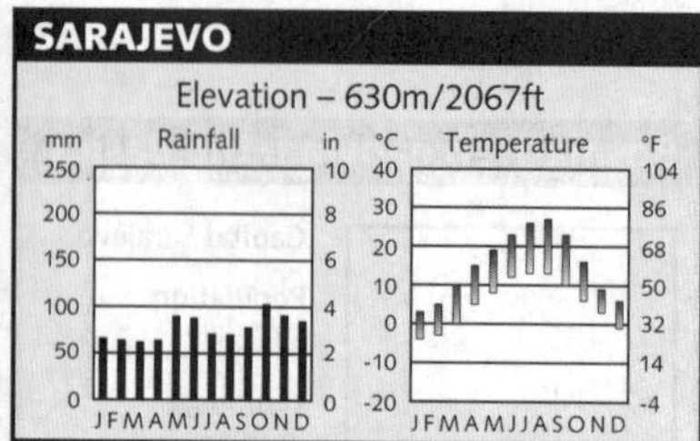

GOVERNMENT & POLITICS

With a practical absence of internal cooperation, Bosnia-Hercegovina is essentially ruled by the West. National elections are planned for late 2002.

POPULATION & PEOPLE

A Bosnian Serb is a Serb living in Bosnia; a Bosnian Croat is a Croat living in Bosnia; and Bosnian Muslims go by the term Bosniak.

LANGUAGE

Bosnian, Croatian and Serbian are essentially the same language. The Federation uses the Latin alphabet; the RS uses Cyrillic. See the Language chapter at the back of the book.

Facts for the Visitor

HIGHLIGHTS

Sarajevo, a major historic site, is recovering its vibrancy. Beautifully situated Mostar deserves a visit for its cobbled old town. Taking the bus through Bosnia's ravaged but slowly recovering countryside is unforgettable.

VISAS & DOCUMENTS

No visas are required for citizens of the USA, Canada and most EU countries. Others can obtain a one-month single-entry tourist visa by sending a personal cheque or money order for approximately UK£20 (ask your embassy for the exact amount in local currency), a passport, a copy of a round-trip plane ticket, a bank statement, and an application to the nearest embassy.

EMBASSIES & CONSULATES

Bosnian Embassies & Consulates

Bosnia-Hercegovina has embassies and/or consulates in the following countries:

Australia (☎ 02-6232 4646, fax 6232 5554) 6 Beale Crs, Deakin ACT 2600
Canada (☎ 613-236 0028, fax 236 1139) Suite 805, 130 Albert St, Ottawa, Ontario K1P 5G4
Croatia *Consulate*: (☎ 01-48 19 420, fax 48 19 418) Pavla Hatza 3, PP27, 10001 Zagreb
Slovenia *Consulate*: (☎ 01-432 23 70, ☎ 319 978) Likozarjeva 6, 1000 Ljubljana
UK (☎ 020-7255 3758) 57 Lexham Gardens, London W8
USA (☎ 202-337 1500, fax 337 1502) 2109 E St NW, Washington DC 20037
Consulate: (☎ 212-593 1042, fax 751 9019) Suite 580, 866 UN Plaza, New York NY 10017

Check out Ⓦ www.mvp.gov.ba for more details about Bosnian embassies/consulates.

Embassies & Consulates in Bosnia-Hercegovina

These embassies are in Sarajevo (area code ☎ 033), and the German consulate is in Banja Luka (area code ☎ 051):

Canada (☎ 447 900, fax 447 901) Logavina 7
Croatia (☎ 444 331, fax 472 434) Mehmeda Spahe 16
Germany (☎ 275 000, fax 652 978) Mejtaš Buka bb
Consulate: (☎ 277 949, fax 217 113) Kralja Karađorđevića 103, Banja Luka
Macedonia (☎/fax 206 004) Emerika Bluma 23
Yugoslavia (☎ 260 090, fax 221 469) Obala Maka Dizdara 3A
Slovenia (☎ 271 260, fax 271 270) Bentbaša 7
UK (☎ 444 429, fax 666 131, Ⓔ britemb@bih.net.ba) Tina Ujevića 8
USA (☎ 445 700, fax 659 722, Ⓔ opabih@pd.state.gov) Alipašina 43

MONEY

The convertible mark (KM) is tied to the euro at 1KM to €0.51129. Most places accept euros as well as convertible marks and sometimes list prices in euros. Conversion rates for major currencies in mid-2002 are listed below.

country	unit		convertible mark
Australia	A$1	=	1.18KM
Canada	C$1	=	1.34KM
Eurozone	€1	=	1.96KM
Japan	¥100	=	1.65KM
NZ	NZ$1	=	1.01KM
UK	UK£1	=	3.04KM
USA	US$1	=	2.06KM

For up-to-the-minute exchange rates check out Ⓦ www.xe.net/ucc/full.shtml.

Travellers cheques can be exchanged at banks in larger cities, though usually not in smaller cities (including Bihać or Travnik). ATMs have sprouted in Sarajevo. MasterCard, Visa, Plus, Maestro, and Cirrus are usually accepted. Have a back-up option lest the machines malfunction.

Tipping is customary in nice restaurants and taxis – round up the bill, or leave 1KM to 2KM extra. Bargaining is sometimes possible in souvenir shops.

POST & COMMUNICATIONS

Post and telephone offices are usually combined. Bosnia-Hercegovina's country code is ☎ 387. To make an international call from Bosnia-Hercegovina, it's cheapest to go to the post office. Dial the international access number (☎ 00), then the country code and number. Unfortunately, phone cards issued in the different entities of Bosnia-Hercegovina are not interchangeable.

Some important telephone numbers are ☎ 900/901/902 for international operator and ☎ 988 for local directory information.

Internet cafés abound in Sarajevo, and other large cities have one or two Internet access spots.

DIGITAL RESOURCES

Bosnia's natural and cultural wonders are talked up at W www.bhtourism.ba, a site administered by the Office of the High Representative. Listings and information on several Bosnian cities, including Sarajevo and Mostar, are at W www.city.ba.

DANGERS & ANNOYANCES

Mines are the greatest danger.

Nationalism runs strong in some parts of the country (notably Republika Srpska and Hercegovina), but this should'nt affect international travellers, who can expect a warm welcome almost everywhere.

PUBLIC HOLIDAYS

Bosnia-Hercegovina observes Independence Day (1 March), May Day (1 May) and the Day of the Republic (25 November). Bajram, a twice-yearly Muslim holiday, is observed in parts of the Federation. Catholic Christmas and Orthodox Christmas are observed by those religious groups.

Emergencies

In the event of an emergency dial ☎ 92 for police, ☎ 93 for the fire department or ☎ 94 for emergency assistance

Warning: Land Mines

Over one million landmines are estimated to be in Bosnia-Hercegovina. All of Sarajevo's suburbs are heavily mined, as are areas around Travnik, Mostar and Bihać. Only about 60% of minefields in the country have been reported. Sarajevo's **Mine Action Centre** *(☎ 033-209-762, fax 209 763; W www.bhmac.org; open 8am-4pm Mon-Fri)* runs valuable mine awareness briefings that visitors can book in advance.

The golden rule for mines and unexploded ordnance is to stick to asphalt surfaces. Avoid areas that look abandoned, and regard every centimetre of ground as suspicious.

ACTIVITIES

Outdoor activities are severely compromised due to mines. However Jahorina and Bjelašnica, Bosnia's ski resorts, are again open; stay on the groomed ski runs as there are mines in the vicinity. Rafting season runs from May to September. The Una River near Bihać is particularly popular.

ACCOMMODATION

Larger towns have a smattering of *pansions* (pensions) that are humbler and more personable than hotels. Breakfast is usually included in the rates. Confusingly, in Sarajevo some pansions now style themselves as 'hotels' or 'motels'.

Private accommodation is easy to arrange in Sarajevo and possible in Mostar. Elsewhere, ask locals at markets or shops.

FOOD & DRINKS

When confronted with the ubiquitous *burek* (a layered meat pie), vegetarians can instead opt for *sirnica* (cheese pie) or *zeljanica* (spinach pie). *Cevapčići*, another favourite, is lamb and beef rolls tucked into a half-loaf of spongy somun bread. For dessert, try baklava or *tufahije* (apple cake).

Good wines include Žilavka (white) and Blatina (red), best sampled in Hercegovina's wineries.

Getting There & Around

Bosnia-Hercegovina's main airport is in Sarajevo. Several airlines serve the country.

Buses are a reliable (if slow) way to enter Bosnia-Hercegovina. Many run from Croatia (Zagreb, Split, Dubrovnik), and more from Germany. The Republika Srpska is closely connected to Yugoslavia. Buses run hourly between Banja Luka and Belgrade; seven more run daily from the Sarajevo suburb of Lukavica (in RS) to Belgrade. Few bus stations offer luggage storage outside Sarajevo and Mostar.

One daily train runs from Sarajevo to Zagreb via Banja Luka, and another runs daily from Sarajevo to Ploče (five hours) via Mostar.

Within the country, trains are generally more comfortable than buses. About 10 daily trains chug out of Sarajevo. Trains from Banja Luka have a limited radius within the RS. Bosnia's bus network is quite comprehensive.

Taxis are readily available and cheap, though outside Sarajevo and Banja Luka they may not have meters. You may want to agree on the price before you set off.

Bosnia

SARAJEVO

☎ 033 • pop 500,000

Before the war, Bosnia-Hercegovina's capital was a microcosm of Yugoslavia, where Muslims, Serbs, Croats, Turks, Jews and others peacefully coexisted for hundreds of years. It's one of Europe's most Eastern cities, retaining the essence of its rich history in its mosques, markets and the picturesque old Turkish bazaar of Baščaršija.

Despite highly visible scars of the recent war, during which over 10,500 of its residents died, Sarajevo is again bursting with energy. Colourful trams run down 'Sniper's Alley', innumerable cafés line the streets, and locals spend leisurely evenings strolling down the main pedestrian street, Ferhadija. The energy poured into Bosnia-Hercegovina's recovery has rendered Sarajevo one of the fastest-changing cities in Europe.

Orientation & Information

From the airport 13km to the west, the main road runs through Novo Sarajevo, then past the turn-off to the bus and train stations and into the town centre. Baščaršija is on the east end of town.

The **Tourist Information Bureau** *(☎ 22 07 24, 532 606, fax 532 281; ul Zelenih Beretki 22; open 9am-4pm Mon-Fri, 9am-1pm & 4pm-6pm Sat)* stocks books, maps and helpful brochures and can answer most questions about the city.

The **Central Profit Banka** *(☎ 533 688; ul Zelenih Beretki 24; open 8am-7pm Mon-Fri, 8am-noon Sat)*, with other branches around town, exchanges travellers cheques for 1% commission. ATMs are sprinkled over the city centre, though some may have 100KM withdrawal limits.

The renovated **central post office** *(ul Obala Kulina Bana 8)* has post and telephone booths. Poste restante is held at the **post office** between the bus and train stations. Two handy 24-hour Internet cafés are at Ferhadija 12 and Pehlivanuša 2 (closed Sunday mornings). Both charge 3KM per hour.

For medical services, try **Koševo Hospital** *(☎ 666 620; ul Bolnioka 25)* or the **City Hospital** *(☎ 664 724; ul Kranjčevića 12)*. Ask your embassy for a list of private doctors.

Things to See & Do

The cobbled **Baščaršija** (the Turkish Quarter) is the heart of Sarajevo. **Morića Han**, now a café along Saraći, was formerly a tavern and stable when Sarajevo was a crossroads between East and West. **Svrzo House** *(Glodžina 6; admission 2KM; open 10am-3pm Tues-Sat, 10am-1pm Sun)*, just above Baščaršija, shows how a well-to-do 18th-century Muslim family would have lived.

In the city centre, places of worship for four different religions lie in close vicinity. These include the **Catholic church** *(Ferhadija)*; the old **Orthodox church** *(ul Mula Mustafe Bašeskije)*; the **Gazi-Husrevbey Mosque** (1531) in the old town; and the old **Jewish synagogue** *(ul Mula Mustafe Bašeskije)*.

The road into the city from the airport was dubbed 'Sniper's Alley' during the war because Serb snipers in the surrounding hills picked off civilians crossing the road. The bright yellow **Holiday Inn** was the wartime home to international journalists. Across the street is the **National Museum** *(open 10am-2pm Tues-Fri & Sun, longer hrs Wed summer)* which has interesting ethnology and archaeology collections. A **History Museum** *(open 9am-2pm Mon-Fri, 9am-1pm Sat & Sun)*, just up the road, displays old photos of Bosnia-Hercegovina and has rotating exhibits, some of which pertain to the recent war.

A **tree line** ringing the city demarcates the former front line. Watch the pavement for **Sarajevo roses**, which are skeletal indentations where a shell exploded. The tiny **War Museum Tunnel** (*☎ 628 591; ul Tuneli 1; admission 5KM*), beyond the airport, allows visitors to walk through an uncollapsed section of Sarajevo's dangerous wartime exit.

Twenty-five kilometres southeast of Sarajevo, the nearly deserted slopes of **Mt Jahorina**, site of the 1984 Winter Olympics, offer some of the best skiing in Europe at bargain-basement prices. There are mines in the area so stay on the groomed ski runs. **Green Visions** *(☎ 033-207 169)*, a Sarajevo tour agency, sometimes organises ski trips.

Special Events

In late August, internationally produced films are shown at the annual **Sarajevo Film Festival** *(☎ 524 127, fax 664 547)*. The **Winter Festival** in February and March features theatre and musical performances. Other festivals include **Baščaršija Noći**, when the old town erupts in song, dance and theatre.

Places to Stay

Prices remain high, and reservations are wise. Private accommodation is a relative bargain at 40KM to 50KM per person, but cheaper rooms are usually farther from the centre. For central, private rooms, contact **Unis Tours**

(☎/fax 209 089; Ferhadija 16; singles/doubles 42/74KM). **Turistička Agencija Ljubičica** (☎ 535 829, ☎/fax 232 109; ul Mula Mustafe Bašeskije 65; rooms 32-62KM), in Baščaršija, has rooms both in the centre and farther out.

The cheapest pansion is **Pansion Konak** (☎ 533 506; Mustafe Bašeskije 48; singles/doubles 30/60KM), a quite basic but acceptable spot in the centre. **Pansion Čobanija** (☎ 441 749, ☎/fax 203 937; ul Čobanija 29; singles/doubles 80/120KM), just past Pizzeria Galija on the south side of the river, is a popular option. Request one of the nicer upstairs rooms.

Places to Eat

On the street behind the cathedral, the **outdoor market** *(ul Mula Mustafe Bašeskije)*, overflows with fruits and vegetables. Its indoor counterpart is across the street in the sandy-coloured building.

For a quick meal, čevapi, burek and 'fast-food' joints are ubiquitous. Sarajevo's restaurants are the domain of internationals, as Bosnians socialise over coffee and eat at home.

To Be or Not to Be *(Čizmedžiluk 5)*, in Baščaršija, has generous, colourful salads in a candlelit setting. Vegetarians can opt for an omelette or spaghetti, while others can enjoy classic Bosnian steaks.

Inat Kuća *(Spite House)*, opposite the National Library, offers fabulous, low-priced Bosnian specialities such as a whopping *zeljanica* (spinach pie; 5KM) in a lively old Turkish setting. Authorities wanted to demolish the old house during library construction,

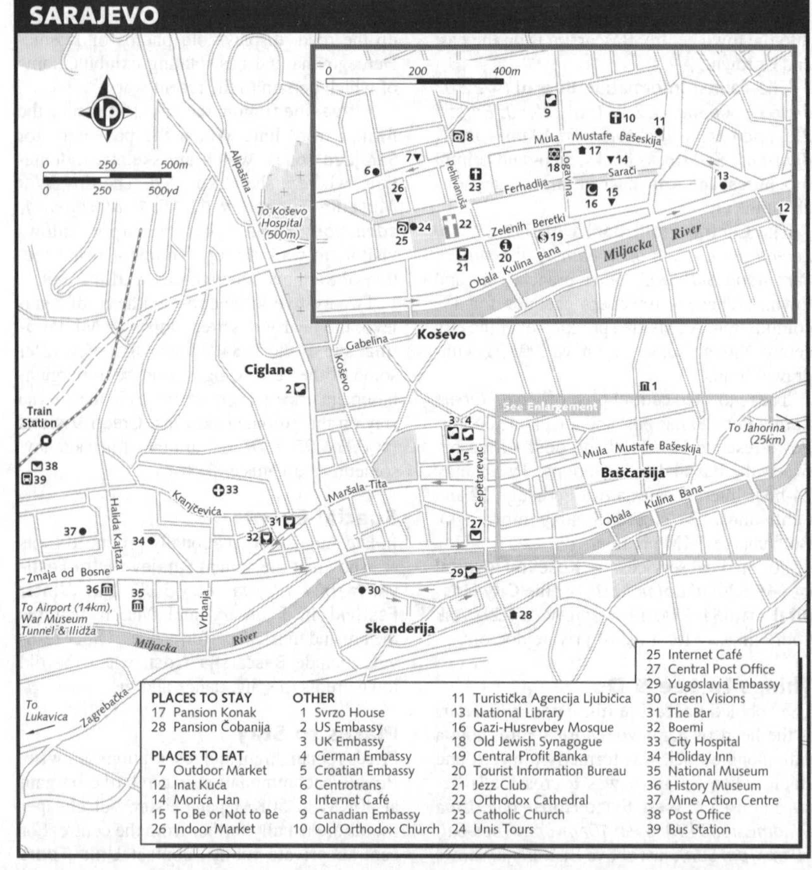

but the owner insisted on having it moved piece by piece across the river and reconstructed – hence the name.

Entertainment

Jezz Club *(Zelenih Beretki 14)*, beside the Jež restaurant, has live jazz on Thursdays and Saturdays. **Boemi** *(Valtera Periša 16)* is the current darling with Sarajevo's fickle disco-lovers.

The Bar *(ul Maršala Tita 7)*, near the intersection with ul Alipašina, is a popular hangout for young Bosnians when they're not at other cafés in town.

Getting There & Away

Three buses a day run to Sarajevo from Zagreb (54KM; eight hours), four from Split (39KM; seven to eight hours) and three from Dubrovnik (8½ hours; four in summer). Three daily buses also go to and from Banja Luka. **Centrotrans** *(☎ 532 874; Niže Banje 1)*, at Mula Mustafe Bašekije, is helpful in providing bus times.

For buses to Belgrade (20KM; seven per day) and the RS, ask a taxi driver to take you to the station (☎ 057-677 377) in Lukavica, a Sarajevo suburb in the RS. The Sarajevo tourist office has a schedule of these buses.

Trains run once a day to Zagreb (single/return 44/71KM; nine hours) via Banja Luka (22/35KM). One train daily goes to Plooe (18/28KM; five hours) via Mostar (12/19KM; 2½ hours).

Getting Around

An efficient tram network runs east-west between Baščaršija and Ilidža. Tram No 4 from Baščaršija peels off at the bus station; tram 1 goes between the bus station and Ilidža. Buy tickets at kiosks near tram stations (1.20KM; 1.50KM if you buy them from the driver). Validate your ticket on board. Buses and trolleybus tickets work the same way.

Sarajevo's ubiquitous taxis all have meters that begin at 2KM and cost about 1KM per kilometre. Call **Radio Taxi** *(☎ 970)*. A taxi from the airport should cost about 15KM.

TRAVNIK

☎ 030

Tucked into a narrow valley only 90km northwest of Sarajevo, Travnik served as the seat of Turkish viziers who ruled Bosnia-Hercegovina from 1699 to 1851. Today, its lovely medieval castle and pristine natural springs are well worth a day trip from Sarajevo or a stopover en route to Banja Luka.

The **medieval fort** at the top of the hill is believed to date from the 15th century. Head up ul Hendek on the east side of town, turn right at the top of the steps and then take another right; you'll see the walkway across to the fort. If the fort's not open, ask in the museum on the right of ul Bosanska for the key. Near the base of ul Hendek lies the famous **Many Coloured Mosque** which allegedly contains hairs from Mohammed's beard. Just east of the mosque are the peaceful springs of **Plava Voda** *(Blue Water)*, a favourite summer spot.

Buses go almost hourly to Sarajevo, and four per day go to Banja Luka.

BANJA LUKA

☎ 05 • pop 239,000

With an almost total lack of traditional tourist attractions, the capital of the Republika Sprska is an excellent spot to catch daily life in action. The large 16th-century **castle** along the Vrbas River is an interesting place to explore. Note the overgrown amphitheatre, whose benches were burned for fuel during the war. Atop the Šehitluci hill, 5km southeast of town stands a huge white stone **WWII memorial**.

If you come across a bare patch of land in Banja Luka, it probably used to be one of the city's 16 destroyed mosques. The most famous was **Ferhadija** (1580), originally built with the ransom money for an Austrian count. Ground has been broken for rebuilding.

Hotel Vidović *(☎ 217 217, fax 211 100; Kozarska 85; rooms 71-87KM)*, a few kilometres from the centre, has clean, fresh rooms (rates are by room, not by person). **Restaurant Kazamat** *(mains 10-15KM)* is tucked inside the castle walls in the former prison. It serves excellent traditional food and has outdoor seating overlooking the Vrbas in summer.

Orthodox Celts *(Stevana Bulajića 12)*, a lively Irish pub that sometimes features live bands, is good for a meal of Guinness.

The train and bus stations lie roughly 3km north of the town centre; a taxi should cost 5KM. Buses run four times a day to Zagreb, three times to Sarajevo (five hours), and hourly to Belgrade (seven hours). There are also four connections to Bihac (four hours). Trains run once a day to Zagreb (4½ hours), Ljubljana (seven hours) and Sarajevo. Trains serve destinations in Republika Srpska; Banja Luka is also on the Sarajevo-Zagreb line.

Hercegovina

MOSTAR

☎ 036 • pop 120,000

Mostar is a beautiful medieval town set in the valley of the Neretva River. Sadly, the town was the scene of intense Muslim-Croat fighting during the recent war, which left many buildings destroyed or scarred. The bridge was destroyed by Croat shelling in November 1993. Once divided only by the Neretva, Mostar is now segregated into Muslim and Croat sectors. Nonetheless, visitors are drifting back to enjoy the medieval buildings, cobbled streets and Turkish souvenir shops that give Mostar its charm.

The **Atlas Travel Agency** *(☎ 326 631, ☎/fax 318 771)* has useful suggestions. In the **tourist agency** *(☎ 551 900)*, on the east side beside the bus station, staff speak English and have information and maps (3KM).

There is an **Internet café** *(Ul Kralja Petra)* just beyond Kralja Tomislava. A small **post office** *(Kralja Tomislava)* also has four computers that are linked to the Internet.

Stari Most *(Old Bridge)*, which is now being slowly rebuilt, is still the heart of the Old Town. The small Crooked Bridge, which spanned a Neretva tributary nearby, was swept away in floods.

The cobbled old town, **Kujundžiluk**, extends on both sides of Stari Most and is filled with small shops selling Turkish-style souvenirs. Along the east side, Mostar's most famous mosque is the **Karadžozbeg Mosque** (1557). The top of its minaret was blown off in the recent war.

Places to Stay & Eat

Many pansion rooms have multiple beds. Reserve a week in advance, because groups occasionally fill the space. **Private accommodation** *(25KM per person)* can be arranged through the east side tourist office.

Omer Lakiše *(☎ 551-627; Mladena Balorde 21A; rooms 15KM)* has eight beds in two rooms and is run by a retired professor who speaks a smattering of English. Breakfast is included in the price and it welcomes students.

Pansion Corić *(☎ 331 077, fax 331 078; ul Fra Didaka Buntića; beds 50KM)* is about a 20-minute walk directly west of Stari Most. Rates include an excellent breakfast, and the friendly proprietors speak German but not English.

Zdrava Hrana *(☎/fax 550 969, 551 444; Trg 1 maja 20; single/double/triple/quad 30/40/60/80KM)*, a short walk uphill on the east side, is a good budget option. A handful of small apartments have very basic cooking equipment.

Čevapi spots are everywhere, and restaurants with divine views of the river cluster along the western riverbank near Stari Most; enjoy a *šopska salata* (lettuce, tomato and grated cheese salad) and a fresh trout there.

Restaurant Taurus overlooks where the Crooked Bridge used to stand and has tables on a covered porch. The food is hearty and traditional.

Entertainment

The **Pavarotti Music Centre** *(☎ 550 7500, fax 552 081; ul Maršala Tita 179)* is the hub of Mostar's cultural activities. The reception desk keeps a schedule of free public concerts and events and the receptionist is bound to be up on the latest hot spots.

Palladium, just off ul Kralja Tvrtka near the west side roundabout, draws flocks of youth in search of disco.

Getting There & Away

Mostar lies between Sarajevo and the coast. Eight buses per day run to Sarajevo, two to Split, one to Dubrovnik and one to Zagreb. Luggage storage is available in the bus station (2KM per item per day). Several bus stops on the west side send buses to Međugorje and other parts of Hercegovina. There's also a daily train from Sarajevo to Ploče that stops in Mostar.

MEĐUGORJE

☎ 036

On 24 June 1981, six teenagers in this dirt-poor mountain village claimed they'd seen an apparition of the Virgin Mary, and Međugorje's instant economic boom began. Two decades later, Međugorje is awash with tour buses, souvenir stands, car-rental offices, travel agencies and pansions.

St James' Church is a hub of activity. An **information booth** *(☎ 651 988; W www.medjugorje.hr)* beside the church has the daily schedule, plus multilingual print outs of the Virgin's monthly message. **Apparition Hill**, where the Virgin was spotted, is near the hamlet of Podbrdo southwest of town. A blue cross marks the spot.

Mt Križerac *(Cross Mountain)* lies about 1.5km southwest of town. The 45-minute hike to the top leads to a white cross planted in 1934.

With 17,000 rooms, Međugorje probably has more accommodation than the rest of Bosnia-Hercegovina combined. Set about 100m back from the street, the whitewashed **Pansion Santa Maria** *(☎ 651 523, fax 651 723; B&B/half-board/full-board 25/36/50KM per person)*, just past the post office, has pleasant rooms. **Pansion Međugorje** *(☎ 651 315, fax 651 452; B&B 20KM, half/full board per person 30/40KM)* is a homy gem on the road to Cross Mountain. The half- or full-board option at the pansions includes a very hearty meat-and-bread meal.

Most visitors come to Međugorje from Croatia. Globtour runs two buses daily from Split (3½ hours), one from Dubrovnik (three hours) and one from Zagreb (nine hours). Four buses run daily between Međugorje and Mostar (40 minutes). Four buses daily come from Sarajevo (three to four hours).

Britain

Little more than a speck in the centre of the map, the humble island of Britain once ruled half the earth. Through an unprecedented combination of commercial prowess and military puissance, the British spread their culture, traditions and language worldwide. Their legacy has inspired a curious mix of resentment and awe, resulting in people around the globe imitating British customs while railing against all that is British. For those whose countries once lay in the shadow of Britain's empire, a visit to the isle can involve a peculiar blend of homecoming and confrontation.

The island is still a cultural mecca, and students of history and the arts will not be disappointed by the homeland of Chaucer and Shakespeare. But to the surprise of many, Britain remains one of the most beautiful islands in the world. The country that inspired Wordsworth, Coleridge and Keats has been immortalised in countless literary works, paintings and pictures that appear exaggerated but are remarkably accurate. Britain is small, but the more you explore the bigger it seems to become.

The sun has set on the British Empire, but nightfall is no obstacle to the British. London's reputation as a nightlife paradise is well deserved, but unexpected rivals such as Glasgow, Manchester, Newcastle and Brighton ensure that that the traveller need not bed down before the wee hours. Remember – this is the country that has presented the world with artists from the Beatles and the Rolling Stones to the Spice Girls. Be prepared.

Whatever corner of Britain your travels bring you to, you may be taken aback by the extraordinary friendliness and hospitality of the English, Scotch and Welsh. Bucking stereotypes of being rigidly formal and aloof, the British themselves may well provide the highlights of your time on the island. Since you already speak the language (well, more or less), don't hesitate to strike up conversations and explore the stories of the region on a personal level.

As an aside, the United Kingdom comprises both Britain (England, Scotland and Wales) and Northern Ireland. For reasons of geographical coherence, Northern Ireland is included in the Ireland chapter.

Britain: the Basics

Capital London

Population
56.9 million

Languages
English, Scottish Gaelic, Welsh

Currency
1 pound sterling (£) = 100 pence

Avoid at all costs Cock-a-leeky soup

Moan over Welsh weather by saying *Mae'n uffernol o oer yma.* (It's hellishly cold out here.)

Facts about Britain

This section covers general, Britain-wide information. For facts about England, Scotland and Wales, see those countries' sections, later in this chapter.

GEOGRAPHY

Britain has an area of 93,000 sq miles (240,000 sq km), about the same size as New Zealand or half the size of France. It is less than 600mi from south to north and under 300mi at its widest point.

The seas surrounding the British Isles are shallow, and also relatively warm because of the influence of the warm North Atlantic Current. This current creates a temperate, changeable, maritime climate with few extremes of temperature but few cloudless sunny days.

CLIMATE

Although the climate is mild and annual rainfall unspectacular (35 inches/912mm), grey skies can make for an utterly depressing atmosphere. Even in midsummer you can go for days without seeing the sun, and showers (or worse) should be expected. The average July temperature in London is 17.6°C (64°F), and the average January temperature is 4°C (39°F); it's generally cooler the farther north you go.

GOVERNMENT & POLITICS

In practice, the supreme body is Parliament's House of Commons. The Queen appoints the leader of the majority party in the House of Commons as prime minister.

POPULATION & PEOPLE

Britain has an average of 236 inhabitants per sq km, making the island one of the most crowded on the planet. Since WWII there has been significant immigration from the ex-colonies, especially the West Indies, Bangladesh, Pakistan and India. Outside London and big northern cities, however, the population is overwhelmingly white.

SOCIETY & CONDUCT

It is difficult to generalise about the British, but there's no doubt they are a creative, energetic and aggressive people whose impact on the world has been disproportionate to their numbers. Britain is also a country of sceptical individualists who resent any intrusion on their privacy or freedom.

LANGUAGE

English may be one of the world's most widely spoken languages, but the language as it's spoken in some parts of Britain can be incomprehensible to overseas visitors.

Facts for the Visitor

HIGHLIGHTS

Of Britain's many attractions, probably the most outstanding are:

Castles Tower of London, Windsor, Dover, Leeds (near Canterbury), Edinburgh

Cathedrals Canterbury, Salisbury, Winchester, York, Durham

Coastline Land's End to St Ives (Cornwall), Ilfracombe (Devon) to Minehead (Somerset), St David's to Cardigan (Wales), the Scottish coastline (particularly the west coast)

Historic Towns Salisbury, Winchester, Bath, Oxford, Cambridge, Shrewsbury, St David's, York, Whitby, Durham, Edinburgh, St Andrews

Houses Blenheim Palace (Oxfordshire), Castle Howard (North Yorkshire)

Museums & Galleries British Museum, Victoria & Albert Museum, Natural History Museum, National Gallery, Tate Galleries (London); HMS Victory (Portsmouth); Castle Museum (York)

National Parks & Nature Regions The Cotswolds, Exmoor National Park, Brecon Beacons National Park, Pembrokeshire Coast National Park, Peak District National Park, Lake District National Park, Scottish Highlands (especially the west coast)

Scottish Islands Orkney, Skye, Lewis and Harris

Other Highlights Avebury complex, Hadrian's Wall

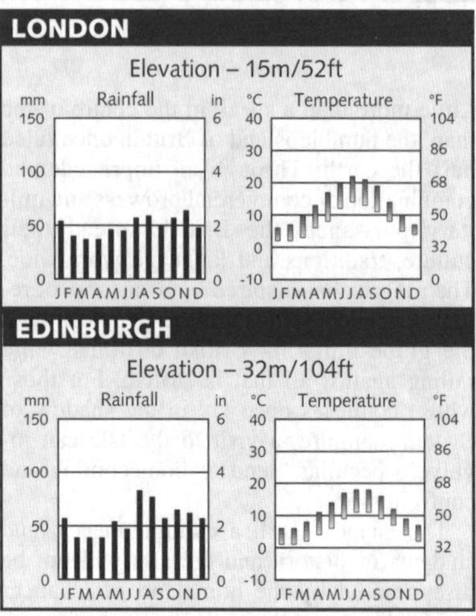

PLANNING

July and August are the busiest months, and should be avoided if possible. You are just as likely to get good weather in spring and autumn, so May to June and September to October are the best times to visit.

TOURIST OFFICES

The British Tourist Authority (BTA) has a remarkably extensive collection of information, quite a lot of it free and relevant to budget travellers. Make sure you contact the BTA before you leave home, because some of the material and discounts are only available for purchase outside Britain.

Tourist Information Centres (TICs) can be found even in small towns. They can give invaluable advice on accommodation and cheap ways of seeing the area, often including excellent guided walking tours.

There are more than 40 BTA offices worldwide. The addresses of some overseas offices are as follows:

Australia (☎ 02-9377 4400, fax 9377 4499) Level 16, The Gateway, 1 Macquarie Place, Circular Quay, Sydney, NSW 2000

Canada (☎ 905-405 1720, fax 405 1835) Suite 120, 5915 Airport Rd, Mississauga, ON L4V 1T1
New Zealand (☎ 09-303 1446, fax 776 965) Level 17, NZI House, 151 Queen St, Auckland 1
South Africa (☎ 011-325 0343) Lancaster Gate, Hyde Lane, Hyde Park, Sandton 2196
USA *Chicago:* (personal callers only) 625 N Michigan Ave, Suite 1001, Chicago IL 60611 *New York:* (☎ 1 800 GO 2 BRITAIN) Suite 701, 7th floor, 551 Fifth Ave, New York, NY 10176-0799

VISAS & DOCUMENTS

Visas

You don't need a visa if you are a citizen of Australia, Canada, New Zealand, South Africa or the USA. Tourists are generally permitted to stay for up to six months, but are prohibited from working. Citizens of the European Union (EU) can live and work in Britain free of immigration control.

Work Permits

EU nationals don't need a work permit, but all other nationalities must have one to work legally. If the *main* purpose of your visit is to work, you basically have to be sponsored by a British company. There are some exceptions for Commonwealth citizens. Inquire at the **Home Office, Immigration & Nationality Department** *(☎ 0870 606 7766; W www.ind.homeoffice.gov.uk; Lunar House, Wellesley Rd, Croydon CR9 2BY; East Croydon train station).*

EMBASSIES & CONSULATES

British Embassies

British embassies in Western Europe are listed in the relevant country chapters in this book. Other UK embassies abroad include:

Australia
British High Commission (☎ 02-6270 6666) Commonwealth Ave, Yarralumla, Canberra, ACT 2600
Canada
British High Commission (☎ 613-237 1530) 80 Elgin St, Ottawa, ON K1P 5K7
Japan
British Embassy (☎ 03-3265 5511) 1 Ichiban-cho, Chiyoda-ku, Tokyo 102
New Zealand
British High Commission (☎ 04-472 6049) 44 Hill St, Wellington 1
South Africa
British High Commission (☎ 21-461 7220) 91 Parliament St, Cape Town 8001
USA
British Embassy (☎ 202-462 1340) 3100 Massachusetts Ave NW, Washington DC 20008

Embassies & Consulates in Britain

Countries with diplomatic representation in Britain include the following:

Australian High Commission (☎ 020-7379 4334) Australia House, The Strand, London WC2; tube Temple
Canadian High Commission (☎ 020-7258 6600) 1 Grosvenor Square, London W1X; tube Bond St
French Consulate (☎ 020-7838 2000) 21 Cromwell Rd, London SW7; tube South Kensington
German Embassy (☎ 020-7824 1300) 23 Belgrave Square, London SW1; tube Hyde Park Corner
Irish Embassy (☎ 020-7235 2171) 17 Grosvenor Place, London SW1; tube Hyde Park Corner
Japanese Embassy (☎ 020-7465 6500) 101–104 Piccadilly, London W1V; tube Green Park
Netherlands Embassy (☎ 020-7590 3200) 38 Hyde Park Gate, London SW7; tube Gloucester Rd
New Zealand High Commission (☎ 020-7930 8422) New Zealand House, 80 Haymarket, London SW1; tube Piccadilly Circus
South African High Commission (☎ 020-7451 7299) South Africa House, Trafalgar Square, London WC2; tube Trafalgar Square
Spanish Consulate (☎ 020-7589 8989) 20 Draycott Place, London SW3; tube Sloane Square
US Embassy (☎ 020-7499 9000) 24 Grosvenor Square, London W1A; tube Bond St

CUSTOMS

As long as tax and duty have been paid somewhere in the EU, there is no prohibition on importing goods that are for individual consumption, from within the EU.

MONEY

Currency

No euros here! The currency is the pound sterling (£), and there are 100 pence (p) in a pound. Coins come in denominations of 1p, 2p, 5p, 10p, 20p, 50p, £1 and £2. Notes come in £5, £10, £20 and £50 denominations. You may also come across notes issued by several Scottish banks, including a £1 note; they are legal tender on both sides of the border, though shopkeepers in England and Wales may be reluctant to accept them.

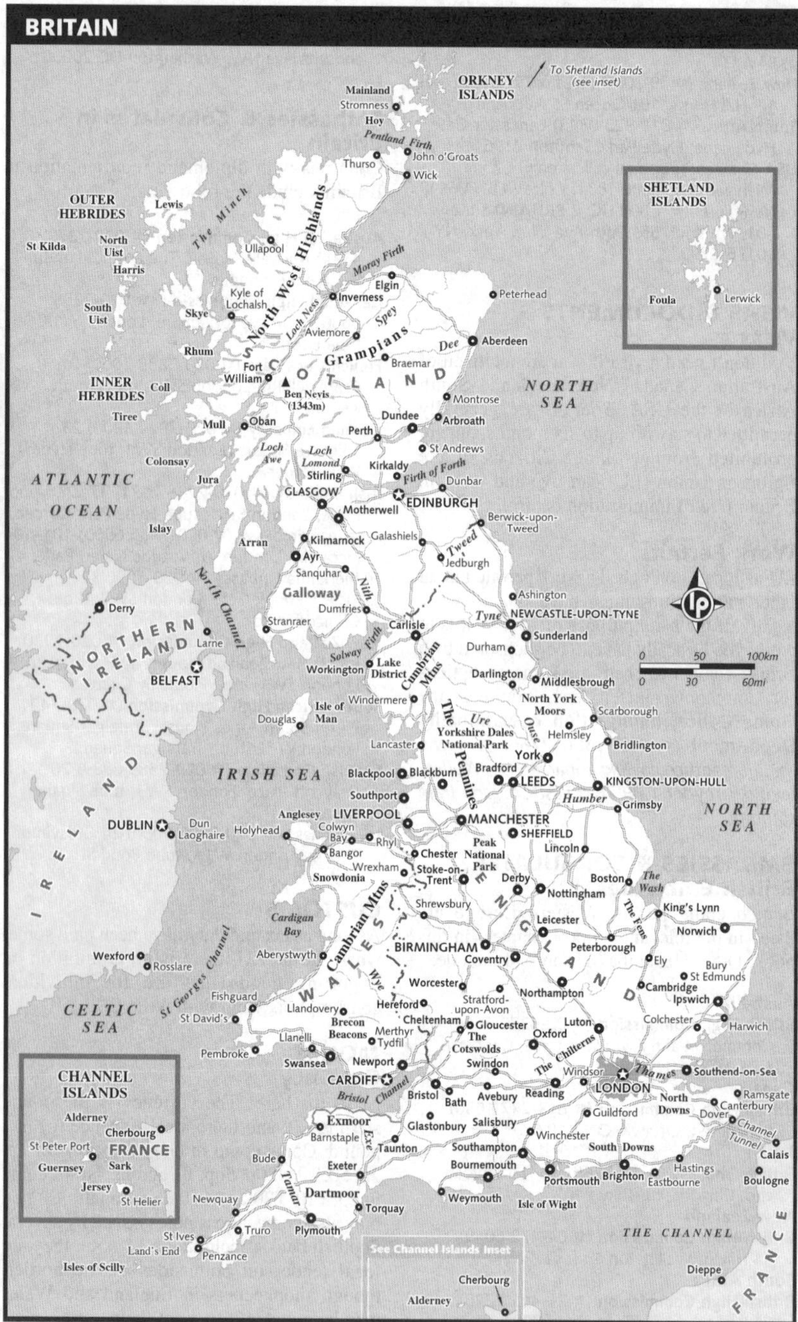
BRITAIN
ORKNEY ISLANDS
To Shetland Islands (see inset)
Mainland
Stromness
Hoy
Pentland Firth
Thurso
John o'Groats
Wick
SHETLAND ISLANDS
Foula
Lerwick
OUTER HEBRIDES
Lewis
The Minch
North West Highlands
St Kilda
North Uist
Harris
Ullapool
Moray Firth
Elgin
Kyle of Lochalsh
Inverness
Peterhead
South Uist
Skye
Loch Ness
Spey
Aviemore
Grampians
Aberdeen
Dee
Rhum
Braemar
SCOTLAND
Fort William
Ben Nevis (1343m)
INNER HEBRIDES
Coll
Montrose
NORTH SEA
Tiree
Dundee
Arbroath
Mull
Oban
Perth
St Andrews
Loch Awe
Loch Lomond
Colonsay
Kirkaldy
Firth of Forth
Stirling
Dunbar
ATLANTIC OCEAN
Jura
GLASGOW
EDINBURGH
Motherwell
Berwick-upon-Tweed
Islay
Galashiels
Arran
Kilmarnock
Tweed
Jedburgh
Ayr
North Channel
Sanquhar
Nith
Galloway
Ashington
Derry
Dumfries
Tyne
NEWCASTLE-UPON-TYNE
Stranraer
Carlisle
Sunderland
NORTHERN IRELAND
Larne
Solway Firth
Durham
BELFAST
Workington
Lake District
Cambrian Mtns
0 50 100km
0 30 60mi
Darlington
Middlesbrough
North York Moors
Windermere
Isle of Man
Douglas
Scarborough
The Pennines
Ure
Yorkshire Dales National Park
Ouse
Helmsley
Lancaster
Bridlington
IRELAND
York
Bradford
IRISH SEA
Blackpool
Blackburn
LEEDS
KINGSTON-UPON-HULL
Humber
Southport
Grimsby
NORTH SEA
Anglesey
LIVERPOOL
MANCHESTER
DUBLIN
Dun Laoghaire
Holyhead
Colwyn Bay
Rhyl
SHEFFIELD
Peak National Park
Lincoln
Bangor
Chester
Wrexham
Stoke-on-Trent
Snowdonia
Derby
Boston
The Wash
Nottingham
Shrewsbury
The Fens
King's Lynn
Cardigan Bay
Leicester
Norwich
ENGLAND
BIRMINGHAM
Peterborough
Wexford
Rosslare
Aberystwyth
Cambrian Mtns
Coventry
Ely
WALES
Bury St Edmunds
St Georges Channel
Wye
Worcester
Northampton
Cambridge
Fishguard
Hereford
Stratford-upon-Avon
Ipswich
CELTIC SEA
St David's
Llandovery
Cheltenham
Gloucester
Luton
Colchester
Brecon Beacons
Merthyr Tydfil
Harwich
Llanelli
The Cotswolds
Oxford
Pembroke
The Chilterns
Swansea
Newport
Swindon
Windsor
Thames
Southend-on-Sea
CARDIFF
LONDON
CHANNEL ISLANDS
Bristol Channel
Bristol
Bath
Avebury
Reading
North Downs
Ramsgate
Canterbury
Alderney
Guildford
Dover
Cherbourg
Exmoor
Glastonbury
Salisbury
Channel Tunnel
St Peter Port
FRANCE
Barnstaple
Exe
Taunton
Winchester
Guernsey
Sark
Bude
Southampton
South Downs
Calais
Jersey
Exeter
Bournemouth
Hastings
St Helier
Tamar
Portsmouth
Brighton
Eastbourne
Boulogne
Newquay
Dartmoor
Torquay
Weymouth
Isle of Wight
Truro
Plymouth
THE CHANNEL
St Ives
Land's End
Penzance
See Channel Islands Inset
Isles of Scilly
Cherbourg
Alderney
Dieppe
FRANCE

Exchange Rates

country	unit		pound sterling
Australia	A$1	=	£0.35
Canada	C$1	=	£0.40
Eurozone	€1	=	£0.65
Japan	¥100	=	£0.50
New Zealand	NZ$1	=	£0.30
USA	US$1	=	£0.65

Exchanging Money

Exchange bureaus frequently levy outrageous commissions and fees. Travellers cheques are rarely accepted outside banks. Visa, MasterCard, Access, American Express and Diners Club cards are widely used, although most B&Bs require cash. ATMs on the Cirrus, Maestro and Plus networks are widespread.

Costs

Britain is extremely expensive and London is horrendous. While in London you will need to budget around £30 to £35 a day just for bare survival. There's not much point visiting if you can't participate in some of the city's life, so add another £15 to £20. Once you start moving around the country, you'll need and extra £20 to £25 per day.

Throughout this chapter admission costs are often given as adult/concession (students and seniors).

Tipping & Bargaining

Taxi drivers and waiters all expect 10% tips. Some restaurants include a service charge (tip) of 10% to 15% on the bill, but this should be clearly advertised. Bargaining is only really expected if you're buying second-hand gear, especially vehicles. Always check for discounts.

Taxes & Refunds

Value-added tax (VAT) is a 17.5% sales tax levied on virtually all goods and services, but not on food and books. Restaurant menu prices must by law include VAT.

In some cases it's possible to claim a refund of VAT paid on goods. If you are leaving the EU within three months of making the purchase, you are eligible.

POST & COMMUNICATIONS

Post office hours can vary, but most are open 9am to 5pm weekdays, and to noon on Saturday.

Most public phone booths are operated by British Telecom (BT). If you're likely to make some calls (especially international), make sure you buy a phonecard. There are numerous cheap phonecards around which massively undercut BT rates on international calls. Take note however that some of these cards can only be used from a private phone. Dial ☎ 100 for a BT operator.

Note that any number that begins with the code 0870 is charged at the national rate; a number that begins with 0845 is charged at the (cheaper) local rate.

Dial ☎ 155 to get the international operator. Direct dialling is cheaper, but some budget travellers prefer operator-connected reverse-charge (collect) calls. To get an international line (for international direct dialling) dial ☎ 00, then the country code, area code (drop the first zero if there is one) and number. Britain's country code is ☎ 44.

To collect email visit one of the growing number of Internet cafés. Some hostels and pubs also offer Internet services. Expect to pay around £2 or £3 per hour. Alternatively many public libraries offer free Internet access, but you often need to book in advance.

DIGITAL RESOURCES

Britain is second to the USA in its number of websites. Attractions, towns, tourist boards, hostels, B&Bs, hotels and transportation companies all have websites. Also see the UK Travel Guide (W www.uktravel.com).

BOOKS

There are countless guidebooks covering every nook and cranny in the British Isles. Look for Lonely Planet's *Britain*, *England*, *Scotland* or *Wales* guidebooks as well as the *London* and *Edinburgh* city guides. *London Condensed* provides essential information in a handy format.

For in-depth information on history, art and architecture, the *Blue Guide* series is excellent.

Hikers and cyclists should check Lonely Planet's *Walking in Britain* and *Cycling Britain* guides.

WOMEN TRAVELLERS

Lone women travellers should have no problems, although common-sense caution should be observed in big cities. Hitching, though, is extremely risky.

The **Council Rape & Crisis Support Group** (*☎ 020-8572 0100*) gives confidential advice and support to women who have been sexually assaulted.

GAY & LESBIAN TRAVELLERS

London, Manchester and Brighton are Britain's main gay and lesbian centres. You'll also find gay and lesbian information centres in most other cities and large towns. Check the listings in *Gay Times*, available from newsagents, for details of major events such as London Pride (end of June or early July).

DISABLED TRAVELLERS

The **Royal Association for Disability and Rehabilitation** (*RADAR; ☎ 020-7250 3222; 12 City Forum, 250 City Rd, London EC1V 8AF*) publishes a useful guide, *Holidays and Travel Abroad: A Guide for Disabled People*, which gives a good overview of facilities available. For disabled travellers in the capital, it also stocks *Access in London* (£8).

SENIOR TRAVELLERS

All senior citizens (over 60) are entitled to discounts on public transport, museum admission fees etc, provided they show proof of their age. Rail companies offer a Senior Citizens' Railcard (£18 for one year) giving a third off fares. Bus companies have similar cards.

DANGERS & ANNOYANCES

Britain is remarkably safe considering its size and the disparities in wealth. However, city crime is certainly not unknown. Pickpockets and bag snatchers operate in crowded public places.

When travelling by tube at night in London, choose well-lit, populated stations and carriages.

Hotel/hostel touts descend on backpackers at London Underground stations such as Earl's Court, Liverpool St and Victoria. Don't accept offers of free lifts. Be careful of unauthorised taxi drivers approaching you at these same stations.

Emergencies

The emergency number for the police, fire brigade and ambulance is ☎ 999. The Europe-wide telephone number ☎ 112 can also be used. See Car & Motorcycle in the introductory Getting Around section later in this chapter for information regarding roadside assistance in the event of breakdown.

BUSINESS HOURS

Offices are open 9am to 5pm weekdays. Shops may be open for longer hours, and all shops are open 9am to 5pm Saturday. Except in rural areas, some shops also open 10am to 4pm Sunday. Late-night shopping is usually possible on Thursday or Friday. Some supermarkets are open 24 hours.

PUBLIC HOLIDAYS & SPECIAL EVENTS

Most banks, businesses and a number of museums and other places of interest are closed on public holidays (also known as Bank Holidays): New Year's Day (1 January), 2 January (Bank Holiday in Scotland), Good Friday, Easter Monday (not in Scotland), May Day Bank Holiday (first Monday in May), Spring Bank Holiday (last Monday in May), Summer Bank Holiday (last Monday in August, first Monday in August in Scotland), Christmas Day (25 December) and Boxing Day (26 December).

There are countless, diverse special events held around the country all year. Even small villages have weekly markets, and many still enact traditional customs and ceremonies, some of which are believed to date back thousands of years. For local special events, see individual city sections.

ACTIVITIES

Cycling

You should be able to hire a three-speed bicycle for around £25 per week, or a mountain bike for £60. Book ahead if you want a bike in July or August.

Bicycles can be taken on most rail services, but the regulations are complex and inconsistent so it is essential to check in advance. The major bus operators (National Express, Citylink etc) don't carry bikes, but most local bus lines do.

The **Cyclists' Touring Club** (*☎ 0870 873 0061; Ⓦ www.ctc.org.uk; Cotterell House, 69 Meadrow, Godalming, Surrey GU7 3HS*) is a national cycling association that can provide a great deal of helpful information.

For ideas on where to tour, check Lonely Planet's *Cycling Britain*.

Walking

This is great walking country. The countryside is crisscrossed by a network of rights of way, or public footpaths, most of them crossing private land. It's often easy to put together walks that connect with public transport and take you from village to village.

For long-distance walks, the best areas include the Cotswolds, Exmoor National Park, North York Moors National Park, Yorkshire Dales National Park, the Lake District, Pembrokeshire Coast National Park and the Scottish islands.

Those intent on a serious walking holiday should contact the **Ramblers' Association** *(☎ 020-7339 8500; Ⓦ www.ramblers.org.uk; Camelford House, 87-90 Albert Embankment, London SE1 7TW)*.

Lonely Planet's *Walking in Britain* details more than a dozen long-distance paths, together with a wide selection of shorter walks and day-hikes.

Boating

Even budget travellers should consider the possibility of hiring a canal boat and cruising part of the extraordinary 2000mi network of canals that has survived the railway era.

Especially if you hire a boat outside the high season, prices are quite reasonable, ranging from about £350 per week in April to £700 in August for a boat that sleeps four. Try **Alvechurch Boat Centres** *(☎ 0121-445 2909)* or **Hoseason's Holidays** *(☎ 01502-501501)*.

The **Inland Waterways Association** *(☎ 01923-711114; PO Box 114, Rickmansworth, Herts WD3 1ZY)* publishes an annual *Directory* (£4) and can provide mail-order maps and guides.

ACCOMMODATION

This will almost certainly be your single largest expense. Even camping can be expensive at official sites. For travel on the cheap, there are really only three options: hostels, B&Bs and some hotels. TICs can help with bookings, sometimes with a fee.

Camping

Free camping is rarely possible, except in Scotland. Camping grounds vary widely but most have reasonable facilities. For an extensive listing, buy *Camping & Caravanning in Britain* published by the **Automobile Association** *(☎ 01256-491524; £9.99)*. Some YHA hostels cater for campers.

Hikers will occasionally find camping barns – usually converted farm buildings – where you can bunk down for between £3.50 to £5 per night. Bunkhouses (from £7) are similar but have a bit more comfort.

Hostels

Hostelling International/Youth Hostel Association *(HI/YHA; ☎ 0870 870 8808, advance bookings ☎ 0870 241 2314; Ⓦ www.yha.org.uk)* membership gives you access to a huge network of hostels throughout England, Wales, Scotland and Ireland. Overseas visitors without an international membership can join through a system of 'welcome stamps', available at most hostels.

All hostels have facilities for self-catering and some have cheap meals. Advance booking is advisable, especially on weekends, Bank Holidays and anytime over the summer months. Once on the hostelling trail, you can use the YHA's free Book A Bed Ahead scheme to reserve your next night's bed at a different hostel.

Overnight prices are in two tiers: under-18s, with prices from £5.50 to £20, but mostly around £8; and adults, with prices from £7 to £24, but mostly around £11.25.

Independent Hostels

Outside London, there are more and more independent backpackers hostels, particularly in the southwest, Scotland and some of the popular walking regions. This growing network offers the opportunity to escape curfews and daytime closures for a price of around £11 per night in a basic bunkroom. *The Independent Hostel Guide* (£4.95) covers Britain and Ireland, but new places are opening fast so it's always worth asking at the TIC.

Universities

Many British universities offer their student accommodation to visitors during the Christmas, Easter and summer holidays. B&B will normally cost from £19 to £28 per person. For more information, contact the **British Universities Accommodation Consortium** *(BUAC; ☎ 0115-846 6444; Ⓦ www.buac.co.uk)*.

B&Bs, Guesthouses & Hotels

B&Bs are a great British institution and the cheapest private accommodation you can find. At the bottom end (£15 to £20 per person) you get a bedroom in a normal house, a shared bathroom and an enormous cooked breakfast. Single rooms are in short supply.

Guesthouses, which are often just large converted houses with half a dozen rooms, are an extension of the idea. They range in price from £15 to £50 per night, depending on the quality of the food and accommodation. Local pubs and inns also often have cheap rooms.

Hotels range from humble pubs to grand old castles. The national tourist boards operate a classification and grading system; participating hotels, guesthouses and B&Bs have a plaque at the front door. The first classification by the national tourist board is 'listed', denoting clean and comfortable accommodation. Better places are indicated by one to five crowns – the more crowns, the more facilities and, generally, the more expensive the room.

FOOD & DRINK

British cuisine used to crop up more often in comedy sketches than on restaurant pages, but fortunately those days are long gone. The days of the 'greasy spoon' café that used to dispense cheap breakfasts (eggs, bacon and sausages) and English tea (strong, sweet and milky) look numbered, their place taken by the ubiquitous café-bars which prefer serving pasta and pesto to beans and burgers. If you're on a tight budget, pubs will often be one of your best sources of cheap nutrition. A filling 'ploughman's lunch' of bread, cheese and pickle costs around £4.50.

British pubs generally serve an impressive range of beers – lagers, bitters, ales and stouts. If you've been raised on lager, a traditional bitter or ale is a bit of a shock – not as cold or as effervescent. Ale is similar to bitter – it's more a regional difference in name than anything else. Stout is a dark, rich, foamy drink; Guinness is the most famous brand. Good wines are widely available and very reasonably priced (except in pubs).

ENTERTAINMENT

For many Brits, the local (pub) is still the main focus for a good night out. For the visitor, the country offers some of the world's best drama, dance and music. A visit to a London theatre is a real must. TICs have lists of nightclubs and discos.

Getting There & Away

Buses are the cheapest, most exhausting method of transport, although discount rail tickets are competitively priced, and budget flights can be good value.

AIR

London is one of the world's most important transport hubs. Most travellers will find that cheap flights all wind up in one of the five London airports: Heathrow, Gatwick, Luton, Stansted and London City.

London is an excellent centre for cheap tickets; the best resource is *TNT Magazine*, but Sunday papers also carry travel ads. You can also pick up bargains with discount carriers such as Easyjet, Ryanair and Go.

Low season one-way/return flights from London bucket shops start at: Amsterdam £20/40, Athens £45/60, Frankfurt £25/45, İstanbul £50/80, Madrid £35/60, Paris £20/40 and Rome £35/65.

People taking flights from Britain need to pay an Air Passenger Duty: those flying to countries in the EU will pay £10; those flying beyond it, £20. This is usually factored into the price of your ticket.

LAND

The Channel Tunnel gives Britain a land link with Europe (albeit rail only), but even without using the tunnel, you can still get to Europe by bus or train – there's just a short ferry ride thrown in. The ferries carry cars and motorcycles.

Bus

Eurolines (*☎ 0870 514 3219; Ⓦ www.eurolines.com; 52 Grosvenor Gardens, Victoria, London SW1 • Paris ☎ 01 49 72 48 00 • Amsterdam ☎ 020-560 8788 • Brussels ☎ 02-203 07 07 • Frankfurt ☎ 069-790 32 40 • Madrid ☎ 091-327 1381 • Rome ☎ 06-884 08 40*), a division of National Express (the largest UK bus line), has an enormous network of European destinations, including Ireland and Eastern Europe.

You can book tickets through any National Express office, including Victoria coach station in London (which is where Eurolines' buses depart and arrive), and at many travel agencies.

The following one-way/return prices and journey times are representative: Amsterdam £32/52 (11 hours), Brussels £32/52 (eight hours), Frankfurt £42/69 (18½ hours), Madrid £77/89 (27 hours), Paris £32/52 (10 hours) and Rome £69/79 (36 hours).

Eurolines Explorer tickets allow travel between 46 major cities and are valid for up to six months. As an example, a 15-day pass costs £90 (€150).

Train

Three options exist for travel between England and Europe: Eurostar, Eurotunnel or train/ferry connections.

Travellers aged under 26 can pick up Billet International de Jeunesse (BIJ) tickets which cut train fares by up to 50%. Various agents issue BIJ tickets in London.

Eurostar The high-speed **Eurostar** *(☎ 0870 518 6186; Ⓦ www.eurostar.com)* passenger train service travels between London and Paris or Brussels via the Channel Tunnel. There are stops in Ashford (England) and in Lille and Calais (France). The London terminal is at Waterloo station. There are between 14 and 20 trains per day from London to Paris (£170 one way, three hours), and from eight to 12 trains daily between London and Brussels (£157, 2¾ hours). Holders of BritRail, Eurail and Euro passes are entitled to discounted fares.

Eurotunnel The **Eurotunnel** *(☎ 0870 535 3535; Ⓔ callcentre@eurotunnel.com; Ⓦ www.eurotunnel.com)* trains carry vehicles and their passengers or freight through the Channel Tunnel between Folkestone in the UK and Calais in France. The specially designed shuttle trains run 24 hours, departing up to four times an hour in each direction between 6am and 10pm, and every hour from 10pm to 6am. A car and its passengers cost between £185 and £220, depending on day and time of travel.

Train & Ferry Connections Rail and ferry links involve trains at either end and a ferry or high-speed catamaran across the Channel. Trains depart from London's Victoria, Liverpool St or Charing Cross stations, depending on the ferry terminal. Rail/ferry links include: Charing Cross–Dover–Calais (France); Charing Cross–Folkestone–Boulogne (France); and Liverpool St–Harwich–Hook of Holland (the Netherlands).

Fares from London depend on where you are travelling to in Europe. For example, London to Amsterdam via Harwich and the Stena Line high-speed catamaran costs £25/79 (7¾ hours). This price example is for an adult; youth tickets and passes are considerably lower. For inquiries concerning European trains, contact **Rail Europe** *(☎ 0870 584 8848; 179 Piccadilly, London W1)*.

SEA

There is a bewildering array of alternatives between Britain and mainland Europe. The entire market is now so competitive there are constant special deals. Return tickets may be much cheaper than two one-way fares. Unless otherwise noted, the prices quoted for cars don't include passengers.

France

On a clear day, you can see across the Channel. A true budget traveller would obviously swim – it's only seven hours and 40 minutes if you match the record.

Dover The shortest ferry link to Europe is between Dover and Calais. **P&O Stena Line** *(☎ 0870 600 0600)* operates ferries roughly every 45 minutes from Dover to Calais (1¼ hours). It charges one-way foot passengers £26; a car plus 2/9 passengers costs from £139/154; motorcycle prices (including driver and passenger) start at £89. Special offers make a big difference.

Hoverspeed *(☎ 0870 240 8070)* uses high-speed catamarans, called Seacats, between Dover and Calais (45 minutes). It charges £24 for either a one-way passenger or for a five-day return. A car plus two/five passengers costs £110/115 for a standard one-way fare, or £137/147 for a five-day return.

Portsmouth Another option to France is a **P&O** *(☎ 0870 242 4999)* ferry to/from either Cherbourg (one to five ferries per day) or Le Havre (two to three per day). The day ferries to Cherbourg take 2¾ to five hours; to Le Havre takes 5½ hours. The night crossings are longer, taking seven to eight hours and 7½ hours, respectively. One-way foot passenger fares start at £12, and a car costs from a bargain £15 to a steep £120.

Brittany Ferries *(☎ 0870 536 0360)* has at least one sailing a day to/from Caen (six hours) and St Malo (8¾ hours).

Belgium, the Netherlands & Germany

There are direct links with Germany but many people prefer to drive to/from the Dutch or Belgian ferry ports.

Dover To Belgium, **Hoverspeed** *(☎ 0870 240 8070)* has regular high-speed ferries sailing daily to Ostend (one to two hours depending on the ferry). The fare for one-way foot passengers is £24.

Harwich Ferries to Hamburg are run by **DFDS Seaways** *(☎ 0870 533 3000)*. **Stena Line** *(☎ 0870 570 7070)* has high-speed ferries to Hook of Holland.

Newcastle Another option for getting to the Netherlands is a **DFDS Seaways** *(☎ 0870 533 3000)* ferry.

Spain

From Plymouth, **Brittany Ferries** *(☎ 0870 536 0360)* operates ferries to Santander. **P&O** *(☎ 0870 242 4999)* operates a service between Portsmouth and Bilbao.

Scandinavia

Until you see the ferry possibilities, it's easy to forget how close Scandinavia and Britain are.

Aberdeen & Lerwick (Shetland) A very interesting possibility is the summer-only link (15 May–early Sept, once a week) between Aberdeen or Shetland and Norway (£97/117 one way in low/high season, 13½ hours) or Shetland to Iceland (via the Faroe Islands, 31 hours). The operator is **Smyril Line Shetland** *(☎ 01595-690845)*.

Newcastle Norway's **Fjord Line** *(☎ 0191-296 1313)* operates ferries year-round to Stavanger, Haugesund and Bergen in Norway. **DFDS Seaways** *(☎ 0870 533 3000)* operates ferries twice a week to Gothenburg in Sweden via Kristiansand in Norway.

Harwich Ferries run by **DFDS Seaways** *(☎ 0870 533 3000)* go to Esbjerg, Denmark.

Getting Around

Although public transport is generally of a high standard, it's not great in national parks and small villages. With a mix of local buses, the occasional taxi, plenty of time, walking and occasionally hiring a bike, you can get almost anywhere.

Buses are nearly always the cheapest way to get around. With discount passes and tickets, trains can be competitive. Ticket types and prices vary considerably, advance purchase often saving you as much as 50% of the full-price fare.

The BTA's excellent brochure, *Getting About Britain for the Independent Traveller*, gives details of bus, train, plane and ferry transport around Britain and into mainland Europe.

BUS

Road transport in Britain is almost entirely privately owned and run. **National Express** *(☎ 0870 580 8080; Ⓦ www.gobycoach.com)* runs the largest national network, but there are often smaller competitors on main routes. In Britain, long-distance express buses are usually referred to as 'coaches'.

For information on the fast-changing and often chaotic timetables, telephone the national public transport information line, **Traveline** *(☎ 0870 608 2608; 8am-8pm)*. A variety of passes and discounts are available. Contact National Express for details.

Hop-On Hop-Off Buses

Stray Travel Network *(Slowcoach; ☎ 020-7373 7737)* is an excellent bus service designed especially for those staying in hostels, but useful for all budget travellers. Buses run on a regular circuit between London, Windsor, Bath, Wales, the Lake District, Edinburgh, York, Stratford-upon-Avon and London, calling at hostels. You can get on and off the bus where you like and catch another one as it comes along (at least twice a week and almost daily in peak season).

There are four ticket options: one day costs £34, three days in two months is £109, four days in two months £129 and six days in four months £159. The price includes some activities and visits en route. Tickets are available from branches of STA Travel.

Postbus

Royal Mail postbuses provide a reliable service to remoter areas and can be useful for walkers. For information and timetables, contact **Customer Services** *(☎ 01246-546329)*.

TRAIN

Britain still has an impressive rail service. There are several particularly recommended trips on beautiful lines through sparsely populated country, the most famous being in Wales and Scotland. The main routes are served by excellent intercity trains that travel at speeds of up to 140mph. Unless otherwise stated, prices quoted in this chapter are for adult one-way tickets. Unfortunately, Eurail passes are not recognised in Britain.

The main railcards are accepted by all the companies, and travellers are able to buy a ticket to any destination from any rail station or from authorised travel agencies.

Passengers can travel only on services provided by the company who issued their ticket, and each company is able to set whatever fare it chooses.

BritRail Passes

For visitors, BritRail passes are the most interesting possibility, but they are *not available in Britain* and must be bought in your country of origin.

A BritRail Classic pass, which allows unlimited travel, can be bought for eight, 15, 22 or 30 days. An eight-day pass for an adult/youth is US$265/215, a 15-day pass is US$399/279, a 22-day pass is US$499/355 and a 30-day pass is US$599/415.

A BritRail plus Ireland pass costs US$399 for five days in a month or US$569 for 10 days in a month and includes unlimited rail travel in both countries and a return ferry trip.

An even more useful deal is the Flexipass, which allows four days (adult/youth US$235/185), eight days (US$339/239) or 15 days (US$515/359) of unlimited travel within two months.

Rail Rovers

The domestic versions of these passes are called BritRail Rovers: a seven-day All Line Rover is £325/215 for an adult/youth, and 14 days is £495/330. There are also regional Rovers.

Railcards

Various railcards, available from major stations, give a third off most tickets and are valid for a year. The Young Person's Railcard (£18) is for people aged from 16 to 25, or for those studying full time. You'll need a passport photo and proof of age (birth certificate or passport) or student status. There are also railcards for seniors (over 60s; £18), disabled people (£14) and families (£20).

Tickets

Like the airlines, each train operating company (TOC) has its own discount scheme and promotional fares. You can just roll up to a station and buy a standard one-way or return ticket on the day you want, but this is the most expensive way to go. If you don't have a pass, the cheapest tickets must be bought at least one week in advance and you have to commit yourself to travelling on specified trains. Contact **National Rail Enquiries** *(☎ 0845 748 4950; W www.nationalrail.co.uk)* for timetables, fares and the numbers to ring for credit-card bookings.

CAR & MOTORCYCLE

Rental is expensive in Britain; often you will be best off making arrangements in your home country. The large international rental companies charge from around £160 per week for a small car (Ford Fiesta, Peugeot 106). **Holiday Autos** *(☎ 0870 400 0000)* operates through a number of rental companies and can generally offer excellent deals.

If you're travelling as a couple or in a group, a camper van is worth considering. **Sunseeker Rentals** *(☎ 020-8960 5747)* has four-berth and two-berth vans from £250 per week (£400 in the high season).

In the event of a breakdown, 24-hour roadside assistance is offered by the **Automobile Association** *(AA; ☎ 0800 887766)* or the **Royal Automobile Club** *(RAC; ☎ 0800 828282)*.

BICYCLE

See Activities in the Facts about the Visitor section, earlier in this chapter.

HITCHING

If you're not worried about safety, hitching is reasonably easy, except around the big cities and built-up areas. It's against the law to hitch on motorways or the immediate slip roads.

BOAT

See the appropriate sections later in this chapter for ferry information, and the Activities section earlier in this chapter for canal boating.

England

The largest section of the British island is also the part that is linked in people's minds with all things which are 'British'. For centuries, the English have buried their identity in that of greater Britain, but as Scotland and Wales devolve, the English are rediscovering themselves.

HISTORY

England had long been settled by small bands of hunters when, around 4000 BC, stone-tool users arrived from Europe. They farmed the chalk hills radiating from Salisbury Plain, and began the construction of stone tombs and, around 3000 BC, the great ceremonial complexes at Avebury and Stonehenge. The next great influx were the Celts. In AD 43, the Romans arrived in force. But by the 4th century the empire was in retreat. The British were left to the mercies of the Angles, Jutes and Saxons. Next, the Norwegian Vikings conquered northern Scotland, Cumbria and Lancashire, and the Danes conquered eastern England. They were finally stopped by Alfred the Great, and he and his successors created a tenuously unified country.

In 1066 the Norman Prince William landed with 12,000 men and defeated Prince Harold at the Battle of Hastings. English aristocrats were replaced by French-speaking Normans, dominating castles were built and the feudal system was imposed.

In the 12th century, disputes over royal succession led to the 1215 signing of the Magna Carta, in which King John ceded many important powers to Parliament. The final victor of the 30-year War of the Roses was Henry VII, the first Tudor king.

Breaking with Rome, Parliament made Henry VIII the head of the Church of England. The 16th century was a golden age of humanism and the arts, seeing both William Shakespeare and Francis Bacon. After Elizabeth I (Henry's daughter), the relationship between Parliament and the Stuart kings deteriorated. Civil war between Catholic royalists and Protestant Puritans broke out in 1642. Parliament found a brilliant leader in Oliver Cromwell; the royalists were defeated and then in 1649 Charles I was executed. Cromwell assumed dictatorial powers, but he also laid the foundation for the British Empire by modernising the army and navy. Two years after his death in 1658, Parliament recalled Charles II from exile.

The Restoration was a period of expansion; colonies stretched down the American coast and the East India Company established its headquarters in Mumbai (Bombay). In the 18th century, Sir Robert Walpole became the first prime minister in all but name. By 1770 France had ceded all of Canada and surrendered all but two of its trading stations in India, while Captain Cook claimed Australia for Britain in 1778. The empire's first major reverse came when the American colonies won their independence in 1783.

Also in the 1780s arose the first developments that would lead to the Industrial Revolution. By the time Queen Victoria took the throne in 1837, Britain was the greatest power in the world. Under prime ministers Disraeli and Gladstone, the worst excesses of the Industrial Revolution were addressed, education became universal and the right to vote was extended to most men.

The old order was shattered by the Great War (WWI). In the late 1920s the world economy slumped, ushering in more than a decade of misery and political upheaval. By mid-1940, most of Europe was either ruled by or under the direct influence of the Nazis, and Britain, under the extraordinary leadership of Winston Churchill, was virtually isolated. Between July and October 1940 the Royal Air Force won the Battle of Britain (43,000 Britons died in the bombing raids of 1940–41).

The postwar years have been challenging. The last of the empire has gained independence, many traditional industries have collapsed and it has had to accept a new role as a partner in the EU. Britain has entered the 21st century as a wealthy and influential country, but no longer a superpower.

London

☎ 020 • pop 7.4 million

Mighty London exudes the splendour of a bygone age. Its majestic architecture, dignified traditions and glorious monuments all point to a nearly unparalleled imperial history. At the same time, though, London has been heralded as the 'coolest, hottest city in the world' – the very image of modernity. Indeed, the capital is a combination of the establishment and the avant-garde. Afternoon tea, pomp and all that was quintessentially English sit comfortably alongside international cuisine, world music and all that is quintessentially contemporary. It's a magnificent juxtaposition.

There's no denying that London is a tug on the purse strings. Unfortunately, the most extortionate prices are slapped on items vital to a traveller – hotels, food and drink. Thankfully, there's plenty to do for free or very little – from big-name museums and galleries to a stroll in the royal parks or watching Covent Garden's quirky street entertainers. And, in the end, you get what you pay for: splash out occasionally and keep your eyes open, and you can't help but get caught up in London's vibrancy.

History

The Romans are credited with founding Londinium in AD 43. In the 9th century, the capital moved from Winchester to London. William the Conqueror raised the White Tower (the core of the Tower of London) and confirmed the city's independence and right to self-government.

Medieval Tudor and Jacobean London were virtually destroyed, first by the Plague of 1665, and then the Great Fire of 1666. But by 1720 there were 750,000 inhabitants, and London, as the seat of Parliament and focal point for a growing empire, was becoming ever more important.

After WWII, ugly housing and low-cost developments were thrown up on bombed sites. The docks recovered only in the 1980s. In 2000, London elected its first true mayor, Ken Livingstone.

Orientation

Walking around is the best way to get a grip on London's geography. But if you're pressed for time, the temperamental Underground railway system (the 'tube') will be your travelling habitat. Each line has its own colour, immortalised in the indispensable Underground map.

Most important sights, theatres, restaurants and even some cheap places to stay lie north of the River Thames within the fairly compact rectangle formed by the tube's Circle Line.

Lonely Planet's *London City Map* has three separate maps at different scales as well as an inset map of Theatreland and an index.

The City & East Once the site of the original London settled by the Romans, the aptly named City is now London's financial heartland. Major sights include the Tower of London and St Paul's Cathedral, Spitalfields market, the Guildhall and the Barbican.

To the east, beyond the Circle Line, is the East End, now a trendy, multicultural melting pot. Farther east again lies the Docklands.

The West West of the City are Holborn (Britain's sedate legal nucleus) and Bloomsbury (synonymous with the literary world). Besides dozens of specialist shops, this is where you'll find that unrivalled treasure chest – the British Museum.

The West End proper lies west of Tottenham Court Rd and Covent Garden. It includes such magnets as Trafalgar Square, the restaurants and clubs of lively and infamous Soho, the West End cinemas and theatres around Piccadilly Circus and Leicester Square, and the elegant shops of Regent and Bond Sts. St James's and Westminster, the political hub, lie to the southwest. To the south of Victoria station lies Pimlico. Earl's Court, South Kensington and Chelsea are in the southwestern corner formed by the Circle Line.

The North Notting Hill is a lively, cosmopolitan district that gets trendier by the day. North of Kensington Gardens and Hyde Park, Bayswater and Paddington are virtual tourist ghettos.

The South The British Airways London Eye observation wheel across from Parliament and the huge Tate Modern gallery on the Thames in Southwark are the most notable of scores of developments that are transforming an ugly, concrete mass of a neighbourhood.

Information

Time Out magazine (out Tuesday; £2.20) is a listings guide covering everything from clubs, music and theatre events, to films, books and comedy nights. It's highly recommended. Free magazines are available at most hostels and from pavement bins, especially in Bayswater, Earl's Court and Islington.

Tourist Offices London's TICs are extremely helpful and packed to the hilt with useful information. They can also offer a range of practical information and advice on travelling to other parts of the UK and the rest of the world.

Britain Visitor Centre (1 Regent St SW1Y 4XT; open daily). A two-minute walk from Piccadilly Circus, this is a one-stop shop for information on London, with the tourist boards of Wales, Scotland and Ireland ready to provide assistance too. If you need further information on Britain or Ireland and aren't able to get to Regent St, then call the British Tourist Authority (BTA) general inquiries line (☎ 8846 9000).

London Tourist Information Centres There are TICs in the Underground concourse of Heathrow Terminals 1, 2 and 3, in the Arrivals Hall at Waterloo International Terminal and at Liverpool St Underground station. There are also information desks at Gatwick, Stansted and Luton airports. The offices are all open daily. Written inquiries should be sent to the London Tourist Board & Convention Bureau, Glen House, Stag Place, London SW1E 5LT (fax 7932 0222).

Money Banks and ATMs abound across central London. All the airports have foreign-exchange offices.

American Express *(main office: ☎ 7930 4411; 6 Haymarket; tube Piccadilly Circus; open 9am-5.30pm Mon-Fri, 9am-4pm Sat & Sun, longer hours June-Sept)* has currency exchange.

Thomas Cook *(main office: ☎ 7853 6400; 30 St James's St SW1; tube Green Park; open 9am-5.30pm Mon, Tues, Thur & Fri, 10am-5.30pm Wed)* has many branches scattered around central London.

Post & Communications Poste-restante mail goes to **Trafalgar Square Post Office** *(24-28 William IV St WC2N 4DL; tube Charing Cross)*. Mail is held for four weeks.

CallShop International *(181a Earl's Court Rd; tube Earl's Court; open 10am-10.30pm daily)* has lower charges than British Telecom (BT) for international calls and also has photocopying and faxing facilities.

There are numerous Internet cafés dotted around the capital, but it's often cheaper to head for the huge 24-hour **easyEverything** outlets. A £1 voucher will usually buy 40 minutes, with some vouchers being transferable between locations. Branches include:

Kensington (☎ 7938 1814) 160-166 Kensington High St W8; tube High St Kensington

Kings Rd 120 Kings Rd SW3; tube Sloane Square

Oxford St (☎ 7491 8986) 358 Oxford St W1; tube Bond St

Tottenham Court Rd (☎ 7436 1771) 9-16 Tottenham Court Rd W1; tube Tottenham Court Rd

Trafalgar Square (☎ 7930 4094) 7 The Strand WC2; tube Charing Cross

Victoria (☎ 7233 8456); 9-13 Wilton Rd SW1; tube Victoria

Travel Agencies Refer to the Sunday papers (especially the *Sunday Times*), *TNT Magazine* and *Time Out* for listings of cheap flights. Long-standing and reliable firms include:

London Flight Centre (☎ 7727 4290) 47 Notting Hill Gate; tube Notting Hill Gate

STA Travel (☎ 7361 6262) 86 Old Brompton Rd SW7; tube South Kensington

Trailfinders (☎ 7938 3939) 194 Kensington High St W8; tube High St Kensington; for travel centre & 1st- & business-class flights; 215 Kensington High St W8; tube High St Kensington; for transatlantic & European flights

Medical & Emergency Services Dial ☎ 999 (free) for fire, police or ambulance. The following hospitals have 24-hour accident and emergency departments:

Chelsea & Westminster Hospital (☎ 8746 8000) 396 Fulham Rd SW10; tube Fulham Broadway

University College Hospital (☎ 7387 9300) Grafton Way WC1; tube Euston Square

Drop-in doctor services or MediCentres have opened in several main line railway stations but their charges can be high. You could try **NHS Direct** *(☎ 0845 4647; 24hr service)* for help with diagnosis and further advice. All pharmacies display the address of the nearest late-night pharmacy in their windows.

Dangers & Annoyances Crime in London shouldn't be downplayed – especially after dark. Your main hazard will be pickpockets, whose haunts include the tube, Oxford St and Leicester Square. Care and attention should also be taken when using ATMs.

Food from mobile street carts, though temptingly cheap, should be treated warily.

Things to See & Do

Walking Tour The centre of London can easily be explored on foot. The following walking tour will introduce you to the West End, the South Bank and Westminster.

Start at one of London's most enduring sites – **St Paul's Cathedral** *(adult/concession/child £6/5/3)*, completed in 1710 – and marvel at Christopher Wren's masterpiece.

From the cathedral, walk down to the Thames. Here you can cross the **Millennium Bridge** directly to the **Tate Modern**. It's difficult to decide whether the exhibits housed in this huge old Bankside Power Station are the expressions of very talented or very disturbed minds.

Walk west along the river past the **Oxo Tower**. It's difficult to miss the 450ft **British Airways London Eye** *(☎ 0870 500 0600; adult/concession/child £11.50/10.50/6)*. On a rare, clear day you can see for 25mi.

Continue under the **Hungerford Bridge** to **County Hall** and visit the famous *Mae West Lips Sofa* at the **Dalí Universe** *(☎ 7620 2720; adult/concession/child £8.50/7.50/4.95)*. Return to and cross the Hungerford Bridge, cut through Charing Cross station and walk east along the Strand to Southampton St and head north to **Covent Garden piazza**. Once London's fruit and vegetable market, the piazza is now home to a colourful variety of street performers and a million and one tourists.

Leave the piazza walking southwest on Long Acre. Continue across Charing Cross Rd (where Long Acre becomes Coventry St) to **Leicester Square**, with its cinemas and statues of Charlie Chaplin and Shakespeare. Continue along Coventry St to **Piccadilly Circus**, the neon capital of London. Regent St curves out of the northwestern corner; at the northeastern corner is Shaftesbury Avenue – a theatregoer's mecca. This eventually runs back into chaotic **Soho**, where it's cheap eats by day, a bouncing red-light and gay district by night.

Continue west along Piccadilly and ogle another Wren offering, **St James's church**. Return to Piccadilly and continue southwest until you reach St James's St on your left. This runs down to **St James's Palace**, the royal home from 1660 to 1837. It's now the home of Prince Charles. Skirt around its eastern side and you come to The Mall.

Trafalgar Square is to the east, **Buckingham Palace** *(☎ 7321 2233; adult/concession/child £11.50/9.50/6; open 9.30am-4.15pm daily in summer only)* to the west. Don't be surprised if the palace's 19 state rooms remind you of a series of ornate hotel lobbies. From mid-April to late July the changing of the guard happens outside Buckingham Palace at 11.30am daily; the rest of the year (weather permitting) it's at 11.30am on alternate days.

Walk across St James's Park, following the lake to its eastern end. Turn right onto Horse Guards Rd, then turn left onto Great George St, which takes you through to stunning Westminster Abbey, the Houses of Parliament and Westminster Bridge. **Westminster Abbey** *(adult/concession/child £6/3/free)* is so rich in history you need a few hours to do it justice. The coronation chair, where all but two monarchs since 1066 have been crowned, is behind the altar, and many greats – from Darwin to Chaucer – have been buried here. It also houses the grave of the Unknown Warrior.

The **Houses of Parliament** *(☎ 7219 4272)* and the clock tower (actually its bell), **Big Ben**, were built in the 19th century in neo-Gothic style. The best way to get into the building is to attend the Commons or Lords visitors' galleries during a parliamentary debate.

Walking away from Westminster Bridge, turn right onto Parliament St, which becomes Whitehall. On your left, the hard-to-see, unspectacular house at **No 10 Downing St** is the official residence of the prime minister.

Finally, you reach **Trafalgar Square** with its many pigeons and Nelson's Column. The **National Gallery** and **National Portrait Gallery**, both free, are on the northern side.

Tower of London Home to the dazzling Crown Jewels, Beefeaters and ravens, the **Tower of London** *(☎ 7709 0765; tube Tower Hill; adult/concession/child £11.50/8.75/7.50; open 9am-5pm Mon-Sat, 10am-5pm Sun)* has been a fortress, royal residence, prison and place of execution. It's one of London's most popular attractions and in summer, it shows. If you want to avoid the inevitable admission queues, buy your tickets in advance at any Underground station.

For some amazing views of London's skyline, be sure to stop at the Gothic spires of **Tower Bridge** *(☎ 7403 3761; adult/concession/child £4.50/3/3; open 9.30am-5pm daily)*.

Greenwich To fully explore Greenwich you need time. It can be reached via the Dockland's Light Railway from Tower Gateway, Bank or Canary Wharf tube stations. At the Cutty Sark stop, turn left out of the station and head west along Creek Road. At the crossroads, turn left down Greenwich Church St and continue until you reach the **Cutty Sark** *(☎ 8858 3445; adult/concession/child £3.90/2.90/2.90)*, the only surviving tea-and-wool clipper and arguably one of the most beautiful

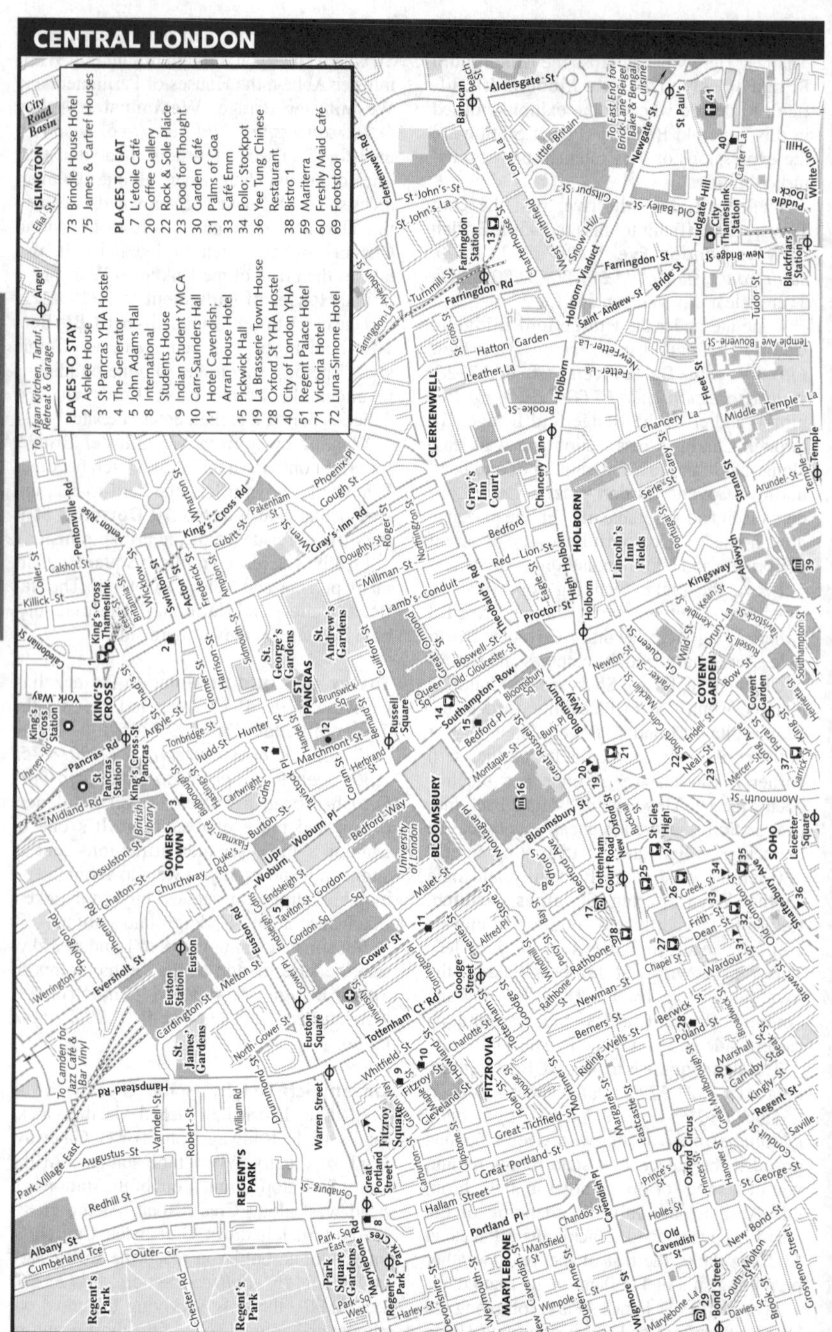
CENTRAL LONDON
PLACES TO STAY
2 Ashlee House
3 St Pancras YHA Hostel
4 The Generator
5 John Adams Hall
8 International Students House
9 Indian Student YMCA
10 Carr-Saunders Hall
11 Hotel Cavendish; Arran House Hotel
15 Pickwick Hall
19 La Brasserie Town House
28 Oxford St YHA Hostel
40 City of London YHA
51 Regent Palace Hotel
71 Victoria Hotel
72 Luna-Simone Hotel
73 Brindle House Hotel
75 James & Cartref Houses
PLACES TO EAT
7 L'etoile Café
20 Coffee Gallery
22 Rock & Sole Plaice
23 Food for Thought
30 Garden Café
31 Palms of Goa
33 Café Emm
34 Pollo; Stockpot
36 Yee Tung Chinese Restaurant
38 Bistro 1
59 Mariterra
60 Freshly Maid Café
69 Footstool
ISLINGTON
KING'S CROSS
SOMERS TOWN
ST PANCRAS
BLOOMSBURY
CLERKENWELL
HOLBORN
FITZROVIA
MARYLEBONE
SOHO
COVENT GARDEN
REGENT'S PARK
To Afgan Kitchen, Tartuf, Retreat & Garage
To Camden for Jazz Café & Bar Vinyl
To East End for Brick Lane Beigel Bake & Bengal Cuisine

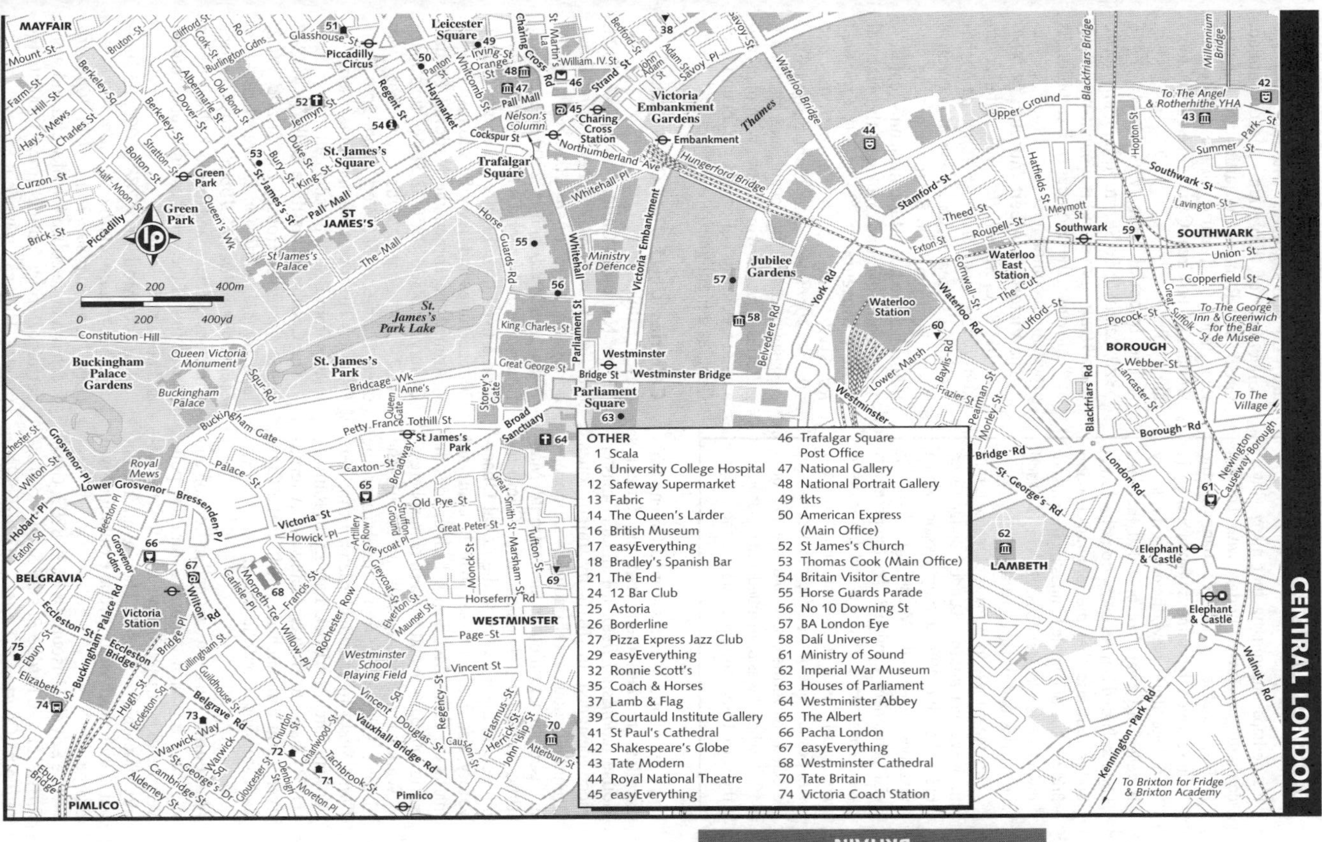
CENTRAL LONDON
OTHER
1 Scala
6 University College Hospital
12 Safeway Supermarket
13 Fabric
14 The Queen's Larder
16 British Museum
17 easyEverything
18 Bradley's Spanish Bar
21 The End
24 12 Bar Club
25 Astoria
26 Borderline
27 Pizza Express Jazz Club
29 easyEverything
32 Ronnie Scott's
35 Coach & Horses
37 Lamb & Flag
39 Courtauld Institute Gallery
41 St Paul's Cathedral
42 Shakespeare's Globe
43 Tate Modern
44 Royal National Theatre
45 easyEverything
46 Trafalgar Square Post Office
47 National Gallery
48 National Portrait Gallery
49 tkts
50 American Express (Main Office)
52 St James's Church
53 Thomas Cook (Main Office)
54 Britain Visitor Centre
55 Horse Guards Parade
56 No 10 Downing St
57 BA London Eye
58 Dalí Universe
61 Ministry of Sound
62 Imperial War Museum
63 Houses of Parliament
64 Westminister Abbey
65 The Albert
66 Pacha London
67 easyEverything
68 Westminster Cathedral
70 Tate Britain
74 Victoria Coach Station

Falling Down, Falling Down

It's perhaps unsurprising that many visitors conflate the Tower Bridge with London Bridge, another structure spanning the Thames, given the former's ubiquitousness in tourist literature. Nevertheless, some savvy travellers are aware not only that the sleek London Bridge is miles away from the Tower Bridge, but also that the 'original' London Bridge – the one made famous by the nursery rhyme – was relocated to Arizona in 1970 and now spans part of Lake Havasu.

But what these folks may not realise is that there was yet *another* London Bridge, even older than the 19th-century version, which was constructed in the Middle Ages. The original 'permanent' London Bridge (predecessors were constructed of wood and burnt down periodically) was finished around 1200 and was possibly one of the ugliest structures ever erected. Nevertheless, it did the job until 1831, when it was dismantled and replaced by the soon-to-be Arizona version of the bridge.

ships ever built. Wander around Greenwich's excellent market, then visit the **Queen's House** *(admission free)*, a Palladian masterpiece designed in 1616 by Inigo Jones. Britain's famous naval traditions are covered in fascinating fashion at the **National Maritime Museum** *(admission free)*. Climb the hill behind the museum to the **Royal Observatory**, also free. A brass strip in the courtyard marks the Prime Meridian, which divides the world into eastern and western hemispheres.

Walk back down the hill and through the historic Greenwich foot tunnel (near the *Cutty Sark*) to Island Gardens. From here you can catch the Docklands Light Railway (DLR) back to Tower Gateway. Alternatively, you can catch the DLR at the Cutty Sark stop and avoid the tunnel.

Museums Museums abound in London and it's easy to reach cultural saturation point very quickly. Listed below are a few that really shouldn't be missed. They're all free but a donation is advised; special exhibitions will charge.

The **British Museum** *(☎ 7323 8299; Great Russell St WC1; tube Russell Square or Tottenham Court Rd; open 10am-5.30pm Sat-Wed, 10am-8.30pm Thur-Fri)* is arguably London's greatest museum. Its large collections of Egyptian, Mesopotamian, Greek and Roman antiquities are unparalleled, and you'll marvel at the architectural wonder of the Great Court. Free gallery tours are available.

The **Imperial War Museum** *(☎ 7416 5320; Lambeth Rd SE1; tube Lambeth North; open 10am-6pm daily)* is thought-provoking and moving; the Holocaust Exhibition is especially recommended.

The **Victoria & Albert Museum** *(☎ 0870 442 0808; Cromwell Rd SW7; tube South Kensington; open 10am-5.45pm daily)* has the world's greatest collection of decorative arts dating from 3000 BC to the present day. It also has the best of the museums' cafés.

A good all-round package, the **Natural History Museum** *(☎ 7942 5000; Cromwell Rd SW7; tube South Kensington; open 10am-5.30pm Mon-Sat, 11am-5.30pm Sun)* consists of a striking facade and interesting galleries. The Darwin Centre, with plant and animal specimens collected by Captain James Cook, is a highlight.

Galleries Check *Time Out* for details of current exhibitions.

The **National Gallery** *(☎ 7747 2885; Trafalgar Square WC2; tube Charing Cross; admission free; open 10am-6pm daily, 10am-9pm Wed)* houses 2300 masterpieces from some of the world's most prolific European artists. Its collection spans the 13th to 20th centuries and never fails to inspire.

Around the corner, the **National Portrait Gallery** *(☎ 7306 0055; 2 St Martin's Place WC2; tube Charing Cross; admission free; open 10am-6pm Sat-Wed, 10am-9pm Thur-Fri)* offers Tudor portraits and some fascinating images from British popular culture.

The **Courtauld Institute Gallery** *(☎ 7848 2546; Somerset House, the Strand WC2; tube Temple; admission £5, free 10am-2pm Mon; open 10am-5.15pm daily)* houses works by Rubens and has a brilliant room stuffed full of the very best in impressionism and postimpressionism.

The **Tate Modern** *(☎ 7887 8000; 25 Sumner St SE1; tube Southwark; admission free; open 10am-6pm Sun-Thur, 10am-10pm Fri-Sat)* has a huge collection of weird and wonderful offerings dating from 1900 to the present. They call it modern art.

The **Tate Britain** *(☎ 7887 8000; Millbank SW1; tube Pimlico; admission free; open 10am-5.50pm daily)* majors in the history of British art from 1500 to the present day.

Other Attractions The largest park in central London is **Hyde Park**. Visit the weird yet wonderful **Serpentine Gallery** *(☎ 7298 1515; admission free; open 10am-6pm daily)*, row a boat on the Serpentine, go **horse riding** *(☎ 7723 2813)*, maybe take a dip in the outdoor swimming pool, or heckle the soapbox orators on Sunday at Speakers' Corner (near Marble Arch).

Regent's Park has an **Open Air Theatre** *(☎ 7486 2431; open May-Sept)* where you can enjoy some interesting interpretations of Shakespeare.

Places to Stay

The price of accommodation in London never fails to shock. To make the most of the cheaper offerings it's wise to book a night or two's accommodation in advance, especially in summer. The official TICs at the airports can arrange last-minute bookings. You can also phone the London Tourist Board's **Accommodation Line** *(☎ 7932 2020)*, or use the private services at Victoria; both services charge £5. It's cheaper to search for accommodation yourself and phone or email hotels direct.

YHA/HI Hostels There are seven hostels in central London affiliated with Hostelling International (HI), known as Youth Hostels Association (YHA) in Britain.

Central London's hostels get very crowded in summer. They all take advance bookings by phone (if you pay by Visa or MasterCard), and once you're on the hostelling trail you can use the YHA's free Book A Bed Ahead scheme to book your next hostel bed. All offer 24-hour access and some have a *bureau de change* and Internet access. Most have facilities for self-catering and some offer cheap meals.

City of London *(☎ 7236 4965, fax 7236 7681; ⓔ city@yha.org.uk; 36 Carter Lane EC4; tube St Paul's; B&B adult/child from £24/20)* was the old choir school for nearby St Paul's Cathedral and is an excellent hostel (193 beds). Rooms are mainly four to eight beds, though there are a few singles and twins. It has a licensed cafeteria but no kitchen. Remember, this part of town is pretty quiet outside working hours.

Earl's Court *(☎ 7373 7083, fax 7835 2034; ⓔ earlscourt@yha.org.uk; 38 Bolton Gardens SW5; tube Earl's Court; dorm beds adult/child £19/16.75)* hostel (159 beds) is a Victorian town house and, like the area it occupies, is shabby but lively. Rooms are mainly six- to 10-bed dorms with communal showers. It has a café, kitchen facilities, foreign exchange and a small garden courtyard for summer barbecues.

Hampstead Heath *(☎ 8458 9054, fax 8209 0546; ⓔ hampstead@yha.org.uk; 4 Wellgarth Rd NW11; tube Golders Green; B&B adult/child £20.40/18)* is a 199-bed hostel situated in a beautiful, if a little isolated, leafy suburb. The dorms are comfortable and each room has a washbasin, some overlooking the pretty garden. There's a licensed café and kitchen.

Holland House *(☎ 7937 0748, fax 7376 0667; ⓔ hollandhouse@yha.org.uk; Holland Walk, Kensington W8; tube High Street Kensington; B&B adult/child £21/18.75)* hostel (201 beds) is built into the Jacobean wing of Holland House in the middle of Holland Park. The location is gorgeous, but care is needed after dark when the park gates shut and access is via a poorly lit side path. The dorms are comfortable and there is a café and kitchen.

Oxford St *(☎ 7734 1618, fax 7734 1657; 14 Noel St W1; tube Oxford Circus or Tottenham Court Rd; adult/child in 3-/4-bed rooms £22/17.25, twins £24)* is the most central of the hostels and has 75 beds. While it's clean, the office-block appearance makes it feel cramped and you can kiss goodbye to a good night's sleep. No meals are served but you can buy a packed breakfast for £3.40. Laundry and locker facilities are also available.

Rotherhithe *(☎ 7232 2114, fax 7237 2919; ⓔ rotherhithe@yha.org.uk; 20 Salter Rd SE16; tube Rotherhithe; B&B adult/child £24/20)* has 320 beds and is modern and functional. It's right by the River Thames and recommended, but the location is a bit quiet. Most rooms have four or six beds, though there are some doubles; all have a bathroom. The hostel has a bar with pool table, a kitchen, restaurant and laundry.

St Pancras *(☎ 7388 9998, fax 7388 6766; ⓔ stpancras@yha.org.uk; 79-81 Euston Rd NW1; tube King's Cross St Pancras; B&B adult/child £24/20)* is central and although modern, also retains an office-block feel. The area isn't great, but the hostel (152 beds) is handy to King's Cross station.

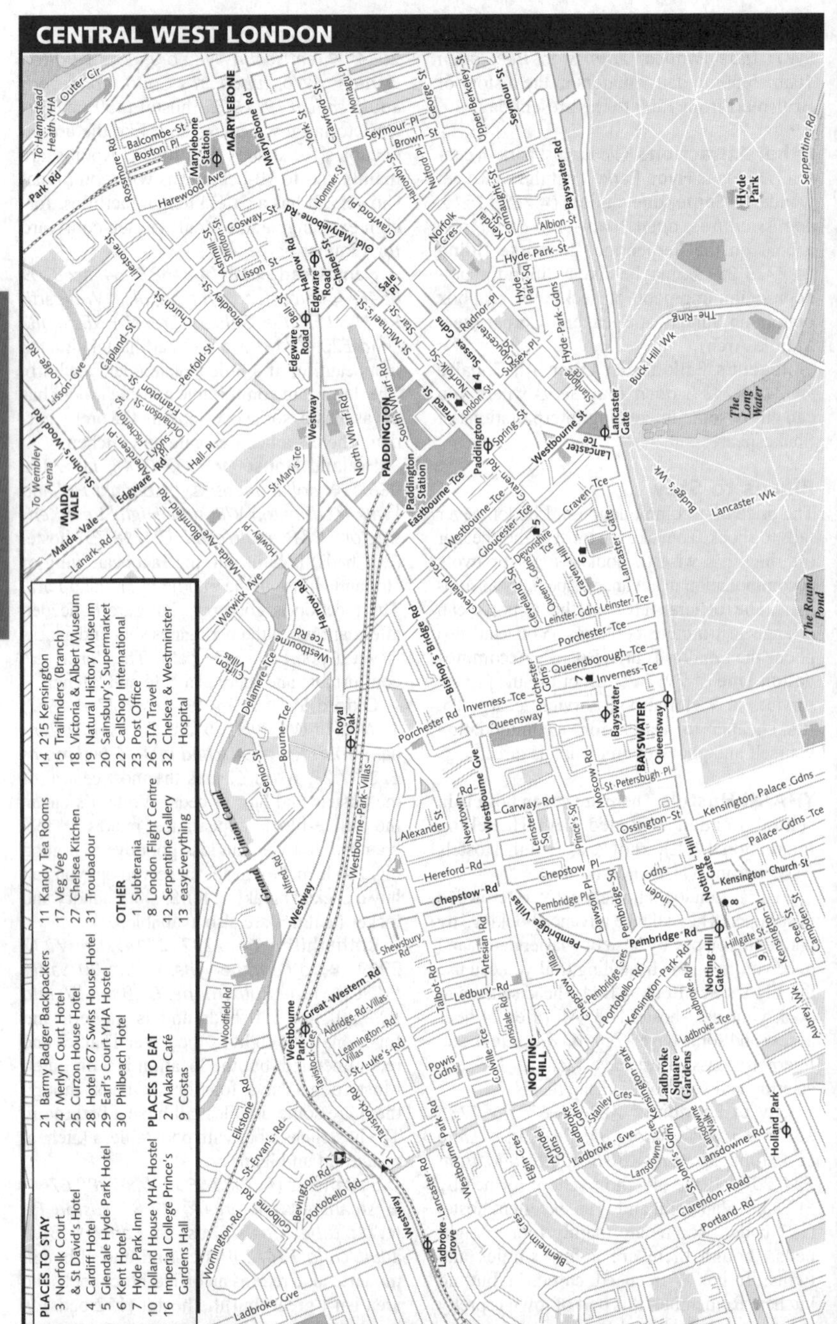
CENTRAL WEST LONDON
PLACES TO STAY
3 Norfolk Court & St David's Hotel
4 Cardiff Hotel
5 Glendale Hyde Park Hotel
6 Kent Hotel
7 Hyde Park Inn
10 Holland House YHA Hostel
16 Imperial College Prince's Gardens Hall
21 Barmy Badger Backpackers
24 Merlyn Court Hotel
25 Curzon House Hotel
28 Hotel 167; Swiss House Hotel
29 Earl's Court YHA Hostel
30 Philbeach Hotel
PLACES TO EAT
2 Makan Café
9 Costas
11 Kandy Tea Rooms
17 Veg Veg
27 Chelsea Kitchen
31 Troubadour
OTHER
1 Subterania
8 London Flight Centre
12 Serpentine Gallery
13 easyEverything
14 215 Kensington
15 Trailfinders (Branch)
18 Victoria & Albert Museum
19 Natural History Museum
20 Sainsbury's Supermarket
22 CallShop International
23 Post Office
26 STA Travel
32 Chelsea & Westminster Hospital
MARYLEBONE
MAIDA VALE
PADDINGTON
BAYSWATER
NOTTING HILL
Hyde Park
The Long Water
The Round Pond
Ladbroke Square Gardens
Grand Union Canal
Marylebone Station
Paddington Station
To Hampstead Heath YHA
To Wembley Arena

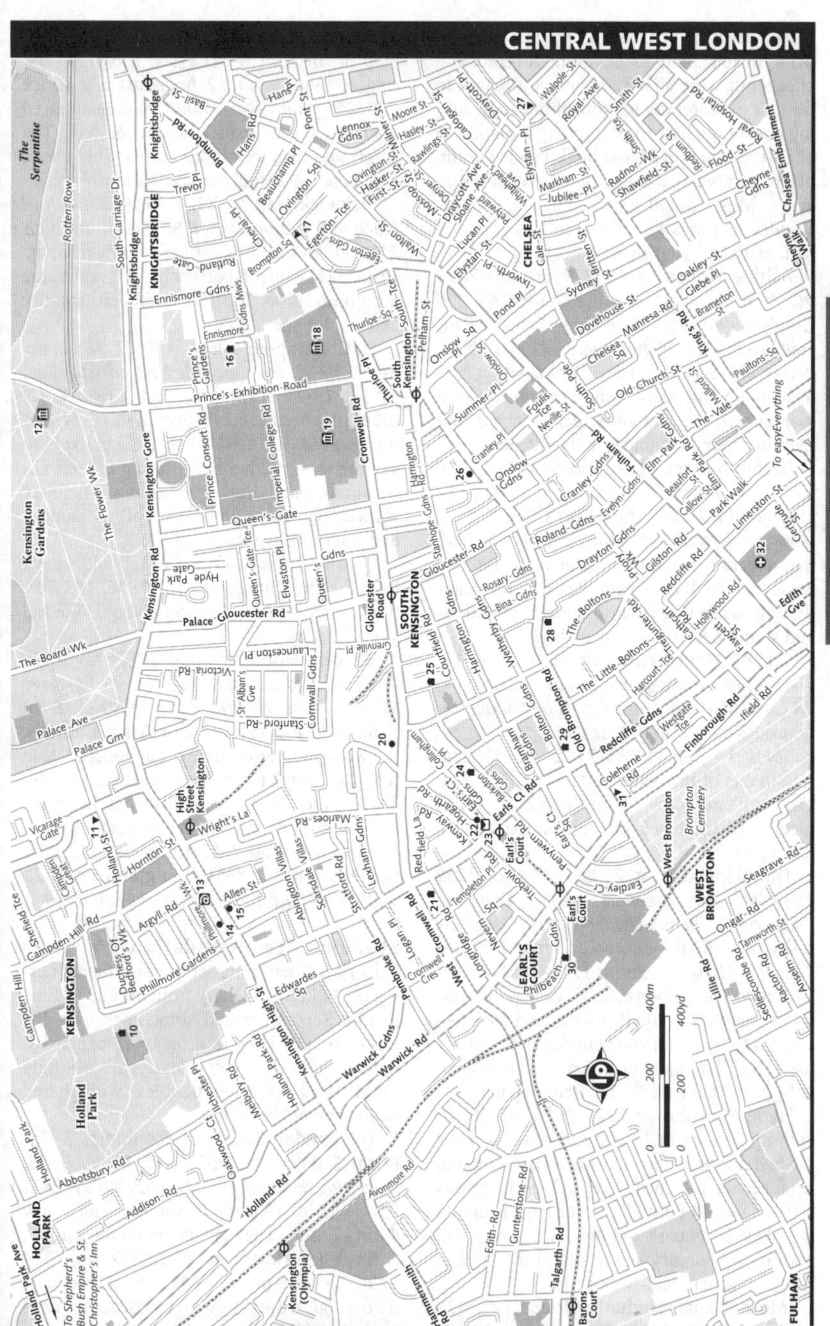
CENTRAL WEST LONDON
The Serpentine
Rotten Row
South Carriage Dr
Kensington Gardens
The Flower Wk
The Board Wk
Holland Park
KNIGHTSBRIDGE
Knightsbridge
Brompton Rd
Basil St
Hans Pl
Hans Rd
Pont St
Trevor Pl
Rutland Gate
Ennismore Gdns
Ennismore Gdns Mws
Prince's Gardens
Prince's Consort Rd
Exhibition Road
Imperial College Rd
Kensington Gore
Kensington Rd
Queen's Gate
Hyde Park Gate
Queen's Gate Tce
Elvaston Pl
Queen's Gdns
Palace Gloucester Rd
Launceston Pl
Victoria Rd
St Alban's Gve
Stanford Rd
Cornwall Gdns
Grenville Pl
Palace Ave
Palace Grn
High Street Kensington
Wright's La
Vicarage Gate
Holland St
Hornton St
Campden Hill Rd
Sheffield Tce
Campden Hill
Argyll Rd
Phillimore Gardens
Duchess Of Bedford's Wk
Allen St
Abingdon Villas
Scarsdale Villas
Stratford Rd
Marloes Rd
Lexham Gdns
Edwardes Sq
Pembroke Rd
Logan Pl
Cromwell Rd
Cromwell Cres
Warwick Gdns
Warwick Rd
Kensington High St
Holland Park Rd
Melbury Rd
Ilchester Pl
Oakwood Ct
Abbotsbury Rd
Addison Rd
Holland Rd
Holland Park Ave
HOLLAND PARK
To Shepherd's Bush Empire & St. Christopher's Inn
Kensington (Olympia)
Avonmore Rd
Hammersmith Rd
Edith Rd
Gunterstone Rd
Talgarth Rd
Barons Court
KENSINGTON
Beauchamp Pl
Ovington Sq
Egerton Tce
Egerton Gdns
Brompton Sq
Cheval Pl
Lennox Gdns
Moore St
Milner St
Ovington St
Hasker St
First St
Hasley St
Rawlings St
Cadogan St
Denyer St
Mossop St
Walton St
Draycott Ave
Draycott Pl
Sloane Ave
Whitehead's Gve
Petyward
Lucan Pl
Elystan St
Elystan Pl
Ixworth Pl
Pond Pl
Thurloe Sq
South Tce
Thurloe Pl
Pelham St
South Kensington
Onslow Sq
Onslow Gdns
Summer Pl
Cranley Pl
Cranley Gdns
Foulis Tce
Neville St
Harrington Rd
Stanhope Gdns
Gloucester Rd
Gloucester Road
SOUTH KENSINGTON
Courtfield Rd
Harrington Gdns
Wetherby Gdns
Rosary Gdns
Bina Gdns
Collingham Pl
Barkston Gdns
Earl's Ct Sq
Earls Ct Rd
Hogarth Rd
Kenway Rd
Redfield La
Templeton Pl
Trebovir Rd
Longridge Rd
Nevern Sq
Penywern Rd
Earl's Court
Earls Court
EARL'S COURT
Philbeach Gdns
Earls Ct Sq
Eardley Cr
Old Brompton Rd
Bolton Gdns
Bramham Gdns
The Boltons
The Little Boltons
Tregunter Rd
Coleherne Rd
Redcliffe Gdns
Westgate Tce
Harcourt Tce
Cathcart Rd
Hollywood Rd
Fawcett St
Finborough Rd
Ifield Rd
Redcliffe Rd
Gilston Rd
Priory Wk
Drayton Gdns
Roland Gdns
Evelyn Gdns
Elm Park Gdns
Elm Park Rd
Beaufort St
Callow St
Park Walk
Limerston St
Gertrude St
Edith Gve
West Brompton
WEST BROMPTON
Brompton Cemetery
Seagrave Rd
Ongar Rd
Tamworth St
Lillie Rd
Sedlescombe Rd
Racton Rd
Anselm Rd
FULHAM
CHELSEA
Cale St
Markham St
Jubilee Pl
Britten St
Sydney St
Dovehouse St
Chelsea Sq
Manresa Rd
South Pde
Old Church St
Fulham Rd
King's Rd
Mallord St
The Vale
Paultons Sq
Bramerton St
Glebe Pl
Oakley St
Cheyne Walk
Cheyne Gdns
Chelsea Embankment
Flood St
Radnor Wk
Shawfield St
Redburn St
Smith Tce
Smith St
Royal Ave
Walpole St
Royal Hospital Rd
To easyEverything
0 200 400m
0 200 400yd

BRITAIN

Independent Hostels London's independent hostels tend to be more relaxed and cheaper than the YHAs, though you'll have to do a bit of searching for something approaching decent quality. Expect to pay a minimum of £10 per night in a basic bunk-bedded dorm, but remember that some don't accept credit cards. Most should have a kitchen, lounge, laundry facilities and if you're lucky, secure lockers (bring your own padlock).

Ashlee House (☎ 7833 9400, fax 7833 9677; ⓔ *info@ashleehouse.co.uk; 261-265 Gray's Inn Rd WC1; tube King's Cross St Pancras; B&B 4- to 16-bed rooms £15-19, bunk bed twins £24)* has an excellent position next to King's Cross station and is clean and well maintained. Dorm rooms feel cramped, but facilities include laundry and a kitchen.

Barmy Badger Backpackers (☎/fax 7370 5213; ⓔ *barmybadger@hotmail.com; 17 Longridge Rd SW5; tube Earl's Court; B&B dorm beds from £15, twins per person £17)* has a variety of dorms. The large kitchen leads to a small courtyard area which catches the sun (when there's any). Laundry facilities and safety deposits are available.

Curzon House Hotel (☎ 7581 2116, fax 7835 1319; ⓔ *info@curzonhousehotel.co.uk; 58 Courtfield Gardens SW5; tube Gloucester Road; B&B 4-/8-bed dorms £18/16, singles/doubles per person £35/21)* is an excellent find in one of the better parts of Earl's Court. The staff are some of the friendliest you'll meet, and there's a kitchen and cable-TV room on offer.

The Generator (☎ 7388 7666, fax 7388 7644; ⓔ *info@the-generator.co.uk; Compton Place, off 37 Tavistock Place WC1; tube Russell Square; B&B 7-/8-bed dorms £21.50/19, beds in 3- to 6-bed dorms £20-22.50, singles £42, twins per person £26.50)* can be summed up in one word – loud! It's fun and sociable, and has to be seen to be believed (particularly the decor). Excellent facilities and a bar (open until 2am) make this immensely popular.

Hyde Park Inn (☎ 7229 0000; *48-50 Inverness Terrace W2; tube Queensway; B&B 10-bed dorms £10, singles £28)* is situated in what seems to be hostel central, with various differing sized dorms. The staff are friendly, the place is relaxed and there's a games and pool room, laundry and a sofa in the kitchen for the ultimate laid-back style.

International Students House (☎ 7631 8310, fax 7631 8315; ⓔ *accom@ish.org.uk; 229 Great Portland St W1; tube Great Portland St; beds in 6- to 8-bed room £11.99, singles/twins with £2 breakfast allowance £31/25; open year-round)* has enamoured readers with its residential college feel. The single and twin rooms are ordinary but clean, and there's a friendly, relaxed atmosphere.

Pickwick Hall (☎ 7323 4958; *7 Bedford Place WC1; tube Russell Square; dorm beds £15, doubles £20)* is a stone's throw from the British Museum and offers basic, good-value accommodation. It offers a kitchen, laundry and TV lounge.

St Christopher's Inn (☎ 7407 1856, fax 7403 7715; ⓔ *bookings@st-christophers.co.uk; 13-15 Shepherd's Bush Green W12; tube Shepherd's Bush; bed in 8-/6-/4-bed dorms £10/17/18.50, twins £23)* is lively to say the least, with a bar offering regular entertainment and drinks promotions. There are showers on every floor, as well as laundry and Internet access.

If you want a roof-top hot tub and sauna, head for **The Village** (☎ *7407 1856; 163 Borough High St; tube London Bridge)*. We kid you not.

Victoria Hotel (☎ 7834 3077, fax 7932 0693; ⓔ *astorvictoria@aol.com; 71 Belgrave Rd SW1; tube Victoria; dorm beds from £15)* is the cleanest and nicest of Astor's hostels, the wooden interior giving it a modern, clean feel. The wooden benches in the eating/cable-TV area are a bit school-hallish, but the dorms are comfortable, mixed and have a sink.

For a list of all **YMCA hostels** in Greater London, contact **YMCA England** (☎ *8520 5599; 640 Forest Rd, London E17 3DZ)*.

Student Accommodation University halls of residence are let to nonstudents during the holidays, usually from the end of June to mid-September and sometimes over the Easter break. They're a bit more expensive than hostels, but you usually get a single room (there are a few doubles) with shared bathroom and breakfast.

The **London School of Economics & Political Science** (☎ *7955 7531; Room B508, Page Bldg, Houghton St, London WC2A 2AE)* lets seven of its halls in summer and a few during Easter. The convenient options are:

Bankside House (☎ *7633 9877, fax 7574 6730; 24 Sumner St SE1; tube Blackfriars; B&B singles £30, singles/twins/quads with bath £43/58/88)* is only open during the summer months but has an enviable location near the Globe Theatre and Tate Modern. It has a laundry and bar.

Carr-Saunders Hall *(☎ 7580 6338, fax 7580 4718; 18-24 Fitzroy St W1; tube Warren St; B&B singles/twins £27/45)* is in a quiet location. Don't be fooled by the dodgy exterior. There are kitchens on each floor, a basement bar and pool and table tennis tables.

Imperial College Prince's Gardens Hall *(☎ 7594 9507, fax 7594 9504; ⓔ accommodationlink@ic.ac.uk; Watts Way, Prince's Gardens SW7; tube South Kensington; B&B singles/twins £39.50/59; open Easter & July–late Sept)* is huge and right in the centre of the action, two minutes from some of London's greatest museums.

John Adams Hall *(☎ 7387 4086, fax 7383 0164; ⓔ jah@ioe.ac.uk; 15-23 Endsleigh St WC1; tube Euston; singles/doubles from £27/48; open Easter & July-Sept)*, belonging to the Institute of Education, is quite a grand residence occupying a row of Georgian houses. Rates vary depending on the time of year.

B&Bs & Hotels Once you've exhausted the hostels, YMCAs and university halls, searching for decent, cheap accommodation in London is like a quest for the Holy Grail. If you find anything below £30/50 for a basic single/double and below £40/60 with private bathroom, you've done well! For some good deals, you might want to check ⓦ www.lastminute.com. Have a credit card handy.

Once you find somewhere suitable, don't be afraid to ask for the 'best' price, particularly if you are staying out of high season or for more than a couple of nights. In July, August and September prices can jump by 25% or more.

The following listings are arranged by neighbourhood and listed in order of price.

Pimlico & Victoria Victoria may not be the most attractive part of London, but the budget hotels are better value than those in Earl's Court. Pimlico is more residential.

Brindle House Hotel *(☎ 7828 0057, fax 7931 8805; 1 Warwick Place North SW1; tube Victoria; B&B singles £35-45, doubles with/without bath £48/44, triples £69)* is cheap for the area and popular with travellers. The rooms are small but clean, and the staff are helpful.

Luna-Simone Hotel *(☎ 7834 5897, fax 7828 2474; 47 Belgrave Rd SW1; tube Victoria; B&B singles/doubles from £40/50, doubles with bath £55-70)*, in a road stuffed full of varying quality B&Bs, is a shining example of good value that's simply done. The rooms are bright, airy and spotless.

James House and **Cartref House** *(☎ 7730 6176, fax 7730 7637; ⓔ jandchouse@cs.com; 108 & 139 Ebury Street SW1; tube Victoria; B&B singles/doubles £52/70, with bath £62/85)* are situated across the street from each other and are run by a very friendly couple with a good knowledge of Victoria. The rooms are simple but clean.

The West End & Covent Garden Here you're in the centre of the action, but you pay for the convenience. **Regent Palace Hotel** *(☎ 0870 400 8703, fax 7734 6435; Piccadilly Circus, W1; tube Piccadilly Circus; singles/doubles Sun-Thur £64/69, Fri & Sat £75/89)* is ripe for renovation but ideally located for those arriving from Heathrow on the tube. This enormous hotel has basic rooms; rates don't include breakfast.

Bloomsbury This area is altogether more sedate and refined, at half the price of the West End. There are lots of places on Gower and North Gower Sts.

La Brasserie Town House *(☎ 7636 2731, fax 7580 1028; ⓔ Labrasserietownhouse@hotmail.com; 24 Coptic St WC1; tube Tottenham Court Rd; B&B singles/doubles £32/60)* is a good French restaurant just off a rather busy street, but its four tidy, stylish rooms and one studio are excellent value.

Hotel Cavendish *(☎ 7636 9079, fax 7580 3609; 75 Gower St WC1; tube Goodge Street; B&B singles/doubles £38/48, with bath £45/66)* is extremely friendly and the rooms are simple but clean. The shaded, walled garden makes a pleasant spot for catching some rays.

Arran House Hotel *(☎ 7636 2186, fax 7436 5328; ⓔ arran@dircon.co.uk; 77-79 Gower St WC1; tube Goodge Street; B&B singles with/without bath £55/45, doubles £55-75, triples £73-93)* grabs attention with its family-run atmosphere, scrupulous attention to detail and peaceful summer rose garden. The windows are sound-proofed, and laundry facilities are also available. It's definitely recommended.

Chelsea, South Kensington & Earl's Court Chelsea and South Kensington are close to museums and restaurants, but the cheapest accommodation is in Earl's Court. The lower end of Earl's Court's hotel market is appalling.

Merlyn Court Hotel *(☎ 7370 1640, fax 7370 4986; 2 Barkston Gardens SW5; tube Earl's Court; B&B singles/doubles £35/55, with bath £45/70, triples with/without bath £75/65)* is cheap accommodation, expertly done. It's ideally placed for the tube and the rooms are small but clean. It has a 24-hour laundry service, and you'll receive a friendly welcome.

Philbeach Hotel *(☎ 7373 1244, fax 7244 0149; 30-31 Philbeach Gardens SW5; tube Earl's Court; B&B singles/doubles £55/70)* is a gay-friendly hotel set in the middle of a sweeping crescent. Its 35 rooms are small, but clean and arty, and its onsite bar and restaurant are renowned.

Swiss House Hotel *(☎ 7373 2769, fax 7373 4983; ⓔ recap@swiss-hh.demon.co.uk; 171 Old Brompton Rd SW5; tube Gloucester Rd; B&B singles £51-71, doubles £89-104)* has a modern, relaxed feel, with small rooms offering a variety of private bathroom facilities. Laminate floors and modern standard lamps provide an uncluttered, contemporary edge.

Bayswater, Paddington & Notting Hill This area is crammed full of hotels, and it's not surprising that it's a tourist hub.

Kent Hotel *(☎ 7402 0254, fax 7402 2468; ⓔ kenthotel@btinternet.com; 41 Lancaster Gate W2; tube Lancaster Gate; B&B singles £30, singles/doubles with bath £45/60)* has 20 simple, clean and functional rooms in a prime location. You'll get plenty of exercise if your room's on the top floor – there's no lift.

Glendale Hyde Park Hotel *(☎ 7706 4441, fax 7479 9273; ⓔ booking@ghphotel.com; 8 Devonshire Terrace W2; tube Lancaster Gate; singles/doubles £35/45)* offers great facilities behind an unassuming exterior. Despite flowery duvets, all 20 rooms have bathroom, satellite TV, phone and minibar. With free Internet access, this is excellent value.

Norfolk Court & St David's Hotel *(☎ 7723 4963, fax 7402 9061; 16-20 Norfolk Square W2; tube Paddington; B&B singles/doubles £39/59, singles/doubles with bath £49/69)* is possibly the friendliest hotel in London and its huge, tasty breakfasts come highly recommended. The rooms are clean and comfortable with some 'interesting' colour schemes.

Cardiff Hotel *(☎ 7723 9068, fax 7402 2342; ⓔ stay@cardiff-hotel.com; 5-9 Norfolk Square W2; tube Paddington; B&B singles £45-55, doubles £79)* is a family-run hotel whose 60 rooms are a good size and neatly decorated. The staff are friendly.

Places to Eat

British food has far surpassed its dire reputation and what's available in London is no exception. Although kebabs and curries remain a national institution, you'll find food from every corner of the globe. Even on a small budget you'll be able to take advantage of lunchtime offers and set dinner menus.

Westminster & Pimlico This area is light on restaurants – it's for recliners rather than diners. **Footstool** *(☎ 7222 2779; St John's, Smith Square SW1; tube Westminster; buffet from £3.50, lunch mains £9.95-11.95, 2-course set dinners £10.95)* is in the crypt of an 18th-century baroque church (now a concert hall) and is a favoured lunchtime retreat of MPs. It offers a buffet with soups and a more formal restaurant for à-la-carte lunches and set dinners on concert evenings.

The West End: Piccadilly, Chinatown & Soho These days Soho is London's gastronomic centralis. You'll find plenty of choice along Old Compton and Dean Sts. Gerrard and Lisle Sts form London's Chinatown and offer set-menu bargains.

Pollo *(☎ 7734 5917; 20 Old Compton St W1; tube Leicester Square; all dishes under £5)* has a massive selection of generous and filling pasta dishes at a bargain £3. It's intimate, noisy and usually crowded, but brilliant value for money.

Stockpot *(☎ 7287 1066; 18 Old Compton St W1; tube Leicester Square; pasta from £3.50, set menu £4.20)* is more country kitchen than Italian chic, but is good value.

Garden Café *(☎ 7494 0044; 4 Newburgh St W1; tube Oxford Circus)*, just off famous Carnaby St, is a yellow-and-pink lunch spot offering simple fare. Jacket potatoes are a reasonable £3.60, but there's plenty of cheap sandwiches and salads on offer, too.

Yee Tung Chinese Restaurant *(☎ 7437 3870; 20 Gerrard St W1; tube Leicester Square; buffets £4.90-7.90)* is one of many stuff-your-face hang-outs in Chinatown, and despite the dodgy decor it does surprisingly edible food. Unlike its neighbours, you won't be hurried out of your seat.

Café Emm *(☎ 7437 0723; 17 Frith St W1; tube Tottenham Court Rd; mains £5.50)* looks a dive from the outside but is home to some of the finest-value food in Soho. It's friendly and intimate, with generous portions.

Palms of Goa *(☎ 7439 3509; 4 Meard St W1; tube Leicester Square; dishes from £5.95)* is on a sneaky little back street away from Soho's crowds. The restaurant isn't huge, but the Goan-inspired dishes are recommended.

Covent Garden & The Strand Covent Garden is packed to the rafters with eateries, and thanks to its proximity to Theatreland has plenty of pretheatre set-menu deals to take advantage of. The following are accessible from Covent Garden tube station unless indicated otherwise.

Food for Thought *(☎ 7836 0239; 31 Neal St WC2; meals around £4)* is a mecca for vegetarians with a café atmosphere upstairs, a more restaurant feel downstairs. Its quiches and stir-fried vegetables with rice are moreish.

Bistro 1 *(☎ 7379 7585; 33 Southampton St WC2; 2-/3-course set menus £5.90/6.90)* is intimate and does European dishes and Mediterranean specials such as vegetable moussaka expertly.

Rock & Sole Plaice *(☎ 7836 3785; 47 Endell St WC2)* looks like a sweaty caff, tastes like a million dollars. For delicious cod and chips from a British chippy institution, expect to pay £7 – divine.

Bloomsbury Though usually thought of as B&B territory, Bloomsbury has a few reasonably priced restaurants and cafés. **Coffee Gallery** *(☎ 7436 0455; 23 Museum St WC1; tube Tottenham Court Rd; pasta around £4, salads £4.90)* has a daily changing menu, 90% of which is vegetarian.

L'etoile Café *(☎ 7387 5400; 45 Fitzroy St W1; tube Warren St; open Mon-Fri)* has a few seats outside but is mainly a takeaway joint. Start the day with a mean full English breakfast (£5), or enjoy filled ciabatta and bagels (around £3).

South Bank Reflecting the development of the area, this part of town offers a mixed bag of workers' caffs and upmarket refinement.

Freshly Maid Café *(☎ 7928 5426; 79 Lower Marsh; tube Waterloo; burger & chips £1.99)* is officially the fourth cheapest café in London, and as long as you're not hoping to rest your legs, you'll get decent enough food at bargain prices.

Mariterra *(☎ 7928 7628; 14 Gambia St SE1; tube Southwark; tapas £4-6.50)* does excellent Spanish food but is overpopulated with office workers in the early evening.

Chelsea, South Kensington & Earl's Court All budgets are well catered for in these areas. At **Chelsea Kitchen** *(☎ 7589 1330; 98 King's Rd SW3; tube Sloane Square; set meal £5.50)* the decor suggests a trucker's café, the food suggests you've found a bargain.

Veg Veg *(☎ 7584 7007; 8 Egerton Gardens Mews SW2; tube South Kensington)* is a small, stylish affair offering Szechuan vegetarian cuisine. The all-you-can-eat lunch buffet (£4.99) is excellent and surprisingly filling.

Troubadour *(☎ 7370 1434; 265 Old Brompton Rd SW5; tube Earl's Court; breakfasts £4.50, mains £7-9)* is a café and music venue, which has played host to Eric Clapton and the Rolling Stones. The atmosphere is still dark and moody, with live music on occasions and good food everyday, especially the breakfasts.

Kensington & Knightsbridge These cosmopolitan 'villages' still cater for their loyal following of well-heeled foodies, but once you get off Kensington High St there's plenty of choice. **Kandy Tea Rooms** *(☎ 7937 3001; 4 Holland St W8; tube High St Kensington; afternoon tea £6.70)* mixes a small, traditional English tearoom with a touch of the oriental and, bizarrely, it works. Readers praise its afternoon tea.

Notting Hill & Bayswater Notting Hill is yet another good eat-out option, with everything from cheap takeaways to good quality restaurants, some quite quirky. **Makan Café** *(☎ 8960 5169; 270 Portobello Rd W10; tube Ladbroke Grove; daily specials £3.50-4, mains £5-6)* has horrific luminous decor but cheap Malaysian-inspired vegetarian cuisine, meat and fish dishes.

Costas *(☎ 7727 4310; 18 Hillgate St W8; tube Notting Hill Gate; open Tues-Sat)* is a down-to-earth fish and chippy with cod or rock salmon and chips at £6.50. It's in need of renovation, but it's still producing some of the best chips in London.

Islington Islington is full of eateries, especially on Upper St. If you can't find what you fancy here, your tastebuds must be dead.

Afgan Kitchen *(☎ 7359 8019; 35 Islington Green N1; tube Angel; mains from around £5.50)* is an old favourite that has first-timers coming back for more. Bland food is spiced up and given a delicious makeover, leaving you wondering how every other London restaurant gets away with their prices. Making a booking is advisable.

Tartuf *(☎ 7288 0954; 88 Upper St N1; tube Angel)* is Alsatian and proud of it. Modern, upbeat and authentic, you'll love its *tarte flambeés* (French thin-bread pizzas), either savoury (£5 to £6) or sweet (£4).

East End If your life's in need of spicing up, Brick Lane (dubbed 'Banglatown' on account of it being lined with Indian and Bangladeshi restaurants) will become your spiritual home.

Brick Lane Beigel Bake *(☎ 7729 0616; 159 Brick Lane E2; tube Shoreditch; open 24 hrs)* provides the ultimate cure for late-night munchies. You won't find cheaper or fresher bagels anywhere else.

Bengal Cuisine *(☎ 7377 8405; 12 Brick Lane E1; tube Aldgate East; mains £4.95-8.95)* is praised by all who eat here for excellent service and authentic taste. Try the Shatkora Chicken (£7.95) for a true taste of Bangladesh.

Greenwich Beautiful Greenwich is great for finding what you want, fast. Its best eateries are packed into a triangle formed by the Market, Greenwich Church St and Nelson Rd. The Cutty Sark DLR station is convenient to all the places here.

Nelson Rd has a few options that'll suit all budgets. **Bar de Musee** *(☎ 8858 4710; mains £11.75-13.50)* at No 17 is a sophisticated bistro, all red and arty.

Entertainment

By day and night, London plays host to a lively mix of welcome distractions. It's rich in contemporary and classical music and theatre, and is home to world-renowned venues that live up to their hype. Most entry charges are anywhere from £5 to £15. Note that the last Underground trains leave between 11.30pm and 12.30am, after which you must figure out the night-bus system or take a taxi. For all event listings, check *Time Out*.

Pubs London is awash in pubs, all of which close at a puritanical 11pm. Unfortunately many are uninspired boozers or charmless chain outlets. But there are still a few gems.

The Albert *(Victoria St SW1; tube St James's Park)* is home to the Division Bell, used to call drinking MPs back to Parliament to vote. It's a popular daytime boozer, with plenty of good pub grub.

Lamb & Flag *(Rose St WC2; tube Covent Garden)* is manic just after office hours, but is beloved by all for its family-like quality.

Bradley's Spanish Bar *(44 Hanway St W1; tube Tottenham Court Rd)* is more pub-like than its name suggests, with an excellent jukebox and wicked staff.

Coach & Horses *(29 Greek St W1; tube Leicester Square)* is a small, busy pub with excellent beer and a regular band of satisfied customers.

The Queen's Larder *(1 Queen Square WC1; tube Russell Square)*, used by Queen Charlotte to store delicacies for George III, now offers a handy retreat, with outside benches and pub grub.

George Inn *(Talbot Yard, 77 Borough High St SE1; tube London Bridge or Borough)* is London's only surviving galleried coaching inn. Dating from 1676, it's in Charles Dickens' *Little Dorrit*. It's also the site of Tabard Inn where the pilgrims gathered in Chaucer's *Canterbury Tales* before setting out.

The Angel *(101 Bermondsey Wall East SE16; tube Bermondsey)* is a riverside pub dating from the 15th century (though the present building harks back to the early 17th century). This is where Captain Cook supposedly prepared for his trip to Australia.

Music & Clubs Major venues for live contemporary music include the **Brixton Academy** *(☎ 7771 2000; 211 Stockwell Rd SW9; tube Brixton)*, **Shepherds Bush Empire** *(☎ 7771 2000; Shepherds Bush Green W12; tube Shepherds Bush)* and **Wembley Arena** *(☎ 8902 0902; Empire Way, Wembley; tube Wembley Park)*.

Smaller places with a more club-like atmosphere which are worth checking out: **12 Bar Club** *(☎ 7916 6989; 22 Denmark Place WC2; tube Tottenham Court Rd)*; **Borderline** *(☎ 7734 2095; Orange Yard, off Manette St WC2; tube Tottenham Court Rd)*; **Garage** *(☎ 7607 1818; 20-22 Highbury Corner N5; tube Highbury & Islington)*, an indie favourite;

and **Subterania** *(☎ 8960 4590; 12 Acklam Rd W10; tube Ladbroke Grove)*. Ring ahead to find out which bands are playing.

If you're into DJ-ing, check out some quality mixing at the occasionally free DJ bars. Excellent haunts include: **Bar Vinyl** *(☎ 7682 7898; 6 Inverness St N1; tube Camden Town; open 7pm-11pm Wed-Sun)* and the über cool **Retreat** *(☎ 7704 6868; 144 Upper St N1; tube Angel; open from 8pm Mon-Sat, from 7pm Sun)*.

The better club venues include: **Fabric** *(☎ 7490 0444; 77a Charterhouse St EC1; tube Farringdon)*, with its bodysonic dance floor; the multifaceted **Fridge** *(☎ 7326 5100; Town Hall Parade SW2; tube Brixton)*; the famous **Ministry of Sound** *(☎ 7378 6528; 103 Gaunt St SE1; tube Elephant & Castle)*; **Pacha London** *(☎ 7834 4440; Terminus Place SW1; tube Victoria)* for Balearic beats; the eclectic **Scala** *(☎ 7833 2022; 278 Pentonville Rd N1; tube King's Cross)*; **The End** *(☎ 7419 9199; 16a West Central St WC1; tube Holborn)* owned by The Shamen's Mr C; and the ever-popular gay haunt **Astoria** *(☎ 7434 9592; 157 Charing Cross Rd WC2; tube Tottenham Court Rd)*.

If you're a jazz fan, keep your eye on **Ronnie Scott's** *(☎ 7439 0747; 47 Frith St W1; tube Leicester Square)*, the **Jazz Café** *(☎ 7916 6060; 5 Parkway NW1; tube Camden Town)* and the **Pizza Express Jazz Club** *(10 Dean St W1; tube Tottenham Court Rd)*.

Theatre Even if it's not your thing, you'll be surprised by the diversity of London's theatre and musicals scene. Some theatres and concert halls sell stand-by tickets 90 minutes before performances.

The South Bank's **National Theatre** *(☎ 7452 3000; tube Waterloo)* is actually three theatres in one – the Olivier, Lyttleton and Cottesloe – and puts on consistently good performances, mixing classic and contemporary works. For cheap tickets, queue at the box office from 10am on the day of the show.

tkts *(tube Leicester Square; open 10am-7pm Mon-Sat, noon-3.30pm Sun)*, on the southern side of Leicester Square, sells half-price tickets (plus £2.50 commission) on the day of performance. The queues can be worse than Harrods' sales.

Don't miss a performance at **Shakespeare's Globe Theatre** *(☎ 7401 9919; 21 New Globe Walk; tube London Bridge; standing £5, tickets £12-27)*, the replica of Shakespeare's 'wooden O', which now dominates Bankside. Many people copy the 17th-century 'groundlings' who stood in front of the stage. The Globe is open to the elements; hence performances are only from May to September.

Getting There & Away

Bus travellers will arrive at **Victoria coach station** *(Buckingham Palace Rd)*, about 10 minutes' walk south of Victoria station. Each of the 10 main line train stations serve various parts of Britain, so the station you arrive at might not be the one you'll leave from.

Getting Around

To/From the Airports Transport to/from London's five airports is as follows:

Heathrow The airport *(☎ 0870 000 0123)* is accessible by bus, Underground (between 5am and 11pm) and main line train.

The Heathrow Express rail link whisks passengers from Paddington station to Heathrow in just 15 minutes. Tickets cost an exorbitant £12 each way. Trains leave every 15 minutes from around 5am to 11.30pm. Many airlines have advance check-in desks at Paddington.

The Underground adult one-way fare is £3.60, or you can use an All Zone Travelcard (£5). The journey time from central London is about 50 minutes – allow an hour.

The **Airbus A2** *(☎ 0870 575 7757; W www.gobycoach.com)* service is prone to traffic congestion. It runs from Heathrow Terminal 4 to King's Cross Cheney Rd every 30 minutes from 5.30am to 9.45pm, and from King's Cross between 4am and 10pm. It takes 1¾ hours and costs £8.

Gatwick The **Gatwick Express train** *(☎ 0870 530 1530)* runs nonstop between the main terminal and Victoria station 24 hours daily. One-way fares are £11 and the journey takes about 30 minutes. The **Connex South Central** *(☎ 01332-387601)* service takes a little longer and costs £8.20.

London City The **airport** *(☎ 7646 0000)* is two minutes' walk from the Silvertown & City Airport train station, which is linked by train to Stratford. A frequent shuttle bus also connects the airport with Liverpool St station (£6, 30 minutes), Canary Wharf DLR and tube (£3, 12 minutes) and Canning Town station (£2, 10 minutes).

Luton The **airport** *(☎ 01582-405100)* is connected by frequent shuttle bus from the Luton Airport Parkway station. Several **trains** *(☎ 0845 748 4950)* an hour go to/from London through the Kings Cross Thameslink station. Fares cost £9.50 and the journey takes about 35 minutes.

Stansted The **airport** *(☎ 0870 0000 303)* is served by the **Stansted Express** *(☎ 0845 730 1530)* from Liverpool St station, which costs £11 and takes 45 minutes. The trains depart every 15 minutes.

There's also the **Airbus A6** *(☎ 0870 575 7747)* service, which runs every 20 minutes at peak times, 30 minutes off-peak, 24 hours a day between the airport and Victoria coach station. It takes 1¾ hours and costs £8.

Bus & Underground For information regarding the bus or Underground networks, call ☎ 7222 1234 or visit the TICs at Victoria coach station and various tube stations.

Prices for bus and tube travel depend on how many zones your journey covers. A ticket good for Zones 1 and 2 should suffice for most visitors. Travelcards are the easiest and cheapest option, and they can be used on all forms of transport – trains in London, the DLR, buses and the tube. A card for Zones 1 and 2 costs £5.30 before 9.30am; £4.10 after.

DLR & Train The monorail-like, driverless Docklands Light Railway (DLR) links the City at Bank and Tower Gateway with Canary Wharf, Stratford, Beckton, Greenwich and Lewisham. It's a quick, convenient way of seeing what some herald as 'new' London. Fares operate the same way as on the tube.

Trains are the primary means of transport to much of London's suburbia. All main line stations interchange with the tube.

Taxi The famous **London black cabs** *(☎ 7272 0272)* can carry five people but are not cheap. Most 'cabbies' expect a tip of 10%. Minicabs can carry four people and tend to be cheaper than the black cabs. Although they are only supposed to be hired by phone, hawkers abound in popular spots at night. Women, particularly if alone, are advised to steer clear. Make sure you barter hard on a price before you get in.

Small minicab companies are based in particular areas – ask a local for the name of a reputable company, or phone one of the large **24-hour minicab operations** *(☎ 7272 2612, 8340 2450, 8567 1111)*. Women could phone **Lady Cabs** *(☎ 7254 3501)*. Gays and lesbians can choose **Freedom Cars** *(☎ 7734 1313)*.

AROUND LONDON

As well as the spots below, the towns of Oxford, Cambridge, Stratford-upon-Avon, Bath and Brighton are also all within easy striking distance from the capital.

Windsor & Eton

☎ 01753

Windsor Castle *(☎ 831118; admission £11.50; open 9.45am-5.15pm daily)* is one of three official residences of the Queen and has been home to English sovereigns for over 900 years. It was built in stages between 1165 and the 16th century on chalk bluffs overlooking the Thames; its majesty is still striking.

Inside the castle, **St George's Chapel** *(closed Sunday)* is a masterpiece of perpendicular Gothic architecture. You can also see Queen Mary's Doll's House and the recently restored State Apartments. The castle can be closed at short notice when members of the royal family are in residence; phone for opening arrangements. In summer, the changing of the guard takes place from Monday to Saturday, weather permitting, at 11am, and on alternate days for the remainder of the year.

A short walk along Thames St and across the river brings you to an enduring symbol of Britain's class system, **Eton College** *(admission £3.50; open to visitors during term 2pm-4.30pm, from 10.30am Easter & summer holidays)*, a famous 'public' (meaning private) school that has educated no fewer than 18 prime ministers and a number of royals. Several buildings date from the mid-15th century, when the school was founded by Henry VI.

South West Trains operates direct services from London's Waterloo to Windsor & Eton Riverside station for £6.30 return.

Southeast England

The southeast is exceptionally rich in beauty and history, and caters to those unshakeable traditional images of England – picturesque villages with welcoming old pubs, spectacular coastlines, impressive castles and magnificent cathedrals. There are also a number of great walks along the South and North Downs.

The main roads and railway lines radiate from London like spokes in a wheel, linking the south-coast ports and resorts with the capital.

Getting Around

For information on all public transport options in Kent, East and West Sussex and Hampshire, ring **Traveline** (*☎ 0870 608 2608*). It is possible to do an interesting rail loop from London via Canterbury East, Dover, Ashford, Rye, Hastings, Battle (via Hastings), Brighton, Arundel, Portsmouth and Winchester.

CANTERBURY

☎ 01227 • pop 36,000

Canterbury's greatest treasure is its magnificent cathedral, the successor to the church St Augustine built after he began converting the English to Christianity in AD 597. In 1170 Archbishop Thomas à Becket was murdered in the cathedral by four of Henry II's knights as a result of a dispute over the church's independence. An enormous cult grew up around the martyred Becket, and Canterbury became the centre of one of the most important medieval pilgrimages in Europe, immortalised by Geoffrey Chaucer in the *Canterbury Tales*.

Canterbury makes a good base for exploring the eastern and northern coastal areas of Kent, namely Herne Bay and Whitstable, Margate, Broadstairs and Sandwich.

Orientation & Information

The two train stations are both a short walk from the centre. The bus station is just within the city walls at the eastern end of High St.

The **TIC** (*☎ 766567, fax 459840; ⓔ canterburyinformation@canterbury.gov.uk; 34 St Margaret's St; open 9.30am-5.30pm Mon-Sat, 10am-4pm Sun*) is in the heart of town. For free Internet access (bookings required), head to the **library** (*☎ 463608; High St*).

Things to See & Do

The **Canterbury Cathedral** (*☎ 762862; adult/concession £3.50/2.50; open 9am-6.30pm Mon-Sat Easter-Sept, 9am-5pm Oct-Easter, shorter hours Sun*) was built in two stages between 1070 and 1184, and 1391 and 1505. It is a massive rabbit warren of a building, with treasures tucked away in corners and a trove of associated stories.

Also not to be missed is the **Roman Museum** (*☎ 785575; Butchery Lane; adult/concession £2.60/1.65; open 10am-5pm Mon-Sat, 1.30pm-5pm Sun June-Oct*), built underground around the remains of a Roman town house. Here you can visit the market-place, smell the odours of a Roman kitchen and handle artefacts.

Places to Stay

Canterbury Youth Hostel (*☎ 0870 770 5744, fax 770 5745; ⓔ canterbury@yha.org.uk; 54 New Dover Rd; dorm beds £11.25, twins £32*) is a mile east of the centre. Another budget option is the **University of Kent** (*☎ 828000, fax 828019; ⓔ d.p.smith@ukc.ac.uk; Tanglewood; B&B per person from £19.50, with bath £27.50; open Apr, June-Sept*), a 20-minute walk from the centre.

Head to London Rd or New Dover Rd for good-value B&Bs such as **Alverstone House** (*☎/fax 766360; 38 New Dover Rd; singles/doubles £20/38*), which has large rooms that look out over a pleasant garden. **Tudor House B&B** (*☎ 765650; 6 Best Lane; singles £20, doubles with/without bath £45/38*), in a slightly eccentric 450-year-old building, is very good value for somewhere so central. It also does canoe and bike hire for guests (£10 per day).

Places to Eat

The Custard Tart (*☎ 785178; 35a St Margaret's St*) charges from £2.75 for delicious baguettes and sandwiches, or £1.75 for take-away.

Three Tuns Hotel (*☎ 456391; 24 Watling St; pub meals around £4.50*) stands on the site of a Roman theatre and dates from the 16th century. It serves good-value pub grub.

Ha!Ha! (*☎ 379800; 7 St Margaret's St; dishes £7*) is a bar with bistro-style food.

Entertainment

The TIC stocks copies of *W3 – What WhereWhen* – a free leaflet to what's on in Canterbury. **The Miller's Arms** (*☎ 456057; Mill Lane*) is a cosy pub near the old locks. **Caseys** (*☎ 463252; 5 Butchery Lane*) has a large selection of Irish ales and stouts.

Getting There & Away

To Canterbury, National Express buses leave every 30 minutes to/from London's Victoria coach station (£7.50/11.50 one-way/return, two hours). The No 115 bus run by **Stagecoach East Kent's** (*☎ 828100*) runs hourly (less on Sunday) from Canterbury to Dover

(£3.25/4 one-way/return, 30 minutes), Deal, Sandwich, Ramsgate, Broadstairs, Margate, Whitstable and back to Canterbury.

Canterbury East train station (for the YHA hostel) is accessible from London's Victoria station, and Canterbury West is accessible from London's Charing Cross and Waterloo stations (£15.90, 1½ hours). There are regular trains between Canterbury East and Dover Priory (£4.40, 45 minutes).

DOVER

☎ 01304 • pop 37,000

Dover may be England's 'Gateway to Europe', but it has just two things going for it: the famous white cliffs and a spectacular medieval hill-top castle. The foreshore of Dover is basically an enormous, complicated and unattractive vehicle ramp for the ferries.

Ferry departures are from the Eastern Docks (accessible by bus) below the castle. Dover Priory train station is off Folkestone Rd, just to the west of the town centre. The bus station is on Pencester Rd. The **TIC** *(☎ 205108, fax 225498; ⓔ tic@doveruk.com; Biggin St; open daily)* is in the town centre.

Dover Castle *(☎ 211067; adult/concession/child £7.50/5.60/3.80; open 10am-6pm daily Apr-Sept, 10am-4pm Oct-Mar)* is a well-preserved medieval fortress with unbelievable views. The excellent tour of **Hellfire Corner** covers the castle's history during WWII, and takes you through the tunnels that burrow beneath the castle.

The **Dover Museum** *(☎ 201066; Market Square; adult/child £1.75/95p; open 10am-5.30pm daily)* is one of the best around.

Places to Stay & Eat

Book well ahead if you intend to be here in July and August. The **Dover Youth Hostel** *(☎ 0870 770 5798, fax 770 5799; ⓔ dover@yha.org.uk; 306 London Rd; adult/under-18 £11.25/8)* is five minutes' walk from Market Square.

There are a few cheap B&Bs on Castle St and Maison Dieu Rd. **East Lee Guest House** *(☎ 210176, fax 206705; ⓔ eastlee@eclipse.co.uk; 108 Maison Dieu Rd; singles/doubles from £35/50)* is friendly and luxurious. **St Martin's Guest House** *(☎ 205938, fax 208229; 17 Castle Hill Rd; singles/doubles £38/45)* is also highly recommended.

Dover is short on decent places to eat. **Riveria Coffee House** *(☎ 201303; 9 Worthington St; light meals from £1.75)* is good value, with cream teas for £2 or sandwiches and light meals from £1.75. **Jermain's** *(☎ 205956; Beaconsfield Rd; meals £4.25)* is near the hostel and has a range of traditional lunches. **Curry Garden** *(☎ 206357; 24 High St)* is a cheap Indian restaurant where prawn korma costs £6.

Getting There & Around

For details on ferries to mainland Europe, see Getting There & Away at the beginning of this chapter.

From Dover, National Express buses leave hourly to/from London's Victoria coach station (£9.50/10.50 one-way/day return, 2¼ hours). **Stagecoach East Kent** *(☎ 0870 243 3711)* has an office on Pencester Rd. Dover to Canterbury (30 minutes) costs £3.25.

There are over 40 trains a day from Dover Priory to London Victoria and Charing Cross stations (£19.15 one way, 1¾ hours).

The ferry companies run complimentary buses every 20 minutes between the docks and train stations.

LEEDS CASTLE

Near Maidstone in Kent, Leeds Castle *(☎ 01622-765400; adult/concession £11/9.50; open 10am-5.30pm daily Mar-Oct, 10am-3pm Nov-Feb)* is one of the world's most famous and most visited castles. It stands on two small islands in a lake, and is surrounded by a park housing an aviary, a maze and a grotto. Unfortunately, it's usually overrun by families and school groups, so if you want to get your money's worth from the rather high admission price, call ahead.

National Express has a bus from Victoria coach station, leaving at 9am and returning at 3.45pm (1½ hours). It must be prebooked, and combined admission and travel is £15.

BRIGHTON

☎ 01273 • pop 180,000

Brighton is deservedly Britain's number one seaside town – a fascinating mixture of seediness and sophistication. Just an hour away from London by train, it's the perfect choice for day-trippers looking for a drop of froth and ozone. It's fine to swim here, though a little on the cool side, and the pebble beach comes as a bit of a shock if you're used to fine sand.

Brighton has a reputation as the club and party capital of the south. There's a bubbly population of students and travellers, excel-

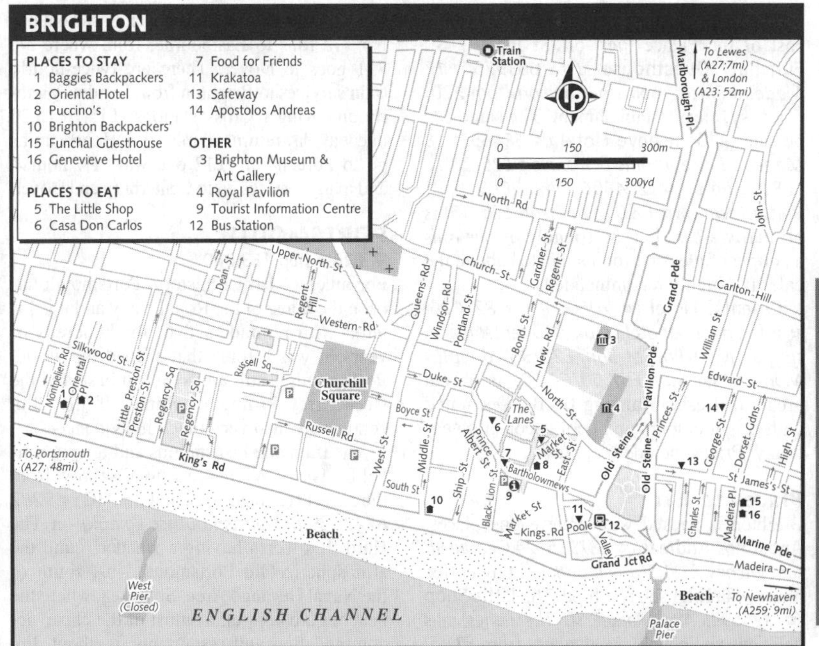

lent shopping, a terrific arts scene and countless restaurants, pubs and cafés. In May, Brighton hosts the largest **arts festival** (☎ *292961;* 🅆 *www.brighton-festival.org.uk)* in Britain outside Edinburgh.

Orientation & Information

Brighton train station is a 15-minute walk north of the beach. The bus station is tucked away in Poole Valley. The interesting part of Brighton is the streets north of North St, including Bond, Gardner, Kensington and Sydney Sts.

The **TIC** *(☎ 0906-711 2255;* 🄴 *brighton-tourism@brighton-hove.gov.uk; 10 Bartholomew Square)* has maps and magazines such as the *Brighton Latest* and *New Insight* (both free) and *The List* (50p). For £2-an-hour Internet access go to **Riki-Tik** *(☎ 683844; 18a Bond St)*.

Things to See

The **Royal Pavilion** *(☎ 290900; adult/concession £4.50/3.25; open 10am-5.15pm daily June-Sept, 10am-4.15pm Oct-May)* is an extraordinary fantasy: Indian palace on the outside, Chinese brothel on the inside – all built between 1815 and 1822 for George IV. The whole edifice is way over the top in every respect.

The **Brighton Museum & Art Gallery** *(☎ 290900;* 🅆 *www.museums.brighton-hove.gov.uk; entry via Royal Pavilion gardens; admission free; open 10am-7pm Tues, 10am-5pm Wed-Sat, 2pm-5pm Sun)* is another must. It reopened in 2002 after a £10 million facelift and houses Art Deco and Art Nouveau furniture, archaeological finds and surrealist paintings (including Salvador Dalí's lip sofa). The nearby **Palace Pier** is the very image of Brighton with its fast food, flashing lights and rides.

Places to Stay

There are loads of accommodation options in Brighton.

Baggies Backpackers *(☎ 733740; 33 Oriental Place; dorm beds £12, doubles £25, key deposit £5)* is more friendly and homey than the other hostels. **Brighton Backpackers** *(☎ 777717;* 🄴 *stay@brightonbackpackers.com; 75 Middle St; dorm beds £11, in seafront annexe £12, doubles £30)* bills itself as 'England's funkiest hostel' – there's loud music and decor to prove it.

The main cluster of cheap B&Bs is to the east of the Palace Pier, off St James's St. **Funchal Guesthouse** *(☎ 603975; 17 Madeira Place; rooms per person from £20)* is a cosy, clean establishment. The same can be said of **Genevieve Hotel** *(☎ 681653; 18 Madeira Place; rooms per person £25-30)*.

Puccino's *(☎ 204656, fax 206915; 1 Bartholowmews; B&B per person £25-35)* is primarily a café but the friendly owner runs a couple of pleasant rooms located above the café. It's highly recommended.

Oriental Hotel *(☎ 205050, fax 821096; e info@orientalhotel.co.uk; 9 Oriental Place; singles Mon-Fri/Sat-Sun £25/35, doubles Mon-Fri/Sat-Sun £57.50/64.50)* is a real breath of fresh air among B&Bs. Decorated with bright colours and cool decor, it's very funky. Prices include breakfast.

BRITAIN

Places to Eat

Brighton is packed with great eating places. **Apostolos Andreas** *(☎ 687935; 24 George St; sandwiches £1-1.50)* is a popular, tiny coffee house with English-style food. **The Little Shop** *(☎ 325594; 48a Market St, The Lanes)* has delicious and chunky sandwiches from £2.35.

Krakatoa *(☎ 719009; 7 Poole Valley; mains £6-9)*, near the bus station, is a small, casual restaurant with a modern Asian fusion menu. It's for serious foodies. **Casa Don Carlos** *(☎ 327177; 5 Union St, The Lanes)* is an intimate Spanish tapas house and restaurant. A big serve of paella costs £4.25.

Vegetarians and vegans have ample choice, including **Food for Friends** *(☎ 202310; 17 Prince Albert St, The Lanes; meals £5; open 8am-10pm)*, a rabbit warren of little rooms where delicious wholefood is served.

If you're self-catering head to **Safeway supermarket** *(St James's St)*.

Entertainment

Ever since the 1960s, Brighton has had a reputation as the club and party capital of the south. Pubs, bars and clubs are constantly opening, closing and changing their themes – check *Brighton Latest*, *New Insight* and bar and café walls for places of the moment. Most of the gay bars and clubs lie around St James's St and the Old Steine.

Getting There & Away

National Express buses leave hourly from London Victoria coach station to Brighton (£8 one way, 1¾ hours). Stagecoach East Kent bus No 712 runs to Eastbourne, from where No 711 goes to Dover. There are twice-hourly train services to Brighton from London Victoria and King's Cross stations (£15.10/15.20 one way/day return, 50 minutes). Hourly trains go to Portsmouth (£12 one way, 1½ hours), and many services go to Canterbury and Dover.

PORTSMOUTH

☎ 023 • pop 183,000

For much of British history, Portsmouth has been the home of the Royal Navy and it is littered with reminders that, for hundreds of years, it was a force that shaped the world. Portsmouth is still a busy naval base and the sleek, grey killing machines of the 20th century are also very much in evidence.

The train and bus stations and ferry terminal for Isle of Wight are a stone's throw from the Naval Heritage Area and the **TIC** *(☎ 9282 6722; e tic@portsmouthcc.gov.uk)* on The Hard. It's worth having a wander round the atmospheric Old Portsmouth, just south of the Naval Heritage Area. Southsea, where the beaches are, as well as most of the cheap accommodation and restaurants, is about 2mi south of Portsmouth Harbour.

Things to See

Portsmouth's centrepiece is the **Naval Heritage Area**. Exploring HMS *Victory*, Lord Nelson's flagship at the Battle of Trafalgar, is about as close as you can get to time travel – a fascinating experience. After 437 years underwater, Henry VIII's favourite ship, the *Mary Rose*, and its time-capsule contents can now be seen in the **Mary Rose Museum**. The **Royal Navy Museum** is really for naval buffs, and HMS *Warrior* does not have the same magic as the *Victory*. Admission is around £7 for each ship; alternatively buy a three-for-two ticket (£13.75), which includes the Royal Navy Museum and the Mary Rose Museum, or a Passport ticket (£18) valid for all attractions in the heritage area.

Places to Stay & Eat

Most budget accommodation is in Southsea. One exception is the **Youth Hostel** *(☎ 0870 770 6002; e portsmouth@yha.org.uk; Old Wymering Lane, Cosham; adult/under-18 £10.25/7)*, about 4mi from the main sights.

Twigs *(☎ 9282 8316; 39 High St; sandwiches £2.40-3.75)* is a small coffee shop with sandwiches, baguettes and baps (rolls). Osborne Rd and Palmerston Rd are the main restaurant strips in Southsea.

Getting There & Away

From Portsmouth, National Express bus No 30 goes via Heathrow to London (£11/12 one-way/day return, 2½ hours). **Stagecoach Coastline** (☎ *01903-237661*) bus No 700 runs between Brighton and Portsmouth every 30 minutes (£3.40 one way) and Stagecoach bus No 69 runs to/from Winchester hourly from Monday to Saturday.

There are over 40 trains a day to/from London's Victoria and Waterloo stations (£20 one way, 1½ hours). There are plenty of trains to/from Brighton (£12, 1½ hours) and Winchester (£7, one hour).

For information on ferries to France and Spain, the Getting There & Away section at the beginning of this chapter. The Continental Ferryport is north of Flagship Portsmouth.

WINCHESTER

☎ 01962 • pop 37,000

Winchester is a beautiful cathedral city on the River Itchen, interspersed with water meadows. It was both the capital of Saxon England and the seat of the powerful Bishops of Winchester from AD 670. Much of the present-day city dates from the 18th century, and its main attraction is its stunning cathedral.

Winchester makes a good base for exploring the south coast (ie, Portsmouth and New Forest) or the country farther west.

The city centre is compact and easily negotiated on foot. The train station is a 10-minute walk to the west of the centre, and the bus and coach station is on Broadway, directly opposite the Guildhall and the **TIC** (☎ *840500;* ⓔ *tourism@winchester.gov.uk; Broadway; open daily May-Sept*).

Things to See

One of the most beautiful cathedrals in the country is **Winchester Cathedral** *(suggested donation £2.50)*, a mixture of Norman, Early English and perpendicular styles. The north and south transepts are a magnificent example of pure Norman architecture. Nearby is **Winchester College** (☎ *621217; tours of chapel & cloisters at 10.45am, noon, 2.15pm & 3.30pm Mon-Sat, 2.15pm & 3.30pm Sun; adult/concession £2.50/2)*, founded in 1382 and the model for the great public schools of England.

Places to Stay & Eat

The **Youth Hostel** (☎ *0870 770 6092, fax 0870 770 6093; 1 Water Lane; adult/under-18 £9.50/6.75)* is in a beautiful 18th-century water mill in the heart of town. B&Bs tend not to hang signs out the front; you'll have to get a list from the TIC. **East View** (☎ *862986; 16 Clifton Hill; singles/doubles from £35/45)* is conveniently located and features three small but comfortable rooms with bathroom.

At **Presto** (☎ *878370; The Square; snacks around £2)*, try an Indian chicken pastie or a huge baguette. The **Cathedral Refectory** (☎ *857258; sandwiches £1.90, cream teas £4.25)*, near the entrance to the cathedral, is a self-service cafeteria with a pleasant terrace.

Getting There & Away

National Express bus No 32 leaves every two hours from to/from London Victoria via Heathrow (£10.50, one hour). **Stagecoach Hampshire Bus** (☎ *0845 121 0180)* has a good network of services linking Salisbury, Southampton, Portsmouth and Brighton. Trains depart about every 15 minutes from London Waterloo (£21.20 one way, one hour), Southampton (£3.80, 18 minutes) and Portsmouth (£7, one hour).

Southwest England

The counties of Wiltshire, Dorset, Somerset, Devon and Cornwall include some of the most beautiful countryside and spectacular coastline in Britain. They are also littered with the evidence of successive cultures and kingdoms that have been swept away by one invader after another.

The region can be divided between Devon and Cornwall out on a limb in the far west, and Dorset, Wiltshire and Somerset, which are more readily accessible in the east.

In the east, the story of English civilisation is signposted by some of its greatest monuments. The east is densely packed with things to see, and the countryside, though varied, is a classic English patchwork of hedgerows, thatch-roofed cottages, stone churches, great estates and emerald-green fields.

Devon and particularly Cornwall were once Britain's 'wild west', and smuggling was rife. These days, the 'English Riviera' is almost too popular for its own good. Land's End – a veritable icon – has been reduced to an overly commercialised tourist trap, and inland much of the peninsula has been devastated by generations of tin and china-clay mining. However, many of the coastal villages retain their charm, especially if you visit out of season.

Activities

Walking The southwest has plenty of beautiful countryside, but walks in Dartmoor and Exmoor national parks, and around the coastline, are the best known. Exmoor covers some of the most beautiful countryside in England, and the coastal stretch from Ilfracombe to Minehead is particularly spectacular.

Two famous walks are the South West Coast Path (Exmoor), following the coastline round the peninsula for 613mi from Poole to Minehead, and the Ridgeway, starting at Avebury and running northeast for 85mi to Ivinghoe Beacon near Aylesbury.

Surfing The capital of British surfing, complete with surf shops, bleached hair and Kombi vans, is Newquay on the west Cornish coast. The surfable coast runs from Porthleven (near Helston) in Cornwall, west around Land's End and north to Ilfracombe. The most famous reef breaks are at Porthleven, Lynmouth and Millbrook.

Cycling Bikes can be hired in most major regional centres, and infrequent bus connections make cycling a more sensible option than in other regions. There's no shortage of hills, but the mild weather and quiet back roads make this excellent cycling country.

Getting Around

Bus Reasonable connections between the main towns, particularly in the east, are provided by National Express buses. However, the farther west you go the more dire the situation becomes. Contact **Traveline** *(☎ 0870 608 2608)* for information on regional bus services.

Train The train services in the east are reasonably comprehensive, linking Bristol, Bath, Salisbury, Weymouth and Exeter. Beyond Exeter a single line follows the south coast as far as Penzance, with spurs to Barnstaple, Gunnislake, Looe, Falmouth, St Ives and Newquay. For rail information, phone ☎ 0845 748 4950. Several regional rail passes are available.

SALISBURY

☎ 01722 • pop 37,000

Salisbury is justly famous for the cathedral and its close, but its appeal also lies in the fact that it is still a bustling market town, not just a tourist trap. Markets have been held in the town centre every Tuesday and Saturday since 1361, and the jumble of stalls still draws a large, cheerful crowd.

The town's architecture is a blend of every style since the Middle Ages, including some beautiful, half-timbered black-and-white buildings. It's a good base for visiting the Wiltshire Downs, Stonehenge, Wilton House and Avebury. Portsmouth and Winchester are also easy day trips.

The town centre is a 10-minute walk from the train station. The bus station is just north of the centre of town, along (not-so) Endless St. The **TIC** *(☎ 334956; ⓔ visitorinfo@salisbury.gov.uk; Fish Row)* is behind the impressive 18th-century Guildhall, located on the southeastern corner of Market Square.

Beautiful **St Mary's Cathedral** *(donation £3.50)* is built in a uniform style known as Early English. This period is characterised by the first pointed arches and flying buttresses, and has a rather austere feel. The spire, at 123m, is the highest in Britain. The adjacent **chapter house** is one of the most perfect achievements of Gothic architecture.

Places to Stay & Eat

Salisbury Youth Hostel *(☎ 0870 770 6018, fax 770 6019; ⓔ salisbury@yha.org.uk; Milford Hill; dorm beds adult/under-18 £11.25/8)* is an attractive old building, a 15-minute walk from the town centre.

Griffin Cottage *(☎ 328259, fax 416928; ⓔ mark@brandonsoc.demon.co.uk; 10 St Edmunds Church St; B&B per person £20)* is a central, peaceful and comfortable B&B.

Fisherton St, running from the centre to the train station, has Chinese, Thai, Indian and other restaurants. For a casual bite, try **Cawardine's** *(☎ 320619, 3 Bridge St)*, a popular local café big on sandwiches and snacks. **Berli's** *(☎ 328923; 14 Ox Row; meals £4.50-6)* is an informal vegetarian restaurant with delicious food and a great view over Market Square.

Getting There & Around

National Express has three buses a day from Salisbury to London via Heathrow to Salisbury (£12 one way, three hours). There are three unlimited travel tickets available in Wiltshire – **Wiltshire Bus Lines** *(☎ 0845 709 0899)* or **Wilts & Dorset** *(☎ 336855)* can tell you more. There are daily buses to Avebury and Stonehenge. If you're going through to Bristol or Bath, via Somerset (Wells, Glastonbury) or Gloucestershire (Cotswolds), get the Badgerline Day Explorer ticket (£5.30). Wilts & Dorset run an hourly bus No X6 to Bath (£5.50, 2¼ hours).

Salisbury is linked by rail to Bath (£10, 50 minutes), Portsmouth (£11.10, 1¾ hours), Exeter (£20.20, 1¾ hours) and London's Waterloo station (£23.10, two hours).

Local buses are reasonably well organised and link Salisbury with Stonehenge (£5.50 return) and Wilton House; phone ☎ 336855 for details.

STONEHENGE & AVEBURY

☎ 01672

Stonehenge is the most famous prehistoric site in Europe – a ring of enormous stones (some of which were brought from Wales), built in stages beginning 5000 years ago. It's 2mi west of Amesbury, and 9mi northwest of Salisbury (the nearest station). Some feel that it's unnecessary to pay the admission (£4.40), because you can get a good view from the road. There are six buses a day from Salisbury (£5.50 return); a Getaway ticket (also £5.50) can be used for the day and allows travel to other destinations so is better value.

Avebury (between Calne and Marlborough) stands at the hub of a prehistoric complex of ceremonial sites, ancient avenues and burial chambers dating from 3500 BC. In scale the remains are more impressive than Stonehenge, and if you visit outside the summer weekends it's quite possible to escape the crowds. **Avebury TIC** *(☎ 01380-729408, fax 730319; ⓔ alltic@kennet.gov.uk)* can help with accommodation. Avebury can easily be reached by frequent buses from Salisbury (Wiltshire Bus Lines No 5, £4, 1½ hours) or from Swindon (No 6, £2, 30 minutes). To travel to/from Bath (£9.40, 1¾ hours) you'll have to change buses at Devizes.

EXETER

☎ 01392 • pop 102,000

Exeter is the heart of the West Country. It was devastated during WWII and, as a result, first impressions are not particularly inspiring; if you get over these, you'll find a lively university city with a thriving nightlife and one of England's most attractive cathedrals. It's a good base for Dartmoor and Cornwall.

Most intercity trains use St David's station, which is a 20-minute walk west of the city centre, and Central station. The **TIC** *(☎ 265700; ⓔ tic@exeter.gov.uk; Civic Centre, Paris St; open Mon-Sat)* is just across the road from the bus station.

Globe Backpackers *(☎ 215521, fax 215531; ⓔ caroline@globebackpackers.freeserve.co.uk; 71 Holloway St; dorm beds £11, doubles £30)* is a thankful addition to the budget scene with its good vibe (and Internet access). There are several B&Bs on St David's Hill; the welcoming **Kellsmoor** *(☎ 211128, fax 211198; ⓔ kellsmoor@exeter81.fsnet.co.uk; 81 St David's Hill; B&B singles/doubles £25/45)* is the pick of the crop.

Coolings *(☎ 434184; 11 Gandy St; mains £6.65)* is a busy brasserie on a medieval, pedestrianised street; it's signposted off High St. **Ship Inn** *(☎ 272040; Martin's Lane)*, down the alley between the cathedral and the High St, was where Sir Francis Drake used to drink.

Nine buses a day run between London, Heathrow airport and Exeter (£18, four hours). From Exeter there are frequent services to Plymouth (£5.35, 1¼ hours) and three direct buses a day to Penzance (£19, 4½ hours). For bus information phone National Express or **Stagecoach** *(☎ 427711)*.

For rail information, phone ☎ 0845 748 4950. Exeter is at the hub of lines running from London's Waterloo and Paddington stations (£51, 2¾ hours, hourly), Bristol (£15.60, 1¾ hours), Salisbury (£20.20, 1¾ hours) and Penzance (£19.10, three hours).

The 39mi branch line to Barnstaple (£9.60, 1¼ hours) gives good views of traditional Devon countryside.

EXMOOR NATIONAL PARK

Exmoor is a small national park (265 sq mi) enclosing a wide variety of beautiful landscapes. In the north and along the coast the scenery is particularly breathtaking, with dramatic humpbacked headlands giving superb views across the Bristol Channel.

There are a number of particularly attractive villages: **Lynton/Lynmouth**, twin villages joined by a water-operated railway; **Porlock**, at the edge of the moor in a beautiful valley; **Dunster**, which is dominated by a castle, a survivor from the Middle Ages; and also

Selworthy, a National Trust village with many classic thatch-roofed cottages.

For walkers, arguably the best and easiest section of the South West Coast Path is the part that's between Minehead and Padstow (sometimes known as the Somerset & North Devon Coast Path).

The National Park Authority (NPA) has five information centres in and around the park, but it's also possible to get information from the TICs at Barnstaple, Ilfracombe, Lynton and Minehead. The **main NPA visitor centre** (*☎ 01398-323841; Fore St, Dulverton; open year-round*) is between Bampton and Minehead. Other NPA centres (*Dunster: ☎ 01643-821835 • Lynmouth: ☎ 01598-752509*) are open from the end of March to November.

CORNWALL COAST

Penzance

☎ 01736 • pop 20,000

At the end of the railway line from London, Penzance is a busy town that has not yet completely sold its soul to tourism. It makes a good base for walking the Coastal Path from Land's End to St Ives, a dramatic 25mi section. The **TIC** (*☎ 362207; ⓔ pztic@penwith.gov.uk*) is just outside the train station. A central place to stay is friendly **Penzance Backpackers** (*☎ 363836, fax 363844; ⓔ pzbackpack@ndirect.co.uk; Alexander Rd; dorm beds £10*).

There are four buses a day from Penzance to Bristol via either Newquay or Truro and Plymouth; three direct buses a day to Exeter (£19, 4½ hours); and five buses a day to London and Heathrow (£30.50, 7½ hours). The train is definitely the civilised, if expensive, way to get to from Penzance to London's Paddington station (£61.70, five hours). There are frequent trains from Penzance to St Ives (£2.90, 20 minutes) and Plymouth (£10.30, two hours).

Land's End

☎ 01736

The coastal scenery on either side of Land's End is some of the finest in Britain, although the development at Land's End itself is shameful. Colourful **Whitesand's Lodge** (*☎ 871776; ⓔ info@whitesandslodge.co.uk; Sennen village; dorm beds £11, doubles with bath £51*) is on the main road, 2mi before Land's End. The closest **Youth Hostel** (*☎ 0870 770 5906, fax 770 5907; St Just*) is just over 3mi from Land's End or 8mi from Penzance.

St Ives

☎ 01736 • pop 9500

St Ives is the ideal to which other seaside towns can only aspire. The omnipresent sea, the harbour, the beaches, the narrow alleyways, steep slopes and hidden corners are captivating, but it gets mighty busy in summer. Artists have long been attracted to St Ives, and in 1993 a branch of London's **Tate Gallery** (*☎ 796226*) was opened here.

The **TIC** (*☎ 796297, fax 798309; ⓔ ivtic@penwith.gov.uk; the Guildhall, Street-an-Pol*) is a short walk from the train station. Busy **St Ives Backpackers** (*☎/fax 799444; ⓔ st.ives@backpackers.co.uk; Lower Stennack; dorm beds £12*) occupies a converted chapel. Of the numerous B&Bs, **Kynance Guest House** (*☎ 796636; ⓔ enquiries@kynance24.co.uk; The Warren; rooms per person £23*) is a sure bet. Restaurants – both cheap and pricey – congregate around the harbour and behind it on Fore St.

St Ives is easily accessible by train from Penzance (£2.90, 20 minutes) and London (£61.70, five hours) via St Erth.

Newquay

☎ 01637 • pop 14,000

Newquay, the original Costa de Cornwall, was drawing them in long before the British learned to say 'Torremolinos.' There are numerous sandy beaches, several of them right in town (including Fistral Beach for board riders). The **TIC** (*☎ 854020; ⓔ info@newquay.co.uk; Marcus Hill*) is near the bus station in the centre of town. The **Original Backpackers** (*☎ 874668; 16 Beachfield Ave; dorm beds from £10*) is in an excellent central position overlooking Towan Beach. **Home Surf Lodge** (*☎ 873387; 18 Tower Rd; dorm beds per night £10, per week in summer £120*) is bigger and brighter.

There are four trains a day between Newquay and Par (£4.30, 45 minutes), which is on the London–Penzance line, and numerous buses to Truro.

BATH

☎ 01255 • pop 85,000

For more than 2000 years Bath's fortune has been linked to its hot springs and tourism. The Romans developed a complex of baths and a temple to Sulis-Minerva. Today, however, Bath's Georgian architecture is an equally important attraction.

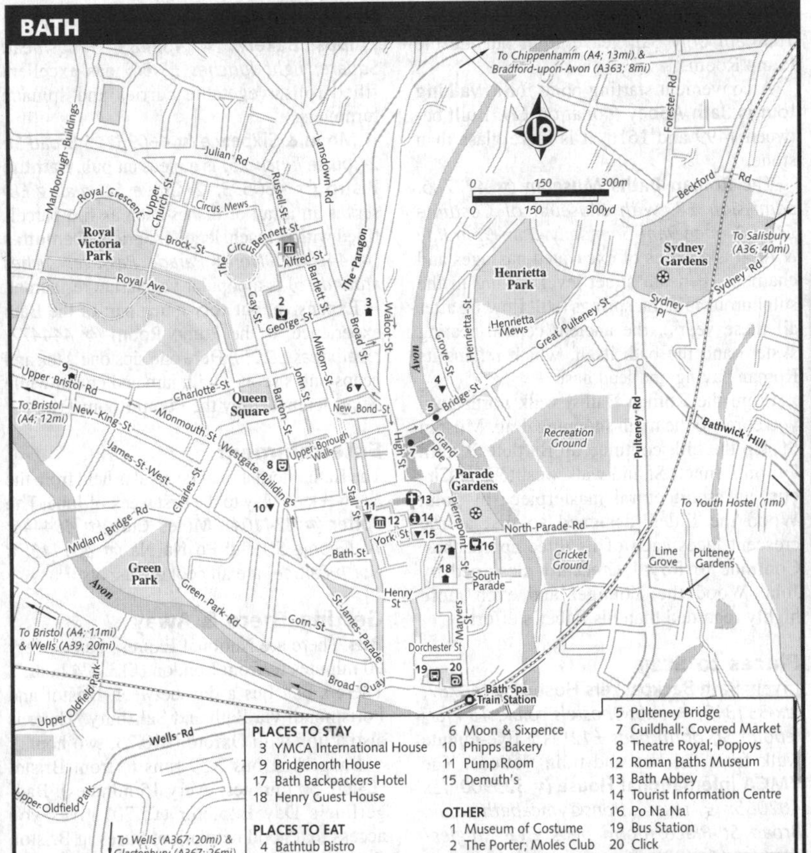

Throughout the 18th century, Bath was the most fashionable haunt of English society. Aristocrats flocked here to gossip, gamble and flirt. Fortunately, they had the good sense and fortune to employ a number of brilliant architects who designed the Palladian terrace that dominates the city.

Like Italy's Florence, Bath is an architectural jewel, with a much-photographed, shop-lined bridge (Pulteney). When sunlight brightens the honey-coloured stone, no-one can deny Bath's exceptional beauty.

Orientation & Information

Bath sprawls more than you'd expect. Fortunately, the centre is compact and easy to get around, although the tangle of streets, arcades and squares can be confusing. The train and bus stations are both south of the TIC, by the river.

The **TIC** *(☎ 477101; ⓔ tourism@bathnes.gov.uk; Abbey Chambers, Abbey Churchyard; open daily)* can help with information. Advance booking of accommodation is essential over Easter, during the Bath International Festival (late May), over summer weekends and throughout July and August. **Click** *(☎ 481008; 13a Manvers St; open 10am-10pm daily; £1 per 20 mins)* provides Internet access.

Things to See & Do

Bath was designed for wandering around. There is a **covered market** located next to the Guildhall, and don't miss the maze of passageways just north of Abbey Churchyard.

Walking tours *(free; 10.30am & 2pm, 10.30am only Sat)* leave from outside the Pump Room.

A convenient starting point for a **walking tour** is **Bath Abbey** *(donation £2)*. Built between 1499 and 1616, it is more glass than stone.

The **Roman Baths Museum** *(☎ 477785; admission £8, with Museum of Costume £10.50; open 9am-5pm daily, 9am-9pm July & Aug)* is a series of excavated passages and chambers beneath street level, taking in the sulphurous mineral springs (still flowing after all these years), the ancient central-heating system and the bath itself, which retains its Roman paving and lead base.

From the Roman Baths, walk north until you come to the main shopping drag, Milsom St. Up the hill, continue up Bartlett St, turn left on Bennett St and walk west to **The Circus**, an architectural masterpiece by John Wood the Elder, designed so that a true crescent faces each of its three approaches. Continue to **Royal Crescent**, designed by John Wood the Younger and even more highly regarded than his father's effort.

Places to Stay

Lively **Bath Backpackers Hostel** *(☎ 446787, fax 331319; ⓔ bath@hostels.co.uk; 13 Pierrepoint St; dorm beds £12)* is a five-minute walk from the bus and train stations. The **YMCA International House** *(☎ 325900, fax 462065; ⓔ reservations@ymcabath.co.uk; Broad St Place; dorm beds £12, singles/doubles £16/32)* offers the next best budget accommodation, but it's heavily booked. Rates include breakfast.

Bath Youth Hostel *(☎ 0870 770 5688, fax 0870 770 5689; ⓔ bath@yha.org.uk; Bathwick Hill; dorm beds £9.75)* is a 25-minute walk from town, or alternatively take First Badgerline bus No 18 from Cc bus stop. The views from the hostel make up for the distance, and the building is magnificent.

Bath's B&Bs are expensive. In summer most charge at least £22/45 for a single/double. The main areas are along Newbridge Rd to the west, Wells Rd to the south and around Pulteney Rd in the east. Considering its central location, **Henry Guest House** *(☎ 424052; 6 Henry St; rooms per person £22)* is a good value. **Bridgenorth House** *(☎ 331186; 2 Crescent Gardens; doubles £44)* is also reasonable.

Places to Eat

Phipps Bakery *(☎ 462483; Kingsmead Square; light lunches £3.50)* has excellent filled rolls, vegetable curries and spinach turnovers.

Moon & Sixpence *(☎ 460962; 6 Broad St; 2-course lunch £5)* is a pleasant pub. **Bathtub Bistro** *(☎ 460593; 2 Grove St; mains £8)* serves an array of dishes such as filo parcels filled with spinach, lentil or apricot. **Demuth's** *(☎ 446059; North Parade Passage; dishes around £5)* is a popular vegetarian restaurant.

Expensive, but very much part of the Bath experience, is the **Pump Room** *(☎ 444477; cream teas £6.25)*. Here one sips one's tea and heaps one's scones with jam and cream while being serenaded by the Pump Room Trio.

Entertainment

The Bath International Festival is held from the last week of May to the first week of June. **The Porter** *(☎ 424104)*, **Moles Club** *(☎ 404445; 14 George St)* and **Po Na Na** *(☎ 401115; 8 North Parade)* are all cool nightspots.

Getting There & Away

Bus There are National Express buses every 90 minutes to/from London (£13, 3¼ hours). There's one bus a day between Bristol and Portsmouth via Bath and Salisbury. There is also a link with Oxford (£10.25, two hours).

Badgerline bus X39 runs to/from Bristol (£3.60, 50 minutes, every 15 minutes). Badgerline's Day Explorer (£5.70) gives you access to a good network of buses in Bristol, Somerset (Wells, Glastonbury), Gloucestershire (Gloucester via Bristol) and Wiltshire (Lacock, Bradford-on-Avon, Salisbury). Maps and timetables are available from the **bus station** *(☎ 464446)*.

Train There are numerous services to/from London's Paddington station (£37.50, 1¾ hours). Plenty of trains also run to Bristol (£4.60, 10 to 20 minutes) for onward travel to Exeter, Cardiff or the north. Trains run hourly to Salisbury (£10, 50 minutes).

GLASTONBURY

☎ 01458 • pop 7000

Legend and history combine at Glastonbury to produce an irresistible attraction for romantics and eccentrics of every description. It's a small market town with the ruins of a 14th-century **abbey**, and a nearby **tor** with superb views.

According to some legends, Jesus travelled here with Joseph of Arimathea and the chalice from the Last Supper, it is the burial place of King Arthur and Queen Guinevere, and the tor is either the Isle of Avalon or a gateway to the underworld. Whatever you choose to believe, a climb to the top of the tor is well worthwhile.

The **Glastonbury Festival** *(☎ 832020; admission £100 by advance ticket only)*, a three-day festival of theatre, music, circus, mime, natural healing etc, is a massive affair with over 1000 acts. It takes place over three days in late June at Pilton, 8mi from Glastonbury.

The **TIC** *(☎ 832954; ⓔ glastonbury.tic@ukonline.co.uk)* can supply maps and accommodation information. There are plenty of B&Bs for around £21 per person. **Glastonbury Backpackers Hostel** *(☎ 833353; ⓔ backpackers@glastonbury/online.com; Crown Hotel, 4 Market Place; dorm beds £10, doubles £26)* has good facilities. Another possibility is **Street Youth Hostel** *(☎ 0870 770 6056, fax 0870 770 6057)*, 4mi south of the city centre.

There are Badgerline buses from Bristol to Wells, Glastonbury and Street. Glastonbury is only 6mi from Wells, so walking or hitching is also feasible. Bus No 163 from Wells continues to Bridgwater, from where there are buses to Minehead (for Exmoor)

Central England

The English heartland covers a vast swathe of territory that includes many of England's highs and lows. Many of the areas around the M1 corridor can look pretty miserable on a wet and windy day, but here you'll also find such lively cities as Nottingham, Leicester, Coventry and Birmingham. What the area lacks in prettiness, it makes up for in personality.

To the west, however, it's a different story. Oxford remains a must for any visitor. The southwest sections of the Chilterns remain largely unspoilt and are accessible to walkers of the Ridgeway.

The Cotswolds, more than any other region, embody the popular image of English countryside. The prettiness can be forced, and the villages are certainly not strangers to mass tourism, but there are also moments when you will be transfixed by the area's beauty. The combination of golden stone, flower-draped cottages, church spires, towering chestnuts and oaks, rolling hills and green, stone-walled fields can be too extraordinarily picturesque to seem quite real.

West again, you reach the Bristol Channel and the wide Severn Valley, a natural border to the counties of Herefordshire and Worcestershire and the region known as the Welsh Marches. The Wye Valley is a famous spot of beauty, popularised by the first Romantic poets in the 18th century.

Bus transport around the region is fairly efficient, and particularly good in the Peak District. There's also a good network of railway lines.

OXFORD

☎ 01865 • pop 115,000

It's impossible to pick up any tourist literature about Oxford without reading about its dreaming spires. Like all great cliches, it's strikingly apt. Looking across the meadows or rooftops to Oxford's golden spires is certainly an experience to inspire purple prose.

These days, however, Oxford battles against a flood of tourists that can dilute the charm during summer. It is not just a university city, but also the home of Morris cars. Rapid expansion has created a city with a bustling heart surrounded by sprawling industrial suburbs.

Oxford University is the oldest university in Britain, but no-one can find an exact starting date. It evolved during the 11th century as an informal centre for scholars and students. The colleges began to appear from the mid-13th century onwards. There are now about 14,500 undergraduates and 36 colleges.

Orientation & Information

The city centre is surrounded by rivers and streams on the eastern, southern and western sides, and can easily be covered on foot. **Carfax Tower** *(admission £1.20; open daily)* at the intersection of Queen St and Cornmarket St/St Aldate's is a useful central marker.

The train station is to the west of the city, with frequent buses to Carfax Tower. The bus station is nearer the centre, on Gloucester 'Green'. A visit to the hectic **TIC** *(☎ 726871, fax 240261; ⓔ tic@oxford.gov.uk; ⓦ www.visitoxford.org; open Mon-Sat, daily in summer)*, also on Gloucester Green, is essential. The *Welcome to Oxford* brochure (£1.30) has a walking tour with college opening times.

For Internet access (£1 for 30 minutes) head to **Mic@s.com** *(☎ 726364; 118 High St; open 9am-11pm daily)*.

Things to See & Do

The colleges remain open throughout the year, but their hours vary; many are closed in the morning. The following walk will give you a taste of Oxford. Starting at Carfax Tower, cross Cornmarket St and walk down the hill, along St Aldate's, to **Christ Church College** *(☎ 276150; admission £4)*, perhaps the most famous college in Oxford. The main entrance is beneath Tom Tower, built by Christopher Wren in 1680, but the usual visitors entrance is farther down the hill via the wrought-iron gates of the War Memorial Gardens and the Broad Walk facing out over Christ Church Meadow. The college chapel, the smallest cathedral in England, is a beautiful example of late Norman (1140–80) architecture.

Return to the Broad Walk, follow the stone wall, then turn left up Dead Man's Walk, through wrought-iron gates, then right onto Merton St. **Merton College** *(☎ 276110; admission free)* was founded in 1264. The present buildings date mostly from the 15th to the 17th centuries. The entrance to the 14th-century Mob Quad, with its medieval library, is on your right.

Turn left onto Merton St, then take the first right onto Magpie Lane, which will take you through the architecturally eclectic High St. Turn right and walk down the hill until you come to **Magdalen College** *(☎ 276000; admission £2)*, just before the river on your left. Magdalen is one of the richest Oxford colleges and has the most extensive and beautiful grounds, with a deer park, river walk, three quadrangles and superb lawns. This was CS Lewis' college and the setting for the film *Shadowlands*. While you're in the area you might want to hire a boat or **punt** *(£10 per hour, £25 deposit; May-Sept only)* which you can do at the Magdalen Bridge.

The **Ashmolean** *(☎ 278000; W www.ashmol.ox.ac.uk; Beaumont St; donation £3; open 10am-5pm Tues-Sat, 2pm-5pm Sun)*, established in 1683, is the country's oldest museum and houses extensive displays of European art (including works by Raphael and Michelangelo) and Middle Eastern antiquities.

Places to Stay

The **Youth Hostel** *(☎ 0870 770 5970, fax 0870 770 5971; e oxford@yha.org.uk; 2a Botley Rd; adult/under-18 in 4-/6-bed rooms £18.50/13.75, twins £41)* is well located in a new building directly behind the train station. It gets booked up very quickly in summer. Rates include breakfast.

B&Bs are expensive and suburban, the two main areas being Abingdon Rd and Cowley/Iffley Rds, both on regular bus routes. **Earlmont** *(☎ 240236, fax 434903; e beds@earlmont.prestel.co.uk; 322 Cowley Rd; singles/doubles £40/60)* is a large and comfortable B&B within walking distance of shops and restaurants. **Sportsview Guest House** *(☎ 244268, fax 249270; e stay@sportsview-guest-house.freeserve.co.uk; 106-110 Abingdon Rd; singles/doubles from £40/62)* is clean, quiet and nonsmoking.

Places to Eat

There are some excellent sandwich bars throughout the centre, and many a student debate has centred on which is the best. **Morton's** *(☎ 200860; 22 Broad St)* can't be faulted for its tasty baguettes and attractive garden; nearby, the relaxed **Heroes** *(☎ 723459; 8 Ship St; sandwiches from £2.15)* builds to order with a fine selection of fillings.

Pubs are also a good bet. There's excellent pub grub at **Turf Tavern** *(☎ 243235; 4 Bath Place)*, a recommended watering hole hidden away down an alley. **Head of the River** *(☎ 721600; Folly Bridge)* has an ideal location and is very popular.

Self-caterers should visit the **covered market**, near Carfax Tower, for fruit and vegetables.

Entertainment

Po Na Na *(☎ 249171; 13 Magdalen St)* is a late night bar-cum-club. **Oxford Playhouse** *(☎ 305305; Beaumont St)* has a mixed bag of theatre, dance and music. **Burton Taylor Theatre** *(☎ 305350; Beaumont St)* presents a more offbeat range of productions.

Getting There & Away

Bus The **Oxford Tube** *(☎ 772250; £9 return ticket valid 2 days; 1¾ hours)* starts at London's Victoria coach station but also stops at Marble Arch, Notting Hill Gate and Shepherd's Bush. The bus service operates 24 hours a day.

National Express has one service a day to/from Bath (£10, two hours) and Bristol (£13, 2¾ hours), and two services to/from Gloucester (£8.25, 1½ hours) and Cheltenham (£8, one hour). From Bristol there are connections to Wales, Devon and Cornwall.

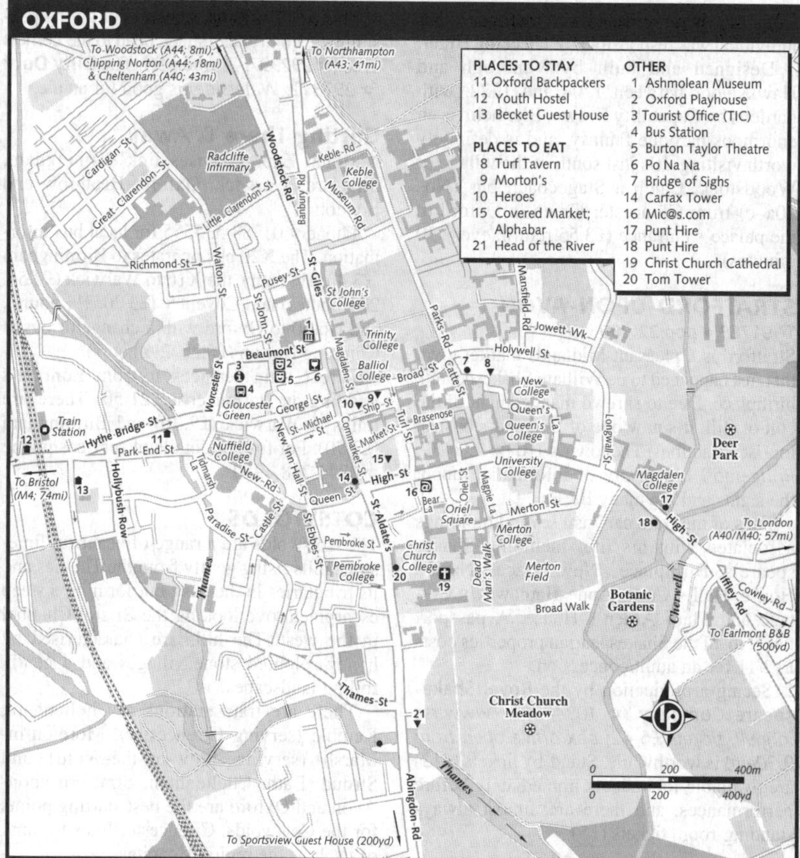

Buses to Shrewsbury, North Wales, York and Durham go via Birmingham.

Oxford Express (☎ *785400)* has frequent departures to London (£8.50 one way, 1¾ hours, every 20 to 30 minutes), Heathrow (£11 one way, 1¼ hours, every 30 minutes) and Gatwick (£18, two hours, hourly).

Stagecoach (☎ *772250)* runs six buses a day to Cambridge and Stratford.

Train There are very frequent trains to/from London's Paddington station (£13.70 one way, 1½ hours). Regular trains run north to Coventry and Birmingham, and northwest to Worcester and Hereford (for Moreton-in-Marsh, Gloucester and Cheltenham in the Cotswolds). Birmingham is the main hub for transport farther north.

To connect with trains to the southwest you have to change at Didcot Parkway (15 minutes). There are plenty of connections to Bath; with a bit of luck the whole trip won't take longer than 1½ hours. Change at Swindon for another line running into the Cotswolds (Kemble, Stroud and Gloucester). For train inquiries, phone ☎ 0845 748 4950.

BLENHEIM PALACE

Blenheim Palace (☎ *01993-811325; adult/concession £10/7.50; house open 10.30am-5.30pm 11 Mar-31 Oct, park open 9am-4.45pm daily year-round)*, one of the largest palaces in Europe, was a gift to John Churchill from Queen Anne and Parliament as a reward for his role in defeating Louis XIV. Curiously, the palace was the birthplace of Winston

Churchill, who perhaps more than any other individual was responsible for checking Hitler.

Designed and built by Vanbrugh and Hawksmoor between 1704 and 1722, with gardens by Capability Brown, Blenheim is an enormous baroque fantasy, and is definitely worth visiting. It's just south of the village of Woodstock. Catch a Stagecoach bus (Nos 20a–c) from Gloucester Green in Oxford to the palace's entrance (£3.55 return, every 30 minutes).

STRATFORD-UPON-AVON

☎ 01789 • pop 22,000

Stratford is a pleasant Midlands market town that just happened to be William Shakespeare's birthplace. Due to shrewd management of the cult of Bill, it's now one of England's busiest tourist attractions. The town's **TIC** *(☎ 293127; Bridgefoot)* has plenty of information about the sights and the many B&Bs.

Fans of the Bard can visit several buildings associated with his life, including Shakespeare's Birthplace, New Place, Nash's House, Hall's Croft, Anne Hathaway's Cottage and Mary Arden's House. A passport ticket to all the Shakespearian properties costs £12/11 for an adult/concession.

Seeing a production by the **Royal Shakespeare Company** *(☎ 403403; w www.rsc.org.uk; tickets £5-42; box office open from 9.30am)* is worthwhile. Stand-by tickets (£12) are available to students immediately before performances, and there are almost always standing-room tickets (£5).

Places to Stay & Eat

Knit the raveled sleave of care at the central **Backpackers Hostel** *(☎/fax 263838; 33 Greenhill St; dorm beds £12)*. The **Youth Hostel** *(☎ 0870 770 6052, fax 0870 770 6053; e stratford@yha.org.uk; Hemmingford House, Alveston; B&B adult/under-18 £16/11.75)* is nearly 2mi out of town – from the TIC, cross Clopton Bridge and follow the B4086, or take bus No 18 from Bridge St near the TIC.

B&Bs are plentiful just west of the centre on Evesham Place, Grove Rd and Broad Walk. In summer, however, many insist on bookings of at least two nights. Head to the neat **Dylan** *(☎ 204819; e thedylan@lineone.net; 10 Evesham Place; per person £25)*, or the delightful **Twelfth Night** *(☎ 414595; 13 Evesham Place; doubles only from £55)*.

Sheep St has a fine selection of dining possibilities. For a cheap snack head to the **Lemon Tree** *(☎ 292997; 2 Union St)*. The **Dirty Duck** *(☎ 297312; Waterside)* is good for an ale.

Getting There & Away

National Express buses link Birmingham, Stratford, Warwick, Oxford, Heathrow and London.

Phone ☎ 01788-535555 for local bus information. The X20 bus operates to Birmingham (£3.40, 1¼ hour), the X16 to Warwick (£2.55, 20 minutes) and Coventry (£3.20, 1½ hours), and No 50 to Oxford with a change of bus at Chipping Norton (£5.25, 2½ hours).

Direct train services to/from London's Paddington station cost £21.50. There are trains to Warwick (£2.70) and Birmingham (£3.70). For further details of services phone ☎ 0845 748 4950.

COTSWOLDS

The Cotswolds are a range of beautiful limestone hills rising gently from the Thames and its tributaries in the east, but forming a steep escarpment overlooking the Bristol Channel in the west. The hills are characterised by honey-coloured stone villages and a gently rolling landscape.

There are train stations at Cheltenham, Kemble (serving Cirencester), Moreton-in-Marsh (serving Stow-on-the-Wold) and Stroud. Bath, Cheltenham, Stratford-upon-Avon and Oxford are the best starting points for the Cotswolds. Cirencester likes to think of itself as the region's capital.

The TICs in surrounding towns all stock information on the Cotswolds, but those dealing specifically with the region are **Cirencester TIC** *(☎ 01285-654180; Market Place)* and **Stow-on-the-Wold TIC** *(☎ 01451-831082; The Square)*. The latter (usually known as 'Stow') is one of the Cotswolds' most impressive towns, with many beautiful villages within a day's hike. Its **Youth Hostel** *(☎ 0870 770 6050, fax 0870 770 6051; e stow@yha.org.uk; The Square; adult/under-18 £12.75/8.75)* is in a 16th-century building.

Getting around the Cotswolds by public transport isn't easy. If you're trying anything ambitious, contact the **Gloucestershire inquiry line** *(☎ 01452-425543)*. Bicycles can be hired in Bath, Oxford and Cheltenham. **Compass Holidays** *(☎ 01242-250642)* has bikes for hire (£12 per day) at Cheltenham station.

BIRMINGHAM

☎ 0121 • pop 1.01 million

Birmingham is Britain's second largest city – culturally vibrant, socially dynamic...but aesthetically challenged. Traditionally it's been thought of as a rather dreary city with no essential sights. More recently, however, things have looked up, with the restoration of the old canal network and the opening of innumerable restaurants and bars in the Brindleyplace area.

The **TIC** *(☎ 693 6300; Victoria Square; open daily)* can help with information, including accommodation options. The **Museum & Art Gallery** *(☎ 303 2834)* has a fine collection of Pre-Raphaelite paintings and overlooks **Victoria** and **Chamberlain squares**, both of them full of interesting statuary. The old **Jewellery Quarter** is also looking much smarter.

New St Station and Digbeth St coach station are both major transport hubs.

PEAK DISTRICT

Squeezed between the industrial Midlands to the south, Manchester to the west and Sheffield to the east, the Peak District seems an unlikely site for one of England's most lovely regions. Even the name is misleading, being derived from the tribes who once lived here, not from the existence of any peaks. Nonetheless, the 542-sq-mi Peak District National Park is a delight, particularly for walkers and cyclists.

The Peak District divides into the green fields and steep-sided dales of the southern White Peak and the bleak, gloomy moors of the northern Dark Peak. Buxton, to the west, and Matlock, to the east, are good bases for exploring the park, or you can stay right in the centre at Bakewell or Castleton. Castleton and nearby Edale are popular villages on the border between the White and Dark Peaks. From Edale, the Pennine Way starts its 250mi meander northwards. From the town of Castleton, the 25mi Limestone Way is a superb day walk covering the length of the White Peak to Matlock. In addition, a number of disused railway lines in the White Peak have been redeveloped as walking and cycling routes.

There are National Park Information Centres at **Edale** *(☎ 01433-670207)*, **Castleton** *(☎ 01433-620679)* and **Bakewell** *(☎ 01629-813227)*. The Peak District is packed with hotels, B&Bs, YHA hostels and a collection of **camping barns** *(☎ 01629-825850)*, together with plenty of convivial pubs and good restaurants. Visitors to Bakewell should make sure to sample Bakewell pudding (not tart).

The regular Transpeak bus service cuts right across the Peak District from Nottingham and Derby to Manchester via Matlock, Bakewell and Buxton.

East England

With the exception of Cambridge, most of the eastern counties – Essex, Suffolk, Norfolk, Cambridgeshire and Lincolnshire – have been overlooked by tourists. East Anglia, as the region is often known, has always been distinct, historically separated from the rest of England by the marshy Fens and the Essex forests. To the east of the Fens, Norfolk and Suffolk have gentle, unspectacular scenery that can still be very beautiful.

Peterborough, Norwich and Lincoln are the most important cities. Harwich is the main port for ferries to Germany, the Netherlands and Scandinavia. The **East of England Tourist Board** *(☎ 01473-822922)* can provide information on the region's various hostels and many B&Bs.

Activities

The **Peddars Way & Norfolk Coast Path National Trail Office** *(☎ 01328-711533; ⓔ peddars.way@dial.pipex.com; 6 Station Rd, Wells-next-the-Sea, Norfolk NR23 1AE)* can supply information about the walks in this region. This is also ideal cycling country; bikes can be hired in Cambridge, and the TIC there can suggest several interesting routes.

Getting There & Away

Harwich, Norwich, King's Lynn and Cambridge are all easily accessible by train from London. For details on ferry services from Harwich to the Netherlands, Germany and Scandinavia, see the Getting There & Away section at the beginning of this chapter.

Getting Around

Bus transport around the region is slow and disorganised. For regional timetables and information, phone **Traveline** *(☎ 0870 608 2608)*. From Norwich you can catch trains to the Norfolk coast and Sheringham, but there's an unfortunate gap between Sheringham and King's Lynn, which prevents a rail loop back to Cambridge.

CAMBRIDGE

☎ 01223 • pop 100,000

Cambridge can hardly be spoken of without reference to Oxford – so much so that the term 'Oxbridge' is used to cover them both. The two cities are not just ancient and beautiful university towns; they embody preconceptions and prejudices that are almost mythical in dimension.

An Oxbridge graduate is popularly characterised as male, private-school educated, intelligent and upper class. The term can be both abusive and admiring: for some it means academic excellence, for others it denotes an elitist club whose members unfairly dominate many aspects of British life.

Cambridge is the newer of the two universities, probably beginning some time in the early 13th century. There is a fierce rivalry between the two cities, and a futile debate over which is better and more beautiful. If you only have time for one, choose Cambridge.

BRITAIN

Orientation & Information

The central area, which lies in a wide bend of the River Cam, is easy to get around on foot or bike. The bus station is in the centre of town, but the train station is a 20-minute walk to the southeast.

Two-hour walking tours are organised by the **TIC** *(☎ 322640, fax 457549; ⓔ tourism@cambridge.gov.uk; Wheeler St; open Mon-Sat, daily Easter-Sept)*. Tours start at 1.30pm and run daily, year-round, with more during summer. There's general mayhem for the 168 hours following exams, the so-called May Week. Most colleges are closed to visitors for the Easter term, and all are closed for exams. Contact the TIC for information. For Internet access head to **ITC Café** *(☎ 377358; 2 Wheeler St)*, opposite the TIC, charging £1 for 30 minutes.

Things to See & Do

Cambridge is an architectural treasure house. Starting at Magdalene Bridge, walk south down Bridge St until you reach the unmistakable **Round Church**, one of only four medieval round churches surviving, dating from the 12th century. Turn right down St John's St (immediately across the road) which is named in honour of **St John's College** (on the right).

Next door, **Trinity College** *(☎ 338400)* is one of the largest and most attractive colleges. It was established in 1546 by Henry VIII on the site of several earlier foundations. The Great Court, Cambridge's largest enclosed court, incorporates buildings from the 15th century. Beyond Great Court is Nevile's Court with one of Cambridge's most important buildings on its western side – Sir Christopher Wren's library, built in the 1680s.

Next comes **Gonville** and **Caius** (pronounced 'keys') College, then **King's College** *(☎ 331100)* and its famous **chapel** *(adult/concession £3.50/2.25)*, one of Europe's greatest buildings. The reason its late Gothic style is described as 'perpendicular' is immediately obvious. The chapel was begun in 1446 by Henry VI, but it was not completed until 1545. Majestic as this building is from the outside, it is its interior, with its breathtaking scale and intricate fan vaulting, that makes the greater impact. Even heavy-metal fans will find choral evensong an extraordinary experience.

Places to Stay

The TIC has an accommodation guide (75p) or you can call its booking service on ☎ 457581.

Cambridge Youth Hostel *(☎ 0870 770 5742, fax 0870 770 5743; ⓔ cambridge@yha.org.uk; 97 Tenison Rd; dorm beds adult/under-18 £12.75/8.75)* has small dorms and a restaurant near the train station. It's very popular – book ahead. Breakfast costs £3.40.

The **YMCA** *(☎ 356998, fax 312749; ⓔ admin@camymca.org.uk; Gonville Place; singles/doubles £23/37, per week £130/224)* is closer to the centre and is good value for weekly stays. Breakfast is included.

There are many B&Bs open year-round, even more during university holidays (late June to late September). B&Bs line Tenison Rd, including cosy **Tenison Towers Guest House** *(☎ 363924, fax 411093; 148 Tenison Rd; rooms per person from £25)*. **Six Steps Guest House** *(☎ 353968, fax 356788; ⓔ sara.dias@ntlworld.com; 93 Tenison Rd; rooms per person from £28)* is much larger and has big, uncluttered rooms. The other B&B area is in the north of the city around Chesterton Rd.

Antoni Guest House *(☎ 357444; 4 Huntingdon Rd; rooms per person £20-25)* is both spacious and comfortable. **Benson House** *(☎/fax 311594; 24 Huntingdon Rd)* has well-equipped doubles and is similarly priced.

Places to Eat & Drink

Cambridge may be a university town, but tourism's cash-cow status is reflected in restaurant prices. There are, however, lots of reasonably priced joints.

A small chain of excellent-value bakeries, **Nadia's** *(☎ 568334; King's Parade • ☎ 568335; Silver St)* offers sandwich and coffee for £1 before 10.30am. A smoked ham and Swiss cheese baguette is £1.85.

Tucked away in a narrow alley is **Rainbow** *(☎ 321551; 9a King's Parade; mains from £6.75; closed Sun)*, a cosy vegetarian/vegan restaurant.

Clowns *(☎ 355711; 54 King St; light meals £3-6)* is informal, popular with students and good value. The nearby **Slug & Lettuce** *(☎ 306051; 41 Green St; mains around £7)* is a trendy new café-bar which draws students galore with its filling burgers, tortilla and pasta dishes.

The **Sainsbury's supermarket** *(Sidney St)* is open daily.

Fort St George *(☎ 354327; Midsummer Common)* is a good riverside pub.

Getting There & Away

Cambridge can easily be visited as a day trip from London. To London there are hourly National Express buses (£8/8.50 one-way/day return, two hours). Four buses a day run to/from Bristol (two stop at Bath). To get to Lincoln or York you'll have to change at Peterborough or Nottingham, respectively. King's Lynn is accessible only via Peterborough. **Jetlink** *(☎ 0870 575 7747)* runs buses to all London airports. **Stagecoach Express** *(☎ 01640-676060)* goes to Oxford (£5.99, 3½ hours, hourly).

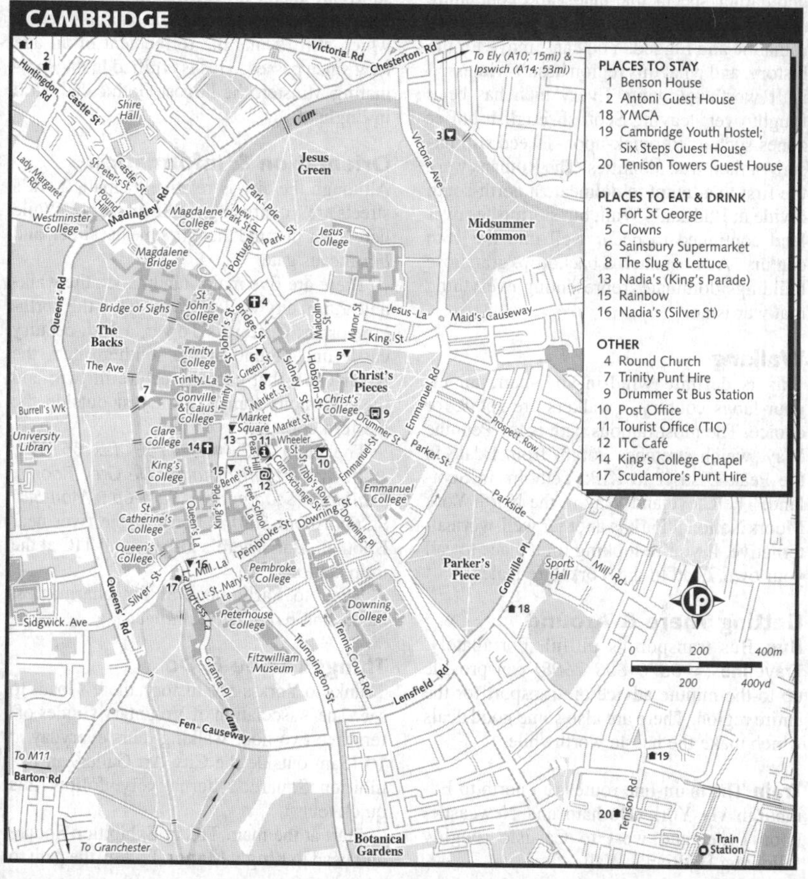

There are trains every half-hour from London's King's Cross and Liverpool St stations (£15.10, 45 minutes). Trains from King's Cross run via Hatfield and Stevenage. There are also regular train connections to Ely (£3.30, 20 minutes), Bury St Edmunds (£5.80, one hour) and King's Lynn (£7.50, one hour). There are connections at Peterborough with the main northbound trains to Lincoln, York and Edinburgh. If you want to head west to Oxford or Bath, you'll have to return to London first. For more information, phone ☎ 0845 748 4950.

Northeast England

Northeast England is a place of contrasts. Its undulating, spectacular landscape, containing three of England's best national parks, is both romantic and rugged. You can't move for the history, and what this region hasn't witnessed isn't worth knowing. Every inch has been fought over, leaving Scottish-English buffer zones such as Berwick-upon-Tweed still unsure of their true identities. The Romans were the first to attempt to delineate a north-south divide in Hadrian's Wall, but skirmishes over land continued to occur well into the 18th century. Against such a backdrop, grandiose buildings dominate, representing everything that war is not.

Walking

This is definite wind-in-your-hair, air-in-your-lungs country – walkers are spoilt for choice. The most famous path is the Pennine Way, which stretches 266mi from Edale in the Peak District to Kirk Yetholm in Scotland. The Cleveland Way in the North York Moors National Park is another well-worn alternative. If you're looking for a place to call your own, head to the Yorkshire Dales.

Getting There & Around

Bus Bus transport is pitiful. Fortunately, **Traveline** *(☎ 0870 608 2608)* can provide up-to-the-minute advice on transport for the entire region. There are also some good deals which make the hassle worthwhile.

Train The main-line routes run north to Edinburgh via York, Durham and Newcastle-upon-Tyne, and west to Carlisle roughly following Hadrian's Wall.

YORK

☎ 01904 • pop 179,305

King George VI declared, 'The history of York is the history of England', and how right he was. In AD 306, Constantine, the first Christian Roman ruler, was reputedly proclaimed emperor on the site of the cathedral. In Saxon times, York became an important centre for Christianity – the first church on the site of the current cathedral was built in 627. York prospered as a political and trading hub after William the Conqueror's initial 'pacification'. In the 15th and 16th centuries, however, it declined economically. It was the arrival of George Hudson and the railway in 1839 that gave York a new lease of commercial life.

The city walls were built during the 13th century and are among the most impressive surviving medieval fortifications in Europe. They enclose a thriving, fascinating centre which still retains the refinement of an age long since passed. This is typified in the dominating Minster, the largest Gothic cathedral in England.

Orientation & Information

Although the city is relatively small, York's streets are a confusing medieval tangle. While here, bear in mind that *gate* means street, and *bar* means gate.

There are five major landmarks: the walkable 2.5mi city wall; the Minster at the northern corner; Clifford's Tower, a 13th-century castle and mound at the southern end; the River Ouse that cuts the centre in two; and the enormous train station just outside the western corner.

The main **TIC** *(☎ 621756, fax 551801; ⓔ tic@york-tourism.co.uk; De Grey Rooms, Exhibition Square; open 9am-6pm Mon-Sat, 9.30am-6pm Sun)* is north of the river near Bootham Bar. There's also a small TIC at the train station.

Head to Parliament St for pharmacies, banks and *bureaux de change*.

Things to See & Do

Thanks to York's rich history, there's loads to see. The Association of Voluntary Guides offers free two-hour walking tours everyday at 10.15am outside the City Art Gallery in Exhibition Square. Alternatively, follow this quick tour.

Start at the main TIC in Exhibition Square and head to **King's Manor**. Follow the path to

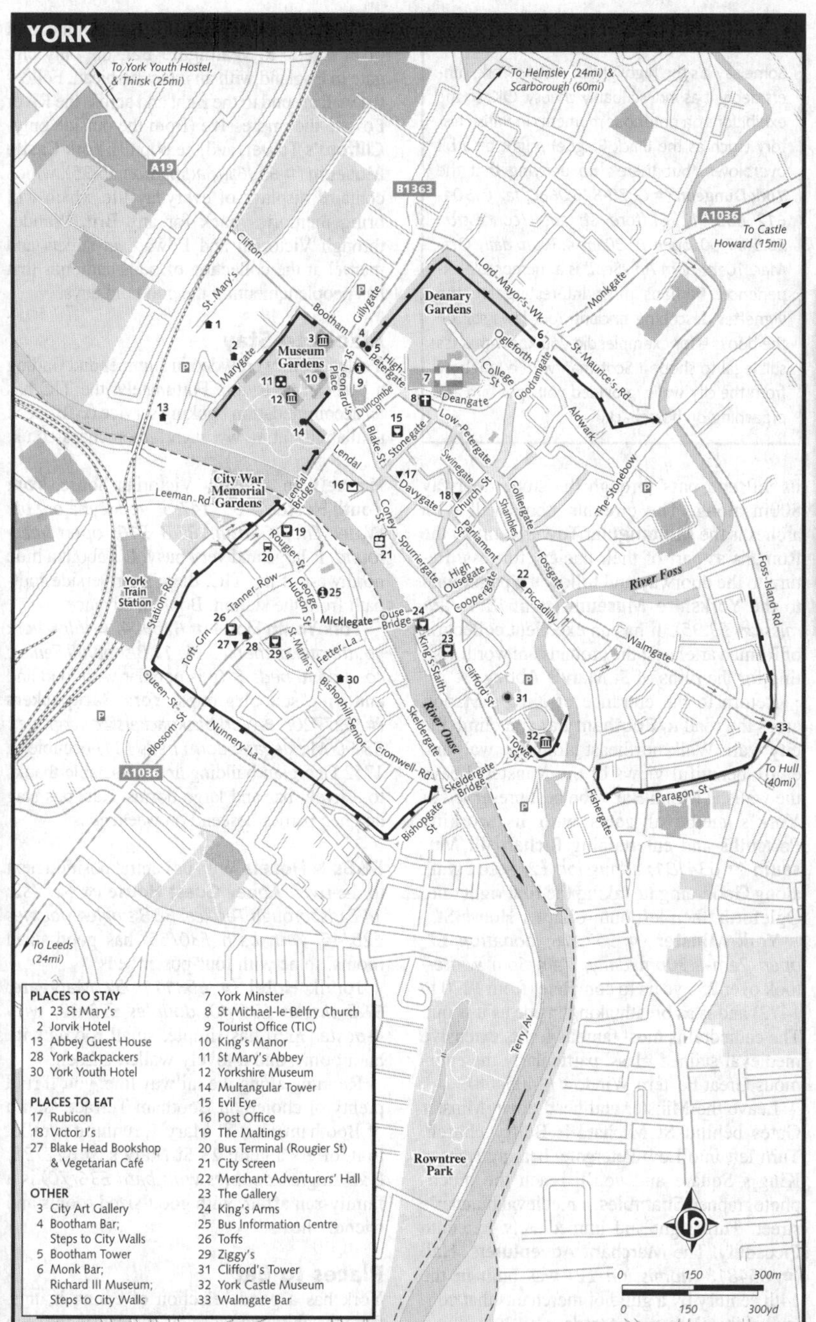
YORK
To York Youth Hostel, & Thirsk (25mi)
To Helmsley (24mi) & Scarborough (60mi)
To Castle Howard (15mi)
To Hull (40mi)
To Leeds (24mi)
A19
B1363
A1036
A1036
Clifton
St Mary's
Marygate
Bootham
Gillygate
High Petergate
St Leonard's Place
Duncombe Pl
Lord-Mayor's-Wk
Monkgate
Ogleforth
Goodramgate
College St
St Maurice's Rd
Aldwark
Deangate
Low Petergate
Blake St
Stonegate
Lendal
Lendal Bridge
Leeman Rd
Station Rd
Rougier St
Tanner Row
Toft Grn
George Hudson St
Micklegate
Ouse Bridge
St Martin's La
Fetter La
Bishophill Senior
Queen St
Blossom St
Nunnery La
Cromwell Rd
Skeldergate
Skeldergate Bridge
Bishopgate St
King's Staith
Clifford St
Tower St
Fishergate
Paragon St
Walmgate
Foss Islands Rd
Piccadilly
Fossgate
Coppergate
High Ousegate
Spurriergate
Coney St
Davygate
Swinegate
Church St
Parliament St
Shambles
Colliergate
The Stonebow
Terry Av
Deanary Gardens
Museum Gardens
City War Memorial Gardens
York Train Station
River Foss
River Ouse
Rowntree Park
0 150 300m
0 150 300yd
PLACES TO STAY
1 23 St Mary's
2 Jorvik Hotel
13 Abbey Guest House
28 York Backpackers
30 York Youth Hotel
PLACES TO EAT
17 Rubicon
18 Victor J's
27 Blake Head Bookshop & Vegetarian Café
OTHER
3 City Art Gallery
4 Bootham Bar; Steps to City Walls
5 Bootham Tower
6 Monk Bar; Richard III Museum; Steps to City Walls
7 York Minster
8 St Michael-le-Belfry Church
9 Tourist Office (TIC)
10 King's Manor
11 St Mary's Abbey
12 Yorkshire Museum
14 Multangular Tower
15 Evil Eye
16 Post Office
19 The Maltings
20 Bus Terminal (Rougier St)
21 City Screen
22 Merchant Adventurers' Hall
23 The Gallery
24 King's Arms
25 Bus Information Centre
26 Toffs
29 Ziggy's
31 Clifford's Tower
32 York Castle Museum
33 Walmgate Bar

A Captivating Experience?

Some say it's the highlight of visiting York; others decry it as indescribably cheesy. OK, so the exhibitions on notorious moments in British history (such as the Black Plague) might be a bit overblown, but there's no denying that the **York Dungeon** (*☎ 0870-846 0666, fax 01904-612 602; 12 Clifford St; adult/concession £8.50/7.50; open 10.30am-4.30pm daily Oct-Mar, 10am-5pm Apr-Sept)* is a memorable experience. Perhaps most interesting are the vignettes describing ancient York laws still on the books – for example, did you know that it's still legal to shoot a Scotsman with a longbow from the city walls, provided you spot him approaching on horseback?

its left and pass through the stone doorway 800m along. The circular stone wall with arches is the **Multangular Tower**, built by the Romans as part of their ancient fortress. Return to the doorway and follow the path round to the **Yorkshire Museum** (*☎ 551800; admission £3.95)*. It has an excellent collection of Roman artefacts; the grounds are worth visiting for the ruins of **St Mary's Abbey**.

Return to the entrance of King's Manor, cross the road to **Bootham Bar** and climb the city wall. Walk northeast along the wall and enjoy beautiful views of the Minster. Leave the walls at Monk Bar – the best preserved of York's medieval gates with its working Portcullis and entertaining **Richard III Museum** (*☎ 634191; admission £2)* – and walk along Goodramgate taking the first right onto Ogleforth, then left onto Chapter House St.

York Minster (*☎ 557216; donation £2; open 7am-8.30pm daily, 7am-6pm winter)* took over 250 years to complete (from 1220 to 1472) and is as breathtaking inside as it is out. The cathedral is most famous for its extensive medieval stained glass, particularly the enormous Great Eastern Window (1405–08).

Leave the Minster and head down Minster Gates behind St Michael-le-Belfry church. Turn left into Low Petergate, bearing right at King's Square and you'll reach the much-photographed **Shambles**, a medieval butcher's street. Turn right and immediately left onto Piccadilly. The **Merchant Adventurers' Hall** (*☎ 654818; admission £2)* was built in the 14th century by a guild of merchants that controlled the cloth export trade.

Continue down Walmgate (the continuation of Fossgate) to **Walmgate Bar**, the only city gate in England with an intact barbican. Follow the wall around to the right and across the River Foss to the impressive (from the outside only) **Clifford's Tower**, and the popular **York Castle Museum** (*☎ 653611; admission £5.95)*, which contains displays of everyday life which will bring memories back for any Brit. Wander through Victorian and Edwardian streets and marvel at the collection of odds and ends that has people lamenting the good old days.

Places to Stay

York gets very crowded in summer and finding a bed can be trying. Fortunately, the TIC has an accommodation booking service (£4); check availability at **w** www.york.roomcheck.co.uk.

Hostels In a lovely Victorian house, **York Youth Hostel** (*☎ 653147; **e** york@yha.org.uk; Water End, Clifton; B&B £16; open year-round)* is large and very busy. It's about a mile northwest of the TIC; there's a riverside footpath from the station. Book in advance.

York Youth Hotel (*☎ 625904; **e** info@yorkyouthhotel.demon.co.uk; 11 Bishophill Senior; coed dorm beds £10)* is popular with loud and annoying school groups. **York Backpackers** (*☎ 627720; **e** yorkbackpackers@cwcom.net; 88-90 Micklegate; dorm beds £11)* occupies a 1752 Georgian building and is sociable thanks to a lively bar and large dorms. Raucous stag and hen parties descend on weekends.

B&Bs & Hotels With its central position next to the river, **Abbey Guest House** (*☎ 627782; 14 Earlsborough Terrace; B&B singles/doubles £25/45, with bath £30/55)* has good-sized rooms, some with four-poster beds.

Jorvik Hotel (*☎ 653111; 52 Marygate; B&B singles £35-40, doubles £29-32, with 4-poster £35)* has simple, small rooms with bathrooms, and a lovely walled garden.

Running along the railway line, you'll find plenty of choice on Bootham Terrace (south of Bootham), but St Mary's, running parallel to it, offers a gem: **23 St Mary's** (*☎ 622738; B&B singles/doubles with bath £36/70)* is a family-run affair, with good-sized rooms and friendly hosts.

Places to Eat

York has a good selection of eating haunts, from the ubiquitous all-you-can-eats to the ultra chic. **Victor J's** *(☎ 673788; 1a Finkle St; mains £5-6)* is a funky, ambient café/bar selling art, absinthe and munchies. Vegetarians will love the excellent **Blake Head Bookshop & Vegetarian Café** *(☎ 623767; 104 Micklegate; lunch mains £5.90)*, and the sophisticated **Rubicon** *(☎ 676076; 5 Little Stonegate; mains £6-8)*.

Entertainment

Head to **City Screen** *(☎ 541155; 13-17 Coney St)* for live music. The limited clubbing 'scene' consists of local favourite **The Gallery** *(Clifford St)*, student-orientated **Toffs** *(Toft Green)* and small and sweaty **Ziggy's** *(Micklegate)*.

Evil Eye *(☎ 640002; above Forever Changes, Stonegate)* is chill, with Internet access (£2 per hour) and excellent cocktails (£3.50). **King's Arms** *(King's Staith)*, does cheap beer and is the pub that famously floods.

The Maltings *(Tanners Moat)*, below Lendal Bridge, has great beers, friendly locals and a toilet in the corner!

Getting There & Away

Bus The main bus terminal is on Rougier St. National Express buses leave from the train station. There are at least three services a day to London (£19.50, five hours), one to Birmingham (£20, 2½ hours) and one to Edinburgh (£26.50, 5¼ hours).

For information on local buses (to Castle Howard, Helmsley, Scarborough, Whitby etc), call ☎ 551400 or drop into the **Bus Information Centre** *(20 George Hudson St)*. Yorkshire Coastliner has buses to Leeds, Malton and Scarborough.

Train There are numerous trains from London's King's Cross (£63.50, two hours) and on to Edinburgh (£51, 2½ hours).

North–south trains also connect with Peterborough (£36, 1½ hours) for Cambridge and other parts of East Anglia. There are a few trains for southwest England, including Oxford, via Birmingham (£53.50, 4¼ hours). Local trains to/from Scarborough take 45 minutes (£9.30). For Whitby it's necessary to change at Middlesbrough (three hours).

NORTH YORK MOORS NATIONAL PARK

The North York Moors *(park headquarters: ☎ 01439-770657, phone inquiries only)* carries every texture in its landscape. Vast expanses of rugged heather moorland and rolling hills are offset by dramatic coastline and secluded dales. If you're a walker, you'll have found your spiritual home. The famous Cleveland Way (110mi) snakes around the edge of the park from Helmsley to Filey, taking in all the contrasting harshness and romanticism. If you don't fancy walking, enjoy nostalgic steam travel on the North Yorkshire Moors Railway (NYMR). The best visitor centre for the park is at **Danby** *(☎ 01287-660654; open daily March-Dec)*. A must for all public transport users is the invaluable *Transport Times for Ryedale District* booklet, available from TICs.

The **Moorsbus** *(☎ 01845-597426)* is a special service that runs daily from mid-July to early September, linking a web of destinations in the Moors. The **North Yorkshire Moors Railway** *(☎ 01751-472508)* cuts through the park from Pickering to Grosmont, which is on the Esk Valley line between Whitby and Middlesbrough. This railway operates from April to early November (£10 all lines).

Helmsley & Around

☎ 01439 • pop 1520

What Helmsley lacks in size, it makes up for in charm. It attracts busloads of tourists (especially on Friday, market day), but unlike in overrun Pickering, they seem to melt into the background. Perhaps it's because the **ruined castle** *(admission £2.50)*, like York Minster, is too dignified to be overrun.

The bustling marketplace is the town's main focus. The **TIC** *(☎ 770173; open daily Apr-Oct, Sat & Sun Nov-Mar)* is located in the town hall.

Duncombe Park and Nunnington Hall are within easy walking distance, but the highlight is the 13th-century remains of **Rievaulx Abbey** *(☎ 798228; admission £3.30)*. The 3.5mi uphill walk to the abbey from Helmsley along the Cleveland Way is well worth it, but the Moorsbus also runs from the town to the site for the less energetic.

Dorm accommodation is available at the excellent and friendly **Helmsley Youth Hostel** *(☎/fax 770433; Carlton Lane; dorm beds £9.50)*. The TIC offers a free booking service for B&Bs.

Scarborough & District has hourly buses (No 128) daily between Helmsley and Scarborough via Pickering (1½ hours).

BRITAIN

DURHAM

☎ 0191 • pop 81,079

Durham is home to over 1000 years of history and the third-oldest university in England. It's like your favourite grandma – old, endearing and reassuringly familiar. Such reassurance is partially provided by the Norman cathedral; its dramatic position on a wooded promontory, high above a bend in the River Wear, keeps it in constant view.

The train station is above and northwest of the cathedral, on the other side of the river. The bus station is also on the western side. The **TIC** *(☎ 384 3720; open daily year-round)* is in the Gala building, just off Claypont. Internet access is available at **Saints**, in the old Market Vaults just off the Marketplace. Rates per hour for members/nonmembers are £3.50/4.50. A one-off membership fee is £1.50.

Durham Cathedral is an architectural masterpiece. The vast interior is all stocky pillars and intricate stonework archways; the stunning Galilee Chapel and a climb up the tower (£2) are obligatory. **Durham Castle** *(guided tours £3 Easter-Oct)* served as the home for the county's prince-bishops. These 11th-century bishops lived like kings and had virtual autonomy over what was essentially a buffer zone between England and Scotland.

Places to Stay & Eat

Several colleges rent rooms during the university holidays (Easter and July to September), but if you would like to feel like a prince-bishop then head straight for **University College** *(☎ 374 3863; B&B per person £20.50)*, in the old Durham Castle.

The TIC makes local bookings for free, but cheap accommodation is difficult to come by; avoid graduation week in late June. **Mrs Koltai** *(☎/fax 386 2026; 10 Gilesgate; singles £16)* is still the cheapest.

Most of the eating options are within a short walk of the market square. **Almshouses** *(☎ 386 1054; Palace Green; lunch mains £5)* makes an ideal refreshment spot after traipsing around the cathedral.

Getting There & Away

There are six National Express buses a day to London (£23, 6½ hours), one to Edinburgh (£18.50, 4½ hours), and three to Newcastle-upon-Tyne (£2, 30 minutes). Arriva X1 runs throughout the day (except Sunday) to Newcastle via Chester-le-Street.

There are numerous trains to York (£14.90, one hour), a good number of which head on to London (£78, three hours) via Peterborough. Frequent trains from London continue through Durham to Edinburgh (two hours).

NEWCASTLE-UPON-TYNE

☎ 0191 • pop 270,500

There's never been a more exciting time to visit Newcastle. Once home to the 'new castle' of Robert Curthose (the eldest son of William the Conqueror), the city thrived as a medieval walled town and was later to become the coal commercial hub of Tyneside.

With WWII and the general decline of manufacturing, Newcastle struggled. It's only recently resurged, with visitors being treated to a mini cultural revolution. The Quayside north of the River Tyne and Gateshead Quays to the south have been transformed into airy, stimulating quarters. The tilting Gateshead Millennium Bridge and Music Centre Gateshead are both visually stunning, while the BALTIC Centre for Contemporary Art seems to define modern Newcastle. What's more, the nightlife is definitely on the up too – no-one parties like the Geordies.

Orientation & Information

The city centre is surprisingly easy to navigate on foot, and the metro or underground railway (for the YHA hostel and B&Bs) is fast and easy to use. The Central train station is just south of the centre and the coach station is just east.

The friendly, helpful **TIC** *(☎ 277 8006; 132 Grainger St; open daily)* also has an office at the train station (closed Sunday). Both offices have a free map, guide and accommodation list. Be sure to pick up the entertainment listings guide *The Crack*. All major banks and *bureaux de change* are dotted around the area of the TIC. Internet access is available at **Internet Exchange** *(26 Market St)*, where £1 will get you 30 minutes.

Things to See & Do

With its five amazing art galleries, the **BALTIC Centre** *(☎ 478 1810; Gateshead Quays; admission free)* could easily absorb a day. If this appeals, you'll also appreciate Thomas Heatherwick's quirky **Blue Carpet** just outside another cultural oasis, the **Laing Art Gallery** *(☎ 232 7734; Higham Place; admission free)*. The 'carpet' actually comprises tiles containing recycled blue glass shreds. Both **St Nicholas Cathedral** and **Castle Garth Keep** are also worth visiting.

Further afield, take the metro to nearby Wallsend with its reconstruction of **Segedunum** *(☎ 295 5757; admission £3.50)*, the last outpost of Hadrian's Wall.

Places to Stay & Eat

Clean and comfortable **Newcastle Youth Hostel** *(☎ 281 2570; ✉ Newcastle@yha.org.uk; 107 Jesmond Rd; dorm beds £11.25; open Feb-Dec, only Fri-Sun in Jan)* is a five-minute walk from Jesmond metro station. **North East YWCA** *(☎ 281 1233; Jesmond House, Clayton Rd; B&B per person £16)* accepts both male and female guests.

There are a number of B&Bs within easy walking distance of West Jesmond station, mostly along Jesmond and Osborne Rds. **Portland Guest House** *(☎ 232 7868; 134 Sandyford Rd; singles/doubles from £18/36)* has large rooms and its rates are cheap for the area.

Good restaurants cluster around Grey St, among them modern, excellent-value **eviva** *(☎ 241 4565; 11 Grey St; pizza & pasta £3.50)*, which has a romantic alcoved lower floor. The bizarrely decorated **JT's** *(☎ 222 0659; 6-10 Leazes Park Rd; mains £4-12; open 24hr)* does a three-course lunch and early evening special for £5.99. **Paradiso** *(☎ 221 1240; 1 Market Lane; 2-course meals £6.95)* has arguably the best Italian food in Newcastle.

Entertainment

Newcastle's nightlife is superb. For bars and late-night drinking head to the Quayside. **Trent House** *(1-2 Leazes Lane)*, with its laid-back feel and free soul classics jukebox has a relaxed vibe. Clubs worth shaking a stick at include the housey **Foundation** *(57-59 Melbourne St)* and the cheaper, funk and hip-hop pumping **World Headquarters** *(7 Marlborough Crescent)*; membership required (£1).

Getting There & Away

There are numerous National Express connections with virtually every major city in the country. The local bus No 505 serves Berwick-upon-Tweed and No 685 Hexham and Haltwhistle for Hadrian's Wall.

There are frequent **trains** *(☎ 0845 748 4950)* to Edinburgh (£33.50, 1¾ hours), London (£83, three hours) and York (£15.50, one hour). Berwick-upon-Tweed and Alnmouth (for Alnwick) are also served.

Regular ferries link Newcastle with Bergen, Kristiansand, Haugesund and Stavanger (Norway), Gothenburg (Sweden) and Amsterdam (Netherlands). See the introductory Getting There & Away section at the beginning of this chapter.

The excellent metro (underground railway) is quicker and more efficient than local buses. Unlimited travel for one day is £3. For advice and information contact **Traveline** *(☎ 0870 608 2608)*.

NORTHUMBERLAND

Northumberland has a haunting beauty about it. It offers a rare opportunity to really get away from everything and everyone. Its plethora of historical sites serves as living testament to England's long, bloody struggle with the Scots.

The most significant site is, of course, Hadrian's Wall. The brainchild of Roman Emperor Hadrian in AD 122, it stretches for 73mi from Newcastle to Bowness-on-Solway near Carlisle and was the northern frontier of the empire for almost 300 years.

Northumberland National Park lies north of Hadrian's Wall, incorporating the sparsely populated Cheviot Hills. There are information centres open from mid-March to October and at weekends in winter. The centres in **Once Brewed** *(☎ 01434-344396)* and **Rothbury** *(☎ 01669-620887)* both handle accommodation bookings, while the one in **Ingram** *(☎ 01665-578248)* is not as well facilitated.

Hadrian's Wall

The most spectacular section of the wall is between Hexham and Brampton. **Chesters Roman Fort & Museum** *(☎ 01434-681379; admission £3)* is in a pleasant valley by the River Tyne. It has an interesting museum, an extraordinary bathhouse and the remains of a massive bridge.

Housesteads Roman Fort *(☎ 01434-344363; admission £3)* is the most dramatic and popular ruin. The well-preserved foundations, including the famous latrine, have amazing views over the Northumbrian countryside.

Vindolanda Fort & Chesterholm Museum *(☎ 01434-344277; admission £3.90)* 2.5mi south is an extensively excavated fort and civil settlement with accompanying museum. If you're lucky, you'll catch chatty archaeologists hard at work.

Birdoswald Roman Fort *(☎ 016977-47602; admission £3)* sits on an escarpment overlooking the picturesque Irthing Valley. It's less inundated with visitors than some of the other sites.

Places to Stay Corbridge, Hexham, Haltwhistle and Brampton make ideal bases for exploring the wall and have a plentiful supply of B&Bs. There is also a number of cheap, convenient YHA hostels.

Starting in the east, **Acomb Youth Hostel** *(☎ 01434-602864; dorm beds £7)* is about 2.5mi north of Hexham and 2mi south of the wall. Catch bus No 880 from Hexham.

Once Brewed Youth Hostel *(☎ 01434-344360; dorm beds £11.25)* is central for both Housesteads Roman Fort (3mi) and Vindolanda (1mi). It's right next door to the Information Centre too. Northumbria bus No 685 (from Hexham or Haltwhistle stations) will drop you at Henshaw, 2mi south; in summer, Hadrian's Wall Bus (AD122) will drop you at the front door. The nearest train station is Bardon Mill, 2.5mi southeast.

Greenhead Youth Hostel *(☎ 016977-47401; dorm beds £9.50)* is a charming chapel conversion 3mi west of Haltwhistle station; it's also served by the trusty bus No 685 and the White Star bus No 185 from Carlisle.

For cheap, basic accommodation with outstanding views, try **Bankshead Camping Barn** *(☎ 01697-73198; beds £4)*. It's close to Banks East Turret and is ideal for exploring Lanercost Priory. Bus No 682 drops you outside.

Getting There & Away The **Newcastle–Carlisle railway line** *(☎ 0845 748 4950)* has stations at Hexham, Haydon Bridge, Bardon Mill, Haltwhistle and Brampton. There are hourly services between Carlisle and Newcastle on **Bus No 685** *(☎ 0870 608 2608)*.

From June to September the hail-and-ride Hadrian's Wall Bus (AD122) runs between Hexham and Haltwhistle train stations, calling at the main sites. For further information, contact **Hexham TIC** *(☎ 01434-652220)*.

Northwest England

The southern part of this region is often dismissed as England's industrial backyard but there are still some beautiful corners. The larger cities are cultural hubs with a legacy of brilliant Victorian architecture and a population that really knows how to have a good time.

The cities of Liverpool and Manchester sprawl into the countryside, burying it under motorways, grim suburbs, power lines, factories and mines. There are, nonetheless, some important exceptions, including walled Chester, which makes a good starting point for North Wales and the Lake District, arguably the most beautiful corner of England.

MANCHESTER

☎ 0161 • pop 460,000

Best known for the soccer team Manchester United and for modern music giants Oasis, The Smiths and New Order, Manchester is also a monument to England's industrial history. In the city centre warehouses and factories rub shoulders with stunning Victorian Gothic buildings and modern apartment blocks, rusting train tracks and motorway overpasses with flashy bars and nightclubs. The longer you stay, the more you'll like Manchester. Not many cities in England can rival it for its vibrancy and nightlife, its gay scene and fantastic sports facilities. England's largest student population gives it that extra spark.

Orientation & Information

The centre of Manchester is easy to get around on foot and with the help of the excellent Metrolink tramway. The University of Manchester lies to the south of the city centre (on Oxford St/Rd). To the west of the university is dodgy Moss Side – keep clear. Victoria train station caps the city in the north. The **TIC** *(☎ 234 3157; Lloyd St, St Peter Square)* is in the town hall extension, with another **branch** at the Castlefield Urban Heritage Park and at the airport. *City Life*, the local 'what's on' magazine, is a compulsory purchase. For cheap Internet access try **easyEverything** *(☎ 832 9200; St Anne's Square)*.

Things to See & Do

Castlefield Urban Heritage Park is an extraordinary landscape made up of the remains of ancient Roman fortresses and newly constructed canalside footpaths, pubs, hotels and a YHA hostel. The area also takes in the excellent **Museum of Science & Industry** *(☎ 832 1830; Liverpool Rd; admission free; open 10am-5pm daily)*.

Dominating Albert Square in the city centre is the enormous Victorian Gothic **town hall**, designed by Albert Waterhouse (of London's Natural History Museum fame) in 1876.

The recently renovated **Manchester Art Gallery** (☎ *234 1456; cnr Nicholas & Mosley Sts; admission free; open 10am-5pm Tues-Sun)* has an impressive collection covering everything from early Italian, Dutch and Flemish painters to Gainsborough, Blake, Constable and the Pre-Raphaelites.

Places to Stay

Most of the cheap options are some distance from the centre. The TIC's free booking service is recommended.

The **Youth Hostel** (☎ *839 9960; dorm beds adult/under-18 £18.50/13.75)*, across the road from the Museum of Science & Industry in the Castlefield area (well signposted), has over 140 beds in comfortable four-bed rooms. From mid-June to mid-September, the University of Manchester rents students' rooms out to visitors from around £13 per person; contact **St Anselm Hall** (☎ *224 7327)* or **Woolaton Hall** (☎ *224 7244)*.

Burton Arms Hotel (☎ *834 3455; 31 Swan St; singles/doubles from £25/40)*, close to the centre of town, is a traditional pub, with a few rooms.

Places to Eat

The most distinctive restaurant zones are Chinatown in the city centre and Rusholme in the south. That said, much of Manchester is experiencing a mini gastronomic boom, with restaurants and cafés springing up throughout the city centre.

Dimitri's (☎ *839 3319; Campfield Arcade; lunches £4)* serves up a mixture of Greek, Italian and Spanish food with a good vegetarian selection.

Rusholme is to the south of the university on Wilmslow Rd, the extension of Oxford St/Rd, and has numerous popular, cheap and very good Indian and Pakistani places.

Chain cafés are big business in Manchester, but for those looking for something less generic, **Earth Vegetarian Café** (☎ *834 1996; 16-20 Turner St; mains £3-7)*, in the Northern Quarter, serves up imaginative vegetarian dishes.

Entertainment

You will be spoiled for choice when it comes to after-dark entertainment. One of the best venues for live jazz, blues and folk is **Band on the Wall** (☎ *832 6625 or 237 5554 for ticket info; 25 Swan St)*. For rock and pop, including big international acts, check out the **Manchester Academy** (☎ *275 2930; 269 Oxford Rd)*, part of the University Students Union.

Dry Bar (☎ *236 9840; 28 Oldham St)*, one of Manchester's first wine-and-cocktail bars, is still cool and drawing in the crowds. **Kro Bar** (☎ *274 3100; 325 Oxford Rd)* is a newcomer and seems popular with the punters. Two historic pubs are **Old Wellington Inn** (☎ *830 1440)* and **Sinclairs Oyster Bar** at the top of New Cathedral St.

There are several places to drink in Castlefield, including **Barça** (☎ *839 7099)* in Catalan Square, and **Dukes 92** (☎ *839 8646)*; both have outdoor seating on sunny days.

Canal St is the centre of Manchester's enormous gay nightlife scene. There are over 20 bars and clubs in the so-called 'Gay Village'. **Paradise Factory** (☎ *273 5422; 114-116 Princess St)* is a cutting edge club, with gay nights on the weekend.

Getting There & Around

There are numerous coach links with the rest of the country. National Express operates out of Chorlton St bus station in the city centre to pretty well anywhere you'll want to go. A return ticket to London's Victoria coach station will set you back £25.50/14.40 adult/concession. Piccadilly is the main station for trains to/from the rest of the country, although Victoria serves Halifax and Bradford. The two stations are linked by **Metrolink** (☎ *0845 748 4950)*.

For general inquiries about local transport, including night buses, phone ☎ 228 7811 (open 8am to 8pm daily).

CHESTER

☎ 01244 • pop 80,000

Despite a steady stream of tourists, Chester remains a beautiful town, ringed by an unbroken, red sandstone city wall that dates back to the Roman era. The 2mi walk along the top of the wall is the best way to see the town. The eye-catching two-level shopping streets may date back to the post-Roman period and certainly make convenient rainproof shopping arcades.

The train station is a 15-minute walk from the city centre; go up City Rd, then turn right onto Foregate at the large roundabout. From the bus station, turn left onto Northgate St. The **TIC** (☎ *402111)* is in the town hall opposite the cathedral. **Chester Visitor Centre** (☎ *351609)* is just outside Newgate, opposite the Roman amphitheatre. Access the Internet at **i-station** *(☎ 401680; Rufus Court)*, which charges £2 for 35 minutes.

The current **Chester Cathedral** *(☎ 324756; donation £2)* was built between 1250 and 1540, but has retained its fine 12th-century cloister. **Dewa Roman Experience** *(☎ 343407; Pierpoint Lane; adult/child under 16 £3.95/2.25; open 9am-5pm daily)*, off Bridge St, gives you a taste of life during Roman times.

Places to Stay & Eat

The **Youth Hostel** *(☎ 680056; 40 Hough Green; dorm beds adult/under-18 £14.50/11.25)* is a mile from the centre, opposite the train station.

There are numerous good-value B&Bs along Hoole Rd, the road into the city from the M53/M56, including **Bawn Park Hotel** *(☎ 324971; 10 Hoole Rd; rooms per person from £15)*. Close to the train station, **Ormonde Guest House** *(☎ 328816; 126 Brook St)* and **Aplas Guest House** *(☎ 312401; 106 Brooke St)* both offer rooms starting at £22 per person. B&Bs can also be found inside the city walls; **Recorder Hotel** *(☎ 326580; 19 City Walls; rooms from £35)*, overlooking the River Dee, is a perfectly positioned option.

On a sun-soaked afternoon, it's hard to beat the beer garden at **BarsLounge** *(cnr Nicholson & Watergate Sts)*, where food is served until 9pm daily. Good, basic pub food can also be found at **Watergates** *(☎ 320515; 11 Watergate St)*.

Alexander's Jazz Theatre *(☎ 313400; Rufus Court by Northgate)* is a wine, coffee and tapas bar that has great music. **Loaf** *(☎ 354041; Music Hall passage, St Werburgh St)* is a sleek addition to Chester's bar scene.

Getting There & Around

Chester has excellent transport connections, especially to/from North Wales. National Express has numerous connections with Chester, including Birmingham (£8.25, 2½ hours) and on to London (£15, 5½ hours), Manchester (£4.50, 1¼ hours), Glasgow (£22.50, six hours), Liverpool (£5, one hour) and Llandudno (£5.50, 1¾ hours). For many destinations in the south or east it's necessary to change at Birmingham; for the north, change at Manchester.

There are numerous trains to Liverpool (£3, 40 minutes) and Manchester (£8.50, 1½ hours); Holyhead (£16.15, two hours), via the North Wales coast, for ferries to Ireland; and London's Euston station (£48, three hours). Phone ☎ 0845 748 4950 for details.

For information on local bus services, ring **Chester City Transport** *(☎ 602666)*. Local buses leave from Market Square behind the town hall.

LIVERPOOL

☎ 0151 • pop 510,000

Of all northern England's cities, Liverpool has perhaps the strongest sense of its own identity, one that is closely tied up with the totems of the Beatles, the Liverpool and Everton soccer teams, and the Grand National steeplechase, run at Aintree since 1839.

Architecturally, the city is a striking mix of grandeur and decay – massive cathedrals, imperious buildings and decrepit streets and boarded-up windows. This juxtaposition, coupled with the city's dramatic site above the broad, mournful Mersey estuary, creates one of the most arresting sights in Britain.

Orientation & Information

Liverpool stretches north–south along the Mersey estuary for more than 13mi. The main visitor attraction is Albert Dock, to the south of the city centre. Lime St, the main train station, is just east of the city centre. The National Express bus station is on the corner of Norton and Islington Sts in the north of the city. The bus station is in the centre on Paradise St.

The main **TIC** *(☎ 0906-680 6886; Queen Square Centre; open daily)* also has a branch at Albert Dock; both offices can book accommodation. Log on to the Internet at **Planet Electra** *(☎ 708 0303; 38 London St)* for £2 per 30 minutes.

Be a bit cautious while in Liverpool. Even in the city centre, wandering the dark sidestreets can make for a hard day's night indeed.

Things to See & Do

The restored **Albert Dock** *(☎ 708 8854; open from 10am daily)* is, deservedly, Liverpool's number one tourist attraction, housing several outstanding modern museums – **Merseyside Maritime Museum**, the **Museum of Liverpool Life** and **Tate Gallery Liverpool**.

The Walker Gallery *(☎ 478 4199; William Brown St; admission free)* contains works by Rubens, Rembrant, Poussin and modern British artists.

The secret command centre for the Battle of the Atlantic in WWII was buried under an undistinguished building behind the town hall in Rumford Square. It's now the **Western Approaches Museum** *(☎ 227 2008; Rumford St; adult/concession £4.75/3.45; open Mon-Thur & Sat Mar-Oct)*.

Yes, this is Beatlemania central. There are numerous sites around town associated with the Fab Four. Both TICs sell tickets to the **Magical Mystery Tour** *(tickets £10.95)*, a two-hour bus trip taking in homes, schools, venues, Penny Lane, Strawberry Fields and many other landmarks. It departs from inside the Albert Dock TIC at 3pm April to October or 2pm November to March, and from the main TIC at 2.40pm or 1.40pm respectively.

Places to Stay

The **YHA Liverpool International** *(☎ 709 8888; ⓔ liverpool@yha.org.uk; Wapping; dorm beds from £16.85)* is right across the road from Albert Dock. The inconspicuous **Embassie Hostel** *(☎ 707 1089; 1 Falkner Square; dorm beds from £12.50)*, to the west of the Anglican Cathedral, has excellent facilities and provides free tea, coffee and toast. The new **International Inn** *(☎ 709 8135; ⓔ info@internationalinn.co.uk; 4 Hunter St; dorm beds £15)* is in a handy position just off Hardman St, close to the city centre. It is well equipped, with a café, kitchen, laundry and Internet facilities.

There are several central hotels on Mt Pleasant, between the city centre and the Metropolitan Cathedral. The basic **Belvedere** *(☎ 709 2356; 83 Mt Pleasant; beds from £20)* is the cheapest.

Places to Eat

There's a plethora of places to eat along Bold St in the city centre. At the eastern end of this street is **Cafe Tabac** *(☎ 709 3735; 124 Bold St; mains around £5)*, a relaxed wine bar which attracts a mixed crowd. **Coffee Union** *(☎ 709 9434; 89 Bold St; snacks from £1.95)* serves cheap snacks and tasty coffee. **Everyman Bistro** *(☎ 708 9545; 5 Hope St)*, found underneath the famous Everyman Theatre, is highly recommended for its variety of good cheap food (eg, pizza slices under £3).

Entertainment

A re-creation of the original venue where the Beatles made its name, the **Cavern Club** *(☎ 236 1964; 10 Mathew St)* hosts live music and DJs and attracts a big crowd.

For nightlife possibilities, the entertainment guide *Itchy Liverpool* (£3) from TICs and major bookshops, is your ticket to ride. Alternatively, take the long and winding road around Mathew St and southwest to Bold, Seel and Slater Sts, and you'll stumble upon an amazing array of clubs and pubs catering to every style. The best-known club is **Cream** *(☎ 709 1693)*, off Parr St, a superclub which rings the changes between samba, house and techno.

Philharmonic Dining Room *(☎ 709 1163; cnr Hope & Hardman Sts)*, built in 1900, is one of Britain's most extraordinary pubs. The interior is resplendent with etched glass, stained glass, wrought iron, mosaics and ceramic tiling. **The Baltic Fleet** *(☎ 709 3116; 33 Wapping)*, next to the YHA hostel, pours a superb traditional ale. Come together for a pint at the pubs around Concert Square, off Wood St, which have chairs outside for al fresco imbibing.

Everyman Theatre *(☎ 709 4776; Hope St)* is one of the best repertory theatres in the country.

Getting There & Around

There are National Express bus services linking Liverpool to most major towns. The journey takes five hours to/from London (£15). Numerous intercity services run to Lime St train station.

Public transport in the region is coordinated by **Merseytravel** *(☎ 236 7676)*. Various zone tickets (such as the £4.30 ticket for buses, trains and ferries) are sold at post offices. Smart Bus Nos 1 and 5 run from Albert Dock through the city centre to the university, and vice versa, every 20 minutes.

The ferry across the Mersey (£1.20) still offers one of the best views of Liverpool. Boats depart from Pier Head ferry terminal, to the north of Albert Dock and next to the Liver Building.

LAKE DISTRICT

The Lake District is arguably the most beautiful corner of England: a combination of perfect green dales, rocky mountains and stunning still lakes. Even the modest Cumbrian Mountains are far more dramatic than their height would suggest. This is Wordsworth country, and his houses, Dove Cottage at Grasmere and Rydal Mount, between Ambleside and Grasmere, are literary shrines.

The two principal bases are Keswick in the north and Windermere/Bowness in the south.

Kendal, Coniston, Ambleside, Grasmere and Cockermouth are less hectic alternatives.

Ullswater, Grasmere, Windermere, Coniston Water and Derwent Water are usually considered the most beautiful lakes, but they also teem with boats. Wastwater, Crummock Water and Buttermere are equally spectacular and less crowded.

Both Windermere and Keswick have decent TICs with free booking services. There are almost 30 YHA hostels in the region, many of which can be linked by foot. Contact the **YHA Central Bookings Service** *(☎ 01629-581061)* for details on the different routes.

Getting There & Away

National Express buses run from Manchester via Preston (three hours) and on to Keswick, and from London via Birmingham and on to Keswick (seven hours). There's a train service from Manchester airport to Windermere (two hours). For all public transport inquiries, contact **Traveline** *(☎ 0870 608 2608)*. Windermere is at the end of a spur off the main railway line between London's Euston station and Glasgow; for Windermere and Kendal, change at Oxenholme.

Windermere & Bowness

☎ 015394 • pop 8500

It's thanks to the railway that the Windermere/Bowness conglomerate is the largest tourist town in the Lake District. The two towns are quite strung out, with lakeside Bowness a 30-minute downhill walk from Windermere. The latter's excellent **TIC** *(☎ 46499; Victoria St, Windermere)* is conveniently located near the train station at the northern end of town. For Internet access try **T2** *(Lake Rd, Bowness)*; it's pricey at £3 per half-hour, but the delicious home-made flapjacks will make you feel better.

Less than two minutes' walk from the train station, **Lake District Backpackers Lodge** *(☎ 46374; High St; dorm beds £12)* offers beds in small dorms. **Windermere YHA** *(☎ 43543; High Cross, Bridge Lane, Troutbeck)* is larger, but 2mi from the station. Numerous buses run past Troutbeck Bridge, and in summer the hostel sends a minibus to meet trains.

Windermere is wall-to-wall B&Bs, most of them costing about £18 per night. **Brendan Chase** *(☎/fax 45638; College Rd; rooms from £20)* is comfortable and close to the train station. There's a healthy smattering of cafés and restaurants in both townships. **The Bowness Kitchen** *(☎ 45529; 4 Grosvenor Terrace, Bowness)* serves tasty toasted sandwiches for £3.

Grasmere

☎ 015394 • pop 2700

Grasmere is a picture-postcard village and a lovely place to stay out of season; in summer it's completely overrun with tourists. The **TIC** *(☎ 35245; Red Bank Rd)* is open daily. The homes of William Wordsworth are the major attractions here. **Dove Cottage & Museum** *(☎ 35544; adult/concession/child £5.50/4.30/2.50; open 9.30am-5.30pm daily; closed 7 Jan-3 Feb)* and **Rydal Mount** *(☎ 33002; Ambleside; adult/student/child £4/3/1.50; open 9.30am-5.30pm daily, shorter hours in winter)* are intriguing time capsules from the poet's life.

Butterlip How Youth Hostel *(☎ 35316; ⓔ grasmere@yha.org.uk; Easedale Rd; dorm beds from £9.25)* is just north of the village. The lovely **How Foot Lodge** *(☎ 35366; rooms from £20)* is ideal for access to Dove Cottage.

Keswick

☎ 017687 • pop 5000

Keswick is an important walking centre, and although the town centre lacks the green charm of Windermere, the lake is beautiful. The **TIC** *(☎ 72645)*, in the middle of the pedestrianised town centre, can book accommodation and also run guided tours of the area.

The **Youth Hostel** *(☎ 72484; dorm beds £11.25)*, a short walk down Station Rd from the TIC, is open most of the year. Station Rd has a number of B&Bs, most charging around £20 per person.

Kendal

☎ 01539

On the eastern outskirts of the Lake District National Park, Kendal is a lively town and makes for a good base from which to explore the region. The **TIC** *(☎ 725758; Highgate)* is in the Town Hall.

Kendal Youth Hostel *(☎ 724066; 118 Highgate; dorm beds adult/under-18 £13/10; open daily mid-Apr–Aug, Tues-Sat Sept-early Apr)* is right next door to the **Brewery**, a wonderful arts complex with a theatre, cinema and bar-bistro.

Kendal is on the branch railway line from Windermere to Oxenholme, with connections to Manchester and to Lancaster and Barrow-in-Furness.

Scotland

No visitor to Britain should miss Scotland. Despite its official union with England in 1707, this bonnie land maintains an independent national identity that goes far beyond the occasional kilt and bagpipes.

Scotland is insanely beautiful. Free from the poor urban planning that plagues its southern neighbour, it is more at liberty to sprawl in a paradoxically cosy manner. Though the dramatic scenery of the Scottish Highlands is hardly a secret, the region is curiously under-appreciated. The islands – Orkney, Shetland and Inner and Outer Hebrides – are some of the most remote places on earth, but Scottish hospitality will make you feel at home. Back in town, Edinburgh, Glasgow and St Andrews are sure to charm you with their energy and aesthetics.

FACTS ABOUT SCOTLAND

History

Despite almost continuous border warfare, it wasn't until a dispute over the Canmore succession that Edward I attempted the conquest of Scotland. The 1328 Treaty of Northampton recognised Robert the Bruce as king of an independent country.

In 1503 James IV, a Stuart king, married the daughter of Henry VII, thereby linking the two families. By the 16th century, Scotland was a nationalistic society with close links to Europe and a visceral hatred for the English. It boasted universities at St Andrews, Glasgow, Edinburgh and Aberdeen (there were only two in England) and a rigorous intellectual climate.

When the childless Queen Elizabeth I died in 1603, Mary Stuart's son united the two crowns as James I of England and James VI of Scotland. In 1707, after complex bargaining (and buying a few critical votes), England's government persuaded the Scottish Parliament to agree to the union of the two countries under a single parliament. After a Stuart rebellion was buried at the Battle of Culloden (1746), the English set out to destroy the clans, prohibiting Highland dress, weapons and military service.

By the end of the 19th century the population was concentrated in the grim industrial towns and cities of the Lowlands. Working-class disillusionment led to the development of fierce left-wing politics.

Geography

Scotland covers 30,414 sq mi and can be divided into three areas: the Southern Uplands, with ranges of hills bordering England; the Central Lowlands, a triangular slice from Edinburgh and Dundee in the east to Glasgow in the west; and the Highlands and Islands that are in the north.

Climate

Scotland has a cool temperate climate, with winds from the Atlantic warmed by the Gulf Stream. The east coast tends to be cool and dry, the west coast milder and wetter. May and June are generally the driest months, but expect rain anytime.

Government & Politics

The Scottish parliament is a single-chamber system with 129 members (known as MSPs) elected through proportional representation, led by a first minister.

Language

Gaelic is spoken by some 80,000 people, mainly in the Highlands and Islands. Lallans, or Lowland Scots, is spoken in the south. Numerous Gaelic and Lallan words linger in everyday English speech.

FACTS FOR THE VISITOR

Planning

The best time to visit Scotland is May to September. April and October are also acceptable weather risks, although many businesses close in October. Edinburgh becomes impossibly crowded during the festivals in August.

Tourist Offices

The **Scottish Tourist Board/Visit Scotland** *(STB; ☎ 0131-332 2433, fax 315 4545; ⓔ info@stb.gov.uk; headquarters: 23 Ravelston Terrace; PO Box 705, Edinburgh EH4 3TP)* deals with postal and telephone inquiries. In London, contact the **STB** *(☎ 020-7930 8661; 19 Cockspur St, London SW1 5BL)*, off Trafalgar Square, for routes, detailed information and reservations. Most towns have TICs.

Business Hours

Banking hours are normally 9.30am to 4pm weekdays, but in remote areas banks may only open for two or three days. Post offices and shops open 9am to 5.30pm weekdays; post offices close at 1pm Saturday. Shops in

BRITAIN

small towns sometimes have an early closing day midweek, while in cities there's often late-night shopping until 7pm or 8pm on Thursday or Friday.

Public Holidays & Special Events

Scottish towns normally have a spring and autumn holiday; dates vary. The Edinburgh International Festival (the world's largest arts festival), the Edinburgh Fringe Festival and the Military Tattoo take place during August each year.

Activities

Long-distance **walking** routes in Scotland include the Southern Upland Way, the West Highland Way, the Fife Coastal Path and the Speyside Way. There's also a network of thousands of miles of paths and tracks. Numerous guidebooks are available, including Lonely Planet's *Walking in Scotland*. **Cycling** is a popular way to see the lochs, forests, glens and hills of central and southern Scotland.

Scotland has a flourishing **skiing** industry; the season runs between December and April. There are several resorts of international standard in the Cairngorms (near Aviemore and Braemar) and around Ben Nevis (Scotland's highest mountain, near Fort William).

The north coast of Scotland, from Thurso to Bettyhill, offers some of the best (and coldest) **surfing** in Britain.

Accommodation

Prices are given per person, per night, unless otherwise noted.

Free wild camping is usually acceptable in unenclosed land, well away from houses and roads. The commercial camping grounds are geared to caravans and vary widely in quality, but usually have tent sites for £4 to £12. The STB's *Scotland: Caravan & Camping* (£3.99), available from TICs, lists many camping grounds. Bothies and camping barns are primitive shelters, often in remote places. There's no charge and you can't book. Users should stay one night only.

There are numerous hostels. The **Scottish Youth Hostel Association** *(SYHA; ☎ 01786-891400, fax 891333; W www.syha.org.uk; 7 Glebe Crescent, Stirling FK8 2JA)* produces a free handbook giving details on over 70 hostels, including transport links. Its hostels are generally cheaper and better than English counterparts. In big cities rates are around £14/12.50 per adult/child; the rest start at £6.50/5. These YHA hostels are supplemented by independent hostels and bunkhouses, most charging between £7 and £11. Check W www.hostel-scotland.co.uk for more details.

B&Bs cost around £18 to £25 per person. The TICs have local booking services (usually costing £1 or £2) and a Book a Bed Ahead scheme (£3). A 10% deposit is also required for most bookings. The service is worth using in July and August.

Many Scottish universities offer their student accommodation to visitors during the holidays (late June to late September).

Food & Drink

You've almost certainly heard of the ubiquitous national dish, haggis, but you may not be aware of its contents. Haggis is a 'delicious' concoction of sheep's lungs and other edible organs, mixed with oats, onions and spices, wrapped in a sheep's stomach (mmm – offal and oats, together at last). If the haggis leaves a funny taste in your mouth, then feel free to sweeten your palate with a deep-fried Mars bar. No kidding.

Perhaps more globally appealing, Scotch whisky is a treat. Great, peaty varieties are available throughout pubs in Scotland.

GETTING THERE & AWAY

Land

Bus Long-distance buses (coaches) are usually the cheapest method of getting to Scotland. The main operators are **National Express** *(☎ 0870 580 8080; W www.gobycoach.com)* and its subsidiary **Scottish Citylink** *(☎ 0870 550 5050; W www.citylink.co.uk)*, with numerous services from London and other points in England and Wales.

Fares on the main routes are competitive, with some operators undercutting National Express. **Silver Choice Travel** *(☎ 0141-333 1400)* offers the cheapest deal for a return ticket from London to Edinburgh or Glasgow (£24, 9½ hours); the ticket must be bought at least seven days prior to departure. Cheap tickets sell out quickly, so book in advance.

Train For timetable and fare information throughout Britain, call the **National Rail Enquiry Service** *(☎ 0845 748 4950)*. **Great North Eastern Railway** *(☎ 0845 722 5225)* runs a regular rail service between London King's Cross and Edinburgh (four hours), or

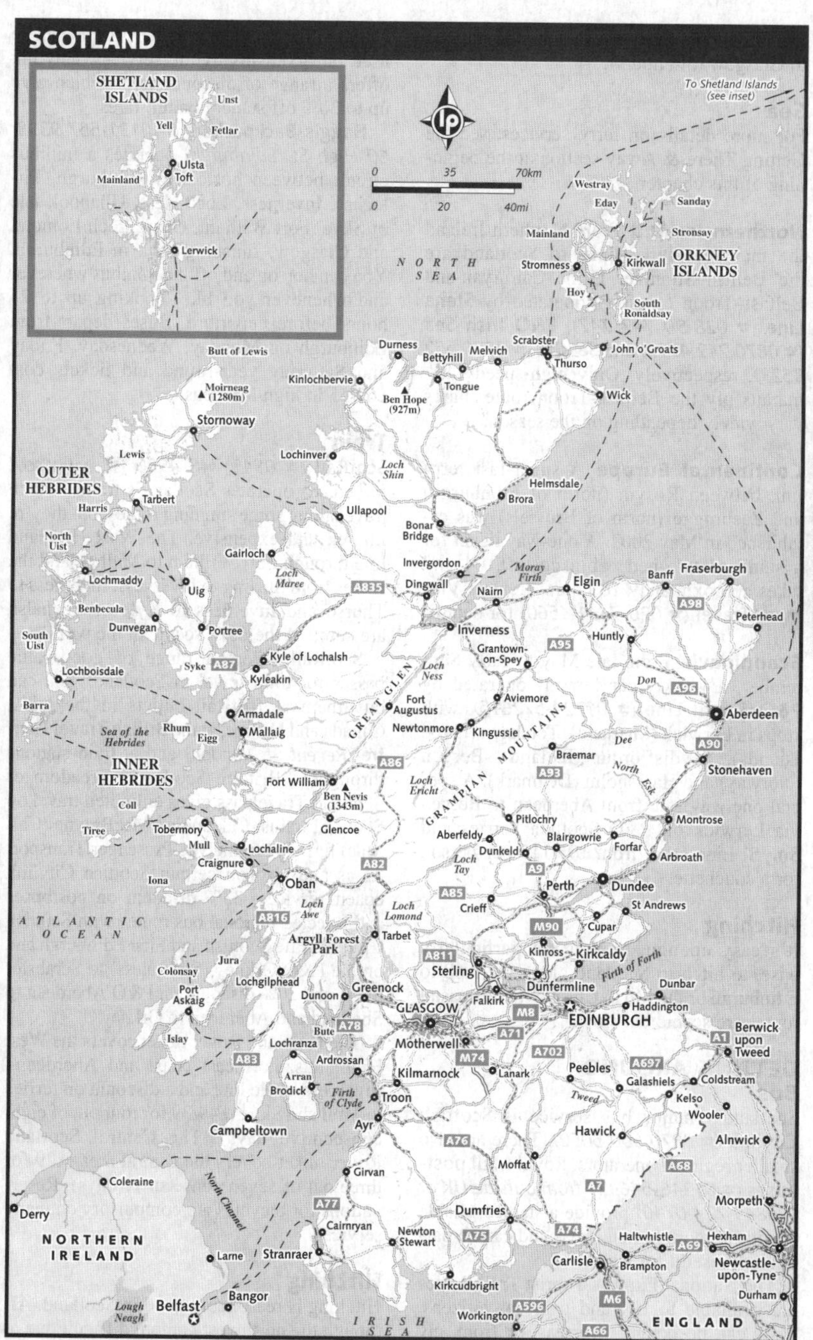
SCOTLAND
SHETLAND ISLANDS
Unst
Yell
Fetlar
Ulsta
Toft
Mainland
Lerwick
To Shetland Islands (see inset)
0 35 70km
0 20 40mi
NORTH SEA
Westray
Eday
Sanday
Stronsay
Mainland
Stromness
Kirkwall
ORKNEY ISLANDS
Hoy
South Ronaldsay
Scrabster
John o' Groats
Thurso
Wick
Butt of Lewis
Durness
Bettyhill
Melvich
Kinlochbervie
Tongue
Ben Hope (927m)
Moirneag (1280m)
Stornoway
Lewis
Lochinver
Loch Shin
Helmsdale
Brora
OUTER HEBRIDES
Harris
Tarbert
Ullapool
Bonar Bridge
North Uist
Gairloch
Loch Maree
Invergordon
Moray Firth
Lochmaddy
Uig
A835
Dingwall
Nairn
Elgin
Banff
Fraserburgh
A98
Benbecula
Dunvegan
Portree
Inverness
Peterhead
Huntly
South Uist
Grantown-on-Spey
A95
Syke
A87
Kyle of Lochalsh
Kyleakin
Loch Ness
Lochboisdale
Don
A96
GREAT GLEN
Fort Augustus
Aviemore
Aberdeen
Barra
Armadale
Rhum
Sea of the Hebrides
Eigg
Mallaig
Newtonmore
Kingussie
GRAMPIAN MOUNTAINS
Dee
A90
INNER HEBRIDES
A86
Braemar
North Esk
A93
Stonehaven
Fort William
Ben Nevis (1343m)
Loch Ericht
Coll
Glencoe
Pitlochry
Montrose
Tiree
Tobermory
Mull
Lochaline
Aberfeldy
Blairgowrie
Forfar
Craignure
Dunkeld
Arbroath
Loch Tay
A82
A9
Iona
Oban
Perth
Dundee
A85
Crieff
Loch Awe
Loch Lomond
St Andrews
ATLANTIC OCEAN
A816
M90
Cupar
Tarbet
Argyll Forest Park
A811
Kinross
Kirkcaldy
Jura
Sterling
Firth of Forth
Colonsay
Lochgilphead
Dunfermline
Port Askaig
Greenock
Falkirk
Dunbar
Dunoon
GLASGOW
EDINBURGH
Haddington
Bute
A78
M8
Islay
A71
Berwick upon Tweed
Lochranza
Motherwell
A702
A1
M74
Ardrossan
A697
A83
Kilmarnock
Lanark
Peebles
Arran
Galashiels
Coldstream
Brodick
Firth of Clyde
Troon
Tweed
Kelso
Wooler
Ayr
Campbeltown
Hawick
Alnwick
A76
Moffat
A68
Coleraine
North Channel
Girvan
A7
A77
Morpeth
Derry
Dumfries
Cairnryan
Newton Stewart
A75
A74
Haltwhistle
Hexham
NORTHERN IRELAND
A69
Larne
Stranraer
Carlisle
Brampton
Newcastle-upon-Tyne
Kirkcudbright
Bangor
M6
Durham
Lough Neagh
Belfast
A596
Workington
IRISH SEA
A66
ENGLAND
BRITAIN

from London's Euston or Paddington stations to Glasgow (5½ hours).

Sea

For more details on ferry services, see the Getting There & Away section at the beginning of this chapter.

Northern Ireland From Northern Ireland the main car ferry links to Scotland are the Belfast–Stranraer, Larne–Cairnryan and Belfast–Troon crossings operated by **Stena Line** (*☎ 028-90 747 747*), **P&O Irish Sea** (*☎ 0870 242 4777*) and **SeaCat** (*☎ 0870 552 3523*), respectively. Only high-speed catamarans ply the Belfast–Troon route. Fares vary widely depending on the season.

Continental Europe A super-fast ferry link between Rosyth (north of Edinburgh) and Zeebrugge (north of Brussels) was established in May 2002. A one-way ticket for a standard two-bed cabin costs £104 and takes approximately 16 hours. Contact **Viamare Travel** (*☎ 020-7431 4560*) for details.

Scandinavia From late May to early September, a weekly car ferry is operated by **P&O/Smyril Line** (*☎ 01224-572615*), with stops in Lerwick (Shetland), Tórshavn (Faroe Islands), Seydisfjördur (Iceland), Bergen (Norway) and Hantsholm (Denmark). A special one-way fare from Aberdeen to Bergen via Lerwick on P&O Scottish Ferries and Smyril Line costs from £95/115 per person for a couchette.

Hitching

It's easy enough, though not particularly wise, to hitch to Scotland along the A68 to Edinburgh or the M6 to Glasgow. The coastal routes are scenic but slow.

GETTING AROUND

Bus

Scotland's major bus service is **Scottish Citylink** (*☎ 0870 550 5050*). There are also smaller regional operators. **Royal Mail postbuses** (*☎ 01246-546329 from outside UK or ☎ 0845 774 0740*) provide a stable, reliable service to more remote areas and can be particularly useful for walkers.

The National Express Tourist Trail Passes are available to UK and overseas citizens. They can be bought overseas, or from any National Express agent in the UK and can be used on Scottish Citylink services. Citylink offers a range of discount cards which give up to 30% off standard adult fares.

Haggis Backpackers (*☎ 0131-557 9393; 60 High St, Edinburgh*) operates a minibus circuit between hostels in Edinburgh, Pitlochry, Inverness, Loch Ness, Ullapool, Isle of Skye, Fort William, Oban, Loch Lomond and Glasgow, finishing back in Edinburgh. You can hop on and off the minibus wherever and whenever you like, booking up to 24 hours before departure. Buses depart from Edinburgh on Monday, Wednesday, Friday and Saturday year-round and tickets cost £69/55 in high/low season.

Train

ScotRail (*☎ 0845 748 4950; W www.scotrail.co.uk*) operates Scotland's trains, which travel along some stunning routes, but they're limited and expensive. The West Highland line through Fort William to Mallaig and the routes from Stirling to Inverness, Inverness to Thurso and Inverness to Kyle of Lochalsh are some of the most scenic in the world.

ScotRail offers a range of good-value passes for train travel in Scotland. You can buy them at BritRail outlets in the USA, Canada and Europe, at the **British Travel Centre** (*Regent St, London*) and at train stations throughout Britain. ScotRail's Freedom of Scotland Travelpass gives unlimited travel on ScotRail trains, Caledonian MacBrayne (CalMac) ferries, Strathclyde Passenger Transport trains and also on certain Scottish Citylink coach services; 33% discount on postbuses and selected regional bus routes with Scottish Citylink, Fife Scottish and First Edinburgh and on the P&O Orkney (Stromness) to Scrabster ferry; and 20% discount on P&O Aberdeen to Shetland and Aberdeen to Orkney.

The Highland Rover ticket covers the West Highlands, northeast coast and Aberdeen–Inverness–Kyle line and a discount on ferries to Mull and Skye (£49/39 for four out of eight consecutive days). The Central Scotland Rover ticket covers the central area (£29 for three out of seven consecutive days). Reservations for bicycles are compulsory on many services.

Hitching

Hitching is reasonably good in Scotland. Although the northwest is more difficult due to the fact that there's less traffic, waits of over two hours are unusual. Public transport isn't scheduled to stop on the A9 (except in villages), though buses will usually stop and rescue you.

Boat

Caledonian MacBrayne *(CalMac; ☎ 0870 565 0000; Ⓦ www.calmac.co.uk)* is the most important ferry operator on the west coast, with services from Ullapool to the Outer Hebrides, and from Mallaig to Skye and on to the Outer Hebrides. Its main west-coast port, however, is Oban, with ferries to the Inner Hebridean islands of Coll, Tiree, Lismore, Mull and Colonsay and the Outer Hebridean islands of Barra and South Uist.

CalMac's Island Rover ticket gives unlimited travel on its ferry services, and costs £43/63 for eight/15 days, plus £210/315 for a car.

P&O Scottish Ferries *(☎ 01224-572615; Ⓦ www.posf.co.uk)* has ferries from Aberdeen and Scrabster to Orkney, and from Aberdeen to Shetland. See those sections for details.

EDINBURGH

☎ 0131 • pop 453,430

Edinburgh has an incomparable location, studded with volcanic hills, on the southern edge of the Firth of Forth. Its superb architecture ranges from extraordinary 16th-century tenements to monumental Georgian and Victorian masterpieces. Sixteen thousand buildings are listed as being architecturally or historically important.

In some ways, however, Edinburgh is the least Scottish of Scotland's cities – partly because of the impact of tourism, partly because of its closeness to England and the links between the two countries' upper classes, and partly because of its multicultural population.

Orientation

The two most distinctive landmarks are Arthur's Seat, the 251m-high rocky peak southeast of the centre, and the castle, which dominates Princes St Gardens. The Old and New Towns are separated by Princes St Gardens and Waverley station.

Buildings are restricted to the northern side of Princes St, which has the usual high-street shops. At the eastern end, Calton Hill is crowned by several monuments, including an incomplete war memorial modelled on the Parthenon, and a tower honouring Nelson. The Royal Mile (Lawnmarket, High St and Canongate) is Princes Street's parallel equivalent in the Old Town.

The bus station is in the New Town, off the southeastern corner of St Andrew Square, north of Princes St.

Information

The busy main **TIC** *(☎ 473 3800; Waverley Market, 3 Princes St EH2 2QP; open daily year-round)* also has a **branch** *(☎ 338 2167)* at Edinburgh airport. Both offices have Scotland-wide information, and sell the useful *Essential Guide to Edinburgh* (£1). The TIC *bureau de change* is open the same hours as the TIC. **American Express** *(☎ 718 2501; 139 Princes St; open 9am-5.30pm Mon-Wed & Fri, 9.30am-5.30pm Thur, 9am-4pm Sat)* can help with currency exchange, as can **Thomas Cook** *(☎ 456 7700; 26-28 Frederick St; open 9am-5.30pm Mon-Wed, Fri & Sat, 10am-5.30pm Thur)*.

You can get Net access at **easyEverything** *(☎ 220 3580; 58 Rose St; open 24hr)* for around £1 per hour.

BRITAIN

Things to See & Do

The best place to start any tour of Edinburgh is **Edinburgh Castle** *(☎ 225 9846; adult/concession/child £8/6/2; open 9.30am-6pm daily Apr-Sept, 9.30am-5pm Oct-Mar)*. The castle, now headquarters for the British army's Scottish Division, is a complex of buildings that were altered many times by war and the demands of the military. The small, 12th-century **St Margaret's Chapel** is the oldest building in Edinburgh. The castle was the seat of Scottish kings, and the royal apartments include the tiny room where Mary Queen of Scots gave birth to the boy who became James VI of Scotland and James I of England. You can also see the **Stone of Destiny**, returned to Scotland in 1996, and the **Scottish Crown Jewels**.

Gladstone's Land *(☎ 226 5856; 477b Lawnmarket; adult/concession £5/3.75; open Apr-Oct)* is a townhouse, originally completed in 1620, which has been skilfully restored, giving a fascinating insight into urban life in the past. **The Writers' Museum** *(☎ 529 4901; Lady Stair's Close, Lawnmarket; admission free; open 10am-5pm Mon-Sat)* contains memorabilia belonging to Robert Burns, Sir Walter Scott and Robert Louis Stevenson.

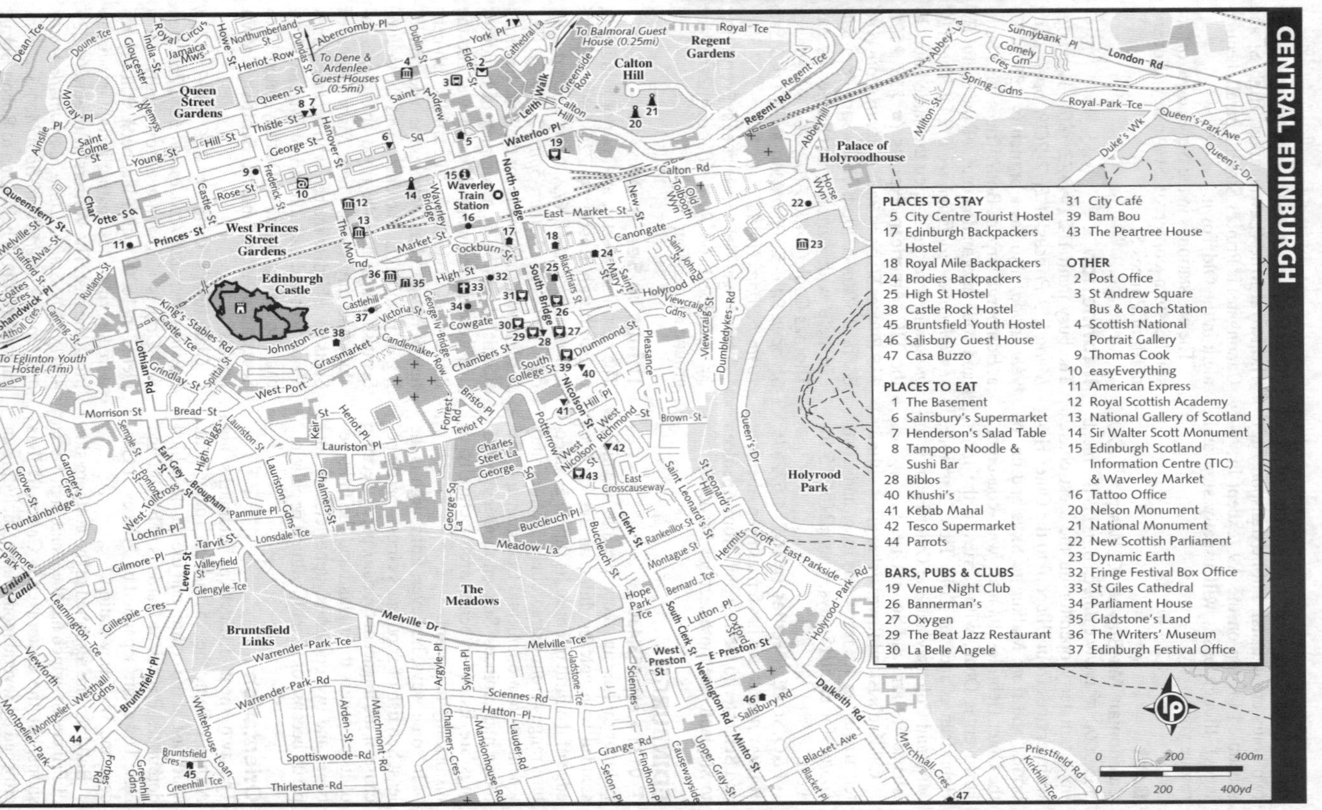
CENTRAL EDINBURGH
PLACES TO STAY
5 City Centre Tourist Hostel
17 Edinburgh Backpackers Hostel
18 Royal Mile Backpackers
24 Brodies Backpackers
25 High St Hostel
38 Castle Rock Hostel
45 Bruntsfield Youth Hostel
46 Salisbury Guest House
47 Casa Buzzo
PLACES TO EAT
1 The Basement
6 Sainsbury's Supermarket
7 Henderson's Salad Table
8 Tampopo Noodle & Sushi Bar
28 Biblos
40 Khushi's
41 Kebab Mahal
42 Tesco Supermarket
44 Parrots
BARS, PUBS & CLUBS
19 Venue Night Club
26 Bannerman's
27 Oxygen
29 The Beat Jazz Restaurant
30 La Belle Angele
31 City Café
39 Bam Bou
43 The Peartree House
OTHER
2 Post Office
3 St Andrew Square Bus & Coach Station
4 Scottish National Portrait Gallery
9 Thomas Cook
10 easyEverything
11 American Express
12 Royal Scottish Academy
13 National Gallery of Scotland
14 Sir Walter Scott Monument
15 Edinburgh Scotland Information Centre (TIC) & Waverley Market
16 Tattoo Office
20 Nelson Monument
21 National Monument
22 New Scottish Parliament
23 Dynamic Earth
32 Fringe Festival Box Office
33 St Giles Cathedral
34 Parliament House
35 Gladstone's Land
36 The Writers' Museum
37 Edinburgh Festival Office
0 200 400m
0 200 400yd

On the Royal Mile is the much-restored 15th-century **St Giles Cathedral**. At the cathedral's rear is **Parliament House**, now the seat of the supreme law courts of Scotland.

The **Palace of Holyroodhouse** *(☎ 556 7371; admission £6; open daily Apr-Oct)* at the eastern end of the Royal Mile is a Stuart palace mostly dating from a reconstruction by Charles II in 1671. Holyroodhouse is the official Scottish residence of the British royal family and is closed when the Queen is in residence – usually around mid-May or mid-June.

Close to Holyroodhouse, the **New Scottish Parliament** was in the final stages of construction at the time of writing and was expected to be completed in early 2003. Opposite is the engaging **Dynamic Earth** *(☎ 550 7800; Holyrood Rd; adult/concession £7.95/4.50; open daily April-Oct, Wed-Sun Nov-Mar)*, an exhibition on the planet's geology and natural history.

Walking along Princes St you'll pass the extravagant 200ft spire of the **Sir Walter Scott Monument**. A farther 200yd along Princes St, on the corner of Princes St and The Mound, the **Royal Scottish Academy** *(RSA; ☎ 558 7097; admission £2-5 for special exhibitions; open 10am-5pm Mon-Sat, 2pm-5pm Sun)* and the **National Gallery of Scotland** *(☎ 624 6200; admission £2-5 for special exhibitions; same opening hours as RSA)* contain collections of paintings, drawings, sculptures and architectural drawings by academy members and European art, from Renaissance to postimpressionism.

Scottish National Portrait Gallery *(☎ 624 6200; 1 Queen St; admission free; open 10am-5pm Tues-Sat)*, in the New Town, contains portraits of famous Scots, from Mary Queen of Scots to Sean Connery.

Special Events

The Edinburgh International Festival is the world's largest, most important arts festival, and the world's premier companies play to packed audiences. The Fringe Festival grew up alongside it, presenting the would-be future stars. It now claims to be the largest such event in the world, with over 500 amateur and professional groups presenting every possible kind of avant-garde performance. Just to make sure that every bed within a 40mi radius is taken, the Edinburgh Military Tattoo is held at the same time.

The festivals take place around mid-August, but the Tattoo finishes earlier, so the last week is less hectic. If you want to attend the International Festival, it's necessary to book; the programme, published in April, is available from the **Edinburgh Festival Office** *(☎ 473 2000; The Hub, Castlehill, Royal Mile, EH1 2NE)*. The Fringe Festival is less formal, and many performances have available seats the day before. Programmes are available from June from the **Festival Fringe Office** *(☎ 226 0026; 180 High St EH1 1QS)*. To book the Military Tattoo, contact the **Tattoo Office** *(☎ 225 1188; 32 Market St EH1 1QB)*.

Edinburgh is *the* place to be in the New Year (Hogmanay), so you'll need to book well ahead if you want to be part of the fun.

Places to Stay

Edinburgh has numerous accommodation options but they fill quickly over New Year, at Easter and also between mid-May and mid-September. Book in advance or use the accommodation services operated by the TIC.

Hostels & Colleges The ever-popular **High St Hostel** *(☎ 557 3984; 8 Blackfriars St; dorm beds from £10.50)* is comfortable and handy for Royal Mile tourist attractions, pubs and clubs. Nearby are two quality hostels: **Royal Mile Backpackers** *(☎ 557 6120; 105 High St; dorm beds from £10.50)* and **Brodies Backpackers** *(☎ 556 6770; 12 High St; dorm beds from £9.90)*. In the shadow of the castle is the excellent **Castle Rock Hostel** *(☎ 225 9666; 15 Johnston Terrace; dorm beds from £10.50)*. The **Edinburgh Backpackers Hostel** *(☎ 220 1717 or 220 2200 for reservations; 65 Cockburn St; dorm beds from £12.50)* is close to all the action and also has a licensed café. **City Centre Tourist Hostel** *(☎ 556 8070; 5 West Register St; dorm beds from £12)* has an equally good location, behind Princes St and close to the bus station, although you will have to negotiate 77 exhausting steps to reach reception.

There are two good SYHA hostels. **Eglinton Youth Hostel** *(☎ 337 1120; 18 Eglinton Crescent; adult/under-18 from £12/10.50)* is west of the city centre, near Haymarket train station. Walk west along Princes St and continue on Shandwick Place, which becomes West Maitland St; veer right at Haymarket along Haymarket Terrace, then turn right onto Coates Gardens, which runs into Eglinton Crescent.

Bruntsfield Youth Hostel *(☎ 447 2994; 7 Bruntsfield Crescent; dorm beds from £11.50)* has an attractive location overlooking Bruntsfield Links about 2.5mi southwest of Waverley train station. Catch bus No 11 or 16 from the garden side of Princes St and get off at Forbes Rd after the gardens on the left.

B&Bs You'll need to hunt around for a good deal; pick up the TIC's free accommodation guide and make some phone calls. Outside festival time you should have no trouble getting something for around £20, although it may be a bus ride away in the suburbs.

Guesthouses are generally £2 or £3 more expensive, and to get a private bathroom you'll have to pay about £25 to £30. The main concentrations are around Pilrig St, Pilrig; Minto St (a southern continuation of North Bridge), Newington; and Gilmore Place and Leamington Terrace, Bruntsfield.

There are two good deals in the New Town: **Dene Guest House** *(☎ 556 2700; 7 Eyre Place; rooms from £23.50)* and next door **Ardenlee Guest House** *(☎ 556 2838; 9 Eyre Place; rooms from £26)*. Both these places are located about a mile north of the city centre.

Pilrig St, off Leith Walk (veer left at the eastern end of Princes St), is a happy hunting ground for guesthouses. **Balmoral Guest House** *(☎ 554 1857; 32 Leith Walk; rooms from £20)* has easy access to the city.

There are also numerous guesthouses on and around Minto St/Mayfield Gardens in Newington, south of the centre, accessed by plenty of buses. This is the main traffic artery from the south and carries traffic from the A7 and A68. The best places are on the streets on either side of the main road. **Casa Buzzo** *(☎ 667 8998; 8 Kilmaurs Rd; doubles from £20)* is east of Dalkeith Rd.

Places to Eat

The wide variety of eating establishments in Edinburgh should keep culinary adventurers very happy.

Tampopo Noodle & Sushi Bar *(☎ 220 5254; 25a Thistle St; mains around £8; open Tues-Sat)* is a tiny place but it's big on authenticity and flavour. **The Basement** *(☎ 557 0097; 10a-12a Broughton St; mains from £5.95; open noon-10.30pm daily)* changes its lunchtime menu daily, but you can rely on Mexican-influenced fare on weekends and Thai-inspired on Wednesday. **Biblos** *(☎ 226 7177; 1a Chambers St; sandwiches from £4, mains from £5.95; open 8am-9pm daily)* joins the burgeoning ranks of cool cafés in Edinburgh's centre. **Khushi's** *(☎ 556 8996; 16 Drummond St; 2-course meal £7.50; open Mon-Sat)* is Edinburgh's original curry house.

Vegetarians should look for **Henderson's Salad Table** *(☎ 225 2131; 94 Hanover St; mains from £4.25; open Mon-Sat)*, an excellent value cafeteria-style restaurant.

The university students' budget favourites can be found between Nicolson St and Bristo Place (at the end of the George IV Bridge). **Kebab Mahal** *(☎ 667 5214; 7 Nicolson Square; kebabs from £3.25)* is a legendary source of cheap sustenance.

For self-caterers, there's a **Sainsbury's** *(St Andrew's Square)* near the bus station, and a **Tesco** *(Nicolson St)*.

Entertainment

The fortnightly magazine *List* (£1.95), giving full coverage of events in Edinburgh (and Glasgow), is essential if you're staying for a few days.

There are several busy pubs on Grassmarket's northern side; they often have live music. Along Cowgate, off Grassmarket's southeast, are some good pubs, including the relaxed **Bannerman's** *(☎ 556 3254)*. For long summer evenings **The Peartree House** *(☎ 667 7533; 38 West Nicolson St)* has a large outdoor courtyard and an equally large student following.

Jazz lovers will gravitate to **The Beat Jazz Basement** *(☎ 225 5209; 1 Chambers St)*. The Friday night improvised jazz jam, sponsored by Blue Note records, is popular.

For a mix of music styles, from hip-hop and house to drum 'n' bass and funk, try **Bam Bou** *(☎ 556 0200; 66/67 South Bridge)*, or **La Belle Angele** *(☎ 225 7536; 11 Hasties Close)*, off Cowgate.

Fashionable young things can be seen at **Oxygen** *(☎ 557 9997; 3-5 Infirmary St)*, where house beats dominate the decks.

City Café *(☎ 220 0125; 19 Blair St)* is a cool, 1950s US-style bar and diner with pool tables. **Venue Night Club** *(☎ 557 3073; 17 Calton Rd)* has dance music on three floors and is worth checking out.

Getting There & Away

Bus Fares from London are competitive and you may be able to get cheap promotional tickets. National Express and Scottish Citylink are the main operators. The journey time is 9½ to 11¼ hours depending on the route, and the cheapest fare with National Express is £28 return (£24 with Silver Choice).

There are links to cities throughout England and Wales, including Newcastle (£21, 2¾ hours) and York (£28.50, six hours). Scottish Citylink has buses to major towns in Scotland. Most west-coast towns are reached via Glasgow to which there are buses every 15 to 20 minutes from Edinburgh (£5 return, 1¼ hours); there are also regular services to Aberdeen (£25, 3¼ hours) and Inverness (£24, four hours).

Train There are up to 20 trains daily to/from London's King's Cross station (4½ to 5½ hours). ScotRail has two northern lines from Edinburgh: one cuts north across the Grampians to Inverness (£37.10, 3¼ hours) and on to Thurso; the other follows the coast north around to Aberdeen (£44.90, 2½ hours) and on to Inverness. There are trains every 15 minutes to Glasgow (£7.50, 50 minutes). For rail inquiries, phone ☎ 0845 748 4950.

Getting Around

There are two main bus companies: **Lothian Regional Transport** *(LRT; ☎ 555 6363)* and **First Edinburgh** *(☎ 663 9233)*. For short trips in the city, fares are 50p to £1.20. After midnight there are special night buses. The free *Edinburgh Travelmap* shows the most important services and is available from the TIC, or during weekdays contact **Traveline** *(☎ 225 3858, 0800 232323)*.

GLASGOW

☎ 0141 • pop 612,000

Glasgow is one of Britain's largest, most interesting cities. It doesn't have the instantly inspiring beauty of Edinburgh, but it does have interesting Georgian and Victorian architecture and some distinguished suburbs of terraced squares and crescents.

Although influenced by thousands of Irish immigrants, this is the most Scottish of cities, with a unique blend of friendliness, urban chaos, black humour and energy. Highlights include excellent art galleries and museums (most free), numerous good-value restaurants, countless pubs and bars, and a lively arts scene.

Glasgow's location is also close to great scenery – Loch Lomond, the Trossachs and the Highlands to the north, the Hebrides to the west and the rolling hills of southern Scotland to the south.

Orientation

The two train stations (Central and Queen St), Buchanan St bus station and the TIC are all within a couple of blocks of George Square, which is the main city square. Running along a ridge in the northern part of the city, Sauchiehall (pronounced sorky-hall) St has a pedestrian mall with numerous high-street shops at its eastern end, and pubs and restaurants to the west. The University of Glasgow and SYHA hostel are northwest of the city centre around Kelvingrove Park.

Information

An accommodation-booking service is provided by the main **TIC** *(☎ 204 4400; 11 George Square; open daily)* for £2. For currency exchange there's **American Express** *(☎ 222 1401; 115 Hope St; open 8.30am-5.30pm Mon-Fri, 9am-2pm Sat)*. The TIC and the **post office** *(cnr Buchanan & St Vincent Sts)*, both have currency-exchange facilities. You are able to access the Internet at **easyEverything** *(☎ 222 2364; 57 St Vincent St)*; the average cost is £1 for 45 minutes.

Things to See & Do

A good starting point is **George Square**, which is surrounded by imposing Victorian architecture, including the post office, the Bank of Scotland and, along its eastern side, the extravagant **City Chambers**.

The current **Glasgow Cathedral** *(☎ 552 6891; open 9.30am-6pm Mon-Sat, 2pm-5pm Sun Apr-Oct & 9.30am-4pm Mon-Sat, 2pm-4pm Sun Nov-Mar)* is a direct descendant of St Mungo's simple church. It was begun in 1238 and is seen as a perfect example of pre-Reformation Gothic architecture. St Mungo's tomb was the focus of a medieval pilgrimage that was believed to be as meritorious as a visit to Rome.

Beside the cathedral, the **St Mungo Museum of Religious Life & Art** *(☎ 552 2557; admission free; open 10am-5pm Mon-Thur & Sat, 11am-5pm Fri & Sun)* is worth visiting. In the main gallery, Dalí's *Christ of St John of the Cross* hangs beside statues of the Buddha and Hindu deities. Outside you'll find Britain's only **Zen garden**. Opposite the cathedral and St Mungo Museum is **Provand's Lordship**

(☎ 553 2557; admission free; open 10am-5pm Mon-Thur & Sat, 11am-5pm Fri & Sat), the oldest dwelling in Glasgow.

There are some superb Art Nouveau buildings designed by famous Scottish architect and designer Charles Rennie Mackintosh. In particular, check the **Glasgow School of Art** *(☎ 353 4500; 167 Renfrew St; open 10am-7pm Mon-Thur, 10am-5pm Fri, 10am-noon Sat)*, which has guided tours from Monday to Saturday (adult/concession £5/3).

Special Events

Like Edinburgh, Glasgow has developed several festivals of its own, starting with a two-week **Celtic Connections** *(☎ 353 8000)* music festival from mid-January. The **West End Festival** *(☎ 341 0844)* of music and the arts runs for two weeks in mid-June and is Glasgow's biggest festival. The excellent **International Jazz Festival** *(☎ 552 3552)* is held in early July. **Glasgay** *(☎ 334 7126)* is a gay performing arts festival, held around October/November.

Places to Stay

Finding a decent B&B in July and August can be difficult, so get into town reasonably early and use the TIC's booking service. Unfortunately, Glasgow's B&Bs are expensive by Scottish standards – you may have to pay up to £35 for a single.

Hostels & Colleges The **Glasgow Youth Hostel** *(☎ 332 3004; 7 Park Terrace; dorm beds adult/child £12.50/10.50)* has mainly four-bed rooms, many with bathroom; book

GLASGOW

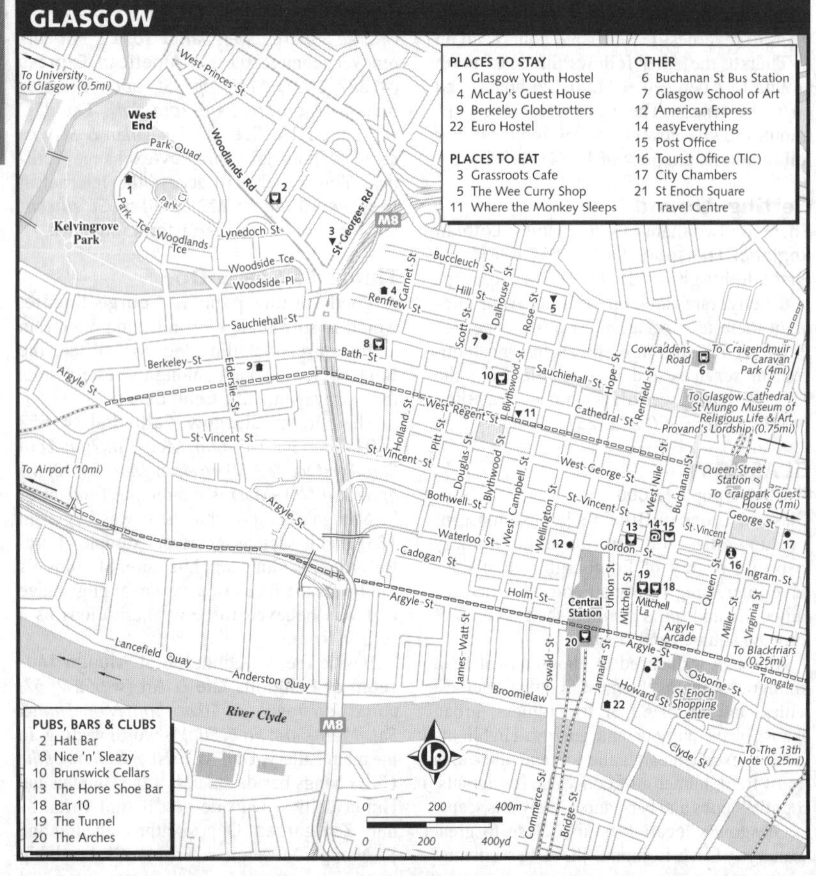

ahead during summer. From Central station take bus No 44 or 59 and ask for the first stop on Woodlands Rd.

Berkeley Globetrotters *(☎ 221 7880; 63 Berkeley St, Charing Cross; dorm beds £8.50-10.50, twins £12.50)* is another option. Phone ahead for bookings.

The 380-bed **Euro Hostel** *(☎ 222 2828; ⓔ info@euro-hostels.com; 318 Clyde St; B&B £13.75-25)* is a former student hall of residence. It has 24-hour reception and Internet access for around £3 per hour. The **University of Glasgow** *(☎ 330 5385; ⓔ vacation@gla.ac.uk; dorm beds per day/week, from £14/84, B&B per room from £35.50; open mid-Mar–mid-Apr & July-Sept)* offers self-catering hostel and B&B accommodation around the city. The **University of Strathclyde** *(☎ 553 4148; ⓔ rescat@mis.strath.ac.uk; Cathedral St; open mid-June–Sept)* also seasonally opens its halls of residence to tourists.

B&Bs Renfrew St, which is located north of Sauchiehall St, has several places. **McLay's Guest House** *(☎ 332 4796; 264-276 Renfrew St; singles/doubles from £24/40)* is excellent value and well placed for city centre attractions.

There's a batch of reasonable-value B&Bs east of the city centre **Craigpark Guest House** *(☎ 554 4160; 33 Circus Drive; singles/doubles from £18/32)* is an acceptable option.

Places to Eat

Glasgow has an excellent range of moderately priced restaurants. Along Sauchiehall St or around the city centre you'll find the ethnic cuisine of your choice. Set lunches offered by many restaurants are usually good value at £4 to £6.

Towards the West End, **Grassroots Cafe** *(☎ 333 0534; 93-97 St Georges Rd; mains £4-8; open 10am-10pm daily)* will keep herbivores happy.

The Wee Curry Shop *(☎ 353 0777; 7 Buccleuch St; mains around £7; open noon-2pm & 5.30pm-10.30pm Mon-Sat)* is popular for its authentic, home-style Indian cooking. It serves a great-value two-course lunchtime special for £4.25. You'll need to book.

Where the Monkey Sleeps *(☎ 226 3406; 182 West Regent St; open 7am-7pm Mon-Fri, 10am-7pm Sat & noon-6pm Sun)* has delicious soups and sandwiches for those on the run.

Entertainment

Some of the best nightlife in Scotland hums in the pubs, bars and clubs of Glasgow. The *List* (£1.95) is Glasgow's comprehensive, invaluable fortnightly entertainment guide.

The city centre is where the club action is focused; West Regent and Bath Sts have a plethora of small, subterranean hang-outs; and Merchant City, to the east along Ingram St, is full of larger, hip joints. The West End offers a cool nightlife alternative.

Pubs & Bars In the centre, **Brunswick Cellars** *(☎ 572 0016; 239 Sauchiehall St)* is a smoky, candlelit, basement bar which is popular with a younger crowd. At **Nice 'n' Sleazy** *(☎ 333 0900; 421 Sauchiehall St)* there's no sleaze in sight, just a laid-back crowd, chill tunes and cheap drinks.

Bar 10 *(☎ 221 8353; 10 Mitchell Lane)* is a stylish but unpretentious place (a rare combination), just off Buchanan St.

The Horse Shoe Bar *(☎ 229 5711; 17 Drury Lane)* has the longest continuous bar in Britain, but its main attraction is the ale and excellent-value food. **Blackfriars** *(☎ 552 5924; 36 Bell St)* is relaxed and friendly, and there's free jazz on weekends.

In the West End, there are numerous pubs on or around Byres Rd. The **Halt Bar** *(☎ 564 1527; 160 Woodlands Rd)* is a popular university pub that hasn't been tarted up. There's a great atmosphere and free live music most nights.

Clubs Clubs charge an entry fee of between £3 and £7. **The Tunnel** *(☎ 204 1000; 84 Mitchell St)* pumps out hard house music to a dressed-up crowd. Friday and Saturday nights at **The 13th Note** *(☎ 243 2177; 50-60 King St)* are seriously funky affairs. **The Arches** *(☎ 221 4001; Midland St, off Jamaica St)* keeps its 2000-plus punters on their toes with house, hard house and trance.

Getting There & Away

Bus All buses arrive and depart from Buchanan St bus station. Fares from London are competitive; **Silver Choice** *(☎ 01355-230403)* offers the best deal at £20/24 one-way/return. There are daily departures at 10pm from both London's Victoria coach station and Glasgow's Buchanan bus station; the run takes 8½ hours.

There are numerous links with other English cities. National Express services include three daily buses from Glasgow to Birmingham (£33.50/36, 5¾ hours), one to Cambridge (£39.50/41, 9¾ hours), numerous to Carlisle (£13/14, two hours), two to Newcastle (£21/22, four hours), and one to York (£23.50/25.50, 7½ hours).

Scottish Citylink operates buses to most major towns in Scotland. There are buses every 20 minutes to Edinburgh (£5 return, 1¼ hours); and frequent buses to Stirling (single/return £3.60/5, 45 minutes), Oban (£11.20/15, three hours), Fort William (£11.80/16, three hours), Inverness (£14/19.50, from 3½ hours), Aberdeen (£15/21, four hours) and Skye (£20/27, 6¼ hours).

There's a twice-daily summer service (late May to September) to Stranraer, connecting with the ferry to Belfast (£29/39, six hours).

First Edinburgh *(☎ 01324-613777)* runs hourly buses to Milngavie (£1.15, 30 minutes), which is the start of the West Highland Way.

Train As a general rule, Central station serves southern Scotland, England and Wales, and Queen St serves the north and east. There are buses every 10 minutes between the two stations (50p, or free with a through train ticket). There are up to eight direct trains daily from London's Euston station; they're not cheap, but they're quicker (five to six hours) than the bus. There are also up to eight direct services to/from London's King's Cross. Fares change name and price constantly, but there are usually return fares in the £30 to £40 range.

ScotRail operates the West Highland line north to Oban and Fort William, and direct links to Dundee (£19.70), Aberdeen (£28) and Inverness (£30.60). There are numerous trains to Edinburgh (£7.50, 50 minutes). For rail inquiries, call ☎ 0845 748 4950.

Getting Around

Located at **St Enoch Square Travel Centre** *(☎ 226 4826; St Enoch Square)*, **Strathclyde Passenger Transport** *(STP; open 8.30am-5.30pm Mon-Sat)* provides information on transport in the Glasgow region.

Bus services are frequent and cheap. You can buy tickets when you board buses, but on some you have to have the exact change. For short trips in the city, fares are 70p. After midnight there are limited night buses from George Square.

There's an extensive suburban train network, which connects with the Underground at Buchanan St station. The circular Underground serves 15 stations in the centre and west (north and south of the river) for 90p one way; a Discovery Ticket (£2.50) gives unlimited travel for one day.

SOUTHWEST SCOTLAND

The tourist board describes this region as 'Scotland's surprising southwest', but it's surprising only if you expect beautiful mountain and coastal scenery to be confined to the Highlands.

Ayrshire, immediately southwest of Glasgow, was the home of Scotland's national poet, Robert Burns, and is also a major horse-racing hub. Dumfries & Galloway covers the southern half of this western elbow, and is where the coast and mountains approach the grandeur of the north. Warmed by the Gulf Stream, this is also the mildest corner of Scotland, and there are some famous gardens.

There are many notable historic and prehistoric attractions linked by the **Solway Coast Heritage Trail** (information from TICs). **Kirkcudbright** is a picturesque town which makes a good base.

The southwest is excellent cycling and walking country, and it is crossed by the coast-to-coast **Southern Upland Way** and a number of cycle trails (pick up brochures from the TICs).

The **Isle of Arran** is described as 'Scotland in miniature' owing to its varied scenery. Its **TIC** *(☎ 302140)*, by the pier in **Brodick** (the main town), has details of accommodation on the island. Arran is an hour's ferry ride from Ardrossan, and is conveniently accessible from Glasgow.

Stranraer (with nearby Cairnryan) is the ferry port to Larne and Belfast in Northern Ireland; it's the shortest link from Britain to Ireland, and takes less than 2½ hours. The area's SYHA hostels are at Ayr, Newton Stewart (Minnigaff), Kendoon, Wanlockhead, and at Lochranza and Whiting Bay on the Isle of Arran.

Getting There & Around

Bus National Express buses travel from London and Birmingham (via Manchester and Carlisle), and Glasgow/Edinburgh to Stranraer. These buses service the main towns and villages along the A75 (including Ayr, Dumfries and Newton Stewart). **Stagecoach Western** *(☎ 01387-253496)* provides local bus service.

Train There are regular services between Ayr and Glasgow (£6.90, 50 minutes) and Stranraer and Glasgow (£14.90, 2½ hours). For rail inquiries call ☎ 0845 748 4950.

Boat Frequent car and passenger ferries between Stranraer and Belfast are operated by **Stena Line** *(☎ 0870 570 7070)*, and between Cairnryan (5mi north of Stranraer) and Larne by **P&O** *(☎ 0870 242 4777)*. **SeaCat** *(☎ 0870 552 3523)* operates a high-speed catamaran between Troon, to the north of Ayr, and Belfast three times a day.

CalMac *(☎ 302166)* runs a daily car ferry between Ardrossan and Brodick on Arran (£4.55 for driver and for each passenger, £25.50/31.50 for car low/high season, 55 minutes, four to six daily).

STIRLING

☎ 01786 • pop 37,000

Occupying the most strategically important location in Scotland, Stirling has witnessed many of the struggles of the Scots against the English. The cobbled streets of the attractive old town surround the castle. The **TIC** *(☎ 0870 720 0620; 41 Dumbarton Rd; open Mon-Sat)* can help with information. There's also a visitor centre next to the castle.

The town is dominated by **Stirling Castle** *(☎ 450000; adult/concession/child £7/5/2; open daily)*, perched dramatically on a rock. This was where Mary Queen of Scots was crowned.

Stirling Youth Hostel *(☎ 473442; St John St; dorm beds from £10/8)* is central and an excellent place to stay. The independent **Willy Wallace Hostel** *(☎ 446773; 77 Murray Place; dorm beds £10)* has Internet access, and free tea and coffee. The excellent **Forth Guest House** *(☎ 471020, fax 447220; 23 Forth Place; B&B £19.50-37.50)* is a short walk north from the train station, just off Seaforth Rd.

There are regular buses to Edinburgh, Glasgow and Aberdeen.

ST ANDREWS

☎ 01334 • pop 13,900

St Andrews is a beautiful and unusual seaside town – an eclectic mix of medieval ruins, golf fanatics, coastal scenery, tourist kitsch and a university where wealthy English undergraduates (including the future King of England, Prince William) rub shoulders with Scottish theology students.

Although St Andrews was once the ecclesiastical capital of Scotland, both its cathedral and castle are now in ruins. These days St Andrews is the headquarters of golf's governing body, the Royal & Ancient Golf Club, and home of the world's most famous golf course, the 16th-century Old Course.

The **TIC** *(☎ 472021; 70 Market St; open daily year-round)* has copies of *Getting Around Fife*, a free guide to public transport.

Things to See

At the eastern end of North St, **St Andrews Cathedral** is the ruined west end of what was once the largest and one of the most magnificent cathedrals in Scotland. Many of the town's buildings are constructed from its stones. **St Andrews Castle & Visitor Centre** *(☎ 477196; joint admission with cathedral adult/concession/child £4/3/1.50; open daily)* has a spectacular cliff-top location. Near the Old Course is the **British Golf Museum** *(☎ 460046; adult/concession/child £4/3/2; open daily Apr–mid-Oct, Thur-Mon mid-Oct–Mar)*.

Places to Stay & Eat

Just five minutes' walk from the bus station, **St Andrews Tourist Hostel** *(☎ 479911; ⓔ info@eastgatehostel.com; Inchape House, St Mary's Place; dorm beds from £12)* is the only hostel in town. Two good-value B&Bs are **Abbey Cottage** *(☎ 473727; ⓔ coull@lineone.net; Abbey Walk; rooms £19-24)*, just south of Abbey St, and **Fairnie House** *(☎ 474094; ⓔ kate@fairniehouse.freeserve.co.uk; 10 Abbey St; rooms £16-30)*. Other central B&Bs and hotels line Murray Park and Murray Place; most charge from around £25.

Ziggy's *(☎ 473686; 6 Murray Place; meals £4.95-15.95)* is popular with students and has burgers and a good range of Mexican, vegetarian and seafood dishes. **The Vine Leaf** *(☎ 477497; 131 South St; 2-course dinner £19.95)* serves gourmet seafood, game, Scottish beef and vegetarian meals.

Getting There & Away

Stagecoach Fife *(☎ 01592-642394)* has a half-hourly bus service from Edinburgh to St Andrews (£5.70, two hours) and on to Dundee (£2.40, 30 minutes).

The nearest train station to St Andrews is Leuchars (one hour from Edinburgh), 5mi away on the Edinburgh, Dundee, Aberdeen,

Inverness coastal line. Bus Nos X59 and X60 leave every half-hour Monday to Saturday to St Andrews, hourly on Sunday.

EASTERN HIGHLANDS

A great elbow of land juts into the North Sea between Perth and the Firth of Tay in the south, and Inverness and Moray Firth in the north. The Cairngorm Mountains are as dramatic and demanding as any of the Scottish ranges, and the coastline, especially from Stonehaven to Buckie, is excellent. The valley of the River Dee boasts sublime scenery.

Aberdeen is the main ferry port for Shetland, and Inverness is the centre for the northern Highlands. There are few coast-to-coast links between Perth and Inverness.

Getting Around

The main bus and train routes from Edinburgh to Inverness run directly north through Perth, or around the coast to Aberdeen and then northwest and inland back to Inverness.

Bus The main towns are linked by Scottish Citylink. Edinburgh to Inverness via Perth takes four hours (£12.50); to Aberdeen, changing at Dundee, also takes four hours (£13.50). There are also regular buses from both Inverness and Aberdeen to Glasgow for much the same price. The bus trip from Aberdeen to Inverness takes three hours (£10) and passes through Elgin.

For detailed information on local bus services, phone **Perth & Kinross** *(☎ 0845 301 1130)*, **Angus** *(☎ 01307-461775)*, **Dundee** *(☎ 01382-433125)* and **Aberdeenshire & Moray** *(☎ 01224-664581)*.

Train The train journey from Perth to Inverness is one of the most spectacular in Scotland, with a beautiful climb through the Cairngorms from Dunkeld to Aviemore. There are up to 10 trains daily Monday to Saturday, and five on Sunday (2¼ hours). There are many trains from Edinburgh and Glasgow to Aberdeen (2½ hours from Edinburgh) and from Aberdeen to Inverness (2¼ hours). Call **ScotRail** *(☎ 0845 748 4950)* for information on the various fares available.

Aberdeen

☎ 01224 • pop 211,250

Aberdeen is an extraordinary symphony in grey: almost everything is built of granite. In the sun, especially after a shower, the stone turns silver and sparkles like fairy-lights, but with low grey clouds and rain scudding in off the North Sea it can be a bit depressing.

Aberdeen is built on a ridge that runs east–west to the north of the River Dee. Union St, the main shopping street, runs along the crest of this ridge. The train and bus stations are next to each other off Guild St. The **TIC** *(☎ 288828; open year-round)* is next door to the Maritime Museum on Shiprow.

The **Aberdeen Youth Hostel** *(☎ 646988; 8 Queen's Rd; dorm beds adults/under-18s £12.25/10.75; open year-round)* is a mile west of the train station. Clusters of B&Bs line Bon Accord St and Springbank Terrace (both close to the centre) and Great Western Rd (the A93, a 25-minute walk from the city centre).

Ashvale Fish Restaurant *(☎ 596981; 42-48 Great Western Rd)* is a fish-and-chip shop well known outside the city. Mushy peas with haddock and chips (from £3.30 takeaway) tastes much better than it sounds. **Lemon Tree** *(☎ 621610; 5 West North St; mains £4.25-6.45; open noon-3pm Wed-Sun)*, an excellent café-bar attached to the theatre of the same name, does great coffee, meals and cakes.

There are daily buses to London with Scottish Citylink, but it's a tedious 12-hour trip. **Stagecoach Bluebird** *(☎ 212266)* is the major local bus operator. Trains from London's King's Cross station take an acceptable seven hours, but they're more expensive than buses.

The passenger-ferry terminal is a short walk east of the train and bus stations. **P&O** *(☎ 572615)* has daily evening departures Monday to Friday for Lerwick (Shetland); the trip takes 14 hours (20 hours via Orkney). A reclining seat costs £55.50/62 in the low/high season, one way. Mid-April to mid-December there are weekly Saturday (plus Tuesday from June to August) departures to Stromness (Orkney); £41.50/45, 10 hours.

WESTERN HIGHLANDS

This is the Highlands of the tour bus, but there are also some unspoilt peninsulas and mountains where you can feel very isolated. Ben Nevis (1343m) is Britain's highest mountain; brooding Glencoe still seems haunted by the massacre of the MacDonalds; the Cowal and Kintyre peninsulas have a magic of their own; and Loch Lomond may be a tourist cliche but is still beautiful.

Orientation & Information

Fort William, at the southern end of the Great Glen, is a major tourist centre, easily reached by bus and train and a good base for the mountains. Oban, on the west coast, is the most important ferry port for the Inner Hebrides (Mull, Coll, Tiree, Colonsay, Jura and Islay) and the Outer Hebridean islands of South Uist and Barra. There's a reasonable scattering of SYHA hostels, including those at Glencoe village, Oban, Tobermory and Crianlarich. There are also independent bunkhouses at Glencoe, Inchree and Corpach (the Fort William TIC has details).

Getting There & Around

Travelling around this region is difficult – many of the roads are single-track, steep and have hairpin bends. From Glasgow, Scottish Citylink provides daily connections to Oban (£11.20, three hours), Fort William (£11.80, three hours) and Inverness (£14, 3½ hours).

The spectacular West Highland rail line runs from Glasgow north to Fort William and Mallaig, with a spur to Oban from Crianlarich. There are up to three trains daily from Glasgow to Oban (£15.50, three hours), and the same number from Glasgow to Fort William (£18, 3¼ hours).

Fort William

☎ 01397 • pop 10,774

Fort William is an attractive little town and an excellent base for exploring the mountains. Its pedestrianised centre, with its small selection of shops, takeaways and pubs, is easy to get around. The **TIC** *(☎ 703781; Cameron Square)* can help with information.

Popular **Fort William Backpackers' Guest House** *(☎ 700711; e fortwilliam@scotlands-top-hostels.com; Alma Rd; dorm beds from £10)* is a short walk from the train station. Three miles from Fort William, up magical Glen Nevis, there's the **Glen Nevis Youth Hostel** *(☎ 702336; dorm beds from £9)* and, just over the river, **Ben Nevis Bunkhouse** *(☎ 702240; e achintee.accom@glennevis.com; Achintee Farm; dorm beds £9.50)*. There are several other independent hostels in the area; the TIC has details.

Scottish Citylink has four daily buses to Glasgow (£11.80, three hours) and two daily buses to Edinburgh (£16.50, 3¼ hours), both via Glencoe, with onward connections to London.

Oban

☎ 01631 • pop 8517

As the most important ferry port on the west coast, Oban gets inundated with visitors, but it's on a beautiful bay and the harbour is interesting. The bus, train and ferry terminals are together beside the harbour. The **TIC** *(☎ 563122; Argyll Square; open Mon-Sat, daily June-Sept)* is in an old church, one block behind the harbour.

Oban Backpackers Lodge *(☎ 562107; e oban@scotlands-top-hostels.com; Breadalbane St; dorm beds £9.50-11.50)* is popular. **Oban Youth Hostel** *(☎ 562025; Corran Esplanade; dorm beds adults/under-18s £12.25/ 10.75; open year-round)* is north of the train station. **Corran Hotel** *(☎ 566040; 1 Victoria Crescent; beds £13-20)* has wonderful views over the harbour.

CalMac *(☎ 566688)* boats link Oban with the Inner Hebridean islands and the Outer Hebridean isle of South Uist (Lochboisdale). Up to seven ferries sail daily to Craignure on Mull (£6.25 return, 45 minutes).

NORTHERN HIGHLANDS & ISLANDS

The Highlands and northern Islands are all about mountains, sea, moors, lochs and wide, empty, exhilarating space. This area is one of Europe's last great wildernesses, and it's mind-blowingly beautiful. It's the north and west, where the mountains and sea collide, that exhaust superlatives.

Information

The **Highlands of Scotland Tourist Board** *(☎ 01997-421160)* publishes free accommodation guides for the Highlands north of Glencoe (including Skye). The **Western Isles Tourist Board** *(☎ 01851-703088)* does the same for the Outer Hebrides (Western Isles). There are also separate tourist boards for **Orkney** *(☎ 01856-872856; w www.visitorkney.com)* and **Shetland** *(☎ 01595-693434; w www.visitshetland.com)*.

Getting There & Around

This is a remote, sparsely populated region, so you need to be well organised and/or have plenty of time if you're relying on public transport. Transport services are drastically reduced after September until late April or early May. Car rentals are available in Inverness, Oban and Stornoway; if you can get a group together, this can be a worthwhile option.

Bus Wick, Thurso, Ullapool and Kyle of Lochalsh can all be reached by regular buses from Inverness, or from Edinburgh and Glasgow via Inverness or Fort William; for advice contact **Scottish Citylink** *(☎ 0870 550 5050)* and **Highland Country** *(☎ 01847-893123)*. In the far northwest, however, there's no straightforward link around the coast between Thurso and Ullapool; Highland Country buses and Royal Mail postbuses are the main options.

Train The Highland lines are justly famous. There are two routes from Inverness: up the east coast to Thurso, and west to Kyle of Lochalsh (see Getting There & Away under Inverness later for details). There's also a regular train from Glasgow to Oban, Fort William and Mallaig (for Skye and the Inner Hebrides). Call ☎ 0845 748 4950 for more information.

Ferry Car and passenger ferries to all the major islands are available through **CalMac** *(☎ 0870 565 0000)*, but it can be expensive, especially if you're taking a vehicle. Consider its Island Rover ticket for unlimited travel between islands for eight or 15 days, or Island Hopscotch tickets that offer various route combinations at reduced rates. Inter-island ferry timetables depend on tides and weather, so check departures with the TIC offices.

Inverness

☎ 01463 • pop 41,800

Inverness, on the Moray Firth, is the capital of the Highlands and the hub for Highlands transport. It's a pleasant place to while away a few days, although it lacks major attractions. In summer it's packed with keen monster hunters on their way to Loch Ness, and visitors on their way to Fort William.

The bus and train stations, the TIC and the hostels are east of the River Ness, all within 10 minutes' walk of each other. The **TIC** *(☎ 234353; Castle Wynd)* is beside the museum, just off Bridge St.

Places to Stay & Eat In high season it's best to book a bed ahead. The Inverness TIC books accommodation.

Only 10 minutes' walk from the train station and just past the castle is the **Inverness Student Hostel** *(☎ 236556; 8 Culduthel Rd; dorm beds £10)*. It's a friendly, cosy place with a great view. **Ho Ho Hostel** *(☎ 221225; 23a High St; dorm beds £8.90-9.90, twins per person £12)* is conveniently positioned, just off the pedestrianised High St.

Along Old Edinburgh Rd and on Ardconnel St are lots of guesthouses and B&Bs, including **Ivybank Guest House** *(☎/fax 232796; ⓔ ivybank@talk21.com; 28 Old Edinburgh Rd; B&B per person from £20)*.

Located near the TIC, **Castle Restaurant** *(☎ 230925; 41 Castle St; mains £4-8)* is a traditional café with plentiful food at low prices. **The Phoenix** *(☎ 233685; 108 Academy St; bar meals from £4.95)* is a comfortable pub in the city centre.

Getting There & Away Many people take tours from Inverness to Loch Ness, and there's a wide variety costing from £7.50.

Bus From the **Inverness bus station** *(☎ 233371)*, Scottish Citylink has bus connections with major centres in England, including London (£28, 13 hours) via Perth and Glasgow. There are numerous daily buses to Glasgow (£14, 3½ hours) and Edinburgh (£14, four hours) via Perth. Buses to Aberdeen (£10, three hours) are run by Stagecoach Bluebird.

There are three or four daily Scottish Citylink services via Wick to Thurso and Scrabster (£10, three hours) for ferries to Orkney. The Citylink bus leaving Inverness at 1.30pm connects at Wick with a Highland Country service to John o'Groats. There are connecting ferries from John o'Groats to Burwick and Kirkwall (both in Orkney). It costs £16 to Burwick, the same price to Kirkwall.

Citylink/Skyeways *(☎ 01599-534328)* operates three buses a day (two on Sunday) from Inverness to Kyle of Lochalsh and Portree (£12.40, three hours), on Skye.

It's possible to head to the northwest through Lairg. **Stagecoach Inverness** *(☎ 239292)* has a Monday to Saturday service to Lairg (Sunday in summer). In summer, daily buses run through to Durness. There's also a Monday to Saturday **postbus service** *(☎ 01246-546329)*, travelling Lairg–Tongue–Durness.

Train The standard one-way fare to/from London costs £90.50 (eight hours). There are direct trains to Aberdeen (£17.80, 2¼ hours), Glasgow (£29.90, four hours) and Edinburgh

Whoa, Nessie!

Delving into the legend of the Loch Ness Monster ('Nessie' to her fans) would require an entire chapter. Fortunately, intrepid British researchers have already done the work for us. Check their list of sightings, catalogues of photographs, and research into the Nessie myths at W www.nessie.co.uk.

(£30.60, four hours). The onward line from Inverness to Kyle of Lochalsh (£14.70, 2½ hours) offers one of the greatest scenic journeys in Britain and leaves you within walking distance of the pier for buses across the Skye Bridge to Kyleakin. The line to Thurso (£12.50, 3½ hours) connects with the ferry to Orkney. There are three trains daily Monday to Saturday on both lines.

John o'Groats

The coast at the island's northeastern tip isn't particularly dramatic, and John o'Groats is little more than an upmarket car park, but there's something inviting about the view across the water to Orkney. **John o'Groats Youth Hostel** *(☎ 01955-611424; dorm beds £8.50/7.25; open Apr-Oct)* is in Canisbay, 3mi west of John o'Groats. There are up to seven buses daily Monday to Saturday from Wick (£2.50, one hour) via Canisbay, and Thurso (£2.50).

Orkney Islands

☎ 01856

Just 6mi off the north coast of Scotland, this magical group of islands is known for its dramatic coastal scenery (which ranges from 300m cliffs to white, sandy beaches) and abundant marine-bird life, and for a plethora of prehistoric sites, including an entire 4500-year-old village at **Skara Brae**. If you're in the area around mid-June, don't miss the St Magnus Arts Festival.

Sixteen of these 70 islands are inhabited. **Kirkwall** (population 6100) is the main town, and **Stromness** the major port; both are on the largest island, which is known as Mainland. Contact the **TIC** *(☎ 872856; 6 Broad St, Kirkwall)* for more information.

There's a good selection of cheap B&Bs and numerous hostels. In Stromness, **Brown's Hostel** *(☎ 850661; 45 Victoria St; dorm beds £9)* is very popular hostel and just five-minutes' walk from the ferry. **Kirkwall Youth Hostel** *(☎ 872243; Old Scapa Rd; dorm beds adults/under-18s £8.75/7.75)* is large and well equipped.

There's a car ferry from Scrabster, near Thurso, to Stromness operated by **P&O Scottish Ferries** *(☎ 01224-572615)*; one-way fares cost £16.50/51 per passenger/car. P&O also sails from Aberdeen to Stromness. **John o'Groats Ferries** *(☎ 01955-611353)* has a passenger ferry from John o'Groats to Burwick (£16 one way) on South Ronaldsay from May to September.

Shetland Islands

☎ 01595 • pop 23,000

Sixty miles north of Orkney, the Shetland Islands remained under Norse rule until 1469, when they were given to Scotland as part of a Danish princess' dowry. Even today, these remote, windswept, treeless islands are almost as much a part of Scandinavia as of Britain. Lerwick, the capital, is less than 230mi from Bergen in Norway.

Much bleaker than Orkney, Shetland is famous for its varied bird life, its rugged coastline and 4000-year-old archaeological heritage. There are 15 inhabited islands. **Lerwick** is the largest town on Mainland Shetland, which is used as a base for the North Sea oilfields. Oil has brought a certain amount of prosperity to the islands – there are well-equipped leisure centres in many villages.

Small ferries connect a handful of the smaller islands. Contact the **TIC** *(☎ 693434)* for information on B&Bs and camping *böds* (barns), or you can stay at **Lerwick Youth Hostel** *(☎ 692114; King Harald St; dorm beds from £9.25; open mid-Apr–Sept)*.

Newly established **NorthLink Ferries** *(☎ 01856 851144; e info@northlinkferries.co.uk)* runs a service from Aberdeen to Lerwick (£63, 14 hours) and Scrabster to Stromness (£30, 1½ hours).

North Coast

The coast from Dounreay, with its nuclear power station, west around to Ullapool is nothing short of spectacular. Everything is on a massive scale: vast emptiness, enormous lochs and snow-capped mountains. Unreliable weather and limited public transport are the only drawbacks.

Getting to Thurso by bus or train is no problem, but from there your troubles start. From June to September, **Highland Country**

BRITAIN

Buses *(☎ 01847-893123)* runs the Northern Explorer bus once daily (except Sunday) from Thurso to Durness, leaving Thurso at 11.30am (£7.25, 2½ hours). The rest of the year, there are Monday to Saturday services from Thurso to Bettyhill.

West Coast

Ullapool is the jumping-off point for the Isle of Lewis; contact its **TIC** *(☎ 01854-612135; 6 Argyle St)*. There is even more brilliant coastline round to Gairloch, along the incomparable Loch Maree and down to the Kyle of Lochalsh and Skye. From there you're back in the land of the tour bus; civilisation (and main roads) can be a shock after all the empty space.

Kyle of Lochalsh ('Kyle') is a small village that overlooks the lovely island of Skye across narrow Loch Alsh. There's a **TIC** *(☎ 01599-534276)* beside the seafront car park; the nearest hostels are on Skye. Kyle can be reached by bus and train from Inverness and also by direct Scottish Citylink buses from Glasgow (£17.50, 5½ hours).

Isle of Skye

pop 8847

Skye is a large, rugged island, 50mi north to south and 25mi east to west. It's ringed by stunning coastline and dominated by the magnificent Cuillin Hills, popular for the sport of 'Munro bagging' – climbing Scottish mountains of 3000ft (914m) or higher. You can contact the **Portree TIC** *(☎ 01478-612137; Bayfielf Rd)* for more information.

Places to Stay & Eat There are more than a dozen SYHA and independent hostels on the island and numerous B&Bs. The SYHA hostels most relevant to ferry users are at **Uig** *(☎ 01470-542211; dorm beds adults/under-18s from £8.25/7; open Apr-Sept)* for the Outer Hebrides (Western Isles); and **Armadale** *(☎ 01471-844260; dorm beds adults/under-18s from £8.25/7; open Apr-Sept)*, for Mallaig. There's also an SYHA hostel at **Kyleakin** *(☎ 01599-534585; dorm beds adults/under-18s from £9/6; open year-round)*.

The pick of the independent hostels is the friendly **Skye Backpackers** *(☎/fax 01599-534510; ⓔ skye@scotlands-top-hostels.com; Kyleakin; dorm beds £10-12)*, a short walk from the Skye Bridge.

In the main centre, Portree, **Bosville Hotel** *(☎ 01478-612846; Bosville Terrace; bar meals £7-12)* and **Portree House** *(☎ 01478-613713; Home Farm Rd; bar meals £7-12)* are two of the best places for a hearty meal.

Getting There & Away The bridge toll on the Skye Bridge is an exorbitant £4.70 one way per car. There are two ferries from the mainland to Skye. Mid-July to August, **CalMac** *(☎ 0147-844248)* operates between Mallaig and Armadale (£2.80 passengers, £15.65 cars, 30 minutes); it's wise to book. There's also a private **Glenelg to Kylerhea service** *(☎ 01599-511302)* from mid-April to late October (not always on Sunday), taking 10 minutes (70p).

From Uig on Skye, CalMac has daily services to Lochmaddy on North Uist and (except Sunday) to Tarbert on Harris; both journeys take 1¾ hours.

Outer Hebrides

The Outer Hebrides (Western Isles) are bleak, remote and treeless. The climate is fierce – the islands are completely exposed to the gales that sweep in from the Atlantic, and it rains more than 250 days of the year. Some people find the landscape mournful, but others find the stark beauty and isolated world of the crofters strangely unique and captivating.

See the preceding Isle of Skye section for details of CalMac ferries to Tarbert and Lochmaddy, and the Oban section for ferries to Lochboisdale. All the TICs open for late ferry arrivals in summer but close between mid-October and early April.

Lewis is reached by ferry from Ullapool; its largest town, Stornoway, has a **TIC** *(☎ 01851-703088)* and several banks. On **Harris** (which can be reached from Uig on Skye), the **TIC** *(☎ 01859-502011)* is in Tarbert. **North Uist** sports a **TIC** *(☎ 01876-500321; open Apr–mid-Oct)* in Lochmaddy, while **South Uist** has one *(☎ 01878-700286)* in Barra.

Wales (Cymru)

There's a remarkably upbeat feeling in Wales today. In 1979 the majority of the people voted against home rule; yet in the 1997 referendum they said yes to a Welsh Assembly, and two years later its first members were elected.

Wales has had the misfortune to be so close to England that it could not be allowed its independence, and yet to be far enough away to be conveniently forgotten. It sometimes feels rather like England's unloved backyard – a suitable place for mines, pine plantations and nuclear power stations. It is almost miraculous that anything Welsh should have survived the onslaught of its dominating neighbour, but Welsh culture and language has proved enduring.

Wales' appeal lies in its countryside – the towns and cities are not particularly inspiring. The best way to appreciate the Great Welsh Outdoors is by walking, cycling, canal boating or hitching, or by some other form of private transport.

FACTS ABOUT WALES

History

The Celts arrived from their European homeland sometime after 500 BC. The Romans invaded in AD 43, and from the 5th century to the 11th, the Welsh were under almost constant pressure from the Anglo-Saxon invaders of England. In 927, faced with the destructive onslaught of the Vikings, the Welsh kings recognised Athelstan, the Anglo-Saxon king of England, as their overlord.

The last doomed Welsh revolt began in 1400 under Owain Glyndwr and was crushed by Henry IV. In 1536 and 1543, the Acts of Union made Wales, for all intents and purposes, another region of England.

From the turn of the 18th century, Wales, with its plentiful coal and iron, became the most important source of Britain's pig iron. By the end of the 19th century, almost a third of the world's coal exports came from Wales.

The 20th century, especially the 1960s, '70s and '80s, saw the coal industry and associated steel industry collapse. Large-scale unemployment persists as Wales attempts to move to more high-tech and service industries. After agriculture, tourism is now the second most important industry. Since 1999, the people of Wales have elected their own Assembly.

Geography

Wales has two major mountain systems: the Black Mountains and Brecon Beacons in the south, and the more dramatic mountains of Snowdonia in the northwest. The population is concentrated in the southeast along the coast between Cardiff (the capital) and Swansea and the old mining valleys that run north into the Brecon Beacons.

Population

Wales has a population of 2.9 million, around 5% of the total population of Britain.

Language

Welsh is spoken by 20% of the population, mainly in the north. At first sight, Welsh looks impossibly difficult to get your tongue around – just try pronouncing Llanfairpwllgwyngyllgogerychwyrndrobwllllantysiliogogogoch (a village in Anglesey reputed to have Britain's longest place name). Alternatively, have a go at the following (pronunciation in brackets):

Bore da (bora-da)	good morning
Shw'mae (shoo-my)	hello
Peint o gwrw (paint-o-guru)	pint of beer
Diolch (diolkh)	thank you
Da boch (da bokh)	goodbye

FACTS FOR THE VISITOR

Activities

Walking Wales has many popular walks; the most challenging are in the rocky Snowdonia National Park (around Llanberis and Betws-y-Coed) and the grassy Brecon Beacons National Park (around Brecon). There are three official National Trails – long-distance paths open to walkers, cyclists and horse riders. These are the Pembrokeshire Coast Path, Offa's Dyke Path (in the east) and Glyndwr's Way. The National Park people publish an accommodation guide (£2.50); phone ☎ 01437-764636 for further details. See Lonely Planet's *Walking in Britain* for more information.

Cycling Much of Wales is excellent for cycling. Two of the best-known routes are Lôn Las Cymru ('the Welsh National Route'), which takes in 260mi from Holyhead to Cardiff; and the 227mi Lôn Getaidd ('the Celtic Trail') from near Chepstow to Fishguard. Pick up the Wales Tourist Board's free *Cycling Wales* publication for an introduction to these and other routes.

GETTING AROUND

With the exception of links around the coast, public transport users have to fall back on infrequent and complicated bus timetables. Sniff out a copy of *Wales Bus, Rail and Tourist Map & Guide*, sometimes available from TICs.

Bus

Some 70 private bus companies operate in Wales. The biggest intercity operators are

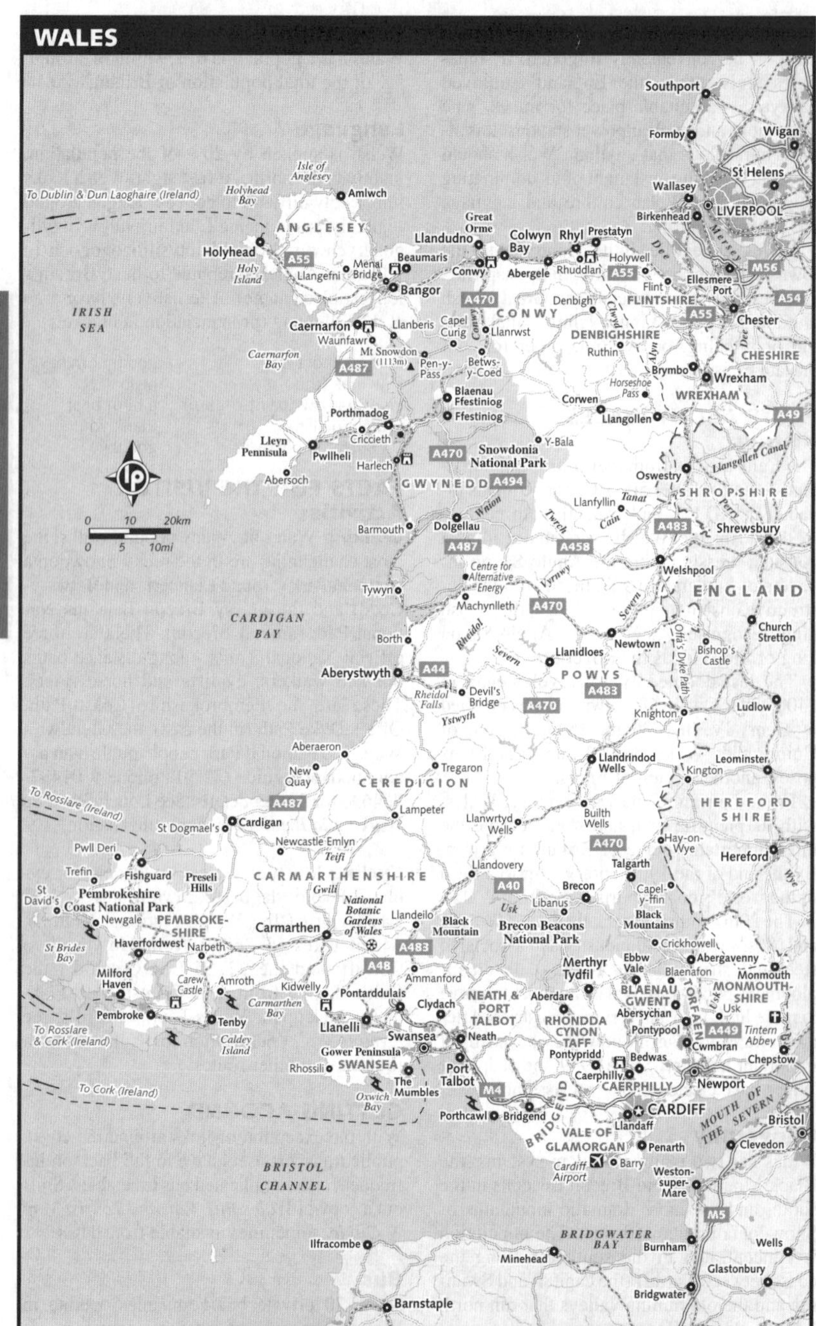
WALES
Southport
Formby
Wigan
St Helens
Wallasey
Birkenhead
LIVERPOOL
Mersey
Dee
Isle of Anglesey
To Dublin & Dun Laoghaire (Ireland)
Holyhead Bay
Amlwch
ANGLESEY
Holyhead
A55
Holy Island
Llangefni
Menai Bridge
Beaumaris
Bangor
Great Orme
Llandudno
Conwy
Colwyn Bay
Abergele
Rhyl
Prestatyn
Rhuddlan
Holywell
A55
Flint
Ellesmere Port
M56
A54
FLINTSHIRE
A55
Chester
IRISH SEA
A470
CONWY
Denbigh
Clwyd
DENBIGHSHIRE
Ruthin
Alyn
Caernarfon
Waunfawr
Llanberis
Capel Curig
Conwy
Llanrwst
Caernarfon Bay
Mt Snowdon (1113m)
Pen-y-Pass
Betws-y-Coed
A487
Brymbo
Wrexham
CHESHIRE
WREXHAM
Horseshoe Pass
Blaenau Ffestiniog
Ffestiniog
Corwen
Llangollen
A49
Porthmadog
Criccieth
Lleyn Pennisula
Pwllheli
Abersoch
Harlech
A470
Snowdonia National Park
Y-Bala
Oswestry
Llangollen Canal
GWYNEDD
A494
SHROPSHIRE
0 10 20km
0 5 10mi
Llanfyllin
Tanat
Wnion
Twrch
Cain
Perry
Barmouth
Dolgellau
A487
A458
A483
Shrewsbury
Centre for Alternative Energy
Vyrnwy
Welshpool
Tywyn
Machynlleth
A470
ENGLAND
CARDIGAN BAY
Severn
Church Stretton
Borth
Rheidol
Severn
Newtown
Offa's Dyke Path
Bishop's Castle
Llanidloes
Aberystwyth
A44
POWYS
A483
Rheidol Falls
Devil's Bridge
A470
Ystwyth
Knighton
Ludlow
Aberaeron
Llandrindod Wells
Leominster
New Quay
Tregaron
Kington
CEREDIGION
To Rosslare (Ireland)
A487
Lampeter
HEREFORDSHIRE
Cardigan
St Dogmael's
Llanwrtyd Wells
Builth Wells
Newcastle Emlyn
Teifi
A470
Hay-on-Wye
Pwll Deri
Hereford
Trefin
Fishguard
Preseli Hills
CARMARTHENSHIRE
Llandovery
Talgarth
Wye
St David's
Pembrokeshire Coast National Park
Gwili
A40
Brecon
Capel-y-ffin
National Botanic Gardens of Wales
Usk
Libanus
Newgale
PEMBROKESHIRE
Carmarthen
Llandeilo
Black Mountain
Brecon Beacons National Park
Black Mountains
St Brides Bay
Haverfordwest
Narbeth
A483
Crickhowell
A48
Merthyr Tydfil
Ebbw Vale
Abergavenny
Milford Haven
Carew Castle
Amroth
Ammanford
Blaenafon
Monmouth
Kidwelly
Pontarddulais
Clydach
NEATH & PORT TALBOT
Aberdare
BLAENAU GWENT
TORFAEN
MONMOUTHSHIRE
Carmarthen Bay
Usk
Pembroke
Tenby
Llanelli
RHONDDA CYNON TAFF
Abersychan
Usk
To Rosslare & Cork (Ireland)
Caldey Island
Swansea
Neath
Pontypool
A449
Tintern Abbey
Gower Peninsula
Cwmbran
Rhossili
SWANSEA
Port Talbot
Pontypridd
Bedwas
Chepstow
The Mumbles
Caerphilly
CAERPHILLY
Newport
To Cork (Ireland)
Oxwich Bay
M4
BRIDGEND
CARDIFF
MOUTH OF THE SEVERN
Porthcawl
Bridgend
Llandaff
Bristol
VALE OF GLAMORGAN
Penarth
Clevedon
Cardiff Airport
Barry
BRISTOL CHANNEL
Weston-super-Mare
M5
BRIDGWATER BAY
Ilfracombe
Burnham
Wells
Minehead
Glastonbury
Bridgwater
Barnstaple

Arriva Cymru *(☎ 0870 608 2608)* for the north and west, **First Cymru** *(☎ 01656-728393)* in the southwest and **Stagecoach** in the southeast.

Arriva has a useful daily TrawsCambria service, known as the 701 (west coast), but there's only one bus a day each way. It runs between Cardiff, Swansea, Carmarthen, Aberystwyth, Porthmadog, Caernarfon, Bangor, Conwy and Llandudno. From Cardiff to Aberystwyth (four hours) costs £10.90; Aberystwyth to Porthmadog (two hours) is £8.

For all bus information call the UK-wide public transport information line, **Traveline** *(☎ 0870 608 2608; open 8am-8pm)*.

Train

Wales has some fantastic rail lines, both main-line services (☎ 0845 748 4950) and narrow-gauge survivors. Apart from the main lines along the north and south coasts to the Irish ferry ports, there are some interesting lines that converge on Shrewsbury. The lines along the west coast and down the Conwy valley are exceptional.

SOUTH WALES

The valleys of the Usk and Wye, with their castles and **Tintern Abbey**, are beautiful, but can be packed with day-trippers. The south coast from Newport to Swansea is heavily industrialised, and the valleys running north into the Brecon Beacons National Park are still struggling to come to grips with the loss of the coal-mining industry.

Even so, the little villages that form a continuous chain along the valleys have their own stark beauty and the people are very friendly. The traditional market town of Abergavenny is also worth a look. The **Big Pit** *(☎ 01495-790311; admission free)*, near Blaenafon, closed as a coal mine in 1980. These days it gives you a chance to experience life underground, and the guided tours by former miners are highly recommended.

The Black Mountains and Brecon Beacons have very majestic, open scenery and their northern flanks overlook some of the most beautiful country in Wales.

Cardiff (Caerdydd)

☎ 029 • pop 285,000

The Welsh are proudly defensive of their capital, which has rapidly been transformed from a dull provincial backwater into a prosperous university city with an increasingly lively arts scene. Stock up on maps and information from the **TIC** *(☎ 2022 7281; ⓔ enquiries@cardifftic.co.uk; open daily)* in the central train station. Free Internet access is available at **Cardiff Central Library** *(☎ 2038 2116; Frederick St)*.

Cardiff Castle *(☎ 2087 8100; Castle St)* is worth seeing for its outrageous Hollywood-esque interior refurbishment. Nearby, the **National Museum & Gallery of Wales** *(☎ 2039 7951; Cathays Park)* packs in everything Welsh but also includes one of the finest collections of impressionist art in Britain. The **Museum of Welsh Life** *(☎ 2057 3500; St Fagan's)*, 5mi from the city centre, is a popular open-air attraction, with reconstructed buildings and craft demonstrations.

The **Youth Hostel** *(☎ 0870 770 5750, fax 770 5751; ⓔ cardiff@yha.org.uk; 2 Wedal Rd, Roath Park; dorm beds £14)* is 2mi from the city centre; take bus No 80B. The lively **Cardiff Backpacker** *(☎ 2034 5577, fax 2023 0404; ⓔ cardiffbackpacker@hotmail.com; 98 Neville St, Riverside; dorm beds from £14)* is less than a mile from the train and bus stations. **Austin's Guest House** *(☎ 2037 7148; ⓔ austins@hotelcardiff.com; 11 Coldstream Terrace; singles/doubles £20/39)* is a cheap, central B&B.

National Express has buses to/from London (£15.50, 3¼ hours) or you can do the trip in two hours by train from London's Paddington station (£36/97 SuperSaver/standard single, hourly).

Swansea (Abertawe)

☎ 01792 • pop 190,000

Swansea is the second-largest town (it would be stretching the definition to call it a city), and the gateway to the **Gower Peninsula** and its superb coastal scenery (crowded in summer). Dylan Thomas grew up in Swansea and later called it an 'ugly, lovely town'. For more information, contact its **TIC** *(☎ 468321; ⓔ tourism@swansea.gov.uk; Plymouth St)*.

Brecon Beacons National Park

The Brecon Beacons National Park covers 519 sq mi of high bare hills, surrounded on the northern flanks by a number of attractive market towns; Llandovery, Brecon, Crickhowell, Talgarth and Hay-on-Wye make good bases. The **National Park Visitor Centre** *(☎ 01874-623366)* is in open countryside near Libanus, 5mi southwest of Brecon.

SOUTHWEST WALES

The coastline northeast of St David's to Cardigan is particularly beautiful and unspoilt, owing to its national park status. The Pembrokeshire Coast Path begins at Amroth, north of Tenby, on the western side of Carmarthen Bay and continues to St Dogmaels to the west of Cardigan.

Carmarthen Bay is often referred to as Dylan Thomas Country; **Dylan's boathouse** (*☎ 01994-427420; adult/concession £3/2*) at Laugharne, where he wrote *Under Milk Wood*, has been preserved exactly as he left it, and it is a moving memorial.

Irish Ferries (*☎ 0990-329129*) leave Pembroke Dock for Rosslare in Ireland; ferries connect with buses from Cardiff and destinations east. **Stena Line** (*☎ 0990-707070*) has ferries to Rosslare from Fishguard; these connect with buses and trains.

Pembroke Dock is an unpleasant ferry port, although nearby **Pembroke Castle** (*☎ 01646-684585*), the home of the Tudors and birthplace of Henry VII, is magnificent.

For **Pembrokeshire Coast National Park**, visit a National Park Information Centre or the TICs at **Tenby** (*☎ 01834-842402*), **St David's** (*☎ 01437-720392*) or **Fishguard** (*☎ 01348-873484*), among others. Get a copy of their free paper, *Coast to Coast*, which has detailed local information.

BRITAIN

NORTH WALES

North Wales is dominated by the Snowdonia Mountains, which loom over the beautiful coastline. This is the holiday playground for much of the Midlands, so the coast is marred by tacky holiday villages and the serried ranks of caravan parks.

From Llandudno and Conwy you can catch buses or trains to Betws-y-Coed or Llanberis, the main centres for exploring Snowdonia National Park. From Betws-y-Coed there's a train to the bleak but strangely beautiful mining town of Blaenau Ffestiniog. One of Wales' most spectacular steam railways runs from Blaenau to the coastal market town of Porthmadog. From Porthmadog you can loop back to Shrewsbury, via Harlech and its castle.

The remote **Lleyn Peninsula** in the west escapes the crowds to a large extent; start from **Caernarfon**, with its magnificent castle, or Pwllheli. Near Porthmadog is whimsical **Portmeirion**, a holiday village built in the Italianate style – it's bizarrely attractive, but crowded in summer. **Holyhead (Caergybi)** is one of the main Irish ferry ports. Both **Irish Ferries** (*☎ 0870 517 1717*) and **Stena Line** (*☎ 0870 570 7070*) run ferries to Dublin.

In the northeast, **Llangollen** is famous for its **International Musical Eisteddfod** (*☎ 01978-862001; w www.international-eisteddfod.co.uk*), a six-day music, song and dance festival held in July which attracts folk groups from around the world.

For transport information call **Traveline** (*☎ 0870 608 2608*).

Llandudno

☎ 01492 • pop 22,000

Llandudno seethes with tourists in summer. It was developed as a Victorian holiday town and has retained much of its 19th-century architecture and antiquated atmosphere. You can enjoy the wonderful **pier** and **promenade**, as well as donkeys on the beach.

Llandudno is dominated by a spectacular limestone headland, the **Great Orme**, with the mountains of Snowdonia as a backdrop. There are hundreds of guesthouses, but it can be hard to find somewhere in the peak July/August season. Contact the town's **TIC** (*☎ 876413; e www.llandudno.tic@virgin.net*).

Snowdonia National Park

Although the Snowdonia Mountains are fairly compact, they loom spectacularly over the coast. The most popular region is in the north around Mt Snowdon, at 1085m the highest peak in Britain south of the Scottish Highlands. Walkers must be prepared to deal with hostile conditions at any time of year.

There are several **National Park Information Centres**, including in **Betws-y-Coed** (*☎ 01690-710426*), **Blaenau Ffestiniog** (*☎ 01766-830360*) and **Harlech** (*☎ 01766-780658*). They all have a wealth of information, and all make B&B bookings.

Bulgaria

What is it about Bulgaria? Odds are that you've underestimated it drastically. This little stick of dynamite often gets short shrift from travellers, but that's to your advantage. Bulgaria boasts long, sandy beaches, plenty of good accommodation, and four major ski resorts with heaps of snow. Sofia is a cosmopolitan and eminently explorable city, while the charming old towns of Plovdiv and Veliko Târnovo, and traditional villages like Koprivshtitsa, exude an infectious historical ambience.

While some hotels, roads and buses may not be up to the standards expected in Western and northern Europe, Bulgaria is excellent value. And because you'll be one of the few foreigners traipsing about, you'll be assured of a cordial welcome.

Bulgaria: the Basics

Local name България

Capital Sofia

Population 7.97 million

Official language Bulgarian

Currency leva (lv) = 100 stotinki

Avoid at all costs Drinking and driving

Make friends on the coast by suggesting *Ha'ide da se syblechem' i da se izky'pem!* (Let's go skinny-dipping!)

Facts about Bulgaria

HISTORY

From about 72 BC, the Romans invaded Greek ports in Bulgaria, but took over 100 years to control the indigenous Thracians. Slavic tribes arrived during the late 5th century. About 200 years later, the fierce Bulgars migrated from Central Asia and integrated with the Slavs and remaining Thracians. The Bulgar leader, Khan (Tsar) Asparukh, was responsible for establishing what became known as the First Bulgarian Empire (681–1018).

The Ottomans started to invade the northern Balkan peninsula in 1362, and within 30 years had conquered all of Bulgaria. Russia's defeat of Turkey during the Russian-Turkish War (1877–78) led the Ottomans to cede 60% of the Balkan peninsula to Bulgaria, but the powers of western Europe later reversed these gains. Between 1878 and WWII each country in the Balkans, including Bulgaria, fought up to six wars over border issues.

Bulgaria's independence was declared on 22 September 1908, but only four years later the First Balkan War (1912) broke out as Bulgaria, Greece and Serbia declared war on Turkey. Squabbling among the victors led to the Second Balkan War (1913), from which Bulgaria emerged a loser.

To avoid a war it could not win, the Bulgarian government joined the Axis side during WWII. A hastily formed coalition government sought peace with the Allies after the war, but to no avail. Russia then invaded Bulgaria, and the People's Republic of Bulgaria was proclaimed on 15 September 1946. Bulgaria became one of the most prosperous countries in the Soviet bloc.

In 1989 an internal Communist Party coup led to the resignation of the ageing president, Todor Zhivkov. The Communist Party subsequently agreed to relinquish its monopoly on power and changed its name to the Bulgarian Socialist Party (BSP). The BSP won the first parliamentary elections in 1990 – so Bulgaria had the dubious honour of being the first country from the former Soviet bloc to elect the communists back into power. They've stuck around ever since.

GEOGRAPHY

Bulgaria (110,912 sq km) lies at the crossroads of Europe and Asia in the heart of the Balkan peninsula. Bulgaria stretches 520km from the Yugoslav border to the Black Sea and 330km from Romania to Greece. About one-third of Bulgaria is mountainous – 5% of the terrain is over 1600m high.

The 378km-long coast of the Black Sea is lined with some of Europe's finest beaches. The mighty Danube River mostly acts as a border with Romania.

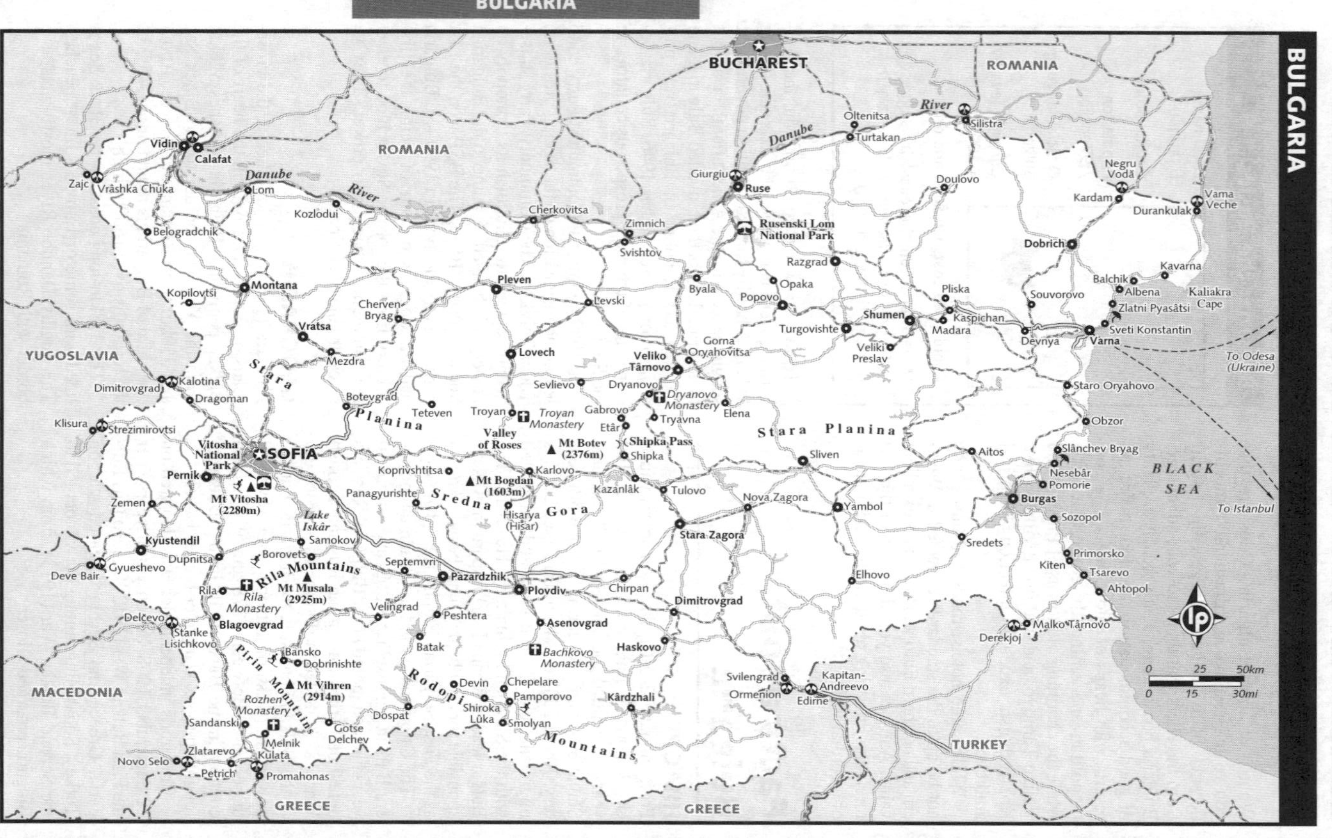
BULGARIA
BUCHAREST
ROMANIA
ROMANIA
Danube
River
Danube
River
YUGOSLAVIA
MACEDONIA
GREECE
GREECE
TURKEY
BLACK SEA
To Odesa (Ukraine)
To Istanbul
0 25 50km
0 15 30mi
Vidin
Calafat
Zajc
Vrâshka Chuka
Lom
Kozlodui
Belogradchik
Montana
Kopilovtsi
Vratsa
Mezdra
Cherven Bryag
Pleven
Levski
Lovech
Cherkovitsa
Zimnich
Svishtov
Giurgiu
Ruse
Rusenski Lom National Park
Oltenitsa
Turtakan
Silistra
Doulovo
Negru Vodă
Kardam
Vama Veche
Durankulak
Dobrich
Kavarna
Balchik
Albena
Kaliakra Cape
Zlatni Pyasâtsi
Sveti Konstantin
Varna
Devnya
Souvorovo
Pliska
Kaspichan
Madara
Shumen
Veliki Preslav
Razgrad
Opaka
Popovo
Byala
Turgovishte
Gorna Oryahovitsa
Veliko Târnovo
Dryanovo
Dryanovo Monastery
Elena
Sevlievo
Gabrovo
Tryavna
Etâr
Shipka Pass
Shipka
Troyan
Troyan Monastery
Teteven
Botevgrad
Stara Planina
Stara Planina
Valley of Roses
Mt Botev (2376m)
Kalotina
Dimitrovgrad
Dragoman
Klisura
Strezimirovtsi
Vitosha National Park
SOFIA
Pernik
Mt Vitosha (2280m)
Koprivshtitsa
Karlovo
Mt Bogdan (1603m)
Panagyurishte
Sredna Gora
Hisarya (Hisar)
Kazanlâk
Tulovo
Stara Zagora
Nova Zagora
Sliven
Yambol
Aitos
Staro Oryahovo
Obzor
Slânchev Bryag
Nesebâr
Pomorie
Burgas
Sozopol
Sredets
Primorsko
Kiten
Tsarevo
Ahtopol
Malko Târnovo
Derekjoj
Elhovo
Zemen
Kyustendil
Dupnitsa
Gyueshevo
Deve Bair
Lake Iskâr
Samokov
Borovets
Rila Mountains
Mt Musala (2925m)
Rila
Rila Monastery
Septemvri
Pazardzhik
Plovdiv
Chirpan
Dimitrovgrad
Velingrad
Peshtera
Asenovgrad
Haskovo
Batak
Bachkovo Monastery
Delčevo
Stanke Lisichkovo
Blagoevgrad
Bansko
Dobrinishte
Pirin Mountains
Mt Vihren (2914m)
Rozhen Monastery
Sandanski
Melnik
Gotse Delchev
Dospat
Rodopi Mountains
Devin
Chepelare
Pamporovo
Shiroka Lûka
Smolyan
Kârdzhali
Svilengrad
Ormenion
Kapitan-Andreevo
Edirne
Zlatarevo
Novo Selo
Petrich
Kulata
Promahonas

BULGARIA

CLIMATE

Generally, Bulgaria has a temperate climate with cold, damp winters and hot, dry summers. The Rodopi Mountains form a barrier to the moderating Mediterranean influence of the Aegean. Northern Bulgaria is open to the extremes of central Europe, while the Black Sea moderates temperatures in the east. Sofia's generally favourable climate is one of its main attributes.

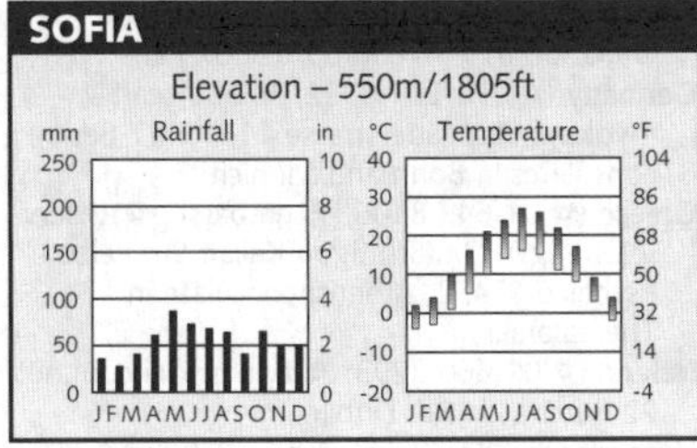

GOVERNMENT & POLITICS

Since 1990, Bulgaria has been a multiparty, democratic republic. The prime minister leads the unicameral National Assembly; the president is head of state.

POPULATION & PEOPLE

Fertility rates are alarmingly low, which is one reason why the population has actually *fallen* by about 503,000 since 1992.

Bulgarians are Slavs and officially constitute 88.3% of the population. The largest minorities are the Turks (8%); Roma (2.6%), commonly known as Gypsies; Macedonians (2.5%); Armenians (0.3%); and Russians (0.2%).

SOCIETY & CONDUCT

Bulgarians shake their head in a curved, almost bouncy, motion to indicate 'yes', and, less often, nod their head to mean 'no'. To add to the confusion, some well-travelled Bulgarians may do the opposite to 'help' confused foreigners. If in doubt, ask *da ili ne* (yes or no)?

When visiting mosques, churches and monasteries, dress conservatively and also act appropriately.

LANGUAGE

Older Bulgarians may speak Russian and a few others may get by speaking French or German, while others, especially those working in tourism and business, are more likely to speak English. Almost everything is written in Cyrillic, so it's essential to learn this alphabet. See the Language chapter of this book for a list of useful Bulgarian words and phrases.

Facts for the Visitor

HIGHLIGHTS

The best museums are the Archaeological Museum in Varna and Sofia's Ethnographical Museum. Of the 160 monasteries throughout the country, the big draw is the Rila Monastery. There are also numerous mosques and churches – none more spectacular than the Alexander Nevski Church in Sofia. The Romans left impressive reminders, such as the Roman Thermae in Varna and the Roman Amphitheatre in Plovdiv. Other must-sees are the traditional village of Koprivshtitsa; Nesebâr, along the Black Sea coast; and the fascinating Old Towns in Veliko Târnovo and Plovdiv.

PLANNING

Spring (particularly April to mid-June) is an excellent time to visit Bulgaria. Summer (mid-June to early September) is ideal for walking and festivals, but is also the peak season for travellers. September can often be perfect: the autumn trees are glorious, fruit and vegetables are plentiful, shoulder-season tariffs are in effect, the tourist hordes have returned home, and you can still swim in the Black Sea and sunbathe on its shores.

The peak season along the Black Sea coast is mid-July to late August; at the ski resorts, it's Christmas/New Year and February to mid-March. If you avoid these times, you may be astounded by how few tourists there are in Bulgaria.

TOURIST OFFICES

The **National Information & Advertising Center** *(☎ 987 9778; Ⓦ www.bulgariatravel.org; ul Sveta Sofia; open Mon-Fri)* is the closest thing to a tourist office in the capital. A number of autonomous, regional tourist information centres (TICs) have also been established throughout Bulgaria, but most are associations of travel agencies. Some offices worth contacting abroad include:

Australia *Consulate-General:* (☎/fax 02-9327 7581; Ⓦ www.users.bigpond.com/bulcgsyd) 4 Carlotta Rd, Double Bay, NSW 2028
Canada (☎ 0613-789 5341, fax 789 3524) 325 Stewart St, Ottawa, Ontario K1N 6K5

BULGARIA

France (☎ 01 45 51 05 32, fax 45 51 78 97) 1 Ave Rapp, 75007 Paris
Germany (☎ 069-295 284, fax 295 286) Eckenhemier Landstrasse 101, 60318 Frankfurt am Main
Netherlands (☎ 070-346 8872, fax 363 6704) Alexander Godelweg 22, 2517 JJ, The Hague
UK (☎ 020-7589 8402, fax 7589 4875) 186 Queen's Gate, London, SW7 5HL
US (☎/fax 0202-332 6609) 1621 22nd St NW, Washington, DC 20008

VISAS & DOCUMENTS

Visas

Currently, citizens of the following countries can obtain a free, 30-day tourist visa at any Bulgarian border, international airport or sea port: all member countries of the EU, Australia, Canada, the Czech Republic, Hungary, Israel, Japan, New Zealand, Poland, Slovakia, Switzerland, the USA and Yugoslavia.

The 30-day tourist visa *cannot* currently be extended within Bulgaria. If you want to stay longer, apply for a 90-day tourist visa, or simply leave Bulgaria for Greece, Turkey or Romania and obtain another 30-day tourist visa on arrival.

At all hotels, hostels, camping grounds and, often, private homes, staff normally take details from your passport, fill out the registration form (in Cyrillic) and give you a copy. In theory, you must then show *all* of these forms to Immigration officials when you leave. However, this requirement is almost never enforced these days.

If you're staying with friends and relatives, or, sometimes, in a private home, you're supposed to personally register with the police within 48 hours.

BULGARIA

Student, Youth & Teacher Cards

Holders of the International Student Identity Card (ISIC), International Youth Travel Card (IYTC) and International Teacher Identity Card (ITIC) can obtain discounts of 10% to 20% at some museums, hotels, hostels, medical and dental clinics, and restaurants. Selective travel agencies also offer card-holders up to 50% off domestic flights and 10% off train and bus tickets.

A brochure (in Cyrillic) listing places that offer these discounts is available from **Orbita** *(☎ 02-987 9128; e orbita@ttm.bg; bul Hristo Botev 48, Sofia)*. Orbita will also issue these cards to anyone with the correct documentation.

EMBASSIES & CONSULATES

Bulgarian Embassies & Consulates

Major Bulgarian diplomatic missions include:

Australia (☎/fax 02-9327 7581; w www.users.bigpond.com/bulcgsyd) 4 Carlotta Rd, Double Bay, NSW 2028
Canada (☎ 0613-789 3215; e mailmn@storm.ca) 325 Stewart St, Ottawa, K1N 6K5; consulate in Toronto
France (☎ 01 45 51 85 90; e bulgamb@wanadoo.fr) 1 Ave Rapp, 75007 Paris
Germany (☎ 030-201 0922; e bbotscaft@myokay.net) Mauerstrasse 11, 10117 Berlin; consulates in Bonn and Munich
Greece (☎ 01-647 8106; e embassbg@athserv.otenet.gr) 33a, Stratigou Kallari Str, Paleo Psychico 15452, Athens; consulate in Thessaloniki
Ireland (☎ 01-660 3293; e bgemb@eircom.net) 22 Burlington Rd, Dublin
Netherlands (☎ 070-350 3051; e bulnedem@xs4all.nl) Duinroosweg 9, 2597 KJ The Hague
Turkey (☎ 0312-426 7455, fax 427 3178) Atatürk Bulvari 124, Kavaklidere, Ankara; consulates in İstanbul and Edirne
UK (☎ 020-7584 9400; e bgembassy@globalnet.co.uk) 186 Queen's Gate, London SW7 5HL
USA (☎ 0202-387 0174; w www.bulgaria-embassy.org) 1621 22nd St NW, Washington, DC 20008; consulate in New York

Embassies & Consulates in Bulgaria

All diplomatic missions detailed here are in Sofia (area code ☎ 02).

France *Embassy:* (☎ 965 1100; w www.ambafrance-bg.org) ul Oborishte 27–29
Germany *Embassy:* (☎ 918 380) ul Frederic Joliot-Curie 25
Greece *Consulate:* (☎ 946 1562) ul Oborishte 19; consulate in Plovdiv
Macedonia *Consulate:* (☎ 705 098) ul Frederic Joliot-Curie 17
Netherlands *Embassy:* (☎ 962 5785) ul Galichitsa 38
Romania *Consulate:* (☎ 973 3510) bul Sitnyakovo 4
Turkey *Embassy:* (☎ 980 2270) bul Vasil Levski 80; Consulates in Burgas & Plovdiv
UK *Embassy:* (☎ 9339 2222) ul Moskovska 9
USA *Embassy:* (☎ 963 2022) ul Kapitan Andreev 1
Yugoslavia *Consulate:* (☎ 943 4590) ul Marin Drimov 17

CUSTOMS

Foreigners are allowed to take in and out 'gifts up to a reasonable amount', as well as souvenirs and articles for personal use.

MONEY

The local currency, leva (lv) – singular lev – comprises of 100 stotinki. Prices are often quoted in US dollars for major purchases, but payments should be in leva.

Currency

Bulgarian banknotes come in denominations of one, two, five, 10, 20 and 50 leva, and coins come in one, two, five, 10, 20 and 50 stotinki. Since January 2002, the lev has been pegged to the euro.

Exchange Rates

Below are the official exchange rates for major currencies at the time of publication.

country	unit		leva
Australia	A$1	=	1.07 lv
Canada	C$1	=	1.25 lv
Eurozone	€1	=	1.96 lv
Japan	¥100	=	1.67 lv
New Zealand	NZ$1	=	1.06 lv
Romania	10,000 lei	=	0.57 lv
Turkey	TL1,000,000	=	1.14 lv
UK	UK£1	=	3.05 lv
USA	US$1	=	1.93 lv
Yugoslavia	10DIN	=	0.32 lv

Exchanging Money

Foreign-exchange offices are found at every city, town and major attraction. Most don't charge commission or fees. The best currencies to take are US dollars, UK pounds and euros. It's also easy to change cash at most larger banks.

Not all foreign-exchange offices and banks in Bulgaria change travellers cheques. Those that do sometimes only accept cheques issued by American Express and Thomas Cook and will charge 3% to 5% commission. Some of the larger banks (eg, Bulbank in Sofia) will change US-dollars travellers cheques into US-dollars cash for a fee (around 2% to 3%). ATMs are an increasingly common sight. Some of the larger banks (and occasional foreign-exchange offices) provide cash advances in leva over the counter with Visa or MasterCard.

Costs

If you stay in budget hotels or private rooms, eat at cheap Bulgarian restaurants and catch public buses and 2nd-class trains, US$17/15 per person per day travelling as a single/double should be enough.

One annoying aspect of travelling around Bulgaria is that foreign tourists are charged considerably more than Bulgarians for accommodation and admission fees to tourist attractions.

Tipping & Bargaining

Waiters and taxi drivers normally round the bill/fare up to the nearest convenient figure. In some restaurants a 10% service charge is already added. If not, and the service is good, add about 10%.

Haggling is not customary. An exception is at the Black Sea resorts, where taxi drivers and landlords of private rooms habitually inflate prices for foreigners.

POST & COMMUNICATIONS

Poste restante is available in Sofia. To ring Bulgaria from abroad, dial the international access code from your home country, add ☎ 359 (the country code for Bulgaria), the area code (minus the first zero) and then the number.

It's (normally) easy to telephone anywhere in the world from public telephone booths, telephone centres, private homes and hotels. Every major settlement throughout the country has a Bulgarian Telecommunications Centre (BTC), normally inside or very near the main post office.

Most telephone booths are operated by Mobika and BulFon and use phonecards, while some Mobika booths also accept Visa and MasterCard for long-distance calls. Mobika and BulFon booths can be used to make calls within Bulgaria, and direct long-distance calls to Europe and North America, but to anywhere else you have to use the international operator (☎ 0123).

Even the smallest town has at least one Internet centre. Competition is fierce and access is remarkably cheap: about 1 lv per 30 minutes.

DIGITAL RESOURCES

Useful English-language websites include: W www.onlinebg.com, good for news, shopping and with great links; W www.dirbg.com, which has excellent search facilities and links; W www.bulgarianspace.com/bmg, for anything cultural; and W www.news.bg, which has all sorts of useful information.

WOMEN TRAVELLERS

If you attract unwanted attention, *Omâzhena sâm* (I am married) will send a pretty firm message.

GAY & LESBIAN TRAVELLERS

Bulgaria is generally far from gay-friendly. Same-sex couples should refrain from overt displays of affection and be discreet when booking into hotels. For details about gay clubs, contact the **Bulgarian Gay Organization Gemini** *(☎ 02-987 6872; W www.bgogemini.org; bul Vasil Levski 3, Sofia)*.

DISABLED TRAVELLERS

Few facilities exist for people with special needs. Uneven and broken pavements make wheelchair mobility problematic, and ramps and special toilets for those in wheelchairs are few and far between.

DANGERS & ANNOYANCES

Bulgaria is as peaceful and trouble-free as Greece, Turkey and Romania. Theft is not much of a problem, but parked cars are prime targets.

LEGAL MATTERS

Bulgaria has harsh drug laws. It's a common route for drugs smuggled across the Black Sea from Russia and Armenia, and from Turkey to the south, so always treat the transport, trade and use of drugs with a *great* deal of caution.

BUSINESS HOURS

Most shops open from around 9am to 7pm weekdays, and about 9am to 1pm on Saturday, but tend to open and close later in summer. Banks are open weekdays between 9am and 4pm, while foreign-exchange offices generally open Monday to Saturday from 9am to 6pm.

Emergencies

In the case of emergency call the following nationwide numbers: for the fire brigade call ☎ 160, Medical Rescue & Ambulance ☎ 150 and police ☎ 166.

If you need roadside assistance outside Sofia call ☎ 146 or mobile ☎ 048 146; within Sofia ☎ 1286.

Many tourist attractions close for one or two days per week, usually between Sunday and Wednesday. Opening times change regularly.

PUBLIC HOLIDAYS & SPECIAL EVENTS

Official public holidays are: New Year's Day (1 January); Liberation Day (3 March), also known as National Day; Orthodox Easter Sunday & Monday (March/April), one week after the Catholic/Protestant Easter; St George's Day (6 May); Cyrillic Alphabet Day (24 May), also known as Day of Bulgarian Culture; Unification (6 September), also known as National Day; Bulgarian Independence Day (22 September); National Revival Day (1 November); Christmas (25 and 26 December).

Bulgaria hosts an inordinate number of festivals, the largest of which is the International Folk Festival held in Koprivshtitsa every five years (next one in 2005). Other marvellous events are held annually in Sofia, Plovdiv, Koprivshtitsa, Veliko Târnovo, Burgas and Varna – see those sections later for details. More information about these and other festivals can be obtained from the relevant regional tourist offices and from W www.bulgariatravel.org and W www.bulgarianspace.com/bmg.

ACTIVITIES

Ski resorts may not be world-class, but the snow is plentiful, the slopes accessible and the prices affordable. The ski season runs from about mid-December to mid-April at four major resorts: Bansko, Borovets, Vitosha National Park and Pamporovo. You can rent equipment and arrange ski instruction at any of the resorts, but it's less easy at Vitosha.

Bulgaria boasts approximately 37,000km of marked hiking trails. Most trails start and/or finish each day at one of the numerous mountain huts, so there's usually no need to bring a tent. By far the best hiking maps, which are available in Sofia, are published by Kartografia.

Beaches along the Black Sea coast are long, wide, clean and developed.

WORK

Most foreigners working in Bulgaria are specialists with contracts arranged *before* they arrived. The frightening amount of paperwork required, and the fees for work permits (1000 lv!), are designed to dissuade foreigners from taking up temporary employment.

ACCOMMODATION

Camping

Many of the few remaining camping grounds in Bulgaria are rundown and close to noisy main roads. Most close between November and April, and some along the Black Sea coast only open from June to early September. Pitching a tent outside a camping ground is technically prohibited, but normally accepted if you're discreet.

Hostels

Most larger hostels and dormitories are only open in summer (June to August), and only cater to Bulgarians on excursions and hiking trips. Getting information is difficult unless you speak Bulgarian or know well-informed locals. No hostel in Bulgaria is part of any international organisation.

Mountain Huts

A dormitory bed in a mountain hut – called a *hizha* – is available to anyone. Most are only open May to October, but those situated at or near major ski slopes are often also open in winter. It's usually not necessary to book a bed in advance, but they can be reserved at the **Bulgarian Tourist Union** *(☎ 02-980 1285; bul Vasil Levski 75, Sofia)*.

Private Rooms

Some families in a few cities, towns and villages offer rooms in private homes to visitors. These rooms are normally comfortable and clean, but bathroom facilities are often communal. The home owners are almost always friendly, but rarely speak English. Rooms can be arranged through accommodation agencies in town/city centres or at bus and train stations. Alternatively, wait to be approached in the street by people offering accommodation or look for relevant signs in shop windows and hanging outside homes.

Hotels

Most smaller and more remote hotels at the ski resorts are closed outside the ski season (ie, closed mid-April to November), while almost nowhere along the Black Sea coast opens in late October to early April. Reserving rooms in Bulgarian hotels is not necessary.

FOOD & DRINKS

Popular Bulgarian main courses include *kebabche* (grilled spicy meat sausages); *kyufte*, which is basically the same thing but round and flat; *musaka*, which is shaped like the Greek equivalent but doesn't contain eggplant (aubergine); *kavarma* (meat and vegetables in a clay pot); and *plakiya* (rich fish stew). Vegetarians will not be disappointed with the number of meatless dishes available, but may be disaffected by the lack of imagination.

The average Bulgarian doesn't seem to be able to function properly without a serious fix of caffeine (and nicotine) each morning. Acceptable espresso coffee can be found everywhere, and many places now also serve cappuccinos.

Bulgaria is the world's fifth-largest exporter of wine. Palatable plonk includes cabernet sauvignon (from around Sliven and Melnik) and sauvignon blanc (from near Varna). Beers produced by the Zagorka, Astika and Kamenitsa breweries are available countrywide, though provincial beers – such as Pirinsko Pivo (from Blagoevgrad) and Shumensko Pivo (from Shumen) – are often better.

ENTERTAINMENT

There are numerous bars in which to enjoy a drink, meet some locals and, maybe, hear bands play traditional Bulgarian folk music or passable versions of foreign pop. Most cities also have grand old theatres where opera, drama and ballet is performed (in Bulgarian).

Getting There & Away

AIR

The national carrier, Balkan Airlines, flies between Sofia and most European cities. Other airlines that fly to Sofia year-round include British Airways (from London), KLM (from Amsterdam), Lufthansa (from Frankfurt and Munich), Air France (from Paris) and Alitalia (from Rome and Milan).

LAND

Border Crossings

Following is a list of major road borders that accept foreigners and are open 24 hours.

Greece Between Kulata (Bulgaria) and Promahonas (Greece) and Svilengrad and Ormenion

Macedonia Between Gyueshevo and Deve Bair; Stanke Lisichkovo and Delčevo; and Zlatarevo and Novo Selo.

Romania Between Vidin and Calafat; Ruse and Giurgiu; Kardam and Negru Vodă; and Durankulak and Vama Veche
Turkey Between Malko Târnovo and Derekjoj; and Kapitan-Andreevo and Edirne
Yugoslavia Between Kalotina and Dimitrovgrad; Vrâshka Chuka and Zajc; and Strezimirovtsi and Klisura

Bus

Greece & Macedonia From outside its office in Sofia, **MATPU** *(☎ 02-953 2481; ul Damyan Gruev 23)* runs a bus that leaves every day at 10.30am for Athens, via Thessaloniki (Greece), while **ATT** *(bul Maria Luisa)* also offers daily buses from outside its office in Sofia to Athens and Thessaloniki. Slightly cheaper buses to Athens leave from the bus terminals to the northwest and northeast of the Princess Hotel in Sofia.

City Local Transportation Co *(☎ 032-624 274; pl Tsentralen)* operates between one and three buses a day from Plovdiv to Thessaloniki, and runs another bus to Athens on Tuesday and Thursday. **Hemus Tours** *(☎ 042-57018; ul Tsar Simeon Veliki)*, in Stara Zagora, also has regular buses to Athens.

MATPU and ATT offer several daily buses from Sofia to Skopje (Macedonia), and **MATPU** *(bul Sveti Dimitâr Solunski)*, opposite the bus terminal in Blagoevgrad, has daily buses to Bitola (Macedonia).

Turkey MATPU and ATT offer daily buses from Sofia to İstanbul, while others depart from the two terminals near the Princess Hotel in Sofia. Also to İstanbul, several private companies at the Yug bus terminal in Plovdiv offer daily buses; **Zlatni Piasaci Travel** *(☎ 052-355 419)*, based at the main bus terminal in Varna, operates regular services; and **Enturtrans** *(☎ 056-844 708; ul Bulair)* in Burgas has daily buses.

Yugoslavia ATT (see previously) offers buses from Sofia to Belgrade via Niš (Yugoslavia). Others to Belgrade and Niš leave from the bus terminals near the Princess Hotel in Sofia.

Train

Tickets for international trains can be purchased at any Rila Bureau (most are open weekdays only) in the cities and major towns and/or at dedicated ticket offices (open daily) at larger train stations that have international connections. You will have to pay for your train tickets in leva.

Greece The *Trans-Balkan Express* travels between Thessaloniki and Budapest (Hungary) every day, via Bucharest, Ruse, Gorna Oryahovitsa, Sofia and Sandanski. The *Sofia-Thessaloniki* service links the two cities every day from the 15 June to 30 September, via Sandanski. There are also daily trains between Svilengrad and Athens.

Romania The *Bulgaria Express* runs between Sofia and Moscow, via Bucharest, Ruse and Pleven, every day. (Between Sofia and Bucharest, this train is called the *Grivitza.*) Also, every day from 15 June to 28 September, a train from Burgas and another from Varna connect with a train leaving Ruse for Bucharest, Budapest, Bratislava (Slovakia) and Prague (the Czech Republic).

Every day in summer (15 June to 28 September), the *Sofia-Saratov* service travels to Bucharest from Sofia, via Gorna Oryahovitsa and Ruse. Every day year-round, the *Bosfor* between İstanbul and Bucharest also passes through Bulgaria, via Stara Zagora, Veliko Târnovo and Ruse. And the *Trans-Balkan Express* (see under Greece earlier) travels between Thessaloniki and Budapest, via Bulgaria and Bucharest.

Turkey To İstanbul, take the *Bosfor* (see Romania) or *Balkan Express* (see Yugoslavia) trains. There are also daily trains between Svilengrad and İstanbul.

Yugoslavia The daily *Balkan Express* between İstanbul and Belgrade travels via Plovdiv, Sofia and Niš and the *Sofia-Beograd* train travels every day between İstanbul and Belgrade, via Niš.

Car & Motorcycle

Drivers of normal-sized cars (and motorbikes) are charged an entrance tax of US$10, with the exception of citizens from the Czech Republic, Denmark, France, Germany, Hungary, Italy, the Netherlands, Spain, Sweden, Switzerland and the UK. Drivers of private cars (and motorbikes) from *all* countries must state on arrival which border they plan to exit and pay a 'highway fee' of US$0.10 per kilometre (minimum of US$5) when they depart Bulgaria. All drivers must also pay a 'disinfection fee' of

US$3 when they enter the country. These fees can be paid in US dollars, euros, leva and most other major European currencies.

Your driving licence from home is valid in Bulgaria. Third-party 'liability insurance' is compulsory and can be purchased at any Bulgarian border.

Getting Around

BUS & MINIBUS

Buses and minibuses link all cities and major towns and connect villages with the nearest transport hub. Buses run by the government are old, uncomfortable and slow, but newer, quicker and more commodious private buses and minibuses are increasingly common.

Seats on private buses can be reserved one or more days in advance. Except for long-distance services at peak times, however, there's no need to book any bus more than a few hours ahead.

Whenever possible take a minibus, because they're quicker and more comfortable than public and private buses.

TRAIN

Trains are generally more comfortable than buses and minibuses and offer far nicer views. Except for the intercity express between Sofia, and Varna and Burgas, standards are not what you'd expect in Western and northern Europe, but trains are reasonably quick, often punctual and astoundingly cheap. Trains are classified as *ekspresen* (express), *bârz* (fast) or *pâtnicheski* (slow passenger). Use a fast or express train unless you absolutely thrive on train travel, or you want to visit a smaller village (and have no choice), or you're travelling on a really tight budget.

For frequent services, such as between Sofia and Plovdiv, there's rarely a problem if you just turn up at the station and buy a ticket for the next train. Advance tickets are sometimes advisable, however, to the Black Sea on the intercity express during a summer weekend. Most Europe-wide rail passes can be used anywhere within Bulgaria.

> **Drink, Drive, Die**
>
> No, we're not being preachy. We are dead serious.
>
> If you get caught drinking and driving in Bulgaria, you get a lengthy prison sentence. If you're convicted of the offence again, they kill you. By firing squad. Seriously.
>
> Don't do it.

CAR & MOTORCYCLE

Smaller Bulgarian rental agencies charge foreigners the same rates as Bulgarians. For a basic Mazda 323, expect to pay from US$24 per day.

Larger, more established Bulgarian rental companies offer more or less the same standard of vehicles and service as the major international agencies but are far cheaper (ie, about 50% more than the rates listed for the smaller rental agencies). Two such reliable agencies in Sofia are **Drenikov** (*☎/fax 02-944 9532; W www.drenikov.com; ul Oborishte 55*) and **Rentaavto** (*☎ 02-929 5005; W www.rentauto-bg.com; ul Stamboliyski 219*).

BICYCLE

Cycling is a viable way of getting around. The downside is that many roads are windy, steep, in poor condition and chock-a-block with traffic, and bikes aren't allowed on highways. On the other hand, traffic is light along routes between villages, and long-distance buses and trains will carry your bike for a small extra fee.

HITCHING

Hitching in rural Bulgaria may be preferable to being restricted by infrequent public transport. Hitching tends to be in fits and starts, however, because cars often only travel to the next village. Oh – and the pretty ladies standing along the major highways near Sofia waving down male drivers are *not* looking for, umm, a lift.

LOCAL TRANSPORT

All cities and major towns have buses, trolleybuses and trams, but they're generally decrepit and overcrowded. Tickets for these can be bought from kiosks (and sometimes from drivers), and don't forget to buy an extra ticket for each piece of large luggage. Newer minibuses operate in some cities, but most visitors will be confused by the ever-changing routes; tickets are available from the driver. Sofia boasts a modern metro (subway) system.

Taxis – which must be painted yellow and equipped with working meters – can be flagged down along most streets in every city and town. Rates vary enormously, so it pays to shop around before jumping in. All taxis must clearly display the rates on their windows: the first line indicates the rate per kilometre between 6am and 10pm, while the last line shows the cost per minute for waiting.

Sofia София

☎ 02 • pop 1.18 million

Sofia, which sits on a 545m-high plateau in western Bulgaria at the foot of the imposing Mt Vitosha mountain range, is the highest capital in Europe. Almost all international flights start and finish here, and the capital is also the hub of much of Bulgaria's bus and rail transport.

Sofia sports enough museums, churches and art galleries to keep most visitors happy, and it's only an hour or so to excellent hiking and skiing spots. It's also an ideal base for organised tours to the Rila Monastery.

Information

Staff members are happy to help and speak English at the **National Information & Advertising Center** *(☎ 987 9778; W www.bulgariatravel.org; ul Sveta Sofia; open Mon-Fri)*, near Goody's restaurant. You will find **foreign-exchange offices** along bul Stamboliyski, bul Maria Luisa and bul Vitosha. Some along upper (northern) bul Maria Luisa are open 24 hours. The best bank for changing cash and travellers cheques, and obtaining cash advances over the counter with Visa and MasterCard, is the **Bulbank** *(cnr ul Lavele & ul Todor Alexandrov)*. Most banks around central Sofia have ATMs that accept all major credit cards.

The **Central Post Office** *(ul General Gurko 6; open 7.30am-8.30pm daily)* has poste restante. Inside the impressive **BTC** office *(ul General Gurko; open 24hr)* are plenty of telephone booths and a service for sending and receiving faxes. BTC also offers Internet access.

Internet access is pleasingly cheap and easy. Try the **Ultima Internet Center** *(ul Lavele 16)*, just down from the entrance to the Odysseia-In Travel Agency; and the **Internet centres** inside, and along the underpass beneath, the NDK National Palace of Culture complex in Yuzhen Park.

The major public hospital for emergencies is **Pirogov Hospital** *(☎ 51 531; bul Gen Totleben 21)*, while **Poliklinika Torax** *(☎ 988 5259; bul Stamboliyski 57)* is a competent, privately run clinic. For police matters (from 8am to 6pm daily), there are special contact numbers where the operators speak English (☎ 988 5239) and French (☎ 982 3028).

Things to See & Do

The best place to start a **walking tour** is **Aleksander Nevski Church** *(pl Aleksander Nevski; admission free; open 7am-7pm daily)*. This massive building was created between 1892 and 1912 as a memorial to the 200,000 Russian soldiers who died fighting for Bulgaria's independence during the Russian-Turkish War (1877–78). Inside, the **Aleksander Nevski Crypt** *(admission 8 lv; open 10.30am-noon & 2pm-6.30pm Wed-Mon)* contains one of Bulgaria's best collections of religious icons.

East of the church, head down bul Vasil Levski and turn right into ul Tsar Osvoboditel, along which is the **Monument to the Liberators**. Detour down ul Panzh to the 6th-century **Church of St Sofia** *(admission free; open 7am-7pm daily)*, the oldest Orthodox church in the capital. Nearby is the **Tomb of the Unknown Soldier** *(admission free; open 24hr)*.

Back on ul Tsar Osvoboditel is **St Nikolai Russian Church** *(admission free; open 7am-7pm daily)*, built in 1912–13 by Russian emigres. Soon you'll stumble across the **National Art Gallery** *(ul Tsar Osvoboditel; admission 2 lv, free Sun; open 10.30am-6.30pm Tues-Sun)*, which features several rooms of Bulgarian art. Sharing this former Royal Palace is the **Ethnographical Museum** *(admission 3 lv; open 10am-5.30pm Tues-Sun)*, which contains fascinating displays about Bulgarian arts and crafts from the last 300 years. From here, walk southwest down ul Vasil Levski to admire the eye-catching neoclassical **Ivan Vazov National Theatre** *(ul Vasil Levski 5)*.

Cut through the **Sofia City Garden** and then head west along trendy ul Sâborna to the magnificent **Sveta Nedelya Cathedral** *(pl Sveta Nedelya; admission free; open 7am-7pm daily)*. Built between 1856 and 1863, this cathedral features an exceptionally ornate interior. The gorgeous 14th-century **Sveta Petka Samardjiiska Church** *(admission 6 lv; open 7am-6pm daily)* is accessible via an underpass from bul Maria Luisa. North along bul Maria Luisa is the unmistakable **Banya Bashi Mosque** *(bul Maria Luisa; admission free; open dawn-dusk daily)*. The walk finishes at the resplendent **Sofia Synagogue** *(ul Ekzarh Yosif 16)*, behind the Central Hali shopping centre.

BULGARIA

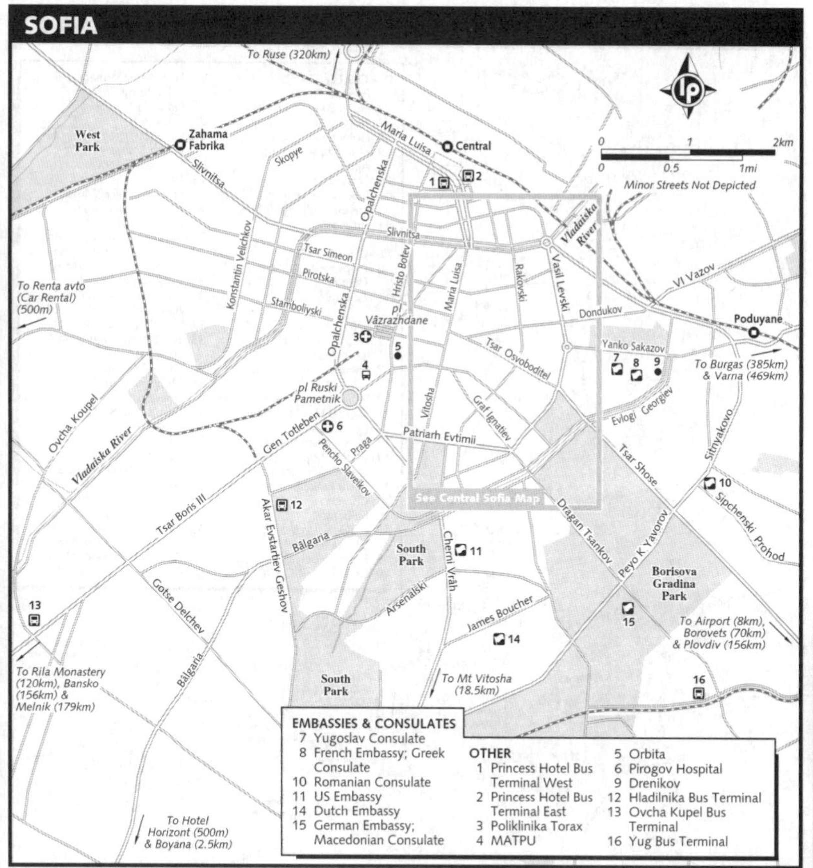

Special Events

St Sofia is the Mother of Hope, Love and Faith, so St Sofia's Day (17 September) is widely celebrated throughout the capital. The associated Sofia Fest (14 to 18 September) includes various cultural events, concerts and exhibitions. The Sofia International Folklore Festival takes places in and around the capital for five days during late August.

Places to Stay

Private Rooms Try the **accommodation agency** *(rooms per person around 35 lv)* at the central train station to find rooms in local homes. The **accommodation agency** *(rooms per person from 30 lv)* at the airport is rarely staffed, but some readers have been impressed with its service and quality of rooms on offer.

Radost Tour Private Lodgings Office *(☎/fax 988 2631; e radostur@bol.bg; bul Vitosha 37; singles/doubles 35/58 lv)* offers a number of private rooms and apartments with TV in central Sofia. Look for the sign (in English) near the Reks Cinema.

A helpful lady runs **Markella Accommodation Agency** *(☎/fax 981 1833; ul Ekzarh Yosif 35; singles/doubles 25/35 lv)*. She is able to show you photos of the available rooms.

Hostels Above a Chinese restaurant, but not well signposted, **Sofia Hostel** *(☎/fax 989 8582; e hostel-sofia@usa.net; ul Pozitano 16; dorm beds with breakfast 25 lv)* offers basic accommodation around a communal kitchen and TV room.

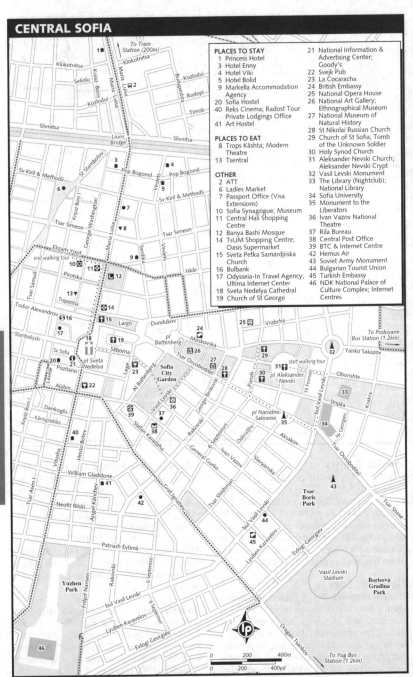

CENTRAL SOFIA

PLACES TO STAY
1 Princess Hotel
3 Hotel Enny
4 Hotel Viki
5 Hotel Bolid
9 Markella Accommodation Agency
20 Sofia Hostel
40 Reks Cinema; Radost Tour Private Lodgings Office
41 Art Hostel

PLACES TO EAT
8 Trops Kâshta; Modern Theatre
13 Tsentral

OTHER
2 ATT
6 Ladies Market
7 Passport Office (Visa Extensions)
10 Sofia Synagogue; Museum
11 Central Hali Shopping Centre
12 Banya Bashi Mosque
14 TsUM Shopping Centre; Oasis Supermarket
15 Sveta Petka Samardjiiska Church
16 Bulbank
17 Odysseia-In Travel Agency; Ultima Internet Center
18 Sveta Nedelya Cathedral
19 Church of St George
21 National Information & Advertising Center; Goody's
22 Svejk Pub
23 La Cocaracha
24 British Embassy
25 National Opera House
26 National Art Gallery; Ethnographical Museum
27 National Museum of Natural History
28 St Nikolai Russian Church
29 Church of St Sofia; Tomb of the Unknown Soldier
30 Holy Synod Church
31 Aleksander Nevski Church; Aleksander Nevski Crypt
32 Vasil Levski Monument
33 The Library (Nightclub); National Library
34 Sofia University
35 Monument to the Liberators
36 Ivan Vazov National Theatre
37 Rila Bureau
38 Central Post Office
39 BTC & Internet Centre
42 Hemus Air
43 Soviet Army Monument
44 Bulgarian Tourist Union
45 Turkish Embassy
46 NDK National Palace of Culture Complex; Internet Centres

To Train Station (200m)
To Poduyane Bus Station (1.2km)
To Yug Bus Station (1.2km)
start walking tour
end walking tour

Art Hostel *(☎ 987 0545; e art-hostel@art-hostel.com; ul Angel Kânchev 21a; dorm beds 22 lv)* is the sort of bohemian place where you will most likely meet fascinating English-speaking locals, but never get any sleep before 3am.

Hotels For basic but comfortable rooms, try **Hotel Viki** *(☎ 983 9746; ul Veslets 56; beds in 3-bed rooms 12 lv)*. Each room has three beds, so a room to yourself will cost 36 lv.

Hotel Bolid *(☎ 983 3002; cnr ul Pop Bogomil & ul Veslets; singles/doubles with shared bathroom 25/45 lv)* is slowly undergoing renovations. The rooms (which have a TV and sink) are small, the ceilings are low and the floors squeak, but it's good value.

Hotel Horizont *(☎ 574 217; ul Gen Mihail Kutuzov 23; rooms with shared bathroom per person 25 lv)* is friendly, family-run and great value, but inconvenient. Contact them about free transport from the bus or train station or airport, or take tram No 5 or 19 from along bul Vitosha.

Hotel Enny *(☎ 983 3002; ul Pop Bogomil 46; singles/doubles with shared bathroom 25/48 lv, doubles with TV & shower but no toilet 70 lv)* is popular, friendly, central and quiet. It's a little overpriced and some rooms are small, but the courtyard is a convivial place to meet fellow travellers.

Places to Eat

With several branches around the city **Trops Kâshta** *(bul Maria Luisa 26; salads 1 lv, mains 3 lv)* is ideal for anyone who wants to try some local nosh without paying through the nose – just point. The most convenient branch is next to the Modern Theatre cinema.

Tsentral *(ul George Washington; mains 3-4.50 lv)* is a folksy outdoor *mehana* (tavern) with a beer-garden setting. It offers Bulgarian dishes and a huge range of salads at reasonable prices. Staff can rustle up a menu in English.

Goody's *(pl Sveta Nedelya; mains 3-4 lv)* is a central landmark. It offers more interesting meals, such as salads and scrumptious club sandwiches, than the usual junk-food place. It's large and clean place, and provides plenty of outdoor seats.

To self-cater, try the **Oasis Supermarket** *(bul Maria Luisa)*, in the northern end of the TsUM shopping centre; the **Central Hali Shopping Centre** *(bul Maria Luisa 25)*; and the chaotic **Ladies Market** *(ul St Stambolov)*.

Entertainment

The best source of information about what's going on (and where and when) is unquestionably the *Sofia Echo*.

The **National Opera House** *(ul Vrabcha)* features the best that Bulgaria has to offer. Performances are at 9pm Tuesday and Saturday from May to September, and at 7pm daily for the rest of the year. The **NDK National Palace of Culture** *(Yuzhen Park)* has a regular programme of cultural events throughout the year, including summer (when most other theatres are closed).

The Library *(bul Vasil Levski)*, also called 'The Biblioteka', offers live music and a karaoke bar. It's in the basement of the National Library.

The smoky **La Cocaracha** *(ul Lege 19)* features a decent wine list and live music, while the **Svejk Pub** *(bul Vitosha 1)* offers an extensive range of beers, as well as meals every day and live music on weekends.

Getting There & Away

Air Refer to the Getting Around section earlier for flights to/from Sofia. The three domestic airlines are **Balkan Airlines** *(☎ 988 3595, 659 517; ul Alabin, NDK underpass)*, **Dandy Airlines** *(☎ 943 3674; ul Shipka 42)* and **Hemus Air** *(☎ 981 8330; ul Rakovski 157)*. Offices for all major international airlines are listed in the *Sofia Echo*.

Bus The two major bus terminals in Sofia are either side of bul Maria Luisa and just north of Princess Hotel. In lieu of any official names for these terminals, we have dubbed them the Princess Hotel Bus Terminal East and the Princess Hotel Bus Terminal West. Both are fairly chaotic and disorganised – thankfully not an indication of bus terminals elsewhere in Bulgaria.

More buses leave from the western terminal, but if you can't find a bus at one terminal simply cross the road and look around at the other. Because there are so many regular departures on public and private buses every day (especially in summer), it's usually easy enough to simply turn up at the western terminal and buy a ticket for a bus leaving within an hour or so.

Train The **Central Train Station** *(bul Maria Luisa)* in Sophia can be overwhelming. Timetables for all domestic and international services are still in Cyrillic, but departures (for the next two hours) and arrivals (for the previous two hours) are listed in English on a large computer screen on the ground floor. You can walk to the station from pl Sveta Nedelya (30 minutes) or go by tram Nos 1, 2 and 7. Counters and offices are open 24 hours, and staff usually understand some English.

Tickets for international trains, and advance tickets for domestic services, are available from the **Rila Bureau** *(☎ 932 3346)* at the central train station and the **Rila Bureau** *(☎ 987 0777; ul General Gurko 5)* in the city centre.

Getting Around

To/From the Airport The Sofia Airport is roughly 12km southeast of the city centre. It can be reached by bus No 84 from opposite Sofia University on bul Vasil Levski, or by minibus No 30 from along bul Maria Luisa and ul Tsar Osvoboditel. A taxi from the city centre should cost no more than 6 lv.

Public Transport All forms of public transport operate from 5am to midnight daily. Most drivers on trams, buses and trolleybuses sell tickets (0.50 lv), but it's far easier and quicker to buy one ticket (or more) from any kiosk along a route before boarding. Minibuses are quicker and more comfortable, but cost a little more. Destinations and fares are indicated (in Cyrillic) on the front of the minibuses, and tickets are bought from the drivers.

Taxi An affordable and more comfortable alternative to public transport is taxis. The ones that wait around the airport, luxury hotels and pl Sveta Nedelya are often unscrupulous and will offer unmetered fares.

Southern Bulgaria

Southern Bulgaria is easily defined as the part of the country between the Sredna Gora Mountains and the borders with Greece and Turkey. In the southeast, between the Sredna Gora Mountains, Rodopi Mountains and Black Sea coast, is an area still known by its historical name of Thrace.

RILA MONASTERY
РИЛСКИ МАНАСТИР

☎ 07054

Bulgaria's largest and most famous monastery is tucked away in a narrow, forested valley of the Rila Mountains, 120km south of Sofia. It's the holiest place in the country and probably *the* major attraction for Bulgarian pilgrims, as well as for foreign tourists.

The Rila Monastery was built in 927. Under adverse conditions, the monastery helped to keep Bulgarian culture and religion alive during centuries of Turkish rule. In 1833, a fire virtually engulfed all of the buildings, but it was rebuilt soon after and extensively restored in 1469.

Many places to stay and eat are within 100m of the eastern **Samokov Gate**, while most cars and buses park near the front (western) **Dupnitsa Gate**.

The monastery grounds are open 6am to 10pm daily. Admission is free, but there is an entrance fee (5lv) to the museum. No photos are allowed inside the Nativity Church.

Things to See

Four levels of colourful balconies, with some 300 monastic cells, as well as storerooms and a refectory, surround the large, irregular courtyard. The top balcony offers outstanding views of the surrounding Rila Mountains.

If you enter the monastery grounds from the Samokov Gate, you'll soon see the 23m-high stone **Hrelyu Tower**, named after a significant benefactor. It is all that remains of the part of the monastery built in 1335.

Standing in the middle of the courtyard is the magnificent **Nativity Church**, probably the largest monastery church in Bulgaria. The main building and its three great domes were built between 1834 and 1837, and now contain 1200 murals.

The two-storey **Ethnographic Museum** *(admission 6 lv; open 8.30am-4.30pm daily)* houses an impressive collection, including the **Rila Cross**, a double-sided cross that Brother Raphael took over 12 years to create during the late 18th century.

Places to Stay & Eat

Rila Monastery *(☎ 2208; rooms per person from 25 lv)* has cheaper rooms in the older western wing with three or four beds. These are sparsely furnished, but clean enough. The communal facilities have toilets, but no showers. **Rila Restaurant** *(mains 5-8 lv)* is in a 120-year-old building a few metres from the Samokov Gate. It has a pleasant outdoor setting and an extensive menu, but gets mixed reviews from travellers.

Getting There & Away

Buses leave Rila village (located 22km to the west) for the Rila Monastery at 7.40am, 12.40pm and 3.50pm; they return to Rila village at 9am, 3pm and 5pm. From Dupnitsa, buses to Rila Monastery leave at 6.40am and 2.15pm, and return from the monastery at 9.40am and 5.15pm.

It's just about possible to make a day trip from Sofia by public transport. Get on any bus that stops at Dupnitsa from the Princess Hotel Bus Terminal West or the Ovcha Kupel Bus Terminal no later than 8am. In Dupnitsa, jump on the 10am (or 11am) bus to Rila village, and then catch the 12.40pm bus to the monastery. To return to Sofia, take the 5.15pm bus to Dupnitsa and one of the hourly buses (or trains) back to the capital. In summer, it's worth finding out from the **Ovcha Kupel Bus Terminal** *(☎ 02-554 033)* about direct buses between Sofia and the monastery.

PLOVDIV РЛОВДИВ

☎ 032 • pop 376,500

Plovdiv is the second-largest transportation hub and economic centre in Bulgaria. It's also the first/last stop for those travelling between Bulgaria and Greece or Turkey. Tourist authorities and travel agencies often use cliches like 'you must see Plovdiv to see Bulgaria' – but, for once, these types of phrases are not overstated at all. This modern, thriving city is based around a majestic Old Town crammed with 18th- and 19th-century homes, as well as dozens of museums, art galleries and churches. And to top it off, Plovdiv is the site of the most remarkable Roman ruin in Bulgaria.

Information

Plenty of foreign-exchange offices can be found along the pedestrian mall, off ul Knyaz Aleksandâr, and ul Ivan Vazov. Several offices along the mall also change travellers cheques and offer cash advances with major credit cards. There are a handful of banks near pl Dzhumaya, such as the United Bulgarian Bank, which has an ATM.

The **Telephone Centre** *(open 6am-11pm daily)* is inside the **Main Post Office** *(pl Tsentralen)*. For 'cyber mail', try **RNet Internet** *(ul Aleksandâr Ekzarh)* or **Net Burger**, just down the steps from the overpass along ul Gladston.

Things to See

The best place to start a walking tour is pl Dzhumaya. The square is dominated by the **Dzhumaya Mosque** *(admission free; open dawn-dusk daily)*, one of 50 or so mosques built during the Turkish occupation.

Head east along ul Sâborna to **Danov House** *(ul Mitropolit Paisii 2; admission 1.50 lv; open 9am-12.30pm & 2pm-4.30pm Mon-Sat)*, dedicated to a famous Bulgarian writer and publisher. Opposite is the huge 19th-century **Church of Sveta Bogoroditsa** *(admission free; open 8am-6pm daily)*, which contains a marvellous array of paintings and murals.

Further along ul Sâborna is the **State Gallery of Fine Arts** *(ul Sâborna 14a; admission Wed-Mon 2.50 lv, free Tues; open 9am-12.30 & 1pm-5.30pm daily)*, housed in a charmingly renovated home built in 1846. A little further up is the **Zlatyo Boyadjiev House** *(ul Sâborna 18; admission 3 lv; open 9am-noon & 1pm-6pm daily Oct-Mar, Mon-Fri Apr-Sept)*, which contains massive works by this local artist.

Before the junction with ul Lavrenov look for the entrance to the charming **Church of St Konstantin & Elena** *(ul Sâborna 24; admission free; open 8am-6pm daily)*. It was constructed in AD 337, but mostly rebuilt in 1832.

Head up ul Dr Chomakov (the extension of ul Sâborna) to the dramatic **Ruins of Eumolpias** *(admission free; open 24hr)*. These remains of a Thracian settlement date from about 5000 BC. On the way down visit the excellent **Ethnographical Museum** *(ul Dr Chomakov 2; admission 3.50 lv; open 9am-5pm daily)*.

Stroll down ul Cyril Nektariev and then follow the 'Ancient Theatre' signs to the magnificent **Roman Amphitheatre** *(admission 2.50 lv; open 8am-6pm daily)*. It was built by the Romans in the early 2nd century AD, and partially restored to hold special events. On the way back to pl Dzhumaya have a look at the remarkable **Roman Stadium** *(ul Knyaz Aleksandâr)*.

Places to Stay

The **Prima Vista Agency** *(☎ 272 778; ul Knyaz Aleksandâr 28; rooms per person 20-25 lv)* has irregular opening hours, but staff are helpful. Look for the black 'accommodation agency' sign (in English) along the mall.

The **Esperantsa** *(☎ 260 653; ul Ivan Vazov 14; rooms per person 25 lv)* accommodation agency can be a bit haphazard, but readers have commented favourably about the quality of rooms on offer.

Tourist Hotel *(Turisticheski Dom; ☎ 633 211; ul PR Slaveikov 5; rooms per person 25 lv)* is a remarkable old place. No-one minds the noisy nightclub at the back, the musty aroma and the saggy beds because it is so convenient and just oozes atmosphere.

Places to Eat

Several stalls along the northern section of ul Rayko Daskalov sell tasty doner kebabs. **Totova Hrana** *(ul Han Kubrat; mains 2 lv)* is an excellent choice for cheap, cafeteria-style food.

I Claudius Cafe *(ul Knyaz Aleksandâr; mains from 3.50 lv)* is so close to the Roman Stadium that it almost touches it. Considering the extraordinary setting, prices here are quite reasonable.

Sportna Sretsha *(ul PR Slaveikov 5; mains 4 lv)* is ideal if you're staying at the Tourist Hotel (at the back) or traipsing around the Old Town.

Entertainment

From late May to early June, special events are often held at the **Roman Amphitheatre**, while the **Open-Air Theatre** *(Bunardjika Park; Hill of the Liberators)* hosts opera, music and drama throughout the summer. The **Nikolai Masalitinov Dramatic Theatre** *(ul Knyaz Aleksandâr 38)* is one of the most respected in the country.

One of the trendiest places to get down is the **Dive Club**, at the end of a lane from pl Dzhumaya – look for the distinctive aquamarine murals on the front wall. To enjoy a drink while admiring views of the Old Town, head to **Rahat Tepe Bar** *(ul Dr Chomakov)* almost at the top of Nebet Tepe hill.

Getting There & Away

Bus Every day from the **Yug bus terminal** *(bul Hristo Botev)*, diagonally opposite the train station, there are two buses each to Burgas (four hours) and Varna (six hours); one to Ruse (six hours); six to Sliven (three hours); eight to Hisarya (one hour); and three to Veliko Târnovo (4½ hours). Buses also run hourly to Karlovo (one hour), Stara Zagora (1½ hours) and Sofia (7.50 lv, 2½ hours). Every day in summer, one or two buses also leave this terminal for most resorts along the Black Sea coast.

The **Rodopi Bus Terminal** is really only accessible on foot through the underpass by the train station. From this bus terminal, four buses a day go to Karlovo, and six to eight leave for Smolyan, via Bachkovo Monastery and Pamporovo.

From the **Sever Bus Terminal** in the northern suburbs (best accessible by taxi), one bus each day goes directly to Ruse, Troyan and Koprivshtitsa.

Train Each day from the **train station** *(bul Hristo Botev)*, there are 19 trains to Sofia (express train 1st/2nd class 7.50/5.80 lv, 2½ hours), five to Burgas, four to Svilengrad, six to Karlovo and Hisarya, and five to Veliko Târnovo. Advance tickets for domestic services are sold upstairs. For international tickets, go to the **Rila Bureau** *(☎ 446 120)*, along a side street parallel to bul Hristo Botev.

Central Bulgaria

This part of the country was historically defined as the region between the Rodopi Mountains to the south and the Stara Planina further north. These days, however, central Bulgaria is determined more by the railway lines and highways between Sofia and Varna, and between Sofia and Burgas.

KOPRIVSHTITSA КОПРИВИЩТИЦА

☎ 07184 • pop 2900

This picturesque village, which is 113km east of Sofia, has been carefully preserved as an open-air museum of the Bulgarian national revival period. It oozes charm and history and boasts nearly 400 buildings of 'architectural and historical' importance (according to the Bulgarian government). Koprivshtitsa is famous as the place where, on 20 April 1876, Todor Kableshkov first proclaimed the national uprising against the Turks.

The **Tourist Information Centre** *(☎/fax 2191; e koprivshtitsa@hotmail.com; pl 20 April)* is helpful.

Six of the old, traditional homes have been turned into 'house-museums'. Admission to each costs 2.50 lv, so a combined ticket (6 lv) for all house-museums is better value. Tickets can be bought at the **souvenir shop** *(ul Gereniloto)*, just up from the tourist office, or directly from one of the house-museums.

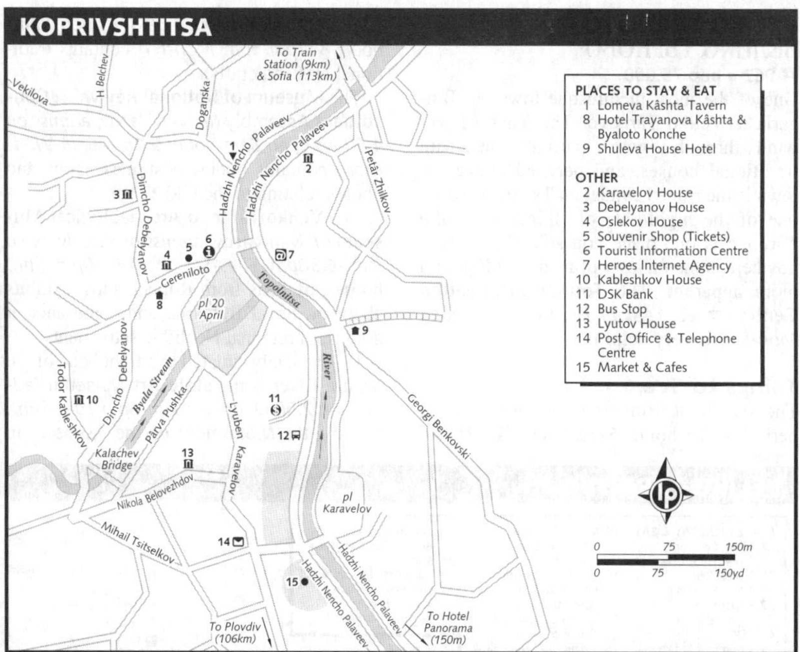

Each is open daily from 9.30am to 5.30pm in summer, but most close for one or two days (often Sunday and/or Monday) in winter.

The most interesting and best-preserved are the three-sectioned **Karavelov House** *(ul Hadzhi Nencho Palaveev 39)*, which includes a printing press; the **Oslekov House** *(ul Gereniloto 4)*, probably the best example of Bulgarian national revival period architecture in the village; and the **Lyutov House** *(ul Nikola Belovezhdov 2)*, reminiscent of the baroque homes found in Plovdiv. You can also check out **Debelyanov House** and **Kableshkov House**.

Places to Stay & Eat

The tourist office can arrange rooms *(per person 20-24 lv)* in private houses.

Shuleva House Hotel *(☎ 2122; ul Hadzhi Nencho Palaveev 37; singles/doubles with bathroom 20/25 lv)* is excellent value. The rooms are large, simple and clean, and readers have commented about the friendly staff.

Hotel Trayanova Kâshta & Byaloto Konche *(☎ 2250; ul Gereniloto 5; singles/doubles from 25/45 lv)* offers huge, quiet rooms crammed with traditional furniture.

Lomeva Kâshta Tavern *(ul Hadzhi Nencho Palaveev 42; mains from 4 lv)* is a cosy place offering traditional cuisine at reasonable prices. The fireplace and low ceilings are reminiscent of a quaint English pub.

Getting There & Away

One bus leaves Koprivshtitsa for Sofia (4.50 lv, 2½ hours) at about 6.30am from Monday to Saturday and at 2pm on Sunday. It returns to Koprivshtitsa from the Princess Hotel Bus Terminal West in Sofia at 4pm (Monday to Saturday) and at 5pm (Sunday). Another bus departs Koprivshtitsa for Plovdiv at 6.30am and returns from the Sever Bus Terminal in Plovdiv at 4.30pm. A bus schedule (in English), and a train timetable (in Bulgarian), are helpfully placed on the window of the **bus stop** *(ul Hadzhi Nencho Palaveev)*.

The train station is located about 9km north of Koprivshtitsa. To and from Sofia, five or six slow passenger trains stop at this station every day, but only one fast train from the capital stops on its way to Burgas, via Karlovo. If you're heading east, change trains at Karlovo for Plovdiv and at Tulovo for Veliko Târnovo.

VELIKO TÂRNOVO
ВЕЛИКО ТЪРНОВО

☎ 062 • pop 75,000

One of the most picturesque towns in Bulgaria is Veliko Târnovo. The Yantra River winds through a gorge, partially lined with traditional houses, and perched above the town is the ruined citadel on Tsarevets Hill – one of the highlights of Bulgaria. Veliko Târnovo is one place you should not miss: nowhere is the majesty of medieval Bulgaria more apparent. The **Tourist Information Centre** *(☎ 22 148; ul Hristo Botev; open Mon-Sat)* is very helpful.

Things to See

The excellent Bulgarian national revival period–style home **Sarafkina Kâshta** *(ul Gurko 88; admission 4.50 lv; open 8am-noon & 1pm-5pm Mon-Fri)* contains traditional arts and crafts.

The **Museum of National Revival & Constituent Assembly** *(ul Ivan Vazov; admission 4.50 lv; open 8am-noon & 1pm-6pm Wed-Mon)* contains books, costumes, icons and photos relating to the Old Town.

The **Veliko Târnovo Archaeological Museum** *(ul Ivan Vazov; admission 4.50 lv; open 8am-6.30pm Tues-Sat, 9am-5.30pm Sun)* houses artefacts from Roman ruins, exhibits about medieval Bulgaria, and some ancient gold from regional Neolithic settlements.

Dramatically situated in a tight bend of the Yantra River is the **State Art Museum** *(admission 2.50 lv; open 10am-6pm Tues-Sun)*. Nearby, the **Monument of the Asens** is an

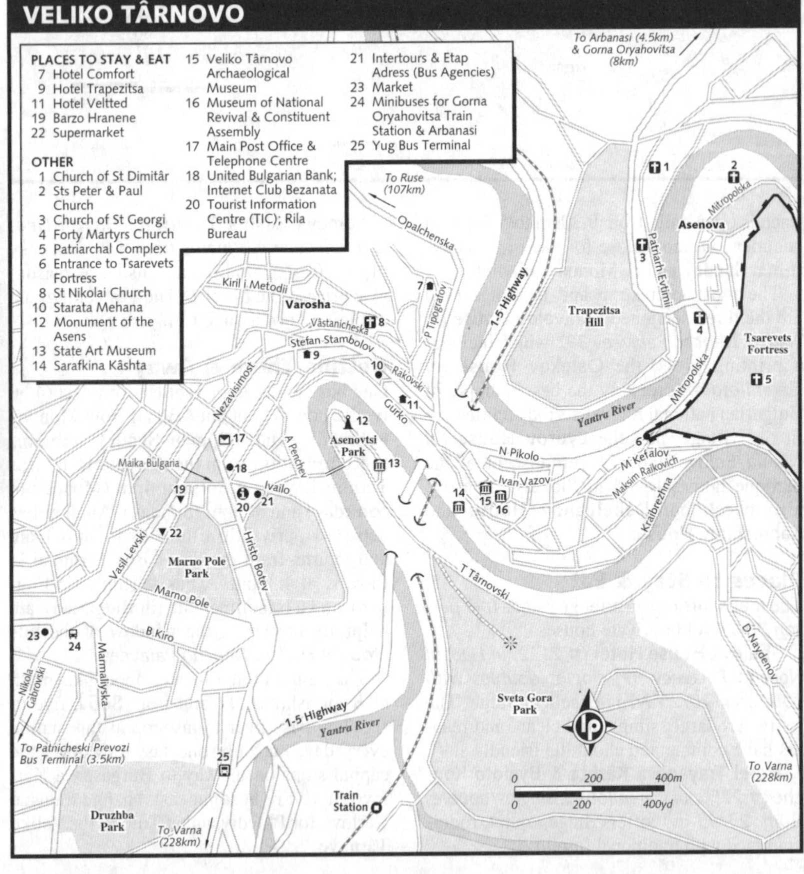

awe-inspiring commemoration of the establishment of the Second Bulgarian Empire.

The **Forty Martyrs Church** *(ul Mitropolska; admission 2 lv)* was originally built in 1230 to celebrate the victory of the Bulgars under Tsar Asen II against the Byzantines. A few blocks north, the 13th-century **Sts Peter & Paul Church** *(ul Mitropolska; admission 4 lv)* features three layers of remarkable murals.

Tsarevets Fortress *(admission 5 lv; open 8am-7pm daily Apr-Sept, 9am-5pm daily Oct-Mar)* should definitely not be missed. The hill was originally settled by the Thracians and then by the Romans, before the Byzantines built the first significant fortress between the 5th and 7th centuries. Archaeologists have so far uncovered remains of over 400 houses and 18 churches, as well as numerous monasteries, dwellings, shops, gates and towers.

The evening **Sound & Light Show** over the fortress is stunning – but it doesn't happen until a minimum of 25 people have paid 12 lv each (or at least 300 lv in total has been collected).

Places to Stay

The tourist office can provide **private rooms** *(per person 15-25 lv)* in local homes. You may also be approached by locals offering private rooms for about the same price.

Hotel Trapezitsa *(☎ 22 061, fax 621 593; ul Stefan Stambolov 79; singles/doubles 15/30 lv, with bathroom 20/40 lv)* is central, clean and outstanding value. Get a room at the back for the awesome views of the gorge.

Hotel Veltted *(☎ 29 788; ul Gurko; singles/doubles 20/30 lv)* may not be the friendliest place in town, but the rooms are lovely and it's in a quiet part of the Old Town. The hotel is accessible by steps that start from near the Starata Mehana restaurant.

Hotel Comfort *(☎/fax 23 525; ul P Tipografov 5; dorm beds 22 lv, singles/doubles with bathroom 33/44 lv)* is a new place in an appealing part of town. The rooms feature huge bathrooms and balconies with marvellous views.

Places to Eat

For a quick, cheap and filling meal it's hard to walk past any place selling doner kebabs along ul Nezavisimost. To self-cater, visit the **supermarket** *(ul Vasil Levski)*.

Barzo Hranene *(ul Vasil Levski; mains 3 lv)* has limited choice, but tasty and cheap food. Pick up a plate, point at a dish and dig in.

Getting There & Away

Bus The **Patnicheski Prevozi Bus Terminal** *(ul Nikola Gabrovski)* is about 4km west of the town centre. Numerous public buses stop here on the way to Varna, Shumen and Sofia (9 lv, four hours). Also, buses regularly leave Veliko Târnovo for Karlovo, Kazanlâk, Stara Zagora, Plovdiv and Ruse.

From the **Yug bus terminal** *(ul Hristo Botev)*, which is a 15-minute walk south of the town centre, private buses leave regularly for Sofia, Varna, Albena, Burgas, Plovdiv, Ruse and Stara Zagora. From outside their offices under Hotel Etâr (ul Ivailo 2), Etap Adress runs buses each day to Sofia, Dobrich, Varna, Albena and Balchik, and Intertours offers daily services to Burgas, Sofia and Kiten.

Train Every day from the train station, about 1km south of central Veliko Târnovo, five slow trains plod along to Plovdiv, via Stara Zagora, and 10 slow trains crawl along to Gorna Oryahovitsa. Gorna Oryahovitsa is one of the largest train stations in Bulgaria and only 8.5km north of Veliko Târnovo. Every day from this station, there are 11 trains (including four express and six fast) to Sofia, four to Varna and 11 to Ruse.

Rila Bureau *(☎ 22 042; ul Hristo Botev 13a)*, near the tourist office in Veliko Târnovo, sells tickets for domestic and international trains departing from Veliko Târnovo and Gorna Oryahovitsa.

Black Sea Coast

Foreigners have been visiting the Black Sea coast of Bulgaria since the 5th millennium BC. Initially, it was marauders from the Thracian, Roman and Greek Empires lured by the attractive coastline and trading opportunities; these days, it's masses of tourists from Germany, Poland, Russia and Britain attracted by the quality of sandy beaches, seemingly perpetual summer sunshine and variety of water sports.

Most hotels, restaurants, bars and cafés in the resorts close between mid-October and early April, while nearly all of those in the cities and larger towns stay open year-round.

BURGAS
БУРГАС

☎ 056 • pop 210,000

Burgas is primarily a port, so it has fewer museums, beaches and parks than its rival to the north, Varna. While Burgas is a fairly relaxed place with good shopping and an abundance of restaurants and outdoor cafés, for most travellers the city is a convenient base for exploring the coast.

Numerous foreign-exchange offices can be found along ul Aleksandrovska and ul Aleko Bogoridi. **Bulbank** *(ul Aleksandrovska)* has an ATM. The **ENet Internet Agency** *(ul Tsar Boris)* is cheap and reliable.

The **Archaeological Museum** *(ul Aleko Bogoridi 21; admission 2.50 lv; open 9am-5pm daily Apr-Sept, Mon-Sat Oct-Mar)* houses a small collection of antiquities and also various bits and pieces from the Roman period. The highlight is probably the wooden tomb of a Thracian king.

The **Ethnographical Museum** *(ul Slavyanska 69; admission 2.50 lv; open 9am-5pm Mon-Fri Oct-Mar, Mon-Sat rest of year)* features period furniture, regional costumes and exquisite jewellery. The small **Art Gallery** *(ul Mitropolit Simeon 24; admission 2.50 lv; open 9am-noon & 2pm-6pm Mon-Fri)* contains an eclectic collection of contemporary Bulgarian art and sculpture, as well as religious icons.

Annual events include the International Folklore Festival (late August), the Burgas Sea Song Festival (July and August) and the Flora Flower Exhibition (April and September).

BULGARIA

Places to Stay & Eat

There are two accommodation agencies in Burgas that offer rooms in private homes. **Primorets Travel** *(☎ 842 727; ul Bulair; open 9.30am-5.30pm Mon-Fri; rooms per person 12 lv)* is in a bright blue-green building opposite the Yug Bus Terminal. **Dim-ant** *(☎ 840 779, fax 843 748; ul Tsar Simeon 15; open 8am-10pm daily; rooms per person 8 lv)* is inconveniently located, but is open at weekends.

Hotel Mirazh *(☎ 838 177; ul Lermontov 48; doubles 45-50 lv)* is convenient and clean. Most of the rooms are large and each features a balcony and seats, but those facing the street are noisy during the day.

BMS *(ul Aleksandrovska; mains 3 lv)* is a cheap and cheerful cafeteria.

Fast Food Beit *(ul Aleko Bogoridi; mains from 2.50 lv)* offers a decent range of continental and Oriental food at reasonable prices. It's ideal for vegetarians who don't want to resort to yet another salad.

Getting There & Away

Most buses and minibuses use the convenient **Yug Bus Terminal** *(ul Aleksandrovska)*. To popular places along the Black Sea coast, such as Sozopol, Nesebâr and Slânchev Bryag, buses and minibuses leave every 30 to 40 minutes throughout the day. To Varna, buses leave every 30 to 40 minutes. Every day, there are also about 10 buses to Sofia (15 lv, eight hours), and regular services to Stara Zagora, Sliven and Plovdiv. **Enturtrans** *(☎ 844 708; ul Bulair)* operates daily buses to Sliven, Veliko Târnovo, Kazanlâk and Varna.

Every day from the **train station** *(ul Ivan Vazov)*, seven trains head to Sofia – five via Plovdiv and two through Karlovo. Tickets for international services are available at **Rila Bureau** *(☎ 820 523; ul Aleksandrovska 106)*, about 350m north of pl Troikata.

NESEBÂR
НЕСЕЪР

☎ 0554 • pop 9500

Perched on a small rocky island connected to the mainland by a causeway, Nesebâr is a glorious town with church ruins along cobblestone streets and a couple of worthwhile museums.

Every second or third shop seems to be a foreign-exchange office. The only bank, **Biochim Commercial Bank** *(ul Mesembria)*, changes travellers cheques and has an ATM. The **Internet Club** *(ul Tsar Simeon 2)* is inside the awkwardly named Hotel the White House.

Things to See

The **Basilica** *(ul Mitropolitska)*, now in ruins, was originally built in the early 6th century. It contained three naves and a spacious interior with high walls and wide windows. The well-preserved 14th-century **Pantokrator Church** *(ul Mesembria)* is renowned for its bell tower and unusually conspicuous urban location.

Probably the most beautiful church in Nesebâr was the **St John Aliturgetos Church** *(ul Mena)*. It was built in the mid-14th century, but mostly destroyed by an earthquake in 1913. The **Church of St John the Baptist** *(ul Mitropolitska)* was built in the 10th century and features some of Bulgaria's best-preserved murals from the 14th and 17th centuries. **St Spa's Church** *(ul Aheloi; admission 2 lv; open 10am-1pm & 2pm-5.30pm Mon-Fri, 10am-1.30pm Sat & Sun)* features more well-preserved murals.

St Stefan Church *(ul Ribarska; admission 2 lv; open 9am-noon & 2pm-6pm daily)* was built between the 10th and 12th centuries. It's almost completely covered inside with murals, and was one of the first churches in Bulgaria to be decorated with ceramics.

The city **beaches** are small and rocky, and the water is often choked with seaweed. The beach at Slânchev Bryag, only 3km away, is far superior.

Places to Stay & Eat

Kentavor 45 Travel Agency *(☎ 45 880; ⓔ tsf@94hotmail.com; rooms in a hotel/private home per person 22/15 lv)* is along a laneway that starts northeast of ul Ribarska.

Hotel Toni *(☎ 42 403; ul Kraybrezhna; doubles with bathroom from 33 lv)* features the same sort of amenities, location and views as other more-expensive hotels nearby.

Neptun Restaurant *(ul Neptun 1; mains from 6 lv)* is one of several excellent restaurants at the end of the main drag, mercifully distant from the noise and crowds.

Getting There & Away

From the bus terminal at the end of the causeway, buses and minibuses go to Burgas every 30 to 40 minutes; to Varna about six times a day; and to Sofia (17 lv, seven hours) about 10 times every day. There are several ways to reach Slânchev Bryag: catch a taxi, take a bus (which leaves every 15 minutes), or jump into a water taxi (every 30 minutes) from a spot north of the fortress walls.

VARNA ВАРНА

☎ 052 • pop 350,000

Varna is an atmospheric city on a bay hemmed in by hills. It boasts the largest and most impressive museum in Bulgaria, a marvellous seaside park, seemingly endless summer festivals, and the most extensive archaeological ruins in the country. **Bulbank** *(ul Slivnitsa)* changes travellers cheques, provides cash advances over the counter with credit cards, and offers an ATM. Oodles of foreign-exchange offices around the city centre offer competitive rates. **Cyber X Internet Club** *(ul Knyaz Boris I)* is around the corner from McDonald's.

Etap Adress and Megatours are both on the ground floor of the Cherno More Hotel complex at ul Slivnitsa 33. They are the best places to book organised tours, buy tickets for boats and private long-distance buses, and ask general questions.

Things to See

The **Roman Thermae** *(ul Khan Krum; admission 2.50 lv; open 10am-5pm Tues-Sun Apr-Sept, Mon-Fri Oct-Mar)* was built in the late 2nd century AD and is now the largest ruins in Bulgaria. The mammoth **Cathedral of the Assumption of the Virgin** *(pl Mitropolitska Simeon; admission 2.50 lv; open 6am-10pm daily)* was built between 1880 and 1886.

Over 100,000 items are housed in the 39 rooms of the magnificent **Archaeological Museum** *(ul Maria Luisa 41; admission 2.50 lv; open 10am-5pm Tues-Sun Apr-Sept, Tues-Sat Oct-Mar)*, one of the highlights of Bulgaria. All exhibits originate from the Varna area.

The **Ethnographic Museum** *(ul Panagyurishte 22; admission 2.50 lv; open 10am-5pm Tues-Sun Apr-Sept, Tues-Sat Oct-Mar)* contains large and varied displays on weaving, wine-making and fishing, as well as exhibits of regional costumes and jewellery. Varna also boasts the best suburban **beach** in Bulgaria.

Special Events

Varna hosts the renowned Varna Summer International Festival between May and October. It features outstanding events including opera, the International Ballet Competition (held in even-numbered years) and choral, jazz and folkloric music.

Places to Stay & Eat

Two agencies inside the train station offer rooms in local homes: **Astra Tour** *(☎ 605 861; ⓔ astratur@mail.vega.bg; singles/doubles 22/33 lv)* and **Isak Accommodation Bureau** *(singles/doubles 22/33 lv)*. The **Voennomorski Club** *(☎ 238 312; ul Maria Luisa 1; doubles 24 lv, singles/doubles with bathroom 25/40 lv)* is in the bright-blue building opposite the cathedral. It offers small, sparsely furnished but clean rooms in an unbeatable location.

Three Dolphins Hotel *(☎ 600 911; ul Gabrovo 27; singles/doubles with bathroom* *from 50/60 lv)* is in a quiet area near the train station. This small, homy guesthouse is great value and rates include breakfast.

Trops Kâshta *(ul Knyaz Boris I; salads 1.50 lv, mains 2.50-4 lv)* is the best place to enjoy a cheap, simple meal without needing to plough through a menu in Cyrillic.

Restaurant Arkitekta *(ul Musala; mains from 3 lv)* is based in a delightful house built during the Bulgarian national revival period. Although the helpings are not huge, it's worth visiting for the service and setting. The menu is in English.

Entertainment

For some culture, find out what's happening at the **Varna Opera House** *(pl Nezavisimost)* or the **Storya Bachvarov Dramatic Theatre** *(pl Mitropolitska Simeon)*, near the clock tower. The Open-Air Theatre and the temporary Summer Theatre, both in Primorski Park, host live music and drama. Otherwise, hit Night Club Danvi, incongruously located under the opera house.

Getting There & Away

Bus & Minibus The main **bus terminal** *(bul Vladislav Varenchik)* is 2km northwest of the city centre. From this terminal, buses to Sofia (16 lv, eight hours) leave every 45 minutes and travel via Shumen and Veliko Târnovo. Every day, there are also regular services to Burgas, Dobrich, Plovdiv, Sliven, Stara Zagora, Ruse and Durankulak (on the Romanian border). Most long-distance services are operated by private buses. Tickets for private buses can be bought at agencies in town (as well as at the bus terminal), but all services depart from the main bus terminal.

Train From the **train station** *(bul Primorski)*, six trains a day travel between Varna and Sofia – four via Gorna Oryahovitsa (for Veliko Târnovo) and Pleven, one through Plovdiv and another via Karlovo. Every day, there are also nine trains to Shumen and two each to Ruse and Dobrich. The **Rila Bureau** *(☎ 226 273; ul Preslav 13)* sells tickets for international trains and advance tickets for domestic trains.

Getting Around

The bus terminal and train station are linked by bus Nos 1, 22 and 41. Bus No 409 connects the airport with Zlatni Pyasâtsi (Golden Sands) every 15 minutes between 6am and 11pm.

Croatia

Crystal-clear seas, lush islands, unspoilt fishing villages, beaches, vineyards, Roman ruins and medieval walled cities are some of the many treasures that make Croatia a traveller's paradise. When Yugoslavia split apart in 1991, no less than 80% of the country's tourist resorts ended up in Croatia, mostly along the Adriatic coast. All told, almost 6000km of coastline winds around innumerable bays and inlets, rising to steep mountainous backdrops or flattening out to shingle beaches.

The war against Yugoslavia disrupted the tourist industry, which had always been Croatia's main source of cash. The country is bounding back from the slow years however and the coast is packed from mid-July to the end of August. Visit outside the peak season and Croatia's many delights are relatively tourist-free.

Croatia: the Basics

Local Name Hrvatska

Capital Zagreb

Population 4.4 million

Language Croatian

Currency 1 kuna (KN) = 100 lipa

Avoid at all costs Visiting abandoned areas in Eastern Slavonia

Protect your health by asking *Imate li kremu za sunčanje sa zaštitnim faktorom trideset?* (Do you have SPF 30 sunscreen?)

Facts about Croatia

HISTORY

With the defeat of the Austro-Hungarian empire in WWI, Croatia became part of the Kingdom of Serbs, Croats and Slovenes (Yugoslavia). After the German invasion in March 1941, a puppet government dominated by the fascist Ustaša movement was set up in Croatia. The Ustaša launched an extermination campaign that murdered 60,000 to 600,000 ethnic Serbs, Jews and Roma (Gypsies), although not all Croats supported these policies. Josip Broz, known as Maršal Tito, was himself of Croat-Slovene parentage, and tens of thousands of Croats fought bravely with his partisans. In all, about a million people died violently in a war that was fought mostly in Croatia and Bosnia-Hercegovina.

After the war, Tito became prime minister of the new Yugoslav Federation. Croatia and Slovenia moved far ahead of the southern republics economically. By Tito's death in 1980, many Croats felt the time had come for autonomy. In the free elections of 1990 the Communist Party was defeated, and on 22 December 1990 a new Croatian constitution was promulgated. However, the constitution's failure to guarantee minority rights stimulated the 600,000-strong ethnic Serb community to demand autonomy. When Croatia declared independence on 25 June 1991, the Serbian enclave of Krajina proclaimed independence from Croatia.

Heavy fighting broke out. The Yugoslav People's Army intervened under the pretext of halting ethnic violence. War between Croatians and Serbs lasted six months, during which 10,000 people died, hundreds of thousands fled and tens of thousands of homes were deliberately destroyed by Serb forces.

The EC, succumbing to pressure from Germany, recognised Croatia in January 1992. In January 1993 the Croatian army suddenly launched an offensive in southern Krajina. The Krajina Serbs vowed never to accept rule from Zagreb and in June 1993 voted overwhelmingly to join the Bosnian Serbs (and eventually Greater Serbia).

On 1 May 1995, the Croatian army and police entered and occupied western Slavonia and seized control of the region. Belgrade's silence made it clear that the Krajina Serbs had lost the support of their Yugoslav sponsors. Encouraged by this, the Croatians moved through the region and forced many Serbs out.

The Dayton agreement of December 1995 recognised Croatia's traditional borders and provided for the return of eastern Slavonia. Although stability has returned, a key provision of the agreement was the promise by the Croatian government to allow the return of Serbian refugees. Housing, local industry and agriculture in Slavonia and the Krajina were devastated by the war, however, making resettlement costly and complicated. Although Serbian refugees face a tangle of bureaucratic obstacles, Croatia's new government is finally acceding to the international community's demands and refugees are slowly trickling back.

GEOGRAPHY

Croatia is half the size of present-day Yugoslavia in area (56,538 sq km) and population. The republic swings from the Pannonian plains of Slavonia between the Sava, Drava and Danube Rivers, across hilly central Croatia to the Istrian Peninsula, then south through Dalmatia along the rugged Adriatic coast. Croatia's 1185 islands and islets are every bit as beautiful as those in Greece.

CLIMATE

The climate varies from Mediterranean along the Adriatic coast to continental inland. The high coastal mountains help to shield the coast from cold northerly winds, making for an early spring and late autumn.

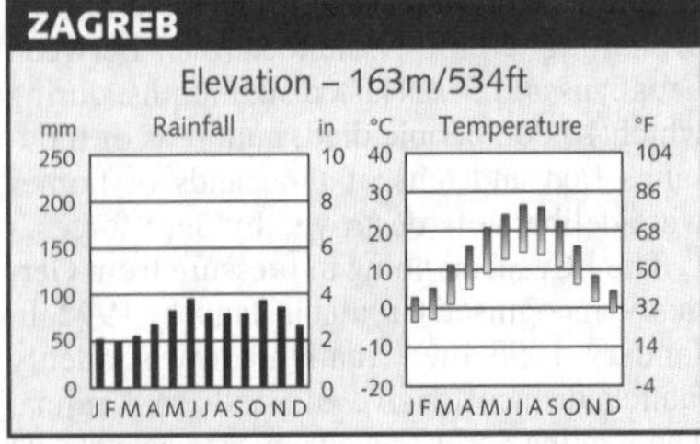

GOVERNMENT & POLITICS

Croatia is a parliamentary democracy with a presidency. Ivica Račan is prime minister and Stipe Mesic is president.

POPULATION & PEOPLE

Before the war, Croatia had a population of nearly five million, of which 78% were Croats and 12% were Serbs. Now it has a population of around 4.4 million with 201,000 Serbs, slightly less than 5%. Most live in Eastern Croatia (Slavonia).

SOCIETY & CONDUCT

The long coastline that spent centuries under Italian domination is infused with a Mediterranean insouciance, while the interior has a Central European sense of orderliness and propriety. The contrasting attitudes create a society that operates efficiently, even though there seem to be few rules and the prevailing spirit is *nema problema* (no problem).

Tidy streets and stylish clothes are rooted in the Croats' image of themselves as Western Europeans – not Yugoslavs, a word that makes Croats wince. Dressing neatly will go a long way towards a traveller gaining acceptance.

LANGUAGE

Before 1991 both Croatian and Serbian were considered dialects of a single language known as Serbo-Croatian. German is the most commonly spoken second language. Most Istrians speak Italian, and English is popular among young people.

For a basic rundown on Croatian and Serbian for travellers, see the Language chapter at the end of this book.

Facts for the Visitor

HIGHLIGHTS

Exquisitely harmonious Dubrovnik is unmissable. Vibrant Split and bustling Zagreb are also worth detours. The coastline is indented with wide bays and cosy coves where you might be tempted to cast off your bathing suit along with the many naturists that flock here each summer. All along the Adriatic coast are white-stone towns with narrow, winding streets enclosed by defensive walls.

PLANNING

May and September are great months to travel along the Adriatic coast. June is also good, but in July and August all of Europe arrives and prices soar. In April and October it may be too cool for camping, but the weather should still be fine along the coast and private rooms will be plentiful and inexpensive.

TOURIST OFFICES

The **Croatian National Tourist Board** (☎ *46 99 333, fax 45 57 827;* ⓔ *info@htz.hr; Iblerov trg 10, Importanne Gallerija, 10000 Zagreb)* is a good source of information. There are regional tourist offices that supervise tourist development, and municipal tourist offices that have free brochures and good information on local events. Some arrange private accommodation.

Tourist information is also dispensed by commercial travel agencies such as **Atlas** (W *http://atlas-croatia.com)*, Croatia Express, Generalturist and Kompas, which also arrange private rooms, sightseeing tours etc. Ask for the schedule for coastal ferries.

Croatian tourist offices abroad include:

UK (☎ 020-8563 7979) Croatian National Tourist Office, 2 Lanchesters, 162–64 Fulham Palace Rd, London W6 9ER
USA (☎ 212-279 8672) Croatian National Tourist Office, Suite 4003, 350 Fifth Ave, New York, NY 10118

VISAS & DOCUMENTS

Visitors from Australia, Canada, New Zealand, the EU and the USA do not require a visa for stays under 90 days. For other nationalities, visas are issued free of charge at Croatian consulates. Croatian authorities require all foreigners to register with the local police when they first arrive in a new area of the country, but this is normally handled by accommodation facilities.

EMBASSIES & CONSULATES

Croatian Embassies & Consulates

Croatian embassies and consulates abroad include:

Australia (☎ 02-6286 6988) 14 Jindalee Crescent, O'Malley, ACT 2601
Canada (☎ 613-562 7820) 229 Chapel St, Ottawa, Ontario K1N 7Y6
Germany (☎ 030-219 15 514) Ahornstrasse 4, Berlin 10787
New Zealand (☎ 09-836 5581) 131 Lincoln Rd, Henderson, Box 83200, Edmonton, Auckland
South Africa (☎ 012-342 1206) 1160 Church St, 0083 Colbyn, Pretoria
UK (☎ 020-7387 2022) 21 Conway St, London W1P 5HL
USA (☎ 202-588 5899) 2343 Massachusetts Ave NW, Washington, DC 20008

Embassies & Consulates in Croatia

The following addresses are in Zagreb (area code ☎ 01), unless otherwise noted:

Australia (☎ 48 36 600) Kršnjavoga 1
Bosnia-Hercegovina (☎ 46 83 761) Torbarova 9
Canada (☎ 48 81 200) Prilaz Gjure Deželića 4
Germany (☎ 61 58 105) Avenija grada Vukovara 64
New Zealand (☎ 65 20 888) Avenija Dubrovnik 15
Poland (☎ 48 34 579) Krležin Gvozd 3
Slovakia (☎ 48 48 941) Prilaz Gjure Deželića 10
UK (☎ 45 55 310) Vlaška 121, Zagreb 21000; (☎ 021-341 464) Obala hrvatskog narodnog preporoda 10, Split 21000; (☎ 020-412 916) Petilovrijenci 2, Dubrovnik 20000
USA (☎ 45 55 500) Andrije Hebranga 2
Yugoslavia (☎ 46 80 552) Mesićeva 19

CUSTOMS

Travellers can bring their personal effects into the country, along with 1L of liquor, 1L of wine, 500g of coffee, 200 cigarettes and 50mL of perfume. The import or export of kuna is limited to 2000 per person.

MONEY

The currency is the kuna. Banknotes are in denominations of 500, 200, 100, 50, 20, 10 and 5. Each kuna is divided into 100 lipa in coins of 50, 20 and 10. Many places exchange money, all with similar rates. Exchange offices may deduct a commission of 1% to change cash or travellers cheques, but some banks do not. Hungarian currency is difficult to change.

Exchange Rates

country	unit		kuna
Australia	A$1	=	4.25KN
Canada	C$1	=	4.94KN
Eurozone	€1	=	7.65KN
Japan	¥100	=	6.53KN
NZ	NZ$1	=	3.65KN
UK	UK£1	=	12.25KN
USA	US$1	=	7.83KN

American Express, MasterCard, Visa and Diners Club cards are widely accepted in large hotels, stores and many restaurants, but don't count on cards to pay for private accommodation or meals in small restaurants. ATMs accepting MasterCard, Maestro, Cirrus, Plus and Visa are available in most bus and train stations, airports, all major cities and most small towns. Many branches of Privredna Banka have ATMs that allow cash withdrawals on an American Express card.

Accommodation takes the largest chunk of a travel budget, and costs vary widely depending on the season. If you travel in March you'll quite easily find a private room for 90KN per person, but prices climb upward to double that in July and August. Count on 25KN for a meal at a self-service restaurant and 35KN to 50KN for an average intercity bus fare. It's not that hard to survive on 250KN daily if you stay in hostels, private rooms or camping grounds.

If you're served well at a restaurant, you should round up the bill, but a service charge is always included. (Don't leave money on the table.) Bar bills and taxi fares can also be rounded up. Tour guides on day excursions expect to be tipped.

A 22% Value Added Tax (VAT) is usually imposed upon most purchases and services, and is included in the price. If your purchases exceed 500KN in one shop you can claim a refund upon leaving the country. Ask the merchant for the paperwork, but don't be surprised if they don't have it.

POST & COMMUNICATIONS

Mail sent to Poste Restante, 10000 Zagreb, Croatia, is held at the post office (open 24 hours) next to the Zagreb train station. A good coastal address to use is c/o Poste Restante, Main Post Office, 21000 Split, Croatia. If you have an American Express card, most Atlas travel agencies will hold your mail.

To call Croatia from abroad, dial your international access code, ☎ 385 (Croatia's country code), the area code (without the initial zero) and the local number. When calling from one region to another within Croatia, use the initial zero.

To make a phone call from Croatia, go to the main post office. You'll need a phonecard to use public telephones. Phonecards are sold according to *impulsa* (units), and you can buy cards of 25 (15KN), 50 (25KN), 100 (40KN) and 200 (70KN) units. These can be purchased at any post office and most tobacco shops and newspaper kiosks.

CROATIA

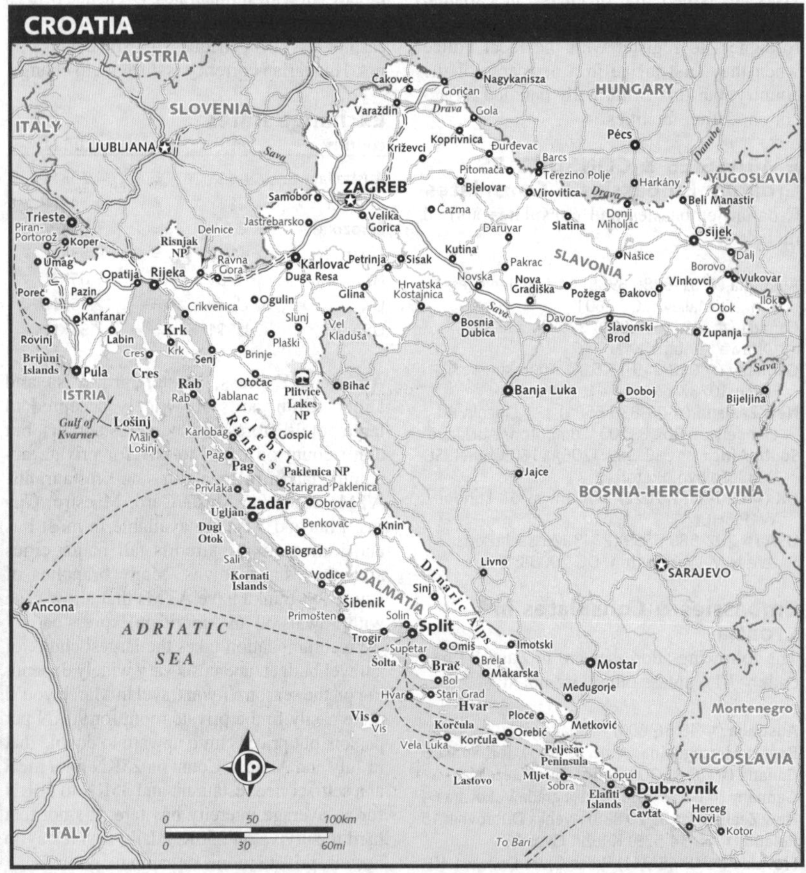

The international access code is ☎ 00. Dial ☎ 901 to place an operator-assisted call.

Internet cafés are becoming increasingly plentiful. The going rate is about 30KN per hour, and connections are usually good.

DIGITAL RESOURCES

Croatian Telecom has an on-line phone directory in English at Ⓦ *http://imenik.hinet.hr*. The useful Ⓦ *www.visit-croatia.co.uk* is a good stop for updated practical information.

BOOKS

For a comprehensive guide to Croatia, pick up Lonely Planet's *Croatia*. There's also Zoë Brân's *After Yugoslavia*, which recounts the author's recent trip through the country.

WOMEN TRAVELLERS

Women on their own usually face no problems but may be harassed and followed in the larger coastal cities. In some local bars and cafés, a woman by herself is likely to be greeted with sudden silence and cold stares. There are few rules about appropriate dress and topless sunbathing is considered acceptable.

GAY & LESBIAN TRAVELLERS

Homosexuality is legal and generally tolerated as long as it remains discreet. Public displays of affection between members of the same sex may meet with hostility, especially outside major cities. A small lesbian and gay community is developing in Zagreb.

DISABLED TRAVELLERS

Because of the number of wounded war veterans, more attention is being paid to the needs of disabled travellers. Public toilets at bus stations, train stations, airports and large public venues are usually wheelchair accessible. Large hotels are wheelchair accessible, but very little private accommodation is. Bus and train stations in Zagreb, Zadar, Rijeka, Split and Dubrovnik are wheelchair accessible, but the local Jadrolinija ferries are not. For further information, contact **Savez Organizacija Invalida Hrvatske** *(☎/fax 01 48 29 394; Savska cesta 3, 10000 Zagreb)*.

SENIOR TRAVELLERS

Although there are no transportation discounts, most museums and attractions offer the same discounts to people aged over 60 as to students. Your passport usually suffices as proof of age.

DANGERS & ANNOYANCES

The former confrontation line between Croat and federal forces is still undergoing de-mining operations. Eastern Slavonia was heavily mined and, outside of the main city of Osijek, de-mining is not yet completed. It would be unwise to stray into fields or abandoned villages.

Personal security including theft are not problems. It's highly unlikely you'll have any problems with police or military.

BUSINESS HOURS

Banking hours are 7.30am to 7pm on weekdays and 8am to noon on Saturday. Many shops are open 8am to 7pm on weekdays and until 2pm on Saturday. Along the coast, life is more relaxed; shops and offices frequently close around 1pm for an afternoon break.

PUBLIC HOLIDAYS & SPECIAL EVENTS

Public holidays are New Year's Day (1 January), Easter Monday (March/April), Labour Day (1 May), Bleiburg and Way of the Cross Victims Day (15 May), Statehood Day (30 May), Day of Antifascist Struggle (22 June), Homeland Thanksgiving Day (5 August), Feast of the Assumption (15 August), All Saints' Day (1 November) and Christmas and Feast of St Stephen (25 and 26 December).

In July and August there are summer festivals in Dubrovnik, Split and Zagreb. Mardi Gras celebrations have recently been revived in many towns with the attendant parades and festivities.

ACTIVITIES

There are countless possibilities for anyone carrying a folding sea kayak, especially among the Elafiti, and Kornati Islands Lopud makes a good launch point to explore the Elafiti Islands – there's a daily ferry from Dubrovnik. Sali on Dugi Otok is close to the

Emergencies

In the event of an emergency call ☎ 92 for police, ☎ 93 for fire, ☎ 94 for emergency medical assistance and ☎ 901 to place an operator-assisted call. Motorists can turn to the **Hrvatski Autoclub** *(HAK; Croatian Auto Club)* for help or advice – contact ☎ 987 HAK *(vučna služba)* for roadside assistance. These numbers can be dialled nationwide.

Kornati Islands and is connected by daily ferry to Zadar.

Risnjak National Park at Crni Lug, 12km west of Delnice between Zagreb and Rijeka, is a good hiking area in summer. Hiking is advisable only from late spring to early autumn. The steep gorges and beech forests of Paklenica National Park, 40km northeast of Zadar, also offer excellent hiking.

The clear waters and varied underwater life of the Adriatic have led to a flourishing dive industry along the coast. Cave diving is the real speciality in Croatia; night diving and wreck diving are also offered and there are coral reefs in some places, but in rather deep water. You must get a permit for a boat dive: go to the harbour captain in any port with your passport, certification card and 100KN. Permission is valid for a year. If you dive with a dive centre, they will take care of the paperwork. Most of the coastal resorts mentioned in this chapter have dive shops. See **Diving Croatia** (*W www.diving.hr*) for contact information.

ACCOMMODATION

Along the Croatian coast, accommodation is priced according to three seasons. Generally October to May are the cheapest months, June and September are mid-priced and peak season runs for a six-week period in July and August. Prices quoted in this chapter are for the peak period, but do not include 'residence tax', which runs from about 4KN to 7.50KN depending on the location and the season. Deduct about 25% if you come in June, the beginning of July and September; about 35% for May and October; and about 50% for all other times. Prices for Zagreb are pretty constant all year. Many hotels on the coast close in winter.

Camping

Nearly 100 camping grounds are scattered along the Croatian coast. Most operate from mid-May to September only, although a few are open in April and October. In May and late September, call ahead to make sure the camping ground is open before beginning the long trek out.

> **Get Nekked!**
>
> Some of the best camping grounds in Croatia are its many nudist sites, marked FKK. Some have secluded locations, which ensure peace and quiet – but those of modest temperaments may wish to look elsewhere, as 'dressing' *au natural* is mandatory.

Hostels

The **Croatian YHA** (*☎ 01-48 47 472, fax 48 47 474; W www.nncomp.com/hfhs/; Dežmanova 9, Zagreb*) operates youth hostels in Dubrovnik, Zadar, Zagreb and Pula open to YHA members. Nonmembers pay an additional 10KN per person daily for a stamp on a welcome card; six stamps entitle you to a membership. Prices in this chapter are for high season in July and August; prices fall the rest of the year. They can also provide information about private youth hostels in Zagreb.

Private Rooms

Private rooms in local homes are the best form of accommodation. Although you may be greeted by offers of *sobe* (rooms) as you step off your bus and boat, rooms are most often arranged by travel agencies. In a two-star room, the bathroom is shared with one other room; in a one-star room, the bathroom is shared with two other rooms or with the owner. Breakfast sometimes can be arranged for an additional 25KN. If you're travelling in a small group, it may be worthwhile getting a small apartment with cooking facilities.

It makes little sense to shop around since prices are fixed by the local tourist association. You'll pay a 30% surcharge for stays less than four nights, and sometimes 50% or even 100% more for a one-night stay, although you may be able to get them to waive the surcharge if you arrive off season. Prices in this chapter assume a four-night stay.

Hotels

Hotels are ranked from one to five stars with the vast majority in the two- and three-star range. One-star hotels have at least a telephone in the room. Prices in this chapter are for the pricey six-week period that begins in mid-July and lasts until the end of August. Breakfast is included in hotel prices.

FOOD & DRINKS

The cheapest dishes are pastas or risottos. Fish dishes are often charged by weight (220KN to 280KN a kilogram). Throughout the former Yugoslavia the breakfast of the people is *burek,* a greasy layered pie made with *mesa* (meat) or *sira* (cheese) and cut on a huge metal tray.

The Adriatic coast excels in seafood, including scampi, *prstaci* (shellfish) and Dalmatian *brodet* (mixed fish stewed with rice), all cooked in olive oil and served with boiled vegetables or *tartufe* (mushrooms) in Istria. In the Croatian interior, watch for *manistra od bobića* (beans and fresh maize soup) or *štrukle* (cottage cheese rolls). A Zagreb speciality is *štrukli* (boiled cheesecake).

It's customary to have a small glass of brandy before a meal and to accompany food with one of Croatia's fine wines. Croatia is also famous for its *šljivovica* (plum brandies), *travarica* (herbal brandies), *vinjak* (cognacs) and liqueurs such as maraschino, a cherry liqueur made in Zadar, or herbal *pelinkovac*. Italian-style espresso is popular in Croatia.

Zagreb's Ožujsko *pivo* (beer) is very good, but Karlovačko beer from Karlovac is even better. You'll probably want to practise saying *živjeli!* (cheers!).

ENTERTAINMENT

Admission to operas, operettas and concerts is reasonable. In the interior cities, winter is the best time to enjoy the theatres and concert halls. The main season at the opera houses of Split and Zagreb runs from October to May. These close for holidays in summer and the cultural scene shifts to the many summer festivals.

Discos operate in summer all over the coastal resorts and all year in the interior cities, but the best way to mix with the local population is to enjoy a leisurely coffee or ice cream in a café. With the first hint of mild weather, Croatians head for an outdoor terrace to drink, smoke and watch the passing parade. In the summer season, various resort hotels will sponsor free dances on their terraces.

Getting There & Away

AIR

Croatia Airlines *(☎ 01-48 19 633; Ⓦ www.croatiaairlines.hr; Zrinjevac 17, Zagreb)* has direct flights from Zagreb to several European cities.

LAND

Bus

Eurolines runs buses from major towns to Vienna, Amsterdam and Brussels. There are daily connections from Sarajevo (€21.50, six hours, daily) and Mostar (€10.50, three hours) to Dubrovnik; from Međugorje, Mostar and Sarajevo to Split (€16.50, seven hours); and from Sarajevo to Zagreb (€26.50, eight hours) and Rijeka (€32).

Deutsche Touring GmbH runs many buses from German cities to Croatia. Slovenia is well connected with the Istrian coast, as is Trieste, Italy (see Ⓦ www.croaziatravel.it).

There's one bus each morning from Zagreb to Belgrade (€25, six hours). The border between Yugoslavia and Croatia is open to visitors, allowing Americans, Australians, Canadians and Brits to enter visa-free.

Train

The *Ljubljana* express travels daily from Vienna to Rijeka (€68.50, eight hours), via Ljubljana, and the EuroCity *Croatia* from Vienna to Zagreb (€62.30, 6½ hours). Both travel via Maribor, Slovenia.

There are three daily trains from Munich to Zagreb (€75, nine hours), via Salzburg and Ljubljana, and a daily train from Berlin to Zagreb (€162, 16 hours).

The four daily trains from Zagreb to Budapest (€21, 6½ hours) also stop in Nagykanizsa, the first main junction inside Hungary (€9). The price is the same for one way and return.

Between Venice and Zagreb (€40, seven hours) there's an overnight direct train and a daily train via Trieste and Ljubljana.

There are seven trains daily between Zagreb and Ljubljana (3853 SIT, three hours) and seven between Rijeka and Ljubljana (2466 SIT, three hours). Five trains daily connect Zagreb with Belgrade (€16.50, six hours).

Car & Motorcycle

The main highway entry/exit points between Croatia and Hungary are Goričan (between Nagykanizsa and Varaždin), Gola (23km east of Koprivnica), Terezino Polje (opposite Barcs) and Donji Miholjac (7km south of Harkány). There are 29 crossing points to/from Slovenia. There are 23 border crossings into Bosnia-Hercegovina and 10 into Yugoslavia.

SEA

Regular boats from several companies connect Croatia with Italy.

Jadrolinija *(Rijeka ☎ 51-211 444, fax 211 485; W www.jadrolinija.hr; Riva 16 • Ancona: ☎ 071-20 71 465 • Bari: ☎ 080-52 75 439)*, Croatia's national boat line, runs car ferries from Ancona to Split (€36.50, 10 hours) and Zadar (€34, seven hours), and a line from Bari to Dubrovnik.

SEM *(Split ☎ 21-338 292, fax 21-338 291; W www.sem-marina.hr; Gat Sv Duje • Ancona ☎ 071-20 40 90)* connects Ancona with Split and Stari Grad.

SNAV *(Ancona: ☎ 071-20 76 116 • Naples: ☎ 081-76 12 348 • Split: ☎ 21 322 253; W www.snavali.com)* has a fast car ferry that links Ancona and Split in four hours and a passenger boat that connects Split, Vela Luka on Korčula and Stari Grad with the Italian cities Pescara, Vasto and Giulianova daily in summer.

La Rivera *(Rome ☎ 06 509 16 061; • Naples: ☎ 081-76 45 808; W www.lariverabus.it)* offers a combination bus and boat trip two or three times a week from Rome and Naples to Korčula (€117, 9¼ hours) and Dubrovnik (€139, 12½ hours).

Adriatica Navigazione *(Venice: ☎ 041-781 611 • Ancona: ☎ 071-20 74 334; W www.adriatica.it)* connects Ancona and Split and runs between Trieste and Rovinj (€15.49, 3½ hours).

Ustica Lines *(Venice: ☎ 041-27 12 646, Trieste: ☎ 040-67 02 711; W www.usticalines.it)* runs boats from Trieste to Pula (€22, two hours). There are also boats between Venice and Rovinj (€40, 2½ hours).

In Croatia, contact Jadroagent in Pula and **Istra Line** *(☎ 52-451 067, Partizansko 2)* in Poreč.

DEPARTURE TAX

There is an embarkment tax of €3 from Italian ports.

CROATIA

Getting Around

BUS

Bus services are excellent. At large stations, bus tickets must be purchased at the office; book ahead to be sure of a seat. Tickets for buses that arrive from somewhere else are usually purchased from the conductor. Buy a one-way ticket only or you'll be locked into one company's schedule for the return. On schedules, *vozi svaki dan* means 'every day' and *ne vozi nedjeljom ni praznikom* means 'not Sunday and public holidays'. Check W www.akz.hr for information on schedules and fares.

TRAIN

Train travel is about 15% cheaper than bus travel and often more comfortable, although slower. Local trains usually have only unreserved 2nd-class seats. Reservations may be required on express trains. 'Executive' trains have only 1st-class seats and are 40% more expensive than local trains.

On posted timetables in Croatia, the word for arrivals is *dolazak* and for departures it's *odlazak* or *polazak*. For train information check out **Croatian Railway** *(W www.hznet.hr)*.

CAR & MOTORCYCLE

Motorists require vehicle registration papers and the green insurance card to enter Croatia. **Hrvatski Autoklub** *(HAK; Croatian Auto Club)* offers help and advice. Contact the nationwide **HAK road assistance** *(vučna služba; ☎ 987)*.

The large car-rental chains represented in Croatia are Avis, Budget, Europcar and Hertz.

HITCHING

Hitching is never entirely safe, and we don't recommend it. Hitchhiking in Croatia is undependable. You'll have better luck on the islands, but in the interior cars are small and usually full.

BOAT

Year-round Jadrolinija car ferries operate along the Bari–Rijeka–Dubrovnik coastal route, stopping at Zadar, Split, and the islands Hvar, Korčula and Mljet. Services are less frequent in winter. The most scenic section is Split to Dubrovnik, which all Jadrolinija ferries cover during the day. Ferries are a lot more comfortable than buses, though considerably more expensive. You must buy tickets in advance at an agency or Jadrolinija office since they are not sold on board.

Local ferries connect the bigger offshore islands with each other and the mainland.

LOCAL TRANSPORT

Zagreb has a well-developed tram system as well as local buses, but in the rest of the country you'll only find buses. In major cities such as Rijeka, Split, Zadar and Dubrovnik, buses run about every 20 minutes, and less often on Sunday. Small medieval towns along the coast are generally closed to traffic and have infrequent links to outlying suburbs.

Taxis are available in all cities and towns, but must be called or boarded at a taxi stand. Prices are high (meters start at 25KN).

Zagreb

☎ 01 • pop 780,000

Zagreb is not a city that dazzles you at first glance – it requires time to appreciate. Spreading up from the Sava River, it sits on the southern slopes of Medvednica mountain and throbs with the energy you would expect from a capital city. The nightlife is good, a wealth of outdoor cafés are packed from the first hint of mild weather, and there's a decent assortment of museums and galleries.

The lower town is all business, with stately Austro-Hungarian buildings housing shops, restaurants and businesses. Parks, fountains and several imposing monuments lighten the sober architecture of the town centre.

Orientation

As you come out of the train station, you'll see a series of parks and pavilions directly in front of you, and the twin neo-Gothic towers of the cathedral in the distance. Trg Josip Jelačića, beyond the northern end of the parks, is the main city square. The bus station is 1km east of the train station. Tram Nos 2 and 6 run from the bus station to the nearby train station, with No 6 continuing to Trg Jelačića.

Information

Tourist Offices The **main tourist office** *(☎ 48 14 051, fax 48 14 056; ⓔ info@zagreb-touristinfo.hr; Trg Jelačića 11; open daily)* distributes city maps and free leaflets. It also sells the Zagreb Card, which costs 60KN and includes 72 hours of free transportation and a 50% discount on museums. The Croatian Auto Club (HAK) has an **information centre** *(☎ 46 40 800; Derenćinova 20)*.

A **park information office** *(☎ 46 13 586; Trg Tomislava 19)* has details on Croatia's national parks. **Jadrolinija** *(☎ 48 73 307; Zrinjevac 20)* has information on coastal ferries.

Money There are ATMs at the bus and train stations and the airport, as well as numerous locations around town. Exchange offices at the bus and train stations change money with 1.5% commission. Both the banks in the train station and the bus station accept travellers cheques.

The American Express representative in Zagreb is **Atlas travel agency** *(☎ 48 13 933; Zrinjevac 17)*.

Post & Communications Poste restante mail is held (for one month) in the post office on the eastern side of the train station. Address letters to Poste Restante, 10000 Zagreb, Croatia. This post office is also the best place to make long-distance telephone calls.

Zagreb's flashiest cybercafé is **Art Net Club** *(☎ 45 58 471; Preradovićeva 25; open 9am-11pm daily)*, which hosts frequent concerts and performances. There's also **Sublink** *(☎ 48 11 329; Teslina 12; open 9am-10pm Mon-Sat, 3pm-10pm Sun)*.

Travel Agencies The travel branch of the Croatian YHA, **Dali Travel** *(☎ 48 47 472, fax 48 47 474; ⓔ hfhs-cms@zg.hinet.hr; Dežmanova 9; open 9am-5pm Mon-Fri)*, can provide information on HI hostels throughout Croatia and make advance bookings. It also sells ISIC student cards (40KN).

Medical Services For medical aid the closest health centre is **KBC Rebro** *(☎ 23 88 888; Kišpatićeva 12; open 24hr)*, east of the city. It charges 200KN for an examination.

Things to See

Kaptol The twin neo-Gothic spires of **St Stephen's Cathedral** (1899) contains elements from the medieval cathedral on this site, destroyed by an earthquake in 1880. Remnants include 13th-century frescoes, Renaissance pews, marble altars and a baroque pulpit. The baroque **Archiepiscopal Palace** surrounds the cathedral, as do 16th-century fortifications constructed when Zagreb was threatened by the Turks.

Gradec From ul Radićeva 5, off Trg Jelačića, there's a pedestrian walkway called stube Ivana Zakmardija leads to the **Lotršćak Tower** *(open Mon-Sat)* and a **funicular railway** (1888), which connects the lower and upper towns (2KN). To the right is the

ZAGREB

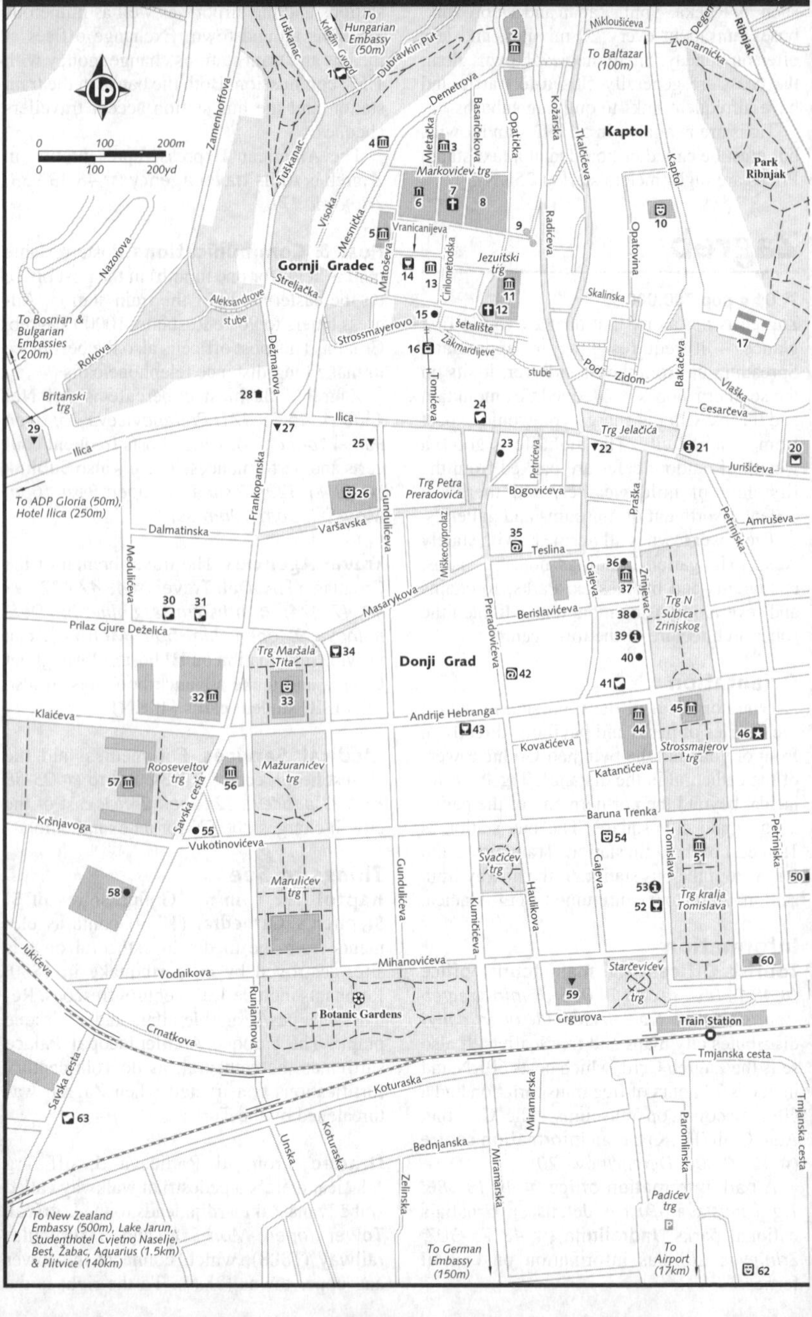

To Hungarian Embassy (50m)
Tuškanac
Krležin Gvozd
Dubravkin Put
Miklouššićeva
Degen
Ribnjak
Zvonarnička
To Baltazar (100m)
Demetrova
Basaričekova
Opatička
Kožarska
Tkalčićeva
Kaptol
Zamenhoffova
0 100 200m
0 100 200yd
Mletačka
Markovićev trg
Kaptol
Park Ribnjak
Visoka
Mesnička
Vranicanijeva
Radićeva
Opatovina
Gornji Gradec
Matoševa
Ćirilometodska
Jezuitski trg
Nazorova
Streljačka
Aleksandrove stube
Skalinska
To Bosnian & Bulgarian Embassies (200m)
Strossmayerovo šetalište
Zakmardijeve stube
Rokova
Dežmanova
Tomićeva
Pod Zidom
Bakačeva
Vlaška
Britanski trg
Ilica
Cesarčeva
Trg Jelačića
Ilica
Petrićeva
Jurišićeva
Frankopanska
Trg Petra Preradovića
Bogovićeva
Praška
Petrinjska
To ADP Gloria (50m), Hotel Ilica (250m)
Gundulićeva
Amruševa
Dalmatinska
Varšavska
Miškecovprolaz
Teslina
Medulićeva
Gajeva
Zrinjevac
Trg N Subica Zrinjskog
Masarykova
Berislavićeva
Prilaz Gjure Deželića
Preradovićeva
Trg Maršala Tita
Donji Grad
Klaićeva
Andrije Hebranga
Kovačićeva
Strossmajerov trg
Rooseveltov trg
Mažuranićev trg
Katančićeva
Savska cesta
Kršnjavoga
Baruna Trenka
Vukotinovićeva
Gundulićeva
Svačićev trg
Gajeva
Haulikova
Kumičićeva
Tomislava
Petrinjska
Marulićev trg
Trg kralja Tomislava
Jukićeva
Mihanovićeva
Vodnikova
Starčevićev trg
Runjaninova
Botanic Gardens
Grgurova
Train Station
Crnatkova
Tmjanska cesta
Savska cesta
Koturaska
Miramarska
Paromlinska
Tmjanska cesta
Unska
Koturaska
Bednjanska
Miramarska
Zelinska
Padićev trg
To New Zealand Embassy (500m), Lake Jarun, Studenthotel Cvjetno Naselje, Best, Žabac, Aquarius (1.5km) & Plitvice (140km)
To German Embassy (150m)
To Airport (17km)

1 2 3 4 5 6 7 8 9 10 11 12 13 14 15 16 17 20 21 22 23 24 25 26 27 28 29 30 31 32 33 34 35 36 37 38 39 40 41 42 43 44 45 46 50 51 52 53 54 55 56 57 58 59 60 62 63

CROATIA

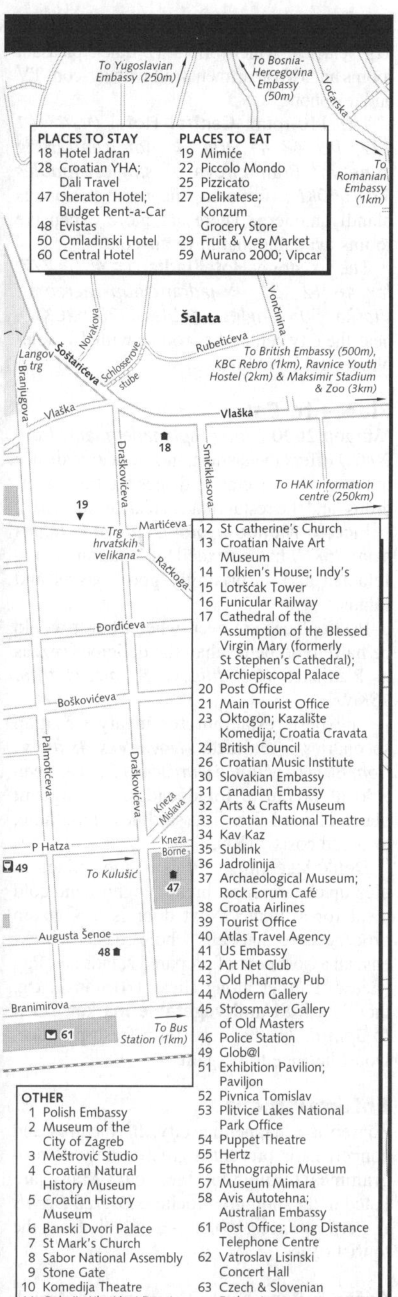

baroque **St Catherine's Church**, with Jezuitski trg beyond. The **Galerija Klovićevi Dvori** *(Jezuitski trg 4; open Tues-Sun)* is Zagreb's premier exhibition hall. Farther north, and to the right, is the 13th-century **Stone Gate**, with a painting of the Virgin.

The colourful painted-tile roof of the Gothic **St Mark's Church** *(☎ 48 51 611; Markovićev trg; open 11am-4pm & 5.30pm-7pm daily)* marks the centre of Gradec. Inside are works by Ivan Meštrović, Croatia's most famous modern sculptor. On the eastern side of St Mark's is the **Sabor** (1908), Croatia's National Assembly. To the west of St Mark's is the 18th-century **Banski Dvori Palace**, the presidential palace.

Nearby is the former **Meštrović Studio** *(☎ 48 51 123; Mletačka 8; adult/concession 20/10KN; open 9am-2pm Tues-Fri, 10am-6pm Sat)*, which now presents an excellent collection of some 100 sculptures, drawings, lithographs and furniture created by the artist. Of the area's many museums, the most interesting is the recently renovated **Museum of the City of Zagreb** *(☎ 48 51 364; Opatička 20; adult/concession 20/10KN; open 10am-6pm Tues-Fri, 10am-1pm Sat & Sun)*, with a scale model of old Gradec.

Lower Town Zagreb really is a city of museums. There are four on the parks between the train station and Trg Jelačića. The yellow **exhibition pavilion** (1897), across the park from the station, presents changing contemporary art exhibitions. The second building north, also in the park, houses the **Strossmayer Gallery of Old Masters** *(☎ 48 95 115; adult/student 20/15KN; open 10am-1pm & 5pm-7pm Tues, 10am-1pm Wed-Sun)*, with Old Master paintings. In the interior courtyard is the **Baška Slab** (1102) from the island of Krk, one of the oldest inscriptions in the Croatian language.

The **Archaeological Museum** *(☎ 48 73 101; Trg Nikole Zrinjskog 19; adult/concession 20/10KN; open 10am-5pm Tues-Fri, 10am-1pm Sat & Sun)* has a fascinating and wide-ranging display of artefacts from prehistoric times through to the medieval era. Behind the museum is a garden of Roman sculpture.

Special Events

During odd-numbered years in April there's the Zagreb Biennial of Contemporary Music,

Croatia's most important music event. Zagreb also hosts a festival of animated films during even-numbered years in JU. Croatia's largest international fairs are the Zagreb spring (mid-April) and autumn (mid-September) grand trade fairs. In July and August, the Zagreb Summer Festival presents a cycle of concerts and theatre performances on open stages in the upper town.

Places to Stay

Budget accommodation is in short supply. Private room-finding agencies are an attractive alternative, but they usually refuse telephone bookings. Since the town centre is the liveliest and most attractive part of the city, it's worthwhile trying to find central accommodation.

Hostels A new and well-run private hostel, **Ravnice Youth Hostel** *(☎/fax 23 32 325; e ravnice-youth-hostel@zg.hinet.hr; Ravnice 38d; tram Nos 4, 7, 11 & 12; beds 99KN)* offers good value in its doubles, quads and 10-bed dorm.

The noisy 215-bed **Omladinski Hotel** *(☎ 48 41 261, fax 48 41 269; Petrinjska 77; dorm beds 65KN, singles/doubles without bath 149/197KN, with bath 202/267KN; checkout 9am, open year-round)* is near the train station.

Studenthotel Cvjetno Naselje *(☎ 45 93 587; tram Nos 4, 5, 14, 16 or 17 southwest on Savska cesta to 'Vjesnik'; singles/doubles 240/360KN, students 165-230KN)* is off Slavonska avenija in the south of the city. The rooms are good, each with a private bathroom. Cvjetno Naselje is available to visitors only from mid-July to the end of September.

Private Rooms Close to the train station is **Evistas** *(☎ 48 39 554, fax 48 39 543; e evistas@zg.tel.hr; Šenoina 28; rooms 254KN, studios from 365KN)*. There's a 10% surcharge for staying only one night. You could also try **ADP Gloria** *(☎ 48 23 567, fax 48 23 571; e gordana.gordic@zg.tel.hr; Britanski trg 5; doubles with private bathroom 257KN, apartments from 365KN)* in the city's west; it's wise to reserve in advance.

Hotels For small hotels, you can't do better than the stylish **Hotel Ilica** *(☎ 37 77 522, fax 37 77 622; e info@hotel-ilica.hr; Ilica 102; singles/doubles 349/449KN, twins 549KN, apartments 749KN)*, two tram stops west from Trg Jelačića, which offers 12 quiet, pleasant rooms and two apartments, all with air-con, TV and telephone.

The 110-room **Central Hotel** *(☎ 48 41 122, fax 48 41 304; e hotelcentral@zg.hinet.hr; Branimirova 3; singles/doubles 380/550KN)*, opposite the train station, is blandly modern. There are more expensive rooms available that have air-con.

The six-storey **Hotel Jadran** *(☎ 45 53 777, fax 46 12 151; e jadran@hup-zagreb.hr; Vlaška 50; singles/doubles 390/520KN)*, near the city centre, has rooms with TV, telephone and breakfast.

Places to Eat

Murano 2000 *(Hotel Esplanade; mains from 90KN)* offers the tastiest, most creative dishes in town. The vegetarian dishes are truly wondrous, and the restaurant specialises in *štrukli*.

Piccolo Mondo *(Hotel Dubrovnik; mains from 35KN)* has an excellent location on Trg Jelačića and surprisingly good pastas and salads.

Pizza places are everywhere, but it would be hard to do better than the delicious pizzas at **Pizzicato** *(Gundulićeva 4; pizzas from 18KN)*.

The best restaurant for meaty Croatian specialties is **Baltazar** *(Nova Ves 4; mains from 60KN)*. **Mimiće** *(Jurišićeva 21)* has been a local favourite for decades, turning out plates of fried fish. Ten sardines and a hunk of bread costs 11KN.

Delikatese *(Ilica 39)* is a good place to pick up cheese, fruit, bread, yoghurt and cold meat for a picnic. Next door is a Konzum grocery store that sells whole roasted chickens, an assortment of prepared salads and Pag cheese. Farther along Ilica at Britanski trg, there's a **fruit and vegetable market** *(open to 3pm daily)* that sells farm fresh produce. Don't hesitate to bargain.

Entertainment

Zagreb is a happening city. Its theatres and concert halls present a great variety of programmes throughout the year. Many are listed in the monthly brochure *Zagreb Events & Performances*, which is available from the tourist office.

Cafés & Bars The liveliest scene in Zagreb is along bar-lined Bogovićeva, just south of

Trg Jelačića, which turns into prime meet-and-greet territory each evening. Tkalčićeva, north of Trg Jelačića, attracts a slightly funkier crowd.

Pivnica Tomislav *(Trg Tomislava 18)*, facing the park in front of the train station, is a good local bar with inexpensive draught beer. **Rock Forum Café** *(Gajeva ul 13; open mid-May–mid-Sept)* occupies the rear sculpture garden of the Archaeological Museum.

One of Zagreb's most pretentious cafés is Kazališna Kavana, known as **Kav Kaz** *(Trg Maršala Tita)*, opposite the Croatian National Theatre.

Old Pharmacy Pub *(Andrije Hebranga 11a)* was once a pharmacy but now dispenses healthy doses of beer and spirits in a congenial environment. For a bit more of an offbeat experience, try **Tolkien's House** *(Vranicanijeva 8)*, decorated in the style of JRR Tolkien's books. Next door, **Indy's** *(Vranicanijeva 4)* presents a dazzling assortment of cocktails on an outdoor terrace.

Discos & Clubs A casual, funky rock club, **Kulušić** *(Hrvojeva 6)* offers occasional live bands, fashion shows and record promos, as well as standard disco fare.

A lot of the night action happens around Lake Jarun in the southwestern corner of the city. Take tram No 17 to the Jarun stop. Try **Best** *(☎ 36 91 601; Horvaćanski zavoj bb; open 10pm-4am Fri & Sat)*, **Žabac** *(Jarunska ul bb)* or **Aquarius** *(☎ 36 40 231; open 10pm-4am Wed-Sun)* on Lake Jarun. In town, **Sokol klub** *(☎ 48 28 510; Trg Maršala Tita 6; admission free before midnight; open 10pm-4am Wed-Sun)*, across the street from the Ethnographic Museum, is a more polished place to dance till dawn. **Glob@l** *(☎ 48 76 146; P Hatza 14)* is a friendly, relaxed spot that welcomes gays and straights.

Theatres Tickets are usually available at the venues, even for the best shows. A small office marked 'Kazalište Komedija' (look for the posters) also sells theatre tickets; it's in the Oktogon, a passage connecting Trg Petra Preradovićeva to Ilica 3.

The neo-baroque **Croatian National Theatre** *(☎ 48 28 532; Trg Maršala Tita 15; box office open 10am-1pm & 5pm-7.30pm Mon-Fri, 10am-1pm Sat, half-hour before performances Sun)* was established in 1895. It stages opera and ballet performances. **Komedija Theatre** *(☎ 48 14 566; Kaptol 9)*, near the cathedral, stages operettas and musicals. The ticket office of **Vatroslav Lisinski Concert Hall** *(☎ 61 21 166)* is just south of the train station.

Concerts also take place at the **Croatian Music Institute** *(☎ 48 30 822; Gundulićeva 6a)* off Ilica.

Getting There & Away

Air See the Getting There & Away section earlier in this chapter.

Bus Zagreb's big, modern bus station has a large, enclosed waiting room and a number of stores, including grocery shops. Buy most international tickets at window Nos 17 to 20. Buy an advance ticket at the station if you're travelling long distances.

The following domestic buses depart from Zagreb:

destination	cost (KN)	duration (hrs)	frequency (per day)
Dubrovnik	195	11	7
Korčula	209	12	1
Krk	126	5	3
Ljubljana	150	2½	5
Osijek	95	4	6
Plitvice	72	2½	19
Poreč	120–155	5	6
Pula	122–147	7	13
Rab	138	6	2
Rijeka	100	4	21
Rovinj	133–146	5–8	8
Split	120–132	7–9	27
Varaždin	50	1¾	20
Zadar	94–110	5	20

Train The following domestic trains depart from Zagreb:

destination	cost (KN)	duration (hrs)	frequency (per day)
Osijek	88	4½	4
Pula	114	5½	2
Rijeka	77	5	5
Split	131	9	3-4
Varaždin	45	3	13
Zadar	131	11	2

Both daily trains to Zadar (131KN, 11 hours) stop at Knin. Reservations are required on fast InterCity (IC) trains and there's a supplement that costs from 5KN to 15KN for fast or express trains.

Getting Around

To/From the Airport The Croatia Airlines bus to Zagreb airport, 17km southeast of Zagreb, leaves from the bus station every half-hour or hour from about 5.30am to 7.30pm, depending on flights, and returns from the airport on about the same schedule (30KN). A taxi costs about 250KN.

Public Transport Public transport is based on an efficient but overcrowded network of trams. Nos 3 and 8 don't run weekends.

Buy tickets at newspaper kiosks for 6KN or from the driver for 7KN. You can use your ticket for transfers within 90 minutes, but only in one direction.

A *dnevna karta* (day ticket), valid on all public transport until 4am the next morning, is available for 16KN at most Vjesnik or Tisak news outlets.

Car Major car-rental companies include **Budget Rent-a-Car** *(☎ 45 54 936)* in the Hotel Sheraton, **Avis Autotehna** *(☎ 48 36 006)* at the Hotel Opera, and **Hertz** *(☎ 48 46 777; Vukotinovićeva 1)*. Local companies usually have lower rates. Try **Vipcar** *(☎ 45 72 148, Mihanovićeva 1)* at the Hotel Esplanade.

Taxi Zagreb's taxis all have meters that begin at a whopping 25KN and then ring up 7KN per kilometre. All day Sunday and other nights from 10pm to 5am there's a 20% surcharge.

Istria (Istra)

Istria, the heart-shaped 3600-sq-km peninsula just south of Trieste, Italy, is graced with 430km of indented shoreline and an interior of green hills, drowned valleys and fertile plains. Italy took Istria from Austria-Hungary in 1919, but then had to give it to Yugoslavia in 1947. Today the Koper-Piran strip belongs to Slovenia, while the rest is held by Croatia. Attractive Rovinj is a good base from which to explore old Roman towns such as Poreč and Pula.

ROVINJ (ROVIGNO)

☎ 052 • pop 14,200

Relaxed Rovinj, with its high peninsula topped by the great 57m-high tower of massive St Euphemia Cathedral, is perhaps the best place to visit in Istria. Wooded hills punctuated by low-rise luxury hotels surround the town, while the 13 green offshore islands of the Rovinj archipelago make for pleasant and varied views. The cobbled, inclined streets within the Old Town are charmingly picturesque. Rovinj is still a very active fishing port, so you will be able to see the local people going about their day-to-day business, and while there you should also try a swim from the rocks in the sparkling water below the Hotel Rovinj (see Places to Stay later).

Orientation & Information

The bus station is in the southeast corner of the Old Town. **Autotrans Travel Agency** changes money. The **tourist office** *(☎ 811 566, fax 816 007; W www.tzgrovinj.hr; Obala Pina Budicina 12; open daily Sept-June)* is just off Trg Maršala Tita. Central **Planet Tourist Agency** *(☎ 840 494; Sv. Križ 1)* has a few computers that you can use to access the Internet. The American Express representative is **Atlas travel agency** *(☎ 813 463)*, next to the **Hotel Park** *(V Nazora bb)*. Phone calls can be made from the post office across from the bus station.

Things to See

The **Cathedral of St Euphemia** *(open 10am-6pm daily mid-June–mid-Sept, Sun only winter)*, which completely dominates the town from its hill-top location, dates from 1736 and is the largest baroque building in Istria. It reflects the period during the 18th century when Rovinj was Istria's most populous town, an important fishing centre and the bulwark of the Venetian fleet. Inside the cathedral, don't miss the tomb of St Euphemia behind the right-hand altar. The saint's remains were brought from Constantinople in AD 800.

Take a wander along the winding narrow backstreets below the cathedral, such as **ul Grisia**, where the local artists sell their work. Each year in mid-August Rovinj's painters stage a big open-air art show in town.

When you think you have seen enough of the town, follow the waterfront down to the south past the Park Hotel to **Punta Corrente Forest Park**, which was afforested in 1890 by Baron Hütterodt, an Austrian admiral who kept a villa on Crveni otok (Red Island).

Special Events

The city's annual events include the Rovinj-Pesaro Regata (early May), the Rovinj Summer concert series (July and August) and the Rovinj Fair (August).

Places to Stay & Eat

The surcharge for a stay of less than three nights in private rooms is 50%, and one-night guests are punished with a 100% surcharge – but you should be able to bargain it away outside July and August.

Natale-Lokva *(☎ 813 365, fax 830 239; ⓔ natale@pu.tel.hr; Via Carducci 4; singles /doubles with shared bath 185/315KN)* is opposite the bus station. You could also try **Futura Travel** *(☎ 817 281; M Benussi 2)* or **Marco Polo** *(☎ 816 616; ⓦ www.marcopolo.hr; Trg Lokva 3)*. All three places have rooms at the same price. Breakfast is an additional 30KN.

Hotel Rovinj *(☎ 811 288, fax 840 757; ⓔ hotel-rovinj@pu.hinet.hr; Svetoga Križa; singles/doubles from 352/487KN)* has a splendid location overlooking the sea.

The cheapest hotel is the 192-room **Hotel Monte Mulin** *(☎ 811 512, fax 815 882; singles/doubles with half-board 241/367KN)*, on the wooded hillside overlooking the bay just beyond Hotel Park. It's about a 15-minute walk south of the bus station.

Most of the fish and spaghetti places along the harbour cater to well-heeled tourists, but **Cantinon** *(obala Alzo Rismondo 18)* sells fresh grilled fish beginning at 25KN to a local crowd. **Veli Jože** *(Svetoga Križa 1)* is a bit more expensive, but has good Isvrian dishes to try.

Picnickers can pick up supplies at the supermarket about 25m downhill from the bus station.

Getting There & Away

There's a bus from Rovinj to Pula (22KN, 1¼ hours) every hour or so. There's eight daily to Rijeka (73KN, 3½ hours), eight daily to Zagreb (140KN, five to eight hours), one daily to Koper (69KN, 1½ hours) and Split (263KN, 11¼ hours), and one daily to Dubrovnik (373KN, 17½ hours) and Ljubljana (128KN, 2½ hours, summer only). The closest train station is Kanfanar, 19km away on the Pula–Divača line.

Eurostar Travel *(☎ 813 144; Obala Pina Budicina 1)* has schedules and tickets for boats to Italy.

Dalmatia (Dalmacija)

Dalmatia occupies the central 375km of Croatia's Adriatic coast. With its Roman ruins, spectacular beaches, old fishing ports, medieval architecture and unspoiled offshore islands, it offers an unbeatable combination of hedonism and historical discovery. The ferry trip from Split to Dubrovnik is one of the classic journeys of Eastern Europe.

Zadar (ancient Zara) is northern Dalmatia's largest town, with some interesting Roman ruins and medieval churches, but most travellers head south to Split where the islands await.

SPLIT (SPALATO)

☎ 021 • pop 188,700

Split, the largest Croatian city on the Adriatic coast, is the heart of Dalmatia. Within the ancient walls of Diocletian's Palace rises the majestic cathedral, surrounded by a tangle of marble streets containing shops and businesses. The entire western end of the peninsula is a vast, wooded mountain park. High coastal mountains set against the blue Adriatic provide a striking frame.

Split achieved fame when the Roman emperor Diocletian (AD 245–313) had his retirement palace built here. When the nearby colony of Salona was abandoned in the 7th century, many of the Romanised inhabitants fled to Split and barricaded themselves behind the high palace walls, where their descendants live to this day.

Orientation & Information

The bus, train and ferry terminals are adjacent on the eastern side of the harbour, a short walk from the Old Town. Obala hrvatskog narodnog preporoda, the waterfront promenade, is your best central reference point.

The **Turistička Zajednica** *(☎/fax 342 606; ⓦ www.visitsplit.com; open Mon-Sat)*, on Peristyle, has several brochures about Split, but little more. The **Turistička Biro** *(☎/fax 342 142; ⓔ turist-birosplit@st.hinet.hr; Obala hrvatskog narodnog preporoda 12)* arranges private accommodation and sells guidebooks.

There are several ATMs around the bus and train station. The American Express representative is **Atlas travel agency** *(☎ 343 055;*

Nepotova 4). You can change money there or at any travel agency. There's also an ATM next to the **Croatia Airlines office** *(Obala hrvatskog narodnog preporoda 9)*.

Poste-restante mail can be collected at window No 7 at the **main post office** *(Kralja Tomislava 9; open 7am-8pm Mon-Fri, to 3pm Sat)*. There's a **telephone centre** *(open 7am-9pm Mon-Sat)* here. **Internet Games** *(☎ 338 548; Obala Kneza Domagoja 3)* caters to backpackers and offers an Internet connection.

Things to See

The Old Town is a vast open-air museum. **Diocletian's Palace** *(enter from Obala hrvatskog narodnog preporoda 22)*, facing the harbour, is one of the most imposing Roman ruins in existence. It was built as a strong rectangular fortress, with walls measuring 215m from east to west and 181m wide at the southernmost point and reinforced by towers. The imperial residence, temples and mausoleum were south of the main street, connecting the east and west gates. Its main features include the **Peristyle**, a picturesque colonnaded square; the **Temple of Jupiter**, now a baptistry; and the **cathedral**, originally Diocletian's mausoleum.

The west palace gate opens onto medieval Narodni trg, dominated by the 15th-century Venetian Gothic **old town hall**. Trg Braće Radića, between Narodni trg and the harbour, contains the surviving north tower of the 15th-century Venetian garrison castle, which once extended right to the water's edge. The east palace gate leads into the market area.

In the Middle Ages, the nobility and rich merchants built residences within the old palace walls; the **Papalic Palace** *(Papalićeva – also known as Žarkova – ul 5)* is now the town museum. Go through the north palace gate to see Ivan Meštrović's powerful **statue** (1929) of 10th-century Slavic religious leader Gregorius of Nin.

Museums & Galleries Most of Split's museums have been closed for the last 10 years awaiting money for renovation.

The **town museum** *(Papalićeva ul 5; adult/concession 10/5KN; open 9am-noon & 6pm-9pm Tues-Fri, 10am-noon Sat & Sun)*, east of Narodni trg, has a broad and well-displayed collection of artefacts, paintings, furniture and clothes from Split. Captions are in Croatian.

The **archaeological museum** *(Zrinjsko-Frankopanska 25; adult/student 10/5KN; open 9am-noon & 5pm-8pm Tues-Fri, 9am-noon Sat & Sun)*, north of town, is worth the walk for its exhibits devoted to burial sculpture and excavations at Salona.

The finest art museum in Split is the **Meštrović Gallery** *(Šetalište Ivana Meštrovića 46; adult/student 15/10KN; open 10am-6pm Mon-Sat, 10am-2pm Sun)*. You'll see a comprehensive, well-arranged collection of works by Ivan Meštrović, Croatia's premier modern sculptor, who built the gallery as his home in 1931–39. Bus No 12 runs to the gallery from Trg Republike every 40 minutes.

Special Events

The Split Summer Festival (mid-July to mid-August) features opera, drama, ballet and concerts on open-air stages. There's also the Feast of St Dujo (7 May), a flower show (May) and the four-day Festival of Popular Music (end of June). The traditional February Carnival has been revived and from June to September a variety of evening entertainment is presented in the Old Town.

Places to Stay & Eat

Budget travellers are out of luck. There's only one one-star hotel in the town centre, and the two-star hotels are a long bus or expensive taxi ride away. For private accommodation, you could try **Turistički Biro** or **Daluma Travel** *(☎/fax 338 439; ⓔ daluma-st@st.tel.hr; Obala Kneza Domagoja 1)*, which has two star singles/doubles for 145/265KN. The 32-room **Slavija** *(☎ 347 053, fax 591 558; Buvinova 3; singles/doubles 190/230KN, with bath 230/280KN)* has the cheapest rooms in town, but they're still overpriced considering the lack of amenities.

The best pizza in town is served at **Galija** *(Tončićeva; pizzas from 26KN)*. The vegetarian salad bar at **Ponoćno Sunce** *(Teutina 15)* is good value at 40KN. It also serves pasta and grilled meat. For excellent Dalmatian specialities at a reasonable price, try **Kod Joze** *(Sredmanuška 4; mains from 40KN)*.

The enormous **supermarket-delicatessan** *(Svačićeva 1)* has a wide selection of meat and cheese for sandwiches. The vegetable market has a wide array of fresh local produce.

Entertainment

In summer, everyone starts the evening at one of the cafés along Obala hrvatskog narodnog preporoda and then heads to the Bačvice complex on the beach. This former public bathroom offers restaurants, cafés, discos and venues for live rock and salsa. During winter, opera and ballet are presented at the **Croatian National Theatre** *(Trg Gaje Bulata; best seats about 60KN)*. It's worth attending a performance for the architecture alone.

Getting There & Away

Bus Advance bus tickets are recommended. There are buses from the main bus station beside the harbour to:

destination	cost (KN)	duration (hrs)	frequency (per day)
Dubrovnik	100	4½	12
Ljubljana	234	10	1
Međugorje	70	3	4
Mostar	74	4	4
Osijek	204	10½	1
Pula	250	10	3
Rijeka	104	8	14
Sarajevo	121	7	11
Zadar	78–88	3	26
Zagreb	130	8	27

Bus No 37 to Solin and Split airport leaves from a local bus station on Domovinskog, 1km northeast of the city centre.

Touring *(☎ 338 503; Obala Domagojeva 10)*, near the bus station represents Deutsche Touring and sells tickets to German cities.

Train There are four trains daily between Split and Zagreb (90KN to 131KN, eight to nine hours), and Split and Šibenik (31KN, 90 minutes).

Boat In the large ferry terminal opposite the bus station, **Jadrolinija** *(☎ 338 333)* handles all car ferry services. For passenger ferries, buy tickets at the Jadrolinija stall on Obala Domagoja near the train station.

Jadroagent *(☎ 338 335)*, in the ferry terminal, represents Adriatica Navigazione for connections between Split and Ancona. There's also an **SMC agency** *(☎ 338 292)* in the terminal for tickets between Ancona and Split, Hvar and Vis, as well as **SNAV** *(☎ 322 252)* for a four-hour connection to Ancona, and other connections to Pescara, Giulianova and Vasto. For information on connections to Italy see the Getting There & Away section at the beginning of this chapter.

HVAR ISLAND

☎ 021 • pop 12,600

Called the 'Croatian Madeira', Hvar receives more sunshine than anywhere else in the country. Yet the island is luxuriantly green, with brilliant patches of lavender, rosemary and heather. The fine weather is so reliable that hotels give a discount on cloudy days and a free stay if you ever see snow.

Hvar Town

Medieval Hvar lies between protective pine-covered slopes and the azure Adriatic, its Gothic palaces hidden among narrow backstreets below the 13th-century city walls. A long seaside promenade, dotted with small, rocky beaches, stretches from either end of Hvar's welcoming harbour. The traffic-free marble streets remind visitors that it was under Venetian rule that Hvar's citizens developed the fine stone-carving skills evident in a profusion of beautifully ornamented buildings.

The town centre is Trg Sv Stjepana, 100m west of the bus station. Passenger ferries tie up on Riva, the eastern quay running south.

The **tourist office** *(☎/fax 742 977, 741 059; ⓔ tzg-hvar@st.tel.hr; ⓦ www.hvar.hr; open daily)* is in the arsenal building on the corner of Trg Sv Stjepana. The travel agencies **Mengola Travel** *(☎/fax 742 099; ⓔ megola-hvar@st.tel.hr)*, on the western side of the harbour, and **Pelegrini** *(☎/fax 742 250)*, on Riva, are generally more informative.

Things to See The full flavour of medieval Hvar is best savoured on the backstreets of the Old Town. At each end of Hvar is a monastery with a prominent tower. The Dominican **Church of St Marko** at the head of the bay was largely destroyed by Turks in the 16th century, but you can visit the local **archaeological museum** *(admission 10KN; open 10am-noon daily)* in the ruins.

At the southeastern end of Hvar, the 15th-century Renaissance **Franciscan monastery** *(open 10am-noon & 5pm-7pm daily July & Aug, plus Christmas week & Holy Week)*, has a collection of Venetian paintings in the church and adjacent **museum** *(admission 10KN; open 10am-noon & 5pm-7pm Mon-Sat)*.

In the middle of Hvar is the imposing Gothic **arsenal**, its great arch visible from afar. Upstairs off the arsenal terrace is Hvar's prize, the first **municipal theatre** *(admission 10KN; open 10am-noon & 5pm-7pm daily)* in Europe (1612).

On the hill top high above Hvar town is a **Venetian fortress** (1551), well worth the climb for sweeping panoramic views.

The best **beach** is in front of the Hotel Amphora, around the western corner of the cove. Most people take a launch to the lovely offshore islands (20KN to 30KN).

Places to Stay Accommodation is extremely tight in July and August. For private accommodation, try Mengola Travel or Pelegrini. Expect to pay from 160KN to 262KN in the town centre.

Jagoda & Ante Bracanović Guesthouse *(☎ 741 416, ☎ 091 520 3796; ⓔ virgilye@yahoo.com; Poviše Škole; singles/doubles 100/190KN)* is a friendly place close to the town centre that offers six spacious rooms with private baths, balconies and kitchen access.

About 1km southwest of the town centre is the two-star **Hotel Croatia** *(☎ 742 707, fax 742 400; ⓔ croatia-hvar@st.tel.hr; singles/doubles 290/510KN)*. The hotel is surrounded by a pine grove and has easy access to a small cove. Half-board is also possible.

In town is **Slavija** *(☎ 741 820, fax 741 147; singles/doubles 444/664KN)*, right on the harbour. Reservations are handled by **Sunčani Hvar** *(☎ 741 026, fax 742 014; ⓦ www.suncanihvar.hr)*.

Places to Eat The pizzerias along the harbour offer predictable but inexpensive eating. **Bounty** *(☎ 742 565; mains from 60KN)*, next to Mengola travel agency, is the cheapest, but it's worthwhile heading upstairs from the northern side of Trg Sv Stjepana to **Macondo** *(☎ 741 851; mains from 50KN)* or, further east, to **Paradise Garden** *(☎ 741 310; mains around 75KN)*.

The **grocery store** *(Trg Sv Stjepana)* is a viable restaurant alternative and there's a morning market next to the bus station.

Getting There & Away The Jadrolinija ferries between Rijeka and Dubrovnik stop in Stari Grad before continuing to Korčula. The **Jadrolinija agency** *(☎ 741 132)* beside the landing sells tickets.

Car ferries from Split call at Stari Grad (32KN, one hour) three times daily (five in July and August) and there's an afternoon passenger boat from Split to Hvar town (23KN) that goes on to Vela Luka on Korčula Island (22KN, one hour). Buses meet all ferries that dock at Stari Grad during July and August, but in winter it's best to check with a travel agency to ensure the bus is running.

KORČULA ISLAND

☎ 020 • pop 16,200

Korčula is the largest island in an archipelago of 48 islets. Rich in vineyards and olive trees, the island was named Korkyra Melaina (Black Korčula) by the original Greek settlers because of its dense woods and plant life. The southern coast is dotted with quiet coves and small beaches linked to the interior by winding, scenic roads.

Korčula Town

With its round defensive towers and compact cluster of red-roofed houses, Korčula (Curzola in Italian) is a typical medieval Dalmatian town. The gated, walled Old Town is crisscrossed by narrow stone streets designed to protect its inhabitants from the winds swirling around the peninsula. If you didn't plan a stop in Korčula, one look from the Jadrolinija ferry will make you regret it.

The ferry drops you off either in the west harbour next to the Hotel Korčula or the east harbour next to Marko Polo Tours. The Old Town lies between the two harbours.

The **Turistička Agencija** *(☎ 711 067, fax 715 067; ⓦ www.korcula.net)* is a good source of information on the west harbour. **Atlas travel agency** *(☎ 711 231)* represents American Express, and the **Jadrolinija office** *(☎ 715 410)* is about 25m up from the west harbour. There are ATMs in town at Splitska Banka and Dubrovačka Banka.

Other than following the circuit of the former city walls or walking along the shore, sightseeing in Korčula centres on Cathedral Square. The Gothic **Cathedral of St Mark** features two paintings by Tintoretto (*Three Saints* on the altar and *Annunciation* to one side). The **treasury** *(☎ 711 049; Trg Sv Marka Statuta; admission 10KN; open 9am-7pm daily June-Aug)*, in the 14th-century Abbey Palace next to the cathedral, is worth a look; even better is the **town museum** *(☎ 711 420; Trg Sv Marka Statuta; admission 10KN; open*

CROATIA

9am-1.30pm Mon-Sat) in the 15th-century Gabriellis Palace opposite. It's said that Marco Polo was born in Korčula in 1254; for 5KN, you can climb the tower of what is believed to have been his house.

Places to Stay Korčula offers a range of accommodation, though prices are high in July and August. Turistička Agencija and Marko Polo Tours arrange private rooms, charging 155/295KN for a single/double with a private bathroom and apartments starting at 335KN.

You may get a better deal from guesthouses who are less likely to insist on a 30% surcharge for short stays. Try **Tarle** *(☎ 711 712, fax 711 243; ⓔ croatia-osiguranje1@du.tel.hr; Stalište Frana Kršinića; doubles with/without kitchen 200/170KN, apartments 440KN)*, next to the Hotel Marko Polo, about 500m southeast of the bus station, which has a pretty enclosed garden and rooms with balconies.

Closer to the Old Town is the residential neighbourhood of Sveti Nikola, about 100m west of the bus station. There you'll find **Depolo** *(☎/fax 711 621; ⓔ tereza.depolo@du .hinet.hr; doubles with/without sea view 200/160KN)*, which has spiffy rooms, some with air-con.

Other guesthouses nearby for about the same price include **Peručić** *(☎/fax 711 458; ⓔ tonci.perucic@du.hinet.hr)*, with great balconies, and the homy **Ojdanić** *(☎/fax 711 708; ⓔ roko-taxi@du.hinet.hr)*. Ratko Ojdanić also has a water taxi and a lot of experience with fishing trips around the island.

The hotel scene is uninspiring. The 330-bed **Hotel Park** *(☎ 726 004, fax 711 746; ⓔ htp-korcula@du.tel.hr; singles/doubles 425/525KN)* is the cheapest.

Places to Eat A reliable choice for fresh fish, **Adio Mare** *(mains around 80KN)* also has a charming maritime decor. **Marco Polo** *(mains from 35KN)* does a good job with Italian-style dishes and is open year-round. **Gradski Podrum** *(mains from 65KN)* serves up local specialities, such as Korčula-style fish boiled with potatoes and topped with tomato sauce. There's a supermarket next to Marko Polo tours.

Entertainment From May to September there's graceful **moreška sword dancing** *(tickets 50KN)* by the Old Town gate every Thursday at 9pm, and more often in July and August. Atlas, the Turistička Agencija or Marko Polo Tours sell tickets.

Getting There & Away There is a daily bus to Dubrovnik and Zagreb, and one bus a week to Sarajevo (145KN, eight hours). There is a regular afternoon car ferry that goes between Split and Vela Luka on the island's western end (35KN, three hours) that stops at Hvar most days. Six daily buses link Korčula town to Vela Luka (24KN, one hour), but services from Vela Luka are reduced on weekends.

Dubrovnik

☎ 020 • pop 43,770

Lord Byron called it 'the pearl of the Adriatic'; Agatha Christie spent her second honeymoon here; George Bernard Shaw said it was 'paradise on earth'. Behind the stone curtain of Dubrovnik's walls lie marble-paved squares, steps and streets ornamented with finely carved fountains and palaces. Churches, monasteries and museums recall an eventful history and a vibrant artistic tradition that is still flourishing. Beyond the walls stretch the crystal-blue waters of the southern Adriatic, sprinkled with tiny islands for the hedonistically inclined.

Founded 1300 years ago by refugees from Epidaurus in Greece, medieval Dubrovnik (Ragusa until 1918) shook off Venetian control in the 14th century and became one of Venice's more important maritime rivals. The deliberate and militarily pointless shelling of Dubrovnik by the Yugoslav army in 1991 sent shockwaves through the international community. But with a substantial amount of international aid, the famous monuments were rebuilt and resculpted, the streets paved and the clay roofs re-tiled. After a steep postwar decline, visitors are once again discovering Dubrovnik's magic.

Orientation

The Jadrolinija ferry terminal and the bus station are at Gruž, several kilometres northwest of the Old Town. There's also a bus stop outside the gates to the Old Town. The main street in the Old Town is Placa, also called Stradun. Most accommodation is on the leafy Lapad Peninsula, west of the bus station.

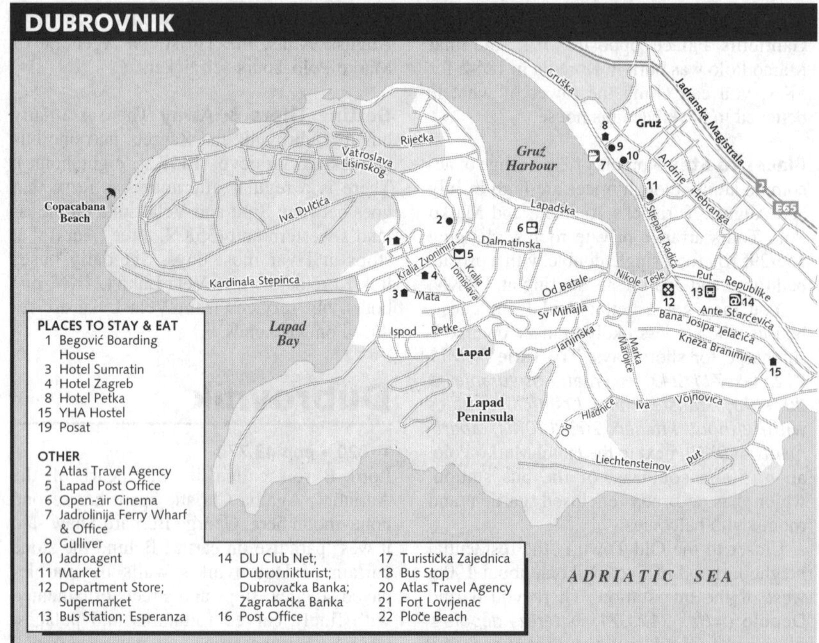

Information

Tourist Offices The main **Turistička Zajednica** *(☎ 427 591, fax 426 253; ⓔ ured.pile@tzdubrovnik.hr; Starčevića 7; open daily)* is right outside Pile gate. There's also a privately run **Tourist Information Centar** *(☎ 323 350, fax 323 351; Placa 1)* across from the Franciscan monastery in the Old Town.

Money You can change money at any travel agency or post office; there's a convenient post office near Turistička Zajednica. There are ATMs just southeast of the bus station at **Dubrovačka Banka** *(Put Republike 9)*, for Visa and Plus, and at **Zagrabačka Banka** *(Put Republike 5)*, for other cards. There are also several ATMs on Placa.

Post & Communications The **main post office** *(cnr Široka & Od Puča)* is in town, and there's another one near the town at Ante Starćevića 2, a block from Pile Gate. There's Internet access at **DU Club Net** *(☎ 356 894; Put Republike 7; open 8am-midnight daily)* and, in town, at the **Library** *(cnr Od Puća & Miha Pracata; open 8am-8.30pm Mon-Fri, 8am-1pm Sat)*.

Travel Agencies The American Express representative is **Atlas travel agency** *(☎ 442 574; Sv Đurđa 1)*, outside Pile gate next to the Old Town. The travel agency closest to the bus station is **Dubrovnikturist** *(☎ 356 959, fax 356 885; ⓔ dubrovnikturist@net.hr; Put Republike 7)* and, in town, there's **Globtour** *(☎ 323 991; Placa)*. Near the Jadrolinija dock, try **Gulliver** *(☎ 313 300, fax 419 119; Radića 32)*. **Jadroagent** *(☎ 419 009, fax 419 029; Radića 32)* handles ticketing for most international boats from Croatia.

Things to See

You'll probably begin your visit at the bus stop outside **Pile Gate**. As you enter the city, the Placa, Dubrovnik's wonderful pedestrian promenade, extends all the way to the clock tower at the other end of town. Just inside Pile Gate is the huge **Onofrio Fountain** (1438) and the **Franciscan monastery**, with a splendid cloister and the third-oldest functioning pharmacy (since 1391) in Europe. The **monastery museum** *(adult/concession 5/3KN; open 9am-4pm daily)* presents a collection of liturgical objects, paintings and pharmacy equipment.

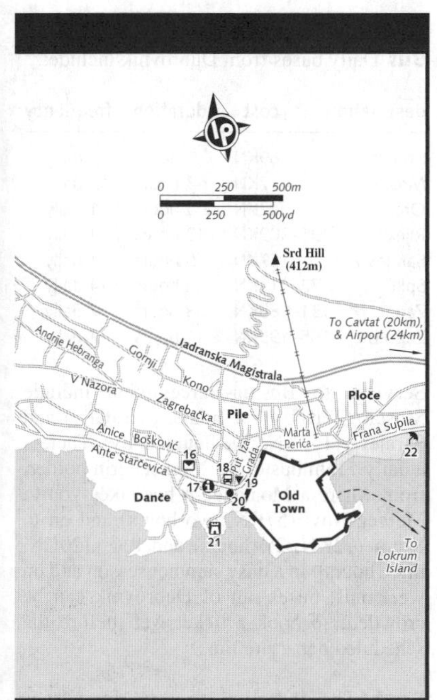

In front of the clock tower, at the eastern end of Placa, you'll find the **Orlando Column** (1419). On opposite sides of Orlando are the 16th-century **Sponza Palace** and **St Blaise's Church**, a lovely Italian baroque building.

At the end of the broad street beside St Blaise, Pred Dvorom, is the baroque **Cathedral of the Assumption of the Virgin** and, between the two churches, the Gothic **Rector's Palace** *(adult/concession 15/10KN; open 9am-2pm Mon-Sat)*, built in 1441.

As you proceed up Placa, make a detour to the **Museum of the Orthodox Church** *(adult/concession 10/5KN; open 9am-1pm Mon-Sat)* for a look at a fascinating collection of 15th- to 19th-century icons.

By this time you'll be ready for a walk around the **city walls** *(adult/concession 15/5KN; open 9am-7pm daily)*, which have entrances just inside Pile Gate, across from the Dominican monastery and near Fort St John. These powerful walls are the finest in the world and Dubrovnik's main claim to fame. The views are great – this walk could be the high point of your visit.

Whichever way you go, you'll notice the 14th-century **Dominican monastery** *(adult/concession 10/5KN; open 9am-6pm daily)* in the northeastern corner of the city, whose forbidding fortress-like exterior shelters a rich trove of paintings from Dubrovnik's finest 15th- and 16th-century artists.

The closest beach to the Old Town, Ploče, is outside Ploče Gate. There are also hotel beaches on the **Lapad Peninsula**.

An even better option is to take the ferry that shuttles half-hourly in summer to lush **Lokrum Island** *(25KN return)*, a national park with a rocky nudist beach, a botanical garden and the ruins of a medieval Benedictine monastery.

Special Events

The Dubrovnik Summer Festival from mid-July to mid-August is a major cultural event, with over 100 performances at different venues in the Old Town. The Feast of St Blaise (3 February) and carnival (February) are also celebrated.

Places to Stay

Hostels & Private Rooms The **YHA hostel** *(☎ 423 241, fax 412 592; B&B/half-board 90/120KN)*, up Vinka Sagrestana from Bana Josipa Jelačića 17, is a party place. Agencies that handle private accommodation include Atlas, Dubrovnikturist, Globtour and Gulliver. The Turistička Zajednica will put you in touch with proprietors, but does not make reservations. In high season, prices are about 93/76KN per person for rooms with private/shared bathroom, with a 30% surcharge for single occupancy.

Hotels The most personal and original accommodation in the Old Town is **Apartments van Bloemen** *(☎ 323 433, ☎ 91 33 24 106; e marc.van-bloemen@du.hinet.hr; Bandureva 1; apartments 680KN)* offering four beautifully decorated apartments, with air-con, that sleep three people.

Most hotels are in Lapad. Bus No 6 runs from the Old Town and the bus station to Lapad. From the Jadrolinija wharf, take bus No 7b. **Begović Boarding House** *(☎ 435 191; Primorska 17; rooms per person 100KN, apartments per person 135KN)* is a friendly establishment that has three rooms with shared bathroom and three small apartments.

Hotel Sumratin *(☎ 436 333, fax 436 006; singles/doubles 278/452KN)*, with a lift and parking, and **Hotel Zagreb** *(☎ 436 146, fax*

436 006; singles/doubles 307/510KN) are near each other in a tranquil part of Lapad.

The renovated **Hotel Petka** *(☎ 418 008, fax 418 058; Obala Stjepana Radića 38; singles/doubles from 320/470KN)*, opposite the Jadrolinija ferry landing, has 104 nondescript rooms with air-con.

Places to Eat

The dining scene in the Old Town is unstupendous. Vegetarians will enjoy the Italian-influenced **Arka** *(Uz Jezuite bb; mains from 40KN)*. **Express** *(Kaboge 1; mains from 16KN)* is a self-service restaurant that serves up freshly prepared food at unbeatable prices. **Posat** *(Uz Posat 1; mains from 50KN)* is the place for a romantic dinner.

The cheapest way to fill up in Dubrovnik is at a local supermarket, such as the one in the department store near the bus station.

Entertainment

Esperanza *(☎ 357 144; Put Republike 30; open 10pm-4am nightly)*, next to the bus station, is a popular disco, and there is Jelačića, dubbed 'Bourbon St' which has a cluster of clubs on either side of the youth hostel. **Troubadur** *(☎ 412 154; Gundulićeva)*, in the Old Town, is a local favourite for live music. Ask at the tourist office about concerts and folk dancing.

Getting There & Away

Bus Daily buses from Dubrovnik include:

destination	cost	duration	frequency
Korčula	69KN	3 hours	1 daily
Mostar	77KN	3 hours	2 daily
Orebić	42KN	2½ hours	1 daily
Rijeka	295–309KN	12 hours	4 daily
Sarajevo	157KN	5 hours	1 daily
Split	72–111KN	4½ hours	14 daily
Zadar	131–185KN	8 hours	7 daily
Zagreb	165–199KN	11 hours	7 daily

Services to Bosnia-Hercegovina include Mostar (77KN, three hours, two daily) and Sarajevo (157KN, five hours, daily). There's a daily 11am bus to the Montenegrin border, from where a Montenegro bus takes you to Merceg-Novi (57KN, two hours) and on to Kotor (72KN, 2½ hours) and Bar (120KN, three hours). In a busy summer season and on weekends, buses out of Dubrovnik can be crowded, so book a ticket well before the scheduled departure time.

Boat The Jadrolinija coastal ferry runs north to Hvar, Split, Zadar and Rijeka. General information on domestic ferries is available from **Jadrolinija** *(☎ 418 000; Obala S Radića 40)*.

Cyprus

Legendary birthplace of Aphrodite, Cyprus is the Mediterranean's third-largest island. While the goddess of love might blanch at the international tension that has divided the island since 1974, the gods of fortune have bestowed the island with a variety of natural and architectural delights. Landscapes are dotted with ancient Greek and Roman ruins, and the beaches are slivers of paradise.

Close to Greece, Turkey, Jordan, Israel and Egypt, Cyprus is a useful stepping stone for those travelling between east and west. The island features an easy-going lifestyle, the crime rate is low and the sun shines a lot. What more could you want?

Cyprus: the Basics

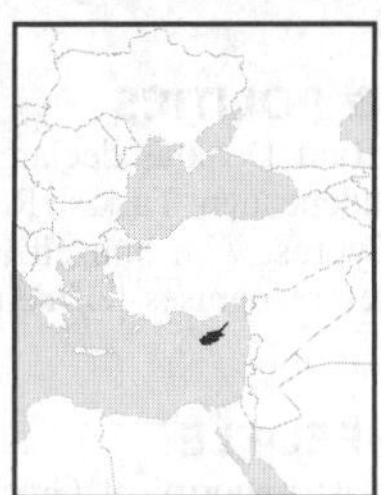

Local name Κύπρος, Kıbrıs

Capital Lefkosia (formerly Nicosia, Lefkoşa in Turkish)

Population 763,000

Languages Greek (Republic), Turkish (Northern Cyprus)

Currency 1 Cypriot pound (CY£) = 100 cents; Turkish lira (TL)

Avoid at all costs The tourist strip in Lemesos

Dispense good advice by declaiming *Pinne krasin kai eche igeian!* (Drink wine and be healthy! – Greek)

Demur on seconds by noting *O kadar çok meze yedim ki patlamak üzereyim.* (I have eaten so much meze that I'm about to burst. – Turkish)

Facts about Cyprus

HISTORY

Cyprus has been an important trading post since ancient times. As part of the Roman Empire, Cyprus enjoyed relative peace and prosperity. Later it came to be torn between the warring Byzantine and Islamic empires. The Turks took over in 1570 and ruled for 300 years. In 1878 the administration of Cyprus was ceded to Britain out of fear of Russia's expansionist policy. In return, Britain promised to aid Turkey in the event of a Russian attack.

By 1925, Cypriots were deeply frustrated by their lack of self-determination, and the first stirrings of the *enosis* movement (which wanted union with Greece) were felt. This led to intercommunal riots between Greeks and Turks. In 1954 Britain prepared a new constitution for Cyprus that was rejected by the separatist National Organisation of Cypriot Freedom Fighters (EOKA), which began guerrilla activities. Finally, in August 1960 the UK granted independence to Cyprus.

On 15 July 1974, Greece overthrew the Cypriot president. The Turks responded by invading Cyprus, and the Greeks soon withdrew. The Turkish troops continued to advance until they occupied the northern third of the island, forcing some 180,000 Greek Cypriots to flee for the safety of southern Cyprus.

Cyprus remains a divided island. From time to time violence between the two sides erupts. Unsuccessful peace talks have been held sporadically, the most recent being extended direct negotiations during the summer of 2002 between the presidents of both communities. As yet, no concrete proposal has been agreed to.

GEOGRAPHY & CLIMATE

Cyprus boasts two mountain ranges: the Kyrenia Mountains in Northern Cyprus and the Troödos Massif in the centre of the Republic in the south. Between them is the Mesaoria Plain. The island enjoys an intense

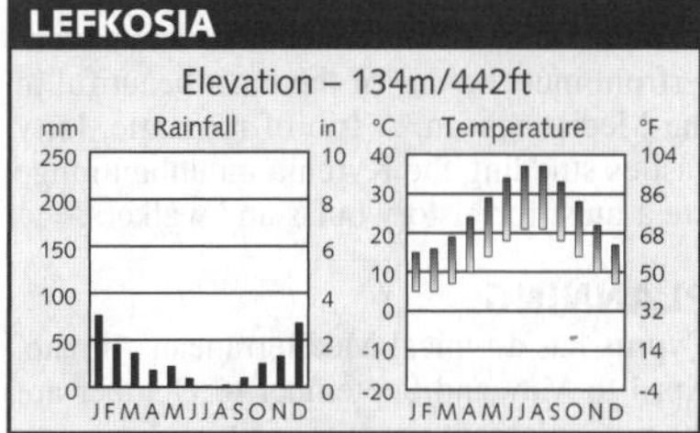

Mediterranean climate with a strongly marked seasonal rhythm. Summers are hot and dry, and last from June until September. Winters are changeable, with cold and warmer weather alternating.

GOVERNMENT & POLITICS

In November 1983, Rauf Denktaş declared northern Cyprus the independent Turkish Republic of Northern Cyprus, with himself as president. Only Turkey recognises this self-styled nation.

POPULATION & PEOPLE

Since partition, the vast majority of Greek Cypriots live in the Republic, while Turkish Cypriots and Turkish mainland colonists live in the north.

SOCIETY & CONDUCT

Cypriots are friendly, honest, patriotic and law-abiding. Family life, marriage and children still play a central role in society, as does religion.

LANGUAGE

Most Cypriots in the Republic speak English. In Northern Cyprus you'll have to brush up on your Turkish. See the Turkish and Greek language guides at the back of the book for pronunciation guidelines and useful words and phrases.

Facts for the Visitor

HIGHLIGHTS

Nine of the frescoed Byzantine churches in the Troödos Massif are deservedly on Unesco's World Heritage List. The Tombs of the Kings, dating back to the 3rd century BC, are a lot more fun than the famous Pafos Mosaics, and only half as crowded.

With the castle at one end, Kyrenia's waterfront must be one of the most beautiful in the Mediterranean. A trio of romantic, lofty castles studding the Kyrenia mountain range are a must for history buffs and walkers.

PLANNING

Cyprus has a typical Mediterranean climate. April to May and September to October are the most pleasant times to visit.

TOURIST OFFICES

The Cyprus Tourism Organisation (CTO) has offices in major towns in the Republic. Its leaflets and maps are excellent. In Northern Cyprus there are tourist offices in North Nicosia (Lefkoşa), Famagusta (Mağusa) and Kyrenia (Girne), which have free country and town maps.

The CTO has branches in most European countries, the USA, Russia, Israel and Japan. Northern Cyprus tourist offices can be found in the UK, Belgium, USA, Pakistan and Turkey; otherwise inquiries are handled by Turkish tourist offices.

VISAS & DOCUMENTS

In both the Republic and Northern Cyprus, nationals of Australia, Canada, Japan, New Zealand, Singapore, USA and EU countries can enter and stay for up to three months without a visa.

It is advisable to get immigration to stamp a separate piece of paper instead of your passport when entering Northern Cyprus.

EMBASSIES & CONSULATES

Cypriot Embassies & Consulates

The Republic of Cyprus has diplomatic representation in 27 countries, including:

Australia (☎ 02-6281 0832) 30 Beale Crescent, Deakin, ACT 2600
Germany (☎ 030-308 6830) Wallstrasse, D-10179 Berlin
Greece (☎ 21 0723 2727) Irodotou 16, GR-10675, Athens
Israel (☎ 03-525 0212) 50 Dizengoff St, 14th floor, Top Tower, Dizengoff Centre, 64322 Tel Aviv
UK & Ireland (☎ 020-7499 8272) 93 Park St, London W1Y 4ET
USA (☎ 202-462 5772) 2211 R St North West, Washington, DC, 20008

The Northern Cyprus Administration has offices in:

Canada (☎ 905-731 4000) 328 Highway 7 East, Suite 308, Richmond Hill, Ontario L4B 3P7
Germany (☎ 026-833 2748) Auf Dem Platz 3, D-53577 Neustadt Wied-Neschen
Japan (☎ 03-203 1313) 4th Floor, 6th Arai Blog-1-4, Kabohi-Cho, Shinytku-Ku, Tokyo 160
Turkey (☎ 0312-437 6031) Rabat Sokak No 20, Gaziosmanpaşa 06700, Ankara
UK (☎ 020-7631 1920) 29 Bedford Sq, London WC1B 3EG

USA (☎ 212-687 2350) 821 United Nations Plaza, 6th floor, New York, NY 10017

Embassies & Consulates in Cyprus

Countries with diplomatic representation in the Republic of Cyprus include:

Australia (☎ 2275 3001) Gonia Leoforos Stasinou 4 & Annis Komninis, 2nd floor, 1060 Lefkosia
Canada (☎ 2245 1630) Office 403, Themistokli Dervi 15, Lefkosia
Germany (☎ 2245 1145) Nikitara 10, 1080 Lefkosia
Greece (☎ 2268 0645) Leoforos Vyronos 8–10, 1513 Lefkosia
Israel (☎ 2266 4195) I Grypari 4, 1500 Lefkosia
UK (☎ 2286 1100) Alexandrou Palli, 1587 Lefkosia
USA (☎ 2277 6400) Gonia Metochiou & Ploutarchou, 2406 Egkomi, Lefkosia

Countries with diplomatic representation in Northern Cyprus include:

Australia (☎ 227 7332) Güner Türkmen Sokak 20, North Nicosia
Germany (☎ 227 5161) Kasım Sokak 15, North Nicosia
Turkey (☎ 227 2314) Bedrettin Demirel Caddesi, North Nicosia
UK (☎ 228 3861) Mehmet Akif Sokak 29, North Nicosia
USA (☎ 227 3930) Şerif Arzik Sokak, Keşluçiftlik, North Nicosia

CUSTOMS

Items which can be imported duty-free into the Republic are 250g of tobacco or the equivalent in cigarettes, 2L of wine or 1L of spirits, and one bottle of perfume not exceeding 600mL. In Northern Cyprus it is 500g of tobacco or 400 cigarettes, and 1L of spirits or 1L of wine.

MONEY

The Republic's currency is the Cyprus pound (CY£). The unit of currency in Northern Cyprus is the Turkish lira (TL).

Banks will exchange all major currencies in either cash or travellers cheques. Most shops, hotels etc in Northern Cyprus readily accept UK pounds, euros and Cyprus pounds. In the Republic you can get a cash advance on major credit cards, and there are plenty of ATMs. In Northern Cyprus cash advances are given on Visa cards at the Vakiflar and Türk banks in North Nicosia and Kyrenia; major banks in large towns have ATMs.

Exchange Rates

Exchange rates for the Turkish lira have not been given because of the high inflation rate.

country	unit		pound
Australia	A$1	=	CY£0.35
Canada	C$1	=	CY£0.40
Eurozone	€1	=	CY£0.58
Israel	NS1	=	CY£0.12
Japan	¥100	=	CY£0.50
New Zealand	NZ$1	=	CY£0.30
Turkey	TL1,000,000	=	CY£0.43
UK	£1	=	CY£0.90
USA	US$1	=	CY£0.62

Cyprus is cheaper than most Western European countries, and in Northern Cyprus costs are slightly lower still. Living frugally, you could just get by on CY£20 a day, or live quite adequately on CY£40.

If a service charge isn't included in restaurants, tip 10%. Taxi drivers and hotel porters always appreciate a small tip. Bargaining is uncommon.

POST & COMMUNICATIONS

There are poste restante services in Lefkosia (south and north), Larnaka, Pafos, Lemesos (also known as Limasill), Kyrenia and Famagusta. Mail to the north must be addressed to Mersin 10, Turkey, *not* Northern Cyprus.

In the Republic, phone booths only take phonecards available from newsagents, some banks or the Republic's telephone company (CYTA). The Republic's country code is ☎ 357.

In Northern Cyprus, most booths only take phonecards bought at a Turkish Telecom administration office or shops. To call Northern Cyprus from abroad, dial ☎ 90 (Turkey), the regional code ☎ 392, and then the actual number.

To call the North from the Republic, dial ☎ 0139 followed by the local number. To call the South from the North, call ☎ 0132 followed by the local number.

There are Internet cafés in all main towns in southern Cyprus and several in the north. The majority open late, close in the early hours of the morning and have become real

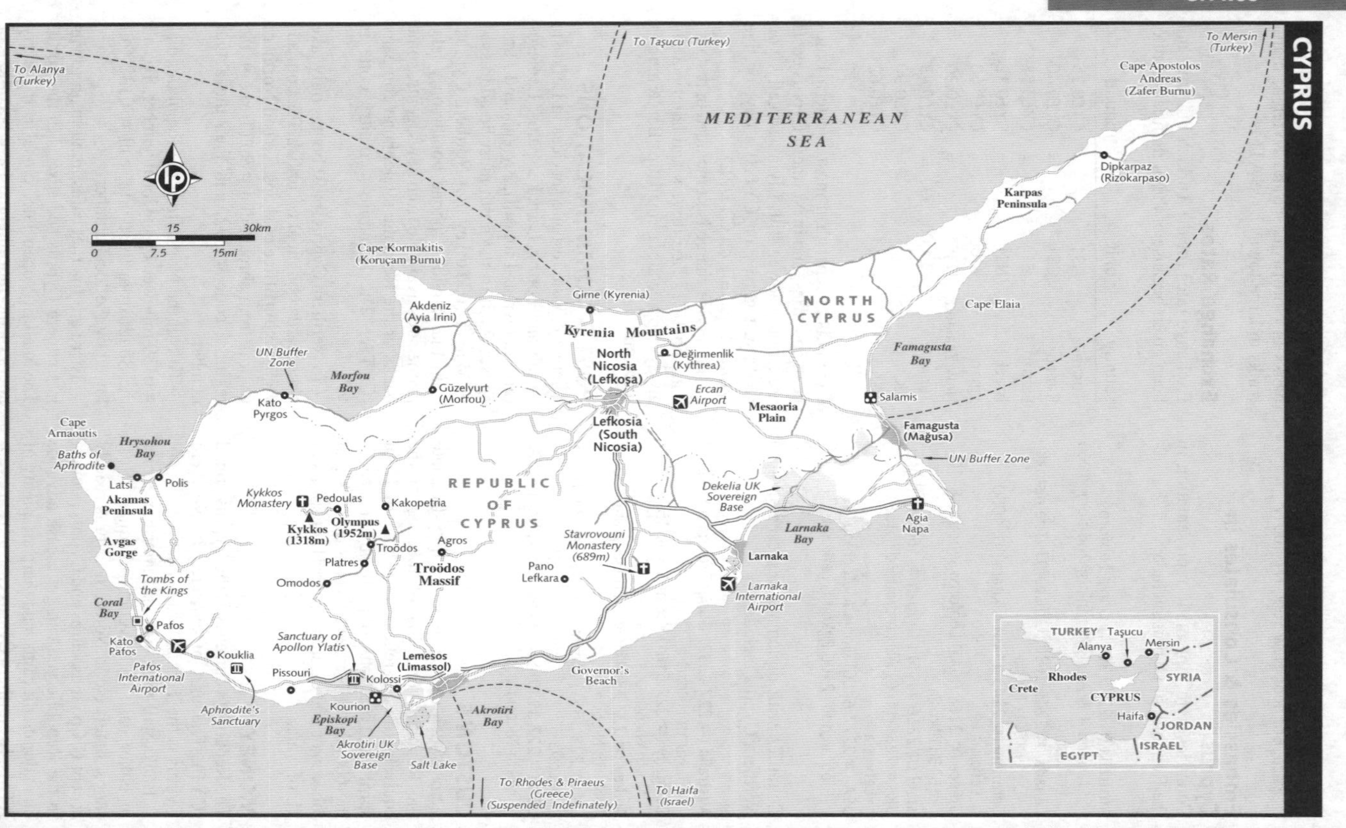
CYPRUS
MEDITERRANEAN SEA
NORTH CYPRUS
REPUBLIC OF CYPRUS
To Alanya (Turkey)
To Taşucu (Turkey)
To Mersin (Turkey)
To Rhodes & Piraeus (Greece) (Suspended Indefinately)
To Haifa (Israel)
Cape Apostolos Andreas (Zafer Burnu)
Dipkarpaz (Rizokarpaso)
Karpas Peninsula
Cape Elaia
Famagusta Bay
Salamis
Famagusta (Mağusa)
UN Buffer Zone
Agia Napa
Larnaka Bay
Larnaka
Larnaka International Airport
Dekelia UK Sovereign Base
Mesaoria Plain
Ercan Airport
Değirmenlik (Kythrea)
Kyrenia Mountains
Girne (Kyrenia)
North Nicosia (Lefkoşa)
Lefkosia (South Nicosia)
Stavrovouni Monastery (689m)
Pano Lefkara
Governor's Beach
Akrotiri Bay
Salt Lake
Akrotiri UK Sovereign Base
Lemesos (Limassol)
Kolossi
Kourion
Episkopi Bay
Sanctuary of Apollon Ylatis
Pissouri
Aphrodite's Sanctuary
Kouklia
Pafos
Pafos International Airport
Kato Pafos
Tombs of the Kings
Coral Bay
Avgas Gorge
Akamas Peninsula
Latsi
Polis
Hrysohou Bay
Baths of Aphrodite
Cape Arnaoutis
Kato Pyrgos
UN Buffer Zone
Morfou Bay
Cape Kormakitis (Koruçam Burnu)
Akdeniz (Ayia Irini)
Güzelyurt (Morfou)
Kakopetria
Agros
Troödos Massif
Troödos
Olympus (1952m)
Platres
Omodos
Pedoulas
Kykkos (1318m)
Kykkos Monastery
0 15 30km
0 7.5 15mi
TURKEY
Taşucu
Alanya
Mersin
SYRIA
Crete
Rhodes
CYPRUS
Haifa
JORDAN
ISRAEL
EGYPT

Emergencies

For urgent emergency assistance call either ☎ 199 or ☎ 112 for ambulance, fire and police services.

social centres. They all charge in the region of CY£2.50/TL1,000,000 for the first hour and CY£1/TL750,000 for subsequent hours.

DIGITAL RESOURCES

The Internet has lots of interesting information on Cyprus, and the most comprehensive site on Northern Cyprus is at W www.cypnet.com/cyradise/cyradise.html. The best site for the South is W www.cyprustourism.org.

BOOKS

Lonely Planet's *Cyprus* provides a comprehensive guide to the whole island.

WOMEN TRAVELLERS

A firm 'no thank you' should be enough to deter any unwanted interest.

GAY & LESBIAN TRAVELLERS

Homosexuality is legal in the Republic, but not in Northern Cyprus.

DISABLED TRAVELLERS

Any CTO can send you the *What the Disabled Visitor Needs to Know about Cyprus* fact sheet, which lists some useful organisations. In Northern Cyprus there are few facilities for the disabled visitor.

PUBLIC HOLIDAYS & SPECIAL EVENTS

Holidays in the Republic are the same as those in Greece, with the addition of Greek Cypriot Day (1 April) and Cyprus Independence Day (1 October). A useful publication is the *Diary of Events* available from any CTO. The Kataklysmos (Deluge) Festival is observed in most coastal cities 50 days after Easter.

Northern Cyprus observes Muslim holidays and the month of Ramadan, which means the north can sometimes shut down for periods of up to a week. It also has National Children's Day (23 April), Victory Day (30 August), Turkish Republic Day (20 October) and the Proclamation of the Turkish Republic of Northern Cyprus Day (15 November).

WORK

Throughout Cyprus, work permits can only be obtained through a prospective employer applying on your behalf. The best place to look for jobs is in the *Cyprus Weekly*. During the tourist season you can sometimes pick up bar or café work in return for bed and board (payment is rare if you don't have a permit).

ACCOMMODATION

There are seven licensed camping grounds in the Republic, mostly with limited opening times. They charge around CY£1.50 a day for a tent space and CY£1 per person per day. In the North there are four camping grounds.

There are four Hostelling International (HI) hostels in the Republic, but none in Northern Cyprus. Contact the **Cyprus Youth Hostel Association** (*☎ 2267 0027; PO Box 1328, 1506 Lefkosia*).

Prices for a double hotel room start at CY£17. Guesthouses cost between CY£10 and CY£32. In southern Cyprus you can sometimes stay overnight in monasteries, ostensibly free of charge, but a donation is expected.

FOOD & DRINKS

Cypriot food is a combination of Greek and Turkish cuisine, based primarily on meat, salad and fruit.

Cypriot wine, which is made in the villages of the Troödos, is excellent. *Zivania* (a strong spirit distilled from grape pressings) is widely available in both the Republic and Northern Cyprus.

Getting There & Around

Never attempt to cross from the North to the South if you entered Cyprus initially via the North (see Visas & Documents, earlier).

The Republic's airports are at Larnaka and Pafos. There are scheduled and charter flights from most European cities and the Middle East. The Republic's passenger ferry port is in Lemesos. Check with a travel agent to see if Salamis or Poseidon Line services to Rhodes, Piraeus (Greece) and Haifa (Israel) have been restored.

From Northern Cyprus there are two routes to mainland Turkey: Famagusta to Mersin (TL50,000,000; students TL37,500,000) and from Kyrenia to Taşucu (TL33,500,000 to TL41,500,000). During peak season there is also a twice-weekly express ferry to Alanya in Turkey (US$30, four to five hours).

On the island, urban and long-distance buses run Monday to Saturday and are operated by a host of private companies. Service taxis, which take up to eight people, are run by a central company called Travel & Express. The fares are competitive with bus travel.

Car and motorbike rental is widely available. Any car or motorcycle license is valid in the Republic. For more information contact the **Cyprus Automobile Association** *(☎ 2231 3131; Hristou Mylona 12, Lefkosia)*.

The Republic of Cyprus

In the Republic, which comprises 63% of the island, you'll find a real mix of Greek, Eastern and Western cultures.

LEFKOSIA ΛΕΥΚΩΣΙΑ, LEFKOŞA

pop 197,800

Lefkosia is bisected by the Green Line, which separates the Republic from Northern Cyprus. According to the sign at the UN-patrolled barrier at Lidras St, this is 'the last divided capital', and a visit is essential to appreciate the island's plight. The city centre is Plateia Eleftherias on the southwestern edge of the 16th-century Venetian wall.

The helpful **CTO** *(☎ 2267 4264; open Mon-Sat)* in the Old Town is in Laïki Yitonia, a fairly touristy, restored area. The **Hellenic Bank** *(Leoforos Konstantinou Paleologou 5; open 8.15am-12.30pm Mon-Fri)* is near the CTO. The **main post office** *(Plateia Eleftherias; open Mon-Sat)* can help with postal requirements. There is a cluster of public phones on Plateia Eleftherias. For Internet access, **Nicosia Palace Arcade** *(☎ 2266 3653; ⓔ n.palace@cytanet.com.cy; Leoforos Kostaki Pantelidi; open daily)* is in the Old Town.

The **police station** *(☎ 2267 1434)* in the Old Town is at the top of Lidras, by the barrier. For medical care, contact Lefkosia's **general hospital** *(☎ 2280 1400; Leoforos Nechrou)*.

Things to See & Do

From Plateia Eleftherias go along Lidras and turn right onto Ippokratous. At No 17 is the **Leventis Municipal Museum** *(admission free; open 10.30am-4.30pm Tues-Sun)*, which traces city history from prehistoric times.

Continue to the end of Ippokratous, turn left onto Thrakis and take the dogleg onto Trikoupi. Soon you'll see the **Omeriye Mosque** on your right, after which you turn right onto Patriarhou Grigoriou. On the right is the 18th-century house of **Dragoman Hatzigeorgakis** *(admission CY£0.75; open 8am-2pm Mon-Fri, 9am-1pm Sat)*, now a museum.

The next left leads to Plateia Arhiepiskopou Kyprianou, dominated by the **Archbishop's Palace** and a colossal statue of Makarios III. Here you'll find the **Byzantine Museum** *(admission CY£1; open 9am-4.30pm Mon-Fri, 9am-1pm Sat)*, with a superb collection of icons. In its grounds is the 1662 **St John's Cathedral** *(open 9am-noon Mon-Sat, 2pm-4pm Mon-Fri)*, which has the most wonderful frescoes. Continue north along Agiou Ioannou and turn right onto Thiseos, which leads to Leoforos N Foka. Turn left and you'll see the imposing **Famagusta Gate**, once the main entrance to the city.

Near the CYTA office, the **Cyprus Museum** *(admission CY£1.50; open 9am-5pm Mon-Sat, 10am-1pm Sun)* has an extraordinary collection of 2000 7th-century BC terracotta figurines found at the sanctuary of Ayia Irini, as well as the original Leda and the Swan mosaic found at Aphrodite's sanctuary near Kouklia.

Places to Stay & Eat

The very pleasant HI **Hostel** *(☎ 2267 4808; Hatzidaki 5; dorm beds CY£5)* is in a quiet part of the new town about six blocks from Plateia Eleftherias. Follow the signs from Tefkrou, off Themistokli Dervi. Solonos is good for inexpensive accommodation. The best is **Tony's Bed & Breakfast** *(☎ 2266 6752, fax 2266 2225; Solonos 13; singles/doubles CY£18/28)*, where the rooms are rather small and cost slightly more with a bathroom.

For a filling *meze* meal, head for **Zanettos Taverna** *(☎ 2276 5501; Trikoupi 65; mains CY£2.50-3)*. Also worth checking out is **1900 Paei Kairos** *(☎ 2266 7668; Pasikratous 11-15; mezes CY£2.20-4.50)*, a Greek-style restaurant where you only order the mezedes you want.

Getting There & Away

Depending on prevailing diplomatic relations between the Republic and Northern Cyprus, you're usually allowed into Northern Cyprus for one day, but check at the CTO first.

Intercity *(☎ 2266 5814; Plateia Solomou)* has seven buses a day to Lemesos (CY£1.50, two on Saturday) and six buses a day to Larnaka (CY£1.50). **Nea Amoroza** *(☎ 2693 6822; Constanza Bastion)* and **Alepa** *(☎ 2266 4636; Tripolis Bastion)* both operate at least one daily bus to Pafos (CY£3), while **Clarios** *(☎ 2275 3234; Constanza Bastion)* runs at least one bus daily to Troödos (CY£1.50) and 12 buses to Kakopetria (CY£1.20). There is also one bus, which runs at noon (Monday to Saturday) by **Solis** *(☎ 2266 6388; Tripolis Bastion)* that goes directly to Polis (CY£5). EMAN goes to Agia Napa (CY£2) Monday to Saturday at 3pm, departing from the Constanza car park.

Travel & Express *(☎ 077 7474; Podocataro Bastion)* has service taxis operating to Larnaka (CY£2.50) and Lemesos (CY£3.50).

LARNAKA ΛΑΡΝΑΚΑ

pop 69,700

Larnaka is a coastal resort built over the ancient city of Kition. Attractions include a city beach, a long waterfront promenade, an old Turkish area and a fort. North of the fort, touristy cafés line the seafront, but the other side is less spoilt and much quieter.

The **CTO** *(☎ 2465 4322; Plateia Vasileos Pavlou; open Mon-Sat)* is at the northern end of town. **Alto Internet Cafe** *(☎ 2465 9625; Grigoriou Afxentiou)* charges CY£2 per hour.

Larnaka's promenade beach is not Waikiki stuff, but the water is clean and fairly shallow. Head about 2km south to **Makenzy Beach** (McKenzie Beach) for a better deal. On Agiou Lazarou, St Lazaros (who rose from the dead) is buried at the ornate Byzantine **church of St Lazaros**. Check out the **museum** *(☎ 2465 2498; admission CY£0.50)*.

The HI **Hostel** *(☎ 2462 1188; N Rossou 27; dorm beds/family room CY£4/5)* is just east of the church. It's fairly basic, but the rooms are clean enough. In a very quiet part of town, 500m west of the fort, is the friendly two-star **Onisillos Hotel** *(☎ 2465 1100, fax 2465 4468; ⓔ onisillos@cytanet.com.cy; Onisillos 17; singles/doubles with bath CY£25/33 including breakfast)*. Rooms all have phone, TV and air-con.

To the south, beside the mosque, is **Prasino Amaxoudi** *(☎ 2462 2939; kebabs CY£2)* where you'll get good-value, freshly prepared souvlaki, doner kebab or haloumi pitta sandwiches. South of the fort on the waterfront is **Militzis Restaurant** *(☎ 2465 5867; Piyale Pasha 28; mains CY£4)* where all the locals eat.

The bus stop for Lefkosia (CY£1.50), Lemesos (CY£1.70) and Agia Napa (CY£1) is almost opposite the Dolphin Cafe Restaurant on the waterfront. On Sunday there is only a service to Agia Napa. **Travel & Express** *(☎ 077 7474)* operates service taxis to Lemesos (CY£3) and Lefkosia (CY£2.50).

LEMESOS ΛΕΜΕΣΟΣ

pop 157,600

Lemesos is Cyprus' second-largest city and the main passenger and cargo port. Behind the bland waterfront to the west is the more attractive Old Town, with crumbling houses, a mosque, old-fashioned artisans' shops and a castle. The **CTO** *(☎ 2536 2756; Spyros Araouzou 115a; open Mon-Sat)* is on the waterfront near the old harbour. There are a number of Internet cafés.

Lemesos's main attraction is the well-restored **Mediaeval Castle & Museum** *(☎ 2533 0419; admission CY£1; open 9am-5pm Mon-Sat, 10am-1pm Sun)*, where Richard the Lionheart married Berengaria of Navarre in 1191. Fourteen kilometres on the road to Pafos is **Kolossi Castle**, and a further 5km away are the extensive remains of **Kourion** and the immensely popular **Sanctuary of Apollon Ylatis**.

The cheapest hotels are clustered in the Old Town, to the east of the castle. One with large, clean rooms is **Luxor Guest House** *(☎ 2536 2265; Agiou Andreou 101; singles/doubles CY£6/12)*. A good place to lunch or snack is **Richard & Berengaria** *(☎ 2536 3863; Irinis 23; lunch CY£5.50)*, a small café just by the castle.

Intercity *(☎ 2266 5814)* has frequent daily services to Lefkosia (CY£1.50) from the Old Port and **Nea Amoroza** *(☎ 2693 6822)* to Pafos (CY£2), via Lemesos, and also from the Old Port. From here there is also a weekday bus at noon to Agros (CY£1) in the Troödos Mountains. **Intercity** *(☎ 2464 3492)* also goes to Larnaka (CY£1.70) from the Old Port.

Travel & Express *(☎ 077 7474)* has service taxis operating to Lefkosia (CY£3.50), Larnaka (CY£3) and Pafos (CY£2.75).

TROÖDOS MASSIF ΤΡΟΟΔΟΣ

The mountains of the Troödos region are beautiful, with their secluded Byzantine monasteries, 15th-century frescoed churches, small winemaking villages, pine forests and numerous walking trails. The **CTO** *(☎ 2542 1316; ⓔ platresinfo@cto.org.cy; open Mon-Sat)* is in the square at Platres. Check at the CTO for suggested walking trails and skiing information.

The **Kykkos Monastery**, 20km west of Pedoulas, is the best-known monastery. Though it dates from the 12th century, all the mosaics, frescoes and stonework are newer. In Pedoulas is the small **Church of Arhangelos**, with frescoes dating from 1474. The key to the church is at a nearby house (signposted). Another fine church is **St Nikolaos of the Roof** *(open 9am-4pm Tues-Sat, 11am-4pm Sun)*, near Kakopetria.

Even though there are hotels or rooms in almost all the villages, in July and August you'd be wise to book. In Troödos, the airy, clean **Troödos HI Hostel** *(☎ 2542 0200; dorm beds 1st/subsequent nights CY£5/4; usually open May-Oct)* is the cheapest option. There's a big common area with a kitchen. Rather more luxurious is two-star **Jubilee Hotel** *(☎ 2542 0107, fax 2267 3951; ⓔ jubilee@cytanet.com.cy; singles/doubles CY£27/38)*, where rates include breakfast. It's about 1km west of the hostel. Eat Anglicised food at **Fereos Restaurant** *(☎ 2542 0114; full kebab CY£5)* on the main drag.

In Platres, the central, clean and unpretentious **Lantern Hotel** *(☎ 9945 2307; Makariou 6; singles/doubles CY£12/18)* is a superb budget choice. Cosy **Minerva Hotel** *(☎ 2542 1731, fax 2542 1075; ⓔ minerva@globalsoftmail.com; singles/doubles CY£18/28)*, including breakfast, is on the top road, a five-minute walk from Platres' centre.

An excellent place for an evening meal is the **Village Tavern** *(☎ 2542 2777; Leoforos Makariou; mains CY£4-5)*, where the *stifado* (rich meat stew) and *kleftiko* (oven-baked lamb with herbs) are just mouth-watering.

Only expensive **taxis** currently link Platres with Lemesos (CY£17). A **bus** *(☎ 9961 8865)* from Lefkosia to Platres (via Pedoulas) runs at 12.15pm (CY£2). From Platres to Lefkosia the bus departs at 6am.

There is an additional **Clarios** *(☎ 2275 3234)* service from Lefkosia to Troödos, which leaves at 11.30am (CY£1.50, Monday to Friday). For the Kykkos Monastery, there is one bus from Lefkosia at midday (CY£1.90, Monday to Saturday), which returns the following day at 6am.

PAFOS ΠΑΦΟΣ, BAF

pop 40,000

Once the capital of Cyprus, Pafos has always been historically and mythologically important. Today it consists of the touristy Kato (lower) Pafos, on the coast, and the more pleasant and authentic Pafos, 1km inland. The **tourist office** *(☎ 2693 2841; Gladstonos 3; open Mon-Sat)* is just down from Pafos' main square. The most convenient Internet café is **Maroushia Internet** *(☎ 2694 7240; Akti Posidonos; open 10am-11pm Mon-Sat, 3pm-10pm Sun)*, just back from the seafront in Kato Pafos.

Most renowned of Pafos' many sights are the **Pafos Mosaics** *(☎ 2694 0217; admission CY£1.50; open 8am-7.30pm daily)*, the well-preserved (if dusty) floors from the villas of 3rd-century Roman nobles. Many emphasise the exploits of Dionysos, the uninhibited god of wine. On the way to the mosaics you pass the remains of a **Byzantine castle** and an **odeion** (ancient music and dance school).

About 2km north of Kato Pafos, on the coastal road to Polis, are the fascinating 3rd-century BC **Tombs of the Kings** *(☎ 2694 0295; admission CY£0.75; open 8.30am-7.30pm daily)*.

The HI **Hostel** *(☎ 2693 2588; Eleftheriou Venizelou 37; dorm beds CY£4-5)* is quite a way north of Ano Pafos centre. To get there, walk up Leoforos Evagora Pallikaridi and it's off on the right. **Trianon Hotel** *(☎ 2693 2193; Arhiepiskopou Makariou III 99; singles/doubles CY£5/12)* has bright and airy rooms, but bathroom and kitchen facilities are shared. Friendly two-star **Axiothea Hotel** *(☎ 2693 2866, fax 2694 5790; Ivis Malioti 2; singles/doubles with bath CY£24/32)* includes breakfast in its rates.

Nikos Tyrimos Fish Tavern *(☎ 2694 2846; Agapinoros 71; fish CY£3.75-8)* is just spectacular. Fish are caught from the owner's boat and served up the same day to discerning palates.

Nea Amaroza Co *(☎ 2693 6822; Evagora Palikaridi 79)* operates around 10 buses a day to Polis (CY£1), one daily service to Lemesos (CY£1.50, 2.30pm) and two daily to Pomos (CY£1.10). **Alepa** *(☎ 2693 4410)* runs one morning bus daily to Lefkosia (CY£3) and buses every 15 to 20 minutes to Coral Beach (CY£0.50) and every 10 to 15 minutes to Kato Pafos (CY£0.50). All buses depart from the Central (Karavella) Bus Station. **Travel &**

Express *(☎ 077 7474)* runs service taxis to Lemesos (CY£2.75).

Northern Cyprus

The Turkish Republic of Northern Cyprus (TRNC) occupies 37% of the island. Almost completely unspoilt by tourism, it has some of the island's best beaches, as well as awe-inspiring monasteries, archaeological sites and castles.

NORTH NICOSIA LEFKOŞA, ΛΕΥΚΩΣΙΑ

pop 40,000

North Nicosia, the capital of Northern Cyprus, is a quiet city with some good examples of Gothic and Ottoman architecture. It's a great place for a day excursion, but budget accommodation options are not so hot.

The city centre is Atatürk Meydanı. Girne Caddesi is the main thoroughfare, running north from Atatürk Meydanı to the well-preserved **Kyrenia Gate** (Girne Kapisi). To the east of the square is the Selimiye quarter, where you'll find most of the interesting places. Inside Kyrenia Gate is an excellent **tourist office**. The easiest Internet outlet to find is **Deep Net City** *(☎ 227 9669; ⓔ deepnetcity@kktc.net; Girne Caddesi 73; open 24hr)*. In an emergency ring ☎ 112 for the hospital, ☎ 155 for the police or ☎ 199 for the fire station.

The **Turkish Museum** *(Mevlevi Tekke Müzesi; admission TL2,500,000; open 7.30am-2pm Mon-Fri)* is at the northern end of Girne Caddesi in a 17th-century Islamic monastery that was used by 19th-century Whirling Dervishes (Muslim ascetics). Extending from the museum is a long, thin mausoleum containing the tombs of 16 sheikhs.

The Old Quarter east of Atatürk Meydanı is dominated by the **Selimiye Mosque** *(Agios Nikolaos Cathedral)*, originally a cathedral built between 1209 and 1326. Next door is the **Bedesten**, a building comprising two churches, which became an Ottoman bazaar.

Most budget accommodation is not recommended for travellers (particularly lone females). Only just passable is **Altin Pansiyon** *(☎ 228 5049; Girne Caddesi 63; singles/doubles UK£6/8)*. The three-star **Saray** *(☎ 228 3115, fax 228 4808; ⓔ saray@northcyprus.net; Atatürk Meydanı; singles/doubles UK£27/41)*, including breakfast, is the best hotel in the Old Town.

On Girne Caddesi are two friendly, low-key kebab restaurants. **Amasyali** *(☎ 228 3294; Girne Caddesi 186; doner TL1,500,000)* serves up staples such as doner kebabs. Close by is the **Umutlar Restaurant** *(☎ 227 3236; Girne Caddesi 51; kebabs TL1,500,000)*.

The **long-distance bus station** *(cnr Atatürk Caddesi & Kemal Aşik Caddesi)* is in the new town. However, it is much easier to catch the frequent minibuses to Kyrenia (TL1,000,000) from the bus stop and İtimat bus station just east of Kyrenia Gate. Local minibuses leave from just west of Kyrenia Gate.

KYRENIA GİRNE, ΚΕΡΥΝΕΙΑ

pop 12,600

Kyrenia is a very attractive town built around a horseshoe-shaped harbour dominated on one side by an impressive Byzantine castle. At the harbour's western end is the **tourist office** *(☎ 815 2145)*. The star attraction is the **Castle & Shipwreck Museum** *(Girne Kalesi; admission TL7,000,000; open 9am-6.45pm daily)*, which houses Cyprus' oldest shipwreck and its cargo. The ship is believed to have sunk in a storm around 3000 BC.

St Hilarion Castle *(admission TL4,500,000)* and **Buffavento Castle**, in the Kyrenia mountain ranges, are fascinating places to visit for lovers of medieval ruins. The views are stupendous.

There's lots of accommodation in Kyrenia, with much of the cheaper options along Ecevit Caddesi and between Hürriyet Caddesi and the harbour.

Bingöl Guest House *(☎ 815 2749; Efeler Sokak; singles/doubles UK£4/10)*, including breakfast, on the main roundabout, is good and central. The **New Bristol Hotel** *(☎ 815 6570, fax 815 7365; Hürriyet Caddesi 114; singles/doubles UK£15/19)* is a bit old-fashioned, but has decent enough rooms.

Little Arif's Restaurant *(☎ 852 0281; Hürriyet Caddesi; full kebab TL5,000,000)* is a bit of an institution and excellent value. Pitched almost exclusively at local clientele, it's unpretentious and cheap.

The long-distance bus station is on Ecevit Caddesi in the south of the New Town. Minibuses and shared taxis to North Nicosia (TL1,000,000) depart from Belediye Meydanı.

There are daily slow ferries (TL33,500,000, seven hours) and express boats (TL41,500,000, three hours) to Taşucu in Turkey. Tickets can be bought from the passenger lounge at the port or from **Fergün Denizcilik Şirketi Ltd** (*☎ 815 2344; Mustafa Çağatay Caddesi 6/2C*). During the peak season there is also an express ferry that runs twice weekly to Alanya in Turkey (US$30, four to five hours).

ANCIENT SALAMIS

Just nine kilometres north of the town of Famagusta is the huge site of Cyprus' most important classical city, Salamis (*Salamis Harabeleri; admission TL4,500,000; open 8am-6pm daily in summer*). Among many other remains are a fully restored Roman amphitheatre; a gymnasium still surrounded by the majority of its marble columns (with adjacent baths); and some mosaics. Be sure to allow at least half a day here as there is also a long sandy beach next to the site. Unfortunately, there are no buses, but a return taxi will cost UK£8.

Czech Republic

Deep in the heart of Europe lie the ancient lands of Bohemia and Moravia, which together make up the Czech Republic. It's one of Europe's most historic countries, full of fairy-tale castles, chateaux, manors and museums.

The Czech Republic is doubly inviting for its cultured, predominantly friendly people and excellent facilities; the transportation network is both cheap and efficient. Although 90% of English-speaking visitors limit themselves to Prague, the clever few who escape the hordes and high prices in the capital soon experience just how helpful the Czech people can be. Indeed, almost everywhere outside Prague and Český Krumlov still feels off the beaten tourist track, yet also comfortably friendly.

Czech Republic: the Basics

Local Name Ceska Republika

Capital Prague

Population 10.3 million

Language Czech

Currency koruna (Kč) = 100 haléřů

Avoid at all costs Pick-up hockey games

Get in the spirit by Requesting Velko pivo, prosím. (A large beer, please.)

CZECH REPUBLIC

Facts about the Czech Republic

HISTORY

In 995 the Czech lands were united as the principality of Bohemia. In 1310, John of Luxembourg annexed the kingdom to the German (and later, Holy Roman) Empire. In 1526 the Austrian Habsburg dynasty ascended to the Bohemian throne. The Thirty Years' War, which devastated central Europe from 1618 to 1648, began in Prague.

The Czechs began rediscovering their linguistic and cultural roots in the early 19th century during the so-called National Revival. After WWI, the Czechoslovak Republic was created, but in 1938 Hitler occupied the country.

After WWII, a power struggle developed between communist and democratic forces. In 1948 the communists deposed their opposition in a February coup d'etat. Many people were imprisoned, and hundreds were executed or died in labour camps.

The 'Prague Spring' was introduced in April 1968 by the new first secretary, Alexander Dubček. Censorship ended, political prisoners were released and decentralisation of the economy began. Moscow sent in 200,000 soldiers to reinstall Stalinism on the night of 20 August 1968.

By 1989, Gorbachev's *perestroika* was sending shock waves through the region. The 'Velvet Revolution' began on 17 November, when an officially sanctioned Prague student march was smashed by police. Weeks later, the communists had fallen. Václav Havel, Prague's best-known 'dissident', took over as the country's interim president by popular demand. The Czechoslovak federation ceased to exist at midnight on 31 December 1992 – the so-called 'velvet divorce' between the Czech Republic and Slovakia.

Despite rapid economic reforms, by 1996 the Czech economy had started slowing down. Among other major problems were corruption, an ineffective judiciary and a lack of openness in business. As the 21st century began, the Czech Republic stood on the threshold of the EU, and in 2004 it's expected to join, along with Poland, Hungary and Slovenia.

GEOGRAPHY

The Czech Republic is a landlocked country of 78,864 sq km. In between its mountain ranges are rolling plains, as well as forests and farm land.

CLIMATE

The Czech climate is temperate, with cool and humid winters, warm summers and clearly defined spring and autumn seasons.

GOVERNMENT & POLITICS

The country is a parliamentary democracy headed by a president who faces election by the bicameral parliament every five years.

CZECH REPUBLIC

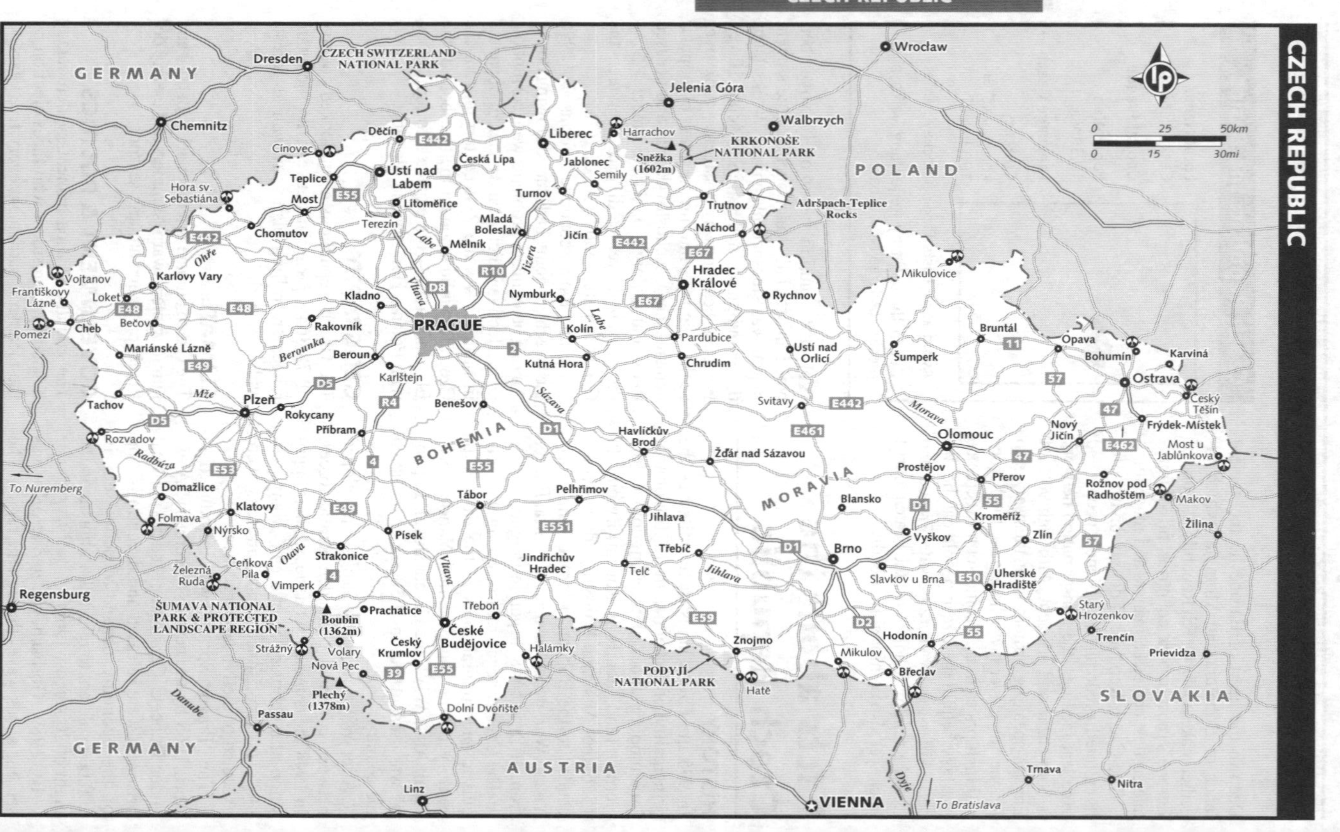

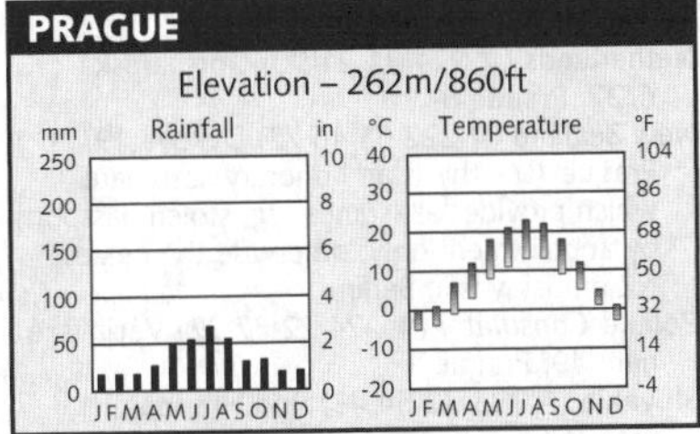

POPULATION & PEOPLE

The Czech Republic is fairly homogeneous; 95% of the people are Czech and 3% are Slovak. A small Polish minority lives in the borderlands near Ostrava.

SOCIETY & CONDUCT

It is customary to say *dobrý den* (good day) when entering a shop, café or quiet bar, and *na shledanou* (goodbye) when leaving. If you are invited to a Czech home, bring fresh flowers and when entering someone's home remember to remove your shoes.

LANGUAGE

German is understood by many Czechs and is useful in most parts of the country, while in the capital you can get by with English.

An English-Czech phrasebook will prove invaluable, so consider Lonely Planet's *Czech phrasebook* or *Eastern Europe phrasebook*. Also see the Language chapter at the back of this book.

Facts for the Visitor

HIGHLIGHTS

Authentic and picturesque historic towns include Prague, Litoměřice, Český Krumlov, Kutná Hora and Telč. There are magnificent castles at Karlštejn, Konopiště and Český Krumlov.

Prague Castle is packed with art treasures, notably the collection of the National Gallery in the Šternberg Palace at the entrance of the castle. The Brewery Museum in Plzeň highlights one of the country's noblest contributions to humanity.

PLANNING

The weather is best in summer, but July and August as well as Christmas–New Year and Easter are very busy, so it's better to visit in May, June or September. During the Prague Spring festival (in May), accommodation in Prague can be tight.

2002 Floods

In the summer of 2002, the Czech Republic, along with neighbouring Austria and Germany, suffered its worst floods in over a century. The country is facing an estimated clean-up bill of around €3 billion. Prague was severely affected with the famous Charles Bridge being threatened at one stage and the Jewish section of town badly damaged.

Visitors to Prague and other affected regions may find some attractions limited by repair work into 2003. The former concentration camp at Terezín in North Bohemia also suffered severely, and may not be fully repaired until 2006. Check with tourist information offices for the latest situation.

TOURIST OFFICES

Local Tourist Offices

Staff at the municipal Prague Information Service (PIS) are very knowledgeable about attractions, eateries and entertainment in the capital. Elsewhere there's a network of *městské informační centrum/středisko* (municipal information centres) in all major tourist areas.

In the Czech Republic there are several youth travel bureaus including CKM (Cestovní kancelář mládeže) in Prague.

Tourist Offices Abroad

The following Czech Tourist Authority (ČCCR) offices abroad provide information about the whole of the Czech Republic, but do not book hotels or transportation.

Canada (☎ 416-363 9928, fax 363 0239, ⓔ ctacanada@iprimus.ca) Czech Airlines Office, 401 Bay St, Suite 1510, Toronto, Ontario M5H 2Y4
France (☎ 01 53 73 00 32, fax 01 53 73 00 33, ⓔ bohmova@czech.cz) rue Bonaparte 19, 75006 Paris
Germany (☎/fax 030-204 4770, ⓔ tourinfo@czech-tourist.de) Karl Liebknecht Strasse 34, 10178 Berlin
UK (☎ 020-7291 9925, fax 7436 8300, ⓔ ctainfo@czechcentre.org.uk) 95 Great Portland St, London W1W 7NY
USA (☎ 212-288 0830, fax 288 0971, ⓔ travelczech@pop.net) 1109-1111 Madison Ave, New York, NY 10028

VISAS & DOCUMENTS

Everyone requires a valid passport. Citizens of EU countries, Switzerland, the USA, Japan and New Zealand can stay for up to 90 days without a visa; for UK citizens the limit is 180 days. Australians, Canadians and South Africans need a visa. Visas are not available at border crossings or Prague's Ruzyně airport; you'll be refused entry if you arrive without one.

Czech visa regulations change frequently, so check the Czech Ministry of Foreign Affairs website (W www.mzv.cz).

All foreign visitors must register with the Czech immigration police within three days of arrival. Hostels, camping grounds and hotels will automatically register you when you check in.

EMBASSIES & CONSULATES

Czech Embassies & Consulates

The Czech Republic has diplomatic representation in the following countries:

Australia *Consulate:* (☎ 02-9371 0860) 169 Military Rd, Dover Heights, Sydney NSW 2030
Canada (☎ 613-562 3875) 251 Cooper St, Ottawa, Ontario K2P 0G2
France (☎ 01 40 65 13 01) 15 ave Charles Floquet, 75343 Paris Cedex 07
Germany (☎ 030-22 63 80) Wilhelmstrasse 44, 10117 Berlin
Ireland (☎ 031-668 1135) 57 Northumberland Rd, Ballsbridge, Dublin 4
Netherlands (☎ 070-346 9712) Paleisstraat 4, 2514 JA The Hague
New Zealand Contact the Australian embassy in Canberra
UK (☎ 020-7243 1115) 26 Kensington Palace Gardens, London W8 4QY
USA (☎ 202-274 9100) 3900 Spring of Freedom St NW, Washington, DC 20008

Embassies & Consulates in the Czech Republic

Most embassies and consulates are open at least 9am to noon Monday to Friday.

Australia (☎ 251 01 83 50) Klimentská 10, Prague 1 – this is an honorary consulate for emergency assistance only (eg, a stolen passport); otherwise contact the Australian embassy in Vienna
Austria (☎ 257 09 05 11) Viktora Huga 10, Prague 5
Canada (☎ 272 10 18 00) Mickiewiczova 6, Prague 6
France (☎ 251 17 17 11) Velkopřerovské nám 2, Prague 2
Germany (☎ 257 11 31 11) Vlašská 19, Prague 1
Ireland (☎ 257 53 00 61) Tržiště 13, Prague 1
Netherlands (☎ 224 31 21 90) Gotthardská 6/27, Prague 6
New Zealand (☎ 222 51 46 72) Dykova 19, Prague 10 – this is an honorary consulate which provides assistance (eg, stolen passport) by appointment only; otherwise the nearest NZ embassy is in Berlin
Poland *Consulate:* (☎ 224 22 87 22) Václavské nám 49, Prague 1
Slovakia (☎ 233 32 54 43) Pod Hradbami 1, Prague 6
UK (☎ 257 40 21 11) Thunovská 14, Prague 1
USA (☎ 257 53 06 63) Tržiště 15, Prague 1

CUSTOMS

Customs officers can be strict about antiques and will confiscate goods that are even slightly suspect. There is no limit to the amount of Czech or foreign currency that can be taken in or out of the country, but amounts exceeding 350,000 Kč must be declared.

MONEY

Currency

The Czech crown, or *Koruna česká* (Kč), is divided into 100 hellers or *haléřů* (h). Banknotes come in denominations of 20, 50, 100, 200, 500, 1000, 2000 and 5000 Kč; coins are of 10, 20 and 50 h and one, two, five, 10, 20 and 50 Kč. Keep a few 2 Kč, 10 Kč and 20 Kč coins handy for use in public toilets, telephones and tram-ticket machines.

Exchange Rates

Conversion rates for major currencies at the time of publication were:

country	unit		Czech crown
Australia	A$1	=	16.74 Kč
Canada	C$1	=	19.68 Kč
Eurozone	€1	=	30.56 Kč
Japan	¥100	=	25.85 Kč
NZ	NZ$1	=	14.48 Kč
UK	UK£1	=	48.38 Kč
USA	US$1	=	30.94 Kč

For up-to-date exchange rates go to W www.xe.net/ucc/full.shtml.

Exchanging Money

There is no longer a black market in currency exchange; anyone who offers to change money in the street is a thief.

There is a good network of ATMs, or *bankomaty,* throughout the country. Most accept

Visa, Plus, MasterCard, Cirrus, Maestro, Euro and EC cards. The main banks – Komerční banka, Česká spořitelna, ČSOB and Živnostenská banka – are the best places to change cash and travellers cheques. They'll also provide a cash advance on Visa or MasterCard.

Many private exchange offices, especially in Prague, charge exorbitant *výlohy* (commissions) or sky-high 'handling fees'. American Express and Thomas Cook offices change their own-brand cheques without commission.

Credit cards are widely accepted in mid-range and top-end hotels and restaurants.

Costs
Food, transport and admission fees are fairly cheap, but accommodation in hotels is expensive, at least in Prague. You might be able to get away with US$15 a day in summer. Staying in private rooms or better pensions, eating at cheap restaurants and using public transport, you should count on US$25 to US$30. Get out of the capital and your costs will drop dramatically.

Tipping & Bargaining
Tipping in restaurants is optional, but if there is no service charge you should certainly round up the bill to the next 10 or 20 Kč (up to 10%). The same applies to tipping taxi drivers.

Taxes & Refunds
Value-added tax (VAT, or DPH in Czech) is 5% on food, hotel rooms and restaurant meals, but 22% on luxury items (including alcohol). This tax is included in the sticker price.

It is possible to claim VAT refunds for purchases worth more than 1000 Kč made in shops displaying the 'Tax-Free Shopping' sticker.

POST & COMMUNICATIONS
General delivery mail can be addressed to Poste Restante, Pošta 1, in most major cities. For Prague, also include: Jindřišská 14, 11000 Praha 1, Czech Republic.

All Czech phone numbers have nine digits – you will have to dial all nine for any call, local or long distance. You can make international telephone calls at main post offices or directly from card-phone booths. The international access code is ☎ 00. The Czech Republic's country code is ☎ 420.

There are Internet cafés in most towns and cities. The usual charge is about 1 Kč to 2 Kč per minute.

DIGITAL RESOURCES
Websites **W** www.prague-info.cz, **W** www.czechsite.com and **W** www.ceskenoviny.cz/news have useful information and links.

BOOKS
Lonely Planet's guides to *Czech & Slovak Republics* and *Prague* cover the area in detail, while LP's *Czech phrasebook* is a good introduction to the language.

The Coasts of Bohemia by Derek Sayer is a very readable exploration of the ironies of Czech history from the 18th century to 1968.

WOMEN TRAVELLERS
Sexual violence has been on the rise in the Czech Republic, but is still much lower than in the West. Women may experience catcalls and whistling.

GAY & LESBIAN TRAVELLERS
The bimonthly gay guide and contact magazine ***Amigo*** (**W** *www.amigo.cz/indexe.htm*) has a few pages in English, and an English-language website. **Gay Guide.Net Prague** (**W** *www.gayguide.net/Europe/Czech/Prague*) is another useful source of information.

DISABLED TRAVELLERS
Ramps for wheelchair users in Prague are becoming more common. Transport is a major problem as most buses and trams have no wheelchair access. For information, contact the **Prague Wheelchair Users Organisation** (*Pražská organizace vozíčkářů;* ☎ *224 82 72 10;* **e** *pov@gts.cz; Benediktská 6, Josefov*).

DANGERS & ANNOYANCES
Theft and pickpocketing are a real problem in Prague's tourist zone. Prague's Ruzyně airport is also a haven for thieves. Another problem is robberies on international trains.

Groups of skinheads occasionally abuse and assault darker-skinned people.

Emergencies
The telephone number for all emergency services is ☎ 112. For state police dial ☎ 158 and for local police ☎ 156. For the fire brigade ring ☎ 150 and for the ambulance call ☎ 155.

Assistance for car breakdowns is available by calling ☎ 1230 and ☎ 1240.

All numbers are valid nationwide.

BUSINESS HOURS

Shops open at around 8.30am and close at 5pm or 6pm Monday to Friday. Outside Prague, almost everything closes on Saturday afternoon and all day Sunday. Most restaurants are open every day.

PUBLIC HOLIDAYS & SPECIAL EVENTS

Public holidays include New Year's Day (1 January), Easter Monday (March/April), Labour Day (1 May), Liberation Day (8 May), Cyril and Methodius Day (5 July), Jan Hus Day (6 July), Czech Statehood Day (28 September), Republic Day (28 October), Struggle for Freedom and Democracy Day (17 November) and Christmas (24 to 26 December).

Festivals include the Prague Spring International Music Festival during the second half of May. Karlovy Vary holds an International Film Festival in July and the Dvořák Autumn Music Festival in September. Brno has an Easter Festival of Spiritual Music and the International Moravian Music Festival in September.

Moravian folk-art traditions culminate at the Strážnice Folk Festival (late June). The Chod Festival at Domažlice (mid-August) is a chance to enjoy the folk songs and dances of South and West Bohemia. Medieval festivals are held in Český Krumlov (June) and Tábor (September).

ACTIVITIES

There are good hiking possibilities in the forests around Karlovy Vary and in the Moravian karst area, north of Brno. The Šumava hills in the southern part of Bohemia offers some of the best hiking in the country, while the Adršpach-Teplice Rocks in East Bohemia has the most spectacular scenery. The whole country is ideal for cycling and cycle touring.

WORK

Unless you speak Czech, the most readily available work is teaching English or assisting in one of the backpacker hostels in Prague or Český Krumlov. It's easier to find a teaching job in provincial towns and your living costs will be much lower. In Prague, look in the Czech advertising paper *Annonce*, the *Prague Post*, and around the expat cafés.

The **Klub mladých cestovatelů** *(KMC, Young Travellers Club; ☎/fax 222 22 03 47; Ⓦ www.kmc.cz; Karolíny Světlé 30, Prague 1)* organises international work camps from June to August.

ACCOMMODATION

Camping

At around 50 Kč to 100 Kč per person, pitching your own tent would have to be the least expensive accommodation option. There are several hundred camping grounds around the Czech Republic, and most of these are open from May to September only. Camping on public land is prohibited.

Hostels

The Hostelling International (HI) handbook lists an impressive network of associate hostels across the Czech Republic. In July and August many student dormitories become temporary hostels, while a number in Prague have been converted into year-round, Western-style hostels. In central Prague, some normal schools also turn into temporary hostels during summer. Český Krumlov is the only place, apart from Prague, with a solid network of backpacker hostels.

Hostelling is controlled by **Klub mladých cestovatelů** *(KMC, Young Travellers Club; ☎/fax 222 22 03 47; Ⓦ www.kmc.cz; Karolíny Světlé 30, Prague 1)*. It's best to book ahead. A HI-membership card is not usually required to stay at hostels, although it will usually get you a reduced rate. An ISIC, ITIC, IYTC or Euro<26 card may also get you a discount. A dorm bed costs around 300 Kč to 400 Kč.

Another category of hostel not connected with HI is *turistické ubytovny* (tourist hostels), which provide very basic and cheap (200 Kč to 300 Kč) dormitory accommodation.

Private Rooms & Pensions

Private rooms (look for signs reading *'privát'* or *'Zimmer frei'*) are usually available in tourist towns, and many tourist information offices can book them for you; expect to pay from 250 Kč to 500 Kč per person outside Prague. Some have a three-night minimum-stay requirement.

In Prague, many private travel agencies offer private rooms, and the service is available daily and during evenings. This is the easiest way to find accommodation in Prague if you don't mind paying at least 500 Kč per person per night.

Hotels

Hotels in Prague and Brno are expensive, whereas those in smaller towns are usually much cheaper. Czechs pay less than half as much as foreigners at some hotels.

Two-star hotels usually offer reasonable comfort for about 500 Kč to 700 Kč with shared bathroom, or 600 Kč to 1000 Kč with private facilities (about 50% higher in Prague).

FOOD & DRINKS

Czech cuisine is strong on sauces and gravies, and weak on fresh vegetables. *Pražská šunka* (smoked Prague ham) is often eaten as a starter with Znojmo gherkins, followed by *bramborová polévka* (potato soup) or *zeleninová polévka* (vegetable soup). *Dršťková polévka* (tripe soup) is a treat not to be missed.

Prague has a good range of vegetarian restaurants; elsewhere, *bezmasá* (vegie) dishes are limited to pizzas, *smažený sýr* (fried cheese) and *knedlíky s vejci* (scrambled eggs with dumplings).

The Czech Republic really is a beer *(pivo)* drinker's paradise – where else could you get two or three 500mL glasses of top-quality Pilsner for under a dollar? Bohemian beer is probably the best in the world – the most famous brands are Budvar (the original Budweiser) and Plzeňský Prazdroj (Pilsner Urquell in German). The South Moravia and Mělník regions produce reasonable white wines *(bílé víno)*.

ENTERTAINMENT

Theatres and concert-hall admission prices are still well below those in Western Europe and most performances are first rate. Most theatres are closed in summer.

Outside Prague, the nightlife is rather limited, although after 9pm there's usually a band playing in the bar of the best hotel in town and at weekends a club will be pumping somewhere, so just ask.

Getting There & Away

AIR

The national carrier, **Czech Airlines** *(ČSA; ☎ 220 10 46 20; V celnici 5; metro Náměstí Republiky)*, has direct flights to Prague from many European cities, and also from the Middle East and North America.

The British airline **Go** *(in Prague ☎ 296 33 33 33)* has direct flights to Prague from London Stansted, Bristol and East Midlands. **KLM** *(in Prague ☎ 233 09 09 33)* is also a good bet for low-cost flights to Prague via Amsterdam.

LAND

Bus

Most international buses are operated by the company **Eurolines-Sodeli CZ** *(☎ 224 23 93 18; W www.eurolines.cz; Senovážné nám 6, Prague 1)* and **Bohemia Euroexpress International** *(☎ 224 21 86 80, W www.bei.cz; Florenc Bus Station, Křižíkova 4-6, Prague 8)*. Prague's main international bus station is Florenc, 600m northwest of the main train station, but some buses use stands at Holešovice train station or Želivského metro station. It's easier to buy a bus ticket from a travel agency such as GTS (see Prague, later).

The peak season for bus travel is from mid-June to the end of September, when there are daily Eurolines buses to Prague from London (UK£61/95 single/return, 23 hours), Paris (€68/122, 15 hours), Frankfurt (€44/69, 9½ hours), Vienna (€24/47, 4¾ hours) and Amsterdam (€73/130, 15 to 19 hours). Two buses a week link Kraków in Poland with Brno (80/130 zł, 6½ hours). Outside peak season, daily services fall to two or three a week.

There are several buses daily to Bratislava from Prague (300 Kč one way, 4¾ hours) and Brno (250 Kč, 1¾ hours), five a week from Prague to Budapest (1100 Kč, 7¼ hours) and three a week from Prague to Warsaw (550 Kč, 10½ hours) via Wrocław (350 Kč, five hours).

Kingscourt Express *(☎ 224 23 45 83; W www.kce.cz; Havelská 8, Prague 1)* runs four buses a week (six in summer) from Brno to London calling at Prague and Plzeň (1850/2900 Kč one way/return from all three Czech cities, 20 hours from Prague). **Capital Express** *(☎ 020-7243 0488; W www.capitalexpress.cz; 57 Princedale Rd, Holland Park, London W11 4NP)* has daily buses (twice daily in summer) from London to Plzeň, Prague (UK£40/60, 21 hours), Brno (UK£43/65, 24 hours), Olomouc and Ostrava.

Train

Train travel is the easiest and the most comfortable way to get from Western Europe to the Czech Republic, but is expensive compared to the bus and even to budget airlines. You can save a bit of money by buying a ticket that terminates at a border town, then continuing with a cheaper, Czech-bought ticket.

In the capital, international trains arrive at Prague's central station (Praha hlavní nádraží, or Praha hl. n.), Holešovice (Praha Hol.), Smíchov (Praha Smv.) or Masarykovo (Praha Mas.) stations.

Prague and Brno are on the main line used by daily express trains from Berlin and Dresden to Bratislava and Budapest, and from Hamburg and Berlin to Vienna. Trains from Frankfurt and Munich pass through Nuremberg, Cheb and Plzeň on the way to Prague. Local railcars shuttle between Cheb and Schirnding (15 minutes) in Germany several times a day. There are also daily express trains between Prague and Warsaw, Poland, via Wrocław or Katowice.

If you're planning to travel between Prague and Budapest, check whether you need a Slovak transit visa (the train goes via Bratislava).

Sample one-way fares to Prague include €130 from Paris (15 hours), UK£95 from London (25 to 30 hours), €42 from Salzburg (eight hours), €122 from Amsterdam (12½ hours), €46 from Berlin (five hours) and €85 from Frankfurt (7½ hours).

One-way fares from Prague include 400 Kč to Bratislava, 750 Kč to Vienna, 1150 Kč to Budapest, 750 Kč to Kraków and 890 Kč to Warsaw.

You can buy tickets in advance from Czech Railways (ČD) ticket offices, ČD travel agencies or other travel agencies. International tickets are valid for two months with unlimited stopovers. Inter-Rail (Zone D) passes are valid in the Czech Republic, but Eurail passes are not. For travel within the Czech Republic only, the Czech Flexipass is available (from US$48 to US$78 for three to eight days' travel in a 15-day period).

Seat reservations are compulsory on international trains. First-class sleepers and 2nd-class couchettes are available on overnight services.

Car & Motorcycle

Motorists can enter the country at one of the many border crossings marked on most road maps. Foreign driving licences are valid for up to 90 days.

You will need to buy a motorway tax coupon *(nálepka)* in order to use Czech motorways. They are on sale at border crossings, petrol stations and post offices.

Getting Around

BUS

Within the Czech Republic, buses are often faster, cheaper and more convenient than the train. Long-distance bus companies include the national carrier ČSAD, Čebus and Bohemia Euroexpress. There are several buses a day from Prague to Brno (140 Kč, 2½ hours), Plzeň (60 Kč, 1½ hours), Karlovy Vary (100 Kč, 2¼ hours) and Český Krumlov (120 Kč, three hours).

Many buses don't operate at weekends. It's best to get to the station at least 15 minutes before the official departure time.

Bus ticketing at main stations such as Prague and Karlovy Vary is computerised, so you can often book a seat ahead and be sure of a comfortable trip. Way stations are rarely computerised and you must line up and pay the driver.

TRAIN

Czech Railways (České dráhy, or ČD) provides efficient train services to almost every part of the country. However, some remote places are difficult or impossible to get to by train. One-way, 2nd-class fares cost around 64/120/224/424 Kč for 50/100/200/400km; 1st-class fares are 50% more expensive.

The clerks at information counters seldom speak English, so try writing down your destination and the date you wish to travel, then point to your watch and pray. Alternatively, check train (and bus) timetables in English on W www.vlak.cz.

Train categories include:

SC (SuperCity) – a few top-quality services with 1st-class coaches only; supplementary charge of 1000 Kč, reservations compulsory

EC (EuroCity) – fast, comfortable international trains, stopping at main stations only, with 1st- and 2nd-class coaches; supplementary charge of 60 Kč, reservations recommended

IC (InterCity) – long-distance and international trains with 1st- and 2nd-class coaches; supplement of 40 Kč, reservations recommended

Ex (express) – as for IC, but no supplementary charge

R *(rychlík)* – the main domestic network of fast trains with 1st- and 2nd-class coaches and sleeper services; no supplement except for sleepers; express and *rychlík* trains are usually marked in red on timetables

Sp *(spěšný)* – slower and cheaper than *rychlík* trains, 2nd class only

Os *(osobní)* – slow trains using older rolling stock that stop in every one-horse town, 2nd-class only

Only SC, EC, IC and express trains include a *restaurační vůz* (dining carriage).

If there is a notice over the timetable or a footnote with the words *'Náhradní autobusová doprava'*, it means that a bus departing outside the train station is replacing the train service.

If you have to purchase a ticket or pay a supplement on the train for any reason, you'll have to pay a fine if you do not tell the conductor *before* you're asked for your ticket.

Some Czech train conductors try to intimidate foreigners by pretending there's something wrong with their ticket. Don't pay any 'fine', 'supplement' or 'reservation fee' unless you first get a *doklad* (written receipt).

CAR & MOTORCYCLE

The main international car-rental chains include A-Rent-Car/Thrifty, Avis, Budget, Europcar and Hertz. A-Rent-Car is the cheapest, charging 1684/9666 Kč per day/week for a Škoda Felicia including unlimited mileage, Collision Damage Waiver and tax.

Small local companies are much cheaper – from 680 Kč a day all inclusive – but are less likely to have English-speaking staff.

BICYCLE

The Czech Republic offers some good opportunities for cycle touring. Theft is a problem, especially in Prague and other large cities, so a good long chain and lock are essential. It's fairly easy to transport your bike on Czech trains and buses.

HITCHING

The Czech Republic is no safer than other European countries when it comes to hitching; many hitchhikers are assaulted or raped, and each year a few are killed.

LOCAL TRANSPORT

City buses and trams operate from around 4.30am to midnight daily. In Prague, buses and trains on some main routes operate every 40 minutes all night long. Tickets – sold at bus and train stations, newsstands and vending machines – must be validated using the time-stamping machines found on buses and trams, and at the entrance to metro stations. Tickets are hard to find at night, at weekends and out in residential areas, so carry a good supply.

Taxis have meters – just make sure they're switched on.

Prague (Praha)

pop 1.21 million

It's no wonder that Goethe called Prague 'the prettiest gem in the stone crown of the world'. Prague has a magical feel about it, like a history lesson come to life. As you walk among the baroque palaces or across the Karlův most (Charles Bridge), with Smetana's Vltava flowing below and pointed towers all around, you'll feel as if history stopped back in the 18th century.

Unlike Warsaw, Budapest and Berlin, which were major battlefields during WWII, Prague escaped almost unscathed. Since 1989, however, central Prague has been swamped by capitalism as street vendors, cafés and restaurants take over pavements, streets and parks. If you're arriving from London, Paris or Rome, the tourist crush may seem normal, but if you've been elsewhere in Eastern Europe, you'll be in for a bit of a shock. Try to overcome your initial astonishment and enjoy this great European art centre for all it's worth.

Orientation

Almost exactly midway between Berlin and Vienna, Prague nestles in a picturesque bend of the Vltava (Moldau) river. The Vltava swings through the centre of the city, separating Malá Strana (Little Quarter) on the west bank from Staré Město (Old Town) on the east. North of Malá Strana is Hradčany, the medieval castle district, while Nové Město (New Town) is a late-Gothic extension of Staré Město to the east and south.

Prague Castle, visible from almost everywhere in the city, overlooks Malá Strana, while the twin Gothic spires of Týn Church dominates the wide open space of Staroměstské nám, the old town square. The broad avenue of Václavské nám (Wenceslas Square) stretches southeast from Staré Město towards the National Museum and the main train station.

Information

Tourist Offices The municipal **Prague Information Service** *(PIS, Pražská informační služba;* ☎ *12444;* Ⓦ *www.prague-info.cz;*

open Mon-Sat daily Apr-Oct) has branches at Na příkopě 20; in the Old Town Hall on Staroměstské nám; in Malá Strana Bridge Tower; and in Praha-hlavní nádraží train station, next to the metro entrance. The monthly *Culture in Prague* booklet in English is an invaluable guide to action in the city.

Money You can change **American Express** *(☎ 222 80 02 37; Václavské nám 56; open 9am-7pm daily)* or **Thomas Cook** *(☎ 221 10 53 71; Národní 28; open 9am-7pm Mon-Fri, 9am-6pm Sat, 10am-6pm Sun)* travellers cheques without commission at their respective offices.

Major banks are the best places for changing cash. Convenient branches include:

Komerční banka (Václavské nám 42) open 8am to 5pm Monday to Friday
Živnostenská banka (Na příkopě 20) open 8am to 4.30pm Monday to Friday
ČSOB (Na příkopě 14) open 8am to 5pm Monday to Friday

Be on guard against exorbitant commission charged by private exchange offices.

Post & Communications Pick up poste restante at the **main post office** *(Jindřišská 14; metro Můstek; open 7am-8pm daily)*. There's a telegraph and 24-hour telephone centre to the left of the right-hand entrance.

The centre is overflowing with Internet cafés. The cheapest place is **Bohemia Bagel** *(☎ 224 81 25 60; Masná 2, Staré Město • ☎ 257 31 06 94; Újezd 16, Malá Strana; both open 7am-midnight Mon-Fri, 8am-midnight Sat & Sun)*, which charges 1 Kč a minute with no minimum.

Travel Agencies The **CKM Travel Centre** *(☎ 222 72 15 95; e ckmprg@login.cz; Mánesova 77, Vinohrady; metro Jiřího z Poděbrad; open 10am-6pm Mon-Thur, 10am-4pm Fri)* makes reservations for accommodation and books air and bus tickets, with discounts for those aged under 26 (it also sells youth cards). A similar agency for young travellers is **GTS International** *(☎ 222 21 12 04; e gts.smecky@gtsint.cz; Ve Smečkách 33; open 8am-6pm Mon-Fri, 11am-3pm Sat)*, which also sells train tickets and youth cards.

People aged under 26 can also buy discounted train and bus tickets to Western Europe or book accommodation in Prague at **Wasteels** *(☎ 224 61 74 54; e wasteels@iol.cz; open 7.30am-8pm Mon-Fri, 8am-3pm Sat)* in Praha-hlavní nádraží train station.

Eurolines-Sodeli CZ *(☎ 24 23 93 18; Senovážné nám 6; open 8am-6pm Mon-Fri)* is the agent for Eurolines. The **Czech Railways Travel Agency** *(CKČD; ☎ 224 21 79 48; Praha-hlavní nádraží; open 8am-6pm daily)* at the main train station sells air, train and bus tickets to points all over Western Europe.

Medical Services Emergency medical aid is available at **Na Homolce Hospital** *(☎ 257 27 11 11, after hours ☎ 257 27 25 27; 5th floor, Foreign Pavilion, Roentgenova 2)*, which has some of the best facilities in the country.

District clinics have after-hours emergency services (from 7pm to 7am, 24 hours at weekends and holidays). The **Polyclinic at Národní** *(☎ 222 07 51 20; Národní 9; metro Národní Třída)* has English-, French- and German-speaking staff.

There are several 24-hour *lékárna* (pharmacies) in the city centre, including **Praha lékárna** *(☎ 224 94 69 82; Palackého 5)* and **Lékárna U sv Ludmily** *(☎ 222 51 33 96; Belgická 37; metro Náměstí Míru)*. For emergency service after hours, ring the bell.

Dangers & Annoyances Pickpockets regularly work the crowds at tourist centres. Sometimes bogus policemen approach tourists and ask to see their money, then run off with it. Being ripped off by taxi drivers is another hazard. Try not to take a taxi from Václavské nám, Národní and other tourist areas.

Hradčany & Prague Castle

Prague's finest churches and museums lie in Hradčany, stretching along a hilltop west of the river. Unless otherwise indicated, museums and galleries are closed on Monday; concession prices are for children under 16 and students.

The easiest way to get to this area is by metro to Malostranská, then tram No 22 up the hill to the fourth stop, Památník Písemnictví. From here Pohořelec and Loretánská slope down to the castle gate.

A passage at Pohořelec 8 leads up to the **Strahov Library** *(adult/concession 50/30 Kč; open 9am-noon & 1pm-5pm daily)*, the largest monastic library in the country. The Philosophy Hall features beautifully carved shelves and a gorgeous frescoed ceiling.

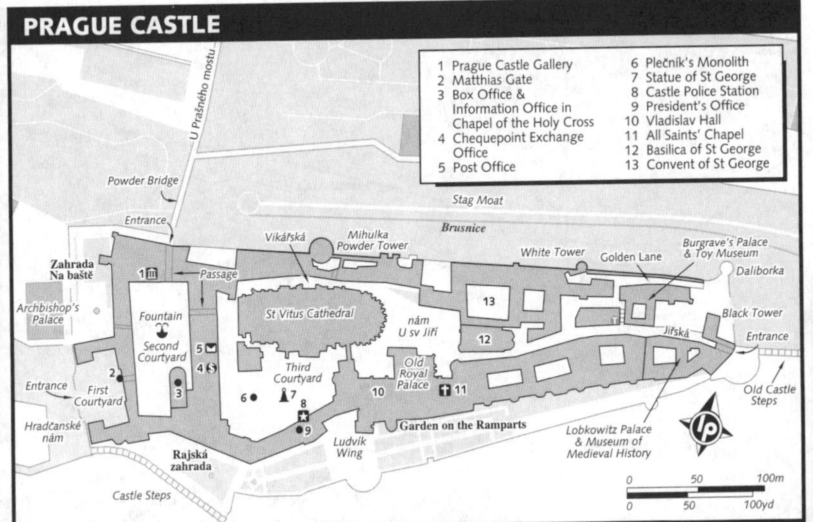

Look for the books on tree-growing bound in the bark of the trees they describe.

Nearby on Loretánské nám is the splendid **Černín Palace** (1687). The exuberantly baroque **Loreta** *(adult/concession 80/60 Kč; open 9.15am-12.15pm & 1pm-4.30pm daily)*, opposite the palace, is a convent housing a fabulous treasure of diamonds, pearls and gold, and a replica of the Santa Casa in the Italian town of Loreto.

Loretánská soon opens onto Hradčanské nám. Off the square at No 15 is the 18th-century Šternberg Palace, the main branch of the **National Gallery** *(adult/concession 60/30 Kč; open 10am-6pm Tues-Sun)*. This houses the country's main collection of 14th- to 18th-century European paintings, including Cranachs and Goyas.

Lovely **Prague Castle** *(☎ 224 37 33 68; adult/concession 220/110 Kč; buildings open 9am-5pm daily Apr-Oct, 9am-4pm Nov-March; grounds open 5am-midnight daily Apr-Oct, 6am-11pm Nov-Mar)* was founded in the 9th century. Always the centre of political power, it's still the official residence of the president. Castle highlights include the **Prague Castle Gallery** *(adult/concession 100/50 Kč; open 10am-6pm daily)*, with a good collection of European baroque paintings; the **tomb of St Wenceslas**, the Czech patron saint; the **Old Royal Palace**; the **Basilica of St George**, Prague's finest Romanesque church; and the **Convent of St George** *(adult/concession 50/20 Kč; open 10am-6pm Tues-Sun)*, which houses the National Gallery's collection of Czech art from the 16th to 18th centuries.

Beyond the basilica, follow the crowd into **Golden Lane**, a 16th-century tradesmen's quarter of tiny houses built into the castle walls. Franz Kafka, who was born in Prague, lived and wrote in the tiny house at No 22.

On the right, just before the gate leading out of the castle, is the **Lobkowitz Palace** *(adult/concession 40/20 Kč; open 9am-5pm)*, which houses a museum of medieval Czech history with replicas of the crown jewels.

Malá Strana

Malá Strana (Small Quarter), sheltered beneath the protective walls of Prague Castle, was built in the 17th and 18th centuries by Catholic clerics and nobles on the foundations of Renaissance palaces.

From Malostranská metro station, follow Valdštejnská around to Valdštejnské nám,

House Cleaning

On 23 May 1618, two Catholic councillors were thrown from the window of a chamber in the Old Royal Palace by irate Protestant nobles. This was the famous 'Defenestration of Prague', which touched off the Thirty Years' War.

CENTRAL PRAGUE

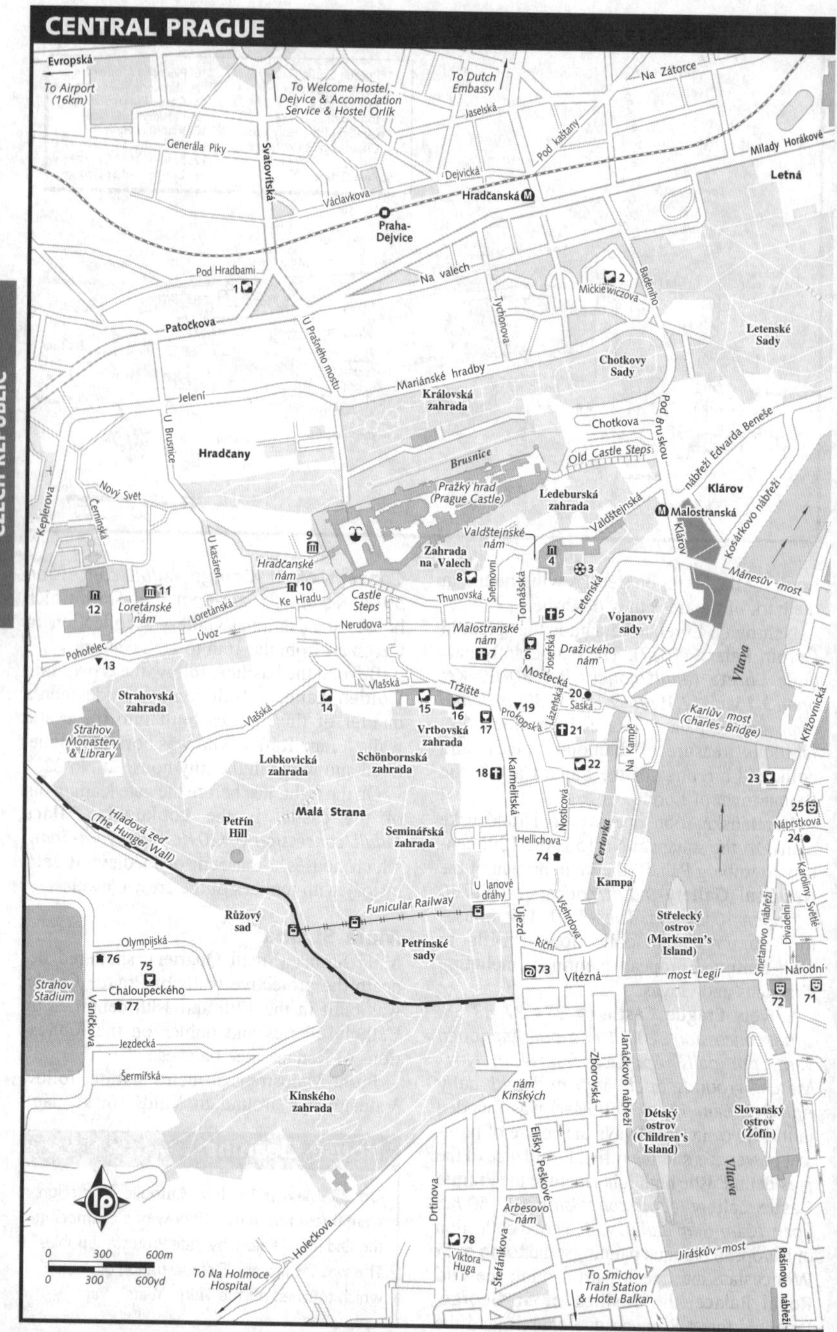

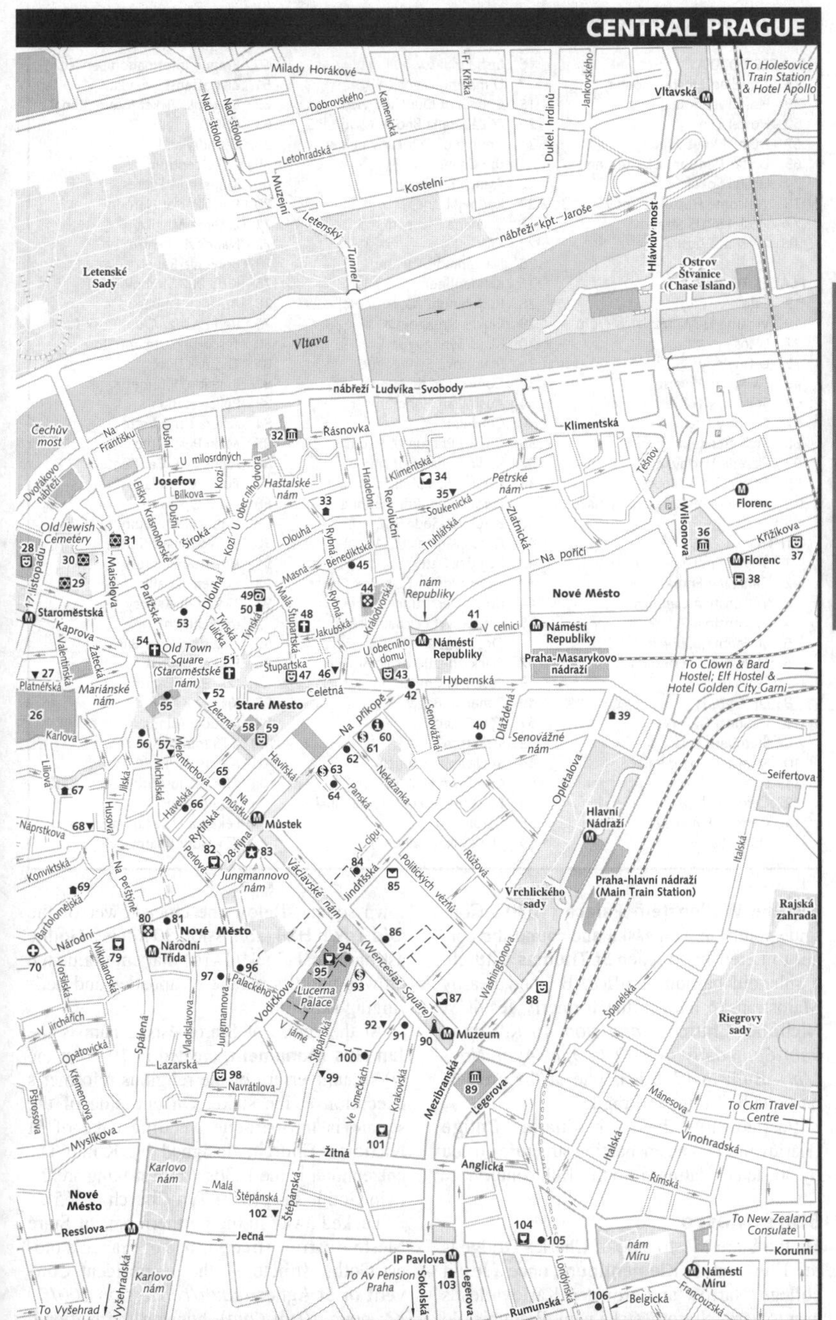
CENTRAL PRAGUE
To Holešovice Train Station & Hotel Apollo
Vltavská
Milady Horákové
Dobrovského
Kamenická
Fr Křížka
Jankovského
Dukel. hrdinů
Nad štolou
Letohradská
Kostelní
Muzejní
Letenský Tunnel
nábřeží kpt. Jaroše
Hlávkův most
Ostrov Štvanice (Chase Island)
Letenské Sady
Vltava
nábřeží Ludvíka Svobody
Čechův most
Na Františku
Dušní
Rásnovka
Klimentská
U milosrdných
Josefov
Haštalské nám
Petrské nám
Těšnov
Florenc
Dvořákovo nábřeží
Bílkova
Soukenická
Hradební
Revoluční
Old Jewish Cemetery
Široká
Dlouhá
Rybná
Truhlářská
Zlatnická
Wilsonova
Křižíkova
Na poříčí
Maiselova
Benediktská
Masná
nám Republiky
Nové Město
17. listopadu
Staroměstská
Pařížská
Kaprova
Valentinská
Žatecká
Old Town Square (Staroměstské nám)
Týnská ulička
Týnská
Malá Štupartská
Jakubská
Králodvorská
V celnici
Náměstí Republiky
U obecního domu
Štupartská
Praha-Masarykovo nádraží
To Clown & Bard Hostel; Elf Hostel & Hotel Golden City Garni
Platnéřská
Mariánské nám
Celetná
Hybernská
Staré Město
Železná
Na příkopě
Senovážná
Dlážděná
Senovážné nám
Karlova
Liliová
Melantrichova
Michalská
Havířská
Nekázanka
Opletalova
Seifertova
Jilská
Husova
Havelská
Na můstku
Můstek
Panská
Hlavní Nádraží
Náprstkova
Rytířská
Perlová
28. října
Jungmannovo nám
V cípu
Politických vězňů
Růžová
Konviktská
Na Perštýně
Jindřišská
Václavské nám
Vrchlického sady
Praha-hlavní nádraží (Main Train Station)
Italská
Rajská zahrada
Bartolomějská
Národní
Nové Město
Národní Třída
Mikulandská
Voršilská
Palackého
(Wenceslas Square)
Lucerna Palace
Vodičkova
Washingtonova
Španělská
V jirchářích
Opatovická
Spálená
Vladislavova
Jungmannova
V jámě
Štěpánská
Muzeum
Riegrovy sady
Lazarská
Navrátilova
Ve Smečkách
Krakovská
Mezibranská
Legerova
Mánesova
To Ckm Travel Centre
Křemencova
Pštrossova
Myslíkova
Žitná
Vinohradská
Anglická
Italská
Římská
Karlovo nám
Malá Štěpánská
Nové Město
Resslova
Ječná
To New Zealand Consulate
nám Míru
Korunní
IP Pavlova
To Av Pension Praha
Sokolská
Náměstí Míru
Karlovo nám
Londýnská
Vyšehradská
To Vyšehrad
Rumunská
Belgická
Francouzská
26
27
28
29
30
31
32
33
34
35
36
37
38
39
40
41
42
43
44
45
46
47
48
49
50
51
52
53
54
55
56
57
58
59
60
61
62
63
64
65
66
67
68
69
70
79
80
81
82
83
84
85
86
87
88
89
90
91
92
93
94
95
96
97
98
99
100
101
102
103
104
105
106
CZECH REPUBLIC

CENTRAL PRAGUE

PLACES TO STAY
- 33 Travellers Hostel Dlouhá
- 39 Hostel Jednota
- 50 Hostel Týn
- 67 Dům U krále Jiřího
- 69 Unitas Pension; Cloister Inn
- 74 Hostel Sokol
- 76 Welcome Hostel Strahov
- 77 Hostel SPUS Strahov
- 103 Pension Březina

PLACES TO EAT
- 13 Sate
- 19 Vinárna U Maltézských rytířů
- 27 Lotos
- 35 U Góvindy
- 46 Pivnice Radegast
- 52 Staroměstská restaurace
- 57 Country Life
- 68 Klub architektů
- 92 Pizzeria Václavka
- 99 Titanic Steak House
- 102 Jihočeská restaurace u Šumavy

OTHER
- 1 Slovak Embassy
- 2 Canadian Embassy
- 3 Wallenstein Gardens
- 4 Wallenstein Palace
- 5 St Thomas Church
- 6 Malostranská beseda
- 7 St Nicholas Church
- 8 UK Embassy
- 9 National Gallery; Šternberg Palace
- 10 Schwarzenberg Palace
- 11 Loreta
- 12 Černín Palace
- 14 German Embassy
- 15 US Embassy
- 16 Irish Embassy
- 17 U malého Glena
- 18 Church of Our Lady Victorious
- 20 Malá Strana Bridge Tower; PIS
- 21 Church of Our Lady Below the Chain
- 22 French Embassy
- 23 Karlovy lázné; Smetana Museum
- 24 KMC
- 25 Na zábradlí Theatre
- 26 Klementinum
- 28 Rudolfinum (Concert Hall)
- 29 Pinkas Synagogue
- 30 Klaus Synagogue
- 31 Staronová Synagogue
- 32 Convent of St Agnes
- 34 Australian Honorary Consulate
- 36 City of Prague Museum
- 37 Karlin Theatre of Music
- 38 Florenc Bus Station; Bohemia Euroexpress International
- 40 Eurolines-Sodeli CZ
- 41 Czech Airlines (ČSA)
- 42 Powder Gate
- 43 Obecni dům; FOK Box Office
- 44 Kotva Department Store
- 45 Prague Wheelchair Users Organisation
- 47 Black Theatre of Jiří Srnec
- 48 St James Church
- 49 Bohemia Bagel
- 51 Týn Church
- 53 Ticketpro
- 54 St Nicholas Church
- 55 Old Town Hall; PIS
- 56 Bohemia Ticket International
- 58 Carolinum
- 59 Stavovské Theatre
- 60 Prague Information Service
- 61 Živnostenská banka
- 62 Bohemia Ticket International
- 63 ČSOB
- 64 Laundryland
- 65 Ticketcentrum
- 66 Kingscourt Express
- 70 Polyclinic at Národní
- 71 Laterna Magika
- 72 National Theatre
- 73 Bohemia Bagel
- 75 Klub 007 Strahov
- 78 Austrian Embassy
- 79 Reduta Jazz Club; Rock Café
- 80 Tesco Department Store
- 81 Thomas Cook
- 82 Batalion; Internet Kafe
- 83 Police Station
- 84 Astera Laundrette
- 85 Main Post Office
- 86 Alimex ČR Car Rental
- 87 Polish Consulate
- 88 State Opera
- 89 National Museum
- 90 St Wencelaus Statue
- 91 American Express
- 93 Komerční banka
- 94 Ticketpro Agency (Melantrich)
- 95 Lucerna Music Bar
- 96 Praha Lékárna (24-Hour Pharmacy)
- 97 Kiwi
- 98 Divadlo Minor
- 100 GTS International
- 101 AghaRTA Jazz Centrum
- 104 Club Radost FX; Radost Café
- 105 Laundryland
- 106 Lékárna U sv Ludmily (24-Hour Pharmacy)

past the **Wallenstein Palace** (1630). Continue south on Tomášská and round the corner to Letenská to reach **St Thomas Church**, a splendid baroque edifice. Beyond nearby Malostranské nám is the formerly Jesuit **St Nicholas Church** *(admission 45 Kč; open 9am-6pm daily Apr-Oct, 9am-4pm Nov-Mar)*. Built in 1755 it is one of the greatest baroque buildings in Prague.

East towards the river, **Charles Bridge** (Karlův most) is an enchanting structure graced by 30 statues dating from the 18th century.

Staré Město

On the Staré Město side of Charles Bridge is the 17th-century **Klementinum**, once a Jesuit college. Narrow and crowded Karlova leads east towards Staroměstské nám, Prague's old town square. Below the clock tower of the **Old Town Hall** *(admission 30 Kč)* is a Gothic astronomical clock (1410) that entertains the crowds with its parade of apostles and bell-ringing skeleton.

At the centre of Staroměstské nám is the **Jan Hus Monument**, erected in 1915 on the 500th anniversary of the religious reformer's execution at the stake. On one side of the square is the baroque wedding cake of **St Nicholas Church**, designed by Kilian Dientzenhofer in the 1730s. More striking are the twin Gothic steeples of **Týn Church** (1365).

Tucked away in the northern part of Staré Město's narrow streets is one of Prague's oldest Gothic structures, the magnificent **Convent of St Agnes** *(adult/concession 100/50 Kč; open 10am-6pm)*, housing the National

Gallery's collection of Czech and central European medieval art.

Josefov

Josefov – the area north and northwest of Staroměstské nám – was once the city's Jewish Quarter. It retains a fascinating variety of monuments, all of which are now part of the **Prague Jewish Museum** *(adult/concession 500/340 Kč; open 9am-5.30pm Sun-Fri)* complex. Men must cover their heads to enter the synagogues. In 1942 the Nazis brought objects here for a planned 'museum of an extinct race', to be opened once their extermination programme was completed.

Vyšehrad

Take the metro to Vyšehrad station, where the concrete **Congress Centre** rises above a deep ravine crossed by the Nuselský Bridge. Pass north of the centre and along Na Bučance to the gates of the 17th-century **Vyšehrad Citadel**, built on a crag above the Vltava. You pass the Romanesque **Rotunda of St Martin** before reaching the twin towers of **SS Peter & Paul Church**, founded in the 11th century. **Slavín Cemetery**, beside the church, contains the graves of many distinguished Czechs, including the composers Smetana and Dvořák.

Places to Stay

If you're visiting during Christmas, Easter or May to September, book a room. The prices quoted are for 'high season', generally May, June, September and October; however, even these rates can increase by up to 15% on certain dates, notably at Christmas to New Year, Easter, and at weekends in May (during the Prague Spring festival). Some hotels, but not all, have slightly lower rates in July and August. November to March is low season.

Accommodation Agencies Dozens of agencies will help you find a place to stay. The **TravelGuide website** *(w www.travelguide.cz)* has a database of almost 400 hostels, pensions and hotels, as well as a straightforward online booking system.

The long-established **AVE** *(☎ 224 22 32 26, reservations ☎ 251 55 10 11, fax 224 22 34 63; w www.avetravel.cz)* has convenient booking offices at Praha-hlavní nádraží and Praha-Holešovice train stations, at Ruzyně airport and in PIS offices (see Tourist Offices earlier in this section).

Welcome Accommodation Service *(☎ 224 32 02 02, fax 224 32 34 89; w www.bed.cz; Zikova 13, Prague 6)* offers rooms in student dormitories, hostels and hotels.

You can also rent a private room from householders who will approach you at train and bus stations. They'll ask from about 300 Kč to 800 Kč per person. Check the location on a map before accepting.

Hostels In Malá Strana, the central **Hostel Sokol** *(☎ 257 00 73 97; e hostel@sokol-cos.cz; 3rd floor, Tyršův dům, Nostícova 2, Prague; dorm beds/doubles 270/1200 Kč)* gets good reports. Take the metro to Malostranská and then tram No 12, 22 or 23 two stops south.

Travellers Hostel Dlouhá *(Roxy; ☎ 224 82 66 62; e hostel@travellers.cz; Dlouhá 33, Prague 1; dorm beds/singles/doubles 370/1120/1240 Kč)*, on the opposite side of the river in Staré Město, has basic but clean accommodation and 24-hour service that includes lockers and Internet access.

Hostel Týn *(☎ 222 73 45 90; e info@itastour.cz; Týnská 19; dorm beds 370 Kč)*, only a few minutes' walk from Staroměstské nám, is another good central place.

Clown & Bard Hostel *(☎ 222 71 64 53; e reservations@clownandbard.com; Bořivojova 102, Prague 3; metro Jiřího z Poděbrad; dorm beds/doubles 250/900 Kč)* is in the heart of Žižkov's pub district. It's a party place so don't come seeking peace and quiet.

Readers have recommended friendly **Hostel Elf** *(☎ 222 54 09 63; e info@hostelelf.com; Husitská 11, Prague 3; dorm beds/doubles 260/840 Kč)*, also in Žižkov.

Student Residences Many *koleje* (student residences) rent out accommodation to tourists year-round. As well as dorms, they offer good-value single, double and triple rooms.

Hostel Jednota *(☎ 224 21 17 73, ☎/fax 224 81 82 00; Opletalova 38, Prague 1; singles/doubles/triples/quads 550/680/1020/1240 Kč)* is central and only five minutes' walk from Praha-hlavní nádraží train station. You can book a bed through **Alfa Tourist Service** *(☎/fax 224 23 00 37; e info@alfatourist.cz)*, based at the same address.

There is plenty of accommodation at the student dormitory complex opposite the Strahov football stadium, west of the centre. The main providers are **Hostel SPUS Strahov**

CZECH REPUBLIC

(☎/fax 283 88 25 72; ⓔ reception@spushostels.cz; Chaloupeckého, Block 4, Prague 6; dorm beds/singles/quads 250/480/1160 Kč) and **Welcome Hostel Strahov** *(☎ 224 32 02 02, fax 224 32 34 89; ⓔ welcome@bed.cz; Vaníčkova, Block 3; dorm beds/singles/doubles 150/350/480 Kč)*. Both offer 10% discount to ISIC card-holders.

There's another concentration of student dorms in Dejvice, only five minutes' walk from Dejvická metro station, including **Hostel Orlík** *(☎ 224 31 12 40; ⓔ praguehotel@atlas.cz; Terronská 6, Prague 6; singles/doubles/triples 550/860/1250 Kč; open July-Aug)* and **Welcome Hostel Dejvice** *(☎ 224 32 02 02, fax 224 32 34 89; ⓔ welcome@bed.cz; Zikova 13, Prague 6; singles/doubles 400/540 Kč)*.

Pensions An interesting place to stay is **Unitas Pension** *(☎ 224 21 10 20, fax 224 21 08 00; ⓔ unitas@cloisterinn.com; Bartolomějská 9, Prague 1; metro Národní třída; singles/doubles 1100/1400 Kč)* in Staré Město. A former convent its cramped rooms were once prison cells (Havel did time here), with shared bathrooms and a generous breakfast included.

Pension Březina *(☎ 296 18 88 88, fax 224 26 67 77; ⓔ info@brezina.cz; Legerova 41, Prague 2; economy singles/doubles 900/1100 Kč, luxury 1800/2000 Kč)* is south of IP Pavlova metro station. The economy rooms have shared bathrooms. Rooms facing the street can be pretty noisy.

AV Pension Praha *(☎ 272 95 17 26, fax 267 91 26 95; ⓔ votava@pension-praha.cz; Malebná 75, Prague 4; singles/doubles with bathroom 1200/1630 Kč)*, southeast of the centre, is a superb eight-room place that's a five-minute walk east of Chodov metro.

Hotels Central Prague has no cheap hotels. The recently redone **Hotel Golden City Garni** *(☎ 222 71 10 08, fax 222 71 60 08; ⓔ hotel@goldencity.cz; Táboritská 3, Prague 3; singles/doubles/triples 1650/2450/2700 Kč)* in Žižkov, three stops east of the main strain station on tram No 5, 9 or 26, is excellent value.

Hotel Balkán *(☎ 257 32 21 50; ⓔ balkan@mbox.dkm.cz; třída Svornosti 28, Prague 4; singles/doubles/triples 2000/2400/2700 Kč)*, two blocks from Anděl metro station, is a good deal. The hotel also has a decent restaurant.

The **Hotel Apollo** *(☎ 284 68 06 28, fax 284 68 45 70; Kubišova 23, Prague 8; singles/doubles/triples 1800/2300/2700 Kč)* is a bland, modern place in a quiet housing estate north of the centre. It is 15 minutes from the centre on tram No 5, 14 or 17.

There are several interesting hotels in Staré Město, including the appealing **Dům U krále Jiřího** *(☎ 222 22 09 25, fax 222 22 17 07; ⓔ krak.jiri@telecom.cz; Liliová 10, Prague 1; singles/doubles 1800/3100 Kč)*. The attic rooms with exposed wooden beams are particularly attractive.

Places to Eat

Tourism has had a heavy impact on the Prague restaurant scene, as cheaper restaurants are disappearing left and right. Insist on a menu with prices. If drink prices aren't listed, expect them to be sky high.

Hradčany & Malá Strana Five minutes' walk west of the castle is **Sate** *(Pohořelec 3; mains 90-110 Kč)*, which serves tasty Indonesian and Malaysian dishes.

Vinárna U Maltézských rytířů *(Prokopská 10; mains 200-400 Kč)* is cosy and romantic and offers top-notch food and professional service.

Bohemia Bagel *(Újezd 18; mains 50-100 Kč)*, in southern Malá Strana, doubles as an Internet café (see Information, earlier). It's also a great informal place to eat, and is one of the few places offering early morning breakfast.

Staroměstské Nám & Around Easily the best of the restaurants on the square is **Staroměstská restaurace** *(Staroměstské nám 19; mains 75-245 Kč)*, which has good Czech food and beer.

Pivnice Radegast *(Templová 2; mains 55-110 Kč)*, off Celetná, has good cheap Czech food; try the tasty *guláš* (goulash).

There are a few good places around Betlémské nám. The popular, subterranean **Klub architektů** *(Betlémské nám 5; mains 100-220 Kč)* serves tasty and inventive dishes, including vegetarian ones.

Václavské Nám & Around In a courtyard through a passage on Václavské nám 48 is the decent **Pizzeria Václavka** *(mains 65-120 Kč)*, with good inexpensive pizzas, pastas and salads.

Titanic Steak House *(Štěpánská 22; mains 90-190 Kč)*, southwest of the square, is a good place to sample the excellent steaks and salads.

Jihočeská restaurace u Šumavy *(Štěpánská 3; mains 95-155 Kč)*, a little bit farther away from the square, serves delicious, inexpensive South Bohemian dishes.

Vegetarian In a passage south of Staroměstské nám, **Country Life** *(Melantrichova 15; mains 75-150 Kč; open Mon-Fri)* has inexpensive salad sandwiches, pizzas, goulash and other vegetarian dishes.

Lotos *(Platnéřská 13; mains 70-150 Kč)*, just north of the Klementinum, does gourmet vegie food with many dishes modelled on Bohemian cuisine.

U Góvindy *(Soukenická 27; open Mon-Sat)*, a cafeteria-style place run by Hare Krishnas, is in the northern part of Nové Město; a donation of at least 50 Kč gets you a hearty meal.

Radost Café *(Bělehrádska 120; mains 110-230 Kč)* in Club Radost FX (see Entertainment, following), where the menu ranges from Mexican to Italian to Thai, has the best vegie food in Prague.

Entertainment

Prague offers an amazing range of entertainment. While it has long been a centre for classical music and jazz, it is now known for its rock and post-rock scenes as well. For the most up-to-date information, refer to the *Prague Post, The Prague Pill, Culture in Prague* and the *Do města – Downtown* freesheet, and keep an eye on posters and bulletin boards.

For classical music, opera, ballet, theatre and some rock concerts – even the most *vyprodáno* (sold-out) events – you can often find a ticket or two on sale at the box office 30 minutes before concert time. In addition, there are plenty of ticket agencies around Prague that will sell the same tickets at a high commission. Touts also sell overpriced tickets at the door. Tickets can cost as little as 30 Kč for standing room; the average price is about 500 Kč.

Ticket Agencies One of the largest agencies is **Ticketpro** *(☎ 296 32 99 99, fax 296 32 88 88; W www.ticketpro.cz; Salvátorská 10, Prague 1; open 9am-12.30pm & 1pm-5.15pm Mon-Fri)*, with branches in PIS offices (see Information, earlier) and many other places, including **Ticketcentrum** *(Rytířská 31; open 8.30am-8.30pm daily)*. The best place to buy tickets for rock concerts is Ticketpro's Melantrich outlet in the Rokoko passage at Václavské nám 38.

Other agencies include **Bohemia Ticket International** *(☎ 224 22 78 32, fax 221 61 21 26; W www.ticketsbti.cz; Malé nám 13; open 9am-5pm Mon-Fri, 9am-2pm Sat • Na příkopě 16; open 10am-7pm Mon-Fri, 10am-5pm Sat, 10am-3pm Sun)* and American Express (see Information, earlier).

Classical concert tickets are also available from the **FOK Box Office** *(☎ 222 00 23 36, fax 222 32 25 01; U obecního domu 2, Prague 1; open 10am-6pm Mon-Fri)* at Obecni dům theatre.

Classical Music & Performance Prague's main concert venues are the Dvořák Hall in the neo-Renaissance **Rudolfinum** *(nám Jana Palacha; metro Staroměstská)*, and the Smetana Hall in the city's wonderful Art Nouveau **Obecní dům** *(nám Republiky 5)*. The latter always hosts the opening concert of the Prague Spring festival. Opera, ballet and classical drama (in Czech) are performed at the neo-Renaissance **National Theatre** *(Národní 2; metro Národní Třída)*. Next door is the modern **Laterna Magika** *(Národní 4)*, established in 1983, which offers a widely imitated combination of theatre, dance and film.

Opera and ballet are also presented at the neo-Renaissance **State Opera** *(Wilsonova; metro Muzeum)*.

Jazz There are dozens of jazz clubs. The **Reduta Jazz Club** *(Národní 20; metro Národní Třída; admission 200 Kč; open 9pm-3am daily)* was founded in 1958 and is one of the oldest in Europe. You can hear live jazz every night at the unpretentious **AghaRTA jazz centrum** *(Krakovská 5; metro Muzeum; open 9pm-midnight daily)* and in the cosy basement at **U malého Glena** *(Karmelitská 23; metro Malostranská; music 9pm-2am daily)*.

Rock & Clubs Adjacent to the Reduta Jazz Club is the **Rock Café** *(Národní 20; open Mon-Sat)*; wear black clothing if you can.

Batalion *(28.října 3; open 24hr)* offers local rock, folk, jazz or blues bands downstairs, while DJs spin discs late at night or when there are no bands playing.

Lucerna Music Bar *(Vodičkova 36)*, inside the Lucerna passage, has live rock bands performing most nights.

Klub 007 Strahov *(Block 7, Chaloupeckého 7, Prague 6)* has underground rock, punk, reggae bands or DJs playing nightly. Another place with inexpensive beer which is popular with students is **Malostranská beseda** *(Malostranské nám 21; metro Malostranská)*, where jazz, folk, country and rock can be heard nightly from 8.30pm.

Club Radost FX *(W www.radostfx.cz; Bělehradská 120, Prague 2; metro IP Pavlova)*, with famous local and European guest DJs, is Prague's prime club venue.

Karlovy lázně *(Novotného lávka, Prague 1)* a complex, near the Smetana Museum, has a nightclub playing anything from 1960s hits to the latest techno on each of its three floors, while the basement hosts live bands.

Getting There & Away

Bus There are buses to Karlovy Vary (100 Kč, 2¼ hours), Brno (140 Kč, 2½ hours) and most other towns in the Czech Republic departing from the **Florenc bus station** *(Florenc ÚAN; Křižíkova 4; metro Florenc)*. Seven express buses a day go from Florenc to Bratislava (300 Kč). They take just 4½ hours, compared to 5½ hours on the train. Reservations are recommended on all these services.

Train Prague has four main train stations. International trains between Berlin and Budapest often stop at **Praha-Holešovice station** *(metro Nádraží Holešovice)* on the northern side of the city. Other important trains terminate at **Praha-hlavní nádraží** *(metro Hlavní Nádraží)* or **Praha-Masarykovo nádraží** *(metro Náměstí Republiky)*, both of which are close to the city centre. Some local trains to the southwest depart from **Praha-Smíchov station** *(metro Smíchovské Nádraží)*.

Praha-hlavní nádraží handles trains to České Budějovice (126 Kč, 2½ hours), Cheb via Plzeň (154 Kč, 3½ hours), Karlovy Vary (138 Kč, four hours), Košice (640 Kč, 10 hours), Kutná Hora (60 Kč, one hour), Plzeň (126 Kč, 1½ hours) and Tábor (80 Kč, 1½ hours). Trains to Brno (242 Kč, three hours) and Bratislava (400 Kč, 5½ hours) may leave from either Praha-hlavní nádraží, Praha-Holešovice or Masarykovo nádraží. Karlštejn (28 Kč, 35 minutes) trains depart from Hlavní nádraží and Smíchov. International tickets, domestic and international couchettes, and seat reservations are sold on level 2 at the even-numbered windows from 10 to 24 to the right of the stairs leading to level 3. Domestic tickets are sold at the odd-numbered windows from 1 to 23 to the left of the stairs.

At Praha-Holešovice, windows marked ARES 1 and 2 are for booking international tickets and couchettes.

Getting Around

To/From the Airport Prague's Ruzyně airport is 17km west of the city centre. City bus No 119 runs between the airport and Dejvická metro station (12 Kč, 20 minutes) daily from 5am to midnight.

Cedaz *(☎ 220 11 42 96, 224 28 10 05)* minibuses depart from nám Republiky every 30 minutes from 5.30am to 9.30pm daily across from the Kotva department store (metro: Náměstí Republiky), and pick up passengers about 30 minutes later at Dejvická metro station on Evropská. Buy your ticket from the driver; they cost 90 Kč per person. To book a return trip to the airport, call at least two hours before your planned departure time.

Airport Cars taxi service, whose prices are regulated by the airport administration, charge 650 Kč (20% discount for return trip) into the centre of Prague.

Public Transport All public transport is operated by **Dopravní podnik Praha** *(DP; ☎ 22 62 37 77; W www.dp-praha.cz)*. Tickets are sold from machines at metro stations and major tram stops, at newsstands, Trafiky snack shops, tobacco kiosks, hotels and DP information offices.

A *jízdenka* (ticket) for one journey is 12 Kč. Validate your ticket by sticking it in the yellow machine in the metro station lobby or on the bus or tram. Once validated, tickets remain valid for 60 to 90 minutes from the time of stamping. Within this period, unlimited transfers are allowed.

The metro operates from 5am to midnight daily. After the metro closes, trams (Nos 51 to 58) and buses (Nos 501 to 512) still rumble across the city about every 40 minutes all night.

Car Local rental companies offer the best prices. Typical rates for a Škoda Felicia are 680 Kč to 1150 Kč per day including unlimited kilometres, Collision Damage Waiver and VAT. Reputable local companies include:

Alimex ČR (☎ 800 150 170, e praha@alimexcr.cz) Václavské nám, Prague 1
Secco Car (☎ 283 87 10 31, e info@seccocar.cz) Přístavní 39, Prague 7
West Car Praha (☎ 235 36 53 07, e auto@westcarpraha.cz) Veleslavínská 17, Prague 6

Taxi The best way to avoid being ripped off is to telephone a reliable taxi company such as **AAA** *(☎ 221 11 11 11)* or **ProfiTaxi** *(☎ 261 31 41 51)*. If you feel you're being overcharged ask for a *účet* (bill). Most taxi trips within the city centre should cost around 100 Kč to 150 Kč.

AROUND PRAGUE

Karlštejn

An easy day trip from Prague is **Karlštejn Castle** *(open 9am-noon & 12.30pm-6pm Tues-Sun July & Aug; 9am-noon & 12.30pm-5pm May, June & Sept; 9am-noon & 1pm-4pm Apr & Oct; 9am-noon & 1pm-3pm Nov-Mar)*, 33km to the southwest. Erected by Emperor Charles IV in the mid-14th century, this towering, fairy-tale castle crowns a ridge above the village. The highlight is the **Chapel of the Holy Rood** in the Great Tower, where the coronation jewels were kept until 1420. Some 128 painted panels by Master Theodoric and numerous precious stones covering the walls make it a veritable gallery of 14th-century art.

The 45-minute guided tours in English on Route I cost 200 Kč. Route II, which includes the chapel, runs from July to November only and must be pre-booked (☎ 274 00 81 54; ⓔ rezervace@spusc.cz) at 300 Kč per person, plus a 20 Kč booking fee.

Trains leave for Karlštejn about once every hour from Praha-hlavní nádraží and Praha-Smíchov train stations (35 minutes).

Konopiště

Midway between Prague and Tábor, and 2km west of Benešov train station, is **Konopiště Chateau** *(open 9am-12.30pm & 1pm-5pm daily May-Aug; 9am-12.30pm & 1pm-4pm daily Sept; 9am-12.30pm & 1pm-3pm Mon-Fri, 9am-12.30pm & 1pm-4pm Sat & Sun Apr & Oct; 9am-12.30pm & 1pm-3pm Sat & Sun Nov)*. The castle dates from the 14th century, but the Renaissance palace it shelters is from the 17th century.

Archduke Franz Ferdinand d'Este, heir to the Austro-Hungarian throne, had Konopiště renovated in 1894 and added a large English park and rose garden. His huge collection of hunting trophies and weapons, on display at the chateau, will disturb animal lovers.

There are three tours of the castle, each covering a different part. Tours I and II last 45 minutes each and in English cost 130 Kč; Tour III (one hour) is 260 Kč.

Twelve fast trains leave Prague's Praha-hlavní nádraží for Benešov (one hour, 49km) daily. Most trains to and from Tábor (one hour, 54km) and České Budějovice (two hours, 120km) also stop here. There are occasional buses from Benešov train station to the castle, otherwise it's a 10-minute walk to the west.

Kutná Hora

pop 21,500

In the 14th century, Kutná Hora, 66km east of Prague, was the second-largest town in Bohemia, owing to the rich veins of silver below the city. During the 16th century, Kutná Hora's boom ended, so the medieval townscape is basically unaltered.

The easiest way to visit Kutná Hora on a day trip is to arrive on the morning express train from Prague's Praha-hlavní nádraží train station, and then walk for 10 minutes from Kutná Hora hlavní nádraží train station to Sedlec to visit **Sedlec Ossuary** *(admission 30 Kč; open 8am-6pm daily Apr-Sept, 8am-noon & 1pm-5pm Oct, 9am-noon & 1pm-4pm Nov-Mar)*. In 1870, František Rint, a local woodcarver, arranged the bones of 40,000 people in the form of bells, a chandelier, monstrances and even the Schwarzenberg coat-of-arms – a truly macabre sight. From there it's another 15-minute walk or a five-minute bus ride to central Kutná Hora. The helpful municipal **information centre** *(☎ 327 51 23 78; ⓔ infocentrum@kutnohorsko.cz; Palackého nám 377)* sells local maps.

From the southern side of St James Church, a narrow cobbled lane leads down and then up to the **Hrádek Mining Museum** *(admission with/without tour of mine 110/60 Kč; open 10am-6pm Tues-Sun July & Aug, 9am-6pm May, June & Sept, 9am-5pm Apr & Oct)*. This 15th-century palace contains an exhibit on the silver mining that made Kutná Hora wealthy. The museum's main attraction is the 45-minute guided tour through 500m of **medieval mine shafts** beneath the town.

Kutná Hora's greatest monument is the **Cathedral of St Barbara** *(admission 30 Kč; open 9am-5.30pm Tues-Sun May-Sept, 10am-11.30am & 1pm-4pm Apr & Oct, 10am-11.30am & 2pm-3.30pm Nov-Mar)*, which was finished in 1547.

Kutná Hora is on the main railway line between Prague and Brno via Havlíčkův Brod, but many express trains don't stop here.

There are seven direct trains daily from Prague's Praha-hlavní nádraží (62 Kč, 55 minutes) to Kutná Hora hlavní nádraží.

There are half-a-dozen buses to Prague (60 Kč, 1¼ hours) Monday to Friday, but far fewer at weekends.

North Bohemia

Tourists tend to be shy of North Bohemia, perceived as little more than an arc of polluted factory towns, but away from the Chomutov-Most-Ústí nad Labem industrial region there are many unspoilt attractions.

LITOMĚŘICE & TEREZÍN

pop 25,100

Under Ferdinand III, Litoměřice's status as a royal seat and bishopric brought it prosperity. Today, the old town centre has a multitude of picturesque baroque buildings and churches, some of which were designed by the 18th-century architect (and hometown kid) Ottavio Broggio.

The **information centre** *(☎ 416 73 24 40; ⓔ info@mulitom.cz; Mírové nám 15; open Mon-Sat daily May-Sept)* is in the distinctive House at the Chalice, the present town hall. Dominating the broad and beautiful main square is the Gothic-turned-baroque **All Saints Church**. Across the street is the **Old Town Hall** with a small town museum, while the thin slice of pink baroque wedding cake at the uphill end of the square is the **House of Ottavio Broggio.**

South of the city, the huge 18th-century fortress town of **Terezín** is better known to history as Theriesenstadt – a notorious WWII concentration camp. It's only 3km from Litoměřice and makes a deeply moving day trip. Hourly buses from Litoměřice drop you off at the main square

The best bargain in town is **Penzion U pavouka** *(☎ 416 73 44 09; Pekařská 7; doubles 550 Kč)*, where the price includes breakfast. The new **Pension U svatého Václava** *(☎ 416 73 75 00; Svatováclavská 12; singles/doubles 600/1000 Kč)* is a bit more posh.

Radniční sklípek *(Mírové nám 21; mains 85-125 Kč; open 10am-11pm daily)* is a good cellar pub and restaurant serving cheap Czech grub.

From Prague, hourly buses (61 Kč, one hour) make the trip from Litoměřice.

West Bohemia

Plzeň is the western gateway to the Czech Republic. All trains from western Germany pass this way and the stately imperial spa of Karlovy Vary is in the region.

KARLOVY VARY

pop 53,900

Karlovy Vary (Charles' Hot Springs) is the largest and oldest of the Czech Republic's spas. According to legend, Emperor Charles IV discovered the hot springs by chance while hunting a stag. From the 19th century on, celebrities from Beethoven to Peter the Great to Yuri Gagarin came here to take the waters. Ludvík Moser began making glassware at Karlovy Vary in 1857, and today Bohemian crystal is prized around the world.

Karlovy Vary still has a definite 19th-century atmosphere despite being crowded with tourists. The elegant colonnades and boulevards complement the many peaceful walks in the surrounding parkland.

Orientation

Karlovy Vary has two train stations. Express trains from Prague and Cheb use Karlovy Vary-horní nádraží, across the Ohře River, just north of the city. Local trains stop at Karlovy Vary Dolní nádraží, which is beside the main ČSAD bus station. The Tržnice city bus station is in front of the *Městská tržnice* (market), three blocks east of Karlovy Vary Dolní nádraží. TG Masaryka, the pedestrian mall in Karlovy Vary's city centre, runs east to the Teplá River. Upstream is the heart of the spa area.

Information

The main information office, **Infocentrum** *(☎ 353 22 40 97; ⓔ infocentrum@email.cz; Lázeňská 1; open daily)*, has maps and brochures. **Česká spořitelna** *(TG Masaryka 14)* has an exchange counter and an ATM. **Incentives CZ** *(☎ 353 22 60 27; Vřídelní 51; open 10am-6pm Mon-Fri, 10am-4pm Sat)* is an American Express representative and has an exchange office.

The **main post office** *(TG Masaryka 1; open 7.30am-7pm Mon-Fri, 7am-1pm Sat, 7am-noon Sun)* includes a telephone centre. You can check email at the **Internet Café** *(open 10am-10pm daily)* in the Hotel Thermal, which charges 80 Kč an hour.

Things to See & Do

As you follow the riverside promenade south, you'll pass the towering concrete **Hotel Thermal & Spa** (1976) and the neoclassical **Mlýnská Kolonáda**. On a nearby hill is the old **Zámecká tower** (1608) on the site of Charles IV's 1358 hunting lodge. Down the hill from the tower is the **House of the Three Moors** *(Dagmar House; Tržiště 25)*, where Goethe stayed.

Opposite this building is a bridge that leads to the pulsing heart of Karlovy Vary, the **Vřídelní Kolonáda**. A modern glass enclosure houses the Vřídlo or Sprudel (geyser), where spring water at 72.2°C spurts 12m into the air. Continue southwest along the river to the **Karlovy Vary Museum** *(Nová Louka 23; admission 30 Kč; open 9am-noon & 1pm-5pm Wed-Sun)*, which has displays on local and natural history. Beyond the park past the museum is the beautifully restored **Lázně I** (Spa No 1) built in 1895.

Relax after your sightseeing with a swim in the large **open-air thermal pool** *(bazén; admission 30 Kč an hour; open 8am-8.30pm Mon-Sat, 9am-9.30pm Sun)* on the cliff top overlooking the Hotel Thermal.

Places to Stay

At weekends accommodation can be tight.

Čedok *(☎ 353 22 33 35; Dr Bechera 21; open 9am-6pm Mon-Fri, 9am-noon Sat)* travel agency and **W-Privat Accommodation Agency** *(☎/fax 353 22 77 68; nám Republiky 5; open 8.30am-5pm Mon-Fri, 9.30am-1pm Sat)* can book private rooms from 350 Kč per person.

A spa tax of 15 Kč per person is added to hotel rates.

Penzión Hestia *(☎ 353 22 59 85, fax 353 22 04 82; Stará Kysibelská 45; beds 350 Kč)* is a hostel-style place that's half-hour walk east of the centre, or you can take bus No 6 from Tržnice bus station. It has clean rooms, with shared facilities.

There are several reasonable pensions located along Zahradní, such as the **Pension Kosmos** *(☎/fax 353 22 31 68; singles/doubles from 450/720 Kč)*, which can be found at No 39.

The two-star **Hotel Kavalerie** *(☎ 353 22 96 13, fax 353 23 61 71; ⓔ kavalerie@volny.cz; TG Masaryka 43; singles/doubles 950/1350 Kč)* is probably the best-value hotel in the town centre.

Places to Eat

P&P Pizzeria *(IP Pavlova 13; mains 75-90 Kč)* is just across Poštovní Bridge. In a back court around the corner is the good **VgR Vegetarian Restaurant** *(IP Pavlova 23)*.

Parlament *(cnr TG Masaryka & Zeyerova; mains 65-85 Kč; open Mon-Sat)* is a good inexpensive place serving pork sauerkraut and dumplings, and other Czech dishes.

There's a good, cheap **buffet** inside the entrance to the market.

Bistro Pupík *(Horova 2)*, next to the Tržnice city bus station, has cheap beer on tap.

Entertainment

Karlovy Vary's main theatre is the **Divadlo Vítězslava Nezvala** *(Divadlo nám)*. From mid-May to mid-September concerts are held in Vřídelní Kolonáda Tuesday to Friday.

Propaganda Music Club *(Jaltská 7)* has occasional live bands or DJs spinning rock and pop music nightly.

Getting There & Away

Five daily buses run to Prague (110 Kč, 2½ hours). The only way to get directly to Plzeň (1½ hours, 84km) and České Budějovice (four hours, 220km) is by bus. Seats on express buses should be reserved in advance at the **ČSAD agency** *(☎ 353 22 36 62; nám Republiky 7; open 6am-6pm Mon-Fri, 7am-noon Sat)* at the Dolní nádraží train station.

There are several direct trains daily from Karlovy Vary to Prague (168 Kč, four hours). Hourly local trains connect Cheb (48 Kč, one hour) to Karlovy Vary. Heading west from Karlovy Vary to Nuremberg, Germany, and beyond, you'll have to change at Cheb.

Getting Around

Bus No 11 runs hourly from Karlovy Vary-horní nádraží to the Tržnice city bus station at the market, then over the hills to Divadlo nám and the Vřídelní Kolonáda. Bus No 2 runs between Tržnice and Grandhotel Pupp (Lázně I) every half-hour or so from 6am to 11pm daily.

PLZEŇ

pop 166,300

The city of Plzeň (Pilsen), midway between Prague and Nuremberg, is the capital of West Bohemia. At the confluence of four rivers, this town was once an active medieval trading centre. Beer has been brewed in Plzeň for 700 years, and the town is famous as the original home of Pilsner. Connoisseurs of the brewer's art will not regret the pilgrimage.

The main train station, Plzeň-hlavní nádraží, is on the eastern side of town. The central bus station is west of the centre on Husova, opposite the Škoda Works. Between these is the old town, centred on nám Republiky. The **city information centre** *(☎ 377 03 27 50; ⓔ infocenter@mmp.plzen-city.cz; open daily)* is on the main square at nám Republiky 41.

Things to See & Do

The Gothic **St Bartholomew Church** *(admission 20 Kč; open 10am-4pm Wed-Sat, noon-7pm Sun Apr-Dec)* in the middle of nám Republiky has the highest **tower** *(admission 20 Kč; open 10am-6pm daily)* in Bohemia, at 102m. On the back of the outer side of the church is an iron grille; touch the angel and make a wish.

To the south on Františkánská is the 14th-century **Assumption Church**. Behind it, around the block, is the **West Bohemian Museum** *(admission 20 Kč; open 9am-5pm Tues-Sun Mar-Jan)* with a collection of porcelain and 17th-century weapons. The neo-Renaissance **Great Synagogue** across Sady Pětatřicátníků is one of Europe's biggest synagogues.

Plzeň's most interesting sight by far is the **Brewery Museum** *(Veleslavínova 6; admission 60 Kč, with guide 100 Kč; open 10am-6pm daily Apr-Dec, 10am-4pm Jan-Mar)*, northeast of nám Republiky. In an authentic medieval malt house, the museum displays a fascinating collection of artefacts related to brewing.

The famous **Pilsner Urquell Brewery** *(☎ 377 06 11 11; tour 100 Kč; open 8am-4pm Mon-Fri, 8am-1pm Sat & Sun)* is only a 10-minute walk east along Pražská over the river. The twin-arched gate, which appears on every genuine Pilsner label, is here. A one-hour tour of the brewing room and fermentation cellar is offered to individuals at 12.30pm Monday to Friday only.

Places to Stay

CKM *(☎ 377 23 63 93, fax 377 23 69 09; ⓔ ckm-plzen@volny.cz; Dominikánská 1; open 9am-5pm Mon-Fri)* youth travel agency can book hostels in summer (from 200 Kč per person), pensions and hotels.

Pension v Solní *(☎ 377 23 66 52; Solní 8; ⓔ pension.solni@post.cz; singles/doubles 510/850 Kč)* is a pleasant little town house close to the square; there are only three rooms, so bookings are a must.

Hotel Slovan *(☎ 377 22 72 56, fax 377 22 70 12; ⓔ hotelslovan@iol.cz; Smetanovy sady 1; singles/doubles 500/750 Kč, with bath & TV 1420/2040 Kč)* is a grand old place with a magnificent central stairway, dating from the 1890s. The cheap rooms are tired-looking.

Places to Eat

S&S Grill *(Sedláčkova 7; chicken per 100g 45-55 Kč)* has great barbecued chicken. **Fénix Bistro** *(nám Republiky 18; mains 35-80 Kč)* is a good, cheap self-service place.

You can get decent, inexpensive pizzas at **Pizzerie** *(Solní 9; pizzas 52-62 Kč)*. Not far from the square is **Pivnice U Salzmannů** *(Pražská 8; mains 80-180 Kč)*, a Plzeň institution known for its good-quality food and beer.

Entertainment

Try JK Tyla Theatre or the ultramodern Dům kultury beside the river. There are also interesting tours of the backstage area, dressing rooms and below the stage of the Tyla Theatre, in Czech only, during July and August (20 Kč).

You can listen to local and foreign rock bands (until 11.30pm) or dance to pop tunes (until 5am) at **Rock Bar Elektra** *(Americká 24)*. **Zach's Pub** *(Palackého nám 2)* serves Guinness and English beers.

Getting There & Away

All international trains from Munich and Nuremberg to Prague stop at Plzeň. There are fast trains from here to České Budějovice (100 Kč, two hours) and Cheb (120 Kč, 1½ hours).

If you're heading for Karlovy Vary, take a bus (80 Kč, 1½ hours). Buses also run to Prague (60 Kč, 1½ hours) and České Budějovice (96 Kč, 2¾ hours).

South Bohemia

South Bohemia has many quaint little towns with a Bavarian or Austrian flavour, mixed with local folk baroque buildings.

ČESKÉ BUDĚJOVICE

pop 98,900

České Budějovice (Budweis), the regional capital of South Bohemia, is a charming medieval city halfway between Plzeň and Vienna. Here the Vltava River meets the Malše and flows north to Prague. Nearby silver mines made the town rich in the 16th century. After a fire in 1641, much of the town was rebuilt in the baroque style. The city is famous as the original home of Budvar (Budweiser) beer.

The town is a good base for day trips to many local attractions, including picturesque little Bohemian towns such as Jindřichův Hradec, Písek, Prachatice, Tábor and Třeboň.

Orientation & Information

It's a 10-minute walk west down Lannova třída, then Kanovnická, from the adjacent bus and train stations to nám Přemysla Otakara II, the main square. The helpful **city information centre** *(☎/fax 386 35 94 80; ⓔ infocb@c-budejovice.cz; nám Přemysla Otakara II 1; open daily)* sells maps and can arrange guides, tickets and accommodation. The commercial **Tourist Information and Map Centre** *(☎/fax 386 35 25 89; ⓔ mapcentrum@mbox.vol.cz; nám Přemysla Otakara II 28; open daily)* sells maps and theatre tickets. **Raiffeisen Bank** *(open 8.30am-5pm Mon-Thur, 8.30am-4.30pm Fri)*, on the main square, changes travellers cheques and has an ATM.

The 24-hour **main post office** *(Pražská 69)* is north of the centre; there's a more convenient **branch post office** *(open 7am-7pm Mon-Fri, 8am-noon Sat)* on Senovážné nám. You can surf the Internet at **Xfiles internet café** *(Senovážné nám; open 10am-10pm Mon-Fri, 4pm-10pm Sat & Sun)*, opposite the post office, for 1 Kč a minute.

Things to See

Nám Přemysla Otakara II, a vast, open square surrounded by 18th-century arcades, is one of the largest of its kind in Europe. At its centre is the **Samsonova Fountain** (1727), and on the western side stands the baroque **town hall** (1731). The allegorical figures of the cardinal virtues – Justice, Wisdom, Courage and Prudence – on the town hall balustrade, stand above four bronze dragon gargoyles. Looming above the opposite corner of the square is the 72m-tall **Black Tower** *(admission 15 Kč; open 10am-6pm daily July & Aug, 10am-6pm Tues-Sun Apr-June, Sept & Oct)*, dating from 1553, with great views from the gallery.

The streets around the square, especially Česká, are lined with old burgher houses. West near the river is the former **Dominican monastery** (1265), with another tall tower and a splendid pulpit. South along the riverside behind the warehouse are the remaining sections of the 16th-century walls. The **Museum of South Bohemia** *(admission 20 Kč; open 9am-12.30pm & 1pm-5pm Tues-Sun)* is just south of the old town.

The **Budweiser Budvar Brewery** *(☎ 387 70 53 41; cnr Pražská & K Světlé; bus No 2; open 9am-5pm daily)* is involved in a long-standing legal tussle with the US brewer Anheuser-Busch over the brand name 'Budweiser', which has been used by both breweries since the 19th century. However, there's no contest as to which beer is superior; one taste of Budvar and you'll be an instant convert. The 2pm tour is open to individual travellers. The brewery's **beer hall** is open 10am to 10pm daily.

Places to Stay

Accommodation can be tight during the regular trade fairs held here throughout the year. Check with the tourist information centre before turning up without a booking.

CKM *(☎ 386 35 12 70; Lannova třída 63; open 9am-5pm Mon-Thur, 9am-3.30pm Fri)* youth travel agency and both tourist information offices can arrange dorm accommodation from 120 Kč per person. **Kolej jihočeské university** *(☎ 387 77 42 01; Studentská 13-19; doubles 240 Kč)*, west of the centre, has beds available from July to September.

Both tourist information offices offer private rooms from around 300 Kč per person. A good place with similarly priced rooms is **CTS Travel Agency** *(☎ 386 35 39 68; nám Přemysla Otakara II 38; open 7.30am-7pm Mon-Thur)*.

Small private pensions around town are a better deal than the hotels. **Pension Centrum** *(☎ 386 35 20 30; Mlýnská stoka 6; doubles 850 Kč)*, just off Kanovnická, has been recommended by readers. Its neighbour, **Pension Na Mlýnské stoce** *(☎/fax 386 35 34 75; ⓔ penzion.garni@mybox.cz; Mlýnska stoka 7; singles 600-800 Kč, doubles 800-950 Kč)*, has also generated good feedback.

Hotel Bohemia *(☎/fax 386 36 06 91; ⓔ hotel-bohemia@volny.cz; Hradební 20; singles/doubles 1290/1690 Kč)*, on a quiet side street, has comfy rooms and a cellar wine bar with plenty of character.

Places to Eat

Try the local carp, which you'll find on many restaurant menus.

Masné krámy *(mains 40-60 Kč)* beer hall in the old meat market (1560), on the corner of Hroznová and 5.května, has been a local institution for centuries. **Na dvorku** *(Kněžská 11; mains 40-60 Kč)* has a more genuine beer-hall atmosphere.

Víno z Panské *(Panská 14; open Mon-Sat)* is good wine bar that serves vegetarian and chicken dishes. Its wine is served straight from the barrel.

The best coffee in town is served up at friendly little **Caffé Bar Piccolo** *(Mlýnská stoka 9; open Mon-Sat)*.

Entertainment

Regular classical music concerts by the Chamber Philharmonic Orchestra of South Bohemia are held at the **Concert Hall** *(Kněžská 6)* in the Church of St Anne, and also at the **Conservatory** *(Kanovnická 22)*.

Jihočeské Theatre, by the river on Dr Stejskala, usually presents plays in Czech, but operas, operettas and concerts are also performed here.

Singer Pub *(Česká 55; open 11am-11pm daily)* is a lively Irish-type pub. Rock bands often play at **Černej velbloud** *(U tří lvů 4; open Mon-Sat)*.

Getting There & Away

There are fast trains from České Budějovice to Plzeň (100 Kč, two hours), Tábor (55 Kč, one hour) and Prague (126 Kč, 2½ hours). You can connect with trains between Prague and Vienna at České Velenice, 50km southeast of České Budějovice.

For shorter trips you're better off travelling by bus. The bus to Brno (182 Kč, four hours) travels via Telč (86 Kč, two hours). Twice a week there's a bus to Linz, Austria (2¼ hours, 125km).

ČESKÝ KRUMLOV

pop 14,600

Český Krumlov, a small medieval town 25km south of České Budějovice, is one of the most picturesque – and touristy – towns in Europe. Its appearance has remained almost unchanged since the 18th century. Its sprawling chateau occupies a ridge above the west bank of the river, while the old town centre sits on the tongue of land inside the loop on the east bank. Český Krumlov's Gothic border castle, rebuilt as a huge Renaissance chateau by 16th-century Italian architects, is second only to Prague Castle in size and splendour.

Orientation & Information

Arriving by bus from České Budějovice, get off at the Český Krumlov Špičák bus stop, the first in town. The train station is 1.5km north of the old town centre. Bus Nos 1, 2 and 3 go from the station to the Špičák bus stop.

The municipal **Infocentrum** *(☎ 380 70 46 22; ⓔ infocentrum@ckrf.ckrumlov.cz; nám Svornosti 2; open daily)* provides information about the town and region. You can check email here for 10 Kč per 10 minutes.

Things to See

Two blocks south of the **Budějovická Gate** (1598) is the **Red Gate**, the main entrance to **Český Krumlov Chateau** *(open 9am-noon & 1pm-6pm daily July & Aug, 9am-noon & 1pm-5pm Apr, May, Sept & Oct)*. The chateau is said to be haunted by a white lady who appears from time to time to forecast doom. Tours in English/Czech cost 140/70 Kč each; however, you are free to wander through the courtyards and grounds without buying a ticket.

Nám Svornosti, the old town square across the river, is overlooked by the plain Gothic **town hall** and a baroque **plague column** (1716), and ringed by some pleasant outdoor cafés. Nearby is the **Regional Museum** *(admission 20 Kč; open 10am-5pm Tues-Sun)*, with a surprisingly interesting collection housed in the old Jesuit seminary (1652).

Places to Stay

Hostels There are plenty of backpacker hostels in town.

Travellers' Hostel *(☎/fax 337 71 13 45; ⓔ krumlov@travellers.cz; Soukenická 43; dorm beds 250 Kč)*, owned by the Prague Travellers Hostel chain, has a lively bar and is popular with the party crowd.

Hostel 99 *(☎ 377 71 28 12; ⓔ hostel99@hotmail.com; Věžní 99; dorm beds 250 Kč, doubles 600 Kč)* is another good place with a cool sun terrace to hang out on.

U vodníka *(☎ 377 71 19 35; ⓔ zukowski3@hotmail.com; Po vodě 55; doubles 600 Kč)*, down a cobbled lane off Rooseveltova, is a much more peaceful spot right next to the river. It has three double rooms, cooking facilities, a small English library and a nice garden out the back.

Private Rooms & Pensions The Infocentrum has private rooms from 400 Kč per

ČESKÝ KRUMLOV

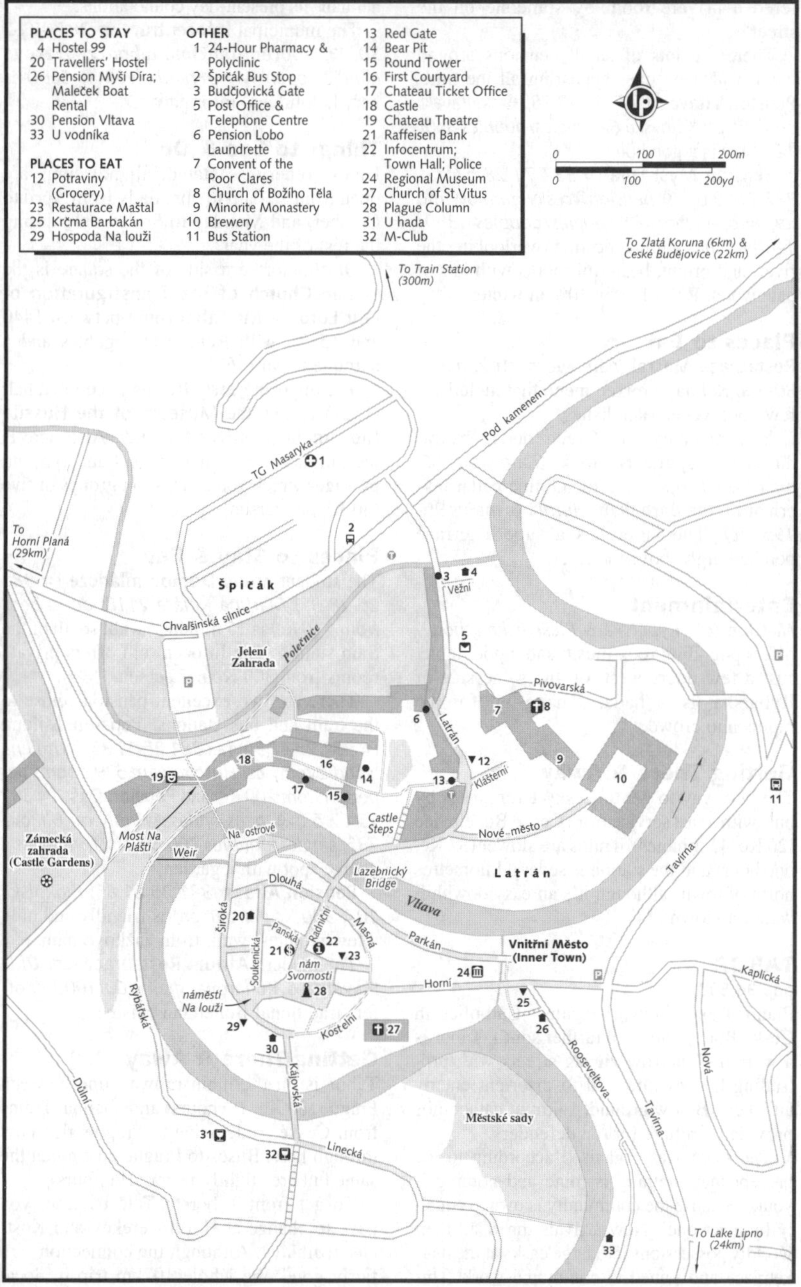

PLACES TO STAY
4 Hostel 99
20 Travellers' Hostel
26 Pension Myší Díra; Maleček Boat Rental
30 Pension Vltava
33 U vodníka

PLACES TO EAT
12 Potraviny (Grocery)
23 Restaurace Maštal
25 Krčma Barbakán
29 Hospoda Na louži

OTHER
1 24-Hour Pharmacy & Polyclinic
2 Špičák Bus Stop
3 Budčjovická Gate
5 Post Office & Telephone Centre
6 Pension Lobo Laundrette
7 Convent of the Poor Clares
8 Church of Božího Těla
9 Minorite Monastery
10 Brewery
11 Bus Station
13 Red Gate
14 Bear Pit
15 Round Tower
16 First Courtyard
17 Chateau Ticket Office
18 Castle
19 Chateau Theatre
21 Raiffeisen Bank
22 Infocentrum; Town Hall; Police
24 Regional Museum
27 Church of St Vitus
28 Plague Column
31 U hada
32 M-Club

person with breakfast. You may also be offered a private room by someone on the street.

There are lots of small pensions around town, with new ones appearing all the time. **Pension Vltava** *(☎ 377 71 19 78; ⓔ ckvltava@ckvltava.cz; Kájovská 62; singles/doubles 850/1200 Kč)* is a good one.

Pension Myší Díra *(☎ 337 71 28 53, fax 337 71 19 00; ⓔ pension@ceskykrumlov-info.cz; Rooseveltova 28; singles/doubles 1390/1480 Kč)* has a great location overlooking the river, and bright, beautiful rooms with lots of pale wood. Rates fall by 40% in winter.

Places to Eat

Restaurace Maštal *(nám Svornosti 2; mains 80-150 Kč)* has a mixed menu that includes a few good vegetarian dishes.

You can enjoy good Czech food at the traditional **Hospoda Na louži** *(Kájovaská 66; mains 60-100 Kč)* and the Gothic cellar tavern of **Krčma Barbakán** *(Horní 26; mains 95-195 Kč)*. The latter has a superb terrace perched high above the river.

Entertainment

M-Club *(cnr Rybářská & Plešivecké schody)* offers pounding rock music and a pool table. Just a few doors west, on the same side of Rybářská, is U hada, a hang-out for the rap/techno crowd.

Getting There & Away

The best way to get to Český Krumlov is by bus, with a fast service from České Budějovice (26 Kč, 45 minutes). Trains are slower (32 Kč, one hour) and the station is several kilometres north of town (although it's an easy downhill walk into town).

TÁBOR

pop 36,800

Planned as a bulwark against Catholics in České Budějovice and farther south, Tábor is a warren of narrow zigzag streets with protruding houses intended to disorient enemy attackers. Below ground, 14km of catacombs provided a refuge for the defenders.

The town was organised according to the precept that 'nothing is mine and nothing is yours, because the community is owned equally by everyone'. New arrivals threw all their worldly possessions into large casks at the marketplace and joined in communal work. This nonconformism helped to give the word 'Bohemian' its present-day connotations.

The municipal **Infocentrum** *(☎ 381 48 62 30; ⓔ infocentrum@mu.tabor.cz; Žižkovo nám 2; open Mon-Fri, daily May-Sept)* is very helpful and informative.

Things to See & Do

Unless otherwise stated, all museums are open from 8.30am to 5pm daily from April to October, and Monday to Friday only during the rest of the year.

On the northern side of the square is the Gothic **Church of the Transfiguration of Our Lord on Mt Tábor** (built between 1440 and 1512), with Renaissance gables and a baroque tower (1677).

The imposing early Renaissance town hall (1521) is now the **Museum of the Hussite Movement** *(admission 40 Kč)*. Also here is the entrance to a 650m stretch of underground passages which you can visit in groups of five (40 Kč per person).

Places to Stay & Eat

The student hostel **Domov mládeže** *(☎ 381 25 28 37; Martina Koláře 2118; dorm beds from 110 Kč)* is 15 minutes' walk south of the train station. The Infocentrum offers private rooms from 300 Kč per person.

There are two excellent pensions close to the train and bus stations: **Pension Milena** *(☎ 381 25 47 55, fax 381 25 11 33; ⓔ milena.sport@volny.cz; Husovo nám 529; rooms per person from 200 Kč)* and **Pension Dáša** *(☎ 381 25 62 53; ⓔ pensiondasa@volny.cz; Bílkova 735; singles/doubles 700/990 Kč)*, which is a deluxe spot with a garden.

Pension Alfa *(☎ 381 25 61 65; Klokotská 107; 300 Kč per person)* is friendly and only a few minutes' walk from Žižkovo nám.

The modern **Atrium Restaurace** *(cnr třída 9.května & Kollárova; mains 60-100 Kč)* offers traditional Bohemian cuisine.

Getting There & Away

Tábor is on the main railway line between Prague (80 Kč, 1½ hours) and Vienna. Trains from České Budějovice to Prague also pass through here. Buses to Prague cost much the same but are slightly faster (1¼ hours).

To get from Tábor to Telč by train you have to change at Horní Cerekev and Kostelec u Jihlavy. Although the connections are fairly good, the whole 107km trip by local train takes three or four hours. Otherwise take a bus to Jihlava (74km) and change there for Telč (29km).

Eastbound buses to Brno (140 Kč, three hours) leave four times a day.

Moravia

The historic land of Moravia – Bohemia's eastern partner in the Czech Republic – is often overlooked. Yet the region has its own history and natural wonders, like the karst area north of the Moravian capital, Brno, and the charming historic town of Telč. South Moravia is also famed for its excellent wines.

TELČ

pop 6000

Telč was founded in the 14th century by the feudal lords of Hradec as a fortified settlement with a castle separated from town by a strong wall. The bus and train stations are a few hundred metres apart on the eastern side of town.

There's an **information office** *(☎ 567 24 31 45; ⓔ info@telc-etc.cz; open Mon-Fri)* in the town hall where you can check your email (1 Kč a minute).

Telč's greatest monument is the Renaissance **Water Chateau** *(open 9am-noon & 1pm-5pm Tues-Sun May-Aug, 9am-noon & 1pm-4pm Apr, Sept & Oct)*, at the town square's northwestern end. Opposite the chateau is the baroque **Church of Jesus' Name** (1655), in the former Jesuit college.

Places to Stay & Eat

The information office can book private rooms (from around 300 Kč per person) and pensions. There are several *'Zimmer frei'* signs east along Štěpnická and on nám Zachariáš e z Hradce.

The friendly **Hotel Pod kaštany** *(☎ 567 21 30 42, fax 567 22 30 65; Štěpnická 409; singles/doubles/triples without bath 400/660/780 Kč)* is just outside the old town. It gives a 10% discount to ISIC card-holders.

Restaurace U Zachariáše *(mains 80-110 Kč)*, on the square, is the place preferred by locals. The restaurant at **Hotel Pod kaštany** is good for Moravian food and beer.

Getting There & Away

Buses travelling between České Budějovice and Brno stop at Telč about twice a day – it's about a 100km, two-hour trip from Telč to either city. Five buses a day run to Prague (100 Kč, 2½ hours).

BRNO

pop 379,200

Halfway between Budapest and Prague, Brno has been the capital of Moravia since 1641; its large fortress was an instrument of Habsburg domination. The botanist Gregor Mendel (1822–84) established the modern science of heredity through his studies of peas and bees at the Augustinian monastery here.

The **tourist office** *(☎ 542 21 10 90, 542 21 07 58; ⓔ info@kicbrno.cz; Radnická 8; open daily)* in the Old Town Hall can book accommodation and help out with other information.

Things to See

Unless otherwise stated, admission to museums and galleries costs 40 Kč, and all are closed on Mondays and Tuesdays.

As you enter the city along Masarykova, turn left into Kapučínské nám to reach the **Capuchin monastery** *(open 9am-noon & 2pm-4.30pm Tues-Sat, 11am-11.45am & 2pm-4.30pm Sun mid-Feb–Apr & mid-Oct–mid-Dec; 9am-noon & 2pm-4.30pm Mon-Sat, 11am-11.45am & 2pm-4.30pm Sun May-Sept)*, dating from 1651. In the ventilated crypt below the church are the intact mummies of monks and local aristocrats deposited here before 1784. At the western end of Kapučínské nám is the Dietrichstein Palace (1760), where the **Regional Moravian Museum** *(open 9am-5pm Tues-Sat)* includes geology exhibits and a mock medieval village.

On Radnická, just off the northern side of Zelný trh, is Brno's 13th-century **Old Town Hall** *(admission 20 Kč; open 9am-5pm daily)*, which has a splendid Gothic portal (1511) below the tower. The town hall's interior includes the Crystal Hall, Fresco Hall

Not on His Watch

In 1645, the Swedish general Torstensson, who was besieging Brno, declared that he would leave if his troops hadn't captured the city by noon. At 11am the Swedes were about to scale the walls when the cathedral bell keeper suddenly rang noon. True to his word, the general broke off the attack. Since that day the cathedral bells have always tolled noon at 11am.

and Treasury. The **Panorama**, another Brno curiosity, is a rare apparatus made in 1890 that offers continuous showings of images of the Czech Republic in 3-D.

On the hill above this gallery is the sinister silhouette of **Špilberk Castle**. Founded in the 13th century and converted into a citadel during the 17th century, it served as a prison for opponents of the Habsburgs until 1855.

From Petrov Hill descend Petrská into Zelný trh and continue on Orlí to Minoritská and the Church of St John (rebuilt in 1733) with fine altarpieces, an organ and painted ceilings. Nám Svobody – the city's broad main square – has a striking plague column (1680). North of the square is the parish church, St James (1473), with a soaring nave in the purest Gothic style.

Places to Stay

Brno hosts international trade fairs year-round, and accommodation is a problem during the main ones in February, March, April, August, September and October.

Čedok and **GTS International** can arrange accommodation in student dormitories during July and August. **Čedok** can arrange private rooms from 550 Kč per person a night. Most are far from the centre, but can easily be reached on public transport. The **Infocentrum** also has private rooms from 350 Kč.

South of the centre, the HI-listed **Hotel Interservis** *(☎ 545 23 42 32; Lomená; beds from 225 Kč)* rents beds in double rooms. Take tram No 12 eastbound from the train station to the end of the line, go through the underpass and continue south on the main road, then turn left along Pompova.

Hotel Pegas *(☎ 542 21 01 04, fax 542 21 43 14; Jakubská 4; singles/doubles 1200/1700 Kč)* is on a quiet street right in the centre of town. Rooms are bright and clean and come with bath and breakfast.

Places to Eat

Vinárna U zlatého meče *(Mečová 3; mains 60-110 Kč)* is an inexpensive and pleasant place to order a bottle of local wine with your meal. Nearby, **Restaurace Pod radničním kole** *(Mečová 5; mains 80-150 Kč)* is a red-brick cellar with good Moravian food and plenty of charming atmosphere.

Haribol *(Lužanecká 4; mains 50-90 Kč; open Mon-Fri)* is a vegetarian restaurant with some Indian dishes on the menu.

Entertainment

Live Performance Brno's theatres are excellent. Opera, operettas and ballet are performed at the modern **Janáček Theatre** *(Janáčkovo divadlo; Sady Osvobození)*. The beautiful neobaroque **Mahenovo Theatre** (Mahenovo divadlo) presents classical drama in Czech and operettas. The **Brno State Philharmonic** *(Komenského nám 8)*, in Besední dům, has regular concerts.

The **Central Booking Office** *(Centrální předprodej; Běhounská 17)* sells tickets to classical, rock and folk concerts at a variety of venues.

Bars & Clubs Popular **Charlie's Hat** *(Kobližná 12)* is a cellar bar with many rooms and a small dance floor where DJs spin anything from heavy rock to dance music. Nearby restaurant and bar **Čtrnačka** *(Jánská 14; open Mon-Sat)* is hugely popular with students.

Stará pekárna *(Štefánikova 8)*, north of the city centre, has live bands playing a variety of styles, including jazz, funk and rock on most nights.

Alterna *(Kounicova 48, block B)* is an alternative *klub* where you can enjoy live rock, punk and jazz. From Česká take trolleybus No 134 or 136 three stops north.

Getting There & Away

Bus The bus to Vienna–Mitte Bahnhof (350 Kč, 2½ hours) departs from platform No 20 at the bus station twice a day. There are also buses to Prague (140 Kč, 2½ hours). For shorter trips such as Telč (86 Kč, two hours) buses are faster and more efficient than trains.

Train All trains travelling between Budapest and Berlin stop at Brno. If you're going to or from Vienna, change trains at Břeclav. To get to or from Košice, change trains at Přerov. There are frequent direct trains from Bratislava (two hours, 141km) and Prague (242 Kč, 2¾ hours). Three overnight trains with couchettes and sleepers travel between Brno and Košice.

Getting Around

You can buy public transport tickets from shops, vending machines and the **MHD Information Office** *(Novobranská 18; open 6am-6pm Mon-Fri, 8am-3.30pm Sat & Sun)*. Tickets valid for 10/40/60 minutes cost 7/12/15 Kč.

Denmark

Unwrap Denmark carefully – it comes in a small package, but it's bursting with alluring attractions. This tiny Scandinavian nucleus holds within its boundaries a compelling mix of buzzing cities, historic provincial towns, sleepy villages, pastoral farmland, peaceful woods and idyllic islands. Copenhagen, Scandinavia's largest and most cosmopolitan capital, is a world-class destination, with superb museums and a vibrant cultural life. Regional capitals, such as Århus and Odense, are sophisticated, friendly university cities.

The sea defines Denmark in every way. The country boasts miles of white sand beaches to match those of the Caribbean – and though temperatures may be a touch more bracing, these are the warmest waters in the Baltic. A wealth of archipelagos and islands adds to the country's marvellous diversity. And although modern Denmark seems to perch precariously atop Germany, lying in the shadow of its northern neighbours, the nation was the ancient heart of Scandinavia and remains home to myriad reminders of a proud Viking past. Underestimate Denmark, or the Danes, at your peril.

Denmark: the Basics

Local name Danmark

Capital Copenhagen

Population 5.3 million

Language Danish

Currency Danish kroner (Dkr) = 100 øre

Avoid at all costs Pricey Legoland

Win instant approval by noting *Danske sild smager I hvert fald bedre end svenske sild.* (Danish herring certainly tastes much better than Swedish herring.)

Facts about Denmark

HISTORY

It is from the arrival of the Danes, thought to have migrated south from Sweden around AD 500, that present-day Denmark traces its linguistic and cultural roots. In the late 9th century, warriors led by the Viking chieftain Hardegon conquered the Jutland Peninsula. The Danish monarchy, Europe's oldest, dates back to Hardegon's son, Gorm the Old. Successive Danish kings went on to invade England and conquer most of the Baltic region.

In 1397 Margrethe I of Denmark established a union between Denmark, Norway and Sweden. Sweden withdrew from the union in 1523 and over the next few hundred years Denmark and Sweden had numerous border skirmishes and a few wars. Norway remained under Danish rule until 1814.

Denmark's golden age was under Christian IV (1588–1648), with Renaissance cities, castles and fortresses flourishing throughout his kingdom. But Denmark's involvement in a series of failed military campaigns resulted in a steady contraction of its borders, culminating in the ceding of the Schleswig and Holstein regions to Germany in 1864.

Denmark remained neutral throughout WWI. However, on 9 April 1940 an unfortified Denmark faced a full-scale invasion by German troops. The Danish government settled for surrender in return for autonomy. In August 1943 the Germans took outright control. The Danish Resistance movement blossomed, and 7000 Jewish Danes were quickly smuggled into neutral Sweden.

Denmark joined NATO in 1949 and the European Community (now the EU) in 1973. The issue of the euro remains controversial, as many Danes fear the loss of local control to a European bureaucracy.

GEOGRAPHY & CLIMATE

Denmark is a small country with a land area of 43,075 sq km, mostly on the peninsula of Jutland. There are 406 islands, 90 of which are inhabited.

Despite its northerly position, Denmark has a relatively mild climate that is moderated by the effects of the warm Gulf Stream Drift.

In midwinter, average daytime maximum temperatures hover around freezing point.

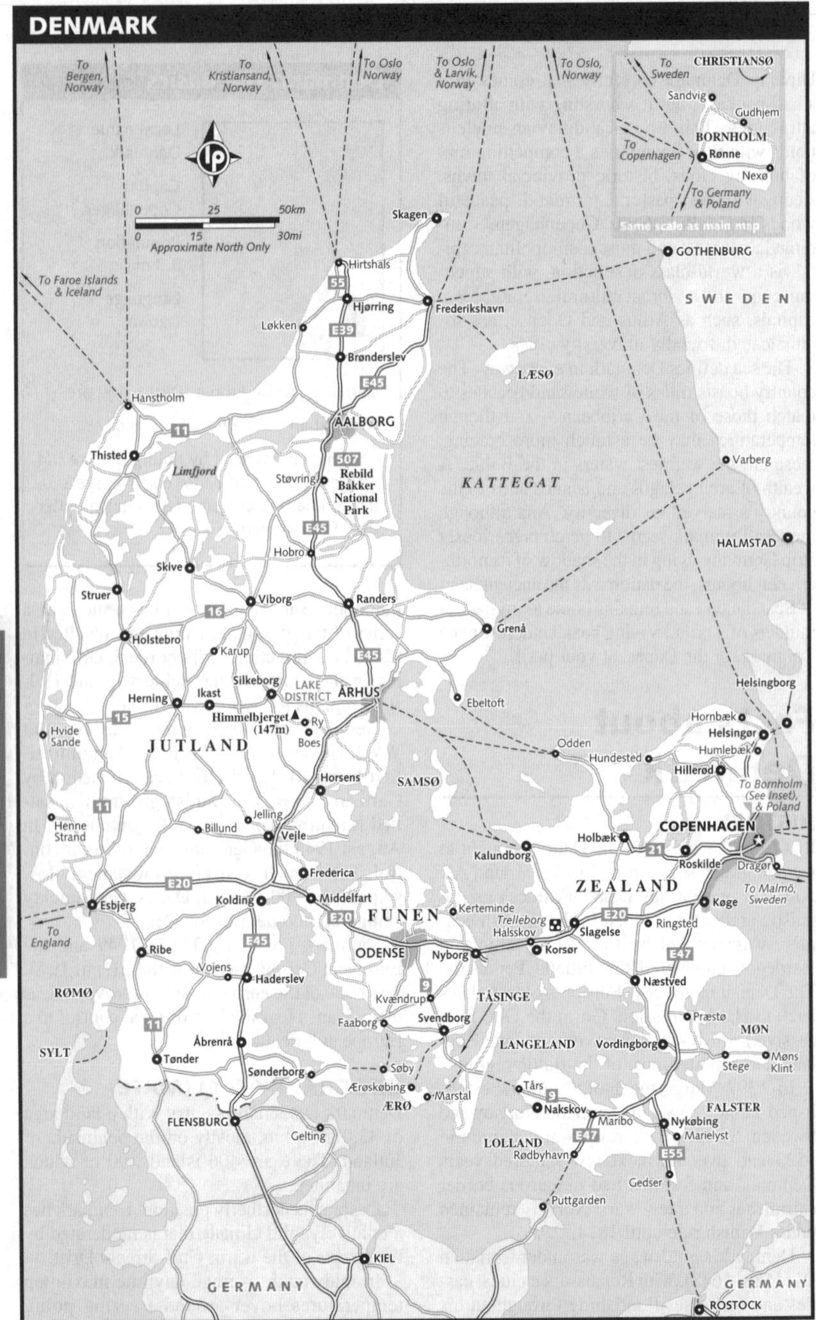
DENMARK
To Bergen, Norway
To Kristiansand, Norway
To Oslo Norway
To Oslo & Larvik, Norway
To Oslo, Norway
0 25 50km
0 15 30mi
Approximate North Only
To Faroe Islands & Iceland
Skagen
Hirtshals
Hjørring
Frederikshavn
Løkken
Brønderslev
LÆSØ
Hanstholm
AALBORG
Thisted
Limfjord
Støvring
Rebild Bakker National Park
KATTEGAT
Hobro
Skive
Struer
Viborg
Randers
Holstebro
Grenå
Karup
Silkeborg
LAKE DISTRICT
ÅRHUS
Herning
Ikast
Himmelbjerget (147m)
Ry
Boes
Ebeltoft
Hvide Sande
JUTLAND
Horsens
SAMSØ
Henne Strand
Billund
Jelling
Vejle
Frederica
Esbjerg
Kolding
Middelfart
FUNEN
Kerteminde
To England
Ribe
Vojens
Haderslev
ODENSE
Nyborg
RØMØ
Kværndrup
Faaborg
Svendborg
TÅSINGE
SYLT
Åbrenrå
Tønder
Sønderborg
Søby
Ærøskøbing
Marstal
ÆRØ
LANGELAND
FLENSBURG
Gelting
KIEL
GERMANY
To Sweden
CHRISTIANSØ
Sandvig
Gudhjem
BORNHOLM
To Copenhagen
Rønne
Nexø
To Germany & Poland
Same scale as main map
GOTHENBURG
SWEDEN
Varberg
HALMSTAD
Helsingborg
Hornbæk
Helsingør
Humlebæk
Odden
Hundested
Hillerød
To Bornholm (See Inset), & Poland
COPENHAGEN
Holbæk
Kalundborg
Roskilde
Dragør
ZEALAND
To Malmö, Sweden
Køge
Trelleborg
Halsskov
Slagelse
Ringsted
Korsør
Næstved
Præstø
MØN
Vordingborg
Stege
Møns Klint
Tårs
Nakskov
Maribo
FALSTER
Nykøbing
Marielyst
LOLLAND
Rødbyhavn
Gedser
Puttgarden
GERMANY
ROSTOCK
55
E39
E45
11
507
16
15
E20
9
21
E47
E55

DENMARK

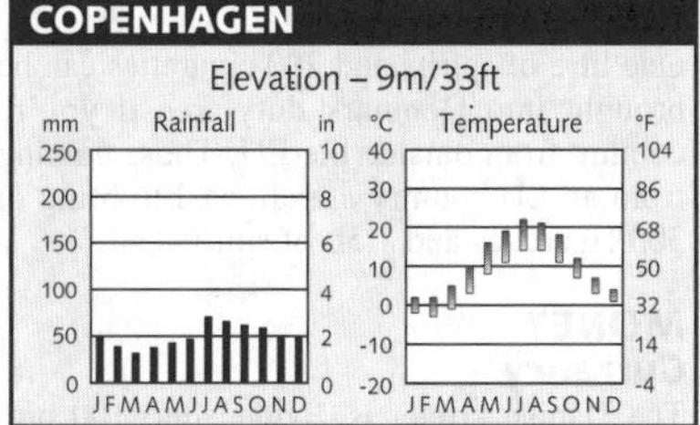

Winter, however, has the highest relative humidity (90%) and the cloudiest weather. Expect rain and grey skies at any time of year.

GOVERNMENT & POLITICS

Denmark is a constitutional monarchy. Queen Margrethe II has been on the throne since 1972, but legislative powers rest with the Folketing, Denmark's elected parliament.

POPULATION & PEOPLE

Denmark's population is about 5.3 million, with 70% living in urban areas. Foreign nationals account for 7.8% of Denmark's population, and 11.8% of Copenhagen's population.

SOCIETY & CONDUCT

Perhaps nothing captures the Danish perspective more than the concept of *hygge,* which, roughly translated, means 'cosy and snug'. It implies shutting out the turmoil and troubles of the outside world and striving for a warm intimate mood.

Danes are refreshingly self-effacing and reserved about themselves and their achievements; the pervasive attitude is that no-one should think of themselves as better than the average, and one should always keep one's feet firmly on the ground.

LANGUAGE

While the majority of Danes speak English, any effort to learn the basics will be greatly appreciated. See the Language Guide at the back of the book for pronunciation guidelines and useful words and phrases.

Facts for the Visitor

HIGHLIGHTS

Denmark has castles aplenty. The most strikingly situated is Egeskov Castle. In Copenhagen the king of castles is Rosenborg.

Ribe, the oldest town in Denmark, has an exquisite historic centre encircling a 12th-century cathedral.

Denmark has many open-air folk museums with period buildings. The most impressive is Den Gamle By in Århus; Odense's folk museum has the most engaging natural setting.

An outstanding art museum is Ny Carlsberg Glyptotek in Copenhagen, while the Viking Ship Museum in Roskilde displays excavated Viking ships and also has an educational centre where Viking ships are being replicated using traditional methods.

PLANNING

May and June can be a delightful and uncrowded time to visit. While autumn can also be pleasant, although the countryside is not so lush and green. July to August is the peak tourist season.

TOURIST OFFICES

Local Tourist Offices

Virtually every sizable town has a local tourist office, usually found in the *rådhus* (town hall) or elsewhere on *torvet* (the central square). Most can load you up with both regional and nationwide brochures. Danish tourist offices abroad include:

France (☎ 01 53 43 26 26, ⓔ paris@dt.dk) Conseil du Tourisme de Danemark, 18 blvd Malesherbes, 75008 Paris

Germany (☎ 40 32 02 10, ⓔ daninfo@dt.dk) Dänisches Fremdenverkehr-samt, Glockengiesserwall 2, 20095 Hamburg

Norway (☎ 22 00 76 46, ⓔ danmark@dt.dk) Danmarks Turistkontor, Tollbugaten 27, Postboks 406 Sentrum, 0103 Oslo

Sweden (☎ 08-611 72 22, ⓔ info@dtab.se) Danmarks Turistråd, Box 5524, 114 85 Stockholm

UK (☎ 020-7259 5959, ⓔ dtb.london@dt.dk) Danish Tourist Board, 55 Sloane St, London SW1X 9SY

USA (☎ 212-885 8700, ⓔ info@goscandinavia.com) Danish Tourist Board, PO Box 4649, Grand Central Station, New York, NY 10163

VISAS & DOCUMENTS

Citizens of the EU, USA, Canada, Australia and New Zealand require a valid passport to enter Denmark, but do not need to have a visa for stays of less than three months. If you wish to apply for a visa make sure that you do so at least three months in advance of your planned arrival.

EMBASSIES & CONSULATES

Danish Embassies

Danish embassies abroad include:

Australia (☎ 02-6273 2195) 15 Hunter St, Yarralumla, ACT 2600
Canada (☎ 613-562 1811) 47 Clarence St, Suite 450, Ottawa, Ontario K1N 9K1
Finland (☎ 9-684 1050) Centralgatan 1A, 00101 Helsinki
France (☎ 01 44 31 21 21) 77 ave Marceau, 75116 Paris
Germany (☎ 5050 2000) Rauchstrasse 1, 10787 Berlin
Iceland (☎ 56 21 230) Hverfisgata 29, 121 Reykjavík
Ireland (☎ 1-475 6404) 121 St Stephen's Green, Dublin 2
New Zealand Contact the embassy in Australia
Norway (☎ 22 54 08 00) Olav Kyrres Gate 7, 0244 Oslo
Sweden (☎ 8-406 75 00) Jakobs Torg 1, 11186 Stockholm
UK (☎ 020-7333 0200) 55 Sloane St, London SW1X 9SR
USA (☎ 202-234 4300) 3200 Whitehaven St NW, Washington DC 20008

Embassies & Consulates in Denmark

Foreign representation in Denmark includes:

Australia (☎ 70 26 36 76) Dampfægevej 26, Copenhagen
Canada (☎ 33 48 32 00) Kristen Bernikows Gade 1, Copenhagen
Finland (☎ 33 13 42 14) Sankt Annæ Plads 24, Copenhagen
France (☎ 33 67 01 00) Kongens Nytorv 4, Copenhagen
Germany (☎ 35 45 99 00) Stockholmsgade 57, Copenhagen
Iceland (☎ 33 18 10 50) Dantes Plads 3, Copenhagen
Ireland (☎ 35 42 32 33) Østbanegade 21, Copenhagen
Netherlands (☎ 33 70 72 00) Toldbodgade 33, Copenhagen
New Zealand Contact the British embassy
Norway (☎ 33 14 01 24) Amaliegade 39, Copenhagen
Poland (☎ 39 46 77 00) Richelius Allé 12, Hellerup
Russia (☎ 35 42 55 85) Kristianiagade 5, Copenhagen
Sweden (☎ 33 36 03 70) Sankt Annæ Plads 15A, Copenhagen
UK (☎ 35 44 52 00) Kastelsvej 36–40, Copenhagen
USA (☎ 35 55 31 44) Dag Hammarskjölds Allé 24, Copenhagen

CUSTOMS

One litre of spirits and 200 cigarettes can be brought into Denmark duty free if you're coming from outside the EU. Those coming from an EU country are allowed to bring in 300 cigarettes and 1.5L of spirits.

MONEY

Currency

The Danish kroner is divided into 100 øre; there are coins for 25 and 50 øre, as well as 1, 2, 5, 10 and 20 kroner. Notes come in denominations of 50, 100, 200, 500 and 1000 kroner. The euro is widely accepted.

Exchange Rates

The following currencies convert at these approximate rates:

country	unit		kroner
Australia	A$1	=	Dkr4.22
Canada	C$1	=	Dkr4.86
Eurozone	€1	=	Dkr7.44
New Zealand	NZ$1	=	Dkr3.70
Norway	Nkr1	=	Dkr1.00
Sweden	Skr1	=	Dkr0.81
UK	UK£1	=	Dkr11.82
USA	US$1	=	Dkr7.60

Exchanging Money

All common travellers cheques are accepted in Denmark. Bank fees for changing money are a hefty Dkr25 to Dkr30 per cheque with a Dkr40 minimum. If you're exchanging cash, there's a Dkr25 fee for any transaction. Travellers cheques command a better exchange rate than cash by about 1%.

Post offices will also exchange foreign currency at comparable rates. Major banks have ATMs that accept Visa, MasterCard and the Cirrus and Plus bank cards.

Visa, Eurocard, MasterCard, American Express (AmEx) and Diners Club credit cards are widely accepted.

Costs

Nothing's particularly cheap. If you camp or stay in hostels and prepare your own meals you might get by on Dkr250 a day. If you stay in even modest hotels and eat at inexpensive restaurants, expect to spend about Dkr500 a day if doubling up, Dkr700 if travelling alone. Staying in private rooms arranged through tourist offices can knock Dkr150 to Dkr200 off this. To this you will need to add local transport, museum admission fees, entertainment and incidentals.

Tipping & Bargaining

Restaurant bills and taxi fares include service charges in the quoted prices, and further tipping is unnecessary. Bargaining is not a common practice.

Taxes & Refunds

Foreign visitors who are not EU citizens can get a refund on the 25% VAT for goods costing more than Dkr300 purchased at stores participating in the 'Tax Free Shopping Global Refund' plan.

POST & COMMUNICATIONS

Denmark has an efficient postal system. You can receive mail c/o poste restante at any post office in Denmark.

There are no telephone area codes within Denmark; you must dial all eight numbers. If you're going to be making many calls, consider buying a phonecard. The country code for calling Denmark is ☎ 45. To make international calls dial ☎ 00 and then the code for the country you're calling.

The larger cities have Internet cafés, which charge an hourly rate of about Dkr20 to Dkr30 to go online. Public libraries also have Internet access.

DIGITAL RESOURCES

The Danish foreign ministry website at **W** www.denmark.org has a wealth of information, including updated weather reports and exchange rates, as well as links to many sites, such as the Danish Tourist Board at **W** www.visit denmark.com.

BOOKS

Lonely Planet's *Denmark* is the most comprehensive all-around guidebook available. *Camping Danmark*, published each year by the Danish Camping Board (Campingrådet), contains detailed information on all camping grounds in Denmark.

WOMEN TRAVELLERS

The **Danish Centre for Information on Women & Gender** *(KVINFO; ☎ 33 13 50 88; **W** www.kvinfo.dk; Christians Brygge 3, Copenhagen)* has information on feminist issues, whereas **Kvindehuset** *(☎ 33 14 28 04; Gothersgade 37, Copenhagen)* is a help centre and meeting place for women. Dial ☎ 112 for rape crisis or other emergencies.

GAY & LESBIAN TRAVELLERS

Denmark is a popular destination for gay and lesbian travellers. Copenhagen in particular has an active, open gay community and lots of nightlife options.

Landsforeningen for Bøsser og Lesbiske *(LBL; ☎ 33 13 19 48; **e** kbh@lbl.dk; Teglgårdstræde 13, Copenhagen)* is the national organisation for gay men and lesbians. A good English-language website with links to LBL and other gay organisations is **W** www.copenhagen-gay-life.dk.

DISABLED TRAVELLERS

Overall, Denmark is a friendly destination for disabled travellers. The Danish Tourist Board publishes *Access in Denmark – a Travel Guide for the Disabled*, which is an English-language booklet with information on accommodation, transportation and sightseeing options for disabled travellers.

SENIOR TRAVELLERS

Senior citizens between the ages of 60 and 65 may be given discounts at most museums by showing proof of age. Transportation is often discounted for seniors; the DSB railway system, for example, gives a 25% to 50% discount to those aged 65 and older.

DANGERS & ANNOYANCES

In cities, you'll need to become accustomed quickly to the busy cycle lanes between vehicle roads and the pedestrian pavement, as these lanes are easy to step into accidentally.

LEGAL MATTERS

Although marijuana and hashish are widely available in Denmark, sometimes quite openly, all forms of cannabis are illegal, as are harder drugs.

You can get free legal advice on your rights from the EU legal aid organisation **EURO-JUS** *(☎ 33 14 41 40)*.

Emergencies

In case of an emergency dial the nationwide number ☎ 112 for police, fire and ambulance emergency services.

BUSINESS HOURS

Office hours are generally 9am to 4pm Monday to Friday. Most banks are open 9.30am to 4pm (Thursday to 6pm) weekdays. Shops are usually open to 5.30pm on weekdays and 2pm on Saturday.

PUBLIC HOLIDAYS & SPECIAL EVENTS

Summer holidays for schoolchildren begin around 20 June and end around 10 August. Many Danes go on holiday during the first three weeks of July. Public holidays in Denmark are New Year's Day (1 January), Maundy Thursday (Thursday before Easter), Good Friday to Easter Monday (March/April), Common Prayer Day (fourth Friday after Easter), Ascension Day (fifth Thursday after Easter), Whit Sunday (fifth Sunday after Easter), Whit Monday (fifth Monday after Easter), Constitution Day (5 June), Christmas Eve (from noon, 24 December), Christmas Day (25 December) and Boxing Day (26 December).

Beginning with Midsummer's Eve bonfires in late June, Denmark buzzes with outdoor activity throughout the summer. Roskilde hosts an internationally acclaimed rock festival, with big international names, on the last weekend of June.

For details on music festivals nationwide, contact **Dansk Musik Informations Center** *(☎ 33 11 20 66; W www.mic.dk; Gråbrødre Torv 16, 1154 Copenhagen K)*.

ACTIVITIES

Cycling is a leading holiday activity in Denmark, and there are thousands of kilometres of established **cycling routes**. The Danish cycling federation, **Dansk Cyklist Forbund** *(DCF; ☎ 33 32 31 21; W www.dcf.dk; Rømersgade 7, 1362 Copenhagen K)*, publishes *Cykelferiekort*, which is a cycling map of the entire country, and also more detailed regional cycling maps.

DCF also publishes *Overnatning i det fri*, which lists hundreds of farmers who provide cyclists with a place to pitch a tent for Dkr15 a night. Cycling maps can be purchased in advance from DCF or from tourist offices and bookshops upon arrival. Tourist offices also have information on packaged cycling holidays.

Even though Denmark does not have substantial forests, there are numerous small tracts of woodland that are crisscrossed by pleasant **walking trails**. The coast in Denmark is public domain and in many areas there are scenic walking tracks along the shoreline.

Canoeing possibilities on Denmark's inland lakes are superb. Such areas as Jutland's Lake District are ideal for canoe touring between lakeside camp sites.

Denmark's remarkable coastline offers terrific **windsurfing**. There is not much swell for conventional surfing but the configuration of headlands and bays and the often windy nature of Danish coastal weather creates ideal conditions for windsurfers.

WORK

Overall, the job situation is generally bleak for non-Danes. Citizens of EU countries are allowed to stay in Denmark for up to three months searching for a job, and it's fairly straightforward to get a residency permit if work is found. Citizens of other countries are required to get a work permit before entering Denmark.

ACCOMMODATION

Camping & Cabins

Denmark's 516 camping grounds typically charge from Dkr50 to Dkr60 per person to pitch a tent. Many places surcharge about Dkr20 for the tent space. Places with the simplest facilities have the cheapest rates. A camping pass is required (Dkr80). If you do not have a seasonal pass you pay an extra Dkr20 a night.

Many camping grounds rent simple cabins that sleep two to six people and cost from Dkr225 to Dkr500 a day. Bedding is rarely provided.

Camping is restricted to camping grounds, or on private land with the owner's permission.

Hostels

Most of Denmark's 100 *vandrerhjem*, belonging to the Danhostel association, have private rooms in addition to dormitory rooms. Dorm beds cost from about Dkr90 to Dkr100, while private rooms range from Dkr180 to Dkr300 for singles, and from Dkr250 to Dkr400 for doubles, depending on the season and facilities. Blankets and pillows are provided at all hostels, but if you don't bring your own sheets you'll have to hire them for around Dkr40. Sleeping bags are not allowed.

Travellers without an international hostel card can buy one in Denmark for Dkr160 or pay Dkr30 extra a night. During the summer, it's a good idea to call ahead for reservations.

All Danish hostels have an all-you-can-eat breakfast for Dkr45 or less and many also provide dinner (Dkr65 maximum). Nearly all hostels also have guest kitchens with pots and pans.

The national HI office is **Danhostel** *(☎ 33 31 36 12; Ⓦ www.danhostel.dk; Vesterbrogade 39, 1620 Copenhagen V)*.

Hotels

Hotels are in the centre of all major towns, with the lower end of the range starting at around Dkr450/600 for singles/doubles. While cheapest places tend to be spartan, they're rarely seedy or unsafe. *Kro*, a name that implies 'country inn', but is more often the Danish version of a motel, is a type of accommodation common along motorways near the outskirts of towns; they are generally cheaper than hotels. Both hotels and *kros* usually include an all-you-can-eat breakfast.

Other Accommodation

Many tourist offices book rooms in private homes for a small fee, or provide a free list of the rooms. Rates vary, averaging about Dkr250/300 for singles/doubles. **Dansk Bed & Breakfast** *(☎ 39 61 04 05; Ⓦ www.bbdk.dk; PO Box 53, 2900 Hellerup)* handles 300 homes throughout Denmark offering private rooms at similar rates.

If you prefer accommodation in the countryside, **Landsforeningen for Landboturisme** *(☎ 86 37 39 00, fax 86 37 35 50; Ⓦ www.bondegaardsferie.dk; Lerbakken 7, Følle, 8410 Rønde)* books stays on farms throughout Denmark – some in rooms in family homes, others in separate flats. Prices vary, but average around Dkr200 a person a day.

FOOD & DRINK

Nothing epitomises Danish food more than *smørrebrød* (literally, 'buttered bread'), an open-faced sandwich that ranges from very basic fare to some elaborate sculpture-like creations. Typically, it's a slice of rye bread topped with either roast beef, tiny shrimps, roast pork or fish fillet and finished off with a variety of garnishes.

The rich pastry known worldwide as a 'Danish' is called *wienerbrød* in Denmark, and nearly every second street corner has a bakery with mouth-watering varieties. For a cheap munch, stop at one of the ubiquitous *pølsemandens*, the wheeled carts that sell a variety of frankfurters for around Dkr15.

Denmark's Carlsberg and Tuborg breweries both produce excellent beers. The most popular spirit in Denmark is caraway-spiced Aalborg aquavit; it's drunk straight down as a shot, followed by a chaser of beer.

ENTERTAINMENT

Denmark's cities have some of the most active nightlife in Europe, with live music wafting through side-street cafés, especially in the university cities of Copenhagen, Århus and Odense. Little begins before 10pm or ends before 3am. Most towns have movie theatres showing first-run, English-language films subtitled in Danish.

Getting There & Away

AIR

Scandinavian Airlines is the largest carrier serving Denmark. Other airlines flying into Copenhagen include Air France, Alitalia, Austrian Airlines, British Airways, British Midland, El Al, Finnair, Iberia, Icelandair, KLM, Lithuanian Airlines, LOT, Lufthansa, Maersk, Cimber Air, Olympic Airways and Virgin Express.

LAND

Three railway lines link Germany and Denmark; 2nd-class fares from Copenhagen to Frankfurt are Dkr1000. **Eurolines** *(☎ 33 88 70 00)* operates buses from Copenhagen to Berlin (Dkr295) and Frankfurt (Dkr680) several times a week.

Trains operate daily between Copenhagen and Oslo; the 2nd-class fare (via Sweden) is Dkr430. Eurolines offers a daily bus service between Oslo and Copenhagen (Dkr220) via Gothenburg.

Trains run many times a day between Denmark and Sweden via the new Øresund Fixed Link, the longest bridge-tunnel of its type in the world. The bridge links Copenhagen with Malmö in Sweden. The 2nd-class train fare from Copenhagen costs Dkr62 to Malmö, Dkr200 to Gothenburg and Dkr370 to Stockholm. If you are travelling by train, the bridge crossing is included in the fare. For those travelling by car, however, there is a Dkr220 per-vehicle toll.

There are numerous buses that travel between Copenhagen and Sweden, including Eurolines buses to Gothenburg (Dkr160) and Stockholm (Dkr346).

SEA

Germany

The frequent Rødbyhavn–Puttgarden ferry takes 45 minutes and is included in rail tickets for those travelling by train; otherwise, the cost per adult/child is Dkr45/25 and for a car with up to five passengers is Dkr345.

Other ferries run from Rømø to Sylt (Dkr35, one hour), Rønne on Borhholm to Sassnitz–Mukran (Dkr130, 3½ hours) and Gedser to Rostock (Dkr60, two hours). See also the respective Getting There & Away sections for more information.

Iceland & the Faroe Islands

Norröna, operated by **Smyril Line** *(☎ 33 16 40 04; W www.smyril-line.dk),* runs every week from Hanstholm to Tórshavn (Faroe Islands) and Seyðisfjörður (Iceland) from mid-May to early September. The boat leaves Hanstholm 8pm Saturday, arriving in Tórshavn 5am Monday. Visitors then have a two-day stopover in the Faroe Islands, departing Tórshavn at 6pm Wednesday and arriving in Seyðisfjörður at 8am Thursday. The return boat departs from Seyðisfjörður at noon Thursday, arriving in Tórshavn at 5am Friday and in Hanstholm at 3pm Saturday.

The midsummer fares to Tórshavn for a couchette are Dkr1638, a bunk in a four-berth cabin, Dkr1766. Fares to Seyðisfjörður for a couchette are Dkr2114, for a four-berth cabin Dkr2707; these fares are 25% less for travel in low season September to April. There is a 25% discount for students under 26. You can transport a bicycle to all destinations for about Dkr75, a motorcycle for about Dkr510 (Faroe Islands) and Dkr850 (Iceland), and a car for Dkr1290 (Faroe Islands) and Dkr2150 (Iceland).

Norway

A daily overnight ferry operates between Copenhagen and Oslo. Ferries also run from Hirtshals to Oslo and Kristiansand; from Hanstholm to Bergen; and from Frederikshavn to Oslo and Larvik. More details are provided in the relevant Getting There & Away sections.

Poland

Polferries *(☎ 33 11 46 45)* operates ferries to Świnoujście from both Copenhagen (Dkr380, 10 hours) and Rønne (Dkr180, 5½ hours).

Sweden

The cheapest and most frequent ferry to Sweden is the shuttle between Helsingør and Helsingborg (Dkr18, 20 minutes); ferries leave opposite the Helsingør train station every 20 minutes during the day and once an hour through the night. Passage for a car with up to five people costs Dkr230.

Other ferries go from Frederikshavn to Gothenburg (Dkr100 to Dkr160, two to 3¼ hours), Rønne to Ystad (Dkr150, 1½ hours) and Grenå to Varberg (Dkr100 to Dkr140, four hours). See also the relevant Getting There & Away sections in this chapter.

UK

DFDS Seaways *(☎ 79 17 79 17)* sails from Esbjerg to Harwich at least three times a week at 6pm year-round. It takes 19 hours. The cost for passage in a chair ranges from Dkr600 in winter to Dkr1140 in midsummer, while a bed in a two-person cabin is between Dkr948 and Dkr1798. Add Dkr116 to Dkr232 for a motorcycle and Dkr406 to Dkr640 for a car. Bikes are carried free.

Getting Around

BUS

All large cities and towns have a local bus system and most places are served by regional buses, many of which connect with trains. There are also a few long-distance bus routes, including from Copenhagen to Aalborg or Århus. The cost of travelling by bus on long-distance routes is about 20% less than travel by train.

TRAIN

With the exception of a few short private lines, the Danish State Railways (DSB) runs all train services in Denmark.

There are two types of long-distance trains. Sleek InterCity (IC) trains have ultramodern comforts and generally require reservations (Dkr20). Inter-regional (IR) trains are older and a bit slower, make more stops and don't require reservations. Both trains charge the same fares, as long as you avoid the cushy

InterCity-Lyn. Rail passes don't cover reservation fees or surcharges.

Overall, train travel in Denmark is not expensive, largely because the distances are short. Standard fares work out to about Dkr1 per kilometre.

Scanrail, Eurail and other rail passes are valid on DSB ferries and trains, but not on the private lines.

CAR & MOTORCYCLE

Denmark's main motoring organisation is **Forenede Danske Motorejere** *(FDM; ☎ 32 66 01 00; Ⓦ www.mst.dk; Firskovvej 32, 2800 Lyngby)*.

You'll generally get the best deal by booking through an international rental agency before you arrive in Denmark. Otherwise, rates for the cheapest cars, including VAT, insurance and unlimited kilometres, begin at about Dkr680 a day, or Dkr520 a day on rentals of two days or more.

BICYCLE

Cycling is a practical way to get around Denmark. There are extensive bike paths linking towns throughout the country and bike lanes through most city centres.

You can rent bikes in most towns for around Dkr60 a day, plus a deposit of about Dkr250. Bikes can be taken on ferries and most trains for a modest cost; make sure you pick up the DSB pamphlet *Cykler i tog*. See also Activities in Facts for the Visitor earlier in this chapter.

HITCHING

Hitching in Denmark is rare, and illegal on motorways.

BOAT

A network of ferries links virtually all of Denmark's populated islands. Where there's not a bridge, there's usually a ferry. Specific ferry information is given under the individual destination sections.

LOCAL TRANSPORT

All cities and towns of any size in Denmark are served by local buses. As a rule, the main local bus terminal is adjacent to the train station or ferry depot. For more details, see the individual destination sections.

Taxi stands can be found at train stations and major shopping areas in Denmark. The fare is typically Dkr21 to Dkr30 flag fall and between Dkr10 and Dkr13 per kilometre, with the higher rates prevailing at night and on weekends.

Copenhagen (København)

pop 1.7 million

Copenhagen is Scandinavia's largest and liveliest city, and one of Europe's most seductive destinations. It began life as a fishing village and developed within the shelter of Slotsholmen, the island that is now dominated by the monumental Christiansborg Palace. Today, Copenhagen sprawls across a flat cityscape. No surrounding hills give it overall context, yet buildings are generally low rise and the skyline is broken by several splendid steeples and towers.

Central Copenhagen has an active nightlife that rolls on well into the early hours, and there's a treasure trove of museums, castles and old churches to explore. The city's famous Tivoli amusement park and garden always draws locals and visitors alike, but much of Copenhagen's allure lies in the irresistible buzz of its central streets and squares and in the liveliness of its bars, cafés, restaurants and music venues.

Orientation

The always bustling train station, Central Station (Hovedbanegården or København H), is flanked on its west by the main hotel zone. To the east of Central Station's main entrance is the Tivoli amusement park. Tivoli is flanked on its northeastern corner by the equally broad and traffic-bound HC Andersens Blvd. Beyond this area lies the spacious Rådhuspladsen, the central city square, main bus transit point, and gateway into the heart of Copenhagen.

From Rådhuspladsen, the narrow opening of Frederiksberggade is the unassuming introduction to Strøget, 'the world's longest pedestrian mall'. The mall is a linked sequence of lively, crowded streets that runs through the heart of the city linking Rådhuspladsen and the other great square of Kongens Nytorv, at the head of the Nyhavn canal. Strøget is made up of Frederiksberggade, Nygade, Vimmelskaftet, Amagertorv and Østergade.

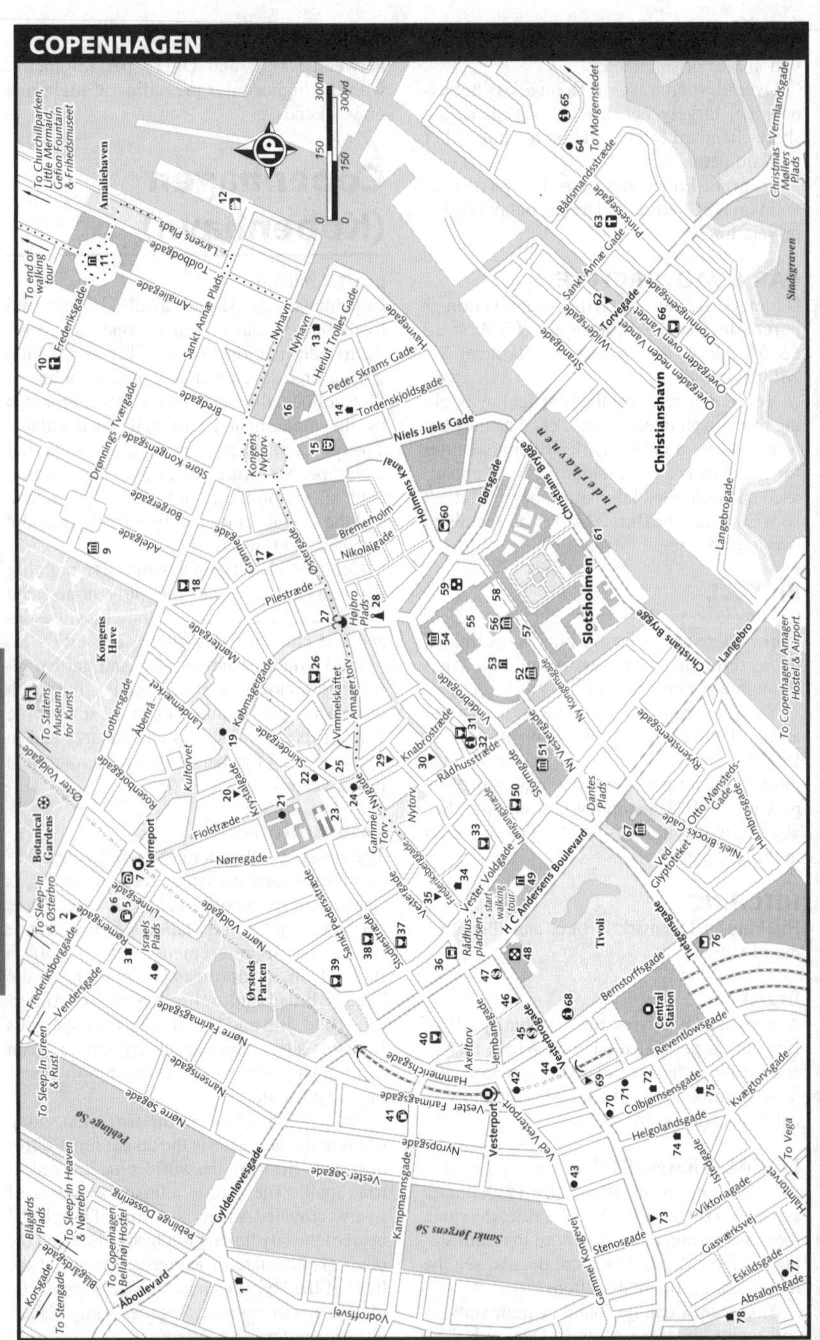
COPENHAGEN
To Churchillparken, Little Mermaid, Gefion Fountain & Frihedsmuseet
Amaliehaven
To end of walking tour
Frederiksgade
Amaliegade
Toldbodgade
Larsens Plads
Sankt Annæ Plads
Nyhavn
Herluf Trolles Gade
Havnegade
Peder Skrams Gade
Tordenskjoldsgade
Niels Juels Gade
Holmens Kanal
Kongens Nytorv
Bredgade
Store Kongensgade
Dronnings Tværgade
Borgergade
Adelgade
Kongens Have
Gothersgade
Østergade
Grønnegade
Bremerholm
Nikolajgade
Pilestræde
Højbro Plads
Amagertorv
Vimmelskaftet
Købmagergade
Møntergade
Landemærket
Åbenrå
Kultorvet
Skindergade
Krystalgade
Fiolstræde
Nørregade
Rosenborggade
Botanical Gardens
Øster Voldgade
To Statens Museum for Kunst
Nørreport
Linnésgade
Israels Plads
Rømersgade
Frederiksborggade
To Sleep-In & Østerbro
Vendersgade
Nørre Voldgade
Ørsteds Parken
Sankt Peders Stræde
Studiestræde
Vestergade
Gammel Torv
Nytorv
Knabrostræde
Rådhusstræde
Vindebrogade
Frederiksberggade
Rådhuspladsen
Vester Voldgade
start walking tour
H C Andersens Boulevard
Longangstræde
Stormgade
Ny Vestergade
Ny Kongensgade
Dantes Plads
Slotsholmen
Christians Brygge
Børsgade
Inderhavnen
Christianshavn
Strandgade
Wildersgade
Torvegade
Sankt Annæ Gade
Prinsessegade
Bådsmandsstræde
To Morgenstedet
Overgaden oven Vandet
Overgaden neden Vandet
Dronningensgade
Langebrogade
Langebro
Stadsgraven
Christmas Møllers Plads
Vermlandsgade
To Copenhagen Amager Hostel & Airport
Rysensteensgade
Hambrosgade
Otto Mønsteds Gade
Niels Brocks Gade
Ved Glyptoteket
Tietgensgade
Tivoli
Bernstorffsgade
Central Station
Reventlowsgade
Kvægtorvsgade
Colbjørnsensgade
Helgolandsgade
Istedgade
Viktoriagade
To Vega
Halmtorvet
Gasværksvej
Eskildsgade
Absalonsgade
Stenosgade
Gammel Kongevej
Vesterbrogade
Jernbanegade
Axeltorv
Hammerichsgade
Vester Farimagsgade
Vesterport
Ved Vesterport
Nyropsgade
Vester Søgade
Kampmannsgade
Sankt Jørgens Sø
Vodroffsvej
Gyldenløvesgade
Peblinge Sø
Nørre Søgade
Nansensgade
Nørre Farimagsgade
To Sleep-In Green & Rust
To Sleep-In Heaven & Nørrebro
Blågårds Plads
Blågårdsgade
Korsgade
To Stengade
To Copenhagen Bellahøj Hostel
Åboulevard
Peblinge Dossering
0 150 300m
0 150 300yd

DENMARK

COPENHAGEN

PLACES TO STAY
1 Cab-Inn Scandinavia
3 Hotel Jørgensen
13 Sømandshjem Bethel
14 Hotel Opera
34 Rainbow Hotel
72 Hotel Ibis
74 Selandia Hotel
75 Saga Hotel
78 City Public Hostel

PLACES TO EAT
2 Supermarket
17 Netto Supermarket
20 Ankara
25 Samos
29 Café Sorgenfri
30 RizRaz
35 Shawarma Grill House
46 Matahari; Italian Corner
62 Christianshavns Bådudlejning
69 Astor Pizza
73 Ankara

OTHER
4 Dansk Cyklist Forbund (Cycling Federation)
5 Petrol Station
6 Fruit/Veg Market
7 Outpost Entertainment
8 Rosenborg Slot
9 Davids Samling
10 Frederikskirke (Marmorkirken)
11 Amalienborg Palace
12 Boats to Oslo & Bornholm
15 Royal Theatre
16 Charlottenborg (Royal Academy of Arts)
18 Kvindvinhuset
19 Rundetårn
21 University Library
22 Kilroy Travels
23 Vor Frue Kirke
24 Wasteels
26 Copenhagen Jazz House
27 Storkespringvandet
28 Bishop Absalon Statue
31 Huset
32 Use It
33 Oscar
36 Main Bus Transit
37 Masken
38 Cosy Bar
39 Never Mind
40 Pumphuset
41 Petrol Station
42 Hertz Car Rental
43 Europcar Car Rental
44 Steno Apotek
45 Nordea
47 Forex
48 Rådhusarkaden Shopping Centre
49 Rådhus (City Hall)
50 Mojo
51 Nationalmuseet
52 Museum of Royal Coaches
53 Christiansborg Palace
54 Thorvaldsens Museum
55 Royal Reception Chambers
56 Teatermuseet
57 Tøjhusmuseet (Royal Arsenal)
58 Folketing (Parliament)
59 Ruins of Absalon's Fortress
60 Netto-Bådene Boats
61 Royal Library; Internet Access
63 Vor Frelsers Kirke
64 Christiania; Loppen
65 Christiania Information Center
66 Sofiekælderen
67 Ny Carlsberg Glyptotek
68 Wonderful Copenhagen (Tourist Office)
70 Danwheel
71 Eurolines Office
76 Main Post Office
77 Laundrette

Information

Tourist Offices The tourist office, **Wonderful Copenhagen** *(☎ 70 22 24 42, fax 70 22 24 52; W www.visitcopenhagen.dk; Bernstorffsgade 1; open Mon-Sat, daily May-Aug)*, north of Central Station, distributes informative brochures and maps. It also sells the Copenhagen Card, which secures unlimited travel on buses and trains around Copenhagen and North Zealand. It gives free or discounted admission to many attractions. An adult card (age 16 upwards) costs Dkr215/375/495 for one/two/three days.

Use It *(☎ 33 73 06 20, fax 33 73 06 49; W www.useit.dk; Rådhusstræde 13; open Mon-Fri, daily mid-June–mid-Sept)* is a 1st-class information centre aimed at young budget travellers but open to all. It books rooms, stores luggage, holds mail, offers free Internet use and provides information on everything.

Money Banks, all of which charge transaction fees, are found in the city centre. At Central Station the **Forex exchange booth** *(open 8am-9pm daily)* has the lowest fees. You'll find 24-hour ATMs that exchange major foreign currencies for Danish kroner, minus a hefty Dkr25 to Dkr30 fee, at the **Den Danske Bank** *(Central Station)* and **Nordea** *(Axeltorv)*.

Post & Communications You can pick up poste-restante mail at the **main post office** *(Tietgensgade 35-39; open 11am-6pm Mon-Fri, 10am-1pm Sat)*. **Outpost Entertainment** *(☎ 33 93 22 63; Frederiksborggade 15)* has Internet access for Dkr30 an hour. If you just want to check your email, **Use It** *(Rådhusstræde 13)*, offers free Internet access, within reasonable time restraints, or you can drop by the Royal Library at the southern side of Slotsholmen, where more than 100 terminals fill the hallways.

Travel Agencies Both **Kilroy Travels** *(☎ 33 11 00 44; Skindergade 28)* and **Wasteels** *(☎ 33 14 46 33; Skoubogade 6)* specialise in student and budget travel.

Medical Services There's a 24-hour emergency ward at **Frederiksberg Hospital** *(☎ 38 16 38 16; Nordre Fasanvej 57)*, west of the city centre. Private doctor visits (☎ 33 93 63

00 for referrals) usually cost around Dkr350. **Steno Apotek** *(Vesterbrogade 6c)*, opposite Central Station, is a 24-hour pharmacy.

Walking Tour

Taking a half-day's walk from Rådhus (City Hall), in busy Rådhuspladsen, to the Little Mermaid is a pleasant way of taking in some central sights.

The **Rådhus** *(☎ 33 66 25 82; open 9.30am-3pm daily)* dates from the late 19th century and reflects a dazzling mix of influences in the decor of its sumptuous rooms. You can take a free look at the rooms or join a guided tour (Dkr30), with commentary in English, at 3pm Monday to Friday and 10am Saturday. **Jens Olsens World Clock** *(adult/child Dkr10/5)*, in a side chamber of the entrance hall, contains 15,448 individual parts and is a staggering expression of Danish ingenuity and precision.

From Rådhus go down Strøget, which, after a couple of blocks, cuts between the cobbled squares of Gammel Torv, the 'Old Square' on the left and Nytorv, the 'New Square' on the right. Strøget enters Nygade and then widens into the lively square of Amagertorv. Ahead is the famous *Storkespringvandet*, the 'Stork Fountain', a popular venue for street entertainers. To the right is Højbro Plads with, at its far end, the great statue of the city founder, Bishop Absalon.

Strøget ends at Kongens Nytorv, a huge square circled by some gracious old buildings including the **Royal Theatre**, home to the Royal Danish Ballet, and **Charlottenborg**, a 17th-century Dutch baroque palace housing the **Royal Academy of Arts** *(admission Dkr20; open 10am-5pm Mon-Sun, 10am-7pm Wed)*.

On the eastern side of Kongens Nytorv is picturesque **Nyhavn** canal, dug 300 years ago to allow traders to bring their wares into the heart of the city. Nyhavn was once the haunt of sailors, local characters and writers, such as Hans Christian Andersen who lived at No 67.

From the northern side of Nyhavn, head north on Toldbodgade, turn right into Sankt Annæ Plads and then turn left along the airy waterfront. When you reach a fountain, turn inland to the great cobbled square of Amalienborg Plads and to **Amalienborg Palace** *(adult/child Dkr40/5; open 10am-4pm daily May-Oct, 11am-4pm Nov-Apr)*, home of the royal family since 1794.

Head inland along Frederiksgade to splendid **Frederikskirken** *(admission free, guided tour of tower adult/child Dkr20/10; open 10am-5pm Mon-Thur, noon-5pm Fri-Sun, tower tour 1pm & 3pm daily mid-June–Aug)*, known as *Marmorkirken* (Marble Church) because of its magnificent marble dome. The panelled and gilded frescoes on the inside of the dome have breathtaking colours.

Back on Amalienborg Plads, head north along Amaliegade to Churchillparken, where you'll find **Frihedsmuseet** *(admission Dkr30, free Wed; open 10am-4pm Tues-Sat, 10am-5pm Sun May–mid-Sep, 11am-3pm Tues-Sat, 11am-4pm Sun mid-Sep–Apr)*, which depicts the history of Danish Resistance against Nazi occupation. Farther along, you pass the spectacular **Gefion Fountain**. Continue north along the waterfront to the forlorn, and somewhat disappointing, statue of the famed **Little Mermaid** (Den Lille Havfrue).

Statens Museum for Kunst

North of the city centre, Denmark's national gallery *(☎ 33 74 84 94; W www.smk.dk; Sølvgade 48-50; adult/child Dkr50/free, free Wed; open 10am-5pm Tues & Thur-Sun, 10am-8pm Wed)* has an enormous collection of superb paintings. The main collection is located on the 2nd floor and includes works by 19th-century Danish masters such as Jens Juel, CW Eckersberg, Constantin Hansen, PS Krøyer and Kristian Zahrtmann, as well as works by the 17th-century Dutch and Flemish masters, Rembrandt and Rubens. Other leading European artists including Matisse, Picasso, Braque, Utrillo and Munch are also well represented.

Slotsholmen

On an island separated from the city centre by a moat-like canal, Slotsholmen is the site of **Christiansborg Palace** *(☎ 33 92 64 92)* and the seat of Denmark's national government. Of the many sites, the grandest is the **Royal Reception Chambers** *(adult/child Dkr40/10; guided tours 11am, 1pm & 3pm daily May-Sept, 11am & 3pm Tues, Thur, Sat & Sun Jan-Apr & Oct-Dec)*, the ornate Renaissance hall where the queen entertains heads of state. The tours have commentary in English.

The **Ruins of Absalon's Fortress** *(adult/child Dkr20/5; open 9.30am-3.30pm daily May-Sep, 9.30am-3.30pm Tues, Thur, Sat & Sun Oct-Apr)* are the excavated foundations of Bishop Absalon's original castle of 1167, those of the original Slotsholmen castle of

DENMARK

1167 and of its successor, Copenhagen Castle. They can be visited in the atmospheric basement of the present palace tower.

Other attractions on the island include the **Royal Coach Museum**, **Thorvaldsens Museum**, the **Royal Arsenal** and the **Teatermuseet**.

Christiania

Christianshavn is the site of the remarkable 'Freetown' of Christiania, an alternative city community of about 1000 residents that has its own commercial life, political structure, education system, radio station and weekly newspaper – as well as a thriving music, theatre and social scene. It also has a relentless hash culture, and hash, grass and skunk are openly, though illegally, sold on Pusher St from a variety of stalls. Passive smoking can be an occupational hazard for deep breathers. Christiania has an **information office** *(☎/fax 32 95 65 07; W www.christiania.org; Nyt Forum, Pusher St; open Mon-Fri)* on the first floor of the music centre of Operæn.

Livin' on the Edge

In the early 1970s an abandoned military barracks on the eastern side of Christianshavn experienced a huge and dynamic influx of squatters, hippies, artists, musicians, political activists and other urban escapees, all fired with the dream of an alternative 'New Society' run by, and for, the community. During the next 10 years, the citizens of Freetown dug in amid sporadic, and often violent, confrontations with the State, especially when elections brought in less sympathetic governance. By the start of the 1980s an acknowledged hard drugs problem resulted in police raids, a moral backlash from some quarters, and much soul-searching within Freetown itself. The result is, that while hash remains an almost Eucharistic feature of life in Freetown, there are tough community rules against the use of hard drugs.

The government eventually agreed to the continuation of Christiania as a 'social experiment' in communal living. Until recently progress was still punctuated by police actions and by bureaucratic conflicts, but Christiania has emerged as a viable community that pays duties from a Common Fund, supports a range of social organisations and businesses, and is, inevitably, a tourist attraction. It is a fascinating place to visit, although some ultra 'free spirits' may be repelled by a certain sense of claustrophobia that such dedicated community living may sometimes engender.

Tivoli

Right in the heart of the city is Copenhagen's century-old amusement park, **Tivoli** *(☎ 33 15 10 01; W www.tivoli.dk; adult/child Dkr50/25; open 11am-11pm Sat-Thur, 11am-1am Fri mid-Apr–mid-June & mid-Aug–mid-Sept, 11am-midnight Sun-Thur, 11am-1am Fri & Sat mid-June–mid-Aug)*. It's a mishmash of gardens, food pavilions, amusement rides, carnival games and various stage shows. Fireworks light up the skies at 11.45pm on Wednesday and Saturday.

Ny Carlsberg Glyptotek

This splendid museum *(☎ 33 41 81 41; Dantes Plad 7, HC Andersens Blvd; adult/child Dkr30/free, free Wed & Sun; open 10am-4pm Tues-Sun)*, housed in a grand period building near Tivoli, has an exceptional collection of Greek, Egyptian, Etruscan and Roman sculpture; a wing of paintings by Gauguin, Monet and Van Gogh; and a complete set of Degas bronzes.

Special Events

The **Copenhagen Jazz Festival** *(☎ 33 93 20 13; W www.cjf.dk)* is the biggest event of the year, with 10 days of music in early July. The festival presents a wide range of Danish and international jazz, blues and fusion music. It's a cornucopia of some 500 indoor and outdoor concerts, with music wafting out of practically every public square, park, pub and café from Strøget to Tivoli.

Places to Stay

Rooms & Booking Services The **tourist office** *(☎ 70 22 24 42; Bernstorffsgade 1)* can book rooms in private homes from Dkr300/500 for singles/doubles. It also books unfilled hotel rooms, often at discounted rates; expect a double room with shared bath to cost around Dkr500. There's a Dkr60 fee per booking. The airport information booth outside customs offers a similar service.

Use It *(☎ 33 73 06 20; Rådhusstræde 13)* is an agency that books private rooms (singles from Dkr175, doubles from Dkr250) free of booking fees, keeps tabs on which hostel beds are available, and is also a good source of information for subletting student housing and other long-term accommodation.

Hostels Copenhagen has two HI hostels, the Bellahøj and Amager, each about 5km from the city centre. Both have laundry facilities and guest kitchens. They often fill early in the summer so it's best to call ahead for reservations. The hostels charge Dkr20 to Dkr40 for hire of sheets

Copenhagen Bellahøj (☎ *38 28 97 15, fax 38 89 02 10;* ⓔ *bellahoej@danhostel.dk; Herbergvejen 8; dorm beds/doubles Dkr95/250; reception 24hr, open 1 Mar-15 Jan)* is in a quiet suburban neighbourhood and has 250 dorm beds and a limited number of family rooms (doubles). You can take bus No 2-Brønshøj from Rådhuspladsen and get off at Fuglsangs Allé. The night bus is 82N.

Copenhagen Amager (☎ *32 52 29 08, fax 32 52 27 08; Vejlands Allé 200, Amager; dorm beds/doubles Dkr95/275; open 15 Jan-30 Nov)*, in an isolated part of Amager just off the E20, is one of the largest hostels in Europe, with 528 beds in two- and five-bed rooms. Take the S-train to Sjælør Station, then change to bus No 100S, which stops in front of the hostel. On weekdays until 5pm, bus No 46 runs from Central Station directly to the hostel.

Even when the HI hostels are full you can nearly always find a bed at one of the city-sponsored hostels. Though the larger ones tend to be a crash-pad scene, they're central and sleeping bags are allowed.

City Public Hostel (☎ *33 31 20 70, fax 33 55 00 85;* ⓔ *info@city-public-hostel.dk; Absalonsgade 8; dorm beds Dkr130; reception 24hr, open early May–mid-Aug)* sleeps 200 people. Breakfast is available for Dkr25, or Dkr20 if it's included with the bed price. From Central Station, walk west for 10 minutes along Vesterbrogade then bear off left at Vesterbro Torv.

The 286-bed **Sleep-In** (☎ *35 26 50 59, fax 35 43 50 58;* ⓔ *copenhagen@sleep-in.dk; Blegdamsvej 132; dorm beds Dkr90; reception 24hr, open end June-31 Aug)*, in the pleasant Østerbro area, is a few kilometres north of the city centre and occupies a sports hall that's partitioned off into 'rooms' with four to six beds. There's a group kitchen, a café and free lockers. This is a busy and popular place. Take bus No 1 or 6 from Rådhuspladsen to Trianglen and walk 300m south on Blegdamsvej. Night buses are 85N and 95N.

Sleep-In Green (☎ *35 37 77 77;* ⓦ *www.sleep-in-green.dk; Ravnsborggade 18; dorm beds Dkr85; open mid-May–mid-Oct)* is in the Nørrebro area, close to cafés and bars. It has 68 dorm beds. Take bus No 5 or 16, or the S-train to Nørreport Station then walk northwest on Frederiksborggade over the canal.

The privately run **Sleep-In Heaven** (☎ *35 35 46 48;* ⓔ *morefun@sleepinheaven.com; Struenseegade 7; dorm beds Dkr120; open year-round)*, in the Nørrebro area, has beds in a basement dorm. There is an age limit of 35 years. Breakfast is available for Dkr35 and sheets for Dkr20. Take bus No 8 to the Kapelvej stop; the night bus is 92N.

Hotels The main hotel area lies in Vesterbro on the western side of Central Station, where rows of six-storey, century-old buildings house one hotel after the other. This is also Copenhagen's red-light district, though the only visible sign is a scattering of porn shops and strip clubs. All rates include breakfast.

Saga Hotel (☎ *33 24 49 44, fax 33 24 60 33;* ⓔ *booking@sagahotel.dk; Colbjørnsensgade 18-20; singles/doubles Dkr650/800, with shared bathroom Dkr450/580)* has pleasant, modernised rooms, all with phone and TV.

Ibis Hotel (☎ *33 22 11 00, fax 33 21 21 86;* ⓔ *star@accorhotel.dk; Colbjørnsensgade 13; singles/doubles Dkr745)* is a modernised hotel that has bright, straightforward rooms.

Selandia Hotel (☎ *33 31 46 10, fax 33 31 46 09;* ⓔ *hotel-selandia@city.dk; Helgolandsgade 12; singles/doubles Dkr775/950, with shared bathroom Dkr525/650)* has reasonably sized and comfortable rooms, although the fittings and decor are not enthralling.

Hotel Rainbow (☎ *33 14 10 20;* ⓦ *www.copenhagen-rainbow.dk; Frederiksberggade 25; rooms with shared bathroom Dkr720-835, one room with bathroom Dkr890)* is a small, friendly and exclusively gay hotel in an excellent location, right near the Rådhus end of Strøget. The hotel is on the top floor and has just a few bright and airy rooms. Use the street-level intercom. It's advisable to book ahead.

Sømandshjem Bethel (☎ *33 13 03 70, fax 33 15 85 70; Nyhavn 22; singles/doubles Dkr595/745)* is in a great location on Nyhavn. It has bright, pleasant rooms and views of Nyhavn's quays from some rooms, although you pay more for a harbour view.

Hotel Jørgensen (☎ *33 13 81 86, fax 33 15 51 05;* ⓔ *hotel@post12.tele.dk; Rømersgade*

11; dorm beds Dkr120, singles/doubles Dkr575/700, with shared bathroom Dkr475/575), near Nørreport Station, is popular with gay travellers but is open to all. The simple rooms have shared bathroom. The hotel also has 13 dorm rooms and 150 beds.

Cab-Inn Scandinavia *(☎ 35 36 11 11, fax 35 36 11 14; ⓔ cabinn@cabinn.dk; Vodroffsvej 57; singles/doubles Dkr510/630)* has 201 compact rooms that resemble cruise-ship cabins. Though small, the rooms are comfortable and have TV and private bathroom. If it's full, try its sister hotel **Cab-Inn Copenhagen** *(☎ 33 21 04 00, fax 33 21 74 09; ⓔ cabinn@cabinn.dk; Danasvej 32-34)*, which costs the same and is a few blocks away.

Places to Eat

Around Central Station An extensive buffet of Middle Eastern dishes, including calamari, chicken, lamb and salads, is offered by **Ankara** *(☎ 33 31 14 99; Vesterbrogade 35; buffet noon-4pm Dkr39, 4pm-midnight Dkr69)*. There's also a fast-food bar with a Dkr20 pitta bread sandwich and drink deal.

For an all-you-can-eat deal there's the **Astor Pizza** *(Vesterbrogade 7; buffet 11am-5pm Dkr49, after 5pm Dkr59)*, just north of Central Station, which has a reasonable pizza-and-salad buffet.

Scala, on Vesterbrogade opposite Tivoli, is a multistorey building with fast-food eateries. Good outlets include Matahari, with wok-cooked dishes for around Dkr50, and Italian Corner, with various pizzas starting at Dkr22 and pasta plates for Dkr42. Rådhusarkaden, a shopping centre on Vesterbrogade near Rådhus, has the Irma grocery store and Conditori Hans Christian Andersen, which offers sandwiches, pastries and coffee.

Around Strøget Greek specialities and salads are available at the excellent buffet at **Samos** *(☎ 33 33 00 25; Skindergade 29; buffet noon-5pm Dkr39, after 5pm Dkr79)*.

At **Riz Raz** *(☎ 33 15 05 75; Kompagnistræde 20; buffet 11.30am-5pm Mon-Fri, 11.30am-4pm Sat & Sun Dkr49, to 11pm daily Dkr59)*, just south of Strøget, you can feast on a Mediterranean-style vegetarian buffet including salads, pasta and felafels.

The corner pub **Café Sorgenfri** *(☎ 33 11 58 80; Brolæggerstræde 8)* features some reasonably priced Danish food. Items such as smørrebrød and pickled herring average Dkr38 to Dkr68, while a generous variety plate of traditional hot and cold dishes costs Dkr125.

Strøget has an abundance of cheap eateries including hot-dog, hamburger and ice-cream stands, and numerous hole-in-the-wall kebab joints selling felafels and kebabs for under Dkr30. The best is **Shawarma Grill House** *(16 Frederiksbeggade; sandwiches Dkr23, kebabs Dkr44; open 11am-10pm daily)*, which is a bustling spot at the western end of Strøget, a two-minute walk from Rådhuspladsen.

Christianshavn & Christiania The **Christianshavns Bådudlejning** *(☎ 32 96 53 53; Overgaden neden Vandet 29; fish or meat mains Dkr110-120)* is a deservedly popular place on a canal-side deck. It does a tasty lunch menu, including sandwiches for Dkr45 and salads for Dkr60 to Dkr70. You can hire rowboats as well – and just drift away.

In the heart of Christiania, **Morgenstedet** *(Langgaden; mains Dkr35)* is a long-running vegetarian and vegan eatery where a main dish and salad will cost you Dkr50. It has a pretty garden and a non-smoking interior. In the style of Christiania, Morgenstedet (which means 'the morning place') is open from a respectable noon to 9pm.

Entertainment

Copenhagen is a 24-hour party city. For free entertainment simply stroll along Strøget, especially between Nytorv and Højbro Plads, which is a bit like an impromptu three-ring circus of musicians, magicians, jugglers and other street performers. In addition, numerous free concerts are held throughout the summer in city parks and squares.

Copenhagen has scores of backstreet cafés with live music. Entry is often free on weeknights, while there's usually a cover charge averaging Dkr60 on weekends.

The free publications *Nat & Dag*, *Musik Kalenderen*, *Film Kalenderen* and *Teater Kalenderen* list concerts and entertainment schedules in detail and are available from Wonderful Copenhagen.

The westside Nørrebro area has a number of good entertainment spots, including **Rust** *(☎ 35 24 52 00; Guldbergsgade 8; admission Dkr30-50)*, which is a multilevel dance venue attracting a college-age crowd. **Stengade 30** *(☎ 35 36 09 38; Stengade 18; admission varies)* is a lively alternative live music and dance scene. **Vega** *(Enghavevej 40)*, in the Vesterbro area, stages hugely popular Friday- and Saturday-night sessions. Big-name rock bands and underground acts play the 'Big Vega' 1500-capacity venue.

Closer to the centre is **Pumphuset** *(☎ 70 15 65 65; Studiestræde 52)*, featuring rock and blues groups. Admission can be anything from Dkr50 to Dkr285 for big names. **Copenhagen Jazz House** *(☎ 33 15 26 00; Niels Hemmingsensgade 10)* is the city's leading jazz spot and it has a terrific ambience. After concerts on Thursday, Friday and Saturday nights, the place becomes a lively disco from 1am to 5am, admission Dkr60. **Mojo** *(☎ 33 11 64 53; Løngangstræde 21)* is a prime spot for blues, with entertainment nightly. **Huset** *(☎ 33 15 20 02; Rådhusstræde 13)* is in the same courtyard as the Use-It information centre and includes a cinema, theatre, café, restaurant and music scene that includes good jazz. Many music events are free, but it's about Dkr50 for special events.

In Christianshavn, an engaging local bar is **Sofiekælderen** *(☎ 32 57 27 87; Sofiegade 1)*. It opens noon and does lunches until 4pm, and there is often live jazz and rock until late. **Loppen** *(☎ 32 57 84 22; Loppebygningen, Christiania; admission Dkr50-70)* is a celebrated venue in Freetown that has live music: from soul to punk rock on various nights and a late disco on Friday and Saturday, from 2am to 5am.

There are numerous cinemas showing first-release movies along Vesterbrogade between Central Station and Rådhuspladsen.

Gay & Lesbian Venues A popular meeting place for gay men is the central **Oscar** *(☎ 33 12 09 99; Rådhuspladsen 77; open noon-2am, kitchen noon-10pm)*, which is near the Rådhus. The long-established **Never Mind** *(Nørre Voldgade 2; open 10pm-6am daily)* is a dance bar for mainly gay men, but also with a dash of transgender folk and lesbians enjoying its kitschy decor. **Kvindehuset** *(Women's House; Gothersgade 37)* stages various dance nights for lesbians and has a café and bar. **Masken** *(Studiestræde 33)* is popular with students at weekends, not least because of special drinks prices. There is also a lesbians-only night in the basement section on Thursdays. Near Masken is **Cosy Bar** *(Studiestræde 24)*, a recently brightened up late-night place for gay men, and with a cruisy ambience.

Getting There & Away

Air Copenhagen's modern international airport is in Kastrup, 10km southeast of the city centre. Most airline offices are located north of Central Station near the intersection of Vester Farimagsgade and Vesterbrogade.

Bus International buses leave from Central Station; advance reservations on most routes can be made at **Eurolines** *(☎ 33 88 70 00; Reventlowsgade 8)*.

Train Long-distance trains arrive and depart from Central Station, a huge complex with eateries and numerous services. There are three ways of buying a ticket, and the choice can be important, depending on how much time you have before your train leaves. Billetautomat are coin-operated machines and are the quickest, if you've mastered the zone system prices. If you're not rushed, then **DSB Billetsalg** *(open 8am-7pm Mon-Fri, 9.30am-4pm Sat)* is best for reservations. There's a numbered ticket queuing system. **DSB Kviksalg** *(open 5.45am-11.30pm daily)* is for quick ticket buying, although the queues can build at busy times.

Car & Motorcycle Agencies **Avis** *(☎ 33 15 22 99; Kampmannsgade)*, **Hertz** *(☎ 33 17 90 20; Ved Vesterport 3)* and **Europcar** *(☎ 33 55 99 00; Gammel Kongevej 13)* have airport booths as well as city branches.

Boat The **DFDS Seaways** *(☎ 33 42 30 00; Sankt Annæ Plads)* ferry to Oslo departs daily at 5pm, while **Bornholmstrafikken's** *(☎ 33 13 18 66)* service to Bornholm departs nightly at 11.30pm. Both leave from Kvæsthusbroen, north of Nyhavn.

Getting Around

To/From the Airport A rail system now links the airport with Central Station three times an hour (Dkr19.50, 12 minutes). If your baggage is light, you could also take local bus No 250S (Dkr19.50), which runs between Rådhuspladsen and the airport terminal – but it's much slower.

The airport is 15 minutes and about Dkr160 from the city centre by taxi.

Bus & Train Copenhagen has an extensive public transit system that consists of a metro rail network called S-train, whose 10 lines pass through Central Station (København H). At the time of writing, a new underground metro system was being constructed in Copenhagen. The new line was scheduled to open in 2003 but it is estimated that only part of the system will be completed and open by then. The metro will mainly be of use to suburban commuters, but for travellers there will be a useful link from Copenhagen airport to train stations at Kongens Nytorv and Nørreport. Copenhagen also has an extensive bus system, whose main terminus is located nearby at Rådhuspladsen.

Buses and trains use a common fare system that is based on the number of zones you pass through. The basic fare of Dkr14 for up to two zones covers most city runs and allows transfers between buses and trains on a single ticket as long as they're made within an hour. In place of a single destination ticket, you can buy a *klippekort* (clip card), good for 10 rides in two zones for adult/child Dkr90/45 or get a 24-hour pass allowing unlimited travel in all zones for adult/child Dk85/42.

On buses, fares are paid to the driver when you board, while on S-trains tickets are purchased at the station and then punched in the yellow time clock on the platform.

Trains and buses operate from about 5am to 12.30am, though buses continue to run through the night (charging double fare) on a few main routes. For schedule information about trains call ☎ 33 14 17 01, and for buses call ☎ 36 13 14 15.

Taxi You can flag down taxis with signs saying *'fri'* or you can phone ☎ 35 35 35 35. The cost is Dkr22 flag fall plus about Dkr10 per kilometre between 6am and 3pm, and Dkr11 between 3pm and 6am (Dkr13 between 11pm to 6am Friday and Saturday). Most taxis accept credit cards.

Bicycle & Scooter At Central Station, Københavns Cykler rents bicycles for Dkr75 a day. For cheaper prices (Dkr40 a day) walk a few blocks northwest to **Danwheel** *(Colbjørnsensgade 3)*.

If you just want to ride in the city centre, look for a free-use City Bike – they've got solid spokeless wheels painted with sponsors' logos. There are about 125 City Bike racks scattered throughout central Copenhagen, although available bikes are often few and far between.

Zealand (Sjælland)

Numerous places on the island of Zealand offer a refreshing break from the Copenhagen's relentless charm. Northern Zealand boasts exhilarating beaches, likeable coastal towns and villages, and a number of breathtaking castles.

NORTH ZEALAND

The northern part of Zealand is a compact region consisting of of wheat fields and beech woodlands interspersed with small towns and tiny hamlets. One of the most popular day trips from Copenhagen is a loop tour taking in Frederiksborg Castle in Hillerød and Kronborg Castle in Helsingør.

Frederiksborg Slot

Hillerød, 30km northwest of Copenhagen, is the site of **Frederiksborg Castle** *(adult/child Dkr50/10; open 10am-5pm daily Apr-Oct, 11am-3pm daily Nov-Mar)*, an impressive Dutch Renaissance castle spread across three islands. The oldest part of the castle dates from Frederik II's time, though most of the present structure was built by his son Christian IV in the early 1600s.

The sprawling castle has a magnificent interior with gilded ceilings, wall-sized tapestries, royal paintings and antiques. The richly embellished **Riddershalen** *(Knights' Hall)* and **coronation chapel**, where Danish monarchs were crowned between 1671 and 1840, are well worth the admission fee.

The S-train (A and E lines) runs every 10 minutes between Copenhagen and Hillerød (Dkr49), a 40-minute ride. From Hillerød Station follow the signs to Torvet and then continue along Slotsgade to the castle, a 15-minute walk in all, or take bus No 701, which can drop you at the gate.

Helsingør (Elsinore)

Helsingør's castle was not the royal residence portrayed in Shakespeare's *Hamlet*, but rather a grandiose tollhouse that wrested taxes from ships for over 400 years. Helsingør itself is a busy and attractive port town, with ferries shuttling across the Øresund Strait to Sweden. The **tourist office** *(☎ 49 21 13 33; Havnepladsen 3; open Mon-Sat)* is opposite the train station. There is an **Internet centre** *(☎ 49 21 52 93; Stengade 28D)* that charges Dkr20 an hour.

Helsingør's top sight is **Kronborg Castle** *(tour Dkr40; open 10.30am-5pm daily Apr-Sep, 11am-3pm Tues-Sun Nov-Mar)*, made famous as Hamlet's Elsinore Castle. The town itself has been taken in hand over the years, and careful preservation work has created a busy and attractive centre. From the tourist office head up Brostræde and along Sanct Anna Gade. This will take you through the **medieval quarter** and past the old cathedral, **Sanct Olai Kirke** *(open 10am-4pm Mon-Sat Apr-Oct, 10am-2pm Mon-Sat Nov-Mar)* and **Karmeliterklostret** *(admission Dkr10; open 10am-3pm Mon-Fri mid-May–mid-Sept, 10am-2pm rest of year)*, one of Scandinavia's best-preserved medieval monasteries.

Danhostel Helsingør *(☎ 49 21 16 40, fax 49 21 13 99; e helsingor@danhostel.dk; Nordre Strandvej 24; dorm beds Dkr100, singles or doubles Dkr250; open Feb-Nov)* is 2km northwest of the centre and is right on the Øresund. The tourist office books **rooms** in private homes from Dkr200 to Dkr300 for singles, and Dkr400 for doubles, plus a Dkr25 booking fee.

Try the **Kødbørsen butchers shop** *(Sudergade 18B)* for cheap and excellent takeaway smørrebrød. **Snack Baren** *(☎ 49 21 10 18; Hovedvagtsstræde 7a; mains Dkr42)* is a worthwhile budget place that does a different lunch dish every day in the solid Danish meat-and-vegetables mode. A good breakfast costs Dkr41.

Trains from Hillerød (Dkr42, 30 minutes) run at least once hourly. Trains from Copenhagen run a few times hourly (Dkr49, 55 minutes). For information on ferries to Helsingborg (Dkr18, 20 minutes) see the introductory Getting There & Away section to this chapter.

DENMARK

ROSKILDE

pop 43,000

Roskilde is ponderous with history, yet, apart from its magnificent cathedral, there is little visible excitement that is left in the town centre's modern buildings to recall a remarkable medieval heritage. Denmark's original capital was a thriving trading port throughout the Middle Ages. Today it's a pleasant, low-profile place, serene and well ordered – even the public toilet in the main square has carpets. It's worth a day trip from buzzing Copenhagen.

Roskilde has a helpful **tourist office** *(☎ 46 35 27 00; w www.destination-roskilde.dk; Gullandsstræde 15; open Mon-Sat)*. There are two ternet cafés side by side: **Net-X** *(Allehelgensgade 15)* and **Netcenter** *(Grønnegade 2)*, both charging about Dkr7 for 15 minutes.

The **cathedral** is on Torvet, 10 minutes northwest of the train station; cut diagonally across the old churchyard and go left along Algade. The harbourside **Viking Ship Museum** is north of the cathedral, a pleasant 15-minute stroll through city parks.

Most of Roskilde's medieval buildings have vanished in fires over the centuries, but **Roskilde Domkirke** *(☎ 46 35 27 00; Domkirkepladsen; adult/child Dkr15/10; open 9am-4.45pm Mon-Sat, 12.30pm-4.45pm Sun Apr-Sept; 10am-3.45pm Tues-Sat, 12.30pm-3.45pm Sun Oct-Mar)* still dominates the city centre. Started by Bishop Absalon in 1170, the Domkirke has been rebuilt and added to so many times that it represents a millennium of Danish architectural styles.

The **Viking Ship Museum** *(☎ 46 30 02 00; Vindeboder 12; adult/child Dkr60/35, winter Dkr45/28; open 9am-5pm daily May-Sept, 10am-4pm daily Oct-Apr)* contains five reconstructed Viking ships (c. 1000), excavated from the bottom of Roskilde Fjord in 1962 and brought to shore in thousands of fragments.

Northern Europe's largest music festival (w www.roskilde-festival.dk) rocks Roskilde each summer (generally during the last weekend in June). This is a major event that draws vast numbers of festival-goers. Past stars include Bob Dylan, the Pet Shop Boys, Robbie Williams and the Chemical Brothers. Roskilde Festival 2003 is scheduled for 26–29 June; 2004 is 1–4 July.

Trains from Copenhagen to Roskilde are frequent (Dkr49, 25 minutes). From Copenhagen by car, route 21 leads to Roskilde; upon approaching the city, exit by route 156, which leads into the centre.

MØN

Møn is celebrated for its spectacular, and totally un-Danish, sea cliffs of white chalk. Stege, the main settlement, is an everyday place, but it is enlivened by its role as the island's gateway town and main commercial centre. **Møn tourist office** *(☎ 55 86 04 00; w www.moen-touristbureau.dk; Storegade 2; open Mon-Sat, daily mid-June–Aug)* is at the entrance to Stege and has good information on the entire island.

The chalk cliffs at Møns Klint were created during the final Ice Ages, when the calcareous deposits from aeons of compressed seashells were lifted from the ocean floor. The gleaming white cliffs rise sharply for 128m above an azure sea, presenting one of the most striking landscapes in Denmark. The woods of Klinteskoven, behind the cliffs, have a network of paths and trails.

Møn has a wealth of prehistoric remains, although many are vestigial burial mounds. The best-preserved sites are the late–Stone Age passage graves of **Kong Asgers Høj** and **Klekkende Høj**. Both are on the west side of the island near the village of Røddinge.

Danhostel Møns Klint *(☎ 55 81 20 30, fax 55 81 28 18; open May-Sept; dorm beds Dkr100, singles or doubles Dkr280)* is in a former lakeside hotel 3km from the cliffs. **Pension Elmehøj** *(☎ 55 81 35 35; ⓔ pension-moen@vip.cybercity.dk; Kirkebakken 39; singles/doubles with shared bathroom Dkr265/430)* is located right next to Elmelunde Kirke. It offers pleasant, simple rooms and is an ideal base for exploring Møn. For terrific smørrebrød, try the cheerful **Stig's Slagterforretning** *(☎ 55 81 42 67; Storegade 59; fish & meat portions Dkr15-32)*.

From Copenhagen take the train to Vordingborg (Dkr92, 1½ hours) from where it's a 45-minute (Dkr32) bus ride to Stege. From late June to mid-August, buses make the 45-minute run (Dkr13) from Stege to Møns Klint a few times a day. The bus stops at the hostel and camping ground en route.

Bornholm

pop 44,000

Bornholm's main town of Rønne is a charming little port with a number of engaging museums and an old quarter of cobbled streets flanked by pretty single-storeyed dwellings. The tourist office **BornholmsVelkomstcenter** *(☎ 56 95 95 00; Nordre Kystvej 3)* is a few minutes' walk from the harbour and has masses of information on all of Bornholm.

Bornholm is no mere day-trip island, but rather a remarkable self-contained little world. Life is satisfyingly slow-paced, but never dull. The island's centre is a lush swathe of wheat fields and forests; the coast is beaded with small fishing villages and stretches of powdery white sand. In the northwest, granite cliffs and reef-lined shores create a striking contrast. Unique among Bornholm's attractions are its four 12th-century **round churches**, splendid buildings whose 2m-thick whitewashed walls are framed by solid buttresses and crowned with black, conical roofs. Each was designed not only as a place of worship, but also as a fortress against enemy attacks.

Gudhjem is a compact and attractive seaside village with half-timbered houses and sloping streets that rattle down to the pleasant harbour front. The harbour was one of the settings for Bornholm novelist Martin Andersen Nexø's Oscar-winning film *Pelle the Conqueror*. The **tourist office** *(☎ 56 48 52 10; Åbogade 7; open Mon-Fri, Mon-Sat mid-June–mid-Aug)* is a block inland from the harbour, alongside the library.

A bike path leads inland 4km south from Gudhjem to **Østerlars Rundkirke**, the most impressive of the island's round churches; bus No 3 goes by the church.

Sandvig is tucked away under Bornholm's rocky northwestern tip of Hammer Odde and boasts an excellent sandy beach to add to its distinctive appeal. Bornholm's best known sight, **Hammershus Slot**, is 3km south on the road to Rønne. The impressive and substantial ruins of this 13th-century castle are the largest of their kind in Scandinavia.

Tiny **Christiansø** is a charmingly preserved, 17th-century fortress island, an hour's sail northeast of Bornholm. A seasonal fishing hamlet since the Middle Ages, Christiansø fell briefly into Swedish hands in 1658, after which Christian V decided to turn the island into an invincible naval fortress. Bastions and barracks were built; a church, school and prison followed.

Places to Stay & Eat

In Gudhejm, **Danhostel Gudhjem** *(☎ 56 48 50 35, fax 56 48 56 35; ⓔ dgh@mail.tele.dk; dorm beds Dkr100, singles/doubles Dkr250/325; open year-round)* is located just up from the harbourside bus stop. Management can book rooms in private homes for Dkr250/350 and handles the pleasant **Therns Hotel** *(Brøddegade 31; singles/doubles Dkr500/700)*.

The waterfront smokehouse **Gudhjem Rogeri** *(☎ 56 48 57 08)* offers an all-you-can-eat buffet for Dkr78. It has live folk, country and rock music most nights in summer.

Getting There & Around

Bornholmstrafikken *(☎ 33 13 18 66; ⓦ www.bornholmstrafikken.dk)* is an agency that operates ferries between Copenhagen and Rønne (adult/child Dk224/112, seven hours, 11.30pm daily in either direction). Add Dkr74 for a dorm bunk, Dkr176 per person for a double cabin, or spread out your sleeping bag in the lounge for free. This is the slowest route, but it also provides a cheap night's sleep. From mid-June to mid-August there's also a day ferry (except Wednesday). Bornholmstrafikken operates the ferry service that runs several times daily between Rønne and Ystad, Sweden (Dkr180 one way or same-day return, 1½ hours) and on a near-daily basis during the summer months from Sassnitz-Mukran in Germany (Dkr130, 3½ hours). Sassnitz-Mukran and Ystad prices can be about 20% less off season.

A quicker option is the train-ferry combination from Copenhagen to Rønne via Ystad, Sweden. This trip goes a few times a day, takes three hours and costs Dkr205. The same route by bus costs Dkr195 and takes 3½ hours.

Bornholms Amts Trafikselskab (BAT) operates a good, inexpensive bus service around the island. Fares are based on a zone system and cost Dkr8.50 per zone, with the maximum fare set at 10 zones.

Cycling is a great way to get around. Bornholm is crisscrossed by more than 200km of bike trails, many built over former rail routes. Rønne tourist office sells a 60-page English-language *Bicycle Routes on Bornholm* (Dkr40), which maps out routes and describes sights along the way. In Ronne, **Bornholms Cykeludlejning** *(☎ 56 95 13 59; e bornholms.cykeludlejning@teliamail.dk; Nordre Kystvej 5)*, which is next to the tourist office, has a large fleet of bikes that can be rented for Dkr60 a day. Bicycles can usually be rented from hostels and camping grounds around the island for about Dkr55 a day.

Funen (Fyn)

pop 472,000

Funen is Denmark's garden island. It is largely rural, with rolling woodlands, pastures and corn fields peppered with old farmhouses and sleepy villages. The unspoilt islands of the South Funen archipelago, especially Langeland and Ærø, are delightful places.

The railway line from Copenhagen runs straight through Odense, Funen's main city, and on westward to Jutland. Store Bælt (Great Belt), the channel that separates Zealand and Funen, was until recently crossed only by boat. It's now spanned by Europe's longest combined road and rail bridge.

ODENSE

pop 184,00

Denmark's third largest city takes great pride in being the birthplace of Hans Christian Andersen, though after an unhappy childhood Andersen left Odense with little regret. It is, however, a friendly university city with busy pedestrianised areas, an interesting cathedral and several worthwhile museums.

The **tourist bureau** *(☎ 66 12 75 20; W www.visitodense.com; open Mon-Sat, daily mid-June–Aug)*, at Rådhus, is a 15-minute walk from the train station. There's free use of the Internet at **Odense Central Library** *(Odense Banegård Center; open 10am-7pm Mon-Thurs, 10am-4pm Fri & Sat)*.

The **HC Andersens Hus** *(☎ 66 14 88 14; Hans Jensens Stræde 37-45; adult/child Dkr35/15; open 9am-7pm daily mid-June–Aug, 10am-4pm Tues-Sun Sept–mid-June)* is amid the now-picturesque little houses of the old poor quarter of Odense. It depicts Andersen's life story through his memorabilia and books. **HC Andersens Barndomshjem** *(Munkemøllestræde 3; adult/child Dkr10/5; open 10am-4pm daily mid-June–Aug, 11am-3pm Tues-Sun Sept–mid-June)* contains a couple of rooms of exhibits in the small house where Hans grew up.

Odense's 13th-century **Sankt Knuds Kirke** *(☎ 66 12 03 92; Flakhaven; admission free; open 9am-5pm Mon-Sat & noon-3pm Sun)* reflects Odense's medieval wealth and stature. It has a handsome rococo pulpit and a dazzling 16th century altarpiece – a gilded wood triptych crowded with over 300 carved figures and said to be one of the finest pieces of religious art in northern Europe.

Delightful open-air museum **Den Fynske Landsby** *(☎ 66 14 88 14; adult/child Dkr55/15; open 10am-5pm daily April-Oct, until 7pm mid-Jun–mid-Aug, 11am-3pm Nov-Mar)* is furnished with period buildings laid out like a small country village, complete with barnyard animals, a duck pond and flower gardens. The museum is in a green zone 4km south of the city centre via bus No 42.

Places to Stay

The 143-bed **Danhostel Odense City** *(☎ 63 11 04 25, fax 63 11 35 20; W www.cityhostel.dk;*

dorm beds Dkr100, singles/doubles Dkr310/360) is a bright, modern place alongside the train and bus stations.

Danhostel Odense Vandrerhjem *(☎ 66 13 04 25, fax 65 91 28 63; Kragsbjergvej 121; dorm beds Dkr94, singles/doubles Dkr376)*, which has 168 beds, occupies a former manor house round a grassy central square, 2km southeast of the centre via bus No 61 or 62.

Good value is the 35-room **Hotel Domir** *(☎ 66 12 14 27, fax 66 12 14 31; W www.domir.dk; Tausensgade 19; singles Dkr420, doubles Dkr495-585)*, with pleasant rooms, but some singles that are a bit cramped.

Places to Eat

There are a number of various eateries along Kongensgade. **China Barbecue** *(Kongensgade 66; lunch buffet noon-3pm Dkr49)* does take-away boxes for Dkr22 to Dkr33, while **Jensen's Bøfhus** *(☎ 66 14 59 59; Kongensgade 10)* serves inexpensive steak and chicken lunches for Dkr39 to Dkr69.

A cheerful place is **Café Biografen** *(☎ 66 13 16 16; Brandts Klædefabrik; brunch Dkr60; open 11am-midnight daily)*, where ducks waddle happily around the terrace tables. It does a good selection of baguettes at Dkr38 and salads at about Dkr60, as well as cakes, pastries, coffees, light meals and beer all at reasonable prices.

The unique **Kærnehuset** *(Nedergade 6)*, a vegetarian collective, located in a 1st-floor room, serves a Dkr40 meal at 6pm Tuesday to Friday and welcomes visitors. Let them know an hour or so beforehand that you'd like a meal.

Entertainment

Ryan's *(Nørregade)* is a friendly Irish-style pub set back from the busy Thomas B Thriges Gade. **Boogies** *(Nørregade 21)*, a dance place downstairs from Birdy's Café, is popular with students; admission is about Dkr35 on Friday and Saturday. Brandts Klædefabrik has an outdoor amphitheatre for free summer weekend concerts.

Kong Graes *(☎ 66 11 18 16; Asylgade 7-9)* is a late-night dance club, and **Jazzhus Dexter** *(☎ 66 13 68 88; Vindegade 65)* has good live groups. **Lambda** *(☎ 66 17 76 92; Vindegade 100)*, Odense's gay and lesbian centre, has a late-night café on Fridays and most Saturdays, and a disco on the first and third Saturdays of each month. It's located in an unsigned, red-brick building.

Getting There & Around

Odense is on the main railway line between Copenhagen (Dkr192, 1½ hours), Århus (Dkr168, 1¾ hours), Aalborg (Dkr257, three hours) and Esbjerg (Dkr151, two hours). Buses leave from the rear of the train station.

In Odense you board city buses at the front and pay the driver (Dkr12) when you get off. Have the correct change. Bicycles can be rented at **Rolsted Cykler** *(☎ 66 17 77 36; Ostre Stationsvej 33; open 10am-5pm Mon & Tues, 10am-7pm Fri, 10am-2pm Sun)* for Dkr85 a day or Dkr500 a week.

EGESKOV CASTLE

Egeskov *(☎ 62 27 10 16; W www.egeskov.com; admission castle grounds adult/child Dkr75/37, plus castle interior Dkr55/28; open 10am-5pm daily May, June, Aug & Sept, 10am-7pm daily July)* is a magnificent Renaissance castle, complete with moat and drawbridge. The grounds include century-old privet hedges, free-roaming peacocks, a topiary, English gardens and an entertaining bamboo grass labyrinth.

Egeskov Castle is 2km west of Kværndrup on route 8. From Odense take the Svendborg-bound train to Kværndrup Station (Dkr45) and continue on foot or by taxi, or for Dkr36 take bus No 801 to Kværndrup Bibliotek, where you can switch to bus No 920, which stops at the castle on its regular run between Faaborg and Nyborg.

Jutland (Jylland)

Most of flat, sandy Jutland's cities are on the sheltered east coast, while most of the island is level farmland whose fields are lushly verdant in spring and drably brown in autumn.

ÅRHUS

pop 285,000

Denmark's second city is one of Scandinavia's most modern and sophisticated regional capitals. Yet this university town retains all the friendliness and ease of a small country town – combined with one of Denmark's best music and entertainment scenes, a well-preserved historic quarter and a wide range of outdoor opportunities.

The helpful **tourist office** *(☎ 89 40 67 00, fax 86 12 95 90; W www.visitaarhus.com; Park Allé; open Mon-Sat, daily mid-June–mid-Sept)*

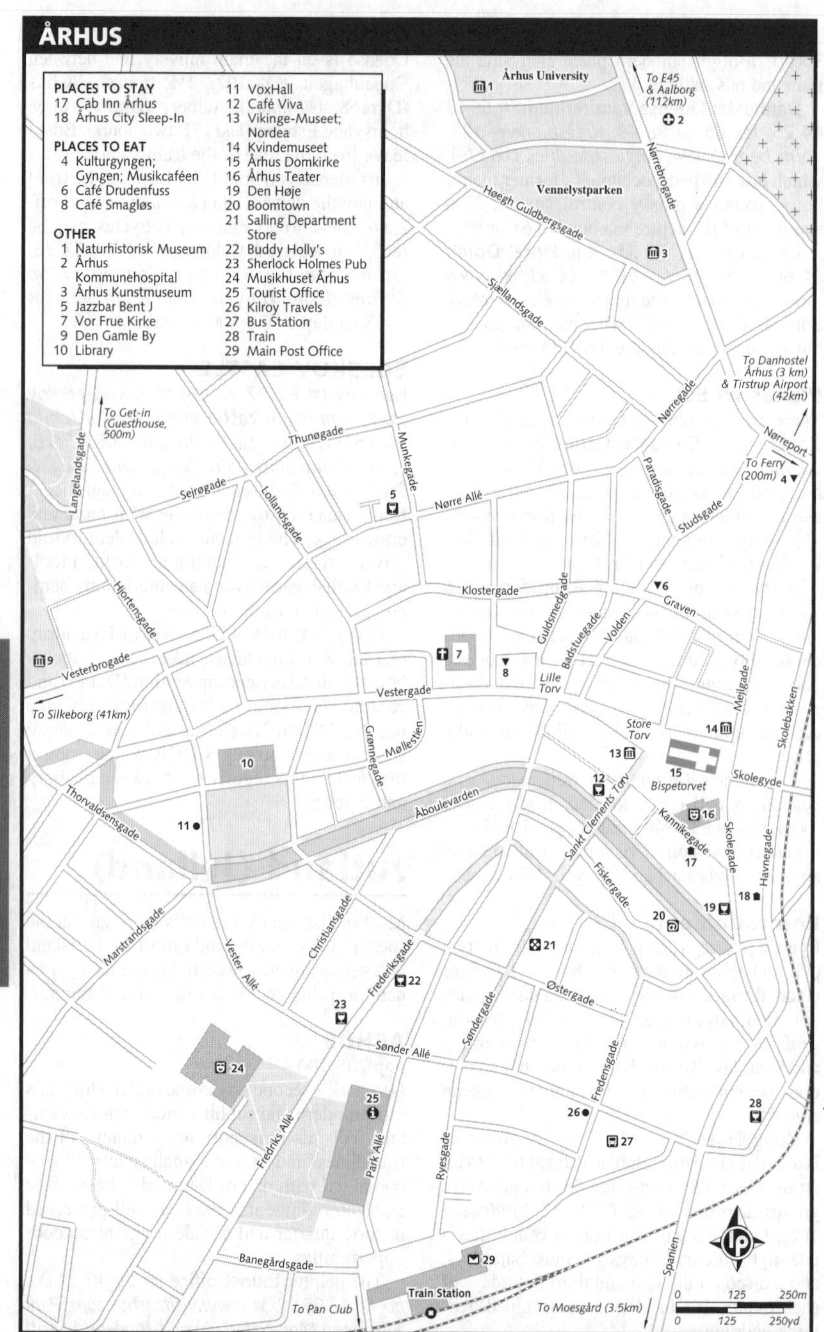
ÅRHUS
PLACES TO STAY
17 Cab Inn Århus
18 Århus City Sleep-In
PLACES TO EAT
4 Kulturgyngen; Gyngen; Musikcaféen
6 Café Drudenfuss
8 Café Smagløs
OTHER
1 Naturhistorisk Museum
2 Århus Kommunehospital
3 Århus Kunstmuseum
5 Jazzbar Bent J
7 Vor Frue Kirke
9 Den Gamle By
10 Library
11 VoxHall
12 Café Viva
13 Vikinge-Museet; Nordea
14 Kvindemuseet
15 Århus Domkirke
16 Århus Teater
19 Den Høje
20 Boomtown
21 Salling Department Store
22 Buddy Holly's
23 Sherlock Holmes Pub
24 Musikhuset Århus
25 Tourist Office
26 Kilroy Travels
27 Bus Station
28 Train
29 Main Post Office
Århus University
Vennelystparken
To E45 & Aalborg (112km)
To Danhostel Århus (3 km) & Tirstrup Airport (42km)
To Ferry (200m)
To Get-in (Guesthouse, 500m)
To Silkeborg (41km)
To Pan Club
To Moesgård (3.5km)
Train Station
Høegh Guldbergsgade
Nørrebrogade
Sjællandsgade
Nørregade
Nørreport
Paradisgade
Studsgade
Thunøgade
Munkegade
Sejrøgade
Langelandsgade
Lollandsgade
Nørre Allé
Klostergade
Guldsmedgade
Graven
Volden
Badstuegade
Hjortensgade
Vesterbrogade
Vestergade
Lille Torv
Store Torv
Mejlgade
Skolebakken
Grønnegade
Møllestien
Bispetorvet
Skolegyde
Thorvaldsensgade
Åboulevarden
Sankt Clemens Torv
Kannikegade
Skolegade
Havnegade
Fiskergade
Marstrandsgade
Vester Allé
Christiansgade
Frederiksgade
Østergade
Søndergade
Sønder Allé
Fredensgade
Fredriks Allé
Park Allé
Ryesgade
Banegårdsgade
Spanien
0 125 250m
0 125 250yd

is in Rådhuset, the city hall. The **main post office** *(Banegardspladsen; open 9.30am-6pm Mon-Fri, 10am-1pm Sat)*, is beside the train station. **Boomtown** *(Åboulevarden 21; open 10am-2am Mon-Thur, 10am-8am Fri & Sat, 11am-midnight Sun)* is part of a city Internet chain; access is Dkr20 for one hour. **Kilroy Travels** *(☎ 86 20 11 44; Fredensgade 40)* specialises in discount and student travel, and has friendly, helpful staff.

Things to See & Do

Den Gamle By *(Old Town; ☎ 86 12 31 88; w www.dengamleby; Viborgvej 2; adult/child Dkr70/25; open 9am-6pm daily June-Aug, 10am-5pm daily April, May, Sept & Oct, 10am-4pm daily Feb, Mar, Nov & Dec, 11am-3pm daily Jan)* is an engaging open-air museum of 75 half-timbered houses brought here from around Denmark and reconstructed as a provincial town, complete with a functioning bakery, silversmith, bookbinder etc. It's on Viborgvej, a 20-minute walk from the city centre. After-hours you can walk through the old streets free. Bus Nos 3, 14, 25 and 55 will take you there.

The impressive **Århus Domkirke** *(☎ 86 12 38 45; Bispetorvet; admission free; open 9.30am-4pm Mon-Fri May-Sept, 10am-3pm Mon-Fri Oct-Apr)* is Denmark's longest cathedral, with a lofty nave that spans nearly 100m. The original Romanesque chapel at the eastern end dates from the 12th century. Like other Danish churches, the cathedral was once richly decorated with frescoes, but after the Reformation, church authorities had them all whitewashed. Many have been uncovered and restored.

Lurking in the bank basement of Nordea is the **Vikinge-Museet** *(☎ 89 42 11 00; Sankt Clements Torv 6; admission free; open 10am-4pm Mon-Wed & Fri, 10am-6pm Thur)*. In this space you will find an exhibition of artefacts from the Viking Age town that were excavated at this site in 1964 during the bank's construction.

There are sandy **beaches** on the outskirts of Århus. The most popular one to the north is Bellevue, about 4km from the city centre (bus No 6 or 16).

Special Events

The 10-day **Århus Festival** *(w www.aarhusfestuge.dk)* in early September turns the city into a stage for nonstop revelry, with jazz, rock, classical music, theatre and dance. The festival is of international significance and in its long history has hosted such bill-toppers as the Rolling Stones, Anne-Sophie Mutter, Ravi Shankar, City of Birmingham Symphony Orchestra, New York City Ballet, Günter Grass and many more.

Places to Stay

The **Danhostel Århus** *(☎ 86 16 72 98, fax 86 10 55 60; e danhostel.aarhus@get2net.dk; Marienlundsvej 10; dorm beds Dkr95, singles or doubles Dkr400; open late Jan–mid-Dec)*, is in a renovated 1850s dance hall at the edge of the Risskov Woods, 4km north of the city centre, reached by bus No 6 or 9.

Århus City Sleep-In *(☎ 86 19 20 55, fax 86 19 18 11; e sleep-in@citysleep-in.dk; Havnegade 20; dorm beds Dkr105, doubles with/without bathroom Dkr360/300; reception open 24hr)*, run by a youth organisation, is in a central former mariners' hotel. It's casual, the rooms are a bit run-down and it can be a noisy (but cheerful) place. Sheets can be hired for Dkr30 and key deposit is Dkr50. There's a TV and pool table, guest kitchen and laundry facilities. Bikes can be hired for Dkr50 a day.

The tourist office books rooms in private homes for Dkr200/300 singles/doubles, plus a Dkr25 booking fee.

The 62-room **Get-in** *(☎ 86 10 86 14, fax 86 10 86 24; e get-in@get-in.dk; Jens Baggesensvej 43; singles/doubles with bathroom Dkr300/400, without bathroom Dkr250/350)* is a guesthouse near Århus University, about 1.5km from the city centre. It has clean and adequate rooms and there's a TV room and guest kitchen. Breakfast is Dkr35. Take bus No 7 from the train station.

Cab Inn Århus *(☎/fax 86 75 70 00; e aarhus@cab-inn.dk; Kannikegade 14; singles/doubles Dkr510/630)* is in an ideal central location opposite the Domkirke. The style is standard Cab Inn with small, but comfy and spotless rooms.

Places to Eat

The narrow streets of the old quarter north of the cathedral are thick with cafés serving Danish and ethnic foods.

The café/restaurant of **Kulturgyngen** *(Mejlgade 53; lunch/dinner Dkr38/75; open 11am-9pm Mon-Sat)*, an alternative cultural and youth complex, has a great atmosphere and pretty good food, including sandwiches for Dkr25 and a choice of vegetarian or meat dishes nightly.

Café Drudenfuss *(☎ 86 12 82 72; Graven 30; brunch Dkr55)* is a pleasant relaxing bar/café with artwork on the walls, photography exhibitions and a good range of sandwiches, starting at Dkr35, and salads for Dkr47.

Café Smagløs *(☎ 86 19 03 77; Klostertorv 7; brunch Dkr65)* is a cosy and down-to-earth place with salads, sandwiches and vegetarian dishes for about Dkr35 to Dkr58.

Entertainment

The monthly free publication *What's On in Århus* lists current happenings and is available at the tourist office and also at other venues around town.

Århus has a vibrant music scene. **Train** *(☎ 86 13 47 22; Toldbodgade 6; open until 5am Thur-Sat)* is one of the biggest venues in Denmark. It stages concerts by international rock, pop and country stars and there's a late-night disco. **Musikcaféen** and the adjacent **Gyngen** *(Kulturgyngen; ☎ 86 76 03 44; Mejlgade 53; open 8.30pm-2am Mon-Sat)* are alternative venues with rock, jazz and world music.

VoxHall *(☎ 87 30 97 97; Vester Allé 15; open 8pm-2am Mon-Sat)* offers a very wide range of music and sometimes features UK bands. **Jazzbar Bent J** *(☎ 86 12 04 92; Nørre Allé 66)* is a long-established, jazz-only bar that has an impressive guest list. Entry is Dkr80 on guest nights.

Sherlock Holmes Pub *(☎ 86 12 40 50; Frederiksgade 76d)* has live music, a big screen for football matches and lots more. Drinks are half-price until 7pm. Just down the road is the three-floor dance and disco venue **Buddy Holly's** *(☎ 86 18 08 55; Frederiksgade 29; open 10am-5am Mon-Thur, from 5pm Fri, from 10pm Sat)*.

Café Viva *(Aboulevarden/Sankte Clemens Strade 22)*, a classy riverside restaurant, transforms into a late-night disco.

There are a number of busy bars in Skolegade. **Den Høje** *(Skolegade 28)* is popular with an easygoing young crowd, not least for its cheap beer.

The main gay and lesbian social scene is at **Pan Club** *(☎ 86 13 43 80; Jægergårdsgade 42)*, south of the train station.

The city concert hall, Musikhuset Århus, presents dance, opera and concerts by international performers.

Getting There & Away

Bus The bus station is on Fredensgade. **Express buses** *(☎ 70 21 08 88)* run a few times daily between Århus and Copenhagen's Valby Station (adult/child/student Dkr210/105/110, three hours). Buses run regularly to Silkeborg (Dkr46, 48 minutes) and Aalborg (Dkr110, two hours).

Train There are trains to Århus, via Odense, leaving Copenhagen on the hour from early morning to 10pm (Dkr267, 3¼ hours) and there's a night train at 2am. There are regular trains to Aalborg (Dkr135, 85 minutes) and Esbjerg (Dkr184, 2¾ hours). There's a ticket-queuing system at the station – red for internal, green for international. For local journeys, unless you have mastered use of the quicker ticket machines, be prepared for long waits at busy times. Friday trains are always very busy and it's advised to reserve a seat for long journeys.

Boat Car ferries are operated by the company **Mols-Linien** *(☎ 70 10 14 18)* between Århus and Odden (adult/child from Dkr135/67.50, car and five passengers Dkr435, 65 minutes) and Kalundborg (2½ hours, adult/child from Dkr135/67.50).

Getting Around

Most in-town buses stop in front of the train station or around the corner on Park Allé. City bus tickets are bought from a machine in the back of the bus for Dkr13 and are good for unlimited rides within the time period stamped on the ticket (about two hours). You can buy tickets and passes at **Århus Sporveje** *(☎ 89 40 10 10; Banegårdspladsen 20; open 8am-6pm Mon-Fri, 10am-1pm Sat)*, the city transport service shop across from the train station.

Taxis wait outside the station and at Store Torv. Expect to pay up to Dkr60 for in-city destinations. The fare to the airport is about Dkr470.

THE LAKE DISTRICT

The Danish Lake District, the closest thing to hill country in Denmark, offers excellent canoeing, biking and hiking amid the woods and on the water. The scenery is placid and pastoral rather than stunning, but the area is delightful and has a distinctive character. The district's biggest town, **Silkeborg**, overcomes its rather bland modern character with a friendly openness. It's an ideal base for exploring the surrounding forests and waterways. The helpful **tourist office** *(☎ 86 82 19 11; w www.silkeborg.com; Åhavevej 2A; open Mon-Sat, daily mid-June–Aug)* is near the harbour and has lots of leaflets and brochures.

Ry is a smaller town in a more rural setting than Silkeborg and is a good place from which to base your exploration of the Lake District. The **tourist office** *(☎ 86 89 34 22; w www.visitry.com; Klostervej 3; open Mon-Sat)* is in the train station.

The Lake District's most visited place is the whimsically named **Himmelbjerget** *(Sky Mountain)*, which, at just 147m, is one of Denmark's highest hills. Another good, half-day outing is to cycle from Ry to **Boes**, a tiny hamlet that has picturesque thatch-roofed houses and vivid flower gardens. From Boes you can continue cross-country to **Øm Kloster** *(☎ 86 89 81 94; adult/child Dkr35/10; open 10am-6pm Tues-Sun July-Aug, 10am-5pm Mar-June & Sept, 10am-4pm Apr & Oct)*, the ruins of a medieval monastery, where glass-topped tombs reveal the 750-year-old bones of Bishop Elafsen of Århus and many of his abbots. The trip from Ry and back is 18km.

Places to Stay & Eat

Danhostel Ry *(☎ 86 89 14 07; e mail@danhostel-ry.dk; Randersvej 88; dorm beds Dkr100, singles/doubles Dkr400)* is 1km north of Ry. To get there from the train station, cross the tracks, turn left and go 2.5km; or take the infrequent bus No 311. The tourist office books rooms in private homes from Dkr200/275 for singles/doubles.

Ry Park Hotel *(☎ 86 89 19 11; e rypark hotel@mail.dk; Kyhnsvej 2; singles/doubles Dkr690/890)* is a modern complex with swimming pool, sauna and restaurant. It has a sizeable coach-tour trade.

Ry's butcher's shop, opposite the train station, offers fried fish and a few other take-away selections. There is a bakery next door. In Skanderborgvej are the cheap eateries Gormand Sandwich and Pizza Express.

Getting There & Around

Hourly trains connect Ry with Silkeborg (Dkr25, 20 minutes) and Århus (Dkr35, 30 minutes). **Ry Cykel** *(☎ 86 89 14 91; Skanderborgvej 19)* rents out bikes.

AALBORG

pop 161,000

People soon warm to Aalborg's unassuming style. This is Jutland's second largest city, an industrial and trading centre without many great buildings or medieval quaintness. Yet Aalborg is a friendly, down-to-earth place that has plenty of good shops and a lively nightlife.

The town centre is a 10-minute walk from the train and bus stations, north on Boulevarden. The helpful **tourist office** *(☎ 98 12 60 22; w www.visitaalborg.com; Østerågade 8; open Mon-Sat)* has masses of information. The office of **Landsforeningen for Bøsser og Lesbiske** *(☎ 98 16 45 07; Toldbodgade 27, PO Box 1244)* is the local branch of the Danish national organisation for gays and lesbians. **Net City** *(Nytorv 13A)* charges Dkr20 per hour of Internet access. Access is free at the city library, **Hovedbiblioteket** *(Rendsburggade 2; open 10am-8pm Mon-Fri, 10am-3pm Sat)*.

Old Town

The whitewashed **Buldolfi Domkirke** marks the centre of the Old Town. About 75m east of the cathedral is the **Aalborg Historiske Museum** *(Algade 48; adult/child Dkr20/10; open 10am-5pm Tues-Sun)*, with interesting artefacts and Renaissance furnishings.

The alley between the museum and church leads to the rambling **Monastery of the Holy Ghost**, which dates from 1431; the tourist office arranges guided tours (Dkr40). Northeast of the cathedral on Østerågade are three noteworthy historic buildings: the **old town hall** (c. 1762), five-storey **Jens Bangs Stenhus** (c. 1624) and **Jørgen Olufsens House** (c. 1616).

Lindholm Høje

On a hill-top pasture overlooking the city, Lindholm Høje *(admission free; open dawn-dusk daily)*, is the site of nearly 700 graves from the Iron Age and Viking Age. Many of the **Viking graves** are marked by stones placed in the outline of a Viking ship, with two larger end stones as stem and stern. There is a compelling atmosphere at the site. Adjacent to the field, a **museum** *(☎ 96 31 04 29; adult/child Dkr30/15; open 10am-5pm daily Apr-Oct)* depicts the site's history in an imaginative way. Lindholm Høje is 15 minutes from Aalborg centre on bus No 6.

Places to Stay

Danhostel Aalborg (*☎ 98 11 60 44, fax 98 12 47 11; e aalborg@danhostel.dk; Skydebanevej 50; dorm beds Dkr100, singles/doubles Dkr460*) is at the marina 4km west of the centre. Take bus No 8. The tourist office books rooms in private homes for Dkr200/300 for singles/doubles, plus a Dkr25 booking fee.

Aalborg Sømandshjem (*☎ 98 12 19 00, fax 98 11 76 97; e hansen@hotel-aalborg.com; Østerbro 27; singles/doubles Dkr500/680*) is about a kilometre east of the centre and has comfortable and quiet rooms.

Park Hotel (*☎ 98 12 31 33, fax 98 13 31 66; e parkhotel@email.dk; Boulevarden 41; singles/doubles from Dkr725/859*) has comfortable rooms and traditional decor, and is just 100m from the rail and bus stations.

Places to Eat

A good place for food, drink and diversion is Aalborg's famous Jomfru Ane Gade, a lively, pedestrian street lined with restaurants and bars. It is the heart of Aalborg's nightlife, and most places are open until the early hours.

Round the corner from Jomfru Ane Gade on Ved Stranden, a gaggle of eateries offers slightly cheaper options. The popular **Café Casa Blanca** (*☎ 98 16 44 45; Ved Stranden 4*) offers brunch or a buffet for Dkr59 between 11am and 4pm and also has a youngsters' menu for Dkr39.

Algade, a pedestrian shopping street a block south of the tourist office, offers inexpensive options, including **Schak Nielsen** (*☎ 98 12 35 92; Algade 23*), a terrific fish shop that has takeaway salmon-burgers and a range of tasty fish specialities.

DENMARK

Entertainment

Jomfru Ane Gade has a number of early hours dance bars and discos. Away from the street of bars, **Huset** (*☎ 98 16 76 66; Hasserisgade 10*) is a cultural centre that stages jazz, folk and world music events. **Pan Aalborg** (*☎ 98 12 22 45; Danmarksgade 27A; open 11pm-2am Thur, 10pm-5am Fri & Sat*) is Aalborg's main gay venue.

Getting There & Around

Trains run at least hourly to Århus (Dkr135, 85 minutes) and every two hours to Frederikshavn (Dkr68, one hour). **Express buses** (*☎ 70 10 00 30*) run daily to Copenhagen (Dkr220, five hours).

City buses leave from Østerågade and Nytorv, near Burger King. The bus fare is Dkr13 to any place in greater Aalborg.

FREDERIKSHAVN

pop 26,000

Frederikshavn is a major ferry town and industrial port with a fairly featureless dockside area, but the town has a pleasant pedestrianised centre with plenty of shops and several attractive bars and restaurants. An overhead walkway leads from the ferry terminal to **Frederikshavn Turistbureau** (*☎ 98 42 32 66; w www.frederikshavn-tourist.dk; Skandiatorv 1; open Mon-Sat, daily July–mid-Aug*). The train station and adjacent bus terminal are a 10-minute walk to the north.

Danhostel Frederikshavn (*☎ 98 42 14 75, fax 98 42 65 22; e frederikshavn@danhostel.dk; Buhlsvej 6; dorm beds Dkr90, singles/doubles Dkr200/270; open Feb–mid-Dec*) is 2km north of the ferry terminal. The tourist office books rooms.

Damsgaard Supermarked (*Havnegade*) beside the tourist office, has a cheap cafeteria with a harbour view.

Frederikshavn is the northern terminus of the DSB rail line. Trains run about hourly south to Aalborg (Dkr71.50) and on to Copenhagen (Dkr310). Nordjyllands Trafikselskab has both a train (40 minutes) and bus service (one hour) north to Skagen (Dkr39).

Stena Line (*☎ 96 20 02 00*) runs ferries from Frederikshavn to Gothenburg, Sweden, six to 10 times daily (adult/child from Dkr80/40 to Dkr160/80, two to 3¼ hours). There are also services to Larvik, Norway (Dkr125 to Dkr300, 6¼ hours) daily in summer, with fewer services in winter. **Color Line** (*☎ 99 56 19 77*) has daily ferries to Larvik, Norway (adult/child from Dkr170/85 to Dkr360/180, 6¼ hours).

SKAGEN

Artists discovered Skagen's luminous light and its colourful heath-and-dune landscape in the mid-19th century, and painters such as Michael and Anna Ancher and Oscar Björck established a vivid figurative style of painting that became known as the 'Skagen School'. Today, Skagen is a major tourist resort, packed to the gills in high summer – but the sense of a more picturesque Skagen survives, and the town's older neighbourhoods are filled with distinctive yellow-washed houses, each with red tile roofs that are painted with distinctive bands of whitewash at their edges. The peninsula is lined with fine beaches.

Sankt Laurentii Vej, Skagen's main street, runs almost the entire length of this long, thin town. The **tourist office** *(☎ 98 44 13 77; w www.skagen-tourist.dk; Sankt Laurentii Vej 22; open daily)* is in the train/bus station. **Skagens Museum** *(☎ 98 44 64 44; Brøndumsvej 4; admission Dkr50; open 10am-5pm or 6pm daily May-Aug, 11am-4pm Tues-Sun April, 1pm-5pm Wed-Fri, 11am-4pm Sat, 11am-3pm Sun Nov-Mar)* displays the paintings of Michael and Anna Ancher and PS Krøyer, and of other artists who flocked to Skagen between 1830 and 1930.

Denmark's most northerly point is the culmination of a long curving sweep of sand at **Grenen**, about 3km northeast of Skagen along route 40. Where the road ends there's a car park, café and souvenir shops, and, in high summer, what seems like everyone in Denmark. Crowds head along the last stretch of beach for the 30-minute walk to the narrow tip where the waters of the Kattegat and Skagerrak clash and you can put one foot in each sea – but not too far (bathing is strictly forbidden).

Places to Stay & Eat

The 112-bed **Danhostel Skagen** *(☎ 98 44 22 00, fax 98 44 22 55; e danhostel.skagen@adr.dk; Rolighedsvej 2; dorm beds Dkr100, singles/doubles from Dkr250/300)* is located 1km west of the centre. The tourist office can book rooms in private homes for around Dkr200/350, plus a Dkr50 booking fee.

Clausens Hotel *(☎ 98 45 01 66; e bestilling@clausenhotel.dk; singles/doubles with bathroom Dkr550/795, without bathroom Dkr495/525)* is just across from the train station and has comfortable rooms.

The harbourside **Skagen Sømandshjem** *(☎ 98 44 25 88; Østre Strandvej 2; singles/doubles with bathroom Dkr550/740, without bathroom Dkr410/630)* has bright, pleasant rooms.

You'll find a couple of pizzerias, a kebab shop, a burger joint and an ice-cream shop clustered near each other on Havnevej. **Super Brugsen** *(Sankt Laurentii Vej 28)*, a grocery shop west of the tourist office, has a bakery.

Getting There & Around

Either a bus or a train leaves Skagen Station for Frederikshavn (Dkr39) about once an hour. The seasonal Skagerakkeren bus (No 99) runs half a dozen times daily between Hirtshals and Skagen (Dkr32.50, 1½ hours) from mid-June to mid-August. The same bus continues on to Hjørring and Løkken.

Cycling is an excellent way of exploring Skagen and the surrounding area. **Skagen Cykeludlejning** *(☎ 98 44 10 70; Banegårdspladsen)* rents bicycles for Dkr75 a day and has a stand on the western side of the train station and at the harbour.

HIRTSHALS

pop 7000

Hirtshals takes its breezy and friendly character from its commercial fishing harbour and ferry terminal. The essentially modern main street, pedestrianised Nørregade, is lined with a mix of cafés and shops, as well as supermarkets that cater to Norwegian shoppers who load up with relatively cheap Danish meats and groceries. The **tourist office** *(☎ 98 94 22 20; e pj@hirtshals-tourist.dk; Nørregade 40; open Mon-Sat, daily mid-July–Aug)* can help you out.

Hirtshals Hostel *(☎ 98 94 12 48; e danhostel.hirtshals@adr.dk; Kystvejen 53; dorm beds Dkr95, singles/doubles Dkr300/400; open Mar-Nov)* is 1km west of the train station. Staff at the tourist office can book rooms in private homes starting at Dkr150 plus a Dkr25 booking fee.

Hotel Hirtshals *(☎ 98 94 20 77; fax 98 94 21 07; e info@hotelhirtshals.dk; Havnegade 2; singles/doubles Dkr645/785)* is right on the main square above the fishing harbour and has bright, comfortable rooms. There are cafés and a good bakery at the northern end of Hjørringgade and a couple of pizza and kebab places on Nørregade.

In summer there's a bus from Hirtshals Station to Hjørring (Dkr19.50) that stops en route at Tornby Strand six times a day. Hirtshals' main train station is 500m south of the ferry harbour, but there's also a stop near the Color Line terminal. The railway, which is operated by a private company, connects Hirtshals with Hjørring (Dkr19.50), 20 minutes to the south. Trains run at least hourly, with the last departure from Hjørring to Hirtshals at 10.25pm. From Hjørring you can take a DSB train to Aalborg (Dkr54) or Frederikshavn (Dkr39).

Color Line *(☎ 99 56 20 00)* runs year-round ferries to the Norwegian ports of Oslo (8½ hours, 10am daily in summer) and Kristiansand

(2½ to five hours, four times daily in summer). Fares on both routes are from Dkr170 midweek in the off season to Dkr400 on summer weekends for passengers, from Dkr150 to Dkr290 for a motorcycle and from Dkr200 to Dkr680 for a car.

RIBE

On Denmark's southeastern coast, Ribe sells its quaintness with great efficiency. Dating from 869, it is said to be the oldest town in Scandinavia and was an important medieval trading centre. The half-timbered 16th-century houses and crooked, cobblestone streets certainly impart a sense of history. Almost everything, including the hostel and train station, is within 10 minutes' walk of Torvet, the town square, which is dominated by a huge Romanesque cathedral. Here, too, is the **tourist office** *(☎ 75 42 15 00; Ⓦ www.ribetourist.dk; open Mon-Fri, Mon-Sat Apr-Jun & Sept-Dec, daily July & Aug)*.

Ribe Domkirke *(☎ 75 42 06 19; Torvet; adult/child Dkr12/5)* dominates the heart of the town and boasts a variety of styles from Romanesque to Gothic. Its monumental presence is literally sunk into the heart of Ribe: the cathedral floor is over a metre below the level of the surrounding streets. **Ribes Vikinger** *(☎ 76 88 11 22; Odins Plads 1; adult/child Dkr50/20; open 10am-6pm daily July & Aug, 10am-4pm rest of year, closed Mon Nov-Mar)*, a substantial museum opposite the train station, has archaeological displays on Ribe's Viking history, with lots of hands-on features. **Ribe Vikingecenter** *(☎ 75 41 16 11; Lustrupvej 4; adult/child Dkr50/20; open 11am-4.30pm daily July & Aug, 11am-4pm daily May, June & Sept)*, 3km south of the centre, is a re-created Viking village complete with working artisans and interpreters decked out in period costumes. Bus No 51 (Dkr15) will take you there from Ribe.

The modern, 140-bed **Danhostel Ribe** *(☎ 75 42 06 20, fax 75 42 42 88; Ⓔ ribe@danhostel.dk; Sct Pedersgade 16; dorm beds Dkr100, singles/doubles Dkr250/295)* has friendly staff and a good, uncrowded location. The tourist office maintains a list of rooms in private homes from Dkr250/350 for singles/doubles. **Weis Stue** *(☎ 75 42 07 00; Torvet; singles/doubles Dkr400/500)* is in a handsome old building, from where you are ushered across the road to the restaurant of Hotel Dagmar for breakfast.

There are several fast-food outlets along Nederdammen, including Kebabhus & Grill, with burgers and kebabs round about Dkr30 to Dkr48, Pizza Expressen, with pizza at Dkr45, and Peking House, offering Chinese lunch specials from Dkr30.

There are trains from Esbjerg to Ribe (Dkr50, 40 minutes) and from Århus to Ribe (Dkr192).

Estonia

Estonia's transition from a Soviet socialist republic to Western-style economy has been little short of miraculous. Even before independence, Estonia was known as the most 'Western' of the Soviet republics, partly because of its links with Finland. These days, it remains more Scandinavian in look and feel than its Baltic neighbours.

However, Estonia's German past lingers and is particularly evident in Tallinn's beautiful medieval Old Town. Although Tallinn may be the hub of Estonian life, the university town of Tartu and coastal resort of Pärnu are also appealing destinations that remain the best-kept secret of Estonians and their Scandinavian neighbours.

Estonia: the Basics

Local name (Eesti)

Capital Tallinn

Population 1.36 million

Languages Estonian, Russian

Currency 1 Kroon (EEK) = 100 sents

Avoid at all costs Making a public spectacle of yourself

Win approval by realising *Vrääkimine on hõbe, vaikus on kuld* (Conversation is silver, silence is golden)

Facts about Estonia

HISTORY

In 1202 the Bishop of Rīga established the Knights of the Sword to convert the pagan region by conquest. By 1346 the German Teutonic Order ruled all Estonia, placing the Estonians under servitude to a German nobility that would last until the early 20th century. Hanseatic trade towns prospered, although many Estonians in rural areas were forced into serfdom.

After the Great Northern War (1700–21), Estonia became part of the Russian Empire. Repressive government and economic control by the ruling powers forged a national self-awareness among native Estonians. Serfs were freed in the 19th century, and improved education and land-ownership rights promoted culture and welfare. During WWI, the Soviet government abandoned the Baltics to Germany, after Estonian nationalists declared independence. In 1920 the USSR renounced territorial claims on Estonia supposedly forever.

Independent Estonia suffered economically even as it bloomed culturally. In 1933, the anti-communist, anti-parliamentary 'Vaps' movement won a referendum, but the prime minister, Konstantin Päts, outflanked it bloodlessly and took over as a moderate benevolent dictator. Occupied by the Soviets, Estonia was 'accepted' into the USSR in 1940 after fabricated elections. Within a year, over 10,000 Estonians were killed or deported. During the German occupation in WWII, about 5500 people died in concentration camps. Between 1945 and 1949, with Stalinism back on course, industry was nationalised and agriculture collectivised, and a further 60,000 Estonians were killed or deported.

As early as 1980, Estonian students were demonstrating against 'Sovietisation', and widespread activism surged under *glasnost* (openness) in the late 1980s. On 23 August 1989, an estimated two million people formed a human chain across Estonia, Latvia and Lithuania.

Independence came suddenly after the Moscow putsch against Gorbachev. Estonia's declaration of full independence on 20 August 1991 was immediately recognised by the West and by the USSR on 6 September.

The following decade saw frequent changes of government and no shortage of scandal. These days, Estonia enthusiastically embraces the ways of the West while cautiously maintaining ties with Russia.

GEOGRAPHY

With an area of 45,227 sq km, Estonia is only slightly bigger than Denmark. It's mainly low-lying, with extensive bogs and marshes. Nearly 50% of the land is forested, and 22% wetlands. Islands make up nearly 10% of the country and there are over 1400 lakes.

CLIMATE

From May to September, maximum temperatures are between 14°C and 22°C. July and August, the warmest months, are also the wettest. May, June and September are more comfortable. Snow is usually visible from December to late March.

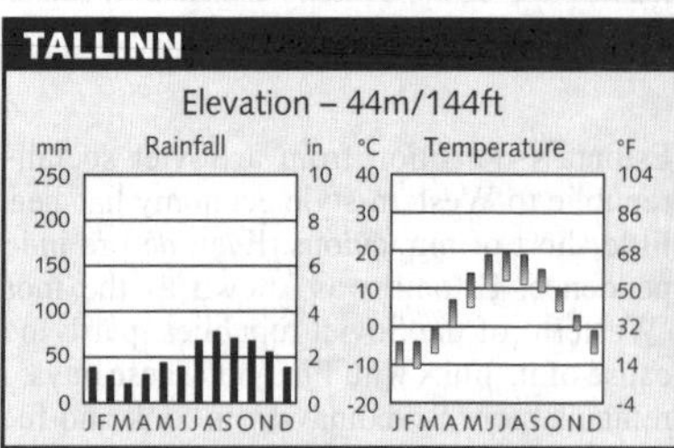

GOVERNMENT & POLITICS

Estonia is an independent parliamentary republic led by a prime minister. The head of state is the president, but his duties are mainly ceremonial. The next presidential elections are due to be held around 2006.

POPULATION & PEOPLE

Estonia's population of 1.36 million is 68% Estonian, 26% Russian, and 3% Ukrainian and Belarussian, with a growing number of resident Finns. The Russian speakers are concentrated in Tallinn and in the industrial northeast, forming around 41% and 96% of the respective populations.

SOCIETY & CONDUCT

The Estonians are a rural people said to be happiest when their neighbours are no closer than 1km away. Many urban-based Estonians retire to cottages outside of the city for as much of the summer as possible.

Estonians have a habit of taking flowers whenever they go visiting or attend any kind of celebration.

LANGUAGE

Estonian is a devilishly difficult Finno-Ugric language. Many Estonians speak at least some English. While only a small, yet growing, number of Russians in Estonia speak Estonian, most Estonians also speak some Russian.

See the Language Guide at the back of the book for pronunciation guidelines and useful words and phrases.

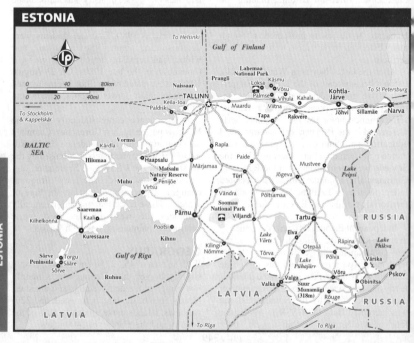

ESTONIA

ESTONIA

Facts for the Visitor

HIGHLIGHTS

Tallinn's Old Town, with its winding cobbled streets and gingerbread-style facades, is a definite highlight of any visit. A trip east to Lahemaa National Park is the best way to experience something more essentially Estonian: solitude and nature.

PLANNING

Between May and September are the best times of the year. You'll see the 'white nights' from mid- to late June, when the skies darken for only a few hours each night.

TOURIST OFFICES

Estonia boasts a well-coordinated tourism infrastructure. The **Estonian Tourist Board** *(☎ 627 9770, fax 626 9777; W www.visitestonia.com; Roosikrantsi tänav 11, Tallinn)* oversees the functioning of individual tourism information centres throughout the country.

VISAS & DOCUMENTS

Make sure your passport extends at least two months after the end of your travels.

Visa regulations are constantly changing, so check with your local Estonian consulate or embassy or directly with the **Estonian Foreign Ministry** *(☎ 631 7600, fax 631 7617; W www.vm.ee; Islandi Väljak 1, Tallinn)*. Note that visas cannot be obtained at the border.

Visa extensions are not readily available and applicants must prove valid grounds for an extension. Contact the Visa Extension Department of the **Citizenship & Immigration Board** *(☎ 612 6963; Endla tänav 13, Tallinn)*.

EMBASSIES & CONSULATES

Estonian Embassies & Consulates

For up to date contact details of Estonian diplomatic organisations, visit W www.vm.ee. Estonian diplomatic representation abroad includes:

Australia (☎ 02-9810 7468, fax 9818 1779) 86 Louisa Road, Birchgrove, Sydney NSW 2041
Canada (☎ 416-461 0764, fax 461 0353) 202-958 Broadview Ave, Toronto, Ontario M4K 2R6
Finland (☎ 9-622 0260, fax 622 02610) Itäinen Puistotie 10, 00140 Helsinki, Suomi
Germany (☎ 30-25 460 600, fax 25 460 101) Hildebrandstrasse 5 10785 Berlin
Consulate: (☎ 40-450 40 26, fax 450 40 515) Badestrasse 38, 20143 Hamburg
Latvia (☎ 781 20 20, fax 781 20 29) Skolas iela 13, Rīga
Lithuania (☎ 5-278 0200, fax 278 0201) Mickeviciaus gatvė 4a, Vilnius
Russia (☎ 095-290 5013, 737 3640, fax 737 3646) Malo Kislovski 5, 103009 Moscow
Consulate: (☎ 812-238 1804, fax 325 4246) Bolsaja Monetnaja 14, St Petersburg
Sweden (☎ 08-5451 2280, fax 5451 2299) Tyrgatan 3, Stockholm
UK (☎ 020-7589 3428, fax 7589 3430) 16 Hyde Park Gate, London SW7 5DG
USA (☎ 202-588 0101, fax 588 0108)
To mid-2003: 1730 M St, Suite 503, NW, Washington, DC 20036
From mid-2003: 2131 Massachusetts Ave, NW, Washington DC 20008
Consulate: (☎ 212-883 0636, fax 883 0648) 660 3rd Ave, 26th floor, New York, NY

Foreign Embassies in Estonia

Following is a list of some of the foreign embassies in Tallinn. For information on other countries, or visa-related inquiries, contact the **Estonian Foreign Ministry** *(☎ 631 7600, fax 631 7617; W www.vm.ee; Islandi Väljak 1, Tallinn)*.

Australia (☎ 650 9308, fax 667 1333) Kopli tänav 25
Canada (☎ 627 3311, fax 627 3312) Toom-Kooli tänav 13
Finland (☎ 610 3200) Kohtu tänav 4
Consulate: (☎ 610 3300, fax 610 3288; W www.finem.ee) Pikk jalg 14
Germany (☎ 627 5300, fax 627 5305) Toom-Kuninga tänav 11
Latvia (☎ 646 1310, fax 631 1366) Tõnismägi tänav 10
Lithuania (☎ 631 4030, visas: ☎ 641 2014, fax 641 2013) Uus tänav 15
Russia (☎ 646 4175, 646 4178) Pikk tänav 19
Consulate in Narva: (☎ 035-60 652, fax 60 654) Rüütli tänav 8
Sweden (☎ 640 5600, fax 640 5695) Pikk tänav 28
UK (☎ 667 4700, fax 667 4724) Wismari tänav 6
USA (☎ 668 8100, fax 668 8134) Kentmanni tänav 20

CUSTOMS

In general, travellers aged over 21 years are allowed to bring into, or take out of, the country up to 200 cigarettes, 1L of hard alcohol and 2L of wine.

There are restrictions on taking out antiques and works of art. Permits can be obtained from the **Division of the Export of Cultural Objects** *(☎ 644 6578; Sakala tänav 14, Tallinn)*.

MONEY

Estonia introduced its own currency, the kroon (EEK; pronounced 'krohn') in June 1992; it's now pegged to the euro. The kroon comes in two, five, 10, 25, 50, 100 and 500EEK notes. One kroon is divided into 100 sents, and there are coins of five, 10, 20 and 50 sents, as well as one and five kroon coins.

The best currencies to bring into Estonia are US dollars or euros, although almost all Western currencies are readily exchangeable. Private exchange bureaus offer the most favourable rates.

All major credit cards are widely accepted, although Visa is the most common. Most banks accept travellers cheques, but their commissions can be unpleasantly high.

At the time of printing the following exchange rates prevailed:

country	unit		kroon
Australia	A$1	=	9.20EEK
Canada	C$1	=	10.70EEK
Denmark	1Dkr	=	2.10EEK
Eurozone	€1	=	15.60EEK
Iceland	Ikr1	=	5.40EEK
Latvia	1Ls	=	27EEK
Lithuania	1Lt	=	4.50EEK
Norway	1Nkr	=	2.10EEK
Sweden	1SKr	=	1.70EEK
UK	UK£1	=	24.50EEK
USA	US$1	=	16.60EEK

Accommodation and food costs constantly rise, particularly in Tallinn, although bus and train services within Estonia remain cheap by Western standards. Students, pensioners and groups should ask about concessions on tickets, which are available for most transport services and sights.

The *käibemaks* consumption tax, levied on most goods and services, ranges from 5% to 18%. Prices for imported goods compare with those in Scandinavia.

Tipping has become traditional in the last few years, but generally no more than 5% to 10% is expected.

POST & COMMUNICATIONS

Mail service in and out of Estonia is quite reasonable. There is a poste-restante bureau, where mail is kept for up to one month, at Tallinn's **central post office** *(Narva maantee 1, Tallinn 10101)*.

To call other cities in Estonia, dial ☎ 0 followed by the area code and telephone number. Tallinn now has no area code and all Tallinn numbers have seven digits. Estonia's country code is ☎ 372.

Public telephones accept chip cards (50EEK or 100EEK), available at post offices, hotels and most kiosks. For placing calls outside Estonia, an international telephone card, available at many kiosks, brings far better value.

See the Tallinn, Tartu and Pärnu sections for details of Internet access points. Most cities and towns in Estonia and even some rural dots on the map have at least one place to log on.

DIGITAL RESOURCES

For background information on Estonia or tips on travel planning, see **w** www.ee/www/welcome.html and **w** www.visitestonia.com. A useful site for tourist services is **w** www.turismiweb.ee. The *In Your Pocket* homepage **w** www.inyourpocket.com is also a good one to try.

BOOKS

Lonely Planet's *Estonia, Latvia & Lithuania* makes a helpful travel companion. For anyone interested in a comprehensive account of the region, *The Baltic Revolution* by Anatol Lieven is essential reading.

WOMEN TRAVELLERS

Western women are unlikely to experience aggravation, but traditional gender-role expectations are somewhat entrenched. Notions of feminism and equal opportunity resonate much more quietly here and acts of chivalry are not uncommon.

GAY & LESBIAN TRAVELLERS

While open displays of same-sex affection are discouraged in Estonia, the overall attitude is more of curiosity than antagonism; the media have run several gay-positive articles since the early 1990s. For more information, contact the **Estonian Gay League** *(PO Box 142 Tallinn, 10502; **e** gayliit@hotmail.com)*.

The **Estonian Union for Lesbian & Bisexual Women** (☎ *055 11 132*) can also be contacted through the Estonian Gay League.

DISABLED TRAVELLERS

For information on all services available in Estonia, contact the **Tallinn Association for the Disabled** (☎ *644 2804; Tatari tänav 14*). The **Invaühing** (☎ *07-366 762*) in Tartu and its **information centre** (☎ *07-401 226*) can also provide information. Specially equipped taxis and minibuses can be ordered in advance in Tallinn through **Linnataxo** (☎ *644 2442*).

DANGERS & ANNOYANCES

Theft from hotel rooms is a danger. Keep valuables with you or in a hotel safe.

Drunks on the streets, around stations and in hotels can be a nuisance.

PUBLIC HOLIDAYS & SPECIAL EVENTS

The biggest occasion is the night of June 23: Jaanipäev (St John's Eve), a celebration of the pagan Midsummer's Night, best experienced out in the country where huge bonfires are lit for all-night parties. June 23 is also the Victory Day holiday (anniversary of Battle of Võnnu, 1919). June 24 is the official Jaanipäev holiday. Good Friday, Christmas, Boxing Day and New Year's Day are celebrated as elsewhere in the West and May 1 is the traditional May Day holiday.

Independence is celebrated twice, on February 24 (Independence Day), the anniversary of the 1918 declaration, and on August 21 (New Independence Day), celebrating the 1991 declaration of independence.

Estonia also has a busy calendar of festivals encompassing all aspects of contemporary and folk culture. The Baltika International Folk Festival (usually mid-July) is a week of music, dance and displays focusing on Baltic and other folk traditions. The All-Estonian Song Festival convenes every four years and culminates in a 30,000-strong traditional choir, due in Tallinn in 2003.

Emergencies

In an emergency call the following countrywide numbers: ☎ 110 for police and ☎ 112 for fire, ambulance and urgent medical advice. Call ☎ 1188 for 24-hour roadside assistance.

ACTIVITIES

Jalgrattakeskus (☎ *623 7799; Tartu maantee 73, Tallinn*) rents bicycles by the hour with deals for long-term rentals. Bicycle tours of Estonia can be arranged through **Alutaguse Matkaklubi** (☎ *051-41 692, fax 23 70 568*), which is based in Kohtla-Järve.

Skiing (predominantly cross-country) is extremely popular. The main skiing centre is Otepää in southeast Estonia where there are several skiing centres that hire out equipment. Contact the Otepää **Tourist Information Centre** (☎ *76-55 364;* ⓔ *otepaa@visitestonia.com*) for more information.

The sauna is an Estonian institution and comes close to being a religious experience. The most common type of sauna here is the dry, Finnish style. Most hotels have saunas; the most luxurious can be experienced at Tallinn's **Hotel Olümpia** (☎ *631 5585*), which has fantastic views. **Kalma Saun** (☎ *627 1811; Vana-Kalamaja 9A; open 10am-11pm daily*) is the best of the public saunas.

ACCOMMODATION

Tallinn Tourist Information Centre (☎ *645 7777, fax 645 7778;* ⓔ *turismiinfo@tallinlv.ee; Raekoja plats 10, Tallinn*) has lists of hotels, camping grounds, motels and guesthouses throughout Estonia. It's worth booking ahead wherever you plan to stay as vacancies, particularly during summer, can be scarce.

There are a few *kämpingud* (camping grounds) that allow you to pitch a tent, but most consist mainly of permanent wooden cabins. Showers and toilets are usually communal. Grounds are generally open from mid-May to early September.

The **Estonian Youth Hostels Association** (☎ *646 1457;* ⓦ *www.baltichostels.net*) takes bookings for hostels located throughout Estonia. Accommodation is mainly in small, two- to four-bed rooms.

Budget hotels are generally bare and dowdy, but usually have tolerably clean rooms. In summer, rooms can be booked out well in advance in major centres and resort towns.

There are a number of homestay organisations that will rent you a room in a private home, which is an excellent way to experience local life. Try **Rasastra** (☎*/fax 661 6921;* ⓦ *www.bedbreakfast.ee; Mere puiestee 4, Tallinn*). The best information about farmstays can be obtained from regional tourist information centres throughout Estonia. Farms offer more than a choice of rooms, in many cases meals, sauna and a wide range of activities are also available.

FOOD & DRINKS

The Estonian diet relies heavily on *sealiha* (pork), red meat, chicken, sausage and potatoes. *Hapukoor*, a favourite Estonian sour-cream condiment, while increasingly less ubiquitous, can still engulf anything from salads to soups. *Forell* (smoked trout) is a good speciality. *Sült* (jellied meat) will likely be served as well. At Christmas, *verivorst* (sausages) are made from fresh blood and wrapped in pig intestine (joy to the world!). Those really in need of a transfusion will also find blood bread and blood dumplings. Delicious and inexpensive freshly baked cakes, breads and pastries are available everywhere.

Õlu (beer) is the favourite alcoholic drink; the best are Saku and A Le Coq. *Viin* (vodka) and *konjak* (brandy) are also popular. Vana Tallinn, the very sweet, very strong liqueur of unknown extraction is an integral part of any Estonian gift pack. Saare Dzinn (gin made from Saaremaa-grown juniper berries) is also well worth trying. A non-alchoholic regional speciality is the Estonian *kali* (cola) and, while it may not taste quite like the real thing, makes a healthier home-grown alternative.

ENTERTAINMENT

The university city of Tartu and resorts of Pärnu and Otepää are giving the capital some serious competition as party centres. At the end of the day Tallinn prevails, with its legions of clubs, pubs, bars, theatres and casinos. Regular free events take place in the Old Town Square over the warmer months.

Classical music, opera and ballet feature strongly in most major centres; festivals of music, dance and theatre are also an integral part of the entertainment and arts calendar. See the individual city sections for more details.

ESTONIA

Getting There & Away

AIR

The national carrier **Estonian Air** *(☎ 640 1101, fax 601 6092; W www.estonian-air.ee)* links Tallinn with many destinations throughout Europe, also via code-share arrangement with SAS and airBaltic. Stockholm and Copenhagen are also served with growing frequency by Finnair.

Western airlines also offer worldwide connections via their hubs. Lauda Air flies direct from Vienna to Tallinn daily.

LAND

Bus

Buses are the cheapest but least comfortable way of reaching the Baltics. **Eurolines** *(☎ 680 0909; W www.eurolines.ee; Lastekodu tänav 46, Tallinn)* runs direct buses daily to Tallinn from several destinations in Germany, with connecting services to cities throughout Western Europe. Direct services connect Tallinn to Rīga (200EEK to 250EEK, six hours, eight daily) and Vilnius (300EEK, 10½ hours, two daily). Some German-bound buses stop at Rīga and either Vilnius or Kaunas.

Buses leave Tallinn for St Petersburg several times daily (200EEK, eight hours). There is also one bus from Tallinn to Kaliningrad daily (300EEK, 15 hours).

Train

The twice-weekly Tallinn–Minsk train passes through Rīga and Vilnius. St Petersburg and Tallinn are serviced by an overnight train on alternate evenings (2nd/3rd class 390/228EEK, nine hours). An overnight train runs every evening between Moscow and Tallinn (2nd class 724EEK, around 14 hours).

Car & Motorcycle

From Finland it's easier to put your vehicle on a Helsinki–Tallinn ferry than to drive via St Petersburg.

SEA

Finland

About 25 ferries and hydrofoils cross between Helsinki and Tallinn daily. Ferries make the crossing in 2½ to 3½ hours. All companies provide some concessions and charge higher prices for weekend travel. Expect to pay around the price of an adult ticket extra to take a car on many services.

Tallink *(☎ 640 9808)* runs several ferries and hydrofoils daily. Ferry tickets start from 235EEK. **Lindaline** *(☎ 641 2412)* makes six hydrofoil crossings each way daily. A one-way trip costs from 310EEK. **Eckerö Line** *(☎ 631 8606)* operates a daily auto catamaran making the crossing in 3½ hours, with one-way tickets starting from 190EEK. **Nordic Jet Line** *(☎ 613 7000)* has several auto catamarans, making the trip in around 1½ hours, several times a day; one-way/return tickets cost from 280EEK to 580EEK. **Silja Line** *(☎ 611 6661)* ferries make the crossing between Tallinn and Helsinki in 1½ hours with worthwhile day-trip packages available to Helsinki. Prices start from 370EEK.

Sweden

Tallink now runs two former Estline ferries daily to Sweden; *Regina Baltica* between Tallinn and Stockholm, (from 650EEK, 15 hours) and the smaller *Baltic Kristina*, from Paldiski, 52km west of Tallinn, to Kappelskär near Stockholm, (from 450EEK, 12 hours). There are slight reductions for students. Tickets should be booked well in advance through the **Tallink city office** *(☎ 640 9808; Pärnu maantee 12)* or **Frihamnen** *(Free Harbour; ☎ 08-667 0001)* in Stockholm.

Getting Around

BUS

Long-distance buses serve all major Estonian towns. Buses are generally cheaper, more frequent, definitely faster and cover many destinations not serviced by trains. For a listing of current bus schedules throughout Estonia visit Ⓦ www.bussireisid.ee.

TRAIN

Trains are slower and rarer than buses; the most frequent trains service the suburbs of Tallinn. Regional train schedules are listed at Ⓦ www.edel.ee.

CAR & MOTORCYCLE

Travelling by car is a good way to see Estonia. An International Driving Permit (IDP) is necessary, as are your vehicle's registration papers and compulsory accident insurance, which can be bought at border crossings.

BICYCLE

Estonia is predominantly flat, with good roads and light traffic, and distances between urban centres are relatively small. As few locals cycle within main cities, be wary of inconsiderate motorists. For organised bike trips through Estonia, see Activities earlier in the chapter.

HITCHING

Hitching is common but never entirely safe or recommended.

LOCAL TRANSPORT

Estonia's cities have good networks of buses, trolleybuses and trams that usually run from 6am to midnight. In Estonia *piletid* (tickets) are sold from street kiosks or can be purchased from the driver. Validate your ticket using the hole-punch inside the vehicle.

Taxis cost a minimum of 7EEK per kilometre and are by far the most efficient in the Baltic region. In Tallinn call **Klubi Takso** *(☎ 638 0638)* or **Raadiotakso** *(☎ 601 1111)*.

ORGANISED TOURS

Local tourist information centres are the best place to find information about organised tours. It's also a good idea to contact your destination directly, especially if your visit extends to a national park. Contact the following for more information:

Biosphere Reserve of the West Estonian Archipelago (BKA; ☎ 46-22 101; Ⓦ www.bka.ee/hiiumaa; Vabriku väljak 1) On the island of Hiiumaa, it can assist with advice on exploring Hiiumaa or connect you with BKA branches covering the island of Saaremaa and places along Estonia's west coast.

Matsalu Nature Reserve (☎ 47-78 114; Ⓔ matsalu@matsalu.ee) in Penijõe. Arranges birdwatching tours in one of Europe's prime migration and breeding grounds.

Tallinn

☎ no code • pop 398,430

The aura of the 14th and 15th centuries survives intact in central Tallinn's judiciously restored jumble of medieval walls and turrets, spires and winding cobbled streets. The city fronts a bay on the Gulf of Finland and is dominated by Toompea, the hill over which it has tumbled since the Middle Ages.

By the mid-14th century Tallinn was a major Hanseatic trading town. Prosperity faded in the 16th century as Swedes, Russians, Poles and Lithuanians fought over the Baltic region. The city grew in the 19th century and by WWI had a population of 150,000. In 1944 Soviet bombing brought massive destruction. After WWII, industry developed and Tallinn expanded quickly,

CENTRAL TALLINN

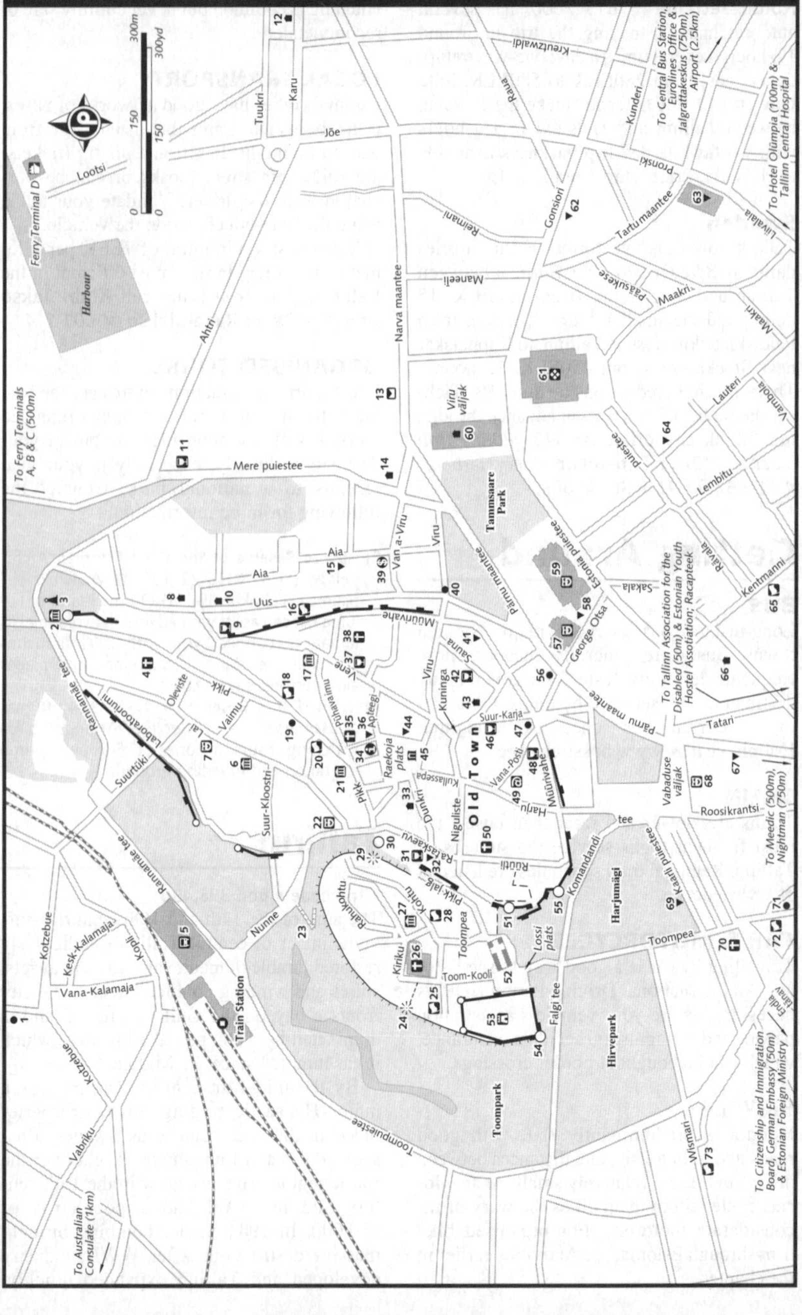

To Ferry Terminals A, B & C (500m)
Ferry Terminal D
Harbour
To Australian Consulate (1km)
Train Station
Old Town
Toompark
Hirvepark
Harjumägi
Tammsaare Park
Viru väljak
Vabaduse väljak
Raekoja plats
Lossi plats
To Tallinn Association for the Disabled (50m) & Estonian Youth Hostel Assotiation; Racapteek
To Central Bus Station, Eurolines Office & Jalgrattakeskus (750m), Airport (2.5km)
To Hotel Olümpia (100m) & Tallinn Central Hospital
To Citizenship and Immigration Board, German Embassy (50m) & Estonian Foreign Ministry
To Meedic (500m), Nightman (750m)

Kotzebue
Vabriku
Vana-Kalamaja
Kesk-Kalamaja
Kopli
Rannamäe tee
Suurtüki
Laboratooriumi
Oleviste
Lai
Vaimu
Pikk
Suur-Kloostri
Nunne
Uus
Aia
Mere puiestee
Ahtri
Tuukri
Karu
Jõe
Lootsi
Pühavaimu
Vene
Apteegi
Rahukohtu
Kiriku
Kohtu
Pikk-jalg
Rataskaevu
Dunkri
Kullassepa
Niguliste
Toompea
Toom-Kooli
Rüütli
Harju
Vana-Posti
Suur-Karja
Müürivahe
Viru
Van a-Viru
Kuninga
Sauna
Narva maantee
Maneeži
Reimani
Raua
Kreutzwaldi
Gonsiori
Pärnu maantee
Estonia puiestee
George Otsa
Sakala
Falgi tee
Komandandi tee
Toompuiestee
Kaarli puiestee
Wismari
Roosikrantsi
Tatari
Rävala
Lembitu
Kentmanni
Lauteri
Vambola
Maakri
Pääsukese
Tartu maantee
Pronski
Kunderi
Liivalaia
Endla tänav

0 150 300m
0 150 300yd

CENTRAL TALLINN

PLACES TO STAY
- 8 Hostel
- 10 Old House
- 12 Dorell
- 14 Rasastra
- 33 Hotel Eeslitall
- 43 Vana Tom
- 60 Hotel Viru

PLACES TO EAT
- 15 Kaubahall
- 32 Vanaema Juures
- 36 Balthasar
- 41 Creperie Sans Nom
- 44 Troika
- 58 Armaada Sandwicherie
- 62 Poliina
- 63 Stockmann
- 64 Eesti Maja
- 67 Peetri Pizza
- 69 Võiroos

OTHER
- 1 Kalma Saun
- 2 Meremuuseum (Maritime Museum); Paks Margareeta (Fat Margaret); Great Coast Gate
- 3 Estonia Ferry Disaster Memorial
- 4 Oleviste Church
- 5 Local Bus Station
- 6 Tarbekunstimuuseum (Applied Art Museum)
- 7 Linnateater (City Theatre)
- 9 Levi'st Väljas
- 11 Spirit
- 13 Central Post Office; Internet Salon
- 16 Lithuanian Embassy
- 17 Linnamuuseum (City Museum)
- 18 Swedish Embassy
- 19 Baltic Tours
- 20 Russian Embassy
- 21 State History Museum
- 22 Nukuteater (Puppet Theatre)
- 23 Patkuli Trepp (Steps)
- 24 Lookout Point
- 25 Canadian Embassy
- 26 Toomkirik
- 27 National Art Museum
- 28 Finnish Embassy
- 29 Lookout Point
- 30 Pikk Jalg Gate Tower
- 31 Von Krahli Baar & Theatre
- 34 Tourist Information Centre
- 35 Pühavaimu Kirik (Holy Spirit Church)
- 37 Kloostri Ait
- 38 Dominican Monastery
- 39 Tavid
- 40 Viru Gate
- 42 X-Baar
- 45 Town Hall; Tristan ja Isolde
- 46 Nimeta Baar
- 47 Estravel
- 48 Hollywood Club; Kino Sõprus
- 49 Arvutisaal
- 50 Niguliste Church
- 51 Neitsitorn
- 52 Alexander Nevsky Cathedral
- 53 Toompea Castle; Riigikogu (Parliament)
- 54 Pikk Hermann
- 55 Kiek-in-de-Kök
- 56 Estonian Holidays; Tallink
- 57 Estonian Drama Theatre
- 59 Estonia Theatre; Concert Hall
- 61 Kaubamaja Shopping Centre; @5
- 65 US Embassy
- 66 Helke; Division of the Export of Cultural Objects
- 68 Russian Drama Theatre
- 70 Kaarli Kirik Church
- 71 Tõnismäe Apteek (24-Hour Pharmacy)
- 72 Latvian Embassy
- 73 UK Embassy

with much of its population growth due to immigration.

Orientation

The medieval town, just south of Tallinn Bay, comprises Toompea (the upper town) and the lower town. The lower town spreads around the eastern foot of Toompea, which is still surrounded by much of its 2.5km defensive wall. Its centre is Raekoja plats (Town Hall Square). Around the Old Town is a belt of green parks that follow the line of the city's original moat defences. On this green belt are a number of places useful for orientation: Vabaduse väljak, the modern centre; Balti jaam, the train station northwest of the Old Town; and the tall slab of Hotel Viru, just outside the eastern edge of the Old Town.

Information

Tourist Offices The **Tallinn Tourist Information Centre** *(☎ 645 7777, fax 645 7778; ⓔ turismiinfo@tallinnlv.ee; Raekoja plats 10; open Mon-Sat Nov-Mar, daily Apr-Oct)* is right in the Old Town's centre and offers a range of services. Here you can purchase the Tallinn Card, which gives free admission to museums and rides on public transport.

Infotelefon *(☎ 626 1111)* can provide information in English 24 hours a day. In summer, the Welcome to Estonia Visitor Centre, a country-wide specialist tourist information office, sets up in Tallinn; check with the main tourist information centre for details.

Money Currency exchange is available at all transport terminals, the post office and inside all banks and major hotels. One of many private exchange bureaus with competitive rates is **Tavid** *(☎ 627 9900; Aia tänav 5; open 9am-7pm Mon-Fri, 10am-5pm Sat & Sun)*.

Most central ATMs also accept major cards. **Estravel** (see Travel Agencies, later) is the official agent for American Express.

Post & Communications The central **post office** *(☎ 625 7300; Narva maantee 1; open 7.30am-8pm Mon-Fri, 8am-6pm Sat)* is on the north side of Viru väljak. Express mail, faxes and telegrams can be sent from here, and there's a postal shop on site. Upstairs is **Internet Salon** *(open 7.30am-8pm*

Mon-Fri, 8am-6pm Sat), which charges 1EEK per minute.

@5 *(Kaubamaja Shopping Centre; open 9am-9pm Mon-Fri, 10am-8pm Sat, 10am-6pm Sun)* is a lively central place to connect with the Net for 40EEK an hour. **Arvutisaal** *(2nd floor, Vana-Posti tänav 2; open 10am-8pm daily)* is ideal for lengthy sessions at 30EEK an hour; every third hour is free.

Travel Agencies City tours, guided trips to provincial Estonia, and accommodation in other towns are all part of most travel agencies' stock in trade. Leading ones include:

Baltic Tours (☎ 630 0400, fax 630 0411, ⓔ baltic.tours@bt.ee) Pikk tänav 31; one of the longest-established firms, with offices in other cities
Estonian Holidays (☎ 631 4106, fax 631 4109, ⓔ holidays@holidays.ee) Pärnu maantee 12
Estravel (☎ 626 6285, fax 626 6202, Ⓦ www.estravel.ee) Suur-Karja tänav 15

Medical Services The **Tallinn Central Hospital** *(☎ 620 7015; Ravi tänav 18)*, south of Liivalaia tänav, has a full range of services, a polyclinic and a 24-hour emergency room. Western in price, service and attitude are Tallinn's privately run medical centres, such as **Meedic** *(☎ 646 3390; Pärnu maantee 48A)*.

All pharmacies sell Western medicines. **Tõnismäe Apteek** *(☎ 644 2282; Tõnismägi 5; open until 8pm daily)* runs a night service (just ring the bell).

Raekoja Plats & Around

Wide Raekoja plats (Town Hall square) has been the centre of Tallinn life since the 11th century. It's dominated by the only surviving Gothic **town hall** (1371–1404) in northern Europe. The **Raeapteek** (Town Council Pharmacy), on the north side of the square, is another ancient Tallinn institution; there's been a pharmacy or apothecary's shop here since at least 1422. An arch beside it leads into narrow Saia käik (White Bread passage), at the far end of which is the lovely, 14th-century Gothic **Pühavaimu Kirik** (Holy Spirit Church). Its clock is the oldest in Tallinn, with carvings from 1684 and a tower bell cast in 1433.

A medieval merchant's home at Vene tänav 17, on the corner of Pühavaimu tänav, houses Tallinn's most interesting museum – the **Linnamuuseum** *(City Museum; ☎ 644 6553; Vene tänav 17; adult/student 25/10EEK; open 10.30am-5.30pm Wed-Mon Apr-Oct, 11am-4.30pm Nov-Mar)*, which traces the development of Tallinn from its beginnings through to 1940.

Also on Vene is a church that is set back from the street. A door leads into the **Dominican Monastery** *(☎ 644 4606; ⓔ kloostri@hot.ee; Vene tänav 16; admission 25/15EEK; open 9.30am-6pm daily mid-May–mid-Sept)*, founded in 1246 as a base for Scandinavian monks. Today the monastery complex houses Estonia's largest collection of **stone carvings**.

The majestic **Niguliste Church** *(☎ 631 4330; admission 35EEK; open 10am-5pm Wed-Sun)*, a minute's walk south of Raekoja plats, is now used to stage concerts and serves as a **museum** of medieval church art.

At the foot of the slope below the Niguliste is the carefully exposed wreckage of the buildings that stood here before the Soviet bombing of Tallinn on the night of 9 March 1944.

Toompea

A regal approach to Toompea is through the red-roofed 1380 **gate tower** at the western end of Pikk tänav in the lower town, and then along Pikk jalg (Long Leg). The 19th-century Russian Orthodox **Alexander Nevsky Cathedral** dominates Lossi plats at the top of Pikk jalg, sited strategically across from **Toompea Castle**, traditionally Estonia's seat of power. The parliament meets in the pink Baroque style **Riigikogu**, an 18th-century addition.

The Lutheran **Toomkirik** (Dome Church) is Estonia's oldest church. At the northern end of Toom-Kooli, it dates from the 14th century. Across from Toomkirik at Kiriku plats 1, an 18th-century noble's house is now the **National Art Museum** *(Kunstimuuseum; ☎ 644 9340; Kiriku plats 1; adult/student 30/20EEK; open 11am-6pm Wed-Sun)*

A path leads down from Lossi plats through an opening in the wall to the **Danish King's Courtyard** where, in summer, artists set up their easels.

Lower Town

Pikk tänav, running north from Raekoja plats to the **Great Coast Gate** – the medieval exit to Tallinn port – is lined with many 15th-century houses of medieval merchants and gentry. Also here are the buildings of several old Tallinn guilds and some museums.

The Great Coast Gate is joined to **Paks Margareeta** *(Fat Margaret)*, the rotund 16th-century bastion that protected this entrance to the Old Town. Inside is the **Meremuuseum** *(Maritime Museum; ☎ 641 1408; adult/student 25/10EEK; open 10am-6pm Wed-Sun; closed July)*. There are great views from the platform on the roof.

At the northern end of Pikk tänav stands a chief Tallinn landmark, the Oleviste Church. The Church is dedicated to the 11th century King Olav II of Norway but linked in local lore with another Olav (Olaf) the church's legendary architect who fell to his death from the 120m-high tower. It's said that a toad and snake then crawled out of his mouth. Just south of the church on Lai tänav 46/48, is the former KGB centre, the basement windows were bricked up to conceal the sounds of interrogations from those on the street above.

While Pikk was a street of traders, **Lai tänav**, running roughly parallel, was the street of artisans, whose traditions are recalled in the **Tarbekunstimuuseum** *(Applied Art Museum; open 11am-6pm Wed-Sun)* in a 17th-century granary at No 17, with excellent ceramics, glass, rugs, metalwork and leatherwork.

Nearby, Suur-Kloostri leads to the longest-standing stretch of the **Lower Town Wall**, with nine towers along Laboratooriumi to the northern end of Lai.

Places to Stay

Hostels The **Estonian Youth Hostels Association** *(☎ 646 1457; w www.baltichostels.net)* has a few good choices in the city. It can also book hostel stays in neighbouring countries.

Vana Tom *(☎ 631 3252; Väike-Karja tänav 1; dorm beds HI member/nonmember 210/225EEK, rooms from 590EEK)* has an unbeatable location – 30 seconds' walk from Raekoja plats. Some rooms may provide a second-hand experience of the strip club upstairs.

Hostel *(☎ 641 1281; Uus tänav 26; dorm beds/singles/doubles 220/500/650EEK)* has a friendly reception and modest but comfortable rooms in a convenient Old Town location.

Hotels A favourite in the Old Town, **Hotel Eeslitall** *(☎ 631 3755; Dunkri tänav 4; singles/doubles 450/585EEK)* is a minute's walk from Raekoja plats. Discounted breakfast is popular from its restaurant downstairs.

Helke *(☎ 644 5802, fax 644 5792; Sakala 14 singles/doubles 400/490EEK)* is a friendly place on the Old Town's southern fringe. Rooms at Helke are comfortable and breakfast is included.

Old House *(☎ 641 1464; e info@oldhouse.ee; Uus tänav 22; singles/doubles 450/650EEK)* is a well-positioned and professional B&B that offers warm and friendly hospitality in clean surroundings.

Dorell *(☎ 626 1200, fax 662 3578; Karu tänav 39; singles/doubles 650/750EEK)* is another good central choice, with clean renovated rooms, sauna access and a bar serving inexpensive meals.

Places to Eat

The **Armaada Sandwicherie** *(Georg Otsa tänav; open 24hr)*, beside the Estonian Drama Theatre, serves hot baguettes often precariously loaded with sour cream. **Peetri Pizza** *(delivery ☎ 641 8203)* has a number of outlets doling out thin-crusted and pan pizzas; there is one at Pärnu maantee 22 (takeaway only).

Self-caterers will find a good selection of groceries inside **Stockmann** *(Liivalaia tänav 53)*, and at **Kaubahall** *(Aia tänav 7)* in the Old Town, open daily from 9am to 9pm.

Restaurants Some fine-dining options offer satisfying rewards for courageous palates and treats for those more timid. Generally, better value can be found over lunch rather than dinner at restaurants in the Old Town.

Eesti Maja *(☎ 645 5252; Lauteri tänav 1; buffet 75EEK, meals 120EEK)* offers genuine Estonian cuisine. The weekday buffet allows for a sampling of some exotic carnivoria without demanding a full-plate commitment.

Vanaema Juures *(Grandma's Place; ☎ 626 9080; Rataskaevu tänav 12; meals 140EEK)* was one of Tallinn's most stylish restaurants in the 1930s and still ranks today as authentic Estonian. **Balthasar** *(☎ 627 6400; Raekoja plats 11; meals 150EEK)* is a haven for garlic lovers.

Troika *(☎ 627 6245; Raekoja plats 11; meals 140EEK)* leads in ambience, with evocative otherworldly decor and authentic Russian meals.

Cafés & Light Meals Fine savoury and dessert crepes are served in tastefully understated surroundings at **Creperie Sans Nom** *(Müürivahe 23A)*. **Poliina** *(Gonsiori tänav 10)* has ready-made salads, tasty meat and vegetable dishes, and some excellent French pastries.

Tristan ja Isolde *(Town Hall building, Raekoja plats)* is an essential stop for lovers of fine coffee in intimate medieval surroundings. **Võiroos** *(Kaarli puiestee 4; open 24hr)*, a Tallinn institution for those with late-night munchies, is a shack serving decent food to an interesting and diverse crowd.

Entertainment

Bars & Clubs Due to a central location, flavoursome meals, a good choice of music, sports telecasts and beers, **Nimeta Baar** *(Bar with No Name; Suur-Karja tänav 4/6)* retains its popularity with both expats and visitors. **Kloostri Ait** *(Vene tänav 14)* is a focal meeting place for an alternative crowd.

Von Krahli Baar *(Rataskaevu tänav 10/12)*, one of the city's best hang-outs, is definitely worth a visit. It often has live bands and is a good place to meet interesting locals.

Levi'st Väljas *(Olevimägi tänav 12)*, which roughly translates as 'out of range', is a cellar space in the Old Town off the tourist path and refreshingly raw. The hot club event in Tallinn is the once-monthly event **Vibe** *(W www.vibe.ee)*, where Tallinners revel under the influence of imported DJs.

Mainstream clubs are the most popular. **Hollywood** *(Vana-Posti tänav 8)*, in the Sõprus cinema, attracts the largest crowds of youth and beauty.

Spirit *(Mere puiestee 6A; W www.spirit.ee)* is a sophisticated Scandinavian-inspired bar with a rave arena upstairs hosting a fluid list of guest DJs.

Nightman *(Vineeri tänav 4)* is Tallinn's main gay and lesbian club, but is also a hang-out for a straight and alternative crowd. **X-Baar** *(Sauna tänav 1)* is a more exclusively gay venue.

Opera, Ballet & Theatre Tallinn has several companies staging dramas in repertory from September until the end of May, sometimes with simultaneous English translation.

The **Estonia Theatre** *(box office ☎ 626 0215; Estonia puiestee 4)* is Tallinn's main theatre, and also houses the Estonian national opera and ballet.

Other theatres include the **Estonian Drama Theatre** *(☎ 680 5555; Pärnu maantee 5)*; the **Russian Drama Theatre** *(☎ 644 3716; Vabaduse väljak 5)*; the **Puppet Theatre** *(Nukuteater; ☎ 667 9555; Lai tänav 1)*; the fringe **Von Krahli Theatre** *(☎ 626 9090; Rataskaevu tänav 10/12)*; and the most beloved theatre in town, **Linnateater** *(City Theatre; ☎ 665 0800; Lai tänav 23)*, which always puts on something memorable.

Getting There & Away

Air Tallinn's **airport** *(☎ 605 8888; W www.tallinn-airport.ee)* is 3km southeast of the city centre on Tartu maantee. See the Getting There & Away section earlier in this chapter for details of flights and carriers.

Bus Buses to within about 40km of Tallinn leave from the local bus station beside the train station. Information and timetables can be had 24 hours via **Harju Linnid** *(☎ 644 1801)*. For detailed bus information and advance tickets for all other destinations, contact the central bus station **Autobussijaam** *(☎ 680 0900; Lastekodu tänav 46)*. Tram No 2 south from Mere puiestee or tram No 4 east from Tammsaare Park will take you there.

Domestic services include Haapsalu (52EEK, 1½ hours, 100km, 20 buses daily), Kärdla (130EEK, 4½ hours, 160km, three buses daily), Kuressaare (Saaremaa Island; 160EEK, 220km, 4½ hours, nine buses daily), Narva (75EEK, four hours, 210km, 15 buses daily), Pärnu (60EEK, two hours, 130km, more than 20 buses daily), Tartu (80EEK, three hours, 190km, around 50 buses daily) and Võru (85EEK, 4½ hours, 250km, 12 buses daily).

Train Tallinn's **Baltic Train station** *(Balti jaam; Toompuiestee 35)* is on the northwestern edge of the Old Town – a short walk from Raekoja plats, or a ride of three stops on tram No 1 or 2 north from Hotel Viru. Services within Estonia include two trains daily to Tartu (70EEK, three to four hours), two daily to Pärnu (40EEK, three hours) and one daily to Narva (70EEK, four hours).

Car & Motorcycle Car rental in Tallinn is spectacularly overpriced. Far better prices can be found with rental agencies in Tartu, Pärnu or Võru (contact tourist information centres in each city).

Boat See the Getting There & Away section at the start of this chapter for information about the services between Tallinn and

Helsinki or Stockholm. Tallinn's sea-passenger terminal is at the end of Sadama, about 1km northeast of the Old Town. Tram Nos 1 and 2 and bus Nos 3, 4 and 8 go to the Linnahall stop (by the Statoil petrol station), five minutes' walk from terminals A, B and C. Terminal D is at the end of Lootsi tänav, which is better accessed from Ahtri tänav. A taxi to and from the centre will cost about 40EEK.

Getting Around

Tallinn airport is on Tartu maantee 3km from the centre. Bus No 2 runs every 30 minutes from the eastern side of the Kaubamaja shopping centre. A taxi from the centre should cost about 80EEK.

The train station and many hotels are an easy walk from the city centre. Buses, trams and minibuses will take you everywhere else.

LAHEMAA NATIONAL PARK

☎ 32

A rocky stretch of the north coast – encompassing 220 sq km of marine area plus 480 sq km of hinterland with 14 lakes, eight rivers and many waterfalls – forms the gorgeous Lahemaa National Park. Roads crisscross the park from the Tallinn–Narva highway, and some places are accessible by bus.

Lahemaa National Park Visitors Centre *(Lahemaa Rahvuspark Külatuskeskus; ☎ 95 555, fax 95 556; ⓔ info@lahemaa.ee; open daily)* is in Palmse, 8km north of Viitna in the park's southeast. It's worth getting in touch with the centre before heading out. For an outstanding guide, contact Anne Kurepalu (ⓔ anne@phpalmse.ee) at Park Hotel Palmse.

There is an unlimited amount of sightseeing, hiking, biking and boating possibilities, as well as remote islands to be explored. The park has several well-signposted nature trails and cycling paths winding through it. The small coastal towns of **Võsu**, **Käsmu** and **Loksa** are popular seaside spots in summer. There are also **prehistoric stone barrows** (tombs) at Kahala, Palmse and Vihula, and a **boulder field** on the Käsmu Peninsula.

The visitors centre arranges accommodation to suit every budget. It can also advise on the best places for camping. **Ojaäärse hostel** *(☎ 34 108; ⓔ sagadi.hotell@rmk.ee; bunk beds 150 EEK; open year-round)* is a converted 1855 farmhouse 1.5km southeast of Palmse. **Viitna Holiday Centre** *(☎ 93 651; dorm bed/singles/doubles/cabins 60/110/150/300EEK)* is in a tranquil wooded area beside a clean lake.

There are some 19 buses daily from Tallinn to Rakvere, which stop at Viitna (30EEK, one hour). For an update on bus services between Tallinn, Käsmu and Võsu, contact the visitor centre.

Southeast Estonia

The focus of southeast Estonia is the historic university town of Tartu, Estonia's second city. Beyond is an attractive region of gentle hills, beautiful lakes and the traditional lands of the Setu people.

TARTU

☎ 7 • pop 101,140

Tartu lays claim to being Estonia's spiritual capital. The Estonian nationalist revival in the 19th century had its origins here, and Tartu was the location for the first Estonian Song Festival in 1869. This is also a classic university town, and students inject vitality into the leafy, serene surroundings.

The university, founded in 1632 during Swedish rule to train Protestant clergy and government officials, developed into one of the foremost 19th-century seats of learning. During the Soviet occupation, Westerners were not allowed to stay overnight in Tartu because of the supposed security risk to a military airfield nearby.

Orientation & Information

Toomemägi Hill and the area of older buildings between it and the Emajõgi River are the focus of Tartu. At the heart of this area are Raekoja plats (Town Hall square) and Ülikooli tänav, the main shopping area.

The Tartu **tourist information centre** *(☎/fax 432 141; ⓔ tartu@visitestonia.com; Raekoja plats 14; open Mon-Sat)* has an excellent range of local maps, books and brochures, and sells the useful booklet *Tartu Today*, which has both entertainment and accommodation listings.

All Hansapanks accept travellers cheques (the central one is in the Kaubahall Shopping Centre next to the main post office). **Estravel** *(☎ 440 300, fax 440 301; ⓔ tartu@estravel.ee; Vallikraavi tänav 2)* is the official agent for American Express.

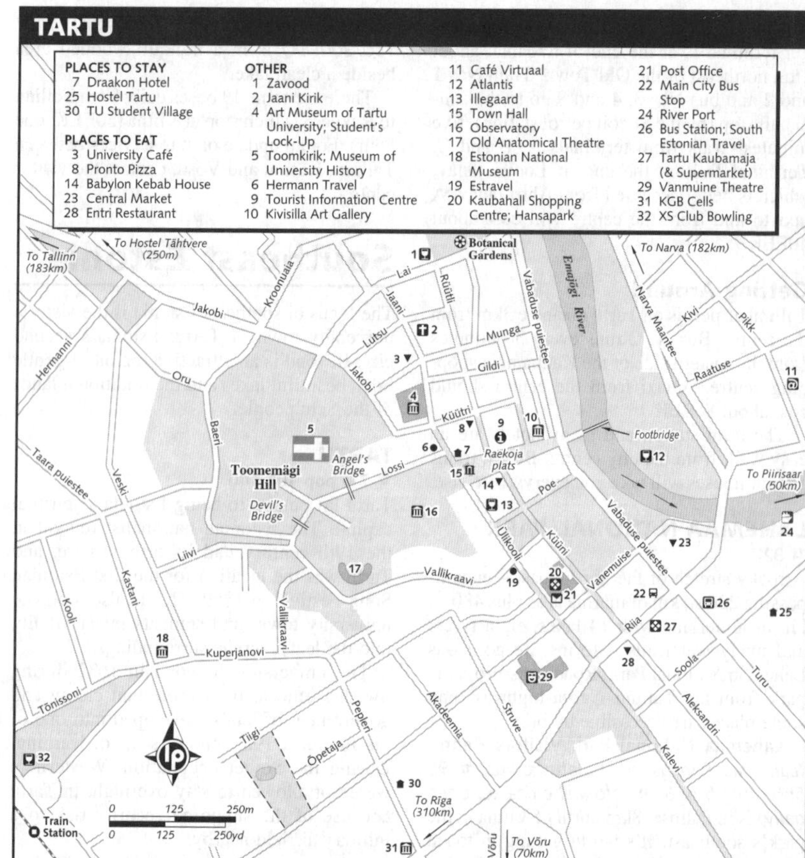

The **central post office** *(Vanemuise tänav 7)* is open Monday to Saturday. Tartu's coolest Internet café is **Café Virtuaal** *(Pikk tänav 40)*, which charges 30EEK/hour.

Travel agencies that can organise tours or arrange bookings include Estravel (see earlier) and also **Hermann Travel** *(☎ 301 444; ⓔ tartu@hermann.ee; Lossi tänav 3)*, which specialises in nature tours. The helpful **South Estonian Travel** *(Lõuna Eesti Reisburoo; ☎ 474 553; ⓔ lets.travel@kiirtee.ee)*, on the 2nd floor of the bus station, sells bus tickets for European destinations and can arrange tours in southern Estonia.

Things to See & Do

At the town centre on Raekoja plats is the beautifully proportioned **town hall** (1782–89), topped by a tower and weather vane. Nearby at No 18, the former home of Colonel Barclay de Tolly (1761–1818) is a wonderfully crooked building housing the **Kivisilla Art Gallery** *(☎ 441 080; Raekoja plats 18; adult/student 10/5EEK; open 11am-6pm Wed-Sun;)*

The main **university building** *(☎ 375 100; Ülikooli tänav 18)* dates from 1803. It houses the **Art Museum of Tartu University** *(☎ 375 384; adult/child 7/4EEK; open 11am-5pm Mon-Fri)* and **Student's Lock-Up** *(adult/child 5/2EEK; open 11am-5pm Mon-Fri)*, where 19th-century students were held for their misdeeds. Further north, the Gothic brick **Jaani Kirik** *(St John's Church)*, founded in 1330, is undergoing extensive restoration after Soviet bombing in 1944. It has rare **terracotta sculptures** around the main portal.

Rising to the west of Raekoja plats is Toomemägi Hill, landscaped in the manner of a 19th-century English park. The 13th-century Gothic cathedral **Toomkirik** at the top was rebuilt in the 15th century, despoiled during the Reformation in 1525, and partly rebuilt in 1804–07 to accommodate the university library, which is now the **Museum of University History** *(☎ 375 677; admission adult/student 20/5EEK; open 11am-5pm Wed-Sun)*.

Also on Toomemägi Hill are the **Angel's Bridge** *(Inglisild; 1838)*, with a good view of the city; the 1913 **Devil's Bridge** *(Kuradisild)*; and the **observatory**.

Tartu, as the major repository of Estonia's cultural heritage, has an abundance of museums. Among them is the country's most interesting museum: the **Estonian National Museum** *(☎ 421 311; W www.erm.ee; Kuperjanovi tänav 9; adults/students 12/5EEK; open 11am-6pm Wed-Sun)*, which traces the history, life and traditions of the Estonian people. The former KGB centre on Riia maantee now house the sombre **KGB Cells** *(☎ 461 717; Riia maantee 15b; adult/student 20/5EEK; open 11am-6pm Tues-Sat)*.

Places to Stay

At **TU Student Village** *(☎ 420 337; Pepleri tänav 14; E telts@ut.ee; dorm beds around 70EEK, apartments per person 150EEK)*, reservations should be made, but in summer it's possible to just show up and ask nicely for a hostel bed.

Hostel Tähtvere *(☎ 421 364; Laulupeo tänav 19; singles/doubles from 200/350EEK)* is a 1km walk west from the centre. Its comfortable rooms come equipped with bathroom, TV, fridge and telephone. Many activities are offered at its adjoining sports complex.

Hostel Tartu *(☎ 432 091; Soola tänav 3; singles/doubles 375/640EEK, with shower 660/990EEK)* does have the location and reasonable rooms – but beware: this charm-free old Soviet place is undergoing large-scale and lengthy renovations.

Places to Eat

Ultra-modern **Entri** *(☎ 306 812; 2nd floor, Riia maantee 4; meals from 70EEK)*, is a restaurant with an airy bright decor, serves delicious meals in its room with a view.

Babylon Kebab house *(☎ 441 295; Raekoja plats 3; meals 90EEK)* offers courtyard dining or the option of a colourful Arabian experience in its restaurant downstairs. **University Café** *(Ülikooli 20)*, an old-world café with beautiful wooden floors, is a must for a light lunch or afternoon tea. It's in the original part of the university (dating from 1632).

Pronto Pizza *(☎ 442 085; Küütri tänav 3)* serves interesting pizza and has a decent salad bar. The **central market**, about 150m northwest of the bus station, is a vast indoor space offering a wide variety of fresh produce.

Entertainment

Attracting an artsy crowd, **Illegaard** *(☎ 434 424; Ülikooli tänav 5, open 5pm-2am daily)* is a New Wave–inspired jazz vault. Check posters around town for live sessions. Another popular spot for late-night carousing, **Zavood** *(☎ 441 321; Lai tänav 30; open 4pm-2am daily)*, offers your best chance to see a student band.

The **Atlantis** *(Narva maantee 2; open 10pm-3am Sun-Thur, 10pm-4am Fri & Sat)* nightclub overlooks the Emajõgi River and remains popular. **XS** *(Vaksali tänav 21)* attracts a very mixed, fun crowd. You can bowl under the same roof until it's time to hit the club.

For theatre selections, check out what's on at the **Vanamuine Theatre** *(☎ 442 272; Vanamuise tänav 6)*; the first Estonian-language theatre troupe performed here when the theatre was founded in 1870.

Getting There & Away

Some 50 buses a day run to/from Tallinn, taking 2½ to 3½ hours depending on the service, and costing around 80EEK. There are also two trains daily.

OTEPÄÄ & AROUND

☎ 76 • pop 2200

The small hill-top town of Otepää, 44km south of Tartu, is the centre of a pretty area much loved by the Estonians for its hills and lakes.

The centre of town is the triangular main 'square', Lipuväljak, with the bus station just off its eastern corner. There is a **tourist information centre** *(☎ 55 364, fax 61 246; E otepaa@visitestonia.com; open daily)*. The post office, bank and main food shop are beside the bus station. Staff at the **Otepää Travel Agency** *(☎ 54 060; E otepaarb@hot.ee)* are efficient and friendly.

Otepää's pretty little 17th-century **church** is on a hill top about 100m northeast of the bus station. It was in this church in 1884 that the Estonian Students' Society consecrated its new blue, black and white flag, which later became the flag of independent Estonia. The best views are along the shores of the 3.5km-long **Pühajärv** (Holy Lake), on the south-western edge of the town. The lake was blessed by the Dalai Lama in 1992.

Otepää is home to many rare species of bird, including the black stork, osprey and the white-backed woodpecker.

Places to Stay & Eat

In the heart of town, **Edgari** *(☎ 54 275; Lipuväljak 3; singles/doubles 200/300EEK)* has clean freshly renovated rooms, a dining area and kitchenette, with TV in a communal lounge.

Setanta Guesthouse *(☎ 68 200; ⓔ setanta@estpak.ee; doubles from 650EEK)* is better known for its Irish Pub, and has views from its terrace over lake Pühajärv that are worth writing home about.

About 25km from Otepää is **Sangaste Loss** *(☎ 79 300; ⓔ sloss@hot.ee; singles/doubles 200/400EEK; museum adult/student 10/5EEK; open 9am-6pm daily)*, a lovely, fairy-tale brick castle modelled on England's Windsor Castle. It sits in parkland close by a river where it's possible to hire boats and bicycles. Three to five buses daily run between Otepää and Sangaste, and one daily to/from Tartu. The castle also opens to visitors.

A quick stroll through the town centre will acquaint you with popular local haunts **Oti Pubi** *(☎ 69 840; Lipuväljak 26; meals 70EEK)* or **Hermanni Pubi** *(☎ 79 241; Lipuväljak 10; meals 60EEK; open 11am-11pm daily)*.

Getting There & Away

Buses are Otepää's only public transport. Daily services to/from Otepää include Tartu (45 minutes to 1½ hours, 11 buses), Tallinn (3½ hours, three buses) and Võru (one bus).

VÕRU

☎ 78 • pop 14,800

Võru, 64km south of Tartu, is a good base for visiting some interesting points in Estonia's far southeast, such as Suur Munamägi (at 318m, the highest point in the Baltics), the lovely, picturesque village of Rõuge, or the area of Setumaa along the Russian border, one of Estonia's culturally most interesting places.

The **tourist information centre** *(☎/fax 21 881; ⓔ info@visitestonia.com; Tartu maantee 31; open Mon-Fri Oct-Apr, daily May-Sept)* generously gives advice on the area's attractions. The **South Estonian Tourism Agency** *(☎ 28 580; ⓔ tourism@wk.ee; Jüri tänav 22a)* can arrange all kinds of tours, including excursions to nearby Haanja Nature Reserve, Setumaa and day trips to Setu lands in Russia.

Hermes Guesthouse *(☎ 21 326; Jüri tänav 32A; singles/doubles/suites 410/520/700-900EEK)* has reasonable rooms, despite a characterless exterior. **Hundijalg** *(☎ 24 073; Jüri tänav 18B; meals 75EEK)* is a local favourite for lunches.

There are about 28 buses to/from Tartu daily (1½ hours), 12 to/from Tallinn (4½ hours) and about four to Rõuge and Haanja. Schedules are posted around the bus station or call ☎ 21 018 for details of other services.

Southwest Estonia

PÄRNU

☎ 44 • pop 45,040

Pärnu is Estonia's leading seaside resort and a magnet for party-loving Estonians and mud-cure–seeking Finns. Those looking for relaxation will enjoy the wide leafy streets and white sandy beaches.

The town lies on either side of the estuary of the Pärnu River, which empties into Pärnu Bay. The **tourist information centre** *(☎ 73 000; ⓔ parnu@visitestonia.com; ⓦ www.parnu.ee; Rüütli tänav 16)* is on the main commercial street in the heart of the Old Town, around 100m south of the bus station.

Ühispank *(Rüütli tänav 40a)*, in the building behind the bus station, cashes travellers cheques and gives cash advances on credit cards; it also has an ATM. Send a postcard at the **central post office** *(Akadeemia 7; open 8am-6pm Mon-Fri, 9am-3pm Sat & Sun)*. **Rüütli Internetipunkt** *(Rüütli tänav 25)* has access to Internauts for 20EEK an hour.

In town, the **Punane Torn** *(Red Tower; Hommiku tänav; adult/student 10/5EEK; open 10am-6pm Mon-Fri, 10am-3pm Sat)* survives from the days of the Knights of the Sword. Parts of the 17th-century Swedish moat and ramparts remain in Vallikäär Park, including the tunnel-like **Tallinna Värav** (Tallinn Gate) at the western end of Kuninga. Local history features at **Pärnu Museum** *(☎ 33 231; Rüütli 53; adult/student 30/15EEK; open 10am-6pm Wed-Sun)*.

The **Pärnu New Art Museum** *(☎ 30 772; ⓔ aip@chaplin.ee; Esplanaadi tänav 10; adult/student 15/10EEK; open 9am-9pm daily)*, southwest of the centre, is among the cultural bright spots in all of Estonia, with its café, bookshop and intriguing exhibitions.

The wide, white-sand beach south of Ranna puiestee, with buildings nearby dating from the first independence, are Pärnu's finest attractions. It is possible to walk west along the coast from here to the 2km stone breakwater that stretches out into the mouth of the river.

Places to Stay & Eat

There are several camping options around the city, all of which have cabins and possibly tent space too. **Linnakämping Green** *(☎ 38 776; Suure-Jõe 50b; cabin per person 95EEK)*, 3km from Pärnu at the rowing centre on the river, offers boat and bike rentals.

Tanni-Vakoma Majutüsburoo *(☎ 31 070; ⓔ tanni@online.ee; Hommiku tänav 5)* organises rooms in local homes. Fresh new **Lõuna Hostel** *(☎ 30 943, fax 30 944; ⓔ hostellouna@hot.ee; Lõuna tänav 2; dorm beds 200-250EEK, doubles 400EEK)* overlooks a park and offers the quality budget accommodation Pärnu so desperately needed. The gleaming new bathrooms will impress.

Pärnu Mudaravila *(☎/fax 25 523; ⓔ info@mudaravila.ee; Sääse tänav 7; singles/doubles 380/500EEK, accommodation with treatments from 460EEK)*, the accommodation arm of the Mudaravila, redefines the notion of bed, bath and breakfast.

For self-catering, try the **central market** *(cnr Karja tänav & Suur-Sepa tänav)*. The beachfront is lined with café-kiosks that serve fast food. **Georg** *(Rüütli tänav 43; meals 50EEK)* is a well-styled café offering good soups, salads and meals.

Väike Klaus *(Supeluse tänav 3; meals 80EEK)*, a hearty, German-inspired pub, is a great place for a meaty lunch to offset those healthy mud treatments. **Pärnu New Art Museum café** *(Esplanaadi tänav 10; open 11am-5pm daily)* serves delicious food daily with an arts ambience. **Steffani Pizzeria** *(Nikolai tänav 24)* does Pärnu's best fast pizza and pasta.

Entertainment

Sunset Club *(Ranna puiestee 3)*, in a grandiose seafront building dating from 1939, brings in the numbers as a club or concert hall for touring musicians. **Tuberkuloited Pub** *(Kuninga tänav 11)* is a fine place for catching local live music; its namesake is one of Estonia's favourite bands.

At **Jazz Café** *(☎ 27 546; Ringi tänav 11)*, jazz, sand and mud make quite an ensemble. Spontaneous live performances here may surprise. **Mirage** *(Rüütli tänav 40; open Fri-Sat)* retains its popularity despite the dazzling Vegas foyer lights and a few shady types in its casino.

Getting There & Away

More than 20 buses daily connect Pärnu with Tallinn (60EEK, two hours). Details on a multitude of other destinations are available at the Pärnu bus station **ticket office** *(open 5am-8.30pm)* nearby on Ringi tänav, across from the bus station.

Finland

For much of the 20th century, Finland was the least visible of the Scandinavian countries; Sweden had ABBA, Norway had those lovely fjords, Denmark had Lego, but Finland stirred few notions in the average traveller's mind.

With the rise of mobile communications and the Internet, though, Finland has hit the world stage. Companies such as Nokia are exploring areas of communications that were once imagined only in science fiction, and as the techno-wave breaks into the 21st century, Finland appears set to play an important role.

In contrast to this hi-tech revolution, Finland is for the most part a land of quietness, where happiness is a ramshackle cottage by a lake and a properly stoked sauna. Finland is also a vast expanse of forests and lakes, punctuated by towns full of people who are genuinely surprised to find tourists visiting them. It's a country waiting to be 'discovered', which is an attraction in itself. Sophisticated Helsinki is deservedly becoming a popular travel destination but is still far from overrun. Working-class Tampere is embedded with quirky museums, and tranquil Savonlinna lies marvellously snuggled between two lakes. Then there's Lapland, with its Santa Claus connections, northern lights and sheer, unadulterated wilderness. Festivals explode everywhere in summer and you could easily plan your trip around them.

Finally, Finns and Finland have a reputation for being quiet and mysterious, but if you look under the surface, you'll find some of the warmest people you'll ever meet.

Finland: the Basics

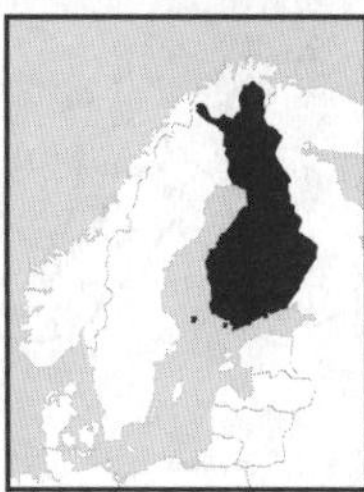

Capital Helsinki

Population 5.2 million

Language Finnish, Swedish

Currency euro (€) = 100 centimes

Avoid at all costs Forgetting to put on sunscreen before summer midnight bike rides

End extended hikes by noting *Olkaa kilttejä ja kohentakaa tulta saunassa!* (Can somebody please stoke the sauna?)

Facts about Finland

HISTORY

Human settlement in Finland dates back almost 10,000 years. After arriving on the Baltic coast from Russia, the Finns' ancestors established themselves in the forests and drove the nomadic Sami people north, where a small number still live.

By the end of the Viking era, Swedish traders had extended their interests throughout the Baltic region, and in 1155 the Swedes made Finland a province. Sweden swiftly imposed its culture, but its heavy-handedness split the country along religious lines, and most Orthodox believers fled to Russia.

In 1809 Sweden ceded Finland to Russia and the capital was moved to Helsinki, but the communist revolution of October 1917 brought the downfall of the Russian tsar and enabled the Finnish senate to declare independence.

Anticommunist violence broke out during the 1930s and relations with the Soviet Union remained uneasy. Finland sought neutrality but Soviet deals with Germany led to demands for Finland's eastern Lakeland (Karelia). In 1939 the Winter War between the Soviet Union and Finland began, in which the massively outnumbered Finns were defeated and Finland was forced to cede territory. When no Western allies would help it against the Soviets, Finland accepted assistance from Germany and resumed hostilities in 1941 with the Soviets to win back large swathes of Karelia in the Continuation War, which cost Finland almost 100,000 lives.

By 1944 growing Soviet strength forced another armistice, under the terms of which Finns turned and fought against German forces entrenched in Lapland.

Finland eventually signed a new treaty which recognised Soviet security concerns and also agreed to Soviet aid in defending the frontier. This treaty allowed Finland to take an independent stance during the Cold War, and with this new sense of security came the

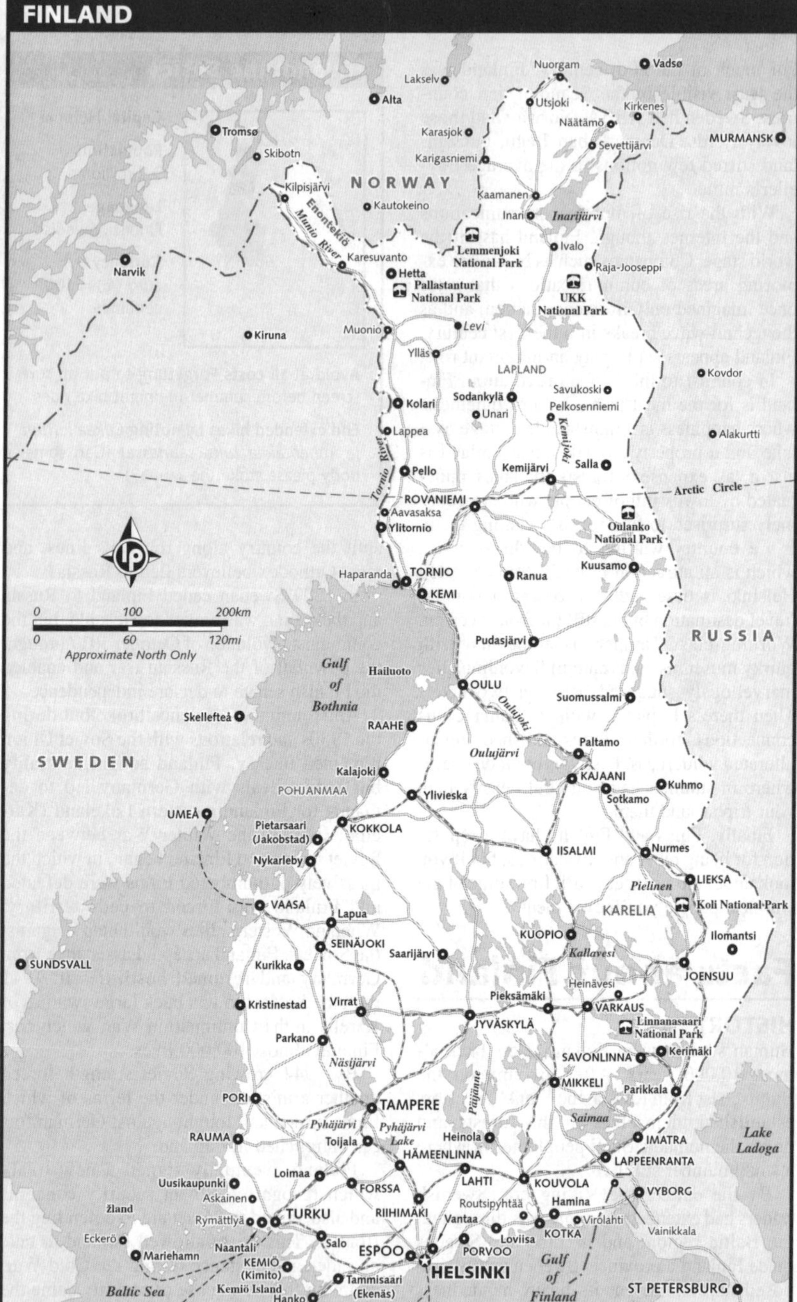
FINLAND
NORWAY
SWEDEN
RUSSIA
LAPLAND
POHJANMAA
KARELIA
Arctic Circle
Gulf of Bothnia
Gulf of Finland
Baltic Sea
Lake Ladoga
Approximate North Only
0 100 200km
0 60 120mi
Nuorgam
Vadsø
Lakselv
Alta
Utsjoki
Kirkenes
Näätämö
Tromsø
Karasjok
Sevettijärvi
MURMANSK
Skibotn
Karigasniemi
Kilpisjärvi
Kautokeino
Kaamanen
Inari
Inarijärvi
Enontekiö
Munio River
Lemmenjoki National Park
Ivalo
Narvik
Karesuvanto
Hetta
Raja-Jooseppi
Pallastanturi National Park
UKK National Park
Muonio
Levi
Kiruna
Ylläs
Kovdor
Savukoski
Kolari
Sodankylä
Pelkosenniemi
Unari
Kemijoki
Lappea
Alakurtti
Tornio River
Pello
Kemijärvi
Salla
ROVANIEMI
Aavasaksa
Ylitornio
Oulanko National Park
Haparanda
TORNIO
Ranua
Kuusamo
KEMI
Pudasjärvi
Hailuoto
OULU
Suomussalmi
Oulujoki
Skellefteå
RAAHE
Paltamo
Oulujärvi
Kalajoki
KAJAANI
Kuhmo
Sotkamo
Ylivieska
UMEÅ
Pietarsaari (Jakobstad)
KOKKOLA
IISALMI
Nurmes
Nykarleby
LIEKSA
Pielinen
Koli National Park
VAASA
Lapua
KUOPIO
Ilomantsi
SEINÄJOKI
Saarijärvi
Kallavesi
SUNDSVALL
Kurikka
JOENSUU
Heinävesi
Kristinestad
Pieksämäki
Virrat
VARKAUS
JYVÄSKYLÄ
Linnanasaari National Park
Parkano
SAVONLINNA
Kerimäki
Näsijärvi
Päijänne
MIKKELI
Parikkala
PORI
TAMPERE
Saimaa
Pyhäjärvi
Pyhäjärvi Lake
RAUMA
Toijala
Heinola
IMATRA
HÄMEENLINNA
LAPPEENRANTA
Loimaa
LAHTI
KOUVOLA
Uusikaupunki
FORSSA
VYBORG
Askainen
Routsipyhtää
Hamina
Žland
TURKU
RIIHIMÄKI
Rymättylä
Vantaa
Virolahti
Vainikkala
Eckerö
Salo
Loviisa
KOTKA
Naantali
ESPOO
PORVOO
Mariehamn
KEMIÖ (Kimito)
HELSINKI
Tammisaari (Ekenäs)
Kemiö Island
Hanko
ST PETERSBURG

opportunity for Finland to develop its economy and welfare system. The Helsinki conferences and accords played a significant part in the end to the Cold War and the dismantling of the USSR. Since then, Finland has recovered from its worst post-war recession, underscoring its new robustness by joining the EU in 1995.

In 1999 Finland adopted the euro – the only Nordic nation to do so – and in 2000 and 2001 was voted one of the least corrupt countries in the world.

GEOGRAPHY
Finland is Europe's seventh-biggest country, with one-third beyond the Arctic Circle. Compared with Sweden and Norway, it's a flat country with a scattering of fells (forested hills) in the northern Lakeland and Lapland areas.

CLIMATE
The four seasons differ enormously in Finland, ranging from continuing darkness in the Arctic winter to a two-month 'day' in northern Lapland's summer. In most parts of the country snow first falls in October and vanishes by the end of March, but in Lapland it lingers from September to late May. Temperatures can be surprisingly warm in summer, especially in the south.

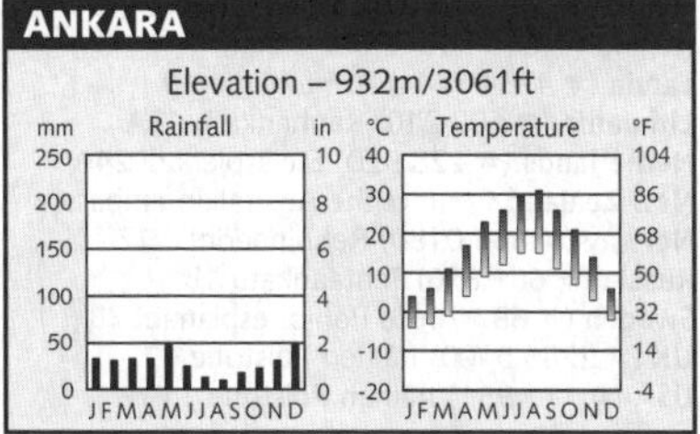

GOVERNMENT & POLITICS
Finland is a presidential republic and a prime minister is elected every four years by the 200-member parliament.

POPULATION & PEOPLE
Finland sports only 17 people per square kilometre. There are around 300,000 Swedish-speaking Finns in the west, and also in communities that are along the coast and on the Åland Islands; and a smaller number of Roma (Gypsies) in the south.

The Sami (Lapp) population of 6500 in the north consists of three distinct groups, each speaking its own dialect. Many Samis look across the border at the more developed Sami community in Norway for a deeper cultural identity.

SOCIETY & CONDUCT
A capacity for silence and reflection is the trait that best sums up the Finnish character (however, get a Finn near a stack of duty-free liquor and see if this remains the case). The image of a log cabin with a sauna by a lake tells much about Finnish culture: independence, endurance (*sisu* or 'guts') and a love of open space and nature.

The Finns are a naturally reserved people, but the seemingly icy front never lasts, and almost every visitor leaves with a story of unexpected kindness from a Finn.

LANGUAGE
Finnish is spoken by just six million people, all but a few of whom live in Scandinavia and Russian Karelia.

You can certainly get by with English in Finland – staff at hotels, hostels and tourist offices generally speak it fluently – but don't assume everyone does. All Finns learn Swedish at school.

See the Language chapter at the back of the book for pronunciation guidelines and useful words and phrases.

Facts for the Visitor

HIGHLIGHTS
Helsinki is the most interesting of Finland's major cities; Kiasma, the city's daring museum of contemporary art, is one place not to be missed. For a further urban fix, gritty **Tampere** is coming into its own as a funky city with a robust nightlife. Of course, much of Finland's charm lies in its **forests** and **lakes**, **castles** and **churches**, **winter sports** and **summer festivals**, so please don't just stick to the cities! You can soak in the world's largest smoke sauna in **Kuopio;** putter through **Savonlinna**, a town nestled between two lakes and home to the mightiest of the northern medieval castles; or head north to Lapland to experience, if there at the right time, the awe-inspiring magic of the aurora borealis.

FINLAND

PLANNING

May to September are the best months to visit. The tourist season in southern and central Finland is in full swing from early June to the end of August, when all attractions, hostels and camping grounds are open, and festivals abound. Tourist infrastructure hibernates the rest of the year.

Lapland's tourist season is different; the mosquitoes are annoying in July, but September is delightful, with its *ruska* (autumn) colours. October and February/March are good times to visit Lapland to view the aurora borealis (northern lights).

TOURIST OFFICES

Every town has a tourist office with English-language brochures, free maps and helpful staff. The **Finnish Tourist Board** *(MEK; ☎ 09-4176 9300; ⓔ mek@mek.fi; Eteläesplanadi 4, Helsinki)* has a mailing address, PO Box 249, 00131 Helsinki. The following overseas offices can assist with tourist material and inquiries but are generally not walk-in offices:

Denmark (☎ 3313 1362, ⓔ finland.dk@mek.fi) Finlands Turistbureau, Nyhavn 43A, 1051 Copenhagen K
Estonia (☎ 06-997 010, ⓔ mek.tal@mek.fi) Soome Turismiar-endamise, Uus 32, 10111 Tallinn
Norway (☎ 2316 2430, ⓔ finland.no@mek.fi) Finlands Turistkontor, Lille Grensen 7, 0159 Oslo 1
Sweden (☎ 08-587 69121, ⓔ finland.se@mek.fi) Finska Turistbyrån Snickarbacken 2, 111 39 Stockholm
UK (☎ 020-7365 2512, ⓔ finlandinfo.lon@mek.fi) Finnish Tourist Board, PO Box 33213, London W68JX
USA (☎ 212-885 9700) Finnish Tourist Board, 655 Third Ave, New York, NY 10017

A better source is the Finnish Tourist Board website (ⓦ www.mek.fi).

VISAS & DOCUMENTS

A valid passport is required to enter Finland. Citizens of EU countries (except Greece), Norway and Iceland can, however, travel with only an identity card. Most Western nationals don't need a tourist visa for stays under three months; South Africans require a Schengen visa. **The Directorate of Immigration** *(☎ 09-476 5500; ⓔ ulkomaalaisvirasto@uvi.fi; Panimokatu 2A, 00580 Helsinki)* handles visas and work permits.

EMBASSIES

Finnish Embassies

Finland maintains embassies in the following countries:

Australia (☎ 02-6273 3800, ⓔ sanoman.can@formin.fi) 10 Darwin Ave, Yarralumla, ACT 2600
Canada (☎ 613-236 2389, ⓔ sanoman.ott@formin.fi) 55 Metcalfe St, Suite 850, Ottawa K1P 6L5
France (☎ 01 44 18 19 20, ⓔ sanomat.par@formin.fi) 1 Place de Finlande, 57007 Paris
Germany (☎ 030-505030, ⓔ sanomat.ber@formin.fi) Rauchstrasse 1, 10787 Berlin
Ireland (☎ 01-478 1344, ⓔ sanomat.dub@formin.fi) Russell House, Stokes Pl, St Stephen's Green, Dublin 2
Netherlands (☎ 070-346 9754, ⓔ sanomat.haa@ formin.fi) Groot Hertoginnelaan 16, 251r EG Den Haag
UK (☎ 020-7838 6200, ⓔ sanomat.lon@formin.fi) 38 Chesham Place, London SW1X 8HW
USA (☎ 202-298 5800, ⓔ sanomat.was@formin.fi) 3301 Massachusetts Ave NW, Washington DC 20008

Embassies & Consulates in Finland

The following embassies are in Helsinki:

Australia *Consulate*: (☎ 447233) Museokatu 25B, Vantaa; nearest embassy is in Stockholm
Canada (☎ 171 141) Pohjoisesplanadi 25B
Denmark (☎ 684 1050) Keskuskatu 1A
Estonia (☎ 622 0288) Itäinen Puistotie 10
France (☎ 618 780) Itäinen Puistotie 13
Germany (☎ 458 580) Krogiuksentie 4
Ireland (☎ 646 006) Erottajankatu 7
Latvia (☎ 4764 7244) Armfeltintie 10
Lithuania (☎ 608 210) Rauhankatu 13A
Netherlands (☎ 228 920) Eteläsplanadi 24A
New Zealand Contact the Australian embassy
Norway (☎ 686 0180) Rehbinderintie 17
Russia (☎ 661 876) Tehtaankatu 1B
Sweden (☎ 687 7660) Pohjoisesplanadi 7B
UK (☎ 2286 5100) Itäinen Puistotie 17
USA (☎ 171 931) Itäinen Puistotie 14A

MONEY

Finland uses the euro. See Money in the Facts for the Visitor chapter for information about currency-exchange rates.

Finland has three national banks with similar rates and charges. In cities independent exchangers such as Forex are a better alternative for exchanging cash and travellers cheques. Finnish ATMs ('Otto') are linked to international networks such as Cirrus, EC, Eurocard, Visa, Plus and MasterCard. Credit cards are widely accepted. Banks open 9am to 4.15pm weekdays.

There's no American Express office that changes travellers cheques in Finland, but Thomas Cook is represented (through Travelex) in Helsinki and Turku.

For the traveller, overall costs are lower than they've been for decades. Finland is still expensive but comparable to much of Western Europe. If you camp or stay in hostels, prepare your own meals, don't move around too much and don't have much nightlife, it's possible to get by on €25 a day. If you stay in guesthouses (or private rooms in hostels) and eat at inexpensive restaurants, expect to pay about €60/50 a day if travelling as a single/double.

Students with valid ID and seniors receive substantial discounts on museum admission and transportation prices quoted in this chapter.

Tipping is not necessary and Finns generally don't do it. However, in cities such as Helsinki the hospitality industry expects it so it's polite to tip for good service at a restaurant. Bargaining isn't common, except at flea markets.

The 22% value-added tax (VAT) can be deducted if you post goods home from the point of sale. At stores showing the 'Tax Free for Tourists' sign, non-EU citizens receive a 12% to 16% refund on items priced over €45.

POST & COMMUNICATIONS

Post offices are generally open from 9am to 5pm weekdays, but stamps can be bought at bus or train stations and R-kiosks (newsagents). Poste restante can be collected at the main post office in cities.

Some public phones accept coins, but most only accept Telecards. In a few cities like Turku there are public telephones that accept only a local telephone card which is completely useless elsewhere.

International calls are much cheaper with a prepaid calling card from any R-kiosk. The cheapest calls are those placed between 10pm and 8am on weekdays and all day on weekends. For national directory assistance dial ☎ 020 202, for international help ☎ 020 208.

Finland has 13 area codes, each starting with a zero. Include the zero when dialling within Finland, but omit it if you are calling from abroad. The country code for calling Finland from abroad is ☎ 358. To make an international call from Finland, first dial an international prefix (☎ 00, 990, 994 or 999) and then the country code for the country you're calling.

All public libraries offer free Internet access, though you may need to book hours or even days in advance. An increasing number of businesses and tourist offices have at least one terminal you can use free for 15 minutes. Internet cafés aren't common.

DIGITAL RESOURCES

A few useful websites include the Finnish Tourist Board at w www.mek.fi, Finnish Youth Hostel Association at w www.srmnet.org, Forest & Park Service (Metsähallitus) at w www.metsa.fi and the Helsinki city tourist office at w www.hel.fi.

BOOKS

Lonely Planet's *Finland* is the most comprehensive guidebook available.

For a readable history, see the paperback *A Short History of Finland* by Fred Singleton. Some great Finnish authors, including Mika Waltari and Väinö Linna, have been translated by American as well as Finnish publishers. *A Way to Measure Time* (from the Finnish Literature Society) contains contemporary work from over 50 authors.

WOMEN TRAVELLERS

The only annoyance you're likely to find is harassment by drunken men. Ignore them, and try to avoid neighbourhood pubs in the evening. **Unioni Naisasialiitto Suomessa** *(Union for Womens Affairs; ☎ 643 158; Bulevardi 11A, Helsinki)* is the national feminist organisation.

GAY & LESBIAN TRAVELLERS

Though you won't find the equivalent of Stockholm's active gay community, Finland is as tolerant as other Nordic countries. There's a growing scene in Helsinki. Current information is available from the Finnish organisation for gay and lesbian equality, **Seksuaalinen tasavertaisus** *(SETA; ☎ 681 2580; w www.seta.fi; Hietalahdenkatu 2B 16, Helsinki)*.

DISABLED TRAVELLERS

By law, most public and private institutions must provide ramps, lifts and special toilets for disabled people, making Finland one of the easiest countries to negotiate. Some national parks offer wheelchair-accessible trails.

DANGERS & ANNOYANCES

Drunken men are the main cause of violence, but even in this regard Finland is remarkably safe. Foreign males of dark complexion run

Emergencies

Dial the following nationwide numbers in case of emergency: police, fire or ambulance ☎ 112, and emergency medical advice (24 hours) ☎ 10023.

the highest risk of being harassed on the street, though reports of race-related violence are becoming less common. In Helsinki it's best to avoid the main train station late at night.

Weather extremes in Lapland can be an unexpected danger at any time of the year. Exposure kills lone trekkers almost every winter, and cold rain can be a problem in summer. If hiking in the wilderness there's the remote possibility of encountering wild animals like bears and wolves, but a bigger problem in summer is insects such as mosquitoes, which grow as big as your hand and swarm relentlessly.

BUSINESS HOURS

Shops generally open from 9am to 5pm weekdays, and to 1pm on Saturday. Banks are open from 9.15am until 4.15pm weekdays. Many supermarkets and Helsinki department stores stay open until 9pm or 10pm on weeknights and open all day on Saturday and Sunday. Town markets begin about 7am on weekdays and Saturday and continue until about 2pm. Public holidays are taken seriously – everything shuts at 6pm on holiday evenings and reopens the morning after the holiday ends.

PUBLIC HOLIDAYS & SPECIAL EVENTS

Finland grinds to a halt twice a year – around Christmas and New Year and during the Midsummer weekend. Plan ahead and avoid travelling during those times. The public holidays are: New Year's Day (1 January), Epiphany (6 January), Good Friday–Easter Monday (March/April), May Day Eve and May Day (30 April and 1 May), Ascension Day (40 days after Easter), Whit Sunday (late May or early June), Juhannus (third weekend in June), All Saints Day (1 November), Independence Day (6 December), Christmas Eve (24 December), Christmas Day (25 December) and Boxing Day (26 December).

Finland has a barrage of festivals between mid-June and mid-August. Most notable are the **Jazz Festival** in Pori, the **Opera Festival** in Savonlinna and the annual **Midnight Sun International Film Festival** in Sodankylä. Midsummer is a big deal, though for most Finns it's family time, when they disappear to their summer cottages. Pick up the *Finland Festivals* booklet in any tourist office or check out 🅦 www.festivals.fi.

Vappu (May Day) is a *big* day for Finns – more alcohol is consumed in the 48 hours surrounding it than over a similar period any other time of year.

ACTIVITIES

What would Finland be without the physically and mentally cleansing sauna? The traditional sauna is made up of a wooden room with benches and a properly stoked wooden stove, although most Finnish saunas now have electrical heating. Temperatures are from 80°C to 100°C, and bathing is done nude. A cold swim afterwards completes the refreshment (fanatics roll in snow or jump into lakes during winter).

Hiking or trekking (often called fell walking) is best from June to September, although in July mosquitoes and other insects can be a problem in Lapland. Wilderness huts line the northern trails (they are free and must be shared) and you're generally allowed to hike in any forested or wilderness area, and camp for a night anywhere outside inhabited, privately owned areas.

Canoes and kayaks can be hired in most towns near a lake, often from camping grounds.

To fish you need a licence, available at banks, post offices and the **Forest and Park Service information office** (🅦 *www.metsa.fi; Eteläesplanadi 20, Helsinki*). Most fishing

She Ain't Heavy, She's My Wife

What began as the uncommendable 19th-century habit of stealing women from neighbouring villages has morphed into a highly entertaining and alcohol-drenched weekend in tiny Sonkajärvi, host of the annual **Wife Carrying World Championships**. Held in July, the race covers 253m over grass, sand, and asphalt, through a water hazard and over two hurdles; dropping your passenger draws a 150-second penalty. The winner earns, among other prizes, the woman's weight in beer. One of the rules of the International Wife Carrying Competition Rules Committee (IWCCR) states that the wife to be carried 'can be your own, the neighbour's or you may have found her farther afield'. All borrowed wives must be returned.

spots are owned privately or by local or national authorities, so you also need a daily or weekly local permit – check tourist offices for information.

Nordic skiing is popular and the season runs from October to April.

WORK

There's little work for foreigners due to high local unemployment, but students can apply for limited summer employment. Au pair arrangements are possible for stays of up to 18 months. Busking is a possible money-earner, and many foreigners find bar work, particularly in Irish pubs in Helsinki, Tampere and Turku.

A work permit is required of all non-EU foreigners, and employment must be secured before applying for the permit.

ACCOMMODATION

Camping is the cheapest way to travel around Finland, but it's less than convenient in the bigger cities. Camp sites are usually near lakes, in forests or on the coast. Most are closed in winter and popular spots are crowded during July.

The **Finnish Youth Hostel Association** *(SRM; ☎ 09-64 0377; ⓔ info@srm.inet.fi; Yrjönkatu 38B, 00100 Helsinki)* operates 133 hostels; about half of these are open all year. Hostel prices quoted in this chapter are without the €2.50 discount given to holders of a valid HI card.

The invaluable free publication *Camping & Hostels*, published by the **Finnish Tourist Board** *(ⓦ www.finland-tourism.com)*, gives a full listing of hostels and camping grounds.

FOOD & DRINKS

Typical Finnish food is heavy on fish, potatoes, dark rye bread and the like. Restaurant meals are generally expensive, particularly dinner. Fortunately, most restaurants offer special lunch menus for around €7, which include salad, bread, milk, coffee and dessert, plus big helpings of hearty fare – sausage, or fish, and potatoes.

Most towns have a *kauppahalli* (covered market) where you can buy cheap sandwiches and snacks. *Grilli* are the venues for takeaway meals of hamburgers or hot dogs for under €3. Turkish kebab joints offer good value, and inexpensive pizzerias are legion.

Local drink specialities include vodka, and cloudberry or cranberry liqueurs.

ENTERTAINMENT

For many Finns, talking and socialising over a few drinks is entertainment enough, but you'll find live music venues for rock, jazz and folk in most major towns. In summer, temporary stages are often set up for live music.

In Helsinki you'll see flyers for large dance parties in all the hipper bars. Nightclubs usually charge €5 after 11pm (minimum age is 18 or 20 years, sometimes 24!).

Getting There & Away

AIR

All major European carriers have flights to/from Helsinki. Cheap flights can also be found from the USA and Asia. From London, consider a cheap flight to Stockholm with Ryanair and the ferry from there to Turku or Helsinki.

Holders of the International Youth Travel Card (IYTC) or International Student Identity Card (ISIC) should also be able to get discount flights; in Finland, contact **Kilroy Travels** in Helsinki, Turku, Tampere, Jyväskylä, Vaasa and Oulu.

LAND

Sweden

There are six crossings from northern Sweden to northern Finland over the Tornionjoki (Torneälv) and Muonionjoki Rivers. From Norway or southern Sweden, there are trains to Boden and buses (train passes are valid) to the Swedish town of Haparanda, from where you can walk across (or take another bus) to the Finnish town of Tornio.

Norway

There are six border crossings by road plus several crossings on wilderness trails. Buses run between Rovaniemi and the Norwegian border, and more buses continue on to the first Norwegian town.

The main Nordkapp route goes from Rovaniemi to Karigasniemi and across the border to Karasjok and Lakselv. Bus services run from Ivalo to Karasjok. The road from the northernmost point of Finland, at Nuorgam, will take you to Tana Bru, with connections to various parts of Finnmark in Norway. Buses take you to the border, 4km from Nuorgam.

Russia

Daily express buses run from Turku and Helsinki, via other cities, to St Petersburg. Check timetables and book tickets at the bus station or a travel agency. A visa is required.

There are three daily trains from Helsinki to Russia, travelling via the Finnish stations of Lahti, Kouvola and Vainikkala.

The *Tolstoi* sleeper departs from Helsinki daily at 5.42pm, arrives in Moscow at 8.30am and costs €83 (2nd class, one way). It departs Moscow at 10.20pm daily.

The *Sibelius* and *Repin* have daily services between Helsinki and St Petersburg (5½ hours). The *Sibelius* departs Helsinki at 7.42am (€44.10, 2nd class, seats only). The *Repin* departs at 3.42pm and has 2nd-class seats for €49.10 or 1st-class sleeping berths for €86.10. From St Petersburg departures are at 4.48pm *(Sibelius)* and 7.48am *(Repin)*.

A Russian visa is needed for all trains. Buy Russian rail tickets in Helsinki at the special ticket counter in the central station. There are discounts for seniors and children, but not students. Check timetables at W www.vr.fi.

SEA

Baltic ferries are some of the world's most impressive seagoing craft and service between major cities is year-round. Book ahead when travelling in July, especially if you have a car.

Many ferries offer 50% discounts for holders of Eurail, Scanrail and Inter-Rail passes. Some services offer discounts for seniors and for those with ISIC and IYTC cards.

Sweden

The Stockholm to Helsinki, Stockholm to Turku and Kapellskär (Sweden) to Mariehamn (Åland) runs are covered by Silja Line and Viking Line (see under Stockholm later for contact details for both lines), with year-round daily departures. Birka Cruises travels between Mariehamn and Stockholm.

Cabins are compulsory on Silja, optional on Viking – you can buy a passenger ticket and sleep in the salons or any spare patch of inside deck. In summer overnight crossings (passenger ticket only) from Stockholm start at €33 to Turku (11 to 12 hours) and €40 to Helsinki (16 hours).

Eckerö Line sails from Grisslehamn to Eckerö in Åland. At three hours and €5.50 (€8.90 in summer) it's the quickest and cheapest crossing from Sweden to Finland.

Estonia

If you're heading to Estonia for onward travel it can be cheaper to get a same day return ticket than a one-way ticket.

Eckerö Line has only one departure daily but is the cheapest with a return fare at €12 from Tuesday to Thursday, except in July and August when it's €22. Tallink (see under Getting There & Away in the Helsinki section later) and Silja Line have several daily departures. Linda Line (see under Helsinki later) is the cheapest – but smallest – fast boat.

Germany

Finnlines *(☎ 09-251 0200 in Helsinki; W www.finnlines.fi)* has year-round service from Helsinki to Travemünde (32 to 36 hours) with bus service to Hamburg. Rates are from €272 one way.

Superfast Ferries *(☎ 09-2535 0640, fax 2535 0601; W www.superfast.com; Melkonkatu 28, Helsinki)* runs a ferry between Rostock and Hanko on the south coast of Finland (22 hours), daily except Sunday. Minimum one-way fare is €138/69 adult/child.

Getting Around

BUS

Buses are the main carriers, outside the railways, travelling 90% of Finland's roads. Buy your ticket on board or book at a bus station or travel agency. Few lines operate Sunday.

Long-distance and express bus travel is handled by **Oy Matkahuolto Ab** *(☎ 09-682 701)* in Helsinki. Private lines operate local services but all share the same ticketing system. National timetables are available from bus stations and at tourist offices.

From Helsinki to Rovaniemi by express bus (13½ hours) costs €82.60 one way. Return tickets are about 10% cheaper than two one-way fares. Discounts are available for students and seniors, though usually only if the ticket is booked and the trip is more than 80km. On some routes, buses accept train passes.

TRAIN

Finnish trains are efficient, fast and much cheaper than in Sweden and Norway. On longer routes there are two- and three-bed sleepers. Rovaniemi is the main northern rail terminus.

VR Ltd Finnish Railways *(☎ 09-707 3519; W www.vr.fi)* in Helsinki has its own travel bureau at main stations and staff can advise on tickets. An open return ticket is valid for 15 days and costs the same as two one-way tickets. Students, seniors and children under 17 pay half fare, and children under six travel free (without a seat).

International rail passes accepted in Finland include the Eurail pass, Eurail Flexipass, ScanRail Pass, Euro Domino and Inter-Rail Ticket.

The Finnrail Pass is a one-month pass good for unlimited rail travel for three/five/10 days; 2nd-class travel costs €114/154/208. These passes may be purchased before arrival in Finland (consult your local travel agent). Check at the train station on arrival for summer and regional special fares.

CAR

For information on road rules, insurance and driving conditions contact Finland's national motoring organisation, **Autoliitto** *(Automobile & Touring Club of Finland; ☎ 09-774 761; W www.autoliitto.fi; Hämeentie 105A, 00550 Helsinki)*.

Rental companies such as **Budget** *(☎ 686 6500)*, **Hertz** *(☎ 0800-112 233)* and **Europcar** *(☎ 09-7515 5300)* have offices in most cities. Rates at airport offices are highest. The smallest car costs from €40 per day plus €0.30 per kilometre.

BICYCLE

Finland is bicycle-friendly, with miles of bike paths. Daily/weekly hire at about €10/50 is possible in most cities. SRM (youth hostel association) offers a cycling and hostel package that takes in the flat south and lakes and costs €249/431 for seven/14 days, including bike rental and accommodation.

New bikes are around €250 for a hybrid, but good second-hand models may cost less than €100.

HITCHING

Hitching in Finland is fairly easy, especially if you try outside the biggest cities and look clean. However, it's relatively uncommon and you can expect long waits on minor roads.

BOAT

Lake and river ferries operate over the summer period. They're more than mere transport – a cruise is a bona fide Finnish experience. Many ferries that run between the islands along the coast are free, especially in Åland.

Helsinki

☎ 09 • pop 560,000

For many travellers, Helsinki *is* Finland. While the nation still struggles to gain the attention of tourists, Helsinki is fast becoming one of Europe's hottest destinations. Although this is Finland's largest and most vibrant city, Helsinki is small and intimate compared to other Scandinavian capitals, and walking or cycling is the best way to appreciate its cafés, parks, markets and nearby islands.

The area has been settled since 1550. While the Swedes were here in the 1700s they erected a fortress on the nearby island of Suomenlinna. After falling to the tsar in 1808, Helsinki became the seat of the Russian Grand Duchy. The monumental buildings of Senaatintori (Senate Square) were designed to give the new city an appropriate measure of oomph.

Orientation

Helsinki occupies a peninsula and is linked by bridge and boat to nearby islands. The city centre surrounds the main harbour, Eteläsatama, and the *kauppatori* (market square); huge international ferry terminals lie either side. The main street axes are the twin shopping avenues of Pohjoisesplanadi and Eteläesplanadi, and Mannerheimintie.

Information

Tourist Offices The helpful **Helsinki City Tourist Office** *(☎ 169 3757; W www.hel.fi/tourism; Pohjoisesplanadi 19; open daily May-Sept, Mon-Sat Oct-Apr)* is near the market square.

The **Finnish Tourist Board** *(☎ 4176 9300; W www.finland-tourism.com; open Mon-Fri year-round, Sat May-Sept)* has an office at Eteläesplanadi 4.

Tikankontti *(☎ 270 5221 or 0203-44 122; W www.metsa.fi; Eteläesplanadi 20; open Mon-Sat)* is the Helsinki office of Metsähallitus, the Finnish Forest and Park Service. It has information and maps for national parks and hiking areas, cabin rentals and fishing.

Kompassi *(☎ 3108 0080; W www.lasipalatsi.fi/kompassi; Mannerheimintie 22-24; open Tues-Fri & Sun)* is a youth information centre offering Euro26 youth cards.

Helsinki Card This pass gives free urban travel and entry to more than 50 attractions in and around Helsinki and discounts on day

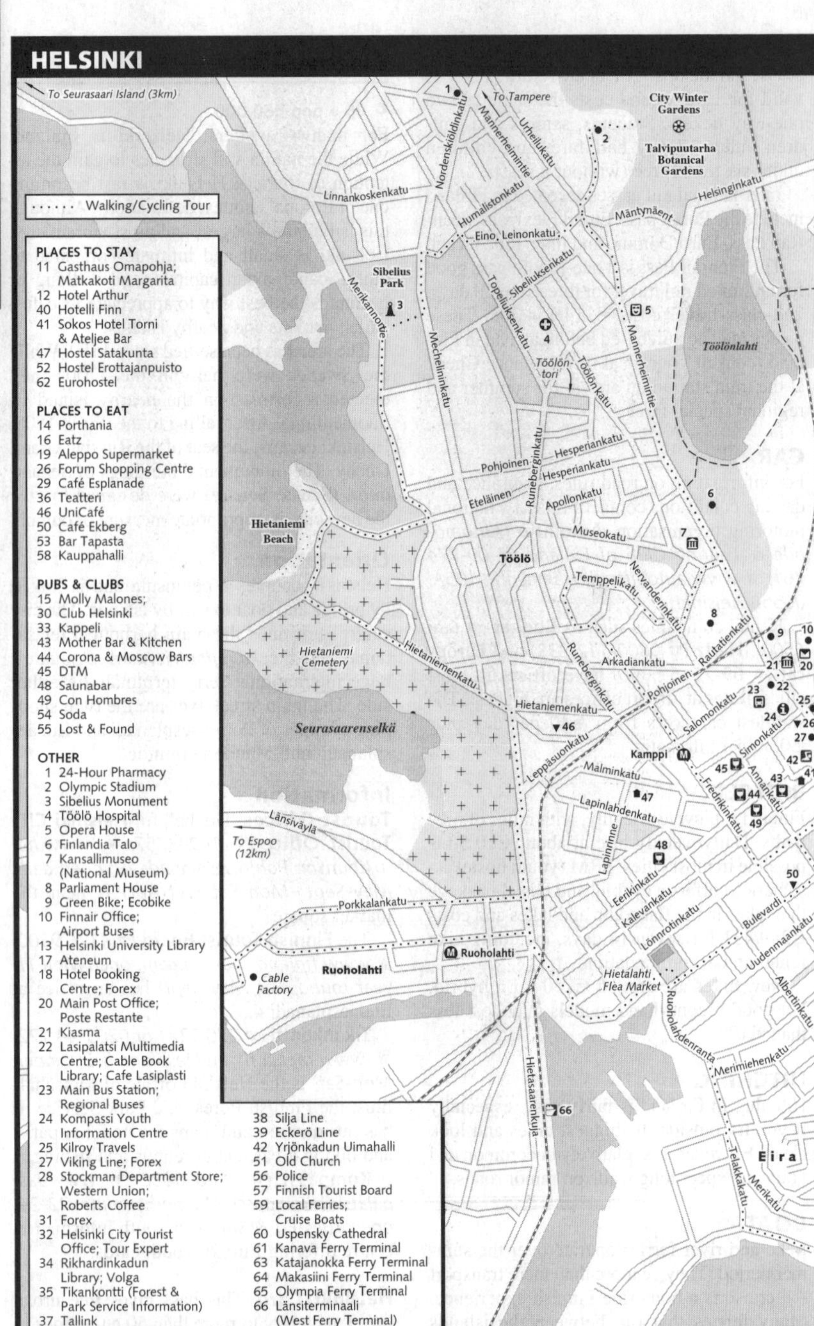

HELSINKI
To Seurasaari Island (3km)
To Tampere
City Winter Gardens
Talvipuutarha Botanical Gardens
Walking/Cycling Tour
PLACES TO STAY
11 Gasthaus Omapohja; Matkakoti Margarita
12 Hotel Arthur
40 Hotelli Finn
41 Sokos Hotel Torni & Ateljee Bar
47 Hostel Satakunta
52 Hostel Erottajanpuisto
62 Eurohostel
PLACES TO EAT
14 Porthania
16 Eatz
19 Aleppo Supermarket
26 Forum Shopping Centre
29 Café Esplanade
36 Teatteri
46 UniCafé
50 Café Ekberg
53 Bar Tapasta
58 Kauppahalli
PUBS & CLUBS
15 Molly Malones; 30 Club Helsinki
33 Kappeli
43 Mother Bar & Kitchen
44 Corona & Moscow Bars
45 DTM
48 Saunabar
49 Con Hombres
54 Soda
55 Lost & Found
OTHER
1 24-Hour Pharmacy
2 Olympic Stadium
3 Sibelius Monument
4 Töölö Hospital
5 Opera House
6 Finlandia Talo
7 Kansallimuseo (National Museum)
8 Parliament House
9 Green Bike; Ecobike
10 Finnair Office; Airport Buses
13 Helsinki University Library
17 Ateneum
18 Hotel Booking Centre; Forex
20 Main Post Office; Poste Restante
21 Kiasma
22 Lasipalatsi Multimedia Centre; Cable Book Library; Cafe Lasiplasti
23 Main Bus Station; Regional Buses
24 Kompassi Youth Information Centre
25 Kilroy Travels
27 Viking Line; Forex
28 Stockman Department Store; Western Union; Roberts Coffee
31 Forex
32 Helsinki City Tourist Office; Tour Expert
34 Rikhardinkadun Library; Volga
35 Tikankontti (Forest & Park Service Information)
37 Tallink
38 Silja Line
39 Eckerö Line
42 Yrjönkadun Uimahalli
51 Old Church
56 Police
57 Finnish Tourist Board
59 Local Ferries; Cruise Boats
60 Uspensky Cathedral
61 Kanava Ferry Terminal
63 Katajanokka Ferry Terminal
64 Makasiini Ferry Terminal
65 Olympia Ferry Terminal
66 Länsiterminaali (West Ferry Terminal)
Linnankoskenkatu
Nordenskiöldinkatu
Mannerheimintie
Urheilukatu
Humalistonkatu
Helsinginkatu
Mäntymäent
Eino Leinonkatu
Sibeliuksenkatu
Topeliuksenkatu
Sibelius Park
Merikannontie
Mechelininkatu
Töölö Hospital
Töölön-tori
Töölönkatu
Töölönlahti
Hesperiankatu
Pohjoinen
Eteläinen
Runeberginkatu
Apollonkatu
Museokatu
Hietaniemi Beach
Töölö
Temppelikatu
Nervanderinkatu
Hietaniemi Cemetery
Hietaniemenkatu
Arkadiankatu
Rautatienkatu
Salomonkatu
Simonkatu
Seurasaarenselkä
Leppäsuonkatu
Kamppi
Malminkatu
Annankatu
Fredrikinkatu
Lapinlahdenkatu
Lapinrinne
Länsiväylä
To Espoo (12km)
Eerikinkatu
Kalevankatu
Lönnrotinkatu
Bulevardi
Uudenmaankatu
Porkkalankatu
Ruoholahti
Cable Factory
Hietalahti Flea Market
Albertinkatu
Ruoholahdenranta
Merimiehenkatu
Hietasaarenkuja
Eira
Telakkakatu
Merikatu

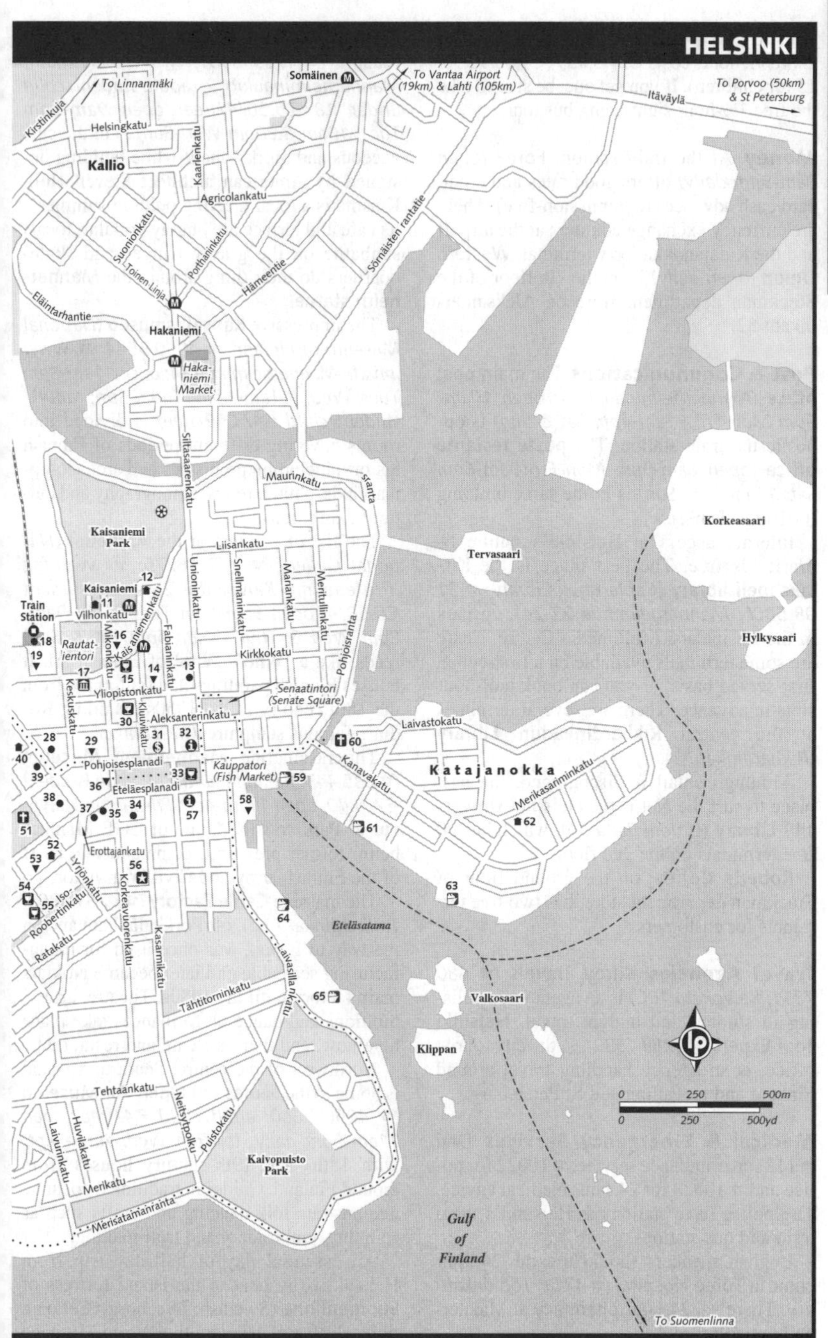
HELSINKI
To Linnanmäki
Somäinen
To Vantaa Airport (19km) & Lahti (105km)
To Porvoo (50km) & St Petersburg
Itäväylä
Kirstinkuja
Helsingkatu
Kallio
Kaarlenkatu
Agricolankatu
Suonionkatu
Porthaninkatu
Toinen Linja
Hämeentie
Sörnäisten rantatie
Eläintarhantie
Hakaniemi
Hakaniemi Market
Siltasaarenkatu
Maurinkatu
Kaisaniemi Park
Liisankatu
Unioninkatu
Snellmaninkatu
Mariankatu
Meritullinkatu
Pohjoisranta
Tervasaari
Korkeasaari
Hylkysaari
Kaisaniemi
Train Station
Vilhonkatu
Rautatientori
Mikonkatu
Kaisaniemenkatu
Fabianinkatu
Kirkkokatu
Keskuskatu
Yliopistonkatu
Senaatintori (Senate Square)
Kluuvikatu
Aleksanterinkatu
Laivastokatu
Pohjoisesplanadi
Kauppatori (Fish Market)
Kanavakatu
Katajanokka
Merikasarminkatu
Eteläesplanadi
Erottajankatu
Yrjönkatu
Iso-Roobertinkatu
Korkeavuorenkatu
Kasarmikatu
Ratakatu
Laivasillankatu
Eteläsatama
Tähtitorninkatu
Valkosaari
Klippan
Tehtaankatu
Neitsytpolku
Puistokatu
Huvilakatu
Laivurinkatu
Merikatu
Kaivopuisto Park
Merisatamanranta
Gulf of Finland
To Suomenlinna
0 250 500m
0 250 500yd
11 12 13 14 15 16 17 18 19 28 29 30 31 32 33 34 35 36 37 38 39 40 51 52 53 54 55 56 57 58 59 60 61 62 63 64 65

tours to Porvoo and Tallinn. A card valid for 24/48/72 hours costs €24/33/39 (€9.50/12.50/15 for children). If you get one, be sure to take the free 1½-hour sightseeing bus tour.

Money At the train station, **Forex** *(open 8am-9pm daily)* offers good rates and credit card cash advances (commission-free). There are currency exchange counters at the airport and the Katajanokka ferry terminal. **Western Union** *(open daily)* is on the 7th floor of the Stockman department store on Aleksanterinkatu 52.

Post & Communications The **main post office** *(Mannerheiminaukio 1; open 10am-7pm Mon-Fri, 11am-4pm Sat & Sun)* is opposite the train station. The **poste restante office** *(open 8am-9pm Mon-Fri, 9am-6pm Sat, 11am-9pm Sun)* is in the same building (00100 Helsinki).

Internet access at Helsinki's public libraries is free. The best place is the **Kirjakaapeli library** *(Cable Book Library; ☎ 31 08 5000; Mannerheimintie 22-24)*, upstairs in the Lasipalatsi Multimedia Centre. There are some terminals available on a first-come, first-served basis, or you can book half-hour slots in advance. There are several terminals at the central **Rikhardinkadun Library** *(Rikhardinkatu 3)*.

Although email is discouraged, the best place to surf the Net is the **Helsinki University Library** *(Unioninkatu 36)*, which has 20 free terminals on the 2nd floor.

Roberts Coffee, on the ground floor of Stockman department store, has two free terminals for customers.

Travel Agencies **Kilroy Travels** *(☎ 680 7811; Kaivokatu 10C)* is an agency specialising in student and budget travel. **Helsinki Tour Expert** *(☎ 2288 1599)*, in the city tourist office, is an agency handling travel around Finland and to Tallinn and St Petersburg.

Medical & Emergency Services Dial ☎ 112 for ambulance service, ☎ 10022 for police and ☎ 10023 for 24-hour medical advice. The police have stations at Helsinki's main train and bus stations.

English speakers should use the 24-hour clinic at **Töölö Hospital** *(☎ 4711; Töölönkatu 40)*. There's a 24-hour **pharmacy** at Mannerheimintie 96.

Things to See & Do

Kiasma *(☎ 1733 6501; W www.kiasma.fi; Mannerheiminaukio 2; adult/student/child under 18 €5.50/4/free; open 9am-5pm Tues, 10am-8.30pm Wed-Sun)* is in the curvaceous and quirky chalk-white building designed by American architect Steven Holl. Kiasma is a local meeting point in summer – its café and terrace are hugely popular, locals sunbathe on the grassy fringes and skateboarders do their thing around the **Mannerheim statue**.

The impressive **Kansallismuseo** *(National Museum of Finland; ☎ 4050 9544; W www.nba.fi; Mannerheimintie 34; open 11am-8pm Tues-Wed, 11am-6pm Thurs-Sun; adult/student/child €4/3.50/free)* is divided into rooms covering different periods of Finnish history, including prehistory and archaeological finds, church relics, ethnography and cultural exhibitions.

The list of painters at the **Ateneum** *(National Gallery; ☎ 173 36275; W www.fng.fi/ateneum; Kaivokatu 2; adult/student €5.50/4; open 9am-6pm Tues & Fri, 9am-8pm Wed & Thur, 11am-5pm Sat & Sun)* reads like a 'Who's Who' of Finnish art. It houses Finnish paintings and sculptures from the 18th century to the 1950s including Rodin's famous sculpture *The Thinker*.

The fascinating **Mannerhiem Museum** *(☎ 635 443; Kalliolinnantie 14; adult/student €7/5.40; open 11am-4pm Fri-Sun)* in Kaivopuisto Park was the home of CGE Mannerheim, former president, commander-in-chief of the Finnish army and Civil War victor.

The massive **Cable Factory** *(☎ 4763 8303; Tallberginkatu 1C)*, off Porkkalankatu and on the way to Espoo, was once used for manufacturing sea cable and later became Nokia's main factory until the 1980s. Theatre, art exhibitions and dance performances take place here now, and there's a café and restaurant.

Northwest of the centre, Seurasaari island is home to the **Seurasaari Open-Air Museum** *(☎ 4050 9660; adult/child €4/free; open 11am-5pm daily, to 7pm Wed, June-Sept)* with 18th- and 19th-century houses from around Finland. Guides in traditional costume demonstrate folk dancing and crafts such as spinning, embroidery and troll-making.

An essential day or half-day trip from Helsinki is by boat to the island fortress of **Suomenlinna** (Swedish: Sveaborg). Set on a tight cluster of islands, the World Heritage

Listed fortress was founded by the Swedes in 1748 to protect the eastern part of the empire against the Russians.

At the bridge connecting the two main islands, Iso Mustasaari and Susisaari, is the **Inventory Chamber Visitor Centre** *(☎ 668 800)* with tourist information, maps and guided walking tours in summer. Also here is the **Suomenlinna Museum** *(adult/student/child €5/4/2.50)*, covering the island's history.

HKL ferries depart every 40 minutes from the passenger quay at the kauppatori. Buy tickets (€2) for the 15-minute trip at the pier. The Helsinki Card is valid for all ferries and attractions at Suomenlinna.

Places to Stay

Book at least a week in advance for hostels and hotels in summer. The **Hotel Booking Centre** *(☎ 2288 1400; e hotel@helsinkiexpert.fi; open 9am-7pm Mon-Fri, 9am-6pm Sat, 10am-6pm Sun June-Aug; 9am-5pm Mon-Sat Sept-May)* can help in a pinch. There's also a branch at the city tourist office.

Hostels Another student apartment building is **Hostel Satakunta** *(☎ 6958 5231, fax 685 4245; e ravintola.satakunta@sodexho.fi; Lapinrinne 1A; dorm beds/singles/doubles/triples/quads €12/36.50/51/58.50/66; open 1 June-31 August)*. The dorms aren't flash but they're the cheapest in Helsinki. Private rooms are clean and have a fridge and buffet breakfast included.

Eurohostel *(☎ 622 0470, fax 655 044; w www.eurohostel.fi; Linnankatu 9; dorm beds €18.50, singles/doubles/triples €32/37/55.50; open year-round, 24hr reception)*, a high-rise place on Katajanokka Island, is a friendly and busy HI hostel. Rates include a morning sauna. Take tram No 4 or 2 from the centre or walk.

Hostel Erottajanpuisto *(☎ 642 169, fax 680 2757; Uudenmaankatu 9; dorm beds €19.50-22.50, singles/doubles €43.50/55; open year-round)* is definitely the most laid-back hostel in Helsinki. It has an unbeatable location on a lively street close to the heart of the city.

Suomenlinna Hostel *(☎ 794 481; w www.leirikoulut.com; dorm beds €20.50, singles/doubles €37.50/55; open year-round)*, in an old red-brick building near the ferry quay on Suomenlinna Island, is a peaceful and interesting alternative to staying in central Helsinki.

Guesthouses Near the train station, **Gasthaus Omapohja** *(☎ 666 211; Itäinen Teatterikuja 3; singles/doubles from €40/60, with bathroom €58/75)* is a fine old guesthouse. Rooms are spotless; management is friendly.

Matkakoti Margarita *(☎ 622 4261; Itäinen Teatterikuja 3; singles/doubles with shared bath €37/50)*, next door, is not quite as charming but it's clean and reasonably good value.

Hotels Near the train station, **Hotel Arthur** *(☎ 173 441, fax 626 880; w www.hotelarthur.fi; Vuorikatu 19; singles/doubles/triples from €89/106/126, weekends & summer €71/88/108)* is a welcoming place.

Hotelli Finn *(☎ 684 4360, fax 6844 3610; w www.hotellifinn.fi; Kalevankatu 3B; singles/doubles €65/80, weekends €55/70)* is a small hotel occupying the top floors of a central city building.

Places to Eat

If you're self-catering, stock up at **Aleppo**, a supermarket in the pedestrian tunnel by the train station. The **kauppahalli** *(Eteläranta 1)* is a brilliant place for cheap filled sandwiches, snacks and fresh produce. The **kauppatori** is good for fish soup and other Finnish snacks.

For everything from Asian noodles to burgers and kebabs, head to the **Forum shopping centre** *(Mannerheimintie 20)*.

Helsinki University has numerous student **caféterias** around the city, where meals cost less than €5. These include **UniCafé** *(Hietaniemenkatu 14)* below Hostel Academica, **Porthania** *(Hallituskatu 11-13)* and the huge **Ylioppilasaukio** *(Mannerheimintie 3B)*.

Café Esplanade *(Pohjoisesplanadi 37; sandwiches €3-5)* serves oversized Danish pastries and Finnish *pulla* (wheat bun) €2, as well as spectacular salads. **Café Ekberg** *(Bulevardi 9; buffet breakfast & lunch €7.20)* is Helsinki's oldest café and one of the best places for breakfast in the city. The lunch buffet is also great value.

Bar Tapasta *(☎ 640 724; Uudenmaankatu 13)* is an intimate place with a welcoming atmosphere and wonderful tapas and salads for €2 to €7. Wash it all down with a jug of sangria (€16.80).

Eatz *(☎ 687 7240; Mikonkatu 15; mains €10-20, sushi €3-8)* manages to serve up everything from Thai to Italian to Japanese. It's also the cornerstone of Helsinki's biggest summer beer terrace.

Entertainment

Helsinki has a lively and sophisticated nightlife scene that's fast becoming the envy of northern Europe. In summer drinking starts early at the many **beer terraces** that sprout up all over town. The biggest is along Mikonkatu at the front of Eatz. Get there early for a seat.

In summer the bright red pub tram, **Spårakoff** *(admission €7, beer €5)* shuttles around the city – the terminus is opposite Eatz restaurant at Mikonkatu.

Kappeli, in the middle of Esplanade Park near the kauppatori, has one of the city's most popular summer terraces, facing a stage where various bands and musicians regularly play in summer. Inside, there's a vault-like brewery-pub in the cellar.

Ateljee Bar *(Yrjönkatu 26)* is a tiny perch on the roof of the Sokos Hotel Torni, and is worth ascending just for the views of the city.

Molly Malone's *(Kaisaniemenkatu 1C)* is one of the best places in Helsinki to meet a variety of people – travellers, expats and Finns. There's live music on most nights upstairs, where it's shoulder-to-shoulder Guinness consumption.

If you're young and/or beautiful (or just trying), **Soda** *(W www.barsoda.fi; Uudenmaankatu 16-20)* is for you; its house and techno music draws shiny happy people most nights. The club above **Teatteri** *(Pohjoisespa 2)* has space for an ultra-chic 300 people.

More down-to-earth is the stylish **Mother Bar & Kitchen** *(☎ 612 3990; Eerikinkatu 2)* which has DJs spinning drum & bass and acid jazz music four nights a week.

Corona *(Eerikinkatu 15)* and **Moscow** next door are run by film makers Aki and Mika Kaurismäki; both attract a savvy, grungy crowd. Corona has about 20 pool tables. Farther down the street, the **Saunabar** *(☎ 685 5550; Eerikinkatu 27)*, downstairs at the rear of the building, is popular with students and does indeed have saunas.

If you're partying late **Club Helsinki** *(Yliopistonkatu 8)* is a popular mainstream dance club open till 4am.

By Scandinavian standards, Helsinki has a low-key gay scene but **Lost & Found** *(☎ 680 1010; Annankatu 6; open until 4am)* and the associated **Hideaway Bar** is a sophisticated place that's open till 4am and gets busy around midnight. More vibrant are **DTM** *(Annankatu 32)*, and the industrial 'eurobar' **Con Hombres** *(☎ 608 826; Eerinkinkatu 14)*.

Getting There & Away

Air There are flights to Helsinki from all major European cities. Vantaa airport, one of Europe's most user-friendly terminals, is 19km north of Helsinki.

Finnair flies to 20 Finnish cities, generally at least once a day but several times daily on routes as such Turku, Tampere, Rovaniemi and Oulu. The **Finnair office** *(reservations ☎ 0203-140160; Asema-aukio 3; open Mon-Sat)*, is near the train station.

Bus Purchase long-distance and express bus tickets at the **main bus station** *(open 7am-7pm Mon-Fri, 7am-5pm Sat, 9am-6pm Sun)*, which is off Mannerheimintie or on the bus itself.

Train A pedestrian tunnel links the train station to Helsinki's metro system. There is a separate counter for buying tickets for the international trains.

Express trains run daily to Turku, Tampere and Lappeenranta, and there's a choice of day and overnight trains to Oulu, Rovaniemi and Joensuu. There are also daily trains to the Russian cities of Vyborg, St Petersburg and Moscow.

Boat International ferries depart from four terminals and travel to Stockholm, Tallinn, and Travemünde in Germany. See this chapter's introductory Getting There & Away section for more details.

Ferry tickets can be bought at the terminals, from the ferry companies' offices in the centre or (in some cases) from the city tourist office. Tickets should be booked in advance in summer.

Silja Line *(☎ 0203-74552)* offices are at Mannerheimintie 2 and in the Olympia terminal. The **Viking Line** *(☎ 123 577)* office is at Mannerheimintie 14 and in the Katajanokka terminal. **Nordic Jet Line** *(☎ 681 770)* is in the Kanava terminal. **Eckerö Line** *(☎ 228 8544)* is at Mannerheimintie 10 and the Länsiterminaali (West Terminal). **Tallink** *(☎ 2282 1222)* is at Erottajankatu 19. A catamaran service to Tallinn departs from Kanava Terminal.

Kanava and Katajanokka terminals are served by bus No 13 and tram Nos 2, 2V and 4; Olympia and Makasiini terminals by tram Nos 3B and 3T; and Länsiterminaali by bus No 15.

Getting Around

To/From the Airport Bus No 615 (€3, 30 minutes; Helsinki Card not valid) shuttles between Vantaa airport (all international and domestic flights) and platform No 10 at Rautatientori (Railway Square) next to the main train station.

Finnair buses (€4.90) depart from the Finnair office at Asema-aukio, also next to the main train station, every 20 minutes from 5am to midnight. There are also door-to-door **airport taxis** *(☎ 10 64 64; Ⓦ www.airporttaxi.fi)* at €16.80 per person.

Public Transport A one-hour flat-fare ticket for the bus, tram, metro, Suomenlinna ferry and local trains within Helsinki's **HKL network** *(Ⓦ www.hel.fi/HKL)* costs €2 when purchased on board, €1.40 when purchased in advance. It allows unlimited transfers but should be validated in the stamping machine on board when you first use it. A single tram ticket (no transfers) is €1.50/1 (on board/in advance).

Tourist tickets are available at €4.20/8.40/12.60 for one/three/five days; 10-trip tickets cost €12.80. The Helsinki Card gives you free travel anywhere within Helsinki (see the Information section earlier for details).

HKL offices at the Rautatientori and Hakaniemi metro stations (open weekdays) sell tickets and passes, as do many of the city's R-kiosks. The *Helsinki Route Map*, available at HKL offices and the city tourist office, is good for making sense of local transport.

Bicycle Helsinki is ideal for cycling. The toursit office has a Helsinki cycling map.

Helsinki provides 300 green 'City Bikes' at stands within a radius of 2km from the kauppatori. Bikes are free: deposit a €2 coin into the stand which locks them, then reclaim it when you return the bike to any stand.

For something more sophisticated, **Greenbike** *(☎ 8502 2850)*, in the old railway goods sheds, rents quality bikes for €10 per day, or €15 for 24 hours. **Ecobike** is a smaller operation in the small yellow hut across the road from parliament house.

AROUND HELSINKI

Porvoo

☎ 019 • pop 45,400

Porvoo (Swedish: Borgå), a picturesque medieval town, makes a perfect day or overnight trip from Helsinki, 50km away.

The HI **Porvoo Hostel** *(☎/fax 523 0012; Ⓦ www.porvoohostel.cjb.net; Linnankoskenkatu 1-3; dorm beds €9.50, singles/doubles €24.50/27, linen hire €4)* is in a lovely old building with spotless rooms and a well-equipped kitchen. You can pitch a tent at **Camping Kokonniemi** *(☎ 581 967; Ⓔ myynti palvelu@lomaliitto.fi; tent sites €15, four-person cabins €62; open June–mid-Aug)*, 2km south of town.

Frequent buses connect Porvoo and Helsinki (€7.90, one hour), as do ferries in summer. Steamship *JL Runeberg* *(☎ 019-524 3331)* sails daily (except Thursday) to/from Helsinki (one way/return €20/29). You can return by bus or, on Saturdays in summer, on the vintage diesel train (combined ferry/boat ticket €27).

Turku

☎ 02 • pop 173,600

Though you might not know it due to its predominantly modern buildings, Turku (Åbo) is the oldest city in Finland, founded in the 1200s, and also the former Swedish capital. For many travellers it's their first taste of Finland due to the ferries from Sweden via the Åland Islands. Turku has a wonderfully active riverside (in summer), an impressive castle and is an ideal base for exploring the south-western archipelago.

Information

The busy city **tourist office** *(☎ 262 7444; Ⓦ www.turkutouring.fi; Aurakatu 4; open daily)* hires out bikes and sells the **Turku Card** (€21/28 for one/two days) which gives free admission to most museums and attractions in the region, and public transport.

Forex *(Eerikinkatu 12; open 8am-7pm Mon-Fri, 8am-5pm Sat)* is the best place to exchange cash and travellers cheques. The **main post office** is at Humalistonkatu 1.

There are several Internet terminals at the **public library** *(Linnankatu 2; open Mon-Sat)*, and there's one terminal (free for 15 minutes) at the tourist office. **Surf City** *(Aninkaistenkatu 3)* is an Internet café charging €2 for 30 minutes, with discounts for students.

Things to See & Do

The city's 50 museums are generally open daily in summer, closed Monday in winter and charge €3.40 admission.

A visit to the **Turku Castle** *(☎ 262 0300; adult/child €6.50/4.50, guided tours €1.50; open 10am-6pm daily mid-May–mid-Sept, shorter hours in winter)*, near the harbour, is a must. Guided tours are given in English throughout the day.

Forum Marinum *(☎ 282 9511; Linnankatu 72; adult/child €10/5)* is an impressive new maritime museum near the castle. As well as a better-than-average exhibition space devoted to Turku's shipping background, it incorporates three **museum ships**: the mine layer *Keihässalmi,* the three-masted barque *Sigyn*; and the impressive 1902 sailing ship *Suomen Joutsen* (Swan of Finland). The ships can be visited independently of the museum for €4/2.

The **Aboa Vetus** and **Ars Nova** *(☎ 250 0552; Itäinen Rantakatu 4-6; adult/child €7/5 to each, combined ticket €9.50/7; open 11am-7pm daily May–mid-Sept, 11am-7pm Thurs-Sun Sept-Dec)*, both museums found under the one roof, are respectively an archaeological exhibition and a modern art collection. The **Titanik** gallery nearby often has great contemporary work.

Archipelago cruises are a popular activity in summer, with daily departures from Martinsilta bridge. The best option is a cruise out to Naantali aboard the steamship **SS *Ukkopekka*** *(☎ 515 3300; W www.ukkopekka.fi)* daily at 10am and 2pm from June to August. The trip takes 1½ hours and costs one way/return €13/18.

Places to Stay & Eat

Interpoint Hostel *(☎ 231 4011, fax 231 2584; Vähä-Hämeenkatu 12a; beds €8.50-10.50)*, open only between 15 July and 15 August, is the cheapest place in Turku but for good reason – 30 mattresses on the floor and one shower!

HI-affiliated **Hostel Turku** *(☎ 231 6578, fax 231 1708; Linnankatu 39; dorm beds €11, singles & doubles €34.50; reception open 6am-10am & 3pm-midnight daily year-round)* is well located on the river close to the town centre and is one of the busiest hostels in Finland. Facilities include a well-equipped kitchen, laundry, lockers and bike hire.

There are plenty of cheap eateries around Turku's market square and in the **kauppahalli** *(open Mon-Sat)*. You can always get a cheap meal at the Turku University Student Café.

Next to the bridge is the ultra-chic **Blanko** *(☎ 233 3966; Aurakatu 1)*, where Turku shakes its booty to DJs on weekend nights; the staff whip up excellent tapas.

Pizzeria Dennis *(☎ 469 1191; Linnankatu 17; dishes €8-11)* serves up a range of pizzas and pasta in cosy rooms.

The riverfront **Vaakahuoneen Paviljonki** *(☎ 515 3324; Linnankatu 38; mains €7-15, fish buffet €8)* is *the* place to go for excellent-value food and entertainment. As well as an à la carte menu of snacks, pasta, pizzas and steak, there's a daily 'archipelago fish buffet' (11am to 10pm), plus a changing buffet of Asian cuisines.

South of the river, **Uusi Apteeki** *(Kaskenkatu 1)* is a wonderful bar in a converted old pharmacy; the antique shelves are filled with hundreds of old beer bottles.

Getting There & Away

From the main terminal at Aninkaistentulli there are hourly express buses to Helsinki (€20.90, 2½ hours), and frequent services to Tampere (€16.80, two hours) and Rauma (€11.40, 1½ hours).

Express trains run to and from Helsinki (€19.80, two hours), Tampere (€16.60, 1¾ hours), Oulu (€60.20, seven hours) and Rovaniemi (€67.40, 10 hours). There are direct train connections from Turku harbour to Helsinki. Bus No 30 shuttles between the centre and the train station.

Silja Line and Viking Line ferries sail from Stockholm (9½ hours) and Mariehamn (six hours). Seawind Line sails to Stockholm via Långnäs (Åland). All three have offices at the harbour, and Silja Line and Viking Line also have offices in the Hansa shopping centre.

AROUND TURKU

Naantali

☎ 02 • pop 13,400

Naantali, 13km west of Turku, is one of Finland's loveliest seaside towns, but the hordes of families descending on the popular **Moomin World theme park** *(day pass €13; open June-Aug)* can distort this image.

The village was developed after the founding of a convent in the 1440s and today the harbour, lined with cafés and restaurants, the delightful cobbled **Old Town** and the huge **Convent Church** are enough incentive to make a day trip here from Turku. Tourist information is available at **Naantali Tourist Service** *(☎ 435 9800, fax 435 0852; Kaivotori 2; open daily June–mid-Aug, Mon-Fri rest of year)*.

Nearby on Luonnonmaa Island sits **Kulturanta**, the summer residence of the president of Finland. Tours are by guide, book through the tourist office.

The exceptional **Naantali Camping** *(☎ 435 0855, 435 0850; Kuparivuori; tent sites €13-17, 2–6-person cabins €30-100; open April-Oct)*, is 400m south of the town centre. **Naantali Summer Hotel** *(☎ 445 5660; Opintie 3; rooms per person €31; open June–mid-Aug)* is a modern hostel-type place near to, and run by, the spa hotel.

Café Antonius *(Mannerheiminkatu 9)* is an unbeatable café in Villa Antonius, with home-made gingerbread and other mouth-watering sweets. The more pricey **Merisali** *(Nunnakatu 1; buffet lunch/dinner €9/10.50, Sun lunch €12)* has a terrace and a mind-blowing smorgasbord for lunch and dinner.

There are buses every 15 minutes from Turku (€3.40, 20 minutes), and in summer the steamship **SS *Ukkopekka*** cruises between Turku and Naantali several times daily (see the Turku section for details).

Åland

☎ 018 • pop 25,400

The Åland Islands are unique and autonomous, with their own flag and culture. Several Swedish dialects are spoken, and few Ålanders speak Finnish. This situation goes back to a 1921 League of Nations' decision after a dispute over sovereignty. Åland took its own flag in 1954 and has issued stamps (prized by collectors) since 1984.

The islands are popular for cycling and camping, and Midsummer celebrations are among the best in Finland. There are medieval parish churches, ruins and fishing villages.

The capital and main (only) town of Åland is Mariehamn. You can take your wheels almost anywhere around the islands using the bridges or the network of bicycle and car ferries.

The main tourist office is **Elands Turistinformation** *(☎ 24000; W www.info.aland.fi; Storagatan 8)* in Mariehamn.

Getting There & Away

The main companies operating between Finland and Åland (and on to Sweden) are **Viking Line** and **Silja Line**, while **Eckerö Line** and **Birka Cruises** operate only between Åland and Sweden.

Viking and Silja Lines have daily ferries to Mariehamn from Turku as part of their links with Stockholm: you can stop off 'between' countries. Viking Line also sails from Kapellskär in Sweden.

Birka Cruises sails only between Stockholm and Mariehamn. Eckerö Line sails from Grisslehamn to Eckerö – the latter is the cheapest and quickest route from Sweden to Åland.

Getting Around

Five main bus lines depart from Mariehamn's regional bus terminal on Torggatan in front of the library. No 1 goes to Hammarland and Eckerö; No 2 to Godby and Geta; No 3 to Godby and Saltvik; No 4 to Godby, Sund and Vårdö (Hummelvik) and No 5 to Lemland and Lumparland (Långnäs).

Free ferries are constantly plying across the shorter straits. There are also three bicycle ferries in summer (€6-9 with bicycle). For timetables ask at the tourist office or **Ålandstrafiken** *(Strandgatan 25, Mariehamn)*.

Bicycle is the best way to see these flat, rural islands. The most scenic roads have separate bike lanes. **Ro-No Rent** *(☎ 12 820)* has bicycles available at Mariehamn and Eckerö harbours starting at €7/35 a day/week (€13/65 for a mountain bike).

MARIEHAMN

☎ 018 • pop 11,000

Mariehamn, the 'town of a thousand linden trees', becomes the town of a thousand tourists in summer but it still manages to retain its village flavour. The main pedestrian street, Torggatan, is a colourful hive of activity, and there are some fine museums.

The town lies on a peninsula and has two harbours, Västra Hamnen (West Harbour) and Östra Hamnen (East Harbour). The main ferry terminals are at Västra Hamnen but the more colourful local marina is at Östra Hamnen.

The **tourist office** *(☎ 24000; W www.info.aland.fi; Storagatan 8)*, on the main east–west Esplanade, has free Internet access, as does the **library**.

Things to See

The **Maritime Museum** *(☎ 19930; Västra Hamnen; adult/child €4.50/2.50; open 9am-5pm daily May-Aug, 9am-7pm daily July, 10am-4pm daily Sept-Apr)* is a kitsch museum of fishing and maritime commerce. Found outside is the museum ship ***Pommern*** *(adult/child €4.50/2.50)*, a beautifully preserved four-masted barque built in Glasgow in 1903. A combined ticket to both is €7/3.50.

The fine **Ålands Museum** and **Åland Art Museum** *(☎ 25426; Stadhusparken; adult/child €2.50/1.70; open 10am-4pm daily, 10am-8pm Tues year-round, closed Mon Sept-April)* are housed jointly. The museum gives an absorbing account of Åland's history and culture, from prehistory to the present.

There are trade and craft displays at the **Köpmannagar** *(Merchant's House; Parkgatan; admission free; open 1pm-3pm Mon-Fri June-Aug)*.

Places to Stay & Eat

Gröna Uddens Camping *(☎ 21121; Osternäsvägen; camp site €17.50; open mid-May–Aug)*, 1km south of town, is the closest camping to Mariehamn.

In the absence of any hostels, the next cheapest accommodation is the shabby **Gästhem Kronan** *(☎ 12617; Neptunigatan 52; singles/doubles June-Aug €37/55)*. Basic but cleanish rooms have a shared bathroom, and the owners also have another guesthouse up the road if Kronan is full.

Café Julius *(Torggatan 10)* opens early and has plenty of cheap sandwiches, pastries and snacks. **Kaffestugan Svarta Katten** *(Norragatan 15)* is a lovely spot to sample the local speciality, Åland pancakes, made with semolina and served with fruit and whipped cream.

On Esplanadgatan **Buffalo After Beach bar** is a chic little open-fronted bar and club popular with the younger crowd.

SUND

☎ 018 • pop 950

Åland's most striking attraction is the medieval **Kastelholm** *(adult/child €5/3.50; open daily June-Aug)* castle, in Sund 20km northeast of Mariehamn. You can visit only on a guided tour, which run frequently from June to August.

Farther east, the ruins of the Russian fortress at **Bomarsund** are accessible all year, as are the cemeteries on **Prästö Island**.

Located near Bomarsund is **Puttes Camping** *(☎ 44016; camp sites per person €2.50; open May-Aug)*, which also rents cabins.

On the Mariehamn–Sund road, near Godby is **Café Uffe på Berget**, which is popular for its view and 30m observation tower.

Tampere

☎ 03 • pop 198,000

Tampere is set between the Näsijärvi and Pyhäjärvi Lakes. Once known for its textile industry, dozens of red-brick chimneys from former factories point skyward in this 19th-century manufacturing centre; most have now been transformed into cultural centres, bars or restaurants. Known as the 'Manchester of Finland', Tampere combines working-class energy with Finnish sophistication.

Information

The **tourist office** *(☎ 3146 6800, fax 3146 6463; W www.tampere.fi; Verkatehtaankatu 2; open daily June–late Aug, Mon-Fri rest of year)* has two free Internet terminals.

There are also free Internet terminals at the **public library** *(☎ 314 614; Pirkankatu 2)*, and the **Vuoltsu Internet Café** *(Vuolteenkatu 13)*.

There's a **Forex** *(Hämeenkatu 1; open daily June-Aug, Mon-Sat Sept-May)*.

Things to See & Do

The tiny **Lenin Museum** *(☎ 276 8100, Hämeenpuisto 28; W www.tampere.fi/culture/lenin; adult/child €4/2; open 9am-6pm Mon-Fri, 11am-4pm Sat & Sun)* gives insight into the work of Russian revolutionary leader.

The **Sara Hildén Art Museum** *(☎ 214 3134; Särkänniemi; adult/child €4/1; open 11am-6pm daily)* concentrates on modern and Finnish art and sculpture. In the basement of the public library is **Moominvalley** *(☎ 3146 6578; Hámeenpuisto 20; adult/child €4/2)* exhibition, based on the children's books of Tove Jansson featuring original drawings from this cultural phenomenon.

Pyynikki Ridge, between Tampere's two lakes, is a forested area of walking trails with fine views on both side. There's an old stone **observation tower** *(open 9am-8pm daily; adult/child €1/0.50)* on the ridge, with a great café serving Tampere's best doughnuts.

Places to Stay & Eat

Tampere has two HI-affiliated hostels at opposite ends of town. **Hostel Tampere YWCA** *(☎ 254 4020, fax 254 4022; Tuomiokirkonkatu 12A; dorm beds €11-12.50, singles/doubles €28.50/39; open June-Aug)* is simple and clean, with kitchen and laundry facilities.

Hostel Uimahallin Maja *(☎ 222 9460, fax 222 9940; Pirkankatu 10-12; dorm beds*

€16.50; open year-round) has a slightly higher standard of room.

One of the best cafés in town is **Pikkupapu** on Tomiokirkonkatu, with espresso, cappuccino, great smoothies and crepes and sandwiches.

Both **Thai Non Khon** *(Hämeenkatu 29; lunch from €6)* and **Tây-Do** *(Hämeenkatu 22; lunch from €6)*, a tiny Vietnamese restaurant across the street, offer some good vegetarian dishes.

Café Europa *(☎ 223 5526; Aleksanterinkatu 29)* is the coolest bar in Tampere, but gets very crowded on weekends. Upstairs is a small dance club called **Attic** which opens at 10pm.

O'Connell's *(Rautatienkatu 24)*, an unpretentious Irish pub with a strong local following, is a good place to meet travellers, expats and locals.

Vanha Posti *(Hämeenkatu 13A)* is a perennial favourite with a good terrace. **Telakka** *(☎ 225 0700; Tullikamarinaukio 3)* is a bohemian bar-theatre-restaurant. There's live music here regularly, theatre performances and a brilliant summer terrace.

Getting There & Around

The **main bus station** *(Hatanpäänvaltatie 7)* is a block from the Koskikeskus shopping centre. Regular express buses run from Helsinki (€23.10, 2½ hours) and Turku (€16.80, two hours).

Express trains run hourly to/from Helsinki (€21.40, two hours). Intercity trains go on to Oulu (€50, five hours); there are direct trains to Turku, Pori, Jyväskylä, Vaasa and Joensuu.

You can cruise down to Hämeenlinna by lake ferry in summer. **Suomen Hopealinja** *(Finnish Silverline; ☎ 212 4804; W www.finnishsilverline.com)* operates cruises from Tampere's Laukontori quay daily (€37 one way, eight hours), and north to Virrat (€42, eight hours).

Bus services are extensive; a one-hour ticket costs €2. A 24-hour Traveller's Ticket is €4.

Oulu

☎ 08 • pop 123,300

Oulu is the largest city north of Tampere and is a lively, fast-growing university town. Technology companies have set up shop in recent years, giving Oulu an affluent, progressive air. The city was rebuilt after a fire in 1822; few old buildings remain. While Oulu lacks any 'must see' sights and suffers a dearth of budget accommodation, its summertime energy, cosmopolitan air and frenetic nightlife make it worth a stop on the road north.

The city **tourist office** *(☎ 5584 1330; W www.oulutourism.fi; open Mon-Sat mid-June–mid-Aug, Mon-Fri rest of year)* is at Torikatu 10.

The **public library** *(open daily)* has eight Internet terminals and a reading room. There are also two terminals at **Pint Netti Baari**, a pub on Rotuaari.

Oulu City Art Museum *(adult/child €3/1, Fri free; open Tues-Sun)* has some intriguing temporary international and Finnish exhibitions.

Visiting **Tietomaa** *(☎ 5584 1340; W www.tietomaa.fi; adult/child €10/8.50; open 10am-6pm daily, 10am-8pm July)*, Scandinavia's largest science museum, can occupy a full day, but it's essentially for kids.

Places to Stay & Eat

Nallikari Camping *(☎ 5586 1350; e nallikari.camping@ouka.fi; Hietasaari; camp sites per person/family €10/15.50, 2/4-bed camping cabins €29, cottages from €58; open year-round)* is Oulu's saviour for budget travellers, especially because it's close to the city centre on Hietasaari Island, 5km northwest of city centre.

Kesähotelli Oppimestari *(☎ 884 8527, fax 884 8772; Nahkatehtaankatu 3; singles/doubles €35/50; open June–early Aug)*, a summer hotel, has the cheapest rooms in Oulu.

Cheap snacks and local specialities can be found in the **kauppatori** and the **kauppahalli** on the southern side of the square.

There are plenty of cheap kebab and pizza places, including **Da Mario's Pizzeria** *(Torikatu 24; pizzas €6)* and **Ristorante Quattro Pizzeria** *(Asemakatu 20)* where you can get pizza, salad and a drink for €5.

Café Bisketti *(Kirkkokatu 8)*, has excellent rolls, croissants, quiche and cakes (€2.50 to €5), and a terrace facing the pedestrian square. Oulu hipsters sip green tea in the Nordic elegance of **Café Kaldi** *(Isokatu 25)*.

Entertainment

Kaarlenholvi Jumpru Pub *(Kauppurienkatu 6)* is an Oulu institution and a great place for meeting locals. It has an enclosed terrace and a warren of cosy rooms inside.

Calling all Airheads

Proving that Finns do indeed have a finely tuned sense of humour, the Air Guitar World Championships (part of the annual Oulu Music Video Festival in August) provide a unique venue for those promoting world peace by having a rockin' good time. The training camp leading up to it offers lectures such as 'How to Maintain Your Instrument'. If you want to compete but didn't win your country's contest, strut your stuff in the qualifying round held the day before. The champion takes home a (real) electric guitar and the adoration of thousands. Well, maybe hundreds. See the 'Festival Fever' special section for details on the competition.

Oluthuone Leskinen *(Saaristonkatu 15)* is where expats working for Nokia start (and often end) their night, so it's a good place to find out where to head next.

Rotuaari is the main pedestrian strip between the kauppatori and Isokatu and along here are plenty of bars and cafés, including **Oulon Panimo & Pub** *(Kauppurienkatu 13)*, a brewery pub with home-grown tap beers and good atmosphere.

On Hallituskatu is a small strip of bars and cafés, including **Never Grow Old**, a reggae bar that hits its stride after 10pm.

Café Milou *(Asemakatu 21)* is a hip bar, packing in students with its cheap beer and bookshelves filled with comics.

The **Giggling Marlin** *(Torikatu 21-22)* is one of a new brand of 'Suomi pop' clubs, featuring two dance floors with contemporary Finnish pop and international music.

Getting There & Away

Trains and buses connect Oulu with all main centres; the fastest direct train from Helsinki takes six hours (€53.40). Bus services include Rovaniemi (€26.70); Tornio (€19.20) and Kajaani (€20.90).

Eastern Finland

Eastern Finland is a romantic region of lakes, rivers, locks and canals, encompassing Karelia and the Savo region of which Savonlinna is the centre. This Lakeland area is a highlight of any trip to Finland and is definitely worth a visit.

LAPPEENRANTA

☎ 05 • pop 58,400

Lappeenranta was a frontier garrison town until the construction of the Saimaa Canal in 1856 made it an important trading centre. Despite the surrounding pulp factories it's one of the most attractive stops on Lake Saimaa, Finland's largest lake. The day cruise along the Saimaa Canal to Vyborg, is one of Lappeenranta's main attractions.

The **main tourist office** *(☎ 667 788; e matkailuoy@lappeenranta.fi; open Mon-Fri year-round)* is on the south side of the market square. A **summer tourist office** at the harbour is open daily from June to late August. The **public library** *(Valtakatu 47)* has free Internet terminals (book ahead), but **I@Café** *(Kauppakatu 63)* at €5 per hour is a better bet.

The day cruise along the Saimaa Canal to Vyborg is one of Lappeenranta's main attractions. The fortifications in **Linnoitus** (Fortress) were started by the Swedes and finished by the Russians in the 18th century. Some of the fortress buildings have been turned into mildly interesting **museums** *(combined ticket adult/student/child €5/4.20/3.40; all open 10am-6pm Mon-Fri, 11am-5pm Sat & Sun June–late Aug; 11am-5pm Tues, Thur, Sat & Sun Sept–late May)*.

Places to Stay & Eat

Huhtiniemi *(☎ 451 5555; w www.huhtiniemi.com; Kuusimäenkatu 18; open mid-May–September; tent & van sites €17.50, cottages for 2/4 people €30/41, apartments €34-74)* is a well-kept, slightly officious camping ground on the shores of Lake Saimaa, 2km west of the centre (bus No 6 runs past). Also here is the **Huhtiniemi Hostel** *(dorm beds €10; open June–mid-Aug)*, with six-bed dorms and the cheapest accommodation in town.

Karelia Park *(☎ 675 211, fax 452 8454; Korpraalinkuja 1; dorm beds €17.50, singles/doubles €40.50/45; open June–late Aug)*, 300m west of Huhtiniemi, is good value. Spotless two-bed rooms each have kitchen facilities and private bathroom.

At the **kauppatori** and the harbour you can try *vety* (meat pie or sandwich with ham, eggs and butter), a Karelian favourite.

Kahvila Majurska *(Kristiinankatu 7)*, in an 18th-century wooden building at the fortress complex, is one of the most charming cafés in Finland and serves up delicious home-made cakes and quiches.

Gram Marie *(☎ 451 2625; Kauppakatu 41; lunch buffet €7.20)* is a 5th-floor lunch restaurant specialising in Finnish food with an all-you-can-eat buffet.

In summer the **SS *Suvi-Saamai*** and the ***Prinsessa Armaada***, at the harbour, serve as busy beer terraces.

Kolme Lyhtyä *(Kauppakatu 21)*, across from Café Wolkoff, is a typical eastern Finland bar, and next door is **Birra** *(Kauppakatu 19)*, an ugly, modern bar where Lappeenranta's student population congregates.

Getting There & Away

Bus and train tickets can be booked at the central office of **Matkahuolto**. Regular bus services include: Helsinki (€26.70, four hours) and Savonlinna (€18.50, three hours via Parikkala).

There are frequent direct trains to/from Helsinki (€33, 2¾ hours), and to Savonlinna (€18.40, 2½ hours; change at Parikkala).

SAVONLINNA

☎ 015 • pop 27,600

Savonlinna grew up between lakes near Olavinlinna Castle in some of the prettiest of Finland's waterscapes.

The **tourist office** *(☎ 517 510; ⓔ savonlinna@touristservice-svl.fi; Puistokatu 1; open Mon-Fri year-round)* is a good place for opera festival information. The **public library** *(☎ 571 5100; Tottinkatu; open 11am-7pm Mon-Fri, 10am-2pm Sat)* has Internet terminals you can book in advance. **Café Knut Posse** *(Olavinkatu 44)*, adjacent to the bookshop of the same name, has one free terminal.

The best-preserved medieval castle in the northern countries is **Olavinlinna** *(☎ 531 164; adult/student & child €5/3.50; open 10am-5pm daily June-Aug, 10am-3pm daily Sept-May)*. It was used by both Swedish and Russian overlords, but is now known as the setting for the month-long Savonlinna Opera Festival. Excellent guided tours are given hourly.

Dozens of 1½-hour **scenic cruises** *(adults €7-10)* leave from the harbour at the kauppatori daily in summer.

Punkaharju, between Savonlinna and Parikkala, is the famous pine-covered sand ridge that is one of the most overrated attractions in Finland. However, the surrounding forest and lakes are beautiful and it's a great area for cycling or walking. Punkaharju can be reached from Savonlinna by train, bus or, in summer, a two-hour cruise (adult/child €7/3.50 one way) to Retretti jetty.

The weird underground art centre, **Retretti** *(☎ 775 2200; adult/senior/student/child €15/12/9/5; open 10am-5pm daily June & Aug, to 6pm July)*, in Punkaharju, has superb summer exhibitions.

The world's largest wooden church – built to seat 3300 – can be found at **Kerimäki**, about 23km east of Savonlinna.

Special Events

The Savonlinna Opera Festival *(☎ 476 750; ⓦ www.operafestival.fi; Olavinkatu 27, 57130 Savonlinna)*, held throughout July, is perhaps the most famous festival in Finland with an international cadre of performers. The setting, in the courtyard of Olavinlinna Castle, is breathtaking. Tickets cost from €37 to €95 (more for premieres), but can be picked up for as little as €20 on some nights. Book tickets over the Internet.

Places to Stay & Eat

Book accommodation well in advance during the opera festival – six months for hotels and several months for hostels. Prices rise by as much as 100% during this time.

During summer the **SS *Heinävesi*** *(☎ 533 120; cabins upper/lower deck per person €19/17)* offers two-person cabin accommodation after its last nightly cruise.

On the kauppatori, **Café Torppa** is a popular student-run kiosk for coffee and late night snacks.

Pizzeria Capero *(Olavinkatu 51; pizza & pasta €6-8)* is the best place in town for a quick pizza. It's open till 10pm.

Liekkilohi *(Flaming Salmon; fishy mains €7-8.50)* is a bright-red, covered pontoon anchored just off the kauppatori. Open till 2am during summer.

A good place for a drink is the brewery-pub **Huvila**, which has the best *sahti* (a high-alcohol sweet Finnish beer) in the country. **Olutravintola Sillansuu**, near the main bridge just off Olavinkatu, is an English-style pub with a vast range of international beers and whiskys.

Juanita *(Olavinkatu 44)* is the place to mix with young Savonlinnans – it's open, and usually jumping, till 4am.

Getting There & Away

Regular buses head to Helsinki (€35.40, 4½ hours), Joensuu (€18.50, two hours), Mikkeli

(€17, 1½ hours), Kuopio (€23.10, two hours) and Kerimäki (€4.20, 30 minutes).

There are trains from Helsinki (€42.20, five hours) via a change at Parikkala. For Kuopio, you need to take a bus to Pieksämäki and a train from there. The main train station is a long walk from the centre; get off at the kauppatori platform instead.

In summer the lake ferry **MS *Puijo*** travels to Kuopio on Monday, Wednesday and Friday at 9.30am (€60, 11½ hours), returning on Tuesday, Thursday and Saturday.

KUOPIO

☎ 017 • pop 87,300

Kuopio is a vibrant place in a beautiful location, surrounded by forest and lakes. Visit on a Tuesday or Friday and you can steam it up in the world's biggest smoke sauna.

The helpful tourist office, **Kuopio Travel Shop** *(☎ 182 585, fax 261 3538; W www.kuopioinfo.fi; Haapaniemenkatu 17; open Mon-Sat July, Mon-Fri Aug-June)* is behind the town hall on the north side of the market square.

In a land as flat as Finland, **Puijo Hill** is highly regarded. Take the lift to the top of the 75m-high **Puijo Tower** (€3).

Don't miss the chance to sweat in the world's largest **smoke sauna** *(Jätkänkämpällä; adult/child €10/5; open 5pm-10pm Tues & Fri year-round)*, near the Rauhalahti Hotel-Spa. This 60-person sauna is mixed and guests are given wraps to wear. If you really want to feel Finnish, bring a swimsuit for a dip in the lake afterwards.

Kuopio's main event is the **Dance Festival** *(☎ 282 1541; W www.kuopiodancefestival.fi)* in mid-June. Open-air classical and modern dances are performed and the town is abuzz.

Places to Stay & Eat

Camping Rauhalahti *(☎ 361 2244; Kiviniementie; tent sites per person/family €10/16, 2–4-person cabins €30-54; open mid-May–Sept)*, is found adjacent to the Rauhalahti spa complex.

The friendly **Hermannin Salit** *(☎ 364 4961, fax 364 4911; Hermanninaukiol 3A; dorm beds €13, singles/doubles €25.50/35)* is Kuopio's cheapest and most central hostel, 1.5km south of the market square.

At Vuorikatu 35, there's a small **guesthouse** *(☎ 580 0569; singles/doubles €36/56)*.

There are indoor and outdoor markets in the main square where you can try *kalakukko*, fish baked inside a rye loaf (eaten hot or cold). The 2nd-floor **Golden Rax Pizza & Pasta** *(Puijonkatu 45; buffet lunch & dinner €7)* serves the usual all-you-can-eat fare.

Burts Café *(☎ 262 3995; Puijonkatu 15)* is the best place in town for coffee and homemade cakes and pastries. **Café-Restaurant Helmi** *(Kauppakatu 2; pizzas €7-10)*, in an old stone building near the harbour, is an atmospheric bar and restaurant specialising in great pizzas. There's often live music in the courtyard at the side.

Most of Kuopio's nightlife is along Kauppakatu, running east from the market square to the harbour. **Wanha Satama** *(☎ 197 304)*, down at the harbour, is a lively pub with a sprawling terrace during summer, and occasional live music.

Henry's Pub *(Käsityökatu 17)* is one of the best in town with live rock Friday and Saturday nights. Around the corner, **Maxims** *(Kauppakatu)*, draws a younger late-night crowd, combining a music bar on two levels, with a club playing house and drum & bass.

Getting There & Away

Kuopio is easily reached by train or bus from Helsinki or Kajaani. The express bus station is north of the train station.

In summer, the lake ferry **MS *Puijo*** departs for Savonlinna on Tuesday, Thursday and Saturday at 9.30am (€60, 8½ hours), going via Heinävesi and Oravi. It returns from Savonlinna on Monday, Wednesday and Friday.

KOLI NATIONAL PARK

The views from the heights of Koli, overlooking Lake Pielinen, are excellent. In summer the park has scenic hiking routes, and there's a ferry service between Koli and Lieksa (less than two hours) or Joensuu (seven hours).

There's a regular bus service from Koli village up to the top of the hill, where the **Ukko-Koli Heritage Centre** *(☎ 688 8400)* has displays and information on the park.

Kolin Lomaranta *(☎ 040-729 5030; Merilänrannantie 15; camp sites €10, cabins €20-34; open June-Aug)* has camp sites and also 'out-buildings' for two to five people.

The family-run **Koli Hostel** *(☎ 673 131; dorm beds from €9.50; open year-round)*, 5km from the bus stop, has a kitchen, smoke sauna and beds. If you call ahead you may be able to arrange a pick-up.

KAJAANI

☎ 08 • pop 36,000

Kajaani is the centre of the Kainuu region, and although a pleasant enough riverside city, for travellers it's mainly a transport hub and stopover between the south and Lapland. The **tourist office** *(☎ 615 5555; Kauppakatu 21)* is just off the town square.

Retkeilymaja Huone ja Aamiainen *(☎/fax 622 254; Pohjolankatu 4; singles/doubles/triples €24.50/35.50/47.50)* has clean rooms that are the cheapest in town. Breakfast and linen is included, and reception opens at 4pm.

Kauppakatu, from the market square to the town square, is the main street and has many restaurants. **Pikantti** *(cnr Kauppakatu & Urho Kekkonenkatu)*, has excellent lunch buffets (€8.60) until 5pm weekdays. When it's warm, the outside chairs at the **Brahe Public house** *(cnr Kauppakatu & Linnankatu)*, in the cute cobbled town square, is Kajaani's best spot to sit with drink and watch the passing parade.

Trains from here connect with Kuopio, Nurmes and Oulu.

Lapland

Lapland is Finland's true wilderness and a place of extremes: continuous daylight in summer and continuous night in winter; and average daytime temperatures that range from -15°C in December to 15°C in June. If you dare brave the Arctic winter, October, February and March are ideal times to see the stunning aurora borealis.

September brings exceptional autumn colours and *kaamos* in the far north, the season of eerie bluish light, begins in late October.

Finnish Lapland is home to some 6500 Sami people, whose culture is best experienced in the villages of Hetta, Inari or Utsjoki.

TORNIO

☎ 016 • pop 23,200

The Swedish town of Haparanda across the Tornionjoki is Tornio's twin, and they're geographically, if not culturally, melded into one.

The **Green Line Centre** *(☎ 432 733; 🅦 www.tornio.fi/tuli/matkailu; open daily June–mid-Aug, Mon-Fri rest of year)* is the tourist office for both towns. There's free Internet access, and a few terminals are at the **public library.**

If midnight golf is your thing, you can tee off at, say, 12.30am and hit the ball into yesterday (ie, Sweden) at the **Green Zone golf course** *(☎ 431 711).*

Camping Tornio *(☎ 445 945; ⓔ sirkka.hyry@pp.inet.fi; Matkailijantie; camp sites €15, cabins €39-54)* is 3km from town on the road to Kemi. Pleasant **STF Youth Hostel** *(☎ 0046 611 71, fax 0046 61784; Strandgatan 26; open year-round)* is in Haparanda. Reception opens at 5pm.

From Kemi, take a bus from the train station. Road No 21 leads from Tornio to the north, and there are frequent buses to Rovaniemi.

ROVANIEMI

☎ 016 • pop 35,400

Rovaniemi is the capital of and gateway to Lapland. Many travellers make a beeline here from Helsinki, either to say they've visited Lapland or to 'cross' the Arctic Circle.

The town is quite modern and relatively uninteresting, built from a plan by Alvar Aalto after its complete destruction in WWII (the main streets radiate out from Hallituskatu in the shape of reindeer antlers). The official Arctic Circle marker and Santa Claus village is 8km away; tour buses thunder by all year.

Information

The tourist office, shamelessly named **Santa Claus Tourist Centre** *(☎ 346 270; 🅦 www.rovaniemi.fi; open daily June–late Aug, Mon-Fri rest of year)* is at Koskikatu 1.

The **post office** is at Koskikatu 9, and the **public library** *(Hallituskatu 9; open Mon-Sat)*, has several Internet terminals. There's an **Internet café** on Poromiehentie.

Things to See & Do

Arktikum *(☎ 317 840; 🅦 www.arktikum.fi; Pohjoisranta 4; adult/student/child €10/8.50/5; open 9am-8pm daily mid-June–mid-Aug, 10am-6pm daily early June–Sept, 10am-4pm daily Oct-Apr)*, with its beautifully designed glass tunnel, is one of the best museums in Finland. Included are displays on Arctic flora and fauna as well as the Sami and other people of Arctic Europe, Asia and North America.

The official **Arctic Circle marker** *(Napapiiri; bus No 8 or 11)* is 8km north of Rovaniemi, and is the site of the 'official' **Santa Claus Village**. The Santa Claus post office receives close to a million letters each year. As tacky as it sounds, it's all good fun. You can send a postcard home with an official Santa stamp (to be delivered at Christmas) and have your picture taken with St Nick.

Places to Stay & Eat

The facilities at **Tervashonka Hostel** *(☎ 344 644; Hallituskatu 16; dorm beds €11.50, singles/doubles €25.50/31; open year-round)* are not flash but the place has plenty of character. Reception is closed from 10am to 5pm, and closes again at 10pm (ring ahead if you're coming in on the night train).

Matkustajakoti Outa *(☎ 312 474; Ukkoherrantie 16; singles/doubles €30/40)* is a cheap no-frills guesthouse with shared bathrooms right in the town centre.

Koskikatu has plenty of inexpensive and mid-range restaurants, which include branches of **Rosso** and **Koti Pizza**. **Café Sandwich** is a good place for cheap takeaways with sandwiches for around €3. The world's northernmost **McDonald's** is also in town.

Mariza *(Ruokasenkatu 2; lunch buffet €5.90-6.50; open for lunch Mon-Fri)* is a simple working-class place offering sensational lunch buffet of home-cooked Finnish food.

In summer lie out under the midnight sun in the open beer terrace of **Oluthuone**.

Rovaniemen Panimo *(Koskikatu 11)* is a popular English-style pub with cosy seating, a small terrace and international beers on tap.

Taso Café & Bar *(Maakuntakatu)* is the trendiest place in Rovaniemi with loungy, lime-green retro furniture, magazines, a hip crowd and quality DJs on weekend evenings.

In the Sokos Hotel Vakuna, **Doris Nightclub** is open till 4am and attracts a slightly older crowd (over 22 only Friday and Saturday).

Getting There & Away

Frequent buses travel to Kemi (€14.60) and Oulu (€26.70) to the south; Muonio, Enontekiö and Kilpisjärvi in the northwest, Kuusamo in the east; and to Sodankylä (€16.80), Ivalo (€30.90) and Inari (€35.60) in the north, continuing on to Norway.

Train is the best way to travel between Helsinki and Rovaniemi (€69.20, 10 to 12 hours). There are daily trains (via Oulu). There's one train connection daily to Kemijärvi (1½ hours).

INARI

☎ 016 • pop 550

As unprepossessing as it seems at first, the village of Inari (Sami: Anár) is the most interesting point of civilisation in far northern Lapland. It's the main Sami community in the region, and a centre for Sami handicrafts – though the galleries and boutique shops have a commercial air, this is the best place to shop for genuine Lappish and Sami handmade textiles, jewellery, silverware and woodwork.

One of the finest conceptual and open-air museums in Finland, **Siida** *(☎ 665 212; W www.samimuseum.fi; adult/student & pensioner/child €7/6/3; open 9am-8pm daily June-Sept, 10am-5pm Tues-Sun Oct-May)* should not be missed. The exhibition successfully brings to life Sami origins, culture, lifestyle and present-day struggles.

There's a 7.5km walking track (starting from the Siida parking area) to the 18th-century **Pielpajärvi wilderness church**, with a nearby hut and sauna. Trekking in winter is not recommended; snow is more than a metre deep and, at the very least, snowshoes are needed.

Uruniemi Camping *(☎ 671 331, fax 671 200; tent sites €11, cottages doubles €17, 4 people €34-42; open Mar–late Sept)*, 2km south of town, is well equipped with cottages, café, sauna, and boats and bikes for hire.

The nearest youth hostel is the HI-affiliated **Hostel Jokitörmä** *(☎ 672 725, fax 672 745; tent sites €12.60, dorm beds €13.20, cabins singles/doubles €16/25.30; open year-round)*, 23km north of Inari. It's a great place with cosy two and four person rooms, and a separate set of cottages – all buses will stop here on request.

Hotel Inari *(☎ 671 026; singles/doubles €33.50/38)* has decent rooms with private bathroom.

Gold Line buses run daily to/from Ivalo with connections south to Rovaniemi.

France

France is the *quoi* in *'je ne sais quoi'*. Sure, it has its share of coiffed, caffeinated croissant-munchers with arrogant sneers at the ready. But it also has its share of warm-hearted souls who are more than willing to debunk national stereotypes with their hospitality and generosity. Endearing, delicious, beautiful, diverse and occasionally maddening, France will test your patience and capture your heart.

The largest country in Western Europe, France stretches from the rolling hills of the north to the seemingly endless beaches of the south; from the wild coastline of Brittany to the icy crags of the Alps, with cliff-lined canyons, dense forest and vineyards in between. Over the centuries, it has received more immigrants than any other country in Europe. From the ancient Celtic Gauls and Romans to the more recent arrivals from France's former colonies in Indochina and Africa, these peoples have introduced their own culture, cuisine and art to an increasingly delightful mix of traditions.

Once the western boundary of Europe, today France stands firmly at the crossroads: between England and Italy, Belgium and Spain, North Africa and Scandinavia. Of course, this is exactly how the French have always regarded their country – at the very centre of things.

France: the Basics

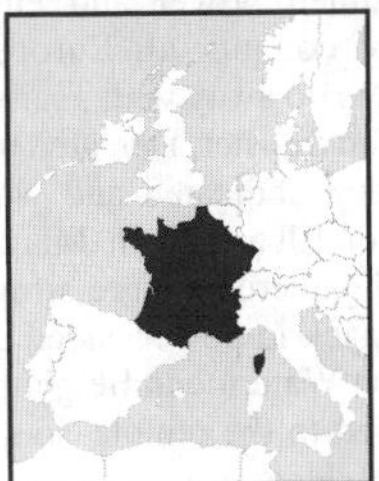

Capital Paris

Population 60.2 million

Language French

Currency euro (€) = 100 centimes

Avoid at all costs Calling your waiter *garçon*

Vent your inevitable frustration by asking *Avez-vous jamais entendu parler du concept de service des clients?* (Have you ever heard of something called 'customer service'?)

Facts about France

HISTORY

The Celtic Gauls moved into what is now France between 1500 and 500 BC. Julius Caesar's Roman legions took control of the territory around 52 BC, and France remained under Roman rule until the 5th century. Two Frankish dynasties ruled from the 5th to the 10th centuries. Charlemagne extended the boundaries of the kingdom and was crowned Holy Roman Emperor in AD 800.

Under William the Conqueror (the Duke of Normandy), Norman forces occupied England, making Normandy a formidable rival of the kingdom of France. In 1420, the English took control of Paris, and two years later Henry IV of England became king of France. But a 17-year-old peasant girl, Jeanne d'Arc (Joan of Arc) rallied the French troops. She was burned at the stake two years later, but her efforts helped to turn the war in favour of the French.

The ideals and aesthetics of the Italian Renaissance were introduced in the 15th century. By the 1530s the Protestant Reformation had been strengthened in France by the ideas of the Frenchman John Calvin, an exile in Geneva. Interdenominational fighting brought the French state close to disintegration. In 1598, Henry of Navarre promulgated the Edict of Nantes, which guaranteed the Huguenots (French Catholics) many civil and political rights.

Louis XIV – also known as Le Roi Soleil (the Sun King) – sought to extend the power of the French monarchy. He was succeeded by Louis XV and then the incompetent Louis XVI. The Seven Years' War (1756–63), fought by France and Austria against Britain and Prussia, was pursued by Louis XV and culminated in the loss of France's colonies in Canada, the West Indies and India to the British.

By the late 1780s, Louis XVI and his queen, Marie Antoinette, had managed to alienate virtually every segment of society. On 14 July 1789, a Parisian mob stormed the Bastille prison. The Revolution began in the hands of the moderate, republican Girondists (Girondins in French), but they soon lost power to the radical Jacobins, led by Robespierre, Danton and Marat. In January 1793, Louis was guillotined; two months later the Jacobins set up the notorious Committee of

Public Safety, which had near-dictatorial control during the Reign of Terror (September 1793 to July 1794).

In 1799, a successful general named Napoleon Bonaparte assumed power and embarked on a quest to conquer all Europe. However, his attempt to do away with Tsarist Russia in 1812 met with disaster. Defeated by allied forces, Napoleon abdicated and was exiled to the island of Elba. But in March 1815, he escaped and gathered a large army. His 'Hundred Days' back in power ended in defeat by the English at Waterloo in Belgium. Napoleon was banished to the remote South Atlantic island of St Helena.

After a chaotic restoration of the Bourbon monarchy and numerous revolutions, Napoleon's undistinguished nephew Louis-Napoleon Bonaparte led a coup d'etat in 1851, after which he was proclaimed Napoleon III, Emperor of the French. But in 1870, the Prussian prime minister Bismarck goaded Napoleon III into declaring war on Prussia and suffering prompt defeat. The emperor was deposed and the Third Republic proclaimed.

Central to France's entry into WWI was the desire to regain Alsace and Lorraine, lost to Germany in 1871. This was achieved but at immense human cost: of the eight million French men who were called to arms, 1.3 million were killed and almost one million crippled. In WWII, France capitulated to Germany by June of 1940, giving rise to the collaborationist Vichy regime.

General Charles de Gaulle, France's undersecretary of war, fled to London and set up a

French government-in-exile. The liberation of France began with the US, British and Canadian landings in Normandy on D-Day (6 June 1944). De Gaulle returned to Paris and set up a provisional government. The Fourth and then Fifth Republics were born.

In 1995, the smooth, irksome Jacques Chirac was elected president. Seven years later, French voters boxed themselves into a corner by setting up National Front right-winger Jean-Marie Le Pen as the only alternative to Chirac, resulting in an overwhelming victory for the not-terribly-popular conservative.

GEOGRAPHY

France (551,000 sq km) is the largest European country after Russia and Ukraine. It's shaped like a hexagon bordered by either mountains or water, except for the relatively flat, northeast frontier that abuts Germany, Luxembourg and Belgium.

CLIMATE

France has a temperate climate with mild winters, except in mountainous areas and Alsace. The Atlantic impacts on the northwest, bringing high humidity, rain and persistent westerly winds. A pleasant Mediterranean climate extends from the southern coast as far inland as the southern Alps, the Massif Central and the eastern Pyrenees.

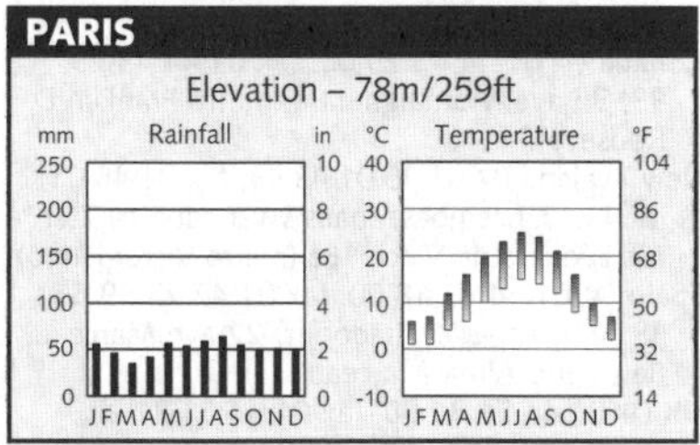

GOVERNMENT & POLITICS

France is led by a powerful president; the legislative body is the National Assembly.

France is a member of the European Union and one of the five permanent members of the UN Security Council. It withdrew from NATO's joint military command in 1966.

POPULATION & PEOPLE

During the last 150 years France has received more immigrants than any other European country. Today, France has around five million foreign-born residents. In recent years, there has been a racist backlash against France's nonwhite immigrant communities.

SOCIETY & CONDUCT

Never address a waiter or bartender as *garçon* (boy) – *s'il vous plaît* is the way it's done nowadays; avoid discussing money; keep off the manicured French lawns; resist handling produce in markets; and always address people as *Monsieur* (Mr/sir), *Madame* (Mrs/madam) and *Mademoiselle* (Miss).

Finally, when you go out for the evening, follow the local custom of dressing relatively well, particularly in a restaurant.

LANGUAGE

In France it tends to be assumed that all decent human beings speak French. Your best bet is always to approach people politely in French, even if the only words you know are *'Pardon, Monsieur/Madame/Mademoiselle, parlez-vous anglais?'* ('Excuse me sir/madam/miss, do you speak English?').

See the Language chapter at the back of this book for pronunciation guidelines and useful words and phrases.

Facts for the Visitor

HIGHLIGHTS

Many of the country's most exceptional museums are in Paris. Besides the rather overwhelming Louvre, Parisian museums not to be missed include the Musée d'Orsay (late-19th and early-20th-century art), the Pompidou Centre (modern and contemporary art), the Musée Rodin (sculpture), and the Musée National du Moyen Age (Museum of the Middle Ages) at the Hôtel de Cluny. Other French cities known for their museums include Nice, Bordeaux, Strasbourg and Lyon.

The royal palace at Versailles is the largest and most grandiose of the hundreds of chateaux throughout the country. Many impressive ones, including Chambord, Cheverny, Chenonceau and Azay-le-Rideau, are in the Loire Valley around Blois and Tours. The cathedrals at Chartres, Strasbourg and Rouen are among the most beautiful in France.

The Côte d'Azur – the French Riviera – has some of the best-known beaches in the world, but you'll also find lovely beaches farther west on the Mediterranean.

PLANNING

France is at its best in spring, though wintry relapses aren't uncommon in April and the beach resorts only begin to pick up in mid-May. Autumn is pleasant, too, but by late October it's a bit cool for sunbathing. Winter is great for snow sports in the Alps and Pyrenees, but Christmas, New Year and the February/March school holidays create surges in tourism. Paris always has all sorts of cultural activities during its rather wet winter.

In summer, the weather is warm and even hot, especially in the south, and the beaches, resorts and camping grounds get packed to the gills. Also, millions of French people take their annual month-long holiday *(congé)* in August – avoid travelling in France during this month if you can.

TOURIST OFFICES

Local Tourist Offices

Every city, town, village and hamlet seems to have either an *office de tourisme* or a *syndicat d'initiative*. Both are excellent resources. Many tourist offices will make local hotel reservations, usually for a small fee.

Tourist Offices Abroad

The French Government Tourist Offices in the following countries can provide brochures and tourist information.

Australia (☎ 02-9231 5244, fax 9221 8682, ⓔ france@bigpond.net.au) 25 Bligh St, 22nd floor, Sydney, NSW 2000

Canada (☎ 514-876 9881, fax 845 48 68, ⓔ mfrance@attcanada.net) 1981 McGill College Ave, Suite 490, Montreal, Que H3A 2W9

UK (☎ 090-6824 4123, fax 020-7493 6594, ⓔ info@mdlf.co.uk) 178 Piccadilly, London W1J 9AL

USA (☎ 212-838 7800, fax 838 7855, ⓔ info@francetourism.com) 444 Madison Ave, New York, NY 10020

VISAS & DOCUMENTS

Citizens of the USA, Canada, Australia and New Zealand and most European countries can enter France for up to three months without a visa. South Africans must have a visa.

If you're not an EU citizen, it's extremely difficult to get a work visa; one of the few exceptions allows holders of student visas to work part-time. Begin the paperwork several months before you leave home.

By law, everyone in France, including tourists, must carry identification with them.

EMBASSIES & CONSULATES

French Embassies & Consulates

French embassies abroad include:

Australia (☎ 02-6216 0100, fax 6216 0127, ⓔ embassy@ambafrance-au.org) 6 Perth Ave, Yarralumla, ACT 2600

Canada (☎ 613-789 1795, fax 562 3704, ⓔ consulat@amba-ottowa.fr) 42 Sussex Dr, Ottawa, Ont K1M 2C9

Germany (☎ 030-206 39000, fax 206 39010, ⓔ consulat.berlin@diplomatie.gouv.fr) Pariser Platz 5, 10117 Berlin

Italy (☎ 06-686 011, fax 860 1360, ⓔ france-italia@france-italia.it) Piazza Farnese 67, 00186 Rome

New Zealand (☎ 04-384 2555, fax 384 2577, ⓔ consulfrance@actrix.gen.nz) Rural Bank Building, 34–42 Manners Street, Wellington

Spain (☎ 91-423 8900, fax 423 8901) Calle de Salustiano Olozaga 9, 28001 Madrid

UK (☎ 020-7073 1000, visa inquiries: ☎ 0891-887 733, fax 7073 1004, ⓔ info-londres@diplomatie.gouv.fr) 58 Knightsbridge, London SW1X 7JT.

USA (☎ 202-944 6060, fax 944 6040, ⓔ info-washington@diplomatie.gouv.fr) 4101 Reservoir Rd, NW Washington, DC 20007

Embassies & Consulates in France

Countries with embassies in Paris include:

Australia (☎ 01 40 59 33 00, fax 01 40 59 33 10, ⓔ information.paris@dfat.gov.au) 4 rue Jean Rey, 15e (metro Bir Hakeim)

Canada (☎ 01 44 43 29 00, fax 01 44 43 29 99) 35 ave Montaigne, 8e (metro Franklin D Roosevelt)

New Zealand (☎ 01 45 01 43 43, fax 01 45 01 43 44, ⓔ nzembassy.paris@wanadoo.fr) 7ter rue Léonard de Vinci, 16e (metro Victor Hugo)

Spain (☎ 01 44 43 18 00, fax 01 47 23 59 55, ⓔ emba.espa@wanadoo.fr) 22 ave Marceau, 8e (metro Alma-Marceau)

UK (☎ 01 44 51 31 00, fax 01 44 51 31 27, ⓔ ambassade@amb-grandebretagne.fr) 35 rue du Faubourg St Honoré, 8e (metro Concorde)

USA (☎ 01 43 12 22 22, fax 01 42 66 97 83, ⓔ citizeninfo@state.gov) 2 rue St Florentin, 1er (metro Concorde)

MONEY

France's currency is the euro. Generally you'll get a better exchange rate for travellers cheques than for cash (see Money in the Facts for the Visitor chapter for more information on exchange rates). Visa (Carte Bleue in France) is more widely accepted than MasterCard

(Eurocard). American Express cards aren't very useful, except to get cash at American Express offices in big cities.

Many post offices make exchange transactions at a very good rate and accept American Express travellers cheques; there's 2.5% commission on cash and 1.5% commission on US-dollar travellers cheques. Commercial banks usually charge a stiff €3 to €5 per foreign currency transaction. In larger cities, exchange bureaus are faster, easier, open longer hours and often give better rates than the banks.

If you stay in hostels, buy provisions from grocery stores and don't travel much, it's possible to survive in France for US$30 a day (US$35 in Paris). A frugal – but less miserable – budget is more like US$55 a day.

It's not necessary to leave a *pourboire* (tip) in restaurants or hotels. However, it's usual to leave €0.50 or €1 for a casual meal, about €1 per person for a more formal meal and about 10% of the bill in a truly posh restaurant. For a taxi ride, the usual tip is about €1 no matter what the fare.

France's sales tax is 19.6% on most goods. Prices that include TVA are often marked TTC *(toutes taxes comprises)*, which means 'all taxes included'. It's possible (although rather complicated) to get a reimbursement for TVA if you meet several conditions.

POST & COMMUNICATIONS

La Poste, the French postal service, is fast, reliable and expensive. Mail to France *must* include the area's five-digit postcode. In Paris, all postcodes begin with 750 and end with the *arrondissement* number, eg, 75004 for the 4th *arrondissement*, 75013 for the 13th etc.

If not addressed to a particular branch, poste restante mail ends up at the town's *recette principale* (main post office). In Paris, this means the **central post office** *(☎ 01 40 28 20 00; 52 rue du Louvre, 1er; metro Sentier or Les Halles)*. There's a €0.46 charge for every poste restante claimed. You can also receive mail care of American Express offices, although if you don't have an American Express card or travellers cheques there's a €0.76 charge each time you check.

Almost all public phones now require *télécartes* (phonecards), which are sold at post offices, *tabacs* (tobacco shops), Paris metro ticket counters and supermarket check-out counters. All telephone cabins can take incoming calls; give the caller the 10-digit number written after the words *'ici le'* on the information sheet next to the phone.

France has five telephone zones and all telephone numbers comprise 10 digits. Paris and Île de France numbers begin with ☎ 01. The other codes are ☎ 02 for the northwest, ☎ 03 for the northeast, ☎ 04 for the southeast (including Corsica) and ☎ 05 for the southwest. Numbers beginning with ☎ 0800 are free. For directory assistance, dial ☎ 12.

The international country code for France is ☎ 33. When dialling from abroad, omit the initial '0' at the beginning of 10-digit phone numbers. To place a direct call, dial ☎ 00 and then the country code, area code and local number.

Email can be sent and received at Internet cafés throughout France. La Poste has set up Internet centres at many post offices around France; a €7 Cybercarte gives you an hour's access, and each €4.50 'recharge' is good for another hour. Commercial Internet cafés charge about €3 for a half-hour's surfing.

DIGITAL RESOURCES

Useful websites in English include the Paris Tourist Office (W www.paris-touristoffice.com), the USA's French Government Tourist Office (W www.francetourism.com) and GuideWeb (W www.guideweb.com), which has information about selected regions in France. Many towns have their own websites.

BOOKS

Lonely Planet's *France* guide has comprehensive coverage of France and includes chapters on Andorra and Monaco. *Paris Condensed* is a pocket companion with short visits in mind. Regional guides include *Provence & the Côte d'Azur*, *The Loire*, *Southwest France*, *Brittany*, *Normandy* and *Corsica*. The *French phrasebook* is a complete guide to *la langue française*.

Paul Rambali's *French Blues* is a series of uncompromising yet sympathetic snapshots of modern France.

WOMEN TRAVELLERS

If you're subject to catcalls or hassled on the street, the best strategy is usually to walk on and ignore the comment. France's national rape crisis hotline, which is run by women's organisation **Viols Femmes Informations** *(☎ 0800 05 95 95; staffed 10am-7pm Mon-Fri)*, can be reached toll-free.

GAY & LESBIAN TRAVELLERS

Centre Gai et Lesbien *(CGL; ☎ 01 43 57 21 47; 3 rue Keller, 11e; metro Ledru Rollin; open 4pm-8pm daily)*, 500m east of place de la Bastille, is headquarters for numerous organisations. Paris' Gay Pride parade is held on the last weekend in June. Gay publications include the monthlies *3 Keller* and *Action*, and the newsstand magazine *Têtu*. The monthly *Lesbia* gives a rundown of what's happening around the country.

A good online resource is the **Queer Resources Directory** *(W www.france.qrd.org)*.

DISABLED TRAVELLERS

France isn't well equipped for *handicapés*. Details of train travel for wheelchair users are available in the French rail company SNCF's booklet *Guide du Voyageur à Mobilité Réduite*. You can also contact **SNCF Accessibilité** *(☎ 0800 15 47 53)*.

Hostels in Paris that cater to disabled travellers include the Foyer International d'Accueil de Paris Jean Monnet and the Centre International de Séjour de Paris Kellermann.

DANGERS & ANNOYANCES

The biggest crime problem for tourists in France is theft – especially of and from cars. Pickpockets are a problem, and women are a common target because of their handbags.

France's laws regarding even small quantities of drugs are very strict, and the police have the right to search anyone at any time.

The rise in support for the extreme rightwing Front National in recent years reflects growing racial intolerance in France.

BUSINESS HOURS

Most museums are closed on either Monday or Tuesday and public holidays; in summer some open daily. Most small businesses open 9am or 10am to 6.30pm or 7pm daily, except Sunday and perhaps Monday, with a break between noon and 2pm or between 1pm and 3pm.

Banks may only change money and travellers cheques in the morning (usually 8.45am to 12.15pm).

Emergencies

Call the following numbers for emergency services assistance: ambulance ☎ 15, fire ☎ 18, police ☎ 17.

PUBLIC HOLIDAYS & SPECIAL EVENTS

National *jours fériés* (public holidays) in France include New Year's Day, Easter Sunday and Monday, May Day (1 May), 1945 Victory Day (8 May), Ascension Thursday, Pentecost/Whit Sunday and Whit Monday, Bastille Day (14 July), Assumption Day (15 August), All Saints' Day (1 November), 1918 Armistice Day (11 November) and Christmas Day.

Some of the biggest and best events in France include: the Festival d'Avignon (early July to early August); Bastille Day celebrations, spread over 13 and 14 July; Francofolies, a six-day dance and music festival held in mid-July in La Rochelle; the Festival Interceltique, a 10-day Celtic festival in early August held in the Breton town of Lorient; Lyon's Biennale de la Danse/d'Art Contemporain is a month-long festival (from mid-September), which is held in even-numbered years; the Carnaval de Nice, held in Nice every spring around Mardi Gras (Shrove Tuesday); and the Nice Jazz Festival in July.

ACTIVITIES

The French Alps have some of the finest (and priciest) skiing in Europe, but there are cheaper, low-altitude ski stations in the Pyrenees; see W www.skifrance.fr.

France has thousands of kilometres of hiking trails. Many paths are run by **Fédération Française de Randonnée Pédestre** *(FFRP; ☎ 01 44 89 93 93, fax 01 40 35 85 67; e info@ffrp.asso.fr)*, which also publishes route guides.

The **Fédération Française de Canoë-Kayak** *(☎ 01 45 11 08 50; e ffck@ffcanoe.asso.fr; 87 quai de la Marne, 94344 Joinville-le-Pont)* can supply information on canoeing and kayaking clubs around the country.

The French take their cycling very seriously, and whole parts of the country almost grind to a halt during the annual Tour de France. Lonely Planet's *Cycling in France* is an essential resource when touring.

WORK

All EU citizens are allowed to work in France. For anyone else it's almost impossible. Working as an au pair is very common in France, especially in Paris. Single young people – particularly women – receive board, lodging and a bit of money in exchange for taking care of the kids. Knowing some French may be a prerequisite. For placements, contact a French consulate or private agencies such as **Agence Nurse Au Pair Placement** *(NAPP; ☎ 01 45 00 33 88, fax 01 45 00 33 99; W www.napp.fr; 16 rue Le Sueur, Paris 75016)*.

ACCOMMODATION

Camping

France has thousands of seasonal and year-round camping grounds. Facilities and amenities, reflected in the number of stars the site has been awarded, determine the price. At the less fancy places, two people with a small tent pay €10 to €15 a night.

Refuges (mountain huts or shelters) are basic dorms operated by national park authorities, the Club Alpin Français and other private organisations. They are marked on hiking and climbing maps. Some open year-round. In general, *refuges* have mattresses and blankets but not sheets. Charges average €10 to €16 per night (more in popular areas), and meals are sometimes available. It's a good idea to call ahead and make a reservation. *Gîtes d'étape*, which are usually better equipped and more comfortable than *refuges*, are found in less remote areas, often in villages. They cost around €9 to €11 per person.

A *chambre d'hôte*, basically a B&B (bed and breakfast), is a room in a private house rented to travellers by the night. Breakfast is included.

Hostels

In the provinces, *auberges de jeunesse* (hostels) generally charge €9 to €12 for a bunk in a single-sex dorm. In Paris and the Côte d'Azur, expect to pay €15 to €20 a night, including breakfast. In the cities, especially Paris, you'll also find *foyers*, student dorms used by travellers in summer. Most of France's hostels belong to one of three Paris-based organisations:

Fédération Unie des Auberges de Jeunesse (FUAJ; ☎ 01 44 89 87 27, fax 01 44 89 87 10, W www.fuaj.org) 27 rue Pajol, 18e, 75018 Paris (metro La Chapelle)

Ligue Française pour les Auberges de la Jeunesse (LFAJ; ☎ 01 44 16 78 78, fax 01 44 16 78 80) 67 rue Vergniaud, 75013 Paris (metro Glacière)

Union des Centres de Rencontres Internationales de France (UCRIF; ☎ 01 40 26 57 64, fax 01 40 26 58 20, W www.ucrif.asso.fr) 27 rue de Turbigo, 2e, 75002 Paris (metro Étienne Marcel)

Only FUAJ is affiliated with the Hostelling International (HI) organisation. HI membership in France for under-26s costs €10.70 and €15.25 for those older than 26.

Hotels

For two people sharing a room, budget hotels are often cheaper than hostels. Doubles tend to cost only marginally more than singles; most hotles have only one bed *(un grand lit)*. Doubles with two beds usually cost a little more. A hall *douche* (shower) can be free or cost between €2 and €3. If you'll be arriving after noon (after 10am at peak times), it's wise to book ahead, though if you call on the day of your arrival, many will hold a room for you until a set hour. Local tourist offices also make reservations, usually for a small fee. Check whether your hotel is part of the Bon Weekend en Ville scheme whereby one night's stay at the weekend gives you a second night free.

The prices listed in this chapter are high-season prices (usually June to August, except in ski areas); discounts of 30% to 50% are possible at other times of year.

FOOD & DRINKS

A fully-fledged traditional French dinner – usually begun about 8.30pm – has quite a few distinct courses: an *apéritif* or cocktail; an *entrée* (first course); the *plat principal* (main course); *salade* (salad); *fromage* (cheese); *dessert*; *fruit* (fruit; pronounced fwee); *café* (coffee); and a *digestif* (liqueur). Most restaurants offer at least one multi-course meal known in French as a *menu*. In general, *menus* cost much less than ordering *à la carte*. Restaurants usually specialise in a particular cuisine while brasseries – which look very much like cafés – serve quicker meals of more standard fare. Sitting in a café to read, write or talk with friends is an integral part of everyday life in France.

Tap water in France is perfectly safe. Make sure you ask for *une carafe d'eau* (a jug of water) or *de l'eau du robinet* (tap water) or you may get costly *eau de source* (mineral water). The French almost always take their meals with wine – *rouge* (red), *blanc* (white) or *rosé*. The least expensive wines cost less per litre than soft drinks.

Alcoholic drinks other than wine include *apéritifs*, such as *kir* (dry white wine sweetened with *cassis* – blackcurrant liqueur), *kir royale* (champagne with *cassis*) and *pastis* (anise-flavoured alcohol drunk with ice and water); and *digestifs* such as brandy or Calvados (apple brandy). A *demi* of beer (about 250ml) is cheaper *à la pression* (on draught) than from a bottle.

Getting There & Away

AIR

Air France and scores of other airlines link Paris with every section of the globe. Other French cities with international air links (mainly to places within Europe) include Bordeaux, Lyon, Marseille, Nice, Strasbourg and Toulouse. For information on Paris' two international airports, Orly and Roissy-Charles de Gaulle, see Getting There & Away in the Paris section later.

In France, inexpensive flights offered by discount airlines and charter clearing houses can be booked through many regular travel agents – look in agency windows and pamphlets advertising **Go Voyages** *(☎ 01 53 40 44 29; Ⓦ www.govoyages.com)* or **Look Voyages** *(☎ 01 55 49 49 60, 0825 82 38 23; Ⓦ www.look-voyages.fr)*. Reliable travel agency chains include the French student travel company **OTU** *(☎ 0820 81 78 17; Ⓦ www.otu.fr)* and **Nouvelles Frontières** *(☎ 0825 00 08 25; Ⓦ www.nouvelles-frontieres.fr)*.

LAND

Britain

The highly civilised **Eurostar** *(UK: ☎ 0870 518 6186 • France: ☎ 0892 35 35 39; Ⓦ www.eurostar.com)* links London's Waterloo Station with Paris' Gare du Nord via the Channel Tunnel, which passes through a layer of chalk marl 25m to 45m below the floor of the English Channel. The journey takes about three hours (including 20 minutes in the tunnel), not including the one-hour time change. Tickets for people aged 25 and under cost UK£40/69 one way/return; return fares booked 14/seven days ahead cost UK£79/95.

Discount return fares start around UK£60. Student travel agencies often have youth fares not available direct from Eurostar.

Eurotunnel shuttle trains *(UK: ☎ 0870 535 3535; • France: ☎ 03 21 00 61 00; Ⓦ www.eurotunnel.com)* whisk buses and cars (and their passengers) from near Folkestone to Coquelles (just west of Calais) in 35 minutes. The regular one-way fare for a car and its passengers ranges from UK£147.50 (February and March) to UK£162.50 (July and August). For promotional fares you must book at least one day ahead.

Elsewhere in Europe

Bus For details on **Eurolines coach services** *(France: ☎ 0836 69 52 52; Ⓦ www.eurolines.fr)* linking France with other European countries, see Getting There & Away in the Paris section.

Train Paris, France's main rail hub, is linked with every part of Europe. Depending on where you're coming from, you sometimes have to change train stations in Paris to reach the provinces. For details on Paris' six train stations, see Getting There & Away in the Paris section later.

People aged 25 or under are eligible for at least 20% discounts on most international 2nd-class rail travel; on some routes discounts are limited to night trains. On the super-fast *Thalys* trains, which link Paris with Brussels, Amsterdam and Cologne, seniors also get significant discounts.

SEA

Ferry tickets are available from almost all travel agents.

Britain & the Channel Islands

Hoverspeed *(UK ☎ 0870 240 8070 • France ☎ 0800 1211 1211; Ⓦ www.hoverspeed.co.uk)* runs giant catamarans (SeaCats) from Folkestone to Boulogne (55 minutes, 17 daily). Foot passengers are charged UK£24 one way (or return if you come back within five days). Depending on the season, a car with up to five passengers is charged UK£115 to UK£189 one way.

The Dover–Calais crossing is also handled by car ferries (one to 1½ hours, 15 daily) run by **SeaFrance** *(UK: ☎ 0870 571 1711 • France: ☎ 0803 04 40 45; Ⓦ www.seafrance.com)* and **P&O Stena** *(UK: ☎ 0870 600 0611 • France: ☎ 0802 01 00 20; Ⓦ www.posl.com)*. Pedestrians pay UK£17/26 with SeaFrance/P&O Stena; cars are charged UK£130 to UK£170 one way.

If you're travelling to Normandy, Hoverspeed's SeaCats (2¼ hours, one to three daily) handle the Newhaven–Dieppe route. Poole is linked to Cherbourg by **Brittany Ferries** *(UK: ☎ 0870 536 0360 • France: ☎ 0825 82 88 28; Ⓦ www.brittany-ferries.com)*, which has one or two 4¼-hour crossings daily; the company also has ferries from Portsmouth to Caen (Ouistreham). On the Portsmouth–Cherbourg route, **P&O Portsmouth** *(UK: ☎ 0870 598 0555 • France: ☎ 0803 01 30 13; Ⓦ www.poportsmouth.com)* has two car ferries daily and, from mid-March to mid-October (UK£117 with car), two faster catamarans daily; the company also links Portsmouth with Le Havre.

If you're going to Brittany, Brittany Ferries links Plymouth with Roscoff (six hours, one to three daily) from mid-March to mid-November; the company also has services from Portsmouth to Saint Malo (8¾ hours). For information on ferries from Saint Malo to Weymouth, Portsmouth and the Channel Islands, see Getting There & Away in the Saint Malo (Brittany) section later.

Ireland

Irish Ferries *(Ireland: ☎ 1890 31 31 31 • Cherbourg: ☎ 02 33 23 44 44; Ⓦ www.irishferries.com)* has overnight runs from Rosslare to either Cherbourg (19½ hours) or Roscoff (17 hours) between six and 13 times a month. Pedestrians pay €60 to €120 (€48 to €96 for students and seniors). Eurailpass holders are charged 50% of the adult pedestrian fare.

Italy

For details on ferries from Italy, see the Corsica section.

North Africa

France's **SNCM** *(☎ 0836 67 21 00; Ⓦ www.sncm.fr)* and the **Compagnie Tunisienne de Navigation** *(CTN; Tunis: ☎ 01-341 777 • Marseille: ☎ 04 91 91 55 71)* link Marseille with Tunis (about 24 hours, three or four a week). The standard adult fare is TD196/356 one way/return.

Sète, 29km southwest of Montpellier, is linked with the Moroccan port of Tangier (Tanger; 36 hours, five to seven a month) by the **Compagnie Marocaine de Navigation** *(Marseille: ☎ 04 91 56 40 88 • Tangier: ☎ 09-94 40 57; Ⓦ www.comanav.co.ma)*. The cheapest one-way berth costs Dh1940. Discounts are available if you're under 26 or in a group of four or more.

Getting Around

BUS

The country has only very limited intercity bus service. However, buses (some run by the SNCF, see the following Train section) are widely used for short distances, especially in rural areas with relatively few train lines (eg, Brittany and Normandy).

TRAIN

Eurail and Inter-Rail passes are valid in France.

France's excellent rail network, operated by the **Société Nationale des Chemins de Fer Français** *(SNCF; Ⓦ www.sncf.com)* reaches almost every part of the country. The most important train lines fan out from Paris like the spokes of a wheel. The SNCF's nationwide telephone number for inquiries and reservations (☎ 0836 35 35 39 in English) costs €0.34 a minute.

The pride and joy of the SNCF is the high-speed TGV network. The TGV Sud-Est and TGV Midi-Mediterranée link Paris' Gare de Lyon with the southeast, including Dijon, Lyon, the Alps, Avignon, Marseille, Nice and Montpellier; the TGV Atlantique Sud-Ouest and TGV Atlantique Ouest link Paris' Gare Montparnasse with western and southwestern France, including Brittany, Tours, La Rochelle, Bordeaux, Biarritz and Toulouse; and the TGV Nord links Paris' Gare du Nord with Arras, Lille and Calais.

Reservation fees are optional unless you're travelling by TGV or want a couchette or special reclining seat. On popular trains (eg, on holiday weekends) you may have to reserve ahead to get a seat. Eurail-pass holders must pay all applicable reservation fees.

Before boarding the train, you must validate your ticket (and your reservation card, if it's separate) by time-stamping it in one of the *composteurs*, the bright orange posts that are located somewhere between the ticket windows and the tracks. Eurail and some other rail passes *must* be validated at a train station ticket window to initiate the period of validity.

Discounts

Passes for Nonresidents of Europe The France Railpass allows unlimited rail travel within France for up to 10 days over the course of a month. In 2nd class, the three-day version costs US$210 (US$171 each for two people travelling together); each additional day of travel costs US$30. The France Youthpass, available if you're 25 or under, costs US$148 for four days of travel in a month; additional days (up to a maximum of six) cost US$18. **Rail Europe** *(USA ☎ 800-456 7245; W www.raileurope.com)* has details.

Passes for Residents of Europe The Euro Domino France flexipass gives European residents who don't live in France three to eight days of midnight-to-midnight travel over a period of one month. The youth version (for people 25 and under) costs €84 for three days, plus about €15 each additional day; the adult version costs €115 for three days, plus about €20 each additional day.

Other Discounts Discounts of 25% on one-way or return travel within France are available at all train station ticket windows for: people aged 12 to 25 (the Découverte 12/25 fare); one to four adults travelling with a child aged four to 11 (the Découverte Enfant Plus fare); people over 60 (the Découverte Senior fare); and, for return travel only, any two people who are travelling together (the Découverte à Deux fare).

No matter what your age, the Découverte Séjour excursion fare gives you a 25% reduction for return travel within France if you meet two conditions: the total length of your trip is at least 200km; and you'll be spending a Saturday night at your destination.

The Découverte J30, which must be purchased 30 to 60 days before the date of travel, offers savings of 45% to 55%. The Découverte J8, which you must buy at least eight days ahead, gets you 20% to 30% off.

CAR & MOTORCYCLE

Travelling by car or motorcycle is expensive. If you don't live in the EU and need a car in France (or Europe) for 17 days (or a bit more) to six months, it's *much* cheaper to 'purchase' one from the manufacturer and then 'sell' it back than it is to rent one. The purchase-repurchase *(achat-rachat)* paperwork is not your responsibility. Both Renault's **Eurodrive** *(USA: ☎ 800-221-1052; W www.eurodrive.renault.com)* and Peugeot's **Vacation Plan/Sodexa** *(USA: ☎ 212-581-3040; W www.sodexa.com)* offer great deals that – incredibly – include insurance with no deductible (excess).

HITCHING

Hitching in France can be difficult, and getting out of big cities like Paris, Lyon and Marseille or travelling around the Côte d'Azur by thumb is well nigh impossible. Remote rural areas are your best bet, but few cars are likely to be going farther than the next large town. Women should not hitch alone.

It's an excellent idea to hold up a sign with your destination followed by the letters *s.v.p.* (for *s'il vous plaît* – 'please'). Some people have reported good luck hitching with truck drivers from truck stops. It's illegal to hitch on autoroutes, but you can stand near the entrance ramps.

FUAJ, the French youth hostel association, has a car-pooling registry that matches drivers and passengers for car journeys within Europe. Check it out at W www.fuaj.org.

Paris

pop 2.2 million,
metropolitan area 10.6 million

Entire forests have been felled to provide all the tourist literature that has been written about France's capital. Everyone has an opinion on Paris, having travelled there or no. Other towns are quick to adopt its moniker: Maastricht styles itself 'the Paris of the Netherlands'; St Pierre in its heyday was known as 'the Paris of the West Indies'; Melbourne is affectionately referred to as 'Paris on the Yarra'; while Bucharest, St Petersburg, Shanghai and Hanoi all lay claim to being 'the Paris of the East'.

Oft imitated, but never duplicated, Paris stands in a class by itself. France's *bijou extraordinaire* remains the benchmark for beauty, culture and class the world over. Even the most cynical traveller, sceptical that any city could live up to Paris' reputation, can't help but be charmed by its magnificent avenues and cosy café life, its unparalleled arts scene and energetic but composed pace. Paris is the Paris of the Parisians, the Paris of France, the one and only Paris. Nothing comes close.

Orientation

In central Paris (Intra-Muros – 'within the walls'), the Rive Droite (Right Bank) is north of the Seine, while the Rive Gauche (Left Bank) is south of the river. For administrative purposes, Paris is divided into 20 *arrondissements* (districts) that spiral out from the centre. Addresses always include the *arrondissement* number, listed here after the street address using the usual French notation (eg, 1er stands for *premier* – 1st – 19e for *dix-neuvième* – 19th – etc. When an address includes the full five-digit postal code, the last two digits indicate the *arrondissement*, eg, 75014 for the 14e.

Lonely Planet's *Paris City Map* includes central Paris, the Métropolitain, Montmartre, a walking tour and an index of all streets and sights.

Information

Tourist Offices Paris' **main tourist office** *(☎ 0836 68 31 12, fax 01 49 52 53 00; e info@paris-touristoffice.com; 127 Ave des Champs-Élysées, 8e; metro Georges V; open daily • branches: Gare de Lyon; open Mon-Sat • base of Eiffel Tower; open daily May-Sept)* is the best source of information on what's going on in the city.

For a small fee (€3 for a one-star hotel), the office can find you accommodation in Paris for that night only.

Money All of Paris' six major train stations have exchange bureaus open daily until at least 7pm. Big exchange-bureau chains like Chequepoint and ExactChange offer much poorer rates. Exchange offices at both airports are open until 10.30pm.

American Express (9e) Paris' landmark American Express office (☎ 01 47 77 77 75, metro Auber or Opéra) at 11 rue Scribe, faces the west side of Opéra Garnier. Exchange services are available 9.30am to 6.30pm (7pm June to September) weekdays, and 9am to 5.30pm on the weekend.

Champs-Élysées (8e) Thanks to fierce competition, the Champs-Élysées is an excellent place to change money. There's a bureau de change inside the tourist office at 127 ave des Champs-Élysées and a Thomas Cook branch next door.

Grands Boulevards (9e) FCO (☎ 01 47 70 02 59, 19 rue du Faubourg Montmartre, metro Grands Boulevards) tends to have decent rates. Open 8.30am to 7pm daily.

Notre Dame (4e & 5e) Société Française de Change (☎ 01 43 26 01 84, 21 rue Chanoinesse, metro Cité) has good rates. It's open 8.30am to 7pm daily.

Post & Communications Paris' **main post office** *(☎ 01 40 28 76 00; 52 rue du Louvre, 1er; metro Sentier or Les Halles; open 24hr)* has foreign exchange available during regular post office hours – 8am to 7pm weekdays, till noon on Saturday.

The cheapest Internet cafés are **EasyInternet** *(31-37 blvd de Sébastopol, 2e; metro Châtelet-Les Halles • 6 rue de la Harpe, 6e; metro St Michel • 15 rue de Rome, 8e; metro St-Lazare; all open 24hr daily)* where you can get a 24-hour Internet access pass for €5. More pleasant, but more expensive, is the cool **Web Bar** *(☎ 01 42 72 66 55; 32 rue de Picardie, 3e; metro Temple or Républic; open 8.30am-2am daily)*, which charges €4 for an hour of Net access.

Also try **Mike's Bike Tours** *(24 rue Edgar Faure, 15e)*, which has English keyboards and a tourist-friendly atmosphere.

Travel Agencies There are 15 outlets around the city of **Nouvelles Frontières** *(☎ 0825 00 08 25; 66 blvd St Michel, 6e; metro Luxembourg; open 9am-7pm Mon-Sat)*. **Voyageurs du Monde** *(☎ 01 42 86 16 00; 55 rue Ste Anne, 2e; metro Pyramides or Quartre Septembre; open 9.30am-7pm Mon-Sat)* is a huge agency.

Medical & Emergency Services An easy *assistance publique* (public health service) to find is the **Hôtel Dieu hospital** *(☎ 01 42 34 82 34; 1 place du Parvis Notre Dame, 4e; metro Cité)* on the northern side of the square. A 24-hour *service des urgences* (emergency service) is provided.

Dangers & Annoyances For its size, Paris is a safe city but you should always use common sense; avoid the large Bois de Boulogne and Bois de Vincennes parks after nightfall. And some stations are best avoided late at night, especially if you are on your own. These include Châtelet and its seemingly endless tunnels, Château Rouge in Montmartre, Gare du Nord, Strasbourg-St Denis, Montparnasse-Bienvenüe and Réaumur-Sébastopol.

Things to See – Left Bank

The Carte Musées et Monuments museum pass gets you into some 60 museums and monuments without having to queue for a ticket. The card costs €15/30/45 for one/three/five consecutive days and is on sale at

FRANCE

CENTRAL PARIS

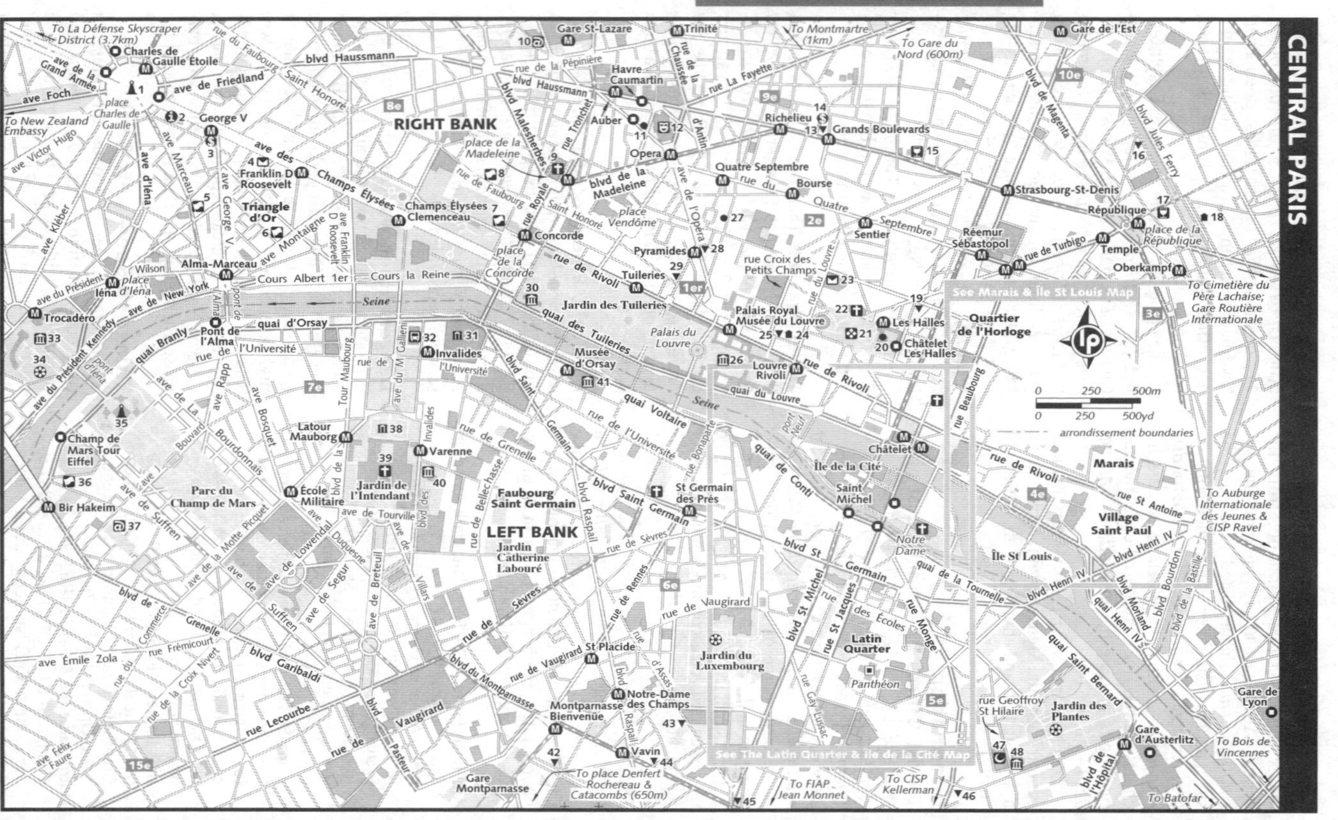

CENTRAL PARIS

PLACES TO STAY
18 Auberge de Jeunesse Jules Ferry
24 Centre International BVJ Paris-Louvre & Laundrette

PLACES TO EAT
13 Chartier
16 Chez Prune
19 Joe Allen
25 Le Petit Mâchon
28 Monoprix Supermarket
29 Food Shops
42 Le Flibustier
43 CROUS Assas
44 Le Caméléon
45 CROUS Bullier
46 Founti Agadir

MUSEUMS
26 Louvre Museum
30 Musée de l'Orangerie
33 Palais de Chaillot (Musée de l'Homme & Musée de la Marine)
40 Musée Rodin
41 Musée d'Orsay
48 Musée d'Histoire Naturelle

OTHER
1 Arc de Triomphe
2 Main Tourist Office; bureau de change
3 24hr Currency exchange machine
4 Post Office
5 Spanish Embassy
6 Canadian Embassy
7 US Embassy
8 UK Embassy
9 La Madeleine Church
10 EasyInternet
11 American Express
12 Opéra Garnier; Musée de l'Opera
14 FCO Currency Exchange
15 De La Ville Café
17 Favela Chic
20 Roue Libre
21 Forum des Halles (Shopping Mall & Park); FNAC Ticket Office
22 Église Saint Eustache
23 Main Post Office
27 Voyageurs du Monde
31 Palais Bourbon (National Assembly Building)
32 Aérogare des Invalides (Buses to Orly)
34 Jardins du Trocadéro
35 Eiffel Tower
36 Australian Embassy
37 Mike's Bike Tours Office
38 Hôtel des Invalides; Musée de l'Armée
39 Église du Dôme
47 Mosquée de Paris; Hammam

the museums and monuments it covers, at some metro ticket windows, at the tourist office and FNAC outlets. Most museums offer discounts for 18- to 25-year-olds and free admission to children; furthermore, many are free the first Sunday of each month.

Île de la Cité (1er & 4e) Paris was founded sometime during the 3rd century BC when members of a tribe known as the Parisii set up a few huts on Île de la Cité. By the Middle Ages the city had grown to encompass both banks of the Seine, though Île de la Cité remained the centre of royal and ecclesiastical power.

Notre Dame (4e) Paris' cathedral (*☎ 01 42 34 56 10; metro Cité or St Michel; admission free; open 8am-6.45pm daily)* is one of the most magnificent achievements of Gothic architecture, begun in 1163 and completed around 1345. Features include the three spectacular rose windows. One of the best views of Notre Dame's ornate flying buttresses can be had from the lovely little park behind the cathedral. The haunting **Mémorial des Martyrs de la Déportation**, in memory of the more than 200,000 people deported by the Nazis and French fascists during WWII, is close by.

Free **guided tours** of Notre Dame in English take place at noon on Wednesday and Thursday and at 2.30pm on Saturday. Concerts held here don't keep to a schedule, but are advertised on posters around town. The **North Tower** *(adult/concession €5.50/3.50)*, from which you can view many of the cathedral's fierce-looking gargoyles, can be climbed via long, spiral steps.

Ste Chapelle (1er) The gem-like upper chapel of Ste Chapelle *(☎ 01 53 73 78 50; metro Cité; adult/concession €5.50/3.50, combination ticket for Ste Chapelle & Conciergerie €8/5; open 9.30am-6pm daily)*, illuminated by a veritable curtain of 13th-century stained glass, is inside the **Palais de Justice** *(Law Courts; 4 blvd du Palais, 1er)*. Consecrated in 1248, Ste Chapelle was built in three years to house a crown of thorns (supposedly worn by the crucified Christ) and other relics purchased by King Louis IX (later St Louis) earlier in the 13th century.

Conciergerie (1er) The Conciergerie was a luxurious royal palace when it was built in the 14th century. During the Reign of Terror (1793–94), it was used to incarcerate 'enemies' of the Revolution before they were brought before the tribunal, which met next door in what is now the Palais de Justice.

Île St Louis (4e) The 17th-century houses of grey stone and the small-town shops lining the streets and quays of Île St Louis create an almost provincial atmosphere, making it a

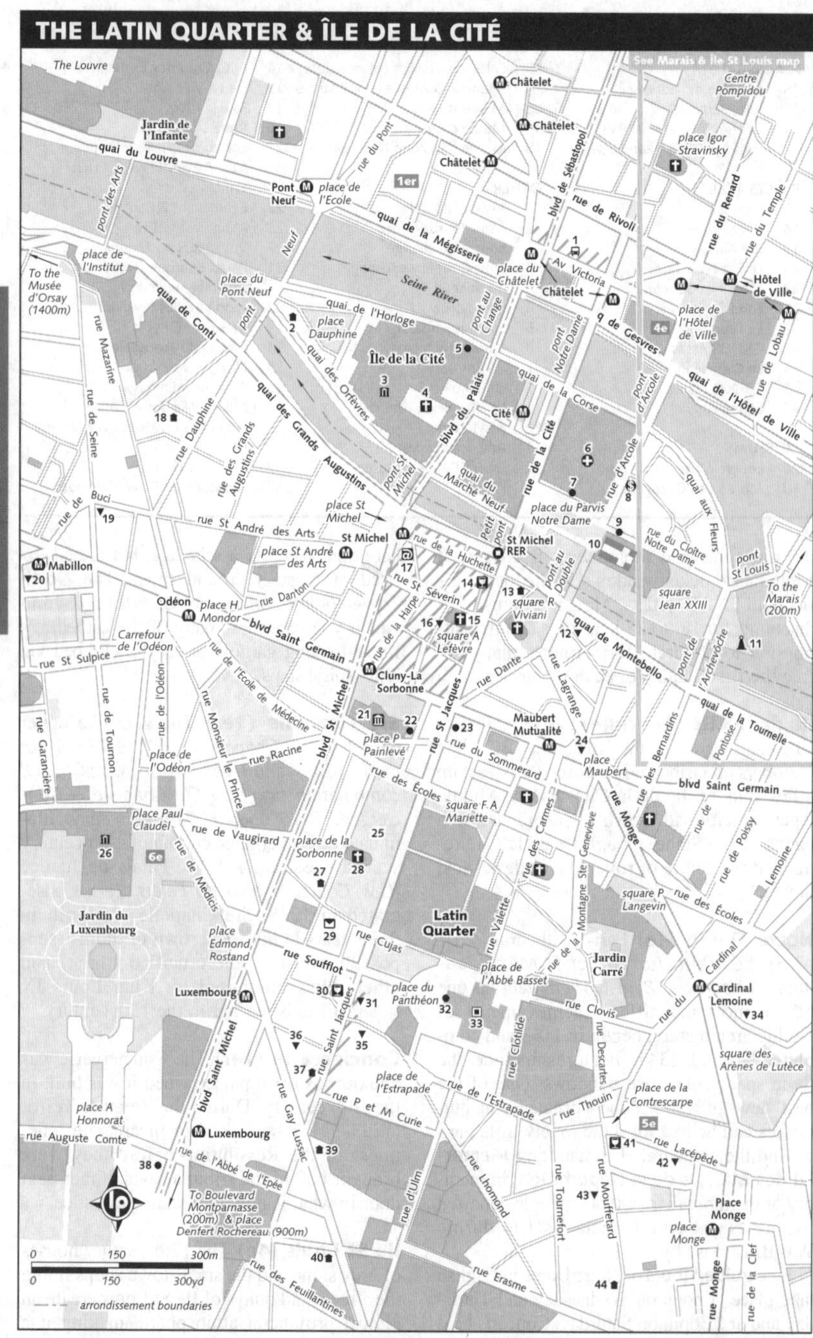
THE LATIN QUARTER & ÎLE DE LA CITÉ
See Marais & Île St Louis map
The Louvre
Jardin de l'Infante
quai du Louvre
pont des Arts
Châtelet
Châtelet
Châtelet
Centre Pompidou
place Igor Stravinsky
rue du Pont
1er
Pont Neuf
place de l'Ecole
blvd de Sébastopol
rue de Rivoli
rue du Renard
rue du Temple
quai de la Mégisserie
Neuf
place de l'Institut
To the Musée d'Orsay (1400m)
Seine River
place du Châtelet
Av Victoria
Châtelet
Hôtel de Ville
place de l'Hôtel de Ville
quai de Conti
place du Pont Neuf
pont
quai de l'Horloge
place Dauphine
pont au Change
pont Notre Dame
q de Gesvres
4e
rue Mazarine
quai des Orfèvres
Île de la Cité
quai de la Corse
pont d'Arcole
quai de l'Hôtel de Ville
rue de Lobau
rue de Seine
rue Dauphine
quai des Grands Augustins
rue des Grands Augustins
blvd du Palais
Cité
rue de la Cité
rue d'Arcole
quai aux Fleurs
pont St Michel
quai du Marché Neuf
rue de Buci
place St Michel
place du Parvis Notre Dame
rue St André des Arts
St Michel
Petit pont
St Michel RER
rue du Cloître Notre Dame
pont St Louis
Mabillon
place St André des Arts
rue de la Huchette
To the Marais (200m)
rue St Séverin
pont au Double
square Jean XXIII
Odéon
place H Mondor
rue Danton
square R Viviani
blvd Saint Germain
rue de la Harpe
square A Lefèvre
Carrefour de l'Odéon
quai de Montebello
pont de l'Archevêché
rue St Sulpice
rue de l'Ecole de Médecine
Cluny-La Sorbonne
rue Dante
rue Lagrange
rue de l'Odéon
rue Monsieur le Prince
rue de Tournon
rue Garancière
blvd St Michel
rue St Jacques
Maubert Mutualité
quai de la Tournelle
place P Painlevé
rue du Sommerard
place de l'Odéon
rue Racine
place Maubert
rue des Bernardins
Pontoise
rue des Écoles
blvd Saint Germain
square F A Mariette
rue Monge
rue de Poissy
place Paul Claudel
rue de Vaugirard
place de la Sorbonne
rue des Carmes
rue Montagne Ste Geneviève
6e
rue de Médicis
square P Langevin
rue des Écoles
rue Lemoine
Jardin du Luxembourg
Latin Quarter
rue Valette
rue de la
place Edmond Rostand
rue Cujas
Jardin Carré
rue Soufflot
place de l'Abbé Basset
rue du Cardinal
Luxembourg
place du Panthéon
Cardinal Lemoine
rue Clovis
rue Saint Jacques
rue Clotilde
rue Descartes
square des Arènes de Lutèce
rue Gay Lussac
blvd Saint Michel
place de l'Estrapade
rue de l'Estrapade
rue Thouin
place de la Contrescarpe
place A Honnorat
rue P et M Curie
5e
rue Auguste Comte
Luxembourg
rue Lacépède
rue de l'Abbé de l'Epée
rue Lhomond
To Boulevard Montparnasse (200m) & place Denfert Rochereau (900m)
rue d'Ulm
rue Tournefort
rue Mouffetard
Place Monge
place Monge
0 150 300m
0 150 300yd
rue Erasme
rue des Feuillantines
rue Monge
rue de la Clef
arrondissement boundaries
1 2 3 4 5 6 7 8 9 10 11 12 13 14 15 16 17 18 19 20 21 22 23 24 25 26 27 28 29 30 31 32 33 34 35 36 37 38 39 40 41 42 43 44

THE LATIN QUARTER & ÎLE DE LA CITÉ

PLACES TO STAY

2 Hôtel Henri IV
13 Hôtel Esmeralda
18 Hôtel de Nesle
27 Hôtel de la Sorbonne
37 Hôtel de Médicis
40 Grand Hôtel du Progrès
39 Hôtel Gay Lussac
44 Y & H Hostel

PLACES TO EAT

12 Le Grenier de Notre-Dame
16 Restaurants ('Bacteria Alley')
19 Food Shops
20 CROUS Mabillon
24 Food Shops
31 Perraudin
34 Le Petit Légume
35 Tashi Delek Tibetan Restaurant
36 Douce France Sandwich Bar
42 Ed l'Épicier Supermarket
43 Le Petit Grec

OTHER

1 Noctambus (All-Night Bus) Stops
3 Palais de Justice & Conciergerie
4 Sainte Chapelle
5 Conciergerie Entrance
6 Hôtel Dieu (Hospital)
7 Hospital Entrance
8 Société Française de Change
9 Notre Dame Tower Entrance
10 Notre Dame Cathedral
11 Mémorial des Martyrs de la Déportation
14 Caveau de la Huchette Jazz Club
15 Église Saint Séverin
17 EasyInternet
21 Musée du Moyen Age (Musée de Cluny)
22 Musée du Moyen Age Entrance
23 Eurolines Bus Office
25 Sorbonne (University of Paris)
26 Palais du Luxembourg (French Senate Building)
28 Église de la Sorbonne
29 Post Office
30 Café Oz
32 Panthéon Entrance
33 Panthéon
38 Nouvelles Frontières
41 La Contrescarpe

great place for a quiet stroll. On foot, the shortest route between Notre Dame and the Marais passes through Île St Louis. For reputedly the best ice cream in Paris, head for **Berthillon** *(31 rue St Louis en l'Île)*.

Quartier Latin (5e & 6e) This area is known as the Latin Quarter because, until the Revolution, all communication between students and their professors here took place in Latin. Whilst the 5e has become increasingly touristy, there's still a large population of students and academics. Shop-lined **blvd St Michel**, known as 'Boul Mich', runs along the border of the 5e and the 6e.

Panthéon (5e) A Latin Quarter landmark, the Panthéon *(☎ 01 44 32 18 00; metro Luxembourg; adult/concession €7/4.50; open 9.30am-5.45pm daily Apr-Sept, 10am-5.15pm daily Oct-Mar)*, at the eastern end of rue Soufflot, was commissioned as an abbey church in the mid-18th century. In 1791, the Constituent Assembly converted it into a mausoleum for the 'great men of the era of French liberty'. Permanent residents include Victor Hugo, Voltaire and Jean-Jacques Rousseau.

Sorbonne (5e) Founded in 1253 as a college for 16 poor theology students, the Sorbonne was closed in 1792 by the Revolutionary government but reopened under Napoleon. **Place de la Sorbonne** links blvd St Michel with **Église de la Sorbonne**, the university's domed 17th-century church.

Jardin du Luxembourg (6e) The gardens' main entrance is opposite 65 blvd St Michel. The **Palais du Luxembourg**, fronting rue de Vaugirard at the northern end of the Jardin du Luxembourg, was built for Maria de Medici, queen of France from 1600 to 1610. It now houses the Sénat, the upper house of the French parliament.

Musée National du Moyen Age (5e) The Museum of the Middle Ages *(☎ 01 53 73 78 16; metro Cluny-La Sorbonne; adult/concession €5.50/4; open 9.15am-5.45pm Wed-Mon)*, which is also known as the Musée de Cluny, houses one of France's finest collections of medieval art. Its prized possession is a series of six late-15th-century tapestries from the southern Netherlands known as La Dame à la Licorne (The Lady and the Unicorn).

Mosquée de Paris (5e) Paris' ornate central mosque *(☎ 01 45 35 97 33; place du Puits de l'Ermite; metro Monge; open 9am-noon & 2pm-6pm Sat-Thur)* was built between 1922 and 1926. The mosque complex includes a small *souk* (marketplace), a *salon de thé* (tearoom), an excellent couscous restaurant and a *hammam* (Turkish bath).

The mosque is opposite the **Jardin des Plantes** (Botanical Gardens), which includes a small **zoo**, as well as the **Musée d'Histoire Naturelle** *(Museum of Natural History; ☎ 01 40 79 30 00; metro Monge; adult/concession €4.6/3.05; open Wed-Mon 10am-5pm)*.

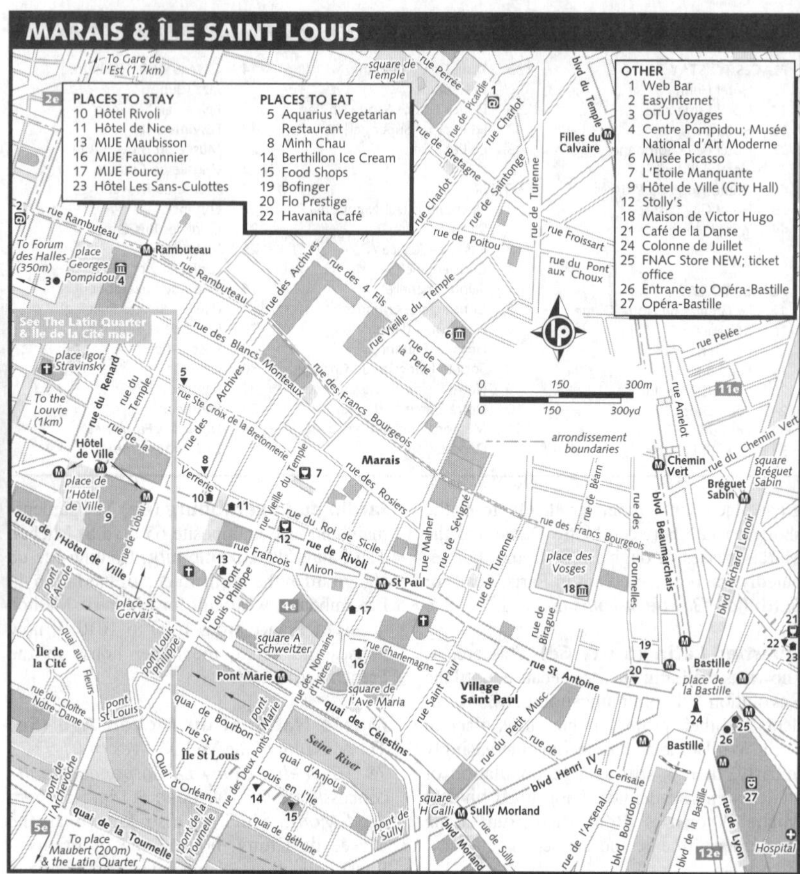

Catacombes (14e) In 1785, the bones of millions of Parisians were exhumed from overflowing cemeteries and moved to the tunnels of three disused quarries. One such ossuary is the Catacombes *(☎ 01 43 22 47 63; metro Denfert Rochereau; adult/student & senior/child €5/3.30/2.60; open 11am-4pm Tues, 9am-4pm Wed-Sun)*. During WWII, these tunnels were used by the Résistance as headquarters. The route through the Catacombes begins from the small green building at 1 place Denfert Rochereau. Take a torch (flashlight).

Musée d'Orsay (7e) The Musée d'Orsay *(☎ 01 40 49 48 48; 1 rue de la Légion-d'Honneur; metro Musée d'Orsay; adult/concession €7/5, all €5 Sun; open 10am-6pm Tues-Wed & Fri-Sat, 10am-9.45pm Thur, 9am-6pm Sun, from 9am summer)* exhibits works of art produced between 1848 and 1914, and is spectacularly housed in a 1900 train station. Tickets are valid all day.

Musée Rodin (7e) The Musée Auguste Rodin *(☎ 01 44 18 61 10; 77 rue Varenne; metro Varenne; adult/concession €5/3; open 9.30am-5.45pm daily Apr-Sept, 9.30am-4.45pm daily Oct-Mar)* is one of the most pleasant museums in Paris. Visiting just the garden (5pm close) costs €1.

Invalides (7e) The **Hôtel des Invalides** *(metro Invalides for Esplanade, metro Varenne or Latour Maubourg for main building)* was built in the 1670s by Louis XIV to provide housing for 4000 disabled veterans *(invalides)*.

It also served as the headquarters of the military governor of Paris, and was used as an armoury. On 14 July 1789 the Paris mob forced its way into the building and took all 28,000 firearms before heading for the Bastille prison.

The **Église du Dôme**, built between 1677 and 1735, is considered one of the finest religious edifices erected under Louis XIV. In 1861 it received the remains of Napoleon, encased in six concentric coffins.

The buildings on either side of the **Cour d'Honneur** (Main Courtyard) house the **Musée de l'Armée** *(☎ 01 44 42 37 72; adult/concession €6/4.50; open 10am-5pm daily, 6pm in summer)*, a huge military museum, which includes the light and airy **Tombeau de Napoléon 1er** (Napoleon's Tomb).

Tour Eiffel (7e) The Eiffel Tower *(☎ 01 44 11 23 23; metro Champ de Mars-Tour Eiffel; open 9.30am-11pm daily Sept–mid-June, 9am-midnight mid-June–Aug)* faced massive opposition from Paris' artistic and literary elite when it was built for the 1889 Exposition Universelle (World's Fair), held on the centenary of the Revolution. It was almost torn down in 1909, but was spared for practical reasons – it proved an ideal platform for newfangled transmitting antennae. The tower is 320m high, including the television antenna at the very tip.

Three levels are open to the public. The lift (west and north pillars) costs €3.70 for the 1st platform (57m), €7 for the 2nd (115m) and €10 for the 3rd (276m). Children three to 12 pay €2.10/3.80/5.30 respectively; there are no other discounts. The escalator in the south pillar to the 1st and 2nd platforms costs €3.

Things to See – Right Bank

Jardins du Trocadéro (16e) The Trocadéro gardens *(metro Trocadéro)*, whose fountain and nearby sculpture park are grandly illuminated at night, are across the pont d'Iéna from the Eiffel Tower. The colonnaded Palais de Chaillot, built in 1937, houses the anthropological and ethnographic **Musée de l'Homme** *(Museum of Mankind; ☎ 01 44 05 72 72; adult/concession €4.60/3.05; open 9.45am-5.15pm Wed-Mon)*; and the **Musée de la Marine** *(Maritime Museum; ☎ 01 53 65 69 69; adult/concession €7/5.50; open 10am-5.50pm Wed-Mon)*, known for its beautiful model ships.

Louvre (1er) The Louvre Museum *(☎ 01 40 20 53 17, recorded message ☎ 01 40 20 51 51; metro Palais Royal-Musée du Louvre; permanent collection admission €7.50, after 3pm & Sun €5; open 9am-6pm Thur-Sun, 9am-9.45pm Mon & Wed)*, which was constructed around 1200 as a fortress and rebuilt in the mid-16th century as a royal palace, became a public museum in 1793. The collections on display have been assembled by French governments over the past five centuries and include works of art and artisanship from all over Europe, as well as important collections of Assyrian, Egyptian, Etruscan, Greek, Coptic, Roman and Islamic art. The Louvre's most famous work is undoubtedly Leonardo da Vinci's *Mona Lisa*.

Ticket sales end 45 minutes before closing time. Admission to temporary exhibits varies. Tickets are valid for the whole day, so you can leave and re-enter as you please. By advance purchasing your tickets at the *billeteries* (ticket office) at FNAC, or other department stores, for an extra €1.10, you can walk straight in without queuing.

For English-language guided tours (€6/4.50; 11am, 2pm and 3.45pm most days) and audioguide tours (€5), go to the mezzanine level beneath the glass pyramid.

Place Vendôme (1er) The 44m-high column in the middle of place Vendôme (metro Opéra or Pyramides) consists of a stone core wrapped in bronze from 1250 cannons captured by Napoleon at the Battle of Austerlitz (1805). The shops around the square are among Paris' most fashionable and expensive.

Musée de l'Orangerie (1er) This museum *(☎ 01 42 97 48 16; metro Concorde)*, usually home to important impressionist works including a series of Monet's spectacular *Nymphéas* (Water Lilies), is being renovated and is due to reopen at the end of 2004.

Place de la Concorde (8e) This vast, cobbled square between the Jardin des Tuileries and the Champs-Élysées was laid out between 1755 and 1775. Louis XVI was guillotined here in 1793 – as were another 1343 people, including his wife Marie Antoinette, over the next two years. The 3300-year-old Egyptian **obelisk** in the middle of the square was given to France in 1829 by the ruler of Egypt, Mohammed Ali.

La Madeleine (8e) The church of St Mary Magdalene *(metro Madeleine)*, built in the style of a Greek temple, was consecrated in 1842 after almost a century of design changes and construction delays.

Champs-Élysées (8e) The 2km-long ave des Champs-Élysées links place de la Concorde with the Arc de Triomphe. Once popular with the aristocracy as a stage on which to parade their wealth, it has, in recent decades, been partly taken over by fast-food restaurants and overpriced cafés. The nicest bit is the park between place de la Concorde and rond-point des Champs-Élysées.

Arc de Triomphe (8e) Paris' second most famous landmark, the Arc de Triomphe *(☎ 01 55 37 73 77; metro Charles de Gaulle-Étoile; viewing platform adult/concession €7/4.50; viewing platform open 10am-11pm daily Apr-Sept, 10am-10.30pm Oct-Mar)* is 2.2km northwest of place de la Concorde in the middle of place Charles de Gaulle. Also called place de l'Étoile, this is the world's largest traffic roundabout and the meeting point of 12 avenues. Commissioned in 1806 by Napoleon to commemorate his imperial victories, it remained unfinished until the 1830s. An Unknown Soldier from WWI is buried under the arch, his fate and that of countless others like him commemorated by a memorial flame lit each evening at around 6.30pm.

The platform atop the arch is accessed by lift going up, and by steps heading down. The only sane way to get to the arch's base is via the underground passageways.

The **Voie Triomphale** (Triumphal Way) stretches 4.5km from the Arc de Triomphe along ave de la Grande Armée to the skyscraper district of **La Défense**, whose best known landmark, the **Grande Arche** (Grand Arch), is a hollow cube (112m to a side).

Centre Georges Pompidou (4e) Thanks in part to its outstanding temporary exhibitions, **Centre Pompidou** *(☎ 01 44 78 12 33; metro Rambuteau or Châtelet-Les Halles)* – also known as Centre Beaubourg – is by far the most frequented sight in Paris. **Place Igor Stravinsky**, south of the centre, and the large square to the west attract all kinds of street artists.

The **Musée National d'Art Moderne** *(National Museum of Modern Art; adult/concession €5.50/3.50; open 11am-9pm Wed-Mon, till 11pm Thur)* on the 4th floor displays France's brilliant collection of modern art, from 1905 to the present. The fee includes admission to Brancusi's studio, reconstructed at the north of the forecourt. The **Bibliothèque Publique d'Information**, a huge, nonlending library, is on the 2nd floor (enter from rue du Renard).

Les Halles (1er) Paris' main wholesale food market, Les Halles, occupied this site from the 12th century until 1969, when it was moved to the suburb or Rungis; a huge underground shopping mall (Forum des Halles) was built in its place. North of the grassy area on top of Les Halles is the mostly 16th-century **Église St Eustache**, noted for its wonderful pipe organ.

Hôtel de Ville (4e) Paris' magnificent city hall *(☎ 01 42 76 50 49; place de l'Hôtel de Ville; metro Hôtel de Ville)* was burned down during the Paris Commune of 1871 and rebuilt (1874–82) in the neo-Renaissance style.

Marais Area (4e) A *marais* (marsh) converted to agricultural use in the 13th century, this area was, during the 17th century – when the nobility erected luxurious but discreet mansions known as *hôtels particuliers* – the most fashionable part of the city. Eventually the Marais was taken over by ordinary Parisians and by the time renovation began in the 1960s, it had become a poor but lively Jewish neighbourhood. In the 1980s the area underwent serious gentrification and today it is the centre of Paris' gay life.

Place des Vosges (4e) Built in 1605 and originally known as place Royal, place des Vosges *(metro Chemin Vert)* is a square ensemble of 36 symmetrical houses. Duels were once fought in the elegant park in the middle. Today, the arcades around place des Vosges are occupied by upmarket art galleries, antique shops and boutiques.

The nearby **Maison de Victor Hugo** *(☎ 01 42 72 10 16; adult/concession €3.50/2.50; open Tues-Sun)* is where the author lived from 1832 to 1848.

Musée Picasso (3e) The Picasso Museum *(☎ 01 42 71 25 21; 5 rue de Thorigny; metro St Paul; adult/concession €5.50/4; open 9.30am-6pm, to 8pm Thur; closes 5.30pm Oct-Mar)* is just northeast of the Marais.

Paintings, sculptures, ceramics, engravings and drawings, that were donated to the French government by the heirs of Pablo Picasso (1881–1973) to avoid huge inheritance taxes, are on display, as is Picasso's personal art collection (Braque, Cézanne, Matisse, Rousseau etc).

Bastille (4e, 11e & 12e) The Bastille is the most famous nonexistent monument in Paris; the notorious prison was demolished shortly after the mob stormed it on 14 July 1789. The site is known today as 'place de la Bastille'. The 52m-high **Colonne de Juillet** in the centre was erected in 1830. There is also the new (though rather drab) **Opéra Bastille** *(☎ 0836 69 78 68; place de la Bastille; metro Bastille)*.

Opéra Garnier (9e) Paris' renowned opera house (see Opera & Classical Music under Entertainment later) was designed in 1860 by Charles Garnier. The **ceiling** of the auditorium was painted by Marc Chagall in 1964. The building also houses the **Musée de l'Opéra** *(adult/concession €6/4; open 10am-5pm daily)*.

Montmartre (18e) During the 19th century Montmartre was a vibrant centre of artistic and literary creativity. Today it's an area of mimes, buskers, tacky souvenir shops and commercial artists.

The **Basilique du Sacré Cœur** *(☎ 01 53 41 89 00; metro Anvers; admission free; open 7am-11pm daily; admission to dome & crypt adult/student €4.50/2.50; dome & crypt open 10am-5.45pm daily)* was built to fulfil a vow taken by Parisian Catholics after the disastrous Franco-Prussian War of 1870–71. The funicular up the hill's southern slope costs one metro/bus ticket each way.

Just west of Église St Pierre, **place du Tertre** is filled with cafés, restaurants, portrait artists and tourists – though the real attractions of the area are the quiet, twisting streets. Look for the **windmills** on rue Lepic and Paris' last **vineyard**, on the corner of rue des Saules and rue St Vincent.

Pigalle (9e & 18e) Just west of Montmartre, the area along blvd de Clichy between the Pigalle and Blanche metro stops is lined with sex shops, striptease parlours and bad nightclubs.

Musée de l'Érotisme *(Museum of Eroticism; ☎ 01 42 58 28 73; 72 blvd de Clichy; metro Blanche; adult/student €7/5; open 10am-2am daily)* tries to raise erotic art, both antique and modern, to a loftier plane – but we know why *you're* going to visit. The **Moulin Rouge** *(☎ 01 53 09 82 82; 82 blvd de Clichy; metro Blanche; tickets from €60)*, founded in 1889, is well known for its thrice-nightly revues of near-naked girls.

Cimetière du Père Lachaise (20e) East of the city, Père Lachaise Cemetery *(☎ 01 55 25 82 10; metro Père Lachaise; admission free; open to at least 5.30pm daily)*, final resting place of such notables as Chopin, Proust, Wilde and Piaf, may be the most visited cemetery in the world. The best known tomb is that of 1960s rock star Jim Morrison, lead singer for The Doors, who died in 1971.

FRANCE

Bois de Vincennes (12e) Highlights of this 9.29-sq-km English-style park include the **Parc Floral** *(Floral Garden; metro Château de Vincennes)*; the **Parc Zoologique de Paris** *(Paris Zoo; ☎ 01 44 75 20 10; metro Porte Dorée)*; and the **Jardin Tropical** *(Tropical Garden; RER stop Nugent-sur-Marne)*.

Château de Vincennes (12e) A *bona fide* royal chateau, the Château de Vincennes *(☎ 01 48 08 31 20; metro Château de Vincennes; open 10am-noon & 1pm-5pm daily)* is at the northern edge of the Bois de Vincennes. You can walk around the grounds for free, but to see the Gothic **Chapelle Royale** and the 14th-century **donjon** (keep), you must take a tour (in French, with an information booklet in English).

Places to Stay

Accommodation Services Directly across the square from the Centre Pompidou, **OTU Voyages** *(☎ 01 40 29 12 12; W www.otu.fr; 119 rue Saint Martin, 4e; metro Rambuteau; open 9.30am-6.30pm Mon-Fri, 10am-5pm Sat)* can find you accommodation for the same or following day for a €3 fee. The staff will give you a voucher to take to the hotel.

The main tourist office (see Information earlier) and its Gare de Lyon annexe can also make same-day bookings.

Camping At the far western edge of the Bois de Boulogne, **Camping du Bois de**

Boulogne *(☎ 01 45 24 30 81, fax 01 42 24 42 95;* ⓔ *resa@mobilhome-paris.com; Allée du Bord de l'Eau, 16e; 2 people & tent with/without vehicle from €17/11)* is Paris' only camping ground. The Porte Maillot metro stop is linked to the camping ground by RATP bus No 244 (6am to 8.30pm) and, April to October, by privately operated shuttle bus (€1.70).

Hostels Many hostels allow a three-night maximum stay, especially in summer. Only official *auberges de jeunesse* (youth hostels) require guests to present Hostelling International (HI) cards or equivalent. Curfew – if enforced – tends to be 1am or 2am. Few hostels accept reservations by telephone.

Louvre Area (1er) There are bunks that are in single- sex rooms at **Centre International BVJ Paris-Louvre** *(☎ 01 53 00 90 90; 20 rue Jean-Jacques Rousseau; metro Louvre-Rivoli; dorm bed €26)* and rates include breakfast.

Marais (4e) The **Maison Internationale de la Jeunesse et des Étudiants** *(MIJE; ☎ 01 42 74 23 45, fax 01 40 27 81 64; dorm beds/singles from €23/38)* runs three hostels that are in attractively renovated 17th- and 18th-century Marais residences. Rates include breakfast. **MIJE Maubisson** *(12 rue des Barres; metro Hôtel de Ville)* is in our opinion the best. **MIJE Fourcy** *(6 rue de Fourcy; metro St Paul)*, the largest hostel, and **MIJE Fauconnier** *(11 rue du Fauconnier; metro Pont Marie)*, two blocks south of MIJE Fourcy, are the other options.

Panthéon Area (5e) The clean and friendly **Y&H Hostel** *(☎ 01 45 35 09 53, fax 01 47 07 22 24;* ⓔ *smile@youngandhappy.fr; 80 rue Mouffetard; metro Monge; dorm beds/doubles €22/50)* has become popular with a younger crowd.

11e & 12e Arrondissements Breakfast is included in the prices at the **Auberge de Jeunesse Jules Ferry** *(☎ 01 43 57 55 60;* ⓔ *auberge@ easynet.fr; 8 blvd Jules Ferry; metro République; dorm beds €18 plus €2.90 without HI card)*.

The clean and friendly **Auberge Internationale des Jeunes** *(☎ 01 47 00 62 00, fax 01 47 00 33 16;* ⓔ *aij@aijparis.com; 10 rue Trousseau, 11e; metro Ledru Rollin; dorm beds Nov-Feb €13, Mar-Oct €14)* attracts a young crowd and gets full in summer. Rates include breakfast.

Breakfast is also included at **Centre International de Séjour de Paris (CISP) Ravel** *(☎ 01 44 75 60 00, fax 01 43 44 45 30;* ⓔ *reservation@cisp.asso.fr; 6 ave Maurice Ravel; metro Porte de Vincennes; beds in 2/4-bed rooms €19.20, singles/doubles €30/48)*.

13e & 14e Arrondissements The **Foyer International d'Accueil de Paris (FIAP) Jean Monnet** *(☎ 01 43 13 17 00, fax 01 45 81 63 91;* ⓔ *fiapadmi@fiap.asso.fr; 30 rue Cabanis; metro Glacière; dorm beds from €22, singles €48.50)* has modern rooms, and rates include breakfast. Rooms specially outfitted for disabled people *(handicapés)* are available. Reservations are accepted.

The **Centre International de Séjour de Paris (CISP) Kellermann** *(☎ 01 44 16 37 38, fax 01 44 16 37 39; 17 blvd Kellermann; metro Porte d'Italie; dorm beds/singles €15.50/22.50)* includes sheets and breakfast in its rates. There are facilities for disabled people on the 1st floor. Reservations are accepted up to 48 hours in advance.

Hotels Marais (4e) Friendly **Hôtel Rivoli** *(☎ 01 42 72 08 41; 44 rue de Rivoli; metro Hôtel de Ville; singles without shower from €26, doubles with bath & toilet €48)* is still a good deal. **Hôtel de Nice** *(☎ 01 42 78 55 29, fax 01 42 78 36 07; 42bis rue de Rivoli; metro Hôtel de Ville; singles/doubles/triples €60/95/115)* is a family-run place; some rooms have balconies.

Bastille (11e) Above the bistro of the same name, **Hôtel Les Sans-Culottes** *(☎ 01 49 23 85 80, fax 01 48 05 08 56; 27 rue de Lappe; metro Bastille; singles/doubles €53/61)* has nine pleasant rooms with TV.

Notre Dame Area (5e) The **Hôtel Esmeralda** *(☎ 01 43 54 19 20, fax 01 40 51 00 68; 4 rue St Julien; metro St Michel; singles €30, doubles with shower & toilet from €60)* is a scruffy but well-loved institution. Its simple rooms are booked well in advance.

Panthéon Area (5e) Good-sized rooms are available at shabby **Hôtel de Médicis** *(☎ 01 43 54 14 66;* ⓔ *hotelmedicis@aol.com; 214* *rue St Jacques; metro Luxembourg; singles/doubles €16/31)*, but they are basic. Triples are available too. Much nicer is **Grand Hôtel du Progrès** *(☎ 01 43 54 53 18, fax 01 56 24 87 80; 50 rue Gay Lussac; metro Luxembourg; singles/doubles from €27/42, with shower & toilet from €54/56)*, which includes breakfast in its rates and has good views from some rooms.

There are some spacious rooms at older-style **Hôtel Gay Lussac** *(☎ 01 43 54 23 96, fax 01 40 51 79 49; 29 rue Gay Lussac; metro Luxembourg; singles/doubles/quads from €55/49/95)*. **Hotel de la Sorbonne** *(☎ 01 43 54 58 08, fax 01 40 51 05 18; e reservation@hotelsorbonne.com; 6 rue Victor Cousin; rooms with shower/bath €79/89)* is a comfortable place near blvd St Michel. Breakfast is an extra €5.

St Germain des Prés (6e) The whimsically decorated **Hôtel de Nesle** *(☎ 01 43 54 62 41; e contact@hoteldenesle.com; 7 rue de Nesle; metro Odéon or Mabillon; singles/doubles from €35/69)* is hospitable, with a tranquil garden. The well-positioned **Hôtel Henri IV** *(☎ 01 43 54 44 53; 25 place Dauphine; metro Pont Neuf; singles/doubles from €22/25, no credit cards)*, at the western end of Île de la Cité, has adequate rooms (hall showers €2.50). Book well ahead.

Montmartre (18e) An attractive place to try is **Hôtel des Arts** *(☎ 01 46 06 30 52, fax 01 46 06 10 83; e hotel.arts@wanadoo.fr; 5 rue Tholozé; metro Abbesses; singles/doubles from €64/78)*, while **Hôtel de Rohan** *(☎ 01 42 52 32 57, fax 01 55 79 79 63; 90 rue Myrha; metro Château Rouge; singles/doubles €19/23, with shower & toilet €28/31)* has recently renovated most of its rooms (hall showers €3).

Places to Eat

Restaurants Except in the very touristy areas, most of the city's thousands of restaurants are pretty good value for money.

Forum des Halles There are Lyon-inspired specialities at **Le Petit Mâchon** *(☎ 01 42 60 08 06; 158 rue St Honoré; metro Palais Royal; menu €15)* bistro. American bar/restaurant **Joe Allen** *(☎ 01 42 36 70 13; 30 rue Pierre Lescot; metro Étienne Marcel; hamburger €12)* promises the best burgers in Paris.

Opéra Area (2e & 9e) Although the food is so-so, **Chartier** *(☎ 01 47 70 86 29; 7 rue du Faubourg Montmartre; metro Grands Boulevards; mains from €6.50, 3-course menu with wine €14)* is worth it for the atmosphere and fabulous *belle époque* dining room.

Marais (4e) Rue des Rosiers (metro St Paul), the heart of the old Jewish neighbourhood, has a few *kascher* (kosher) restaurants. **Minh Chau** *(10 rue de la Verrerie; metro Hôtel de Ville; mains around €4.50)* is tiny but welcoming, and has tasty Vietnamese/Chinese dishes. Head to **Aquarius** *(☎ 01 48 87 48 71; 54 rue Ste Croix de la Bretonnerie; metro Rambuteau; 2-course lunch €11, 3-course dinner €15.40; closed Sun)* for tasty vegetarian dishes like soy sausages and tofu omelette.

République (10e) On the Canal St Martin, **Chez Prune** *(☎ 01 42 41 30 47; 36 rue Beaurepaire; metro République; lunch around €10)* is a hip café with tasty French food.

Bastille (4e, 11e & 12e) The area around Bastille has many ethnic and traditional restaurants. Rue de Lappe, a happening strip since the 17th century, has heaps of eateries and bars. **Havanita Café** *(☎ 01 43 55 96 42; mains €10-17)*, at No 11, is a loud, brassy lounge serving Cuban-inspired food and drinks.

Bofinger *(☎ 01 42 72 87 82; 5-7 rue de la Bastille; metro Bastille; lunch/dinner menus €20/30; open daily)* is a brasserie with an Art Nouveau interior and seafood specialities.

Latin Quarter (4e, 5e & 6e) This area has plenty of good Greek, North African and Middle Eastern restaurants – but avoid rue de la Huchette (aka 'bacteria alley') and its nearby streets, unless you're after shwarma (€4), available at several places.

The Moroccan **Founti Agadir** *(☎ 01 43 37 85 10; 117 rue Monge; metro Censier Daubenton; lunch menus €12 & €14)* has some of the best couscous, grills and tajines on the Left Bank. Or, if you fancy classics like *bœuf bourguignon* (€12.20), try **Perraudin** *(☎ 01 46 33 15 75; 157 rue St Jacques; metro Luxembourg; open Mon-Fri)*, a reasonably priced traditional French restaurant.

Le Petit Légume *(☎ 01 40 46 06 85; 36 rue des Boulangers; metro Cardinal Lemoine; menus €8, €10.50 & €13)* is a great choice for organic vegetarian fare.

Some of the best crepes in Paris are sold at **Le Petit Grec** *(68 rue Mouffetard; crepes about €3)*, which has upgraded from the cart it used to operate over the street. **Tashi Delek** *(☎ 01 43 26 55 55; 4 rue des Fossés St Jacques; metro Luxembourg; dinner menus €17.50, vegetarian dishes €6.40-8.40)* offers good, cheap, Tibetan fare. **Douce France** *(7 rue Royer Collard; metro Luxembourg)* is a popular hole-in-the-wall selling great sandwiches for €2.20 each.

Le Grenier de Notre-Dame *(☎ 01 43 29 98 29; 18 rue de la Bûcherie; menu €12)* is a vegetarian restaurant with dishes like lasagna and cassoulet.

Montparnasse (6e & 14e) One of many Breton-style creperies along rue d'Odessa and rue du Montparnasse is **Le Flibustier** *(☎ 01 43 21 70 03; 20 rue d'Odessa; crepes around €6)*. **Mustang Café** *(☎ 01 43 35 36 12; 84 blvd du Montparnasse; metro Montparnasse-Bienvenüe; platters & chilli from €10; open to 5am)* serves passable Tex-Mex.

For innovative food in a traditional setting, try **Le Caméléon** *(☎ 01 43 20 63 43; 6 rue de Chevreuse, 6e; metro Vavin)*; the lobster ravioli (€16) alone is worth a visit.

Montmartre (9e & 18e) Restaurants around place du Tertre tend to be touristy and overpriced – but there are alternatives. An old favourite is **Chez des Fondus** *(☎ 01 42 55 22 65; 17 rue des Trois Frères; metro Abbesses; open 7pm-2am daily)*, where €15 buys an apéritif, wine, and either cheese or meat fondue. **Le Mono** *(☎ 01 46 06 99 20; 40 rue Véron; dishes €8-12)*, is another option, serving West African fare.

Le Bateau Lavoir *(☎ 01 42 54 23 92; 8 rue Garreau; entrees/mains €7/14)* is an atmospheric and traditional French restaurant.

University Restaurants Paris has 17 *restaurants universitaires* (student cafeterias) run by the **Centre Régional des Œuvres Universitaires et Scolaires** *(CROUS; ☎ 01 40 51 37 01)*. Students with ID pay €2.40. Opening times vary, so check the schedule outside any of the following: **Assas** *(☎ 01 46 33 61 25; 92 rue d'Assas, 6e; metro Port Royal or Notre Dame des Champs)*; **Bullier** *(☎ 01 43 54 93 38; 39 ave Georges Bernanos, 5e; metro Port Royal)*; **Châtelet** *(☎ 01 43 31 51 66; 10 rue Jean Calvin, 5e; metro Censier Daubenton)*, just off rue Mouffetard; and **Mabillon** *(☎ 01 43 25 66 23; 3 rue Mabillon, 6e; metro Mabillon)*.

Self-Catering Supermarkets are always cheaper than small grocery shops. The **Monoprix supermarket** *(23 ave de l'Opéra)* opposite metro Pyramides is convenient for the Louvre area, or try **Ed l'Épicier** *(37 rue Lacépède; metro Monge)* if you're in the Latin Quarter. For a different shopping experience altogether, head to **Fauchon** *(☎ 01 47 42 91 10; 26 place de la Madeleine; metro Madeleine)*, Paris' most famous gourmet-food shop.

Food Markets Paris' **marchés découverts** *(open-air markets; open 7am-2pm)* pop up in various squares and streets two or three times a week. There are also **marchés couverts** *(covered markets; open 8am-about 1pm & 4pm-7pm Tues-Sun)*. Ask at your hotel for the location of the nearest market.

Notre Dame Area (4e & 5e) There are a number of *fromageries* and **groceries** along rue St Louis en l'Île *(metro Pont Marie)* and place Maubert hosts a **food market** *(open Tues, Thur & Sat)* and various other food shops.

St Germain des Prés (6e) Food shops are clustered on **rue de Seine** and **rue de Buci** *(metro Mabillon)* and at rue **St Jacques**. The covered **Marché St Germain** *(rue Lobineau)*, just north of the eastern end of Église St Germain des Prés, has a huge array of produce and prepared foods.

Marais (4e) **Flo Prestige** *(10 rue St Antoine; metro Bastille; open 8am-11pm daily)* has fancy picnic supplies and, more importantly, delectable pastries and baked goods.

Montmartre (18e) Most of the food shops in this area are along rue Lepic and rue des Abbesses, which is about 500m southwest of Sacré Cœur.

Entertainment

It's virtually impossible to sample the richness of Paris' entertainment scene without consulting *Pariscope* (€0.40; includes an English-language insert from Time Out) or *L'Officiel des Spectacles* (€0.35), both published on Wednesday and available at any newsstand. Look out for *LYLO*, a free listings zine.

Tickets Tickets can be reserved and bought at the ticket outlets in **FNAC stores** *(☎ 01 43 42 04 04; 4 place Bastille, 12e; metro Bastille • ☎ 01 40 41 40 00; 3rd underground level, Forum des Halles shopping mall, 1 rue Pierre Lescot, 1er; metro Châtelet-Les Halles)* and in the **Virgin Megastores** *(☎ 01 49 53 50 00; 52 ave des Champs-Élysées, 8e; metro Franklin D Roosevelt • ☎ 01 44 50 03 10; 99 rue de Rivoli, 1er; metro Pont Neuf)*.

Bars A gay/mixed bar with funky art, **L'Étoile Manquante** *(☎ 01 42 72 47 47; 34 rue Vieille du Temple, 4e; metro St Paul)* also serves meals. The anglophone, and always crowded, **Stolly's** *(☎ 01 42 76 06 76; 16 rue de la Cloche Percée, 4e; metro Hôtel de Ville)* is on a tiny street just off rue de Rivoli.

De La Ville Café *(☎ 01 48 24 48 09; 36 blvd Bonne Nouvelle, 10e; metro Bonne Nouvelle)* is a fashionable but welcoming bar. **Café Oz** *(☎ 01 43 54 30 48; 18 rue St Jacques; metro Luxembourg)* is a casual and friendly pub that has Fosters on tap.

Relaxed **La Contrescarpe** *(☎ 01 43 36 82 88; 57 rue Lacépède, 5e)*, on place Contrescarpe, is as nice for morning coffee or cocktail hour.

Clubs The clubs and other dancing venues favoured by the Parisian 'in' crowd change frequently, and many are officially private, which means bouncers can deny entry to whomever they don't like the look of. For example, single men may not be admitted; women, on the other hand, get in free of charge some nights.

Favela Chic *(☎ 01 40 21 38 14; 18 rue du Faubourg du Temple, 9e; metro République; admission free; open Tues-Sat 7.30pm-2am)* morphs at night from a Brazilian restaurant into a heaving dance spot.

Batofar *(☎ 01 45 83 33 06; quai de la Gare, 13e; metro Bibliothèque Nationale)* is the best known place out of a number of floating barges, all of which host parties and concerts.

Café de la Danse *(☎ 01 47 00 57 59; 5 passage Louis Philippe; metro Bastille)* is a good venue with a varied line-up. It's off 21 rue de Lappe. Pick up a program at Web Bar (see Email & Internet Access earlier).

Jazz Caveau de la Huchette *(☎ 01 43 26 65 05; 5 rue de la Huchette, 5e; metro St Michel; adult/student €10.50/9 Mon-Fri, all €13 Sat-Sun; open 9.30pm-2am, later Sat-Sun)* is touristy but still a favourite place for live jazz.

Opera & Classical Music Paris plays host to dozens of concerts each week. The **Opéra National de Paris** *(☎ 0892 69 78 68; W www.opera-de-paris.fr)* splits its performances between **Opéra Garnier**, its original home built in 1875, and the modern **Opéra Bastille**, which opened in 1989. Both opera houses also stage ballets and concerts. Opera tickets (available from September to July only) cost €7 to €109; ballets €8 to €67; and concerts €7 to €39. Unsold tickets are offered 15 minutes prior to showtime to students and under 25s for about €15 – ask for the *tarif spécial*.

FRANCE

Getting There & Away

Air Paris has two major international airports. **Aéroport d'Orly** *(flight & other information ☎ 01 49 75 15 15, 0836 25 05 05)* is 14km south of central Paris. **Aéroport Charles de Gaulle** *(☎ 01 48 62 22 80, 0836 25 05 05)*, also known as Roissy-Charles de Gaulle (it's in the suburb of Roissy), is 23km northeast of central Paris.

Telephone numbers for information at Paris' airline offices are:

Air France (☎ 0836 68 10 48)
Air Liberté (☎ 0825 80 58 05)
Air New Zealand (☎ 01 40 53 82 23)
Air UK (☎ 01 44 56 18 08)
American Airlines (☎ 0810 87 28 72)
British Airways (☎ 0825 82 54 00)
Continental (☎ 01 42 99 09 09)
Lufthansa (☎ 0802 02 00 30)
Northwest Airlines (☎ 0810 55 65 56)
Qantas (☎ 0820 82 05 00)
Singapore Airlines (☎ 01 53 65 79 01)
Thai (☎ 01 44 20 70 15)
United (☎ 0801 72 72 72)

Bus Eurolines terminal, **Gare Routière Internationale** *(☎ 0836 69 52 52; Porte de Bagnolet, 20e; metro Gallieni)*, is on the eastern edge of Paris. There is also a **ticket office** *(☎ 01 43 54 11 99; 55 rue St Jacques, 5e; metro Cluny-La Sorbonne; open 9.30am-6.30pm Mon-Fri, 10am-1pm & 2pm-6pm Sat)* in town. There is no domestic, intercity bus service to or from Paris.

Train Paris has six major train stations *(gares)*, each handling traffic to different destinations. For information in English call ☎ 0836 35 35 39, 7am to 10pm. The metro station attached to each train station bears the same name as the *gare*. Paris' major train stations are:

Gare d'Austerlitz (13e) Loire Valley, Spain and Portugal and non-TGV trains to southwestern France.
Gare de l'Est (10e) Parts of France east of Paris (Champagne, Alsace and Lorraine), Luxembourg, parts of Switzerland (Basel, Lucerne, Zürich), southern Germany (Frankfurt, Munich) and points farther east.
Gare de Lyon (12e) Regular and TGV Sud-Est trains to places southeast of Paris, including Dijon, Lyon, Provence, the Côte d'Azur, the Alps, parts of Switzerland (Bern, Geneva, Lausanne), Italy and points beyond.
Gare Montparnasse (15e) Brittany and places between (Chartres, Angers, Nantes) and the terminus of the TGV Atlantique serving Tours, Nantes, Bordeaux and other destinations in southwestern France.
Gare du Nord (10e) Northern suburbs of Paris, northern France, the UK, Belgium, northern Germany, Scandinavia, Moscow etc; terminus of the TGV Nord (Lille and Calais), and the Eurostar to London.
Gare St Lazare (8e) Normandy, including Bayeaux, Rouen, Dieppe, Le Havre and Cherbourg.

Getting Around

Paris' public transit system, most of which is operated by the **RATP** *(Régie Autonome des Transports Parisians; ☎ 0836 68 77 14; English information ☎ 0892 68 41 14)* is cheap and efficient.

To/From Orly Airport Orly Rail is the quickest way to reach the Left Bank and the 16e. Take the free shuttle bus to the Pont de Rungis-Aéroport d'Orly RER station, which is on the C2 line, and get on a train heading into the city. Another fast way into town is the Orlyval shuttle train (€7, 35 to 40 minutes); it stops near Orly-Sud's Porte F and links Orly with the Antony RER station, which is on line B4. Orlybus (€5.50, 30 minutes) takes you to the Denfert-Rochereau metro station, 14e. Air France buses (€7.50) go to/from Gare Montparnasse, 15e, (every 15 minutes) along Aérogare des Invalides in the 7e. RATP bus No 183 (one bus/metro ticket) goes to Porte de Choisy, 13e, but is very slow. Jetbus, the cheapest option, links both terminals with the Villejuif-Louis Aragon metro stop (€4.50, 15 minutes). All services between Orly and Paris run every 15 minutes or so (less frequently late at night) from 5.30am or 6.30am to 11pm or 11.30pm. A taxi to/from Orly costs about €45 to €55, plus €0.90 per piece of luggage over 5kg.

To/From Charles de Gaulle Airport Roissybus links the city with both of the airport's train stations (€8, 50 minutes). To get to the airport, take any line B train whose four letter destination code begins with E (eg, EIRE). Regular metro ticket windows can't always sell these tickets, so you may have to buy one at the RER station where you board. Trains run every 15 or 20 minutes from 6am to around 11pm.

Air France bus No 2 will take you to Porte Maillot and the corner of ave Carnot near the Arc de Triomphe for €10; bus No 4 to Gare Montparnasse costs €11.50.

RATP bus No 350 (€3.90 or three bus/metro tickets) links both *aérogares* (air terminals) with Porte de la Chapelle, 18e, and stops at Gare du Nord and Gare de l'Est, both in the 10e. RATP Bus No 351 goes to ave du Trône, on the eastern side of place de la Nation in the 11e, and runs every half-hour or so until 8.20pm (9.30pm from the airport to the city). The trip costs €3.90 or three bus/metro tickets.

A taxi to/from Charles de Gaulle costs about €38 to €42.

Bus Short trips cost one bus/metro/RER ticket (see Metro & RER below), while longer rides require two. Travellers without tickets can purchase them from the driver. Whatever kind of ticket *(coupon)* you have, you must cancel it in the little machine next to the driver. The fines are hefty if you're caught without a ticket or without a cancelled ticket. If you have a Carte Orange or Paris Visite pass, just flash it at the driver – do not cancel it in the machine.

After the metro shuts down at around 12.45am, the Noctambus network, whose symbol is a black owl silhouetted against a yellow moon, links the Châtelet-Hôtel de Ville area with most parts of the city. Noctambuses begin their runs from ave Victoria, 4e, between the Hôtel de Ville and place du Châtelet between 1am and 5.30am seven days a week. A single ride costs €2.40 and allows one transfer onto another Noctambus.

Metro & RER Paris' underground rail network consists of two separate but linked systems: the Métropolitain, known as the metro, which now has 14 lines and over 300 stations, and the suburban commuter rail network, the RER, which, along with certain SNCF lines, is divided into eight concentric zones. The whole system has been designed so that no point in Paris is more than 500m from a metro stop.

Each metro train is known by the name of its terminus; trains on the same line have different names depending on which direction they are travelling in. On lines that split into several branches and thus have more than one end-of-the-line station, the final destination of each train is indicated on the front, sides and interior of the train cars. In the stations, white-on-blue *sortie* signs indicate exits and black-on-orange *correspondance* signs show how to get to connecting trains. The last metro train sets out on its final run at 12.30am. Plan ahead so as not to miss your connection. The metro starts up again at 5.30am.

The same tickets are valid on the metro, the bus and, for travel within the Paris city limits, the RER's 2nd-class carriages. They cost €1.30 if bought individually and €9.30 (half for children aged four to 11) for a *carnet* of 10. One ticket lets you travel between any two metro stations, including stations outside of the Paris city limits, no matter how many transfers are required. You can also use it on the RER system within zone 1.

For travel on the RER to destinations outside the city, purchase a special ticket *before* you board the train or you won't be able to get out of the station and could be fined. Always keep your ticket until you reach your destination and exit the station.

The cheapest and easiest way to travel the metro is with a Carte Orange, a bus/metro/RER pass that comes in weekly and monthly versions. You can get tickets for travel in up to eight urban and suburban zones; the basic ticket – valid for zones 1 and 2 – is probably sufficient.

The weekly ticket costs €13.25 for zones 1 and 2, and is valid Monday to Sunday. Even if you'll be in Paris for only three or four days, it may very well work out cheaper than purchasing a *carnet* – you'll break even at 15 rides – and it will certainly cost less than buying a daily Mobilis or Paris Visite pass. The monthly Carte Orange ticket (€44.35 for zones 1 and 2) begins on the first day of each calendar month. Both are on sale in metro and RER stations and at certain bus terminals.

To get a monthly Carte Orange, bring a passport-size photograph of yourself to the ticket counter (automatic photo booths are in most stations). You don't need a photo for a weekly *carte*.

Mobilis and Paris Visite passes, designed for tourists, are on sale in many metro and train stations and international airports. The Mobilis card (and its *coupon*) allows unlimited travel for one day in two to eight zones (€5 to €17.95). Paris Visite transport passes, providing discounts on entries to certain museums and activities as well as transport, are valid for one/two/three/five consecutive days of travel in either three, five or eight zones. One–three zones cost €8.35/13.70/18.25/26.65 for one/two/three/five days. Children aged four to 11 pay half-price. Tickets can be bought at larger metro and RER stations, at SNCF bureaus in Paris and at the airports.

Taxi The *prise en* charge (flag fall) is €2. Within the city limits, it costs €0.60 per kilometre for travel 7am to 7pm Monday to Saturday (tariff A). At night and on Sunday and holidays (tariff B), it's €1 per kilometre. An extra €2.45 is charged for taking a fourth passenger, but most drivers refuse to take more than three people because of insurance constraints. Luggage over 5kg costs €0.90 extra and for pick-up from SNCF mainline stations there's a €0.70 supplement. The usual tip is 10% no matter what the fare.

There are 500 taxi stands *(tête de station)* in Paris. Radio-dispatched taxis include **Taxis Bleus** *(☎ 01 49 36 10 10)* and **G7 Taxis** *(☎ 01 47 39 47 39)*. If you order a taxi by phone, the meter is switched on as soon as the driver gets your call.

Car & Motorcycle Driving in Paris is nerve-wracking but not impossible. The fastest way to get across Paris is usually via the Périphérique, the ring road that encircles the city.

Renting a small car (Opel Corsa 1.2) for one day with insurance and 250km costs about €85, but cheaper deals are often available.

Rental agencies in Paris include:

Avis (☎ 0820 05 05 05, 01 43 48 29 26)
Budget (☎ 01 45 44 62 00)
Europcar (☎ 0825 35 23 52)
Hertz (☎ 01 39 38 38 38)
National/Citer (☎ 01 42 06 06 06)

Bicycle There are 130km of bicycle lanes running throughout Paris. Some of the paths aren't particularly attractive or safe, but cyclists may be fined about €40 for failing to use them. The tourist office distributes a free brochure-map called *Paris à Vélo*.

Paris à Vélo (*☎ 01 43 37 59 22; 2 rue du Fer á Moulin arrondissement; metro Censier Daubenton)* rents bikes for €12.20/30.50 for one/three days, and offers tours of the city. Also try the RATP-sponsored **Roue Libre** *(☎ 0810 44 15 34; 1 passage Mondétour arrondissement)*.

Around Paris

The region surrounding Paris is known as the Île de France (Island of France) because of its position between the rivers Aube, Marne, Oise and Seine.

DISNEYLAND PARIS

It took US$4.4 billion to turn the beet fields 32km east of Paris into the much heralded Disneyland Paris *(adult/child 3-11 years €39/29 Apr-early Jan, €29/25 early Jan-Mar; open 9am-8pm daily, to 11pm July-Aug)*, which is now the most popular tourist attraction in Europe. Three-day passes are available.

VERSAILLES

pop 95,000

Versailles served as the country's political capital and the seat of the royal court from 1682 until 1789. After the Franco-Prussian War of 1870–71, the victorious Prussians proclaimed the establishment of the German empire from the chateau's Galerie des Glaces (Hall of Mirrors), and in 1919 the Treaty of Versailles was signed in the same room, officially ending WWI.

The chateau is often jam-packed with tourists, particularly on weekends, in summer and most especially on summer Sundays. If you can, it is worth arriving early to avoid the worst of the queues; or beat most of the queues by prebuying (or buying on arrival) a guided tour ticket, which includes general admission to Versailles.

The **tourist office** *(☎ 01 39 24 88 88; ⓔ tourisme@ot-versailles.fr; 2bis ave de Paris; open daily)* is just north of the Versailles-Rive Gauche train station.

Château de Versailles

The enormous Château de Versailles *(☎ 01 30 83 78 00, 01 30 83 77 77)* was built in the mid-17th century during the reign of Louis XIV (the Sun King). The chateau essentially consists of four parts: the main palace building; the vast 17th-century gardens; the late-17th-century Grand Trianon; and the mid-18th-century Petit Trianon.

The main building opens 9am to 5.30pm (6.30pm April to October) Tuesday to Sunday. Admission to the **Grands Appartements** (State Apartments), including the 73m-long **Galerie des Glaces** (Hall of Mirrors) and the **Appartement de la Reine** (Queen's Suite), costs €7.50 (after 3.30pm €5.30, free for under 18s). Tickets are on sale at Entrée A (Entrance A) off to the right from the equestrian statue of Louis XIV as you approach the building. You won't be able to visit other parts of the main palace unless you take one of the guided tours (see Guided Tours later). Entrée H has facilities for the disabled, including a lift.

The **Grand Trianon** *(€5, €3 reduced rate; admits to Petit Trianon too)* opens noon to 6.30pm daily April to October; the rest of the year it closes at 5.30pm. The **Petit Trianon** is open the same days and hours.

The **gardens** *(€3)* are open 8am (9am in winter) to nightfall daily (except if it's snowing). On Saturday, July to September, and Sunday early April to early October, the baroque fountains 'perform' the **Grandes Eaux** *(☎ 01 30 83 78 78; €5.50; times vary)*.

A 'passport' (€21.20) includes admission to the Chateau, audio tour, the Grand Trianon, Petit Trianon and the garden; it's available from FNAC stores and some SNCF stations.

Guided Tours To make a reservation go to Entrées C or D. A one-hour tour costs €4.20 in addition to the regular entry fee; 80-minute audio- guide tours are available at Entrée A for €3.50.

Getting There & Away

Bus No 171 (€1.30 or one metro/bus ticket, 35 minutes) links Pont de Sèvres in Paris with the place d'Armes and Versailles, but it's faster to go by train. Each of Versailles' three train stations is served by RER and/or SNCF trains coming from a different group of Paris stations.

RER line C4 takes you from Paris' Left Bank RER stations to Versailles-Rive Gauche station (€2.20). From Paris, catch any train whose four-letter code begins with the letter 'V'. There are up to 70 trains daily (around 35 on Sunday), and the last train back to Paris leaves shortly before midnight.

RER line C5 links Paris' Left Bank with Versailles-Chantiers station (€2.20). From Paris, take any train whose code begins with 'S'. Versailles-Chantiers is also served by some three dozen SNCF trains daily (20 on Sunday) from Gare Montparnasse (€2.20, 15 minutes); all trains on this line continue on to Chartres.

From Paris' Gare St Lazare (€3) and La Défense (€2), the SNCF has about 70 trains daily to Versailles-Rive Droite, which is 1200m from the chateau. The last train to Paris leaves a bit past midnight.

CHARTRES

pop 42,059

The impressive 13th-century cathedral of Chartres rises spectacularly from the fields 88km southwest of Paris. The amenable town is an easy place to spend a day or two.

The medieval sections of Chartres are situated along the Eure River and the hillside to the west. The cathedral is about 500m east of the train station. The **tourist office** *(☎ 02 37 18 26 26; ⓔ chartres.tourism@wanadoo.fr)* is across place de la Cathédrale from the cathedral's main entrance. The **post office** *(place des Épars)* handles money exchange.

Cathédrale Notre Dame

There have been churches on this site since the 4th century. The current 13th-century cathedral *(☎ 02 37 21 75 02; open 8am-8pm Easter-Oct, 8.30am-7.30pm Nov-Easter, except during services)* has a high degree of architectural unity, having been built in 30 years after a Romanesque cathedral on this site was destroyed by fire in 1194. Unlike so many of its contemporaries, this early Gothic masterpiece has not been significantly modified, apart from a 16th-century steeple.

Fascinating **tours** *(☎ 02 37 28 15 58; €5.50, students €4)* are conducted by Englishman Malcolm Miller from Easter to November; audioguides (€2.50-5.65) are available from the cathedral bookshop. The 112m-high **Clocher Neuf** *(new bell tower; adult/concession 18-25 years €4/2.50)* is well worth the ticket price and the long, spiral climb.

Inside, the cathedral's most exceptional feature is its 172 **stained-glass windows**, most of which are 13th-century originals. The **trésor** *(treasury)* displays a piece of cloth said to have been worn by the Virgin Mary.

The early-11th-century Romanesque **crypt**, the largest in France, can be visited by a half-hour guided tour in French (with a written English translation) for €2.30.

Old City

Streets with buildings of interest include **rue de la Tannerie**, which runs along the Eure, and **rue des Écuyers**, midway between the cathedral and the river. **Église St Pierre** *(place St Pierre)* has a massive bell tower dating from around 1000 and some fine (often overlooked) medieval stained-glass windows.

Places to Stay

The pleasant and calm **Auberge de Jeunesse** *(☎ 02 37 34 27 64, fax 02 37 35 75 85; 23 ave Neigre; dorm beds €10.50; reception open 2pm-10pm daily)* includes breakfast in its prices. To get here from the train station, take bus No 5 (direction Mare aux Moines) to the Rouliers stop.

It's fair to say that **Hôtel de l'Ouest** *(☎ 02 37 21 43 27, fax 02 37 21 47 80; 3 place Pierre Sémard; singles/doubles from €15/23)* is pretty dingy. Better is **Hôtel Jehan de Beauce** *(☎ 02 37 21 01 41, fax 02 37 21 59 10; ⓔ jehan_de_beauce@club-internet.fr; 1st floor, 19 ave Jehan de Beauce; singles/doubles from €37/45)*.

Le Boeuf Couronné *(☎ 02 37 18 06 06, fax 02 37 21 72 13; 15 place Châtelet; singles/doubles from €26/29)* is quiet but central with a decent restaurant on site.

Places to Eat

Across from the south porch of the cathedral is **Café Serpente** *(☎ 02 37 21 68 81; 2 rue du Cloître Notre Dame; mains €13-18)*.

Le Vesuve *(☎ 02 37 21 56 35; 30 place des Halles; pizzas €6.50-9.50)* serves light meals. There's a **Monoprix supermarket** *(21 rue Noël Ballay)* northeast of place des Épars.

Getting There & Away

There are three dozen trains daily (20 on Sunday) to/from Gare Montparnasse in Paris (€11.40, 55 to 70 minutes) also stopping at

Chantiers station in Versaille (€9.70, 45 to 60 minutes). The last train travelling back to Paris leaves Chartres a little bit after 9pm (7.55pm on Saturday, after 10pm on Sunday and holidays).

Alsace & Lorraine

The charming Alsace region, long a meeting place of Europe's Latin and Germanic cultures, nestles between the Vosges Mountains and the Rhine River, which marks the Franco-German border.

Most of Alsace became part of France in 1648 (Strasbourg, the region's largest city, retained its independence until 1681), but French rule did little to dampen German enthusiasm for a foothold on the west bank of the Rhine. The region (along with part of Lorraine) was twice annexed by Germany – from the Franco-Prussian War (1871) until the end of WWI, and again between 1940 and 1944.

STRASBOURG

pop 451,000

Strasbourg, just a few kilometres west of the Rhine, is Alsace's intellectual and cultural capital. Towering above the restaurants and pubs of the lively old city is the marvellous cathedral, near which you'll find one of the finest ensembles of museums in France.

When it was founded in 1949, the Council of Europe decided to base itself in Strasbourg as a symbol of Franco-German (and pan-European) co-operation. The city is also the seat of the European Parliament (the legislative branch of the EU) at Palais de l'Europe; hence, many signs are in French, German and English.

Today, Strasbourg has acquired something of a reputation as a flashpoint for street crime, an issue currently dominating French politics. Around tram intersection place de l'Homme-de-Fer, travellers should keep their wits about them.

Orientation

The train station is 400m west of the Grande Île (Large Island), the city centre, delimited by the Ill river to the south and the Fossé du Faux Rempart to the north. Place Kléber, the main public square on the Grande Île, is 400m northwest of the cathedral. Grand Rue is the main pedestrian thoroughfare; most nightlife is across the river in the Krutenau quarter.

Information

The **main tourist office** *(☎ 03 88 52 28 28, fax 03 88 52 28 29; W www.strasbourg.com; 17 place de la Cathédrale; open daily)* has **branch offices** *(☎ 03 88 32 51 49 • ☎ 03 88 61 39 23; both open daily)* at level -1 in the underground complex beneath the train station and at Pont de l'Europe respectively. Offices exchange money and sell the three-day **Strasbourg Pass** *(€9.90)*, which offers sightseeing discounts.

The **main post office** *(5 ave de la Marseillaise; open 8am-noon & 1pm-5.30pm Mon-Fri, 8am-noon Sat)* has exchange services and Cyberposte; there's a branch in place de la Cathédrale.

The **Best Coffee Shop** *(☎ 03 88 35 10 60; 10 quai des Pêcheurs; open 8am-7pm Mon-Fri, 9.30am-5pm Sat)* offers one hour of Net access for €3 with a compulsory drink. **L'Utopie** *(☎ 03 88 23 89 21; 21 rue du Fossé des Tanneurs)*, off the cinema-lined rue du 22 Novembre, has the same rate.

Things to See

Grande Île is about bustling public squares and pedestrianised areas with upmarket shopping. Work started on Strasbourg's lacy Gothic cathedral, **Cathédrale Notre Dame** *(open 7am-11.30am & 12.40pm-7pm daily)* in 1176. The west facade was completed in 1284; the spire (its southern companion was never built) not until 1439. The **astronomical clock** *(adult/concession €0.80/0.60)* goes through its paces at 12.30pm daily. You are able to visit the 66m-high **platform** *(adult/concession €3/2.30; open 9am-7pm)* above the facade (from which the tower and its spire soar another 76m) via 332 steep steps.

Crisscrossed by narrow lanes, canals and locks, **Petite France**, in the southwest corner of the Grande Île, is a fairy-tale area of half-timbered houses.

Tours of the **Palais de l'Europe** *(☎ 03 88 17 20 07)* and the **Conseil de l'Europe** *(Council of Europe; ☎ 03 88 41 20 29)* – both about 2km northeast of the cathedral – have been scaled down for security reasons. Group tours are still possible; phone ahead for reservations.

Place de la Gare hosts a huge flea market every Saturday.

Museums

The outstanding **Musée de l'Œuvre Notre Dame** *(3 place du Château; open 10am-6pm Tues-Sun)* displays one of France's finest collections of sculpture, including many of the cathedral's original statues. The **Palais Rohan** *(2 place du Château; open Wed-Mon 10am-6pm)*, built between 1732 and 1742 as a residence for the city's princely bishops, now houses three museums (a combined ticket costs adult/concession €6/3): the **Musée Archéologique**, **Musée des Arts Décoratifs** and the **Musée des Beaux-Arts**.

The superb **Musée d'Art Moderne et Contemporain** *(☎ 03 88 23 31 31; 1 place Hans Jean Arp; adult/concession €4.40/3; open 11am-7pm Tues-Sun, until 10pm Thur)* has a extensive collection of works from Rodin to Picasso.

The **Musée Alsacien** *(23-25 quai Saint-Nicolas; adult/concession €3/1.50; open 10am-6pm Wed-Sun)* glimpses Alsatian life throughout history.

Organised Tours

Call to reserve a free brewery tour of **Kronenbourg** *(☎ 03 88 27 41 59; 68 route d'Oberhausbergen; tram stop Duc d'Alsace)* or **Heineken** *(☎ 03 88 19 57 50; 4 rue Saint-Charles; bus No 4 to Schiltigheim Mairie)*. Both are in suburbs about 2.5km from the city centre (northwest and north, respectively).

Places to Stay

It's *extremely* difficult to find accommodation from Monday to Thursday, when the European Parliament is in plenary session (one week monthly, except August, and twice in October). Many hotels, however, offer good deals at weekends.

Camping The grassy **Camping de la Montagne Verte** *(☎ 03 88 30 25 46; 2 rue Robert Forrer; open Mar-Dec; 2-person sites €10.90)* is a few hundred metres from the Auberge de Jeunesse René Cassin (see Hostels, below). Rates include breakfast.

Hostels The modern **CIARUS** *(☎ 03 88 15 27 88, fax 03 88 15 27 89; 7 rue Finkmatt; bus No 4, 2 or 10 to place de Pierre stop; dorm beds from €16 including breakfast)* is about 1km northeast of the train station.

The 286-bed **Auberge de Jeunesse René Cassin** *(☎ 03 88 30 26 46, fax 03 88 30 35 16; 9 rue de l'Auberge de Jeunesse; dorm beds €13 including breakfast)* is 2km southwest of the train station. Take tram B or C to Montagne Verte stop then bus No 12, 13 or 15 to Auberge de Jeunesse stop.

Hotels Opposite the train station, **Hôtel du Rhin** *(☎ 03 88 32 35 00, fax 03 88 23 51 92; 7-8 place de la Gare; doubles with washbasin/shower & toilet from €41/58)* has decent but unwelcoming rooms. A better option, a few minutes' walk along rue du Maire Kuss, is refurbished **Hôtel Le Grillon** *(☎ 03 88 32 71 88, fax 03 88 32 22 01; ⓔ contact@grillon.com; 2 rue Thiergarten; singles/doubles €38/49)*, which offers clean rooms, a €6.50 buffet breakfast and Net access (€1 for 15 minutes).

Opposite, **Hôtel Le Colmar** *(☎ 03 88 32 16 89, fax 03 88 21 97 17; 1 rue du Maire Kuss; singles/doubles from €24/27)* has cheap, simple rooms.

The dark, rustic **Hôtel Patricia** *(☎ 03 88 32 14 60, fax 03 88 32 19 08; ⓔ hotelpatricia@hotmail.com; 1a rue du Puits; rooms with/without bathroom €38/29)* has ordinary rooms but great views of Petite France.

The two-star **Hôtel de l'Ill** *(☎ 03 88 36 20 01, fax 03 88 35 30 03; 8 rue des Bateliers; singles/doubles €34/40)* has a quiet location away from tourist hordes.

Places to Eat

A *winstub* (pronounced **veen**-shtub) is typically Alsatian, serving hearty fare; try **Winstub Le Clou** *(3 rue du Chaudron; mains €12-20; closed Wed lunch, Sun & holidays)*.

Rue de l'Écurie is the best spot for cheap eats. It has several decent restaurants offering good value *menus* which – rare for Strasbourg – open on Sunday too. At No 4, **La Robe des Champs** *(☎ 03 88 22 36 82)* has huge €10 salads, while **Le Petit Ours** *(☎ 03 88 32 13 21)* at No 3 has filling lunch options.

Of Petite France's tourist-oriented restaurants, **Au Pont St Martin** *(15 rue des Moulins; menu €7)* has a few vegetarian options.

Self-service vegetarian-organic food is on offer at **Adan** *(☎ 03 88 35 70 84; 6 rue Sédillot; open noon-2pm Mon-Sat)*. Self-caterers can head for **Monoprix supermarket** *(47 rue des Grandes Arcades; open 8.30am-8pm Mon-Sat)*.

Café La Chaine d'Or *(134 Grand Rue)* is a great place to read the papers over a coffee.

STRASBOURG

PLACES TO STAY
1 CIARUS Hostel
14 Hôtel du Rhin
15 Hôtel Le Grillon
17 Hôtel Le Colmar
28 Hôtel de l'Ill
35 Hôtel Gutenberg
45 Hôtel Patricia

PLACES TO EAT
22 Monoprix Supermarket
23 Winstub Le Clou
36 Café La Chaine d'Or
44 Au Pont St Martin
46 Le Petit Ours
47 La Robe des Champs
52 Adan Vegetarian Restaurant

MUSEUMS
29 Palais Rohan (Musée Archéologique, Musée des Arts Décoratifs & Musée des Beaux-Arts)
30 Musée de l'Œuvre Notre Dame
42 Musée d'Art Moderne et Contemporain
48 Musée Alsacien

PUBS & CLUBS
26 La Salamandre
27 Rock City
38 The Irish Times
39 Académie de la Bière
41 L'Abattoir

TRAM STOPS
3 Parc du Contades Tram Stop
5 République Tram Stop
11 Ancienne Synagogue Les Halles Tram Stop
12 Gare Centrale (Underground Tram Stop)
19 Homme de Fer Tram & Bus Hub
24 Gallia Tram Stop
37 Langstross Grand' Rue Tram Stop
40 Faubourg National Tram Stop
43 Musée d'Art Moderne Tram Stop
49 Porte de l'Hôpital Tram Stop

OTHER
2 Église Saint Pierre-le-Jeune (Catholic)
4 Synagogue de la Paix
6 Église Saint Paul
7 Main Post Office
8 Banque de France
9 Hôtel de Police
10 Église Saint Pierre-le-Jeune (Protestant)
13 Tourist Office Annexe (Galerie de l'En-Verre)
16 Velocation Bike Hire
18 Église Saint Pierre-le-Vieux (Catholic & Protestant)
20 L'Utopie Internet
21 CTS Bus Information Office
25 Best Coffee Shop
31 Post Office
32 Cathédrale Notre Dame
33 Main Tourist Office
34 Buses to Kehl
50 Hôpital Civil
51 Eurolines Bus Office

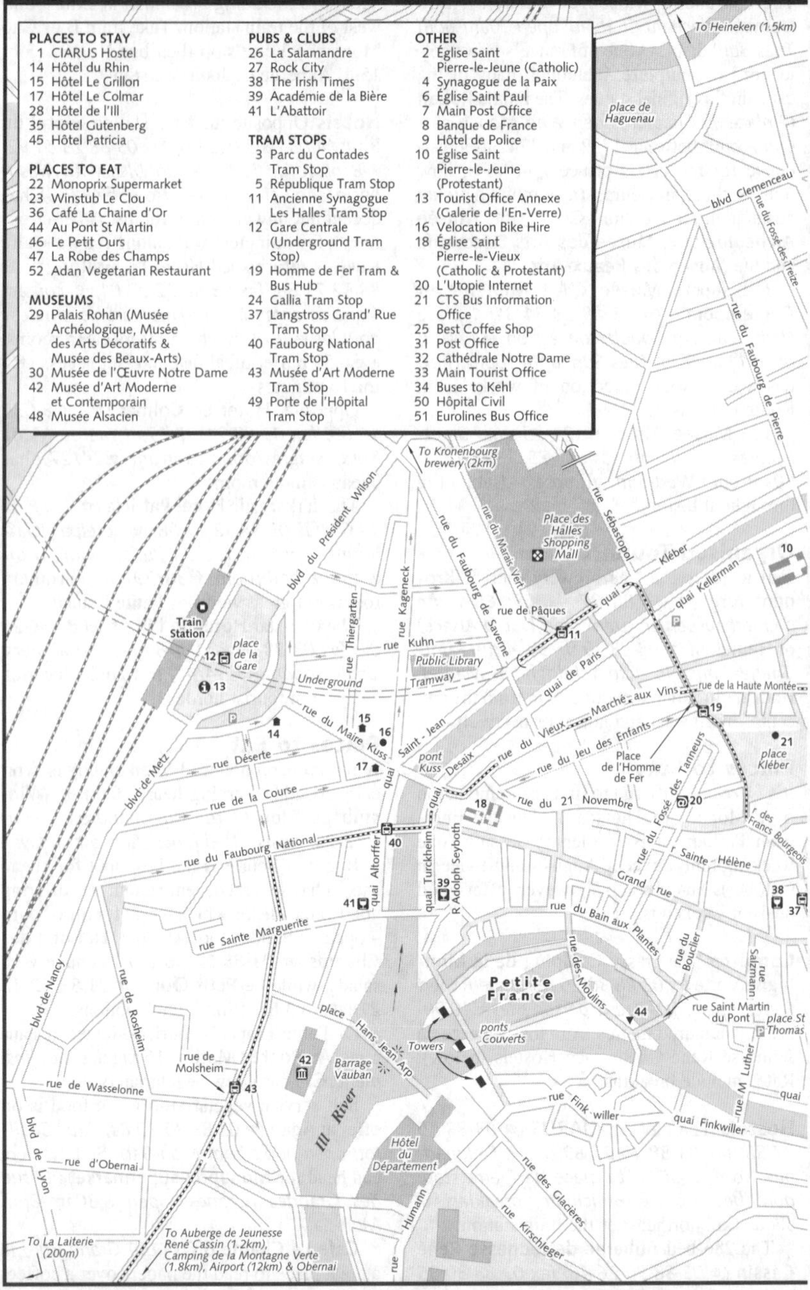

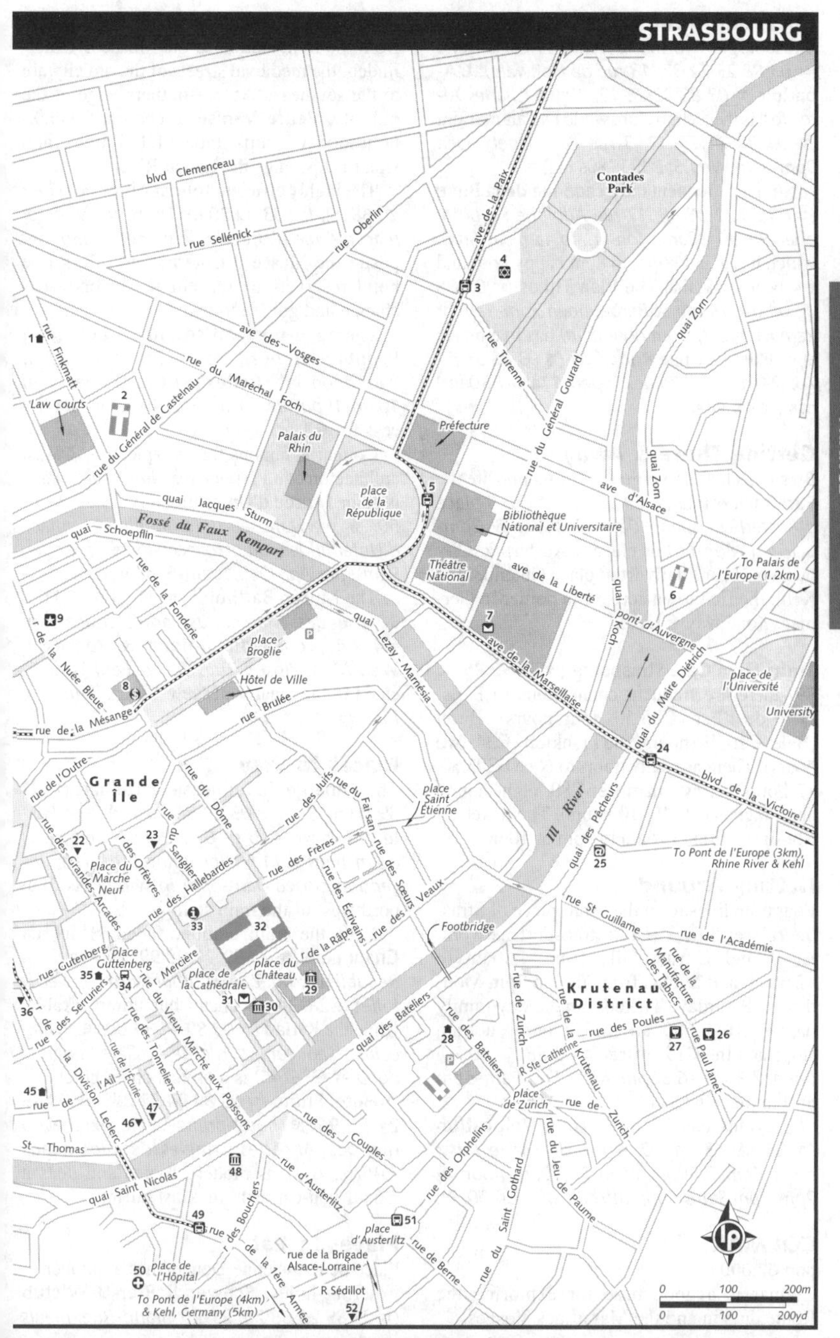
STRASBOURG
blvd Clemenceau
rue Sellénick
rue Oberlin
ave de la Paix
Contades Park
4
3
quai Zorn
rue Turenne
ave des Vosges
rue du Maréchal Foch
rue Finkmatt
1
2
Law Courts
rue du Général de Castelnau
rue du Général Gourard
Préfecture
Palais du Rhin
place de la République
5
quai Zorn
ave d'Alsace
Bibliothèque National et Universitaire
quai Jacques Sturm
Fossé du Faux Rempart
quai Schoepflin
Théâtre National
ave de la Liberté
To Palais de l'Europe (1.2km)
6
rue de la Fonderie
9
r de la Nuée Bleue
quai Lezay-Marnésia
7
quai Koch
pont d'Auvergne
place Broglie
ave de la Marseillaise
quai du Maire Dietrich
place de l'Université
University
8
Hôtel de Ville
rue Brulée
rue de la Mésange
24
rue de l'Outre
Grande Île
rue du Dôme
rue des Juifs
rue du Fai san
place Saint Étienne
blvd de la Victoire
Ill River
quai des Pêcheurs
rue des Grandes Arcades
22
23
r des Orfèvres
rue du Sanglier
Place du Marché Neuf
rue des Hallebardes
rue des Frères
rue des Écrivains
rue des Soeurs
rue des Veaux
25
To Pont de l'Europe (3km), Rhine River & Kehl
rue St Guillame
rue de l'Académie
33
32
Footbridge
rue de la Manufacture des Tabacs
rue Gutenberg
place Gutenberg
35
34
r Mercière
place de la Cathédrale
place du Château
r de la Râpe
29
rue de Zurich
Krutenau District
36
rue des Serruriers
31
30
rue du Vieux Marché aux Poissons
quai des Bateliers
rue des Bateliers
28
rue des Poules
27
26
rue Paul Janet
rue des Tonneliers
rue de l'Écurie
rue de la Krutenau
R Ste Catherine
45
rue de l'Ail
47
46
rue de la Division Leclerc
place de Zurich
rue de Zurich
St Thomas
rue des Couples
rue des Orphelins
rue du Jeu de Paume
48
rue d'Austerlitz
quai Saint Nicolas
rue des Bouchers
rue du Saint Gothard
49
rue de la 1ère Armée
51
place d'Austerlitz
rue de la Brigade Alsace-Lorraine
rue de Berne
50
place de l'Hôpital
To Pont de l'Europe (4km) & Kehl, Germany (5km)
R Sédillot
52
0
100
200m
0
100
200yd
FRANCE

Entertainment

Strasbourg's live music venue is **La Laiterie** *(☎ 03 88 23 72 37; 13 rue de Hohwald)*; **L'Abattoir** *(☎ 03 88 32 28 12; 1 quai Charles Altorffer)* is the techno club, while **La Salamandre** *(☎ 03 88 25 79 42; 3 rue Paul Janet; open 9pm-3am Wed-Sat)* has '80s nights.

Students frequent the **Académie de la Bière** *(☎ 03 88 22 38 88; 17 rue Adolphe Seyboth; open 9am-2.30am Mon-Fri, to 4am Sat-Sun)*, which has a daily 6pm to 8pm happy hour and €4 beer cocktails. **The Irish Times** *(☎ 03 88 32 04 02; 19 rue St Barbe; open 2pm-1am or 2am Mon-Sat, from noon Sun)* has live music at weekends, while **Rock City** *(☎ 03 88 36 54 76; 24 rue des Poules; open 11am-1.30am)* has a rock vibe.

Getting There & Away

Bus Coaches arrive/depart from opposite the **Eurolines office** *(☎ 03 90 22 14 60; 6 place d'Austerlitz; open 10am-12.30pm & 2pm-6.15pm Mon-Fri)* in place d'Austerlitz. City bus No 21 runs daily from place Gutenberg to Kehl, the first town across the border in Germany (one way €1.10).

Train From **Gare Strasbourg** *(☎ 08 92 35 35 39)* there are frequent connections to Paris' Gare de l'Est (€25.50, four hours), Basel (Bâle; €16, 1½ hours) and Frankfurt (€34, two hours). There are daily trains to Nice (€93.30, 12 hours), Amsterdam (€65.80, eight hours) and Prague (€91.10, 10 hours). The ticket office opens from 5.15am to 9pm or 10pm.

Getting Around

Four tram lines form the centrepiece of Strasbourg's excellent public transport network. A, B and C run daily from 4.30am to 12.30am and D runs from 7am to 7pm Monday to Saturday. Tickets (single/day/family pass €1.10/3/3.80) are sold on buses, at tram stops and the **CTS office** *(☎ 03 88 77 70 70; open 7.30am-6.30pm Mon-Fri, 9am-5pm Sat)* in place Kléber.

Bicycles can be hired from **Velocation** *(☎ 03 88 43 64 30; 4 rue de Marie Kuss; open 6am-7.30pm Mon-Fri, 9am-noon & 2pm-7pm Sat & Sun; full/half-day €4.50/3)*.

COLMAR

pop 67,000

Colmar is a good base for exploring the Route du Vin and the Massif des Vosges.

Ave de la République stretches from 1km from the train station to the Musée d'Unterlinden; the medieval streets of the old city are to the southeast. At the southern edge of the old city, **Petite Venise**, a charming neighbourhood of half-timbered buildings and street cafés, hugs the Lauch River.

The highly efficient **tourist office** *(☎ 03 89 20 68 92, fax 03 89 20 69 14; 🅦 www.ot-colmar.fr; 4 rue d'Unterlinden; open daily)*, opposite the Musée d'Unterlinden, offers free hotel reservations via email, currency exchange and guided tours.

There's a **post office** *(36-38 ave de la République; open 8am-6.30pm Mon-Fri, 8am-noon Sat)*; **Reflex** *(41 Grand Rue; open 10am-10pm daily)* has one hour of Net access for €3.

Colmar is famous for its typically Alsatian architecture, and *Issenheim Altarpiece*, which is in the **Musée d'Unterlinden** *(☎ 03 89 20 15 50; 🅦 www.musee-unterlinden.com; place d'Unter linden; adult/concession €7/5; open 9am-6pm Apr-Oct, 10am-5pm Nov-Mar)*.

The **Musée Bartholdi** *(☎ 03 89 41 90 60; 30 rue des Marchands; adult/concession €4/2.50; open 10am-noon & 2pm-6pm Wed-Mon; closed Tues Jan & Feb)* is dedicated to the creator of New York's *Statue of Liberty*.

Places to Stay

The **Auberge de Jeunesse Mittelhart** *(☎ 03 89 80 57 39, fax 03 89 80 76 16; 2 rue Pasteur; bus No 4, 5 or 6 to Pont-Rouge stop; dorm beds €11.50 including breakfast; reception closed 9am-5pm in winter)* is 2km northwest of the train station.

Near the train station, faded **Hôtel La Chaumière** *(☎ 03 89 41 08 99; 74 ave de la République; doubles without/with shower & toilet €28/34)* is cheap but unremarkable, while the **Kyriad** *(☎ 03 89 41 34 80; 🅔 kyriad colmar@aol.com; 1 rue de la Gare; singles/doubles €36/45)* is a typical chain hotel.

Hôtel Primo *(☎ 03 89 24 22 24, fax 03 89 24 55 96; 🅔 hotel-primo-99@calixo.net; 5 rue des Ancêtres; singles/doubles/quads €45/52/61)* has modern rooms and does a €6 all-you-can-eat breakfast buffet.

Places to Eat

Place de l'Ancienne Douane has a number of watering holes; **Schwendi Bier-U-Wistub** *(☎ 03 89 23 66 26; 23-25 Grand-Rue; meals* *from €9, beers from €3; open 10am-1am daily)*, an Alsacian beer hall with a large terrace, is a good bet. Most restaurants tend to cater to tourists but **Le Flamm's** *(☎ 03 89 41 56 85; Passage Saint-Martin)* is a good-value hidden gem, tucked away down a passageway off rue des Serruriers.

There's a **Monoprix supermarket** *(open 8am-8pm Mon-Sat)* across the square from the Musée d'Unterlinden.

Getting There & Around

Colmar is served by frequent trains from Strasbourg (€9.10, every 30 minutes). Many Route du Vin and Massif des Vosges destinations are accessible by local bus; ask the tourist office for details. The office also arranges guided Route du Vin **bus tours** in summer *(half/full day €25/35)*. **Colmarvélo** *(place Rapp; open Apr-Oct)* hires out bicycles (half/full day €3/4.50).

Euro Regio *(☎ 03 89 24 65 65)* runs seven weekday (plus four Saturday, three Sunday) **buses** to the German university city of Freiburg (€6.15, 75 minutes).

NANCY

pop 99,351

Nancy has an air of refinement unique in Lorraine, the region that borders Alsace to the west. The gilded **place Stanislas** (the central square) and shop windows filled with fine glassware give the former capital of the dukes of Lorraine an opulent feel.

The heart of Nancy is place Stanislas; the train station, at the bottom of busy rue Stanislas, is 800m to the southwest. The **tourist office** *(☎ 03 83 35 22 41, fax 03 83 35 90 10; ⓔ tourisme@ot-nancy.fr; open daily)* is inside the **Hôtel de Ville** *(place Stanislas)*. It charges €2 for hotel reservations and offers currency exchange on weekends only.

The **post office** *(open 8am-7pm Mon-Fri, 8am-noon Sat)* is behind the tourist office on rue Pierre Fourier and has Cyberposte. For a small town, Nancy has an excellent Internet café, **e-café** *(☎ 03 83 35 47 34; 11 rue des Quatre-Églises; open 9am-9pm daily, to 8pm Sun)*, which charges €5.34 for an hour of Net access and offers student discounts.

The **Musée de l'École de Nancy** *(☎ 03 83 40 14 86; 36-38 rue du Sergent Blandan; bus No 123 to Nancy Thermal stop; adult/concession €4.60/2.30, students free Wed; open 10.30am-6pm Wed-Sun)* is home to a superb collection of works from the Art Nouveau movement. The renovated **Musée des Beaux-Arts** *(Fine Arts Museum; ☎ 03 83 85 30 72; 3 place Stanislas; adult/concession €5.34/3.05, free Wed for students; open 10am-6pm Wed-Mon)* is absorbing.

Places to Stay & Eat

The 60-bed **Auberge de Jeunesse Remicourt** *(☎ 03 83 27 73 67, fax 03 83 41 41 35; 149 rue de Vandœuvre in Villers-les-Nancy; bus No 122 to Grand Corvée stop; dorm beds €9 including breakfast)*, located in an old chateau, is 4km south of the centre.

Two blocks southwest of place Stanislas, **Hôtel de l'Académie** *(☎ 03 83 35 52 31, fax 03 83 32 55 78; 7bis rue des Michottes; singles/doubles with shower from €22.50/25.50)* is cheap and welcoming. The two-star **Hôtel des Portes d'Or** *(☎ 03 83 35 42 34, fax 03 83 32 51 41; 21 rue Stanislas; singles/doubles €40/45)* has smart rooms with upholstered doors.

Rue des Maréchaux is lined with restaurants; **Le Pitchoun** at No 14 *(☎ 03 83 30 45 33; lunch menu €14; open Tues-Sat)* is one of the best. **La Romana** *(☎ 03 83 37 35 43; 10 Grand Rue; open Tues-Sat & Mon dinner)* is a friendly, good-value pizzeria.

Self-caterers should head for the **covered market** *(place Henri Mangin; open 7am-6pm Tues-Sat)* and the **Monoprix supermarket** *(open 8.30am-8.30pm Mon-Sat)* inside the St Sébastien shopping centre.

For drinks, **cafés** line place Stanislas; the **Blue Note** *(3 rue des Michottes; open 11pm-4am Wed-Sun)* is a Latin-style club.

Getting There & Away

Gare Nancy *(☎ 08 92 35 35 39; place Thiers)* has direct services to Strasbourg (€17.30, 80 minutes), Paris' Gare de l'Est (€32.90, 2½ hours), Épernay (€21.30, two hours) and Lyon (€38, four hours).

Far Northern France

Le Nord de France (ⓦ www.cdt-nord.fr) is made up of three historical regions: Flanders (Flandre or Flandres), Artois and Picardy (Picardie). Traditionally an industrial area, this is not one of the best-known corners of France. Most travellers will pass through this area on the way from England, via Calais.

FRANCE

CALAIS

pop 78,000

Calais, a grim and desperate town, is only 34km from the English town of Dover. Though it was long a popular port for passenger travel between the UK and continental Europe, the 1994 opening of the Channel Tunnel at Coquelles, 5km southwest of the town centre, heralded the end of Calais' dominance over trans-Channel transport. Calais now relies on the bawdy booze-cruise trade and offers poor value for money.

Orientation & Information

Calais is centred on place d'Armes with Calais-Ville train station to the south. The car ferry terminal is 1.7km northeast of place d'Armes; the hoverport is 1.5km farther out. Hotels and eateries are located near the harbour off rue Royale.

The **tourist office** *(☎ 03 21 96 62 40, fax 03 21 96 01 92; W www.ot-calais.fr; 12 blvd Clémenceau; open daily)* fields visitor inquiries. **Banks** line rue Royale. The **post office** *(place de Rheims; open 8.30am-6pm Mon-Fri, 9am-noon Sat)* has currency exchange and Cyberposte. **Spicey Café** *(☎ 03 21 96 84 20; 68 rue Royale)* charges €4 for one hour of Net access.

Things to See

A cast of Auguste Rodin's famous bronze statue of six emaciated but proud figures, known in English as **The Burghers of Calais**, stands in front of the Flemish Renaissance-style Hôtel de Ville, which is topped with an ornate 75m clock tower.

Opposite, the **Musée de la Guerre** *(☎ 03 21 34 21 57; Parc St Pierre; adult/concession €4.50/3.80; open 10am-5.15pm May-Aug, 11am-4.45pm Apr & Sept, 11am-4.15pm 15 Feb-31 Mar, noon-4.15pm 1 October-15 Nov; closed Tues)* has WWII artefacts housed in a 94m-long concrete bunker.

Places to Stay

Modern **Auberge de Jeunesse** *(☎ 03 21 34 70 20, fax 03 21 96 87 80; ave Maréchal De Lattre de Tassigny; bus No 3 to Pluviose stop; 2-bed doubles per person €14.33, singles €16 including breakfast)*, also called the Centre Européen de Séjour, is 200m from the beach.

Hôtel-Pension L'Ovale *(☎/fax 03 21 97 57 00; 38-40 ave Wilson; singles or doubles €25, triples €30.50)*, near the train station, has adequate rooms with private shower and televisions receiving UK TV channels. The central **Hôtel Bristol** *(☎/fax 03 21 34 53 24; 15 rue du Duc de Guise; singles & doubles €25, with shower & toilet €31/36, 4/5-bed rooms €59/70)* has simple rooms.

Places to Eat

Histoire Ancienne *(☎ 03 21 34 11 20; 20 rue Royale; menus €10-28; open Tues-Sat, & Mon lunch)* is a cosy bistro. Show a ferry or shuttle ticket for a free bottle of takeaway wine. The rustic **Au Coq d'Or** *(☎ 03 21 34 79 05; 31 place d'Armes; menus €10.10-38.30; open Thur-Tues)* serves grilled meat dishes and seafood.

Au Tonnaire de Brest *(☎ 03 21 96 95 35; 16 place d'Armes)* is a bright and friendly creperie with good value (€6) pancakes. **Bouddha Bar** *(☎ 03 21 34 63 67; 7 rue Royale)* is a decent spot for a beer and a snack.

For self-caterers, place d'Armes is host to a **food market** on Wednesday and Saturday mornings and the **Match supermarket** *(opens until 7.30pm & Sun morning in summer)*.

Getting There & Away

For details on Channel Tunnel and ferry schedules, see Britain under Land and Sea in the Getting There & Away section.

Bus The express buses of **BCD** *(☎ 03 21 83 51 51)* operate from Boulogne to Calais (€6.40, 35 minutes, four on weekdays and two on Saturday) and on to Dunkerque (€7, 45 minutes, nine weekdays and three on Saturday). There's no service on Sunday and holidays.

Train Calais has two train stations: Gare Calais-Fréthun, which is 10km southwest of town near the Channel Tunnel entrance, and **Gare Calais-Ville** *(☎ 08 92 35 35 39)*; they are connected by Opale Bus No 7 (€1.50).

Calais-Ville handles non-TGV trains to Paris' Gare du Nord (€29.20, three hours, three to six daily), Boulogne (€6.30, 35 minutes, hourly), and Lille-Flandres (€13.40, 1½ hours, seven to 15 daily). Calais-Fréthun handles TGVs only to Paris' Gare du Nord (€34.30, 1½ hours, two daily) and Eurostar to London (from €75, 1½ hours, three or four daily).

Car To reach the Channel Tunnel's vehicle loading area, follow road signs on the A16 to 'Tunnel Sous La Manche'.

Boat P&O Stena and SeaFrance Sealink car ferries to/from Dover dock at the busy Terminal Est, just over 1km northeast of place d'Armes.

P&O Ferries *(☎ 08 20 01 00 20; Ⓦ www.posl.com; 41 place d'Armes; open 8.30am-6pm Mon-Fri, 8.30am-5pm Sat)* sells tickets. **SeaFrance Sealink's office** *(☎ 08 25 04 40 45; Ⓦ www.seafrance.com; 9.30am-12.30pm & 1.30pm-6pm Mon-Fri, 9am-12.30pm Sat in summer only)* is nearby at No 2.

SeaCats to/from Dover, operated by **Hoverspeed** *(☎ 0800 12 11 12 11; Ⓦ www.hoverspeed.com)*, use the hoverport, 3km northeast of the town centre. For more details on ferry services, see the main Getting There & Away section.

Getting Around

To reach the car ferry terminal, free shuttles run by SeaFrance Sealink and P&O Stena stop round the corner from Calais-Ville train station (turn left out of the station) and outside each company's office on place d'Armes. Last buses leave around 9pm.

Hoverspeed runs free buses to the hoverport from the train station roughly 45 minutes before each departure.

Normandy (Normandie)

Normandy derives its name from the Norsemen (Vikings) who took control of the area in the early 10th century. Modern Normandy is the land of the *bocage*, farmland subdivided by hedges and trees.

ROUEN

pop 107,000

The city of Rouen, for centuries the lowest bridging point on the Seine, is known for its many spires, church towers and half-timbered houses, not to mention its Gothic cathedral and excellent museums. Rouen can be visited on a day or overnight trip from Paris.

The train station (Gare Rouen-Rive Droite) is at the northern end of rue Jeanne d'Arc, the major thoroughfare running south to the Seine.

The **tourist office** *(☎ 02 32 08 32 40, fax 02 32 08 32 44; Ⓔ www.rouen-online.com; 25 place de la Cathédrale; open daily)* is the departure point for guided city tours (adult/concession €6/4) in summer at 2.30pm daily. **Place Net** *(37 rue de la République; open daily)* offers Internet access for €6 an hour.

Things to See

Rouen's main street, rue du Gros Horloge, runs from the cathedral to **place du Vieux Marché**, where 19-year-old Joan of Arc was burned at the stake for heresy in 1431. You'll learn more about her life from its stained-glass windows at the adjacent **Église Jeanne d'Arc** than at the tacky **Musée Jeanne d'Arc** across the square at No 33.

Rouen's **Cathédrale Notre Dame**, the subject of a series of paintings by Claude Monet, is a masterpiece of French Gothic architecture. There is a guided visit at 3pm daily during the summer months and on weekends the rest of the year.

The **Musée Le Secq des Tournelles** *(rue Jacques Villon; adult/concession €2.30/1.55; open Wed-Mon)*, located opposite 27 rue Jean Lecanuet, is devoted to the blacksmith's craft, and displays some 12,000 locks, keys and tongs made between the 3rd and 19th centuries.

The **Musée des Beaux-Arts** *(Fine Arts Museum, 26bis rue Jean Lecanuet; adult/concession €3/2; open Wed-Sun)* facing the square, features some major paintings from the 16th to 20th centuries, including some of Monet's cathedral series.

La Tour Jeanne d'Arc *(rue du Donjon)*, south of the train station, is the tower where Joan of Arc was imprisoned before her execution. There are two **exhibition rooms** *(adult/concession €1.50/0.75; open Wed-Mon)*.

Places to Stay

The spotless **Hôtel Normandya** *(☎ 02 35 71 46 15; 32 rue du Cordier; singles €19-25, doubles €2 more)* is on a quiet street 300m southeast of the train station. Some singles have a shower. The very French **Hostellerie du Vieux Logis** *(☎ 02 35 71 55 30; 5 rue de Joyeuse; rooms from €15)*, 1km east of the train station, has a pleasantly frayed atmosphere and a lovely garden out the back. The **Hôtel Le Palais** *(☎ 02 35 71 41 40; 12 rue du Tambour; singles/doubles from €20/25, with shower €25/38)* is between the Palais de Justice and the Gros Horloge.

Places to Eat

There's a **covered market** *(place du Vieux Marché; open 6am-1.30pm Tues-Sun)* for

FRANCE

self-caterers. The bistro-style **Les Maraîchers** *(menus from €15, dinner menus from €16)* at No 37 is the pick of the Vieux Marché's many restaurants, with its terrace and varied *menus*.

Gourmand'grain *(☎ 02 35 98 15 74; 3 rue du Petit Salut; menus from €8)* behind the tourist office, is a lunchtime eatery catering for vegetarians.

Entertainment

Café Curieux *(3 rue des Fossés Louis VIII; admission €3; open Fri & Sat from 9pm)* is a small and intimate nightclub in the heart of the old city. **Alexander Pub** *(85 rue Martainville)* is a pleasant English-style pub open until 2am daily.

Getting There & Away

The **bus station** *(☎ 02 35 52 92 00; 9 rue Jeanne d'Arc)* is near the Théâtre des Arts. Buses tend to be slower and more expensive than the train.

There are at least 20 trains daily to/from Paris' Gare St Lazare (€16.50, 70 minutes), as well as services to Caen (€18.20) and Bayeux (€20.60). For train information, call ☎ 0836 35 35 39.

Getting Around

TCAR operates the local bus network and metro line. The metro links the train station with the Théâtre des Arts before crossing the Seine into the southern suburbs. Bus tickets cost €1.20, or €10 for a magnetic card good for 10 rides.

BAYEUX

pop 15,000

Bayeux is celebrated for two trans-Channel invasions: the AD 1066 conquest of England by William the Conqueror (an event chronicled in the Bayeux Tapestry) and the Allied D-Day landings of 6 June 1944; Bayeux was the first town in France to be liberated from the Nazis.

Today Bayeux is an attractive – though fairly touristy – town with several excellent museums. It's also a good base for visiting the D-Day beaches. The cathedral, Bayeux's central landmark, is 1km northwest of the train station. The **tourist office** *(☎ 02 31 51 28 28, fax 02 31 51 28 29; Pont St Jean; open daily)* is just off the northern end of rue Larcher.

Things to See

The world-famous **Bayeux Tapestry** – a 70m-long strip of coarse linen decorated with woollen embroidery – was commissioned by Odo, bishop of Bayeux and half-brother to William the Conqueror, for the consecration of the cathedral in Bayeux in 1077. The tapestry recounts the story of the Norman invasion of 1066 – from the Norman perspective. Halley's Comet, which visited our solar system in 1066, also makes an appearance. The tapestry is housed in the **Musée de la Tapisserie de Bayeux** *(rue de Nesmond; adult/student €6.40/2.60; open 9am-6.30pm daily, closed at lunch off season)*.

Bayeux's **Cathédrale Notre Dame** is an exceptional example of Norman-Gothic architecture, dating from the 13th century.

The **Musée Mémorial 1944 Bataille de Normandie** *(blvd Fabien Ware; adult/student €5.40/2.50)*, Bayeux's huge war museum, displays a haphazard collection of photos, uniforms, weapons and life-like scenes associated with D-Day and the Battle of Normandy. An excellent 30-minute film is shown in English.

The **Bayeux War Cemetery** *(blvd Fabien Ware)*, a British cemetery a few hundred metres west of the museum, is the largest of the 18 Commonwealth military cemeteries in Normandy. Many of the headstones are inscribed with poignant epitaphs.

Places to Stay

Hostels The **Family Home hostel and guesthouse** *(☎ 02 31 92 15 22, fax 02 31 92 55 72; 39 rue du Général de Dais; dorm beds HI members/nonmembers €16/18)*, in three old buildings, is an excellent place to meet other travellers. There's a kitchen, or you can have a multicourse French dinner (with wine) for €9.15. The modern, if slightly sterile, **Centre d'Accueil Municipal** *(☎ 02 31 92 08 19; 21 rue des Marettes; singles €11.90)* is 1km southwest of the cathedral and has good-value singles.

Hotels The old but well-maintained **Hôtel de la Gare** *(☎ 02 31 92 10 70, fax 02 31 51 95 99; 26 place de la Gare; singles/doubles from €16/22)* is opposite the train station. A few hundred metres north, **Hôtel Le Maupassant** *(☎ 02 31 92 28 53; 19 rue St Martin; singles/doubles from €26/33.55)* has decent rooms (most with shower). **Hotel Reine Mathilde** *(☎ 02 31 92 08 13; 23 rue*

Larcher; rooms from €45) is slightly more upmarket, with congenial motel-style rooms and friendly staff.

Places to Eat

There are **food markets** on rue St Jean (Wednesday morning) and on place St Patrice (Saturday morning).

Le Petit Normand *(☎ 02 31 22 88 66; 35 rue Larcher; menus from €9; open daily July & Aug, Thur-Sat & Sun dinner Sept-June)* specialises in traditional Norman food and has simple *menus*.

Le Pommier *(☎ 02 31 21 52 10; 38 rue des Cuisiniers; lunch/dinner menus from €11.50; closed Tue & Wed)* offers Norman fare at its best, including a vegetarian *menu*. **Milano** *(☎ 02 31 92 15 10; 18 rue St Martin; open daily June-Aug, Mon-Sat Sept-May)* serves good pizza from €6 to €10.

Getting There & Away

The **train station office** *(☎ 02 31 92 80 50; open 7am-8.45pm daily)* sells tickets. Trains serve Paris' Gare St Lazare (€27, via Caen), Cherbourg, Rennes and points beyond.

D-DAY BEACHES

The D-Day landings were the largest military operation in history. Early on the morning of 6 June 1944, swarms of landing craft – part of a flotilla of almost 7000 boats – ferried ashore 135,000 Allied troops along 80km of beaches north of Bayeux. The landings on D-Day were followed by the 76-day Battle of Normandy that began the liberation of Europe from Nazi occupation.

Things to See

Arromanches In order to unload the vast quantities of cargo necessary for the invasion, the Allies established two prefabricated ports. The remains of one of them, Port Winston, can be seen at Arromanches, a seaside town 10km northeast of Bayeux.

The **Musée du Débarquement** *(Landing Museum; ☎ 02 31 22 34 31; adult/concession €6/4; open 9am-7pm daily in summer, 9.30am-12.30pm & 1.30pm-5.30pm in low season)* explains the logistics and importance of Port Winston and makes a good first stop before visiting the beaches.

Omaha Beach The most brutal combat of 6 June was fought 20km west of Arromanches at Omaha Beach. Today, little evidence of the war remains except the bunkers and munitions sites of a German fortified point to the west (look for the tall obelisk on the hill).

American Military Cemetery The remains of the Americans who lost their lives during the Battle of Normandy were either sent back to the USA or buried in the American Military Cemetery at Colleville-sur-Mer, which contains the graves of 9386 American soldiers and a memorial to 1557 others whose bodies were never found.

Organised Tours

Tours of the D-Day beaches are offered by **Bus Fly** *(☎ 02 31 22 00 08)*, based at the Family Home hostel in Bayeux (see Places to Stay in Bayeux earlier). An afternoon tour to major D-Day sites costs adult/concession €35/31, including museum entry fees. There are three other tour operators, all offering their own variations on the war cemetery theme – the tourist office can provide more details.

Getting There & Away

Bus With an office (closed weekends and in July) opposite Bayeaux's train station, **Bus Verts** *(☎ 02 31 92 02 92)* sends bus No 70 west to the American cemetery at Colleville-sur-Mer and Omaha Beach. Bus No 74 serves Arromanches, and Gold and Juno beaches. In July and August only, Bus No 75 goes to Caen via Arromanches, Gold, Juno and Sword beaches and the port of Ouistreham. Timetables are posted in the train station and at place G Despallières. Canadians wishing to visit the Canadian war cemetery at Courseulles-sur-Mer should consider renting a car, as public transport options are limited.

Car For three or more people, renting a car can actually be cheaper than a tour. **Lefebvre Car Rental** *(☎ 02 31 92 05 96; blvd d'Eindhoven)* in Bayeux charges €65 per day with 200km free.

MONT SAINT MICHEL

pop 42

It is difficult not to be impressed by Mont St Michel and its massive abbey anchored at the summit of a rocky island. Around the base are the ancient ramparts and a jumble of buildings that house the handful of people who still live there.

At low tide, Mont St Michel looks out over bare sand stretching into the distance. At high tide – about six hours later – this huge expanse of sand is under water, though only the very highest tides cover the 900m causeway that connects the islet to the mainland. The French government is currently spending millions to restore Mont St Michel to its former glory, so parts of it may be scaffolded.

The Mont's major attraction is the **Abbaye du Mont St Michel** *(☎ 02 33 89 80 00; adult/concession €7/4.50; open 9am-5.30pm daily, 9.30am-5pm Oct-Apr)*, at the top of the Grande rue, up the stairway. It's worth taking the guided tour (in English) included in the ticket price. There are also self-paced evening tours (adult/concession €9/6.50) at 9pm or midnight (except Sunday) of the illuminated and music-filled rooms.

The nearest town, **Pontorson**, is located 9km south and is the base for most travellers. Route D976 from Mont St Michel runs right into Pontorson's main thoroughfare, rue du Couësnon.

Information

The **tourist office** *(☎ 02 33 60 14 30, fax 02 33 60 06 75; ⓔ ot.mont.saint.michel@wanadoo.fr; open Mon-Sat, daily Easter-Sept)* is up the stairs to the left as you enter Mont St Michel at Porte de l'Avancée. There's another **tourist office** *(open daily, Mon-Sat in low season)* in Pontorson.

Places to Stay

Camping On the road to Pontorson (D976), 2km from the Mont, is **Camping du Mont St Michel** *(☎ 02 33 60 09 33, fax 02 33 60 20 02; Route du Mont-Saint-Michel; sites per tent/person €4.65/3, 2-person bungalows with shower & toilet low/high season €34.60/42.40; open mid-Feb–mid-Nov)*. It also offers hotel rooms (single/double from €45.60/55) and breakfast.

Hostels & Hotels Pontorson's **Centre Duguesclin** *(☎ 02 33 60 18 65; dorm beds €8/8.40 members/nonmembers; closed 10am-6pm, no curfew)* operates as a 10-room hostel from Easter to mid-September. The hostel is 1km west of the train station on rue du Général Patton, which runs parallel to the Couësnon River north of rue du Couësnon. The hostel is on the left side in a three-storey stone building opposite No 26.

In Pontorson, across place de la Gare from the train station, there are a couple of cheap hotels, including **Hôtel de l'Arrivée** *(☎ 02 33 60 01 57; 14 rue du Docteur Tizon; rooms with/without shower €25/15.40)*.

Places to Eat

The tourist restaurants around the base of the Mont have lovely views but tend to be mediocre; *menus* start at about €12. A few places along the Grande rue sell sandwiches, quiches and the like. The nearest **supermarket** to the Mont is next to Camping du Mont St Michel on the D976.

In Pontorson, **La Crêperie du Couësnon** *(☎ 02 33 60 16 67; 21 rue du Couësnon)* has crepes and *galettes* (savoury pancakes) for €1.50 to €6.10. **La Tour de Brette** *(☎ 02 33 60 10 69; 8 rue du Couësnon; menus from €9.80)*, across from the river, has good *menus*.

Getting There & Around

STN *(☎ 02 33 58 03 07)* sends bus No 15 from Pontorson's train station to Mont St Michel daily year-round; most of the buses connect with trains travelling to/from Paris, Rennes and Caen.

There are trains to Pontorson from Caen (via Folligny) and Rennes (via Dol). From Paris, take the train to Caen (from Gare St Lazare), Rennes (from Gare Montparnasse) or direct to Pontorson via Folligny (Gare Montparnasse).

Bikes can be rented from **Couësnon Motoculture** *(☎ 02 33 60 11 40; 1bis rue du Couësnon)*, which charges €7/12 per half-day/day for mountain bikes.

Brittany (Bretagne, Breizh)

Brittany, the westernmost region of France, is famous for its rugged countryside and wild coastline. Traditional costumes, including extraordinarily tall headdresses worn by the women, can still be seen at *pardons* (religious festivals) and other local festivals.

The indigenous language of Brittany is Breton, which, to the untrained ear, sounds like Gaelic with a French accent. It can sometimes still be heard in western Brittany and especially in Cornouaille, where perhaps a third of the population understands it.

QUIMPER

pop 63,200

Situated at the confluence of two rivers, the Odet and the Steïr, Quimper (cam-**pair**) has managed to preserve its Breton architecture and atmosphere, and is considered by many to be the cultural capital of Brittany. Some even refer to the city as the 'soul of Brittany'.

The Festival de Cornouaille, a showcase for traditional Breton music, costumes and culture, is held here every year between the third and fourth Sundays in July.

Orientation & Information

The largely pedestrianised old city is to the west and northwest of the cathedral. The train station is 1km east of the city centre on ave de la Gare; the bus station is to the right as you exit, in the modern-looking building.

The **tourist office** *(☎ 02 98 53 04 05, fax 02 98 53 31 33; ⓔ office.tourisme.quimper@ouest-mediacap.com; place de la Résistance; open Mon-Sat, daily mid-June–Sept)* can help with information. **Cyber Vidéo** *(51 blvd Kerguélen)* has Internet facilities for €4.50 per hour.

Things to See

The old city is known for its centuries-old houses, which are especially in evidence on **rue Kéréon** and around **place au Beurre**.

The **Cathédrale St Corentin** *(place Saint-Corentin)*, built between 1239 and 1515, incorporates many Breton elements, including (on the western facade between the spires) an equestrian statue of King Gradlon, the city's mythical 5th-century founder.

The **Musée Départemental Breton** *(1 rue du Roi Gradlon; adult/concession €3.80/2.50; open Tues-Sat & Sun afternoon, to 7pm daily in summer)*, next to the cathedral in the former bishop's palace, houses exhibits on the history, costumes, crafts and archaeology of the area.

The **Musée des Beaux-Arts** *(Museum of Fine Art; adult/concession €3.85/2.30; open daily July-Aug, Wed-Mon Sept-June)* in the **Hôtel de Ville** *(40 place St Corentin)* has a wide collection of European paintings from the 16th to early 20th centuries.

Faïenceries HB Henriot *(☎ 02 98 90 09 36; rue Haute)* has been turning out *faïence* (glazed earthenware) since 1690. Tours of the factory (adult/concession €3.05/2.30), southwest of the cathedral, are held from 9am to 11.15am and 1.30pm to 4.15pm weekdays (to 4.45pm in July and August).

Places to Stay

It's extremely difficult to find accommodation during the Festival de Cornouaille in late July. The tourist office makes bookings in Quimper (€0.30) and elsewhere in Brittany (€0.76), and has a list of **private rooms**.

Found just over 1km west of the old city is **Camping Municipal** *(☎ 02 98 55 61 09; ave des Oiseaux; bus No 1 from train station to Chaptal stop; sites per person/tent €2.90/0.63; open year-round)*.

The **Auberge de Jeunesse** *(☎ 02 98 64 97 97, fax 02 98 55 38 37; 6 ave des Oiseaux; bus No 1 or 8 to Chaptal stop; dorm beds €8)* is about 1km west of the old city. Rooms are basic but clean.

The spotless **Hôtel TGV** *(☎ 02 98 90 54 00; 4 rue de Concarneau; rooms from €27.50)* has large, basic rooms with shower and toilet. **Hôtel de la Gare** *(☎ 02 98 90 00 81; 17bis ave de la Gare; singles/doubles with shower €31/40, €40/46 at peak periods)* is another option. **Hôtel Le Celtic** *(☎ 02 98 55 59 35; 13 rue Douarnenez; doubles with/without shower €30.50/25)* is 100m north of Église St Mathieu.

Places to Eat

There's a **Monoprix supermarket** *(quai du Port au Vin; open Mon-Sat)* near the **covered market**. Opposite the market is **C.Com Café** *(9 quai du Port au Vin)*, a cheerful daytime eatery with sandwiches and salads (€2.60 to €7.60). Crepes, a Breton speciality, are your best bet for a cheap and filling meal. You'll find **creperies** everywhere, particularly along rue Ste Catherine across the river from the cathedral. Otherwise, there are several decent **restaurants** on rue Le Déan not far from the train station.

Getting There & Away

A half-dozen companies operate out of the **bus station** *(☎ 02 98 90 88 89)*. Destinations include Brest, Pointe du Raz, Roscoff (for ferries to Plymouth, England), Concarneau and Quimperlé.

Inquire at the train station for SNCF buses to Douarnenez, Camaret-sur-Mer, Concarneau and Quiberon. A one-way ticket on the TGV train to Paris' Gare Montparnasse costs €59.70 to €69.80 (4½ hours). You can also reach Saint Malo by train via Rennes. For rail information call ☎ 0836 35 35 39.

Getting Around

At **Airbike** *(☎ 02 98 90 88 02; 128 ave de la Libération; open Mon-Sat)* you can hire mountain bikes for €12 per day.

AROUND QUIMPER

Concarneau (Konk-Kerne)

pop 19,500

Concarneau, 24km southeast of Quimper, is France's third-most important trawler port. It's slightly scruffy and a bit touristy, but also refreshingly unpretentious and near several decent beaches. The **Ville Close** (walled city), built on a small island measuring 350m by 100m and fortified between the 14th and 17th centuries, is reached via a footbridge from place Jean Jaurès.

The **tourist office** *(☎ 02 98 97 01 44, fax 02 98 50 88 81; W www.concarneau.org; quai d'Aiguillon; open Mon-Sat, daily Apr-June)* is 200m north of the main (west) gate to the Ville Close.

Places to Stay & Eat About 600m southeast of the Ville Close is **Camping Moulin d'Aurore** *(☎ 02 98 50 53 08; 49 rue de Trégunc; open Apr-Sept)*. The **Auberge de Jeunesse** *(☎ 02 98 97 03 47, fax 02 98 50 87 57; quai de la Croix; dorm beds €9; reception open 9am-noon & 6pm-8pm)* is on the water next to the Marinarium. From the tourist office, walk south to the end of quai Peneroff and turn right. **Hôtel des Halles** *(☎ 02 98 97 11 41, fax 02 98 50 58 54; place de l'Hôtel de Ville; singles/doubles €32/34, with shower €40/45)* has doubles with shower and TV.

L'Escale *(☎ 02 98 97 03 31; 19 quai Carnot; menu from €14.20; open Mon-Fri, & Sat lunch)* is popular with local Concarnois, and has a hearty lunch or dinner. For excellent home-style crepes, give the unpretentious **Crêperie du Grand Chemin** *(17 ave de la Gare)* a try.

Getting There & Away The bus station is in the parking lot north of the tourist office. **Caoudal** *(☎ 02 98 56 96 72)* runs up to four buses daily (three on Sunday) between Quimper and Quimperlé (via Concarneau and Pont Aven). The trip from Quimper to Concarneau costs €4 and takes 30 minutes.

SAINT MALO

pop 52,700

The Channel port of Saint Malo is one of the most popular tourist destinations in Brittany – and with good reason. It has a famous walled city and good nearby beaches, and is an excellent base for day trips to Mont St Michel (see the earlier Normandy section).

Orientation & Information

Saint Malo consists of the resort towns of St Servan, Saint Malo, Paramé and Rothéneuf. The old city, signposted as 'Intra-Muros' and also known as the Ville Close, is connected to Paramé by the Sillon Isthmus. The train station is 1.2km east of the old city along ave Louis Martin.

The **tourist office** *(☎ 02 99 56 64 48, fax 02 99 56 67 00; e office.de.tourisme.saint-malo@wanadoo.fr; esplanade St Vincent; open Mon-Sat, daily July & Aug)* is just outside the old city. **Cybercom** *(26bis blvd des Talards; open 9am-noon & 2pm-6pm Mon-Fri, 9am-noon Sat)* charges €1.60 per half-hour of Web surfing.

Things to See & Do

Old City During the fighting of August 1944, which drove the Germans from Saint Malo, 80% of the old city was destroyed. After the war, the main historical monuments were lovingly reconstructed, but the rest of the area was rebuilt in the style of the 17th and 18th centuries. The **ramparts**, built over the course of many centuries, are largely original and afford superb views in all directions.

The **Musée de la Ville** *(adult/concession €4.40/2.20; open 10am-noon & 2pm-6pm daily in summer, Tues-Sun in winter)*, in the Château de Saint Malo at Porte St Vincent, deals with the history of the city and the Pays Malouin, the area around Saint Malo.

Built into the walls of the old city next to place Vauban, the **Aquarium Intra-Muros** *(adult/concession €5.50/4)* has over 100 tanks. Europe's first circular aquarium, **Le Grand Aquarium Saint Malo** *(ave Général Patton; adult/concession €12/9)* is 1.5km south of the train station. Take bus No 5 from the train station and hop off at the La Madeleine stop.

Île du Grand Bé You can reach the Île du Grand Bé, where the 18th-century writer Chateaubriand is buried, on foot at low tide via the Porte des Bés. Be warned – when the tide comes rushing in, the causeway is impassable for about six hours.

Saint Servan St Servan's fortress, **Fort de la Cité**, was built in the mid-18th century and served as a German base during WWII. The **Musée International du Long Cours Cap-Hornier** *(esplanade Menguy; adult/concession €4.40/2.20, combined ticket with Musée de la Ville €11/5.50; closed Mon low season)*, housed in the 14th-century Tour de Solidor, has interesting seafaring exhibits.

Beaches To the west, just outside the old city walls, is **Plage de Bon Secours**. The **Grande Plage**, which stretches northeastward from the Sillon Isthmus, is spiked with tree trunks that act as breakers.

Places to Stay

Camping At the northern tip of St Servan is **Camping Municipal Cité d'Aleth** *(☎ 02 99 81 60 91; sites for 1 or 2 people plus tent €10.50; open year-round)*, next to Fort de la Cité. In summer take bus No 1; at other times your best bet is bus No 6.

Hostels About 2km northeast of the train station (bus No 5) there's **Auberge de Jeunesse** *(☎ 02 99 40 29 80, fax 02 99 40 29 02; 37 ave du Père Umbricht; bus No 2 or 5 from train station; beds per person in 2–3/5–6-bed room €14.90/12.20; singles/doubles €20/15; reception open 24hr)* where prices include breakfast.

Hotels Across the roundabout from the train station is **Hôtel de l'Europe** *(☎ 02 99 56 13 42; 44 blvd de la République; singles/doubles from €25/28, with shower & toilet €34/40)*. Rooms are modern, nondescript and a third cheaper in winter.

Hôtel Armoricaine *(☎ 02 99 40 89 13, fax 02 99 49 46 42; 4 rue du Boyer; rooms from €31)* is in the old city. The friendly, family-run **Hôtel Aux Vieilles Pierres** *(☎ 02 99 56 46 80; 4 rue des Lauriers; singles/doubles from €25/40)* is in a quiet part of the old city. Hall showers are free.

Places to Eat

Tourist restaurants, creperies and pizzerias are chock-a-block in the area between Porte St Vincent, the cathedral and the Grande Porte, but if you're after better food, and better value, avoid this area completely.

As good as any for seafood is **La Pomme d'Or** *(☎ 02 99 40 90 24; 4 place du Poids du Roy; menus €11-34)*. If you overindulge you might consider staying in one of the rooms upstairs (from €45.20). Or try the more intimate **Grain de Sable** *(☎ 02 99 56 68 72)* at No 2, which serves an excellent fish soup (€4.50). In St Servan, **Crêperie du Val de Rance** *(11 rue Dauphine)* serves Breton-style crepes and *galettes* (€1.50 to €6).

Getting There & Away

Bus The bus station, served by several operators, is at esplanade St Vincent. Many of the buses departing from here also stop at the train station.

Courriers Bretons *(☎ 02 99 19 70 70)* has regular services to regional destinations, including Mont St Michel (€8.80, one hour). The first daily bus to Mont St Michel leaves at 10am and the last one returns around 4.30pm.

TIV *(☎ 02 99 40 82 67)* has buses to Dinan (€6.40) and Rennes (€9.40). Buses to Dinard run about once an hour until around 7pm.

Train From the **train station** *(☎ 0836 35 35 39)* there is a direct service to Paris' Gare Montparnasse (€49.60 to €59.80, 3¼ hours). Some go via Rennes (€10.70). There are local services to Dinan (€7.30) and Quimper (€31).

Boat Ferries link Saint Malo with the Channel Islands, Weymouth and Portsmouth in England. There are two ferry terminals: hydrofoils, catamarans and the like depart from Gare Maritime de la Bourse; car ferries leave from the Gare Maritime du Naye. Both are south of the walled city.

From Gare Maritime de la Bourse, **Condor** *(☎ 02 99 20 03 00)* has catamaran and jetfoil services to Jersey (one-day excursion €46) and Guernsey (€46) from mid-March to mid-November. Condor's service to Weymouth (one way from €46, four hours) operates daily from late May to mid-October – discount prices are sometimes available.

Émeraude Lines *(☎ 02 23 18 01 80)* has ferries to Jersey, Guernsey and Sark from Gare Maritime du Naye. Service is most regular between late March and mid-November. **Brittany Ferries** *(☎ 0825 82 88 28)* has boats to Portsmouth from the Gare Maritime du Naye.

The Bus de Mer ferry (run by Émeraude Lines) links Saint Malo with Dinard (€3.40/5.40 single/return, 10 minutes) from April to September. In Saint Malo, the dock is just outside the Porte de Dinan; the Dinard quay is at 27 ave George V.

AROUND SAINT MALO

Dinard

pop 10,400

Whereas Saint Malo's old city and beaches are geared towards middle-class families, Dinard attracts a well-heeled clientele – especially among those from the UK. Indeed, Dinard has the feel of an early-20th-century beach resort, with its candy-cane bathing tents and carnival rides.

Beautiful seaside trails extend along the coast in both directions from Dinard. The famous **promenade du Clair de Lune** (Moonlight Promenade) runs along the Baie du Prieuré. The town's most attractive walk is the one that links the promenade du Clair de Lune with Plage de l'Écluse via the rocky coast of **Pointe du Moulinet**. Bikes are not allowed.

The **tourist office** *(☎ 02 99 46 94 12, fax 02 99 88 21 07; ⓔ dinard.office.de.tourime@wanadoo.fr; 2 blvd Féart; open Mon-Sat)* is in the colonnaded building. Staying in Dinard can strain the budget, so consider making a day trip from Saint Malo.

Loire Valley

From the 15th to 18th centuries, the fabled Loire Valley (Vallée de la Loire) was the playground of kings and nobles who expended vast fortunes and the wealth of the nation to turn it into an enormous neighbourhood of lavish chateaux. Today, this region is a favourite destination of tourists seeking architectural glories from the Middle Ages and the Renaissance.

The earliest chateaux were medieval fortresses, thrown up in the 9th century to fend off marauding Vikings. As the threat of invasion diminished by the 15th century, chateau architecture changed: fortresses gave way to pleasure palaces as the Renaissance ushered in whimsical, decorative features. From the 17th century onwards, grand country houses – built in the neoclassical style amid formal gardens – took centre stage.

BLOIS

pop 49,300

The medieval town of Blois (pronounced 'blwah') was a hub of court intrigue between the 15th and 17th centuries, and in the 16th century served as a second capital of France. Some dramatic events involving some of France's most important kings and historical figures took place inside the outstanding Château de Blois. The old city, seriously damaged by German attacks in 1940, retains its steep, twisting medieval streets.

Several of the Loire Valley's most rewarding chateaux, including Chambord and Cheverny, are a pleasant 20km-or-so cycle ride from Blois.

Orientation

Almost everything of interest is within walking distance of the train station, which is at the western end of ave Dr Jean Laigret. The old city lies south and east of Château de Blois, which towers over place Victor Hugo.

Information

The **tourist office** *(☎ 02 54 90 41 41, fax 02 54 90 41 49; ⓔ blois.tourism@wanadoo.fr; 3 ave Dr Jean Laigret; open daily)* can help with information. **Banque de France** *(4 ave Dr Jean Laigret; open 9am-12.15pm & 1.45pm-3.30pm Mon-Fri)* is one of a number of banks. Several commercial banks face the river along quai de la Saussaye, near rond-point de la Résistance.

Send mail at the **post office** *(rue Gallois; open 8.30am-7pm Mon-Fri, 8am-noon Sat)*, which has Cyberposte. You will find speedy Internet access at **Planet Info** *(☎ 02 54 55 99 41; 1 rue Jeanne d'Arc; open 10am-noon, 2pm-6pm Mon-Fri)* for the princely sum of €1.50 for every 10 minutes.

Things to See

Château de Blois The château *(☎ 02 54 74 16 06; adult/concession €6/4)* has a compellingly bloody history and an extraordinary mixture of architectural styles. Its four distinct sections are: early Gothic (13th century); Flamboyant Gothic (1498–1503), dating to the reign of Louis XII; Renaissance (1515–24), from the reign of François I; and neoclassical (17th century). The chateau also houses an **archaeological museum** and the **Musée des Beaux-Arts** (Museum of Fine Arts), both open 9am to noon and 2pm to 5pm, mid-October to

FRANCE

mid-March; and 9am to 6.30pm (8pm in July and August), the rest of the year. The chateau's evening **sound-and-light show** *(adult/concession €9.50/4.50)* runs May to September. For a chateau visit *and* show, buy the combination ticket (€11.50/5).

Opposite, the **Maison de la Magie** *(House of Magic; ☎ 02 54 55 26 26; 1 place du Château; adult/12-17 yrs/6-11 yrs €7.30/6.40/5.20; open 10.30am-12.30pm & 2pm-6.30pm daily July-Aug, 10am-noon & 2pm-6pm Tues-Sun Apr-June, 10am-noon & 2pm-6pm Wed-Thur & Sat-Sun Sept-Mar)* has magic shows, interactive exhibits and displays of clocks invented by the Blois-born magician Jean-Eugène Robert-Houdin (1805–71), after whom the great Houdini named himself.

Old City Large brown signs in English pinpoint tourist sights around the predominantly pedestrianised old city. **Cathédrale St-Louis** is named after an ancestor of Louis XIV, who had it rebuilt after a hurricane in 1678. There is a great view of Blois and the River Loire from the lovely **Jardins de l'Évêché** (Gardens of the Bishop's Palace), which is behind the cathedral.

The 15th-century **Maison des Acrobates** *(House of Acrobats; 3bis rue Pierre de Blois)* is one of Blois' few medieval houses to survive the bombings of WWII. It's named after the cheeky characters carved in its timbers.

Places to Stay

Camping A two-star site in Vineuil is **Camping des Châteaux** *(☎ 02 54 78 82 05; 2 adults, tent & car €8; open July-Sept)*, about 4km south of Blois. There is no bus service from town except in July and August (phone the camp site or the tourist office for details).

Hostels The **Auberge de Jeunesse Les Grouëts** *(☎/fax 02 54 78 27 21; 18 rue de l'Hôtel Pasquier; bus No 4 from place de la République; dorm beds €7; closed 10am-6pm, open Mar–mid-Nov)* in Les Grouëts, is 4.5km southwest of Blois train station. Call first – it's often full.

Hotels Near the train station, your best bet is **Hôtel St-Jacques** *(☎ 02 54 78 04 15, fax 02 54 78 33 05; 7 rue Ducoux; singles/doubles from €21.50/23, with shower from €26/28)*, which has basic doubles. Opposite at No 6, family-run **Hôtel Le Savoie** *(☎ 02 54 74 32 21, fax 02 54 74 29 58; singles/doubles from €36/39)* has well-kept rooms with shower, toilet and TV.

North of the old city is 12-room **Hôtel du Bellay** *(☎ 02 54 78 23 62, fax 02 54 78 52 04; 12 rue des Minimes; rooms €22.10-24.40, with shower & toilet €30.50)*.

Places to Eat

In the old city, **Le Rond de Serviette** *(☎ 02 54 74 48 04; 18 rue Beauvoir; menu €8)* claims to be Blois' most humorous and cheapest restaurant; its *menu* is unbeatable. Nearby, tuck into pasta and pizza at **La Scala** *(☎ 02 54 74 88 19; 8 rue des Minimes)*. Its leafy summer terrace gets full fast.

La Mesa *(☎ 02 54 78 70 70; 11 rue Vauvert; menus from €11.50)* is a busy Franco-Italian joint, up an alleyway from 44 rue Foulerie. Its lovely courtyard is perfect for dining alfresco.

There's a **food market** *(place Louis XII; open Tues, Thur & Sat to 1pm)* and an **Intermarché supermarket** *(ave Gambetta)* near the station.

Entertainment

L'Étoile Tex *(9 rue du Bourg Neuf)* is a busy bar/Tex-Mex place full of very young people. Several pubs overlook place Ave Maria.

Getting There & Away

The train station is at the western end of ave Dr Jean Laigret. Up to 16 direct trains go daily to Paris' Gare d'Austerlitz (€19.60, 1½ to two hours); there are several more if you change at Orléans. Frequent trains go to/from Tours (€8, 40 minutes, 11 to 17 daily) and its TGV station, St-Pierre des Corps (€7.70, 25 to 35 minutes, hourly). Most trains on the Blois-Tours line stop at Amboise (€5.30, 20 minutes).

Getting Around

Run by TUB, all buses within Blois (except No 4) stop at the train station and tickets cost €1 (€6.70 for a *carnet* of 10). Tickets and information are available from the **Point Bus information office** *(☎ 02 54 78 15 66; 2 place Victor Hugo)*.

Hire a bicycle from **Cycles Leblond** *(☎ 02 54 74 30 13; 44 Levée des Tuileries)*, which charges upwards of €12.20/80 per day/week. To get here, walk eastwards along promenade du Mail.

BLOIS AREA CHATEAUX

Blois is surrounded by some of the Loire Valley's finest chateaux in countryside that are perfect for cycling around. Spectacular Chambord, magnificently furnished Cheverny and charmingly situated Chaumont are each located about 20km from Blois, as is the modest but more personal Beauregard. The chateau-crowned town of Amboise (see the Tours Area Chateaux section) is also easily accessible from Blois. Travellers who try to cram too many into one day risk catching 'chateau sickness'.

Organised Tours

Without your own wheels, an organised tour is the best way to see more than one chateau in a day. From mid-May to 31 August, Blois-based **TLC** *(☎ 02 54 58 55 55)* runs two bus tours daily from Blois to Chambord and Cheverny (adult/concession €10/8); prices don't include entry fees. Tickets are sold on the bus and from the tourist office. Buses pick up passengers in Blois at the Point Bus information office.

Getting There & Away

TLC runs limited bus services in the vicinity of Blois. Buses depart from place Victor Hugo (in front of the Point Bus office) and from the bus station to the left of the train station as you exit.

Château de Chambord

The 440-room Château de Chambord *(☎ 02 54 50 50 02; W www.chambord.org; adult/18-25s/child €7/4.50/free; open 9am-6.30pm daily Apr-Sept, 9am-5.15pm daily Oct-Mar)*, begun in 1519 by François I (1515–47), is the largest and most visited chateau in the Loire Valley. Its Renaissance architecture and decoration, grafted onto a feudal ground plan, may have been inspired by Leonardo da Vinci. The emblems of François I – a royal monogram of the letter 'F' and a fierce salamander – adorn parts of the building. Beset by financial problems, which even forced him to leave his two sons unransomed in Spain, the king managed to keep 1800 workers and artisans at work on Chambord for 15 years. At one point he demanded that the River Loire be rerouted so it would pass by Chambord.

The chateau's famed **double-helix staircase**, attributed by some to Leonardo, consists of two spiral staircases that wind around the same central axis but never meet. It leads to an Italianate **rooftop terrace**, where you're surrounded by towers, cupolas, domes, chimneys, dormers and slate roofs with geometric shapes. Visitors already in the chateau can stay 45 minutes after ticket sales end.

Chambord is 16km east of Blois and 20km northeast of Cheverny. During the school year, TLC bus No 2 averages three return trips (two on Saturday, one on Sunday) from Blois to Chambord (€3.25, 45 minutes). In July and August, your only bus option is TLC's guided tour (see Organised Tours earlier in this section).

Château de Cheverny

Completed in 1634, Château de Cheverny *(☎ 02 54 79 96 29; e chateau.cheverny@wanadoo.fr; adult/concession €5.80/4; open 9.15am or 9.30am-6.15pm Apr-June & Sept, to 6.30pm July & Aug, 9.15am or 9.30am-noon & 2.15pm-5.30pm Oct & Mar, to 5pm Nov-Feb)* is the most magnificently furnished of the Loire Valley chateaux and is still privately owned. Visitors can wander through sumptuous rooms that are outfitted with the finest canopied beds, tapestries, paintings, painted ceilings and walls covered with embossed Córdoba leather. Three dozen panels illustrate the story of *Don Quixote* in the downstairs dining room.

The lush grounds shelter an 18th-century **Orangerie** where Leonardo da Vinci's *Mona Lisa* was hidden during WWII. The stables now house a mediocre **Tintin museum** *(adult/concession €10/8.20, includes entry to chateau)* that might appeal to kids and diehard fans. The antlers of almost 2000 stags cover the walls of the **Salle des Trophées**, while the kennels keep a pack of 100 hunting hounds – their daily meal at 5pm, called the 'soupe des chiens', is worth a glimpse.

Cheverny is 16km southeast of Blois and 20km southwest of Chambord. The TLC bus No 4 from Blois to Villefranche-sur-Cher stops at Cheverny (€3, 25 to 35 minutes). Buses leave Blois at 12.25pm Monday to Friday. Returning to Blois, the last bus leaves Cheverny at 6.58pm. Departure times can vary and are different on Sunday and holidays; check schedules first.

Château de Beauregard

Built in the 16th century as a hunting lodge for François I, Beauregard *(☎ 02 54 70 36 74; adult/student & child €6.50/4.50; open*

9.30am-noon & 2pm-5pm or 6.30pm daily Apr-Sept, 9.30am-noon & 2pm-5pm or to 6.30pm Thur-Tues Oct-Mar) is most famous for its **Galerie des Portraits**, which displays 327 portraits of notable faces from the 14th to 17th centuries.

Beauregard is 6km south of Blois or a pleasant 15km cycle ride through forests from Chambord. There's road access to the chateau from the Blois-Cheverny D765 and the D956 (turn left at the village of Cellettes).

The TLC bus from Blois to St-Aignan stops at Cellettes (€1.45), 1km southwest of the chateau, Monday to Friday at 7.50am. On Wednesday, Friday and Saturday the first bus from Blois to Cellettes leaves at 12.25pm. Unfortunately, there's no afternoon bus back except for the Châteauroux-Blois line operated by **Transports Boutet** *(☎ 02 54 34 43 95)*, which passes through Cellettes around 6pm daily.

Château de Chaumont

Château de Chaumont *(☎ 02 54 51 26 26; adult/18-25s/child €5.50/3.50/free; open 9.30am-6.30pm daily mid-Mar–mid-Oct, 10am-4.30pm daily mid-Oct–mid-Mar)*, set on a bluff overlooking the Loire, resembles a feudal castle. Built in the late 15th century, it served as a booby prize for Diane de Poitier when her lover, Henry II, died in 1559, and hosted Benjamin Franklin several times when he served as ambassador to France after the American Revolution.

Its luxurious **stables** are the most famous feature, but the **Salle du Conseil** (Council Chamber) on the 1st floor, with its majolica tile floor and tapestries, and **Catherine de Medici's bedroom** overlooking the chapel, are also remarkable.

Château de Chaumont is 17km southwest of Blois and 20km northeast of Amboise in Chaumont-sur-Loire. The path leading up to the chateau begins at the intersection of rue du Village Neuf and rue Maréchal Leclerc (D751). Local trains run from Blois to Onzain (€2.70, 10 minutes, eight or more daily), which is a 2km walk across the river from the chateau.

TOURS

pop 270,000

Lively Tours has the cosmopolitan and bourgeois air of a miniature Paris, with wide 18th-century avenues and café-lined boulevards. Tours was devastated by German bombardment in June 1940, but much of the city has been rebuilt since. The French spoken in Tours is said to be the purest in France.

Orientation

Tours' focal point is place Jean Jaurès, where the city's major thoroughfares – rue Nationale, blvd Heurteloup, ave de Grammont and blvd Béranger – join up. The train station is 300m east along blvd Heurteloup. The old city, centred on place Plumereau, is about 400m west of rue Nationale.

Information

The **tourist office** *(☎ 02 47 70 37 37, fax 02 47 61 14 22; ⓔ info@ligeris.com; 78-82 rue Bernard Palissy; open daily)* can help with information. **Banque de France** *(2 rue Chanoineau)* is open 8.45am to noon on weekdays. Commercial banks overlook place Jean Jaurès, and ATMs are easily found throughout the city's centre.

The **post office** *(1 blvd Béranger; open 8am-7pm Mon-Fri, 8am-noon Sat)* has Cyberposte. **Alli@nce Micro** *(☎ 02 47 05 49 50; 7ter rue de la Monnaie)*, and **Le Cyberspace** *(☎ 02 47 66 29 96; 27 rue Lavoisier; open 2pm-5am)* both charge around €4 per hour to surf the Web; the latter is housed in a pub so you can sip a quiet ale while you surf.

Things to See

Tours offers some lovely quarters for strolling, including the **old city** around place Plumereau, surrounded by half-timbered houses, as well as **rue du Grand Marché** and **rue Colbert**. The interior of the **Cathédrale St-Gatien**, which was built between 1220 and 1547, is well known for its 13th- and 15th-century stained glass. Its Renaissance **cloister** can be visited.

The **Musée de l'Hôtel Goüin** *(25 rue du Commerce; adult/concession €3.50/2.60)* is an archaeological museum, housed in a splendid Renaissance mansion built around 1510. The **Musée du Compagnonnage** *(Guild Museum; 8 rue Nationale; adult/concession €4/2.50)*, overlooking the courtyard of **Abbaye St-Julien**, is a celebration of the skill of the French artisan. The **Musée des Vins de Touraine** *(Museum of Touraine Wines; adult/concession €2.50/2)* at No 16 is in the 13th-century wine cellars of Abbaye St-Julien.

The **Musée des Beaux-Arts** *(Museum of Fine Arts; 18 place François Sicard; adult/concession €4/2)* has a good collection of works from the 14th to 20th centuries.

Most museums in Tours close Tuesday.

Places to Stay

Hostels About 500m north of the train station, **Le Foyer** *(☎ 02 47 60 51 51, fax 02 47 20 75 20; ⓔ fjt.tours@wanadoo.fr; 16 rue Bernard Palissy; singles/doubles €17/26; reception open Mon-Sat)* is a workers' dormitory that sometimes has rooms available that travellers can use.

Hotels Recently spruced up **Hôtel Val de Loire** *(☎ 02 47 05 37 86, fax 02 47 64 85 54; 33 blvd Heurteloup; singles/doubles with washbasin & bidet €16.50/26, with shower, toilet & TV €30/40)* has rooms that may be spartan, but they're clean and comfortable.

Hôtel Français *(☎ 02 47 05 59 12; 11 rue de Nantes; singles/doubles/triples/quads with washbasin & bidet €20/20/25/29, with shower & TV €25/29/34/37, with shower, TV & toilet €27/33/36/47)* provides a cold welcome but is good for penny-pinchers. A hall shower costs €2 and breakfast €5.

Mon Hôtel *(☎ 02 47 05 67 53, fax 02 47 05 21 85; 40 rue de la Préfecture; singles/doubles from €17/20, with shower & toilet €30/35)* is 500m north of the train station. Cheerful **Hôtel Vendôme** *(☎/fax 02 47 64 33 54; ⓔ hotelvendome.tours@wanadoo.fr; 24 rue Roger Salengro; rooms from €20, with shower & toilet from €30.50)* is run by a friendly couple. It has simple but decent rooms.

Places to Eat

In the old city, place Plumereau and rue du Grand Marché are loaded with places to eat. **Le Serpent Volant** *(54 rue du Grand Marché)* is a quintessential French café, while **Le Café** *(39 rue du Dr Bretonneau)* is a contemporary, funky favourite.

Simple but attractive **Le Bistroquet** *(☎ 02 47 05 12 76; 17 rue Blaise Pascal; menus €10.30-15)* specialises in paella but has French food *menus*. **Les Tanneurs** is a university restaurant-cum-café near the main university building on rue des Tanneurs. To dine you need a student ticket.

Sandwich stalls selling well-filled baguettes and pastries fill the **Grand Passage shopping mall** *(18 rue de Bordeaux)*. There's a **covered market** *(place Gaston Pailhou; open to 7pm Mon-Sat, to 1pm Sun)*.

Entertainment

Old-city café nightlife is centred on place Plumereau. **Les 3 Orfèvres** *(☎ 02 47 64 02 73; 6 rue des Orfèvres)* has live music starting at 11pm most nights. Student nightlife abounds down tiny rue de la Longue Échelle and the southern strip of adjoining rue Dr Bretonneau.

Live jazz venues include alternative café-theatre **Le Petit Faucheux** *(☎ 02 47 38 67 62; 23 rue des Cerisiers)* and brilliant **Bistro 64** *(☎ 02 47 38 47 40; 64 rue du Grand Marché)*, which has Latin, blues and *musique française* in a 16th-century interior.

Getting There & Away

Bus There's a **Eurolines** *(☎ 02 47 66 45 56; 76 rue Bernard Palissy; open Mon-Sat)* ticket office next to the tourist office.

The **Tours bus station** *(☎ 02 47 05 30 49; place du Général Leclerc)*, opposite the train station, serves local destinations. It has an **information desk** *(☎ 02 47 05 30 49; open 7.30am-noon & 2pm-6.30pm Mon-Sat)*. You can visit the chateaux Chenonceau and Amboise in a day using CAT bus No 10 (study the schedules carefully).

Train Tours train station is on place du Général Leclerc. Several Loire Valley chateaux can be easily accessed by rail.

Paris' Gare Montparnasse is about 1¼ hours away by TGV (€33.50 to €43.60, up to 20 daily), often with a change at St-Pierre des Corps. Other services include to/from Paris' Gare d'Austerlitz (€24.30, 2½ hours), Bordeaux (€35.40, 2½ hours) and Nantes (€23.80, 1½ hours).

Getting Around

Local buses are run by **Fil Bleu** *(information office ☎ 02 47 66 70 70; 5bis rue de la Dolve)*.

From April to September, **Amster' Cycles** *(☎ 02 47 61 22 23, fax 02 47 61 28 48; 5 rue du Rempart)* rents out road and mountain bikes for €14/54 per day/week.

TOURS AREA CHATEAUX

Several chateaux around Tours can be reached by train, SNCF bus or bicycle. Several companies offer English-language tours of the chateaux – reserve at the Tours tourist office or contact the company directly.

Services Touristiques de Touraine *(STT; ☎/fax 02 47 05 46 09; W www.stt-millet.fr)* runs coach tours April to mid-October costing €34 (including admission fees to three or four chateaux).

In summer, you can make an all-day circuit by public bus from Tours to Chenonceaux and Amboise by taking the 10am bus to Chenonceaux (€2.10), then the 12.40pm bus from Chenonceaux to Amboise (€1.05, 25 minutes). Return buses from Amboise to Tours (€2.10) leave at 4.25pm, 5.25pm and 6.20pm. Double-check times and schedules before departing.

Château de Chenonceau

With its stylised moat, drawbridge, towers and turrets straddling the River Cher, 16th-century Chenonceau *(☎ 02 47 23 90 07; e chateau.de.chenonceau@wanadoo.fr; adult/concession €7.60/6.10; open 9am-around 4.30pm mid-Nov–Jan, 9am-around 7pm mid-Mar–mid-Sept)* is everything a fairy-tale castle should be, although its interior is only of moderate interest.

Of the many remarkable women who created Chenonceau, Diane de Poitiers, mistress of King Henri II, planted the garden to the left (east) as you approach the chateau. After Henri's death in 1559, his widow Catherine de Médicis laid out the garden to the right (west) as you approach the castle.

Between 1940 and 1942, the demarcation line between Vichy-ruled France and the German-occupied zone ran down the middle of the Cher: the castle itself was under direct German occupation, but the southern entrance to the 60m-long **Galerie** was in the area controlled by Marshal Pétain. For many trying to escape to the Vichy zone, this room served as a crossing point.

Château de Chenonceau, in the town of Chenonceaux, is 34km east of Tours, 10km southeast of Amboise and 40km southwest of Blois. Chenonceaux SNCF train station is in front of the chateau. Between Tours and Chenonceaux there are four to six trains daily (€5.20, 30 minutes); alternatively, trains on the Tours–Vierzon line stop at Chisseaux (€5.20, 24 minutes, six daily), which is 2km east of Chenonceaux. In summer, you can take CAT bus No 10 to/from Tours (€2.10, 1¼ hours, one daily).

Château d'Azay-le-Rideau

Built on an island in the River Indre, Azay-le-Rideau *(☎ 02 47 45 42 04; adult/concession €5.50/3.50; open 9.30am-6pm Apr-June & Sept, 9am-7pm July & Aug, 10am-12.30pm & 2pm-5.30pm Oct-Mar)* is among the most elegant of Loire chateaux. The highlight of the 14 renovated rooms open to the public are a few 16th-century Flemish tapestries, and it's one of the few chateaux that allows picnicking in its beautiful park.

Azay-le-Rideau, 26km southwest of Tours, is on SNCF's Tours–Chinon line (four or five daily Monday to Saturday, one on Sunday). From Tours, the 30-minute trip (50 minutes by SNCF bus) costs €4.30; the station is 2.5km from the chateau.

Amboise

pop 11,000

Picturesque Amboise, is an easy day trip from Tours. **Château d'Amboise** *(☎ 02 47 57 00 98; adult/concession €6.50/5.50; open 9am-noon & 2pm-4.45pm or 5.30pm Nov-Mar, 9am-6.30pm Apr-June, Sept & Oct, 9am-7pm July & Aug)* is perched on a rocky outcrop overlooking the town. The remains of Leonardo da Vinci (1452–1519), who lived in Amboise for the last three years of his life, are said to be under the chapel's northern transept.

Inside the chateau walls, opposite 42 place Michel Debré, is the innovative **Caveau des Vignerons d'Amboise**, a wine cellar where you can taste (free) regional Touraine wines, Easter to October.

Da Vinci, who came to Amboise at the invitation of François I in 1516, lived and worked in **Le Clos Lucé** *(☎ 02 47 57 62 88; 2 rue du Clos Lucé; adult/concession €6.50/5.50; open 9am-7pm Mar-June, Sept-Dec, 9am-8pm July & Aug, 10am-5pm Jan, 9am-6pm Feb)*, a 15th-century brick manor house 500m southeast of the chateau along rue Victor Hugo. The building contains restored rooms and scale models of some 40 of Leonardo's fascinating inventions.

Amboise **tourist office** *(☎ 02 47 57 09 28, fax 02 47 57 14 35; e tourisme.amboise@wanadoo.fr; open Mon-Sat, daily Easter-Oct)* is next to the river, opposite 7 quai du Général de Gaulle.

Several daily trains run to Amboise from both Tours (€4.20, 20 minutes) and Blois (€5.40, 20 minutes). From Tours, you can also take CAT bus No 10 (€2.10, 30 to 50 minutes).

Southwestern France

The southwestern part of France is made up of a number of diverse regions, ranging from the Bordeaux wine-growing area, near the beach-lined Atlantic seaboard, to the Basque Country and the Pyrenees mountains in the south. The region is linked to Paris, Spain and the Côte d'Azur by convenient rail links.

LA ROCHELLE

pop 120,000

La Rochelle, a lively port city midway down France's Atlantic coast, is popular with middle-class French families and students on holiday. The ever-expanding Université de La Rochelle, opened in 1993, adds to the city's vibrancy. The nearby Île de Ré is ringed by long, sandy beaches.

The old city is north of the Vieux Port (old port), which is linked to the train station – 500m southeast – by ave du Général de Gaulle. The **tourist office** *(☎ 05 46 41 14 68; w www.ville-larochelle.fr; open Mon-Sat, daily June-Sept)* is in Le Gabut, the quarter on the south side of the Vieux Port.

Things to See

To protect the harbour at night and defend it in times of war, a chain used to be stretched between the two 14th-century stone towers at the harbour entrance, the 36m **Tour St Nicolas** and **Tour de la Chaîne**; the latter houses displays on local history. West along the old city wall is **Tour de la Lanterne**, long used as a prison. All three towers are open daily; admission to each costs adult/concession €4/2.50 (€8.50 for combined ticket).

The **Musée Maritime Neptunea** *(Bassin des Chalutiers; adult/concession €7.60/5.30)*, an excellent maritime museum, is also the permanent home of Jacques Cousteau's research ship *Calypso*. The entry fee includes tours of a *chalutier* (fishing trawler). Next door, the vast **Aquarium La Rochelle** *(☎ 05 46 34 00 00; bassin des Grands Yachts; adult/concession €10/7; open 10am-8pm Oct-Mar, 9am-8pm Apr-June & Sept, 9am-11pm July & Aug)* features some 10,000 of the sea's flora and fauna species.

Île de Ré This flat, 30km-long island, fringed by beaches, begins 9km west of La Rochelle. It's connected to the mainland by a 3km toll bridge.

In July and August, and on Wednesday, weekends and holidays in June, city bus No 1 or 50 (known as No 21 between the train station and place de Verdun) go to Sablanceaux (€2.50, 25 minutes). Year-round, **Rébus** *(☎ 05 46 09 20 15; St Martin de Ré)* links La Rochelle (the train station and place de Verdon) with St Martin de Ré and other island towns.

Places to Stay

Camping du Soleil *(☎ 05 46 44 42 53; ave Marillac; bus No 10; open mid-May–mid-Sept)*, about 1.5km south of the city centre, is often full.

The **Centre International de Séjour-Auberge de Jeunesse** *(☎ 05 46 44 43 11, fax 05 46 45 41 48; ave des Minimes; dorm beds €12.50)* is 2km southwest of the train station. To get here take bus No 10 and ask for the Lycée Hôtelier stop. Rates include breakfast.

In the pedestrianised old city, the friendly, 24-room **Hôtel Henri IV** *(☎ 05 46 41 25 79, fax 05 46 41 78 64; place de la Caille; rooms from €34, with shower & toilet €45)* has spacious doubles.

A few blocks from the train station, the 32-room **Terminus Hôtel** *(☎ 05 46 50 69 69, fax 05 46 41 73 12; e terminus@cdl-lr.com; 7 rue de la Fabrique; singles/doubles €31-55/35-60)* offers comfortable doubles, with rates depending on the season. One block north, the 22-room **Hôtel de Bordeaux** *(☎ 05 46 41 31 22, fax 05 46 41 24 43; e hbordeaux@free.fr; 43 rue St Nicolas; singles/doubles from €27.50/29, with shower & toilet from €30.50/33)* has quiet, pastel rooms (also at variable rates), and breakfast is included.

Near the bus station, **Hôtel de la Paix** *(☎ 05 46 41 33 44; 14 rue Gargoulleau; singles/doubles from €40/43, room for up to 5 people from €60)* is another pleasant, friendly option.

Places to Eat

Rustic **Le Petit Rochelais** *(25 rue St Jean du Perot; mains from €12.20; open daily July & Aug, Thur-Mon Sept-June)* serves traditional fare in a warm, inviting atmosphere. Bustling **Les Comédiens** *(15 rue de la Chaîne; menus from €10)*, derives its name from the theatre above it and serves contemporary French cuisine. There are dozens of other eateries along the northern side of the port and on nearby streets, many specialising in seafood.

Loan Phuong *(quai du Gabut; lunch/dinner buffet €11/12)* has an all-you-can-eat Chinese and Vietnamese buffet. Couscous is on offer at **Shéhérazade** *(35 rue Gambetta; open Tues-Sun, & Mon dinner)*.

There's a lively **covered market** *(place du Marché; open 7am-1pm daily)* and a **Prisunic supermarket** *(30 rue du Palais; open Mon-Sat)* in the old city.

Getting There & Away

Eurolines ticketing is handled by **Citram Littoral** *(☎ 05 46 50 53 57; 30 cours des Dames; open Mon afternoon, Tues-Fri, & Sat morning)*.

You can take a TGV to Paris' Gare Montparnasse (€50.60 to €61.10, three hours). Other destinations include Bordeaux (€21.10, two hours) and Tours (€29).

Getting Around

The innovative local transport system, **Autoplus** *(☎ 05 46 34 02 22)*, has its main bus hub at place de Verdun. Most lines run until sometime between 7.15pm and 8pm.

Autoplus' *Le Passeur* (€0.60) ferry service links Tour de la Chaîne with the Avant Port. It runs whenever there are passengers – just press the red button on the board at the top of the gangplank – until midnight in summer, and until 10pm at other times.

Les Vélos Jaunes, a branch of the public transport company, Autoplus, will furnish you with a bike (lock included) free for two hours (€1 per hour after that).

BORDEAUX

pop 735,000

Bordeaux is known for its neoclassical (if somewhat grimy) architecture, wide avenues and well-tended public parks. The city's cultural diversity (including 60,000 students), excellent museums and untouristy atmosphere make it much more than just a convenient stop between Paris and Spain. The marketing and export of Bordeaux wine are the town's most important economic activities.

Orientation

Cours de la Marne stretches for about 2km from the train station northwestward to place de la Victoire, which is linked to the tourist office area (1.5km farther north) by the pedestrians-only rue Ste Catherine. The city centre lies between place Gambetta and the Garonne River. The city's peripheral road is called the *rocade*.

Information

The **main tourist office** *(☎ 05 56 00 66 00, fax 05 56 00 66 01; W www.bordeaux-tourisme.com; 12 cours du 30 Juillet; open daily)* can help with information. **Banque de France** *(15 rue de l'Esprit des Lois)* is open 9am to noon on weekdays. There are commercial banks near the tourist office on cours de l'Intendance, rue Esprit des Lois and cours du Chapeau Rouge. **American Express** *(☎ 05 56 00 63 36; 14 cours de l'Intendance; open Mon-Fri Oct-May, Mon-Fri & Sat morning June-Sept)* has a branch here.

Currency exchange and Cyberpostes are offered at both the **main post office** *(37 rue du Château d'Eau; open 8.30am-6.30pm Mon-Fri, 8.30am-12.30pm Sat)* and the **branch post office** *(place St Projet; open to 6.30pm Mon-Fri, to noon Sat)*. **Cyberstation** *(☎ 05 56 01 15 15; 23 cours Pasteur; open 11am-2am Mon-Sat, 2pm-midnight Sun)* has Internet access for €2 per hour.

Things to See

The following sights are listed roughly north to south. Admission to each museum costs €4/2.50 (free for students and on the first Sunday of the month).

The **Musée d'Art Contemporain** *(Museum of Contemporary Art; ☎ 05 56 00 81 50; Entrepôt 7, rue Ferrére; open 11am-6pm Tues-Sun, to 8pm Wed, closed Mon)* has excellent displays on recent artists. The **Jardin Public**, an 18th-century English-style park, is along cours de Verdun and includes Bordeaux's **botanical garden** and **Musée d'Histoire Naturelle** *(Natural History Museum; ☎ 05 56 48 26 37; 5 place Bardineau; open 11am-6pm Mon-Fri, 2pm-6pm Sat-Sun, closed Tues)*.

The most prominent feature of **esplanade des Quinconces**, a vast square laid out in 1820, is a towering fountain-monument to the Girondins, a group of moderate, bourgeois legislative deputies executed during the French Revolution.

The neoclassical **Grand Théâtre** *(☎ 05 56 00 85 95; place de la Comédie; closed Sun & Mon)* was built in the 1770s. **Porte Dijeaux**, which dates from 1748, leads from **place Gambetta**, which has a garden in the middle, to the pedestrianised commercial centre. A few blocks south, the **Musée des Arts Décoratifs** *(Museum of Decorative Arts; ☎ 05 56 00 72 50; 39 rue Bouffard; open 2pm-6pm Wed-Mon, temporary exhibits from 11am Mon-Fri)* specialises in *faïence*, porcelain, silverwork, glasswork, furniture and the like.

In 1137, the future King Louis VII married Eleanor of Aquitaine in **Cathédrale St André**. Just east of the cathedral, there's the 15th-century, 50m-high belfry, **Tour Pey-Berland** *(place Jean Moulin; adult/concession €3.95/2.45; open 10am-6.30pm daily June-Sept, 10am-12.30pm & 2pm-5.30pm daily Oct-May)*. The **Centre National Jean Moulin** *(Jean Moulin Documentation Centre; ☎ 05 56 79 66 00; admission free; open 11am-6pm Tues-Fri, 2pm-6pm Sat & Sun)*, facing the north side of the cathedral, has exhibits on France during WWII.

The **Musée des Beaux-Arts** *(Museum of Fine Art; ☎ 05 56 10 20 56; 20 cours d'Albret; open Wed-Sat 11am-6pm)* occupies two wings of the 18th-century Hôtel de Ville and houses a large collection of paintings, including 17th-century Flemish, Dutch and Italian works. The outstanding **Musée d'Aquitaine** *(☎ 05 56 01 51 00; 20 cours Pasteur; open 11am-6pm Tues-Sun)*, illustrates the history and ethnography of the Bordeaux area.

The **Synagogue** *(rue du Grand Rabbin Joseph Cohen; open generally 9am-noon & 2pm-4pm Mon-Thur)*, just west of rue Ste Catherine, and dating from 1882, is a mixture of Sephardic and Byzantine styles. During WWII the Nazis turned the complex into a prison. Ring the bell marked *gardien* at 213 rue Ste Catherine.

Places to Stay

Auberge de Jeunesse *(☎ 05 56 91 59 51; 22 cours Barbey; members/nonmembers €16/17.50)*, about 700m west of the train station, is well-appointed if somewhat cold. Take bus No 7 or 8 from the station to the Meunier stop.

North of the centre near place de Tourny (from the station take bus No 7 or 8), friendly **Hôtel Touring** *(☎ 05 56 81 56 73, fax 05 56 81 24 55; 16 rue Huguerie; singles/doubles with shower from €24.30/29, with shower & toilet €35.10/38.10)* has rather gigantic and spotless rooms. Nearby, **Hôtel Studio** *(☎ 05 56 48 00 14, fax 05 56 81 25 71; W www.hotel-bordeaux.com; 26 rue Huguerie)* and three affiliated hotels offer charmless singles/doubles with shower, toilet and (in most cases) cable TV starting at an absolute minimum of €16/20. The hotel's mini Internet café charges guests €2.25 an hour.

A few blocks southwest of place Gambetta, the quiet **Hôtel Boulan** *(☎ 05 56 52 23 62, fax 05 56 44 91 65; 28 rue Boulan; singles/doubles from €17/20, with shower €20/23)* has decent rooms.

Just east of place Gambetta is **Hôtel de la Tour Intendance** *(☎ 05 56 81 46 27, fax 05 56 81 60 90; 16 rue de la Vieille Tour; singles €35, doubles €41-52)*, where you're assured of a warm welcome.

Places to Eat

La Chanterelle *(3 rue de Martignac; lunch/dinner menus €12/16; open Mon, Tues, Fri & Sat, & Wed lunch)* serves moderately priced traditional French and regional cuisine. Bistro-style cuisine and southwestern French specialities are on offer at **Claret's** *(☎ 05 56 01 21 21; place Camille Julien; lunch menu €10, dinner menus €16 & €20; open Mon-Fri, & Sat dinner)*.

The popular **Le Bistrot d'Édouard** *(16 place du Parlement; lunch menu Mon-Sat €11, dinner menus €16 & €26)* purveys French bistro-style meat and fish dishes. There are a host of eateries along nearby rue du Parlement Ste Catherine, rue des Piliers de Tutelle and rue St Rémi.

Restaurant Baud et Millet *(19 rue Huguerie; open Mon-Sat)* serves cheese-based cuisine (most dishes are vegetarian), including all-you-can-eat *raclette* (a block of melted cheese eaten with potatoes and cold meats) for €17.50. Slightly more upmarket is **Restaurant Brasserie V. Hugo** *(160 cours Victor Hugo; entrées €6.50-11.50, mains €10-12)*, where a meal will cost you €25, not including wine.

The inexpensive cafés and restaurants around place de la Victoire include the **Cassolette Café** *(20 place de la Victoire; small/large cassolettes €2.20/6.50; open daily)*, which serves family-style French food on *cassolettes* (terracotta plates).

There's a **Champion supermarket** *(place des Grands Hommes; open Mon-Sat)* in the basement of the mirror-plated Marché des Grands Hommes. Near **Marché des Capucins** *(open 6am-1pm Tues-Sun)*, a covered food market just east of place de la Victoire, you'll find super-cheap **fruit and vegetable stalls** *(open to 1pm Mon-Sat)* along rue Élie Gintrec.

Entertainment

Cinephiles will love **Cinéma Utopia** *(☎ 05 56 52 00 03; 5 place Camille)*, where new and old films are shown in their original language. A bistro serves a €10 lunch menu and drinks until late.

Bordeaux has a hopping nightlife scene. **The Down Under** *(104 cours Aristide Briand)*, run by an ex-Aucklander, is an Anglophone favourite. One of the really hot venues is a Cuban-style bar called **Calle Ocho** *(24 rue des Piliers de Tutelle; open Mon-Sat)*.

Among the best of the late-late dancing bars is tropical-beach-themed **La Plage** *(☎ 05 56 49 02 46; 40 quai de la Paludate; open Wed-Sat)* along the river east of the train station.

Getting There & Away

Buses to places all over the Gironde and nearby departments leave from the **Halte Routière** *(☎ 05 56 43 68 43)*, in the northeast corner of esplanade des Quinconces; schedules are posted.

Bordeaux's train station, **Gare St Jean** *(☎ 0836 35 35 39)*, is about 3km southeast of the city centre at the end of cours de la Marne. It occasionally has attractive special fares worth asking for. By TGV it takes only about three hours to/from Paris' Gare Montparnasse (€64 to €66.10). The trip to Bayonne (€23) takes 1¾ hours.

BORDEAUX VINEYARDS

The Bordeaux wine-producing region, 1000 sq km in extent, is subdivided into 57 production areas called *appellations*, whose climate and soil impart distinctive characteristics to the wines grown there.

Over 5000 chateaux (also known as *domaines*, *crus* and *clos*) produce the region's highly regarded wines, which are mainly reds. Many smaller chateaux accept walk-in visitors (some are closed during the October grape harvest); the larger and better-known ones usually require that you phone ahead.

Each vineyard has different rules about tasting – at some it's free, others charge entry fees, and others don't serve wine at all. Look for signs reading *dégustation* (wine tasting), *en vente directe* (direct sales), *vin à emporter* (wine to take away) and *gratuit* (free).

Opposite Bordeaux's main tourist office, the **Maison du Vin de Bordeaux** *(☎/fax 05 56 00 22 66; ⓦ www.vins-bordeaux.fr; open Mon-Fri year-round, & Sat summer)* has details on vineyard visits. It can also supply information on the many local *maisons du vin* (special wine-oriented tourist offices).

From May to October, the Bordeaux tourist office runs five-hour bus tours in French and English to local wine chateaux, with wine tastings included (adult/concession €26/22.50).

St Émilion

pop 2500

Medieval St Émilion, 39km east of Bordeaux, is surrounded by vineyards renowned for their full-bodied, deeply coloured red wines. The most interesting historical sites – including the **Église Monolithe**, carved out of solid limestone from the 9th to the 12th centuries – can be visited only on the 45-minute guided tours (€5.05/3.05) run by the **tourist office** *(☎ 05 57 55 28 28; place des Créneaux; open daily)*. The 50 or so wine shops include the cooperative **Maison du Vin** *(☎ 05 57 55 50 55; place Pierre Meyrat; open daily)*, around the corner from the tourist office, owned by the 250 chateaux whose wines it sells.

From Bordeaux, St Émilion is accessible by train (€6.80, 35 minutes, two or three daily) and bus (at least once daily, except on Sunday and holidays from October to April). The last train back usually departs at 6.27pm.

BAYONNE

pop 40,000

Bayonne is the most important city in the French part of the Basque Country (Euskadi in Basque, Pays Basque in French), a region straddling the French-Spanish border.

Its most important festival is the annual Fêtes de Bayonne, beginning on the first Wednesday in August. The festival includes a running of the 'bulls' (like Pamplona's), except that here they use cows.

Orientation & Information

The Adour and Nive Rivers split Bayonne into three: St Esprit, north of the Adour; Grand Bayonne, the oldest part of the city, on the west bank of the Nive; and the very Basque Petit Bayonne to its east.

The **tourist office** *(☎ 05 59 46 01 46, fax 05 59 59 37 55; ⓔ info@bayonne-tourisme.com; place des Basques; open Mon-Sat, daily July & Aug)* can help visitors. Its free brochure *Fêtes de Bayonne* is useful for cultural and sporting events, while *Fêtes en Pays-Basque* also free, describes the region more generally.

The office organises guided tours of the city at 3pm on Saturday (€4.60).

You can log on at **Cyber Net Café** *(☎ 05 59 55 78 98; place de la République; open 7am-11pm Mon-Sat, noon-11pm Sun)*; it charges €4.50 per hour until noon, and €6.80 per hour thereafter.

Things to See & Do

Construction of the Gothic **Cathédrale Ste Marie** *(place Monseigneur Vansteenberghe)* began in the 13th century and was completed in 1451. The entrance to the beautiful 13th-century **cloister** is on place Louis Pasteur.

The **Musée Bonnat** *(5 rue Jacques Laffitte; adult/concession €5.50/3; open 10am-12.30pm & 2.30pm-6.30pm Wed-Mon)*, in Petit Bayonne, has a diverse collection, including a whole gallery of Rubens' paintings.

Places to Stay

Hostels The **Auberge de Jeunesse d'Anglet** *(☎ 05 59 58 70 00, fax 05 59 58 70 07; ⓔ biarritz@fuaj.fr; 19 route des Vignes; tent sites €8.30 per person, B&B €14.90 1st night, €12.20 per night thereafter; open mid-Feb–mid-Nov)* in Anglet comes complete with a Scottish pub. Popular with surfers, reservations are essential in summer. You can also pitch a tent here, and rates include breakfast. Membership costs €2.90. There's a minimum one-week stay in July and August, when the hostel is often booked out.

From Bayonne, catch bus No 2 to Cinq-Cantons, then bus No 7 and get off at Moulin Barbot, a 10-minute walk away. From Biarritz town or station, take bus No 9.

Hotels You can tumble off the train into hyperfriendly **Hôtel Paris-Madrid** *(☎ 05 59 55 13 98, fax 05 59 55 07 22; singles from €15, doubles with/without shower from €23/21, quads with shower & toilet from €39)*, beside the station. It has singles, pleasant doubles, and big rooms with bathroom and cable TV that can take up to four. Nearby, **Hôtel Monte Carlo** *(☎ 05 59 55 02 68; 1 rue Ste Ursule; basic rooms from €19, 2-4 person rooms €26-39)* has simple rooms and larger ones with bathroom for two to four people.

In Petit Bayonne, **Hôtel des Basques** *(☎ 05 59 59 08 02; 4 rue des Lisses; rooms with washbasin €21.50-26, with bathroom €28-30.50)*, in a quiet location on place Paul Bert, has large, pleasant rooms.

The mid-range **Hôtel des Basses-Pyrénées** *(☎ 05 59 59 00 29, fax 05 59 59 42 02; 12 rue Tour de Sault; doubles/triples with toilet & shower from €46/58; open Feb-Dec)* is built around a 17th-century tower, and offers private parking.

Places to Eat

Nowhere in town is more Basque than **Restaurant Euskalduna Ostatua** *(61 rue Pannecau; mains €6.80; open lunch Tue-Sat)*, near Hôtel des Basques, where the main dishes are a bargain. Over the Nive River, the family-run **Bar-Restaurant du Marché** *(39 rue des Basques; open lunch)*, where the cooking's homely and the owner's wife mothers everyone, will fill you to bursting for about €12.

The central market, **Les Halles** *(open Mon-Sat morning)* is on the west quay (quai Amiral Jauréguiberry) of the Nive River.

Entertainment

The greatest concentration of pubs and bars is in Petit Bayonne, especially along rue Pannecau and quai Galuperie. **Chai Ramina** *(☎ 05 59 50 33 01; 9 rue de la Poissonerie; open 9.30am-8pm Mon-Thu & until 2am Fri & Sat)* is a friendly bar that opens late on Friday and Saturday nights, with a discotheque next door open until dawn.

Getting There & Away

Bus The **ATCRB buses** *(☎ 05 59 26 06 99)* that run to St-Jean de Luz (€3.60, 40 minutes, 10 daily) leave from place des Basques with connections for the border town of Hendaye (€5.60, one hour). Two Transportes Pesa buses run to Irún and San Sebastián in Spain (€6.20, 1¾ hours, daily except Sunday).

From the train station car park, **RDTL** *(☎ 05 59 55 17 59)* runs services northwards into Les Landes. For beaches north of Bayonne, such as Mimizan Plage and Moliets Plage, get off at Vieux Boucau (€6.40, 1¼ hours). **TPR** *(☎ 05 59 27 45 98)* has three buses daily to Pau (€13.20, 2¼ hours).

Bayonne is one of three hubs in southwest France for Eurolines, whose buses stop in place Charles de Gaulle, opposite the **Eurolines office** *(☎ 05 59 59 19 33)* at No 3.

Train The train station is just north of pont St Esprit bridge. TGVs run to/from Paris' Gare Montparnasse (€67.81 to €76.80, five hours). Two daily non-TGV trains go overnight to

Paris' Gare d'Austerlitz (€61.50 or €76 with couchette, eight hours).

There's a frequent service to Biarritz (€2, 10 minutes), St-Jean de Luz (€3.80, 25 minutes) and St-Jean Pied de Port (€7.20, one hour), plus the Franco-Spanish border towns of Hendaye (€5.60, 40 minutes) and Irún (€5.90, 45 minutes).

Trains also run to destinations such as Bordeaux (€23, 2¾ hours, about 12 daily), Lourdes (€16.90, 1¾ hours, six daily) and Pau (€13.10, 1¼ hours, six daily).

BIARRITZ

pop 30,000

The classy coastal town of Biarritz, 8km west of Bayonne, has fine beaches and some of Europe's best surfing. Unfortunately, it can be a real budget-buster – consider making it a day trip from Bayonne, as lots of French holiday-makers do. Many surfers camp or stay at one of the two excellent youth hostels – in Biarritz and in Anglet (see the Bayonne section earlier).

Biarritz's Festival International de Folklore is held in early July.

Orientation & Information

Place Clemenceau, at the heart of Biarritz, is just south of Grande Plage, the main beach. The **tourist office** (*☎ 05 59 22 37 10, fax 05 59 24 14 19; e biarritz.tourisme@biarritz.tm.fr; 1 square d'Ixelles; open daily*) is one block east of the square. It publishes *Biarritzcope*, a free monthly guide to what's on. In July and August it has a branch at the train station.

Check your emails at **Génius Informatique** (*☎ 05 59 24 39 07; 60 ave Édouard VII*) for €8 an hour.

Things to See & Do

The **Grande Plage**, lined in season with striped bathing tents, stretches from the Casino Bellevue to the stately Hôtel du Palais. North of the hotel is **Plage Miramar** and the 1834 **Phare de Biarritz**. Beyond this lighthouse, the superb surfing beaches of **Anglet** extend for 4km (take bus No 9 from place Clemenceau).

The **Musée de la Mer** (*adult/concession €7.20/4.60*), Biarritz' sea museum, is on Pointe Atalaye overlooking **Rocher de la Vierge**, an islet reached by a short footbridge which offers sweeping coastal views. The museum has a 24-tank aquarium plus seal and shark pools.

Places to Stay

Hostels For Biarritz's **Auberge de Jeunesse** (*☎ 05 59 41 76 00, fax 05 59 41 76 07; e aubergejeune.biarritz@wanadoo.fr; 8 rue Chiquito de Cambo; B&B €15.50 1st night, €12.80 thereafter, meals €8*), follow the railway westwards from the train station for 800m. The otherwise expensive **Hôtel Barnetche** (*☎ 05 59 24 22 25, fax 05 59 24 98 71; 5 ave Charles Floquet; dorm beds €20*) has dorm bunks.

Hotels Nowhere is cheap in Biarritz, but prices drop by up to 25% outside summer.

In the Vieux Port area is the trim **Hôtel Palym** (*☎ 05 59 24 16 56; 7 rue du Port Vieux; rooms with toilet & shower low/high season €40/47*). In the centre of town, **Hôtel Au Saint James** (*☎ 05 59 24 06 36; 15 rue Gambetta; singles/doubles low season €29/37, high season €45/55*) has small but charming rooms, with full and half-board available in the hotel restaurant.

Hôtel Etche-Gorria (*☎ 05 59 24 00 74; 21 ave du Maréchal Foch; rooms low/high season €31/40 , with bathroom €40/45*) is an attractive option.

Places to Eat

Popular **Le Bistroye** (*☎ 05 59 22 01 02; 6 rue Jean Bart; mains from €7.35; open Mon-Tues, Wed lunch, Thur-Sat*) has delicious fare. Next door, **La Mamounia** (*☎ 05 59 24 76 08*) doles out couscous from €12.50 and other Moroccan specialities from €15.

There are a few decent restaurants around Les Halles, such as **Bistrot des Halles** (*☎ 05 59 24 21 22; 1 rue du Centre; 2-course meal about €20*). There's a **covered market** (*open 7am-1.30pm daily*) off ave Victor Hugo.

Entertainment

Popular bar areas include the streets around rue du Port Vieux, the covered market area and around place Clemenceau. Two central discos are **Le Caveau** (*4 rue Gambetta*) and **Le Flamingo** inside the Casino Bellevue.

Getting There & Away

Most local STAB buses stop beside the Biarritz town hall, from where Nos 1 and 2 go to Bayonne's town hall and station.

Biarritz-La Négresse train station is 3km south of the centre and served by bus Nos 2 and 9. There's a downtown office of **SNCF** (*☎ 05 59 24 00 94; 13 ave du Maréchal Foch*).

AROUND BIARRITZ

St-Jean Pied de Port

pop 1500

The walled Pyrenean town of St-Jean Pied de Port, 53km southeast of Bayonne, was once (and remains) the last stop in France for pilgrims heading for the Spanish pilgrimage city of Santiago de Compostela. Nowadays it's a popular departure point for latter-day hikers and bikers, and can be hideously crowded in summer. The climb to the 17th-century **Citadelle** merits the effort with fine views.

The **tourist office** *(☎ 05 59 37 03 57; place Charles de Gaulle)* helps with information. Riverside **Camping Municipal Plaza Berri** *(☎ 05 59 37 11 19; ave du Fronton; 2 people & tent €5.50; open Easter–mid-Oct)* has tent sites. **Hôtel des Remparts** *(☎ 05 59 37 13 79; 16 place Floquet; singles/doubles with bathroom from €34/39)* is a cheerful place.

For lunch, **Chez Dédé** *(☎ 05 59 37 16 40; menu du €10, mains from €8)*, just inside the porte de France, has as many as seven good-value, tasty *menus*.

Half the reason for coming to St-Jean Pied de Port is the scenic train trip from Bayonne (€7.20, one hour, up to four daily).

LOURDES

pop 15,000

In 1858, 14-year-old Bernadette Soubirous saw the Virgin Mary within a small grotto in a series of 18 visions, later confirmed as bona fide apparitions by the Vatican. This simple peasant girl, who lived out her short life as a nun, was canonised as Ste Bernadette in 1933.

Today, some five million pilgrims annually, including many seeking cures for their illnesses, converge on Lourdes from all over the world. In counterpoint to the fervent, almost medieval piety of the pilgrims is a tacky display of commercial exuberance.

Orientation & Information

Lourdes' two main east-west streets are rue de la Grotte and, 300m north, blvd de la Grotte. Both lead to the Sanctuaires Notre Dame de Lourdes. The principal north-south thoroughfare connects the train station with place Peyramale and the **tourist office** *(☎ 05 62 42 77 40, fax 05 62 94 60 95; ⓔ lourdes@sudfr.com; open Mon-Sat)*.

The office sells the **Visa Passeport Touristique** *(€30)*, allowing entry to five museums in Lourdes.

Things to See

The huge religious complex, which has grown around the cave where Bernadette saw the Virgin, is just west of the town centre. The main Pont St Michel entrance is open from 5am to midnight.

Major sites include the **Grotte de Massabielle**, where Bernadette had her visions, its walls today worn smooth by the touch of millions of hands; the nearby **pools** in which 400,000 people immerse themselves each year; and the **Basilique du Rosaire** (Basilica of the Rosary). Dress modestly.

From the Sunday before Easter until mid-October, solemn **torch-lit processions** leave nightly at 9pm from the Grotte de Massabielle, while the **Procession Eucaristique** (Blessed Sacrament Procession) is at 5pm daily.

Places to Stay

Camping Tiny **Camping de la Poste** *(☎ 05 62 94 40 35; 26 rue de Langelle; sites per person/tent €2.50/3.60, rooms with/without shower €25/22; open Easter–mid-Oct)* is a few blocks east of the tourist office. It is small and friendly, and the rooms, though spartan, are good value.

Hotels Lourdes has plenty of budget hotels. Near the train station is the friendly **Hôtel d'Annecy** *(☎ 05 62 94 13 75; 13 ave de la Gare; singles/doubles/triples/quads with washbasin €14/23/27/28, with bathroom €21/29.50/32.50/33.50; open Easter-Oct)*. In the town centre, **Hôtel St Sylve** *(☎/fax 05 62 94 63 48; 9 rue de la Fontaine; singles/doubles €12.50/22, with shower €20/28; open Apr-Oct)* has large rooms.

Places to Eat

Restaurants close early in this pious town. **Restaurant Le Magret** *(10 rue des Quatre Frères Soulas; menus €13, €23 & €31; open Tues-Sun)*, opposite the tourist office, has excellent value *menus*. Next door, **La Rose des Sables** *(open Tues-Sun)* specialises in couscous (from €11). The **covered market** *(place du Champ Commun)* is south of the tourist office.

Getting There & Away

The bus station, down rue Anselme Lacadé east of the covered market, serves regional towns including Pau (€7.20, 1¼ hours, four to six daily). SNCF buses to the Pyrenean towns of Cauterets (€5.90, one hour, five daily) and

Luz-St-Sauveur (€6.30, one hour, six daily) leave from the train station's car park.

The train station is 1km east of the sanctuaries. Trains connect Lourdes with many cities including Bayonne (€16.90, 1¾ hours, up to six daily), Bordeaux (€27.30, 2½ hours, six daily), Pau (€6, 30 minutes, over 10 daily) and Toulouse (€19.70, 2¼ hours, seven daily). There are five TGVs daily to Paris' Gare Montparnasse (€72.40 to €81.40, six hours) and one overnight train to Gare d'Austerlitz (€66.20, nine hours).

The Dordogne

The Dordogne (better known as Périgord in France) was one of the cradles of human civilisation, and a number of local caves – including the world-famous Lascaux – are adorned with extraordinary prehistoric paintings. The region is also renowned for its cuisine, which makes ample use of those quintessential French delicacies, *truffes du Périgord* (black truffles) and *foie gras*, the fatty liver of force-fed geese.

PÉRIGUEUX

pop 33,000

Founded over 2000 years ago on a curve in the gentle Isle River, Périgueux has one of France's best museums of prehistory, the **Musée du Périgord** *(22 cours Tourny; adult/concession €3.50/1.75; open Wed-Mon; closed holidays)*.

The old city, known as **Puy St Front**, lies between blvd Michel Montaigne and the Isle River. The **tourist office** *(☎ 05 53 53 10 63, fax 05 53 09 02 50; ⓔ tourisme.perigueux@perigord.tm.fr; 26 place Francheville; open Mon-Sat, daily mid-June–mid-Sept)* is next to a fortified, medieval tower called **Tour Mataguerre**.

Don't Trifle with Truffles

The humble truffle, a kind of underground mushroom, is worth thousands of dollars per kilogram. It can't be farmed and is only found in the wilds of Périgord Noir (Black Perigord) by dogs or pigs specially trained for the purpose. Truffle season doesn't last long, and the fungus remains fresh only for a couple of weeks, but its rich flavours are famous the world over, even in preserved form.

Places to Stay

About 600m south of the cathedral is the **Foyer des Jeunes Travailleurs** *(☎ 05 53 53 52 05; rue des Thermes Prolongée; dorm beds €11.50)*, just off blvd Lakanal. Rates include breakfast. Near the train station, the cheapest hotel is the family-run, 16-room **Hôtel des Voyageurs** *(☎ 05 53 53 17 44; 26 rue Denis Papin; doubles with/without shower €17/14)* with basic but clean rooms. Reception may be closed on weekend afternoons (hours posted).

Getting There & Away

The **bus station** *(☎ 05 53 08 91 06; place Francheville)*, just southwest of the tourist office, has buses to Sarlat (€8.15, 1½ hours, one or two daily) via the Vézère Valley town of Montignac (€5.30, 55 minutes).

The **train station** *(☎ 0836 35 35 39; rue Denis Papin)*, about 1km northwest of the tourist office, is served by local buses Nos 1, 4 and 5. Destinations offered include Bordeaux (€15.40, 1¼ hours), Les Eyzies de Tayac (€6.10, 30 minutes, two to four daily), Paris' Gare d'Austerlitz (€42.90, four to five hours) and Sarlat (€11.60).

SARLAT-LA-CANÉ DA

pop 10,000

This beautiful town, situated between the Dordogne and Vézère Rivers, is graced by numerous Renaissance-style, 16th and 17th-century stone buildings. On Saturday morning there's a colourful market on place de la Liberté and along rue de la République – edible (though seasonal) offerings include truffles, mushrooms, geese and parts thereof.

The main drag is known as rue de la République where it passes through the heart-shaped old town. The **tourist office** *(☎ 05 53 59 27 67; ⓔ info@ot-sarlat-perigord.fr; rue Tourny)* can organise hotel bookings (€2 within the *département* or €3 outside it).

Places to Stay

Modest but friendly, 15-bed **Auberge de Jeunesse** *(☎ 05 53 59 47 59, 05 53 30 21 27; 77 ave de Selves; tent sites per person €5, plus €0.50 for 1st night, dorm beds €9, plus €1 for 1st night; open mid-Mar–Nov)* has cooking facilities. Call ahead to check availability.

Doubles start at €40 at **Hôtel de la Mairie** *(☎ 05 53 59 05 71; 13 place de la Mairie; open Feb-Dec)*, in the medieval city and **Hôtel**

Les Récollets *(☎ 05 53 31 36 00, fax 05 53 30 32 62; ⓔ otelrecol@aol.com; 4 rue Jean-Jacques Rousseau)*, up an alley west of rue de la République, both are two-star hotels.

Getting There & Away

There are one or two buses daily (fewer in July and August) from place de la Petite Rigaudie to Périgueux (€8.15, 1½ hours) via the Vézère Valley town of Montignac (35 minutes).

Sarlat's tiny **train station** *(☎ 0836 35 35 39)* is linked to Bordeaux (€18.80, 2½ hours), Périgueux (€11.60) and Les Eyzies de Tayac (€7.20, 50 minutes, two daily).

VÉZÈRE VALLEY

Périgord's most important prehistoric sites are about 45km southeast of Périgueux and 20km northwest of Sarlat in the Vézère Valley, mainly between Les Eyzies de Tayac and Montignac. Worthwhile caves not mentioned below include the **Grotte du Grand Roc** and **La Roque St Christophe**. For details on public transport, see Getting There & Away under Périgueux and Sarlat earlier.

Les Eyzies de Tayac

pop 850

This dull, touristy village offers one of the region's best introductions to prehistory, the **Musée National de la Préhistoire** *(adult/concession €4.50/3; open Wed-Mon Sept-June, daily July & Aug)*, built into the cliff above the tourist office. **Abri Pataud** *(adult/concession €4.60/2.50; open Tues-Sun Sept-June, daily July & Aug)* is an impressive Cro-Magnon rock shelter in the cliff face.

The **Grotte de Font de Gaume**, a cave with 230 sophisticated polychrome figures of bison, reindeer and other creatures, and the **Grotte des Combarelles**, decorated with 600 often-superimposed engravings of animals, are 1km and 3km respectively northeast of Les Eyzies de Tayac on the D47. **Tours** *(☎ 05 53 06 86 00; adult/18-25/under 18s €6/4/free; Sun-Fri)* must be reserved in advance.

Les Eyzies' **tourist office** *(☎ 05 53 06 97 05, fax 05 53 06 90 79; open Mon-Sat, daily Mar-Sept)* is on the town's main street.

Montignac

pop 3100

Montignac, 25km northeast of Les Eyzies, achieved sudden fame thanks to the **Lascaux Cave**, 2km to the southeast, discovered in 1940 by four teenage boys who, it is said, were out searching for their dog. The cave's main room and a number of steep galleries are decorated with 15,000-year-old figures of wild oxen, deer, horses, reindeer and other creatures depicted in vivid reds, blacks, yellows and browns.

Lascaux has long been closed to the public to prevent deterioration, but you can get a good idea of the original at **Lascaux II** *(open 10am-noon & 2pm-5.30pm Mon-Sat Sept-June, 9am-7pm daily July & Aug; closed 3 weeks in Jan)*, a meticulous replica of the main gallery. The last tour begins about an hour before closing time. Tickets, which from April to October are sold *only* in Montignac (next to the tourist office), cost €7.70 (children €4.50).

Burgundy & the Rhône

DIJON

pop 230,000

Dijon, the prosperous capital of the dukes of Burgundy for almost 500 years, is one of France's most appealing provincial cities, combining elegant Renaissance buildings with a youthful university-town feel.

Dijon is a good starting point for visits to the vineyards of the Côte d'Or, arguably the greatest wine-growing region in the world (unless you come from Bordeaux).

Orientation & Information

Ave Maréchal Foch links the train station with the tourist office. Rue de la Liberté, Dijon's main thoroughfare, runs easterly onwards.

The main **tourist office** *(☎ 03 80 44 11 44, fax 03 80 42 18 83; ⓦ www.ot-dijon.fr; open daily)* is 300m east of the train station at place Darcy. The **tourist office annexe** *(34 rue des Forges; open Mon-Sat May–mid-Oct, Mon-Fri mid-Oct–Apr)* faces the north side of the Palais des Ducs. Both sell **wine country bus tour** tickets *(half/full day €45/95)*.

Rue de la Liberté is lined with **banks**. The **main post office** *(place Grangier; open 8am-7pm Mon-Fri, 8am-noon Sat)* also offers exchange and Cyberposte. Situated in the bus station, **Multi Rezo** *(☎ 03 80 42 13 89; open 10am-midnight Mon-Sat, 2pm-10pm Sun)* charges €1 for 12 minutes of Net access.

Things to See

Dijon's major museums open daily except Tuesday (except for the Musée National Magnin, which closes Monday). Except where noted, entry is free for under 18s and students and, on Sunday, for everyone. The **Dijon Card** *(24/48/72 hours €8/12/14)*, available at tourist offices, offers free museum and transport access.

The **Palais des Ducs et des États de Bourgogne**, once home to the dukes of Burgundy, now houses the **Musée des Beaux-Arts** *(Fine Arts Museum; ☎ 03 80 74 52 09; adult €3.40; open 9.30am-6pm May-Oct, 10am-5pm Nov-Apr)*, one of France's most renowned fine arts museums.

Many great figures of Burgundy's history are buried in the Burgundian-Gothic **Cathédrale St Bénigne**, built in the late 13th century. Next door, the **Musée Archéologique** *(☎ 03 80 30 88 54; 5 rue du Docteur Maret; adult €2.20; open 9am-6pm)* houses rare Gallo-Roman artefacts.

Just off place de la Libération, the **Musée National Magnin** *(☎ 03 80 67 11 10; 4 rue des Bons Enfants; adult €3; open 9am-noon & 2pm-6pm)* contains around 2000 works of art.

Dijon has been associated with producing the world's finest mustard since the 13th century, a heritage celebrated at the **Amora Musée de la Moutarde** *(☎ 03 80 44 11 44; 48 quai Nicolas Rolin; 3 guided tours at 3pm Mon-Sat mid-June–mid-Sept, Wed & Sat Oct-May)*. Bookings are mandatory.

Places to Stay

Camping The two-star **Camping du Lac** *(☎ 03 80 43 54 72; 3 blvd Chanoine Kir; open 8.30am-8pm Apr–mid-Oct)* is 1.2km west of the train station; take bus No 12 (direction Fontaine d'Ouche) to stop Hôpital des Chartreux.

Hostels The 260-bed **Centre de Rencontres Internationales et de Séjour de Dijon** *(CRISD; ☎ 03 80 72 95 20, fax 03 80 70 00 61; ⓔ reservation@auberge-cri-dijon.com; 1 blvd Champollion; dorm beds €17.50 including breakfast)* is 2.5km northeast of the centre. Take bus No 5 (direction Épirey) from place Grangier.

Hotels Three blocks south of rue de la Liberté, **Hôtel Monge** *(☎ 03 80 30 55 41, fax 03 80 30 30 15; 20 rue Monge; singles/doubles with shower & toilet €32.50/34.50)* is the cheap-and-cheerful option. Further down the road at No 64, **Hôtel Le Sauvage** *(☎ 03 80 41 31 21, fax 03 80 42 06 07; singles/doubles with bathroom €43/46)* is smarter with tasteful rooms built around a lively courtyard restaurant.

A hidden gem in Dijon is the **Hôtel Le Jacquemart** *(☎ 03 80 60 09 60, fax 03 80 60 09 69; ⓦ www.hotel-lejacquemart.fr; 32 rue Verrerie; singles/doubles with washbasin from €25.50/27)* which has smart and clean rooms available.

Just north of Église St Michel, **Hôtel Le Chambellan** *(☎ 03 80 67 12 67, fax 03 80 38 00 39; 92 rue Vannerie; rooms with washbasin/shower from €28/37)* has comfortable rooms with a rustic feel.

Hôtel Lamartine *(☎ 03 80 30 37 47, fax 03 80 30 03 43; 12 rue Jules Mercier; singles/doubles with washbasin €27.20/30.40)*, on a narrow street off rue de la Liberté, has clean if a little threadbare rooms.

Places to Eat

Head for rue Monge and rue Berbisey for cheap eats. **Alice's** *(☎ 03 80 50 19 51; 2 rue Monge; lunch menus €10)* is a nice spot.

Breton crepes (€5 to €7) are the speciality at **Crêperie Kerine** *(36 rue Berbisey)*; the small but friendly **Le Petit Charlois** *(☎ 03 80 49 81 60)* at No 106 has a €14.80 dinner *menu* on offer, which includes an all-you-can-eat salad buffet.

For cheap student eats, the **Restaurant Universitaire Maret** *(3 rue du Docteur Maret; open 11.40am-1.15pm & 6.40pm-8pm Mon-Fri; closed during university holidays)* requires student ID for its €2.40 meal tickets (sold on the ground floor weekday lunchtime).

The **Halles du Marché** *(open to 1pm Tues, Thur-Sat)* covered market, 150m north of rue de la Liberté, is ideal for picnics, while **Chez Nous** *(6 impasse Quentin)*, down an alley from the market, serves excellent €7 Burgundian *plat du jour* from noon in a divey café with an anarchist squat vibe. Get there early.

The **Monoprix supermarket** *(open 8.30am-8pm Mon-Sat)* is in the Centre Commercial Dauphine off rue Bossuet. **Moulot et Petitjean** *(13 place Brossuet)* is a long-established sweet shop; **Maille** *(30 rue de la Liberté)* has all those essential mustard souvenirs.

Entertainment

The nightlife area lies north of place de la République with techno club **L'An-Fer** *(w www.an-fer.com; 8 rue Marceau; admission €8 with drink after 11pm, €6.50 before, open until 5am Wed-Sat)*, and Latin bar/club **Coco-Loco** *(18 ave Garibaldi; open until 2am Tues-Sat)* the main attractions.

Getting There & Away

Transco buses *(☎ 03 80 42 11 00)* link the bus station (next to the train station) with wine-making villages along the Côte d'Or via bus No 60 (€6.40 round trip); No 44 goes direct to Beaune (€6.40).

The train station, **Gare Dijon-Ville** *(☎ 0892 35 35 39)* has TGV services to/from Paris' Gare de Lyon (€35.80 to €40.80, 1½ hours). There are non-TGV trains to Lyon (€22.80, two hours) and Nice (€70.40, six hours).

Getting Around

STRD shuttle buses *(☎ 03 80 30 60 90; €3 ticket bought on the bus)*, connecting with Buzz flights from London, run from **Dijon-Bourgogne airport** *(☎ 03 80 67 67 67)* to behind the place Darcy tourist office.

The **STRD office** *(place Grangier; open 6.30am-7.15pm Mon-Sat)* has details of Dijon's urban bus network. A day ticket will cost you €2.70.

Eurobike *(☎ 03 80 45 32 32; 4 rue du Faubourg Raines; half/full day €9.15/15.25)* hires out bikes.

CÔTE D'OR

Burgundy's finest vintages come from the vine-covered Côte d'Or, the eastern slopes running for about 60km south from Dijon. The northern section, known as the Côte de Nuits, incorporates Gevrey-Chambertin, Vougeot, Vosne-Romanée and Nuits St Georges, known for their fine reds; the southern section, the Côte de Beaune, includes Pommard, Volnay, Meursault and Puligny-Montrachet.

Beaune

pop 22,000

Beaune, a sleepy little town about 40km south of Dijon, makes for an ideal day trip. It's known for its wine cellars and the **Hôtel-Dieu**, France's most opulent medieval charity hospital *(adult/concession €5.10/4.10)*.

The **tourist office** *(☎ 03 80 26 21 30, fax 03 80 26 21 39; w www.ot-beaune.fr; place de la Halle; open daily)*, 1km west of the train station, is opposite the Hôtel-Dieu. It sells the **Pass Beaune** *(€14.50)*, which offers a variety of tourist discounts, and advises on visits to *caves* (wine cellars).

Alternatively, hire bikes from the friendly **Bourgogne Randonnées** *(☎ 03 80 22 06 03; ave du 8 Septembre; €15 per day; open 9am-noon & 1.30pm-7pm Mon-Sat, from 10am Sun)*.

There are 18 wine cellars in town. The two best known are the **Marché aux Vins** *(☎ 03 80 25 08 20; 2 rue Nicolas Rolin)*, behind the tourist office, which offers a daily sampling of 18 wines for €9, and **Patriarche Père et Fils** *(☎ 03 80 24 53 78; 5-7 rue du Collège)*, which has visits (including sampling 13 wines for €9) from 9.30am to 11.30am and 2pm to 5.30pm.

The **Musée du vin de Bourgogne** *(☎ 03 80 22 08 19; 6 rue d'Enfer; adult/concession €5.10/3.10; open 9.30am-6pm daily, to 5pm Jan-Mar)* incorporates the Musée Marey and Musée des Beaux Arts.

Places to Stay & Eat The best deal in town is **Hôtel Rousseau** *(☎ 03 80 22 13 59; 11 place Madeleine; singles/doubles from €23/29, 5-person room €61.50)*. It has large, old-fashioned rooms off a tranquil garden and is run by a charismatic woman. Opposite the station, **Hôtel de France** *(☎ 03 80 24 10 34, fax 03 80 24 96 78; 35 ave du 8 Septembre; singles/doubles from €43/49)* has clean, modern rooms.

Place Madeleine is graced with eateries; many close Sunday and Monday. The best place to eat is **Caves Madeleine** *(☎ 03 80 22 93 30; 8 rue du Faubourg Madeleine; menus €12 & €19.20; open noon-2pm & 6pm-9.30pm Mon-Wed, Fri & Sat)*, a very friendly wine bar, which encourages people to sit together at long tables and chat – ideal for lone travellers.

There's a **Petit Casino supermarket** *(6 rue Carnot)*, and café **Jean Ourvois** *(8 rue Carnot)* is a nice coffee spot.

Getting There & Away Beaune has direct train connections to Dijon (€5.70, 25 minutes, roughly every 40 minutes) and Paris (€38.40, two hours, three daily).

Transco *(☎ 03 80 42 11 00)* runs bus No 60 through wine-making villages along the Côte d'Or (€3.20) and bus No 44 direct to Dijon (€6.40).

LYON

pop 450,000

Lyon forms part of a prosperous urban area of almost two million people, France's second-largest conurbation. Founded by the Romans over 2000 years ago, it has spent the last 500 years as a commercial, industrial and banking powerhouse. Lyon boasts outstanding museums and a dynamic cultural life, and it's among France's greatest gastronomic capitals.

Orientation

The city centre is on the Presqu'île, a peninsula bounded by the Rhône and Saône Rivers. Place Bellecour is 1km south of place des Terreaux and 1km north of place Carnot, next to one of Lyon's train stations, Gare de Perrache. The main station, Gare de la Part-Dieu, is 2km east of the Presqu'île in a commercial district called La Part-Dieu. Vieux Lyon (old Lyon) sprawls across the Saône's west bank, but offers little by way of good-value hotels or eateries.

Information

The efficient **tourist office** *(☎ 04 72 77 69 69, fax 04 78 42 04 32; Ⓦ www.lyon-france.com; place Bellecour; open daily)* sells the **Lyon City Card** *(1/2/3 days €15/25/30)*, which offers free museum entry and use of public transport. Tickets must be validated before transport use. An **SNCF reservations desk** *(2 place Bellecour; open 9am-7pm Mon-Sat)* is nearby.

Thomas Cook exchange offices grace both train stations; **banks** dot rue Victor Hugo and rue de la République. The **central post office** *(10 place Antonin Poncet; open 8am-7pm Mon-Fri, 8am-12.30pm Sat)* has exchange and Cyberposte. Specialist travel bookshop and relaxed Internet café **Raconte-Moi La Terre** *(☎ 04 78 92 60 20; 38 rue Thomassin)* is one of the best traveller resources you could hope to find. It stocks a superb map selection and charges €3.80/6 for 30 minutes/one hour of Net access (student discounts available).

Connectick *(☎ 04 72 77 98 85; 19 quai St Antoine; open 11am-7pm Mon-Sat)* charges €7 for one hour online.

Things to See & Do

Vieux Lyon The old city, with its cobbled streets, restored houses and famous *traboules* (hidden connecting passageways), lies at the base of Fourvière hill.

In summer, guided rooftop tours of the **Basilique Notre Dame de Fourvière** are held daily (Wednesday and Sunday in low season) at 2.30pm and 4pm (adult/concession €4/2.50).

Fourvière Two thousand years ago, the Romans built the city of Lugdunum on Fourvière's slopes. Today the hill – topped by the **Tour Métallique** (1893), a sort of stunted Eiffel Tower – offers spectacular views of Lyon, its two rivers and, on clear days, Mont Blanc. The easiest way to the top is to ride the funicular railway (between 6am and 10pm) from rue Vieux Lyon station. Use a bus/metro ticket or buy a €1.20 funicular ticket.

The **Musée de la Civilisation Gallo-Romaine** *(☎ 04 72 38 81 90; 17 rue Cléberg; adult/concession €3.80/2.30, free to all Thur; open 9am-12.30pm & 2pm-5pm Tues-Sun)* is neighboured by two **Roman theatres**, which host rock and classical music concerts during **Les Nuits de Fourvière** *(Ⓦ www.nuits-de-fourviere.org)*, a summer festival held mid-June to mid-September.

Presqu'île The centrepiece of **place des Terreaux** is a monumental 19th-century fountain by Bartholdi, sculptor of New York's *Statue of Liberty*. Fronting the square is the **Hôtel de Ville** (1655). Its south side is dominated by Lyon's **Musée des Beaux-Arts** *(Fine Arts Museum; ☎ 04 72 10 17 40; adult/concession €3.80/2; open 10.30am-6pm Wed-Mon)*, which showcases sculptures and paintings from every period of European art.

The **statue of a giant on roller skates** on place Louis Pradel, northeast of the **Opéra House**, was sculpted from scrap metal by

The Lyonnais Bouchon

Lyon has a healthy gastronomic life of which its *bouchons* are the most famous exponent. Traditionally, these are simple unpretentious restaurants serving hearty country-style fare at reasonable prices. They are most renowned, however, for serving up dishes based on tripe and offal. No part of the pig goes to waste in a *bouchon* – vegetarians should stay well clear. One of the best dishes is *andouillette* – a beefy sausage made from pig intestines.

The problem now is that the concept is so famous in Lyon that just about every eatery in town claims to be a *bouchon*. The real *bouchons*, however, are worth seeking out. Many close at weekends and over holiday periods.

LYON

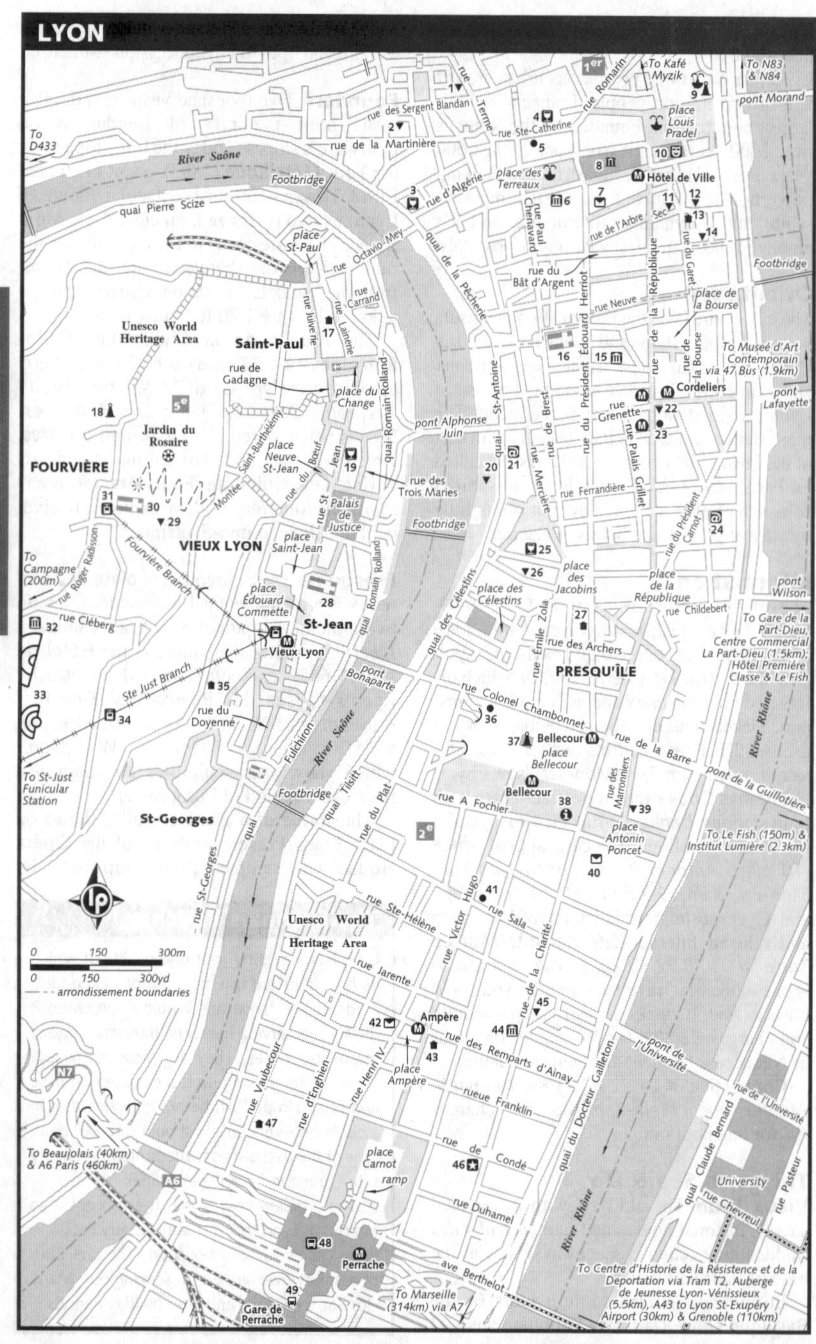
To Kafé Myzik
To N83 & N84
1er
rue Romarin
rue Terme
rue des Sergent Blandan
rue de la Martinière
rue Ste-Catherine
place Louis Pradel
pont Morand
To D433
River Saône
Footbridge
quai Pierre Scize
rue d'Algérie
place des Terreaux
Hôtel de Ville
rue Paul Chenavard
rue de l'Arbre Sec
rue du Garet
place St-Paul
rue Octavio Mey
quai de la Pêcherie
rue du Bât d'Argent
rue Carrand
rue Juiverie
rue Lainerie
rue Neuve
rue de la République
place de la Bourse
rue de la Bourse
Unesco World Heritage Area
Saint-Paul
rue de Gadagne
place du Change
quai Romain Rolland
quai St-Antoine
rue du Président Édouard Herriot
To Musée d'Art Contemporain via 47 Bus (1.9km)
pont Lafayette
Cordeliers
rue Grenette
rue Palais Grillet
rue de Brest
5e
Jardin du Rosaire
FOURVIÈRE
Montée Saint-Barthélemy
place Neuve St-Jean
rue du Boeuf
rue St Jean
pont Alphonse Juin
rue des Trois Maries
rue Mercière
rue Ferrandière
Palais de Justice
Footbridge
rue du Président Carnot
To Campagne (200m)
rue Roger Radisson
Fourvière Branch
VIEUX LYON
place Saint-Jean
place Édouard Commette
St-Jean
Vieux Lyon
quai des Célestins
place des Célestins
place des Jacobins
place de la République
rue Childebert
pont Wilson
rue Cléberg
rue Émile Zola
rue des Archers
PRESQU'ÎLE
To Gare de la Part-Dieu, Centre Commercial La Part-Dieu (1.5km); Hôtel Première Classe & Le Fish
Ste Just Branch
pont Bonaparte
rue du Doyenné
rue Colonel Chambonnet
rue de la Barre
Bellecour
place Bellecour
River Rhône
pont de la Guillotière
quai Fulchiron
River Saône
To St-Just Funicular Station
Footbridge
quai Tilsitt
rue du Plat
rue A Fochier
rue des Marronniers
place Antonin Poncet
St-Georges
2e
To Le Fish (150m) & Institut Lumière (2.3km)
quai St-Georges
rue Victor Hugo
rue Sala
rue Ste-Hélène
rue de la Charité
Unesco World Heritage Area
0 150 300m
0 150 300yd
arrondissement boundaries
rue Jarente
Ampère
rue des Remparts d'Ainay
pont de l'Université
quai du Docteur Gailleton
rue de l'Université
N7
rue Vaubecour
rue d'Enghien
rue Henri IV
place Ampère
rue Franklin
rue Claude Bernard
To Beaujolais (40km) & A6 Paris (460km)
place Carnot
rue de Condé
quai Claude Bernard
University
rue Pasteur
A6
ramp
rue Duhamel
River Rhône
rue Chevreul
Perrache
ave Berthelot
Gare de Perrache
To Marseille (314km) via A7
To Centre d'Historie de la Résistence et de la Deportation via Tram T2, Auberge de Jeunesse Lyon-Vénissieux (5.5km), A43 to Lyon St-Exupéry Airport (30km) & Grenoble (110km)
FRANCE

LYON

PLACES TO STAY
13 Hôtel Iris
17 Hôtel St Paul
27 Hôtel Élysée
35 Auberge de Jeunesse du Vieux Lyon
43 Hôtel d'Ainay
47 Gîtes de France

PLACES TO EAT
1 La Randonnée
2 Les Halles de la Martinière (Covered Food Market)
11 Bistro Pizay
12 Café 203
14 Alyssaar
20 Outdoor Food Market
22 Monoprix Supermarket
26 Notre Pain
29 Restaurant de Fourvière
39 Chabert et Fils
45 Petit Grain

MUSEUMS
6 Musée des Beaux-Arts
15 Musée de l'Imprimerie
32 Musée de la Civilisation Gallo-Romaine
44 Musée des Tissus; Musée des Arts Décoratifs

OTHER
3 Le Voxx
4 Le Shamrock
5 Laundrette
7 Branch Post Office
8 Hotel de Ville
9 Skater Statue
10 Opéra House
16 Église St-Nizier
18 Tour Métallique
19 St James Pub
21 Connectick Internet Centre
23 TCL Info Office
24 Raconte-Moi La Terre
25 Café Tombé du Ciel
28 Cathédrale Saint Jean
30 Basilique Notre Dame de Fourvière
31 Fourvière Funicular Station
33 Roman Theatres
34 Minimes Funicular Stop
36 SNCF Office
37 Louis XIV Statue
38 Tourist Office
40 Central Post Office
41 Laundrette
42 Branch Post Office
46 Police Station
48 Bus Terminal; Centre d'Échange
49 Airport Bus (Satobus)

Marseille-born sculptor César (1921–98). Skaters buzz around its feet. To the south, **rue de la République** is the main thoroughfare for shops and cinemas.

The **Musée des Tissus** *(☎ 04 78 38 42 00; 34 rue de la Charité)*, where Lyonnais silks are displayed, also houses the **Musée des Arts Décoratifs** (Decorative Arts Museum). Adult/concession is €4.60/2.30 and both open 10am to 5.30pm Tuesday to Sunday.

The history of printing, a technology established in Lyon in the 1480s, is illustrated by the **Musée de l'Imprimerie** *(☎ 04 78 37 65 98; 13 rue de la Poulaillerie; adult/concession €3.80/2; open 9.30am-noon & 2pm-5.30pm Wed-Sun)*.

Other Attractions Inspirational **Musée d'Art Contemporain** *(Contemporary Art Museum; ☎ 04 72 69 17 18; Ⓦ www.moca-lyon.org; 81 quai Charles de Gaulle; adult/concession €3.80/2; open noon-7pm Wed-Sun)* borders the river and hosts fantastically daring modern art exhibitions. The museumx also houses a multimedia centre devoted to digital art.

The **Institut Lumière** *(☎ 04 78 78 18 95; Ⓦ www.institut-lumiere.org; 25 rue du Premier-Film; adult/concession €5.34/4.42; open 11am-7pm Tues-Sun)* brings to life the work of the motion-picture pioneers Auguste and Louis Lumière.

Lyon's role as the centre for the WWII resistance movement is recorded in arguably the city's most important exhibition, the **Centre d'Histoire de la Résistance et de la Deportation** *(☎ 04 78 72 23 11; 14 ave Berthelot; adult/concession €3.80/2; open 9am-5.30pm Wed-Sun)*. Housed in the former Gestapo headquarters where Klaus Barbie operated until 1944, it's a thought-provoking experience.

Places to Stay

Hostels In Vieux Lyon, the **Auberge de Jeunesse du Vieux Lyon** *(☎ 04 78 15 05 50, fax 04 78 15 05 51; Ⓔ lyon@fuaj.org; 41-45 montée du Chemin Neuf; dorm beds €12.20 including breakfast; reception open 24hr)* requires non-HI affiliates to buy membership (€14.20).

Auberge de Jeunesse Lyon-Vénissieux *(☎ 04 78 76 39 23, fax 04 78 77 51 11; Ⓔ lyonvenissieux@fuaj.fr; 51 rue Roger Salengro; dorm beds €11.30 including breakfast; reception open 7.30am-12.30am)* is 5.5km southeast of Gare de Perrache in the Vénissieux district. Bus No 35 from place Jean Macé stops outside.

Chambres d'Hôtes B&B-type accommodation around Lyon is arranged by **Gîtes de France** *(☎ 04 72 77 17 55, fax 04 78 38 21 15; 1 rue Général Plessier)*, which has lists of *gîtes* (self-catering farms and cottages) to rent on a weekly basis; prices range from €50 to €80 per night for two people with breakfast.

Hotels Near the station, **Hôtel d'Ainay** *(☎ 04 78 42 43 42, fax 04 72 77 51 90; 14 rue des Remparts d'Ainay; singles/doubles €32/34 with shower & TV)* has rooms that are basic but functional.

The best bet for tasteful but budget accommodation is **Hôtel Élysée** *(☎ 04 78 42 03 15, fax 04 78 37 76 49; 92 rue du Président Édouard Herriot; singles/doubles from €43/59)*, with the bonus of being the only hotel listed here that is in the Bon Weekend en Ville scheme, whereby one night's stay at the weekend gives you a second night free. Just off place des Terreaux, **Hôtel Iris** *(☎ 04 78 39 93 80, fax 04 72 00 89 91; 36 rue de l'Arbre Sec; singles/doubles €37/40)* is dark but centrally located.

In Vieux Lyon, **Hôtel St Paul** *(☎ 04 78 28 13 29, fax 04 72 00 97 27; 6 rue Lainerie; rooms from €43)* is the pick of the bunch.

Around Gare Part-Dieu, head for **Hôtel Première Classe** *(☎ 04 72 36 86 62, fax 04 72 36 89 57; 75 blvd Vivek Merle; rooms from €40)* for a quick stopover.

Places to Eat

Piggy-part cuisine is the speciality of the traditional Lyonnais *bouchon*, a small, unpretentious bistro-style restaurant. It's now hard to find genuine *bouchons* that haven't sold out to coach-party catering, but rue des Marronniers and rue Mercière are still good places to look. **Chabert et Fils** *(☎ 04 78 37 01 94; 11 rue des Marronniers)* has a decent €10.50 lunch *menu*, as does **Bistro Pizay** *(☎ 04 78 28 37 26; 4 rue Verdi)*, near place Louis Pradel.

Many restaurants close Sunday. One of Lyon's hidden gems which doesn't is the arty **Café 203** *(☎ 04 78 28 66 65; 9 rue de Garet; open 7am-midnight, 3pm-midnight Sun)*, a buzzy place, deservedly popular for its excellent €10 *menus*. Round the corner, Syrian **Alyssaar** *(☎ 04 78 29 57 66; 29 rue du Bât d'Argent)* has spicy €12/14/18 *menus*.

La Randonnée *(☎ 04 78 27 86 81; 4 rue Terme)* offers vegetarian dishes and lunchtime/evening €6.50/12.50 *menus*, while the Vietnamese **Petit Grain** *(☎ 04 72 41 77 85; 19 rue de la Charité)* has salad platters from €7.50.

In Vieux Lyon, the **Restaurant de Fourvière** *(☎ 04 78 25 21 15; 9 place Fourvière)* has an €11.50 lunch *menu* and also feature great panoramic views.

For coffee, **Notre Pain** *(☎ 04 78 37 03 16; 1 rue de l'Ancienne Préfecture)* is a mellow bakery – get there around opening time (9am) for warm patisserie fresh from the oven.

Self-Catering Fresh produce, cheeses and bread are piled high at the **outdoor morning food market** *(quai St Antoine; open Tues-Sun)*; **Les Halles de la Martinière** *(covered food market; 24 rue de la Martinière; closed Sun afternoon & Mon)* in the northern Presqu'île is also good for self-caterers. The **Monoprix supermarket** is at the intersection of rue de la République and rue Grenette.

Entertainment

Rue Ste-Catherine is lined with bars. The long established **Le Shamrock pub** *(☎ 04 78 27 37 82)*, at No 15, opens late; another popular Irish bar is the **St James pub** *(☎ 04 78 37 36 70; 19 rue St Jean)*, in Vieux Lyon, which has an all-night happy hour on Thursday. North of place Louis Pradel, close to Croix Paquet metro, bands play at **Kafé Myzik** *(☎ 04 72 07 04 26; 20 Montée St-Sébastien)*, a hole-in-the-wall club.

On the Saône's left bank, bar **Le Voxx** *(☎ 04 78 28 33 87; 1 rue d'Algérie)* lures lively bands and patrons. Lively in a seedy late-night-dive way is café **Tombé du Ciel** *(☎ 04 78 42 69 30; 9 rue du Port du Temple)*.

The city's big night out is the club-on-a-boat **Le Fish** *(☎ 04 72 84 98 98; opp 21 quai Victor Augagneur; open Wed-Sat 10pm-5am)*.

Getting There & Away

Bus Intercity and international buses depart from the terminal next to Gare de Perrache. Timetables are available from the **TCL information office** *(☎ 04 78 71 70 00; open 7.30am-6.30pm Mon-Fri, 9.30am-noon & 1.30pm-7pm Sat)* on the middle level of the Centre d'Échange. Tickets are sold on the bus.

Satobus runs **airport shuttles** *(☎ 04 72 68 72 17)* to/from Perrache to Lyon Ste Exupéry airport (€8, one hour, every 20 minutes).

Train Lyon is a major rail hub. There are up to 30 trains daily to/from Paris (€50.30, two hours). Rather confusingly, trains can terminate at either of Lyon's stations. Generally, Part-Dieu (the larger and more blessed with facilities) handles TGV and international traffic, and Perrache handles local trains. Check, however, where trains are stopping as it's a €15 taxi ride between the stations, or a change at Charpennes metro station.

Getting Around

Lyon's efficient and musical metro system has four lines (A to D), running 5am to midnight. Tickets (€1.30) are valid for buses, the funicular and metro for one hour after time-stamping. A *carnet* of 10 tickets/day pass (€10.40/3.74), can be bought at ticket machines, and at **TCL information offices** *(☎ 04 78 71 70 00; Centre d'Échange, 43 rue de la République • Vieux Lyon metro station)*.

The French Alps

The French Alps constitute one of the most awe-inspiring mountain ranges in the world. In summer, visitors can take advantage of hundreds of kilometres of hiking trails, while in winter the area's ski resorts attract enthusiasts from around the world.

If you're going to ski or snowboard, expect to pay at least €45 a day (including equipment hire, lifts and transport) at low-altitude stations, which operate December to March. Larger, high-altitude stations cost €55 to €65 a day. There are good deals in January between the school holiday periods.

CHAMONIX

pop 10,109

Chamonix sits in a valley surrounded by the most spectacular scenery in the French Alps, an area almost Himalayan in its awesome scenery, with Mont Blanc soaring almost four vertical kilometres above the valley floor.

There are some 330km of hiking trails in the Chamonix area. In winter, the valley offers superb skiing, with dozens of ski lifts and over 140km of downhill and cross-country ski runs. The population swells to 100,000 in peak season and the town takes on an Ibiza *sur neige* feel, accompanied by giant music festivals.

Information

The **tourist office** *(☎ 04 50 53 00 24, fax 04 50 53 58 90; W www.chamonix.com; 85 place du Triangle de l'Amitié; open daily)* has brochures on ski-lift hours and costs, *refuges*, camping grounds and parapente schools. In winter it sells a range of ski passes, valid for bus transport and ski lifts in the valley.

The **Maison de la Montagne** *(109 place de l'Église)*, opposite the tourist office, houses the **Office de Haute Montagne** *(☎ 04 50 53 22 08; open Mon-Sat)*, which has information and maps for walkers and mountaineers.

There are **exchange** machines on place Balmat opposite the **post office** *(open 8.30am-noon & 2pm-6pm Mon-Fri, 8.30am-noon Sat)* and ave Michel Croz. The **cyBar** *(☎ 04 50 53 64 80; 80 rue des Moulins)* and **El Dorado** *(75 ave de l'Aiguille)* both charge €1 for 10 minutes of Internet access.

Things to See & Do

The **Musée Alpin** *(☎ 04 50 53 25 93; admission €4; open 2pm-7pm June–mid-Oct, 3pm-7pm Christmas-Easter, closed end May & June)*, just off ave Michel Croz, illustrates the history of Alpine sports.

Aiguille du Midi A lone spire of rock, the Aiguille du Midi (3842m) is 8km from the summit of Mont Blanc. The **téléphérique** *(€33; operates 6am-4.45pm July & Aug, 8am-3.45pm rest of year)* from Chamonix to the Aiguille du Midi is the highest and probably scariest cable car in the world. Arrive before 9am for better visibility and to avoid the tourist buses.

A ride from Chamonix to the cable car's halfway point, **Plan de l'Aiguille** (2308m) – an excellent place to start hikes in summer – costs €12/14 one way/return.

Between April and September, you can take a second cable car, depending on the winds, from the Aiguille du Midi across the glacier to **Pointe Helbronner** (3466m) and down to the Italian ski resort of Courmayeur (€79.50 round trip).

Le Brévent The highest peak on the valley's west side, Le Brévent (2525m) is known for its views of Mont Blanc. It can be reached from Chamonix by a combination of **téléphérique** and **télécabine** *(gondola; ☎ 04 50 53 13 18; €12/15 single/return; operates 9am-4pm in winter, 8am-5pm rest of year)*. Hiking trails back to the valley can be picked up at Le Brévent or at the cable car's midway station, **Planpraz** (1999m; €8/10 one way/return).

Mer de Glace The second-largest glacier in the Alps, Mer de Glace (Sea of Ice) is 14km long, 1950m across at its widest point, and up to 400m deep. It is a popular tourist destination due to a cog-wheel railway, which has an upper terminus at an altitude of 1913m.

FRANCE

The train, which runs year-round (weather permitting), leaves from **Gare du Montenvers** *(☎ 04 50 53 12 54; €10/13 single/return)* in Chamonix. A combined ticket valid for the train, the gondola to the ice cave and entry to the cave costs €19.60.

Activities

Hiking From mid-June to October, Chamonix has some of the most spectacular hiking trails anywhere in the Alps. The combined map and guide, *Carte des Sentiers du Mont Blanc* (Mountain Trail Map, €12.5) is ideal for day hikers. Lonely Planet publishes *Walking in France*, a useful guide for walks throughout the whole country. The **Grand Balcon Sud** trail, which traverses the Aiguilles Rouges (western) side of the valley at about 2000m, offers great views of Mont Blanc and the glaciers to the east and south. If you'd prefer to avoid 1km of hard uphill walking, take either the Planpraz or La Flégère lift (both €8 one way).

From Plan de l'Aiguille, the midway point on the Aiguille du Midi cable car, the **Grand Balcon Nord** takes you to the Mer de Glace, from where you can hike down to Chamonix.

Skiing & Snowboarding The Chamonix area has 140km of marked ski runs, 42km of cross-country trails and 64 ski lifts of all sorts. Count on paying around €13/60 per day/week for regular skis or boots, and €20/100 for a snowboard. Ask the tourist office for a list of dealers.

Places to Stay

Camping There are some 14 camp sites in the Chamonix region. In general, camping costs €5.50 per person and €4 for a tent site. **L'Île des Barrats** *(open May-Sept)* is near the base of the Aiguille du Midi cable car. The three-star **Les Deux Glaciers** *(route des Tissières; open mid-Dec–mid-Nov)* is in Les Bossons, 3km south of Chamonix. To get there, take the train to Les Bossons or Chamonix bus to the Tremplin-le-Mont stop.

Refuges The **Mountain refuges** *(€10 per night; open June–mid-Sept)* are accessible to hikers. Easy-to-reach *refuges* include **Plan de l'Aiguille** *(☎ 04 50 53 55 60)* at 2308m, the intermediate stop on the Aiguille du Midi cable car, and **La Flégère** *(☎ 04 50 53 06 13)* at 1877m. Book ahead.

Hostels The **Auberge de Jeunesse** *(☎ 04 50 53 14 52, fax 04 50 55 92 34; e chamonix@fuaj.org; 127 Montée Jacques Balmat; dorm beds €13)* is located two train stops before Chamonix at Les Pelérins and operates a free ski shuttle bus. In winter, six-day packages including bed, food, ski pass and ski hire cost €406 to €441.

The Scottish-run **Red Mountain Lodge** *(☎ 04 50 53 94 97; e redmountainlodge@yahoo.com; 435 rue Joseph Vallot; dorm/doubles €16/23 including breakfast; open Apr-Oct only)* organises mountain biking tours. **Gîte Le Vagabond** *(☎ 04 50 53 15 43, fax 04 50 53 68 21; 365 ave Ravanel le Rouge; dorm beds €12.5, with half-board €25.76)* has a guest kitchen, bar/restaurant with Internet access, a climbing wall and parking.

Further out, **Chalet Gîte Ski Station** *(☎ 04 50 53 20 25; 6 Route des Moussoux; dorm beds €10.70; closed 10 May-20 June & 20 Sept-20 Dec)* is next to the Planpraz/Le Brévent *télécabine* station. The semi-rustic **Gîte Le Chamoniard Volant** *(☎ 04 50 53 14 09; 45 route de la Frasse; €13)* is rather cramped on the northeastern outskirts of town. The nearest bus stop is La Frasse.

Hotels The lively **Hôtel El Paso** *(☎ 04 50 53 64 20, fax 04 50 53 64 22; e cantina@cantina.fr; 37 impasse des Rhododendrons; rooms with/without bathroom from €43/36, dorm beds €15, negotiable in low season)* has the whole package, incorporating **La Cantina** Tex-Mex restaurant, Net access and a nightclub.

Places to Eat

Rue des Moulins is the place to go for nightlife. **Munchies** *(☎ 04 50 53 45 41)* at No 87 has excellent €15 dinner *menus* and is surrounded by bars. By the station, **1904** *(259 ave Michel Croz)* has good €12 lunch *menus*; **Goophey** at No 239 is smarter for dinner and drinks.

Le Sanjon *(☎ 04 50 53 56 44; 5 ave Ravanel le Rouge; open daily)* serves €11 *raclette* in a picturesque wooden chalet.

For snacks, **Poco Loco** *(47 rue du Docteur Paccard)* has hot sandwiches/sweet crepes from €4/3; **Le Gouthé** *(95 rue des Moulins)* is an excellent patisserie.

Supermarket **Super U** *(117 rue Joseph Vallot; open 8.15am-7.30pm Mon-Sat, 8.15am-*

noon Sun) is well stocked, as is the **Petit Casino** *(ave Michel Croz)* near the station.

For après-ski, Cham Sud is the downmarket party zone, with the Swedish-run **South Bar** *(place de Chamonix Sud)* running happy hour promotions and **Le Garage** *(200 ave de l'Aiguille du Midi)*, a cheesy nightclub, open *very* late.

Getting There & Away

Bus Chamonix' bus station is next to the train station. **SAT Autocar** *(☎ 04 50 53 01 15)* has buses to Annecy (€14.45, three hours), Geneva (€29, two hours) and Grenoble (€30, 3½ hours).

Train The **Mont Blanc Express** from St Gervais takes 30 minutes to Chamonix (stopping at eight towns in the Chamonix Valley) before heading towards Martigny, Switzerland (36km north of Chamonix); change trains at the Swiss border.

Chamonix-Mont Blanc train station *(☎ 08 92 35 35 39)*, on the east side of town, has connections to Paris' Gare de Lyon (€70, up to 10 hours), Lyon (€29, 3½ hours) and Geneva (€15, two hours via St Gervais). Most journeys require a change at St Gervais, which has connections across France.

Getting Around

Bus transport in the valley is handled by **Chamonix Bus** *(☎ 04 50 53 05 55)*, which has an office located at place de l'Église opposite the tourist office. The town is easily accessible on foot.

Provence

Provence was settled by the Ligurians, the Celts and the Greeks, but it was after its conquest by Julius Caesar in the mid-1st century BC that the region really began to flourish and prosper.

Many well-preserved amphitheatres, aqueducts and other buildings from the Roman period can still be seen in Arles and Nîmes (see the Languedoc-Roussillon section later). During the 14th century, the Catholic Church, then led by a series of French-born popes, moved its headquarters from feud-riven Rome to Avignon, thus beginning the most resplendent period in that city's history.

MARSEILLE

pop 797,491

The cosmopolitan and much maligned port of Marseille, France's second-largest city and third-most populous urban area, isn't the least bit prettified for the benefit of tourists. Its urban geography and atmosphere derive from the diversity of its inhabitants, the majority of whom are immigrants (or their descendants) from the Mediterranean basin, West Africa and Indochina. Although Marseille is notorious for organised crime and racial tensions, the city is a vibrant and interesting place to explore.

Orientation & Information

The city's main street, La Canebière, stretches eastward from the Vieux Port. The train and bus stations are north of La Canebière at the top of blvd d'Athènes. The city centre is around rue Paradis, which becomes more fashionable as you move south.

The **tourist office** *(☎ 04 91 13 89 00, fax 04 91 13 89 20; ⓔ accueil@marseille-tourisme.com; 4 La Canebière; open daily)* is next to the Vieux Port. There are **annexes** *(open Mon-Fri, Mon-Sat July & Aug)* at the train station and place des Pistoles.

Info-Café *(☎ 04 91 33 74 98; 1 quai de Rive Neuve; open 9am-10pm Mon-Sat, 2pm-7pm Sun)* charges €3.60 an hour for Net access, and has over 50 computer terminals, fast connections, a bar and harbour views.

Despite its fearsome reputation, Marseille is probably no more dangerous than other French cities. At night it's advisable to avoid the Belsunce area – the neighbourhood southwest of the train station and streets bordering La Canebière.

Things to See & Do

Marseille grew up around the **Vieux Port**, where Greeks from Asia Minor established a settlement around 600 BC. The quarter north of quai du Port (around the Hôtel de Ville) was blown up by the Germans in 1943 and rebuilt after the war. The lively **place Thiars** pedestrian zone, with its many late-night restaurants and cafés, is south of the quai de Rive Neuve.

For panoramic views and overwrought mid-19th-century architecture, take Bus No 60 1km south of the Vieux Port to the **Basilique Notre Dame de la Garde**, the city's highest point.

Museums Unless otherwise noted, the museums listed are open 10am to 5pm Tuesday to

Sunday, with extended hours in summer; all charge €2 to €3 for admission and admit students for half-price. The **Carte Privilèges** *(€15.25/22.87/30.49 for 1/2/3 days)* includes admission to all museums, boat fare to Le Château d'If and all public transport. It's only a good deal if you're going to the islands.

The **Centre de la Vieille Charité** *(☎ 04 91 14 58 80; 2 rue de la Charité)* is home to Marseille's **Museum of Mediterranean Archaeology** and has superb permanent exhibits on ancient Egypt and Greece. It's in the mostly North African Panier quarter (north of the Vieux Port).

The **Musée Cantini** *(☎ 04 91 54 77 75; 19 rue Grignan)*, off rue Paradis, hosts modern art exhibitions.

Roman history buffs will love the **Musée d'Histoire de Marseille** *(☎ 04 91 90 42 22; ground floor, Centre Bourse shopping mall; open noon-7pm Mon-Sat)*, just north of La Canebière. Its exhibits include the remains of a merchant ship dating to the late 2nd century AD.

Château d'If This chateau *(☎ 04 91 59 02 30; admission €4; open 9am-7pm Tues-Sun Apr-Sept, 9am-7.30pm Tues-Sun Oct-Mar)* is the 16th-century island fortress-turned-prison made infamous by Alexandre Dumas' *The Count of Monte Cristo*. Boats (€8 return, 20 minutes each way) depart from quai des Belges in the Vieux Port and continue to the nearby **Îles du Frioul** (€13 return for both islands).

Cité Radieuse Le Corbusier Finished in 1952, Le Corbusier's apartment building *(☎ 04 91 77 14 07; 280 blvd Michelet, 8e; bus No 21 from La Canebière)* has been much imitated but rarely with the famous architect's careful dimensions. Ask at the 3rd floor hotel (see Places to Stay) about **tours** *(€5; minimum 3 people)*.

Places to Stay

Hostels In the Montolivet neighbourhood, 4.5km east of the city centre, is **Auberge de Jeunesse Château de Bois Luzy** *(☎ 04 91 49 06 18, fax 04 91 49 06 18; Allées des Primevères, 12e; bus No 8 from La Canebière; dorm beds €8)*. HI cards are required.

The **Auberge de Jeunesse de Bonneveine** *(☎ 04 91 17 63 30, fax 04 91 73 97 23; ⓔ ajemb@freesurf.fr; impasse du Docteur Bonfils, 8e; dorm beds €12-16.40; open Feb-Dec)* is 4.5km south of the Vieux Port. Take bus No 44 from the rond-point du Prado metro stop and get off at place Louis Bonnefon.

Hotels Two-star **Hôtel d'Athènes** *(☎ 04 91 90 12 93, fax 04 91 90 72 03; 37-39 blvd d'Athènes, 1er; rooms with shower & toilet/bath €38.15/34.30)* is at the foot of the grand staircase leading from the train station into town. The well-kept rooms are comfortable but can be noisy.

Guests can arrive 24 hours a day at clean, simple **Hôtel Ozea** *(☎/fax 04 91 47 91 84; 12 rue Barbaroux, 1er; doubles with/without shower €27/23; hall shower €3)*. At night just ring the bell to wake up the night clerk. **Hôtel Pied-à-Terre** *(☎ 04 91 92 00 95; 18 rue Barbaroux, 1er; singles/doubles with/without shower €45/40)* has well-kept rooms.

More expensive but worth the money is the homy **Hôtel Lutetia** *(☎ 04 91 50 81 78, fax 04 91 50 23 52; 38 allées Léon Gambetta; singles/doubles €40/45, with bath €44/49)* with smallish rooms equipped with TV and phone.

Hôtel Corbusier *(☎ 04 91 16 78 00, fax 04 91 16 78 28; ⓔ hotelcorbusier@wanadoo.fr; 280 blvd Michelet, 8e; doubles €38)* has simple but stylish rooms in a famous apartment block.

Places to Eat

Fresh fruit and vegies are sold at the **Marché des Capucins** *(place des Capucins; open Mon-Sat)*, one block south of La Canebière.

Restaurants along pedestrianised cours Julien, a few blocks south of La Canebière, offer an incredible variety of cuisines: Antillean, Pakistani, Thai, Lebanese, Tunisian and even French.

Restaurant Antillais *(10 cours Julien; mains from €6.50, menu with house wine €16)* features West Indian cuisine. **Le Chalet Berbere** *(☎ 04 96 12 08 47; 94 cours Julien; mains from €7; open Tues-Sun lunch, Mon-Sat dinner)* is a small but smart Algerian couscous place.

Restaurants line the streets around place Thiars on the south side of the Vieux Port. Many offer bouillabaisse, the rich fish stew for which Marseille is famous.

Entertainment

Listings magazines such as *Vox Mag*, *Ventilo* and *Cesar* are distributed free at the tourist office. *Sortir* comes out with the Friday edition of *La Provence* newspaper; look out for *PAF*, a monthly one-page gig guide.

Le Web Bar *(☎ 04 96 11 65 11; 114 rue République)* hosts all kinds of funky music events, including brunch concerts.

Atmospheric **La Caravelle** *(☎ 04 91 90 36 64; 34 quai du Port)* is a jazzy bar with views of the port. On the other side of the water is **O'Malleys Irish pub** *(9 quai de Rive Neuve)*.

Getting There & Away

Bus The **bus station** *(☎ 04 91 08 16 40; place Victor Hugo)*, 150m to the right as you exit the train station, offers services to Aix-en-Provence, Avignon, Cannes, Nice, Nice airport and Orange, among others.

Eurolines *(☎ 04 91 50 57 55)* has buses to Spain, Italy, Morocco, the UK and other countries. Its counter in the bus station is open from 9am to noon and 2pm to 5.30pm (closed Sunday).

Train Marseille's passenger train station, served by both metro lines, is called **Gare St Charles** *(☎ 0836 35 35 39)*. Services along Voie A (Platform A) include a busy ticket office, sparkling **toilets** *(entry €0.40; open 6am-midnight daily)* and **left luggage** *(from €3 per piece of luggage for 72hr; open 7.15am-10pm)*. There's a **tourist information annexe** out the side door at the top of the platform.

From Marseille there are trains to more or less any place in France. Some sample destinations are Paris' Gare de Lyon (€77.10, 3¼ hours by TGV, 18 daily), Avignon via Arles (€17.10, one hour, 20 daily), Lyon (€32.90, 3½ hours), Nice (€25, 1½ hours), Barcelona (€60.40, 8½ hours) and Geneva (€49.50, 6½ hours).

Ferry The **Société Nationale Maritime Corse-Méditerranée** *(SNCM; ☎ 0836 67 95 00, fax 04 91 56 35 86)* runs ferries from the *gare maritime* (passenger ferry terminal) at the foot of blvd des Dames. There's also an **SNCM office** *(61 blvd des Dames; open Mon-Sat)*. For ferries to Corsica (see also the Corsica Getting There & Away section), Italy and Sardinia call ☎ 0891 70 18 01, and for Algeria and Tunisia call ☎ 0891 70 28 02.

Getting Around

Marseille has a trolleybus line and an extensive bus network, which operate from 5am to 9pm. Night buses and tram No 68 run from 9pm to 1am (12.30am Saturday and Sunday). Two easy-to-use metro lines run until about 9pm (12.30am Friday to Sunday). Tickets (single/*carnet* of six €1.40/6.50) are valid on all services for one hour. Time-stamp your ticket when you board the bus. For more information, visit the **Espace Infos RTM** *(☎ 04 91 91 92 10; 6-8 rue des Fabres)*.

AROUND MARSEILLE

Aix-en-Provence

pop 134,324

One of the most appealing cities in Provence, Aix owes its atmosphere to the students who make up over 20% of the population. The city is renowned for its *calissons* (almond-paste confectionery) and for being the birthplace of postimpressionist painter Cézanne. Aix hosts the Festival International d'Art Lyrique each July.

The **tourist office** *(☎ 04 42 16 11 61, fax 04 42 16 11 62; ⓔ infos@aixenprovence tourism.com; place Général de Gaulle)* has walking-tour brochures. Aix is easy to see on a day trip from Marseille, and frequent trains (€4.10) make the 35-minute trip.

The mostly pedestrianised old city is a maze of tiny streets full of ethnic restaurants and specialist food shops, intermixed with elegant 17th- and 18th-century mansions. Aix also has several interesting museums, the finest of which is the **Musée Granet** *(place St Jean de Malte; admission varies; open Wed-Mon)*. The collection includes paintings from the 16th to 19th centuries, including some lesser-known Cézanne works. Slow-moving renovations mean that the museum may be only partially open.

Places to Stay About 2km southeast of town is **Camping Arc-en-Ciel** *(☎ 04 42 26 14 28; route de Nice; camp sites €17.10; open Apr-Sept)* at Pont des Trois Sautets. Take bus No 3 to Les Trois Sautets stop. **Auberge de Jeunesse du Jas de Bouffan** *(☎ 04 42 20 15 99, fax 04 42 59 36 12; 3 ave Marcel Pagnol; beds €14 including breakfast & sheets)* is almost 2km west of the centre. Rooms are locked between 9am and 5pm. Take bus line No 4 from La Rotonde to the Vasarely stop. **Hôtel Cardinal** *(☎ 04 42 38 32 30, fax 04 42 26 39 05; 24 rue Cardinale; singles/doubles €46/58, self-catering suites €73)* has large rooms with shower, toilet and a mix of modern and period furniture. Small self-catering suites are in its annexe at 12 rue Cardinale.

Places to Eat Pop your head in **Les Deux Garçons** *(53 cours Mirabeau)*, the café where everyone from Cézanne to Sartre drank and chatted. **Restaurant Gu et Fils** *(3 rue Frédéric Mistral)* serves delicious regional meals.

AVIGNON

pop 85,937

Avignon acquired its ramparts and its reputation as a city of art and culture during the 14th century, when Pope Clement V and his court, fleeing political turmoil in Rome, established themselves here. From 1309 to 1377 huge sums of money were invested in building and decorating the popes' palace. Even after the pontifical court returned to Rome amid bitter charges that Avignon had become a den of criminals and brothel-goers, the city remained an important cultural centre.

Today, Avignon maintains its tradition as a patron city of the arts, most notably through its annual performing-arts festival. The world-famous Festival d'Avignon in July attracts hundreds of artists who put on some 300 performances of all sorts each day.

Orientation

The main avenue in the walled city runs northward from the train station to place de l'Horloge; it's named cours Jean Jaurès south of the tourist office and rue de la République north of it. Rue des Teinturiers, in the south-eastern segment of the walled city, is dotted with cool cafés, galleries and shops. The island that runs down the middle of the Rhône between Avignon and Villeneuve-lès-Avignon is known as Île de la Barthelasse.

Information

The **tourist office** *(☎ 04 32 74 32 74, fax 04 90 82 95 03; ⓔ information@ot-avignon.fr; 41 cours Jean Jaurès; open daily)* is 300m north of the train station. There's an annexe at pont St Bénézet (open April to October).

The **main post office** *(cours Président Kennedy)* can be accessed via Porte de la République from the train station.

Cyberdrome *(☎ 04 90 16 05 15; ⓔ cyberdrome@wanadoo.fr; 68 rue Guillaume Puy; open 7am-1am)* is a decent Internet café charging €4.60 an hour for Net access.

Things to See & Do

Palais des Papes & Around Avignon's leading tourist attraction is the fortified Palace of the Popes *(adult/concession €11/7.50 including admission to pont St Bénézet; open 9am-7pm daily Apr-June, 9am-8pm July-Sept, 9.30am-5.45pm Oct-Mar)*, built during the 14th century. The seemingly endless halls, chapels, corridors and staircases were once sumptuously decorated, but these days they are nearly empty except for a few damaged frescoes.

At the far northern end of place du Palais, the **Musée du Petit Palais** *(adult/concession €4.50/2.50; open 9.30am-1pm & 2pm-5.30pm Wed-Mon Oct-May, 10am-1pm & 2pm-6pm Wed-Mon June-Sept)* houses an excellent collection of 13th- to 16th-century Italian religious paintings.

Pont St Bénézet Originally built in the 12th century to link Avignon and Villeneuve-lès-Avignon, this is the **'pont d'Avignon'** *(same hours as Palais des Papes)* mentioned in the French nursery rhyme. Once 900m long, the bridge was repaired and rebuilt several times until all but four of its 22 spans were washed away in the 17th century.

Museums Housed in an 18th-century mansion, the **Musée Calvet** *(☎ 04 90 86 33 84; 65 rue Joseph Vernet; adult/concession €5/3; open Wed-Mon)* has a collection of ancient Egyptian, Greek and Roman artefacts, as well as paintings from the 16th to 20th centuries. Its annexe, the **Musée Lapidaire** *(27 rue de la République; adult/concession €5/3; open Wed-Mon)* houses sculpture and statuary from the Gallo-Roman, Romanesque and Gothic periods.

The **Collection Lambert** *(☎ 04 90 16 56 20; 5 rue Violette; adult/concession €5/4; open Tues-Sun)* is a new contemporary art museum displaying the astonishing collection of art dealer Yvon Lambert.

The **Musée Angladon** *(☎ 04 90 82 29 03; 5 rue Laboureur; adult/concession €5/3; open 1pm-6pm Wed-Sun, also Tues mid-June–mid-Oct)* was once a private home but it now exhibits 19th- and 20th-century paintings to the public. It is the only place in the region where you are able to see a Van Gogh painting.

Villeneuve-lès-Avignon Avignon's picturesque sister city can be reached by foot or bus No 10 from the main post office. A pass for the following attractions costs €6.86.

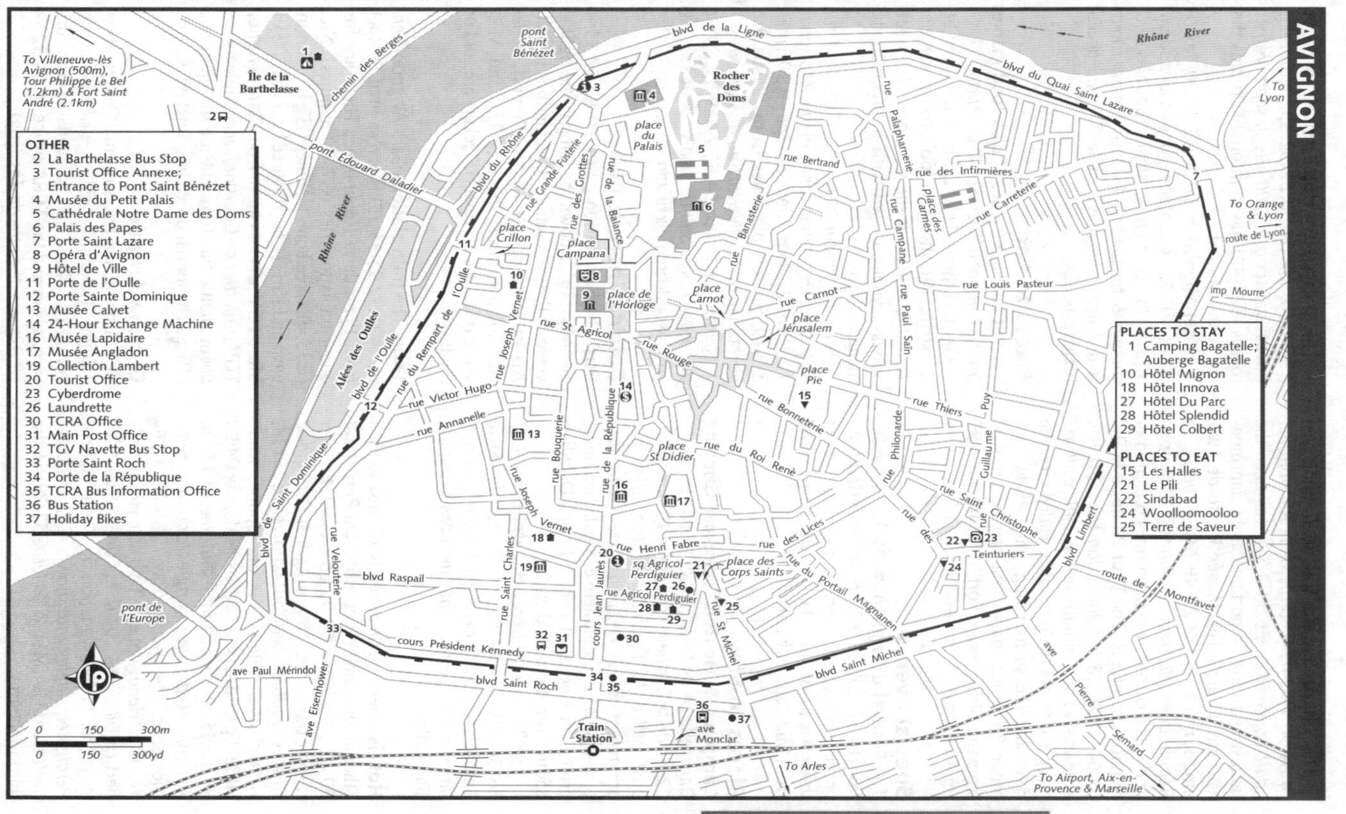
AVIGNON
OTHER
2 La Barthelasse Bus Stop
3 Tourist Office Annexe; Entrance to Pont Saint Bénézet
4 Musée du Petit Palais
5 Cathédrale Notre Dame des Doms
6 Palais des Papes
7 Porte Saint Lazare
8 Opéra d'Avignon
9 Hôtel de Ville
11 Porte de l'Oulle
12 Porte Sainte Dominique
13 Musée Calvet
14 24-Hour Exchange Machine
16 Musée Lapidaire
17 Musée Angladon
19 Collection Lambert
20 Tourist Office
23 Cyberdrome
26 Laundrette
30 TCRA Office
31 Main Post Office
32 TGV Navette Bus Stop
33 Porte Saint Roch
34 Porte de la République
35 TCRA Bus Information Office
36 Bus Station
37 Holiday Bikes
PLACES TO STAY
1 Camping Bagatelle; Auberge Bagatelle
10 Hôtel Mignon
18 Hôtel Innova
27 Hôtel Du Parc
28 Hôtel Splendid
29 Hôtel Colbert
PLACES TO EAT
15 Les Halles
21 Le Pili
22 Sindabad
24 Woolloomooloo
25 Terre de Saveur
To Villeneuve-lès Avignon (500m), Tour Philippe Le Bel (1.2km) & Fort Saint André (2.1km)
Île de la Barthelasse
chemin des Berges
pont Saint Bénézet
Rhône River
Rocher des Doms
blvd de la Ligne
blvd du Quai Saint Lazare
To Lyon
To Orange & Lyon
route de Lyon
imp Mourre
pont Édouard Daladier
Allées des Oulles
blvd de l'Oulle
blvd du Rhône
rue du Rempart de l'Oulle
blvd de Saint Dominique
pont de l'Europe
ave Paul Mérindol
ave Eisenhower
rue Velouterie
blvd Raspail
cours Président Kennedy
blvd Saint Roch
blvd Saint Michel
blvd Limbert
route de Montfavet
ave Pierre Sémard
To Airport, Aix-en-Provence & Marseille
To Arles
Train Station
ave Monclar
place du Palais
place Crillon
place Campana
place de l'Horloge
place Carnot
place Jérusalem
place Pie
place St Didier
place des Carmes
place des Corps Saints
sq Agricol Perdiguier
rue Agricol Perdiguier
rue Grande Fusterie
rue des Grottes
rue de la Balance
rue Banasterie
rue Bertrand
rue Palapharnerie
rue des Infirmières
rue Carreterie
rue Campane
rue Paul Saïn
rue Louis Pasteur
rue Carnot
rue St Agricol
rue Rouge
rue Bonneterie
rue Thiers
rue Philonarde
rue Guillaume Puy
rue Saint Christophe
rue des Teinturiers
rue du Roi René
rue des Lices
rue du Portail Magnanen
rue Henri Fabre
rue St Michel
cours Jean Jaurès
rue de la République
rue Bouquerie
rue Joseph Vernet
rue Victor Hugo
rue Annanelle
rue Saint Charles
0 150 300m
0 150 300yd

FRANCE

The **Chartreuse du Val de Bénédiction** *(☎ 04 90 15 24 24; 60 rue de la République; adult/concession €5.50/3.50)* was once the largest and most important Carthusian monastery in France. The **Musée Pierre de Luxembourg** *(☎ 04 90 27 49 66; 3 rue de la République; adult/concession €3/1.90; open Tues-Sun; closed Feb)* has a fine collection of religious paintings. The **Tour Philippe le Bel** *(☎ 04 32 70 08 57; admission €1.60/0.90)*, a defensive tower built in the 14th century, has great views of Avignon's walled city, the river and the surrounding countryside. Another Provençal panorama can be enjoyed from the 14th-century **Fort St André** *(☎ 04 90 25 45 35; adult/concession €4/2.50)*.

Special Events

The **Festival d'Avignon** *(☎ 04 90 14 14 60, fax 04 90 27 66 83; W www.festival-avignon.com)* is held every year during the last three weeks of July. Tickets can be reserved from mid-June onwards.

Places to Stay

Camping & Hostels Three-star **Camping Bagatelle** *(☎ 04 90 86 30 39, fax 04 90 27 16 23; Île de la Barthelasse; bus No 10 from main post office to Barthelasse stop; sites per adult/tent €4/3; reception open 8am-9pm year-round)* is an attractive, shaded camping ground just north of pont Édouard Daladier, 850m from the walled city.

The 210-bed **Auberge Bagatelle** *(☎ 04 90 86 30 39, fax 04 90 27 16 23; Île de la Barthelasse; dorm beds €10.50)* is part of a large, park-like area that includes Camping Bagatelle.

Hotels There are three hotels all close to each other on the same street. **Hôtel Du Parc** *(☎ 04 90 82 71 55, fax 04 90 85 64 86; e hotelsurparc@aol.com; 18 rue Agricol Perdiguier; singles/doubles without shower €29/34, with shower €36/42)* is one option, while **Hôtel Splendid** *(☎ 04 90 86 14 46, fax 04 90 85 38 55; e contacthotel@infonie.fr; 17 rue Agricol Perdiguier; singles/doubles with shower €34/43, with shower & toilet €36/46)* is a friendly place. Two-star **Hôtel Colbert** *(☎ 04 90 86 20 20, fax 04 90 85 97 00; e colberthotel@wanadoo.fr; 7 rue Agricol Perdiguier; singles with shower €42, doubles/triples with shower & toilet €52/79)* is the third in the trio.

The always busy **Hôtel Innova** *(☎ 04 90 82 54 10, fax 04 90 82 52 39; e hotel.innova@wanadoo.fr; 100 rue Joseph Vernet; rooms €23-41)* has comfortable rooms that are soundproofed.

Hôtel Mignon *(☎ 04 90 82 17 30, fax 04 90 85 78 46; e hotel.mignon@wanadoo.fr; 12 rue Joseph Vernet; singles/doubles with shower & toilet €37/43)* has spotless rooms with English-language cable TV and decent breakfasts (€4).

Places to Eat

For self-catering try **Les Halles food market** *(place Pie; open Tues-Sun 7am-1pm)*.

On the other side of town, in a groovy little strip, **Woolloomooloo** *(16bis rue des Teinturiers; lunch menu €11; open Tues-Sat)* draws a young crowd with its international menu.

Terre de Saveur *(☎ 04 90 86 68 72; 1 rue St Michel; vegetarian lunch menu €13; open 11.30am-2.30pm Tues-Sat, 7pm-9.30pm Fri & Sat)*, just off place des Corps Saints, has vegetarian dishes like *tortilla da quinoa*.

Nearby, **Le Pili** *(☎ 04 90 27 39 53; 34-36 place des Corps Saints; meals about €8)* has good wood-fired pizza and steaks.

Getting There & Away

Bus The **bus station** *(☎ 04 90 82 07 35; 5 ave Monclar)* is down the ramp to the right as you exit the train station. Destinations include Aix-en-Provence (€12, 1¼ hours), Arles (€7.80, one hour), Nice (€27), and Marseille (€15.20, 2½ hours). Tickets are sold on the buses.

Train The **train station** *(Gare Avignon Centre; ☎ 0893 35 35 35)* is across blvd St Roch from Porte de la République. There are frequent trains to Arles (€7, 20 minutes), Nice (€35.40, three hours), Nîmes (€7.10, 35 minutes) and Paris (€63.70, three hours via TGV). Most TGV services leave from **Gare Avignon TGV** *(Quartier de Courtine)*, accessible by frequent shuttle bus from outside the main post office. The tourist office has timetables.

Getting Around

TCRA municipal buses operate 7am to about 7.40pm. Tickets cost €1 or €7.80 for a *carnet* of 10 tickets; they're available from drivers, tabacs and the **TCRA office** *(☎ 04 32 74 18 32; ave de Latre de Tassigny)*.

Holiday Bikes (*☎ 04 90 27 92 61, fax 04 90 95 66 41; e motovelo@provencebike.com; 52 blvd St Roch; open 9am-6.30pm daily*) rents road bikes (€14/day) and scooters (from €30).

Côte d'Azur

The Côte d'Azur, which includes the French Riviera, stretches along France's Mediterranean coast from Toulon to the Italian border. Many of the towns here – budget-busting St Tropez, Cannes, Antibes, Nice and Monaco – have become world-famous thanks to the recreational activities of the tanned and idle rich. The reality is rather less glamorous, but the Côte d'Azur still has a great deal to attract visitors: sunshine, 40km of beaches, all sorts of cultural activities and, sometimes, even a bit of glitter.

Unless you're camping or hostelling, your best bet is to stay in Nice, which has a generous supply of cheap hotels, and make day trips to other places. Note that theft from backpacks, pockets, cars and even laundrettes is a serious problem along the Côte d'Azur, especially at train and bus stations.

NICE

pop 343,123

Known as the capital of the Riviera, the fashionable yet relaxed city of Nice makes a great base from which to explore the entire Côte d'Azur. The city, which did not become part of France until 1860, has plenty of relatively cheap accommodation and is only a short train or bus ride from the rest of the Riviera. Nice's beach may be nothing to write home about, but the city has some fine museums.

Orientation

Ave Jean Médecin runs from near the train station to place Masséna. Vieux Nice is the area delineated by the quai des États-Unis, blvd Jean Jaurès and the 92m hill known as Le Château. The neighbourhood of Cimiez, home to several very good museums, is north of the town centre.

Information

The **main tourist office** (*☎ 04 93 87 07 07, fax 04 93 16 85 16; e info@nicetourism.com; open daily*) is at the train station. There's an **annexe** (*☎ 04 92 14 48 00; 5 promenade des Anglais; open Mon-Sat*) near the beach. The **main post office** (*23 ave Thiers*) is one block from the train station.

Opposite the train station, **Le Change** (*☎ 04 93 88 56 80; 17 ave Thiers; open 7.30am-9pm*), to the right as you exit the terminal, offers decent rates. **American Express** (*☎ 04 93 16 53 53; 11 promenade des Anglais; open Mon-Sat*) also has currency exchange.

Access the Net for €5 an hour at **Société Sencom** (*☎ 04 97 03 23 10; cnr Paganini & rue Belgique; open 10am-8pm daily*).

Things to See

An excellent-value **museum pass** (*€8/25 for one/seven days*), available at tourist offices and participating museums, gives free admission to some 60 Côte d'Azur museums. A cheaper one is available for Nice's museums. Unless otherwise noted, the following places are open Wednesday to Monday from around 10am to 5pm or 6pm (sometimes with a break for lunch in the off season), and entry is around adult/concession €4/2.

Musée d'Art Moderne et d'Art Contemporain (*Museum of Modern and Contemporary Art; ave St Jean Baptiste; bus Nos 3, 5, 7, 16 & 17*) displays conceptual works by artists such as Arman and Nice-born Yves Klein.

Vivid paintings of Old Testament scenes dominate the **Musée Marc Chagall** (*☎ 04 93 53 87 20; ave Docteur Ménard opp No 4; adult/concession €5.50/4*). Ask at the ticket counter for your free bus ticket to Cimiez.

A 17th-century Genoese villa houses the **Musée Matisse** (*☎ 04 93 81 08 08; 164 ave des Arènes de Cimiez*) in Cimiez. Bus No 15 is convenient; get off at the Arènes stop.

The **Musée Archéologique** (*Archaeology Museum; ☎ 04 93 81 59 57; 160 ave des Arènes de Cimiez*) and nearby **Gallo-Roman ruins** (which include public baths and an amphitheatre) are next to the Musée Matisse.

Nice's **Russian Orthodox Cathedral of St Nicholas** (*admission €2; open Mon-Sat, & Sun afternoon; closed noon-2.30pm*), crowned by six onion-shaped domes, was built between 1903 and 1912. Shorts, short skirts and sleeveless shirts are forbidden.

Special Events

Nice parties in Nice include the Festin des Cougourdons (gourd feast) in March, a jiving Jazz Festival in July and the Vineyard Festival in September.

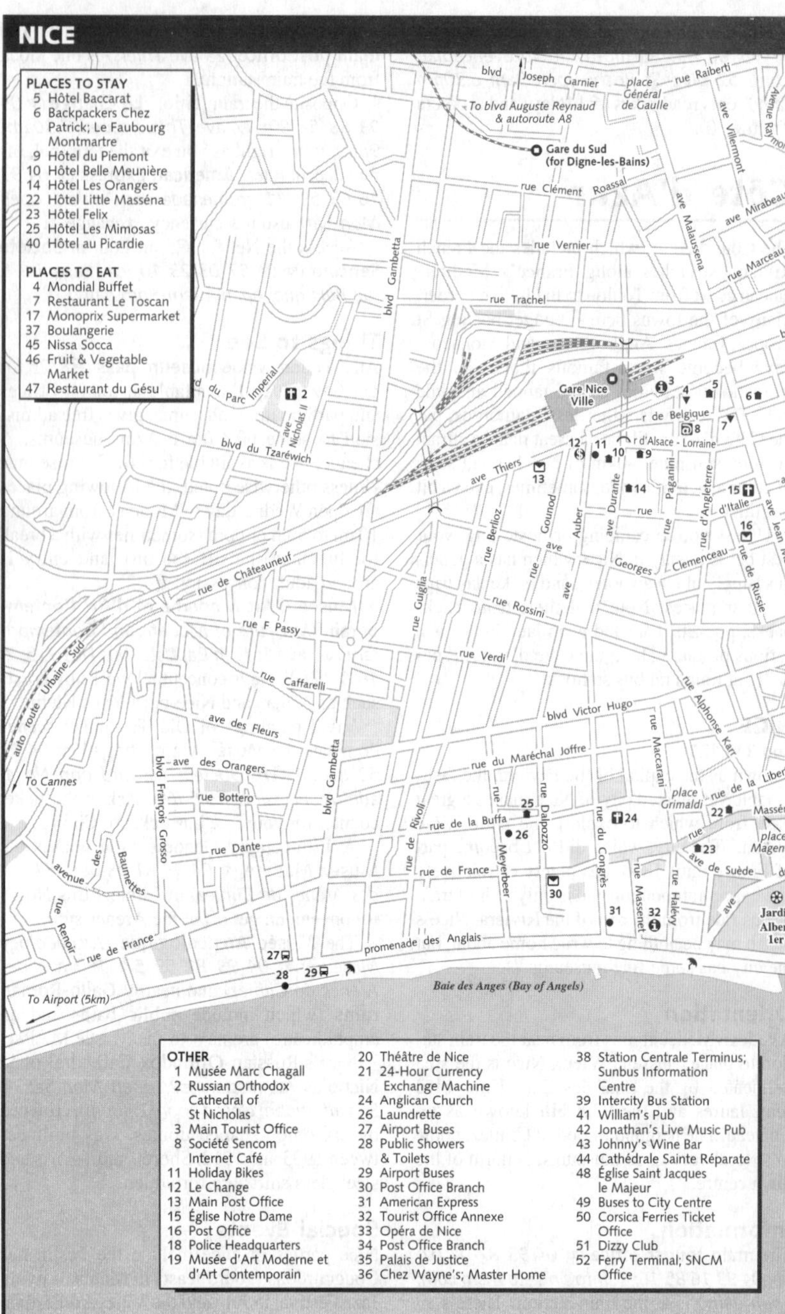
NICE
PLACES TO STAY
5 Hôtel Baccarat
6 Backpackers Chez Patrick; Le Faubourg Montmartre
9 Hôtel du Piemont
10 Hôtel Belle Meunière
14 Hôtel Les Orangers
22 Hôtel Little Masséna
23 Hôtel Felix
25 Hôtel Les Mimosas
40 Hôtel au Picardie
PLACES TO EAT
4 Mondial Buffet
7 Restaurant Le Toscan
17 Monoprix Supermarket
37 Boulangerie
45 Nissa Socca
46 Fruit & Vegetable Market
47 Restaurant du Gésu
OTHER
1 Musée Marc Chagall
2 Russian Orthodox Cathedral of St Nicholas
3 Main Tourist Office
8 Société Sencom Internet Café
11 Holiday Bikes
12 Le Change
13 Main Post Office
15 Église Notre Dame
16 Post Office
18 Police Headquarters
19 Musée d'Art Moderne et d'Art Contemporain
20 Théâtre de Nice
21 24-Hour Currency Exchange Machine
24 Anglican Church
26 Laundrette
27 Airport Buses
28 Public Showers & Toilets
29 Airport Buses
30 Post Office Branch
31 American Express
32 Tourist Office Annexe
33 Opéra de Nice
34 Post Office Branch
35 Palais de Justice
36 Chez Wayne's; Master Home
38 Station Centrale Terminus; Sunbus Information Centre
39 Intercity Bus Station
41 William's Pub
42 Jonathan's Live Music Pub
43 Johnny's Wine Bar
44 Cathédrale Sainte Réparate
48 Église Saint Jacques le Majeur
49 Buses to City Centre
50 Corsica Ferries Ticket Office
51 Dizzy Club
52 Ferry Terminal; SNCM Office
blvd Joseph Garnier
place Général de Gaulle
rue Raiberti
Avenue Raymond
To blvd Auguste Reynaud & autoroute A8
Gare du Sud (for Digne-les-Bains)
ave Villermont
rue Clément Roassal
ave Malaussena
ave Mirabeau
rue Vernier
rue Marceau
blvd Gambetta
rue Trachel
blvd
Gare Nice Ville
r de Belgique
r d'Alsace - Lorraine
blvd du Parc Imperial
ave Nicholas II
blvd du Tzaréwich
ave Thiers
rue Berlioz
rue Gounod
ave Auber
ave Durante
rue Paganini
rue d'Angleterre
ave d'Italie
ave Jean Médecin
rue de Russie
ave Georges Clemenceau
rue de Châteauneuf
rue Guiglia
rue Rossini
rue F Passy
rue Verdi
rue Caffarelli
rue Alphonse Karr
auto route Urbaine Sud
blvd Victor Hugo
ave des Fleurs
rue du Maréchal Joffre
rue Maccarani
ave des Orangers
To Cannes
blvd François Grosso
rue Bottero
place Grimaldi
rue de la Liberté
Masséna
place Magenta
rue de la Buffa
rue Dalpozzo
rue du Congrès
rue de Rivoli
rue Meyerbeer
rue Dante
avenue des Baumettes
rue de France
rue Massenet
rue Halévy
ave de Suède
Jardin Albert 1er
rue Renoir
promenade des Anglais
Baie des Anges (Bay of Angels)
To Airport (5km)

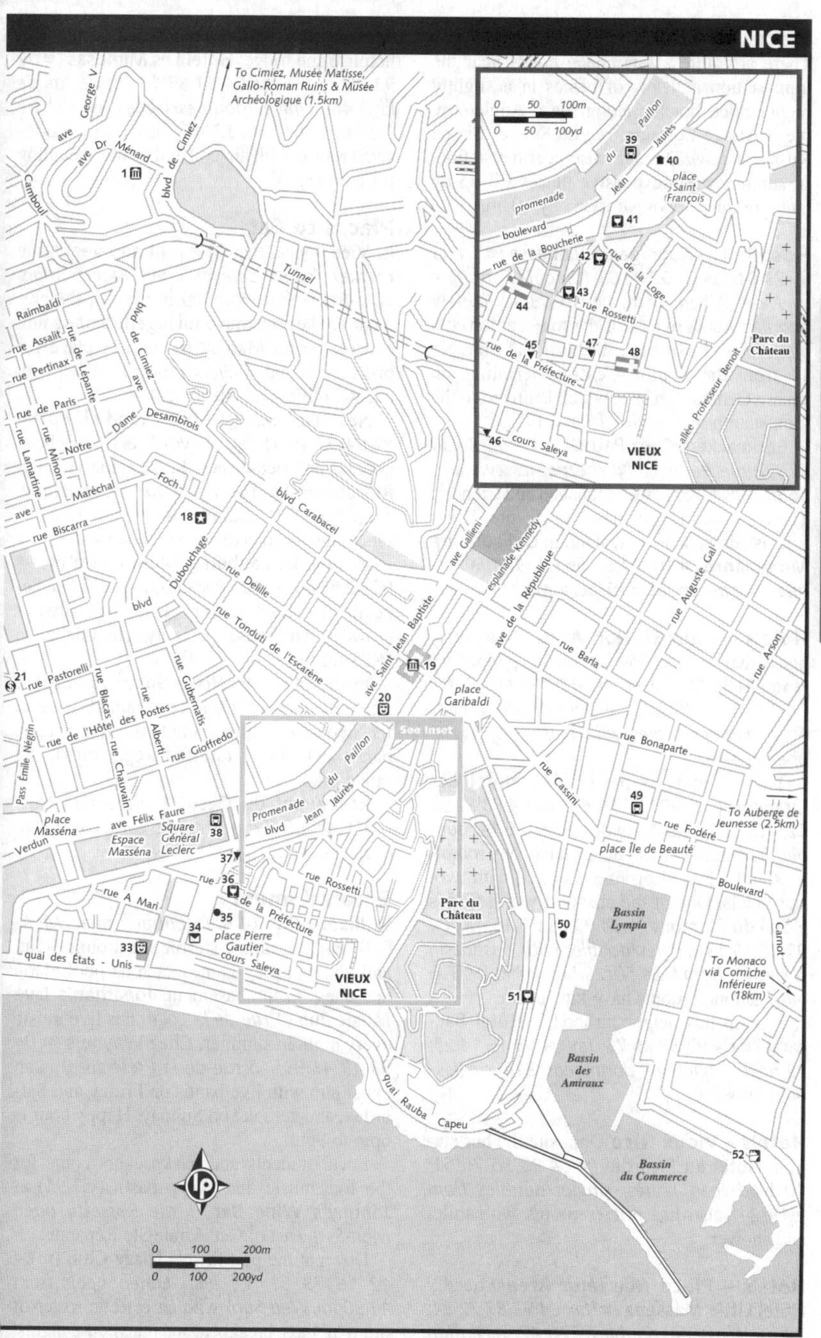
NICE
To Cimiez, Musée Matisse, Gallo-Roman Ruins & Musée Archéologique (1.5km)
ave George V
ave Dr Ménard
blvd de Cimiez
Camboul
Tunnel
Raimbaldi
rue Assalit
rue de Lépante
rue Pertinax
blvd de Cimiez
ave Notre Dame
rue de Paris
rue Lamartine
rue Minon
Desambrois
ave Maréchal Foch
rue Biscarra
blvd Dubouchage
blvd Carabacel
rue Delille
rue Tonduti de l'Escarène
rue Pastorelli
rue Blacas
rue Alberti
rue Gubernatis
rue de l'Hôtel des Postes
rue Gioffredo
rue Chauvain
Pass Émile Négrin
place Masséna
Verdun
ave Félix Faure
Espace Masséna
Square Général Leclerc
Promenade du Paillon
blvd Jean Jaurès
See Inset
rue A Mari
rue de la Préfecture
rue Rossetti
place Pierre Gautier
cours Saleya
quai des États - Unis
VIEUX NICE
Parc du Château
quai Rauba Capeu
ave Gallieni
esplanade Kennedy
ave de la République
ave Saint Jean Baptiste
place Garibaldi
rue Barla
rue Auguste Gal
rue Arson
rue Bonaparte
rue Cassini
rue Fodéré
place Île de Beauté
Boulevard Carnot
To Auberge de Jeunesse (2.5km)
To Monaco via Corniche Inférieure (18km)
Bassin Lympia
Bassin des Amiraux
Bassin du Commerce
0 100 200m
0 100 200yd
0 50 100m
0 50 100yd
promenade du Paillon
boulevard Jean Jaurès
place Saint François
rue de la Boucherie
rue de la Loge
rue Rossetti
rue de la Préfecture
cours Saleya
allée Professeur Benoit
1
18
19
20
21
33
34
35
36
37
38
39
40
41
42
43
44
45
46
47
48
49
50
51
52
FRANCE

FRANCE

Places to Stay

There are quite a few cheap hotels near the train station and lots of places in a slightly higher price bracket along rue d'Angleterre, rue d'Alsace-Lorraine, rue de Suisse, rue de Russie and ave Durante, also near the station. In summer the inexpensive places fill up by late morning – book your bed by 10am.

Hostels The **Auberge de Jeunesse** *(☎ 04 93 89 23 64, fax 04 92 04 03 10; route Forestière de Mont Alban; dorm beds €13.40; curfew midnight)* is 4km east of the train station. It's often full so be sure to call ahead. Take bus No 14 from the Station Centrale terminus on square Général Leclerc, which is linked to the train station by bus Nos 15 and 17.

Backpackers Chez Patrick *(☎ 04 93 80 30 72; 32 rue Pertinax; ⓔ chezpatrick@viola.fr; dorm beds €18)* is well managed and friendly. There's no curfew or daytime closure. If it's full, ask downstairs at restaurant **Le Faubourg Montmartre** *(☎ 04 93 62 55 03; 32 rue Pertinax; rooms about €15/person)*.

Hotels – Train Station Area For a cruisy place that attracts lots of young people try **Hôtel Belle Meunière** *(☎ 04 93 88 66 15, fax 04 93 82 51 76; 21 ave Durante; dorm beds €13, doubles/triples with bath €79/94.50; open Feb-Nov)*.

The welcome is patchy, but **Hôtel Les Orangers** *(☎ 04 93 87 51 41, fax 04 93 82 57 82; 10bis ave Durante; dorm beds €14, doubles from €34)* has some great balcony rooms.

Rue d'Alsace-Lorraine is dotted with two-star hotels. One of the cheapest you'll find is **Hôtel du Piemont** *(☎ 04 93 88 25 15, fax 04 93 16 15 18; singles/doubles with washbasin & shower from €24.50/28.50)*, at No 19. The old-fashioned rooms have kitchenettes.

Also in this neighbourhood is **Hôtel Baccarat** *(☎ 04 93 88 35 73, fax 04 93 16 14 25; 39 rue d'Angleterre; dorm beds €14, singles/doubles €29/36)*.

Hotels – Vieux Nice Opposite the bus station, **Hôtel au Picardie** *(☎ 04 93 85 75 51; 10 blvd Jean Jaurès; singles/doubles from €19/24)* also has pricier rooms with toilet and shower.

Hotels – Place Masséna Area Friendly **Hôtel Little Masséna** *(☎/fax 04 93 87 72 34; 22 rue Masséna; doubles €26-42; reception open to 8pm)* offers rooms that come with hotplate and fridge. **Hôtel Les Mimosas** *(☎ 04 93 88 05 59, fax 04 93 87 15 65; 26 rue de la Buffa; singles/doubles/triples with share facilities €30.50/37/48)* has clean, good-sized rooms with air-con and a cute sheepdog for company.

Places to Eat

In Vieux Nice, there's a **fruit and vegetable market** *(cours Saleya; open 6am-5.30pm Tues-Sat & Sun morning)* in front of the prefecture. The no-name **boulangerie** at the south end of rue du Marché is the best place for pizza slices and *michettes* (bread stuffed with cheese, olives and anchovies).

Near the train station, **Mondial Buffet** *(☎ 04 93 16 15 51; 7 ave Thiers)* has cheap noodles and rice dishes. In the same vicinity, **Restaurant Le Toscan** *(1 rue de Belgique; open Tues-Sat)*, a family-run Italian place, offers large portions of home-made ravioli.

Nearby, **Le Faubourg Montmartre** *(☎ 04 93 62 55 03; 32 rue Pertinax; menu €11)*, beneath the Backpackers Hotel, is always crowded. The house speciality is bouillabaisse (€28 for two).

In the old city, **Nissa Socca** *(5 rue Ste Reparate; menu €13)* is a perennial favourite. Its Niçois specialities include *socca* (chickpea pancakes), *farcis* (stuffed vegetables) and ratatouille.

Restaurant du Gésu *(1 place du Jésus; pasta about €7; no credit cards)* is local, cheap and loud.

Entertainment

William's Pub *(4 rue Centrale; open Mon-Sat)* has live music starting at around 9pm, and you can play games such as pool, darts and chess in the basement. **Jonathan's Live Music Pub** *(1 rue de la Loge)* has live music every night in summer. **Chez Wayne's** *(☎ 04 93 13 46 99; 15 rue de la Préfecture)* is an expat pub with live bands on Friday and Saturday, and karaoke on Sunday. Happy hour is 6pm to 9pm.

Local students and backpackers come for the live music and cheap pasta (€7.95) at **Johnny's Wine Bar** *(1 rue Rossetti; open Mon-Sat)*, east of Cathédrale Ste Réparate.

Down at the port there's **Dizzy Club** *(☎ 04 12 16 78 81; 26 quai Lunel; open from 11.30pm Wed-Sun)* with an eclectic roster of drum 'n' bass, breakbeat and pure house nights.

Getting There & Away

Bus The **intercity bus station**, opposite 10 blvd Jean Jaurès, is served by some two dozen bus companies. There are slow but frequent services daily until about 7.30pm to Cannes (€5.70, 1½ hours), Antibes (€4.50, 1¼ hours), Monaco (€3.70 return, 45 minutes), and Menton (€4.90 return, 1¼ hours).

Train Nice's main train station, **Gare Nice Ville**, is 1.2km north of the beach on ave Thiers. There are fast, frequent services (up to 40 daily trains) that travel to points all along the coast, including Monaco (€2.90, 20 minutes), Cannes (€5, 40 minutes) and Marseille (€25.10, 2¾ hours).

About six daily TGVs link Nice with Paris' Gare de Lyon (€80 to €90, six hours; discounts available). SNCF trains go to Spain as well.

Trains for Digne-les-Bains (€17, 3¼ hours) make the scenic trip five times daily from Nice's **Gare du Sud** *(☎ 04 93 82 10 17; 4bis rue Alfred Binet)*.

Getting Around

Local buses, run by Sunbus, cost €1.30/4 for a single ticket/daily pass (available on the bus). The **Sunbus information office** *(☎ 04 93 16 52 10; ave Félix Faure)* is at the Station Centrale. From the train station to Vieux Nice and the bus station, take bus No 2, 5 or 17. Bus No 12 links the train station with the beach. Bus Nos 9 and 10 go to the port (for details of ferries to Corsica, see the Corsica Getting There & Away section).

Holiday Bikes *(☎ 04 93 16 01 62; 34 ave Auber)* rents bicycles (€12/day) and motor scooters (from €30/day).

CANNES

pop 67,406

The harbour, the bay, Le Suquet hill, the beachside promenade and the sun-worshippers on the beach provide more than enough natural beauty to make Cannes worth at least a day trip. It is also interesting to watch the rich drop their money with such fashionable nonchalance.

Cannes is renowned for its many festivals and cultural activities, the most famous being the International Film Festival, which runs for two weeks in mid-May. People come to this town all year long, but the main tourist season runs from May to October.

Orientation

From the train station, follow rue Jean Jaurès west and turn left onto rue Vénizélos, which runs west into the heart of the Vieux Port. Place Bernard Cornut Gentille (formerly place de l'Hôtel de Ville), where the bus station is located, is on the northwestern edge of the Vieux Port. Cannes' most famous promenade, the magnificent blvd de la Croisette, begins at the Palais des Festivals and continues eastward around the Baie de Cannes to Pointe de la Croisette.

Information

The **main tourist office** *(☎ 04 93 39 24 53, fax 04 92 99 84 23; e semoftou@palais-festivals-cannes.fr; open daily)* is on the ground floor of the **Palais des Festivals**. There's an **annexe** *(☎ 04 93 99 19 77; open Mon-Fri)* at the train station; turn left as you exit the station and walk up the stairs next to Buffet de la Gare.

The main **post office** *(22 rue Bivouac Napoléon)* is not far from the Palais des Festivals. There are Internet terminals for €4/7 for 30 minutes/one hour at **Mondego Café** *(☎ 04 93 68 19 21; 15 square Merimée)*, opposite Palais des Festivals.

Things to See & Do

Vieux Port Some of the largest yachts you'll ever see are likely to be sitting in the Vieux Port, a fishing port now given over to pleasure craft. The streets around the old port are particularly pleasant on a summer's evening, when the many cafés and restaurants light up the area.

The hill just west of the Vieux Port, **Le Suquet**, affords magnificent views of Cannes. The **Musée de la Castre** *(☎ 04 93 38 55 26; Le Suquet; adult/student €3/free; open 10am-1pm & 2pm-5pm Tues-Sun Dec-Oct)*, housed in a chateau atop Le Suquet, has Mediterranean and Middle Eastern antiquities, as well as objects of ethnographic interest from all over the world.

Beaches Each of the fancy hotels that line blvd de la Croisette has its own private section of the beach. You can pay to roast alongside the hotel guests; a sunlounge at the Hotel Carlton beach starts at €21. There's a small strip of public sand near the Palais des Festivals. Other free public beaches – the **Plages du Midi** and **Plages de la Bocca** – stretch several kilometres westward from the old port.

Îles de Lérins The eucalyptus and pine-covered **Île Ste Marguerite**, where the man in the iron mask (made famous in the novel by Alexandre Dumas) was held captive during the late 17th century, is just over 1km from the mainland. The island is crisscrossed by many trails and paths. The smaller **Île St Honorat** is home to Cistercian monks who welcome visitors to their monastery, the ruins of a cloister and the small chapels dotted around the island. Bring a picnic to eat on the rocky shores of this tiny island.

Compagnie Maritime Cannoise *(CMC; ☎ 04 93 38 66 33)* is among several companies running ferries to Île Ste Marguerite (€8 return, 15 minutes). The ticket offices are at the Vieux Port near the Palais des Festivals. Ferries to St Honorat are less common, but you'll find one at the same port. Many companies offer day trips to Monaco and St Tropez (about €27).

Places to Stay

Tariffs can be up to 50% higher in July and August than in winter. During summer you'll be lucky to find a room at any price. Hotels are ususally booked up to a year in advance for the film festival.

Hostels The pleasant **Le Chalit** *(☎/fax 04 93 99 22 11; ⓔ le_chalit@libertysurf.fr; 27 ave du Maréchal Galliéni; dorm beds €20; open year-round, no curfew, reception closed 10.30am-5pm)* is a five-minute walk northwest of the station.

Hotels The very friendly **Hôtel Florella** *(☎ 04 93 38 48 11, fax 04 93 99 22 15; ⓔ reservations@hotelflorella.com; 55 blvd de la République; singles/doubles/triples/quads with shower & toilet €30/35/45/60)* is run by an Irish couple.

Villa Elodie *(☎/fax 04 93 39 39 91; ⓔ villaelodie@wanadoo.fr; 35 ave de Vallauris; 2-person studio/8-person apartment €39/80)* is about 400m northeast of the train station. There's a two-night minimum and you need to call ahead because there's no reception. To get there, follow blvd de la République for 300m and ave de Vallauris runs off to the right.

Hôtel de Bourgogne *(☎ 04 93 38 36 73, fax 04 92 99 28 41; 11 rue du 24 Août; singles/doubles with washbasin €24/31, with bath & toilet €45)* is another option, or you could try **Hôtel National** *(☎ 04 93 39 91 92, fax 04 92 98 44 06; ⓔ hotelnationalcannes@wanadoo.fr; 8 rue Maréchal Joffre; singles/doubles with shower & TV from €40/55)*.

Places to Eat

Morning **food markets** *(open Tues-Sun, daily in summer)* are held on place Gambetta, and at the **Marché Forville** north of place Bernard Cornut Gentille.

There are a few budget restaurants around the Marché Forville and many small (but not necessarily cheap) restaurants along rue St Antoine, which runs northwest from place Bernard Cornut Gentille.

A good choice is popular **Au Bons Enfants** *(80 rue Meynadier; open Mon-Sat; menu €15.50)* with regional dishes. **La Crêperie** *(☎ 04 92 99 00 00; 66 rue Meynadier; menu €9; open Mon-Sat)* has dozens of buckwheat crepe options.

Getting There & Away

Buses to Nice (€5.10, 1½ hours) and other places, most operated by Rapides Côte d'Azur, leave from place Bernard Cornut Gentille.

From the **train station** *(☎ 0836 35 35 39)* there are regular services to Nice (€5, 40 minutes), Marseille (€20.90, two hours) and St Raphaël (€5.30, 20 minutes), where you can pick up a bus to St Tropez.

Getting Around

Bus Azur *(☎ 04 93 45 20 08; place Bernard Cornut Gentille)* has an office in the same building as Rapides Côte d'Azur. It serves Cannes and destinations up to 7km from town. Tickets cost €1.22.

Alliance Location *(☎ 04 93 38 62 62; 19 rue des Frères Pradignac)* rents mountain bikes/scooters for €15/26 a day.

SAINT TROPEZ

pop 19,858

Since 1956, when the small fishing village of St Tropez found fame through the patronage of French actor Brigitte Bardot and her acolytes, things have never been the same. The once isolated fishing village now draws in thousands of visitors a year. If you can, come by boat since the road traffic into and out of the town can be horrendous. If watching the rich dining on yachts is not your flute of Moët, then head for the backstreets where men still play *pétanque* and you might spy a famous face or two.

The **tourist office** *(☎ 04 94 97 45 21, fax 04 94 97 82 66; ⓔ tourisme@saint-tropez.st; quai Jean Jaurès; open daily)* offers guided tours. You might care to visit the **Musée de l'Annonciade** *(place Grammont)*, a disused chapel in the Old Port that contains an impressive collection of modern art, including works by Matisse, Bonnard, Dufy, Derain and Rouault. The **Musée Naval** in the dungeon of the citadel at the end of montée de la Citadelle has displays on the town's maritime history and the Allied landings in 1944. For a decent beach you need to get 4km out of town to the excellent **Plage de Tahiti**.

Accommodation isn't cheap, even if you camp. St Tropez's cheapest hotel is the dingy **Hôtel La Méditerranée** *(☎ 04 94 97 00 44, fax 04 94 97 47 83; 21 blvd Louis Blanc; singles/doubles €63/99)*. Extremely tasteful is **Café Sud** *(☎ 04 94 97 71 72; 12 rue Étienne Berny; mains around €22)*, tucked down a narrow street off places des Lices. Tables are outside in a star-topped courtyard.

The **bus station** *(ave Général de Gaulle)* is on the southwestern edge of town on the main road out of town. Frequent taxi boats run to Port Grimaud nearby and excursion boats run regularly to and from St Maxime and St Raphaël.

MENTON

pop 28,792

Reputed to be the warmest spot on the Côte d'Azur, Menton is encircled by mountains. The town is renowned for lemons and holds a two-week Fête du Citron (Lemon Festival) each year between mid-February and early March. The helpful **tourist office** *(☎ 04 92 41 76 76; 8 ave Boyer)* is in the Palais de l'Europe.

It's pleasant to wander around the narrow, winding streets of the Vieille Ville (old town) and up to the cypress-shaded **Cimetière du Vieux Château**, with the graves of English, Irish, North Americans, New Zealanders and others who died here during the 19th century. The view alone is worth the climb.

Église St Michel, the grandest baroque church in this part of France sits perched in the centre of the Vieille Ville. The **beach** along the promenade du Soleil is public and, like Nice's, carpeted with smooth pebbles. Better private beaches lie east of the old city in the port area, the main one being **Plage des Sablettes**.

Places to Stay

One kilometre northeast of the train station, **Camping St Michel** *(☎ 04 93 35 81 23, fax 04 93 57 12 35; plateau St Michel; adult/tent/car from €3.20/3.70/3.50; open April-Oct)* is up steep steps. Terraced sites are interspersed with olive trees, and the facilities are clean. The adjacent **Auberge de Jeunesse** *(☎ 04 93 35 93 14, fax 04 93 35 93 07; ⓔ menton@fuaj.org; plateau St Michel; dorm beds €11.50; open Feb-Oct)* takes HI members only.

Hôtel St Michel *(☎ 04 93 57 46 33, fax 04 93 57 71 19; 1684 promenade du Soleil; rooms from €65)* has some rooms overlooking the water.

Getting There & Away

The **bus station** *(☎ 04 93 28 43 27)* has services to Monaco (€2 return, 30 minutes) and Nice (€4.90 return, 1¼ hours). Take the train to get to Ventimiglia in Italy.

Monaco

pop 30,000

The Principauté de Monaco (Principality of Monaco), a sovereign state whose territory covers only 1.95 sq km, has been ruled by the Grimaldi family for most of the period since 1297. Prince Rainier III (born in 1923), whose sweeping constitutional powers make him far more than a figurehead, has reigned since 1949. The citizens of Monaco (Monégasques), of whom there are only 5000 out of a total population of 30,000, pay no taxes. The official language is French, although efforts are being made to revive the country's traditional dialect. As there are no border formalities, Monaco makes a perfect day trip from Nice if you're wealthy, but can be a bit depressing if you can't keep up with the high rollers.

Orientation

Monaco consists of four principal areas: Monaco Ville, also known as the old city or the Rocher de Monaco, perched atop a 60m-high crag overlooking the Port de Monaco; Monte Carlo, famed for its casino and its Grand Prix motor race, north of the harbour; La Condamine, the flat area surrounding the harbour; and Fontvieille, an industrial area southwest of Monaco Ville and the Port de Fontvieille.

Information

Tourist Offices The **Direction du Tourisme et des Congrès de la Principauté de Monaco** *(☎ 92 16 61 66, fax 92 16 60 00; ⓔ dtc@monaco-tourisme.com; 2a blvd des Moulins; open daily)* is across the public gardens from the casino. There's a helpful counter at the train station open the same hours; several tourist office kiosks operate around the principality in summer.

Money Unsurprisingly, there are lots of **banks** in the vicinity of the casino. **American Express** *(☎ 93 25 74 45; 35 blvd Princesse Charlotte; open Mon-Fri)* is near the main tourist office.

Post & Communications Monégasque stamps are valid only within Monaco. The **main post office** *(1 ave Henri Dunant)* is inside the Palais de la Scala. Calls between Monaco and the rest of France are treated as international calls. Monaco's country code is ☎ 377. To call France from Monaco, dial ☎ 00 and France's country code (☎ 33). This applies even if you are only making a call from the east side of blvd de France (in Monaco) to its west side (in France)!

Stars 'n' Bars *(☎ 97 97 95 95; 6 quai Antoine, 1er; open 11am-midnight Tues-Sun)* is an American-style bar and restaurant charging €6 for 30 minutes of Net access.

Things to See & Do

Palais du Prince The changing of the guard takes place outside the **Prince's Palace** *(adult/concession €6/3; open 9.30am-6.20pm daily June-Oct)* daily at 11.55am. About 15 state apartments are open to the public. Guided tours (35 minutes) in English leave every 15 or 20 minutes. Some of Napoleon's personal effects are displayed in the **Musée des Souvenirs Napoléoniens** *(adult/concession €4/2)*, in the palace's south wing.

Musée Océanographique If you're going to go to one aquarium on your whole trip, it should be the world-famous Oceanographic Museum *(ave St Martin in Monaco Ville; adult/concession €11/6; open 9am-7pm daily, to 8pm July & Aug)*, with its 90 seawater tanks.

Cathédrale de Monaco The unspectacular 19th-century cathedral *(4 rue Colonel)* has one major attraction – the grave of Grace Kelly (1929–1982). The Hollywood star married Prince Rainier III in 1956, but was killed in a car crash in 1982. The remains of other members of the royal family, buried in the church crypt since 1885, rest behind Princess Grace's tomb.

Jardin Exotique The steep slopes of the wonderful Jardin Exotique *(bus No 2 from tourist office to end of line; adult/concession €6.40/3.60)* are home to some 7000 varieties of cacti and succulents from all over the world. The spectacular view is worth at least half the admission fee, which also gets you into the **Musée d'Anthropologie Préhistorique** and includes a half-hour guided visit to the **Grottes de l'Observatoire**, a system of caves 279 steps down the hillside.

Places to Stay

Monaco's HI hostel, **Centre de la Jeunesse Princesse Stéphanie** *(☎ 93 50 83 20, fax 93 25 29 82; ⓔ info@youthhostel.asso.mc; 24 ave Prince Pierre; dorm beds €16)* is 120m uphill from the train station. You must be aged between 16 and 31 to stay here. Beds are allocated mornings on a first-come, first-served basis; you can book ahead with a deposit.

Two-star **Hôtel de France** *(☎ 93 30 24 64, fax 92 16 13 34; ⓔ hotel-france@monte-carlo.mc; 6 rue de la Turbie; singles/doubles €67/85)* has rooms with shower, toilet and TV.

Places to Eat

There are a few cheap restaurants in La Condamine along rue de la Turbie. Lots of touristy restaurants can be found in the streets leading off from place du Palais. The flashy **Stars 'n' Bars** *(☎ 93 50 95 95; 6 quai Antoine, 1er; open Tues-Sun, food until midnight)* does Tex-Mex, burgers and salads.

One of the few affordable restaurants offering in Monégasque dishes is **U Cavagnetu** *(☎ 93 30 35 80; 14 rue Comte Félix-Gastaldi; lunch/dinner menus from €13/18)*.

Getting There & Away

There is no single bus station in Monaco – intercity buses leave from various points around the city.

The flash **train station** *(☎ 0836 35 35 39; ave Prince Pierre)* is part of the French SNCF network. There are frequent trains to Menton (€2, 10 minutes), Nice (€2.90, 20 minutes) and Ventimiglia in Italy (€3, 25 minutes).

FRANCE

Languedoc-Roussillon

Languedoc-Roussillon stretches in an arc along the coast from Provence to the Pyrenees. The plains of Bas Languedoc (Lower Languedoc) extend to the coast, where beaches are generally broad and sandy. The wine – Languedoc is France's largest wine-producing area – is red, robust and cheap. Inland are the rugged, sparsely populated mountains of Haut Languedoc (Upper Languedoc), a region of bare limestone plateaus and deep canyons.

Transport is frequent between cities on the plain, but buses in the interior are about as rare as camels. For train information throughout the region, ring ☎ 0836 35 35 39.

MONTPELLIER

pop 229,000

Montpellier is one of the nation's fastest-growing cities. It's also one of the youngest, with students making up nearly a quarter of its population. The city hosts a popular theatre festival in June and a two-week international dance festival in June/July.

Montpellier's Centre Historique has at its heart place de la Comédie, an enormous pedestrianised square. Westward from it sprawls a network of lanes between rue de la Loge and rue Grand Jean Moulin. The **main tourist office** *(☎ 04 67 60 60 60; open daily)* is at the south end of esplanade Charles de Gaulle. To snack and surf, visit the **Dimension 4 Cybercafé** *(11 rue des Balances; open 10am-1am daily)*, which charges €4 per hour.

Musée Fabre *(39 blvd Bonne Nouvelle)* shows one of France's richest collections of French, Italian, Flemish and Dutch works of art from the 16th century onwards. **Musée Languedocien** *(7 rue Jacques Cœur)* displays the region's archaeological finds. Both charge adult/concession €5.50/3.

The closest beach is at **Palavas-les-Flots**, 12km south of the city. Take bus No 17 or 28.

Places to Stay

Hostels The **Auberge de Jeunesse** *(☎ 04 67 60 32 22, fax 04 67 60 32 30; ⓔ montpellier@fuaj.org; 2 impasse de la Petite Corraterie; beds €8; open mid-Jan–mid-Dec)* is just off rue des Écoles Laïques. Take the tram to the Louis Blanc stop.

Hotels Off place de la Comédie is **Hôtel des Touristes** *(☎ 04 67 58 42 37, fax 04 67 92 61 37; 10 rue Baudin; singles/doubles/triples with shower from €25/30/50)* with spacious rooms. **Hôtel des Étuves** *(☎/fax 04 67 60 78 19; 24 rue des Étuves; singles/doubles with bathroom from €28/34)* is friendly. Close by, **Hôtel Majestic** *(☎ 04 67 66 26 85; 4 rue du Cheval Blanc; singles/doubles €18/23, doubles/triples/quads with bathroom €29/46/53)* has basic rooms and rooms with bathrooms.

Places to Eat

Eating places abound in Montpellier's old quarter. **Tripti Kulai** *(20 rue Jacques Cœur; menus €10.50 & €14.50)* is vegetarian. **La Tomate** *(6 rue Four des Flammes; menus from €8)* does great regional dishes, salads the size of a kitchen garden, plus dessert.

Entertainment

For a drink, try the bars flanking rue En-Gondeau, off rue Grand Jean Moulin. **Mash Disco Bar** *(5 rue de Girone)* is a popular student hang-out. For more entertainment options, look out for a free copy of *Sortit à Montpellier* in restaurants and shops.

Getting There & Away

Montpellier's **bus station** *(☎ 04 67 92 01 43)* is immediately southwest of the train station, itself 500m south of place de la Comédie.

Rail destinations include Paris' Gare de Lyon (€63.10/77.10 weekdays/weekends, four to five hours by TGV, about 10 daily), Carcassonne (€17.70, 1½ hours, at least 10 daily) and Nîmes (€7.20, 30 minutes, 15 or more daily).

NÎMES

pop 133,000

Nîmes has some of Europe's best-preserved Roman buildings. **Les Arènes** *(the amphitheatre; adult/child €4.50/3.20)*, built about AD 100 to seat 24,000 spectators, is used to this day for theatre performances, music concerts and bullfights.

The rectangular **Maison Carrée**, a well-preserved 1st-century Roman temple, survived the centuries as a meeting hall, private residence, stable, church and archive.

Time your trip to coincide with one of Nîmes' three wild *férias* (festivals) – Féria Primavera (Spring Festival) in February, Féria de Pentecôte (Whitsuntide Festival) in June, and the Féria des Vendanges coinciding with the grape harvest in September. The **main tourist office** *(☎ 04 66 58 38 00; 6 rue Auguste)* can help with information.

To check your email, log on at **Netgames** *(25 rue de l'Horloge)*, right beside the Maison Carrée, which charges €3 an hour.

Places to Stay & Eat

Domaine de la Bastide *(☎/fax 04 66 38 09 21; tent sites for 2 people with car €11.30; open year-round)* is 4km south of town on route de Générac (the D13). Take bus D and get off at La Bastide, the terminus.

Hôtel de la Maison Carrée *(☎ 04 66 67 32 89, fax 04 66 76 22 57; 14 rue de la Maison Carrée; singles/doubles with washbasin €22/26; singles with bathroom €28-37, doubles with bathroom €34-43, triples/quads €50/53)* is a welcoming, highly recommended place.

La Truye qui Filhe *(9 rue Fresque; menu €8.40; open noon-2pm Mon-Sat; closed Aug)*, beneath the vaults of a restored 14th-century inn, is a self-service format restaurant with a warm atmosphere and a superb-value changing daily *menu*.

Getting There & Away

Nîmes' bus station is beside the train station. Destinations include Pont du Gard (€5.40, 45 minutes, five to six daily), Avignon (€7.10, 30 minutes, 10 or more daily) and Arles (€5.25, 30 to 45 minutes, four to eight daily).

The train station is at the southeastern end of ave Feuchères. Destinations include Paris' Gare de Lyon (€62.50, four hours by TGV, seven daily), Avignon (€7.10, 30 minutes, 10 or more daily), Marseille (€15.30, 1¼ hours, 12 daily) and Montpellier (€7.20, 30 minutes, 15 or more daily).

AROUND NÎMES

Pont du Gard

The Roman general Agrippa slung the mighty Pont du Gard over the Gard River around 19 BC. You won't be alone; this three-tier aqueduct, 275m long and 49m high, receives over two million visitors a year.

There's a tourist kiosk on each bank and a brand new information centre on the left bank, set back from the river.

Buses from Avignon (26km) and Nîmes (23km) stop 1km north of the bridge.

CARCASSONNE

pop 46,250

From afar, the old walled city of Carcassonne looks like a fairy-tale medieval city. Once inside the fortified walls, however, the magic rubs off. Luring some 200,000 visitors in July and August alone, Carcassonne can be a tourist hell in high summer. Purists may sniff at its 'medieval' Cité – whose impressive fortifications were extensively renovated and rebuilt in the 19th century – but what the heck; it *is* magic, one of France's greatest skylines.

The 1.7km-long double ramparts of **La Cité** (spectacularly floodlit at night) are spiked with 52 witches' hat towers. Within are narrow, medieval streets and the 12th-century **Château Comtal** (Count's Castle), visited by guided tour only (adult/concession €4.50/3.50). A 40-minute tour in English departs up to five times daily, according to season.

The Ville Basse (lower town), a more modest stepsister to camp Cinderella up the hill, has cheaper eating places and accommodation and also merits a browse. The Aude River separates the Ville Basse from the Cité on its hillock. The **main tourist office** *(☎ 04 68 10 24 30)* is in the Ville Basse opposite square Gambetta. **Alerte Rouge** *(Red Alert; 73 rue Verdun; open 10am-11pm daily)* is an Internet café charging €4.80 per hour.

Places to Stay & Eat

In the heart of the Cité, the large, cheery **Auberge de Jeunesse** *(☎ 04 68 25 23 16; rue Vicomte Trencavel; dorm beds €12.20 with breakfast)* has a snack bar offering light meals and a great outside terrace. The B&B at the **Centre International de Séjour** *(☎ 04 68 11 17 00; 91 rue Aimé Ramon; dorm beds €8)* in the Ville Basse is another option.

Handy for the train station is recommended **Hôtel Astoria** *(☎ 04 68 25 31 38; 18 rue Tourtel; singles/doubles from €18/20, with bathroom from €27)*.

Prices at the welcoming **Relais du Square** *(☎ 04 68 72 31 72; 51 rue du Pont Vieux; 1–3-person room €30)* couldn't be simpler: all large rooms, for one to three people, cost the same, whatever their facilities. In summer arrive early if you want your own bathroom.

L'Italia *(32 route Minervoise)*, handy for the station, is a pizza-plus joint that also does takeaways. Next door you'll find the more stylish **Restaurant Gil** *(menus from €14)* with Catalan-influenced cuisine.

Getting There & Away

The train station is at the northern end of pedestrianised rue Georges Clemenceau in the Ville Basse. Carcassonne is on the main line linking Toulouse (€11.70, 50 minutes, 10 or more daily) with Béziers (€11.10, 50 minutes, five daily) and Montpellier (€17.70, 1½ hours, 10 or more daily).

TOULOUSE

pop 690,000

Toulouse, France's fourth largest city, is renowned for its high-tech industries, especially aerospace; local factories have built the Caravelle, Concorde and Airbus passenger planes, and the Ariane rocket. Like Montpellier, it's a youthful place; indeed, it houses over 110,000 students – more than any other French provincial city.

Most older buildings in the city centre are in rose-red brick, earning the city its nickname *la ville rose* (the pink city).

Orientation & Information

The heart of Toulouse is bounded to the east by blvd de Strasbourg and its continuation, blvd Lazare Carnot and, to the west, by the Garonne River. Its two main squares are place du Capitole and, 300m eastwards, place Wilson.

The busy **tourist office** *(☎ 05 61 11 02 22; open daily)* is in the Donjon du Capitole, a 16th-century tower on square Charles de Gaulle. Online time at Internet café **Résomania** *(85 rue Pargaminières; open until midnight daily)* is €3 per hour before noon and €4 between midday and midnight.

Major annual events include Festival Garonne with riverside music, theatre and dance (July), Musique d'Été with music of all definitions around town (July and August) and Jazz sur Son 31, an international jazz festival (October).

Things to See & Do

Cité de l'Espace *(Space City; ☎ 05 62 71 48 71; adult/concession €12/10)* is a truly mind-boggling interactive space museum and planetarium. To get there, take bus No 15 from allées Jean Jaurès to the end of the line, from where it's a 600m walk.

The **Galerie Municipale du Château d'Eau** *(place Laganne; open 1pm-7pm Wed-Mon; adult/concession €2.30/1.50)* is a world-class photographic gallery inside a 19th-century water tower at the western end of pont Neuf, which is located just across the Garonne River.

Musée des Augustins *(21 rue de Metz; adult/student €2.20/free)* has a superb collection of paintings and stone artefacts.

Within the magnificent Gothic **Église des Jacobins**, the remains of St Thomas Aquinas (1225–74), an early head of the Dominican order, are interred on the north side.

The **Basilique St Sernin** is France's largest and most complete Romanesque structure. It's topped by a magnificent eight-sided 13th-century **tower**.

Places to Stay & Eat

Try to avoid the cheap hotels near the train station; most are fairly sordid.

The exceptionally friendly **Hôtel Beauséjour** *(☎/fax 05 61 62 77 59; 4 rue Caffarelli; basic rooms from €20, doubles/triples with bath €25/33)*, off allées Jean Jaurès, is a great value. **Hôtel Splendid** *(☎/fax 05 61 62 43 02; basic rooms from €13.72, singles/doubles/triples with bath €21.40/24.40/33.55)* is at No 13.

Fill yourself at lunchtime, when there are some amazing deals. Many places have lunch *menus* for €8 to €10. Unmissable and an essential Toulouse experience are the small, spartan, lunchtime-only **restaurants** on the 1st floor of Les Halles Victor Hugo covered market (great in itself for atmosphere and fresh produce). They serve up generous quantities of hearty fare for €9 to €20.

Place St Georges is almost entirely taken over by café tables. Both blvd de Strasbourg and place du Capitole are lined with restaurants and cafés.

Entertainment

For what's on where, pick up a copy of *Toulouse Hebdo* (€0.90) or *Intramuros* (free from selected restaurants and bars). For life after dark, ask at the tourist office for its free listing *Toulouse By Night*.

Cafés around place St-Pierre beside the Garonne River pull in a mainly young crowd. Nearby, the **Why Not Café** *(5 rue Pargaminières)* has a beautiful terrace while **Café des Artistes** *(13 place de la Daurade)* is an art-student hang-out.

Two hot discos near the centre are **La Strada** *(4 rue Gabriel Péri)* and **L'Ubu** *(16 rue St-Rome)*.

Getting There & Away

Toulouse's **bus station** *(☎ 05 61 61 67 67)*, just north of the train station, serves mainly regional destinations including Andorra (€20, four hours, one to two daily). For longer distance travel, both **Intercars** *(☎ 05 61 58 14 53)* and **Eurolines** *(☎ 05 61 26 40 04)* have offices in Toulouse.

The train station, Gare Matabiau, is on blvd Pierre Sémard, about 1km northeast of the city centre.

Destinations served by multiple daily direct trains include Bayonne (€31, 3¾ hours), Bordeaux (€26.10, 2½ hours) and Carcassonne (€11.70, 50 minutes).

The fare to Paris is €56 by Corail (6½ hours, Gare d'Austerlitz) and €70.40 to €80 by TGV (5½ hours, Gare Montparnasse via Bordeaux).

SNCF *(5 rue Peyras)* provides information and ticketing.

Corsica (Corse)

Corsica, the most mountainous and geographically diverse of all the Mediterranean islands, has spent much of its history under foreign rule. From the 13th century it remained under Genoese control until the Corsicans, led by the extraordinary Pasquale Paoli, declared the island independent in 1755. But France took over in 1769 and has ruled Corsica since – except in 1794–96, when it was under English domination, and during the German and Italian occupation of 1940–43.

The island has 1000km of coastline, soaring granite mountains that stay snowcapped until July, a huge national park, flatland marshes, an uninhabited desert in the northwest and a 'continental divide' running down the middle of the island. It's a popular holiday destination for the French and increasingly for foreign travellers who come for its exceptional hiking and diving opportunities.

AJACCIO (AIACCIU)

pop 52,850

Port city Ajaccio, birthplace of Napoleon Bonaparte (1769–1821), is a great place to begin a visit to Corsica and a fine place for walking. The many museums and statues dedicated to Bonaparte speak volumes – not about Napoleon himself, but about how the people of his native town prefer to think of him.

Ajaccio's main street is cours Napoléon, which stretches from place du Général de Gaulle northward to the train station and beyond. The old city is south of place Foch. The ferry port is central to both the old and new town.

Information

The **tourist office** *(☎ 04 95 51 53 03, fax 04 95 51 53 01; ⓔ ajaccio.tourisme@wanadoo.fr; 1 place Foch; open daily)* is boosted by a **chamber of commerce counter** *(☎ 04 95 23 56 56; open daily)* at the airport. **Gare.Net** *(☎ 04 95 50 72 79; 2 ave de Paris)* charges €5 for an hour's Internet access. Money can be exchanged at the **main post office** *(13 cours Napoléon)*.

The **Maison d'Information Randonnées** *(☎ 04 95 51 79 00, fax 04 95 21 88 17; ⓔ infos@parc-naturel-corse.com; 2 rue du Sergent Casalonga; open 8.30am-12.30pm & 2pm-6pm Mon-Thur, to 5pm Fri)* provides information on the Parc Naturel Régional de la Corse and its hiking trails.

Things to See & Do

Museums The house where Napoleon was born and raised, **Maison Bonaparte** *(☎ 04 95 21 43 89; rue St Charles; adult/concession €4/2.60; open 10am-noon & 2pm-4.45pm Oct-Mar; 9am-noon & 2pm-6pm Apr-Sept; closed Mon morning year-round)*, in the old city, was sacked by Corsican nationalists in 1793, but rebuilt later in the decade.

The sombre **Salon Napoléonien** *(☎ 04 95 21 90 15; 1st floor, Hôtel de Ville, place Foch; admission €2.29; open 9am-11.45am & 2pm-4.45pm Mon-Fri mid-Sept–mid-June, 9am-11.45am & 2pm-5.45pm Mon-Sat mid-June–mid-Sept)* exhibits memorabilia of the emperor.

The **Musée A Bandera** *(☎ 04 95 51 07 34; 1 rue Général Lévie; adult/concession €3.85/2.30; open 9am-7pm Mon-Sat, 9am-noon Sun July–mid-Sept, 9am-noon & 2pm-6pm Mon-Sat mid-Sept–June)* deals with Corsican military history.

Musée Fesch *(☎ 04 95 21 48 17; 50 rue du Cardinal Fesch; adult/concession €5.34/3.81; open 1.30pm-6pm Mon, 9am-6.30pm Tues-Thur, 9am-6.30pm & 9pm-midnight Fri, 10.30am-6pm Sat & Sun July-Aug, shorter hours Sept-June, closed Sun & Mon Oct-Mar)* houses an awesome assembly of 14th- to 19th-century Italian paintings collected by Napoleon's uncle.

Places to Stay

Efficient **Hôtel Kallisté** *(☎ 04 95 51 34 45, fax 04 95 21 79 00; ⓔ hotelkalliste@cyrnos.com; 51 cours Napoléon; singles/doubles with shower & toilet €56/69)* has classy rooms with terracotta tiles. Prices drop by a third in low season. Breakfast (€6.50) is served in your room.

Only 200m from the ferry terminal, **Hôtel Le Dauphin** *(☎ 04 95 21 12 94, fax 04 95 21 88 69; 11 blvd Sampiero; singles/doubles with shower & toilet €49/60)* includes breakfast in the price.

Places to Eat

Most of Ajaccio's restaurants are seasonal. Cafés can be found along blvd du Roi Jérôme, quai Napoléon and the north side of place de Gaulle. **Café de Paris** and the neighbouring **Dolce Piacere**, on the west side of place du Général de Gaulle, both have giant terraces with sea views.

The best pizza is served at **La Pizza** *(☎ 04 95 21 30 71; 2 rue des Anciens Fosées; pizza €8.50-10.50)*. Try the *quatre saisons*, drizzled with chilli-laced olive oil.

The popular **U Scampi** *(☎ 04 95 21 38 09; 11 rue Conventionnel Chiappe; menus from €13; open Mon-Thur, Fri lunch & Sat dinner year-round)* dishes up a host of Corsican specialities – including octopus stew – on a flower-filled terrace.

Da Mamma *(☎ 04 95 21 39 44; Passage de la Guinguetta; menus from €10.50)*, tucked away off cours Napoléon, does paella, pasta and Corsican specialities.

There's an open-air **Marché Municipal** *(square Campinchi; open 8am-noon Tues-Sun)* and a **Monoprix supermarket** *(33 cours Napoléon; open Mon-Sat)* for supplies.

Getting There & Away

Bus The Terminal Maritime et Routier on quai l'Herminier houses Ajaccio's bus station. **Eurocorse** *(☎ 04 95 21 06 30; open 8.30am-4pm Mon-Sat)* is responsible for most lines. Destinations include Bastia (€18, three hours), Bonifacio (€19.50, four hours), Corte (€10.50, 1½ hours), Porto and Ota (€10.50, 2½ hours), Calvi (€22, via Porto), and Sartène (€11.50, two hours). Sunday services are minimal.

The bus station's **information counter** *(☎ 04 95 51 55 45; open 7am-7pm daily)* can provide schedules.

Train The **train station** *(☎ 04 95 32 80 60; blvd Sampiero)* is a 15-minute walk from the old town. Destinations include Bastia via Corte (€19.90, 3½ hours) and Calvi via Ponte Leccia (€24.40, 4½ hours).

Ferry The Terminal Maritime is on quai l'Herminier next to the bus station. SNCM's **ticketing office** *(☎ 04 95 29 66 99; 3 quai l'Herminier; open 8am-6pm Mon, 8am-8pm Tues-Fri, 8am-1pm Sat)* is across the street. Ajaccio is connected to the mainland (Toulon or Marseille, €62 in high season, including departure tax; Nice, €50 in high season including departure tax) by at least one daily ferry; the **SNCM bureau** *(open 7am-8pm Mon-Sat)* in the ferry terminal also opens two hours before the scheduled departure time on Sunday.

Corsica Ferries *(☎ 04 95 50 78 82, fax 04 95 50 78 83; ⓦ www.corsicaferries.com)* runs cheaper but less frequent services to Ajaccio from Toulon and Nice (€35 in high season, including tax). Its office is at the Terminal Maritime.

Getting Around

Local bus tickets cost €1.15 (€4 to the airport). Pick up maps and timetables at the **TCA Boutique** *(☎ 04 95 23 29 41; 75 cours Napoléon; open 8am-noon & 2.30pm-6pm Mon-Sat)*.

There's a taxi rank on place du Général de Gaulle, or call **ABC Taxis Ajacciens** *(☎ 06 62 55 71 38)*.

BASTIA

pop 37,880

Pleasant, bustling Bastia, Corsica's most important commercial centre, has rather an Italian feel to it. It was the seat of the Genoese governors of Corsica from the 15th century, when the *bastiglia* (fortress) from which the city derives its name was built. There's not all that much to see or do, but Bastia makes a good base for exploring **Cap Corse**, the wild, 40km-long peninsula to the north.

The **tourist office** *(☎ 04 95 54 20 40, fax 04 95 54 20 41; place St Nicolas; open daily)* dispenses information. The **main post office** *(cnr ave Maréchal Sébastiani & blvd Paoli)* is a block west of place St Nicolas. **Le Cyber** *(☎ 04 95 34 30 34; 6 rue Jardins; open 9am-late)* has drinks and snacks and provides Internet access for €3.10 an hour.

Things to See & Do

Bastia's **place St Nicolas**, a palm- and plane tree–lined esplanade, was laid out in the late 19th century. The narrow streets and alleyways of **Terra Vecchia**, which is centred on place de l'Hôtel de Ville, lie just south. The 16th-century **Oratoire de l'Immaculée Conception** is opposite 3 rue Napoléon and was decorated in rich baroque style in the early 18th century.

The picturesque, horseshoe-shaped **Vieux Port** is between Terra Vecchia and the **Citadelle** and is the most colourful part of Bastia with its crumbling buildings and lively restaurants.

Places to Stay

Book ahead because Bastia's hotels fill up with business travellers.

Hôtel Le Riviera *(☎ 04 95 31 07 16, fax 04 95 34 17 39; 1bis rue du Nouveau Port; doubles with shower & toilet €58)* is very close to the ferry. The family-run **Hôtel Central** *(☎ 04 95 31 71 12, fax 04 95 31 82 40; ⓔ infos@centralhotel.fr; 3 rue Miot; singles/doubles with shower & toilet €40/50; with kitchenette €75/90)* has recently renovated its rooms.

Don't be discouraged by the dingy stairs – once you get inside, the rooms are fresh and comfortable at **Hôtel Le Forum** *(☎ 04 95 31 02 53, fax 04 95 31 65 60; ⓔ hotel_leforum@wanadoo.fr; 20 blvd Paoli; rooms with shower & toilet from €60)*. Prices drop by about €10 outside July and August.

Places to Eat

Cafés and brasseries line the western side of place St Nicolas. There are more restaurants at the Vieux Port, on quai des Martyrs de la Libération and on place de l'Hôtel de Ville in Terra Vecchia, where the **Café Pannini** sells great jumbo sandwiches.

A delightful **food market** *(place de l'Hôtel de Ville; open 8am-1pm Tues-Sun)* takes place in Terra Vecchio, and there's a **Spar supermarket** *(cnr rue César Campinchi & rue Capanelle)*.

Getting There & Away

Bus The afternoon bus to Calvi run by **Les Beaux Voyages** *(☎ 04 95 65 02 10)* leaves from outside the train station. **Rapides Bleus** *(☎ 04 95 31 03 79; 1 ave Maréchal Sébastiani)* has buses to Porto-Vecchio (€16.30, three hours) and handles tickets for Eurocorse buses to Corte and Ajaccio.

Train The **train station** *(☎ 04 95 32 60 06)* is at the northern end of ave Maréchal Sébastiani. Destinations include Corte (€9.40, two hours), Ajaccio (€19.90, 3½ hours) and Calvi via Ponte Leccia (€15, 4½ hours).

Ferry Bastia is linked by ferry to both France and Italy. The ferry terminal is at the eastern end of ave Pietri. **SNCM's office** *(☎ 04 95 54 66 81; open 7.15am-6.30pm Mon-Fri, 8am-11.45am Sat)* handles ferries to mainland France. The SNCM counter in the ferry terminal opens two hours before each sailing.

Corsica Ferries *(☎ 04 95 32 95 95, fax 04 95 32 14 71; 15bis rue Chanoine Leschi; open 8.30am-noon & 2pm-6pm Mon-Sat)* runs to Toulon, Nice and Italy. For more Italian destinations, try **Mobylines** *(☎ 04 95 34 84 94, fax 04 95 32 17 94; 4 rue du Commandant Luce de Casabianca; open 8am-noon & 2pm-6pm Mon-Fri, 8am-noon Sat)*, 200m north of place St Nicolas. Mobylines and Corsica Ferries also have ticket windows in the ferry terminal with restricted hours.

Standard low/high season fares to/from mainland France are around €30/15 for passengers over/under 25 years of age, including departure tax.

CALVI

pop 6219

Calvi, where Admiral Horatio Nelson lost his eye, is both a military town and an upmarket holiday resort. The Citadelle, garrisoned by a crack regiment of the French Foreign Legion, sits atop a promontory at the western end of a beautiful half-moon-shaped bay. Also known as the Haute Ville (upper town), it's northeast of the port. Blvd Wilson, the main thoroughfare in the Basse Ville (lower town), is up the hill from quai Landry and the marina.

Information

The **tourist office** *(☎ 04 95 65 16 67, fax 04 95 65 14 09; open Mon-Sat, daily June-Sept)* is near the marina. **Crédit Lyonnais** *(7 blvd Wilson; open 8.15am-noon & 2pm-5pm Mon-Fri)* is on the same street as the **main post office**, about 100m to the south. **Café de L'Orient** *(☎ 04 95 65 00 16; quai Landry)* has Internet-connected computers for €1 plus €0.10 a minute.

Things to See & Do

The **Citadelle**, set atop an 80m-high granite promontory and enclosed by massive Genoese ramparts, affords great views of the surrounding area. The 13th-century **Église St Jean Baptiste** was rebuilt in 1570; inside is a miraculous ebony icon of Christ. West of the church, a marble plaque marks the site of the house where, according to local tradition, Christopher Columbus was born. The imposing 13th-century **Palais des Gouverneurs** (Governors' Palace) is above the entrance to the citadel, which is now known as Caserne Sampiero. It serves as a barracks and mess hall for officers who serve the French Foreign Legion.

Calvi's 4km-long **beach** begins just south of the marina and stretches around the Golfe de Calvi. Other nice beaches, including one at **Algajola**, are west of town. The port and resort town of L'Île Rousse (Isula Rossa) east of Calvi is also endowed with a long, sandy beach with incredibly clean water.

Places to Stay

Camping & Bungalows Just under 1km southeast of town is **Camping La Clé des Champs** *(☎/fax 04 95 65 00 86; ⓔ camagni@wanadoo.fr; route de Pietra Maggiore; sites per adult/tent/car €5.35/1.55/1.55, bungalows from €185 a week for 2 people; open Apr-Oct)*.

Hostels & Hotels The 130-bed **Auberge de Jeunesse BVJ Corsotel** *(☎ 04 95 65 14 15, fax 04 95 65 33 72; ave de la République; dorm beds €20.60; open late Mar-Oct)* has beds in two to eight-person rooms, and rates include a filling breakfast.

A cheap option is **Hôtel du Centre** *(☎ 04 95 65 02 01; 14 rue Alsace-Lorraine; rooms with showers €31-42; open 1 June-5 Oct)*.

Places to Eat

Calvi's attractive marina is lined with expensive restaurants, but there are several budget places on rue Clemenceau, which runs parallel to blvd Wilson. **Best Of**, at the south end of the street, sells good sandwiches (around €4.50).

It doesn't have sea views, but **U Fornu** *(☎ 04 95 65 27 60; impasse du blvd Wilson; mains €15-19)* has the best Corsican food in town. You'll find it up the stairs next to Banque Lyonnais on blvd Wilson.

The tiny **Marché Couvert** *(open 8am-noon daily)* is near Église Ste Marie Majeure. The **Super U supermarket** *(ave Christophe Colomb)* is south of the town centre.

Getting There & Away

Buses to Bastia are run by **Les Beaux Voyages** *(☎ 04 95 65 15 02; place de la Porteuse d'Eau)*. From mid-May to mid-October **Autocars SAIB** *(☎ 04 95 26 13 70)* trundles to Porto (€16, 2½ hours) along Corsica's spectacular western coast.

Calvi's **train station** *(☎ 04 95 65 00 61)* is just off ave de la République. From mid-April to mid-October, *navettes* (one-car trains) make 19 stops between Calvi and L'Île Rousse (€6, 45 minutes).

SNCM ferries *(☎ 04 95 65 01 38)* sail to Calvi from Nice and Marseille, but during winter they can be very infrequent. **Corsica Ferries** *(☎ 04 95 65 43 21)* links Calvi with Nice and Savone, Italy, about once a week (more in summer).

PORTO (PORTU)

pop 460

The pleasant seaside town of Porto, nestled among huge outcrops of red granite and renowned for its sunsets, is an excellent base for exploring some of Corsica's natural wonders. **Les Calanques**, a spectacular mountain landscape of red and orange granite outcrops, towers above the azure waters of the Mediterranean slightly south of Porto along route D81. The **Gorges de Spelunca**, Corsica's most famous river gorge, stretches almost from the town of Ota, which is located around 5km east of Porto, to the town of Evisa, 22km away.

Orientation & Information

The marina is around 1.5km downhill from Porto's pharmacy – the local landmark – on the D81. The area, which is known as Vaïta, is spread out along the road linking the D81 to the marina. The Porto River just south of the marina is linked by an arched pedestrian bridge to a eucalyptus grove and small pebble beach.

The **tourist office** *(☎ 04 95 26 10 55, fax 04 95 26 14 25; open Mon-Fri, daily July & Aug)* is near the marina. The only ATM between Ajaccio and Calvi is here at Porto – it's outside the post office, halfway between the pharmacy and the marina.

Things to See & Do

A short trail leads to the 16th-century **Genoese tower** *(admission €2.50; open 10am-12.30pm & 3pm-7pm Apr-Oct)* on the outcrop above the town.

From March to November, **Nave Va** *(☎ 04 95 26 15 16)* runs boat excursions (€25.50) to the fishing village of Girolata (passing by the Scandola Nature Reserve). Occasionally excursions are also run to Les Calanques in the evenings (€12).

Places to Stay

Friendly **Funtana al' Ora** *(☎ 04 95 26 11 65, fax 04 95 26 10 83; ⓔ info@porto-tourisme.com; sites per tent/person/car €2.15/5.20/2.15, bungalows from €183 a week; open 15 April-Oct)* is 2km east of Porto on the road to Évisa.

In the nearby village of Ota, **Gîte d'Étape Chez Félix** *(☎/fax 04 95 26 12 92)* and **Gîte d'Étape Chez Marie** *(☎/fax 04 95 26 11 37)* both open year-round and charge €11 for a dorm bed.

There are plenty of hotels in Vaïta and at the marina, but most are closed between November and March. One of the best deals is the **Hôtel du Golfe** *(☎/fax 04 95 26 13 33; doubles/triples with shower & toilet €40/49)*. **Hôtel Monte Rosso** *(☎ 04 95 26 11 50, fax 04 95 26 12 30; doubles with shower & toilet €51)* is nearby.

Getting There & Away

Autocars SAIB *(☎ 04 95 22 41 99)* has two bus services daily (Sunday service July to mid-September only) linking Porto and nearby Ota with Ajaccio (€10.50, 2½ hours). From mid-May to mid-October a bus also goes from Porto to Calvi (€16, 2½ hours).

CORTE (CORTI)

pop 6335

When Pasquale Paoli led Corsica to independence in 1755, he made Corte, a fortified town at the centre of the island, the country's capital. To this day, the town remains a potent symbol of Corsican independence. In 1765, Paoli founded a national university there, but it was closed when his short-lived republic was taken over by France in 1769. The Università di Corsica Pasquale Paoli was reopened in 1981 and now has about 4000 students, making Corte the island's liveliest and least touristy town.

Ringed with mountains, snowcapped until as late as June, Corte is an excellent base for hiking; some of the island's highest peaks rise west of the town.

Information

The **tourist office** *(☎ 04 95 46 26 70, fax 04 95 46 34 05; ⓔ corte.tourisme@wanadoo.fr; La Citadelle; open Mon-Fri, Mon-Sat May-Sept)* has helpful staff.

There are several **banks** with ATMs along cours Paoli. The **post office** *(ave Baron Mariani)* also has an ATM.

There's Internet access for €3.50 an hour at **Grand Café du Cours** *(22 cours Paoli)*.

Things to See & Do

The **Citadelle**, built in the early 15th century and largely reconstructed during the 18th and 19th centuries, is perched on top of a hill, with the steep and twisted alleyways and streets of the **Ville Haute** and the Tavignanu and Restonica river valleys below.

The **Château** – the highest part, also known as the Nid d'Aigle (Eagle's Nest) – was built in 1419 by a Corsican nobleman and expanded by the French.

The outstanding **Museu di a Corsica** *(Musée de la Corse; ☎ 04 95 45 25 45; adult/concession €5.34/3.05; open 10am-6pm Tues-Sun, to 8pm July & Aug)* houses exhibitions on Corsican folk traditions, crafts, agriculture, economy and anthropology. It also hosts temporary art exhibitions.

The **Gorges de la Restonica**, a deep valley cut through the mountains by the Restonica River, is a favourite with hikers. The river passes Corte, but some of the choicer trails begin about 16km southwest of town at the Bergeries Grotelle sheepfolds.

Places to Stay

Camping & Hostels Just south of pont Restonica is **Camping Alivetu** *(☎ 04 95 46 11 09, fax 04 95 46 12 34; ⓔ camping.alivetu@laposte.net; Faubourg de St Antoine; sites per tent/adult/car €6/2.50/2.50; open 1 Apr-15 Oct)*.

Very rural and pretty is **Gîte d'Étape U Tavignanu** *(☎ 04 95 46 16 85, fax 04 95 61 14 01; chemin de Baliri; dorm beds with breakfast/full pension €14/34.30, camping per tent/adult €1.90/3.80; open year-round)*. From pont Tavignanu (the first bridge on allée du 9 Septembre), walk westward along chemin de Baliri and follow the signs and orange paint splodges for almost 1km. There's parking down below.

Hotels The 135-room **Hôtel HR** *(☎ 04 95 45 11 11, fax 04 95 61 02 85; ⓔ hr2b@aol.com; 6 allée du 9 Septembre; singles/doubles from €21/25)* has clean, utilitarian rooms. **Hôtel de la Poste** *(☎ 04 95 46 01 37; 2 place Padoue; rooms with shower/shower & toilet €29/41.50)* has spacious, simple rooms.

The atmospheric **Hôtel du Nord et de L'Europe** *(☎ 04 95 46 00 68, fax 04 95 46 03 40; ⓔ info@hoteldunord-corte.com; 22 cours Paoli; rooms with shower & toilet €55)* has recently been renovated.

Places to Eat

Corte's best restaurant is **U Museu** *(☎ 04 95 61 08 36; Rampe Ribanella; 2/3-course menus €11.50/13.60)*. Tasty local fare includes *civet de sanglier aux myrtes sauvages* (wild boar stew with myrtle).

Restaurant Le Bip's *(☎ 04 95 46 06 26; 14 cours Paoli; menus from €12; open Sun-Fri)* is a nice cellar restaurant at the bottom of the flight of stairs beside **Brasserie Le Bip's** *(☎ 04 95 46 04 48)*.

Nearby, **Grand Café du Cours** *(22 cours Paoli; open 7am-2am daily)* is a cruisy student bar with Internet machines. It serves light snacks.

There's a **Spar supermarket** *(7 ave Xavier Luciani)* and a **Casino supermarket** *(allée du 9 Septembre)*.

Getting There & Away

Corte is on Eurocorse's Bastia–Ajaccio route, served by two buses daily in each direction (no Sunday service). The stop is at 3 ave Xavier Luciani where a schedule is posted.

The **train station** *(☎ 04 95 46 00 97; open 6.25am-8pm Mon-Sat, 8.50am-11.20am & 3.30pm-8.25pm Sun)* is at the eastern end of allée du 9 Septembre.

BONIFACIO (BUNIFAZIU)

pop 2661

The famed **Citadelle** of Bonifacio sits 70m above the translucent waters of the Mediterranean, atop a long, narrow and easily defensible promontory – 'Corsica's Gibraltar'. On all sides, limestone cliffs sculpted by the wind and the waves drop almost vertically to the sea; the north side looks out on 1.6km-long Bonifacio Sound, at the eastern end of which is the **marina**. The southern ramparts afford views of the coast of Sardinia, 12km away.

Bonifacio was long associated with the Republic of Genoa. The local dialect – unintelligible to other Corsicans – is Genoese, and many local traditions (including cooking methods) are Genoa-based.

Information

The **tourist office** *(☎ 04 95 73 11 88, fax 04 95 73 14 97; ⓔ tourisme.bonifacio@wanadoo.fr; 2 rue Fred Scamaroni; open Mon-Sat, daily May-Oct)* is in the Citadelle.

The **Société Générale** *(38 rue St Érasme; open Mon-Fri)*, outside the Citadelle, has poor exchange rates, charges €5.30 plus a percentage commission, and has the only ATM in town. In summer, there are exchange bureaus along the marina.

Things to See & Do

Looking down the dramatic cliffs to the sea is a delight; the best views are to be had from **place du Marché** and from the walk west towards and around the cemetery. Don't miss **Porte de Gênes**, which is reached by a tiny 16th-century drawbridge, or the Romanesque **Église Ste Marie Majeure**, the oldest building in Bonifacio. **Rue des Deux Empereurs** (Street of the Two Emperors) is so-called because both Charles V and Napoleon slept there; look for the plaques at Nos 4 and 7. The **Foreign Legion Monument** east of the tourist office was brought back from Algeria in 1963 when that country won its independence.

Places to Stay

The olive-shaded **Camping Araguina** *(☎ 04 95 73 02 96, fax 04 95 73 01 92; ⓔ camping.araguina@wanadoo.fr; ave Sylvère Bohn; sites per person/tent €6.25/1.90, bungalows €53.50; open mid-Mar–Oct)* is 400m north of the marina.

In the Citadelle, **Hôtel Le Royal** *(☎ 04 95 73 00 51, fax 04 95 73 04 68; rue Fred Scamaroni; rooms from €92 Aug, from €69 July & Sept, €39 Nov-Mar)* is a friendly place with restaurant attached.

Places to Eat

In the Citadelle, **Pizzeria-Grill de la Poste** *(☎ 04 95 73 13 31; 5 rue Fred Scamaroni)* has Corsican dishes, pizza (from €7) and pasta (€8 to €20). **Cantina Doria** *(☎ 04 95 73 50*

49; 27 rue Doria) is a rustic hole-in-the-wall popular with locals. The enormous *soupe Corse* (€6) is enough for two people.

Super Marché Simoni *(93 quai Jérôme Comparetti)* is at the marina.

Getting There & Away

For buses to Ajaccio via Sartène (€19.50, four hours, two or three daily with some Sunday services) and Porto-Vecchio (€6, 30 minutes, two buses daily, four in summer), there's **Eurocorse** *(Bastia: ☎ 04 95 31 73 76; 1 rue du Nouveau Port)*. All buses leave from the parking lot next to the Eurocorse kiosk at the east end of the marina.

From Bonifacio's ferry port, both **Saremar** *(☎ 04 95 73 00 96)* and **Moby Lines** *(☎ 04 95 73 00 29)* offer car and passenger ferry service year-round to Santa Teresa (50 minutes, two to seven per day).

Saremar charges €6.71/8.52 for a one-way passenger fare in low/high season while Moby Lines charges €8.50/12. There's an additional €3.10 port tax.

FRANCE

Germany

No-one can ignore Germany. The country that bequeathed the world some of its most glorious works of literature, philosophy and music was also a key architect of the 20th century's most horrifying tragedies. This central European powerhouse sits on a fascinating, complicated past that has shaped events around the globe, fashioning a national history that attracts visitors in droves. Not to be forgotten, though, is that Germany is a country of sheer physical beauty, both natural and created. Outdoor activity is a way of life, and cities boast a huge variety of museums, architecture and cultural draws. And the worldwide fame of Germany's frothy beer, heady wine and hearty food is well deserved.

Germany's reunification in 1990 – still at the forefront of many Germans' minds – began another intriguing chapter. Today, visitors can continue to experience the cultural, social and economic differences of the formerly separate Germanys, enjoying their individual charms.

Germany: the Basics

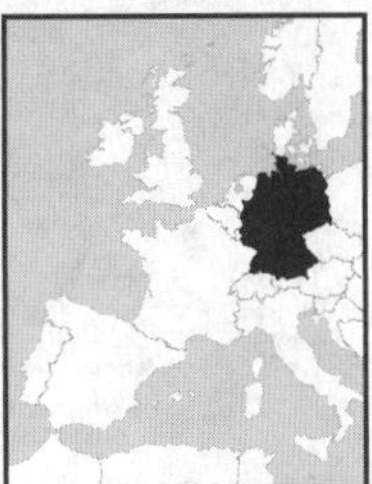

Local name Deutschland

Capital Berlin

Population 83 million

Language German

Currency euro (€1) = 100 centimes

Avoid at all costs Overpriced cuckoo clocks

Break the ice in the local bars by saying *Ihr Hosegeschmack ist sehr wagemutig.* (You have very daring taste in pants.)

Facts about Germany

HISTORY

Most of Germany was part of the Roman Empire, but the legions never managed to subdue the warrior tribes beyond the Rhine and Main. After the Romans, the Frankish conqueror Charlemagne conquered the land, which was incorporated into the Holy Roman Empire following his death. The Habsburgs, ruling from Vienna, took nominal control of the shrinking empire in the 13th century.

In 1517 a scholar named Martin Luther shook Europe to its core. His *95 Theses*, nailed to the Wittenberg church door, outlined his opposition to the Catholic Church's system of selling 'indulgences', which automatically absolved sinners. In 1521 Luther translated the Bible into a German vernacular. This Bible was printed on presses developed by Gutenberg in Mainz and was read widely to the masses. Luther's efforts gained widespread support, sparking the Protestant movement and the Reformation.

During the Thirty Years' War (1618–48) between Protestants and Catholics, Germany became the battlefield for the great powers of Europe, losing over a third of its population and many of its towns and cities. The 1648 Peace of Westphalia established the rights of both faiths in Germany but also sealed the country's political division.

In the 18th century the Kingdom of Prussia began expanding eastwards at the expense of Poland, Lithuania and Russia. Even Napoleon never managed to subdue Prussia, which became the centre of German resistance. After Napoleon's downfall, Austria took control of Germany. But the well-oiled Prussian civil and military machine eventually smashed this arrangement. In 1866 Otto von Bismarck (the Iron Chancellor) annexed northern Germany. Bismarck succeeded in uniting all Germany by 1871 under King Wilhem I, who became *Kaiser* (emperor).

Germany's rapid growth led to mounting tensions with England, Russia and France. When war broke out in 1914, only a weakened Austria-Hungary was its ally. Gruelling trench warfare on two fronts sapped the nation, and by late 1918 Germany sued for peace. A new republic, which became known as the Weimar Republic, was proclaimed. The government was seriously hampered by the 1919 Treaty of Versailles, which chopped huge areas off Germany and also imposed impossible reparation payments. Subsequent hyperinflation and miserable economic conditions paved the way for Adolf Hitler.

GERMANY
0
50
100km
0
30
60mi
DENMARK
SWEDEN
COPENHAGEN
Bornholm
BALTIC SEA
NORTH SEA
Sylt Island
Amrum Island
North Frisian Islands
East Frisian Islands
Rügen Island
Sassnitz
Binz
Schleswig
Heide
Kiel
SCHLESWIG-HÖLSTEIN
Stralsund
Warnemünde
Rostock
Wismar
Lübeck
Cuxhaven
Wilhelmshaven
Hamburg
HAMBURG
Schwerin
MECKLENBURG-WESTERN POMERANIA
A24
A241
A19
A1
A7
Bremen
BREMEN
NETHERLANDS
Elbe River
A11
POLAND
A31
LOWER SAXONY
BRANDENBURG
Oder
SAXONY-ANHALT
A1
A10
BERLIN
Frankfurt/Oder
Hanover
Potsdam
BERLIN
A12
A2
A2
River
A30
Hameln
Magdeburg
A13
Badenwerder
Goslar
Lutherstadt Wittenberg
NORTH RHINE-WESTPHALIA
Wernigerode
Clausthal-Zellerfeld
Quedlinburg
Dessau
Rhine
A15
A44
A9
Dortmund
Göttingen
A13
Halle
A7
Nordhausen
Leipzig
Kassel
THURINGIA
Meissen
A4
Görlitz
Düsseldorf
Naumburg
Dresden
Erfurt
Eisenach
Weimar
Cologne
A4
A4
Aachen
A45
Marburg
Bonn
SAXONY
A5
61
A9
BELGIUM
HESSE
River
A72
Cochem
Koblenz
Frankfurt/Main
A3
A48
St Goau
A7
Wiesbaden
PRAGUE
RHINELAND-PALATINATE
Bacharach
Bullay
Hanau
Rüdosheim
Mainz
LUXEMBOURG
Trier
Würzburg
Bamberg
Marktredwitz
A3
River
CZECH REPUBLIC
Moselle
SAARLAND
Mannheim
Heidelberg
Nuremberg
Saarbrücken
Rothenburg ob der Tauber
Steinach
Ansbach
BAVARIA
A6
Dinkelsbühl
A9
Regensburg
Karlsruhe
A3
Rhine River
Baden-Baden
Stuttgart
Nördlingen
Danube
Ingolstadt
River
Passau
A8
Freudenstadt
A92
A5
BADEN-WÜRTTEMBERG
Triberg
Ulm
Augsburg
Schramberg
FRANCE
Furtwangen
A81
A7
Munich
AUSTRIA
Freiburg
Donaueschingen
Titisee
A95
A8
Constance
Lake Constance
Lindau
Füssen
Berchtesgaden
Garmisch-Partenkirchen
Oberstdorf
LIECHTENSTEIN
SWITZERLAND

Hitler's Nazi Party staged an abortive coup in 1923, landing Hitler in prison (where he wrote *Mein Kampf*). Meanwhile, the Nazis took advantage of economic depression and gained political dominance. Out of prison, Hitler was appointed chancellor and assumed control as *Führer* (leader). He reoccupied the Rhineland in 1936 and in 1938 annexed Austria and parts of Czechoslovakia. Racism in Germany was growing, and laws were enacted depriving Jews and Roma (Gypsies) of citizenship and other rights. On 9 November 1938, the horror escalated into the *Reichspogromnacht* (also known as *Kristallnacht*), during which synagogues and Jewish cemeteries, property and businesses across Germany were desecrated, burnt or demolished.

In September 1939 Hitler attacked Poland, which led to war with Britain and France. Germany quickly invaded large parts of Europe, but after 1942 began to suffer heavy losses. Massive bombing reduced Germany's cities to rubble, and the country lost 10% of its population. Meanwhile, 'concentration camps' exterminated some six million Jews and a million more Roma, communists, homosexuals and others in what is now known as the Holocaust, history's first 'assembly-line' genocide. Germany surrendered in May 1945, soon after Hitler's suicide. The Allies (the USSR, USA, the UK and Commonwealth countries, China, Poland and France) redrew German borders, further shrinking it. Some 6.5 million ethnic Germans migrated or were expelled to Germany from Eastern Europe, where they had lived for centuries. Germany was divided into four occupation zones, and Berlin was occupied jointly by the four victors.

In the Soviet zone, the communists began a rapid nationalisation of industry. In June 1948 the Soviet Union stopped all land traffic between Germany's western zones and Berlin, which forced the Western allies to mount the Berlin Airlift, to bring supplies to West Berlin by plane until the Soviets lifted the blockade in May 1949. In September the Federal Republic of Germany (FRG) was created out of the three western zones; in response, the communist German Democratic Republic (GDR) was founded in the Soviet zone, with (East) Berlin as its capital.

As the West's bulwark against communism, the FRG received massive injections of US capital. Meanwhile, the GDR had to pay US$10 billion in war reparations to the Soviet Union and rebuild itself from scratch. To prevent emigration of skilled workers, in 1961 the GDR built a wall around West Berlin and sealed its border with the FRG.

Events in 1989 rapidly overtook the stodgy East German government. As mass demonstrations mounted, the Politburo permitted direct travel to the west on 9 November 1989. This was mistakenly interpreted as the immediate opening of all borders with West Germany, resulting in thousands of people streaming past stunned guards that same night. Millions followed in the next few days, and dismantling of the Berlin Wall began soon thereafter. In 1990 East Germans voted clearly for reunification. The wartime Allies ended the post-war system of occupation zones, and the countries were unified on 3 October 1990.

It's believed that another 10 years will be necessary to achieve parity between the two Germanys. Unemployment in some eastern states is above 20%, occasionally there have been violent attacks on foreigners and the German 'economic miracle' seems to be losing steam. Still, Germany is more confident and democratic than it was under division, and it has assumed a more assertive role in world affairs, strongly bound to the EU but also focusing attention on the East.

GEOGRAPHY

Germany covers 356,866 sq km and can be divided from north to south into several geographical regions, including the Northern Lowlands, the Central Uplands (Germany's heartland), the Alpine Foothills and the Alps.

CLIMATE

German weather can be variable. The most reliable weather is from May to October. Shoulder periods (late March to May and September to October) can bring fewer tourists and surprisingly pleasant weather. Camping season is May to September.

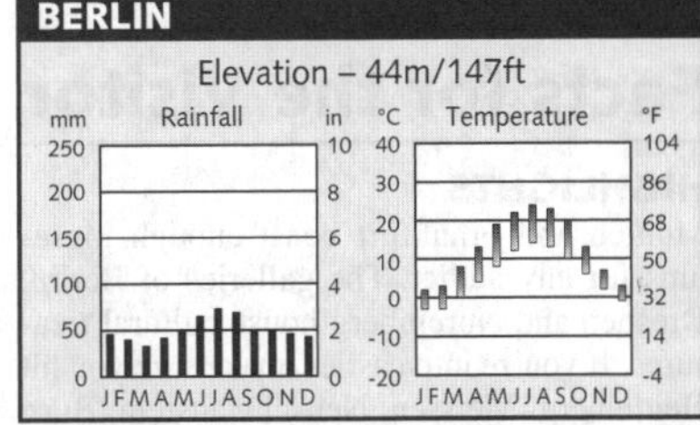

GOVERNMENT & POLITICS

Germany is a bicameral parliamentary democracy. The Bundesländer (states) exert influence through the *Bundesrat* (upper house), while the *Bundestag* (lower house) is elected by direct universal suffrage.

In the 2002 elections, Social Democrat Gerhard Schröder, in coalition with the Greens, narrowly retained power in the closest election since WWII.

POPULATION & PEOPLE

With 83 million people, Germany is the most populous country in Europe after Russia. In effect, immigration compensates for the very low birth rate among the established German population. Over seven million foreigners now live in Germany, most in the west.

SOCIETY & CONDUCT

Far from the common strict and humourless reputation, Germans are on the whole relaxed, personable and interested in enjoying life. But manners remain important. When making a phone call, you'll find people more helpful if you first introduce yourself by name. Germans sometimes shake hands when greeting or leaving. Hugging and cheek kissing is common between males and females who know one another.

The Holocaust and WWII should be discussed with tact and understanding in Germany. The Germans understandably take great offence at the presumption that fascist ideas are somehow part of or even compatible with their national culture.

LANGUAGE

The official language, *Hochdeutsch* (High German), is universally understood. English is widely understood by young or educated Germans, but not out of the big cities, especially in eastern Germany. See the Language chapter at the back of the book for pronunciation guidelines and useful words and phrases.

Facts for the Visitor

HIGHLIGHTS

Munich and Frankfurt boast enough museums for any addict. The galleries of Berlin, Dresden and Nuremberg house cultural treasures. If you're into castles, make sure you hit Heidelberg, Meissen, Neuschwanstein, Burg Rheinfels on the Rhine River, Burg Eltz on the Moselle, the medieval Königstein and Wartburg Castles, Renaissance Wittenberg Castle, baroque Schloss Moritzburg and romantic Wernigerode Castle. Captivating historical towns include Goslar and Regensburg. Lübeck is one of Europe's true gems.

Oh – you wanted to party? The Big Three towns in which to burn the midnight oil, and beyond, are Berlin, Munich and Hamburg.

PLANNING

Germany is best visited from April to October. If you don't mind slushy, bitterly cold and bleak weather, a winter visit has its charms; large cities and the Baltic coast can be blessedly free of tourists. Central Uplands regions, like the Harz Mountains and Black Forest, are good places to hike and relax year-round, especially at higher altitudes.

TOURIST OFFICES

Before your trip you might consult the **German National Tourist Office** *(Deutsche Zentrale für Tourismus, DZT; ☎ 069-97 46 40, fax 75 19 03; Ⓦ www.visits-to-Germany.com; Beethovenstrasse 69, 60325 Frankfurt/Main)*. For local information, head for the *Verkehrsamt* (tourist office) or *Kurverwaltung* (resort administration), listed for each town. German National Tourist Office representatives abroad include the following:

Australia & New Zealand (☎ 02-9267 8148, fax 9267 9035, ⓔ gnto@germany.org.au) P.O. Box A 980, Sydney, NSW 1235
Canada (☎ 416-968 1570, fax 968 1986, ⓔ gnto@aol.com) 175 Bloor St East, North Tower, 6th Floor, Toronto, Ont M4W 3R8
South Africa (☎ 011-643 1615, fax 484 2750) c/o Lufthansa Airlines, PO Box 10883, Johannesburg 2000
UK (☎ 020-7317 09 08, fax 7495 61 29) PO Box 2695, London W1A 3TN
USA (☎ 212-661 7200, fax 661 7174, ⓔ gntony@aol.com) 122 East 42nd St, 52nd floor, New York, NY 10168-0072

Other offices are in Amsterdam, Brussels, Copenhagen, Helsinki, Hong Kong, Madrid, Milan, Moscow, Oslo, Paris, Stockholm, Tel Aviv, Tokyo, Vienna and Zürich.

VISAS

Americans, Australians, Britons, Canadians, Israelis, Japanese, New Zealanders and Singaporeans require no visa. Citizens of the EU and some other Western European countries can enter on an official identity card. Three months is the usual limit of stay; less for citizens of some developing countries.

EMBASSIES & CONSULATES

German Embassies & Consulates

Diplomatic representation abroad includes:

Australia (☎ 02-6270 1911, fax 6270 1951) 119 Empire Circuit, Yarralumla, ACT 2600
Canada (☎ 613-232 1101, fax 594 9330) 1 Waverley St, Ottawa, ON K2P 0T8
Ireland (☎ 01-269 3011, fax 269 3946) 31 Trimleston Ave, Booterstown, Dublin
New Zealand (☎ 04-473 6063, fax 473 6069) 90–92 Hobson St, Wellington
UK (☎ 020-7824 1300, fax 7824 1435) 23 Belgrave Square, London SW1X 8PZ
USA (☎ 202-298 4000, fax 298 4249) 4645 Reservoir Rd, NW Washington, DC 20007-1998

Embassies & Consulates in Germany

The area code for Berlin is ☎ 030.

Australia (☎ 880 08 80, fax 880 08 80 351) Friedrichstrasse 200, 10117 Berlin
Canada (☎ 20 31 20, fax 20 31 25 90) Friedrichstrasse 95, 10117 Berlin
Ireland (☎ 22 07 20, fax 22 07 22 99) Friedrichstrasse 200, 10117 Berlin
New Zealand (☎ 20 62 10, fax 20 62 11 14) Friedrichstrasse 60, 10117 Berlin
South Africa (☎ 82 52 711, fax 82 66 543) Friedrichstrasse 60, 10117 Berlin
UK (☎ 20 45 70) Wilhelmstrasse 70–71, 10117 Berlin
USA (☎ 238 51 74, fax 238 62 90 1) Neustädtische Kirchstrasse 4–5, 10117 Berlin

CUSTOMS

Most items you will need for personal use during a visit are duty-free. In Germany, the usual allowances apply to duty-free and duty-paid goods if you are coming from a non-EU country.

MONEY

In 2002 the euro replaced the beloved Deutschmark. See under Money in the Facts for the Visitor chapter for information about currency exchange rates.

Exchanging Money

The easiest places to change cash in Germany are banks or foreign-exchange counters at airports and train stations, particularly those of the Reisebank. Main banks in larger cities generally have money-changing machines for after-hours use, though they don't often give good rates. The Reisebank charges a flat €2.50 to change cash. Some local Sparkasse banks have good rates and low charges.

There are ATMs virtually everywhere in Germany; most accept Visa, MasterCard, American Express (AmEx), Eurocard and bankcards linked to the Plus and Cirrus networks. Typically, withdrawals over the counter against cards at major banks cost a flat €5 per transaction.

Travellers cheques can be cashed at any bank; the most widely accepted are AmEx, Thomas Cook and Barclays. A percentage commission (usually a minimum of €5) is charged by most banks on any travellers cheque, even those issued in euros. The Reisebank charges 1% or a minimum of €5 (€2.50 on amounts below €50) and €3.75 for AmEx. AmEx charges no commission on its own cheques.

Credit cards are especially useful for emergencies, although they are often not accepted by budget hotels and restaurants outside major cities. Most widely accepted are Eurocard (linked to Access and MasterCard), Visa and AmEx.

For emergencies, the Reisebank (Western Union) and Thomas Cook (MoneyGram) offer ready and fast international cash transfers through agent banks, but commissions are costly.

Costs

A tight budget can easily blow out in Germany. Minimise costs by staying in hostels or private rooms, eat midday restaurant specials or self-cater, and visit museums on free days. Campers can expect to pay around €7.50 per night, less if there are two of you. Add another €10 for self-catering expenses and a beer or two from the supermarket, and your food, drinks and accommodation costs will be around €17.50 per day. If travelling on a rail pass, but allowing for public transport costs and occasional expenses such as toiletries, €22.50 per day should be sufficient. Local public transit passes for tourists often offer discounts to museums and attractions.

Tipping & Bargaining

Apart from restaurants and taxis, tipping is not widespread in Germany. In restaurants, tip when you pay by stating a rounded-up figure or saying *es stimmt so* (that's the right amount). A tip of 10% is more than sufficient. Bargaining is usual only at flea markets.

Taxes & Refunds

Most German goods and services include *Mehrwertsteuer* (value-added tax or VAT) of 16% (7% for books and anything else involving copyright). Non-EU residents leaving the EU can have this tax refunded for any goods (not services) they buy.

POST & COMMUNICATIONS

Standard post office hours are 8am to 6pm Monday to Friday and to noon on Saturday. Many train station post offices stay open later or offer limited services outside these hours. Mail can be sent *Postlagernde* (poste restante) to the main post office in your city. There's no fee for collection, but German post offices will hold mail for two weeks only.

Most pay phones in Germany accept only phonecards, available for €6 and €25 at post offices and some news kiosks, tourist offices and banks.

To ring abroad from Germany, dial ☎ 00 followed by the country code, area code and number. Germany's country code is ☎ 49.

Home direct services for reverse-charge (collect) calls are only possible to some countries. The prefix is ☎ 0800 followed by the home number. For the USA dial ☎ 888 225 5388 (AT&T) or ☎ 888 00 13 (Sprint); for Canada ☎ 080 10 14; for Australia ☎ 080 00 61 (Telstra); for Britain dial ☎ 080 00 44.

For directory assistance within Germany call ☎ 11833 (☎ 11837 in English); both cost €1 for the first minute and €0.49 after that. International information is ☎ 11834 (€1.48/first minute, €0.97 after that).

Internet cafés exist in most large cities. Locations change frequently, so check at tourist offices. The price in an Internet café is anything from around €3 to €10 per hour. If you wish to plug in your own laptop, you'll need a telephone plug adapter.

DIGITAL RESOURCES

For up-to-date information about Germany on the Internet, try the German Information Centre website at Ⓦ www.germany-info.org. Most of the information is in English. Try Ⓦ www.visits-to-germany.com, which targets tourists. It's in English and has useful links. Individual cities and regions also have websites.

BOOKS

For a more detailed guide to the country, pick up a copy of Lonely Planet's *Germany*. Lonely Planet also publishes *Bavaria*, and *Berlin* and *Munich* city guides.

WOMEN TRAVELLERS

Women should not encounter particular difficulties, and most large cities have women-only organisations. If you are a victim of either harassment or violence, contact **Frauenhaus München** (*☎ 089-354 83 11, 24-hour service ☎ 089-35 48 30, Munich*) or **LARA – Krisen und Beratungszentrum für vergewaltigte Frauen** (*Crisis and Counselling Centre for Raped Women; ☎ 030-216 88 88*), in Berlin.

GAY & LESBIAN TRAVELLERS

Germans are generally fairly tolerant of homosexuality, but gays (who call themselves *Schwule*) and lesbians (*Lesben*) still don't enjoy quite the same social acceptance as in certain other northern European countries. Most progressive are the large cities, particularly Berlin and Frankfurt. The age of consent is 18 years. Larger cities have many gay and lesbian bars as well as other meeting places for homosexuals. The Berlin Pride festival is held in June. Other Pride festivals are held in Bielefeld, Bochum, Hamburg, Mannheim and Wurzburg in June, and in July in Cologne.

DISABLED TRAVELLERS

Germany caters reasonably well to the needs of *Behinderte* (disabled) travellers, with access ramps for wheelchairs or lifts where necessary in most public buildings, including toilets, train stations, museums, theatres and cinemas. Assistance is usually required when boarding public transport. On Deutsche Bahn distance services, you can arrange this when buying your ticket.

DANGERS & ANNOYANCES

Although the usual cautions should be taken, theft and other crimes against travellers are relatively rare in Germany. In the event of problems, the police are helpful and efficient.

Emergencies

Nationwide emergency numbers are ☎ 110 for police and ☎ 112 for fire brigade and ambulance.

Africans, Asians and southern Europeans may encounter racial prejudice, especially in eastern Germany. The animosity is directed against immigrants, not tourists.

LEGAL MATTERS

Police in Germany are well trained and usually treat tourists with respect. You are required by law to prove your identity if asked by the police, so always carry your passport, or an identity card if you're an EU citizen.

BUSINESS HOURS

Shops are generally open from 8am or 9am to 6pm Monday to Friday and possibly a few hours on weekends. Banking hours are generally 8.30am to 1pm and 2.30pm to 4pm Monday to Friday, but many banks remain open all day, and until 5.30pm on Thursday. Government offices close for the weekend at 1pm or 3pm on Friday. Museums are generally closed on Monday. Restaurants usually open 11am to midnight (the kitchen often closes at 10pm), often closing from 3pm to 6pm. All shops and banks are closed on public holidays.

PUBLIC HOLIDAYS & SPECIAL EVENTS

Public holidays include New Year's Day; Good Friday to Easter Monday; 1 May (Labour Day); Whit Monday, Ascension Day, Pentecost, Corpus Christi (10 days after Pentecost); 3 October (Day of German Unity); 1 November (All Saints' Day); 18 November (Day of Prayer and Repentance); and usually Christmas Eve to the day after Christmas.

There are many festivals, fairs and cultural events throughout the year. Some famous and worthwhile ones are:

January

Carnival season (Shrovetide, known as 'Fasching') Many carnival events begin in large cities, most notably Cologne, Munich, Düsseldorf and Mainz; the partying peaks just before Ash Wednesday.

February

International Toy Fair Held in Nuremberg
International Film Festival Held in Berlin

March

Frankfurt Music Fair and **Frankfurt Jazz Fair**
Thuringian Bach Festival
Spring Fairs Held throughout Germany

April

Stuttgart Jazz Festival
Munich Ballet Days
Mannheim May Fair
Walpurgisnacht Festivals Held the night before May Day in the Harz Mountains

May

International Mime Festival Held in Stuttgart
Red Wine Festival Held in Rüdesheim
Dresden International Dixieland Jazz Festival
Dresden Music Festival Held in last week of May into first week of June

June

Händel Festival Held in Halle
Sailing regatta Held in Kiel
Munich Film Festival
International Theatre Festival Held in Freiburg

July

Folk festivals Held throughout Germany
Berlin Love Parade
Munich Opera Festival
Richard Wagner Festival Held in Bayreuth
German-American Folk Festival Held in Berlin
Kulmbach Beer Festival
International Music Seminar Held in Weimar

August

Heidelberg Castle Festival
Wine festivals Held throughout the Rhineland area

September-October

Oktoberfest Held in Munich
Berlin Festival of Music & Drama

October

Frankfurt Book Fair
Bremen Freimarkt
Gewandhaus Festival Held in Leipzig
Berlin Jazzfest

November

St Martin's Festival Held throughout Rhineland and Bavaria

December

Christmas fairs Held throughout Germany, most famously in Munich, Nuremberg, Berlin, Essen and Heidelberg

ACTIVITIES

Germany is ideal for hiking and mountaineering. Well-marked trails crisscross the country, especially popular areas like the Black Forest, the Harz Mountains, the so-called Saxon Switzerland area and the Thuringian Forest. The Bavarian Alps are the centre of mountaineering in Germany. Good sources of information on hiking and mountaineering are

Verband Deutscher Gebirgs-und Wandervereine *(Federation of German Hiking Clubs; ☎ 0561-93 87 30, fax 938 73 10; Ⓦ www.wanderverband.de; Wilhelmshöher Allee 157-9, 34121 Kassel)* and **Deutscher Alpenverein** *(German Alpine Club; ☎ 089-14 00 30, fax 140 03 98; Ⓦ www.alpenverein.de; Von-Kahr-Strasse 2-4, 80997 Munich)*.

The Bavarian Alps are the most extensive area for winter sports. Cross-country skiing is also good in the Black Forest and Harz Mountains. Ski equipment starts at around €12 per day; daily ski-lift passes start at around €13. Local tourist offices are the best sources of information.

Eastern Germany has much to offer cyclists in the way of lightly travelled back roads, especially in the flat and less-populated north. There's also an extensive cycling trail along the Elbe River. Islands such as Amrum and Rügen are also good for cycling.

ACCOMMODATION

Germany's accommodation is well organised, though some cities are short on budget hotels; private rooms are one option in such situations. Accommodation usually includes breakfast. Look for signs saying *Zimmer frei* (rooms available) or *Fremdenzimmer* (tourist rooms) in house or shop windows. In nearly every town, tourist offices offer a room-finding service *(Zimmervermittlung)*, which costs from nothing to €3. If you're looking for rooms in private homes, this is the way to go. **TIBS** *(☎ 0761-88 58 10, fax 885 81 19; ⓔ email@TIBS.de)* handles accommodation bookings throughout Germany.

GERMANY

Camping

There are over 2000 organised camping grounds in Germany . Most are open April to September, but several hundred stay open year-round. Facilities range from primitive to overequipped. In eastern Germany camping grounds often rent out small bungalows. Get permission before camping on private property. The best source of information is the **Deutscher Camping Club** *(☎ 089-380 14 20, fax 33 47 37; Ⓦ www.camping-club.de; Mandlstrasse 28, 80802 Munich)*.

Hostels

The **Deutsches Jugendherbergswerk** *(DJH; ☎ 05231-740 10, fax 05231-74 01 49; DJH Service GmbH, 32754 Detmold)* coordinates all Hostelling International (HI) hostels in Germany. Almost all German hostels are open all year. Guests must be members of an HI-affiliated organisation or join the DJH when checking in. The annual fee is €10/17.50 for juniors/seniors (above/below 26 years of age). A dorm bed costs €12 to €20 for juniors and €15 to €23 for seniors. If you don't have a hostel-approved sleeping sheet, it usually costs from €2.50 to €3.50 to hire one (some hostels insist you hire one anyway). Breakfast is always included.

In practice prior booking or arrival determines who gets rooms. In Bavaria, the strict maximum age is 26. Most hostels have a curfew, which may be as early as 10pm in small towns. The curfew is rarely before 11pm in large cities; several have no curfew.

The DJH's *Jugendgästehäuser* (youth guesthouses) offer some better facilities, freer hours and two-bed to four-bed dormitory rooms from €12.50 to €22.50 per person, including sleeping sheet.

Pensions, Guesthouses & Hotels

Pensions offer the basics of hotel comfort without asking hotel prices. Many are private homes, often a bit out of the centre of town. Some proprietors are a little sensitive about who they take in and others are nervous about telephone bookings – you may have to give a time of arrival and stick to it (many visitors have lost rooms by turning up late). If you're having difficulty finding a cheap place to sleep, head for the tourist office and use the room-finding service (see earlier in this section).

Cheap hotel rooms are a bit hard to find during summer, but there is usually not much seasonal price variation. The cheapest hotels have rooms with shared toilets (and showers) in the corridor. Average budget prices are €30 for a single and €45 for a double (without bathroom). Rates usually include breakfast.

FOOD & DRINKS

This is truly a meat-and-potatoes kind of country, although vegetarians will usually find suitable restaurants or fast-food places. Students can often eat cheaply at *mensas* (university cafeterias).

Wurst (sausage), in its hundreds of forms, is by far the most universal main dish. Regional favourites include *Bratwurst* (spiced sausage), *Weisswurst* (veal sausage) and *Blutwurst* (blood sausage). Other popular main dishes include *Rippenspeer* (spare ribs), *Rotwurst* (black pudding), *gegrilltes Fleisch* or *Rostbrätl* (grilled meat), *Putenbrust* (turkey breast) and many forms of *Schnitzel* (breaded pork or veal cutlet). Many restaurants serve at least one fish dish; vegetarian dishes may be harder to find. Potatoes feature prominently in German meals, either *Bratkartoffeln* (fried), *Kartoffelpüree* (mashed), Swiss *Rösti* (grated then fried), or *Pommes Frites* (french fries). Germans are keen on rich desserts. Popular choices are the *Schwarzwälder Kirschtorte* (Black Forest cherry cake), as well as endless varieties of *Apfeltasche* (apple pastry). In the north you're likely to find berry *mus*, which is a sort of compote.

The most popular nonalcoholic drinks are mineral water and soft drinks, coffee and fruit or black tea. Order water *ohne Kohlensäure* if you're bothered by fizz.

Beer is a cultural phenomenon that must be adequately explored. The beer is excellent and relatively cheap. Beer-drinking has its own vocabulary. *Vollbier* is 4% alcohol by volume, *Export* is 5% and *Bockbier* is 6%. *Helles Bier* is light, while *dunkles Bier* is dark. Export is similar to, but much better than, typical international brews, while the *Pils* is more bitter. *Alt* is darker and more full-bodied. A speciality is *Weizenbier*, which is made with wheat instead of barley malt and served in a tall, half-litre glass with a slice of lemon.

German wines are exported around the world, and for good reason. They are fairly inexpensive and typically white, light and intensely fruity. The Rhine and Moselle Valleys are classic wine-growing regions.

ENTERTAINMENT

The standard of theatre performances, concerts and operas is among the highest in Europe. Berlin is unrivalled when it comes to concerts and theatre and Dresden is famed for its opera. Tickets can usually be purchased at short notice from tourist offices and directly from box offices.

The variety of pubs is enormous, ranging from vaulted-cellar bars through to theme pubs, Irish pubs, historic student pubs and clubs offering music or performances. Beer gardens are especially common in the south.

Large cities throb with club and disco sounds. Berlin is a world techno capital, but you'll find a variety of lively clubs in most major cities.

Getting There & Away

AIR

The main arrival and departure points in Germany are Frankfurt, Munich, Düsseldorf and Berlin. Flights to Frankfurt are usually cheaper than to other German cities.

From the US, Lufthansa Airlines, United Airlines, Air Canada, Delta Air Lines and Singapore Airlines have the most frequent flights. You can often get the best fare by flying with another European carrier and changing planes for Germany at their home-country hub. Asian carriers offer the cheapest – but often the most indirect – flights from Australia and New Zealand.

Lufthansa has many flights to the Eastern European nations, but the region's national carriers are cheaper.

LAND

Bus

It's generally cheaper to get to/from Germany by bus than by train or plane, but you trade price for speed. Eurolines is a consortium of national bus companies operating throughout the continent. Some sample one-way fares and travel times for routes include:

London-Frankfurt	€72	14¼ hours
Amsterdam-Frankfurt	€36	6 hours
Paris-Hamburg	€55	12½ hours
Paris-Cologne	€34	7¼ hours
Prague-Berlin	€35	6½ hours
Barcelona-Frankfurt	€85	20 hours

Eurolines has a youth fare for those aged under 26 that saves around 10%. Tickets can be bought in Germany at most train stations. For information (but not bookings), contact **Deutsche-Touring GmbH** (*☎ 069-79 03 50, fax 790 32 19;* W *www.deutsche-touring.com; Am Römerhof 17, 60486 Frankfurt/Main*).

Train

Trains are a lot more comfortable (albeit more expensive) than buses. Long-distance trains between major German cities and other countries are called EuroCity (EC) trains. The main German hubs with the best connections to/from major European cities are Hamburg (Scandinavia); Cologne (France,

Belgium and the Netherlands, with Eurostar connections from Brussels or Paris going on to London); Munich (southern and southeastern Europe); and Berlin (Eastern Europe). Frankfurt-am-Main has the widest range of, but not always the quickest, international connections.

Generally the longer international routes are served by at least one day train and often a night train as well. Many night trains only carry sleeping cars, but a bunk is more comfortable than sitting up in a compartment and only adds from €21/14 to the cost of a 2nd-class ticket in four/six-berth compartments.

Car & Motorcycle

Germany is served by an excellent highway system. If you're coming from the UK, the quickest option is via the Channel Tunnel. Ferries take longer but are cheaper. Choices include taking a hovercraft from Dover, Folkestone or Ramsgate to Calais in France. You can be in Germany three hours after the ferry docks.

You must have third-party insurance to enter Germany with a car or motorcycle.

Hitching & Ride Services

Lonely Planet does not recommend hitching, but should you decide to try it you may encounter delays getting to Germany via the main highways.

Aside from hitching, the cheapest way to get to Germany from elsewhere in Europe is as a paying passenger in a private car. Such rides are arranged by *Mitfahrzentrale* (ride-sharing agencies) in many German cities. You pay a reservation fee to the agency and a share of petrol and costs to the driver. Local tourist offices can direct you to local agencies, or call the city area code and ☎ 194 40 in large German cities.

SEA

If you're heading to or from Scandinavia or the UK, the German port options are Hamburg, Lübeck, Rostock, Sassnitz, and Kiel. In eastern Germany, there are five ferries in each direction daily year-round between Trelleborg (Sweden) and Sassnitz near Stralsund (see the Rügen Island section later in this chapter for more information). There are daily services between Kiel and Gothenburg (Sweden) and Oslo. More ferries run to other destinations in Scandinavia, including Helsinki.

Getting Around

BUS

The bus network functions primarily in support of the train network, going where trains don't. Bus stations or stops are usually near the train station in any town. Schedule and route information is usually posted. Consider buses when you want to cut across two train lines and avoid long train rides to and from a transfer point. A good example of this is in the Alps, where the best way to follow the peaks is by bus.

Deutsche Bahn (DB) agents have information on certain key regional services, otherwise check with tourist offices. **Eurolines** operates within Germany as Deutsche-Touring GmbH, a subsidiary of the German Federal Railways (Deutsche Bahn). Eurolines services include the Romantic and Castle Roads buses in southern Germany, as well as organised bus tours of Germany lasting a week or more. See the Romantic Road section later in this chapter for details, or contact **Deutsche-Touring GmbH** *(☎ 069-79 03 50; W www.deutsche-touring.com)*, in Frankfurt/Main.

TRAIN

Operated almost entirely by the **Deutsche Bahn** *(DB; W www.bahn.de)*, the German train system is arguably the best in Europe. Information is on its website.

Schedules are integrated throughout the country so that connections between trains are tight, often only five minutes. This means, of course, that when a train is late connections are missed. Put some slack in your itinerary so you won't miss a connection and be stranded.

German trains fall into specific classifications; *Zuschlag* (supplements) for faster trains are built into fares. From fastest to slowest, these include InterCityExpress (ICE) trains, InterCity (IC) or EuroCity (EC) trains, InterRegio (IR) trains, RegionalExpress (RE) trains, StadtExpress (SE) trains, RegionalBahn (RB) trains and S-Bahn trains (not to be confused with U-Bahns, which are run by local authorities who don't honour rail passes). EN, ICN and D trains are generally night trains.

It's always better to buy your ticket before boarding; buying from a conductor carries a penalty (€1.50 to €4.50). Ticket agents cheerfully accept credit cards, as do most machines. During peak travel periods, a seat reservation (€2.50) on a long-distance train can mean the difference between squatting near the toilet or relaxing in your own seat. If you don't have a reservation, try the end carriages.

A host of special train fares offered by DB allow you to cut costs for journeys. Most ticket agents are quite willing to help you find the cheapest options for your intended trip. For schedule and fare information (available in English), you can call ☎ 01805-99 66 33 from anywhere in Germany (€0.13/minute).

Travel agents outside Germany sell German Rail Passes valid for unlimited travel on all DB trains for a given number of days within a 30-day period. Eurail and Inter-Rail passes are also valid in Germany.

CAR & MOTORCYCLE

Although having a vehicle can be a great way to tour the country, it's expensive. For information, contact Munich-based **Allgemeiner Deutscher Automobil Club** *(ADAC; ☎ 089-767 60, fax 76 76 28 01)*; it has offices in all major cities. Call the **ADAC road patrol** *(☎ 0180-222 22 22)* if your car breaks down.

BICYCLE

Radwandern (bicycle touring) is very popular in Germany. Favoured routes include along the Rhine, Moselle, Elbe and Danube Rivers and around the Lake Constance area. Cycling is strictly *verboten* (forbidden) on autobahns. There are well-equipped cycling shops in almost every town, and a fairly active market for used touring bikes. Simple three-gear bicycles can be hired from around €8/32 per day/week, and more robust mountain bikes from €10/48. The DB publishes *Bahn&Bike*, an excellent handbook covering bike rental and repair shops, routes, maps and other resources.

A separate ticket must be purchased whenever you carry your bike on most trains (generally €3-6). Most trains (excluding ICEs) have a 2nd-class carriage at one end with a bicycle compartment.

The central office for the main cycling organisation in Gemany is the **Allgemeiner Deutscher Fahrrad Club** *(ADFC; ☎ 0421-34 62 90, fax 346 29 50; Ⓦ www.adfc.de)* in Bremen.

BOAT

Boats are most likely to be used for basic transport when travelling to or between the Frisian Islands, although tours along the Rhine and Moselle Rivers are also popular.

LOCAL TRANSPORT

Local transport is excellent within big cities and small towns, and is generally based on buses, Strassenbahn (trams), S-Bahn and/or U-Bahn (underground train system). The systems integrate all forms of transit; fares are determined by the zones or the time travelled, or sometimes both. Multiticket strips or day passes are generally available and offer better value than single-ride tickets.

In some cases you will have to validate your ticket in a little time-stamp machine on the platform or once aboard. The fine for not having a ticket is a non-negotiable €30.

Berlin

☎ 030 • pop 3.45 million

Berlin has more to offer visitors than almost any city in Europe: bustling pubs; peerless cultural life; worldly wise, tolerant attitude and indomitable spirit. No other city has been so dramatically split (then reintegrated so completely and quickly). The eastern neighbourhoods near the wall are now centres of artistic and cultural activity, although some outlying areas remain as bleak as ever.

The centre of 19th-century Prussian military and industrial might, this great city reached maturity in the 1920s, only to be bombed into rubble in WWII. After hibernating for decades, Berlin is now reassuming its role as the heart of Germany. It's an exciting time to visit Berlin, once again the nation's capital and one of Europe's most dynamic cities.

Orientation

Berlin sits in the middle of the region known from medieval times as the Mark and is surrounded by the state of Brandenburg. Roughly one-third of the city's municipal area is made up of parks, forests, lakes and rivers. There are more trees here than in Paris and more bridges than in Venice. Much of the natural beauty of rolling hills and quiet shorelines is in the southeast and southwest of the city.

The Spree River winds across the city for over 30km, from the Grosser Müggelsee in the east to Spandau in the west. North and south of Spandau, the Havel River widens into a series of lakes from Tegel to Potsdam. A network of canals links the waterways to the Oder River.

Most travellers visit only eight of the 23 *Bezirken* (the administrative districts) within

GERMANY

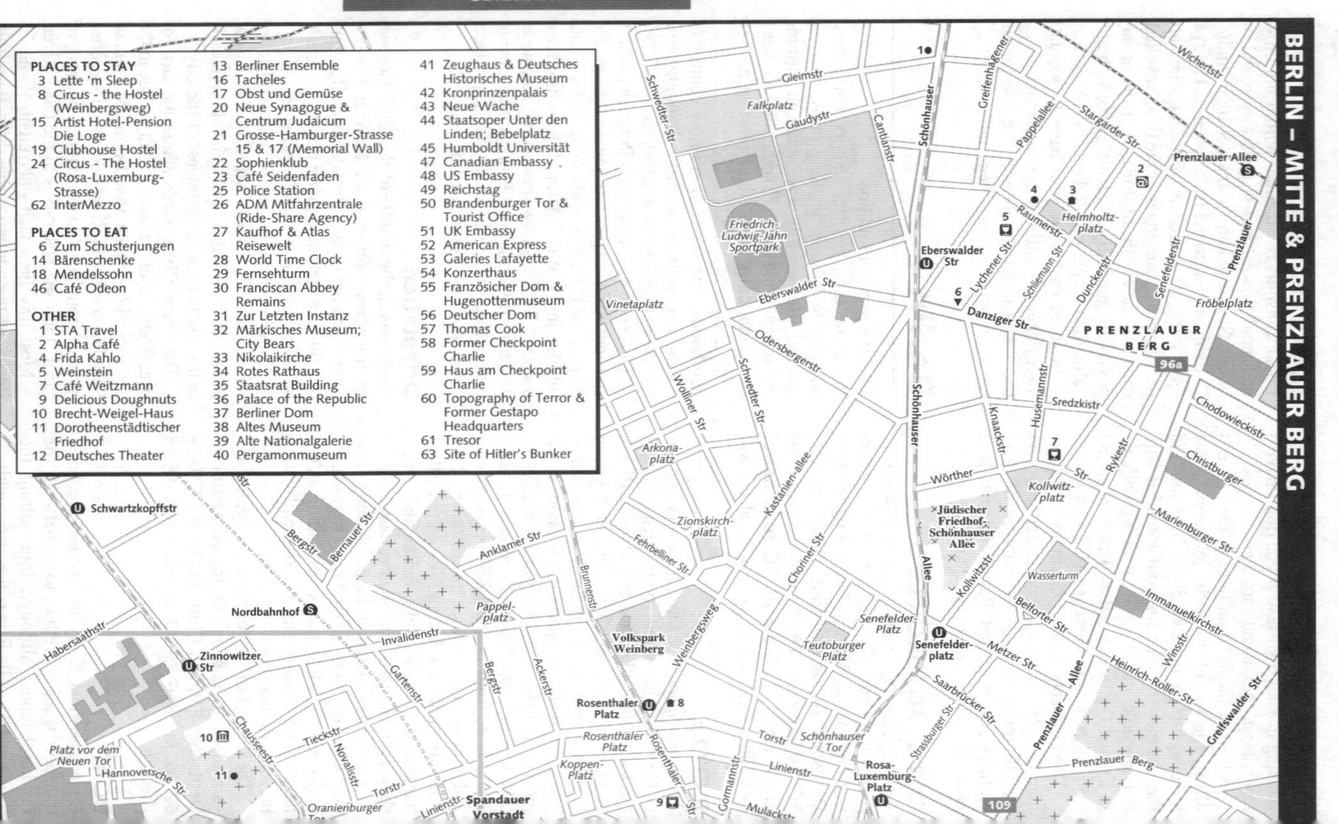
BERLIN – MITTE & PRENZLAUER BERG
PLACES TO STAY
3 Lette 'm Sleep
8 Circus - the Hostel (Weinbergsweg)
15 Artist Hotel-Pension Die Loge
19 Clubhouse Hostel
24 Circus - The Hostel (Rosa-Luxemburg-Strasse)
62 InterMezzo
PLACES TO EAT
6 Zum Schusterjungen
14 Bärenschenke
18 Mendelssohn
46 Café Odeon
OTHER
1 STA Travel
2 Alpha Café
4 Frida Kahlo
5 Weinstein
7 Café Weitzmann
9 Delicious Doughnuts
10 Brecht-Weigel-Haus
11 Dorotheenstädtischer Friedhof
12 Deutsches Theater
13 Berliner Ensemble
16 Tacheles
17 Obst und Gemüse
20 Neue Synagogue & Centrum Judaicum
21 Grosse-Hamburger-Strasse 15 & 17 (Memorial Wall)
22 Sophienklub
23 Café Seidenfaden
25 Police Station
26 ADM Mitfahrzentrale (Ride-Share Agency)
27 Kaufhof & Atlas Reisewelt
28 World Time Clock
29 Fernsehturm
30 Franciscan Abbey Remains
31 Zur Letzten Instanz
32 Märkisches Museum; City Bears
33 Nikolaikirche
34 Rotes Rathaus
35 Staatsrat Building
36 Palace of the Republic
37 Berliner Dom
38 Altes Museum
39 Alte Nationalgalerie
40 Pergamonmuseum
41 Zeughaus & Deutsches Historisches Museum
42 Kronprinzenpalais
43 Neue Wache
44 Staatsoper Unter den Linden; Bebelplatz
45 Humboldt Universität
47 Canadian Embassy
48 US Embassy
49 Reichstag
50 Brandenburger Tor & Tourist Office
51 UK Embassy
52 American Express
53 Galeries Lafayette
54 Konzerthaus
55 Französicher Dom & Hugenottenmuseum
56 Deutscher Dom
57 Thomas Cook
58 Former Checkpoint Charlie
59 Haus am Checkpoint Charlie
60 Topography of Terror & Former Gestapo Headquarters
61 Tresor
63 Site of Hitler's Bunker
PRENZLAUER BERG
Prenzlauer Allee
Schönhauser Allee
Eberswalder Str
Danziger Str
Senefelderplatz
Friedrich-Ludwig-Jahn Sportpark
Jüdischer Friedhof Schönhauser Allee
Kollwitzplatz
Helmholtzplatz
Teutoburger Platz
Zionskirchplatz
Arkonaplatz
Vinetaplatz
Falkplatz
Volkspark Weinberg
Rosenthaler Platz
Rosa-Luxemburg-Platz
Zinnowitzer Str
Nordbahnhof
Schwartzkopffstr
Spandauer Vorstadt
Platz vor dem Neuen Tor
Kastanienallee
Schwedter Str
Brunnenstr
Bernauer Str
Chausseestr
Invalidenstr
Torstr
Greifswalder Str
96a
109

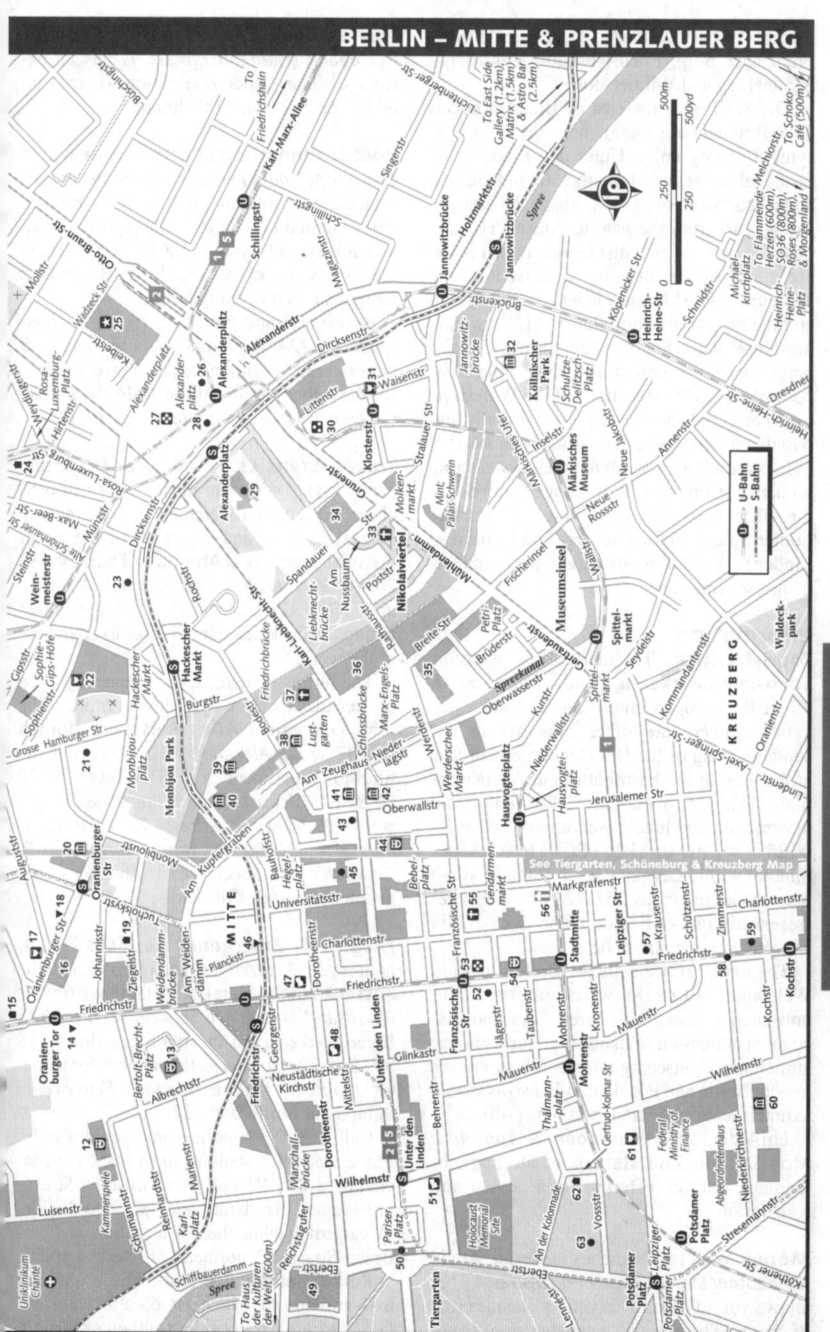

BERLIN – MITTE & PRENZLAUER BERG
To Friedrichshain
Karl-Marx-Allee
Otto-Braun-Str
Mollstr
Wadzeck Str
Keibelstr
Schillingstr
Singerstr
Magazinstr
Lichtenberger Str
To East Side Gallery (1.2km), Matrix (1.5km) & Astro Bar (2.5km)
Holzmarktstr
Jannowitzbrücke
Spree
Alexanderplatz
Alexanderstr
Dircksenstr
Littenstr
Waisenstr
Klosterstr
Grunerstr
Stralauer Str
Brückenstr
Köllnischer Park
Schultze-Delitzsch-Platz
Heinrich-Heine-Str
Köpenicker Str
Schmidstr
Michael-kirchplatz
Heinrich-Heine-Platz
To Flammende Herzen (600m), SO36 (800m), Roses (800m) & Morgenland
To Schoko-Café (500m)
Melchiorstr
Dresdner
Rosa-Luxemburg-Platz
Rosa-Luxemburg-Str
Weydingerstr
Hirtenstr
Max-Beer-Str
Alte Schönhauser Str
Münzstr
Steinstr
Weinmeisterstr
Rochstr
Spandauer Str
Karl-Liebknecht-Str
Liebknecht-brücke
Am Nussbaum
Poststr
Rathausstr
Nikolaiviertel
Molkenmarkt
Mint; Palais Schwerin
Mühlendamm
Märkisches Ufer
Inselstr
Märkisches Museum
Neue Jakobstr
Annenstr
Neue Rossstr
Wallstr
Fischerinsel
Museumsinsel
U-Bahn
S-Bahn
Gipsstr
Sophie-Gips-Höfe
Sophienstr
Grosse Hamburger Str
Hackescher Markt
Burgstr
Friedrichbrücke
Bodestr
Lustgarten
Schlossbrücke
Marx-Engels-Platz
Breite Str
Brüderstr
Petri-Platz
Gertraudenstr
Spreekanal
Oberwasserstr
Kurstr
Spittelmarkt
Seydelstr
Kommandantenstr
Axel-Springer-Str
KREUZBERG
Waldeckpark
Oranienstr
Lindenstr
Monbijouplatz
Monbijou Park
Am Zeughaus
Niederlagstr
Werderstr
Werderscher Markt
Niederwallstr
Hausvogteiplatz
Jerusalemer Str
Oberwallstr
Monbijoustr
Am Kupfergraben
Bauhofstr
Hegelplatz
Bebelplatz
See Tiergarten, Schöneburg & Kreuzberg Map
Gendarmenmarkt
Markgrafenstr
Charlottenstr
Auguststr
Oranienburger Str
Tucholskystr
Universitätsstr
Französische Str
Leipziger Str
Krausenstr
Schützenstr
Zimmerstr
Friedrichstr
Kochstr
MITTE
Johannisstr
Ziegelstr
Weidendammbrücke
Am Weidendamm
Planckstr
Dorotheenstr
Jägerstr
Taubenstr
Stadtmitte
Kronenstr
Mohrenstr
Mauerstr
Oranienburger Tor
Bertolt-Brecht-Platz
Albrechtstr
Georgenstr
Neustädtische Kirchstr
Mittelstr
Unter den Linden
Glinkastr
Behrenstr
Thälmannplatz
Gertrud-Kolmar Str
Wilhelmstr
Federal Ministry of Finance
Abgeordnetenhaus
Niederkirchnerstr
Kammerspiele
Schumannstr
Reinhardtstr
Marienstr
Karlplatz
Luisenstr
Marschallbrücke
Pariser Platz
Holocaust Memorial Site
An der Kolonnade
Vossstr
Potsdamer Platz
Leipziger Platz
Stresemannstr
Köthener Str
Ebertstr
Lennéstr
Tiergarten
Reichstagufer
Schiffbauerdamm
To Haus der Kulturen der Welt (600m)
Uniklinikum Charité

Berlin – Charlottenburg, Tiergarten, Mitte, Prenzlauer Berg, Friedrichshain, Kreuzberg, Schöneberg and Wilmersdorf.

The Wall once ran east of Brandenburger Tor (Brandenburg Gate); now the gate is a symbol of city unity. Unter den Linden, the fashionable avenue of aristocratic old Berlin, and its continuation, Karl-Liebknecht-Strasse, extend east from the gate to Alexanderplatz, once the heart of socialist Germany. En route are some of Berlin's finest museums, on Museumsinsel (Museum Island) in the Spree, and the monstrous Fernsehturm (TV tower, a most useful landmark). The former Checkpoint Charlie is now almost lost amid new construction. A few sections of the Wall have been preserved, but otherwise it's virtually impossible to tell where the barrier once stood.

In central Berlin, street numbers usually run sequentially up one side of the street and down the other (important exceptions are Martin-Luther-Strasse in Schöneberg, and Unter den Linden). A continuous street may change names several times.

Information

Tourist Offices The main office of **Berlin Tourismus Marketing** *(Budapester Strasse 45)*, in the Europa-Center, handles hotel reservations. There are other branches in the southern wing of the Brandenburger Tor and at the base of the Fernsehturm at Alexanderplatz. All are open daily. For telephone information and hotel reservations, call ☎ 25 00 25 or ☎ 1900-01 31 16 (€0.45 to €1.20 per minute) within Germany, or ☎ 1805-75 40 40 outside Germany; fax 25 00 24 24; or ⓔ hotel-reservation@t-online.de. The website is ⓦ www.berlin-tourism.de.

The tourist office sells the Berlin-Potsdam Welcome Card (€18), which entitles you to unlimited transport for three days and discounted admission to major museums, shows, attractions, sightseeing tours and boat cruises in both Berlin and Potsdam. It is also available at hotels and public transport ticket offices.

EurAide *(open 8am-noon & 1pm-4pm Mon-Sat)*, in Zoo station, is an English-language service offering train advice and reservations.

Money With two branches in Berlin, **AmEx** *(Bayreuther Strasse 37 • Friedrichstrasse 172)* allows you to cash its travellers cheques free of charge. There is also an exchange office of **Thomas Cook** *(Friedrichstrasse 56, Mitte)*. **Reisebank** *(Hardenbergplatz 1)* has an exchange office outside Zoo station. There is another branch inside Ostbahnhof.

Post & Communications The **main post office** *(open daily)* is in Joachimstalerstrasse, a block south of Zoo station. Poste restante letters should be marked 'Hauptpostlagernd' and addressed to you at 10612 Berlin. There are dozens of post offices all over Berlin with more restricted opening hours.

easyEverything *(☎ 88 70 79 70; Kurfürstendamm 224)* has hundreds of terminals for your Internet-surfing pleasure. You could also try the rather smoky **Alpha Café** *(☎ 447 90 67; Dunckerstrasse 72, Prenzlauer Berg)*.

Travel Agencies Travel agencies offering cheap flights advertise in the *Reisen* (travel) classified section *(Kleinanzeigen)* of the city magazines *Zitty* and *Tip*. One of the better discount operators is **Alternativ Tours** *(☎ 881 20 89; Wilmersdorfer Strasse 94, Wilmersdorf; U7 to Adenauerplatz)*, which specialises in unpublished, discounted fares to anywhere in the world.

The following agencies are generally open on weekdays and on Saturday mornings. The most convenient **Atlas Reisewelt branch** *(☎ 247 57 60; Alexanderplatz 9)* is inside the **Kaufhof** department store. **STA Travel** *(☎ 28 59 82 64; Gleimstrasse 28, Prenzlauer Berg • ☎ 311 09 50, Goethestrasse 73, Charlottenburg • ☎ 310 00 40; Hardenbergstrasse 9, Charlottenburg)* specialises in travel for young people and issues ISIC cards.

Medical & Emergency Services For 24-hour medical aid, advice and referrals, call the **Kassenärztliche Bereitschaftsdienst** *(Public Physicians' Emergency Service; ☎ 31 00 31)*. If you need a pharmacy after hours, dial ☎ 118 80. The general emergency number for a doctor *(Notarzt)* or fire brigade *(Feuerwehr)* throughout Berlin is ☎ 112.

Call ☎ 110 for police emergencies only. There are police stations all over the city, including a **City Wache** *(Joachimstaler Strasse 15)* south of Ku'damm and near Zoo Station. In eastern Berlin, there's a station at Otto-Braun-Strasse 27, northeast of Alexanderplatz.

Police headquarters and the municipal **lost-and-found office** *(☎ 69 95; Platz der Luftbrücke 6)* are beside Tempelhof airport.

Things to See & Do

Among Berlin's 170 museums, the **State museums** (denoted in this section by 'SMB') are among the highlights. Unless otherwise noted, SMB museums are closed Monday, admission is by day-pass (€6/3 adult/concession), valid for all SMB museums on that day, and is free the first Sunday of each month. Serious museumgoers may invest in the Drei-Tages-Touristenkarte (€10/5), offering free entry to over 50 museums over three consecutive days (ask at tourist offices).

Central Berlin Soaring above Berlin is the restored 368m **Fernsehturm** *(☎ 242 33 33; Panoramastrasse 1A; adult/concession €6/3; open 10am-1am daily)*. The best thing about the view is that it is the one place in the city where you can't see the tower! On the opposite side of the elevated train station is **Alexanderplatz** (or, affectionately, 'Alex'), the square named after Tsar Alexander I, who visited Berlin in 1805. It was bombed in WWII and rebuilt in the 1960s Soviet style. The **World Time Clock** (1969) is nearby.

Berlin's famed **Museumsinsel** (Museum Island) is a scene of heavy construction as its grand buildings are restored. On an island west of the Fernsehturm is the GDR's **Palace of the Republic** (1976), which occupies the site of the bombed, baroque Berliner Schloss. During the communist era, the Volkskammer (People's Chamber) used to meet in this monstrosity. On the southern side is the former **Staatsrat** *(Council of State)* building, constructed in 1964 with a portal from the old city palace incorporated in the facade. North of Marx-Engels-Platz looms the great neo-Renaissance **Berliner Dom** (1904), a former court church of the Hohenzollern family. The 1930 SMB **Pergamonmuseum** *(☎ 20 90 55 55; Am Kupfergraben)* is a feast of classical Greek, Babylonian, Roman, Oriental and Islamic antiquity. The world-renowned Ishtar Gate from Babylon (580 BC), the reconstructed Pergamon Altar from Asia Minor (160 BC) and the Market Gate from Greek Miletus (Asia Minor, 2nd century AD) are among the beautiful Middle Eastern artefacts. Other good museums include the SMB **Alte Nationalgalerie** *(Old National Gallery; ☎ 20 90 58 01; Bodestrasse 1-3)*, with classical sculpture and paintings by European masters; and Karl Friedrich Schinkel's 1829 neoclassical SMB **Altes Museum** (☎ 20 90 52 01; Am Lustgarten), with its famed rotunda area featuring statues of the Greek divinities.

The rebuilt, 13th-century **Nikolaikirche** stands amid the forced charms of the **Nikolaiviertel** *(Nikolai quarter)*, conceived and executed under the GDR's Berlin restoration programme. The monumental **Rotes Rathaus** (Red Town Hall), a neo-Renaissance structure from 1860, has been proudly restored and is once again the centre of Berlin's municipal government. Across Grunerstrasse, the remains of the bombed-out shell of the late 13th-century **Franciscan Abbey** mark the position of the former Spandauer Tor as well as the earliest town wall.

Several interesting sights can be covered from the Märkisches Museum U-Bahn station. The collections of the **Märkisches Museum** *(☎ 30 86 60; Am Köllnischen Park 5; adult/concession €4/2, free on Wed; open Tues-Sun)* cover Berlin's history, art and culture. The brown bears housed behind the main museum are the official city mascots.

A stroll west of Museumsinsel along Unter den Linden takes in the greatest surviving monuments of the former Prussian capital. The **Deutsches Historisches Museum** in a former *Zeughaus* (armoury) built in 1706, offers a collection on German history from AD 900 to the present under a new glass roof built by architect IM Pei. Opposite the museum is the beautiful colonnaded **Kronprinzenpalais** *(Crown Princes' Palace; ☎ 20 30 40; admission free; open Thur-Tues)*. Next to the museum is Schinkel's **Neue Wache** *(admission free; open daily)*, a memorial to the victims of fascism and despotism. To the west, **Bebelplatz** was the site of the Nazis' first book-burning on 10 May 1933. Just south lies Gendarmenmarkt, an elegant square containing a trio of magnificent buildings. At the southern end of the square, the **Deutscher Dom** *(German Cathedral; ☎ 22 73 04 31; admission free; open Tues-Sun)* boasts a museum with an excellent exhibit on German history from 1800 to the present. The **Französischer Dom** (French Cathedral) contains the **Hugenottenmuseum** *(Huguenot Museum; ☎ 229 17 60; adult/concession €1.50/1; open Tues-Sun)*, covering the French Protestant contribution to Berlin life. Completing the picture is the statuesque **Konzerthaus** *(Concert Hall)*.

Europe's busiest square until WWII, **Potsdamer Platz** was occupied by the Wall and death strip until reunification. Now, it's one

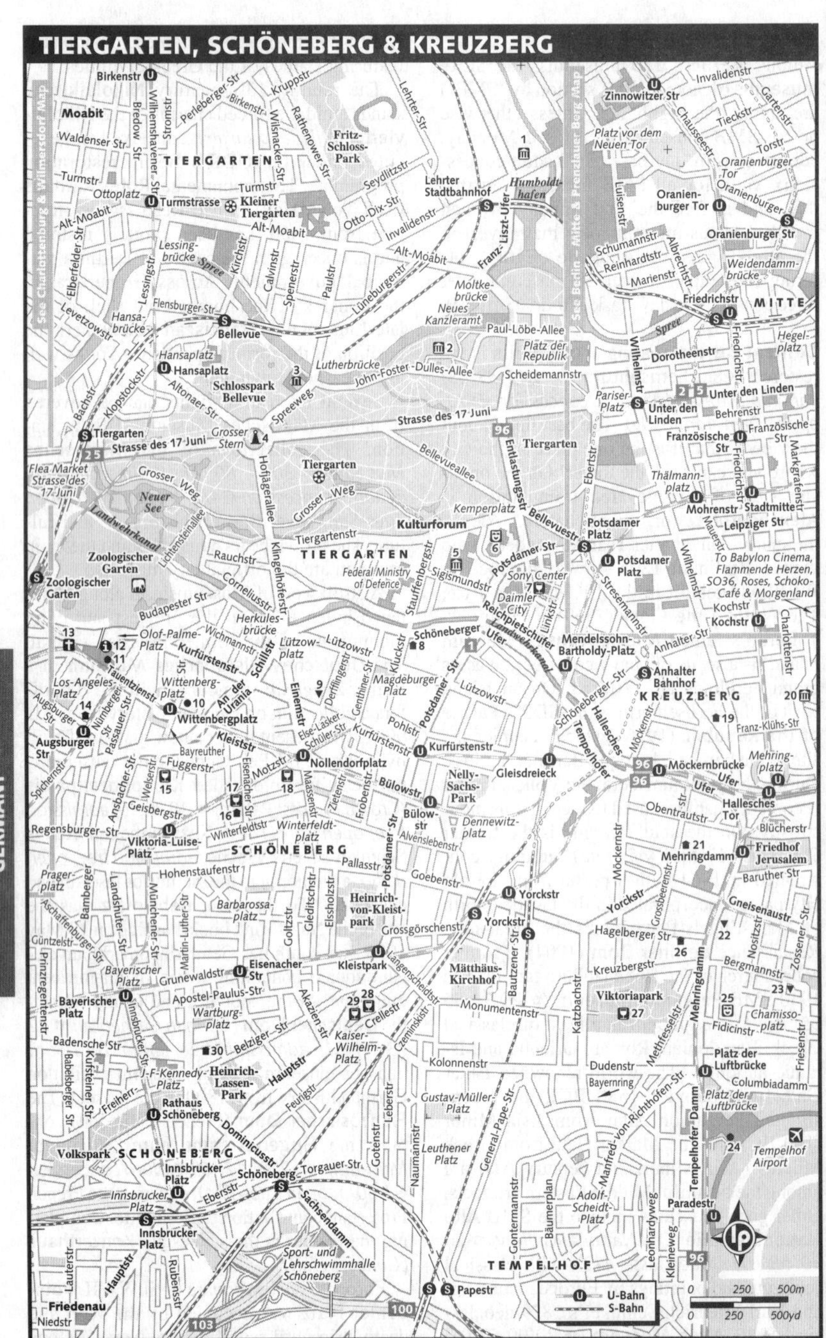
TIERGARTEN, SCHÖNEBERG & KREUZBERG
See Charlottenburg & Wilmersdorf Map
See Berlin – Mitte & Prenzlauer Berg Map
Birkenstr
Moabit
Waldenser Str
Turmstr
Ottoplatz
Turmstrasse
Alt-Moabit
Elberfelder Str
Bredow Str
Wilhelmshavener Str
Stromstr
Perleberger Str
Birkenstr
Kruppstr
Wilsnacker Str
Rathenower Str
Fritz-Schloss-Park
Lehrter Str
TIERGARTEN
Kleiner Tiergarten
Seydlitzstr
Otto-Dix-Str
Invalidenstr
Lehrter Stadtbahnhof
Humboldt-hafen
Lessing-brücke
Spree
Kirchstr
Calvinstr
Spenerstr
Paulstr
Lüneburgerstr
Alt-Moabit
Franz-Liszt-Ufer
Moltke-brücke
Neues Kanzleramt
Paul-Löbe-Allee
Platz der Republik
Scheidemannstr
Lessingstr
Levetzowstr
Flensburger Str
Hansa-brücke
Bellevue
Hansaplatz
Schlosspark Bellevue
Lutherbrücke
John-Foster-Dulles-Allee
Altonaer Str
Spreeweg
Bachstr
Klopstockstr
Tiergarten
Strasse des 17 Juni
Grosser Stern
Flea Market Strasse des 17 Juni
Grosser Weg
Neuer See
Landwehrkanal
Lichtensteinallee
Hofjägerallee
Tiergarten
Bellevueallee
Entlastungsstr
Ebertstr
Kemperplatz
Bellevuestr
Kulturforum
Tiergartenstr
Klingelhöferstr
Zoologischer Garten
Rauchstr
TIERGARTEN
Federal Ministry of Defence
Stauffenbergstr
Sigismundstr
Potsdamer Str
Sony Center
Daimler City
Linkstr
Potsdamer Platz
Corneliusstr
Budapester Str
Herkules-brücke
Lützow-platz
Lützowstr
Schöneberger Ufer
Reichpietschufer
Olof-Palme-Platz
Wichmannstr
Kurfürstenstr
Schillstr
Tauentzienstr
Wittenberg-platz
An der Urania
Los-Angeles-Platz
Augsburger Str
Nürnberger Str
Passauer Str
Wittenbergplatz
Einemstr
Derfflingerstr
Genthiner Str
Kluckstr
Magdeburger Platz
Lützowstr
Pohlstr
Else-Lasker-Schüler-Str
Kurfürstenstr
Kleiststr
Bayreuther Str
Fuggerstr
Eisenacher Str
Motzstr
Nollendorfplatz
Maassenstr
Zietenstr
Frobenstr
Bülowstr
Nelly-Sachs-Park
Gleisdreieck
Dennewitz-platz
Alvenslebenstr
Spichernstr
Ansbacher Str
Welserstr
Geisbergstr
Regensburger Str
Viktoria-Luise-Platz
Winterfeldtstr
Winterfeldt-platz
SCHÖNEBERG
Pallasstr
Hohenstaufenstr
Prager-platz
Aschaffenburger Str
Bamberger Str
Landshuter Str
Münchener Str
Barbarossa-platz
Goltzstr
Gleditschstr
Elssholzstr
Heinrich-von-Kleist-park
Goebenstr
Grossgörschenstr
Yorckstr
Güntzelstr
Prinzregentenstr
Martin-Luther-Str
Bayerischer Platz
Grunewaldstr
Eisenacher Str
Kleistpark
Langenscheidtstr
Matthäus-Kirchhof
Bautzener Str
Apostel-Paulus-Str
Akazienstr
Wartburg-platz
Crellestr
Kaiser-Wilhelm-Platz
Czeminskistr
Monumentenstr
Badensche Str
Belziger Str
Babelsberger Str
Kufsteiner Str
Innsbrucker Str
J-F-Kennedy-Platz
Heinrich-Lassen-Park
Hauptstr
Kolonnenstr
Freiherr-
Rathaus Schöneberg
Feurigstr
Gustav-Müller-Platz
Dominicusstr
Volkspark
SCHÖNEBERG
Innsbrucker Platz
Schöneberg
Torgauer Str
Gotenstr
Leberstr
Naumannstr
Leuthener Platz
General-Pape-Str
Ebersstr
Sachsendamm
Sport- und Lehrschwimmhalle Schöneberg
Lauterstr
Rubensstr
Friedenau
Niedstr
Papestr
TEMPELHOF
Gontermannstr
Bäumerplan
Adolf-Scheidt-Platz
Leonhardyweg
Kleineweg
Manfred-von-Richthofen-Str
Invalidenstr
Zinnowitzer Str
Gartenstr
Platz vor dem Neuen Tor
Chausseestr
Tieckstr
Torstr
Oranienburger Tor
Luisenstr
Oranienburger Str
Schumannstr
Reinhardtstr
Albrechtstr
Marienstr
Weidendamm-brücke
Friedrichstr
MITTE
Spree
Wilhelmstr
Dorotheenstr
Hegel-platz
Pariser Platz
Unter den Linden
Behrenstr
Französische Str
Thälmann-platz
Mohrenstr
Stadtmitte
Markgrafenstr
Leipziger Str
Mauerstr
To Babylon Cinema, Flammende Herzen, SO36, Roses, Schoko-Café & Morgenland
Kochstr
Stresemannstr
Mendelssohn-Bartholdy-Platz
Anhalter Str
Anhalter Bahnhof
Charlottenstr
KREUZBERG
Schöneberger Str
Möckernstr
Franz-Klühs-Str
Halleschesufer
Tempelhofer Ufer
Möckernbrücke
Mehring-platz
Hallesches Tor
Obentrautstr
Blücherstr
Mehringdamm
Friedhof Jerusalem
Baruther Str
Grossbeerenstr
Gneisenaustr
Yorckstr
Hagelberger Str
Nostitzstr
Zossener Str
Kreuzbergstr
Bergmannstr
Katzbachstr
Viktoriapark
Methfesselstr
Chamisso-platz
Fidicinstr
Friesenstr
Dudenstr
Platz der Luftbrücke
Columbiadamm
Bayernring
Tempelhofer Damm
Tempelhof Airport
Paradestr
U-Bahn
S-Bahn
0 250 500m
0 250 500yd

GERMANY

TIERGARTEN, SCHÖNEBERG & KREUZBERG

PLACES TO STAY
8 Jugendherberge Berlin International
14 Pension Fischer
16 Hotel Gunia
19 Hotel am Anhalter Bahnhof
21 Pension Kreuzberg
26 Hotel Transit
30 Studentenhotel Meininger 10

PLACES TO EAT
9 Café Einstein
22 Seerose
23 Barcomi's

OTHER
1 Hamburger Bahnhof Museum
2 Haus der Kulturen der Welt
3 Schloss Bellevue
4 Siegessäule
5 Gemäldegalerie
6 Berliner Philharmonie
7 Blu Discothek
10 American Express
11 Europa-Center
12 Berlin Tourismus Marketing
13 Kaiser-Wilhelm-Gedächtniskirche (Memorial Church)
15 Connection Disco
17 Tom's Bar; Hafen
18 KitKat Club
20 Jüdisches Museum
24 Municipal Lost & Found Office
25 Friends of Italian Opera
27 Golgatha
28 Leuchturm
29 Café Mirell

of the city's main tourist attractions, with striking buildings by world-famous architects including Renzo Piano, Arata Isozaki, Rafael Moneo and Helmut Jahn.

North of Oranienburger Tor U-bahn station is the neighbourhood known as the Scheunenviertel, one of Berlin's most vibrant. Behind the Brecht-Weigel Gedenkstätte, where socialist playwright Bertolt Brecht lived, is **Dorotheenstädtischer Friedhof**. The graveyard (the one closer to Brecht's house) houses tombs of philosopher Georg Friedrich Hegel, poet Johannes Becher and Brecht. Don't miss the magnificent **Neue Synagogue**, which these days houses the **Centrum Judaicum** *(☎ 88 02 83 16; Oranienburger Strasse 28-30; adult/concession €3/2; open 10am-6pm Sun-Thur, 10am-2pm Fri)*.

Tiergarten & Kreuzberg At the western end of Unter den Linden is the **Brandenburger Tor** *(Brandenburg Gate)*, built in 1791 by Karl Gotthard Langhans, the symbol of Berlin and once the boundary between east and west. It is crowned by the winged Goddess of Victory and a four-horse chariot.

Beside the Spree River, north of the Brandenburger Tor, is the **Reichstag** *(admission free; open 8am-midnight daily, last admission 10pm)*, where at midnight on 2 October 1990 the reunification of Germany was enacted. Again the home of the German parliament, the Reichstag has become Berlin's number one attraction, thanks to Sir Norman Foster's stunning reconstruction completed in 1999. Tours can be arranged by writing to Deutscher Bundestag, Besucherdienst, 11011 Berlin.

West of the Reichstag, along the Spree River, is the **Haus der Kulturen der Welt** *(House of World Cultures; ☎ 39 78 70; John Foster Dulles-Allee 10; adult/concession €4/2; open 10am-9pm Tues-Sun)*, built in 1957 and nicknamed the 'pregnant oyster' for its shape. Photo and art exhibitions often have Third World themes.

The huge city park, **Tiergarten**, stretches west from the Brandenburger Tor towards Zoo station. Strasse des 17 Juni (named after the 1953 workers' uprising in East Berlin) leads from the Brandenburger Tor through the park. In the middle of this street, the **Siegessäule** *(Victory Column; adult/concession €1/0.50)* commemorates 19th-century Prussian military adventures. Just northeast is **Schloss Bellevue** (1785), the official Berlin residence of the German president.

The SMB **Gemäldegalerie** *(Gallery of Paintings; ☎ 20 90 55 55; Matthäiskirchplatz 4/6)* is the Kulturforum area's star attraction, focusing on European works from the 13th to 18th centuries; its collection includes works by Dürer, Rembrandt, Botticelli and Goya. The area abounds with stunning museums – check at the tourist office for details.

Parallel to a section of the Wall is the site of the former SS-Gestapo headquarters, where the open-air **Topography of Terror** *(☎ 25 48 67 03; Niederkirchnerstrasse 8; admission free; open 10am-6pm daily in summer, until dusk in winter)* exhibition documents Nazi crimes.

Almost nothing remains of the famous **Checkpoint Charlie**, a major crossing between east and west during the Cold War. However, the Wall's history is commemorated nearby in the fascinating **Haus am Checkpoint Charlie** *(☎ 253 72 50; Friedrichstrasse 43-45; adult/concession €7/4; open 9am-8pm daily)*.

The longest surviving stretch of the **Berlin Wall** is just west of the Warschauer Strasse terminus of the U1. This 300m section was

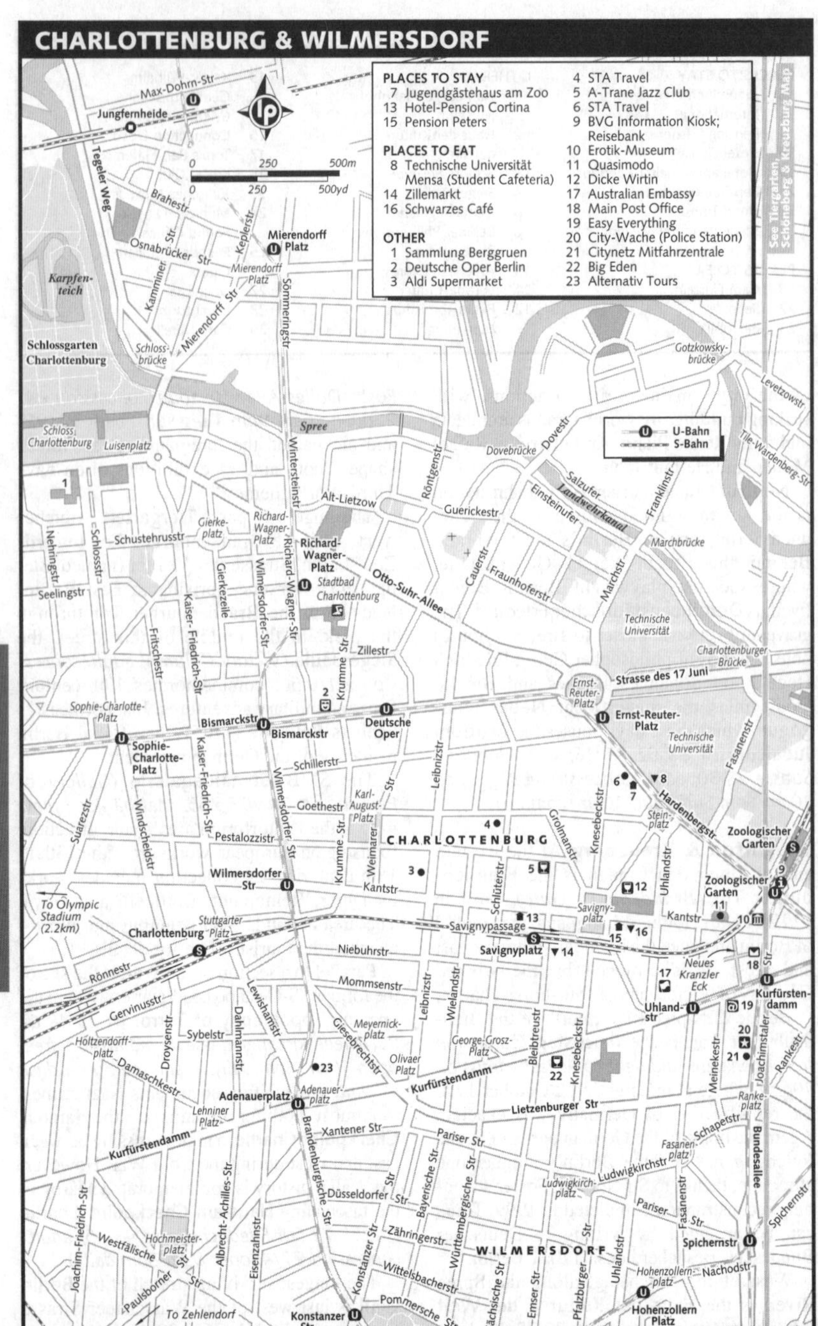
CHARLOTTENBURG & WILMERSDORF
PLACES TO STAY
7 Jugendgästehaus am Zoo
13 Hotel-Pension Cortina
15 Pension Peters
PLACES TO EAT
8 Technische Universität Mensa (Student Cafeteria)
14 Zillemarkt
16 Schwarzes Café
OTHER
1 Sammlung Berggruen
2 Deutsche Oper Berlin
3 Aldi Supermarket
4 STA Travel
5 A-Trane Jazz Club
6 STA Travel
9 BVG Information Kiosk; Reisebank
10 Erotik-Museum
11 Quasimodo
12 Dicke Wirtin
17 Australian Embassy
18 Main Post Office
19 Easy Everything
20 City-Wache (Police Station)
21 Citynetz Mitfahrzentrale
22 Big Eden
23 Alternativ Tours
U-Bahn
S-Bahn
0 250 500m
0 250 500yd
See Tiergarten, Schöneberg & Kreuzburg Map
Max-Dohrn-Str
Jungfernheide
Tegeler Weg
Brahestr
Kamminer Str
Osnabrücker Str
Keplerstr
Mierendorff Platz
Mierendorffstr
Sömmeringstr
Karpfenteich
Schlossgarten Charlottenburg
Schlossbrücke
Spree
Schloss Charlottenburg
Luisenplatz
Wintersteinstr
Röntgenstr
Dovebrücke
Dovestr
Salzufer
Landwehrkanal
Einsteinufer
Franklinstr
Gotzkowskybrücke
Levetzowstr
Tile-Wardenberg-Str
Alt-Lietzow
Guerickestr
Richard-Wagner-Platz
Stadtbad Charlottenburg
Otto-Suhr-Allee
Cauerstr
Fraunhoferstr
Marchstr
Marchbrücke
Technische Universität
Nehringstr
Schlossstr
Schustehrusstr
Gierkeplatz
Gierkezeile
Seelingstr
Kaiser-Friedrich-Str
Wilmersdorfer Str
Richard-Wagner-Str
Fritschestr
Zillestr
Krumme Str
Charlottenburger Brücke
Strasse des 17 Juni
Ernst-Reuter-Platz
Sophie-Charlotte-Platz
Bismarckstr
Deutsche Oper
Schillerstr
Leibnizstr
Fasanenstr
Hardenbergstr
Goethestr
Karl-August-Platz
Weimarer Str
Grolmanstr
Knesebeckstr
Steinplatz
Zoologischer Garten
Suarezstr
Windscheidstr
Pestalozzistr
CHARLOTTENBURG
Schlüterstr
Uhlandstr
Kantstr
Savignyplatz
To Olympic Stadium (2.2km)
Stuttgarter Platz
Charlottenburg
Savignypassage
Niebuhrstr
Neues Kranzler Eck
Rönnestr
Mommsenstr
Gervinusstr
Lewishamstr
Kurfürstendamm
Uhlandstr
Meyernickplatz
Holtzendorffplatz
Sybelstr
Droysenstr
Dahlmannstr
Giesebrechtstr
George-Grosz-Platz
Bleibtreustr
Damaschkestr
Olivaer Platz
Adenauerplatz
Lehniner Platz
Lietzenburger Str
Meinekestr
Joachimstaler Str
Rankestr
Rankeplatz
Xantener Str
Pariser Str
Brandenburgische Str
Bayerische Str
Württembergische Str
Schaperstr
Fasanenplatz
Ludwigkirchstr
Ludwigkirchplatz
Bundesallee
Joachim-Friedrich-Str
Albrecht-Achilles-Str
Düsseldorfer Str
Eisenzahnstr
Konstanzer Str
Zähringerstr
Westfälische Str
Hochmeisterplatz
WILMERSDORF
Spichernstr
Wittelsbacherstr
Sächsische Str
Emser Str
Pfalzburger Str
Hohenzollernplatz
Nachodstr
Paulsborner Str
To Zehlendorf
Konstanzer Str
Pommersche Str
Hohenzollern Platz
GERMANY

Use the Magic Word, Bitte

Berliners are known for their quick, sometimes cutting, wit. Witness the following very brief conversation, overheard on a Berlin street:

Foreigner: Ah! Do you know the way to the Reichstag?
Berliner: *Ja.* (Walks away.)

turned over to artists who created the **East Side Gallery**, a permanent, open-air art gallery along the side facing Mühlenstrasse. The area can be a bit seedy, although it's improving with gentrification.

Even before it opened in 2001, the zinc-clad shell of the Daniel Libeskind-designed **Jüdisches Museum** *(Jewish Museum; ☎ 25 99 33 00; Lindenstrasse 9-14; adult/concession €5.50/2.75; open 10am-8pm daily except Jewish high holidays and Christmas Eve)* drew thousands of visitors. Now its collection covers 1000 years of Jewish history in Germany in a manner that's both admiring and wistful.

Kurfürstendamm & Charlottenburg

Once the commercial heart of West Berlin, the 'Ku'damm' is showing a touch of age as creative and commercial energies are focused elsewhere. The area around Zoo station can become a tourist ghetto in summer. The stark and haunting ruins of the **Kaiser-Wilhelm-Gedächtniskirche** (1895) in Breitscheidplatz, engulfed in the roaring commercialism all around, are a world-famous landmark. A British bombing on 22 November 1943 left only the broken west tower standing. South of Zoo station is the **Erotik-Museum** *(☎ 866 06 66; Joachimstalerstrasse 4; adult/concession €5/4; open 9am-midnight daily)*, a surprisingly highbrow creation of Beate Uhse, the German porno and sex-toy queen.

Originally a summer residence for Queen Sophie Charlotte, **Schloss Charlottenburg** *(☎ 0331-969 42 02; Luisenplatz; day card adult/concession €7.50/5)* is an exquisite baroque palace (U-Bahn to Sophie-Charlotte-Platz or bus No 145 from Zoo station). The winter chambers of Friedrich II, upstairs in the new wing (1746) to the east, are highlights, as well as the Schinkel Pavilion, the neoclassical Mausoleum and also the rococo Belvedere pavilion. It may be difficult to get a ticket on weekends and holidays in summer.

Nearby is the SMB **Sammlung Berggruen** *(☎ 32 69 58 15; Schlossstrasse 1)*, showing a collection called 'Picasso and His Time' on loan until 2006. You'll also be treated to works by Cézanne, Van Gogh, Gauguin, Braque and Klee.

Built by Hitler for the 1936 Olympic Games in which African-American runner Jesse Owens won four gold medals, the 85,000-seat **Olympic Stadium** *(☎ 301 11 00; Olympischer Platz 3; adult/concession €2.50/1; guided tours €5/person)* lies southwest of Schloss Charlottenburg. One of the best examples of Nazi-era neoclassical architecture, it's still very much in use – the finals of the 2006 World Cup will be played here.

Organised Tours

Guide yourself for the price of a bus ticket (€2.10) on bus No 100, which passes 18 major sights on its way from Zoo station to Michelangelostrasse in Prenzlauer Berg via Alexanderplatz. The public-transport company Berliner Verkehrsbetriebe (BVG; see Getting Around later in this section) puts out a special brochure describing the route.

Among the best walking tours are **Berlin Walks** *(☎ 301 91 94; W www.berlinwalks.com; €10/7.50 for over/under 26)*, **Insider Tours** *(☎ 692 31 49; W www.insidertour.com; walking tour €12/9, bike tour €20/17 including bicycle)* and **Brewer's Best of Berlin Walking Tour** *(☎ 70 13 10 37; W www.brewersberlin.com; all tours €10)*.

Special Events

Berlin's calendar is filled with events. The best are as follows:

February

International Film Festival Berlin Also known as the Berlinale, this is Germany's answer to the Cannes and Venice film festivals and attracts its own stable of stars (few) and starlets (plenty). For info call ☎ 25 48 90.

June

Berlin Pride Held on the last weekend in June, this is by far the largest gay event in Germany.

July

Love Parade The largest techno party in the world wends its way through the streets of Berlin in the middle of the month. It attracts a million people and is quickly challenging Oktoberfest as Germany's premier party event.

Places to Stay

If you're travelling to Berlin on weekends and between May and September, especially during big events, be sure to make reservations several weeks ahead of time. From November to March, on the other hand, visitor numbers plunge significantly (except during the Christmas and New Year holidays) – be sure to ask your travel agent about cheap deals.

The city's tourist information office, **Berlin Tourismus Marketing** *(BTM; ☎ 25 00 25, fax 25 00 24 24)*, handles hotel reservations for €3.

DJH Hostels Berlin's hostels are very popular and often full. None offer guests cooking facilities, but breakfast is included. Reserve several weeks in advance (ⓔ djh-berlin-brandenburg-zr@jugendherberge.de; Deutsches Jugendherbergswerk Zentralreservierung, Kluckstrasse 3, 10785 Berlin).

The only DJH hostel within the city centre is the institutional 364-bed **Jugendherberge Berlin International** *(☎ 261 10 98, fax 265 03 83; Kluckstrasse 3; dorm beds junior/senior €18.50/22.60, doubles €23/27.10)*. It's in Schöneberg, near the Landwehrkanal (U1 to Kurfürstenstrasse).

Jugendherberge am Wannsee *(☎ 803 20 34, fax 803 59 08; Badeweg 1; beds junior/senior €18/22.10)*, on the corner of Kronprinzessinnenweg, is pleasantly located on Grosser Wannsee, the lake on the way to Potsdam. It's a 10-minute walk from Nikolassee S-Bahn station (S1 and S7) via the footbridge.

Jugendherberge Ernst Reuter *(☎ 404 16 10, fax 404 59 72; Hermsdorfer Damm 48-50; beds junior/senior €14.40/18)* is in the far northwest of Berlin. Take the U6 to Alt-Tegel, then bus No 125 right to the door.

Independent Hostels & Guesthouses

The hostels listed here don't have curfews. Breakfast costs extra unless indicated. Some of the hostels give discounts to students with ID.

In Charlottenburg, **Jugendgästehaus am Zoo** *(☎ 312 94 10, fax 312 54 30; Hardenbergstrasse 9a; dorm beds €18, singles/doubles €25/44)*, just three blocks from Zoo station, has handsome, wooded communal spaces. Add €3 if you're aged over 27.

In Mitte, **Circus – The Hostel** *(☎ 28 39 14 33, fax 28 39 14 84; ⓔ info@circus-berlin.de; Rosa-Luxemburg-Strasse 39 & Weinbergsweg 1a; dorm beds/singles/doubles/triples €14/30/46/60)* has two hugely popular, well-run hostels. You'll find similarly helpful, friendly staff at **Clubhouse Hostel** *(☎ 28 09 79 79, 28 09 79 77; ⓔ info@clubhouse-berlin.de; Kalkscheune 4-5; dorm beds/doubles/triples from €14/45/60)*, near Friedrichstrasse and Tacheles.

Despite its name, **Studentenhotel Meininger 10** *(☎ 78 71 74 14, fax 78 71 74 12; ⓔ info@studentenhotel.de; Meininger Strasse 10; dorm beds/singles/doubles €12.50/33/46)* offers its rooms to anyone (U4 to Rathaus Schöneberg).

In the heart of Prenzlauer Berg's nightlife is **Lette 'm Sleep** *(☎ 44 73 36 23, fax 44 73 36 25; ⓔ info@backpackers.de; Lettestrasse 7; dorm beds €15-19, doubles €48)*. Doubles have kitchenettes.

Two moderately priced hotels close to the Mehringdamm station in Kreuzberg (U6 or U7) have dorm accommodation. Friendly **Pension Kreuzberg** *(☎ 251 13 62, fax 251 06 38; Grossbeerenstrasse 64; dorm beds/singles/doubles €22.50/40/52)* has plain rooms and garden views out back. **Hotel Transit** *(☎ 789 04 70, fax 78 90 47 77, ⓔ info@hotel-transit.de; Hagelberger Strasse 53-54; dorm beds/singles/doubles €19/52/60, including breakfast)* is in a former factory that oozes character. Most rooms have showers.

Hotels The **Hotel-Pension Cortina** *(☎ 313 90 59, fax 312 73 96; Kantstrasse 140; singles/doubles with shared toilet from €31/50)*, in Charlottenburg, has plenty of basic rooms, some with in-room shower cabinets. Mitte's **Artist Hotel-Pension Die Loge** *(☎/fax 280 75 13; ⓔ die-loge@t-online.de; Friedrichstrasse 115; singles/doubles from €40/60)* has far more personality than your average hotel and boasts a clientele that includes actors and artists.

New **InterMezzo** *(☎ 22 48 90 96, fax 22 48 90 97; ⓦ www.hotelintermezzo.de; Gertrud-Kolmar-Strasse 5; singles/doubles €40/67)* is a spotless place between Brandenburger Tor and Potsdamer Platz, exclusively for women (and their children). Gay men might try **Hotel Gunia** *(☎ 218 59 40, fax 218 59 44; ⓔ info@hotelgunia.de; Eisenacher Strasse 10; singles €45, singles/doubles with bath €50/70)*, with simple but well-kept rooms near Nollendorfplatz, the heart of the gay district.

Readers have recommended cheery **Pension Peters** *(☎ 312 22 78, fax 312 35 19; ⓔ penspeters@aol.com; Kantstrasse 146;*

singles/doubles from €58/78) for service above the call.

In Kreuzberg, **Hotel am Anhalter Bahnhof** *(☎ 251 03 42, fax 251 48 97; ⓔ hotel-aab@t-online.de; Stresemannstrasse 36; singles/doubles from €45/70, with facilities €65/90)* has simple, reasonably priced digs. Schöneberg's **Pension Fischer** *(☎ 21 91 55 66, fax 21 01 96 14; ⓔ hotelpensionfischer@t-online.de; Nürnberger Strasse 24a; singles/doubles from €60/70)* was recently handsomely renovated.

Places to Eat

Berlin is paradise for snackers on the go, with international *Imbiss* (snack) **stands** throughout the city. They cluster along Budapester Strasse in Tiergarten, at the eastern end of Kantstrasse near Zoo station, on Wittenbergplatz in Schöneberg, on Alexanderplatz in Mitte and around Schlesisches Tor station in Kreuzberg. To prepare your own food, try the discount Aldi, Lidl or Penny Markt **supermarket** chains. There are also **farmers markets** around town, the most famous (although not necessarily cheapest) of which is held on Wednesday and Saturday on Schöneberg's Winterfeldtplatz.

Berliners love eating out. There's no need to travel far, since every neighbourhood has its own clutch of eateries running the gamut of cuisines. The blocks around Savignyplatz in Charlottenburg, Prenzlauer Berg's Kollwitzplatz, and south of Winterfeldtplatz in Schöneberg are great places to browse for good restaurants with character.

Anyone may eat at the 1st-floor **Technische Universität Mensa** *(Hardenbergstrasse 34; 3-course lunch €3-5 for students, €2 extra for nonstudents; open 11am-2.30pm)*, three blocks from Zoo station. The **Humboldt Universität Mensa** *(Unter den Linden 6)*, in Mitte, has the same hours.

For good German fare, head for Charlottenburg, where you'll find the Art Nouveau **Zillemarkt** *(☎ 881 70 40; Bleibtreustrasse 48a; mains €8-12.50)*, serving huge portions at fair prices. In Mitte, **Bärenschenke** *(☎ 282 90 78; Friedrichstrasse 124; mains €3-10)* has a long bar and local specialities. For hearty home-style basics, head for the corner **Zum Schusterjungen** *(☎ 442 76 54; Danziger Strasse 9; mains €4.50-9)* in Prenzlauer Berg.

Homy **Seerose** *(☎ 69 81 59 27; Mehringdamm 47; mains €4.20-6.20)* in Kreuzberg (U6 or U7 to Mehringdamm) has takeaway or eat-in vegetarian fare. Most Asian restaurants will make vegetarian dishes too, including several Indian places on Goltzstrasse, south of Winterfeldtplatz in Schöneberg.

Cafés The number and variety of cafés in Berlin is simply astonishing. They're wonderful places to relax over coffee and cake. Many also honour the great Berlin tradition of serving breakfast all day.

Elegant **Café Einstein** *(☎ 261 50 96; Kurfürstenstrasse 58; mains €5-21.50)* is a Viennese-style coffee house in a rambling villa. The nonstop rock-and-roll **Schwarzes Café** *(☎ 313 80 38; Kantstrasse 148; dishes €4.50-9; open 24hr)*, in Charlottenburg, is open around the clock. The footpath benches at **Mendelssohn** *(☎ 281 78 59; Oranienburger Strasse 39)* are pleasant places to slurp *Milchkaffee* (milk coffee) and people-watch on a sunny morning. **Barcomi's** *(☎ 694 81 38; Bergmannstrasse 21; baked goods from around €1)* in Kreuzberg is a hole-in-the-wall café loved by locals for coffee and bagels.

Beneath the S-Bahn near Museumsinsel, **Café Odéon** *(☎ 208 26 00; Georgenstrasse, S-Bahn arch 192; dishes €1.80-6.90)* serves light meals like quiche Lorraine and vegetable lasagne. Balmy summer nights are the best time to be at the **Café am Neuen See** *(☎ 254 49 30; Lichtensteinallee 1; dishes €3-11.50)*, right in Tiergarten park.

Entertainment

Berliners take culture and fun seriously. Options are always changing, so put your faith in word-of-mouth tips for the most cutting-edge scenes.

Kreuzberg – around Mehringdamm, Gneisenaustrasse and Bergmannstrasse – is mostly alternative but with trendy touches, while along Oranienstrasse and Wiener Strasse it has a grungy, slightly edgy feel. Around Winterfeldtplatz in Schöneberg, you'll find few tourists and lots of thirty-somethings with alternative lifestyles and young families. In the eastern districts nightlife is far more earthy and experimental. The most dynamic scenes are in Prenzlauer Berg and Friedrichshain, where the feel is energetic and slightly gritty. More established are the nightclubs and cafés/pubs in Mitte along Oranienburger Strasse, Rosenthaler Platz, Hackescher Markt and adjacent streets in the Scheunenviertel.

Pubs & Bars Gentrifying Kreuzberg is **Morgenland** (*☎ 611 31 83; Skalitzer Strasse 35*), good for long conversations at oddly shaped, designer tables. A longtime hang-out is **Flammende Herzen** (*Flaming Hearts; ☎ 615 71 02; Oranienstrasse 170*), which is dark, knick-knack filled and, occasionally, gay.

Plenty of popular café-pubs cluster around Kollwitz-Platz and Helmholtz-Platz in Prenzlauer Berg, including the contemporary **Café Weitzmann** (*Husemannstrasse 2*), Mexican-themed **Frida Kahlo** (*☎ 445 70 16; Lychener Strasse 37*) and the cosy wine bar **Weinstein** (*☎ 441 18 42; Lychener Strasse 33*). Dark and retro, **Astro** (*☎ 29 66 16 15; Simon-Dach-Strasse 40*) is a cool techno bar in Friedrichshain. In Schöneberg there are lots of interesting pubs and cafés around Akazienstrasse and on lovely Crellestrasse, including the inexpensive, tropical **Café Mirell** (*☎ 782 04 57; Crellestrasse 46*) and **Leuchturm** (*Lighthouse; Crellestrasse 41*), which has walls plastered in kitsch oil paintings. **Obst und Gemüse** (*☎ 282 96 47; Oranienburger Strasse 49*) in Mitte is a hip and popular bar.

Typical Berlin pubs have their own tradition of hospitality: good food, beer and *Schlagfertigkeit* (quick-wittedness). In Charlottenburg, **Dicke Wirtin** (*☎ 314 49 52; Carmerstrasse 9*) is an earthy place and sports bar off Savignyplatz. Historic **Zur letzten Instanz** (*The Final Authority; ☎ 242 55 28; Waisenstrasse 14*) in Mitte claims traditions dating back to the 1600s and is next to a chunk of medieval town wall.

As soon as the last winter storms have blown away, pallid Berliners reacquaint themselves with the sun in beer gardens. The open-air **Golgatha** (*☎ 785 24 53; Viktoriapark*), in Kreuzberg, is an institution. In the southwestern district of Zehlendorf is **Loretta am Wannsee** (*☎ 803 51 56; Kronprinzessinenweg 260*), a huge garden with seating for over 1000 (S-bahn to Wannsee).

GERMANY

Clubs Berlin has a reputation for unbridled and very late nightlife. Not much starts before 11pm, except for some new 'after-work' clubs and raves. Cover charges range from €2.50 to €10.

Berlin *is* techno, and you'll be hard pressed to find a nightclub that plays anything else. One of the oldest techno temples is Mitte's **Tresor** (*☎ 609 37 02; Leipziger Strasse 126a*). Also popular is **Delicious Doughnuts** (*☎ 28 09 92 74; Rosenthaler Strasse 9*), an acid jazz club in Mitte. **SO 36** (*☎ 61 40 13 07; Oranienstrasse 190*), in Kreuzberg, is one of Berlin's longest-running nightclubs, with theme nights including punk and gay and lesbian. In Friedrichshain, **Matrix** (*☎ 29 49 10 47; Warschauer Platz 18*) has several dance floors beneath U-Bahn arches.

Technoed-out? At Mitte's **Sophienklub** (*☎ 282 45 52; Sophienstrasse 6*), you'll hear Brazilian, house and reggae. The hot-spot on busy Potsdamer Platz is **Blu** (*☎ 25 59 30 30; Marlene-Dietrich-Platz 4*), with three floors of dancing plus city views.

A great example of the wilder side of Berlin is the **KitKat Club** (*Bessemerstrasse 2-14; W www.kitkatclub.de*), in the Tempelhof-Schöneberg area. On Friday and Saturday nights you get in by wearing your 'sexual fantasy outfit' (erotic or basically no clothes!), and women choose who's admitted.

The nightclubs around the Ku'damm are generally packed with tourists. Typical is **Big Eden** (*☎ 882 61 20; Kurfürstendamm 202*).

Gay & Lesbian Venues Berlin is about the gayest city in Europe. Consult the gay and lesbian freebie *Siegessäule* or strictly gay *Sergej* magazine, or contact **Mann-O-Meter** (*☎ 216 80 08; Bülowstrasse 106*), in Schöneberg.

Hafen (*☎ 214 11 18; Motzstrasse 19*), near Nollendorfplatz, is full of gay yuppies fortifying themselves before they move on to legendary **Tom's Bar** (*☎ 213 45 70; Motzstrasse 19*). Multi-roomed **Connection** (*☎ 218 14 32; Fuggerstrasse 33*) is the biggest and arguably the busiest gay nightclub in town.

Interesting places in Kreuzberg include the over-the-top, kitschy **Roses** (*☎ 615 75 70; Oranienstrasse 187*) and **Schoko-Café** (*☎ 615 15 61; Mariannenstrasse 6*), a convivial meeting place for lesbians. **Café Seidenfaden** (*☎ 283 27 83; Dircksenstrasse 47*), near Häckische Höfe, is a pleasant lesbian café.

Live Performance The **Berliner Philharmonie** (*☎ 25 48 81 32; Herbert-von-Karajan Strasse 1*) is famous for its supreme acoustics. All seats are excellent. The lavish **Konzerthaus** (*☎ 25 00 25; Gendarmenmarkt*), in Mitte, is home to the world-renowned Berlin Symphony Orchestra.

Berlin has around 150 theatres. In the former eastern section, they cluster around Friedrichstrasse; in the western part they're concentrated along Ku'damm. The historic **Deutsches Theater** *(☎ 25 00 25; Schumannstrasse 13a)* offers classic as well as modern productions. Nearby, the **Berliner Ensemble** *(☎ 282 31 60; Bertolt-Brecht-Platz 1)* performs works by Brecht and other 20th-century Europeans. **Friends of Italian Opera** *(☎ 691 12 11; Fidicinstrasse 40)*, in Kreuzberg, is Berlin's only English-language theatre venue.

The **Staatsoper Unter den Linden** *(☎ 20 35 34 55; Unter den Linden 5-7)*, in Mitte, hosts lavish opera productions. The **Deutsche Oper Berlin** *(☎ 343 84 01; Bismarckstrasse 35, Charlottenburg)* has classical works of mostly Italian and French composers, plus contemporary works.

The **A-Trane** *(☎ 313 25 50; Bleibtreustrasse 1; cover €5-10)*, in Charlottenburg, is still *the* place in Berlin for jazz. On some nights (usually Tuesday and Wednesday) admission is free. **Quasimodo** *(☎ 312 80 86; Kantstrasse 12a)* has live jazz, blues or rock acts in the basement every night. The stylish café on the ground floor is a good place for a pre-show drink.

Getting There & Away

Air Depending on the airline, you're likely to fly first into a European city such as Frankfurt, Amsterdam, Paris or London and catch a connecting flight from there. Tegel airport, which serves domestic and European destinations, will soon be closed, leaving Schönefeld as the airport hub. Berlin-Tempelhof became famous as the landing hub for Allied airlifts during the Berlin blockade of 1948–49.

Bus Berlin is well connected to the rest of Europe by long-distance bus. Most utilise the **Zentraler Omnibusbahnhof** *(ZOB; ☎ 302 53 61; Masurenalee 4-6)* in Charlottenburg, opposite the stately Funkturm radio tower (U2 to Kaiserdamm or S45 to Witzleben). Tickets are available from many travel agencies in Berlin or at the bus station.

Train ICE and IC trains have hourly services to every major city in Germany. There are night trains to the capitals of most major central European countries. Until the opening of the huge, new, centralised Lehrter Bahnhof (scheduled for 2007), visitors may find train services confusing.

Zoo station is the principal station for long-distance travellers going to/from the west. It has scores of lockers (from €1) and a large *Reisezentrum* (reservation and information office). Ostbahnhof (the former main station) is gaining importance, while Lichtenberg generally handles trains to/from the old east and countries beyond, as well as night trains.

Many trains serving Zoo station also stop at Ostbahnhof and may also stop at Friedrichstrasse and Alexanderplatz. Check schedules carefully and be aware that you may need to switch stations, usually easily done via S-Bahn. The S5 and S7 travel directly between Zoo and Lichtenberg (35 to 45 minutes); several additional lines serve the rest.

Conventional train tickets to and from Berlin are valid for all trains on the S-Bahn, which means that you can use your train ticket to ride the S-Bahn to/from your train station.

Hitching Lonely Planet does not encourage hitching. If you want to hitch, it's best to head to one of the autobahn service areas. If your destination is Leipzig, Nuremberg, Munich and beyond, make your way to the Dreilinden service area on the A115. For Dresden, take the S9 or S45 to Altglienicke and stand near the autobahn on-ramp. Those headed to Hamburg or Rostock should go to the former border checkpoint Stolpe by catching the U6 to Alt-Tegel and then bus No 224 to Stolpe.

Mitfahrzentralen (ride-share agencies) organise lifts and charge a fixed amount payable to the driver, plus commission from €6 to €10.50. Sample fares (including commission) are Leipzig €13.50, Hanover €17, Frankfurt/Main, Munich or Cologne €28.50. **ADM Mitfahrzentrale** *(☎ 194 40)* has two branches: in Zoo station on the Vinetastrasse platform of the U2 *(open 9am-8pm Mon-Fri & 10am-6pm Sat & Sun)* and in the Alexanderplatz U-Bahn station as you cross from U2 to U8 *(open 10am-6pm Mon-Fri, 11am-4pm Sat & Sun)*. Another agency, **Citynetz** *(☎ 194 44)*, is at Joachimstalerstrasse 17.

Getting Around

To/From the Airports Tegel airport is connected by bus No 109 to Zoo station (€2.10), a route that travels via Kurfürstendamm and Luisenplatz. JetExpress Bus TXL (€3.10) goes via Unter den Linden, Potsdamer Platz and the Reichstag. The trip between the airport and the western centre takes 30 minutes. A taxi between Tegel and Zoo station costs about €19.

Schönefeld airport is easily reached in 29 minutes by Airport Express trains leaving from Zoo station every 30 minutes. The train also stops at the rest of the stations along the central train line. A taxi to Zoo station costs between €25 and €35.

Tempelhof airport is reached by the U6 (Platz der Luftbrücke) and by bus No 119 from Kurfürstendamm via Kreuzberg. A taxi to/from Zoo station will cost about €16.

Public Transport Berlin's public transport system offers services jointly provided by **Berliner Verkehrsbetriebe** *(BVG; ☎ 194 49)*, which operates the U-Bahn, buses, trams and ferries; and the **Deutsche Bahn** *(DB)*, which runs the S-Bahn and regional RE, SE and RB trains (rail-pass holders can use the DB trains for free). One type of ticket is valid on all forms of transport (with the few exceptions noted in the following text). BVG has information kiosks at major entry points. For information on S-Bahn, RE and RB connections, visit the Reisezentrum office inside Zoo station.

Unless you're venturing to Potsdam or the very outer suburbs, you'll need only the AB zone ticket. Taking a bicycle in specially marked carriages of the S-Bahn or U-Bahn costs €1.25. On the U-Bahn, bikes are allowed only between 9am and 2pm and from 5.30pm to closing time on weekdays (any time on the weekend). Tickets range from *Kurzstrecke* (Short Trip – three stops by U-/S-Bahn, six stops by bus or tram; €1.20) to *Tageskarte* (Day Pass; €6.10). Bus drivers sell single and day tickets, but tickets for U-/S-Bahn trains and other multiple day tickets must be purchased in advance. Most types of tickets are available from vending machines; they must be stamped (validated) in a red or yellow machine *(Entwerter)* at the platform entrances to U-/S-Bahn stations, at bus stops before boarding, or as you enter the bus or tram. If you're using a timed ticket, validate it just as your train or bus arrives to ensure full value.

The most efficient way to travel around Berlin is by U-/S-Bahn. Services operate from 4am until just after midnight, but most S-Bahns continue to operate hourly between midnight and 4am on Saturday and Sunday. Some 70 bus lines operate between 1am and about 4am *(Nachtbus)*, when regular service resumes. Buses leave from the major nightlife areas such as Zoo station, Hackescher Markt in Mitte and Nollendorfplatz in Schöneberg, and cover the entire Berlin area.

Taxi stands are located throughout the city. Flag fall is €2.50 to €3, then €1.53 per kilometre; short trips (under 2km) cost €3. You can call a **taxi** on ☎ 194 10, ☎ 21 01 01 or ☎ 21 02 02.

Fahrradstation is the largest bicycle-rental agency, with branches all over the city, including at the **left-luggage office** *(☎ 29 74 93 19)* in Zoo station. Bikes cost from €10 a day with a €50 deposit.

Around Berlin

Many Berliners will warn you not to stray too far afield in the 'Wild East'. There are still occasional violent attacks against African and Asian foreigners in some small Brandenburg towns. However, the city-slickers are mainly being paranoid, and the region's two key attractions – Potsdam and Sachsenhausen – are worth a visit.

POTSDAM

☎ 0331 • pop 130,500

Potsdam, capital of Brandenburg state, was devastated by British bombers in 1945. Fortunately, most of the spectacular palaces in Sanssouci Park escaped undamaged. The Allies chose Schloss Cecilienhof for the Potsdam Conference of August 1945, which set the stage for the division of Berlin and Germany.

Only 24km from central Berlin and easily accessible by S-Bahn, Potsdam is an ideal day trip. Its main train station and last stop for the S-Bahn from Berlin is Potsdam Hauptbahnhof. The town is an interesting mix of newly restored buildings exuding charm, bad GDR-era architecture and old classics that have been mouldering away for decades.

Potsdam-Information *(☎ 27 55 80, fax 27 55 99; Friedrich-Ebert-Strasse 5; open daily)* is beside the Alter Markt. For details on the park palaces go to **Sanssouci-Information** *(☎ 969 42 02; W www.spsg.de; An der Historischen Mühle)*, near the old windmill northwest of Schloss Sanssouci.

The main attraction is **Sanssouci Park** *(admission free; open dawn-dusk daily)*, with myriad palaces and outbuildings. A ticket good for two consecutive days offers admission to all the park sites (Premium *Tageskarte*) and costs €15. Attractions sprawl across several

GERMANY

kilometres and include Georg Wenzeslaus von Knobelsdorff's **Schloss Sanssouci** *(compulsory tours depart 9am-5pm Tues-Sun Apr–mid-Oct & 9am-4pm Tues-Sun Nov-May; adult/concession €8/5)*, the celebrated 1747 rococo palace with glorious interiors; the imposing late-baroque **Neues Palais** (1769), the summer residence of the royal family; the **Bildergalerie** (1764), with an extensive collection of 17th-century paintings; and the unmissable **Schloss Charlottenhof** (1826).

Potsdam boasts scores of other marvels of architecture and art. The staff at the tourist office can fill you in. A particularly notable historical attraction is in Neuer Garten, the winding lakeside park on the west bank of the Heiliger See. Here stands **Schloss Cecilienhof** *(admission €2; open daily)*, site of the 1945 Potsdam Conference.

Potsdam's proximity to Berlin and the dearth of cheap accommodation make staying overnight an unappealing option. **Pension Auf dem Kiewitt** *(☎ 90 36 78, fax 967 87 55; Auf dem Kiewitt 8; singles/doubles €48/69)* is kindly despite the GDR high-rises surrounding it. For meals, try the classic **Café Heider** *(☎ 270 55 96; Friedrich-Ebert-Strasse 29; dishes €4.80-9.80)*, a lively meeting and eating place adjacent to Nauener Tor. Brandenburger Strasse has several nice cafés, shops and snack shops.

The Hauptbahnhof (main train station) in Potsdam is just southeast of the town centre across the Havel River. It's served by ICE and IC trains linking Berlin with points west. Bus No 695 goes past Schloss Sanssouci, the Orangerieschloss and the Neues Palais from the south exit of Potsdam Hauptbahnhof. Change to bus No 692 for Schloss Cecilienhof. To reach Schloss Charlottenhof and the Neues Palais, take bus No 606.

SACHSENHAUSEN

In 1936 the Nazis opened a 'model' concentration camp near Oranienburg, about 35km north of Berlin. By 1945 about 220,000 men from 22 countries had passed through the gates of Sachsenhausen. About 100,000 died here. After the war, the Soviets and the communist leaders of the GDR used the camp for *their* undesirables.

Plan on spending at least two hours at Sachsenhausen *(☎ 03301-20 02 00; admission free; open 8.30am-6pm daily Apr-Sept, open 8.30am-4.30pm daily Oct-Mar)*, which is easily reached from Berlin. Among the many museums and monuments are **Barracks 38 and 39**, which contain excellent displays of the camp's history. At the front gate you may rent a chilling audio guide in English (€2.50), and an **information office** that sells maps, brochures and books.

From Berlin take the S1 to Oranienburg (€2.40, 40 minutes). The camp is an easy 2km northeast of the station.

Eastern Germany

Along with Mecklenburg-Western Pomerania in the north, the three states of Saxony, Thuringia and Saxony-Anhalt constituted the former GDR. Saxony (Sachsen) is eastern Germany's most densely populated and industrialised region. The Elbe River cuts through a picturesque area known as 'Saxon Switzerland' as it heads towards Saxony's tragic capital, Dresden. Leipzig, a great educational and commercial centre, rivals Dresden for history. Beautiful little towns such as Görlitz and Meissen punctuate this colourful, accessible corner of Germany.

Thuringia (Thüringen) occupies the German heartland. Although lively Erfurt is its capital, its humanist traditions reside in Weimar, birthplace of the post-WWI republic. Saxony-Anhalt boasts a varied geography and alluring historical towns such as Quedlinburg and Wernigerode. Meanwhile, Lutherstadt-Wittenberg attracts lovers of Martin Luther.

DRESDEN

☎ 0351 • pop 463,500

In the 18th century the Saxon capital was famous throughout Europe as 'the Florence of the north', as Italian artists, musicians, actors and master craftsmen flocked to the Dresden court, bestowing countless masterpieces upon the city. But in February 1945, carpet-bombing Allied aircraft levelled Dresden. At least 35,000 people died at a time when the city was jammed with refugees and the war was almost over.

Many of Dresden's great baroque buildings have been restored, but the city's former architectural masterpiece, the Frauenkirche, is still being laboriously reconstructed. In spite of modern rebuilding, this city invariably wins visitors' affections with its numerous museums and many fine baroque palaces.

Dresden's two train stations are Dresden-Hauptbahnhof, on the southern side of town and Dresden-Neustadt, in the Neustadt section of town north of the River Elbeř. From Dresden Hauptbahnhof, the pedestrian mall of Prager Strasse leads northwards past some classic GDR monoliths into the old centre. **Dresden-Information** *(☎ 49 19 20, fax 49 19 21 16; Ⓦ www.dresden.de; Prager Strasse 10; open Mon-Sat)* has its main office near the Hauptbahnhof. An **information counter** *(open daily)* is in the Schinkelwache near the Semperoper (opera house). The offices sell the Dresden-City-Card (€16 for 48 hours), which includes local public transport and free admission to many leading museums.

Reisebank has a branch in the main train station. There are **post offices** near the Prager Strasse tourist office and on Köningsbrücker Strasse in Neustadt. Surf the net at Neustadt's **twindot.com** *(☎ 802 06 02; Alaunstrasse 19)*.

Things to See & Do

The Altmarkt area is the historic hub of Dresden. To the east you'll see the rebuilt **Kreuzkirche** (1792), famous for its boys' choir, and in the distance the 1912 **Neues Rathaus** (New Town Hall).

Cross the wide Wilsdruffer Strasse to the **Stadtmuseum** *(City History Museum; ☎ 49 86 60; adult/concession €2/1; open 10am-6pm Tues-Sun)*. Northwest along Landhausstrasse is Neumarkt and the site of the ruined **Frauenkirche** (Church of Our Lady), built in 1738. The remaining rubble on display is a moving reminder of the bombings.

Leading northwest from Neumarkt is Augustusstrasse, with the stunning 102m-long **Procession of Princes** porcelain mural covering the outer wall of the old royal stables. Augustusstrasse leads directly to Schlossplatz and the baroque Catholic **Hofkirche** (1755). Just south of the church is the Renaissance **Schloss** *(adult/concession €2.60/1.50; open Tues-Sun)*, which is being reconstructed as a museum.

On the western side of the Hofkirche is Theaterplatz, with Dresden's glorious opera house, the neo-Renaissance **Semperoper**. The Dresden opera has a tradition going back 350 years, and many works by Richard Strauss, Carl Maria von Weber and Richard Wagner premiered here.

The baroque **Zwinger** (1728) and its museums are among Dresden's stars; they occupy the southern side of Theaterplatz. You can buy a day pass to all these museums for €6.10/3.60 per adult/concession. The superb **Historisches Museum** *(Rüstkammer; adult/concession €1.50/1; open Tues-Sun)* has a collection of ceremonial weapons. Housed in opposite corners of the complex with separate entrances are the **Mathematisch-Physikaler Salon** *(adult/concession €1.50/1; open Fri-Wed)*, with scientific instruments and timepieces, and the **Museum für Tierkunde** *(zoological museum; adult/concession €3/1.50; open Wed-Mon)*, with natural-history exhibits.

East of the Augustusbrücke is the **Brülsche Terrasse**, a pleasant, elevated, riverside promenade with the overwrought moniker of 'the Balcony of Europe'. At the eastern end of the promenade is the **Albertinum** (1885). Here you will find the **Gemäldegalerie Alte Meister** *(open Tues-Sun)*, which boasts Raphael's *Sistine Madonna*; **Gemäldegalerie Neue Meister** *(open Wed-Mon)*, with renowned 19th- and 20th-century paintings; and **Grünes Gewölbe** *(Green Vault; open Wed-Mon)*, hosting a collection of jewel-studded precious objects. You can visit all three with a combined ticket (adult/concession €4.50/2.50).

Places to Stay

The **tourist office** *(☎ 49 19 22 22 for bookings)* can arrange private rooms for a €3 fee. In a former communist party training centre, **Jugendgästehaus Dresden** *(☎ 49 26 20, fax 492 62 99; Maternistrasse 22; beds junior/senior from €17.50/21)* is a 15-minute walk northwest of Hauptbahnhof (or take tram No 7, 9, 10 or 26 to the corner of Ammonstrasse and Freiberger Strasse). The non-DJH **Jugendherberge Rudi Arndt** *(☎ 471 06 67, fax 472 89 59; Hübnerstrasse 11; beds junior/senior €16.80/19.50)* is 10 minutes' walk south of the main train station.

In Neustadt are **Hostel Mondpalast Dresden** *(☎/fax 8 04 60 61; Ⓔ mondpalast@t-online.de; Katherinenstrasse 11-13; dorm beds €13, singles/doubles €23/34)*, in the centre of Neustadt's nightlife, and **Die Boofe** *(☎ 801 33 61, fax 801 33 62; Ⓔ info@boofe.com; Hechtstrasse 10; beds from €14.50/person)*, north of Neustadt station.

Hotel prices are among the highest in Germany. Pickings south of the Elbe are especially slim. In Neustadt, **Pension Edith** *(☎/fax 802 83 42; Priesnitzstrasse 63; singles/*

GERMANY

doubles €41/61), in a quiet backstreet, has a few rooms with private shower; book well ahead. **Hotel Rothenburger Hof** *(☎ 88 12 60, fax 812 62 22; ⓔ kontakt@dresden-hotel.de; Rothenburger Strasse 15-17; singles/doubles from €64/85)* is clean and bright.

Places to Eat

Head straight to Neustadt, Dresden's nightlife centre, for food and fun. **Raskolnikoff** *(Böhmische Strasse 34; mains €3-12)* serves dishes from the four corners of central Europe. Alaunstrasse has loads of Italian places, including comfortable **Trattoria Vecchia Napoli** *(☎ 802 90 55; Alaunstrasse 33; mains €4.50-14.90)*, where wood-oven-baked pizzas and enticing pastas demand to be washed down with red wine. You'll also find scores of late-night restaurant-bars nearby. **Café Europa** *(☎ 804 48 10; Königsbrücker Strasse 68; mains €4-18.20)* stays open 24 hours. **El Perro Borracho** *(☎ 803 67 23; Alaunstrasse 70; dishes €2.80-10.20)* serves tapas and other Spanish fare in an avant-garde courtyard.

Café Antik Kunst *(☎ 498 98 36; Terrassengasse)* combines an antique shop with excellent coffee. Other popular cafés include **Max** *(☎ 563 59 96; Louisenstrasse 65)* and **Blumenau** *(☎ 802 65 02; Louisenstrasse 67)*, next door. There are several supermarkets in Neustadt, including a **Plus** at Königsbrückerstrasse south of Louisenstrasse.

Entertainment

The comprehensive *Sax* (€1.25) is a German-language guide that's available at newsstands.

Dresden is synonymous with opera performances at the **Semperoper**. Its two other great theatres are the **Staatsschauspiel** *(☎ 491 35 55)*, also near the Zwinger, and the **Staatsoperette** *(☎ 207 99 29; Pirnaer Landstrasse 131)*, in Leuben. Tickets for all can be bought from Dresden-Information, or an hour before each performance at the theatre's box office. Many theatres close from mid-July to the end of August.

A variety of musical events are presented in the austere **Kulturpalast** *(☎ 486 60; Schlossstrasse 2)*. **Jazzclub Tonne** *(☎ 802 60 17; Königstrasse 15; cover charge €6-10)* has live jazz five nights per week.

For a drink, the choices in the café-laden blocks around Alaunstrasse and Louisenstrasse are many. Gay visitors might start at the cocktail bar **Roses** *(☎ 802 42 64; Jordanstrasse 10)* or amid a young-ish crowd at the club **Queens** *(☎ 803 16 50; Görlitzerstrasse 3)*. *Gegenpol* magazine has gay and lesbian listings.

Getting There & Away

Hourly trains link Dresden to Leipzig (ICE, €24, 1¼ hours; IR, €16.80, 1¾ hours) and Berlin-Ostbahnhof (€30.60, two hours). IR trains running every two hours to Hanover (€54.40, 4½ hours) allow more connection possibilities. There's a **Mitfahrzentrale** *(☎ 194 40)* at Dr-Friedrich-Wolfsstrasse 2, across from Neustadt station.

AROUND DRESDEN

Meissen

☎ 03521 • pop 32,000

Just 27km northwest of Dresden, Meissen is a perfectly preserved, old German town and the centre of a rich wine-growing region. It straddles the Elbe, with the old town on the western bank and the train station on the eastern bank. In the central square you'll find **Meissen-Information** *(☎ 419 40, fax 41 94 19; Markt 3; open Mon-Sat, daily Apr-Oct)*. Also on Markt, the 15th-century **Frauenkirche** *(☎ 45 38 32; open 10am-noon, 1pm-5pm daily May-Oct)* boasts a tower well worth climbing for fine views; pick up the key in the church or from the adjacent Pfarrbüro (parish office).

Various steeply stepped lanes lead up to **Albrechtsburg** *(☎ 45 24 90; adult/concession €2/1.50; open daily)*. Beside the cathedral is the remarkable 15th-century Albrechtsburg **castle** *(adult/concession €3.50/2.50; open daily 1 Feb-9 Jan)*. Constructed with an ingenious system of internal arches, it was the first palace-style castle built in Germany.

Meissen has long been famous for its chinaware, with its trademark blue crossed-swords insignia. The **porcelain factory** *(☎ 46 87 00; Talstrasse 9; open daily)* is 1km southwest of town.

Pension Burkhardt *(☎ 45 81 98, fax 45 81 97; Neugasse 29; singles/doubles from €25/50)* has attractive rooms with full facilities. At **Goldener Löwe** *(☎ 441 10; Heinrichsplatz 6; mains €6.75-15.25)* you can sit on the square and people-watch. Around the Markt are grocers, bakers, *eiscafés* and butchers selling **snacks**.

Half-hourly S-Bahn trains travel to Meissen from both of Dresden's train stations (€4.40, 40 minutes).

Görlitz

☎ 03581 • pop 63,000

Situated 100km east of Dresden on the Neisse River, Görlitz is an important stop on the way to Poland. The city emerged from WWII with its beautiful old town undamaged. Of particular interest are the **Rathaus** (1537), the **Peterskirche** (1497) and the 16th-century **Dreifaltigkeitskirche** on Obermarkt. The **tourist office** *(☎ 475 70, fax 47 57 27; Obermarkt 29; open 9am-6.30pm Mon-Fri, 10am-4pm Sat, 10am-1pm Sun)* has a free room-finding service.

The **DJH hostel** *(☎ 40 65 10, fax 66 17 75; ⓔ jugendherbergegoerlitz@t-online.de; Goethestrasse 17; juniors/seniors €12.50/15)* is south of the station. **Gästehaus Lisakowski** *(☎ 40 05 39, fax 31 30 19; Landeskronstrasse 23; singles/doubles €23/46)* offers simple rooms near the train station. **Zum Flyns** *(☎ 40 06 97; Langenstrasse 1; mains €6.50-14.50)* serves local specialities amid vaulted ceilings and tiny nooks.

Frequent trains run to/from Dresden (€14.80, 1½ hours). There are a few nonstop trains daily to/from Berlin (€30, three hours).

GERMANY

LEIPZIG

☎ 0341 • pop 437,000

Since the discovery of rich silver mines in the nearby Erzgebirge (Ore Mountains) in the 16th century, Leipzig has enjoyed almost continual prosperity. Today it's the second-largest city in eastern Germany, offering plenty for book and music lovers as well as pub-crawlers.

Leipzig-Information *(☎ 710 42 60, fax 710 42 71; ⓦ www.leipzig.de; Richard-Wagner-Strasse 1; open daily)* is directly opposite the train station (Germany's largest). You can buy the Leipzig Card here (one/three days €9.90/21) for unlimited local transport and discounts at attractions and some restaurants.

There is a **Reisebank** at the main train station, while the main **post office** is at Augustusplatz 1. You can surf the Internet for €3 per hour at **Le Bit** *(☎ 998 20 20; Friedrich-List-Platz)*, east of the Hauptbahnhof.

Things to See & Do

The Renaissance **Altes Rathaus** *(1556; Markt)* is one of Germany's most beautiful town halls. Behind it is the **Alte Börse** (1687), with a **monument** to Goethe (1903). Between Markt and Augustusplatz, The remarkable **Nikolaikirche** *(☎ 960 52 70; Nikolaikirchhof 3)*, was built in 1165 and was the local meeting point of the 'Gentle Revolution', which helped overthrow the communist regime.

Just southwest of Markt is **Thomaskirche** *(☎ 960 28 55; Thomaskirchhof 18)*, built in 1212 with Bach's tomb in front of the altar. Bach worked in Leipzig from 1723 until his death in 1750, and the St Thomas Boys' Choir, which he once led, is still going strong. Opposite the church is the **Bach Museum** *(☎ 964 41 33; Thomaskirchhof 16; adult/concession €3/2; open daily 10am-5pm)*.

Along Dittrichring is the former East German *Stasi* (secret police) headquarters, diagonally opposite the Schauspielhaus. Now it houses the **Museum in der Runden Ecke** *(☎ 961 24 43; admission free; open 10am-6pm daily)*, outlining Stasi methods of investigation and intimidation. A new museum, the **Zeitgeschichtliches Forum** *(Forum of Contemporary History; ☎ 222 00; Grimmaishce Strasse 6; admission free; open 9am-6pm Tues-Fri, 10am-6pm Sat-Sun)*, gives a history of the GDR that's both fact-filled and wrenching. Across the street are the temporary quarters of Leipzig's finest museum, **Museum der bildenden Künste** *(Museum of Fine Arts; ☎ 21 69 90; Grimmaische Strasse 1-7; adult/concession €2.50/1.25)*, with an excellent collection of old masters.

The **Deutsche Bücherei** *(German Library; ☎ 227 13 24; Deutscher Platz 1; admission free; open 9am-4pm Mon-Sat)* houses millions of books (including most titles published in German since 1913). Farther to the southeast is Leipzig's most impressive sight, the **Völkerschlachtdenkmal** *(Battle of Nations Monument; ☎ 878 04 71; Prager Strasse; adult/concession €3/2; open 10am-6pm daily Apr-Oct, 10am-4pm daily Nov-Mar)*, a 91m-high monument erected in 1913 to commemorate the decisive victory by combined Prussian, Austrian and Russian armies over Napoleon's forces here in 1813.

Places to Stay

During trade fairs many of Leipzig's hotels raise their prices and are often full. The **Jugendherberge** *(☎ 245 70 11, fax 245 70 12; Volksgartenstrasse 24; junior/senior €14.30/17)* is about 3km from the centre. Take tram No 17, 27 or 31 (direction: Schönefeld) to Löbauer Strasse. The new **Hostel Sleepy Lion** *(☎ 993 94 80, fax 993 94 82; ⓔ info@hostel-leipzig.de; Käthe-Kollwitz-Strasse 3; dorms* *from €14, singles/doubles €24/36)* is central and popular.

South of the centre, **Pension Christin** *Kochstrasse 4; singles/doubles from €29/41)* offers plain but spotless rooms on a handsome sidestreet. Take tram No 10 or 11 to Kochstrasse. **Zill's Tunnel** *(☎ 960 20 78, fax 960 19 69; ⓔ info@zillstunnel.de; Barfussgasschen 9; doubles from €67)* is a real find – a couple of lovely rooms with private facilities above Leipzig's pub district.

Stay amid what's often called Leipzig's second best art collection at **Galerie Hotel Leipziger Hof** *(☎ 697 40, fax 697 41 50; Hedwigstrasse 1-3; singles/doubles from €55/65)*, about 1.2km east of the centre. Or sleep like a politburo member at the GDR-era **Hotel Mercure Leipzig** *(☎ 214 60, fax 960 49 16; ⓔ mercure_leipzig@t-online.de; Augustusplatz 5-6; singles/doubles from €61/77)*, with large rooms.

Places to Eat

Try food such as *Mutti* (mother) used to make at **Paulaner** *(☎ 211 31 15; Klostergasse 3 & 5; mains €5.40-14.90)*. Luther's favourite pub was **Thüringer Hof** *(☎ 994 49 99; Burgstrasse 19; mains €6.90-13.15)*, with great dishes. Another place with a long tradition is **Zill's Tunnel** *(mains €6.60-13.60)*, with typical German specialities (see Places to Stay for contact details). Founded in 1525, **Auerbachs Keller** *(☎ 21 61 00; Grimmaischerstrasse 3-4; mains €7.10-18.90)*, in the Mädler Passage just south of the Altes Rathaus, featured in Goethe's *Faust*.

Barfussgässchen is the centre of Leipzig's exaggeratedly named **pub mile**, with casual cafés and restaurants. The **Hauptbahnhof** is also filled with eateries and supermarkets.

Entertainment

Dating back to 1743, the **Neues Gewandhaus** *(☎ 127 02 80; Augustusplatz 8)* has Europe's longest established civic orchestra. Leipzig's modern **Opernhaus** is just across the square. The **Schauspielhaus** *(☎ 126 81 68; Bosestrasse 1)*, a few blocks to the west of Markt, mixes classic theatre with modern works.

Moritz-Bastei *(☎ 70 25 90; Universitätsstrasse 9)*, spread over three underground floors, has live music or disco most nights, but in summer it really comes into its own as a cultural venue.

Spizz *(☎ 960 80 43; Markt 9)* is a trendy café by day and slick place for drinking and dancing by night. **Blaue Trude** *(☎ 212 66 79; Katharinenstrasse 17)* is Leipzig's gay club of the moment.

Getting There & Around

Leipzig is linked by fast and frequent trains to all major German cities, including Dresden (€24, 1¼ hours), Berlin (€33.40, 1¾ hours) and Munich (€76, five hours). Ride sharers can visit the **Mitfahrzentrale** *(☎ 194 40; Goethestrasse 7-10)*.

Trams are the main form of public transport in Leipzig, with the most important lines running via Willy-Brandt-Platz in front of the train station. A 15-minute ticket in the inner city is €1 while an hour ticket on the whole system is €1.30. Strip tickets valid for four rides are €4/4.90 for short/long trips. Day tickets are €4.

ERFURT

☎ 0361 • pop 215,000

The capital of Thuringia was only slightly damaged during WWII and boasts numerous burgher town houses, churches and monasteries gracing its surprisingly well-preserved medieval quarter. In April 2002 Erfurt became the unlikely focus of national grief when a disgruntled former student shot dead 16 people and himself at a local high school.

The friendly and efficient **tourist office** *(☎ 664 00; ⓔ service@erfurt-tourist-info.de; Benediktsplatz 1; open 10am-4pm Sat & Sun Jan-Mar)* is just east of Fischmarkt and the Rathaus. It sells the three-day Erfurt Card (€14), which allows unlimited use of public transport and entry to museums. There's a **Reisebank** at Erfurt's Hauptbahnhof, and the main **post office** is on Anger. **Internet Café** *(Fischmarkt 5)* charges €4 an hour.

The numerous interesting backstreets and laneways in Erfurt's surprisingly large Altstadt make this a fascinating place to explore. Don't miss the 13th-century Gothic **Dom St Marien** and **Severikirche**, which stand together on a hillock dominating the central square of Domplatz. The wooden stools (1350) and stained glass (1410) in the choir, and figures on the portals, make the cathedral one of the richest medieval churches in Germany.

The eastbound street beside the Rathaus leads to the medieval restored **Krämerbrücke** (1325), which is lined on each side with timber-framed shops. This is the only such bridge north of the Alps. Further north, on the same side of the River Gera, is **Augustinerkloster** *(☎ 576 60; Augustinerstrasse 10; adult/concession €3.50/2.50; open 9am-noon, 2pm-5pm Mon-Sat, 11am Sun Apr-Oct; 10am-noon, 2pm-4pm Mon-Sat, 11am Sun Nov-Mar)*, a late-medieval monastery that was home to Martin Luther early in the 16th century.

Places to Stay & Eat

The tourist office arranges private accommodation costing around €20/40 for doubles/singles (plus a booking fee of 10%). Erfurt's **Jugendherberge** *(☎ 562 67 05, fax 562 6706; ⓔ jh-erfurt@djh-thueringen.de; Hochheimer Strasse 12; juniors/seniors €15/18)* is southwest of the centre. Take tram No 5 from Erfurt train station to Steigerstrasse. **Pension Schuster** *(☎ 373 50 52; Rubenstrasse 11; rooms €40 with bathroom)* has sunny, spotless rooms 10 minutes from the train station. Stay among the nuns at the historic **Protestant Augustiner Priory** *(☎ 57 66 00, fax 576 60 99; ⓔ AK-efurt@augustinerkloster.de; Augustinerstrasse 10; singles/doubles €40/70)*, which offers fully-renovated but simple lodgings.

Erfurt has a lively restaurant and eatery scene. **Suppen und Salatinsel** *(Marktstrasse 45; dishes €2-7)* is a simple place that serves up soups, vegetarian fare and German goodies. **Erfurter Brauhaus** *(☎ 562 58 27; Anger 21; mains €5-10)* is a microbrewery that serves its own beer, and has a good selection of regional specialties.

Descend into the middle ages at **Luther Keller** *(☎ 568 82 05; Futterstrasse 15-16; mains €8-12)*, where there's cheap, traditional food, lusty wenches and tankards full of frothy brew.

Entertainment

Small bars such as **Otto L** *(Pergamentergasse 30)* and **Tiko** *(Michaelistrasse 35)* huddle throughout the Andreasviertel, northwest of Fischmarkt. The focus here is **P33** *(Pergamentergasse 33)*, a popular live music venue. The **Jazzkeller** *(Fischmarkt 12-13)* makes Thursday night its own with live jazz from 8.30pm. Try **Museumskeller** *(Juri-Gagarin-Ring 140a)* for rock music, **DASDIE Live** *(Marstallstrasse 12)* for Kabarett and variety, and, for Latin and blues, **Presseklub** *(Dalbersweg 1)*. The tourist office sells the monthly *Erfurt Magazine* (€0.50), which outlines entertainment happenings.

Getting There & Away

Every two hours a direct IR train runs between Erfurt and Frankfurt (€37, 2½ hours). The same train goes to and from Berlin (€49, 3½ hours), Weimar (€4, 15 minutes) and Eisenach (€15.20, 27 minutes). Cheaper but slower regional trains also run between Weimar and Eisenach. ICE trains link Erfut with Leipzig (€23.60, 1¾ hours) every two hours.

WEIMAR & AROUND

☎ 03643 • pop 62,000

As a repository of German humanistic traditions, Weimar is unrivalled. Those who lived or worked here include Lucas Cranach the Elder, Johann Sebastian Bach, Friedrich Schiller, Johann Wolfgang von Goethe, Franz Liszt, Walter Gropius, Wassily Kandinsky, and Paul Klee. From 1919 to 1925 it was the focal point of the Bauhaus architectural movement. Weimar is also known as the place where the German republican constitution was drafted after WWI. The ruins of the Buchenwald concentration camp nearby are haunting evidence of the terrors of the Nazi regime.

The town centre is a 20-minute walk south of the Hauptbahnhof. The **tourist office** *(☎ 240 00; ⓔ tourist-info@weimar.de; Markt 10; open daily)* is very helpful. There is a smaller office inside the Hauptbahnhof. Both sell the three-day Weimar Card (€10), providing entry to most of Weimar's museums, unlimited travel on city buses and other benefits. The central **post office** is on the corner of Heinrich-Heine-Strasse and Schwanseestrasse.

Central Weimar

Except where otherwise noted, attractions are closed Monday.

A good place to begin is on Herderplatz. The **Herderkirche** (1500) has an altarpiece (1555) by Lucas Cranach the Elder and his son, Lucas Cranach the Younger. A block east of Herderplatz towards the Ilm River is the **Schlossmuseum** *(☎ 54 60; Burgplatz 4; adult/concession €4/2.50; open 10am-6pm Tues-Sun Apr-Oct, 10am-4.30pm Tues-Sun Nov-Mar)*. The large collection, with masterpieces by Cranach, Dürer and others, occupies three floors of this castle. North of the centre, the **Neue Museum Weimar** *(☎ 54 60; Weimarplatz; adult/concession €3/2; open*

10am-6pm Tues-Sun Apr-Oct, 10am-4.30pm Tues-Sun Nov-Mar) houses, among other pieces, one of Germany's most important private collections of contemporary art.

Platz der Demokratie, with the renowned music school founded in 1872 by Franz Liszt, is south of the Sclossmuseum. This square spills over into Markt, where you'll find the neo-Gothic **Rathaus** (1841) and the **Cranachhaus**, in which Lucas Cranach the Elder died (in 1553). West of Markt via some narrow lanes is the **German National Theatre**, where the Weimar Republic constitution was drafted in 1919. On this same square is the **Bauhaus Museum** *(☎ 54 51 02; Theaterplatz; adult/concession €3/2; open 10am-6pm Tues-Sun Apr-Oct, 10am-4.30pm Tues-Sun Nov-Mar)*, which documents the evolution of this influential artistic and architectural movement.

From here, the elegant Schillerstrasse curves around to Schillers Wohnhaus; Goethes Wohnhaus, where *Faust* was written; and the **Goethe-Nationalmuseum** *(☎ 54 51 02; Frauenplan 1; adult/concession €2.50/2; open 9am-6pm Tues-Sun Apr-Oct, 9am-4pm Tues-Sun Nov-Mar)*, with exhibits on Schiller, Goethe and their life and times. The **Liszthaus** *(☎ 54 51 02; Marienstrasse 17; adult/concession €2/1.50; open 9am-1pm, 2pm-6pm Tues-Sun Apr-Oct, 10am-1pm, 2pm-4pm Tues-Sun Nov-Mar)*, by the edge of Park an der Ilm, was where Liszt wrote his *Hungarian Rhapsody* and *Faust Symphony*. In the yellow complex across the road from the Liszthaus, Walter Gropius laid the groundwork for modern architecture. His buildings now house Weimar's **Bauhaus Universität**.

The tombs of Goethe and Schiller lie side by side in a neoclassical crypt in the **Historischer Friedhof** (Historical Cemetery), two blocks west of the Liszthaus.

Weimar boasts three large parks, each replete with monuments, museums and attractions. Most accessible is **Park an der Ilm**, which runs right along the eastern side of Weimar.

Buchenwald

Buchenwald museum and concentration camp *(☎ 43 02 00; Ettersburg Hill; admission free; open 9.45am-6pm Tues-Sun May-Sep, 9.45am-5pm Tues-Sun Oct-Apr)* is 10km north of Weimar. You first pass the memorial with mass graves of some of the 56,500 WWII victims from 18 nations, including German antifascists, Jews, and Soviet and Polish prisoners of war. The concentration camp and museum are 1km beyond. Many prominent German communists and Social Democrats, Ernst Thälmann and Rudolf Breitscheid among them, were murdered here. On 11 April 1945, as US troops approached, the prisoners overcame the SS guards and liberated themselves.

After the war the Soviet victors turned the tables by establishing Special Camp No 2, in which thousands of (alleged) anticommunists and former Nazis were worked to death.

Last entry is 45 minutes before closing. Bus No 6 runs via Goetheplatz and Weimar train station to Buchenwald every 40 minutes.

Places to Stay & Eat

For €2.50 the tourist office arranges private rooms (from about €20 per person). Weimar has four DJH hostels, but the most central are **Jugendherberge Germania** *(☎ 85 04 90, fax 85 04 91; ⓔ jh-germania@djh-thueringen.de; Carl-August-Allee 13)*, in the street running downhill from the station, and also **Am Poseckschen Garten** *(☎ 85 07 92, 85 07 93; ⓔ jh-posgarten@djh-thueringen.de; Humboldtstrasse 17)*, near the Historischer Friedhof. Both charge €15/18 for juniors/seniors.

Pension and hotel prices include breakfast. Cheapest is **Am Poseckschen Garten** *(☎ 51 12 39; ⓔ koenig-weimar@t-online.de; Am Poseckschen Garten 1; singles/doubles €18/34)*, which has reasonable rooms. **Pension Savina II** *(☎ 866 90, fax 86 69 11; ⓔ savina@pension-savina.de; Meyerstrasse 60; singles/doubles with shower & toilet €40/70)* is a comfortable option near the train station. Its sister **Savina I** *(same contact details; Rembrandtweg 13; singles/doubles with shared facilities €34/52)* is more basic. **Pension Am Theater** *(☎ 889 40, fax 88 94 32; Erfurterstrasse 10; singles/doubles with bathroom €45/65)* is about the friendliest accommodation you'll find anywhere – and the rooms aren't bad either. **Hotel Zur Sonne** *(☎ 80 04 10, fax 86 29 32; Rollplatz 2; singles/doubles from €51/77)* offers good value in a central location.

ACC *(☎ 85 11 61; Burgplatz 2; mains €6-10)* has an interesting menu and a palatable price range. In a restored late-19th-century winter garden, **Anno 1900** *(☎ 90 35 71; Geleitstrasse 12a; mains €6-11)* pulls a good crowd with its well-priced fare of pastas, steaks, fish and vegetarian. **Zum Zwiebel** (☎ *50 23 75; Teichgasse 6; mains €6-13)* serves hearty regional dishes. Southwest of the centre, ever-popular **Felsenkeller** *(☎ 85 03 66; Humboldstrasse 37; mains €6-13)* has brewed its own Felsenbräu since 1889, and serves it liberally with cheap, traditional German food.

Entertainment

The **German National Theatre** *(☎ 75 53 34; Theaterplatz)* is the main stage for Weimar's cultural activities. Buy tickets at the tourist office. The **Kasseturm** *(Goetheplatz 1)*, a beer cellar in a round tower, has live music, disco or cabaret most nights. **SchutzeNgasse** *(Schutzengasse 2)* is a relaxed bar that packs in the student crowd.

Getting There & Away

There are frequent direct IR trains to Berlin-Zoo (€38.40, three hours) via Naumburg and Halle, and to Frankfurt/Main (€40, three hours) via Erfurt and Eisenach. ICE trains go to Dresden (€37, two hours) and Leipzig (€21.20, one hour).

EISENACH

☎ 03691 • pop 44,000

The birthplace of Johann Sebastian Bach, Eisenach is a small, picturesque city on the edge of the Thuringian Forest. Its main attraction is Wartburg castle, from where the landgraves (German counts) ruled medieval Thuringia. Martin Luther went into hiding here after excommunication.

Eisenach-Information *(☎ 194 33; e tourist-info@eisenach-tourist.de; Markt 2; open daily)* is friendly and well organised. Its three-day Classic-Card (€14) provides you with free admission to the castle and most museums, and use of public transport.

At world-famous **Wartburg** *(☎ 770 73; tour adult/concession €6/3; open 8.30am-5pm Mar-Oct, 9am-3.30pm Nov-Feb)* Martin Luther translated the New Testament into German while in hiding, contributing greatly to the development of the written German language. You can visit the castle's interior with a guided tour (in German), which includes the museum, Luther's study room and the amazing Romanesque great hall; arrive early to avoid the crowds. A free English-language leaflet set out in the sequence of the tour is available.

Jugendherberge Artur Becker *(☎ 74 32 59, fax 74 32 60; e jh-eisenach@djh-thueringen.de; Mariental 24; juniors/seniors €14/17)* is in the valley below Wartburg. Take bus No 3 to Liliengrund. **Gasthof Storchenturm** *(☎ 73 32 63, fax 73 32 65; Georgenstrasse 43; beds per person €18)* has bare, clean rooms with facilities. **Pension Mahret** *(☎ 74 27 44, fax 750 33; e pension.mahret@t-online.de; Neustadt 30; singles/doubles €35/52)* offers pleasant, self-contained apartments near the town centre.

In a cave-like cellar, **Brunnenkeller** *(☎ 21 23 58; Markt 13; dishes €6-8)* has a cosy feel and cheap Thuringian specialities. **Kartoffelhaus** *(Sophienstrasse 44)* offers all things spud for around €8.

Use the cheap, frequent RB/RE services to Erfurt (€8.10, 50 minutes) and Weimar (€10.70, 70 minutes) rather than the IC. IR services run direct to Frankfurt/Main (€29) and ICE to Berlin-Zoo (€56.60).

QUEDLINBURG

☎ 03946 • pop 26,000

One of Germany's true gems, Quedlinburg dates back over 1000 years. Almost all buildings in its centre are half-timbered, street after cobbled street. **Quedlinburg-Information** *(☎ 90 56 24, fax 90 56 29; e Q.T.M@t-online.de; Markt 2; open Mon-Sat, daily Apr-Oct)* books rooms at no cost.

The focal point for visitors is the hill with the old castle district, known as **Schlossberg**. The area features the 1129 Romanesque **Church of St Servatii** *(Dom; ☎ 70 99 00; Am Dom; adult/concession €3/2; open 10am-6pm Tues-Fri, 10am-4pm Sat, noon-6pm Sun May-Oct, 10am-4pm Mon-Sat, noon-4pm Sun Nov-Apr)*, with a 10th-century crypt and priceless reliquaries and early Bibles. In 1938 SS meetings were held in the Dom.

To get in some hiking, take a bus or train 10km southwest to **Thale**, blessed with a landscape of rugged cliffs and the starting point for hikes along the lovely Bode Valley in the Harz Mountains. Also worthwhile is a visit to Gernrode and its delightful **Church of St Cyriakus**, just 8km south of Quedlinburg.

For accommodation, central **Familie Klindt** *(☎ 70 29 11; Hohe Strasse 19; €12, breakfast €4)* is a great deal, with comfy rooms. **Hotel am Dippeplatz** *(☎ 77 14 11, fax 77 14 47; Breite Strasse 16; singles/doubles from €49/59)* is bright and clean.

Kartoffelhaus No 1 *(☎ 70 83 34; Breite Strasse 37; mains €5.10-11.60)* serves filling meals and snacks for all budgets. **Brauhaus Lüdde** *(☎ 70 52 06; Blasiistrasse 14; dishes €8.50-14.50)* has hearty pub food and brews its own pilsener, *Altbier*.

You can change trains in Magdeburg (€10.70, 1¼ hours) for long distance routes. To Wernigerode (€6.60, one hour), trains connect via Halberstadt.

WERNIGERODE

☎ 03943 • pop 35,000

Flanked by the foothills of the Harz Mountains, Wernigerode is crowned by a romantic ducal castle rising above the old town. Summer throngs of tourists and their cash has all but erased any trace of the old GDR.

The **tourist office** *(☎ 194 33, fax 63 20 40; Nicolaiplatz 1; open daily)* is near Markt. The **Rathaus** (1277), with its pair of pointed black-slate towers, is a focal point. From here it's just a short climb to the neo-Gothic **castle**. Built in the 12th century, the castle has been renovated and enlarged over the centuries. Try **hiking** the beautiful deciduous forest behind the castle. The more serious might tackle the 30km route (marked by blue crosses) from Mühlental southeast of the town centre to Elbingerode; Königshütte, with its 18th-century wooden church; and the remains of medieval Trageburg castle at Trautenstein. The tourist office can make suggestions.

Wernigrode has a new DJH **Jugendherberge** *(☎ 60 61 76, fax 60 61 77; ⓔ JH-Wernigrode@djh-sachsen-anhalt.de; Am Eichberg 5; juniors/seniors €15/17.70)*, with a discotheque and sauna. It's a 35-minute walk from the centre. Rooms booked through the tourist office's free room-finding service cost around €25. The central **Hotel zur Tanne** *(☎ 63 25 54, fax 67 37 35; Breite Strasse 57-59; singles/doubles from €41/49)* has basic rooms. **Pension Schweizer Hof** *(☎/fax 63 20 98; Salzbergstrasse 13; singles/doubles from €35/50)* is quiet and away from the centre, catering to hikers.

Altwernigerode Kartoffelhaus *(☎ 94 92 90; Marktstrasse 14; dishes €2.50/14.50)* serves well-priced traditional dishes. **Restaurant Am Nicolaiplatz** *(☎ 63 23 28; Breite Strasse 17; mains €6.90-13.50)* is a local favourite for regional specialties. There are lots of **cafés** around the Markt.

Frequent trains run to Goslar (€6.60, 40 minutes) and Hanover (€18.60, two hours). Change trains in Halberstadt for Magdeburg (€12.40, 1¼ hours), from where you can catch longer-distance trains.

LUTHERSTADT-WITTENBERG

☎ 03491 • pop 53,000

Wittenberg is where Martin Luther did most of his work, including launching the Protestant Reformation in 1517 (he even referred to the Vatican as a 'gigantic, bloodsucking worm'). **Wittenberg-Information** *(☎ 49 86 10, fax 49 86 11; Ⓦ www.wittenberg.de; Schlossplatz 2; open Mon-Sat, daily Mar-Oct)* is very well organised and offers an excellent audio guide to the town (€5).

The **Lutherhaus** *(☎ 420 30; Collegienstrasse 54; adult/concession €5/3)*, inside Lutherhalle (a former monastery), is a Reformation museum. Luther stayed here in 1508 while teaching at Wittenberg University and made it his home after returning in 1511.

The large altarpiece in **Stadtkirche St Marien** *(☎ 40 44 15; Jüdenstrasse 35; open 9am-5pm Mon-Sat, 11.30am-5pm Sun May-Oct, 10am-4pm Mon-Sat, 11.30am-4pm Sun Nov-Apr; admission free)* was created jointly by Renaissance painter Lucas Cranach the Elder and his son in 1547. It shows Luther, his friend and supporter Melanchthon and other Reformation figures, as well as Cranach the Elder himself, in Biblical contexts. Luther preached in this church and was married here. **Luthereiche** *(Luther's Oak; cnr Lutherstrasse & Am Bahnhof)* is where Luther burnt the papers that threatened his excommunication. Imposing **monuments** to both Luther and Melanchthon stand in front of the impressive **Altes Rathaus** (1535) on Markt. Also on Markt, the **Cranachhaus** is where Louis Cranach the Elder lived and worked. At the western end of town is the **Schloss** on whose church door Luther allegedly nailed his *95 Theses* on 31 October 1517. His tombstone lies below the pulpit, and Melanchthon's is opposite.

The often-mobbed **Jugendherberge** *(☎ 40 32 55, fax 40 94 22; ⓔ Jugendherberge@wittenberg.de; Schloss; beds junior/senior €12/14.70)* is upstairs in the Schloss (sheets €3.50). Wittenberg-Information finds private rooms from €25 per person. **Hotel-Garni Am Schwanenteich** *(☎ 41 10 34, fax 40 28 07; Töpferstrasse 1; singles/doubles from €31/59)* is central and has charming staff. For a room with a brew, **Im Beyerhof** *(☎ 43 31 30, fax 43 31 31; ⓦ www.brauhaus-wittenberg.de; Markt 6; singles/doubles €50/70)* has comfy rooms above a brewery. Most of the town's food options face Collegienstrasse.

Wittenberg is on the main train line between Leipzig (€15.80, 30 minutes) and Berlin (€23.60, one hour). Be sure you buy tickets to 'Lutherstadt-Wittenberg' – *not* Wittenberge.

Bavaria

For many visitors to Germany, Bavaria (Bayern) is a microcosm of the whole country. Here you will find fulfilled the German stereotypes of *Lederhosen*, beer halls, oompah bands and romantic castles. Bavaria draws visitors all year. If you only have time for one part of Germany, this is it. Munich, the capital, is the heart and soul, and the Bavarian Alps, Nuremberg and the medieval towns on the Romantic Road are other important attractions.

MUNICH

☎ 089 • pop 1.3 million

Munich (München) is the Bavarian mother lode – a beer-quaffing, sausage-eating city that's as cosmopolitan as anywhere in Europe. Munich residents have figured out how to enjoy life and are perfectly happy to show outsiders, as a visit to a beer hall will confirm.

Munich almost starved during WWI, the Nazis got their start here in the 1920s and WWII brought bombing and more than 6000 civilian deaths. The town has rebounded fantastically, and today it's the centre of Germany's burgeoning high-tech industries and boasts a world-class set of museums. And did we mention the beer?

GERMANY

Orientation

The main train station is west of the centre. From the station, head east along Bayerstrasse, through Karlsplatz, and then along Neuhauser Strasse and Kaufingerstrasse to Marienplatz, the hub of Munich.

North of Marienplatz are the Residenz (former royal palace), Schwabing (the famous student section) and the parklands of the Englischer Garten. East of Marienplatz is the Platzl quarter for beer houses and restaurants, as well as Maximilianstrasse, fun for strolling and window-shopping.

Information

Tourist Offices The tourist office's **main branch** *(☎ 23 33 03 00; ⓔ tourismus@ems.muenchen-tourist.de; Hauptbahnhof; open daily)* is at the main train station. Its room-finding service is free; call ☎ 23 33 03 00 or write to Fremdenverkehrsamt München, D-80313 München. Another **branch** on Marienplatz, beneath the Neues Rathaus (new town hall) is open Monday to Saturday. Both offices sell the Munich Welcome Card (€15.50), which allows three days unlimited travel on public transport, plus discounts for many attractions.

EurAide *(☎ 59 38 89; ⓔ euraide@compuserve.com; Hauptbahnhof; open daily)*, near platform 11 at the main train station, is an excellent source of travel and accommodation information in English. Another useful office for young people is the **Jugendinformationszentrum** *(Youth Information Centre; ☎ 51 41 06 60; Paul-Heyse-Strasse 22; open Mon-Fri)*, offering cheap Internet access as well.

The excellent *Young People's Guide* (€0.50) is available from information offices. The English-language monthly *Munich Found* (€3) is also useful, as is the annual *Visitors' Guide* (free), available at the tourist offices. A useful website is ⓦ www.munich-tourist.de.

Money At the main train station, **Reisebank** has two offices; if you show a EurAide newsletter, *The Inside Track*, your commission will be 50% cheaper. You'll find **AmEx** at Promenadeplatz 6 and **Thomas Cook** at Kaiserstrasse 45 in Schwabing.

Post & Communications Munich's **main post office** *(Bahnhofplatz 1)* is open Monday to Saturday. The poste-restante address is Hauptpostlagernd (Poste Restante), Bahnhofplatz 1, 80074 Munich. Sharing the building is **easyEverything**, where Internet access is €2 for 80 minutes. It's open 24 hours and normally packed with cyber surfers. **Savic Internet Point** *(☎ 55 02 89 88; Schillerstrasse 17)* charges €3 per hour and lets you download and print files and burn CDs.

Medical & Emergency Services Medical help is available at the **Home Medical Service** *(☎ 55 17 71, 72 42 001)*. For **ambulances** call ☎ 112. At the main train station there is an English-speaking **pharmacy**, as well as a **police station** on the Arnulfstrasse side (emergency number ☎ 110).

Dangers & Annoyances Be wary of pickpockets around the touristy areas, near the Hauptbahnhof, and during major festivals such as Oktoberfest and the Christkindlmarkt. A common trick is to steal your gear if you strip off in the Englischer Garten (don't let that stop you, just watch your stuff!).

Things to See & Do

Dominating Marienplatz is the towering neo-Gothic **Neues Rathaus** (new town hall), with its incessantly photographed Glockenspiel (carillon). Also on the square are two important churches – **Peterskirche** and **Heiliggeistkirche**. Head west along the shopping street Kaufingerstrasse to the late-Gothic **Frauenkirche** *(Church of Our Lady; ☎ 42 34 57; Frauenplatz; tower adult/concession €3/1.50)*, the landmark church of Munich. Climb the tower for majestic views. Continue west to the large, grey **Michaelskirche** *(☎ 609 02 24; Kaufingerstrasse)*, Germany's grandest Renaissance church. Farther west is the **Richard Strauss Fountain**, then the medieval **Karlstor**, an old city gate. Off Hermann-Sack-Strasse is the **Stadtmuseum** *(☎ 233; St-Jakobs-Platz 1; adult/concession €2.50/1.50; open 10am-6pm Tues-Sun)*, where the outstanding exhibits cover beer brewing, fashion, musical instruments, photography and puppets.

Palace enthusiasts have to check out the huge **Residenz** *(Max-Joseph-Platz 3)*, which housed Bavarian rulers from 1385 to 1918. The **Residenzmuseum** *(☎ 29 06 71; enter from Max-Joseph-Platz 3; adult/concession €4/2; open 9am-6pm, to 8pm Thur)* has an extraordinary array of 100 rooms containing the Wittelsbach house's belongings. The **Schatzkammer** *(☎ 29 06 71; Max-Joseph-Platz 3; open 9am-6pm, to 8pm Thur; adult/concession €4/2)* exhibits a ridiculous quantity of jewels, crowns and ornate gold.

One of the largest city parks in Europe, the **Englischer Garten**, west of the city centre, is a great place for strolling, especially along the Schwabinger Bach. In summer, nude sunbathing is the rule; if people aren't sunning themselves *au naturale*, they're probably drinking merrily at one of the park's popular three beer gardens (see Entertainment later in this section).

Museums & Galleries

Except where noted, museums and galleries are closed on Monday.

A vast science and technology museum, the **Deutsches Museum** *(☎ 217 91; Theresienhöhe 14a; adult/concession €6/4; open 9am-5pm)* is like a combination of Disneyland and the Smithsonian Institution. You can explore anything from the depths of coal mines to the stars, but it's definitely too large to see everything. Reach it via the S-Bahn to Isartor or tram No 18 to Deutsches Museum.

The **Glyptothek** *(☎ 28 61 00; Königsplatz 3; adult/concession €3/1.75; open 10am-5pm, to 8pm Thur)* and **Antikensammlungen** *(☎ 59 83 59; Königsplatz 1; adult/concession €3/1.75; open 10am-5pm, to 8pm Wed)* have some of Germany's best antiquities collections (mostly Greek and Roman). To visit both is €5.

North of the city, automobile-fetishists can thrill to the **BMW Museum** *(☎ 38 22 33 07; Petuelring 130; adult/concession €2.75/2; open 9am-5pm)*. Take the U3 to Olympiazentrum.

The **Alte Pinakothek** *(☎ 23 80 52 16; Barer Strasse 27; adult/concession €5/3.50, Sunday free; open 10am-5pm Tues-Sun, to 10pm Thur)* is a treasure house of European masters from the 14th to 18th centuries. Highlights include Dürer's *Self Portrait* and *Four Apostles*, van der Weyden's *Adoration of the Magi* and Botticelli's *Pietà*. Immediately north is the **Neue Pinakothek** *(☎ 23 80 51 95; Barer Strasse 29; adult/concession €5/3.50, Sunday free; open 10am-5pm Wed-Sun, to 10pm Thur)*, which contains mainly 19th-century works, including Van Gogh's *Sunflowers*. A combined card (€8/5) gets you into both.

Dachau

Dachau *(☎ 08131-17 41; Alte-Roemer-Strasse 75; admission free; open 9am-5pm Tues-Sun)* was the first Nazi concentration camp, built in March 1933. Over 200,000 Jews, political prisoners, homosexuals and others deemed 'undesirable' by the Third Reich were sent here; more than 30,000 of them died at Dachau or at other camps. An English-language documentary is shown at 11.30am and 3.30pm. Take the S2 to Dachau (20 minutes) and then bus No 726 or 724 to the camp. A Gesamtnetz (total area) ticket (€9) is needed for the trip.

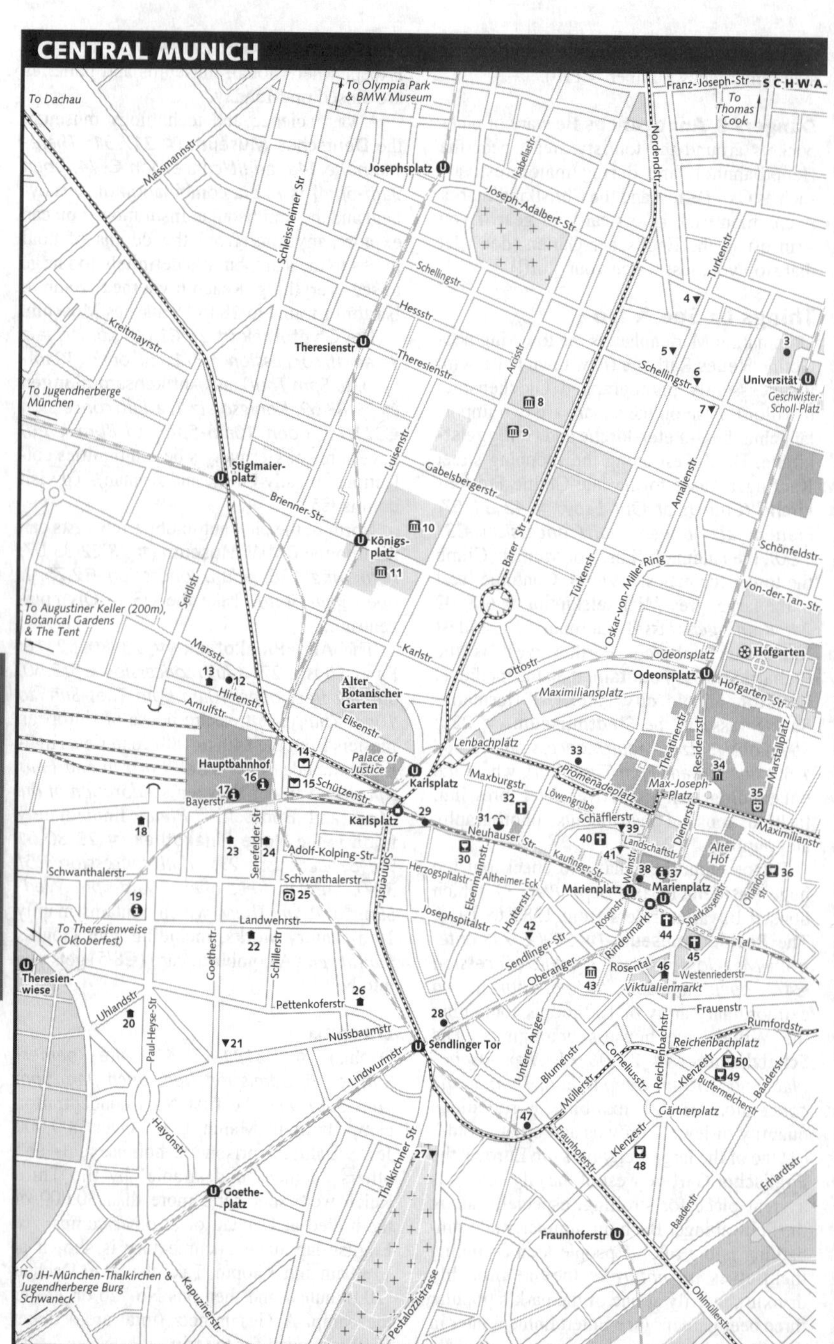
CENTRAL MUNICH
To Olympia Park & BMW Museum
To Dachau
Franz-Joseph-Str
SCHWA
To Thomas Cook
Massmannstr
Schleissheimer Str
Josephsplatz
Isabellastr
Nordendstr
Joseph-Adalbert-Str
Schellingstr
Türkenstr
Hessstr
Kreitmayrstr
Theresienstr
Theresienstr
Arcisstr
Schellingstr
Universität
Geschwister-Scholl-Platz
To Jugendherberge München
Luisenstr
Gabelsbergerstr
Amalienstr
Stiglmaier-platz
Brienner-Str
Königs-platz
Barer Str
Schönfeldstr
Oskar-von-Miller Ring
Türkenstr
Von-der-Tan-Str
To Augustiner Keller (200m), Botanical Gardens & The Tent
Seidlstr
Karlstr
Hofgarten
Marsstr
Ottostr
Odeonsplatz
Odeonsplatz
Hirtenstr
Alter Botanischer Garten
Maximiliansplatz
Hofgarten-Str
Arnulfstr
Elisenstr
Lenbachplatz
Hauptbahnhof
Palace of Justice
Karlsplatz
Promenadeplatz
Theatinerstr
Residenzstr
Marstallplatz
Maxburgstr
Max-Joseph-Platz
Bayerstr
Schützenstr
Löwengrube
Karlsplatz
Schäfflerstr
Maximilianstr
Neuhauser Str
Landschaftstr
Dienerstr
Alter Hof
Adolf-Kolping-Str
Senefelder Str
Sonnenstr
Herzogspitalstr
Altheimer Eck
Kaufinger Str
Weinstr
Schwanthalerstr
Schwanthalerstr
Eisenmannstr
Marienplatz
Marienplatz
Orlando str
Josephspitalstr
Hotterstr
Rosenstr
Sparkassenstr
To Theresienweise (Oktoberfest)
Landwehrstr
Rindermarkt
Tal
Sendlinger-Str
Goethestr
Schillerstr
Oberanger
Rosental
Westenriederstr
Theresien-wiese
Viktualienmarkt
Pettenkoferstr
Uhlandstr
Frauenstr
Unterer Anger
Rumfordstr
Paul-Heyse-Str
Nussbaumstr
Sendlinger Tor
Reichenbachstr
Reichenbachplatz
Corneliusstr
Lindwurmstr
Blumenstr
Klenzestr
Buttermelcherstr
Baaderstr
Müllerstr
Gärtnerplatz
Haydnstr
Thalkirchner Str
Fraunhoferstr
Klenzestr
Erhardtstr
Goethe-platz
Baaderstr
Fraunhoferstr
To JH-München-Thalkirchen & Jugendherberge Burg Schwaneck
Kapuzinerstr
Pestalozzistrasse
Ohlmüllerstr
GERMANY

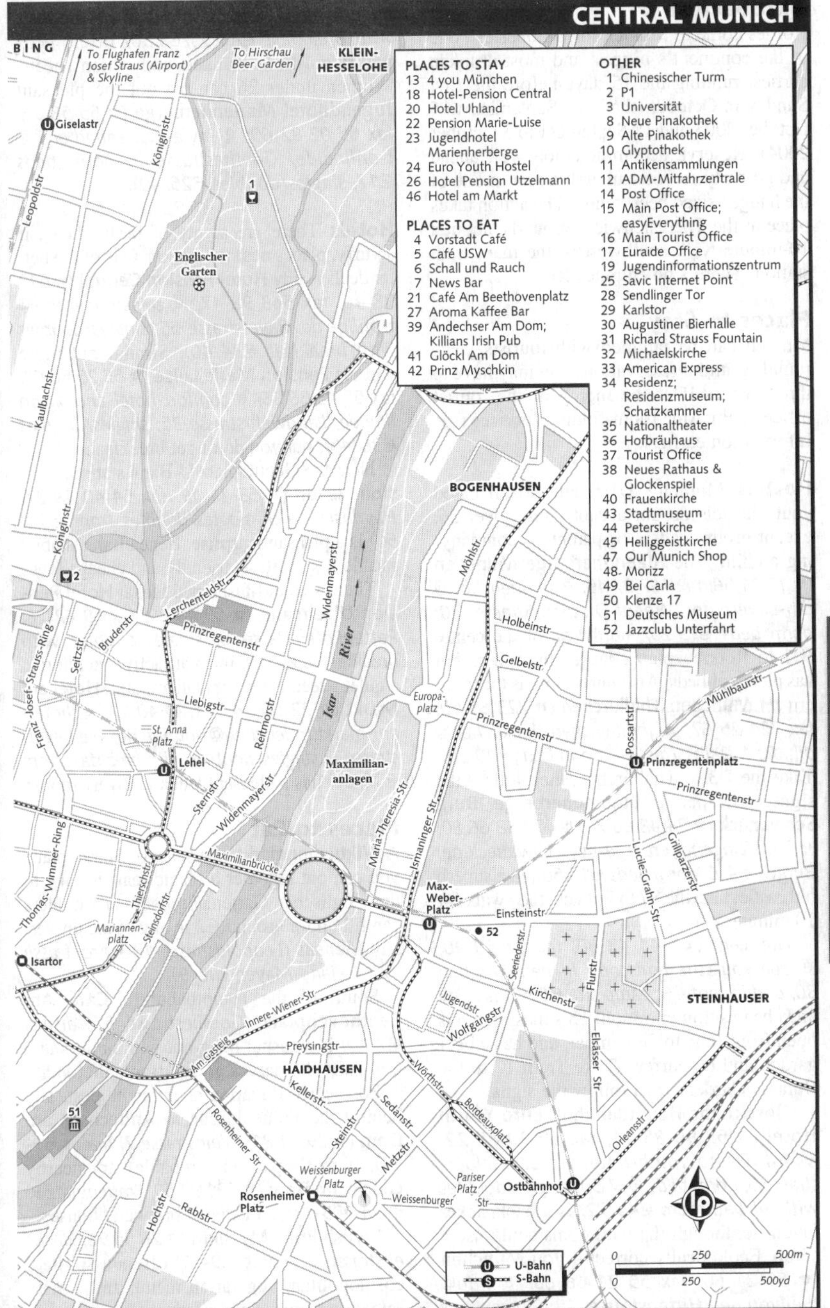
CENTRAL MUNICH
PLACES TO STAY
13 4 you München
18 Hotel-Pension Central
20 Hotel Uhland
22 Pension Marie-Luise
23 Jugendhotel Marienherberge
24 Euro Youth Hostel
26 Hotel Pension Utzelmann
46 Hotel am Markt
PLACES TO EAT
4 Vorstadt Café
5 Café USW
6 Schall und Rauch
7 News Bar
21 Café Am Beethovenplatz
27 Aroma Kaffee Bar
39 Andechser Am Dom; Killians Irish Pub
41 Glöckl Am Dom
42 Prinz Myschkin
OTHER
1 Chinesischer Turm
2 P1
3 Universität
8 Neue Pinakothek
9 Alte Pinakothek
10 Glyptothek
11 Antikensammlungen
12 ADM-Mitfahrzentrale
14 Post Office
15 Main Post Office; easyEverything
16 Main Tourist Office
17 Euraide Office
19 Jugendinformationszentrum
25 Savic Internet Point
28 Sendlinger Tor
29 Karlstor
30 Augustiner Bierhalle
31 Richard Strauss Fountain
32 Michaelskirche
33 American Express
34 Residenz; Residenzmuseum; Schatzkammer
35 Nationaltheater
36 Hofbräuhaus
37 Tourist Office
38 Neues Rathaus & Glockenspiel
40 Frauenkirche
43 Stadtmuseum
44 Peterskirche
45 Heiliggeistkirche
47 Our Munich Shop
48 Morizz
49 Bei Carla
50 Klenze 17
51 Deutsches Museum
52 Jazzclub Unterfahrt
To Flughafen Franz Josef Straus (Airport) & Skyline
To Hirschau Beer Garden
KLEIN-HESSELOHE
Giselastr
Königinstr
Leopoldstr
Englischer Garten
Kaulbachstr
Königinstr
BOGENHAUSEN
Möhlstr
Widenmayerstr
Isar River
Lerchenfeldstr
Prinzregentenstr
Bruderstr
Seitzstr
Franz-Josef-Strauss-Ring
Holbeinstr
Gelbelstr
Liebigstr
St. Anna Platz
Reitmorstr
Europaplatz
Prinzregentenstr
Mühlbaurstr
Possartstr
Prinzregentenplatz
Prinzregentenstr
Lehel
Maximiliananlagen
Maria-Theresia-Str
Ismaninger Str
Sternstr
Widenmayerstr
Maximilianbrücke
Thomas-Wimmer-Ring
Thierschstr
Steinsdorfstr
Mariannenplatz
Max-Weber-Platz
Einsteinstr
Lucile-Grahn-Str
Grillparzerstr
Isartor
Seeriederstr
Kirchenstr
Flurstr
STEINHAUSER
Jugendstr
Wolfgangstr
Innere-Wiener-Str
Am Gasteig
Preysingstr
HAIDHAUSEN
Elsässer Str
Kellerstr
Wörthstr
Bordeauxplatz
Sedanstr
Rosenheimer Str
Steinstr
Metzstr
Orleansstr
Weissenburger Platz
Pariser Platz
Ostbahnhof
Rosenheimer Platz
Weissenburger Str
Rablstr
Hochstr
U-Bahn
S-Bahn
0 250 500m
0 250 500yd

GERMANY

Oktoberfest

Hordes come to Munich for Oktoberfest, one of the continent's biggest and most drunken parties, running the 15 days before the first Sunday in October (that's 20 September to 5 October 2003 and 18 September to 3 October 2004). Reserve accommodation well ahead and go early so you can grab a seat in one of the hangar-sized beer 'tents'. The action takes place at the Theresienwiese grounds, about a 10-minute walk southwest of the main train station. There's no entrance fee.

Places to Stay

Munich can be jammed with tourists year-round. Without reservations you may have to throw yourself at the mercy of the tourist office or EurAide room-finding services (see Information earlier).

Hostels Munich's DJH- and HI-affiliated youth hostels do not accept guests over 26, except group leaders or parents accompanying a child. The **Jugendherberge München** *(☎ 13 11 56, fax 167 87 45; ⓔ jhmuenchen@djh-bayern.de; Wendl-Dietrich-Strasse 20; dorm beds €19.20)*, northwest of the centre (U1 to Rotkreuzplatz), lacks atmosphere but has plenty of beds. Also fairly close is the modern **JH München-Thalkirchen** *(☎ 723 65 50, fax 724 25 67; ⓔ jhmuenchen-thalkirchen@djh.de; Miesingstrasse 4; dorm beds €19.20)*. Take the U3 to Thalkirchen, then follow the signs. Cheaper is **Jugendherberge Burg Schwaneck** *(☎ 74 48 66 70, fax 74 48 66 80; ⓔ info@jugendherberge-burgschwaneck.de; Burgweg 4-6; dorm beds €15.50)*, in a superb old castle; take the S7 to Pullach, then walk for 10 minutes.

The Tent *(☎ 141 43 00, fax 17 50 90; ⓔ see-you@the-tent.com; In den Kirschen 30; bed in tent €9, camp site €5.50)* is a fun and cheap summer option. This mass camp is open from June to September, and has a beer garden and no curfew. Take Tram 17 to the Botanic Gardens then follow the signs.

Close to the Hauptbahnhof, **Euro Youth Hotel** *(☎ 59 90 88 11, fax 59 90 88 22; ⓔ info@euro-youth-hotel.de; Senefelderstrasse 5; dorm beds €17.50, singles/doubles without bathroom €45/72)* is a backpacker favourite, though the bathrooms could use a scrub. Ecologically correct **4 you München** *(☎ 55 21 60, fax 55 21 66 66; ⓔ info@the4you.de; Hirtenstrasse 18; dorm beds under/over 27s €16.50/17.50, singles/doubles with breakfast €43.50/68.50)* offers beds with wool-fibre blankets and cotton sheets. Women under 26 can try out the pleasant **Jugendhotel Marienherberge** *(☎ 55 58 05, fax 55 02 82 60; ⓔ invia-marienherberge@t-online.de; Goethestrasse 9; dorm beds €17, singles/doubles €25/40)*.

Hotels There are plenty of fairly cheap, if scruffy, places near the station. One of the better deals is tidy **Hotel Pension Central** *(☎ 543 98 46, fax 543 98 47; ⓔ pensioncentral@t-online.de; Bayerstrasse 55; singles/doubles with breakfast €34/40)*. Similar but more worn is **Pension Marie Luise** *(☎ 55 25 56 60, fax 55 45 56 66; ⓔ comfort-hotel-andi@t-online.de; Landwehrstrasse 35; singles/doubles €30/45)*, but you don't get breakfast.

Near the Goetheplatz U-Bahn station, **Pension Haydn** *(☎ 53 11 19, fax 54 40 48 27; Haydnstrasse 9; singles/doubles from €35/50)* is a pleasant surprise. Beneath the shabby facade it's spotless, friendly and cheap.

There's an old-fashioned feel at **Hotel Pension Utzelmann** *(☎ 59 48 89, fax 59 62 28; Pettenkoferstrasse 6; singles/doubles with breakfast €33/53)*, in an attractive building in a quiet street. Near Viktualienmarkt, **Hotel am Markt** *(☎ 22 50 14, fax 22 40 17; ⓔ hotel-am-markt.muenchen@t-online.de; Heiliggeistrasse 6; singles/doubles with breakfast from €38/68)* has a pleasant feel and lovely rooms.

Places to Eat

At **Viktualienmarkt**, just south of Marienplatz, you can put together a picnic feast to take to the Englischer Garten. Student-card holders can fill up for around €2 in any of the university **Mensas** *(Leopoldstrasse 13 • Arcistrasse 17 • Helene-Mayer-Ring 9)*.

South of the Hauptbahnhof, **Café Am Beethovenplatz** *(Goethestrasse 51; dishes €7-10)* is a casual hang-out with no airs and graces. It also serves great, affordable food.

For hearty Bavarian chow at its best, slip behind the Frauenkirche to **Andechser am Dom** *(☎ 29 84 81; Weinstrasse 7; mains €9-14)*. If that's packed (probable), try nearby **Glöckl am Dom** *(☎ 291 94 50; Frauenplatz 9; mains €5-13)*, a medieval bratwurst house.

Stylish **Prinz Myshkin** *(☎ 26 55 96; Hackenstrasse 2; mains €9-13)* offers a spirited, cosmopolitan, vegetarian menu, and a tasty selection of pizza and pasta.

Most of Munich's café culture centres on Schwabing, the university haunt. Here you'll find plenty of little spots filled with laid-back laureates and lively lingo. For the ultimate cool hang-out, head to unpretentious **Schall und Rauch** *(Schellingstrasse 22)*, where problems are solved over coffee. Or join the mellow gang around the corner at **Café USW** *(Turkenstrasse 55)*. Nearby, **Vorstadt Café** *(Turkenstrasse 83)* is busy and trendy, while at the modern **News Bar** *(Amalienstrasse 54)*, an entire wall is dedicated to the latest magazines and newspapers (some in English). South of Sendlinger Tor, cramming 30 people into a shoebox isn't easy, so the coffee must be good at **Aroma Kaffee Bar** *(Pestalozzistrasse 24)*.

Entertainment

Beer Halls & Gardens Beer drinking is an integral part of Munich's entertainment scene. Germans drink an average of 130L each per year; Munich residents manage to drink much more than this!

Several breweries run their own beer halls, so try at least one large, frothy litre mug (called a *Mass*) before heading off to another hall. Most famous is the enormous **Hofbräuhaus** *(Am Platzl 9)*. A tourist trap it may be, but it's still a rollicking good time – singing, drinking and general merriment is encouraged. Less prominent but no less enjoyable is the **Augustiner Bierhalle** *(Neuhauser Strasse 27)*, an authentic example of an old-style Munich beer hall, filled with laughter, smoke and clinking glasses.

On a summer day there's nothing better than sitting and sipping at one of Munich's beer gardens. In the Englischer Garten is the classic **Chinesischer Turm**, although nearby **Hirschau** on the banks of the Kleinhesseloher See is less crowded. The **Augustiner Keller** *(Arnulfstrasse 52)*, five minutes from the Hauptbahnhof, has a large leafy beer garden.

Pubs & Clubs The *Young People's Guide* (see under Information earlier in this section) keeps abreast of Munich's hot spots. **Klenze 17** *(Klenzestrasse 17)* has a great crowd and an extensive whisky selection, while in a cellar behind the Frauenkirche, **Killians Irish Pub** *(Frauenplatz 11)* is a cosy, casual drinking hole. If you can get past the goons at the door, **P1** *(Prinzregentenstrasse 1)* is a classy club with a high celebrity quotient. In northern Schwabing, **Skyline** *(Leopoldstrasse 82)* plays hip-hop on the top floor of the Hertie department store.

Much of Munich's gay and lesbian scene is in the area just south of Sendlinger Tor, especially around Gärtnerplatz. *Our Munich* is a monthly guide to gay and lesbian life available at **Our Munich Shop** *(☎ 26 01 85 03; Müllerstrasse 36)*. Resembling a Paris bar, **Morizz** *(Klenzestrasse 43)* is a popular haunt for gay men. **Bei Carla** *(Buttermelcherstrasse 9)* is an exclusively lesbian bar-café with a friendly atmosphere and lots of regulars.

Live Performance Munich is one of the cultural capitals of Germany. The **Nationaltheater** *(☎ 21 85 19 20; Max-Joseph-Platz 2)* is the home of the Bavarian State Opera and the site of many cultural events (particularly during the opera festival in July). You can buy tickets at the box office or book by telephone.

Munich's ripping jazz scene is led by **Jazzclub Unterfahrt** *(☎ 448 27 94; Kirchenstrasse 42-44)*, near Max-Weber-Platz U-Bahn station. It has live music every night from 7.30pm and open jam sessions on Sunday nights.

Getting There & Away

Munich is second in importance only to Frankfurt for international and national connections. Flights will take you to all major destinations worldwide. Main German cities are serviced by at least half a dozen flights daily.

Train services are excellent. There are rapid connections at least every two hours to all major cities in Germany, as well as frequent EC trains to other European cities such as Innsbruck (two hours), Vienna (five hours), Prague (six hours), Zürich (4¼ hours), Verona (5½ hours) and Paris (eight hours). The high-speed ICE services include Frankfurt (€75.60, 3½ hours), Hamburg (€127, six hours) and Berlin (€142.40, 6½ hours).

Munich is linked to the Romantic Road by the Deutsche-Touring (or Europabus) Munich-Frankfurt service. **Deutsche-Touring** *(☎ 545 87 00, fax 54 58 70 21; ⓔ service@deutsche-touring.com)*, is near platform 26 of the main train station, about its international services to destinations such as Prague and Budapest. Buses stop along the northern side of the train station.

For arranged rides, **ADM-Mitfahrzentrale** *(☎ 194 40)* is near the main train station at Lämmerstrasse 6. Destinations include Berlin (€32), Frankfurt (€25) and Hamburg (€39).

Getting Around

Munich's gleaming Flughafen Franz Josef Strauss airport is connected by the S8 and the S1 to Marienplatz and the main train station (€8). The service takes 40 minutes and runs every 20 minutes from 4am until around 12.30am. The airport bus also runs at 20-minute intervals from Arnulfstrasse on the north side of the main train station (€9, 45 minutes) between 6.50am and 7.50pm.

Most places of interest to tourists (except Dachau and the airport) are within the 'blue' *Innenraum* (inner public-transport zone). MVV tickets are valid for the S-Bahn, U-Bahn, trams and buses, but must be validated before use. The U-Bahn shuts down around 12.30am on weekdays and 1.30am on weekends, but there are some later buses and S-Bahns. Rail passes are valid only on the S-Bahn.

Kurzstrecke (short rides) cost €1 and are good for four stops on buses and trams, two stops on the U- and S-Bahns. Longer trips cost €2. It's cheaper to buy a *Mehrfahrtenkarte* (strip-card of 10 tickets) for €9 and stamp one strip per adult on short rides, two strips for longer rides in the inner zone. *Tageskarte* (day passes) for the inner zone cost €4.50, while three-day tickets cost €11, or €15 for two adults.

Taxis are expensive and not much more convenient than public transport. **Radius Bike Rental** *(☎ 59 61 13)* rents out two-wheelers from €14/43 per day/week.

GERMANY

AUGSBURG

☎ 0821 • pop 262,000

Originally established by the Romans, Augsburg later became a centre of Luther's Reformation and is now a lively provincial city. For some it will be a day trip from Munich, for others an ideal base (especially during Oktoberfest). Augsburg has two **tourist offices** *(☎ 502 07 22; Bahnhofstrasse 7; open Mon-Fri • ☎ 502 07 35; Rathausplatz; open daily)*. The onion-shaped towers of the modest **St Maria Stern Kloster** in Elias-Holl-Platz started a fashion that spread throughout southern Germany. More impressive are those on the **Rathaus**, the adjacent **Perlachturm** and the soaring tower of **St Ulrich und Afra Basilika** (on Ulrichsplatz near the southern edge of the old town). One of Luther's more colourful antipapal documents was posted on the **Dom Mariae Heimsuchung**, on Hoher Weg north of Rathausplatz. Dramatist Bertolt Brecht's family home on the stream is now the **Bertolt-Brecht-Gedänkstätte** *(☎ 324 27 79; Am Rain 7; adult/concession €1.50/1; open 10am-4pm Wed-Sun)*, a museum dedicated to Brecht and the work of young artists.

Augsburg's seedy **DJH Hostel** *(☎ 33 909, fax 15 11 49; ⓔ jugendherberge@kvaugsburg-stadt.bvk.de; Beim Pfaffenkeller 3; dorm beds from €12.30)*, just east of St Mary's Cathedral, needs a serious spruce-up. **Jakoberhof** *(☎ 51 00 30, fax 15 08 44; Jakobstrasse 39-41; singles/doubles €25/32.50)* is a simple place with a good Bavarian restaurant downstairs. **Der Andechser** *(☎ 349 79 90; Johannisgasse 4; mains €5-12)* is cosy and serves hearty German fare.

Trains between Munich and Augsburg are frequent (€9, 40 minutes). Regular ICE/IC trains also serve Ulm (€12.40, 50 minutes), Stuttgart (€33.80, 1½ hours) and Nuremberg (€19.20, 1½ hours). Connections to/from Regensburg take two hours via Ingolstadt. The Romantic Road bus stops at the train station.

THE ROMANTIC ROAD

The popular Romantic Road (Romantische Strasse) links a series of picturesque Bavarian towns and cities, running north-south through western Bavaria from Würzburg to Füssen, and passing through Rothenburg ob der Tauber, Dinkelsbühl and Augsburg. Locals get their cut of the Romantic Road hordes through, among other things, scores of good-value private accommodation offerings. Look for the *Zimmer Frei* signs and expect to pay around €15 to €25 per person. Tourist offices are efficient at finding accommodation in almost any price range. DJH hostels in this section accept only people under 27, except group leaders or parents accompanying a child.

In the north of the route, Würzburg is well-served by trains. To start at the southern end, take the hourly RE train from Munich to Füssen (€18.20, two hours). Rothenburg is linked by train to Würzburg, Nuremberg and Munich via Steinach. To reach Dinkelsbühl, take a train to Ansbach and from there a frequent bus onwards. Nördlingen has train connections to Stuttgart and Munich. There are four daily buses between Füssen and Garmisch-Partenkirchen (€7; all stop at Hohenschwangau and Oberammergau), as well as several connections between Füssen and

Oberstdorf (€8.10; via Pfronten). **Deutsche-Touring GmbH** (*☎ 069-79 03 50, fax 069-79 03 219; ⓔ service@deutsche-touring.com; Am Römerhof 17, 60486 Frankfurt/Main)* runs a daily 'Castle Road' coach service in each direction between Mannheim and Rothenburg via Heidelberg (€29, 5½ hours).

It is possible to do this route using train connections, local buses or by car (just follow the brown 'Romantische Strasse' signs), but most train pass-holders prefer to take the Deutsche-Touring (or Europabus) bus. From April to October Deutsche-Touring runs one coach daily in each direction between Frankfurt and Munich (12 hours), and another in either direction between Dinkelsbühl and Füssen (4½ hours). You can break the journey at any point and continue the next day (reserve a seat as you disembark). The full fare from Frankfurt to Füssen is €74 (change buses at Rothenburg). Eurail and German Rail passes are valid, and Inter-Rail pass-holders receive a 50% discount, while those under 26 save 10%. For information and reservations, contact Deutsche-Touring.

Rothenburg ob der Tauber

☎ 09861 • pop 12,000

It's soon obvious why this charmingly preserved medieval town is continually under siege from tourists. It's an enchanting place of twisting cobbled lanes and strikingly pretty architecture enclosed by towered stone walls. From November to March, the town's museums open only in the afternoon. The **tourist office** *(☎ 404 92; ⓔ info@rothenburg.de; Markt 1)* is open Monday to Saturday.

The **Rathaus on Markt** was commenced in Gothic style in the 14th century but completed in Renaissance style. The tower (€1) gives a majestic view over the town and the Tauber Valley.

The **Puppen und Spielzeugmuseum** *(Doll & Toy Museum; ☎ 73 30; Hofbronnengasse 13; adult/concession €4/2.50; open 9.30am-6pm Mar-Dec, 11am-5pm Jan & Feb)* has the largest private doll and toy collection in Germany. The **Reichsstadt Museum** *(☎ 93 90 43; Klosterhof 5; adult/concession €3/1.50; open 10am-5pm Apr-Oct, 1pm-4pm Nov-Mar)*, in the former convent, features the superb *Rothenburger Passion.* Get a gruesome glimpse of the past at the **Krimminalmuseum**, *(☎ 53 59; Burggasse 3-5; adult/concession €3.20/1.70; open 10am-5pm Apr-Oct, 1pm-4pm Nov-Mar)*, which houses all manner of devices with which to torture and shame medieval miscreants.

Selflessness in Action

According to legend, Rothenburg was saved during the Thirty Years' War (1618–48) when the mayor won a challenge by the Imperial general Tilly and downed more than 3L of wine at a gulp. The **Meistertrunk** scene is re-enacted by the clock figures on Rothenburg's tourist office building (eight times daily in summer).

Rothenburg's jammed **Youth Hostel** *(☎ 941 60, fax 94 16 20; ⓔ jhrothenburg@djh.bayern.de; Mülacker 1; dorm beds €15.10)* is housed in two enormous renovated old buildings in the south of the old town. **Das Lädle** *(☎/fax 61 30; ⓔ das-laedle-pension-hess@t-online.de; Spitalgasse 18; singles/doubles with breakfast €22/40)* is a good cheapie, with casual and comfortable rooms in a central location.

Vine-covered and impossibly cosy, **Altfrankische Weinstube** *(☎ 64 04; Klosterhof 7; mains €6-13)* is justifiably popular, with a varied and well-priced menu and fantastic atmosphere. Resist the temptation to try a disgusting *Schneeball.*

Nördlingen

☎ 09081 • pop 20,000

Nördlingen is encircled by its original 14th-century walls and lies within the basin of the **Ries**, a huge crater created by a meteor more than 15 million years ago. The crater is one of the largest in existence (25km in diameter); the **Rieskrater Museum** *(☎ 273 82 20; Eugene-Shoemaker-Platz 1; adult/concession €3/1.50; open 10am-noon, 1.30pm-4.30pm Tues-Sun)* provides details. You'll find the local **tourist office** *(☎ 43 80; ⓔ verkersamt@noerdlingen.de; Marktplatz 2)* very helpful.

Füssen

☎ 08362 • pop 14,000

Just short of the Austrian border, Füssen has a monastery, castle and splendid baroque architecture, but it is primarily visited for the two castles in nearby Schwangau. Its **tourist office** *(☎ 938 50; ⓔ tourismus@fuessen.de; Kaiser-Maximillian-Platz 1)* is open Monday to Saturday.

The castles provide a fascinating glimpse into King Ludwig II's state of mind (or lack thereof). More interesting than Hohenschwangau is **Neuschwanstein** *(☎ 810 35; adult/concession €7/6; open 9am-6pm, 9am-8pm Thur Apr-Oct, 10am-4pm Oct-Apr)*, which the king himself created. There is plenty of evidence of Ludwig's twin obsessions: swans and Wagnerian operas. The sugary pastiche of architectural styles reputedly inspired Disney's Fantasyland castle. Take the bus from Füssen train station (€2.80 return), share a taxi (☎ 77 00; €8.50) or walk the 5km. The only way to enter the castles is with a 35-minute guided tour, purchased from the ticket centre at Alpseestrasse 12, near Hohenschwangau.

Füssen's **Youth Hostel** *(☎ 77 54, fax 27 70; ⓔ jhfuessen@djh-bayern.de; Mariahilferstrasse 5; dorm beds €13.30)* is a 10-minute walk from the train station. A pavilion near the tourist office has a computerised list of vacant rooms in town from €12 per person. Central **Sonne Café** *(Reichenstrasse 37; dishes €3-15)* has great baguettes, salads and schnitzels.

WÜRZBURG

☎ 0931 • pop 130,000

Surrounded by forests and vineyards, charming Würzburg straddles the upper River Main. Rebuilt after the war, it's a centre of art, beautiful architecture and delicate wines. The **tourist office** *(☎ 37 23 98; ⓔ tourismus@wuerzburg.de; Oberer Markt; open Mon-Sat, daily May-Oct)* is in the rococo masterpiece Haus zum Falken. In the same building, **Stadtbücherei** *(☎ 37 34 38)* offers Internet access for €0.50 for 10 minutes.

GERMANY

The magnificent baroque **Residenz** *(☎ 35 51 70; Balthasar-Neumann-Promenade; adult/concession €4/3; open 9am-6pm Apr-Sept, 10am-4pm Oct-Mar)* took a generation to build. The open Hofgarten at the back is a favourite spot. The **Dom St Kilian** interior and the adjacent **Neumünster** in the old town continue the baroque themes.

Reach the **Marienberg** fortress, across the river on the hill, by crossing the 15th-century stone **Alte Mainbrücke** from the city and walking up Tellstiege, a small alley. It encloses the **Fürstenbau Museum** *(☎ 438 38; adult/concession €3/1.50; open 9am-6pm Tues-Sun Apr-Sept, 10am-4pm Tues-Sun Oct-Mar)* and regional **Mainfränkisches Museum** *(☎ 430 16; adult/concession €3/1.50; open 10am-6pm Tues-Sun Apr-Sept, 10am-4pm Tues-Sun Oct-Mar)*. For a dizzy thrill, look down the well in the courtyard.

Jugendgästehaus Würzburg *(☎ 425 90, fax 41 68 62; ⓔ jhwuerzburg@djh-bayern.de; Burkarderstrasse 44; dorm beds €17.70)* is below the fortress (tram No 3 or 5 from the train station). Simple and friendly **Pension Spehnkuch** *(☎ 547 52, fax 547 60; ⓔ spehnkuch@web.de; Röntgenring 7; singles/doubles/triples from €29/52/75)* offers spotless rooms and welcoming hosts.

Just south of the Friedensbrücke, **Pane e Vino** *(Dreikronenstrasse 2; dishes €6-15)* is a sunny lunch spot with views of the vine-covered hills. Insanely popular **Bürgerspital** *(☎ 35 28 80; Theaterstrasse 19; mains €5-18)* is in a labyrinthine, former medieval hospice. The atmosphere, food and local wines are all first class.

Würzburg is two hours by frequent RE train from Frankfurt (€19.20) and an hour from Nuremberg (€14.40). It's a major stop for the Hamburg–Munich ICE trains. It is also on the Deutsche-Touring Romantic Road bus route (2½ hours to/from Rothenburg by bus).

BAMBERG

☎ 0951 • pop 70,000

Tucked away from the main routes in northern Bavaria, Bamberg is practically a byword for magnificence – an untouched monument to the Holy Roman Emperor Heinrich II (who conceived it), to its prince-bishops and clergy and to its patriciate and townsfolk. The **tourist office** *(☎ 87 11 61; ⓔ info@bamberg.de; Geyerswörthstrasse 3; open Mon-Sat, daily May-Oct)* is on an island in the River Regnitz.

Bamberg's main appeal is its fine buildings. Most are spread on either side of the River Regnitz, but the colourful **Altes Rathaus** is actually in it, precariously perched on its own islet. The princely and ecclesiastical district is centred on Domplatz, where the Romanesque and Gothic **cathedral**, housing the statue of the chivalric king-knight, the *Bamberger Reiter*, is the biggest attraction. The **Kirche St Michael** is a definite must-see for its baroque art and the herbal compendium painted on its ceiling.

Jugendherberge Wolfsschlucht *(☎ 560 02, fax 552 11; ⓔ jh-bamberg@stadt.bamberg.de; Oberer Leinritt 70; dorm beds €14.60; closed mid-Dec–mid-Jan)* is on the river's west bank; take bus No 18 to Rodelbahn, walk northeast to the riverbank, then turn left. **Gasthof Fässla** *(☎ 265 16, fax 20 19 89; ⓔ kaspar_schultz@t-online.de; Hallstadter Strasse 174; singles/*

doubles €34/52) offers a drinker's dream – a clean and comfy bed in a brewery.

Wirsthaus zum Schlenkerla *(Dominikanerstrasse 6; mains €7-12)* has brewed its extraordinary *Rauchbier* since 1678. The dark-red concoction with a smoky flavour accompanies a menu of Franconian specialties.

There are hourly RE and RB trains to/from both Würzburg (€14) and Nuremberg (€9), taking one hour. Bamberg is also served by ICE trains running between Munich (€45.20, 2½ hours) and Berlin (€68.80, 4½ hours) every two hours.

NUREMBERG

☎ 0911 • pop 500,000

Though the flood of tourists to historical Nuremberg (Nürnberg) never seems to cease, it's still worth the trip. Nuremberg played a major role during the Nazi years and was the scene of the war-crimes trials afterwards. The city was rebuilt after Allied bombs reduced it to rubble on 2 January 1945.

The main artery, mostly pedestrianised Königstrasse, takes you through the old town and its major squares. The **main tourist office** *(☎ 233 61 32; ⓔ tourismus@nuernberg.de; Königstrasse 93; open Mon-Sat)* is near the train station. A smaller **branch** *(☎ 233 61 35; Hauptmarkt 18; open Mon-Sat, daily May-Sept)* operates on the city's main square. Both sell the two-day Kultour Ticket (€14.50), which provides free public transport and entry to most museums and attractions. The main **post office** *(Bahnhofplatz 1)* is by the station and a **Reisebank** operates inside the station. **M@x Internet-Café** *(☎ 23 23 84; Färberstrasse 11)* offers one hour of surfing for €2.50.

Things to See

The spectacular **Germanisches Nationalmuseum** *(☎ 133 10; Kartäusergasse 1; adult/concession €4/3, free 6pm-9pm Wed; open 10am-5pm Tues-Sun, to 9pm Wed)* is the most important museum of German culture. It displays works by German painters and sculptors, an archaeological collection, arms and armour, musical and scientific instruments and toys. Close by, the sleek and remarkably harmonious **Neues Museum** *(☎ 24 02 00; Luitpoldstrasse 5; adult/concession €3.50/2.50; open 10am-8pm Tues-Fri, 10am-6pm Sat & Sun)* contains a superb collection of contemporary art and design.

The scenic **Altstadt** is easily covered on foot. The **Handwerkerhof**, an overpriced re-creation of the crafts quarter of old Nuremberg, is opposite the main train station. On Lorenzer Platz is the **St Lorenzkirche**, noted for the 15th-century tabernacle that climbs like a vine up a pillar.

To the north is bustling **Hauptmarkt**, where the most famous *Christkindlesmarkt* (Christmas market) in Germany is held from the Friday before Advent up to Christmas Eve. Near the Rathaus is the 13th-century **St Sebalduskirche**, Nuremberg's oldest church.

It's not a bad climb up Burgstrasse to the enormous **Kaiserburg complex** *(☎ 22 57 26; Burg 13; adult/concession €5/4; open 9am-6pm daily Apr-Sept, 10am-4pm Oct-Mar)* for a good view of the city. You can visit the palace complex, chapel, well, tower and museum on the one ticket. Nearby is the renovated **Albrecht-Dürer-Haus**, *(☎ 231 25 68; Albrecht-Dürer-Strasse 39; adult/concession €4/2; open 10am-5pm Tues-Sun, to 8pm Thur)*, where Dürer, Germany's renowned Renaissance draughtsman, lived from 1509 to 1528.

The Nazis chose Nuremberg as their propaganda centre and for mass rallies, which were held at **Luitpoldhain**, a (never completed) sports complex of megalomaniac proportions. After the war, the Allies chose Nuremberg as the site for the trials of Nazi war criminals. A new museum called **Dokumentationzentrum** *(☎ 231 56 66; Bayernstrasse 110; adult/concession €5/2.50; open 9am-6pm Mon-Fri, 10am-6pm Sat & Sun)* deals with the reality and aftermath of the Nazi regime. Take tram No 9 to Luitpoldhein.

Places to Stay & Eat

In historic Kaiserstallung next to the castle, **Jugendherberge Nürnberg** *(☎ 230 93 60, fax 23 09 36 11; ⓔ jhnuernberg@djh-bayern.de; Burg 2; dorm beds with linen €17.70)* has more character than most. Another good, central backpacker option is **Lette'm Sleep** *(☎ 99 28 128, fax 99 28 130; Frauentormauer 42; dorm beds €13, doubles from €22)*. Family-run, no-frills **Pension Vater Jahn** *(☎ 44 45 07, fax 43 15 236; Jahnstrasse 13; singles/doubles from €25/39)* is friendly, offering clean rooms with shared facilities. **Pension Sonne** *(☎ 22 71 66; Königstrasse 45; singles/doubles with breakfast €30/50)* has bright, cheery rooms up a steep flight of stairs.

Don't leave Nuremberg without trying its famous *Bratwurstl* (small grilled sausages). The best place is the **Bratwursthäusle** (☎ *22 76 95; Rathausplatz 2; 10 for €8.30*), where they're flame-grilled, scrumptious, and served with *Meerettich* (horseradish) and *Kartoffelsalat* (potato salad).

Getting There & Around

IC trains run hourly to/from Frankfurt (€37.20, 2¼ hours) and Munich (€38, 1½ hours). IR trains run every two hours to Stuttgart (€28, two hours) and ICE trains every two hours to Berlin (€78.20, five hours). Several daily EC trains travel to Vienna (seven hours) and Prague (5½ hours). Buses to regional destinations leave from the station just east of the main train station.

Tickets on the bus, tram and U-Bahn system cost €1.35/1.75 for each short/long ride in the central zone.

REGENSBURG

☎ 0941 • pop 143,000

On the Danube River, Regensburg lacks the packaged feel of some other German cities. It escaped the carpet bombing, and here, as nowhere else in Germany, you enter the misty ages between the Roman and the Carolingian.

The **tourist office** (☎ *507 44 10;* Ⓔ *tourismus@info.regensburg.baynet.de; open daily*) is in the Altes Rathaus. **Surf City** (*Speichergasse 1*) charges €3 for 30 minutes on the Internet.

Dominating the skyline are the twin spires of the Gothic **Dom St Peter** (☎ *597 10 02; Domplatz; admission free; tours in German adult/concession €2.50/1.50*), built during the 14th and 15th centuries from unusual green limestone. It has striking original stained-glass windows above the choir on the eastern side. The **Altes Rathaus** was progressively extended from medieval to baroque times and remained the seat of the Reichstag for almost 150 years. The **Roman wall**, with its **Porta Praetoria** arch, follows Unter den Schwibbögen onto Dr-Martin-Luther-Strasse.

For budget beds, the **Youth Hostel** (☎ *574 02, fax 524 11;* Ⓔ *jhregensburg@djh-bayern.de; Wöhrdstrasse 60; dorm beds €16.60*) can be reached on bus No 3 to the Eisstadion stop. Central **Hotel Am Peterstor** (☎ *545 45, fax 545 42; Fröliche-Türken-Strasse 12; singles/doubles €40/50*) is good value, with clean, basic rooms. By far the best spot for a snack of Bratwurstl in bread is the **Historische Wurstküche** (*Thundorferstrasse; €6*), on the banks of the roaring Danube.

Regensburg is on the train line between Nuremberg (€19, one hour) and Austria; there are EC/IC trains in both directions every two hours, as well as RB/RE trains to Munich (€19.20, 1½ hours). Regensburg is a major stop on the Danube bike route.

BAVARIAN ALPS

While not quite as high as their Austrian counterparts, the Bavarian Alps (Bayerische Alpen) rise dramatically from the rolling hills of southern Bavaria. Stretching westward from Germany's southeastern corner to the Allgäu region near Lake Constance, the Alps take in most of the mountainous country fringing the southern border with Austria.

The Bavarian Alps are extraordinarily well organised for outdoor pursuits, with skiing, snowboarding and hiking being the most popular. The ski season usually runs from mid-December to April. Ski gear is available for hire in all the resorts. In warmer months, activities include hiking, canoeing, rafting, biking and paragliding.

Most resorts have plenty of reasonably priced guesthouses and private rooms, though it's a good idea to reserve accommodation. Try tourist offices or look for *Zimmer Frei* signs. Rates can be higher in July and August.

While the public transport network is very good, there are few direct routes between main centres; sometimes a short cut via Austria is quicker (such as between Füssen and Oberstdorf). Regional RVO bus passes giving free travel on the network between Füssen, Garmisch and Mittenwald are excellent value (☎ 089-55 16 40).

Berchtesgaden

☎ 08652 • pop 8200

Berchtesgaden is perhaps the most romantically scenic place in the Bavarian Alps. The helpful **tourist office** (☎ *96 70;* Ⓔ *info@berchtesgaden.de; Königsseer Strasse 2; open Mon-Sat, daily in summer*) is just across the river from the train station.

Tours of the **Salzbergwerk** (☎ *600 20; Bergwerkstrasse 83; adult/concession €12/6.50; open 9am-5pm May–mid-Oct; 12.30pm-3.30pm Mon-Sat mid-Oct–Apr*) combine history with a carnival. Visitors descend down into the salt mine for a 1½-hour tour. Nearby, the **Obersalzberg** is a deceptively innocent-looking place with a creepy legacy as the second seat of government for the Third Reich. Hitler, Himmler, Goebbels and the rest of the Nazi hierarchy all maintained homes here.

The **Dokumentation Obersalzberg museum** *(☎ 94 79 60; Salzbergstrasse 41; adult/concession €2.50/1.50; open 9am-5pm Tues-Sun May-Nov, 10am-3pm Tues-Sun Nov-May)* documents the evil bunch's time in the area. The fee also gets you into **Hitler's bunker**. Catch bus No 9538 (€3.70 return) from the Nazi-constructed Berchtesgaden train station to Obersalzberg-Hintereck. **Kehlstein** *(☎ 29 69; admission €12; buses run 7.40am-4.25pm; open May-Oct)* is a spectacular meeting house built for, but seldom used by, Hitler. The views are stunning and the history bracing. Entrance includes transport on special buses linking the summit with Hintereck/Obersalzberg as well as the 120m lift through solid rock to the peak.

Alternatively, you can forget the horrors of war at the **Königssee**, a beautiful alpine lake 5km south of Berchtesgaden (linked by hourly buses in summer).

The wilds of Berchtesgaden National Park unquestionably offer some of the best **hiking** in Germany. A good introduction to the area is a 2km path up from St Bartholomä beside the Königssee to the Watzmann-Ostwand, a massive 2000m-high rock face where scores of ambitious mountaineers have died.

Berchtesgaden has five major **skiing** resorts, and you can buy five-day lift passes that cover all (€98). Rossfeld is the cheapest for day passes (€13), while Götschen, with a permanent half-pipe, is the destination for snowboarders (€20 a day).

The pleasant **Youth Hostel** *(☎ 943 70, fax 94 37 37; ⓔ jhberchtesgaden@djh-bayern.de; Gebirgsjägerstrasse 52; dorm beds €13.10)* is closed in November and December. Take bus No 9539 to Jugendherberge. Lovely **Hotel Watzmann** *(☎ 20 55, fax 51 74; Franziskanerplatz 2; singles/doubles from €28/50)* is decorated in traditional upper-Bavarian style, and has comfortable rooms and an excellent outdoor terrace with top food (mains €9 to €11). If you have an itch for schnitzel, head to **Alt Berchtesgaden** *(☎ 45 19; Bahnhofstrasse 3; schnitzel €4.99)*, with 15 kinds to choose from.

Both RB and RE trains run to Munich and cost €24.80.

Baden-Württemberg

Baden-Württemberg is one of Germany's main tourist regions. With recreational centres such as the Black Forest and Lake Constance, medieval towns such as Heidelberg, and the health spa of Baden-Baden, it's one of the most varied parts of Germany.

STUTTGART

☎ 0711 • pop 590,000

Stuttgart started life in 950 as a horse stud. However, as capital of Baden-Württemberg it led Germany's economic recovery from the ravages of WWII. Eighty per cent of the city centre was destroyed in the war, but there are still some fine historical buildings left, along with huge expanses of parkland, vine-covered hills and an air of relaxed prosperity.

Opposite the main train station, the **tourist office** *(☎ 22 280; ⓔ info@stuttgart-tourist.de; Königstrasse 1a; open daily)* reserves rooms at no cost. The office sells the three-day StuttCard (€14), which allows free public transport and free entry to some museums. The main **post office** is at Bolzstrasse 3. There's a **Reisebank** at the main train station. **Surf Inn** *(Königstrasse 6)*, located on the top floor of Kaufhof department store, charges €1.50 for 30 minutes on the Internet. **Netbox** *(Lautenschlager Strasse 21)* is free.

Things to See & Do

The **tower** at the main train station is an excellent vantage point for the sprawling city and surrounding hills. Stretching southwest from the Neckar River to the city centre is the **Schlossgarten**, an extensive strip of parkland complete with ponds, swans, street entertainers and modern sculptures. At their southern end the gardens encompass the sprawling baroque **Neues Schloss** and the Renaissance **Altes Schloss**, which houses a regional **museum** *(☎ 279 34 00; Schillerplatz 6; adult/concession €2.60/1.50; open 10am-1pm Tues, 10am-5pm Wed-Sun)*.

Next to the Altes Schloss is the city's oldest square, **Schillerplatz**. Adjoining the park you'll find the **Staatsgalerie** *(☎ 212 40 50; Konrad-Adenauer-Strasse 30; adult/concession €4.50/2.50; open 10am-6pm, to 9pm Thur)*, housing an excellent collection from the Middle Ages to the present. Next door is the

Haus der Geschichte *(House of History; ☎ 212 39 50; Urbansplatz 2; admission €3)*. This eye-catching, modern museum covers the past 200 years of Baden-Württemburg in film, photography, documents and multimedia displays.

The motor car was first developed by Gottlieb Daimler and Carl Benz at the end of the 19th century. The impressive **Mercedes-Benz Museum** *(☎ 172 25 78; Mercedesstrasse 137; admission free; open 9am-5pm Tues-Sun)* is in the suburb of Bad-Cannstatt; take S-Bahn No 1 to Neckarstadion. Mercedes-Benz also runs free weekday tours of its Sindelfingen plant, but you must reserve a spot in advance (☎ 07031-907 04 03). For even faster cars, cruise over to the **Porsche Museum** *(☎ 911 56 85; Porschestrasse 42; admission free; open 9am-4pm Mon-Fri, 9am-5pm Sat & Sun)*; take S-Bahn No 6 to Neuwirtshaus. Neither place offers free samples.

Places to Stay & Eat

It's a steep climb to the **DJH Hostel** *(☎ 24 15 83, fax 23 61 041; ⓔ info@jugendherberge-stuttgart.de; Haussmannstrasse 27; juniors/seniors €13.35/16.05)*, a signposted, 15-minute walk from the train station. You might prefer the spacious, bright non-DJH **Jugengästehaus** *(☎ 24 11 32, fax 23 61 110; ⓔ JGH.Stuttgart@internationaler-bund.de; Richard-Wagner-Strasse 2; singles/doubles/triples €21/36/48)*. Take the U15 to Bubenbad.

Gasthof Alte Mira *(☎ 22 29 502, fax 22 29 50 329; ⓔ altemira@web.de; Büchenstrasse 24; singles/doubles from €31/52)* offers clean and simple rooms with shared facilities. Around the corner, **Museumstube** *(☎/fax 29 68 10; Hospitalstrasse 9; singles/doubles €32/50)* offers similar lodgings.

Pack a picnic at **Markthalle** *(Dorotheen strasse 4; open 7am-6.30pm Mon-Fri, to 4pm Sat)*, an excellent Art Nouveau–style market that's packed with fresh fare. Alternatively, fill up for around €2.50 at the university **Mensa** *(Holzgartenstrasse 11)*, which has a downstairs cafeteria for the uneducated masses. Vegetarians can try **iden** *(Eberhardtsrasse 1; meals from €1.53)*, a cheap, self-serve salad and soup spot. **Alte Kanzlei** *(☎ 29 44 57; Schillerplatz 5b; dishes €6-10)* is excellent for a sunny lunch, with pastas, wraps and salads.

Stuttgart is a great place to sample Swabian specialties such as *Spätzle* (like doughy pasta) and *Maultaschen* (similar to ravioli). The best spot is cosy **Zur Kiste** *(☎ 24 40 02; Kanalstrasse 2; mains €8-15)*, in the Bohnenviertel (Bean Quarter).

Entertainment

Lift Stuttgart is a comprehensive guide to local entertainment and events (€1). Home of the famous Stuttgart Ballet, the **Staatstheater** *(☎ 20 20 90; Oberer Schlossgarten 6)* holds regular symphony, ballet and opera performances.

The grandly named **Palast de Republic** *(Friedrichstrasse 27)* is a tiny bar that pulls a huge crowd of laid-back drinkers. There are several funky drinking holes around Hans-im-Glück-Platz, a small square that's often packed with party-goers. Nearby, **Bar Code** *(Theodore-Heuss-Strasse 30)* is a cool, modern bar with a young crowd. For leafy fun, there's a **beer garden** in the Mittlerer Schlossgarten, northeast of the main train station.

Getting There & Around

Stuttgart's international airport is south of the city and is served by S2 and S3 trains (30 minutes from the main train station). There are frequent train departures for all major German and many international cities. ICE trains run to Frankfurt (€45.20, 1½ hours), Berlin (€127, 5½ hours) and Munich (€44.60, two hours). Regional and long-distance buses leave from the station next to the main train station.

Single fares on Stuttgart's public transport network are €1.10/5.30 for short/long trips. A four-ride strip ticket costs €5.80 and a central-zone day pass is €4.70.

HEIDELBERG

☎ 06221 • pop 140,000

The French destroyed Heidelberg in 1693; they may have been the last visitors to dislike this charming town on the Neckar River. Its magnificent castle and medieval centre are irresistible drawcards for most travellers. Mark Twain recounted his observations of Heidelberg in *A Tramp Abroad*, and the city inspired JMW Turner to produce some of his finest landscape paintings. Today, its sizable student population keeps Heidelberg a lively city.

The **main tourist office** *(☎ 194 33; ⓔ cvb@heidelberg.de; Willy-Brandt-Platz 1; open Mon-Sat, daily Apr-Nov)* is outside the train station. The €12 Heidelberg Card offers unlimited public transport and free admission to many sights. There's a **post office** branch to the right as you leave the train station.

Office Shop GmbH *(Plock 85)* charges €1.30 for 15 minutes on the Internet.

Things to See & Do

Heidelberg's imposing **Schloss** *(☎ 53 84 14; adult/concession €2/1; open 8am-5.30pm)* is one of Germany's finest examples of grand, Gothic-Renaissance architecture. The building's half-ruined state actually adds to its romantic appeal. You can take the funicular railway to the castle from the lower Kornmarkt station (adult/concession €3/2 return) or enjoy an invigorating 10-minute walk up steep, stone lanes.

Dominating Universitätsplatz are the 18th-century **Alte Universität** and the **Neue Universität**. Nearby is the **Studentenkarzer** *(student jail; ☎ 54 21 63; Augustinergasse 2; adult/concession €2.50/2; open 10am-noon & 2pm-5pm Tues-Sat Apr-Oct, 10am-2pm Tues-Fri Nov-Mar)*, used from 1778 to 1914 to incarcerate uproarious students. Sentences were earned for such heinous crimes as drinking, singing and womanising. The **Marstall** is the former arsenal, now a student mensa. The **Kurpfälzisches Museum** *(Palatinate Museum; ☎ 58 34 02; Hauptstrasse 97; adult/concession €2.50/1.50; open 10am-5pm Tues-Sun, to 9pm Wed)* contains paintings, sculptures and the jawbone of the 600,000-year-old Heidelberg Man.

Places to Stay & Eat

Finding accommodation in high season can be difficult. Arrive early in the day or book ahead. The local **DJH hostel** *(☎ 41 20 66, fax 40 25 59; ⓔ jh-heidel berg@t-online.de; Tiergartenstrasse 5; juniors/seniors €13.35/16.05)* is across the river from the train station. From the station or Bismarckplatz, take bus No 33 towards Ziegelhausen. The labyrinthine backpacker favourite **Pension Jeske** *(☎ 237 33, fax 65 91 23; Mittelbadgasse 2; beds €20, doubles from €50)* has new owners, beds and bathrooms, but it's still the cheapest place in the Altstadt.

The **Mensa** *(Univsersitätsplatz; meals for students/guests €2/3)* has budget feeds whether you're the studious type or not. In the Altstadt there are two decent, cheap, Indian takeaways: **Raja Rani** *(Mittelbadgasse 5; meals from around €3)* and also **Lahori** *(Heiliggeistrasse 9a; meals from around €3)*. You can grab a feed at many student pubs (see Entertainment) for around €8.

Entertainment

You won't have to go far to find a happening backstreet bar. Laid-back, intimate **Hörnchen** *(Heumarkt)* is the perfect place to start an evening out. At **Destille** *(Untere Strasse 16)*, there's an eclectic mix of loud chat, louder music and board games. Also popular is modern **iPunkt** *(Untere Strasse 30)*. Heidelberg's famous historic student pubs **Zum Roten Ochen** *(Hauptstrasse 217)* and **Zum Sepp'l** *(Hauptstrasse 213)* don't get much more than a tourist trade these days.

For live jazz and blues, head to **Cave54** *(Krämergasse 2)*, an underground stone cellar that oozes character and once hosted Louis Armstrong. It's big on Thursday, Friday and Saturday.

Getting There & Around

Heidelberg is on the Castle Road route from Mannheim to Nuremberg. From mid-May until the end of September **Deutsche-Touring GmbH** *(☎ 089-59 38 89, fax 550 39 65; ⓔ service@deutsche-touring.com; Am Römerhof 17, 60486 Frankfurt/Main)* has a daily coach service, with one bus in either direction between Heidelberg and Rothenburg ob der Tauber (€29, five hours).

There are hourly ICE/IC trains to/from Frankfurt (€22.80, one hour), Stuttgart (€19.60, 40 minutes) and Munich (€53.40, three hours). Mannheim, 12 minutes to the west by frequent trains, has connections to cities throughout Germany.

The bus and tram system in Heidelberg is extensive and efficient. Single tickets cost €1.80 and a 24-hour pass costs €5.90.

BADEN-BADEN

☎ 07221 • pop 50,000

Baden-Baden's natural hot springs have attracted visitors since Roman times, but this small city only really became fashionable in the 19th century when the likes of Victor Hugo came to bathe in and imbibe its therapeutic waters. Today Baden-Baden is Germany's ritziest health spa.

The **tourist office** *(☎ 27 52 00; ⓔ info@baden-baden.com; Kaiserallee 3; open daily)* is in the ornate and grand Trinkhalle *(pump room; Kaiserallee 3)*. Collect some info and sample the local drop: You can have a free drink of the spa water piped in hot right from the ground. There is a spa tax of €2.50, entitling you to a discount Kurkarte from your hotel. The tax doesn't apply to those staying at the hostel.

The **Merkur Cable Car** *(€4; 10am-10pm daily)* takes you up to the 660m hill summit, where there are fine views and many walking trails (bus No 204 or 205 from Leopoldplatz takes you to the cable-car station). A good hiking tour is to the wine-growing area of **Rebland**, 6km to the west.

On either side of Römerplatz are the two places where you can take to the waters. The 19th-century **Friedrichsbad** *(☎ 27 59 20; Römerplatz 1; bathing programme €21; open 9am-10pm Mon-Sat, noon-8pm Sun)* is decadently Roman in style and offers you a muscle-melting Roman-Irish bathing programme. No clothing is allowed inside, so leave your modesty at the reception desk. Modern **Caracalla-Therme** *(☎ 27 59 40; Römerplatz 11; 2 hours €11; open 8am-10pm)* is a vast complex of outdoor and indoor pools, hot- and cold-water grottoes and many more delights. You must wear a bathing costume and bring your own towel.

Baden-Baden's **DJH hostel** *(☎ 522 23, fax 600 12; ⓔ info@jugendherberge-baden-baden.de; Hardbergstrasse 34; juniors/seniors €13.35/16.05)* lies 3km northwest of the centre; take bus No 201 to Grosse Dollenstrasse then walk for 10 minutes. Central **Hotel Zur Altstadt** *(☎ 30 22 80, fax 302 28 28; Baldreitstrasse 1; singles/doubles with bathroom from €34/64)* is a good deal, with rooms that are pleasant and ample.

For a light bite, head to **Leo's** *(☎ 380 81; Luisenstrasse 8; meals €8)*, a trendy spot with outdoor tables and tasty, well-presented dishes.

Baden-Baden is on the busy Mannheim-Basel train line. Fast trains in either direction stop every two hours. Frequent local trains serve Karlsruhe and Offenburg, from where you can make connections to much of Germany. The station is 7km from the town centre; frequent public transport makes the run.

BLACK FOREST

Home of the cuckoo clock, the Black Forest (Schwarzwald) gets its name from its dark canopy of evergreens. The fictional Hansel and Gretel encountered their wicked witch in these parts, but modern-day hazards are more likely to include packs of tourists. However, a 20-minute walk from even the most crowded spots will put you in quiet countryside dotted

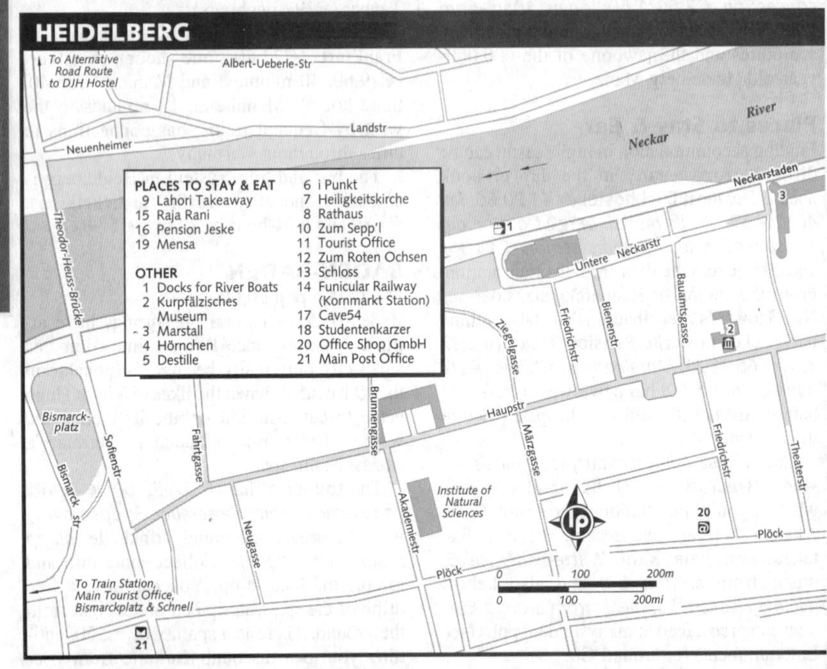

with huge, traditional farmhouses and patrolled by amiable dairy cows.

The Black Forest lies east of the Rhine between Karlsruhe and Basel. It's roughly triangular in shape, about 160km long and 50km wide. Baden-Baden, Freudenstadt, Titisee and Freiburg act as convenient information posts for excursions. Even smaller towns in the area generally have tourist offices.

Freudenstadt's **tourist office** *(☎ 07441-86 40; ⓔ touristinfo@freudenstadt.de; Am Marktplatz; open daily)* is a good place for information on the northern section. **Titisee's office** *(☎ 07651-98 04 0; ⓔ touristinfo@titisee.de; Strandbadstrasse 4; open Mon-Fri, also Sat & Sun May-Oct)*, inside the Kurhaus, also covers the southern Black Forest. The **Feldberg office** *(☎ 07655-80 19; ⓔ tourist-info@feldberg-schwarzwald.de; Kirchgasse 1; open Mon-Fri all year, also Sat Jun-Sept, Sun July & Aug)* also supplies ski information.

Things to See & Do

Along the Schwarzwald-Hochstrasse (Black Forest Hwy), the first major tourist sight is the **Mummelsee**, south of the Hornisgrinde peak. It's a small, deep lake inhabited, it is said, by an evil sea king. Farther south, **Freudenstadt** is mainly used as a base for excursions into the countryside.

The area between Freudenstadt and Freiburg is (overpriced) cuckoo-clock country. A few popular stops are Schramberg, Triberg and Furtwangen. In Furtwangen, visit the **Deutsches Uhrenmuseum** *(German Clock Museum; ☎ 07723-92 01 17; Gerwigstrasse 11; adult/concession €3/2.50; open 9am-6pm daily, from 10am Nov-Mar)* for a look at traditional clock-making.

With over 7000km of marked trails, **hiking** possibilities are endless. Any tourist office can set you off on anything from easy, one-hour jaunts to multiday treks. Three classic, long-distance hiking trails run south from the northern Black Forest city of Pforzheim as far as the Swiss Rhine: the 280km Westweg to Basel; the 230km Mittelweg to Waldhut-Tiengen; and the 240km Ostweg to Schaffhausen.

The southern Black Forest, especially around the 1493m **Feldberg summit**, offers some of the best hiking; small towns such as Todtmoos or Bonndorf can serve as bases. The 10km **Wutachschlucht** (Wutach Gorge) outside Bonndorf is justifiably famous. You

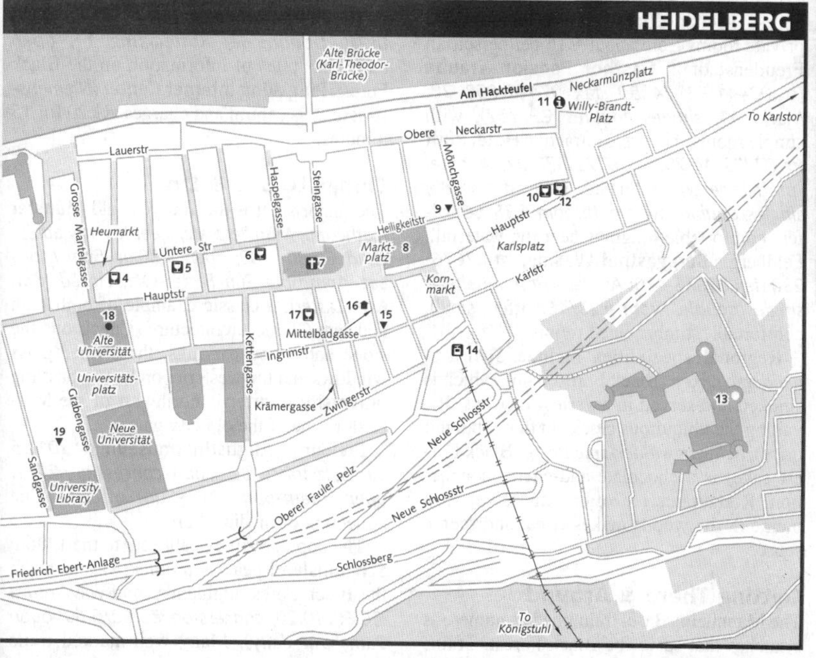

can also windsurf, go boating or swim at the highland **lakes.** Titisee boasts several beaches.

The Black Forest ski season runs from late December to March. While there is some good downhill **skiing**, the area is more suited to cross-country skiing. The Titisee area is the main centre for winter sports, with uncrowded downhill runs at Feldberg (day passes €20) and numerous, graded, cross-country trails. In midwinter, **ice skating** is also possible on the Titisee and the Schluchsee. For winter sports information, check with the Feldberg or Titisee tourist offices.

Places to Stay & Eat

Away from the major towns you can find scores of simple, warm, cheap guesthouses. The DJH hostel net is extensive in the southern Black Forest but limited in the north. Some convenient hostels are in **Freudenstadt** *(☎ 07441-77 20; ⓔ info@jugendherberge-freudenstadt.de; Eugen-Nägele-Strasse 69)*, **Triberg** *(☎ 07722-41 10; ⓔ info@jugendherberge-triberg.de; Rohrbacher Strasse 3)* and **Zuflucht** *(☎ 07804-611; ⓔ info@jugendherberge-zuflucht.de; Schwarzwaldhochstrasse)*. All charge €13.35/16.05 for juniors/seniors.

Lodges may outnumber cows in the Black Forest. Tourist offices can also direct you to private rooms from about €16 per person. In Freudenstadt is **Gasthof Pension Traube** *(☎ 07441-91 74 50, fax 07441-853 28; Markt 41; singles/doubles €30/57)*, with simple rooms. Triberg's attractive **Hotel Pfaff** *(☎ 07722-44 79, fax 07722-78 97; ⓔ hotel-pfaff-triberg@t-online.de; Hauptstrasse 85; singles/doubles with bathroom €38/66)* offers comfortable lodgings near the waterfall. Feldberg's **Berggasthof Wasmer** *(☎ 07676-230, fax 07676-430; An der Wiesenquelle 1; singles/doubles from €23/46)* offers small, comfortable, timber-lined rooms.

Regional specialities include *Schwarzwälderschinken* (Black Forest ham), which is smoked and served in a variety of ways. Rivalling the ubiquitous clocks in fame (but not price), *Schwarzwälderkirschtorte* (Black Forest cake) is a chocolate-and-cherry concoction. Restaurants are often expensive, so a picnic in the woods makes fiscal and scenic sense.

Getting There & Around

The Mannheim-Basel train line has numerous branches that serve the Black Forest. Trains for Freudenstadt and the north leave from Karlsruhe. Triberg is on the busy line linking Offenburg and Constance. Titisee has frequent services from Freiburg, with some trains continuing to Feldberg and others to Neustadt, where there are connections to Donaueschingen.

The rail network is extensive, and where trains don't go, buses do. Check the schedules at bus stops or consult with the tourist offices. To reach Feldberg, take one of the frequent buses from the train stations in Titisee or Bärental.

FREIBURG

☎ 0761 • pop 200,500

The gateway to the southern Black Forest, Freiburg is a fun place thanks to the city's large, thriving university community. Major reconstruction of Freiburg's old sights was needed following severe bombing damage during WWII. The monumental 13th-century cathedral is the city's key landmark, but the real attractions are the vibrant cafés, bars and street life, plus the local wines. The best times for tasting are early July during *Weinfest* (Wine Festival), or early August for the nine days of *Weinkost* (loosely, 'wine as food').

The **tourist office** *(☎ 388 18 80; ⓔ touristik@fwt-online.de; Rotteckring 14; open daily)* has piles of information on the Black Forest. **PingWing Internet Center** *(Niemensstrasse 3)* is central and charges €1.20 for 15 minutes.

Things to See & Do

The major sight is the 700-year-old **Münster** *(cathedral; Münsterplatz; steeple entry adult/child €1.30/0.80; open 9.30am-5pm Mon-Sat, 1pm-5pm Sun Easter-Oct, closed Mon Nov-Easter)*, a classic example of both high and late-Gothic architecture. Check out the stone and wood carvings, the stained-glass windows and the western porch. The bustling **university quarter** is northwest of the Martinstor (one of the old city gates).

Freiburg's **Augustinermuseum** *(☎ 201 25 31; Salzstrasse 32; adult/concession €2/1; open 10am-5pm Tues-Sun)* offers a fine collection of medieval art.

The popular trip by cable car to the 1286m **Schauinsland** peak is a quick way to reach the Black Forest highlands *(one-way/return €6.60/10.20, concession €3.60/5.60; open 9am-5pm daily)*. Many well-marked trails make the Schauinsland area ideal for day walks. From Freiburg take tram No 4 south to Günterstal and then bus No 21 to Talstation.

Places to Stay & Eat

The modern **DJH Hostel** *(☎ 67 565, fax 60 367; ⓔ jh-freiburg@t-online.de; Karthäuserstrasse 151; juniors/seniors €14.90/17.60)* isn't very convenient. Take Tram No 1 to Römerhof (direction: Littenweiler).

Ten minutes' walk south of the centre, friendly **Hotel Sonne** *(☎ 40 30 48, fax 40 98 856; Basler Strasse 58; singles/doubles €35/52)* has decent, simple rooms and a magnificent breakfast buffet. The charming **Hotel Rappen** *(☎ 313 53, fax 38 22 52; ⓔ rappen@t-online.de; Münsterplatz 13; singles/doubles from €55/70)* has lovely rooms with close-up views of the Münster.

Freiburg guarantees cheap eats and a lively restaurant scene. University-subsidised **Mensas** *(Rempartstrasse 18 • Hebelstrasse 9a)* have salad buffets and other filling fodder. You may be asked to show student ID. Most of the student bars serve good, cheap meals for between €3 and €8 (see Entertainment). **UC Uni Café** *(☎ 38 33 55; Niemensstrasse 7; meals €3-7)* is a popular hang-out that serves light bites on its outdoor terrace. **Warsteiner Keller** *(☎ 32 929; Niemensstrasse 13; meals €7.50)* is a bar/café that oozes atmosphere. At self-serve **Salatstuben** *(Löwenstrasse 1; 100g salad €1.20, hot meal €4.10)* there's a great range of cheap vegetarian dishes.

Entertainment

Schlappen *(Lowenstrasse 2)* is where it happens with the student crowd most nights. It's a large, sprawling bar with a lively vibe, a budget menu and late closing. **Galerie** *(Milchstrasse 7)* is an intimate watering hole with a nice courtyard and cheap Spanish eats. Mellow, candlelit **Cohibar** *(Milchstrasse 9)* is a nearby cocktail bar that doesn't close till 3am on weekends. **Alter Simon** *(Konviktstrasse 43)* has a laid-back feel, and is a good stopover on your way back from **Greiffenberg-Schlössle** *(Schlossbergring 3)*, a hilltop beer garden with stunning views.

Freiburg's **Konzerthaus** *(☎ 388 85 52; Konrad-Adenauer-Platz 1)* hosts an impressive range of orchestral performances, while nearby the **Jazzhaus** *(☎ 34 973; Schnewlinstrasse 1)* has live jazz every night. Admission (from €6) depends on who's playing.

Getting There & Around

Freiburg lies on the Mannheim-Basel train corridor. The trains to Titisee leave every 30 minutes (€9). The regional bus station is next to Track 1. For ride-sharing information contact the **Citynetz Mitfahr-Service** *(☎ 194 44; Belfortstrasse 55)*. Single rides on the efficient local bus and tram system cost €1.75. A 24-hour pass costs €4.60.

ULM

☎ 0731 • pop 165,000

Ulm is famous for its Münster tower, the highest cathedral spire in Europe. Oh…and it's also the birthplace of Albert Einstein. Greater Ulm is actually two cities in two states: Ulm proper, on the Danube's northern bank, is more interesting than Bavaria's Neu Ulm. The **tourist office** *(☎ 16 12 830; ⓔ info@tourismus.ulm.de; Münsterplatz; open Mon-Sat, daily May-Oct)* is very helpful. **Albert's Café** *(Kornhausplatz 5)* offers free Internet access.

The huge **Münster** *(cathedral; Münsterplatz; steeple climb adult/concession €3/2; open 9am-5pm Sept-May, longer hours June-Aug)* is noted for its 161m-high steeple, the world's tallest. It took over 500 years for the entire structure to be completed. A stained-glass window above the entrance recalls the Holocaust.

Schwörmontag (Oath Monday), on the second-last Monday in July, has been celebrated since 1397. After the mayor takes an oath at the **Schwörhaus** (Oath House), the populace moves down to the old Fischerviertel quarter for a raucous procession of rafts and barges, followed by all-night partying. The next day is a local holiday.

Reach the **DJH hostel** *(☎ 38 44 55, fax 38 45 11; ⓔ jh-ulm@t-online.de; Grimmelfinger Weg 45; juniors/seniors €13.35/16.05)* by taking the S1 to Ehinger Tor, then bus No 4 or 8 to Schulzentrum; from here it's five minutes' walk. Over in Neu-Ulm is the **Rose** *(☎ 778 03, fax 977 17 68; ⓔ u.hilpert@t-online.de; Kasernstrasse 42a; singles/doubles €22/44)*, with tidy, spacious rooms and friendly hosts. Near the Münster, **Hotel Bäumle** *(☎ 622 87, fax 602 26 04; Kohlgasse 6; singles/doubles from €30/45)* is terrific value, with lovely, timber-lined rooms and a snug downstairs restaurant with regional fare (mains €7 to €14). **Drei Kannen** *(☎ 677 17; Hafenbad 31; mains €4-11)* brews its own dark beer and serves hearty German tucker.

Ulm is a major transport hub, with trains in all directions.

LAKE CONSTANCE

Lake Constance (Bodensee) is a perfect cure for travellers stranded in landlocked southern Germany. This giant bulge in the sinewy course of the Rhine River offers a choice of water sports, relaxation or cultural pursuits. The lake adds special atmosphere to the many historic towns around its periphery. The lake's southern side belongs to Switzerland and Austria, whose snow-capped mountains provide a perfect backdrop when viewed from the northern shore. The German side features three often-crowded tourist centres in Constance, Meersburg and the island of Lindau.

The tourist booklet *Rad Urlaub am Bodensee* details bike routes and rental places, and a wealth of other information for the region. In Constance, **Velotours** *(☎ 07531-982 80; Fritz-Arnold-Strasse 2b; bike rental €11/52 daily/weekly)* rents out bikes and organises cycling tours.

Fortunately, excellent hostel and camping facilities exist around the lake. For reservation information, contact the **Constance tourist information office** *(☎ 13 30 30; ⓔ info@ti.konstanz.de; Bahnhofplatz 13)*.

Constance has train connections every one to two hours to Offenburg (€25.40) and Stuttgart (€34). Meersburg is easily reached by bus No 7395 from Friedrichshafen (€6.40, every 30 minutes), or by **Weisse Flotte** *(☎ 07531-28 13 98)* boats from Constance (€3.40, several times a day in season). Lindau has trains to/from Ulm (€17.80), Munich (€28) and Bregenz, Austria (€2.10).

Trains link Lindau, Friedrichshafen and Constance, and buses fill in the gaps. The most enjoyable, albeit slowest, way to get around is on the Weisse Flotte boats, which, from Easter to late October, call several times a day at the larger towns along both sides of the lake; there are discounts for rail-pass holders.

GERMANY

Western Germany

The western section of Germany comprises the states of Rhineland-Palatinate, Saarland, Hesse and also North Rhine–Westphalia. Rhineland-Palatinate (Rheinland-Pflaz) is rugged and beautiful, dotted by wineries and medieval castles. Saarland, western Germany's poorest region, does not lie on most travellers' itineraries. Hesse is home to the quite un-German city of Frankfurt, a major transport hub and a good base to explore the region. Finally, North Rhine–Westphalia (Nordrhein-Westfalen) shelters a quarter of Germany's population. Although the area is dominated by bleak industrial centres connected by a maze of train lines and autobahns, some of the cities are steeped in history and warrant an extensive visit.

THE MOSELLE VALLEY

Exploring the vineyards and wineries of the Moselle (Mosel) Valley is an ideal way to get a taste of German culture and people – and, of course, the wonderful wines. Take the time to slow down and do some sipping.

The Moselle Valley is bursting at the seams with historical sites and picturesque towns built along the river below steep rocky cliffs planted with vineyards (they say locals are born with one leg shorter than the other so that they can easily work the vines). It's one of the country's most romantically scenic regions, with stunning views rewarding the intrepid hikers who brave the hilly trails. Tourist offices sell good maps showing trails and paths, and usually have tips on short hikes.

There are camping grounds, hostels and rooms with classic views all along the Moselle Valley. Many wine-makers also have their own small pensions. In May, on summer weekends or during the local wine harvest (mid-September to mid-October), accommodation is hard to find. The most scenic section of the Moselle Valley runs 195km northeast from Trier to Koblenz; it's most practical to begin your Moselle Valley trip from either of these two hubs.

Local and fast trains run every hour between Trier and Koblenz (€16, 1½ hours), but the only riverside stretch of this line is between Cochem and Koblenz. Apart from this run, travellers must use buses, ferries, bicycles, or cars to travel between Moselle towns. **Moselbahn** *(☎ 0651-14 77 50)* runs eight buses on weekdays (fewer on weekends) between Trier and Bullay (three hours each way). Buses leave from outside the train stations in Trier, Traben-Trarbach and Bullay. Frequent buses run between Kues (Alter Bahnhof) and the Wittlich main train station (€3.60, 30 minutes each way), connecting with trains to Koblenz and Trier.

A great way to explore the Moselle in the high season is by boat. Between early May and mid-October, **Köln-Düsseldorfer (KD) Line** *(☎ 0221-208 8318)* ferries sail daily between Koblenz and Cochem (€20.20 one way, 4½ hours), and the **Gebrüder Kolb Line** *(☎ 02673-15 15)* runs boats upriver from Cochem to Trier and then back via Traben-Trarbach and Bernkastel. Various, smaller ferry companies also operate on the Moselle. Eurail and German Rail passes are valid for all normal KD Line services, and travel on your birthday is free.

The Moselle is a popular area among cyclists, and for much of the river's course there's a separate 'Moselroute' bicycle track. **Touren-Rad** *(☎ 0261-911 60 16; Hohenzollernstrasse 127)*, six blocks from the main train station in Koblenz, rents out quality mountain and touring bicycles from €6/10 per day. It has a deal with the rental shop at Trier's main **train station** *(☎ 0651-14 88 56)*, so you can pick up or return bikes at either. In Bernkastel, **Fun-Bike Team** *(☎ 06531-940 24; Schanzstrasse 22)*, rents standard bikes from €8 per day.

TRIER

☎ 0651 • pop 100,000

Trier is touted as Germany's oldest town. Although settlement of the site dates back to 400 BC, Trier itself was founded in 15 BC as Augusta Treverorum, the capital of Gaul, and was second in importance only tothe city of Rome in the Western Empire. You will find more Roman ruins here than anywhere else north of the Alps.

From the main train station head west along Bahnhofstrasse and Theodor-Heuss-Allee to the Porta Nigra, where you'll find Trier's **tourist office** *(☎ 97 80 80; e info@tit.de; open Mon-Sat, daily Apr-Oct)*. Ask here about daily, guided, city walking tours (€6) and the three-day Trier-Card (€9), a combined ticket for the city's main sights, museums and public transport. From Porta Nigra, walk along Simeonstrasse's pedestrian zone to Hauptmarkt, the heart of the old city.

The town's chief landmark is the **Porta Nigra** *(adult/concession €2.10/1.60; open 9am-6pm daily Apr-Sept, till 5pm Oct-Mar)*, the imposing 2nd-century gate on the northern edge of the town centre. The interesting **Rheinisches Landesmuseum** *(Weimarer Allee 1; admission €5.50; open 9.30am-5pm Tues-Fri, 10.30am-5pm Sat & Sun)* has works of art dating from Palaeolithic, Roman and modern times.

Trier's massive Romanesque **Dom** shares a 1600-year history with the nearby and equally impressive **Konstantin Basilika**. Also worth visiting are the ancient Amphitheater, Kaiserthermen and Barbarathermen *(Roman baths)*. The early-Gothic **Dreikönigenhaus** *(Simeonstrasse 19)* was built around 1230 as a protective tower. History buffs and nostalgic socialists can visit the **Karl Marx Haus Museum** *(☎ 97 06 80; Brückenstrasse 10; adult/concession €2/1; open daily)*, in the house where a star was born.

Places to Stay & Eat

The **DJH Jugendgästehaus** *(☎ 14 66 20; e jh-trier@djh-info.de; An der Jugendherberge 4; dorm beds/doubles/singles per person €16/21/29)* is down by the river. **Hotel Hochwald** *(☎ 758 03, fax 743 54; Bahnhofplatz 5; singles €26, singles/doubles with bath €36/60)*, opposite the train station, has austere but clean rooms.

Trier is a great place to sample some Franco-German cooking. **Astarix** *(☎ 722 39; Karl-Marx-Strasse 11)* is a favourite student hang-out in an arcade. It serves large salads and main dishes for under €6 (open till late). The weinstube of the **Weingut Reichsgraf von Kesselstadt** *(☎ 411 78; Liebfrauenstrasse 10; mains from €7)* offers a limited menu and superlative wines in a casual outdoor setting.

Plus *(Brotstrasse 23)* is a central supermarket. The narrow Judengasse, near Markt, has several bars and cafés for tipples and nibbles, whereas a slicker crowd gravitates towards a cluster of bars on Viehmarktplatz.

Getting There & Away

Trier has hourly local and fast trains to Koblenz (€15.60, 1½ hours), as well as services to Luxembourg (€7.40, 45 minutes) and Metz (in France; €18.20, 2½ hours). For information on river ferries, see the Moselle Valley section earlier.

RHINE VALLEY – KOBLENZ TO MAINZ

A trip along the Rhine is on the itinerary of most travellers. Spring and autumn are the best times to visit; in summer it's overrun and in winter most towns go into hibernation.

This section of the Rhine Valley is great for wine tasting, with Bacharach, 45km south of Koblenz, being one of the top choices for sipping. Hiking along the Rhine Valley is also excellent.

Koblenz and Mainz are the best starting points for trips. The Rhine Valley is also easily accessible from Frankfurt on a long day trip. The **Köln-Düsseldorfer (KD) Line** *(☎ 0221-20 88 318)* earns its bread and butter on the Rhine, with many slow and fast boats daily between Koblenz and Mainz. The most scenic stretch is between Koblenz and Rüdesheim; the journey takes about four hours downstream, about 5½ hours upstream (€23.20). Train services operate on both sides of the Rhine River, but are more convenient on the west bank.

Mainz

☎ 06131 • pop 183,000

Though it can't compare to the compact beauty of the nearby towns along the Rhine, Mainz impresses with its massive **cathedral** *(Domstrasse; admission free; open daily)* and **St Stephanskirche** *(Weissgasse 12; admission free; open daily)*. Museums include the **Gutenberg Museum** *(☎ 26 40; Liebfrauenplatz 5; adult/concession €3/1.30; open Tues-Sun)*, which contains two precious copies of the first printed Bible, produced by Mainz's most famous son. For more information, visit the **tourist office** *(☎ 28 62 10; e tourist@info-mainz.de; Brückenturm am Rathaus)*. **C@fé Enterprise** *(Bilhildisstrasse 2, Münsterplatz)* has Internet facilities.

St Goar/St Goarshausen

☎ 06741/06771 • pop 3500

Where the slopes along the Rhine aren't covered with vines, you can bet there are castles. One of the most impressive is **Burg Rheinfels** *(☎ 06741-383; adult/concession €4/2; open 9am-5pm daily Apr-Oct, 10am-4pm Sat & Sun in good weather Nov-Mar)* in St Goar. An absolute must-see, the labyrinthine ruins reflect the greed and ambition of Count Dieter V of Katzenelnbogen, who built the castle in 1245 to help levy tolls on passing ships. Across the river, just south of St Goarshausen, is the Rhine's most famous sight: the **Loreley Cliff**. Legend has it that a maiden sang sailors to their deaths against its base. It's worth the trek to the top, but try to get there early.

FRANKFURT/MAIN

☎ 069 • pop 650,000

It is called 'Bankfurt', 'Mainhattan' and much more. Frankfurt-am-Main is indeed on the Main (pronounced 'mine') River, and it is known as 'Frankfurt', although there's another large city called Frankfurt an der Oder near the Polish border. It's the financial and geographical centre of western Germany, as well as the host of important trade fairs. Thanks to generous funding in the 1980s and early 1990s, it also has some excellent museums.

Frankfurt is also Germany's most important transport hub for air, train and road connections, so you'll probably end up here at some point. Don't be surprised if you find this cosmopolitan melting pot much more interesting than you expected.

Orientation

The airport is 11 minutes by train southwest of the city centre. The Hauptbahnhof is on the western side of the city, but within walking distance of the old city centre.

The safest route to the city centre through the sleazy train-station area is along Kaiserstrasse. This leads to Kaiserplatz and then to a large square called An der Hauptwache. The area between the former lockup (Hauptwache) and the Römerberg, in the tiny vestige of Frankfurt's original old city, is the centre of Frankfurt. The Main River runs just south of the Altstadt, with several bridges leading to one of the city's livelier areas, Sachsenhausen. Its old northeastern corner, behind the youth hostel, is known as Alt Sachsenhausen.

Information

Tourist Offices Frankfurt's most convenient **tourist office** *(☎ 21 23 88 00; open daily)* is in the main hall of the train station. Its efficient room-finding service costs €2.50. In the city centre, the **Römer tourist office** *(☎ 21 23 88 00; Römerberg 27; open daily)* occupies the northwest corner of Römerberg square. Another conveniently located branch is **City-Info Zeil** *(☎ 21 23 88 00; cnr Stiftstrasse & Ziel; open daily)*. The head office of the **German National Tourist Office** *(☎ 97 46 4, fax 75 19 03; w www.deutschland-tourismus.de; Beethovenstrasse 69)* has brochures on all areas of the country.

One/two-day Frankfurt cards (€7.50/11) give 50% reductions on admission to all of the city's important museums, the airport terraces,

GERMANY

the zoo and Palmengarten, as well as unlimited travel on public transport.

Money The main train station has a **Reisebank** *(open 6.30am-10pm daily)* near the southern exit of platform No 1. There are banks and numerous ATMs at the airport, including a **Reisebank** *(open 6am-11pm daily)* in Terminal 1, arrival hall B. **AmEx** and **Thomas Cook** are opposite each other on Kaiserstrasse at Nos 10 and 11, respectively.

Post & Communications The **main post office** *(Zeil 90)* is on the ground floor of the Karstadt department store (standard shop hours). Inside the Hauptbahnhof is another **post office** *(open Mon-Sat)*. The airport **post office** *(open 7am-9pm daily)* is in the waiting lounge, departure hall B.

Telebistro *(☎ 61 99 11 87; Poststrasse 2)*, right across from the train station, charges €2.10 for a half-hour online.

Medical Services The **Uni-Klinik** *(☎ 630 10; Theodor Stern Kai; open 24 hrs)* is in Sachsenhausen. For medical queries, contact the doctor service on ☎ 192 92, 24 hours a day.

Dangers & Annoyances The area around the main train station is a base for Frankfurt's sex and illegal-drugs trades. Frequent police patrols keep things under control, but it's advisable to exercise 'big city' sense.

Things to See & Do

Eighty per cent of the old city was wiped off the map by two Allied bombing raids in March 1944, and post-war reconstruction was subject to the demands of the new age. Rebuilding efforts were more thoughtful in the **Römerberg**, the old, central area west of the cathedral, where restored 14th- and 15th-century buildings provide a glimpse of the beautiful city this once was. The stepped-gabled old Römer (town hall) is in the north-western corner of Römerberg.

East of Römerberg is the **Dom**, the coronation site of Holy Roman Emperors from 1562 to 1792. It's dominated by the elegant, 15th-century Gothic tower – one of the few structures left standing after the 1944 raids. The small **Wahlkapelle** (Voting Chapel) on the cathedral's southern side is where the seven electors of the Holy Roman Empire chose the emperor from 1356 onwards.

Anyone with an interest in German literature should visit **Goethe Haus** *(☎ 13 88 00; Grosser Hirschgraben 23-25; adult/concession €5/3; open 9am-6pm Mon-Fri Apr-Sept, 9am-4pm Mon-Fri Oct-Mar, 10am-4pm Sat & Sun year-round)*, where Johann Wolfgang von Goethe was born in 1749.

Most of Frankfurt's museums are closed Monday and offer free entry Wednesday. Unless otherwise indicated, the ones listed here are open 10am to 5pm Tuesday to Sunday, to 8pm Wednesday. The **Museum für Moderne Kunst** *(☎ 21 23 04 47; Domstrasse 10; adult/concession €5/2.50)*, north of the cathedral, features works of modern art by Joseph Beuys, Claes Oldenburg and many others. Also on the north bank is the **Jüdisches Museum** *(Jewish Museum; ☎ 21 23 50 00; adult/concession €2.60/1.30, free Sat)*.

Numerous museums line the south bank of the Main River along the Museumsufer (Museum Embankment). Pick of the crop is the **Städelsches Kunstinstitut** *(☎ 605 09 80; Schaumainkai 63; adult/concession €6/5; open till 8pm Thur)*, with a world-class collection of paintings by artists ranging from the Renaissance to the 20th century, including Botticelli, Dürer, Van Eyck, Rembrandt, Rubens, Vermeer, Cézanne and Renoir.

Places to Stay

In this city, 'cheap' can mean paying over €60 for a spartan double room. During the many busy trade fairs even that price is unrealistic. The big, bustling and crowded **Haus der Jugend** *(☎ 610 01 50, fax 61 00 15 99; Deutschherrnufer 12; beds €14.50/18 under/over 20 years; curfew 2am)* is within walking distance of the city centre and Sachsenhausen's nightspots. From the train station take bus No 46 to Frankensteinerplatz, or take S-Bahn No 2, 3, 4, 5 or 6 to Lokalbahnhof, then walk north for 10 minutes.

Most of Frankfurt's budget accommodation is in the sleazy Bahnhofsviertel surrounding the station. **Hotel Eden** *(☎ 25 19 14, fax 25 23 37; Münchener Strasse 42; singles/doubles €45/60)* has reasonable rooms with toilet and shower. **Hotel Münchner Hof** *(☎ 23 00 66, fax 23 44 28; Münchener Strasse 46; singles/doubles €49/65)* has fairly good basic offerings with toilet and shower. **Hotel Carlton** *(☎ 23 20 93, fax 23 36 73; Karlstrasse 11; singles/doubles €57/73)* and the neighbouring **Concorde Hotel**

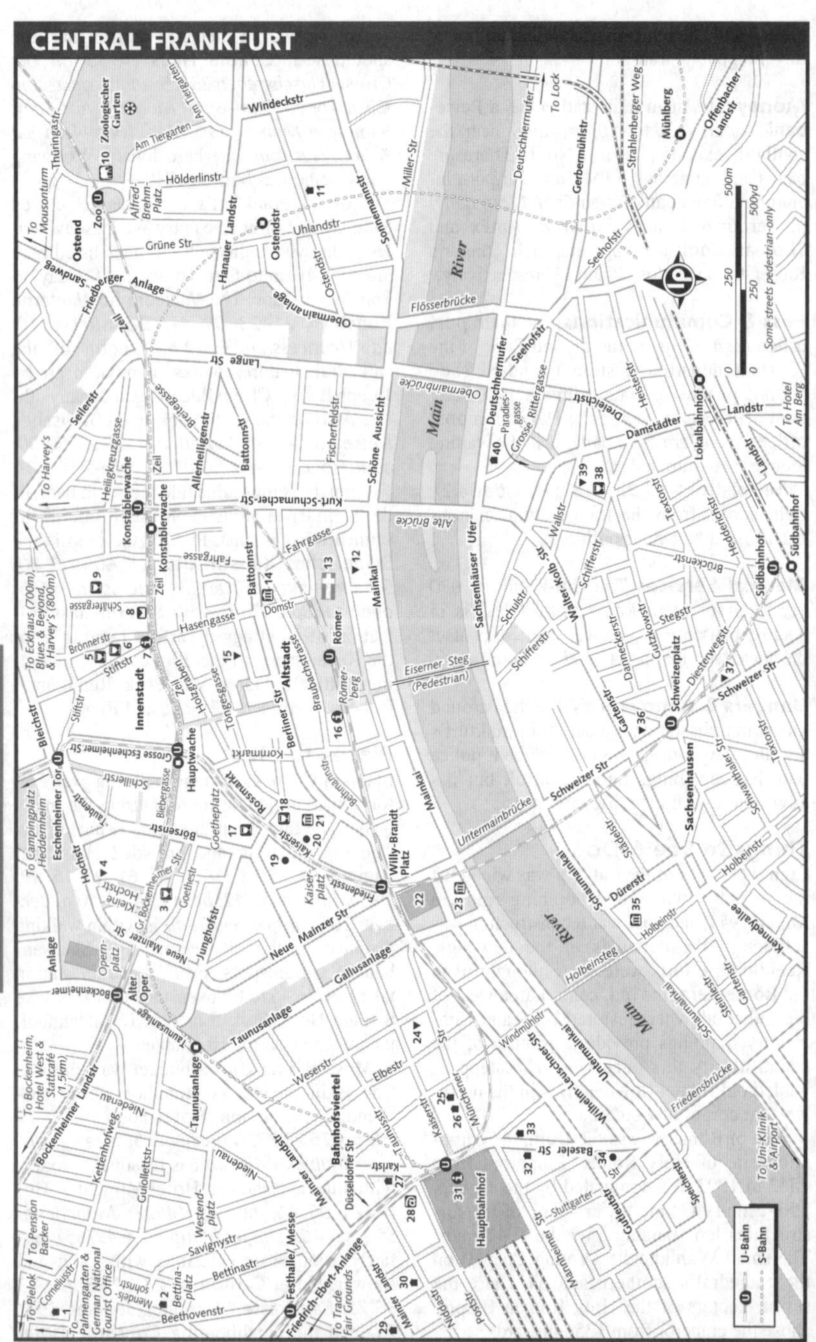
CENTRAL FRANKFURT
Zoologischer Garten
Am Tiergarten
Thüringastr
Windeckstr
Hölderlinstr
Alfred-Brehm-Platz
Zoo
Ostend
To Mousonturm
Grüne Str
Uhlandstr
Ostendstr
Hanauer Landstr
Sonnemannstr
Miller-Str
Deutschherrnufer
To Lock
Gerbermühlstr
Strahlenberger Weg
Mühlberg
Offenbacher Landstr
Sandweg
Friedberger Anlage
Obermainanlage
Flösserbrücke
River
Main
Seehofstr
Zeil
Lange Str
Obermainbrücke
Schöne Aussicht
Fischerfeldstr
Battonnstr
Allerheiligenstr
Breitegasse
Sellerstr
Heiligkreuzgasse
To Harvey's
Konstablerwache
Kurt-Schumacher-Str
Alte Brücke
Paradiesgasse
Grosse Rittergasse
Dreieichstr
Heisterstr
Damstädter
Landstr
Lokalbahnhof
To Hotel Am Berg
Textorstr
Wallstr
Walter-Kolb-Str
Schifferstr
Hedderichstr
Brückenstr
Südbahnhof
Fahrgasse
Domstr
Römer
Römerberg
Braubachstrasse
Altstadt
Berliner Str
Töngesgasse
Hasengasse
Holzgraben
Schäfergasse
Brönnerstr
Stiftstr
Innenstadt
To Eckhaus (700m), Blues & Beyond, & Harvey's (800m)
Mainkai
Sachsenhäuser Ufer
Eiserner Steg (Pedestrian)
Schulstr
Dannenckerstr
Gutzkowstr
Stegstr
Diesterwegstr
Schweizerplatz
Schweizer Str
Gartenstr
Bleichstr
Eschenheimer Tor
Grosse Eschenheimer Str
Hauptwache
Biebergasse
Schillerstr
Taubenstr
Börsenstr
Goetheplatz
Rossmarkt
Kornmarkt
Bethmannstr
Kaiserstr
Kaiserplatz
Willy-Brandt Platz
Untermainbrücke
Sachsenhausen
Schwanthaler Str
Holbeinstr
Dürerstr
Schaumainkai
Hochstr
Kleine Hochstr
Gr Bockenheimer Str
Goethestr
Junghofstr
Neue Mainzer Str
Friedensstr
Opernplatz
Alter Oper
Bockenheimer Anlage
To Campingplatz Heddernheim
Gallusanlage
Taunusanlage
Holbeinsteg
Kennedyallee
Windmühlstr
Untermainkai
Wilhelm-Leuschner-Str
Friedensbrücke
Steinlestr
To Uni-Klinik & Airport
To Bockenheim, Hotel West & Stattcafé (1.5km)
Bockenheimer Landstr
Niedenau
Weserstr
Elbestr
Münchener Str
Taunusstr
Bahnhofsviertel
Mainzer Landstr
Düsseldorfer Str
Karlstr
Hauptbahnhof
Baseler Str
Gutleutstr
Speicherstr
Stuttgarter Str
Mannheimer Str
Kettenhofweg
Guiollettstr
Westendplatz
Savignystr
Bettinastr
Bettinaplatz
Mendelssohnstr
Beethovenstr
Cornelisstr
To Pension Backer
To Pielok
To Palmengarten & German National Tourist Office
Festhalle/Messe
Friedrich-Ebert-Anlage
To Trade Fair Grounds
Niddastr
Poststr
U-Bahn
S-Bahn
0 250 500m
0 250 500yd
Some streets pedestrian-only

CENTRAL FRANKFURT

PLACES TO STAY
1 Hotel-Pension Gölz; Hotel Beethoven
2 Hotel-Pension Bruns
11 Hotel-Garni Diplomat
25 Hotel Eden
26 Hotel Münchner Hof
27 Hotel Carlton; Concorde Hotel
29 Hotel Glockshuber
30 Hotel Topas
32 Hotel Tourist
33 Hotel Wiesbaden
40 Haus der Jugend

PLACES TO EAT
4 Blaubart Gewölbekeller
12 Metropol
15 Kleinmarkthalle
24 India Curry House
36 HL Supermarket
37 Zum Gemalten Haus
39 Fichte-Kränzi

OTHER
3 Jazzkeller
5 The Cave
6 Sinkkasten
7 CityInfo Zeil
8 Main Post Office; Karstadt Department Store
9 Zum Schwejk
10 Zoo
13 Dom
14 Museum für Moderne Kunst
16 Römer Tourist Office
17 U60311
18 Cooky's
19 American Express
20 Thomas Cook
21 Goethe Haus
22 Städtische Bühnen/ Frankfurter Oper
23 Jüdisches Museum
28 Telebistro
31 Tourist Office
34 ADM-Mitfahrzentrale
35 Städelsches Kunstinstitut
38 Stereo Bar

(☎ 242 42 20, fax 24 24 22 88; Karlstrasse 9; singles/doubles €50/65) both have rooms with facilities. **Hotel Tourist** *(☎ 23 30 95/96/97, fax 23 69 86; Baseler Strasse 23-25; singles/doubles €55/75)* is similar. **Hotel Wiesbaden** *(☎ 23 23 47, fax 25 28 45; Baseler Strasse 52; singles/doubles from €65/75)* is one of the better options.

Hotel Glockshuber *(☎ 74 26 28, fax 74 26 29; Mainzer Landstrasse 120; singles/doubles from €35/60)*, north of the main train station, is another pleasant option. **Hotel Topas** *(☎ 23 08 52, fax 238 05 82 60; Niddastrasse 88; singles/doubles €64.50/68)* has quite nice rooms with bathroom.

Sachsenhausen has few budget places. **Hotel Am Berg** *(☎ 61 20 21, fax 61 51 09; Grethenweg 23; singles/doubles without bath from €33/55)* is in quiet backstreets a few minutes' walk southeast from Südbahnhof.

Some of the best pensions are in the posh Westend. **Pension Backer** *(☎ 74 79 92, fax 74 79 00; Mendelssohnstrasse 92; singles/doubles €25/40)* is basic. **Hotel-Pension Bruns** *(☎ 74 88 96, fax 74 88 46; Mendelssohnstrasse 42; singles/doubles without bath €40/50)* has simple rooms in a spacious house. The pleasant **Hotel-Pension Gölz** *(☎ 74 67 35, fax 74 61 42; ⓔ info@hotel-goelz.de; Beethovenstrasse 44; singles/doubles with bath €45/70)* has basic rooms.

In Bockenheim, **Hotel West** *(☎ 247 90 20, fax 707 53 09; Gräfstrasse 81; singles/doubles €60/80)* has quite good rooms with facilities. East of Konstablerwache, friendly **Hotel-Garni Diplomat** *(☎ 430 40 40, fax 430 40 22; Ostendstrasse 24-26; singles/doubles €50/70)* has passable rooms a short walk from the Ostend S-Bahn station.

Places to Eat

The area around the main train station has lots of ethnic options. Baseler Strasse in particular has a Middle Eastern tone. **India Curry House** *(Weserstrasse 17; mains from €5)* has savoury curries.

Known as Fressgass (Munch-Alley), the Kalbächer Gasse and Grosse Bockenheimer Strasse area, between Opernplatz and Börsenstrasse, has some medium-priced restaurants and fast-food places with outdoor tables in summer. **Blaubart Gewölbekeller** *(Kaiserhofstrasse 18; mains from €6)* serves well-priced, hearty dishes in a beer-cellar atmosphere.

The **Kleinmarkthalle**, off Hasengasse, is a great produce market with loads of fruit, vegetables, meats and hot food. **Metropol** *(Weckmarkt 13-15; mains from €7.20)*, near the Dom, serves well-priced and filling salads, casseroles and the like until late, but the service is notoriously slow.

Apple-wine taverns are a Frankfurt eating and drinking tradition, serving *Ebbelwoi* (Frankfurt dialect for 'Apfelwein'), along with local specialities such as *Handkäse mit Musik* (literally, 'hand-cheese with music') – cheese soaked in oil and vinegar and topped with onions. Your bowel supplies the music. Some good *Ebbelwoi* places are found in Alt-Sachsenhausen – the area behind the DJH hostel – which bulges with eateries and pubs. **Fichte-Kränzi** *(Wallstrasse 5; mains from €7)* is highly recommended for its friendly atmosphere and well-priced food. **Zum Gemalten**

Haus *(Schweizer Strasse 67; mains from €7)* is a lively place full of paintings of old Frankfurt. **Zur Sonne** *(☎ 45 93 96; Berger Strasse 312; open from 4pm daily)*, in Bornheim, is authentic and has a gorgeous yard for summer tippling. Take the U-4 to Bornheim-Mitte.

Wallstrasse and the surrounding streets in Alt-Sachsenhausen also have lots of mid-priced, ethnic restaurants.

Another good place for ravenous hunters and gatherers is the cosmopolitan Berger Strasse and Nordend areas north of the Zeil. **Eckhaus** *(Bornheimer Landstrasse 45; meals from €6)* is a relaxed restaurant and bar that serves well-priced salads and main dishes in the evening. For both of these, take the U-4 to Merianplatz.

In Bockenheim, **Stattcafé** *(Grempstrasse 21; dishes from €6)* offers vegetarian and meat dishes, as well as good coffee and cakes. **Pielok** *(Jordanstrasse 3; mains around €7)* looks like your grandmother had a hand in the decorations; the food is filling and very popular with students.

Fresh-produce **markets** are held 8am to 6pm on Thursday and Friday at Bockenheimer Warte and Südbahnhof respectively. There is a **supermarket** in the basement of Karstadt on Zeil. A HL **supermarket** is in the basement of Woolworths on Schweizer Strasse in Sachsenhausen.

Entertainment

The Cave *(Brönnerstrasse 11)* is a club that spins Goth and features occasional live concerts. **U60311** *(Rossmarkt)* has techno and house music. **Cooky's** *(Am Salzhaus 4)* stays open until the wee hours, delivering a winning combination of hip-hop and house nights and live indie bands. **Stereo Bar** *(Abtgässchen 7)*, in Sachsenhausen, has a 1970s feel. A popular gay bar is **Zum Schwejk** *(Schäffergasse 20)*, while **Harvey's** *(Friedberger Platz)*, a restaurant and bar, is a favoured meeting place for Frankfurt's gay and lesbian yuppies.

Ballet, opera and theatre are strong features of Frankfurt's entertainment scene. For information and bookings, ring **Städtische Bühnen** *(☎ 134 04 00; Willy-Brandt-Platz)* or **Karstadt concert and theatre-booking service** *(☎ 29 48 48; Zeil 90; commission charged)*. *Journal Frankfurt* (€1.50) and *Fritz* have listings of what's on.

Frankfurt also has a couple of very good jazz venues. **Blues & Beyond** *(☎ 46 99 09 87; Berger Strasse 159)* is a small venue for blues and jazz bands; the **Jazzkeller** *(☎ 28 85 37; Kleine Bockenheimer Strasse 18a)* gets top acts. **Sinkkasten** *(☎ 28 03 85; Brönnerstrasse 5)* has a mix of acoustic shows and '80s-themed dance nights. **Mousonturm** *(☎ 40 58 95 20; Waldschmidtstrasse 4)*, in Bornheim, offers arty rock, dance performances and politically oriented cabaret.

Getting There & Away

Flughafen Frankfurt/Main *(☎ 69 01)* is Germany's largest airport, with the highest freight and second-highest passenger turnover in Europe. Departure and arrival halls A (Lufthansa), B and C are in Terminal 1; halls D and E are in the new Terminal 2. The airport train station has two sections: platforms 1 to 3 (below Terminal 1, hall B) handle regional and S-Bahn connections, whereas IR, IC and ICE connections are in the long-distance train station. Hourly IC or EC trains go to Cologne (€33.80, two hours) and Nuremberg (€38.80, 2½ hours), and ICEs run to/from Hamburg on weekdays (€100, four hours).

Long-distance buses leave from the southern side of the main train station, where there's a **Deutsche-Touring/Eurolines office** *(☎ 79 03 50; Mannheimer Strasse 4)* that handles bookings.

The Hauptbahnhof handles more departures and arrivals than any other German station. For information, call ☎ 01805-99 66 33. The **DB Lounge** *(open 6am-11pm daily)*, above the information office, is a comfortable retreat for anyone with a valid train ticket.

All main car-rental companies have offices in the main hall of the train station and at the airport. The **ADM-Mitfahrzentrale** *(☎ 194 40; Baselerplatz)* is three minutes' walk south of the train station.

Getting Around

The S-Bahn's S8/S9 train runs every 15 minutes between the airport and Frankfurt Hauptbahnhof (11 minutes), usually continuing via Hauptwache and Konstablerwache to Offenbach; a fixed fare of €5.90 applies. Taxis (about €25) or the frequent airport bus No 61 (from Südbahnhof; €3.10) take longer.

Frankfurt's excellent transport network (RMV) integrates all bus, tram, S- and U-Bahn lines. Single or day tickets can be purchased from automatic machines. Press *Einzelfahrt*

Frankfurt for destinations in zone 50, which takes in most of Frankfurt. *Kurzstrecken* (peak-period, short-trip tickets) cost €1.05; single tickets cost €1.60; a *Tageskarte* (24-hour ticket) is €4.35 without a trip to the airport, €6.65 with.

For a taxi, ring ☎ 23 00 01, ☎ 25 00 01 or ☎ 54 50 11.

COLOGNE

☎ 0221 • pop 1 million

Located at a major crossroads of European trade routes, Cologne (Köln) was an important city even in Roman times, when it was Germania's capital and housed 300,000 inhabitants. In later years it remained one of northern Europe's main cities, and it's still the centre of the German Roman Catholic church.

Situated on the Rhine River, Cologne is Dom-inated by its cathedral. The pedestrianised Hohe Strasse runs straight through the middle of the old town from north to south. The main train station is just north of the cathedral.

Information

The helpful **tourist office** *(☎ 22 12 33 45; e koelntourismus@stadt-koeln.de; Unter Fettenhennen 19; open daily)* is opposite the cathedral's main entrance. *Monatsvorschau*, the monthly what's-on booklet, is a good investment at €1.20. The room-finding service (€3) is a bargain when the city is busy with trade fairs.

There is a **Reisebank** *(open 8am-10pm daily)* at the train station. Offices of **AmEx** *(Burgmauer 14)* and **Thomas Cook** *(Burgmauer 4)* are near the tourist office. The **post office** *(open 6am-10pm Mon-Sat, 7am-10pm Sun)* is in Ludwig im Bahnhof bookshop near track 6 inside the main train station. **Future Point** *(☎ 206 72 51; Richmodstrasse 13; open 8am-1am Mon-Sat, 10am-1am Sun)* charges €1.50 per 30 minutes online.

Things to See

The heart and soul of central Cologne is its **Dom** *(open 7am-7.30pm daily)*. The sheer size of the structure, with 157m spires, is overwhelming. Building began in 1248 in the French Gothic style. The huge project was stopped in 1560 but started again in 1842 as a symbol of Prussia's drive for unification. It was finally finished in 1880. Miraculously, it survived WWII's heavy night bombing intact. Inside, you'll be overwhelmed by the magnificent stained-glass windows; the Magi's Shrine (circa 1150–1210), believed to contain the remains of the Three Wise Men; and the 15th-century Adoration of the Magi altarpiece. Guided tours in English are held at 10.30am and 2.30pm Monday to Saturday (at 2.30pm only on Sunday) and cost adult/concession €4/2. The church's 24-tonne Peter Bell is the largest working bell in the world.

When done with the Dom, hop over to inspect Cologne's fascinating museums. The **Römisch-Germanisches Museum** *(Roman Germanic Museum; Roncalliplatz 4; adult/concession €4/2; open 10am-5pm Tues-Sun)*, next to the cathedral, displays artefacts from the Roman settlement in the Rhine Valley. The **Wallraf-Richartz-Museum** *(Martinstrasse 39; adult/concession €6.60/4.10; open 10am-6pm Wed-Fri, 10am-8pm Tues, 11am-6pm Sat & Sun)* has a fantastic collection including paintings by Rubens, Rembrandt and Monet. **Museum Ludwig** *(Bischofsgartenstrasse 1; adult/concession €7.70/4.10; open 10am-6pm Tues-Fri, to 8pm Tues, 11am-6pm Sat & Sun)* uses natural light to brilliant effect, displaying prime pieces from Kirchner, Kandinsky and Max Ernst, as well as pop-art works by both Rauschenberg and Andy Warhol.

The former church of St Cecilia houses the **Schnütgen Museum** *(Cäcilienstrasse 29; adult/concession €2.50/1.25; open 10am-5pm Tues-Fri, 11am-5pm Sat & Sun)*, featuring an overwhelming display of church riches, including many religious artefacts and early ivory carvings.

You can give yourself a free tour of ancient and medieval Cologne by walking around its restored monuments with a free city-sights map from the tourist office. These **historical walks** will lead you past several sites dating from Roman and medieval times.

Special Events

Try to visit Cologne during the wild and crazy period of the Cologne *Karneval* (Carnival), rivalled only by Munich's Oktoberfest. People dress in creative costumes, clown suits, as popular personalities and whatever else their alcohol-numbed brains may invent. The streets explode with activity on the Thursday before the seventh Sunday before Easter. Got that? The action lasts through to Monday.

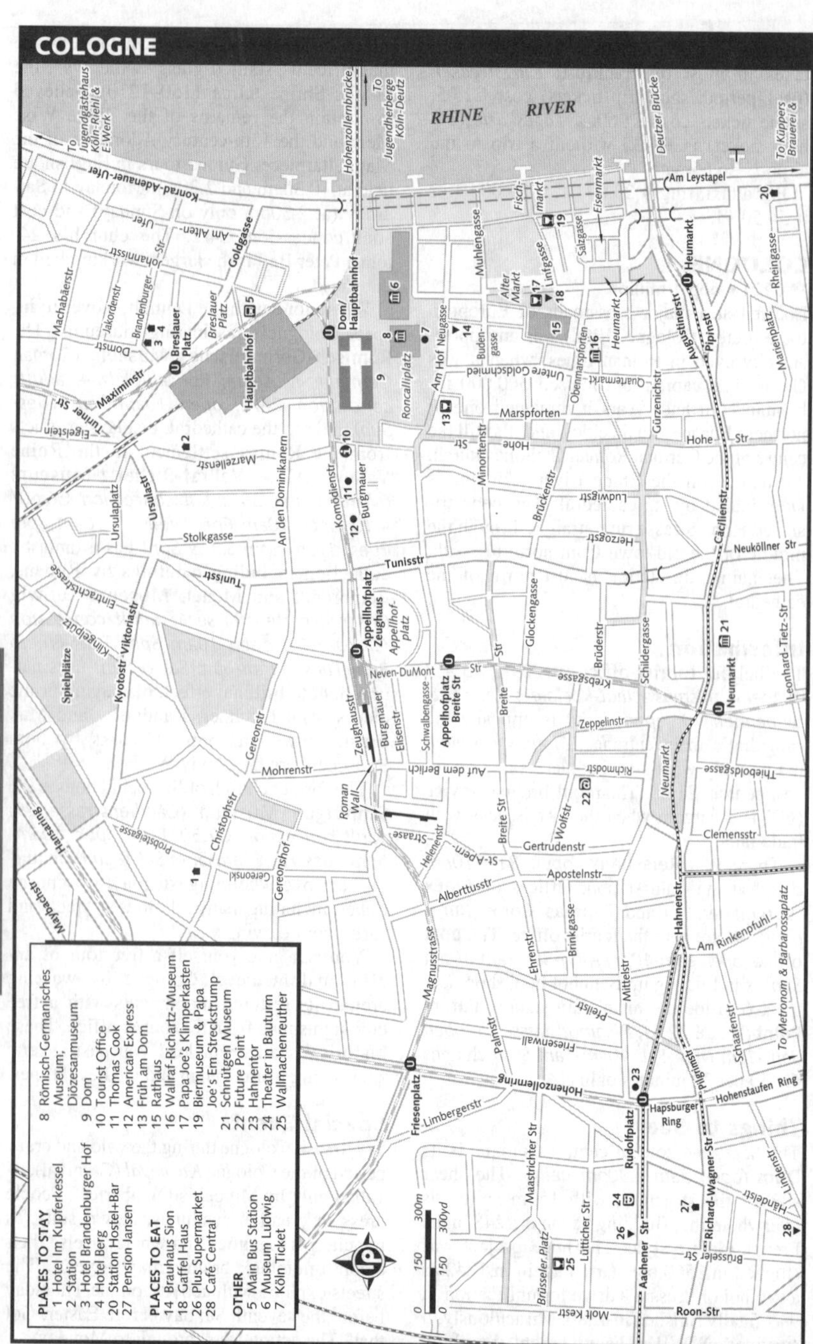
COLOGNE
RHINE RIVER
PLACES TO STAY
1 Hotel Im Kupferkessel
2 Station
3 Hotel Brandenburger Hof
4 Hotel Berg
20 Station Hostel+Bar
27 Pension Jansen
PLACES TO EAT
14 Brauhaus Sion
18 Gaffel Haus
26 Plus Supermarket
28 Café Central
OTHER
5 Main Bus Station
6 Museum Ludwig
7 Köln Ticket
8 Römisch-Germanisches Museum; Diözesanmuseum
9 Dom
10 Tourist Office
11 Thomas Cook
12 American Express
13 Früh am Dom
15 Rathaus
16 Wallraf-Richartz-Museum
17 Papa Joe's Klimperkasten
19 Biermuseum & Papa Joe's Em Streckstrump
21 Schnütgen Museum
22 Future Point
23 Hahnentor
24 Theater in Bauturm
25 Wallmachenreuther
To Jugendgästehaus Köln-Riehl & E-Werk
To Jugendherberge Köln-Deutz
To Küppers Brauerei &
To Metronom & Barbarossaplatz
Hohenzollernbrücke
Deutzer Brücke
Dom/Hauptbahnhof
Hauptbahnhof
Breslauer Platz
Appellhofplatz Zeughaus
Appellhofplatz Breite Str
Neumarkt
Heumarkt
Friesenplatz
Rudolfplatz
Roman Wall

Places to Stay

Cheap accommodation is limited to a couple of good pensions. You should be able to get private rooms unless there's a trade fair on, during which prices jump 20%.

Cologne has two DJH hostels. The bustling **Jugendherberge Köln-Deutz** *(☎ 81 47 11; ⓔ jh-koeln-deutz@djh-rheinland.de; Siegesstrasse 5a; beds junior/senior €17/19.50)*, in Deutz, is a 15-minute walk east from the main train station over the Hohenzollernbrücke, or three minutes from Bahnhof Köln-Deutz (sometimes called Messe-Osthallen). The more pleasant **Jugendgästehaus Köln-Riehl** *(☎ 76 70 81; ⓔ jh-koeln-riehl@djh-rheinland.de; An der Schanz 14; rooms €21-34 per person)* is north of the city. Take the U15 or U16 to Boltensternstrasse. The backpackers' hostel **Station** *(☎ 912 53 01, fax 912 53 03; ⓔ station@hostel-cologne.de; Marzellenstrasse 44-48; dorm beds €14, singles €25)* is an easy walk from the main train station. **Station Hostel+Bar** *(☎ 221 23 02 47; ⓔ station2@hotel-cologne.de; Rheingasse 34-36; dorm beds €16.50, singles €25)*, the Station hostel's other branch, is closer to Cologne's pubs.

Pension Jansen *(☎ 25 18 75, fax 25 18 75; Richard-Wagner-Strasse 18; singles/doubles from €31/62)* provides basic rooms and is convenient to the restaurant quarter. **Hotel Im Kupferkessel** *(☎ 13 53 38, fax 12 51 21; Probsteigasse 6; singles/doubles from €26/49)* has recently remodelled rooms and is a 15-minute walk west of the train station.

A lot of other budget hotels cluster in the streets just north of the main train station. **Hotel Brandenburger Hof** *(☎ 12 28 89, fax 13 53 04; Brandenburger Strasse 2; singles/doubles from €27/48)* has basic rooms. **Hotel Berg** *(☎ 12 11 24, fax 139 00 11; ⓔ hotel@hotel-berg.com; Brandenburger Strasse 6; singles/doubles from €41/49)* has fairly good rooms and offers Internet access.

Places to Eat

Cologne's beer halls serve cheap and filling (although often bland) meals to go with their home brew. **Brauhaus Sion** *(Unter Taschenmacher 9)* is a big beer hall, and is justifiably packed most nights of the week. You'll eat your fill for well under €15 here, including a couple of beers. **Gaffel Haus** *(Alter Markt 20-22)* is another nice place to eat and sample the local brew.

The Belgisches Viertel (Belgian Quarter) around and west of Hahnentor is packed with restaurants of all descriptions. You'll find a couple of moderately priced **Asian eating houses** on Händelstrasse.

Café Central *(Jülicher Strasse 1)*, on the corner of Händelstrasse, is open till late and has an adjoining restaurant called **o.T.** *(mains €6.50-9.50)*.

To put together a picnic, visit a **market**; the biggest is held on Tuesday and Friday at Aposteln-Kloster near Neumarkt. The supermarket **Plus** *(Aachener Strasse 64)* is in the Belgisches Viertel.

Entertainment

Evenings and weekends in the Altstadt are like miniature carnivals, with bustling crowds and lots to do.

Papa Joe's Klimperkasten *(Alter Markt 50)* is a lively jazz pub with a wonderful pianola. **Papa Joe's Em Streckstrump** *(Buttermarkt 37)* is more intimate. **Metronom** *(☎ 21 34 65; Weyerstrasse 59)*, near the Kwartier Latäng (Latin Quarter), is Cologne's most respected evening bar for jazz enthusiasts, with live performances mainly weekdays.

Wallmachenreuther *(Brüsseler Platz 9)* is an off-beat bar in the Belgisches Viertel that also serves food. The gay scene also centres on the Belgisches Viertel.

E-Werk *(☎ 96 27 90; Schanzenstrasse 37)*, in a converted power station in Mülheim, is Cologne's usual venue for rock concerts. It turns into a huge techno club on Friday and Saturday nights.

Köln Ticket *(☎ 28 02 80; Roncalliplatz)*, next to the Römisch-Germanisches Museum, has tickets and information on classical music and theatre performances in town. **Theater im Bauturm** *(☎ 52 42 42; Aachener Strasse 24)* is one of Cologne's more innovative theatres.

As in Munich, beer reigns supreme. There are more than 20 local breweries, all producing the light, bitter Kölsch. **Früh am Dom** *(Am Hof 12-14)* is famous for its own-brew beer. The **Biermuseum** *(Buttermarkt 39)* – beside Papa Joe's – has 18 varieties on tap. **Küppers Brauerei** *(☎ 934 78 10; Alteburger Strasse 157)* is in Bayenthal, south of the city (take the U16 to Bayenthalgürtel).

Getting There & Around

Deutsche Touring's Eurolines *(☎ 13 52 52)*, at the train station, offers overnight trips to

Paris (€34, 6½ hours). There are frequent rail services to both nearby Bonn (€7, 18 minutes) and Düsseldorf (€8.10, 20 minutes), as well as to Aachen (€10.70, one hour). Frequent direct IC/EC (€47.80, 3¼ hours) and ICE (€53.40, 2¾ hours) trains connect Cologne with Hanover. There are ICE links with Frankfurt/Main (€39, 2¼ hours) and Berlin (€97.60, 4½ hours). The Thalys high-speed train links Paris with Cologne via Aachen and Brussels (€74.60/67.10 weekdays/weekends, four hours).

Cologne offers a convenient and extensive mix of buses, trams and local trains – trams go underground in the inner city, and trains handle destinations up to 50km around Cologne. Ticketing and tariff structures are complicated. The best ticket option is the one-day pass, which costs €5.15 if you're staying near the city. To order a taxi call ☎ 194 10 or ☎ 28 82.

BONN

☎ 0228 • pop 293,000

This friendly, relaxed city became West Germany's temporary capital in 1949 and is mainly an administrative centre now that Berlin's back in black. Settled in Roman times, Bonn was the seat of the electors of Cologne in the 18th century, and some of their baroque architecture survived the ravages of WWII and the post-war demand for modern government buildings. Classical music buffs can pay homage to Bonn's most famous son, Ludwig van Beethoven.

The **tourist office** *(☎ 77 50 00, 194 33, fax 77 50 77; e bonninformation@bonn.de; open daily)* is behind the Karstadt department store in Windeckstrasse, a three-minute walk along Poststrasse from the Hauptbahnhof.

Bonn lives and breathes Beethoven. You can visit the **Beethoven-Haus** *(☎ 981 75; Bonngasse 20; adult/concession €4/3; open 10am-6pm Mon-Sat Apr-Oct, 10am-5pm Mon-Sat Nov-Mar, 11am-4pm Sun year-round)*, where the composer was born in 1770. The house contains much memorabilia concerning his life and music, including his last piano, specially made with an amplified sounding board to accommodate his deafness. The annual Beethoven Festival is held in September/October.

There are frequent trains to Cologne (€7, 18 minutes) in the north and to Koblenz (€15.40, 30 minutes) in the south.

GERMANY

DÜSSELDORF

☎ 0211 • pop 571,000

Although not particularly strong in historical sights, the elegant and wealthy capital of North Rhine-Westphalia is an important centre for fashion and commerce. The **tourist office** *(☎ 17 20 20; e tourist@duesseldorf.de; open daily)* is opposite the train station's main exit. The **main post office** is across the street. **Internet Café World** *(Worringer Platz 21)*, three blocks north of the train station, charges €2 for a half-hour online.

The swish lifestyle of Düsseldorf revolves around the famed Königsallee, or 'Kö', with its stylish boutiques and arcades. City museums include the **Kunstmuseum Düsseldorf** *(☎ 899 24 60; adult/concession €4/2; open 10am-6pm Tues-Sun)*, with a comprehensive European collection that includes Rubens' *Venus and Adonis*. Also here is the **Glasmuseum Hentrich** *(open 10am-6pm Tues-Sun)*. The expansive modern-art collection of the **Kunstsammlung Nordrhein-Westfalen** is displayed in two different galleries: **K20** *(☎ 838 11 30; Grabbeplatz 5; adult/concession €6.50/4.50; open 10am-6pm Tues-Fri, 11am-6pm Sat & Sun)* and **K21** *(☎ 838 16 00; Ständehausstrasse 1; adult/concession €6.50/4.50)*. A combined ticket costs €10/8. The **Goethe-Museum Düsseldorf** *(☎ 899 62 62; Jacobistrasse 2; adult/concession €2/1; open 11am-5pm Tues-Fri & Sun, 1pm-5pm Sat)*, in Schloss Jägerhof, pays tribute to the life and work of one of Europe's great men of letters. The large collection includes books, first drafts, letters, medals and much more.

Places to Stay & Eat

The **Jugendgästehaus** *(☎ 55 73 10, fax 57 25 13; e jgh-duesseldorf@t-online.de; Düsseldorfer Strasse 1; dorm beds €20.20)* is in posh Oberkassel, across the Rhine from the Altstadt. Take U-Bahn No 70, 74, 75, 76 or 77 from the main train station to Luegplatz. From there it's a short walk.

Düsseldorf's frequent trade shows inflate already high hotel and pension prices. **Hotel Komet** *(☎ 17 87 90, fax 178 79 50; e info@hotelkomet.de; Bismarckstrasse 93; singles/doubles €33/44)* has reasonable rooms with bathroom. A good-value alternative is **Hotel Haus Hillesheim** *(☎ 38 68 60, fax 386 86 33; e rezeption@hotel-hillesheim.de; Jahnstrasse 19; singles/doubles without bath €40/55, with bath €60/70)*.

Ratinger Strasse is home to a couple of pub-style places where you can eat and drink. **Zum Schlüssel** *(Bolkerstrasse 43-7; dishes €5-11)* is popular for its beer, but also has good food. **Anadolou** *(Mertensgasse 10; mains from €4)* serves delicious Anatolian sit-down and takeaway food including vegetarian dishes.

Entertainment

Besides walking around and museum-hopping, one of the best things to do when in Düsseldorf is (surprise!) drink beer. The Altstadt is affectionately referred to as the 'longest bar in the world'. On evenings and weekends, the best places overflow onto the streets. Favoured streets include Bolkerstrasse, Kurze Strasse, Andreasstrasse and the surrounding side streets.

The beverage of choice is Alt, a dark and semisweet brew. Try Gatzweilers Alt in **Zum Schlüssel** (see Places to Stay & Eat). The spartan **Zum Uerige** *(Berger Strasse)* is the only place where you can buy Uerige Alt beer, which flows so quickly that the waiters just carry around trays and give you a glass when you're ready (and sometimes even when you're not!).

Night-Live *(Bolkerstrasse 22)* has live bands; downstairs is **dä Spiegel**, a popular bar.

Getting There & Around

Düsseldorf is part of a dense S-Bahn and train network in the Rhine-Ruhr region. Regular IC/EC services run to/from Hamburg (€63.20, 3¾ hours); ICE services run to Hanover (€48.80, 2¾ hours) and Frankfurt (€47.20, 2½ hours); and trains service Cologne (€6.60, 30 minutes) and most of the other major German cities.

Buy public-transport tickets from the orange machines at stops (bus drivers will sell singles). A short-trip ticket up to 1.5km costs €2. A single ticket for zone A, which includes all of Düsseldorf proper, is €3.30. Better value is the 24-hour TagesTicket for €12, valid for up to five people in zone A.

AACHEN

☎ 0241 • pop 244,000

Charlemagne was so impressed by Aachen's thermal springs that he made this town the capital of his empire in 794. Ever since, Aachen has held special significance among the icons of German nationhood. It is now an industrial and commercial centre and home to the country's largest technical university.

Aachen's compact old centre is contained within two ring roads that roughly follow the old city walls. Pick up an excellent free city map from the DB **Service Point** counter in the train station. The efficient **tourist office** *(☎ 1 80 29 60/1; ⓔ mail@aachen-tourist.de; Kapuzinergraben; open daily)* is at Atrium Elisenbrunnen. The **bus station** is at the northeastern edge of Grabenring on the corner of Kurhausstrasse and Peterstrasse. Surf until late at **The Web** *(Kleinmarschierstrasse 74-76)*, where a half-hour of Internet time costs €2.

Things to See & Do

Aachen's drawing card is its cathedral **Dom** *(Kaiserdom or Münster; open 7am-7pm daily)*, whose subtle grandeur, its historical significance and interior serenity make a visit almost obligatory. No fewer than 30 Holy Roman emperors were crowned here from 936 to 1531. The heart of the cathedral is a Byzantine-inspired octagon, built on Roman foundations. Charlemagne lies buried here in the golden shrine. His white-marble throne is on the upper gallery of the octagon on the western side, where the nobles sat.

North of the cathedral, the 14th-century **Rathaus** *(adult/concession €1.50/0.75; open 10am-5pm Mon-Fri, 10am-1pm & 2pm-5pm Sat & Sun)* overlooks Markt, a lively gathering place in summer. The eastern tower of the Rathaus, the Granusturm, was once part of Charlemagne's palace.

Foremost among Aachen's worthwhile museums is the **Ludwig Forum for International Art** *(☎ 180 70; Jülicherstrasse 97-109; adult/concession €3/1.50; open 10am-4pm Tues & Thur, 10am-7:30pm Wed & Fri, 11am-4.30pm Sat & Sun)* with works by Warhol, Lichtenstein, Baselitz and others.

Aachen was known for its thermal springs as early as Roman times. A visit to the city-owned **Carolus Thermen** *(☎ 18 27 40; ⓦ www.carolus-thermen.de; Passstrasse 79)* costs €8 for two hours (€15 with the sauna). It's in the city garden, northeast of the centre.

Places to Stay & Eat

The DJH **Jugendgästehaus** *(☎ 71 10 10; Maria-Theresia-Allee 260; dorm beds €20.50, singles/doubles €33.80/38.80)* is 4km southwest of the train station on a hill

GERMANY

overlooking the city. Take bus No 2 to Ronheide, or bus No 12 to the closer Colynshof at the foot of the hill.

To arrange a private room in advance, call Aachen's room reservation line Monday to Friday on ☎ 180 29 50/1. **Hotel Marx** *(☎ 375 41, fax 267 05; e info@hotel-marx.de; Hubertusstrasse 33-35; singles/doubles €34/62, with bath from €49/67)* offers good, cheap rooms, but you'll have to perform your ablutions acrobatically in the basin. The central **Hotel Drei Könige** *(☎ 483 93, fax 361 52; Büchel 5; singles/doubles from €35/55)* has a few basic rooms.

As a university town, Aachen is full of spirited cafés, restaurants and pubs, especially along Pontstrasse, referred to by locals as the 'Quartier Latin'. **Café Kittel** *(Pontstrasse 39; mains around €6)* is a cosy hang-out with a lively garden area. It serves reasonably priced light meals, including vegetarian dishes. **Gaststätte Labyrinth** *(Pontstrasse 156-158; dishes €7-11)* is a rambling beer-hall type place that lives up to its name and serves good, filling meals. **Plus** *(Bahnhofstrasse 18)* is a fairly central supermarket for self-caterers.

GERMANY

Entertainment

The best source of information on bars, clubs and restaurants in the region is the free *Euroview* in English – the tourist office keeps copies. **Domkeller** *(Hof 1)* has been a student pub since the 1950s and usually features jazz or blues on Monday. **B9** *(Blondelstrasse 9)* is one club that gets a young crowd. The style changes nightly. **Club Voltaire** *(Friedrichstrasse 9)* attracts an older, mixed crowd.

The **City Theatre** *(☎ 478 42 44; Theaterplatz)* has concerts and opera most nights; **Aachen Ticket** *(☎ 180 29 65)* in the tourist office has information and sells tickets.

Getting There & Around

Fast trains run almost every hour to Cologne (€10, 43 minutes) and Liège (€9.90, 40 minutes). The high-speed Thalys passes through seven times daily on its way to Brussels and Paris. There's also a frequent bus service to Maastricht (€5, 55 minutes).

The Aachen city centre is covered easily on foot. City bus tickets bought from the driver cost €1.20 each. A 24-hour Familienkarte und Gruppenkarte is valid for up to five people and costs €4.85. You can buy it on buses and from machines and outlets.

Bremen & Lower Saxony

Among the more popular attractions of this beautiful region are the scenic Harz Mountains, the old student town of Göttingen, and the picturesque towns along the so-called Fairy-Tale Road.

BREMEN

☎ 0421 • pop 550,000

Bremen is Germany's second-largest harbour. Its Hanseatic past and congenial Altstadt area around Am Markt and Domsheide make it an enjoyable place to explore on foot, and Bremen's vibrant student population ensures the fun continues long after dark.

The heart of the city is Am Markt, but its soul is the port. The **tourist office** *(☎ 30 80 00; w www.bremen-tourism.de; open daily)* is before the main train station. There is also a **booth** at the Rathaus opposite the Unser Lieben Frauen Kirche. City walks (English explanations provided) leave at 2pm daily from the tourist office at the station (€6). A Bremen tourist card (from €8.50 for two days) offers unlimited public transport and substantial discounts on city sights. The **main post office** is also on Domsheide and there's another one near the train station.

Things to See & Do

Around Am Markt don't miss the splendid and ornate **Rathaus**; the cathedral **St-Petri-Dom**; and the large **statue of Roland**, Bremen's sentimental protector, erected in 1404.

Walk down **Böttcherstrasse**, a must-see recreation of a medieval alley, complete with tall brick houses, shops, galleries, restaurants and two **museums** *(adult/concession combined ticket €6/3; open 11am-6pm Tues-Sun)*. The **Paula Modersohn-Becker Museum**, at No 8, has works by its namesake contemporary painter, and varied exhibits of the Bernhard Hoetger Collection. The **Museum im Roselius-Haus** is at No 6, with a collection of paintings and applied arts from the 12th through to the 19th centuries. The **Glockenspiel**, active in summer hourly from noon to 6pm (in winter at noon, 3pm and 6pm), plays an extended tune between rooftops.

Beck's Brewery *(☎ 50 94 5555; Am Deich 18-19; tram No 1 or 5 to Westerstrasse)* runs its English-language tours at 1.30pm Tuesday to Sunday. The tour costs €3 and includes a tasting.

Places to Stay & Eat

Jugendgästehaus Bremen *(☎ 17 13 69, fax 17 11 02; Kalkstrasse 6; beds junior/senior €17/19.70)* is across from Beck's brewery. Take tram No 1, 3 or 5 from the train station to Am Brill. The friendly **Hotel Garni Gästehaus Walter** *(☎ 55 80 27, fax 55 80 29; Buntentorsteinweg 86-88; singles/doubles from €25/40)* has pleasant rooms, some with shower and toilet. Take tram No 4 or 5 from the main train station. Basic accommodation is available at **Hotel-Pension Weidmann** *(☎ 498 44 55; Am Schwarzen Meer 35; singles/doubles €21/41)*; take tram No 2 from Domsheide or No 10 from the station.

A prowl around Ostertorsteinweg (near Am Dobben) will offer all sorts of gastronomic possibilities. **Casablanca** *(Ostertorsteinweg 59; mains €5-12)* is known for its breakfasts; it also has cheap pastas and soups. **Piano** *(Fehrfeld 64)*, just east of Am Dobben, serves huge Mediterranean-inspired salads and tasty baked casseroles for around €5.50 to €7.50.

The long **courtyard** of Auf den Höfen, north of Ostertorsteinweg, has several restaurants and bars and serves as one of the epicentres of Bremen's nightlife.

Bremen's **Ratskeller** has 650 varieties of wine but no Beck's beer. The **Penny Markt** *(Ostertorsteinweg)* supermarket is one that's convenient.

Getting There & Around

There are frequent regional and IC trains servicing Hamburg (€16.80, one hour). Hourly IC trains run to Cologne (€46.60, three hours). A couple of ICE trains run direct to Frankfurt (€88.40, 3½ hours) and Munich (€124, six hours) daily. Change trains in Hanover for Berlin (€135, 3½ hours). For Amsterdam (€54, four hours), change in Osnabrück.

To get to Am Markt follow the tram route from directly in front of the train station. The tourist office has good public transport maps. Short trips on buses and trams cost €1.85, a four-trip transferable ticket €5.60 and a day pass €4.50.

HANOVER

☎ 0511 • pop 523,000

Hanover (Hannover), capital of Lower Saxony, has close links with the English-speaking world. In 1714 the eldest son of Electress Sophie of Hannover – a granddaughter of James I of England and VI of Scotland – ascended the British throne as King George I. This Anglo-German union lasted through several generations until 1837. Savaged by heavy bombing in 1943, Hanover was rebuilt into a prosperous city known throughout Europe for its trade fairs.

The **tourist office** *(☎ 16 84 97 11; Ernst-August-Platz 2; open Mon-Sat)* is next to the main post office and near the main train station. The HannoverCard, which entitles you to unlimited public transport and discount admission to museums and other attractions, costs €8 for one day, €12 for three days.

Things to See & Do

One way to find most city sights on foot is to follow the numbered attractions with the help of the *Red Thread Guide* (€2) from the tourist office. The chief attractions are the glorious parks of **Herrenhäuser Gärten** *(☎ 16 84 77 43; open 9am-sunset year-round)*, especially the baroque **Grosser Garten** and the **Berggarten** *(admission €3; open till 8pm on summer evenings)*, with its newly installed rainforest exhibit. The gardens also include two museums. The **Fürstenhaus** *(adult/concession €3.30/1.50; open Tues-Sun)* shows how royalty lived in the 1700s, and the **Wilhelm-Busch-Museum** *(adult/concession €4.50/2.50; open Tues-Sun)* contains the work of Busch and other satirical artists. To reach the gardens, take tram No 4 or 5.

The respected **Sprengel Museum** *(☎ 16 84 38 75; Kurt-Schwitters-Platz; adult/concession €3.50/1.80; open Tues-Sun, till 8pm Tues)* exhibits contemporary works, the highlights being Picasso and Max Beckmann.

At Am Markt in the old town, the 14th-century **Marktkirche**, apart from its truncated tower, is characteristic of the northern red-brick Gothic style; the original stained-glass windows are particularly beautiful. Around **Burgstrasse** are some half-timbered houses.

On Breite Strasse near the corner of Osterstrasse, the ruin of the **Aegidienkirche** – smashed in 1943 – is an eloquent memorial; the peace bell inside is a gift from one of Hanover's sister-cities, Hiroshima.

Places to Stay & Eat

Tourist office staff will find you a private room only during trade fairs, but can arrange

The Stuff of Legend

The road from Hanau to Bremen is known as the Fairy-Tale Road (Märchenstrasse), owing to the number of myths that have sprung up from the region. The road's most historical section is the stretch between Hanover and Göttingen. In the town of **Hamelin** (Hameln), you can visit the Rattenfängerhaus (Rat-Catcher's, or Pied Piper's, House). Legend says that in 1284, 130 local children were led out of town by a piper wearing multi-coloured clothes, never to be seen again.

Another birthplace of tall tales is Bodenwerder's Rathaus, supposedly where the renowned Baron von Münchhausen was born. The baron achieved legendary status by telling outrageous stories, such as the one about the time he rode a cannonball through the air (sceptics can see the cannonball itself at the Rathaus) or when he rode half a horse through the country (a statue outside confirms this story).

For more information contact Hamelin's **information centre** *(☎ 05151-930 00, fax 93 00 33; Deisterallee 1).*

a hotel room year-round for €6.50. The **Jugendherberge** *(☎ 131 76 74, fax 185 55; Ferdinand-Wilhelm-Fricke-Weg 1; beds junior/senior €13.50/16)* is 3km out of town. Take the U3 or U7 from Hauptbahnhof to Fischerhof, then cross the river on the Lodemannbrücke and turn right. **Hotel Flora** *(☎ 38 39 10, fax 383 91 91; Heinrichstrasse 36; singles/doubles from €36/62, with bath €46/72)* provides quite pleasant rooms. **Hotel Gildehof** *(☎ 36 36 80, fax 30 66 44; Joachimstrasse 6; singles/doubles €41/65, with bath €57/75)* has clean rooms, some with bathroom. The restaurant downstairs serves well-priced traditional dishes.

The Altstadt area behind Marktkirche has plenty of good-value restaurants offering German cuisine. The **Markthalle** *(cnr Karmarschstrasse & Leinestrasse)* is a gourmand's paradise – it roughly keeps normal shopping hours and has lots of budget, ethnic food stalls, some vegetarian offerings and fresh produce. Hanover institution **Brauhaus Ernst August** *(Schmiedestrasse 13A; mains €5-17)* brews its own Hannöversch beer and serves German dishes.

Getting There & Around

Hanover's spruced-up train station is a major hub. ICE trains to/from Hamburg (€34.40, 1½ hours), Munich (€110, 4½ hours), Frankfurt (€72, 2½ hours) and Cologne (€53.40, 2¾ hours) leave hourly, and every two hours to Berlin-Zoo (€51.80, 1¾ hours). A web of regional services fills in the gaps locally.

Single journeys on the combined tram/U-Bahn system for one zone cost €1 and day passes cost €3.10. The S5 connects the airport with the fairgrounds via the main train station in 25 minutes. For the Messe, the U8 also runs to Messe Nord from the main train station.

GÖTTINGEN

☎ 0551 • pop 130,000

This leafy university town is an ideal stopover between Munich and Hamburg. Though small, Göttingen is lively, mostly because of its large student population. A legion of notables, including Otto von Bismarck and the Brothers Grimm, studied and worked here, and the university has produced over 40 Nobel Prize winners.

The **main tourist office** *(☎ 49 98 00; ⓔ tourismus@goettingen.de; Markt 9; open Mon-Sat, daily in summer)* is in the old Rathaus. There's a **post office** just to the left. Check your email at **Computerwerk** *(Düsterestrasse 20)*, where a half-hour of Internet time costs €2.

Things to See

At Markt, don't miss the **Rathaus' Great Hall**, where colourful frescoes cover every inch of wall space. Just outside, students and punk rockers mill about the **Gänseliesel** fountain, the town's symbol. The bronze beauty has a reputation as 'the most kissed girl in the world', because every student who obtains a doctor's degree must plant a kiss on her cheek.

The 15th-century **Junkernschänke** *(Barfüsserstrasse 5)*, with its colourful carved facade, is the most stunning of the town's half-timbered buildings. A walk on top of the old **town wall** along Bürgerstrasse takes you past **Bismarckhäuschen** *(admission free; open 10am-1pm Tues, 3pm-5pm Wed, Thur & Sat)*, a modest building where the Iron Chancellor lived in 1833 during his wild student days.

Places to Stay & Eat

To reach the **Jugendherberge** *(☎ 576 22, fax 438 87; Habichtsweg 2; beds junior/senior*

€14.80/20.70), take bus No 6 to the Jugendherberge stop. The friendly **Hotel Garni Gräfin von Holtzenorff** *(☎ 639 87, fax 63 29 85; Ernst-Ruhstrat-Strasse 4; singles/doubles from €26/45)* has basic rooms. Take bus No 13 to Florenz-Sartorius-Strasse. **Berliner Hof** *(☎ 38 33 20, fax 383 32 32; ⓔ info@berlinerhof.de; Weender Landstrasse 43; singles/doubles €36/52)* is across from the university. **Hotel Kasseler Hof** *(☎ 720 81, 770 34 29; Rosdorfer Weg 26; singles/doubles from €34/67)*, on the edge of the old town, has simple rooms. **Hotel Central** *(☎ 571 57, fax 571 05; Jüdenstrasse 12; singles without bath from €40, singles/doubles with bath €52/80)* is conveniently situated in the middle of town.

Nikolaistrasse and Goethe Allee offer loads of **takeaway** options. The **Mensa Am Turm** *(Gosslerstrasse 12b)*, just east of campus, is the most pleasant of the dirt-cheap student cafeterias. There's another, more-convenient Mensa on Wilhelmsplatz. **Salamanca** *(Gartenstrasse 21b; mains €5-10; open from 6pm Mon-Fri, from 1pm Sat & Sun)* offers tasty, well-priced food in a prototypical leftist twentysomething café. **Plus** *(cnr Prinzenstrasse & Stumpfebiel)* is a convenient supermarket.

Entertainment

Göttingen's bars and clubs give this small town a big-city atmosphere. **Apex** *(Burgstrasse 46)* is a nice place for a nibble and drink. The **Irish Pub** *(Mühlenstrasse 4)* offers a few dishes and has live music. The salsa, hip-hop, and funk dance nights at the **Blue Note** *(Wilhelmsplatz 3)* are popular with students and nonstudents alike; **Tangente** *(☎ 463 76; Goetheallee 8a)* gets an older student crowd. **Sechs Million Dollar Club** *(Neustadt 1)* has a cool, retro feel and stiff cocktails. The tiny **Elektroosho** *(Weender Strasse 38)*, Göttingen's hippest dance club, specialises in house music. Things don't get started there until late.

Getting There & Away

Hourly ICE trains pass through on their way to/from Hanover (€26.20, 30 minutes), Berlin (€62.60, 2¼ hours), Hamburg (€53, two hours), Frankfurt (€48.20, two hours) and Munich (€92.60, 4½ hours). Direct RB trains depart every two hours from Göttingen for Goslar in the Harz Mountains (€12.40, 1¼ hours).

GOSLAR

☎ 05321 • pop 48,000

Charming, millennium-old Goslar is a centre for Harz Mountains tourism, offering tranquil beauty even during the tourist season. The **tourist office** *(☎ 780 60; ⓔ goslarinfo@t-online.de; Markt 7; open Mon-Sat, daily May-Oct)* can offer help when accommodation is packed. For information on the Harz Mountains, visit the **Harzer Verkehrsverband** *(☎ 3 40 40, fax 34 04 66; ⓔ info@harzinfo.de; Marktstrasse 45; open 8am-4pm Mon-Thur, 8am-1pm Fri)*.

The **Marktplatz** has several photogenic houses. The **Kaiserpfalz** *(Kaiserbleek 6; adult/concession €4.50/2.50; open daily)* is a reconstructed, 11th-century, Romanesque palace usually jammed with tour-bus visitors. Just below is the restored **Domvorhalle**, which displays the 11th-century 'Kaiserstuhl' throne, used by German emperors. At the **Rammelsberger Bergbaumuseum** *(adult/concession €8.50/5.50; open 9am-6pm daily)*, about 1km south of the town centre on Rammelsberger Strasse, you can literally delve into the 1000-year mining history of the area.

The pretty **Jugendherberge** *(☎ 222 40, fax 413 76; Rammelsberger Strasse 25; beds junior/senior €15.40/18.10)* is behind the Kaiserpfalz (take bus 803 to Theresienhof from the train station). Another option is **Hotel und Campingplatz Sennhütte** *(☎ 225 02; Clausthaler Strasse 28; tent sites €2.50 plus €3.30/2 per person/car, singles/doubles from €20/40; open Fri-Wed)*, 3km south on Route B241. Take bus No 830 from the train station to Sennhütte. The clean, simple rooms sport nice views, and you'll find lots of trails nearby. **Gästehaus Schmitz** *(☎ 234 45, fax 30 60 39; Kornstrasse 1; singles/doubles €30/40, apartments from €30)* offers the best value, with bright, cheerful rooms. **Gästehaus Verhoeven** *(☎ 238 12; Hoher Weg 12; singles/doubles from €32/50)* has clean, simple rooms.

The **Altdeutsches Kartoffelhaus** *(Breite Strasse; mains €4-11)*, in the Kaiserpassage shopping arcade, has generous potato dishes. **Brauhaus Wolpertinger** *(Marstallstrasse 1; mains €5-15)* is a pleasant restaurant with whimsical decor.

Goslar is regularly connected by train to Göttingen (€12.40, 1¼ hours), Hanover (€12.40, one hour) and Wernigerode (€5.50, 30 minutes).

WESTERN HARZ MOUNTAINS

Known mostly to Germans and Scandinavians, the Harz Mountains (Harzgebirge) don't have the dramatic peaks and valleys of the Alps, but they offer a great, four-seasons, sports getaway without tackiness and tourism. For weather reports and winter snow information (in German), contact the **Harzer Verkehrsverband** *(☎ 05325-340 40)* in Goslar. Local tourist offices include those in **Hahnenklee** *(☎ 05325-510 40; Kurhausweg 7)*, **Bad Harzburg** *(☎ 05322-753 30; Herzog-Wilhelm-Strasse 86)* and **Clausthal-Zellerfeld** *(☎ 05323-810 24; Bahnhofstrasse 5a)*. All have information on the 500km of beautifully groomed **hiking trails** in National Park Harz. **Cycling** is popular in summer among those seeking a hilly challenge, and in winter the Harz Mountains offers excellent conditions for **cross-country skiing**. **Downhill skiing** can be quite good in Hahnenklee, St Andreasberg and Braunlage.

Many of the 30 or so camping grounds in the Harz Mountains are open all year. There is no shortage of budget rooms in hotels and pensions. Goslar is the most popular base for the region.

Northern Germany

Most travellers journey up north to visit the happening and hopping city of Hamburg. Apart from this town, Germany's far north is home to the states of Schleswig-Holstein and Mecklenburg–Western Pomerania. The former, bordering Denmark at the southern end of the Jutland Peninsula, broke away from Denmark in the mid-17th century. Since then, Germany and Denmark have fought three wars over the region. Travellers will appreciate why the region was so hotly contested after sampling the attractions of the North Frisian Islands and the lovely historical city of Lübeck. Stretching from Schleswig-Holstein to Poland, Mecklenburg–Western Pomerania (Mecklenburg-Vorpommern), is home to some of Germany's most untouched spots, such as Poel Island, and resorts such as Rügen.

HAMBURG

☎ 040 • pop 1.7 million

Historic Hamburg strode confidently into the 20th century, but WWI stopped all its trade and WWII demolished it. The city spent the remainder of the 20th century climbing back to the top of the ladder, and today it's a sprawling port city with a stylish shopping district, numerous waterways (featuring more bridges than Venice) and even a beach.

Orientation & Information

The Hauptbahnhof is very central, near Aussenalster lake and fairly close to most of the sights. These cluster south of Aussenalster and north of the Elbe River, which runs all the way from the Czech Republic to Hamburg before flowing into the North Sea. The port is west of the city centre, facing the Elbe.

The small **tourist office** *(☎ 30 05 12 00; ⓔ info@hamburg-tourism.de; open 7am-11pm daily)* is in the main train station at the Kirchenallee exit and offers a room-finding service (€4). There's also a **tourist office** *(ⓦ www.hamburg-tourism.de; open daily)* at St Pauli harbour, between piers 4 and 5. Both offices stock the Hamburg Card, which offers unlimited public transport and free or discounted admission to numerous attractions, museums and cruises.

There is a **Reisebank** *(open 7.30am-10pm daily)* above the Kirchenallee exit of the main train station. A small **post office** *(open 8am-8pm Mon-Fri, 9am-6pm Sat, 10am-6pm Sun)* offers a poste-restante service close to the Kirchenallee exit of the train station. The **main post office** *(cnr Dammtorstrasse & Stephansplatz)* is close to the Stephansplatz U-Bahn stop. **Cyberb@r** *(Mönchebergstrasse 16)*, on the third floor of the Karstadt department store, charges €1.50 for 30 minutes online.

Things to See & Do

The Altstadt centres on Rathausmarkt, where the large **Rathaus** and huge clock tower overlook the lively square. This is one of the most interesting city halls in Germany, and the 35-minute tour is worthwhile (€1/0.50). It's in English hourly from 10.15am to 3.15pm Monday to Thursday, to 1.15pm Friday to Sunday.

It is a moving experience to visit the remaining tower of the devastated **St-Nikolai-Kirche**, now an antiwar memorial, nearby on Ost-West-Strasse. From there, walk a few blocks west to the baroque **Hauptkirche St Michaelis** and take the lift up the tower *(adult/concession €2.50/1.25; open 10am-6pm daily Apr-Oct, till 5pm Nov-Mar)*.

After exploring the Altstadt, stroll down to one of the busiest ports in the world. If you're in the area early on a Sunday (5am to 10am), head for **Fischmarkt** (fish market) in St Pauli, right on the Elbe. Hamburg's oldest market (established 1703) is popular with locals and tourists alike, and everything under the sun is sold here. Cap your morning with a visit to the live-music session at the **Fischauktionshalle** *(Fish Auction Hall; Grosse Elbstrasse 9)*.

Among Hamburg's biggest tourist attractions is the famous **Reeperbahn** red-light district, heart of the St Pauli entertainment district. In recent years, sex establishments have been gradually replaced by popular restaurants and bars, with a dwindling number of peep shows and sex shops. If you venture into one of these haunts, make sure you understand costs before going in. Entry is sometimes free or €2 to €5, but there will likely be a minimum purchase of €25 or more. **Herbertstrasse** is the notorious street where the prostitutes pose in windows offering their wares. Men under 18 and women are not allowed in.

For more wholesome pastimes, visit Hamburg's **Kunsthalle** *(Glockengiesserwall)*, with old masters and a large collection of German paintings from artists of the 19th and 20th centuries. Contemporary art is is on disply next door in the modern **Galerie der Gegenwart** *(adult/concession for both museums €7.50/5; both open 10am-6pm Tues-Sun, 10am-9pm Thur)*. **Harry's Hamburger Hafen Basar** *(Bernhard-Nocht-Strasse 89-91; adult/concession €2.50)* is the life's work of Harry, a bearded character known to seamen all over the world, who for decades bought trinkets and souvenirs from sailors and others. The **Erotic Art Museum** *(Nobistor 10a; adult/concession €8/5; open 10am-midnight Sun-Thur, 10am- 1am Fri & Sat)* contains around 1800 paintings, drawings and sculptures by artists from Delacroix to Picasso.

Places to Stay

Call the **Hamburg-Hotline** *(☎ 30 05 13 00; operates 8am-8pm daily)* for availability and reservations.

Hamburg's two DJH hostels are large. **Auf dem Stintfang** *(☎ 31 34 88; ⓔ jh-stintfang@t-online.de; Alfred-Wegener-Weg 5; junior/senior €15.25/19.25)* has a wonderful view of the Elbe. Take the U- or S-Bahn to St Pauli-Landungsbrücken. **Horner Rennbahn** *(☎ 651 16 71; ⓔ jgh-hamburg@t-online.de; Rennbahnstrasse 100; junior/senior €16.75/19.50)* is less convenient. Catch the U3 to Horner Rennbahn and walk 10 minutes north past the racecourse and leisure centre. The private hostel **Schanzenstern** *(☎ 439 84 41, fax 439 34 13; ⓔ info@schanzenstern.de; Bartelsstrasse 12; dorm beds €17, singles/doubles/triples €35/50/60)* is ideally located in the lively Schanzenviertel.

Many budget hotels are along Steindamm and a few blocks east of the main train station along Bremer Reihe, but the concentration of junkies and prostitutes makes the streets feel unsafe. **Hotel Eden** *(☎ 24 84 80, fax 24 15 21; Ellmenreichstrasse 20; singles/doubles €41/62, with bath €72/103)* is just far enough removed from the sleaze to be comfortable.

Lange Reihe is less grubby than other streets in St Georg. **Hotel-Pension Alpha** *(☎ 24 53 65, fax 24 37 94; singles/doubles €36/62)* has bare-bones rooms, all with shower. Welcoming **Hotel-Pension von Blumfeld** *(☎ 24 58 60, fax 24 32 82; Lange Reihe 54; singles/doubles €31/46, with bath €41/56)* has nice, basic rooms and a friendly parrot called Jakob. **Galerie-Hotel Sarah Petersen** *(☎/fax 24 98 26; Lange Reihe 50; singles/doubles from €45/65)* is a classic art-scene Hamburg hotel, with rooms decorated in different styles.

The family-run **Hotel Imperial** *(☎ 319 60 21, fax 31 56 85; ⓔ info@hotel-imperial-hamburg.de; Millerntorplatz 3-5; singles/doubles weekdays €50/77, weekends from €60/85)* has rates that vary from week to weekends. Spacious, well-furnished rooms face away from the Reeperbahn.

Places to Eat

Self-caterers should head for one of the **Penny Markt** budget groceries. There's one on Baumeisterstrasse, one on the corner of Lange Reihe and Schmilinskystrasse to the east of the main train station, and one near the corner of Königstrasse and Holstenstrasse at the western end of the Reeperbahn. Marvellous fresh fare is offered at **Grossneumarkt** on market days (Wednesday and Saturday).

Kantine im Schauspielhaus *(Kirchenallee; lunches €6)* downstairs in the Deutsches Schauspielhaus, is one of the best-kept secrets in the Hauptbahnhof area, with plain but filling lunches. The student **Café Urlaub** *(Lange Reihe 63; dishes around €7; open breakfast until 2am)* provides good salads and pasta dishes. **Café Gnosa** *(Lange Reihe 93; mains from €6.20)* is especially popular among gays and lesbians. It features good

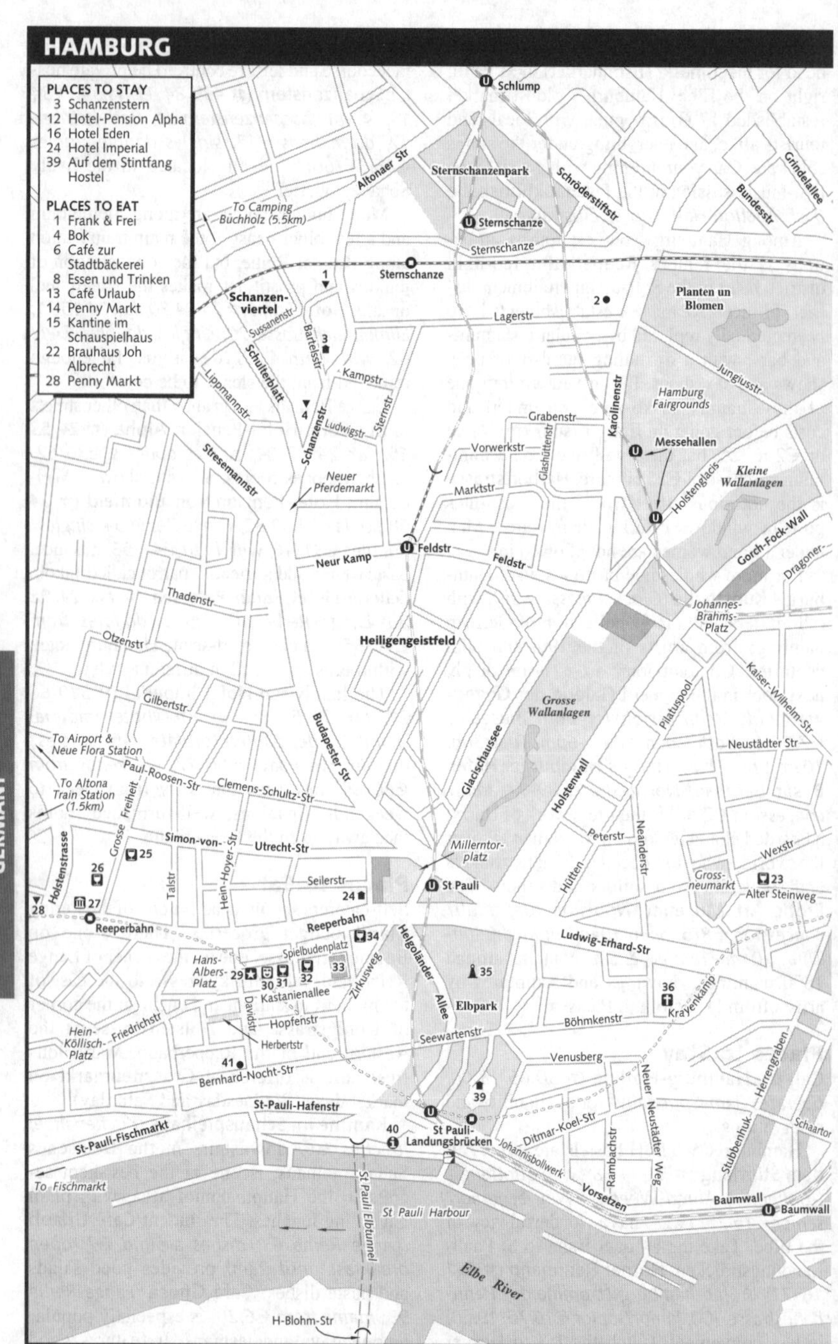

HAMBURG
PLACES TO STAY
3 Schanzenstern
12 Hotel-Pension Alpha
16 Hotel Eden
24 Hotel Imperial
39 Auf dem Stintfang Hostel
PLACES TO EAT
1 Frank & Frei
4 Bok
6 Café zur Stadtbäckerei
8 Essen und Trinken
13 Café Urlaub
14 Penny Markt
15 Kantine im Schauspielhaus
22 Brauhaus Joh Albrecht
28 Penny Markt
Schlump
Sternschanzenpark
Sternschanze
Altonaer Str
Schröderstiftstr
Bundesstr
Grindelallee
To Camping Buchholz (5.5km)
Schanzenviertel
Planten un Blomen
Lagerstr
Sussanenstr
Bartelsstr
Kampstr
Schulterblatt
Lippmannstr
Ludwigstr
Sternstr
Schanzenstr
Jungiusstr
Hamburg Fairgrounds
Grabenstr
Karolinenstr
Vorwerkstr
Glashüttenstr
Messehallen
Neuer Pferdemarkt
Stresemannstr
Marktstr
Kleine Wallanlagen
Holstenglacis
Gorch-Fock-Wall
Feldstr
Neur Kamp
Thadenstr
Otzenstr
Heiligengeistfeld
Johannes-Brahms-Platz
Dragoner-
Gilbertstr
Kaiser-Wilhelm-Str
Grosse Wallanlagen
Pilatuspool
Neustädter Str
To Airport & Neue Flora Station
To Altona Train Station (1.5km)
Paul-Roosen-Str
Clemens-Schultz-Str
Budapester Str
Glacischaussee
Holstenwall
Grosse Freiheit
Simon-von-
Utrecht-Str
Millerntorplatz
Peterstr
Neanderstr
Wexstr
Holstenstrasse
Talstr
Hein-Hoyer-Str
Seilerstr
St Pauli
Hütten
Grossneumarkt
Alter Steinweg
Reeperbahn
Ludwig-Erhard-Str
Spielbudenplatz
Hans-Albers-Platz
Kastanienallee
Zirkusweg
Helgoländer Allee
Elbpark
Krayenkamp
Davidstr
Hopfenstr
Böhmkenstr
Hein-Köllisch-Platz
Friedrichstr
Herbertstr
Seewartenstr
Venusberg
Herrengraben
Bernhard-Nocht-Str
St-Pauli-Hafenstr
Neuer Neustädter Weg
St-Pauli-Fischmarkt
St Pauli-Landungsbrücken
Ditmar-Koel-Str
Rambachstr
Stubbenhuk
Schaartor
Johannisbollwerk
Vorsetzen
To Fischmarkt
St Pauli Elbtunnel
St Pauli Harbour
Baumwall
Elbe River
H-Blohm-Str
GERMANY

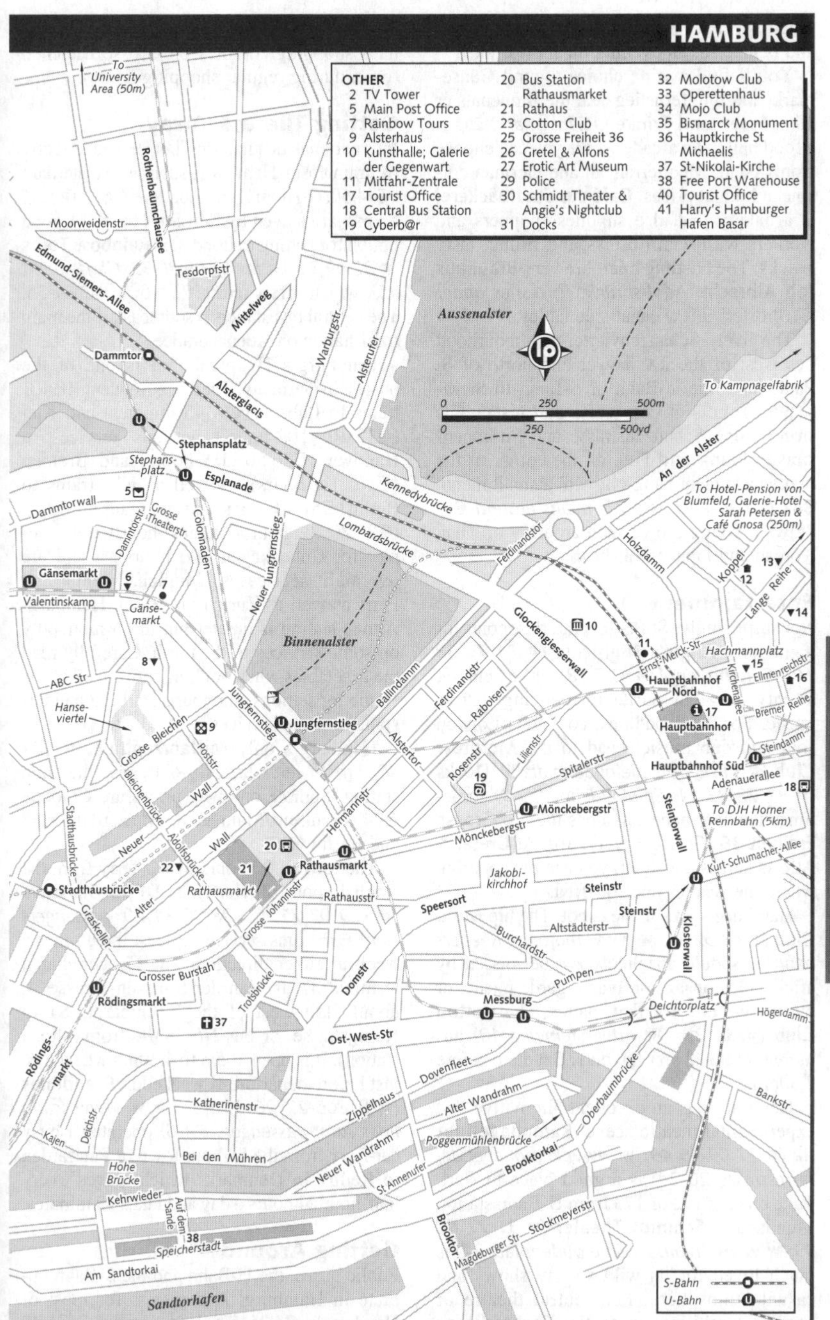
HAMBURG
OTHER
2 TV Tower
5 Main Post Office
7 Rainbow Tours
9 Alsterhaus
10 Kunsthalle; Galerie der Gegenwart
11 Mitfahr-Zentrale
17 Tourist Office
18 Central Bus Station
19 Cyberb@r
20 Bus Station Rathausmarket
21 Rathaus
23 Cotton Club
25 Grosse Freiheit 36
26 Gretel & Alfons
27 Erotic Art Museum
29 Police
30 Schmidt Theater & Angie's Nightclub
31 Docks
32 Molotow Club
33 Operettenhaus
34 Mojo Club
35 Bismarck Monument
36 Hauptkirche St Michaelis
37 St-Nikolai-Kirche
38 Free Port Warehouse
40 Tourist Office
41 Harry's Hamburger Hafen Basar
To University Area (50m)
To Kampnagelfabrik
To Hotel-Pension von Blumfeld, Galerie-Hotel Sarah Petersen & Café Gnosa (250m)
To DJH Horner Rennbahn (5km)
Aussenalster
Binnenalster
Sandtorhafen
Dammtor
Stephansplatz
Gänsemarkt
Jungfernstieg
Rathausmarkt
Stadthausbrücke
Rödingsmarkt
Hauptbahnhof Nord
Hauptbahnhof
Hauptbahnhof Süd
Mönckebergstr
Messburg
Steinstr
S-Bahn
U-Bahn
0 250 500m
0 250 500yd

GERMANY

lunch specials, wonderful homemade cakes, and is nice for an evening meal or drink.

You'll find a wide choice around Gänsemarkt and Jungfernstieg near the Binnenalster lake. **Essen und Trinken** *(Gänsemarkt 21)* is a food hall in an arcade where you can choose from Asian, Mediterranean and German cuisine at budget prices. **Café zur Stadtbäckerei** is a bakery that also supplies shoppers and workers with warm drinks and filling, tasty snacks. The bustling microbrewery **Brauhaus Joh Albrecht** *(Adolfsbrücke 7; dishes under €10)* offers a few canal-side tables.

The lively Schanzenviertel neighbourhood lies west of the TV Tower and north of St Pauli (take the U-Bahn or S-Bahn to Sternschanze). Lots of cosy cafés and restaurants string along Schanzenstrasse and Susannenstrasse; **Frank and Frei**, on the corner of the two, is a student hang-out with a small menu. **Bok** *(Schanzenstrasse 27; mains around €8)* draws a young crowd with an array of Thai, Korean and Japanese dishes.

Entertainment

Not surprisingly, St Pauli is the flashpoint for nightclubs. **Angie's Nightclub** *(☎ 31 77 88 16; Spielbudenplatz 27-28)* is a classy, sweaty, local favourite for dancing to live music. For indie oddities, cool '60s London soul and dub music, head to the **Molotow Club** *(☎ 31 08 45; Spielbudenplatz 5)*. **Docks** *(☎ 31 78 83 11; Spielbudenplatz 19)* sometimes has live bands, as does the hip **Grosse Freiheit 36** *(Grosse Freiheit 36)*. At **Gretel & Alfons** across the street, you can have a drink where the Beatles once quaffed.

Hamburg's jazz scene is hot. The hip **Mojo Club** *(☎ 43 52 32; W www.mojo.de; Reeperbahn 1)* should absolutely *not* be missed by aficionados of jazz or avante-garde music, or by anyone else for that matter. The **Cotton Club** *(☎ 34 38 78; Alter Steinweg 10)* has more traditional jazz flavours. Get there before 8.30pm.

Hamburg has an excellent alternative and experimental theatre scene. **Kampnagelfabrik** *(☎ 27 09 49 49; W www.kampnagel.de; Jarrestrasse 20-24)* is a good place to start. Take bus No 172 or 173 from U-Bahn station Mundsburg. **Schmidt Theater** *(☎ 31 77 88 99; W www.tivoli.de; Spielbudenplatz 27)* is much loved for its wild variety shows and casual atmosphere. For central theatre or concert bookings, go to the **Theaterkasse** *(☎ 35 35 55)* in the basement of the Alsterhaus shopping complex on Grosse Bleichen (open during regular shopping hours).

Getting There & Away

International destinations not served directly by train from Hamburg, such as Amsterdam (€44.50, 6½ hours) and London (€61.50, 17½ hours), are served by Eurolines buses. A good option for getting to London is **Rainbow Tours** *(☎ 32 09 33 09, fax 32 09 30 99; Gänsemarkt 45)*, which offers return trips from only €55. The central bus station is southeast of the main train station on Adenauerallee.

Hamburg's Hauptbahnhof is one of the busiest in Germany. There are frequent RE/RB trains to Lübeck (€9, 45 minutes) and Kiel (€15.20, 1¼ hours), various services to Hanover (€26.50, 1½ hours) and Bremen (€16, 1¼ hours), as well as ICE trains to Berlin (€51.40, 2½ hours) and Frankfurt/Main (€98.20, 3½ hours). Almost-hourly trains depart for Copenhagen (4½ hours). There are overnight services to Munich, Vienna and Paris as well as Zurich via Basel. Hamburg-Altona station is quieter but has a monopoly on some services to the north. Carefully read the timetables when booking to/from all of the Hamburg stations. Hamburg-Harburg handles some regional services.

Hamburg's only **Mitfahrzentrale** *(☎ 194 40; Ernst-Merck-Strasse 8)* is near the train station. Sample one-way prices are Cologne €24, Frankfurt/Main €28, Amsterdam €33 and Berlin €17.

The town is 20 hours by car ferry from the English port of Harwich. **DFDS Seaways** *(☎ 389 03 71, fax 38 90 31 20; passengers from €35)* runs services at least three times a week in either direction. The Fischereihafen terminal is at Van-der-Smissen-Strasse 4, about 1km west of the Fischmarkt (S1 to Königstrasse, or bus No 383 to/from Altona station). It is open 10am to 4.30pm weekdays, just before departure at weekends. **Scandlines** *(☎ 01805-72 26 35 46 37; W www.scandlines.com; passengers €3-6)* operates a busy car ferry from the harbour town of Puttgarden to Redby in Denmark, which leaves every half-hour 24 hours a day and takes 45 minutes.

Getting Around

Public buses, the U-Bahn and the S-Bahn operate in Hamburg. A day pass for most of Hamburg is €4.25. Single journeys cost €1.40

for the city tariff area. A three-day pass is €12.25. Hamburg's bike tracks are extensive and reach almost to the centre of the city.

LÜBECK

☎ 0451 • pop 215,000

Medieval Lübeck was known as the Queen of the Hanseatic League, as it was the capital of this association of towns that ruled Baltic Sea trade from the 12th to 16th centuries. This beautiful city, with its red-stone buildings, is a highlight of the north. Its old town is set on an island ringed by the canalised Trave River, a 15-minute walk east from the main train station. **Lübeck-Information** *(☎/fax 1 22 54 19; Breite Strasse 62; open daily)* is near the Rathaus. The private **room-finding office** *(☎ 86 46 75, fax 86 30 24)* at the train station charges €3 (free by phone). See Ⓦ www.luebeck-info.de. The Lübeck Happy Day Card (€5 for 24 hours) entitles you to unlimited travel and discounts on cruises, museums, cinema and other attractions.

The **central post office** *(Königstrasse 46)* is across from the Katarinenkirche. For Internet access, visit **PC & Internet Café** *(Am der Untertrave 103)*, near the Holstentor.

Things to See & Do

The landmark **Holstentor** *(☎ 122 41 29; adult/concession €5/3; open Tues-Sun)*, a fortified gate with huge twin towers, serves as the city's symbol as well as its museum. For a literary kick, visit the recently refurbished **Buddenbrookhaus** *(Mengstrasse 4; adult/concession €4.10/2.60; open daily)*, birthplace of Thomas Mann, who made this place famous in his novel *Buddenbrooks*. The must-see **Marienkirche** *(Markt)* contains a stark reminder of WWII: A bombing raid brought the church bells crashing to the stone floor, and the townspeople have left the fragments in place. A small sign reads 'A protest against war and violence'. Also on Markt is the imposing **Rathaus**, which covers two full sides of the square.

Lübeck's **Marionettentheater** *(Puppet Theatre; ☎ 700 60; cnr Am Kolk & Kleine Petersgrube; performances €4-11; open Tues-Sun)* is an absolute must. Usually there is a daily afternoon performance for children and an evening performance for adults on Saturday, but the schedule varies. It's best to book.

The tower lift at the partly restored **Petrikirche** *(adult/concession €2/1.20; open 9am-7pm daily May-Oct, closed Jan & Feb)* affords a superb view over the Altstadt.

Places to Stay & Eat

Lübeck has two DJH hostels. The **Jugendgästehaus Lübeck** *(☎ 702 03 99; Mengstrasse 33; dorm beds juniors/seniors €17.40/20.10)* is clean, comfortable and well situated in the middle of the old town. The **Jugendherberge 'Vor dem Burgtor'** *(☎ 334 33, fax 345 40; Am Gertrudenkirchhof 4; juniors/seniors €15.40/18.10)* is a little outside the old town – take bus No 1, 3, 11, 12 or 31 to Gustav-Radbruch-Platz. The YMCA's centrally located **Sleep-Inn** *(☎ 719 20, fax 789 97; Grosse Petersgrube 11; dorm beds €10, doubles €30; open mid-Jan–mid-Dec)* charges €4 extra for breakfast and €4.50 extra for sheets. **Hotel Stadt Lübeck** *(☎ 838 83, fax 86 32 21; Am Bahnhof 21; singles/doubles €43/63)* is just outside the main train station. Fairly good rooms come with shower and toilet.

The best eating and drinking options are in the area directly east of the Rathaus. The fun **Tipasa** *(Schlumacherstrasse 12-14; mains from €4.40)* serves everything from tandoori to tacos. It's also a great place to eat and drink in the evening. **Hieronymus** *(☎ 706 30 17; Fleischhauerstrasse 81; mains €4.50-19.40)* is a relaxed and rambling restaurant spread over three floors of a 15th-century building. Lunch specials are good value.

Save room for a dessert or some marzipan, which was invented in Lübeck (local legend has it that the town ran out of flour during a long siege and resorted to grinding almonds to make bread). **JG Niederegger** *(Breite Strasse 89)*, a shop and café directly opposite the Rathaus, is Lübeck's marzipan mecca. The supermarket **Sky** *(Sandstrasse 24)* is located conveniently near Kohlmarkt.

Getting There & Around

Lübeck is close to Hamburg, with at least one train every hour (€9, 45 minutes). There are also frequent services to Kiel (€12.40, 1¼ hours) and Schwerin (€10.70, 1¼ hours). Trains to/from Copenhagen also stop here. The central bus station is next to the main train station. Services to/from Wismar stop here, as well as Autokraft buses to/from Kiel, Hamburg, Schwerin, Rostock and Berlin.

Frequent double-decker buses run to Travemünde (€3.50, 45 minutes) from the central bus station. City buses also leave from here; a single journey costs €1.35.

KIEL

☎ 0431 • pop 246,000

Quickly and effectively rebuilt after WWII, these days the capital of Schleswig-Holstein is a vibrant and modern city. At the end of a modest firth, it has long been one of Germany's most important Baltic Sea harbours and was the host of Olympic sailing events in 1936 and 1972. The **tourist office** *(☎ 67 91 00; W www.kiel-tourist.de; Andreas-Gayk-Strasse 31; open Mon-Sat)* is five minutes by foot from the main train station. **Cyber Treff** *(Bergstrasse 17)* is a good place to surf the Web until late.

Kiel's most famous attraction is the **Kieler Woche** (Kiel Week), a festival revolving around a series of yachting regattas attended by over 4000 of the world's sailing elite and half a million spectators. It takes place the last full week in June. Even if you're not into sailing, the atmosphere is electric – just make sure you book a room in advance.

Kiel is also the point at which the shipping canal from the North Sea enters the Baltic Sea. Some 60,000 ships pass through every year and the **locks** *(Schleusen; ☎ 360 30; adult/concession €1.50/1)* at Holtenau, 6km north of the city centre, are worth a visit.

GERMANY

Places to Stay & Eat

The tourist office charges €2.50 to make bookings, and stocks an excellent free brochure listing private rooms and apartments. The **Jugenherberge** *(☎ 73 14 88, fax 73 57 23; Johannesstrasse 1; juniors/seniors €14.90/16.90)* is in the suburb of Gaarden. You can walk across the pretty drawbridge behind the train station or take bus No 11 from the main train station to Kieler Strasse. **Hotel Runge** *(☎ 733 33 96, 73 19 92; Elisabethstrasse 16; singles/doubles from €34/56)*, in Gaarden, is one of the area's cheapest options. The central **Hotel Schweriner Hof** *(☎ 614 16, fax 67 41 34; Königsweg 13; singles €36, singles/doubles with shower & toilet €57/77)* has good rooms.

The **Ratskeller** *(Fleethörn 9; mains €8.40-17.90)*, in the Rathaus, serves typical German cuisine with an emphasis on fish. The **Klosterbrauerei** *(Alter Markt 9; lunch specials €7.40)* is a private brewery with good beer, well-priced food and a great atmosphere. You'll find lots of cheap takeaway options in the Turkish quarter around the hostel in Gaarden.

Getting There & Around

Regional buses run to Lübeck, Schleswig and Puttgarden from the bus station on Auguste-Viktoria-Strasse. Numerous RE trains run daily between Kiel and Hamburg-Altona or Hamburg Hauptbahnhof (€15.20, 1¼ hours). Trains to Lübeck leave every hour (€12.40, 1¼ hours). For arrangements for ride-sharing, contact the **ADM Mitfahrzentrale** *(☎ 194 40; Sophienblatt 52a)*.

The daily Kiel-Gothenburg ferry (13½ hours) leaves from Schwedenkai and is run by **Stena Line** *(☎ 0431-90 99; W www.stenaline.de; passengers €38-74)*. **Color Line ferries** *(☎ 730 03 00; W www.colorline.com; passengers €64-72 mid-June–mid-Aug only, cabins €84-116)* run direct to/from Kiel and Oslo daily (19½ hours). There are 50% off-peak student concessions. Ferries depart from the Norwegenkai across the fjord in Gaarden (use the footbridge).

City buses leave from Sophienblatt, in front of the train station. To get to the North-Baltic Sea Canal and the locks, take bus No 11 to Wik; the locks are about five minutes' walk from the terminus.

NORTH FRISIAN ISLANDS

Sylt ☎ 04651 • pop 21,600
Amrum ☎ 04682 • pop 2100

The Frisian Islands reward those who make the trek with sand dunes, sea, pure air and, occasionally, even sunshine. North Friesland (Nordfriesland) is the western coastal area of Schleswig-Holstein up to and into Denmark. The sea area forms the National Park of Wattenmeer. The most popular of the North Frisian Islands is the glamorous resort of Sylt; the neighbouring islands of Föhr and Amrum are far more relaxed and less touristy.

Nature is the prime attraction on the North Frisian Islands. The different moods of the rough North Sea and the placid Wattenmeer lend the region its unique character. Beautiful dunes stretch out for miles, red and white cliffs border wide beaches, and the skies teem with birds. After WWII, the German jet-set invaded the island, which explains the abundance of luxury homes, cars and expensive restaurants.

Sylt's excellent **tourist office** *(☎ 99 88; open Mon-Sat, daily June-Sept)*, inside the

Westerland train station, can help with information and accommodation. On Amrum, the friendly **tourist office** *(☎ 940 30)* is at the harbour car park. All communities charge visitors a *Kurtaxe*, a resort tax of about €3 a day. Payment gets you a *Kurkarte*, which you need on Sylt even to get onto the beach.

Sylt is connected to the mainland by a scenic, train-only causeway right through the Wattenmeer. Around seven trains leave from Hamburg-Hauptbahnhof daily for Westerland (€33, 3¼ hours). To get to Amrum and the island of Föhr, you must board a ferry in Dagebüll Hafen. Take the Sylt-bound train from Hamburg-Altona and change in Niebüll. A day-return from Dagebüll costs €17.50, which allows you to visit both islands. Five bus lines cover Sylt; for other islands, local buses and ferries are the way to go.

SCHWERIN

☎ 0385 • pop 105,000

Surrounded by numerous lakes, Schwerin is one of eastern Germany's most genteel, picturesque towns. This former seat of the Grand Duchy of Mecklenburg – now the capital of Mecklenburg–Western Pomerania – is an interesting mix of renovated 16th- and 17th-century half-timbered houses and 19th-century architecture.

Down the hill east of the Hauptbahnhof is Pfaffenteich, the rectangular lake whose southern end is at the beginning of Schwerin's main street, Mecklenburgstrasse. Markt is southeast of here. Farther southeast, around Alter Garten on the Schweriner See, are the monumental Marstall (the former royal stables), the Schloss (ducal castle), and parks, museums, tour boats and other treats. Go to **Schwerin-Information** *(☎ 592 52 13, fax 55 50 94; ⓔ stadtmarketing-schwerin@t-online.de; Am Markt 10; open daily)* to buy the Schwerin-Ticket, which covers local transport and discounted admissions (adult/child €6/4).

Above Markt rises the tall 14th-century Gothic **Dom** *(☎ 56 50 14; Am Dom 1; adult/concession €1/0.50; open 11am-5pm Mon-Sat & noon-5pm Sun May-Oct, shorter hours Nov-Apr)*, a superb example of north German red and glazed-black brick architecture. To the southeast of Alter Garten, over a causeway, is Schwerin's neo-Gothic **Schloss** *(☎ 56 57 38; Lennéstrasse 1; adult/concession €4/2.50; open 10am-6pm Wed-Sun Apr-Oct, 10am-5pm Wed-Sun Nov-Mar)*, with superb interiors and lake country views. On the city side of Alter Garten is the **Staatliches Museum** *(☎ 595 80; Alter Garten 3; adult/concession €3/2; 10am-8pm Tues & 10am-6pm Wed-Sun Apr-Oct, 10am-5pm Tues-Sun Nov-Mar)*, with an excellent collection of works by old Dutch masters.

Places to Stay & Eat

There's a nifty computerised accommodation system in front of the Hauptbahnhof. Schwerin-Information can book private rooms from about €25 per person.

The **Jugendherberge Schwerin** *(☎ 326 00 06, fax 326 03 03; Waldschulweg 3; beds junior/senior €14.30/17)* is lakeside, about 4km south of the city centre (take bus No 14 from Marienplatz). Tiny, central **Pension Wilk** *(☎ 550 70 24; Buschstrasse 13; €18/person)* has basic rooms without private facilities (breakfast €5 extra). Historic **Zur Guten Quelle** *(☎ 56 59 85, fax 500 76 02; ⓦ www.zur-guten-quelle.de; Schusterstrasse 12; singles/doubles from €51/70)* has nice rooms and a good restaurant.

Friedrich's *(☎ 55 54 73; Friedrichstrasse 2; mains €8.90-12.50)* serves traditional dishes in a warm, historic atmosphere. **Café Prag** *(☎ 56 59 00; Schlossstrasse 17; mains €6.10-10.40)* is a popular coffee and cake destination. There's a food court in the **Schlosspark Center**. The **Schlemmermarkt food hall**, across the street in *Der Wurm* shopping centre, has cheap Asian and German chow. Self-caterers can visit **Neukauf supermarket** *(cnr Schmiedestrasse & Buschstrasse)*.

Getting There & Away

Various fast trains serve Rostock (€12.40, 1¼ hours), Stralsund (€22.40, 2½ hours) and Hamburg (€17.60, 1¼ hours). Most travel to/from Berlin (€33.40, two hours) requires a change at Wittenberge or Ludwigslust.

ROSTOCK & WARNEMÜNDE

☎ 0381 • pop 210,000

Rostock, the largest city in lightly populated northeastern Germany, is a major Baltic port and shipbuilding centre. In the 14th and 15th centuries it was an important Hanseatic city. Rostock University, founded in 1419, was the first in northern Europe.

The years after reunification were difficult in Rostock – unemployment soared and neo-Nazis attacked foreign workers, bringing national and worldwide condemnation. Now, however, the city centre along Kröpeliner Strasse and the former dock area on the Warnow River have been redeveloped into pleasant pedestrian quarters. Rostock hosts the **IGA** *(International Garden Show;* **W** *www.iga.de)* from April to October 2003, cause for even more sprucing up.

The town's chief suburb is the beach resort and fishing village of Warnemünde, 12km north. In winter this popular getaway offers a picturesque accommodation alternative, while on warm days it's jammed with Berlin's fun-seekers. The IGA site is between central Rostock and Warnemünde.

Rostock-Information *(☎ 194 33, 381 22 22, fax 381 26 01;* **W** *www.rostock.de; Neuer Markt 3-8; open Mon-Fri Oct-Apr, daily May-Sept)* is located about 1.5km from the Hauptbahnhof (tram No 11 or 12). The tourist office sells the 48-hour Rostock Card (€8), which entitles holders to a free walking tour (in German), various reductions for sights and performances, and free public transport (including the S-Bahn to/from Warnemünde).

Things to See & Do

Rostock's splendid 13th-century **Marienkirche** *(☎ 45 33 25; Am Ziegenmarkt; adult/concession €1/0.50; open 10am-5pm Mon-Sat, 11.15am-5pm Sun)* survived WWII unscathed. This huge brick edifice contains a functioning astronomical clock (1472), a Gothic bronze baptismal font (1290), a Renaissance pulpit (1574) and a baroque organ (1770). For a bird's-eye view of town, visit the **Petrikirche** *(☎ 211 01; Alter Markt; open 10am-5pm daily Apr-Oct, 10am-4pm Mon-Fri Nov-Mar)* and scale the stairs.

Kröpeliner Strasse, a broad pedestrian mall lined with 15th- and 16th-century burgher houses, runs west from the **Rathaus** on Neuer Markt to the 14th-century **Kröpeliner Tor** *(☎ 45 41 77; Kröpeliner Strasse; adult/concession €3/1; open 10am-6pm Wed-Sun)*, near a stretch of old city wall. Halfway along, off the southwestern corner of Universitätsplatz, is the **Kloster 'Zum Heiligen Kreuz' Museum** *(☎ 20 35 90; Klosterhof; adult/concession €2/1; open 10am-6pm Tues-Sun)*, in an old convent (1270).

At Warnemünde's north end, a broad, sandy **beach** stretches west from the **lighthouse** (1898). It's chock-a-block with bathers on hot summer days and its promenade makes for a nice stroll.

Places to Stay & Eat

Rostock-Information can book private rooms from around €15, plus a €2.50 fee. In summer, however, rooms are about as scarce as hen's teeth. The new **Jugendherberge** *(☎ 54 81 70, fax 548 17 23;* **e** *jh-warnemuende@t-online.de; Parkstrasse 47, Warnemünde; juniors/seniors €19.30/23.30)* is just two minutes' walk to the beach and sporting activities. Back in central Rostock, the small **City-Pension** *(☎ 459 07 04, fax 25 22 60; Krönkenhagen 3; singles/doubles from €44/67)* is central, quiet and homey. In Warnemünde, finding good, cheap accommodation is easy in winter and makes a wonderful alternative to Rostock.

In central Rostock, **Kölsch & Altbierhaus** *(☎ 490 38 62; Wokrenter Strasse 36; dinner mains €5-14)* has a woodsy, pub atmosphere; lunches and pub selections are cheaper. For those looking to explore Rostock's Swedish heritage, **Tre Kronor** *(☎ 490 42 60; Lange Strasse 11; mains €7.50-15.80)* offers you salmon, reindeer and elk. Quick bites are available in the **Rostocker Hof** shopping centre, off Universitätsplatz.

In Warnemünde, along **Alter Strom**, the picturesque fishing harbour, stallholders sell the daily catch – fresh, smoked or in bread rolls...it's delicious! Fish restaurants abound.

Getting There & Around

Frequent trains run from Berlin-Zoo (€33.40, 2¾ hours), Stralsund (€10.70, one hour), Schwerin (€12.40, 1¼ hours) and Hamburg (€28, 2¼ hours).

Vehicle-passenger ferries cross to Trelleborg (Sweden) and Gedser (Denmark) from Rostock Seaport (bus No 19 or 20). **Scandlines** *(***W** *www.scandlines.de; passengers €14-19)* has services daily between Rostock and Trelleborg (5¾ hours). Trips to Gedser cost €5 to €8 per person and take up to two hours. **TT-Line** *(☎ 040-360 14 42, fax 360 14 07;* **W** *www.TTLine.de; passengers €40)* departs from Rostock for Trelleborg several times daily using fast and slow boats (three to six hours).

For local transport *Tageskarte* (day tickets) cost €3.15. For two zones (covering Rostock and Warnemünde), single rides cost €1.70; for one zone it's €0.90. The double-decker

S-Bahn north to Warnemünde departs from Rostock Hauptbahnhof every 15 minutes during the day, every 30 minutes in the evenings, and hourly from midnight to dawn.

STRALSUND

☎ 03831 • pop 61,500

Stralsund, an enjoyable city on the Baltic Sea north of Berlin, is almost completely surrounded by water. It was a Hanseatic city in the Middle Ages and later was under Swedish control. Today it's an attractive, historic town with fine museums and buildings, pleasant walks and a restful, uncluttered waterfront. The island of Rügen is just across the sound, the Strelasund, and in summer the ferry to Hiddensee Island leaves from here.

Stralsund Tourismuszentrale *(☎ 246 90; e info@stralsund-tourismus.de; Alter Markt 9; open Mon-Sat, daily May-Sept)* is near the northern focus of the old town. Pick up a pamphlet guide to the city's Gothic architecture (€0.50). The **post office** *(Neuer Markt)* is opposite the Marienkirche.

Things to See & Do

On Alter Markt is the medieval **Rathaus**, where you can stroll through the vaulted and pillared structures and around to the impressive **Nikolaikirche** *(☎ 29 71 99)*. The 14th-century **Marienkirche** *(☎ 29 35 29; Neuer Markt; open 10am-noon Mon-Sat, 2pm-4pm Sat, 11.30am-noon Sun)* is a massive, red-brick edifice typical of north German Gothic architecture.

There are two excellent museums on Mönchstrasse. **Deutsches Meeresmuseum** *(German Oceanographic Museum; ☎ 265 00; Katharinenberg 14-20; adult/concession €4.50/3; open 9am-6pm daily July & Aug, 10am-5pm rest of year)* is an oceanic complex in a 13th-century convent church. Some exhibits contain tropical fish and coral, while others display creatures of the Baltic and North Seas. The **Kulturhistorisches Museum** *(Cultural History Museum; ☎ 287 90; Mönchstrasse 25-27; adult/concession €3/1.50; open 10am-5pm Tues-Sun)* has a collection housed in the cloister of an old convent.

Many fine buildings have been restored on the showpiece **Mühlenstrasse** near Alter Markt. The old harbour is close by, and you can stroll along the sea wall, then west along the waterfront park for a great view of the skyline of Stralsund.

Places to Stay & Eat

The excellent Stralsund **Jugendherberge** *(☎ 29 21 60, fax 29 76 76; e jh-stralsund@t-online.de; Am Kütertor 1; juniors/seniors €14.30/17)* is in the 17th-century waterworks at the western edge of the Altstadt. **Jugendherberge Devin** *(☎ 49 02 89, fax 40 02 91; e jh-devin@djh-mv.de; Strandstrasse 219; juniors/seniors €14.30/17; open Mar-Nov)* is by the sea, 8km east of town in the village of Devin. To get there take bus No 3 from Stralsund Hauptbahnhof.

Herwig's Hotel *(☎ 266 80, fax 26 68 23; w www.herwigs.de; Heilgeiststrasse 50; singles/doubles from €50/70)* has quite good rooms with facilities. The new **Hotel Kontorhaus** *(☎ 28 90 00, fax 28 98 09; e info@kontorhaus-stralsund.de; Am Querkanal 1; singles/doubles from €55/65)* offers flash rooms and flashier city or harbour views.

Torschliesserhaus *(☎ 29 30 32; Am Kütertor; mains €7.40-14.90)* is a cosy pub in the old gatekeeper's house next to the youth hostel. The **Hansekeller** *(☎ 70 38 40; Mönchstrasse 48; mains €7-12.30)* serves hearty, regional dishes in a vaulted cellar. There's also a selection of *imbisse* (snack stands) around Apollonienmarkt.

Getting There & Away

Frequent IR trains run to/from Rostock (€10.70, 50 minutes), Berlin (€35, three hours), Schwerin (€22.40, two hours) and Hamburg (€38.20, 3¼ hours). International trains between Berlin and Stockholm or Oslo use the car ferry connecting Sassnitz Mukran harbour on Rügen Island with Trelleborg and Malmö (Sweden). Two or three daily connections to Stockholm are available.

From Stralsund there are about 20 daily trains to Sassnitz (€8.10, one hour) on Rügen Island, most of which connect at Bergen for Binz (€8.10, one hour). In summer you can also catch **Weisse Flotte ferries** *(☎ 0180-321 21 50; €0.18 per minute)* to Hiddensee Island.

RÜGEN ISLAND

Germany's largest island is just northeast of Stralsund, connected by a causeway. Once the summer haunt of Germany's leading thinkers, politicos and businesspeople (including Einstein), it fell on hard times during the war and GDR eras, but since reunification it's being brought back to life.

The island's highest point is the 117m **Königsstuhl**, reached by car or bus from Sassnitz. The **chalk cliffs** that tower above the sea are the main attraction. Much of Rügen and its surrounding waters are either national park or protected nature reserves. The **Bodden** inlet area is a bird refuge popular with bird-watchers. **Kap Arkona**, on Rügen's north shore, is famous for rugged cliffs and two lighthouses.

The main resort area is in eastern Rügen, around the towns of Binz, Sellin and Göhren. A lovely **hike** from Binz to Sellin skirts the cliffs above the sea through beech and pine forest and offers great coastal views. Another destination is **Jagdschloss Granitz** (1834), which is also surrounded by lush forest. **Prora**, up the coast from Binz, is the site of a 2km-long workers' retreat built by Hitler before the war, now housing several museums.

Tourismus Verband Rügen (☎ *03838-807 70;* Ⓦ *www.ruegen.de; Am Markt 4)* in Bergen, the administrative centre, publishes a huge booklet listing all accommodation on the island and other useful information. Otherwise, Rügen has dozens of tourist offices, both municipal and private. **Tourismusgesellschaft Binz** (☎ *038393-134 60;* Ⓔ *tourismusAG@binz.de; Hauptstrasse 1, Binz)* is especially helpful.

Rügen has 21 **camping grounds**; the largest concentration is found at Göhren. The island's only **Jugendherberge** (☎ *038393-325 97, fax 325 96;* Ⓔ *jugendherberge-binz@t-online.de; Strandpromenade 35; beds junior/senior €18.30/22.30)* is across from the beach in Binz. Binz is the island's top resort, with lodgings known for their distinctive *Bäderarkitektur* (spa architecture) of whitewashed wooden balconies. **Hotel Villa Neander** (☎ *038393-42 90, fax 038393-529 99;* Ⓔ *glasner@binz.de; Hauptstrasse 16; rooms from €41 per person)* has warm rooms and friendly owners. At **Lohme** (☎ *038302-9221; Dorfstrasse 35, Lohme)*, on the island's northern side, you can dine on regional specialties while watching the sun set over Kap Arkona.

Local trains run almost hourly from 8am to 9pm between Stralsund and Sassnitz (€8.10, one hour) or Binz via Bergen (€8.10, one hour). A fun narrow-gauge train links Putbus to Göhren via Binz.

Fares for Baltic ferries vary with the season. **Scandlines** (Ⓦ *www.scandlines.de)* runs five passenger-vehicle ferries daily from Sassnitz Mukran ferry terminal, 5km south of town, to/from Trelleborg, Sweden (€10-15 one way). Scandlines also has at least two services weekly to/from Ronne on Bornholm, Denmark (daily in summer; €12-17). To reach the ferries by train, make sure you go to Sassnitz Mukran station. Otherwise, catch a bus or walk from Sassnitz.

Greece

If you're going to Greece, you're in great company. The first travel guide to Greece was written 1800 years ago by the geographer and historian Pausanias. Since then, millions of visitors have come to revel in the splendour of this legendary land, cradle of Western civilisation and birthplace of its culture. You'll be far from solitary on your wanderings, whether you're exploring tiny Byzantine churches or kicking back on an idyllic Mediterranean beach. But we know you're unique.

Greece's enduring attraction is its archaeological sites; those who travel through Greece journey not only through the landscape but also through time, witnessing the legacy of Europe's greatest ages – the Mycenaean, Minoan, classical, Hellenistic and Byzantine. You cannot wander far without stumbling across a broken column or a crumbling bastion, perhaps neglected and forgotten but still retaining an aura of former glory.

Contemporary Greek culture is a unique blend of East and West, inherited from the long period of Ottoman rule. The mountainous countryside is a walker's paradise crisscrossed by age-old donkey tracks leading to stunning vistas.

The magnetism of Greece is also due to less tangible attributes – the dazzling clarity of the light, the floral aromas that permeate the air, and perhaps most subtly, the spirit of places. There is hardly a grove, mountain or stream that is not sacred to a deity, and the ghosts of the past still linger. But they are benevolent spirits, and they have infused their land and people with a warmth – both physical and psychological – that is as apparent today as it was millennia ago.

Greece: the Basics

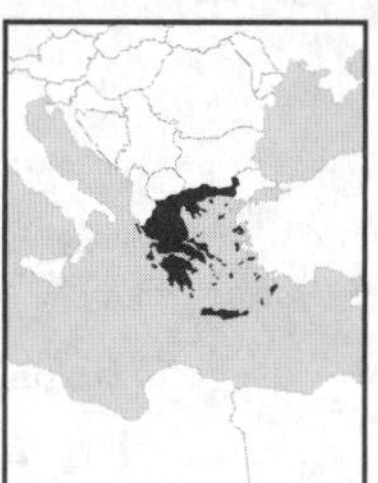

Local name Ελλάδα (Ellada)

Capital Athens

Population 10.9 million

Language Greek

Currency euro (€) = 100 centimes

Avoid at all costs Bar touts and scams

Attempt to vary your diet by claiming *Ime allergikos sto eleolado.* (I'm allergic to olive oil.)

Facts about Greece

HISTORY

During the Bronze Age, which lasted from 3000 to 1200 BC in Greece, the advanced Cycladic, Minoan and Mycenaean civilisations flourished. The Mycenaeans were eventually replaced by the Dorians, who introduced Greece to the Iron Age. The next 400 years are often referred to as the Dark Ages, a period about which very little is known. Homer's *Odyssey* and *Iliad* were composed at this time.

By 800 BC, when Homer's works were first written down, Greece was undergoing a cultural and military revival with the evolution of the city-states, the most powerful of which were Athens and Sparta. The unified Greeks repelled the Persians twice, at Marathon (490 BC) and Salamis (480 BC). Victory over Persia was followed by a period of unparalleled growth and prosperity known as the classical (or golden) age. This is the period when the Parthenon was commissioned by Pericles, Sophocles wrote *Oedipus the King*, and Socrates taught young Athenians to think. The golden age ended with the Peloponnesian War (431–404 BC). So embroiled were the Greeks in this war that they failed to notice the expansion of Macedonia under King Philip II, who easily conquered the city-states. Philip's ambitions were surpassed by those of his son Alexander the Great, who marched triumphantly into Asia Minor, Egypt, Persia and what are now parts of Afghanistan and India.

Roman incursions began in 205 BC, and by 146 BC Greece and Macedonia had become Roman provinces. In AD 395, Greece became part of the eastern (Byzantine) Empire, based at Constantinople. The end of the Byzantine Empire came in 1453, when Constantinople fell to the Turks. Most of Greece soon became part of the Ottoman Empire. By the 19th century the long-lived Ottoman Empire had become the 'sick man of Europe'. The Greeks, seeing nationalism sweep through Europe,

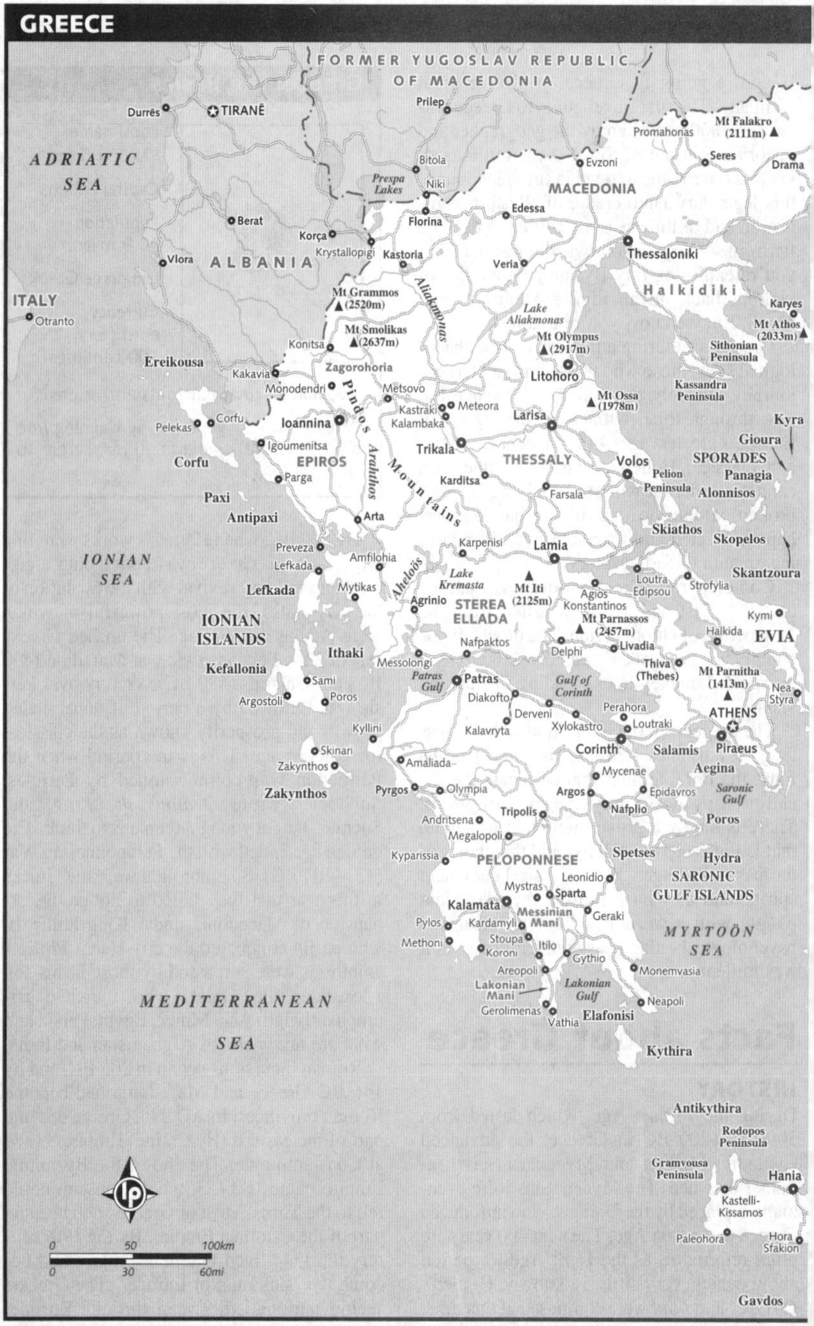

GREECE

FORMER YUGOSLAV REPUBLIC OF MACEDONIA
Prilep
Durrës
TIRANË
ADRIATIC SEA
Bitola
Prespa Lakes
Niki
Berat
Florina
Korça
Krystallopigi
Kastoria
Vlora
ALBANIA
ITALY
Otranto
Promahonas
Mt Falakro (2111m)
Evzoni
Seres
Drama
MACEDONIA
Edessa
Thessaloniki
Veria
Halkidiki
Karyes
Mt Athos (2033m)
Sithonian Peninsula
Kassandra Peninsula
Mt Grammos (2520m)
Aliakmonas
Lake Aliakmonas
Mt Olympus (2917m)
Mt Smolikas (2637m)
Konitsa
Zagorohoria
Litohoro
Ereikousa
Kakavia
Monodendri
Pindos
Metsovo
Kastraki
Meteora
Kalambaka
Mt Ossa (1978m)
Larisa
Pelekas
Corfu
Ioannina
Igoumenitsa
Trikala
Corfu
EPIROS
Arahthos
Mountains
THESSALY
Volos
Pelion Peninsula
Kyra
Gioura
SPORADES
Panagia
Alonnisos
Parga
Karditsa
Farsala
Paxi
Antipaxi
Arta
Skiathos
Skopelos
Preveza
Karpenisi
Lamia
IONIAN SEA
Lefkada
Amfilohia
Lake Kremasta
Mt Iti (2125m)
Loutra Edipsou
Strofylia
Skantzoura
Lefkada
Mytikas
Aheloös
Agrinio
STEREA ELLADA
Agios Konstantinos
Kymi
IONIAN ISLANDS
Mt Parnassos (2457m)
Halkida
EVIA
Nafpaktos
Delphi
Livadia
Ithaki
Messolongi
Thiva (Thebes)
Mt Parnitha (1413m)
Kefallonia
Patras Gulf
Patras
Gulf of Corinth
Sami
Nea Styra
Argostoli
Poros
Diakofto
Derveni
Perahora
ATHENS
Xylokastro
Loutraki
Kyllini
Kalavryta
Piraeus
Corinth
Salamis
Skinari
Zakynthos
Amaliada
Aegina
Mycenae
Zakynthos
Pyrgos
Olympia
Argos
Epidavros
Saronic Gulf
Nafplio
Tripolis
Poros
Andritsena
Megalopoli
Spetses
Kyparissia
PELOPONNESE
Hydra
Leonidio
SARONIC GULF ISLANDS
Mystras
Sparta
Kalamata
Messinian Mani
Geraki
Pylos
Kardamyli
MYRTOÖN SEA
Methoni
Stoupa
Itilo
Koroni
Gythio
Areopoli
Monemvasia
Lakonian Mani
Lakonian Gulf
MEDITERRANEAN SEA
Neapoli
Gerolimenas
Vathia
Elafonisi
Kythira
Antikythira
Rodopos Peninsula
Gramvousa Peninsula
Hania
Kastelli-Kissamos
Paleohora
Hora Sfakion
Gavdos
0 50 100km
0 30 60mi

GREECE

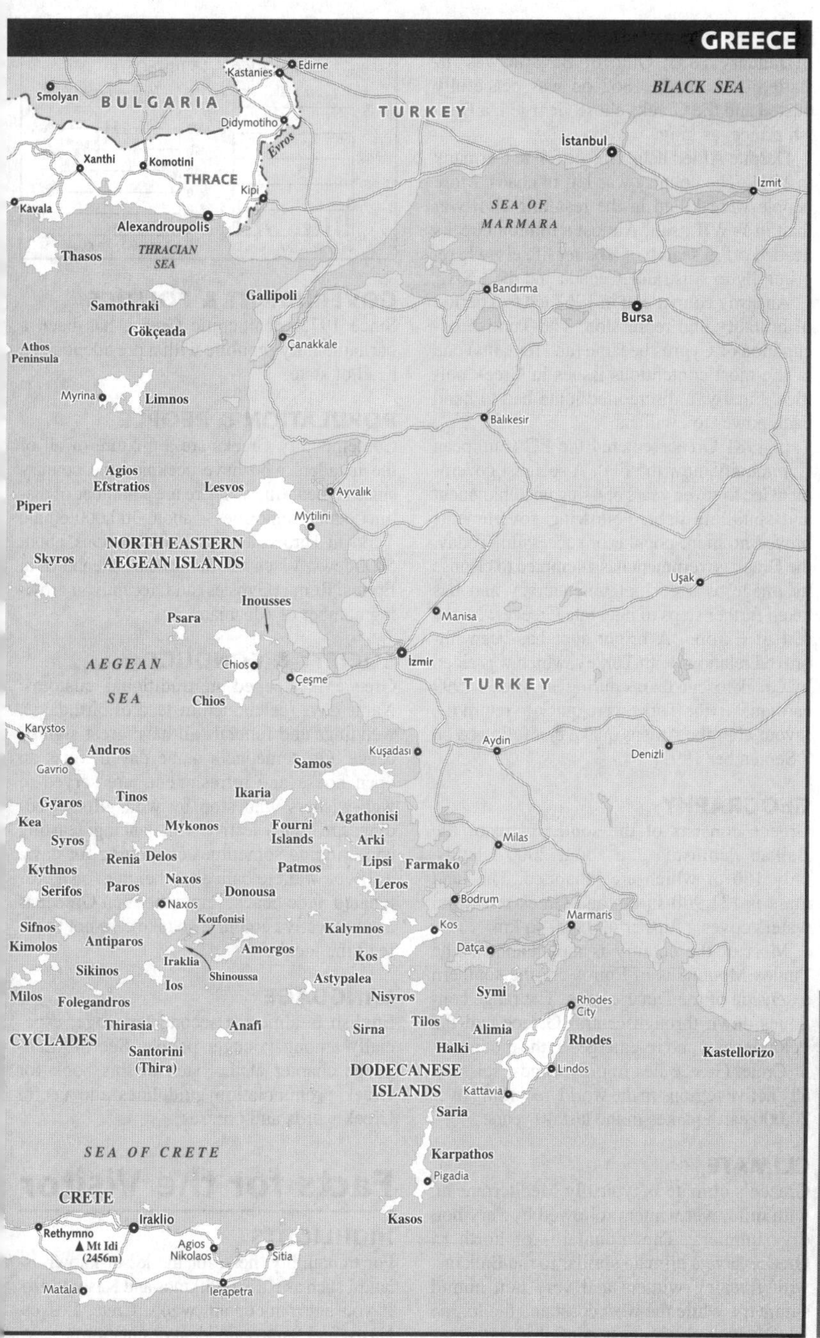

GREECE

fought the War of Independence (1821–32). In January 1833, Otho of Bavaria was installed as king. In 1862 he was peacefully ousted and the Greeks chose George I, a Danish prince, as king.

Despite Allied help, Greece fell to Germany in 1941. The country was left in chaos. More people were killed in the resulting civil war than in WWII itself. Almost a million Greeks headed off in search of a better life elsewhere, primarily to Australia, Canada and the USA.

An army coup d'etat in 1967 led to a period of brutality and repression. The Turkish occupation of Cyprus became (and remains) one of the most contentious issues in Greek politics. Finally, a discredited junta had to hand back power to civilians.

In 1981 Greece entered the EC (European Community, now the EU). A socialist government led to seven years of rising unemployment and spiralling debt. Following governments proved no more popular or successful. Today, the Greek government has attempted to cleanse its image as a corrupt bureaucracy and has taken further steps to integrate Greece with the rest of Europe. A bright spot has been improved relations with Turkey, which was aided by Greek rescue teams during an August 1999 earthquake (the Turks were quick to return the favour after the Athens quake that followed on 7 September 1999).

GEOGRAPHY

Greece consists of the southern tip of the Balkan Peninsula and about 2000 islands, only 166 of which are inhabited. The land mass is 131,900 sq km and Greek territorial waters cover a further 400,000 sq km.

Most of the country is mountainous. The Pindos Mountains in Epiros are the southern extension of the Dinaric Alps. The range continues down through central Greece and the Peloponnese, and re-emerges in the mountains of Crete. Greece lies in one of most seismically active regions in the world, recording over 20,000 earthquakes in the last 40 years.

CLIMATE

Greece's climate is typically Mediterranean, with mild, wet winters followed by very hot, dry summers. The mountains of northern Greece have a climate similar to the Balkans, with freezing winters and very hot, humid summers, while the west coast and the Ionian Islands have the highest rainfall.

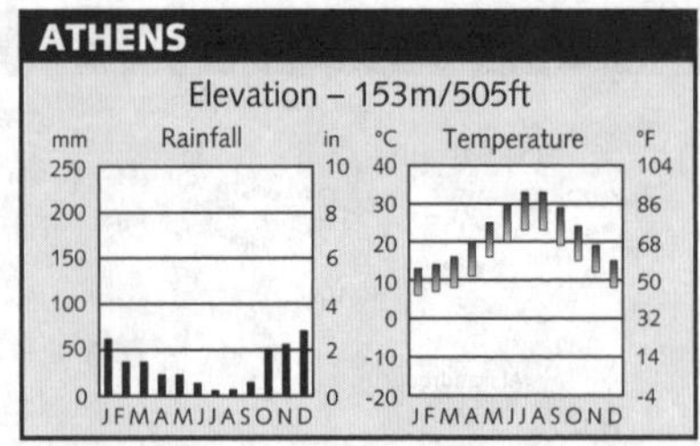

GOVERNMENT & POLITICS

Since 1975, democratic Greece has been a parliamentary republic with a president as its head of state.

POPULATION & PEOPLE

Contemporary Greeks are a mixture of all of the invaders who have occupied the country since ancient times. There are a number of distinct ethnic minorities – about 300,000 ethnic Turks in Thrace, about 100,000 Britons, about 5000 Jews, Vlach and Sarakatsani shepherds in Epiros, Roma (Gypsies) and, recently, a growing number of Albanians.

SOCIETY & CONDUCT

Greece is steeped in traditional customs. Name days (celebrated instead of birthdays), weddings and funerals all have great significance. On someone's name day there is an open house and refreshments are served to well-wishers who stop by with gifts. Weddings are highly festive with dancing, feasting and drinking sometimes continuing for days.

If you want to bare all, other than on a designated nude beach, remember that Greece is a conservative country, so take care not to offend the locals.

LANGUAGE

English is almost a second language, especially among younger people. See the Language chapter at the back of this book for Greek pronunciation guidelines and useful Greek words and phrases.

Facts for the Visitor

HIGHLIGHTS

For tranquillity, head for the lesser-known islands, such as Kassos, Sikinos and Kastellorizo. If you enjoy mountain walks, Crete, Lesvos, Naxos and Samos are ideal destinations.

Greece has more ancient sites than any other country in Europe. The big-time ones are the Acropolis, Delphi, Knossos and Olympia. The leading museum is the National Archaeological Museum in Athens. The Thessaloniki Museum contains treasures from the graves of the Macedonian royal family, and the Iraklio Museum houses a vast collection from the Minoan sites of Crete.

Two of Greece's most spectacular Byzantine cities are in the Peloponnese: the ghostly city of Mystras and Monemvasia. There are some stunning towns on the islands. Rhodes is the finest surviving example of a fortified medieval town in Europe, while Naxos' *hora* (main village or town) is a maze of narrow, stepped alleyways of whitewashed Venetian houses, their tiny gardens ablaze with flowers.

PLANNING

Spring and autumn are the best times to visit. Outside the major cities, winter is pretty much a dead loss – unless you're going to take advantage of the cheap skiing. The islands go into hibernation between late November and early April. The cobwebs are dusted off in time for Easter, and conditions are perfect until the end of June. From July until mid-September, it's on for young and old as northern Europe heads for the Mediterranean en masse.

TOURIST OFFICES

The Greek National Tourist Organisation (GNTO) is known as EOT in Greece. There is either an EOT office or a local tourist office in almost every town of consequence and on many of the islands. Most do no more than give out brochures and maps. Popular destinations have tourist police, who can often help in finding accommodation.

Local Tourist Offices

The **EOT main tourist office** *(☎ 21 0331 0561/0562, fax 21 0325 2895; W www.gnto.gr; Amerikis 2, Athens 105 64)* can help with information. Other tourist offices are listed throughout this chapter.

Tourist Offices Abroad

Australia (☎ 02-9241 1663) 51–57 Pitt St, Sydney, NSW 2000
Canada (☎ 416-968 2220) 91 Scollard St, Toronto, Ontario M5R 1G4
(☎ 514-871 1535) 1170 Place Du Frere Andre, Montreal, Quebec H3B 3C6
France (☎ 01-42 60 65 75) 3 Ave de l'Opéra, Paris 75001
Germany (☎ 069-236 561) Neue Mainzerstrasse 22, 60311 Frankfurt
(☎ 089-222 035) Pacellistrasse 5, 2W 80333 Munich
(☎ 040-454 498) Neurer Wall 18, 20254 Hamburg
(☎ 030-217 6262) Wittenbergplatz 3A, 10789 Berlin 30
Italy (☎ 06-474 4249) Via L Bissolati 78-80, Rome 00187
(☎ 02-860 470) Piazza Diaz 1, 20123 Milan
Japan (☎ 03-350 55 917) Fukuda Bldg West, 5th Floor 2-11-3 Akasaka, Minato-ku, Tokyo 107
UK (☎ 020-7734 5997) 4 Conduit St, London W1R ODJ
USA (☎ 212-421 5777) Olympic Tower, 645 5th Ave, New York, NY 10022
(☎ 312-782 1084) Suite 160, 168 North Michigan Ave, Chicago, Illinois 60601
(☎ 213-626 6696) Suite 2198, 611 West 6th St, Los Angeles, California 92668

VISAS & DOCUMENTS

Nationals of Australia, Canada, EU countries, Israel, New Zealand and the USA are allowed to stay in Greece for up to three months without a visa. For longer stays, apply at a consulate abroad or at least 20 days in advance to the **Aliens Bureau** *(☎ 21 0770 5711; Leoforos Alexandras 173, Athens)* at Athens Central Police Station. Elsewhere in Greece, apply to the local police authority.

In the past, Greece has refused entry to those whose passport indicates that they have visited Turkish-occupied North Cyprus, although there are reports that this is less of a problem now. To be on the safe side, however, ask the North Cyprus immigration officials to stamp a piece of paper rather than your passport.

The most widely recognised (and thus the most useful) form of student ID is the International Student Identity Card (ISIC). Holders qualify for half-price admission to museums and ancient sites, and for discounts at some budget hotels and hostels.

EMBASSIES & CONSULATES

Greek Embassies Abroad

Greece has diplomatic representation in the following countries:

Australia (☎ 02-6273 3011) 9 Turrana St, Yarralumla, ACT 2600
Canada (☎ 613-238 6271) 76–80 Maclaren St, Ottawa, Ontario K2P 0K6

France (☎ 01-47 23 72 28) 17 Rue Auguste Vaquerie, 75116 Paris
Germany (☎ 0228-83010) An Der Marienkapelleb 10, 53 179 Bonn
Italy (☎ 06-854 9630) Via S Mercadante 36, Rome 3906
Japan (☎ 03-340 0871/0872) 3-16-30 Nishi Azabu, Minato-ku, Tokyo 304-5853
New Zealand (☎ 04-473 7775) 5–7 Willeston St, Wellington
South Africa (☎ 12-437 351/352) 1003 Church St, Hatfield, Pretoria 0028
Turkey (☎ 312-436 8860) Ziya-ul-Rahman Caddesi 9–11, Gazi Osman Pasa 06700, Ankara
UK (☎ 020-7229 3850) 1A Holland Park, London W11 3TP
USA (☎ 202-939 5818) 2221 Massachusetts Ave NW, Washington, DC, 20008

Embassies in Greece

The following countries have diplomatic representation in Greece:

Australia (☎ 21 0645 0404) Dimitriou Soutsou 37, Athens 115 21
Canada (☎ 21 0727 3400) Genadiou 4, Athens 115 21
France (☎ 21 0361 1663) Leoforos Vasilissis Sofias 7, Athens 106 71
Germany (☎ 21 0728 5111) Dimitriou 3 & Karaoli, Kolonaki 106 75
Italy (☎ 21 0361 7260) Sekeri 2, Athens 106 74
Japan (☎ 21 0775 8101) Athens Tower, Leoforos Messogion 2–4, Athens 115 27
New Zealand (☎ 21 0687 4701) Kifissias 268, Halandri 152 32; honorary consulate
South Africa (☎ 21 0680 6645) Kifissias 60, Maroussi, Athens 151 25
Turkey (☎ 21 0724 5915) Vasilissis Georgiou 8, Athens 106 74
UK (☎ 21 0723 6211) Ploutarhou 1, Athens 106 75
USA (☎ 21 0721 2951) Leoforos Vasilissis Sofias 91, Athens 115 21

CUSTOMS

Duty-free allowances in Greece are the same as for other EU countries. The export of antiques is prohibited.

MONEY

Greece uses the euro. Banks will exchange all major currencies, in either cash or travellers cheques and also Eurocheques (see Money in the Facts for the Visitor chapter for more information on exchange rates). Post offices charge a lower commission than banks, but won't cash travellers cheques. All major credit cards are accepted, but only in larger establishments. You'll find ATMs everywhere, particularly in tourist areas.

Greece is still a cheap country by northern European standards, but it is no longer dirt-cheap. A rock-bottom daily budget would be €25. Allow at least €50 per day if you want your own room and plan to eat out regularly, as well as see the sights.

In restaurants the service charge is included on the bill, but it is the custom to leave a small tip – just round off the bill. Accommodation, which eats up a large part of the daily budget, is generally about 25% cheaper outside the high season, especially if you are staying more than one night. Souvenir shops are another place where you can bargain for substantial savings.

Value-added tax (VAT) varies from 15% to 18%. A tax-rebate scheme applies at a restricted number of shops and stores; look for a Tax Free sign in the window.

POST & COMMUNICATIONS

Post offices are usually open from 7.30am to 2pm. In major cities they stay open until 8pm and are also open 7.30am to 2pm on Saturday. Mail can be sent poste restante to any main post office and is held for up to one month.

The phone system is modern and efficient. All public phone boxes use phonecards, sold at Organismos Tilepikoinonion Ellados (OTE) telephone offices and *periptera* (street kiosks). It's also possible to use these phones using a growing range of discount-card schemes, such as Kronokarta and Teledome, which involve dialling an access code and then punching in your card number. The cards come with instructions in Greek and English.

If you're calling Greece from abroad, the country code is ☎ 30. If you're making an international call from Greece, the international access code is ☎ 00.

Greece was slow to embrace the wonders of the Internet, but is now striving to make up for lost time. Internet cafés are springing up everywhere. Charges vary radically – from less than €3.50 per hour in big cities up to €15 per hour on Mykonos.

DIGITAL RESOURCES

There has been a huge increase in the number of websites providing information about Greece. A good place to start is the 500 Links to Greece listed at www.viking1.com/corfu/link.htm. One site that it doesn't provide a link to is www.greektravel.com, the front door for an assortment of interesting sites by Matt Barrett.

The Greek Ministry of Culture has put together an excellent site at www.culture.gr, which has loads of information about museums and ancient sites. Other websites include www.gogreece.com/travel and www.aegean.ch.

BOOKS

Lonely Planet's *Greece* contains more comprehensive information on all the areas covered by this chapter, as well as coverage of less-visited areas, particularly in central and northern Greece. *Greek Islands* is especially tailored for island-hoppers. If you want to concentrate on specific regions, pick up Lonely Planet's guides to *Athens*, *Corfu & the Ionians*, *Crete*, *Rhodes & the Dodecanese,* and *Peloponnese* will be published in 2003.

The ancient Greek traveller Pausanias is acclaimed as the world's first travel writer. His *Guide to Greece* was written in the 2nd century AD and still makes fascinating reading.

WOMEN TRAVELLERS

Violent offences are very rare. Women travelling alone in rural areas are usually treated with respect. In rural areas it's sensible to dress conservatively, but it's perfectly OK to wear shorts, short skirts etc in touristy places.

GAY & LESBIAN TRAVELLERS

Homosexuality is generally frowned upon. It is wise to be discreet and to avoid open displays of togetherness. This has not prevented Greece from becoming a popular destination for gay travellers. Athens has a busy gay scene, but most people head for the islands – Mykonos and Lesvos in particular. Paros, Rhodes, Santorini (Thira) and Skiathos also have their share of gay hang-outs.

DISABLED TRAVELLERS

The hard fact is that most hotels, museums and ancient sites are not wheelchair accessible.

SENIOR TRAVELLERS

There are some good deals available for EU nationals. For starters, those over 60 qualify for a 50% discount on train travel plus five free journeys per year. Take your ID card or passport to a Greek Railways (OSE) office and you will be given a Senior Card. Pensioners also get a discount at museums and ancient sites.

Emergencies

The emergency number for the police is ☎ 100, tourist police ☎ 171, fire brigade ☎ 199 and ambulance (Athens only) ☎ 166. The Europe-wide emergency telephone number ☎ 112 can also be used. See Car & Motorcycle in the introductory Getting Around section later in this chapter for information regarding roadside assistance in the event of breakdown.

DANGERS & ANNOYANCES

Greece has the lowest crime rate in Europe. Athens is developing a bad reputation for petty theft and scams, but elsewhere crimes are most likely to be committed by other travellers.

LEGAL MATTERS

Greek drug laws are the strictest in Europe. Greek courts make no distinction between possession and pushing. Possession of even a small amount of marijuana is likely to land you in jail.

BUSINESS HOURS

Banks are open from 8.30am to 2.30pm Monday to Thursday, and 8.30am to 2pm Friday. Some city banks also open from 3.30pm to 6.30pm and on Saturday morning. Shops are open from 8am to 1.30pm and 5.30pm to 8.30pm on Tuesday, Thursday and Friday, and 8am to 2.30pm on Monday, Wednesday and Saturday, but these times are not always strictly adhered to. *Periptera* are open from early morning to midnight. All banks and shops, and most museums and archaeological sites, close during public holidays.

PUBLIC HOLIDAYS & SPECIAL EVENTS

Public holidays are as follows: New Year's Day (1 January), Epiphany (6 January), First Sunday in Lent (February), Greek Independence Day (25 March), Good Friday/Easter Sunday (March/April), Spring Festival/Labour Day (1 May), Feast of the Assumption (15 August), Okhi Day (28 October), Christmas Day (25 December) and St Stephen's Day (26 December).

Easter is Greece's most important festival, with candle-lit processions, feasting and firework displays. The Orthodox Easter is 50 days after the first Sunday in Lent.

A number of cultural festivals are also held during the summer months. The most important is the Athens Festival, when plays, operas, ballet and classical music concerts are staged at the Theatre of Herodes Atticus.

ACTIVITIES

Windsurfing & Surfing

Sailboards are widely available for hire, priced from €12. The top spots for windsurfing are Hrysi Akti on Paros, and Vasiliki on Lefkada, which is reputedly one of the best places in the world to learn.

Sailing facilities are harder to find, although the same locations recommended previously for windsurfing are all also ideal for sailing.

Hrysi Akti on Paros and Mylopotas Beach on Ios are two of the best locations. Hire charges for Hobie cats (catamarans) range from €20 to €25, depending on the gear and the location.

Skiing

Greece offers some of the cheapest skiing in Europe. There are 16 resorts dotted around the mainland, most in the north. They have all the basic facilities and are a pleasant alternative to the glitzy resorts of northern Europe.

The season depends on snow conditions, but runs approximately from January to the end of April. You'll find information about the latest snow conditions on the Internet at w www.snowreport.gr.

Hiking

The mountainous terrain of the Greek countryside is perfect for trekkers who want to get away from the crowds. The popular routes are well marked and well maintained, including the E4 and E6 trans-European treks, which both end in Greece.

A number of companies run organised treks. **Trekking Hellas** *(☎ 21 0323 4548, fax 21 0325 1474; w www.trekking.gr; Filellinon 7, Athens 105 57)* operates treks on the islands as well as on the mainland, while **Alpin Club** *(☎ 21 0729 5486, fax 21 0721 2773; w www.alpinclub.gr; Mihalakopoulou 39, Athens 115 28)* concentrates on the Peloponnese and central Greece.

WORK

Your best chance of finding work is to do the rounds of the tourist hotels and bars at the beginning of the season. The few jobs available are hotly contested, despite the menial work and dreadful pay. EU nationals don't need a work permit, but everyone else does.

ACCOMMODATION

There is a range of accommodation in Greece. All places to stay are subject to strict price controls set by the tourist police. By law, a notice must be displayed in every room, which states the category of the room and the price for each season. If you think you've been ripped off, contact the tourist police. Prices quoted in this book are for the high season; they're about 40% cheaper between October and May.

Greece has almost 350 camping grounds, a lot of them in great locations. Standard facilities include hot showers, kitchens, restaurants and minimarkets – and quite often there is a swimming pool. Prices vary according to facilities, but reckon on €4.50 per adult and €3 for a small tent.

Greece has 55 mountain refuges, which are listed in the booklet *Greece Mountain Refuges & Ski Centres*, available free of charge at EOT and EOS (Ellinikos Orivatikos Syndesmos, the Greek Alpine Club) offices.

You'll find youth hostels in most major towns and on half a dozen islands. The only place affiliated to Hostelling International (HI) is the excellent **Athens International Youth Hostel** *(☎ 21 0523 4170)*; see Places to Stay under Athens, later.

Most other youth hostels in Greece are run by the **Greek Youth Hostel Organisation** *(☎ 21 0751 9530, fax 21 0751 0616; e y-hostels@otenet.gr; Damareos 75, Athens 116 33)*. There are affiliated hostels in Athens, Olympia, Patras and Thessaloniki on the mainland, and on the islands of Crete and Santorini. Most charge €7 to €8, and you don't have to be a member to stay in any of them.

Domatia are the Greek equivalent of British B&Bs, minus the breakfast. Once upon a time, *domatia* consisted of little more than spare rooms that families would rent out in summer to supplement their income. Nowadays many *domatia* are purpose-built appendages to the family house. Rates start at about €18/25 for singles/doubles.

Hotels are classified as deluxe, A, B, C, D or E class. The ratings seldom seem to have much bearing on the price, but expect to pay €18/25 for singles/doubles in D and E class, and from €35/45 to €60/80 for singles/doubles in a decent C-class place with private bathroom. Some places are classified as *pensions* and are rated differently. Both are allowed to levy a 10% surcharge for stays of less than three nights, but they seldom do. It normally works the other way – you can bargain a cheaper rate if you're staying more than one night.

FOOD & DRINKS

Greece has a great range of fast-food options for the inveterate snacker. Foremost among them are the *gyros* and the *souvlaki*. The *gyros* is a giant skewer laden with seasoned meat that grills slowly as it rotates. *Souvlaki* are small, individual kebabs. Both are served wrapped in pitta bread with salad and lashings of *tzatziki* (a yogurt, cucumber and garlic dip).

Greece is famous for its appetisers, known as *mezedes* (literally, 'tastes'; meze for short). Standards include *tzatziki*, *melitzanosalata* (aubergine or eggplant dip), *taramasalata* (fish-roe dip), *dolmades* (stuffed vine leaves), *fasolia* (beans) and *oktapodi* (octopus). A selection of three or four starters represents a good meal and can be a good option for vegetarians.

You'll find moussaka (layers of aubergine and mince, topped with bechamel sauce and baked) on every menu, alongside a number of other taverna staples. They include *moschari* (oven-baked veal and potatoes), *keftedes* (meatballs), *stifado* (meat stew), *pastitsio* (baked dish of macaroni with mincemeat and bechamel sauce) and *yemista* (either tomatoes or green peppers stuffed with mincemeat and rice). The most popular fish are *barbouni* (red mullet) and *sifias* (swordfish), but they don't come cheap. Fortunately for vegetarians, salad is a mainstay of the Greek diet.

Bottled mineral water is cheap and available everywhere, as are soft drinks and packaged juices. Greece is traditionally a wine-drinking society. If you're spending a bit of time in the country, it's worth acquiring a taste for *retsina* (resinated wine).

Mythos and Alpha are two Greek beers to look out for.

ENTERTAINMENT

The busy nightlife is a major attraction for many travellers. Nowhere is the pace more frenetic than on the islands in high season. Discos abound in all resort areas, and Ios and Paros especially are famous for their raging discos and bars. If you enjoy theatre and classical music, Athens and Thessaloniki are the places to be.

Getting There & Away

AIR

Eleftherios Venizelos International Airport in Athens handles the vast majority of international flights, including all intercontinental flights. Most flights are with the national carrier, Olympic Airways, or the flag carrier of the country concerned.

Olympic Airways has daily flights to Athens from New York and up to three a week from Boston. Delta also has daily flights from New York. Apex fares range from US$960 to US$1550. It's worth shopping around for cheaper deals from the major European airlines. You should be able to get to Athens from Toronto and Montreal for about C$1150 or from Vancouver for C$1500. Olympic has up to five flights a week to Athens from Toronto via Montreal.

Olympic flies to Athens twice a week from Sydney via Melbourne. Fares range from A$1695 to A$2400.

Flying is the fastest, easiest and cheapest way of getting to Greece from northern Europe. What's more, scheduled flights are so competitively priced that it's hardly worth hunting around for charter cheapies.

Olympic Airways and British Airways both offer 30-day return tickets from London for about UK£240 (mid-week departures) in high season, as well as returns to Thessaloniki for about UK£225. At the time of writing, the cheapest fares were being offered by **EasyJet** *(☎ 0870 600 0000)*, which had flights from London (Stansted) to Athens from UK£69 one way.

LAND

Overland travel between northern Europe and Greece is virtually a thing of the past. All too often, direct travel from this region is prohibitively expensive and difficult.

The Hellenic Railways Organisation (OSE) has buses from Athens to Istanbul

(€67.50, 22 hours) at 7pm from Thursday to Tuesday, and to Tirana (€35.20, 21 hours) at 7pm daily.

There are daily trains between Athens and Istanbul for €58.70, leaving Athens from Larisis train station at 11.15pm. The trip takes 23 hours.

The crossing points into Turkey are at Kipi and Kastanies, the crossings into the Former Yugoslav Republic of Macedonia (FYROM) are at Evzoni and Niki, and the Bulgarian crossing is at Promahonas. All are open 24 hours a day. The crossing points to Albania are at Kakavia and Krystallopigi.

If you're thinking of hitchhiking to Turkey, look for a through-ride from Alexandroupolis, because you cannot hitchhike across the border.

SEA

Italy

The most popular crossing is from Brindisi to Patras (18 hours), via Corfu (nine hours) and Igoumenitsa (10 hours). There are numerous services. Deck-class fares start at about €35 one way in low season and €45 one way in high season. Eurail pass-holders can travel free with Blue Star Ferries and Hellenic Mediterranean. You still need to make a reservation and pay port taxes.

There are also ferries to Patras from Ancona, Bari, Trieste and Venice, stopping at either Corfu or Igoumenitsa on the way. In summer you can get ferries from Bari and Brindisi to Kefallonia.

Turkey

There are five regular ferry services between the Greek Islands and Turkey: Lesvos–Ayvalık, Chios–Çeşme, Samos–Kuşadası, Kos–Bodrum and Rhodes–Marmaris. All are daily services in summer, dropping to weekly in winter. Tickets must be bought a day in advance and you will be asked to hand over your passport. It will be returned on the boat.

Cyprus & Israel

Salamis Lines and Poseidon Lines operate services from Piraeus to the Israeli port of Haifa, via Rhodes and Lemessos (formerly Limassol) on Cyprus. Deck-class fares from Piraeus are €70.50 to Lemessos and €106 to Haifa.

Students and travellers aged under 30 qualify for a 20% discount on these fares.

Departure Taxes

Port taxes are €5.50 to Italy and €8.80 to Turkey, Cyprus and Israel.

Getting Around

AIR

Most domestic flights are operated by **Olympic Airways** (W *www.olympic-airways.gr*) and its offshoot, Olympic Aviation. They offer a busy schedule in summer with flights from Athens to 25 islands and a range of mainland cities. **Aegean Airlines** (W *www.aegeanair.com*) provides competition on a few major routes.

BUS

Buses are the most popular form of public transport. They are comfortable, they run on time and there are frequent services on all major routes. Almost every town on the mainland (except in Thrace) has at least one bus a day to Athens. Local companies can get you to all but the remotest villages. Reckon on paying about €4 per hour of journey time.

TRAIN

Trains are generally looked on as a poor alternative to bus travel. The main problem is that there are only two main lines: to Thessaloniki and Alexandroupolis in the north, and to the Peloponnese. If there are trains going in your direction, they are a good way to travel. Be aware that there are two distinct levels of service: the painfully slow, dilapidated trains that stop at all stations, and the faster, modern intercity trains.

Inter-Rail and Eurail passes are valid in Greece, but you still need to make reservations.

CAR & MOTORCYCLE

Greece recognises all national driving licences, provided the licence has been held for at least one year. It also recognises an International Driving Permit, which should be obtained before you leave home.

The Greek automobile club, ELPA, offers reciprocal services to members of other national motoring associations. If your vehicle breaks down, dial ☎ 104.

Car hire is expensive, especially from the multinational hire companies. High-season weekly rates with unlimited mileage start at about €380 for the smallest models, dropping to €300 in winter – and that's without

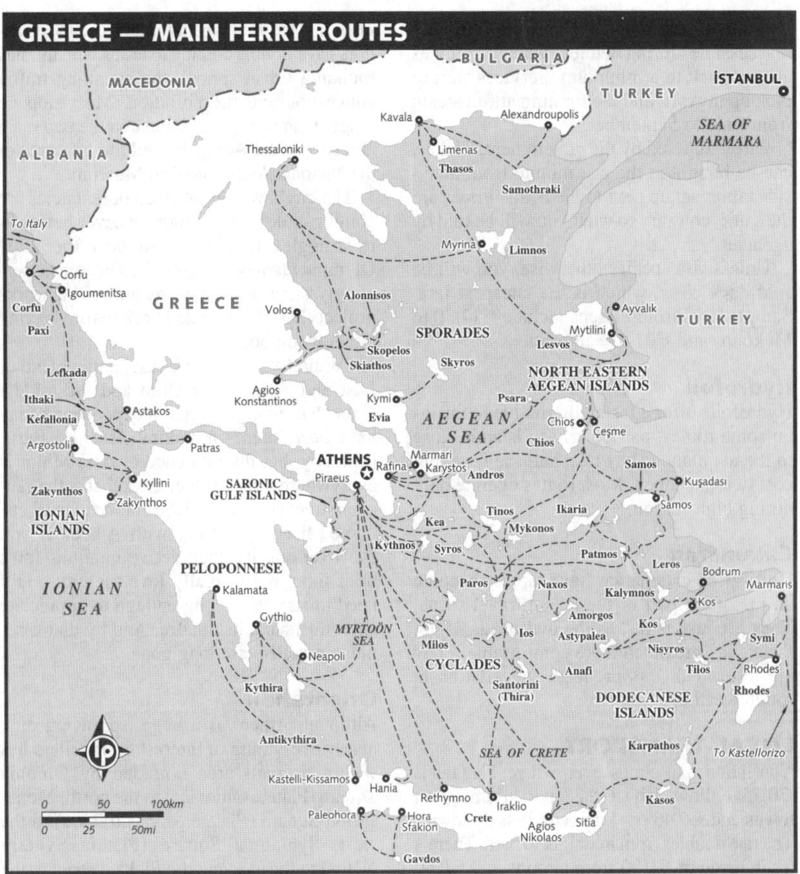

tax and extras. You can generally do much better with local companies. Mopeds, however, are cheap and available everywhere. Most places charge about €15 per day.

BICYCLE

Cycling is becoming a popular way to visit Greece. Bicycles are an ideal way to explore some of the larger islands, and they are carried free on ferries. The Peloponnese is another favourite cycling destination, but you need strong leg muscles to tackle the mountainous terrain.

HITCHING

The farther you are from a city, the easier hitching becomes. Getting out of major cities can be hard work, and Athens is notoriously difficult. In remote areas, people may stop to offer a lift even if you aren't hitching.

BOAT

Ferry

Every island has a ferry service of some sort. They come in all shapes and sizes, from the state-of-the-art 'superferries' that run on the major routes to the ageing open ferries that operate local services to outlying islands.

The hub of the vast ferry network is Piraeus, the main port of Athens. It has ferries to the Cyclades, Crete, the Dodecanese, the Saronic Gulf Islands and the northeastern Aegean Islands. Patras is the main port for ferries to the Ionian Islands, while Volos and Agios Konstantinos are the ports for the Sporades.

Some of the smaller islands are virtually inaccessible during winter, when schedules are cut back to a minimum. Services start to pick up in April and are running at full steam from June to September.

Fares are fixed by the government. Tickets can be bought at the last minute from quayside tables set up next to the boats. Prices are the same, contrary to what you will be told by agencies.

Unless you specify otherwise, you will be sold deck class, which is the cheapest fare. Sample fares from Piraeus include €17.30 to Mykonos and €21 to Santorini.

Hydrofoil

Hydrofoils offer a faster alternative to ferries on some routes, particularly to islands close to the mainland. They take half the time, but cost twice as much. Most routes operate only during high season.

Catamaran

High-speed catamarans have rapidly become an important part of the island travel scene. They are just as fast as the hydrofoils, if not faster, and are much more comfortable. They are also much less prone to cancellation in rough weather.

LOCAL TRANSPORT

You'll find taxis almost everywhere. Flag fall is €0.75, followed by €0.23 per kilometre in towns and €0.46 per kilometre outside towns. The rate doubles from midnight to 5am. There's a surcharge of €0.90 from airports and €0.60 from ports, bus stations and train stations. Luggage is charged at €0.30 per item over 10kg.

Taxis in Athens and Thessaloniki often pick up extra passengers along the way (yell out your destination as they cruise by; when you get out, pay what's on the meter, minus what it read when you got in, plus €0.75).

In rural areas taxis don't have meters, so make sure you agree on a price with the driver before you get in.

Athens Αθήνα

pop 3.7 million

Ancient Athens outranks Rome and Jerusalem for its glorious past and mighty influence on Western civilisation, but the modern city is a place that few people fall in love with. However inspiring the monuments might be, most visitors have trouble coming to terms with the surrounding urban sprawl, the appalling traffic congestion and the pollution. Most stop no longer than is required to take in the two main attractions: the Acropolis and the treasures of the National Archaeological Museum.

The city's well-publicised deficiencies are coming under the spotlight as never before as it struggles to prepare to host the 2004 Olympic Games. Progress has been exasperatingly slow, and some major public works projects have been scaled back before leaving the drawing board.

Culturally, Athens is a fascinating blend of East and West. King Otho and the middle class that emerged after independence may have been intent on making Athens a European city, but the influence of Asia Minor is everywhere – the coffee, the kebabs, the raucous street vendors and the colourful markets.

You'll enjoy a fling with Athens if you can overlook its unattractive qualities for a brief time, but to really love the city you'd need to stay there long enough to appreciate and understand its culture. And by that time, most travellers are long gone.

Orientation

Although Athens is a huge, sprawling city, nearly everything of interest to travellers lies within a small area bounded by Omonia Square (Plateia Omonias) to the north, Monastiraki Square (Plateia Monastirakiou) to the west, Syntagma Square (Plateia Syntagmatos) to the east and the Plaka district to the south. The city's two major landmarks, the Acropolis and Lykavittos Hill, can be seen from just about everywhere in this area.

Syntagma is the heart of modern Athens. Flanked by luxury hotels, banks and fast-food restaurants, the square is dominated by the old royal palace – home of the Greek parliament since 1935.

Omonia has developed a sorry reputation for sleaze in recent years, but this is set to change with the announcement of a plan to transform Plateia Omonias from a traffic hub into an expanse of formal gardens. This is guaranteed to create traffic chaos, since all the major streets of central Athens meet here. Panepistimiou (El Venizelou) and Stadiou run parallel southeast to Syntagma, while Athinas leads south to the market district of Monastiraki. Monastiraki is in turn linked to

Syntagma by Ermou – home to some of the city's smartest shops – and Mitropoleos.

Mitropoleos skirts the northern edge of Plaka, the delightful old quarter which was virtually all that existed when Athens was declared the capital of independent Greece. Its labyrinthine streets are nestled on the northeastern slope of the Acropolis, and most of the city's ancient sites are close by. It may be touristy, but it's the most attractive and interesting part of Athens.

Information

Tourist Offices Athens' main **EOT tourist office** *(☎ 21 0331 0561/0562, fax 21 0325 2895; Ⓦ www.gnto.gr; Amerikis 2; open Mon-Fri)* is close to Syntagma. It has a free map of Athens, as well as information about public transport, including ferry departures from Piraeus. There's also an EOT office at the airport *(☎ 21 0353 0445; open daily)*.

The **tourist police** *(☎ 21 0920 0724; Veikou 43, Koukaki; trolleybus No 1, 5 or 9 from Syntagma; open 24hr)* have a 24-hour **information service** *(☎ 171)*.

Money Most of the major banks have branches around Syntagma. The **National Bank of Greece** *(cnr Karageorgi Servias & Stadiou)* is open extended hours for foreign-exchange dealings only. It also has an ATM.

For money exchange try **American Express** *(AmEx; ☎ 21 0324 4975; Ermou 2)* or **Eurochange** *(☎ 21 0322 0155; Karageorgi Servias 4)*, which has an office nearby. It changes Thomas Cook travellers cheques without commission.

Acropole Foreign Exchange *(Kydathineon 23; open 9am-midnight daily)* is in Plaka. The airport also has several ATMs.

Post & Communications The **Athens Central Post Office** *(Eolou 100, postcode 102 00, Omonia)* is where mail addressed to poste restante will be sent unless specified otherwise. If you're staying in Plaka, it's best to get mail sent to the Syntagma post office (postcode 103 00) on the corner of Plateia Syntagmatos and Mitropoleos.

The main **OTE telephone office** *(28 Oktovriou-Patission 85)* is open 24 hours.

Internet cafés are popping up like mushrooms all over Athens. Most charge from €4 to €6 per hour of computer time, whether you log on or not. Try the following places.

Bits and Bytes Internet Café Akadimias 78, Exarhia; open 24 hours

Museum Internet Café Oktovriou-Patission 46, Omonia (next to the National Archaeological Museum); open 9am to 3am daily

Plaka Internet World Pandrosou 29, Monastiraki; open 11am to 11pm daily

Skynet Internet Centre Cnr Voulis & Apollonos, Plaka; open 9am to 11pm Monday to Saturday

Sofokleous.com Internet Café Stadiou 5, Syntagma (behind Flocafé); open 10am to 10pm Monday to Saturday, 1pm to 9pm Sunday

Travel Agencies The bulk of the city's travel agencies are around Plateia Syntagmatos, particularly in the area just south of the square on Filellinon, Nikis and Voulis.

Reputable agencies include **STA Travel** *(☎ 21 0321 1188, 21 0321 1194; ⓔ statravel@robissa.gr; Voulis 43)* and **USIT-Etos Travel** *(☎ 21 0324 0483, fax 21 0322 8447; ⓔ usit@usitetos.gr; Filellinon 7)*. Both these places also issue ISIC cards.

Medical & Emergency Services For emergency medical treatment, ring the **tourist police** *(☎ 171)* and they'll tell you where the nearest hospital is. Hospitals give

Scammy Scams, Bar None

Lonely Planet receives a steady flow of letters warning about bar scams, particularly around Syntagma. The most popular version runs something like this: friendly Greek approaches solo male traveller and discovers that the traveller knows little about Athens; friendly Greek then reveals that he, too, is from out of town. Why don't they go to this great little bar that he's just discovered and have a beer? They order a drink, and the equally friendly owner then offers another drink. Women appear, more drinks are provided and the visitor relaxes as he realises that the women are not prostitutes, just friendly Greeks. The crunch comes at the end of the evening when the traveller is presented with an exorbitant bill and the smiles disappear. The con men who cruise the streets playing the role of the friendly Greek can be very convincing – some people have been taken in more than once.

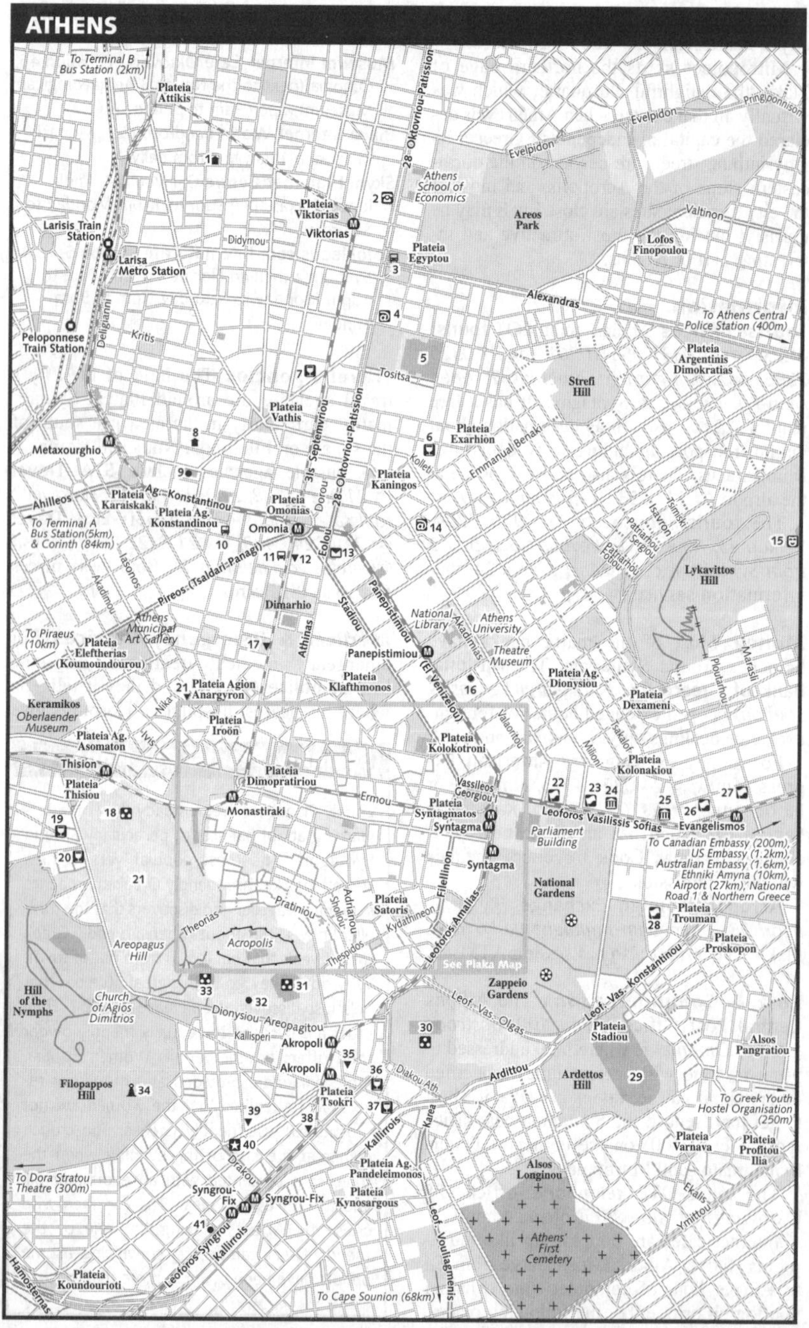

ATHENS

To Terminal B Bus Station (2km)
Plateia Attikis
1
28 Oktovriou-Patission
Pringiponnison
Evelpidon
Athens School of Economics
Areos Park
2
Plateia Viktorias
Viktorias
Larisis Train Station
Larisa Metro Station
Didymou
Plateia Egyptou
3
Valtinon
Lofos Finopoulou
Alexandras
4
To Athens Central Police Station (400m)
Peloponnese Train Station
Deligianni
Kritis
5
Plateia Argentinis Dimokratias
7
Tositsa
Strefi Hill
Plateia Vathis
3is Septemvriou
28 Oktovriou-Patission
8
Metaxourghio
6
Plateia Exarhion
Kolleti
Emmanual Benaki
9
Plateia Kaningos
Ahilleos
Plateia Karaiskaki
Ag. Konstantinou
Plateia Ag. Konstandinou
Plateia Omonias
Dorou
To Terminal A Bus Station(5km), & Corinth (84km)
Omonia
14
Tsimiski
Isavron
Patriarhou Sergiou
Patriarhou Foiou
15
10
11
12
13
Eolou
Iasonos
Akadimou
Pireos (Tsaldari Panagi)
Dimarhio
Stadiou
Panepistimiou
Lykavittos Hill
Athens Municipal Art Gallery
National Library
Athens University
Akadimias
To Piraeus (10km)
Plateia Eleftherias (Koumoundourou)
17
Athinas
Panepistimiou
(El Venizelou)
Theatre Museum
Plateia Klafthmonos
16
Plateia Ag. Dionysiou
Ploutarhou
Marasli
21
Plateia Agion Anargyron
Plateia Dexameni
Keramikos
Oberlaender Museum
Nika
Plateia Iroon
Valaoritou
Ivis
Plateia Ag. Asomaton
Plateia Kolokotroni
Tsakalof
Milioni
Thision
Plateia Kolonakiou
Plateia Dimopratiriou
Vassileos Georgiou I
22
23
24
Plateia Thisiou
Ermou
25
26
27
18
Monastiraki
Plateia Syntagmatos
Syntagma
Leoforos Vasilissis Sofias
Evangelismos
19
Parliament Building
To Canadian Embassy (200m), US Embassy (1.2km), Australian Embassy (1.6km), Ethniki Amyna (10km), Airport (27km), National Road 1 & Northern Greece
20
Syntagma
21
Filellinon
National Gardens
Adrianou
Sholiou
Plateia Satoris
Pratiniou
Kydathineon
Plateia Trouman
28
Theorias
Leoforos Amalias
Plateia Proskopon
Acropolis
Thespidos
Areopagus Hill
See Plaka Map
Leof. Vas. Konstantinou
33
31
Zappeio Gardens
Hill of the Nymphs
Church of Agios Dimitrios
32
Leof. Vas. Olgas
Dionysiou Areopagitou
Kallisperi
Plateia Stadiou
Akropoli
30
Alsos Pangratiou
35
Akropoli
36
Diakou Ath
Ardittou
Ardettos Hill
29
Filopappos Hill
34
Plateia Tsokri
37
Karea
To Greek Youth Hostel Organisation (250m)
39
38
Kallirrois
Plateia Varnava
Plateia Profitou Ilia
40
Drakou
Alsos Longinou
To Dora Stratou Theatre (300m)
Plateia Ag. Pandeleimonos
Syngrou-Fix
Syngrou-Fix
Plateia Kynosargous
Ekalis
Leof. Vouliagmenis
Ymittou
41
Leoforos Syngrou
Kallirrois
Athens' First Cemetery
Hamosternas
Plateia Koundourioti
To Cape Sounion (68km)

GREECE

free emergency treatment to tourists. For hospitals with outpatient departments on duty, call ☎ 106. For first-aid advice, ring ☎ 166.

Dangers & Annoyances A major problem in Athens is pickpockets. Their favourite hunting grounds are the metro system and the crowded streets around Omonia, particularly Athinas. The Sunday market on Ermou is another place where it pays to take extra care of your valuables.

Working in league with some overpriced C-class hotels around Omonia, some taxi drivers have become a problem. The scam involves taxi drivers picking up late-night arrivals, particularly at the airport and Bus Terminal A, and persuading them that the hotel they want to go to is full.

Acropolis

Most of the buildings now gracing the Acropolis *(combined site & museum admission €12; site open 8am-6.30pm daily, museum open 8am-6.30pm Tues-Sun, noon-6.30pm Mon Apr-Oct; site & museum open 8am-2.30pm daily Nov-Mar)* were commissioned by Pericles during the golden age of Athens in the 5th century BC. The site had been cleared for him by the Persians, who destroyed an earlier temple complex on the eve of the Battle of Salamis.

The entrance to the Acropolis is through the **Beule Gate**, a Roman arch that was added in the 3rd century AD. Beyond this is the **Propylaia**, the monumental gate that was the entrance to the city in ancient times. It was damaged by Venetian bombing in the 17th century, but it has since been restored. To the south of the Propylaia is the small, graceful **Temple of Athena Nike**, which is not accessible to visitors.

Standing supreme over the Acropolis is the monument which more than any other epitomises the glory of ancient Greece – the **Parthenon**. Completed in 438 BC, this building is unsurpassed in grace and harmony. To achieve perfect form, its lines were ingeniously curved to counteract cacophonous optical illusions. The base curves upward slightly towards the ends, and the columns become slightly narrower towards the top, with the overall effect of making them both look straight.

Above the columns are the remains of a Doric frieze, which was partly destroyed by Venetian shelling in 1687. The best surviving pieces are the controversial Elgin Marbles, carted off to Britain by Lord Elgin in 1801. The Parthenon, dedicated to Athena, contained an 11m-tall gold-and-ivory statue of the goddess completed in 438 BC by Phidias of Athens (only the statue's foundations exist today).

To the north is the **Erechtheion** and its much-photographed Caryatids, the six maidens who support its southern portico. These are plaster casts – the originals (except for the one taken by Lord Elgin) are in the site's **museum**.

The €12 admission charge buys a collective ticket that also gives entry to all the other significant ancient sites: the Ancient Agora, the Roman Agora, the Keramikos, the Temple of Olympian Zeus and the Theatre of Dionysos. The ticket is valid for 48 hours, otherwise individual site fees apply.

ATHENS

PLACES TO STAY
1 Hostel Aphrodite
8 Athens International Youth Hostel

PLACES TO EAT
12 Marinopoulos (Supermarket)
17 Fruit & Vegetable Market
35 Oinomageireion ton Theon
38 To 24 Hours
39 Veropoulos (Supermarket)

OTHER
2 OTE Telephone Office
3 Mavromateon Bus Terminal
4 Museum Internet Café
5 National Archaeological Museum
6 AN Club
7 Rodon Club
9 OSE Office
10 Bus No 051 to Bus Terminal A
11 Bus No 049 to Piraeus
13 Athens' Central Post Office
14 Bits and Bytes Internet Café
15 Lykavittos Theatre
16 OSE Office
18 Temple of Hephaestus
19 Stavlos
20 To Lizard
21 Ancient Agora
22 French Embassy
23 Italian Embassy
24 Benaki Museum
25 Goulandris Museum of Cycladic & Ancient Greek Art
26 German Embassy
27 British Embassy
28 Turkish Embassy
29 Roman Stadium
30 Temple of Olympian Zeus
31 Theatre of Dionysos
32 Stoa of Eumenes
33 Theatre of Herodes Atticus
34 Monument of Filoppapos
36 Lamda Club
37 Granazi Bar
40 Tourist Police
41 Olympic Airways Head Office

Ancient Theatres

The importance of theatre in the life of the Athenian city-state can be gauged from the dimensions of the enormous **Theatre of Dionysos** *(enter from Dionysiou Areopagitou; admission €2; open 8am-7pm Tues-Fri, 8.30am-3pm Sat-Sun Apr-Oct; 8.30am-3pm daily Nov-Mar)*, just south of the Acropolis. Built between 342 and 326 BC on the site of an earlier theatre, in its time it could hold 17,000 people spread over 64 tiers of seats, of which about 20 tiers survive.

The **Stoa of Eumenes**, built as a shelter and promenade for theatre audiences, runs west from the Theatre of Dionysos to the **Theatre of Herodes Atticus**, which was built in Roman times. It is used for performances during the Athens Festival, but is closed at other times.

Temple of Olympian Zeus

Begun in the 6th century BC, this massive temple *(admission €2; open 8.30am-3pm Tues-Sun)* took more than 700 years to complete. Emperor Hadrian eventually finished the job in AD 131. It was the largest temple in Greece, impressive for the sheer size of its 104 **Corinthian columns** (17m high with a base diameter of 1.7m). The site is just southeast of Plaka, and the 15 remaining columns are a useful landmark.

Roman Stadium

The stadium, just east of the Temple of Olympian Zeus, hosted the first Olympic Games of modern times in 1896. It was originally built in the 4th century BC as a venue for the Panathenaic athletic contests. The seats were rebuilt in Pentelic marble by Herodes Atticus in the 2nd century AD, and faithfully restored in 1895.

Ancient & Roman Agoras

The **ancient agora** *(admission €4; open 8am-7pm daily Apr-Oct; 8.30am-3pm Tues-Sun Nov-Mar)* was the marketplace of ancient Athens and the focal point of civic and social life. Socrates spent much time here expounding his philosophy. The main monuments are the well-preserved **Temple of Hephaestus**, the 11th-century **Church of the Holy Apostles** and the reconstructed **Stoa of Attalos**, which houses the site's museum.

The Romans built their **agora** *(admission €2; open 8.30am-2.30pm Tues-Sun)* just west of its ancient counterpart. Its principal monument is the wonderful **Tower of the Winds**, built in the 1st century BC by a Syrian astronomer named Andronicus. Each side represents a point of the compass, and has a relief carving depicting the associated wind.

Museums

Athens has no fewer than 28 museums, displaying everything from ancient treasures to old theatre props. You'll find a complete list at the tourist office, but three are unmissable. First comes the star of the show: the **National Archaeological Museum** *(28 Oktovriou-Patission 44; admission €6; open 12.30pm-7pm Mon, 8am-7pm Tues-Sun Apr-Oct; 10.30am-5pm Mon, 8.30am-3pm Tues-Sun Nov-Mar)*, unquestionably the most important museum in the country, with finds from all the major sites. The crowd-pullers are the magnificent, exquisitely detailed gold artefacts from Mycenae and the spectacular Minoan frescoes from Santorini, which are here until a suitable museum is built on the island.

Second place goes to the **Benaki Museum** *(cnr Vasilissis Sofias & Koumbari; admission €5.90; open 9am-5pm Mon, Wed, Fri & Sat, 9am-midnight Thurs, 9am-3pm Sun)*, which houses the collection of Antoine Benaki, the son of an Alexandrian cotton magnate named Emmanual Benaki. The collection includes ancient sculpture, Persian, Byzantine and Coptic objects, Chinese ceramics, icons, two El Greco paintings and a superb collection of traditional costumes.

Rounding out the triumvirate is the **Goulandris Museum of Cycladic & Ancient Greek Art** *(Neofytou Douka 4; admission €2.95; open 10am-4pm Mon & Wed-Fri, 10am-3pm Sat)*. This private museum was custom-built to display a fabulous collection of Cycladic art, with an emphasis on the early Bronze Age. Particularly impressive are the beautiful marble figurines. These simple, elegant forms, mostly of naked women with arms folded under their breasts, inspired 20th-century artists such as Brancusi, Epstein, Modigliani and Picasso.

Special Events

The annual Hellenic Festival is the city's most important cultural event, running from mid-June to late September. It features a line-up of international music, dance and theatre at the Theatre of Herodes Atticus. The setting is superb, backed by the floodlit Acropolis. Information and tickets are available from the

Athens Festival Box Office *(Stadiou 4)*. You'll find details at Ⓦ www.greekfestival.gr.

Places to Stay

Hostels There are a few places around town making a pitch for the hostelling market by tagging 'youth hostel' onto their name. There are some dreadful dumps among them.

There is only one youth hostel worth knowing about: the HI-affiliated **Athens International Youth Hostel** *(☎ 523 4170, fax 523 4015; Ⓔ info2002yh@yahoo.com; Victor Hugo 16; dorm beds HI members €8.40)*. Apart from its location, the place is almost too good to be true. The spotless rooms, each with bathroom, sleep two to four. You need to become a HI member; if you're not a member the joining fee is €12.35, or €2.05 for a daily stamp.

Hotels Athens is a noisy city and Athenians keep late hours, so an effort has been made to select hotels in quiet areas. Plaka is the most popular place to stay, and it has a good choice of accommodation right across the price spectrum. Rooms fill up quickly in July and August, so it's wise to make a reservation.

Plaka Most backpackers head to the **Student & Travellers' Inn** *(☎ 21 0324 4808, fax 21 0321 0065; Ⓔ students-inn@ath.forthnet.gr; Kydathineon 16; dorm beds €18, singles/doubles with shared bathroom €32/42, singles/doubles with private bathroom €36/52)*. Facilities include a courtyard with big-screen TV, Internet and a travel service.

Festos Youth & Student Guest House *(☎ 21 0323 2455, fax 21 0321 0907; Ⓔ consolas@hol.gr; Filellinon 18)* is the main budget alternative.

Hotel Adonis *(☎ 21 0324 9737, fax 21 0323 1602; Kodrou 3; singles/doubles from €39/55.70)*, opposite the Acropolis House Pension, is a comfortable modern hotel with air-con rooms.

Monastiraki The friendly, family-run **Hotel Tempi** *(☎ 21 0321 3175, fax 21 0325 4179; Ⓔ tempihotel@travelling.gr; Eolou 29; singles with shared bathroom €28, doubles/triples with private bathroom €42/50)* is a quiet place on the pedestrian precinct part of Eolou. Rooms at the front overlook a small square with a church and a flower market. It has a small communal kitchen where guests can prepare breakfast.

Omonia Area There are dozens of hotels around Omonia, but most of them are either bordellos masquerading as cheap hotels or uninspiring, overpriced C-class places.

Hostel Aphrodite *(☎ 21 0881 0589, fax 21 0881 6574; Ⓔ hostel-aphrodite@ath.forthnet.gr; Einardou 12; dorm beds €17, singles/doubles/triples with shared bathroom €30/40/54; singles/doubles with private bathroom €32/42)* is a fair way north of Omonia, but it's only 10 minutes from the train stations. It offers Internet access and there's a bar.

Places to Eat

Plaka For most people, Plaka is the place to be. It's hard to beat the atmosphere of dining out beneath the floodlit Acropolis. You do, however, pay for the privilege – particularly at the outdoor restaurants around the square on Kydathineon. The best of this bunch is **Byzantino** *(☎ 21 0322 7368; Kydathineon 20; mains €3.50-12)*, which prices its menu more reasonably and is popular with Greek family groups.

Eden Vegetarian Restaurant *(☎ 21 0324 8858; Lyssiou 12; mains €8-12; open Wed-Mon)* is one of only two vegetarian restaurants, which are thin on the ground in Athens. The Eden has been around for years, substituting soy products for meat in tasty vegetarian versions of moussaka and other Greek favourites.

South of the Acropolis A new place just five minutes' walk from Plaka, **Oinomageireion ton Theon** *(☎ 21 0924 3721; Makrigianni 23-27; mains €4-9)* has a great selection of meze, priced from €2, as well as tasty versions of favourites such as beef *stifado* and moussaka. There are good views of the Acropolis from the window seats.

To 24 Hours *(☎ 21 0922 2749; Syngrou 44; mains €4-6.50)* is a great favourite with Athenian night owls. As the name suggests, it's open 24 hours. It calls itself a *patsadakia*, which means that it specialises in *patsas* (tripe soup), but it always has a wide selection of taverna dishes.

Syntagma Fast food is the order of the day around busy Syntagma with an assortment of Greek and international offerings.

Furin Kazan Japanese Fast-Food Restaurant *(☎ 21 0322 9170; Apollonos 2; mains €5-16; open 11am-11pm Mon-Sat)* is the place to head for anyone suffering from a surfeit of Greek salad and *souvlaki*. It's reassuring to see that the Furin Kazan is always full of Japanese visitors. Follow your nose to the **Brazil Coffee Shop** *(Voukourestiou 2)* for the best coffee in town.

Entertainment

The weekly *Athens News* carries a 16-page entertainment guide listing weekly events, while the *Kathimerini* supplement that accompanies the *International Herald Tribune* has daily listings.

Clubs & Bars Clubs operate in central Athens only between October and April. In summer, the action moves to the coastal suburbs of Glyfada and Ellinikon.

Most bars around Plaka and Syntagma are places to avoid, especially if there are guys outside touting for customers.

Brettos *(Kydathineon 41)*, a delightful old family-run place right in the heart of Plaka, is one bar that's recommended. Huge old barrels line one wall, and the shelves are stocked with an eye-catching collection of coloured bottles.

Most bars in Athens have music as a main feature. Thisio is a good place to look, particularly on Iraklidon. **Stavlos** *(Iraklidon 10)* occupies an amazing old rabbit warren of a building.

Gay Venues The greatest concentration of gay bars is to be found on the streets off Syngrou, south of the Temple of Olympian Zeus. Popular spots include the long-running **Granazi Bar** *(Lembesi 20)* and the more risque **Lamda Club** *(Lembesi 15)*. These places don't open until after 10pm, and don't warm up until after midnight.

To Lizard *(Apostolou Pavlou 31)*, in Thisio, is a party bar which operates Friday to Sunday nights from 11pm. The crowd is mostly lesbian, with a few gays and the occasional straight.

Rock & Jazz Concerts Local bands play at the **AN Club** *(Solomou 20, Exarhia)*, while **Rodon Club** *(Marni 24)*, north of Omonia, hosts touring international rock bands.

Folk Dancing Performances by **Dora Stratou Dance Company** *(☎ 21 0921 6650; tickets €11.75)* are presented on Filopappos Hill

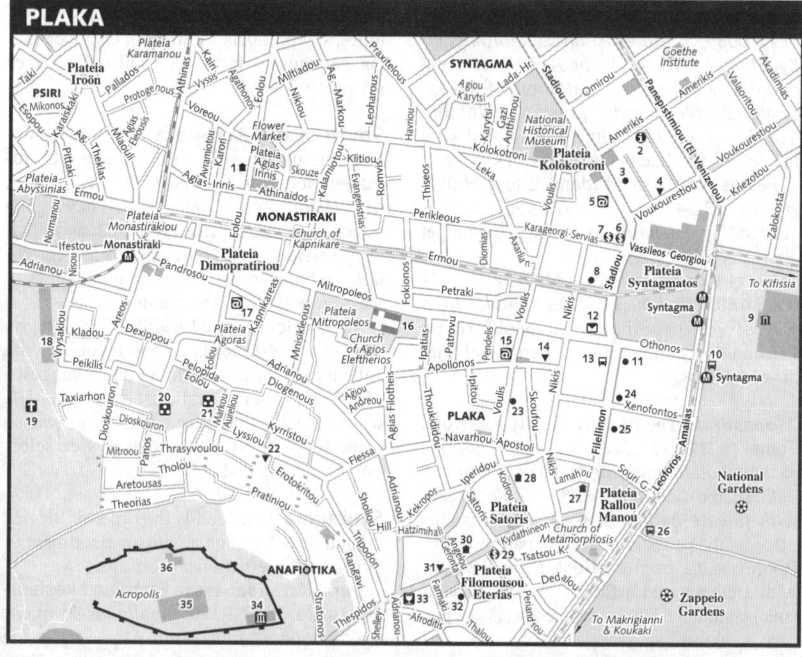

at 10.15pm every night from mid-May to October, with additional performances at 8.15pm on Wednesday. Filopappos Hill is west of the Acropolis, off Dionysiou Areopagitou. Bus No 230 from Syntagma will get you there.

Getting There & Away

Air Athens is served by gleaming Eleftherios Venizelos International Airport at Sparta, 27km east of Athens.

For Olympic Airways flight information ring ☎ 21 0936 3363; for all other airlines ring ☎ 21 0969 4466/4467. The head office of **Olympic Airways** *(☎ 21 0926 7251/4)* is at Leoforos Syngrou Andrea 96. The most central **Olympic Airways branch office** *(☎ 21 0926 7444, international ☎ 21 0926 7489)* is at Filellinon 13, just off Plateia Syntagmatos.

Bus Athens has two main intercity bus stations. EOT gives out schedules for both stations detailing departure times, journey times and fares.

Terminal A *(Kifissou 100)*, northwest of Omonia, has departures to the Peloponnese, the Ionian Islands and western Greece. To get to Terminal A, take bus No 051 from the junction of Zinonos and Menandrou, near Plateia Omonia. Buses run every 15 minutes from 5am to midnight.

Terminal B *(off Liossion)* is north of Omonia and has departures to central and northern Greece, as well as to Evia. To get to Terminal B, take bus No 024 from outside the main gate of the National Gardens on Amalias. EOT misleadingly gives the terminal's address as Liossion 260, which turns out to be a small workshop. Liossion 260 is where you should get off the bus. Turn right onto Gousiou and you'll see the terminal at the end of the road.

Buses for Attica leave from the Mavromateon bus terminal at the junction of Alexandras and 28 Oktovriou-Patission, north of Omonia.

Train Athens has two train stations, about 200m apart on Deligianni, approximately 1km northwest of Omonia. Trains to the Peloponnese leave from the Peloponnese station, while trains to the north leave from Larisis station – as do all international services.

Services to the Peloponnese include eight trains to Patras, four of which are intercity express (€10, 3½ hours), while services north include 10 trains a day to Thessaloniki, five of which are intercity express (€27.60, six hours). The 7am service from Athens is express right through to Alexandroupolis, arriving at 7pm. There are also trains to Volos and Halkida in Evia. The easiest way to get to the stations is on Metro Line 2 to Larisa, outside Larisis station. The Peloponnese station is across the footbridge at the southern end of Larisis station. Tickets can be bought at the stations, or at **OSE offices** *(Sina 6 • Karolou 1)*.

Hitching Athens is the most difficult place in Greece to hitchhike from. Your best bet is to ask the truck drivers at the Piraeus cargo wharves. Otherwise, for the Peloponnese, take a bus from Panepistimiou to Dafni,

PLAKA

PLACES TO STAY
1 Hotel Tempi
27 Festos Youth & Student Guest House
28 Hotel Adonis
30 Student & Travellers' Inn

PLACES TO EAT
4 Brazil Coffee Shop
14 Furin Kazan Japanese Fast-Food Restaurant
22 Eden Vegetarian Restaurant
31 Byzantino

OTHER
2 EOT Main Tourist Office
3 Athens Festival Box Office
5 Sofokleous.com Internet Café
6 Eurochange
7 National Bank of Greece
8 American Express
9 Parliament Building
10 Bus E95 to Airport
11 USIT-Etos Travel
12 Syntagma Post Office
13 Bus No 040 to Piraeus
15 Skynet Internet Centre
16 Athens Cathedral
17 Plaka Internet World
18 Stoa of Attalos
19 Church of the Holy Apostles
20 Roman Agora
21 Tower of the Winds
23 STA Travel
24 Trekking Hellas
25 Olympic Airways Branch Office
26 Bus 024 to Bus Terminal B
29 Acropole Foreign Exchange
32 Laundrette
33 Brettos
34 Acropolis Museum
35 Parthenon
36 Erechtheion

where National Rd 8 begins. For northern Greece, take the metro to Kifissia, then a bus to Nea Kifissia and walk to National Rd 1.

Ferry See Piraeus, later in this chapter, for information on ferries travelling to and from the islands.

Getting Around

To/From the Airport There are two special express-bus services operating between the airport and the city, as well as a service between the airport and Piraeus.

Bus service E94 operates between the airport and the eastern terminus of Metro Line 3 at Ethniki Amyna, which is about 10km northeast of the city centre. According to the official timetable there are departures every 16 minutes between 6am and midnight. The journey takes about 25 minutes.

Service E95 operates between the airport and Plateia Syntagmatos. This line operates 24 hours a day with services approximately every 30 minutes. The bus stop is outside the National Gardens on Vasilissis Amalias on the eastern side of Plateia Syntagmatos. The journey takes between an hour and 90 minutes, depending on traffic conditions.

Service E96 operates between the airport and Plateia Karaïskaki in Piraeus. This line also operates 24 hours, with services approximately every 40 minutes.

Tickets for all these services cost €2.95. The tickets are valid for 24 hours, and can be used on all forms of public transport in Athens – buses, trolleybuses and the metro.

Taxi fares vary according to the time of day and level of traffic, but you should expect to pay €15 to €20 from the airport to the city centre, and €20 to €25 from the airport to Piraeus.

Bus & Trolleybus Blue-and-white suburban buses operate from 5am to midnight. Route numbers and destinations, but not the actual routes, are listed on the free EOT map. The map does mark the routes of the yellow trolleybuses, making them easy to use. They also run from 5am to midnight.

Special buses operate 24 hours a day to Piraeus. Bus No 040 leaves from the corner of Syntagma and Filellinon, and No 049 leaves from the Omonia end of Athinas. They run every 20 minutes from 6am to midnight, then hourly.

Tickets for all these services cost €0.45, and must be purchased before you board – either from a ticket booth or from a *periptero*. The same tickets can be used on either buses or trolleybuses and must be validated as soon as you board.

Metro The opening of the first phase of the long-awaited new metro system has transformed travel around central Athens. Coverage is still largely confined to the city centre, but that's good enough for most visitors. The following is a brief outline of the three lines that make up the network:

Line 1 This line is the old Kifissia–Piraeus line. Until the opening of lines 2 and 3, this was the metro system. It is indicated in green on maps and signs. Useful stops include Piraeus (for the port), Monastiraki and Omonia (city centre), Plateia Viktorias (National Archaeological Museum) and Irini (Olympic Stadium). Omonia and Attiki are transfer stations with connections to Line 2; Monastiraki will eventually become a transfer station with connections to Line 3.

Line 2 This line runs from Sepolia in the northwest to Dafni in the southeast. It is indicated in red on maps and signs. Useful stops include Larisa (for the train stations), Omonia, Panepistimiou and Syntagma (city centre) and Akropoli (Makrigianni). Attiki and Omonia are transfer stations for Line 1, while Syntagma is the transfer station for Line 3.

Line 3 This line runs northeast from Syntagma to Ethniki Amyna. It is indicated in blue on maps and signs. Useful stops are Evangelismos (for the museums on Vasilissis Sofias) and Ethniki Amyna (buses to the airport). Syntagma is the transfer station for Line 2.

Travel on lines 2 and 3 costs €0.75; Line 1 is split into three sections: Piraeus–Monastiraki, Monastiraki–Attiki and Attiki–Kifissia. Travel within one section costs €0.60, and a journey covering two or more sections costs €0.75. The same conditions apply everywhere though: tickets must be validated at the machines at platform entrances before travelling. The penalty for travelling without a validated ticket is €23.50.

The metro operates between 5am and midnight. Trains run every three minutes during peak periods, dropping to every 10 minutes at other times.

Taxi Athenian taxis are yellow. Flag fall is €0.75, and there's an additional surcharge of €0.60 from ports and train and bus stations, as well as a €0.90 surcharge from the airport. After that, the day rate (tariff 1 on the meter) is €0.23/km. The rate doubles between midnight and 5am (tariff 2 on the meter). Baggage is charged at the rate of €0.30 per item over 10kg. The minimum fare is €1.50, which covers most journeys in central Athens.

Around Athens

PIRAEUS ΠΕΙΡΑΙΑΣ

pop 171,000

Piraeus has been the port of Athens since classical times. These days it's little more than an outer suburb of the space-hungry capital, linked by a mish-mash of factories, warehouses and apartment blocks. The streets are every bit as traffic-clogged as Athens, and behind the veneer of banks and shipping offices most of Piraeus is pretty seedy. The only reason to come here is to catch a ferry or hydrofoil.

Orientation & Information

Piraeus consists of a peninsula surrounded by harbours. The most important of them is the Great Harbour (Megas Limin). All ferries leave from here, as do hydrofoil and catamaran services to Aegina and the Cyclades. There are dozens of shipping agencies around the harbour, as well as banks and a post office.

Zea Marina (Limin Zeas), on the other side of the peninsula, is the main port for hydrofoils to all the Saronic Gulf Islands, except Aegina. Northeast of here is the picturesque Mikrolimano (Small Harbour), which is lined with countless fish restaurants. There's an **EOT tourist office** *(☎ 21 0452 2586)* at Zea Marina.

Getting There & Away

Bus There are two 24-hour bus services between central Athens and Piraeus. Bus No 049 runs from Omonia to the Great Harbour, and bus No 040 runs from Syntagma to the tip of the Piraeus peninsula. No 040 is the service to catch for Zea Marina – get off at the Hotel Savoy on Iroön Polytehniou – and leave plenty of time as the trip can take over an hour in bad traffic. The fare is €0.45 for each service.

E96 buses to the airport leave from the southern side of Plateia Karaïskaki.

Metro The fastest and most convenient link between the Great Harbour and Athens is the metro. The station is close to the ferries, at the northern end of Akti Kalimassioti. There are metro trains every 10 minutes from 5am to midnight.

Train All services to the Peloponnese from Athens start and terminate at Piraeus, although some schedules don't mention it. The station is next to the metro.

Ferry The following information is a guide to departures between June and mid-September. Schedules are similar in April, May and October, but are radically reduced in winter – especially to smaller islands. The main branch of EOT in Athens has a reliable schedule, which is updated weekly.

Crete There are two boats a day to Iraklio; daily services to Hania and Rethymno; and three a week to Agios Nikolaos and Sitia.

Cyclades There are daily ferries to Amorgos, Folegandros, Ios, Kimolos, Kythnos, Milos, Mykonos, Naxos, Paros, Santorini, Serifos, Sifnos, Sikinos, Syros and Tinos; two or three ferries a week to Iraklia, Shinoussa, Koufonisi, Donousa and Anafi; none to Andros or Kea.

Dodecanese There are daily ferries to Kalymnos, Kos, Leros, Patmos and Rhodes; three a week to Karpathos and Kasos; and weekly services to the other islands.

Saronic Gulf Islands There are daily ferries to Aegina, Poros, Hydra and Spetses year-round.

North Eastern Aegean Islands There are daily ferries to Chios, Lesvos (Mytilini), Ikaria and Samos; and two a week to Limnos.

The departure points for the various ferry destinations are shown on the map of Piraeus. Note that there are two departure points for Crete. Check where to find your boat when you buy your ticket. See Boat under Getting Around, earlier in this chapter, and Getting There & Away sections for each island, for more information.

Hydrofoil & Catamaran Minoan Lines operate Flying Dolphins (hydrofoils) and high-speed catamarans to the Cyclades from early April to the end of October, and year-round services to the Saronic Gulf Islands.

All services to the Cyclades and Aegina leave from Great Harbour. Some services to Poros, Hydra and Spetses also leave from here, but most leave from Zea Marina.

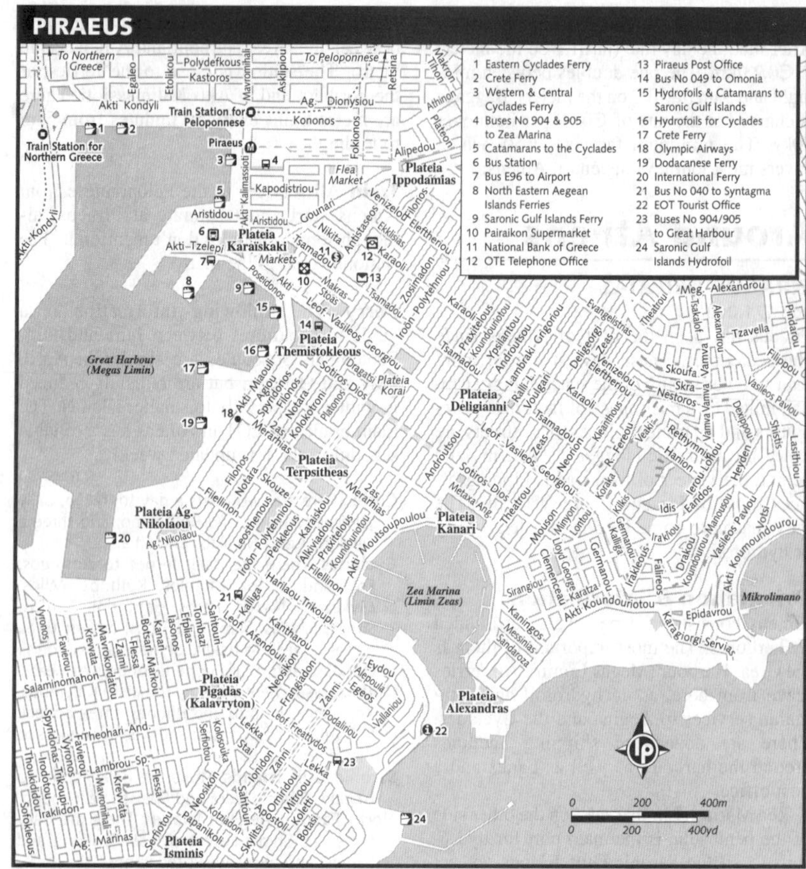

DELPHI ΔΕΛΦΟΙ

pop 2400

As with so many of Greece's ancient sites, the setting at Delphi – overlooking the Gulf of Corinth from the slopes of Mt Parnassos – is stunning. The Delphic oracle is thought to have originated in Mycenaean times, when the earth goddess Gaea was worshipped here. By the 6th century BC, Delphi had become the Sanctuary of Apollo and thousands of pilgrims came to consult the oracle, who was always a peasant woman of 50 years or more. She sat at the mouth of a chasm which emitted fumes. These she inhaled, causing her to gasp, writhe and shudder in divine frenzy. The pilgrim, after sacrificing a sheep or goat, would deliver a question, and the priestess' incoherent mumbling was then translated by a priest. Wars were fought, voyages embarked upon and business transactions undertaken on the strength of these prophecies.

The bus station, post office, OTE, National Bank of Greece and **tourist office** *(☎ 2265 082 900; Vasileon Pavlou 44; open 7.30am-2.30pm Mon-Fri)* are all on modern Delphi's main street, Vasileon Pavlou. The ancient site is 1km east of modern Delphi.

The **Sacred Way** leads up from the entrance of the site to the **Temple of Apollo** *(admission €6 site only, €9 site and museum; open 7.30am-7.15pm Mon-Fri, 8.30am-2.45pm Sat, Sun & public holidays)*. It was here that the oracle supposedly sat, although no chasm, let alone vapour, has been detected. The path continues to the theatre and stadium. Opposite this sanctuary is the **Sanctuary of Athena** *(admission free)* and the much-photographed **Tholos**, a 4th-century BC columned rotunda of Pentelic marble.

There are lots of hotels in the modern town, catering for the many tour groups who stop overnight. **Hotel Tholos** *(☎/fax 2265 082 268; Apollonos 31; singles/doubles with bathroom €15/30; open daily Mar-Nov, Fri & Sat only Dec-Mar)* is great value for rooms with air-con and TV. **Hotel Parnassos** *(☎ 2265 082 321; Vasileon Pavlou & Frederikis 32; singles/doubles €30/38)* is another good choice, and rates include buffet breakfast.

Taverna Vakhos *(☎ 2265 083 186; Apollonos 31; mains €4.80-10.50)*, next to the Hotel Tholos, turns out tasty taverna dishes such as lamb in lemon sauce with rice and potatoes (€5.60).

There are five buses a day to Delphi from Athens (€10.20, three hours).

SARONIC GULF ISLANDS ΝΗΣΙΑ ΤΟΥ ΣΑΡΩΝΙΚΟΥ

The Saronic Gulf Islands are the closest island group to Athens. Not surprisingly, they are a very popular escape for residents of the congested capital. Accommodation can be hard to find between mid-June and September, and at weekends year-round. The closest island to Athens is **Aegina**. Oddly popular with British travellers is unremarkable **Poros**, while **Hydra** is the most stylish and familiar to the jet-setting crowd. Pine-covered **Spetses** is probably the most beautiful of the group. Tourist offices have information on all the islands.

The Peloponnese Η Πελοπόννησος

The Peloponnese is the southern extremity of the rugged Balkan peninsula. It's linked to the rest of Greece only by the narrow Isthmus of Corinth, and this has long prompted people to declare the Peloponnese to be more an island than part of the mainland. It technically became an island after the completion of the Corinth Canal across the isthmus in 1893, and it is now linked to the mainland only by road and rail bridges.

The Peloponnese is an area rich in history. The principal site is Olympia, which is the birthplace of the Olympic Games. Epidavros, Corinth and Mycenae in the northeast are all within easy striking distance of the pretty Venetian town of Nafplio.

In the south are the magical old Byzantine towns of Monemvasia and Mystras. The rugged Mani Peninsula is famous for its spectacular wildflowers in spring, as well as for the bizarre tower settlements sprinkled across its landscape.

PATRAS ΠΑΤΡΑ

pop 153,300

Patras is Greece's third-largest city and the principal port for ferries to Italy and the Ionian Islands. It's not particularly exciting, and most travellers hang around only long enough for transport connections. The city is easy to negotiate and is laid out on a grid stretching uphill from the port to the old *kastro* (castle). Most services of importance to travellers are to be found along the waterfront, which is known as Othonos Amalias, in the middle of town, and Iroön Politehniou to the north. The train station is right in the middle of town on Othonos Amalias, and the main bus station is close by.

The **EOT tourist office** *(☎ 261 062 0353)* is inside the port fence, off Iroön Politehniou, and the **tourist police** *(☎ 261 045 1833)* are upstairs in the embarkation hall. The **National Bank of Greece** *(Plateia Trion Symahon)* has a 24-hour ATM. You can send mail at the **post office** *(cnr Zaïmi & Mezonos)*. There's an OTE telephone office opposite the tourist office at the port. For Internet access, try **Internet Café Paradise** *(Zaïmi 7; open 5am-1am daily)*.

Pension Nicos *(☎ 261 062 3757; cnr Patreos & Agiou Andreou 121; singles/doubles/triples with bathroom €18/30/40)*, just up from the waterfront, is where most travellers head. **Europa Centre** *(Othonos Amalias 10; meals from €3.50)* is a convenient cafeteria-style place close to the international ferry dock.

Getting There & Away

The best way to travel to Athens is by train. The buses may be faster, but they drop you a long way from the city centre at Terminal A on Kifissou. The trains take you close to the city centre, five minutes from Syntagma on the new metro system (see also Getting There & Away in the Athens section).

There are buses to Athens (€12.25, three hours) that run every 30 minutes from the main bus station, with the last at 9.45pm. There are also 10 buses a day to Pyrgos (for Olympia).

Buses to Kefallonia leave from the corner of Othonos Amalias and Gerokostopoulou, and buses to Zakynthos leave from Othonos Amalias 58. These services travel by ferry from Kyllini.

There are eight trains a day to Athens. Four are slow trains (€5.30, five hours) and five are intercity express trains (€10, 3½ hours). The last intercity train leaves at 6.30pm. Trains also run south to Pyrgos and Kalamata.

There are daily ferries to Kefallonia (€10, 2½ hours), Ithaki (€10.90, 3¾ hours) and Corfu (€17.90, seven hours). Services to Italy are covered in under Getting There & Away at the start of this chapter. Ticket agencies line the waterfront.

CORINTH ΚΟΡΙΝΘΟΣ

pop 27,400

Modern Corinth is an uninspiring town which gives the impression that it has never quite recovered from the devastating earthquake of 1928. It is, however, a convenient base from which to visit nearby ancient Corinth.

The ruins of **ancient Corinth** *(admission €3.55; open 8am-7pm May-Oct, 8am-5pm Nov-Mar)* lie 7km southwest of the modern city. Corinth was one of ancient Greece's wealthiest and most wanton cities. When Corinthians weren't clinching business deals, they were paying homage to Aphrodite in her temple, which meant they were frolicking with the temple's sacred prostitutes. The only ancient Greek monument remaining here is the imposing **Temple of Apollo**; the others are Roman. Towering over the site is **Acrocorinth** *(admission free; open 8am-6pm daily)*, the ruins of an ancient citadel built on a massive outcrop of limestone.

Hotel Apollon *(☎ 2741 022 587, fax 2741 083 875; Pirinis 18; singles/doubles with bathroom €23.50/35.20)*, near the train station, is the best of modern Corinth's budget hotels. The rooms are equipped with air-con and TV. **Restaurant To 24 Hours** *(☎ 2741 083 201; Agiou Nikolaou 19; mains €3.50-8)* never closes, turning out an ever-changing selection of taverna favourites 24 hours a day.

Buses to Athens (€5.70, 1½ hours) leave every half-hour from opposite the train station at Dimocratias 4. This is also the departure point for buses to ancient Corinth (€0.80, 20 minutes, hourly) and Lecheon. Buses to Nafplio leave from the junction of Ethnikis Antistaseos and Aratou. There are 14 trains a day to Athens, five of which are intercity services. There are also trains to Kalamata, Nafplio and Patras.

NAFPLIO ΝΑΥΠΛΙΟ

pop 11,900

Nafplio is easily one of Greece's prettiest towns. The narrow streets of the old quarter are filled with elegant Venetian houses and neoclassical mansions. The **municipal tourist office** *(☎ 2752 024 444; 25 Martiou; open daily)* is about as unhelpful as tourist offices get. The bus station is on Syngrou, the street that separates the Old Town from the new. There are hourly buses to Athens (€8.50, 2½ hours) via Corinth, as well as services to Argos (for Peloponnese connections), Mycenae and Epidavros.

There are terrific views of the Old Town and the surrounding coast from magnificent hill-top **Palamidi Fortress** *(admission €4; open 8am-6.45pm Apr-Oct, 8am-5pm Nov-Mar)*, built by the Venetians at the beginning of the 18th century. The climb is strenuous – there are almost 1000 steps – so start early and take water with you.

The cheapest rooms are in the new part of town along Argous, the road to Argos. **Hotel Argolis** *(☎/fax 2752 027 721; Argous 32; singles/doubles with bathroom €18/25)* is a good place to start. It normally discounts rooms to a bargain €8/16 for singles/doubles. If you're arriving by bus, ask to let off at the Thanasenas stop, right opposite the hotel.

Dimitris Bekas *(☎ 2752 024 594; Efthimiopoulou 26; singles/doubles/triples with shared bathroom €15/21/24)* offers top value for a great location above the Catholic church on the slopes of the Akronafplia. The rooftop terrace has great views over the Old Town.

Mezedopoleio O Noulis *(☎ 2752 025 541; Moutzouridou 21; meze €1.50-7.35)* serves a fabulous range of meze which can easily be combined into a meal. Check the *saganaki flambé*, ignited with Metaxa (brandy) as it reaches your table.

MYCENAE ΜΥΚΗΝΕΣ

Mycenae *(admission €6; open 8am-7pm daily Apr-Oct; 8am-5pm daily Nov-Mar)* was the most powerful influence in Greece for three centuries until about 1200 BC. The rise and fall of Mycenae is shrouded in myth, but the site was settled as early as the sixth millennium BC. Historians are divided as to whether the city's eventual destruction was wrought by invaders or internal conflict. Described by Homer as 'rich in gold', Mycenae's entrance, the **Lion Gate**, is Europe's oldest monumental sculpture.

Excavations have uncovered the palace complex and a number of tombs. The so-called **Mask of Agamemnon**, discovered by Heinrich Schliemann in 1873, now holds pride of place at the National Archaeological Museum in Athens, along with other finds from the site. Most people visit on day trips from Nafplio. There are buses to Mycenae from Argos and Nafplio.

SPARTA ΣΠΑΡΤΗ

pop 14,100

The bellicose Spartans sacrificed all the finer things in life to military expertise and left no monuments of any consequence. Ancient Sparta's forlorn ruins lie amid olive groves at the northern end of town. Modern Sparta is a neat, unspectacular town, but it's a convenient base from which to visit Mystras.

Sparta is laid out on a grid system. The main streets are Palaeologou, which runs north-south through the town, and Lykourgou, which runs east-west. The **tourist office** *(☎ 2731 024 852; open 8am-2.30pm Mon-Fri)* is in the town hall on Plateia Kentriki.

Hotel Cecil *(☎ 2731 024 980, fax 2731 081 318; Palaeologou 125; singles/doubles with bathroom €30/40)* is a family-run place and one of the many good hotels back in town. Rooms here have TV. **Restaurant Elysse** *(☎ 2731 029 896; Palaeologou 113; mains €4.50-8.80)* offers Lakonian specialities such as chicken *bardouniotiko*, which is chicken cooked with onions and feta cheese.

The bus terminal is at the eastern end of Lykourgou. There are 10 buses a day to Athens (€12.65, four hours), three to Monemvasia and two to Kalamata. There are also frequent buses to Mystras (€0.80, 30 minutes).

MYSTRAS ΜΥΣΤΡΑΣ

Mystras *(admission €5; open 8am-6pm Apr-Oct, 8am-3.30pm Nov-Mar)*, 7km from Sparta, was once the shining light of the Byzantine world. Its ruins spill from a spur of Mt Taygetos, crowned by a mighty fortress built by the Franks in 1249. The streets of Mystras are lined with palaces, monasteries and churches, most of them dating from the period between 1271 and 1460, when the town was the effective capital of the Byzantine Empire.

MONEMVASIA ΜΟΝΕΜΒΑΣΙΑ

Monemvasia is no longer an undiscovered paradise, but mass tourism hasn't lessened the impact of one's first encounter with this extraordinary Old Town – nor the thrill of exploring it.

Monemvasia occupies a great outcrop of rock that rises dramatically from the sea opposite the village of Gefyra. It was separated from the mainland by an earthquake in AD 375, and access is by a causeway from Gefyra. From the causeway, a road curves around the base of the rock for about 1km until it comes to a narrow L-shaped tunnel in the massive fortifying wall. You emerge, blinking, into the **Byzantine town**, hitherto hidden from view.

The cobbled main street is flanked by stairways leading to a complex network of stone houses with tiny walled gardens and courtyards. Signposted steps lead to the ruins of the **fortress** built by the Venetians in the 16th century. The views are great, and there is the added bonus of being able to explore the Byzantine **Church of Agia Sophia**, perched precariously on the edge of the cliff.

There is no budget accommodation in Monemvasia, but there are *domatia* in Gefyra, as well as cheap hotels. **Hotel Monemvasia** *(☎ 2732 061 381, fax 2732 061 707; singles/doubles with bathroom €25/38)* is a small modern hotel 500m north of Gefyra on the road to Molai. It has large balconies looking out to Monemvasia, and prices include breakfast.

Overlooking the port, **Taverna O Botsalo** is the place to go for a hearty meal in Gefyra, while **To Kanoni**, on the right of the main street in Monemvasia, has an imaginative menu.

There are four buses a day to Athens (€18.65, six hours), travelling via Sparta, Tripolis and Corinth. In July and August, there are at least two hydrofoils a day to Piraeus via the Saronic Gulf Islands.

GYTHIO ΓΥΘΕΙΟ

pop 4900

Gythio, once the port of ancient Sparta, is an attractive fishing town at the head of the Lakonian Gulf. It is the gateway to the rugged Mani Peninsula to the south.

The main attraction is the picturesque islet of **Marathonisi**, linked to the mainland by a causeway. According to mythology, this islet is ancient Cranae, where Paris (a prince of Troy) and Helen (the wife of Menelaus of Sparta) consummated the love affair that sparked the Trojan War. An 18th-century tower on the islet has been turned into a **museum** of Mani history.

You'll find plenty of *domatia* signs around town. They include **Xenia Rooms to Rent** *(☎ 2733 022 719; singles/doubles with bathroom €15/20)* opposite the causeway to Marathonisi. The nearby **Saga Pension** *(☎ 2733 023 220, fax 2733 024 370; singles/doubles €25/30)* is another good choice and rooms have TV. The waterfront is lined with countless fish tavernas.

There are five buses a day to Athens (€15.10, 4¼ hours) via Sparta (€2.60, one hour), five to Areopoli (€1.70, 30 minutes), two to Gerolimenas (€3.70, 1¼ hours) and one to the Diros Caves (€2.30, one hour).

ANEN Lines operates ferries to Kastelli–Kissamos on Crete (€15.60, seven hours) via Kythira (€7.10, 2½ hours), three times a week between June and September. The schedule is subject to constant change, so check with **Rozakis Travel** *(☎ 2733 022 207, fax 2733 022 229; e rosakigy@otenet.gr)* before coming here to catch a boat.

THE MANI Η ΜΑΝΗ

The Mani is divided into two regions: the Lakonian (inner) Mani in the south, and Messinian (outer) Mani in the northwest below Kalamata.

Lakonian Mani

The Lakonian Mani is wild and remote, its landscape dotted with the dramatic stone-tower houses that are a trademark of the region. They were built as refuges from the clan wars of the 19th century. The best time to visit is in spring, when the barren countryside briefly bursts into life with a spectacular display of wildflowers.

The region's principal village is **Areopoli**, about 30km southwest of Gythio. There are a number of fine towers on the narrow, cobbled streets of the Old Town at the lower end of the main street, Kapetan Matepan.

Just south of here are the magnificent **Diros Caves** *(admission €10.90; open 8am-5.30pm June-Sept, 8am-2.30pm Oct-May)*, where a subterranean river flows.

Gerolimenas, 20km farther south, is a tiny fishing village built around a sheltered bay. **Vathia**, a village of towers built on a rocky peak, is 11km southeast of Gerolimenas. Beyond Vathia, the coastline is a series of rocky outcrops sheltering pebbled beaches.

Most of the accommodation in the Lakonian Mani is in Areopoli. **Tsimova Rooms** *(☎ 2733 051 301; singles/doubles €22/36)* has cosy rooms tucked away behind the Church of Taxiarhes on Kapetan Mapetan. **Pyrgos Kapetanakas** *(☎ 2733 051 233, fax 2733 051 401; singles/doubles €30/45)* occupies the tower house built by the powerful Kapetanakas family at the end of the 18th century. It's signposted to the right at the bottom of Kapetan Matepan. **Hotel Akrotenaritis** *(☎ 2733 054 205; singles/doubles €18/35)*, in Gerolimenas, is a good budget option.

Nicola's Corner Taverna *(☎ 2733 051 366; Plateia Athanaton; mains €3-6.50)* is a popular spot on Areopoli's central square, with a good choice of tasty taverna staples.

Areopoli is the focal point of the local bus network. There are four buses a day to Gythio and Sparta, two to Gerolimenas and Itilo, and one to the Diros Caves. Crossing to the Messinian Mani involves changing buses at Itilo.

Messinian Mani

The Messinian Mani runs north along the coast from Itilo to Kalamata. The beaches here are some of the best in Greece, set against the dramatic backdrop of the Taygetos mountains.

Itilo, the medieval capital of the entire Mani area, is split by a ravine that is the traditional dividing line between inner and outer Mani.

The picturesque coastal village of **Kardamyli**, 37km south of Kalamata, is a favourite destination for trekkers. It's well set up, with a network of colour-coded trails that crisscross the foothills of the Taygetos Mountains behind the village. Many of the walks incorporate the spectacular Vyros Gorge. **Stoupa**, 10km south of Kardamyli, has a great beach and is a popular package destination in summer.

Kardamyli has a good choice of accommodation to suit all budgets, starting with several *domatia*. **Olympia Koumounakou** *(☎ 2721 073 623; singles/doubles €20/25)* is a good place to try; it's signposted opposite the post office. The popular Taverna Perivolis is one of nine tavernas around the village.

There are two buses a day from Kalamata to Itilo, stopping at Kardamyli and Stoupa.

OLYMPIA ΟΛΥΜΠΙΑ

The site of ancient Olympia lies 500m beyond the modern town, surrounded by the green foothills of Mt Kronion. There is a well-organised **municipal tourist office** *(open Mon-Sat, daily June-Sept)* on the main street that also changes money.

In ancient times, Olympia was a sacred place of temples, priests' dwellings and public buildings, as well as being the venue for the quadrennial Olympic Games. The first Olympics were staged in 776 BC, reaching the peak of their prestige in the 6th century BC. The city-states were bound by a sacred truce to stop fighting for three months and compete.

The site *(admission €6 site only, site & museum €9; open 8am-7pm daily Apr-Oct; 8am-5pm Mon-Fri, 8.30am-3pm Sat-Sun Nov-Mar; open 8am-7pm Mon-Fri, 8.30am-3pm Sat & Sun)* is dominated by the immense, ruined **Temple of Zeus**, to whom the games were dedicated. There's also a **museum** *(admission €6)*, north of the archaeological site, which keeps similar hours.

Youth Hostel *(☎ 2624 022 580; Praxitelous Kondyli 18; dorm beds €7)* has free hot showers. There are two more good budget options around the corner on Stefanopoulou: **Pension Achilleys** *(☎ 2624 022 562; Stefanopoulou 4; singles/doubles with shared bathroom €15/20)* and **Pension Posidon** *(☎ 2624 022 567; Stefanopoulou 9; singles/doubles with bathroom €18/28)*.

Taverna To Steki tou Vangeli *(Stefanopoulou 13; mains €4-6.50)* represents better value than most of the tavernas around town.

There are four buses a day to Olympia from Athens (€19.05, 5½ hours). There are also regular buses to Pyrgos, 24km away on the coast.

Northern Greece

Northern Greece covers the regions of Epiros, Thessaly, Macedonia and Thrace. It includes some areas of outstanding natural beauty, such as the Zagoria region of northwestern Epiros.

IGOUMENITSA ΗΓΟΥΜΕΝΙΤΣΑ

pop 6800

Igoumenitsa, opposite the island of Corfu, is the main port of northwestern Greece. Few people stay here any longer than it takes to buy a ticket out. The bus station is on Kyprou. To get there from the ferries, follow the waterfront (Ethnikis Antistasis) north for 500m and turn up El Venizelou. Kyprou is two blocks inland and the bus station is on the left.

If you get stuck for the night, you'll find signs for domatia around the port. The D-class **Egnatia** *(☎ 2665 023 648; Eleftherias 2; singles/doubles with bathroom €30/40)* has comfortable rooms.

Bus services include nine buses a day to Ioannina (€6.20, two hours), and four a day to Athens (€28.45, 8½ hours). There are international ferry services to the Italian ports of Ancona, Bari, Brindisi, Trieste and Venice. Ticket agencies are opposite the port. Ferries to Corfu (€4.20, 1½ hours) operate every hour between 5am and 10pm.

IOANNINA ΙΩΑΝΝΙΝΑ

pop 90,000

Ioannina is the largest town in Epiros, sitting on the western shore of Lake Pamvotis. In Ottoman times, it was one of the most important towns in the country. The town centre is around Plateia Dimokratias, where the main streets of the new town meet. All facilities of importance to travellers are nearby. The **EOT office** *(☎ 2651 041 142; Dodonis 39; open Mon-Sat)* is about 600m south of Plateia Dimokratias. **Robinson Travel** *(☎ 2651 074 989; ⓔ activities@robinson.gr; 8th Merarhias Gramou 10)* specialises in treks in the Zagoria region. There are lots of Internet cafés in town, including **Armos Internet Café** *(☎ 2651 071 488; Harilaou Trikoupi 40)*, 300m west of Plateia Dimokratias.

The **Old Town** juts out into the lake on a small peninsula. Inside the impressive fortifications lies a maze of winding streets flanked by traditional Turkish houses. The **Nisi** (island) is a serene spot in the middle of the lake, with four monasteries set among the trees. Ferries (€0.80) to the island leave from just north of the Old Town. They run half-hourly in summer and hourly in winter.

Most travellers end up staying either at the no-frills **Agapi Inn** *(☎ 2651 020 541; Tsirigoti 6; doubles €18)* near the bus station, or at the co-owned **Hotel Paris** *(singles/doubles €20/30)* next door. There are several restaurants outside the entrance to the Old Town. **To Manteio Psistaria** is recommended.

The main bus terminal is 300m north of Plateia Dimokratias on Zossimadon, the northern extension of Markou Botsari. Services include 12 buses a day to Athens (€24.85, seven hours), nine to Igoumenitsa, five to Thessaloniki and three to Trikala via Kalambaka.

ZAGORIA & VIKOS GORGE

The Zagoria (Ζαγώρια) region covers a large expanse of the Pindos Mountains north of Ioannina. It's a wilderness of raging rivers, crashing waterfalls and deep gorges. Snowcapped mountains rise out of dense forests. The remote villages that dot the hillsides are famous for their impressive grey-slate architecture.

The fairytale village of **Monodendri** is the starting point for treks through the dramatic Vikos Gorge, with its awesome sheer limestone walls. It's a strenuous 7½-hour walk from Monodendri to the twin villages of **Megalo Papingo** and **Mikro Papingo**. The trek is very popular and the path is clearly marked. Ioannina's EOT office has information. Other walks start from **Tsepelovo**, near Monodendri.

There are some wonderful places to stay, but none is particularly cheap. The options in Monodendri include the cosy **To Kalderimi** *(☎ 2653 071 510; doubles €35)*. **Haradra tou Vikou** *(☎ 2653 071 559)* specialises in *pittes* (pies). Try its excellent *tyropitta* (cheese pies), or *hortopitta* (wild-greens pies).

Buses to the Zagoria leave from the main bus station in Ioannina. There are buses to Monodendri Monday to Friday at 6am and 4.15pm; to Tsepelovo on Monday, Wednesday and Friday at 6am and 3pm; and to the Papingo villages on Monday, Wednesday and Friday at 6am and 2.30pm.

METEORA ΜΕΤΕΩΡΑ

Meteora is an extraordinary place. The massive, sheer columns of rock that dot the landscape were created by wave action millions of years ago. Perched precariously atop these seemingly inaccessible outcrops are monasteries that date back to the late 14th century.

Meteora is just north of the town of Kalambaka, on the Ioannina–Trikala road. The rocks behind the town are spectacularly floodlit at night. **Kastraki**, 2km from Kalambaka, is a charming village of red-tiled houses just west of the monasteries. There were once monasteries on each of the 24 pinnacles, but only six are still occupied. They are **Megalou Meteorou** *(Grand Meteora; open 9am-1pm & 3pm-6pm Wed-Mon)*, **Varlaam** *(open 9am-1pm & 3.30pm-6pm Sat-Thur)*, **Agiou Stefanou** *(open 9am-1pm & 3pm-5pm daily)*, **Agias Triados** *(Holy Trinity; open 9am-5pm Fri-Wed)*, **Agiou Nikolaou** *(open 9am-5pm daily)* and **Agias Varvaras Rousanou** *(open 9am-6pm Thur-Tues)*. Admission is €2 for each monastery; free for Greeks.

Kastraki is the best base for visiting Meteora. There are several domatia in town, charging from €20/30 for singles/doubles.

There are hourly buses to Trikala and two a day to Ioannina. Local buses shuttle constantly between Kalambaka and Kastraki; five a day continue to Grand Meteora. Trikala is the region's major transport hub. It has eight buses a day which run to Athens (€18.20, 5½ hours). There are trains between Kalambaka and Volos. These trains connect with services from Athens and Thessaloniki at Paleofarsalos.

THESSALONIKI ΘΕΣΣΑΛΟΝΙΚΗ

pop 750,000

Thessaloniki, also known as Salonica, is Greece's second-largest city. It's a bustling, sophisticated place with good restaurants and a busy nightlife. It was once the second city of Byzantium, and there are some magnificent Byzantine churches, as well as a scattering of Roman ruins.

Thessaloniki is laid out on a grid system. The main thoroughfares – Tsimiski, Egnatia and Agiou Dimitriou – run parallel to Nikis, on the waterfront. Plateias Eleftherias and Aristotelous, both on Nikis, are the main squares. The city's most famous landmark is the White Tower (which is no longer white) at the eastern end of Nikis. The train station is on Monastiriou, the westerly continuation of Egnatia beyond Plateia Dimokratias.

The **EOT office** *(☎ 231 027 1888; Plateia Aristotelous 8; open Mon-Sat)* can help with inquiries, or try the **tourist police** *(☎ 231 055 4871; Dodekanisou 4, 5th floor; open daily)*. There are numerous banks around the city centre, all with ATMs. The branch of the **National Bank of Greece** *(Tsimiski 11)* is open Saturday and Sunday for currency exchange. Send mail at the **main post office** *(Aristotelous 26)*, and make calls at the **OTE telephone office** *(Karolou Dil 27)*. **E-Global** *(Vas Irakliou 40)* is the most central of the city's many Internet cafés. It's open 24 hours.

The **archaeological museum** *(admission €4.40; open 8am-7pm Tues-Fri, 12.30pm-7pm Mon)*, at the eastern end of Tsimiski, houses a superb collection of treasures from

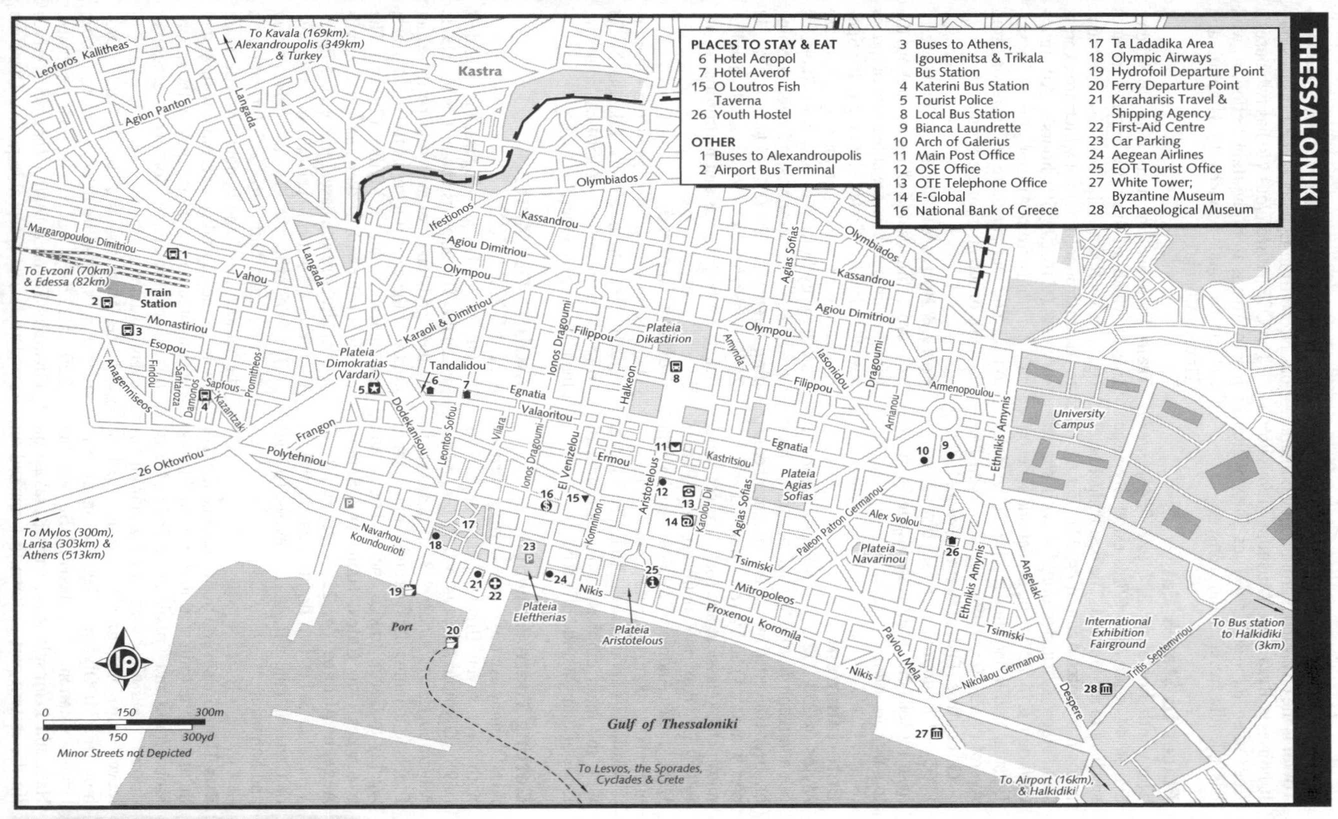
THESSALONIKI
PLACES TO STAY & EAT
6 Hotel Acropol
7 Hotel Averof
15 O Loutros Fish Taverna
26 Youth Hostel
OTHER
1 Buses to Alexandroupolis
2 Airport Bus Terminal
3 Buses to Athens, Igoumenitsa & Trikala Bus Station
4 Katerini Bus Station
5 Tourist Police
8 Local Bus Station
9 Bianca Laundrette
10 Arch of Galerius
11 Main Post Office
12 OSE Office
13 OTE Telephone Office
14 E-Global
16 National Bank of Greece
17 Ta Ladadika Area
18 Olympic Airways
19 Hydrofoil Departure Point
20 Ferry Departure Point
21 Karaharisis Travel & Shipping Agency
22 First-Aid Centre
23 Car Parking
24 Aegean Airlines
25 EOT Tourist Office
27 White Tower; Byzantine Museum
28 Archaeological Museum
To Kavala (169km), Alexandroupolis (349km) & Turkey
Kastra
To Evzoni (70km) & Edessa (82km)
Train Station
Plateia Dimokratias (Vardari)
Plateia Dikastirion
Plateia Agias Sofias
Plateia Navarinou
Plateia Eleftherias
Plateia Aristotelous
University Campus
International Exhibition Fairground
To Bus station to Halkidiki (3km)
To Mylos (300m), Larisa (303km) & Athens (513km)
Port
Gulf of Thessaloniki
To Lesvos, the Sporades, Cyclades & Crete
To Airport (16km) & Halkidiki
0 150 300m
0 150 300yd
Minor Streets not Depicted

the royal tombs of Philip II. The **White Tower** is the city's most prominent landmark. It houses a **Byzantine Museum** *(admission free; open 8am-2.30pm Tues-Sun)*, which has splendid frescoes and icons.

Places to Stay & Eat

The **youth hostel** *(☎ 231 022 5946; Alex Svolou 44; dorm beds €8)* is extremely basic and hard to recommend. The best budget hotel in town is **Hotel Acropol** *(☎ 231 053 6170; Tandalidou 4; singles/doubles with shared bathroom €16/20.50)*, on a quiet side street off Egnatia. You'll find similar prices at the **Hotel Averof** *(☎ 231 053 8498; Leontos Sofou 24)*.

O Loutros Fish Taverna *(☎ 231 022 8895; M Koundoura 5; fish dishes €6-9)* hasn't lost its cult following despite its move to a new location.

Entertainment

Mylos *(☎ 231 052 5968; Andreou Georgiou 56; admission free)* is a huge old mill which has been converted into an entertainment complex with an art gallery, restaurant, bar and live music club (classical and rock). To get there, follow 26 Oktovriou southwest from Plateia Dimokratias; Andreou Georgiou is on the right after about 700m, opposite a small park.

Music bars abound in the Ta Ladadika area, with the main emphasis on music and all kinds of draught and bottled beer.

Getting There & Away

Air Olympic Airways and Aegean Airlines both have seven flights a day to Athens (€96). **Olympic Airways** *(☎ 231 036 8666; Navarhou Koundourioti 1-3)* also has daily flights to Ioannina, Lesvos and Limnos; three weekly to Corfu, Iraklio and Mykonos; and two weekly to Chios, Hania and Samos. **Aegean Airlines** *(☎ 231 028 0050; El Venizelou 2)* has two flights a day to Iraklio on Crete, and daily flights to Lesvos, Rhodes and Santorini.

Bus There are several bus terminals, most of them near the train station. Buses to Athens, Igoumenitsa and Trikala leave from Monastiriou 65 and 67; buses to Alexandroupolis leave from Koloniari 17; and buses to Litihoro (for Mt Olympus) leave from the Katerini bus station, Promitheos 10. Buses to the Halkidiki Peninsula leave from Karakasi 68 (in the eastern part of town; it's marked on the free EOT map). To get there, take local bus No 10 from Egnatia to the Botsari stop.

The **OSE** *(Aristotelous 18)* has two buses a day to Athens from the train station, as well as international services to Istanbul and Tirana (Albania).

Train There are nine trains a day to Athens, five of which are intercity express services (€27.60, six hours). There are also five trains to Alexandroupolis, two of which are express services (€16.20, 5½ hours). All international trains from Athens stop at Thessaloniki. You can get more information from the OSE office or from the train station.

Ferry & Hydrofoil There's a Sunday ferry to Lesvos, Limnos and Chios throughout the year. In summer there are at least three ferries a week to Iraklio (Crete), stopping in the Sporades and the Cyclades on the way. There are also daily hydrofoils to Skiathos, Skopelos and Alonnisos. **Karaharisis Travel & Shipping Agency** *(☎ 231 052 4544, fax 231 053 2289; Navarhou Koundourioti 8)* handles tickets for both ferries and hydrofoils.

Getting Around

There is no bus service from the Olympic Airways office to the airport. Take bus No 78 from the train station (€0.50). A taxi from the airport costs about €8.

MOUNT OLYMPUS
ΟΛΥΜΠΟΣ ΟΡΟΣ

Mt Olympus is Greece's highest and mightiest mountain. The ancients chose it as the abode of their gods and assumed it to be the exact centre of the earth. Olympus has eight peaks, the highest of which is Mytikas (2917m). The area is popular with trekkers: most use the village of **Litohoro** as a base. Litohoro is 5km inland from the Athens–Thessaloniki highway.

The **EOS office** *(☎ 2352 084 544; Plateia Kentriki; open Mon-Sat)* has information on the various treks and conditions. The main route to the top takes two days with a stay overnight at one of the refuges on the mountain. Good protective clothing is essential, even in summer.

Hotel Markisia *(☎ 2352 081 831; Dionysou 5; singles/doubles with bathroom €20.50/23.50)* is a good, clean budget choice. **Olympus Taverna** *(Agiou Nikolaou)* serves standard fare at reasonable prices. There are four **refuges** *(open May-Sept)* on the mountain at altitudes ranging from 940m to 2720m.

There are eight buses a day to Litohoro from Thessaloniki (€6.10, 1½ hours), and three from Athens (€24.80, 5½ hours).

Cyclades Κυκλάδες

The Cyclades, named after the rough circle they form around Delos, are quintessential Greek Islands, with brilliant white villages, dazzling light and azure waters. Delos, the most important historic island of the group, is uninhabited. The inhabited islands of the archipelago are Mykonos, Syros, Tinos, Andros, Paros, Naxos, Ios, Santorini, Anafi, Amorgos, Sikinos, Folegandros and the tiny islands of Koufonisi, Shinousa, Iraklia and Donousa, lying east of Naxos.

Some of the Cyclades, such as Mykonos, Ios and Santorini, have seized tourism, stuffing their coastlines with bars and their beaches with sun lounges. Others, such as Anafi, Sikinos and the tiny islands east of Naxos, are little more than clumps of rock, each with a village, secluded coves and curious tourists.

Doing justice to islands is impossible in a single chapter. For more detailed information, see Lonely Planet's *Greek Islands*.

MYKONOS ΜΥΚΟΝΟΣ

pop 6170

Polished Greek island perfection, Mykonos is perhaps the most visited – and expensive – of the archipelago. It has the most sophisticated nightlife and is a mecca for gay travellers. The **tourist police** *(☎ 2289 022 482)* are at the port, in the same building as the **hotel reservation office** *(☎ 2289 024 540)*, which has free tourist maps; the **Association of Rooms and Apartments** *(☎/fax 2289 026 860)*; and the **camping information office** *(☎ 2289 022 852)*.

Island Mykonos Travel *(☎ 2289 022 232; ⓔ islandmykonos@1net.gr)* on Taxi Square, where the port road meets the town, is a hectic but helpful agency with tourist and travel information. The post office is near the southern bus station. **Double Click** *(Florou Zouganeli)*, off Taxi Square, has expensive Internet access.

Summer crowds consume the island's capital and port, shuffling through snaking streets of chic boutiques and blinding white walls with balconies of cascading flowers.

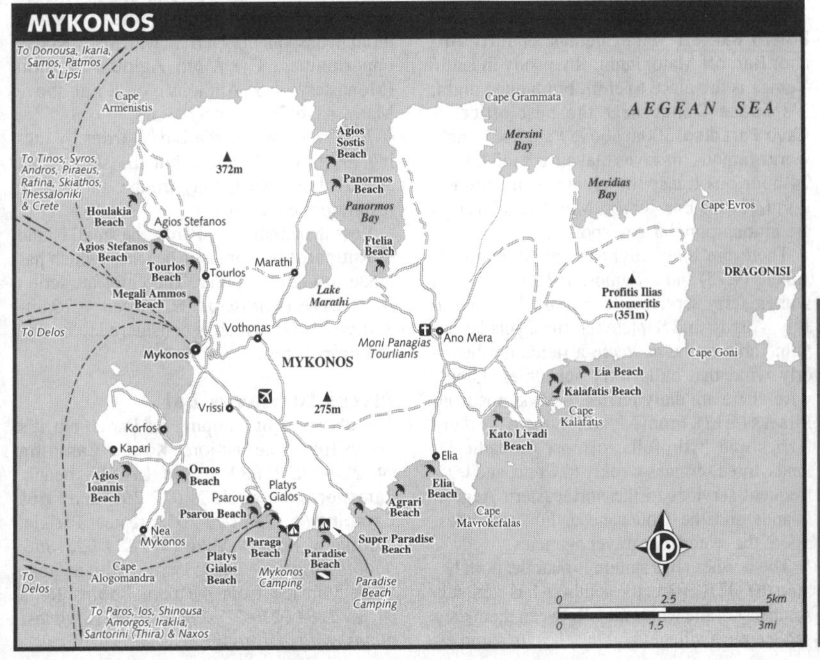

GREECE

The most popular beaches are **Platys Gialos** (wall-to-wall sun lounges), the often nude **Paradise Beach** and mainly gay **Super Paradise**, **Agrari** and **Elia**. The less squashy ones are **Panormos**, **Kato Livadi** and **Kalafatis**.

Paradise Beach Camping *(☎ 2289 022 852; ⓔ paradise@paradise.myk.forthnet.gr; camping per person/tent €7/3.50, sleeping bag area €7)* is skin-to-skin mayhem in summer, bursting with facilities and a party atmosphere. **Mykonos Camping** *(☎/fax 2289 024 578; ⓔ info.mykcamp.gr; camping per person/tent €7/3.50)*, near Platys Gialos beach, also parties. Minibuses from both meet the ferries and buses jog regularly into town. Rooms fill up quickly in high season so it's wise to go with the first *domatia* owner who accosts you. Outside July and August, rooms are cheap as chips.

Seduce someone over dinner in **Little Venice** on the western waterfront – it's bound to work. Busy **Niko's Taverna**, near the Delos quay, serves good seafood. **Sesame Kitchen**, behind the maritime museum, is a vegetarian's friend. Popular with locals are intimate **Avra** *(cnr Kalogera & Florou Zouganeli)* for gourmet Greek food and **Antonini's Taverna** on Taxi Square.

For house and Latin vibes, there's chic **Bolero Bar**, off Malamatenias, or flirty **Anchor Bar**, off Matogianni. Rhapsody in Little Venice is the place to chill. For a huge night, it's **Space Dance** near the post office or **Cavo Paradiso**, 300m above Paradise Beach, world-famous for raves that attract top DJs. A 24-hour bus transports clubbers in summer. Porta, Kastro Bar, Icaros, Manto and Pierro's are among popular gay spots.

There are daily flights from Mykonos to Athens (€75) and to Santorini (Thira; €58). In winter, ferry services sleep most days and in July, August and September, the Cyclades are vulnerable to the *meltemi*, a fierce northeasterly wind that culls ferry schedules. Otherwise, there are daily ferries to Mykonos from Piraeus (€17). From Mykonos, there are daily ferries and hydrofoils to most Cycladic islands, three services weekly to Crete, and less-frequent services to the northeastern Aegean Islands and the Dodecanese. For schedules, ask at the waterfront travel agencies.

The northern bus station is near the port, behind the OTE office; the southern bus station is southeast of the windmills. Between them they service most villages and beaches. In summer, caïques (small fishing boats) from Mykonos town and Platys Gialos putter to Paradise, Super Paradise, Agrari and Elia Beaches.

PAROS ΠΑΡΟΣ

pop 9591

Paros is an attractive island with softly contoured and terraced hills that culminate in Mt Profitis Ilias. It has fine swimming beaches and is famous for its pure white marble from which the *Venus de Milo* was created. Paros' main town and port is Parikia, on the west coast. Agora, also known as Market St, is Parikia's main commercial thoroughfare running from the main square, Plateia Mavrogenous (opposite the ferry terminal).

One of the most notable churches in Greece is Parikia's **Panagia Ekatontapyliani** *(Our Lady of the Hundred Gates; open 7am-9pm daily)* for its beautiful, ornate interior. Visitors must dress modestly (ie, no shorts). On the northeast coast, **Naoussa** is still a sweet fishing village, despite a deluge in tourism, and there's good swimming nearby: **Kolimvythres** has Wild West rock formations; tiny **Monastiri** has a pumping beach bar; and **Santa Maria** a dive-instruction centre.

Take a bus to the peaceful inland villages of **Lefkes**, **Marmara** and **Marpissa** for walks through unspoilt hilly terrain with many Kodak opportunities. The **Moni Agiou Antoniou** (Monastery of St Anthony), on a hill above Marpissa, offers soaring views.

You can visit the **marble quarries** by taking the bus to Marathi, but the steep walk and marble powder may trouble those with respiratory conditions.

Less than 2km from Paros, the small island of **Antiparos** has fantastic beaches, which has made it wildly popular. The chief attraction is its **cave** *(admission €2; open 9.30am-3.30pm daily)*, which is considered to be one of Europe's best.

Places to Stay & Eat

There's loads of camping on Paros, but it's away from the action. **Koula Camping** *(☎ 2284 022 081)* is on Livadia beach. **Parasporas** *(☎/fax 2284 022 268)* and **Krios Camping** *(☎ 2284 021 705)* are near Parikia.

Mike at **Rooms Mike** *(☎ 2284 022 856; doubles/triples €30/45)* is a brilliant host. Walk 50m left from the port. **Rooms Rena** *(☎/fax 2284 021 427; singles/doubles/triples/quads with bathroom €29/38/44/55)* is a friendly place with spotless rooms featuring balcony and fridge. To get there turn left from the pier, then right at the ancient cemetery.

On Plateia Mavrogenous, trust **Zorba's** *gyros* for a quick fix, or **Restaurant Argonauta** for tasty Greek fare in cheery surrounds. Ephesus, on the street behind the yacht marina, is dip delicious.

Entertainment

Mellow **Pirate** jazz-and-blues bar is tucked away in the Old Town. The far southern end of Parikia's waterfront has **Pebbles** bar for classical music, and **Mojo** and **Black Bart's** for upbeat vibes. Further along you'll find **The Dubliner** (which is three bars in one) and **Sex Club**, for dancing, not topless Playboy bunnies. Pounda Beach has two rave clubs; **Pounda Beach Club** and **Viva Pounda**.

Getting There & Around

There is one flight daily to and from Athens (€69.75). Paros is a major ferry hub with daily connections to Piraeus (€16), frequent ferries and daily catamarans to Naxos, Ios, Santorini and Mykonos, and less-frequent ones to Amorgos. The Dodecanese and the northeastern Aegean Islands (via Syros) are also well serviced from here.

The bus station, 100m left from the port, has frequent services to the entire island. In summer, there are also excursion boats and caïques from Parikia.

NAXOS ΝΑΞΟΣ

pop 16,703

Naxos is the biggest and greenest of the Cyclades, but what it lacks in small-town allure, it makes up for with excellent beaches and a striking interior. Naxos town *(hora)*, on the west coast, is the island's capital and port. Court Square is also known as Plateia Protodikiou.

Privately-owned **Naxos Tourist Information Centre** *(NTIC; ☎ 2285 025 201, fax 2285 025 200; open daily)*, directly opposite the port, offers help with accommodation and tours. To find the post office, turn right from the port, walk 700m, cross Papavasiliou and take the left branch where the road forks. Reliable Internet access is at the cool **M@trix Cyber Café**, off Court Square, towards the police station.

Things to See & Do

Naxos town twists and curves up to a crumbling 13th-century **Kastro** and well-stocked **archaeological museum** *(admission €3; open 8.30am-3pm Tues-Sun)*.

The town beach of **Agios Georgios** is 10 minutes' walk from the town; turn right from the port. Beyond it, wonderful sandy beaches as far as **Pyrgaki Beach** become progressively less crammed. **Agia Anna Beach** is a sublime 3km stretch.

A day trip to **Apollonas** on the north coast reveals a dramatic landscape. The **Tragaea region** is a vast Arcadian olive grove with tranquil villages in valleys and dome churches atop rocky crests.

Filoti, the largest settlement, perches on the slopes of **Mt Zeus** (1004m). It's a tough three-hour trail to the summit.

In Apollonas you'll find the mysterious 10.5m **kouros** (naked male statue), constructed c. 7th century, lying abandoned and unfinished in an ancient marble quarry.

The old village of **Apiranthos** is a gem, with paved marble streets and few tavernas.

There is a string of **minor islands** off the east coast of Naxos. Of the seven, only Ano Koufonisi, Donousa, Shinousa and Iraklia are inhabited. Intrepid visitors will find few amenities, but each has some *domatia*. They are served by two to three ferries per week from Piraeus via Naxos, some of which continue on to Amorgos.

Places to Stay & Eat

Studios Stratos *(☎/fax 2285 025 898; doubles/triples with bathroom €35/45)*, in the back streets around Agios Georgios, has immaculate, lovingly decorated rooms with mini-kitchen. Call ahead to be met at the ferry. **Dionyssos Hostel** *(☎ 2285 022 331; dorm beds €7, doubles with shared bathroom €30)* and pretty **Hotel Anixis** *(☎ 2285 022 932, fax 2285 022 112; ⓔ info@hotel-anixis.gr; singles/doubles €40/50)*, where rates include breakfast, can be found near the quiet Kastro; ask NTIC for directions or call ahead.

Taverna O Apostolis is a good place to try for ouzo and *mezedes*; go up the street adjacent to the NTIC and Zas Travel and spot the signs. You can't avoid the waffles, ice cream and crepes around the waterfront – just surrender.

Entertainment

The **Venetian Museum** by the Kastro holds twilight concerts. Nightlife clusters around the southern end of the waterfront. There's the tropical **Med Bar**, crowd-pleasing **Veggera** and **Day & Night** for Greek pop and rock. **The Ocean** club opens at 11pm but goes wild after midnight.

Getting There & Around

Naxos has six flights weekly to Athens (€70.40). There are daily ferries to Piraeus (€16.35) and good ferry and hydrofoil connections to most Cycladic islands. Boats go once a week to Crete, Thessaloniki and usually Rhodes, and to Samos two to three times per week. Check with travel agencies.

Buses travel to most villages regularly (including Apollonas and Filoti) and the beaches towards Pyrgaki. The bus terminal is in front of the port.

IOS ΙΟΣ

pop 2000

In high season, Ios is the spoilt brat of the islands, with little to offer beyond beach baking all day and drinking all night. The island is reasonably popular with the older set – anyone over 25 – but the two groups tend to be polarised. The young stay in the *hora* (Ios town) and the others at Ormos port. Non-ravers should avoid the village from June to September. The locals wish they could, too.

Gialos Beach near the port is crowded. **Koubara Beach**, a 20-minute walk west of Gialos, is less crazy. Stumble 1km east of the village to **Milopotas** to recover, but **Manganari** is the magnet, with four sandy crescent beaches on the south coast.

Orientation & Information

The capital, Ios town, also known as 'the village' or *hora*, is 2km inland from the port. The **bus stop** *(Plateia Emirou)* in Ormos is straight ahead from the ferry quay. The bus trundles regularly to the village, otherwise it's a nasty, steep hike. There is no EOT tourist office, but **Acteon Travel** *(☎ 2286 091 343, fax 2286 091 088; e acteon@otenet.gr)* has five offices in Ios to keep busy. Internet access is scattered between hotels (Francesco's Hotel and Far Out Village Hotel), cafés and bars (Fun Pub, Café Cyclades), and Acteon Travel.

Places to Stay & Eat

Clearly visible just right of the port are **Camping Ios** *(☎ 2286 091 050; tents €8)* and **Hotel Poseidon** *(☎ 2286 091 091, fax 2286 091 969; doubles €67)*, which has an enticing communal area and pool. **Francesco's** *(☎/fax 2286 091 223; e fragesco@otenet.gr; dorm beds €15, doubles with bathroom €50)*, in the village, is a lively meeting place with superlative views from its terrace bar.

Milopotas Beach parties hard from noon until midnight with up to 3000 people. **Camping Stars** *(☎ 2286 091 302; tents €7.50, bungalows with bathroom per person €19)* has a pool, bar and live music. **Far Out Camping Club** *(☎ 2286 091 468; e camping@faroutclub.com; camping per person €8, bungalows & dorms per person €18)* has tons of facilities and bungy jumping.

In the village, **The Nest** is the cheapest taverna for hungry backpackers, or try **Ali Baba's** near the gym for huge meals and funky ambience. **Lord Byron Taverna** and **Pithari** are cosy nooks for Greek fare.

Entertainment

At night, the village erupts with bars to explore and you'll have to elbow your way nicely to the other side. Perennial favourites include **Red Bull**, **Slammers** and **Blue Note**. Opposite the central car park, **Sweet Irish Dreams** is a crowd pleaser with table dancing. For clubbing, head to **Scorpions**.

GREECE

Getting There & Around

Mercifully, Ios has daily connections to Piraeus (€16.50) and there are frequent hydrofoils and ferries to the major Cycladic islands. For schedules, visit Acteon Travel (see under Orientation & Information, earlier).

There are buses every 20 minutes between the port, the village and Milopotas Beach until early morning, and two to three per day to Manganari Beach (45 minutes).

SANTORINI (THIRA) ΣΑΝΤΟΡΙΝΗ (ΘΗΡΑ)

pop 9360

Around 1450 BC, the volcanic heart of Santorini exploded and sank, leaving an extraordinary landscape. Today, the startling sight of the submerged caldera almost encircled by sheer cliffs remains – this is certainly the most dramatic of all the islands. It's possible that the catastrophe destroyed the Minoan civilisation, but neither this theory nor the claim that the island was part of the lost continent of Atlantis has been proven.

The capital, Fira, perches on top of the caldera on the west coast. The port of Athinios is 12km away. The bus station and taxi station are just south of Fira's main square Plateia Theotokopoulou. There is no EOT tourist office or tourist police, but there are several travel agencies on the square and the helpful **Dakoutros Travel** *(☎ 2286 022 958, fax 2286 022 686)* opposite the taxi station. The post office is one block south of the taxi station. The best-value Internet café on the square is **PC Club**, above Santo Volcano Tours & Travel.

The shameless commercialism of Fira has not quite reduced its all-pervasive dramatic aura. The best of the town's museums is the exceptional **Museum of Prehistoric Thira** *(admission free; open 8.30am-3pm Tues-Sun)*, which has wonderful displays of artefacts, mainly from ancient Akrotiri. To get there, walk south from the main square, past the bus station and take the next street on the right.

Excavations in 1967 uncovered the remarkably well-preserved Minoan settlement of **Akrotiri**, with its remains of two- and three-storey buildings, and evidence of a sophisticated drainage system. Until construction of a new shelter to protect the ruins is complete (around 2007), artefacts have been moved to the Museum of Prehistoric Thira. Without a guided tour, the site is just rubble. Dakoutros Travel conducts tours for €20.

Moni Profiti Ilia, a monastery built on the island's highest point, can be reached along a path from the site of **Ancient Thira**; the walk takes about one hour.

The flawless village of **Oia** (pronounced *ee*-ah), famed for its postcard sunsets, is less hectic than Fira and a must-visit. Its caldera-facing tavernas are dreamy spots for brunch.

Santorini's **beaches** of black volcanic sand sizzle – beach mats are essential. **Kamari**, **Perissa** and **Monolithos** get crowded, but those near Oia are quieter. **Red Beach**, a 15-minute walk from Akrotiri, is very popular.

Of the surrounding islets, only **Thirasia** is inhabited. At **Palia Kameni** you can bathe in hot springs and on **Nea Kameni** you can clamber around on volcanic lava. A six-hour tour to these three islands by caïque or glass-bottomed boat costs €17. Tickets are available from most travel agencies.

Places to Stay & Eat

Beware aggressive accommodation owners who meet boats and buses and claim that their rooms are in Fira when they're actually in Karterados, a 20-minute walk or short bus ride into town. Always ask to see a map. Dakoutros Travel can help with a range of accommodation in Fira (and Oia) and organises pick-ups from its office.

Santorini Camping *(☎ 2286 022 944; ⓔ santocam@otenet.gr; camping per person/tent €6/3)*, 400m east of the main square, has a restaurant and swimming pool. **Thira Hostel** *(☎ 2286 023 864; dorm beds €11, doubles/triples with bathroom €35/40)*, 200m north of the square, is a spacious, run-down old monastery. Some may enjoy its decaying appeal! It also has a cheap restaurant.

Pension Petros *(☎ 2286 022 573, fax 2286 022 615; doubles €60)* is 250m east of the square. Its owners meet the ferries.

Effusive **Mama's Cyclades**, up the top end of town past the youth hostel, offers a hearty breakfast. On the square, **Lucky's Souvlakis** cares for the budget conscious. You'll find excellent-value meals at **Naoussa** on Erythrou Stavrou, not far from the cable-car station, and **Stani Taverna**, next to the Koo Club.

Entertainment

Bars and clubs are clustered along one street, Erythrou Stavrou. From the main square, facing north, turn left at George's Snack Corner, then take the first right.

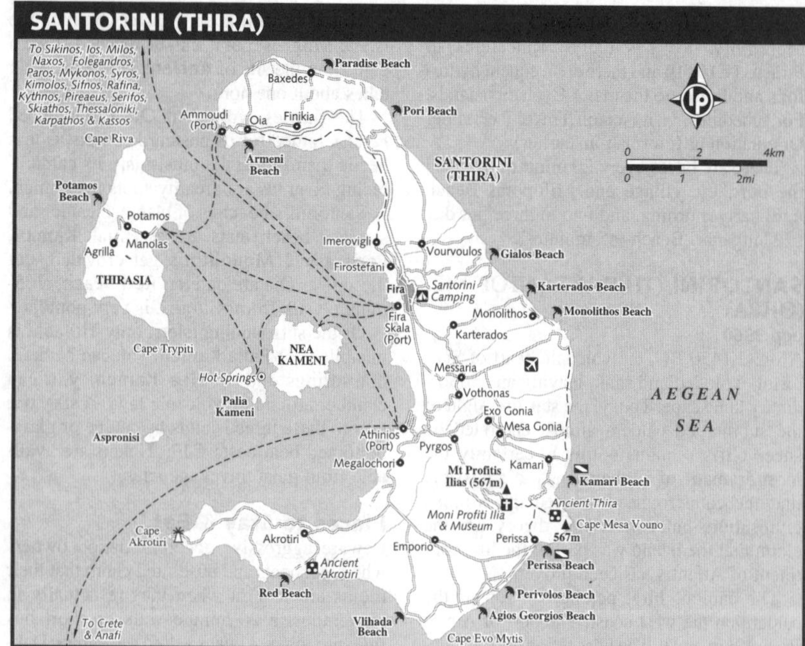

Koo Club, **Enigma** and **Murphys** are all big. The dimly lit **Kira Thira Jazz Bar** is a cosy alternative. The **Dubliner Irish Pub**, next to the youth hostel, rocks till late.

Getting There & Around

There are regular flights to Athens (€78.40), Rhodes (€80.40), Mykonos (€57.40) and Iraklio (Crete; €59.40). Book through the travel agencies on the main square. There are daily ferries to Piraeus (€23.90), daily connections in summer to Mykonos, Ios, Naxos, Paros and Iraklio, and three ferries per week to Anafi, Sikinos, Folegandros, Sifnos, Serifos, Kimolos and Milos. More? Ask at travel agencies.

Large ferries use Athinios port, where they are met by buses (€1.20) and taxis. Small boats use Fira Skala port, where the modes of transport are by donkey or cable car (€3); otherwise it's a clamber up 600 steps.

There are daily boats from Athinios and Fira Skala to Thirasia and Oia. The islets surrounding Santorini can be visited only on excursion from Fira.

Buses go frequently to Oia, Kamari, Perissa, Akrotiri, Ancient Thira and Monolithos. Port buses usually leave Fira, Kamari and Perissa 90 minutes to an hour before ferry departures.

Crete Κρήτη

Crete, Greece's largest island, hosts a quarter of all visitors to the country. All of Crete's major towns are on the north coast and it's here that the package-tourism industry thrives. You can escape the hordes by visiting the undeveloped west coast or by heading into the villages. The mountainous interior offers rigorous trekking and climbing.

Crete was the birthplace of Minoan culture, Europe's first advanced civilisation, which flourished from 2800 to 1450 BC. Very little is known of Minoan civilisation, which came to an abrupt end, possibly destroyed by Santorini's volcanic eruption. For more detailed information, see Lonely Planet's *Crete*.

IRAKLIO ΗΡΑΚΛΕΙΟ

pop 127,600

Iraklio, the capital of Crete, is a noisy, polluted, unavoidable transport hub and the main connection to the Cyclades. Apart from its archaeological museum and proximity to Knossos, there's no reason to linger here. The **tourist police** *(☎ 281 028 3190; Dikeosynis 10)* are helpful with maps and information. Banks, travel agencies and Olympic Airways are on 25 Avgoustou. There's a central **post office** *(Plateia Daskalogiani)* and Internet access at **Cyber SportC@fe** *(25 Avgoustou)*.

Iraklio's **archaeological museum** *(adult/student €6/3; open 12.30pm-7pm Mon, 8am-7pm Tue-Sun)* has an outstanding collection second only to the national museum in Athens.

Places to Stay & Eat

Rent Rooms Hellas *(☎ 281 028 8851; Handakos 24; dorm beds €8, doubles/triples €27/34)* is by far the best budget choice and is popular with backpackers. It's clean, with packed dorms, a rooftop bar and a bargain breakfast. **Hotel Lena** *(☎ 281 022 3280; Lahana 10; singles with private bathroom €32, doubles with shared bathroom €33)* has large, dull rooms, while nearby **Ilaira Hotel** *(☎ 281 022 7103; Epimenidou 1; singles/doubles €35/42)* has compact ones with nice views from the rooftop bar.

There's a bustling, colourful market all the way along 1866 for self-caterers. **Giakoumis Taverna** is the best of a bunch of cheap tavernas in the area around 1866. **Pagopeion**, by Agios Titos church, is a super-cool café and bar with exceptional food at OK prices. (Check out the toilets!)

Getting There & Away

It's easy to leave Iraklio. There are several flights a day to Athens and, in summer, daily flights from Iraklio to Thessaloniki, and three flights a week to Rhodes and Santorini.

There are daily ferries to Piraeus (€24), as well as boats most days to Santorini that continue on to other Cycladic islands. In summer, a boat sails twice weekly from Iraklio to Marmaris in Turkey, via Rhodes. For boat schedules, **Skoutelis Travel Bureau** *(☎ 281 028 0808, fax 281 033 2747; 25 Avgoustou 20)* seems friendly, or try some of the other agencies on this strip.

Iraklio has two bus stations. Bus Station A, just inland from the new harbour, serves eastern Crete (Agios Nikolaos, Ierapetra, Sitia, Malia and the Lasithi Plateau). The Hania and Rethymno terminal is opposite Bus Station A, across the street. Bus Station B, 50m

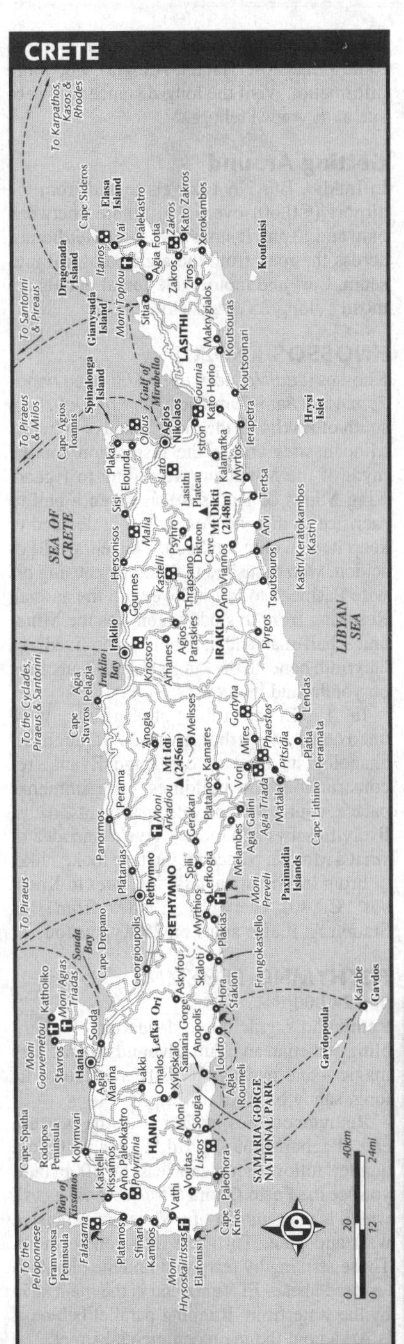

beyond the Hania Gate, serves the southern route (Phaestos, Matala, Anogia). For more information, visit the long-distance bus website at w www.ktel.org.

Getting Around

In Iraklio, Bus No 1 travels to and from the airport (€0.60) every 15 minutes between 6am and 11pm. It stops at Plateia Eleftherias, across the road from the archaeological museum. Car- and motorcycle-rental outlets are mostly along 25 Avgoustou.

KNOSSOS ΚΝΩΣΟΣ

Knossos *(adult/concession €6/3; open noon-7pm Mon, 8am-7pm Tues-Sun Apr-Oct)*, 5km south of Iraklio, is the most famous of Crete's Minoan sites and is the inspiration for the myth of the Minotaur. According to legend, King Minos of Knossos was given a bull to sacrifice to the god Poseidon, but decided to keep it, as would anybody. This enraged Poseidon, who punished the king by causing his wife Pasiphae to fall in love with the animal. Resulting from this odd union was the Minotaur – half-man and half-bull – who lived in a labyrinth beneath the king's palace, munching on youths and maidens.

In 1900, the ruins of Knossos were uncovered by Arthur Evans. Although archaeologists tend to disparage Evans' reconstruction, the buildings – an immense palace, courtyards, private apartments, baths, lively frescoes and more – give a fine idea of what a Minoan palace might have looked like.

From Iraklio, local bus No 2 goes to Knossos (€0.80) every 10 minutes from Bus Station A; it also stops on 25 Avgoustou.

RETHYMNO ΡΕΘΥΜΝΟ

pop 24,000

Rethymno's gracious old quarter of crumbling Venetian and Turkish buildings radiates magic – and package tourists who crowd its long, sandy beachfront.

Rethymno's bus station is at the western end of Igoumenou Gavriil. To reach the old quarter, follow Igoumenou east for 700m until you see the **Porto Guora** *(Ethnikis Andistasis)*, which is the remnant of a Venetian defensive wall and gate. Turn left and you're there. Those arriving by ferry will find the old quarter dead ahead. El Venizelou is the main strip by the waterfront. Running parallel behind it is Arkadiou, the main commercial street.

GREECE

The **municipal tourist office** *(☎ 2831 029 148; open 8am-2.30pm Mon-Fri)* is on the beach side of El Venizelou, in the same building as the **tourist police** *(☎ 2831 028 156)*. **Ellotia Tours** *(☎ 2831 051 981; e elotia@ret.forthnet.gr; Arkadiou 155)* will answer all transport and tour inquiries. The **post office** *(Moatsou 21)* is in the new town, one block back from the main square **Plateia Martyron** *(cnr Igoumenou Gavriil & Ethnikis Andistasis)*. There's 24-hour Internet access at **G@meNet-Café** opposite Plateia Martyron.

The **Venetian Fortress** *(admission €2.90; open 9am-6pm Tues-Sun)* affords great views across the town and mountains. Opposite is the **archaeological museum** *(admission €1.50; open 8.30am-3pm Tues-Sun)*. The **historical and folk art museum** *(Vernardou; admission €3; open 9.30am-2.30pm, 6pm-9pm Mon-Sat)* proudly displays Cretan crafts.

Places to Stay & Eat

Youth Hostel *(☎ 2831 022 848; e reservations@yhrethymno.com; Tombazi 45; dorm & roof beds €6)* is a well-run place with crowded dorms. **Olga's Pension** *(☎ 2831 028 665; Souliou 57; singles/doubles/triples with bathroom €30/35/45)* is central with colourful, cosy rooms of intriguing taste and a wild rooftop garden.

Taverna Kyria Maria *(Diog Mesologiou 20)* is tucked behind the Rimondi fountain under a lush canopy. **Gounakis Restaurant & Bar** *(Koroneou 6)* has live Cretan music and reasonably priced food. East of the Rimondi fountain, Arabatzoglou and Radamanthios have upmarket eateries of bewitching ambience.

Getting There & Away

Ferries travel daily from Piraeus to Rethymno (€24). For schedules, visit **ANEK** *(Arkadiou 250)* by the old Venetian harbour or Ellotia Tours *(☎ 2831 051 981; Arkadiou 155)*. Buses depart regularly to Iraklio (€5.90, 1½ hours), Hania (€5.30, one hour), Agia Galini, Moni Arkadiou and Plakas.

HANIA ΧΑΝΙΑ

pop 65,000

Lovely Hania, the old capital of Crete, lures tourists in droves with its softly hued Venetian buildings, snug location near idyllic beaches, and a glorious mountain interior. Hania is a place to amble wide-eyed for a couple of days, enjoying its vital signs and plotting side trips. For information, try the **tourist police** *(2821 053 333; Kydonias 29; open Mon-Fri)*, near Plateia 1866. Send your mail at the **central post office** *(Tzanakaki 3)*. **Vranas Studios** *(Agion Deka)* has a comfortable Internet set up.

The **archaeological museum** *(Halidon 30; admission €1.50; open 8.30am-3pm Tues-Sun)* was formerly the Venetian Church of San Francesco, until it was converted by the Turks into a mosque.

Pension Fidias *(☎ 2821 052 494; Sarpaki 6; dorm beds/doubles/triples €8/15/21)*, behind the Orthodox Cathedral, is still the budget choice and renovations are planned. **Ifigenia II** *(☎ 2821 094 357, fax 2821 036 104; Angelou 18; doubles €35-40)* has a range of excitingly eccentric rooms, some with four-poster beds. **Rooms for Rent George** *(☎ 2821 088 715; Zambeliou 30; singles/doubles/triples €15/24/33)* is an atmospheric relic.

The food market off Plateia Markopoulou is a self-caterers' paradise. **To Ayho Toy Kokkopa** *(Agion Deka)*, beneath Vranas Studios, does crisp salads and sandwiches.

Many restaurants play live Cretan music, but **Café Kriti** is the authentic experience. Harbour tavernas are packed at sunset. After dark, **Neorio Café**, **Bora Bora** and **Cocktails Galini** attract a younger crowd. For shots and dancing on the bar, it's **Nota-Bene**.

If you must leave Hania, there are several flights a day to Athens and two flights a week to Thessaloniki. Daily ferries run to Piraeus (€22) from the port of Souda, 10km east of town. The travel agencies on Halidon can help with all schedules and ticketing. Frequent buses plough daily to Iraklio, Rethymno and Kastelli-Kissamos; less-frequent buses go to Paleohora, Omalos, Hora Sfakion and Elafonisi from the main bus station on Kydonias. Buses for Souda (the port) leave frequently from outside the food market. Buses for the beaches west of Hania leave from the south-eastern corner of Plateia 1866.

SAMARIA GORGE ΦΑΡΑΓΓΙ ΤΗΣ ΣΑΜΑΡΙΑΣ

Samaria Gorge *(☎ 2825 067 179; admission €3.50; open 6am-3pm daily May–mid-Oct)* is one of Europe's most spectacular – and tramped upon – gorges. Rugged footwear, food, water and sun protection are essential for this strenuous six-hour trek, which is not recommended for inexperienced walkers. You can do the walk independently by taking the Omalos bus from the main bus station in Hania (€5, one hour, three daily) to the head of the gorge at Xyloskalo and walking the length of the gorge (16km) to Agia Roumeli, from where you take a boat to Hora Sfakion (€4.40, two daily) and then a bus back to Hania (€5.10; two hours; four daily). Too much? You could join one of the easier daily excursions from Hania that walk about 4km into the gorge. Check out the travel agencies on Halidon in Hania for information.

PALEOHORA ΠΑΛΑΙΟΧώΡΑ

☎ 2823

Paleohora, discovered by hippies back in the 1960s, is a relaxing if overrated resort favoured by backpackers. There's a welcoming **tourist office** *(☎ 2823 041 507)* three blocks south of the bus stop.

Camping Paleohora *(☎ 2823 041 120; camping per person/tent €4/3)* is 1.5km northeast of town, near the pebble beach. There's also a restaurant and nightclub here. **Homestay Anonymous** *(☎ 2823 042 098; singles/doubles/triples €12/17/20)*, in Paleohora, is a great place for backpackers with its warm service and communal kitchen.

Domatia and taverna dot the harbourfront. Readers recommend **Calypso** near the pebble beach. Near the sandy beach, try **The Third Eye** for vegetarian, or **The Small Garden** for international fare.

There are at least five buses daily between Hania and Paleohora (€5, 1¼ hours). No road links the coastal resorts but if you can't swim (kidding) daily boats from Paleohora to Elafonisi, Agia Roumeli and Hora Sfakion connect the resorts in summer.

SITIA ΣΗΤΕΙΑ

pop 9000

Back on the northeastern coast, package tourism gathers momentum as it advances eastwards, reaching a crescendo in Agios Nikolaos. Attractive Sitia, further east on a hotel-lined bay flanked by mountains, is an easy place to unwind and has good connections to the Dodecanese islands. The main square, Plateia El Venizelou, is at the northern end of Karamanli. The **municipal tourist office** *(open Mon-Fri)* is on the waterfront just before the town beach. **Tzortzakis Travel Agency** *(☎ 2843 025 080; ⓔ tzortzakis@sit.forthnet.gr; Kornarou 150)* is good for tickets and accommodation advice.

The **post office** *(Dimokratou)* is off El Venizelou. The ferry port is about 800m away, signposted from the square.

There is no shortage of *domatia* behind the waterfront. **Hotel Arhontiko** *(☎ 2843 028 172; Kondylaki 16; doubles/triples €23/27.60)* is basic, but immaculate. To find it, walk towards the ferry quay along El Venizelou, turn left up Filellinon and then right onto Kondylaki.

Just inland the tavernas **Kali Kardia** *(Foundalidhou 22)* and **O Mixos** *(Kornarou 15 • harbourside)* are popular with the locals. At the port end of Kornarou, you'll find **Murphy's Irish Pub**.

There are daily ferries from Piraeus to Sitia (€24), three ferries per week to Rhodes and four to Karpathos. In summer, there's one ferry per week to Santorini. Visit Tzortzakis Travel Agency for tickets and schedules.

There are five buses daily to Ierapetra, and five to Iraklio, via Agios Nikolaos. In peak season, there are four buses daily to Vaï Beach.

Dodecanese Δωδεκάνησα

The Dodecanese are more verdant and mountainous than the Cyclades and have comparable beaches. Here you get a sense of Greece's proximity to Asia. Ancient temples, massive crusader fortifications, mosques and imposing Italian-built neoclassical buildings stand juxtaposed, vestiges of a turbulent past. There are 16 inhabited islands in the group; the most visited are Rhodes, Kos, Patmos and Symi.

RHODES ΡΟΔΟΣ

According to mythology, the sun god Helios chose Rhodes as his bride and bestowed light, warmth and vegetation upon her. The blessing seems to have paid off, for Rhodes produces more flowers and sunny days than most Greek islands.

The ancient sites of Lindos and Kamiros are legacies of Rhodes' importance in antiquity. In 1291, the Knights of St John, having fled Jerusalem under siege, came to Rhodes and established themselves as masters. In 1522, Süleyman I, sultan of the Ottoman Empire, staged a massive attack on the island and took Rhodes City. The island, along with the other Dodecanese islands, then became part of the Ottoman Empire.

Rhodes City

pop 43,500

Rhodes' capital and port is Rhodes City, on the northern tip of the island. Almost everything of interest lies in the Old Town, enclosed within massive walls. The main thoroughfares are Sokratous, Pythagora, Agiou Fanouriou and Ipodamou, with a clump of spaghetti streets in between. The new town to the north is a monument to package tourism.

The main port, Commercial Harbour, is east of the Old Town, and north of here is Mandraki Harbour, the supposed site of the Colossus of Rhodes, a giant bronze statue of Apollo (built in 292–280 BC) and one of the Seven Wonders of the Ancient World. The statue stood for a mere 65 years before being toppled by an earthquake.

Orientation & Information The **EOT tourist office** *(☎ 2241 023 255; e eot-rodos@otenet.gr; cnr Makariou & Papagou; open Mon-Fri)* is next door to the **tourist police** *(☎ 2241 027 423; open daily)*. In summer there is also a **municipal tourist office** *(☎ 2241 035 945; Plateia Rimini; open daily)*. For ticketing and tour information, see **Triton Holidays** *(☎ 2241 021 690; e info@triton dmc.gr; 1st floor, Plastira 9)* in the new town. In the Old Town, try **Castellania Travel** *(☎ 2241 075 860; e castell@otenet.gr)*, which faces the clock tower in front of the Castellania Fountain. It's tucked in the right-hand back corner of the square.

Send mail at the **main post office** *(Mandrak Harbour)*. There is a tiny Internet café in the Old Town, **Cosmonet** *(Plateia Martyron Evreon)*, on the west corner of the square.

Things to See & Do The Old Town is reputedly the world's finest surviving example of medieval fortification. The 12m-thick walls are closed to the public, but you can take a **guided walk** *(€6; 2.45pm Tues & Sat)* along them starting in the courtyard of the Palace of the Knights.

Odos Ippoton (Avenue of the Knights) is lined with magnificent medieval buildings, the most imposing of which is the **Palace of the Knights** *(Ippoton; admission €6; open 12.30pm-7pm Mon, 8am-7pm Tues-Sun)*, restored, but never used, as a holiday home for Mussolini.

The 15th-century Knight's Hospital is a splendid building. Restored by the Italians, it is now the **archaeological museum** *(Plateia Mousiou; admission €4; open 8.30am-7pm Tues-Sun)* with an impressive collection that includes the ethereal marble statue the *Aphrodite of Rhodes*.

The 18th-century **Turkish Baths** *(Plateia Arionos; admission €1.50; open 11am-6pm Wed-Fri, 8am-6pm Sat)* – signposted from Ipodamou – offers a rare opportunity to bathe Turkish-style in Greece. Bring your own soap and towel.

Places to Stay The EOT can help with accommodation in the new town, but get there early; they're frantic in summer.

Rodos Youth Hostel *(☎ 2241 030 491; Ergiou 12; roof/dorm beds €6/8, doubles with/without bathroom €22/18)*, off Agio Fanouriou in the Old Town, has a lovely garden but lumpy mattresses. Ask about the new studios out back.

Sunlight Hotel *(☎/fax 2241 021 435; Ipodamou 32; doubles/triples with bathroom €40/45)* is above sociable Stavros Bar; rooms have a fridge.

Hotel Andreas *(☎ 2241 034 156; ⓔ andreasch@otenet.gr; Omirou 28D; rooms €33-59)* has small, pleasant rooms with varied facilities and terrific views from its terrace.

For fresh, basic rooms try **Pink Elephant Pension** *(☎/fax 2241 022 469; ⓔ pinkelephantpension@yahoo.com; Timaxida; doubles €32-53)*, signposted off Irodotou, and **Spot Hotel** *(☎ 2241 034 737; ⓔ spothot@otenet.gr; Perikleous 12; singles/doubles/triples with bathroom €35/44/68)*.

Places to Eat Away from the venues with tacky photo menus, you'll find some good eateries. Head to **Kringlan Swedish Bakery** *(I Dragoumi 14)* in the new town for exceptional sandwiches and light snacks. **Taverna Kostas** *(Pythagora 62)*, **Yiannis Taverna** *(Platanos)* and **Ta Synaxaria** *(Aristofanous)* are authentic Greek places with family service.

If you're tired of Greek food, there are some excellent options. **Kasbah** *(Platanos 4)* serves huge Moroccan-influenced meals in a refined atmosphere. **Mandala** *(Sofokleous)* is very relaxed, with a healthy choice of stir-fries and pasta.

Entertainment The **Greek Folk Dance Theatre** *(☎ 2241 029 085; Andronikou; adult/concession €12/8; performances from 9.20pm Mon, Wed & Fri)* gives a first-rate show. Go Zorba!

The Old Town has some classy, less-chaotic bars for a cruisy night out, as well as leafy squares with live Greek music. In the new town, the drink-till-you-drop crowd goes bar hopping on Orfanidou in the city's northwest.

Around the Island

The **Acropolis of Lindos** *(admission €6; open 12.30pm-7pm Mon, 8am-7pm Tues-Sun)*, 47km from Rhodes City, is Rhodes' most important ancient city and is spectacularly perched atop a 116m-high rocky outcrop. Below the site is Lindos town, a touristy tangle of streets with elaborately decorated 17th-century houses. The bus to Lindos (€3.20) departs from Rhodes City's east-side station.

The extensive ruins of **Kamiros** *(admission €3; open 8.30am-7pm Tues-Sun)*, an ancient Doric city on the west coast, are well preserved, with the remains of houses, baths, a cemetery and a temple, but the site should be visited as much for its lovely setting on a gentle hillside overlooking the sea.

Getting There & Away

There are daily flights from Rhodes to Athens (€87) and Karpathos (€29). In summer there are regular flights to Iraklio, Mykonos, Santorini and Kastellorizo. Contact Triton Holidays or Castellania Travel (see Orientation & Information under Rhodes City, earlier).

There are daily ferries from Rhodes to Piraeus (€29). Most sail via the Dodecanese north of Rhodes, but at least three times a week there is a service via Karpathos, Crete and the Cyclades. The EOT gives out a schedule. Kiriacoulis Maritime holds the hydrofoil schedules.

Excursion boats (€18 return) and hydrofoils (€12 one way) trip daily to Symi. Ferries travel less often (€8 one way). Similar services also run to Kos, Kalymnos, Nisyros, Tilos, Patmos and Leros.

Between April and October, there are regular boats from Rhodes to Marmaris in Turkey (€36 one way). There is an additional US$15 Turkish port tax each way.

From April to August, there are regular ferries to Israel (€100) via Cyprus (€71). Prices do not include foreign port tax. For information, contact Triton Holidays, Castellania Travel, or other travel agencies in the New Market area.

Getting Around

There are frequent buses between the airport and Rhodes City's west-side bus station (€2). Or you could catch a taxi for about €13.

Rhodes City has two bus stations. The west-side bus station, next to the New Market, serves the airport, the west coast, Embona and Koskinou; the east-side bus station at Plateia Rimini serves the east coast and the inland southern villages. The EOT has a schedule.

SYMI ΣΥΜΗ

pop 2332

Symi town is outstandingly attractive, with pastel-coloured neoclassical mansions surrounding the harbour and hills. The island is swamped by day trippers from Rhodes, so it's worth staying over to enjoy Symi.

The town is divided into Gialos, the harbour, and above it the tranquil Horio, which is accessible by taxi, bus or 360 steps from the harbour. The best source of information is the free and widely available English-language *Symi Visitor* newspaper, which includes maps of the town. Excursion boats to other parts of the island also run guided walks. **Kalodoukas Holidays** *(☎ 2246 071 077; ⓔ information@kalodoukas.gr)* has a book of trails that you can do independently. An excellent website is ⓦ www.symivisitor.com.

Budget accommodation is scarce, but digs in the village are cheaper; ask at Kalodoukas Holidays. Located in the two streets opposite the excursion boats, **Hotel Albatros** *(☎ 2246 071 829, fax 2246 072 257; ⓔ fabienne@otenet.gr; doubles €50)* and **Hotel Kokona** *(☎ 2246 071 549, fax 2246 072 620; doubles €50)* both have spotless, bright doubles.

From the ferry dock, the bulk of restaurants are to the left, past the central square. **Meraklis** is a cheap and cheery taverna. **Sunflower** offers excellent sandwiches and savoury vegetarian. Up in the Horio, **Kali Strata Bar** *(Kali Strata)* provides perfect sunset moments.

There are frequent ferries and hydrofoils between Rhodes and Kos that also call at Symi, as well as less-frequent services to Tilos, Nisyros, Kalymno, Leros and Patmos. The bus and taxi stop is at the east end of the harbour, past the restaurants.

KOS ΚΩΣ

pop 26,379

Kos is the birthplace of Hippocrates, the father of medicine, but that's as Greek as this place gets. With its ruins and Turkish buildings on a backdrop of pretty palm-lined streets, neon cafés, pulsing clubs and tourist trains, Kos town exudes a very Vegas-esque aura. It's well located for day trips to several islands and Turkey.

Kos town, on the northeast coast, is the main town and port. The **municipal tourist office** *(☎ 2242 024 460; ⓔ dotkos@hol.gr; open Mon-Sat)*, on the waterfront just past the police station, provides maps and accommodation information. The post office is on Vasileos Pavlou. The **tourist police** *(☎ 2242 022 444)* and regular police live together, opposite the quay. **Café Del Mare** *(Megalou Alexandrou 4)* is the best-equipped Internet café. To get to the **bus station** *(Kleopatras)* walk 350m up Vasileos Pavlou from the harbourfront and turn right.

Things to See & Do

The focus of the **archaeological museum** *(Plateia Eleftherias; admission €3; open 8am-2.30pm Tues-Sun)* is sculpture from excavations around the island. The ancient agora, with the ruins of the **Shrine of Aphrodite** and **Temple of Hercules**, is just off Plateia Eleftherias. It's free but has zero data.

On a pine-clad hill, 4km from Kos town, stand the extensive ruins of the renowned healing centre of **Asklipion** *(admission €4; open 8.30am-6pm Tues-Sun)*, where Hippocrates practised medicine. Farther south is Kefalos Bay, a long stretch of beach swamped in sun lounges and rippling with water sports.

Places to Stay & Eat

Kos Camping *(☎ 2242 023 910; camping per adult/tent €6/3.50)* is 3km along the eastern waterfront, with good shade and a minimart. Hop on any of the buses from the harbourfront going to Agios Fokas.

Pension Alexis *(☎ 2242 028 798, fax 2242 025 797; Irodotou 9; doubles/triples with shared bathroom €26/32)* is a convivial place. It's noisy, but Alexis is an admirable host. To find it, turn right from the port and walk about 300m to the port police, turn left and then take the first right.

Hotel Afendoulis *(☎ 2242 025 321; Evripilou 1; doubles/triples with bathroom €36/45)* is a superior hotel with well-kept rooms in a quieter area. To get there, turn left from the ferry, walk about 500m to Evripilou and turn right.

Among the glut of uninspired tourist tavernas, **Filoxenia Taverna** *(cnr Pindou & Alikarnassou)* and **Barba's Grill**, opposite Hotel Afendoulis, are happy exceptions.

Entertainment

There are a dozen clubs catering to the different music moods of the crowd around the streets of Diakon and Nafklirou. Head for **Kalua**, 400m past the ferry quay, for foam parties and dance mania.

Getting There & Around

There are daily flights to Athens (€80.40) from Kos's international airport.

There are frequent ferries from Rhodes that continue on to Piraeus (€29.75), via Kalymnos, Leros and Patmos, and less-frequent connections to Nisyros, Tilos, Symi, Samos and Crete. Daily excursion boats visit Nisyros, Kalymnos, Patmos and Rhodes.

In summer, ferries depart daily for Bodrum in Turkey (€15 one way, €25 return). Port tax costs €10.

For tickets and scheduling information, visit the efficient **Exas Travel** *(☎ 2242 029 900; ⓔ exas@exas.com; Antinavarhou Ioannini)*.

Next to the tourist office is a mini blue train that leaves hourly for Asklipion (€3) and a mini green train that does city tours (€2). Buses for Agios Fokas leave from opposite the town hall on the harbourfront; all other buses (including those to Kefalos Bay) leave from the bus station on Kleopatras.

PATMOS ΠΑΤΜΟΣ

pop 2663

Starkly scenic Patmos gets crowded in summer, but somehow remains remarkably tranquil. Orthodox and Western Christians have long made pilgrimages to this holy island for its world-class sites. The **tourist office** *(open Mon-Fri)*, post office and police station are in the white building at the island's port and capital of Skala. Buses leave regularly for the *hora*, 4.5km inland. Blue Bay Hotel, 200m left from the port (facing inland), has limited Internet access.

The **Cave of the Apocalypse** *(admission free; open 8am-1.30pm Mon-Sat, 8am-noon Sun, 4pm-6pm Tues, Thurs & Sun)*, where St John wrote the *Book of Revelations*, is halfway between the port and *hora*. Take a bus or make the pilgrimage via the **Byzantine path**. To do this, walk up the Skala–Hora road, take the steps to the right 100m beyond the far side of the football field. The path begins opposite the top of the steps.

The **Monastery of St John the Theologian** *(admission monastery/treasury free/€5)*, which is open the same hours as the cave, exhibits monastic treasures: early manuscripts, embroidered robes, incredible carvings and an El Greco painting. Dress modestly (ie, no shorts) for the holy sites.

Patmos' coastline provides secluded coves, mostly with pebble beaches. The best is **Psili Ammos**, in the south, reached by excursion boat from Skala port.

Stefanos Camping *(☎ 2247 031 821)* is on Meloi Beach, 2km northeast of Skala. Try **Travel Point Holidays** *(☎ 2247 032 801; ⓦ www.travelpoint.gr)*, on the road to the *hora*, for budget *pensions* such as **Pension Maria Paskeledi** *(☎ 2247 032 152, fax 2247 033 346; doubles/triples with bathroom €32/45)*. **Grigoris Taverna**, opposite the port's passenger-transit gate, is popular.

Frequent ferries travel between Patmos and Piraeus (€20.40), and to Rhodes (€17) via Leros, Kalymnos and Kos. Visit GA Ferries, inland from the central square, for schedules. In summer, there are daily Flying Dolphin hydrofoils to Leros, Kalymnos, Kos, Rhodes, Fourni, Ikaria, Agathonisi and Samos. See Apollon Travel on the waterfront, near the quay, for bookings.

Northeastern Aegean Islands

There are seven major islands in this neglected group: Chios, Ikaria, Lesvos, Limnos, Samos, Samothraki and Thasos. The distance between them makes island hopping tricky, but these neighbours reward exploration with wonderful hiking, crowd-free beaches and unique villages.

LESVOS ΛΕΣΒΟΣ

Fertile Lesvos, also known as Mytilini, is the third-largest Greek island. It has always been a centre of philosophy and artistic achievement, and still attracts creative types on sabbatical. Spoil yourself with its prized olive oil, ouzo, sardines and therapeutic hot springs. An excellent source of information on the island is ⓦ www.greeknet.com.

Mytilini

pop 23,970

The capital and main port, Mytilini, is a large, dreary working town. The **tourist police** *(☎ 2251 022 776)* are at the entrance to the quay. The **EOT** *(☎ 2251 042 511; open Sun-Fri)*, 50m up Aristarhou by the quay, offers brochures and maps, but is too busy for tourists! Try **Manos Centre** *(☎ 2251 048 124; Kountourioti 47)*, 400m from the ferry on the waterfront, for travel arrangements.

Mytilini's museums are exceptional. The neoclassical **archaeological museum** *(admission €3; open 8.30am-7pm Tues-Sun)* has a fascinating collection from Neolithic to Roman times. The **new archaeological museum** *(same admission & hours)* displays spectacular mosaics from ancient households. Both are on 8 Noemvriou, signposted from the ferry. **Theophilos Museum** *(admission €2; open 9am-2.30pm & 6pm-8pm Tues-Sun)*, 4km from Mytilini in Varia village, is a shrine to the prolific folk painter, Theophilos.

Central, budget accommodation choices are **Arion Rooms** *(☎ 2251 042 650; Arionos 4; doubles €25)* for basic rooms with mythical frescoes and **Alkaios Rooms** *(☎/fax 2251 047 737; Alkaiou 16; doubles €24)* in an old mansion. To get there, face inland from the waterfront and take Alkaiou to the right of Therapon church; Arion is on the first left, Alkaios is another 100m straight ahead.

There are daily flights to Athens (€78) and to Thessaloniki (€80), five per week to Limnos (€36.25) and two per week to Chios (€28.25), but don't rush to leave. In summer, there are daily boats to Piraeus (€24), some via Chios, Mykonos and Syros, and one boat per week to Thessaloniki (€28). There are four ferries per week to Ayvalik in Turkey (€38 one way, €45 return, including taxes). Stop by Manos Centre for ticketing and schedules.

Mytilini has two bus stations. For local buses, walk about 400m from the ferry to the harbourfront station where buses leave regularly for Loutra Yera and Varia.

For long-distance buses, walk 600m from the ferry along the waterfront to El Venizelou and turn right until you reach Agia Irinis park, which is next to the station. There are regular services in summer to Mithymna, Petra, Agiasos, Skala Eresou, Mantamados and Agia Paraskevi.

Mithymna

pop 1333

The gracious, preserved town of Mithymna (known by locals as Molyvos), is 62km north of Mytilini. Cobbled streets canopied by flowering vines are lined with cosy tavernas and genteel stone cottages. You'll be tempted never to leave this scenic place.

From the bus stop, walk straight ahead towards the town to a fork in the road. Take the right fork onto 17 Noemvriou, the main thoroughfare, or continue straight ahead to reach the colourful fishing port. The **municipal tourist office** *(☎ 2253 071 347; open daily)* is 50m from the bus stop. There are three Internet cafés and an open-air cinema along the port road.

The noble **Genoese castle** *(admission €2; open 8am-7pm Tues-Sun)* hosts a drama festival in summer. **Eftalou hot springs** *(admission €2.50; open 9am-1pm & 3pm-7pm Mon-Sat)*, 3km from town on the beach, is a tiny bathhouse with a whitewashed dome and a nice steaming, pebbled pool. **Mithymna Beach** gets crowded. Nearby **Eftalou**, **Skala Sykaminias** and **Petra** are better options.

There are over 50 *domatia* in Mithymna; 17 Noemvriou is a good place to start. The tourist office also offers accommodation advice. **Nassos Guest House** *(☎ 2253 071 432; ⓔ nassosguesthouse@hotmail.com; doubles with shared bathroom €29)* is an airy, friendly, traditional place with communal kitchen and rapturous views. To get there, head up 17 Noemvriou and take the second right (a sharp switchback).

At the end of the port road, **Captain's Table** does Greek fare with flair. Upstairs at **Dilino** is ideal for breakfast. Head up the port road for night-time action.

For cruisy blues and nightcaps, drop by **Pirates Café**. **Café Del Mare** and **Christine's Bar** are good primers for a big night out at **Med Bar** dance club.

In summer, buses go regularly to Petra Beach and Eftalou. Excursion boats leave the port daily for Skala Sykaminias. Faonas Travel at the port has schedules.

Around the Island

East of Mithymna, the traditional picturesque villages surrounding **Mt Lepetymnos** – Sykaminia, Mantamados and Agia Paraskevi – are worth your time.

Sensuous Sappho

Of course you were already aware of this, but the resemblance between the name 'Lesvos' and the term 'lesbian' is no coincidence. One of Greece's great ancient poets, Sappho, was born on Lesvos during the seventh century BC in the town of Eresos. Sappho's poetry quickly became famous for its lyrically evocative style and richly sumptuous imagery. Most of Sappho's work was devoted to love and desire, and the objects of her affection were often female. Owing to this last fact, her name and birthplace have come to be associated with female homosexuality.

Sappho's prodigious talent and massive body of work led her to be championed as a genius – even a muse – by her contemporaries. Although few of her works have survived in their entirety, she has inspired several modern poets and artists, and remains something of an icon for several admirers.

The southwestern beach resort of **Skala Esrou**, built over ancient Eresos, is the birthplace of Sappho (see 'Sensuous Sappho'). It has become a popular destination for the lesbian travellers who come on a kind of pilgrimage to honour her.

Southern Lesvos is dominated by **Mt Olympus** (968m) and the pretty day-trip destination of **Agiasos**, which has good artisan workshops.

Sporades Σποράδες

The Sporades group comprises the lush, pine-forested islands of Skiathos, Skopelos and Alonnisos, and far-flung Skyros, off Evia. The main ports for these islands are Volos and Agios Konstantinos on the mainland.

SKIATHOS ΣΚΙΑΘΟΣ

pop 4100

Crowded and expensive with a happening nightlife, Skiathos has a universal beach-resort feel, but no charm. There are loads of good beaches awash with water sports on the south coast, particularly Koukounaries.

There is a tourist-information booth to the left as you leave the port. Harried travel agencies along the waterfront spit out tour and travel information.

Skiathos town's main thoroughfare is Papadiamanti, running inland opposite the port. Here you'll find the post office, **tourist police** (*☎ 2427 023 172*) and Draft-Net Internet café. The bus stop is at the far end of the harbour; turn right from the ferry.

Nightlife sprawls along Politehniou; to find it, turn left off Papadiamanti and walk 70m up Evangelistrias.

Places to Stay & Eat

There is a Rooms to Let bookings kiosk on the waterfront. Package-tour operators book accommodation solid for July and August when *domatia* owners drop value for money. Off peak, rooms are up to 50% cheaper. **Camping Koukounaries** (*☎ 2427 049 250; camping per person/tent €6/3*) is 30 minutes away by bus at Koukounaries Beach.

Hotel Karafelas (*☎ 2427 021 235, fax 2427 023 307; singles/doubles with bathroom €30/53*), in town at the end of Papadiamanti on your left, has generous rooms with balconies.

Hotel Marlton (*☎ 2427 022 552, ☎/fax 2427 022 878; doubles/triples with bathroom €40/48*) is friendly and has fresh, pine-furnished rooms. To get there from Papadiamanti, turn right onto Evangelistrias and walk 50m.

On the waterfront, **Zio Peppe's** yummy pizza cures hangovers. On Papadiamanti, try reasonably priced **Niko's Café Bar**.

Getting There & Around

In summer, there are five flights per week from Athens to Skiathos (€69.35) and one a week to Skyros (€34.55).

There are frequent ferries to the mainland ports of Volos (€11) and Agios Konstantinos (€10.10), and frequent hydrofoils each day to Skopelos (€8.80) and Alonnisos (€12). In summer, there are two boats a week to Thessaloniki.

Crowded buses ply the south-coast road between Skiathos town and Koukounaries every 20 minutes, stopping at all the beaches along the way. Many south-coast beaches are only accessible by caïque from the port.

SKOPELOS ΣΚΟΠΕΛΟΣ

pop 5000

Skopelos has the appeal of a mountain-lake resort, with its thick forests of scruffy pine and jade-green pebble beaches. **Thalpos Leisure**

& Services *(☎ 2424 022 947; ⓔ thalpos@otenet.gr)* on the waterfront is handy for accommodation and tours. It's a few doors past Pension Kir Sotos on the first floor.

Attractive **Skopelos town**, with its dazzling white, hillside homes, is a maze of narrow streets and stairways where the kissing balconies of cascading flowers and bright window shutters burst with colour. Take time to wander – you'll find stone churches with glittering interiors tucked around many corners.

Glossa, the island's other inland town, is quite ordinary but it's a pleasant drive there with marvellous views.

Velanio Beach is the island's nudie spot. Pebbled **Panormos Beach**, with its sheltered emerald bay surrounded by pine forest is superb. The 2km stretch of **Milia Beach**, a few kilometres further on, is considered the island's best.

Thalpos Leisure & Services and **Madro Travel** *(☎ 2424 022 145; ⓔ enquiries@madrotravel.com)* offer boat excursions and walking tours. Madro is at the end of the northern waterfront, about 70m before the church.

Places to Stay & Eat

In high season, rooms are engulfed by package tourists, so it pays to sift through the *domatia* owners who meet the boats. Thalpos Leisure & Services has an accommodation-finding service. Opposite the port entrance, the Rooms & Apartments Association of Skopelos has a brochure of *domatia*, but doesn't make bookings.

Pension Kir Sotos *(☎ 2424 022 549, fax 2424 023 668; doubles/triples with bathroom €35/49)*, in the middle of the waterfront, has spacious rooms in an enchanting building. There's also a communal kitchen and courtyard.

Pension Soula *(☎ 2424 022 930/024 631; doubles/studios from €24/27)*, a 10-minute walk out of town, is welcoming place with airy rooms; you'll awake in rural bliss to donkeys braying and birdsong. To find it, walk left from the port and turn left at Hotel Amalia. Follow the road, bearing right after about 200m; it's on your right.

Zio Peppe, on the waterfront, is the best place for a pizza fix. **Taverna Fikinas** has imaginative dishes; follow the signs from the middle of the waterfront – getting there is a treasure hunt!

Entertainment

The crowd-pleasing **Dancing Club Kounos** never fails. Nearby, try **Panselinos** for Greek *rembetika* music and **Metro Club** for Greek pop and rock.

For a sultry mood, it's **La Costa** bar, opposite the bus station, or the so-laid-back-it's-falling-over **Platanos Jazz Bar** at the northern end of the waterfront.

Getting There & Away

In summer, there are daily ferries to Volos (€10.60) and Agios Konstantinos (€25.40) that also call at Skiathos. Flying Dolphin hydrofoils dash several times a day to Skiathos, Alonnisos, Volos and Agios Konstantinos. All boats leave from the same port, but in rough weather they may depart from Agnontas Beach, southwest of town. Most hydrofoils also call in at Loutraki, the port below Glossa. For schedules and tickets, see Kosifis Travel opposite the port.

There are frequent buses from Skopelos town to Glossa, stopping at all beaches along the way.

ALONNISOS ΑΛΟΝΝΗΣΟΣ

pop 3000

Green, serene Alonnisos is the least visited of the Sporades. The area surrounding the island has been declared a marine park and is the cleanest in the Aegean. The restful port village of **Patitiri** has two main thoroughfares; facing inland from the ferry quay, Pelasgon is to the left and Ikion Dolopon is to the far right. The bus stop is on the corner of Ikion Dolopon and the waterfront.

The tiny *hora*, **Old Alonnisos**, is a few kilometres inland. Its streets sprout a profusion of plant life, alluring villas of eclectic design and dramatic vistas.

Alonnisos is ideal for walking. Waterfront travel agencies offer guided tours, and an excellent trail guide called *Alonnisos on Foot: A Walking & Swimming Guide*, by Bente Keller & Elias Tsoukanas, is available at newsstands. **Patitiri Beach** is OK for a dip; **Kokkinokastro** and **Hrysia Milia**, on the east coast, are better.

The **Rooms to Let service** *(☎/fax 2424 065 577)*, right of the quay, books accommodation all over the island.

Camping Rocks *(☎ 2424 065 410)* is a shady, basic site. It is a steep hike about 1.5km from the port; go up Pelasgon and take the first road on your left. **Ikaros Camping** *(☎ 2424 065 258)* is smaller than Camping Rocks and is on the beach at the teensy fishing village of Steni Vala.

Villa Gallini *(☎ 2424 065 573, fax 2424 065 094; doubles/triples with bathroom €45/72)* has exceptional rooms, a pool and bar. It's 400m up Pelasgon on your left.

Fantasia House *(☎ 2424 065 186; doubles €35)* in Old Alonnisos has sweet rooms and a verdant terrace. From the bus stop, it's on the road towards town.

In Patitiri, **To Kamaki Ouzeri** and **Kavari Ouzeri** on Ikion Dolopon offer delectably prepared fare. Get there early!

Cruisy **Café Dennis**, near the quay, and **Rahati** (signposted from Ikion Dolopon) with its moody interior and shady terrace, are the places to sip and lounge.

There are daily ferries from Alonnisos to Volos, and two a week to Agios Konstantinos, via Skiathos and Skopelos. Flying Dolphins hydrofoils travel several times a day to Volos and Agios Konstantinos and between the islands.

The local bus runs to the *hora* every hour and to Steni Vala twice a day.

Car- and scooter-hire outlets are on Pelasgon and Ikion Dolopon, but only one main road spans the island! In summer, taxi boats leave Patitiri every morning for the east-coast beaches.

Ionian Islands
Τα Ιόνια Νησιά

The Ionian Islands stretch down the west coast of Greece from Corfu in the north to remote Kythira, situated off the southern tip of the Peloponnese.

CORFU ΚΕΡΚΥΡΑ

pop 107,592

Corfu is the most important island in the group and has the largest population. Wedged between two fortresses, the Old Town of Corfu, occupies a peninsula on the island's east coast. The narrow alleyways of high-shuttered tenements in mellow ochres and pinks are an immediate reminder of the town's long association with Venice.

The town's old fortress (Palaio Frourio) stands on an eastern promontory, separated from the town by an area of parks and gardens known as the Spianada. The new fortress (Neo Frourio) lies to the northwest. Ferries dock at the new port, just west of the new fortress. The **long-distance bus station** *(Avrami)* is just inland from the port.

The **EOT office** *(☎ 2661 037 520; Rizospaston Voulefton)* is between the OTE and the post office; alternatively, contact the **tourist police** *(☎ 2661 030 265; Samartzi 4)*.

The **archaeological museum** *(Vraili 5; admission €2.35; open 8.30am-3pm Tues-Sun)* houses a collection of finds from Mycenaean to classical times. The star attraction is the pediment from the Temple of Artemis, decorated with gorgons. The **Church of Agios Spiridon**, Corfu's most famous church, has an elaborately decorated interior. Pride of place is given to the remains of St Spiridon, displayed in a silver casket; four times a year it is paraded around the town.

There's hardly anywhere on the island that hasn't made its play for the tourist dollar, but the north is totally over the top. The only real attraction there is the view from the summit of **Mt Pantokrator** (906m), Corfu's highest mountain. There's a road to the top from the village of **Strinila**.

The main resort on the west coast is **Paleokastritsa**, which is built around a series of pretty bays. Further south, there are good beaches around the small village of **Agios Gordios**. Between Paleokastritsa and Agios Gordios is the hill-top village of **Pelekas**, supposedly the best place on Corfu to watch the sunset.

Places to Stay & Eat In Corfu town near the fruit-and-vegetable market, **Hotel Hermes** *(☎ 2661 039 268, fax 2661 031 747; G Markora 14; singles/doubles with shared bathroom €26.40/30.80, with private bathroom €30.80/38.15)* has a certain shabby charm and is popular with backpackers.

Pink Palace *(☎ 2661 053 103/04, fax 2661 053 025; ⓔ pink-palace@ker.forthnet.gr; rooms from €22 per person)*, a huge complex of restaurants, bars and budget rooms that tumbles down a hillside outside Agios Gordios, is where most backpackers head. Rates include bed, breakfast and dinner. Debauchery is the main item on a menu designed for young travellers who want to party hard. A hotel bus meets the ferries in Corfu.

Getting There & Around

Three flights daily to Athens are offered by both **Olympic Airways** *(☎ 2661 038 694; Polila 11, Corfu town)* and **Aegean Airlines** *(☎ 2661 027 100)*. Olympic also flies to Thessaloniki three times a week.

There are daily buses to Athens (€27.90, 11 hours) and Thessaloniki (€25.70, nine hours) from the Avrami terminal in Corfu town. Fares include the ferry to Igoumenitsa.

There are hourly ferries to Igoumenitsa (€4.10, 1½ hours) and a daily ferry to Paxi. In summer, there are daily services to Patras (€17.90, 10 hours) on the international ferries that call at Corfu on their way from Italy.

Buses for villages close to Corfu town leave from Plateia San Rocco. Services to other destinations leave from the bus terminal on Avrami.

ITHAKI ΙΘΑΚΗ

pop 3100

Ithaki is the fabled home of Odysseus, the hero of Homer's *Odyssey*, who pined for his island during his journeys to far-flung lands. It's a quiet place with some isolated coves. From the main town of Vathy you can walk to the **Fountain of Arethousa**, the fabled site of Odysseus' meeting with the swineherd Eumaeus on his return to Ithaki. Take water with you, as the fountain dries up in summer.

Ithaki has daily ferries to the mainland ports of Patras and Astakos, as well as daily services to Kefallonia and Lefkada.

KEFALLONIA ΚΕΦΑΛΛΟΝΙΑ

pop 32,500

After years of drifting along in relative obscurity, quiet Kefallonia found itself thrust into the international spotlight following the success of Louis de Bernières novel *Captain Corelli's Mandolin*. Publicity reached fever pitch in the summer of 2001 with the release of the movie. But visitors who come to the island's capital, Sami, hoping to wander the old Venetian streets depicted in the movie, will be disappointed to learn that it was all a cleverly constructed set. The originals were destroyed by a major earthquake in 1953.

Kefallonia is the largest of the Ionians, and tourism remains fairly low key outside the resort areas near the capital and on the beaches in the southwest. Public transport is very limited, apart from regular services between Argostoli and the main port of Sami, 25km away on the east coast.

There's an **EOT** *(☎ 2671 022 248)* on the waterfront in Argostoli. **Kyknos Studios** *(☎ 2671 023 398, fax 2671 025 943, M Geroulanou 4; double studios €35.20)*, in Argostoli close to the main square, Plateia Vallianou, is a good place to check out.

Hotel Melissani *(☎/fax 2674 022 464; singles/doubles €38.20/49.90)*, in Sami, is a pleasant older-style hotel offering such comforts as TV and fridge. It's signposted from the eastern end of the waterfront.

Delfinia *(☎ 2674 022 008; mains €4-10.50)* is a popular waterfront spot favoured by local diners.

There is a daily flight to Athens from the airport, which is 9km south of Argostoli. There are daily ferries from Sami to Patras (€10, 2½ hours), as well as from Argostoli and the southeastern port of Poros to Kyllini in the Peloponnese. There are also ferry connections to the islands of Ithaki, Lefkada and Zakynthos.

ZAKYNTHOS ΖΑΚΥΝΘΟΣ

pop 32,560

Zakynthos, or 'Zante', is a beautiful island surrounded by great beaches – so it's hardly surprising that the place is completely overrun by package groups. Its capital and port, Zakynthos town, is an imposing old Venetian town that has been painstakingly reconstructed after being levelled by an earthquake in 1953.

Some of the best beaches are around the huge **Bay of Laganas** in the south, which is where endangered loggerhead turtles come ashore to lay their eggs in August – at the peak of the tourist invasion. Conservation groups are urging people to stay away, and the Greek government has declared this area a national marine park.

There are regular ferries between Zakynthos and Kyllini in the Peloponnese.

Hungary

Hungary is just the place to kick off an Eastern European trip. Just a short hop from Vienna, the land of Franz Liszt and Béla Bartók, Romani (Gypsy) music and the romantic Danube (Duna) River continues to entice and enchant visitors. The allure of imperial Budapest is apparent on arrival, but other cities and the countryside prove equally entrancing. In Hungary you'll find much of the glamour and excitement of Western Europe – at half the cost.

Hungary: the Basics

Local name Magyarország

Capital Budapest

Population 10.2 million

Language Hungarian (Magyar)

Currency forint (Ft)

Avoid at all costs Budapest 'cocktail girls'

Invoke a national passion by asking *Lenne szíves elmagyarázni a vízilabda szabályait?* (Could you explain the rules of water polo?)

Facts about Hungary

HISTORY

Until the early 5th century AD, all of today's Hungary west of the Danube (Transdanubia) was part of Roman Pannonia. The Romans were forced to abandon Pannonia in 451 by Attila's Huns. The subsequent occupants were subdued by Charlemagne in 796.

Exactly a century later, seven Magyar tribes swept in. The Magyars terrorised much of Europe until they were stopped at the battle of Augsburg in 955. Hungary's first king and patron saint, Stephen (István), was crowned on Christmas Day in 1000, marking the foundation of the Hungarian state.

Medieval Hungary was a powerful state, but in 1526 the Turks defeated the Hungarian army at Mohács. After the Turks' expulsion from Buda in 1686 the Habsburgs began full-scale domination. Under the 'enlightened absolutism' of Maria Theresa (r. 1740–80) and her son Joseph II (r. 1780–90), the country made great steps forward economically and culturally.

After WWI and the collapse of the Habsburg Empire, Hungary became independent, but the 1920 Trianon Treaty stripped the country of more than two-thirds of its territory. Hungary's ambition to recover its lost territories drew the nation into WWII on the Axis side. When leftists tried to negotiate a separate peace in 1944, the Germans occupied Hungary and brought the fascist Arrow Cross Party to power. The Arrow Cross immediately began deporting hundreds of thousands of Jews to Auschwitz.

By early April 1945, all of Hungary had been liberated by the Soviet army. In 1947 the communists took complete control of the government and began dividing estates among the peasantry, and nationalising industry.

On 23 October 1956, student demonstrators demanding the withdrawal of Soviet troops were fired upon. Soviet tanks moved into Budapest, and by the end of the fighting, over 25,000 people had died.

Hungary began moving towards full democracy in 1989. The Republic of Hungary was proclaimed in October, and democratic elections were scheduled for March 1990. The last Soviet troops left the country in June 1991.

The painful transition to a market economy resulted in declining living standards for most people, but the end of the 20th century saw astonishing economic growth.

Hungary became a full member of NATO in 1999 and hopes to join the EU by 2004.

GEOGRAPHY

Hungary occupies the Carpathian Basin in the centre of Eastern Europe. It covers just over 93,000 sq km and shares borders with Austria, Slovakia, Ukraine, Romania, Yugoslavia, Croatia and Slovenia. The Danube separates the Great Plain (Nagyalföld, or *puszta*) in the east and Transdanubia (Dunántúl) in the west.

CLIMATE

Hungary has a temperate continental climate with Mediterranean and Atlantic influences. Winters are cold, cloudy and damp or windy,

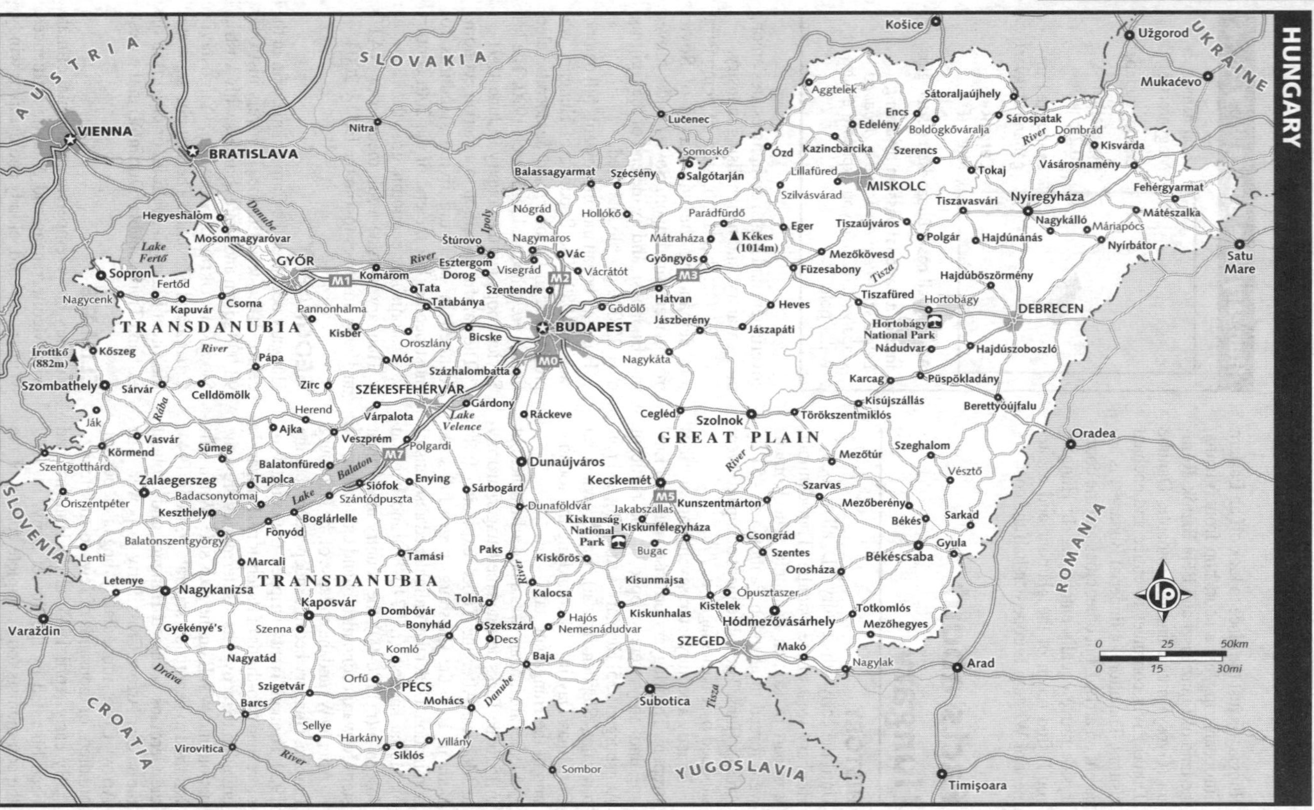
HUNGARY
AUSTRIA
SLOVAKIA
UKRAINE
ROMANIA
YUGOSLAVIA
CROATIA
SLOVENIA
0 25 50km
0 15 30mi
VIENNA
BRATISLAVA
Nitra
Lučenec
Košice
Užgorod
Mukaćevo
Satu Mare
Oradea
Arad
Timişoara
Subotica
Sombor
Virovitica
Varaždin
BUDAPEST
GREAT PLAIN
TRANSDANUBIA
MISKOLC
DEBRECEN
SZEGED
PÉCS
GYŐR
SZÉKESFEHÉRVÁR
Nyíregyháza
Kecskemét
Szolnok
Békéscsaba
Hódmezővásárhely
Kaposvár
Zalaegerszeg
Szombathely
Sopron
Nagykanizsa
Veszprém
Eger
Dunaújváros
Tatabánya
Aggtelek
Sátoraljaújhely
Encs
Sárospatak
Edelény
Boldogkőváralja
Dombrád
Kisvárda
Kazincbarcika
Szerencs
Ózd
Somoskő
Tokaj
Vásárosnamény
Lillafüred
Fehérgyarmat
Szilvásvárad
Tiszavasvári
Mátészalka
Nagykálló
Máriapócs
Polgár
Hajdúnánás
Nyírbátor
Balassagyarmat
Szécsény
Salgótarján
Nógrád
Hollókő
Parádfürdő
Mátraháza
Kékes (1014m)
Tiszaújváros
Mezőkövesd
Füzesabony
Hajdúböszörmény
Gyöngyös
Hegyeshalom
Mosonmagyaróvár
Lake Fertő
Štúrovo
Nagymaros
Vác
Esztergom
Visegrád
Vácrátót
Komárom
Dorog
Szentendre
Tata
Hatvan
Tiszafüred
Hortobágy
Hortobágy National Park
Nádudvar
Hajdúszoboszló
Fertőd
Nagycenk
Kapuvár
Csorna
Pannonhalma
Gödöllő
Heves
Jászberény
Jászapáti
Kisbér
Oroszlány
Bicske
Írottkő (882m)
Kőszeg
Pápa
Mór
Nagykáta
Karcag
Püspökladány
Százhalombatta
Sárvár
Celldömölk
Zirc
Gárdony
Lake Velence
Kisújszállás
Berettyóújfalu
Herend
Várpalota
Ráckeve
Cegléd
Törökszentmiklós
Ják
Ajka
Vasvár
Körmend
Sümeg
Polgárdi
Szeghalom
Mezőtúr
Szentgotthárd
Balatonfüred
Lake Balaton
Tapolca
Siófok
Enying
Vésztő
Szántódpuszta
Sárbogárd
Őriszentpéter
Badacsonytomaj
Keszthely
Boglárlelle
Dunaföldvár
Jakabszállás
Kunszentmárton
Szarvas
Mezőberény
Kiskunság National Park
Kiskunfélegyháza
Békés
Sarkad
Fonyód
Csongrád
Balatonszentgyörgy
Bugac
Gyula
Lenti
Paks
Kiskőrös
Szentes
Marcali
Tamási
Orosháza
Letenye
Kisunmajsa
Kalocsa
Ópusztaszer
Tolna
Kistelek
Totkomlós
Hajós
Kiskunhalas
Dombóvár
Nemesnádudvar
Mezőhegyes
Gyékényé's
Szenna
Bonyhád
Szekszárd
Decs
Komló
Makó
Nagyatád
Baja
Nagylak
Orfű
Szigetvár
Barcs
Mohács
Sellye
Harkány
Villány
Siklós
Danube
Tisza
Ipoly
Rába
Dráva
River
M0
M1
M2
M3
M5
M7

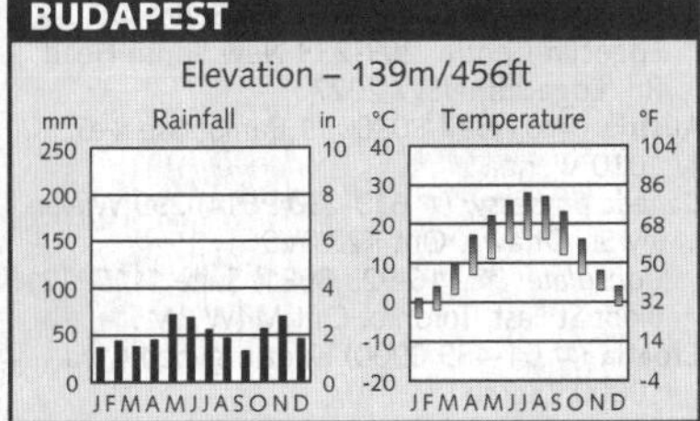

and summers are warm, and sometimes very hot. March, April and November are the wettest months.

GOVERNMENT & POLITICS

Hungary works under a parliamentary system headed by a prime minister. The president is the head of state.

POPULATION & PEOPLE

The Ugric Hungarians were the last major ethnic group to arrive in Europe during the period of the Great Migrations. Ethnic Magyars make up some 98% of the population. The number of Roma is officially put at 1.4% of the population (or 132,600 people), though some sources have it as high as 3%.

SOCIETY & CONDUCT

In general, Hungarians are a reserved, somewhat formal people. The overall mood is one of *honfibú*, literally 'patriotic sorrow', but really it's a penchant for the blues. Family is very important. If you're invited to someone's home, bring a bunch of flowers and/or a bottle of good local wine.

LANGUAGE

Hungarians speak Magyar, which is related very distantly to Finnish and Estonian. Many older Hungarians understand German and many young people, particularly in Budapest, speak some English. See the Language chapter at the back of the book for useful words and phrases.

Unfamiliar Waters

Unlike the vast majority of tongues you'll hear in Europe, Hungarian is not an Indo-European language. Neither Germanic, Romantic nor Slavic, it is something of a linguistic orphan and proves fiendishly difficult for visitors to master. Helpful English cognates (sound-alike words) are nearly nonexistent: for example, 'wine' is *bor* and 'beer' is *söröző*. Tread carefully, and pick up Lonely Planet's *Eastern European Phrasebook* for some much-needed assistance.

Facts for the Visitor

HIGHLIGHTS

Budapest is an architecture-buff's delight. Beautiful historic towns include Eger, Győr and Veszprém. Sopron and Kőszeg, in the far west, are among the few towns with a strong medieval flavour. The greatest monuments of the Turkish period are in Pécs.

Hungary's most famous castles are in Eger, Kőszeg and Siklós. Although in ruins, the citadel at Visegrád still evokes strong images and the power of medieval Hungary. The Festetics Palace at Keszthely is among the finest in the land.

PLANNING

Although it can be wet in April and May, spring is mild and the crowds have not yet arrived. Summer is warm, sunny and unusually long. Budapest comes to a grinding halt in August. Autumn is beautiful, particularly in the hills around Budapest and in the north. Avoid the cold, bleak and desolate winter.

TOURIST OFFICES

Local Tourist Offices

The Hungarian National Tourist Office (HNTO) has a chain of 120 Tourinform information bureaus across the country, and these are the best places to ask general questions and pick up brochures. The main **Tourinform** office (*☎ 1-438 8080, fax 318 9059; W www.hungarytourism.hu; V Vigadó utca 6)* in Budapest is open 24 hours.

If you require information about private accommodation, flights or international train travel, you may have to seek the advice of a commercial travel agency. The oldest, Ibusz, is arguably the best for sorting out private accommodation. Other tourist agencies include Cooptourist and Vista. Express, with branches in many Hungarian cities, issues student, youth, teacher and hostel cards (1600Ft) and sells discounted Billet International de Jeunesse (BIJ) train tickets and cheap airfares.

Tourist Offices Abroad

The HNTO has offices in 19 countries, including the following:

Austria (☎ 01-585 20 1213, fax 585 20 1214, ⓔ htvienna@hungarytourism.hu) Opernring 5/2, A-1010 Vienna
Czech Republic (☎ 02-2109 0135, fax 2109 0139, ⓔ htpragaue@hungarytourism.hu) Rumunská 22, 22537 Prague 2
France (☎ 01 53 70 67 17, fax 47 04 83 57, ⓔ htparis@hungarytourism.hu) 140 ave Victor Hugo, 75116 Paris
Germany (☎ 030-243 146 0, fax 243 146 13, ⓔ htberlin@hungarytourism.hu) Karl Liebknecht Strasse 34, D-10178 Berlin
Netherlands (☎ 070-320 9092, fax 327 2833, ⓔ htdenhaga@hungarytourism.hu) Laan van Nieuw Oost Indie 271, 2593 BS The Hague
UK (☎/fax 020-7823 1032, fax 7823 1459, ⓔ htlondon@hungarytourism.hu) 46 Eaton Place, London SW1X 8AL
USA (☎ 212-355 0240, fax 207 4103, ⓔ htnewyork@hungarytourism.hu) 33rd floor, 150 East 58th St, New York, NY 10155-3398

In countries without an HNTO office, contact Malév Hungarian Airlines.

VISAS & DOCUMENTS

To enter Hungary, everyone needs a valid passport or (for citizens of certain European countries) a national identification card. Citizens of virtually all European countries, the USA, Canada, Israel, Japan and New Zealand do not require visas to visit Hungary for stays of up to 90 days. UK citizens do not need a visa for a stay of up to six months. Nationals of Australia and now South Africa (among others) require visas. Check out the current visa requirements at a consulate, any HNTO or Malév office, or on the Foreign Ministry's website at ⓦ www.kum.hu, as the requirements can change without notice.

Visas are issued at Hungarian consulates or missions, most international highway border crossings, Ferihegy airport and the International Ferry Pier in Budapest. However, visas are never issued on trains and rarely on buses.

EMBASSIES & CONSULATES

Hungarian Embassies & Consulates

Hungarian embassies around the world include the following:

Australia *Embassy:* (☎ 02-6282 2555) 17 Beale Crescent, Deakin, ACT 2600
Consulate: (☎ 02-9328 7859) Suite 405, Edgecliff Centre, 203-233 New South Head Rd, Edgecliff, NSW 2027
Austria (☎ 01-537 80300) 1 Bankgasse 4–6, 1010 Vienna
Canada *Embassy:* (☎ 613-230 9614) 299 Waverley St, Ottawa, Ont K2P 0V9
Consulate: (☎ 416-923 8981) Suite 1115, 121 Bloor St East, Toronto, Ont M4W 3M5
Croatia (☎ 01-489 0900) Krlezin gvozd 11/a, 10000 Zagreb
Germany *Embassy:* (☎ 030-203 100) Unter den Linden 76, 10117 Berlin
Consulate: (☎ 089-911 032) Vollmannstrasse 2, 81927 Munich
Ireland (☎ 01-661 2902) 2 Fitzwilliam Place, Dublin 2
Romania (☎ 01-311 0062) Strada Jean-Louis Calderon 63–65, Bucharest 70202
Slovakia (☎ 02-544 30541) ul Sedlárska 3, 81425 Bratislava
Slovenia (☎ 01-512 1882) Konrada Babnika ulica 5, 1210 Ljubljana-Sentvid
South Africa (☎ 012-430 3030) 959 Arcadia St, Hatfield, 0083 Pretoria
UK *Embassy:* (☎ 020-7235 5218) 35 Eaton Place, London SW1X 8BY
Consulate: (☎ 020-7235 2664) 35/b Eaton Place, London SW1X 8BY
Ukraine (☎ 044-212 4134) ul Rejtarskaja 33, Kiev 01034
USA *Embassy:* (☎ 202-362 6730) 3910 Shoemaker St NW, Washington, DC 20008
Consulate: (☎ 212-752 0661) 223 East 52nd St, New York, NY 10022
Consulate: (☎ 310-473 9344) Suite 410, 11766 Wilshire Blvd, Los Angeles, CA 90025
Yugoslavia (☎ 011-444 0472) ul Ivana Milutinovica 74, Belgrade 11000

Embassies & Consulates in Hungary

Countries with diplomatic representation in the city of Budapest (phone code ☎ 1) include the following:

Australia (☎ 457 9777) XII Királyhágó tér 8–9
Austria (☎ 352 9613) VI Benczúr utca 16
Canada (☎ 392 3360) XII Budakeszi út 32
Croatia (☎ 354 1315) VI Munkácsy Mihály utca 15
Germany (☎ 488 3500) I Úri utca 64–66
Ireland (☎ 302 9600) V Szabadság tér 7–9
Romania (☎ 352 0271) XIV Thököly út 72
Slovakia (☎ 460 9010) XIV Stefánia út 22–24
Slovenia (☎ 438 5600) II Cseppkő utca 68
South Africa (☎ 392 0999) II Gárdonyi Géza út 17
UK (☎ 266 2888) V Harmincad utca 6
Ukraine (☎ 355 2443) XII Nógrádi utca 8
USA (☎ 475 4400) V Szabadság tér 12
Yugoslavia (☎ 322 9838) VI Dózsa György út 92/b

CUSTOMS

You can bring the usual personal effects, 200 cigarettes, 1L of wine or champagne and 1L of spirits. You are not supposed to export valuable antiques without a special permit; this should be available from the place of purchase. You must declare the import/export of any amount of cash exceeding the sum of 1,000,000Ft.

MONEY

Currency

The unit of currency is the Hungarian forint (Ft). Coins come in denominations of one, two, five, 10, 20, 50 and 100Ft, and notes are denominated 200, 500, 1000, 2000, 5000, 10,000 and 20,000Ft.

Exchange Rates

Exchange rates at the time of going to press were:

country	unit		forint
Australia	A$1	=	139Ft
Canada	C$1	=	163Ft
Eurozone	€1	=	245Ft
Japan	¥100	=	206Ft
New Zealand	NZ$1	=	120Ft
UK	UK£1	=	378Ft
USA	US$1	=	247Ft

Exchanging Money

You'll find ATMs accepting most credit and cash cards throughout the country; all banks mentioned in this chapter have them unless indicated otherwise. It's always prudent to carry a little foreign cash, preferably euros or US dollars, and perhaps some travellers cheques.

Banks and bureaux de change generally don't charge commission, but exchange rates vary tremendously; private agencies are always the most expensive. The national bank, Országos Takarékpenztár (OTP), has branches everywhere and offers among the best rates; Ibusz is also a good bet. Many banks, including K&H and Postabank (at post offices nationwide), give cash advances on most credit cards. The use of credit cards is gaining ground, especially Visa, MasterCard and American Express (AmEx).

Costs

Hungary remains a bargain destination. If you stay in private rooms, eat at medium-priced restaurants and travel on public transport, you should get by on US$30 a day without scrimping. Those staying at hostels, dormitories or camping grounds and eating at food stalls or self-catering will cut costs substantially. Many hotels quote their rates in euros, as does the national rail company.

Tipping

Hungarians routinely tip waiters, hairdressers, taxi drivers and even doctors, dentists and petrol station attendants about 10%. In restaurants, do this on payment of the bill; leaving money on the table is rude. Some upmarket places add a 10% service charge to the bill, which makes tipping unnecessary.

Taxes & Refunds

ÁFA, a value-added tax of between 11% and 25%, covers the purchase of all new goods. Check whether it's included in the price. Visitors can claim refunds for purchases of more than 50,000Ft on one receipt as long as they take the goods out of the country within 90 days. The ÁFA receipts (available from the shops where you made the purchases) should be stamped by customs at the border.

Budapest-based **Global Refund Hungary** *(☎/fax 1-468 2965, fax 468 2966; W www.globalrefund.com; XIV Zászlós utca 54)* can help you with refunds for a fee.

POST & COMMUNICATIONS

Letters addressed to poste restante will go to the main post office *(főposta)*. Look for the sign *postán maradó küldemények*. If you hold an AmEx credit card or are carrying their travellers cheques, you can have your mail sent to **American Express** *(Deák Ferenc utca 10, 1052 Budapest)*.

Public telephones take coins or phonecards (800/1800Ft), available from post offices, newsagents, hotels and petrol stations. Telephone booths with a black-and-white arrow and red target with the word *'Visszahívható'* display a telephone number, so you can be phoned back.

For an intercity call, dial ☎ 06 and wait for a second dial tone. Then dial the area code and phone number. To make an international call, dial ☎ 00, followed by the country code, the area code and then the number. Useful phone numbers include domestic (☎ 198) and international (☎ 199) operator/directory inquiries. Hungary's country code is ☎ 36.

Internet cafés have sprouted in Budapest, and all of the capital's year-round hostels offer access. Public Internet connections in the provinces are more difficult to find, though most major towns now have a Matáv Pont outlet.

DIGITAL RESOURCES

Tourinform's informative W www.hungarytourism.hu should be your first portal of call. Check out W www.youthhostels.hu for hostel accommodation and W www.camping.hu for camping sites.

The best overall site for Budapest is W www.budapestinfo.hu. Budapest Week Online, with events, music and movie listings, is at W www.budapestweek.com.

BOOKS

If you plan to spend a lot of time in Hungary, an excellent resource is Lonely Planet's *Hungary*, while the *Budapest* guide takes an in-depth look at the capital. *An Illustrated History of Hungary* by István Lázár is an easy introduction to the nation's past.

WOMEN TRAVELLERS

Women should not experience any particular problems. For assistance ring the **Women's Line** *(Nővonal; ☎ 06-80 505 101)* or contact **Women for Women against Violence** *(NANE; ☎ 1-267 4900)*.

GAY & LESBIAN TRAVELLERS

For up-to-date information, pick up *Na végre!* (At Last!) at gay venues in Budapest or email e navegre@hotmail.com. Useful websites include W www.gayguide.net/europe/hungary/budapest, W www.masprogram.freeweb.hu, W www.english.gay.hu and W www.pride.hu.

For one-to-one contact, ring either **Gay Switchboard** *(☎ mobile 06-30 932 3334 or 351 2015; open 4pm-8pm Mon-Fri)* or **Háttér Gay & Lesbian** Association *(☎ 329 3380; open 6pm-11pm daily)*.

DISABLED TRAVELLERS

Facilities are virtually nonexistent, although audible traffic signals are becoming more common and there are Braille markings on the higher-denominated forint notes. For more information, contact the **Hungarian Disabled Association** *(MEOSZ; ☎ 1-388 5529 or 388 2387; e meosz@matavnet.hu; San Marco utca 76, Budapest 1035)*.

Emergency Services

In the event of an emergency anywhere in Hungary, phone the central emergency number on ☎ 112 (English spoken).

For police call ☎ 107, for fire ☎ 105 and for ambulance ☎ 104. The English-language crime hotline is ☎ 1-438 8000.

Car assistance (24 hours) is available by calling ☎ 188.

DANGERS & ANNOYANCES

Hungary is not a violent or dangerous society, but racially motivated attacks against Roma, Africans and Arabs are not unknown. Beware of pickpockets and taxi louts.

BUSINESS HOURS

Nyitvatartás (opening hours) are posted on front doors; *nyitva* means 'open' and *zárva* 'closed'. Grocery stores and supermarkets open from about 7am to 6pm or 7pm on weekdays, and department stores 10am to 6pm. Most shops stay open until 8pm Thursday, but on Saturday they close at 1pm. Main post offices open 8am to 6pm weekdays, to noon or 1pm Saturday. Banking hours are usually 8am to about 4pm Monday to Thursday and to 1pm Friday.

Most places have a 'nonstop' convenience store, which opens late, and many of the hyper-supermarkets open on Sunday.

PUBLIC HOLIDAYS & SPECIAL EVENTS

Hungary's public holidays are: New Year's Day (1 January), 1848 Revolution Day (15 March), Easter Monday (March/April), International Labour Day (1 May), Whit Monday (May/June), St Stephen's Day (20 August), 1956 Remembrance Day (23 October), All Saints' Day (1 November) and Christmas and Boxing Days (25 and 26 December).

The most outstanding annual events include the Budapest Spring Festival (March); Balaton Festival based in Keszthely (May); Sopron Festival Weeks (late June to mid-July); Győr Summer Cultural Festival (late June to late July); Hortobágy International Equestrian Days (July); Szeged Open-Air Festival (July); Kőszeg Castle Theatre Festival (mid- to late July); Sziget (Island) Music Festival on Hajógyár Island in Budapest (late July to early August); Hungaroring Formula-1 races at Mogyoród, held 24km northeast of

Budapest (mid-August); and, lastly the Budapest Autumn Festival (mid-October to early November).

ACTIVITIES

More than 100 thermal baths are open to the public. The thermal lake at Hévíz is Hungary's most impressive.

The main water-sport spots are Lake Balaton and Lake Velence. Many canoe and kayak trips are available. The HNTO publishes *Water Tours in Hungary*, a gold mine of information for planning itineraries and rentals and learning the rules and regulations.

Hungary now counts 2500km of dedicated bicycle lanes around the country, with more on the way. For information and advice in Budapest contact the helpful **Hungarian Bicycle Touring Association** *(MKTSZ; ☎ 1-311 2467; ⓔ mktsz@dpg.hu; VI Bajcsy-Zsilinszky út 31)*. Also in the capital, the enthusiastic **Friends of Nature Bicycle Touring Association** *(TTE; ☎ 1-316 5867; II Bem rakpart 51)* can help organise bike tours and supply guides.

You can enjoy good hiking in the forests around Visegrád, Esztergom, Badacsony, Kőszeg and Budapest. North of Eger are the Bükk Hills and south of Kecskemét the Bugac Puszta, both with marked trails. Maps are available from **Cartographia** *(☎ 1-312 6001; ⓦ www.cartographia.hu; VI Bajcsy-Zsilinszky út 37; open 9am-5pm Mon-Wed, 9am-6.30pm Thur, 9am-3.30pm Fri)* in Budapest (see Orientation in the Budapest section).

The Magyars say they were 'created by God to sit on horseback'. Book horse riding through a local tourist office or the **Hungarian Equestrian Tourism Association** *(MLTSZ; ☎ 1-456 0444, fax 456 0445; ⓦ www.equi.hu; IX Ráday utca 8)* in Budapest.

WORK

Travellers on tourist visas in Hungary are forbidden from taking employment, but some end up teaching or even working for foreign firms without permits.

Check the English-language telephone book or ads for English schools in the *Budapest Sun*; there are also job listings but the pay is generally low. You can do much better teaching privately (2000Ft to 4000Ft per hour).

ACCOMMODATION

Many cities and towns levy a local tourist tax of around 250Ft per person per night, although sometimes only after the first 48 hours. People under 18 years or staying at camping grounds may be exempt. Breakfast is usually included in hotel or hostel prices.

Camping

Hungary has more than 400 camping grounds. Small, private ones are usually preferable to the large, noisy, 'official' sites. Prices vary widely and sites around Lake Balaton can be exorbitant in summer.

A Camping Card International will sometimes get you a 10% discount. Camping 'wild' is prohibited. Tourinform's *Camping Hungary* map/brochure lists every camp site in Hungary.

Hostels & Student Dormitories

Despite all the places listed in the Budapest-based **Hungarian Youth Hostel Association** *(MISZSZ; ☎ 1-413 2065, fax 321 4851; ⓦ www.youthhostels.hu; VII Baross tér 15, 3rd floor)*, a hostel card isn't particularly useful as most associated hostels are remote. Generally the only year-round hostels are in Budapest.

From 1 July to around 20 August, the cheapest rooms are in vacant student accommodation (dorm beds and sometimes private rooms too).

Private Rooms

Private rooms are usually assigned by travel agencies. In Budapest, individuals at train stations approach anyone looking vaguely like a traveller and offer private rooms. You're probably better off getting a room from an agency.

There's usually a 30% supplement on the first night if you stay less than four nights, and single rooms are hard to come by.

In resort areas look out for houses with signs that read *'szoba kiadó'* or the German *'Zimmer frei'*.

Pensions & Hotels

Quaint, often family-run, *panziók* (pensions) are abundant. Pensions are really just little hotels. They are usually new and clean, and often have a restaurant attached.

Hotels, called *szállók* or *szállodák*, run the gamut from luxurious five-star palaces to rundown old communist-era hovels. A cheap hotel will be more expensive than a private room, but it may be the answer if you're only staying one night or if you arrive too late to get a private room through an agency. Two-star hotels usually have rooms with a bathroom: it's always down the hall in a one-star place.

FOOD & DRINKS

Inexpensive by Western European standards and served in huge portions, traditional Hungarian food is heavy and rich. The most famous traditional meal is *gulyás* (or *gulyásleves*), a thick beef soup cooked with onions and potatoes. *Pörkölt* (stew) is closer to what we call 'goulash'. Another Hungarian favourite is *halászlé* (fisherman's broth), which is a rich mixture of several kinds of poached freshwater fish, tomatoes, green peppers and paprika.

Some dishes for vegetarians are *rántott sajt* (fried cheese), *gombafejek rántva* (fried mushroom caps), *gomba leves* (mushroom soup), *gyümölcs leves* (fruit soup), *sajtos kenyer* (sliced bread with soft cheese) and *túrós csusza* (Hungarian pasta with cheese). *Lángos* (a deep-fried dough with various toppings) is a cheap meatless snack sold on streets.

Excellent wine is available everywhere. A popular spirit is *pálinka* (a strong brandy distilled from a variety of fruits). Hungarian beers include Dreher and Kőbanyai, as well as a host of local brews.

ENTERTAINMENT

Hungary is a paradise for culture vultures. In Budapest there are several musical events every night, and excellent opera tickets cost between 600Ft and 7000Ft. Besides traditional opera, operetta and classical concerts, there are rock and jazz concerts, folk dancing, pantomime, puppet shows, movies in English, clubs, floor shows and circuses to keep you entertained.

Excellent cultural performances can also be seen in such provincial towns as Eger, Győr, Kecskemét, Pécs, Szeged, Veszprém and Szombathely, all of which have fine theatres. Information about these events is readily available at Tourinform offices and in the monthly *Programme in Ungarn/in Hungary* and *Pesti Est* listings magazines, which are also available at Tourinform offices and entertainment venues everywhere.

Many theatres close from mid-June to late September or October. Summer opera, operetta and concert programmes designed for tourists are more expensive than the normal productions.

Getting There & Away

AIR

Malév Hungarian Airlines (*www.malev.hu*) flies nonstop to Budapest's Ferihegy airport from North America, the Middle East and many cities in continental Europe and the British Isles. It has links to Asia and Australia via its European gateways.

An air-passenger duty of between 8000Ft and 10,000Ft is levied on all airline tickets written in Hungary. The one exception is JFK airport in New York, which attracts a tax of 20,000Ft.

LAND

Hungary has excellent land-transport connections with its seven neighbours. Most departures are from Budapest, although other cities and towns closer to the various borders can also be used as springboards.

Bus

Most international buses are run by **Eurolines** (*☎ 1-219 8080; www.eurolines.hu*) or its Hungarian associate, **Volánbusz** (*☎ 1-485 2162; www.volanbusz.hu*). Eurolines has passes valid for 15/30/60 days that allow unlimited travel between 32 European cities, including Budapest. Adults pay €189/269/339 in the low season (mid-September to May) and €249/369/429 in the high season. Passes for under-26s and seniors cost €159/269/339 and €209/299/329.

Buses run to Amsterdam (25,900Ft, 19 hours), Berlin (19,900Ft, 15 hours), London (33,900Ft, 26 hours), Paris (27,900Ft, 22 hours), Rome (23,500Ft, 15 hours) and Vienna (6390Ft, 3½ hours), via an array of European cities. To Romania, there are regularly scheduled buses on Saturday year-round to Arad (4000Ft, seven hours, 282km) and Timi¢oara (Hungarian: Temesvár; 4900Ft, eight hours).

Other useful international buses include those to Bratislava (Pozsony; 3100Ft, four hours, 213km, daily); Prague (8900Ft, eight hours, 535km, three to five weekly); Belgrade (4100Ft, nine hours, 422km, daily) via Subotica (Szabatka; 3300Ft, four hours, 227km); Pula (9900Ft, 14½ hours, 775km, Friday from late June to early September) via Rijeka (7900Ft, 10 hours, 546km); and Krákow

(6900Ft, 10 hours, Saturday) via Zakopane (5600Ft, 8½ hours, 387km).

Train

Magyar Államvasutak *(Hungarian State Railways; MÁV; www.mav.hu)* links up with the European rail network in all directions, running trains as far as London (via Cologne and Brussels), Paris (via Frankfurt), Stockholm (via Hamburg and Copenhagen), Moscow, Rome and Istanbul (via Belgrade).

In Budapest, international trains arrive and depart from three different train stations (see Getting There & Away in that section for details). For 24-hour information on international train services call ☎ 1-461 5500 in Budapest. For domestic schedules, ring ☎ 1-461 5400.

You can buy tickets at the three international train stations in Budapest, but it's easier at MÁV's central ticket office in Budapest (see Getting There & Away in that section).

The following are sample one-way 2nd-class fares from Budapest (return trip is double): Amsterdam €387.20; Berlin (via Prague) €182.80; London €444; Munich €162; Rome (via Croatia) €237.60; and Vienna €39.20. Three daily EuroCity (EC) trains to Vienna and points beyond charge a supplement of 1000Ft to 1500Ft. The 1st-class seats are usually 50% more expensive than 2nd class. Costs for sleepers depend on the destination, and how many beds are in the carriage. Eurail passes are valid, but not sold in Hungary.

Car & Motorcycle

For the most up-to-date list of border crossings check out Tourinform's website (www.hungarytourism.hu).

Walking & Cycling

Many border guards frown on walking or cycling across borders, particularly in Romania, Yugoslavia and Ukraine. If you're heading north, there are three crossings to/from Slovakia where you shouldn't have any problems. Bridges link Esztergom with Štúrovo and Komárom with Komárno. At Sátoraljaújhely, northeast of Miskolc, there's a highway border crossing over the Ronyva River that links the centre of town with Slovenské Nové Mesto.

RIVER

A hydrofoil service on the Danube between Budapest and Vienna (5½ hours, 282km) with the possibility of disembarking at Bratislava (on request) operates daily from April to early November. Adult one-way/return fares for Vienna are €65/89, for Bratislava €59/83. Students with ISIC cards pay €51/75.

For information and tickets, contact **Mahart PassNave** *(☎ 1-484 4010; www.mahart tours.com)* at the Belgrád rakpart in Budapest and **Mahart PassNave Wien** *(☎ 01-72 92 161, 72 92 162; Handelskai 265/3/517)* in Vienna.

Getting Around

BUS

Volán buses are a good alternative to trains, and fares are only slightly more expensive than comparable 2nd-class train fares. Bus fares average 994/1992/2974Ft per 100/200/300km.

In southern Transdanubia or parts of the Great Plain, buses are virtually essential. For short trips on the Danube Bend or Lake Balaton areas, buses are also recommended.

Timetables are posted at stations and stops. Some footnotes you could come across include *naponta* (daily), *hétköznap* (weekdays), *munkanapokon* (on workdays), *munkaszüneti napok kivételével naponta* (daily except holidays), *szabadnap kivételével naponta* (daily except Saturday), *szabad és munkaszüneti napokon* (on Saturday and holidays), *munkaszüneti napokon* (on holidays), *iskolai napokon* (on school days) and *szabadnap* (on Saturday).

A few large bus stations have luggage rooms, but they generally close by 6pm.

TRAIN

MÁV operates reliable, comfortable train services on its 8000km of track. Second-class train fares are 302Ft for 50km, 732Ft for 100km, 1482Ft for 200km and 2390Ft for 400km. If you buy your ticket on the train rather than in the station, there's a 500Ft surcharge (1500Ft on InterCity trains). Seat reservations may be compulsory (indicated on the timetable by an 'R' in a box), mandatory on trains departing from Budapest (an 'R' in a circle) or simply available (just a plain 'R').

There are several types of train. The InterCity Express (ICE) and InterCityRapid (ICR) trains levy a supplement of 250Ft to 400Ft, which includes a seat. IC trains stop at main centres only and are the fastest and most comfortable trains. *Gyorsvonat* (fast trains) and *sebesvonat* (swift trains) – indicated on the timetable by bold-face type, a thicker route line and/or an 'S' – often require a seat reservation (110Ft). *Személyvonat* (passenger trains) are the real milk-runs and stop at every city, town, village and hamlet along the way.

If you plan to do a lot of travelling by train, get yourself a copy of *Menetrend* (MÁV's official timetable), which is available at most large stations and at the MÁV office in Budapest for 650/1350Ft in small/large format.

CAR & MOTORCYCLE

Third-party insurance is compulsory. If your car is registered in the EU, it's assumed you have it. Other motorists must show a Green Card or buy insurance at the border.

The so-called 'Yellow Angels' of the Hungarian Automobile Club do free basic breakdown repairs if you belong to an affiliated organisation such as AAA in the USA or AA in the UK. You can call 24 hours a day on ☎ 188 nationwide.

All the big international car-rental firms have offices in Budapest, and there are scores of local companies throughout the country, but don't expect many bargains.

HITCHING

In Hungary, hitchhiking is legal except on motorways. A service in Budapest matches drivers and passengers – see Getting There & Away in the Budapest section.

BOAT

In summer there are regular passenger ferries on Lake Balaton and on the Danube from Budapest to Szentendre, Visegrád and Esztergom. Details are given in the relevant sections.

LOCAL TRANSPORT

Public transport is efficient and cheap, with city bus and, in many towns, trolleybus services. Four cities, including Budapest and Szeged, also have trams, and there's an extensive metro (underground or subway) and a suburban commuter railway in Budapest. Purchase all tickets at newsstands or ticket windows before travelling and validate them once aboard.

Taxis are plentiful and very reasonably priced. Flag-fall varies, but a fair price is 150Ft to 200Ft, with the charge per kilometre about the same. The best places to find taxis are in ranks at bus and train stations, near markets and around main squares.

Budapest

☎ 1 • pop 1.8 million

There's no other Hungarian city like Budapest. Home to almost a fifth of the national population, the *főváros* (capital) is also the country's administrative, business and cultural centre. For better or for worse, virtually everything in Hungary starts or finishes in Budapest.

But it is the beauty of the city that makes it stand apart. More romantic than Warsaw and more cosmopolitan than Prague, Budapest straddles a gentle curve in the Danube, with the Buda Hills to the west and the start of the Great Plain to the east. Architecturally, it is a gem. Add to this parks brimming with attractions, museums filled with treasures, boats sailing upriver to the scenic Danube Bend and Turkish-era thermal baths, and you have one of Europe's most delightful cities. There's no doubt that the 'Queen of the Danube' will be among the highlights of your trip to Eastern Europe.

Orientation

The Danube, the city's traditional artery, is spanned by nine bridges that link hilly, historic Buda with bustling, commercial and very flat Pest. Two ring roads link three of the bridges across the Danube and essentially define central Pest. The most central square in Pest is Deák tér. Buda is dominated by Castle and Gellért Hills; the main square is Moszkva tér. Lonely Planet's *Budapest City Map* covers the town in detail.

Information

Tourist Offices The best source of information about Budapest is **Tourinform** *(☎ 438 8080, fax 356 1964; Ⓦ www.hungarytourism.hu; V Vigadó utca 6; open 24hr)*. It has a nearby **branch** *(☎ same number; Sütő utca 2; open daily)* and an **information hotline** *(☎ 06-80 66 0044)*. Both branches sell a variety of discount cards for attractions and transport.

Money Among the best exchange rates for cash and travellers cheques are offered by **OTP Bank** *(V Nádor utca 6; open 7.45am-5pm Mon, 7.45am-4pm Tues-Fri)*. **K&H** *(V Váci utca 40; open 8am-5pm Mon, 8am-4pm Tues-Thur, 8am-3pm Fri)* often offer good rates, too. There are ATMs all around the city.

American Express *(☎ 235 4330; V Deák Ferenc utca 10; open 9am-5.30pm Mon-Fri,*

9am-2pm Sat) changes its own travellers cheques without commission, but its rates are poor. Its commission on converting US-dollar travellers cheques into cash dollars is 7%.

Tribus (see Private Rooms under Places to Stay) is handy if you arrive late at night and need to change money.

Post & Communications The **main post office** *(V Petőfi Sándor utca 13-15 or V Városház utca 18; open 8am-8pm Mon-Fri, to 2pm Sat)* is a few minutes' walk from Deák tér and the Tourinform branch office. The best place to make international telephone calls is from a phone box with a phonecard.

Email & Internet Access Budapest abounds in Internet cafés. Among the most central are:

Ami Internet Coffee (☎ 267 1644, W www.amicoffee.hu) V Váci utca 40. Open 9am to 2am daily, this very central place has 50 terminals and charges 200/400/700Ft for 15/30/60 minutes. Five/10 hours costs 3250/6400Ft.

Budapest Net (☎ 328 0292, fax 328 0294, e info@budapestnet.hu) V Kecskeméti utca 5. With more than 50 terminals, this place attracts students from ELTE university nearby. It charges 150/350/700Ft for 10/30/60 minutes, and 2400/4600Ft for five/10 hours. It's open 10am to 10pm daily.

Vista Internet Café (☎ 429 9950, fax 429 9951, e icafe@vista.hu; VI Paulay Ede utca 7) Open 10am to 10pm Monday to Friday and 10am to 8pm Saturday, this café at the Vista Visitor Centre (see Travel Agencies) charges 11/660Ft per minute/hour.

Most of the year-round hostels (see Places to Stay, later) offer Internet access.

Travel Agencies The main office of **Ibusz** *(☎ 485 2723, 485 2767; W www.ibusz.hu; V Ferenciek tere 10; open 8.15am-5.30pm Mon-Fri, 9am-1pm Sat in summer, 8.15am-4.30pm Mon-Fri in winter)* supplies travel brochures, changes money, books all types of accommodation and accepts credit-card payments. Its nearby **branch** *(☎ 322 7214; VII Dob utca 1)* is good for booking train tickets.

The main office of **Express** *(☎ 317 8600; W www.express-travel.hu; V Semmelweiss utca 1-3; open 8am-6pm Mon-Fri, 9am-1pm Sat)* can book accommodation in Budapest, particularly hostels and colleges, while the **Express branch** *(☎ 311 6418; V Zoltán utca 10; open 8.30am-4.30pm Mon-Thur, 8.30am-4pm Fri)* books international and domestic trains, Eurolines buses and sells cheap airline tickets.

An excellent one-stop shop for all your outbound needs (air tickets, package tours etc) is the massive **Vista Travel Center** *(☎ 429 9760; W www.vista.hu; VI Andrássy út 1; open 9am-6.30pm Mon-Fri, 9am-2.30pm Sat)*. The **Vista Visitor Center** *(☎ 268 0888; VI Paulay Ede utca; open 9am-8pm Mon-Fri, 10am-6pm Sat)* handles tourist information, room bookings and organised tours. There's a popular café and Internet centre here, too.

Medical & Emergency Services The **American Clinics** *(☎ 224 9090; I Hattyú utca 14, 5th floor; open 8.30am-7pm Mon-Thur, 8.30am-6pm Fri, 8am-noon Sat, 10am-2pm Sun)* can help you in an emergency; a basic consultation costs 28,600Ft.

If you need to report a crime or a lost or stolen passport or credit card, first call the **emergency police** *(☎ 107)*.

Buda

Most of what remains of medieval Budapest is on **Castle Hill** (Várhegy), perched above the Danube. The easiest way to get there from Pest is to stroll across Chain Bridge and board the **funicular railway** *(uphill/downhill ticket adult 450/250Ft, child 2-10 years 350/250Ft; open 7.30am-10pm daily)* from Clark Ádám tér up to Szent György tér near the Royal Palace.

At the **Vienna Gate**, turn west (right) onto Petermann bíró utca and walk past the **National Archives**, with its majolica-tiled roof, to Kapisztrán tér. The **Magdalen Tower** is all that's left of a Gothic church destroyed here during WWII. Walk southeast along Tóth Árpád sétány, the ramparts promenade, and to the east you'll catch a glimpse to the east of the neo-Gothic tower of **Matthias Church** *(☎ 489 0717; Szentháromság tér; adult/child 300/150Ft; open 9am-5pm Mon-Fri, 9am-1pm Sat, 1pm-5pm Sun)*. The church, rebuilt in 1896, has a colourful tiled roof and lovely murals inside.

Just south of the church is an equestrian **statue of St Stephen** *(977–1038)*, Hungary's first king. Behind it is **Fishermen's Bastion** *(adult/child 250/120Ft; open 8.30am-11pm daily)*, a neo-Gothic structure built in 1905 with stunning views of Pest and the Parliament building.

CENTRAL PEST

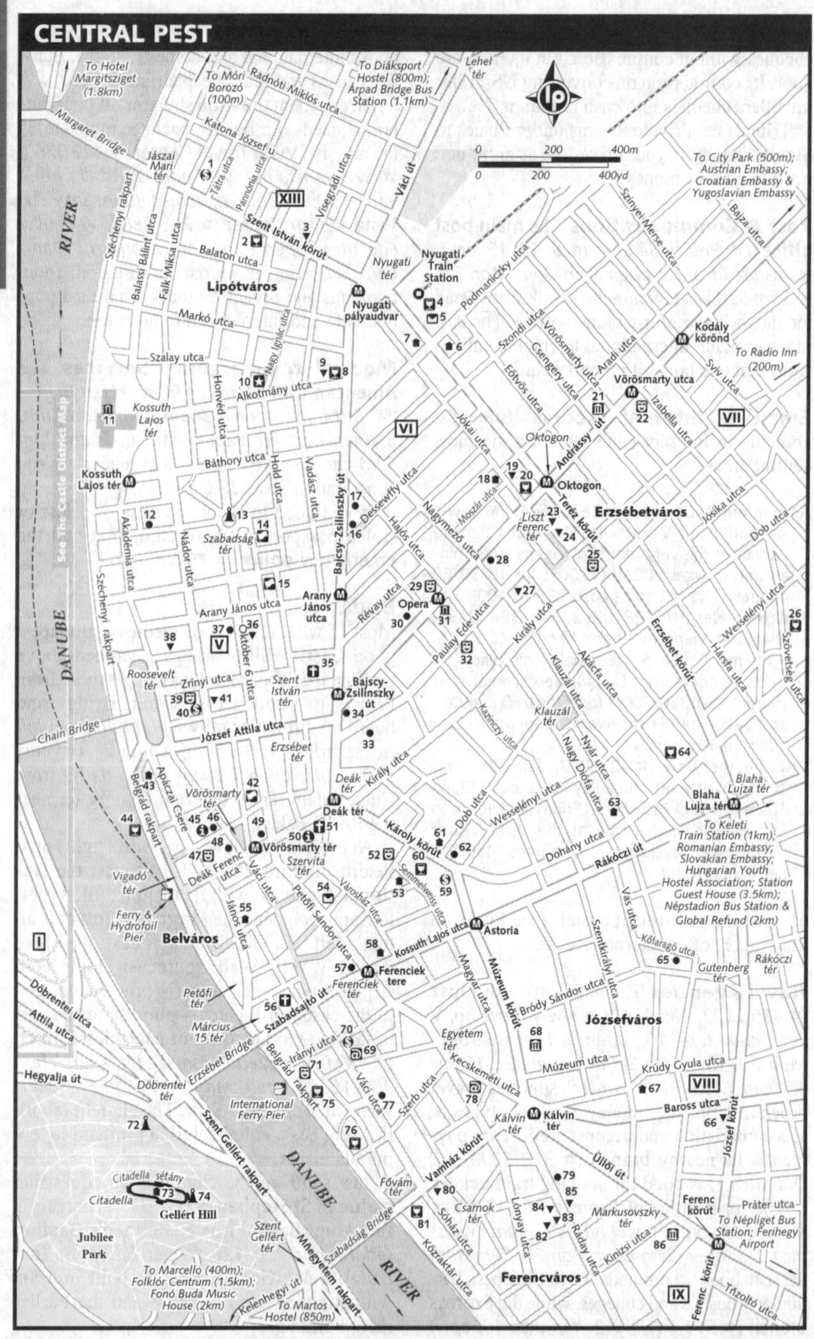

CENTRAL PEST

PLACES TO STAY
- 6 Best Hostel
- 7 Yellow Submarine Youth Hostel
- 18 Hotel Medosz
- 43 Inter-Continental Hotel
- 53 Red Bus Hostel
- 55 Tribus Nonstop Hotel Service
- 58 Leo Panzió
- 61 Carmen Mini Hotel
- 63 Hostel Marco Polo
- 67 Museum Guest House
- 73 Citadella Hotel

PLACES TO EAT
- 3 Wabisabi
- 9 Semiramis
- 19 Teaház a Vörös Oroszlánhoz
- 23 Fortuca
- 24 Café Vian
- 27 Felafel Faloda
- 36 Kisharang
- 38 Gandhi
- 41 Coquan's
- 66 Stex Alfred
- 80 Nagycsarnok (Great Market)
- 82 Shiraz
- 83 Shiraz Gyros Takeaway
- 84 Coquan's
- 85 Pink Cadillac

BARS & CLUBS
- 2 Trocadero
- 4 Face Music Club
- 8 Beckett's Irish Pub
- 20 Cactus Juice
- 26 Angyal
- 44 Columbus Irish Pub
- 60 Café Eklektika
- 64 Old Man's Music Pub
- 75 Capella Café
- 76 Limo Café
- 81 Közgáz Pince Klub

OTHER
- 1 OTP Bank
- 5 Post Office
- 10 District V Police Station
- 11 Parliament
- 12 Express Branch (Transport Tickets)
- 13 Soviet Army Memorial
- 14 US Embassy
- 15 Irish Embassy
- 16 Hungarian Bicycle Touring Association
- 17 Cartographia Map Shop
- 21 House of Terror
- 22 Bábszínház (Budapest Puppet Theatre)
- 25 Liszt Academy of Music
- 28 MÁV Ticket Office
- 29 Hungarian State Opera House
- 30 Ticket Express
- 31 Drechsler House
- 32 New Theatre
- 33 Vista Internet Café & Visitor Centre
- 34 Vista Travel Center
- 35 St Stephen's Basilica
- 37 To-Ma Travel Agency
- 39 Duna Palota
- 40 OTP Bank
- 42 UK Embassy
- 45 Tourinform (24 Hours)
- 46 Malév Ticket Office
- 47 Pesti Vigadó (Concert Hall)
- 48 Vigadó Jegyiroda (Ticket Office)
- 49 American Express
- 50 Tourinform Branch
- 51 Lutheran Church
- 52 Merlin Theatre
- 54 Main Post Office
- 56 Inner Town Parish Church
- 57 Ibusz Main Office
- 59 K&H Bank
- 62 Ibusz Branch
- 65 Kenguru (Car Pooling)
- 68 National Museum
- 69 Ami Internet Coffee
- 70 K&H Bank
- 71 Kalamajka Táncház & Aranytíz Youth Centre
- 72 St Gellért Statue
- 74 Independence Monument
- 77 Folkart Centrum
- 78 Budapest Net
- 79 Hungarian Equestrian Tourism Association
- 86 Museum of Applied Arts

From the **Holy Trinity statue** in the centre of Szentháromság tér, Tárnok utca runs southeast to Dísz tér and the **Royal Palace**. The palace enjoyed its greatest splendour under King Matthias in the second half of the 15th century and has been destroyed and rebuilt half a dozen times since then. Today it contains several important museums, including the **National Gallery** (*☎ 375 7533; Wings B, C & D, Szent György tér 6; adult/child 600/300Ft; open 10am-6pm Tues-Sun Mar-Nov, 10am-4pm Tues-Sun Dec-Feb)* and the **Budapest History Museum** (*☎ 375 7533; Wing E, Szent György tér 2; admission adult/child, student & senior/family 600/300/1000Ft; open 10am-6pm Wed-Mon Mar–mid-May & mid-Sept–Oct, 10am-6pm daily mid-May–mid-Sept, 10am-4pm Nov-Feb)*.

Pest

The most attractive boulevard in Budapest is leafy Andrássy út, which stretches northeast from Bajcsy-Zsilinszky út to Heroes' Square (Hősök tere) and City Park, and is home to many important sights, including the neo-Renaissance **Hungarian State Opera House** (*☎ 332 8197; VI Andrássy út 22)*, completed in 1884.

Many of the other great buildings along this section of Andrássy út date from Budapest's Golden Age, including **Drechsler House** *(VI Andrássy út 25)*, now being turned into a hotel, and the sublime Art Nouveau **New Theatre** *(VI Paulay Ede utca 35)* around the corner.

A bit farther afield, Budapest's newest museum, the **House of Terror** (*☎ 374 2600; Andrássy út 60; adult/child 1000/500Ft; open 10am-6pm Tues-Sun)*, in what was once the headquarters of the dreaded ÁVH secret police, focuses on the crimes and atrocities committed by Hungary's fascist and Stalinist regimes.

The neo-Renaissance dome of **St Stephen's Basilica** (*☎ 311 0839; V Szent István tér; treasury adult/child 200/150Ft; open 9am-7pm*

Mon-Sat, 1pm-4pm Sun), dating from 1905, looms some 96m over Bajcsy-Zsilinszky út. The mummified right hand – the so-called Holy Right or Holy Dexter – of St Stephen is kept in the chapel at the rear of the church; take the passage on the left of the main altar.

To the northwest of the basilica, through stately Szabadság tér, is the neo-Gothic **Parliament** *(☎ 441 4904; V Kossuth Lajos tér 1-3; adult/student 1700/800Ft; English-language tours at 10am, noon and 2pm daily)*, which was built in 1902 and houses the Crown of St Stephen, the nation's most important national icon.

Of Pest's several other museums, especially worthwhile are the **National Museum** *(☎ 338 2122; VIII Múzeum körút 14-16; adult/student 600/300Ft; open 10am-6pm Tues-Sun mid-Mar–mid-Oct, 10am-5pm Tues-Sun mid–Oct-mid-Mar)*, which contains the nation's most important collection of historical relics, and the **Museum of Fine Arts** *(☎ 363 2675, 469 7100; adult/student & child 6-12 yrs 700/350Ft; open 10am-5.30pm Tues-Sun)*, which houses Hungary's richest collection of foreign art. The collection of Old Masters is the most complete in the museum, and there are more works by El Greco in this museem than anywhere else outside Spain.

Organised Tours

Highly recommended is **Absolute Walking Tours** *(mobile ☎ 06-30 211 8861)*, which charges 3500Ft for adults and 3000Ft for students and people under 26 years old.

CASTLE DISTRICT

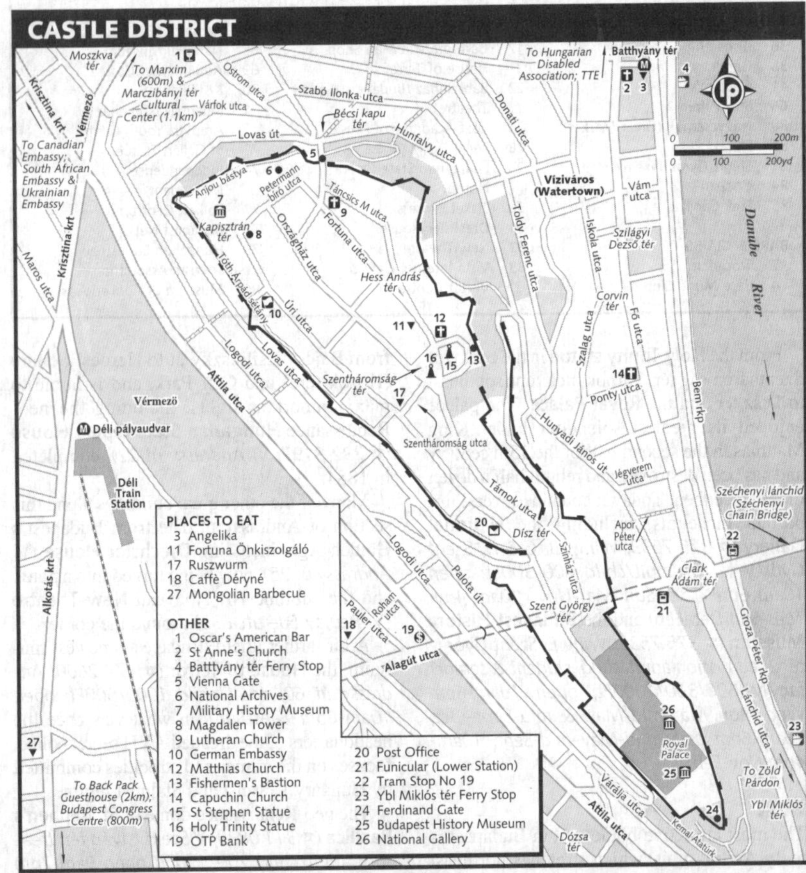

PLACES TO EAT
3 Angelika
11 Fortuna Önkiszolgáló
17 Ruszwurm
18 Caffè Déryné
27 Mongolian Barbecue

OTHER
1 Oscar's American Bar
2 St Anne's Church
4 Batthyány tér Ferry Stop
5 Vienna Gate
6 National Archives
7 Military History Museum
8 Magdalen Tower
9 Lutheran Church
10 German Embassy
12 Matthias Church
13 Fishermen's Bastion
14 Capuchin Church
15 St Stephen Statue
16 Holy Trinity Statue
19 OTP Bank
20 Post Office
21 Funicular (Lower Station)
22 Tram Stop No 19
23 Ybl Miklós tér Ferry Stop
24 Ferdinand Gate
25 Budapest History Museum
26 National Gallery

Places to Stay

Hostels There are two types of hostel in Budapest: year-round private hostels, many in old apartments in or near central Pest, and student dormitories open to travellers during the summer holidays (July to late August). Year-round hostels generally have laundry facilities (about 1000Ft per load), a fully equipped kitchen, storage lockers, TV lounge, no curfew and computers for accessing the Internet. Dormitory accommodation in both year-round and summer hostels ranges from 1700Ft to 3300Ft; expect to pay from 2800Ft to 4700Ft for doubles (book these in advance). High season usually means April to October. Prices almost always include breakfast. Express is the best travel agency to approach for hostel information (see Travel Agencies under Information earlier).

HI-affiliated **Mellow Mood** *(☎ 413 2062 or 215 0660; w www.hostels.hu)* runs many summer hostels in student accommodation. Its booths at Keleti train station *(☎ 343 0748; open 7.30am-11pm daily in summer, 7.30am-9pm daily rest of year)* make bookings and may arrange to transport you there. All the hostels are open 24 hours a day, and there's no curfew. An HI card is not required, but having one usually gets you a 10% discount.

Year-round hostels in Buda include **Back Pack Guesthouse** *(☎ 385 8946; w www.backpackbudapest.hu; XI Takács Menyhért utca 33; dorm beds 1800-2300Ft, doubles 2800Ft)*, a colourful place with 50 beds and a friendly, much-travelled manager. There are dorms with between five and 11 beds and one small double, a lovely garden and very laid-back clientele. Get there on the black-numbered bus No 7 or 7A from Keleti train station, tram No 49 from the little ring road in central Pest, or tram No 19 from Batthyány tér in Buda.

Citadella Hotel *(☎ 466 5794; w www.citadella.hu; XI Citadella sétány; dorm beds 2200Ft)*, in the fortress atop Gellért Hill, has a room with 14 beds, as well as hotel rooms. To get there catch bus No 27 from XI Móricz Zsigmond körtér in Buda.

Student accommodation is available year-round at **Martos Hostel** *(☎ 209 4883, fax 463 3650; e reception@hotel.martos.bme.hu; XI Sztoczek utca 5-7; singles 3500FT, doubles/triples/quads per person 2200Ft)*.

In Pest, Mellow Mood has two year-round hostels. The more central (and expensive) is **Hostel Marco Polo** *(☎ 413 2555; w www.marcopolohostel.com; VII Nyár utca 6; bed in 12-bed dorm €17/19 and singles €46/51 low/high season, doubles/triples/quads per person €31/26/22 low season, €34/29/24 high season)*. It's almost like a mid-range hotel, with telephones in the rooms, a lovely courtyard and bar and restaurant (set meals 1000Ft). The other is the 131-bed **Diáksport Hostel** *(☎ 340 8585, 413 2062; XIII Dózsa György út 152; bed in 6-bed dorms 3300Ft, singles & doubles with bath 4600Ft per person, doubles/triples & quads with shared bath from 3600/3500Ft per person)*. This is definitely a party place, so go elsewhere for rest. Student, youth and hostel card-holders get a 10% discount.

Another rocking place with a great atmosphere is the **Station Guesthouse** *(☎ 221 8864; w www.stationguesthouse.hu; XIV Mexikói út 36/b; bed in 14-/8-bed dorms 1700/2400Ft, doubles & triples/quads 3200/2700Ft per person)*. It boasts a 24-hour bar, pool table and occasional live entertainment. HI card-holders get 200Ft off and rates drop by 100Ft a night from the second to sixth night of stay. Get here on the M1 metro (stop: Mexikói út) or red-numbered bus No 7 from Keleti train station.

For a central, well-managed place, look no farther than **Red Bus Hostel** *(☎/fax 266 0136; e redbusbudapest@hotmail.com; V Semmelweiss utca 14, 1st floor; dorm beds 2700Ft, singles 6000/7000Ft winter/summer, doubles 7000Ft)*, with large airy rooms and exceptionally friendly management.

Close to the restaurants and bars of Ráday utca is friendly **Museum Guest House** *(☎ 318 9508; e museumgh@freemail.C3.hu; VIII Mikszáth Kálman tér 4, 1st floor; dorm beds 2800Ft)*.

Two similar places close to Nyugati train station almost face one another on Teréz körút and Podmaniczky utca. **Yellow Submarine Hostel** *(☎/fax 331 9896; w www.yellowsubmarinehostel.com; VI Teréz körút 56, 3rd floor; dorm beds 2500Ft, doubles/quads 3750/2800Ft per person)* overlooks one of Pest's busiest boulevards. **Best Hostel** *(☎ 332 4934; e bestyh@mail.datanet.hu; VI Podmaniczky utca 27, 1st floor; dorm beds 2800Ft, doubles/quads 4000/3400Ft)* is a bit dearer, but the rooms are bigger, airier and quieter.

Private Rooms Private rooms in Budapest generally cost from 3600Ft to 5000Ft for a single, 5000Ft to 7000Ft for a double and 8000Ft to 14,000Ft for a small apartment, with a 30% supplement if you stay fewer than four nights. To get a room in the centre of town, you may have to try several offices. There are lots of rooms, and even in July and August you'll most likely be able to find something. You'll probably need an indexed city map to find the flat housing your room.

Among the best places to try for private rooms are Ibusz and Vista (see Travel Agencies under Information earlier). Another good place is **To-Ma** *(☎ 353 0819; W www.tomatour.hu; V Október 6 utca 22; open 9am-noon & 1pm-8pm Mon-Fri, 9am-5pm Sat & Sun)*, with extended opening hours. After hours try **Tribus Nonstop Hotel Service** *(☎ 318 3925 or 318 4848; W www.tribus.hu; V Apáczai Csere János utca 1; open 24hr)* southwest of the Vörösmarty metro station.

Hotels In Buda, **Büro Panzió** *(☎ 212 2929, fax 212 2928; e buro-panzio@axelero.hu; II Dékán utca 3; singles/doubles with shower 9000/13,500Ft)*, a pension just a block off the north side of Moszkva tér, sports 10 comfy rooms with TVs and telephones.

In Pest, the most central cheap place is **Hotel Medosz** *(☎ 374 3000, fax 332 4316; VI Jókai tér 9; singles/doubles/triples 10,000/13,000/15.5000Ft)*, right near Oktogon metro station and the restaurants and bars of Liszt Ferenc tér. The 70 rooms are well worn, but have bath and satellite TV.

Near Deák tér, **Carmen Mini Hotel** *(☎ 352 0798, fax 318 3865; e carmen@axelero.hu; Károly körút 5/b, 2nd floor; singles/doubles €50/60)* has nine large and spotless rooms all protected from the noise of the little ring road by double-glazing.

Excellent value for its location and immaculate 14 rooms is **Leo Panzió** *(☎ 266 9041, fax 266 9042; e panzioleo@mail.datanet.hu; V Kossuth Lajos utca 2/a, 2nd floor; singles €45-66, doubles €69-82)*.

Up by leafy Andrássy út, **Radio Inn** *(☎ 342 8347, fax 322 8284; e radioinn@elender.hu; VI Benczúr utca 19; singles €43-48, doubles €48-65)* is a real find, with 33 large suites with bath, kitchen and bed (or beds).

Hotel Margitsziget *(☎ 329 2949, fax 340 4846; e hotelmargitsziget@axelero.hu; XIII Margitsziget; singles €43-45, doubles €43-54)*, on Margaret Island, is good value and almost feels like a budget resort, with free use of tennis courts, swimming pool and sauna.

Places to Eat

Buda For a cheap and quick weekday lunch while in the Castle District, try the **Fortuna Önkiszolgáló** *(☎ 375 2401; I Hess András utca 4; open 11.30am-2.30pm Mon-Fri)*, a self-service place above the Fortuna restaurant. **Nagyi Palacsintázója** *(Granny's Palacsinta Place; ☎ 201 8605, 212 4866; I Hattyú utca 16; menús 568-888Ft; open 24hr)* serves Hungarian pancakes – both savoury (148Ft to 248Ft) and sweet (78Ft to 248Ft) – throughout the day.

The **Aranyszarvas** *(☎ 375 6451; I Szarvas tér 1; mains 1500-2500Ft)* is set in an old 18th-century inn at the foot of Castle Hill and serves game dishes.

Near Moszkva tér, **Marxim** *(☎ 316 0231; II Kisrókus utca 23; pizzas 490-950Ft)* is a temple of Communist memorabilia and campy Stalinist decor. For more serious (but affordable) Italian fare head for **Marcello** *(☎ 466 6231; XI Bartók Béla út 40; pizza & pasta 720-850Ft; open Mon-Sat)*.

South of Déli train station, the **Mongolian Barbecue** *(☎ 353 6363; XII Márvány utca 19/a; buffet before/after 5pm 1990/3690Ft)* is another one of those all-you-can-eat pseudo-Asian places that includes as much beer and wine as you can sink too.

The perfect place for coffee and cakes in the Castle District is the very crowded **Ruszwurm** *(☎ 375 5284; I Szentháromság utca 7; open 10am-7pm daily)*. Two other charming cafés are **Angelika** *(☎ 212 3784; I Batthyány tér 7; open 9am-midnight daily)* and the untouristed **Caffè Déryné** *(☎ 212 3864; I Krisztina tér 3; open 8am-10pm Mon-Fri, 8am-9pm Sat, 9am-9pm Sun)*.

Pest The **Nagycsarnok** *(Great Market; IX Fővám tér)* is Budapest's biggest, although it has become a bit of a tourist trap. Still, plenty of locals head there for fruit and vegetables, deli items, fish and meat. There are good food stalls on the upper level. Large supermarkets are everywhere in Pest.

American fast-food joints proliferate, but much better are the wonderful little *étkezde* serving simple dishes that change every day. A central one is **Kisharang** *(☎ 269 3861; V Október 6 utca 17; mains 500-820Ft)*.

An inexpensive place to nosh Israeli-style is **Falafel Faloda** *(☎ 267 9567; VI Paulay Ede utca 53; large/small sandwiches 450/270Ft, salads 420-1050Ft; open Mon-Sat)*. Cheaper

Middle Eastern food can be found at **Semiramis** *(☎ 311 7627; V Alkotmány utca 20; open Mon-Sat)*.

For good, old-fashioned Hungarian home-cooking try the **Móri Borozó** *(☎ 349 8390; XIII Pozsonyi út 37; mains 500-750Ft; open Mon-Fri)*, a little wine bar–restaurant just a short walk north of Szent István körút.

Stex Alfred *(☎ 318 5716; VIII József körút 55-57; mains 710-1980Ft)* is a big, noisy place that's open almost 24 hours. The extensive menu includes soups, sandwiches, pasta, fish and meat dishes, and it transforms into a lively bar late at night.

Two pedestrian areas in Pest popular with Budapest's youth are Ráday utca and Liszt Ferenc tér. On or near the former, try the upbeat **Pink Cadillac** *(☎ 216 1412; IX Ráday utca 22; pizzas 650-1055Ft)* for pizza or **Shiraz** *(☎ 218 0881; IX Mátyás utca 22; mains 1350-1950)*, a Persian restaurant with a **gyros takeaway** *(☎ 217 4547; IX Ráday utca 21; gyros 460-550Ft)* around the corner.

Of the many places on Liszt Ferenc tér, **Café Vian** *(☎ 268 1164; VI Liszt Ferenc tér 9)*, with an eight-page drinks menu, is a good choice. **Fortuca** *(☎ 413 1612; VI Liszt Ferenc tér 10; pizza & pasta 990-1290Ft)* is the recommended new kid on the block.

Budapest has some decent vegetarian restaurants. **Gandhi** *(☎ 269 1625; V Vigyázó Ferenc utca 4; menú small/large 980/1680Ft; open Mon-Sat)*, in a cellar near Chain Bridge, serves up a daily Sun and Moon plate set menu as well as wholesome salads, soups and desserts. **Wabisabi** *(☎ 412 0427; XIII Visegrádi utca 2; mains 1080-1480Ft; open Mon-Sat)* serves up wonderful Asian-inspired vegan dishes.

Budapest has a growing number of hip modern cafés and teahouses whose patrons take their hot beverages very seriously indeed. For the former, try **Coquan's** *(☎ 215 2444; IX Ráday utca 15; open Mon-Sat)*, with a long list of brews, cakes and bagels. Among the best teahouses is **Teaház a Vörös Oroszlánhoz** *(Teahouse at the Red Lion; ☎ 269 0579; VI Jókai tér 8)*, with an Asian vibe.

Entertainment

Vigádo Jegyiroda *(☎ 327 4322; V Vörösmarty tér 1; open 9am-7pm Mon-Fri, 10am-5pm Sat)* sells tickets for all types of concerts, dance performances and theatre. **Ticket Express** *(for information ☎ 312-0000, for bookings mobile ☎ 06-30 303 0999; W www.tex.hu)* has half a dozen outlets, including a **District VI branch** *(VI Andrássy út 18; open 9.30am-6.30pm Mon-Fri, 9am-1pm Sat)*.

Classical Music & Opera The *Koncert Kalendárium* lists all concerts in town each month. Major venues include the **Liszt Academy of Music** *(☎ 342 0179; VI Liszt Ferenc tér 8)* in Pest and the **Budapest Congress Centre** *(☎ 372 57000; XII Jagelló út 1-3)* in Buda. The **Pesti Vigadó** *(☎ 318 9167; V Vigadó tér 2)* usually has light classical music and touristy musical revues. Concerts are also held regularly in the city's churches, including **Matthias Church** on Castle Hill.

You should pay at least one visit to the **Hungarian State Opera House** *(☎ 332 7914; W www.opera.hu; VI Andrássy út 22)* to see a performance and the incredible internal decor.

Folk & Traditional Performance Authentic folk-music workshops (*táncház*, literally 'dance house') are held at various locations throughout the week but less frequently in summer. Venues in Buda include the **Fonó Buda Music House** *(☎ 206 6296; W www.fono.hu; XI Sztregova utca 3)*, the **Folklór Centrum** *(☎ 203 3868; XI Fehérvári út 47)* in the Municipal Cultural House and the **Marczibányi tér Cultural Centre** *(☎ 212 2820; W www.marczi.hu; II Marczibányi tér 5/a)*.

In Pest there's the wonderful **Kalamajka Táncház** *(☎ 317 5928; V Molnár utca 9)* at the Aranytíz Youth Centre.

Hungária Koncert *(☎ 317 1377)* organises folk and Gypsy concerts featuring the Hungarian State Folk Ensemble and two other groups at the **Duna Palota** *(V Zrínyi utca 5)* and the **Bábszínház** *(Budapest Puppet Theatre; VI Andrássy út 69)* throughout the year. Tickets cost 5600Ft (5100Ft for students).

Pubs & Clubs Budapest has a number of 'Irish' pubs on offer, including **Becketts** *(☎ 311 1035; V Bajcsy-Zsilinszky út 72)* and **Columbus** *(☎ 266 9013)*, which sits on a boat moored in the Danube opposite the Inter-Continental hotel. Also in Pest, **Cactus Juice** *(☎ 302 2116; VI Jókai tér 5)* is in 'American rustic' drag and a good place to sip and sup with no distractions. **Old Man's Music Pub** *(☎ 322 7645; VII Akácfa utca 13)* pulls in the best live blues and jazz acts in town.

In Buda, **Oscar's American Bar** *(☎ 212 8017; I Ostrom utca 14)*, with film memorabilia on the wood-panelled walls and leather director's chairs on the floor, is a cocktail oasis.

A wonderful spot to chill out along the banks of the Danube is **Zöld Párdon** *(W www.zp.hu)*, an outdoor dancing and drinking venue on the Buda side of Petőfi Bridge. The 'world's longest summer festival' runs daily from May to September. Concerts begin at 8pm and then DJs take over till dawn.

Face Music Club *(☎ 414 5025; VI Teréz körút 55; open Thur-Sat)*, in the south wing of Nyugati train station next to McDonald's, has a floor with international hits and another with Hungarian pop music and concerts. The **Közgáz Pince Klub** *(☎ 218 6855; IX Fővám tér 8; open Mon-Sat)* has fewer frills and charges cheap covers.

Trocadero *(☎ 311 4691; VI Szent István körút 15; open Tues-Sat)* attracts one of the most diverse crowds in Budapest with its great canned Latin, salsa and concert nights.

Budapest's flagship gay club is **Angyal** *(☎ 351 6490; VII Szövetség utca 33; open Fri-Sun)*, which welcomes grrlz on Friday and Sunday. **Capella Café** *(☎ 318 6231; V Belgrád rakpart 23; open Thur-Sat)* and its new extension, **Limo Café** *(☎ 266 5455; V Belgrád rakpart 9)* are twin clubs frequented by gays, lesbians and fellow travellers. The only real lesbian venue is **Café Eklektika** *(☎ 266 3054; V Semmelweis utca 21)*, although even it attracts a mixed crowd.

Getting There & Away

Air In Budapest, the main ticket office for **Malév Hungarian Airlines** *(☎ 235 3534, 235 3417; W www.malev.hu; V Dorottya utca 2; open 8.30am-5.30pm Mon-Wed & Fri, 8.30am-6pm Thur)* is near Vörösmarty tér.

Budapest's **Ferihegy airport** *(☎ 296 9696)*, 24km southeast of the city centre, has two modern terminals side by side.

Bus All international buses and some buses to/from southern Hungary arrive at and depart from Pest's new **Népliget bus station** *(☎ 264 3939; IX Üllői út 131; metro Népliget)*. The **ticket office** *(open 6am-6pm Mon-Fri, 6am-4pm Sat & Sun)* is upstairs. **Eurolines** *(☎ 219 8080 or 219 8000; W www.eurolines.hu)* is represented here, as is its Hungarian associate, **Volánbusz** *(☎ 1-485 2162; W www.volanbusz.hu)*.

Népstadion bus station *(☎ 252 4498; XIV Hungária körút 48-52; metro Népstadion)* in Pest now serves most buses to domestic destinations. You should find the **ticket office** *(open 6am-6pm Mon-Fri, 6am-noon Sat & Sun)* here.

Most buses to the Danube Bend and parts of Northern Hungary (eg, Balassagyarmat, Szécsény etc) arrive at and leave from the **Árpád Bridge bus station** *(☎ 329 1450, off XIII Róbert Károly körút; metro Árpád híd; ticket office open 7am-4pm Mon-Fri)* in Pest. The small **Széna tér bus station** *(☎ 201 3688; I Széna tér 1/a; metro Moszkva tér)* in Buda handles some traffic to and from the Pilis Hills and towns northwest of the capital, with some departures to Esztergom.

Train The three main train stations are each on a metro line. **Keleti station** *(Eastern; ☎ 333 6342 or 313 6835; VIII Kerepesi út 2-4; metro Keleti pályaudvar)* handles most international trains, plus domestic trains to/from the north and northeast. For some Romanian and German destinations, as well as domestic ones to/from the Great Plain and the Danube Bend, head for **Nyugati station** *(Western; ☎ 349 0115; VI Nyugati tér; metro Nyugati pályaudvar)*. For trains bound for Transdanubia and Lake Balaton, go to **Déli station** *(Southern; ☎ 375 6293 or 355 8657; I Krisztina körút 37/a; metro Déli pályaudvar)*. Some trains to/from Western and Southern Transdanubia also pass through Budapest's 'fourth' station – Kelenföld in Buda. Most of these services start or end at Déli or Keleti stations. Check where the train leaves from when you buy a ticket.

The **MÁV ticket office** *(☎ 461 5500 or 461 5400; e informacio@mav.hu; VI Andrássy út 35; open 9am-6pm Mon-Fri Apr-Sept, 9am-5pm Mon-Fri Oct-Mar)* sells international train tickets and can make advance seat reservations for domestic express trains for the same price you would pay at the station. It accepts credit cards.

MÁV, Express (see Travel Agents under Information) and **Wasteels** *(☎ 210 2802; open 8am-7pm Mon-Fri, 8am-1pm Sat)* in Keleti station sell BIJ train tickets to those aged under 26, giving a 25% to 50% discount on fares to Western Europe. You must show your passport as proof of age.

Car & Motorcycle One of the cheapest companies for renting cars is **Inka Rent a Car**

(☎ 456 4666, fax 456 4699; ⓔ mail@inkarent.hu; IX Könyves Kálmán körút; open 8am-7pm Mon-Sat, 8am-2pm Sun). One of their Opel Corsas costs €20 a day plus €0.20 per kilometre (or €250 a week with up to 800km a day included).

Hitching For a fee, **Kenguru** *(☎ 266 5837; ⓦ www.kenguru.hu; VIII Kőfaragó utca 15; open 8am-6pm Mon-Fri, 10am-2pm Sat & Sun)* matches up drivers and riders. Destinations and approximate one-way fares include Amsterdam (13,800Ft), London (15,200Ft), Munich (7300Ft), Paris (14,400Ft), Prague (5400Ft) and Vienna (2800Ft).

Boat Hydrofoils link Budapest with Vienna via Bratislava daily between April and early November; see River in the introductory Getting There & Away section of this chapter.

Mahart ferries link Budapest with the towns of the Danube Bend. In Budapest, boats leave from below Vigadó tér on the Pest side. The first stop is at Batthyány tér in Buda.

Getting Around

To/From the Airport The **Airport Minibus Service** *(☎ 296 8555, fax 296 8993)* ferries passengers in eight-seat vans from the airport directly to their hotel, hostel or residence. The fare is 1800/3300Ft one way/return. You need to book your journey *to* the airport 24 hours in advance.

The cheapest but most time-consuming method to get into town is to take the airport bus (look for the stop marked 'BKV Plusz Reptér Busz' on the pavement between terminals 2A and 2B), which terminates at Kőbánya-Kispest metro station. From there take the blue metro line (M3) into the centre. The total cost should be 190Ft.

If you want to take a taxi, call **Tele 5** *(☎ 355 5555)* as they have a flat fare of 2800Ft to or from the airport from Pest (3200Ft from Buda).

Public Transport Public transport is run by **BKV** *(☎ 342 2335; ⓦ www.bkv.hu)*. The three underground metro lines meet at Deák tér. The HÉV above-ground suburban railway, which runs north from Batthyány tér, is almost like a fourth metro line. There's also an extensive network of buses, trams and trolleybuses.

The metro operates from 4.30am until 11.30pm. There are also some 17 night buses (marked with an 'É' after the designated number) running every half-hour or so along the main routes.

The basic fare for all forms of transport is 106Ft (1000/1910Ft for a block of 10/20 tickets), allowing you to travel as far as you like on the same metro, bus, trolleybus or tram line without changing. A ticket allowing unlimited stations with one change within 90 minutes costs 190Ft. Various other tickets and passes are available.

Taxi Overcharging is common. Never get into a taxi that does not have a yellow licence plate, the logo of a reputable taxi firm, and a posted table of fares.

Between 6am and 10pm the maximum flag-fall allowed is 200Ft, the per-kilometre fee is 200Ft, and the waiting fee is 50Ft a minute. From 10pm to 6am, the maximum charges are 280/280/70Ft.

Following are the telephone numbers of reliable taxi firms in order of preference: **City** *(☎ 211 1111)*, **Fő** *(☎ 222 2222)* and **Tele 5** *(☎ 355 5555)*.

The Danube Bend

Between Vienna and Budapest, the Danube breaks through the Pilis and Börzsöny Hills in a sharp bend. Here medieval kings once ruled Hungary from majestic palaces overlooking the river at Esztergom and Visegrád. East of Visegrád, the river divides, with Szentendre and Vác facing different branches and long, skinny Szentendre Island in the middle. Today the historic monuments, easy access, good facilities and forest trails combine to put this scenic area at the top of any visitor's list.

SZENTENDRE

☎ 26 • pop 21,400

Szentendre is a pretty little town 19km north of Budapest on an arm of the Danube, and is an easy day trip from the capital. With its, Serbian Orthodox churches, charming old centre, art and craft galleries, and easy accessibility from the capital, the place swells with tourists during the summer.

Tourinform *(☎ 317 965; ⓔ szentendre@tourimform.hu; Dumtsa Jenő utca 22; open Mon-Fri, daily in summer)* has brochures and information. The **OTP bank** *(Dumtsa Jenő utca 6)* is just off Fő tér.

Begin your sightseeing at Fő tér, the town's central focus. Many of the buildings around this colourful square date from the 18th century, as does the **memorial cross** (1763) in the centre and the 1752 **Blagoveštenska Church** *(☎ 310 554; admission 100Ft; open daily mid-Mar–Oct)*, the Greek Orthodox church on the northeast corner.

Narrow stepped lanes lead up from between Fő tér 8 and 9 to Castle Hill and the **Parish Church of St John** (rebuilt in 1710), from where you get splendid views of the town. Just north, the tall red tower of the 1764 Serbian **Belgrade Cathedral** *(Pátriárka utca)* casts its shadow over the **Serbian Ecclesiastical Art Collection** *(☎ 312 399; adult/child 200/100Ft; open 10am-6pm Tues-Sun May-Oct, 10am-4pm Tues-Sun Mar & Apr, 10am-4pm Fri-Sun Jan & Feb)* next door.

Take a bus from stand No 7 at the station to the very large **Hungarian Open-Air Ethnographic Museum** *(☎ 502 500; adult/child 600/300Ft, guided tours in English, French & German 7000Ft; open 9am-5pm Tues-Sun Apr-Oct, 9am-7pm July & Aug)*, which includes reassembled houses and buildings from around the country.

For those who wish to stay in town, either find **private houses** west of the town centre around the Dunakanyar körút ring road, or stay in central **Bükkös Hotel** *(☎ 312 021, fax 310 782; Bükkös part 16; singles/doubles €40/45)*. In a tourist hub such as Szentendre, you're not going to starve. **Régimódi** *(☎ 311 105; Dumtsa Jenő utca 2)*, just down from the Margit Kovács Museum, has a filling Hungarian set menu for 1500Ft.

Getting There & Away

Take the HÉV from Budapest's Batthyány tér metro station to the end of the line (40 minutes). The last train leaves Szentendre for Budapest at 11.10pm. Some HÉV trains run only as far as Békásmegyer, where you cross the platform for the Szentendre train.

Buses from Budapest's Árpád Bridge bus station, which is on the blue metro line, also run to Szentendre frequently. Some buses continue on to Visegrád (eight buses daily) and Esztergom (17 daily).

From April to late September, at least one daily ferry plies the Danube between Budapest's Vigadó tér and Szentendre. In the high season, regular ferries go to Visegrád and Esztergom. The riverboat terminal is 1km northern part of town at the end of Czóbel Béla sétány.

VISEGRÁD

☎ 26 • pop 1540

Visegrád is superbly situated on the Danube's abrupt loop between the Pilis and Börzsöny Hills. After the 13th-century Mongol invasions, Hungarian kings built mighty **Visegrád Citadel** *(adult/child 500/250Ft; open 9.30am-6pm daily mid-Mar–mid-Oct, weekends only rest of year)* on the hilltop and a **Royal Palace** *(☎ 398 026; Fő utca 29; adult/child 400/200Ft; open 9am-4.30pm Tues-Sun)* on the flood plain at the foot of the hills.

Visegrád Tours *(☎ 398 160; Rév utca 15)*, near the bank, can organise private rooms starting at 4000/5900Ft for singles/doubles. Many houses along Fő utca and Széchenyi utca in the main centre have signs advertising 'Zimmer frei'. **Haus Honti** *(☎ 398 120, fax 397 274; Fő utca 66; singles/doubles 7000/8000Ft)* is a friendly pension with homely rooms. **Gulás Csárda** *(☎ 398 329)*, in town at the start of Mátyás király utca, serves reliable Hungarian standards for around 1000Ft.

Buses are very frequent from Budapest's Árpád Bridge station, the Szentendre HÉV station and Esztergom. Between late May and early September, three daily Mahart ferries shuttle between Budapest and Visegrád via Szentendre, and continue to Esztergom.

ESZTERGOM

☎ 33 • pop 29,300

Esztergom is one of Hungary's most historically important cities. The 2nd-century Roman emperor-to-be Marcus Aurelius wrote his famous *Meditations* while he camped here. Stephen I, founder of the Hungarian state, was born and crowned at Esztergom, and it was the royal seat from the late 10th to the mid-13th centuries.

Gran Tours *(☎/fax 502 000; Széchenyi tér 25; open 8am-6pm Mon-Fri, 9am-noon Sat)* is the best source of information in town. Ask here about private rooms (from 2000Ft) or apartments (6000Ft).

You can't miss **Esztergom Basilica** *(☎ 411 895; admission free; open 7am-6pm daily)*. Built on a hill high above the Danube, it's the largest church in Hungary. The white and red marble **Bakócz Chapel** (1510) on the south side was moved here from an earlier church. At the southern end of the hill is the **Castle**

Museum *(☎ 415 986; adult/child 400/200Ft; open 9am-4.30pm Tues-Sun Apr-Oct, 10am-4pm Nov-Mar)* with partially reconstructed remnants of the medieval royal palace (1215).

From July to late August, dormitory rooms become available at the **trade school** *(☎ 411 746; Budai Nagy Antal utca 38; dorm beds 1200Ft)* near the train station, and at the **László Kőrösy College** *(☎ 400 005; Szent István tér 16; dorm beds 2700Ft per person)*, opposite the cathedral.

The large, plain **Platán Panzió** *(☎ 411 355; Kis-Duna sétány 11; doubles from 4200Ft)* is central and relatively cheap. Comfortable **Alabárdos** *(☎/fax 312 640; Bajcsy-Zsilinszky utca 49; singles/doubles 6000/9000Ft)* is close to the basilica.

Anonim *(☎ 411 880; Berényi Zsigmond utca 4; mains 1000-2400Ft; open until 10pm daily)*, in a historical town house, serves small but excellent dishes.

Getting There & Away

Buses to/from Budapest's Árpád Bridge bus station run about every half-hour until 6.30pm. Buses to Visegrád and Szentendre depart almost hourly from 6am to 8.40pm and to Sopron and Győr once daily.

Trains to Esztergom depart from Budapest's Nyugati train station (1½ hours) up to 13 times a day. To get to western Transdanubia from Esztergom, take one of the three daily trains to Komárom (1½ hours).

Mahart riverboats travel to/from Budapest via Visegrád and Szentendre at least once a day from late May to late September.

Western Transdanubia & Lake Balaton

Beyond the Bakony Hills lies western Transdanubia, bounded by the Danube and the Alps. Conquered by the Romans but never fully occupied by the Turks, this enchanting corner of Hungary contains picturesque small towns and cities with a decidedly Central European air.

Lake Balaton, 77km long, is the largest freshwater lake in Europe outside Scandinavia. The southeastern shore is shallow and in summer the warm, sandy beaches are a favourite holiday spot. Better scenery, more historic sites and deeper water are found on the northwestern side. But Balaton's popularity is its drawback, with the southeastern shore particularly crowded in July and August.

GYŐR

☎ 96 • pop 129,500

Győr (pronounced 'jyeur') is Hungary's third-largest industrial centre, but you'd never know it standing in its charming old centre. Its large neo-baroque City Hall (1898) rises up across from the train station. Baross Gábor utca, which leads to the old town and the rivers, lies diagonally across from City Hall. Much of central Győr is pedestrianised, making parking difficult but walking the city a real pleasure.

There's a **Tourinform** office *(☎ 311 771; e gyor@tourinform.hu; Árpád út 32; open Mon-Sat)* on the corner of Árpád út and Baross Gábor utca. **OTP bank** *(Baross Gábor 16)* has a branch on the main pedestrian street. There are several ATMs around the town centre.

The enchanting **Carmelite church** (1725) and many fine baroque palaces line Bécsí kapu tér. On the northwest side of the square are the fortifications built in the 16th century to stop the Turks. The solid baroque **Cathedral** *(open 10am-noon & 2pm-5pm daily)* on Chapter Hill (Káptalandomb) was originally Romanesque, but most of what you see inside dates from the 17th and 18th centuries. Don't miss the Gothic **Héderváry Chapel** on the church's south side of the church. At the bottom of the hill on Jedlik Ányos utca is the **Ark of the Covenant**, an outstanding baroque statue dating from 1731.

Széchenyi tér is the heart of Győr and features the **Column of the Virgin** (1686) in the middle. **St Ignatius Church** (1641) is the finest church in the city with a superb pulpit, pews and ceiling frescoes.

The **Jesuit Pharmacy** *(☎ 320 954; Széchenyi tér 9; admission free; open 7.30am-4pm Mon-Fri)* is a fully operational baroque institution. If you have a half-day to spare, it's worth visiting **Pannonhalma Abbey** *(☎ 570 191; tours in Hungarian with foreign language text adult/child 1000/300Ft, tours in foreign languages 2000/1000Ft; open 8.30am-6pm daily June-Sept & 8.30am or 9.30am-4.30pm or 5pm Tues-Sun Oct-May)*, on top of a 282m hill some 21km south of Győr.

Places to Stay & Eat

Private rooms are available from the friendly **Ibusz** *(☎ 311 700; Kazinczy utca 3)* office from 2000Ft per person. Dormitory accommodation is available year-round at the huge **István Széchenyi University** *(☎ 503 447; Héderváry út 3; dorm beds around 1000Ft)* north of the town centre.

Convenient to the train and bus stations is **Hotel Szárnyaskerék** *(☎ 314 629; Révai Miklós utca 5; doubles with/without bath 6900/4650Ft)*, a large place with an institutional feel. Only four rooms have en suite baths.

For a cheap, filling meal, try **Rábaparti** *(Zechmeister utca 15; mains from 700Ft)*, an unpretentious (though rather gloomy) restaurant. For the cheaper option head to **Márka** *(☎ 320 800; Bajcsy-Zsilinszky út 30; salads & mains around 430Ft; buffet open 11am-5pm Mon-Sat)*, which has self-service.

Entertainment

The celebrated Győr Ballet and the city's opera company and orchestra all perform at the modern **Győr National Theatre** *(☎ 314 800; Czuczor Gergely utca 7)*. A month-long festival of music, theatre and dance is held from late June to late July.

Captain Drakes Pub *(Radó sétány)* on the little island in the Rába River is a great spot for a drink on balmy summer evenings. **Amnesia** *(Hédervárу utca 16)* is a club/bar north of city centre that attracts a student crowd.

Getting There & Away

Buses run to Budapest (hourly), Esztergom (one daily), Keszthely (five daily), Pécs (two daily) and Vienna (one to three daily). To get to Fertőd, you must take the Sopron bus to Kapuvár (up to 12 a day) and change there.

Győr is well connected by express train to Budapest's Déli, Kelenföld and Keleti train stations (1½ hours) and to Sopron (1½ hours). To go to Lake Balaton take one of the six trains daily heading south to Veszprém (2½ hours) via Pannonhalma.

For Vienna's Westbahnhof you may have to change trains at Hegyeshalom. Another route to Austria requires a change at Sopron.

SOPRON (ÖDENBURG)

☎ 99 • pop 55,000

Sopron sits right on the Austrian border, only 69km south of Vienna. In 1921 the town's residents voted in a referendum to remain part of Hungary, while the rest of Bürgenland (the region to which Sopron used to belong) went to Austria. The Mongols and Turks never got this far, so numerous medieval structures remain intact.

Előkapu (Front Gate) and **Hátsókapu** (Back Gate) are the two main entrances to the old town and Fő tér, the town's central square. **Tourinform** *(☎/fax 338 892; ⓔ sopron@tourinform.hu; Előkapu 11; open daily)* is right near the 60m-high **Fire Tower** *(☎ 311 327, Fő tér; adult/child 300/150Ft; open 10am-6pm Tues-Sun Apr-Oct)*. The 2m-thick square base, built on a Roman gate, dates from the 12th century; the middle cylindrical and arcaded balcony were built in the 16th century; and the baroque spire was added in 1680. In the centre of Fő tér is the magnificent **Holy Trinity Column** (1701) and beyond this the 13th-century **Goat Church**, whose name comes from the heraldic animal of its chief benefactor. Below the church is **Chapter Hall** *(☎ 338 843; Templom utca 1; admission free; open 10am-noon, 2pm-5pm Tues-Sun May-Sept)*, part of a 14th-century Franciscan monastery with frescoes and stone carvings.

Of the excellent museums on Fő tér, two stand out (both open 10am to 6pm Tuesday to Sunday April to September, and 10am to 2pm Tuesday to Sunday the rest of the year). **Fabricius House** *(☎ 311 327; adult/child 300/150Ft)* at No 6 is a historical museum. Rooms on the upper floors are devoted to domestic life in the 17th and 18th centuries and there's impressive Roman sculpture in the Gothic cellar. **Storno House** *(☎ 311 327; adult/child 500/250Ft)* at No 8 is a famous Renaissance palace (1560) that is now a museum and gallery of Romanesque and Gothic decorative art.

Places to Stay & Eat

Ciklámen Tourist *(☎ 312 040; Ógabona tér 8)* travel agency has private rooms for about 3000/4000Ft a single/double, although singles are scarce in summer.

A good bet is **Jégverem** *(☎/fax 510 113, ⓔ haspart@axelero.hu; Jégverem utca 1; singles/doubles 4000/8000Ft)*, with five large rooms in an 18th-century ice warehouse and cellar, in the Ikva district.

Bástya *(☎ 325 325, fax 334 061; Patak utca 40; singles/doubles 6000/8000Ft)* has 16 modern rooms and is a 10-minute walk north of the old town. Another wise choice – though it's out near the Lővér Hills – is **Diana** *(☎ 329 013; Lővér körút 64; singles/doubles 5400/8000Ft)*. Its eight rooms are large and comfortable, and there's a restaurant.

The burgers at **Speedy Burger** *(Várkerület 36; burgers 260-380Ft)* are filling and arrive before you know it. A great place for an inexpensive lunch or light meal is **Cézár Pince** *(☎ 311 337; Hátsókapu 2; open until 11pm daily; dishes 330-690Ft)*, in a medieval cellar off Orsolya tér. For self-catering, head for the **Smatch supermarket** *(Várkerület 100)*.

Entertainment

The **Hungarian Cultural House** *(Széchenyi tér)* is the place for music and other cultural events. The beautiful **Petőfi Theatre** *(☎ 511 700; Petőfi tér 1)*, with its National Romantic-style decor, is in constant use. Its **ticket office** *(☎ 511 730; open 9am-5pm Mon-Fri, 9am-noon Sat)* is at Széchenyi tér 17.

For less highbrow entertainment, head to the **Music Cafe** *(Várkerület 49)*, which often has live jazz in the evenings. Before leaving town be sure to sample Sopron's wines in the deep, deep cellar of **Gyógy-gődőr** *(Fő tér 4)*.

Getting There & Away

There are hourly buses (sometimes more) to Fertőd and Győr, and less frequent buses to Budapest (four), Esztergom (two), Hévíz and Keszthely (three), Kőszeg (eight), Pécs (one) and Szombathely (nine). There is an 8am bus to Vienna daily, with extra departures Monday, Thursday and Friday. Two buses a week make the trip to Munich and Stuttgart (8.05pm Thursday and 9.05pm Sunday).

Express trains to Vienna's Südbahnhof pass through Sopron up to nine times daily; five local services a day to depart for Wiener Neustadt in Austria (where you can transfer for Vienna). There are eight express trains a day for Budapest via Győr and Komárom.

KESZTHELY

☎ 83 • pop 23,000

Keszthely (pronounced 'kest-hay') is the only town on Lake Balaton with a life of its own. It's a fairly large old town that boasts the incredible Festetics Palace, good facilities and boat services on the lake from June to early September.

The bus and train stations are fairly close to the ferry pier. From the stations follow Mártírok útja up the hill, then turn right onto Kossuth Lajos utca into town. **Tourinform** *(☎/fax 314 144; ⓔ keszthely@tourinform.hu; Kossuth Lajos utca 28; open Mon-Sat)* is an excellent source of information on the whole Balaton area. There's a huge **OTP bank** that faces the park, which is south of the Catholic church.

Keszthely's most impressive sight is the 1745 **Festetics Palace** *(☎ 312 190; Kastély utca 1; adult/student 1500/750FT; open 9am-6pm daily June-Aug, 9am-5pm Tues-Sun Sept-May)*, the one-time residence of the wealthy Festetics family. The palace boasts 100 rooms, but only the **Helikon Palace Museum** and the renowned **Helikon Library**, in the baroque south wing, are open to visitors.

Places to Stay & Eat

Vajda Hostel *(☎ 311 361; Gagarin utca 4; dorm beds 1000-1200Ft per person; open mid-June–late Aug)* is what János Vajda College becomes over the summer break. Private rooms are available from **Keszthely Tourist** *(☎ 312 031; Kossuth utca 25)*; a double room should cost around 4000Ft. Alternatively, look for *szoba kiadó* or *Zimmer frei* signs on Móra Ferenc utca, to the east of the town centre near the lake.

In the off season it's worth checking for specials at the hotels along the lakefront. **Phoenix Hotel** *(☎ 312 631; Balatonpart 5; singles/doubles €20-24/25-40)* is a two-star place with low off-season rates. **Párizsi Udvar** *(☎/fax 311 202; Kastély utca 5; rooms from 6900Ft)* pension is a good choice near Festetics Palace. Its 14 large rooms were originally part of the palace complex.

Burgers, salads and outdoor seating are available at **Hamburger Saláta Bár** *(Erzsébet királyné utca; burgers from 300Ft)*. **Oázis** *(☎ 311 023; Rákóczi tér 3; mains 650-950Ft; open 11am-4pm Mon-Fri)* incredibly serves only vegetarian dishes.

Entertainment

At 8.30pm on Sunday from July to mid-August, you can see Hungarian folk dancing in the courtyard of the **Károly Goldmark Cultural Centre** *(☎ 314 286; Kossuth Lajos utca 28)*.

There are several interesting places for a drink along Kossuth Lajos utca. **Easy Rider** at No 79 is popular with youth. **Dick Turpin's Pub** *(Városház utca 2)* plays the best music and is more central.

Getting There & Away

There are about 10 daily buses to Hévíz and Veszprém; one to Szombathely and two to Siófok. Other towns served by bus include

Badacsony (three daily), Budapest (six), Győr (two), Pécs (three) and Sopron (three).

Keszthely is on a branch rail line linking Tapolca and Balatonszentgyörgy, from where up to 17 daily trains continue along the southern shore to Siófok and Budapest. To reach Szombathely or towns along Lake Balaton's northern shore by train, change at Tapolca.

Mahart ferries link Keszthely with most places on the lake from late May to early September.

Southern Transdanubia

Southern Transdanubia is generally flatter than Western Transdanubia, with the Mecsek and Villány Hills rising in isolation from the plain.

PÉCS

☎ 72 • pop 166,500

Pécs (pronounced 'paich') was for 400 years the capital of Roman Lower Pannonia. By the 9th century, the town was known as Quinque Ecclesiae for its five churches (it's still called Fünfkirchen in German). The first Hungarian university was founded here in the mid-14th century. The Turks left their greatest monuments at Pécs and these – together with imposing churches and a lovely synagogue, over a dozen museums, possibilities for hiking through the Mecsek Hills and a lively student atmosphere – make Pécs the perfect place to spend a couple of days.

A dozen streets meet at Széchenyi tér, the centre of the old town. **Tourinform** *(☎ 213 315; ⓔ baranya-m@tourinform.hu; Széchenyi tér 9; open daily)* has copious amounts of information on Pécs and Baranya County. Unless otherwise indicated, museums and other sites are open 10am to 6pm Tuesday to Saturday and 10am to 4pm Sunday from April to October (10am to 4pm the rest of the year) and cost 200Ft to 400Ft for adults and 100Ft to 200Ft for children.

There are plenty of ATMs scattered around town. The **OTP bank** *(Rákóczi út)* has a currency-exchange machine. **M&M Exchange** *(Király utca 16; open 8.30am-5pm Mon-Fri, 8.30am-1pm Sat)* offers decent rates. The **main post office** *(Jókai Mór utca 10)* is in a beautiful Art Nouveau building (1904). **Mac Cafe** inside the Dante Cafe (see Entertainment later) charges 500Ft for Internet connections.

Things to See

Széchenyi tér is the bustling heart of Pécs, dominated on the north by the former Gazi Kassim Paça Mosque, the largest Turkish building in Hungary. Today it's known as the **Mosque Church** *(☎ 321 976; open 10am-4pm Mon-Sat, 11.30am-4pm Sun mid-Apr–mid-Oct, 10am-noon Mon-Sat, 11.30am-2pm Sun mid-Oct–mid-Apr)*. Islamic elements inside, such as the *mihrab* (prayer niche) on the southeastern side, are easy to spot.

Southwest from Széchenyi tér is another important Turkish building, the 16th-century **Hassan Jakovali Mosque** *(Rákóczi út 2)*. It comes complete with minaret and a small museum of Ottoman history.

From the Hassan Mosque, head northeast to Szent István tér, where you'll find an excavated 4th-century **Christian tomb** *(☎ 312 7190)* with striking frescoes of Adam and Eve, and Daniel in the lion's den. The **Roman mausoleum** *(Apáca utca 14)*, a little farther south, and the **Jug mausoleum** *(Dom tér)*, to the north, are other fine examples of underground tombs. A stone's throw east of the Christian tomb is the **Csontváry Museum** *(☎ 310 544; Janus Pannonius utca 11)*, displaying the work of the incomparable painter Tivadar Kosztka Csontváry (1853–1919).

Dóm tér is dominated by the enormous four-towered **Basilica of St Peter**. The oldest part of the building is the 11th-century crypt, but the entire complex was rebuilt in a neo-Romanesque style in 1881. West of the **Bishop's Palace** (1770), which stands in front of the cathedral, is a 15th-century **barbican**, the only stone bastion to survive from the old city walls.

Káptalan utca, which climbs northeast from here, is lined with museums. Behind the **Endre Nemes Museum** *(☎ 310 172; open 10am-2pm Tues-Sun)* at No 5 is Erzsébet Schaár utca, a complete artistic street environment in which the sculptor has set her whole life in stone.

Attractions in the eastern part of the city include the neo-rococo **National Theatre** and **Church of St Stephen** (1741), both on Király utca. If you turn right from Király utca into Felsőmalom utca, you'll find an excellent **City History Museum** *(☎ 310 165; open 10am-4pm Tues-Sat)* at No 9.

The city's beautifully preserved **synagogue** *(☎ 315 881; Kossuth tér; adult/child*

150/50Ft; open 9am-5pm Sun-Thur, to 4pm Fri May-Oct) is south of Széchenyi tér.

Places to Stay

In July and August, central **Mátyás Kollégium** *(☎ 315 846; Széchenyi tér 11; dorm beds around 1200Ft)* and **János Kollégium** *(☎ 251 234; Szánto Kovács János utca 1/c; dorm beds around 1000Ft)*, to the west of the centre, accommodate travellers in dorm rooms. **Ibusz** *(☎ 212 157; Apáca utca 1)* arranges private rooms from 2000Ft per person.

Centrum *(☎/fax 311 707; Szepessy Ignác utca 4; singles/doubles 4500/5600Ft)* has seven not particularly modern rooms, but it's a friendly place and very central. Another central place is **Főnix Hotel** *(☎ 311 682, fax 324 113; Hunyadi János út 2; singles/doubles 4790/7290Ft)*, with 15 accommodating rooms.

Just south of the synagogue is the friendly **Diana** *(☎ 328 594, fax 333 373; Tímár 4a; dorm beds 2000Ft per person, singles/doubles 5600/8600Ft)*, with eight excellent hotel-style rooms, and dorm rooms that sleep up to four.

The big 1960s-style **Hotel Laterum** *(☎ 252 108, fax 252 131; Hajnóczy utca 37-39; bus No 4; dorm beds 2000-2500Ft, doubles 5500-8000Ft)* is on the far west side of town. Dorm-bed rates depend on the season and doubles on the amenities.

Places to Eat

Király utca is lined with eateries. **Dóm Snack** *(Király utca 3; dishes around 700Ft)* has pizza and pasta. Farther east at No 17 is **Oázis** *(kebabs and dishes 500-800Ft)*, a small takeaway spot (it also has pavement seating) serving Middle Eastern dishes at the right price. **Az Elefánthoz** *(☎ 215 026; Jókai tér 6; mains around 1000Ft)* is a bustling Italian restaurant with excellent pizza, pasta and meal-sized salads. There are several **nonstop grocery stores**, including one at Rákóczi út 8.

Entertainment

The biweekly freebie *Pécsi Est* will tell you what's on in Pécs and surrounding towns. Pécs also has well-established opera and ballet companies. If tickets to the **National Theatre** *(☎ 310 539; Király utca)* are sold out, check for cancellations an hour before the performance. The **Artists' House** *(☎ 315 388; Széchenyi tér 7-8)* advertises its classical-music programmes outside. Another venue is the **Ferenc Liszt Concert Hall** *(☎ 311 557; Király utca 83)*, east of the centre.

Pubs and bars line Király utca. **Murphy's Pub** *(Király utca 2)* is a poor attempt at an Irish pub, but it attracts the crowds. **Dante Cafe** *(Janus Pannonius 11)*, occupying the ground floor of the Csontváry Museum, is a good place to meet local students.

Clubs worth checking out include **Boccaccio** *(Bajcsy-Zsilinszky utca 45)*, a large place with three dance floors, and **Soul 6** *(Czindery utca 6)*, a small but popular venue.

Getting There & Away

In summer, hourly buses run to Abaliget and Orfű in the Mecsek Hills, but only seven to 10 a day in winter. Other destinations include Hévíz (two daily), Keszthely (three), Kecskemét (two), Siklós (12 or more), Siófok (four), Sopron (one) and Szeged (seven). Buses run three to four times a day between Barcs on the border and Zagreb in Croatia. There are also three buses a day (at 11.50am, 4.30pm and 4.45pm) from Pécs to Osijek, Croatia.

Up to 13 trains a day connect Pécs with Budapest. You can reach Nagykanizsa and other points northwest via a rather circuitous but scenic line along the Dráva River. One early morning express (at 5.35am) follows this route from Pécs all the way to Szombathely. Two daily trains run from Pécs (10.50am and 1pm) to Osijek.

The Great Plain

The Great Plain (Nagyalföld) of southeastern Hungary is a wide expanse of level *puszta* (prairie) drained by the Tisza River. For centuries it has appeared in poems, songs, paintings and stories. Parts of the plain have been turned into farmland, but other regions are little more than grassy, saline deserts.

Visitors to the region are introduced to the lore of the Hungarian horse, cow and shepherds and their unique animals: Nonius horses, long-horned grey cattle and *racka* sheep. Two national parks, Kiskunság in the Bugac Puszta and Hortobágy in the Hortobágy Puszta, protect this unique environment.

KECSKEMÉT

☎ 76 • pop 108,500

Exactly halfway between Budapest and Szeged, Kecskemét is a clean, leafy city, famous for its apricots, potent *barack pálinka* (apricot brandy), fine architecture and level *puszta*.

Tourinform (☎ *481 065;* e *kecskemet@tourinform.hu; Kossuth tér 1; open Mon-Fri, daily July-Aug)* is on the west side of the Town Hall, which dominates the central square. It has a list of colleges offering accommodation. The travel agency **Ibusz** *(☎ 486 955; Kossuth tér 3)* has private rooms from 1500Ft to 2500Ft per person. For a fab place, try **Fábián Pension** *(☎ 477 677, fax 477 175; Kápolna utca 14; singles/doubles 5500/7500Ft)*.

Good eating choices include **Boston Grill** *(☎ 484 444; Kápolna utca 2)* and **X-Burger** *(Kisfaludy utca 4; in a small mall)*, both with burgers from around 250Ft and open late daily.

There are buses almost hourly to Budapest, every couple of hours to Szeged and at least two a day to Pécs and Eger. Kecskemét is on the rail line that links Budapest's Nyugati station with Szeged. To get to Debrecen and beyond, you must change at Cegléd.

SZEGED (SEGEDIN)

☎ 62 • pop 175,500

Szeged, the most important city on the southern Great Plain, straddles the Tisza River just before it enters Yugoslavia. The Maros River from Romania enters the Tisza just east of the centre.

Tourinform *(☎ 488 690;* e *szeged@tourinform.hu; Dugonics tér 2; open Mon-Fri)* is tucked away in a quiet courtyard. Start your tour in Dom tér, dominated by the twin-towered **Votive Church**, an ugly brown brick structure. The **Szeged Open-Air Festival** is held here from mid-July to late August. Running along three sides of the square is the **National Pantheon** – statues and reliefs of 80 Hungarian notables.

Inside the 1778 **Serbian Orthodox Church** *(adult/child 100/80Ft)*, located behind the 13th-century Votive Church, have a look at the fantastic iconostasis – a central gold 'tree' with 60 icons hanging off its 'branches'. Get the key at Somogyi utca 3 (flat I/5). Don't miss the **Reök Palace** *(Kölcsey utca)*, a mind-blowing Art Nouveau (1907) structure.

The **Great Synagogue** *(☎ 423 849; Gutenberg utca 13; adult/child 200/100Ft; open 10am-noon & 1pm-5pm Sun-Fri Apr-Sept, 9am-2pm Sun-Fri Oct-Mar)*, is the most beautiful Jewish house of worship in Hungary.

Plenty of student accommodation is open to travellers in July and August, including the central **István Apáthy College** *(☎ 545 896; Eötvös utca 4; dorm beds 1250ft, rooms per person from 2500Ft)*. Contact **Szeged Tourist** *(☎ 420 428; Klauzál tér)* for **private rooms** *(2000-3000Ft per person)*. If you arrive by bus you'll be within walking distance of comfortable **Pölös Panzió** *(☎/fax 498 208; Pacsirta utca 17a; singles/doubles 4500/5500Ft)*.

Jumbo Grill *(Mikszáth Kálmán utca 4; dishes from 270Ft)*, with salads and excellent grilled chicken, is a good spot for a cheap meal.

Your best sources of information in this culturally active city are the **Cultural Centre** *(☎ 479 566; Vörösmarty utca 3)* and the free biweekly *Szegedi Est*. The cover charge for clubs here ranges from free entry to 500Ft. The clubs generally open till 4am almost daily. There's a vast array of bars, clubs and other nightspots, especially around Dugonics tér. **JATE Club** *(Toldy utca 1)* is the best place to meet students. **Sing Sing Disco** *(cnr Mars tér & Dr Baross József utca; open Wed-Sat)* has lots of rave parties, while **Soho Music Club** *(Londoni körút 3)* is best for drum 'n' bass.

Buses run to Budapest (seven daily), Eger (two), Győr (two), Kecskemét (10) and Pécs (seven). For Romania, daily buses run to Arad and three go weekly to Timi¢oara. Buses head for Novi Sad, Yugoslavia, once daily and to Subotica three times daily. A 9.30am Friday bus departs for Vienna.

Szeged is on the main train line to Nyugati station in Budapest.

Northern Hungary

Northern Hungary is the most mountainous part of the country. **Eger**, a lovely baroque city full of historic buildings that includes Eger Castle, offers an ideal base for sightseers and wine-tasters. Egri Bikavér (Eger Bull's Blood) wine is known the world over. The friendly staff at **Tourinform** *(☎ 36-517 715, fax 518 815;* e *eger@tourinform.hu; Bajcsy-Zsilinszky utca 9; open Mon-Sat, daily June-Aug)* can supply all the information you need.

To the northeast is **Tokaj**, celebrated for its legendary sweet wines. Its **Tourinform** *(☎ 552 070, fax 352 259;* e *tokaj@tourinform.hu; Serház utca 1; open Mon-Fri)* is just off Rákóczi út.

Iceland

Nowhere are the powerful forces of nature more evident than in Iceland. This poorly monikered island offers glaciers, hot springs, geysers, active volcanoes, icecaps, tundra, snowcapped peaks, vast lava deserts, waterfalls, craters and even Snæfell – Jules Verne's gateway to the centre of the earth. On the high cliffs that characterise much of the coastline are some of the most densely populated seabird colonies in the world, and the lakes and marshes teem with waterfowl. The island is also a backdrop for the sagas, considered by literary scholars to be the finest of all Western medieval works.

Iceland: the Basics

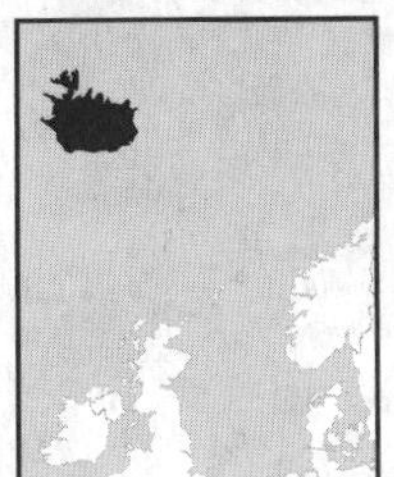

Local name Ísland

Capital Reykjavík

Population 286,575

Language Icelandic

Currency króna (Ikr) = 100 aurar

Avoid at all costs Putrefying shark flesh

End extended hikes by noting *Ég hef nú séð alveg nóg af lunda.* (I have definitely seen enough puffins.)

Facts about Iceland

HISTORY

The Age of Settlement is traditionally defined as the period between AD 874 and 930, when political strife on the Scandinavian mainland caused many Nordic people to flee westward. Early Icelanders decided against a Scandinavian-style monarchy in favour of the world's first democratic parliamentary system. But in the early 13th century, after 200 years of peace, violent feuds and raids ravaged the countryside, and the chaos eventually led to the cession of control to Norway in 1281, then to Danish rule in 1397.

Starting at the end of the 16th century, Iceland was devastated by a series of natural disasters including harsh winters and the eruption of Lakagígar. Tens of thousands of islanders perished. By 1874, Iceland had drafted its own constitution. The Republic of Iceland was established on 17 June 1944.

During WWII British troops occupied the island to defend its strategic position. When the British withdrew in 1941, the government allowed US troops to move in. Despite protests up to the 1980s by the government and people, the USA continues to operate a NATO military base at Keflavík.

GEOGRAPHY

Covering an area of 103,000 sq km, Iceland is the second-largest island in Europe. The bulk of the population and agriculture is concentrated in the southwest, between Reykjavík and Vík.

Iceland is prone to earthquakes and volcanic eruptions because of its position on the mid-Atlantic ridge.

CLIMATE

Warm Gulf Stream waters and prevailing southwesterly winds give the southern and western coasts mild temperatures. This warm air meets cold polar seas and mountainous coastlines, causing nearly continuous rain.

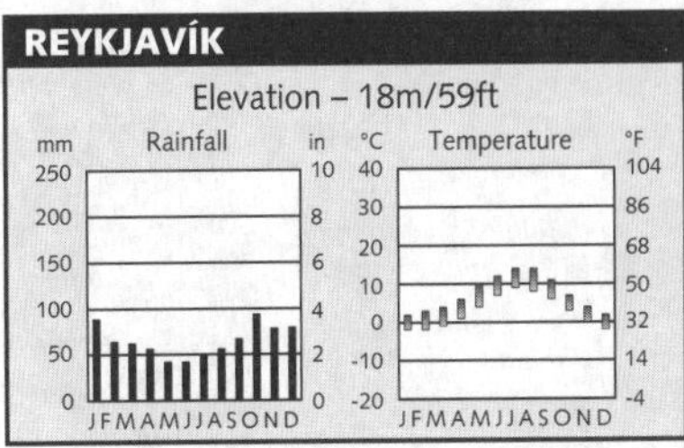

GOVERNMENT & POLITICS

Since 1944 Iceland has been a democratic republic with a president elected to four-year terms by majority vote. Legislative powers rest with the Alþing (parliament). Executive functions are performed by the prime minister and a cabinet of ministers.

POPULATION & PEOPLE

The majority of Icelanders are descended from the early Scandinavian and Celtic settlers.

ICELAND

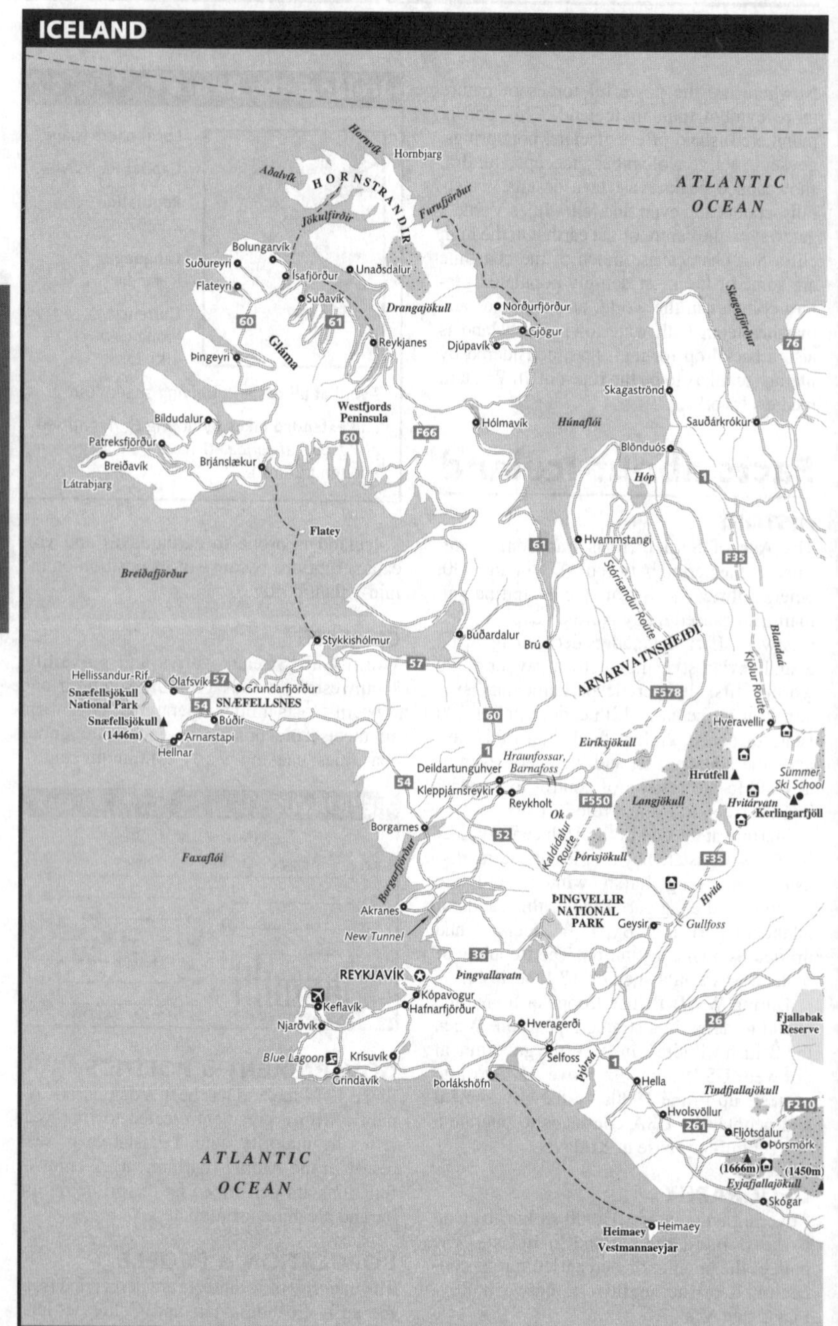

Hornvík
Hornbjarg
Aðalvík
HORNSTRANDIR
Jökulfirðir
Furufjörður
ATLANTIC OCEAN
Bolungarvík
Suðureyri
Ísafjörður
Unaðsdalur
Flateyri
Súðavík
Drangajökull
Norðurfjörður
60
61
Gjögur
Glàma
Reykjanes
Djúpavík
Þingeyri
Skagafjörður
76
Skagaströnd
Westfjords Peninsula
Bíldudalur
Hólmavík
Húnaflói
Sauðárkrókur
Patreksfjörður
F66
Breiðavík
Brjánslækur
Blönduós
Látrabjarg
Hóp
1
Flatey
Hvammstangi
Breiðafjörður
Stórisandur Route
F35
Blandaá
Stykkishólmur
Búðardalur
Brú
ARNARVATNSHEIÐI
Kjölur Route
57
Hellissandur-Rif
Ólafsvík
Grundarfjörður
Snæfellsjökull National Park
SNÆFELLSNES
54
F578
Snæfellsjökull
(1446m)
Búðir
Arnarstapi
Hellnar
Hveravellir
Eiríksjökull
Hraunfossar, Barnafoss
Deildartunguhver
Hrútfell
Summer Ski School
Kleppjárnsreykir
Reykholt
F550
Langjökull
Hvítárvatn
Kerlingarfjöll
Ok
Borgarnes
52
Kaldidalur Route
Faxaflói
Þórisjökull
Borgarfjörður
ÞINGVELLIR NATIONAL PARK
Hvítá
Akranes
Geysir
Gullfoss
New Tunnel
36
REYKJAVÍK
Þingvallavatn
Kópavogur
Keflavík
Hafnarfjörður
Njarðvík
Hveragerði
26
Fjallabak Reserve
Blue Lagoon
Krísuvík
Selfoss
Þjórsá
Grindavík
Þorlákshöfn
Hella
Tindfjallajökull
F210
Hvolsvöllur
261
Fljótsdalur
Þórsmörk
(1666m)
(1450m)
Eyjafjallajökull
Skógar
Heimaey
Vestmannaeyjar

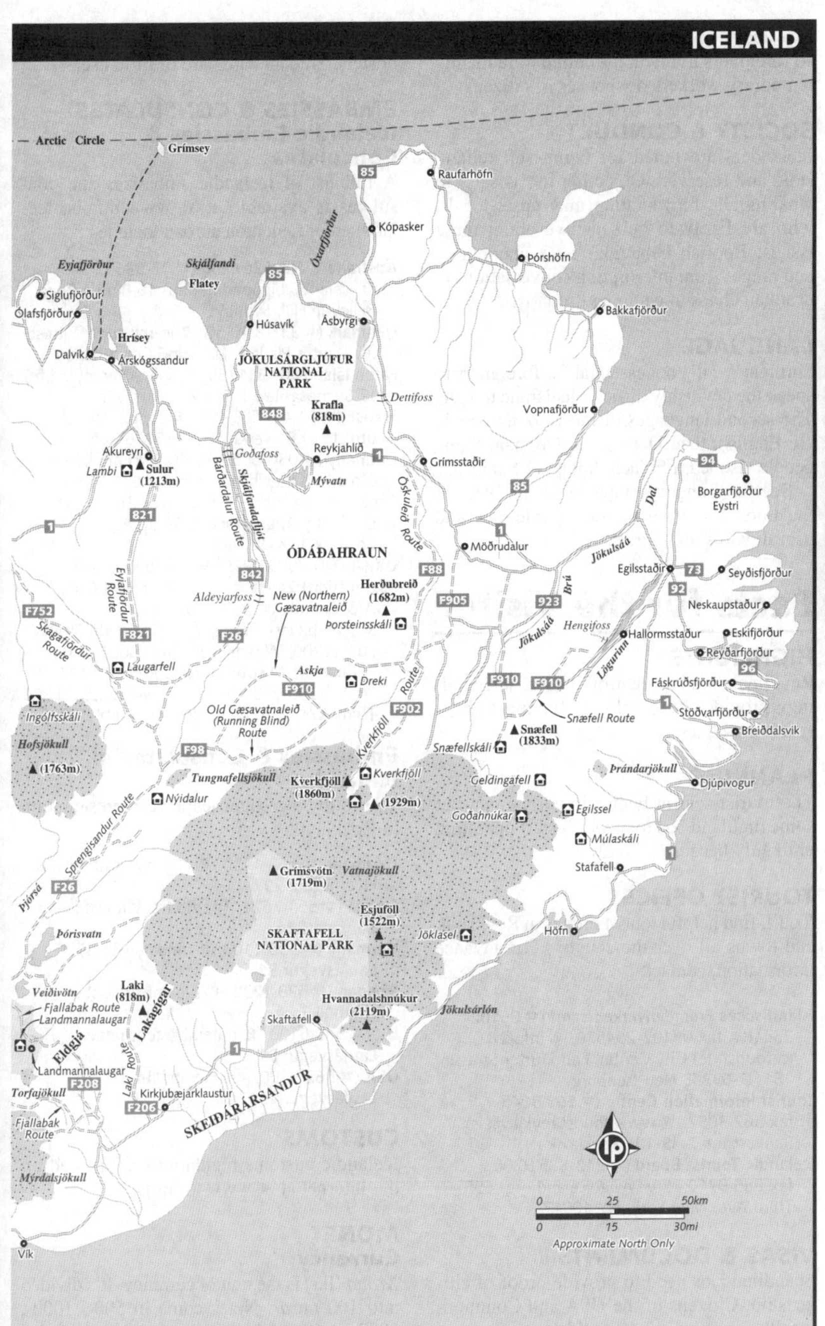
ICELAND
Arctic Circle
Grímsey
Raufarhöfn
Kópasker
Öxarfjörður
Þórshöfn
Bakkafjörður
Eyjafjörður
Skjálfandi
Flatey
Siglufjörður
Ólafsfjörður
Hrísey
Dalvík
Árskógssandur
Húsavík
Ásbyrgi
JÖKULSÁRGLJÚFUR NATIONAL PARK
Dettifoss
Krafla (818m)
Vopnafjörður
Akureyri
Sulur (1213m)
Lambi
Goðafoss
Reykjahlíð
Mývatn
Grímsstaðir
Borgarfjörður Eystri
Dal
Skjálfandafljót
Bárðardalur Route
Öskuleið Route
Möðrudalur
Jökulsá á
ÓDÁÐAHRAUN
Egilsstaðir
Seyðisfjörður
Eyjafjörður Route
Aldeyjarfoss
New (Northern) Gæsavatnaleið
Herðubreið (1682m)
Brú
Neskaupstaður
Þorsteinsskáli
Hengifoss
Hallormsstaður
Eskifjörður
Skagafjörður Route
Jökulsá á
Lögurinn
Reyðarfjörður
Laugarfell
Askja
Dreki
Fáskrúðsfjörður
Route
Ingólfsskáli
Old Gæsavatnaleið (Running Blind) Route
Snæfell Route
Stöðvarfjörður
Hofsjökull
Snæfell (1833m)
Breiðdalsvík
Kverkfjöll
Snæfellsskáli
(1763m)
Tungnafellsjökull
Kverkfjöll (1860m)
Kverkfjöll
Geldingafell
Þrándarjökull
Djúpivogur
Nýidalur
(1929m)
Egilssel
Goðahnúkar
Sprengisandur Route
Múlaskáli
Stafafell
Grímsvötn (1719m)
Vatnajökull
Þjórsá
Esjufjöll (1522m)
SKAFTAFELL NATIONAL PARK
Jöklasel
Höfn
Þórisvatn
Laki (818m)
Veiðivötn
Fjallabak Route
Landmannalaugar
Lakagígar
Hvannadalshnúkur (2119m)
Jökulsárlón
Skaftafell
Eldgjá
Landmannalaugar
Laki Route
Torfajökull
Kirkjubæjarklaustur
SKEIÐARÁRSANDUR
Fjallabak Route
Mýrdalsjökull
Vík
85
848
1
821
842
F88
F905
923
94
73
92
F752
F821
F26
F910
F910
F910
96
F902
F98
F26
F208
F206
0 25 50km
0 15 30mi
Approximate North Only

Nowadays, immigration is strictly controlled, so foreigners living in the country are mainly temporary workers or spouses of citizens.

SOCIETY & CONDUCT

Icelanders are noted for being self-reliant, stoic and reserved. Objecting too vocally to whaling and bird hunting may upset locals, who are likely to be sensitive about these issues. Boorish behaviour isn't uncommon and ranges from interrupting conversations to drunken chaos at camping grounds.

LANGUAGE

Fortunately, it's not essential for foreigners to speak the devilishly difficult Icelandic tongue. The second languages of most young people are English, then Danish and German. Some people also learn French, Italian or Spanish.

See the Language chapter at the back of the book for pronunciation guidelines and useful words and phrases.

Facts for the Visitor

HIGHLIGHTS

Reykjavík and its beautiful natural surroundings provide the highlights for most shoestring travellers.

PLANNING

The tourist season begins in early June, but some highland bus tours don't start operating until July because of snow.

TOURIST OFFICES

You'll find helpful tourist offices in Reykjavík and towns all over the country. For advance information, contact:

Isländisches Fremdenverkehrsamt (☎ 06102-254484, fax 06102-254570, ⓔ info@icetourist.de) City Center, Frankfurter Strasse 181, D-63263 Neu-Isenburg
Tourist Information Centre (☎ 562 3045, fax 562 3057, Ⓦ www.tourist.reykjavik.is) Bankastræti 2, IS-101 Reykjavík
Icelandic Tourist Board (☎ 212-885 9700, fax 885 9710, Ⓦ www.goiceland.org) 655 Third Ave, New York, NY 10017

VISAS & DOCUMENTS

Scandinavians need to provide proof of citizenship. Citizens of the USA and Commonwealth countries need a valid passport.

HI hostel cards give discounts of Ikr350 at hostels. Student cards are of little use.

EMBASSIES & CONSULATES

Icelandic Embassies & Consulates

A full list of Icelandic embassies and consulates is available at Ⓦ www.mfa.is. Icelandic representation abroad includes:

Australia & New Zealand (☎ 02-9365 7345, ⓔ iceland@bigpond.net.au) 16 Birriga Road, Bellevue Hill, Sydney
Denmark (☎ 33 18 10 50, ⓔ icemb.coph@utn.stjr.is) Dantes Plads 3, DK-1556 Copenhagen V
Faroe Islands (☎ 311155, ⓔ solva@faroeyard.fo) JC Svabosgøta 31, Box 65, Tórshavn
France (☎ 01 44 17 32 85, ⓔ icemb.paris@utn.stjr.is) 8 ave Kléber, F-75116 Paris
Germany (☎ 030-5050 4000, ⓔ icemb.berlin@utn.stjr.is) Rauchstrasse 1, D-10787 Berlin
Greenland (☎ 981293, ⓔ arcwon@greennet.gl) c/o Hotel Angmagssalik, Sulup Aqq B725, Postbox 117, Tasiilaq
UK (☎ 020-7599 3999, ⓔ icemb.london@utn.stjr.is) 2a Hans St, London SW1X 0JE
USA & Canada (☎ 202-265 6653, ⓔ icemb.wash@utn.stjr.is) 1156 15th St NW, Suite 1200, Washington, DC 20005-1704
Permanent Mission of Iceland to the UN: (☎ 212-593 2700, ⓔ icecon.ny@utn.stjr.is) 800 Third Ave, 36th floor, New York, NY 10022

Embassies & Consulates in Iceland

The following countries have representation in Reykjavík:

Denmark (☎ 562 1230, ⓔ ambdan@mmedia.is) Hverfisgata 29
France (☎ 551 7621, ⓔ amb.fran@itn.is) Túngata 22
Germany (☎ 530 1100, ⓔ embager@li.is) Laufásvegur 31
Sweden (☎ 520 1230, ⓔ sveamb@itn.is) Lágmúli 7
UK (☎ 550 5100, ⓔ britemb@centrum.is) Laufásvegur 31
USA (☎ 562 9100, ⓔ amemb@itn.is) Laufásvegur 21

CUSTOMS

Icelandic customs regulations are posted on the Internet at Ⓦ www.tollur.is.

MONEY

Currency

Króna (Ikr) is the unit of currency. It's divided into 100 *aurar*. Notes come in 500-, 1000-, 2000- and 5000-krónur denominations. Coins come in one-, five-, 10-, 50- and 100-krónur denominations.

Exchange Rates

At the time of printing the following exchange rates prevailed:

country	unit		krónur
Australia	A$1	=	Ikr47.99
Canada	C$1	=	Ikr54.74
Denmark	Dkr1	=	Ikr11.49
Eurozone	€1	=	Ikr85.29
Japan	¥100	=	Ikr70.29
New Zealand	NZ$1	=	Ikr41.84
Norway	Nkr1	=	Ikr11.59
Sweden	Skr1	=	Ikr9.27
UK	UK£1	=	Ikr135.63
USA	US$1	=	Ikr86.86

Exchanging Money

Travellers cheques, postal cheques and banknotes may be exchanged for Icelandic currency at banks for a small commission (there's no commission at Landsbanki Íslands). Other exchange offices charge commissions up to 8.75%, and exchange rates are lower.

Cash can be withdrawn from banks using a MasterCard, Visa or Cirrus ATM card. Maestro, EDC and Electron debit cards are widely accepted.

MasterCard and Visa can be used at many retail outlets; Diners Club and American Express (AmEx) are rarely accepted.

Costs

If you must get by on less than Ikr1500 a day, you'll have to camp, self-cater and hitchhike, cycle or walk. Otherwise, count on spending at least Ikr4500 a day.

Student card-holders get substantial discounts on flights, museum admissions and bus fares (in winter). Students and Iceland bus-pass holders receive a 5% to 10% discount on most camping fees, sleeping-bag accommodation at Edda hotels and some restaurants.

Tipping & Bargaining

Tipping isn't required in Iceland; restaurants automatically add service charges to the bill. If you want to tip for particularly good or friendly service, no-one will be furious. Bargaining isn't standard practice.

Taxes & Refunds

The 24.5% Icelandic *söluskattur* (VAT) is included in marked prices.

If you spend over Ikr4000 in a shop with the sign 'Iceland Tax-Free Shopping', you'll get a tax-refund coupon worth up to 15% of the cost price.

POST & COMMUNICATIONS

Poste restante to Reykjavík should be addressed with your name to Poste Restante, Central Post Office, Pósthússtræti 5, IS-101 Reykjavík, Iceland.

International direct dialling is available via satellite. The international access code is ☎ 00. Iceland's country code is ☎ 354 and there are no area codes.

Internet access is available in public libraries around the country (usually closed at weekends); you have to pay in Reykjavík (around Ikr200 per half-hour). There are also rather expensive Internet cafés in Reykjavík.

DIGITAL RESOURCES

The **Icelandic Tourist Board** *(W www.icetourist.is)* has detailed country information.

BOOKS

Lonely Planet's *Iceland, Greenland & the Faroe Islands* is the guide for in-depth travel. A great history is provided by Gunnar Karlsson in *Iceland's 1100 Years*.

WOMEN TRAVELLERS

Drunken Icelandic men can be a nuisance. The **Womens' Crisis Centre** *(☎ 561 1205)* is available 24 hours a day.

GAY & LESBIAN TRAVELLERS

Icelanders generally hold a fairly open attitude towards gays and lesbians. Contact the gay and lesbian organisation **Samtökin '78** *(☎ 552 7878, fax 552 7820; e office@samtokin78.is; Reykjavík Gay Centre, Laugavegur 3, IS-101 Reykjavík)* or check out W www.gayiceland.com.

DISABLED TRAVELLERS

For details, contact the tourist information centre in Reykjavík, or the organisation for the disabled, **Sjálfsbjörg** *(☎ 552 9133; W www.sjalfsbjorg.is; Hátún 12, IS-105 Reykjavík)*.

Emergencies

In Iceland, dial ☎ 112 (police, ambulance and fire) in case of emergency.

DANGERS & ANNOYANCES

Be careful when using taxis; there have been reports from readers and travellers of rip-offs.

BUSINESS HOURS

Weekday shopping hours are 9am to 6pm, although some shops may open at 8am and close at 4pm or later. Shops usually open at 9am or 10am and close between 1pm and 4pm on Saturday. Some shops in Reykjavík open on Sunday. Post offices have variable opening hours.

PUBLIC HOLIDAYS & SPECIAL EVENTS

The following public holidays are observed in Iceland: New Year's Day (1 January), Maundy Thursday (Thursday before Easter), Good Friday to Easter Monday (March/April), First Day of Summer (April), Labour Day (1 May), Ascension Day (May), Whit Sunday & Whit Monday (May), Independence Day (17 June), Shop & Office Workers' Holiday (First Monday in August), Christmas Eve (24 December), Christmas Day (25 December), Boxing Day (26 December) and New Year's Eve (31 December).

Every two years Reykjavík hosts an **arts festival** *(W www.listahatid.is)* in May (even-numbered years), with a wide range of events, including painting exhibitions, song and dance.

The first day of summer, or Sumardagurinn fyrsti, is celebrated in carnival style on the third Thursday in April, with the biggest bash staged in Reykjavík.

Sjómannadagurinn, celebrated on the first Sunday in June, is dedicated to seafarers.

Midsummer is celebrated around 24 June in Iceland, but with less fervour than on the Scandinavian mainland.

On a Saturday in mid-August, there's the Culture Night in Reykjavík; it's great fun, with art, music, dance and a finale of fireworks.

ACTIVITIES

Most visitors to Iceland agree that the best way to see the country is on foot. The best months for walking are July, August and September. For details on hiking and mountaineering, contact **Ferðafélag Íslands** *(☎ 568 2533; W www.fi.is; Mörkin 6, IS-108 Reykjavík)*, or **Íslenski Alpaklúbburinn** *(☎ 581 1700; Mörkin 6, IS-108 Reykjavík)*.

Skiers will find some pleasant no-frills skiing in Iceland. **Reykjavík** and **Akureyri** have winter resorts for downhill skiing, and a summer ski school operates at **Kerlingarfjöll** near Hofsjökull in central Iceland.

WORK

Most foreign workers find themselves gutting fish eight hours a day for mediocre wages. However, some companies include food and/or accommodation in the deal; your best chances are in spring. If you intend to work in Iceland, you'll need a job offer before you arrive in the country, then apply for a work permit.

ACCOMMODATION

Camping

Camping provides the most effective relief from high accommodation prices. To camp on a private farm, ask the owner's permission first. Otherwise, apart from national parks and reserves where camping is either forbidden or restricted, you're free to camp anywhere.

Organised camping grounds *(tjaldsvæði)* charge about Ikr400 to Ikr700 per person.

Emergency Huts

The Lifesaving Association and the Icelandic Automobile Association maintain orange-coloured emergency huts on high mountain passes, remote coastlines and other places subject to life-threatening conditions. They're stocked with food, fuel and blankets and must be used only in emergencies.

Mountain Huts

Ferðafélag Íslands, the Icelandic Touring Club and smaller local clubs maintain a system of *sæluhús* (mountain huts). For more information, contact **Ferðafélag Íslands** *(☎ 568 2533; E fi@fi.is; Mörkin 6, IS-108 Reykjavík)*.

Útivist *(☎ 562 1000; W www.utivist.is; Laugavegur 178, IS-105 Reykjavík)* operates huts at Goðaland and Fimmvörðuháls along the Þórsmörk to Skógar route.

Hostels

Icelandic HI hostels, called *farfuglaheimili*, which translates into something like 'little home for migrating birds'. All hostels have hot water, duvets and pillows, cooking facilities, luggage storage and opportunities to meet other travellers. There are normally no curfews. Sleeping bags are welcome. For more information contact the **Icelandic Hostel Association** *(Bandalag Íslenskra Farfugla; ☎ 553 8110, fax 588 9201; W www.hostel.is; Sundlaugavegur 34, IS-105 Reykjavík)*.

Guesthouses

There are many types of *gistiheimilið* (guesthouses), from private homes to elaborate institutions. Most guesthouses are only open seasonally; between October and May, room rates are significantly cheaper than June to September. A cold breakfast is usually served buffet style.

Rooms are always cheaper if they are booked through a travel agent abroad.

Hotels

Most summer hotels, including **Edda Hotels** (*w www.hoteledda.is*), run by Icelandair Hotels, are schools that are used as tourist accommodation during summer holidays (early June to late August). Some offer sleeping-bag accommodation in rooms or classrooms, in addition to more conventional lodging.

Regular hotels are expensive.

FOOD & DRINKS

Icelanders make a staple of *harðfiskur*, haddock that's cleaned and dried in the open air. It's torn into strips and eaten with butter as a snack. Icelanders also eat broiled *lundi*, or puffin, which looks and tastes like calf liver. A unique treat is the delicious yoghurt-like concoction *skyr*, made of pasteurised skimmed milk and bacteria culture.

The only nonalcoholic traditional drink (though it may be spiked with alcohol) is *jólaöl* or 'Christmas brew'. British travel writer Tony Moore disparagingly described the taste as 'de-alcoholised Guinness seasoned with Marmite'. Considerably better is the do-it-yourself mixture of malt extract and orangeade.

The traditional Icelandic alcoholic brew is *brennivín* (burnt wine), a sort of schnapps made from potatoes and caraway. Its nickname, *svarti dauði* or 'black death', may offer some clues about its character, but it's actually quite palatable.

Jaws' Worst Nightmare

Iceland boasts some 'delicacies' that may remind foreigners of the nightmare feast in *Indiana Jones and the Temple of Doom*. Top of the list is *hákarl* – putrefied shark meat that has been buried in sand and gravel for three to six months to ensure sufficient decomposition. It reeks of a cross between ammonia and old road kill. Some people take ill due to the foul stench alone!

Other primeval oddities include *súrsaðir hrútspungar* – rams' testicles pickled in whey and pressed into a cake, and *svið* – singed sheep's head (complete with eyes but minus the brain) sawn in two, boiled and eaten either fresh or pickled.

Getting There & Away

AIR

Icelandair (*w www.icelandair.net*), Iceland's national carrier, offers short-stay 'cheap' tickets.

Flugfélag Íslands (*Air Iceland;* ☎ *570 3030;* *w www.airiceland.is*) and **Atlantic Airways** (*w www.atlantic.fo*) fly between Reykjavík and the Faroe Islands. Flugfélag Íslands also flies year-round from Kulusuk (Greenland) to Reykjavík.

In summer other airlines serve Iceland from France and Germany, including **LTU** (*in Germany* ☎ *0211-941 8466, in Reykjavík* ☎ *587 1919;* *w www.ltu-airways.com*).

Combined air/ferry tickets to Iceland are now available from the UK and Scandinavia.

SEA

Travelling by ferry from the European mainland is expensive and time-consuming. For information, contact **Smyril Line** (☎ *298-345900;* *e office@smyril-line.fo; Jónas Broncksgøta 37, PO Box 370, FO-110 Tórshavn, Faroe Islands*).

The Icelandic cargo-shippers, **Eimskip** (*w www.eimskip.com*), can take up to four passengers each on its vessels *Dettifoss* and *Goðafoss* to mainland Europe via the Faroe Islands. The trip to or from Rotterdam costs €470/660 for singles/doubles each way (full board). To/from Hamburg takes four days and costs €560/790 for singles/doubles.

Getting Around

BUS

Destination Iceland (☎ *591 1000, fax 591 1050;* *w www.dice.is; BSÍ bus station, Vatnsmýrarvegur 10, IS-101 Reykjavík*) covers the country. Many buses stop running in September and don't resume until June.

CAR & MOTORCYCLE

Bringing a vehicle or renting one is prohibitively expensive. Some readers have reported illegal dual pricing, with tourists being charged more than locals.

BICYCLE

In Iceland the wind, rough roads, gravel, river crossings, intimidating vehicles, sandstorms and horrid weather conspire against cyclists. Come prepared to pack up your bike and travel by bus when things become intolerable.

In areas best suited to cycling, such as in Mývatn or urban Reykjavík and Akureyri, bicycles can be hired for around Ikr1500 per day, plus deposit.

HITCHING

Summer hitching is possible but can be inconsistent. Long waits are common in most areas.

LOCAL TRANSPORT

Reykjavík, Hafnarfjörður and Akureyri have good local bus and taxi services; the bus service in Ísafjörður is more limited. Taxis with English- or German-speaking drivers are available in most towns.

Reykjavík

pop 178,030

Reykjavík is the world's most northerly capital city and also one of its smallest. By European standards, Reykjavík is historically and architecturally unexciting, but politically, socially, culturally, economically and psychologically, it dominates the country.

Reykjavík was the first place in Iceland to be intentionally settled. The original settler, Ingólfur Arnarson, tossed his high-seat pillars (a bit of pagan paraphernalia) overboard in 874, and built his farm near where they washed ashore. He called the place Reykjavík (Smoky Bay) because of the steam rising from nearby geothermal features.

Orientation & Information

Reykjavík's heart is still between Tjörnin and the harbour, and many old buildings remain. Nearly everything in the city lies within walking distance of the old settlement.

The main tourist information centre, **Upplýsingamiðstöð Ferðamála** *(☎ 562 3045; ⓔ tourinfo@tourinfo.is; Bankastræti 2; open daily)* is near Lækjargata. A second branch is at the **Raðhus** *(City Hall; ☎ 563 2005; Tjarnargata 11)*.

Banks cluster on Austurstræti and Bankastræti. After-hours banking is available at **The Change Group** *(Keflavík International Airport)*, open for flight arrivals and departures. Head for **Landsbanki Íslands** *(Austurstræti)* for a better deal.

Reliable postal services are available at the **Central Post Office** *(fax 580 1191; Posthússtræti 5; open 9am-4.30pm Mon-Fri year-round)*. Free Internet access isn't available unless you buy a library card for Ikr1000. The best libraries for Internet access are **Borgarbókasafn** *(Tryggvagata 15; open 10am-8pm Mon-Thur, 11am-7pm Fri, 1pm-5pm Sat & Sun)* charging Ikr200/300 per 30/60 minutes and **Kringlusafn** *(Kringlan shopping centre)* where the cost is Ikr200 per half-hour.

The 24-hour emergency ward is at the **city hospital** *(☎ 525 1000; Fossvogur)*, near Áland. There's also a 24-hour pharmacy, **Háaleitis Apotek** *(☎ 581 2101; Háaleitisbraut 68)*.

Things to See

Old Reykjavík The **old town** of Reykjavík includes the area bordered by Tjörnin, Lækjargata, the harbour and the nearby suburb of Seltjarnarnes. The historical centre of the city includes the east bank of Tjörnin and both sides of Lækjargata.

Old Reykjavík grew up around **Tjörnin**, the pleasant lake in the centre of town. The octagonal gazebo, **Hljómskálinn**, was built in 1922 as a rehearsal hall for the Reykjavík Brass Band.

Reykjavík's new **Raðhus** *(City Hall; ☎ 563 2005; open 8am-7pm Mon-Fri, 10am-6pm Sat & Sun)*, on the northern bank of Tjörnin, could be described as a sort of postmodern floating palace.

Stjórnarráðið, the white building opposite Lækjartorg, contains government offices. It's one of the city's oldest buildings, originally an 18th-century jail. On nearby **Árnarhóll** (Eagle Hill) there's a statue of the first settler, Ingólfur Arnarson.

Sheriff Skúli Magnússon's weaving shed *(Aðalstræti 10)* is the oldest building in Reykjavík, originally built around 1752. Although the shed burnt down in 1764, it was immediately replaced on the same foundation and now contains a pub.

Þjóðmenningarhúsið *(Culture House; ☎ 545 1400; Hverfisgata 15; adult/child Ikr300/200; open 11am-5pm daily)* has impressive temporary exhibits about Vikings and Icelandic cultural heritage. There's a permanent exhibit of original saga manuscripts.

New Reykjavík Reykjavík's most imposing structure, the immense church **Hallgrímskirkja** *(☎ 510 1000; Skólavörðuholt; open 10am-5pm daily)* was consecrated in 1986 and was unashamedly designed to resemble a mountain of basaltic lava. The stark, light-filled interior is enhanced by the great view from its 75m tower. The lift costs Ikr300/50 per adult/child. Outside the church, there's a **statue of Leifur Eiríksson**, presented by the USA in 1930.

The extraordinary **Icelandic Phallological Museum** *(☎ 566 8668; Laugavegur 24; admission Ikr400; open 2pm-5pm Tues-Sat May-Aug, 2pm-5pm Tues & Sat Sept-Apr)* claims to be the only museum in the world with a collection of penises from all local mammals – with one exception. Although the offerings currently lack a *Homo sapiens* specimen, as of late 2002 a human had promised to donate his unit for member-ship.

Iceland's **Nordic House** *(☎ 551 7030; Sæmundargata; exhibition admission Ikr300; open noon-5pm daily during exhibitions)*, south of Tjörn, serves as a Scandinavian cultural centre and offers a cafeteria, travelling exhibitions, concerts, lectures, films based on Nordic themes and a library of Scandinavian literature.

To appreciate Vestmannaeyjar or Mývatn, visit the excellent **Volcano Show** *(☎ 551 3230; Hellusund 6a; admission Ikr950/750 for 2/1-hour show)*. Filmed by locals, the show offers an insight into the volcanic spectre under which Icelanders live. Daily two-hour shows (in English) begin at 11am, 3pm and 8pm in July and August; shows are once or twice daily September to June.

The **National Museum** *(☎ 552 8888; Suðurgata 41; admission Ikr400; open 11am-5pm Tues-Sun mid-May–mid-Sept, shorter hrs mid-Sept–mid-May)* is obligatory for anyone interested in Norse culture and Icelandic history. The most renowned artefact is the c. 1200 **Valþjófsstaður church door** (from east Iceland), which depicts a Norse battle scene.

The impressive **Kjarvalsstaðir** *(☎ 552 6131; Flókagata; adult/child Ikr500/free, admission free Mon; open 10am-5pm daily)* displays the work of Jóhannes Kjarval, one of Iceland's most popular artists. The surrealism that defines his work was derived from the ethereal nature of the distinctive Icelandic landscape.

Near Hallgrímskirkja is the cube-shaped **Einar Jónsson Museum** *(☎ 551 3797; Njarðargata; adult/child Ikr400/free; open 2pm-5pm Tues-Sun June–mid-Sept, 2pm-5pm Sat & Sun mid-Sept–May)*, a worthwhile exhibit of work by Iceland's foremost 20th-century sculptor that includes his apartment and sculpture garden.

The well-respected igloo-shaped **Ásmundur Sveinsson Museum** *(☎ 553 2155; Sigtún; adult/child Ikr500/free, admission free Mon; open 10am-4pm daily May-Sept, 1pm-4pm daily Oct-Apr)* features massive but graceful concrete sculptures on Icelandic saga and folklore themes by Ásmundur Sveinsson, plus smaller works in wood and various metals.

On the shore near the bay end of Klapparstígur stands the astonishing **Sun-Craft sculpture**, which resembles a distinctly porous Viking ship and certainly merits a photo.

Activities

Spreading out southeast of Elliðavatn lake immediately southeast of Reykjavík is **Heiðmörk** (Heath Woods), a 2800-hectare city park. There are lots of hiking tracks, picnic sites and forested areas; ask the tourist office for a map.

Viðey, 1km north of Reykjavík's Sundahöfn harbour (near Laugardalur), is served by daily ferries. From the ferry landing, walk uphill to the **church** and the **farmhouse**, which dates from 1755 and is the oldest original building in Iceland.

Places to Stay

Finding a place to stay in summer may be difficult. Bring a tent or book accommodation in advance if you'd rather not risk being left out in the cold.

Hostels & Guesthouses Reykjavík proudly sports the clean and environmentally friendly, award-winning **Reykjavík HI Hostel** *(☎ 553 8110, fax 588 9201; ⓔ info@hostel.is; Sundlaugavegur 34; beds HI members/nonmembers Ikr1500/1850, private rooms per person with en suite Ikr2000-3150; open year-round)*. Breakfast is Ikr700. The excellent facilities include a wide-screen TV and two PCs with Internet access (Ikr400 per half-hour). Book well in advance.

The cheapest guesthouse is the no-frills **Salvation Army Guesthouse** *(☎ 561 3203; e guesthouse@guesthouse.is; Kirkjustræti 2; sleeping-bag accommodation Ikr1700-2200, singles Ikr3700-4000, doubles Ikr5100-5500)*, which has shared bathrooms and cooking facilities; breakfast is Ikr800 extra. The bright and clean **Gistiheimilið Jörð** *(☎ 562 1739, fax 562 1735; Skólavörðustígur 13a; singles Ikr3000-4000, doubles Ikr4000-6000)* has shared bathrooms and breakfast is Ikr600.

About 10 minutes' walk from the BSÍ bus station, the smart and friendly hostel-style **Central Guesthouse** *(☎ 552 2822; e central guesthouse@visir.is; Bólstaðarhlíð 8; sleeping-bag accommodation Ikr1400-1800, singles Ikr2400-3600, doubles Ikr3600-4800)* offers shared bathrooms. Internet access costs Ikr200 per half-hour and breakfast is Ikr700 (but cooking facilities are available).

The architecturally bizarre **Tower Guesthouse** *(☎ 896 6694; e towerguesthouse@hotmail.com; Grettisgata 6; doubles Ikr7900-9300)* welcomes gay travellers.

Hotels On the university campus, **Icelandic Hotel Garður** *(☎ 551 5656; e hotelgardur@icelandichotels.is; Hringbraut; sleeping-bag accommodation Ikr2300, B&B singles/doubles Ikr6900/8100; open 25 May-26 Aug)*, is a straightforward 43-room student residence hall with shared bathrooms.

Fosshótel Höfði *(☎ 552 6477; bokun@foss hotel.is; Skipholt 27; B&B singles/doubles Ikr6900/8900; open June-Aug)* has reasonable deals and a variety of rooms.

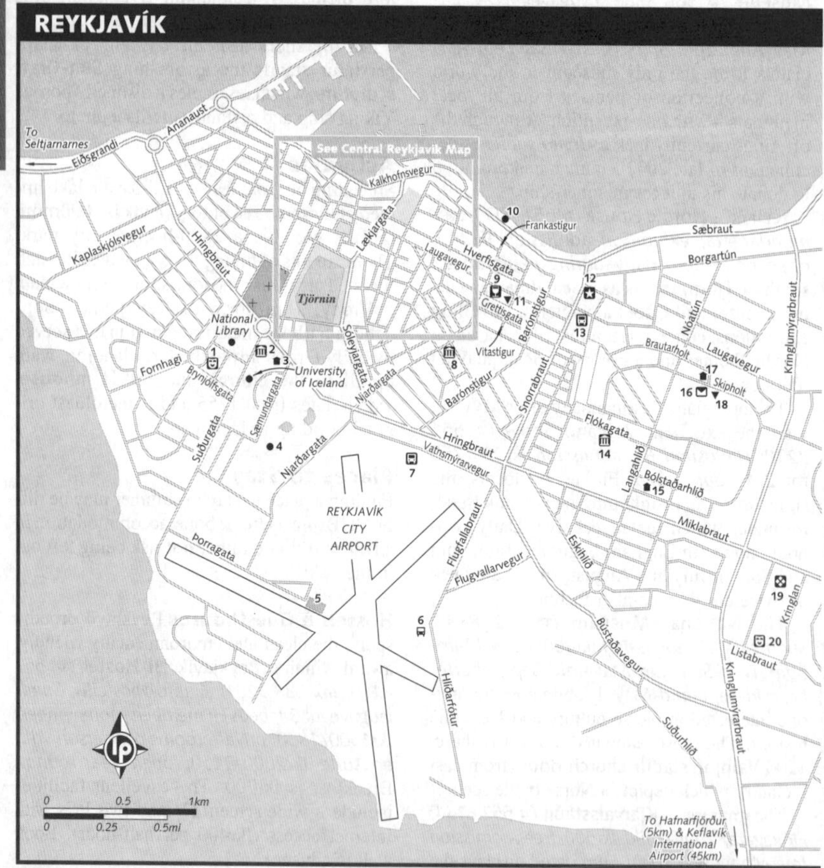

Places to Eat

For a quick bite on the run, nothing beats the **snack kiosks** on Hafnarstræti and the Austurstræti mall. **Nonnabiti** *(Hafnarstræti 18; dishes Ikr280-640)* serves burgers and fried snacks, and **Kebabhúsið** *(Lækjargata 2; kebabs from Ikr640)* dishes up kebabs and tasty fish and chips (Ikr770). Thai meals are delicious and filling and are served at the cafeteria-style **Núðluhúsið** *(Vitastígur 10; mains Ikr780-950)*. For a change, try the great pita sandwiches at **Pítan** *(Skipholt 50c; sandwiches Ikr550-760)*.

Pizza 67 *(Tryggvagata 26; pizzas Ikr650-2510)* is a pleasant, hippy-theme pizza-pub, which also serves burgers, sandwiches and desserts. **Ítalía** *(☎ 562 4630; Laugavegur 11; pasta dishes Ikr1350-1650, pizzas about Ikr1450)* rustles up a good Icelandic variation on Italian food. The recommended **Pasta Basta** *(☎ 561 3131; Klapparstígur 38; lunch buffet Ikr1190, mains Ikr1530-2980)* has a generous buffet lunch, including soup, bread, homemade pasta, vegetables and salad.

A basic Chinese option is **Kína Húsið** *(Lækjargata 8; specials from Ikr750)*. The excellent vegetarian restaurant **Á næstu grösum** *(Laugavegur 20b; meals Ikr750, daily special lunch/dinner Ikr900/990; open lunch & dinner Mon-Sat, dinner Sun)* serves macrobiotic and standard vegetarian meals. **Grænn Kostur** *(Skolavörðustígur 8; veg special Ikr800)* does two great vegetarian daily specials. **Restaurant Salatbarinn** *(Pósthússtræti 13; veg & non-veg buffet before/after 5pm Ikr980/1290; open 11am-9pm daily)* offers a rather good eat-all-you-like buffet including soups,

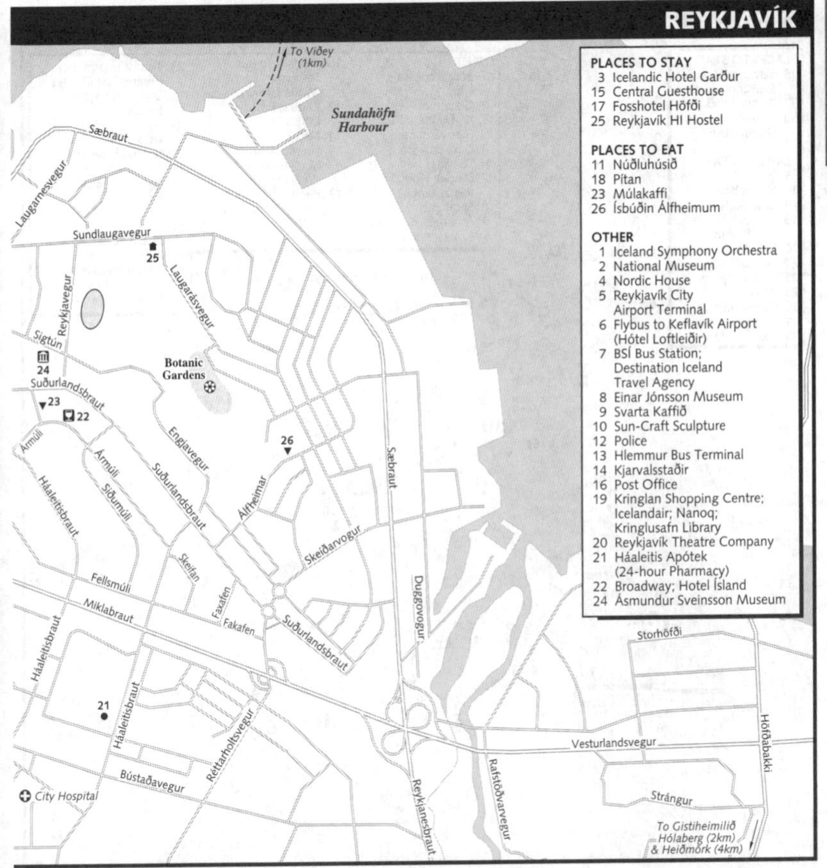

two hot courses, 20 different salads, yoghurt, fruit and drinks.

There are several pub-style cafés serving inexpensive food. At the popular but stuffy **Café Paris** *(Austurstræti 14; light lunches Ikr450-870)* you'll get a coffee for Ikr220 and light continental lunches. Iceland's only bohemian café (complete with art gallery) is the intriguing **Hús Málarans** *(Bankastræti 7a)*.

The funky **Svarta Kaffið** *(Laugavegur 54)*, which serves up great light meals, including home-made soup in bread-roll bowls (Ikr690, including 500mL beer) is recommended.

The no-frills workers' cafeteria **Múlakaffi** *(Hallarmúli; meals Ikr890-1290)* offers a decent soup and salad buffet, with filling fish, beef or lamb mains and coffee included. Inexpensive sandwiches are also available.

The best ice cream in Reykjavík is at **Ísbúðin Álfheimum** *(Álfheimar 2)*; delectable gigantic cones with dip cost from Ikr130.

Entertainment

Clubs For an unforgettable cultural experience, try a Friday- or Saturday-night crawl with the beautiful youth through Reykjavík's 'in' bars and clubs. Cover charges average Ikr1000 and there are huge queues weekend evenings. The city rocks until 5am or later and central streets are thronged with inebriated clubbers all night long. For an up-to-date listing, see *Reykjavík this month*. Avoid the strip joints: the 'dancers' aren't locals and most of them work under dubious conditions.

NASA *(Austurvöllur)* is the latest hot spot, popular with people in their 20s; you'll get

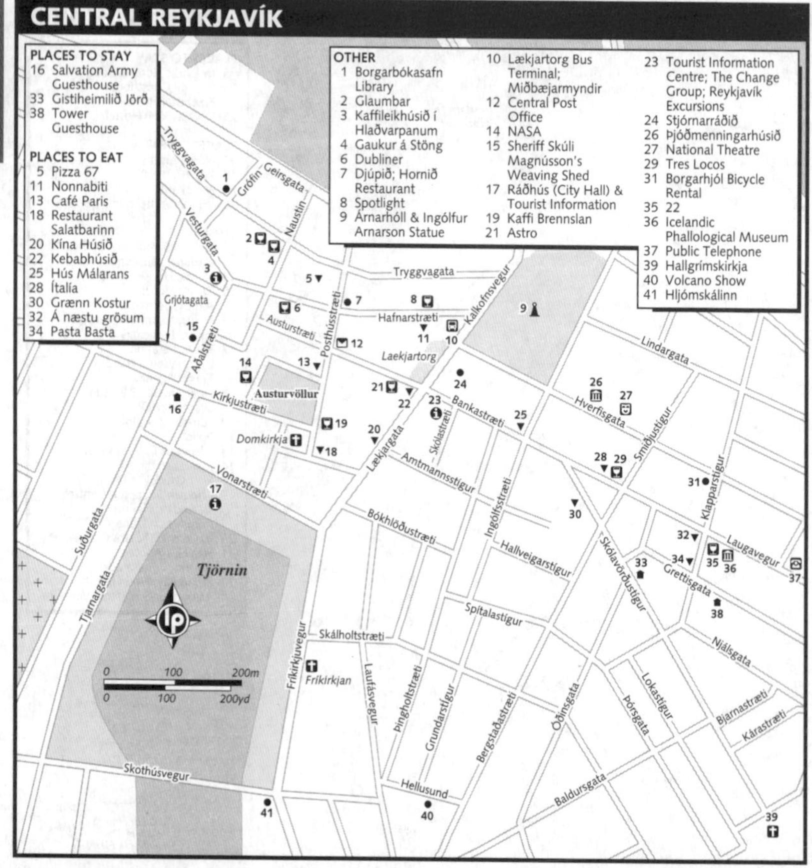

dance music and chart sounds here. Other popular places include **Astro** *(Austurstræti 22)*, with techno and dance music; the enduring **Gaukur á Stöng** *(Tryggvagata 22)*, which features live music most nights; the wild gay bar/club **Spotlight** *(Hafnarstræti 17)*; and the more sedate **Broadway** *(Ármúli 9)* in Hótel Ísland.

Pubs Some of the best pubs include sporty **Glaumbar** *(Tryggvagata 20)*, **22** *(Laugavegur 22)* and the Irish-style, wood-panelled **Dubliner** *(Hafnarstræti 4)*. Also recommended is the salsa bar at **Tres Locos** *(Laugavegur 11)*, and the quiet **Djúpið** *(Hafnarstræti 15)*, in the cellar of the Hornið restaurant. Another option is **Kaffi Brennslan** *(Pósthússtræti 9)*, which boasts up to 62 varieties of beer.

The pub/café **Svarta Kaffið** *(Laugavegur 54)* serves some of the cheapest beer in Reykjavík, between 6pm and 9pm daily (Ikr400 for 500mL).

Theatre There are several theatre groups, an opera, a symphony orchestra and a dance company. Important box offices are: the **National Theatre** *(☎ 551 1200; Hverfisgata 19)*, the **Iceland Symphony Orchestra** *(☎ 545 2500; Hagatorg)*, the **Reykjavík Theatre Company** *(☎ 568 8000; Listabraut 3, Kringlan)* and the **Kaffileikhúsið í Hlaðvarpanum** *(☎ 551 9030; Vesturgata 3b)*. For other venues, check the daily listings in papers for information or contact the tourist information centre for details and tickets.

Getting There & Away

Air Reykjavík city airport serves all domestic destinations, the Faroe Islands and Greenland. All other flights operate through Keflavík International Airport, 50km west of Reykjavík. **Icelandair** *(☎ 505 0300/0100; Kringlan shopping centre)* has an office in Kringlan.

Bus From early June to mid-September, bus services run daily between Reykjavík's **BSÍ bus station** *(☎ 591 1000; Vatnsmýrarvegur 10)* and, essentially, between every other city in the country.

Getting Around

To/From the Airport The Flybus to Keflavík international airport leaves Hótel Loftleiðir two hours prior to international departures (Ikr900, 50 minutes). The first bus leaves from the Reykjavík HI hostel daily at 5am (year-round), then picks up at all main hotels. Buses from Keflavík airport into town leave about 35 minutes after the arrival of an international flight.

Bus Reykjavík's excellent **city bus system** *(☎ 551 2700; W www.bus.is)* runs from 7am to midnight, with night buses at weekends. Buses pick up and drop off passengers only at designated stops (marked with the letter S). The two central terminals are at Hlemmur near the corner of Laugavegur and Rauðarárstígur, and on Lækjargata near Lækjartorg. The fare is Ikr200 (no change given), but *skiptimiði* (transfer tickets) are available.

Taxi There are four taxi companies in the Reykjavík area: **Hreyfill-Bæjarleiðir** *(☎ 588 5522)*, **BSR** *(☎ 561 0000)*, **Borgarbíll** *(☎ 552 2440)* and **BSH** *(☎ 555 0888)*. Taxis are only moderately expensive, and there's no tipping.

Bicycle Bikes may be hired from **Borgarhjól** *(☎ 551 5653; Hverfisgata 50)* and Reykjavík HI Hostel. Both charge Ikr1750/10,500 per day/week.

Boat Ferries to Viðey depart three to five times daily from **Sundahöfn harbour** *(☎ 892 0099; bus No 4 from Lækjartorg)*; Ikr500 return.

AROUND REYKJAVÍK

Blue Lagoon (Bláa Lónið)

The Blue Lagoon isn't a lagoon, but rather a pale-blue, 20°C pool of effluent from the Svartsengi power plant, about 50km southwest of Reykjavík. Its deposits of silica mud, combined with an organic soup of dead algae, have been known to relieve psoriasis. However, its over-zealous promotion attracts many more visitors than it deserves.

Even so, a swim can be an ethereal experience, with clouds of vapour rising and parting at times to reveal the stacks of the power plant and moss-covered lava in the background. Bring enough shampoo for a number of rinses or your hair will become a brick-like mass afterwards.

You can use the **pool** *(adult/child Ikr880/440; open 9am-9pm daily June-Aug, shorter hrs Sept-May)* for a maximum of three hours.

From the BSÍ bus station in Reykjavík, take one of four daily Grindavík buses (Ikr850 one way) to Blue Lagoon.

The Golden Triangle

The 'Golden Triangle' refers to Gullfoss, Geysir and Þingvellir, the 'Big Three' destinations for Icelandair's stopover visitors. If Iceland has a star attraction, it's **Gullfoss**, where the Hvitá River drops 32m in two falls. On sunny afternoons, you may see a rainbow through the spray.

Ten kilometres down the road is Geysir, after which all the world's spouting hot springs are named. The **Great Geysir** died in the mid-20th century, plugged by debris tossed in by tourists. However, it now erupts irregularly up to 15m as a result of ground movements during the powerful earthquakes in June 2000. There's also the faithful stand-in **Strokkur** (Butter Churn), which spouts up to 35m approximately every eight minutes. There's a good exhibition of volcanic, geysir, earthquake, folk and natural history exhibits at the **Geysisstofa Geocentre** *(☎ 486 8915; adult/child Ikr400/200; open 10am-7pm daily June-Sept, noon-5pm daily Oct-May)*.

Þingvellir is Iceland's most significant historical site, since the Alþing was established here in AD 930. The site was selected because of its topography, acoustics and proximity to population. In 1928 its history and wealth of natural attractions led to the creation of Iceland's first national park.

The popular Reykjavík Excursions and Destination Iceland Golden Circle day tours to Gullfoss, Geysir and Þingvellir cost Ikr5900, without lunch. They depart from the BSÍ bus station in Reykjavík at 8.40am daily throughout the year.

Destination Iceland buses run between Reykjavík, Gullfoss and Geysir, departing at 8.30am and 12.30pm daily (June to August) from BSÍ (Ikr3740 round-trip). Public buses between Reykjavík and Þingvellir depart from the BSÍ bus station at 1.30pm daily; they cost Ikr1700 for a return.

Þórsmörk

Þórsmörk (Woods of Thor), about 130km southeast of Reykjavík, is one of the most beautiful places in Iceland, a glacial valley with scrub birch, flowers, braided rivers and clear streams surrounded by snowy peaks and glaciers.

There's great **hiking** but on summer weekends it gets busy and noisy, with considerable drunken disorder. The three Þórsmörk area huts – **Þórsmörk** *(☎ 568 2533; ⓔ fi@fi.is; Ferðafélag Íslands)*, **Básar** *(☎ 562 1000; ⓔ utivist@utivist.is; Útivist)* and **Húsadalur** *(☎ 545 1717; ⓔ austurleid@austurleid.is; Austurleið)* – are often crowded in summer. Tent sites at any of the three centres cost Ikr500 per person. There's also a cosy, turf-roofed **HI hostel** *(☎ 487 8498; beds HI members/non-members Ikr1000/1350)* at nearby Fljótsdalur.

During summer (June to mid-September), buses run between Reykjavík and Húsadalur (over the hill from Þórsmörk) once or twice daily (Ikr3200 one way). To reach Fljótsdalur, get off the Ring Road bus at Hvolsvöllur, then walk or hitch the 27km along route 261. Mid-July to mid-August, the Syðri Fjallabaksleið bus (Ikr250) runs once daily from Reykjavík to Fljótsdalur via Hvolsvöllur.

Ireland

Ireland is everywhere. From the literary traditions of geniuses such as Yeats and Joyce, to the crooning of modern-day stars such as U2 and the Corrs, to the pub named 'O'Flanagan's' (or something like that) down the street from your house, Irish culture has permeated nearly every corner of the globe. Not bad for one of Western Europe's least-populated and least-industrialised – as well as least-spoilt – countries.

Perhaps the world's affection for Ireland stems in part from sympathising with its long, tragic history. Stone Age ring forts and medieval castles placed Ireland on the map early in the course of human events, while centuries of domination by foreign powers have bequeathed its people a confidence and love of their land that transcends any challenge the world can throw at them.

Chances are that you're already familiar with Ireland's famous images – rolling green countryside, gregarious pub life, the Blarney Stone – but you may be surprised by the torrid pace of its major cities, the ethereal otherworldliness of its prehistoric monuments, and the forward-looking vitality that infuses the nation. So pull up a stool, grab a pint, and open your ears: Ireland has several stories to share with you.

Ireland: the Basics

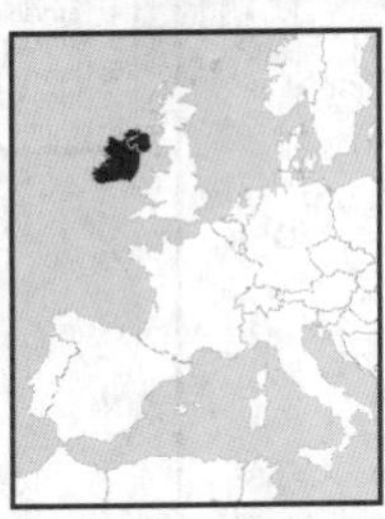

Capitals Dublin (Ire), Belfast (NI)

Populations 3.9 million (Ire), 1.6 million (NI)

Languages English, Irish, Gaelic

Currency euro (€) = 100 centimes (Ire); pound sterling (£) = 100 pence (NI)

Avoid at all costs Religious debates

Toast your new friends by saying *Sláinte!* (Cheers!)

Facts about Ireland

For convenience, this chapter includes both the Republic of Ireland and Northern Ireland. The latter, often known as 'the North' or Ulster, is administered by the UK.

HISTORY

Celtic warriors reached Ireland around 300 BC. Christian monks, including St Patrick, arrived around the 5th century AD, and Ireland became an outpost of European civilisation, a land of saints, scholars and missionaries.

In 1169 the Norman conquest of England spread to Ireland. In the 1500s under Elizabeth I, oppression of the Catholic Irish got seriously under way. Huge swathes of land were given to Protestant settlers, and by the early 18th century, the dispirited Catholics held less than 15% of the land and suffered brutal restrictions in employment, education, land ownership and religion. In 1800 the Act of Union, joining Ireland with Britain, was passed.

Following the successful campaign of Catholic (and thus ineligible) leader Daniel O'Connell for parliament, Britain passed the 1829 Act of Catholic Emancipation, granting Catholics the right to be elected as MPs. O'Connell died as Ireland was suffering its greatest tragedy, the Great Famine. Successive failures of potato crops between 1845 and 1851 resulted in mass starvation and emigration. Inadequate and ill-conceived relief schemes from Britain and the Irish ruling classes, many of whom profited from inflated food prices, were a national disgrace. As a result, about one million people died from disease or starvation, and another million emigrated.

In the early 20th century Ireland might have moved slowly but peacefully towards some sort of autonomy but for a bungled uprising in 1916. The so-called Easter Rising was, in fact, heavy with rhetoric, light on planning and lacking in public support. The British response was just as badly conceived. After the insurrection had been put down, a series of trials and executions (15 in all) transformed the ringleaders from troublemakers to martyrs and roused international support for Irish independence.

In the 1918 general election, Irish republicans under the banner of Sinn Féin (We Ourselves or Ourselves Alone) won a majority

IRELAND
Counties
1 Derry
2 Antrim
3 Tyrone
4 Fermanagh
5 Armagh
6 Down
7 Donegal
8 Leitrim
9 Sligo
10 Mayo
11 Roscommon
12 Galway
13 Longford
14 Cavan
15 Monaghan
16 Westmeath
17 Meath
18 Louth
19 Offaly
20 Kildare
21 Dublin
22 Clare
23 Kerry
24 Limerick
25 Tipperary
26 Ladis
27 Kilkenny
28 Carlow
29 Wicklow
30 Cork
31 Waterford
32 Wexford
Belfast
Dublin
North Channel
Rathlin Island
Giant's Causeway
Portstewart
Inishowen Peninsula
Bushmills
Carrick-a-Rede Island
Ballycastle
Downhill
Portrush
Coleraine
Cushendun
Cushendall
Muff
Lough Foyle
A37
Glens of Antrim
Glenariff
To Cairnryan & Fleetwood
Derry
Letterkenny
A29
A26
A6
Ballymena
Larne
To Liverpool, Heysham, Isle of Man, Troon & Stranraer
Strabane
NORTHERN IRELAND
Glencolumbcille
Ardara
N15
Carrickfergus
Carrick
Killybegs
Donegal
A5
A505
BELFAST
Donegal Bay
Omagh
Cookstown
Lough Neagh
Bangor
Newtownards
Ballyshannon
Irvinestown
A29
Lisburn
Strangford Lough
Belleek
Lower Lough Erne
A4
Dungannon
A3
Portaferry
Belmullet
Killala Bay
Killala
Sligo Bay
SLIGO
N16
Enniskillen
ARMAGH
Downpatrick
Dundrum
Bangor
Monaghan
A28
A1
Strangford
Achill Island
Ballina
Upper Lough Erne
Newry
Mountains of Mourne
Dundrum Bay
N17
N4
Belturbet
N2
Lough Conn
Carrickmacross
Keel
Mulrany
Charlestown
Boyle
Carrick on Shannon
Cavan
DUNDALK
Clare Island
Castlebar
IRISH SEA
Louisburgh
Westport
N5
N3
Ardee
N1
Inishbofin Island
N59
Lough Mask
Longford
Kells
Slane
DROGHEDA
Cleggan
Roscommon
Lanesborough
Navan
Newgrange
Leenane
Cong
N4
Tara
Clifden
Connemara
Tuam
Mullingar
Trim
N2
N1
To Holyhead, Mostyn, Isle of Man & Liverpool
Recess
Lough Corrib
Malahide
Oughterard
ATHLONE
Moate
N3
N4
DUBLIN
Rossaveal
GALWAY
Maynooth
Brittas Bay
North Sound
Spiddal
Salthill
N6
Clonmacnois
Tullamore
DUN LAOGHAIRE
Inishmór
Galway Bay
N18
N7
Naas
Enniskerry
Bray
Aran Islands
Inishmaan
Kinvarra
REPUBLIC OF IRELAND
Powerscourt
Inisheer
Doolin
Lisdoonvarna
Birr
Kildare
Glendalough
South Sound
Kilfenora
Portlaoise
Wicklow
Cliffs of Moher
The Burren
Ennistymon
N9
Mt Lugnaquilla (924m)
Roscrea
Rathdrum
Nenagh
N7
N11
ATLANTIC OCEAN
Ennis
Durrow
CARLOW
Arklow
N8
Kilrush
Thurles
Gorey
Shannon
LIMERICK
KILKENNY
Loop Head
Tarbert
Foynes
N24
Cashel
Callan
N10
Thomastown
Enniscorthy
Mouth of the Shannon
Tipperary
To Fishguard & Pembroke (Britain), Roscoff & Cherbourg (France)
N21
N20
Castlegregory
TRALEE
Rathluirc (Charleville)
Kilmallock
Cahir
CLONMEL
Carrick-on-Suir
New Ross
Wellington Bridge
WEXFORD
Blasket Islands
Dingle Peninsula
N86
Dingle Bay
N22
Mitchelstown
Waterford
N25
Passage East
Ballyhack
Rosslare Harbour
Killorglin
Mallow
N8
Glenbeigh
Dunquin
Dingle
Killarney
Fermoy
Cahirciveen
N70
Mt Carrantuohill (1038m)
Dungarvan
Valentia Island
Ring of Kerry
St George's Channel
Iveragh Peninsula
Kenmare
N22
Blarney
CORK
Youghal
Ardmore
Waterville
Sneem
N71
Ringaskiddy
Cobh
Skellig Michael Island
Kenmare River
Beara Peninsula
Glengarriff
Bandon
CELTIC SEA
Allihies
Bantry
Bantry Bay
Kinsale
Ferry to Swansea (Britain) & Roscoff (France)
Sheep's Head
Schull
Skibbereen
Clonakilty
Mizen Head
Roaringwater Bay
Baltimore
Fastnet Rock
Cape Clear Island
0
25
50km
0
15
30mi
To Ringaskiddy Town & Roscoff (France)

of Irish seats. The newly elected deputies declared Ireland independent and formed the first Dáil Éireann (Irish assembly or lower house). The resulting Anglo-Irish War (1919–21) pitted Sinn Féin and its military wing, the Irish Republican Army (IRA), against the British. The increasingly brutal responses of Britain's hated Black and Tans infantry further roused anti-British sentiment, and atrocity was met with atrocity. Michael Collins, a charismatic and ruthless leader, masterminded the IRA's campaign. After months of negotiations, a 1921 treaty gave 26 counties of Ireland independence and allowed six largely Protestant counties in Ulster the choice to opt out (a foregone conclusion).

Under the Anglo-Irish Treaty, the British monarch remained the (nominal) head of the new Irish Free State and Irish MPs were required to swear allegiance. To many Irish Catholics, these compromises were a betrayal of republican principles, and civil war broke out. By 1923 the war had ground to a halt, and for nearly 50 years development was slow and relatively peaceful. A new constitution in 1937 abolished the oath of British allegiance and claimed sovereignty over the six counties of Ulster. In 1948 the Irish government declared the country a republic and, in 1949, left the British Commonwealth.

In the North, the Protestant majority systematically excluded Catholics from power. In January 1969 civil rights marchers walked from Belfast to Derry to demand a fairer division of jobs and housing. Just outside Derry a Protestant mob attacked the mostly Catholic marchers. In August British troops were sent to Derry and, two days later, Belfast, to maintain law and order. The peaceful civil rights movement lost ground and the IRA found itself with new and willing recruits for an armed independence struggle.

The so-called Troubles rolled throughout the 1970s and the 1980s. Passions reached fever pitch in 1972 when 13 unarmed Catholics were shot dead by British troops in Derry on 'Bloody Sunday' (30 January), then again in 1981 when 10 IRA prisoners fasted to death. The waters were further muddied by the IRA splitting into 'official' and 'provisional' wings, from which sprang even more violent republican organisations. Protestant paramilitary organisations such as the Ulster Volunteer Force (UVF) sprang up in response, and violence was met with violence.

In 1985 the Anglo-Irish Agreement gave the Dublin government an official consultative role in Northern Irish affairs for the first time. In August 1994 a 'permanent cessation of violence' by the IRA was announced by Sinn Féin's leader Gerry Adams. It was matched by a Protestant cease-fire in October 1994.

The British government refused to allow all-party talks until the IRA decommissioned its weapons. An IRA bomb in London shattered the negotiations in February 1996. But the peace process regained momentum with the landslide victory in May 1997 of Britain's Labour Party. Soon afterward, on 20 July 1997, the IRA declared another cease-fire.

To worldwide acclaim, these talks produced the Good Friday Agreement on 10 April 1998. This complex agreement allows the people of Northern Ireland to decide their political future by majority vote, and commits its signatories to 'democratic and peaceful means of resolving differences on political issues'. In May 1998, the agreement was approved by 71% of voters in referendums held simultaneously on both sides of the Irish border. Since the Good Friday Agreement, though, the peace process has stopped and started, largely over wrangles about how and when the IRA should 'decommission' its weapons stockpiles.

Despite all this there's an underlying sense of optimism in the whole of Ireland. An apology in the summer of 2002 from the IRA to noncombatants affected by its actions during the troubles, although dismissed as posturing by hard-line loyalists, was yet another example of a gesture that would have been unimaginable a few years ago.

Although it often seems bickering of one sort or another will continue forever, most agree (with fingers crossed perhaps) that the 'war' is over.'

GEOGRAPHY & ECOLOGY

Ireland measures 84,421 sq km (about 83% is the Republic) and stretches 486km north to south and 275km east to west. The jagged coastline extends for 5631km. The midlands of Ireland are flat, generally rich farmland with huge swaths of brown peat (which is rapidly being depleted for fuel).

CLIMATE

Ireland has a relatively mild climate with a mean annual temperature of 10°C. In January and February, average temperatures range

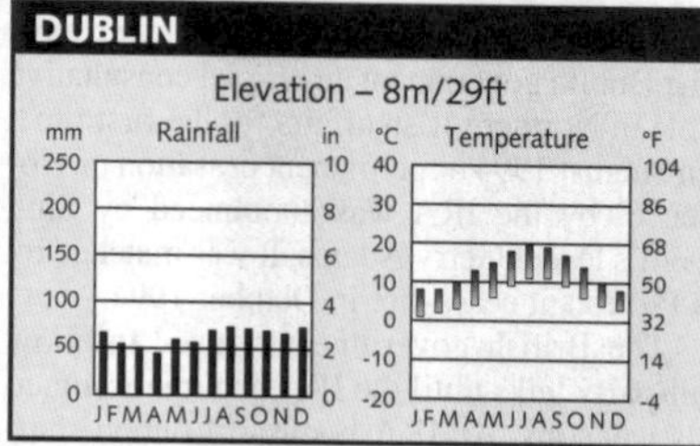

from 4° to 7°C. Average maximums in July and August are from 14° to 16°C. June, July and August are the sunniest months; December and January are the gloomiest. The sea around Ireland is surprisingly warm for the latitude. Snow is relatively scarce – perhaps one or two flurries in winter in higher areas.

It can rain a lot in Ireland. Annual rainfall is about 1000mm.

GOVERNMENT & POLITICS

The Republic of Ireland has a parliamentary system of government. The prime minister's official title is Taoiseach (pronounced 'tea shock'). The president *(an tuachtaran)* of Ireland is elected for seven years.

Northern Ireland, governed from London since 1972, elected a new parliament in 1998 as part of the Good Friday Agreement.

POPULATION & PEOPLE

Prior to the 1845–51 Great Famine the population of Ireland was around eight million; death and emigration reduced it to around six million, and emigration continued at a high level for the next 100 years. It wasn't until the 1960s that Ireland's population finally began to recover. The total population of Ireland is currently around 5.5 million: 3.9 million in the Republic and 1.6 million in Northern Ireland.

A Ruinous Glossary

You may encounter the following terms during your explorations of Ireland's history:

cashel – a stone ring fort or *rath*
dolmen – a portal tomb or Stone-Age grave consisting of stone 'pillars' supporting a stone roof or capstone
ogham stone – a memorial stone of the 4th to 9th centuries, marked on its edge with groups of straight lines or notches to represent the Latin alphabet
passage tomb – a megalithic mound-tomb with a narrow stone passage leading to a burial chamber
ring fort or *rath* – a circular fort, originally constructed of earth and timber, later made of stone
round tower – a tall tower or belfry built as a lookout and place of refuge from the Vikings

SOCIETY & CONDUCT

The Irish are an easy-going, loquacious, fun-loving people. They are used to tourists and there are few social taboos. In Northern Ireland people discuss the troubles more openly than before but it can still be a sensitive topic. Do not take humorous Irish scepticism or sarcasm too seriously.

RELIGION

Religion has always played a major role in Irish history. Almost everybody is either Catholic or Protestant, with the Republic 95% Catholic and Northern Ireland about 60% Protestant. The Jewish community in Ireland is tiny but long-established.

The Catholic Church has always opposed attempts to liberalise laws governing contraception, divorce and abortion. Today, condom machines can be found in all parts of Ireland and divorce is legal, but abortion remains illegal in the Republic. The Catholic Church's once considerable political and social power in the Republic is waning, owing to increased secularism and to the waves of sexual and physical abuse scandals that have convulsed the Church during the past decade.

LANGUAGE

Officially the Republic is bilingual. English is spoken throughout the island, but there are still parts of western and southern Ireland known as the Gaeltacht where Irish Gaelic is still the native language.

Facts for the Visitor

HIGHLIGHTS

Among Ireland's most scenic areas are around the Ring of Kerry, the Beara and Dingle Peninsulas, the barren stretches of the Burren, the rocky Aran Islands, and, in Northern Ireland, the Glens of Antrim. Favourite stretches of coast include the Cliffs of Moher, the Connemara and Donegal coasts, and the Causeway Coast of Northern Ireland.

In Dublin, Trinity College's Old Library with the ancient *Book of Kells* is a must-see, and there are extensive collections at the National Museum and National Gallery. Belfast has the Ulster Museum and, just outside the city, the Ulster Folk Museum.

Ireland is littered with castles and ancient ring forts. The Stone Age forts on the Aran Islands are of particular interest. Prime examples of castles can be found at Kilkenny, Blarney, and in Northern Ireland, Dunluce and Carrickfergus.

Early Christian churches and ruined monastic sites, some well over 1000 years old, are scattered throughout Ireland. Jerpoint Abbey and the Rock of Cashel are good options. If the weather allows, the tiny early-Christian monastery atop the jagged isle of Skellig Michael is an amazing place to visit.

PLANNING

The tourist season lasts from the weekend before the much-celebrated St Patrick's Day (17 March) to September. In July and August the crowds are at their biggest and prices at their highest. Many tourist facilities close or have shorter opening hours in the winter months.

TOURIST OFFICES

The Irish tourist board, Bord Fáilte (pronounced 'bord fawlcha'), and the Northern Ireland Tourist Board (NITB) operate separate offices, although they share a useful website: W www.tourismireland.com. Every town big enough to have half-a-dozen pubs will have a tourist office, although the smaller ones close in winter. Most will find you a place to stay for a small fee.

Overseas offices of Bord Fáilte include:

Australia (☎ 02-9299 6177) 5th Floor, 36 Carrington St, Sydney, NSW 2000
Canada (☎ 416-487 3335) 120 Eglington Ave East, Suite 500, Toronto, Ont M5P 1E2
Netherlands (☎ 020-504 0689) Spuistraat 104, 1012 VA Amsterdam
New Zealand (☎ 09-379 8720) Dingwall Bldg, 87 Queen St, Auckland 1
UK (☎ 0207-493 9065) Irish Tourist Board, Ireland House, 150 New Bond St, London W1Y OAQ
USA (☎ 1800 223 6470) 345 Park Ave, New York, NY 10154

Tourist information for Northern Ireland abroad is usually handled by the British Tourist Authority (BTA), though there are a few offices of the NITB:

Canada (☎ 1800 223 6470) 2 Bloor St West, Suite 1501, Toronto, Ont M4W 3E2
New Zealand (☎ 09-977 2255) 18 Shortland St, Private Bag 92136, Auckland 1
UK (☎ 0800 03 9700) British Travel Centre, 12 Lower Regent St, London SW1Y 4PQ
USA (☎ 800 233 6470) 551 5th Ave, Suite 701, New York, NY 10176

VISAS & DOCUMENTS

For citizens of the EU and most other Western countries, no visa is required to visit Ireland. EU nationals are allowed to stay indefinitely, while other visitors can usually remain for three to six months.

UK nationals born in Britain or Northern Ireland do not need a passport, but it's better to carry some form of identification.

EMBASSIES & CONSULATES

Irish Embassies & Consulates

Irish diplomatic offices overseas include:

Australia (☎ 02-6273 3022) 20 Arkana St, Yarralumla, ACT 2600
Canada (☎ 613-233 6281) 130 Albert St, Ottawa, Ontario, K1A 0L6
Japan (☎ 03-3263 0695) 2-10-7 Kojimachi, Chiyoda-ku, Tokyo 102
New Zealand (☎ 09-302 2867) 6th Floor, 18 Shortland St, 1001 Auckland
South Africa (☎ 012-342 5062) Tubach Centre, 1234 Church St, 0083 Colbyn, Pretoria
UK (☎ 020-7235 2171) 17 Grosvenor Place, London SW1X 7HR
USA (☎ 202-462 3939) 2234 Massachusetts Ave NW, Washington DC 20008. In addition there are consulates in Boston, Chicago, New York and San Francisco.

Foreign Embassies in Ireland

Foreign embassies in Dublin include:

Australia (☎ 01-676 1517) 2nd floor, Fitzwilton House, Wilton Terrace, Dublin 2
Canada (☎ 01-478 1988) 65–68 St Stephen's Green, Dublin 2
France (☎ 01-260 1666) 36 Ailesbury Rd, Dublin 4
New Zealand (☎ 01-660 4233) 37 Leeson Park, Dublin 6
UK (☎ 01-205 3700) 29 Merrion Rd, Dublin 4
USA (☎ 01-668 9946) 42 Elgin Rd, Dublin 4

In Northern Ireland, nationals of most countries other than the USA should contact their embassy in London.

USA (☎ 028-9032 8239) Queens House, 14 Queen St, Belfast, BT1 6EQ

MONEY

The Republic uses the euro. The British pound sterling (£) is the Northern Irish currency (see Money in the Britain chapter). Banks offer the best exchange rates. Exchange bureaus are open longer, but the rate is not as good and the commission higher. Most post offices provide currency-exchange facilities.

In Northern Ireland several banks issue Northern Irish pound notes, which are equivalent to sterling but not readily accepted in Britain. Many Northern Irish shops and businesses accept payment in euros. Most major currencies and types of travellers cheques are readily accepted in Ireland. Eurocheques can also be cashed here.

Ireland is an expensive place, marginally more costly than Britain, but prices vary around the island. Entry prices to sites and museums are usually 20% to 50% lower for children, students and senior citizens (OAPs). For the budget traveller, €60 per day should cover hostel accommodation, getting around and a meal in a restaurant leaving just enough for a pint at the end of the day.

Major credit cards, particularly Visa and MasterCard, are widely accepted, even at B&Bs. You can obtain cash advances on cards from banks and ATMs.

Fancy hotels and restaurants usually add a 10% or 15% service charge onto the bill. Simpler places usually do not add service; if you decide to tip, just round up the bill (or add 10% at most). Taxi drivers do not have to be tipped.

Value-added tax (VAT) of 20% applies to most goods and services. Non-EU visitors can claim back VAT on purchases taken out of the EU. Stores displaying Cashback stickers will give you a voucher that can be refunded at most international airports or stamped at ferry ports and mailed back for refund.

POST & COMMUNICATIONS

Post offices (An Post) in the Republic are open 9am to 5.30pm weekdays, 9am to 1pm Saturday; smaller offices close for lunch. Hours in Northern Ireland are the same as in Britain. Mail can be addressed to poste restante at post offices, but is officially held for only two weeks. Writing on it 'hold for collection' on the envelope may help.

Phonecards are essential in the Republic, where Eircom sells Callcards of 10/20/50 units for €2.50/4.50/10.20. Post offices also sell the Swift low-cost international phone cards for €7/15/25/30. In Northern Ireland, telephone booths accepting British Telecom (BT) phonecards are few and far between outside Belfast. International calls can be dialled directly from pay phones.

The Republic's country code is ☎ 353. To call Northern Ireland, use the UK country code (☎ 44). To call the North from the Republic, dial ☎ 028 and then the local number.

Internet access is available in almost every town, with typical hourly rates of about €6 per hour.

DIGITAL RESOURCES

For an overview of travelling and tourism in Ireland you can try **W** www.visitdublin.com, **W** www.ireland.travel.ie or **W** www.discovernorthernireland.com.

Useful travel websites for the south and north respectively are **W** www.cie.ie and **W** www.translink.co.uk. The site for the Irish Government is at **W** www.gov.ie and for the Northern Ireland Office at **W** www.nio.gov.uk. The *Irish Times* has an award-winning site at **W** www.irish-times.ie with Irish news, and arts features.

BOOKS

Lonely Planet's *Ireland*, *Dublin*, *Dublin Condensed* and *Walking in Ireland* guides offer comprehensive coverage of the island and its most visited city. One of the better books about Irish history is *The Oxford Companion to Irish History* (1998) edited by SJ Connolly.

WOMEN TRAVELLERS

Women travellers will find that there is little risk of being hassled on the street or anywhere else in Ireland. Nonetheless, walking alone at night, especially in certain parts of Dublin, is unwise. Hitching is not recommended, even though it's probably safer than anywhere else in Europe.

GAY & LESBIAN TRAVELLERS

Only Dublin, and to a certain extent Belfast and Cork, have open gay communities. The *Gay Community News*, a free tabloid published monthly in Dublin, is available at bars and cafés or by subscription to **GCN** *(☎ 01-671 0939/9076; **W** www.gcn.ie; Unit 2, Scarlet Row, Temple Bar, Dublin 8)*. The bi-monthly events magazine *In Dublin* (*W www.indublin.ie*) has a gay and lesbian section with club and resource-centre listings. Information is also available from:

Northern Ireland Gay Rights Association (NIGRA; ☎ 028-9066 4111) PO Box 44, Belfast
Outhouse Community Centre (☎ 01-873 4932; ⓔ info@outhouse.ie) 105 Capel St, Dublin 1

DISABLED TRAVELLERS

Bord Fáilte's accommodation guides indicate which places are wheelchair accessible, and the NITB publishes *Accessible Accommodation in Northern Ireland*. Comhairle also publishes detailed accessibility information in the Republic and Northern Ireland.

Comhairle (☎ 01-874 7503; ⓦ www.comhairle.ie) 44 North Great George's St, Dublin 1
Disability Action (☎ 028-9049 1011; ⓦ www.disabilityaction.org) 2 Annadale Ave, Belfast BT7 3JH

DANGERS & ANNOYANCES

Drug-related crime is on the increase, and Dublin has its fair share of pickpockets. Look after your things when visiting pubs and cafés. Dublin is notorious for car break-ins and petty theft. Car theft is also a problem in Belfast. Cyclists should always lock their bicycles and be cautious about leaving bags attached.

BUSINESS HOURS

Offices are open 9am to 5pm weekdays, shops a little later. On Thursday or Friday, shops stay open later. Many are also open on Saturday. In winter, tourist attractions are often open shorter hours, fewer days per week or may be shut completely. In Northern Ireland some tourist attractions are closed on Sunday morning.

PUBLIC HOLIDAYS & SPECIAL EVENTS

Public holidays in Ireland (IR), Northern Ireland (NI) or both are New Year's Day (1 January); St Patrick's Day (17 March); Good Friday and Easter Monday; May Holiday (IR), first Monday in May; May Bank Holidays (NI), first and last Mondays in May; June Bank Holiday (IR), first Monday in June; Orangemen's Day (NI), 12 July, or 13th if 12th is a Sunday; August Holiday (IR), first Monday in August; August Bank Holiday (NI), last Monday in August; October Holiday (IR), last Monday in October; Christmas Day (25 December); St Stephen's Day/Boxing Day (26 December).

Emergencies

The emergency number in both the Republic and Northern Ireland for police, ambulance and fire brigade is ☎ 999.

The All-Ireland hurling and football finals both take place in Dublin in September. There are some great regional cultural events around the island, like the Galway Arts Festival in late July. In Dublin, Leopold Bloom's Joycean journey around the city is marked by various events on Bloomsday (16 June). The Dublin International Film Festival in April is also a highlight. In Northern Ireland, July is marching month and every Orangeman in the country hits the streets on the 'glorious 12th'. Other events include the Ould Lammas Fair at Ballycastle in August, and the Belfast Festival at Queen's in November.

ACTIVITIES

Ireland is a great place for outdoor activities, and the tourist boards put out a wide selection of information sheets covering bird-watching (the Hook area of County Wexford is recommended), surfing (great along the west coast), scuba diving, hang-gliding, trout and salmon fishing, ancestor tracing, horse riding, sailing, canoeing and many other activities.

Walking is particularly popular, but come prepared for wet weather. There are now well over 20 way-marked trails, varying in length from the 26km Cavan Way to the 900km Ulster Way.

WORK

At present Ireland is good for casual employment; many pubs and restaurants advertise positions in their windows. Citizens of EU countries can work in Ireland without special papers. For information contact an Irish embassy or consulate in your own country.

ACCOMMODATION

Bord Fáilte's dedicated guides to camping grounds, B&Bs, hotels etc cost €3 and €4. There are also a great many excellent places that aren't 'tourist-board approved'. NITB publishes free B&B and hotel guides. Its camping and caravanning guide costs 50p.

Bord Fáilte offices book local accommodation for a fee of €1.50 (or €2.54 to book in another town). The NITB provides a similar booking service. Accommodation for the Republic and the North may also be booked online, via the **Gulliver booking service** *(w www.gulliver.ie)*. A deposit of 10% and a €4 fee is payable.

All accommodation prices in this chapter are high-season rates (generally June to August); at other times of year, subtract 15% to 25% from the listed prices.

Camping

There are plenty of camping grounds in Ireland, although they are not as common as elsewhere in Europe. Some hostels also have space for tents. At commercial camping grounds, costs are typically €9 to €14 for a tent and two people.

Hostels

In summer hostels can be heavily booked. **An Óige** *(Youth; ☎ 01-830 4555; w www.irelandyha.org; 61 Mountjoy St, Dublin 7)*, the Irish branch of Hostelling International (HI), has 31 hostels scattered round the country, and there are another 10 in Northern Ireland administered by **Hostelling International Northern Ireland** *(HINI; ☎ 048-9031 5435; w www.hini.org.uk; 22-32 Donegall Rd, Belfast)*. These hostels are open to members of HI, members of An Óige/HINI (annual membership €15/£10), or to any overseas visitor for a small, additional nightly charge.

Two other hostel associations include the **Independent Holiday Hostels** *(IHH; ☎ 01-836 4700; w www.hostels-ireland.com; 57 Gardiner St Lower, Dublin 1)*, a cooperative group, with about 140 hostels in both Northern Ireland and the Republic; and the **Independent Hostels Owners** *(IHO; ☎ 073- 30130; w www.holidayhound.com/ihi; Dooey Hostel, Glencolumbcille, County Donegal)* association, with more than 100 members around Ireland.

From June to September nightly costs at most hostels are about €20, except for the more expensive hostels in Dublin, Belfast and a few other places. Rates are cheaper in the low season.

B&Bs

The bed and breakfast is as Irish a form of accommodation as there is. You'll stumble upon them in the most unusual and remote locations. Typical costs are around €30 per person a night. In summer they can quickly fill up. Irish B&B breakfasts almost inevitably include 'a fry', which means fried eggs, bacon and sausages, the ubiquitous black pudding (a blood sausage), plus toast and butter.

FOOD & DRINKS

Traditional meals (such as Irish Stew, often found in pubs) are hearty and cheap. Fast food is everywhere, from traditional fish and chips to more recent arrivals such as burgers, pizzas and kebabs. A bowl of soup and some excellent soda or brown bread can be a cheap lunch. Seafood is often excellent, especially in the west, and there are some good vegetarian restaurants.

In Ireland a drink means a beer. Stout is usually Guinness, although in Cork it can mean a Murphy's or a Beamish. A wide variety of lagers is available, including Harp and Smithwicks. Simply asking for a Guinness will get you a pint (570ml, €3 to €4 in a pub). If you want a half-pint (285mL, around €2), ask for a 'glass' or a 'half'.

ENTERTAINMENT

Listening to traditional music in a pub while nursing a pint of Guinness is a popular form of entertainment (and easy to while away a few pleasant hours). If someone suggests visiting a pub for its good 'crack' (from the Irish *craic*), it means a good time, convivial company, sparkling conversation and scintillating music.

Up for Grabs

No, it's not what you do after a night of too much Guinness. Hurling is an indigenous Irish sport that probably had its origins back in the days of yore (BC). Along with Gaelic football, it enjoys massive popularity on the island and almost no publicity anywhere else in the world.

Played on a field about 1½ times as long as a soccer pitch, hurling is a ball sport that vaguely resembles field hockey. Each team, made up of 15 players, tries to hit the small round *sliothar* (ball) through the enemy's goal, whether over the crossbar (one point) or under it (three points). To accomplish this, they whack it about with a *hurley*, a wooden stick that's curved at one end.

As with Gaelic football, hurling is a fast-paced and exciting sport. The season runs through the summer. See local newspapers for schedules and ticket information.

IRELAND

A useful website is Ⓦ www.entertainment ireland.ie, which has reviews, festival information and listings for music, clubs, theatre, exhibitions and comedy.

Getting There & Away

AIR

Aer Lingus *(Ⓦ www.aerlingus.com)* has international connections to other countries in Europe and to the USA. Budget airline **Ryanair** *(Ⓦ www.ryanair.com)* is the next largest Irish carrier, and has many routes that go to Europe and the USA.

Competition is fierce on UK/Irish routes. Dublin, Shannon and Cork are linked to many cities in Britain. A number of budget airlines, including Ryanair and **easyjet** *(Ⓦ www.easyjet.com)*, offer advance-purchase fares for £50 or less. Belfast is also linked with several cities in Britain, including London (Heathrow), via British Airways. Other UK airlines include **British Midland** *(☎ 0870-607 0555)* and **British European** *(☎ 0870-567 6676)*.

Dublin is connected with other major centres in Europe; there are also flights to Cork, Shannon and Belfast. From Paris to Belfast or Dublin fares range from €150 to €550, sometimes more in peak times. From Paris, Frankfurt and Brussels Ryanair flies to Dublin and/or Shannon. Easyjet flies between Amsterdam and Belfast.

Aer Lingus (from New York and other centres) and Delta (from Atlanta) fly direct to Dublin and Shannon. It can be cheaper to fly to London first.

Advance-purchase excursion fares from Australia or New Zealand to Britain (see the Britain chapter) can have a return flight to Dublin tagged on at no extra cost.

LAND

Because of cheap flights, getting to Ireland by land (including ferry) is less popular. Bus Éireann and National Express operate services direct from London and other UK centres to Dublin, Belfast and other cities. For details in London, contact **Eurolines** *(☎ 0870-514 3219)*, or **National Express** *(☎ 0870-580 8080)*. They share a website at Ⓦ www.gobycoach.com. London to Dublin by bus takes about 12 hours and costs £20/37 one-way/return. It's 13 hours to Belfast, and slightly more expensive.

SEA

There's a great variety of ferry services from Britain and France to Ireland. Prices vary drastically, depending on season, time of day, day of the week and length of stay. One-way fares for an adult foot passenger can be as little as £20, but nudge close to £50 in summer. For a car plus driver and up to four adult passengers, prices can range from £130 to £210. There are often special deals, discounted return fares and other money savers worth investigating.

Britain

There are ferry services from Scotland (Troon, Cairnryan and Stranraer), England (Fleetwood, Heysham, Mostyn and Liverpool), Wales (Fishguard, Holyhead, Pembroke and Swansea) and the Isle of Man (Douglas) to ports in the Republic (Dublin, Cork, Rosslare Harbour and Dun Laoghaire) and Northern Ireland (Belfast and Larne).

Following is a list of shipping lines:

Irish Ferries (☎ 0870-517 1717) Services from Holyhead to Dublin (3¼ hours by ferry), and Pembroke to Rosslare Harbour (1¾ to 4 hours by ferry)

Isle of Man Steam Packet Company and SeaCat Services (☎ 0870-552 3523) Catamaran services from Douglas (Isle of Man) to Belfast (2¾ hours, May to September) and Dublin (2¾ hours, May to September); Liverpool to Dublin (3¾ hours); and Heysham (four hours), and Troon (2½ hours) to Belfast

Norse Merchant Ferries (☎ 028-9077 9090) Services from Liverpool to Belfast (8½ hours by ferry)

P&O European Ferries (☎ 0870-242 4777) Services from Cairnryan to Larne (one hour by fast ferry, 1¾ hours by ferry), Fleetwood to Larne (eight hours by ferry), and Mostyn (near Chester) to Dublin (six hours by ferry)

Stena Line (☎ 0870-570 7070) Services from Holyhead to Dublin (3¼ hours by fast ferry) and Dun Laoghaire (1¾ hours by fast ferry), Fishguard to Rosslare Harbour (3½ hours by ferry, 1¾ hours by catamaran), and Stranraer to Belfast (3¼ hours by ferry, 1¾ hours by catamaran)

Swansea Cork Ferries (☎ 01792-456116) Services from Swansea to Ringaskiddy (10 hours, mid-May to mid-September)

France

Eurail passes are valid for ferry crossings between Ireland and France on Irish Ferries only; Inter-Rail passes give reductions of 75%.

Irish Ferries run from Roscoff and Cherbourg to Rosslare Harbour, April to January, taking 14 and 18½ hours respectively.

Brittany Ferries *(Cork ☎ 021-27 7801; 🅦 www.brittanyferries.com)* sails from Roscoff to Cork once weekly, the trip taking 14 hours (Friday from Roscoff, Saturday from Cork), from April to the end of September.

Getting Around

In Ireland, A to B is seldom a straight line, and public transport can be expensive, infrequent or both. For these reasons having your own transport can be a major advantage.

PASSES & DISCOUNTS

Eurail passes are valid for train travel in the Republic of Ireland, but not in Northern Ireland, and entitle you to a reduction on Bus Éireann's three-day Irish Rambler tickets. They are also valid on some ferries between France and the Republic. Inter-Rail passes offer a 50% reduction on train travel within Ireland and discounts on some ferries to/from France and Britain.

For €10 students can have a Fairstamp affixed to their ISIC card by any Usit Travel agency. This gives a 50% discount on Iarnród Éireann (Irish Rail) services. Irish Rambler tickets are available from Bus Éireann for bus-only travel in the Republic. They cost €45 (for travel on three out of eight consecutive days), €100 (eight out of 15 days) or €145 (15 out of 30 days).

For train-only travel within the Republic, the Irish Explorer ticket (€98) is good for five travel days out of 15. In Northern Ireland, the Freedom of Northern Ireland pass allows unlimited travel on Ulsterbus and Northern Irish railways for one day (£11), three days (£27.50) or seven consecutive days (£40). The Irish Rover ticket combines services with Bus Éireann and Ulsterbus for three days (€60), eight days (€135) or 15 days (€195).

BUS

Bus Éireann *(☎ 01-836 6111; 🅦 www.buseireann.ie)* offers services all over the Republic and into Northern Ireland. Fares are much cheaper than regular rail fares. Returns are usually only slightly more expensive than one-way fares, and special deals are often available. Most intercity buses in Northern Ireland are operated by Ulsterbus.

TRAIN

Iarnród Éireann *(☎ 01-836 3333)* operates trains on routes that fan out from Dublin. Fares are often twice as expensive as the bus, but travel times can be dramatically reduced. A midweek return ticket is often not much more than the single fare.

Northern Ireland Railways *(☎ 028-9089 9411)* has four routes from Belfast, one of which links up with the Republic's rail system.

CAR & MOTORCYCLE

The **Automobile Association** *(AA; Dublin ☎ 01-677 9481 • Cork ☎ 021-50 5155; breakdowns Republic ☎ 1800 667788, breakdowns Northern Ireland ☎ 0800 88 7766)* has various offices. In Northern Ireland, members of the **Royal Automobile Club** *(RAC; information ☎ 028-9033 1133, breakdowns ☎ 0800 82 8282)* can phone for assistance.

Car rental is expensive, so you will often be better off booking a package deal from your home country. In the off season prices are often around 25% cheaper. International companies such as Avis, Budget and Hertz have offices all over Ireland. There are many Dublin-based operators with rates from as low as €230 a week, including **Murray's Europcar** *(☎ 01-614 2800)*, **Argus Rent-A-Car** *(☎ 01-490 4444)* and **Malone Car Rental** *(☎ 01-670 7888)*.

BICYCLE

A large number of visitors explore Ireland by bicycle. Although distances are relatively short, the weather is often wet and the terrain hilly. Despite these drawbacks, it's a great place for cycling, and facilities are good.

Typical rental costs are €10 to €20 a day or €70 to €80 a week. **Raleigh Rent-a-Bike** *(☎ 01-465 9659; Unit 1, Finches Park, Longmile Rd, Dublin 12)* has dozens of outlets around the country, some of which offer one-way rentals for €80 a week.

Bicycles can be transported on some Bus Éireann and Ulsterbus routes; the charges vary. By train the costs start from €2.25 for a one-way journey, depending on the distance.

HITCHING

In Ireland hitching is common and generally hassle-free. The major exceptions are in busy tourist areas where the competition from other hitchers is stiff. Women shouldn't travel alone. Hitching is not a particularly safe practice anywhere and we do not recommend it.

ORGANISED TOURS

Bord Fáilte has details of general tour operators and specialist companies that include angling, walking, cycling, cultural holidays and tours for the disabled. Ulsterbus and Bus Éireann run day trips to major tourist sites.

Tír na nÓg Tours *(☎ 01-836 4684; ⓔ info@tirnanogtours.com; 57 Gardiner St Lower, Dublin 1)* specialises in off-the-tourist-trail tours. Prices start at €127 (for three days) and include transport, accommodation and site entry fees.

Dublin (Baile Átha Cliath)

☎ 01 • pop 1.1 million

Although it's one of the smallest capitals in the EU, Dublin is a bustling place that is growing at a furious pace. It may not be Europe's most elegant city, but it has been busy sprucing itself up and making the most of its physical charms. Those who haven't visited Dublin in a few years should be favourably struck by its vibrantly painted buildings and the ever-growing numbers of smart new restaurants and bars.

In spite of the development, Dublin remains a city of character and characters. Its rich literary past seems to bump against you at every corner, much of it associated with the many excellent pubs. A good number remain classic, unreconstructed Dublin boozers, where regulars happily enjoy a blether over a leisurely pint of Guinness.

Orientation

Dublin is divided by the River Liffey into the more affluent south side and the grubbier north side. North of the river, important landmarks are O'Connell St, the major shopping thoroughfare, and Gardiner St, with its many B&Bs and guesthouses. Pedestrianised Henry St, running west off O'Connell St, is the main shopping area.

Immediately south of the river is the bustling, sometimes raucous, Temple Bar district, Dame St, Trinity College and just below it, lovely St Stephen's Green. The pedestrianised Grafton St and its surrounding streets and lanes are crammed with shops.

Information

Tourist Offices The **Dublin Tourism Centre** *(☎ 1850 230330; ⓦ www.visitdublin.com; open Mon-Sat Sept-June, daily July & Aug)* is in the de-sanctified **St Andrew's Church** *(Suffolk St)*, west of Trinity College. Services include accommodation bookings, car rentals, maps, tours, tickets and more. There are also Dublin Tourism offices at the airport and on the waterfront at Dun Laoghaire.

The head office of **Bord Fáilte** *(Baggot St Bridge; open Mon-Fri)* has an information desk and is much less crowded. The **NITB** *(☎ 679 1977; ⓦ www.discovernorthernireland.com; 16 Nassau St; open Mon-Sat)* office offers information and booking services.

Money American Express has an exchange bureau in the Dublin Tourism Centre. The Central Bank offers the best exchange rates; the airport and ferry terminal bureaus offer the worst.

Post & Communications Dublin's famous **General Post Office** *(O'Connell St)* is located north of the river. South of the river there are post offices on Anne St South and St Andrew's St.

For Internet access, **Planet Cyber Café** *(13 St Andrew's St; open to at least 10pm daily)* charges about €5 per hour. **Does Not Compute** *(☎ 670 4464; Essex St West)*, and **Global Internet Café** *(☎ 878 0295)*, just north of the O'Connell Bridge, are alternatives.

Travel Agencies The **Usit Travel** *(☎ 679 8833; 19 Aston Quay; open 9.30am-5pm, later Mon-Sat)* office is near O'Connell Bridge.

Medical & Emergency Services The **Eastern Health Board Dublin Area** *(☎ 679 0700; Doctor Stevens Hospital, 138 Thomas St, Dublin 8)* can advise you from 9am to 5pm weekdays. There is also a **Well Women clinic** *(☎ 872 8051; 35 Lower Liffey St)*.

For emergency assistance phone ☎ 999 or ☎ 112 for *gardai* (police), ambulance or fire brigade.

Trinity College & Book of Kells

Trinity is the University of Dublin's sole college. Until 1793 its students were all Protestants, but today the majority of its 9500 students are Catholic. In summer, **walking tours** *(☎ 608 1827)* depart regularly from the

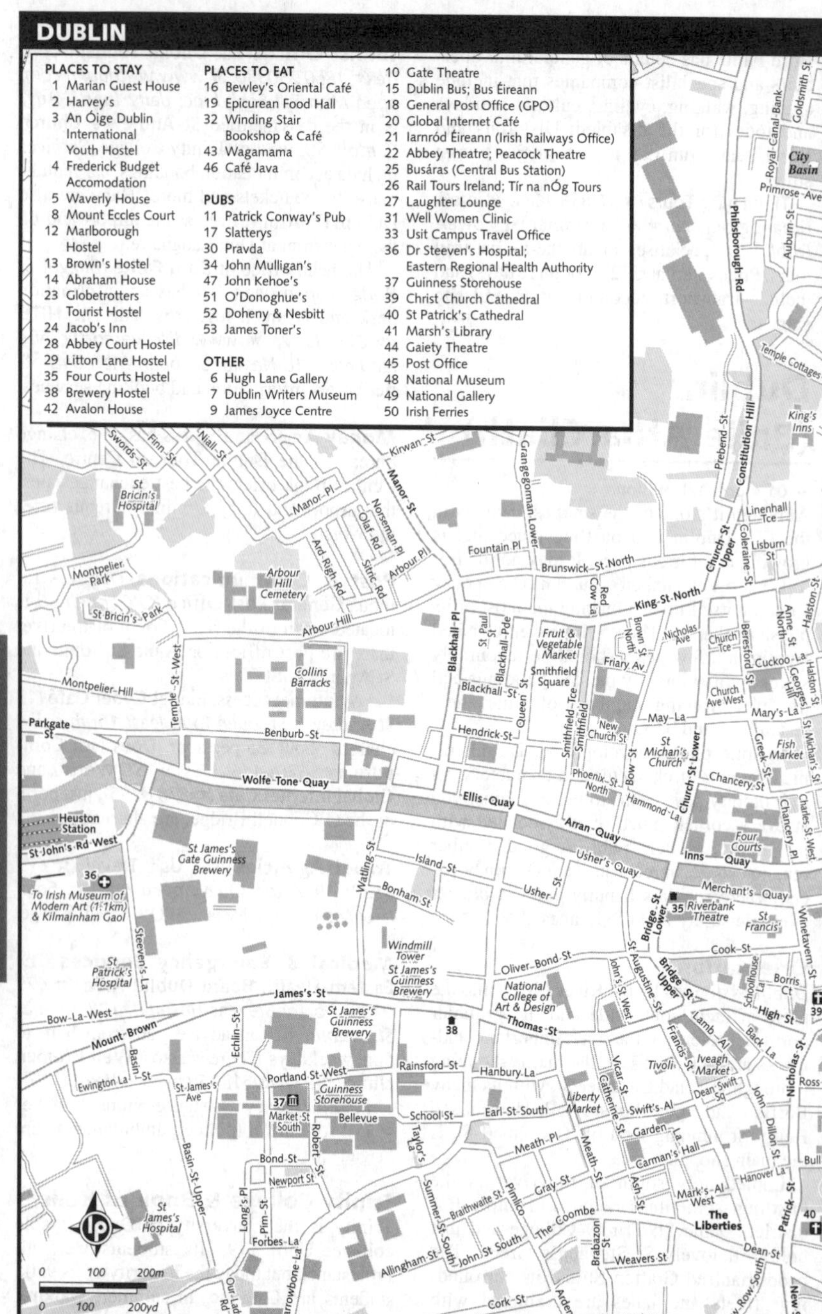
DUBLIN
PLACES TO STAY
1 Marian Guest House
2 Harvey's
3 An Óige Dublin International Youth Hostel
4 Frederick Budget Accomodation
5 Waverly House
8 Mount Eccles Court
12 Marlborough Hostel
13 Brown's Hostel
14 Abraham House
23 Globetrotters Tourist Hostel
24 Jacob's Inn
28 Abbey Court Hostel
29 Litton Lane Hostel
35 Four Courts Hostel
38 Brewery Hostel
42 Avalon House
PLACES TO EAT
16 Bewley's Oriental Café
19 Epicurean Food Hall
32 Winding Stair Bookshop & Café
43 Wagamama
46 Café Java
PUBS
11 Patrick Conway's Pub
17 Slatterys
30 Pravda
34 John Mulligan's
47 John Kehoe's
51 O'Donoghue's
52 Doheny & Nesbitt
53 James Toner's
OTHER
6 Hugh Lane Gallery
7 Dublin Writers Museum
9 James Joyce Centre
10 Gate Theatre
15 Dublin Bus; Bus Éireann
18 General Post Office (GPO)
20 Global Internet Café
21 Iarnród Éireann (Irish Railways Office)
22 Abbey Theatre; Peacock Theatre
25 Busáras (Central Bus Station)
26 Rail Tours Ireland; Tír na nÓg Tours
27 Laughter Lounge
31 Well Women Clinic
33 Usit Campus Travel Office
36 Dr Steeven's Hospital; Eastern Regional Health Authority
37 Guinness Storehouse
39 Christ Church Cathedral
40 St Patrick's Cathedral
41 Marsh's Library
44 Gaiety Theatre
45 Post Office
48 National Museum
49 National Gallery
50 Irish Ferries
Goldsmith St
Royal Canal Bank
City Basin
Primrose Ave
Auburn St
Phibsborough Rd
Temple Cottages
King's Inns
Prebend St
Constitution Hill
Swords St
Finn St
Niall St
Kirwan St
St Bricin's Hospital
Manor St
Manor Pl
Norseman Pl
Olaf Rd
Ard Righ Rd
Sitric Rd
Arbour Pl
Grangegorman Lower
Fountain Pl
Linenhall Tce
Lisburn St
Coleraine St
Church St Upper
Montpelier Park
Arbour Hill Cemetery
Brunswick St North
Red Cow La
King St North
Halston St
Anne St North
St Bricin's Park
Arbour Hill
Blackhall Pl
St Paul St
Blackhall Pde
Fruit & Vegetable Market
Smithfield Square
Brown St North
Nicholas Ave
Church Tce
Beresford St
Friary Av
Cuckoo La
Georges Hill
Temple St West
Collins Barracks
Montpelier Hill
Blackhall St
Queen St
Smithfield Tce
Smithfield
Church Ave West
Mary's La
May La
Parkgate St
Benburb St
Hendrick St
New Church St
St Michan's Church
Greek St
Fish Market
St Michan's St
Church St Lower
Bow St
Wolfe Tone Quay
Ellis Quay
Phoenix St North
Hammond La
Chancery St
Charles St West
Chancery Pl
Heuston Station
Arran Quay
Four Courts
St John's Rd West
St James's Gate Guinness Brewery
Inns Quay
Usher's Quay
Island St
Watling St
36
To Irish Museum of Modern Art (1.1km) & Kilmainham Gaol
Bonham St
Usher St
Merchant's Quay
Bridge St Lower
35 Riverbank Theatre
St Francis
Winetavern St
Steeven's La
Windmill Tower
St James's Guinness Brewery
Cook St
St Patrick's Hospital
Oliver Bond St
St Augustine St
John's St West
Bridge St Upper
Schoolhouse La
Borris Ct
National College of Art & Design
James's St
High St
39
Bow La West
St James's Guinness Brewery
38
Thomas St
Lamb Al
Back La
Mount Brown
Echlin St
Francis St
Iveagh Market
Nicholas St
Basin St
Rainsford St
Hanbury La
Tivoli
Vicar St
Ross
Ewington La
St James's Ave
Portland St West
37
Guinness Storehouse
Liberty Market
Catherine St
Dean Swift Sq
Swift's Al
John Dillon St
Market St South
Earl St South
Garden La
School St
Bellevue
Robert St
Taylor's La
Meath Pl
Carman's Hall
Bull
Basin St Upper
Bond St
Meath St
Hanover La
Newport St
Long's Pl
Pim St
Summer St South
Braithwaite St
Pimlico
Gray St
Ash St
Mark's Al West
Patrick St
St James's Hospital
The Coombe
The Liberties
40
Forbes La
Allingham St
John St South
Brabazon St
Dean St
Weavers St
0 100 200m
0 100 200yd
Marrowbone La
Our Lady's Rd
Cork St
Arden St
Newmarket
New Row South
New St

IRELAND

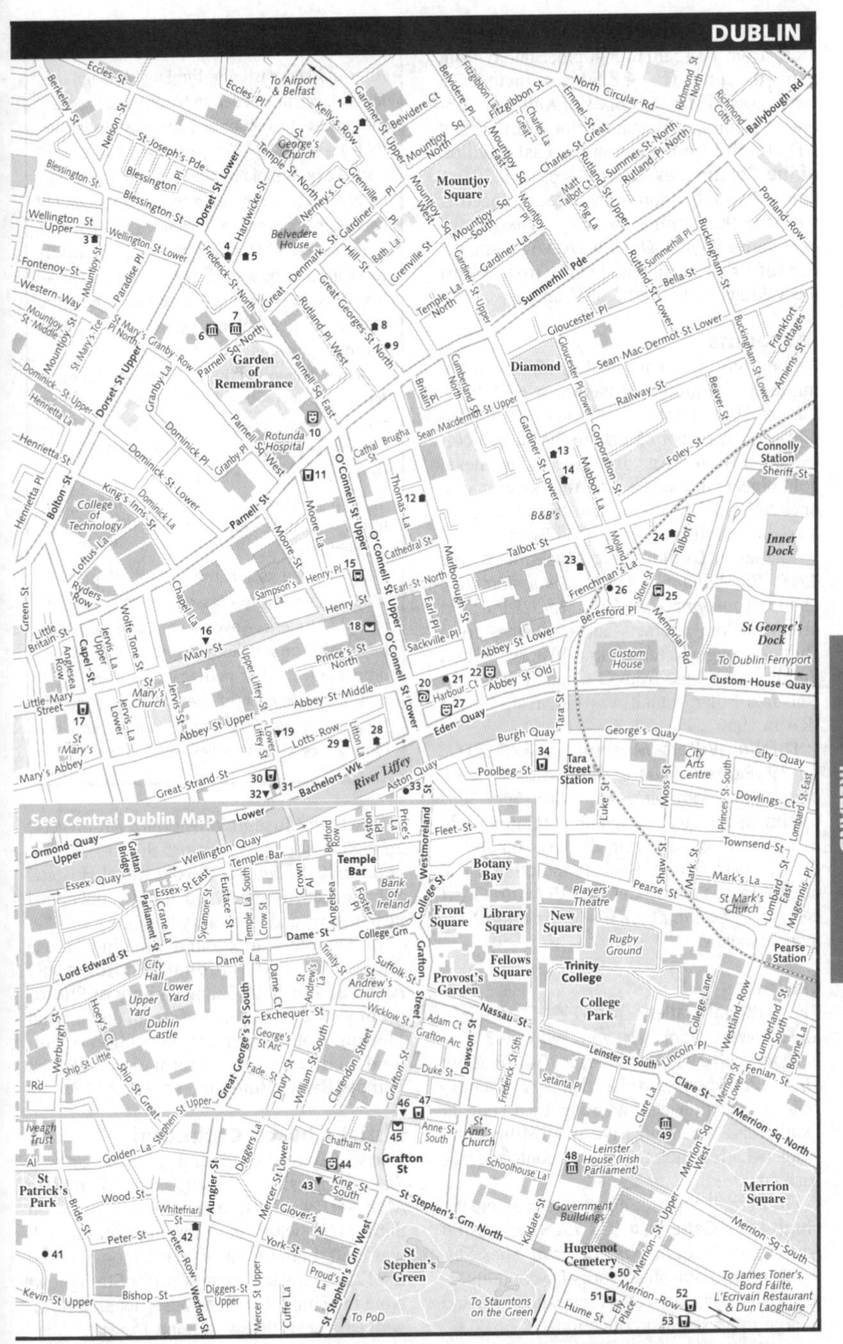
DUBLIN
To Airport & Belfast
Eccles St
Eccles Pl
Berkeley St
Nelson St
St Joseph's Pde
Blessington St
Blessington
Wellington St Upper
Wellington St Lower
Fontenoy St
Mountjoy St
Western Way
Paradise Pl
Mountjoy St Middle
St Mary's Tce
St Mary's Pl North
Dorset St Lower
Dorset St Upper
Hardwicke St
Temple St North
Frederick St North
Granby Row
Granby La
Dominick St Upper
Henrietta La
Henrietta St
Henrietta Pl
Bolton St
College of Technology
King's Inns St
Dominick St Lower
Dominick La
Dominick Pl
Granby Pl
Loftus La
Ryders Row
Green St
Little Britain St
Capel St
Anglesea Row
Little Mary Street
St Mary's Abbey
Mary's Abbey
Jervis La Upper
Jervis La Lower
Wolfe Tone St
Jervis St
St Mary's Church
Chapel La
Mary St
Upper Liffey St
Lower Liffey St
Abbey St Upper
Abbey St Middle
Great Strand St
Bachelors Wk
Lotts Row
Litton La
Parnell Sq North
Parnell Sq West
Parnell Sq East
Parnell St
Garden of Remembrance
Rotunda Hospital
Moore La
Moore St
Henry Pl
Sampson's La
Henry St
Prince's St North
O'Connell St Upper
O'Connell St Lower
Cathal Brugha St
Thomas La
Cathedral St
Earl St North
Earl Pl
Sackville Pl
Marlborough St
Harbour Ct
Abbey St Lower
Abbey St Old
Eden Quay
River Liffey
Aston Quay
Gardiner St Upper
Gardiner St Lower
Kelly's Row
St George's Church
Belvidere Ct
Belvedere Pl
Belvedere House
Mountjoy Sq North
Mountjoy Sq West
Mountjoy Sq South
Mountjoy Sq East
Mountjoy Square
Mountjoy Pl
Fitzgibbon La
Fitzgibbon St
Charles La
Great Charles St
Charles St Great
Nerney's Ct
Grenville Pl
Grenville St
Great Denmark St
Gardiner Pl
Gardiner La
Hill St
Bath La
Great Georges St North
Rutland Pl West
Temple La North
Britain Pl
Cumberland St North
Sean Macdermot St Upper
Sean Mac Dermot St Lower
Summerhill Pde
Diamond
Gloucester Pl
Gloucester Pl Lower
Railway St
Corporation St
Mabbot La
B&B's
Talbot St
Talbot Pl
Moland Pl
Frenchman's La
Store St
Beresford Pl
Memorial Rd
Custom House
Custom House Quay
To Dublin Ferryport
St George's Dock
Inner Dock
Connolly Station
Sheriff St
Foley St
Beaver St
Buckingham St Lower
Buckingham St Upper
Amiens St
Frankfort Cottages
Bella St
Summerhill Pl
Rutland St Lower
Rutland St Upper
Matt Talbot Ct
Pig La
Rutland Pl North
Summer St North
Emmet St
North Circular Rd
Richmond St North
Richmond Cotts
Ballybough Rd
Portland Row
Burgh Quay
Tara St
Tara Street Station
George's Quay
City Quay
Poolbeg St
City Arts Centre
Luke St
Moss St
Prince's St South
Dowlings Ct
Lombard St East
Townsend St
Shaw St
Mark St
Mark's La
Pearse St
St Mark's Church
Lombard St East
Magennis Pl
Pearse Station
See Central Dublin Map
Ormond Quay Upper
Lower
Grattan Bridge
Wellington Quay
Essex Quay
Essex St East
Temple Bar
Parliament St
Crane La
Sycamore St
Eustace St
Temple La South
Crow St
Crown Al
Anglesea St
Bedford Row
Aston Pl
Price's La
Fleet St
Westmoreland St
Temple Bar
Bank of Ireland
Foster Pl
College St
College Grn
Botany Bay
Front Square
Library Square
New Square
Players' Theatre
Rugby Ground
Dame St
Dame La
Lord Edward St
City Hall
Lower Yard
Upper Yard
Dublin Castle
Werburgh St
Hoey's Ct
Ship St Little
Ship St Great
Dame Ct
St Andrew's La
Trinity St
Suffolk St
St Andrew's Church
Grafton Street
Provost's Garden
Fellows Square
Trinity College
College Park
Exchequer St
Wicklow St
Nassau St
George's St Arc
Adam Ct
Grafton Arc
Great George's St South
Fade St
Drury St
William St South
Clarendon Street
Grafton St
Duke St
Dawson St
Frederick St Sth
Rd
St Stephen St Upper
Leinster St South
Lincoln Pl
College Lane
Westland Row
Cumberland St South
Boyne La
Fenian St
Setanta Pl
Clare St
Clare La
Merrion Sq Lower
Merrion Sq North
Iveagh Trust
Golden La
Al
Diggers La
Aungier St
Mercer St Lower
Chatham St
Anne St South
St Ann's Church
Schoolhouse La
Leinster House (Irish Parliament)
Merrion Sq West
King St South
Grafton St
St Patrick's Park
Wood St
Bride St
Whitefriar St
Peter Row
Peter St
Glover's Al
St Stephen's Grn North
St Stephen's Grn West
Kildare St
Government Buildings
Merrion St Upper
Merrion Square
Merrion Sq South
York St
Proud's La
St Stephen's Green
Huguenot Cemetery
Merrion Row
Ely Place
Hume St
Kevin St Upper
Bishop St
Diggers St Upper
Mercer St Upper
Cuffe La
Wexford St
To PoD
To Stauntons on the Green
To James Toner's, Bord Fáilte, L'Ecrivain Restaurant & Dun Laoghaire
1
2
3
4
5
6
7
8
9
10
11
12
13
14
15
16
17
18
19
20
21
22
23
24
25
26
27
28
29
30
31
32
33
34
41
42
43
44
45
46
47
48
49
50
51
52
53

main gate on College Green, Monday to Saturday from 10.15am to 3.40pm, Sunday from noon to 3pm. The €8.50 fee includes a viewing of the famous *Book of Kells*, an elaborately illuminated manuscript from around AD 800. It's on display in the **East Pavilion of the Colonnades** *(adult €7; open 9.30am-5pm Mon-Sat, noon-4.30pm Sun)* together with the 9th-century *Book of Armagh*, the even-older *Book of Durrow* (AD 675) and the harp of Brian Ború, who led the Irish against the Vikings in the Battle of Clontarf.

Museums

Among the highlights of the exhibits at the impressive **National Museum** *(☎ 667 7444; Kildare St; admission free; open 10am-5pm Tues-Sat, 2pm-5pm Sun)* are the superb collection of Bronze Age, Iron Age and medieval gold objects in the treasury, the skeleton of a once tall, mighty Viking and the slighter but incredibly well-preserved 'Bog Body'.

The small **Dublin Civic Museum** *(☎ 679 4260; 58 William St South; admission free; open 10am-6pm Tues-Sat, 11am-2pm Sun)* offers random artefacts and curiosities from Dublin's long and tumultuous history, including the stone head from O'Connell St's Lord Nelson's Pillar, which was blown up by the IRA in 1966.

Dublin Writers Museum *(☎ 872 2077; 18-19 Parnell Square; admission €5.50; open 10am-5pm Mon-Sat, 11am-5pm Sun)* celebrates the city's long and continuing role as a literary centre, with displays on Joyce, Swift, Yeats, Wilde, Beckett and others. The nearby **James Joyce Centre** *(35 North Great George's St; admission €4.50)* is a must for avid Joyceans.

IRELAND

Galleries

The **National Gallery** *(☎ 661 5133; Merrion Square West; admission free; open 9.30am-5.30pm Mon-Wed, Fri & Sat, 9.30am-8.30pm Thur, 12pm-5pm Sun)* has displays of an excellent collection with a strong Irish content. Don't miss the impressive new Millennium wing, which focuses on more contemporary Irish art.

On Parnell Square, north of the river, the **Hugh Lane Gallery** *(☎ 874 1903; admission free; open 9.30am-5pm or 6pm Tues-Sat, 9.30am-5pm Sun)* has works by contemporary Irish artists, as well as retrospectives and a large impressionist collection.

Portrait of the Writer

After quickly mastering the English language, James Joyce proceeded to blow it apart, and in the process revolutionised the way stories are told. Joyce (1882–1941) was raised in a strict Catholic household but lost his faith in college; he drew extensively upon this childhood in his earliest major work, *A Portrait of the Artist as a Young Man*. This was the piece in which Joyce introduced a stream-of-conscious narrative, which describes a protagonist's thoughts and free associations rather than simply chronicling events.

Joyce developed this technique in his masterpiece, *Ulysses*, which focuses on a day in the life of two Irishmen – one a Catholic, the other a Jew. His last major work, *Finnegans Wake*, stretches the limits of the English language by introducing new, often nonsensical terms and apparently discarding the idea of plot entirely.

Joyce's works are the delight of many a college literature professor and the bane of many a student. Anyone who tells you that he or she understands *Finnegans Wake* is probably lying. But perhaps after downing a pint or two in each of the Dublin pubs Joyce frequented, you'll begin to understand his writing…or at least believe that you do.

The **Irish Museum of Modern Art** *(IMMA; admission free; open 10am-5.30pm Tues-Sat, noon-5.30pm Sun)*, at the old Royal Hospital Kilmainham, is renowned for its conceptual installations and temporary exhibits.

In Temple Bar, around Meeting House Square, is the **National Photographic Archive** *(☎ 603 0200)* and **Gallery of Photography** *(☎ 671 4654)*. In fact, in and around Meeting House Square is a cauldron of cultural activities. For information call the **Temple Bar Culture Line** *(☎ 671 5717)*.

Christ Church Cathedral

Christ Church Cathedral *(Christ Church Place; admission €3; open 9.45am-5pm Mon-Sat)* was a simple structure of wood until 1169, when the present stone church was built. In the south aisle is a monument to the 12th-century Norman warrior Strongbow. Note the church's precariously leaning north wall (it's been that way since 1562).

St Patrick's Cathedral & Around

A church stood on the site of St Patrick's Cathedral *(Patrick's Close; admission €3.50; open 9am-6pm daily)* as early as the 5th century, but the present building dates from 1191. The cathedral is closed during worship. Satirist Jonathan Swift, author of *Gulliver's Travels*, was dean of St Patrick's from 1713 to 1745. Swift and his beloved companion Stella (Esther Johnson) are both interred here. Swift's death mask is on display just south of the cathedral in **Marsh's Library** *(☎ 454 3511; admission €2.50; open 10am-12.45pm & 2pm-5pm Mon & Wed-Fri, 10.30am-12.45pm Sat)*. Dating from 1701, this lovely building boasts some rare manuscripts.

Dublin Castle

Although much of it has been rebuilt over the centuries, Dublin Castle (*☎ 677 7129; admission €3.35 by guided tour only; open 10am-5pm Mon-Fri, 2pm-5pm Sat & Sun*), off Dame St, more a palace than a castle, dates back to the 13th century, from when it was the centre of British power. The city got its modern name from the black pool (dubh linn) beneath the castle gardens.

Guinness Brewery

The excellent **Guinness Storehouse** *(☎ 453 8364; Market St; adult/concession €12/8; open 9.30am-5pm daily)* sits in the midst of the malty fug of the mighty Guinness brewery southeast of the city centre. The production and marketing processes of Dublin's world-famous black stuff are presented with sensory verve inside seven floors. The city views from the glass-walled bar are unbeatable on a clear day, and you won't get better Guinness anywhere than the complementary pint served up here. Catch bus No 51B or 78A from Aston Quay, or No 123 from O'Connell St.

Kilmainham Gaol

The grey, sombre Kilmainham Gaol *(☎ 453 5984; Inchicore Rd; admission €4.40; open 9.30am-4.45pm daily Apr-Sept, 9.30am-4pm Mon-Fri, 10am-4.45pm Sun Oct-Mar)* played a key role in Ireland's struggle for independence and was the site of mass executions following the 1916 Easter Rising. The tour includes a great audiovisual introduction to the prison from its opening in 1796 until its closure in 1924. Catch bus No 51B, 79 or 79A from Aston Quay.

Places to Stay

At weekends and other unexpected times Dublin can be bedless for a radius of up to 60km. Book in advance, even for hostels. Dublin Tourism offices can find and book accommodation for €2.50 plus a deposit of 10% for the first night's stay.

Hostels – North of the Liffey A stone's throw from the Busáras bus and Connolly train stations is the 212-bed **Jacobs Inn** *(☎ 855 5660; 21-28 Talbot Place; dorm beds from €16/18 Fri/Sat, doubles/triples/quads per person from €36/32/30)*, which has a café and cooking facilities.

Gardiner St Lower has three places worth considering. At No 47, the welcoming IHH **Globetrotters Tourist Hostel** *(☎ 873 5893; dorm beds low/high season €16.50/21.50)* is a modern, secure place. Rates include a full Irish breakfast. The IHH **Abraham House** *(☎ 855 0600; dorms from €12, doubles weekday/weekend from €75/96)* is at No 82. At No 90, **Brown's Hostel** *(☎ 855 0034; dorm beds from €20)* is smart and modern, and offers Internet access as well as a light breakfast.

If you don't mind street noise, the pleasant, central **Abbey Court Hostel** *(☎ 878 0700; 29 Bachelor's Walk; dorm beds from €26, doubles €88)* overlooks the River Liffey and has new facilities, good security, and a friendly vibe. Just around the corner and off the main road, **Litton Lane Hostel** *(☎ 872 8389; 2-4 Litton Lane; dorm beds from €16)* is a former recording studio.

The friendly IHH **Marlborough Hostel** *(☎ 874 7629; 81-82 Marlborough St; dorm beds weekday/weekend from €14/16.50, private rooms €51)* offers austere dorms and can be noisy. IHH **Mount Eccles Court** *(☎ 873 0826; 42 North Great George's St; dorm beds from €14, doubles €60 plus €3 weekend supplement)* is a sprawling 100-bed hostel that's located in an old Georgian townhouse.

An Óige's creaking 363-bed **Dublin International Youth Hostel** *(☎ 830 1766; 61 Mountjoy St; dorm beds weekday/weekend from €19/22, twins/triples €57/81.90)* is being renovated. Although the hostel is safe, after dark it's an unsavoury walk from the city centre. From Dublin airport, bus No 41A stops on Dorset St Upper, a short walk away. Rates include light breakfast.

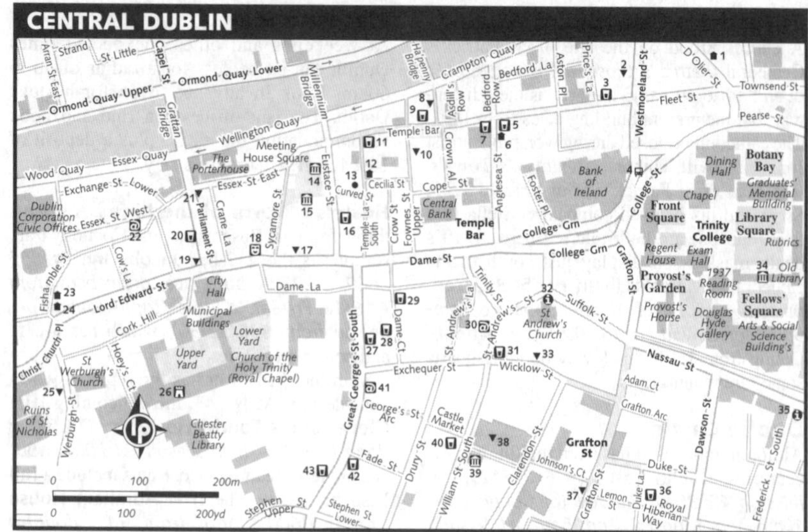

Hostels – South of the Liffey One of the best hostels in this area is the friendly, smart, 230-bed **Four Courts Hostel** *(☎ 672 5839; 15-17 Merchant's Quay; dorm beds from €16.50, twins from €64)*, which occupies a handsome Georgian mansion facing the Liffey.

The big IHH **Kinlay House** *(☎ 679 6644; 2-12 Lord Edward St; beds in 4-bed dorms €22.50, singles/doubles €36/57)*, beside Christ Church Cathedral, is central, but dorms need updating and can be noisy. Cooking facilities are available.

IHH's **Avalon House** *(☎ 475 0001; 55 Aungier St; dorm beds weekday/weekend €15/17, twins weekday/weekend €32/35)* is a popular place in a renovated Georgian building just west of St Stephen's Green. Beds are in standard dorms, and rates include continental breakfast.

Just north of Trinity College is pleasant **Ashfield House** *(☎ 679 7734; 19-20 D'Olier St; dorm beds €17, singles/doubles €50/80)*. It has all the amenities of a semideluxe hotel but it fills up rather quickly. Breakfast is included in the rates.

Staying in the Temple Bar district is fun and convenient, but street noise is a serious drawback. A good choice is the IHH **Barnacles Temple Bar House** *(☎ 671 6277; 19 Temple Lane; dorm beds from €16.50, twins or doubles from €74)*. **Oliver St John Gogarty Hostel** *(☎ 671 1822; 18-21 Anglesea St; dorm beds from €23, twins €56)* adjoins a boisterous pub but is surprisingly quiet.

The IHH **Brewery Hostel** *(☎ 453 8600; 22-23 Thomas St; dorm beds from €20, doubles from €75)* is close to the Guinness Hopstore and it has top-drawer facilities, including a secure car park, although the neighbourhood is scruffy and is a fair way from the centre.

B&Bs & Hotels If you want something close to the city centre, Gardiner Sts Upper and Lower are the places to look. They're not the prettiest parts of Dublin and can be noisy, but they are relatively cheap.

Harvey's *(☎ 874 8384; 11 Gardiner St Upper; singles/doubles €40/45)* is a friendly place. There are several more B&Bs nearby. The cheapest is **Marian Guest House** *(☎ 874 4129; 21 Gardiner St Upper; singles €30, rooms per person sharing €27)*.

Hardwicke St, close to Gardiner St Upper, has a few B&Bs including the Joycean haunt **Waverley House** *(☎ 874 6132; 4 Hardwicke St; singles/doubles €30/64)*, which was then known as 'The Boarding House'.

Harding Hotel *(☎ 679 6500; e harding.hotel@usitworld.com; Fishamble St; singles/twins or triples €60/90)* offers good value for groups of three.

Pleasant, modern **Frederick Budget Accommodation** *(☎ 878 6689; 48 Hardwicke

CENTRAL DUBLIN

PLACES TO STAY
1 Ashfield House
6 Oliver St John Gogarty Hostel
12 Barnacles Temple Bar House
23 Harding Hotel
24 Kinlay House

PLACES TO EAT
2 Bewley's Oriental Café
8 La Paloma
10 Cafe Irie
17 Gruel
19 Da Pino
21 Zaytoon's
25 Leo Burdock's
33 Cornucopia
37 Bewley's Oriental Café
38 Blazing Salads

PUBS
3 Palace Bar
5 Oliver St John Gogarty Bar
7 Auld Dubliner
9 Quays Bar
11 Temple Bar
16 Switch
20 Front Lounge
27 The Globe
28 Rí Rá
29 Stag's Head
31 International Bar
36 Cocoon
40 Grogan's Castle Lounge
42 Hogan's
43 The Long Hall

OTHER
4 Nitelink Buses
13 Temple Bar Music Centre
14 National Photographic Archive
15 Gallery of Photography
18 Olympia Theatre
22 Does Not Compute
26 Dublin Castle
30 Planet Cyber Cafe
32 Dublin Tourism Centre; American Express
34 Book of Kells (East Pavilion of the Colonnades)
35 Northern Irish Tourist Board
39 Dublin Civic Museum
41 Planet Cyber Cafe

Street; singles/doubles from €40/60) has en suite rooms with TV.

Places to Eat

Restaurants Dublin serves up a variety of treats to keep your palate pleased.

Around Temple Bar This district probably holds the largest and best concentration of restaurants. Generous, cheap portions of pizza and pasta are on offer at **Da Pino** *(38-40 Parliament Street; mains around €10)*. At the other end of Parliament St, **Zaytoon's** *(cnr Essex & Parliament Sts; mains €7)* serves tasty, flat breads, kebabs and Iranian dishes in smart café-style surroundings. The interior is dull at **Gruel** *(☎ 670 7119; 68a Dame St; mains around €5)* but the sandwiches and lovely home-made desserts are far from it.

Small **Café Irie** *(upstairs 12 Fownes St)* is good for cheap, tasty sandwiches and snacks.

La Paloma *(Asdill's Row)*, around the corner from the Quays Bar, has a wide range of Spanish tapas from €4.

Although it's not quite in Temple Bar, **Leo Burdock's** *(2 Werburgh St)* serves Dublin's best takeaway fish and chips.

Around Grafton St Popular **Café Java** *(5 Anne St South)* does good brunches and lunches (around €8). **Cornucopia** *(19 Wicklow St; dishes under €9; open Mon-Sat)* is a justly popular veggie café, catering for special diets with all sorts of creative concoctions.

Blazing Salads *(42 Drury St; open Mon-Sat)* offers crunchy, inventive takeaway salads for around €3 to €5. **Wagamama** *(South King St; mains €9)* serves cheap noodles and ramen in modern surroundings.

Cafés There are three branches of **Bewley's Oriental Cafés** *(78 Grafton St; open to 1am Mon-Sat, to 7pm Sunday • 11-12 Westmoreland St; open to 9pm daily • 40 Mary St)* around the centre, with Grafton St being the flagship store. Something of a Dublin institution, Bewley's serves above-average cafeteria-style breakfasts (€6), sandwiches (up to €5) and full meals (up to €8).

Winding Stair Bookshop & Café *(Ormond Quay Lower)*, north of the Liffey, opposite Ha'penny Bridge, is a rambling bookshop with teas, pastries and sandwiches.

The excellent **Epicurean Food Hall** *(open 8.30am-7pm Mon-Sat, 10am-6pm Sun)*, with entrances on Lower Liffey and Middle Abbey Sts, has several good delis, celebrating world food from Japanese to eastern European and several cafés.

Entertainment

For events and club listings, get a free copy of the fortnightly *Event Guide* (W www.eventguide.ie), from venues, cafés, hostels etc.

The **Temple Bar Music Centre** *(☎ 670 9202; Curved St)* is a venue to watch. There is music seven days a week, with something to suit most tastes.

Pubs Dublin has some 850 pubs, so you're always close to a Guinness. The Temple Bar district is crammed with pubs that feature live music. Notables include the **Temple Bar** *(Temple Lane)*, the restored **Oliver St John Gogarty Bar** *(57-58 Fleet St)*, the **Quays Bar** overlooking Temple Square, and the **Auld Dubliner** *(24-25 Temple Bar)*.

Other atmospheric spots for a pint include the **Stag's Head** *(Dame Court)*, **The Long Hall** *(South Great George's St)*, the **Palace Bar** *(Fleet St)*, **John Kehoe's** *(Anne St South)*, **John Mulligan's** *(8 Poolbeg St)*, **Grogan's Castle Lounge** *(cnr William & Castle Sts)*, **James Toner's** *(Baggot St)*, and **Doheny & Nesbitt** *(Baggot St)* – also popular for lunch.

Pubs with live music from blues to rock to traditional Irish include the **International Bar** *(23 Wicklow St)* and touristy but still pleasant **O'Donoghue's** *(15 Merrion Row)*.

North of the river, **Slatterys** *(Capel St)* is a busy music pub. **Patrick Conway's Pub** *(70 Parnell St)* has music some nights.

Hipster spots include **Front Lounge** *(Parliament St)*, **The Globe** *(South Great George's St)* and **Hogan's** *(South Great George's St)*, and the northside's USSR-style **Pravda** *(Liffey St)*. **Cocoon** *(Hibernian St)* is another pre-club flocking place for the beautiful people.

Clubs Check club listings or just ask around. Some stayers include **Rí Rá** *(Dame Court)*, with funk leanings, and the legendary 'Place of Dance' – **PoD** *(35 Harcourt St)*. **Switch** *(☎ 670 7655; 11 Eustace St)* is a small, relaxed place boasting some accomplished local DJs.

Theatre & Classical Music Near the river are the famous **Abbey Theatre** *(☎ 878 7222; Abbey St Lower)* and smaller **Peacock Theatre** *(Abbey St Lower)*. The **Gate Theatre** *(☎ 874 4045; Parnell Square East)* is another choice. The **Olympia Theatre** *(☎ 677 7744; Dame St)* has plays and international music acts, and there's also the **Gaiety Theatre** *(☎ 677 1717; King St South)*. **The Laughter Lounge** *(Abbey St Middle)* has stand-up comedy most nights.

Concerts take place at the **National Concert Hall** *(☎ 671 1888; Earlsfort Terrace)*, just south of St Stephen's Green.

Getting There & Away

Air For flight information contact **Aer Lingus** *(reservations ☎ 886 8888, flight information ☎ 886 6705)* or **Ryanair** *(☎ 0818-303030)*.

Bus Just north of the Liffey, **Busáras** *(☎ 836 6111; Store St;* Ⓦ *www.buseireann.ie)* is at Bus Éireann's central bus stationt. Standard one-way fares from Dublin include Cork (€17.10, 3½ hours, every two hours 8am to 6pm), Galway (€11.40, 3¾ hours, five daily) and Rosslare Harbour (€12.70, three hours, six daily). Buses to Belfast (€16.50) depart from the Busáras up to seven times a day Monday to Saturday (three times on Sunday).

Slightly cheaper private bus companies have many services daily to Galway, but are less frequent to other locations. Try **City Link** *(☎ 626 6888)*.

Train Just north of the Liffey, **Connolly station** *(☎ 836 6222)* is the station for Belfast, Derry, Sligo, other points north and Wexford. **Heuston station**, south of the Liffey and well west of the centre, is the station for Cork, Galway, Killarney, Limerick, Waterford and most other points to the west, south and southwest. For travel information and tickets, contact the **Iarnród Éireann Travel Centre** *(☎ 836 6222;* Ⓦ *www.irishrail.ie; 35 Abbey St Lower)*. Regular one-way fares from Dublin include Belfast (€26.60, 2¼ hours, six daily), Cork (€44.40, 3¼ hours, up to eight daily) and Galway (€20.90, three hours, four daily).

Boat There are two direct services from Holyhead on the northwestern tip of Wales, one to Dublin Port, and the other to Dun Laoghaire at the southern end of Dublin Bay. **Stena Lines** *(☎ 204 7777)*, in Dun Laoghaire, and **Irish Ferries** *(office/information line ☎ 638 3333/661 0715;* Ⓦ *www.irishferries.com; 2-4 Merrion Row)* are the main carriers. See the Getting There & Away section earlier in this chapter for more details.

Getting Around

To/From the Airport & Ferry Terminals

Ten kilometres north of the centre is **Dublin airport** *(☎ 814 1111)*. There's an Airlink Express service to/from Busáras and to/from Heuston train station for €4.50 (both 30 to 40 minutes). Alternatively, the slower bus (one hour) Nos 41 and 41A (the latter on weekends only) cost €1.40. A taxi to the centre should cost about €16.50.

Buses go to Busáras from the **Dublin Ferryport terminal** *(☎ 855 2296; Alexandra Rd)* after all ferry arrivals. Buses also run from Busáras to meet ferry departures. To travel between Dun Laoghaire's ferry terminal and

Dublin, take bus No 46A to Fleet St in Temple Bar, bus No 7 to Eden Quay, or bus No 7A or 8 to Burgh Quay. Alternatively, take the Dublin Area Rapid Transport (DART) rail service to Pearse station (for south Dublin) or Connolly station (for north Dublin).

Local Transport Contact **Dublin Bus** *(Bus Átha Cliath; ☎ 873 4222; 59 O'Connell St)*. Buses cost from €0.75 for one to three stages, up to a maximum of €1.65. These tickets give you two trips valid for a month, and single fares can be bought on the bus. One-day passes cost €4.50 for bus only, or €7.20 for bus and DART. Late-night Nitelink buses (€4 to €6) operate from the College St/Westmoreland St/D'Olier St triangle until 3am on Friday and Saturday nights.

DART provides quick rail access to the coast as far north as Howth (€1.50) and south to Bray (€1.70). Pearse station is handy for central Dublin. Bicycles cannot be taken on the DART but may travel on suburban trains.

Taxis in Dublin are expensive with flagfall at €2.50. Try **National Radio Cabs** *(☎ 677 2222)*.

Car All the major companies have offices at Dublin airport and in the city centre. Three cheaper options are **Murray's Europcar** *(☎ 614 2800)*, **Argus Rent-A-Car** *(☎ 490 4444; W www.argusrentals.com)*, with a desk at the Dublin Tourism Centre, and **Malone Car Rental** *(☎ 670 7888; 26 Lombard St East)*. The cheapest rates are around €230 per week.

Bicycle Most rental places open during high season. Daily rental costs around €14 per day. Try **Dublin Bike Tours** *(☎ 670 0899; Lord Edward St)* near Kinlay House.

AROUND DUBLIN

Dun Laoghaire

☎ 01

Dun Laoghaire (pronounced 'dun leary') is a popular resort and a busy harbour with ferry connections to Britain. On the southern side of the harbour is the **Martello Tower**, where James Joyce's epic novel *Ulysses* opens; it's now the **James Joyce Museum** *(☎ 280 9265; admission €5.50; open 10am-1pm & 2pm-5pm Mon-Sat, 2pm-6pm Sun early Apr-Oct)*.

Bus No 7, 7A, or 8 or the DART rail service (€1.50, 20 minutes), will take you from Dublin to Dun Laoghaire.

The Southeast

WEXFORD & ROSSLARE HARBOUR

☎ 053 • pop 44,000

Little remains of Wexford's Viking past – apart from its narrow streets and name, Waesfjord, or 'Ford of Mud Flats'. Cromwell was in one of his most destructive moods when he included Wexford on his 1649–50 Irish tour, destroying the churches and 'putting to the sword' three-quarters of the town's 2000 inhabitants. These days, the town makes a convenient stopover for those travelling to France or Wales via the Rosslare Harbour ferry port, 21km southeast of Wexford.

The train and bus stations are at the northern end of town, on Redmond Place. Follow the River Slaney 700m south along the waterfront quays to reach the **tourist office** *(☎ 23111; The Crescent; open Mon-Sat)*. The curiously tight North Main and South Main Sts are a block inland and parallel to the quays. The main post office is between the quays and North Main St on Anne St. Internet access is available for €5 per hour at the **Westgate Computer Centre** *(☎ 46291; Westgate Yard, Westgate)*.

Of the six original town gates, only the 14th-century **West Gate** *(Slaney St)* survives. Nearby **Selskar Abbey** is in a ruinous state as a result of Cromwell's visit in 1649. The **Bullring** *(cnr Cornmarket & North Main St)* was the site of one of Cromwell's massacres.

Rosslare Harbour has frequent ferry services to France and Wales. There is no reason to linger, so catch the first bus or train to Wexford or beyond. The local **tourist office** *(☎ 33622)* is in Kilrane, 500m from Rosslare Port on the N25.

IRELAND

Places to Stay & Eat

The IHH **Kirwan House** *(☎ 21208; e kirwanhostel@eircom.net; 3 Mary St; dorm beds from €12, private rooms €32)* is a small and friendly hostel with Internet access. From the tourist office, go right at Henrietta St, then right at South Main St, take a quick left at Allen St, right at High St and left at Mary St.

The Blue Door *(☎ 21047; e bluedoor@indigo.ie; Georges St; doubles from €60)* is a clean, friendly, tastefully decorated B&B opposite White's Hotel. Rooms have en suites and TV. There's a row of better-quality B&B's in lovely period houses, near the station on Auburn Terrace, along Redmond Rd including **McMenamin's** *(☎ 46442; ⓔ mcmem@indigo.ie)* and **O'Brien's** *(☎ 23605; ⓔ mary@obriensauburnhouse.com)*. Both charge around €30 per person.

North and South Main Sts have something for most tastes, including a delicious range of picnic supplies at **Greenacres Food Hall** *(54 North Main St)*; and pub grub at **Tim's Tavern** *(51 South Main St)*. **Finegan's Bar** *(74 South Main St)* is a smartly furnished bar with some good outdoor seating and a decent snack menu.

Entertainment

Many of Wexford's pubs are strung along North and South Main Sts. Just around the corner is the small **Thomas Moore Tavern** *(Cornmarket)*, where the poet's mother was born. For music try **Wren's Nest** *(Customs House Quay)*, **Mooney's** *(12 Commercial Quay)*, **Tack Room** *(South Main St)* or tiny **Crown Bar** *(Monck St)*. **The Sky and the Ground**, on the far end of South Main Street, is one of the town's most popular bars.

Getting There & Away

O'Hanrahan train station *(☎ 22522; ⓦ www.irishrail.ie)*, on the Dublin-Rosslare line, is served by three trains daily in each direction; the three-hour trip to Dublin costs €14.60. There are also trains to Rosslare Harbour (€4.45, 30 minutes, three daily). **Bus Éireann** *(☎ 33114)* runs from the train station to Rosslare Harbour (€3.35, 25 minutes, every 45 minutes Monday to Saturday, 10 on Sunday), Dublin (€10.15, 2¼ hours, 10 daily Monday to Saturday, eight on Sunday) and beyond.

KILKENNY (CILL CHAINNIGH)

☎ 056 • pop 18,700

Kilkenny is perhaps the most attractive large town in the country. Even though Cromwell ransacked it, it retains some of its medieval ground plan. There's an excellent selection of eating, drinking and accommodation options and a vibrant arts and music scene. Overlooking a sweeping bend in the river, and nestling in expansive grounds, Kilkenny Castle is a must for visitors.

Most places of interest lie close to Parliament St and its continuation (High St), which runs parallel to the River Nore; or along Rose Inn St, which changes its name to John St and leads away from the river to the northeast. The **tourist office** *(☎ 51500; Shee Alms House, Rose Inn St; open Mon-Sat)* is a short walk from the castle. Internet access is plentiful; **Kilkenny E-centre** *(☎ 60093; 26 Rose St)* is central.

Things to See

Stronghold of the powerful Butler family, **Kilkenny Castle** *(☎ 21450; compulsory guided tour €4.40; open 10am-7pm daily summer, shorter hours rest of year)* has a history dating back to 1172, when the legendary Anglo-Norman Strongbow built a wooden tower on the site. The **Long Gallery**, with its vividly painted ceiling and extensive portrait collection of Butler family members over the centuries, is quite remarkable.

The approach on foot to **St Canice's Cathedral** *(admission €3)* from Parliament St leads over Irishtown Bridge and up **St Canice's Steps**, which date from 1614. Beside the cathedral is a round tower. Although the present cathedral dates from 1251, it has a much longer history and contains some remarkable tombs and monuments.

Places to Stay

The IHH **Kilkenny Tourist Hostel** *(☎ 63541; 35 Parliament St; open year-round; dorm beds from €12, twins €31)* is central and has helpful staff. **Rose Inn** *(☎ 70061; 9 Rose Inn; dorm beds €13, private rooms €20)*, just opposite the tourist office, is good value, central and throws in a light breakfast.

There are plenty of B&Bs, especially south of the city along Patrick St and north of the city on Castlecomer Rd. The central **Bregagh Guesthouse** *(☎ 22315; Dean St; rooms per person from €38)*, with comfortable en suite rooms, is near St Canice's Cathedral.

The Kilford Arms *(☎ 61018; ⓔ kilfordarms@indigo.ie; John St; rooms per person weekday/weekend €35/60)* offers good-quality large, new hotel rooms at B&B prices on weekdays.

Places to Eat

The Kilkenny Design Centre *(☎ 22118; Castle Yard; mains around €6)* is one of the best lunch spots in town. Opposite the castle, it offers cheap, home cooked food in appealing, spacious surroundings. It's closed evenings. **Key Largo** *(1-2 Canal Square; mains around €10)* offers reasonable Italian fare with a view of the river. **Dunn's Stores** *(St Kieran's St)* is Kilkenny's most convenient supermarket.

Entertainment

The best pub for traditional Irish music is **Maggie's** *(St Keiran St)*. Other traditional-music joints include **Ryan's** *(Friary St)* and **John Cleere's** *(Parliament St)*, which also has a theatre staging occasional comedy and more contemporary bands. **The Pumphouse** is popular with travellers and locals alike. **The Marble City Bar** *(66 High St)* is a tastefully modernised bar with a good atmosphere.

The **Watergate Theatre** *(☎ 61674; Parliament St)* is host to musical and theatrical productions throughout the year.

Getting There & Around

McDonagh train station *(☎ 22024; Dublin Rd)* is east of the town centre via John St. Four trains a day (five on Monday and Friday, three on Sunday) travel from Dublin's Heuston station to Kilkenny (€15.80) and then on to Waterford (€6.90).

Bus Éireann *(☎ 051-87 9000)* operates out of the train station. There are six buses a day (five on Sunday) to Dublin (€8.85), three to Cork (€13.95), up to six to Galway (€19.05) and one or two to Wexford, Waterford and Rosslare Harbour.

JJ Wall *(☎ 21236; 88 Maudlin St)* rents bikes for €15 a day (plus €40 deposit) from April to August.

AROUND KILKENNY

Cashel

☎ 062

The **Rock of Cashel** *(☎ 61437)* is one of Ireland's most striking archaeological sites. On the outskirts of town rises a huge lump of limestone bristling with ancient fortifications. Mighty stone walls encircle a complete round tower, a roofless abbey and the country's finest 12th-century **Romanesque chapel** *(admission €4.40; open 9am-3.45pm daily Oct–mid-Mar, 9am-4.45pm mid-Mar–June, 9am-6.45pm July-Sept)*.

Six buses on line 8 (Dublin to Cork) pass through Cashel daily.

The Southwest

CORK

☎ 021 • pop 180,000

Lively and friendly Cork (Corcaigh), the Republic's second-largest city, is increasingly rivalling Dublin as a place to party but lacking the capital's sometimes edgy feel. Cork prides itself on a great mix of pubs, cafés, restaurants, and love of the arts. The Cork International Jazz Festival and the International Film Festival both take place in October.

The Black and Tans were at their most brutal in Cork. The city was also a centre for the civil war that followed independence (leader Michael Collins was ambushed and killed near Macroom).

Orientation & Information

The city centre is an island between two channels of the River Lee. Oliver Plunkett St and the curve of St Patrick's St are the main shopping/eating/drinking areas. The train station and several hostels are north of the river; MacCurtain St and Glanmire Rd Lower are the main thoroughfares there.

The **tourist office** *(☎ 425 5100; Grand Parade; open Mon-Sat Sept-June, daily July & Aug)* is helpful. There is a **post office** *(Oliver Plunkett St)*. Internet access is available at the **Internet Exchange** *(☎ 425 4666; 5 Wood Street; open 10am-midnight daily)*.

Central Cork

Cork's notable churches include the fairytale riot of spires and buttresses of the 1879 Protestant **St Finbarr's Cathedral**, south of the centre. North of the river there's a fine view from the tower of the 18th-century **St Anne's Church, Shandon** *(☎ 450 5906; admission €5; open 10am-5pm Mon-Sat)*. Admission entitles you to climb the tower, ring the Shandon Bells and watch an audiovisual presentation about the Shandon area. The **Cork Public Museum** *(☎ 427 0679; admission Mon-Fri free, Sun afternoon €1.50)* should be worth a visit when it opens its new €1.8million extension.

Cork City Gaol *(☎ 430 5022; admission €5; open 9.30am-6pm daily Mar-Oct, shorter hours Nov-Feb)* received its first prisoners in 1824 and its last in 1923, including many prominent independence fighters. The impressive 35-minute taped tour around the restored cells is worthwhile.

The brick, glass and steel **Crawford Art Gallery** *(☎ 427 3377; admission free; open 10am-5pm Mon-Sat)* is an impressive example of cutting-edge architecture blending into an existing 18th-century building. The permanent collection has works by Irish artists like Jack Yeats and Seán Keating.

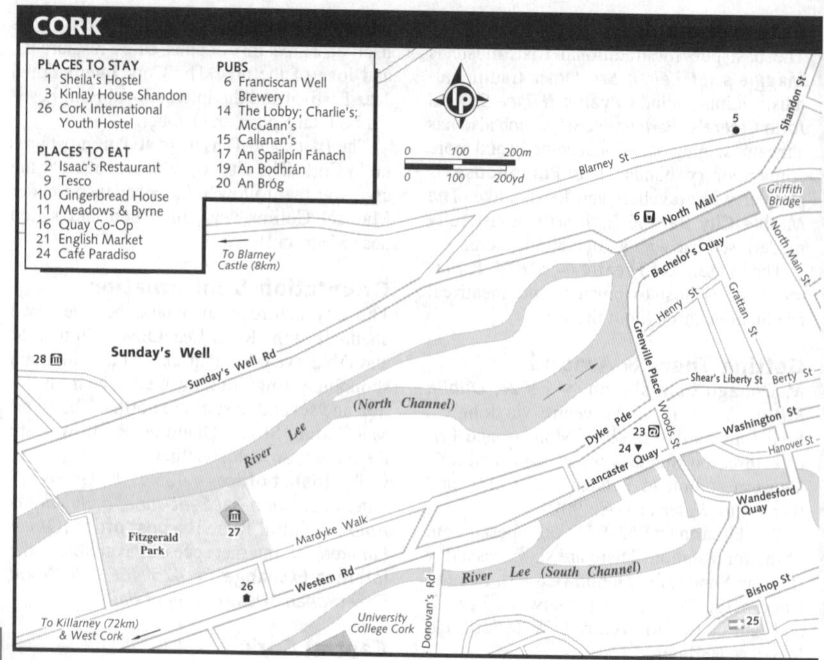

Places to Stay

Back from MacCurtain St, off Wellington Rd, is clean, friendly **Sheila's Hostel** *(☎ 450 5562; e info@sheilashostel.ie; 4 Belgrave Place; dorm beds from €12, doubles from €36)*. Facilities include foreign exchange, a café, laundry, bicycle hire and a sauna.

Behind St Anne's Church is the modern **Kinlay House Shandon** *(☎ 450 8966; Bob & Joan's Walk; dorm beds €11, doubles €40)*. Beds are in basic mixed dorms of up to 12 people. A light breakfast is included.

Out by the university, to the west of the centre, the An Óige **Cork International Youth Hostel** *(☎ 454 3289; 1-2 Western Rd; dorm beds weekday/weekend €15/17, twins €37)* has had an expensive makeover. Bus No 8 from the bus station stops outside the hostel.

Glanmire Rd Lower, a short distance east of the train station, is lined with economical B&Bs. **Kent House** *(☎ 450 4260; 47 Glanmire Rd Lower; singles/doubles from €28/52)* is clean and cheap, although the rooms are small.

Places to Eat

For self-catering, head for the well-stocked food stalls inside the **English Market**.

Between St Patrick's St and pedestrianised Paul St are several narrow lanes packed with restaurants. For coffees and light meals, try the popular **Gingerbread House** *(Carey's Lane)*, which also does cheap breakfasts. **Meadows & Byrne** *(French Church St)* is often full.

For vegetarians, **Café Paradiso** *(Lancaster Quay; open Tues-Sat)*, opposite Jury's Hotel, has friendly staff, good coffee and inventive dishes. The popular **Quay Co-Op** *(24 Sullivan's Quay; evening menus from €10; open Mon-Sat)* also caters for vegetarians.

Entertainment

In Cork, locally brewed Murphy's is the stout of choice. Entertainment goes further than pints though; *Cork's List*, a free fortnightly publication available from pubs, cafés and the like, lists it all.

On Union Quay **The Lobby**, **Charlie's** and **McGann's** are all side by side, and at least one of them has live music most nights.

An Bodhrán *(42 Oliver Plunkett St)* regularly features music, as does **An Bróg** *(78 Olive Plunkett St)*. More subdued is **An Spailpín Fánach** *(28 South Main St)*, with traditional music four nights a week. For a

IRELAND

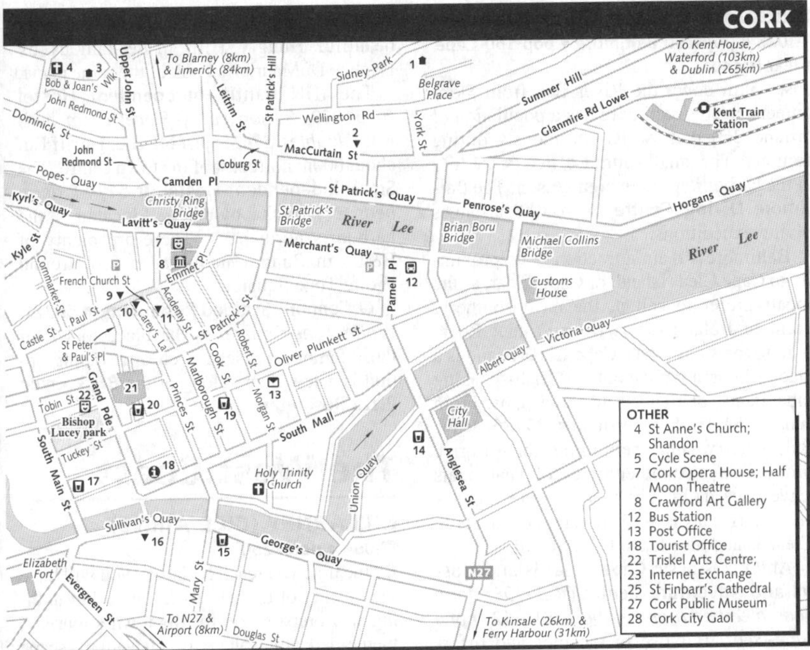

real Cork drinking experience visit tiny **Callanan's** *(George's Quay)*.

The splendid new **Franciscan Well Brewery** *(☎ 421 0130; 14B North Mall)* serves its own ales brewed in the gleaming copper vats behind the bar and a fine selection of guest ales, lagers and stouts.

Cork's cultural institutions include the **Cork Opera House** *(☎ 427 0022; Emmet Place)*, the **Half Moon Theatre** *(☎ 427 0022)* behind it, which hosts live bands and dance music, and the **Triskel Arts Centre** *(Tobin St)*, just off South Main St.

Getting There & Around

The **bus station** *(☎ 450 8188; cnr Merchants Quay & Parnell Place)* is east of the centre. You can get to almost anywhere in Ireland from Cork: Dublin (€17.10, 3½ hours, six daily), Killarney (€11.80, two hours, 11 daily), Wexford and more.

Kent train station *(☎ 450 6766; Glanmire Rd Lower)* is across the river. Trains go to Dublin (€44.40), Kilkenny (€30.40) and Galway (€40).

Cork's ferry terminal is at Ringaskiddy, about 15 minutes southeast of the city centre along the N28. Bus Éireann runs frequent daily services to the terminal (45 minutes).

You can hire a bike for €20 per day from **Cycle Scene** *(☎ 430 1183; 396 Blarney St)*.

AROUND CORK

Blarney (An Bhlarna)

Just northwest of Cork, Blarney is a village with one reason to visit: the tall, imposing walls of 15th-century **Blarney Castle** *(☎ 438 5252; admission €5.50; open 9am-6.30pm or 7pm Mon-Sat, 9.30am-5.30pm Sun)*. If you don't mind putting your lips where millions have also been, you can kiss the castle's legendary **Blarney Stone** on the high battlements. In winter the castle closes at sundown Monday to Saturday.

Buses run regularly from the Cork bus station (€2.50 return, 30 minutes).

WEST COUNTY CORK

Travelling west by public transport from Cork can be tough. There are at least two daily bus services (more in summer) connecting towns. The trick is to plan ahead at Cork, have the timetables committed to memory, and be prepared to change buses and backtrack.

Baltimore & Cape Clear Island

☎ 028 • pop 260 Baltimore • pop 150 Cape Clear Island

Just 13km down the River Ilen from Skibbereen, sleepy Baltimore has a population of around 260 that swells enormously during summer. The small **tourist office** *(☎ 21766)* at the harbour opens in high season. The **Baltimore Diving Centre** *(☎ 20300)* arranges diving expeditions.

Baltimore's main attraction is its proximity to Cape Clear Island, or Cape Clear, as the locals prefer to call it, the most southerly point of Ireland (apart from Fastnet Rock, 6km to the southwest). Cape Clear Island is a Gaeltacht area with about 150 Irish-speaking inhabitants, one shop and three pubs. From June to September, **ferries** *(☎ 39135)* leave Baltimore (weather permitting) three to five times a day. At other times of year boats leave once daily. The trip takes 45 minutes and return fare is €12. In summer, boats to Clear Island also leave from Schull.

An Óige's basic **Cape Clear Island Hostel and Adventure Centre** *(☎ 39198; dorm beds members/nonmembers €10/12; open June–Sept)* is close to the pier and offers kayaking, snorkelling and archery. Further up the road is the friendly **Ard Na Goithe B&B** *(☎ 39160; rooms per person €28)*.

Baltimore shelters the excellent IHH **Rolf's Hostel** *(☎ 20289; dorm beds from €12, doubles €44)*; follow the signs up a hill 700m east of town. Rolf's cheap, terrific café and restaurant is the place to eat in town.

IRELAND

Bantry & the Beara Peninsula

☎ 027 • pop 2940

Famed for its mussels and wedged between hills and the waters of Bantry Bay, Bantry is a good base for coastal explorations. Its **tourist office** *(☎ 50229; open Mar-Nov)* is on the east end of Wolfe Tone Square. Frequent buses to Cork (three daily), Killarney, Glengarriff and beyond stop just off the main square at Barry Murphy's pub.

From Bantry the N71 follows the coast northwest to Glengarriff, from where the R572 runs southwest to the Beara Peninsula, a wild, handsome, rocky landscape ideal for exploring by foot or bike. The Beara is far less on the tourist trail than the Ring of Kerry or the Dingle and is a great place to spend a few relaxing days. If you're driving or cycling don't miss the beautiful Healy Pass. Walkers might like to tackle the ruggedly beautiful Hungry Hill, made famous by Daphne DuMaurier's book of the same name.

The IHH **Bantry Independent Hostel** *(☎ 51050; Bishop Lucey Place; dorm beds €10, doubles €24)* is just off Glengarriff Rd, about 600m northeast of the town centre. The **Small Independent Hostel** *(☎ 51140; dorm beds €11)* is shabby but well located on the harbour's north bank. There are plenty of B&Bs in Bantry, including a few around Wolfe Tone Square.

O'Connor's Seafood Restaurant *(☎ 50221; Wolfe Tone Square)* is the place to go for those famous mussels. A cheaper dining option is a few doors along at the **Brick Oven Pizza Restaurant**.

The West Coast

KILLARNEY (CILL AIRNE)

☎ 064 • pop 7250

By the time you reach Killarney you will have seen plenty of touristy Irish towns, but nothing will prepare you for the town's touristy, theme-park atmosphere. If you want to escape the crush, head for the national park or three lakes nearby. Killarney is also convenient for touring the Ring of Kerry.

Killarney's **tourist office** *(☎ 31633; Beech Rd; open Mon-Sat Sept-May, daily June-Aug)* is busy. Send mail at the **main post office** *(New St)*. **Web Talk** *(High St; open daily)* and the newer **Ri-Ra** *(Plunkett St; open daily)* provide Internet access.

Things to See & Do

Most of Killarney's attractions are just outside the town. The 1855 **St Mary's Cathedral** *(Cathedral Place)* is worth a look.

The picture-perfect backdrop of mountains (well, big hills) beyond town are in fact part of the 10,236-hectare **Killarney National Park**. Within the park are beautiful Lough Leane, Muckross Lake and the Upper Lake. As well as ruins and ex-gentry housing, the park offers rewards exploring by foot, bicycle or boat. The *Killarney Area Guide* has some ideas.

In summer the **Gap of Dunloe**, a heather-clad valley at the foot of Purple Mountain (832m), is Killarney tourism at its worst. Consider hiring a bike and cycling to **Ross Castle**. From here take a boat across to **Lord Brandon's Cottage** and cycle down through the

Gap and back into town via the N72 and a path through the golf course. Including bicycle hire, this should cost you about €23. The 90-minute boat ride alone justifies the trip.

Places to Stay

Wherever you plan to stay, book ahead from June to August. Just off Park Rd and closest to the bus and train station is the modern and well-equipped **Killarney Railway Hostel** *(☎ 35299; ⓔ railwayhostel@eircom.net; dorm beds €12, doubles €36)*. Off New St, in the town centre, Bishop's Lane leads to **Neptune's Hostel** *(☎ 35255; dorm beds from €11, singles/doubles €32/34)*.

Small, friendly **Súgán** *(☎ 33104; Lewis Rd; dorm beds €12)* has a big kitchen, a cosy dining room, bikes for hire and a rack of guitars. There are only two toilets and an outdoor shower.

An Óige's large **Killarney International Hostel** *(☎ 31240; ⓔ anoige@killarney.iol.net; dorm beds €12, doubles €44)* is an excellent bet apart from its location about 4km west of town. It offers plenty of double rooms and pick-up from the train station.

In high season finding accommodation can be tricky, so it's worth paying the booking fee so the tourist office can do the work. Within easy walking distance of the town centre is **Ashville Guest House** *(☎ 36405; Rock Rd; doubles from €56)* and **Rathmore B&B** *(☎ 32829; Rock Rd; doubles from €56)*. The Muckross road is also lined with B&Bs.

Places to Eat

It's easy to eat badly or expensively in Killarney. The exceptions include **L'Artista** *(☎ 38744; Bohereen Cael; mains €8)*, tucked away from High St, with very reasonably priced pizza and pasta. **Busy Bee's Bistro** *(Old Market Lane)* is cheap and cheerful. Duck down Flemings Lane, off High St, to the appealing **Stonechat** *(Flemings Lane)*, which has a good choice of home-made soups, sandwiches and cakes and a courtyard if the weather is kind.

Entertainment

Killarney has plenty of music pubs, but much of what's played is tourist-oriented, like at **The Laurels** *(Main St)*. Pubs with more authentic music and often a better buzz include the **Danny Mann Inn** *(New St)* and **Courtney's**, just off High St. But the most popular is the **Killarney Grand** *(Main St)*, which has nights of poetry readings. **Kube** *(East Avenue Rd)*, beneath the Killarney Towers Hotel, is an ultra-modern bar/nightclub where dressed-up locals go to party.

Getting There & Around

Bus Éireann *(☎ 30011)* operates from outside the small train station (☎ 31067), with regular services to Cork (€11.90), Galway (via Limerick, €17.10), Dublin (€19) and Rosslare Harbour (€20.20). Travelling by train to Cork (€17.70) usually involves changing at Mallow, but there is a direct route to Dublin (€45) via Limerick Junction.

Killarney Rent A Bike *(☎ 32578)* beside the Laurel Pub rents bikes for €10.

THE RING OF KERRY

☎ 066

The Ring of Kerry, a 179km circuit around the Iveragh Peninsula, is one of Ireland's premier tourist attractions. Most travellers tackle the Ring by bus on a guided day trip from Killarney. However, the **Ballaghbeama Pass** cuts across the peninsula's central highlands and has spectacular views and remarkably little traffic. The shorter **Ring of Skellig**, at the end of the peninsula, has fine views of the Skellig Rocks and is less touristy. You can forgo roads completely by walking the **Kerry Way**, which winds through the Macgillycuddy's Reeks mountains past Carrantuohill (1038m), Ireland's highest mountain.

Things to See

Daniel O'Connell was born near **Cahirciveen**, one of the Ring's larger towns. The excellent **Barracks Heritage Centre** *(☎ 947 2777; admission €4; open Mar-Sept)*, off Bridge St, has exhibits on Daniel O'Connell and moving material on the local impact of the famine.

South of Cahirciveen, the R565 branches west to the 11km-long **Valentia Island**, a jumping-off point for one of Ireland's most unforgettable experiences: the **Skellig Rocks**, two tiny islands 12km off the coast. The vertiginous climb up uninhabited Skellig Michael inspires a mild terror and an awe that monks could have clung to life in the beehive-shaped stone huts that stand on the only flat strip of land on top. On a clear day the views from the summit are astounding.

Calm seas permitting, boats run from spring to late summer from Portmagee, just before the bridge to Valentia, to Skellig Michael. The standard fare is €32 return. Booking is essential; contact **Joe Roddy** *(☎ 947 4268)* or **Des Lavelle** *(☎ 947 6124)*.

The pretty pastel-coloured town of **Kenmare** is an excellent alternative base for exploring the Ring of Kerry. Kenmare is somewhat touristy, but it's nothing like Killarney.

Places to Stay

Book your next night as you make your way around the Ring. Ring of Kerry hostels typically charge €11 to €14 for dorm beds.

Cycling hostel-to-hostel around the Ring, there's the IHH **Laune Valley Farm** *(☎ 976 1488)*, 2km east of Killorglin; the IHO **Caitin Baiters Hostel** *(☎ 947 7614)* in Kells; the meagre IHH **Sive Hostel** *(☎ 947 2717)* in Cahirciveen; the IHO **Ring Lyne Hostel** *(☎ 947 6103)* in Chapeltown and large **Royal Pier Hostel** *(☎ 947 6144)* in Knightstown on Valentia Island; and the An Óige **Baile an Sceilg** *(☎ 947 9229)* in Ballinskelligs.

An Óige's **Black Valley Hostel** *(☎ 064-34712; open Mar-end Oct)* in the Macgillycuddy's Reeks mountains is a good starting point for walking the Kerry Way.

Getting There & Around

If you're not up to cycling, **Bus Éireann** *(☎ 064-30011)* operates a Ring of Kerry bus service daily from mid-May to mid-September. In June buses leave Killarney at 8.30am, 1.30pm and 3.45pm (Sunday at 9.40am and noon), stopping at Killorglin, Glenbeigh, Kells, Cahirciveen, Waterville, Caherdaniel and Sneem before returning to Killarney. (The 3.45pm service terminates at Waterville.)

Travel agents in Killarney, including **Destination Killarney Tours** *(☎ 064-32638; East Avenue Rd)*, offer daily tours of the Ring for about €20. Hostels in Killarney arrange tours for around €16.

THE DINGLE PENINSULA

☎ 066

The Dingle Peninsula is just as beautiful as, and far less crowded than, the Ring of Kerry, with narrow roads that discourage any bus traffic. The region's main hub, Dingle Town (An Daingean), is a workaday fishing village with a dozen good pubs. The western tip of the peninsula, noted for its extraordinary number of ring forts and high crosses, is predominantly Irish speaking.

From Tralee the N86 heads west along the coast. The 'quick' route to Dingle Town is southwest from Camp via Anascaul and the N86. The scenic route follows the R560 northwest and crosses the wildly scenic **Connor Pass** (456m). Heading west from Dingle Town, follow signs for the 'Slea Head Drive', a scenic coastal stretch of the R559. To the southwest, **Slea Head** offers some of the peninsula's best views.

The going rate for a dorm bed in and around Dingle is €12 to €15. In Dingle Town, the inviting **Grapevine Hostel** *(☎ 915 1434; Dykegate St)* has beds in dorms and four-bed rooms. For a more rural setting try the popular **Rainbow Hostel** *(☎ 915 1044)*, 1km west of town (call for free pick-up from the bus stop); camping is also available. East along the Tralee road, the IHH **Ballintaggart Hostel** *(☎ 915 1454)*, in a spacious 19th-century house, has a free shuttle service to/from town, plus bicycle hire.

Hostels east of Dingle include the IHH **Fuchsia Lodge** *(☎ 915 7150; open year-round)* in Anascaul; and the IHH **Connor Pass Hostel** *(☎ 713 9179; open mid-Mar–Nov)* in Stradbally.

West of Dingle, look for An Óige's **Dunquin Hostel** *(☎ 915 6121; open year-round)* near the Blasket ferry, the pleasant **Ballybeag Hostel** *(☎ 915 9876; ⓔ balybeag@iol.ie)* in Ventry and the IHO **Black Cat Hostel** *(☎ 915 6286; open year-round)* in Ballyferriter.

Buses stop outside the car park at the back of the Super Valu store in Dingle Town. Buses for Dingle Town leave Tralee four times daily from Monday to Saturday. Two buses daily depart from Killarney for Dingle in the summer. Note that there are few services on Sunday.

There are several bike-rental places in Dingle. **Paddy Walsh** *(☎ 915 2311; Dykegate St)*, near Grapevine Hostel, hires bikes for €7.

THE BURREN

County Clare's greatest attraction is the haunting Burren, a harsh and bleakly beautiful area. The word *boireann* is Irish for 'Rocky Country', and the name is no exaggeration. One of Cromwell's generals concluded that in the Burren there was 'neither water enough to drown a man, nor a tree to hang him, nor soil enough to bury him'.

The Burren is an area of major interest, with many ancient dolmens, ring forts, round towers and high crosses. There's also some stunning scenery, a good collection of hostels and some of Ireland's best music pubs.

From Galway both **Lally Coaches** *(☎ 091-56 2905)* and **O'Neachtain Tours** *(☎ 091-55 3188)* arrange guided bus tours to the Burren and Cliffs of Moher for €25, leaving the Galway tourist office at 10am daily and returning by 5.30pm. **Rambler Guided Walks** *(☎ 091-58 2525)* explores the Burren by bus and foot.

Doolin

☎ 065

Tiny Doolin, famed for its quality music pubs, is a convenient base for exploring the Burren and the awesome Cliffs of Moher. It's also a gateway for boats to Inisheer, easternmost and smallest of the Aran Islands. In summer it can be difficult to get a bed, so book ahead. Some of the hostels and **Doolin Bike Rental** rent bicycles for around €8 a day plus deposit.

Doolin's hostels charge around €11 for dorm beds. **Paddy Moloney's Doolin Hostel** *(☎ 707 4006; doubles €33)*, a large and noisy but basic IHH hostel in the lower village, has two doubles. The upper village has three IHH hostels: 16-bed **Rainbow Hostel** *(☎ 707 4415; ⓔ rainbowhostel@eircom.net)*, which also has some cheap B&B rooms; 30-bed **Aille River Hostel** *(☎ 707 4260)*, the nicest of the bunch; and 24-bed **Flanagan's Village Hostel** *(☎ 707 4564)*. There are plenty of B&Bs, including the excellent, modern, spacious **Doolin Activity Lodge** *(☎ 707 4888; ⓔ info@doolinlodge.com)*. Doolin's three pubs serve basic, cheap pub food.

There are direct buses to Doolin from Limerick, Ennis, Galway and even Dublin; the main Bus Éireann stop is across from Paddy Moloney's Doolin Hostel. See the Aran Islands section later in this chapter for details of ferries to and from the islands.

Cliffs of Moher

Eight kilometres south of Doolin are the towering Cliffs of Moher, one of Ireland's most famous natural features. In summer the cliffs are overrun by day-trippers, so consider staying in Doolin and hiking along the Burren's quiet country lanes, where the views are just as good and crowds are never a problem. Either way, be careful walking along these sheer cliffs, especially in wet or windy weather.

Near the **Cliffs of Moher visitor centre** *(☎ 065-708 1171; open daily)* is **O'Brien's Tower**. Apparently, local landlord Cornelius O'Brien (1801–57) raised it to impress 'lady visitors'. From here walk south or north and the crowds soon disappear.

GALWAY (GAILLIMH)

☎ 091 • pop 57,000

Galway is a pleasure, with its narrow streets, fast-flowing river, ramshackle shop-fronts, and good restaurants and pubs. On weekends people come from as far as Dublin for the nightlife, and during the city's festivals the streets are bursting. Galway is also a departure point for the rugged Aran Islands.

Galway's tightly packed town centre is spread evenly on both sides of the River Corrib. The bus and train stations are within a stone's throw of Eyre Square. The **tourist office** *(☎ 56 7700; Forster St; open Mon-Sat Oct-Easter, daily Easter-Sept)* is a short way off Eyre Square. Send mail at the **main post office** *(Eglington St)* and access the Net at **Celtel e-centre**, near the entrance to Kinlay House.

Things to See

A copy of the *Galway Guide*, available from the tourist office, points out many curiosities. Eyre Square is the uninspired focal point of the centre's eastern part. In the square is **Kennedy Park**, honouring a visit by John F Kennedy in 1963. To the north of the square is a controversial statue to the Galway-born writer and hell-raiser Pádraic O'Conaire (1883–1928). Southwest of the square, **St Nicholas Collegiate Church** *(Shop St)* dates from 1320 and has several interesting tombs.

Also on Shop St, parts of **Lynch Castle**, now a bank, date back to the 14th century. Lynch, so the story goes, was a mayor of Galway in the 15th century who, when his son was condemned for murder personally acted as hangman. The stone facade that is the **Lynch Memorial Window** *(Market St)* marks the spot of the sorrowful deed.

Across the road, in the Bowling Green area, is the **Nora Barnacle House Museum** *(☎ 56 4743; admission €2; open Mon-Sat June-Aug)*, the former home of the wife and life-long muse of James Joyce.

Little remains of Galway's old city walls: only the **Spanish Arch**, by the river mouth.

Special Events

The Galway Arts Festival (ⓦ www.galwayartsfestival.com) in July is a huge event.

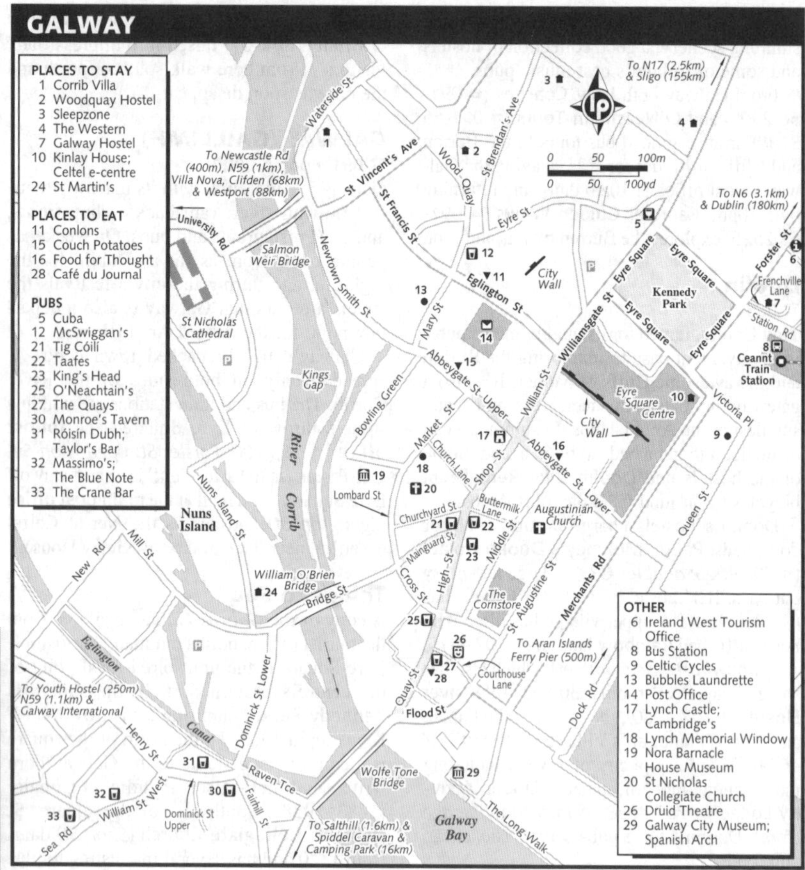

Places to Stay

There are plenty of hostels in and around Galway. All are open year-round except for the An Óige hostel. It's wise to book your hostel during summer, festivals and on weekends.

Sleepzone *(☎ 56 6999; ⓔ info@sleepzone.ie; Bóthar na mBán, Wood Quay; dorm beds from €18, singles/doubles from €50/56)* is Galway's newest and by far best hostel. The facilities are excellent, including laundry, secure parking, Internet access and safety deposit boxes. A light breakfast is included. The 50-bed **Galway Hostel** *(☎ 56 6959; Frenchville Lane; dorm beds €15, doubles €25)* is a cheerful place. Prices include a light breakfast.

The IHH **Kinlay House** *(☎ 56 5244; dorm beds from €14.50, singles/doubles from €38/43)*, a little off Eyre Square, is well equipped and offers a light breakfast. Near the Salmon Weir Bridge, **Corrib Villa** *(☎ 56 2892; 4 Waterside St; dorm beds €15)* is in a three-storey townhouse with good kitchen facilities and powershowers but cramped dorms. The independent **Woodquay Hostel** *(☎ 56 2618; 23-24 Wood Quay; dorm beds €15)* has a decent kitchen and eating area, but cramped washrooms and rickety bunks.

Continue northwest from Upper Dominick St along Henry and St Helen Sts, then turn left onto St Mary's Rd to reach An Óige's 200-bed **Galway International Youth Hostel** *(☎ 52 7411; open late June-Aug; dorm beds €12.70)*. It's on the St Mary's College campus; ring before you make the journey out there. Bus 1 leaves for the college from Eyre Square.

Expect to pay €30 to €40 per person for B&B accommodation. It's worth trying the small but popular **St Martin's** *(☎ 56 8286; 2 Nuns Island St; singles/doubles €35/64)*, which is situated right on the Corrib. **The Western** *(☎ 56 2834; e info@thewestern.ie; 33 Prospect Hill; singles/doubles €40/70)* with off-street parking just off Eyre Square is another reasonable option.

Places to Eat

Among old books and library lighting, **Café du Journal** *(Quay St)* serves light but filling meals and good espresso. Across the road, **Couch Potatoes** has big spuds stuffed with all manner of fillings for about €6.

Food for Thought *(Lower Abbeygate St)* is a budget wholefood restaurant that also serves veggie options, chicken and fish. Nobody does fish and chips (from €7) better than **Conlons** *(Eglington St)*.

Entertainment

The free weekly *Galway Edge* has listings of what's on in and around Galway. Pick up a copy at hostels, cafés and pubs.

Galway has dozens of good pubs, among them **O'Neachtain's** *(17 Upper Cross St)*, which is over 100 years old. **King's Head** *(High St)* has music most nights in summer. Almost next door, the enormously popular and much-recommended **Taafes** is a music and sports bar. Just across the way, **Tigh Cóilí** *(Mainguard St)* is a small, snug pub with music year-round.

McSwiggan's *(Daly's Place; meals from €12)* is big, always busy, and has good meals. **The Quays** *(Quay St)* draws a crowd on weekends and in summer and has an eclectic mix of music.

Across the river the spot for traditional music is **Monroe's Tavern** *(cnr Dominick St Upper & Fairhill St)*. Nearby **Róisín Dubh** is good for alternative music and often has international acts. **Taylor's Bar** next door and, around the corner, **The Crane Bar** *(Sea Rd)*, have music in summer. **Massimo** *(William St West)* and **The Blue Note** *(William St West)* both favour dance music with DJs.

The small **Druid Theatre** *(☎ 56 8617; Chapel Lane)* usually puts on two or three, often experimental, productions per year. **Cuba** at the northwestern edge of Eyre Square is a large bar, nightclub, live music and comedy venue.

Getting There & Around

The **bus station** *(☎ 56 2000)* is behind the Great Southern Hotel, off Eyre Square, next to the **Ceannt train station** *(☎ 56 4222)*. Bus Éireann has services to Doolin (€10.70), Dublin (€11.40), Killarney (€17.10), Limerick, Sligo and beyond. The Dublin services operate up to eight times daily.

Private bus companies, generally cheaper than Bus Éireann, operate from Galway. **Bus Nestor** *(☎ 1800 42 4248)* runs five buses a day (seven on Friday) to Dublin's Tara St (€10) DART station via Dublin airport (€15). **Citylink Express** *(☎ 56 4163)* has similar deals.

From Galway there are four or more trains to and from Dublin (one way €20.90 Monday to Thursday, €29.20 Friday to Sunday, 2¾ hours). Connections with other train routes can be made at Athlone.

Celtic Cycles *(☎ 56 6606; Queen St)* rents bicycles for €13/64 per day/week.

ARAN ISLANDS

☎ 099

In recent years the windswept, starkly beautiful Aran Islands have become one of western Ireland's major attractions. Apart from natural beauty, the islands have some of the country's oldest Christian and pre-Christian ruins.

On the islands the Irish passion for stone walls is almost absurd, with countless kilometres of stone separating even the tiniest patches of rocky land. There are three main islands in the group, all inhabited by Irish-speaking people year-round. Most visitors head for the long and narrow Inishmór (or Inishmore). Inishmaan and Inisheer are much smaller and receive far fewer visitors.

The islands get crowded at holiday times (St Patrick's Day, Easter) and in July and August, when accommodation is at a premium and advance reservations are advised.

The **tourist office** *(☎ 61263)* operates year-round on the waterfront at Kilronan, the arrival point and major village of Inishmór. You can change money there and at some of the local shops. A couple of hundred metres to the north is a small post office and a Wednesday-only branch of the Bank of Ireland (no ATMs). There's Internet access at the **Ionad Árann** heritage centre.

Inishmór

The 'Big Island' has four impressive stone forts of uncertain age, though 2000 years is a good guess. Halfway down the island, about 8km west of Kilronan, semicircular **Dún Aengus** *(☎ 61008; admission €1.25; open 10am-6pm summer, 10am-4pm rest of year)*, perched terrifyingly on the edge of the sheer southern cliffs, is the best known of the four. If you see only one sight on Inishmór, let it be Dún Aengus.

About 1.5km north is **Dún Eoghanachta**, while halfway back to Kilronan is **Dún Eochla**; both are smaller but perfectly circular ring forts. Directly south of Kilronan and dramatically perched on a promontory is another fort, **Dún Dúchathair**.

Hostels charge €10 to €15 for dorm beds and most open year-round. In Kilronan, the modern, justly popular **Kilronan Hostel** *(Tí Joe Mac's Hostel; ☎ 61255)* is near the pier. **St Kevin's Hostel** *(open summer)* is a bit rundown; ask at **Dormer House B&B** *(☎ 61125)* opposite. Just out of town is **The Artist's Hostel Lodge** *(☎ 61457)*. A few kilometres northwest of Kilronan, the IHO **Mainistir House Hostel** *(☎ 61169, 61322)* needs redecorating but does excellent breakfasts and has transport that meets the ferry.

The many B&Bs in and around Kilronan include the large **Dormer House** *(☎ 61125; rooms per person from €20; open year-round)*, behind Tí Joe Mac's. **Tí Eithne** *(☎ 61303)* charges €19 per person sharing or €25 for a single.

Eating options are not great. **Mainistir House Hostel** has a great-value evening 'almost veggie' buffet (booking essential). **The Bayview Guesthouse** has a café.

Inishmaan & Inisheer

The least visited of the three islands is Inishmaan (Inis Meáin, or 'Middle Island'). High stone walls border its fields, and it's a delight to wander along the lanes. The main archaeological site is **Dún Chonchúir**, a massive oval-shaped stone fort built on a high point.

The smallest island, only 8km off the coast from Doolin, is Inisheer (Inis Oírr, or 'Eastern Island'). The 15th-century **O'Brien Castle** (Caislea'n Uí Bhriain) overlooks the beach and harbour.

Getting There & Away

Inishmór is served year-round two or three times daily by **Island Ferries** *(Galway ☎ 091-56 8903)*, charging €19/15 return per adult/student (40 minutes). Unfortunately the boat leaves from Rossaveal, 37km west of Galway. It's an extra €4 to catch an Island Ferries bus from outside the tourist office in Galway. Ferry tickets cost €15 from the Galway tourist office. Buses are scheduled to meet arriving ferries. If you have a car you can go straight to Rossaveal. **Inishmor Ferries** *(☎ 091 56 6535)* runs similar services from Rossaveal.

Between June and September, **O'Brien's Shipping** *(☎ 091-567676)* sails daily direct to the islands from Galway's docks (€15.10 return). The 46km sea crossing takes 1½ hours, which can be a bit hard on sensitive stomachs.

Another option is to leave from Doolin in County Clare. **Doolin Ferries** *(Doolin ☎ 065-7074455; W www.doolinferries.com)* operates some ferry services from mid-April to September and runs to all three islands at least once daily from mid-May to the end of August. Be aware that the ferry does not always call at Inishmaan or Inisheer if it has a full load of passengers for Inishmór.

Inter-island services are extremely limited in winter.

CONNEMARA

☎ 095

The northwest corner of County Galway is the wild and barren region known as Connemara. It's a stunning patchwork of bogs, lonely valleys, pale-grey mountains and shimmering small lakes. Connemara's isolation has allowed Irish to thrive, and the language is widely spoken here.

By car or bicycle the most scenic routes through Connemara are Oughterard-Recess (via the N59), Recess-Kylemore Abbey (via the R344) and Leenane-Louisburgh (via the R335). From Galway, **Lally Coaches** *(☎ 091-56 2905)* and **O'Neachtain Tours** *(☎ 091-55 3188)*, and from Clifden **Michael Nee Coaches** *(☎ 095-51082)*, arrange day-tours of Connemara for around €25.

Things to See

Aughanure Castle *(☎ 55 2214; admission €2.50; open daily mid-June–mid-Sept)*, 3km east of Oughterard, is a 16th-century tower house on a rocky outcrop over Lough Corrib.

Just west of **Recess** (Straith Salach) on the N59, the turn north at the R334 takes you through the stunning Lough Inagh Valley. At the end of the R334 is the equally scenic **Kylemore Abbey** *(☎ 41146; admission €5; some sections open daily year-round)* and its adjacent lake. The neo-Gothic 19th-century abbey is run by nuns.

From Kylemore you can take the N59 east to Leenane (An Líonán), then detour north on the R335 to Louisburgh and onwards to Westport, or you can travel southwest along the N59 to **Clifden** (An Clochán), Connemara's largest town. Clifden is quiet, pleasant and has a few good pubs and restaurants. The **Clifden Walking Centre** *(☎ 21379; Island House, Market St)* runs guided walking trips for around €20.

Places to Stay

Oughterard has numerous B&Bs and a good hostel. **Canrawer House Hostel** *(☎ 552388; dorm beds from €11)* is a very good, attractive place at the Clifden end of town, just over 1km down a signposted turning. It has bike hire. In town, the **Jolly Lodger** *(☎ 552682; B&B per person from €22)* offers cheap B&B.

An Óige's excellent **Ben Lettery Hostel** *(☎ 51136; dorm beds €12; open Easter-Sept)* is on the N59 between Recess and Clifden.

In Clifden, the IHH **Clifden Town Hostel** *(☎ 21076; Market St; dorm beds €12, doubles €32)* is in the town centre. The IHH/IHO **Brookside Hostel** *(☎ 21812; Hulk St; dorm beds €11.50, doubles €30; open Jan-end Oct)* is down by the Owen Glin River. **The Arch B&B** *(☎ 22241; B&B per person €25)* is opposite the Clifden Town Hostel.

Getting There & Away

Buses link Clifden with Galway via Oughterard and Maam Cross, or via Cong and Leenane. In summer there are three express buses a day to/from Galway.

The Northwest

County Sligo and County Donegal comprise Ireland's rural northwestern corner. The coastal scenery is unparalleled, yet its distance from Dublin (and lack of convenient rail links) keeps crowds to a minimum. Tourism in the northwest, especially County Donegal, is extremely seasonal, and many attractions and tourist offices close from October to March.

SLIGO (SLIGHEACH)

☎ 071 • pop 18,000

William Butler Yeats (1865–1939) was educated in Dublin and London, but his poetry is muddied with the county of his mother's family. He returned to Sligo many times, and there are plentiful reminders in this sleepy town and the rolling green hills around it.

The **tourist office** *(☎ 61201; Temple St; open Mon-Fri Sept-June, daily July & Aug)* is just south of the centre. The **main post office** *(Wine St)* is east of the train and bus station. **Cygo Internet Café** *(19 O'Connell St)* has Internet access.

Sligo's two major attractions are outside town. **Carrowmore**, 5km to the southwest, is the site of a **megalithic cemetery** *(☎ 61534; admission €1.90; open Easter-end Oct)* with over 60 stone rings, passage tombs and other Stone Age remains. It's the largest Stone Age necropolis in Europe.

If it's a fine day, don't miss the hill-top cairn-grave **Knocknarea**, a few kilometres northwest of Carrowmore. About 1000 years younger than Carrowmore, the huge cairn is said to be the grave of the legendary Maeve, 1st-century AD Queen of Connaught.

The IHH **White House Hostel** *(☎ 45160; Markievicz Rd; dorm beds €10)* is just north of the town centre. About 1km northeast of the centre is the comfortable **Harbour House** *(☎ 71547; ⓔ harbourhouse@eircom.ie; Finisklin Rd; dorm beds €15, twins €36)*. The facilities include bicycle hire, family rooms and a laundry. **The Railway Hotel** *(☎ 44530; 1 Union Place; dorm beds €10, doubles €26)* is a small, recently refurbished place with free tea and coffee.

Sligo's less-expensive B&Bs are on the various approaches to town. **Renate House** *(☎ 62014; Upper John St; singles/doubles from €33/48)*, in the centre, is a small B&B.

Bus Éireann *(☎ 60066)* has four services a day to/from Dublin (€12.20, four hours). There's also a Galway-Sligo-Donegal-Derry service at least three times daily. Buses operate from below the **train station** *(☎ 69888)*, which is just west of the centre along Lord Edward St. Trains leave four times a day for Dublin via Boyle, Carrick-on-Shannon and Mullingar.

Hire a bike from **Gary's Cycles** *(☎ 45418; Lower Quay St)*.

DONEGAL & AROUND

☎ 073 • pop 3000

Donegal Town (Dún na nGall) is not the major centre in County Donegal, but it's a pleasant and laid-back place and well worth a visit. The triangular Diamond is the centre of

Donegal; a few steps south along the River Eske is the **tourist office** *(☎ 21148; open Mon-Fri June-Sept)*. **Donegal Castle** *(admission €3.80; open daily Mar-Oct)*, on a rocky outcrop over the River Eske, stands in ruins but is impressive all the same.

The awe-inspiring cliffs at **Slieve League**, dropping 300m into the Atlantic Ocean, are a recommended side trip from Donegal. To drive to the cliff edge, take the Killybegs-Glencolumbcille road (R263) and, at Carrick, take the turn-off signposted 'Bunglas'. Continue beyond the track signposted for Slieve League (this trail is good for hikers) to the signpost for Bunglas. Starting from Teelin, experienced walkers can spend a day walking via Bunglas and the somewhat terrifying One Man's Path to Malinbeg, near Glencolumbcille. **McGeehan's Coaches** *(☎ 075-46150)* serves Carrick and Kilcar once daily (more frequently in summer) on its Dublin-Donegal-Glencolumbcille route. Otherwise, there are daily Bus Éireann coaches from Donegal to Killybegs, with buses to Kilcar and Carrick.

The comfortable IHH/IHO **Donegal Town Independent Hostel** *(☎ 22805; tent sites per person €5, dorm beds €10.50, rooms per person €12; open year-round)* is 1km northwest of town on the Killybegs road (N56).

The **Blueberry Tearoom** *(meals from €8)* is busy and often smoky, but has good meals. The **Atlantic Restaurant** *(Main St; meals from €7)* and **Errigal Restaurant** *(meals from €7)*, further east, are inexpensive.

From Donegal there are **Bus Éireann** *(☎ 21101)* connections to Derry, Enniskillen and Belfast to the north; Sligo and Galway to the west; and Limerick and Cork. The bus stop is on the Diamond, outside Abbey Hotel. **McGeehan's Coaches** *(☎ 075-46150)* does a Donegal-Dublin return trip three times a day (more in summer) departing from the police station opposite the tourist office.

Northern Ireland

☎ 028

More than a quarter-century of internal strife has seriously affected tourism in Northern Ireland, although wanton violence was never a serious threat to visitors. In 1995, following the declaration of the first IRA cease-fire, the numbers of visitors from abroad jumped dramatically.

Northern Ireland has plenty going for it: the Causeway Coast road, the Glens of Antrim, the old walls of Derry, cosmopolitan Belfast. But even with the coming of peace and the end of military roadblocks, the signs of the Troubles can't be ignored; street murals in Belfast and Derry, shuttered shopfronts, fortified police-stations and sporadic unrest are still as much a part of Northern Ireland as green fields and smoke-filled pubs.

BELFAST (BÉAL FEIRSTE)

pop 279,240

There's been a real buzz about Belfast in recent years as it tentatively recovers from 30 years of sectarian violence and the dwindling of its once mighty industrial base. Today there's little sign of the daily tension once engendered by bomb threats and army checkpoints. Belfast has so far reaped the dividend of the peace process, and massive inward investment has seen the creation of new entertainment venues and upmarket hotels.

Belfast has not shaken its past altogether, however. You'll still see armoured vans patrolling, hear the buzz of surveillance helicopters overhead, and notice the ubiquitous murals and propaganda in certain areas. Sporadic rioting (far from the city centre) and sectarian gangsterism still form a dark, and largely unseen, backdrop to the growing prosperity and optimism here. But Belfast is safer crimewise than other European cities. Dive in and let the locals teach you how to party.

Orientation & Information

The city centre is a compact area with the imposing City Hall as the central landmark. To the south lies the Golden Mile, a restaurant and pub-filled stretch of Dublin Rd, Shaftesbury Square, Bradbury Place and Botanic Ave.

The **Belfast Welcome Centre** *(☎ 9024 6609, fax 9031 2424; W www.gotobelfast.com; 47 Donegall Place)* is efficient and extremely helpful. **Bord Fáilte** *(☎ 9032 7888; 53 Castle St)* has information about the Irish Republic. **Hostelling International Northern Ireland** *(HINI; ☎ 9032 4733; 22-32 Donegall Rd)* has its offices at the Belfast International Youth Hostel.

Send mail at the **main post office** *(Castle Place)* or the **smaller branch** at the top end of Botanic Avenue by Shaftesbury Square. **Bronco's Web Café** *(122 Great Victoria St)* has Internet access.

Around the City

At the northeastern corner of **City Hall** (1906) is a statue of Sir Edward Harland, the Yorkshire-born engineer who founded Belfast's Harland & Wolff shipyards. His famous yellow twin cranes **Samson and Goliath** tower above the city. The yard's most famous construction was the ill-fated *Titanic*, the 'unsinkable' boat that sank in 1912.

The famed **Crown Liquor Saloon** *(Great Victoria St)* was built by Patrick Flanagan in 1885 and displays Victorian architecture at its most extravagant. The Crown was lucky to survive a 1993 bomb that devastated the (now fully restored) **Grand Opera House** nearby.

Ulster Museum *(☎ 9038 3000; admission free; open 10am-5pm Mon-Fri, 1pm-5pm Sat, 2pm-5pm Sun)* in the **Botanic Gardens** near the university has excellent exhibits on Irish art, wildlife, dinosaurs, steam and industrial machines, and more. The gardens themselves are well worth a wander.

Falls & Shankill Roads

The Catholic Falls Rd and the Protestant Shankill Rd have been battlefronts since the 1970s. Even so, these areas are quite safe and worth venturing into, if only to see the large **murals** expressing the local political and religious passions.

The best way to visit the sectarian zones of the Falls and Shankill Rds is by what is known locally as the 'people taxi'. These former black London cabs run a bus-like service up and down their respective roads from terminuses in the city. Shankill Rd taxis go from North St, Falls Rd taxis from Castle St. They typically charge around £8 per person for a one-hour tour that takes in the main points of interest. The Belfast Welcome Centre has leaflets.

Ulster Folk & Transport Museum

Belfast's biggest tourist attraction is also one of Northern Ireland's best museums *(☎ 9042 8428; joint admission £5; open daily)*, 11km northeast of the centre beside the Bangor road (A2) near Holywood. The 30 buildings on this 60-hectare site range from city terrace-homes to thatched farm-cottages. A bridge crosses the A2 to the Transport Museum, which contains various Ulster-related vehicles. From Belfast take Ulsterbus No 1 or any Bangor-bound train that also stops at Cultra station.

Special Events

For three weeks in late October and early November Belfast hosts the UK's second largest arts festival at the **Festival at Queen's** *(☎ 9066 7687)*, in and around Queen's University. Also worth checking out is the **Cathedral Quarter Arts Festival** *(W www.cqaf.com)* in early May, which has been attracting a good range of writers, comedians, musicians and artists and theatre productions. The **Summerfest** *(☎ 9032 0202)*, also in May, offers classical music, community events and the Lord Mayor's Show.

Places to Stay

Hostels Friendly, if scruffy, **Arnie's Backpackers** *(☎ 9024 2867; 63 Fitzwilliam St; dorm beds £7-8.50)* has small dorms, laundry and cooking facilities, but with only 22 beds, demand for space far exceeds supply.

The HINI **Belfast International Youth Hostel** *(☎ 9031 5435; 22-32 Donegall Rd; dorm beds up to £9, singles/twins £16/24)* is large, modern and very clean. There's a small café, laundry and kitchen.

The Ark *(☎ 9032 9626; 18 University St; dorm beds £8.50-9.50, twins per person £16)* has 31 squeaky beds. At the other (north) end of the central city area is **The Linen House Hostel** *(☎ 9058 6400; 18-20 Kent St; dorm beds £6.50-8.50, singles/doubles £15/24)*. It's well past its prime and probably popular owing only to its location near the city centre and the increasingly cool Cathedral Quarter.

Queen's Elms *(☎ 9038 1608; 78 Malone Rd; rooms UK/international students £8.50/10, nonstudents £12.40, twins £44.40; open June-Sept)*, run by the university, offers excellent accommodation. There are cooking and laundry facilities.

B&Bs & Hotels The **Belfast Welcome Centre** *(☎ 9024 6609)* makes B&B reservations for a minimal fee. Many B&Bs are in the university area, which is close to the centre, safe and well-stocked with restaurants and pubs. Botanic Ave, Malone Rd, Wellington Park and Eglantine Ave are good hunting grounds.

Clean, friendly **Queen's House** *(☎ 9028 2091; e queenshouse127@hotmail.com; 127 University St; singles/doubles £20/40)*, opposite Holiday Inn Express, is good value, with a weekly rate of £100 per person. Rooms at the **Botanic Lodge Guesthouse** *(☎ 9032 7682; 87 Botanic Ave; singles/doubles £25/40)* have

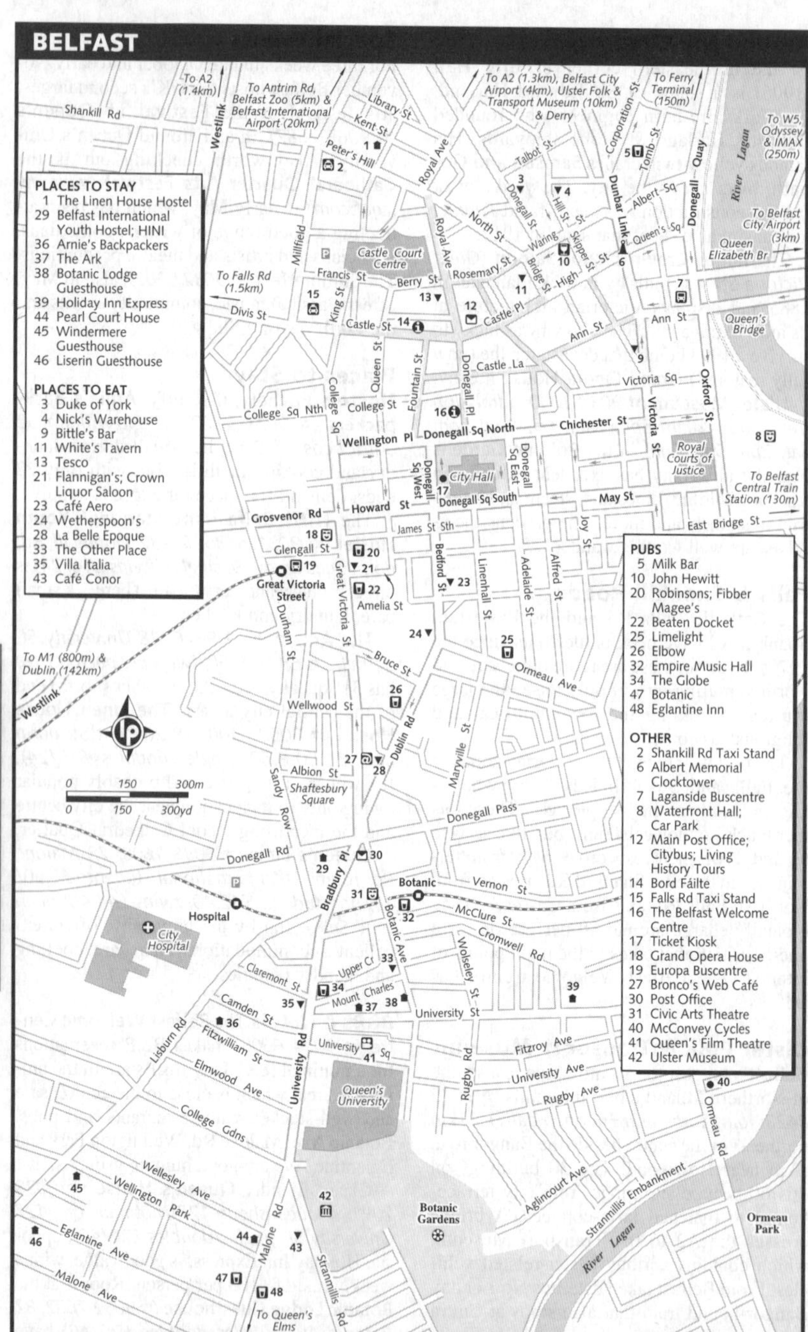
BELFAST
PLACES TO STAY
1 The Linen House Hostel
29 Belfast International Youth Hostel; HINI
36 Arnie's Backpackers
37 The Ark
38 Botanic Lodge Guesthouse
39 Holiday Inn Express
44 Pearl Court House
45 Windermere Guesthouse
46 Liserin Guesthouse
PLACES TO EAT
3 Duke of York
4 Nick's Warehouse
9 Bittle's Bar
11 White's Tavern
13 Tesco
21 Flannigan's; Crown Liquor Saloon
23 Café Aero
24 Wetherspoon's
28 La Belle Epoque
33 The Other Place
35 Villa Italia
43 Café Conor
PUBS
5 Milk Bar
10 John Hewitt
20 Robinsons; Fibber Magee's
22 Beaten Docket
25 Limelight
26 Elbow
32 Empire Music Hall
34 The Globe
47 Botanic
48 Eglantine Inn
OTHER
2 Shankill Rd Taxi Stand
6 Albert Memorial Clocktower
7 Laganside Buscentre
8 Waterfront Hall; Car Park
12 Main Post Office; Citybus; Living History Tours
14 Bord Fáilte
15 Falls Rd Taxi Stand
16 The Belfast Welcome Centre
17 Ticket Kiosk
18 Grand Opera House
19 Europa Buscentre
27 Bronco's Web Café
30 Post Office
31 Civic Arts Theatre
40 McConvey Cycles
41 Queen's Film Theatre
42 Ulster Museum
To A2 (1.4km)
To Antrim Rd, Belfast Zoo (5km) & Belfast International Airport (20km)
To A2 (1.3km), Belfast City Airport (4km), Ulster Folk & Transport Museum (10km) & Derry
To Ferry Terminal (150m)
To W5, Odyssey & IMAX (250m)
To Belfast City Airport (3km)
To Falls Rd (1.5km)
To Belfast Central Train Station (130m)
To M1 (800m) & Dublin (142km)
To Queen's Elms
Castle Court Centre
City Hall
Royal Courts of Justice
Queen Elizabeth Br
Queen's Bridge
River Lagan
Great Victoria Street
Shaftesbury Square
Botanic
Hospital
City Hospital
Queen's University
Botanic Gardens
Ormeau Park
0 150 300m
0 150 300yd
IRELAND

TV. Also in the university area, the **Windermere Guesthouse** *(☎ 9066 2693; Wellington Park; rooms per person £24)* has small but comfy rooms overlooking a quiet street.

Pearl Court House *(☎ 9066 6145; ⓔ pearlcourtgh@hotmail.com; 11 Malone Rd; singles/doubles £26/48)* offers basic accommodation. Or try **Liserin Guesthouse** *(☎ 9066 0769; 17 Eglantine Ave; singles/doubles £22/40)* has rooms with shower and TV.

At the **Holiday Inn Express** *(☎ 9031 1909, fax 9031 1910; 106A University St; rooms weekday/weekend £60/55)*, rates include continental breakfast. Its weekend rate is great value.

Places to Eat

Pubs The **Duke of York** *(lunches around £5.50)* is not only a great old-fashioned Belfast boozer, it also serves sandwiches starting from £1.50 and excellent solid lunches. It's hidden away down Commercial Court, off Donegall St.

Bittle's Bar is a small pub entered from 70 Upper Church Lane. It specialises in traditional dishes such as sausages and *champ* (an Ulster speciality of mashed potatoes and spring onions).

White's Tavern (Wine Cellar entry between Rosemary and High Sts) is one of Belfast's most historic taverns and a popular lunchtime meeting spot.

Above the Crown Liquor Saloon, **Flannigan's** *(☎ 9027 9901)* does cheap, hearty pub grub and mammoth, cheap breakfasts for around £5. The huge new **Wetherspoon's** *(Bedford St; mains around £5)* has some very cheap lunch deals.

Restaurants More and more decent places are opening in the city centre and around the Cathedral Quarter, although the greatest concentration of budget restaurants is along the Golden Mile from Dublin Rd south to University Rd and Botanic Ave.

Nick's Warehouse *(☎ 9043 9690; 34-39 Hill St; meals £7-14)* is a lovely bustling place with a varied menu, great seafood, a buzzing atmosphere and a good wine list.

Central places include **Café Aero** *(☎ 9024 4844; 44 Bedford St; mains from £6)*, a small, bright new place with an inventive menu; and **La Belle Epoque** *(61 Dublin Rd; lunch specials £6.25; open Mon-Sat)*, which serves basic French fare.

Around the university and golden mile **Villa Italia** *(37-41 University Rd; open dinner)*, a vibrant Italian restaurant and pizzeria, is perennially popular.

Botanic Ave has lots of cafés. **The Other Place** *(79 Botanic Ave)* is lively and good for coffee. **Café Conor** *(11A Stranmillis Rd)*, formerly the studio of artist William Conor, makes a lovely, light-filled spot for a coffee or post–Ulster Museum meal.

Entertainment

Belfast's main guide to what's on is the *Big List*, available at cafés and pubs or at ⓦ www.thebiglist.co.uk. The pubs along the Golden Mile are abuzz after dark most nights.

Two great Belfast city-centre institutions include **Robinsons** *(Great Victoria St)*, connected directly through double doors with **Fibber Magee's** *(Blackstaff Square)*. Across the road, the often-rowdy **Beaten Docket** *(Great Victoria St)* is also busy at night. Legendary **Crown Liquor Saloon** *(Great Victoria St)* is a splendid place with fine, ostentatious late-Victorian architecture and discreet panelled snugs.

The student-filled **Globe** *(36 University Rd)* has a good atmosphere but can get packed. Further south and facing each other are the **Eglantine Inn** *(Malone Rd)* and the **Botanic** *(Malone Rd)*, the 'Egg and Bott'. Of the two the Botanic is probably the more beloved by students past and present. If you crave a quiet pint try the **Elbow** *(Dublin Rd)*.

Limelight *(17 Ormeau Ave)* is a stayer in the Belfast nightclub and live-music world. **Empire Music Hall** *(42 Botanic Ave)*, a barn-like pub inside a former church, has live music three nights a week and a stand-up comedy night. Larger classical and pop music events are staged at impressive **Waterfront Hall** *(☎ 9033 4455; 2 Lanyon Place)*.

The Milk Bar *(☎ 9027 8876; Tomb St)* attracts top-name electronica DJs and has music nightly. The **John Hewitt** *(☎ 9023 3768; 51 Donegall St)*, in the nearby Cathedral Quarter, is a lively, pleasant place for pre-clubbing drinks.

The **Queen's Film Theatre** *(toll-free ☎ 0800 3 28 28 11; University Square Mews)* has independent, classic, cult and art house films. There's often a musical, opera or ballet on at the **Grand Opera House** *(☎ 9024 1919)*, and something less formal at the **Civic Arts Theatre** *(☎ 9031 6900; Botanic Ave)*.

Getting There & Away

For security reasons there are no left-luggage facilities at Belfast train or bus stations. For all Ulsterbus, Northern Ireland Railways (NIR) and local bus information call ☎ 9089 9411. Train and bus information is also available from **Translink** *(☎ 9066 6630; W www.translink.co.uk)*.

Bus Belfast has two separate bus stations. The smaller of the two is the **Laganside Buscentre** *(Oxford St)*, near the river, with bus connections to counties Antrim, Down and Derry. Buses to everywhere else in Ireland and the Larne ferries leave from the bigger **Europa Buscentre** *(Glengall St)*. Regional bus timetables are free at the bus stations.

There are seven daily Belfast-Dublin buses (five on Sunday) that take about three hours and start at £10.30 one way. For connections to Derry and Donegal, contact the **Lough Swilly Bus Company** *(☎ 7126 2017)* in Derry.

Train Belfast has two main train stations – **Great Victoria Street**, next to the Europa Buscentre, and **Belfast Central** *(East Bridge St)*, east of the city centre.

Destinations served from Belfast Central include Derry and Dublin. Dublin-Belfast trains (£20/30 one way/return, two hours) run up to six times a day (three on Sunday). From Belfast Central a free (with your bus or train ticket) Centrelink bus to Donegall Square in the city centre leaves every 10 minutes. A local train also connects with Great Victoria Street.

Great Victoria St station has services to Derry and Larne Harbour.

For tickets and information contact the **NIR** *(☎ 9089 9411; open 9am-5pm Mon-Fri, 9am-noon Sat)* at Great Victoria Steet station.

Boat From Belfast there are three main ferry routes connecting Belfast to Liverpool, the Isle of Man and Stranraer.

Belfast's ferry terminal, on Donegall Quay a short walk north of the city centre, is used by boats going to Troon, Heysham and the Isle of Man.

Norse Merchant Ferries *(☎ 9077 9090)* to Liverpool leave from Victoria terminal, 5km north of central Belfast; take a bus from Europa Buscentre or catch a taxi (£7 to £10). Stena Line services to Stranraer leave from nearby Corry Road.

Getting Around

A short bus trip costs 50p to 90p. Most local bus services depart from Donegall Square, near the City Hall, where there is a ticket kiosk. If driving, be fastidious about where you park; car theft is a serious problem here.

McConvey Cycles *(☎ 9033 0322; 182 Ormeau Rd)* rents bicycles for £10/40 per day/week. A £50 deposit is required.

THE BELFAST – DERRY COASTAL ROAD

Ireland isn't short of fine stretches of coast, but the Causeway Coast from Portstewart in County Derry to Ballycastle in County Antrim, and the Antrim Coast from Belfast to Ballycastle are as magnificent as they come.

From late May to late September, Ulsterbus' Antrim Coaster bus No 252 operates twice daily (except Sunday) between Belfast and Coleraine (four hours), stopping at all the main tourist sights. An open-topped Bushmills Bus (No 177) runs from the Giant's Causeway to Coleraine five times daily in July and August. The trip takes just over an hour. Bus No 162 runs year-round along the Antrim coast between Larne and Cushendun.

Carrickfergus

Only 13km northeast of Belfast is Carrickfergus and its impressive Norman **castle** *(☎ 9335 1273; admission £2.70; open 10am-6pm Mon-Sat, 2pm-6pm Sun Apr-Sept, 10am-4pm Mon-Sat Oct-Mar)*, which was built in 1180 by John de Courcy and overlooks the harbour where William III landed in 1690.

Glens of Antrim

Between Larne and Ballycastle, the nine Glens of Antrim are extremely picturesque stretches of woodland and downland where streams cascade into the sea. The picture-perfect port of **Cushendall** has been dubbed the 'Capital of the Glens', while **Glenariff**, a few kilometres to the south, lays claim to the title 'Queen of the Glens'. Between Cushendun and Ballycastle, eschew the main A2 road for the narrower and more picturesque B92, and take the turn-off down to sweeping Murlough Bay.

A good bet for a budget bed, and possibly a bedtime story, is at the modern **Ballyeamon Camping Barn** *(☎ 2175 8451; W www.taleteam.demon.co.uk; dorm beds £8)*, close to Cushendall on the B14. The proprietor is a professional storyteller.

IRELAND

Carrick-a-Rede Island

The 20m **rope bridge** *(admission free; open April-Sept)* connecting Carrick-a-Rede Island to the mainland is fun to stagger across, swaying some 25m above pounding waves. The island is the site of a salmon fishery and a nesting ground for gulls and fulmars. The bridge is closed when the wind is too strong.

Giant's Causeway (Clochán an Aifir)

Chances are you've seen pictures of Northern Ireland's main tourist attraction. The hexagonal basalt columns, all 38,000 of them (that's counting the ones underwater) are amazingly uniform. According to one of the legends, the giant Finn McCool fancied a female giant on the Scottish island of Staffa and built some stepping stones to the island where similar rock formations are found. The more prosaic explanation is that lava erupted from an underground fissure and crystallised some 60 million years ago.

About four buses a day (more in summer, fewer on Sunday) between Portrush and Ballycastle pass the Giant's Causeway. To reach the causeway, take one of two circular footpaths that start from outside the visitors centre.

A recommended walk is from the Giant's Causeway 16km east along the coast (not the highway), past Dunseverick Castle to the beach at Whitepark Bay. A great place to crash at the end is the terrific, modern HINI **Whitepark Bay Hostel** *(☎ 2073 1745; dorm beds from £11, singles/twins from £13/26; open year-round)*, with bay views and smart dorms and rooms with en suite.

Bushmills

About 4km southwest of the Giant's Causeway, Bushmills is a small town off the A2 between Portrush and Ballycastle. The real attraction, 500m south of the main square, is **Old Bushmills Distillery** *(☎ 2073 3272; admission £4)*. After a noisy tour of the industrial process (it's quieter on weekends, when production is halted), there's a whiskey-tasting session.

Portstewart, Portrush & Downhill

These seaside resorts are only a few kilometres apart. The pleasant Portstewart has a slightly decayed, early-20th-century feel to it, while Downhill boasts a lovely long stretch of beach. Portstewart's **Causeway Coast Hostel** *(☎ 7083 3789; 4 Victoria Terrace; dorm beds £7, private rooms £17)* is at the eastern end of town.

Harder to get to, but well worth the effort is the lovely independent **Downhill Hostel** *(☎ 7084 9077; ⓔ downhillhostel@hotmail.com; 12 Mussenden Rd, Downhill; dorm beds £7.50, doubles £20)*, a friendly place with open fires, and a good library, in a solid converted period house overlooking the beach. Pick-ups can be arranged from Castlerock train station. The No 134 bus also passes nearby on its way between Coleraine and Limavady.

DERRY/LONDONDERRY (DOIRE)

pop 72,330

Even choosing what you call Northern Ireland's second-largest city can be a political statement. In practice it's better known as Derry, whatever your politics. Doire, the original Irish name, means 'oak grove', and the 'London' prefix was added after settlers were granted much of the land in the area by James I.

Resentment at the long-running domination of the city council by Protestants boiled over in the civil rights marches of 1968. Simultaneously, perceived attacks by the RUC on the Catholic Bogside district began, leading to days of rioting. On 14 August 1968 British troops entered Derry. In January 1972, 'Bloody Sunday' saw the deaths of 14 unarmed Catholic civil rights marchers in Derry at the hands of the British army.

Today Derry is as safe to visit as anywhere else in Northern Ireland. The arts are alive, and festivals, such as the Foyle Film Festival, draw crowds from everywhere. Halloween is widely and enthusiastically celebrated.

Orientation & Information

The old centre of Derry is the small, walled city on the west bank of the River Foyle. The heart of the walled city is The Diamond, intersected by four main roads: Shipquay St, Ferryquay St, Bishop St Within and Butcher St. The Catholic Bogside area is below the walls to the northwest. To the south is a Protestant estate known as the Fountain. The Waterside district across the river is mostly Protestant.

Derry's **NITB office** *(☎ 7126 7284)* and **Bord Fáilte** *(☎ 7136 9501)* share an impressive, modern stone office just outside the walled city at the **Tourist Information Centre** *(44 Foyle St)*. Together they cover the whole of Ireland. The **main post office** *(Custom*

House St) is just north of the Tower Museum. At **Central Library** *(☎ 7127 2300; 35 Foyle St)* you can access the Internet free until 1pm (£2.50 per hour after).

Things to See & Do

Until the mid-1990s, the presence of the army and protective iron gates made Derry's magnificent **city walls** hard to appreciate. The gates are still there, but they're open and it's possible to walk all round the walls, built between 1613 and 1618. A major highlight for the traveller, and a must-walk, the gates give an excellent overview of Bogside (itself worth a closer look) and its defiant **murals**, one notably proclaiming 'You Are Now Entering Free Derry'.

Just inside Coward's Bastion to the north, O'Doherty's Tower houses the excellent **Tower Museum** *(☎ 7137 2411; admission £4.20; open 10am-5pm Tues-Sat Sept-June, 10am-5pm Mon-Sat, 2pm-5pm Sun July & Aug)*, which traces the story of Derry from the days of St Columbcille to the present. The fine red-brick **Guildhall** was originally built in 1890, just outside the city walls, and is noted for its stained-glass windows. Austere **St Columb's Cathedral** *(admission £1)* dates from 1628 and stands at the southern end of the walled city, off Biship St Within.

Places to Stay

There are only two hostels in Derry, so book ahead. The larger is the HINI **Derry City Hostel** *(☎ 7128 0280; 6 Magazine St; dorm beds £10-13, doubles £35)*, in the walled city near Butcher's Gate, just 150m from the bus station. Not as formal is **Steve's Backpackers** *(☎ 7137 7989; 4 Asylum Rd; dorm beds £9, private rooms per person £12; open year-round)*, a small, basic but friendly hostel north of the walled city. There is no check-out time, a light breakfast and Internet access are included in rates and the fifth night is free.

Within walking distance of the bus station is friendly **Acorn House** *(☎ 7127 1156; 17 Aberfoyle Terrace, Strand Rd; singles/doubles from £20/32)*. **Clarence House** *(☎ 7126 5342; e clarencehouse@zoom.co.uk; 15 Northland Rd; singles/doubles £19/50)* is a friendly place in a pleasant period house with good (and varied) buffet breakfasts.

Places to Eat

Just outside the Ferryquay Gate, southeast of the walled city, modern **Fitzroy's** has entrances at 3 Carlisle Rd and 2–4 Bridge St, and moves from cool café to sophisticated mains at night. **The Sandwich Company** *(The Diamond)* is handy for a simple lunch or coffee break. Just opposite, the new Wetherspoon's-owned **Diamond** serves very good-value pub grub until 10pm nightly.

In the made-for-tourists **Craft Village** *(Shipquay St)*, **Thran Maggies** *(mains from £4.95; open to at least 9.15pm)* serves cheap, basic Irish dishes and is one of the few places to eat in the walled city after dark. Whenever it's sunny the outdoor tables are packed. **Indigo** *(☎ 7127 1011; 27 Shipquay Street; mains £4.50)* is a modern restaurant/café serving cuisine from around the world.

Entertainment

Derry's liveliest pubs are situated along Waterloo St: **The Gweedore Bar**, **Tracy's** and **Peadar O'Donnell's**, which is good for traditional music. **McGinley's** *(Foyle St)* also has live music six nights a week. The **Metro Bar** *(3-4 Bank Place)*, just inside the walls, is Derry's trendiest (and most crowded) pub.

There are several theatres in Derry, with something for most tastes. The newest and spiffiest is **The Millennium Forum** *(☎ 7126 4455; w www.millenniumforum.co.uk; New Market St)* with several performance spaces for theatre, dance, musicals, comedy and concerts.

Getting There & Away

The **Ulsterbus station** *(☎ 7126 2261; Foyle St)* is just outside the city walls, near the Guildhall. There are frequent services between Belfast and Derry. Bus No 212, the *Maiden City Flyer*, is the fastest (one way £7.80, one hour 40 minutes). There are also semifrequent connections to Portrush and Portstewart. At 9am daily a bus leaves Derry for Cork in the Republic, arriving at 7.15pm. Bus Éireann operates a Derry-Galway service three times daily, via Donegal and Sligo.

Lough Swilly Bus Service *(☎ 7126 2017)*, with an office upstairs at the Ulsterbus station, serves County Donegal across the border, and has an £22 eight-day unlimited travel offer from May to September.

Derry's **Waterside train station** *(☎ 9066 6630)* is across the River Foyle from the centre, but is connected to it by a free Linkline bus. There are seven trains daily to Belfast (three on Sunday; three hours) via Portrush.

Italy

Tell people you're going to Italy and they'll sigh, even if they haven't been there. A place of myth, history, artistic achievement, romantic imagery and all manner of cliches, Italy stirs peoples' hearts with its simplicity and complexity. As Luigi Barzini wrote in *The Italians*: 'Italy is still a country of limitless opportunities. It offers stage settings for all kinds of adventures, licit or illicit loves, the study of art, the experience of pathos, the weaving of intrigues. It can be gay, tragic, mad, pastoral, archaic, modern, or simply *dolce'*. Many come to Italy to escape their daily lives and to feel more alive in the process. Soak up what's on offer – this is a country that understands you.

Italy: the Basics

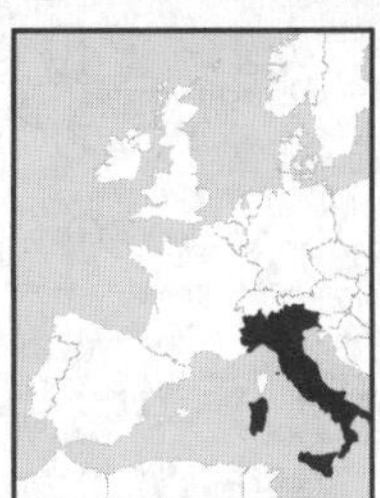

Local name Italia

Capital Rome

Population 57.8 million

Language Italian

Currency euro (€) = 100 centimes

Avoid at all costs Dishevelled children with cardboard.

Avoid unwanted attention by saying *Aspetto per mio marito/fratello/padre.* (I'm waiting for my husband/brother/father.)

Facts about Italy

HISTORY

The traditional date for the founding of Rome by Romulus is 753 BC, but the country had already been inhabited for thousands of years. By the start of the Bronze Age, around 2000 BC, the peninsula had been settled by several Italic tribes. From about 900 BC the Etruscan civilisation developed; the Romans overwhelmed the last Etruscan city at the end of the 3rd century BC.

The new Roman republic expanded into southern Italy and claimed Sicily following the Second Punic War in 241 BC. Rome defeated Carthage in 202 BC and a few years later claimed Spain and Greece. Under Julius Caesar, Rome conquered Gaul and Egypt. After Caesar's assassination, Caesar's adopted son Octavius defeated rivals Mark Antony and Cleopatra, establishing the Roman Empire in 27 BC and adopting the title of Augustus Caesar.

By the end of the 3rd century AD, the empire was so big that Emperor Diocletian divided it between east and west. His successor, Constantine, ruled from Byzantium (Constantinople) and was the first Christian emperor. From the 5th to 9th centuries the empire was beset by Goths, Huns and Arabs from the south.

The Middle Ages were marked by the development of powerful city-states in the north. In the 15th century the Renaissance spread throughout the country, fostering geniuses such as Brunelleschi, Donatello, Bramante, Botticelli, da Vinci, Masaccio, Lippi, Raphael and Michelangelo. By the early 16th century much of the country was under Habsburg rule. After the invasion by Napoleon in 1796, a degree of unity was introduced into Italy, for the first time since the fall of the Roman Empire. In the 1860s Italy's unification movement (The Risorgimento) gained momentum, and in 1861 the Kingdom of Italy was declared under the rule of King Vittorio Emanuele.

In 1921 Benito Mussolini's Fascist Party took control. Mussolini was a German ally in WWII. After several military disasters, the king led a coup against Mussolini and had him arrested. The Germans rescued him, but Italian partisans killed him in April 1945. A year later the monarchy was abolished.

Italy was a founding member of the European Economic Community in 1957. The country enjoyed significant economic growth through the 20th century, but the 1990s heralded a period of crisis for the country, both economically and politically. National bribery scandals rocked the nation. Investigations implicated thousands of politicians, public officials and businesspeople, and left the main parties in tatters after the 1992 elections. A programme of fiscal austerity was ushered in to guarantee Italy's entry into Europe's economic and monetary union (EMU). Italy also moved decisively against the Sicilian Mafia, prompted by the 1992 assassinations of prominent anti-Mafia judges.

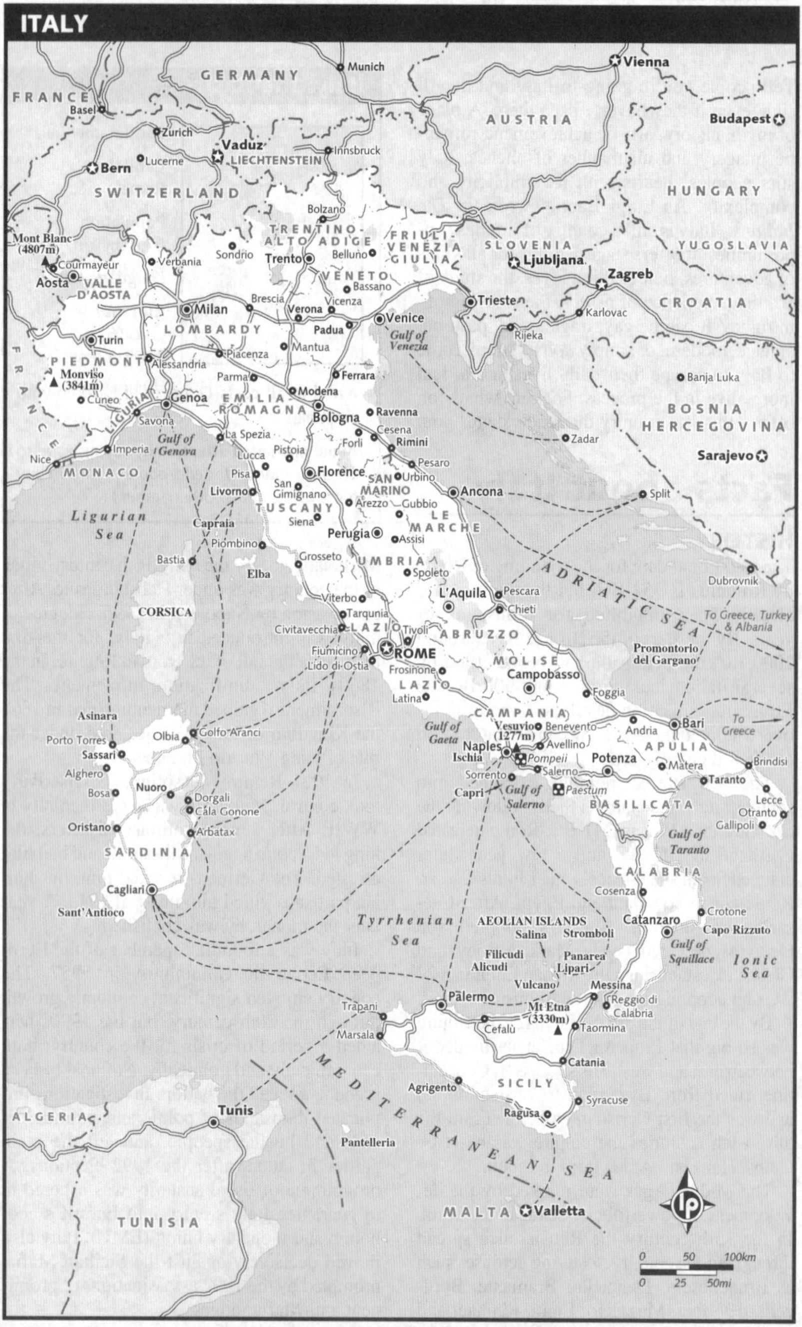

ITALY

GERMANY
Munich
Vienna
FRANCE
Basel
AUSTRIA
Budapest
Zurich
Vaduz
Innsbruck
Lucerne
LIECHTENSTEIN
Bern
SWITZERLAND
HUNGARY
Bolzano
TRENTINO-ALTO ADIGE
FRIULI-VENEZIA GIULIA
SLOVENIA
YUGOSLAVIA
Mont Blanc (4807m)
Sondrio
Trento
Belluno
Ljubljana
Courmayeur
Verbania
VENETO
Zagreb
Aosta
VALLE D'AOSTA
Bassano
Brescia
Vicenza
Trieste
CROATIA
Milan
Verona
Venice
Karlovac
LOMBARDY
Padua
Gulf of Venezia
Rijeka
Turin
Mantua
PIEDMONT
Piacenza
Alessandria
Monviso (3841m)
Parma
Ferrara
Banja Luka
FRANCE
Cuneo
Genoa
Modena
EMILIA-ROMAGNA
Bologna
Ravenna
BOSNIA HERCEGOVINA
LIGURIA
Savona
Cesena
Gulf of Genova
La Spezia
Rimini
Zadar
Forli
Imperia
Pistoia
Nice
Lucca
Pesaro
Sarajevo
MONACO
Pisa
Florence
SAN MARINO
Urbino
San Gimignano
Ancona
Livorno
Split
Arezzo
Gubbio
TUSCANY
LE MARCHE
Ligurian Sea
Capraia
Siena
Perugia
Assisi
Piombino
Bastia
Grosseto
UMBRIA
Spoleto
Elba
ADRIATIC SEA
Dubrovnik
L'Aquila
Pescara
Viterbo
CORSICA
Chieti
Tarquinia
To Greece, Turkey & Albania
Civitavecchia
LAZIO
Tivoli
ABRUZZO
Fiumicino
ROME
Lido di Ostia
MOLISE
Promontorio del Gargano
Frosinone
Campobasso
LAZIO
Foggia
Latina
CAMPANIA
Asinara
Gulf of Gaeta
Vesuvio (1277m)
Benevento
Andria
Bari
To Greece
Porto Torres
Olbia
Golfo Aranci
Naples
Avellino
Sassari
Ischia
Pompeii
APULIA
Potenza
Brindisi
Alghero
Salerno
Matera
Sorrento
Gulf of Salerno
Taranto
Bosa
Nuoro
Capri
Paestum
Dorgali
Lecce
Cala Gonone
BASILICATA
Otranto
Gallipoli
Oristano
Arbatax
Gulf of Taranto
SARDINIA
CALABRIA
Cosenza
Cagliari
Sant'Antioco
Crotone
Tyrrhenian Sea
AEOLIAN ISLANDS
Catanzaro
Capo Rizzuto
Salina
Stromboli
Gulf of Squillace
Filicudi
Panarea
Ionic Sea
Alicudi
Lipari
Vulcano
Messina
Palermo
Mt Etna (3330m)
Reggio di Calabria
Trapani
Cefalù
Taormina
Marsala
Catania
MEDITERRANEAN SEA
SICILY
Agrigento
Syracuse
Ragusa
ALGERIA
Tunis
Pantelleria
TUNISIA
MALTA
Valletta
0 50 100km
0 25 50mi

The current prime minister is Silvio Berlusconi, a controversial right-wing politico whose party, Forza Italia, has proved popular in many quarters with its desire to make Italian bureaucracy more efficient (at the expense of state welfare). He also owns *a lot* of the Italian media, which is a sore point for a great many people.

GEOGRAPHY

The boot-shaped country, incorporating Sicily and Sardinia, is bound by the Adriatic, Ligurian, Tyrrhenian and Ionian Seas. About 75% of the peninsula is mountainous, with the Alps dividing the country from France, Switzerland and Austria, and the Apennines forming a backbone that extends from the Alps into Sicily. There are four active volcanoes: Stromboli and Vulcano (in the Aeolian Islands), Vesuvius (near Naples) and Etna (Sicily).

CLIMATE

Italy lies in a temperate zone, but the climates of the north and south vary. Summers are uniformly hot. Winters can be severely cold in the north, whereas they are mild in the south.

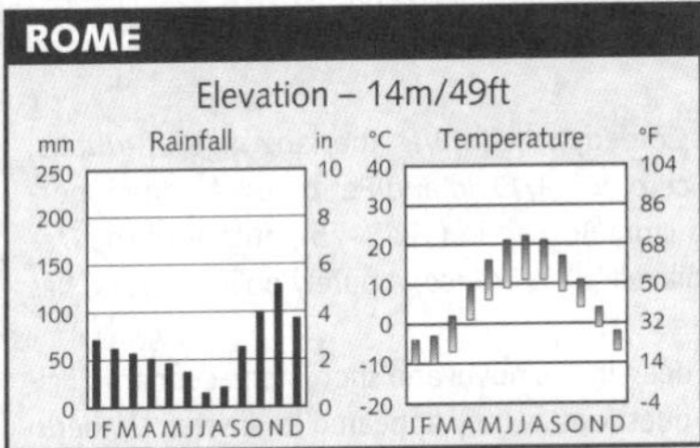

GOVERNMENT & POLITICS

The country is a parliamentary republic, headed by a president who appoints the prime minister.

POPULATION & PEOPLE

Surprisingly, Italy has the lowest birthrate in Europe. People remain fiercely protective of regional dialects and cuisine.

SOCIETY & CONDUCT

It is difficult to make blanket assertions about Italian culture. Many Italians tend to identify more strongly with their region, or home town, than with the nation.

In some parts of Italy, especially in the south, women might be harassed if they wear skimpy clothing. Modest dress is expected in all churches. Major tourist attractions, such as St Peter's in Rome, strictly enforce dress codes (no hotpants, low-cut tops, bare shoulders, shorts or see-through garments).

LANGUAGE

English is most widely understood in the north, particularly in major centres such as Milan, Florence and Venice. You will be better received if you attempt to communicate in Italian. Many older Italians expect to be addressed by the second person formal – *Lei* instead of *Tu*. It is not polite to use *ciao* when addressing strangers, unless they use it first; use *buongiorno* and *arrivederci*. See the Language chapter at the back of this book for pronunciation guidelines and useful words and phrases.

Facts for the Visitor

HIGHLIGHTS

Coming up with a highlight list for Italy is no easy task, given the wealth of must-see sights. Italian food and wine must come at the top of the list. The beauty of Florence and majestic ruins of Rome, Pompeii and Paestum are next. Venice is an enchanting reminder of past glory, while Siena oozes medieval character. Lovers of natural beauty won't want to miss the Amalfi Coast, Cinque Terre, Aeolian Islands or Dolomites. Finally, Palermo's mosaics and architecture will captivate you.

PLANNING

The best time to visit is April to June and September to October, when the weather is good, prices are lower and there are fewer tourists. During July and August (the high season) it is very hot, prices are inflated, the country swarms with tourists and hotels are usually booked out. Many hotels and restaurants in seaside areas close down for winter.

TOURIST OFFICES

Local Tourist Offices

There are three main categories of tourist office: regional, provincial and local. Provincial offices are sometimes known as the Ente Provinciale per il Turismo (EPT) or the Azienda di Promozione Turistica (APT). The Azienda Autonoma di Soggiorno e Turismo (AAST) and Informazioni e Assistenza ai Turisti (IAT) offices usually have information only on the

Le Belle Arti

Italy has often been called a living museum. Art is everywhere around you as you walk through Italian cities. The 15th and early 16th centuries in Italy saw one of the most remarkable explosions of artistic and literary achievement in recorded history – *il Rinascimento* (the Renaissance).

Architecture, Painting & Sculpture

Patronised mainly by the Medici family in Florence and the popes in Rome, painters, sculptors, architects and writers flourished during the Renaissance. The High Renaissance (about 1490–1520) was dominated by three men – Leonardo da Vinci (1452–1519), Michelangelo Buonarrotti (1475–1564) and Raphael (1483–1520). The baroque period (17th century) was characterised by sumptuous, often fantastic architecture and richly decorative painting and sculpture. In Rome there are innumerable works by the great baroque sculptor and architect Gianlorenzo Bernini (1598–1680) and many works by Michelangelo Merisi da Caravaggio (1573–1610). Neoclassicism produced the sculptor Canova (1757–1822).

Of Italy's modern artists, Amedeo Modigliani (1884–1920) is perhaps the most famous. The early 20th century also produced an artistic movement known as the Futurists, who rejected the sentimental art of the past and were infatuated by new technology, including modern warfare. Fascism produced its own style of architecture in Italy, characterised by the EUR satellite city and the work of Marcello Piacentini (1881–1960).

Music

Italian artists have taken a dominant place in the realms of opera and instrumental music. Antonio Vivaldi (1675–1741) created the concerto in its present form. Verdi, Puccini, Bellini, Donizetti and Rossini, composers from the 19th and early 20th centuries, are all stars of the modern operatic era. Tenor Luciano Pavarotti (1935–) has recently had his crown as 'King of Mother's Day CD Sales' taken by Andrea Bocelli (1958–), who soared to international stardom in the 1990s.

Literature

Before Dante wrote his *Divina Commedia* (Divine Comedy), Latin was the language of writers. Among the greatest writers of ancient Rome were Cicero, Virgil, Ovid and Petronius. A contemporary of Dante's was the poet Petrarch (1304–74). Giovanni Boccaccio (1313–75), author of the *Decameron*, is considered the first Italian novelist. Machiavelli's *The Prince*, a purely political work, has proved a lasting Renaissance piece.

Italy's richest contribution to modern literature has been in the novel and short story. Leonardo Sciascia's taut writings on Sicilian themes posed as many questions as they appeared to answer. Umberto Eco's best-known work *The Name of the Rose* is a high-brow murder mystery of the first order.

---

town itself. In some very small towns and villages the local tourist office is called a Pro Loco. At most offices you should be able to get an *elenco degli alberghi* (a list of hotels), a *pianta della cittá* (map of the town) and information on the major sights. Staff speak English in larger towns. Tourist offices are generally open between 8.30am to 12.30pm or 1pm and 3pm to 7pm weekdays and on Saturday morning. Hours are usually extended in summer.

The Centro Turistico Studentesco e Giovanile (CTS) has offices all over Italy and specialises in discounts for students and young people. It's also useful for travellers looking for cheap flights and sightseeing discounts. You can get a student card here if you have documents proving that you are a student.

Tourist Offices Abroad

Information about Italy can be obtained at Italian State Tourist Offices (W www.enit.it):

Australia (☎ 02-9262 1666, fax 9262 5745) c/o Italian Chamber of Commerce, Level 26, 44 Market St, Sydney, NSW 2000
Canada (☎ 416-925 4882, fax 925 4799) Suite 907, South Tower, 175 Bloor St East, Toronto M4W 3R8
UK (☎ 020-7355 1557, fax 7493 6695, e enitlond@globalnet.co.uk) 1 Princes St, London W1R 9AY

USA *Chicago:* (☎ 312-644 0996, fax 644 3019, ⓔ enitch@italiantourism.com) Suite 2240, 500 N Michigan Ave, Chicago, IL 60611; *Los Angeles:* (☎ 310-820 1898, fax 820 6357, ⓔ enitla@earthlink.net) Suite 550, 12400 Wilshire Blvd, Los Angeles, CA 90025; *New York:* (☎ 212-245 5095, fax 586 9249, ⓔ enitny@italiantourism.com) Suite 1565, 630 Fifth Ave, New York, NY 10111

Sestante CIT (Compagnia Italiana di Turismo), Italy's national travel agency, has offices throughout the world (known as CIT outside Italy). It can provide extensive information on Italy, and also books tours, accommodation and trains. Offices include:

Australia *Melbourne:* (☎ 03-9650 5510) Level 4, 227 Collins St, Melbourne 3000; *Sydney:* (☎ 02-9267 1255) Level 2, 263 Clarence St, Sydney, NSW 2000

Canada *Montreal:* (☎ 514-845 9101, toll-free 800-361 7799) Suite 901, 666 Sherbrooke St West, Montreal, Quebec H3A 1E7; *Toronto:* (☎ 905-415 1060, toll-free 800-387 0711) Suite 401, 80 Tiverton Court, Markham, Toronto, Ontario L3R 0G4

France (☎ 01 44 51 39 51) 5 Blvd des Capucines, Paris 75002

UK (☎ 020-8686 0677, 8686 5533) Marco Polo House, 3–5 Lansdowne Rd, Croydon, Surrey CR9 1LL

USA (☎ 212-730 2121) Level 10, 15 West 44th St, New York, NY 10036

VISAS & DOCUMENTS

EU citizens require a national identity card or passport to stay in Italy for as long as they like. Citizens of many other countries including the USA, Australia, Canada and New Zealand don't need visas if they are entering as tourists. Visitors are technically obliged to report to a *questura* (police station) if they plan to stay at the same address for more than one week. Tourists staying in hotels or hostels are not required to do this since proprietors need to register guests with the police. A *permesso di soggiorno* is necessary (for non-EU citizens) if you plan to study, work (legally) or live in Italy.

EMBASSIES & CONSULATES

Italian Embassies & Consulates

Italian diplomatic missions abroad include:

Australia *Embassy:* (☎ 02-6273 3333, fax 6273 4223, ⓔ ambital2@dynamite.com.au) 12 Grey St, Deakin, Canberra, ACT 2601; *Consulate:* (☎ 03-9867 5744, fax 9866 3932, ⓔ itconmel@netlink.com.au) 509 St Kilda Rd, Melbourne, Vic 3004; *Consulate:* (☎ 02-9392 7900, fax 9252 4830; ⓔ itconsyd@armadillo.com.au) Level 45, Gateway, 1 Macquarie Place, Sydney, NSW 2000

Canada *Embassy:* (☎ 613-232 2401, fax 233 1484, ⓔ ambital@italyincanada.com) Level 21, 275 Slater St, Ottawa, Ontario K1P 5H9; *Consulate:* (☎ 514-849 8351, fax 499 9471, ⓔ cgi@italconsul.montreal.qc.ca) 3489 Drummond St, Montreal, Quebec H3G 1X6; *Consulate:* (☎ 416-977 1566, fax 977 1119, ⓔ consolato.it@toronto.italconsulate.org) 136 Beverley St, Toronto, Ontario M5T 1Y5

France *Embassy:* (☎ 01 49 54 03 00, fax 01 45 49 35 81, ⓔ ambasciata@amb-italie.fr) 7 rue de Varenne, Paris 75007; *Consulate:* (☎ 01 44 30 47 00, fax 01 45 25 87 50, ⓔ italconsulparigi@mailcity.com) 5 Blvd Emile Augier, Paris 75116

New Zealand *Embassy:* (☎ 04-473 5339, fax 472 7255, ⓔ ambwell@xtra.co.nz) 34 Grant Rd, Thorndon, Wellington

UK *Embassy:* (☎ 020-7312 2200, fax 7312 2230, ⓔ emblondon@embitaly.org.uk) 14 Three Kings Yard, London W1Y 4EH; *Consulate:* (☎ 020-7235 9371, fax 7823 1609) 38 Eaton Place, London SW1X 8AN

USA *Embassy:* (☎ 202-612 4400, fax 518 2154) 3000 Whitehaven St NW, Washington DC 20008; *Consulate:* (☎ 310-826 6207, fax 820 0727, ⓔ cglos@conlang.com) Suite 300, 12400 Wilshire Blvd, West Los Angeles, CA 90025; *Consulate:* (☎ 212-7737 9100, fax 249 4945, ⓔ italconsulnyc@italconsulnyc.org) 690 Park Ave, New York, NY 10021

Embassies & Consulates in Italy

The headquarters of most foreign embassies are in Rome, although there are generally British and US consulates in other major cities. The following addresses and phone numbers are for Rome:

Australia (☎ 06 85 27 21) Via Alessandria 215, 00198

Canada (☎ 06 44 59 81) Via G B de Rossi 27, 00161

France *Embassy:* (☎ 06 68 60 11) Piazza Farnese 67, 00186; *Consulate:* (☎ 06 68 80 21 52) Via Giulia 251, 00186

Germany (☎ 06 49 21 31) Via San Martino della Battaglia 4, 00185

New Zealand (☎ 06 441 71 71) Via Zara 28, 00198

UK (☎ 06 42 20 00 01) Via XX Settembre 80a, 00187

USA (☎ 06 467 41) Via Veneto 119a, 00187

For a complete list of all foreign embassies in Rome and other major cities throughout Italy, look in the local telephone book under *ambasciate* or *consolati,* or ask for a list at the tourist office.

CUSTOMS

Travellers coming from outside the EU can import, duty-free: 200 cigarettes, 1L of spirits, 2L of wine and other goods up to a total value of €175.

MONEY

Italy uses the euro (see the Facts for the Visitor chapter under Money for currency exchange rates). A combination of travellers cheques and credit cards is the best way to take your money. If you buy travellers cheques in euros there should be no commission charged. There are exchange offices at all major airports and train stations.

Major credit cards, including Visa, MasterCard and American Express, are widely accepted and can be used for purchases or payment in hotels and restaurants (smaller places might not accept them). They can also be used to get money from *bancomats* (ATMs) or, if you don't have a PIN, over the counter in major banks.

A *very* parsimonious traveller could get by on €45 per day. You can save on transport costs by buying tourist or day tickets for city bus and underground services. Museums and galleries usually give discounts to students, but you will need a valid student card. Other discounts (around 50%) are offered to EU citizens aged between 18 and 25. EU citizens under 18 and over 65 years of age are generally admitted free of charge. A basic breakdown of costs during an average day could be: accommodation €15 (youth hostel) to €40; breakfast (coffee and croissant) €1.75; lunch (sandwich and mineral water) €3.20; daily public transport ticket €6; admission for one museum €4.50 to €6.50; a sit-down dinner €8 to €25.

You are not expected to tip in restaurants, but it's common to leave a small amount, around 10%. In bars leave small change. You can tip taxi drivers if you wish. Bargaining is common in flea markets, but not in shops.

POST & COMMUNICATIONS

Main post offices in the bigger cities are generally open from around 8am to 6pm. Many open on Saturday morning too.

Italy's country code is ☎ 39. Area codes are an integral part of the telephone number, even if you're dialling a local number. Calls can be made from public phones, or from a Telecom office. Italy's rates are among the highest in Europe. Most public phones accept only phonecards, sold in denominations of €2.50, €5 and €25 at tobacconists and newsstands, or from Telecom office vending machines. Off-peak hours for domestic calls are between 10pm to 8am. For international calls it's 10pm to 8am and all Sunday.

To make a reverse-charge (collect) call from a public telephone, dial ☎ 170. For European countries call ☎ 15. All operators speak English. For international directory inquiries call ☎ 176. You can transmit faxes from specialist fax/photocopy shops, post offices, Internet cafés and some *tabacchi* (tobacconists).

Italy has a growing number of Internet cafés, where you can send and receive email or surf the Net for around €2 to €5 an hour.

DIGITAL RESOURCES

CTS at **W** www.cts.it has useful information (in Italian only) from Italy's leading student travel organisation. A good cultural site is **W** www.beniculturali.com, which has museum information and online reservation options. Nature lovers can get Italian national park information at **W** www.parks.it.

The Vatican site (**W** www.vatican.va) has detailed information about Vatican City. If you are looking for train information, check out **W** www.trenitalia.it for details about timetables and services.

BOOKS

For a more comprehensive guide to Italy, pick up a copy of Lonely Planet's *Italy*. If you want to concentrate on specific regions, pick up Lonely Planet's *Rome, Florence, Venice, Tuscany, Milan, Turin & Genoa* and *Sicily* guides. Also useful are the *Italian phrasebook, World Food Italy, Rome City Map* and *Florence City Map*. If you're a hiking enthusiast, a good companion is Lonely Planet's *Walking in Italy*.

For a potted history of the country, try the *Concise History of Italy* by Vincent Cronin. Interesting introductions to travelling in Italy include *A Traveller in Italy* by HV Morton.

WOMEN TRAVELLERS

Women travelling alone may find themselves recipients of unwanted attention from men. It is best simply to ignore the catcalls, hisses and whistles. Avoid walking alone in dark and deserted streets; look for central hotels that are within easy walking distance of places where you can eat at night. Women should never hitchhike alone.

GAY & LESBIAN TRAVELLERS

Homosexuality is generally well tolerated, though overt displays of affection might get a negative response in smaller towns and villages, particularly in the south. The age of consent for men and women is 16. The national organisation for gays (men and women) is **Arcigay** *(☎ 051 649 30 55, fax 051 528 22 26; ⓦ www.arcigay.it; Via Don Minzoni 18)* in Bologna.

DISABLED TRAVELLERS

The Italian travel agency CIT can advise on hotels that have special facilities. The UK-based **Royal Association for Disability and Rehabilitation** *(RADAR; ☎ 020-7250 3222; ⓦ www.radar.org.uk; 12 City Forum, 250 City Rd, London EC1V 8AF)*, publishes a useful guide called *Holidays & Travel Abroad: A Guide for Disabled People*.

SENIOR TRAVELLERS

Senior travellers who plan to use the train as their main mode of transport should look into the *Carta Argento* (€25), which gives the over-60s reductions of up to 40% on full-price train fares.

DANGERS & ANNOYANCES

Theft is the main problem for travellers in Italy, mostly in the form of petty thievery and pickpocketing, especially in the bigger cities. Pickpockets operate in crowded areas, such as markets and on buses headed for major tourist attractions.

Watch out for groups of dishevelled-looking kids, who can be lightning fast as they empty your pockets. Motorcycle bandits are a minor problem in Rome, Naples, Palermo and Syracuse. If you're using a shoulder bag, make sure that you wear the strap across your body and have the bag on the side away from the road. Never leave anything in a parked car. Car theft is a major problem in Rome and Naples.

BUSINESS HOURS

Business hours vary, but generally shops and businesses are open 8.30am to 1pm and 5pm to 7.30pm Monday to Saturday, and some are also open on Sunday morning. Banks are generally open 8.30am to 1.30pm and from 2.30pm to 4.30pm on weekdays, but hours vary between banks and cities. Large post offices are open 8am to 6pm or 7pm Monday to Saturday. Most museums close on Monday, and restaurants and bars are required to close for one day each week.

Emergencies

Nationwide emergency numbers are as follows: Carabinieri (police with military and civil duties) ☎ 112; Police ☎ 113; Fire brigade (Vigili del Fuoco) ☎ 115; Automobile Club d'Italia (ACI) ☎ 116; Ambulance ☎ 118

PUBLIC HOLIDAYS & SPECIAL EVENTS

National public holidays include: Epiphany (6 January), Easter Monday, Liberation Day (25 April), Labour Day (1 April), *Ferragosto* or Feast of the Assumption (15 August), All Saints' Day (1 November), Feast of the Immaculate Conception (8 December), Christmas Day (25 December), and Feast of St Stephen (26 December).

Individual towns also have public holidays to celebrate the feasts of their patron saints. Some of these are: the Feast of St Mark in Venice on 25 April; the Feast of St John the Baptist on 24 June in Florence, Genoa and Turin; the Feast of St Peter and St Paul in Rome on 29 June; the Feast of St Rosalia in Palermo on July 15; the Feast of St Januarius in Naples on 19 September; and the Feast of St Ambrose in Milan on 7 December.

Annual events that are worth keeping in mind include:

Carnevale During the 10 days before Ash Wednesday, many towns stage carnivals (one last binge before Lent!). The one held in Venice is the best known, but there are also others, including at Viareggio in Tuscany and Ivrea near Turin.

Holy Week There are important festivals the week before Easter everywhere in Italy, in particular the colourful and sombre traditional festivals of Sicily. In Assisi the rituals of Holy Week attract thousands of pilgrims.

Scoppio del Carro Literally 'Explosion of the Cart', this colourful event held in Florence in Piazza del Duomo on Easter Sunday features the explosion of a cart full of fireworks and dates back to the Crusades. If all goes well, it is seen as a good omen for the city.

Corso dei Ceri One of the strangest festivals in Italy, this is held in Gubbio (Umbria) on 15 May, and features a race run by men carrying enormous wooden constructions called *ceri*, in honour of the town's patron saint, Sant'Ubaldo.
Il Palio On 2 July and 16 August, Siena stages this extraordinary horse race in Siena's main piazza.

ACTIVITIES

Trails are well marked and there are plenty of *refuges* in the Alps, in the Alpi Apuane in Tuscany and in the northern parts of the Apennines. The Dolomites provide spectacular walking and trekking opportunities. On Sardinia, head for the coastal gorges between Dorgali and Baunei. Sicily's Mt Etna is also a popular hiking destination.

The numerous excellent ski resorts in the Alps and the Apennines usually offer good skiing conditions from December to April.

Cycling is a good option if you can't afford a car but want to see the more isolated parts of the country. Classic cycling areas include Tuscany and Umbria.

ACCOMMODATION

There is generally a fair degree of price fluctuation throughout the country, depending on the season. Prices usually rise by 5% to 10% each year, although sometimes they remain fixed for years, or even drop.

Camping

Facilities throughout Italy are usually reasonable and vary from major complexes with swimming pools, tennis courts and restaurants to simple camping grounds. Average prices are around €6 per person and €6 or more for a site. Lists are available at tourist information offices. The Touring Club Italiano (TCI) publishes an annual book on all camping sites in Italy, *Campeggi e Villaggi Turistici* (€18). Free camping is forbidden in many of the more beautiful parts of Italy, although the authorities seem to pay less attention in the off season.

Hostels

Hostels are called *ostelli per la gioventú* and are run by the Associazione Italiana Alberghi per la Gioventú (AIG), which is affiliated with HI. Prices, including breakfast, range from €10 to €15. Closing times vary, but are usually from 9am to 3pm or 5pm, and curfews are around midnight. Men and women are often segregated.

An HI card is not always required, but is recommended. Cards can be purchased at major hostels, from CTS offices and from AIG offices throughout Italy. Pick up a list of all hostels in Italy, with details of prices, locations etc from the **AIG office** *(☎ 06 487 11 52, fax 488 04 92; Via Cavour 44, Rome; open 9am-5pm Mon-Fri)*.

Pensioni & Hotels

Establishments are required to notify local tourist boards of prices for the coming year and by law must adhere to those prices. The best advice is to confirm hotel charges before you put your bags down, since many proprietors employ various methods of bill padding. These include a compulsory breakfast (up to €7.75 in the high season) and compulsory half or full board, although this can often be a good deal.

Single rooms are uniformly expensive in Italy (from around €30) and quite a number of establishments do not even bother to cater for the single traveller. There is often no difference between an establishment that calls itself a *pensione* and one that calls itself an *albergo* (hotel); in fact, some use both titles. *Locande* (similar to pensioni) and *alloggi*, sometimes also known as *affittacamere*, are generally cheaper, but not always.

Agriturismo

This is basically a farm holiday and is becoming increasingly popular in Italy. Traditionally, the idea was that families rented out rooms in their farmhouses. For detailed information on all facilities contact **Agriturist** *(☎ 06 685 23 42; W www.agriturist.it; Corso Vittorio Emanuele 101, 00186 Rome)*. It publishes *Agriturist* (€14) listing establishments throughout Italy.

Refuges

Before you go hiking in any part of Italy, obtain information about *rifugi* (refuges) from the local tourist offices. Some refuges have private rooms, but many offer dorm-style accommodation, especially those in more isolated areas. Average prices are from €10 to €25 per person for B&B. A meal costs around the same as at a trattoria. Locations of refuges are marked on good hiking maps and most open only from late June to September. The alpine refuges of CAI (Italian Alpine Club) offer discounts to members of associated foreign alpine clubs.

FOOD & DRINKS

Eating is one of life's great pleasures for Italians. Cooking styles vary notably from region to region. In the north the food is rich and often creamy; in central Italy the locals use a lot of olive oil and herbs and regional specialities are noted for their simplicity, fine flavour and the use of fresh produce. As you go further south the food becomes hotter and spicier and the *dolci* (cakes and pastries) sweeter and richer. Vegetarians will have no problems.

A full meal will consist of an antipasto, which can vary from *bruschetta,* a type of garlic bread with various toppings, to fried vegetables, or *prosciutto e melone* (ham wrapped around melon). Next comes the *primo piatto,* a pasta dish or risotto, followed by the *secondo piatto* of meat or fish. Italians often then eat an *insalata* (salad) or *contorni* and round off the meal with dolci and *caffé,* often at a bar.

Italian wine is justifiably world-famous. You'll rarely pay more than €7.75 for a bottle of very drinkable wine and as little as €3.10 will buy something reasonable. Try the famous *chianti* and *brunello* in Tuscany, and the *vernaccia* of San Gimignano, the *barolo* in Piedmont, the *lacrima christi* or *falanghina* in Naples and the *cannonau* in Sardinia.

ENTERTAINMENT

Italians make the most of entertainment, so visitors can indulge in opera, theatre, classical music recitals, rock concerts and traditional festivals. Major entertainment festivals are also held, such as the Festival of Two Worlds in June/July at Spoleto, Umbria Jazz in Perugia in July, Rome's Estate Romana in July, and the Venice Biennale every odd-numbered year. Operas are performed in Verona and Rome during summer (for details see the Entertainment sections under both cities) and at various times of the year throughout the country, notably at the opera houses in Milan and Rome.

Getting There & Away

AIR

The national carrier is Alitalia. Examples of high-season Alitalia fares at the time of writing are: Rome–Paris €311 return; Rome–London €271 return; and Rome–Amsterdam €311 return. Another option is to travel on charter flights. Try the **Charter Flight Centre** *(☎ 020-7828 1090; Ⓦ www.charterflights.co.uk; 19 Denbigh St, London SW1),* which specialises in such flights and also organises regular scheduled flights.

LAND

Eurolines *(Ⓦ www.eurolines.com)* is the main international bus carrier in Europe, with representatives in Italy and throughout the continent. In Italy the main bus company operating this service is **Lazzi** *(☎ 055 35 10 61; Piazza Adua 1, Florence, ☎ 06 884 08 40; Via Tagliamento 27b, Rome).* Buses leave from Rome, Florence, Milan, Turin, Venice and Naples, as well as numerous other Italian towns, for major cities throughout Europe including London, Paris, Barcelona, Madrid, Amsterdam, Budapest, Prague, Athens and Istanbul. Some ticket prices are: Rome–Paris €82 (€148 return), Rome–London €116 (€179 return) and Rome–Barcelona €102 (€183 return).

Eurostar (ES) and Eurocity (EC) trains run from major destinations throughout Europe direct to major Italian cities. On overnight hauls you can book a *cuccetta* (known outside Italy as a couchette or sleeping berth – worth booking!). Travellers under 26 can take advantage of the Inter-Rail Pass, Eurail Pass Youth and Europass Youth (see Ⓦ www.eurail.com). You can book tickets at train stations or at CTS, Sestante CIT and most travel agencies. Eurostar and Eurocity trains carry a supplement (determined by the distance you are travelling and the type of train).

To rent a car or motorcycle, you'll need a valid EU driving licence, an International Driving Permit, or your driving permit from your own country. If you're driving your own car, you'll need an international insurance certificate, known as a Carta Verde (Green Card), which can be obtained from your insurer.

Hitching is never safe in any country and we don't recommend it. Your best bet is to inquire at hostels throughout Europe, where you can often arrange a lift. **The International Lift Centre** *(☎ 055 28 06 26)* in Florence and **Enjoy Rome** *(☎ 06 445 18 43)* might be able to help organise lifts. It is illegal to hitch on the autostrade.

SEA

Ferries connect Italy to Spain, Croatia, Greece, Turkey, Tunisia and Malta. There are also services to Corsica (from Livorno) and

Albania (from Bari and Ancona). See Getting There & Away under Brindisi (for ferries to/from Greece), Ancona (to/from Greece, Albania and Croatia), Venice (to/from Greece) and Sicily (to/from Malta and Tunisia).

Getting Around

BUS

Numerous bus companies operate within Italy. It is usually necessary to make reservations only for long trips, such as Rome-Palermo or Rome-Brindisi. Buses can be a cheaper and faster way to get around if your destination is not on major rail lines, for instance from Umbria to Rome or Florence, and in the interior areas of Sicily and Sardinia.

TRAIN

Train travel is easy, relatively cheap and generally efficient. The Ferrovie dello Stato (FS) is the partially privatised state train system, and there are several private railway services.

There are several types of trains: Regionale (R), which usually stop at all stations and can be very slow; interRegionale (iR), which run between the regions; intercity (IC) or Eurocity (EC), which service only the major cities; and Eurostar Italia (ES), which serves major Italian and European cities. To go on the Intercity, Eurocity and Eurostar Italia trains, you have to pay a *supplemento,* an additional charge determined by distance and type of train.

All tickets *must* be validated in the yellow machines at the entrance to all train platforms.

The FS offers its own discount passes for travel within Italy. These include the Carta Verde for those aged between 12 and 26 years. It costs €26, is valid for one year, and entitles you to a 20% discount on all train travel. You can also buy a *biglietto chilometrico*, which is valid for two months and allows you to cover 3000km, with a maximum of 20 trips. It costs €117 (2nd class), and you must pay the supplement if you catch an Intercity or Eurostar train. Its main attraction is that it can be used by up to five people, either singly or together.

Some examples of 2nd-class fares (including the IC supplement) are Rome–Florence €21.95 and Rome–Naples €16.53.

CAR & MOTORCYCLE

Roads are generally good and there's an excellent system of *autostrade* (freeways). Helmets are compulsory for every motorcycle and moped rider and passenger – although you won't necessarily see evidence of this.

Some Italian cities, including Rome, Bologna, Florence, Milan and Turin have introduced restricted access to cars in their historical centres. The restrictions do not apply to vehicles with foreign registrations. *Motorini* (mopeds) and scooters (such as Vespas) are able to enter the zones without any problems. Petrol prices are high.

BICYCLE

Bikes are available for rent in many Italian towns – and cost around €10 a day or €60 a week. Bikes can travel in the baggage compartment of some Italian trains (not on Eurostars or Intercity trains).

BOAT

Navi (large ferries) service Sicily and Sardinia, and *traghetti* (smaller ferries) and *aliscafi* (hydrofoils) service areas such as Elba, the Aeolian Islands, Capri and Ischia. The main embarkation points for Sicily and Sardinia are Genoa, La Spezia, Livorno, Civitavecchia, Fiumicino and Naples. **Tirrenia Navigazione** (W *www.tirrenia.it*) is the major company servicing the Mediterranean, and it has offices throughout Italy. Most long-distance services travel overnight and all ferries carry vehicles (bicycles free of charge).

Rome (Roma)

postcode 00100 • pop 65 million

A phenomenal concentration of history, legend and monuments coexists in chaotic harmony in Rome, as well as an equally phenomenal concentration of people busily going about their everyday lives.

Rome's origins date to a group of Etruscan, Latin and Sabine settlements, but it is the legend of Romulus and Remus (the twins raised by a she-wolf) that has captured the popular imagination. The myth says Romulus killed his brother, then established the city. From the legend grew an empire that eventually controlled almost the entire world known to Europeans.

Rome was home to the two great empires of the Western world: the Roman Empire and the Catholic Church. On the one hand is the Forum and Colosseum, on the other St Peter's and the Vatican. In between lies so many layers of history that what you see is only the tip of the iceberg.

ORIENTATION

Rome is a vast city, but the historical centre is relatively small. Most of the major sights are within walking distance of the central train station, Stazione Termini. Lonely Planet's *Rome City Map* is handy.

The main bus terminus is in Piazza del Cinquecento, directly in front of the train station. Many intercity buses arrive and depart from the Piazzale Tiburtina, in front of the Stazione Tiburtina, accessible from Termini on the Metropolitana Linea B.

INFORMATION

Tourist Offices

There is an **APT tourist information office** *(☎ 06 48 90 63 00; open daily)* at Stazione Termini. It's in the central courseway and has multilingual staff, as well as 'roaming' staff who may approach you in the station (ID is visible). The great main **APT office** *(☎ 06 36 00 43 99; Via Parigi 5; open Mon-Sat)* is northwest from Stazione Termini, through Piazza della Repubblica. It has information on hotels and museum opening hours and entrance fees. Staff can also provide maps and printed information about provincial and intercity bus services.

Another good source of information and assistance is **Enjoy Rome** *(☎ 06 445 18 43, fax 06 445 68 90; W www.enjoyrome.com; Via Marghera 8a; open daily)*, five minutes northeast of the station. A privately run tourist office, it offers a free hotel-reservation service. You can book great three-hour walking tours that cover all sorts of interests and are conducted by native English speakers or art and history specialists.

Money

Banks are open 8.45am to 1.30pm and 2.45pm to 4pm weekdays. You'll find banks and exchange offices at Stazione Termini. There is also an exchange office at Fiumicino airport.

Numerous other exchange offices are scattered throughout the city, including **American Express** *(☎ 06 676 41; Piazza di Spagna 38)* and **Thomas Cook** *(☎ 06 482 81 82; Piazza Barberini 21)*.

Otherwise, go to any one of the dozens of banks in the city centre.

Post & Communications

The **main post office** *(Piazza San Silvestro 19; open 8.30am-6.30pm Mon-Fri & 8.30am-1pm Sat)* is off Via del Tritone. *Fermo posta* (poste restante) is available; use the postcode 00186. The **Vatican post office** *(☎ 06 69 88 34 06; St Peter's Square; open 8.30am-7pm Mon-Fri & 8.30am-6pm Sat)* offers faster and more reliable service (no *fermo posta* though).

There is a small Telecom office at Stazione Termini, from where you can make international calls. Another office is near the station, on Via San Martino della Battaglia opposite Hotel Lachea-Dolomiti.

There are dozens of Internet cafés scattered throughout the city. The biggest and most convenient is **easyEverything** *(Via Barberini 2; open 24hr)*, which has hundreds of terminals and charges around €1 for 30 minutes, depending on the time of day.

Travel Agencies

At **Sestante CIT** *(☎ 06 46 20 31 44; Piazza della Repubblica 65)* you can make bookings for planes, trains and ferries. The staff speak English and there's information on fares for students and young people, plus tours of Rome and surrounds. The student tourist centre, **CTS** *(☎ 06 462 04 31; W www.cts.it; Via Genova 16)*, off Via Nazionale, offers similar services.

Medical & Emergency Services

Emergency medical treatment is available in the *pronto soccorso* (casualty section) at public hospitals, including **Ospedale San Gallicano** *(☎ 06 588 23 90; Via di San Gallicano 25/a, Trastevere)*, specialising in skin and venereal diseases; **Ospedale San Giacome** *(☎ 06 362 61; Via Canova 29)* near Piazza del Popolo; and **Policlinico Umberto I** *(☎ 06 499 71; Via del Policlinico 155)*, close to Stazione Termini.

There is a **24-hour pharmacy** *(☎ 06 488 00 19; Piazza del Cinquecento 51)* near Stazione Termini. All pharmacies post a list in their windows of others open at night nearby.

Report thefts at **police headquarters** *(questura; ☎ 06 468 61; Via San Vitale 11; open 24hr daily)*. Its **Foreigners Bureau** *(Ufficio Stranieri; ☎ 06 46 86 29 77; Via Genova 2)* is around the corner. For immediate police attendance call ☎ 113.

Dangers & Annoyances

Thieves are active in the areas in and around Stazione Termini, at major sights such as the

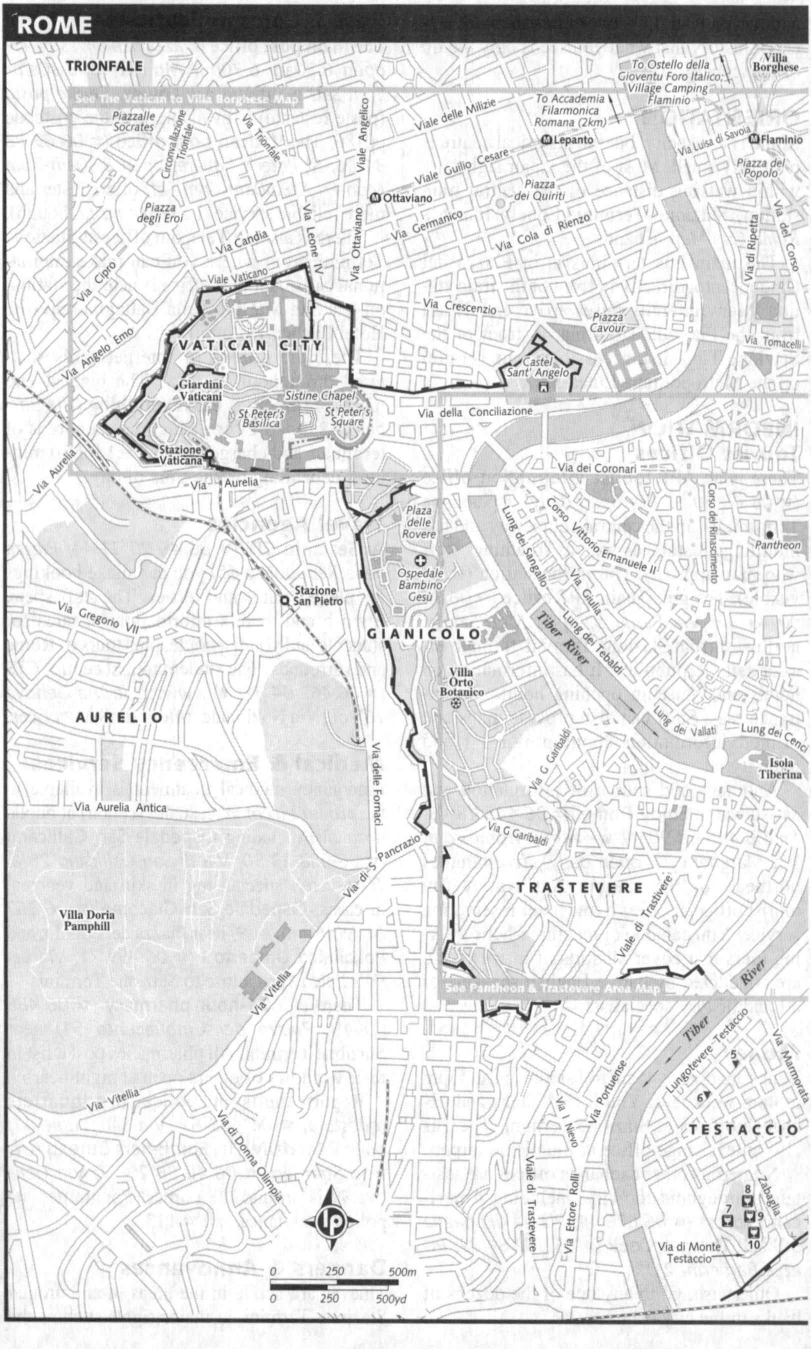

ROME

TRIONFALE

See The Vatican to Villa Borghese Map

To Ostello della Gioventu Foro Italico; Village Camping Flaminio

Villa Borghese

To Accademia Filarmonica Romana (2km)

Piazzalle Socrates

Circonvallazione Trionfale

Via Trionfale

Viale Angelico

Viale delle Milizie

Lepanto

Via Luisa di Savoia

Flaminio

Viale Guilio Cesare

Piazza del Popolo

Piazza degli Eroi

Via Leone IV

Via Ottaviano

Ottaviano

Piazza dei Quiriti

Via Germanico

Via Cola di Rienzo

Via di Ripetta

Via del Corso

Via Candia

Via Cipro

Viale Vaticano

Via Crescenzio

Piazza Cavour

Via Angelo Emo

VATICAN CITY

Via Tomacelli

Castel Sant' Angelo

Giardini Vaticani

Sistine Chapel

St Peter's Basilica

St Peter's Square

Via della Conciliazione

Stazione Vaticana

Via Aurelia

Via dei Coronari

Via Aurelia

Corso Vittorio Emanuele II

Corso del Rinascimento

Lung dei Sangallo

Plaza delle Rovere

Pantheon

Ospedale Bambino Gesù

Via Giulia

Stazione San Pietro

Via Gregorio VII

Lung dei Tebaldi

Tiber River

GIANICOLO

Villa Orto Botanico

AURELIO

Lung dei Vallati

Lung dei Cenci

Via G Garibaldi

Isola Tiberina

Via delle Fornaci

Via Aurelia Antica

Via G Garibaldi

Via di S Pancrazio

TRASTEVERE

Viale di Trastevere

Villa Doria Pamphill

River

See Pantheon & Trastevere Area Map

Via Vitellia

Tiber

Lungotevere Testaccio

Via Marmorata

5

6

Via Portuense

Via Vitellia

Via I Nievo

TESTACCIO

Via di Donna Olimpia

Viale di Trastevere

Via Ettore Rolli

Zabaglia

8

7

9

10

Via di Monte Testaccio

0 250 500m

0 250 500yd

ITALY

ROME

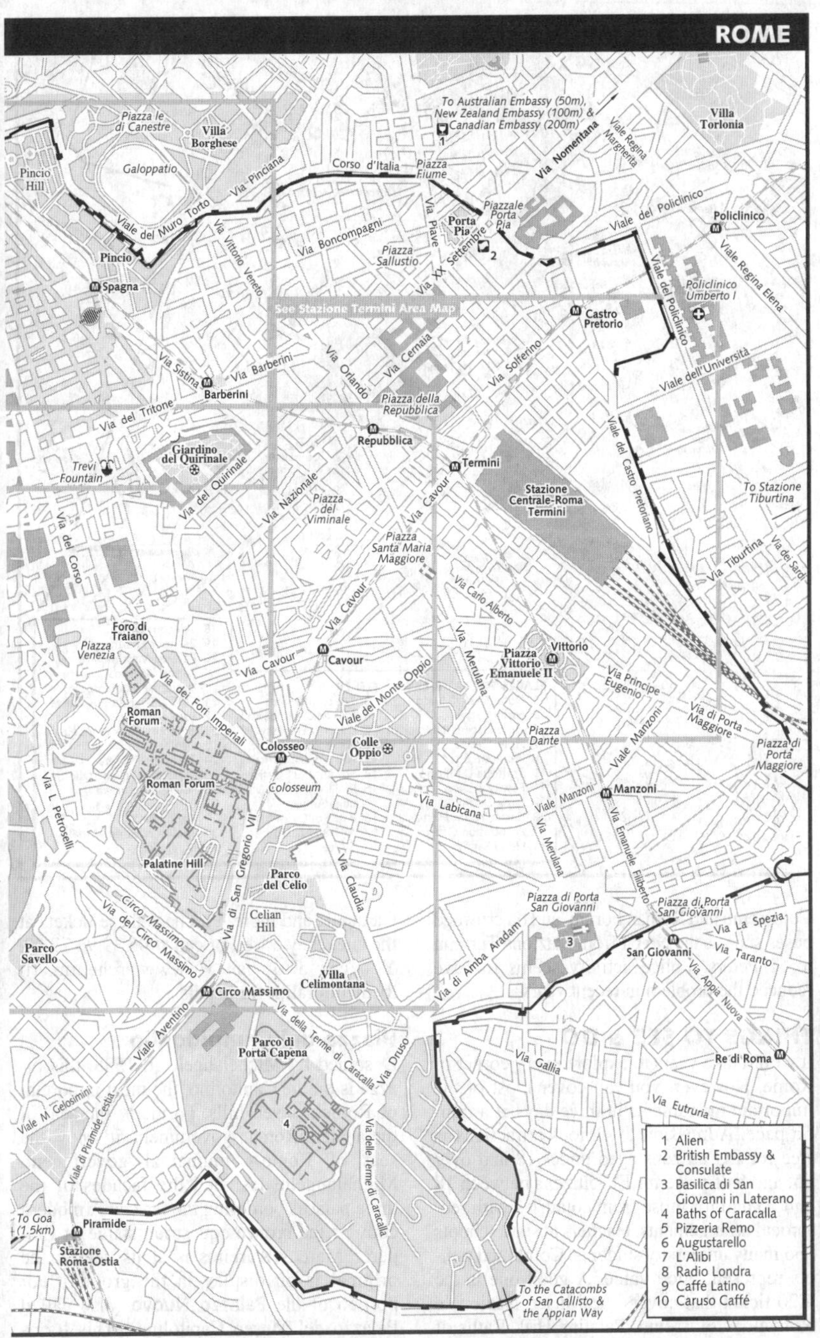
To Australian Embassy (50m), New Zealand Embassy (100m) & Canadian Embassy (200m)
Villa Torlonia
Piazza le di Canestre
Villa Borghese
Galoppatio
Pincio Hill
Pincio
Spagna
Corso d'Italia
Piazza Fiume
Via Nomentana
Viale Regina Margherita
Piazzale Porta Pia
Porta Pia
Viale del Policlinico
Policlinico
Policlinico Umberto I
Viale Regina Elena
Viale del Muro Torto
Via Pinciana
Via Vittorio Veneto
Via Boncompagni
Piazza Sallustio
Via Piave
Via XX Settembre
See Stazione Termini Area Map
Castro Pretorio
Viale dell'Università
Via Sistina
Barberini
Via Barberini
Via Orlando
Via Cernaia
Piazza della Repubblica
Via Solferino
Via del Tritone
Repubblica
Giardino del Quirinale
Trevi Fountain
Via del Quirinale
Termini
Stazione Centrale-Roma Termini
Viale del Castro Pretoriano
To Stazione Tiburtina
Via Nazionale
Piazza del Viminale
Via Cavour
Via del Corso
Piazza Santa Maria Maggiore
Via Tiburtina
Via dei Sardi
Via Carlo Alberto
Foro di Traiano
Piazza Venezia
Cavour
Via Merulana
Piazza Vittorio Emanuele II
Vittorio
Via dei Fori Imperiali
Via del Monte Oppio
Via Principe Eugenio
Roman Forum
Colosseo
Colle Oppio
Piazza Dante
Viale Manzoni
Via di Porta Maggiore
Piazza di Porta Maggiore
Via L Petroselli
Colosseum
Manzoni
Via Labicana
Via Emanuele Filiberto
Palatine Hill
Via di San Gregorio VII
Parco del Celio
Via Claudia
Piazza di Porta San Giovanni
Celian Hill
Via Circo Massimo
Via del Circo Massimo
Via di Amba Aradam
Via La Spezia
San Giovanni
Via Taranto
Parco Savello
Villa Celimontana
Via Appia Nuova
Circo Massimo
Via della Terme di Caracalla
Viale Aventino
Parco di Porta Capena
Via Druso
Via Gallia
Re di Roma
Viale M Gelosimini
Viale di Piramide Cestia
Via delle Terme di Caracalla
Via Eutruria
To Goa (1.5km)
Piramide
Stazione Roma-Ostia
To the Catacombs of San Callisto & the Appian Way
1 Alien
2 British Embassy & Consulate
3 Basilica di San Giovanni in Laterano
4 Baths of Caracalla
5 Pizzeria Remo
6 Augustarello
7 L'Alibi
8 Radio Londra
9 Caffé Latino
10 Caruso Caffé
ITALY

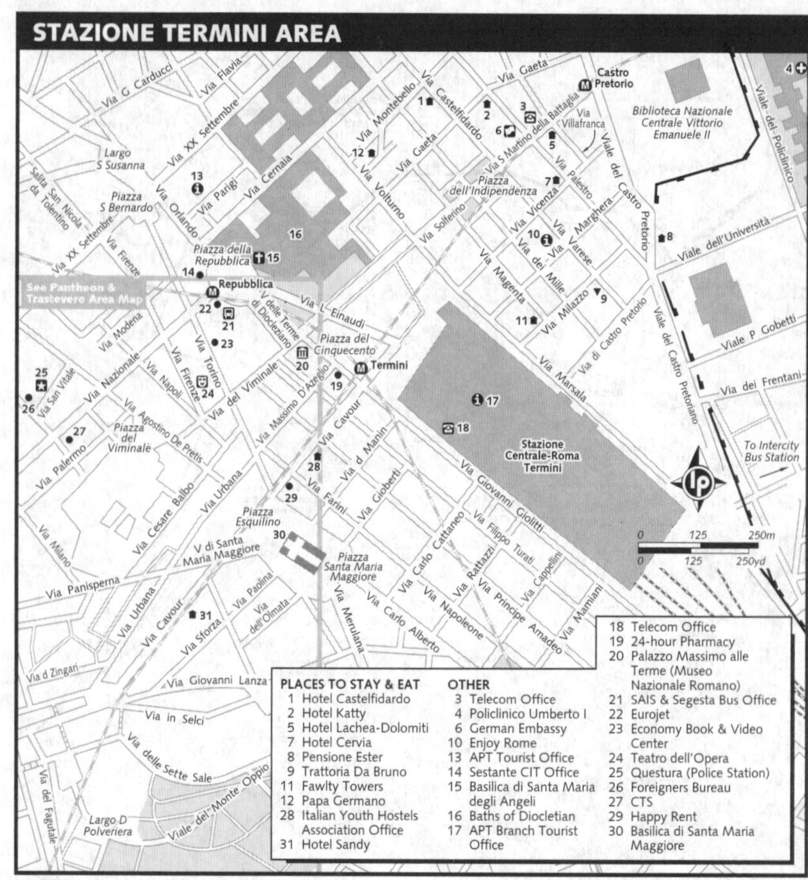

Colosseum and Roman Forum, and on crowded buses such as the No 64 from Stazione Termini to St Peters. Police activity seems to have reduced the problem in recent years.

THINGS TO SEE & DO

It would take years to explore every corner of Rome. However, you can cover most of the important monuments in three days at a frantic pace. Admission to various attractions is free for EU citizens aged under 18 and over 65, and half-price for EU citizens between 18 and 25 and for those from countries with reciprocal arrangements, teachers at state schools and many university students. Combined tickets represent good value. A good one is the €20 ticket that covers the Museo Nazionale Romano, Colosseum, Palatine Hill, Baths of Caracalla and more. Purchase these tickets at the sites they cover, or call ☎ 06 39 96 77 00. You can also visit W www.archeorm.arti.beniculturali.it for details.

Piazza del Campidoglio

Designed by Michelangelo in 1538, this piazza is on the Capitolino, the most important of Rome's seven hills. Formerly the seat of the ancient Roman government, it's now the seat of Rome's municipal government. Michelangelo designed the facades of the three palaces bordering the piazza. A modern copy of the bronze equestrian statue of Emperor Marcus Aurelius is at its centre; the original is on display in the ground-floor portico of the **Palazzo Nuovo** (also called Palazzo del Museo Capitolino). This forms part of the **Musei Capitolini** *(☎ 06 67 10 20 71; admission €6.20; open 9am-8pm Tues-Sun)*, well worth a visit for its collections of ancient Roman sculptures.

Walk to the right of the Palazzo del Senato to see a panorama of the Roman Forum. Walk to the left of the same building to reach the ancient Roman Carcere Mamertino, where it's believed St Peter was imprisoned.

Piazza Venezia

This piazza is overshadowed by the neoclassical **Monumento Vittorio Emanuele II**, often referred to by Italians as the *macchina da scrivere* (typewriter) due to its appearance. Built to commemorate Italian unification, the piazza incorporates the **Altare della Patria** and the tomb of the unknown soldier, as well as the **Museo del Risorgimento**. Also in the piazza is the 15th-century **Palazzo Venezia**, which was Mussolini's official residence.

Roman Forum & Palatine Hill

The commercial, political and religious centre of ancient Rome, the Roman Forum *(☎ 06 699 01 10; admission to Forum free, to Palatine Hill with Colosseum €8; open 9am-1hr before sunset)* stands in a valley between the Capitoline and Palatine (Palatino) hills. The area became a centre for political rallies, public ceremonies and senate meetings. The area was systematically excavated in the 18th and 19th centuries. You can enter the Forum from Via dei Fori Imperiali, which leads from Piazza Venezia to the Colosseum.

As you enter, to your left is the **Tempio di Antonino e Faustina**, erected by the senate in AD 141 and transformed into a church in the 8th century. To your right are the remains of the **Basilica Aemilia**, built in 179 BC and plundered for marble during the Renaissance. The Via Sacra, which traverses the Forum from northwest to southeast, runs in front of the basilica. Towards the Campidoglio is the **Curia**, once the meeting place of the Roman senate and converted into a church. The Curia was restored in the 1930s. In front of the Curia is the **Lapis Niger**, a large piece of black marble which legend says covered the grave of Romulus.

The **Arco di Settimo Severo** was erected in AD 203 in honour of this emperor and his sons, and is considered one of Italy's major triumphal arches. A circular base stone beside the arch marks the *umbilicus urbis*, the symbolic centre of ancient Rome.

South along the Via Sacra is the **Tempio di Saturno**, one of the most important temples in ancient Rome. The **Basilica Giulia**, in front of the temple, was the seat of justice. Nearby is the **Tempio di Giulio Cesare** (Temple of Julius Caesar), erected by Augustus in 29 BC. It's the spot where Mark Antony read his famous speech.

In the area southeast of the temple is the **Chiesa di Santa Maria Antiqua**, the oldest Christian church in the Forum. Back on the Via Sacra is the **Case delle Vestali**, home of the virgins who tended the sacred flame in the adjoining **Tempio di Vesta**.

Climb the Palatine, where wealthy Romans built their homes and where Romulus supposedly founded the city. This hill was home to the area's earliest settlements. Worth a look is the impressive **Domus Augustana**, which was the private residence of the emperors; the **Domus Flavia**, the residence of Domitian; the **Tempio della Magna Mater**, built in 204 BC to house a black stone connected with the Asiatic goddess Cybele; and the fresco-adorned **Casa di Livia**, thought to have been the house of the wife of Emperor Augustus.

Colosseum & Arch of Constantine

Originally known as the Flavian Amphitheatre, Rome's most famous monument *(☎ 06 700 42 61; admission with Palatine €8; open 9am-1hr before sunset)* was begun by Emperor Vespasian in AD 72. The massive structure could seat 80,000 and featured bloody gladiatorial combat and wild beast shows that resulted in thousands of human and animal deaths.

In the Middle Ages the Colosseum became a fortress and was later used as a quarry for travertine and marble. Restoration works have been under way since 1992. Avoid having your photo taken with the muscly dudes dressed as gladiators, who will make extortionate demands for money.

On the west side of the Colosseum is the triumphal arch built to honour Constantine following his victory over his rival Maxentius at the battle of Milvian Bridge in AD 312. Its decorative reliefs were taken from earlier structures.

Baths of Caracalla

The huge Terme di Caracalla complex *(☎ 06 575 86 26; Viale delle Terme di Caracalla 52; admission €5; open 9am-1hr before*

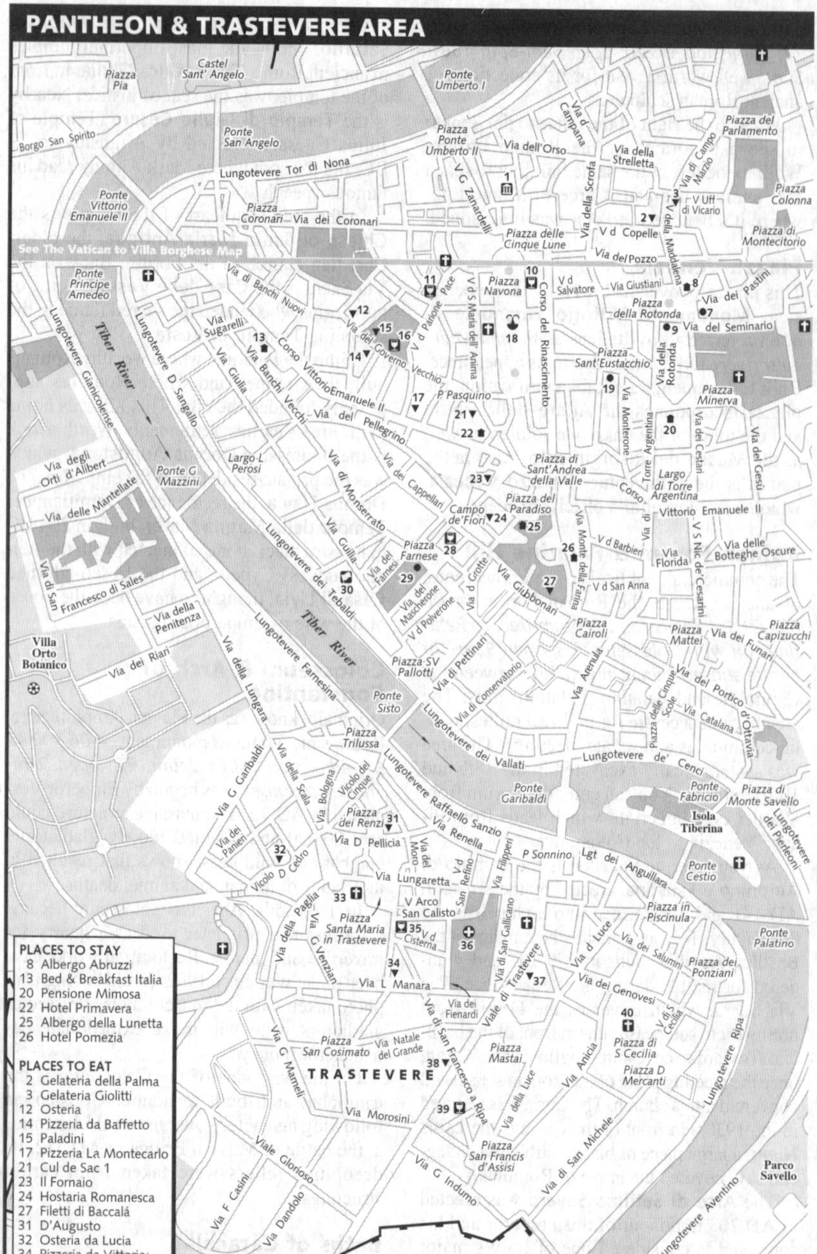

PANTHEON & TRASTEVERE AREA

See The Vatican to Villa Borghese Map

TRASTEVERE

PLACES TO STAY

- 8 Albergo Abruzzi
- 13 Bed & Breakfast Italia
- 20 Pensione Mimosa
- 22 Hotel Primavera
- 25 Albergo della Lunetta
- 26 Hotel Pomezia

PLACES TO EAT

- 2 Gelateria della Palma
- 3 Gelateria Giolitti
- 12 Osteria
- 14 Pizzeria da Baffetto
- 15 Paladini
- 17 Pizzeria La Montecarlo
- 21 Cul de Sac 1
- 23 Il Fornaio
- 24 Hostaria Romanesca
- 27 Filetti di Baccalá
- 31 D'Augusto
- 32 Osteria da Lucia
- 34 Pizzeria da Vittorio; Capo de Ferro
- 37 Fonte della Salute
- 38 Frontoni

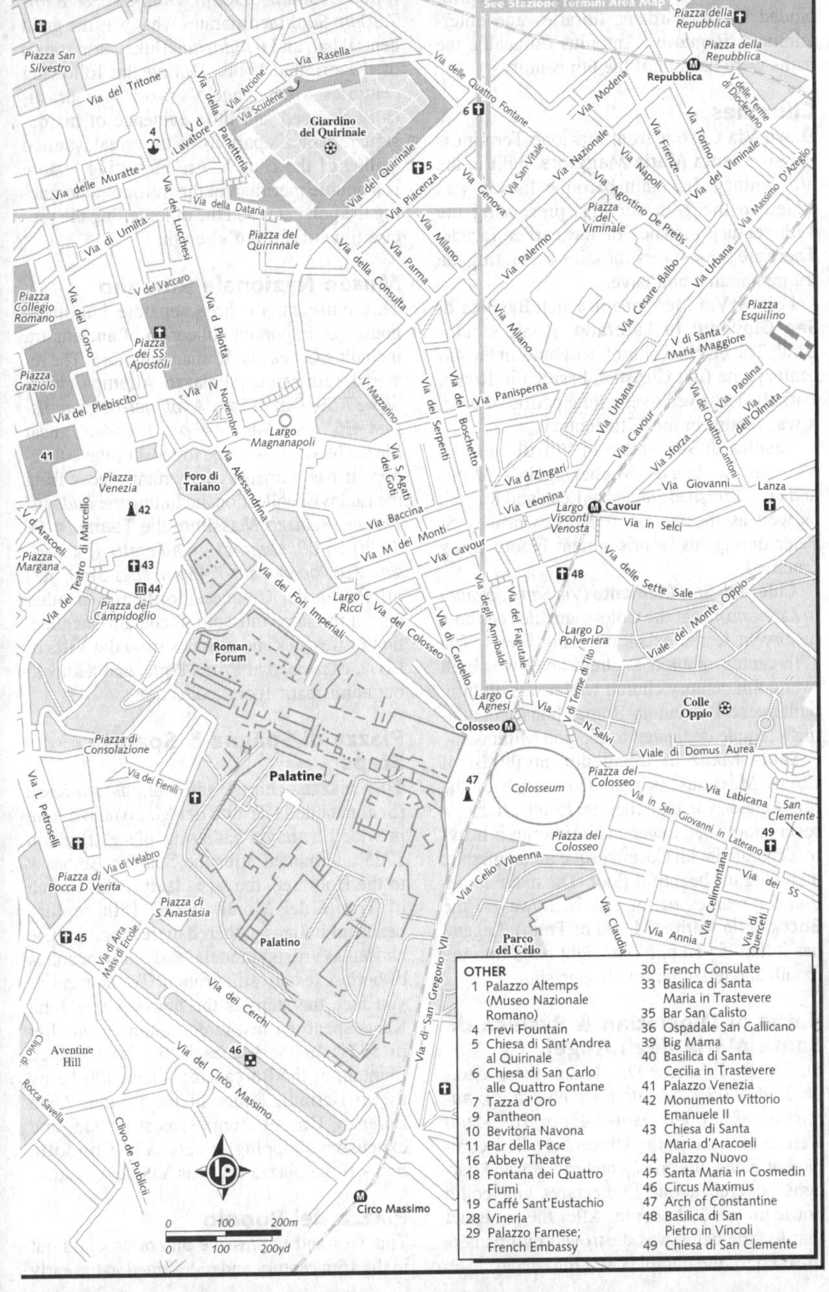
PANTHEON & TRASTEVERE AREA
See Stazione Termini Area Map
Piazza San Silvestro
Via del Tritone
Via Rasella
Via Arcione
Via Scuderie
Via della Panetteria
V d Lavatore
Giardino del Quirinale
Via delle Quattro Fontane
Piazza della Repubblica
Repubblica
V delle Terme di Diocleziano
Via Modena
Via Torino
Via Firenze
Via Nazionale
Via San Vitale
Via Napoli
Via del Viminale
Via Massimo D'Azeglio
Via Agostino De Pretis
Piazza del Viminale
Via Genova
Via Piacenza
Via del Quirinale
Via delle Muratte
Via della Dataria
Via dei Lucchesi
Piazza del Quirinale
Via di Umiltà
Via Milano
Via Parma
Via della Consulta
Via Palermo
Via Urbana
Via Cesare Balbo
Piazza Esquilino
V di Santa Maria Maggiore
Piazza Collegio Romano
V del Vaccaro
Via del Corso
Piazza dei SS Apostoli
Via d Pilotta
Piazza Graziolo
Via del Plebiscito
Via IV Novembre
Largo Magnanapoli
V Mazzarino
Via dei Serpenti
Via del Boschetto
Via Panisperna
Via Paolina
Via dell'Olmata
Via del Quattro Cantoni
Via Cavour
Via Storza
Via S Agati dei Goti
Piazza Venezia
Foro di Traiano
Via Alessandrina
Via d Zingari
Via Giovanni Lanza
Via Leonina
Largo Visconti Venosta
Cavour
Via in Selci
Via Baccina
Via M dei Monti
V d Aracoeli
Via del Teatro di Marcello
Piazza Margana
Via dei Fori Imperiali
Via delle Sette Sale
Piazza del Campidoglio
Largo C Ricci
Via del Colosseo
Via degli Annibaldi
Via del Fagutale
Via di Cardello
Largo D Polveriera
Viale del Monte Oppio
Roman Forum
Via di Terme di Tito
Largo G Agnesi
Via N Salvi
Colle Oppio
Colosseo
Piazza di Consolazione
Viale di Domus Aurea
Via dei Fienili
Palatine
Piazza del Colosseo
Colosseum
Via Labicana
Via in San Giovanni in Laterano
San Clemente
Via L Petroselli
Via di Velabro
Piazza di Bocca D Verita
Via Celio Vibenna
Via Celimontana
Via dei SS Quattro
Piazza di S Anastasia
Via Claudia
Via Annia
Via di Querceti
Via di Arra Mass di Ercole
Palatino
Parco del Celio
Via dei Cerchi
Via di San Gregorio VII
Clivo di
Aventine Hill
Via del Circo Massimo
Rocca Savella
Clivo de Publicii
Circo Massimo
0 100 200m
0 100 200yd
OTHER
1 Palazzo Altemps (Museo Nazionale Romano)
4 Trevi Fountain
5 Chiesa di Sant'Andrea al Quirinale
6 Chiesa di San Carlo alle Quattro Fontane
7 Tazza d'Oro
9 Pantheon
10 Bevitoria Navona
11 Bar della Pace
16 Abbey Theatre
18 Fontana dei Quattro Fiumi
19 Caffé Sant'Eustachio
28 Vineria
29 Palazzo Farnese; French Embassy
30 French Consulate
33 Basilica di Santa Maria in Trastevere
35 Bar San Calisto
36 Ospadale San Gallicano
39 Big Mama
40 Basilica di Santa Cecilia in Trastevere
41 Palazzo Venezia
42 Monumento Vittorio Emanuele II
43 Chiesa di Santa Maria d'Aracoeli
44 Palazzo Nuovo
45 Santa Maria in Cosmedin
46 Circus Maximus
47 Arch of Constantine
48 Basilica di San Pietro in Vincoli
49 Chiesa di San Clemente

sunset Tues-Sun & 9am-2pm Mon), covering 10 hectares, could hold 1600 people and included shops, gardens, libraries and entertainment. Begun by Antonius Caracalla, the baths were used until the 6th century.

Churches

Down Via Cavour from Stazione Termini is massive **Santa Maria Maggiore**, built in the 5th century. Its main baroque facade was added in the 18th century, preserving the 13th-century mosaics of the earlier facade. There are 5th-century mosaics decorating the triumphal arch and nave.

Follow Via Merulana to reach **Basilica di San Giovanni in Laterano**, Rome's cathedral. The original church was built in the 4th century, the first Christian basilica in Rome. Largely destroyed over a long period of time, it was rebuilt in the 17th century.

Basilica di San Pietro in Vincoli, just off Via Cavour, houses Michelangelo's *Moses* and his unfinished statues of Leah and Rachel, as well as the *vincoli* (chains) worn by St Peter during his imprisonment before being crucified.

Chiesa di San Clemente *(Via San Giovanni in Laterano)*, near the Colosseum, defines how history in Rome exists on many levels. The 12th-century church at street level was built over a 4th-century church which was, in turn, built over a 1st-century Roman house containing a temple dedicated to the god Mithras.

Santa Maria in Cosmedin, northwest of Circus Maximus, is regarded as one of the finest medieval churches in Rome. It has a seven-storey bell tower and its interior is heavily decorated with Cosmatesque inlaid marble, including the beautiful floor. The main attraction for masses of tourists is, however, the **Bocca della Veritá** (Mouth of Truth). Legend has it that if you put your right hand into the mouth and tell a lie, it will snap shut.

Baths of Diocletian & Basilica di Santa Maria degli Angeli

Started by Emperor Diocletian, these baths *(☎ 06 488 05 30; Viale E De Nicola 79; admission €5; open 9am-7.45pm Tues-Sun)* were completed in the 4th century. The complex of baths, libraries, concert halls and gardens covered about 13 hectares and could house up to 3000 people. After the aqueduct that fed the baths was destroyed by invaders in AD 536, the complex fell into decay.

Designed by Michelangelo, the basilica *(open 7.30am-6.30pm Mon-Sat & 8am-7.30pm Sun)* incorporates what was the great central hall and *tepidarium* (lukewarm room) of the original baths. During the following centuries Michelangelo's work was drastically changed and little evidence of his design remains, apart from the great vaulted ceiling of the church. An interesting feature is a double meridian in the transept, one tracing the polar star and the other telling the precise time of the sun's zenith.

Museo Nazionale Romano

This museum, in three separate buildings, houses an important collection of ancient art, including Greek and Roman sculpture. The restored 15th-century **Palazzo Altemps** *(☎ 06 683 37 59; Piazza Sant'Apollinare 44; admission €5; open 9am-7.45pm Tues-Sun)*, near Piazza Navona, is home to most of the collection. It has numerous important pieces from the Ludovisi collection, including the *Ludovisi Throne*. **Palazzo Massimo alle Terme** *(☎ 06 48 90 35 00; Largo di Villa Peretti 1; admission €6; open 9am-7.45pm Tues-Sun)*, just off Piazza dei Cinquecento, houses another part of the same museum. It contains a collection of frescoes and mosaics from the Villa of Livia, excavated at Prima Porta, and a knockout numismatic (coin) collection.

Piazza di Spagna & Spanish Steps

This piazza, church and famous staircase (Scalinata della Trinitá dei Monti) have long provided a major gathering place. Built in 1725 and named after the Spanish Embassy to the Holy See, the steps lead to the church of Trinitá dei Monti. In the 18th century beautiful Italians gathered there, hoping to be chosen as artists' models, and many beauties of both sexes are still around. To the right as you face the steps is the house where John Keats spent the last three months of his life in 1821. In the piazza is the boat-shaped fountain of the **Barcaccia**, believed to be by Pietro Bernini, father of the famous Gian Lorenzo. One of Rome's most elegant and expensive shopping streets, **Via Condotti**, runs off the piazza towards Via del Corso.

Piazza del Popolo

This vast and impressive piazza was laid out in the 16th century and redesigned in the early

19th century by Giuseppe Valadier. The piazza is also home to Santa Maria del Popolo, where two magnificent Caravaggio paintings (one of St Peter and one of St Paul) are housed. The piazza is at the foot of the **Pincio Hill**, from where there is a wonderful panoramic view of the city, especially in the early hours.

Villa Borghese

This beautiful park was once the estate of Cardinal Scipione Borghese. His 17th-century villa houses the **Museo e Galleria Borghese** *(☎ 06 32 81 01; admission €6.50, booking fee €1.03; open 9am-9pm Tues-Sat)*, a collection of important paintings and sculptures gathered by the Borghese family; bookings are essential. Outside the park is **Galleria Nazionale d'Arte Moderna** *(☎ 06 32 29 81; Viale delle Belle Arti 131; admission €6.50; open 8.30am-7.30pm Tues-Sun)*. The Etruscan museum, **Museo Nazionale Etrusco di Villa Giulia** *(admission €4; open 8.30am-7.30pm Tues-Sun)*, is on the same street in Piazzale di Villa Giulia, in the former villa of Pope Julius III.

Trevi Fountain

The high-baroque Fontana di Trevi was designed by Nicola Salvi in 1732. Its water was supplied by one of Rome's earliest aqueducts. The custom is to throw a coin into the fountain (over your shoulder while facing away) to ensure your return to Rome. If you throw a second coin you can make a wish.

Pantheon

The Pantheon *(Piazza della Rotonda; admission free; open 8.30am-7.30pm Mon-Sat, 9am-6pm Sun)* is the best-preserved building of ancient Rome. The original temple was built in 27 BC by Marcus Agrippa, son-in-law of Emperor Augustus, and dedicated to the planetary gods. Agrippa's name remains inscribed over the entrance.

Over the centuries the temple was consistently plundered and damaged. The gilded-bronze roof tiles were removed by an emperor of the eastern empire, and Pope Urban VIII had the bronze ceiling of the portico melted down to make the canopy over the main altar of St Peter's and 80 cannons for Castel Sant' Angelo. The Pantheon's extraordinary dome is considered the most important achievement of ancient Roman architecture. The Italian kings Vittorio Emanuele II and Umberto I and the painter Raphael are buried there.

Piazza Navona

This vast and beautiful square, lined with baroque palaces, was laid out on the ruins of Domitian's stadium and features three fountains. In its centre is Bernini's masterpiece, **Fontana dei Quattro Fiumi** (Fountain of the Four Rivers). Relax on one of the stone benches or the expensive cafés and watch the artists who gather in the piazza to work.

Campo de' Fiori

Lined with bars and trattorias that get packed at night, the piazza was a place of execution during the Inquisition. Nowadays a flower and vegetable market is held here Monday to Saturday. So much for respect.

The **Palazzo Farnese** (Farnese Palace), in the piazza of the same name, is just off Campo de' Fiori. A magnificent Renaissance building, it was started in 1514 by Antonio da Sangallo, work was carried on by Michelangelo and it was completed by Giacomo della Porta. Built for Cardinal Alessandro Farnese (later Pope Paul III), the palace is now the French embassy. The piazza has two fountains, which were enormous granite baths taken from the Baths of Caracalla.

Trastevere

You can wander through the narrow medieval streets of this area, which, despite the many foreigners who live here, retains the air of a typical Roman neighbourhood. It is especially beautiful at night and is a wonderful area for bar-hopping or a meal.

Of particular note here is the **Basilica di Santa Maria in Trastevere**, in the lovely piazza of the same name. It is believed to be the oldest church dedicated to the Virgin in Rome. Although the first church was built on the site in the 4th century, the present structure was built in the 12th century and features a Romanesque bell tower and facade, with a mosaic of the Virgin. Its interior was redecorated during the baroque period, but the vibrant mosaics in the apse and on the triumphal arch date from the 12th century. Also take a look at the **Basilica di Santa Cecilia in Trastevere**.

Catacombs

There are several catacombs in Rome, consisting of miles of tunnels carved out of volcanic rock, which were the meeting and burial places of early Christians. The largest are along the Via Appia Antica, just outside the

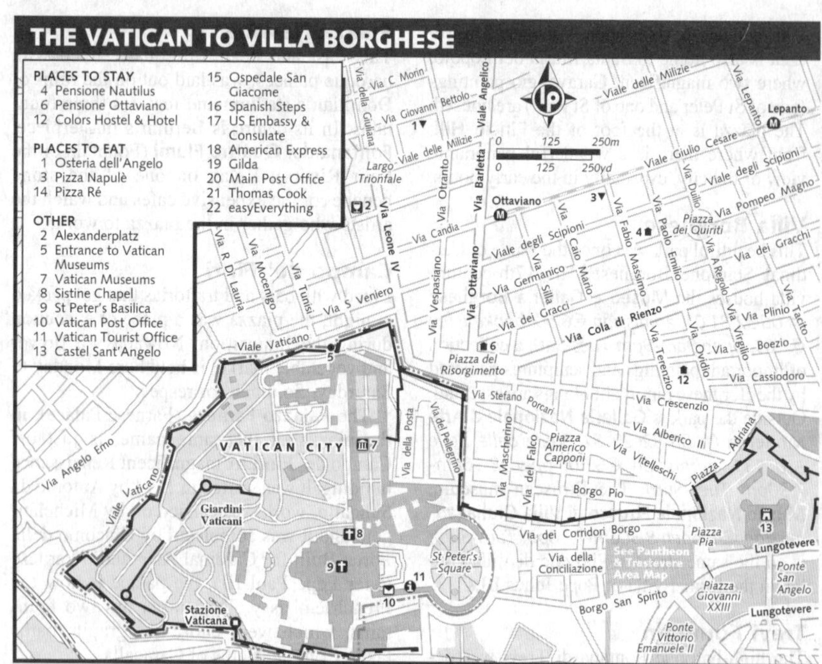

city and accessible on Metropolitana Linea A to Colli Albani, then bus No 660. The **Catacombs of San Callisto** *(admission only with guide €5; open 8.30am-noon & 2.30pm-5pm Thur-Tues Mar-Jan)* and **Catacombs of San Sebastiano** *(admission €5; open 8.30am-noon & 2.30pm-5pm Mon-Sat 10 Dec-10 Nov)* are almost next to each other.

Vatican City

In 1929, Mussolini, under the Lateran Treaty, gave the pope full sovereignty over what is now the world's smallest country.

The **tourist office** *(☎ 06 69 88 16 62; Piazza San Pietro; open Mon-Sat)* is to the left of the basilica. Guided tours of the Vatican City gardens (€10) can be organised here. In the same area is the **Vatican post office** *(☎ 06 69 88 34 06; open 8.30am-7pm Mon-Fri & 8.30am-6pm Sat)*. The city has its own postal service, newspaper, radio station, train station and army of Swiss Guards.

St Peter's Basilica & Square The most famous church, but no longer largest, in the Christian world, **St Peter's** *(San Pietro; open 7am-7pm daily Apr-Sep, 7am-6pm daily Oct-Mar)* stands on the site where St Peter was buried. The first church on the site was built during Constantine's reign in the 4th century, and in 1506 work started on a new basilica, designed by Bramante.

It is generally held that St Peter's owes its grandeur and power to Michelangelo, who took over the project in 1547 at the age of 72. The cavernous interior contains numerous treasures, including Michelangelo's superb *Pietà*, sculpted when he was only 24 years old and the only work to carry his signature.

The extraordinary baroque *Baldacchino* (a heavily sculpted bronze canopy over the papal altar), by Bernini, stands 29m high. Another point of note is the red porphyry disc near the central door, which marks the spot where Charlemagne and later emperors were crowned by the pope.

Entrance to Michelangelo's soaring dome is to the right as you climb the stairs to the atrium of the basilica. Make the entire climb on foot for €4, or pay €5 and take the elevator for part of the way.

Dress rules and security are stringently enforced – no shorts, miniskirts or sleeveless tops, and expect to have your bags searched.

THE VATICAN TO VILLA BORGHESE

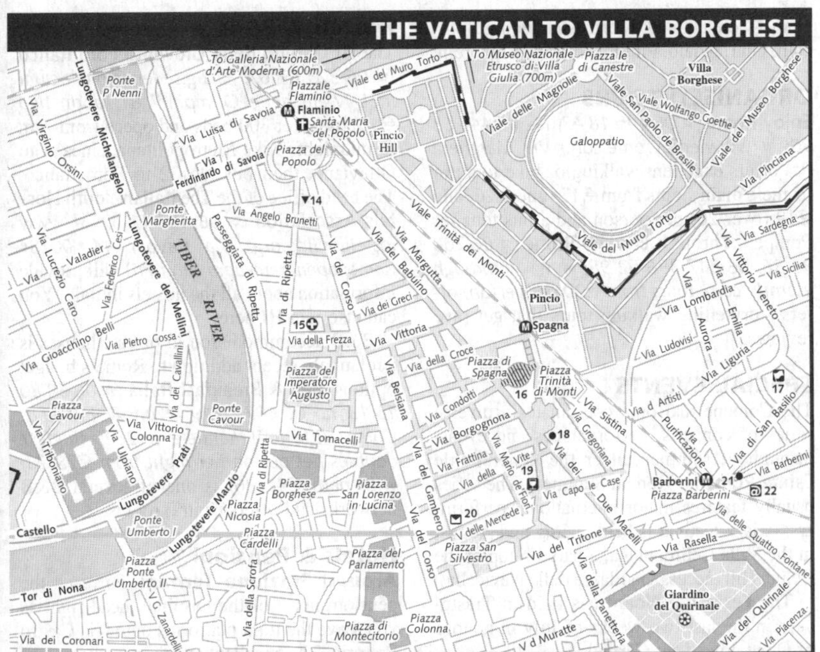

Bernini's **Piazza San Pietro** (St Peter's Square) is rightly considered a masterpiece. Laid out in the 17th century, the immense piazza is bound by two semicircular colonnades, each of which is made up of four rows of Doric columns. In the centre of the piazza is an obelisk that was brought to Rome by Caligula from Heliopolis (in ancient Egypt). The Pope usually gives a public audience at 10am every Wednesday in the Papal Audience Hall or St Peter's Square. You must make a booking, either in person or by fax to the **Prefettura della Casa Pontifica** *(☎ 06 69 88 46 31, fax 06 69 88 38 65)*, between 9am and 1pm on the Monday or Tuesday before the audience. Go through the bronze doors under the colonnade to the right as you face the basilica.

Vatican Museums From St Peter's follow the wall of Vatican City (to the right as you face the basilica) to the museums *(admission €10, free last Sun of month; open 8.45am-4.45pm Mon-Fri, 8.45am-1.45pm Sat & last Sun of month)*. Call ☎ 06 69 88 44 66 to book guided visits to the Vatican gardens (€10).

The Vatican museums contain an incredible collection of art and treasures, and you'll need several hours (at least) to see the most important areas and museums. The Sistine Chapel comes towards the end of a full visit; otherwise, you can walk straight there and then work your way back through the museums.

The **Museo Pio-Clementino**, containing Greek and Roman antiquities, is on the ground floor near the entrance. Through the tapestry and map galleries are the **Stanze di Rafaello**, once the private apartments of Pope Julius II, decorated with frescoes by Raphael. Of particular interest is the magnificent **Stanza della Segnatura**, which features **Raphael's masterpieces** *The School of Athens* and *Disputation on the Sacrament*.

From Raphael's rooms, go down the stairs to the sumptuous **Appartamento Borgia**, decorated with frescoes by Pinturicchio, then go down another flight of stairs to the **Sistine Chapel**, the private papal chapel built in 1473 for Pope Sixtus IV. Michelangelo's wonderful frescoes of the *Creation* and *Last Judgement* have been superbly restored to their original brilliance. It took Michelangelo four years, at the height of the Renaissance, to paint the *Creation*; 24 years later he painted the extraordinary *Last Judgement*. The other walls of the chapel were painted by artists including Botticelli, Ghirlandaio, Pinturicchio and Signorelli.

ORGANISED TOURS

Enjoy Rome *(☎ 06 445 18 43, fax 06 445 68 90; ⓦ www.enjoyrome.com; Via Marghera 8a)* offers excellent walking or bike tours of Rome's main sights from €13 (under 26) and €19 (over 26) per person and a bus tour for Pompeii. **Through Eternity Rome** *(☎ 06 700 93 36, 06 347 336 52 98; ⓦ www.througheternity.com; tours from €20 per person)* offers storytelling walking tours that get rave reviews.

SPECIAL EVENTS

The Comune di Roma coordinates a diverse series of concerts, performances and events throughout summer under the general title **Estate Romana** (Roman Summer). The series usually features major international performers. A jazz festival is held in July and August in the Villa Celimontana, a park on top of the Celian Hill (access via Piazza della Navicella).

The **Festa de' Noantri** is held in Trastevere in the last two weeks of July in honour of Our Lady of Mt Carmel.

At **Christmas** the focus is on the many churches of Rome, each setting up its own nativity scene. Among the most renowned is the 13th-century crib at Santa Maria Maggiore. During **Holy Week**, at Easter, events include the famous procession of the cross between the Colosseum and the Palatine on Good Friday, and the Pope's blessing of the city and the world in St Peter's Square on Easter Sunday.

The Spanish Steps become a sea of pink azaleas during the **Spring Festival** in April. Around mid-April, **Italian Cultural Heritage Week** sees many galleries, museums and tourist attractions open free of charge.

PLACES TO STAY

Camping

By public transport **Village Camping Flaminio** *(☎ 06 333 14 29; ⓦ www.villageflaminio.com; Via Flaminia Nuova 821; per person/tent €9.50/12)* is about 15 minutes north of the centre. Tents and good bungalows are available for rent (there's a fairly frustrating 4pm check-in and 10am check-out for bungalows). Catch the Metropolitana Linea A from Termini station to Flaminio and change to the Prima Porta Linea, getting off at the Due Ponti station (ring the bell).

ITALY

Hostels & B&Bs

The HI **Ostello della Gioventu Foro Italico** *(☎ 06 323 62 67; ⓔ aig.sedenazionale@uni.net; Viale delle Olimpiadi 61; dorm bed €15)* has over 300 beds and opens from 7am to midnight. Take Metropolitana Linea A to Ottaviano, then bus No 32 to Foro Italico. The head office of the The **Italian Youth Hostels Association** *(☎ 06 487 11 52; ⓦ www.ostellionline.org; Via Cavour 44, 00184 Rome; open 9am-5pm Mon-Fri)* will provide information about all the hostels in Italy. You can also join HI here.

B&B accommodation in private houses is a relatively recent addition to Rome's budget options. **Bed & Breakfast Italia** *(☎ 06 68 80 15 13, fax 06 687 86 19; ⓔ info@bbitalia.it; Corso Vittorio Emanuele II 282; singles/doubles per person per night from €28/23, with bath €41/36)* is one of several B&B networks and offers central rooms.

Hotels & Pensioni

Around Stazione Termini To reach the pensioni north of the terminal, head right as you leave the train platforms onto Via Castro Pretorio. The excellent and frequently recommended **Fawlty Towers** *(☎ 06 445 48 02; Via Magenta 39; dorm bed €18, with bath €23)* offers hostel-style accommodation and lots of information about Rome. Added bonuses are the sunny terrace and lack of curfew.

Nearby in Via Palestro are several reasonably priced hotels. **Hotel Cervia** *(☎ 06 49 10 57, fax 06 49 10 56; ⓔ hotelcervia@wnt.it; Via Palestro 55; dorm bed €20, singles €35)* has tidy rooms and a ground floor location. **Hotel Katty** *(☎ 06 444 12 16; Via Palestro 35; singles/doubles €47/62, singles with bath €73, doubles with bath €83-93)* has basic rooms and some other better ones, plus a friendly owner who'll chat your ear off. Around the corner is the clean and comfy **Pensione Ester** *(☎ 06 495 71 23; Viale Castro Pretorio 25; doubles €52)*.

Hotel Lachea-Dolomiti *(☎ 06 495 72 56; ⓔ lachea@hotel-dolomiti.it; Via San Martino della Battaglia 11; singles/doubles/triples €47/68/73, with bath €68/104/124)* has large, quiet, spotlessly clean rooms with all mod-cons. **Papa Germano** *(☎ 06 48 69 19; ⓔ info@hotelpapagermano.com; Via Calatafimi 14a; singles/doubles €47/68, with bath €62/93)* is one of the more popular two-star places in the area.

Hotel Castelfidardo *(☎ 06 446 46 38, fax 06 494 13 78; ⓔ castelfidardo@italmarkey.it; Via Castelfidardo 31; singles/doubles/triples €42/60/77, with bath €52/70/93)* is a well-run and often recommended place with lovely rooms and a 5% discount for cash payments.

South of the terminal is a bit seedier, but prices remain the same. As you exit to the left of the station, follow Via Gioberti to Via G Amendola, which becomes Via F Turati. This street, and the parallel Via Principe Amedeo, harbours a concentration of budget pensioni, so you should easily find a room. The area improves as you get closer to the Colosseum and Roman Forum. **Hotel Sandy** *(☎ 06 488 45 85; Via Cavour 136; dorm bed €18)* has dorms with lockers, no curfew, not-great bathrooms and a party atmosphere for the young crowd.

City Centre The **Albergo Abruzzi** *(☎ 06 679 20 21; Piazza della Rotonda 69; singles €65, doubles €73-95)* overlooks the Pantheon – which explains the noise. Rooms are adequate and bookings are essential year-round.

Pensione Mimosa *(☎ 06 68 80 17 53, fax 06 683 35 57; ⓔ hotelmimosa@tin.it; Via Santa Chiara 61; singles/doubles €77/93, with bath €93/108)*, off Piazza della Minerva, has rooms of varying quality and a great location. Service varies too, depending on who's at the front desk.

A solid, decent choice is **Albergo della Lunetta** *(☎ 06 686 10 80, fax 06 689 20 28; Piazza del Paradiso 68; singles/doubles/triples €52/83/115, with bath €62/109/145)*. You'll definitely need to reserve in advance, or check for cancellations.

The welcoming and well-kitted out **Hotel Pomezia** *(☎/fax 06 686 13 71; Via dei Chiavari 12; singles/doubles €50/85, with bath €105/205)* includes breakfast in the rates, which can drop by 30% in the low season.

Near St Peter's & the Vatican Bargains are rare in this area, but it is comparatively quiet and reasonably close to the main sights. Bookings are a necessity. The simplest way to reach the area is on the Metropolitana Linea A to Ottaviano. Bus No 64 from Termini stops at St Peter's.

A long-standing bargain is **Pensione Ottaviano** *(☎ 06 39 73 72 53; ⓔ gi.costantini@agora.stm.it; Via Ottaviano 6; dorm bed €18, doubles/triples €62/70)*, near Piazza Risorgimento, which has simple rooms and English-speaking staff. A classy new addition to the cheaper end is **Colors Hostel & Hotel** *(☎ 06 687 40 30; Via Boezio 31; dorm bed €18.50, doubles without/with bath €76/83)*. It has tidy rooms, great management and cooking facilities. **Pensione Nautilus** *(☎ 06 324 21 18; Via Germanico 198; singles/doubles €52/79, with bath €78/93)* offers basic, tidy rooms, though things can seem a little dark at times.

PLACES TO EAT

Rome bursts at the seams with trattorias, pizzerias and restaurants. Eating times are generally from 12.30pm to 3pm and 8pm to 11pm. Most Romans head out for dinner around 9pm, so it's better to arrive earlier to claim a table. Prices in this guide reflect the cost per person of two courses with wine, plus a dessert or side dish.

Antipasto dishes are particularly good and many restaurants allow you to make your own mixed selection. Typical pasta dishes include *bucatini all'Amatriciana* (large, hollow spaghetti with a salty sauce of tomato and bacon), *penne all'arrabbiata* (penne with a hot sauce of tomatoes, peppers and chilli) and *spaghetti carbonara* (pancetta, eggs and cheese). Romans also love dishes prepared with offal – try *paiata* (pasta with veal intestines). *Saltimbocca alla Romana* (slices of veal and ham) is a classic meat dish, as is *straccetti con la rucola,* fine slices of beef tossed in garlic and oil and topped with fresh rocket. In winter you can't go past *carciofi alla Romana* (artichokes stuffed with garlic and mint or parsley).

Good options for cheap, quick meals are the hundreds of bars, where *panini* (sandwiches) cost €1.20 to €2.60 if taken *al banco* (at the bar), or takeaway pizzerias, usually called *pizza a taglio*, where a slice of freshly cooked pizza, sold by weight, can cost as little as €1.10. Bakeries are numerous and are another good choice for a cheap snack.

Try **Paladini** *(Via del Governo Vecchio 29)* for sandwiches, and **Il Fornaio** *(Via Baullari 6)* for mouth-watering pastries and bread.

There are numerous outdoor markets, notably the lively and colourful daily market in Campo de' Fiori. Other, cheaper food markets are held in Piazza Vittorio Emanuele, near the station, and off Viale delle Millizie, north of the Vatican. There's a well-stocked 24-hour supermarket underneath the main concourse of Stazione Termini, which is handy for self-caterers.

Restaurants, Trattorias & Pizzerias

Avoid the overpriced, substandard restaurants near Stazione Termini. The side streets around Piazza Navona and Campo de' Fiori harbour many budget trattorias and pizzerias, and the areas of San Lorenzo (to the east of Termini, near the university) and Testaccio (across the Tiber near Piramide) are popular local eating districts. Trastevere offers an excellent selection of rustic eating places hidden in tiny piazzas, and pizzerias where it doesn't cost the earth to sit at a table on the street.

City Centre The **Pizzeria La Montecarlo** *(☎ 06 686 18 77; Vicolo Savelli 12; meal about €11)* has paper sheets for tablecloths, a high turnover (queues form around 9.30pm) and a long list of tasty pizzas. **Pizza Ré** *(☎ 06 321 14 68; Via di Ripetta 13; meal about €15)* gets packed despite its size (and with good reason) by lovers of Naples-style pizza.

Are there any geniuses left in Rome? Yep: they're making pizza at **Pizzeria da Baffetto** *(☎ 06 686 16 17; Via del Governo Vecchio 114; pizza about €7)*. Expect to join a queue and share a table if you arrive after 9pm. Farther along the street is an **osteria** *(Via del Governo Vecchio 18; meal about €13)*, where you can eat an excellent lunch in simple surrounds. Back along the street towards Piazza Navona is **Cul de Sac 1** *(☎ 06 68 80 10 94; Piazza Pasquino 73; meal about €15)*, a wine bar which also has great meals, including hearty soups.

Hostaria Romanesca *(☎ 06 686 40 24; Piazza Campo de' Fiori; meals about €17)* is tiny, so arrive early in winter and get your fill of the generous pasta dishes. In summer there are numerous tables outside.

In cod we trust, and just off Campo de' Fiori is **Filetti di Baccalá** *(☎ 06 686 40 18; Largo dei Librari 88; meal about €9)* which serves only deliciously deep-fried cod fillets in cheap and cheerful surrounds.

West of the Tiber On the west bank of the Fiume Tevere (Tiber River), good-value restaurants are concentrated in Trastevere and the Testaccio district, past the Piramide metro stop. Many establishments around St Peter's and the Vatican are very expensive. There are, however, some good options. Try **Pizza Napul'è** *(☎ 06 63 23 10 05; Viale Giulio Cesare 91; meals about €12)* or the handy and inexpensive **Osteria dell'Angelo** *(Via G Bettolo 24)*, along Via Leone IV from the Vatican City, where you can gorge on cheap pasta for about €4.

In Trastevere, try **Frontoni** *(Viale di Trastevere 54)*, near Piazza Mastai, for fantastic panini. **D'Augusto** *(Piazza dei Renzi 15; meal about €15)*, just around the corner from the Basilica di Santa Maria in Trastevere (turn right as you face the church and walk to Via della Pelliccia), is a very popular cheap eating spot. The atmosphere, especially in summer with tables outside in the piazza, is traditionally Roman. **Osteria Da Lucia** *(Vicolo del Mattinato 2; meals about €20)* is more expensive, but the food is much better and the owners are lovely.

For a good pizza dinner, try **Pizzeria da Vittorio** *(Via San Cosimato 14; meals about €15)*. You'll have to wait for an outside table if you arrive after 8.30pm, but the atmosphere is great, and the bruschetta is worth trying too. Next door is Capo de Ferro, where the meals are about the same price and the same Trastevere atmosphere reigns.

You won't find a cheaper, noisier, more chaotic pizzeria in Rome than **Pizzeria Remo** *(Piazza Santa Maria Liberatrice 44; meal about €10)* in Testaccio on the east of the Tiber, when Friday and Saturday nights are filled with party types. **Augustarello** *(Via G Branca 98; meal about €15)*, off the piazza, specialises in the very traditional Roman fare of offal dishes, which taste better than they sometimes sound.

Dessert

Both **Gelateria Giolitti** *(Via degli Uffici del Vicario 40)* near the Pantheon and **Gelateria della Palma** *(Via della Maddalena 20)* just around the corner have a huge selection of flavours and get big crowds – get the *fichi* (fig) or pistachio at Della Palma dribbling down your chin. In Trastevere, **Fonte della Salute** *(Via Cardinale Marmaggi 2-6)* also has excellent gelato.

ENTERTAINMENT

Rome's best entertainment guide is the weekly *Roma C'è* (€1.03), available at all newsstands. It has an English-language section. *La Repubblica* and *Il Messagero* are daily newspapers with cinema, theatre and concert listings.

Wanted in Rome is a fortnightly magazine for Rome's English-speaking community

(€0.75). It has good cultural listings and is available at outlets including the **Economy Book & Video Center** *(Via Torino 136)*, and at newsstands in the city centre, including Largo Argentina.

Nightclubs

Among the more interesting and popular live music clubs is **Radio Londra** *(☎ 06 575 00 44; Via di Monte Testaccio 67)*, in the Testaccio area. On the same street are the more sedate music clubs Caruso Caffé at No 36 and Caffé Latino at No 96, both generally offering jazz or blues, with some Latin DJ-ing thrown in for dancing. More jazz and blues can be heard at **Alexanderplatz** *(☎ 06 39 74 21 71; Via Ostia 9)* and **Big Mama** *(☎ 06 581 25 51; Via San Francesco a Ripa 18)* in Trastevere.

Discos are pants-wettingly expensive (up to €20). Popular stayers include **Alien** *(☎ 06 841 22 12; Via Velletri 13)*, for those who like the more mainstream end of house and techno; **Goa** *(☎ 06 574 82 77; Via Libetta 13)*, with a groovy ethnic decor and glam crowd but a distant location south of the centre near metro stop Garbatella; and **Gilda** *(☎ 06 679 73 96; Via Mario de' Fiori 97)*, which attracts a slightly older crowd. The best gay disco (according to many reports) is **L'Alibi** *(☎ 06 574 34 48; Via di Monte Testaccio 44)*.

Live Performance

From December to June, opera is performed at the **Teatro dell'Opera** *(☎ 06 48 16 02 55, 800 01 66 65; Piazza Beniamino Gigli)*. A season of concerts is held in October and November at the **Accademia di Santa Cecilia** *(☎ 06 68 80 10 44; Via della Conciliazione 4)* and the **Accademia Filarmonica Romana** *(Teatro Olimpia, Piazza Gentile da Fabriano 17)*.

Cafés & Bars

Remember that prices skyrocket as soon as you sit at a table, particularly near major tourist attractions. The same cappuccino taken at the bar will cost less.

For great coffee head for **Tazza d'Oro** *(Via degli Orfani)* just off Piazza della Rotonda; and **Caffè Sant'Eustachio** *(Piazza Sant'Eustachio 82)*, where you might want to pipe up if you don't want any sugar in your espresso. Try the *granita di caffè* at either one in summer.

Campo de' Fiori is a popular spot to bar-hop and socialise. **Vineria** *(☎ 06 68 80 32 68; Campo de' Fiori 15)* has a tempting selection of wine and beer, plus outdoor tables in warm weather. **Bar della Pace** *(Via della Pace 3-7)* is big with the trendy crew. **Bevitoria Navona** *(☎ 06 68 80 10 22; Piazza Navona 72)* has wine by the glass and makes for a charming early evening spot to have a drink (inside or out). In Trastevere, the slacker-alternative set chooses to hang at **Bar San Calisto** *(Piazza San Calisto)* – drinks aren't extortionate and the clientele is frequently interesting. Near Piazza Navona **Abbey Theatre** *(Via del Governo Vecchio 51)* is a popular but intimate-feeling Irish pub.

GETTING THERE & AWAY

Air

The main airline offices are in the area around Via Veneto and Via Barberini, north of Stazione Termini. Qantas, British Airways and Alitalia are all on Via Bissolati. Cathay Pacific, Singapore Airlines and Thai International Airways are on Via Barberini. The main airport is Leonardo da Vinci, at Fiumicino (see Getting Around later in this chapter).

Bus

The main terminal for intercity buses is in Piazzale Tiburtina, in front of the Stazione Tiburtina. Catch the Metropolitana Linea B from Termini to Tiburtina. Buses connect with cities throughout Italy. For information about which companies operate services to which destinations and from where, go to the APT office, or Enjoy Rome (see Tourist Offices earlier). There are ticket offices for all of the companies at Tiburtina station. COTRAL (also known as Linee Laziali) buses, which service Lazio, depart from numerous points throughout the city, depending on their destinations.

Some useful bus lines are:

Cotral (☎ 800 43 17 84) Via Volturno 65 – services throughout Lazio
Lazzi (☎ 06 884 08 40) Via Tagliamento 27b – services to other European cities (with Eurolines) and northern and central Italy
Marozzi (information at Eurojet on ☎ 06 474 28 01, Piazza della Repubblica 54) – services to Bari, Brindisi, Sorrento, the Amalfi Coast and Pompeii, as well as to Matera in Basilicata
SAIS & Segesta (☎ 06 481 96 76) Piazza della Repubblica 42 – services to Sicily
SENA (information at Picarozzi on ☎ 06 440 44 95, Via Guido Mazzoni) – services to Siena
SULGA (information at Trioviaggi on ☎ 06 440 27 38, Circumvallazione Nomentana; or Sulga Perugia on ☎ 075 575 96 41) – services to Perugia, Assisi and Romagna

Train

Almost all trains arrive at and depart from Stazione Termini. There are regular connections to all major cities in Italy and throughout Europe. For train **timetable information** *(☎ 06 848 88 80 88; open 7am-9pm)*, call or go to the information office at the station (English is spoken). Timetables can be bought at most newsstands in and around Termini. Services at Termini include telephones, money exchange (see the earlier Information section), tourist information, post office, shops and **luggage storage** *(open 7am-midnight daily; €3.10 per piece first 5hr, €0.52 per hr per piece thereafter)*. Some trains depart from the stations at Ostiense and Tiburtina.

Car & Motorcycle

Car rental offices at Stazione Termini in Rome include **Avis** *(☎ 06 481 43 73)*, **Hertz** *(☎ 06 474 03 89)* and **Maggiore** *(☎ 06 488 00 49)*. All have offices at both airports. **Happy Rent** *(☎ 06 481 81 85; Ⓦ www.happyrent.com; Via Farini 3)*, rents scooters (from €38 per day).

Boat

Tirrenia and the Ferrovie dello Stato (FS) ferries leave for various points in Sardinia (see Sardinia's Getting There & Away section) from Civitavecchia. A Tirrenia fast ferry leaves from Fiumicino, near Rome, and Civitavecchia in summer only. Bookings can be made at Sestante CIT, or any travel agency displaying the Tirrenia or FS sign. You can also book directly with **Tirrenia** *(☎ 06 42 00 98 03; Via San Nicola da Tolentino 5, Rome)*; or at the Stazione Marittima (ferry terminal) at the ports. Bookings can be made at Stazione Termini for FS ferries.

GETTING AROUND

To/From the Airport

The main airport is **Leonardo da Vinci** *(☎ 06 65 95 36 40 for flight information)*, at Fiumicino. Access to the city is via the Leonardo Express train service (follow the signs to the station from the airport arrivals hall), which costs €8.78 one way. The train arrives at and leaves from platform Nos 25–29 at Termini. The trip takes 35 minutes. The first train leaves the airport for Termini at 6.37am and the last at 11.37pm. Another train makes stops along the way, including at Trastevere and Ostiense, and terminates at Stazione Tiburtina (€4.65). The trip takes about 50 minutes. A night bus runs every 45 minutes from Stazione Tiburtina to the airport from 12.30am to 3.45am, stopping at Termini at the corner of Via Giolitti about 10 minutes later. Taxis are prohibitively expensive (at least €45).

The other airport is Ciampino, which is used for most domestic and international charters.

Bus

The city bus company is **ATAC** *(☎ 06 800 43 17 84 for information in English, 8am-6pm)*. Details on which buses head where are available at the ATAC information booth in the centre of Piazza dei Cinquecento. Another central point for main bus routes in the centre is Largo Argentina, on Corso Vittorio Emanuele south of the Pantheon. Buses run from 5.30am to midnight, with limited services throughout the night on some routes. A fast tram service, the No 8, connects Largo Argentina with Trastevere, Porta Portese and the suburb of Monte Verde.

Rome has an integrated public transport system, so you can use the same ticket for the bus, Metro, tram and suburban railway. Tickets cost €0.77 and are valid for 75 minutes. They must be purchased *before* you get on the bus and validated in the orange machine as you enter. Tickets can be purchased at any tobacconist, newsstand, metro station or at the main bus terminals. Daily tickets cost €3.10 and weekly tickets cost €12.40.

The new, private **'J' buses** *(☎ 800 07 62 87)* cover some routes of interest to tourists (J2, J4, J5), and you can buy tickets on board, although they are more expensive than ATAC buses. Tickets cost €1 for 75 minutes, €2.45 per day and €9.30 per week. They can also be purchased at tobacconists and newsstands.

Metro

The Metropolitana (Metro) has two lines, A and B. Both pass through Stazione Termini. Take Linea A for Piazza di Spagna, the Vatican (Ottaviano) and Villa Borghese (Flaminio), and Linea B for the Colosseum, Circus Maximus and Piramide (for Testaccio and Stazione Ostiense). Tickets are the same as for city buses (see Bus earlier in this section). Trains run approximately every five minutes between 5.30am and 11.30pm (12.30am on Saturday).

Car & Motorcycle

Negotiating Roman traffic by car is hard enough, but you're in for high stress if you ride a motorcycle or Vespa in the city. If your car goes missing after being parked illegally, check with the **traffic police** *(☎ 06 676 91)*.

Taxi

Cooperativa Radio Taxi Romana *(☎ 06 35 70)* and **La Capitale** *(☎ 06 49 94)* are two of many operators. Major taxi ranks are at the airports, Stazione Termini and Largo Argentina in the historical centre (look for the orange-and-black taxi signs). There are surcharges for luggage (€1.03 per item), night service (€2.58), Sunday and public holidays (€1.03) and travel to/from Fiumicino airport (€7.23/5.94). The flagfall is €2.32 (for the first 3km), then €0.62 for every kilometre. There is a €2.58 supplement from 10pm to 7am and €1.03 from 7am to 10pm on Sunday and public holidays.

Around Rome

OSTIA ANTICA

The Romans founded this port city at the mouth of the Tiber in the 4th century BC and it became a strategically important centre of defence and trade. It was populated by merchants, sailors and slaves, and the ruins of the city provide a fascinating contrast to a place such as Pompeii. It was abandoned after barbarian invasions and the appearance of malaria, but Pope Gregory IV re-established the city in the 9th century. The Rome APT office or Enjoy Rome can provide information about the ancient city, or call the ticket office on ☎ 56 35 80 99.

Of particular note in the **excavated city** *(☎ 06 56 35 80 99; admission €4; open 8.30am-4pm Tues-Sun winter, to 6pm summer)* are the mosaics of the **Terme di Nettuno** (Baths of Neptune); a **Roman theatre** built by Augustus; the **forum** and **temple**, dedicated to Jupiter, Juno and Minerva; and the **Piazzale delle Corporazioni**, where you can see the offices of Roman merchants, distinguished by mosaics depicting their trades.

To get to Ostia Antica take the Metropolitana Linea B to Magliana and then the Ostia Lido train (getting off at Ostia Antica). By car, take the SS8bis (aka Via del Mare) or Via Ostiense.

TIVOLI

postcode 00019 • pop 53,000

Set on a hill by the Anio River, Tivoli was a resort town of the ancient Romans and became popular as a summer playground for the Renaissance wealthy. Today it draws people for the terraced gardens and fountains of the Villa d'Este and the ruins of Villa Adriana, built by the Roman emperor Hadrian. The local **tourist office** *(☎ 0774 33 45 22)* is in Largo Garibaldi near the COTRAL bus stop.

Hadrian built his spectacular summer villa, **Villa Adriana** *(☎ 0774 53 02 02; admission €6.20; open 9am-1hr before sunset daily)* in the 2nd century. It was successively plundered by barbarians and Romans for building materials and many of its original decorations were used to embellish the Villa d'Este. Enough remains to give an impression of the incredible size and magnificence of the villa.

The Renaissance **Villa d'Este** *(admission €6.20; open 9am-1hr before sunset Tues-Sun)* was built in the 16th century for Cardinal Ippolito d'Este on the site of a Franciscan monastery. The villa's wonderful gardens are decorated with numerous fountains, which are its main attraction.

Tivoli is about 40km east of Rome and accessible by COTRAL bus. Take Metropolitana Linea B from Stazione Termini to Ponte Mammolo; the bus leaves from outside the station every 20 minutes. The bus also stops near the Villa Adriana, about 1km from Tivoli. Otherwise, catch local bus No 4 from Tivoli's Piazza Garibaldi to Villa Adriana.

TARQUINIA

postcode 01016 • pop 15,300

Believed to have been home of the Tarquin kings, who ruled Rome before the creation of the republic, Tarquinia was an important economic and political centre of the Etruscan League. The major attractions here are the painted tombs of its *necropoli* (burial grounds), although the town itself is quite pretty. It's an easy day trip from Rome. There is a **IAT tourist information office** *(☎ 0766 85 63 84; Piazza Cavour 1; open Mon-Sat)*.

The 15th-century Palazzo Vitelleschi houses the **Museo Nazionale Tarquiniense** *(admission €4 or €6.50 with Necropolis; open 8.30am-7.30pm Tues-Sun)* and an excellent collection of Etruscan treasures, including frescoes removed from the tombs. Keep an eye out for a few red-and-black plates featuring acrobatic sex acts. The **necropolis** *(open 8.30am-6.30pm Tues-Sun)* is a 15- to 20-minute walk away (or catch one of four daily buses). Ask at the tourist office for directions.

For a meal try **Trattoria Arcadia** *(Via Mazzini 6; meals about €15)*, a friendly joint with good *salsicce* (sausages), near the museum.

To get there, take a Cotral bus (roughly every 45 minutes) to Civitavecchia from Via Lepanto in Rome, near the Metropolitana Linea A Lepanto stop; change for a regular service to Tarquinia (every 45 minutes or so).

Northern Italy

Italy's affluent north is capped by the Alps and bound by the beaches of Liguria and lagoons of Venice, with the gently undulating Po River plain at its heart. Venice is the jewel in the crown, but gems are to be found throughout Piedmont, Lombardy, Emilia-Romagna and the Veneto.

GENOA (GENOVA)

postcode 16100 • pop 628,800

Genoa is, in turn, aristocratic, seedy, grandiose and dingy. A busy port, and regional capital of Liguria, it retains an exuberance that the city's most famous son, Christopher Columbus (1451–1506), would recognise. From the murky streets around the port to the grand thoroughfares and noble palaces, the once mighty maritime republic is compelling, worthy of its historical title, La Superba. Recent events, however, left a bloody mark as the city hit the headlines as host of the G8 summit in the summer of 2001. Violent rioting culminated in police shooting dead a 23-year-old demonstrator.

Orientation & Information

Most trains stop at Genoa's two main stations, Principe and Brignole. The area around Brignole is closer to the city centre and a better bet for accommodation than Principe, which is closer to the port (a spot women travelling alone should avoid at night).

From Brignole walk straight ahead along Via Fiume to get to Via XX Settembre and the historical centre. On the waterfront is an **IAT information kiosk** *(☎ 010 24 87 11, fax 010 246 76 58; open daily)* opposite the aquarium. There are further branches at Stazione Principe *(open Mon-Sat)*, Stazione Marittima *(opening hours depend on ship arrival and departure times)* and at the airport *(open Mon-Sat)*. **Genova Informa** *(Piazza Matteotti; daily)* also provides information.

The **main post office** *(Via Dante 4a)*, is just off Piazza de Ferrari while the **Telecom office** *(Piazza Verdi; open 8am-9pm daily)* is to the left of Stazione Brignole as you approach it on foot. For Internet access try **Internet Point** *(Via di Ravecca 39)* where an hour online costs €6.20.

Things to See & Do

Genoa claims to have the biggest historical centre in Europe. Any tour of the city should start in the backstreets around the old port, which teem with activity – some of it nefarious, most of it entertaining. Search out the 12th-century, black-and-white marble **Cattedrale di San Lorenzo** and the huge **Palazzo Ducale** in Piazza Matteotti. The palaces of the Doria family, one of the city's most important in the 14th and 15th centuries, can be found in **Piazza San Matteo**. Along **Via Garibaldi** are further grand palaces, several of which are open to the public and contain art galleries, including the 16th-century **Palazzo Bianco** and 17th-century **Palazzo Rosso**. Italian and Flemish Renaissance works are displayed in the **Galleria Nazionale di Palazzo Spinola** *(Piazza Superiore di Pellicceria 1; admission €4; open 8.30am-7.30pm Tues-Sat, 1pm-8pm Sun)*.

Genoa's star attraction is, however, its **aquarium** *(Ponte Spinola; admission €11.60; open 9.30am-7.30pm Mon-Wed & Fri, 9.30am-10pm Thur, 9.30am-8.30pm Sat & Sun)*, on the waterfront. As Europe's biggest, it is well worth a visit.

Places to Stay

The HI **Ostello Genova** *(☎ 010 242 24 57; ⓔ hostelge@iol.it; Via Costanzi 120; B&B €13-18; evening meal €7.25)*, in Righi, is just outside Genoa. To get there catch bus No 40 from Stazione Brignole.

On the 3rd floor of a gracious old palazzo near Stazione Brignole, **Carola** *(☎ 010 839 13 40; Via Gropallo 4; singles/doubles/triples €26/42/57, doubles/triples with bath €52/68)* offers simple rooms and a warm welcome. A few doors up at No 8, **Albergo Rita** *(☎/fax 010 87 02 07; singles/doubles/triples €31/47/60, doubles/triples with bath €52/70)* has pleasant enough rooms. Tucked away in the historic centre, **Hotel Major** *(☎ 010 247 41 74, fax 010 246 98 98; Via Garibaldi; singles/*

doubles €31/41, with bath €41/52) is a tight squeeze but the owners are friendly.

Splash out a little at **Hotel Bel Soggiorno** *(☎ 010 54 28 80, fax 010 58 14 18; Via XX Settembre 19; singles/doubles with bath €73/93)*, where the rooms are all chintz and chandeliers.

Places to Eat

Don't leave without trying *pesto genovese*, *pansoti* (ravioli in walnut sauce), *farinata* (a Tuscan torte made with chickpea flour) and, of course, focaccia. Plenty of shops sell sandwiches and pizza by the slice in the Brignole and port areas. For seafood, head to the Via Sottoripo arcades on the waterfront; at No 113 you'll pay €5 for a bag of freshly fried calamari and zucchini.

The basic **Trattoria Da Maria** *(Vico Testa d'Oro 14; meals about €7)*, off Via XXV Aprile, is something of an institution, where good, cheap food is served in an amiably chaotic environment. Hidden away in the Old Town, **La Santa** *(Vico degli Orefici 5; set menu €10.50)* specialises in Ligurian cooking.

Entertainment

The Genoa Theatre Company performs at the **Politeama Genovese** *(☎ 010 839 35 89)* and the **Teatro di Genova** *(☎ 010 534 22 00)*. **Teatro della Tosse in Sant'Agostino** *(☎ 010 247 07 93; Piazza R Negri 4)* has a season of diverse shows from January to May. Opera buffs should head to **Teatro Carlo Felice** *(☎ 010 58 93 29)* near Piazza De Ferrari.

Getting There & Away

There are regular domestic and international connections from **Cristoforo Colombo airport** *(☎ 010 601 54 10; Sestri Ponente)*, 6km west of the city.

Buses for Rome, Florence, Milan and Perugia leave from Piazza della Vittoria, south of Stazione Brignole. Eurolines coaches leave from the same piazza for Barcelona, Madrid and Paris. Book at **Geotravels** *(☎ 01058 71 81)* in the piazza. Genoa is connected by train to major cities; call ☎ 848 88 80 88 for details.

The city's busy port is a major embarkation point for ferries to Sicily, Sardinia and Corsica. Major companies are **Corsica Ferries** *(☎ 019 21 55 11)* in Savona; **Moby Lines** *(☎ 254 15 13)* at Ponte Asserato (for Corsica); **Tirrenia** *(☎ 010 199 12 31 99, 800 82 40 79)* at the Stazione Marittima, Ponte Colombo (for Sicily and Sardinia); and **Grandi Navi Veloci** and **Grandi Traghetti** *(☎ 010 58 93 31; Via Fieschi 17)*, for Sardinia, Sicily, Malta and Tunisia. For more information, see the Getting There & Away sections under Sicily and Sardinia, and in the Corsica section in the France chapter.

RIVIERA DI LEVANTE

The Ligurian coast from Genoa to La Spezia (on the border with Tuscany) is quite spectacular, rivalling the Amalfi Coast in its beauty. Summer can be trying, so try to go in spring and autumn when the weather is more amenable to walking and smaller crowds make sightseeing easier.

To explore the region, your best bet is to use either Santa Margherita Ligure in the north as a base or, further south, La Spezia. Tourist information is available in Santa Margherita at the **IAT tourist office** *(☎ 0185 28 74 85, fax 0185 28 30 34; Via XXV Aprile 4)* in the town centre; and in La Spezia near the waterfront at the other **IAT tourist office** *(☎ 0187 77 09 00, fax 77 09 08; Via Mazzini 45)*.

Things to See & Do

From pretty Santa Margherita Ligure you can explore the nearby resorts of **Portofino**, a haunt of the rich and famous, and **Camogli**, a fishing village turned resort town. The medieval Benedictine monastery of **San Fruttuoso** is a 2½-hour hilly walk from Camogli or Portofino, with sensational views along the way; you may want to catch the ferry back.

Further south, the tiny coastal villages of the **Cinque Terre** national park – Riomaggiore, Manorola, Corniglia, Vernazza and Monterosso – are easily reached by train from La Spezia. They are linked by a 12km path known as the *Via dell'Amore* (Lovers' Lane). The remarkable scenery is well worth the €3 toll.

Places to Stay & Eat

Santa Margherita's **Nuova Riviera** *(☎/fax 0185 28 74 03; ⓔ info@nuovariviera.com; Via Belvedere 10; singles/doubles with bath €75/90)* is a lovely family-run hotel not far from the sea. Nearby, **Albergo Annabella** *(☎ 0185 28 65 31; Via Costasecca 10; singles/doubles €43/75)* has large, airy rooms.

The orderly and well-run **Ostello 5 Terre** *(☎ 0187 92 02 15; ⓔ ostello@cdh.it; Via B Riccobaldi 21; dorm bed €19)* in Manorola offers an evening meal for €11. Be sure to book well ahead.

In La Spezia, **Albergo Parma** *(☎ 0187 74 30 10, fax 74 32 40; Via Fiume 143; singles/doubles €25/42, with bath €32/57)* has decent rooms opposite the station.

La Spezia's many good trattorias include **La Tavernetta** *(Via Fiume 57; meals about €18)*, and **I Gabbiani** *(Molo Italia; meals around €15)*, a restaurant floating in the port.

Getting There & Away

The entire coast is served by train, and all points are accessible from Genoa. Buses leave from Santa Margherita's Piazza Martiri della Libertà for Portofino.

In the summer, **Servizio Marittimo del Tigullio** *(☎ 0185 28 46 70)* runs ferries from Santa Margherita to Portofino, San Fruttuoso and the Cinque Terre. From La Spezia there are numerous ferry routes along the coast, but for the Cinque Terre a cheaper option is a *biglietto giornaliero Cinque Terre* (a one-day rail pass; €5.20) valid for unlimited travel between Monterosso and La Spezia.

TURIN (TORINO)

postcode 10100 • pop 898,400

More noted for its factories than its palaces, Turin is, in fact, a rather grand old city. Formerly the capital of Italy (until 1945) and seat of the House of Savoy, it feels like a place that was once great but still counts (thanks to Fiat and the most loved/hated football team in Italy, Juventus). Towering buildings line the busy boulevards in this baroque city, which will host the Winter Olympics in 2006.

Orientation & Information

Porta Nuova train station is the arrival point for most travellers. To reach the city centre, cross Corso Vittorio Emanuele II and walk straight, through the grand Carlo Felice and San Carlo piazzas, before reaching Piazza Castello. The spire of the Mole Antonelliana will be on your right. There's a **tourist office** *(☎ 011 53 51 81, fax 011 53 00 70; ⓔ info@turismotorino.org; Piazza Castello 161; open daily)* and branches at the **Porta Nuova train station** *(☎ 011 53 13 27, fax 011 561 70 95; open daily)* and the **airport** *(☎ 011 567 81 24)*.

Things to See

Museum enthusiasts should consider the *Torino Card* (€14), a 48-hour pass valid for all public transport in the city and many of the city's museums.

Start at Piazza San Carlo, known as Turin's drawing room and capped by the baroque churches of **San Carlo** and **Santa Cristina**. Nearby, the majestic **Piazza Castello** features the sumptuous **Palazzo Madama**, home to the **Museo Civico d'Arte Antica** and the 17th-century **Palazzo Reale** (Royal Palace) where the gardens were designed in 1697 by Louis le Nôtre, who is better known for his work at Versailles.

Not far away in the **Cattedrale di San Giovanni Battista**, west of the Palazzo Reale, lies one of the Catholic Church's great curiosities: the **Turin Shroud**, the linen cloth believed to have been used to wrap the crucified Christ. Carbon dating places this cloth in the 13th century, but the faithful continue to come.

Turin's enormous **Museo Egizio** *(☎ 011 561 77 76; Via Accademia delle Scienze 6; admission €6.50; open 8.30am-7.30pm Tues-Sun)* is considered one of the best museums of ancient Egyptian art after those in London and Cairo.

Places to Stay & Eat

Turin has plenty of cheap, if a little rundown, accommodation.

In the hills east of the River Po there is **Campeggio Villa Rey** *(☎ 011 819 01 17; Strada Superiore Val San Martino 27; €3.65/6 per person/tent; open Mar-Oct)* and **Ostello Torino** *(☎ 011 660 29 39; Via Alby 1; dorm bed €12)*. To get to the hostel, catch bus No 52 from Porta Nuova station (No 64 on Sunday). Evening meals cost €8.

The one-star **Canelli** *(☎ 011 54 60 78; Via San Dalmazzo 5b; singles/doubles €14/19, singles/doubles/triples with bath €22/30/38)* is reminiscent of a dusty university faculty building – all yellowing corridors and torn posters. Near the station the two-star **Bologna** *(☎ 011 562 02 90, fax 011 562 01 93; Corso Vittorio Emanuele II 60; singles/doubles with bath €55/76)* is deservedly popular. In a great location, **San Carlo** *(☎ 011 562 78 46, fax 53 86 53; Piazza San Carlo 197; singles/doubles €35/55, with bath €59/70)* has rooms with old-world style.

For a lunchtime bite try **La Grangia** *(Via Garibaldi 21; meal about €7)* and mingle with the city centre crowd. During the evening, the pizzas at **Pizzeria alla Baita dei 7 Nani** *(Via A Doria 5; meals about €10)* are sought after. For gelati and chocolate you're spoiled for choice, but the ice cream at **Caffè**

Fiorio *(Via Po 8)* was good enough for the father of Italian unification, Cavour.

Getting There & Around

Intercity, national and international buses terminate at the bus terminal on Corso Castelfidardo. Buses serve the Valle d'Aosta, most of the towns and ski resorts in Piedmont and major Italian cities. Regular trains connect with Milan, Aosta, Venice, Genoa and Rome.

The city is well serviced by a network of buses and trams. A map of public-transport routes is available from the station information office.

MILAN (MILANO)

postcode 20100 • pop 1,302,000

Milan is all about money, looks and shopping. Capital of Italy's finance and fashion industries, this surprisingly scruffy city offers the best in Italian theatre, nightlife and clothes – and not a lot else. Milan closes down almost completely in August, when most of the city's inhabitants take their annual holidays.

From Milan's central train station (Stazione Centrale), it's easy to reach the centre of town on the efficient underground railway (known as the Metropolitana Milanese, or MM). Most sights are in the centre. Use the Duomo (cathedral) and the Castello Sforzesco as your points of reference; the main shopping areas and sights are around and between the two.

Information

Tourist Offices The main branch of the **APT tourist office** *(☎ 02 72 52 43 00, fax 02 72 52 43 50; Via Marconi 1; open daily)* is in Piazza del Duomo. The **branch office** *(☎ 02 72 52 43 60; Stazione Centrale; open daily)*, near the Telecom office, has useful listings in English posted outside. There are also branches at Linate and Malpensa airports.

Money Banks in Milan open 8.30am to 1.30pm and 2.45pm to 3.45pm on weekdays. On Piazza Duomo, Banca Ponti at No 19 has an automatic change machine, and there are exchange offices open daily at Stazione Centrale. There is also an **American Express office** *(☎ 02 720 03 694; Via Brera 3; open 9am-5.30pm Mon-Fri)*.

Post & Communications The **main post office** *(Via Cordusio 4; open 8am-7pm Mon-Fri, 8.30am-noon Sat)* is off Via Dante, near Piazza del Duomo. There are also post offices at the station and at Linate airport. The somewhat squalid **Telecom office** *(open 8am-9.30pm daily)* on the upper level of Stazione Centrale, has international telephone directories, while the **office** *(open 8am-9.30pm daily)* in the Galleria Vittorio Emanuele II has Internet access (€0.10 for 70 seconds), a fax machine and phonecards.

The **Hard Disk Café** *(e info@hdc.it; Corso Sempione 44)* was Milan's first Internet café and is one of Europe's biggest. **Terzomillennio** *(Via Lazzaretto 2)* is a more modest outfit, charging €1 for five minutes and €3.50 for half an hour.

Medical & Emergency Services For an ambulance call ☎ 118. The public hospital, **Ospedale Maggiore Policlinico** *(☎ 02 5 50 31; Via Francesco Sforza 35)* is close to the centre, and there is an all-night **pharmacy** *(☎ 02 669 07 35)* in Stazione Centrale.

The **questura** *(police headquarters; ☎ 02 6 22 61; Via Fatebenefratelli 11)* is near the **Ufficio Stranieri** *(Foreigners' Office; ☎ 02 6 22 61; Via Montebello 26)* where English is spoken. For lost property call the **Milan City Council** *(☎ 02 54 66 81 18; Via Friuli 30)*.

Dangers & Annoyances Milan's main shopping areas are popular haunts for groups of thieves, who are lightning-fast. They use the technique of waving cardboard or newspaper in your face to distract you while they head for your pockets or purse. Be particularly careful in the piazza in front of the Stazione Centrale.

Things to See & Do

Start with the extraordinary **Duomo**, the city's unique landmark. The cathedral was commissioned in 1386 to a lunatic French Gothic design and finished 600 years later. The resulting spiky marble facade is an unforgettable mass of statues, pinnacles and pillars.

Take a *passeggiata* (stroll) through the magnificent **Galleria Vittorio Emanuele II** to **La Scala**, the world's most famous opera house, currently closed for a makeover. At the end of Via Dante is the immense **Castello Sforzesco** *(admission free; open 9.30am-5.30pm Tues-Sun)*, originally a Visconti fortress and entirely rebuilt by Francesco Sforza in the 15th century. Its museum collections include furniture, artefacts and sculpture, notably Michelangelo's unfinished *Pietà Rondanini*.

MILAN

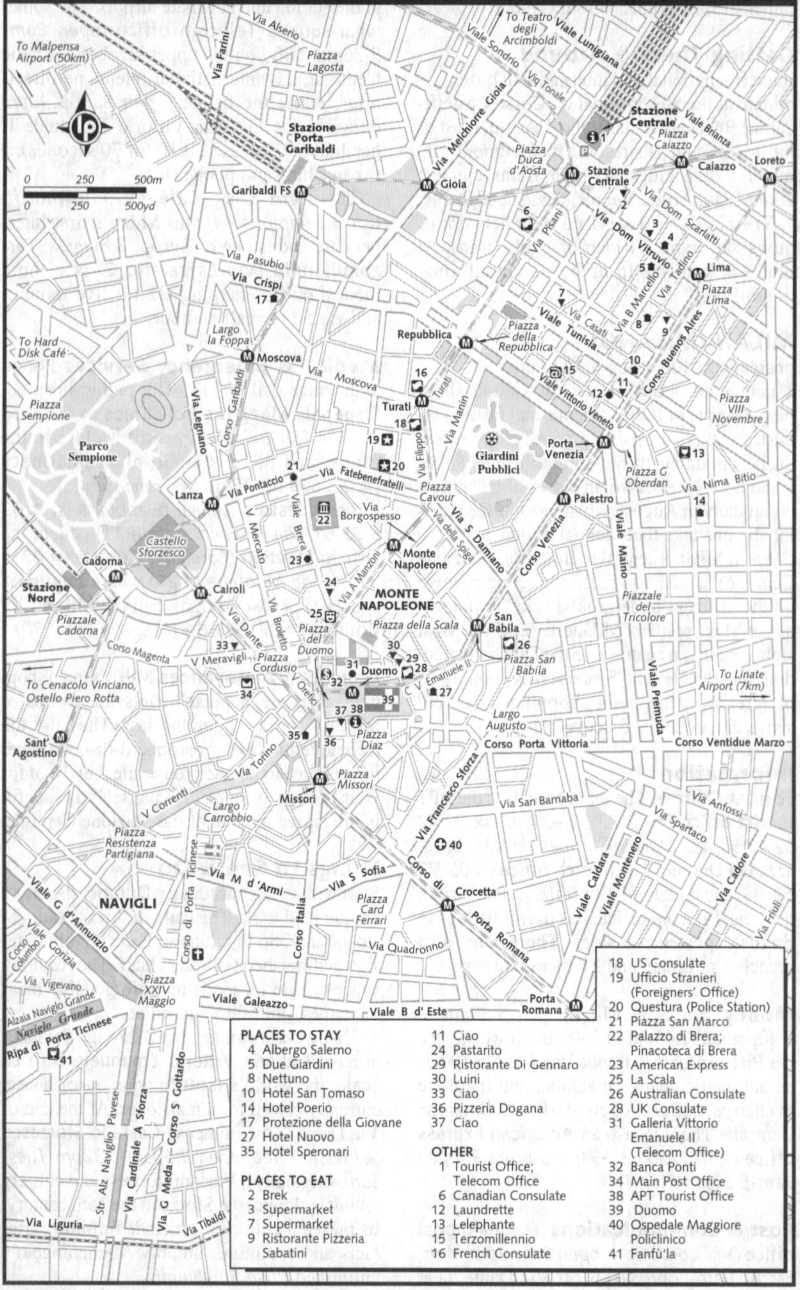

PLACES TO STAY
- 4 Albergo Salerno
- 5 Due Giardini
- 8 Nettuno
- 10 Hotel San Tomaso
- 14 Hotel Poerio
- 17 Protezione della Giovane
- 27 Hotel Nuovo
- 35 Hotel Speronari

PLACES TO EAT
- 2 Brek
- 3 Supermarket
- 7 Supermarket
- 9 Ristorante Pizzeria Sabatini
- 11 Ciao
- 24 Pastarito
- 29 Ristorante Di Gennaro
- 30 Luini
- 33 Ciao
- 36 Pizzeria Dogana
- 37 Ciao

OTHER
- 1 Tourist Office; Telecom Office
- 6 Canadian Consulate
- 12 Laundrette
- 13 Lelephante
- 15 Terzomillennio
- 16 French Consulate
- 18 US Consulate
- 19 Ufficio Stranieri (Foreigners' Office)
- 20 Questura (Police Station)
- 21 Piazza San Marco
- 22 Palazzo di Brera; Pinacoteca di Brera
- 23 American Express
- 25 La Scala
- 26 Australian Consulate
- 28 UK Consulate
- 31 Galleria Vittorio Emanuele II (Telecom Office)
- 32 Banca Ponti
- 34 Main Post Office
- 38 APT Tourist Office
- 39 Duomo
- 40 Ospedale Maggiore Policlinico
- 41 Fanfu'la

Nearby on Via Brera is 17th-century Palazzo di Brera, home to the **Pinacoteca di Brera** *(admission €6.20; open 8.30am-7.15pm Tues-Sun)*. The gallery's vast collection displays Mantegna's masterpiece, the *Dead Christ*.

To view Leonardo da Vinci's *Last Supper* in the **Cenacolo Vinciano** *(☎ 02 89 42 11 46; Piazza Santa Maria delle Grazie 2; admission €6.50; open 8am-7.30pm Tues-Sun)*, you'll need to book by phone.

St Ambrose's Day (7 December) is Milan's major festival, with celebrations at the Fiera di Milano.

Places to Stay

The HI **Ostello Piero Rotta** *(☎/fax 02 39 26 70 95; Viale Salmoiraghi 1; dorm bed €16; closed 9am-3.30pm, curfew 12.30am)* is northwest of the city centre. Take the MM1 to the QT8 stop. **Protezione della Giovane** *(☎ 02 29 00 01 64; Corso Garibaldi 123; beds €22)* is run by nuns for single women aged 16 to 25 years. Booking is required.

Milan's hotels are among the most expensive and heavily booked in Italy. There are numerous budget hotels around Stazione Centrale, but the quality varies.

Stazione Centrale & Corso Buenos Aires One of Milan's nicest one-star hotels is **Due Giardini** *(☎ 02 29 52 10 93, fax 02 29 51 69 33; Via B Marcello 47; singles/doubles with bath €55/85)*, with rooms overlooking a tranquil back garden. To get there turn right off Via D Scarlatti, which is to the left as you leave the station.

On busy Via Dom Vitruvio, off Piazza Duca d'Aosta, there are many hotels. **Albergo Salerno** *(☎/fax 02 204 68 70; doubles without/with bath €60/77)* at No 18, is a good option with clean, simple rooms.

Nettuno *(☎ 02 29 40 44 81; Via Tadino 27; singles/doubles/triples €34/52/70, with bath €47/70/88)* is a modest outfit with some of the cheapest rates around. Near Piazza della Repubblica, you might be able to bargain the rates down at **Verona** *(☎ 02 66 98 30 91; Via Carlo Tenca 12; singles/doubles with bath €70/110)*, depending on the time of year.

Hotel San Tomaso *(☎ 02 29 51 47 47; ⓔ hotelsantomaso@tin.it; Viale Tunisia 6; singles/doubles/triples €41/72/100, doubles with bath €82)*, just off Corso Buenos Aires, is the friendlyprovides a TV and phone in every room. On the other side of Corso Buenos Aires, in a quiet(ish) street **Hotel Poerio** *(☎ 02 29 52 28 72; Via Poerio; singles €31, singles/doubles with bath €42/62)*, offers rooms at the basic end of the basic scale.

The Centre Right in the heart of things, near Piazza del Duomo, **Hotel Speronari** *(☎ 02 86 46 11 25, fax 02 72 00 31 78; Via Speronari 4; singles/doubles/triples €47/73/88, with bath €62/104/130)* has rooms that are decent enough. **Hotel Nuovo** *(☎ 02 86 46 05 42, fax 02 72 00 17 52; Piazza Beccaria 6; singles/doubles €31/51, doubles/triples with bath €93/124)*, just off Corso Vittorio Emanuele II and the Duomo, is a good deal with cheap rates and simple rooms.

Places to Eat

There are plenty of fast-food outlets and sandwich bars in the station and Duomo areas, extremely popular during the lunchtime rush. There are two supermarkets at Stazione Centrale, one on the upper level and one on the western side, as well as those close by at Via D Vitruvio 32 and Via Casati 30. The popular fast-food outlet **Luini** *(Via Santa Radegonda 16)*, just off Piazza del Duomo, is a meeting point for students skipping school.

If you're looking for a traditional trattoria, try the side streets south of the station and along Corso Buenos Aires. Anything but traditional, the **Ciao outlet** *(Corso Buenos Aires 7; meal about €7)* is part of a self-service chain (there are a multitude of others, including those surrounding the Duomo and at Via Dante 5), but the food is pretty good and relatively cheap. The Brek chain is a similar but slightly more expensive alternative.

Ristorante Pizzeria Sabatini *(☎ 02 29 40 28 14; Via Boscovich 54; meals about €15)*, around the corner from Corso Buenos Aires, is a large, characterless place which nevertheless churns out tasty pizzas. Pasta is also available.

The **Ristorante Di Gennaro** *(☎ 02 805 61 08; Via Santa Radegonda 14; pizza from €5)* is reputed to be one of the city's first pizzerias, and the pizzas and focaccias are good. **Pizzeria Dogana** *(☎ 02 805 67 66; cnr Via Capellari & Via Dogana; pizza from €5, meal about €26)* serves standard dishes within spitting distance of the Duomo.

Near La Scala, **Pastarito** *(☎ 02 86 22 10; Via Verdi 6; pasta meal about €10)* makes up for its lack of atmosphere with huge portions and reliable quality.

Entertainment

Music, theatre and cinema dominate Milan's entertainment calendar. The opera season at La Scala runs from 7 December through July, but due to restoration work, which is expected to finish in December 2004, performances are being staged at the modern **Teatro degli Arcimboldi** *(☎ 02 8 87 91; Viale dell'Innovazione)*, in the city's northern reaches. The **box office** *(☎ 02 72 00 37 44)* has been moved to the subterranean pedestrian passage in the Duomo underground station.

Nightlife of the pub/club variety is centred on, but not limited to, Brera and, further south, Navigli. Try **Fanfù'la** *(Ripa di Porta Ticinese 37)* which is fun and, on Friday nights, heaving. Alternatively, and in an altogether quieter area, **Lelephante** *(Via Melzo 22)* is a darkly coloured bar ideal for discussing the woes of the world.

Getting There & Away

Most international flights use Malpensa airport, about 50km northwest of Milan. For arrivals or departures call **flight information** *(☎ 02 74 85 22 00)*.

Bus stations are scattered throughout the city, although some national and international operators use Piazza Castello as a terminal. Check with the APT. Regular trains go from Stazione Centrale to Venice, Florence, Bologna, Genoa, Turin and Rome, as well as major cities throughout Europe. For **timetable information** *(☎ 848 88 80 88; open 7am-9pm)* call or go to the busy office in Stazione Centrale (English is spoken). Regional trains stop at Stazione Porta Garibaldi and Stazione Nord in Piazzale Cadorna on the MM2 line.

Getting Around

The Malpensa Shuttle and Malpensa Bus Express both depart from Piazza Luigi di Savoia every 20 minutes between 4.30am and 12.15am (€4.13-5.16 depending on which operator, 50 to 60 minutes). The Malpensa Express train connects Malpensa airport with Cadorna underground station in the centre of Milan. Trains depart from Cadorna from 5.50am to 8.20pm, after which buses take over until 11.10pm. Tickets cost €9.30 and the journey takes 40 minutes.

Milan's public transport system is extremely efficient, with underground (MM), tram and bus services. Tickets are €1, valid for one underground ride and/or 75 minutes on buses and trams. You can buy tickets in the MM stations, as well as at authorised tobacconists and newsstands.

Taxis simply will not stop if you hail them in the street – head for the taxi ranks, all of which have telephones, or call a radio taxi company. Numbers include ☎ 4040, 5251, 5353, 8383, 8585.

If your car is clamped or towed away call the **Polizia Municipale** *(☎ 02 772 72 59)*. Hertz, Avis, Maggiore and Europcar all have offices at Stazione Centrale.

MANTUA (MANTOVA)

postcode 24100 • pop 48,000

Mantua is a pretty town on the shores of Lake Superior. Closely associated with the Gonzaga family, who ruled from the 14th to 18th centuries, its sumptuous palaces were built on a grand scale. The town is a traditional stronghold of Umberto Bossi's separatist *Lega Nord* party and makes a good day trip.

The **APT tourist office** *(☎ 0376 32 82 53, fax 0376 36 32 92; e aptmantova@iol.it; Piazza Andrea Mantegna 6; open daily)* is a 10-minute walk from the station along Corso Vittorio Emanuele, which becomes Corso Umberto 1.

Piazza Sordello is surrounded by impressive buildings, including the eclectic **cattedrale**, combining a Romanesque tower, baroque facade and Renaissance interior. The piazza is dominated by the massive **Palazzo Ducale** *(admission €6.50; open 8.45am-7.15pm Tues-Sun)*, former seat of the Gonzaga family. The palace has some 500 rooms and 15 courtyards, but its showpieces are the Gonzaga apartments and art collection, and the **Camera degli Sposi** (Bridal Chamber), with frescoes by Mantegna.

Down by the lake the Gonzaga's lavishly decorated summer palace, **Palazzo del Tè** *(admission €8; open 9am-6pm Tues-Sun & 1pm-6pm Mon)* was completed in 1534.

In town, opposite the train station, **Albergo ABC** *(☎ 0376 32 33 47; Piazza Don Leoni 25; singles/doubles with bath €62/83)* has rooms with breakfast included. For a casual pizza, head for **Il Girasole** *(☎ 0376 22 58 80; pizzas about €6)* in the elegant Piazza Erbe. **La Masseria** *(☎ 0376 36 53 03; Piazza Broletto 8; pizza €7, pasta €7.50)* has a good reputation and interesting menu.

Mantua is accessible by train and bus from Verona (about 40 minutes), and by train from Milan and Bologna with a change at Modena.

VERONA

postcode 37100 • pop 256,100

Verona is widely and justifiably regarded as one of Italy's most beautiful cities. Forever associated with Romeo and Juliet, the city was an important Roman centre long before the Della Scala (also known as the Scaligeri) family took the reins in the 13th and 14th centuries, a period noted for the savage family feuding on which Shakespeare based his tragedy.

Orientation & Information

Buses leave for the historical centre from outside the train station; otherwise, it's a 20-minute walk. The main **APT tourist office** *(☎ 045 806 86 80; ⓔ info@tourism.verona.it; Via degli Alpini 9; open daily)* faces Piazza Brà. There are also branches at the train station *(☎ 800 08 61; open Mon-Sat)* and airport *(☎ 045 861 91 63; open Mon-Sat)*.

The **post office** *(Piazza Viviani)* is central, while Internet access is available at **Internet Train** *(☎ 045 801 33 94; Via Roma 19)* where 15 minutes costs €1.50.

Things to See & Do

Piazza Brà's stunning pink marble Roman amphitheatre, known as the **Arena**, dates from the 1st century and is the third largest in existence. It is now Verona's opera house.

Walk along Via Mazzini to Via Cappello and **Casa di Giulietta** (Juliet's House), where the balcony overlooks a courtyard covered with lovers' graffiti. Further along the street is **Porta Leoni**, one of the gates to the old Roman Verona; **Porta Borsari**, the other city gate, is north of the Arena at Corso Porta Borsari.

Piazza delle Erbe, former site of the Roman forum, is lined with marble palaces and filled with market stalls selling the usual tourist tat. Just off the square is the elegant, and much quieter, **Piazza dei Signori**, flanked by the medieval town hall, the Renaissance **Loggia del Consiglio** and the della Scala (Scaligeri) residence, partly decorated by Giotto and nowadays known as the **Governor's Palace**. Take a look at the **Duomo** *(Via Duomo)*, for its Romanesque main doors and Titian's glorious *Assumption*.

Places to Stay & Eat

The excellent **Ostello Villa Francescatti** *(☎ 045 59 03 60, fax 045 800 91 27; Salita Fontana del Ferro 15; B&B €12.50)* offers an evening meal for €7.50. A HI or student card is necessary. To get there catch bus No 73 from the station.

Pensione al Castello *(☎/fax 045 800 44 03; Corso Cavour 43; singles/doubles €52/83, with bath €88/99)* is a stone's throw from the river; the entrance is around the corner.

Albergo Ciopeta *(☎ 800 68 43; ⓔ ciopeta@iol.it; Vicolo Teatro Filarmonico 2; singles/doubles €44/73)*, just off Piazza Brà, has air-conditioned rooms.

Hidden in a side street near Piazza delle Erbe, **Hotel Mazzanti** *(☎ 045 800 68 13, fax 045 801 12 62; Via Mazzanti 6; singles/doubles with bath €61/98)* provides simple rooms, although some are a little poky.

Boiled meats are a Veronese speciality, as is the crisp Soave white wine. The Castello, Ciopeta and Mazzanti hotels all have reasonable restaurants. At the Mazzanti save room for the tiramisu – it's devilishly good. To get away from the crowds, cross the river and try the **Trattoria All'Isolo** *(☎ 045 59 42 91; Piazza dell'Isolo 5a; set menu €12)* where they have an interesting boiled meat dish. For pizza on the hoof you'll find no bigger or better slice than at **Pizza Doge** *(Via Roma 21b; slice about €3.50)*.

Entertainment

Verona hosts musical and cultural events throughout the year, culminating in a season of opera and drama from July to September at the **Arena** *(tickets from €21.50)*. There is a lyric-symphonic season in winter at the 18th-century **Teatro Filarmonico** *(☎ 045 800 28 80; Via dei Mutilati 4)*. For more information check ⓦ www.arena.it, or ask at the tourist office. Booking is through the **box office** *(☎ 045 800 51 51; Via Dietro Anfiteatro 6b)* or website.

Getting There & Around

The main bus station is in the piazza, in front of the train station, which is known as Porta Nuova. Buses leave for surrounding areas, including Mantua, Ferrara and Brescia. Verona is on the Brenner Pass railway line to Austria and Germany, and it is directly linked by train to the cities of Milan, Venice, Florence and Rome.

Bus Nos 11, 12, 13 and 14 (Nos 91, 92 and 98 on Sunday), connect the train station with Piazza Brà, and Nos 72 and 73 go to Piazza delle Erbe.

PADUA (PADOVA)

postcode 35100 • pop 211,500

There is one compelling reason to come to Padua and, although thousands of pilgrims would disagree, it is not to visit the tomb of St Anthony. Rather, it's to marvel at Giotto's recently restored frescoes in the Cappella degli Scrovegni (Scrovegni Chapel), considered by many one of the world's greatest works of figurative art. Masterpieces apart, Padua is a lively city thanks to its university, one of the oldest in Europe, and, as is the norm in these parts, it is porticoed and pretty.

Orientation & Information

It's a 15-minute walk from the train station to the centre of town, or you can take bus Nos 3 or 8 along Corso del Popolo (which becomes Corso Garibaldi).

There is an **IAT tourist office** *(☎ 049 875 20 77, fax 049 875 50 08; open daily)* at the station, another **IAT** *(☎ 049 876 79 27, fax 049 836 33 16; Galleria Pedrocchi; open Mon-Sat)* in the centre and a third **IAT** *(☎ 049 875 30 87; open Apr-Oct)* in the Piazza Del Santo.

The **post office** *(Corso Garibaldi 33)* is on the main road from the station to the centre.

Things to See

If you're planning a couple of days in the city the *padovacard* (€13) is a good investment. Giving significant reductions on museum admission and free transport, it is valid for one adult and one child under 12.

The **Cappella degli Scrovegni** *(☎ 049 20 100 20; W www.giottoagliscrovegni.it; Piazza Eremitani 8; admission €11; open 9am-6pm Mon-Fri, 9am-1pm Sat)* houses Giotto's emotionally charged frescoes. Painted between 1303 and 1305, the 38 transcendent panels depict the life of Christ. Booking is now required, and it's advisable to reserve a few days in advance. The ticket also gives access to the **Musei Civici agli Eremitani** *(open 9am-6pm Tues-Sun winter, to 7pm rest of year)* next door to the chapel.

Thousands of pilgrims arrive in Padua every year to visit the **Basilica di Sant'Antonio** (St Anthony's Basilica) in the hope that St Anthony, patron saint of Padua and of lost things, will help them find whatever it is they are looking for. The saint's gaudy tomb is in the basilica, along with artworks including the 14th-century frescoes and bronze sculptures by Donatello that adorn the high altar. Donatello's bronze equestrian statue, known as the *Gattamelata* (Honeyed Cat), is outside the basilica.

Nature lovers shouldn't miss Padua's botanical gardens, **Orto Botanico** *(Via Orto Botanico 15; admission €2.58; open 9am-1pm & 3pm-6pm Mon-Sat Apr-Oct, 9am-1pm Nov-Mar)*, which date from 1545 and contain many rare plants.

Places to Stay & Eat

Padua has no shortage of budget hotels, but they fill up quickly in summer. The non-HI **Ostello della Città di Padova** *(☎ 049 875 22 19, fax 049 65 42 10; Via A Aleardi 30; dorm B&B €15.50)* is a five-minute bus ride from the station. Take bus No 3, 8 or 12 to Prato della Valle.

The shockingly pink **Junior** *(☎ 049 61 17 56; Via Faggin 2; singles/doubles with bath €37/70)* is in a flowery residential street and has simple rooms. The two-star **Sant'Antonio** *(☎ 049 875 13 93, fax 049 875 25 08; Via Santo Fermo 118; singles/doubles with bath €57/74)*, near the river, provides comfortable rooms with TV and phone. Not a stone's throw from the basilica, **Al Fagiano** *(☎/fax 049 875 00 73; Via Locatelli 45; singles/doubles/triples with bath €52/73/83)* offers large and airy rooms.

Fight through the lunchtime frenzy at **Dalla Zita** *(Via Gorizia 16; panini from €2.30)*, off Piazza Pedrocchi, where the menu of more than 100 sandwich fillings completely covers the walls. **Birroteca da Mario** *(Via Breda 3; pizza from €3.40)*, off Piazza della Frutta, is a good choice for a pub-style snack. **Trattoria al Pero** *(☎ 049 875 87 94; Via Santa Lucia 72; meal about €16)*, attracts a mix of locals and tourists and serves the most enormous plate of fried fish. Daily food markets are held in Piazza delle Erbe and Piazza della Frutta.

Getting There & Away

Padua is directly linked by train to Milan, Venice and Bologna, and is easily accessible from most other major cities. Regular buses serve Venice, Milan, Trieste and surrounding towns. The **bus terminal** *(Piazzale Boschetti)* is off Via Trieste, which is near the train station. There is a large public car park in Prato della Valle, a massive piazza near the Basilica del Santo.

VENICE (VENEZIA)

postcode 30100 • pop 272,100

Venice is extraordinary. In no other city is fantasy and reality so artfully combined – picture delivery boats vying for space with gondolas or a €20 bill for afternoon tea in Piazza San Marco. Ever since Casanova set the romance myth rolling, travellers, writers and even dictators have been beguiled by La Serenissima (the Most Serene Republic). Byron waxed lyrical, Henry James commented, and Napoleon described San Marco's as the finest drawing room in Europe.

The secret to discovering Venice's beauty is to *walk*. Parts of Dorsoduro and Castello see few tourists even in the high season (July to September), and it's here that you'll appreciate just how seductive Venice can be. It's easy to happily lose yourself for hours in the narrow winding streets between the Accademia and the train station, where the signs pointing to San Marco and the Rialto never seem to make any sense – but who's complaining?

Following centuries of Byzantine rule, Venice enjoyed a period of independence that lasted 1000 years. It was the point where east met west, and the city grew in power to dominate half the Mediterranean, the Adriatic and the trade routes to the Levant.

Today, Venice is increasingly being left to the tourists – the regular floods (caused by high tides) and sky-high property prices make it a difficult place to live. Most of the 'locals' live in industrial Mestre, which is linked to the city by the 4km-long bridge across the lagoon.

Orientation

Venice is built on 117 small islands and has some 150 canals and 400 bridges. Only three bridges cross the Canal Grande (Grand Canal): the Rialto, the Accademia and, at the train station, the Scalzi. The city is divided into six *sestieri* (quarters): Cannaregio, Castello, San Marco, Dorsoduro, San Polo and Santa Croce. A street can be called a *calle*, *ruga* or *salizzada*; a street beside a canal is a *fondamenta*; a canal is a *rio*; and a quay is a *riva*. The only square in Venice called a *piazza* is San Marco – all the others are called *campos*.

If all that isn't confusing enough, Venice also has its own style of street numbering. Addresses become virtually meaningless to anyone who's not a Venetian postie. There are no cars and all public transport is via the

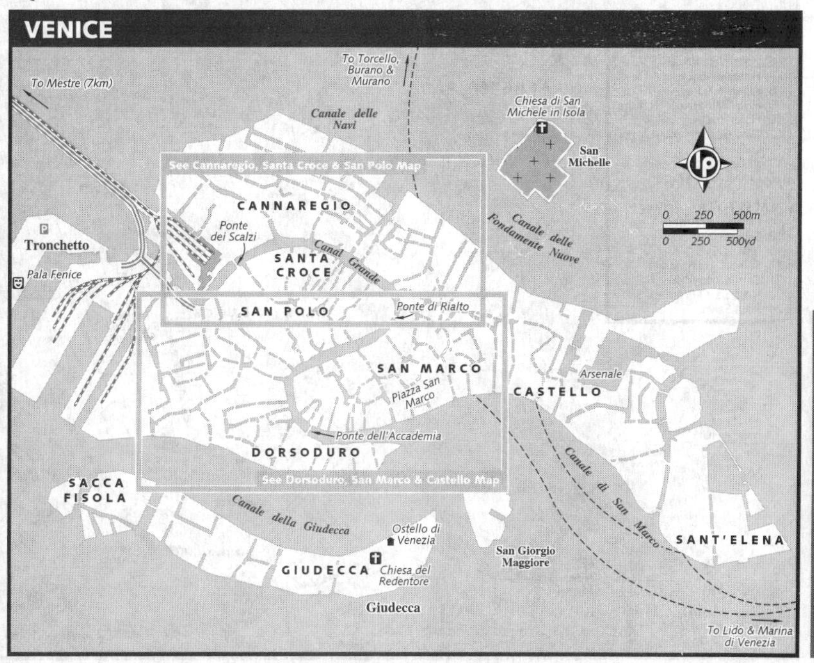

canals, on *vaporetti* (water buses). To cross the Grand Canal between the bridges, use a *traghetto* (basically a public gondola, but much cheaper). The other mode of transportation is *a piedi* (on foot).

To walk from the *ferrovia* (train station) to San Marco along the main thoroughfare, Lista di Spagna (whose name changes several times), will take a good half-hour – follow the signs to San Marco. From San Marco the routes to other main areas, such as the Rialto, the Accademia and the ferrovia, are well signposted but can be a little confusing to find your way around, particularly in the Dorsoduro and San Polo areas.

It's worth buying the yellow street-referenced *Venezia* map published by FMB, as the free tourist office map is not great.

Information

Tourist Offices Central Venice has three APT tourist office branches: at the train station (open daily), Piazza San Marco 71f (open Monday to Saturday) and the Venice Pavilion (open daily) on the waterfront next to the Giardini Ex Reali (turn right from San Marco). There are also offices at Piazzale Roma (open 8am to 8pm daily), the Lido and airport. Pick up the useful guide *Un Ospite di Venezia*. For telephone information call ☎ 041 529 87 11.

Visitors between 14 and 29 can buy a **Rolling Venice card** *(☎ 041 899 90 90 90; €2.58)*, which offers significant discounts on food, accommodation, shopping, transport and admission to museums. It is available from various outlets; check at the tourist offices for details. City planners have also introduced the

Venice Card, a multipurpose pass for museums, public transport, car parks and restrooms. It comes in two forms, one costing €7 and the other €16. For more information go online at W www.venicecard.it.

Money Most of the main banks have branches in the area around the Rialto and San Marco. The **American Express office** *(☎ 041 520 08 44; Salizzada San Moisè 1471; open 9am-5.30pm Mon-Fri, 9.30am-12.30pm Sat & Sun)* will exchange money without charging commission; exit from the western end of Piazza San Marco onto Calle Seconda dell'Ascensione. There's an ATM for card-holders. Additionally, there's a **Thomas Cook** *(☎ 041 522 47 51; Piazza San Marco 141; open 9am-7pm Mon-Sat, 9.30am-5pm Sun)*, and at the train station a **change office** *(open 7am-9pm daily)* on the main concourse opposite platform four.

Post & Communications The main **post office** *(Salizzada del Fontego dei Tedeschi)*, near the Ponte di Rialto (Rialto Bridge), is on the main thoroughfare to the station. Stamps are sold at windows No 1 to No 4 in the central courtyard. There are several Telecom offices in the city, including those at the post office, near the Rialto and on Strada Nova.

Log on at **Nethouse** *(☎ 041 277 11 90; Campo Santo Stefano 2967; open 24hr)*, which has 60 screens, printing and fax facilities. Rates are €3 for 20 minutes, €9 per hour. **Netgate** *(☎ 041 244 02 13; Calle dei Preti Crosera 3812, Dorsoduro; open 10.15am-8pm*

CANNAREGIO, SANTA CROCE & SAN POLO

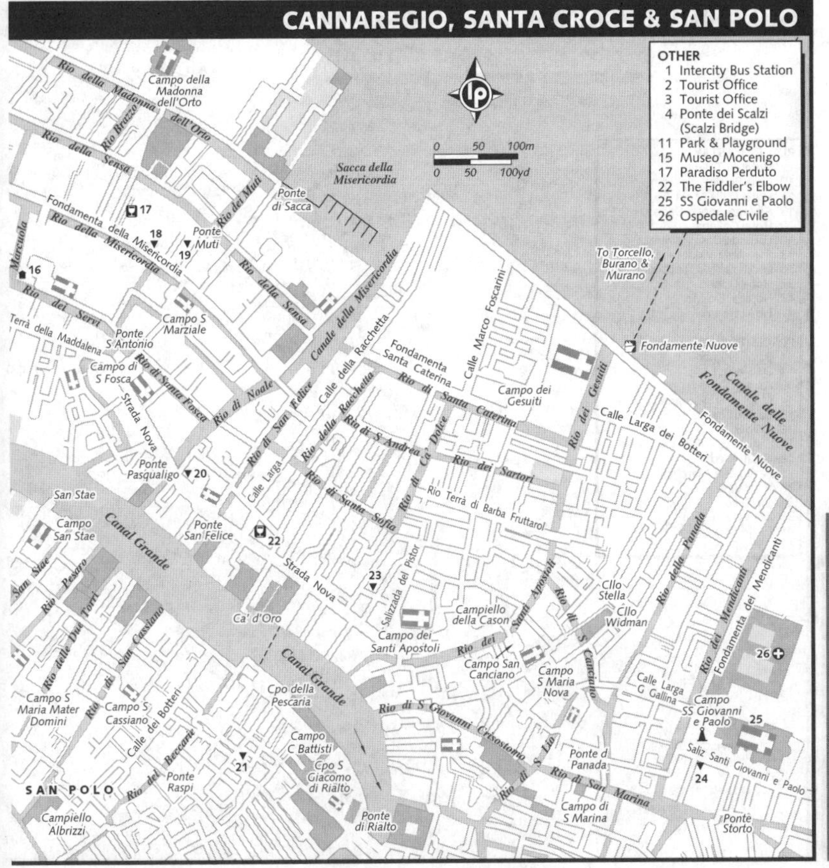

Mon-Fri, 10.15am-10pm Sat & 2.15pm-10pm Sun) offers 11 minutes for €1.29 and one hour for €3.99.

Medical & Emergency Services If you need a hospital, there is the **Ospedale Civile** *(☎ 041 529 41 11; Campo SS Giovanni e Paolo)*. The **questura** *(☎ 041 271 55 11; Fondamenta di San Lorenzo 5056)* is in Castello. An emergency service in foreign languages is run by the carabinieri; call ☎ 112.

Things to See & Do

Before you visit Venice's principal monuments, churches and museums, you should catch the No 1 vaporetto along the Grand Canal, lined with Gothic, Moorish, Renaissance and rococo palaces. Then stretch your legs by taking a long walk: start at **San Marco** and either delve into the tiny lanes of tranquil **Castello** or head for the **Ponte dell'Accademia** (Accademia Bridge) to reach the narrow streets and squares of **Dorsoduro** and **San Polo**.

Remember that most, but not all, museums are closed on Monday.

Piazza & Basilica di San Marco San Marco's dreamlike, 'can this be real' quality has you pinching yourself no matter how many times you visit. The piazza is enclosed by the basilica and the elegant arcades of the **Procuratie Vecchie** and **Procuratie Nuove**. While you're standing gob-smacked you might be lucky enough to see the bronze *mori* (Moors) strike the bell of the 15th-century **Torre dell'Orologio** (clock tower).

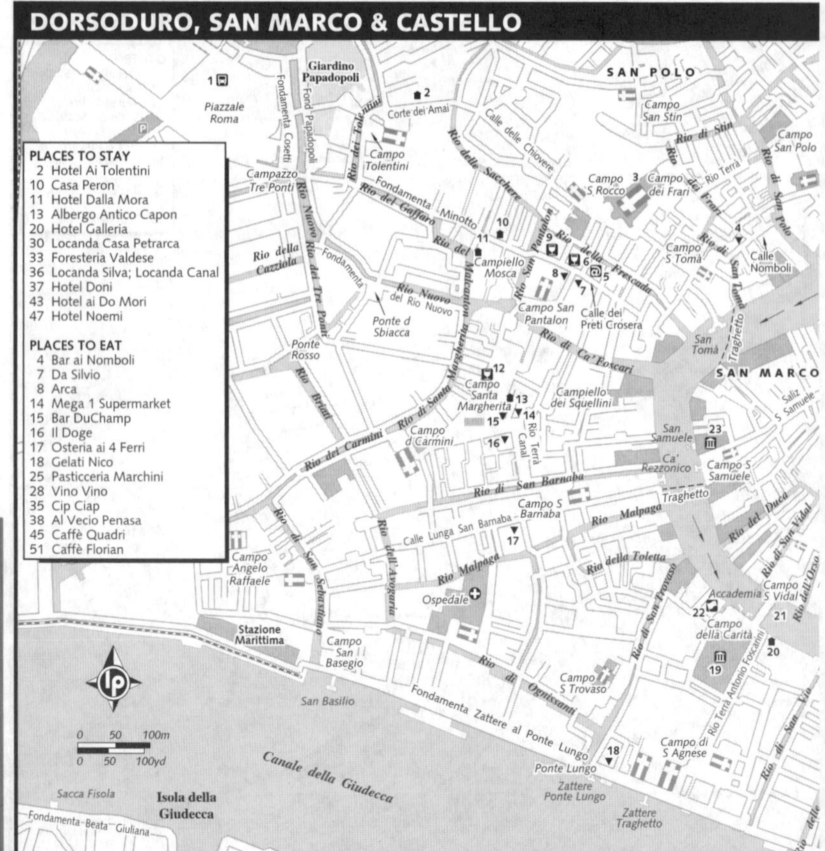

With its spangled spires, Byzantine domes and seething facade of mosaics and marble, the **Basilica di San Marco** (St Mark's Basilica) is the Western counterpart of Istanbul's Santa Sophia. The elaborately decorated basilica was built to house the body of St Mark, stolen from its burial place in Egypt by two Venetian merchants and carried to Venice in a barrel of pork. The saint has been reburied several times in the basilica (at least twice the burial place was forgotten), and his body now lies under the high altar. The present basilica was built in the 11th century and richly decorated with mosaics, marbles, sculpture and a jumble of other looted embellishments over the ensuing five centuries. The bronze horses prancing above the entrance are replicas of the famous statues liberated in the Sack of Constantinople in 1204. The originals can be seen in the basilica's **Galleria** *(admission €1.55)*.

Don't miss the **Pala d'Oro** *(admission €1.55)*, a stunning gold altarpiece decorated with silver, enamels and precious jewels. It is behind the basilica's altar.

The basilica's 99m freestanding **campanile** *(bell tower; admission to top €6)* dates from the 10th century, although it suddenly collapsed on 14 July 1902 and had to be rebuilt.

Palazzo Ducale The official residence of the doges and the seat of the republic's government, this palace *(admission €9.50; open 9am-7pm daily Apr-Oct, 9am-5pm daily Nov-Mar)* also housed many government officials and the prisons. The original palace was built in the 9th century and later expanded,

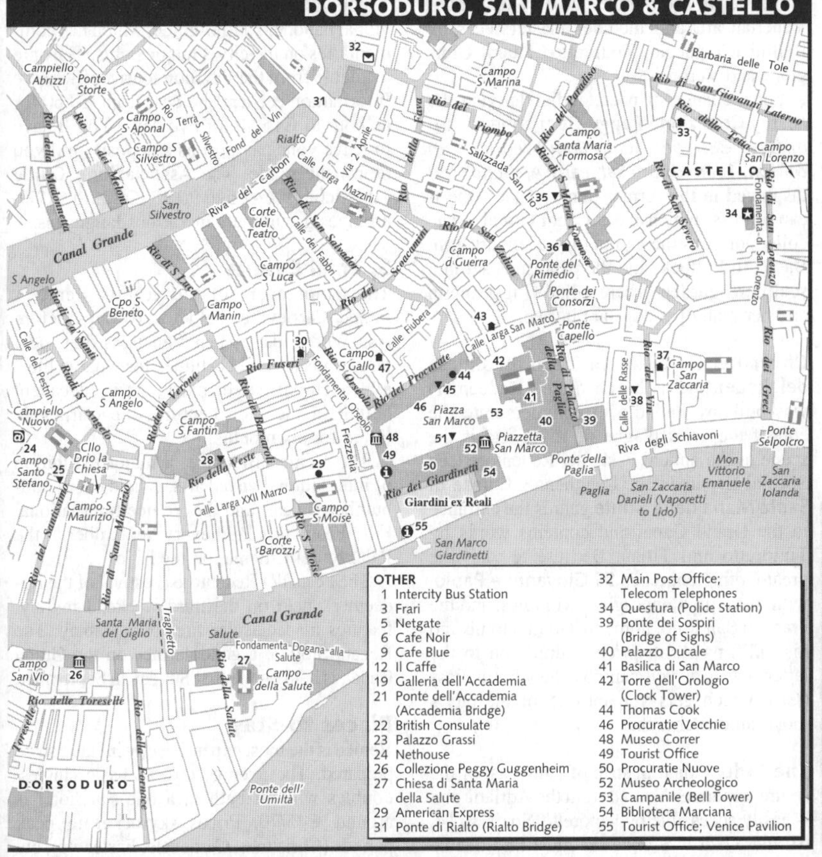

remodelled and given a Gothic tracery facade. Visit the **Sala del Maggior Consiglio** to see the paintings by Tintoretto and Veronese. The ticket office closes 1½ hours before palace closing time; admission also covers admission to the nearby Museo Correr, Biblioteca Marciana and Museo Archeologico. For an additional €6 you can extend the ticket to cover the Palazzo Mocenigo (San Stae area), and Burano and Murano museums.

The **Ponte dei Sospiri** (Bridge of Sighs) connects the palace to the old prisons. The bridge evokes romantic images, probably because of its association with Casanova, a native of Venice who spent time in the dungeons.

Galleria dell'Accademia & Guggenheim The Academy of Fine Arts' collection *(admission €6.50; open 8.15am-7.15pm Tues-Sun, 8.15am-2pm Mon)* traces the development of Venetian art, and includes masterpieces by Bellini, Carpaccio, Tintoretto, Titian, Giorgione and Veronese.

For a change of pace, and style, visit the nearby **Collezione Peggy Guggenheim** *(admission €8; open 10am-6pm Wed-Fri, Sun & Mon, 10am-10pm Sat, early Apr–end Oct)* displayed in the former home of the American heiress, which faces Canal Grande. The collection runs the gamut of modern art from Bacon to Pollock, and the palazzo is set in a sculpture garden where Miss Guggenheim and her many pet dogs are buried.

Churches On Giudecca Island the **Chiesa del Redentore** (Church of the Redeemer) was built by Palladio to commemorate the end of the great plague of 1576, and is the scene of the annual Festa del Redentore (see Special Events later). Longhena's **Chiesa di Santa Maria della Salute** guards the entrance to the Grand Canal and contains works by Tintoretto and Titian. Be sure to visit the great Gothic churches **SS Giovanni e Paolo**, with glorious stained-glass windows, and the **Frari**, in San Polo, home to Titian's tomb and his uplifting *Assumption*. Admission to the latter is €2, or you can buy the Chorus Pass (€8), which gets you into 15 of the city's most famous churches.

The Lido This thin strip of land, east of the centre, separates Venice from the Adriatic and is easily accessible by vaporetto Nos 1, 6, 14, 61 and 82. It was once *the* most fashionable beach resort, and it's still almost impossible to find a space on its long beach in summer.

Islands The island of **Murano** is the home of Venetian glass. Tour a factory for a behind-the-scenes look at its production, or visit the Glassworks Museum to see some exquisite historical pieces. **Burano**, still today a relatively sleepy fishing village, is renowned for its lace and pastel-coloured houses. **Torcello**, the republic's original island settlement, was abandoned due to malaria. Just about all that remains on the hauntingly deserted island is the Byzantine cathedral, its exquisite mosaics intact. Excursion boats travel to the three islands from San Marco (€15 return). Vaporetto No 12 goes to all three from Fondamenta Nuove.

Organised Tours

A popular new choice is to pick up an individual handheld audio-guide, which has commentaries on the city's major sights. They are available from the Pavilion tourist office (see Information earlier) and cost from €3.60 for an hour to €15.50 for two days. You'll have to leave your passport as a deposit until you return the guide. The **Associazione Guide Turistiche** *(☎ 041 520 90 38; Castello 5327)*, arranges group tours in various languages.

Special Events

The major event of the year is Venice's famed **Carnevale**, held for 10 days before Ash Wednesday, when Venetians don spectacular masks and costumes for what is literally a 10-day street party. At its decadent height in the 18th century, the Carnevale lasted for six months!

The Venice Biennale, a major exhibition of international visual arts, is held every odd-numbered year, and the Venice International Film Festival is held every September at the Palazzo del Cinema, on the Lido.

The Festa del Redentore (Festival of the Redeemer), held on the third weekend in July, features a spectacular fireworks display. The Regata Storica, a gondola race on the Grand Canal, is held on the first Sunday in September.

Places to Stay

Venice is the most expensive city in Italy, so be prepared. The average cost of basic singles/doubles without bath in a one-star hotel is around €45/70. Prices skyrocket in peak periods (Christmas, Carnevale, Easter etc), but do drop at other times of the year. It's always advisable to book, but if you arrive with nothing lined up try the **Associazione Veneziana Albergatori** *(☎ 800 84 30 06)*, which runs a hotel reservation office at the train station.

Camping Litorale del Cavallino, northeast of the city along the Adriatic coast, has numerous camping grounds, many with bungalows. The tourist office has a full list, but you could try **Marina di Venezia** *(☎ 041 530 09 55, fax 041 96 60 36; ⓔ camping@marinadivenezia.it; Via Montello 6, Punta Sabbioni; €7.50/19 per person/tent; open mid-Apr–end Aug)*.

Hostels The HI **Ostello di Venezia** *(☎ 041 523 82 11, fax 041 523 56 89; Fondamenta delle Zitelle 86; dorm bed €16; curfew 11.30pm)* is on the island of Giudecca. It is open to members only, though you can buy a card there. Evening meals are available for €7.75. Take vaporetto No 41, 42 or 82 from the station and get off at Zitelle.

Foresteria Valdese *(☎/fax 041 528 67 97; Castello 5170; dorm bed €20, doubles €54, doubles with bath €70)* has a number of dormitory and double-room options. Follow Calle Lunga from Campo Santa Maria Formosa. Students will feel at home at **Ostello Santa Fosca** *(☎ 041 71 57 75; ⓔ cpu@iuav.unive.it; Cannaregio 2372; dorm beds €18, singles/doubles €21; check-in 5pm-8pm daily)*, which is less than 15 minutes from the station through Campo Santa Fosca.

Hotels Not surprisingly, bargain hotels are few and far between in Venice.

Cannaregio The two-star **Edelweiss Stella Alpina** *(☎ 041 71 51 79, fax 041 72 09 16; ⓔ stelalpina@tin.it; Calle Priuli detta dei Cavalletti 99d; singles/doubles €62/104, with bath €130/171)*, down the first street on the left after the Scalzi church, has decent rooms. The next street on the left is Calle della Misericordia, with two recommended hotels. **Hotel Santa Lucia** *(☎ 041 71 51 80, fax 041 71 06 10; ⓔ hotelstlucia@libero.it; singles/doubles without bath €60/70, doubles/triples/quads with bath €110/140/170)* at No 358 has a friendly owner and all rates include breakfast. At No 389, **Hotel Villa Rosa** *(☎/fax 041 71 65 69; ⓔ villarosa@venetuno.it; singles/doubles/triples/quads with bath €82/113/142/165)* is pretty and pink with pleasant, well-furnished rooms.

On Lista di Spagna, the main drag, **Albergo Adua** *(☎ 041 71 61 84, fax 041 244 01 62; singles/doubles €70/75, with bath €100/114)* at No 233a has simple rooms. Across the road at No 230, **Hotel Minerva & Nettuno** *(☎ 041 71 59 68; ⓔ lchecchi@tin.it; singles/doubles €50/61, with bath €58/92)* has modest rooms. **Hotel Rossi** *(☎ 041 71 51 64, fax 041 71 77 84; ⓔ rossihotel@interfree.it; Calle de la Procuratie; singles/doubles/triples/quads with bath €65/89/108/126)* is just off Lista di Spagna (via a Gothic archway) down a tiny side street. Rooms are clean and straightforward. Around the corner, **Casa Gerotto and Alloggi Calderan** *(☎/fax 041 71 53 61; Campo San Geremia 283; dorm bed €20, singles/doubles/triples €36/62/83, with bath €46/88/108)* has something for everyone in a pleasantly ramshackle atmosphere. **Al Gobbo** *(☎ 041 71 50 01, fax 041 71 47 65; singles/doubles €52/75, with bath €78/93)*, at No 312 in the same campo, is somewhat gloomy inside but has an enthusiastic owner.

San Marco Although this is the most touristy area of Venice, it has some surprisingly good-quality pensioni. **Hotel Noemi** *(☎ 041 523 81 44; ⓔ info@hotelnoemi.com; Calle dei Fabbri 909; doubles without/with bath €87/139)* is somewhat characterless but only a few steps from Piazza San Marco.

Locanda Casa Petrarca *(☎ 041 520 04 30; Calle delle Schiavine 4386; singles €44, doubles without/with bath €88/110)* is run by a chatty English-speaking lady full of useful tips.

Just off Piazza San Marco and up some alarmingly steep stairs, **Hotel ai Do Mori** *(☎ 041 520 48 17, fax 041 520 53 28; Calle Larga San Marco 658; doubles without/with bath €87/129)* has some rooms with views of St Mark's basilica.

Castello This atmospheric area is to the east of Piazza San Marco and is far less touristy. **Locanda Silva** *(☎ 041 522 76 43, fax 041 528 68 17; Fondamenta del Rimedio 4423; singles/doubles €47/78, with bath €67/104)* has rather basic rooms and **Locanda Canal** *(☎ 041 523 45 38, fax 041 241 91 38; doubles without/with bath €83/110)*, next door at No 4422c, is much the same. To get there, head off from Campo Santa Maria Formosa towards San Marco.

Hotel Doni *(☎/fax 041 522 42 67; Calle del Vin 4656; singles/doubles €50/80, doubles with bath €105)* gives pride of place to a room with an original fresco.

Dorsoduro, San Polo & Santa Croce Off Fondamenta Tolentini heading down from the station, **Hotel Ai Tolentini** *(☎ 041 275 91 40, fax 041 275 32 66; Corte dei Amai 197g; singles/doubles with bath €70/120)* has reasonable rooms and a helpful owner. At the characterful **Casa Peron** *(☎/fax 041 71 10 38; Salizzada San Pantalon 84; singles/doubles €45/70, doubles with bath €85)* you may well be met by a huge green parrot. To get here from the station, cross Ponte dei Scalzi and follow the signs to San Marco and Rialto till you reach Rio delle Muneghette, then cross the wooden bridge. Nearby, **Hotel Dalla Mora** *(☎ 041 71 07 03, fax 041 72 30 06; ⓔ hotel dallamora@libero.it; Santa Croce 42a; singles/doubles/triples/quads with bath €57/88/108/129)* is on a small canal just off Salizzada San Pantalon and is justifiably popular.

In one of the liveliest squares in Venice, **Albergo Antico Capon** *(☎/fax 041 528 52 92; Campo Santa Margherita 3004b; singles/doubles with bath €88)* provides airy rooms.

Pick of the one-stars **Hotel Galleria** *(☎ 041 523 24 89, fax 041 520 41 72; ⓔ galleria@tin.it; Dorsoduro 878a; singles/doubles €62/93, doubles with bath €104)* has elegant rooms in a 17th-century palace facing the Grand Canal at Ponte dell'Accademia.

Mestre Mestre makes an economical but drab alternative to staying in Venice. There are a number of good hotels as well as plenty of cafés and places to eat around the main square. If you're travelling by car, the savings on car-parking charges are considerable. The two-star **Albergo Roberta** *(☎ 041 92 93 55, fax 041 93 09 83; Via Sernaglia 21; singles/doubles with bath €68/104)* includes breakfast in the rates and the one-star **Albergo Giovannina** *(☎ 041 92 63 96, fax 041 538 84 42; Via Dante 113; singles €36, doubles with bath €72)* is a decent option.

ITALY

Places to Eat

Wherever you choose to eat in Venice it'll be expensive, but quality can vary enormously.

Bars serve a wide range of panini, *tramezzini* (sandwiches) and rolls with every imaginable filling. They start at €2 if you eat them standing at the bar. Head for one of the many *bacari* (traditional wine bars), for wine by the *ombra* (glass) and interesting *cicheti* (bite-sized snacks). The staples of the Veneto region's *cucina* are rice and beans. Try the *risi e bisi* (risotto with peas), which is best followed by a glass of *fragolino*, the Veneto's fragrant strawberry wine.

For fruit and vegetables, as well as delicatessens, head for the market in the streets on the San Polo side of the Rialto Bridge, or on the Rio Terrà San Leonardo in Cannaregio. There's a Standa supermarket on Strada Nova and a Mega 1 supermarket just off Campo Santa Margherita.

Restaurants Avoid the tourist traps around San Marco and near the train station.

Cannaregio Tucked away down a tiny alleyway is **Hosteria Ai Promessi Sposi** *(☎ 041 522 86 09; Calle De L'Oca 4367; meals about €20)* where the mixed fish antipasti is a thing of wonder. It's all shuffling efficiency here as the old boys bring your food between sips. Winning a growing reputation is **Sahara** *(☎ 041 72 10 77; Fondamenta della Misericordia; meals about €19)* where you feast on genuine Syrian grub. A few doors down, **Iguana** *(☎ 041 71 35 61; meals about €11)* represents Venice's Tex-Mex scene.

Around San Marco & Castello The popular bar/osteria **Vino Vino** *(☎ 041 523 70 27; San Marco 2007; meals about €17)* is at Ponte Veste near Teatro La Fenice. Wine is sold by the glass. Just off Campo Santa Maria Formosa and over Ponte del Mondo Novo, **Cip Ciap** *(pizza slice €2.30)* provides welcome sustenance.

Dorsoduro, San Polo & Santa Croce This is the best area for small, authentic trattorias and pizzerias. The pizzas are usually good at **Pizzeria all'Anfora** *(☎ 041 524 03 25; pizzas from €4.80)* across the Ponte dei Scalzi from the station at Lista dei Bari 1223.

Cantina do Mori *(Sottoportego dei do Mori)*, off Ruga Rialto, is a small, very popular wine bar which also serves sandwiches.

The bustling **Arca** *(☎ 041 524 22 36; Calle San Pantalon 3757; set menu €13, pizzas from €5)*, past Campo San Pantalon, has a warm and lively feel and opposite is **Da Silvio** *(☎ 041 20 58 33; Calle San Pantalon 3748)*, which offers more or less the same dishes at the same prices.

If you're looking for a typical osteria try **Osteria ai 4 Ferri** *(☎ 041 520 69 78; Calle Lunga San Barnaba; meals about €17)*, off Campo San Barnaba. You'll need to book.

Cafés & Bars If you can cope with the idea of paying at least €7 for a cappuccino, spend an hour or so sitting at an outdoor table in Piazza San Marco, listening to the orchestra at either **Caffè Florian** or **Caffè Quadri**. For a cheaper alternative, try Campo Santa Margherita's **Bar DuChamp**, a student favourite where panini cost around €1.30 and there's Tetley's on tap.

Bar ai Nomboli *(cnr Calle dei Nomboli & Rio Terrà dei Nomboli)* between Campo San Polo and the Frari, has a huge selection of sandwiches, while in the Castello area you can choose from an extensive range of cheap panini at the bar **Al Vecio Penasa** *(Calle delle Rasse 4585)*.

Desserts Some of the best gelato in Venice continues to be served at **Gelati Nico** *(Fondamenta Zattere ai Gesuati 922)*. Join the locals along the fondamenta or take a seat at an outside table. **Il Doge** *(Campo Santa Margherita)* also has excellent ice cream. A popular place for cakes and pastries is **Pasticceria Marchini** *(Calle del Spezier 2769)*, just off Campo Santo Stefano, where the display of goodies is, to put it mildly, tempting. **Rosa Salva** *(Campo SS Giovanni e Paolo)* is frequented by locals for its gelati and pastries.

Entertainment

The free weekly booklet *Un Ospite di Venezia* has entertainment listings, or you can buy a copy of the monthly *Venezia News* from newsagents for €2.07. The tourist office also has brochures listing events for the entire year.

Venice lost its opera house, the magnificent Teatro La Fenice, to a fire in January 1996. Reconstruction continues, and in the interim performances are held at **PalaFenice** *(☎ 041 78 65 11)*, a tentlike structure on the car-park island of Tronchetto.

Major art exhibitions are held at **Palazzo Grassi** (San Samuele vaporetto stop), and smaller exhibitions at various venues in the city throughout the year.

For less highbrow pursuits, in Cannaregio, **Paradiso Perduto** *(Fondamenta della Misericordia 2539; happy hour 6.30pm-7.30pm)* has live music and sangria. And where would Venice be without an Irish pub? We'll never know because **The Fiddler's Elbow** *(Corte dei Pali 3847)* does the job. In Dorsoduro, there's **Café Blue** *(Salizzada San Pantalon 3778)*, a pub-like drinking den near trendy Campo Santa Margherita, or **Café Noir** *(Calle San Pantalon 3805)*, a laid-back, student hang-out. On Campo Santa Margherita, **Il Caffè** is perennially popular.

Getting There & Away

ACTV buses *(☎ 041 899 90 90 90)* leave from Piazzale Roma for surrounding areas, including Mestre and Chioggia, a fishing port at the southernmost point of the lagoon. Buses also go to Padua and Treviso. Tickets and information are available at the office in Piazzale Roma.

The train station, **Stazione Santa Lucia** *(☎ 848 88 80 88)*, is directly linked to Padua, Verona, Trieste, Milan and Bologna, and so is easily accessible for Florence and Rome. You can also head to major points in France, Germany, Austria, Switzerland, Slovenia and Croatia. The Venice Simplon *Orient Express* runs between Venice and London, via Innsbruck, Zurich and Paris, twice weekly. Ask at any travel agent or phone the headquarters in London (☎ 020-7805 5100).

You can catch ferries to Greece four times a week in winter and daily in summer from the company **Minoan Lines** *(☎ 041 240 71 01; Porto Venezia, Zona Santa Marta)*. High-season tickets cost from €72 one way.

Getting Around

Vaporetti are the city's mode of public transport. From Piazzale Roma, vaporetto No 1 zigzags its way along the Grand Canal to San Marco and then to the Lido. There is the faster No 82 if you are in a hurry to get to St Mark's. The No 12 vaporetto leaves from Fondamenta Nuove for the islands of Murano, Burano and Torcello. A full timetable is available at vaporetto ticket offices (€0.50). A single vaporetto ticket costs €3.10 (plus €3.10 for luggage), even if you only ride to the next station; a return is €5.16. A 24-hour ticket is €9.30 for unlimited travel, a 72-hour ticket is €18.08 (worthwhile) and a one-week ticket costs €30.99.

If you fancy taking a water taxi, be warned that prices are exorbitant.

FERRARA

postcode 44100 • pop 131,600

Ferrara's wonderfully evocative medieval centre retains much of the character of its heyday when, as seat of the Este family (1260–1598), the town was a force to be reckoned with. The imposing **Castello Estense** remains the dominant landmark in this charming town.

The tourist information office *(☎ 0532 20 93 70; ⓔ infotur.comfe@fe.nettuno.it; open daily)* is inside the Castello Estense.

Things to See

The small historical centre encompasses medieval Ferrara, to the south of the **Castello Estense**. The castle – complete with moat and drawbridges – was begun by Nicolò II d'Este in 1385. It is partly open to the public and has a suitably chilling atmosphere.

The pink-and-white striped cathedral, the **Duomo**, dates from the 12th century, with Gothic and Renaissance additions and an unusual triple facade. Its museum has a superb collection of Renaissance art. The Renaissance Palazzo dei Diamanti, along Corso Ercole I d'Este, contains the **Pinacoteca Nazionale** *(☎ 0532 20 58 44; admission €4; open 9am-2pm Tues, Wed, Fri & Sat, 9am-7pm Thurs, 9am-1pm Sun)* and exhibitions of modern art.

The **Palazzo Schifanoia** *(☎ 0532 20 99 88; Via Scandiana 23; admission €4.20; open 9am-6pm Tues-Sun)* is one of the city's earliest major Renaissance buildings and another of the Este palaces. It features the 'Room of the Months', decorated with Ferrara's finest Renaissance frescoes.

Special Events

Every May since 1289, Ferrara has celebrated the **Palio**, considered the oldest in Italy, which culminates in a horse race between the eight town districts. Less dramatic is the **Buskers Festival** held in August, which attracts street performers from all over the world.

Places to Stay & Eat

Ferrara is a cheap alternative to Bologna and can be used as a base for visiting Venice. Hidden in the cobbled streets, **Albergo Centro Storico** *(☎ 0532 20 33 74; Via Vegri 15; singles/doubles €26/36)* has basic rooms. South of the cathedral is the modest **Pensione Artisti** *(☎ 0532 76 10 38; Via Vittoria 66; singles €21, doubles without/with bath €37/52).* Better rooms are available at two-star **Albergo Nazionale** *(☎ 0532 20 96 04; Corso Porta Reno 32; singles/doubles with bath €42/63).*

Pizzeria il Ciclone *(☎ 0532 21 02 62; Via Vignatagliata 11; pizzas from €5.15, meals about €17)* serves local specialities. Closer to the cathedral, **Il Brindisi** *(☎ 0532 20 91 42; Via Adelardi 11; set menu from €10.30)* claims to be the oldest hosteria in the world, dating back to the 15th century. Next door, **Pappagallo** *(☎ 0532 204 796; meals about €8)* is self-service. In the medieval quarter, **Locanda degli Eventi** *(☎ 0532 76 13 47; Via Mayr Carlo 21; meal about €20)* is a quaint local trattoria.

Getting There & Away

Ferrara is on the Bologna-Venice train line, with regular trains to both cities. It is 40 minutes from Bologna and 1½ hours from Venice. Regular trains also run directly to Ravenna. Buses run from the train station to Modena (also in the Emilia-Romagna region).

BOLOGNA

postcode 40100 • pop 380,300

Bologna is vibrant, beautiful and red. And there can't be many cities where the predominant colour of the architecture so accurately reflects the traditional politics of its citizens. The regional capital of Emilia-Romagna, Bologna is home to the oldest university in Europe and it is to the large student population that the city owes much of its dynamism. But it is food for which Bologna is most famous. Other than the eponymous spaghetti bolognese, known as *spaghetti al ragù*, the Bolognese have gifted the world with tortellini, lasagne and mortadella.

The main **IAT tourist office** *(fax 051 23 14 54; Piazza Maggiore 1; open daily)* is complemented by branch offices at the train station *(open Mon-Sat)* and airport *(open daily)*. The main post office is in Piazza Minghetti. Log on at the Internet café **Net Arena** *(☎/fax 051 22 08 50; Via de' Giudei 3b)* for €3.10 per hour.

Things to See & Do

Bologna's porticoed streets are ideal for a stroll. The best starting point is the traffic-free centre formed by **Piazza Maggiore**, the adjoining **Piazza del Nettuno** and **Fontana del Nettuno** (Neptune's Fountain), sculpted in bronze by the French artist who became known as Giambologna, and **Piazza di Porta**

Ravegnana, with its two leaning towers to rival Pisa's (originally there were 42).

The **Basilica di San Petronio** in Piazza Maggiore is dedicated to the city's patron saint, Petronius. It was here that Charles V was crowned emperor by the pope in 1530. The incomplete red-and-white marble facade displays the colours of Bologna, and the chapels inside contain notable works of art. The adjacent **Palazzo Comunale** (town hall) is a huge building combining several architectural styles in remarkable harmony.

The **Basilica di Santo Stefano** is a medieval religious complex of four churches (originally there were seven) and includes the 11th-century Chiesa del Crocefisso, which houses the bones of San Petronio.

The **Basilica di San Domenico**, erected in the early 16th century, houses the elaborate sarcophagus of St Dominic, the founder of the Dominican order. The chapel was designed by Nicoló Pisano, and its shrine features figures carved by a young Michelangelo.

The **Museo Civico Archeologico**, **Pinacoteca Nazionale** and French Gothic **Basilica di San Francesco** are also well worth a visit.

Places to Stay

Budget hotels are difficult to come by and finding a single room can be a nightmare, so always book in advance.

A good option is the HI **Ostello Due Torri** *(☎/fax 051 50 18 10; Via Viadagola 5; dorm bed €12)*. Take bus No 93 or 20b from Via Irnerio (off Via dell'Indipendenza south of the station), and ask the bus driver where to alight.

Right in the historic centre, **Albergo Garisenda** *(☎ 051 22 43 69, fax 051 22 10 07; Via Rizzoli 9, Galleria del Leone 1; singles/doubles/triples €42/62/83)* has some rooms overlooking the two towers and the busy Via Rizzoli. Slightly further out, **Albergo Marconi** *(☎ 051 26 28 32; Via G Marconi 22; singles/doubles €34/53, with bath €43/68)* provides functional but characterless rooms. **Albergo Panorama** *(☎ 051 22 18 02; Via Livraghi 1; singles/doubles/triples/quads €47/62/78/88)* has light and airy rooms. **Accademia** *(☎ 051 23 23 18, fax 051 26 35 90; Via delle Belle Arti 6; singles/doubles €82/113)* offers good two-star rooms and a grumpy owner. Closer to the station the three-star **Donatello** *(☎ 051 24 81 74, fax 051 24 47 76; Via dell'Indipendenza 65; singles/doubles €60/80)* offers discounts if there are no trade fairs on.

Places to Eat

Pizzeria La Bella Napoli *(☎ 051 55 51 63; Via San Felice 40; pizza from €5)* serves popular and reasonably priced pizzas. A few doors away **Trattoria da Danio** *(☎ 051 55 52 02; Via San Felice 50a; meal about €15)* is a pearl, full of large locals who like their food. **Pizzeria Altero** *(Via Ugo Bassi 10; pizza slice from €1)* is the place for a quick lunchtime bite. For more of a pub feel, join the students at the **Osteria Dell'Orsa** *(☎ 051 23 15 76; Via Mentana 1G; panini from €4, mains about €7)* in the university quarter.

Shop at **Mercato Ugo Bassi** *(Via Ugo Bassi 27; open Mon-Sat)*, a covered market offering all the local fare, or at the supermarket **Pam** *(Via Marconi 28a)*.

Getting There & Around

Bologna is a major transport junction and trains from all over the country stop here. National and international coaches to major cities depart from the terminal in Piazza XX Settembre, around the corner from the train station in Piazza delle Medaglie d'Oro.

The bus system is efficient. To get to the city centre from the train station take bus No 25 or 27.

RAVENNA

postcode 48100 • pop 138,900

Ravenna's exquisite mosaics, relics of the time it was capital of the Western Roman Empire and western seat of the Byzantines, are the big drawcards. But Ravenna is also the last resting place of Dante, who died here in 1321. Easily accessible from Bologna, this perfectly manicured, stress-free town is worth a day trip at the very least. There is an **IAT tourist office** *(☎ 0544 3 54 04, fax 0544 48 26 70; Via Salara 8; open daily)*.

The pick of Ravenna's mosaics are found in the **Basilica di Sant'Apollinare Nuovo**, the **Basilica di San Vitale**, the **Mausoleo di Galla Placidia** (these are the oldest) and the **Battistero Neoniano**. These buildings are all in the town centre and an admission ticket to the four, as well as to the **Museo Arcivescovile**, costs €6. The mosaics in the **Basilica di Sant'Apollinare in Classe**, 5km away, are also notable. To get there take bus No 4 or 44 from the train station. In town, **Dante's Tomb** is open to the public daily and is free.

Ravenna hosts a music festival from late June to early August, featuring world-renowned artists, while an annual theatre and literature festival is held in September in honour of Dante. In winter, opera and dance are staged at the **Teatro Alighieri** *(box office ☎ 0544 24 92 44; Piazza Garibaldi 5)*.

Places to Stay & Eat

The HI **Ostello Dante** *(☎ 0544 42 11 64; Via Aurelio Nicolodi 12; B&B €12.50, family rooms per person €14)* is 1km out of town. Take bus No 1 from Viale Pallavacini, to the left of the train station. **Al Giaciglio** *(☎/fax 0544 394 03; Via Rocca Brancaleone 42; singles/doubles €30/42, with bath €36/51)* has very blue rooms and a restaurant with a set menu for €12.20. Two-star **Ravenna** *(☎ 0544 21 22 04, fax 0544 21 20 77; Via Maroncelli 12; singles/doubles with bath €42/62)* provides anonymous rooms just outside the train station. In the heart of the city's historic centre, the three-star **Hotel Centrale Byron** *(☎ 0544 3 34 79, fax 0544 3 41 14; Via IV Novembre 14; singles/doubles with bath from €53/83)* offers all the mod cons and a chatty owner.

For a quick lunch, you could try the Bizantino self-service restaurant in the city's fresh-produce market in Piazza Andrea Costa. There is a fixed menu for €7.30, excluding drinks, but it is closed at weekends. **Cá de Vén** *(☎ 0544 3 01 63; Via Corrado Ricci 24; meal about €25)* offers regional dishes and wine in monastic surroundings.

Getting There & Around

Ravenna is accessible by train from Bologna, sometimes with a change at Castel Bolognese. The trip takes around 1½ hours.

Cycling is a popular way to get around, especially as there are no hills in sight. Rental is €7.75 per day or €1.03 per hour from COOP San Vitale, Piazza Farini, outside the station. The tourist office also has some bikes to lend in spring and summer. They don't charge, but phone ahead to check availability.

SAN MARINO

postcode 47890 • pop 28,000

The world's oldest surviving republic, San Marino was founded in AD 300 by a stonemason said to have been escaping religious persecution; at least according to one legend. The tiny state (only 61 sq km) is an unashamed tourist trap but offers splendid views of the mountains and coast. You can wander along the city walls and visit the two fortresses.

The **tourist office** *(☎ 0549 88 29 98; Contrada Omagnano 20; open daily)* is in the Palazzo del Turismo. San Marino is accessible from Rimini by bus.

The Dolomites

The limestone Dolomites stretch across Trentino-Alto Adige and into the Veneto. Characterised by the reddish glow of the rock formations which jut into the sky like jagged teeth, this spectacular Alpine region is the Italians' favoured area for skiing and, in summer, hiking.

Information about Trentino-Alto Adige can be obtained in Trent (Trento) at the **APT del Trentino** *(☎ 0461 83 90 00, fax 26 02 45; ⓔ info@trentino.to; Via Romagnosi 11)*; in Rome *(☎ 06 36 09 58 42, fax 320 24 13; Via del Babuino 20)*; and in Milan *(☎ 02 86 46 12 51, fax 72 00 21 88; Piazza Diaz 5)*. Bolzano's **tourist office** *(☎ 0471 30 70 00; ⓔ info@bolzano-bozen.it; Piazza Walther 8)* also has information on the region. The **APT Dolomiti** *(☎ 0436 32 31/2/3, fax 0436 32 35)* at Cortina can provide information on trekking and skiing in the Veneto.

Skiing

The Dolomites' numerous ski resorts range from expensive and fashionable Cortina d'Ampezzo in the Veneto to family-oriented resorts such as those in the Val Gardena in Trentino-Alto Adige. All the resorts have helpful tourist offices with information on facilities, accommodation and transport.

Most resort areas offer their own passes for unlimited use of lifts at several resorts for a nominated period. Prices vary depending on the resort but expect to pay around €123 to €154 for six days. The **Superski Dolomiti pass** *(ⓦ www.dolomitisuperski.com)*, which allows access to 464 lifts and 1220km of ski runs in 12 valleys for six days, costs €175.

Trekking

Without doubt, the Dolomites provide the most breathtaking opportunities for walking in the Italian Alps – from a half-day stroll with the kids to demanding treks that require mountaineering skills. The walking season runs from the end of June to the end of September. Alpine *rifugi* (refuges) usually close around 20 September.

Buy a map of the hiking trails with Alpine refuges marked. The best are the Tabacco 1:25,000 series, which are widely available at bookshops throughout the region. Lonely Planet's *Walking in Italy* outlines several treks in detail and the *Italy* guide also details some suggested hikes.

Hiking trails are generally well marked with numbers on red-and-white painted bands on trees and rocks along the trails, or by numbers inside different-coloured triangles for the Alte Vie (the four High Routes through the Dolomites which link a chain of *rifugi* and can take up to two weeks to walk – the APT in Trent has details).

Recommended hiking areas include:

Alpe di Siusi A vast plateau above the Val Gardena, at the foot of the spectacular Sciliar.
Cortina area Featuring the magnificent Parco Naturale di Fanes-Sennes-Braies.
Pale di San Martino Accessible from San Martino di Castrozza.

Even in summer the weather is extremely changeable in the Alps; though it may be sweltering when you set off, you should be prepared for very cold and wet weather on even the shortest of walks. Essentials include a pair of good-quality, worn-in walking boots, an anorak or pile/wind jacket, a lightweight backpack, a warm hat and gloves, a waterproof poncho, light food and plenty of water.

Getting There & Away

The region has an excellent public transport network – the two principal bus companies are **SAD** *(☎ 800 84 60 409)* in Alto Adige and the Veneto, and Atesina in Trentino. There's a network of long-distance buses operated by a number of companies (eg, Lazzi, SITA, Sena, STAT and ATVO) connecting the main towns and ski resorts with major cities such as Rome, Florence, Venice, Bologna, Milan and Genoa. Information is available from tourist offices and *autostazioni* (bus stations) in the region. For long-distance travel information, try **Lazzi Express** *(☎ 06 884 08 40; Via Tagliamento 27b)* in Rome, and *(☎ 055 28 71 18; Piazza Stazione 47r)* in Florence. There is a **SITA office** *(☎ 055 29 49 55; Via Santa Caterina da Siena 15)* in Florence.

Getting Around

Hitchhiking is no problem in the warmer months, especially near the resort towns. The areas around the major resorts are well serviced by local buses, and tourist offices will be able to provide information on routes. During winter, most resorts have 'ski bus' shuttle services from the towns to the main ski facilities.

CORTINA D'AMPEZZO

postcode 32043 • pop 6570

The ski resort for Italy's beautiful people, Cortina is excruciatingly fashionable and correspondingly expensive. It is also one of the best equipped and most picturesque resorts in the Dolomites. The area is very popular for trekking and climbing, with well-marked trails and numerous *rifugi*. The **main APT tourist office** *(☎ 0436 32 31/32/33)* has information on Cortina's accommodation options.

CANAZEI

postcode 38032 • pop 1780

Set in the Fassa Dolomites, the resort of Canazei has more than 100km of trails and is linked to the challenging network of runs known as the Sella Ronda. Canazei also offers cross-country and summer skiing on Marmolada, which at 3342m is the highest peak in the Dolomites.

Spend a cheap night at the Marmolada **camping ground** *(☎ 0462 60 16 60; €7.75/7.75 per person/tent; open year-round)*, or contact the **APT tourist office** *(☎ 0462 60 11 13, fax 0462 60 25 02; Via Roma 34)* for further details on accommodation. The resort is accessible by Atesina bus from Trent and SAD bus from Bolzano.

VAL GARDENA

This is one of the most popular skiing areas in the Alps, due to its reasonable prices and first-class facilities. There are superb walking trails in the Sella Group and the Alpe di Siusi. The Vallunga, behind Selva, is great for family walks and cross-country skiing.

The valley's main towns are Ortisei, Santa Cristina and Selva, all offering plenty of accommodation and easy access to runs. Each town has a **tourist office** *(Ortisei: ☎ 0471 79 63 28, fax 0471 79 67 49; • Santa Cristina ☎ 0471 79 30 46, fax 0471 79 31 98; • Selva ☎ 0471 79 51 22, fax 0471 79 42 45)* and all have extensive information on accommodation and facilities. Staff speak English and will send details on request. The Val Gardena is accessible from Bolzano by SAD bus, and is connected to major Italian cities by coach services (Lazzi, SITA and STAT).

SAN MARTINO DI CASTROZZA

postcode 38058 • pop 700

In a sheltered position beneath the Pale di San Martino, this resort is popular among Italians and offers good ski runs, as well as cross-country skiing and a toboggan run. The **APT office** *(☎ 0439 76 88 67, fax 0439 76 88 14)* will provide a full list of accommodation. **Hotel Suisse** *(☎ 0439 680 87; Via Dolomiti 1; B&B from €30)* is a pleasant one-star option. Buses travel regularly from Trent, Venice and Padua.

Central Italy

Miraculously, the rolling green landscape and soft golden light of Tuscany, and rugged hill towns of Umbria and the Marches (Le Marche) seem virtually unchanged today. In each of the regions there is a strong artistic and cultural tradition, and even the smallest medieval town can harbour a masterpiece or two.

FLORENCE (FIRENZE)

postcode 50100 • pop 375,500

Italy has been successfully selling itself on the back of Florence for centuries. And although everything they claim is true – it is a beautiful city with an artistic heritage unrivalled anywhere else in the world – it can also be disheartening. For most of the year, you're more likely to overhear conversations in English than in Italian, and, especially in summer, the heat, car fumes and crowds can be stifling. But, gripes aside, Florence remains one of the most enticing cities in Italy. Cradle of the Renaissance, home of Dante, Machiavelli, Michelangelo and the Medici – the wealth of art, culture and history continues to overwhelm.

Florence was the strategic Roman garrison settlement of Florentia. In the Middle Ages the city developed a flourishing economy based on banking and commerce, which sparked a period of building and growth previously unequalled in Italy. But Florence truly flourished in the 15th century under the Medici, reaching the height of its cultural, artistic and political development as it gave birth to the Renaissance.

Following unification, Florence was the capital of the new kingdom of Italy from 1865 to 1871. During WWII parts of the city were destroyed by bombing, including all of the bridges except the Ponte Vecchio, and in 1966 a devastating flood destroyed or severely damaged many important works of art.

Orientation

Whether you arrive by train, bus or car, the main train station, Santa Maria Novella, is a good reference point. Budget hotels and pensioni are concentrated around Via Nazionale to the east of the station, and Piazza Santa Maria Novella to the south. The main thoroughfare to the centre is Via de' Panzani and then Via de' Cerretani, about a 10-minute walk. You'll know you've arrived when you first glimpse the Duomo.

Once at Piazza del Duomo you will find Florence easy to negotiate, with most of the major sights within easy walking distance. Many museums are closed on Monday, but you won't waste your time by just strolling through the streets. Take the city ATAF buses for longer distances such as to Piazzale Michelangelo or the nearby suburb of Fiesole, both of which offer panoramic views of the city.

Information

Tourist Offices The Comune di Firenze (Florence City Council) operates a **tourist information office** *(☎ 055 21 22 45, fax 055 238 12 26; Piazza della Stazione 4; open daily)* opposite the main train station, next to the Chiesa di Santa Maria Novella; and another **office** *(☎ 055 234 04 44, fax 055 226 45 24; Borgo Santa Croce 29r; open daily)* southeast of the Duomo. The **main APT office** *(☎ 055 29 08 32/33, fax 055 276 03 83; e infoturismo@provincia.fi.it; Via Cavour 1r; open daily)* is just north of the Duomo. At the airport the **branch office** *(☎/fax 055 31 58 74; open daily)* has the usual wealth of material. The **Consorzio ITA** *(open 8.45am-8pm daily)*, inside the station on the main concourse, helps book hotel rooms for a small fee.

A good map of the city, on sale at newsstands, is the one with the white, red and black cover called *Firenze: Pianta della Città*.

Money Major banks are concentrated around Piazza della Repubblica. The **American Express office** *(☎ 055 5 09 81; Via Dante Alighieri 22r; open 9am-5.30pm Mon-Fri, 9.30am-12.30pm Sat)* is near the Duomo. Be wary of poor exchange rates at the station.

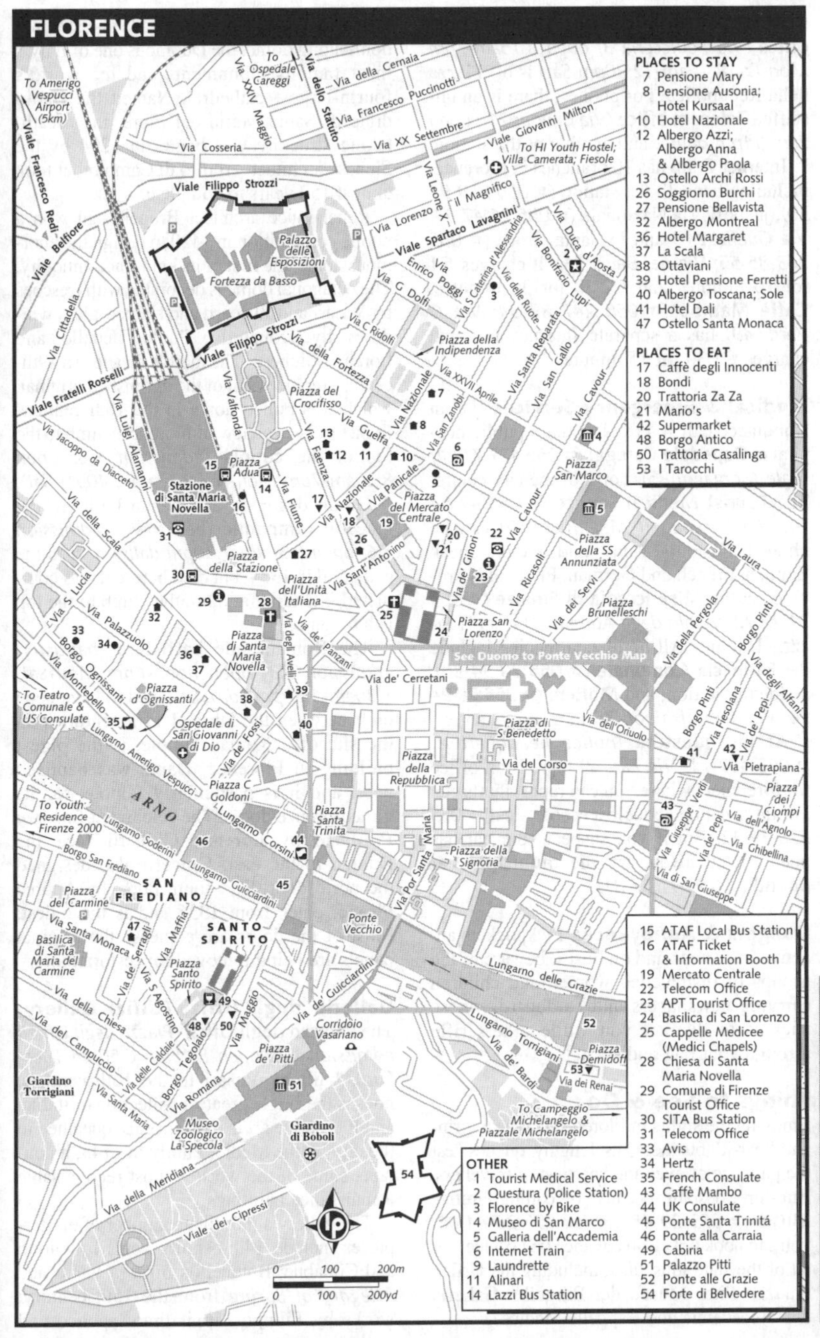
FLORENCE
PLACES TO STAY
7 Pensione Mary
8 Pensione Ausonia; Hotel Kursaal
10 Hotel Nazionale
12 Albergo Azzi; Albergo Anna & Albergo Paola
13 Ostello Archi Rossi
26 Soggiorno Burchi
27 Pensione Bellavista
32 Albergo Montreal
36 Hotel Margaret
37 La Scala
38 Ottaviani
39 Hotel Pensione Ferretti
40 Albergo Toscana; Sole
41 Hotel Dali
47 Ostello Santa Monaca
PLACES TO EAT
17 Caffè degli Innocenti
18 Bondi
20 Trattoria Za Za
21 Mario's
42 Supermarket
48 Borgo Antico
50 Trattoria Casalinga
53 I Tarocchi
OTHER
1 Tourist Medical Service
2 Questura (Police Station)
3 Florence by Bike
4 Museo di San Marco
5 Galleria dell'Accademia
6 Internet Train
9 Laundrette
11 Alinari
14 Lazzi Bus Station
15 ATAF Local Bus Station
16 ATAF Ticket & Information Booth
19 Mercato Centrale
22 Telecom Office
23 APT Tourist Office
24 Basilica di San Lorenzo
25 Cappelle Medicee (Medici Chapels)
28 Chiesa di Santa Maria Novella
29 Comune di Firenze Tourist Office
30 SITA Bus Station
31 Telecom Office
33 Avis
34 Hertz
35 French Consulate
43 Caffè Mambo
44 UK Consulate
45 Ponte Santa Trinitá
46 Ponte alla Carraia
49 Cabiria
51 Palazzo Pitti
52 Ponte alle Grazie
54 Forte di Belvedere
To Amerigo Vespucci Airport (5km)
To Ospedale Careggi
To HI Youth Hostel; Villa Camerata; Fiesole
To Teatro Comunale & US Consulate
To Youth Residence Firenze 2000
To Campeggio Michelangelo & Piazzale Michelangelo
See Duomo to Ponte Vecchio Map
Via della Cernaia
Via XXIV Maggio
Via dello Statuto
Via Francesco Puccinotti
Via Cosseria
Via XX Settembre
Viale Giovanni Milton
Viale Francesco Redi
Viale Belfiore
Viale Filippo Strozzi
Via Lorenzo il Magnifico
Via Leone X
Viale Spartaco Lavagnini
Via Duca d'Aosta
Via Bonifacio Lupi
Via S Caterina d'Alessandria
Via delle Ruote
Via Enrico Poggi
Via G Dolfi
Via C Ridolfi
Palazzo delle Esposizioni
Fortezza da Basso
Via Cittadella
Viale Fratelli Rosselli
Via della Fortezza
Piazza della Indipendenza
Via XXVII Aprile
Via Santa Reparata
Via San Gallo
Via Cavour
Via Valfonda
Piazza del Crocifisso
Via Guelfa
Via Nazionale
Via San Zanobi
Via Luigi Alamanni
Via Jacoppo da Diacceto
Via Faenza
Piazza Adua
Stazione di Santa Maria Novella
Via Fiume
Via Panicale
Piazza del Mercato Centrale
Piazza San Marco
Via della Scala
Piazza della Stazione
Via Sant'Antonino
Via de' Ginori
Via Ricasoli
Piazza della SS Annunziata
Via Laura
Piazza dell'Unità Italiana
Via dei Servi
Piazza Brunelleschi
Via S Lucia
Via Palazzuolo
Piazza di Santa Maria Novella
Via degli Avelli
Via de' Panzani
Piazza San Lorenzo
Via della Pergola
Borgo Pinti
Via degli Alfani
Borgo Ognissanti
Via Montebello
Piazza d'Ognissanti
Via de' Cerretani
Ospedale di San Giovanni di Dio
Via de' Fossi
Piazza di S Benedetto
Via dell'Oriuolo
Via Fiesolana
Via de' Pepi
Lungarno Amerigo Vespucci
Piazza della Repubblica
Via del Corso
Via Pietrapiana
Piazza dei Ciompi
ARNO
Piazza C Goldoni
Lungarno Corsini
Piazza Santa Trinita
Via Por Santa Maria
Via Giuseppe Verdi
Via dell'Agnolo
Via Ghibellina
Lungarno Soderini
Borgo San Frediano
Piazza della Signoria
Via di San Giuseppe
Lungarno Guicciardini
SAN FREDIANO
Piazza del Carmine
SANTO SPIRITO
Ponte Vecchio
Via Santa Monaca
Basilica di Santa Maria del Carmine
Via de' Serragli
Via Maffia
Piazza Santo Spirito
Via S Agostino
Lungarno delle Grazie
Via de' Guicciardini
Via della Chiesa
Via del Campuccio
Via Maggio
Corridoio Vasariano
Lungarno Torrigiani
Via de' Bardi
Piazza Demidoff
Via dei Renai
Via delle Caldaie
Borgo Tegolaio
Piazza de' Pitti
Giardino Torrigiani
Via Santa Maria
Via Romana
Museo Zoologico La Specola
Giardino di Boboli
Via della Meridiana
Viale dei Cipressi
0 100 200m
0 100 200yd

ITALY

Post & Communications The **main post office** *(Via Pellicceria 3; open 8.15am-7pm Mon-Fri, 8.15am-12.30pm Sat)* is off Piazza della Repubblica. For phones, there is an unstaffed **Telecom office** *(Via Cavour 21r; open 7am-11pm daily)*, and another at the station.

Internet Train has 10 branches in Florence, including beneath the station *(☎ 055 239 97 20)*, just off Via Nazionale *(☎ 055 21 47 94; Via Guelfa 24r)* and in Santa Croce *(☎ 055 263 85 55; Via dei Benci 36)*. It charges €1 for 10 minutes and €2.30 for 30 minutes. **Caffè Mambo** *(☎ 055 247 89 94; Via G Verdi 49)* has a separate Internet area and charges €1.30 for 15 minutes.

Medical & Emergency Services For an ambulance call ☎ 118. The main public hospital is **Ospedale Careggi** *(☎ 055 427 71 11; Viale Morgagni 85)*, north of the city centre. The **Tourist Medical Service** *(☎ 055 47 54 11; Via Lorenzo il Magnifico 59)* can be phoned 24 hours a day, and doctors speak English, French and German. First aid is provided at the **Misericordia di Firenze** *(☎ 055 21 22 22; Vicolo degli Adimari 1)* just off Piazza Duomo. All-night pharmacies include the **Farmacia Comunale** *(☎ 055 28 94 35)*, inside the station; and **Molteni** *(☎ 055 28 94 90; Via dei Calzaiuoli 7r)* in the city centre.

At the **questura** *(police headquarters; ☎ 055 497 71; Via Zara 2)* there is an office for foreigners where you can report thefts etc. For information about lost property call ☎ 055 328 39 42. But if you suspect your car has been towed away, try the **municipal car pound** *(☎ 055 41 57 81)*.

Dangers & Annoyances Pickpockets are active in crowds and on buses: beware of the groups of dishevelled women and children carrying newspapers and cardboard, whose trick is to distract you while others rifle through your bag and pockets.

Things to See & Do

Enjoying the sights in Florence can be a 'grin-and-bear-it' business, as lengthy queues test the patience of even the heartiest of travellers. But don't despair, because by calling **Firenze Musei** *(☎ 055 29 48 83, fax 055 26 44 06)* you can book tickets in advance (€1.55 fee) for all of the state museums, including the Uffizi, Palazzo Pitti, Museo del Bargello, Galleria dell'Accademia and Cappelle Medicee.

Duomo With its nougat facade and skyline-dominating dome, the Duomo is one of Italy's most famous monuments and the world's fourth-largest cathedral. Named the Cattedrale di Santa Maria del Fiore, the breathtaking structure was begun in 1294 by the Sienese architect Arnolfo di Cambio but took almost 150 years to complete.

Renaissance architect Brunelleschi won a public competition in 1420 to design the enormous dome, the first of its kind since antiquity. The octagonal dome is decorated with frescoes by Vasari and Zuccari, and stained-glass windows by Donatello, Paolo Uccello and Lorenzo Ghiberti. The marble facade is a 19th-century replacement of the unfinished original, which was pulled down in the 16th century. For a bird's-eye view of Florence, climb to the top of the **cupola** *(admission €6; open 8.30am-7pm Mon-Fri, 8.30am-5.40pm Sat)*.

Giotto designed and began building the graceful **campanile** *(bell tower; admission €6; open 8.30am-7.30pm daily)* next to the cathedral in 1334, but died before it was completed. Standing at 82m, the climb to the top is a tough one.

The Romanesque **battistero** *(baptistry; admission €3; open noon-6pm Mon-Sat, 8.30am-1.30pm Sun)*, believed to have been built between the 5th and 11th centuries on the site of a Roman temple, is the oldest building in Florence. Dante was baptised here, and it is particularly famous for its gilded-bronze doors. The celebrated *Gates of Paradise* by Lorenzo Ghiberti face the Duomo to the east; Ghiberti also designed the north door. The south door, by Andrea Pisano, dates from 1336 and is the oldest. Most of the doors are copies – the original panels are being removed for restoration.

Galleria degli Uffizi (Uffizi Gallery) The **Palazzo degli Uffizi** *(Piazza degli Uffizi; admission €8; open 8.15am-6.50pm Tues-Sun)*, built by Vasari in the 16th century, houses the single greatest collection of Italian and Florentine art in existence. Bequeathed to the city by the Medici family in 1743, it contains some of the world's most recognisable Renaissance paintings.

The gallery's inordinate number of masterpieces include 14th-century gems by Giotto and Cimabue; Botticelli's *Birth of Venus* and *Allegory of Spring* from the 15th century; works by Filippo Lippi, Fra Angelico and

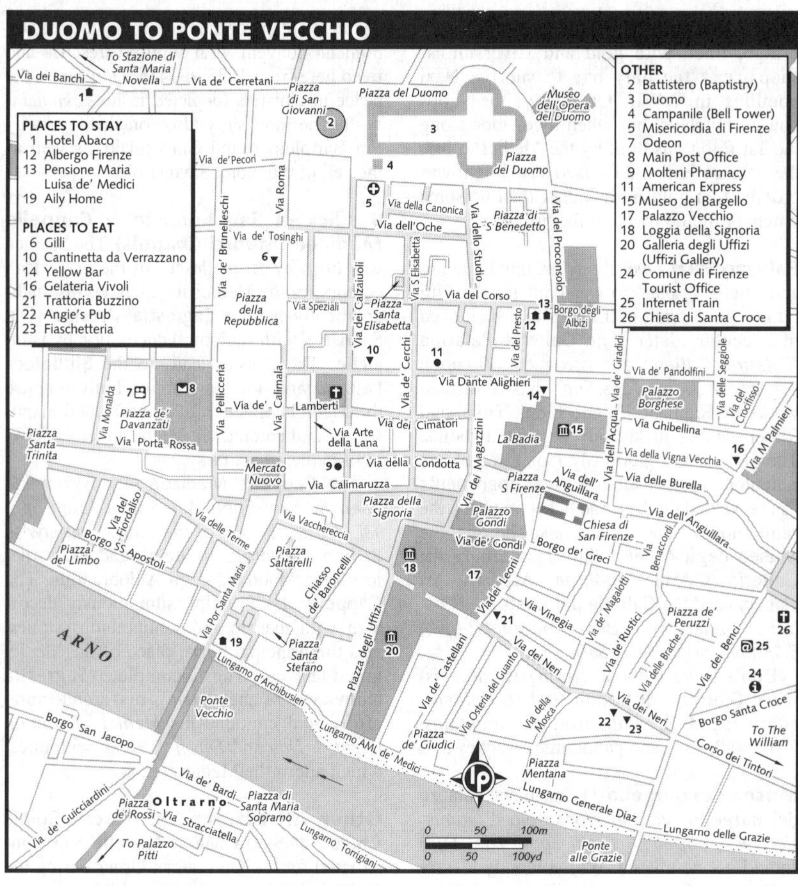

Paolo Uccello. *The Annunciation* by Leonardo da Vinci is also here, along with Michelangelo's *Holy Family,* Titian's *Venus of Urbino* and renowned works by Raphael, Andrea del Sarto, Tintoretto, Caravaggio and Tiepolo.

Piazza della Signoria & Palazzo Vecchio
Designed by Arnolfo di Cambio and built between 1298 and 1340, Palazzo Vecchio *(admission €5.70; open 9am-7pm Tues, Wed & Sat, 9am-11pm Mon & Fri, 9am-2pm Thur, in summer, otherwise 9am-7pm Mon-Wed & Fri-Sat, 9am-2pm Thur)* is the traditional seat of the Florentine government. In the 16th century it became the ducal palace of the Medici (before they moved to the Palazzo Pitti) and was given an interior facelift by Vasari. Visit the Michelozzo courtyard just inside the entrance and the lavishly decorated apartments upstairs.

The palace's turrets, battlements and bell tower form an imposing backdrop to Piazza della Signoria, scene of many pivotal political events in Florence's history, including the execution of religious and political reformer Savonarola; a bronze plaque marks where he was burned at the stake in 1498. The **Loggia della Signoria**, which has recently been thoroughly cleaned up and stands at right angles to the Palazzo Vecchio, displays sculptures such as Giambologna's *Rape of the Sabine Women.* Cellini's famous *Perseus* has, however, been relocated to the Uffizi. The statue of *David* is a fine copy of Michelangelo's masterpiece; the original was installed on the site in 1504 and is now safely indoors at Galleria dell'Accademia.

Ponte Vecchio This famous 14th-century bridge, lined with gold and silversmiths' shops, was the only one to survive Nazi bombing in WWII. Originally, the shops housed butchers, but when a corridor along the 1st floor was built by the Medici to link the Palazzo Pitti and Palazzo Vecchio, it was ordered that goldsmiths rather than noisome butchers should trade on the bridge.

Palazzo Pitti Over the river, this immense and imposing palazzo was built for the Pitti family, great rivals of the Medici, who moved in a century later. The **Galleria Palatina** *(Palatine Gallery; admission €6.50; open 8.15am-6.50pm Tues-Sun)* has collected works by Raphael, Filippo Lippi, Titian and Rubens, hung in lavishly decorated rooms. The gallery and gloriously (some might say ridiculously) over-the-top **royal apartments** can be visited on the same ticket and keep the same hours. The palace also houses the **Museo degli Argenti** (Silver Museum), the **Galleria d'Arte Moderna** (Modern Art Gallery) and the **Galleria del Costume** *(Costume Gallery; all three museums open 8.15am-1.50pm Tues-Sat)*.

Don't leave without visiting the Renaissance **Giardino di Boboli** *(Boboli Gardens; admission €2)*, with grottoes, fountains, leafy walkways and panoramic city views.

Museo del Bargello The medieval **Palazzo del Bargello** *(Via del Proconsolo 4; admission €4; open 8.15am-5pm Tues-Sun)* should not be missed. With a bloody history as the seat of the chief magistrate and, later, as a police station, the palace now houses Florence's rich collection of sculpture. Here you'll marvel at Michelangelo's *Bacchus*, Donatello's bronze *David*, Giambologna's *Mercury* and works by Benvenuto Cellini.

Galleria dell'Accademia Arguably the most famous sculpture in the Western world, Michelangelo's *David* is housed in this gallery *(Via Ricasoli 60; admission €6.50; open 8.15am-6.50pm Tues-Sun)*, as are four of the artist's unfinished *Slaves*. Early Florentine works are on show in the gallery upstairs.

Museo di San Marco The **Museo di San Marco** *(admission €4; open 8.15am-1.50pm Mon-Fri, 8.15am-6.50pm Sat, 8.15-7pm Sun)* pays homage to the work of Fra Angelico, who decorated many of the cells in this former Dominican convent with sublime frescoes and lived here from 1438 to 1455. Don't miss the peaceful cloisters (depicted in his *Annunciation*). The monastery also contains works by Fra Bartolomeo and Ghirlandaio, as well as the cell of the monk Savonarola.

Basilica di San Lorenzo & Cappelle Medicee (Medici Chapels) The basilica was built by Brunelleschi in the early 15th century for the Medici and includes his mathematically precise **Sagrestia Vecchia** (Old Sacristy), with sculptural decoration by Donatello. The cloister leads to the **Biblioteca Laurenziana**, the huge library built to house the Medici collection of some 10,000 manuscripts and entered via Michelangelo's flowing Mannerist stairway.

The **Cappelle Medicee** *(admission €6; open 8.15am-5pm Mon-Sat, 8.15am-5pm 1st, 3rd & 5th Sun of the month, otherwise 8.15am-1.50pm Sun)* are around the corner in Piazza Madonna degli Aldobrandini. The **Cappella dei Principi**, sumptuously decorated with marble and semiprecious stones, was the principal burial place of the Medici grand dukes. The incomplete **Sagrestia Nuova** was Michelangelo's first architectural effort, and contains his *Medici Madonna*, *Night & Day* and *Dawn & Dusk* sculptures, which adorn the Medici tombs.

Other Attractions The Tuscan Gothic **Chiesa di Santa Maria Novella** was constructed for the Dominican Order during the 13th and 14th centuries; its white-and-green marble facade was designed by Alberti in the 15th century. The church features Masaccio's *Trinity*, a masterpiece of perspective, and is decorated with frescoes by Ghirlandaio (who perhaps was assisted by a very young Michelangelo). **Cappella di Filippo Strozzi** has frescoes by Filippo Lippi, and those in the cloisters are by Paolo Uccello.

Head to **Piazzale Michelangelo** for unparalleled views of Florence. To reach the piazzale from the city centre, cross the Ponte Vecchio, turn left and walk along the river, then turn right at Piazza Giuseppe Poggi; if you're footsore, take bus No 13 from the station.

Special Events

Major festivals include the **Scoppio del Carro** (Explosion of the Cart), held in front of the

Duomo on Easter Sunday; and, on 24 June, the **Festa di San Giovanni** (Feast of St John, Florence's patron saint) and the lively **Calcio Storico**, which features soccer matches played in 16th-century costume. **Maggio Musicale Fiorentino**, Italy's longest-running music festival, runs from April to June. For information call the **Teatro Comunale** *(☎ 800 11 22 11)*.

Places to Stay

Always ask the full price of a room before putting your bags down as hotels and pensioni in Florence are becoming notorious for bill-padding, particularly in summer. Prices listed are high season.

Camping The **Campeggio Michelangelo** *(☎ 055 681 19 77, fax 055 68 93 48; Viale Michelangelo 80; €7.50/4.80 per person/tent)* is near Piazzale Michelangelo. Take bus No 13 from the station. **Villa Camerata** *(☎ 055 60 14 51; Viale Augusto Righi 2-4; €6/5 per person/tent)* is next to the HI hostel of the same name (see the following section).

Hostels The HI **Ostello Villa Camerata** *(☎ 055 60 14 51, fax 055 61 03 00; Viale Augusto Righi 2-4; dorm bed €15; closed 9am-2pm)* is beautifully situated. Dinner costs €8 and there is a bar. Take bus No 17, which leaves from the right of the station as you exit the platforms and takes about 30 minutes. It is open to HI members only; reservations can be made by mail (essential in summer).

The private **Ostello Archi Rossi** *(☎ 055 29 08 04, fax 055 230 26 01; Via Faenza 94r; dorm bed €16)* is another good option for a bed in a six- or nine-bed dormitory. **Ostello Santa Monaca** *(☎ 055 26 83 38; Via Santa Monaca 6; dorm bed €15.50)* is a 20-minute walk from the station: go through Piazza Santa Maria Novella, along Via de' Fossi, across the Ponte alla Carraia, directly ahead along Via de' Serragli, and Via Santa Monaca is on the right. Further west, **Youth Residence Firenze 2000** *(☎ 055 233 55 58; ⓔ european@dada.it; Viale Raffaello Sanzio 16; doubles with bath from €62)* lacks atmosphere and is not cheap, but its warm indoor pool is a big plus.

Hotels With more than 150 budget hotels in Florence, there is usually a room available somewhere, but it is still a good idea to book. Arrive by late morning to claim your room.

Around the Station Recently renovated **Pensione Bellavista** *(☎ 055 28 45 28, fax 055 28 48 74; Largo Alinari 15; singles/doubles €50/80, doubles with bath €90)*, at the start of Via Nazionale, has bright rooms and a loo with a view. **Albergo Azzi** *(☎/fax 055 21 38 06; Via Faenza 56; singles/doubles €42/62, doubles with bath €78)* is one of three basic hotels in the same building; upstairs are Albergo Anna and Albergo Paola.

Across Via Nazionale, the easy to miss **Soggiorno Burchi** *(☎ 055 41 44 54; Via Faenza 20; doubles without/with bath €50/60)* is a private house with old-fashioned rooms. Nearby at the **Hotel Nazionale** *(☎ 055 238 22 03, fax 055 238 17 35; Via Nazionale 22; singles/doubles €47/75, with bath €57/85)* some rooms have the dream view of the Duomo.

A few doors up at No 24, **Pensione Ausonia** *(☎ 055 49 65 47, fax 055 462 66 15; singles/doubles €48/82, singles/doubles/triples/quads with bath €62/116/143/170)* can cater to most requests and is run by a helpful couple; downstairs in their two-star **Hotel Kursaal** *(☎ 055 49 63 24; doubles €90)*, prices are the same except for the doubles without bath, and rooms have balcony, air-con and satellite TV. **Pensione Mary** *(☎/fax 055 49 63 10; Piazza dell'Indipendenza 5; singles/doubles €52/73, with bath €68/93)* is a little scruffy and the owner laid-back to the point of indifference.

Around Piazza Santa Maria Novella Via della Scala, which runs northwest off the piazza, is lined with pensioni. **La Scala** *(☎ 055 21 26 29; singles/doubles €52/77, doubles with bath €88)* at No 21 is a cheerfully unpretentious place.

A few doors down, at No 25, **Hotel Margaret** *(☎ 055 21 01 38; singles/doubles €50/70, doubles/triples with bath €90/120)* has newly refurbished rooms, as does **Albergo Montreal** *(☎ 055 238 23 31, fax 055 28 74 91; singles/doubles €40/60, doubles/triples/quads with bath €75/100/120)*, which is at No 43.

At **Sole** *(☎/fax 055 239 60 94; Via del Sole 8; singles €38, singles/doubles/triples with bath €46/77/104)*, ask for a quiet room as the street below can be noisy. **Albergo Toscana** *(☎/fax 055 21 31 56; singles/doubles with bath €70/114)*, in the same building, has pretty rooms.

Further north, the family-run **Hotel Pensione Ferretti** *(☎ 055 238 13 28, fax 055 21 92 88; Via delle Belle Donne 17; singles/doubles/triples €46/74/97, with bath €57/93/116)* has comfortable rooms and a charming address. Near the Duomo, the much recommended **Hotel Abaco** *(☎ 055 238 19 19, fax 055 28 22 89; Via dei Banchi 1; singles/doubles €60/70, doubles with bath €85)* offers 13th-century Florentine decor and double glazing; one room even has a fireplace.

Ottaviani *(☎ 055 239 62 23, fax 055 29 33 55; Piazza Ottaviani 1; singles without/with bath €59/69, doubles €59)*, just off Piazza Santa Maria Novella, has reasonable rates with breakfast included.

The Duomo to Ponte Vecchio This area is a 15-minute walk from the station and is right in the heart of old Florence. One of the best deals in town is the small **Aily Home** *(☎ 055 239 65 05; Piazza Santo Stefano 1; singles/doubles €25/40)*, overlooking the river. **Albergo Firenze** *(☎ 055 21 42 03, fax 21 23 70; Piazza dei Donati 4; singles/doubles with bath €62/83)*, just south of the Duomo, offers simple rooms, while those at **Pensione Maria Luisa de' Medici** *(☎/fax 055 28 00 48; Via del Corso 1; doubles without/with bath €67/82)* are large enough to cater for up to five people. Further east **Hotel Dali** *(☎/fax 055 234 07 06; Via dell'Oriuolo 17; singles/doubles €40/60, doubles with bath €75)* has sunny rooms and free parking for guests.

Places to Eat

Tuscan cuisine is based on the quality of its ingredients and the simplicity of its recipes. At its most basic, how can you beat a thick slice of crusty bread drizzled with olive oil and downed with a glass of Chianti? Local specialities include *ribollita*, a very filling soup of vegetables and white beans, and *bistecca alla Fiorentina* (steak Florentine), usually served in slabs sufficient for two.

You can stock up on supplies at the **food market** *(open 7am-2pm, Mon-Sat)* in San Lorenzo or at the supermarket on the western side of the train station, or at Via Pietrapiana 94, east of Piazza Duomo.

Restaurants In the centre, a popular place for pizza is the **Yellow Bar** *(☎ 055 21 17 66; Via del Proconsolo 39r; pizza meal about €10)*, which has plenty of seating but is still usually full. At **Trattoria Buzzino** *(☎ 055 239 80 13; Via dei Leoni 8; meals €25, tourist menu €13)* you'll be served hearty food, possibly by the waiter whose technique bears more than a passing resemblance to that of Basil Fawlty's hapless helper Manuel. At No 35r on the same street, Angie's Pub has a huge list of panini from €2.50 and refreshingly cold beer and **Fiaschetteria** *(Via dei Neri 17r; pastas from €3.50)* offers good value for money.

Around San Lorenzo, tiny but popular **Mario's** *(Via Rosina 2r; meals around €10; open lunch only)*, near Mercato Centrale, serves delicious pasta. Around the corner at Piazza del Mercato Centrale 24, **Trattoria Za Za** *(☎ 055 21 54 11, meals about €20)* is another favourite, with outdoor seating and an imaginative menu. **Bondi** *(Via dell'Ariento 85)* specialises in focaccia and pizza slices from €1.55.

In the Oltrarno, a bustling place popular with the locals is **Trattoria Casalinga** *(☎ 055 21 86 24; Via dei Michelozzi 9r; meals about €16)*. The food is great and the pace frenetic. **I Tarocchi** *(☎ 055 234 39 12; Via de' Renai 16; pizza from €5, meals about €13)* serves good pizza and huge portions of pasta. In trendy Piazza Santo Spirito, **Borgo Antico** *(☎ 055 21 04 37; meals about €22)* is a cool summer spot for alfresco dining.

Cafés, Snacks & Dessert Perhaps the city's grandest café is the wonderfully intact *belle époque* **Gilli** *(Piazza della Repubblica)*. If you can't resist the bountiful display of mouthwatering sweet and savoury delights, you'll save cash, if not calories, by eating and drinking at the bar.

Caffè degli Innocenti *(Via Nazionale 57)*, near the Mercato Centrale, has a good selection of panini and cakes for around €1.55 to €2.85. The streets between the Duomo and the Arno harbour many pizzerias where you can buy cheap takeaway pizza by the slice.

The **Cantinetta da Verrazzano** *(Via dei Tavolini 18r)* wine bar/café is a tight fit. All hanging hams and dark wood, this is the place to sip that Chianti.

South of Via Ghibellina, **Gelateria Vivoli** *(Via dell'Isola delle Stinche 7)* is widely considered the city's best. Don't be surprised to find a queue.

Entertainment

Listings to look out for include the bimonthly *Florence Today* and the monthly *Florence*

Information, which should be available at tourist offices. *Firenze Spettacolo,* the definitive monthly entertainment guide, is sold at newsstands for €1.55.

Concerts, opera and dance are performed year-round at the **Teatro Comunale** *(Corso Italia 16)*. For reservations contact the **box office** *(☎ 800 11 22 11)*.

Original language films are screened at the **Odeon** *(☎ 055 21 40 68; Piazza Strozzi; tickets €7.20)* on Monday and Tuesday.

For a pint, head to **The William** *(Via Magliabechi 7r),* which is lively and loud, or across the river to the tiny Cabiria bar in Piazza Santo Spirito, itself a good place to hang out, especially in summer.

A more sedate pastime is the evening *passeggiata* (promenade) in Piazzale Michelangelo, overlooking the city.

Getting There & Away

Galileo Galilei airport *(☎ 050 84 92 02)* is just under an hour away from Florence near Pisa, but is one of northern Italy's main international and domestic airports.

The **SITA bus station** *(☎ 800 37 37 60; Via Santa Caterina da Siena 17)* is just west of the train station. Buses leave for Siena, San Gimignano and Volterra. **Lazzi** *(☎ 055 35 10 61; Piazza Adua 1),* next to the station, runs services to Rome, Pistoia and Lucca.

Florence is on the main Rome-Milan rail line. Many of the trains are the fast Eurostars, for which booking is necessary. Regular trains also go to/from Venice (three hours) and Trieste. For train information ring ☎ 848 88 80 88.

Getting Around

Regular trains to Pisa airport leave from platform five at Santa Maria Novella station daily from 6.46am to 5pm; journey time is 1½ hours. Check your bags in at the air terminal (☎ 21 60 73) near platform five, at least 15 minutes before train departure time.

ATAF buses service the city centre and Fiesole. The terminal for the most useful buses is in a small piazza to the left as you go out of the station onto Via Valfonda. Bus No 7 leaves from here for Fiesole and also stops at the Duomo. Tickets must be bought before you get on the bus and are sold at most tobacconists and newsstands or from automatic vending machines at major bus stops (€1 for one hour, €1.80 for three hours, €4 for 24 hours).

To rent a car, try **Hertz** *(☎ 055 239 82 05; Via M Finiguerra 33r),* or **Avis** *(☎ 055 21 36 29; Borgo Ognissanti 128r)*. For bikes and scooters try **Alinari** *(☎ 055 28 05 00; Via Guelfa 85r),* or **Florence by Bike** *(☎/fax 055 48 89 92; Via Zanobi 120/122r)* which also runs bike tours.

You can find taxis outside the station, or call ☎ 4798 or ☎ 4390 to book one.

PISA

postcode 56100 • pop 92,000

No city in Italy can lay claim to as beautiful a construction cock-up as Pisa. Its leaning tower is one of the must-see sights in Italy and a godsend to producers of tourist kitsch. Once a maritime power to rival Genoa and Venice, Pisa has an important university and was the home of Galileo Galilei (1564–1642). It was devastated by the Genoese in the 13th century, and its history eventually merged with that of Florence. The city today retains its charm despite the many day-trippers.

Orientation & Information

The focus for visitors is the Campo dei Miracoli, a 1.5km walk from the train station across the Arno. The medieval town centre around Borgo Stretto is a kilometre or so from the station.

There are several APT tourist information offices: at the **station** *(☎ 050 4 22 91; open daily)*, the airport, and west of **Campo dei Miracoli** *(☎ 050 56 04 64; Via Carlo Cammeo 2; open daily)*. Internet access is available at **InternetSurf** *(Via Carducci 5)* near the Campo dei Miracoli, where 15 minutes costs €0.50.

Things to See & Do

The Pisans can justly claim that their **Campo dei Miracoli** (Field of Miracles) is one of the most beautiful squares in the world, whether by day or by night. A welcome expanse of well-kept lawns provides the perfect setting for the dazzling white marble cathedral, baptistry and bell tower – all of which lean to varying degrees.

The striped Pisan-Romanesque **cathedral** *(admission €2),* begun in 1063, has a graceful facade of tiered arches and a cavernous column-lined interior. The transept's bronze doors, facing the leaning tower, are by Bonanno Pisano. The 16th-century bronze doors of the main entrance are by Giambologna. The cathedral's cupcake-like **battistero** *(baptistry;*

admission €5), which started in 1153 taking two centuries to complete, contains a pulpit sculpted by Nicola Pisano.

The *campanile*, better known as the **Leaning Tower** *(Torre Pendente; admission €15)*, found itself in trouble from the start because of the marshy nature of the land on which it was built. Its architect, Bonanno Pisano, managed to complete only three of the tower's eventual seven tiers before it started to tilt. It has continued to lean by an average 1mm a year, and today is almost 4.1m off the perpendicular despite 11 years of ground-levelling work. Visits are limited to groups of 30 people, so admission times are staggered and waits inevitable.

To save on admission to the Campo's monuments and museums, you can choose from a number of ticket options: for example, admission to one museum and one monument costs €5, two museums and the cathedral €8. Admission to the Leaning Tower is always separate.

After taking in the Campo dei Miracoli, wander down Via Santa Maria, along the Arno and into the Borgo Stretto to explore the old city, which includes the impressive Piazza dei Cavalieri.

Places to Stay & Eat

Pisa has a range of reasonably priced hotels. Many budget places double as residences for students during the school year, so it can sometimes be difficult to find a cheap room.

The non-HI **Ostello per la Gioventù** *(☎/fax 050 89 06 22; Via Pietrasantina 15; dorm bed €15)* is closed during the day. Take bus No 3 from the station. **Albergo Serena** *(☎/fax 050 58 08 09; Via Cavaica 45; singles/doubles €28/41)* is tucked away near Piazza Dante Alighieri and provides simple rooms. The three-star **Hotel di Stefano** *(☎ 050 55 35 59, fax 050 55 60 38; Via Sant'Apollonia 35; singles/doubles €45/60, singles/doubles/triples/quads with bath €70/85/110/120)* offers tastefully decorated rooms and a lovely breakfast terrace. Just outside the station, **Albergo Milano** *(☎ 050 2 31 62, fax 050 4 42 37; Via Mascagni 14; singles/doubles €37/47, doubles/triples/quads with bath €65/87/97)* is a modest but welcoming joint.

Being a university town, Pisa has a number of cheap eating places. For a whopping great pizza **Pizzeria Del Borgo** *(Vicolo del Tinti 15; meals about €11.50)*, just off Via Oberdan, is just the job; plus one of the waiters does impressions. **Antica Trattoria il Campano** *(☎ 050 58 05 85; Vicolo Santa Margherita; meals about €25)* serves Tuscan grub in a medieval atmosphere. In the same price range **Spaghetteria alle Bandierine** *(☎ 050 50 00 00; Via Mercanti 4; meals about €20)* has a rustic feel and continues to win plaudits for its seafood. Head to **La Bottega del Gelato** *(Piazza Garibaldi)* and join the queue for gelati, or for fruit try the open-air food **market** *(Piazza delle Vettovaglie)*, off Borgo Stretto.

Getting There & Away

The airport, with domestic and European flights, is only a few minutes away by train, or by bus No 3 from the station. **Lazzi** *(☎ 050 462 88)* buses run to Florence via Lucca; somewhat surprisingly, there's an original Keith Haring mural opposite its office in Piazza Vittorio Emanuele. **CPT** *(☎ 050 50 55 11)* runs buses to Livorno via Tirrenia. Pisa is linked by direct train to Florence, Rome and Genoa. Local trains head for Lucca and Livorno.

SIENA

postcode 53100 • pop 54,000

To bypass Siena would be to miss one of Italy's most captivating towns. Built on three hills and surrounded by medieval ramparts, it features a labyrinthine centre jam-packed with majestic Gothic buildings in various shades of the colour known as burnt sienna; it's also usually crammed to bursting with visitors.

According to legend, Siena was founded by the sons of Remus. In the Middle Ages the city became a free republic, but its success and power led to serious rivalry with Florence. Painters of the Sienese School produced significant works of art, and the city was home to St Catherine and St Benedict.

Each year 10 of the city's 17 districts are chosen to compete in the Palio, a tumultuous horse race and pageant held in the Piazza del Campo on 2 July and 16 August.

Orientation & Information

Leaving the train station, cross the concourse to the bus stop opposite and catch bus No 3, 9 or 10 to Piazza Gramsci, then walk into the centre along Via dei Termini (it takes about 10 minutes to reach Piazza del Campo). At the **APT office** *(☎ 0577 28 05 51, fax 0577 27 06 76; ⓔ aptsiena@siena.turismo.toscana.it; Piazza del Campo 56; open daily)*, grab the useful guide *Terre di Siena* and a map of the town.

The **post office** *(Piazza Matteotti 1)* is to the north of the centre, and there are phones at the **Telecom offices** *(Via dei Termini 42 • Via di Città 113)*. Check your email at the **Internet Train** *(Via di Città 121)*, with 20 screens. For 15 minutes you'll pay €1.55, for one hour €5.16.

Things to See

Siena's uniquely shell-shaped **Piazza del Campo** (known as Il Campo) has been the city's focus since the 14th century. The piazza's sloping base is formed by the nobly proportioned **Palazzo Pubblico** *(Town Hall, also known as Palazzo Communale; admission €6.50; open 10am-7pm daily mid-Mar–end Oct, 10am-5.30pm end Nov–mid-Feb, 10am-6.30pm rest of the year)*, considered one of Italy's most graceful Gothic buildings. Its Sienese art treasures include Simone Martini's *Maestà* and Ambrogio Lorenzetti's *Allegories of Good & Bad Government*. Pay an extra €5.50 to enter the 102m-high **Torre del Mangia** (bell tower); a combined ticket costs €9.50.

The spectacular **Duomo** is another Gothic masterpiece, and one of the most enchanting cathedrals in Italy. Begun in 1196 and largely completed by 1215, extravagant plans for further construction were stymied by the arrival of the Black Death in 1348. Its black-and-white striped marble facade has a Romanesque lower section, with carvings by Giovanni Pisano, and the inlaid-marble floor features 56 panels depicting biblical stories. The marble and porphyry **pulpit** was carved by Nicola Pisano, father of Giovanni; other artworks include a bronze statue of St John the Baptist by Donatello, and statues of St Jerome and Mary Magdalene by Bernini.

A door in the north aisle leads to the **Libreria Piccolomini** *(admission €1.50)*, built by Pope Pius III to house the magnificent illustrated books of his uncle, Pope Pius II. It features frescoes by Pinturicchio and a Roman statue of the Three Graces.

The **Museo dell'Opera Metropolitana** *(Duomo Museum; admission €5.50; open 9am-7.30pm daily mid-Mar–Sept, 9am-6pm daily Oct, 9am-1.30pm daily Nov–mid-Mar)* is in Piazza del Duomo. Its many works of art formerly adorned the cathedral, including the *Maestà* by Duccio di Buoninsegna and the 12 marble statues by Giovanni Pisano, which once graced the Duomo's facade; other works

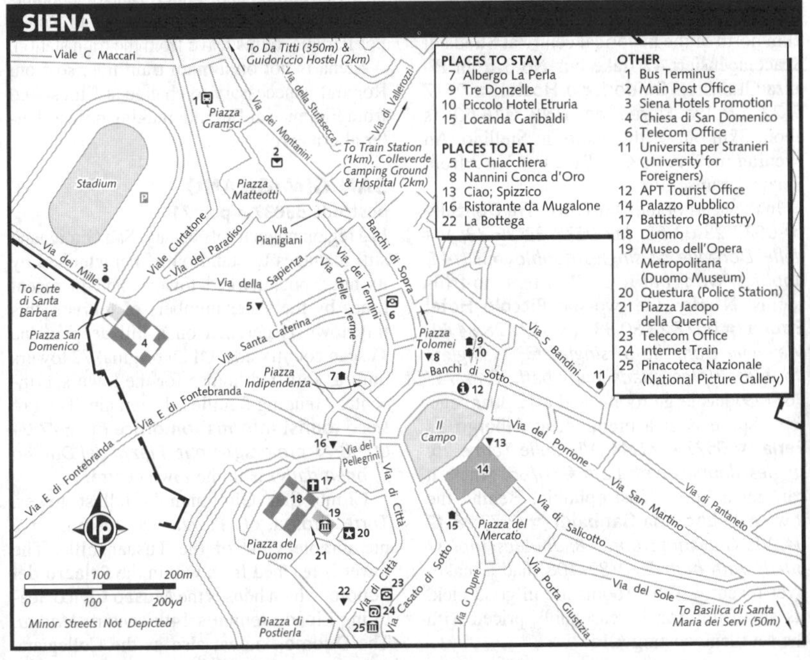

include those by Ambrogio Lorenzetti, Simone Martini and Taddeo di Bartolo.

The **battistero** *(baptistry; admission €2.50; open 9am-7.30pm daily mid-Mar–Sept, 9am-6pm daily Oct, 10am-1pm & 2.30pm-5pm daily Nov–mid-Mar)*, behind the cathedral, has a Gothic facade and is decorated with 15th-century frescoes. The highlight is the font by Jacopo della Quercia, with sculptures by Donatello and Ghiberti.

The 15th-century Palazzo Buonsignori houses the **Pinacoteca Nazionale** *(National Picture Gallery; admission €4; open 8.15am-7.15pm Tues-Sat, 8.30am-1.30pm Mon, 8.15am-1.15pm Sun)*, whose Sienese masterpieces include Duccio di Buoninsegna's *Madonna dei Francescani, Madonna col Bambino* by Simone Martini and a series of Madonnas by Ambrogio Lorenzetti.

Places to Stay

It is always advisable to book in advance, but for August and during the Palio, it's imperative. For help with bookings try **Siena Hotels Promotion** *(☎ 0577 28 80 84; ⓔ info@hotel siena.com; Piazza San Domenico 2)*.

Colleverde camping ground *(☎ 0577 28 00 44, fax 0577 33 32 98; per person/tent €7.75/7.75; open late Mar–early Nov)* is 2km north of the historical centre at Strada di Scacciapensieri 47 (take bus No 3 from Piazza Gramsci). **Guidoriccio Hostel** *(☎ 0577 5 22 12; Via Fiorentina; B&B €16.50)* is about 3km out of the centre in Stellino. An evening meal costs €9. Take bus No 3 from Piazza Gramsci.

In the heart of the Old Town, **Tre Donzelle** *(☎ 0577 28 03 58, fax 0577 22 39 33; Via delle Donzelle 5; singles/doubles €31/44, doubles with bath €57)* offers no-frills rooms. Nearby, the two-star **Piccolo Hotel Etruria** *(☎ 0577 28 80 88, fax 0577 28 84 61; Via delle Donzelle 3; singles €39, singles/doubles/triples/quads with bath €44/73/96/119)* has large rooms and a 12.30am curfew. Space is at a premium at **Albergo La Perla** *(☎ 0577 4 71 44; Via delle Terme 25; singles/doubles with bath €50/65)* where it can get a little claustrophobic. Behind the town hall, **Locanda Garibaldi** *(☎ 0577 28 42 04; Via Giovanni Dupré 18; doubles/triples/quads with bath €70/89/108)* had a makeover recently so the rooms are in good nick. Its small trattoria is reasonably priced with the set menu costing €15.

Agriturismo is well organised around Siena. The tourist office can provide a list of establishments.

Places to Eat

The ubiquitous self-service Ciao and fast food Spizzico are right on the Campo at No 77. **Ristorante da Mugalone** *(☎ 0577 28 32 35; Via dei Pelligrini 8; meals about €25)* is a good place for local specialities.

Tiny **La Chiacchiera** *(☎ 0577 28 06 31; Costa di Sant'Antonio 4; meals about €18)*, off Via Santa Caterina, has a rustic feel with wooden stools and handwritten menus and is ideal for lunch. There are several trattorias further north, in a quieter neighbourhood. **Da Titti** *(☎ 0577 4 80 87; Via di Camollia 193; meals about €15)* is one, serving standard Tuscan grub in simple surroundings.

Supermarket **La Bottega** *(Via di Città 152-6)* and **Nannini Conca d'Oro** *(Banchi di Sopra 22)*, one of Siena's finest cafés and a good place to stock up on *panforte*, are both central.

Getting There & Away

Regular Tra-In buses run from Florence to Siena, arriving at Piazza Gramsci. Buses also go to San Gimignano, Volterra and other points in Tuscany, and there's a daily bus to Rome. For Perugia, buses leave from the train station.

Siena is not on a main train line, so from Rome it is necessary to change at Chiusi and from Florence at Empoli, making buses a better alternative.

SAN GIMIGNANO

postcode 53037 • pop 7100

In a region noted for its beauty, San Gimignano still manages to stand out. Characterised by its huge pockmarked towers, and in recent times by the sheer numbers of tourists, this tiny town is perched on a hill deep in the Tuscan countryside. Of an original 72 towers built as fortified homes for the town's 11th-century feuding families, 13 remain. The Pro Loco **tourist information office** *(☎ 0577 94 00 08; ⓔ prolocsg@tin.it; Piazza del Duomo 1; open daily)* is in the town centre.

Climb San Gimignano's tallest tower, **Torre Grossa**, off Piazza del Duomo, for a memorable view of the Tuscan hills. The tower is reached from within the **Palazzo del Popolo**, which houses the **Museo Civico**, featuring Lippo Memmi's 14th-century *Maestà*. The **Duomo**, known also as the Collegiata, has a Romanesque interior, frescoes by Ghirlandaio in the **Cappella di Santa Fina** and a particularly gruesome *Last Judgment* by Taddeo di Bartolo. The city's most impressive piazza is **Piazza della Cisterna**, named for the 13th-century well at its centre.

San Gimignano offers few options for budget travellers. At the time of writing the youth hostel was closed with no scheduled reopening date, so for a cheap bed your best bet is the **Foresteria Monastero di San Girolamo** *(☎ 0577 94 05 73; Via Folgore 32; B&B €25)*. There are numerous rooms for rent in private homes, and agriturismo is well organised in this area. For further information, contact the tourist office.

For a plate of pasta and sip of the local wine, **Il Castello** *(☎ 0577 94 08 78; Via del Castello 20; pastas about €5.50)* is as good a spot as any. A fresh-produce market is held on Thursday morning in Piazza del Duomo.

Regular buses connect San Gimignano with Florence and Siena. They arrive at Porta San Giovanni and timetables are posted outside the tourist office. Enter through the Porta and continue straight ahead to reach Piazza del Duomo.

PERUGIA

postcode 06100 • pop 158,200

Perugia is a well-preserved medieval hill town that offers sweeping panoramas at every turn. Best known for its University for Foreigners, established in 1925, which attracts thousands of international students, the city is also famous for the Umbria Jazz Festival in July (and for chocolate).

Lowlights of Perugia's history, bloody even by medieval standards, have included the vicious internal feuding of the Baglioni and Oddi families, wars waged against neighbours and the death of at least two popes. However, art and culture have thrived: it was the home of the painter Perugino, and Raphael, his student, also worked here.

Orientation & Information

Perugia's hub is the Old Town's main drag, Corso Vannucci, running north-south from Piazza Italia, through Piazza della Repubblica and ending at Piazza IV Novembre and the Duomo.

The **IAT tourist office** *(☎ 075 573 64 58, fax 075 573 93 86; ⓔ info@iat.perugia.it; Piazza IV Novembre 3; open daily)* is opposite the Duomo. The main post office is in Piazza Matteotti and **Internet Train** *(Via Ulisse Rocchi 30)* has cheap Internet access. The monthly magazine *Viva Perugia: What, Where, When* (€0.52 at newsstands) has events listings and other useful information.

Things to See

Perugia's austere **Duomo** has an unfinished facade in red-and-white marble, while inside are frescoes and decorations by artists from the 15th to 18th centuries, as well as the Virgin Mary's wedding ring, which is unveiled every 30 July. The **Palazzo dei Priori**, nearby on Corso Vannucci, is a rambling 13th-century palace that houses the impressively frescoed **Sala dei Notari** and the **Galleria Nazionale dell'Umbria**, with works by Perugino and Fra Angelico. Between the two buildings, in Piazza IV Novembre, is the 13th-century **Fontana Maggiore**, designed by Fra Bevignate in 1278 and carved by Nicola and Giovanni Pisano.

At the other end of Corso Vannucci is the **Rocca Paolina** (Paolina Fortress), the ruins of a massive 16th-century fortress. Built by Pope Paul III over a medieval quarter formerly inhabited by some of Perugia's most powerful families, notably the Baglioni, the fortress was destroyed by the Perugians after Italian unification in 1860. A series of escalators pass through the underground ruins which are often used to host exhibitions. Raphael's fresco *Trinity with Saints*, some say his first, can be seen in the **Chiesa di San Severo**, Piazza San Severo, along with frescoes by Perugino.

Etruscan remains in Perugia include the **Arco Etrusco** (Etruscan Arch), near the university, and the **Pozzo Etrusco** (Etruscan Well), near the Duomo.

Places to Stay

Perugia has a good selection of reasonably priced hotels, but you could have problems if you arrive unannounced in July or August. **Centro Internazionale per la Gioventù** *(☎/fax 075 572 28 80; ⓔ ostello@ostello.perugia.it; Via Bontempi 13; dorm bed €12; closed 9.30am-4pm daily; closed mid-Dec–mid-Jan)* is a well-located non-HI place. Sheets (for the entire stay) are an extra €1.50. Its TV room has a frescoed ceiling and the terrace has some of Perugia's best views.

Pensione Anna *(☎/fax 075 573 63 04; Via dei Priori 48; singles/doubles €30/46, with bath €40/62)*, off Corso Vannucci, is full of character and antiques, while the two-star **Morlacchi** *(☎/fax 075 572 03 19; Via Tiberi 2; singles €40, singles/doubles with bath €51/60)* nearby is a little smarter but similarly priced.

Pensione Paola *(☎ 075 572 38 16; Via della Canapina 5; singles/doubles €28/42)* is down the escalator from Via dei Priori, and offers eight rooms with the use of a kitchen. Off the Piazza Italia end of Corso Vannucci, **Hotel Eden** *(☎ 075 572 81 02, fax 075 572 03 42; Via Cesare Caporali 9; singles/doubles with bath €36/57)* is excellent value with its blazingly white minimalist rooms.

Places to Eat

A student town, Perugia offers many budget eating options. Good pizza places include **Tit-Bit Pub** *(☎ 075 573 54 97; Via dei Priori 105; pizza meals about €10)*; **Il Segreto di Pulcinella** *(☎ 075 573 62 84; Via Larga 8; pizza from €5.50)*; and **Pizzeria Mediterranea** *(☎ 075 572 63 12; Piazza Piccinino 11/12; pizzas from €4.20)*. There's also a tiny but popular **pizza takeaway** *(Via dei Priori 3)*, near the Duomo.

Osteria del Turreno *(☎ 075 572 19 76; Piazza Danti 16; meals about €10)* serves panini as well as simple, hearty fare. For unforgettable panoramic views and an equally stunning antipasto spread, head for **Ristorante del Sole** *(☎ 075 573 50 31; Via Oberdan 28; meals about €25)*.

Sandri *(Corso Vannucci 32)*, by now a Perugian institution, has the best cakes in town, as well as free chocolate nibbles at the bar. To buy your own supplies of chocolate and other edibles there's a Coop supermarket at Piazza Matteotti 15, near the covered market.

Getting There & Around

Perugia is not on the main Rome–Florence railway line, but there are some direct trains from both cities. Most services require a change, either at Foligno (from Rome) or Terontola (from Florence). Intercity buses leave from Piazza dei Partigiani (at the bottom of the Rocca Paolina escalators) for Rome, Fiumicino airport, Florence, Siena and towns throughout Umbria, including Assisi, Gubbio and nearby Lake Trasimeno. Timetables for trains and buses are available from the tourist office.

The main train station is a couple of kilometres downhill from the historical centre. Catch any bus heading for Piazza Italia. Tickets cost €0.80 and can be bought from the ticket office on your left as you leave the station.

ASSISI

postcode 06081 • pop 25,500

Birthplace and spiritual home of the animal world's favourite saint, Assisi is a major port of call for millions of visitors who swarm to retrace the footsteps of St Francis. Somehow this small town perched halfway up Mt Subasio manages to cope while maintaining an air of tranquillity, particularly in the lanes off the central streets.

In September 1997 an earthquake rocked the town, causing considerable damage to the upper church of the Basilica di San Francesco, but five years on it's business as usual.

The APT **tourist office** *(☎ 075 81 25 34; ⓔ info@iat.assisi.pg.it; Piazza del Comune; open daily)* has plenty of useful information.

Things to See

If you're coming to Assisi to visit the religious sites, look the part. Dress rules are applied rigidly – absolutely no shorts, miniskirts or low-cut dresses/tops are allowed.

The **Basilica di San Francesco** is composed of two churches, one built on top of the other. The lower church is decorated with frescoes by Simone Martini, Cimabue and a pupil of Giotto, and contains the crypt where St Francis is buried. The Italian Gothic upper church has a stone-vaulted roof, and was decorated by the great painters of the 13th and 14th centuries, in particular Giotto and Cimabue. The frescoes in the apse and entrance received the most damage in the 1997 earthquake.

The impressively frescoed 13th-century **Basilica di Santa Chiara** (St Clare's Basilica) contains the remains of St Clare, friend of St Francis and founder of the Order of Poor Clares.

For spectacular views of the valley below, head to the massive 14th-century **Rocca Maggiore** fortress. You'll easily be able to spot the huge **Basilica di Santa Maria degli Angeli**, built around the first Franciscan monastery. St Francis died in its **Cappella del Transito** in 1226.

Places to Stay & Eat

Assisi is geared for tourists, and there are numerous budget hotels and *affittacamere* (rooms for rent). Peak periods, when you will need to book well in advance, are Easter, August and

September, and the Feast of St Francis on 3 and 4 October. The tourist office has a full list of *affittacamere* and religious institutions.

The small HI **Ostello della Pace** *(☎/fax 075 81 67 67; Via Valecchi 177; B&B €13)* is on the bus line between Santa Maria degli Angeli and Assisi. The non-HI hostel **Fontemaggio** *(☎ 075 81 36 36, fax 075 81 37 49; Via Eremo delle Carceri 8; dorm bed €18.50)* also has camping facilities. From Piazza Matteotti, at the far end of town from the basilica, it's a 30-minute uphill walk along Via Eremo delle Carceri.

Heading into town from Piazza Matteotti you'll pass **Pensione La Rocca** *(☎/fax 075 81 22 84; Vicolo della Fortezza; singles/doubles with bath €33.50/40)* in a quiet corner. Some of its sunny rooms have views that overlook the valley below.

For a cheap slice of pizza, head for Pizza Vincenzo, just off Piazza del Comune at Via San Rufina 1a. A good self-service in the same area is **Il Foro Romano** *(Via Portico 23)*. **Il Pozzo Romano** *(☎ 075 81 30 57; Via Santa Agnese 10; set menu €12.50)*, off Piazza Santa Chiara, serves simple dishes and is good value for money. To dine under ancient architraves try **Dal Carro** *(☎ 075 81 33 07; Vicolo dei Nepis 2; set menu €12.50)*, off Corso Mazzini, where the pasta dishes win good reviews.

Getting There & Away

Buses connect Assisi with Perugia, Foligno and other local towns, leaving from Piazza Matteotti. Buses for Rome and Florence leave from Piazzale dell'Unità d'Italia. Assisi's train station is in the valley, in the suburb of Santa Maria degli Angeli. It's on the same line as Perugia and a shuttle bus runs between Piazza Matteotti and the station.

ANCONA

postcode 60100 • pop 98,100

Ancona, a largely unattractive and industrial port city in the Marches, is unlikely to be high on your wish list, but you may well find yourself here waiting for a ferry to Croatia, Greece or Turkey.

The easiest way to get from the train station to the port is by bus No 1. If you're stuck here, there are a couple of options for dining and accommodation. Many backpackers choose to bunk down at the ferry terminal, although the city has many cheap hotels. The relatively new **Ostello della Gioventú** *(☎/fax 071 422 57; Via Lamaticci 7; dorm bed €12)* is not far from the train station; while for a bite to eat, the **Caffé Lombardo** *(Corso Giuseppe Mazzini 130; sandwiches from €2.60)* is a popular spot.

Buses depart from Piazza Cavour for towns throughout the Marches region. Rome is served by **Marozzi** *(☎ 071 280 23 98)*. Ancona is on the Bologna–Lecce train line and thus easily accessible from major towns throughout Italy. It is also linked to Rome via Foligno.

Ferry operators have information booths at the ferry terminal, off Piazza Kennedy. Most lines offer discounts on return fares. Prices listed here are for one-way deck class in the high season.

Companies include **Superfast** *(☎ 071 207 02 40)* to Patras in Greece (€78), **Minoan Lines** *(☎ 071 20 17 08)* to Igoumenitsa and Patras (€68) and **Adriatica** *(☎ 071 20 49 15)* to Durrës in Albania (€86) and to Split in Croatia (€47).

URBINO

postcode 61029 • pop 6000

This town can be difficult to reach – but, as the pride of the Marches, it is worth the effort. Birthplace of Raphael and Bramante, Urbino is still a centre of art, culture and learning. The **IAT tourist office** *(☎ 0722 26 13, fax 0722 24 41; Piazza Duca Federico 35; open Mon-Sat)* is conveniently situated in the centre of town. To stock up on cash the **Banca Nazionale del Lavoro** *(Via Vittorio Veneto)* has an ATM, as do most banks spread about the town centre. There is a **main post office** *(Via Bramante 18)* and **Telecom offices** *(Via Puccinotti 4 • Piazza San Francesco 1)*.

The dominating sight in Urbino is **Palazzo Ducale** *(admission €4.15; open 8.30am-7.15pm Tues-Sun, 8.30am-2pm Mon)*, designed by Laurana and completed in 1482. The best view is from Corso Garibaldi to the west, from where you can appreciate the size of the building and see its towers and loggias. Enter the palace from Piazza Duca Federico and visit the **Galleria Nazionale delle Marche**, featuring works by Raphael, Paolo Uccello and Verrocchio. Also visit the **Casa di Raffaello** *(Via Raffaello 5; admission €2.60)*, where the artist Raphael was born, and the **Oratorio di San Giovanni Battista** *(admission €1.55)*, with 15th-century frescoes by the Salimbeni brothers.

Most cheap beds are taken by students during the school year. The tourist office has a full list of *affittacamere*. You could try **Pensione Fosca** *(☎/fax 0722 32 96 22; Via Raffaello 61; singles/doubles €21/35)* with its simple rooms.

There are numerous bars around Piazza della Repubblica in the town centre and near the Palazzo Ducale that sell good panini. Go to **Pizzeria Galli** *(Via Vittorio Veneto 19)*, for takeaway pizza by the slice, or sit down at **Ristorante Da Franco** *(☎ 0722 24 92; Via del Poggio 1; meals about €10)*, which has a good-value self-service section.

There is no train service to Urbino, but it is connected by Soget and Bucci buses on weekdays to cities including Ancona, Pesaro and Arezzo. There is a bus link to the train station at the town of Fossato di Vico, on the Rome-Ancona line, or take a bus to Pesaro which is on the Bologna-Lecce line. There are also buses to Rome twice a day. All buses arrive at Piazza Mercatale, down Via Mazzini from Piazza della Repubblica. The tourist office has timetables for all bus services.

Southern Italy

Although noticeably poorer than the north, the land of the *mezzogiorno* (midday sun) is rich in history and cultural traditions. The attractions of the area are straightforward: the people seem more passionate; myths, legends and history are intertwined; and the food is magnificent. Campania, Apulia and Basilicata are relatively untouristed in many parts and Naples is like no other city on earth.

NAPLES (NAPOLI)

postcode 80100 • pop 1.5 million

Beautifully positioned on the Bay of Naples and overshadowed by Mt Vesuvius, Naples, the capital of the Campania region, is one of the most densely populated cities in Europe. Love it or hate it, Naples is a truly unforgettable city, with an energy that will either sweep you along or swamp you.

Both the Stazione Centrale and the main bus terminal are just off the vast Piazza Garibaldi. The main shopping thoroughfare into the historical centre, Spaccanapoli, is Corso Umberto I, which heads southwest from Piazza Garibaldi to Piazza Bovio. West on the bay are Santa Lucia and Mergellina, both fashionable and picturesque and quite a contrast with the chaotic historical centre. In the hills overlooking the bay is the Vomero district, a natural balcony across the city and bay to Vesuvius.

Information

Tourist Offices The **EPT office** *(☎ 081 26 87 79; www.ept.napoli.it; open daily)*, at the station, will make hotel bookings and has information on the region. Ask for *Qui Napoli* (Here Naples), published monthly in English and Italian, which lists events in the city, as well as information about transport and other services.

There's a good **AAST office** *(☎ 081 552 33 28; open daily)* in Piazza del Gesú Nuovo. **CTS** *(☎ 081 552 79 60; Via Mezzocannone 25)* is a student travel centre.

Money There are plenty of exchange booths throughout the city, which often offer lower rates than the banks. Banks with ATMs are plentiful too. **Every Tour** *(☎ 081 551 85 64; Piazza Municipio 5)* is the agent for American Express.

Post & Communications The **main post office** *(Piazza G Matteotti; open 8.15am-7pm Mon-Sat)* is off Via Armando Diaz. There is a **Telecom office** *(Via A Depretis 40; open 9am-1pm & 2-5.30pm Mon-Fri)*. **Aexis Telecom** *(Piazza Gesú Nuovo 52; open 8am-10pm daily)* has phones, faxes and Internet access (€3 per hour).

Medical & Emergency Services For an ambulance call ☎ 081 06 96 or ☎ 112. Each city district has a Guardia Medica (after hours medical service); check in *Qui Napoli* for details. The **Ospedale Loreto-Mare** *(☎ 081 254 27 01; Via A Vespucci)* is on the waterfront, near the station. There's a **pharmacy** *(open 8am-8pm daily)* in the central station.

The **questura** *(police station; ☎ 081 794 11 11; Via Medina 75)* is just off Via A Diaz, and has an office for foreigners where you can report thefts and so on. To report a stolen car call ☎ 081 794 14 35.

Dangers & Annoyances The city's home-grown mafia, the Camorra, is a pervasive local force, but one that won't affect you as a tourist. However, the petty crime rate in Naples is very high, and bag-snatchers and pickpockets

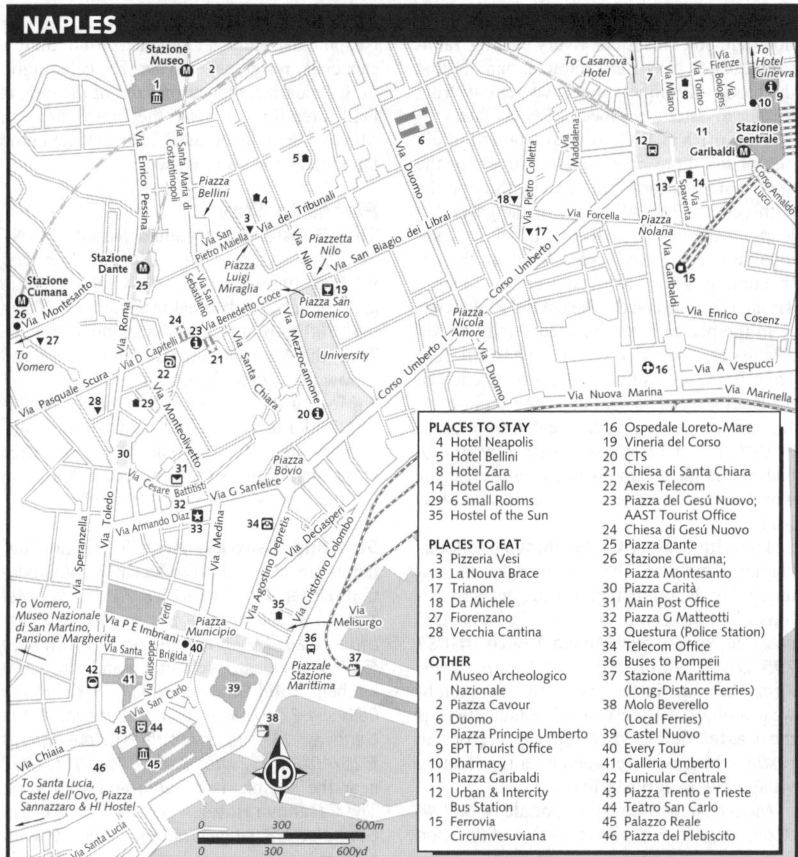

abound. Car theft is also a major problem. Keep your wits about you at night near the station, Piazza Dante, the area west of Via Toledo and as far north as Piazza Caritá.

Naples' legendary traffic means you need the power of prayer when crossing roads.

Things to See & Do

A good investment is the **Napoli artecard** *(☎ 800 60 06 01; W www.napoliartecard.com)* which gives access to six museums at reduced rates and public transport for €13. You can buy it at the airport, train and metro stations and selected museums.

Spaccanapoli, the historic centre of Naples, is a great place to start your sightseeing. From the station and Corso Umberto I turn right onto Via Mezzocannone, which takes you to Via Benedetto Croce, the bustling main street of the quarter. To the left is spacious Piazza del Gesú Nuovo, with the 15th-century rusticated facade of **Chiesa di Gesú Nuovo** and the 14th-century **Chiesa di Santa Chiara**, restored to its original Gothic-Provençal style after it was severely damaged by bombing during WWII. The beautifully tiled **Chiostro delle Clarisse** *(Nuns' Cloisters; admission €3.10; open 9.30am-1pm & 2pm-5.30pm Mon-Fri, 9.30am-1pm Sat)* is also worth visiting.

The **Duomo** has a 19th-century facade but was built by the Angevin kings at the end of the 13th century, on the site of an earlier basilica. Inside is the **Cappella di San Gennaro**, which contains the head of St Januarius (the city's patron saint) and two vials of his congealed blood. The saint is said to have saved the city from plague, volcanic eruptions and other disasters. Every year the faithful gather to pray for a miracle, namely that the blood will liquefy and save the city from further disaster (see Special Events later).

Turn off Via Duomo onto **Via Tribunali**, one of the more characteristic streets of the area, and head for Piazza Dante, through the 17th-century **Port'Alba**, one of the gates that leads to the city. Via Roma, the most fashionable street in old Naples, heads to the left (becoming Via Toledo) and ends at Piazza Trento e Trieste and the **Piazza del Plebiscito**.

In the piazza is the **Palazzo Reale** *(☎ 081 794 40 21; admission €4.50; open 9am-8pm Thur-Tues)*, the former official residence of the Bourbon and Savoy kings, now a museum. Just off the piazza is the **Teatro San Carlo** *(☎ 081 797 23 31; w www.teatrosancarlo.it)*, one of the most famous opera houses in the world thanks to its perfect acoustics and lavish interior.

The 13th-century **Castel Nuovo** overlooks Naples' ferry port. The early Renaissance triumphal arch commemorates the entry of Alfonso I of Aragon into Naples in 1443. It is possible to visit the **Museo Civico** *(☎ 081 795 20 03; admission €5.50; open 9am-7pm Mon-Sat)* in the castle. Situated southwest along the waterfront at Santa Lucia is the **Castel dell'Ovo**, originally a Norman castle, which is surrounded by a tiny fishing village, the **Borgo Marinaro**.

Museo Archeologico Nazionale *(☎ 081 44 0166; Piazza 17; admission €6.50; open 9am-8pm Wed-Mon)*, north of Piazza Dante, contains one of the most important collections of Greco-Roman artefacts in the world, mainly the rich collection of the Farnese family, and the art treasures discovered at Pompeii and Herculaneum. Don't forget to book a (free) tour to see the *gabinetto segreto* (secret cabinet) to see some of the racier artworks, which may well leave your cheeks (facial) flushed.

Catch the **Funicolare Centrale** (funicular), on Via Toledo, to the relative tranquillity of **Vomero** and the Certosa di San Martino, a 14th-century Carthusian monastery, rebuilt in the 17th century in Neapolitan-baroque style. It houses the **Museo Nazionale di San Martino** *(Piazza San Martino 5; admission €6; open 8.30am-7.30pm Tues-Sun)*. The monastery's church is worth visiting, plus its terraced gardens, with spectacular views of Naples and the bay.

Special Events

Neapolitans really get into the spirit of things, especially religious festivals. The celebration of St Januarius, the patron saint of the city, is held three times a year (the first Sunday in May, 19 September and 16 December) in the Duomo, and it's a must-see.

Places to Stay

The HI **Ostello Mergellina Napoli** *(☎ 081 761 23 46; Salita della Grotta 23; dorm bed €13.50; open year-round)* is modern, safe and soulless, with breakfast included. Even with 200 beds, it fills up during busy periods. Take the Metropolitana to Mergellina and follow the sign to the hostel.

Most of the cheap hotels are near the station and Piazza Garibaldi in a rather unsavoury area. You can ask the tourist office at the station to recommend or book a room (let them know your budget though).

Stazione Centrale Area The following hotels are safe and offer decent accommodation. **Hotel Zara** *(☎ 081 28 71 25; e hotelzar@tin.it; Via Firenze 81; singles/doubles/triples €26/47/73, doubles/triples with bath €57/83)* is clean, welcoming and also has a kitchen. **Hotel Ginevra** *(☎ 081 28 32 10, fax 081 554 17 57; e info@hotelginevra.it; Via Genova 116; singles/doubles/triples/quads €25/40/66/65, with bath €40/50/70/80)*, near the station, is reliable and well kept. The **Casanova Hotel** *(☎ 081 26 82 87; Corso Garibaldi 333; singles/doubles €18/39, with bath €26/52)* sounds like a brothel, but it's quiet, safe and friendly in a good way. **Hotel Gallo** *(☎ 081 20 05 12, fax 081 20 18 49; Via Spaventa 11; singles/doubles/triples with bath €57/83/109)*, to the left of the train station, has nice clean rooms with rates that include breakfast.

Around Spaccanapoli The excellent **6 Small Rooms** *(☎ 081 790 13 78; e info@at6smallrooms.com; Via Diodato Lioy 18; dorm bed €15)* is a friendly and sociable hostel, with cheery rooms, spacious kitchen (breakfast included) and rave reviews from many travellers. Ask about the 'beer witch' if you're feeling thirsty.

Hotel Bellini *(☎ 081 45 69 96, fax 081 29 22 56; Via San Paolo 44; singles/doubles with bath €42/68)* has well-appointed rooms (TV, fridge, phone) and a central location.

Other Areas The new **Hostel of The Sun** *(☎/fax 081 420 63 93; W www.hostelnapoli.com; Via Melsurgo 15; dorm bed €16, doubles with/without bath €61/45)* is close to the port, but on the 7th floor. It's tidy and laundry facilities are available.

Just near the Vomero funicular station, **Pensione Margherita** *(☎ 081 556 70 44; Via D Cimarosa 29; singles/doubles with bath €32/58)* is a decent place (some rooms offer bay views). You'll initially need a coin for the lift.

Places to Eat

Naples is the home of pasta and pizza. A true Neapolitan pizza, topped with fresh tomatoes, oregano, basil and garlic, will leave other pizzas looking decidedly wrong. Try *calzone*, a stuffed version of pizza, or *mozzarella in carozza* (mozzarella deep-fried in bread), which is sold at street stalls, along with *misto di frittura* (deep-fried vegetables). Don't leave town without trying the *sfogliatelle* (light, flaky pastry filled with ricotta). Heavenly fried goodies are on offer at bargain prices at **Fiorenzano** *(Piazza Montesanto)*. Naples has many *alimentari* (grocery shops) and food stalls scattered throughout the city.

There are numerous places to eat in and around Naples' centre. Reputedly the best pizza in Naples (and therefore the world) is at **Da Michele** *(☎ 081 553 92 04; Via Cesare Sersale 1; pizza €5-7)*. You can test this by taking a number and waiting for a bubbling, sizzling masterpiece. **Trianon** *(☎ 081 553 94 26; Via Pietro Colletta 46; pizza €5-10)* near Via Tribunali, is also great, with a wider selection and marble-topped tables. **La Nouva Brace** *(☎ 081 26 12 60; Via Spaventa 14; tourist menu €8.50)* is very easy on the pocket, and has tasty local dishes, plus poetry (in dialect) on the walls. **Vecchia Cantina** *(☎ 081 552 02 26; Via San Nicola alla Carita; meal about €12)* boasts a convivial atmosphere with great pasta dishes (the pasta with zucchini is delicious – €4.50). **Pizzeria dei Vesi** *(Via Tribunali 388; pizza €4.50-12)* is a homy, good-value place in the old quarter, with locals flocking to enjoy both sit-down and takeaway delights.

Entertainment

The monthly *Qui Napoli* and the local newspapers are the only real guides to what's on. In May the city organises Maggio dei Monumenti, with concerts and cultural events (mostly free) around town. Ask at the tourist office for details. The **Teatro San Carlo** *(☎ 081 797 21 11; W www.teatrosancarlo.it; tickets from €8)* has performances of opera, ballet and concerts year-round and is definitely worth visiting.

There are a handful of good **bars** in Piazza Gesú Nuovo, which go off on weekend nights and can also provide daytime coffee to ease the hangover. **Vineria del Corso** *(Via Paladino 8a)* is a great little bar, with good lighting, charming decor and low-key electronica played at a polite volume. There is also a good wine list here.

Getting There & Away

Some 5km northeast of the city centre, **Capodichino airport** *(☎ 081 789 61 11, 800 88 87 77; Viale Umberto Maddalena)* has connections to most Italian and several European cities. Bus No 14 or 14R leaves from Piazza Garibaldi every 30 minutes for the airport (20 minutes).

Buses leave from Piazza Garibaldi, just outside the train station, for destinations including Salerno, the Amalfi Coast, Caserta and Bari, Lecce and Brindisi in Apulia. Signage is limited, so you might have to ask at the booths for detailed information.

Naples is a major rail-transport centre for the south, and regular trains for most major Italian cities arrive and depart from the Stazione Centrale. There are over two dozen trains daily for Rome.

Traghetti (ferries), *aliscafi* (hydrofoils) and *navi veloci* (fast ships) leave for Sorrento and the islands of Capri, Ischia and Procida from Molo Beverello, in front of Castel Nuovo. Some hydrofoils leave for the bay islands from Mergellina, and ferries for Ischia and Procida also leave from Pozzuoli. All operators have offices at the various ports from which they leave. Hydrofoils cost around double the price of ferries but take half the time. **Tirrenia** *(☎ 081 199 12 31 99)* operates ferries to Palermo and Cagliari while **Siremar** *(☎ 081 580 03 40, 081 199 12 31 99)* services the Aeolian Islands. Ferries leave from the Stazione Marittima on Molo Angioino, next to Molo Beverello (see the Getting There & Away sections under Sicily and Sardinia). **SNAV** *(☎ 081 761 23 48)* runs regular ferries and, in summer, hydrofoils to the Aeolian Islands.

Getting Around

You can make your way around Naples by bus, tram, Metropolitana (underground) and funicular. City buses leave from Piazza Garibaldi in front of the central station bound for the centre of Naples and Mergellina. Tickets cost €0.77 for 1½ hours (€2.32 for 24 hours) and are valid for buses, trams, the Metropolitana and funicular services. Useful buses include No 14 or 14R to the airport; the R1 to Piazza Dante; the R3 to Mergellina; and No 110 from Piazza Garibaldi to Piazza Cavour and the archaeological museum. Tram No 1 leaves from east of Stazione Centrale for the city centre. To get to Molo Beverello and the ferry terminal from the train station, take bus No R2 or the M1.

The Metropolitana station is downstairs at the train station. Trains head west to Mergellina, stopping at Piazza Cavour, Piazza Amedeo and the funicular to Vomero, and then head on to the Campi Flegrei and Pozzuoli. Another line, still under construction in parts, will connect Piazza Garibaldi, the cathedral, Piazzas Bovio, Carita and Dante, the Museo Archeologico Nazionale and Piazza Vanvitelli.

The main funicular connecting the city centre with Vomero is the Funicolare Centrale in Piazza Duca d'Aosta, next to Galleria Umberto I, on Via Toledo.

The Ferrovia Circumvesuviana operates trains for Herculaneum, Pompeii and Sorrento. The station is about 400m southwest of Stazione Centrale, in Corso Garibaldi (take the underpass from Stazione Centrale). The Ferrovia Cumana and the Circumflegrea, based at Stazione Cumana in Piazza Montesanto, operate services to Pozzuoli, Baia and Cumae every 20 minutes.

AROUND NAPLES

From Naples it's only a short distance to the **Campi Flegrei** (Phlegraean Fields) of volcanic lakes and mud baths, which inspired both Homer and Virgil in their writings. The area is dirty and overdeveloped, but still worth a half-day trip. The Greek colony of **Cumae** is certainly worth visiting, particularly to see the Cave of the Cumaean Sybil, home of one of the ancient world's greatest oracles. Also in the area is **Lake Avernus**, the mythical entrance to the underworld, and **Baia** with its submerged Roman ruins visible from a glass-bottomed boat.

Reached by CPTC bus from Naples' Piazza Garibaldi or by train from the Stazione Centrale is the wonderful **Palazzo Reale** *(☎ 0823 44 74 47; admission €6.50; open 9am-7pm Tues-Sun)*, at Caserta. Built in the 18th century under the Bourbon king Charles III, this imposing 1200-room palace is set in elegant gardens.

Pompeii & Herculaneum

Buried under a layer of lapilli (burning fragments of pumice stone) during the devastating eruption of Mt Vesuvius in AD 79, **Pompeii** *(☎ 081 857 53 47; Via Villa dei Misteri 2; admission €10, with Herculaneum €18; open 8.30am-7.30pm Apr-Oct & 8.30am-5pm Nov-Mar)* provides a truly fascinating insight into the lives of ancient Romans. Once a resort town for wealthy Romans, the vast ruins include impressive temples, a forum, one of the largest known Roman amphitheatres, and streets lined with shops and luxurious houses. Many of the site's original mosaics and frescoes are housed in Naples' Museo Archeologico Nazionale (see that entry earlier). The exception is the Villa dei Misteri, where the frescoes remain *in situ*. Various houses and shops are closed, and details are provided at the entrance to the site. Bring a hat or umbrella, depending on the weather.

There are **tourist offices** *(☎ 081 850 72 55; Via Sacra 1)* in the new town, and just outside the excavations *(☎ 800 01 33 50; Piazza Porta Marina Inferiore 12)*, near the Porta Marina entrance. Both offer information, notes on guided tours and a simple map.

Catch the Ferrovia Circumvesuviana train from Naples and get off at the Pompeii Scavi-Villa dei Misteri stop; the Porta Marina entrance is nearby.

Herculaneum *(Ercolano; Corso Resina; admission €10, with Pompeii €18 for 3 days; open 8.30am-7.30pm, last entrance 6pm, Apr-Oct & 8.30am-5pm, last entrance 3.30pm, Nov-Mar)* is closer to Naples and also a good point from which to visit Mt Vesuvius. Legend says the city was founded by Hercules. First Greek, then Roman, it was also destroyed by the AD 79 eruption, buried under mud and lava. The ruins here are smaller and the buildings, particularly the private houses, are remarkably well preserved. Here you can see better examples of the frescoes, mosaics and furniture that used to decorate Roman houses.

Herculaneum is also accessible on the Circumvesuviana train from Naples (get off at

Ercolano Scavi; €1.55 one way). If you want to have a look into the huge crater of Mt Vesuvius, catch the **Trasporti Vesuviani bus** *(☎ 739 28 33)* from in front of the Ercolano Scavi train station or from Pompeii's Piazza Anfiteatro. The return ticket costs €3.10 from Ercolano and €5.16 from Pompeii. The first bus leaves Pompeii at 9.30am and takes 40 minutes to reach Herculaneum. You'll then need to walk about 1.5km to the summit, where you must pay €5.16 to be accompanied by a guide to the crater. The last bus returns to Pompeii from Herculaneum's Quota 1000 car park at 3pm, and there are only three buses to the crater (from Pompeii at 9.30am, 11am and 12.10pm).

SORRENTO

postcode 80067 • pop 17,450

A resort town in a beautiful area, Sorrento in summer is overcrowded with middle-aged, middle-class, middle-brow tourists and the trinket shops that cater to them. However, it is handy to the Amalfi Coast and Capri, and pleasant out of season.

The centre of town is Piazza Tasso, a short walk from the train station along Corso Italia. The very helpful **AAST tourist office** *(☎ 081 807 40 33; W www.sorrentotourism.it; Via Luigi de Maio 35; open Mon-Sat)* is inside the Circolo dei Forestieri complex.

There is a **post office** *(Corso Italia 210)* and **Telecom telephone office** *(Piazza Tasso 37)*. The **Deutsche Bank** *(Piazza Angelina Laura)* has an ATM. Internet access is available at **Blu Online** *(Via Fuorimura 20)*, near the train station, for €5 per hour.

Ostello delle Sirene *(☎ 081 807 29 25; Via degli Aranci 156; dorm bed €14, with bath €16)*, near the train station, is a good lodging option, with breakfast included. **Hotel Nice** *(☎ 081 878 1650, fax 081 878 30 86; Corso Italia 257; singles/doubles with bath €52/65)* has pleasant rooms, but traffic noise is a problem. **Pensione Linda** *(☎ 081 878 29 16; Via degli Aranci 125; singles/doubles with bath €26/47)* is a charming place with sweet service and bargain rates.

A cheap feed can be had at **Self-Service Angelina Lauro** *(☎ 081 807 40 97; Piazza Angelina Lauro 39; meals about €6)*. **Giardinello** *(☎ 081 878 46 16; Via dell'Accademia 7; pizzas about €5-6)* has a good menu and friendly service, plus a nice courtyard for summer dining. The supermarket at Corso Italia 223 has plenty of groceries.

Sorrento is accessible from Naples on the Circumvesuviana train line. SITA buses leave from outside the train station for the Amalfi Coast. Hydrofoils and ferries leave from the port, along Via de Maio and down the steps from the tourist office, for Capri and Napoli and Ischia. The tourist office hands out comprehensive timetables.

CAPRI

postcode 80073 • pop 7250

This beautiful island, an hour by ferry from Naples, retains the mythical appeal that attracted Roman emperors, including Augustus and Tiberius, who built 12 villas here. Very popular in summer, Capri wears its jet-set exclusivity well, like a cashmere sweater jauntily tied over bronzed shoulders. A short bus ride takes you to Anacapri, the town uphill from Capri, which also has accommodation. The island, famous for its grottoes, is also a good place for walking. There are tourist offices at Marina Grande *(☎ 081 837 06 34; open daily)*, where boats arrive; in Piazza Umberto I *(☎ 081 837 06 86; open daily)*, in the centre of town; and in Anacapri *(☎ 081 837 15 24; Piazza Vittoria 4)*. Online information can be found at W www.capri.it.

Things to See & Do

There are boat tours of the grottoes, including the famous **Grotta Azzurra** (Blue Grotto). Boats leave from Marina Grande and a return trip costs €14.10 (which includes the cost of a motorboat to the grotto, rowing boat into the grotto and entrance fee). On Sunday and public holidays it's a ludicrous €30. It's cheaper to catch a bus from Anacapri (although the rowboat and entrance fee still cost €8.10). You can swim into the grotto before 9am and after 5pm, but do so only in company and when the sea is very calm.

You can walk to most of the interesting points on the island. Sights include the **Giardini d'Augusto**, in the town of Capri, and **Villa Jovis** *(admission €2; open 9am-1hr before sunset daily)*, the ruins of one of Tiberius' villas, along the Via Longano and Via Tiberio. The latter is a one-hour walk uphill from Capri. The beautiful **Villa San Michele** *(☎ 081 837 14 01; Viale Axel Munthe; admission €5; open 9am-6pm daily May-Sept, 9.30am-5pm Mar-Apr & Oct, 10.30am-3.30pm Nov-Feb)* at Anacapri, was the home of Swedish writer Dr Axel Munthe.

Places to Stay & Eat

Stella Maris *(☎ 081 837 04 52, fax 081 837 86 62; Via Roma 27; singles/doubles €45/80)*, just off Piazza Umberto I, is right in the noisy heart of town. In Anacapri, there is the above-average **Loreley** *(☎ 081 837 14 40, fax 081 837 1399; Via G Orlandi 16; singles/doubles with bath €67/108)*, with low-season reductions available.

In Capri, **La Cisterna** *(☎ 081 837 56 20; Via M Serafina 5; meals about €15)* is a good spot to assuage hunger pangs. In Anacapri, **Il Saraceno** *(☎ 081 837 20 99; Via Trieste e Trento 18; meal about €17)* has a lovely family atmosphere and great home-made *limoncello* (lemon liqueur).

Getting There & Around

Getting to Capri is not a problem as there are hydrofoils and ferries that leave virtually every hour from Naples' Molo Beverello and Mergellina, especially during the high season. The Naples daily *Il Mattino* lists all the sailing times.

Several companies make the trip, including **Caremar** *(☎ 081 551 38 82; Ⓦ www.caremar.it)*, which runs ferries/fast ferries for €5.42/10.33 one way from Beverello; and **NLG** *(☎ 081 552 72 09; Ⓦ www.navlib.it/)*, also in Beverello, whose hydrofoils cost €11 one way.

From Marina Grande, the funicular directly in front of the port takes you to the town of Capri, which is at the top of a steep hill up a winding road some 3km from the port. Tiny local buses connect the port with Capri, Anacapri and other points around the island. Tickets for the funicular and buses (buy on board) cost €1.30 each trip or €6.71 per daily ticket.

AMALFI COAST

The 50km-stretch of the Amalfi Coast attracts the world's wealthy in summer, and prices skyrocket. Nevertheless, it's a coastline and landscape of inspiring natural beauty. Visit in spring or autumn and you'll find reasonably priced accommodation and a peaceful atmosphere.

There are tourist information offices in the individual towns, including in Positano *(☎ 089 87 50 67; Via Saracino 2; open daily July-Aug, Mon-Sat rest of year)*, and Amalfi *(☎ 089 87 11 07; Corso Roma 19; open Mon-Sat)*, on the waterfront.

Positano & Around

postcode 84017 • pop 3900

Positano is the most beautiful and fashionable town on the coast, with corresponding prices for the most part. The hills behind Positano offer some great walks, and the tourist office at Positano may have a brochure listing options. You can buy walking guides in town. Visit **Nocelle**, a tiny, isolated village above Positano, accessible by walking track from the end of the road from Positano. Have lunch at **Trattoria Santa Croce** *(☎ 089 81 12 60; meals about €20)*, which has panoramic views. It opens for lunch and dinner in summer, but at other times check in advance. Nocelle is accessible by local bus from Positano, via Montepertuso.

On the way from Positano to Amalfi is the town of **Praiano**, which is not as scenic but has more budget options, including the only camping ground on the Amalfi Coast. **La Tranquillitá** *(☎ 089 87 40 84; Ⓔ contraq@contraqpraiano.com; per person per camp site €13, double bungalows per person with breakfast €43)* has a pensione, bungalows and a small camping ground. The SITA bus stops outside.

Back in Positano, **Villa delle Palme** *(☎ 089 87 51 62; Via Pasitea 134; doubles with bath €78)* is a very good hotel, with English-speaking staff and all the usual mod-cons in each room. Next door is the great pizzeria **Il Saraceno d'Oro** *(pizza about €6)*, which is a cut above most of the tourist-trap joints in town.

Amalfi

postcode 84011 • pop 5520

One of the four powerful maritime republics of medieval Italy, Amalfi is a popular tourist resort. It has an impressive **Duomo**, and nearby is the **Grotta dello Smeraldo**, a rival to Capri's Grotta Azzurra.

In the hills behind Amalfi is delightful **Ravello**, accessible by bus from Amalfi and worth a visit to see the magnificent 11th-century **Villa Rufolo** *(admission €4; open 9am-6pm daily)*, once the home of popes and later of the German composer Wagner. The 20th-century **Villa Cimbrone** is set in beautiful gardens, which end at a terrace offering a spectacular view of the Gulf of Salerno. There are numerous walking paths in the hills between Amalfi and Ravello. Pick up *Strade e Sentieri* (€6.50), a guide to walks in the area.

The HI **Ostello Beato Solitudo** *(☎/fax 089 82 50 48; Piazza G Avitabile 4; dorm bed

€9.50) is in Agerola San Lazzaro, a village just 16km west of Amalfi. Regular buses leave from Amalfi throughout the day, the last at about 8.45pm. For a room in Amalfi try **Pensione Proto** *(☎ 089 87 10 03, fax 089 873 61 80; Via dei Curiali 4; singles/doubles €44/ 70)*, which has clean, decent quarters. The delightful **Hotel Lidomare** *(☎ 089 87 13 32, fax 089 87 13 94; ⓔ lidomare@amalficoast.it; Largo Duchi Piccolomini 9; singles/doubles with bath €39/88)* has romantic rooms and friendly service. Just follow the signs from Piazza del Duomo.

Pizzeria al Teatro *(Via E Marini 19; pizza about €7)* offers good food in attractive surrounds. Follow the signs to the left from Via Pietro Capuana, the main shopping street off Piazza del Duomo. There's a minimarket next to Pensione Proto. The best pastries are nibbled at **Pasticceria Andrea Pansa** *(Piazza Duomo 40)*, which is an old-fashioned place with luxe charm.

Getting There & Away

The coast is accessible by regular SITA buses, which run between Salerno (a 40-minute train trip from Naples) and Sorrento (accessible from Naples on the Circumvesuviana train line). Buses stop in Amalfi at Piazza Flavio Gioia, from where you can catch a bus to Ravello.

Hydrofoils and ferries also service the coast between April and mid-September daily, leaving from Salerno and stopping at Amalfi and Positano. There are also boats between Positano and Capri.

PAESTUM

postcode 84063

The sight that launched a thousand postcards, the three Greek temples standing in fields of red poppies are well worth making an effort to visit. The **temples** *(admission €4.50; open 9am-1hr before sunset daily)*, just south of Salerno, are among the world's best-preserved monuments of the ancient Greek world. A **tourist office** *(☎ 0828 81 10 16; open daily)* and an interesting **museum** *(☎ 0828 81 10 23; admission €4.50; open 9am-7pm daily, closed 1st & 3rd Monday of month)* are at the site.

Paestum is accessible from Salerno by CSTP bus No 34 from Piazza della Concordia or by train. Buses are frequent from Monday to Saturday, almost nonexistent on Sunday.

MATERA

postcode 75100 • pop 57,300

This ancient city of the Basilicata region still trades on haunting images of a peasant culture that existed until the 1960s. Its famous *sassi* (the stone houses built in the two ravines that slice through the city) were home to more than half of Matera's population until the 1950s, when the local government built a new residential area just out of Matera and relocated 15,000 people. The wards are a Unesco World Heritage site – a far cry from the days when Matera struggled against poverty and malaria.

There's a **tourist office** *(☎ 0835 33 19 83; Via de Viti De Marco 9; open Mon-Sat)* off the main Via Roma. **Itinera** *(☎/fax 0835 26 32 59; ⓔ arrtir@tin.it)* can organise guided tours in English for between one and 10 people (two to three hours) for €60. **Sassi Urban Network** *(SUN; ☎ 0835 31 98 06; Via Casalnuovo 15)* organises visits to the *sassi* churches (from €2.10) and provides maps. Its information offices are scattered throughout the wards.

Things to See

The two main *sassi* wards, known as **Barisano** and **Caveoso**, had no electricity, running water or sewerage until well into the 20th century. The oldest *sassi* are at the top of the ravines, and the dwellings that appear to be the oldest were established in the 20th century. As space ran out in the 1920s, the population turned troglodyte and started moving into hand-hewn or natural caves. The *sassi* zones are accessible from Piazza Vittorio Veneto and Piazza del Duomo in the centre of Matera. Be sure to see the rock churches, **Santa Maria d'Idris** and **Santa Lucia alla Malve**, both with well-preserved Byzantine frescoes. The 13th-century Apulian-Romanesque **cathedral**, overlooking Sasso Barisano, is also worth a visit.

Parts of the wards have been restored and some people have moved back to the area. Excavations in Piazza Vittorio Veneto have revealed the ruins of parts of **Byzantine Matera**, including a castle and a rock church decorated with frescoes. Worth visiting is **Casa Grotta di Vico Solitario** *(☎ 0835 31 01 18; Piazza San Pietro Caveoso; admission €1.50)*, an authentic *sassi* dwelling (English brochures available).

Places to Stay & Eat

Accommodation is best booked in advance. **Albergo Roma** *(☎/fax 0835 33 39 12; Via Roma 62; singles/doubles €21/31)* has simple rooms but a central location in town. **Sassi Hotel** *(☎ 0835 33 10 09, fax 0835 33 37 33; ⓔ hotel sassi@virgilio.it; Via San Giovanni Vecchio 89; dorm bed €15.50, singles/doubles with bath €52/78)* is the most atmospheric place to stay, as it's in – you guessed it – the *sassi*.

L'Osteria *(☎ 0835 33 33 95; Via Fiorentini 58; meal about €14)* is a tiny place with mouth-watering local dishes. There's a fresh produce market near Piazza V Veneto, on Via A Persio.

Getting There & Away

SITA buses connect Matera with Taranto and Metaponto. The town is on the private Ferrovie Apulo-Lucane train line, which connects with Bari, Altamura and Potenza. There are also three Marozzi buses a day between Rome and Matera (€30). Buses arrive in Piazza Matteotti, a short walk down Via Roma to the town centre. Buy tickets at **Biglietteria Manicone** *(☎ 0835 332 86 21; Piazza Matteoti 3)*.

APULIA

The province of Apulia, the thin heel of the Italian peninsula, has long been dismissed as a rural backwater with endemic poverty and it retains a sense of isolation from the rest of Italy. Yet for centuries, the 400km-long coastline was fought over by virtually every major colonial power, from the Greeks to the Spanish – all intent on establishing a strategic foothold in the Mediterranean. Each culture left its distinctive architectural mark, still in evidence today, albeit often crumbling.

Brindisi

postcode 72100 • pop 93,020

The highlight of no-one's trip to Italy, Brindisi swarms with travellers in transit, as it's the major embarkation point for ferries to Greece (bring a pack of playing cards!). Backpackers gather at the train station or at either of the two ports. The train station and the old port are connected by Corso Umberto I – which becomes the pedestrianised Corso Garibaldi. The new port, known as Costa Morena, is 7km from the train station, with free bus connections linking the two.Watch your possessions (and not just around locals), especially in the area around the train station and the ports.

Turn left off Corso Umberto I onto Via S Lorenzo da Brindisi to get to the bog-standard but inexpensive **Hotel Venezia** *(☎ 0831 52 75 11; Via Pisanelli 4; singles/doubles €13/25)*.

There's a **supermarket** *(Piazza Cairoli 30)* between the train station and the old port.

Getting There & Away Marozzi runs several buses a day to/from Rome's Stazione Tiburtina, leaving from Viale Arno. **Appia Travel** *(☎ 0831 52 16 84; Viale Regina Margherita 8-9)* sells tickets (€34; nine hours). There are rail connections to major cities in northern Italy, as well as to Bari, Lecce, Ancona, Naples and Rome.

Ferries leave Brindisi for destinations such as Corfu, Igoumenitsa, Patras and Kefallonia. Major ferry companies are **Hellenic Mediterranean Lines** *(HML; ☎ 0831 52 85 31; Corso Garibaldi 8)*; **Blue Star** *(☎ 0831 51 44 84; Corso Garibaldi 65)*; **Italian Ferries** *(☎ 0831 59 08 40; Corso Garibaldi 96)*; and **Med Link Lines** *(☎ 0831 52 76 67; Corso Garibaldi 49)*.

HML is the most expensive, but also the most reliable. HML also officially accepts Eurail and Inter-Rail passes, which means you pay only €12 to travel deck class. If you want to use your Eurail or Inter-Rail pass, it is important to reserve some weeks in advance in summer. Even with a booking in summer, you must still go to your boat company's embarkation office (ask them for details when you buy) to have your ticket checked.

Discounts are available for travellers under 26 years of age and holders of some Italian rail passes. Note that fares and services increase in July and August. Full prices in the 2002 high season for deck class were: HML to Corfu, Igoumenitsa, Cefalonia or Patras €46 (€37 return); Med Link to Patras €45 (€36 return); Blue Star to Corfu and Igoumenitsa €48. Bicycles can be taken aboard free, but the average high-season fare for a motorcycle is €18 and for a car around €48. A good website for trip planning is ⓦ www.ferries.gr, which has details of fares and timetables from Brindisi to Greece in English.

Be wary of any too-good-to-be-true offers from fly-by-night operators claiming your Eurail and Inter-Rail pass is accepted by them or invalid with anyone else. We get numerous letters from travellers who have been stung for two lots of ferry tickets.

The port tax is €6, payable when you buy your ticket. It is essential to check in at least two hours prior to departure. To get to the new port of Costa Morena from the train station, take the free Portabagagli bus, which departs a handy two hours before boat departures.

Lecce

postcode 73100 • pop 97,450

If baroque means 'architectural marzipan' to you, you're in for a sweet surprise in Lecce. The style here is so refined and particular to the city that Italians call it Barocco Leccese, and the city is known as the 'Florence of the South'. The numerous bars and restaurants are a pleasant discovery in such a small city, thanks to Lecce's university students.

There is a dozy **APT information office** *(☎ 0832 24 80 92; Via Vittorio Emanuele 24)* near Piazza Duomo. Take bus No 1, 2 or 4 from the station to the town centre, or a five-minute walk.

The most famous example of Lecce baroque is the **Basilica di Santa Croce**. Artists worked for 150 years to decorate the building, creating an extraordinarily ornate facade. In the **Piazza del Duomo** are the 12th-century **cathedral** (completely restored in the baroque style by Giuseppe Zimbalo of Lecce) and its 70m-high **bell tower**; the **Palazzo del Vescovo** (Bishop's Palace); and the **Seminario**, with its elegant facade and baroque well in the courtyard. The piazza is particularly beautiful at night, when the lights really show the buildings at their best. In Piazza Sant'Oronzo are the remains of a **Roman amphitheatre**.

Lecce's **Hotel Cappello** *(☎ 0832 30 88 81; Via Montegrappa 4; singles/doubles with bath €28/44)* is near the station and *'un buon mercato'* (a good price). For a taste of faded glory, try **Grand Hotel** *(☎ 0832 30 94 05; Viale Quarta 28; singles/doubles with bath €48/84)* just near the train station.

Ristorante Re Idomeneo *(Via Libertini 44; meal about €13)* is near Piazza del Duomo and has hearty, inexpensive pasta dishes, beloved by locals. **Fiaschetteria** *(Via d'Aragone 2; meal about €12)* is just near Chiesa di San Matteo and serves tasty local dishes with excellent bread.

For a small, seemingly sedate town, Lecce has some great little bars in its historic centre. Try **Caffe Letterario** *(Via Paladini 46)*, where you can enjoy wine by the glass in colourful surrounds.

STP buses connect Lecce with towns throughout the Salentine peninsula, leaving from Via Adua. Lecce is directly linked by Ferrovie dello Stato (FS) train to Brindisi, Bari, Rome, Naples and Bologna. The Ferrovie del Sud Est (FSE) runs trains to major points in Apulia.

Sicily (Sicilia)

Sicily is a land of Greek temples, Norman churches and fortresses, Arab domes, Byzantine mosaics and splendid baroque architecture. Its landscape, dominated by Mt Etna (3330m) on the east coast, ranges from fertile coast to mountains in the north to a vast, dry plateau at its centre.

With a population of about five million, Sicily has a mild climate in winter and a relentlessly hot summer. The best times to visit are in spring and autumn, when it's warm but quieter.

Most ferries from Italy arrive at Sicily's capital, Palermo, which is a convenient jumping-off point. If you're short on time, spend a day in Palermo and then perhaps head for Taormina, Syracuse or Agrigento.

Getting There & Away

Bus & Train Bus services from Rome to Sicily are run by **Segesta/Interbus** *(☎ 091 616 90 39, 616 79 19 in Palermo or ☎ 06 481 96 76 in Rome)*, which depart from Rome's Piazza Tiburtina. Buses service Messina (€27, 9¼ hours), Catania (€30, 11 hours) Palermo (€35, 12 hours) and Syracuse (€32.50, 11½ hours).

One of the cheapest ways to reach Sicily is to catch a train to Messina. The cost of the ticket covers the 3km-ferry crossing from Villa San Giovanni (Calabria) to Messina.

Boat Sicily is accessible by ferry from Genoa, Livorno, Naples, Reggio di Calabria and Cagliari, and also from Malta and Tunisia. The main companies servicing the Mediterranean are **Tirrenia** *(☎ 091 602 11 11 in Palermo, ☎ 06 42 00 98 03 in Rome; W www.gruppotirrenia.it)* and **Grimaldi** *(☎ 091 58 74 04 in Palermo, ☎ 010 2 54 65 in Genoa; W www.grimaldi.it)*, which runs Grandi Navi Veloci. Prices are determined by season and are highest from July to September. Timetables can change each year and it's best to check at a travel agency that takes ferry bookings. Book well in advance during summer, particularly if you have a car.

At the time of writing, high-season fares for a *poltrona* (airline-type chair on a ferry) were Genoa-Palermo (€100, 20 hours) and Livorno-Palermo (€94, 17 hours) with Grimaldi's Grandi Navi Veloci, and Naples-Palermo (€45, 9¾ hours) and Cagliari-Palermo (€39, 13½ hours) with Tirrenia.

Cosa Nostra

Of the many avatars of the omnipresent Italian Mafia, the Sicilian version – Cosa Nostra (Our Thing) – is by far the oldest and most powerful. With roots extending back to the 13th century, it has developed a complicated system of justice based on the code of silence known as *omertà*.

From the devastation of WWII, after Mussolini's efforts to stamp the Mafia into the ground, a new version of Cosa Nostra emerged. It has spread its tentacles worldwide and is far more ruthless and powerful than its predecessors. It's involved in drug-trafficking and arms deals, as well as finance, construction and tourist development, not to forget public-sector projects and politics. Few Italians doubt that the Mafia's influence extends into almost every part of the country, and well beyond.

In recent years, the central government has renewed its efforts to clamp down on Mafia activity. Major arrests in the 1990s were followed by confessions elicited from *pentiti* (turncoats), many of whose relatives paid the ultimate price for this behaviour. Despite the crackdown, Cosa Nostra is alive and well, and rumours circulate of influential leaders running Mob cells from prison cells.

Sicilians are often justifiably offended that the image of their proud island is one portrayed in blood. The 'men of honour' are not interested in your travellers cheques, so don't worry about getting into a Godfather-style shoot-out, unless you go looking for trouble.

Virtu Ferries (*w www.virtuferries.com)* serves Sicily-Malta. For information on ferries going from the mainland directly to Lipari, see Getting There & Away under Aeolian Islands later in this chapter.

Getting Around

Bus is the most common (and often the most convenient) mode of public transport in Sicily. Numerous companies run services between Syracuse, Catania and Palermo, as well as to Agrigento and towns in the interior. The coastal train service between Messina and Palermo and Messina to Syracuse varies from efficient and reliable to delayed and unpredictable.

PALERMO

postcode 90100 • pop 680,000

An Arab emirate and later the seat of a Norman kingdom, Palermo was once regarded as the grandest and most beautiful city in Europe. Today, parts of it are in a remarkable state of decay, due to neglect and heavy bombing during WWII, yet enough evidence remains of its golden days to make Palermo one of the most fascinating cities in Italy. Thankfully, some much-needed EU funds are actually beginning to make it to the areas that need it too.

Palermo is a large but easily manageable city. The main streets of the historical centre are Via Roma and Via Maqueda, which extend from the central station to Piazza Castelnuovo, a vast square in the modern part of town.

ITALY

Information

Tourist Offices There is a main **APT tourist office** *(☎ 091 58 38 47; w www.palermotourism.com; Piazza Castelnuovo 34; open Mon-Fri)* and branch offices at the Stazione Centrale *(☎ 091 616 59 14; open Mon-Fri)* and at the airport *(☎ 091 59 16 98; open daily)*.

Money An **exchange office** *(open 8am-8pm daily)* is at the Stazione Centrale. American Express is represented by **Ruggieri & Figli** *(☎ 091 58 71 44; Via Emerico Amari 40)*, near the Stazione Marittima. Otherwise, there is no shortage of banks with ATMs in the city.

Post & Communications The **main post office** *(Via Roma 322; open 8.30am-6.30pm Mon-Sat)* also has a fax service. The main (and grotty) **Telecom telephone office** *(Piazza G Cesare; open 8am-9.30pm daily)* is opposite the station. You can use the Internet (€3.10 per hour), send faxes and make calls at **Aexis Telecom** *(Via Maqueda 347)*.

Medical & Emergency Services For an ambulance call ☎ 091 30 66 44. The public hospital is **Ospedale Civico** *(☎ 091 666 11 11; Via Carmelo Lazzaro)*. A night pharmacy, **Lo Cascio** *(☎ 091 616 21 17; Via Roma 1)*, is near the train station. The **questura** *(☎ 091 21 01 11; Piazza della Vittoria)* is open 24 hours a day. You can also call the **foreigners office** *(ufficio stranieri; ☎ 091 651 43 30; Piazza della Vittoria)*. If your car has been towed, call ☎ 091 656 97 21 to find out where to collect it.

Dangers & Annoyances Contrary to popular opinion, Palermo isn't a hotbed of thievery, but it pays to watch your valuables, which may attract pickpockets and bag snatchers. The historical centre can be a bit dodgy at night, especially for women walking alone. You may also wish to avoid walking alone in the area northeast of the station, between Via Roma and the port (though there is safety in numbers).

Things to See

The intersection of Via Vittorio Emanuele and Via Maqueda marks the **Quattro Canti** (four corners of historical Palermo). The four 17th-century Spanish baroque facades are each decorated with a statue. Nearby **Piazza Pretoria** has a beautiful fountain, **Fontana Pretoria**, created by Florentine sculptors in the 16th century and once known as the Fountain of Shame because of its nude figures. Also in the piazza are the baroque **Chiesa di Santa Caterina** and the **Palazzo del Municipio** (town hall). Just off this piazza is Piazza Bellini and Palermo's famous church, **La Martorana** *(☎ 091 616 16 92; admission free; open 8am-1pm & 3.30pm-5.30pm Mon-Sat)*, with a beautiful Arab-Norman bell tower and Byzantine mosaics inside. Next to it is the Norman **Chiesa di San Cataldo** *(admission free; open 9am-3.30pm Mon-Fri, 9am-1pm Sat & Sun)*, which mixes Arab and Norman styles.

The huge **cattedrale** *(☎ 091 33 43 76; Corso Vittorio Emanuele; admission free; open 7am-7pm Mon-Sat, 8am-1.30pm & 4pm-7pm Sun)* retains vestiges of Norman architecture. At Piazza Indipendenza is Palazzo Reale, also known as the Palazzo dei Normanni, now the seat of the government. Step inside to see the **Cappella Palatina** *(☎ 091 705 48 79; admission free; open 9am-11.45am & 3pm-4.45pm Mon-Fri, 9am-11.45am Sat, 9am-9.45am & noon-12.45pm Sun)*, a truly jaw-dropping example of Arab-Norman architecture, built during Roger II's reign and lavishly decorated with Byzantine mosaics. King Roger's former bedroom, **Sala di Ruggero** *(☎ 091 705 70 03; admission free; open 9am-noon Mon, Fri & Sat)*, is decorated with 12th-century mosaics; you can only visit the room with a guide (free).

Take bus No 389 from Piazza Indipendenza to the nearby town of **Monreale** to see the magnificent mosaics in the world-famous 12th-century **Duomo** *(☎ 091 640 44 13; admission free; open 8am-6pm daily)*, plus its **cloisters** *(admission €4.50; open 9am-7pm Mon-Sat)*.

Places to Stay

The best camping ground is **Trinacria** *(☎/fax 091 53 05 90; Via Barcarello 25; per person/camp site €4.10/7.50)*, at Sferracavallo by the sea. Catch bus No 628 from Piazzale Alcide de Gasperi, which can be reached by bus No 101 or 107 from the station.

Casa Marconi *(☎ 091 645 11 16, fax 091 657 03 10; ⓔ casamarconi@iol.it; Via Monfenera 140; singles/doubles with bath €26 per person)* offers cheap, good-quality rooms. To get there, take bus No 246 from the station. Get off at Piazza Montegrappa; the hostel is a short walk.

Near the train station, the basic, anecdote-inducing **Albergo Orientale** *(☎ 091 616 57 27; Via Maqueda 26; singles/doubles €21/31)* has a decaying palazzo courtyard entrance and no heating in winter. *Lifestyles of the Rich & Famous* it ain't, but it's cheap and close to the action. Around the corner is sweet and spotless **Albergo Rosalia Conca d'Oro** *(☎ 091 616 45 43; Via Santa Rosalia 7; singles/doubles €27/40)*, which is a tad more upmarket.

Hotel Sicilia *(☎/fax 091 616 84 60; Via Divisi 99; singles/doubles with bath €39/62)*, on the corner of Via Maqueda, has decent rooms and friendly management but it can be noisy.

Hotel Florio *(☎/fax 091 609 08 52; Via Principe di Belmonte 33; singles/doubles with bath €45/65)* is a new and appealing addition to Palermo's accommodation options, and it's in a nice part of town too.

Places to Eat

A popular Palermitan dish is *pasta con le sarde* (pasta with sardines, fennel, peppers, capers and pine nuts). Locals are late eaters and restaurants rarely open for dinner before 8.30pm. **Osteria Lo Bianco** *(Via E Amari 104; meals about €12)*, at the Castelnuovo end of town, serves tasty staples amid bright lights, wood panelling, plastic and warm smiles. The wonderful **Trattoria Stella** *(Via Alloro 104)* is in the La Kalsa quarter. Try the *pesce spada* (swordfish) and listen to the lilting Arabic-influenced songs coming out of the kitchen.

Palermo has numerous open-air markets, but the best two are the Vucciria, held daily except Sunday in the narrow streets between Via Roma, Piazza San Domenico and Via Vittoria Emanuele, and Il Ballaro, held in the Albergheria quarter, off Via Maqueda. There's a wealth of fruit and vegetables, seafood and dairy to choose from, and the atmosphere is unbeatable.

Getting There & Away

The main (intercity) terminal for destinations throughout Sicily and the mainland is in the area around Via Paolo Balsamo, to the right (east) as you leave the station. Offices for the various companies are all in this area, including **SAIS Trasporti** *(☎ 091 616 11 41; Via Balsamo 16)*, **SAIS Autolinee** *(☎ 091 616 60 28; Via Balsamo 18)* and **Segesta** *(☎ 091 616 90 39; Via Balsamo 26)*.

Regular trains leave the Stazione Centrale for Milazzo, Messina, Catania, Syracuse and Agrigento as well as for nearby towns such as Cefalú. Direct trains go to Reggio di Calabria, Naples and Rome.

Boats leave from the port (Molo Vittorio Veneto) for Sardinia and the mainland (see the introductory Sicily Getting There & Away section). The **Tirrenia office** *(☎ 091 602 11 11)* is at the port.

Getting Around

Most of Palermo's buses stop outside or near the train station. Bus No 101 or 107 runs along Via Roma from the train station to near Piazza Castelnuovo in a loop. Bus No 139 goes from the station past the port. You must buy tickets before you get on the bus; they cost €0.77 (for 1½ hours) or €2.58 (24 hours).

AEOLIAN ISLANDS

Also known as the Lipari Islands, the seven islands of this archipelago just north of Milazzo are volcanic in origin. They range from the well-developed tourist resort of Lipari and the understated jet-set haunt of Panarea, to the rugged Vulcano, the spectacular scenery of Stromboli (and its fiercely active volcano), the fertile vineyards of Salina, and the solitude of Alicudi and Filicudi, which remain relatively undeveloped. The islands have been inhabited since the Neolithic era, when migrants sought the valuable volcanic glass, obsidian. The Isole Eolie (Aeolian Islands) are so named because the ancient Greeks believed they were the home of Aeolus, the god of wind.

The main **AAST tourist information office** *(☎ 090 988 00 95; Via Vittorio Emanuele 202; open Mon-Sat)* for the islands is on Lipari. Other offices are open on Vulcano, Salina and Stromboli during summer.

Things to See & Do

On **Lipari** visit the **castello** *(citadel; admission €4.50; open 9am-1.30pm & 3pm-7pm Mon-Sat)*, with its archaeological park and museum. The island also offers excellent walks. Catch a local bus from Lipari Town to the hill-top village of Quattrocchi for a great view of Vulcano. The tourist office has information on boat trips and excursions to the other islands.

Vulcano, with its pungent sulphurous odour, is a short boat trip from Lipari. The main volcano, Vulcano Fossa, is still active, though the last recorded period of eruption was 1888–90. You can make the one-hour hike to the crater, or take a bath in the therapeutic hot muds.

Stromboli is the most spectacular of the islands. Climb the volcano (924m) at night to see the Sciara del Fuoco (Trail of Fire) – lava streaming down the side of the volcano, and the volcanic explosions from the crater. Many people make the trip (four to five hours) without a guide during the day, but at night you should go with a guided group. Contact **AGAI** *(☎ 090 98 62 11; Piazza San Vincenzo)* to organise a guide (they only depart if groups are large enough) or the privately owned **Strómbolania information office** *(☎ 090 98 63 90; w www.strombolania.it; open daily Easter-Sept)* under the Ossidiana Hotel at Scari port, can help organise climbs and other island tours.

Places to Stay & Eat

Camping facilities are available on Salina and Vulcano. Most accommodation in summer is booked out well in advance on the smaller islands, particularly on Stromboli, and many places close during winter.

Lipari Lipari provides the best accommodation options, with numerous budget hotels, *affittacamere* (room rentals) and apartments, and the other islands are easily accessible by regular hydrofoil. Accommodation touts at Lipari port are worth checking because offers are usually genuine. The island's camping ground, **Baia Unci** *(☎ 090 981 19 09; e baiaunci@tin.it; €7.75/14 per person/camp site)*, is at Canneto, about 3km out of Lipari town.

Diana Brown *(☎ 090 981 25 84, fax 090 981 32 13; e dbrown@netnet.it; Vico Himera 3; singles/doubles with bath €62/68)* has well-appointed rooms with a homy feel. She can also arrange excursions around the islands.

At **Nenzyna** *(Via Roma 2; meal about €20)* you'll find a tiny, aqua-coloured dining area where your seafood desires will be more than satisfied.

Stromboli & Vulcano Popular **Casa del Sole** *(☎ 090 98 60 17; Via Soldato Cincotta; singles/doubles €21/42)*, on the road to the volcano, has decent rooms and a good kitchen.

On Vulcano, try **Pensione La Giara** *(☎ 090 985 22 29; Via Provinciale 18; B&B €58 per person with bath)*, a pleasant pensione with good rooms and staggering discounts outside August. It closes late October to early April.

Alicudi & Filicudi If you want seclusion, head for Alicudi or Filicudi. The former offers **Ericusa** *(☎ 090 988 99 02, fax 090 988 96 71; Via Regina Elena; doubles €62, half-board €60 per person)*, while Filicudi has the truly delightful **La Canna** *(☎ 090 988 99 56, fax 090 988 99 66; ⓔ vianast@tin.it; Via Rosa 43; singles/doubles with bath €39/78; half-board €68 per person)*. There are restaurants at both these hotels.

Getting There & Away

Ferries and hydrofoils depart for the islands from Milazzo (accessible by train from Palermo and Messina). All ticket offices are along Corso dei Mille at the port. SNAV runs hydrofoils (€10 one way). Siremar also operates hydrofoils, but its ferries are half the price. If arriving at Milazzo by train, you'll need to catch a bus to the port. Giunta buses from Milazzo stop at the port. SNAV also runs hydrofoils between the islands and Palermo (summer only).

You can travel directly to the islands from the mainland. Siremar runs regular ferries from Naples and SNAV runs hydrofoils from Naples (see the Naples Getting There & Away section earlier in this chapter), Messina and Reggio di Calabria. Occasionally the sea around the islands can be very rough and sailings are cancelled, especially in winter.

Getting Around

Regular hydrofoil and ferry services operate between the islands. Both Siremar and SNAV have booths at Lipari's port, where you can get full timetable information.

TAORMINA

postcode 98039 • pop 10,700

Spectacularly atop a hill overlooking the sea and Mt Etna, Taormina was long ago discovered by the European jet set, which has made it one of the more expensive and touristy towns in Sicily. Its magnificent setting, Greek theatre and nearby beaches remain as seductive now as they were for the likes of Goethe and DH Lawrence. The **AAST tourist office** *(☎ 0942 2 32 43; ⓦ www.taormina-ol.it; open Mon-Sat)* in Palazzo Corvaja, just off Corso Umberto, has extensive information on the town.

Things to See & Do

The **Greek theatre** *(admission €4.50; open 9am-6.30pm daily)* was built in the 3rd century BC and later greatly expanded and remodelled by the Romans. Concerts, theatre and festivals are staged here in summer, and there are wonderful views of Mt Etna. From the beautiful **Villa Comunale** (also known as Trevelyan Gardens) there's a panoramic view of the sea. Along Corso Umberto is the **Duomo**, with a Gothic facade. The postcard-perfect local beach is **Isola Bella**, accessible by *funivia* (cable car), which costs €2.70 return.

Trips to Mt Etna can be organised through **CST** *(☎ 0942 262 60 88; Corso Umberto 101)*.

Places to Stay & Eat

Bare-bones style **Campeggio San Leo** *(☎ 0942 2 46 58; Via Nazionale; €4.20/14.50 per person/camp site per night)* is accessible from the train station by the bus to Taormina – ask the driver to drop you off.

The tourist office has a list of *affittacamere* in Taormina. **Odyssey Youth Hostel B&B** *(☎ 0942 2 45 33, fax 0942 2 32 11; ⓦ www.taorminaodyssey.it; Via G Martino 2; dorm bed €15.50)* is a friendly, small place, with pleasant rooms. To get here, follow the signs from Porta Messina along Via Cappuccini and head down Via Fontana Vecchia (about 10 minutes).

The HI **Ostello della Gioventu 'Ulisse'** *(☎ 0942 2 31 93; Vicolo San Francesco di Paola 9; dorm bed €14.50 with breakfast)* is reasonable enough, although restrictions on kitchen use and hot water plus a lock-out make it a bit of a pain.

Pensione Svizzera *(☎ 0942 2 37 90; ⓔ svizzera@tao.it; Via Pirandello 26; singles/doubles/triples/quads with bath €52/72/108/120)*, on the way from the bus stop to the town centre, is a delightful place to treat yourself (or someone else).

Gambero Rosso *(Via Naumachie 11; pizza €4.65-8)* has smart service and nice outdoor seating. **Mamma Rosa** *(Via Naumachie 10;*

pizza about €5.20-7.20) has standard dishes and expensive seafood, but then again, eating in Taormina is rarely cheap! For a good, stiff drink **Arco Rosso** *(Via Naumachie 7)* just can't be beaten.

There's a **Standa supermarket** *(Via Apollo Arcagetta 19)* near the Ulisse hostel and Porta Catania.

Getting There & Away

Bus is the easiest way to get to Taormina. SAIS buses leave from Messina, Catania and also from the airport at Catania. Taormina is on the main train line between Messina and Catania, but the station is on the coast and regular buses will take you to Via Pirandello, near the centre; bus services are reduced on Sunday.

ETNA

Dominating the landscape in eastern Sicily between Taormina and Catania, Mt Etna (3330m) is Europe's largest live volcano. It has four live craters at its summit and its slopes are littered with crevices and extinct cones. Eruptions of slow lava flows can occur, but are not really dangerous. Etna's most recent eruption was in 2001, which destroyed large parts of its surroundings. You can climb to the summit (about a seven-hour hike), but the handiest way is to take the 4WD minibus with **SITAS** *(☎ 095 91 11 58)* from the Rifugio Sapienza (the south side), or with **Le Betulle/STAR** *(☎ 095 64 34 30)* from Piano Provenzana (the north side). Both companies charge €38.

Mt Etna is best approached from Catania by **AST bus** *(☎ 095 746 10 96)*, which departs from Via L Sturzo (in front of the train station) at about 8am, leaving from Rifugio Sapienza at about 4.45pm (€4.65 return). The private **Circumetnea train line** *(☎ 095 54 12 50)* circles Mt Etna from Catania to Giarre-Riposto. It starts from Catania just near Stazione Borgo, Via Caronda 352a (take a Metro train from Catania's main train station, or any bus going up Via Etnea and get off at the Metro stop named 'Borgo'). From Taormina, you can take an FS train to Giarre, where you can catch the Circumetnea.

In Catania, **Natura e Turismo** *(NeT; ☎ 095 33 35 43; e natetur@tin.it; Via Quartararo 11)* organises tours of the volcano with a volcanologist or expert guide.

A handy accommodation option in Catania is party-central **Agora Hostel** *(☎ 095 723 30 10; e agorahostel@hotmail.com; Piazza Curro 6; dorm bed €15.50, doubles €48)*, which has regular shindigs. It's close to La Pescheria market, which is good for those wishing to self-caterer.

SYRACUSE

postcode 96100 • pop 125,700

Once a powerful Greek city to rival Athens, Syracuse (Siracusa) is one of the highlights of a visit to Sicily. Founded in 743 BC by colonists from Corinth, it became a dominant sea power in the Mediterranean, prompting Athens to attack the city in 413 BC. Syracuse was the birthplace of Archimedes, and Plato attended the court of the tyrant Dionysius, who ruled from 405 to 367 BC.

The main sights of Syracuse are in two areas: on the island of Ortygia and at the archaeological park 2km across town. There are two tourist information offices: an **AAT** *(☎ 0931 46 42 55; Via Maestranza 33; open Mon-Sat)* on Ortygia and an **APT** *(☎ 0931 677 10; Via San Sebastiano 45; open Mon-Sat)*.

Things to See

Ortygia The island of Ortygia has eye-catching baroque palaces and churches. The **Duomo** was built in the 7th century on top of the Temple of Athena, incorporating most of the original columns in its three-aisled structure. The splendid **Piazza del Duomo** is lined with baroque palaces. Walk down Via Picherali to the waterfront and the **Fonte Aretusa** (Fountain of Arethusa), a natural freshwater spring. According to Greek legend, the nymph Arethusa, pursued by the river-god Alpheus, was turned into a fountain by the goddess Diana here. Undeterred, Alpheus turned himself into the river that feeds the spring.

Neapolis-Parco Archeologico To get to this archaeological zone *(☎ 0931 6 62 06; admission €4.50; open 9am-1hr before sunset daily)*, catch bus No 1 or 2 from Riva della Posta on Ortygia. The main attraction here is the 5th-century BC **Greek theatre**, its seating area carved out of solid rock. Nearby is the **Orecchio di Dionisio**, an artificial grotto in the shape of an ear which the tyrant of Syracuse, Dionysius, used as a prison. The 2nd-century **Roman amphitheatre** is impressively well preserved.

The excellent **Museo Archeologico Paolo Orsi** *(☎ 0931 46 40 22; admission €4.50; open 9am-1pm Tues-Sat)*, about 500m east of the archaeological zone, off Viale Teocrito, contains Sicily's best-organised and most interesting archaeological collection.

Places to Stay & Eat

Hotel Aretusa *(☎/fax 0931 2 42 11; Via Francesco Crispi 75; singles/doubles €27/42, with bath €32/48)* is close to the train station and has clean, albeit spartan, rooms. **Hotel Milano** *(☎ 0931 6 69 81; Corso Umberto 10; singles/doubles €19/37, with bath €37/66)* has a little more on offer (TV, fridge) and is closer to Ortygia.

Ortygia is the best area for eating in Syracuse. Try **Pizzeria Nonna Margherita** *(☎ 0931 6 53 64; Via Cavour 12; pizzas €2.60-11.40)*, a casual place with great pizza – from simple, tasty Neapolitan to more elaborate affairs. At **Pasticceria Tipica Catanese** *(Corso Umberto 46)* you can try scrumptious Sicilian sweets while planning your next trip to the dentist.

There is an open-air, fresh produce market in the streets behind Riva della Poata, daily (except Sunday) until 1pm. There are alimentari and supermarkets along Corso Gelone.

Getting There & Away

Interbus *(☎ 0931 6 67 10)* leaves from near the office at Via Trieste 28 (just behind Riva della Posta) for Catania, Palermo, Enna and surrounding towns. The service for Rome also leaves from here, connecting with the Rome bus at Catania. **AST** *(☎ 0931 4 62 71)* buses service the town and the surrounding area from Riva della Posta. Syracuse is easy to reach by train from Messina and Catania.

AGRIGENTO

postcode 92100 • pop 55,500

Founded in approximately 582 BC as the Greek Akragas, Agrigento retains several Greek temples in the valley below it. There's an **AAST tourist office** *(☎ 0922 2 04 54; Via Cesare Battisti 15; open Mon-Fri)*.

Agrigento's **Valley of the Temples** *(Collina dei Templi; admission €4.50, with museum €6; open 8.30am-9pm, Tempio di Giove area open 8.30am-6.30pm)* is one of the major Greek archaeological sights in the world. Its five main Doric temples, constructed in the 5th century BC, are in various states of ruin because of earthquakes and vandalism by early Christians. The only temple to survive relatively intact was **Tempio della Concordia**, which was transformed into a church. **Tempio di Giunone**, a short walk uphill to the east, has an impressive sacrificial altar. **Tempio di Ercole** is the oldest of the structures. Across the main road that divides the valley is the huge **Tempio di Giove**, one of the most imposing buildings of ancient Greece. It used to cover an area measuring 112m by 56m, with columns 18m high. *Telamoni*, colossal statues of men, were also used in the structure. The remains of one of them are in **Museo Archeologico** *(admission €4.50, with temples €6; open 9am-1.30pm & 2pm-7.30pm Tues-Sat, 9am-1.30pm Sun & Mon)*, just north of the temples on Via dei Templi. Nearby is the **Tempio di Castore e Polluce**, which was partly reconstructed in the 19th century. Get to the temples from the town, catch bus No 1, 2 or 3 from the train station.

The friendly **Bella Napoli** *(☎ 0922 2 04 35; Piazza Lena 6; singles/doubles/triples with bath €22/54/75)*, off Via Bac Bac at the end of Via Atenea, has clean, comfortable rooms. Good simple food can be had at **La Forchetta** *(Piazza San Francesco 9; meal about €13)*.

Intercity buses leave from Piazza Rosselli, just off Piazza Vittorio Emanuele, for Palermo, Catania and surrounding towns.

Sardinia (Sardegna)

The second-largest island in the Mediterranean, Sardinia was colonised by the Phoenicians and Romans, followed by the Pisans, Genoese and lastly, by the Spaniards. It is often said that the Sardinians were never really conquered – they simply retreated into the hills. Despite this, their hospitality is notable.

The landscape of the island ranges from the 'savage, dark-bushed, sky-exposed land' described by DH Lawrence to the beautiful gorges and valleys near Dorgali and the unspoiled coastline between Bosa and Alghero. Try to avoid the island in August.

Getting There & Away

Sardinia is accessible by ferry from Genoa, Livorno, Fiumicino, Civitavecchia, Naples, Palermo, Trapani, Bonifacio (Corsica) and Tunis. Departure points in Sardinia are Olbia, Golfo Aranci and Porto Torres in the north, Arbatax on the east coast and Cagliari in the south.

The main company, Tirrenia, runs a service between Civitavecchia and Olbia, Arbatax or Cagliari, and between Genoa and Porto Torres,

Olbia, Arbatax or Cagliari. There are fast ferries between Fiumicino and Golfo Aranci/ Arbatax and Civitavecchia and Olbia (both summer only). The national railway, Ferrovie dello Stato (FS), also runs a service between Civitavecchia and Golfo Aranci. **Moby Lines** (*W www.mobylines.it, Italian only)* and **Sardinia Ferries** (*W www.sardiniaferries.com*), also known as Elba and Corsica Ferries, both operate services from the mainland to Sardinia, as well as to Corsica and Elba. They depart from Genoa, Livorno, Civitavecchia and arrive at Olbia, Cagliari or Golfo Aranci. **Grandi Navi Veloci** (*W www.gnv.it)* runs a service between Genoa and Olbia (from June to September) or Porto Torres (year-round). Most travel agencies in Italy have brochures on the various companies' services.

Timetables change and prices fluctuate with the season. Prices for a *poltrona* (airline-type chair) on Tirrenia ferries in the 2002 high season were: Genoa to Cagliari (€54, 20 hours); Genoa to Porto Torres or Olbia (€46, 13 hours); Naples to Cagliari (€41, 16¼ hours); Palermo to Cagliari (€39, 13½ hours); Civitavecchia to Olbia, (€25, eight hours); and Civitavecchia to Cagliari (€41, 14½ hours).

To check departures, timetables and fares, visit the Tirrenia website at W www.tirrenia.com for information (in Italian only).

Getting Around

The two main bus companies are the state-run ARST, which runs extensive services through the island, and the privately owned PANI.

The main FS train lines link Cagliari with Oristano, Sassari and Olbia. The private railways that link smaller towns throughout the island can be *very* slow. However, the *trenino verde* (little green train), which runs from Cagliari to Arbatax through the Barbagia, is a very relaxing and lovely way to see part of the interior (see the Cagliari Getting There & Away section later in this chapter).

The best way to explore Sardinia properly is by road. Car rental agencies are listed under Cagliari and some other towns around the island. Hitchhiking can be laborious away from the main towns because of light traffic. Women definitely should not hitchhike alone in Sardinia.

CAGLIARI

postcode 09100 • pop 163,000

Cagliari is an attractive, friendly city offering a beautifully preserved medieval section, the delightful beach of Poetto, and salt lakes with a population of pink flamingos.

If you arrive by bus, train or boat, you will find yourself at the port area. The main street along the harbour is Via Roma, and the old city stretches up the hill behind it to the castle. Most of the budget hotels and restaurants are in the area near the port, not a great place in most cities, but perfectly safe and pleasant here.

Information

There is an **AAST information office** (*☎ 070 66 92 55; Piazza Matteotti 9; open Mon-Sat)* and information offices at the airport and in the Stazione Marittima. The **Ente Sardo Industrie Turistiche office** (*ESIT; ☎ 070 6 02 31, 800 01 31 53; Via Goffredo Mameli 97; open Mon-Sat*), which has information on the whole island.

The **main post office** (*☎ 070 6 03 11; Piazza del Carmine 27)* is up Via La Maddalena from Via Roma. The **Telecom office** (*Via G M Angioj 6)* is north of Piazza Matteotti. You can use the Internet at **Web Travel Point** (*☎ 070 65 93 07; Via Maddalena 34)* for €2.60 for 30 minutes.

For medical attention, go to the **Ospedale San Giovanni di Dio** (*☎ 070 66 32 37; Via Ospedale*). For police help, head for the **questura** (*☎ 070 6 02 71; Via Amat 9)*.

Things to See

The **Museo Archeologico Nazionale** (*☎ 070 65 59 11; Piazza Arsenale; admission €4; open 9am-8pm Tues-Sun)*, in the Citadella dei Musei, has a fascinating collection of Nuraghic bronzes. The bronzes were found in this local civilisation's stone constructions, which you can see all over Sardinia.

It's enjoyable to wander through the medieval quarter. The Pisan-Romanesque **Duomo** (*☎ 070 66 38 37; Piazza Palazzo)* was built in the 13th century and it has an interesting Romanesque pulpit.

There are good sea and city views from **Bastione di San Remy** in Piazza Costituzione, in the town's centre. It once formed part of the fortifications of the old city.

The Pisan **Torre di San Pancrazio** (*Piazza Indipendenza; open 9am-5pm Tues-Sun)* is also worth a look. The **Roman amphitheatre** (*Viale Buon Cammino; open 9am-5pm Tues-Sun)* is considered the most important Roman monument in Sardinia. During summer opera is performed here.

Places to Stay & Eat

There are numerous hotels near the port. Worth a stay is **AeR Hotel Bundes Jack/Vittoria** (*☎/fax 070 66 79 70; Vià Roma 75; singles/doubles with bath €43/63*), with lovely, spotless rooms and a warm welcome. **Hotel Miramare** (*☎/fax 070 66 40 21; Via Roma 59; singles/doubles €32/42, with bath €37/47*) has OK rooms. **Albergo La Perla** (*☎ 070 66 94 46; Via Sardegna 18; singles/doubles/triples €30/39/53*) has a few different retro decorating styles in evidence, but it's decent.

Reasonably priced trattorias can be found in the area behind Via Roma, particularly around Via Sardegna and Via Cavour. **Trattoria da Serafino** (*Via Lepanto 6; meals about €12*), on the corner of Via Sardegna, has very good food at excellent prices. **Trattoria Gennar-Gentu** (*☎ 070 67 20 21; Via Sardegna 60; meals about €13*) is a friendly place. Try the *spaghetti bottarga* (spaghetti with dried tuna roe) for a true Sardinian flavour. **Trattoria Ci Pensa Cannas** (*Via Sardegna 37; meals about €12*) is cheap and cheerful.

Getting There & Away

Departing from Piazza Matteotti are **ARST buses** (*☎ 070 409 83 24, 800 86 50 42*) servicing nearby towns, the Costa del Sud and Costa Rei. **PANI buses** (*☎ 070 65 23 26*) leave from Stazione Marittima for towns such as Sassari, Oristano and Nuoro. The main train station is also in Piazza Matteotti. Regular trains leave for Oristano, Sassari, Porto Torres and Olbia. The private **Ferrovie della Sardegna** (*FdS; ☎ 070 49 13 04*) train station is in Piazza della Repubblica.

Ferries arrive at the port adjacent to Via Roma. Bookings for Tirrenia can be made at the Stazione Marittima in the port area (☎ 070 66 60 65). See the introductory Sardinia Getting There & Away section for more details.

For rental cars or motorcycles try **Hertz** (*☎ 070 66 81 05; Piazza Matteotti 1*), also at the airport; or **Autonoleggio Cara** (*☎ 070 66 34 71*), which can deliver your scooter or bike to your hotel.

CALA GONONE

postcode 08022 • pop 1000

This attractive seaside resort is an excellent base to explore the coves along the eastern coastline, as well as the Nuraghic sites and rugged terrain inland. Major points are accessible by bus and boat, but you'll need a car to explore.

At the **Pro Loco office** (*☎ 0784 9 36 96; Viale del Blu Marino*) you can pick up maps, a list of hotels and information (generally from May to September). There is also a good **tourist office** (*☎ 0784 9 62 43; Via Lamarmora 181; open Mon-Fri*) in nearby Dorgali. Also in Dorgali, **Coop Ghivine** (*☎/fax 0784 9 67 21; w www.ghivine.com; Via Montebello 5*) organises excellent guided treks in the region from €30 per person.

Things to See & Do

From Cala Gonone's tiny port, catch a boat (€7) to the **Grotta del Bue Marino** (*admission €5.50*), where a guide will take you on a 1km walk to see vast caves with stalagmites, stalactites and lakes. Sardinia's last colony of monk seals once lived here, but they have not been sighted in years. Boats also leave for **Cala Luna**, an isolated beach where you can spend the day by the sea or take a walk along the fabulous gorge called **Codula di Luna**. However, the beach is packed with day-tripping tourists in summer. The boat trip to visit the grotto and beach costs around €18. A **walking track** along the coast links Cala Fuili, about 3.5km south of Cala Gonone, and Cala Luna (about two hours one way).

If you want to descend the impressive **Gorropu Gorge**, ask for information from the team of expert guides based in Urzulei – **Societá Gorropu** (*☎ 0782 64 92 82, 0347 775 27 06; e francescomurru@virgilio.it*). They also offer a wide range of guided walks in the area at competitive prices. It is necessary to use ropes and harnesses to traverse the Gorropu Gorge.

Places to Stay & Eat

Camping Gala Gonone (*☎ 0784 9 31 65, fax 0784 9 32 55; w www.campingcalagonone.it; Via Collodi; per person/camp site €15, 4-bed bungalows €110; open Apr-Oct*) has good-quality camping facilities, including a pool and restaurant.

Hotels include the attractive **Piccolo Hotel** (*☎ 0784 9 32 32; Via Cristoforo Colombo 32; singles/doubles with bath €32/53*) near the port, and **Pop Hotel** (*☎ 0784 9 31 85, fax 0784 9 31 58; e lfancel@box1.tin.it; singles/doubles with bath €57/93*), which is right on the water and has a decent restaurant.

Getting There & Away

Catch a PANI bus to Nuoro from Cagliari, Sassari or Oristano and then take an ARST bus to Cala Gonone (via Dorgali). If you are travelling by car, you will need a proper road map of the area.

ALGHERO

postcode 07041 • pop 40,600

A popular tourist resort Alghero is on the west coast, an area known as the Coral Riviera. The town is a good base from which to explore the magnificent coastline linking it to Bosa in the south, and the famous Grotte di Nettuno (Caves of Neptune) on the Capocaccia to the north. The best time to visit is in spring or autumn, when it's less crowded.

Information

The **train station** *(Via Don Minzoni)* is some distance from the centre, and is connected by a regular bus service to the centre of town. The very helpful **AAST tourist office** *(☎ 079 97 90 54; Piazza Porta Terra 9; open Mon-Sat)* is near the port and just across the gardens from the bus station. The old city and most hotels and restaurants are in the area west of the tourist office.

There is a **main post office** *(Via XX Settembre 108)*. There is a bank of **public telephones** *(Via Vittorio Emanuele)* at the opposite end of the gardens from the tourist office.

In an emergency ring the police on ☎ 113; for medical attention ring ☎ 079 98 71 61, or go to the **Ospedale Civile** *(☎ 079 99 62 33; Via Don Minzoni)*.

Things to See & Do

The narrow streets of the old city and around the port are worth exploring. The most interesting church here is the **Chiesa di San Francesco** *(Via Carlo Alberto; open 9am-noon & 4pm-7pm daily)*. The city's **cathedral** has been ruined by constant remodelling, but its bell tower remains a fine example of Gothic-Catalan architecture.

Near Alghero at the beautiful **Capocaccia** are the **Grotte di Nettuno**, accessible by boat (€10, hourly 8am to 7pm June to September, four daily April to May and October) from the port, or three times a day by the FS bus from Via Catalogna (€3.25 return, 50 minutes, 1 June to 30 Sepember).

If you have private transport, don't miss **Nuraghe di Palmavera** *(☎ 079 95 32 00; admission €2.05)*, a ruined palace about 10km out of Alghero on the road to Porto Conte.

The coastline between Alghero and Bosa is picturesque. Rugged cliffs fall down to solitary beaches, and near **Bosa** is one of the last habitats of the griffon vulture. If you want to rent a bicycle (from €9 per day) or motorcycle (from €70) to explore the coast, try **Cicloexpress** *(☎ 079 98 69 50; Via Garibaldi)* at the port.

Special Events

In summer Alghero stages the Estate Musicale Algherese (Alghero's Summer Music Festival) in the cloisters of the church of San Francesco, Via Carlo Alberto. A festival, complete with fireworks display, is held for the Feast of the Assumption on 15 August.

Places to Stay & Eat

Finding a room in August without a reservation from months ago is a nightmare. At other times of the year you'll be fine. Camping facilities include **Calik** *(☎/fax 079 93 01 11; W www.campeggiocalik.it; open 1 Jun-30 Sep; per person/camp site €12)* in Fertilia, which is about 6km out of town on the SS127bis. The HI **Ostello dei Giuliani** *(☎/fax 079 93 03 53; e ostellodeigiuliani@ticalinet.it; Via Zara 1; dorm bed €10; open year-round)* is also in Fertilia and is in good condition. Take the hourly bus 'AF' from Via Catalogna to Fertilia. Breakfast is included in the rates and a meal costs €7.75.

In the Old Town is the excellent **Hotel San Francesco** *(☎/fax 079 98 03 30; e hotsfran@tin.it; Via Ambrogio Machin 2; singles/doubles with bath €43/75)*, with a charming cloistered courtyard shared with the church of the same name.

A popular eating choice is stone-ceilinged **Trattoria Il Vecchio Mulino** *(☎ 079 97 72 54; Via Don Deroma 7; meal about €12)*, with a good range of pizza. For coffee, wine and cake, head to **Caffe Costantino** *(Piazza Civica 30)*.

Getting There & Away

Alghero is accessible from Sassari by train or bus. The main bus station is on Via Catalogna, next to the public park. **ARST** *(☎ 079 95 01 79)* buses leave for Sassari and Porto Torres. **FdS buses** *(☎ 079 95 04 58)* also service Sassari, Macomer and Bosa. **PANI buses** *(☎ 079 23 69 83)* serve Cagliari, Nuoro and Macomer from Sassari.

Latvia

Latvia, the man in the middle for far too long, is making heads turn at last. Never mind its gorgeous natural sights, fabulous castles and hopping city life – what's really got the competition worrying is Latvia's scooping of the 2002 Eurovision Song Contest. Foreign visitors, however, might be more entranced by Latvia's vibrant capital Rīga, the Baltic's largest and most cosmopolitan city; the sandy white beaches within striking distance; the inspiringly beautiful Gauja National Park; and a rash of palaces evocative of the former Soviet republic's often painful past. Looking ahead, this small Baltic nation is charting a steady course towards Europe – EU membership is slated for 2004. The cognoscenti know not to ask whether Latvia is ready for Europe, but rather whether Europe is ready for Latvia.

Latvia: the Basics

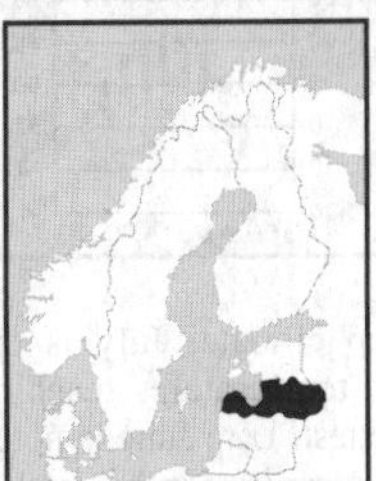

Local name Latvija

Capital Rīga

Population 2.4 million

Language Latvian

Currency lats (Ls) = 100 santīmi

Avoid at all costs Walking under a killer icicle

Hit on people at midsummer by saying *Nāc' man līdzi meklēt papardziedu!* (Come with me to look for the fern flower!)

Facts about Latvia

HISTORY

Agricultural peoples arriving from the south Baltic around 2000 BC eventually grouped into what are called the Baltic tribes. The Knights of the Sword, or Livonian Order, were founded in Rīga in AD 1202 and subjugated Latvia. By 1290 they controlled the seaboard from modern Poland to Estonia, plus inland Latvia.

The region fell under Polish control in 1561 after the Livonian Order appealed to Poland-Lithuania for protection from Ivan the Terrible. In the 1620s Sweden took control until the Great Northern War (1700–21), after which Latvia became part of the Russian empire. The idea of Latvia as a discrete political entity did not arise until the late-19th century, which was marked by an awakening of Latvian national consciousness.

After WWI, fighting among the nationalists (who had declared independence in November 1918), pro-Russian Bolsheviks and lingering German occupation forces continued until 1921, when Moscow signed a peace treaty with the independent Latvian parliamentary republic. But by 1941, Latvia had undergone occupation by Soviet troops, a Communist 'election' victory, incorporation into the USSR, nationalisation, mass killings and about 35,000 deportations. Latvia was occupied partly or wholly by Nazi Germany from 1941 to 1945, and its Jewish population was virtually wiped out. Conquest by the Red Army was followed by farm collectivisation. An estimated 175,000 Latvians were killed or deported.

In the late 1980s, a nationalist reawakening led to mass demonstrations. After the new Latvia Popular Front won a big majority in Latvia's Supreme Soviet (now the parliament), the pre-WWII constitution was reinstated. On 20 January 1991 Soviet troops stormed Rīga. But the communists were on their way out, and Latvia declared full independence on 21 August. It was recognised first by the West, then by the USSR. Latvia's first democratic elections were held in June 1993.

It was not until 1998 that anyone in Latvia – irrespective of ancestry – could apply for citizenship. By April 2002 Latvia had naturalised 50,386 people – but 55% of Russians remained noncitizens.

Latvia started accession talks with the EU in December 1999 and hopes to become a fully fledged member by 2004. Its entry into NATO is slated for the end of 2002.

GEOGRAPHY & CLIMATE

Green and rolling, Latvia embraces 64,600 sq km made up of four regions: Kurzeme (west); Zemgale (south); Vidzeme (east), which includes Gaiziņkalns (312m), the country's highest point; and Latgale (southeast), with over 40% of Latvia's several thousand lakes.

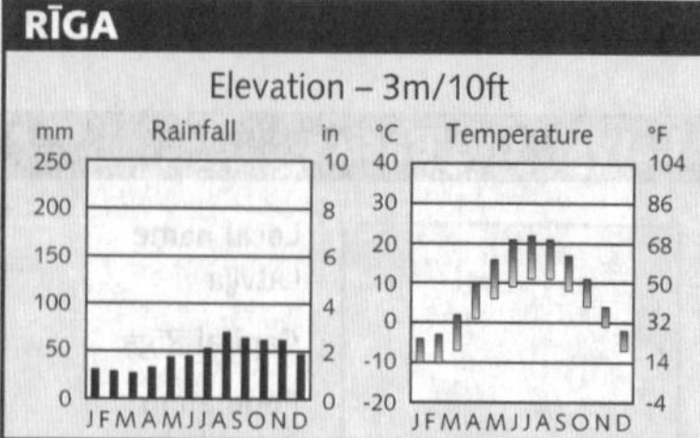

Latvia has a damp climate. July is the warmest month, with temperatures reaching 28°C, but also the wettest. Late June is noted for thunderstorms. Winter starts in November and lasts until late March, with temperatures rarely above 4°C.

GOVERNMENT & POLITICS

Over 40 political parties jostle for seats in Latvia's 100-seat parliament, first elected in June 1993 by proportional representation. The president is elected every four years by parliament.

POPULATION & PEOPLE

Latvia's population is 2.4 million. Only 57.7% is ethnic Latvian, and Latvians are a minority in all the major cities. Russians account for 29.6% of the national population. Latvians (along with Lithuanians) are the only surviving members of the Baltic ethnic family, an Indo-European but non-Slavic group whose third branch – the old Prussians – was exterminated by the Teutonic Knights.

SOCIETY & CONDUCT

It's hard to define the Latvian character without reference to bordering nationalities: they're more emotional and romantic than Estonians but less so than Lithuanians; they're more gregarious and less cautious than Estonians but again not to the degree of Lithuanians etc. One reason for this difficulty in pinning down the Latvians may be the fact that their roots are so entangled, having at one time or another come under the domain of Lutheran Germans and Swedes, Catholic Poles and Orthodox Russians. All these elements are combined in Rīga, the giant among Baltic cities, and itself a force in the shaping of national character.

Flowers are a common gift – but give only odd-numbered bouquets (even-numbered offerings, including 12 red roses, are appropriate for mournful occasions).

LANGUAGE

Latvian is one of two languages of the Baltic branch of the Indo-European language family, making its language something of an endangered species. English is widely spoken in Rīga and other large cities, but not at all in the countryside. See the Language Guide at the back of the book for useful words and phrases.

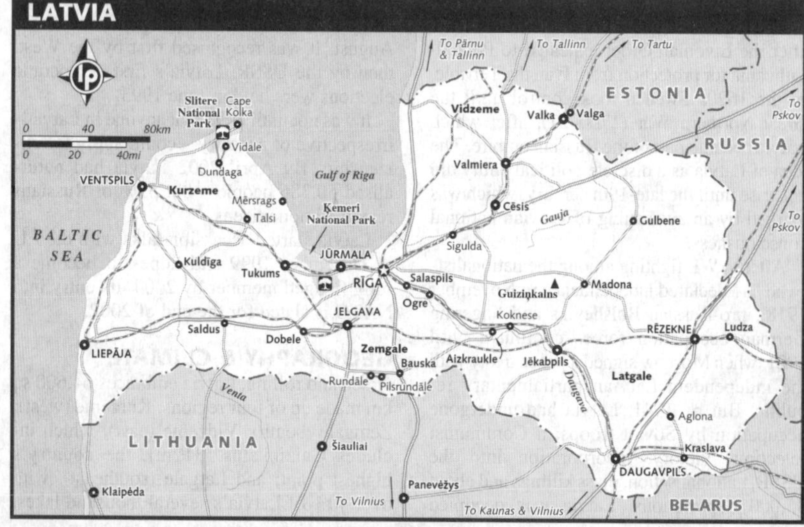

Facts for the Visitor

HIGHLIGHTS

Rīga comes first, but don't miss the Gauja Valley. Take a canoe trip down the Gauja River, hike in the park or bungee jump from Sigulda's cable car.

PLANNING

Summer and spring are the best times to visit. Avoid winter and the slushy March thaw.

TOURIST OFFICES

The **Latvian Tourism Development Agency** (*☎ 722 99 45, fax 708 53 93; Ⓦ www.latviatourism.lv; Pils laukums 4, LV-1050 Rīga)* has an office in most towns and cities. Staff generally speak English.

Latvian tourist offices in **Finland** *(☎ 09-278 47 74; Ⓔ latviatravel@kolumbus.fi; Mariankatu 8B, SE-00170 Helsinki)* and **Germany** *(☎ 0251-215 07 42; Ⓦ www.baltic-info.de; Salzmannstrasse 152, D-48159 Münster)* assist Latvia-bound travellers.

VISAS

Check the latest developments at Latvia's **Ministry of Foreign Affairs** (*Ⓦ www.mfa.gov.lv/en)*. In mid-2002, nationalities that could travel visa-free included citizens of Austria, Belgium, Croatia, Denmark, France, Germany, Greece, Hungary, Ireland, Italy, Japan, Netherlands, Norway, Portugal, Spain, Sweden, Switzerland, UK and the USA.

Australia and New Zealand passport holders still need a visa, available on the spot at Rīga's airport for 12 Ls. To extend a visa once in Latvia, contact the **Department of Immigration & Citizenship** *(☎ 721 96 39; Ⓦ www.pmlp.gov.lv; Raiņa bulvāris 5, LV-1181 Rīga)*.

EMBASSIES & CONSULATES

Latvian Embassies & Consulates Abroad

Latvian representations abroad include:

Australia (☎ 02-9744 5981) 32 Parnell St, Strathfield 2135, Sydney
Belarus (☎ 0172-84 93 93) 6a Doroshevica St, BY-220013 Minsk
Canada (☎ 613-238 6014) Suite 300, 208 Albert St, Ottawa, K1P 5G8 Ontario
Estonia (☎ 646 13 13) Tõnismägi 10, EE10119 Tallinn
Finland (☎ 09-476 472 44) Armfeltintie 10, SF-00150 Helsinki
France (☎ 01 53 64 58 10) 6 Villa Saïd, F-75116 Paris
Germany (☎ 030-826 00 211) Reinerzstrasse 40-41, D-14193 Berlin
Lithuania (☎ 2-231 260) Čiurlionio 76, LT-2600 Vilnius
Russia (☎ 095-925 27 03) ulitsa Chapligina 3, RUS-103062 Moscow
Sweden (☎ 08-700 63 00) Odengatan 5, Box 19167, S-10432 Stockholm
UK (☎ 020-731 20 040) 45 Nottingham Place, London W1U 5LR
USA (☎ 202-726 82 13) 4325 17th Street NW, Washington, DC 20011

Embassies & Consulates in Latvia

The following diplomatic offices are in Rīga:

Australia (☎ 733 63 83) Alberta iela 13
Belarus (☎ 732 34 11) Jēzusbaznīcas iela 12
Canada (☎ 722 63 15) Doma laukums 4
Estonia (☎ 781 20 20) Skolas iela 13
Finland (☎ 733 20 05) Kalpaka bulvāris 1
France (☎ 703 66 00) Raiņa bulvāris 9
Germany (☎ 722 90 96) Raiņa bulvāris 13
Lithuania (☎ 732 15 19) Rūpniecības iela 24
Netherlands (☎ 732 61 47) Torņa iela 4
Poland (☎ 732 16 17) Elizabetes iela 2a
Russia (☎ 733 21 51) Antonijas iela 2
Sweden (☎ 733 87 70) Andreja Pumpura iela 8
UK (☎ 777 47 00) Alunāna iela 5
USA (☎ 703 62 00) Raiņa bulvāris 7

CUSTOMS

People over 18 can bring in and take out 1L of alcohol and 200 cigarettes, 20 cigars or 200g of tobacco without paying duty. You can import and export any amount of hard currency.

MONEY

The lats (plural: lati) comes in 1 and 2 Ls coins, and 5, 10, 20, 50, 100 and 500 Ls notes. One lats is divided into 100 santīmi; coins come in denominations of 1, 2, 5, 10, 20 and 50 santīmi. Latvia could adopt the euro after 2006 if strict economic criteria are met.

Latvijas Bankas *(Latvian Bank; Ⓦ www.bank.lv)* posts the lats' daily exchange rate on its website. In 2002 exchange rates were as follows (continued on next page):

country	unit		lati (Ls)
Australia	A$1	=	0.35
Belarus	1000BR	=	0.34
Canada	C$1	=	0.40
Estonia	10EEK	=	0.37
Eurozone	€1	=	0.57

country	unit		lati (Ls)
Lithuania	1Lt	=	0.16
Poland	1zł	=	0.15
Russia	10R	=	0.20
UK	UK£1	=	0.91
USA	US$1	=	0.62

European currencies can be exchanged easily. Tattered notes will be refused. ATMs accepting Visa and/or MasterCard/Eurocard are widespread. Credit cards are commonly accepted in hotels, restaurants and shops.

Accommodation in Rīga will be your biggest cost. Eating out in the capital is likewise approaching Western norms. Overland travel remains pleasantly affordable.

POST & COMMUNICATIONS

Stamps are sold at *pasts* (post offices). The poste-restante desk at Rīga's train-station post office holds mail; see Information in the Rīga section for details.

Public phones accept chip cards worth 2, 3 or 5 Ls, sold at kiosks, shops and post offices. Latvian telephone numbers have seven digits. Mobile telephone numbers start with 9. To make an international call, dial the international-access code (☎ 00), the country and city codes, followed by the subscriber's number. Latvia's country code is ☎ 371. **ZL Hotline** (*W www.7770777.lv*) is an online telephone directory.

Internet cafés – many open 24 hours – are abundant in Rīga, large towns and seaside resorts. Access costs around 0.50 Ls per hour.

DIGITAL RESOURCES

Start your virtual trip with the **Latvian Tourism Development Agency** (*W www.latviatourism.lv*), which oozes oodles of cultural, historical and practical information. Cheeky hotel, restaurant, bar and nightclub listings make **Riga In Your Pocket** (*W www.inyourpocket.com*) worth a click.

BOOKS

If you're following a Baltic route and want more detail, pick up Lonely Planet's *Estonia, Latvia & Lithuania*.

WOMEN TRAVELLERS

Women are not likely to receive aggravation from men in Latvia, although unaccompanied women should avoid a few of the sleazier bars. Those who are scantily dressed risk being treated as prostitutes.

GAY & LESBIAN TRAVELLERS

Rīga is fairly gay-friendly, but open displays of same-sex affection remain rare. **Latvian Gay & Lesbian** (*☎ 959 22 29; W www.gaybaltics.com; Pastkasteiela 380, Rīga*) offers advice.

DANGERS & ANNOYANCES

Pickpockets and car thieves are rife in the Latvian capital, and you're sure to hear about the 'mafia' when in town. But Latvia is generally a fairly safe place, and the mafia doesn't bother with dull tourists.

LEGAL MATTERS

It is illegal to buy alcohol anywhere between 10pm and 8am except restaurants, cafés, bars and clubs.

PUBLIC HOLIDAYS & SPECIAL EVENTS

Latvia's national holidays are New Year's Day (1 January), Good Friday (March/April), Labour Day (1 May), Mother's Day (second Sunday May), Ligo (Midsummer Festival; 23 June), Jāni (St John's Day; 24 June), Day of Proclamation of the Latvian Republic, 1918 (18 November), Christmas Eve and Day (24–25 December), Boxing Day (26 December), New Year's Eve (31 December).

Key events include the Baltika International Folk Festival, which Latvia hosts every three years, and the All-Latvian Song and Dance Festival, held every five years. Both should fall in 2003.

Smaller annual festivals include Gadatirgus, a folklore fair held the first weekend of June at Rīga's Open-air Ethnography Museum; and Rīga Summer – a festival of symphonic and chamber music – in July. Sigulda hosts an Opera Music Festival every July. The international film festival, Arsenāls, takes place in the capital in mid- September. Cultural events are online at W www.km.gov.lv.

ACTIVITIES

Berrying and bird-watching, skiing and sweating it off in a steaming sauna are fun ways to discover Latvia's wild side.

Emergencies

The nationwide emergency phone number for police is ☎ 02 and for ambulance is ☎ 03.

A cycling track runs from Rīga to Jūrmala. The Gauja, Salaca and Abava Rivers offer uninterrupted routes of several days' duration. Organised expeditions are 3km to 85km long and cost 10 Ls to 39 Ls per boat, including equipment and transportation to the tour's starting point. Makars in Sigulda, Valmiera's Sporta Bāze Baiļi and Hostelis Eži all run trips (see the Eastern Latvia section).

The Gauja Valley is Latvia's winter sports centre. Hire equipment once you arrive.

ACCOMMODATION

Latvian *kempings* (camping grounds) usually have wooden cottages as well as space for tents.

The hostelling scene is undeveloped. **Hostelling Latvia** *(☎ 921 85 60, fax 722 40 30; W www.hostellinglatvia.com; Ciekurkalna iela 1-7, LV-1026 Rīga)* is the only association. In Rīga, several agencies organise B&B with or without a local host. **Lauku Ceļotājs** *(☎ 761 76 00, fax 783 00 41; W www.traveller.lv; Ku-u iela 11, Rīga)* arranges rural B&B for 5 Ls to 16 Ls a night in farmhouses, manor houses, palaces and guesthouses in rural Latvia.

Rīga has a vast choice of hotels, but most are prohibitively expensive. Elsewhere, decent modern hotels tout reasonable rates, alongside a handful of cheap, concrete Soviet dinosaurs.

Overseas, **American-International Homestays** *(☎ 303-258 3234; W www.aihtravel.com/homestays; PO Box 1754, Nederland, CO 80466, USA)* and **Gateway Travel** *(☎ 02-9745 3333; W www.russian-gateway.com.au; 48 The Boulevarde, Strathfield, NSW 2135, Australia)* organise homestays in Latvia. Rīga-based **Patricia** *(☎ 728 48 68, 923 82 67, fax 728 66 50; W www.rigalatvia.net; Elizabetes iela 22)* arranges rooms/apartments from 12.50/23 Ls per person.

FOOD & DRINKS

The Latvian diet leans on fatty dairy products, grains and fish, though meat is common. *Šprotes* (sprats) crop up as a starter in many places. You may also find *siļe* (herring), *līdaka* (pike) and *lasis* (salmon). *Cepts*, fish or meat, is fried; *kūpīnats* is smoked. *Zupa* (soups) and *desa* (sausage) are popular. Throughout Latvia you will find a mouth-watering choice of freshly baked cakes, breads and pastries.

The best *alus* (beer) is produced by Aldaris. A Latvian speciality for the brave-hearted is Rīga Black Balsam, a thick, dark liquid. Revolting on its own, it's better when mixed equally with vodka, in coffee, or best of all with white grape juice.

ENTERTAINMENT

Rīga has a well-developed nightlife: theatres and cinemas abound, and its symphony orchestra and opera are highly regarded. Elsewhere, evening entertainment rarely extends beyond a handful of bars and cafés.

Getting There & Away

AIR

Rīga is served by several international carriers. National carrier **AirBaltic** *(W www.airbaltic.com)* works in partnership with SAS. Several Baltic and central/Eastern European cities are linked by daily scheduled flights with Rīga.

LAND

For travel through Russia or Belarus, look into the visa situation well ahead of departure.

Bus

Eurolines *(☎ 721 40 80; W www.eurolines.lv; Prāgas iela 1)* runs several daily buses to Tallinn, Vilnius, St Petersburg, Kaliningrad and Berlin; an overnight bus to Warsaw; several buses weekly to various German cities; and once a week to Prague. Buses to Paris, Amsterdam, Brussels, Stuttgart and Bremen, Minsk, Moscow and Kyiv are handled by **Ecolines** *(☎ 721 45 12; www.ecolines.lv)*. **TAK Reisid** *(☎ 721 24 02)* operates a twice-weekly bus to Kiel, via Berlin and Hamburg.

At the time of writing, a single fare from Rīga to Amsterdam/Brussels/St Petersburg cost 60/63/11 Ls. One-way fares to Tallinn (six hours, five daily) and Vilnius (six hours, four daily) were 7 Ls to 8.50 Ls and 6 Ls respectively.

Train

Latvia is not covered by any European rail-ticket network. The easiest way to travel to Latvia's neighbouring Baltic capitals is by bus, although there is a snail-slow overnight train service to/from Vilnius (6/8/11 Ls for a seat/couchette/ bunk in four-bed compartment, 7½ hours) via Kaunas. The *Baltija* travels overnight between Rīga and St Petersburg (10/20/31/50 Ls for a seat/couchette/bunk in four-bed compartment/1st class, 12 hours), and the *Latvijas Ekspresis* and *Jūrmala* travel to/from Moscow (11/23/36/61 Ls for a seat/couchette/compartment/1st class, 16½ hours)

Other rail services serving Rīga include a twice-weekly train to/from Lviv and Odesa via Gomel.

Car & Motorcycle

Accident insurance is mandatory for drivers in Latvia. Insurance policies with limited compensation rates can be bought at Latvian borders.

SEA

Rīga's **ferry terminal** (*☎ 732 98 82; www.rop.lv; Eksporta iela 1)* is about 1.5km downstream of Akmens Bridge. Tickets for the twice-weekly Kiel ferry are sold at **Hanza Maritime Agency** (*☎ 732 35 69; www.hanza.lv; Eksporta iela 3a*). There is also a twice-weekly ferry to Lübeck.

Between mid-April and mid-September **Rīgas Jūras Līnija** (*☎ 720 54 60; www.rigasealine.lv; Eksporta iela 3a)* sails every second day to/from Nynashamn, 60km south of Stockholm.

Getting Around

BUS

The country is well served by buses, although services to off-the-beaten-track villages are infrequent. Bus stations in towns and cities have information windows with staff who speak some English. Very occasionally they charge for their services. Updated timetables are online at www.autoosta.lv. Domestic bus fares average 1.50 Ls per 100km.

TRAIN

An excellent network of suburban trains provides the best transport option for many places within about 50km of Rīga. Regular long-distant rail services link major cities and towns. *Elektrovilcienci* (suburban trains) are slower and make more frequent stops than *dizeļvilcienci* (long-distance trains).

On the Internet at www.ldz.lv you can access Latvian Railways updated timetable. Train tickets for a bum-numbing seat in 'general seating' cost around 1.20 Ls per 100km. For longer journeys a bunk in couchette class costs about 3 Ls per 100km.

CAR & MOTORCYCLE

Main roads linking the cities and towns are generally good, distances are not great and traffic is light. You must have your headlights switched on when driving on highways, even during the day.

BICYCLE

Latvia is flat and easy to pedal. Seek advice from the **Latvian Bicycle Tourism Information Centre** (*VIC; ☎ 750 70 41, fax 750 70 42; vic@velokurjers.lv; Jēkabpils iela 19a, LV-1003 Rīga*).

LOCAL TRANSPORT

A mixture of trams, buses and trolleybuses (buses run by electricity from overhead wires) provides thorough public transport around towns and cities. Most run from about 5.30am to 12.30am. Tickets cost 0.20 Ls and must be punched once aboard the bus, tram or trolleybus.

Rīga

pop 753,000

Rīga is the big boy of the Baltics. During the 1930s it was the West's major post for listening to 'the Russian bear', and the city was a thrumming mix of diplomats, traders and intrigue. Today, Rīga's historic old quarter is a Unesco World Heritage site, and its city-wide collection of stunning Art Nouveau architecture is Europe's finest.

A fascinating mix of Latvian, Russian and German influences, Rīga has changed dramatically since independence. Office blocks and swanky hotels are sprouting, the restaurant scene is thriving and nightlife is glitzy.

Fewer than half of Rīgans are ethnic Latvians (41% in 2001), with Russians accounting for 43% of the population. However, ethnic harmony presides.

Orientation

Rīga straddles the Daugava River. On the eastern bank you'll find Old Rīga (Vecrīga), the city's historic heart, dominated by three steeples: St Peter's, Dome Cathedral and St Jacob's. East of the old city is a ring of parks and boulevards. The train and bus stations are five minutes' walk apart on the southeastern edge of Old Rīga. The ferry terminal is about 500m north of Old Rīga.

Information

The **tourist office** *(☎ 703 79 00, fax 703 79 10; Ⓦ www.rigatourism.com; Rātslaukums 6; open 10am-7pm daily)*, inside the House of Blackheads, sells the Riga Card (8/12/16 Ls for one/two/three days) which gets you into many museums for free. There are exchange offices at Rīga airport and throughout the centre. **Bastejkubs** *(Bastēja bulvāris 12; open 24hr)* is on the old-town fringe. ATMs abound in central Rīga. Banks change travellers cheques and Eurocheques.

The **central post office** *(Brīvības bulvāris 19)* is not far from Milda (as the Freedom Monument is known). The train-station **post office** *(Stacijas laukums 1)* keeps mail for one month. Address letters to Poste Restante, Rīga 50, LV-1050, Latvia.

Internet access at **Arēna** *(☎ 731 45 14; Ģertrūdes iela 46; open 24hr)* and **Dual Net Café** *(☎ 781 44 40; Peldu iela 17; open 24 hrs)* costs 0.50 Ls an hour. **Poligons** *(☎ 724 22 12; Dzirnavu iela 55; open 24 hrs)* charges 0.40 Ls an hour.

Latvia Tours *(☎ 708 50 01; ⓔ hq@latviatours.lv; Kaļķu iela 8)* offers a bounty of services, including issuing and replacing American Express travellers cheques. Other agencies include **World Travel Service** *(☎ 733 22 33; K Valdemāra iela 33)* and **Via Rīga** *(☎ 728 59 01; Ⓦ www.viariga.lv; K Barona iela 7-9)*. International Student Identity Cards (ISIC) are handled by **Student & Youth Travel Bureau** *(SJCB; ☎ 728 48 18; Ⓦ www.sjcb.lv; Lāčplēsa iela 29)*.

For medical needs, **ARS Clinic** *(☎ 720 10 06/7/8, fax 728 87 69; ⓔ ars@delfi.lv; Skolas iela 5)* offers a 24-hour English-speaking service and an **emergency home service** *(☎ 720 10 03)*. **Rīgas vecpilsētas aptieka** *(☎ 721 33 40; Audēju iela 20)* is a 24-hour pharmacy.

Old Rīga

The World Heritage–listed Old Town retains whole squares of German buildings that have stood since the 17th century or earlier. **Dome Cathedral** is a 13th- to 18th-century blend of architecture. Its old stone tombs were inundated by a 1709 flood that was blamed for a cholera and typhoid outbreak. The cathedral's 1880s organ is the world's fourth largest. Rīga's oldest museum, the **Museum of the History of Rīga & Navigation** *(Palasta iela 4; adult/concession 1/0.50 Ls; open 11am-5pm Wed-Sun)*, is in a cloister next to the cathedral.

Parts of **Rīga Castle** *(Pils laukums 3)* date from 1330. Now it's home to Latvia's president and a **Museum of Foreign Art** *(adult/concession 1.20/0.70 Ls; open 11am-5pm Tues-Sun)*.

St Saviour's Church *(Anglikāņu iela 2a)* was built in 1857 by a small group of British traders on 30ft of British soil brought over as ballast. **St Jacob's Cathedral** *(Jēkaba iela)* is the seat of Rīga's Roman Catholic archbishop. Latvia's Saeima (Parliament) sits next door.

Picturesque **Swedish Gate** *(cnr Torņa & Aldaru iela)* was built onto the city walls in 1698. The round 14th-century Powder Tower, at the end of Torņa iela, houses a **War Museum** *(Smilšu iela 20; adult/concession 0.50/0.25 Ls; open 10am-6pm Wed-Sun May-Sept, 10am-5pm Wed-Sun Oct-Apr)*.

South of Kaļķu iela, Gothic **St Peter's Church** *(adult/concession 1.60/0.50 Ls; open 10am-6pm Tues-Sun May-Sept, 10am-5pm Tues-Sun Oct-Apr)* dominates the southern half of Old Rīga. Don't miss the view from its famed 123m spire, originally built in the 1660s.

The **Occupation Museum** *(Strēlnieku laukums; admission free; open 11am-5pm daily)*, inside an ugly bunker, gives a moving account of the Soviet and Nazi occupations of Latvia between 1940 and 1944 and the ensuing deportations to Siberia.

Parks & Boulevards

East of Old Rīga's jumbled streets, the city's old defensive moat – now a canal – snakes through parks between wide 19th-century boulevards. On Brīvības bulvāris is the central landmark, the **Freedom Monument**, topped by a bronze statue of Liberty holding aloft three stars representing the historic regions of Kurzeme, Latgale and Vidzeme. During the Soviet years the Freedom Monument was off limits. Since 1992 the guard of honour that stood at the monument before WWII has been revived. Come here to watch the changing of the guards every hour on the hour 9am to 6pm daily.

In Bastejkalns, west of the monument, five red stone slabs lie as **Memorials to the Victims of 20 January 1991**, killed here when Soviet troops stormed the nearby Interior Ministry.

The 19th-century **Russian Orthodox Cathedral** is on Brīvības bulvāris. The **State Museum of Art** *(K Valdemāra iela 10a; adult/concession 1.20/0.70 Ls; open 11am-5pm Wed-Mon)* houses Russian and Latvian work.

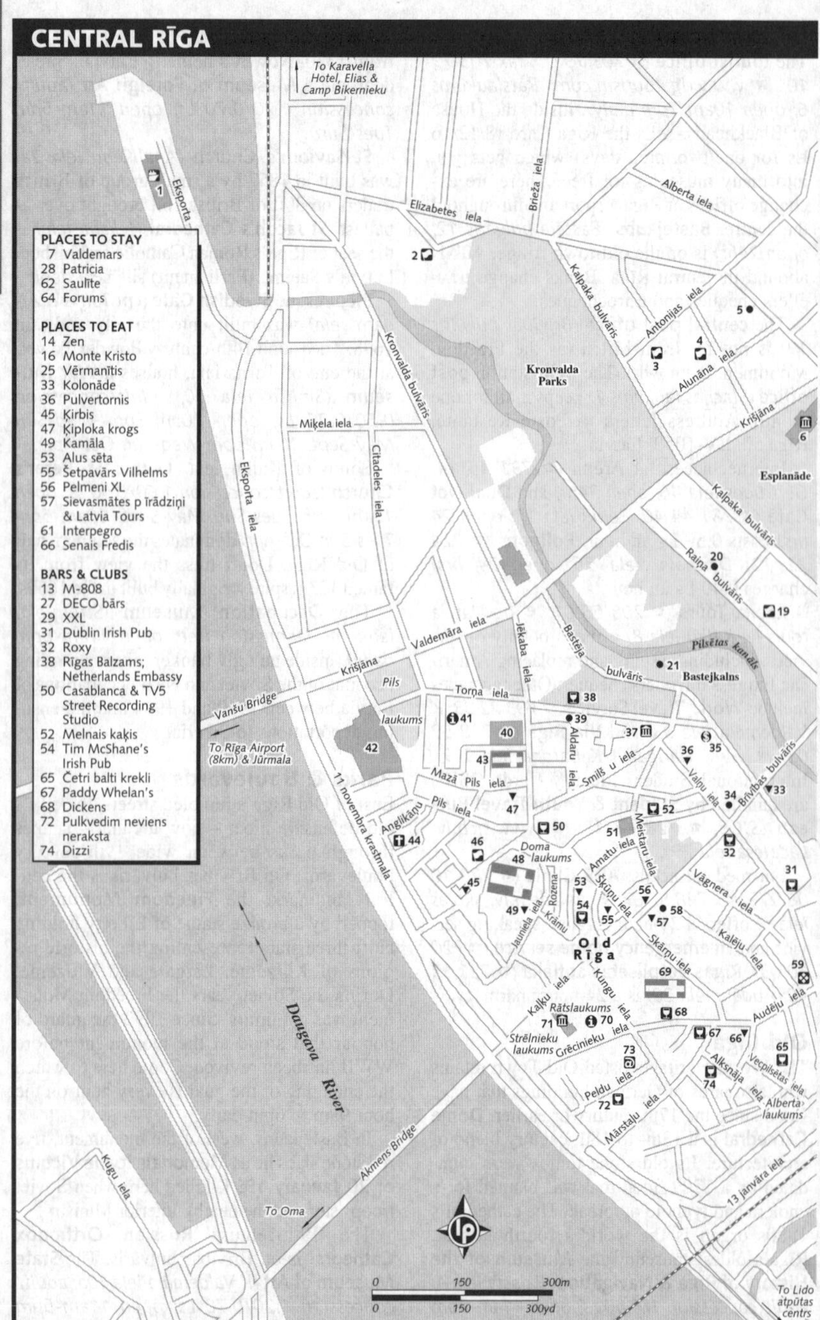
CENTRAL RĪGA
PLACES TO STAY
7 Valdemars
28 Patricia
62 Saulīte
64 Forums
PLACES TO EAT
14 Zen
16 Monte Kristo
25 Vērmanītis
33 Kolonāde
36 Pulvertornis
45 Ķirbis
47 Ķiploka krogs
49 Kamāla
53 Alus sēta
55 Šetpavārs Vilhelms
56 Pelmeni XL
57 Sievasmātes p īrādziņi & Latvia Tours
61 Interpegro
66 Senais Fredis
BARS & CLUBS
13 M-808
27 DECO bārs
29 XXL
31 Dublin Irish Pub
32 Roxy
38 Rīgas Balzams; Netherlands Embassy
50 Casablanca & TV5 Street Recording Studio
52 Melnais kaķis
54 Tim McShane's Irish Pub
65 Četri balti krekli
67 Paddy Whelan's
68 Dickens
72 Pulkvedim neviens neraksta
74 Dizzi
To Karavella Hotel, Elias & Camp Bikernieku
Eksporta iela
Elizabetes iela
Brieža iela
Alberta iela
Kalpaka bulvāris
Antonijas iela
Alunāna iela
Krišjāņa
Kronvalda bulvāris
Kronvalda Parks
Esplanāde
Miķela iela
Citadeles iela
Raiņa bulvāris
Valdemāra iela
Jēkaba iela
Bastėja bulvāris
Pilsētas kanāls
Bastejkalns
Vanšu Bridge
Pils laukums
Torņa iela
Aldaru iela
Smilšu iela
Vaļņu iela
Brīvības bulvāris
To Rīga Airport (8km) & Jūrmala
Mazā Pils iela
Pils iela
Anglikāņu
11 novembra krastmala
Doma laukums
Amatu iela
Meistaru iela
Vāgnera iela
Rozena
Krāmu
Jaunielа
Šķūņu iela
Skārņu iela
Kalēju iela
Old Rīga
Kungu iela
Kaļķu iela
Rātslaukums
Strēlnieku laukums
Grēcinieku iela
Audēju iela
Vecpilsētas iela
Alksnāja iela
Alberta laukums
Peldu iela
Mārstaļu iela
13 janvāra iela
Daugava River
Akmens Bridge
Kugu iela
To Oma
0 150 300m
0 150 300yd
To Lido atpūtas centrs

CENTRAL RĪGA

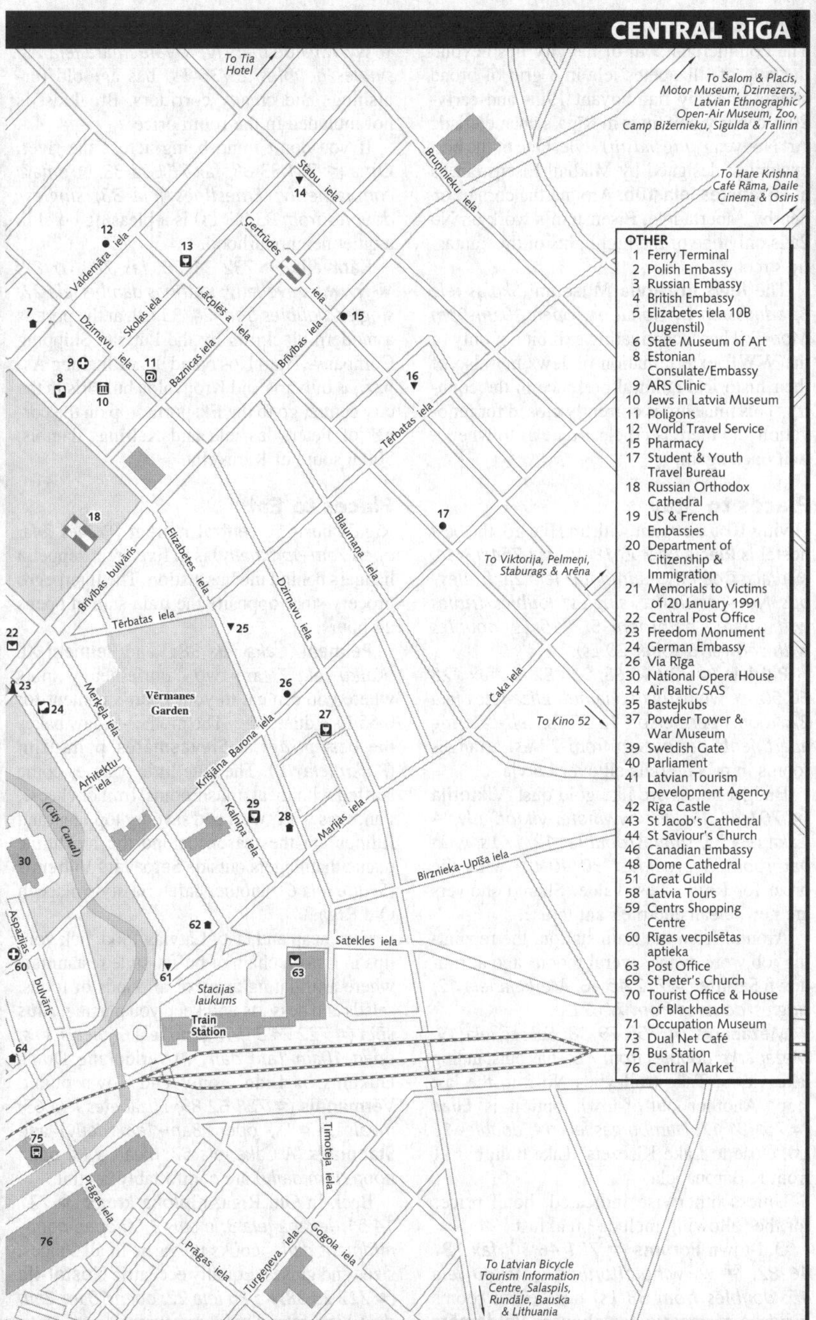

To Tia Hotel
To Šalom & Placis, Motor Museum, Dzirnezers, Latvian Ethnographic Open-Air Museum, Zoo, Camp Bižernieku, Sigulda & Tallinn
To Hare Krishna Café Rāma, Daile Cinema & Osiris
To Viktorija, Pelmeņi, Staburags & Arēna
To Kino 52
To Latvian Bicycle Tourism Information Centre, Salaspils, Rundāle, Bauska & Lithuania
Stabu iela
Bruņinieku iela
Ģertrūdes iela
Valdemāra iela
Skolas iela
Lāčplēša iela
Dzirnavu iela
Baznīcas iela
Brīvības iela
Tērbatas iela
Blaumaņa iela
Brīvības bulvāris
Elizabetes iela
Dzirnavu iela
Tērbatas iela
Merķeļa iela
Vērmanes Garden
Krišjāņa Barona iela
Čaka iela
Arhitektu iela
(City Canal)
Kalniņa iela
Marijas iela
Birznieka-Upīša iela
Aspazijas bulvāris
Satekles iela
Stacijas laukums
Train Station
Timoteja iela
Prāgas iela
Prāgas iela
Turgeņeva iela
Gogola iela
OTHER
1 Ferry Terminal
2 Polish Embassy
3 Russian Embassy
4 British Embassy
5 Elizabetes iela 10B (Jugenstil)
6 State Museum of Art
8 Estonian Consulate/Embassy
9 ARS Clinic
10 Jews in Latvia Museum
11 Poligons
12 World Travel Service
15 Pharmacy
17 Student & Youth Travel Bureau
18 Russian Orthodox Cathedral
19 US & French Embassies
20 Department of Citizenship & Immigration
21 Memorials to Victims of 20 January 1991
22 Central Post Office
23 Freedom Monument
24 German Embassy
26 Via Rīga
30 National Opera House
34 Air Baltic/SAS
35 Bastejkubs
37 Powder Tower & War Museum
39 Swedish Gate
40 Parliament
41 Latvian Tourism Development Agency
42 Rīga Castle
43 St Jacob's Cathedral
44 St Saviour's Church
46 Canadian Embassy
48 Dome Cathedral
51 Great Guild
58 Latvia Tours
59 Centrs Shopping Centre
60 Rīgas vecpilsētas aptieka
63 Post Office
69 St Peter's Church
70 Tourist Office & House of Blackheads
71 Occupation Museum
73 Dual Net Café
75 Bus Station
76 Central Market

New Rīga

The commercial soul of the city lies beyond the ring of Elizabetes iela in a grid of broad streets lined by flamboyant 19th- and early-20th-century buildings in Rīga's characteristic Art Nouveau *(Jugendstil)* style. One of the best examples, designed by Mikhail Eisenstein, is at **Elizabetes iela 10b**. Around the corner, on nearby Alberta iela, Eisenstein's work on No 2a is only one of the highlights of this fantastic street.

The **Jews in Latvia Museum** *(Skolas iela 6; admission by donation; open 10am-5pm Mon-Fri)* has a captivating exhibit not only of the WWII extermination of Jews but also of their historical cultural presence in the country. This museum is currently closed for renovation and there is no clear date as to when it will open again.

Places to Stay

Giving 10% discount with an HI card, the best hostel is **Placis** *(☎ 755 18 24, fax 754 13 44; e placis@delfi.lv; Laimdotas iela 2a; trolleybus No 4 to Teika; singles/doubles/triples with shared bathroom 5/7/15 Ls, doubles with shower & toilet 20 Ls)*.

Patricia *(☎ 728 48 68, 923 82 67, fax 728 66 50; w www.rigalatvia.net; Elizabetes iela 22; rooms per person 12.50 Ls, self-catering apartments per person from 23 Ls)* arranges rooms in private flats all over Latvia.

Budget hotels are like gold dust. **Viktorija** *(☎ 701 41 11; w www.hotel-viktorija.lv; A Čaka iela 55; singles/doubles 12/17 Ls, with bathroom & breakfast 30/40 Ls)* wins the prize for Rīga's best value. Shared showers are new, clean and pleasant to use.

Around from the train station, the repainting job wore away several moons ago at rundown **Saulīte** *(☎ 722 45 46; Merķeļa iela 12; singles/doubles from 7/16 Ls)*.

Mežaparks *(☎ 755 79 88; Sakses iela 19, Mežaparks; doubles from 7 Ls)* has outstanding lake views. Take trolleybus No 2 to the last stop. Another out-of-town option is **Elias** *(☎ 751 81 17; Hamburgas iela 14; doubles 16 Ls)*, close to Lake Ķisezers. Take tram No 11 from K Barona iela.

Unless otherwise indicated, hotel prices for the following include breakfast.

Old-town **Forums** *(☎ 781 46 80, fax 781 46 82; w www.hotelforums.lv; Vaļņu iela 45; doubles from 33 Ls)* has decent rooms inside a terracotta townhouse. **Valdemārs** *(☎ 733 44 62, 733 21 32, fax 733 30 01; w www.valde mars.lv; K Valdemāra iela 23; singles/doubles 25/35 Ls)* has age-old furnishings and creaky corridors. Breakfast is not included in the room price.

If you don't mind being across the river, **Oma** *(☎ 761 33 88, fax 761 32 33; e oma@com.latnet.lv; Ernestīnes iela 33; singles/doubles from 33/43 Ls)* is a pleasing hotel in a quiet neighbourhood.

Karavella *(☎ 732 31 30, fax 783 01 87; w www.karavella.lv; Katrīnas dambis iela 27; singles/doubles from 24/33 Ls)*, at the port, is a modern block run by the Latvian Shipping Company. Tram Nos 5 and 9, north along Aspazijas bulvāris and Kronvalda bulvāris in the city centre, go to the Eksporta stop on the corner of Pētersalas iela and Katrīnas dambis, 500m south of Karavella.

Places to Eat

Rīga's bustling **central market** *(Prāgas iela; open 7am-4pm daily)* is in five great zeppelin hangars behind the bus station. The Interpegro grocery store opposite the train station opens 24 hours.

Pelmeņi *(Čaka iela 38a)* and **Pelmeņi XL** *(Kaļķu iela 7)* are two calorie-heavy spots where you can eat to your heart's content for 0.55 Ls a dumpling. The mother-in-law bakes the best *pīrāgi* at **Sievasmātes p īrādziņi** *(Kaļķu iela 10)*. The cute little pastries come stuffed with meat, mushrooms, fruit or cheese. Pancakes with sweet and savoury toppings and fillings are the reason behind the lunchtime queue that lingers outside **Šetpavārs Vilhelms** *(Šķūņu iela 6)*, another cafeteria-style place in Old Rīga.

For cheap and tasty Latvian food, lick your lips in Lido, a chain of buffet-style restaurants where a titillating array of all kinds of foods, salads and desserts will keep you purring. **Alus sēta** *(☎ 722 24 31; Tirgoņu iela 6; meals 3 Ls; open 10am-1am daily)*, overlooking Doma laukums, is Lido's only Old Town outlet. **Vērmanītis** *(☎ 728 62 89; Elizabetes iela 65; meals 2-3 Ls; open 8am-1am daily)* and **Staburags** *(A Čaka iela 57; meals 3 Ls; open noon-1am daily)* are comfortably central.

Back in Old Rīga, **Ķiploka krogs** *(☎ 721 14 51; Jēkaba iela 3; meals 3 Ls; open noon-midnight daily)* cooks up garlic in all shapes, sizes and guises. Equally eccentric **Nostal-ija** *(☎ 722 23 38; Kaļķu iela 22; open 10am-2am daily)* is a retro Soviet restaurant.

Exuding spiritualism is vegetarian **Kamāla** *(☎ 721 13 32; ⓔ kamala@delfi.lv; Jauniela 14; meals 5 Ls; open 8.30am-midnight daily)*, named after the wife of Vishnu. **Rāma** *(K Barona iela 56; open 9am-midnight Mon-Sat, 11am-7pm Sun)*, the Hare Krishna café, dishes up a healthy, gut-busting vegetarian meal for 1.50 Ls. **Ķirbis** *(The Pumpkin; Doma laukums 1; open 9am-11pm Mon-Fri, 10am-11pm Sat & Sun)* is the other vegetarian rave.

Favoured for its coffee beans and cake range is **Monte Kristo** *(Ģertrūdes iela 27; open 9am-9pm Mon-Sat, noon-9pm Sun)*. The tea equivalent is laid-back **Zen** *(Stabu iela 6; open noon-midnight daily)*, where you can loll on floor cushions and watch – for a thirsty 20 minutes – your tea being prepared.

Old café favourites include **Kolonāde** *(Brīvības bulvāris 26)*, with a terrace garden overlooking the opera house; and **Senais Fredis** *(Audēju iela 5)* in the Old Town. **Pulvertornis** *(Valņu iela 3; soup/salad/meat dishes from 0.17/0.19/0.75 Ls; open 8am-8pm Mon-Fri, 9am-6pm Sat & Sun)* is a dirt-cheap café.

Entertainment

The *Baltic Times* and the website *Riga In Your Pocket* list upcoming events.

Pubs generally open 11am to midnight Sunday to Thursday, and until 2am Friday and Saturday. Most clubs throb until 5am weekends. Anglophones kick off the night at **Dickens** *(Grēcinieku iela 9/1)*, where a pint of Guinness/Kilkenny costs 1.70/1.60 Ls. After that, there's a trio of Irish pubs – **Paddy Whelan's** *(Grēcinieku iela 4)*, **Dublin** *(Vāgnera iela 16)* and **Tim McShane's** *(Tirgoņu iela 10)* – to drink away a Friday night.

Party animals end up at **Pulkvedim neviens neraksta** *(Nobody Writes to the Colonel; Peldu iela 26-28)*, an off-beat dance bar. Watch the sun rise at **Melnais kaķis** *(Meistaru iela 10-12; open 9pm-7am daily)*, where punters play pool, eat or bask in the early-morning sun with pint in hand. Ordering anything other than Black Balsams at **Rīgas Balzams** *(Torņa iela 4)* is sacrilege. **DECO bārs** *(Dzirnavu iela 84)* has a slick industrial decor, chic pavement terrace and ultra-hip dance floor come the early hours.

Music clubs include **M-808** *(ⓦ m.808.lv; Lāčplēša iela 5)* where techno and house beats; house-music hideout **Dizzi** *(Mārstaļu iela 10)*; and **Četri balti krekli** *(ⓦ www.krekli.lv; Vecpilsētas iela 12)*, where the best Latvian bands play. Mainstream nightclubs include **Roxy** *(Kaļķu iela 24)* and flash brash **Casablanca** *(ⓦ www.casablanca.lv; Smilšu iela 1-3)*, next to TV5's recording studio. The only gay club, generically replete with Tom of Finland drawings and a darkroom, is **XXL** *(☎ 728 22 76; Kalniņa iela 4)*.

The **National Opera House** *(☎ 707 37 77; ⓦ www.opera.lv; Aspazijas bulvāris 3)* is home to the highly rated Rīga Ballet, where Mikhail Baryshnikov made his name. The concert hall of the renowned Latvia National Symphonic Orchestra is the **Great Guild** *(Lielā -ilde; Amatu iela 6)*.

Getting There & Away

Air International flights fly into **Rīga airport** *(Lidosta Rīga; ☎ 720 70 09; ⓦ www.riga-airport.com)*, 8km west of the city centre. **Air-Baltic** *(☎ 720 77 77; ⓦ www.airbaltic.com; Kaļķu iela 15)* has offices at the airport too.

Bus All buses use the **bus station** *(ⓦ www.autoosta.lv; Prāgas iela 1)*. Timetables are displayed in the station and on its website. Staff in the **information office** *(☎ 900 00 09; open 6am-11pm daily)* speak English. Bus services within Latvia include:

destination	price (Ls)	duration (hrs)	frequency (times/day)
Cēsis	1.30	2	26
Daugavpils	3	4	up to 7
Jelgava	0.55-0.78	1	1-2
Kolka	2.35-2.98	5¾	3
Kuldīga	2.20	3-4	6-10 daily
Liepāja	2.98	4-6	about 20
Sigulda	0.90	1	12
Talsi	1.65	2½	about 12
Valmiera	1.30	2½	about 12

Train Rīga's **train station** *(centrālā stacija; ☎ 583 30 95; Stacijas laukums)* enjoyed a US$5.5 million facelift in 2002–03. Tickets are sold in the main departures hall: window Nos 1 to 6 sell tickets for international trains, window Nos 7 to 9 sell tickets for mainline services, and window Nos 10 to 13 sell tickets for slower suburban trains, including Sigulda, Cēsis, Valmiera, Jelgava and Jūrmala. Services include Daugavpils (2.42 Ls to 3 Ls, four hours) Liepāja (2.45 Ls, five hours) and Valga (via Sigulda, Cēsis & Valmiera; 2 Ls, three hours).

Getting Around

Bus No 22 runs about every 20 minutes between the airport and the stop opposite the bus station. Tickets (0.20 Ls) are sold by the bus driver. A taxi to the centre should cost no more than 8 Ls.

All bus, trolleybus and tram routes are clearly marked on Jāņa sēta's *Rīga City Map*. Tickets (0.20 Ls) are sold at news kiosks and by drivers. City transport runs 5.30am to 12.30am daily.

Hire bicycles from **Antīvās atpūtas** *(☎ 955 41 55; Pāvu iela 2)* for under 2 Ls an hour.

AROUND RĪGA

Jūrmala

pop 56,000

Jūrmala (Seashore) is a string of resorts stretching 30km west along the coast. Its sandy beaches, backed by dunes and pine woods, have seduced holiday-makers since the 19th century. Of its 14 townships, the 4km stretch between Bulduri and Dubulti is the hub. Jomas iela – the pedestrian street in Majori – is key Sunday strolling territory. Ķemeri, 6km inland, is the starting point for bog walks in **Ķemeri National Park** *(☎/fax 776 53 87; e nacionalparks@kemeri.apollo.lv; Meža māja; open May–mid-Oct)*. The highest dunes are at Lielupe. In Vaivari, the **Nemo Water Park** *(☎ 773 63 92; e nemo@apollo.lv; Atbalss iela 1)* has slides, a sauna and large pool. In Majori is the country cottage where the poet Jānis Rainis died in 1929, now a **museum** *(Plieksāna iela 5-7; open 11am-6pm Wed-Sun)*.

Kempings Nemo *(☎ 773 63 92; e nemo@apollo.lv; Atbalss iela 1; cottage beds 12.50 Ls, tent sites per person 1 Ls)*, at the water park, has little cottages and sites you can pitch your tent.

In Majori, **Dārta***(☎ 766 23 91; e darta@latnet.lv; Jūras iela 59; singles/doubles/triples 12/18/26 Ls)*, with shared bathroom and breakfast, and **Elina** *(☎/fax 776 16 65; Lienes iela 43; doubles Sept-May 15 Ls, June-Aug 25 Ls)* both offer good-value accommodation in typical wooden houses.

Jomas iela offers dozens of eating and drinking options. Stop at **Salmu krogs** *(Jomas iela 70-72)* for a beer and *ķiploku grauzdiņi* (Latvian black-bread garlic sticks). **Jūras Zaķis** *(Sea Rabbit; Vienibas prospkets 1)*, 30m from Bulduri beach, is a good place for local fish.

Two to five trains hourly go from Rīga to Jūrmala. All stop at Dubulti (0.52 Ls, 35 minutes), but not all at Majori (0.51 Ls, 40 minutes) and other stations.

Salaspils

Between 1941 and 1944, an estimated 45,000 Jews from Rīga and approximately 55,000 other people, including Jews from other Nazi-occupied countries and prisoners of war, were murdered in the concentration camp at Salaspils, 15km southeast of Rīga, on the Daugava River. Giant, gaunt sculptures stand on the site as a memorial, and there's a small museum inside the huge concrete bunker. The inscription reads 'Behind this gate the earth groans'.

From Rīga take a suburban train (10 daily) on the Ogre-Krustpils line to Dārziņi (not Salaspils) station. A path leads from the station to the memorial – a 15-minute walk.

Rundāle Palace

The 18th-century **Rundāle Palace** *(Rundāles pils; ☎ 396 21 97; w www.rpm.apollo.lv; adult/concession 1.50/1 Ls; open 10am-6pm daily May-Oct, 10am-5pm daily Nov-Apr)*, in Pilsrundāle, 77km south of Rīga, is the architectural highlight of provincial Latvia. It was designed and built for the Baron Ernst Johann von Bühren (1690–1772), duke of Courland, by Bartolomeo Rastrelli, the baroque genius from Italy who created many of St Petersburg's finest buildings. Some 40 of the palace's 138 rooms are open to visitors, as are the gardens.

Unless you have your own transport, the best way to reach Rundāle is from the town of Bauska, whose **bus station** *(☎ 392 24 77; Slimnīcas iela 11)* is served by hourly buses between 5.30am and 5.30pm to/from Rīga (1.20 Ls, 1¼ hours) – then take a bus west to Rundālespils (not Rundāle).

Eastern Latvia

Two of the country's three historic regions lie east of Rīga. Vidzeme, Latvia's most scenically varied region, is dominated by the beautiful Gauja Valley. Dubbed the 'Switzerland of Latvia', the valley is partly protected by a national park and bespeckled with castles. The small towns of Sigulda, Cēsis and Valmiera all make excellent bases for delving into its scenic depths. Valmiera lures outdoor enthusiasts with its ski resort and canoeing centre, both managed by **Sporta Bāze Baiļi** *(☎ 422 18 61)*. In town, Latvia's best-run hostel is **Hostelis Eži** *(☎ 428 17 64, 420 72 63; W www.ezi.lv; Valdemāra iela 1; dorm beds 5 Ls)*.

Scenic Vidzeme is also home to a long sandy stretch of largely unspoilt coast along the Gulf of Rīga; Latvia's highest terrain known as the Vidzeme Upland; and to one of Europe's oddest border towns, Valka, split between Latvia and Estonia.

Southeast languishes industrial Latgale, whose far southeastern corner is blessed with the Latgale Upland, a scenic lake district. Some of the best scenery is around Lake Rāzna. On Ascension Day (15 August) thousands flock to Aglona Basilica, built on the shores of Lake Egles in 1699.

SIGULDA

postcode 2150 • pop 10,855

Pretty Sigulda stands on the southern edge of a steep-sided, wooded section of the Gauja Valley and is spanned by a string of medieval castles and legendary caves. A minor health resort and winter sports centre, the town boasts an Olympic bobsled run and is the primary gateway to the beautiful Gauja National Park.

Accommodation, guided tours and a wealth of outdoor activities are arranged by the park **visitors centre** *(☎ 797 13 45, fax 797 13 44; W www.gnp.lv; Baznīcas iela 3; open 9.30am-5pm Mon, 9.30am-6pm Tues-Sun)*. The **tourist office** *(☎/fax 797 13 35; W www.sigulda,lv; Pils iela 6; open 10am-7pm daily May-Oct, 10am-5pm daily Nov-Apr)* also stocks reams of information.

Little remains of **Sigulda Castle** (1207–26), but its ruins are perhaps all the more evocative for this. On the way from town you will pass the 1225 **Sigulda Church**, which was rebuilt in the 18th century.

The centrepiece of Sigulda's **Turaida Museum Reserve** *(Turaidas muzejrezervats; ☎/fax 797 14 02; W www.turaida-muzejs.lv; admission 1 Ls Mon & Tues, 1.20 Ls Wed-Fri, 1.50 Ls Sat & Sun May-Oct, 1 Ls daily Nov-Apr; open 9.30am-8pm daily May-Oct, 10am-5pm Nov-April)* is **Turaida Castle** (Turaidas pils), a red-brick archbishops' castle founded in 1214 on the site of a Liv stronghold. The museum offers an interesting account of the Livonian state from 1319 to 1561.

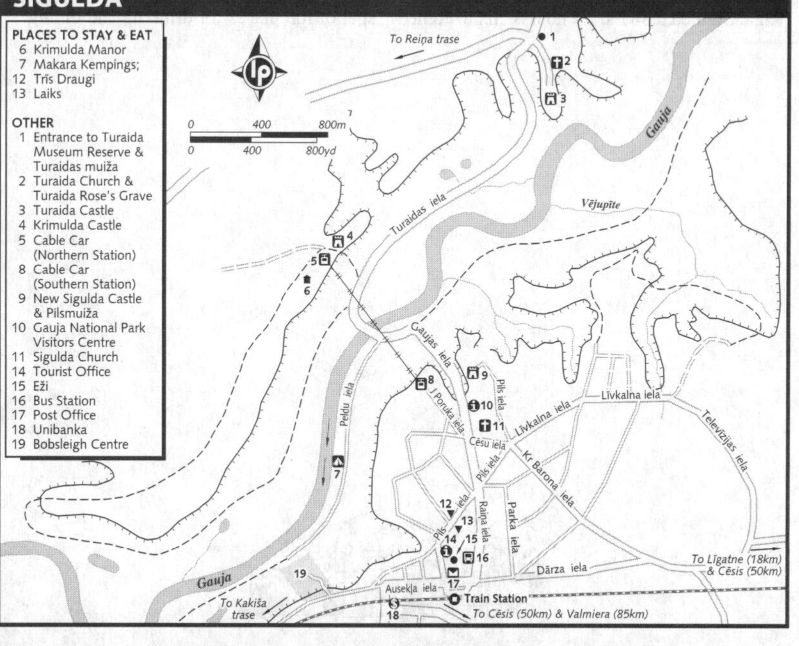

Cheap-thrill-seekers can fly down Sigulda's 16-bend **bobsled track** *(☎ 797 38 13; Sveices iela 13; open 11am-6pm Sat & Sun)* at 80km/h. **Makars** (at Makara Kempings; see Places to Stay) organises rafting and canoeing trips along the Gauja River. In winter it rents equipment for cross-country and downhill skiing.

Places to Stay & Eat

Makara Kempings *(☎ 924 49 48, 797 37 24; w www.makars.lv; Peldu iela 1; person, tent or car/caravan 1/2 Ls; open 15 May-15 Sept)* is a riverside site in the national park. Hostel-seekers should head for **Krimulda Manor** *(☎ 797 22 32; e krimulda@ls.lv; camping per tent 1 Ls, beds from 5 Ls)*.

Canteen-style **Trīs Draugi** *(Pils iela 9)* is the place to fill up on the cheap. **Laiks** *(Pils iela 8)*, opposite, cooks up light dishes in a pub-style setting. **Pilsmuiža** *(☎ 797 13 95; Pils iela 16; meals 3.50 Ls; open noon-2am daily)*, overlooking the ruins of the castle, is a feast for the eyes. Ask the waiter for the key to the castle tower.

Getting There & Away

Ten daily trains on the Rīga–Sigulda–Cēsis–Valmiera line stop at Sigulda train station (Rīga–Sigulda 0.86 Ls, 1¼ hours). Six to eight buses daily trundle between Sigulda and Rīga (0.90 Ls, two hours).

Western Latvia

Kurzeme (Courland in English), the entire western region of Latvia, is one of Latvia's least densely settled regions, and the northern part – crowned by stunning Cape Kolka where the Baltic Sea majestically meets the Gulf of Rīga – is still heavily forested. The largely untouched Baltic coast, lined with white-sand beaches and fishing villages, is home to Latvia's tiny ethnic minority, the Livs. The Slītere National Park, with its **information centre** *(☎ 324 92 11, 328 10 66; w www.slitere.gov.lv)* inside a lighthouse, protects spectacular sand dunes and forests on the northern tip.

Inland, pretty **Talsi**, 75km south, is wedged between two lakes in a shallow valley. **Kuldīga**, 75km farther southwest, is a small town on the Venta River with a clutch of 16th- to 18th-century buildings, a charming Old Town and Europe's widest waterfall. It was the first capital of the Duchy of Courland, albeit briefly (1561–73). **Liepāja** is Latvia's second port, with a pleasant beachfront and a spat of fun places for drinking and dining.

Liechtenstein

Blink and you might miss Liechtenstein: the country measures just 25km from north to south and an average of 6km from west to east. Lose concentration and you might not realise that you're outside Switzerland: the Swiss franc is the currency, travel documents valid for Switzerland are also valid for Liechtenstein, and the only border regulations are on the Austrian side. Switzerland even represents Liechtenstein abroad.

Perhaps eager to underscore its independent status, Liechtenstein sometimes takes a different route from its big sister – seemingly just to be difficult. Although the countries share the Swiss postal system, Liechtenstein issues its own stamps. Unlike Switzerland, Liechtenstein joined the UN (1990) and, in 1995, the European Economic Area (EEA). But the 'border' between Liechtenstein and Switzerland remains open, and Liechtenstein has no plans to seek full EU membership.

There's not much for the budget traveller in this prosperous country other than a museum, some skiing and bragging rights.

Liechtenstein: the Basics

Capital: Vaduz

Population: Heinrich, Wilhelm & 32,526 other people

Language: German

Currency: Swiss franc (Sfr) = 100 centimes

Avoid at all costs: Lunchtime rush hour

Keep in touch by saying: *Vilech chöi mer üs mal zum Briefmärkele träffe?* (Maybe we could swap stamps sometime?)

Facts about Liechtenstein

Liechtenstein achieved full sovereign independence in 1866. Even today the prince retains the power to dissolve parliament and must approve every act before it becomes law. Prince Franz Josef II was the first ruler to live in the castle above Vaduz. He died in 1989 after a reign of 51 years, and was succeeded by his son, Prince Hans-Adam II, who has since clashed with the government over proposed constitutional reforms that would limit government power.

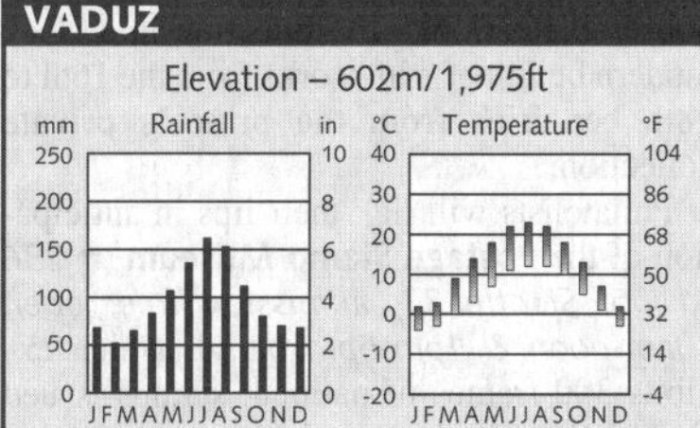

Liechtenstein's 80-man army was disbanded in 1868. It is best known for wine production, postage stamps, dentures (an important export) and its status as a tax haven. In 2000, Liechtenstein's institutions were rocked by allegations that money laundering was rife. In response to international outrage, banks agreed to stop allowing customers to deposit money anonymously.

Despite its size, Liechtenstein has two political regions (upper and lower) and three distinct geographical areas: the Rhine valley in the west, the edge of the Tirolean Alps in the southeast, and the northern lowlands. A third of the population is foreign residents.

For practical details see the Switzerland chapter.

Getting There & Around

Liechtenstein has no airport (the nearest is in Zürich), and only a few trains stop within its borders, at Schaan. Getting there by postbus is easiest. There are usually three buses an hour from the Swiss border towns of Buchs (Sfr2.40) and Sargans (Sfr3.60) that stop in Vaduz. Buses run every 30 minutes from the Austrian border town of Feldkirch; you sometimes have to change at Schaan to reach

Vaduz (the Sfr3.60 ticket is valid for both buses).

By road, route 16 from Switzerland passes through Liechtenstein via Schaan and terminates at Feldkirch. The N13 follows the Rhine along the Swiss-Liechtenstein border; minor roads cross into Liechtenstein at each motorway exit.

Postbus travel within Liechtenstein is cheap and reliable; all fares cost Sfr2.40 or Sfr3.60, and a weekly/monthly pass is only Sfr10/20 (half-price for students and seniors). The only drawback is that some services finish early; the last of the hourly buses from Vaduz to Malbun, for example, leave at 6.20pm. Grab a timetable from the post office.

The Whole Damn Country

Many tourists come to Liechtenstein for the stamps – in the passport for you and on a postcard for the folks back home. But it's also worthwhile heading for the hills, with some 400km of hiking trails through alpine scenery; see the tourist office for the Liechtenstein Hiking Map 1:25,000 (Sfr15.50).

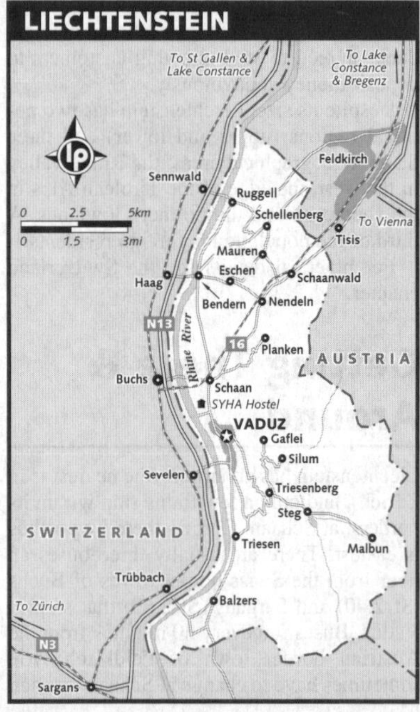

Emergencies

The same emergency numbers apply as in Switzerland. Dial ☎ 117 for the police, ☎ 144 for an ambulance, or ☎ 118 in the event of a fire. Liechtenstein's telephone country code is ☎ 423, and there are no regional telephone codes.

VADUZ

pop 4930

Vaduz is really little more than a village. Two adjoining streets beneath the castle, Äulestrasse and pedestrian-only Städtle, enclose the town centre. Everything of importance is within this small area.

Liechtenstein Tourism (*☎ 239 63 00; e touristinfo@liechtenstein.li; Städtle 37; open Mon-Fri, daily May-Sept*) has plenty of useful information; for Sfr2, staff will stamp your passport with a souvenir entry stamp. Send postcards at the **post office** (*Äulestrasse 38; open 7.45am-6pm Mon-Fri, 8am-11am Sat*). The **Telecom FL shop** (*☎ 237 74 74; Austrasse 77; open 9am-noon & 1.30pm-6.30pm Mon-Fri, 9am-1pm Sat*), 1km south of Vaduz, provides free Internet access.

For medical attention, contact the hospital, **Liechtensteinisches Landesspital** (*☎ 235 44 11; Heiligkreuz 25*).

Things to See & Do

Although the **Vaduz Castle** is not open to the public, you can climb the hill for a closer look. There are views of Vaduz and the mountains, and a network of marked walking trails along the ridge.

Liechtenstein Kunstmuseum (*☎ 235 030 00; Städtle 32; w www.kunstmuseum.li; adult/student/child Sfr8/5/5; open 10am-5pm Tues-Wed & Fri-Sun, 10am-8pm Thur*) houses the national art collection in a sleek modern building, with works from the 16th to 18th centuries from the prince's private collection.

Philatelists will lick their lips in anticipation of the **Postage Stamp Museum** (*☎ 236 61 05; Städtle 37; admission free; open 10am-noon & 1pm-5pm daily*), which exhibits 300 frames of national stamps issued since 1912. The **National Museum** (*Städtle

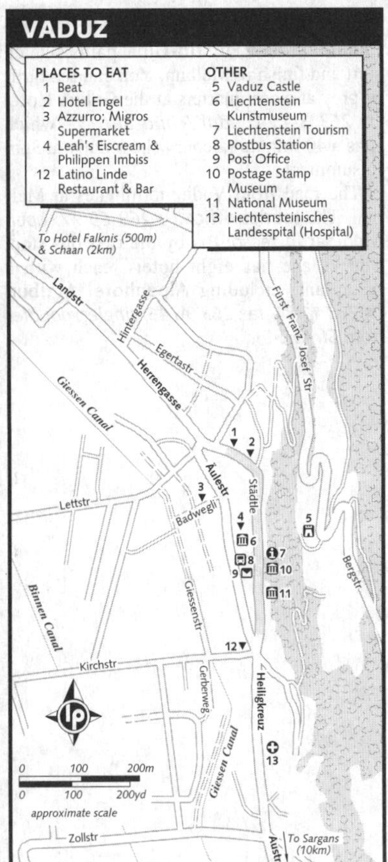

43) reopens after major renovations are complete in spring 2003.

Look out for processions and fireworks on 15 August, Liechtenstein's national holiday. Bands performing at the **Little Big One** *(W www.littlebigone.com)* open-air music festival sweep into town on the third June weekend.

Places to Stay

You can base yourself anywhere and still be within easy cycling or postbus distance of the centre. Ask the tourist office for a list of private rooms and chalets outside Vaduz.

Triesenberg, located on a hillside terrace that overlooks the Rhine valley, has **Camping Mittagspitz** *(☎ 392 26 86; adult/child/tent/car Sfr8.50/4/5/4, dorm beds for adult/child Sfr22/13)*. The **SYHA hostel** *(☎ 232 50 22, fax 232 58 56; e schaan@youthhostel.ch; Untere Rütigasse 6; dorm beds from Sfr29, doubles without/with toilet Sfr75/87; open mid-Mar–Nov)* is in a quiet rural setting between Vaduz and nearby Schaan. Take the postbus to the Muhleholz stop; it's a five-minute walk (signposted) from there.

Another cheapie outside Vaduz is **Hotel Falknis** *(☎ 232 63 77; Landstrasse 92; singles/doubles Sfr55/110)*, a 20-minute walk from the centre (or take the postbus). There's a pub below and, above, there are basic rooms with hall showers.

Places to Eat

The pedestrian-only Stadtle street has a clutch of pavement restaurants and cafés to choose from. Popular options include **Hotel Engel** *(Städtle 13)*, with standard international fare; and **Beat** *(Städtle 5)*, a stylish eatery for local suits.

For an odd but delicious mix of authentic Filipino dishes and home-made ice cream, there's **Leah's Eiscream & Philippen Imbiss** *(☎ 232 72 00; Städtle 28; dishes Sfr9.50, ice cream from Sfr2)*, behind the Kunstmuseum.

Latino Linde Restaurant & Bar *(☎ 233 10 05; Kirchstrasse 2; dishes Sfr17.50-25)* is a local haunt with bamboo screens and South American rugs, serving burgers and Tex-Mex snacks.

For a quick bite, there's **Azzurro** *(☎ 232 48 18)*, next to the Migros supermarket, a stand-up eatery with kebabs and small pizzas from Sfr7.50.

AROUND VADUZ

Northern Liechtenstein is dotted with small, tranquil communities with pleasant village churches. **Schellenberg** has a Russian monument, commemorating the night in 1945 when a band of 500 heavily armed Russian soldiers crossed the border.

Triesenberg, on a terrace above Vaduz, commands excellent views over the Rhine valley. It has a pretty onion-domed church and the **Heimatmuseum** *(☎ 262 19 26; adult/student Sfr2/1; open 1.30pm-5.30pm Tues-Sat year-round, 2pm-5pm Sun June-Aug)*, which is devoted to the Walser community, whose members came from Switzerland's Valais to settle here in the 13th century. Apparently, the Walser dialect is still spoken here. **Balzers**, in the extreme south of the country, is dominated by the soaring sides of Gutenberg Castle.

MALBUN

Liechtenstein's ski resort, Malbun, perches at 1600m in the southeast. It has some good mountain runs for novices (and two ski schools), as well as more difficult runs. A one-day pass for all ski lifts costs Sfr35 (students/seniors Sfr29). Skis, shoes and poles cost Sfr43 for a day, and can be hired from the **sports shop** *(☎ 263 37 55)*.

In summer, skis give way to mountain boots as the hiking fraternity hits town. Worthwhile treks in the area include the **Panorama** and **Furstin-Gina** paths, which start and finish in Malbun. You can see birds of prey at close quarters at the **Galina Hotel** *(☎ 263 34 24; adult/child Sfr6/3)*, which runs a 40-minute falconry show daily at 3pm in summer.

The road from Vaduz terminates at Malbun. The **tourist office** *(☎ 263 65 77; open Mon-Sat in season)* is by the first bus stop. The village has eight hotels, each with a restaurant, including **Alpenhotel Malbun** *(☎ 263 11 81, fax 263 96 46; singles/doubles from Sfr45/90)*.

Lithuania

Tenacious little Lithuania stunned the world when it played David and Goliath with the might of the Soviet Union – and won its independence just over a decade ago. But this Baltic big sister is no stranger to triumph, formerly possessing an empire stretching from the Baltic to the Black Sea. Raw pagan roots fuse with fervent Catholicism, the Polish inheritance that sets Lithuania apart from Latvia and Estonia, as the nation looks once again to Europe.

Enigmatic and eccentric, Lithuania is one of Europe's best-kept secrets. Opulent, baroque Vilnius draws fans of the beautiful and eccentric, while natural treasures such as the Curonian Spit (Neringa) glitter enticingly by the sea. Alternately triumphant and browbeaten, Lithuania is on the rise once again.

Lithuania: the Basics

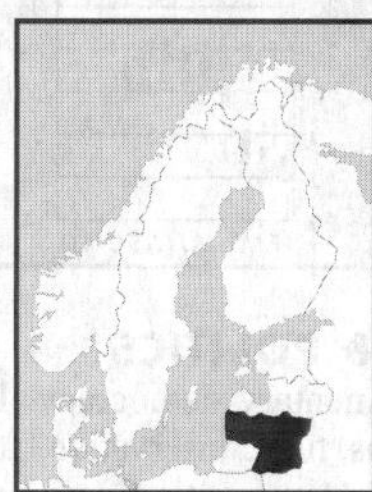

Local name Lietuva

Capital Vilnius

Population 3.7 million

Language Lithuanian

Currency 1 litas (Lt) = 100 centų

Avoid at all costs Insulting Frank Zappa

Obtain necessary ventilation in hotel rooms by saying *Aš negaliu atidaryti lango.* (I can't open the window.)

Facts about Lithuania

HISTORY

Lithuania's troubled history is one of riches to rags – and back again. Lithuania became a powerful state in the 14th to 16th centuries, then disappeared off the maps as a subservient cousin of Poland. In the 18th century, the state was carved up by Russia, Austria and Prussia.

Vilnius became a focus of uprisings against Russian rule, and Lithuanian nationalists declared independence on 16 February 1918. In 1940 Lithuania was forced into the USSR. Within a year 40,000 Lithuanians were killed or deported. Up to 300,000 more people, mostly Jews, died in concentration camps and ghettos during the 1941–44 Nazi occupation. The USSR returned with a vengeance in 1945. An estimated 200,000 people were murdered or deported to Siberia.

In the late 1980s Lithuania led the Baltic push for autonomy. Lithuania was the first Soviet state to legalise noncommunist parties, and on 11 March 1990 the new majority party declared independence. Moscow marched troops into Vilnius and cut off Lithuania's fuel supplies. In January 1991 Soviet troops stormed key buildings in Vilnius. Fourteen people were killed at the TV tower, and Lithuanians barricaded their parliament (Seimas). Caving in to heavy condemnation from the West, the Soviets recognised Lithuanian independence on 6 September, and the first ex-USSR republic was born.

Since the last Soviet troops left on 31 August 1993, Lithuania has struggled with the highs and lows of independence. Domestic and foreign policy has been focused on the West. The country is expected to join NATO in November 2002 and the EU by 2004. The litas was pegged to the euro in February 2002, and there is growing optimism for the future, with foreign investment and EU aid pouring in.

GEOGRAPHY

Lithuania can be described in two words: flat and fertile. The largest of the Baltics is 65,300 sq km, dotted with lush forests, 4000 lakes and a 100km-wide lowland centre. Retreating glaciers left higher areas in the northwest, across the southeast and in the east. Forest covers a third of the country.

Half of Lithuania's short Baltic Coast lies along the mesmerising Curonian Spit (Kuršių Nerija), a 4km-wide sand bar stretching 98km with 60m-high sand dunes.

CLIMATE

From mid-November to mid-March temperatures barely rise above freezing. Beautiful, fleeting summers between June and August bring temperatures of 20°C – and rain.

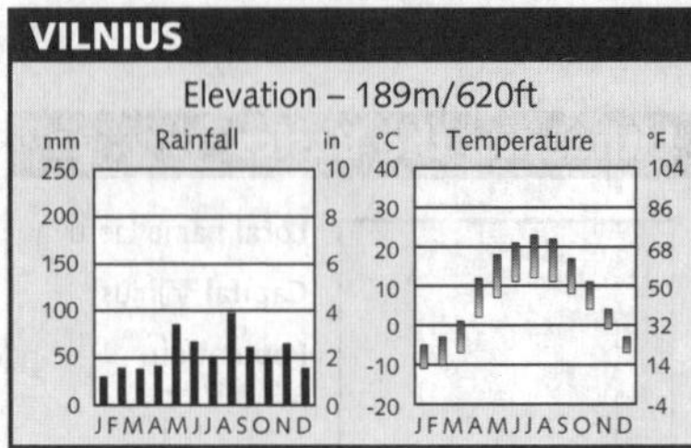

GOVERNMENT & POLITICS

Lithuania is a parliamentary democracy. In October 2000 elections, the Conservative faction lost to the Social Democratic Coalition, which won 31% of the vote and holds 52 seats in the Seimas, headed by former president, Algirdas Brazauskas.

POPULATION & PEOPLE

Lithuanians form 81% of the population. The main minority groups are Russians (8%), Poles (7%) and Jews (0.1%).

SOCIETY & CONDUCT

Lithuanians are emotional people with a tendency towards mysticism. They are fiercely proud of their national identity.

Make sure only to give odd numbers of flowers as a gift, keep eye contact when making a toast, and never, ever shake hands across a doorway if you want to stay friends with your exuberant hosts.

LANGUAGE

Lithuanian is one of the only two surviving languages of the Baltic branch of the Indo-European language family (the other is Latvian). Most Lithuanians, both young and old, speak Russian, and outside Vilnius it's used more than English. See the Language chapter for useful words and phrases.

Facts for the Visitor

HIGHLIGHTS

Wander the cobbled streets of charming Vilnius Old Town flanked by colourful baroque creations. Wonder at the natural magic of the Curonian Spit's towering sand dunes and whispering pine trees. Discover the strength of Lithuanian spirit at the strange Hill of Crosses near Šiauliai, and see Lenin strike a pose at the unique Soviet Sculpture Park in the south.

PLANNING

The best time to catch those fragile Baltic rays is between May and September.

TOURIST OFFICES

Tourist information sources abroad include Lithuanian embassies and specialist travel agencies. In Lithuania there are tourist information centres (TICs) dotted around the country. They are coordinated by the **Lithuanian Tourist Board** (*☎ 5-262 2610; w www.tourism.lt; Vilniaus gatvė 4/35, Vilnius*).

VISAS & DOCUMENTS

Double check before you leave as more countries sign visa-free agreements with Lithuania. The **Foreign Ministry** (*w www.urm.lt*) has up-to-date details.

A valid passport is the only entry requirement for citizens of many countries, including Lithuania's Baltic sisters, Nordic countries, Europe, Australia, Canada, Iceland, Ireland, Israel, Japan, New Zealand, the UK and USA. Lithuania no longer issues visas at its border points. Visas issued are generally for stays of up to 90 days within a period of either six or 12 months.

If you're travelling on to, or via, Poland check whether your bus or train passes through Belarus as you will need to have a Belarusian transit visa.

To extend your Lithuanian visa see the **immigration department** (*imigracijos tarnyba; ☎ 5-271 7749; Verkių gatvė 3, Vilnius*).

EMBASSIES & CONSULATES

Lithuanian Embassies & Consulates

Lithuania has representatives in the following countries:

Australia (☎ 02-9498 2571) 40B Fiddens Wharf Rd, Killara, NSW 2071

Canada (☎ 613-567 5458, e litemb@storm.ca) 130 Albert St, Suite 204, Ottawa, Ontario K1P 5G4

Estonia (☎ 2-631 4030, e amber@anet.ee) Uus tn 15, Tallinn

Finland (☎ 09-608 210, e embassylt@kolumbus.fi) Rauhankatu 13a, Helsinki 20180

France (☎ 01 48 01 00 33, e amb.lituanie@magic.fr) 14 blvd Montmartre 75009, Paris

Germany (☎ 030-890 6810, e botschaftlitauen@t-online.de) Katharinenstrasse 9, 10711 Berlin

Latvia (☎ 2-732 1519, e lithemb@ltemb.vip.lv) Rūpniecibas iela 22, 1010 Rīga

Poland (☎ 022-625 3368, ⓔ konslt@waw.pdi.net) aleje Jana Chrystiana Szucha 5, Warsaw
Russia (☎ 095-291 1698, ⓔ unic13@glasnet.ru) Borisoglebsky per 10, Moscow 121069
Consulate: (☎ 0112-551 444) ul Proletarskaya 133, Kaliningrad
Sweden (☎ 08-667 5455, ⓔ litemb@telia.com) Strandvagen 53, 11523 Stockholm
UK (☎ 020-7486 6402, ⓔ lralon@globalnet.co.uk) 84 Gloucester Place, London W1H 3HN
USA (☎ 202-234 5860, ⓔ info@ltembassy.org) 2622 16th St NW, Washington, DC 20009

Embassies & Consulates in Lithuania

The following embassies and consulates are in Vilnius. The area code for Vilnius is ☎ 5.

Australia (☎ 266 0730, ⓔ aust.con.vilnius@post.omnitel.net) Vilniaus gatvė 23
Belarus (☎ 266 2200, ⓔ bpl@post.5ci.lt) Mindaugo gatvė 13
Canada (☎ 249 6853, ⓔ vilnius@canada.lt) Gedimino prospektas 64
Estonia (☎ 278 0200, ⓔ sekretar@estemb.lt) A Mickevičiaus gatvė 4a
Finland (☎ 212 1621, ⓔ sanomat.vil@formin.fi) Klaipėdos gatvė
Germany (☎ 265 0272, ⓔ germ.emb@takas.lt) Sierakausko gatvė 24
Latvia (☎ 213 1260, ⓔ lietuva@latvia.balt.net) MK Čiurlionio gatvė 76
Poland (☎ 270 9001, ⓔ ambpol@tdd.lt) Smėlio gatvė 20a
Russia (☎ 272 1763, ⓔ rusemb@rusemb.lt) Latvių gatvė 53/54
Sweden (☎ 268 5010, ⓔ ambassden.vilnius@foreign.ministry.se) Didžioji gatvė 16
UK (☎ 212 2070/1, ⓔ be-vilnius@britain.lt) Antakalnio gatvė 2
USA (☎ 266 5500, ⓔ mail@usembassy) Akmenų gatvė 6

CUSTOMS

Customs regulations are subject to change. In Vilnius, check with the **customs department** *(☎ 5-212 6415; ⓦ www.cust.lt; Jakšto gatvė 1/25)* about the regulations.

Lithuania has limits on amber exports, but a few souvenirs are fine providing their value doesn't exceed €266.

MONEY

Currency

Lithuania's currency, the litas (plural: litų; Lt), is pegged to the euro at 3.4528 Lt to €1. The litas comes in 10, 20, 50, 100, 200 and 500 Lt notes and one, two and five litų coins. One litas is 100 centų (ct); these are virtually worthless.

Most currencies can be exchanged but US dollars, euros or British pounds are best. At the time of printing exchange rates were:

country	unit		litų
Australia	A$1	=	1.90 Lt
Canada	C$1	=	2.32 Lt
eurozone	€1	=	3.45 Lt
Japan	¥100	=	2.80 Lt
Sweden	1Skr	=	0.46 Lt
UK	£1	=	5.52 Lt
USA	$1	=	3.8 Lt

Budget travellers staying at camp sites and hostels can spend €20 to €30 a day including food and transport. Student cards get discounts on museums and travel fares.

POST & COMMUNICATIONS

Lithuania's post is quick and cheap. Letters/postcards cost 1.70/1 Lt internationally and 1/0.80 Lt internally. Mail to America takes 10 days, to Europe about a week.

All telephone access codes were changed in 2002. If you are in doubt about a code check on the website ⓦ www.telecom.lt. To call cities within Lithuania, dial ☎ 8, wait for the tone, then dial the area code and telephone number. To make an international call dial ☎ 00 before the country code. To call Lithuania from abroad, dial ☎ 370 then the area code, followed by the city code and telephone number.

All blue public phones are card-only; cards are sold in denominations of 50/75/100/200 units costing 9/13/16/30 Lt.

Internet cafés have grown like mushrooms across Vilnius (2 to 8 Lt per hour). Outside the capital, prices and speed are higher and lower, respectively.

DIGITAL RESOURCES

Check the cheeky online version of *In Your Pocket* (ⓦ www.inyourpocket.com) to *Vilnius* and *Klaipėda/Kaunas*. For news and views go to ⓦ www.baltictimes.com.

BOOKS

Lonely Planet's guide to *Estonia, Latvia and Lithuania* is useful; *Of Gods & Holidays: The Baltic Heritage* (1999), edited by Jonas Trinkūnas, has details on Lithuania's pagan roots.

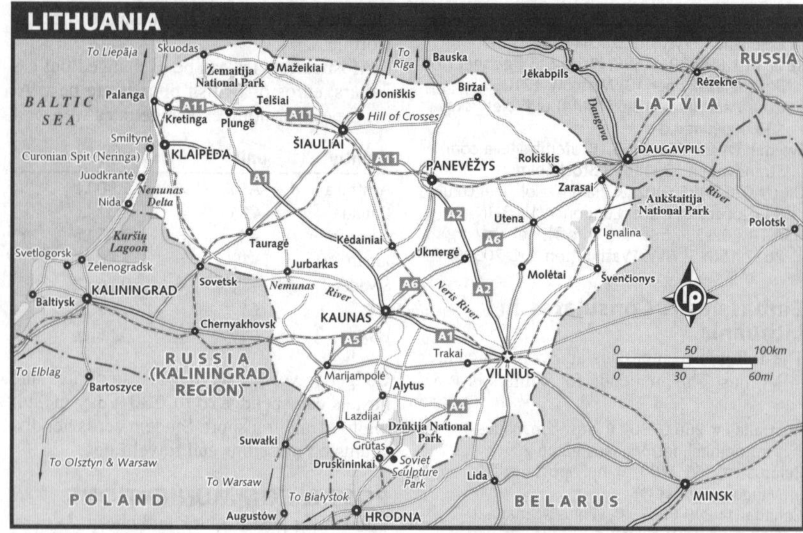

GAY & LESBIAN TRAVELLERS

The scene is still low-key. For general information and guides go to www.gay.lt or call the **Gay Information Line** *(☎ 5-233 3031)*.

The country's first gay club only opened in 2000 in Vilnius: **Men's Factory** *(☎ 5-231 0687; Žygimantų 1)*.

DISABLED TRAVELLERS

The **Association of Invalids** *(☎ 5-275 7716; Saltoniškių gatvė 29/3, Vilnius)* can help direct you to local services.

DANGERS & ANNOYANCES

There have been disturbing reports of anti-Semitic attacks, both verbal and physical, in Lithuania. Gay people and those from non-European backgrounds are also targets.

PUBLIC HOLIDAYS & SPECIAL EVENTS

Lithuania's national holidays are New Year's Day (1 January), Independence Day (16 February, anniversary of 1918 independence declaration), Restoration of Lithuania's 11 March Independence, Good Friday and Easter Monday (April), Labour Day (1 May), State Holiday (6 July), All Saints' Day (1 November), Christmas Day (25 December) and Boxing Day (26 December).

Annual festivals include Lithuania Song Festival, which will take place 1 to 7 July 2003; Baltic Folk Festival in mid-July; Kaunas International Jazz Festival in April; week-long Life Theatre Festival in Vilnius in late May; Vilnius Summer Music Festival throughout July; Vilnius City Masks Festival celebrating the autumnal equinox at the end of September; and theVilnius International Jazz Festival held in October.

In Vilnius, the **Lithuanian Folk Culture Centre** *(☎ 5-261 2594; www.lfcc.lt; Barboros Radvilaitės gatvė 8)* has information on cultural events.

Emergencies

Nationwide emergency numbers are ☎ 01 for fire, ☎ 02 for police and ☎ 03 for ambulance.

ACTIVITIES

The pagan roots of Lithuanians are revealed by their love of nature. Travellers can hike into the wilderness, sweat in traditional saunas and experience the frozen joys of ice-fishing or skiing the slopes.

Lithuanian Ornithological Society *(☎ 5-213 0498; birdlife@post.5ci.lt; Naugarduko gatvė 47/3)* is based in Vilnius. **Krantas Travel** *(www.krantas.lt)*, with offices in several cities, organises tours of the western Nemunas Delta wetlands, which are rich in birdlife.

There are new cycling tracks around Vilnius with bike hire from the **TIC** *(Vilniaus gatvė 22)* for 1 Lt/day. Most towns/cities have bike hire either from Litinterp, the TICs or private hotels/guest houses.

Mushrooming is a relic of Lithuania's traditional way of life. There are deadly poisonous varieties so only eat what you know is safe.

ACCOMMODATION

Lithuanian *Kempingas* (camping grounds) are basic, cheap (5 to 20 Lt to pitch a tent, 15 to 30 Lt for a wooden cabin) and rundown. National parks have basic camp sites, and there are also private ones dotted around Palanga and Trakai.

The **Lithuanian Hostels Association** *(☎ 5-215 4627, fax 212 0149; ⓔ filaretai@post.omnitel.net; Filaretų gatvė 17, Vilnius)* is based at the largest hostel it runs. The association runs a second hostel in Vilnius Old Town, and has an affiliated hostel in Klaipėda. A bed in a shared room costs 32 Lt a night.

Litinterp offers B&Bs and self-catering facilities in Vilnius, Klaipėda, Kaunas and Palanga. In Vilnius prices start at around 80 Lt per person, while outside the capital they start at around 70 Lt.

Tourist centres are able to book countryside homestays from 100 Lt a double.

FOOD & DRINKS

Long, miserable winters are to blame for the waist-widening Baltic diet. Lithuanian food is epitomised in *cepelinai*, an airship-shaped parcel of thick potato dough, filled with cheese, meat or mushrooms. Artery-furring staples are *bulvinai blynai*, pancakes made of grated potato stuffed with dairy products, including *varške* (curd) and *rūgusis pienas* (sour milk), though meat and other vegetables are standard. Another good stand-by is *koldūninė*, small ravioli-like dumplings stuffed with cheese, mushrooms or meat.

The best local *alus* (beers) are Utenos and Kalnapilis. No drink would be complete without *kepta duona* (bar snacks), which reaches new fattening heights. Bread is deep-fried and drowned in garlic.

Lithuanians drink *midus* (mead), such as Žalgiris and Suktinis, which are as much as 60% alcohol, and *gira*, made from fermented grains or fruit and brown rye bread. Wine is *vynas*, tea *arbata*, coffee *kava* and mineral water *mineralinis vanduo*.

Getting There & Around

Lithuania has cheap bus and rail links with Warsaw, which in turn has flights, trains and cheap buses to/from many Western European cities. You can also easily reach Lithuania overland through Latvia or by sea from Germany and Sweden.

AIR

Lithuanian Airlines *(Lietuvos Avialinijos; LAL; ⓦ www.lal.lt)* flies to many European cities. The Latvian state airline, airBaltic, flies from Vilnius to Rīga three times weekly. Estonian Air flies to Tallinn on weekdays.

LAND

Three buses run daily between Vilnius and Rīga (40 Lt) and two run daily to Tallinn (90 Lt). **Eurolines** *(☎ 5-215 1377, fax 215 1376; ⓦ www.eurolines.lt)* is based inside Vilnius bus station. It sells tickets for mainland Europe, Scandinavia, UK and Moscow.

There's one train daily between Vilnius and Rīga (46 Lt, eight hours, 300km), the Warsaw-bound train on even days to Šeštokai (three hours, 198km), and one to three trains daily to Moscow (14 hours, 944km). The excellent website ⓦ www.litrail.lt has details in English. There are two to five daily trains from Vilnius to Kaliningrad (seven hours), one to three daily to St Petersburg (15 to 17 hours) and several weekly to Lviv.

Motorists can wait two minutes or two days at Kalvarija and Lazdijai, on the Lithuanian-Polish borders. Lithuanian-Belarusian border crossings are notoriously slow.

SEA

Lisco and Scandlines ferries sail from Klaipėda to/from Kiel (Germany) daily (31 to 33 hours). Lisco has services to/from Mukran (Germany) daily except Monday (19 hours) and to/from Karlshamn (Sweden) three times weekly (17 hours). For tickets and schedules contact **Krantas Travel** *(☎ 46-395 111; ⓔ travel@krantas.lt; Lietuvininkų aikštė 5, Klaipėda)*.

WITHIN LITHUANIA

Lithuania boasts a cheap, efficient and plentiful supply of long-distance buses linking it internally and to its Baltic sisters. Cheaper, slower and rarer than buses, trains are the dinosaurs of Lithuanian transport. Only bother if you're an anorak-wearing trainspotter.

Vilnius

☎ 5 • pop 600,000

Bizarre, beautiful and bewitching, Vilnius seduces visitors with its baroque Old Town, a skyline of church spires and underlying eccentricity. Where else but this devilishly attractive city could house the world's only statue of psychedelic musician Frank Zappa? Or a self-proclaimed independent republic of artists?

Crumbling archways frame the life of the narrow, cobbled streets. Change is under way, but new infrastructure won't disguise the curious charm of this soulful town.

History

According to legend, Vilnius was founded in the 1320s by Duke Gediminas after a dream. Sixteenth-century Vilnius was one of the biggest cities in Eastern Europe. It blossomed with buildings in late-Gothic and Renaissance styles as Lithuanian monarchs occupied the Polish-Lithuanian throne.

In the 17th and early 18th centuries Vilnius suffered war, famine and plague, and shrank in population and importance. It was devastated during WWI and the subsequent Bolshevik-Polish-Lithuanian fighting. When the fighting ended, Vilnius found itself in Poland, where it remained till 1939. By then it had developed into one of the world's major centres of Jewish culture and scholarship, earning it the nickname 'Jerusalem of Lithuania'. WWII saw Vilnius' Jews slaughtered in its ghetto or at the Paneriai death camp.

Orientation

The heart of Vilnius is Katedros aikštė, the cathedral square, with Gediminas Hill rising behind it. Southwards are the streets of the Old Town; to the west Gedimino prospektas is the axis of the newer part of the city. The train and bus stations are 1.5km south of Katedros aikštė.

Information

Tourist Offices Vilnius **Tourist Information Centre** *(☎ 262 9660, fax 262 8169; w www.vilnius.lt; Vilniaus gatvė 22; open Mon-Fri)* has a touch-operated info kiosk with information in English and German. There's a **smaller branch** *(☎ 262 6470; Pilies gatvė 42; open daily)* that will move to the Old Town Hall. Both offer accommodation bookings, excursions to Trakai and car and bike rental.

Kelvita Tourist Information *(☎/fax 231 0229; Geležinkelio gatvė 16; open Mon-Fri)* is in the international hall of the train station and sells visas for Belarus, Russia and Ukraine.

Money There is a handily located **24-hour currency exchange** *(Parex Bankas; ☎ 213 5454; Geležinkelio gatvė 6)* on your left as you exit the train station.

Vilniaus Bankas *(☎ 268 2093; Gedimino prospektas 12 • ☎ 268 2811; Gedimino prospektas 60 • ☎ 268 1414; Jogailos gatvė 9a)* transfers money, accepts Thomas Cook and American Express travellers cheques, and has Visa ATMs.

Hansa Bankas *(☎ 239 0600; Gedimino prospektas 26 • Pilies gatvė 9 • Vilniaus gatvė 16)* has MasterCard ATMs, as do the **Bankas Snoras kiosks** dotted over town.

Post & Communications The **central post office** *(☎ 262 5468; Gedimino prospektas 7; open 7am-7pm Mon-Fri, 9am-4pm Sat)* has an Internet section as well as stamps, faxes and telegrams service, and the state-run **Express Mail Service** *(EMS; ☎ 261 6759)*.

VOO2 *(☎ 279 1866; e ianplinka@post.5ci.lt; Ašmenos gatvė 8)* boasts a resident iguana and good Internet access. **Bazė** *(☎ 249 7701; e info@base.lt; Gedimino prospektas 50/2)* is speedy and cheap.

Travel Agencies For countryside farmstays, **Baltic Travel Service** *(☎ 212 0220, fax 212 2196; e lcc@bts.lt; Subačiaus gatvė 2; open Mon-Sat)* is the place to inquire. **Lithuanian Student & Youth Travel** *(☎ 239 7397; e info@jaunimas.lt; Basanavičiaus gatvė 30/13)* has a cheap range of fares for ISIC-holders, while **West Express** *(☎ 212 2500, fax 261 9436; e office@westexpress.lt; Stulginskio gatvė 5)* offers good all-round service.

Medical & Emergency Services The **Baltic-American Medical and Surgical Clinic** *(☎ 234 2020; e bak@takas.lt; Antakalnio* *gatvė 124; open 24hr)*, inside Vilnius University Antakalnis hospital, offers a service that is English-speaking. There is a **24-hour pharmacy** *(☎ 261 0135)* at Gedimino prospektas 27.

The **International Police Commission** *(☎ 272 6159, 271 6221)* has English, French and German-speaking staff for foreign crime victims. Ring ☎ 02 in an emergency.

Katedros aikštė & Around

Gedimino Tower is on top of 48m **Gedimino kalnas** (Gedimino Hill), behind the cathedral. Inside the red-brick tower is a **museum** *(open 11am-5pm Tues-Sun Nov-Apr, 10am-7pm May-Oct)*. Katedros aikštė is where the human chain from Tallinn to Vilnius in 1989, protesting Soviet occupation, ended.

Gedimino Hill is dominated by **Vilnius Cathedral**, built on an ancient pagan site. The remains and a centuries-old **ritual stone** were discovered when the foundations were dug. The 5m **bronze statues** of St Helene, St Stanislav and St Casimir on top of the cathedral were levelled in 1956 but resurrected following restoration work. The interior showpiece is the **Chapel of St Casimir**, created between 1623 and 1636, which boasts a bizarre laughing Madonna.

Farther along Arsenalo gatvė are the **National Museum** *(☎ 262 9426; Arsenalo gatvė 1; adult/concession 4/2 Lt; open 10am-5pm Wed-Sun)* and the **Applied Arts Museum** *(☎ 262 8080; Arsenalo gatvė 3; admission 8 Lt; open 11am-6pm Tues-Sat, 11am-4pm Sun)* at No 3, which features an exhibition of jewels discovered hidden in the cathedral walls in 1985. This exhibition will continue until at least the end of 2003.

East of Gediminas Hill

The white **Three Crosses** atop Three Crosses Hill are old Vilnius landmarks said to have stood here since the 17th century in memory of three monks who were crucified at this spot. The existing ones are replicas of three that were knocked down and buried by Soviet authorities.

Inside **St Peter & Paul Church** at the far end of Kosciuškos gatvė is a treasure trove of sparkling white stucco sculptures of real and mythical people, animals and plants, created by Italian sculptors between 1675 and 1704. Catch trolleybus No 2, 3 or 4 from the Arkikatedra stop near the cathedral.

Old Town

Pilies gatvő & Around The largest Old Town in Europe stretches 1.5km south of Katedros aikštė, along Pilies gatvė, Didžioji gatvė and Aušros Vartų gatvė. **Vilnius University** occupies the block between Pilies gatvė and Universiteto gatvė. Founded in 1579, it was one of the greatest centres of Polish learning in the 17th and early 19th centuries. The history faculty hosts the world's first **Centre for Stateless Cultures** *(☎ 268 7293; ⓔ statelesscultures@centras.lt)*, including Yiddish, Roma and Karaimic cultures. The southern gate on Šv Jono gatvė brings you into the Didysis or Skarga Courtyard, in early 17th-century Mannerist style, and **St John's Church** (Šv Jono bažnyčia), which features an outstanding 18th-century baroque facade. The arch through the 16th-century building opposite St John's leads to a two-domed **observatory**, its late 18th-century facade adorned with zodiac reliefs.

East of Pilies gatvė, the old rooms of Polish romantic poet Adam Mickiewicz (1798–1855) are now the **Mickiewicz museum** *(☎ 261 8836; Bernardinų gatvė 11; open 10am-5pm Tues-Fri, 10am-2pm Sat & Sun)*. Mickiewicz grew up near Vilnius and studied at its university (1815–19) before being exiled for anti-Russian activities.

Across Maironio gatvė is the fine 1581 brick facade of **St Anne's Church** (Šv Onos bažnyčia), a Gothic architectural masterpiece. Farther down Maironio, at No 12, stands a lovely Russian Orthodox cathedral – **Church of the Holy Mother of God** (1346) – which was damaged in the late 17th century and reconstructed.

Didžioji gatvė & Around Southern Didžioji gatvė widens into a plaza that was the centre of Vilnius life from the 15th century. **St Casimir's Church** (Šv Kazimiero bažnyčia) is Vilnius' oldest baroque church. It was built by Jesuits (1604–15) and under Soviet rule was a museum of atheism.

Aušros Vartų gatvė was once the start of the Moscow road. On the eastern side of the street is the big, pink 17th-century **Holy Spirit Church** (Šv Dvasios bažnyčia), Lithuania's chief Russian Orthodox church. The preserved bodies of three 14th-century martyrs lie in a chamber in front of the altar. The Catholic **St Teresa's Church** (Šv Teresės bažnyčia) is early baroque outside and more elaborate late baroque inside.

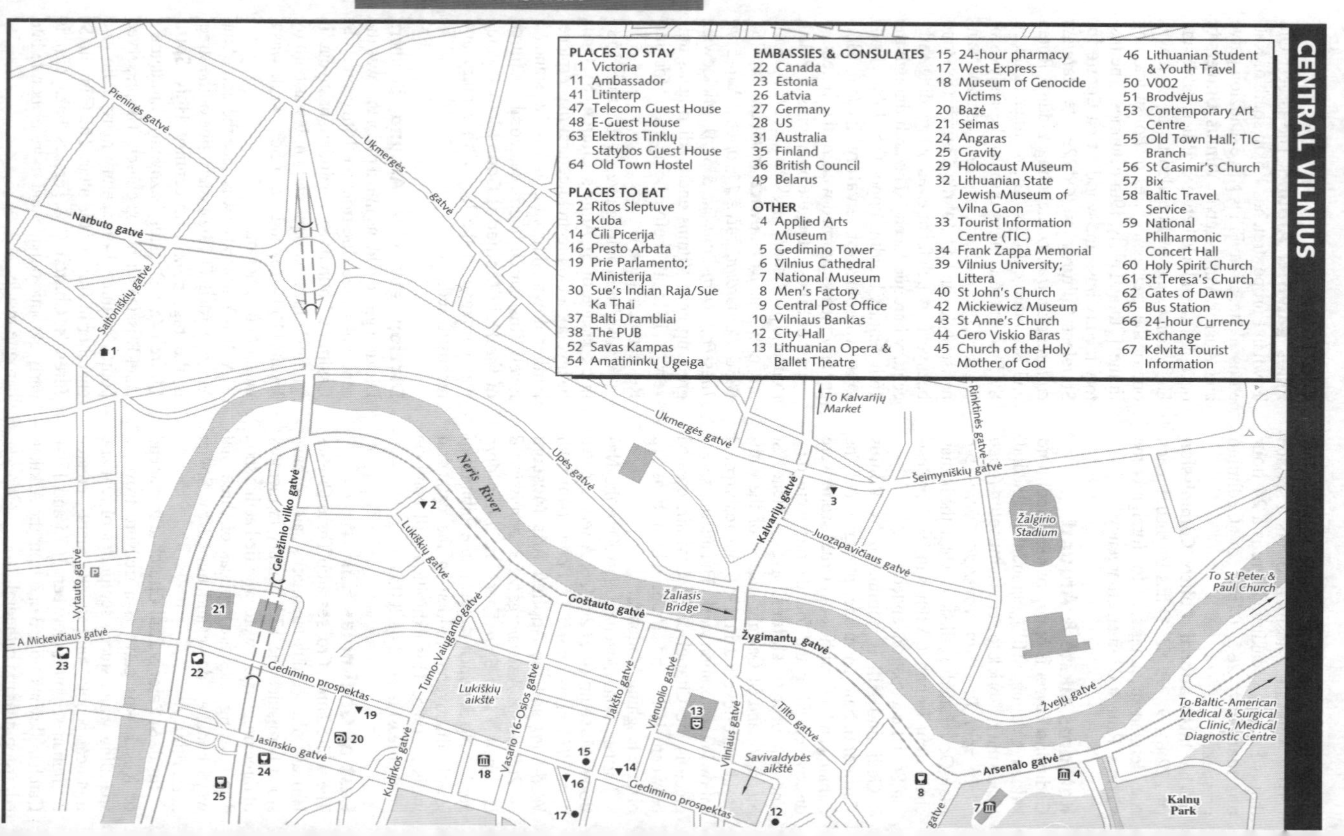
CENTRAL VILNIUS
PLACES TO STAY
1 Victoria
11 Ambassador
41 Litinterp
47 Telecom Guest House
48 E-Guest House
63 Elektros Tinklų Statybos Guest House
64 Old Town Hostel
PLACES TO EAT
2 Ritos Sleptuve
3 Kuba
14 Čili Picerija
16 Presto Arbata
19 Prie Parlamento; Ministerija
30 Sue's Indian Raja/Sue Ka Thai
37 Balti Drambliai
38 The PUB
52 Savas Kampas
54 Amatininkų Ugeiga
EMBASSIES & CONSULATES
22 Canada
23 Estonia
26 Latvia
27 Germany
28 US
31 Australia
35 Finland
36 British Council
49 Belarus
OTHER
4 Applied Arts Museum
5 Gedimino Tower
6 Vilnius Cathedral
7 National Museum
8 Men's Factory
9 Central Post Office
10 Vilniaus Bankas
12 City Hall
13 Lithuanian Opera & Ballet Theatre
15 24-hour pharmacy
17 West Express
18 Museum of Genocide Victims
20 Bazė
21 Seimas
24 Angaras
25 Gravity
29 Holocaust Museum
32 Lithuanian State Jewish Museum of Vilna Gaon
33 Tourist Information Centre (TIC)
34 Frank Zappa Memorial
39 Vilnius University; Littera
40 St John's Church
42 Mickiewicz Museum
43 St Anne's Church
44 Gero Viskio Baras
45 Church of the Holy Mother of God
46 Lithuanian Student & Youth Travel
50 V002
51 Brodvėjus
53 Contemporary Art Centre
55 Old Town Hall; TIC Branch
56 St Casimir's Church
57 Bix
58 Baltic Travel Service
59 National Philharmonic Concert Hall
60 Holy Spirit Church
61 St Teresa's Church
62 Gates of Dawn
65 Bus Station
66 24-hour Currency Exchange
67 Kelvita Tourist Information
Pieninės gatvė
Ukmergės gatvė
Narbuto gatvė
Saltoniškių gatvė
To Kalvarijų Market
Rinktinės gatvė
Šeimyniškių gatvė
Upės gatvė
Neris River
Kalvarijų gatvė
Juozapavičiaus gatvė
Žalgirio Stadium
To St Peter & Paul Church
Geležinio vilko gatvė
Lukiškių gatvė
Goštauto gatvė
Žaliasis Bridge
Žygimantų gatvė
Vytauto gatvė
A Mickevičiaus gatvė
Gedimino prospektas
Tumo-Vaižganto gatvė
Lukiškių aikštė
Vasario 16-Osios gatvė
Jakšto gatvė
Vienuolio gatvė
Vilniaus gatvė
Tilto gatvė
Savivaldybės aikštė
Žvejų gatvė
To Baltic-American Medical & Surgical Clinic, Medical Diagnostic Centre
Jasinskio gatvė
Kudirkos gatvė
Arsenalo gatvė
Kalnų Park

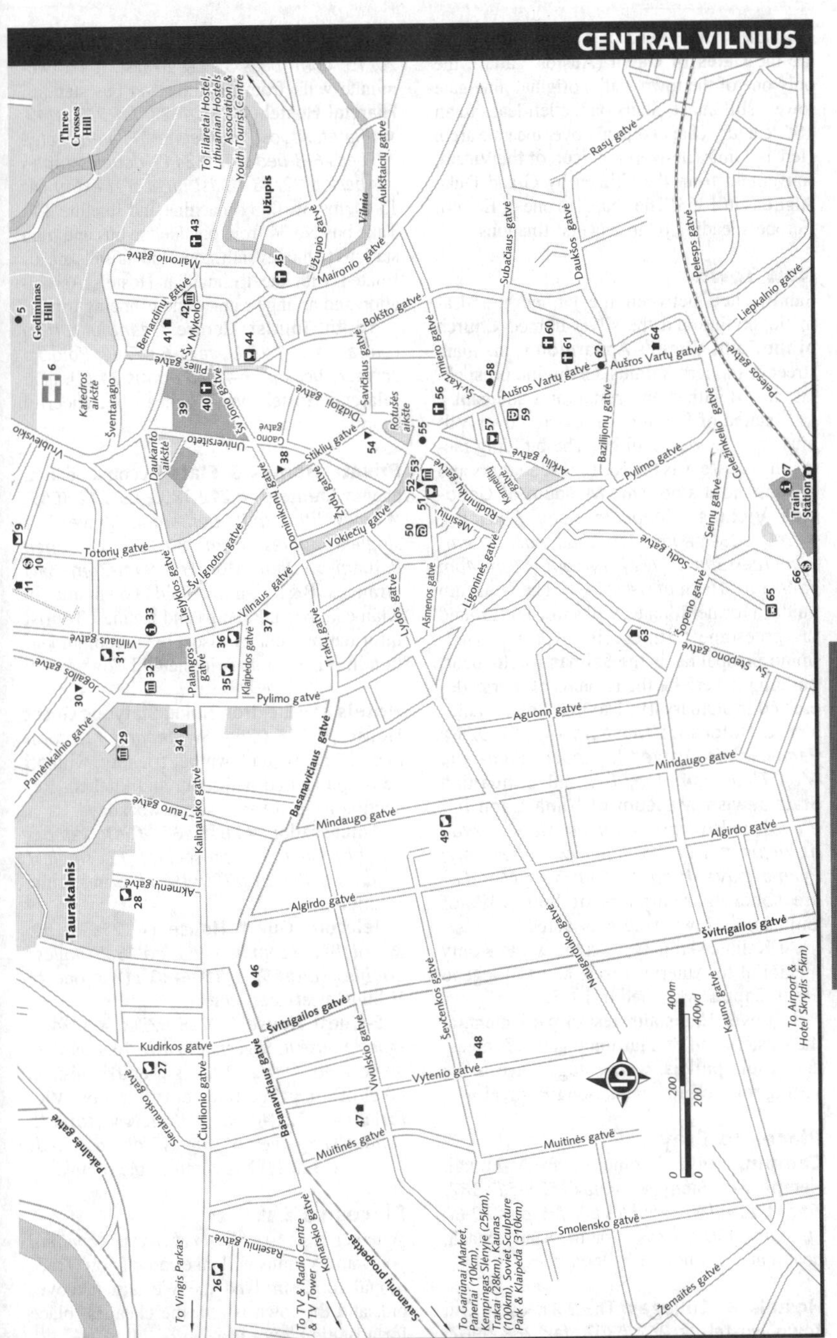
CENTRAL VILNIUS
Three Crosses Hill
To Filaretai Hostel, Lithuanian Hostels Association & Youth Tourist Centre
Užupis
Vilnia
Aukštaičių gatvė
Užupio gatvė
Maironio gatvė
Rasų gatvė
Subačiaus gatvė
Daukšos gatvė
Pelesos gatvė
Liepkalnio gatvė
Gediminas Hill
Bernardinų gatvė
Šv Mykolo
Pilies gatvė
Bokšto gatvė
Savičiaus gatvė
Šv Kazimiero gatvė
Aušros Vartų gatvė
Katedros aikštė
Šventaragio
Vrublevskio
Didžioji gatvė
Rotušės aikštė
Šv Jono gatvė
Gaono gatvė
Universiteto
Daukanto aikštė
Stiklių gatvė
Dominikonų gatvė
Žydų gatvė
Bazilijonų gatvė
Arklių gatvė
Pylimo gatvė
Geležinkelio gatvė
Train Station
Rūdininkų gatvė
Kėdainių gatvė
Mėsinių
Vokiečių gatvė
Totorių gatvė
Šv Ignoto gatvė
Liejyklos gatvė
Vilniaus gatvė
Sodų gatvė
Seinų gatvė
Ligoninės gatvė
Ašmenos gatvė
Lydos gatvė
Trakų gatvė
Klaipėdos gatvė
Palangos gatvė
Šopeno gatvė
Šv Stepono gatvė
Jogailos gatvė
Pamėnkalnio gatvė
Aguonų gatvė
Basanavičiaus gatvė
Kalinausko gatvė
Tauro gatvė
Mindaugo gatvė
Algirdo gatvė
Taurakalnis
Akmenų gatvė
Naugarduko gatvė
Švitrigailos gatvė
Kauno gatvė
To Airport & Hotel Skrydis (5km)
Kudirkos gatvė
Čiurlionio gatvė
Vivulskio gatvė
Ševčenkos gatvė
Vytenio gatvė
Sierakausko gatvė
Pakalnės gatvė
Muitinės gatvė
Smolensko gatvė
Žemaitės gatvė
Raseinių gatvė
Konarskio gatvė
Savanorių prospektas
To Vingis Parkas
To TV & Radio Centre & TV Tower
To Gariūnai Market, Paneriai (10km), Kempingas Slėnyje (25km), Trakai (28km), Kaunas (100km), Soviet Sculpture Park & Klaipėda (310km)
0 200 400m
0 200 400yd
LITHUANIA

At the southern end of Aušros Vartų gatvė are the **Gates of Dawn** (Aušros Vartai), the only one of the town wall's original nine gate towers still intact. Stairs on the left leads to an 18th-century chapel directly over the gate arch. Here is a 'miracle-working' **icon of the Virgin**, souvenired from the Crimea by Grand Duke Algirdas in 1363. The chapel is one of Eastern Europe's leading pilgrimage destinations.

New Town

Sandwiched between the cathedral's dramatic skyline and the silver-domed **Church of the Saint Virgin's Apparition** is the main street of modern Vilnius, Gedimino prospektas, dotted with shops, restaurants and banks.

A statue of Lenin once towered over Vilnius from Lukiškių aikštė. The building facing the square was the KGB headquarters and prison, and it's now the **Museum of Genocide Victims** *(Genocido Aukų Muziejus; ☎ 249 6264; admission 2 Lt; open 10am-6pm Tues-Sun 15 May-14 Sept, 10am-4pm Tues-Sun 15 Sept-14 May)*. The museum guide, a former inmate, will show you around the gruesome torture cells. North of Gedimino prospektas is the **Seimas** (parliament) building, where lie the remains of barricades erected in January 1991 to halt Soviet tanks.

The **Holocaust Museum** *(☎ 262 0730; Pamėnkalnio gatvė 12; open 9am-5pm Mon-Thur, 9am-4pm Fri)* and **Lithuanian State Jewish Museum of Vilna Gaon** *(Lietuvos valstybinis Vilniaus Gaono žydų muziejus; ☎ 261 7907; w www.litjews.org; Pylimo gatvė 4; open 10am-5pm Mon-Fri)* are sobering reminders of how 94% of Lithuania's Jews were massacred.

At Kalinuasko gatvė 1 is the world's only memorial to American rock and roll legend **Frank Zappa**, who died in 1993.

Just over 1km southwest of parliament, at the western end of Čiurlionio gatvė, is pleasant **Vingis parkas**, whose huge stage is the setting for the Lithuanian Song Festival.

Places to Stay

Camping Five kilometres from Trakai, **Kempingas Slėnyje** *(☎/fax 528-51 387; Totoriškes village; doubles 60 Lt, triples 70-80 Lt, suites 130 Lt)* has a sauna, sandy beach, boat rental and hot-air balloon rides.

Hostels & Colleges The 25 beds at **Old Town Hostel** *(☎ 262 5357, fax 268 5967; e oldtownhostels@delfi.lt; Aušros Vartų gatvė 20/15; dorm beds 32 Lt)* go fast. It's a two-minute walk from the train and bus stations. **Filaretai Hostel** *(☎ 215 4627, fax 212 0149; e filaretai@post.omnitel.net; Filaretų gatvė 17; beds 6-8-bed dorms 24 Lt, doubles/triples per person 32/28 Lt, 1st night 5 Lt extra)* has 13 rooms, washing machine and satellite TV. Take bus No 34 from outside the bus and train stations to the seventh stop. Both hostels are affiliated with the Lithuanian Hostels Association and arrange saunas and canoeing trips.

Youth Tourist Centre *(Jaunųjų turistų centras; ☎ 261 1547, fax 262 7742; Polocko gatvė 7; beds in 3-4-bed dorms 24 Lt)*, near Filaretai Hostel, has 16 cheap but cheerful rooms.

Private Homes & Flats Accommodation agency **Litinterp** *(☎ 212 3850, fax 212 3559; w www.litinterp.lt; Bernardinų gatvė 7-2; singles/doubles from 80/120 Lt; open 8.30am-5.30pm Mon-Fri, 9am-3pm Sat)* arranges B&Bs in the Old Town and in Klaipėda, Nida, Palanga and Kaunas. Tourist information centres also book accommodation in private homes in the Old Town.

Hotels The **Elektros Tinklų Statybos Guest House** *(☎ 216 0254; Šv Stepono 11; dorm beds 24 Lt)* is rundown but friendly, with 55 beds and shared bathroom and kitchen. Reception is open 8am to 3pm weekdays.

Ambassador *(☎ 261 5460; e info@ambassador.lt; Gedimino prospektas 12; singles/doubles/suites 240/280/360 Lt)* is in a prime location.

Telecom Guest House *(☎ 236 7150; e hotel@telecom.lt; Vivulskio 13a; singles/doubles/suites 250/300/430 Lt)* is one of Vilnius' best-kept secrets.

E-Guest House *(☎ 266 0730; w www.e-guest house.lt; Ševèenkos gatvė 16; doubles/apartments 180/240 Lt)* is a quirky hi-tech hotel offering free Internet connection. **Victoria** *(☎ 272 4013; e hotel@victoria.lt; Saltoniškių gatvė 56; singles/doubles/quads 192/232/320 Lt)* has comfortable rooms.

Places to Eat

Whether it's curry, *kepta duona* or *cepelinai* you want, Vilnius will take care of you. Traditional food survived the Western takeover bid, and the town is still the cheapest place for a Baltic blow-out.

Fresh milk straight from the cow's udder, honey and smoked eels are just some of the culinary delights to be found at **Kalvarijų market** *(open 7am-noon Tues-Sun)*.

In the Old Town, **Savas Kampas** *(☎ 212 3203; Vokiečių gatvė 4)* does lunch for 10 Lt and has lively night-time dining.

Balti Drambliai *(☎ 262 0875; Vilniaus gatvė 41; meals 15-20 Lt)* is vegetarian heaven. So too is **Sue's Indian Raja/Sue Ka Tai** *(☎ 262 3802; Jogailos gatvė 11/2; meals 40-70 Lt)*.

Who says the English can't cook? **The PUB** *(☎ 261 8393; Dominikonų gatvė 9; meals 13-20 Lt)* serves good old shepherd's pie and fish and chips.

Prie Parlamento *(☎ 249 6606; Gedimino prospektas 46; meals 25-35 Lt)* is a more upmarket, expat haunt. Its divine chocolate brownies, juicy steaks and full English breakfasts cure all homesickness.

Ritos Slėptuvė *(☎ 262 6117; Gostauto gatvė 8; meals 25-40 Lt)* is an underground, all-American diner serving tortillas, steaks and burgers with as much coffee as you can drink.

Amatininkų Užeiga *(☎ 261 7968; Didžioji gatvė 19/2; meals 30 Lt)* serves hearty Lithuanian stews and creamy pancakes until dawn.

For light meals, **Presto Arbata** *(☎ 262 1967; Gedimino prospektas 32a; snacks 3.60-8 Lt; open Mon-Sat)* has salads, frothy coffee and blackcurrant cheesecake. **Čili Picerija** *(☎ 231 2462; Didžioji 5; Gedimino prospektas 23; pizzas 15 Lt)* has 21 varieties of pizza.

Kuba *(☎ 279 0526; Šeimyniškių 3a; dishes by weight, meals 10 Lt)* is a classy canteen.

Entertainment

Bars & Clubs Nightlife begins in Vokiečių gatvė. which, come summer, is awash with young, trendy things enjoying a beer. Aside from Prie Parlamento, which has the popular club **Ministerija**, try hanging out at **Bix** *(Etmonų gatvė 6)*, a favourite among the city's young and fun crowd, or **Gero Viskio Baras** *(Pilies gatvė 28)*. The **Contemporary Art Centre** *(Vokiečių 2)* has a smoky hideout bar filled with arty Lithuanian luvvies.

Or get your dancing gear on for some clubbing. **Gravity** *(Jasinskio gatvė 16; admission 25 Lt)* has happening DJs, exotic cocktails and thumping house until 6am Thursday, Friday and Saturday nights. Dress smart. **Angaras** *(Jasinskio gatvė 14)* moves with live bands and a loud crowd until 6am at weekends. Two bars, local DJs and live music make **Brodvėjus** *(Mėsinių 4; admission 10 Lt)* a relaxed place.

Trendy gay dudes head to **Men's Factory** *(Žygimantų gatvė2)*.

Classical Music, Opera & Ballet The State Symphony, Lithuania Chamber Orchestras and Lithuanian Philharmonic have prestigious reputations. Concert halls include the sublime **National Philharmonic** *(☎ 262 6802; Aušros Vartų gatvė 5)*.

The **Lithuanian Opera & Ballet Theatre** *(☎ 262 0636; Vienuolio gatvė 1)* stages classical productions; bargain tickets cost from 12 to 30 Lt.

Getting There & Away

See the introductory Getting There & Away section earlier in this chapter for international connections.

Air If you are 26 or under, try **Lithuanian Student and Youth Travel** *(☎ 239 7397; Basanavičiaus gatvė 30/13)*. Most major airlines – including **Estonian Air** *(☎ 273 9022)*, **LAL** *(☎ 213 3345; W www.lal.lt)*, **Finnair** *(☎ 233 0810)*, **SAS** *(☎ 239 5500)* and **Lufthansa** *(☎ 230 6031)* – have an office at the airport. **LOT** *(☎ 273 9020)* is at Room 104, Hotel Skrydis at the airport, while **Austrian Airlines** *(☎ 231 3137)* is at Basanavičiaus 11/1.

In town, **West Express** and **Baltic Travel Service** travel agencies arrange flights and check prices. Check the *oro uostas* (airport) on ☎ 230 6666 for departures and arrivals.

Bus The **bus station** *(Autobusų Stotis; ☎ 216 2977; Sodų gatvė 22)* is south of the Old Town next to the train station. Windows one to six are open between 5.30am and 5.30pm. Timetables are displayed on a large board. If you're still confused, head to the **information centre** *(open 6am-9pm)*, with English-speaking staff in the ticket hall.

Selling tickets for international destinations and for ferries **Eurolines** *(☎ 215 1377; W www.eurolines.lt; open 5.30am-9.30pm Mon-Sat, 5.30am-11am & 2pm-9.30pm Sun)* is based inside the main hall.

Timetables change frequently so check W www.autobusai.lt.

Buses to places within the Baltics include the following:

Druskininkai 14.50 Lt, two hours, 125km, four direct buses daily
Kaunas 11.50 Lt, two hours, 100km, about 20 daily (also regular microbuses)
Klaipėda 38 Lt, five to seven hours, 310km, eight daily
Palanga 41 Lt, six hours, 340km, about nine daily
Šiauliai 23 to 27 Lt, 4½ hours, 220km, 12 daily
Trakai 3 Lt, 45 minutes, 28km, about 30 daily

Train The **train station** *(Geležinkelio Stotis; ☎ 233 0087, 233 0086; Geležinkelio 16)* is next to the bus station. There are 13 to 16 daily trains to Kaunas (9.80 Lt, 1¼ to two hours), three to Klaipėda (25.40 Lt, five hours), five to Šiauliai (24.10 Lt, four hours) and seven to Trakai (2.80 Lt, 40 minutes).

Car & Motorcycle Cars and minibuses are rented at **Litinterp** *(☎ 212 3850; Bernardinų gatvė 7/2)* from 210 Lt a day. **Rimas** *(☎/fax 277 6213; ⓔ rimas.cars@is.lt)* has cheap self-drive rental cars from 80 Lt a day. **Avis** *(☎ 230 6820; ⓔ avis@avis.lt; Dariaus ir Girėno 32a)* and **Hertz** *(☎ 272 6940; ⓔ hertz@hertz.lt; Kalvarijų 14)* have offices at the airport.

Getting Around

Vilnius airport is 5km south of the city at Rodūnė skelias 2. Bus No 1 runs between the airport and train station; bus No 2 runs between the airport and Lukiškių aikštė. A taxi to the city centre should cost 15 Lt.

Trolleybuses run from 5.30am to midnight. Bus and trolleybus tickets cost 0.80 Lt from kiosks, 1 Lt when bought from the driver. Validate your ticket by punching it in a machine on the bus or trolleybus. Unpunched tickets warrant a 20 Lt on-the-spot fine. Minibuses shadow most routes; expect to pay about 2 Lt. Check ⓦ www.vilniustransport.lt.

Taxis charge 1 to 1.30 Lt per kilometre. There are ranks outside the train station, in front of the old Town Hall on Didžioji gatvė and outside the Radisson SAS Astorija hotel. The cheapest taxis are those you call by telephone (☎ 215 0505, 261 6161 or 277 7777).

AROUND VILNIUS

Paneriai

Between July 1941 and July 1944, 100,000 people were killed in the Nazi death camp at Paneriai, 10km southwest of central Vilnius. From the entrance a path leads to the small **Paneriai Museum** *(☎ 264 1847; Agrastų gatvė 15; open 11am-6pm Wed-Sat)*. Paths lead to grassed-over pits where the Nazis burnt the bodies of their victims to hide evidence of their crimes.

There are about 20 suburban trains daily (some terminating in Trakai or Kaunas) from Vilnius to Paneriai station (0.90 Lt, 20 minutes). From the station, it is a 1km walk southwest along Agrastų gatvė straight to the site.

Trakai

☎ 528 • pop 6111

Trakai's two lakeside castles were built to fend off German knights. Today the spot between two vast lakes is a popular weekend or day trip. From the train station, follow Vytauto gatvė north to the bus station, then continue north to Karaimų gatvė and the castles.

The **Tourist Information Centre** *(☎/fax 51 934; ⓔ trakaiTIC@is.lt; Vytauto gatvė 69; open Mon-Sat)* sells maps, and books accommodation. **Trakai National Park Information Bureau** *(☎ 55 776; Karaimų 5; open Mon-Fri)* does guided tours and issues fishing permits.

Among the wooden cottages on Karaimų gatvė, at No 30 is an early 19th-century **Kenessa** (prayer house) of the Karaites (see the boxed text 'The Karaites of Trakai'). Check out the **Karaite Ethnographic Exhibition** *(Karaimų gatvė 22; open 10am-6pm Wed-Sun)*.

The remains of Trakai's **Peninsula Castle** are towards the northern end of town, in a park close to the shore of Lake Luka. The painstakingly restored Gothic, red-brick **Island Castle** *(open 10am-6pm daily)* probably dates from around 1400. It stands east of the northern end of the peninsula, linked to the shore by footbridges. The moated main tower has a cavernous central court and a range of galleries,

The Karaites of Trakai

One peculiarity of the Trakai area is the presence of the Karaites or Karaimai, a mixed Judaic and Hebrew sect originating in Baghdad who adhere to the Torah (rejecting the rabbinic Talmud) and who were known for their awesome physical stature. Some Karaites were brought to Trakai from the Crimea by Vytautas around 1400 to serve as bodyguards. Of the 10,000 Karaites left in the world, 200 live in Lithuania (12 families in Trakai).

halls and rooms, some housing the **Trakai History Museum** *(adult/child 8/3.50 Lt)*.

Galvė *(☎ 51 345; Karaimų gatvė 41; beds 24-28 Lt)* is a wooden home in Trakai with lake views.

More than 30 buses daily, between 6.55am and 10pm, run from Vilnius bus station to Trakai and back (3 Lt, 45 minutes). There are seven trains daily (2.80 Lt, 40 minutes).

Druskininkai

☎ 313 • pop 21,700

Spa town Druskininkai, 130km south of Vilnius, is the most famous health resort in Lithuania, but it's the nearby **Soviet Sculpture Park** *(Grūto Parkas; ☎ 55 511; ⓔ hesona@druskininkai.omnitel.net; adult/child 5/2 Lt; open 9am-sunset daily)* that draws visitors. With its defunct Lenins and Stalins and Soviet observation towers, the park has provoked accusations of trivialising Lithuanian history.

There are four direct buses (14.50 Lt, two hours, 125km) daily between Vilnius and Druskininkai. You can ask to be let off at the village and walk the 1.5km to the park.

Central Lithuania

KAUNAS

☎ 37 • pop 415,800

Kaunas has a reputation as a hotbed of post-Soviet mafia activity. Actually, it's a thriving cultural centre with a big student population, a historic old town and fine museums and galleries. The most attractive part is its historic heart, Rotušės aikštė (City Hall Square), between the rivers at the western end of the centre. The new town is focused on pedestrianised Laisvės alėja, farther east. The bus and train stations are about 1km south of the eastern end of Laisvės alėja, down Vytauto prospektas.

The **tourist information centre** *(☎ 323 436; ⓔ turizmas@takas.lt; Laisvės alėja 36; open Mon-Sat)* can help with accommodation. There's a 24-hour currency exchange at **Lietuvos Taupomasis Bankas** *(☎ 322 460; Laisvės alėja 79)*. The **central post office** *(☎ 401 368; Laisvės alėja 102; open 7.30am-6.30pm Mon-Fri, 7.30am-4.30pm Sat)* will assist with telecommunications. **Kavinė Internetas** *(☎ 225 364; Vilniaus gatvė 26; open 10am-10pm daily)* charges 5 Lt/hour before noon (7 Lt afterwards).

Rotušės aikštė

The old **central square** is surrounded by 15th- and 16th-century German **merchants' houses**. The 18th-century white baroque former **city hall** is now the Palace of Weddings and ceramics museum.

In the southwestern corner of Rotušės aikštė stands a **statue of Maironis**, the Kaunas priest and writer whose works were banned by Stalin but who is now Lithuania's national poet. The **Lithuanian Literary Museum** is behind. The square's southern side is dominated by an 18th-century twin-towered Jesuit church. Nearby is the **Lithuanian Sports Museum** *(Muziejaus gatvė 7)*.

Located just off the southeastern corner of the square is the curious 16th-century brick **Perkūno namas** *(House of Perkūnas; Aleksotas gatvė 6)*, built as offices on the site of a temple to Perkūnas, Lithuanian god of thunder. Backing onto the river is Lithuania's biggest church, **Vytautas church** (Vytauto bažnyčia).

Kaunas Cathedral, on the square's northeastern corner retains its early 15th-century Gothic windows. **Maironis' tomb** is found outside the south wall. A reconstructed tower is all that remains today of the 13th-century **Kaunas Castle**.

New Town

Towards the end of the 2km pedestrianised Laisvės alėja (Freedom Avenue) stands a **statue of Vytautas**. The blue, neo-Byzantine **St Michael the Archangel Church** (1893) is on Nepriklausomybės aikštė (Independence Square). Worshippers leaving the church are met with the infamous **Man statue**, in front of the **Mykolas Žilinskas Art Museum** *(Nepriklausomybės aikštė 12)*.

Straddling Donelaičio gatvė, a block north of Laisvės alėja, is Vienybės aikštė (Unity Square). Here the **Freedom Monument** *(Vienybes aikštė)*, dated 16 February 1918 (the day Lithuania declared independence), was erected in 1928, hidden during the Stalin era, and put back in place on 16 February 1989. Nearby, the **Military Museum of Vytautas the Great** *(Donelaičio gatvė 64)* recounts Lithuania's history. Of particular interest is the wreck of the aircraft in which two of Lithuania's greatest modern heroes, Darius and Girėnas (pictured on the 10 Lt note), attempted to fly nonstop from New York to Kaunas in 1933.

Next door is **M-K Čiurlionis Museum** *(Putvinskio gatvė 55)*, with an extensive collection of the symbolic paintings of Čiurlionis (1875–1911), Lithuania's greatest artist and composer. The fascinating **Devil Museum** *(Velnių Muziejus; Putvinskio gatvė 64)* has a bizarre collection of 2000 devil statuettes gathered by landscape artist Antanas Žmuidzinavičius (1876–1966).

Ninth Fort

Built in the late 19th century, the Ninth Fort *(☎ 377 750; admission 4 Lt; open 10am-4pm Wed-Sun winter, 10am-6pm Wed-Mon rest of year)*, 7km from central Kaunas, was used by the Russians in WWI to defend their western frontier against Germany. In WWII the Nazis used it as a death camp. An estimated 80,000 people, mostly Kaunas' Jewish population, were murdered here. Take bus No 35 or 23 from the bus station.

Places to Stay & Eat

The tourist information centre can save you 30% on hotel prices – handy, as there are no hostels. **Litinterp** *(☎ 228 718; ⓔ kaunas@litinterp.lt; Gedimino prospektas 28; singles/doubles/triples from 70/120/180 Lt; open Mon-Sat)* comes to the rescue with B&B rooms. At the yacht club is **Baltosios Bure** *(☎ 370 422; ⓔ jachtklubas@ takas.lt; Gimbutienės gatvė 35; rooms 50-180 Lt)*. Take trolleybus No 5 to the end of the route then walk the 1.5km to the lakeside. **Lietuva** *(☎ 205 992; ⓔ metropol@takas.lt, Daukanto gatvė 21; singles/doubles with breakfast 120/160 Lt)* is a former Soviet dream hotel. **Takioji Neris** *(☎ 306 100; ⓔ takneris@takas.lt; Donelaičio gatvė 27; singles/doubles from 180/220 Lt)* has more upmarket rooms.

Kuba *(☎ 209 932; Laisvės alėja 79; meals 10-15 Lt)* is a split-level canteen and bar. **Miesto Sodas** *(☎ 424 424; Laisvės alėja 93; meals 20-30 Lt)* is trendy, with cool club **Siena** in the basement. **Pas Pranciška** *(☎ 203 875; Zamenhofo gatvė 11; meals 15-25 Lt)* serves delicious Lithuanian dishes in a traditional setting. **Arbatinė** *(☎ 323 732; Laisvės alėja 100; 15 Lt; open Mon-Sat)* will set vegan pulses racing with its dairy/meat-free policy.

Entertainment

Cool hang-outs include **Fortas** *(Donelaičio gatvė 65)*, an Irish bar that is open to the wee hours, and studenty bar **BO** *(Muitinės gatvė 9)*. **Skliautai** *(Rotušės aikštė 26)* has a tiny courtyard filled with local bohemians.

The **Los Petrankos** nightclub *(Savanorių prospektas 124)* has a state-of-the-art sound system for 1500 clubbers. You can have a beer while bowling at **Straikas** *(☎ 409 000; Draugystės gatvė 6a)*.

Getting There & Away

From the **long-distance bus station** *(☎ 409 060; Vytauto prospektas 24)*, **Kautra bus company** *(☎ 409 060)* runs buses to Paris, Minsk, St Petersburg, Kaliningrad, Rīga, Tallinn, Berlin and other destinations in Germany. Other buses travel to Vienna, Warsaw, Prague and Amsterdam. There are many daily domestic connections to Vilnius, Klaipėda and Palanga.

From Kaunas **train station** *(☎ 372 260; Čiurlionio gatvė 16)* about 14 trains make the trip to/from Vilnius daily (9.80 Lt, two hours). Four daily Kaunas-Šeštokai trains connect with the Šeštokai-Suwałki train into Poland. There are also two daily trains travelling to/from Klaipėda (23.40 Lt, six hours), one to/from Rīga (22 Lt, five hours), three to/from Šiauliai (14.10 Lt, three hours) and a daily Moscow train.

There's a summer cruise (from 15 May to 1 October) along the Nemunas River to the **Open Air Museum** at Rumšiškės *(☎ 346-47 392)*. The boat leaves **Kaunas Sea Terminal** (Kaunas Marios Prieplauka) at 11am, returning at 4pm (12 Lt for adults, children under the age of seven go free).

ŠIAULIAI & AROUND

☎ 41 • pop 147,000

Lithuania's fourth-largest city is overshadowed by the legendary Hill of Crosses. But despite this – and plague, fires and battles – Šiauliai has survived to become the eccentric main centre of the northwestern region of Žemaitija.

The main north-south street is Tilžės gatvė, with the bus station to the south and SS Peter & Paul's Church northwards. The main east-west axis is Vilniaus gatvė.

The **Tourist Information Centre** *(☎ 523 110; ⓔ tourinfo@siauliai.sav.lt; Vilniaus gatvė 213; open Mon-Sat)* can arrange excursions to the Hill of Crosses. **Vilniaus Bankas** *(Tilşės gatvė)* and **Šiaulių Bankas** *(Tilşės gatvė)* offer currency exchange. There is a **Bankas Snoras** ATM at the bus station.

Send mail at the **post office** *(Aušros alėja 42)*. **West Express** *(☎ 523 333, fax 524 978; Vasario 16-osios gatvė 48)* handles train and air tickets.

About 10km north of Šiauliai, 2km east off the road to Joniškis and Rīga, the strange **Kryžių kalnas** (Hill of Crosses) is a place of national pilgrimage. It's a two-hump hillock blanketed by thousands of crosses. Some are devotional, others are memorials and a few are finely carved folk-art masterpieces. You can get there from Šiauliai by taxi or bus. There are about 16 buses daily from Šiauliai bus station. Get off at the Domantai stop and walk the 2km track to the hill. Look for the sign 'Kryžių kalnas 2'. A one-way taxi costs about 25 Lt.

Šiauliai boasts some of the country's stranger museums, including the **Cat Museum** *(☎ 523 883; Žuvininkų gatvė 18)* – one of only two in the world! – and the **Water Supply Museum** *(☎ 525 571; Vytauto gatvė 103)*.

Jaunųjų Turistų Centro Nakvynės Namai hostel *(☎ 523 992; Rygos gatvė 36; dorm beds 15 Lt)* has dorm beds. **Šiauliai** *(☎ 434 5549; Draugystės prospektas 25; singles/doubles 60/80 Lt)* is a spectacularly ugly Soviet masterpiece.

Daily services include: Kaunas (17.50 Lt, three hours, about 20 buses); Klaipėda, (20 Lt, 2½ hours, six buses); Rīga (14.50 Lt, three hours, eight buses); Tallinn (8½ hours, one bus); and Vilnius (24 to 27 Lt, four hours, about 12 buses).

From the **train station** *(Dubijos gatvė 44)* each day there are six trains travelling to Vilnius (24.10 Lt, four hours), six to Klaipėda (14.50 Lt, four hours), three to Kaunas (14.10 Lt, four hours) and one to three trains to/from Rīga (2½ hours).

Western Lithuania

KLAIPĖDA

☎ 46 • pop 202,500

Sea port Klaipėda is the gateway to the lush natural beauty of the Curonian Spit. However, Lithuania's third-largest city has some little gems of its own. Most notably it was once the German town of Memel, and some Germanic architecture remains, including the famous bell tower.

The Danės River flows west across the city centre to the Curonian (Kuršių) Lagoon, 4km from the Baltic Sea. The main street, running roughly north-south, is Manto gatvė, which becomes Tiltų gatvė south of the river. The Old Town is centred on Tiltų gatvė. Most of the hotels, restaurants and banks, and the train and bus stations are north of the river.

The **tourist information centre** *(☎ 412 186, 412 181; e kltic@takas.lt; Tomo gatvė 2; open Mon-Sat)* is the traveller's saviour. **Taupomasis Bankas** *(Manto gatvė 4)* offers currency exchange and has an ATM overlooking Teatro aikštė. The **post office** *(☎ 315 014; Liepų gatvė 16; open 8am-7pm Mon-Fri, 9am-4pm Sat)* and **telephone & fax centre** *(☎ 411 033; Manto gatvė 2; open 9am-10pm daily)* are on the north side of the river. Get surfing at **Bitas Internet** *(☎ 411 049; Šaulių gatvė 4)* for 2 Lt per hour.

Things to See

An important landmark on Teatro aikštė (Theatre Square), south of the river, is the 1818 **Klaipėda Theatre**. North of the river, there's a **riverside park**, immediately east of Manto gatvė bridge. Klaipėda **Picture Gallery** *(☎ 213 319; Liepų gatvė 33; adult/child 3/1.50 Lt; open noon-6pm Tues-Sun)* also has a sculpture garden.

The quirky **Clock & Watch Museum** *(☎ 410 415; Liepų gatvė 12; adult/child 4/2 Lt; open noon-6pm Tues-Sat, noon-5pm Sun)* has clocks from Gothic to nuclear. The neighbouring **post office** (1893) has a unique 48-bell carillon inside its bell tower, making it the largest musical instrument in Lithuania.

Smiltynė is just across the thin strait that divides Klaipėda from its achingly beautiful coastal sister, Neringa. It shelters one of nature's best playgrounds, with beaches, high dunes and pine forests. The more adventurous can have a traditional sauna (5 Lt) on the Baltic coast.

Smiltynė's biggest crowd-pleaser (after the nudist beaches) is the **Maritime Museum, Aquarium & Dolphinarium** *(☎ 490 751; e olga@juru.muziejus.lt; adult/student 6/3 Lt; open 10.30am-6.30pm Tues-Sun June-Aug, 10.30am-5.30pm Wed-Sun May & Sept, 10.30am-4.30pm Sat & Sun Oct-Apr)*. Sea lion performances (admission 4 Lt) are at 11.15am and 1.15pm, and dolphin shows (adult/child 10/5 Lt) are at noon and 3pm. Free ferries run every half hour from the old castle port.

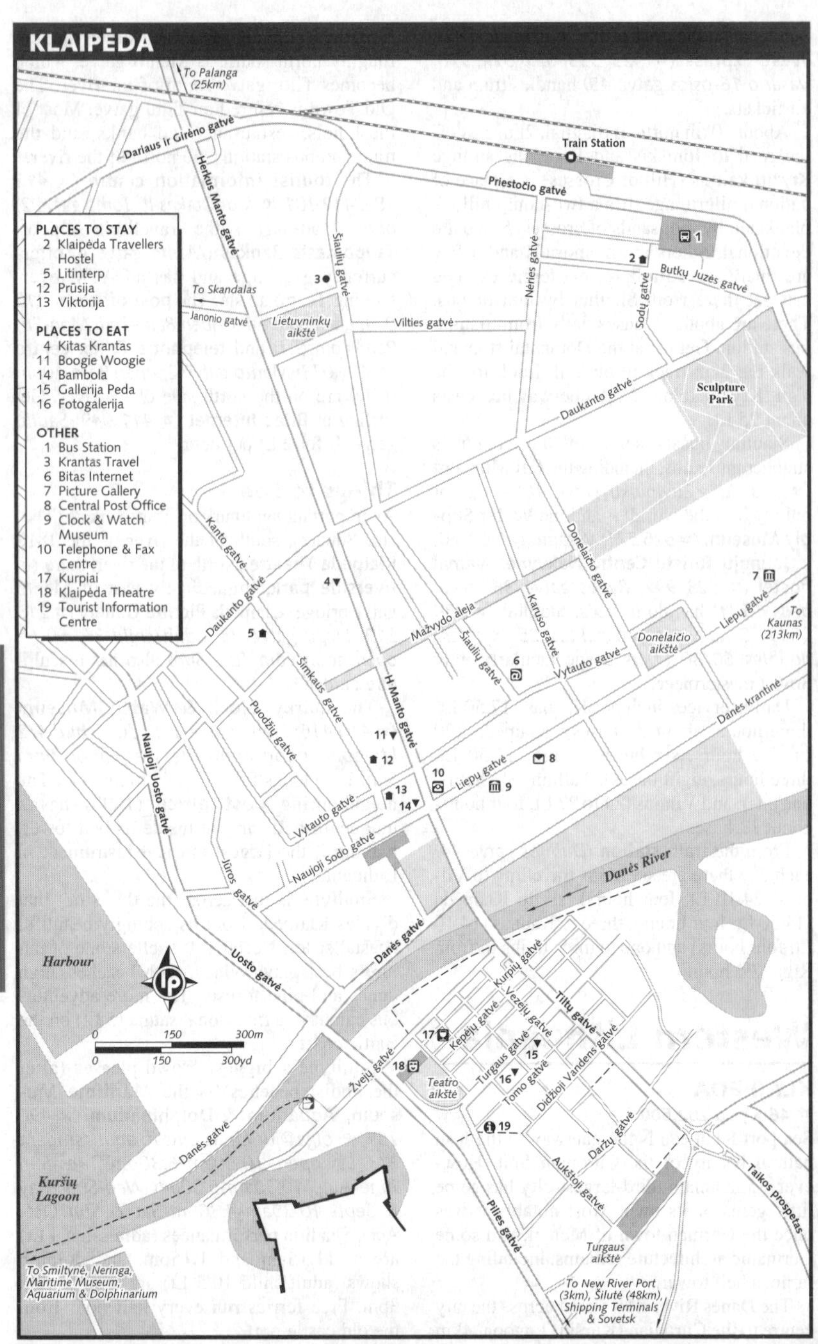
KLAIPĖDA
PLACES TO STAY
2 Klaipėda Travellers Hostel
5 Litinterp
12 Prūsija
13 Viktorija
PLACES TO EAT
4 Kitas Krantas
11 Boogie Woogie
14 Bambola
15 Gallerija Peda
16 Fotogalerija
OTHER
1 Bus Station
3 Krantas Travel
6 Bitas Internet
7 Picture Gallery
8 Central Post Office
9 Clock & Watch Museum
10 Telephone & Fax Centre
17 Kurpiai
18 Klaipėda Theatre
19 Tourist Information Centre
To Palanga (25km)
Train Station
Dariaus ir Girėno gatvė
Priestočio gatvė
Herkus Manto gatvė
Šiaulių gatvė
Nėries gatvė
Sodų gatvė
Butkų Juzės gatvė
To Skandalas
Janonio gatvė
Lietuvninkų aikštė
Vilties gatvė
Sculpture Park
Daukanto gatvė
Kanto gatvė
Donelaičio gatvė
Karuso gatvė
Mažvydo alėja
Liepų gatvė
To Kaunas (213km)
Donelaičio aikštė
Vytauto gatvė
Šimkaus gatvė
H Manto gatvė
Puodžių gatvė
Danės krantinė
Naujoji Uosto gatvė
Naujoji Sodo gatvė
Jūros gatvė
Danės River
Danės gatvė
Uosto gatvė
Harbour
Kurpių gatvė
Vežėjų gatvė
Tiltų gatvė
Kepėjų gatvė
Turgaus gatvė
Tomo gatvė
Didžioji Vandens gatvė
Žvejų gatvė
Teatro aikštė
Danės gatvė
Daržų gatvė
Aukštoji gatvė
Pilies gatvė
Taikos prospektas
Turgaus aikštė
Kuršių Lagoon
To Smiltynė, Neringa, Maritime Museum, Aquarium & Dolphinarium
To New River Port (3km), Šilutė (48km), Shipping Terminals & Sovetsk
0 150 300m
0 150 300yd
LITHUANIA

Places to Stay & Eat

Klaipėda Travellers Hostel *(☎ 211 879; ⓔ jskuodaite@yahoo.com; Butkų Juzės gatvė 7/4; dorm beds 32 Lt)* is a budget option.

Litinterp *(☎ 411 814; ⓔ klaipeda@litin terp.lt, Šimkaus gatvė 21/4; singles/doubles from 70/140 Lt; open 8.30am-5.30pm Mon-Fri, 10am-3pm Sat)* can arrange B&B accommodation for you.

Viktorija *(☎ 400 055; Šimkaus gatvė 2; singles/doubles/triples/quads with shared bathroom 40/60/80/85 Lt, doubles with private bathroom 120 Lt)* is shabby. Up the street, **Prūsija** *(☎ 412 081; Šimkaus gatvė 6; singles/doubles 160/180 Lt)* is cosier.

Fotogalerija *(Tomo gatvė 7; meals 15-25 Lt)*, in the heart of the Old Town, serves light Lithuanian pancakes. **Galerija Peda** *(☎ 410 710; Turgaus gatvė 10; meals 8-18 Lt)* is a stylish restaurant option.

On Manto gatvė there are several eating places. **Bambola** *(☎ 312 213; Manto gatvė 1)* is a fantastic pizzeria, while **Boogie Woogie** *(☎ 411 844; Manto gatvė 5; meals 30 Lt; open to 2am daily)* is hugely popular and serves European fodder. **Kitas Krantas** *(☎ 217 365; Manto gatvė 11; meals 25 Lt)* is where trendy young things sip cocktails.

Kurpiai *(☎ 410 555; Kurpių gatvė 1a)* is Lithuania's best bar, with good food and live jazz every night.

Getting There & Away

Find international ferry connection information in the Getting There & Away section at the start of this chapter. Daily, there are eight buses to Vilnius, 10 to Kaunas, two to Rīga and two to Nida. From Smiltynė one bus travels down the Curonian Spit to Kaliningrad. There are frequent Smiltynė-Nida buses.

NERINGA

☎ 469 • pop 2528

The scent of ozone and pine are at their headiest on this thin tongue of sand, much of which is a 4km-wide national park. Waves from the Baltic Sea pound one side, the Curonian Lagoon laps the other. The winds and tree-felling have sculpted the dunes on the fragile Curonian Spit (Kursių Nerija). The northern half is Lithuanian, the southern Russian, and a road runs the full 97km length into the Kaliningrad Region.

The main settlement is **Nida** (Nidden), a popular resort near the Russian border where amber is washed up on the shores after storms. The German writer Thomas Mann had a house – now a **museum** *(☎ 52 260; Skruzdynės gatvė 17; admission 2 Lt)* – here in the 1930s. Head up Naglių gatvė and climb up the **Parnidis Dune** (52m) to the sundial and take in the stupendous views of the 'Lithuanian Sahara'.

North of Nida is **Juodkrantė** (Schwarzort) where the **Witches' Hill** is not to be missed – fairytale Lithuanian wooden sculptures scattered throughout a fine stretch of forest that is inhabited by elk.

There's a **tourist information bureau** in Nida *(☎ 52 345; ⓔ agilainfo@is.lt; open daily)* and another in Smiltynė *(☎ 391 177; ⓔ kinfo@takas.lt; Smiltynės plentas 11; open Mon-Fri)*.

In Nida, **Medikas** *(☎ 52 985; Kuverto gatvė 14; rooms per person winter 25 Lt, doubles/triples rest of year 120/130 Lt)* is a good option for bargain hunters. In Juodkrantė, **Santauta** *(☎ 53 167; Kalno gatvė 36; singles/doubles/triples 60/90/150 Lt)* has minimalist rooms.

Seklyčia *(☎ 52 945; Lotmiškio gatvė 1; meals 50-70 Lt; open 9am-midnight daily)* has views of the dunes of Nida and the best *kepta duona* in Lithuania. Alternatively, try the **smoked fish outlets** near the bus station. They line the main street, Liudviko Rėzos, in Juodkrantė.

A passenger ferry departs every half hour from the Old Castle Port in Klaipėda for the northern tip of Neringa. Motorists use the vehicle ferry at the **New River Port** *(Nemuno gatvė 8)*.

Luxembourg

The diminutive Grand Duchy of Luxembourg has long been a transit land. For centuries ownership passed from one European superpower to another, and for decades travellers wrote it off as merely an expensive stepping stone to other destinations. While it's true that this tiny country is more a tax shelter for financial institutions than a budget haven for travellers, many people miss out totally by rushing through. Luxembourg's beautiful countryside is dotted with feudal castles, deep river valleys and quaint wine-making towns, while the capital, Luxembourg city, is often described as the most dramatically situated in Europe. And the nation may be small, but it's no Liechtenstein.

> **Luxembourg: the Basics**
>
> 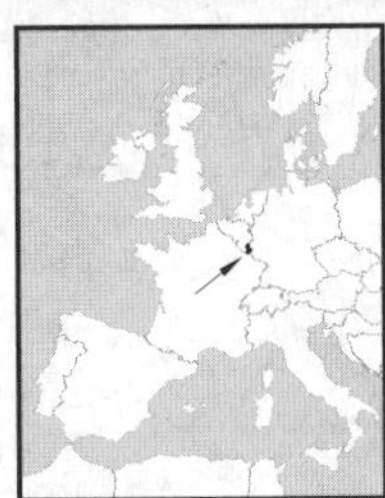
>
> **Local names** Luxemburg, Lëtzebuerg
>
> **Capital** Luxembourg
>
> **Population** 440,000
>
> **Languages** French, German, Letzeburgesch
>
> **Currency** euro (€) = 100 centimes
>
> **Avoid at all costs** Saying that size does matter
>
> **Look knowledgable in the fog by proclaiming** *Ech wees datt e Schloss hei an der Geegend ass.* (I know there's a castle around here somewhere.)

Facts about Luxembourg

HISTORY

By the end of the Middle Ages, the strategically placed, fortified Luxembourg city was much sought after by warring European powers. Besieged, devastated and rebuilt more than 20 times in 400 years, it became the strongest fortress in Europe after Gibraltar.

Listed as a French 'forestry department' during Napoleon's reign, Luxembourg was included in the newly formed United Kingdom of the Netherlands, along with Belgium, in 1814. It was cut in half 16 years later when Belgium seceded and Luxembourg was split between the two countries. In 1839 the Dutch portion achieved independence.

GEOGRAPHY

On the maps of Europe, Luxembourg commonly gets allocated a 'Lux' tag – and even that abbreviation can be too big to fit the space it occupies. At only 82km long, 57km wide, and riddled with rivers, its 2586 sq km are divided between the forested Ardennes highlands to the north and farming and mining country to the south.

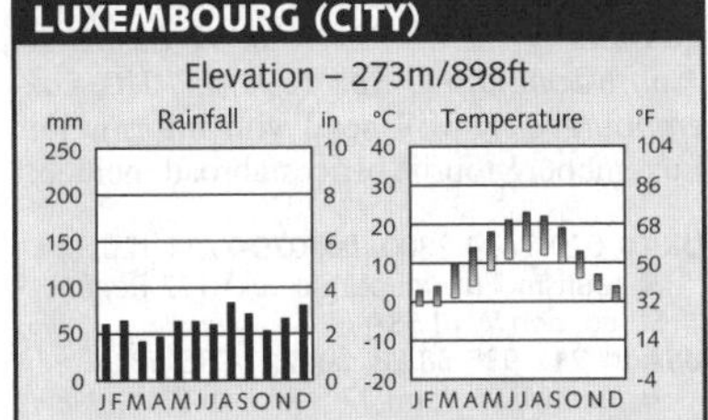

CLIMATE

Luxembourg has a temperate climate with warm summers and cold winters. The sunniest months are May to August, although April and September can be fine also.

GOVERNMENT & POLITICS

Luxembourg is a constitutional monarchy headed by a grand duke. In time-honoured Luxembourg tradition, the throne is passed to the oldest male in the royal family.

POPULATION & PEOPLE

Its 440,000 inhabitants are a confident, proud lot who have no problem with the fact that they live in a seriously minuscule country. A motto occasionally seen carved in stone walls sums up their character: *Mir wëlle bleiwe wat mir sin* – We want to remain what we are.

LANGUAGE

There are three official languages in Luxembourg: French, German and Letzeburgesch.

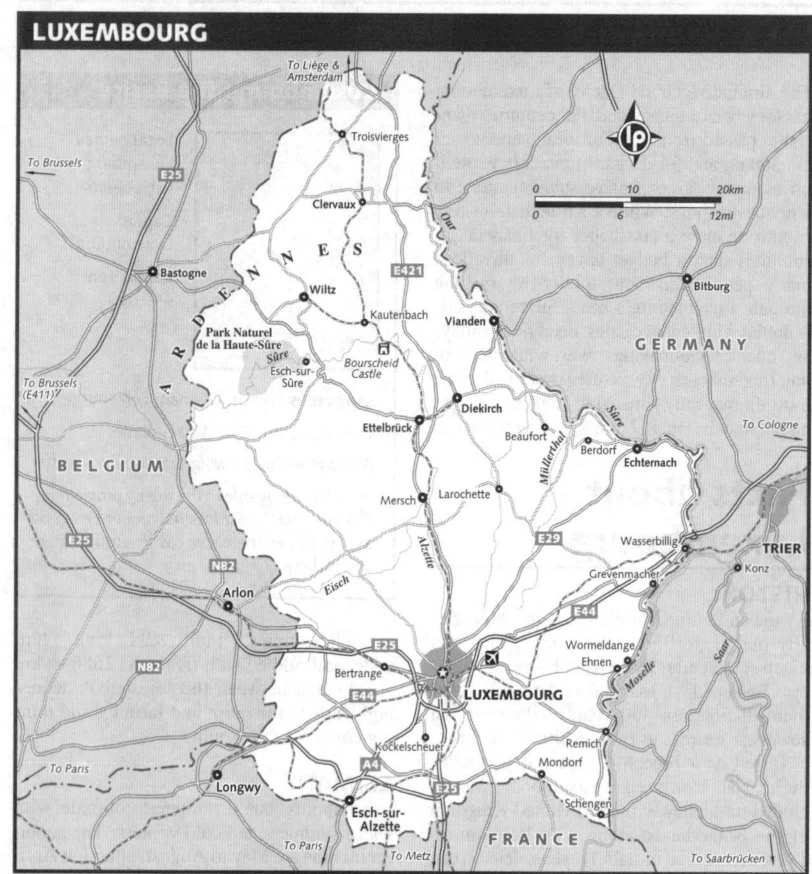

The latter is most closely related to German and was proclaimed as the national tongue in 1984. English is widely spoken in the capital and by younger people around the countryside.

Luxembourgers speak Letzeburgesch to each other but generally switch to French when talking to foreigners.

Facts for the Visitor

HIGHLIGHTS

Luxembourg's highlights include strolling along the capital's Chemin de la Corniche, spending a lazy afternoon visiting wineries along the Moselle Valley, hiking in the Müllerthal region and taking in the expansive view from Bourscheid Castle.

PLANNING

The countryside in spring is a riot of wildflowers and blossoms, summer is the warmest time and, in autumn, wine-making villages celebrate their grape harvests.

TOURIST OFFICES

The **Office National du Tourisme headquarters** (*☎ 42 82 82 1, fax 42 82 82 38;* *e info@ont.lu; PO Box 1001, L-1010, Luxembourg city)* will send you information. Luxembourg tourist offices abroad include:

UK (☎ 020-7434 2800, fax 020-7734 1205, e tourism@luxembourg.co.uk) 122 Regent St, London W1B 5SA

USA (☎ 212-935 88 88, fax 212-935 58 96, e luxnto@aol.com) 17 Beekman Place, New York, NY 10022

VISAS & DOCUMENTS

Visitors from many countries need only a valid passport for three-month visits. Requirements are basically the same as for entering the Netherlands (for more details, see the Facts for the Visitor section in that chapter).

EMBASSIES

Luxembourg Embassies

In countries where there is no representative, contact the Belgian or Dutch diplomatic missions. Luxembourg embassies include:

UK (☎ 020-7235 6961, fax 7235 9734) 27 Wilton Crescent, London SW1X 8SD
USA (☎ 202-265 4171/72, fax 328-8270) 2200 Massachusetts Ave, NW Washington, DC 20008

Embassies in Luxembourg

The nearest Australian, Canadian and New Zealand embassies are in Belgium (see the Belgium Facts for the Visitor section). The following embassies are all in Luxembourg city:

Belgium (☎ 44 27 46 1, fax 45 42 82) 4 Rue des Girondins, L-1626
France (☎ 45 72 71 1, fax 45 72 71 227) 8b Blvd Joseph II, L-1840
Germany (☎ 45 34 45 1, fax 45 56 04) 20–22 Ave Émile Reuter, L-2420
Ireland (☎ 45 06 10, fax 45 88 20) 28 Route d'Arlon, L-1140
Netherlands (☎ 22 75 70, fax 40 30 16) 5 Rue CM Spoo, L-2546
UK (☎ 22 98 64, fax 22 98 67) 14 Blvd Roosevelt, L-2450
USA (☎ 46 01 23, fax 46 14 01) 22 Blvd Emmanuel Servais, L-2535

CUSTOMS

The usual allowances apply to duty-free goods if you are coming from a non-EU country and to duty-paid goods if you're arriving from within the EU.

MONEY

Luxembourg uses the euro.

Banks are the main exchange bureaus and charge a minimum of €3.70 commission. All major credit cards are commonly accepted; ATMs are at Findel airport and in the train station in Luxembourg city. Prices are slightly more expensive than in Belgium. Tipping is not obligatory and bargaining is downright impossible.

Emergencies

In the event of an emergency, call ☎ 113 for the police or ☎ 112 for medical assistance. In the event of a breakdown contact the **Automobile Club of Luxembourg** *(☎ 45 00 45)*.

Value-added tax (abbreviated in French as TVA) is calculated at 15%, except for hotel, restaurant and camping-ground prices, which enjoy only a 3% levy. The procedure for claiming the tax back is tedious unless you buy from shops affiliated with the Tax Cheque Refund Service.

POST & COMMUNICATIONS

There's a €0.45 fee (sometimes waived) for poste restante – letters should be addressed to: Post Office, Poste Restante, L-1118 Luxembourg 2. For making international telephone calls to Luxembourg, the country code is ☎ 352. To telephone abroad, the international access code is ☎ 00. There are no telephone area codes in Luxembourg.

Public Internet access facilities are limited to Internet cafés in Luxembourg city. Expect to pay €1.25 to €3 per half hour.

DIGITAL RESOURCES

Upcoming tourist events in Luxembourg city are listed on the web at Ⓦ www.luxembourg-city.lu/touristinfo. For general information – such as weather, cinema listings, regional events – head to Ⓦ www.luxweb.lu.

WOMEN TRAVELLERS

In the event of attack, contact the women's crisis organisation **Waisse Rank** *(☎ 40 20 40; 84 Rue Adolphe Fischer, Luxembourg city)*.

GAY & LESBIAN TRAVELLERS

Luxembourg's national homosexual and lesbian organisation is **Rosa Lëtzebuerg** *(☎ 021 41 28 12; 252 Ave Gaston Diderich, L-1420 Luxembourg-Belair)*. Attitudes towards homosexuality are quite relaxed. Luxembourg Pride is a small festival held in mid-June.

DISABLED TRAVELLERS

Lifts are not commonplace in Luxembourg, ramps are few, and pavements are uneven. For information it's best to contact **Info-Handicap** *(☎ 36 64 66, fax 36 08 85; 20 Rue de Contern, L-5955 Itzig)*.

BUSINESS HOURS

Trading hours are 9am to 5.30pm weekdays (except Monday when some shops open about noon), and a half or full day on Saturday. Many shops close for lunch between noon and 2pm. Banks have shorter hours: 8.30am to 4.30pm Monday to Friday and, in the capital, on Saturday mornings – country branches close for lunch.

PUBLIC HOLIDAYS & SPECIAL EVENTS

Public holidays include New Year's Day, Easter Monday, May Day (1 May), Ascension Day, Whit Monday, National Day (23 June), Assumption Day (15 August), All Saints' Day (1 November) and Christmas Day.

For a small country, Luxembourg is big on festivals. Pick up the tourist office's monthly *Agenda* brochure for local listings. The biggest national events are Carnival, held six weeks before Easter, and Bonfire Day (Bürgsonndeg), one week later. National Day is held on 23 June; however, festivities take place on the evening of 22 June. In July the Festival Européen de Théâtre en Plein Air et de Musique transforms the town of Wiltz into an open-air stage for theatre, jazz and classical music.

ACTIVITIES

With a 5000km network of marked walking paths, the Grand Duchy is a hiker's haven. National routes are indicated by yellow signposts. Tracks, marked by white triangles, connect the 11 Hostelling International (HI) hostels.

WORK

Seasonal grape picking is possible in the Moselle Valley for about six weeks from mid-September. No permit is needed, but the work is popular with locals.

ACCOMMODATION

In summer it's wise to reserve all accommodation. The national tourist office has free hotel, B&B, camping and farm-stay brochures and will book accommodation for a €0.50 fee.

Camping grounds are abundant, although mainly in the central and northern regions. There are three categories of camping grounds but the bulk fall into the well-equipped 'Category 1' – expect to pay between €3 and €5 per adult.

There are 11 hostels operated by **Hostelling International** *(HI; ☎ 26 29 35 00, fax 26 29 35 03; ⓔ information@youthhostels.lu; 24-26 Place de la Gare, Galerie Kons, L-1616 Luxembourg city)*. Most close irregularly throughout the year, so ring ahead. The nightly dorm rate, including breakfast and sheets, varies from €13.60 to €15.50 for members. Nonmembers must buy a 'welcome stamp' (€2.75 per night) for the first six nights, after which they become an HI member. Many hostels offer rooms for a supplement of €7.50/2.50 per person for singles/doubles.

B&Bs are a rare breed. The few you'll find dotted around the countryside go for between €18 and €22 per person. The cheapest hotels charge €25/40 for basic singles/doubles, including breakfast.

FOOD & DRINKS

Luxembourg's cuisine is similar to that of Belgium's Wallonia region – plenty of pork, freshwater fish and game meat – but with a German influence in local specialities like liver dumplings with sauerkraut. The national dish is *judd mat gaardebounen* (smoked pork with beans).

ENTERTAINMENT

Nightlife outside Luxembourg city is very tame. In summer terrace cafés take over town squares and are the place for people-watching, especially during local festivals.

Getting There & Away

LAND

The Benelux Tourrail pass (see the Belgium Getting Around section) costs €174/116 for a 1st/2nd-class ticket for people over 26 years and €87 (2nd-class only) for those 26 years and under. It's also valid for travelling on national (CFL) buses.

Train services include to Brussels (€24 for a one-way 2nd-class ticket, 2¾ hours, hourly), Amsterdam (€42.80, 5½ hours, hourly), Paris (€39.20, four hours, six trains daily) and Trier in Germany (€7.40, 40 minutes, 11 daily). The **station office** *(☎ 49 90 49 90; open 24hr)* is in Luxembourg city train station.

RIVER

From Easter to September it's possible to take a cruise boat from points along the Moselle to destinations in Germany (Remich to Trier costs €11.50 and takes 4¼ hours). See the Moselle Valley section for more details.

Getting Around

BUS & TRAIN

Luxembourg does not have an extensive rail system, so getting around once you leave the main north–south train line can take time. The bus network (operated by CFL) is comprehensive and the fare system for both train and bus is simple: €1.10 for a 'short' trip of about 10km or less (this ticket is valid for one hour), or €4.40 for a 2nd-class unlimited day ticket (known as a Billet Reseau), which is also good for travelling on inner-city buses. It's valid from the time of purchase until 8am the next day. A book of 10 short-trip tickets costs €8.80 and a book of five Billet Reseau costs €17.60.

More information can be obtained from either the **CFL bus information kiosk** *(☎ 49 90 55 44)* or **train information office** *(☎ 49 90 49 90)*, both inside the Luxembourg city train station.

CAR & MOTORCYCLE

For motoring information contact **Club Automobile de Luxembourg** *(☎ 45 00 45 1; 54 Route de Longwy, L-8007 Bertrange)*.

Car rentals start at about €75 per day (including insurance, value-added tax and unlimited kilometres) for a small Peugeot.

BICYCLE

Cycling is a popular pastime. Bikes can be hired for €20/37.50/75 per day/weekend/week in Luxembourg city. At **Vélo en Ville** *(☎ 47 96 23 83; 8 Rue Bisserwé)* they cost €5 per hour or €12.50/20 per half-day/day (20% off the day rental rate for under-26s). It costs €1.10 to take your bike on a train.

HITCHING

Hitching is not common and it's illegal on motorways.

BOAT

Special train-boat-bus combo tickets (€10.30) are available on weekends (Easter until 31 September) to tour the Moselle Valley. From Luxembourg city, take the train to Wasserbillig, then a boat to Remich and return to the capital by bus. For more specific details ask at the luggage office at the train station in Luxembourg city.

LOCAL TRANSPORT

Luxembourg city has a good local bus network. Elsewhere there is little public transport besides taxis. Taxis cost €0.80 per kilometre plus a 10% night surcharge; it is 25% extra on Sunday.

Luxembourg City

pop 82,000

Strikingly situated high on a promontory overlooking the Pétrusse and Alzette Valleys, the Grand Duchy's 1000-year-old capital is a composed blend of old and new. One of Europe's financial leaders, it's a wealthy city with an uncommonly tranquil air and unusually clean streets.

The historical value of the city's remaining fortifications and older quarters is a major draw.

Orientation

The city centre has three main sections – the largely pedestrianised Old Town, the train station area and the Grund.

The Old Town is northwest of the valleys and based around two large squares – Place d'Armes and Place Guillaume II. To the south – across Pont Adolphe and Pont Passerelle, two impressive bridges that span the Pétrusse Valley – is the train station quarter. The station itself is 1.25km from Place d'Armes. The Grund, or lower town, is a picturesque, cobblestone quarter built well below the fortifications and is now home to some brisk nightlife.

Across the Alzette Valley rise the modern towers of the European Centre (Centre Européen) on the Kirchberg Plateau.

Information

Tourist Offices The **Luxembourg city tourist office** *(☎ 22 28 09, fax 46 70 70; ⓔ touristinfo@luxembourg-city.lu; Place d'Armes; open daily)* offers free city maps, a comprehensive walking tour pamphlet and the handy *Bonjour Luxembourg*, a weekly events guide.

The **national tourist office** *(☎ 42 82 82 20, fax 42 82 82 30; ⓔ info@ont.lu; open daily)*

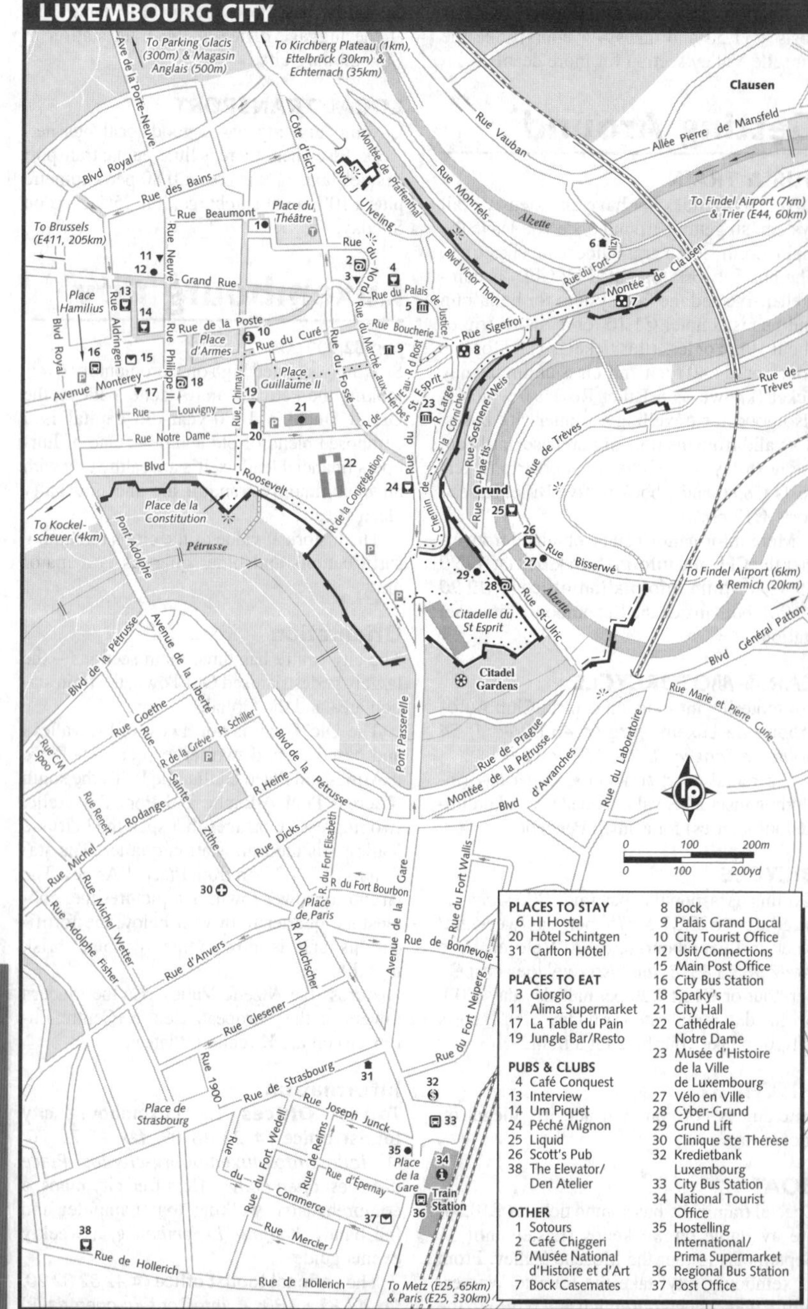
LUXEMBOURG CITY
To Parking Glacis (300m) & Magasin Anglais (500m)
To Kirchberg Plateau (1km), Ettelbrück (30km) & Echternach (35km)
Clausen
To Brussels (E411, 205km)
To Findel Airport (7km) & Trier (E44, 60km)
To Findel Airport (6km) & Remich (20km)
To Kockelscheuer (4km)
To Metz (E25, 65km) & Paris (E25, 330km)
Place du Théâtre
Place Hamilius
Place d'Armes
Place Guillaume II
Place de la Constitution
Grund
Citadelle du St Esprit
Citadel Gardens
Place de Paris
Place de Strasbourg
Place de la Gare
Train Station
Pétrusse
Alzette
PLACES TO STAY
6 HI Hostel
20 Hôtel Schintgen
31 Carlton Hôtel
PLACES TO EAT
3 Giorgio
11 Alima Supermarket
17 La Table du Pain
19 Jungle Bar/Resto
PUBS & CLUBS
4 Café Conquest
13 Interview
14 Um Piquet
24 Péché Mignon
25 Liquid
26 Scott's Pub
38 The Elevator/ Den Atelier
OTHER
1 Sotours
2 Café Chiggeri
5 Musée National d'Histoire et d'Art
7 Bock Casemates
8 Bock
9 Palais Grand Ducal
10 City Tourist Office
12 Usit/Connections
15 Main Post Office
16 City Bus Station
18 Sparky's
21 City Hall
22 Cathédrale Notre Dame
23 Musée d'Histoire de la Ville de Luxembourg
27 Vélo en Ville
28 Cyber-Grund
29 Grund Lift
30 Clinique Ste Thérèse
32 Kredietbank Luxembourg
33 City Bus Station
34 National Tourist Office
35 Hostelling International/ Prima Supermarket
36 Regional Bus Station
37 Post Office
0 100 200m
0 100 200yd

is inside the train station. It provides city and national information and reserves rooms.

At the Luxembourg city train station and at main highway entrances there are interactive touch screens for national information.

Money Near the station, **Kredietbank Luxembourg** *(Place de la Gare)* is a convenient bank. Outside banking hours, exchange offices (with poorer rates) are open at the train station (8.30am to 9pm daily) and at the airport (6am to 10pm daily).

Post & Communications Send mail from the **main post office** *(25 Rue Aldringen; open 7am-7pm Mon-Fri, 7am-5pm Sat)*. There's a **post office branch** *(38 Place de la Gare; open 6am-7pm Mon-Fri, 6am-noon Sat)* near the train station.

For Internet access, there are a few options. **Sparky's** *(☎ 26 20 12 23; 11a Ave Monterey; open 8am-8pm Mon-Fri, 11am-8pm Sat)* is a smoky bar with a handful of terminals for €0.10 per minute. For a bit more atmosphere head to **Café Chiggeri** *(☎ 22 82 36; 15 Rue du Nord; open to 1am Mon-Fri, to 3am Sat & Sun)*. This stylish café has just one computer terminal and charges €2.50 per half hour. A new option in the Grund is **Cyber-Grund** *(☎ 262 39 55; 2 Rue St Ulric; open noon-2pm & 5pm-9pm Tues-Fri, 2pm-5pm Sat)*, a nonprofit organisation working to revitalise the Grund area, which has Net access for €1.25 per half hour.

Travel Agencies Recommended travel agencies include **Sotours** *(☎ 46 15 14 1; 15 Place du Théâtre)* and **Usit/Connections** *(☎ 22 99 33; 70 Grand Rue)*.

Medical Services In the case of a medical emergency call ☎ 112. For a hospital, head to **Clinique Ste Thérèse** *(☎ 49 78 81; Rue Ste Zithe)*.

Things to See & Do

Luxembourg seems made for leisurely wandering. From Place d'Armes, head south down Rue Chimay to **Place de la Constitution** for excellent views over the Pétrusse Valley and the spectacular bridges that span it. Sitting firmly in the background on Place de la Constitution is **Cathédrale Notre Dame**, the city's main church. Architecturally it's an ugly hotchpotch, but it's worth a peek to see the nation's most revered idol is the Lady Comforter of the Afflicted, a small, elaborately dressed statue of the Virgin and child. East along Blvd Roosevelt, the gardens that cover the 17th-century **Citadelle du St Esprit** offer superb panoramas up both valleys and over the **Grund** district, which lies directly below. The Grund is easily reached by a free **lift** dug in the cliff here at Place du St Esprit.

Follow the natural curve north to the **Chemin de la Corniche** – a pedestrian promenade that is hailed as 'Europe's most beautiful balcony' – which winds along to the **Bock**, the cliff on which Count Sigefroi built his mighty fort. The castle and much of the fortifications were dismantled between 1867 and 1883 following the treaty of London. There's not very much left – the main attractions are the view and the nearby entrance to the **Bock Casemates**, an extensive 23km network of underground passages spared from destruction because of the passages' delicate position in relation to the town.

From the Bock, it's just a short walk west to Rue du Marché aux Herbes to the city's **Palais Grand Ducal** *(adult/concession €5.45/2.75; open 15 July-31 Aug)*. The nearby **Place Guillaume II** is lined with formal government edifices.

The **Musée d'Histoire de la Ville de Luxembourg** *(☎ 47 96 30 61; 14 Rue du St Esprit; adult/concession €5/3.75; open 10am-6pm Tues-Sun, to 8pm Thur)* is a state-of-the-art complex covering the history of the city. Take the glass elevator between the six floors to appreciate the rocky geology of this part of the Old Town.

The **Musée National d'Histoire et d'Art** *(☎ 47 93 30 1; Place Marché aux Poissons; admission €5; open 10am-5pm Tues-Sun)* contains a mixture of Roman and medieval relics, fortification models and art from the 13th century up to the present day. However, 80% of it was closed for renovations at the time of research, but the museum was to be completely reopened in November 2002.

Special Events

Two festivals worth catching are: Octave, a Catholic pilgrimage held from the third to fifth Sunday after Easter, which climaxes with a street parade headed by the Grand Duke; and Schueberfouer, a fortnight-long funfair in late August, during which decorated sheep take to the streets.

Places to Stay

Luxembourg city has a dearth of cheap options. The HI **hostel** *(☎ 22 68 89, fax 22 33 60; ⓔ luxembourg@youthhostels.lu; 2 Rue du Fort Olizy; dorm beds €15.50, singles/doubles €23/36; open year-round)* is in a valley below the Old Town. Bus No 9 from the airport or train station stops nearby; otherwise it's a 30-minute walk from the station.

The big, old **Carlton Hôtel** *(☎ 29 96 60, fax 29 96 64; ⓔ carlton@pt.lu; 9 Rue de Strasbourg; singles/doubles €24/41, with shower €44/49)* has clean rooms; breakfast is €4 extra. **Hôtel Schintgen** *(☎ 22 28 44, fax 46 57 19; ⓔ schintgen@pt.lu; 6 Rue Notre Dame; singles/doubles/triples from €65/80/87)* is well located and has decent rooms.

Places to Eat

The **Jungle Bar/Resto** *(☎ 22 58 12; 32 Place Guillaume II; meals from €12)* is good for those on a tight budget. It's relatively cheap, has terrace tables overlooking one of the city's main squares and serves interesting French-African cuisine. **Giorgio** *(☎ 22 38 18; 11 Rue du Nord; pizzas €8-11)* is one of the Grand Duchy's best-known pizzerias.

A convivial café-cum-bakery with non-smoking surroundings is **La Table du Pain** *(☎ 24 16 08; 19 Ave Monterey)*. It extends over two floors, has a pleasant terrace section and serves salads (€11) and half-baguette sandwiches (€4).

For picnic supplies, try either the **Prima supermarket** *(Galerie Kons)*, located opposite the train station, or the **Alima supermarket** *(Rue Neuve)*.

Entertainment

The Grund area is one of the most popular nightlife spots and, when the cliffs are lit up in summer, it's a pleasant stroll down to the taverns that huddle here (open from about 5pm to 1am). **Liquid** *(Rue de Trèves)* has a great line-up of international beers and occasional live music. **Scott's Pub** *(Rue Bisserwé)* is popular with lovers of loud blues and rock on weekends; it's calmer during the week.

In the old centre, **Pêché Mignon** *(17 Rue du St Esprit)* is a trendy café with regular musical and literary evenings. The raw **Interview** *(19 Rue Aldringen)* is popular with a younger crowd while, nearby, the **Um Piquet** *(30 Rue de la Poste)* has a cosier feel. The city's gay scene revolves around lively **Café Conquest** *(7 Rue du Palais de Justice; closed Sun)*. A nightclub worth checking out is **The Elevator** *(54 Rue de Hollerich)*, part of Den Atelier, a popular venue for local and visiting bands.

Getting There & Around

Turn left as you leave the train station to find CFL buses heading to towns within Luxembourg. City buses depart from in front of the train station and from Place Hamilius in the Old Town. Free bus-route maps are handed out at the tourist office.

For car rental try **Autolux** *(☎ 22 11 81; 33 Blvd Prince Henri)* or **Avis** *(☎ 43 51 71)*, **Budget** *(☎ 43 75 75)* and **Hertz** *(☎ 43 46 45)* in Findel airport.

Rent a bike from **Vélo en Ville** *(☎ 47 96 23 83; 8 Rue Bisserwé)* for €5 per hour or €12.50/20 per half-day/day (20% off the day rental rate for under 26s).

Around Luxembourg

MOSELLE VALLEY

Less than half an hour's drive east of the capital, the Luxembourg section of the Moselle Valley is one of Europe's smallest wine regions. More than a dozen towns line the **Route du Vin** (Wine Road), which follows the Moselle from Wasserbillig, through the region's capital at Grevenmacher, past the popular, waterfront playground of Remich, to the small, southern border town of Schengen.

There are only two tourist offices en route: **Grevenmacher tourist office** *(☎ 75 82 75; 10 Route du Vin; open Mon-Fri)*, and **Remich tourist office** *(☎ 69 84 88; Esplanade; open daily July-Aug)*. Wine tasting is the obvious attraction, and there are several *caves* (cellars) where you can sample the fruity, white vintages. Try the **Caves Bernard-Massard** *(☎ 75 05 45 1; 8 Rue du Pont, Grevenmacher)* or **St Martin** *(☎ 69 97 74; Route de Stadtbredimus, Remich)*, which has tours for €2.50 and €2.23 respectively. Both are open daily from April to October.

From Easter to September, it's possible to enjoy a **cruise** on the Moselle aboard the *Princesse Marie-Astrid*. For details contact **Entente Touristique de la Moselle Luxembourgeoise** *(☎ 75 82 75; 10 Route du Vin, Grevenmacher)*.

Wine festivals start in August and they climax with November's 'New Wine' festival in Wormeldange; each village celebrates nearly all stages of the wine-making process.

Remich has several riverfront hotels. The cheapest of these is **Beau Séjour** *(☎ 23 69 81 26, fax 23 66 94 82; 30 Quai de la Moselle; singles/doubles €33/52, with private bathroom €47/70)*.

The region is difficult to explore without your own transport. Trains stop at Wasserbillig only; buses from Luxembourg city go to Grevenmacher (twice daily) from where there are connections to other towns.

CENTRAL LUXEMBOURG

While there's not much to keep you in central Luxembourg, the area can make a good exploration base. The town of Ettelbrück is the nation's central rail junction and from here it's easy to get a train to the nearby town of Diekirch, which is home to the country's main wartime museum.

The Diekirch **tourist office** *(☎ 80 30 23; ⓔ tourisme@diekirch.lu; 3 Place de la Libération; open Mon-Sat, daily July-15 Aug)* is a 10-minute walk from the station.

Diekirch's **Musée National d'Histoire Militaire** *(☎ 80 89 08; 10 Rue Barmertal; adult/concession €5/3; open 10am-6pm daily Apr-Nov, 2pm-6pm daily Nov-Mar)* details the 1944 Battle of the Bulge and the liberation of Luxembourg by US troops. Its excellent collection of wartime artefacts is well presented. With a car, it's well worth taking the winding drive northwest of Diekirch to the 1000-year-old **Bourscheid Castle** *(☎ 99 05 70; admission €3/1.50; open daily Apr-Oct, Sat & Sun Nov-Mar)*.

Diekirch offers a decent choice of accommodation but if you're looking for hostel accommodation you will need to head for the Ettelbrück **hostel** *(☎ 81 22 69, fax 81 69 35; ⓔ ettelbruck@youthhostels.lu; Rue G D Joséphine-Charlotte; dorm beds €13.60, singles/doubles €7.50/2.50; open Feb-Dec)*, which is a 20-minute walk from the station. **B&B Weber-Posing** *(☎ 80 32 54, fax 26 80 06 54; 74 Rue Principale; rooms per person €18)*, in Gilsdorf, is about 2km west from central Diekirch and has large, old-fashioned rooms to offer.

Hourly trains from Luxembourg city to Ettelbrück take 30 minutes; to Diekirch, it takes 40 minutes.

MÜLLERTHAL

The Müllerthal region lies northeast of the capital, based around the old, Christian town of **Echternach**. The area is riddled with fascinating sandstone plateaus and is often referred to as *Petite Suisse* (Little Switzerland), owing to its extensive woodlands. Outdoor enthusiasts love this area – it's great for hiking, cycling and rock climbing.

The Echternach **tourist information office** *(☎ 72 02 30; Porte St Willibrord; open Mon-Fri, daily July & Aug)* is in front of the basilica. There are smaller offices in the villages of **Beaufort** *(☎ 83 60 99; 87 Grand Rue)* and **Berdorf** *(☎ 79 06 43; 7 An der Laach)*.

If you happen to be in Echternach on Whit Sunday, look for the handkerchief pageant in honour of St Willibrord, a missionary who died in the town centuries ago. If not, you can visit the **basilica**, the country's most important religious building, where St Willibrord's remains lie in a white, marble sarcophagus. Immediately west of Echternach, walking paths wind through wonderful rocky chasms and past waterfalls to **Berdorf**, situated on the tableland 6km away, and on to the hidden **Beaufort castle** *(adult/concession €2/1.25; open 9am-6pm daily Apr-Oct)*.

There are two **hostels** *(☎ 72 01 58, fax 72 87 35; ⓔ echternach@youthhostels.lu; 9 Rue André Duchscher, Echternach • ☎ 83 60 75, fax 86 94 67; ⓔ beaufort@youthhostels.lu; 6 Rue de l'Auberge, Beaufort; dorms €13.60)*. Echternach hostel is particularly nice and situated right in the heart of the town. Hotels are plentiful in Echternach. **Aigle Noir** *(☎ 72 03 83, fax 72 05 44; 54 Rue de la Gare; singles/doubles €32.50/40)*, about 40 steps from the bus station, has basic accommodation.

Only buses connect Echternach with Luxembourg city – the trip takes approximately 40 minutes. From Echternach, buses head out to other towns.

THE ARDENNES

The Grand Duchy's northern region is known as the Luxembourg Ardennes. It is spectacular country – winding valleys with fast-flowing rivers cut deep through green plateaus and crowned by castles. Of the three main towns, **Clervaux**, in the far north, is the most accessible; while **Vianden**, in the east, is arguably Luxembourg's most touristy town. To the west is **Wiltz**, the nominal capital of the Ardennes. It's best visited during July when the Grand

Duchy's biggest musical event – an open-air festival of theatre, jazz and classical music – takes over the otherwise quiet little town. Near Wiltz, the tiny hamlet of **Esch-sur-Sûre** attracts a staggering number of tourists simply because of its picturesque location.

Clervaux

Clervaux's **tourist office** *(☎ 92 00 72; open Mon-Fri Easter-June & Sept-Oct; daily July-Aug)* is ensconced in its castle.

The town has two main sights: its feudal **castle**, in the town centre, and the turreted **Benedictine abbey**, high in the forest above. The castle houses Edward Steichen's famous photography collection, **Family of Man** *(☎ 92 96 57; adult/concession €3.75/2; open 10am-6pm Tues-Sun Mar-Dec, 10am-6pm daily Apr-Sept)*.

Vianden

Vianden's **tourist office** *(☎ 83 42 57; 1a Rue du Vieux Marché; open Mon-Fri, daily Apr-Oct)* is in the lower part of town, down by the river.

The town's most noted feature is its impeccably restored **chateau** *(☎ 83 41 08; adult/concession €4.50/3.50; open 10am-4pm daily Oct-Mar, 10am-6pm daily Apr-Sept)*. The chateau's striking position can be photographed from the **télésiège** *(chair lift; tickets €4.20; operates 10am-5pm daily Easter–mid-Oct)*, which climbs the nearby hill.

The **Maison de Victor Hugo** *(☎ 478 66 16; 37 Rue de la Gare; adult/concession €3/2; open 11am-5pm Tues-Sun July-Aug, Easter & Christmas holidays)*, across the river from the tourist office, was home to author Victor Hugo during his exile from France in 1870–71. It opened as a museum in 2002 and houses memorabilia related to his time here.

Wiltz

Built on the side of a small plateau, Wiltz is more spacious, but less picturesque, than Clervaux or Vianden. It's divided in two: the Ville Haute (High Town), where most of the sights are found, is situated on a crest, while the Ville Basse and the train station flank the river below.

The **tourist office** *(☎ 95 74 44; open Mon-Sat, daily June-Aug)* is in the rather sterile **chateau** *(☎ 95 74 42; adult/concession €1.50/0.75; open 10am-noon & 1.30pm-5.30pm daily June-Aug)*, which sits on the edge of the Ville Haute and is home to an exhibition on the 1944 Battle of the Bulge. Nearby, on the main road to the Ville Basse, an unusual stone-sculpted **tower** commemorates those who died or were sent to concentration camps as a result of an anti-Nazi strike in 1942.

Esch-sur-Sûre

The tiny village of Esch-sur-Sûre is off the Wiltz-Ettelbrück road. It's built on a rocky peninsula skirted by the Sûre River and is lorded over by steep cliffs and a ruined castle. It's all very picturesque and, in summer, tourists come here in droves.

A worthwhile detour is to the **Maison du Parc Naturel**, which contains a wonderful working collection of old looms and other textile-making machines, as well as environmental displays.

Places to Stay

In Clervaux **Hôtel du Parc** *(☎ 92 06 50, fax 92 10 68; ⓔ hduparc@pt.lu; 2 Rue du Parc; singles/doubles from €44/70)* occupies an old mansion and has seven presentable rooms.

Vianden's **hostel** *(☎ 83 41 77, fax 84 94 27; ⓔ vianden@youthhostels.lu; 3 Montée du Château; dorm beds €13.60)* sits in the shadow of the chateau. It has rooms with between two and 16 beds. There are heaps of hotels in Vianden, many open from Easter to October only. For something cheap try the friendly **Auberge de l'Our** *(☎ 83 46 75, fax 84 91 94; 35 Rue de la Gare; singles/doubles from €24/40, doubles with private bathroom €50)*. It's by the river and has bright rooms.

Wiltz' **hostel** *(☎ 95 80 39, fax 95 94 40; ⓔ wiltz@youthhostels.lu; 6 Rue de la Montagne; dorm beds €13.60)* is a 1km climb from the train station, behind the Ville Haute.

Getting There & Away

There are trains every two hours to Clervaux from Luxembourg city (one hour). If you want to get to Vianden, catch the Luxembourg city–Ettelbrück train and then take a connecting bus. To get to Wiltz (1½ hours) take the Luxembourg city–Clervaux train to Kautenbach, and another train from there.

Macedonia

Sandwiched in the mountainous centre of the Balkan Peninsula, the Former Yugoslav Republic of Macedonia (FYROM) has often served as a political powder keg. A mix of Islamic and Orthodox influences is evidence of a centuries-long political struggle for cultural hegemony across the region. Despite a chequered history, though, Macedonia managed to avoid altogether recent warfare in the Baltics and has emerged from the turbulent period unscathed.

For travellers Macedonia is a land of contrasts, ranging from Skopje, with its time-worn Turkish bazaar and lively cafés, to the many medieval monasteries around Ohrid. With its fascinating blend of Orthodox mystery and the exotic Orient, together with Lake Ohrid's world-class beauty, Macedonia offers an unexpected variety of opportunities for relaxation and exploration.

Despite military confrontations between Albanian Macedonian militants and Slav Macedonian security forces in the summer of 2001, the situation has eased and the country is quite safe to travel in once more.

Macedonia: the Basics

Local name Република Македонија

Capital Skopje

Population 2.05 million

Language Macedonian

Currency 1 Macedonian denar (MKD) = 100 deni

Avoid at all costs Deriving inspiration from Skopje's architecture

Get ready for the evening by saying *Turi mi uste malku rakija, se osekam sreken vecerva!* (Pour me some more raki, I feel lucky tonight!)

Facts about Macedonia

HISTORY

Historical Macedonia (from where Alexander the Great set out in the 4th century BC) is today contained mostly in present-day Greece. The Romans subjugated the region, and when the empire was divided it became part of the Byzantine Empire. Slav tribes settled in the 7th century. In the 9th century the region was conquered by the Bulgaria. This ushered in a long period when Macedonia passed back and forth between Byzantium, Bulgarian and Serbian rule. The Balkans were overrun by the Ottoman Empire in 1389.

Five centuries later, in 1893 Macedonian nationalists formed the Internal Macedonian Revolutionary Organisation (IMRO) to fight for Independence. Although the nationalist leader Goce Delčev died before the revolt, he has become the symbol of Macedonian nationalism. IMRO continued the nationalist struggle against royalist Serbia, which took over in 1913. In 1943 Macedonia gained full republic status in Yugoslavia.

Over the next 40 years Yugoslavia as a state 'prospered' in comparison with the other Eastern European states. There was a relative freedom of movement of Yugoslavs to and from the country, which was quite open as a tourist destination.

In January 1992 the country declared full Independence. Belgrade cooperated by ordering all federal troops to withdraw, and, because the split was peaceful, road and rail links were never broken.

Greece delayed diplomatic recognition, alleging that the term Macedonia implied territorial claims on northern Greece. The country was thus forced to use the 'temporary' title FYROM for UN admission in 1993. When the USA recognised FYROM in 1994, Greece declared an economic embargo and closed the port of Thessaloniki. The embargo was lifted in November 1995 after Macedonia changed its flag and agreed to discuss its name with Greece. To date, there has been no resolution of this thorny issue.

In August 2001 fighting broke out between Macedonian forces and Albanian would-be separatists. The fighting stopped when both sides agreed to talks that would allow a greater participation by minority groups in the political life of the country. Steps were implemented by May 2002 and tensions have since eased.

GEOGRAPHY

Much of 25,713-sq-km Macedonia is a plateau between 600m and 900m high. The Vardar River cuts across the middle of the country. Ohrid and Prespa Lakes in the southwest drain into the Adriatic Sea via Albania; at 294m, Lake Ohrid is the deepest lake on the Balkan Peninsula. In the northwest the Šar Planina marks Macedonia's border with Kosovo; Titov Vrv (2748m) in this range is Macedonia's highest peak.

CLIMATE

Macedonia's summers are hot and dry. In winter, warm Aegean winds blowing up the Vardar Valley moderate the continental conditions prevailing further north. Macedonia receives a lot of snowfall, though.

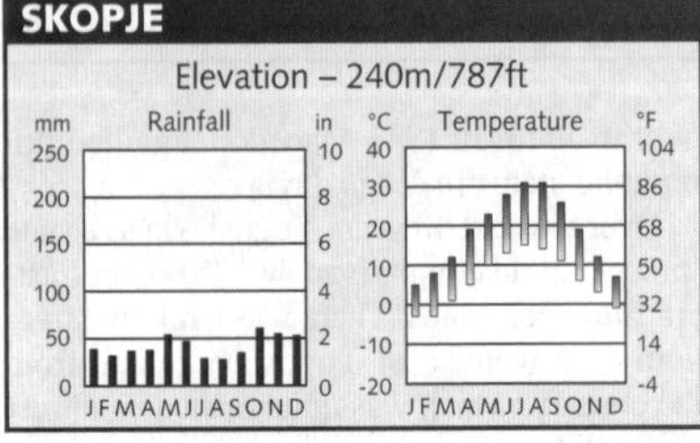

GOVERNMENT & POLITICS

Macedonia is a presidential parliamentary democracy. Elections were last held in September 2002. The main opposition party is now led by former prime minister and leader of VMRO Mr Ljubčo Georgievski.

POPULATION & PEOPLE

Of the republic's two million-plus population, 66.6% are Macedonian Slavs. The largest minority groups are ethnic Albanians (22.7%), Turks (4%), Roma (2.2%) and Serbs (2.1%).

SOCIETY & CONDUCT

Show respect to your hosts by learning a few words of Macedonian. Dress and behave worshipfully in churches and mosques.

Be careful when talking politics: The name issue and Albanian minority question are sensitive topics.

LANGUAGE

Macedonian is a South Slavic language, which is closely related to Bulgarian. The Cyrillic alphabet is used almost exclusively, so it's a good idea to learn it before you go. For useful words and phrases, see the Language chapter at the end of this book.

Facts for the Visitor

HIGHLIGHTS

The Byzantine monasteries of Ohrid, particularly Sveti Sofija and Sveti Kliment, are worth a visit. Lake Ohrid is simply beautiful. The Čaršija (old Turkish bazaar) in Skopje is very colourful.

PLANNING

The best time to enjoy Macedonia is between May and September, though the peak season of mid-July to mid-August could be avoided as most Macedonians take their holidays then. Winters can be cold and wet, though there will always be accommodation in both Ohrid and Skopje.

VISAS & DOCUMENTS

Citizens of EU countries and New Zealanders do not need visas to enter Macedonia, but visas are required of citizens of most countries. For US citizens and Australians the visa is issued free at your port of entry. Canadians and South Africans must buy visas for approximately US$12; these are obtainable either before you go or at the border.

EMBASSIES & CONSULATES

Macedonian Embassies & Consulates

Macedonian embassies are found in the following countries:

Albania (☎ 042-330 36, fax 325 14) Rruga Lek Dukagjini, Vila 2, Tirana
Canada (☎ 613-234 3882, fax 233 1852) 130 Albert St, Suite 1006, Ottawa ON, K1P 5G4
Turkey (☎ 012-446 9204, fax 446 9206) Filistin sokak 30-2/3, Gaziosman Paşa, Ankara
UK (☎ 020-7499 5152, fax 499 2864) 19a Cavendish Square, London, W1M 9AD
USA (☎ 202-337 3063, fax 337 3093) 3050 K Street NW, Washington DC, 20007
Yugoslavia (☎ 011-633 348, fax 182 287) Gospodar Jevremova 34, 11000 Belgrade

Embassies & Consulates in Macedonia

The following countries have diplomatic representation in Skopje (area code ☎ 02):

Albania (☎ 614 636, fax 614 200) ul H T Karpoš 94a
Australia (☎ 361 114, fax 361 834) ul Londonska 11b
Bulgaria (☎ 116 320, fax 116 139) ul Zlatko Šnajder 3
Canada (☎ 125 228, fax 122 681) ul Mitropolit Teodosie Gologanov 104
Germany (☎ 110 507, fax 117 713) ul Dimitri Čupovski 26
Greece (☎ 130 198, fax 115 718) ul Borka Talevski 6
Turkey (☎ 113 270, fax 117 024) ul Slavej Planina bb
UK (☎ 116 772, fax 117 005) ul Dimitri Čupovski 26
USA (☎ 116 180, fax 117 103) Bulevar Ilindenska
Yugoslavia (☎ 129 298, fax 129 427) Pitu Guli 8

CUSTOMS

Customs checks are generally cursory, though travellers with private cars may attract attention on land borders.

MONEY

Macedonian denar (MKD) notes come in denominations of 10, 50, 100, 500, 1000 and 5000, and there are coins of one, two and five denar. The denar is nonconvertible outside Macedonia. Restaurants, hotels and some shops will accept payment in euros (usually) and US dollars (sometimes); prices are often quoted in these currencies.

Conversion rates for major currencies are listed below:

country	unit		denar
Australia	A$1	=	37MKD
Canada	C$1	=	43.30MKD
Eurozone	€1	=	61MKD
Japan	¥100	=	52MKD
NZ	NZ$1	=	27.15MKD
UK	UK£1	=	99.20MKD
USA	US$1	=	69MKD

Small, private exchange offices throughout central Skopje and Ohrid exchange cash for a rate that is only slightly better than what you can get at the banks, but banks cash travellers cheques as well. A handful of ATMs can be found in central Skopje; these offer the best exchange rates.

Except for accommodation in Skopje, Macedonia is not an expensive country. If you stay in a private room in Skopje, you might keep costs to 1800MKD to 2100MKD a day; outside Skopje, frugal travellers may spend 1200MKD to 1500MKD per day.

It is common practice in Macedonia to round up restaurant bills and taxi fares to the nearest convenient figure.

Emergencies

For urgent service you should call the following countrywide numbers for ambulance ☎ 94, police ☎ 92 and highway assistance ☎ 987. Roadside assistance is ☎ 987.

POST & COMMUNICATIONS

Mail services to and from Macedonia are efficient. Poste-restante services available at the major post offices.

Macedonia's country code is ☎ 389. Long-distance phone calls cost less at main post offices than in hotels. Drop the initial zero in city codes when calling Macedonia from abroad. For outgoing calls the international access code in Macedonia is ☎ 99. You can purchase phonecards in 100- (200MKD), 200- (300MKD), 500- (650MKD), or 1000- (1250MKD) unit denominations from post offices. You can often make cheap international phone calls at Internet cafés, which abound in Skopje and Ohrid.

DIGITAL RESOURCES

Virtual Macedonia at W www.vmacedonia.com has useful background and practical information.

BOOKS

The Lonely Planet *Mediterranean Europe phrasebook* will help with the language.

WOMEN TRAVELLERS

Other than possible cursory interest from men, travel is hassle-free and easy.

GAY & LESBIAN TRAVELLERS

Given homosexuality's tenuous social acceptability in Macedonia, it's probably best for visitors to maintain a low profile.

DISABLED TRAVELLERS

Few public buildings or streets have facilities for wheelchairs, but some newer buildings provide wheelchair ramps.

DANGERS & ANNOYANCES

Travellers should be on the lookout for pickpockets in bus and train stations.

BUSINESS HOURS

Businesses are generally open 8am to 8pm on weekdays and 8am to 2pm Saturday.

PUBLIC HOLIDAYS & SPECIAL EVENTS

Public holidays in Macedonia are New Year (1 and 2 January), Orthodox Christmas (7 January), International Woman's Day (8 March), Easter Monday and Tuesday (March/April), Labour Day (1–2 May), Sts Cyril and Methodius Day (24 May), Ilinden or Day of the 1903 Rebellion (2 August), Republic Day (8 September) and 1941 Partisan Day (11 October).

ACTIVITIES

Macedonia's top ski resort is Popova Šapka (1845m), on the southern slopes of Šar Planina west of Tetovo near the border with Kosovo. Mavrovo in western Macedonia comes a close second. Hiking in any of the three national parks (Galičica and Pelister in the south, and Mavrovo) is a good way to get to know the countryside.

ACCOMMODATION

Skopje's hotels are expensive, but there are camping grounds and private-room agencies in Ohrid and Skopje. Skopje's convenient HI hostel is open all year. Beds are available at student dormitories in Skopje in summer.

FOOD & DRINKS

Turkish-style grilled mincemeat is available almost everywhere and there are self-service cafeterias in most towns for the less adventurous. Balkan *burek* (cheese or meat pie) and yogurt makes for a cheap breakfast. Look out for a sign sporting *burekdžilnica* (burek shop). Macedonian *tavče gravče* (beans in a skillet) and Ohrid trout, which is priced according to weight, are also worth looking out for.

Other dishes are *teleška čorba* (veal soup), *riblja čorba* (fish soup), *čevapčinja* (kebabs), *mešena salata* (mixed salad) and the *šopska salata* (mixed salad with grated white cheese).

Skopsko Pivo is the local beer. It's strong and reasonably cheap. There are a good number of commercially produced wines of average to better quality. The national firewater is *rakija,* a strong distilled spirit made from grapes. *Mastika,* an ouzo-like spirit, is also popular.

ENTERTAINMENT

Entertainment for Macedonia's youth consists of hanging out in smart, smoky cafés and bars. Live traditional Macedonian music can often be heard in restaurants and Skopje has some fine jazz and rock bars.

Getting There & Away

AIR

A host of airlines services Skopje's **Petrovac Airport** *(☎ 02-235 156)*. Any of the innumerable travel agencies in Skopje or Ohrid can book flights.

LAND

Macedonia is surrounded by land borders with four countries – Greece, Albania, Bulgaria and Yugoslavia – and one UN-monitored territory, Kosovo. Access is generally trouble-free and unrestricted, though there may still be some tension at the Debar crossing with Albania. The Lake Ohrid crossings with Albania are no problem. Visas are not necessary for travel to Kosovo.

Bus

Skopje has two international bus stations: one is next to the City Museum, while the other station is on Kej 13 Noemvri next to the river. Buses travel to Sofia (640MKD, six hours, three times each day), İstanbul (1860MKD, 14 hours, three to four every day), Belgrade (800MKD, six hours, three times daily), Frankfurt (6100MKD, 24 hours, once a week) and Zagreb (2560MKD, 15 hours, four a week). Buses also travel to Budapest, Vienna, and Sarajevo.

Buses between Skopje and Prishtina, the capital of Kosovo, are fairly frequent. To/from Albania you can travel between Tetovo and Tirana by bus (five to six hours, two per day), or walk across the border at Sveti Naum (see the Ohrid section for details) or Kafa San.

Train

From Skopje's grim and dim train station trains run between Skopje and Belgrade via Niš (1209MKD, eight to nine hours, twice daily). Sleepers are available. One train goes daily to Ljubljana in Slovenia (2690MKD, 12 hours) Two trains run daily between Skopje and Thessaloniki (700MKD, six hours) – one at 7.15am and the other at 5.18pm. Note that Thessaloniki in Macedonian is 'Solun'.

You will have to understand Cyrillic to make any sense of timetables. The staff at the Information desk will be of limited use so come prepared with your phrasebook.

Car & Motorcycle

There are several main highway border crossings into Macedonia from neighbouring countries. You will need a green card endorsed for Macedonia to bring a car into the country.

Taxi

There is at least one enterprising international taxi driver who offers transport to Thessaloniki (€120, up to four persons) and Sofia (€85, up to four persons) from Skopje or the Kosovo border. Contact **Sašo Trajkovski** *(☎ 070 279 449; ⓔ saso_taxi@yahoo.com)*. The Thessaloniki service is a through-run, while the Sofia service involves a pre-arranged change of taxi at the border.

DEPARTURE TAX

The airport departure tax at Skopje and Ohrid is about US$18; this is normally included in your ticket.

Getting Around

Bus travel is well developed in Macedonia with frequent services from Skopje to Ohrid. The domestic bus fleet is getting old and creaky, but it is still serviceable.

Rail destinations include Bitola; Kichevo, in the west of the country; Veles, south of Skopje; Tabanovce, on the border with Yugoslavia; and Gevgelija, on the Greek border north of Thessaloniki.

Skopje is awash with rental-car agencies, from the large ones (Hertz and Avis) to the smaller local companies. The tourist office has a complete listing.

A quick way of getting around the country if buses are not convenient is by taxi, especially if there are two or more to share the cost. A half-hour trip should cost around 350MKD. Taxis are a convenient way to get to Kosovo:

640MKD will get you to the Macedonia-Kosovo border, where taxis are waiting on the other side to whisk you to Prishtina.

Skopje Скопје

☎ 02 • postcode 1000 • pop 600,000

OK, so Skopje isn't a particularly attractive place. However, chalk it up to both a devastating earthquake that destroyed most of the city in the early 1960s and the fact that a small regional town of former Yugoslavia has been forced into the role of national capital. Skopje does boast a flourishing restaurant and nightlife scene and a busy bazaar, but that's about it.

Strategically set on the Vardar River Skopje is at a crossroads of Balkan routes, almost midway between Tirana and Sofia. Thessaloniki, Greece, is 260km southeast. Most of central Skopje is a pedestrian zone, with the 15th-century Turkish **Kamen Most** (stone bridge) over the Vardar River linking the Old and new towns. South of the bridge is Ploštad Makedonija (Macedonia Square), which leads into ul Makedonija leading south. The train station is a 15-minute walk southeast of the stone bridge. The domestic bus station is just north of the stone bridge. Further north is Čaršija, the old Turkish bazaar.

Information

The poorly equipped **tourist information office** *(☎ 116 854; open Mon-Sat)* has rather indifferent staff who may or who may not speak English.

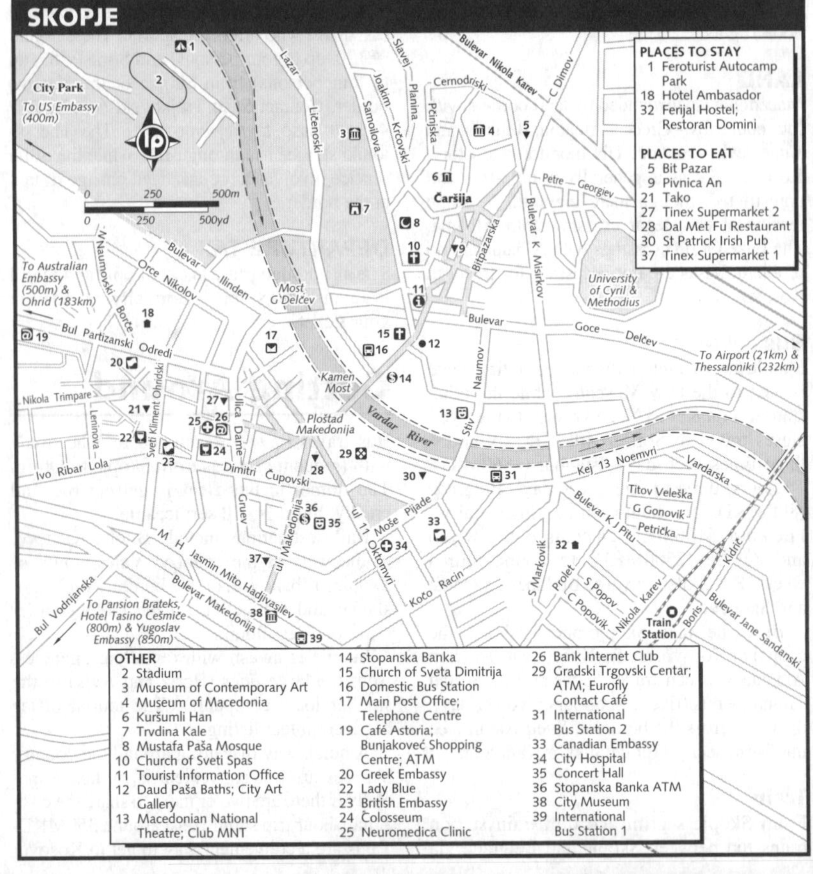

There are many private exchange offices scattered throughout the Old and new towns where you can change your cash at good rates. Skopje has a limited number of ATMs, including one in the Bunjakoveć Shopping Centre, two in the Gradksi Trgovski Centar off Ploštad Makedonija and another at the Stopanska Banka on ul Makedonija.

The **telephone centre** *(open 24hr)*, which is in the **main post office** *(☎ 141 141; ul Orce Nikolov 1; open 7am-7.30pm Mon-Sat, 7.30am-2.30pm Sun)*, is 75m north of Ploštad Makedonija, along the river.

There are at least three Internet cafés in the central business district. The newest (and most expensive) is smoke-free **Contact Café** *(☎ 296 365; 2nd Floor, Gradksi Trgovski Centar; 120MKD per hour)*. The **Bank Internet Club** *(☎ 221 133; ul Dame Gruev 9; 60MKD per hour)* is quite modern and efficient. Oldest of the bunch is **Café Astoria** *(Bunjakoveć Centar; bul Partizanski Odredi 27a; 100MKD per hour)*.

Skopje abounds with travel agencies. A good bet for buying airline tickets is the modern **Eurofly** *(☎ 136 619, fax 136 320; 1st Floor, Gradksi Trgovski Centar)*, where ticket prices are listed boldly by the door in both euros and US dollars.

For medical attention, try the **city hospital** *(☎ 130 111; cnr ul 11 Oktomvri & Moše Pijade)* or the **Neuromedica private clinic** *(☎ 222 170; ul Partizanski 3-1-4)*.

Things to See

There is very little of interest in the new town, with the bizarre exception of the **old train station**, with its **clock** frozen at 5.17 on the morning of 27 July 1963, the moment the earthquake struck.

Walk north from the Turkish bridge into the Old Town and you'll see the **Daud Paša Baths** (1466) on the right, once the largest Turkish baths in the Balkans. The **City Art Gallery** *(☎ 133 102; open 9am-3pm, Tues-Sun)* now occupies its six domed rooms. Almost opposite this building is the functioning Orthodox church of **Sveta Dimitrija**.

North again is **Čaršija**, the old market area. Steps on the left lead to the tiny **Church of Sveti Spas** *(☎ 163 812; 60MKD; open 9am-4pm Tues-Fri, 9am-1pm Sat-Sun)*, with a finely carved iconostasis created in 1824. It's half buried, because when it was constructed no church was allowed to be higher than a mosque. In the courtyard is the **Tomb and Museum of Goce Delčev**, killed by the Turks in 1903.

Beyond the church is the **Mustafa Paša Mosque** *(☎ 117 412)*, with an earthquake-cracked dome. It was built in 1492 In the park across the street are the ruins of the city fort, **Tvrdina Kale**, with an 11th-century Cyclopean wall and good views of Skopje. Higher on the same hill is the **Museum of Contemporary Art** *(☎ 117 735; Samoiliva bb; admission 100MKD; open 9am-3pm Tues-Sun)*.

The lane on the north side of Mustafa Paša Mosque leads back down to Čaršija and the **Museum of Macedonia** *(☎ 116 044; Čurčiska 86; 100MKD; open 9am-3pm)*. Its large collection covers the history of the region fairly well, but explanations are only in Macedonian. The museum is housed in the modern white building behind the **Kuršumli Han** (1550), a caravanserai or inn used by traders during the Turkish period. Skopje's old **Oriental bazaar district** is among the largest and most colourful of its kind left in Europe.

Places to Stay

Accommodation prices are high. The **tourist information office** *(☎ 116 854)* can theoretically arrange rooms in **private homes** starting at 1150MKD per person, but in practice they are not too helpful. Insist on something near the centre.

You can pitch a tent at **Feroturist Autocamp Park** *(☎ 228 246, fax 162 677; sites per tent & adult around 200MKD; open Apr–mid-Oct)*, just a 15-minute walk upstream from the Turkish stone bridge along the river's right (south) bank.

Situated not far from the train station, the HI **Ferijal Hostel** *(☎ 114 849, fax 165 029; ul Prolet 25; singles members/nonmembers 1280/1590MKD, doubles per person 935/1280MKD; open 24hr year-round)* has very tidy and clean, air-conditioned individual rooms. Breakfast is included. Tidy, clean **Pansion Brateks** *(☎ 176 606, 070 243 232; ul Aco Karomanov 3; singles/doubles 1920/3200MKD)*, in a pleasant neighbourhood near the Yugoslav embassy, is a 20-minute walk to the centre. The **Hotel Ambasador** *(☎ 215 510, fax 121 383; ul Pirinska 36; singles/doubles 2800/4340MKD)*, next to the Russian embassy, has simple but pleasant rooms; breakfast is included in the rates.

The expansive **Hotel Tasino Češmiče** *(☎/fax 177 333, 178 329; ul Belgradska 28; singles/doubles 4400/6300MKD)* is south of the city centre. It has decent, if small, rooms with a fridge, TV and phone, and prices include breakfast.

Places to Eat

The **Bit Pazar** next to the Čaršija is a colourful and lively outdoor market. There are two well-stocked **Tinex Supermarkets** *(ul Dame Gruev • ul Makedonija 3)*.

The smart but budget-priced **Restoran Domini** *(☎ 115 519; ul Prolet 5; snacks 120MKD)*, in the basement of the Ferijal Hostel, is an excellent choice.

St Patrick Irish Pub *(☎ 220 431; Kej 13 Noemvri; mains 280MKD)* is a plush, wood-clad establishment serving full Irish breakfasts from 7.30am onwards and meals such as beef in Guinness or Gaelic steak. A pint of very passable Irish ale goes for 180MKD.

From the bridge, **Dal Met Fu Restaurant** *(☎ 112 482; Ploštad Makedonija)* is fairly obvious on the south side of the main square. This place is good for pizza and pasta.

Tako *(☎ 114 808; Sveti Kliment Ohridski; meals 45-75MKD)* is a small smoke-free spot for burritos, fajitas and other Mexican delicacies. It's fast and cheap and has an English-language menu.

Pivnica An *(☎ 212 111; Čaršija; mains 270-300MKD)*, nearby, is a beer house with a wide range of traditional Macedonian dishes. It is an atmospheric place for a relaxing evening meal and is popular with the expat crowd.

Entertainment

Check the **Concert Hall** *(ul Makedonija 12)* for performances. **Club MNT** *(☎ 220 767)*, downstairs below the Macedonian National Theatre, cranks up at around 10pm. The kingpin of the disco scene is **Colosseum** *(Dimitri Čupovski)*. Live jazz, blues and rock music can be heard at **Lady Blue** *(cnr Ivo Ribar Lola & Sveti Kliment Ohridski)*.

The liveliest expat bar is without doubt **St Patrick Irish Pub** (see Places to Eat earlier).

Getting There & Away

The slightly chaotic domestic **bus station** *(☎ 236 254)* is on the north side of the river close to the walls of the Trvdina Kale. Buses to all domestic destinations as well as Kosovo depart from here.

There are two bus routes from Skopje to Lake Ohrid: the 167km route through Tetovo (300MKD, three hours) is much faster and more direct than the 261km route that goes via Veles and Bitola. Book a seat to Ohrid the day before if you're travelling in high season (May to August).

See Getting There & Away for details on international bus and train travel.

Getting Around

There are no buses to the airport, so you'll be at the mercy of the airport 'taxi mafia', which charges 1290MKD to 2200MKD for a ride into town. Do not get into a taxi that has no official taxi sign. It's better to request your accommodation to help arrange pick-up in advance. Taxis to the airport from the centre cost about 660MKD.

Inner-suburban city buses in Skopje cost 15MKD to 30MKD per trip, depending on what kind of bus and whether you buy your ticket on the bus or in advance.

Skopje's taxi system is excellent – once you get beyond the airport area. The first few kilometres are a flat 50MKD, then it's 15MKD per kilometre.

Southern Macedonia

OHRID ОХРИД

☎ 046 • pop 50,000

Ohrid is *the* Macedonian tourist mecca and is popular with visitors from Macedonia and neighbouring countries. Some 30 'cultural monuments' keep visitors busy. The steep, narrow, cobbled streets of the Old Town make for some pleasant, if occasionally strenuous walking, while the long lakeside promenade is popular with walkers and joggers. A Roman amphitheatre has been restored in the Old Town, while a scattering of Byzantine churches, most with vivid frescoes, make for a couple of days of fascinating sightseeing.

Under Byzantium, Ohrid became the episcopal centre of Macedonia. The archbishopric of Ohrid's Independence from the Serbian Orthodox Church in 1967 was an important step on the road to nationhood.

Lake Ohrid, a natural tectonic lake that is shared with Albania, is the deepest lake in the Balkans (294m) and one of the world's oldest. Nestled amid mountains at an altitude of 695m, the Macedonian section of the lake is the more beautiful, with striking vistas of the water from the beach and hills.

Orientation & Information

The Old Town of Ohrid is easy to get around on foot. To the south is Lake Ohrid. There's no official tourist office, but travel agencies provide information and have assorted guided tours. **Generalturist** *(☎ 261 071, fax 260 415; ul Partizanska 6)* is a good place to start. If you would like a personal guide try the voluble **Jana Poposka** *(☎ 263 875)*, who speaks good English and knows Ohrid thoroughly. She is usually found at the church of Sveti Kliment.

Ohridska Banka *(ul Sveti Kliment Ohridski)* changes money and offers Visa advances, less the commission. Exchange bureaus have proliferated, though few post exchange rates. You can also change money at the **post office**. There is one ATM, at the **Balkanska Banka** *(ul Dimitar Vlahov)*.

The **telephone centre** *(open 7am-8pm Mon-Sat, 9am-noon & 6pm-8pm Sun)* is round the corner from the modern **post office**. You can make overseas calls for 15MKD per minute at **Cybercity** *(☎ 231 620; Ⓦ www.cybercity.com.mk; 3rd floor, ul Sveti Kliment Ohridski)* and it also offers Internet access for 60MKD per hour. On the same floor is Pal Net, while just 50m away is **Asteroida** *(ul Dimitar Vlahov bb)*, where access rates are similarly inexpensive.

Things to See

The picturesque Old Town rises from ul Sveti Kliment Ohridski, the main pedestrian mall. A gnarled 900-year-old **plane tree** stands guard at the northern end. A medieval town wall isolates the Old Town from the surrounding valley. Head along Car Samoil as far as the 1827 **National Museum** *(☎ 267 173; Car Samoil 62; adult/student 100/50MKD; open 10am-3pm Tues-Sun)*.

Further along is the 11th-century **Church of Sveti Sofija** *(adult/student 100/30MKD)*. Aside from the frescoes there's an unusual Turkish *mimbar* (pulpit), which remains from the church's days as a mosque. An English-speaking guide is usually on hand.

Near here ul Ilindenska climbs to the **Upper Gate** (Gorna Porta); to the right is the 13th-century **Church of Sveti Kliment** *(admission 100MKD; open 9am-5pm)*, almost covered inside with vividly restored frescoes of biblical scenes. Opposite this church is an **icon gallery** *(open 9am-3pm)*. The restored walls of the 10th-century **citadel** to the west offer splendid views.

In the park below the citadel are the ruins of an early Christian **basilica** with 5th-century mosaics covered by protective sand. Nearby is the shell of **Sveti Pantelejmon**, Ohrid's oldest church.

The very small 13th-century **Church of Sveti Jovan Bogoslov Kaneo**, which overlooks the lake, displays Armenian as well as Byzantine elements.

Special Events

The five-day Balkan Festival of Folk Dances & Songs, held in early July, draws folkloric groups from around the Balkans. The Ohrid Summer Festival has a variety of music and theatre performances. An international poetry festival replete with food and drink in the streets is held annually in nearby Struga on 25 and 26 August. Ohrid hosts a swimming marathon each August, when swimmers race the 30km from Sveti Naum to Ohrid.

Places to Stay

Private rooms or apartments are your best bet in Ohrid. They can be organised either through Generalturist or other local agencies and should cost around 400MKD to 600MKD per person. Rooms in the Old Town are more expensive.

For generous hospitality and Macedonian home cooking, it's hard to beat the rooms of **Stefan Kanevče** *(☎ 070-212 352, 234 813; rooms 600MKD)* in Kaneo. Stefan's friendly wife Anita (or mama) cooks hearty breakfasts for 160MKD and pan-fried 'small fish' (sardines) from the lake.

One of the best options is **Mimi Apartments** *(☎/fax 250 103; Ⓔ mimioh@mail.com.mk; ul Strašo Pinđur 2; rooms 800MKD)*. Affable owner Mimi Apostolov has eight comfortable, heated rooms all with a fridge and satellite TV. Rates include breakfast.

A bit more upmarket and roomier are **Apartments Čekređi** *(☎ 261 733, 070 570 717; Kej Maršal Tito 27; doubles/triples 1500/2700MKD)*. These immaculate spacious quarters close to the lake are good for a stay of a few days as you can self-cater.

Close to the centre and overlooking the lake is the modern and friendly **Hotel Riviera** *(☎ 268 735, fax 254 155; Kej Maršal Tito 4;*

singles/doubles 1680/2640MKD). The rooms are very comfortable.

Places to Eat

Picnic-minded travellers can stock up on fresh vegetables at the busy Popular Market just north of the old plane tree. Buy fresh bread and croissants at **Zhito Leb**, *(ul Kliment Ohridski bb)*.

Several fast-food and pizza joints speckle the Old Town. Try cosy **Pizzeria Leonardo** *(☎ 260 359; Car Samoil 31)*. An individual pizza and half a litre of draft wine costs around 250MKD.

About 100m west of the old plane tree is the traditional-style **Restoran Neim** *(☎ 254 504; Goce Delčev 71)*, which serves some good *musaka* or *polneti piperki* (stuffed peppers).

On the lakefront, **Restaurant Dalga** *(☎ 31 948; Kosta Abrash bb)* is popular, has a glorious lake view and offers the now rather rare lake *letnica* (trout), approximately 2000MKD for a good-sized portion of two trout.

Getting There & Away

No fewer than 10 buses travel between Ohrid and Skopje every day (300MKD, three hours, 167km), via Kičevo. Another three go via Bitola. The first route is shorter, faster, more scenic and cheaper. During the summer rush, it pays to book a seat the day before.

There is a daily bus to Sofia from Ohrid (900MKD, 10 to 12 hours) that departs at 7am. There are buses at 5am and 3.30pm from Ohrid to Belgrade (1220MKD, 14 hours), via Bitola. To go to Albania catch a bus or boat to Sveti Naum monastery, which is very near the border crossing. In summer there are six buses a day running from Ohrid to Sveti Naum (80MKD, 29km), in winter three daily. The bus continues on to the border post. From Albanian customs it's 6km to Pogradec; taxis are waiting and should charge only US$6 to US$10 for the ride.

There are no direct transport links between Ohrid and Greece. You need to take a bus to Bitola and a taxi from there to the Greek border at Medžitlija/Niki.

Malta

Malta, Gozo and Comino may be specks on the map, but you'll be amazed by how much they have to offer the traveller. Strategically placed in the Mediterranean, the islands have proven a tempting target for explorers and invaders, leaving Malta with a unique, eclectic mix of influences. The islands' pleasant climate and scenic coastline have earned them a bucket-and-spade reputation, but beyond the beaches lurk 3000 years of history to explore. Despite a vast degree of development, the Maltese sense of tradition is still very strong, and the warmth of the people matches the climate.

Malta: the Basics

Capital Valletta

Population 390,000

Languages Malti, English

Currency Maltese lira (Lm) = 100 cents

Avoid at all costs Old-age pensioners on coach tours

Make friends with the locals by Drinking with them well into the early hours of the morning – singing optional.

Facts about Malta

HISTORY

Malta's oldest monuments are the beautiful megalithic temples built between 3800 and 2500 BC – the world's oldest surviving free-standing structures. From around 800 to 218 BC, Malta was colonised by the Phoenicians and Carthage. After Rome's defeat of Hannibal in 208 BC, Malta became part of the Roman Empire. In AD 60 St Paul was shipwrecked on the island, where (according to folklore) he converted the islanders to Christianity. Arabs arrived in 870, introducing citrus fruits and cotton. Afterwards came a succession of Normans, Angevins (French), Aragonese and Castilians (Spanish).

In 1530 the islands were given to the Knights of the Order of St John, a religious Crusader organisation. The Knights expelled invading Turks in 1565 and were considered 'saviours of Europe'. Soon afterward, though, the order declined and surrendered to Napoleon in 1798 without a fight. The British helped liberate the island in 1800 and began to develop Malta into a major naval base. The new member of the British empire suffered greatly from WWII bombing.

In 1947 the devastated island was given a measure of self-government, and independence was granted in 1964. Relations with the UK were further reduced as Malta signed agreements with Libya, the USSR and North Korea. Recent elections have seesawed between the pro-EU Nationalist Party and anti-union Labour Party.

In recent decades, the Maltese have achieved considerable prosperity, thanks largely to tourism but increasingly because of shipping, trade and light industries.

GEOGRAPHY & CLIMATE

The Maltese archipelago comprises three islands: Malta (246 sq km), Gozo (67 sq km) and Comino (2.7 sq km). Malta enjoys an excellent climate – temperatures reach 30°C in summer. Rainfall, only 580mm each year, occurs mainly between November and February.

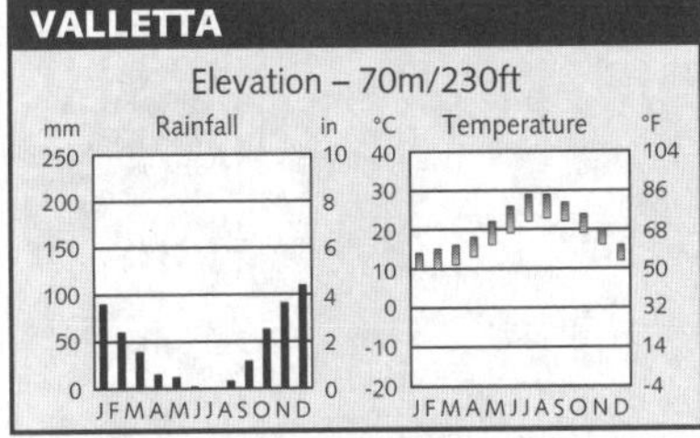

GOVERNMENT & POLITICS

Executive power lies with the prime minister and the cabinet, the latter chosen from the majority party in the 65-member parliament.

SOCIETY & CONDUCT

Despite an easy blend of Mediterranean and British culture existing throughout the islands, there is still a strong feeling of tradition. The people remain fairly conservative in outlook and family values are held in high regard.

Females should cover up modestly in places of worship and men should opt for long trousers rather than shorts.

Smoking is permitted almost everywhere although you should refrain from lighting up on public transport, unless of course you'd like to be ejected before your designated stop.

LANGUAGE

The official languages are English and Maltese (Malti), which is Arabic in grammar and construction but has Romantic components. Most people speak English. See the Language chapter at the back of the book for pronunciation guidelines and useful words and phrases.

Facts for the Visitor

HIGHLIGHTS

Unmissables include the magnificent Hypogeum in Paola, the evocative Ħagar Qim prehistoric temples and the medieval town of Mdina and Gozo. Check out the striking megalithic temples at Ġgantija and enjoy the stunning coastline by taking a boat trip around the island.

PLANNING

Try to avoid the summer months of July and August, when it can get unbearably hot and overrun with tourists. The *festi* season runs from June to September – outside these months, accommodation costs can fall by up to 40%.

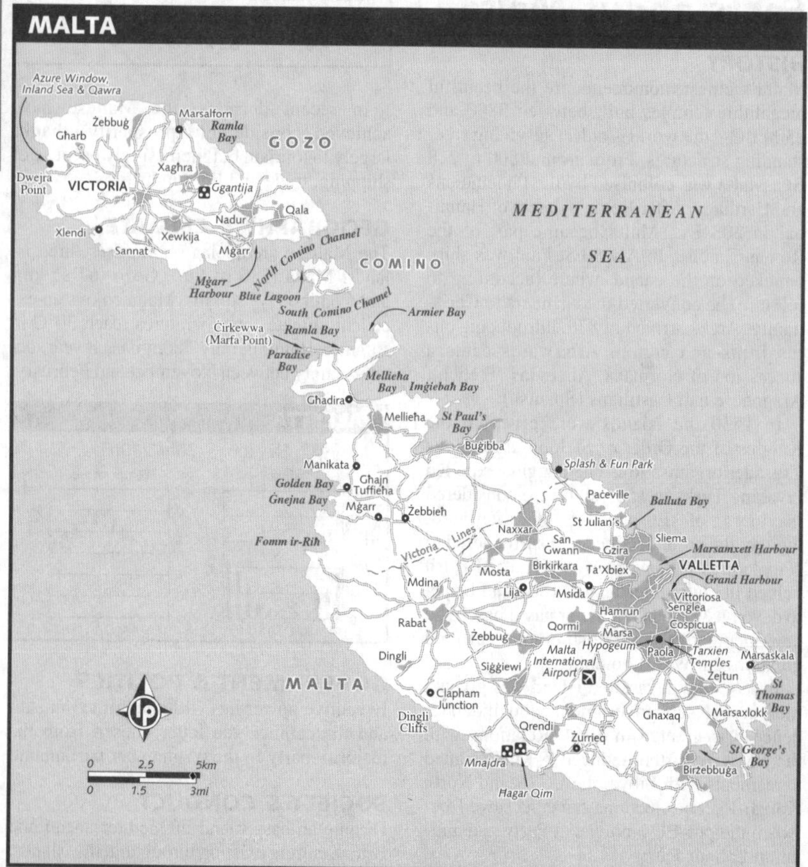

TOURIST OFFICES

The **Malta Tourist Authority** *(MTA; ☎ 216 996073, Malta international airport, open 24hr daily • ☎ 21237747, 1 City Arcade, Valletta • ☎ 21556114, Marr Harbour, Gozo • ☎ 21565171 Independence Square, Victoria)* can provide a range of brochures, hotel listings and maps. The **MTA** *(☎ 020 7292 4900, fax 020 7734 1880; W www.visitmalta.com; Malta House, 36–38 Piccadilly, London, W1V 0PP)* has its main overseas office in London. See the website for other international representation. Embassies and Air Malta offices can also provide information.

VISAS

Entry visas are not required for visits of up to three months by nationals of Australia, Canada, the UK or the USA. See the MTA's official website for details and useful links.

EMBASSIES & CONSULATES

Maltese Embassies & Consulates

Malta has diplomatic missions in the following countries:

Australia (☎ 02-6290 1724) 38 Culgoa Circuit, O'Malley, ACT 2606
France (☎ 01 56597590) 92, Ave des Champs-Elysees, Paris 75008
Italy (☎ 06 687 99 47) 12 Lungotevere Marzio, Rome 00186
UK (☎ 020-7292 4800) 36–38 Piccadilly, London W1V 0PQ
USA (☎ 202-462 3611) 2017 Connecticut Ave, NW Washington, DC 20008

Embassies & Consulates in Malta

The following countries have embassies in Malta:

Australia (☎ 21338201) Ta'Xbiex Terrace, Ta'X-biex MSD 11
Canada (☎ 21233121) 103 Archbishop St, Valletta
Germany (☎ 2133157) 5 Vilhena St, Floriana
Tunisia (☎ 21345866) 144/2 Tower Rd, Sliema
UK (☎ 21233134) 7 St Anne St, Floriana
USA (☎ 21235960/65) Development House, 3rd floor, St Anne St, Floriana

CUSTOMS

Items for personal use are not subject to duty. One litre of spirits, 1L of wine and 200 cigarettes can be imported duty-free. Duty is charged on any gifts over Lm50 intended for local residents.

MONEY

Currency

The Maltese lira is divided into 100 cents. There are one, two, five, 10, 25, 50 cent and Lm1 coins; and Lm2, Lm5, Lm10 and Lm20 notes.

country	unit		Maltese lira
Australia	A$1	=	Lm0.25
Canada	C$1	=	Lm0.29
Eurozone	€1	=	Lm0.42
Japan	¥100	=	Lm0.36
NZ	NZ$1	=	Lm0.22
UK	UK£1	=	Lm0.65
USA	US$1	=	Lm0.44

Banks usually offer the best exchange rates. The 24-hour bureau at the airport is available to passengers only. There are no exchange facilities at the ferry port. ATMs are widespread.

By European standards, Malta is a good-value destination. If you are travelling on a budget, reckon on around Lm10 per day.

Restaurants and taxis expect a 10% tip.

POST & COMMUNICATIONS

Post offices inhabit most towns and villages. Public telephones accept coins or phonecards, available at post offices and shops. For local inquiries, call ☎ 1182; for overseas inquiries, call ☎ 1152. The international direct dialling code is ☎ 00. To call Malta from abroad, dial the international access code, Malta's country code (☎ 356) and the number.

Internet access is widely available throughout the islands.

DIGITAL RESOURCES

There's stacks of information on the official MTA website at W www.visitmalta.com and SearchMalta at W www.searchmalta.com.

BOOKS

For more detailed information check out Lonely Planet's *Malta*. Leonard Mahoney's *5000 Years of Architecture in Malta* is a well-illustrated study.

WOMEN TRAVELLERS

Men are friendly towards female travellers but rarely threatening or imposing. Dress conservatively if you are visiting churches or historical buildings – legs and shoulders should be covered modestly.

GAY & LESBIAN TRAVELLERS

There are no predominantly gay areas, but there are several openly gay-and-lesbian bars. For more information contact the **Malta Gay Rights Movement** *(☎ 9949 9909)* or visit W www.gaymalta.org.

DISABLED TRAVELLERS

The **National Commission for Persons with Disability** *(☎ 21487789, fax 21484609)* has information about facilities and transport. Wheelchair-bound travellers may experience problems in Valletta due to uneven footpaths, steep inclines and endless stone steps.

Emergencies

For police emergencies, telephone ☎ 191; for medical emergencies, ☎ 196.

BUSINESS HOURS

Shops are open 9am to 1pm, and 3.30pm or 4pm to 7pm. Banks are open 8.30am to 12.30pm or 12.45pm Monday to Friday; some banks also open in the afternoon. On Saturday banks open 8.30am to noon.

Between 1 October and 30 June, offices are open from 8am to 1pm and 2.30pm or 3pm to 5.30pm Monday to Friday, and from 8.30am to 1pm on Saturday; from July to September offices open 7.30am to 1.30pm Monday to Saturday.

PUBLIC HOLIDAYS & SPECIAL EVENTS

There are fourteen national public holidays in Malta: New Year's Day (1 January); St Paul's Shipwreck (10 February); St Joseph's Day (19 March); Good Friday; Freedom Day (31 March); Labour Day (1 May); commemoration of 1919 Independence riots (7 June); Feast of Sts Peter & Paul, and Harvest Festival (29 June); Feast of the Assumption (15 August); Feast of Our Lady of Victories (8 September); Independence Day (21 September); Feast of the Immaculate Conception (8 December); Republic Day (13 December); and Christmas (25 December).

Each village also has a *festa* (feast day) honouring their patron saint. You can't avoid getting caught up in the excitement, as the whole community gets involved. Festivities start days before the event. If there's a festa going on, don't miss it.

ACTIVITIES

Water bugs are well catered for. **Diving** conditions are excellent, and there are around 30 licensed schools. The MTA can provide listings. All divers must provide a certificate from their own doctor or a local doctor (Lm3, available through dive centres). People who want to dive unaccompanied will also need a local diving permit (Malta C-Card; Lm2), which is granted on presentation of a medical certificate, proof of qualification (minimum CMAS two-star) and two passport-sized photographs.

A PADI open-water dive course starts at Lm125. One escorted shore dive with equipment hire costs about Lm15. **Maltaqua** *(☎ 21571873; W www.maltaqua.com; St Paul's Bay)*, **Divecare** *(☎ 21319994; St Julian's, Malta)* and **Calypso Diving** *(☎ 2156 1757; W www.calypsodivers.com; Marina St, Marsalforn, Gozo)* have been recommended by readers. Favourite dive spots include Ċirkewwa on Malta and Dwejra Blue Hole on Gozo.

The best sandy **beaches** are Ġnejna Bay; **Għajn Tuffiħea** and Golden Bay (bus Nos 47, 51 and 652); Paradise Bay (bus Nos 45, 48 and 645); Ramla Bay; Armier Bay (bus No 50); **Mellieħa Bay** (bus Nos 44, 45 and 48); and St George's Bay (bus Nos 64 and 67). Gozo's best beaches are Ramla Bay (bus No 42) and Xlendi Bay (bus No 87). All buses on Gozo originate and terminate at the bus station in Victoria. Buses on Malta originate from the City Gate Bus Terminal.

ACCOMMODATION

The MTA can provide listings. Camping is forbidden, but cheap hostel beds abound. Most places offer significantly reduced rates during off-peak periods and for stays of multiple nights. Another option is to board with a family. This can be arranged through NSTS (see Getting There & Away later).

FOOD & DRINKS

Most restaurants offer cheap pizzas and pastas, and there's a good variety of vegetarian options on almost every menu. The national dish is *fenech* (rabbit), fried or baked in a casserole; it's invariably cooked to perfection. Try the locally caught fish and seafood. Other local favourites are the savoury pasties, known as *pastizzi* (filled with cheese or mushy peas), and *bragioli* (spicy beef rolls).

Local beers, such as Cisk, are good. The locally produced pinot grigio is certainly worth a tipple.

ENTERTAINMENT

There's plenty to do in the evenings, with most bars and restaurants staying open until the early hours. The Maltese tend to eat late, so don't be surprised if things seem quiet in the early evening.

Getting There & Away

AIR

Malta is well connected to Europe and North Africa. Some bargains are available through **NSTS** *(☎ 244983, fax 230330; e e@nsts.org; 220 St Paul St, Valletta)*, the representative for most student travel organisations and an associate member of HI. **Air Malta** *(☎ 21662211; w www.airmalta.com)* has scheduled flights to many destinations.

SEA

Malta has regular sea links in summer with Sicily (Palermo, Pozzallo, Syracuse and Catania) and northern Italy (Genoa and Livorno). The Italy-Malta ferry services change schedules frequently, so it is best to confirm information with a travel agent such as **SMS Agency** *(☎ 21232211; 311 Republic St, Valletta)*.

Virtú Ferries *(☎ 21318854)* runs fast catamaran services to Sicily (Catania, Pozzallo and Licata). The journey to Catania takes three hours and costs Lm41 for an open return. Other companies operate regular car ferry services to Italian and Tunisian ports. The journey to Catania takes around 12 hours and a deck passenger is charged Lm20 (cars cost Lm69). Book with **MA.RE.SI Shipping** *(Head Office at SMS Agency)*. **Grimaldi Ferries** *(☎ 21226873)* runs services between Malta and Salerno.

Ferries do not have exchange facilities, and there are none at Malta's port.

DEPARTURE TAX

All passengers departing by sea are required to pay Lm4 departure tax, which should be added by the travel agent when you buy your ticket.

Getting Around

BUS

Malta and Gozo are served by buses run by the Malta Public Transport Authority (ATP). Most services originate from the chaotic **City gate terminus** *(☎ 21250007)* just outside Valletta's city gates. Fares are cheap – from 15c to 50c. Services are regular, and more popular routes run until 11pm. Ask at the tourist office or an ATP kiosk for a timetable.

Bus No 45 runs regularly from Valletta to Ċirkewwa to connect with the ferry to Gozo. On Gozo, the bus terminus is in Victoria, just south of Republic St. Bus No 25 runs from the ferry port of Mġarr to Victoria.

TAXI

Taxis are expensive; establish a price in advance. From Valletta to St Julian's it's around Lm5. **Wembley Motors** *(☎ 21374141; St Andrews)* offers a 24-hour service.

CAR & MOTORCYCLE

Unless you're an extremely confident driver, driving is hardly worth the stress. All the rental companies are at the airport, but rates vary so shop around. In 2002, **Hertz** *(☎ 2131 4636; 66 Gzira Rd, Gzira)* was offering a weekly summer rate of Lm72 for a small car (Lm58 a week in the low season). Local garages charge less. **La Ronde** *(☎ 21322962; Belvedere St, Gzira)* hires out motorcycles from Lm10 per day.

Hitchhiking is unusual and frowned upon.

BICYCLE

Gozo is a better option than Malta for cyclists as it is much smaller and quieter. **Marsalforn Hotel** *(☎ 21556147)* hires out bikes to suit all ages from Lm2 per day.

BOAT

Malta and Gozo are linked by a regular ferry service between Ċirkewwa (Malta) and Mġarr (Gozo). The crossing takes about 30 minutes and runs every 45 minutes between 6am and 11.30pm (extended at weekends). It costs Lm5.75 return for a car with a driver, and Lm1.75 for each additional passenger. All ferries are run by the **Gozo Channel Company** *(☎ 21556016 for information)*.

Ferries *(☎ 2133 8981; 35c one way)* run from Valletta and Sliema, (7.30am to 6.15pm) and depart from the Strand in Sliema.

Valletta, Sliema & St Julian's

Valletta, city of the Knights of the Order of St John, is steeped in history and renowned for its architectural excellence. The quiet back streets are where you'll really get a feel for everyday life. Valletta overlooks the impressive Grand Harbour to the southeast and the Marsamxett Harbour to the northwest. Vittoriosa, Senglea and Cospicua, collectively known as the Three Cities, lie to the southeast. The modern and fashionable areas of Sliema, St Julian's and Paċeville lie to the north of Valletta, crammed with high-rise hotels, apartment blocks, shops, restaurants, bars and nightclubs.

The airport is just southwest of the capital. Ferries from Italy dock in the Grand Harbour below Valletta. It's a steep 15-minute climb to the City Gate bus terminus.

Information

The **local tourist office** *(☎ 21237747; 1 City Arcade, Valletta)* can help with any of your visitor inquiries. There are a number of banks in Valletta's main street, Republic St, including branches of **HSBC Bank** at Nos 15 and 233. You can also change money at the **Thomas Cook office** *(☎ 21233629; 20 Republic St, Valletta • ☎ 21340750; il-Piazzetta, Tower Rd, Sliema)*.

The **YMCA** *(☎ 21240680; 178 Merchants St, Valletta; open Mon-Sat)* offers Internet access at 75c for half an hour. At the **Għall Kafé** *(☎ 21319694; 118 St George's Rd, Paċeville)* you'll pay 50c for 20 minutes.

Things to See

A walk around the city walls features some spectacular views. **St John's Co-Cathedral** *(St John's St; admission by donation)* dominates the centre of the town with its grave exterior design and impressive clock tower. Its baroque interior is quite breathtaking. The cathedral's **museum** *(admission Lm1; open Mon-Sat)* houses two magnificent works by the Italian painter Caravaggio (see the boxed text 'Cavalier Caravaggio').

The **Grand Master's Palace** *(Republic St)* is now the seat of the Maltese parliament and open to the public when parliament is not in session. The corridors are lined with paintings of the Grand Masters.

Cavalier Caravaggio

St John's Co-Cathedral Museum features works by Michelangelo Merisi, better known as Caravaggio. Caravaggio's dramatic style, which provoked plenty of criticism, became a key element in the development of baroque painting. Controversial and realistic, it challenged traditional portrayals of religious subjects, using light and shadow for emphasis and drama. *The Beheading of St John* is considered his finest masterpiece.

Caravaggio led a wild life in Rome. He had to flee to Naples (after he lost a game of tennis and murdered his opponent) where he stayed for several months before moving to Malta in 1607. After being made a Knight of the Order of St John he was arrested for an unspecified crime and imprisoned in Fort St Elmo. He fled to Sicily and was expelled from the Order. On the run, he died of exhaustion and fever before reaching his 38th birthday.

Fort St Elmo *(admission 50c; open 1.10pm-4.30pm Sat, 9am-4.30pm Sun)* was built in 1552 by the Knights of St John. Each month the Malta re-Enactment Society stages a military demonstration. Next door is an informative and moving **war museum** *(admission Lm1; open 7.45am-2pm daily summer, 8.15am-5pm daily winter)*. It is here that the George Cross, presented to the Maltese people for their bravery during WWII, is proudly displayed.

Another highlight is the **Manoel Theatre** *(☎ 21246389; 115 Old Theatre St; theatre tours Lm1.65; open 10am-1pm & 5pm-7pm Mon-Fri, 10am-noon Sat)*. One of the oldest theatres in Europe, it was built by Grand Master Manoel de Vilhena in 1731.

The **National Museum of Archaeology** *(Republic St; admission Lm1; open 7.45am-2pm daily mid-June–Sept; 8.15am-5pm Mon-Sat, 8.15am-4.15pm Sun Oct–mid-June)* is housed in the Auberge de Provence. The museum has a notable collection of Tarxien style figurines – fat ladies with interchangeable heads. Look for the Sleeping Lady, thought to date back to 3000 BC.

Places to Stay

Hostels The NSTS (see Getting There & Away) runs several hostels and also has agreements with guesthouses. It also offers a

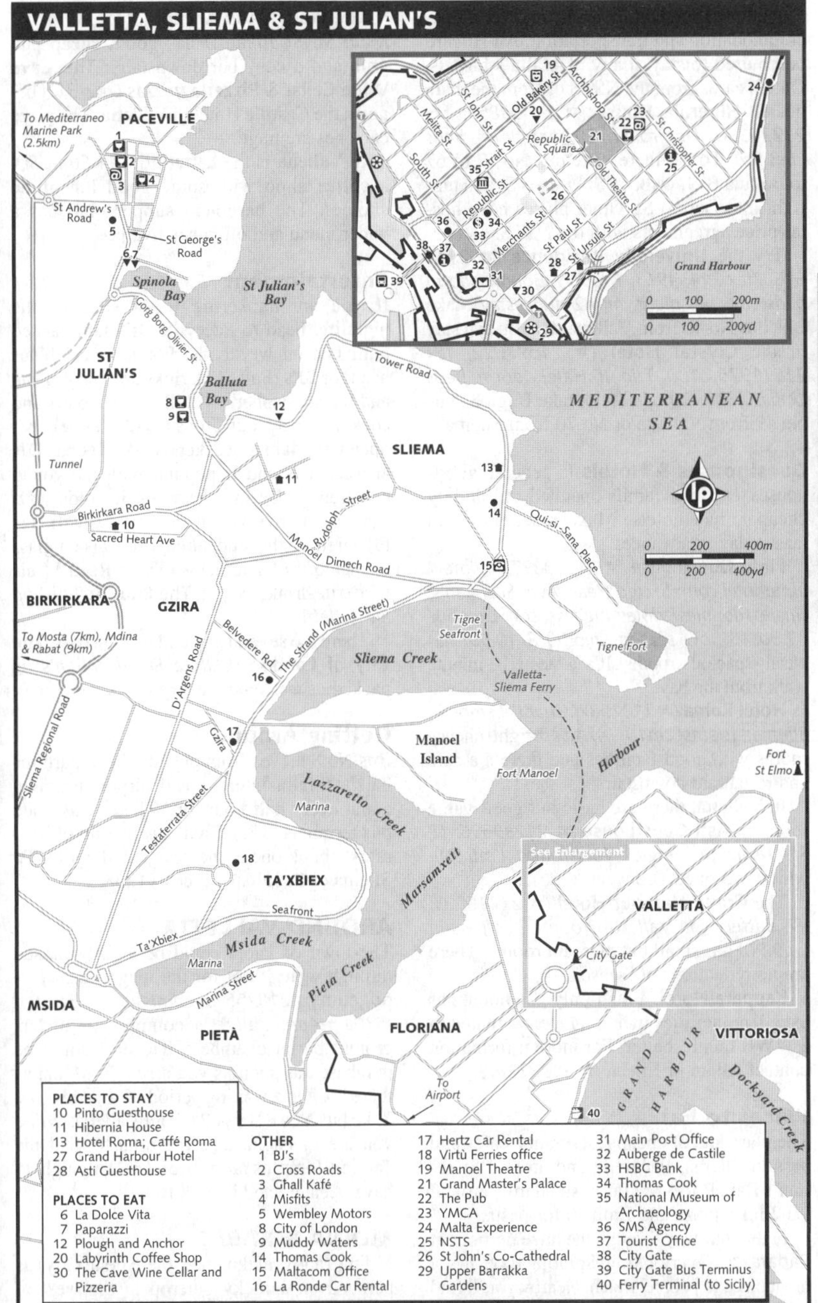

VALLETTA, SLIEMA & ST JULIAN'S
To Mediterraneo Marine Park (2.5km)
PACEVILLE
St Andrew's Road
St George's Road
Spinola Bay
St Julian's Bay
Gorg Borg Olivier St
ST JULIAN'S
Balluta Bay
Tower Road
Tunnel
SLIEMA
MEDITERRANEAN SEA
Birkirkara Road
Sacred Heart Ave
Rudolph Street
Manoel Dimech Road
Qui-si-Sana Place
BIRKIRKARA
GZIRA
To Mosta (7km), Mdina & Rabat (9km)
Belvedere Rd
The Strand (Marina Street)
Tigne Seafront
Tigne Fort
Sliema Creek
Valletta-Sliema Ferry
D'Argens Road
Sliema Regional Road
Gzira
Manoel Island
Fort Manoel
Harbour
Fort St Elmo
Lazzaretto Creek
Marina
Testaferrata Street
Marsamxett
TA'XBIEX
Seafront
Ta'Xbiex
Msida Creek
Marina
Marina Street
Pieta Creek
See Enlargement
VALLETTA
City Gate
MSIDA
PIETÀ
FLORIANA
VITTORIOSA
GRAND HARBOUR
Dockyard Creek
To Airport
St John St
Old Bakery St
Archbishop St
Melita St
Republic Square
St Christopher St
South St
Strait St
Old Theatre St
Republic St
Merchants St
St Paul St
St Ursula St
Grand Harbour
MALTA
PLACES TO STAY
10 Pinto Guesthouse
11 Hibernia House
13 Hotel Roma; Caffé Roma
27 Grand Harbour Hotel
28 Asti Guesthouse
PLACES TO EAT
6 La Dolce Vita
7 Paparazzi
12 Plough and Anchor
20 Labyrinth Coffee Shop
30 The Cave Wine Cellar and Pizzeria
OTHER
1 BJ's
2 Cross Roads
3 Ghall Kafé
4 Misfits
5 Wembley Motors
8 City of London
9 Muddy Waters
14 Thomas Cook
15 Maltacom Office
16 La Ronde Car Rental
17 Hertz Car Rental
18 Virtù Ferries office
19 Manoel Theatre
21 Grand Master's Palace
22 The Pub
23 YMCA
24 Malta Experience
25 NSTS
26 St John's Co-Cathedral
29 Upper Barrakka Gardens
31 Main Post Office
32 Auberge de Castile
33 HSBC Bank
34 Thomas Cook
35 National Museum of Archaeology
36 SMS Agency
37 Tourist Office
38 City Gate
39 City Gate Bus Terminus
40 Ferry Terminal (to Sicily)

special package that includes one week's accommodation and transportation. An HI card is required to stay at any of Malta's hostels. Obtain cards from the NSTS or from the main hostel, **Hibernia House** *(☎ 21333859, fax 21230330; Depiro St, Sliema; dorm beds Lm3.95)*. To get there, take bus No 62 or 67 to Balluta Bay, walk up St Francis St and turn right into Depiro St. Other places have hostel-price agreements with the NSTS.

Try the **University Residence** *(☎ 2143 6168, fax 21434963; Triq R.M.Bonnici; dorm beds Lm6 per night; min 2-night stay)*; take Lija bus No 40 from Valletta. Or you can stay in the **Crystal Hotel** *(☎ 21573022, fax 21571975; 100 Triq Il Halel; dorm beds Lm5.50; min 3-night stay)*; take Buġibba bus No 49 from Valletta or No 70 from Sliema.

Guesthouses & Hotels In general, guesthouses tend to be family operated and slightly cheaper than hotels. Make reservations at least a day in advance.

Pinto Guesthouse *(☎ 21313897; ⓔ info@pintohotel.com; Sacred Heart Ave, St Julian's; singles/doubles/triples high season Lm8.50/13.50/15, low season Lm5.50/8/10.50)* has clean, spacious rooms. It's a steep 10-minute walk from the bay.

Hotel Roma *(☎ 2131587; Ghar Il-Lembi St, Sliema; rooms Lm10-14)* has bright cheery rooms with good facilities and there's a café and restaurant downstairs.

In Valletta, there are basic but good-value rooms at **Asti Guesthouse** *(☎ 21239506; 18 St Ursula St; singles year-round Lm5.50)*, which was once a convent.

The **Grand Harbour Hotel** *(☎ 21246003; 47 Battery St, Valletta; rooms per person Lm9.90)* has small but pleasant rooms. There are no reductions off season.

Kappara Hotel, a men-only gay hotel, has excellent facilities including a bar situated in a WWII bomb shelter. For more information contact Allain or Eileen *(☎ 21387297)*.

Places to Eat

There are lots of cheap restaurants, cafés and bars in Sliema, Paċeville and around St Julian's Bay. Prices are fairly standard – around Lm2 for a pizza and Lm2.50 for pasta.

Fight your way through the huge portions at **Paparazzi**. Overlooking Spinola Bay, it's a great place to people-watch. Nearby you'll find **La Dolce Vita**, the best place for fresh fish.

The Plough and Anchor *(☎ 21334725; 1 Main St, St Julian's)* has good, cheap pub grub and a cosy bar downstairs. **The Cave Wine Cellar & Pizzeria** *(pizzas Lm2-3)* is beneath the Castille Hotel in Valletta. The pizza calzones are huge.

In Valletta is the **Labyrinth** *(44 Strait St)*, a coffee shop with some good lunchtime choices. The basement supper club has a wider menu and often has live jazz.

Entertainment

If you are hankering for a slice of the nightlife, head to Paċeville. It's jam-packed until late on weekends. For jazz and blues head for **BJ's** *(Ball St)*. Drinks are fairly cheap and the atmosphere is chill. For shooters and cocktails check out **Cross Roads**, a lively bar open until 4am at weekends. **Misfits** has DJs at weekends and is popular with the young and trendy. During the week it holds jazz, film and alternative nights. **Muddy Waters** is favoured by the student crowd. Raise a glass in memory of late actor Oliver Reed in his favourite drinking spot, **The Pub** *(Archbishop St, Valletta)*.

There are several gay and lesbian bars. **The City of London** *(Balluta St, St Julian's)* is packed at weekends (everyone is welcome).

Getting Around

Bus No 8 leaves from outside the departures hall at Malta international airport terminal about every half hour for Valletta City Gate bus terminus (15c). Taxis operate on official rates – book one at the designated booth. To Sliema or St Julian's it costs Lm8.

AROUND VALLETTA

The town of Paola could be swiftly passed through were it not for the magnificent **Hypogeum** *(☎ 21825579; admission Lm3; open 8.30am-4pm daily)*, a complex of underground burial chambers. Tickets should be purchased as soon as you arrive in Malta, as there is often a waiting period of several days. Take bus Nos 8, 11 or 27 from Valletta. While you are in Paola, take the time to visit the **Tarxien Temples** *(admission Lm1)*, thought to have been erected in 3000BC.

MDINA & RABAT

Mdina (aptly nicknamed the Silent City) is perched on a rocky outcrop in the west of Malta. Fortified for over 3000 years, it was

Malta's old political centre. Rabat is the town settlement outside the walls.

Mdina's main piazza is dominated by the **cathedral**, worth visiting to see the huge fresco of St Paul's shipwreck. In Rabat you can visit **St Paul's Church** and **St Paul's grotto** (where Paul is said to have preached). Nearby are **St Agatha's Catacombs** *(admission 50c; open Mon-Sat, closed Sat afternoon)*, an underground complex of burial chambers boasting amazing Byzantine frescoes. There are plenty of places to eat and drink in Mdina and Rabat, but you can't beat **Baron snack bar** for the interesting local clientele and cheap, simple food.

Catch bus Nos 80 or 81 from Valletta to reach Mdina and Rabat.

SOUTH COAST

The views are fantastic from the top of **Dingli Cliffs**. Farther inland you can see a good example of prehistoric **cart ruts**. The origin of these topographical features remains a mystery. This collection has been nicknamed **Clapham Junction** by British visitors, after a notoriously complicated London train station.

To the south, you'll find the village of Qrendi and the nearby prehistoric temples of **Ħagar Qim** *(admission Lm1; open daily)* and **Mnajdra**. Built between 3600 and 3000 BC, these megalithic structures have been partially restored. Unfortunately, Mnajdra has been defaced by vandals.

Gozo & Comino

The island of Gozo is much more tranquil than its big sister Malta. If you *really* want to get away from it all, head to virtually uninhabited Comino. **Comino Hotel** *(☎ 2152 9821; W www.cominohotels.com)* runs a ferry service between Mġarr Harbour and Comino (Lm2).

VICTORIA

Victoria, also known as Rabat, is Gozo's commercial centre. There are no hotels but plenty of other facilities. The helpful **tourist office** *(☎ 21565171; Independence Square)* can provide information. The square is a hive of activity, with open-air cafés, treasure-trove craft shops and traders peddling fresh produce. All bus routes originate and terminate at the station just south of Republic St.

Victoria is crowned by the **Citadel** (Il-Kastell or Citadella). A stroll around it offers breathtaking views, but beware the well-worn steps and walkways. The **Cathedral of the Assumption's** elegant design is marred only by the fact that funds ran out before completion and the structure remained flat-topped. This cannot be detected from inside due to an elaborate trompe l'oeil painted on the ceiling.

MARSALFORN

Marsalforn, the summer-tourist favourite, is built around a picturesque cove. Just to the east you'll find some interesting salt pans and strangely eroded cliffs.

Several diving shops are dotted around. You can also book boat trips at the harbourfront kiosk – the best way to see features such as the **Azure Window** and **Inland Sea**. A half-day tour of Gozo and Comino costs Lm6 per person.

Comfortable **Atlantis Hotel** *(☎ 21554685; e info@atlantisgozo.com; Qolla St; inland rooms low/high season per person Lm6/14)* is family run. You can hire cars and jeeps and take advantage of excellent leisure facilities here.

Marsalforn Hotel *(☎ 21556147; B&B per person Lm7)* is a bright green-and-white guesthouse on a road junction. It also has spacious **self-catering flats** that sleep up to six people, costing Lm18/15 per night in high/low season. Contact Joseph & Maria Bugeja *(☎ 21553630; e bugejajoe@vol.net.mt)* for details.

Il-Kartell is a solid seafood restaurant on the western side of the bay. Another good choice is **Il-Forno** *(☎ 21565140; 25 Marina St)*, on the opposite side of the bay. It serves appetising home-cooked food, including Maltese specialities.

You can catch bus No 21 from Victoria's main terminus.

XAGĦRA

For such a small town, there's quite a lot to see in Xagħra. To the south of the main street is **Ta'Kola Windmill** *(admission Lm1, including entrance to Ġgantija; open 7.45am-2pm daily mid-June–Sept; 8.15am-5pm Mon-Sat, 8.15am-4pm Sun Oct–mid-June)*. Climb to the top to examine the original 18th-century mechanical fittings.

Close by are the megalithic temples of **Ġgantija** *(open 8.30am-4.30pm Mon-Sat, 8.30am-3pm Sun)*, dating back to 3600 BC. Little is known about the people who built them, but evidence of sacrificial offerings has been discovered.

Xerri's Grotto *(☎ 21552733; admission 50c; open daily)* and **Nino's Cave** *(admission 35c; open daily)*, both of which boast astounding stalactites and stalagmites, are to the north of the main street. Access is gained through private houses, open at the owners' discretion (usually 9am-6pm in summer). It's not far to one of the best beaches on Gozo: **Ramla Bay**.

Xaghra Lodge *(☎ 21562362; e xaghra lodge@waldonet.net.mt; Dun Gorg Preca St; high/low season per person Lm10/8)* has comfortable guesthouse accommodation. Facilities include a swimming pool, bar and Chinese restaurant.

Oleander's *(☎ 21557230; open noon-3pm & 7pm-10pm Tues-Sat)* is on the main square. It's a great place for pastas, steaks and Maltese dishes.

Morocco

Morocco, or *Al-Maghreb al-Aqsa* ('farthest land of the setting sun') in Arabic, lies at the western extremity of the Muslim and Arab world. Although it may not be strictly European, it's easier to get to Morocco from Europe than it is from the rest of Africa. Morocco is becoming more attractive as an exotic stopover for those 'doing' the Mediterranean, and has a lot to offer the independent traveller. Nothing in Europe can prepare you for the cultural feast that awaits across the strait.

Most travellers from Europe treat Morocco as a week-long diversion; hence, this chapter covers the main destinations easily accessible from Europe, concentrating on the Mediterranean and Atlantic coasts, the Middle Atlas and the Rif mountains, as well as Marrakesh. For full coverage of the country, including the south, check the latest edition of Lonely Planet's *Morocco*.

Morocco: the Basics

Capital Rabat

Population 30.6 million

Languages Arabic, French, Berber

Official language Arabic

Currency 1 dirham (Dh) = 100 centimes

Avoid at all costs Hustlers and sketchy salesmen

Dodge said sketchy salesmen by saying *Désolé, mais je suis allergique aux tapis.* (Sorry, but I'm allergic to carpets.)

Facts about Morocco

HISTORY

Most modern Moroccans are the descendants of Berber settlers who came to the region thousands of years ago. The Berbers were well established by the time the Phoenicians and the Romans started showing an interest in North Africa. Both faded away before the arrival of Islam in the 7th century, when Arab armies took over the whole North African coast and much of Spain.

Tribal divisions soon reasserted themselves, and the Berbers developed their own brand of Islamic Shi'ism, known as Kharijism. By 829 the Kharijites had established a stable Idrissid state with its capital at Fès, dominating all of Morocco. But by the 11th century the region had fragmented. France took over in 1912, handing Spain a token zone in the north. Rabat was made the capital and Casablanca developed as a major port.

By 1934 the last opposition from Berber mountain tribes had been crushed, but Moroccan resistance moved into political channels with the Istiqlal (independence) party. After WWII, violent opposition resurfaced, and in 1956 independence was granted.

The Spanish withdrew around the same time but still retained the coastal enclaves of Ceuta and Melilla. Sultan Mohammed V became king, succeeded by his son Hassan II, who despite moves towards democracy and several coup attempts, retained all effective power until his death in July 1999.

The new king, Mohammed VI, has adopted a reformist agenda, vowing to tackle the huge developmental problems in Morocco, and achieved huge popularity as well as breaking tradition with his highly publicised marriage in 2002.

GEOGRAPHY

One of Africa's most geographically diverse areas, Morocco is spectacularly beautiful. It is traversed by four mountain ranges: the Rif, the Middle Atlas, the High Atlas and the Anti-Atlas. Certain peaks of the High Atlas remain snowcapped all year and are among the highest in Africa. Between the mountain ranges themselves, and between these ranges and the Atlantic Ocean, are plateaus and plains.

CLIMATE

Weather in Morocco's coastal regions is generally mild, but can become cool and wet, particularly in the north. Average temperatures in Tangier and Casablanca range from 12°C (54°F) in winter to 25°C (77°F) and above in

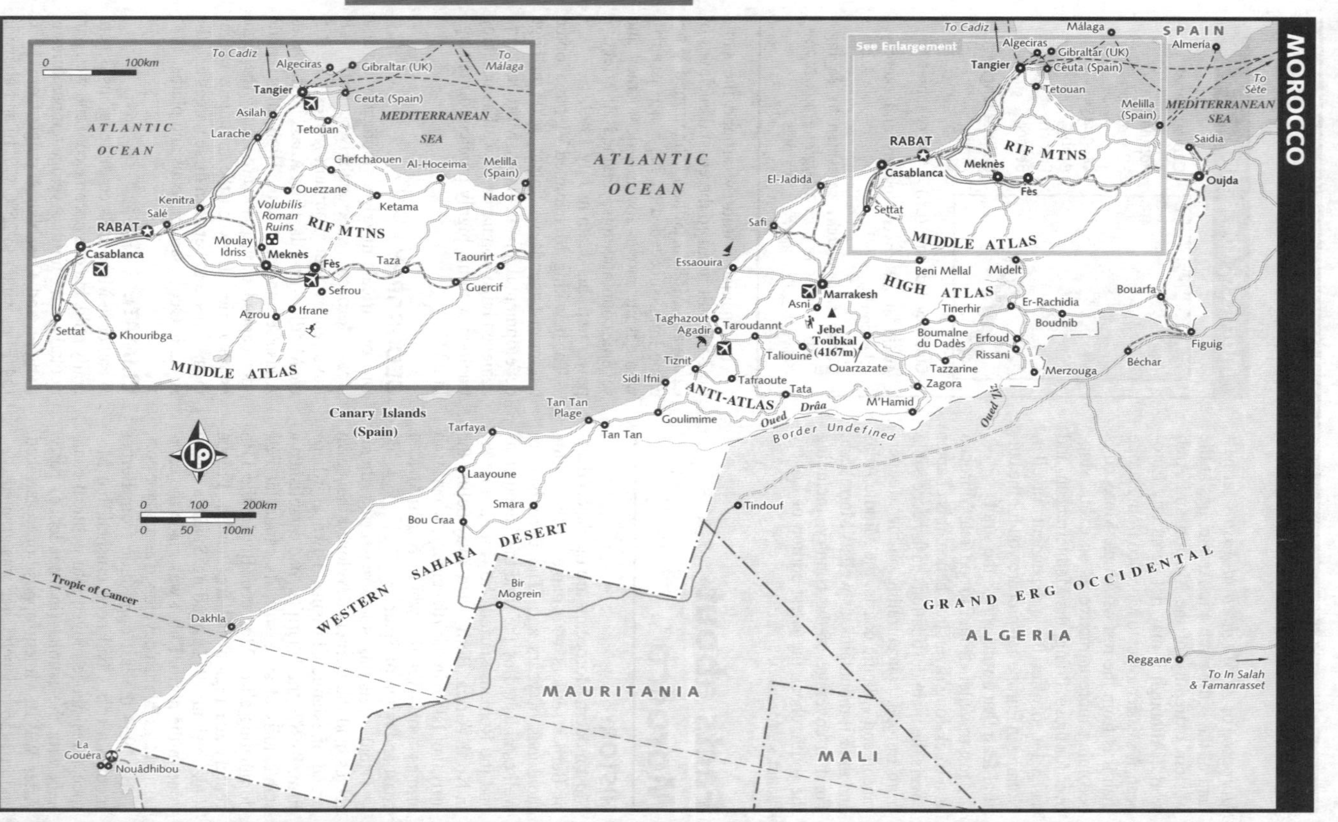
MOROCCO
To Cadiz
Málaga
SPAIN
Almeria
See Enlargement
Algeciras
Gibraltar (UK)
Tangier
Ceuta (Spain)
Tetouan
To Sète
Melilla (Spain)
MEDITERRANEAN SEA
Saidia
RABAT
Casablanca
RIF MTNS
Meknès
Fès
Oujda
Settat
MIDDLE ATLAS
ATLANTIC OCEAN
El-Jadida
Safi
Essaouira
Beni Mellal
Midelt
HIGH ATLAS
Marrakesh
Asni
Bouarfa
Er-Rachidia
Tinerhir
Boudnib
Taghazout
Agadir
Taroudannt
Jebel Toubkal (4167m)
Boumalne du Dadès
Erfoud
Rissani
Figuig
Béchar
Taliouine
Ouarzazate
Tazzarine
Merzouga
Tiznit
Sidi Ifni
Tafraoute
Tata
Zagora
ANTI-ATLAS
M'Hamid
Oued Drâa
Oued Ziz
Tan Tan Plage
Goulimime
Tan Tan
Border Undefined
Tarfaya
Canary Islands (Spain)
Laayoune
Smara
Bou Craa
Tindouf
0 100 200km
0 50 100mi
WESTERN SAHARA DESERT
Tropic of Cancer
Bir Mogrein
Dakhla
GRAND ERG OCCIDENTAL
ALGERIA
Reggane
To In Salah & Tamanrasset
MAURITANIA
MALI
La Gouéra
Nouâdhibou
0 100km
To Cadiz
Algeciras
Gibraltar (UK)
To Málaga
Tangier
Ceuta (Spain)
Asilah
ATLANTIC OCEAN
Larache
Tetouan
MEDITERRANEAN SEA
Chefchaouen
Al-Hoceima
Melilla (Spain)
Ouezzane
Nador
Kenitra
Salé
RABAT
Volubilis Roman Ruins
Ketama
RIF MTNS
Moulay Idriss
Meknès
Fès
Taza
Taourirt
Casablanca
Sefrou
Guercif
Azrou
Ifrane
Settat
Khouribga
MIDDLE ATLAS

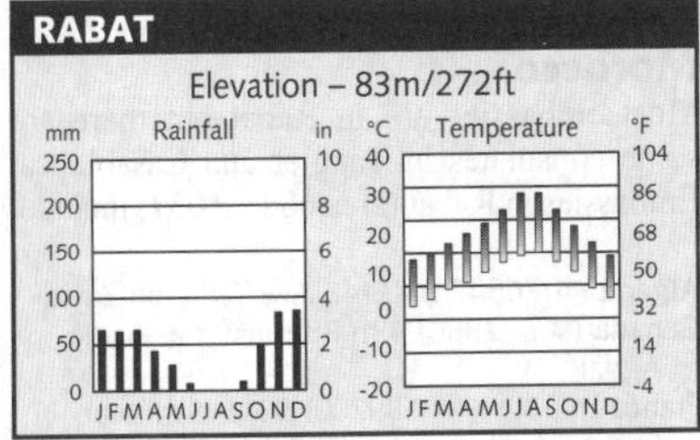

summer. Rainfall is highest in the Rif and northern Middle Atlas, where only the summer months are dry. The Atlantic coast remains agreeable year-round, cooled by sea breezes.

The rainy season is from November to January, but can go on as late as April. During winter the mountains can get as cold as -20°C (-4°F; without taking the wind-chill factor into account), with snow often blocking mountain passes.

GOVERNMENT & POLITICS

Morocco is ruled by King Mohammed VI, who came to the throne in July 1999. Despite some democratic moves, Morocco remains essentially an absolute monarchy.

POPULATION & PEOPLE

The bulk of Morocco's population is made up of Arab and Berber peoples who have intermarried over the centuries. Morocco once hosted a large population of Jews, but the vast majority left after the foundation of Israel in 1948. Trade with trans-Saharan Africa brought a population of black Africans into Morocco, many of whom originally arrived as slaves.

SOCIETY & CONDUCT

Despite extensive Westernisation, Morocco remains a largely conservative Muslim society. As a rule, a high degree of modesty is demanded of both sexes in dress as well as behaviour, and even in the liberal cities scant clothing will stand out a mile. Women in particular are well advised to keep their shoulders and upper arms covered and to opt for trousers or long skirts. You should always ask permission before taking photographs.

If invited into a Moroccan home, remove your shoes before stepping onto the carpet. The left hand should not be used to eat with or to touch any common source of food or water, or to hand over money or presents.

All mosques and religious buildings in active use are off-limits to non-Muslims. Cemeteries are pretty much no-go areas, too.

LANGUAGE

Moroccan Arabic *(darija)* is the official language, but French and Berber are widely spoken. Spanish is spoken in former Spanish-held territory, and some English is understood in the main tourist centres.

Pick up a copy of Lonely Planet's *Moroccan Arabic phrasebook* for more detailed coverage. For pronunciation guidelines and useful words and phrases, see the Language chapter at the back of this book.

Facts for the Visitor

HIGHLIGHTS

The imperial cities of Fès, Meknès, Rabat and Marrakesh are the best places to discover the characteristic medieval vibe of the medina, packed with all the arts, crafts, monuments, sights and smells of traditional Morocco. For a glimpse of modern Islam, don't miss the amazing Hassan II Mosque in Casablanca.

Elsewhere you can explore the breathtaking Rif Mountains around Chefchaouen, experience the sedate and seedy sides of Tangier and Tetouan, expose yourself to some sun in the relaxed Spanish enclaves of Ceuta and Melilla, or just bask on the Atlantic beaches at Asilah and Larache.

PLANNING

The most pleasant times to explore Morocco are during spring (April to May) and autumn (September to October). Midsummer can be very enjoyable on the coast but viciously hot in the interior. It is also the high season, so prices (especially for accommodation) are higher, but there are more services, such as ferries, for travellers. During winter it gets surprisingly cold across the northwestern part of the country.

TOURIST OFFICES

The national tourist body, **Office National du Tourisme Marocain** *(ONMT; head office ☎ 037-730562; W www.tourism-in-morocco.com; Rue al-Abtal, Rabat)*, has offices (usually called Délégation Régionale du Tourisme) in the main cities. A few cities also have local offices known as *syndicats*

MOROCCO

d'initiative; these are often less helpful than ONMT offices, but all have brochures and simple maps to dispense.

The ONMT maintains offices in Australia (Sydney), Belgium (Brussels), Canada (Montreal), France (Paris), Germany (Düsseldorf), Italy (Milan), Japan (Tokyo), Portugal (Lisbon), Spain (Madrid), Sweden (Stockholm), Switzerland (Zürich), the UK (London) and the USA (New York and Orlando).

VISAS

Most visitors to Morocco do not need a visa and on entry are granted leave to remain in the country for 90 days. Exceptions include nationals of Israel, South Africa and Zimbabwe. Visa requirements can change, so check with the Moroccan embassy or a reputable travel agent before travelling. Entry requirements for Ceuta and Melilla are the same as for Spain (see that chapter).

If 90 days just simply aren't enough, the easiest thing is to leave (for example, go to the Spanish enclaves) and return a few days later. Your chances improve if you re-enter by a different route.

People on visas may, however, prefer to try for an extension, which may take up to two weeks. Go to the nearest police headquarters, or Préfecture, with your passport, four photos, proof of sufficient funds and preferably a letter from your embassy requesting a visa extension on your behalf.

MOROCCO

EMBASSIES & CONSULATES

Moroccan Embassies & Consulates

Australia (☎ 02-9922 4999) Suite 2, 11 West St, North Sydney, NSW 2060

Canada (☎ 613-236 7391) 38 Range Rd, Ottawa K1N 8J4

France (☎ 01 45 20 69 35) 5 Rue Le Tasse, Paris 75016

Germany (☎ 030-20 61 24 0) Niederwallstrasse 39, 10117 Berlin

Japan (☎ 03-478 3271) Silva Kingdom 3, 16-3, Sendagaya, Shibuya-ku, Tokyo 151

Spain (☎ 91-563 1090) Calle Serrano 179, 28002 Madrid

The Netherlands (☎ 70-346 9617) Oranjestraat 9, 2514 JB, The Hague

Tunisia (☎ 01-782 775) 39 Avenue du 1er Juin, Mutuelleville, Tunis

UK (☎ 020-7581 5001) 49 Queen's Gate Gardens, London SW7 5NE

USA (☎ 202-462 7979) 1601 21st St NW, Washington, DC 20009

Embassies & Consulates in Morocco

Most embassies are in Rabat but there are some consulates in Tangier and Casablanca. Embassies in Rabat (area code ☎ 037) include:

Algeria (☎ 765474) 46-48 Ave Tariq ibn Zayid

Canada (☎ 672880) 13b Rue Jaafar as-Sadiq, Agdal

France *Embassy:* (☎ 689700) 3 Rue Sahnoun
Service de Visas: (☎ 702404) Rue Ibn al-Khatib

Germany (☎ 709662) 7 Rue Madnine

Japan (☎ 631782) 39 Ave Ahmed Balafrej Souissi

Spain *Embassy:* (☎ 768989) 3-5 Rue Madnine
Consulate: (☎ 704147) 57 Rue du Chellah

The Netherlands (☎ 733512) 40 Rue de Tunis

Tunisia (☎ 730636) 6 Ave de Fès

UK (☎ 720905) 17 Blvd de la Tour Hassan

USA (☎ 762265) 2 Ave de Marrakesh

CUSTOMS

You can import up to 200 cigarettes and 1L of spirits duty-free.

MONEY

The unit of currency is the dirham (Dh), equal to 100 centimes. The importation or exportation of local currency is prohibited. The Spanish enclaves of Ceuta and Melilla use the euro.

Exchange Rates

country	unit		dirham
Australia	A$1	=	Dh6.00
Canada	C$1	=	Dh6.90
Eurozone	€1	=	Dh10.57
Japan	¥100	=	Dh8.69
New Zealand NZ	$1	=	Dh5.25
UK	UK£1	=	Dh16.76
USA	US$1	=	Dh10.74

Exchanging Money

Banking services are generally quick and efficient. Many banks have separate bureaux de change, but it is becoming more difficult to change travellers cheques – branches of the Banque Populaire or the BMCI are your best bet. Australian, Canadian and New Zealand dollars are not quoted in banks and are not usually accepted.

Major credit cards are widely accepted in the main tourist centres, although their use often attracts a surcharge. American Express (AmEx) is represented by the travel agency Voyages Schwartz, which can be found in Rabat, Casablanca and Tangier.

Guichets automatiques (ATMs) are now a common sight; many accept Visa, MasterCard, Electron, Cirrus, Maestro and InterBank. BMCE and Crédit du Maroc ATMs are a good bet.

Costs

Moroccan prices are refreshingly reasonable. With a few small tips here and there plus admission to museums and the like, you can get by on US$15 to US$20 a day if you stay in cheap hotels, eat at cheap restaurants and are not in a hurry. Hot showers, the occasional splurge and a taxi or two can take this up to US$30 to US$35 a day.

Tipping & Bargaining

Practically any service can warrant a tip, but don't be railroaded. A few dirham for a service willingly rendered can make your life a lot easier. Between 5% and 10% of a restaurant bill is about right.

When souvenir hunting, decide beforehand how much you are prepared to spend on an item (to get an idea of prices, visit the Ensemble Artisanal in any major city), but be aware that carpet vendors often start with hugely inflated prices. Wait until the price has been reduced considerably before making your first (low) offer, then approach your limit slowly.

POST & COMMUNICATIONS

The Moroccan post is fairly reliable and offers poste restante. Be sure to take your passport to claim mail. There's a small charge for collecting letters. Outgoing parcels are inspected by customs at the post office, so save yourself the hassle and don't turn up with a sealed parcel. Nifty flat-pack boxes are available.

The telephone system is good. Private *téléboutiques*, which are marked on maps throughout this chapter, are widespread and efficient; attendants sell *télécartes* (phonecards) and provide change. Phonecards for public phones are available from kiosks and some post offices. Reverse charge (collect) calls to most countries are possible.

When calling overseas from Morocco, dial ☎ 00, the country code and then the city code and number. Morocco's country code is ☎ 212.

Internet cafés have sprung up all over Morocco. One hour on the Internet costs between Dh5 and Dh15. Internet access is fairly reliable, though connections are better in the north and usually quicker in the morning.

DIGITAL RESOURCES

There are numerous Internet sites about Morocco – W www.mincom.gov.ma, W www.marweb.com, W www.morocco.com and W www.i-cias.com/mor.htm will get you started.

BOOKS

For more detailed information on Morocco, see Lonely Planet's *Morocco*. *The Moors: Islam in the West* by Michael Brett & Werner Forman details Moorish civilisation at its height, with superb colour photographs.

WOMEN TRAVELLERS

Harassment is generally of the leering, verbal variety. In the bigger cities especially, female travellers will receive hopeful greetings from every male over the age of 13. Ignore them entirely. Women will save themselves a great deal of grief by dressing modestly and avoiding anything skin-tight. It's wise not to walk around alone at night.

GAY & LESBIAN TRAVELLERS

Homosexual acts are officially illegal in Morocco – in theory you can go to jail and/or get fined. However, although not openly admitted or shown, male homosexuality remains relatively common. Male homosexuals are advised to be discreet; aggression towards gay male travellers is not unheard of.

Gay women shouldn't encounter any particular problems, though it's commonly believed by Moroccans that there are no lesbians in their country.

DANGERS & ANNOYANCES

Morocco's era as a hippy paradise is long past. Plenty of fine *kif* (dope) is grown in the Rif Mountains, but drug busts are common and Morocco is not a good place to investigate prison conditions! The majority of shakedowns and rip-offs in Morocco are drug-related; a common ploy is to get you stoned, sell you a piece the size of a house brick and then turn you in to the police (or threaten to).

Those disembarking (and embarking) the ferry in Tangier should expect some hassle from touts and hustlers trying to pull you one way or the other (usually to a hotel/ferry ticket office where they get commission). Ceuta and Melilla are far more pleasant ports of entry.

On the more popular tourist routes you may come across professional hitchhikers and people pretending that their cars have

EMERGENCIES

In case of emergency call the following nationwide telephone numbers: For ambulance or fire ☎ 15, police ☎ 19 and for roadside assistance ☎ 177.

broken down. Once you stop to assist them various scams unfold.

Morocco has its share of pickpockets and thieves, but they're not a major problem.

Guides

A few years ago the Brigade Touristique (tourist police) was set up in the principal tourist centres to clamp down on Morocco's notorious *faux guides* (false guides) and hustlers. This has reduced, but not eliminated, the problem of the *faux guides*. You'll still find plenty hanging around the entrances to the big city medinas and outside bus and train stations. Friendly overtures are the usual ploy to get your attention; the more direct line 'one mosquito better than thousand mosquitoes' is a Tangier favourite! Most will go away if you ignore them and don't stop, but some can be persistent and even unpleasant – stay calm and polite, and head for a café or taxi. If you end up with one of these people remember their main interest is the commission gained from certain hotels or on articles sold to you in the *souqs*.

Official guides can be engaged through tourist offices and hotels at the fixed price of Dh120 per half-day (plus tip). It's worth taking a guide in the larger medinas; their local knowledge is extensive and they'll save you from being hassled by others. If you don't want a shopping expedition included in your tour, make this clear beforehand.

BUSINESS HOURS

Banking hours are usually from 8.30am to 11.30am and from 2.30pm to 4.30pm weekdays, with Friday lunchtime lasting from 11.15am to 3pm. During Ramadan hours are from 9am to 3pm. In some tourist areas exchange offices keep longer hours and open over the weekend. Post offices generally keep similar hours, but don't close until around 6pm. *Téléboutiques* are open until around 10pm, Internet cafés are often open later. Many museums and some monuments are closed on Tuesday.

PUBLIC HOLIDAYS & SPECIAL EVENTS

All banks, post offices and most shops are shut on the main public holidays. Major secular holidays are New Year's Day (1 January), Independence Manifesto (11 January), Labour Day (1 May), Feast of the Throne (30 July), Allegiance of Wadi-Eddahab (14 August), Anniversary of the King's and People's Revolution (20 August), Anniversary of the Green March (6 November) and Independence Day (18 November).

In addition to secular holidays there are many national and local Islamic holidays and festivals, all tied to the lunar calendar.

Probably the most important of these is the Aïd al-Fitr, held at the end of the month-long Ramadan fast, which is fairly strictly observed by most Muslims. The festivities generally last four or five days, during which just about everything grinds to a halt.

Another important Muslim festival is Aïd al-Adha, which marks the end of the Islamic year. Again, most things shut down for four or five days. The third main religious festival, known as Mawlid an-Nabi (or simply Mouloud), celebrates the Prophet Mohammed's birthday.

Local festivals, mostly in honour of *marabouts* (saints) and known as *moussems* or *amouggars*, are common among the Berbers and usually held in the summer months.

ACTIVITIES

With thousands of kilometres of Atlantic coastline, Morocco has some great surfing spots – the **Oudayas Surf Club** *(☎ 037-260683)* in Rabat is a good place for information.

The area around Chefchaouen offers some good trekking opportunities, although most travellers head straight for the High Atlas (see the Marrakesh section). Early spring is the best time to go.

ACCOMMODATION

Camping

You can camp anywhere in Morocco if you have permission from the landowner. There are also many official camping grounds, where you'll pay around Dh10 per person plus Dh10 to pitch a tent, with extra charges for vehicles, electricity and hot water.

Hostels

There are *auberges de jeunesse* (hostels) in Casablanca, Chefchaouen, Fès, Meknès, Rabat and Tangier. If you're travelling alone, they are among the cheapest places to stay. The Moroccan Ministry of Youth and Sports also has reception centres in many major cities, which can be booked by travellers: beds at **Centres d'Acceuil** *(information & reservations ☎ 037-670192, fax 670175; 6 Rue Soumaya, Rabat)* cost Dh50, and advance booking is essential.

Hotels

Cheap, unclassified hotels of varying quality tend to be clustered within the medinas of most cities. Singles/doubles cost from Dh20/40. Showers are often cold, but there are always *hammams* (traditional bathhouses) nearby.

For a little more money, you can often find better unclassified or one-star hotels outside the medinas. At one-star places, single/double rooms with shower start at around Dh60/120; rooms in two-star places start at around Dh150/200. Prices can include breakfast, which is hardly ever a good deal – coffee and a croissant is Dh7 to Dh10 in a café.

The extra star in the three-star category (from Dh200/250) should get you a TV and a telephone.

Prices given here are for high season and include tax; always check the price you are quoted is TTC (all taxes included).

FOOD & DRINKS

At its best, Moroccan food is superb. Influenced by Berber, Arabic and Mediterranean (particularly Spanish and French) traditions, the cuisine features a sublime use of spices and fresh local produce.

Typical dishes include *tajine*, a meat and vegetable stew cooked slowly in an earthenware dish, and couscous, fluffy steamed semolina served with tender meat and vegetables. The preparation of couscous is laborious and many restaurants only serve it on Friday. *Harira*, a thick soup made from lamb stock, lentils, chickpeas, onions, tomatoes, fresh herbs and spices, is usually eaten as a first course in the evening, but is substantial enough to make a meal on its own. In a cheap restaurant a bowl costs around Dh5.

Pastilla, a Fès speciality, is a rich and delicious dish made from pigeon meat, lemon-flavoured eggs, almonds, cinnamon, saffron and sugar, encased in layer upon layer of very fine *ouarka* pastry.

Vegetarians shouldn't have any problems – fresh fruit and vegetables are widely available, as are a range of pulses such as lentils and chickpeas. When ordering couscous or *tajine*, ask for your dish to be served *sans viande* (without meat).

A breakfast of *bessara* (pea soup with spices and olive oil), fresh bread and mint tea is cheap. You'll find stalls near the markets in most towns. Morocco is also full of patisseries which produce excellent French and Moroccan pastries.

Mint tea, the legendary 'Moroccan whisky', is everywhere. It's made with Chinese gunpowder tea, fresh mint and copious sugar. English tea is usually served black and known as *thé Lipton*. Fruit juices, especially fresh orange, are also common; however, the French *jus* is often used to refer to smoothie-like fruit concoctions, which are popular and frequently delicious.

It's not advisable to drink tap water in Morocco. Bottled water is available everywhere.

Beer is easy to find in the *villes nouvelles* (new towns). The local Stork or Flag brands typically cost from Dh11 to Dh15 in bars (more than double that in fancy hotels). Reasonably palatable Moroccan wines can be had for around Dh35 in liquor stores; the whites and rosés are better than the reds.

ENTERTAINMENT

Morocco isn't big on nightlife. Bars and clubs are usually male preserves and tend to be dubious, expensive or both. Many hotels and restaurants provide traditional music to accompany dinner; the real thing, however, is best heard at the annual festivals and *moussems* (festivals in honour of a holy man or saint).

Getting There & Away

AIR

Morocco is well served by air travel options from Europe, the Middle East and West Africa. The main entry point is Mohammed V international airport, 30km southeast of Casablanca. International flights also land at Tangier, Marrakesh and Fès. Air France and Royal Air Maroc (RAM) are the major carriers; other airlines operating to Morocco include Alitalia, British Airways, Gulf Air, Iberia, KLM and Lufthansa.

In the high season, scheduled flights (valid for one month) between London and Casablanca cost as much as UK£350. It is much cheaper to fly to Málaga in Spain for as little as UK£69 one way and then catch a ferry.

Royal Air Maroc and TWA offer direct flights from New York to Casablanca (around US$800); fares from other US and Canadian cities (via Europe) will cost at least an extra US$200. It may be more economical to fly to a European city such as Paris, Amsterdam or London and continue from there. There are no direct flights between Australia or New Zealand and Morocco.

LAND

Bus

Eurolines and the Moroccan national bus line Compagnie des Transports Marocains (CTM) operate buses between Morocco and many European cities. A one-way/open-return ticket from London to Marrakesh costs UK£102/177 (UK£81/141 for under-25s). These fares usually include the cost of the ferry. Regular buses to Paris and other European cities run from major Moroccan terminals; one-way tickets start at Dh450 (Málaga), rising to Dh1200 (Paris). The land border between Morocco and Algeria is closed.

Train

Trains offer couchettes and the option of breaking your trip along the way, though for the price of a train ticket from London to Paris you could fly to Málaga. A one-way/return ticket to Algeciras on the Eurostar, valid for two months, costs UK£207/308 (30% less for under-26s). These tickets don't usually include the ferry fare. Heading the other way, a one-way ticket from Casablanca to London starts at around Dh2000, less with a student card.

The Moroccan rail system is part of the Inter-Rail network. A two-zone pass allowing one month of unlimited travel in France, Belgium, the Netherlands, Spain and Morocco costs UK£265 (UK£189 for under-26s). The cheapest single-zone pass, covering Spain and Morocco, costs UK£169/119 for 12 days. However, in order to qualify for these passes you need to have lived in Europe for six months.

The Eurail pass (US$486 for 15 days) will get you as far as Algeciras, but does not cover Morocco.

SEA

The main ferry operators are Trasmediterranea, Limadet, Buquebus and Euroferrys. The most popular route is Algeciras–Tangier; other routes include Algeciras/Málaga–Ceuta, Almería/Málaga–Melilla, Gibraltar–Tangier and Tarifa–Tangier. Hydrofoils are commonly used between Spain and Spanish Morocco; the Tangier runs use ferries.

Algeciras–Tangier

There's a ferry roughly every hour between 7am and 10pm in high season; the crossing takes 2½ hours. Adult one-way fares cost €26.77 (Dh250); children under 12 travel for half-price. Transporting the average car costs €69.38 (Dh648).

Algeciras & Málaga–Ceuta

There are up to 17 hydrofoils per day between Algeciras and Ceuta. One-way fares for the 35-minute trip are around €20; cars cost from €32. Buquebus usually runs a Málaga–Ceuta hydrofoil (€30, cars €90; 90 minutes) twice daily in summer.

Almería & Málaga–Melilla

Trasmediterranea operates six overnight services a week between Almería or Málaga and Melilla. The crossings take 6½ to eight hours and 7½ to 10 hours respectively. The cheapest one-way fare on both services is €26.31; cars cost €69.50 and cabin space is available from €43.76 per person.

Gibraltar–Tangier

FRS runs five weekly services. The 70-minute voyage costs UK£18 (Dh260) one way; cars cost UK£46 (Dh730).

Tarifa–Tangier

FRS offers up to six daily services (35 minutes) in high season. Fares are €21 (Dh200) one-way; cars are €69 (Dh645).

Getting Around

BUS

There is a good network of bus routes all over the country, and departures are frequent and tickets cheap. Compagnie des Transports Marocains (CTM) is really the only national company, though other smaller companies such as SATAS can be just as good. On major intercity routes CTM runs 1st- and 2nd-class services; there are more of the former, so you will often pay the higher fare (about 25% more) unless you are very flexible about departure times. It is advisable to book in advance, especially in smaller towns that have few services. In many places, CTM has its own terminal.

Some examples of 1st-class CTM fares are:

from	to	fare (Dh)
Casablanca	Fès	80
Casablanca	Tangier	110
Tangier	Fès	80

There is an official baggage charge on CTM buses (Dh5 per pack). On other lines baggage handlers usually ask for Dh3 to Dh5.

TRAIN

Morocco has one of the most modern rail systems in Africa, with a choice of 1st or 2nd class and *ordinaire* or *rapide* trains. Most trains are now *rapide*, but there are still a few cheaper *ordinaire* services on overnight routes. Couchettes are available on night trains between Marrakesh and Tangier. There are refreshment trolleys and sometimes buffet cars on the longer journeys.

The shuttle trains (TNR) between Rabat, Casablanca and Mohammed V international airport are particularly fast (eg, Rabat to Casablanca in 55 minutes) and comfortable. Second-class fares are roughly comparable to bus fares.

Timetables are prominently displayed in train stations, and a free book of timetables, *Indicateur Horaires*, is sometimes available at stations.

Supratours runs luxury buses in conjunction with trains to destinations not on the rail network, including Tetouan and Nador.

CAR & MOTORCYCLE

An International Driving Permit (IDP) is officially required, but most national licences are sufficient. The expanding motorway network now stretches from Casablanca to Tangier and from Rabat to Fès. Tolls are payable (Dh8 minimum) and the speed limit on the motorway is 120km/h – elsewhere it's 100km/h (40km/h to 60km/h in built-up areas).

You'll find all the major rental companies in Moroccan cities, plus plenty of local companies. Renault 4s and Fiat Unos are the cheapest option (around Dh1400, plus 20% tax, for three days with unlimited kilometres; insurance costs extra). You may be asked to leave a deposit of at least Dh3000 if not paying by credit card, and you need to be at least 21 years old. Shop around and always haggle for discounts.

BICYCLE

Distances are great, roads narrow and dusty, and you'll need to carry all supplies with you (including any spare parts you may need, food and plenty of drinking water) – but the rewards can justify the effort. You can transport bikes on trains (minimum charge Dh20) and buses, but pack them well.

HITCHING

Hitching in Morocco is possible but demands a thick skin and considerable diplomatic expertise because of aggressive hustlers; negotiate petrol money in advance. Women should never hitch alone.

LOCAL TRANSPORT

Most cities have reasonable and useful local bus networks. A ride costs about Dh2.50.

Petits taxis (small taxis used in cities) are equally useful and cheap; most drivers use the meter without question. Fares around a town shouldn't be more than Dh10, but rise by about 50% after 8pm. *Petits taxis* won't leave the city limits or take more than three passengers.

Grands taxis (larger, long-distance taxis) work a little like buses. Usually ageing Mercedes, they take six or even seven passengers to a fixed destination for a standard fare and leave again when full. They are quicker than buses and can leave more frequently, but are more expensive and often less comfortable!

The Mediterranean Coast & the Rif

TANGIER

☎ 039

Sadly, most people's first impression of Tangier is as an unpleasant port of entry plagued by touts and hustlers. The Brigade Touristique has done a lot to alleviate the hassling that gave the city its dubious image, but travellers tend not to stick around for the time it takes to learn the ins and outs of this deceptively vibrant city.

Historically, Tangier has been prized for millennia as a strategic site commanding the Strait of Gibraltar. Settled as a trading port by the ancient Greeks and Phoenicians, the city has been occupied by all manner of peoples, all of whom left their mark in some way. The defining moment in Tangier's history, however, was the period known as the 'InterZone years', when the city and surrounding countryside were declared an international zone controlled by the resident diplomatic agents of Belgium, Britain, France, Italy, the Netherlands, Portugal, Spain, Sweden and the USA.

During this time Tangier became a fashionable resort, renowned for its high-profile gay scene and popularity with artists, writers, bankers, exiles and all kinds of dodgy characters, as well as being an infamous haven for paedophiles. The zone was abolished with independence in 1956, but many places (and people!) retain a certain louche nostalgia.

Orientation

Like many large Moroccan towns, Tangier is divided between the convoluted, hectic streets of the old medina and the wide, ordered boulevards of the ville nouvelle (new town). The modern shops and offices and most of the restaurants and better hotels are in the ville nouvelle, while the medina has markets, craft shops, cheaper hotels and smaller restaurants. The tiny square known as the Petit Socco is the heart of the medina; the larger Grand Socco, in front of the medina walls, marks the meeting point of new and old.

MOROCCO

Information

The **tourist office** *(Délégation Régionale du Tourisme; ☎ 948050; 29 Blvd Pasteur)* can arrange official guides and offers a limited range of brochures.

There are plenty of banks along Blvd Pasteur and Blvd Mohammed V, most with ATMs and some with change booths.

The **main post office** *(Blvd Mohammed V)* has a poste restante service (c/o Tangier Principale 90000). The parcel counter is around the back of the building. Internet services are available all over town for about Dh10 an hour. Try **Club Internet 3000** *(☎ 945106; Rue al-Antaki)* or **Espace Net** *(16 Rue du Mexique)*.

Things to See

In the heart of the medina, the **Petit Socco**, with its cafés and restaurants, is the focus of activity. Back in the days of the InterZone this was the sin and sleaze centre, but it now looks largely harmless.

Heading north from the Petit Socco, Rue des Almohades takes you to the **kasbah**, built on the city's highest point. You enter from Bab el-Assa at the end of Rue ben Raissouli in the medina. The gate opens onto a large courtyard leading to the 17th-century **Dar el-Makhzen** *(admission Dh10; open daily)*, the former sultan's palace. It's now a museum housing beautiful craftwork.

The **American Legation Museum** *(admission free; open Mon-Fri)*, a fascinating reminder that Morocco was the first country to recognise US independence, houses an excellent collection of paintings and prints. Knock on the door.

The **Musée de la Fondation Lorin** *(44 Rue Touahine; admission free; open Sun-Fri)* documents Tangier's local history from 1890 to 1960 and is well worth a look.

In the ville nouvelle, the **Musée d'Art Contemporain** *(Rue d'Angleterre; admission Dh10; open Wed-Mon)* displays work by modern Moroccan artists.

Places to Stay

Hostels The **youth hostel** *(☎ 946127; 8 Rue al-Antaki; dorm beds Dh30/33 members/nonmembers)* offers decent accommodation, but there have been complaints from women travellers. Showers cost Dh5.

Hotels & Pensions There are numerous small hotels in the medina, particularly between the Petit Socco and the port area, but the European-style places in the ville nouvelle are generally more comfortable, with most offering substantial discounts out of season.

Medina There are plenty of cheap pensions, though many are now filled with West African refugees. Room prices start at around Dh30 per person. Not all pensions have showers, but there are several *hammams* around the Petit Socco and one at 80 Rue des Almohades.

Ave Mokhtar Ahardan has countless options: **Pension Palace** *(☎ 936128)* and **Hôtel Olid** *(☎ 931310)* are both OK at Dh40 per person. Hot showers cost an extra Dh10.

Across from the Olid, the upmarket **Hôtel Mamora** *(☎ 934105; singles/doubles Dh305/352)* offers some beautiful views over the Great Mosque. However, **Hôtel Continental**

(☎ 931024, fax 931143; 36 Dar Baroud; singles/doubles Dh339/420) rules the roost in the top-end price range. Perched above the port, it was used for some scenes in the film of Paul Bowles' *The Sheltering Sky*, and still oozes character. Rates include breakfast.

Ville Nouvelle Rue Salah Eddine el-Ayoubi houses an overflow of cheapies from the medina, all similarly priced; there are public showers at the southern end of the road. **Pension Atou** *(☎ 936333; no showers)* and **Pension Talavera** *(☎ 931474)* are probably the cheapest at Dh30 per person. **Pension Le Détroit** *(☎ 934838)* charges a little more but is still a good choice.

The stretch of Ave des FAR leading into Rue al-Antaki is packed with hotels of various categories. **Hôtel L'Marsa** *(☎ 932339; 92 Ave des FAR; rooms per person Dh50)* and **Hôtel Excelsior** *(☎ 066-564787; 17 Rue Magellan; singles/doubles Dh50/80)* are reasonable value at the bottom end of the scale; showers cost Dh5 and Dh10, respectively. Nearby, **Hôtel Magellan** *(☎ 372319; 16 Rue Magellan; singles/doubles Dh40/80)* is another great cheap option with excellent views.

Directly opposite each other on Rue Magellan, hotels **El Muniria** *(☎ 935337; Dh130/150)* and **Ibn Batouta** *(☎ 939311; No 8; rooms Dh150-250)* couldn't be more different. William Burroughs wrote *The Naked Lunch* at El Muniria, which is quiet and slightly run-down but still full of character. Its neighbour, by contrast, is modern and lively, boasting satellite TV and a resident crowd of touts and hangers-on, as well as suspiciously variable room prices!

Up another price notch, the nearby **Hôtel Biarritz** *(☎ 932473; 102 Ave des FAR)* and **Hôtel Nabil** *(☎ 375407; 11 Rue Magellan)* seem to be in direct competition, both charging Dh205/232 for singles/doubles.

For a bit more cash, **Hôtel El Djenina** *(☎ 942244, fax 942246; 8 Rue al-Antaki; singles/doubles Dh249/295)* has immaculate, nicely furnished rooms with bathroom and TV.

Places to Eat

Medina Area For really cheap food, head to the covered markets and food stalls close to the Grand Socco. Numerous small cafés and restaurants here and around the Petit Socco also offer cheap traditional fare.

Just down the hill from Hôtel Continental, the unsigned **Restaurant Ayasi** *(7 Rue Dar el-Baroud)* serves *bessara* in the morning and fish, chicken and *tajines* later on. On the eastern side of the Grand Socco, the tiny **Restaurant Economique** offers *harira*, *bessara* and *brochettes* all day.

Restaurant Ahlan *(Ave Mokhtar Ahardan)* is a popular spot for lunch. Nearby, just north of the Petit Socco, **Restaurant Andalus** *(7 Rue du Commerce; meals around Dh35-45)* is a pleasant hole-in-the-wall serving low-budget meals, including liver and swordfish.

To watch the world go by over coffee or mint tea, try the pleasantly faded **Cafe Tingis** *(Petit Socco)*.

Ville Nouvelle Sandwich Cervantes and Sandwich Genève, opposite each other on Rue Salah Eddine el-Ayoubi, offer filled rolls for around Dh10.

Farther down the same street are several restaurants, most with set menus for around Dh45. **Restaurant Africa** *(☎ 935436; 83 Rue Salah Eddine el-Ayoubi)* is as good as any, and happens to be licensed.

The unique **Restaurant Populaire Saveur** *(☎ 336326; Rue Oualili; set menus Dh100-150)* is a real experience. While the almost compulsory set menus are a tad pricy, the food is excellent (especially the seafood *tajine*) and there are copious extras – not least of these is the service, which is friendly, personal and delightfully eccentric!

For Spanish-style fish, try **Restaurant Romero** *(☎ 932277; 12 Rue du Prince du Moulay Abdallah; mains Dh50-75; open until 3.30am)*, which has a wide-ranging menu.

There are innumerable cafés and patisseries around Place de France and down Blvd Pasteur. Try the cakes at **Le Petit Prince** *(34 Blvd Pasteur)*, or a fancy mint tea at the high-class **Porte du Nord** *(☎ 370545; Rue ibn Rochd)*.

The well-stocked liquor store **Casa Pepé** *(9 Rue ibn Rochd)* also has a decent delicatessen counter.

Entertainment

Tangier offers a bit more nightlife than many other Moroccan cities its size, although much of it is slightly seedy and not advisable for women travellers.

Bars & Clubs Some particularly lively and colourful local bars include the **Trou dans le**

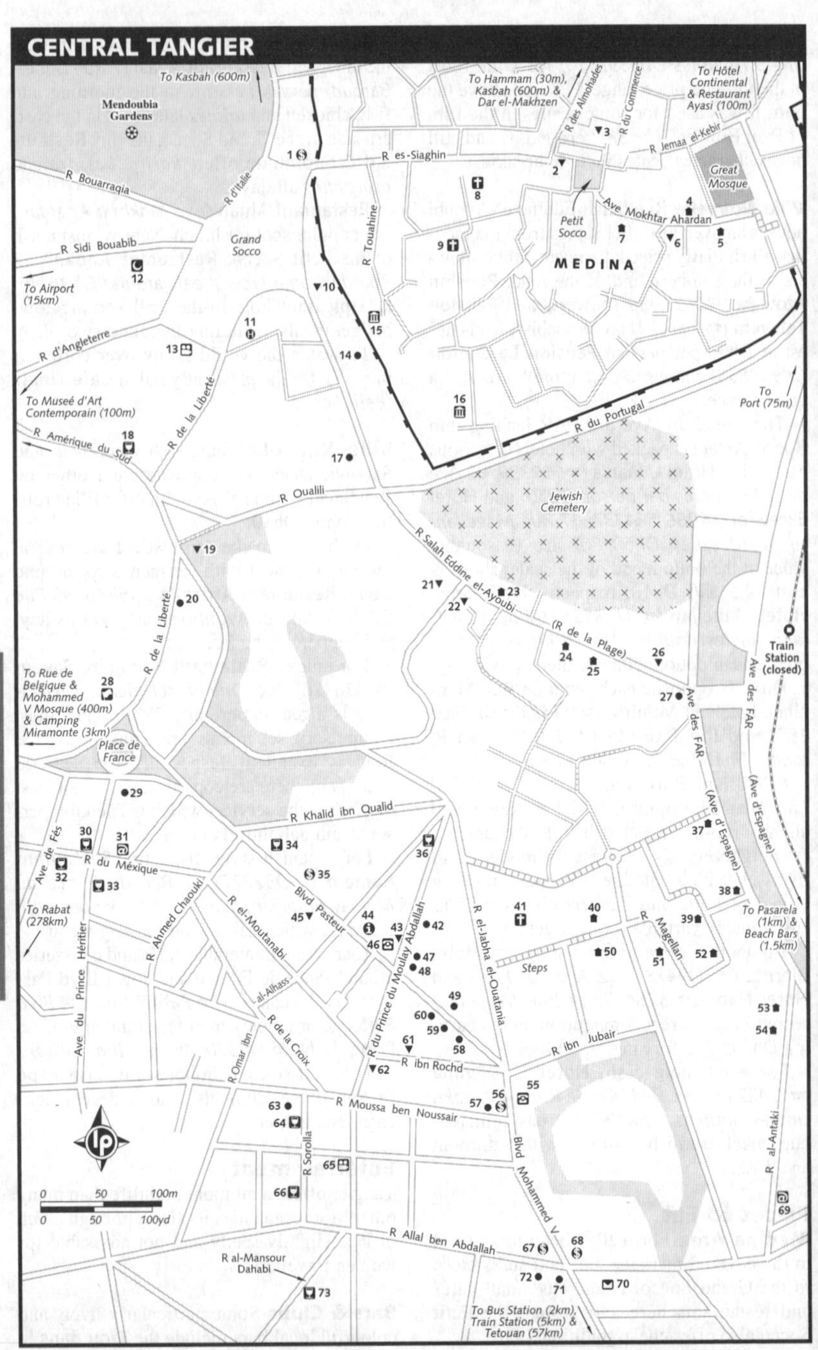
CENTRAL TANGIER
To Kasbah (600m)
Mendoubia Gardens
To Hammam (30m), Kasbah (600m) & Dar el-Makhzen
To Hôtel Continental & Restaurant Ayasi (100m)
R des Almohades
R du Commerce
R Jemaa el-Kebir
R es-Siaghin
Great Mosque
R Bouarraqia
R d'Italie
Petit Socco
Ave Mokhtar Ahardan
R Sidi Bouabib
Grand Socco
R Touahine
MEDINA
To Airport (15km)
R d'Angleterre
To Port (75m)
To Museé d'Art Contemporain (100m)
R de la Liberté
R du Portugal
R Amérique du Sud
Jewish Cemetery
R Oualili
R Salah Eddine el-Ayoubi
(R de la Plage)
Train Station (closed)
Ave des FAR
To Rue de Belgique & Mohammed V Mosque (400m) & Camping Miramonte (3km)
Place de France
(Ave d'Espagne)
R Khalid ibn Qualid
Ave de Fés
R du Méxique
Blvd Pasteur
To Rabat (278km)
R Ahmed Chaouki
R el-Moutanabi
R du Prince Moulay Abdallah
R el-Jabha el-Ouatania
R Magellan
To Pasarela (1km) & Beach Bars (1.5km)
Steps
Ave du Prince Héritier
al-Alhass
R de la Croix
R Omar ibn
R ibn Rochd
R ibn Jubair
R Moussa ben Noussair
R Sorolla
Blvd Mohammed V
R al-Antaki
0 50 100m
0 50 100yd
R Allal ben Abdallah
R al-Mansour Dahabi
To Bus Station (2km), Train Station (5km) & Tetouan (57km)
MOROCCO

CENTRAL TANGIER

PLACES TO STAY
- 4 Hôtel Mamora
- 5 Hôtel Olid
- 7 Pension Palace
- 23 Pension Atou
- 24 Pension Talavera
- 25 Pension Le Détroit
- 37 Hôtel l'Marsa
- 38 Hôtel Biarritz
- 39 Hôtel Excelsior
- 40 Hôtel El Muniria & Tanger Inn
- 50 Hôtel Ibn Batouta
- 51 Hôtel Magellan
- 52 Hôtel Nabil
- 53 Hôtel El Djenina
- 54 Youth Hostel

PLACES TO EAT
- 2 Cafe Tingis
- 3 Restaurant Andalus
- 6 Restaurant Ahlan
- 10 Restaurant Economique
- 19 Restaurant Populaire Saveur
- 21 Sandwich Genève
- 22 Sandwich Cervantes
- 26 Restaurant Africa
- 43 Restaurant Romero
- 45 Le Petit Prince
- 61 Casa Pepé (Liquor Store)
- 62 Porte du Nord

OTHER
- 1 BMCE Bank (ATM)
- 8 Church of the Immaculate Conception
- 9 Spanish Church
- 11 Hammam
- 12 Mosque
- 13 Cinéma Rif
- 14 Covered Market
- 15 Musée de la Fondation Lorin
- 16 American Legation Museum
- 17 Covered Market
- 18 Dean's Bar
- 20 British Airways
- 27 Public Showers
- 28 French Consulate
- 29 Royal Air Maroc
- 30 Negrescu English Bar
- 31 Espace Net
- 32 Pilo
- 33 Trou dans le Mur Bar
- 34 Paname Bar
- 35 BMCE (Late Bank & ATMs)
- 36 Les Ambassadeurs
- 41 Church
- 42 Budget
- 44 Tourist Office
- 46 Telephone & Fax Office
- 47 Limadet Office
- 48 Trasmediterranea Office
- 49 Iberia Airlines
- 55 Téléboutique
- 56 Crédit du Maroc
- 57 Le Palace Disco (Hôtel Tanjah-Flandria)
- 58 Voyages Schwartz (American Express)
- 59 Avis
- 60 Librairie des Colonnes
- 63 Paris Pressing (Laundry)
- 64 The Pub
- 65 Cinéma Goya
- 66 Chico's Pub
- 67 Banque Populaire
- 68 Wafabank
- 69 Club Internet 3000
- 70 Main Post Office
- 71 Hertz
- 72 Cady Loc (Car Rental)
- 73 London's

Mur *(Hole in the Wall; Ave du Prince Héritier)*, the **Paname** *(15 Blvd Pasteur)* and **Les Ambassadeurs** *(Rue du Prince du Moulay Abdallah)*.

Pub lovers will find themselves well catered for: **Chico's Pub** *(10 Rue Sorolla)*, **London's** *(Rue al-Mansour Dahabi; live music most nights)*, **The Pub** *(☎ 934789; 2 Rue Sorolla)* and **Negrescu English Bar** *(Rue du Méxique)* offer a varied range of drinking opportunities.

Pilo *(Ave de Fès)*, just past the intersection with Rue du Méxique, is a relaxed place, with excellent tapas and good views of the twilight zone outside.

The much-reduced European gay population still frequents some of the beach bars south of town. Popular places include the Macumba, Miami Beach and Coco Beach.

Some remnants of Tangier's seedy Inter-Zone days have survived. Tiny **Tanger Inn** *(Rue Magellan; open 9pm-late)*, next to Hôtel El Muniria, and the famous **Dean's Bar** *(Rue Amérique du Sud)* still attract the occasional curious traveller, but on many nights calling them 'quiet' would be charitable!

The three most popular nightclubs in town are Pasarela, down by the beach on Ave des FAR; Olivia Valere in the Ahlan Hôtel, about 5km along the road to Rabat; and Le Palace disco in Hôtel Tanjah-Flandria. Entry to all these clubs is around Dh100; drinks start at Dh40.

Getting There and Away

Air The **Royal Air Maroc** *(☎ 979501, fax 932681)* has daily flights to Casablanca (Dh813 one way), plus direct flights to Amsterdam, Brussels, London, Madrid and Paris. Regional Airlines flies to Málaga, **Iberia** *(Rue de la Liberté)* flies to Madrid and **British Airways** *(Blvd Pasteur)* flies to London.

Bus & Grand Taxi Most CTM buses leave from the CTM office near the port entrance. Others (and some of CTMs 2nd-class services) leave from the *gare routière* on Place Jamia el-Arabia, a Dh8 *petit taxi* ride away. Most non-CTM buses also leave from here, heading to hundreds of destinations. Regular CTM departures include Tetouan (Dh13.50), Rabat (Dh83), Fès (Dh85) and Casablanca (Dh110). *Grands taxis* leave from the bus station; there are frequent departures to Tetouan (Dh20), Asilah (Dh20) and Fnideq (Dh25).

Train Tangier's only functional train station, Tangier Morora, is about 5km southeast of town; a *petit taxi* costs about Dh13. *Rapide* trains heading south from Tangier split at Sidi Kacem to Rabat (Dh89.50, five hours), Casablanca (Dh116.50, six hours) and Marrakesh (Dh188.50, nine to 10 hours), or to Meknès (Dh79.50, four hours) and Fès (Dh95.50, five hours). The only cheap southbound *ordinaire* service (Fès Dh71 and Marrakesh Dh142.50) leaves at 11pm daily.

Boat If you're heading to Spain or Gibraltar by boat, you can buy tickets from virtually any travel agency. You'll find plenty on Ave des FAR; the Limadet and Trasmediterranea offices are on Rue du Prince du Moulay Abdallah. It's possible to get tickets from the port, but the entrance is a hot spot for touts and the process can turn into a real hassle – be firm and make sure you know what you're doing.

Getting Around

Few local bus services in Tangier are any use to the traveller. Local departures, such as they are, leave from outside Mohammed V Mosque on Rue de Belgique. *Petits taxis* are metered and cost under Dh10 around town.

TETOUAN

☎ 039

Set against the dramatic backdrop of the Rif Mountains, Tetouan was originally settled by Arab-Berber and Jewish refugees from Muslim Andalucía in the 16th century, and was subsequently occupied by the Spanish during the protectorate years. Even as a sprawling urban zone, the city retains a distinctly Spanish air, especially around the classic whitewashed medina.

Tetouan can sometimes have a slightly intimidating atmosphere, particularly at night; while much of the former hassle has disappeared, it's still a place to be on your guard.

Information

The **tourist office** *(☎ 961916; 30 Ave Mohammed V)* has helpful staff who speak English. There are plenty of banks along Ave Mohammed V. Copious Internet access is available around town at Dh10 an hour – check out **Magic Internet** *(Rue 10 Mai)*, **Cyber Primo** *(Place Moulay el-Mehdi)* or the stylishly ultraviolet **Cyber Élégance** *(☎ 711843; Rue du P Sidi Mohammed)*.

Things to See

The bustling **medina** is the main point of interest for visitors; it's best entered through Bab er-Rouah. Outside, **Place Hassan II**, the grand main square linking the old and new parts of the city, is another focus for all kinds of local activity.

Just inside the eastern gate of Bab el-Okla, the excellent **Musée Marocain** *(admission Dh10; open Wed-Mon)* has well-presented exhibits of everyday Moroccan and Andalucían life. The small **Archaeology Museum** *(admission Dh10; open Mon-Fri)*, off Place al-Jala, has a good collection originating largely from the Roman ruins of Lixus, near Larache.

Outside Bab el-Okla is the **Artisanal School** *(admission Dh10; open Mon-Fri)*, where children learn traditional crafts. The building itself is worth a visit.

Places to Stay

The nearest camping ground is **Camping Alboustane** *(☎ 688822)* on the beach at Martil, 8km from the town.

There are plenty of cheap, basic pensions, although some of those around Place Moulay el-Mehdi are best avoided. **Hôtel Bilbao** *(7 Ave Mohammed V; singles/doubles Dh31/52)* is one of the cheapest options. A bit better is **Pension Iberia** *(☎ 963679; 5 Place Moulay el-Mehdi; singles/doubles Dh50/80)*, with some nice views, and showers for Dh5.

Hôtel Príncipe *(☎ 962795; 20 Rue ben Tachfine; singles/doubles Dh60/74, with shower Dh70/100)* is OK, though some of the bathrooms are barely functional.

Hôtel Oumaima *(☎ 963473; Rue 10 Mai; singles/doubles Dh200/236)* is getting slightly tatty but has decent rooms with bathroom and phone; **Hôtel Regina** *(☎ 962113; Rue Sidi Mandri; singles/doubles Dh205/246)* has a bit more character and good low-season discounts.

Places to Eat

There are loads of cheap eats in and around the medina. In the ville nouvelle, **Yousfi Snack** *(Rue ben Tachfine)* is a good bet for a munch, and **Supermercado La Española** *(Rue 10 Mai)* has plenty of supplies, including booze.

Restaurant Saigon *(Rue Mohammed ben Larbi Torres)* is good value and has friendly, if slightly scatty, service. Two courses and a drink should cost around Dh35. The licensed Restaurant Restinga, just off Ave Mohammed V, is also good.

For those with more Italian tastes, **Pizza Sicilienne** *(☎ 993184; Rue al-Horuba)* serves its namesake for around Dh25. Watch out for the rowdy pool hall next door!

Café Pâtisserie SMIR *(Ave Mohammed V)* is currently shrouded in scaffolding but still serves excellent pastries, as does the local branch of **Pâtisserie Rahmouni** *(10 Rue ben Tachfine)*.

Getting There & Away

CTM buses depart from the **long-distance bus station** *(cnr Rue Sidi Mandri & Rue Moulay Abbas)* to Casablanca (Dh105), Chefchaouen (Dh16.50), Fès (Dh70), Rabat (Dh80) and Tangier (Dh13). Other companies have buses to these and other destinations, including Marrakesh (Dh130). Local buses to Martil (Dh2.50) leave from Rue Moulay Abbas.

Grands taxis to Chefchaouen (Dh25) and Tangier (Dh20) leave from Rue al-Jazeer. *Grands taxis* for the Ceuta border (Dh20) leave from Ave Sidi Driss, down the steps opposite the bus station.

CHEFCHAOUEN

☎ 039

Nestled on the slopes of the Rif Mountains, picturesque Chefchaouen is deservedly popular with travellers. The air is cool and clear and the atmosphere relaxed. While the people are well aware of their home's appeal, any hassle is friendly and unpressured.

The town, originally called Chaouen, was founded in 1471 after a huge influx of Muslim and Jewish refugees from Andalucía, who gave the town its unique Hispanic look of whitewashed houses. Surprisingly, the striking pale blue that the town is so famous for dates only back to the 1930s – before then doors and window frames were a traditional Muslim green.

Information

There are various banks around town, but not many ATMs; the Banque Populaire kiosk on Plaza Uta el-Hammam changes travellers cheques (Dh10.70 commission per cheque).

The **post office** *(Ave Hassan II)* is on the main street. Good Internet access is available at **Groupe Chaouni Info** *(Ave Abdelkrim el-Kattabi)*, near Plaza Mohammed V at the western end of the ville nouvelle, for Dh10 an hour; **Kouera Computer** *(☎ 987284; Ave Abi Hassan Mandri)* has slower machines but cheaper rates, and also has a PlayStation!

Things to See & Do

The old **medina** is easy to navigate – all the painted streets are dead ends. The centre of activity is **Plaza Uta el-Hammam**, a spacious cobbled area full of cafés, which is dominated by the 15th-century **kasbah** *(admission to museum & gardens Dh10)* and the **Great Mosque**. This is also where you will undoubtedly be offered *kif* (marijuana) – in a very friendly manner, of course.

A lively **market** is held in the new town on Monday and Thursday.

The mountains around the town provide some excellent **trekking**. Contact the president of the **Association Randonnée et Culture** *(☎ 986153)*, just off Plaza Uta el-Hammam, at **Casa Hassan** *(22 Rue Targui)*, which is just off Plaza Uta el-Hammam.

Places to Stay

The pleasant camping ground **Azilan** *(☎ 986 979; sleeping out Dh10 per person)* is north of town, a steep 30-minute walk up the hill.

There is a great range of cheap hotels in the medina, many with roof terraces where you can sleep if the weather's nice. Receptionists often seem to sleep for most of the morning, so be gentle with them.

The cheapest hotel options are the very basic **Pension Ibn Battouta** *(☎ 986044; 31 Rue Abi Khancha; Dh20 per person)* and the popular **Pension Mauritania** *(☎ 986184; 15 Rue Kadi Alami; singles/doubles Dh25/40)*. A shower at either will cost you Dh5.

Pension La Castellana *(☎ 986295; 4 Rue Bouhali; singles/doubles Dh30/60, terrace Dh15)* is a popular choice even out of season, largely thanks to its wonderful roof terrace. **Pension Valencia** *(☎ 062-147119; Rue Hassan I; rooms Dh30 per person, terrace Dh20)* is similarly well endowed up top, but the inside rooms are less desirable. **Pension Znika** *(☎ 986624; Rue Znika; rooms Dh35 per person)* is another good option, with hot showers included.

Outside the medina, **Hôtel Marrakech** *(☎ 987113; Ave Hassan II; singles/doubles Dh50/80, with bathroom Dh80/120)* offers a variety of rooms and has a popular terrace and restaurant. Nearby on Ave Hassan II, **Hôtel Rif** *(☎ 986982; singles/doubles Dh60/90, with bathroom Dh97/140)* and **Hôtel Madrid** *(☎ 987496, fax 987498; singles/doubles Dh180/261, double with 4-poster bed & TV Dh298)* cater for more upscale tastes. Both have excellent views; Hôtel Madrid also has some luxury rooms and probably the only power showers in Morocco.

Places to Eat

Produce can be bought from the market or various transient sellers around the medina; the local goats' cheese is excellent. Snack stalls also appear sporadically on Plaza Uta el-Hammam or just outside Bab al-'Ain.

The clusters of small restaurants and cafés on Plaza Uta el-Hammam are frequented by just about everyone in town at some point. They're all pretty much of a muchness, with Moroccan and Spanish dishes going for around Dh25; Cafe Snack Mounir is worth a look.

Restaurant Assada *(dishes around Dh18)*, near Bab al-'Ain to the north, is a tiny local spot offering good-value standards.

Outside the medina, up the hill from the Bab al-'Ain, popular Restaurant Moulay Ali ben Rachid is also a good option.

For a bit more money there are some excellent set menus at **Salon Aladin** *(set menu Dh45)* and its new rival **Khasba** *(☎ 883397; set menu Dh43)*, off Place Uta el-Hammam. The Aladin is a quiet, relaxed upstairs space away from the square, while Khasba is a more flamboyant, overfriendly spot at street level (it's a favourite with touts and dealers). Hands-down winner in this class, however, is **Restaurant Tissemlal** *(set menu Dh50)* at Casa Hassan, which has just a touch of real inspiration in its decor and menu.

Pâtisserie Daifa *(☎ 988433; Ave Hassan II)*, outside Bab al-'Ain, does good pastries and bread.

Many hotels also have terrace restaurants, which are expensive but offer superb views free of charge.

Getting There & Away

The bus station is a 15-minute downhill walk southwest of the Old Town. Many of the CTM and other buses are through services and often arrive already full, so it's a good idea to book a seat in advance. If you're not having any luck getting a bus to Fès (Dh50, four hours), try for Meknès (Dh45, three hours) and take a bus or *grand taxi* from there.

In addition to the numerous buses to Tetouan (Dh15, one hour) and Tangier (Dh33, two hours), there are departures to Fnideq (near the Ceuta border), Rabat, Casablanca and Nador (Dh86, eight hours).

Grands taxis going northwest to Tetouan (Dh25) and occasionally Tangier (Dh50) leave from just off Plaza Mohammed V. Taxis heading south and east leave from Ave Allal ben Abdallah.

Spanish Morocco

The towns of Ceuta and Melilla constitute Spanish Morocco. About 70% of the towns' inhabitants are Spanish; both are administered as city provinces of Spain, but are currently waiting to be granted full autonomous status on an equal footing with the other provinces. Morocco occasionally campaigns for their return, but Spain's increasing importance as a trading partner has prevented these tiny enclaves from becoming a serious point of contention.

The main function of the towns is to supply Spanish troops stationed there. The principal trade is in tax-free goods; however, Morocco's Free Trade Agreement with the European Union (EU) may remove the need to smuggle goods out to the rest of Africa, seriously affecting the local economy.

Both Ceuta and Melilla keep Spanish time and use the euro. Direct overseas dialling is cheaper than in Morocco. Note that calls into both enclaves require the international dialling code for Spain (☎ 34), not Morocco; the area code is also necessary within the towns themselves.

CEUTA

☎ 956

Ceuta is the larger and more Spanish of the two remaining Spanish-run towns on Moroccan soil. Known as 'Sebta' in Morocco, it offers a couple of days' distraction but it's not cheap. If you're heading for Morocco, you could catch an early fast-ferry from Algeciras and go straight through to Tangier, Tetouan or Chefchaouen.

The **tourist office** *(☎ 501401; open Mon-Sat)*, beside the dock near the end of Avenida Muelle Cañonero Dato, has an accommodation list.

Plenty of banks line Paseo de Revellín and its continuation, Calle Camoens; the **BBVA** *(Plaza de los Reyes)* is your best bet for changing travellers cheques. There's no need to buy dirham here – you can do so at the border as long as you have cash.

The **main post office** *(correos y telégrafos; Plaza de España)* can handle most postal requirements. There are plenty of public phones, which accept coins, phonecards and credit cards. **Indy Net** *(☎ 524076; 6 Calle Isabel Cabral)*, the only Internet café in town, charges €3 per hour.

The **Museo de la Legión** *(Paseo de Colón; admission free, including guided tour)* is dedicated to and run by the Spanish Legion and holds a staggering array of military paraphernalia. Opened in May 1995, the **Maritime Park** (Parque Marítimo del Mediterráneo) is a huge complex on the seafront, complete with a manufactured beach, pools, restaurants, bars and casino.

Places to Stay & Eat

Finding accommodation can be tricky, especially during the annual Carnival in mid-March, so it's worth trying to book in advance. Not everywhere is signed; look out for the blue or green F (for *fondas,* or inn), HR (for *hostal-residencia*) and CH (for *casas de huéspedes,* or boarding houses) signs close to the entrances.

There aren't many genuinely cheap places in town, although **Pensión Revellín** *(☎ 516762; 2 Paseo de Revellín; singles/doubles €7.20/13.20, showers €1.80)* just about fits the bill. Up the street, **Pensión La Bohemia** *(☎ 510615; 16 Paseo de Revellín; rooms €20 per person)* is much more pleasant, but more expensive.

Also nearby, **Hostal Central** *(☎ 516716; 15 Paseo del Revellín; singles/doubles €24/45)* is excellent value. Its small rooms come with bathroom and TV, and the staff speak some English.

There are plenty of eating and drinking options around town, including two Chinese restaurants and an Irish pub, as well as places selling the ubiquitous *bocadillos* (sandwiches) and tapas. **Cafetería La Campana** *(13 Calle Real)* does a good breakfast. To mix with a lively Spanish set, try the tiny bar **Méson Planta Baja** *(19 Tte Pacheco)* in the evening.

On the other side of the yacht harbour, **Club Nautico** *(☎ 514440; Calle Edrisis; mains from €6)* is good for a civilised fish dinner.

Getting There & Away

To get to Morocco proper, the No 7 bus runs every ten minutes or so between Plaza de la Constitución and the *frontera* (border; €0.54). If you arrive by ferry and want to head for the border, there's a stop just up from the tourist office on Calle Edrisis. Once through the border, there are plenty of *grands taxis* to Tetouan (Dh20) and to nearby Fnideq (Dh5), where you can easily find taxis or buses to Tangier (whatever the touts say!).

For those heading to mainland Spain, the ferry terminal is 800m west of the centre. There are frequent fast-ferries (hydrofoils) as well as cheaper ferry departures to Algeciras. Two hydrofoil services per day head to Málaga in the high season.

MELILLA

☎ 952

Melilla is smaller and more out of the way than its sister Ceuta and has more of a Moroccan flavour, even amid the imposing colonial architecture.

There is a well-stocked **tourist desk** *(☎ 675 444; Calle Fortuny)* in the Palacio de Congresos y Exposiciones. Most banks are on Avenida de Juan Carlos I Rey, where you can buy and sell dirham. There's a Banque Populaire on the Moroccan side of the border (cash exchanges only); local moneychangers don't offer great rates. **Locutorio Fon-net** *(☎ 680974; Calle Ejército Español)* has telephones, as well as Internet access for €1 an hour.

The medieval fortress of **Melilla la Vieja** is pretty quiet these days but still very impressive, and offers some great views. Within the walls, tucked away in the maze of winding Castilian streets, are the **Iglesia de la Concepción**, the **Museo Municipal** and the **Museo Militar**. The main entrance to the fortress is through the massive **Puerta de la Marina**.

Places to Stay & Eat

Be warned – accommodation in Melilla is expensive. The cheapest by far is **Pensión del Puerto** *(☎ 681270; 1 Calle Santiago; rooms €10 per person)*, off Avenida General Macías.

It's a big jump in price to the next step up at **Hostal Rioja** *(☎ 682709; 10 Calle Ejército Español; singles/doubles €19/28, plus €3 in summer)*. Perhaps the best option is the friendly **Hostal Cazaza** *(☎ 684648; 6 Calle Primo de Rivera; singles/doubles €23/35)*, which has nice rooms with TV, bathroom and balcony.

There are plenty of good snack stops along Calle Castelar, not far from the Mercado Municipal. **Anthony Pizzeria** *(1 Calle Cándido)* is still a popular spot for Italian food. For a proper Spanish munch, try the €6 set menu at Cafe Central, by the entrance to the Parque Hernandez.

In the evening, head to La Onubense and La Cervecería, opposite each other on Calle O'-Donell, for some excellent tapas (and maybe a beer or two).

Getting There & Away

To Morocco proper, the No 2 bus (marked Aforos) runs from Plaza de España to the *frontera* (€0.48) every 30 minutes from 7.30am to 10pm. On the Moroccan side there are frequent buses (Dh2.30) and *grands taxis* (Dh10) to Nador, the major transport hub for the region. Buses depart until about 8pm daily.

Trasmediterranea runs daily ferries to Málaga and Almería, Spain. Buy your tickets at its office on Plaza de España or at the ferry terminal. Spanish rail and coach tickets can be booked at travel agencies in town. There are also several flights to Málaga.

The Middle Atlas

Morocco's Middle Atlas region is extremely diverse. From mountain skiing to Roman-ruin exploring to desert trekking, the area provides the traveller with a brief précis of the variety that North Africa has to offer.

MEKNÈS

☎ 055

Meknès is perhaps the most underrated of the imperial cities, generally receiving less attention than its larger neighbours. However, the city was Alawite sultan Moulay Ismail's capital for 55 years in the 17th century, and it still houses an enormous palace complex. Unfortunately, an earthquake in 1755 severely damaged Meknès, and little was done to restore it until the onset of mass tourism revealed its economic potential. It's now a relaxed and pleasant alternative (or antidote) to the hustle and bustle of Fès.

The Oued Boufekrane (Boufekrane River) divides the new and old towns. The **tourist office** *(☎ 524426)* is next to the main post office, facing Place de France. Banks with ATMs are concentrated in the ville nouvelle. A BMCE exchange office is on Ave des FAR. Internet cafés are very cheap, if not always fast, at Dh5 an hour. Try **NetWhyNot** *(Ave Mohammed V)*, or Cyber Paris and EasyEverything, either side of Pizza Fongue (see Places to Eat).

Things to See

Unless stated otherwise, admission to sights is Dh10.

Located at the heart of the Old Town, Place el-Hedim is a busy square facing **Bab el-Mansour**, one of the most impressive monumental gateways in Morocco. To the north of the square are the **medina** and the major *souqs*; to the east you'll find the old and new **mellahs** (Jewish quarters).

Enter the medina through the arch next to the **Dar Jamaï Museum** – along the main covered street you'll find the beautiful 14th-century **Medersa Bou Inania** *(open daily)* and the **Great Mosque**.

To visit the **Imperial City**, start from Bab el-Mansour and follow the road through the gate around to the small **Koubbat as-Sufara'**, where foreign ambassadors were formally received. Beside it is the entrance to an enormous underground granary.

Opposite and a little to the left, through another gate, is the **Mausoleum of Moulay Ismail** *(admission free; open Sat-Thur)*, one of the few Islamic monuments in the country open to non-Muslims.

From the mausoleum, the road follows the walls of the **Dar el-Makhzen** (Royal Palace) to reach the **Agdal basin**, a grand artificial lake, and the spectacular **Heri es-Souani** granaries and stables *(open daily)*.

Places to Stay

Camping Agdal *(☎ 555396; sites per person/tent Dh20/10)* is in a lovely site near the Agdal basin, a long way from the ville nouvelle. The **youth hostel** *(☎ 524698; dorm beds Dh30)* is close to the posh Hôtel Transatlantique, about 1km from the ville nouvelle centre.

There are dozens of cheap hotels along Rue Dar Smen and Rue Rouamzine in the medina. **Hôtel Regina** *(☎ 530280; singles/doubles Dh60/90)* and **Hôtel Maroc** *(☎ 530075; singles/doubles Dh60/120)* are both reasonable and have pleasant courtyards.

Found in the ville nouvelle, **Hôtel Toubkal** *(☎ 522218; Rue Mohammed V; singles/doubles Dh50/100)* is cheap but very basic, with a dubious electricity supply. **Hôtel Touring** *(☎ 522351; 34 Ave Allal ben Abdallah; singles/doubles Dh75/117)* is a slightly better option.

Hôtel Majestic *(☎ 522035; 19 Ave Mohammed V; singles/doubles Dh146/172)* is a good mid-range choice with a nice roof terrace; it's currently being refurbished, so avoid the third floor. The quirky **Hôtel Excelsior** *(☎ 521900; 57 Ave des FAR; singles/doubles Dh120/140)* is also worth a look.

Next door, **Hôtel Akouas** *(☎ 515967, fax 515994; 27 Rue Amir Abdelkader; singles/doubles Dh308/375)* tops the comfort league with rooms of varying quality, and a decent bar, restaurant and terrace.

Places to Eat

There is a market and a liquor store in the ville nouvelle. As usual, there are plenty of simple restaurants in the medina, particularly along Rue Dar Smen. The aptly named **Restaurant Économique** *(123 Rue Dar Smen)* is good, as is Snack Bounania, in its own courtyard near the *medersa*.

There's an excellent view and more expensive traditional fare at **Collier de la Colombe** *(67 Rue Driba; set menu Dh75)*, near the Imperial City. The ville nouvelle has some cheap eateries and lots of rotisseries, mainly along and around Ave Mohammed V. **Restaurant Marhaba** *(☎ 521632)*, a tiny tiled place, does a decent *tajine* for Dh30. **Pizza Fongue** *(Zankat Accra; pizzas Dh20)* is another good option.

Classier and far more Western, **Pizzeria Le Four** *(☎ 520857; 11 Rue Ibn Khaldoun; pizzas from Dh40)* is licensed and popular with travellers; 14% tax is added. Across the road, **Montana** *(☎ 520568; mains from Dh45)* offers Western staples, and a bar downstairs.

For breakfast or coffee, join the lively mixed crowds at Cafe Bekkam or Salon de Thé Printemps, in shopping precincts either side of Ave Mohammed V.

Entertainment

Most of the bars in town are attached to hotels and restaurants – **La Coupole** *(☎ 522483; Rue Ghana)* and Pizzeria Le Four are two of the better (but quieter) places. Men could try the 8-Ball if they're feeling tough. The best discos are in Hôtel Bab Mansour at 38 Rue el-Amir Abdelkader (just past Hôtel Akouas) and at Hôtel Akouas.

Getting There & Away

The CTM bus station is on Ave des FAR; the main bus station (where CTM buses also stop) is just outside Bab el-Khemis. Destinations include Fès (one hour), Rabat (2½ hours), Casablanca (four hours), Chefchaouen (five hours), Tangier (six hours) and Marrakesh (seven hours). Local buses and *grands taxis* to the same destinations also leave from here.

Train passengers should head for the more convenient El-Amir Abdelkader station, just west of Ave Mohammed V. All trains to Fès (Dh16.50, one hour), Rabat (Dh55.50, 2½ hours), Casablanca (Dh81, 3½ hours), and Marrakesh (Dh153.50, seven hours) stop here.

AROUND MEKNÈS

About 33km from Meknès, the **Volubilis** *('Oualili' in Arabic; admission Dh20; open sunrise-sunset daily)* site contains the best-preserved Roman ruins in Morocco. Dating largely from the 2nd and 3rd centuries AD, the site was actually originally settled by Carthaginian traders in the 3rd century BC. It is noted for its mosaic floors, many of which have been left *in situ*.

To get there, take a *grand taxi* (Dh7 per person) or bus (Dh6) from Place de la Foire in Meknès and hop out at the turn-off to Moulay Idriss. From there it's a pleasant half-hour walk. Going back, you can hitch or walk to Moulay Idriss and wait for a bus or *grand taxi*. If you have a group, you could hire a *grand taxi* for a half-day trip – don't pay more than Dh300.

FÈS

☎ 055

Fès is the oldest of Morocco's imperial cities, founded shortly after the Arabs swept across North Africa following the death of the Prophet Mohammed. Its magnificent buildings reflect a rich heritage of Arab-Berber imagination and artistry. While Rabat and Marrakesh are more important on paper, Fès is still widely seen as the cultural and spiritual capital of Morocco.

The medina of Fès el-Bali (Old Fès) is one of the largest medieval cities in the modern world. Its narrow, winding alleys and covered bazaars are crammed with workshops, restaurants, mosques, *medersas*, markets and tanneries; the exotic smells, the hammering of metalworkers, the call of the muezzin and the jostling crowds are an amazing and unforgettable experience.

Orientation & Information

Fès consists of three distinct parts. The original walled city of Fès el-Bali is in the east;

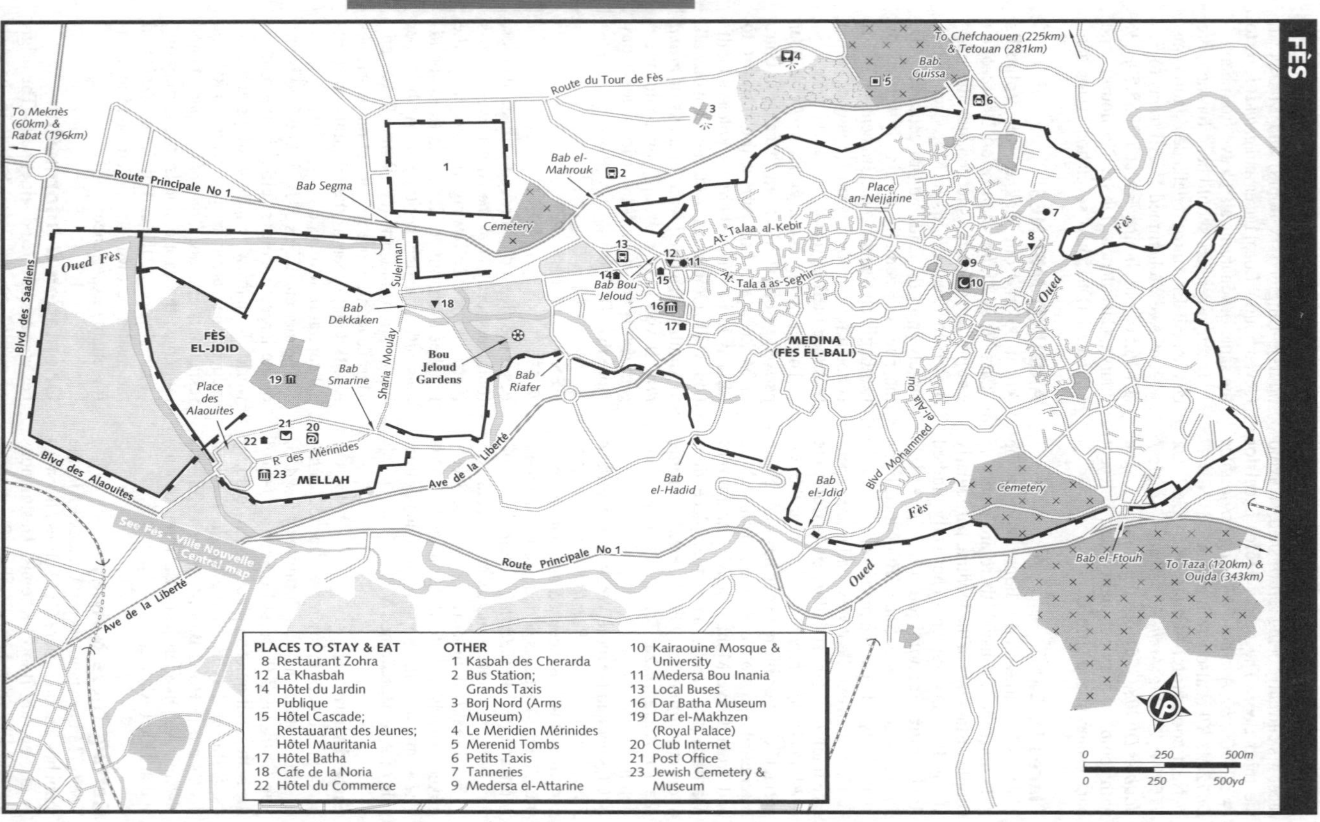
FÈS
PLACES TO STAY & EAT
8 Restaurant Zohra
12 La Khasbah
14 Hôtel du Jardin Publique
15 Hôtel Cascade; Restaurant des Jeunes; Hôtel Mauritania
17 Hôtel Batha
18 Cafe de la Noria
22 Hôtel du Commerce
OTHER
1 Kasbah des Cherarda
2 Bus Station; Grands Taxis
3 Borj Nord (Arms Museum)
4 Le Meridien Mérinides
5 Merenid Tombs
6 Petits Taxis
7 Tanneries
9 Medersa el-Attarine
10 Kairaouine Mosque & University
11 Medersa Bou Inania
13 Local Buses
16 Dar Batha Museum
19 Dar el-Makhzen (Royal Palace)
20 Club Internet
21 Post Office
23 Jewish Cemetery & Museum
MEDINA (FÈS EL-BALI)
FÈS EL-JDID
MELLAH
Bou Jeloud Gardens
Place an-Nejjarine
Place des Alaouites
At-Talaa al-Kebir
At-Tala a as-Seghir
Bab Guissa
Bab el-Mahrouk
Bab Bou Jeloud
Bab Segma
Bab Dekkaken
Bab Smarine
Bab Riafer
Bab el-Hadid
Bab el-Jdid
Bab el-Ftouh
Cemetery
Cemetery
Oued Fès
Oued Fès
Oued Fès
Route du Tour de Fès
Route Principale No 1
Route Principale No 1
Blvd Mohammed el-Alaoui
Ave de la Liberté
Ave de la Liberté
Sharia Moulay Suleiman
R des Mérinides
Blvd des Alaouites
Blvd des Saadiens
To Chefchaouen (225km) & Tetouan (281km)
To Taza (120km) & Oujda (343km)
To Meknès (60km) & Rabat (196km)
See Fès - Ville Nouvelle Central map
0 250 500m
0 250 500yd

MOROCCO

southwest is the French-built ville nouvelle with most of the restaurants and hotels; and the Merenid walled city of Fès el-Jdid lies between the two.

The **ONMT office** *(☎ 623460; Place de la Résistance)* is in the ville nouvelle. Official guides are available here or through hotels at Dh120/150 for a half/full day. Plenty of unofficial guides hang around and will guide you for a lot less – they can be useful, especially in stopping other would-be guides from hassling you. Fès also has a **syndicat d'initiative** *(Place Mohammed V; open daily)*.

The main post office is in the ville nouvelle, as are most banks with ATMs. Internet cafés all over town charge from Dh7 to Dh15 per hour. **Club Internet** *(Rue des Mérinides)* has good, fast connections at Dh10 per hour; **SIBED** *(☎ 941383; Rue Arabie Saoudite; open until midnight)* charges Dh8 per hour.

Things to See

Fès el-Bali The old **medina** is an incredible maze of twisting alleys, arches, mosques, shrines, fountains, workshops and markets. Unfortunately, most of the religious sites are closed to non-Muslims; admission to the exceptions cost Dh10.

The most convenient entry point to the medina is **Bab Bou Jeloud**; close by is the **Medersa Bou Inania**, built by the Merenid sultan Bou Inan between 1350 and 1357. Its carved woodwork is magnificent.

In the guts of the city, you can only take a peek into the **Kairaouine Mosque**, one of the largest mosques in Morocco. Founded between 859 and 862 for Tunisian refugees, it has one of the finest libraries in the Muslim world. Nearby, the **Medersa el-Attarine** *(open daily)*, built by Abu Said in 1325, displays some beautiful Merenid craftsmanship.

On the boundary between Fès el-Bali and Fès el-Jdid, the **Dar Batha Museum** *(Place de Batha; open Wed-Mon)* was built as a palace over 100 years ago, and now houses historical and artistic artefacts from ruined or decaying *medersas*, as well as Fassi embroidery, tribal carpets and ceramics.

Fès el-Jdid Built by the Merenids in the 13th century, Fès's 'other' walled city is not as lively or interesting as Fès el-Bali. It contains the old Jewish quarter (*mellah*) and a couple of mosques and synagogues (one housing a **Jewish Cemetery & museum**). The **Dar el-Makhzen** (Royal Palace) has 80 hectares of grounds, but it's uncharitably closed to the public.

At the northern end of the main street, Sharia Moulay Suleiman, is the enormous **Bab Dekkaken**, formerly the main entrance to the **Dar el-Makhzen** Between it and Bab Bou Jeloud are the **Bou Jeloud Gardens**, through which flows the Oued Fès, the city's main water source.

Borj Nord & Merenid Tombs For a spectacular view of Fès, walk or take a taxi up to the Borj Nord fortress and the Merenid tombs, where you can see the whole of Fès sprawled at your feet. The 16th-century Borj Nord, built by the Saadian sultan Ahmed al-Mansour, houses the **Arms Museum** *(open Wed-Mon)*. The tombs, mostly ruins, are dramatic against the city backdrop; sunrise and sunset are spectacular, but don't go alone.

Places to Stay

Camping & Hostels The shady **Camping Diamant Vert** *(☎ 608369; sites per person/tent Dh20/15)*, 6km south off the Ifrane road, sits in a valley with a clean stream. Take bus No 17 to 'Ain Chkef from Place de Florence.

Camping International *(☎ 731439, fax 731554; sites per adult/child Dh40/30)*, 3km down the Sefrou road, has more extensive facilities. Take bus No 38 from Place Atlas.

The **youth hostel** *(☎ 624085; 18 Rue Abdeslam Serghini; dorm beds/doubles Dh45/55 members, Dh50/60 nonmembers)* in the ville nouvelle is a lovely, quiet little place with its own courtyard, TV, hot showers and tortoise! Rates include breakfast.

Hotels – Medina The most colourful hotels are around Bab Bou Jeloud. They are basic and not all have showers, but there are copious *hammams* in the area.

Hôtel du Jardin Publique *(☎ 633086; singles/doubles Dh40/60)*, outside the gate, has large, clean rooms. Inside the gate, **Hôtel Mauritania** *(singles/doubles Dh50/80)* is OK; and **Hôtel Cascade** *(☎ 638442; singles/doubles Dh50/100)* is popular and well touted, but the fantastic roof terraces are nicer than the rooms. With the medina crowds right outside, all these places can get quite noisy.

Fès el-Jdid doesn't offer the full-on medina experience, but it is central and relatively quiet. The best place is probably **Hôtel**

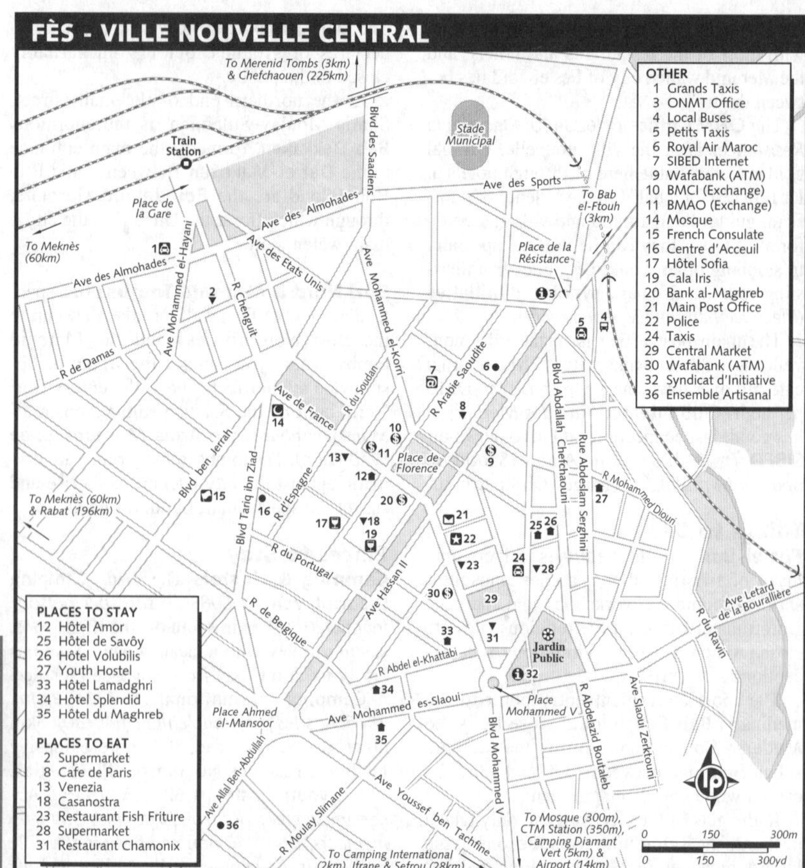

du Commerce *(Place des Alaouites; singles/doubles Dh40/60)*.

The only mid-range choice in the medina is **Hôtel Batha** *(☎ 741077, fax 741078; Place de Batha; singles/doubles with bath Dh190/240)*, overlooking Dar Batha Museum. It has a bar, restaurant and pool.

Hotels – Ville Nouvelle Near the student area, **Hôtel de Savoy** and **Hôtel Volubilis** charge the same (singles/doubles Dh50/70) and are both of a reasonable standard, but rooms facing the road can be noisy.

Hôtel du Maghreb *(☎ 621567; 25 Ave Mohammed es-Slaoui; singles/doubles Dh60/100)* is a slightly better option. Showers are included.

The three-star **Hôtel Amor** *(☎ 622724; 31 Rue Arabie Saoudite; singles/doubles Dh164/198)* has bright, clean rooms with bathroom availabe, as well as a restaurant and bar. It's worth staying here just for the Mr Men shower curtains!

In the same price range, **Hôtel Lamadghri** *(☎ 620310; 10 Rue Abasse El Mssadi; rooms with shower/bath Dh154/200)* is light and quiet, with a pleasant courtyard.

One step closer to the top end, **Hôtel Splendid** *(☎ 622148, fax 654892; 9 Rue Abdelkrim el-Khattabi; singles/doubles Dh281/342)* goes a bit overboard on the 'traditional' trappings, but the rooms are great and it has a superb pool and terrace.

Places to Eat

Supermarkets inhabit the areas near the train station and opposite the central market.

There are multiple eating options in the popular Bab Bou Jeloud area: you can get a filled roll from a snack stall for about Dh10. Alternatively, try one of the tourist-oriented terrace restaurants for a larger feed. The Restaurant des Jeunes, near Hôtel Cascade, and the pushy La Khasbah, nearby, do meals for around Dh50. Both are right near the gate at Bab Bou-Jeloud.

In the ville nouvelle, there are a number of food stores located on Blvd ben Jerrah. You will find countless snack bars along Ave de France and around Place de Florence, as well as a few cheap eats around Blvd Mohammed V and the central market. The popular **Venezia** *(Ave de France; meals Dh12-20)* is one of the best.

For something more substantial, **Restaurant Chamonix** *(set menu Dh50)*, near the central market, offers the usual plus pizza. Nearby, **Restaurant Fish Friture** *(Blvd Mohammed V; meals from Dh40)* serves cheap seafood and pizza.

Sparky **Casanostra** *(☎ 932841; 16 Rue Arabie Saoudite; dishes around Dh40)* is a good approximation of a cheap Western pizza/pasta joint. The service is friendly and it's popular with Moroccan families.

Restaurant Zohra *(☎ 637699; 3 Derb Ain Nass Blida; set menus from Dh70)*, in the medina, is the cheapest and least touristy of the 'traditional' restaurants.

There's a multitude of cafés and patisseries in the ville nouvelle, particularly along Ave Hassan II/Ave de la Liberté. Cafe de Paris has a nice *salon de thé*, but you can basically take your pick. For sheer tranquillity, however, the Cafe de la Noria in the Bou Jeloud Gardens in the medina is unbeatable.

Entertainment

There are a few bars scattered around the ville nouvelle. The European-looking **Cala Iris** *(Ave Hassan II)* is a good place to start, as are the hotel bars. Some of the bigger hotels have nightclubs – try the discos in the Sofia and Le Meridien Mérinides hotels.

Getting There & Away

Fès airport *(☎ 674712)* is at Saiss, 15km to the south. **Royal Air Maroc** *(☎ 625516; 54 Ave Hassan II)* has regular flights to Casablanca (45 minutes) and Paris (three hours).

CTM buses *(☎ 732384)* originate at the **main bus station** *(Place Baghdadi)* near Bab el-Mahrouk, and call in at the ville nouvelle terminus half an hour later. There are daily departures to Tangier (Dh80, six hours), Marrakesh (Dh130, nine hours), and Casablanca (Dh80, five hours) via Rabat (Dh50, four hours) and Meknès (Dh15, one hour). The cheaper buses run more regularly. *Grands taxis* to Meknès (Dh15), Rabat (Dh60) and Casablanca (Dh100) depart from the main bus station.

The train station is in the ville nouvelle, 10 minutes' walk from the town centre. There are daily departures to Tangier (Dh95.50, five hours), Marrakesh (Dh171, 7½ hours), and Casablanca (Dh97, 4½ hours) via Rabat (Dh72, 3½ hours) and Meknès (Dh16.50, one hour).

Getting Around

Fès has good local bus services (with fares around Dh2), although the buses are like sardine cans at times. Useful routes include the following:

No 9 Place de l'Atlas–Ave Hassan II–Dar Batha
No 12 Bab Bou Jeloud–Bab Guissa–Bab el-Ftouh
No 16 train station–airport
No 47 train station–Bab Bou Jeloud

The red *petits taxis* are metered: expect to pay about Dh10 from the train station to Bab Bou Jeloud. Only *grands taxis* go out to the airport (Dh80).

AROUND FÈS

Sefrou

Set against jagged mountain bluffs and rich farmland, the picturesque Berber town of Sefrou makes a fine contrast to the intensity of Fès, which is just 28km away. Accommodation options here are limited, but it's worth a quick trip. The town boasts a small walled **medina** and **mellah**, with a lively market on Thursday; the best points of entry/exit are Bab Taksebt, Bab Zemghila and the Bab Merba. There's a **waterfall** about 1.5km west of town.

Sadly, the hustle endemic to Fès has now started to spread to Sefrou – expect some (mostly friendly) attention from local guides and bolshie children.

Regular buses (Dh5) and *grands taxis* (Dh8) between Fès and Sefrou drop off at Place Moulay Hassan, in front of the Bab M'Kam and Bab Taksebt, and pick up just round the corner.

North Atlantic Coast

The towns of Morocco's Atlantic coast exhibit a dramatically different personality from that of the more insular settlements inland. Long used to the sight of foreigners, the people of the coast are cosmopolitan and urbane, and nowhere more so than in Morocco's urban behemoth, Casablanca.

ASILAH

☎ 039

The small port of Asilah has enjoyed a history far more tumultuous than its size would indicate. Settled by the Carthaginians and taken over by the Romans, it came under Portuguese and Spanish control in the 15th and 16th centuries. Early this century, Asilah became the residence of the bandit Er-Raissouli, who effectively controlled northeastern Morocco until he was imprisoned in 1925. Unfortunately, the proximity of Tangier has rubbed off slightly on Asilah, bringing a number of touts into the tourist trade; the hassle is generally friendly though.

The 15th-century Portuguese **ramparts** are still intact; access is limited, but the views are excellent. The **Palais de Raissouli**, **Hassan II International Center** and the tower of **El Kamra** are the focus of the annual Cultural Moussem in early August; the last two venues also house art exhibitions throughout the year. Several decent **beaches** stretch north of the town, while **Paradise Beach**, a local favourite, is 3km south.

Places to Stay & Eat

Camping As-Saada and Camping Echrigui are a few hundred metres north of town. Both are secure, have decent facilities and fill up in summer; rates are around Dh15 to Dh20 per person.

Budget accommodation is scarce in Asilah, although touts will try and steer you into the medina. **Hôtel Marhaba** *(☎ 417144; Rue Abdel M ben Ali; rooms Dh50 per person)* is simple and clean, with showers for Dh5, and has a great roof terrace. **Hôtel Sahara** *(☎ 417185; 9 Rue Tarfaya; singles/ doubles Dh98/126)* has a good range of rooms, although they pack the beds in a bit. Showers cost Dh5. Out of season, room prices drop by about Dh25. **Hôtel Mansour** *(☎ 417390, fax 416272; 56 Ave Mohammed V; singles/doubles Dh195/240)* is a quiet, friendly place; its rates are cheaper in winter.

If you have a little spare cash, stay at the fantastically stylish Spanish-run **Hôtel Patio de la Luna** *(☎ 416074; 12 Plaza Zelaya; singles/doubles Dh200/300)*.

Fish is *the* option here. There's a whole line of restaurants and cafés along Ave Hassan II, with main courses costing around Dh30, or some more expensive places across from Bab Kasaba. **Casa García** *(☎ 417465)*, **Restaurante Oceano Casa Pepe** *(☎ 417395)* and **Restaurant de la Place** *(☎ 417326)* all offer dishes for around Dh50.

Getting There & Away

The best way to reach Asilah is by bus (Dh10) or *grand taxi* from Tangier (Dh20) or Larache (Dh12). Regular buses leave for Rabat, Casablanca, Fès and Meknès. There are trains, but the station is 1.5km north of town.

LARACHE

☎ 039

Larache may be a big working town, but it's often almost entirely devoid of tourists, making it a more relaxed place than Asilah.

The post office and many of the banks are on Blvd Mohammed V; only the Banque Populaire changes travellers cheques (with commission). There are several Internet cafés around town, charging Dh10 an hour.

At one time the town was completely walled; the **kasbah** and **ramparts** are now mostly ruins, but the old **medina**, the fortress **Casbah de la Cigogne** and a Spanish-built citadel housing the **Archaeological Museum** *(admission Dh10; open Wed-Mon)* are still largely intact.

While the town itself is still worth a wander, particularly along the seafront on Ave Moulay Ismail and Rue de Casablanca, most people come to Larache to visit the Roman ruins of **Lixus** *(admission free)*. Situated 3km to 4km north of town, overlooking the Loukkos estuary and the Tangier-Larache highway, the scattered and overgrown remains of an amphitheatre, temples, mosaics and public baths are strangely impressive. Bus Nos 4 and 5 run past the gate and you can come by *petits taxis*.

Places to Stay

There are plenty of cheap hotels in central Larache. Prices tend to rise in summer by

MOROCCO

10%. **Pension Atlas** *(☎ 912014; 154 Rue 2 Mars; singles/doubles Dh25/50)*, in the medina, is easy to find and has small, moderately clean rooms, and showers for Dh5.

In the ville nouvelle, **Pension Amal** *(☎ 912788; 10 Ave Abdallah ben Yassine; singles/doubles Dh40/65)* is good value and very clean, with showers for Dh6. One street down, **Pension Palmera** *(☎ 500641; 8 Passage beni Mellal; singles/doubles Dh30/60)* is cheaper and not as spotless, but has a Western toilet. Showers go for Dh5.

Hôtel Hay Essalam *(☎ 916822; 9 Ave Hassan II; singles/doubles Dh90/116, with bathroom Dh116/133)* is excellent mid-range value, with immaculate rooms, some with TV and balcony.

Faded **Hôtel España** *(☎ 913195, fax 915628; 3 Ave Hassan II; singles/doubles Dh122/163, with bathroom Dh204/245)* is still just about clinging on to its former grandeur. Rooms have TV and phone.

Places to Eat

Numerous snack stalls and carts appear in the area around Ave Hassan II and the medina every evening, offering a variety of very cheap Moroccan and Spanish-style food. It's even possible to find *churros* (Spanish dunking doughnuts) in the late afternoon.

There are also plenty of decent restaurants around the Place de la Libération, most serving mains for around Dh25; Restaurant Comercial has a pleasant upstairs seating area.

Patisserie-wise, **Salon de Thé Lacoste** *(Ave Mohammed ben Abdallah)* and **Le Sourire** *(Ave Hassan)*, next to Hôtel España, are both top-notch. **Café Central** *(Place de la Libération)* is a popular place for coffee.

Getting There & Around

Larache is most easily reached by bus, but booking is not always possible on the way out, so turn up in the morning and get the first available service. CTM buses run to Tangier (Dh29), Casablanca (Dh82) via Rabat (Dh56), and Fès (Dh89) via Meknès (Dh61). There are also non-CTM buses to these destinations and Asilah (Dh10), Tetouan (Dh20) and Ceuta (Dh25). *Grands taxis* to Asilah (Dh12) leave from outside the bus station.

For the beach or the Lixus ruins catch bus No 4 or 5 opposite the Casbah de la Cigogne, or take a *petit taxi* (around Dh15, but you may have to haggle).

RABAT

☎ 037

Rabat's current role as Morocco's capital began during the French protectorate, but its history goes back 2500 years. The Phoenicians and the Romans both had short-lived interests in the area, but the city itself came to prominence only under the Almohad sultan Yacoub al-Mansour in the 12th century. He used the kasbah as a base for campaigns in Spain, and built the magnificent Almohad Bab Oudaia and the unfinished Tour Hassan. However, the city rapidly declined after his death in 1199.

In the early 17th century, Muslims expelled from Spain resettled the city and neighbouring Salé, ushering in the colourful era of the Sallee Rovers. These corsairs plundered thousands of merchant vessels returning to Europe from Asia, West Africa and the Americas, spawning a whole clutch of popular legends.

French rule brought capital status and a new sense of respectability; independence brought the newly wealthy middle class. Casablanca may be the economic heavyweight, but Rabat is the serious older brother, maintaining a definite air of French sophistication and maturity. It's a relaxed place, even in the *souqs*, and it's worth staying a few days.

Information

The **ONMT office** *(☎ 730562; Rue al-Abtal)* is inconveniently located in Agdal, west of the city; take bus No 3 from Blvd Hassan II. Banks are found along Ave Mohammed V and Ave Allal ben Abdalla. The majority have exchange booths and ATMs. There is a useful BMCE office at Rabat Ville train station.

The parcel ('Colis postaux') and EMS ('Poste Rapide') offices are to the right of the **main post office** *(cnr Rue Soekarno & Ave Mohammed V)*. *Téléboutiques* can be found all over town; **Phobos** *(Blvd Hassan II)* also has Internet access. There are numerous Internet cafés, all charging Dh10 an hour. Among the best are **Comète Cyber** *(4 Rue Tihama; open until 1am)*, and the friendly **Cybercountry** *(☎ 261195; Rue le Caire; open 9am-11pm)*.

Things to See

The 17th-century **medina** is a far cry from the dense medieval mazes of Fès or Tangier, but it's definitely worth exploring, as it's hard to get lost. Excellent carpet shops and jewellery stores dot the area. Follow Rue Souika, then head north up Rue des Consuls (where there's an informal morning carpet *souq* on Tuesday and Thursday) to get to the **Kasbah des Oudaias**, ancient fortifications overlooking the Atlantic Ocean. The main entry is the impressive **Almohad Bab Oudaia**, built in 1195.

The kasbah houses a palace built by Moulay Ismail which now contains the **Museum of Moroccan Arts** *(admission Dh10; open daily)*.

Southeast of the medina, past the dazzling white of the French **St Pierre Cathedral**, is Rabat's most famous landmark, the **Tour Hassan**. This incomplete minaret is the last remnant of the great mosque begun by Yacoub al-Mansour, which was levelled by the 1755 earthquake. On the same site is the **Mausoleum of Mohammed V**, the present king's grandfather.

The impressive **Bab ar-Rouah** (Gate of the Winds) guards the southern entrance to the ville nouvelle near the Royal Palace. Farther on, beyond the city walls, is the **Chellah** *(admission Dh10; open daily)*, a former Berber city turned Merenid necropolis, which also encompasses the remains of the ancient Roman city of **Sala**.

Rabat's **Archaeology Museum** *(23 Rue al-Brihi; admission Dh10; open Wed-Mon)* is interesting, but the marvellous Roman bronzes are sometimes away on loan.

For more active pursuits, there's the King's own **Oudayas Surf Club** *(☎ 260683)*, perched in a stylish clubhouse above the Atlantic, west of the kasbah.

MOROCCO

Places to Stay

Camping & Hostels At Salé beach, **Camping de la Plage** *(sites per person/2-person tent/car Dh15/22/12, camper vans Dh30)*, is well signposted. It costs Dh15 for power and water, plus Dh10 per hot shower. There's not much shade, but it's pretty friendly.

The **youth hostel** *(☎ 725769; 43 Rue Marassa; dorm beds Dh30)*, opposite the medina walls, is pleasant enough. Cold showers are included, but there are no cooking facilities.

Hotels There are countless cheap deals in the medina, particularly around the central market and off Ave Mohammed V. **Hôtel Al Maghrib Al Jadid** *(☎ 732207; 2 Rue Sebbahi; singles/doubles Dh60/100)* and its annexe Hôtel Marrakech are good traveller-oriented places, with clean, very pink rooms. A hot shower at both costs Dh7.50. Slightly farther away, **Hôtel Taroudannt** *(☎ 720521; 18 Rue Tajine; singles/doubles Dh45/80)* could be cleaner, but has a pleasant internal courtyard. Take a shower for Dh7.

Hôtel Dorhmi *(☎ 723898; 313 Ave Mohammed V; singles/doubles Dh80/120)* has comfortable rooms with huge beds, showers for Dh7, and a nice terrace.

In the ville nouvelle, **Hôtel Berlin** *(☎ 703 435; 261 Ave Mohammed V; singles/doubles Dh60/92)* is a fair option, tucked away above a decent Chinese restaurant. Showers are Dh6.

More expensive is **Hôtel Velleda** *(☎ 769 531; 106 Ave Allal ben Abdallah; singles/doubles Dh126/162)*, a nicely furnished place on the 4th floor (use the lift). Most of the rooms have bathrooms, small balconies and good views. **Hôtel Splendid** *(☎ 723283; 8 Rue Ghazza; singles/doubles Dh102/124, with bathroom Dh157/183)* has some great en suite rooms and a lovely courtyard. Prices are due to rise, however.

The friendly three-star **Hôtel d'Orsay** *(☎ 202277; 11 Ave Moulay Youssef; singles/doubles Dh211/264)*, near the train station, has nice rooms with good facilities.

Looking out over the medina walls, **Hôtel Majestic** *(☎ 722997; 121 Blvd Hassan II; singles/doubles Dh232/275)* is a classy middle-bracket choice. It has large, well-equipped rooms with bathroom, some with balconies. Having a TV will cost you an extra Dh10.

Places to Eat

For self-caterers the grocery stalls around the market are a good bet, although foodstuffs are cheaper from the stalls along Rue Souika. There is a supermarket and liquor store on Rue Dimachk.

There are plenty of good, cheap places to eat in the medina; you should be able to get a decent meal for as little as Dh20. **Er Jamahir** *(215 Ave Mohammed V; mains Dh12-18)* is a tiny locals' place; look out for the cut-out of a chef with a *tajine*. The pleasant Moroccan-style **Restaurant El Bahia** *(☎ 734504; Blvd Hassan II; mains around Dh38)* is built into the walls of the medina.

There are plenty of restaurants in the ville nouvelle. **Restaurant Taghzout** *(Rue Jeddah Ammane)* is an excellent low-budget option frequented by locals, with fish dishes and *tajine* for Dh25. **Restaurant La Clef** *(☎ 701972; Ave Moulay Youssef; meals around Dh50, set menu Dh65)* has a good selection of Moroccan standards, as well as some French dishes and a set menu.

For die-hard Europeans, **La Mamma** *(☎ 707329; 6 Rue Zankat Tanta; pizzas Dh50)* has good authentic pizzas and does deliveries, while the stylish **Weimar Club Restaurant** *(☎ 732650; 7 Rue Sana'a; meals around Dh50)*, in the Goethe Institut, serves excellent German/French cuisine.

There are numerous cafés along and around Ave Mohammed V – **Pâtisserie Majestic** *(Ave Allal ben Abdallah)* and **Pâtisserie Tilal** *(8 Rue le Caire)* are both excellent. In the southeastern corner of the Kasbah des Oudaias, the quiet and shady Café Maure overlooks the estuary to Salé.

Entertainment

At night central Rabat is generally a quiet and sensible place, without much riotous nightlife. Some cafés double as bars, such as **Henry's** *(Ave M Abdallah)*, but close early. The **Blue-Note** *(Rue Al Yamama)* is a typically dark hideout for Moroccan males, but may be worth a look.

Getting There & Away

The INTERCITY bus station is inconveniently situated 5km from the centre of town. Take local bus Nos 30 and 17 or a *petit taxi* (Dh20) to the centre. CTM offers a comprehensive service; cheaper non-CTM buses are also available for most destinations. *Grands taxis* for Casablanca (Dh27) leave from outside the *gare routière.* Taxis for Salé (Dh3), Meknès (Dh40) and Fès (Dh55) leave from near the main local city **bus station** *(Blvd Hassan II).*

Rabat Ville train station *(Ave Mohammed V)* is conveniently located in the centre of town. There are 22 trains to Casablanca (Dh29.50, 50 minutes); half are shuttle services linking Rabat with Mohammed V international airport (Dh55, two hours) via Casa Port. There are also frequent departures to Tangier (Dh89.50, five hours), and Fès (Dh72, five hours) via Meknès (Dh55.50, 2½ hours).

Getting Around

The No 16 bus leaves from the **main local city bus station** *(Blvd Hassan II)* for Salé, and No 3 goes to Agdal. Bus Nos 30 and 17 run past Rabat's intercity bus station; they leave from a stop just inside Bab al-Had. *Petits taxis* can usually be found around the station, but the meters go around pretty fast.

CASABLANCA

☎ 022

Casablanca is by far Morocco's largest city and its industrial centre. Although its history goes back many centuries (including over 200 years of Portuguese occupation), Casablanca had declined into insignificance by the mid-1880s, and it only reached its current size and status under French rule.

The key to this renaissance was the decision of the French resident-general, Lyautey, to develop the city as a commercial centre. It was largely his ideas that gave Casablanca its wide boulevards, public parks, fountains and imposing Mauresque civic buildings (a blend of French colonial and traditional Moroccan styles), as well as firmly establishing it at the heart of Morocco's economic well-being.

Amid the 1930s architecture, the Art Deco touches and the very Western pedestrian precincts, cosmopolitan Morocco is alive, well and totally fashionable. Casablanca has ingrained 'attitude', its own style and a gritty edge that gives it a very different air from Rabat or Tangier; as a city, it remains an excellent barometer of liberal Islam.

Information

The **ONMT office** *(☎ 271177; 55 Rue Omar Slaoui; open Mon-Fri)* is generally helpful. There's also a **syndicat d'initiative** *(98 Blvd Mohammed V; open daily)* nearer the centre of town.

Most of the principal banks have branches on Ave des FAR or Blvd Mohammed V, usually with ATMs and exchange offices. The **Crédit du Maroc** *(Blvd Mohammed V)* and **Banque Populaire** *(Ave des FAR)* change travellers cheques. There are independent change counters and banks with ATMs at Mohammed V international airport. AmEx is represented by **Voyages Schwartz** *(☎ 222947; 112 Rue Prince Moulay Abdallah; open Mon-Sat).*

The **main post office** *(Place Mohammed V)* has a poste-restante service. The parcel office is just left of the main entrance. There are plenty of Internet cafés scattered around town, with an hourly rate of between Dh10 and Dh15. **Euro Net** *(51 Rue Tata)* is a good option, as is **First Cyber** *(☎ 492017; 62 Rue Allah ben Abdellah)*, which also sells mobile phones.

Things to See

The stunning **Hassan II Mosque** *(guided tours adult/student Dh100/50, tours Sat-Thur)* is

Casablanca's principal landmark, overlooking the ocean just north of the medina. The third biggest religious monument in the world, it was built as recently as 1993! Unusually, it's open to non-Muslims; the guided tours are offered in various languages.

The central **ville nouvelle** around Place Mohammed V has some of the best examples of Mauresque architecture: the *hôtel de ville* (town hall), the *palais de justice* (law courts) and the post office are all impressive edifices in their own right, and the sadly neglected **Cathédrale du Sacré Cœur** is still an extraordinary sight. Contrary to expectations, Casablanca has some wonderful architecture, so try to look around you occasionally.

Casablanca's **beaches**, such as they are, are west of town along the Blvd de la Corniche and beyond, in the suburb of 'Ain Diab. It's a trendy area and crowded in summer. Take bus No 9 from Place Oued al-Mahazine, just west of Place des Nations Unies.

Places to Stay

Camping & Hostels About 5km southwest of town is **Camping de l'Oasis** *(☎ 253367; sites per person, tent & car Dh15)*; bus No 31 runs past it. The **youth hostel** *(☎ 220551, fax 226777; 6 Place Ahmed El Bidaoui; dorm beds Dh45, doubles/triples Dh120/180)* is in the medina, just off Blvd des Almohades. It's clean and comfortable; showers and breakfast are included.

MOROCCO

Hotels A number of small hotels populate the medina, particularly around Rue Centrale. Most charge around Dh45, but unless you're a *hammam* junkie the ville nouvelle options are much better.

In the ville nouvelle, the cheap places tend to be near the central market, around Rue Allal ben Abdallah. **Hôtel Miramar** *(☎ 310308; 22 Rue Léon L'Africain; singles/doubles Dh62/76)* is about the cheapest, if not the nicest, and is conveniently close to the CTM bus station. Showers at the Miramar cost Dh6. Just around the corner, **Hôtel Mon Rêve** *(☎ 311439; 7 Rue Chaoui)* charges the same rates and also has sizeable triples for Dh110. Showers cost Dh7, but there's no hot water in the rooms.

Hôtel Colbert *(☎ 314241; 38 Rue Chaoui; singles/doubles Dh68/83, with bathroom Dh84/100)*, opposite the central market, is well liked by travellers, offering a choice of rooms with or without bathroom (hot showers cost Dh10). **Hôtel Rialto** *(☎ 275122; 9 Rue Salah ben Bouchaib; singles/doubles Dh84/120)* is generally an amenable place, but the showers could be cleaner.

South of the centre, **Hôtel du Palais** *(☎ 276121; 68 Rue Fahrat Hachad; singles/doubles Dh140/200)* has gone slightly upmarket, with a corresponding hike in price. It's still reasonable value in this range, however, and now has hot water.

Built in 1936, the characterful **Hôtel Plaza** *(☎ 297698; 18 Blvd Houphouet-Boigny; singles/doubles with bathroom & breakfast Dh284/365)* offers rooms with balcony and sea views, as well as cheaper rooms without bathrooms. It also has a bar.

Places to Eat

Fresh food is cheapest in the medina, but there is also a fine delicatessen in the central market. There are a few cheap restaurants around the clock tower entrance to the medina, including the popular **Restaurant Widad** *(Rue de Fes)*, which serves decent Moroccan dishes.

Outside the medina, the best place for good, cheap food is along Rue Chaoui, where there are plenty of good rotisseries and restaurants offering meals for around Dh25. **Snack Saigon** *(Rue Salah ben Bouchaib; meals Dh15-30)* is a tiny place serving proper Moroccan standards to a mainly local crowd. The marked prices can fluctuate.

Despite its vaguely South Pacific decor, **La Grotte** *(Rue Léon L'Africain; meals Dh25-30)* serves good honest *tajines* and pizza to a varied set of mainly young locals.

There are a number of reasonable restaurants along Blvd Mohammed V – **Le Buffet** *(☎ 222344; 99 Blvd Mohammed V; mains Dh70-80, set menu Dh75)* is popular with local couples and has an excellent set menu.

For seafood, head to the popular **Taverne du Dauphin** *(☎ 221200; 115 Blvd Houphouet-Boigny; mains from Dh50)*, built into the medina wall. A 20% tax is added to the bill, so if you don't fancy a full meal try the bar for a relaxed drink or snack.

The city centre is filled with French-style cafés. **Pâtisserie de l'Opéra** *(50 Blvd du 11 Janvier)* is a tranquil, women-friendly place, while **Glacier Fiori** *(☎ 261 967; Rue Omar Slaoui)* is popular with businessmen for a quiet read of *L'Opinion* over a morning coffee.

For delicious home-made ice cream visit the **Swiss Ice Cream Factory** *(Rue Ech-Charif*

Amziane). It's a women-friendly spot deservedly popular with the young and trendy.

There are many options for self-caterers, such as the grocery store on Ave Houmane el-Fetouaki.

Entertainment

Central Casablanca has a large red-light district and plenty of seedy bars and cabaret places, so it can be hard to find a 'normal' place for a drink or a dance. Apparently, even the sailors' bars in the port can be friendlier than some local dives! Women should be particularly mindful of this after dark.

Au Petit Poucet, next to the restaurant of the same name, is a die-hard relic of 1920s France (complete with chain-smoking male clientele) and less forbidding than most. Saint-Exupéry, the French author and aviator, used to spend time here between mail flights. **La Bodéga** *(☎ 541842; 129 Rue Allal ben Abdallah)* is a Spanish-style tapas bar and restaurant. It's expensive but women-friendly and good fun, with regular live music. The trendiest clubs and bars are to be found in the wealthy beachside suburb of 'Ain Diab, west of town.

Getting There & Away

From Mohammed V international airport in Casablanca (30km southeast of the city), there are regular connections to Western Europe, the rest of Africa and the Middle East. Internally, you can get to any destination directly from Casablanca with Royal Air Maroc. There are eight weekly flights to Fès (Dh842, 45 minutes) and at least six to Tangier (Dh827, 50 minutes).

The flash **CTM bus station** *(☎ 449224; Rue Léon L'Africain)* has daily departures to Rabat (one hour), Meknès (four hours), Fès (five hours), Tetouan (five hours) and Tangier (six hours). CTM also operates **international buses** *(☎ 458000)* to Belgium, France, Germany, Italy and Spain from Casablanca. Ouled Ziane is the bus station for almost all non-CTM services – unfortunately, it's some distance from the city centre. Take a taxi (Dh10), or catch bus No 10 from Blvd Mohammed V. *Grands taxis* to Rabat (Dh27) leave from Blvd Hassan Seghir, near the CTM bus station; there's also a rank on Ave des FAR.

Most long-distance rail departures to destinations across the country leave from Casa Voyageurs station, 4km east of the city. A *petit taxi* costs Dh10, or catch local bus No 30. Shuttle trains to Mohammed V international airport (via Casa Voyageurs, Dh30, 38 minutes) and north to Rabat (Dh29.50, 50 minutes) leave from the central Casa Port station.

Getting Around

To/From the Airport Shuttle trains (TNR) run from Mohammed V international airport to Casa Voyageurs and Casa Port (Dh25, 24 minutes). A *grand taxi* to the airport costs Dh150 (Dh200 after 8pm).

Bus Useful local bus routes include the following:

No 9 From the terminal to 'Ain Diab and the beaches
No 10 From Place de la Concorde to Ouled Ziane bus station via Blvd Mohammed V
No 15 From the terminal to Hassan II Mosque
No 30 From Blvd Ziraoui to Casa Voyageurs train station via Ave des FAR and Blvd Mohammed V

Taxi There's no shortage of *petits taxis* in Casablanca. Expect to pay Dh5 for a ride within the city centre with the meter on.

Marrakesh

☎ 044

Basking in the clear African light of the south, Marrakesh has an entirely different feel from its sister cities to the north. It remains unmistakably more African than cosmopolitan Casablanca, more Moroccan than sanitised Rabat, and more Berber than proud and aloof Fès.

Positioned on an important crossroads, Morocco's fourth-largest city is still regarded as the southern capital, attracting merchants and traders from the surrounding plains, High Atlas and the Sahara. Just as the colour blue is synonymous with Fès, green with Meknès and white with Rabat, red is Marrakesh's colour. A local Berber legend says that when the minaret of the Koutoubia Mosque was planted in the city's heart, it poured so much blood that all the walls, houses and roads turned this colour. At dusk, in the last rays of the setting sun, you could almost believe the blood is flowing again as the city's ramparts turn crimson.

Orientation

The old city and the ville nouvelle of Marrakesh are roughly the same size. It takes about 30 minutes to walk from the centre of

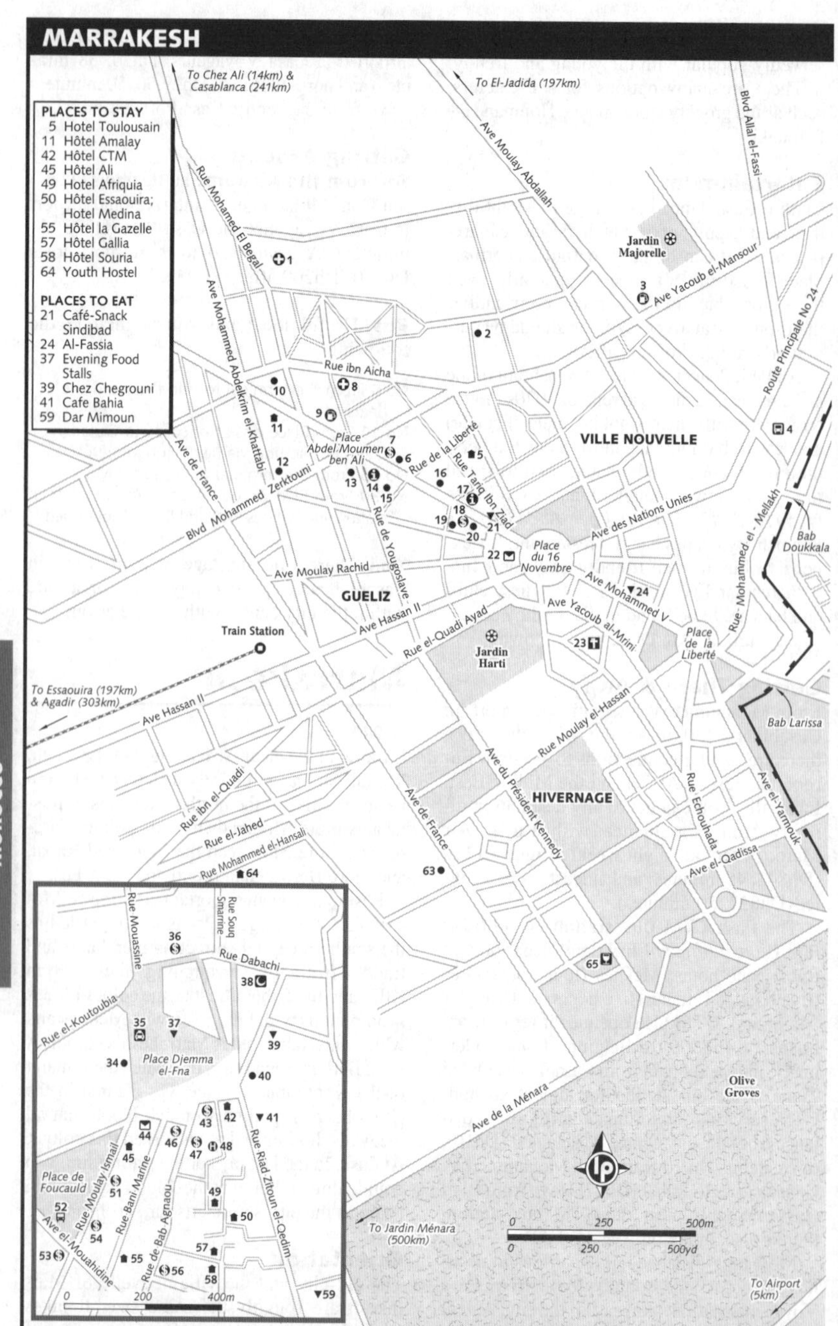
MARRAKESH
PLACES TO STAY
5 Hotel Toulousain
11 Hôtel Amalay
42 Hôtel CTM
45 Hôtel Ali
49 Hotel Afriquia
50 Hôtel Essaouira; Hotel Medina
55 Hôtel la Gazelle
57 Hôtel Gallia
58 Hôtel Souria
64 Youth Hostel
PLACES TO EAT
21 Café-Snack Sindibad
24 Al-Fassia
37 Evening Food Stalls
39 Chez Chegrouni
41 Cafe Bahia
59 Dar Mimoun
To Chez Ali (14km) & Casablanca (241km)
To El-Jadida (197km)
To Essaouira (197km) & Agadir (303km)
To Jardin Ménara (500km)
To Airport (5km)
VILLE NOUVELLE
GUELIZ
HIVERNAGE
Jardin Majorelle
Jardin Harti
Train Station
Place Abdel Moumen ben Ali
Place du 16 Novembre
Place de la Liberté
Bab Doukkala
Bab Larissa
Olive Groves
Place Djemma el-Fna
Place de Foucauld
MOROCCO

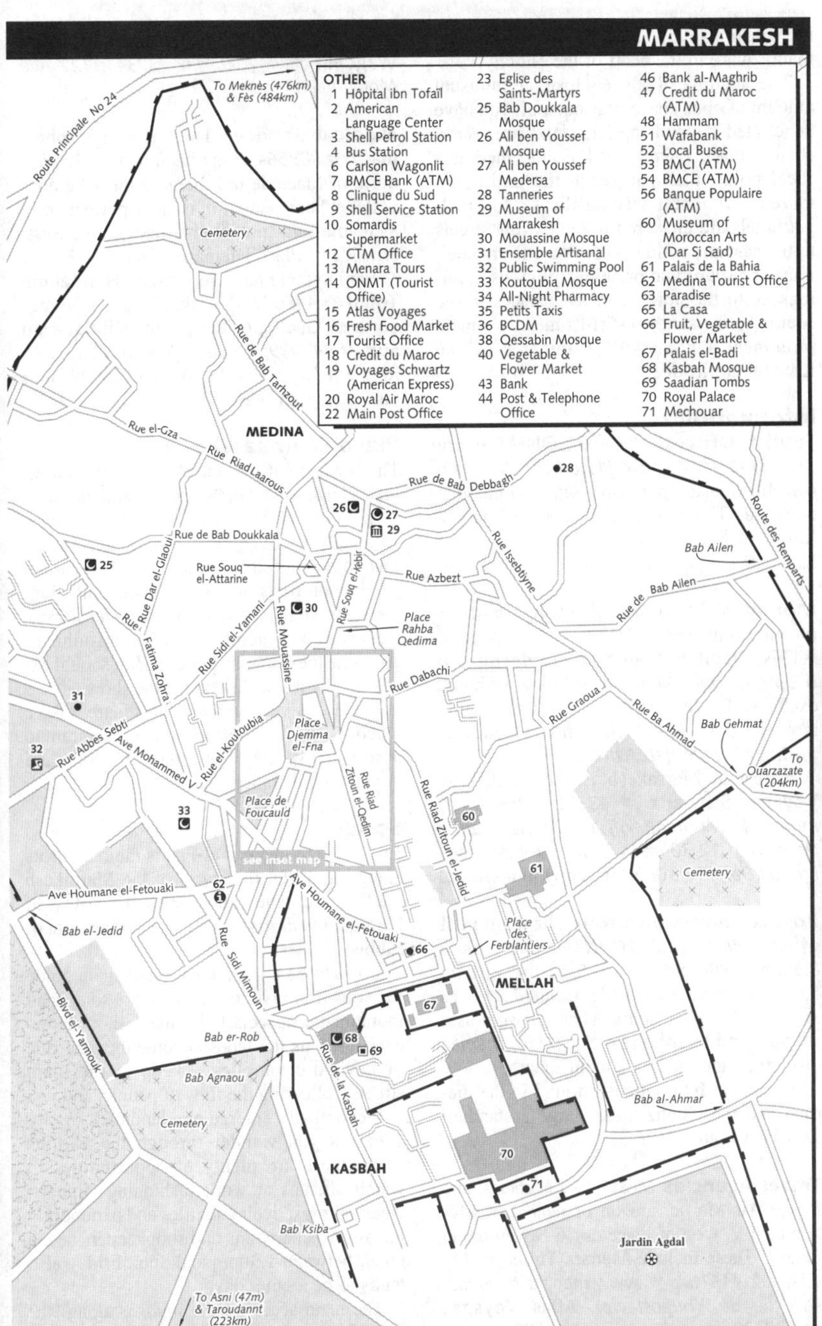
MARRAKESH
OTHER
1 Hôpital ibn Tofaïl
2 American Language Center
3 Shell Petrol Station
4 Bus Station
6 Carlson Wagonlit
7 BMCE Bank (ATM)
8 Clinique du Sud
9 Shell Service Station
10 Somardis Supermarket
12 CTM Office
13 Menara Tours
14 ONMT (Tourist Office)
15 Atlas Voyages
16 Fresh Food Market
17 Tourist Office
18 Crèdit du Maroc
19 Voyages Schwartz (American Express)
20 Royal Air Maroc
22 Main Post Office
23 Eglise des Saints-Martyrs
25 Bab Doukkala Mosque
26 Ali ben Youssef Mosque
27 Ali ben Youssef Medersa
28 Tanneries
29 Museum of Marrakesh
30 Mouassine Mosque
31 Ensemble Artisanal
32 Public Swimming Pool
33 Koutoubia Mosque
34 All-Night Pharmacy
35 Petits Taxis
36 BCDM
38 Qessabin Mosque
40 Vegetable & Flower Market
43 Bank
44 Post & Telephone Office
46 Bank al-Maghrib
47 Credit du Maroc (ATM)
48 Hammam
51 Wafabank
52 Local Buses
53 BMCI (ATM)
54 BMCE (ATM)
56 Banque Populaire (ATM)
60 Museum of Moroccan Arts (Dar Si Said)
61 Palais de la Bahia
62 Medina Tourist Office
63 Paradise
65 La Casa
66 Fruit, Vegetable & Flower Market
67 Palais el-Badi
68 Kasbah Mosque
69 Saadian Tombs
70 Royal Palace
71 Mechouar
To Meknès (476km) & Fès (484km)
Route Principale No 24
Cemetery
MEDINA
Rue de Bab Tarhzout
Rue el-Gza
Rue Riad Laarous
Rue de Bab Debbagh
Rue de Bab Doukkala
Rue Dar el-Glaoui
Rue Souq el-Attarine
Rue Souq el-Kebir
Rue Azbezt
Rue Issebtiyne
Route des Remparts
Bab Ailen
Rue de Bab Ailen
Rue Mouassine
Rue Sidi el-Yamani
Rue Fatima Zohra
Place Rahba Qedima
Rue Dabachi
Rue Graoua
Rue Ba Ahmad
Bab Gehmat
To Ouarzazate (204km)
Place Djemma el-Fna
Rue el-Koutoubia
Rue Abbes Sebti
Ave Mohammed V
Rue Riad Zitoun el-Qedim
Rue Riad Zitoun el-Jedid
Place de Foucauld
see inset map
Ave Houmane el-Fetouaki
Bab el-Jedid
Rue Sidi Mimoun
Place des Ferblantiers
MELLAH
Cemetery
Blvd el-Yarmouk
Bab er-Rob
Bab Agnaou
Rue de la Kasbah
Bab al-Ahmar
Cemetery
KASBAH
Bab Ksiba
Jardin Agdal
To Asni (47m) & Taroudannt (223km)
MOROCCO

the ville nouvelle to Place Djemaa el-Fna, the main square in the heart of the old city.

The medina walls enclose an unusual amount of open space. It is not until you have penetrated beyond the large and irregularly shaped Place Djemaa el-Fna, the medina's focal point, that you reach the traditional maze of *souqs* and twisting alleys. Most budget hotels are clustered in the narrow streets to the east and southeast of Place Djemaa el-Fna. The *souqs* and principal religious buildings lie to the north, and the palaces to the south. To the southwest rises the city's most prominent landmark, the minaret of the Koutoubia Mosque.

Information

Tourist Offices The main **ONMT office** *(☎ 436131, fax 436057; Place Abdel Moumen ben Ali, Gueliz; open Mon-Sat)* is in the ville nouvelle. There is also a separate medina **tourist office** *(open Mon-Fri)* south of the Koutoubia.

Money Most banks will change cash or travellers cheques and there's no shortage of ATMs. **Crèdit du Maroc** *(open 8.45am-1pm & 3pm-6.45pm Mon-Sat)* offers after-hours exchange facilities at its branches in the ville nouvelle *(215 Ave Mohammed V)* and the medina *(Rue de Bab Agnaou)*.

AmEx in Marrakesh is represented by **Voyages Schwartz** *(☎ 433321; 2nd floor, Immeuble Moutaouakil, 1 Rue Mauritanie; open 9am-12.30pm & 3pm-6.30pm Mon-Fri, Sat 9am-12.30pm)* in the ville nouvelle.

Post & Communications The **main post office** *(Place du 16 Novembre; open 8.30am-6.30pm Mon-Fri, 8.30am-11.30am Sat)* is in the ville nouvelle. Limited services are available after hours. There's also a useful **post and telephone office** *(Place Djemaa el-Fna)* on the medina's main square.

The many Internet cafés found in the medina and the Gueliz area charge a standard Dh10 per hour.

Travel Agencies Most travel agencies, and Royal Air Maroc, are on or near Ave Mohammed V, west of Place du 16 Novembre in Gueliz. These include **Menara Tours** *(☎ 446 654, fax 446107; W www.menara-tours.ma; 41 Rue de Yougoslavie)*, **Atlas Voyages** *(☎ 430333, fax 447963; W www.atlasvoyages.com; 131 Ave Mohammed V)* and **Carlson Wagonlit** *(☎ 447076, fax 432341; 122 Ave Mohammed V)*.

Medical Services There is a night **pharmacy** *(☎ 389564; Rue Khalid ben el-Oualid)*, north of Place de la Liberté in the ville nouvelle, where a doctor is also permanently available, and another pharmacy on the western side of Place Djemaa el-Fna.

For anything more serious, try **Hôpital Ibn Tofaïl** *(☎ 448011; Rue Abdelouahab Derraq)* north of Gueliz, or the private **Clinique du Sud** *(☎ 447999; 2 Rue de Yougoslavie)*, also in the ville nouvelle. Both offer 24-hour emergency services.

Place Djemaa el-Fna

The focal point of Marrakesh is Djemaa el-Fna, a huge square in the medina and the backdrop for one of the world's greatest spectacles. Although it's lively all the time, Djemaa el-Fna comes into its own at dusk. The curtain goes up on rows of open-air food stalls, jugglers, storytellers, snake charmers, musicians, the occasional acrobat and benign lunatics consume the remaining space. You should expect to pay a few dirham for the show.

Once you've wandered the square, take a balcony seat in a rooftop café or restaurant to absorb the spectacle at a more relaxing and voyeuristic distance.

Souqs

Just as Place Djemaa el-Fna is famous for its energy and life, the *souqs* of the Marrakesh medina are renowned for their variety of high-quality crafts, as well as a fair amount of rubbish.

It might be a good idea to engage a guide for your first visit to the medina's *souqs* and monuments, especially if time is short. However tortuous the lanes become the first rule of navigation applies – keep to the main streets, following the flow of people, and you will eventually emerge at a landmark or city gate. As you wander through the various *souqs* there are plenty of opportunities to watch artisans at work fashioning slippers, weaving rugs, dyeing textiles and hammering metals. Most artisans and shopkeepers take a break between 1.30pm and 3pm. Friday also tends to be a quiet day.

The main access to the *souqs* is along Rue Souq Smarrine, beneath the white arch on the eastern side of Place Bab Fteuh. At its southern end it's flanked by textile shops and souvenir stalls, interspersed by big-name carpet sellers. Keep an eye out on the left for the entrance to the first of several *qissaria* (covered markets).

Just before Rue Souq Smarrine forks into Rue Souq el-Kebir and Rue Souq al-Attarine, a narrow lane to the right leads to Place Rahba Qedima, a small square given over mainly to carpets and apothecary stalls with all kinds of ingredients for magical potions –including caged iguanas. To the north of the square is the carpet *souq*, also known as the Criée Berbère. It was in this area that slaves were auctioned off until the French put a stop to the trade in 1912.

Back on Rue Souq Smarrine, you could take either fork. Both more or less lead to the Ali ben Youssef Mosque and Medersa, though the right-hand Rue Souq el-Kebir is the slightly more straightforward option. As you head northwards you'll first encounter jewellers among the souvenir stalls, then more *qissaria*, stocked with Westernised goods, which give way to leatherwork shops.

Taking the left fork, on the other hand, you pass the entrance to the *babouche* (leather slipper) *souq* on your right, while off to the left multicoloured skeins hang drying in the dyers *souq*. You eventually end up among carpenters and blacksmiths, who pay tourists scant attention. With a bit of luck, you'll emerge at the Ali ben Youssef Mosque. An alternative route back to Place Djemaa el-Fna could take you to the west via the Mouassine Mosque.

Mosques & Medersas

Like their counterparts elsewhere, mosques and working *medersas* (theological colleges) are generally closed to non-Muslims. The only mosque that has a perspective you can really appreciate is the **Koutoubia Mosque**, southwest of Place Djemaa el-Fna. At 70m, its minaret is visible for miles. It is particularly memorable at night when illuminated against the velvety-black desert sky. When first built, the Koutoubia was covered with painted plaster and brilliantly coloured *zellij* (tilework), but this decoration has all disappeared. What can still be seen, however, are the decorative panels, which are different on each face and practically constitute a textbook of Islamic design.

The largest of the mosques inside the medina is the **Ali ben Youssef Mosque**, first built in the second half of the 12th century. It's the oldest surviving mosque in Marrakesh, but the building itself is fairly recent. Next door is the **Ali ben Youssef Medersa** *(admission Dh20; open 9am-6pm daily)* of the same name. Although undergoing a painstaking restoration, it is a beautiful and still peaceful and meditative place with some absolutely stunning examples of stucco decoration.

The other big mosque in the medina is the **Mouassine Mosque**, built in the 16th century by the Saadians on land formerly occupied by the Jewish community. Its most notable features are the three huge doorways and the elaborate fountain to the northeast. The fountain has three sections: two arched bays for animals and one for humans.

Palaces

The most famous of the city's palaces is the **Palais el-Badi** *(admission Dh10; open 8.30am-11.45am & 2.30pm-5.45pm daily)*, south of Place Djemaa el-Fna. Built by Ahmed al-Mansour between 1578 and 1602, at the time of its construction it was reputed to be one of the most beautiful in the world (and was known as 'the Incomparable'). It included marble from Italy and other precious building materials from as far away as India. Unfortunately, the palace is now largely a ruin, having been plundered by Moulay Ismail in 1696 for its materials, which were used to build his new capital at Meknès. The easiest way to get to the palace is to take Ave Houmane el-Fetouaki south from the Koutoubia Mosque to Place des Ferblantiers. Go through the large gate and turn right.

The **Palais de la Bahia** *(admission Dh10; open 8.30am-11.15am & 2.30pm-5.45pm Sat-Thur, 8.30am-11.30am & 3pm-5.45pm Fri)* was built towards the end of the 19th century as the residence of Si' Ahmed ben Musa, the Grand Vizier of Sultan Moulay al-Hassan I. Upon Bou Ahmed's death it was ransacked, but much has since been restored. It's a rambling structure with fountains, elaborate reception rooms, living quarters, pleasure gardens and numerous secluded, shady courtyards. To get here from the Palais el-Badi, take the road heading northeast from Place des Ferblantiers and you'll soon come to the entrance on your right.

Farther north of the Palais de la Bahia and again off to the right (it's signposted), the **Dar Si Said** *(admission Dh10; open 9am-11.45am & 2.30pm-5.45pm Mon, Wed, Thur, Sat & Sun, 9am-11.30am & 3pm-5.45pm Fri)*, which now houses the Museum of Moroccan Arts, is well worth a visit. The museum has one of the finest collections in the country including jewellery, carpets, oil lamps, pottery and leatherwork.

Museum of Marrakesh

Inaugurated in 1997, the Omar Benjelloun Foundation's museum *(adult/child Dh30/10; open 9.30am-6pm daily)* is housed in a beautifully restored 19th-century *riad* (lavish old-style townhouse) with some very impressive *zellij* work. Not only does the house have a glorious central courtyard with fountains around which galleries display artworks, it also allows the visitor an insight into household features such as the original *hammam*.

Saadian Tombs

Alongside the Kasbah Mosque is this necropolis *(admission Dh10; open 8.30am-11.45am & 2.30pm-5.45pm daily)*, started by the Saadian sultan Ahmed al-Mansour in the late 1500s. Unlike the Palais el-Badi, another of al-Mansour's projects, the tombs escaped Moulay Ismail's depredations – possibly because he was superstitious about plundering the dead. Instead he sealed the tombs and, as a result, they still convey some of the opulence and superb artistry that must also have been lavished on the palace. The tombs are signposted down a narrow alleyway at the southern edge of the Kasbah Mosque.

Jardin Majorelle & Museum of Islamic Art

Now owned by the French couturier Yves Saint-Laurent, these lush gardens *(admission gardens Dh20, museum Dh15; open 8am-noon & 2pm-5pm daily, 8am-noon & 3pm-7pm summer)* provide a wonderful haven. They were designed by the French painter Jacques Majorelle, who lived here from 1922 to 1962. Among the cacti, bamboo and cascades of bougainvillaea is a deep-blue villa, now housing the museum. It contains one of those Moroccan collections you'd love to scoop up and take home to decorate your house with. Exhibits, including carpets, wedding curtains, belts, jewellery and manuscripts are labelled in Arabic and French.

Organised Tours

Menara Tours (see Travel Agencies earlier in this section) offers day trips to the Ourika Valley (from Dh270); Asni, Ouirgane and Tahanaoute (from Dh270); Telouet in the High Atlas (from Dh500); and the Cascades d'Ouzoud (waterfalls; from Dh400). Another agency with a good reputation is **Pampa Voyages** *(☎ 431052, fax 446455; Ⓦ www.pampamaroc.com; 213 Ave Mohammed V)*. It specialises in longer tailor-made tours into the Atlas Mountains and the Drâa Valley. Among other things, it organises excursions into the desert with camels and bivouacs.

While Hôtel Ali (see Places to Stay) is no longer the trekking centre it once was, it remains your best bet for information on the High Atlas. You can arrange treks (Dh350 per person per day) or join an organised tour through its associated travel agency **Sahara Expedition** *(☎ 427977, fax 427972; Ⓦ www.saharaexpe.ma; Angle Ave el-Mouahidine & Rue Bani Marine)*.

Special Events

If you happen to be in Marrakesh in June (the dates change), inquire about the two-week **Festival of Folklore** *(information ☎ 446114)*. Performances take place principally in the Palais el-Badi.

Places to Stay

Hostels The **youth hostel** *(☎ 447713; Rue Mohammed el-Hansali; dorm beds Dh40; open 8am-9am & 1pm-10pm daily)* is not far from the train station, so it could be a first stop. It's also spotless, has hot showers for Dh5 and boasts a kitchen. However, there's an 11.30pm curfew and for the same price you can stay closer to the action in a medina budget hotel. You'll need your HI membership card.

Hotels – Medina There are dozens of budget hotels in the lanes immediately south of Place Djemaa el-Fna between Rue de Bab Agnaou and Rue Riad Zitoun el-Qedim. Many have rooms set around cheerful little courtyards, and roof terraces for soaking up the sun and views. Apart from that, its cleanliness and the shower situation, there's often not much between them. The best places fill up quickly, so it's worth calling ahead. Some spots will let you sleep on the terrace for around Dh25 if you're really stuck.

Hôtel Essaouira *(☎ 443805, fax 426323; 3 Derb Sidi Bouloukat; singles/doubles Dh50/80)* is among the most appealing. It has a tiled central courtyard, terrace café and basic but clean rooms. Bathroom facilities are limited, and hot showers cost Dh5. Follow the signs from Rue Riad Zitoun el-Qedim.

Hôtel Afriquia *(☎ 442403; 45 Derb Sidi Bouloukat; singles/doubles/triples Dh50/ 100/150; doubles with bathroom Dh150)* is larger than many budget hotels. Plus points include a lovely, tree-filled courtyard and the psychedelically tiled and tiered terrace affording panoramic views.

Hôtel la Gazelle *(☎ 441112, fax 445537; 12 Rue Bani Marine; singles/doubles Dh70/120)* lies southwest of the main budget-hotel area. It's a spruce, friendly little place and from the terrace there are fine views to the square, Koutoubia Mosque and mountains.

Hôtel Souria *(☎ 067 482131, ⓔ hotel souria@yahoo.fr; 17 Rue de la Recette; doubles Dh120)*, near the Hôtel el-Atlal, is delightfully homey – the female owners even invite you to share their small kitchen. Prices are slightly above average, but you get a tidy little room, either around a cool and tranquil courtyard or on the terrace. Hot showers cost Dh10.

Hôtel Ali *(☎ 444979, fax 440522; ⓔ hotel ali@hotmail.com; Rue Moulay Ismail; dorm beds or roof terrace sleeping Dh40, singles/ doubles/triples Dh100/150/200)* is a stalwart of the budget scene and much favoured by trekking groups. Regulars swear by its cheap rates and friendly and efficient service, not to mention its sweeping views over the square and Koutoubia Mosque to the Atlas from the terrace. It's got everything the traveller needs: Internet, exchange (cash and travellers cheques), restaurant, café, bike rental, laundry service and baggage store. In addition, car rental, tours and trekking are available through the affiliated Sahara Expedition (see Organised Tours). There's even a wide range of accommodation, from rooms with bathroom and air-con (some with a semi-private terrace or balcony), to basic dorm beds or a mattress on the roof. Rates include a dull breakfast.

Hôtel Gallia *(☎ 445913, fax 444853; ⓔ hotelgalliamarrakech@menara.co.ma; 30 Rue de la Recette; singles/doubles Dh230/ 360)* is one of the medina's most appealing hotels. It has two lovely courtyards and the entire place is scrubbed from top to toe daily. Most rooms have air-con, while the central heating is welcome in winter. Rates include an excellent breakfast. Needless to say, you'll need to book (by fax) several weeks in advance.

Hotels – Ville Nouvelle The ville nouvelle is a bit short of cheap hotels. The few that exist can be found around Ave Mohammed V, west of Place du 16 Novembre.

Hôtel Toulousain *(☎ 430033, fax 431446; 44 Rue Tariq ibn Ziad; singles/doubles Dh110/160, with bathroom Dh150/ 190)* is your best option. It's a nice quiet place around two courtyards, one of them home to a venerable banana palm. Rooms on the 1st floor are more airy. Prices include breakfast; hot showers cost Dh5.

Hôtel Amalay *(☎ 448685, fax 431554; 87 Ave Mohammed V; singles/doubles Dh339/ 415)* makes up for lack of character with its friendly welcome and handy location. It also boasts air-con in the rooms (those on the front can be noisy), plus a bar and restaurant.

Places to Eat

Medina The liveliest, cheapest and most entertaining place to eat is Place Djemaa el-Fna. By the time the sun sets, much of the square is taken over by stalls, each specialising in certain dishes – the busiest are usually the best. You can eat your fill for Dh25 or less and wash it down with a Dh2.50 orange juice from a nearby juice stand.

At lunchtime, before the stalls on Place Djemaa el-Fna itself get going, you'll find much the same fare in the *qissaria* on the square's northern side. Here several vendors sharing a central kitchen will do you a meal for under Dh20.

Chez Chegrouni *(4-6 Place Djemaa el-Fna; salads Dh5, mains around Dh40)* is probably the best budget restaurant on the square. It's best known for its excellent *tajines*, including a melt-in-the-mouth lamb version. At busy times you squeeze up at trestle tables inside or on a small roadside terrace; get here early for a front-row seat.

Chez Bahia *(Rue Riad Zitoun el-Qedim; tajine Dh15)* dishes up some of the cheapest *tajines* in town. To fill up, try a *pastilla* (sweet or savoury pies) or some of the bite-sized flaky-pastry triangles known as *briouat*.

Hôtel Ali *(☎ 444979; Rue Moulay Ismail; set menus from Dh50, buffet Dh60 or Dh50 for hotel guests)* is a major hang-out for travellers stocking up on the Ali's no-nonsense fodder. If you fancy a real pig-out, wait until 6.30pm, when you can load your plate as many times as you like from the buffet of Moroccan fare, vegetables, salad, fruit and dessert.

Dar Mimoun *(☎ 443348; 1 Derb ben Amrane; salads Dh25, mains around Dh50-60, set menus from Dh120; open 9am-11pm daily)*, with its lovely salons around a leafy courtyard, offers the *riad* experience at affordable prices. The selection of Moroccan salads is a meal in itself. You can also breakfast here – a perfect place to start (or end) the day.

You'll find plenty of stalls selling fresh produce in the souqs. Alternatively, try the markets on Ave Mohammed V or on the east side of Place Djemaa el-Fna.

Ville Nouvelle There are many inexpensive places to eat in the ville nouvelle. You'll find a good selection on or around Ave Mohammed V and Blvd Mohammed Zerktouni.

For bottom-rung local food, head for a group of hole-in-the-wall places on Rue ibn Aicha, where a solid meal of rotisserie chicken or *brochettes* (skewered meat), chips and salad will cost around Dh25 to Dh30.

Café-Snack Sindibad *(3 Ave Mohammed V; mains Dh25-35)* looks a bit down-at-heel, but the food – everything from pizzas and salads to couscous, *kefta* and *tajines* – is as cheap and tasty as ever.

Al-Fassia *(☎ 434060; 232 Ave Mohammed V; mains around Dh100, lunch set menu Dh154)* is one of the few Moroccan-style restaurants in the ville nouvelle dishing up quality local cuisine. It's a very attractive place with a cool, peaceful garden and a cushioned pavilion. The lunchtime set menu offers excellent value.

Entertainment

Bars & Clubs The majority of bars are dire, male-oriented places filled with prostitutes. One reasonable option, particularly if you get a table outside, is the top-floor bar of the **Hôtel Tachfine** *(Blvd Mohammed Zerktouni)*, offering stunning views.

If you want to party on, there are some decent nightclubs, many attached to hotels, in the ville nouvelle. Entry varies from Dh80 to Dh150, which includes the first drink. Most offer the standard musical fare: Arab pop interspersed with techno, club, dance etc. Dress to impress. Most places don't get going until around 1am. **La Casa** *(☎ 448226; Ave du Président Kennedy; open 7pm-1.30am daily)*, in the Hôtel el-Andalous, starts out as a tapas bar/restaurant before the DJ cranks up the music at 9.30pm and everyone hits the dance floor. **Paradise** *(☎ 339100; Ave de France; entry Dh150; open 10.30pm-4am daily)* is the biggest and most expensive but also the prettiest of the city-centre nightclubs.

Folkloric Shows The only folkloric show of any real interest is **Chez Ali** *(☎ 307730; dinner & show Dh400; 8pm-11pm nightly)*, out on the Safi road, which offers a sampler of traditional singing and dancing and ends up with an enactment of a *fantasia* (musket-firing cavalry charge). You can buy tickets (including transport and dinner) through hotels or tour agencies.

Getting There & Away

Air Six kilometres southwest of town is the **Ménara airport** *(☎ 447865)*. **Royal Air Maroc** *(☎ 446444, fax 446002; 197 Ave Mohammed V)* offers several flights daily to and from Casablanca (Dh828, 40 minutes), as well as international flights to Geneva, London and Paris. Other carriers include British Airways and Air France.

Bus The **main bus station** *(☎ 433933)* is just outside the city walls by Bab Doukkala, a 20-minute walk or roughly Dh15 taxi ride from Place Djemaa el-Fna. The majority of buses leave between 4am and 5pm. It's advisable to get tickets for early-morning departures the day before.

Buses run to dozens of towns, including Rabat (Dh80, six hours, every half-hour 5am to midnight) via Casablanca (Dh44, four hours), Meknès (from Dh100, six hours, at least three daily), Fès (from Dh103, eight hours, at least six daily) and Tangier (Dh150, 11 hours, 8am daily).

You can also buy tickets for any of the above services at **CTM's Gueliz booking office** *(☎ 448328; Blvd Mohammed Zerktouni)*. This is also the arrival and departure point for their international buses, including Paris (Dh1100) and Madrid (Dh800), both twice weekly.

Train The **train station** *(☎ 446569; Ave Hassan II)* lies on the western side of Gueliz. Take a taxi or city bus (Nos 3, 8, 10 and 14, among others; Dh3) into the centre. There are eight trains to Casablanca (2nd-class *rapide* Dh76, three hours) and Rabat (Dh100, four hours).

There are six direct trains to Fès (Dh171, eight hours) via Meknès (Dh154, seven hours). Overnight trains to Tangier (Dh143) leave once daily; if you want a couchette (Dh193), it's advisable to book at least two days in advance.

Getting Around

To/From the Airport A taxi to Marrakesh from the airport (6km) should be Dh50, but you'll need to establish the fare before getting in. Bus No 11 runs irregularly to Place Djemaa el-Fna.

Bus There are **local buses** *(☎ 335272)*, charging Dh3 for all fares, that run from Place de Foucauld, near Place Djemaa el-Fna, to the following destinations:

Nos 1 & 20 Ave Mohammed V–Gueliz
Nos 3 & 10 Bab Doukkala–main post office–train station–Douar Laskar
No 8 Bab Doukkala–main post office–train station–Douar Laskar
No 11 Ave Ménara–airport
No 14 train station

Taxi The creamy-beige *petits taxis* that dart around town cost between Dh5 and Dh10 per journey. The drivers are all supposed to use their meters, but you may need to insist.

Moscow & St Petersburg

No longer as forbidding or enigmatic as it was once portrayed, Russia remains a fascinating and rewarding destination. The world's largest country is more accessible today than at any other time in its turbulent history.

The very different characters of Russia's two historical capitals represent where Russia is today and where it's heading. Moscow is bold, brash and mercantile; St Petersburg is cultured, elegant and hedonistic. Centres of the country's economic, political, cultural and social life, both cities will leave a lasting impression.

Despite the Western media's tendency to emphasise Russia's problems, travellers are unlikely encounter any special difficulties. Crime levels in the major cities are comparable to those in other large European cities and, while patience is needed for dealing with ever-present bureaucracy and minor hassles, this is more than compensated for by the open-hearted spirit of the locals and Russia's natural beauty, architectural splendour and larger-than-life sense of history.

Russia: the Basics

Capital Moscow

Population 147 million

Language Russian

Currency Rouble (R) = 100 kopecks

Avoid at all costs Drinking St Petersburg's tap water

Slow things down by saying *Ya by khotel(a) tolko chut-chut vodki, pozhaluysta.* (I would like only a little vodka, please.)

Facts about Russia

HISTORY

The migrants who were to give Russia its predominant character were the Slavs, who expanded rapidly to the east, west and south from the vicinity of present-day northern Ukraine and southern Belarus.

The founding of Novgorod in AD 862 by Rurik of Jutland is taken as the birth of the Russian nation, but until 1480 Mongolian warlords (Genghis Khan and his successors) controlled the area. The beginning of the Romanov dynasty in 1613 saw huge expansion of Russian territory and, under the rule of Peter the Great (1696–1725), the founding of a navy and a new capital city, St Petersburg, in 1703.

A workers' revolution in 1905 paved the way for the abdication and eventual murder of the last tsar, Nicholas II, in 1917, and two revolutions that resulted in Vladimir Lenin's Bolshevik party taking control. After a devastating civil war, the communists established the Union of Soviet Socialist Republics (USSR) in 1922.

After the barbarous reign of Josef Stalin, the calamities of WWII (in which an estimated 26 million Russians died) and the decades-long Cold War, the USSR was on the brink of collapse. Mikhail Gorbachev's *glasnost* ushered in Boris Yeltsin's moderately democratic government of the 1990s. Free-market reforms created considerable upheaval and economic disparity: Russians were now free to travel and to buy anything they liked, but the vast majority hadn't the means to do so. The crash of the rouble in 1998 caused even more suffering.

In April 2000, with the economy on a sounder footing, Vladimir Putin was elected president. Despite ongoing conflict in renegade Chechnya, government interference with the media, and national unease over the sinking of the Kursk submarine in 2001, Putin remains popular and Russia continues to experience healthy economic growth.

GEOGRAPHY & CLIMATE

The world's largest country is an astounding 17 million sq km. Moscow and St Petersburg

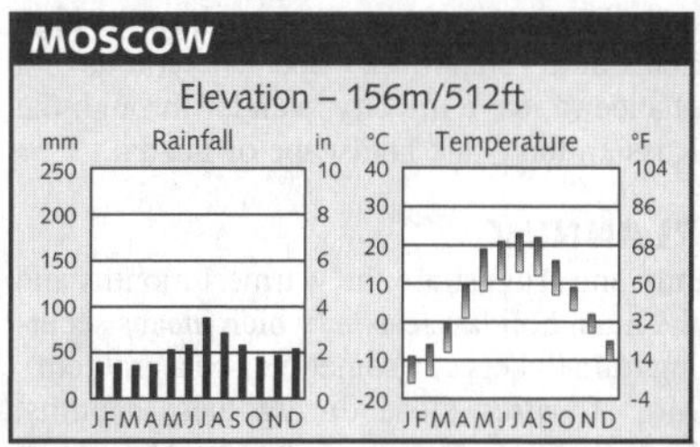

lie in the mainly flat European section, west of the Ural Mountains. Both cities are warm from about mid-May to early September, but drag themselves through dreary, dark and long winters.

GOVERNMENT & POLITICS

Russia is governed by an executive president with broad powers and a two-house parliament (Duma).

POPULATION & PEOPLE

Much of Russia's population is ethnically Russian; there are also dozens of smaller ethnic groups, mainly scattered across Siberia and the north, all with their own languages, traditions and religions.

SOCIETY & CONDUCT

If you are invited into someone's home, you can expect to be regaled with stories, to receive many vodka toasts and to be stuffed with food. Take along a gift and remove your shoes indoors.

LANGUAGE

Almost everyone speaks Russian, and English is little used or understood outside the major cities (and sometimes even in them). For pronunciation guidelines and useful words and phrases, see the Language chapter at the back of this book. In this chapter we've used the following abbreviations: ul for *ulitsa* (street), pr for *prospekt* (avenue), per for *pereulok* (lane), nab for *naberezhnaya* (embankment) and pl for *ploshchad* (square). *Vokzal* is a train station.

Facts for the Visitor

HIGHLIGHTS

You can't visit Moscow without taking in the Kremlin. Paying your respects to Vladimir Ilyich in Red Square is a memorable experience. Don't miss your chance to hear the high notes at a Tchaikovsky opera. If you have a chance to leave the city, wander through the Russian fairy-tale landscape of Suzdal.

PLANNING

July and August are the warmest months and the main holiday season (which means securing train tickets can sometimes be a problem). Most theatres close during these months. Early summer features 'white nights', when the sun never sets completely and it stays light all night long. The highlight of early autumn is the colourful foliage.

TOURIST OFFICES

Tourist offices of the kind that you may be used to in the West do not exist in Russia (St Petersburg is an exception but even that's not great). Instead you're dependent for information mainly on hotel receptionists and administrators, service bureaus and travel firms.

VISAS & DOCUMENTS

All foreigners visiting Russia need visas, which must be obtained outside Russia. Your visa is an exit permit too, so if you lose it (or overstay), leaving the country can be harder than getting in.

All Russian visas must be registered with OVIR (Otdel Viz i Registratsii) within three working days of your arrival in Russia. Usually your hotel or hostel will take care of it, but you can also register it yourself at a local OVIR office. Some hotels will register your visa for the fee of one night in their cheapest room.

Of the six types of visa available, the most common are single or multi-entry tourist and business visas. Tourist visas, which are valid for three months, are issued if you have a confirmed booking in a hotel or hostel. More flexible business visas, valid for up to a year, are available with an invitation from a registered Russian company. Some travel agencies can arrange this as well.

Since February 2002, Russia has been running a trial scheme whereby tourists from Schengen countries, Britain, Switzerland or Japan who wish to visit St Petersburg and Moscow for less than 72 hours can obtain visas upon arrival. Travellers must apply at an authorised tour operator in their home country 48 hours before departure. Check with your local Russian consulate for details.

EMBASSIES & CONSULATES

Russian Embassies & Consulates

Check W www.russianembassy.net for more listings of Russian embassies abroad.

Australia *Embassy:* (☎ 02-6295 9033/9474, fax 6295 1847) 78 Canberra Ave, Griffith, ACT 2603 *Consulate:* (☎ 02-9326 1188, fax 9327 5065) 7 Fullerton St, Woollahra, NSW 2025

Canada *Embassy:* (☎ 613-235 4341, fax 236 6342, *Visa section:* (☎ 613-336 7220, fax 238 6158) 285 Charlotte St, Ottawa, Ontario, KIN

8L5 *Consulate:* (☎ 514-843 5901/5343, fax 842 2012) 3685 Ave Du Musée, Montreal, Quebec, H3G 2EI

Finland *Embassy:* (☎ 09-66 14 49, fax 66 18 12) Tehtaankatu 1B, FIN-00140 Helsinki

Germany *Embassy:* (☎ 030-220 2821, 226 6320, fax 229 9397) Unter den Linden 63-65, 10117 Berlin *Consulate:* (☎ 0228-312 085, fax 312 164) Waldstrasse 42, 53177 Bonn

UK *Embassy:* (☎ 020-7229 3628, fax 7727 8625) 13 Kensington Palace Gardens, London W8 4QX *Consular Section:* (☎ 020-7229 8027, visa information message ☎ 0891-171 271, fax 020-7229 3215) 5 Kensington Palace Gardens, London W8 4QS

USA *Embassy:* (☎ 202-939 8907, fax 483 7579, Ⓦ www.russianembassy.gov) 2641 Tunlaw Rd NW, Washington DC 20007 *Visa Department:* (☎ 202-939 8907, fax 939 8909) 1825 Phelps Place NW, Washington DC 20008

Embassies & Consulates in Russia

Embassies in Moscow The telephone area code for Moscow is ☎ 095. For a full list of embassies check Ⓦ www.themoscowtimes.ru/travel/facts/embassies.html.

Australia (☎ 956 60 70, fax 956 61 70) Kropotkinsky per 2

Canada (☎ 956 66 66, fax 232 99 48) Starokonyushenny per 23

France (☎ 937 15 00, fax 937 15 77) ul Bolshaya Yakimanka 45

Germany (☎ 937 95 00, fax 936 21 43) ul Mosfilmovskaya 56 *Consular section:* (☎ 936 24 01) Leninsky pr 95A

Poland (☎ 255 00 17, visa section ☎ 254 36 21) ul Klimashkina 4

UK (☎ 956 72 00, fax 956 72 01) Smolenskaya nab 10

USA (☎ 728 50 00, fax 728 50 90) Novinsky bul 19/23

Consulates in St Petersburg The telephone area code for St Petersburg is ☎ 812.

France (☎ 312 11 30, fax 311 72 83) nab reki Moyki 15

Germany (☎ 327 24 00, fax 327 31 17) Furshtadtskaya ul 39

UK (☎ 320 32 00, fax 325 31 11) pl Proletarskoy Diktatury 5

USA (☎ 275 17 01, fax 110 70 22) Furshtadtskaya ul 15

CUSTOMS

You may be asked to fill in a declaration form *(deklaratsia)* upon arrival – keep this form until your departure from Russia. If the total value of what you've listed is US$1500 or more, you must go through a red lane and have the form stamped by a customs official, who may also check your luggage.

When you're leaving the country, anything vaguely 'arty', such as manuscripts, instruments, coins, jewellery or antiques, must be assessed by the **Ministry of Culture** *(Committee for Culture; ☎ 921 32 58; ul Neglinnaya 8/10, room 298, Moscow • ☎ 311 51 96; Malaya Morskaya ul 17, St Petersburg)*.

MONEY

The official currency is the rouble (R). Rouble notes come in denominations of R10, R50, R100 and R500, and are divided into 100 kopecks. Most prices in this chapter are listed in roubles.

US dollars and euros are the easiest currencies to exchange. ATMS, known as *bankomat* in Russian, are now quite common in Moscow and St Petersburg.

country	unit		roubles
Australia	A$1	=	R17.04
Canada	C$1	=	R19.92
Eurozone	€1	=	R31.16
Japan	¥100	=	R26.53
NZ	NZ$1	=	R14.63
UK	UK£1	=	R49.51
USA	US$1	=	R31.56

Moscow and St Petersburg are the two most expensive cities in Russia. With the aid of serious economising (self-catering, staying in hostels) you could scrape by on US$30 a day. But if you visit museums, take excursions and go out at night you could easily head towards US$100 a day.

Tipping is not widespread. Generally 5% to 10% of the total is fine. Tipping or offering a small gift to your guide is accepted practice.

Prices in stores are usually fixed. In markets and souvenir stalls, you might make a counterbid, but don't expect protracted haggling.

POST & COMMUNICATIONS

Moscow and St Petersburg have all the services travellers are used to, such as regular and express mail, email and all modes of telecommunication. The country code for Russia is ☎ 7. To make an international call from Russia, dial ☎ 8, wait for the second tone, then dial ☎ 10 plus the country code, city code and number. Omit any zeros from the city code.

DIGITAL RESOURCES

Useful sites include Bucknell University's award-winning site W www.departments.bucknell.edu/Russian, which has links to just about any topic on Russia you can imagine. Another good site is W http://russia-tourism.com, an encyclopaedia of tourism-related sites with links on a myriad subjects, including travel agents, hotels and much more.

WOMEN TRAVELLERS

Discrimination and domestic violence are hard facts of life for many Russian women. Foreign women are likely to be propositioned on the streets, although this interest is rarely dangerous. Women should certainly avoid taking private taxis alone at night.

GAY & LESBIAN TRAVELLERS

Open displays of same-sex love are not condoned. However, newspapers such as the *Moscow Times* and the *St Petersburg Times* feature articles and listings on the gay and lesbian scene. See also W www.gay.ru/english which has up-to-date information and good links, and can put you in touch with personal guides for Moscow and St Petersburg.

DISABLED TRAVELLERS

Inaccessible transport, lack of ramps and lifts, and no centralised policy for people with physical limitations make Russia a challenging destination for wheelchair-bound visitors.

SENIOR TRAVELLERS

Travellers over the age of 60 can expect senior citizen discounts from Russian ticket agents.

DANGERS & ANNOYANCES

Moscow and St Petersburg's streets are about as safe, or as dangerous, as those of New York, London or Amsterdam. On crowded transport, beware of pickpockets, who often work in gangs. The Russian mafia should be of no concern to tourists.

Frightening reports of racial violence against Jewish and darker-skinned people appear from time to time in the media. It's a sure thing that if you have dark skin you'll be targeted with suspicion by many people (and in particular by the police).

Emergencies

Call the following numbers (Russian-language only) for emergency services assistance: police ☎ 02, ambulance ☎ 03 and fire ☎ 01.

BUSINESS HOURS

Government offices and banks are usually open 9am to 5pm or 6pm Monday to Saturday, with a one-hour break for lunch. Shops often stay open until 7pm or 8pm without a lunch break. Most restaurants are open from noon to midnight daily. Museum hours vary widely and change often, as do their weekly days off.

PUBLIC HOLIDAYS & SPECIAL EVENTS

The main public holidays are New Year's Day (1 January), Russian Orthodox Christmas Day (7 January), International Women's Day (8 March), International Labour Day/Spring Festival (1 and 2 May), Victory (1945) Day (9 May), Russian Independence Day (12 June), and Day of Reconciliation and Accord (the rebranded Revolution Day; 7 November).

Other days that are widely celebrated are Defenders of the Motherland Day (23 February), Easter Monday and Constitution Day (12 December). Much of Russia shuts down during the first half of May.

ACCOMMODATION

Moscow and St Petersburg each have several youth or backpackers' hostels, all more or less in the international mould and able to offer visa support. Otherwise, with most hotels you get what you pay for.

FOOD & DRINKS

The local cuisine is undoubtedly on the fat-loaded side, but delicious *bliny* (pancakes) and hearty meat dishes are available. The highlight of Russian cuisine is its soups, such as *solyanka* (salty cucumber soup), *borshcht* (beetroot soup) and *ukha* (fish soup). There are also plenty of good restaurants and cafés serving a variety of other cuisines.

If you think you can get by in Russia without downing a shot of vodka, you are fooling yourself. Do not drink the tap water.

ENTERTAINMENT

Nightlife is one of the main attractions in both Moscow and St Petersburg. Bars and nightclubs can be just about as wild as you are willing to go. These cultural capitals also offer great bargains on classical music, opera and ballet. The theatres themselves are gorgeous, performances spectacular, and tickets (apart from the tourist-trap Bolshoi) cheap.

Getting There & Away

AIR

You'll most likely fly into Moscow's Sheremetyevo-2 airport, but there are also daily services from several European cities to St Petersburg. Two Russian airlines are Aeroflot and Transaero. International carriers such as British Airways, Delta, KLM and SAS offer direct flights to Moscow and/or St Petersburg.

LAND

Bus

In St Petersburg, **Eurolines** *(☎ 168 27 48; 🅦 www.eurolines.ru; ul Shkapina 10)* operates four or five daily buses to Tallinn (R270 to R330, seven to eight hours), and daily buses to Tartu (R300, eight hours) and Rīga (R500, 11 hours).

Finnord *(☎ 314 89 51; Italyanskaya ul 37)* runs buses from its office in St Petersburg to Helsinki via Vyborg and Lahti. A one-way ticket costs R1050. **Sovavto** *(☎ 123 51 25; 🅦 www.pohjolanliikenne.fi)* has daily coaches to Helsinki (R1200) and Turku via Lappeenranta, as well as a service between Vyborg and Lappeenranta.

Stat Express *(☎ 168 20 03, fax 316 24 31; ul Shkapina 10)* has twice-weekly buses to Germany, stopping in 20 cities and towns. Eurolines has some additional routes to Germany.

Train

There are trains between St Petersburg and Tallinn (R710, eight hours, alternate days), Rīga (R968, 13 hours, daily) and Vilnius (R630, 14 hours, alternate days). There are nightly trains between Moscow and Tallinn (R1260, 16 hours), Rīga (R3000, 15 hours) and Vilnius (R3000, 15 hours).

There are two daily trains from Helsinki to St Petersburg (R2500, five hours) and one to Moscow (R3450, 16 hours).

From St Petersburg, there are direct trains to Warsaw (30 hours), Berlin (39 hours), Kiev (24 hours) and Minsk (16 hours). Moscow also has direct connections with Warsaw (21 hours), Prague (35 hours), Vienna (34 hours), Budapest (40 hours), Kiev (14 hours) and Minsk (10 hours).

Car & Motorcycle

The generally poor condition of Russian roads and the frequency of traffic police pull-overs should make any motorist pause before deciding to drive to or through Russia. If you do drive there, make sure you have a valid International Driving Permit and your passport handy, as well as legal and insurance documents for your vehicle.

Getting Around

AIR

There are numerous domestic connections from both Moscow and St Petersburg.

TRAIN

Russia is crisscrossed with an extensive train network. Suburban or short-distance trains are called *elektrichkas* and do not require advance booking – you can buy your ticket at the *prigorodny poezd kassa* (suburban train ticket offices) at train stations. The regular long-distance service is a fast train, or *skory poezd*. First *(myagki)* class will get you a place in a two-person sleeping carriage, while 2nd *(kupeyny)* class will get you a place in a four-person car. *Platskartny* compartments, while cheaper, have open bunk accommodations and are not great for those who value privacy. *Obshchiy* (general) class simply has bench or aeroplane-style seating.

BUS

Buses are a cheap and reliable (though sometimes very slow) way of getting around or between cities. For medium-distance travel (up to 150km), suburban trains are usually the best way to go.

HITCHING

In Russian cities, hitching rides is called 'hailing a cab', no matter what type of vehicle stops. In the countryside, hitching is common. Rides are hailed by flagging passing vehicles with a low, up-and-down wave (not an extended thumb). You're expected to pitch in for petrol.

LOCAL TRANSPORT

Both Moscow and St Petersburg have impressive metro systems, and a network of buses, trams, trolleybuses, express buses and taxi-buses. Fares on these range from R5 to R10, with multitrip cards being available for the metro, which make it even cheaper. Public transport usually runs from around 5.30am to about 12.30am.

ORGANISED TOURS

Once you're in Russia, you'll find many travel agencies that specialise in city tours and excursions throughout the country. Sometimes these are the best way to visit out-of-the-way sights. Some travel agencies are listed in the relevant city section later in this chapter.

Moscow Москва

☎ 095 • pop 9 million

Some people love Moscow, some hate it. Most do both. It's glittering and grey, friendly and surly, beautiful and bleak, pious and hedonistic. It's the epicentre of the new Russia, with shops, restaurants and nightlife that most provincial Russians can still only dream about. It also epitomises the seamier side of post-communist Russia, with growing street crime and rising prices, widespread corruption and lots of beggars. As never before, Moscow is a city of excitement and opportunity where anything can happen.

Orientation

Picture Moscow as four road rings that spread out from the centre. Radial roads spoke out across the rings, and the Moscow River meanders across everything from northwest to southeast. The Kremlin, a north-pointing triangle with 750m sides, is at Moscow's heart. Red Square lies along its eastern side, the Moscow River flows to the south.

Information

Visa & Documents If your hotel does not register your visa, make sure you register yourself at a local visa office or OVIR. It's a fairly straightforward process at the city's central visa and registration office, which is called **OVIR** *(Otdel Viz i Registratsii; ☎ 200 84 97; ul Pokrovka 42; open 9am-1pm & 2pm-6pm Mon-Fri)*.

Money Among the more established banks in Moscow is **Alfa Bank** *(open 8.30am-8pm Mon-Sat)*, which has locations all over the city. ATMs at Alfa Bank branches dispense both roubles and dollars. **American Express** *(☎ 933 66 36, fax 933 66 35; ul Usacheva 33)*, in the city's south, is the most reliable place to cash AmEx travellers cheques.

Post & Communications The convenient **Central Telegraph** *(Tsentralny Telegraf; ul Tverskaya 7; postal counters open 8am-10pm daily, telephone office open 24hr)* offers telephone, fax and Internet services. Pay phones in Moscow operate with cards, which are widely available in shops, kiosks and metro stations.

Email & Internet Access On the lower level of the Okhotny Ryad shopping mall near Red Square, **Time Online** *(☎ 363 00 60; W www.timeonline.ru; open 24hr)* charges R30 to R60 per hour and claims to be the largest Internet café in Eastern Europe. After hours, enter from the Kuznetsky Most metro station. Similar rates and drinks are also available at the equally central **Internet Klub** *(☎ 924 21 40; Kuznetsky Most 12; open 9am-midnight daily)*.

Digital Resources The official Moscow government website, W www.moscow-guide.ru, is frequently updated with information on a wide range of topics from transport to culture.

Travel Agencies South of the centre, **Infinity Travel** *(☎ 234 65 55, fax 234 65 56; e info@infinity.ru; W www.infinity.ru; Komsomolsky pr 13)* is a great source of cheap airline tickets and other services.

Capital Tours *(☎ 232 24 42; W www.capitaltours.ru; Gostiny Dvor Bldg, ul Ilyinka 4)* offers a twice-daily Moscow city tour (adults/children US$18/10) and a Kremlin/Armoury tour (US$30/20), all of which are recommended.

Medical & Emergency Services Several expensive, foreign-run health services are available in Moscow, including the **American Medical Center** *(☎ 933 77 00, fax 933 77 01; Grokholsky per 1)*, which features an English-speaking **pharmacy** *(open 8am-8pm Mon-Fri, 9am-5pm Sat & Sun)*. The best Russian facility is **Botkin Hospital** *(☎ 945 0045; 2-y Botkinsky proezd 5)*.

Kremlin

The first fortified stronghold around Moscow was built in the 1150s. The Kremlin grew with the importance of Moscow's princes and in the 1320s became the headquarters of the Russian Orthodox Church, which shifted from Vladimir. Between 1475 and 1516, Ivan the Great brought master builders from Pskov and Italy to supervise the construction of new walls and towers, three great cathedrals and more.

Before entering the Kremlin *(☎ 203 03 49; Ⓦ www.kremlin.museum.ru; adult/student R200/100; open 10am-6pm Fri-Wed)*, deposit your bags at the **left-luggage office** *(R60 per bag; open 9am-6.30pm)*, beneath the Kutafya Tower, just north of the main ticket office. The ticket office, in the Aleksandrovsky Garden, closes at 4.30pm. The ticket covers admission to all buildings except the Armoury and Diamond Fund Exhibition (see later). A photography permit is R50.

Northern & Western Buildings From the Kutafya Tower, which forms the main visitors' entrance, walk up the ramp and pass through the Kremlin walls beneath the **Trinity Gate Tower** (Troitskaya bashnya). The lane to the right (south) passes the 17th-century **Poteshny Palace** (Poteshny dvorets) where Stalin lived. The bombastic marble, glass and concrete **Kremlin Palace of Congresses** (Kremlyovksy Dvorets Syezdov) houses a concert and ballet auditorium.

North of the Palace of Congresses, the 18th-century **Arsenal** is ringed by 800 captured Napoleonic cannons. The offices of the president of Russia are in the yellow, triangular former **Senate** (Senat) building. Next door is the 1930s **Supreme Soviet** (Verkhovny Soviet) building.

Sobornaya ploshchad On the northern side of Sobornaya ploshchad is the 15th-century **Assumption Cathedral** (Uspensky sobor), the focal church of prerevolutionary Russia. It's the burial place of most of the heads of the Russian Orthodox Church from the 1320s to 1700. The tombs are against the north, west and south walls.

The iconostasis dates from 1652, but its lowest level contains some older icons, including the *Virgin of Vladimir* (Vladimirskaya Bogomater), an early 15th-century Rublev School copy of Russia's most revered image. The 12th-century original, now in the Tretyakov Gallery, stood in the Assumption Cathedral from the 1480s to 1930. One of the oldest Russian icons, the 12th-century red-clothed *St George* (Svyatoy Georgy) from Novgorod, is positioned by the north wall.

With its two golden domes rising above the eastern side of Sobornaya ploshchad, the 16th-century **Ivan the Great Bell Tower** (Kolokolnya Ivana Velikogo) is the Kremlin's tallest structure. Beside the bell tower stands the world's biggest bell, the **Tsar-kolokol**, a 202-tonne monster that cracked before it ever rang. North of the bell tower is the mammoth **Tsar Cannon** (Tsar-pushka), cast in 1586, but never shot.

Back on Sobornaya ploshchad, the 1508 **Archangel Cathedral** (Arkhangelsky sobor), at the square's southeastern corner, was for centuries the coronation, wedding and burial church of tsars. The tombs of Moscow's rulers from the 1320s to the 1690s are here bar one (Boris Godunov, who was buried at Sergiev Posad).

Dating from 1489, the **Annunciation Cathedral** (Blagoveshchensky sobor), at the southwest corner of Sobornaya ploshchad, contains the celebrated icons of master painter Theophanes the Greek. He probably painted the six icons at the right-hand end of the deesis row, the biggest of the six tiers of the iconostasis. *Archangel Michael* (the third icon from the left on the deesis row) and the adjacent *St Peter* are ascribed to Andrey Rublev.

Armoury & Diamond Fund In the southwestern corner of the Kremlin, the **Armoury** *(Oruzheynaya palata; adult/student R300/175)* is a numbingly opulent collection of treasures accumulated over centuries by the Russian State and Church. Your ticket will specify a time of entry. Highlights include the Fabergé eggs in room 2 and the reams of royal regalia in rooms 6 and 9.

If the Armoury hasn't sated your diamond lust, there are more in the separate **Diamond Fund Exhibition** *(Vystavka almaznogo fonda; adult/student R300/175; closed for lunch 1pm-2pm)* in the same building.

Alexandrovsky Garden The first public park in Moscow, the Alexandrovsky Garden (Alexandrovsky Sad) sits along the Kremlin's western wall. Colourful flowerbeds and impressive Kremlin views make it a favourite spot for Muscovites and tourists alike to stroll in.

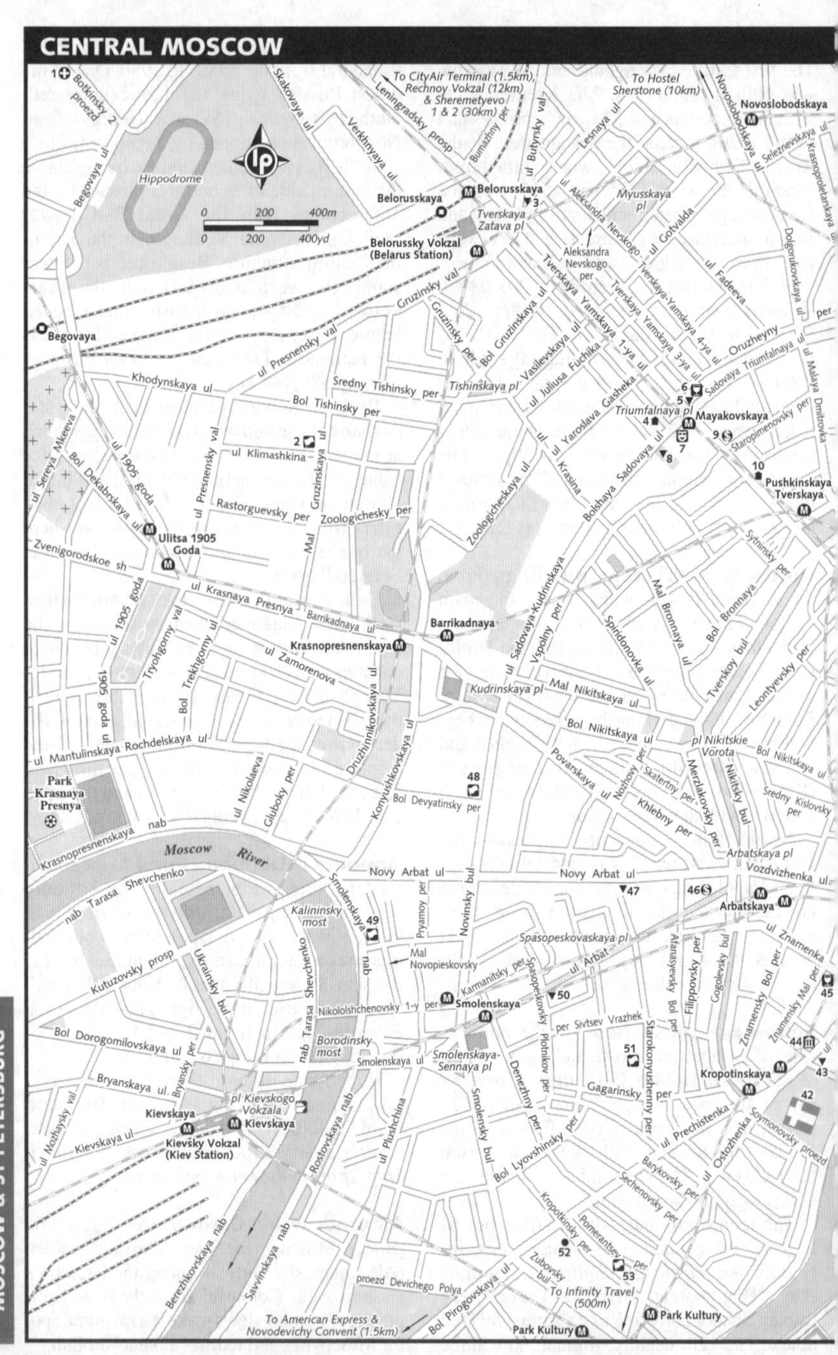
CENTRAL MOSCOW
To CityAir Terminal (1.5km), Rechnoy Vokzal (12km) & Sheremetyevo 1 & 2 (30km)
To Hostel Sherstone (10km)
Hippodrome
Belorusskaya
Belorussky Vokzal (Belarus Station)
Tverskaya Zatava pl
Novoslobodskaya
Begovaya
Ulitsa 1905 Goda
Mayakovskaya
Triumfalnaya pl
Pushkinskaya
Tverskaya
Barrikadnaya
Krasnopresnenskaya
Kudrinskaya pl
Park Krasnaya Presnya
Moscow River
Novy Arbat ul
Arbatskaya
Arbatskaya pl
Smolenskaya
Kalininsky most
Borodinsky most
Smolenskaya-Sennaya pl
Kievskaya
Kievsky Vokzal (Kiev Station)
pl Kievskogo Vokzala
Kropotinskaya
Park Kultury
To Infinity Travel (500m)
To American Express & Novodevichy Convent (1.5km)
pl Nikitskie Vorota
Spasopeskovaskaya pl
ul Arbat
Kutuzovsky prosp
Leningradsky prosp
Krasnopresnenskaya nab
Berezhkovskaya nab
Rostovskaya nab
Savvinskaya nab
proezd Devichego Polya
Bol Pirogovskaya ul
Zubovsky bul
Smolensky bul
Novinsky bul
Nikitsky bul
Gogolevsky bul
Tverskoy bul
ul Prechistenka
ul Ostozhenka
Bolshaya Sadovaya ul
ul Sadovaya-Kudrinskaya
ul Krasnaya Presnya
Zvenigorodskoe sh
ul Presnensky val
Gruzinsky val
Povarskaya ul
Bol Nikitskaya ul
Mal Nikitskaya ul
Vozdvizhenka ul
ul Znamenka
Mal Bronnaya ul
Bol Bronnaya ul
Spiridonovka ul
Zoologicheskaya ul
Tverskaya-Yamskaya 1-ya ul
Mal Gruzinskaya ul
Druzhinnikovskaya ul
Konyushkovskaya ul
ul Mantulinskaya
Rochdelskaya ul
Bol Devyatinsky per
Kutuzovsky prosp
Ukrainsky bul
Bol Dorogomilovskaya ul
Bryanskaya ul
Kievskaya ul
ul Plyushchina
Smolenskaya nab
nab Tarasa Shevchenko
Denezhny per
Gagarinsky per
Starokonyushenny per
per Sivtsev Vrazhek
Bol Lyovshinsky per
Kropotkinsky per
Pomerantsev per
Barykovsky per
Sechenovsky per
Soymonovsky proezd
Khodynskaya ul
Bol Tishinsky per
Sredny Tishinsky per
Tishinskaya pl
Begovaya ul
Botkinsky 2 proezd
Skakovaya ul
Verkhnyaya ul
Lesnaya ul
Butyrsky val
Novoslobodskaya ul
Myusskaya pl
Dolgorukovskaya ul
Sadovaya Triumfalnaya ul
Malaya Dmitrovka
0 200 400m
0 200 400yd

CENTRAL MOSCOW

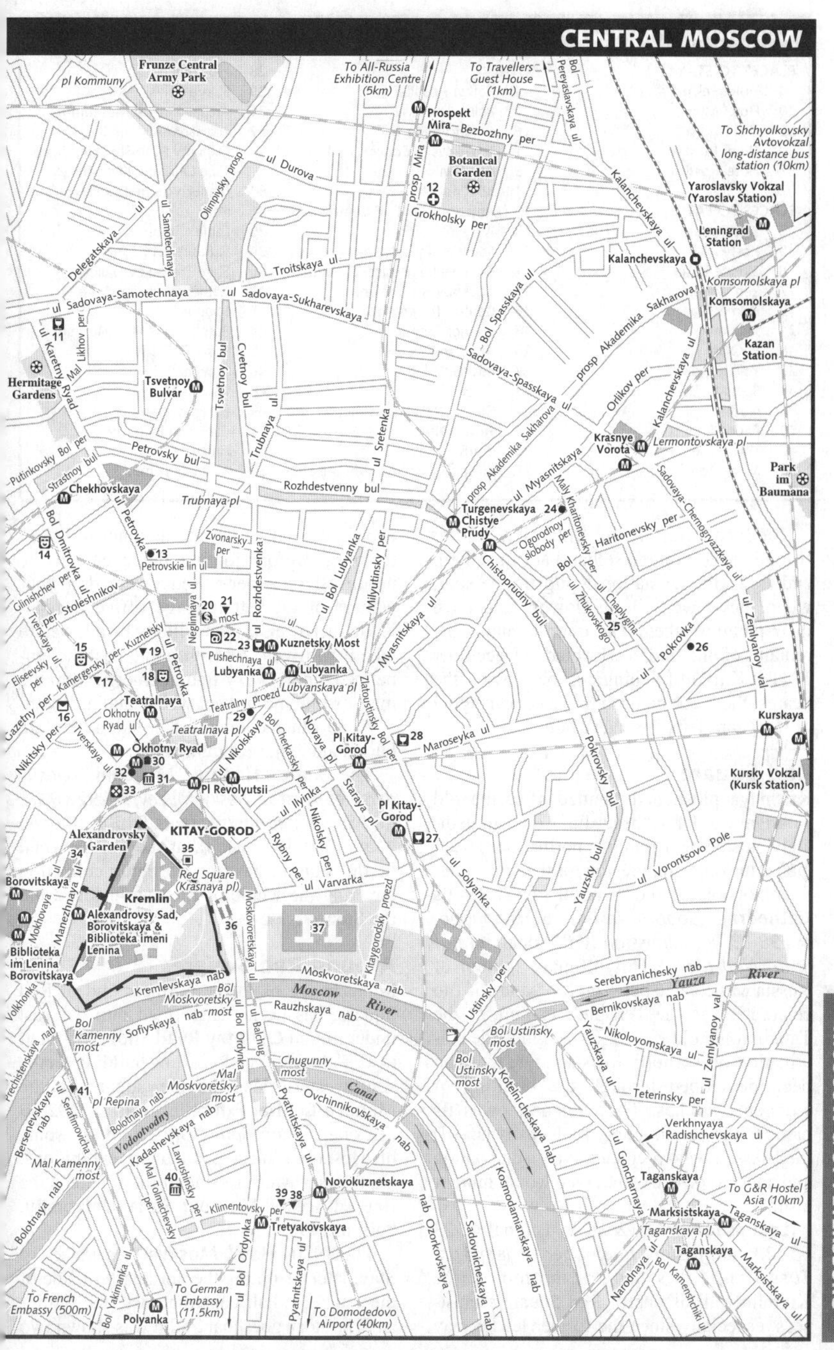

CENTRAL MOSCOW

PLACES TO STAY
- 4 Hotel Pekin
- 10 Hotel Minsk
- 25 Galina's Flat
- 30 Hotel Moskva
- 37 Hotel Rossiya

PLACES TO EAT
- 3 Zen Coffee
- 5 Rostiks
- 8 Starlite Diner
- 17 Zen Coffee
- 19 Pelmeshka
- 21 Jagannat
- 38 PirOGI
- 39 Yolki-Palki
- 41 Spets-Bufet No 7
- 43 Patio Pizza
- 47 Yolki-Palki
- 50 Moo-Moo

OTHER
- 1 Botkin Hospital
- 2 Polish Embassy
- 6 American Bar & Grill
- 7 Tchaikovsky Concert Hall
- 9 Alfa Bank
- 11 BB King
- 12 American Medical Centre
- 13 Aeroflot
- 14 Stanislavsky & Nemirovich-Danchenko Musical Theatre
- 15 Chekhov Art Theatre
- 16 Central Telegraph
- 18 Bolshoi Theatre
- 20 Alfa Bank
- 22 Internet Club
- 23 Duck
- 24 Central Railway Agency Ticket Office
- 26 OVIR
- 27 Kitaysky Lyotchik Dzhao-Da
- 28 Propaganda
- 29 Starye Polya
- 31 Archaeological Museum
- 32 Transaero Airlines
- 33 Okhotny Ryad Shopping Mall; Time Online; Infinity Travel
- 34 Manezh Central Exhibition Hall
- 35 Lenin's Tomb
- 36 St Basil's Cathedral
- 40 State Tretyakov Gallery
- 42 Cathedral of Christ the Saviour
- 44 Pushkin Fine Arts Museum
- 45 Rosie O'Grady's
- 46 Alfa Bank
- 48 US Embassy
- 49 UK Embassy
- 51 Canadian Embassy
- 52 Finnair
- 53 Australian Embassy

The lone **Tomb of the Unknown Soldier** (Mogila neizvestnogo soldata) at its northern end is a kind of national pilgrimage spot, where newlyweds bring flowers and have their pictures taken. The tomb contains the remains of one soldier who died in December 1941 at Km 41 of Leningradskoe shosse – the nearest the Nazis came to Moscow. Changing of the guard happens every hour.

Red Square

Krasnaya ploshchad (named after the old Russian word for 'beautiful') lies immediately outside the Kremlin's northeastern wall. No picture can prepare you for the crazy confusion of colours and shapes that is **St Basil's Cathedral** *(Sobor Vasilia Blazhennogo; ☎ 298 33 04; admission R100; open 11am-5pm Wed-Mon)*. This ultimate symbol of Russia was created between 1555 and 1561 to celebrate Ivan the Terrible's capture of the Tatar stronghold Kazan. Its design is the culmination of a wholly Russian style that had been developed through the building of wooden churches. The cathedral owes its name to the barefoot holy fool Vasily (Basil) the Blessed, who predicted Ivan's damnation and added (correctly) that Ivan would murder a son.

Lenin's tomb *(Mavzoley V I Lenina; ☎ 923 55 27; admission free; open 10am-1pm Tues-Thur, Sat & Sun)*, at the foot of the Kremlin wall, is one of Red Square's must-sees, especially since the former leader may eventually end up beside his mum in St Petersburg. Before joining the queue at the northwestern corner of Red Square, drop your camera at the left luggage office beneath Kutufya Tower, as you will not be allowed to take it with you. After trooping past the embalmed, oddly waxy figure, emerge from the mausoleum and inspect where Stalin, Brezhnev and other communist heavy hitters are buried along the Kremlin wall.

The **State History Museum** *(Gosudarstvenny Istorichesky Muzey; ☎ 292 40 19; Red Square; adults/students R150/75; open 11am-7pm Wed-Mon)*, at the northern end of the square, has an enormous collection covering the whole of Russian history from the Stone Age on.

Around Red Square

Manezhnaya pl, at the northern end of Red Square, has been transformed into the vast underground **Okhotny Ryad Shopping Mall** *(☎ 737 84 09)*. The long, low building on the southwestern side of the square is the **Manezh Central Exhibition Hall** *(☎ 202 89 76; open 11am-8pm daily)*, home to some of Moscow's most popular art exhibitions. On the northwestern side of the square is the fine edifice of **Moscow State University**, built in 1793.

The 1930s **Hotel Moskva** (see Places to Stay, later), fronting the northeastern side of the square, is half constructivist, half Stalinist. The story goes that Stalin was shown two possible designs for the hotel. Not realising they were alternatives, he approved both of them. The builders didn't dare point out his error and built half in each style, with predictably incongruous results.

The entrance to the new **Archaeological Museum** *(☎ 292 41 71; Manezhnaya pl 1; admission R30; open 10am-6pm Tues-Sun)* is at the base of the hotel facing the square.

Teatralnaya pl opens out on both sides of Okhotny ryad, 200m from Manezhnaya pl. The northern half of the square is dominated by the **Bolshoi Theatre**, where Tchaikovsky's *Swan Lake* was premiered (unsuccessfully) in 1877.

The narrow old streets east of Red Square are known as Kitai Gorod, which literally means 'Chinatown'. It actually refers to the palisades that reinforced the earthen ramp around this early Kremlin suburb. Along Teatralnaya proezd at **Starye Polya** (Old Fields), archaeologists uncovered parts of the 16th-century fortified wall that used to surround Kitai Gorod, as well as the foundations of the 1493 Trinity Church.

Pushkin Museum & Around

Moscow's premier foreign art museum is just a skip from the southwestern corner of the Kremlin. The Pushkin Museum *(☎ 203 74 12; ul Volkhonka 12; metro Kropotkinskaya; adult/student R160/60, audio guide R100; open 10am-6pm Tues-Sun)* is famous for its impressionist and post-impressionist paintings, but also has a broad selection of European works from the Renaissance onward, mostly appropriated from private collections after the revolution.

Nearby is the gigantic **Cathedral of Christ the Saviour** *(Khram Khrista Spasitelya; ☎ 201 38 47; open 10am-5pm daily)*, rebuilt at an estimated cost of US$360 million by Mayor Luzhkov on the site of the original destroyed by Stalin, and in place of what was once the world's largest swimming pool.

State Tretyakov Gallery

This gallery *(Gosudarstvennaya Tretyakovskaya galereya; ☎ 951 13 62; Lavrushinsky per 10; adult/student R220/110, audio tour R120; open 10am-6.30pm Tues-Sun)* has the world's best collection of Russian icons and an outstanding collection of other prerevolutionary Russian art, particularly the 19th-century Peredvizhniki.

The Great Red Square Rip-off

Red Square is a prime location for policemen to stop unsuspecting tourists to 'check' their documents. These diligent law enforcers will invariably find something wrong with their victim's visa or registration (even if they are really in perfect order). The policeman may present the option of appearing at the police station to pay the fine, but only if he knows it is impossible for the tourist to do so. He may even furnish you with a (totally meaningless) receipt for your troubles.

So here's how to beat these crooked coppers:

- Get your visa registered in Moscow, even if it has already been registered in another city. As a rule, you can never have too many stamps and signatures.
- Never volunteer your time or date of intended departure, so you can insist on paying the fine at the station.
- Before handing over your documents, ask to see the officer's identification and write down the seven-digit number. Make sure he knows that you know who he is.
- Show the officer a photocopy of your passport and visa (made after you arrive in Moscow, so that your visa registration is visible). Do not give up your passport.
- If you have a cell phone, tell the officer you would like to ring your embassy to have somebody meet you at the station. One reader writes: 'This exact situation has happened to me four times. Once it cost me 1500 roubles; since the mobile it has cost nothing at all.'

Novodevichy Convent

A cluster of sparkling domes behind turreted walls on the Moscow River, Novodevichy Convent *(Novodevichy monastyr; ☎ 246 85 26; admission R30; open 10am-5pm Wed-Mon)* is resplendent with history and treasures. Founded in 1524 to celebrate the re-taking of Smolensk from Lithuania, it is notorious as the place where Peter the Great imprisoned his half-sister Sofia for her part in the Streltsy Rebellion.

You enter the convent under the red-and-white Moscow baroque **Transfiguration Gate-Church**. The oldest and dominant building in the grounds is the white **Smolensk Cathedral** (1524–25). **Sofia's tomb** lies among others in the south nave. The **bell tower** against the convent's east wall, completed in 1690, is generally regarded as Moscow's finest. The adjacent **Novodevichy Cemetery** contains the tombs of Khrushchev, Chekhov, Gogol, Mayakovsky, Stanislavsky, Prokofiev, Eisenstein, Gromyko, Raisa Gorbachev and other Russian and Soviet notables.

VDNKh

About 7km north of the Kremlin, no other place sums up the rise and fall of the Soviet dream quite so well as the All-Russia Exhibition Centre (VVTs). The old initials by which it's still commonly known, VDNKh, stand for Vystavka Dostizheny Narodnogo Khozyaystva SSSR, or USSR Economic Achievements Exhibition.

VDNKh was created in the 1950s and '60s to impress upon one and all the success of the Soviet economic system. Two kilometres long and 1km wide, it is composed of wide pedestrian avenues and grandiose pavilions, glorifying every aspect of Socialist construction. The pavilions represent a huge variety of architectural styles, symbolic of the contributions from diverse ethnic and artistic movements to the common goal. Here you will find the kitschest Socialist realism, the most inspiring socialist optimism and – now – the tackiest of capitalist consumerism. Today the VVTs is a commercial centre, its pavilions given over to sales of the very imported goods that were supposed to be inferior.

The soaring 100m titanium obelisk beside VDNKh metro is a monument to Soviet space flight. In its base is the **Cosmonautics Museum** *(Muzey kosmonavtiki; ☎ 283 79 14; admission R30; open 10am-7pm Tues-Sun)*, a high-concept series of displays from the glory days of the Soviet space exploration programme.

Places to Stay

Guesthouses On the top floors of an old hotel, **G&R Hostel Asia** *(☎ 378 00 01, fax 378 28 66; w www.hostels.ru; ul Zelenodolskaya 2/3; dorm beds/singles/doubles with breakfast US$16/30/44)*, 10km southeast of the centre, is one of the best budget options. The management runs a travel agency that can book train tickets and the like. Leave Ryazansky Prospekt metro from the end of the train and look for the tallest building around.

Galina's Flat *(☎ 921 60 38; e galinas.flat@mtu-net.ru; ul Chaplygina 8, No 35; dorm beds/singles/doubles US$8/15/20)* is just that – a private flat with a few extra rooms that Galina rents out. A kitchen and Internet facilities are available.

Hostel Sherstone *(☎/fax 797 80 75; w www.sherstone.ru; Gostinichny proezd 8/1; dorm beds/singles/doubles US$14/25/40)* is a branch of the G&R 10km north of the centre. Services include visa support, free transfers from the train station and discounts for IYHF cards. It is a 10-minute walk from Vladykino metro.

Travellers Guest House *(☎ 951 40 59, fax 280 76 86; e tgh@glasnet.ru; ul Bol Pereyaslavskaya 50, floor 10; dorm beds US$18, rooms with shared/private bathroom US$48/55)* calls itself Moscow's 'first and only' budget accommodation. Perhaps the first, but no longer the only, this lacklustre place is a 10-minute walk north of Prospekt Mira metro.

Hotels Occupying the whole block between Manezhnaya pl and Teatralnaya pl, **Hotel Moskva** *(☎ 960 20 20, fax 960 59 38; Okhotny Ryad ul 2; singles/doubles R1600/2500)* has tolerable rooms, some with marvellous views of the Kremlin.

Hotel Minsk *(☎ 299 12 13, fax 299 03 62; ul Tverskaya 22; singles/doubles R700/1050)* has shabby rooms and disagreeable staff, but a prime location. The ticket office in the lobby is useful for train and air tickets.

Hotel Rossiya *(☎ 232 60 46, 232 62 48; singles/doubles from R1500/1600)* has literally thousands of rooms. The Rossiya gets a bad rap because it is so big and ugly, but some swear by the place for its unbeatable location and reasonable prices.

Hotel Pekin *(☎ 209 22 15, fax 200 14 20; w www.hotelpekin.ringnet.ru; ul Bolshaya Sadovaya 5/1; doubles from US$62)* is better than it looks, with its cheesy Oriental decor and noisy casino. However, the staff are helpful, rooms are comfortable, and the location is convenient.

Places to Eat

If you want to eat like a Muscovite, you'll buy your food, take it home and cook it there. **Sedmoy Kontinent supermarkets** *(Seventh Continent; open 24hr)* carry mainly local brands but some Western ones as well.

Fast Food & Cafeterias An omnipresent local chain endorsed (and, coincidentally, co-owned) by Mayor Luzhkov, **Russkoe Bistro** serves cheap, traditional goodies such as *pirozhki* (pies) and *bliny*.

Rostik's *(☎ 251 49 50; 1-ya Tverskaya-Yamskaya ul 2/1; open 9am-9pm daily; meals R100)* is a chain that serves American food, including burgers and fried chicken. **Patio Pizza** *(☎ 201 56 26; ul Volkhonka 13a; pizzas from R200)* also has branches all over town.

Moo-Moo *(☎ 241 13 64; ul Arbat 45/23 • ☎ 245 78 20; Komsomolsky pr 26; meals R150; open 10am-11pm)* offers an easy serve-yourself approach to Russian standards such as *borscht*, *pelmeni* and violently coloured desserts. Dig that spotted-cow decor.

Pelmeshka *(☎ 292 83 92; ul Kuznetsky Most 4/3; meals R100; open 11am-midnight)*, clean and modern, serves the most filling of Russian favourites: *pelmeni*.

Restaurants & Cafés An excellent country-cottage style Russian chain that specialises in simple, traditional dishes, **Yolki-Palki** *(☎ 953 9130; Klimentovsky per 14 • ☎ 291 68 88; ul Novy Arbat 11; meals R150, salad bar R120; open 11am-midnight)* has outlets all over town. The beer is cheap and there's a good salad bar.

Spets-Bufet No 7 *(☎ 959 31 35; ul Serafimovicha 2; meals R300; open noon-6am)* is in the basement of a once-prestigious apartment block that was home to many Communist Party apparatchiks. This 'Special Buffet' recreates the forum where the bigwigs may have eaten. The food is decidedly mediocre (thus making the place more authentic).

For those who need their vitamins, **Jagannat** *(☎ 928 35 80; Kuznetsky Most 11; mains R150)* is a funky vegetarian café, restaurant and store. Service is slow but sublime. The food is worth the wait.

The original **Starlite Diner** *(☎ 290 9638; ul Bolshaya Sadovaya 16; open 24hr)*, the quintessential burger and milkshake diner, has a wonderful, leafy outdoor seating area.

Zen Coffee *(☎ 234 17 84; ul Lesnaya 1/2; open 9am-11pm • ☎ 292 51 14; Kamergersky per 6; open 9am-11pm)* has several outlets. The first of these modern, pleasant cafés is opposite Belarusskaya Vokzal; the second is on the popular pedestrian boulevard leading off from Tverskaya to Kuznetsky Most.

PirOGI *(☎ 951 7596; ul Pyatnitskaya 29/8; open 24hr)* is a low-key, bohemian place, serving coffee, beers and even books, which you can buy or just peruse while you have a drink.

Entertainment

The key to finding out what's on is the comprehensive weekly entertainment section in Thursday's *Moscow Times*. For a laugh, you can also try *The Exile*.

Live Performance The largest concert venue is **Tchaikovsky Concert Hall** *(☎ 299 03 78; Triumfalnaya pl 4/31)*, which seats over 1600 and is the home of the famous State Symphony Orchestra.

An evening at the **Bolshoi** *(☎ 292 00 50; W www.bolshoi.ru; Teatralnaya pl 1)* is still one of the most romantic places in Moscow. Tickets are hard to come by unless you hang around the theatre before the performance and buy them from a tout.

Another gorgeous theatre, **Stanislavsky & Nemirovich-Danchenko Musical Theatre** *(☎ 229 06 49; W www.stanislavsky.ru; ul Bolshaya Dmitrovka 17)* has a similar classical repertoire and high-quality performances. Tickets are readily available and relatively cheap.

Chekhov Art Theatre *(☎ 229 87 60; W www.art.theatre.ru; Kamergersky per 3)* is also known as MkhAT. It's where method acting was founded over 100 years ago. Watch for English-language versions of Russian classics performed here by the **American Studio** *(☎ 292 09 41)*.

Bars & Clubs In a basement close to Kitay-Gorod metro, **Kitaysky Lyotchik Dzhao-Da** *(☎ 924 56 11; Lubyansky proezd 25; cover charge R150)* is one of the best and most relaxed club/restaurants, often with live music.

Proekt OGI *(☎ 229 54 89; Potapovsky per 8/12; cover charge R50-80; open 8am-11pm)* is a vaguely hippy, but definitely hip, place for student types. Enter through the unmarked door in the corner of the courtyard. There is live music most nights.

Propaganda *(☎ 924 57 32; Bol Zlatoustinsky per 7)* is a happening place, especially on Thursdays. DJs spin a cool mix for the beautiful people to dance to.

Duck *(☎ 923 61 58; ul Pushechnaya 9/6; cover charge varies; open noon-6am daily)* is a successor to the Hungry Duck, a bar that was often described as the wildest in Europe.

BB King *(☎ 299 82 06; ul Sadovaya-Samotechnaya 4/2; open noon-2am)* is the best venue for live jazz and blues. Concerts and jam sessions go into the wee hours.

As for expat bars, you can't go far wrong at either **American Bar and Grill** *(☎ 250 95 25; 1-ya Tverskaya-Yamskaya ul 2/1; open 24hr)* or **Rosie O'Grady's** *(☎ 203 90 87; ul Znamenka 9/12; open noon-1am)*, both of which are pretty self-explanatory.

Getting There & Away

Air Of Moscow's five airports, the most frequently used are Sheremetyevo-1, Sheremetyevo-2 and Domodedovo. You can purchase domestic airline tickets at most travel agencies and **Aeroflot offices** *(☎ 753 55 55; ul Petrovka 20/1; open 9am-7pm Mon-Sat, 9am-3.30pm Sun)* all over town. **Transaero Airlines** *(☎ 241 4800; Okhotny Ryad 2; open 9am-9pm daily)* also has several ticket offices, including a very convenient one in the corner of Hotel Moskva. International airline offices in Moscow include:

Air France (☎ 937 3839) ul Korovy Val 7
British Airways (☎ 363 2525) Business Centre Parus, ul 1-ya Tverskaya-Yamskaya 23
Delta Air Lines (☎ 937 9090) Gogolevsky bul 11
Finnair (☎ 933 0056) Kropotinsky per 7
KLM-Royal Dutch Airlines (☎ 258 3600) ul Usacheva 33/2
Lufthansa Airlines (☎ 737 6400) Renaissance Moscow Hotel, Olimpiysky prosp 18

Bus Buses run to a number of towns and cities within about 700km of Moscow, but they tend to be crowded. However, they are usually faster than the *prigorodny* (suburban) trains, and are convenient for some destinations. To book a seat you have to go to the long-distance bus terminal, the Shchyolkovsky Avtovokzal beside Shchyolkovskaya metro station.

Train All train lines lead to Moscow. There are daily connections with most parts of Russia and the countries of the former Soviet Union, as well as numerous countries in Eastern and Western Europe, and China and Mongolia. There are nine train stations in Moscow, each serving specific destinations.

Besides the train stations proper, tickets are sold throughout the city at **Central Railway Agency ticket offices** *(Tsentralnoe Zheleznodorozhnoe Agentstvo; ☎ 262 25 66; Mal Kharitonevsky per 6; open 8am-1pm & 2pm-7pm daily)*. Alternatively, travel agencies and other ticket offices *(kassa zheleznoy dorogi)* also sell tickets, sometimes for a small commission, but it's worth it.

Boat The Moscow terminus for cruises to St Petersburg is the **Northern River Station** *(Severny Rechnoy Vokzal; ☎ 459 74 76; Leningradskoe shosse 51)*. Take the metro to Rechnoy Vokzal, then walk 15 minutes due west, passing under Leningradskoe shosse and through a nice park.

Getting Around

To/From the Airport There are minibuses from Sheremetyevo-1 and Sheremetyevo-2 to Rechnoy Vokzal metro. Minibuses also link Domodedovo airport to Domodedovskaya metro, and Vnukovo airport to Yugo-Zapadnaya metro. Suburban trains run between Bykovo train station, 400m from the Bykovo airport, and Kazan station.

To book a taxi to/from the airport, call **Logus 88** *(☎ 911 97 47)* or **Taxi Bistro** *(☎ 324 99 74, 324 51 44)*. It costs R500/800 to/from the Sheremetyevo airports with Logus 88 or R450 with Taxi Bistro.

Metro The metro is the easiest, quickest and cheapest way of getting around Moscow. The 150-plus stations are marked outside with big 'M' signs. Magnetic tickets are sold at ticket booths for one, two or more rides. Each ride costs R5, unless you buy in bulk (10 rides for R35, 20 for R70, 60 for R150).

Taxi To book a taxi in advance, call the **Central Taxi Reservation Office** *(☎ 927 0000; open 24hr)*.

St Petersburg Санкт Петербург

☎ 812 • pop 4.6 million

It's almost impossible to believe that just three centuries ago St Petersburg was little more than a giant swamp – such is the visual power of this handsome city (created by Peter the Great as his 'window on the West') with a history and European savoir-faire that no other place in Russia possesses.

Apart from the seamless architectural ensemble at the heart of St Petersburg, threaded through with languorous canals, the city is home to world-class museums and stunningly opulent palaces. 'Piter', as it's affectionately known to residents, also has a lively club and music scene and prides itself on the quality of its performing arts. It's a city that demands to be savoured.

Orientation

St Petersburg sprawls across and around the delta of the Neva River, at the end of the easternmost arm of the Baltic Sea, known as the Gulf of Finland.

The heart of St Petersburg spreads south and east from the Winter Palace and the Admiralty on the Neva's south bank. Nevsky pr, stretching east–southeast from the Admiralty, is the main street.

The north side of the city has three main areas. The westernmost is Vasilevsky Island, at whose east end is the Strelka, where many of the city's fine early buildings still stand; the middle is the Petrograd Side; and the eastern is the Vyborg Side.

Information

Foreigner admission prices are listed in roubles for all the attractions listed in this section; foreign students get in for half price unless otherwise stated.

Visas & Documents You can register your visa at **OVIR** *(☎ 278 24 81; Kirochnaya ul 4; open 9am-5pm Mon-Fri)*.

Tourist Offices The official **tourist office** *(☎ 311 28 43; W www.spb.ru/eng/)* can help with individual queries, but they don't book accommodation and there's nothing in the way of official literature. A city walking tour from here is US$25.

More helpful are the staff at either the International Holiday Hostel or the HI St Petersburg Hostel (see Places to Stay, later).

Money There are currency exchange offices all along Nevsky pr. ATMs are inside every metro station, in hotels and department stores, in main post offices and along major streets.

American Express *(☎ 326 45 00, fax 326 45 01; Malaya Morskaya ul 23; open 9am-5pm Mon-Fri)* only offers travel services. You can pick up forwarded mail here; correspondents should send mail care of American Express, PO Box 87, SF53501, Lappeenranta, Finland. Mail is then forwarded from Finland to the St Petersburg office.

Post & Communications The **central post office** *(glavpochtamt; ☎ 312 83 02; Pochtamtskaya ul 9)* is open daily. You can call direct from any of the card-operated phone booths all over the city. Cards can be purchased from metro stations and telephone offices. Rouble-coin-operated phones are inside every metro station.

Email & Internet Access There are Internet cafés all over the city, one of the most prominent being **Quo Vadis?** *(Nevsky pr 24; open 24 hr)*, which charges R60 per hour. It has 65 terminals and a free library with foreign newspapers and magazines.

Kro Magnon *(Nevsky pr 81)* is cheaper (R40 per hour); their office is on the right-hand side of the courtyard, on the 2nd floor.

Travel Agencies A student and discount air-ticket office, **Sindbad Travel** *(☎ 327 83 84; W www.sindbad.ru; 3-ya Sovietskaya ul 28)* is located at the HI St Petersburg Hostel. **Ost-West Kontaktservice** *(☎ 327 34 16; W www.ostwest.com; Nevsky pr 105)* can also help with any travel needs.

Medical & Emergency Services Treatment is available at the **American Medical Center** *(AMC; ☎ 326 17 30; Serpukhovskaya ul 10)*, which offers 24-hour emergency care. Consultations cost at least US$100, often much more. **Poliklinika No 2** *(☎ 316 62 72; Moskovsky pr 22)* is also recommended – and much cheaper. Two 24-hour pharmacies are **Apteka Petrofarm** *(Nevsky pr 22)* and **Apteka** *(Liteyny pr 56)*.

The Historic Heart

The western end of Nevsky pr begins with a knockout: **Dvortsovaya Ploshchad** (Palace Square), where the baroque/rococo **Winter Palace** (Zimny dvorets) appears like a mirage under the archway at the start of ul Bolshaya Morskaya. The palace was commissioned from Bartolomeo Rastrelli in 1754 by Empress Elizabeth, and some of its 1057 rooms now house part of the **Hermitage** *(☎ 311 34 65; W www.hermitagemuseum.org; adults R300, students & children free; open 10.30am-6pm*

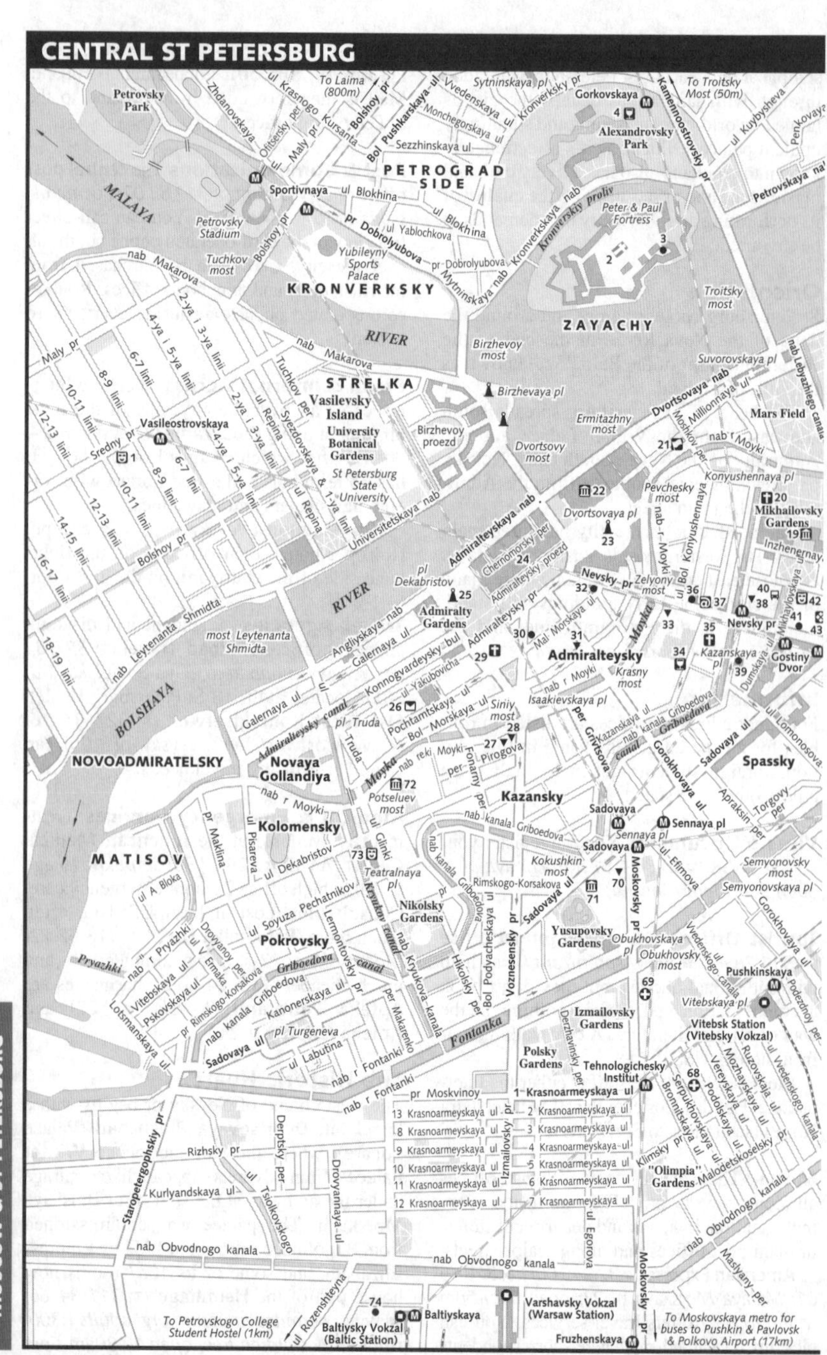
CENTRAL ST PETERSBURG
Petrovsky Park
Zhdanovskaya
ul Krasnogo Kursanta
To Laima (800m)
Bolshoy pr
Bol Pushkarskaya ul
Vvedenskaya ul
Sytninskaya pl
Kronverksky pr
Gorkovskaya
Kamennoostrovsky pr
To Troitsky Most (50m)
ul Kuybysheva
Alexandrovsky Park
Monchegorskaya ul
Ofitsersky per
Maly pr
Sezzhinskaya ul
PETROGRAD SIDE
Sportivnaya
ul Blokhina
Petrovskaya nab
MALAYA
Petrovsky Stadium
pr Dobrolyubova
ul Yablochkova
Kronverksky proliv
Peter & Paul Fortress
Yubileyny Sports Palace
Mytninskaya nab
Kronverkskaya nab
Tuchkov most
nab Makarova
KRONVERKSKY
Troitsky most
ZAYACHY
RIVER
Birzhevoy most
Maly pr
2-ya i 3-ya linii
4-ya i 5-ya linii
6-7 linii
8-9 linii
10-11 linii
12-13 linii
Tuchkov per
STRELKA
Vasilevsky Island
Birzhevaya pl
Suvorovskaya pl
nab Lebyazhiego kanala
University Botanical Gardens
Birzhevoy proezd
Dvortsovaya nab
Millionnaya ul
Mars Field
Ermitazhny most
Vasileostrovskaya
Sredny pr
Dvortsovy most
nab r Moyki
St Petersburg State University
Syezdovskaya & 1-ya linii
ul Repina
Universitetskaya nab
Pevchesky most
Konyushennaya pl
Dvortsovaya pl
Mikhailovsky Gardens
Admiralteyskaya nab
Chernomorsky per
Admiralteysky proezd
Inzhenernaya
14-15 linii
16-17 linii
Bolshoy pr
pl Dekabristov
Nevsky pr
Zelyony most
Bol Konyushennaya
RIVER
Admiralty Gardens
Admiralteysky pr
Mal Morskaya ul
Moyka
Nevsky pr
Gostiny Dvor
nab Leytenanta Shmidta
most Leytenanta Shmidta
Angliyskaya nab
Galernaya ul
Konnogvardeysky bul
Admiralteysky
Kazanskaya pl
18-19 linii
ul Yakubovicha
Krasny most
Dumskaya ul
Mikhaylovskaya ul
BOLSHAYA
Galernaya ul
Admiralteysky canal
pl Truda
Pochtamtskaya ul
Bol Morskaya ul
Siniy most
Isaakievskaya pl
per Grivtsova
Kazanskaya ul
nab kanala Griboedova
ul Lomonosova
NOVOADMIRATELSKY
Novaya Gollandiya
Truda
nab reki Moyki
per Pirogova
Fonarny per
Gorokhovaya ul
Sadovaya ul
Spassky
Moyka
Potseluev most
Kazansky
Apraksin per
Torgovy per
Kolomensky
nab r Moyki
pr Maklina
ul Pisareva
ul Glinki
nab kanala Griboedova
Sadovaya
Sennaya pl
Sennaya pl
Sadovaya
ul Efimova
MATISOV
ul Dekabristov
Teatralnaya pl
Kokushkin most
Rimskogo-Korsakova
Moskovsky pr
Semyonovsky most
Semyonovskaya pl
ul A Bloka
ul Soyuza Pechatnikov
Kryukov canal
Nikolsky Gardens
Sadovaya ul
Gorokhovaya ul
Pryazhki
nab r Pryazhki
ul V Ermaka
Drovyanoy per
Pokrovsky
Lermontovsky pr
Griboedova canal
nab Kryukova kanala
Nikolsky per
Bol Podyacheskaya ul
Voznesensky pr
Yusupovsky Gardens
Obukhovskaya pl
Obukhovsky most
Vvedenskogo canala
Pushkinskaya
Vitebskaya ul
Pskovskaya ul
pr Rimskogo-Korsakova
nab kanala Griboedova
Kanonerskaya ul
per Makarenko
Vitebskaya pl
Podezdnoy per
Lotsmanskaya ul
pl Turgeneva
Fontanka
Izmailovsky Gardens
Derzhavinsky per
Vitebsk Station (Vitebsky Vokzal)
Sadovaya ul
ul Labutina
nab r Fontanki
Polsky Gardens
Tehnologichesky Institut
Serpukhovskaya ul
Bronnitskaya ul
Mozhayskaya ul
Vereyskaya ul
Podolskaya ul
Ruzovskaya ul
ul Vvedenskogo kanala
nab r Fontanki
pr Moskvinoy
1 Krasnoarmeyskaya ul
13 Krasnoarmeyskaya ul
2 Krasnoarmeyskaya ul
8 Krasnoarmeyskaya ul
3 Krasnoarmeyskaya ul
9 Krasnoarmeyskaya ul
4 Krasnoarmeyskaya ul
10 Krasnoarmeyskaya ul
5 Krasnoarmeyskaya ul
11 Krasnoarmeyskaya ul
6 Krasnoarmeyskaya ul
12 Krasnoarmeyskaya ul
7 Krasnoarmeyskaya ul
Izmailovsky pr
Klimsky per
Malodetskoselsky pr
"Olimpia" Gardens
Staropetergophskiy pr
Rizhsky pr
Derptsky per
Kurlyandskaya ul
ul Tsiolkovskogo
Drovyannaya ul
ul Egorova
nab Obvodnogo kanala
nab Obvodnogo kanala
nab Obvodnogo kanala
Maslyany per
Moskovsky pr
ul Rozenshteyna
Baltiyskaya
Baltiysky Vokzal (Baltic Station)
Varshavsky Vokzal (Warsaw Station)
Fruzhenskaya
To Petrovskogo College Student Hostel (1km)
To Moskovskaya metro for buses to Pushkin & Pavlovsk & Polkovo Airport (17km)

CENTRAL ST PETERSBURG

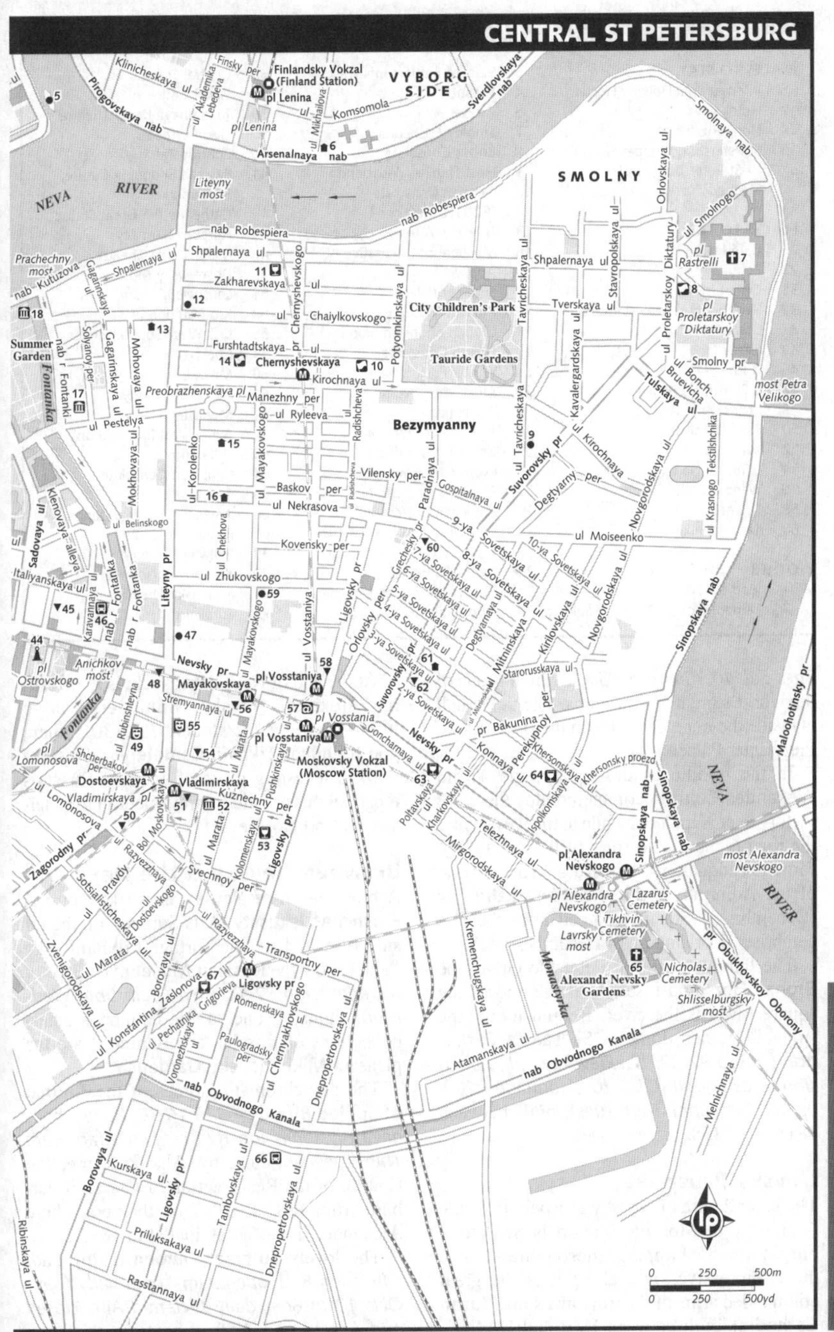

CENTRAL ST PETERSBURG

PLACES TO STAY
6 International Holiday Hostel
12 Hotel Neva
14 Hotel Rus
15 St Petersburg Puppet Hostel
57 HI St Petersburg Hostel; Sindbad Travel

PLACES TO EAT
26 Café Idiot
27 Popugay
30 Orient
32 Strogonoff Yard Restaurant
37 Laima
43 Circus
45 Gushe
47 U Tyoshi Na Blinakh
48 Kuznechny Market
50 Bliny Domik
52 Kafe Kat
54 U Tyoshi Na Blinakh
56 Wendy's Baltic Bread
58 Orient
68 Kafe Adzhika

OTHER
1 Teatr Satiry
2 Cathedral of SS Peter & Paul
3 Start of Battlements walk
4 Par.spb
5 Cruiser Aurora
7 Smolny Cathedral
8 British Consulate
9 Host Families Association
10 German Consulate
11 JFC Jazz Club
13 US Consulate
16 Musuem of Decorative & Applied Arts
17 Summer Palace
18 Russian Museum
19 Church of Spilled Blood
20 French Consulate
21 Winter Palace; Hermitage
22 Alexander Column
23 Admiralty
24 The Bronze Horseman
25 Central Post Office; Express Mail Service
28 St Isaac's Cathedral
29 American Express
31 Central Airline Ticket Office
33 Tinkoff
34 Kazan Cathedral
35 Apteka Petrofarm
36 Quo Vadis?
38 Central Train Ticket Office
39 Teatralnaya Kassa Theatre Ticket Office
40 Bolshoy Zal
41 Passazh Shopping Centre; Supermarket
42 Catherine the Great Statue
44 Apteka Pharmacy
46 Maly Drama Theatre
49 Dostoevsky Museum
51 Lensoviet Theatre
53 Kro Magnon
55 Ost-West Contaktservice
59 Che
60 Moloko
61 Alexandr Nevsky Monastery
62 Avtovokzal (Bus Station)
63 Griboedov
64 Canadian Consulate
65 69 Club
66 American Medical Center
67 Poliklinika No 2
69 Railway Museum
70 Yusupov Palace
71 Mariinsky Theatre
72 Eurolines

Tues-Sat, 10.30am-5pm Sun), which is one of the world's great art museums. The ticket hall is inside the main entrance on the river side of the Winter Palace.

In the middle of the square, the 47.5m **Alexander Column** commemorates the 1812 victory over Napoleon, while to the west across the road is the gilded spire of the **Admiralty**, former headquarters of the Russian navy. West of the Admiralty is **Ploshchad Dekabristov** (Decembrists' Square), named after the Decembrists' Uprising of 14 December 1825.

The famous statue of Peter the Great, the **Bronze Horseman**, stands at the end of the square towards the river. Behind looms the splendid golden dome of **St Isaac's Cathedral** *(☎ 315 97 32; Isaakievskaya pl; admission to cathedral R250, to colonnade R100; open 11am-6pm Thur-Tues)*, built between 1818 and 1858.

Nevsky Prospekt

The inner 2.5km of Nevsky prospekt from the Admiralty to Moscow Station is St Petersburg's main shopping thoroughfare. The most impressive sight along it is the great colonnaded arms of the truly awesome **Kazan Cathedral**, built between 1801 and 1811.

At the end of Nevsky prospekt is the working **Alexandr Nevsky Monastery** *(larva; ☎ 274 04 09, adult/student R50/30)*, where you'll find the **Tikhvin Cemetery** *(admission R50)*, last resting place of some of Russia's most famous artistic figures, including Tchaikovsky and Dostoevsky.

Between Nevsky & the Neva

A block north of Nevsky Prospekt metro is **Ploshchad Iskusstv** (Arts Square), on the far side of which is the former Mikhailovsky Palace, now the **Russian Museum** *(☎ 311 14 65; admission R240; open 10am-5pm Wed-Mon)*, housing one of the country's finest collections of Russian art. Behind it are the pleasant **Mikhailovsky Gardens**.

The polychromatic domes of the **Church of Spilled Blood** *(☎ 315 16 36; Konyushennaya pl; admission R240; open 11am-6pm Thur-Tues)* are close by. Also known as the Church of the Resurrection of Christ, it was built from 1887 to 1907 on the spot where Alexander II was assassinated in 1881.

The lovely **Summer Garden** *(Letny Sad; admission R10; open 9am-10pm daily May-Oct; 10am-6pm daily Oct–mid-Apr; closed mid-Apr to end Apr)* is between the open space of Mars Field (Marsovo Pole) and the Fontanka River. Laid out for Peter the Great with fountains and pavilions along a geometrical plan, it's a great place in which to relax.

East of the Fontaka River is the **Museum of Decorative and Applied Arts** *(☎ 273 32 58; Solyanoy per 13; admission R150; open 11am-5pm Tues-Sat)*. There's an exquisite collection of objects here, but the real draw is the restored halls, each in a different style.

The greatest thing about the unmistakable Rastrelli-designed **Smolny Cathedral** *(Smolenksy sobor; ☎ 278 55 96; pl Rastrelli; admission R100; open 11am-5pm Fri-Wed)*, 3km east of the Summer Garden, is the sweeping view from atop one of its 63m-high belfries.

South & West of Nevsky Prospekt

Just over 1km southwest of Nevsky along the Moyka River is the delightful **Yusupov Palace** *(☎ 314 98 83; nab reki Moyki 94; admission R150; open 11am-4pm daily)*. Notorious as the scene of Rasputin's grisly murder in 1916, the palace has a particularly attractive set of rooms.

Across the meandering kanala Griboedova and the Fontanka, east of the palace, is Sennaya pl, the heart of Dostoevskyville. The author lived in several flats around here, and many of the locations turn up in *Crime and Punishment*. To find out more head to the small but interesting **Dostoevsky Museum** *(☎ 164 69 50; Kuznechny per 5/2; admission R30; open 11am-5.30pm Tues-Sun)* in the house where the writer died in 1881.

West of Sennaya pl, train buffs and kids will be enchanted by the large collection of models at the **Railway Museum** *(Zheleznaya Doroga Muzey; ☎ 168 80 05; Sadovaya ul 50; admission R20; open 11am-5pm Sun-Thur)*. The museum was established in 1809, 28 years before Russia had its first working train!

Petrograd Side

Petrograd Side refers to the cluster of delta islands between the Malaya Neva and Bolshaya Nevka channels. The principal attraction here is the **Peter & Paul Fortress** *(Petropavlovskaya krepost; ☎ 238 45 50; admission to grounds free, admission to all buildings R120; open 10am-5pm Thur-Mon, 10am-4pm Tues)*. Founded in 1703, its main use up to 1917 was as a political prison: famous residents include Peter's own son Alexey, as well as Dostoevsky, Gorky and Trotsky. At noon every day a cannon is fired from the **Naryshkin Bastion**, scaring the daylights out of tourists. It's fun to walk along the **battlements** *(adult/student R50/30; open 10am-10pm daily)*. Most spectacular of all is the **Cathedral of Sts Peter & Paul**, with its landmark needle-thin spire and magnificent baroque interior.

East along Petrovskaya nab you'll come to the cruiser **Aurora** *(admission free; open 10.30am-4pm Tues-Thur, Sat & Sun)*, which fired the (blank) shot that signalled the start of the 1917 revolution.

Places to Stay

Homestays & Private Flats The **Host Families Association** *(HOFA; ☎/fax 275 19 92; ⓔ alexei@hofak.hop.stu.neva.ru; Tavricheskaya ul 5/25)* is a reliable agency for finding private accommodation. It has four programmes, starting with basic B&B (singles/doubles from US$25/40) for central flats.

Ost-West Kontaktservice (see Travel Agencies, earlier) can also arrange homestays and apartment rentals from about US$30 a day. Cheaper still are the private flats offered by old women to travellers arriving off major trains at Moscow station. Check how far from the city centre their place is before accompanying them (ask to see it on a map).

Hostels & Hotels The long-running **HI St Petersburg Hostel** *(☎ 329 80 18, fax 329 90 19; ⓔ ryh@ryh.ru; 3-ya Sovetskaya ul 28; dorm beds/doubles US$19/48)*, a five-minute walk from Moscow station, is popular and prices include breakfast. Spotless dorms have three to six beds and there's one double; all are slightly cheaper in the winter and for holders of ISIC and HI cards.

Some people prefer **International Holiday Hostel** *(☎/fax 327 10 70, 327 10 33; ⓔ info@hostel.spb.ru; Arsenalnaya nab 9; dorm beds/singles/doubles US$14/37/38)*, a convivial place just south of Finland station on the Vyborg Side. It's quiet and a little out of the way, but does have the advantage of a terrace overlooking the Neva. Rates include breakfast.

St Petersburg Puppet Hostel *(☎ 272 54 01, fax 272 83 61; ⓦ www.hostelling-russia.ru; ul Nekrasova 12; dorm beds/doubles US$16/42)* is a great option – central, friendly, cosy and clean. Rates include breakfast.

Petrovskogo College Student Hostel *(☎ 252 75 63, fax 252 65 12; ul Baltiyskaya 26; doubles/triples US$4/6)* is the cheapest deal, but it's not at all central. Reserve in advance, though, as it's often full. From metro Narvskaya walk left (south), down pr Stachek away from the Narva Arch to ul Baltiyskaya, where you turn left and continue another 500m.

Hotel Rus *(☎ 273 46 83, fax 279 36 00; ul Artilleryskaya 1; singles/doubles including breakfast US$44/63)* is central. **Hotel Neva** *(☎ 278 05 04, fax 273 25 93; ul Chaykovskogo 17; singles/doubles US$36/52)*, might have once been a fancy bordello, but the cheapest rooms are basic and drab. Still, it's only a short bus or trolleybus ride from Nevsky.

Places to Eat

For fresh produce head to the city's liveliest food market, **Kuznechny** *(Kuznechny per 3)*, next to Vladimirskaya metro. There's a well-stocked supermarket in the basement of the **Passazh** shopping centre *(Nevsky pr 48; open 10am-10pm daily)*. For breakfast supplies and bakery items, try **Wendy's Baltic Bread** *(Grechesky pr 25)*.

Fast Food The following three self-service operations are open 24 hours, and a meal at one of them won't cost much over R100. **Laima** *(☎ 232 44 28; kanala Griboedova 14 • ☎ 315 55 45; Bol pr 88, Petrograd Side)* has a vast menu that includes oodles of salads, soups, main dishes and drinks. Similar are **Orient** *(☎ 277 57 15; Suvorovsky pr 1/8 • ☎ 314 64 43; Bolshoya Morskaya ul 25; dishes under US$3; open 24hr)* and **U Tyoshi Na Blinakh** *(Zagorodny pr 18 • Ligovsky pr 25)*, which specialises in *bliny*.

Restaurants Practically every traveller drops by **Café Idiot** *(☎ 315 16 75; nab reki Moyki 82)* with good reason: the vegetarian food and atmosphere are great, although the prices are on the high side. Nearby is the cheaper **Popugay** *(☎ 311 5971; 1 Fornary per)*, a new hangout with a laid-back reggae vibe that's popular with overseas students.

For quality, keenly priced Russian cuisine you won't go wrong at blissful **Bliny Domik** *(☎ 315 99 15; Kolokolnaya ul)*. **Circus** *(☎ 310 1077; 4 Malaya Sadovaya ul)* is an imaginatively decorated basement space where you're likely to be treated to a complimentary shot of vodka.

Kafe Kat *(☎ 311 33 77; Stremyannaya ul 22)* is a cosy Georgian restaurant with a good reputation. Also well worth checking out is the friendly and colourfully decorated **Kafe Adzhika** *(☎ 310 26 27, Moskovsky pr 7)*, which is open 24 hours.

The Stroganoff Yard *(☎ 315 2315; Nevsky pr 17)*, found in the courtyard of the Stroganoff Palace, has telephones on each table so you can call up strangers while grazing on the good-value US$5 lunch buffet (US$8 at night).

Vegetarians will be delighted by both the centrally located **Gushe** *(☎ 113 24 05; Vladimirsky pr 5)* and **Troitsky Most** *(☎ 326 82 21; Mal Posadskaya ul 2 • ☎ 232 66 93; Konversky pr 9/2)* over on the Petrograd Side.

Entertainment

Check the *St Petersburg Times* and *Pulse* for listings of what's on.

Performing Arts September to early summer is the main performing season. Most concert halls and theatres are closed Monday.

The Kirov Ballet and Opera are at the **Mariinsky Theatre** *(☎ 114 52 64; W www.kirovballet.com; Teatralnaya pl 1)*. Tickets can be bought at the theatre or any Teatralnaya Kassa, but be aware that the eagle-eyed babushkas at the door will demand you pay the foreigner price, which is 10 times the Russian price.

The renowned **Maly Drama Theatre** *(☎ 113 20 49; ul Rubinshteyna 18)* often stages experimental and unforgettable pieces. Also worth checking out is whatever's playing at the **Lensoviet Theatre** *(☎ 113 21 91; Vladimirsky pr 12)* and the clever, off-beat plays at **Teatr Satiry** *(☎ 314 70 60; Sredny pr 48, Vasilevsky Island)*.

For classical music, the St Petersburg Philharmonia play at **Bolshoy Zal** *(☎ 110 42 57; ul Mikhailovskaya 2)*.

Bars & Clubs The microbrewery **Tinkoff** *(☎ 314 8485; ul Kazanskaya 7)* serves very drinkable ales in a hip beer hall. **Che** *(☎ 277 76 00; Poltavskaya ul 3)* is a Euro-trendy space and serves good coffee and wine.

For the following clubs expect cover charges of at least R150 at the weekends. **JFC Jazz Club** *(☎ 272 98 50, ul Shpalernaya 33)* is a cosy, New York–style space offering some of the city's best jazz and blues.

Moloko *(☎ 274 94 67; Perekupnoy per 12; open 7pm-midnight Thur-Sun)* is in a dimly lit cellar and is the best bet for live rock bands.

Griboedov *(☎ 164 43 55; Voronezhskaya ul 2A)* is in an artfully converted bomb shelter and has a policy of no pop music. Weekends get stiflingly crowded here – the best nights are Wednesday and Thursday.

Par.spb *(☎ 233 3374; Alexandrovsky Park 5B)* is a hip club of the moment; the music changes each night. It has a strict door policy.

Mono *(☎ 164 36 78; Kolomenskaya ul 4; cover charge men R20-50, women R100; open 10pm-6am daily)* is a gay-friendly place. The dance floor is tiny, but drinks are reasonably priced. Thursday is for women, when the cover prices are reversed.

Getting There & Away

Air St Petersburg has direct air links with most major European capitals. Tickets can be purchased at the **Central Airline Ticket Office** *(☎ 311 80 93; Nevsky pr 7)* and at travel agencies such as Sindbad Travel.

Bus The bus station **Avtovokzal** *(☎ 166 57 77; nab Obvodnogo Kanala 36)* is 1km from Ligovsky Prospekt metro in the city's south. It serves Tampere, Vyborg, Pskov, Novgorod, Moscow and other smaller destinations.

For buses to central and Eastern Europe, **Eurolines** *(☎ 168 27 40; ul Shkapina 10)* runs several daily buses to Tallinn, Tartu and Rīga, and has weekly services to Germany. For service to/from Finland, **Finnord** *(☎ 314 89 51)* and **Sovavto** *(☎ 123 51 25)* have daily buses. A one-way ticket to Helsinki costs about US$40.

Train St Petersburg has three major long-distance train stations. **Finland station** *(Finlyandsky vokzal; ☎ 168 76 87; pl Lenina, Vyborg Side* has two daily trains to Helsinki; **Moscow station** *(Moskovsky vokzal; ☎ 168 43 74; pl Vosstaniya, Nevsky pr)*, handles trains to/from Moscow (at least 11 daily), the far north, the Urals, Siberia, Crimea and the Caucasus; and **Vitebsk station** *(Vitebsky vokzal; ☎ 055; Zagorodny pr 52)* deals with the Baltic states, Eastern Europe, Ukraine and Belarus. **Baltic station** *(Baltiysky vokzal; ☎ 168 28 59)* is for suburban trains.

Tickets can be purchased at the train stations, the **Central Train Ticket Office** *(☎ 162 33 44, nab kanala Griboedova 24)*, the **Central Airline Ticket Office** (see under Air, earlier) and Sindbad Travel.

Getting Around

Tokens for the metro cost R6, and a variety of magnetic-strip cards are also available from the booths in the stations, which open around 5.30am and close just after midnight every day. Tickets for buses, trolleybuses and tramways (R5 to R10, depending on the service) are bought inside from controllers. To order a taxi, call **New Service** *(☎ 327 42 00)* or **Taxi na Zakaz** *(☎ 100 00 00)*.

The Netherlands

A small country with a big reputation for liberalism, the Netherlands swims in a sea of familiar images. Central to most travellers' experience is the once radical, still exuberant capital of Amsterdam, famous for its 'anything goes' vibe. Outside the big city the nation is still a land of bikes, dikes, blazing flower fields and windmills. Town-hoppers will appreciate the deeply historic cities of Leiden, Haarlem and Delft, cosmopolitan Rotterdam and the lively student towns of Groningen and Maastrict. Escapists can head directly for the vast beaches of the northern islands. And the countryside's endlessly flat landscape is a cyclist's nirvana.

No matter where you journey, you'll discover that the Dutch people are not only proud of their hard-won country, but eager to share its delights with visitors. Lucky you!

The Netherlands: the Basics

Local Name Nederland

Capitals Amsterdam & the Hague

Population 16.1 million

Languages Dutch, Frisian

Currency euro (€) = 100 centimes

Avoid at all costs Dog crap on the sidewalks

Get the 'stuff' by asking *Hoeveel is de best stof?* (How much is your best smoke?)

Facts about the Netherlands

HISTORY

Until the 16th century, the Netherlands, Belgium and Luxembourg were grouped together as the Low Countries. Originally the land was inhabited by tribal groups: The Germanic Batavi drained the sea lagoons while the Frisii lived on mounds in the remote north.

In the late-16th century, the northern provinces united to fight the Spanish. Led by Prince William of Orange, the Revolt of the Netherlands lasted 80 years, ending in 1648 with a treaty that recognised the 'United Provinces' as an independent republic. The Schelde River was closed to all non-Dutch ships, a blow to the port city of Antwerp, but a boon to its rival, Amsterdam.

During the Netherlands' Golden Age (about 1580 to 1740), the Dutch East India Company sent merchant ships to the Far East, to colonise the Cape of Good Hope and Indonesia and establish trading posts throughout Asia. Later, the West Indies Company sailed to West Africa and the Americas, creating colonies in Surinam, the Antilles and New Amsterdam (today's New York). Meanwhile, Amsterdam's bourgeoisie indulged in fine, gabled canal houses and paintings of themselves. The latter stimulated the arts and brought renown to painters such as Rembrandt.

In 1795 the French invaded and Napoleon appointed his brother Louis as king. When French occupation came to an end, the United Kingdom of the Netherlands – incorporating Belgium and Luxembourg – was born. The first king, William I of Orange, was crowned in 1814, and the House of Orange rules to this day. In 1830 the Belgians won independence; Luxembourg did the same soon after.

While the Netherlands stayed neutral in WWI, it was unable to do so in WWII. The Germans invaded on 10 May 1940, obliterating much of Rotterdam in a bombing blitz. Although a sound Dutch resistance movement formed, only a small minority of the country's Jews survived the war.

In 1949 Indonesia won independence. Surinam followed much later, gaining sovereignty peacefully in 1975. The Antilles still have close ties with the Netherlands but are self-ruled.

In 1953 a severe storm breached the dikes in Zeeland, drowning 1835 people. To prevent future tragedy, a network of dams and dikes was constructed under the Delta Plan (see the Delta Region section later in this chapter).

The social consciousness of the 1960s found fertile ground in the Netherlands, and Amsterdam became the radical heart of Europe. The riotous squatter's movement stopped the demolition of much of the cheap inner-city

> **Not the Same**
>
> Just as England and Britain aren't the same thing, 'the Netherlands' and 'Holland' aren't interchangeable. 'Holland' refers to all but one province (albeit the lion's share) of the country, while 'the Netherlands' refers to the nation as a whole.

housing, the lack of which is a problem that has continued into the 21st century.

The Netherlands is very much a part of the European Union: it was in Maastricht that members of the European Community signed the treaty that created the EU in 1992.

GEOGRAPHY

The Netherlands occupies 33,920 sq km, much of which has been reclaimed from the sea over many centuries. More than half of the flat country lies below sea level. The southwest province of Zeeland is the combined delta area of the Schelde, Maas, Lek and Waal Rivers; the Lek and Waal are branches of the Rhine. The mighty Rhine itself peters out in a pathetic little stream at the coast near Katwijk.

CLIMATE

The Netherlands has a temperate maritime climate with cool winters and mild summers. The wettest months are July and August. The sunniest months are May to August, and the warmest are June to September.

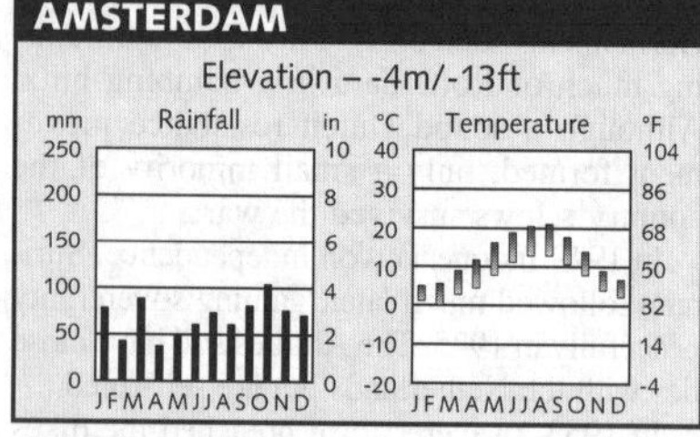

GOVERNMENT & POLITICS

Against the European trend, the Netherlands developed from a republic to a constitutional monarchy, headed today by Queen Beatrix. The three main parties have traditionally been the socialist PvdA, the conservative Liberal VVD and the Catholic Protestant CDA. However, the country was shocked when right-wing politician Pim Fortuyn was assassinated right before the May 2002 election. His party, Lijst Pim Fortuyn (LPF), went on to win the second-largest number of seats in the election, behind the CDA. The CDA's leader, Jan Peter Balkenende, is the new prime minister.

POPULATION & PEOPLE

Western Europe's most densely populated country has 16.11 million people and a lot of Frisian cows. This concentration is intensified in the Randstad, the western hoop of cities that includes Amsterdam, The Hague and Rotterdam.

SOCIETY & CONDUCT

The Dutch are well known for their tolerance, stemming from a Dutch tradition of 'agreeing to disagree'. It's customary to greet shopkeepers and bar/café owners when entering their premises. In red-light districts, 'no photo' stickers should be taken seriously.

LANGUAGE

Almost all Dutch people you meet will speak at least some English. Knowing some Dutch may be useful in the countryside, however; see the Language chapter at the back of the book for pronunciation guidelines and useful words and phrases.

Facts for the Visitor

HIGHLIGHTS

Amsterdam, Amsterdam, Amsterdam! (In between bouts of partying, check out the Rijksmuseum and Van Gogh Museum.) When you're done with that, visit the Randstad's Keukenhof gardens and take in Rotterdam's architecture. Groningen is a fun university town, and Maastricht's medieval streets and great nightlife make a winning combination. The island of Texel provides a relaxing break from the cities.

PLANNING

When to Go

Spring is the ideal time to visit, as there's less rain and the bulbs are in bloom – daffodils from about early to late April, tulips from about late April to mid-May.

Maps

Lonely Planet's *Amsterdam City Map* is a handy reference. Excellent road maps include those produced by Michelin with a scale of

1:400,000, and the Royal Dutch Touring Association (ANWB) with a scale of 1:300,000. The ANWB also puts out provincial maps detailing cycling paths and picturesque road routes (1:100,000).

TOURIST OFFICES

Local Tourist Offices

The ubiquitous VVV – the national tourist organisation – sells brochures on everything and maps for everywhere. Staff will book accommodation, sometimes for nothing and up to €12 a booking. Most VVV offices have telephone numbers prefixed by ☎ 0900 (for about €0.55 a minute) – wait for the automated Dutch message to end to be answered personally.

The **Netherlands Board of Tourism** *(NBT; e info@nbt.nl; Vlietweg 15, Postbus 458, 2260 MG Leidschendam)* takes postal and email inquiries only.

Tourist Offices Abroad

NBT's overseas offices include the following:

Belgium (☎ 02-543 0800, e info@nbt.be) Louizalaan 89, 1050 Brussels
Canada (☎ 416-363 1577) suite 710, 25 Adelaide St East, Toronto, Ont M5C 1Y2
France (☎ 01 43 12 34 27, e balie@hollande-tourisme.fr) 9 rue Scribe, 75008 Paris
Germany (☎ 0221-9257 1727) Friesenplatz 1, Postfach 270580, 50672 Cologne 1
Japan (☎ 03-3222 1112) NK Shinwa Building 5F, 5-1 Kojimachi, Chiyoda-ku, Tokyo 102-0083
UK (☎ 020-7539 7950, e information@nbt.org.uk) PO Box 30783, London, WC2B 6DH
USA (☎ 212-370 7360, e info@goholland.com) 355 Lexington Ave, New York, NY 10017

VISAS & DOCUMENTS

Travellers from Australia, Canada, the EU, Israel, Japan, New Zealand, the USA and many other countries don't require a visa for a stay of up to three months. Nationals of most other countries need a Schengen Visa valid for 90 days. After three months, you can apply for an extension through the Vreemdelingenpolitie, but you'll need a good reason.

EMBASSIES & CONSULATES

Dutch Embassies & Consulates

The following Dutch diplomatic associations are represented abroad:

Australia (☎ 02-6273 3111) 120 Empire Circuit, Yarralumla, Canberra, ACT 2600
Canada (☎ 613-237 5030) Suite 2020, 350 Albert St, Ottawa, Ont K1R 1A4
New Zealand (☎ 04-471 6390) 10th fl, Investment House, corner Ballance and Featherston Sts, Wellington
UK (☎ 020-7590 3200) 38 Hyde Park Gate, London SW7 5DP
USA (☎ 202-244 5300) 4200 Linnean Ave, NW Washington, DC 20008

Embassies & Consulates in the Netherlands

Embassies (in The Hague) and consulates (in Amsterdam) of other countries in the Netherlands include:

Australia (☎ 070-310 82 00) Carnegielaan 4, 2517 KH The Hague
Belgium (☎ 070-312 34 56) Alexanderveld 97, 2584 DB The Hague
Canada (☎ 070-311 16 00) Sophialaan 7, 2514 JP The Hague
France (☎ 070-312 58 00) Smidsplein 1, 2514 BT The Hague
Consulate: (☎ 020-530 69 71) Vijzelgracht 2, 1017 HR Amsterdam
Germany (☎ 070-342 06 00) Groot Hertoginnelaan 18, 2517 EG The Hague
Consulate: (☎ 020-673 62 45) De Lairessestraat 172, 1075 HM Amsterdam
Ireland (☎ 070-363 09 93) Dr Kuyperstraat 9, 2514 BA The Hague
New Zealand (☎ 070-346 93 24) Carnegielaan 10, 2517 KH The Hague
UK (☎ 070-427 04 27) Lange Voorhout 10, 2514 ED The Hague
Consulate: (☎ 020-676 43 43) Koningslaan 44, 1075 AE Amsterdam
USA (☎ 070-310 92 09) Lange Voorhout 102, 2514 EJ The Hague
Consulate: (☎ 020-575 53 09) Museumplein 19, 1071 DJ Amsterdam

CUSTOMS

In the Netherlands, the usual allowances apply to duty-free goods if you are coming from a non-EU country, and to duty-paid goods if you're arriving from within the EU.

MONEY

The Netherlands' currency is the euro.

Exchanging Money

Banks and post offices offer fair exchange rates and commissions – as does the national exchange organisation, De Grenswisselkantoren (GWK), which has branches at major border posts and train stations. In larger cities there are many private exchange bureaus that close late but generally ask high commissions or offer lousy rates. Although

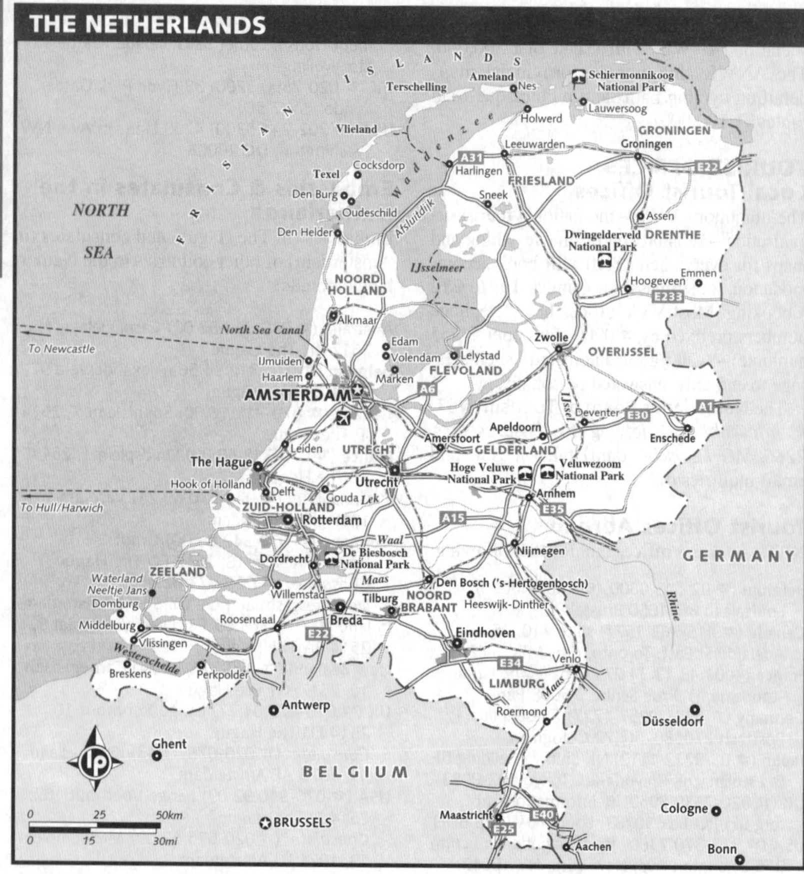

all major credit cards are recognised, the Netherlands is still very much a cash-based society. The best way to change money is through the ubiquitous ATMs.

Costs

Staying in hostels, eating in cheap cafés and going to the occasional museum, you'll be spending at least €35 a day, though to increase your comfort level you could easily spend up to €50. Avid museumgoers should buy the Museumjaarkaart (Museum Year Card; adult/under-25 €35/15), which gives free entry into more than 400 museums and art galleries. It's issued at participating museums (you'll need a passport photo). Most museums mentioned in this chapter are free with the Museumjaarkaart.

Tipping & Bargaining

Tipping is not compulsory, but rounding up the bill is always appreciated in taxis, restaurants and pubs with table or pavement service. Forget about bargaining.

Taxes & Refunds

The value-added tax (BTW in Dutch) is 19% for most goods except consumer items, for which you pay 6%. Travellers from non-EU countries can have it refunded on goods over €175. To claim back the tax, ask the shop owner to provide an export certificate. Get the form endorsed by the Dutch customs, then send the certificate to the supplier, who refunds the tax by cheque or money order. Some shops can give you a stamped Tax Refund Cheque which can be cashed at your port of exit. You'll need to show the customs officers the goods, the bill and your passport.

POST & COMMUNICATIONS

In general, post offices are open 9am to 5pm or 6pm Monday to Friday, and until 1.30pm Saturday.

The Netherlands' country code is ☎ 31. To telephone abroad, the international access code is ☎ 00. Local telephone calls are time-based. Numbers prefixed with ☎ 0900 are more expensive, while those starting with ☎ 0800 are free.

Telephones take €5 and €10 phonecards and, sometimes, credit cards. Coin-operated telephones are rare. International calls can be made from public phones and post offices, using phonecards designed specifically for international calls.

International faxes can be sent from post offices.

There are plenty of Internet cafés in Amsterdam and at least one in most major towns. The local *bibliotheek* (library) is a reliable option for Internet access at reasonable rates.

INTERNET RESOURCES

The Dutch are digital-media leaders. The best place to start a virtual visit is the site of the **Netherlands Board of Tourism** *(W www.visitholland.com)* and the **Amsterdam city site** *(W www.amsterdam.nl)*.

BOOKS

Lonely Planet's *The Netherlands* guide is a must for those intending on in-depth exploration. For those concentrating on the capital, grab Lonely Planet's *Amsterdam* city guide. *Amsterdam Condensed* has all the essentials for a weekend break and fits easily in your pocket. For a humorous look at Dutch ways, pick up *The UnDutchables*, by Colin White & Laurie Boucke or, more seriously, *Culture Shock! Netherlands*, by Hunt Janin.

WOMEN TRAVELLERS

Women travellers will find *vrouwen* (women's) cafés, bookshops and help centres in many cities in the Netherlands. **Het Vrouwenhuis** *(Women's House; ☎ 020-625 20 66; e info@vrouwenhuis.nl; Nieuwe Herengracht 95, 1011 RX Amsterdam)* is well known. Unwanted male attention is not a big problem in the Netherlands. However, in the event of rape or attack, **De Eerste Lijn** *(☎ 020-613 02 45; open 10.30am-11pm Mon-Fri, 4pm-11pm Sat & Sun)* is an Amsterdam-based help line.

GAY & LESBIAN TRAVELLERS

The Netherlands is the most liberal country in Europe where attitudes to homosexuality are concerned. The age of consent is 16, discrimination on the basis of sexual orientation is illegal, and gay and lesbian couples can legally marry. Most provincial capitals have at least one gay and lesbian bar or café, as well as a branch of COC, a gay and lesbian information service. In Amsterdam, contact **COC** *(☎ 020-626 30 87; Rozenstraat 14)*.

The best place for information on gay or lesbian venues is the **Gay & Lesbian Switchboard** *(☎ 020-623 65 65; help line staffed 2pm-10pm daily)*. *Gay & Night* and *Gay News*, available free at COC and bars, list gay hotels, bars etc throughout the Netherlands. The Amsterdam Pride parade is on the first weekend of August.

DISABLED TRAVELLERS

The Netherlands is well equipped to meet specialised needs. Many buildings have lifts and/or ramps. Several trains and some taxis have wheelchair access, and most train stations have lifts and a toilet for the disabled. You can call (☎ 030 230 55 66) in advance of your journey to arrange assistance. For the blind, train timetables are published in Braille.

For more information contact the **Nederlands Instituut voor Zorg & Welzijn** *(☎ 030-230 66 03, fax 231 96 41; W www.nizw.nl; Postbus 19152, 3501 DD Utrecht)*.

SENIOR TRAVELLERS

Senior travellers should encounter few problems when travelling around the Netherlands. Many buildings have lifts or ramps, and public transport is quite accessible. Most museums offer discounts to over 65s.

DANGERS & ANNOYANCES

Pickpockets proliferate in Amsterdam. Keep your hands on your valuables, especially at Centraal Station, the post office and other

Emergencies

Phone the following nationwide number for emergency police, ambulance & fire brigade services: ☎ 112.

tourist strongholds. The stolen-bicycle racket is also rife. Locals use two chains to lock up their bikes, and even that's no guarantee.

LEGAL MATTERS

No, drugs are *not* legal. Possession of more than 5g of marijuana or hash can get you a large fine and/or land you in jail. Hard drugs mean prison time. Small amounts of 'soft' drugs for personal use are unofficially tolerated, but could complicate matters if you're already in trouble with the police. Don't buy drugs from street dealers – you'll end up getting ripped off or mugged.

Police in the Netherlands are generally polite and helpful. If you've broken the law, they can hold you for six hours for questioning. Should you need legal assistance, the **Buro voor Rechtshulp** *(☎ 020-520 51 00; Spuistraat 10, Amsterdam)* can give free legal advice during business hours.

BUSINESS HOURS

The working week starts around lunchtime Monday. The rest of the week most shops open at 8.30am or 9am and close at 5.30pm or 6pm, except Thursday when many close at 9pm, and on Saturday at 5pm. In Amsterdam and tourist centres many shops open Sunday, too. Supermarkets often have extended trading hours. Banks are generally open 9am to 4pm or 5pm Monday to Friday. Many museums are closed on Monday.

PUBLIC HOLIDAYS & SPECIAL EVENTS

Public holidays are New Year's Day, Good Friday, Easter Sunday and Monday, Queen's Day (30 April), Ascension Day, Whit Sunday and Monday, Christmas Day (25 December) and Boxing Day (26 December).

The Holland Festival brings many top names in music, opera, dance and theatre to Amsterdam for performances throughout June. Another big event in Amsterdam is Koninginnedag (Queen's Day), the 30 April national holiday held on former Queen Juliana's birthday. The whole central city becomes a huge street-market/party where people sell whatever they've dug out of their attics.

ACTIVITIES

Cycling, windsurfing, sailing, boating and hanging out at the beach are some of the most popular Dutch pastimes, especially in the waterlogged provinces of Fryslân and Zeeland.

ACCOMMODATION

Rarely cheap and often full, accommodation is best booked ahead, especially in Amsterdam or the Randstad during Keukenhof season. You can book hotels (no deposit required) through the **Netherlands Reservation Centre** *(W www.hotelres.nl)*, or via the **Amsterdam Reservation Center** *(☎/fax 777 000 888; e reservations@amsterdamtourist.nl)*. Once you're in the country, VVV tourist offices and GWK money-exchange offices usually handle bookings for a fee.

Camping grounds are copious but prices vary – on average €4.50/4/2.50 per adult/tent/car. The NBT has a selective list of sites, or there's the ANWB's annual camping guide (€11), both of which are available from some VVVs or bookshops.

The country's official hostel organisation is the **Nederlandse Jeugdherberg Centrale** *(NJHC; ☎ 020-551 31 55, fax 639 01 99; W www.njhc.org; Prof Tulpstraat 2, 1018 HA Amsterdam)*. Dorm rooms cost between €16.50 and €28, with a €2.50 discount for members. Some hostels have private rooms – expect to pay €40 to €75 for a double. In Amsterdam you'll find similarly priced unofficial hostels.

B&Bs start at €17 per person. Local VVVs have lists, or you can book through **Bed & Breakfast Holland** *(☎ 020-615 75 27, fax 669 15 73; W www.bbholland.com)*. If you go this route, you must book for at least two nights and there's a €5 booking fee; you also pay €5 for each place you stay at.

Hotels start at €25/50 for basic single/double rooms, with continental breakfast included. Prices occasionally rise in high season (roughly 15 March to 15 November).

FOOD

While gastronomical delights are not a Dutch forte, you won't go hungry. What traditional cuisine lacks in taste sensation, it makes up for in quantity. Thanks also to sizable Indonesian, Surinamese and Turkish communities, there are plenty of spicy or interesting options. Vegetarians will find that many *eetcafés* (eating pubs) have at least one meat-free dish.

The national fast food is *frites* – chips or French fries – usually sold from a *frituur* (fries vendor). *Kroketten*, or croquettes (crumbed fried concoctions), are sold hot from vending machines; *broodjes* (open sandwiches) are everywhere; and mussels, raw herrings and deep-fried fish are popular coastal snacks. As for sweets, *appelgebak* (apple pie) ranks up there with *frites*, while *poffertjes* (miniature pancakes sprinkled with icing sugar) are surefire tourist food, as are *pannekoeken* (pancakes) and *stroopwafels* (hot wafers glued together with syrup).

Dinner traditionally comprises thick soups and meat, fish or chicken dishes fortified with potatoes. Most restaurants have a *dagschotel* (dish of the day) for €8 to €15, while *eetcafés* serve meals or cheap snacks. Otherwise, the Indonesian *rijsttafel* (rice table) of boiled rice with oodles of side dishes costs about €24 per person and is worth a try, as are Zeeland mussels, best during months with an 'r' in their name (or so local tradition has it).

Beer is the staple alcoholic drink, served cool and topped by a two-finger-thick head of froth. Popular brands include Heineken and Amstel. Many Belgian beers – such as Duvel and Westmalle Triple – have become popular.

Dutch *genever* (gin) is made with juniper berries; a common combination, known as a *kopstoot* (head butt), is a glass of genever with a beer chaser. There are plenty of indigenous liqueurs, including *advocaat* (a kind of eggnog) and the herb-based Beerenburg.

ENTERTAINMENT

You'll rarely have to search for nightlife. Bars and cafés abound, from popular pavement terraces to old 'brown' cafés thick with conversation and smoke. In summer, parks come alive with festivals while city squares reverberate with the sounds of street musicians.

Getting There & Away

AIR

The Netherlands has just one main international airport: Schiphol, 18km southwest of central Amsterdam. It's one of Western Europe's major international hubs, and services flights from airlines worldwide. Most foreign airlines have offices in Amsterdam (see the Amsterdam Getting There & Away section). The airport is linked directly to the Dutch rail network.

LAND

Bus

Eurolines is the main international bus company servicing the Netherlands. It has regular buses from Amsterdam to a crop of European destinations, as well as to North Africa. Depending on the service, there are stops in Breda, Rotterdam, The Hague and Utrecht. Eurolines buses cross the Channel either on ferries departing from Calais in France or via the Eurotunnel. Members of Hostelling International (HI) get a 10% discount on Eurolines tickets.

Train

Nederlandse Spoorwegen *(Netherlands Railways; international train information & reservations ☎ 0900-92 96)* operates efficient train services to neighbouring countries. You can call their hotline for €0.25 per minute.

The main line south from Amsterdam passes through The Hague and Rotterdam to Antwerp (€26.10, two hours, hourly) and Brussels (€29.50, 2¾ hours, hourly) in Belgium. The line southeast runs to Cologne (€45.30, 2¾ hours, every two hours) and farther into Germany. The line east goes to Berlin, with a branch north to Hamburg. All these fares are one way in 2nd class; people under 26 get a 25% discount (bring your passport). The *Weekendretour* (weekend return) ticket gives a 40% discount on return fares to Belgium or Germany when travelling between Friday and Monday.

The high-speed **Thalys** *(W www.thalys.com)* train runs five times per day between Amsterdam and Paris-Nord (€78 Monday to Friday, €67 Saturday and Sunday, 4¼ hours). Those under 26 get a 45% discount, and seniors with a Rail Plus card are entitled to a discount on return fares, although you need to book well in advance.

The only train-ferry route to the UK is via Hook of Holland (Hoek van Holland) near Rotterdam to Harwich in England and on to London. The Channel is crossed using Stena Line's high-speed vessel *Stena HSS*. The fare is €82/41 for adults/children, and the total journey takes six hours. Alternatively, you can get a train to Brussels and connect there with *Eurostar* trains going through the Channel Tunnel. From Amsterdam, the one-way trip to London's Waterloo station takes about six hours and starts at €114. Those under 26 pay €54. There are nine services per day.

Car & Motorcycle

The main entry points to the Netherlands from Belgium are the E22 (Antwerp–Breda) and E25 (Liège–Maastricht). From Germany the main links are the E40 (Cologne–Maastricht), E35 (Düsseldorf–Arnhem) and A1 (Hannover–Amsterdam). For details about car ferries from England, see the following Sea section.

SEA

Three companies operate car/passenger ferries between the Netherlands and England. For information on train-ferry combos, see the earlier Train section. Most travel agencies have information on the following services.

Stena Line's *(☎ UK 08705-707 070; Ⓦ www.stenaline.com)* high-speed *Stena HSS* sails from Hook of Holland to Harwich in 3¾ hours. Return fares for a car with up to five passengers range from UK£120 to UK£200. Foot passenger tickets start at UK£50.

P&O/North Sea Ferries *(UK ☎ 08701-296 002; Ⓦ www.ponsf.com)* operates an overnight boat (14 hours) between Europoort (near Rotterdam) and Hull. Basic one-way adult/student/child/car tickets start from UK£71/58/46/64. Return fares start from UK£104 per adult, plus UK£135 for a car. The prices include a cabin (no seat option available).

DFDS Seaways *(☎ UK 08705-333 000; Ⓦ www.dfdsseaways.co.uk)* sails daily from Ijmuiden (near Amsterdam) to Newcastle. The journey takes 15 hours. Return fares start at UK£114 per adult plus UK£110 for a car and include reclining seats (cabins extra).

Getting Around

The Netherlands' public transport system is excellent; call ☎ 0900-92 92 (€0.50 per minute) for national train, bus and tram information.

BUS

Buses are used for regional transport rather than long distances, which are better travelled by train. They provide a vital service, especially in parts of the north and east, where trains are less frequent or nonexistent. The national *strippenkaart* (see Local Transport, later) is used on many regional buses.

TRAIN

NS trains are fast and efficient, with at least one intercity train every 15 minutes between major cities, and half-hourly trains on branch lines. Most train stations have small/large luggage lockers that cost €2/4 respectively for 24 hours. If you're returning the same day, it's cheaper to buy a *dagretour* (day return) rather than two single tickets.

There's a melange of discount fares but you'd have to live on the trains to make most of them worthwhile. A One-Day Ticket gives unlimited 2nd-class travel and costs €35.60. With this ticket you can also buy a Public Transport Day Card for €4 that gives unlimited use of city buses, trams and metros. If there's a couple of you travelling around the country, the Summer Tour can be good value. It entitles adults to three days' travel within 10 days for €45/59 for one/two persons.

CAR & MOTORCYCLE

Foreign drivers need to have a Green Card as proof of insurance. Watch out for cyclists. The maximum permissable blood-alcohol concentration is 0.05%. For other information about motoring, contact the **Royal Dutch Touring Association** *(ANWB; ☎ 020-673 08 44; Museumplein 5, 1071 DJ Amsterdam)*.

Hitching is no longer common and is not permitted on motorways.

BICYCLE

With 10,000km of cycling paths, a *fiets* (bicycle) is the way to go. The ANWB publishes cycling maps for each province. Major roads have separate bike lanes, and, except for motorways, there's virtually nowhere bicycles can't go. Taking a bicycle on a train (not allowed in peak hours) costs €6 for a *dagkaart* (day card). Bikes are abundantly available for hire. In most cases you'll need to show your passport and leave an imprint of your credit card or a deposit (from €25 to €100). Private operators charge about €7.50/30 per day/week. Hire shops at train stations charge about €5.50/25. You must return the bike to the same station.

It may work out cheaper to buy a 'second-hand' bike from a street market for upwards of €15, although bear in mind that it's probably part of the stolen-bike racket.

BOAT

Ferries connect the mainland with the five Frisian Islands (see The North section for details) and are also used as road connections in Zeeland.

LOCAL TRANSPORT

Bus & Tram

Buses or trams operate in most cities, and Amsterdam and Rotterdam also have metro systems. Fares operate nationally. Buy a *strippenkaart* (strip card), valid throughout the country, and stamp off a number of strips depending on how many zones you cross. The ticket is then valid on all buses, trams, metro systems and city trains for an hour, or longer depending on the number of strips you've stamped. Around central Amsterdam, for example, you'll use two strips – one for the journey plus one for the zone. A zone further will cost three strips, and so on. When riding on trams there may be a conductor, otherwise it is up to you to stamp your card; on buses the driver stamps the strips as you get on. Bus and tram drivers sell two-strip cards for €1.40. More economical are 15/45-strip cards for €5.90/17.40, which you must purchase in advance at train or bus stations, post offices or some VVV offices. Otherwise you can invest in a *dagkaart* (day card), available in some large cities.

Taxi

Usually booked by phone (officially you're not supposed to wave them down on the street), taxis also hover outside train stations and hotels and cost roughly €10 for 5km. Some places have *treintaxis* (train taxis), which charge a flat rate of €3.50 a person to anywhere within a certain radius of the train station.

Amsterdam

☎ 020 • pop 731,000

Personal freedom, liberal drug laws, the gay centre of Europe – these are images that have been synonymous with the Dutch capital since the heady '60s and '70s, when it was unquestionably Europe's most radical city. These days, Amsterdam's cutting-edge nature has been slightly blunted, but it remains a progressive town. Tolerance is still a guiding principle that even serious social problems such as a chronic housing shortage have failed to dent. Just as enduring has been the rich and lively mix of the historical and contemporary that you'll experience when exploring the many museums, relaxing in the canal-side cafés or enjoying summer-time open-air entertainment.

ORIENTATION

By capital-city standards, Amsterdam is small. Its major sights, accommodation and nightlife are scattered around a web of concentric canals known as the 'canal belt', which gives the city an initially confusing, yet ultimately orderly and unique feel. The centre, easily covered on foot, has two main parts: The medieval core and the 'newer' 17th-century canal-lined quarters surrounding it. Corked to the north by Centraal Station, the old city centre is encased by the Kloveniersburgwal and Singel canals. After Singel come Herengracht, Keizersgracht and Prinsengracht, dug to cope with Amsterdam's Golden Age expansion. The city's central point is Dam Square, straight down Damrak from Centraal Station. Main streets bisect the canal belt like spokes in a wheel.

INFORMATION

Tourist Offices

The **VVV** *(☎ 0900-400 40 40; ⓔ info@amsterdamtourist.nl; Centraal Station platform 2; open 8am-8pm Mon-Sat, 9am-5pm Sun • Stationsplein 10; open 9am-5pm daily • Leidseplein; open 9am-5pm daily)* has three offices around town. During peak summer months, opening hours may be extended. There's also an office at Schiphol airport. You can call their information line between 9am and 5pm Monday to Friday for €0.55 per minute.

Money

There is a **GWK office** *(open midnight-10.30pm)* at Schiphol airport. There's also a main Centraal Station branch *(☎ 627 27 31; open 7am-10.45pm daily)*. Another GWK office *(open 8am-11pm daily)* is next to the VVV at Leidseplein. Otherwise, there's a throng of midnight-trading *bureaux de change* along Damrak and Leidsestraat. The main post office handles foreign exchange at reasonable rates. ATMs are sprinkled liberally around the city.

American Express *(Damrak 66; lost or stolen cards ☎ 504 80 00, travellers cheques ☎ 0800-022 01 00)* and **Thomas Cook** *(lost or stolen cheques ☎ 0800-022 86 30 • ☎ 620 32 36; Damrak 1-5 • ☎ 626 70 00; Leidseplein 31A)* are centrally located.

Post & Communications

The **main post office** *(☎ 330 05 55; Singel 250)* has an ATM and fax facilities.

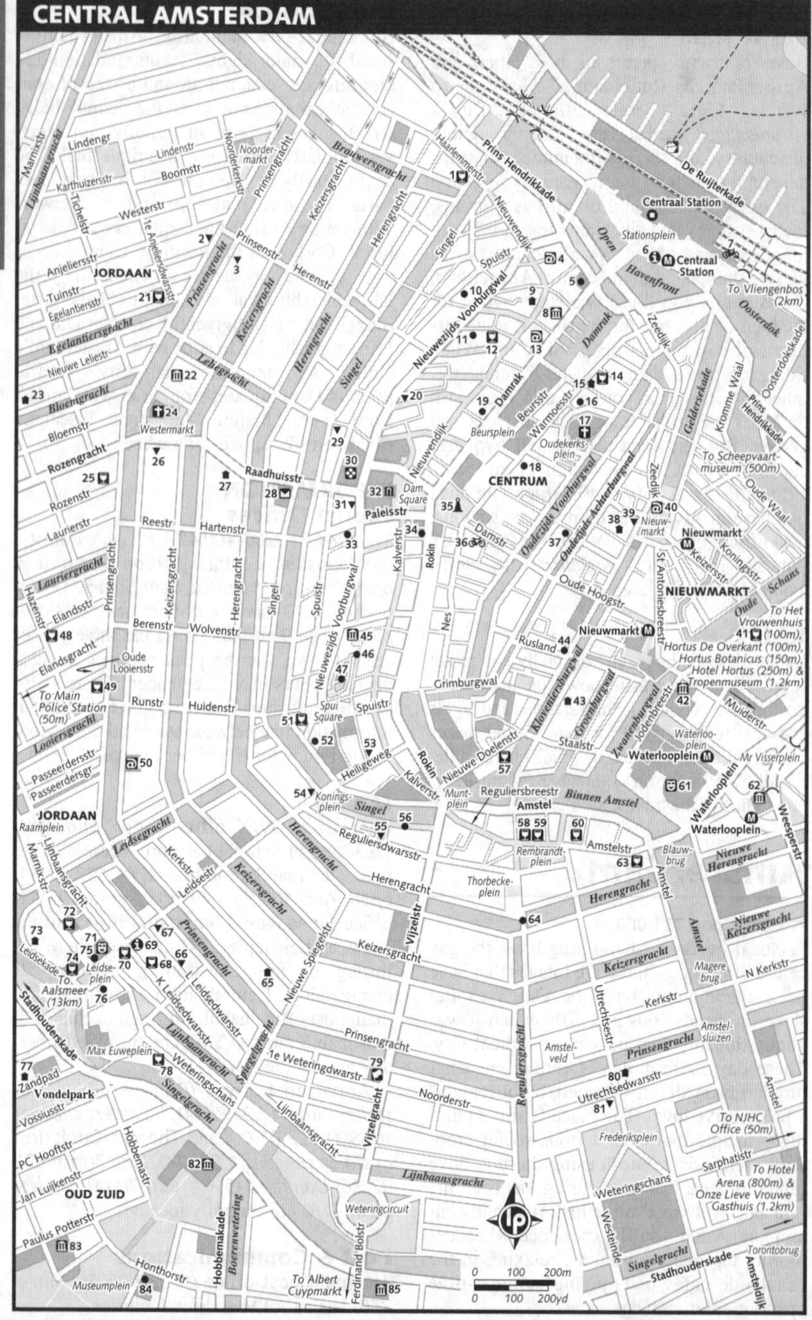
CENTRAL AMSTERDAM
Marnixstr
Lijnbaansgracht
Lindengr
Lindenstr
Noorderkerkstr
Noorder-markt
Prinsengracht
Brouwersgracht
Haarlemmerstr
Prins Hendrikkade
De Ruijterkade
Karthuizersstr
Boomstr
Tichelstr
Westerstr
1e Anjeliersdwarsstr
Keizersgracht
Herengracht
Singel
Nieuwendijk
Centraal Station
Stationsplein
Open Havenfront
Centraal Station
To Vliegenbos (2km)
Oosterdok
Oosterdokskade
Prinsenstr
Herenstr
Spuistr
Anjeliersstr
JORDAAN
Tuinstr
Egelantiersstr
Egelantiersgracht
Nieuwe Leliestr
Leliegracht
Nieuwezijds Voorburgwal
Damrak
Zeedijk
Geldersekade
Kromme Waal
Prins Hendrikkade
Bloemgracht
Bloemstr
Westermarkt
Rozengracht
Rozenstr
Lauriestr
Raadhuisstr
Beursstr
Warmoesstr
Beursplein
Oudekerksplein
To Scheepvaart-museum (500m)
Oude Waal
CENTRUM
Dam Square
Paleisstr
Reestr
Hartenstr
Kalverstr
Rokin
Damstr
Oudezijds Voorburgwal
Oudezijds Achterburgwal
Nieuwmarkt
Koningsstr
Keizersstr
St Antoniesbreestr
Lauriergracht
Prinsengracht
Hazenstr
Elandsstr
Berenstr
Wolvenstr
Spuistr
Nes
Oude Hoogstr
NIEUWMARKT
Oude Schans
To Het Vrouwenhuis (100m), Hortus De Overkant (100m), Hortus Botanicus (150m), Hotel Hortus (250m) & Tropenmuseum (1.2km)
Elandsgracht
Oude Looiersstr
Rusland
Nieuwmarkt
To Main Police Station (50m)
Runstr
Huidenstr
Grimburgwal
Kloveniersburgwal
Groenburgwal
Zwanenburgwal
Jodenbreestr
Muiderstr
Spui Square
Looiersgracht
Heiligeweg
Nieuwe Doelenstr
Staalstr
Waterlooplein
Waterlooplein
Mr Visserplein
Passeerdersstr
Passeerdersgr
Koningsplein
Kalverstr
Muntplein
Reguliersbreestr
Binnen Amstel
Amstel
Waterlooplein
Weesperstr
JORDAAN
Raamplein
Leidsegracht
Reguliersdwarsstr
Rembrandt-plein
Amstelstr
Blauwbrug
Nieuwe Herengracht
Kerkstr
Leidsestr
Herengracht
Thorbecke-plein
Herengracht
Amstel
Vijzelstr
Nieuwe Keizersgracht
Leidsekade
Leidse-plein
To Aalsmeer (13km)
Keizersgracht
Keizersgracht
Magere brug
N Kerkstr
Stadhouderskade
K Leidsedwarsstr
L Leidsedwarsstr
Nieuwe Spiegelstr
Utrechtsestr
Kerkstr
Max Euweplein
Lijnbaansgracht
Spiegelgracht
Prinsengracht
Amstel-veld
Prinsengracht
Amstel-sluizen
Zandpad
Weteringschans
1e Weteringdwarsstr
Reguliersgracht
Vondelpark
Singelgracht
Noorderstr
Utrechtsedwarsstr
Amstel
Vossiusstr
Hobbemastr
Lijnbaansgracht
Vijzelgracht
To NJHC Office (50m)
PC Hooftstr
Frederiksplein
Jan Luijkenstr
Lijnbaansgracht
Sarphatistr
To Hotel Arena (800m) & Onze Lieve Vrouwe Gasthuis (1.2km)
OUD ZUID
Weteringschans
Weteringcircuit
Hobbemakade
Boerenwetering
Paulus Potterstr
Westeinde
Singelgracht
Stadhouderskade
Torontobrug
Amsteldijk
Honthorststr
Museumplein
To Albert Cuypmarkt
Ferdinand Bolstr
0 100 200m
0 100 200yd

CENTRAL AMSTERDAM

PLACES TO STAY
9 Flying Pig Downtown Hostel
15 The Greenhouse Effect
23 Hotel van Onna
27 Hotel Pax
38 The Shelter
43 City Hostel Stadsdoelen
65 Hans Brinker Hostel
73 Quentin Hotel
77 City Hostel Vondelpark
80 Hotel Prinsenhof

PLACES TO EAT
2 Bolhoed
3 Pancake Bakery
20 La Strada
26 Koh-I-Noor
29 Villa Zeeźicht
31 Albert Heijn Supermarket
39 Albert Heijn Supermarket
53 Vlaams Frites Huis
54 Albert Heijn Supermarket
55 Gary's Muffins
66 Bojo
67 Shwarma/Felafel Eateries
81 Pata Negra

ENTERTAINMENT
1 Rokerij
12 In de Wildeman
14 Getto
21 Café 't Smalle
25 COC Café
41 Bimhuis
48 Saarein II
49 La Tertulia
51 Hoppe
57 Café de Jaren
58 Escape
59 Café-Restaurant De Kroon
60 Vivelavie
61 Het Muziektheater
63 iT
68 Jazz Café Alto
70 The Bulldog
71 Stadsschouwburg
72 Melkweg
74 Café Americain
78 Paradiso

OTHER
4 The Internet Cafe
5 Thomas Cook
6 Tourist Office; GVB
7 Rijwiel Shop
8 Sexmuseum
10 Buro voor Rechtshulp
11 Yellow Bike
13 easyEverything
16 Prostitution Information Centre
17 Oude Kerk
18 Condomerie Het Gulden Vlies
19 American Express
22 Anne Frankhuis
24 Westerkerk; Statue of Anne Frank
28 Main Post Office
30 Magna Plaza
32 Koninklijk Paleis
33 De Bierkoning
34 Eurolines Amsterdam
35 Nationaal Monument
36 Rent-a-Bike Damstraat
37 Cannabis College
40 In de Waag
42 Rembrandthuis
44 The Book Exchange
45 Amsterdams Historisch Museum
46 Schuttersgalerij
47 Begijnhof
50 Openbare Bibliotheek
52 Kilroy Travels
56 Bloemenmarkt
62 Joods Historisch Museum
64 Bridge of 15 Bridges
69 Tourist Office; GWK Office
75 Amsterdam Uit Buro
76 Thomas Cook
79 French Consulate
82 Rijksmuseum
83 Van Gogh Museum
84 Royal Dutch Touring Association (ANWB)
85 Heineken Experience

Book a free Internet session at **Openbare Bibliotheek** *(Public Library; ☎ 523 09 00; Prinsengracht 587; open 1pm-9pm Mon, 10am-9pm Tues-Thur, 10am-5pm Fri-Sat, 1pm-5pm Sun)*. **Internet Café** *(☎ 627 10 52; Martelaarsgracht 11; open 9am-1am Sun-Thur, 9am-3am Fri-Sat)*, close to Centraal Station, charges €1 for 20 minutes, as well as a compulsory drink purchase. **easyEverything** *(🅦 www.easyeverything.com; Damrak 33; open 7.30am-9.30pm)* has all the ambience of an examination hall but does offer reasonable rates for longer-term use. Rates are €1 for 20 minutes, €5 for 24 hours and €8 for 7 days.

Travel Agencies
Amsterdam is a major European centre for cheap fares to anywhere in the world. Shop around (eg, along the Rokin) or try **Kilroy Travels** *(☎ 524 51 00; 🅦 www.kilroytravels.com; Singel 143)*.

Medical & Emergency Services
The **Central Doctors Service** *(☎ 0900-503 20 42)* handles 24-hour medical, dental and pharmaceutical emergencies and inquiries. A central hospital is **Onze Lieve Vrouwe Gasthuis** *(☎ 599 91 11; 1e Oosterparkstraat 279)*, near the Tropenmuseum. The national emergency number is ☎ 112; alternatively, contact the **main police station** *(☎ 559 91 11; Elandsgracht 117)*.

THINGS TO SEE & DO
The best place to start a walking tour is **Dam Square** (the 'Dam'), where the Amstel River was dammed in the 13th century, giving the city its name. Today it's the intersection of the pedestrianised Kalverstraat and Nieuwendijk shopping streets. Here, too, is the **Nationaal Monument**, a 22m-high obelisk dedicated to those who died in WWII, and, on the western side, the **Koninklijk Paleis** (Royal Palace).

Heading west along Raadhuisstraat, you'll cross the main canals to the **Westerkerk**, whose 85m-high tower is the city's highest. In the church's shadow stands a **statue of Anne Frank**. Across Prinsengracht spreads the **Jordaan**, an area built up in the 17th century to

A Portrait of Courage

Born in 1929, Anne Frank moved with her family to Amsterdam from Germany in 1933. Seven years later, the Nazis invaded the Netherlands and began segregating Jews. When Nazi authorities summoned Anne's sister Margot to a concentration camp in 1942, the girls' father, Otto, was prepared. He transferred his family into a 'Secret Annex' to his office building that he had prepared beforehand. For the next two years, the Franks lived in hiding, never emerging from the annex. During the entire period, Anne confided her innermost thoughts to her diary. Her words paint a moving portrait of a sensitive girl struggling with the trials impending womanhood under unimaginable circumstances. The fullness of Anne's emotional development and personal growth contrast starkly with the physical confinement she was forced to endure.

The Franks were betrayed by a Dutch cohort in 1944. Anne herself died of typhus in Germany's Bergen-Belsen camp, at the age of 15 – two weeks before the British liberation of the camp. Her father, the sole survivor of the ordeal, found her diary and published the words of his daughter, who had always wished to be a writer so that the world would remember her.

house the city's lower class. Today its renovated gabled houses sit atop canal-front cafés in Amsterdam's trendiest quarter.

South of the Dam, on Nieuwezijds Voorburgwal, visit the impressive **Amsterdams Historich Museum** and then exit through the **Schuttersgalerij** (Civic Guard Gallery), a glass-covered passageway adorned with enormous group portraits of Dutch dignitaries from the 16th to 18th centuries. From here walk through one of the inner city's most tranquil spots, the **Begijnhof**. Such *hofjes*, or groupings of almshouses, were built across the Low Countries in the Middle Ages to house Catholic women, the elderly and poor. The Begijnhof is tucked in behind quaint **Spui Square**.

Continuing southwest from Spui, Leidsestraat ends where the city's nightlife takes off at **Leidseplein**. From there it's just a few minutes' walk southeast past **Vondelpark** – a summer-long entertainment venue – to the ever-inundated **Museumplein**, where you'll find the Rijksmuseum and Van Gogh Museum (see Museums & Galleries, following). Follow Singelgracht two blocks east to the **Heineken Experience**.

Back across the canals at the northern end of Vijzelstraat, the Muntplein tower maks the colourful **Bloemenmarkt** (flower market). Southeast is **Rembrandtplein**, a nightlife hub, and the **Bridge of 15 Bridges**, so-called because from here you can see 15 bridges (best at night). Further north, the sleaze of the **red-light district** extends along the parallel OZ Voorburgwal and OZ Achterburgwal canals past **Oude Kerk**, the city's oldest church, to **Zeedijk**, once the heroin nerve centre. It's had a face-lift in the last decade, but plenty of drugs are still going down in the alleys leading to the stark **Nieuwmarkt**.

Southeast of here is the city's Jewish quarter, or **Jodenhoek**, and the **Joods Historisch Museum** *(☎ 626 99 45)*. The nearby Rembrandthuis and Waterlooplein market attract hordes. Further east, the **Hortus Botanicus** (Botanical Garden) is home to the world's oldest pot plant.

Museums & Galleries

If you intend visiting several museums and galleries, it's worth buying the Museumjaarkaart (see Money in the Facts for the Visitor section, earlier).

Rijksmuseum *(☎ 674 70 00; Stadhouderskade 42; W www.rijksmuseum.nl; adult/child €8.50/free; open 10am-5pm daily)* has the Netherlands' largest art collection, spotlighting Rembrandt's famous *Night Watch*. It's the best introduction to Dutch art. Most of the museum will be closed from October 2003 until 2006 – the popular Dutch masters' works will still be displayed in the southern wing.

The **Van Gogh Museum** *(☎ 570 52 00; Paulus Potterstraat 7; W www.vangoghmuseum.nl; adult/child 13-17 €7/2.25; open 10am-6pm daily)* boasts the world's largest collection of Vincent's works. Highlights include the dour *Potato Eaters*, famous *Sunflowers* and ominous *Wheatfield with Crows*. Check the website for special events during 2003, the 150th anniversary of Van Gogh's birth.

The **Anne Frankhuis** *(☎ 556 71 00; Prinsengracht 263; adult/child 10-17 €6.50/3; open 9am-9pm daily Apr-Aug, 9am-7pm Sept-Mar)* is arguably the city's most famous canal house; come early or late to avoid the queues. This is where Anne wrote her famous diary (see the boxed text 'A Portrait of Courage').

The **Rembrandthuis** *(☎ 520 04 00; Jodenbreestraat 4-6; metro to Waterlooplein; adult/student/child 6-16 €7/5/1.50; open 10am-5pm Mon-Sat, 1pm-5pm Sun)* displays sketches by the Dutch master in his former home, which has been restored to its 17th-century glory.

The **Amsterdams Historisch Museum** *(☎ 523 18 22; Kalverstraat 92; adult/child 6-16 €6/3; open 10am-5pm Mon-Fri, 11am-5pm Sat & Sun)* explores the city's rich history via an impressive and surprisingly interesting collection of paintings, models and archaeological finds.

The highlight of the excellent **Scheepvaartmuseum** *(Shipping Museum; ☎ 523 22 22; Kattenburgerplein 1; bus No 22; adult/child 6-17 €7/4; open 10am-5pm Tues-Sat; 10am-5pm daily mid-June–mid-Sept)* is the superb replica of the 18th-century East Indiaman, *Amsterdam*, moored alongside. It also houses one of the largest collections of maritime memorabilia in the world.

Beer production stopped in 1988, but the **Heineken Experience** *(☎ 523 96 66; Stadhouderskade 78; admission €5; open 10am-6pm Tues-Sun)*, in a 135-year-old former brewery building, still attracts beer buffs for its self-guided tours (which end with three glasses of beer).

The **Prostitution Information Centre** *(☎ 420 73 28; Enge Kerksteeg 3; open 11am-7.30pm Tues, Wed, Fri & Sat)*, run by a former prostitute, provides intelligent information about the red-light district as well as souvenirs and supplies. The **Cannabis College** *(☎ 423 44 20; OZ Achterburgwal 124; admission free)* displays its own cannabis indoor garden. The **Sexmuseum** *(☎ 622 83 76; Damrak 18; over 16s only €2.50; open 10am-11.30pm daily)* is worth a visit for its eclectic collection of pornographic material, from Roman stone phalluses to 1870 studio photos of graphic sex.

ORGANISED TOURS

For a bicycle tour contact **Yellow Bike** *(☎ 620 69 40; Nieuwezijds Kolk 29)*. Yellow Bike organises bicycle tours of the city (€17, three hours) or a countryside tour taking in a windmill and clog factory (€22.50, six hours). Tours run from April to November only.

PLACES TO STAY

Amsterdam is popular all year but in peak times it's overrun – bookings are essential. All hostels in this section have Internet facilities. Hotel rates include breakfast.

Old City Centre

Accurately advertised as the 'cheapest B&B in town', **The Shelter** *(☎ 625 32 30, fax 623 22 82; ⓔ reservations@city.shelter.nl; Barndesteeg 21; dorm beds €15; open until midnight Mon-Thur, 1am Fri & Sat)* is a Christian hostel in the red-light district. It has clean, single-sex dorms, free email access and huge 'Jesus Loves You' signs.

City Hostel Stadsdoelen *(☎ 624 68 32, fax 639 10 35; Kloveniersburgwal 97; dorm beds €20.65; open 24 hrs)*, a bustling NJHC hostel near the red-light district, has 20-bed dorms, free lockers and a no-smoking policy.

Flying Pig Downtown *(☎ 420 68 22; ⓦ www.flyingpig.nl; Vossiusstraat 46; dorm beds from €19-25, singles/doubles €36/72; open 24 hrs)* takes some advance bookings (via Internet only), but most of the beds are for those who turn up that day. This relaxed hostel caters mostly to young backpackers. Rooms are cramped, but you can't beat the location.

The Greenhouse Effect *(☎ 623 74 62, fax 624 49 74; ⓦ www.the-greenhouse-effect.com; Warmoesstraat 55; singles/doubles from €50/75)* is one for smokers. You get a discount on dope and drinks in the café downstairs, and the themed rooms are well worn but trippy. Try your own Red Light room or some Turkish Delight.

Beyond the City Centre

The closest camping ground is **Vliegenbos** *(☎ 636 88 55, fax 632 27 23; Meeuwenlaan 138; tent/person/car €7.10/7.50/7; open Apr-Sept)*, a few minutes from Centraal Station on bus No 32.

The NJHC **City Hostel Vondelpark** *(☎ 589 89 99, fax 589 89 55; ⓦ www.njhic.org/vondelpark; Zandpad 5; dorm beds €22-28, doubles €76; open 24 hrs)* is one of Europe's largest hostels. Rooms are sunny, and all have bathrooms and well-spaced bunks. Facilities include lifts, a bar, two restaurants and bike hire.

The 550-bed **Hans Brinker Hotel** *(☎ 622 06 87, fax 638 20 60; ⓦ www.hans-brinker.com; Kerkstraat 136-8; dorm beds €21-24, doubles €70; open 24 hrs)* has corridors of spartan rooms and allows smoking. A nightly disco hums in the busy bar.

Hotel Hortus *(☎ 625 99 96, fax 625 39 58; W www.hotelhortus.com; Plantage Parklaan 8; singles/doubles/triples €25/50/75)* is full of young, happy stoners who love that cooked breakfast and huge TV screen. You may get a shower in your room.

Hotel Pax *(☎ 624 97 35; Raadhuisstraat 37; singles/doubles/triples from €39/65/110)* is a good budget option on hotel-lined Raadhuisstraat. Breakfast isn't included.

Hotel Prinsenhof *(☎ 623 17 72, fax 638 33 68; e info@hotelprinsenhof.com; Prinsengracht 810; singles/doubles from €40/60, doubles with bath €80)* is in a beautiful old canal house and has spacious rooms and a nifty electric luggage hoist.

In the Jordaan, the efficient **Hotel van Onna** *(☎ 626 58 01; W www.netcentrum.com/onna; Bloemgracht 104; singles/doubles €40/80)*, on a pretty canal, has simple, tidy rooms. Bring your earplugs if night-time church bells are likely to keep you awake.

Quentin Hotel *(☎ 626 21 87, fax 622 01 21; Leidsekade 89; singles/doubles €35/75, with bath €75/90)* has bright, spacious rooms decorated with wooden furniture and white linen. It's a favourite with lesbians, and musicians and actors performing close by. Breakfast is €7.

PLACES TO EAT

If you tire of Dutch cuisine, other choices abound. All listings included here are open daily unless otherwise specified.

Albert Heijn supermarkets *(NZ Voorburgwal 226; open 8am-10pm Mon-Sat, 11am-7pm Sun • Nieuwmarkt 18 • Koningsplein 6)* are dotted around town.

Amsterdam's favourite fries vendor is hole-in-the-wall **Vlaams Frites Huis** *(Voetboogstraat 33; open to 6pm daily)* – the green peppercorn sauce is a winner. There's a clutch of little **shwarma/felafel eateries** on Leidsestraat. Most are open until about 4am and do excellent felafels for about €4.

For late-night munchies, try **Gary's Muffins** *(Reguliersdwarsstraat 53; open noon-2am Sun-Thur, noon-4am Fri-Sat)*; the chocolate brownies are delicious. The best apple cake in town is at **Villa Zeezicht** *(Torensteeg 7; open from 8am-9.30pm Mon-Fri, 9am-9.30pm or later Sat & Sun)* where the generous serves go for €2.50.

There are inexpensive, authentic **Chinese** and **Thai eateries** at Nieuwmarkt, and **Surinamese cafés** near Albert Cuypmarkt. Greek and Italian cuisine compete fiercely with steak houses and Dutch fare in the streets off Leidseplein.

Pata Negra *(☎ 422 62 50; Utrectstraat 124; tapas about €4.50; open noon-11.30pm)* is a beautifully tiled place with fine tapas that's filled with a fun and boisterous crowd at the weekends.

Pancake Bakery *(Prinsengracht 191; mains about €9; open noon-9pm)* is one of the best places to get delicious, filling pancakes in a very Dutch environment.

Bojo *(☎ 622 74 34; Lange Leidsewarsstraat 51; mains about €9; open 5pm-2am Mon-Thur & Sun, 5pm-4am Fri-Sat)* is a busy Indonesian eatery with tasty and generous serves; it's one of the few places open until the wee hours.

The interior might be gaudy, but the Indian food at **Koh-I-Noor** *(☎ 623 31 33; Westermarkt 29; mains about €12.50; open 5pm-11.30pm)* is as good as it gets in Amsterdam.

La Strada *(☎ 625 02 76; Nieuwezijds Voorburgwal 93-95; mains about €12; open 4pm-1am Wed-Sun)* attracts a mixed lesbian, gay and hetero crowd with its pleasant ambience and Euro-style food.

Bolhoed *(☎ 626 18 03; Prinsengracht 60-62; mains about €12.50, 3-course meals €19; open noon-10pm)* is a colourful vegetarian haunt serving excellent organic and vegan food.

ENTERTAINMENT

The infamous 'smoking' coffee shops and red-light district live on, and zillions of cafés, bars and nightclubs give the city a constant vitality. There's also top-notch classical music, theatre and ballet. Pick up the monthly *Day to Day* guide from the VVV or from the **Amsterdam Uit Buro** *(AUB; ☎ 0900-01 91; Leidseplein 26)* for details of what's on.

Gay nightlife in Amsterdam is centred on Reguliersdwarsstraat, Kerkstraat, Warmoesstraat, and the streets off Rembrandtplein. Free gay Amsterdam maps are available from **COC** *(☎ 626 30 87; Rozenstraat 14)* as is *Gay & Night* magazine.

Pubs & Cafés

Pubs, bars, brown cafés – call them what you like, but places to drink abound. They're usually open until 1am Sunday to Thursday, and 2am on Friday and Saturday nights.

For the friendly and intimate atmosphere of the old brown café, try **Hoppe** *(☎ 420 44 20;*

Spui 18), where beers have been downed for more than 300 years. **In de Wildeman** *(Kolksteeg 3)* attracts beer connoisseurs with its menu of more than 200 beers; it also has a nonsmoking section.

In the Jordaan, **Café 't Smalle** *(Egelantiersgracht 12)* is a gorgeous café dating back to the 18th century with a tiny floating terrace. **Café-Restaurant De Kroon** *(☎ 625 20 11; Rembrandtplein 17)* is a classy grand café overlooking Rembrandtplein from a covered terrace. The huge **Café de Jaren** *(☎ 625 57 71; Nieuwe Doelenstraat 20)* has a great sun deck and English newspapers.

The Art Deco **Café Americain** *(☎ 556 32 32; American Hotel; Leidsekade 97; open 11am-11pm daily)* is the oldest (1902) and most stylish grand café in Amsterdam.

Saarein II *(☎ 623 49 01; Elandsstraat 119; open Tues-Sun)*, dating from the early 1600s, is a favourite meeting place for lesbians, as is the lively **Vivelavie** *(☎ 624 01 14; Amstelstraat 7)*.

COC Café *(☎ 623 40 79; Rozenstraat 14)* holds gay, lesbian and mixed club nights every weekend.

Getto *(☎ 421 51 51; Warmoesstraat 51; open 4pm-1am Tues-Sat, 4pm-midnight Sun)* is a fun gay bar-restaurant with a variety of nightly entertainment (tarot readers, DJs, cocktail happy hours).

Live Music

Bimhuis *(☎ 623 13 61; Oude Schans 73; tickets about €12)* is Amsterdam's main jazz venue and attracts local and international greats. It's moving to the Eastern Docklands in early 2004 (west of the ship passenger terminal).

Jazz Café Alto *(☎ 626 32 49; Korte Leidsedwarsstraat 115; open 9pm-3am Sun-Thur, 9pm-4am Fri-Sat)* is a cosy brown café that attracts fans of live jazz and blues.

Melkweg *(Milky Way; ☎ 531 81 81; Lijnbaansgracht 234a)* is a legendary cinema, theatre, and music venue that shakes from late until early with live rock, reggae and African rhythm. The equally hallowed **Paradiso** *(☎ 626 45 21; Weteringschans 6)*, a former church, has been the city's premier rock venue since the 1960s.

'Smoking' Coffee Shops

You'll have little difficulty pinpointing the 350-odd coffee shops whose trade is marijuana and hash rather than tea and tart. One of the most famous, and expensive, is **The Bulldog** *(☎ 627 19 08; Leidseplein 13-17)* with five branches around town. **La Tertulia** *(cnr Prinsengracht & Oude Looiersstraat)* is candid and colourful. **Rokerij** *(Singel 8)* has cool African and South American vibes. **Hortus De Overkant** *(☎ 422 19 49; Nieuwe Herengracht 71)* has well-priced hash and grass in a bright, modern environment.

Nightclubs

The trendy **Escape** *(Rembrandtplein 11)* is capable of drawing 2000 people on a Saturday night with top DJs and house music.

iT *(Amstelstraat 24; open 11pm-4am or 5am Thur-Sun)* is the largest gay and mixed nightclub – there's usually a queue. Saturday night is gay night.

The club at **Hotel Arena** *(☎ 694 74 44; 's Gravesandestraat 51)* has rock, house and techno on Friday and Saturday nights.

Theatre & Dance

Premier performing arts venues are the **Stadsschouwburg** *(☎ 624 23 11; Leidseplein 26; tickets from €19)* for large-scale productions, dance and musicals in the city's most beautiful theatre, and the **Het Muziektheater** *(☎ 551 89 11; Waterlooplein 22; tickets from €11)*, home of the renowned Netherlands Opera and National Ballet.

GETTING THERE & AWAY

Air

Amsterdam has long been known for its cheap air tickets (see Travel Agencies, earlier). Airline offices in Amsterdam include **British Airways** *(☎ 346 95 59)*, **KLM** *(☎ 474 77 47)* and **Qantas** *(☎ 023-569 82 83, call centre)*.

Bus

Eurolines operates from Amstel Station, which is connected to Centraal Station by metro. Buy tickets at the Eurolines office there or in central Amsterdam *(☎ 560 87 88; Rokin 10)*. To London (€55, 10 to 11 hours) there are four services per day, with buses also collecting passengers at Utrecht, The Hague, Rotterdam and Breda. Other Eurolines services include Antwerp (€15, three hours), Brussels (€15, four hours), Copenhagen (€75, 13 hours) and Paris (€39, eight hours).

Train

The international information and reservations office at Centraal Station is open between

6.30am and 10pm daily; for all international information call ☎ 0900-92 96 or go to the information centre on platform 2A. For national information, ask at the ticket windows or call ☎ 0900-92 92.

For information on trains to neighbouring countries, including train/ferry services to London, see the Getting There & Away section earlier in this chapter.

Car

Local companies usually have the cheapest car rental rates – about €40 per day plus kilometre fees. Car rental companies include: **Avis** *(☎ 683 60 61; Nassaukade 380)*, **Diks Autohuur** *(☎ 662 33 66; Van Ostadestraat 278)*, **Europcar** *(☎ 683 21 23; Overtoom 197)* and **Budget** *(☎ 612 06 66; Overtoom 121)*.

Ferry

For details on train-ferry services to the UK, see the Getting There & Away section, earlier in this chapter.

GETTING AROUND

Try to avoid insanely expensive taxis.

To/From the Airport

There are trains every 10 minutes between Schiphol and Amsterdam Centraal Station (€2.90, 20 minutes). Taxis cost about €40.

Bus, Tram & Metro

Amsterdam's comprehensive public transport network is operated by the **Gemeentevervoerbedrijf** *(GVB; open 7am-9pm Mon-Fri, 8am-9pm Sat & Sun)*, which has an information office next to the VVV in Stationsplein. Pick up the free transport map and *Tourist Guide to Public Transport Amsterdam*.

Buses, trams and the metro use strip cards (see Local Transport in the Getting Around section, earlier in this chapter); you can buy oneday cards for €5.20. All services run from 5am or 6am until midnight, when the more limited night buses takes over. The Circle Tram 20 is designed to meet the needs of tourists and operates 9am to 7.30pm daily, departing every 12 minutes from Centraal Station.

For all information, ring the **national public transport number** *(☎ 0900-92 92)*.

Car & Motorcycle

A 17th-century city enmeshed by waterways is hardly the place for cars. Access and parking are severely limited. Motorcycles can usually be parked on pavements providing they don't obstruct pedestrians, but security is a big problem. For queries, contact the **Parking Control Department** *(☎ 553 03 33)*.

Bicycle

Tram tracks and the other 600,000 bikes are the only real obstacle to cycling. It's advisable to book rental bikes ahead in summer. Try **Rent-a-Bike Damstraat** *(☎ 625 50 29; Damstraat 20-22)*, which charges €7/31 per day/week plus a €25 deposit or credit-card imprint; or the **Rijwielshop** *(☎ 624 83 91)*, to the left just out of Centraal Station, which charges €5.70 per day with a €100 deposit and no credit-card imprint option.

Canal Transport

Canal cruises (about €8 an hour) leave from in front of Centraal Station, along Damrak and Rokin and near the Rijksmuseum. They're very touristy but also a great way to see the city from a different perspective; night cruises are especially enchanting.

If you want to travel around by boat, the **Canal Bus** *(☎ 623 98 86)* stops at the tourist enclaves between Centraal Station and the Rijksmuseum, and has a day ticket for €12.50. The **Museumboot** *(☎ 530 10 90)* offers a €13.50 day ticket good for unlimited travel.

In summer, **canal bikes** *(☎ 626 55 74)* can be hired from kiosks at Centraal Station and Leidseplein for €6 per person.

AROUND AMSTERDAM

The world's biggest **flower auction** is held Monday to Friday at **Aalsmeer** *(☎ 0297 39 39 39; Legmeerdijk 313; bus No 172 from Centraal Station; admission adult/child €4/3.50)*, south of Amsterdam. Bidding starts early, so arrive between 7.30am and 9am.

To get to the tourist-filled fishing village of **Volendam**, take bus No 110 from Centraal Station (35 minutes). To visit the similar village and former island of **Marken**, now connected to the mainland by a dike, get bus No 111 (45 minutes) or go to Volendam and take the ferry.

The **Alkmaar cheese market** *(Waagplein, Alkmaar; open 10am Fri Apr-Sept)* is staged in the town's main market square and attracts droves. Arrive early if you want to get more than a fleeting glimpse of the famous round cheeses. There are two trains per hour from

Centraal Station (€5.40, 30 minutes) and it's a 15-minute walk at the other end.

The Randstad

The Netherlands' most densely populated region, the Randstad (literally, 'Urban Agglomeration') spreads in a circle from Amsterdam and incorporates The Hague, Rotterdam and Utrecht, plus smaller towns such as Haarlem, Leiden, Delft and Gouda. A compact area, it features sights highlighted by the bulb fields which explode in intoxicating colours between March and May.

HAARLEM

☎ 023 • pop 147,873

Haarlem is a small but vibrant town, with a wealth of historic buildings and posh shops. The Haarlem **VVV** *(☎ 0900-616 16 00, fax 534 05 37; ⓔ info@vvvzk.nl; Stationsplein 1; open 9.30am-5.30pm Mon-Fri, 10am-2pm Sun Oct-Mar, 10am-4pm Apr-Sept)* is next to the train station.

The **Frans Hals Museum** *(☎ 511 57 75; Groot Heiligland 62; open 11am-5pm Tues-Sat, midday-5pm Sun; adult/child under-13 €5.40/free)* features portraits by the master himself, as well as other great artists – a must-see for fans of Dutch painting. The **Teyler Museum** *(☎ 531 90 10; Spaarne 16; adult/child 5-18 €4.50/1; open 10am-5pm Tues-Sat, midday-5pm Sun)* is the country's oldest museum (1778), with an eclectic mix of fossils, mineral crystals, scientific gadgets and paintings, including drawings by Michelangelo and Raphael. Also worth a look is the Gothic cathedral of **St Bavo** *(☎ 553 20 40; Grote Markt; adult/child over 15 €2/1; open 10am-4pm Mon-Sat)*, housing the stunning Müller organ played by Handel and 10-year-old Mozart. **Molen de Adrian** *(☎ 545 02 59; Papentorenvest 1a; adult/child 4-15 €2/1; open 10am-4pm Fri-Sun)* is Haarlem's newest attraction, a reconstructed 18th-century windmill, with a more modern feel. Knowledgable volunteers can show you around.

From Amsterdam, there are trains every 15 minutes to Haarlem (€2.90, 15 minutes).

KEUKENHOF

Near the town of Lisse between Haarlem and Leiden, the **Keukenhof** *(☎ 0252-46 55 55; Ⓦ www.keukenhof.nl; adult/child 4-11 €11/5.50; open late-Mar–late May)* is the world's largest garden. It attracts a staggering 800,000 people in a mere eight weeks every year. Its beauty is something of an enigma, combining nature's talents with artificial precision to create a garden where millions of bulbs – tulips, daffodils and hyacinths – bloom every year, perfectly in place and exactly on time.

From Amsterdam, the Keukenhof can be reached either by a bus tour or by train to Leiden, from where you pick up bus No 54 (a bus and entrance pass costs €15).

LEIDEN

☎ 071 • pop 118,500

Home to the country's oldest university, Leiden is an effervescent town with an intellectual aura generated largely by the 15,000 resident students. The university was William of Orange's gift to the town for withstanding a long Spanish siege in 1574; a third of the townsfolk starved before the Spaniards retreated on 3 October, now the date of Leiden's biggest festival. Encircled by canals, bursting with cafés and restaurants, and with miles of car-free paved walkways, it's a very civilised place to kick back.

Most of the sights lie within a network of central canals, about a 10-minute walk from the train station. The helpful **VVV** *(☎ 0900-222 23 33, fax 516 12 27; ⓔ leiden@hollandrijnland.nl; Stationsweg 2D; open 9.30am-6pm Mon-Fri, 10am-4.30pm Sat)* has walking-tour booklets guiding you through the town's many *hofjes* (almshouses) and another on the trail of Rembrandt who was born here. The **main post office** *(Schipholweg 130)* is about 300m northeast of the station. For Internet access, head to the **Centrale Bibliotheek** *(library; ☎ 514 99 43; Nieuwstraat 4; open 1pm-5pm Sun & Mon, 11am-5pm Tues-Sat, 7pm-9pm Mon, Wed & Thur)*. Internet access is €2.30 per 30 minutes.

Things to See & Do

Canal cruises *(☎ 513 49 38; Beestenmarkt; adult/child 4-12 €4.40/2.50; daily Apr-Sept, weather dependent Oct-Mar)* cut a lap of the town and offer a taped commentary. To tour the town's many *hofjes* (almshouses), pick up the walking-tour booklet from the VVV.

The **Rijksmuseum van Oudheden** *(National Museum of Antiquities; ☎ 516 31 63; Rapenburg 28; adult/child 6-18 €6/5.50; open 10am-5pm Tues-Fri, noon-5pm Sat &*

Sun) tops Leiden's list of museums. Its striking entrance hall contains an Egyptian temple and it displays its ancient Egyptian, Greek, Near East and Dutch collections with style.

The 17th-century **Museum De Lakenhal** *(Cloth Hall; ☎ 516 53 60; Oude Singel 28; adult/child €4/free; open 10am-5pm Tues-Sat, noon-5pm Sun)* houses works by old masters. The first floor has been restored to reflect its appearance during the peak of Leiden's cloth-trade prosperity.

Leiden's landmark windmill, **De Valk** *(Falcon; ☎ 516 53 53; Binnenvestgracht 1; adult/child 6-15 €2.50/1.50; open 10am-5pm Tues-Sat, 1pm-5pm Sun)* will blow away notions that windmills were a Dutch invention.

Places to Stay & Eat

At Warmond, a few kilometres north of Leiden, is **Camping De Wasbeek** *(☎ 301 13 80; Wasbeeklaan 5b; adult/tent/car €2.50/2.50/1.20; open mid-Apr–mid-Oct)*.

Pension Witte Singel *(☎ 512 45 92, fax 514 28 90; ⓔ wvandriel@pension-ws.demon.nl; Witte Singel 80; singles/doubles from €31/46.50)*, on a peaceful canal south of the centre, is 25 minutes' walk from the station. The ultra-casual **Rose Hotel** *(☎ 514 66 30, fax 521 70 96; Beestenmarkt 14; singles/doubles €50/80)* has basic rooms that are popular with young travellers.

Oudt Leyden Pannekoekenhuysje *(☎ 513 31 44; Steenstraat 51; mains €7; open Mon-Sat 11am-9pm, 2pm-9pm Sun)* does enormous pancakes in a traditional Dutch café. The predominantly vegetarian **Splinter Eethuis** *(☎ 514 95 19; Noordeinde 30; mains €11; open 5pm-9.30pm, Thur-Sun)* offers organic two-course meals.

De Waterlijn *(☎ 512 12 79; Prinsessekade 5; mains about €3; open 10am-10pm daily)* is a floating café popular with locals craving a coffee or cake. Behind that austere black door is **Augustinos** *(☎ 516 23 36; Rapenburg 24; mains €4; open 5.30pm-8.15pm Mon-Fri)*. It's hugely popular with students so book ahead. Self-caterers will find a **Super De Boer** supermarket opposite the train station.

Entertainment

Next to the remains of a 12th-century citadel is **De Burcht** *(☎ 514 23 89; Burgsteeg 14; open 5pm-1.30am Mon-Thur, 4pm-3am Fri, 2pm-3am Sat, 2pm-2am Sun)*, a literary bar. **La Bota** *(☎ 514 63 40; Herensteeg 9; mains about €10; meals 5pm-10pm, bar open until midnight)* is a friendly, down-to-earth, student pub, good for a meal and a beer.

Getting There & Away

There are trains every 15 minutes from Leiden to Amsterdam (€6.10, 35 minutes), Haarlem (€4.40, 30 minutes, every seven minutes), The Hague (€2.50, 15 minutes, every four minutes) and to Schiphol (€4.40, 17 minutes, every 15 minutes).

THE HAGUE (DEN HAAG)

☎ 070 • pop 445,000

The Hague, – known in Dutch as Den Haag and officially 's-Gravenhage – is the country's seat of government and residence of the royal family. The city has a refined air, created by the stately mansions and palatial embassies that line its green boulevards. It's known for its prestigious art galleries, a huge jazz festival held annually near the seaside suburb of Scheveningen, and the silly miniature town of Madurodam.

Information

Trains stop at Station Hollands Spoor (HS), a 20-minute walk south of the city, or at Centraal Station, five minutes east of the centre. The area between Spui and Centraal Station has experienced a massive facelift in order to create a prestigious commercial and residential area.

The **VVV** *(☎ 0900-340 35 05, fax 352 04 26; ⓔ info@vvvscheveningen.nl; Koningin Julianaplein 30; open 9am-5.30pm Tues-Sat, 10am-2pm Sun July & Aug)* has a free monthly magazine detailing events and action around town. It also organises a two-hour guided tour of the city's architecture (adult/child €20/free) every Saturday between May and August.

The **main post office** *(Kerkplein 6; open 7.30am-6.30pm Mon-Wed, 7.30am-8pm Thur, 7.30am-6pm Fri, 7.30am-4pm Sat)* has the longest opening hours in the Netherlands.

Internet users should head to the atmospheric **Café Tweeduizendvijf** *(Denneweg 7f; open 8am-1am Sun-Wed, 9am-2am Thur-Sat)* where access costs €1 for 15 minutes, or to the bank of terminals at the **Centrale Bibliotheek** *(Spui 68; open 10am-9pm Mon-Fri, 11am-5pm Sat May-Aug, midday-5pm Sun Sept-Apr)* where you can log on for €1.50 for 30 minutes.

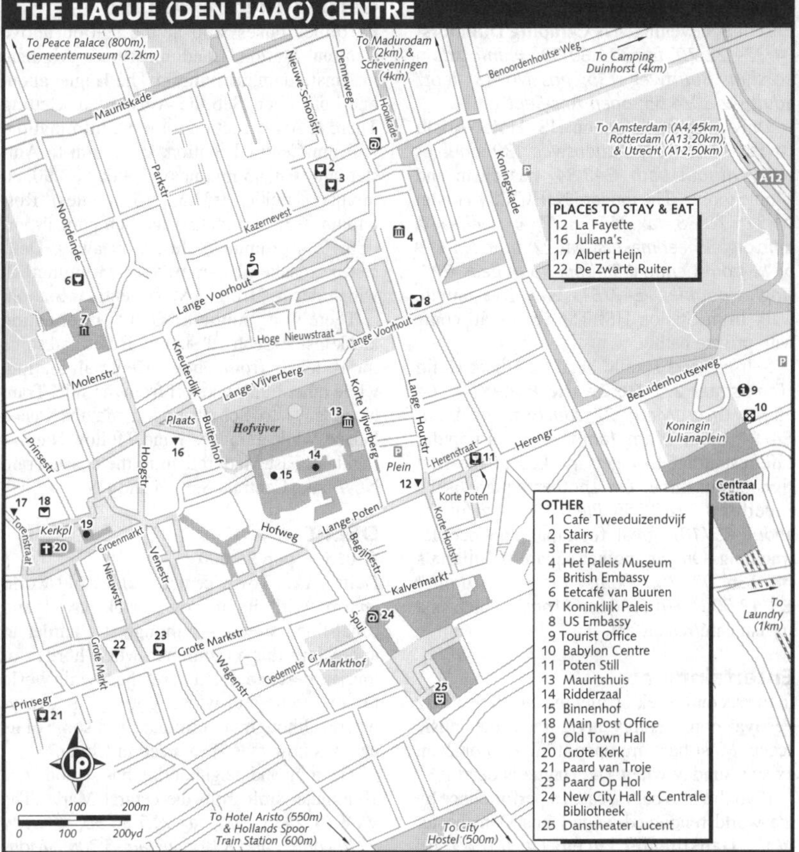

Things to See

The museum showpiece is the **Mauritshuis** *(☎ 302 34 35; Korte Vijverberg 8; adult/child €7/free; open 10am-5pm Tues-Sat, 11am-5pm Sun)*, an exquisite 17th-century mansion packed with superb Dutch and Flemish masterpieces, including works by Vermeer and Rembrandt.

Admirers of De Stijl, and in particular of Piet Mondrian, won't want to miss the **Gemeentemuseum** *(Municipal Museum; ☎ 338 11 11; Stadhouderslaan 41; tram No 17 or bus No 14; adult/child 13-18 €6.80/2.25; open 11am-5pm Tues-Sun)*.

The parliamentary buildings, or **Binnenhof** *(Inner Court; ☎ 364 61 44; Binnenhof 8a; adult/child 6-12 €5.30/4.30; open 10am-3.45pm Mon-Sat)* have long been the heart of Dutch politics, although nowadays the parliament actually meets in a building outside the Binnenhof. One-hour tours take in the 13th-century **Ridderzaal** (Knight's Hall).

Of the three royal palaces, the only one you can visit is the 18th-century **Het Paleis Museum** *(☎ 362 40 61; Lange Varhout 74; adult/child €5.70/free; open 11am-5pm Tues-Sun)*, which stages temporary art exhibitions. Home of the International Court of Justice, the **Peace Palace** *(Vredepaleis; Carnegieplein; tram No 17 or bus No 4 from Centraal Station; adult/child €3.50/1.80; tours 10am-5pm Mon-Fri)* can be visited by guided tours only – book at the VVV.

It's not worth visiting the miniature Netherlands in Madurodam when you can so easily see the real thing.

Places to Stay & Eat

East of Scheveningen is **Camping Duinhorst** *(☎ 324 22 70, fax 324 60 53; ⓔ info@duinhorst.nl; Buurtweg 135; bus No 43; tent/adult €2.30/4.55; open Apr-Sept)*.

Only 50m from Station HS, **Hotel Aristo** *(☎/fax 384 04 01; Stationsweg 139; doubles with/without bath €48/34)* has clean and simple rooms. The modern NJHC **City Hostel** *(☎ 315 78 88, fax 315 78 77; ⓔ denhaag@njhc.org; Scheepmakerstraat 27; tram No 1, 9 or 12 from Centraal Station; dorm beds €23, singles/doubles €47/61)* is a five-minute walk from Station HS. The rooms all come with private bath.

Self-caterers should head to **Albert Heijn** *(Torenstraat 27)*. **De Zwarte Ruiter** *(☎ 364 95 49; Grote Markt 27; lunch/mains about €4/14; open 11am-1am daily)* is a popular café/restaurant that gets packed at the first sign of sunshine. On another square is **La Fayette** *(☎ 392 36 55; Plein 15; lunch/mains about €5/10)*, great for tapas and people-watching. On yet another square is **Juliana's** *(☎ 365 02 35; Plaats 11; lunch/dinner €8/13.50; open 9.30am-11pm)*, which is a stylish café/restaurant.

Entertainment

In the second week of July the North Sea Jazz Festival considerably invigorates the music scene. Most bars are open until 1am or 2am, except Sunday when The Hague is dead.

If you're into ballet, catch a performance by the world renowned Nederlands Danstheater in the **Danstheater Lucent** *(☎ 360 49 30; ⓦ www.ldt.nl; Spui; tickets about €18)*. There are no performances in July and August.

Frenz *(☎ 362 6657; Kazernestraat 106)* flies the rainbow flag with DJs Friday and Saturday nights. Close by is **Stairs** *(☎ 364 81 91; Nieuwe Schoolstraat 21)*, a gay bar/disco.

Eetcafé van Buuren *(Noordeinde 90)* has a good selection of beers and live music on Thursday nights. **Poten Still** *(Herenstraat 15)* is a small Irish pub on a grungy nightlife street.

Paard van Troje *(☎ 360 16 18; Prinsegracht 12)* is The Hague's answer to Amsterdam's Melkweg and Paradiso 'cultural activity centres'. It's expected to reopen in mid-2003 after extensive renovations. In the meantime it's operating as **Paard Op Hol** *(☎ 360 18 38; Grote Markstrat 25; admission about €6)* with dance nights and concerts.

Getting There & Around

Eurolines buses stop at the station above Centraal Station. London services originate in Amsterdam, arriving in The Hague about one hour later. See the Amsterdam Getting There & Away section for more information.

From Centraal Station, trains run to Amsterdam (€8, 45 minutes), Gouda (€3.90, 20 minutes), Leiden (€2.50, 15 minutes), Rotterdam (€3, 20 minutes) and Schiphol airport (€6.10, 40 minutes). Just 9km away, Delft can be reached by tram No 1 (30 minutes), which departs from next to Centraal Station.

There's a public-transport information kiosk inside Centraal Station. Buses and some trams leave from above Centraal Station, while other trams take off from the side. Tram No 8 goes to Scheveningen via the Peace Palace, while tram Nos 1 and 9 follow Nieuwe Parklaan past Madurodam to the coast. Tram No 9 links Centraal Station and HS.

DELFT

☎ 015 • pop 96,000

Delft's Old Town centre exudes old-world charm, with its narrow, brick-paved and canal-lined streets – although it's harder to appreciate this in summer when hordes of tourists descend. Delftware, the town's world famous blue-and-white pottery is everywhere, although in a circular twist some of its china is now mass-produced in China.

The train and neighbouring bus station are a 10-minute stroll from the central Markt. The **VVV** *(☎ 213 01 00, fax 215 86 95; ⓦ www.delft.com; Markt 85; open 9am-5.30pm Mon-Sat year-round, 11am-3pm Sun summer)* will book accommodation at no cost. The **library** *(Centrale Bibliotheek; ☎ 212 34 50; Kruisstraat 71)* has Internet access for €2.40 per hour.

Things to See

See the delftware artisans as they work at the central studio and shop **Atelier de Candelaer** *(☎ 213 18 48; Kerkstraat 14; open 9am-5.30pm Mon-Fri, 9am-5pm Sat, 9am-4.30pm Sun, closed Sun winter)*. Outside the city centre, **De Porceleyne Fles** *(☎ 251 20 30; Rotterdamseweg 196; bus No 63, 121 or 129 from train station; open 9am-5pm Mon-Sat, 9.30am-5pm Sun, closed Sun winter)* has been producing delftware since 1653. Guided tours are €2.50/0.50 for adults/children.

The 14th-century **Nieuwe Kerk** *(Markt; adult/concession €2/0.75; open 9am-6pm*

Mon-Sat Nov-Mar, 11am-4pm Mon-Fri, 11am-5pm Sat Apr-Oct) houses the crypt of the Dutch royal family as well as the ornate mausoleum of William of Orange. The Gothic **Oude Kerk** *(Heilige Geestkerkhof)*, with a distinctive 2m tilt in its tower, houses the (very plain) plaque of Delft artist Johannes Vermeer. Admission is included in the Nieuwe Kerk ticket.

The **Prinsenhof** *(St Agathaplein 1; adult/concession €3.50/3; open 10am-5pm Tues-Sat, 1pm-5pm Sun)* is where William of Orange held court until he was assassinated in 1584 – you can still see the bullet holes. It now houses a rich collection of mostly 17th-century art.

Places to Stay & Eat

Delftse Hout *(☎ 213 00 40, fax 213 12 93; ⓔ info-delftsehout@tours.nl; Korftlaan 5; bus No 64 from station; 2-person tent site €22, camping huts for up to 4 people €30; open year-round)* is a neat camping ground opposite a large park, 15 minutes from the city centre.

Hotel Les Compagnons *(☎ 215 82 55, fax 212 01 68; Markt 61; singles & doubles €65)* has pink decor, hard towels and no customer service, but it does offer clean rooms overlooking the Markt.

Albert Heijn Supermarket *(Brabantseturfmarkt 41; open 8am-8pm Mon-Thur, 8am-9pm Fri)* should be able to satisty the needs of self-caterers.

Eetcafé De Ruif *(☎ 214 22 06; Kerkstraat 23; mains about €14; open 5.30pm-9.30pm daily)* is a rustic café with a popular bar. Try the salmon, cod and lobster tails wrapped in filo pastry.

The bustling **Kleyweg' Stads Koffyhuis** *(☎ 212 46 25; Oude Delft 133; mains about €4; open 9am-7pm Mon-Fri, 9am-6pm Sat)* sells award-winning sandwiches, as well as tasty soups and pancakes, and has a magazine table.

Arrive early or book at **De Zaag en de Fries** *(☎ 213 70 15; Vrouw Juttenland 17; mains about €14; open 5.30pm-9pm Wed-Sun)*, an ever-popular vegetarian restaurant.

Entertainment

Big, multilevel **Speakers** *(☎ 212 44 46; Burgwal 45; admission about €7; open until at least 2am)* has jazz, rock, comedy and DJs on different nights. For a slightly quieter haunt head round the corner to **Kobus Kuch** *(Beestenmarkt 1; open until 2am)*. Beer connoisseurs should aim for the cosy **Trappistenlokaal** *(Vlamingstraat 4; open until 2am)*.

Getting There & Away

It's 14 minutes by train to Rotterdam (€2.50) and 10 minutes to The Hague (€1.90). Tram No 1 leaves for The Hague (30 minutes) every 15 minutes from in front of the train station.

ROTTERDAM

☎ 010 • pop 593,000

Rotterdam is not your quintessential Dutch city. Bombed to oblivion in 1940, its centre is now ultra-modern, with mirrored skyscrapers and some extraordinarily innovative buildings. The city prides itself on this experimental architecture, as well as having the world's largest port. The nightlife is good, a large immigrant community adds diversity and the museums are excellent.

Rotterdam is sprawling by Dutch standards; its hub is the pedestrianised shopping streets based around Lijnbaan. The **VVV** *(☎ 414 00 00, fax 413 31 24; ⓔ info@vvv.rotterham.nl; Coolsingel 67; open 9.30am-6pm Mon-Thur & Sat, 9.30am-9pm Fri)* sells the Rotterdam Card (€25), providing entry to sights and discounted accommodation. **Use-It** *(☎ 240 91 58, fax 240 91 59; ⓔ use-it@jip.org; Conradstraat 2; 9am-5pm Tues-Sat mid-Sep–mid-May, 9am-6pm Tues-Sun mid-May–mid-Sept)*, right next to Central Station, is a tourist service aimed at budget travellers. Services include free day lockers, email access, hotel information and discounts. There's Internet access at the **library** *(☎ 281 61 00; open 10am-8pm Mon-Fri, 10am-5pm Sat year-round, 11am-5pm Sun Sept-May)*, which costs €3.40 per hour.

Things to See

Rotterdam's sights lie within a region bordered by the old town of Delfshaven, the Maas River and the Blaak district. The city's museums are lorded over by the **Boijmans van Beuningen** *(☎ 441 94 00; Museumpark 18; tram Nos 4 & 5, metro to Eendrachtsplein; adult/child €6/free; open 10am-5pm Tues-Sat, 11am-5pm Sun)*, a rich gallery of 14th-century to contemporary art. It has a superb Old Masters collection including work by Bosch, van Eyck, Rembrandt, Monet, van Gogh, Mondrian and Dalí.

Het Schielandshuis *(☎ 217 67 67; Korte Hoogstraat 31; metro to Beurs; adult/child 4-16 €2.70/1.35; open 10am-5pm Tues-Fri, 11am-5pm Sat & Sun)* was the only central 17th-century building to survive the bombing. It's now a museum housing an eclectic mix of exhibits, including some footage of the bombardment.

The **Kijkkubus** *(Cube Houses; ☎ 414 22 85; Overblaak 70; metro to Blaak; adult/child 4-12 €1.75/1.25; open 11am-5pm daily)* is a cube-shaped display house that was an innovative 1970s response to traditional architecture.

Delfshaven, Rotterdam's old town, is most famed for its **Oude Kerk** *(Aelbrechtskolk 20; metro to Delfshaven)* where the Pilgrim Fathers prayed before setting sail to the New World.

Places to Stay & Eat

The **Stadscamping** *(☎ 415 34 40, fax 437 32 15; Kanaalweg 84; bus No 33; tent/adult/car €3.50/4.50/2.50)* is 40 minutes' walk northwest of the station.

The **NJHC hostel** *(City Hostel Rotterdam; ☎ 436 57 63, fax 436 55 69; W www.njhc.org/rotterdam; Rochussenstraat 107; metro to Dijkzigt; dorm beds/singles/doubles from €19/28/47)* has a bar and basic rooms; it's a 20-minute walk from the station.

Friendly **Hotel Bienvenue** *(☎ 466 93 94, fax 467 74 75; Spoorsingel 24; singles from €43, doubles & apartments from €70)* is the pick of the budget hotels. Close to a small park, it overlooks a canal and is two blocks straight up from the rear entrance of Centraal Station.

Hotel Bazar *(☎ 206 51 51, fax 206 51 59; Witte de Withstraat 16; tram No 5 from Centraal Station; singles/doubles from €60/65)*, in the heart of town, has rooms decked out in Middle Eastern and South American style. A bonus when you stay here is the fantastic **Restaurant Bazar**.

Self-caterers can stock up at **Volume Markt supermarket** *(Nieuwe Binnenweg 30a)*.

The **Wester Paviljoen** *(☎ 436 26 45; Nieuwe Binnenweg 136; mains about €11; open 8am-1am or 2am daily)* is a large, smoky café with a down-to-earth atmosphere, and a great outside terrace.

Tampopo Noodle Bar *(☎ 225 15 22; Gravendijkwal 128; mains about €14)* is a trendy and stylish Asian restaurant with a good reputation.

Entertainment

Check the monthly *R'uit* guide (free from the VVV and cafés) for listings of what's on. The many terrace cafés on Stadhuisplein and at Oude Haven near the Kijk-Kubus are popular. Coffeeshop indulgers can imbibe in the selection of shops available along Nieuwe Binneweg.

Getting There & Around

Eurolines buses stop at Conradstraat (to the right as you leave the train station), where there is a **Eurolines office** *(☎ 412 44 44)* at No 20. Services to London leave from Amsterdam, arriving in Rotterdam 1½ hours later (€55/83 one way/return, 8½ hours). If you're under 26, tickets on the *Eurostar* to London via Brussels cost €54 return. For over 26's, fares start at €116.

Trains run every 15 minutes to Amsterdam (€10.80, one hour), Delft (€2.50, 10 minutes), The Hague (€3.40, 20 minutes) and Utrecht (€7, 40 minutes). Half-hourly services run to Middelburg (€15.60, 1½ hours), Gouda (€3.40, 18 minutes) and Hook of Holland (€3.90, 30 minutes).

For information on ferries to England, see the Getting There & Away section at the beginning of this chapter. P&O/North Sea Ferries' bus leaves at 4pm daily from Conradstraat (next to Centraal Station) to connect with the ferry at Europoort.

Trams leave from in front of the train station; the metro from underneath. Both run until about midnight; on Friday and Saturday, night buses then take over. A one-day public transport card costs €6.

AROUND ROTTERDAM

The **Kinderdijk**, the Netherlands' picture-postcard string of 19 working windmills, sits between Rotterdam and Dordrecht near Alblasserdam. On Saturday afternoons in July and August the mills' sails are set in motion. One windmill is open daily from 1 April to 30 September – get the metro to Zuidplein then bus No 154 (1¼ hours).

GOUDA

☎ 0182 • pop 73,000

Think Dutch cheese and you'll think Gouda (or Edam). This pretty little town, 25km northeast of Rotterdam, is well known for its cheese market, held at 10am every Thursday morning in July and August. Enormous rounds of cheese – some weighing up to 25kg – are brought to the

Markt. For more information, contact the **VVV** *(☎ 0900-468 32 888, fax 0182-583 210; Markt 27; open 9am-5pm Mon-Sat, also noon-5pm Sun June-Aug)*.

Regular trains connect Gouda with Rotterdam (€3.80, 18 minutes) and Amsterdam (€8.50, one hour).

UTRECHT

☎ 030 • pop 236,000

Lorded over by the Dom, the country's tallest church tower, Utrecht is an antique frame surrounding an increasingly modern interior. Its 14th-century sunken canals, once-bustling wharfs and cellars now brim with chic restaurants and cafés, and the large student population adds plenty of buzz. You see none of this when arriving at the train station, which lies behind Hoog Catharijne, a shopping-mall monstrosity.

The **VVV** *(☎ 0900-128 87 32, fax 236 00 37; ⓔ info@vvvutrecht.nl; Vinkenburgstraat 19; open 9.30am-6.30pm Mon-Wed & Fri, 9.30am-9pm Thur, 9.30am-5pm Sat Oct-Apr, 10am-2pm Sun May-Sept)*, between Neude and Oudegracht, is 10 minutes' walk east from the train station. They have an information line that charges €0.55 a minute.

Time2Surf *(Oudegracht 112)* has 150 terminals for €2.50 per hour; or try the **library** *(☎ 286 18 00; Oudegracht 167; open 1pm-9pm Mon, 11am-6pm Tues-Fri, 10am-2pm Sat)* which costs €1.20 per 30 minutes.

Things to See & Do

You can see for miles from the 112m-high **Dom Tower** *(adult/child €6/3; open 10am-5pm Mon-Sat, noon-5pm Sun)* once you make the 465-step climb to the top.

The **Museum Van Speelklok tot Pierement** *(☎ 231 27 89; Buurkerkhof 10; adult/child 4-12 €6/4; open 10am-5pm Tues-Sat, noon-5pm Sun)* has a colourful collection of musical clocks and street organs from the 14th century onwards, demonstrated with gusto on hourly tours.

Het Catharijneconvent Museum *(Nieuwegracht 63; adult/child 3-17 €6/3; open 10am-5pm Tues-Fri, 11am-5pm Sat & Sun)* winds through a 15th-century convent and has the country's largest collection of medieval Dutch art.

Places to Stay & Eat

For keen campers **Camping De Berekuil** *(☎ 271 38 70; Ariënslaan 5; bus No 57 from station; tent sites/per person €4/4; open year-round)* is 1.5 km from the centre.

Strowis Hostel *(☎ 238 02 80, fax 241 54 51; ⓔ info@strowis.nl; Boothstraat 8; dorm beds €11-13.50, doubles €41)*, in a lovingly restored 17th-century building, has friendly, helpful staff and services include free email access and bike hire. It's a 15-minute walk from Centraal Station; or take bus No 3, 4, 8 or 11 to Janskerkhof.

Acu *(☎ 231 45 90; Voorstraat 71; 3-course meals €6; open 5pm-2am Sun-Thur, 9pm-4am Fri-Sat; meals available 6pm-7.30pm Sun-Thur)*, around the corner from Strowis, has good vegetarian food, and live music after 10pm.

The Oudegracht is lined with outdoor restaurants and cafés. The best of them is **Oudaen** *(☎ 231 18 64; Oudegracht 99; mains about €16; open 10am-10pm Mon-Sat)* set in a restored 13th-century banquet hall which also brews its own beer.

Shwarma (pitta-bread) eateries are plentiful along Voorstraat. For self-caterers, there's an **Albert Heijn Supermarket** in Hoog Catharijne.

Getting There & Around

Connexion buses stop at the back of the train station; buy tickets at the office or on the bus. As Utrecht is the national rail hub, there are frequent trains to Amsterdam (€8, 30 minutes), Arnhem (€5.30, 40 minutes), Gouda (€4.40, 22 minutes), Maastricht (€19.70, two hours), Rotterdam (€7, 40 minutes) and The Hague (€8, 45 minutes).

Local buses leave from underneath Hoog Catharijne (the shopping complex adjoining the train station).

Arnhem & the Hoge Veluwe

☎ 026 (Arnhem), 031 (Hoge Veluwe) • pop 134,650

About an hour's drive east of Amsterdam, the Hoge Veluwe is the Netherlands' best-known national park and home of the prestigious Kröller-Müller Museum. To the south, Arnhem was the site of fierce fighting between the Germans and British and Polish airborne troops during the failed Operation Market Garden. Today, it's a bland and uninspiring town but the closest base to the nearby war museum and national park.

The **VVV** (*☎ 0900-202 40 75, fax 442 26 44; e info@vvvarnhem.nl; Willemsplein 8)* is one block to the left of Arnhem's train station. Buses leave from the right as you exit the station.

Outside Arnhem is Oosterbeek's wartime **Airborne Museum Hartenstein** (*☎ 333 77 10; Utrechtseweg 232; trolleybus No 1 from Arnhem station; adult/child 5-16 €4/3; open 10am-5pm Mon-Sat Apr-Oct; 11am-5pm Mon-Sat Nov-Mar, noon-5pm Sun year-round)*, which does an excellent job of explaining the battle of Arnhem.

HOGE VELUWE NATIONAL PARK

Stretching for nearly 5500 hectares, this national park (*☎ 859 16 37; w www.hogeveluwe.nl; Apeldoornseweg 250; combined park & museum ticket adult/child 6-12 €10/5, plus cars €5; park open 9am-5.30pm Nov-Mar, 8am or 9am-sunset Apr-Oct, visitors centre open 10am-5pm daily)* is a mix of forests and woods, shifting sands and heathery moors. It's home to red deer, wild boar, moufflon (a Mediterranean goat) and the **Kröller-Müller Museum** (*☎ 859 10 41; open 10am-5pm Tues-Sun)*, a world-class collection of Van Gogh paintings.

The park is best seen on foot or bicycle – the latter are available free of charge at the park entrances or from the visitors centre inside the park. To get there, take bus 107 which leaves from Stationsplein in Arnhem at least four times daily from 1 April to 30 October.

PLACES TO STAY & EAT

North of town is **Hostel Alteveer Arnhem** (*☎ 442 01 14, fax 351 48 92; e arnhem@njhc.org; Diepenbrocklaan 27; bus No 3; dorm beds/singles/doubles €22/30/53)*.

Pension Parkzicht (*☎ 442 06 98, fax 443 62 02; Apeldoornsestraat 16; singles/doubles €25/50)* has basic rooms and is 10 minutes' walk from the station.

De Campaen (*☎ 443 66 06, mobile 06 517 14 274; e reijmers@planet.nl; singles/doubles €37/58)* is a beautifully restored, wood-lined boat with cosy cabins. It's moored on the Rhine and is 10 minutes from the station. Book ahead as it's sometimes used for charter trips.

Terrace cafés rim the Korenmarkt. **Wampie** (*☎ 445 67 05; Korenmarkt 18; lunch about €3.50; open 10am-1am Mon-Fri, 10am-2am Sat & Sun)* has been operating for more than 30 years.

GETTING THERE & AWAY

Trains to Amsterdam (€11.80, 65 minutes, every 15 minutes) and Rotterdam (€14.40, 75 minutes, every five minutes) go via Utrecht (€8, 40 minutes, every 10 minutes), while the line south passes Den Bosch (€8, 45 minutes, every five minutes) and continues to Maastricht (€17, two hours).

The Delta Region

The Netherlands' aptly named province of Zeeland (Sea Land) makes up most of the Delta region. Spread over the southwest corner of the country, it was until recent decades a solitary place, where isolated islands were battered by howling winds and white-capped seas, and where little medieval towns were lost in time. But after the 1953 flood, it was decided to defend Zeeland from the sea. One by one the islands were connected by causeways and bridges, and the Delta Project (see the Around Middelburg section, later) became a reality.

MIDDELBURG

☎ 0118 • pop 45,000

Middelburg is the long-time capital of Zeeland. It makes for a pleasant overnight stop and has a handful of worthy sights. The **VVV** (*☎ 65 99 00, fax 65 99 10; e vvvmid@zeelandnet.nl; Nieuwe Burg 40; open 9.30am-5.30am Mon-Fri, 9.30am-5pm Sat, noon-3pm Sun)* has a free brochure with discount passes.

Nearby is the Gothic **Stadhuis** (*Town Hall; ☎ 67 54 52; guided tours adult/child 5-12 €2.75/2.25; open 11am-5pm Mon-Sat, noon-5pm Sun Apr-Oct)* which, like much of the central district, was destroyed during the German blitz that flattened Rotterdam. Dating back to the mid-15th century, it's convincingly restored and has several sumptuous ceremonial rooms. A few streets away is the huge complex of the **Abdij** (*Abbey; ☎ 61 35 96; open 11am-5pm Mon-Sat, noon-5pm Sun Apr-Oct)*, housing three churches, two museums and a 91m tower, **Lange Jan** (*adult/child 5-12 €2.25/1.60)*.

The nearest NJHC hostel, **Kasteel Westhove** (*☎ 58 12 54, fax 58 33 42; e domburg@njhc.org; Duinvlielweg 8; bus No 53; dorm* *beds €23; open mid-Mar–mid-Oct)*, is in a medieval castle – complete with moat – about 15km west between the villages of Domburg and Oostkapelle.

Hotel Roelant *(☎ 62 76 59, fax 62 89 73; Koepoortstraat 10; singles/doubles €60/70)* has functional rooms, a pleasant garden and an excellent restaurant. Across from the station, **Grand Hotel du Commerce** *(☎ 63 60 51, fax 62 64 00; ⓔ info_ducommerce@fletcher.nl; Loskade 1; singles/doubles €60/80)* has small, nicely furnished rooms.

Vriend Schap *(Markt 75; mains €7; open lunch 11.30am-5pm daily)* is one of several cafés good for people-watching. **De Mug** *(☎ 61 48 51; Vlasmarkt 54; mains about €16.50; open 4pm-11pm daily)* is justifiably famous for its menu of dishes prepared with unusual Dutch beers.

Trains from Middelburg run hourly to Amsterdam (€23.80, 2½ hours) and Rotterdam (€13.20, 1½ hours).

AROUND MIDDELBURG

The disastrous 1953 flood was the impetus for the Delta Project, in which the southwest river deltas were blocked using a network of dams, dikes and a remarkable 3.2km storm-surge barrier, which generally remains open to allow normal tidal movements and the survival of the region's shellfish. Finished in 1986, the project is explained at **Waterland Neeltje Jans** *(☎ 0111-65 27 02; adult/child 4-12 €11/8.50 summer, €7.50/5 winter; open 10am-5.30pm Apr-Oct, 10am-5pm Wed-Sun Nov-Mar)*.

To get there from Middelburg, take bus No 104 (€5.90 or combined bus and admission ticket €15, 30 minutes, twice hourly). If you are driving or hitching, head onto the N57 in the direction of 'Burgh-Haamstede'. From Rotterdam, take the metro to Spijkenesse Centraal and then bus No 104 (2¼ hours).

The North

The Netherlands' northern region is made up of several provinces, including Fryslân and Groningen, and is capped by the Frisian (or Wadden) Islands, five islands including Texel and Ameland that are popular escapes for stressed southerners. The region's shores are washed by the shallow Waddenzee, home to a small number of seals and the unique Dutch sport of *wadlopen* (mud walking; see the Groningen section, later). The lake-land province of Fryslân is a bit 'different' from the rest of the Netherlands. The people here have their own flag, anthem and language – Frysk (Frisian).

LEEUWARDEN

☎ 058 • pop 90,500

The capital of Fryslân, Leeuwarden packs just enough action to provide interest. The city developed from three *terp* (artificial dwelling mound) settlements used as homes by the first Frisians in the 15th century. Its most famous daughter is WWI spy Mata Hari.

The **VVV** *(☎ 0900-202 40 60, fax 234 7551; ⓔ vvvleeuwarden@vvvleeuwarden.nl; Sophialaan 4; open 9am-5.30pm Mon-Fri, 10am-4pm Sat)* sells a city map detailing three walking tours for €1.15. The **Fries Museum** *(☎ 255 55 00; Turfmarkt 11; adult/child 13-18 €5/2.50, free Wed; open 11am-5pm Tues-Sun)* traces the development of Frisian culture and has a huge collection of silver, as well as a look at Mata Hari's life in Leeuwarden and as a dancer of notoriety in Paris.

Pottery lovers will adore the **Princessehof** *(☎ 212 74 38; Grote Kerkstraat 11; adult/child 13-18 €5/2.50; open Tues-Sun 11am-5pm)*, the national museum for ceramics. The collection of Dutch, Asian and Middle Eastern tiles and other works is most impressive.

Hotel De Pauw *(☎ 212 36 51, fax 216 07 93; Stationsweg 10; singles/doubles from €27/47)*, close to the train and bus stations, has birds chirping in the foyer and faded but comfy rooms. More central is **Hotel 't Anker** *(☎ 212 52 16, fax 212 82 93; Eewal 69; singles/doubles €34/44, with bathroom €52/60)*, which has a good bar downstairs.

From Amsterdam there are hourly trains to Leeuwarden (€22.40, 2¼ hours), or you can take bus No 350 from Alkmaar across the Afsluitdijk.

GRONINGEN

☎ 050 • pop 175,000

This lively provincial capital has been an important trading centre since the 13th century. Its prosperity increased with the 1614 founding of the country's second oldest university and, later, the discovery of natural gas. The **VVV** *(☎ 0900 202 30 50, fax 311 38 55; ⓔ info@vvvgroningen.nl; Grote Markt 25; open 9am-6pm Mon-Fri, 9am-8pm Thur, 10am-5pm Sat* *year-round, 11am-5pm Sun July-Aug)* provides free bookings.

The city's colourful and inspired **Groninger Museum** *(☎ 366 65 55; Museumeiland 1; adult/child 5-16 €6/3; open 10am-5pm Tues-Sun)* hosts an exquisite collection of silver tea and coffee pots, works by Groningen artists and a kaleidoscope of interesting temporary exhibitions.

Groningen is the best place to arrange **wadlopen**, or mud walking. It's a serious pastime – strenuous and at times dangerous – involving kilometres-long, low-tide walks in mud that can come up to your thighs. To get down and dirty, contact **Wadloopcentrum** *(☎ 0595-528 300; ⓔ info@wadlopen.com)*, at Pieterburen to the north of town; walks cost from €7.30 to €30.

Clean **Simplon Jongerenhotel** *(☎ 313 52 21, fax 360 31 39; ⓔ simplon-jongerenhotel@xs4all.nl; Boterdiep 73-2; bus No 1 from train station; dorm beds from €10.20, singles/doubles from €24.95/38.85)*, a hostel with themed rooms (try heaven) and huge dorms, is just outside the city centre. Rooms are more basic at the somewhat run-down **Hotel Friesland** *(☎/fax 312 13 07; Kleine Pelsterstraat 4; singles/doubles €23.50/43.50)*, but it's more central.

De Kostery *(☎ 314 19 78; Grote Markt)* has location, location, location in a corner of the 16th-century Martinikerk; it features the usual assortment of sandwiches, soups etc.

Hourly trains depart from Amsterdam to Groningen (€26.10, 2½ hours) and from Groningen to Leeuwarden (€12.50, 50 minutes).

TEXEL

☎ 0222 • pop 13,000

Texel's 30km of beach can seem overrun in summer, especially so in June when it's the site of the world's largest catamaran race. The biggest village is Den Burg, where you'll find the **VVV** *(☎ 31 28 47, fax 31 41 29; ⓔ info@texel.net; Emmalaan 66; 9am-6pm Mon-Fri, 9am-5pm Sat Nov-Mar; 9am-9pm Fri Apr-Oct, 10am-1.30pm Sun July-Aug)*, which sells good maps of the island (€3) and will make accommodation bookings for a hefty €12.

There are 11 camping grounds, including **De Krim** *(☎ 39 01 11, fax 39 01 21; ⓔ info@krim.nl; Roggeslootweg 6; tent & up to 4 adults €25.50; open year-round)*, a five-star camping ground in Cocksdorp that also has hiking huts. The main NJHC hostel is **Panorama** *(☎ 31 54 41, fax 31 38 89; Schansweg 7, Den Burg; dorm beds/triples €21/67)*, in a pretty thatched house.

Trains from Amsterdam to Den Helder (€10.80, 1¼ hours) and buses from Leeuwarden (€11.80, 1¾ hours) are met by a bus that whips you to the awaiting, hourly Teso car ferry *(☎ 36 96 00)* which takes 20 minutes (adult/child 4 to 11 €4/2 return, bicycles €2.70). It's worthwhile buying the all-day €3.50 bus ticket, available at the ferry terminal or on the bus.

AMELAND

☎ 0519 • pop 3400

Ameland has four quaint villages and a distinct holiday feel. Nes is its prettiest and best-preserved village, and home to the **VVV** *(☎ 54 65 46, fax 54 29 32; ⓔ vvv@ameland.nl; Bureweg 2; open 9am-12.30pm & 1.30pm-6pm Mon-Fri, 10am-3.30pm Sat)*, which for a fee can book accommodation.

Camping Duinoord *(☎ 54 20 70, fax 54 21 46; ⓦ www.duinoord.net; Jan van Eijckweg 4; tents/adults €2.60/4.10)* is 2km from Nes and one of six camping grounds. The **NJHC Waddencentrum Ameland** *(☎ 55 53 53, fax 55 53 55; ⓔ ameland@njhc.org; Oranjeweg 59; bus No 130 from ferry or Nes; dorm beds/singles/doubles €20/26/50)* is by the beach and below the lighthouse at Hollum.

Hotel Restaurant de Jong *(☎ 54 20 16, fax 54 20 24; Reeweg 29; singles/doubles from €30/60)* has simple but pleasant rooms in the heart of Nes.

From Leeuwarden, take bus No 66 to the ferry at Holwerd (nine strip tickets, 40 minutes). From Monday to Friday there are six boats a day; Saturday and Sunday have four (hourly services June to August). Returns cost €10.40 per person and €4.75 for bikes.

The Southeast

Sprinkled with woods, heather and the odd incline, the Netherlands' southeastern corner is made up of the North Brabant and Limburg provinces. Its two main towns, Den Bosch and Maastricht, are intimate and energetic.

DEN BOSCH

☎ 073 • pop 127,200

Den Bosch ('The Duke's Forest', officially known as 's-Hertogenbosch) is the capital of

North Brabant. Its pedestrianised centre is based around the Markt, a 10-minute walk east of the train station.

The **VVV** *(☎ 0900-112 23 34, fax 612 89 30; Markt 77; ⓔ info@vvvs_hertogenbosch.nl; open 1pm-6pm Mon, 9am-6pm Tues, Wed & Fri, 9am-9pm Thur, 9am-5pm Sat)* is housed in the town's oldest building.

The **St Janskathedraal** *(Choorstraat 1; admission free; open 9.30am-4pm Nov-Mar, 8am-5pm Apr-Oct)* is the Netherlands' finest Gothic church. It's a few minutes' walk from the Markt at the end of Kerkstraat. The **Noordbrabants Museum** *(Verwersstraat 41; adult/child 6-18 €5.70/3; open 10am-5pm Tues-Fri, noon-5pm Sat & Sun)* features exhibits on Brabant life and art from earlier times. It has works by Bosch as well as a few early Van Goghs.

Near the station, **Hotel Terminus** *(☎ 613 06 66, fax 613 07 26; Boschveldweg 15; singles/doubles/triples €26.50/50/72)* boasts decent rooms as well as a great bar. The **Euro Hotel** *(☎ 613 77 77, fax 612 87 95; ⓔ eurohotel@bestwestern.nl; singles/doubles €60/75)* has standard business rooms and friendly staff.

Cafés line up alongside the cathedral. **Café Cordes** *(☎ 412 42 24; Parade 4)* is one of the better ones. **Javaanse Jongens Eetcafé** *(☎ 613 41 07; Korte Putstraat 27; mains about €16)* has good Indonesian food and a decor of carved wooden tigers; it's in a street of quality restaurants.

Trains run regularly to Amsterdam (€10.80, one hour, two hourly) via Utrecht (€6.10, 30 minutes, six hourly), and to Arnhem (€8, 45 minutes, three hourly) and also Maastricht (€15.60, 1½ hours, hourly).

MAASTRICHT

☎ 043 • pop 120,000

The Netherlands' oldest city, Maastricht sits at the bottom end of the thin finger of land jutting between Belgium and Germany – and is influenced by both countries. Capital of the largely Catholic Limburg province, its history stretches back as far as 50 BC, when the Romans set up camp on a bank of the Maas River. Today, this lively city has a reputation of being a little 'foreign'.

The Maas' west bank is the city's main hub. Here you'll find the old centre, with restaurants, hotels and churches. On the east bank is the Wyck, an area of 17th-century houses, intimate cafés and bars and, further south, Céramique, the modern showpiece quarter.

The particularly helpful **VVV** *(☎ 325 21 21; cnr Kleine Staat & Jodenstraat; open 9am-5pm or 6pm Mon-Sat Nov-Apr, 11am-3pm Sun May-Oct)* offers guided walks in summer (€3) and has a brochure on self-guided walks (€1) for other months.

There's a **GWK** *(open 8am-10pm Mon-Fri, 9am-5pm Sat, 9am-10pm Sun)* at the train station, and, in the centre, the **main post office** *(Grote Staat 5)*. For Internet access try the **Stadsbibliotheek** *(library; ☎ 350 56 00; Ave Céramique 50; open 10.30am-5pm Mon & Wed, later Tues & Fri, 10am-3pm Sat, 1pm-5pm Sun)*, where you can buy an Internet card for €2, then it's €1.50 per hour.

Things to See

The premier museum, **Bonnefanten** *(☎ 329 01 90; Ave Céramique 250; adult/child 13-17 €7/6; open 11am-5pm Tues-Sun)* features medieval sculpture and contemporary art by Limburg artists. The 10th-century **Sint Servaasbasiliek** *(Keizer Karelplein, Vrijthof; adult/child 12-17 €2/0.50; open 10am-5pm, 10am-6pm July & Aug)* is barn-like and somewhat stark, but is a rich treasure house of religious artefacts.

Further south, on the Onze Lieve Vrouweplein, is **Onze Lieve Vrouwebasiliek** *(open 9am-5.30pm daily; treasury open 10am-5pm daily)*, a smaller Gothic structure where you can light candles or explore the treasury for €1.60.

Places to Stay

The closest camping ground is the posh **De Dousberg** *(☎ 343 21 71, fax 343 0556; ⓔ dousbergcamping@dousberg.nl; Dousbergweg 102; tents/adults €4.40/4.05; open Mar-Oct)*, with access to swimming pools and tennis courts. It's 700m from the **NJHC City-Hostel de Dousberg & Budget-Hotel de Dousberg** *(☎ 346 67 77, fax 346 67 55; ⓔ dousberghotel@dousberg.nl; Dousbergweg 4; dorm beds/singles/doubles €18/46.50/53.50)*. Bus No 11 runs to the front door and on to the camping ground. At night a Call-Bus from the station will get you there.

Botel *(☎ 321 9023; Maasboulevard 95; singles/doubles €34/51)* has compact rooms on an old boat on the Maas. **Hotel Le Guide** *(☎ 321 61 76, fax 325 99 13; Stationsstraat 17a; singles/doubles €55/65)* has basic rooms with bath which are decorated with plastic tulips; it is close to the station.

Places to Eat

Thanks mainly to neighbouring Belgium and Germany, Maastricht ranks high among the Dutch where cuisine is concerned. In the centre, Platielstraat is lined with restaurants and cafés. **Café van Bommel** *(☎ 321 44 00; Platielstraat 15; lunch about €6; kitchen open 11am-6pm daily)*, in a 17th-century building, is one of the best.

For cheap, filling and tasty food, **'t Witte Bruudsje** *(☎ 321 00 57; Platielstraat 12; mains about €3; open 10am-2am Sun-Thur, 10am-3am Fri-Sat)* has fresh salads, sandwiches and tapas.

Café Sjiek *(☎ 321 01 58; St Pieterstraat 13; mains about €13; kitchen open 5pm-11pm)* is a smoky and atmospheric little *eetcafé* packed with locals who reckon it's got the best food in town.

In 't Knijpke *(☎ 321 65 25; St Bernardusstraat 13; mains about €12; kitchen open 6pm-10pm)* is a restaurant, cheese cellar and film theatre rolled into one; it's fire is popular in winter. **Servaas Café** *(☎ 321 76 69; Cöversplein 10; mains about €12; kitchen open 11am-9pm)* has a relaxed ambience and great Belgian food.

Entertainment

All the cafés mentioned in the Places to Eat section stay open until 1am or 2am serving drinks. For details of music, concerts, films pick up the weekly *Week In Week Uit*, available in many cafés. If the weather's good, Vrijthof is taken over by people-watching terrace cafés. **In Den Ouden Vogelstruys** *(☎ 321 48 88; Vrijthof 15; open 9.30am-2am daily)* is housed in the city's oldest building (1309).

Across the river in Wyck, there are plenty of rustic cafés including **Take One** *(☎ 321 64 23; Rechtstraat 28; open 4pm-10pm Wed-Mon)*, a beer specialist's haven. **John Mullins** (*☎ 350 01 41; Wijckerbrugstraat 50; open until 2am or 3am*) has music, atmosphere and smooth Guinness.

Getting There & Around

Within the Netherlands, major train lines include those to Amsterdam (€25, 2½ hours, hourly) and Den Bosch (€23.80, 1½ hours, hourly). Major international connections include those to Liège in Belgium (€9.10, 30 minutes, one train hourly), Cologne in Germany (€23.60, 1½ hours, hourly) and Luxembourg City (34.50, three hours, hourly). For national information call ☎ 0900-92 92; for international information call ☎ 0900-92 96.

Stadsbus buses run local routes, as do Call-Buses (evening minibuses), which must be booked by telephone. For information or bookings for either, call ☎ 350 57 07. The main bus station is next to the train station. Bikes can be hired at **Aon de Stasie** *(☎ 321 11 00; Stationsplein 26; open 6am-noon daily)*, to the left as you exit the train station, from €7 per day.

Norway

Ruggedly beautiful Norway is Scandinavia at its purest. This most western and northern of Scandinavian countries is a realm of high mountains, deep fjords and icy blue glaciers. The mainland stretches 2000km from beach towns in the south to treeless Arctic tundra in the north. The country offers incredible wilderness hiking, year-round skiing and some of the most scenic ferry, bus and train rides imaginable. Summer days are delightfully long – indeed, in the northernmost parts, the sun doesn't set for weeks on end. In addition to the lure of the spectacular western fjords, Norway offers pleasantly low-key cities, unspoiled fishing villages and rich historical sites that include Viking ships and medieval stave churches. True adventurers will be hard-pressed to resist the draw of this last northern frontier.

Norway: the Basics

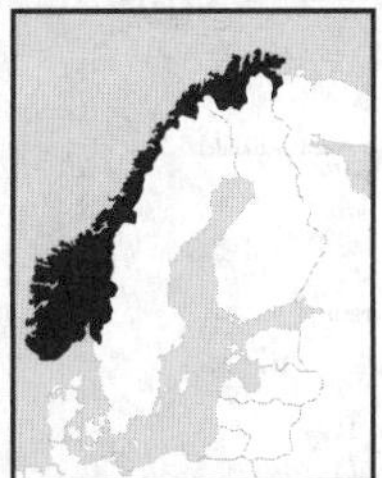

Local name Norge

Capital Oslo

Population 4.5 million

Language Norwegian

Currency krone (Nkr) = 100 øre

Avoid at all costs Hell

Evoke laughter by wondering *Er Norske barn virkelig født med ski på bena?* (Are Norwegian babies really born with skis already on?)

Facts about Norway

HISTORY

Norway's greatest impact on history was in the Viking Age, a period usually dated from the plundering of England's Lindisfarne monastery by Nordic pirates in 793. Over the next century, the Vikings made raids throughout Europe. The Viking leader Harald Hårfagre (Fairhair) unified Norway in 872. However, Norwegian naval power was finished off when Alexander III, King of Scots, defeated a Viking naval force at the Battle of Largs in 1263.

In 1397, Norway was absorbed into a union with Denmark that lasted over 400 years. Denmark's defeat in the Napoleonic Wars resulted in its ceding of Norway to Sweden in January 1814. Tired of forced unions, on 17 May 1814 a defiant Norway adopted its own constitution. In 1884, a parliamentary government was introduced and a growing nationalist movement eventually led to peaceful secession from Sweden in 1905.

Norway stayed neutral during WWI. It was attacked by the Nazis on 9 April 1940. King Håkon set up a government in exile in England and placed most of Norway's merchant fleet under the command of the Allies. Although Norway remained occupied until the end of the war, it had an active resistance movement. The royal family returned to Norway in June 1945.

Norway joined the European Free Trade Association (EFTA) in 1960, but has been reluctant to forge closer bonds with other European nations. In 1972, Norwegians voted against joining the European Community (EC) amid a divisive national debate. Sentiments continue to favour staying outside the EU.

GEOGRAPHY

Norway, occupying the western part of the Scandinavian peninsula, shares borders with Sweden, Finland and Russia. The country is long and narrow, with a coastline deeply cut by fjords – long, narrow inlets of the sea bordered by high, steep cliffs. Mountains, some capped with Europe's largest glaciers, cover more than half of the landmass. Only 3% of the country is arable.

CLIMATE

The typically rainy climate of mainland Norway is surprisingly mild for its latitude and,

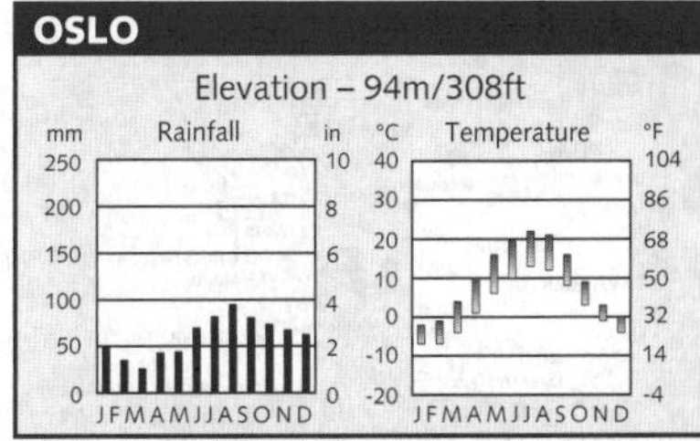

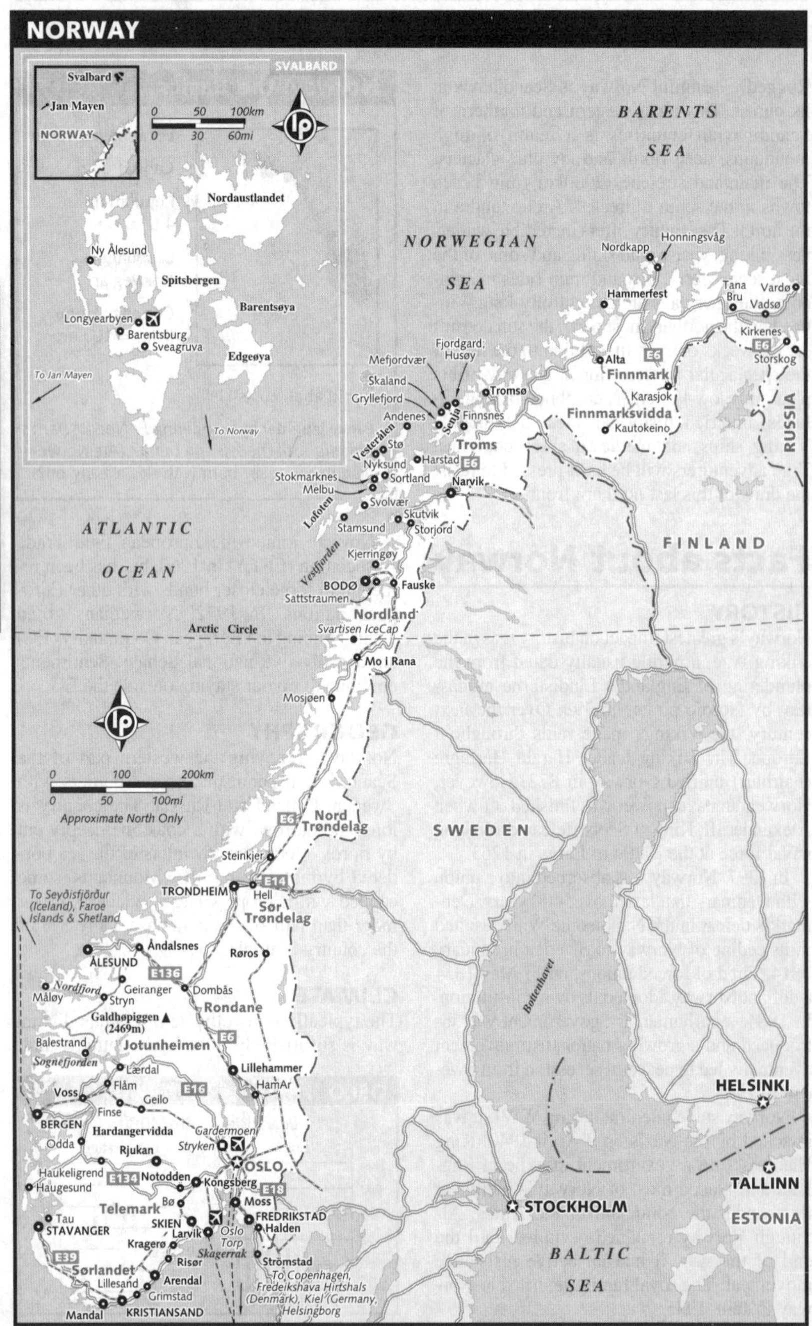
NORWAY
SVALBARD
Svalbard
Jan Mayen
NORWAY
0 50 100km
0 30 60mi
Nordaustlandet
Ny Ålesund
Spitsbergen
Barentsøya
Longyearbyen
Barentsburg
Sveagruva
Edgeøya
To Jan Mayen
To Norway
BARENTS SEA
NORWEGIAN SEA
Nordkapp
Honningsvåg
Hammerfest
Tana Bru
Vardø
Vadsø
Kirkenes
Storskog
Alta
Finnmark
Karasjok
Finnmarksvidda
Kautokeino
RUSSIA
Fjordgard; Husøy
Mefjordvær
Skaland
Gryllefjord
Tromsø
Andenes
Senja
Finnsnes
Vesterålen
Stø
Troms
Nyksund
Harstad
Stokmarknes
Sortland
Melbu
Narvik
Lofoten
Svolvær
Skutvik
Stamsund
Storjord
ATLANTIC OCEAN
FINLAND
Vestfjorden
Kjerringøy
BODØ
Fauske
Sattstraumen
Nordland
Arctic Circle
Svartisen IceCap
Mo i Rana
Mosjøen
0 100 200km
0 50 100mi
Approximate North Only
E6
Nord Trøndelag
SWEDEN
Steinkjer
TRONDHEIM
E14
Hell
To Seyðisfjörður (Iceland), Faroe Islands & Shetland
Sør Trøndelag
Åndalsnes
ÅLESUND
Røros
E136
Nordfjord
Geiranger
Måløy
Stryn
Dombås
Rondane
Galdhøpiggen (2469m)
Bottenhavet
Balestrand
Jotunheimen
Sognefjorden
Lillehammer
Lærdal
Flåm
HamAr
E16
Voss
Geilo
Finse
HELSINKI
BERGEN
Hardangervidda
Gardermoen
Odda
Stryken
Rjukan
OSLO
Haukeligrend
E134
Notodden
Kongsberg
TALLINN
Haugesund
E18
Bø
Moss
Telemark
FREDRIKSTAD
STOCKHOLM
Tau
SKIEN
Halden
ESTONIA
STAVANGER
Larvik
Oslo Torp
Kragerø
Skagerrak
E39
Risør
Strömstad
Sørlandet
Arendal
To Copenhagen, Fredeikshava Hirtshals (Denmark), Kiel (Germany), Helsingborg
Lillesand
BALTIC SEA
Grimstad
Mandal
KRISTIANSAND
NORWAY

thanks to the Gulf Stream (a relatively warm ocean current originating in the Gulf of Mexico), all its coastal ports remain ice-free throughout the year.

Average July temperatures are 16°C in the Oslo area and 11°C in the north. However, temperature extremes are also possible, even in the Arctic region.

GOVERNMENT & POLITICS

Norway is a constitutional monarchy, but it also enjoys a parliamentary democratic government.

POPULATION & PEOPLE

Norway has one of the lowest population densities in Europe. Immigration is strictly controlled and only bona fide refugees admitted.

SOCIETY & CONDUCT

Norwegians tend to be an independent and outdoor-oriented people. Most Norwegians are straightforward and easy-going, and nothing out of the ordinary is expected of visitors. As a guest in a Norwegian home, remove your shoes at the front door. Don't touch your drink before your host makes the toast *'skål'*, which you should return.

LANGUAGE

Norway has two official languages. Bokmål (Book-language) is the urban-Norwegian variety of Danish, used by more than 80% of the population. The other language is Nynorsk. It has a rural base and is the dominant language in the western fjord and central mountain districts. English is widely understood and spoken, especially in the urban areas and in most tourist destinations.

See the Language Guide at the back of the book for pronunciation guidelines and useful words and phrases in Bokmål.

Facts for the Visitor

HIGHLIGHTS

Norway's finest train trip, the 470km Oslo–Bergen railway, is a scenic journey through snow-capped mountains and the windswept Hardanger plateau.

Oslo's Bygdøy Peninsula holds a fascinating collection of explorers' ships. Highly recommended is a visit to one of the 31 remaining medieval stave churches.

Nothing typifies the country more than its glacier-carved fjords, and travelling by public ferry along these inland waterways is Norway's top sightseeing activity. The Geirangerfjord has the most spectacular waterfalls, whereas Nærøyfjorden provides the most stunning scenery in the Bergen region.

PLANNING

Norway is at its best and brightest from May to September. Late spring is a particularly pleasant time – fruit trees are in bloom, daylight hours are long, and most hostels and sights are open but uncrowded.

Midnight-sun days, when the sun never drops below the horizon, extend from 13 May to 29 July at Nordkapp and from 28 May to 14 July in Lofoten. Even southern Norway has full daylight from 4am to 11pm in midsummer.

Norway's cold dark winters are not the prime time to visit.

TOURIST OFFICES

There are tourist offices in nearly every town of any size in Norway, usually near the train station, dock or town centre. In smaller towns they may be open only during peak summer months, while in cities they're open year-round. For general brochures and books on travel in Norway, contact **Norges Turistråd** *(Norwegian Tourist Board, formerly NORTRA; ☎ 24 14 46 00, fax 24 14 46 01; e norway@ntr.no; w www.visitnorway.com; PO Box 722 Sentrum, N-0105 Oslo)*.

Offices abroad include the following:

Australia (☎ 02-6273 3444, e emb.canberra@mfa.no) Royal Norwegian Embassy, 17 Hunter St, Yarralumla, ACT 2600
Denmark (☎ 33 19 36 09, e denmark@ntr.no) Norges Turistråd, Amaliegade 39, DK-1256 Copenhagen K
France (☎ 01-53 23 00 50, e france@ntr.no) Office National du Tourisme de Norvége, PB 47, F-75366 Paris
Germany (☎ 0180-500 1548, e germany@ntr.no) Norwegisches Fremdenverkehrsamt, Postfach 113317, D-20433 Hamburg
Sweden (☎ 08-791 8300, e sweden@ntr.no) Norges Turistråd, PO Box 3363, SE-10367 Stockholm
UK (☎ 0906-302 2003, e greatbritain@ntr.no) Norwegian Tourist Board, 5th Floor, Charles House, 5 Lower Regent St, London, SW1Y 4LR (no personal callers)
USA & Canada (☎ 212-885 9700, e usa@ntr.no) Norwegian Tourist Board, 655 Third Ave, Suite 1810, New York, NY 10017

VISAS & DOCUMENTS

Citizens of the USA, Canada, the UK, Ireland, Australia and New Zealand need a valid passport, but do not need a visa for stays of less than three months. The same is true for EU and EEA countries, most of Latin America and most Commonwealth countries (except South Africa and several other African and Pacific countries).

A HI (Hostelling International) card saves Nkr25 per overnight stay in hostels. Students with an International Student Identity Card (ISIC) or an International Youth Travel Card (IYTC) can get discounts on transport, museum admission and meals in some student restaurants.

NORWAY

EMBASSIES & CONSULATES

Norwegian Embassies

There's an up-to-date listing of Norwegian embassies and consulates at www.embassies.mfa.no.

Australia (☎ 02-6273 3444, emb.canberra@mfa.no) 17 Hunter St, Yarralumla, ACT 2600
Canada (☎ 613-238 6571, emb.ottawa@mfa.no) Royal Bank Centre, 90 Sparks St, Suite 532, Ottawa, Ontario K1P 5B4
Denmark (☎ 33 14 01 2, emb.copenhagen@mfa.no) Amaliegade 39, DK-1256 Copenhagen K
Finland (☎ 09-171234, emb.helsinki@mfa.no) Rehbinderintie 17, FIN-00150 Helsinki
France (☎ 01-53 67 04 00, emb.paris@mfa.no) 28 Rue Bayard, F-75008 Paris
Germany (☎ 030-505 050, emb.berlin@mfa.no) Rauchstrasse 1, D-10787 Berlin
Ireland (☎ 01-662 1800, emb.dublin@mfa.no) 34 Molesworth St, Dublin 2
Sweden (☎ 08-665 6340, emb.stockholm@mfa.no) Skarpögatan 4, SE-11593 Stockholm
UK (☎ 020-7591 5500, emb.london@mfa.no) 25 Belgrave Square, London, SW1X 8QD
USA (☎ 202-333 6000, emb.washington@mfa.no) 2720 34th St NW, Washington DC 20008

Embassies & Consulates in Norway

Australia (☎ 22 47 91 70) Jernbanetorget 2, N-0106 Oslo
Canada (☎ 22 99 53 00) Wergelandsveien 7, N-0167 Oslo
Denmark (☎ 22 54 08 00) Olav Kyrres gate 7, N-0273 Oslo
Finland (☎ 22 43 04 00) Thomas Heftyes gate 1, N-0264 Oslo
France (☎ 23 28 46 00) Drammensveien 69, N-0271 Oslo
Germany (☎ 22 27 54 00) Oscars gate 45, N-0258 Oslo
Ireland (☎ 22 01 72 00) Haakon VIIs gate 1, N-0244 Oslo
New Zealand (☎ 66 77 53 30) Billingstadsletta 19B, Postboks 113, N-1376 Billingstad
Russia (☎ 22 55 32 78) Drammensveien 74, N-0271 Oslo
Sweden (☎ 24 11 42 00) Nobelsgata 16A, N-0244 Oslo
UK (☎ 23 13 27 00, britemb@online.no) Thomas Heftyes gate 8, N-0264 Oslo
USA (☎ 22 44 85 50) Drammensveien 18, N-0255 Oslo

CUSTOMS

Alcohol is expensive in Norway, so you might want to bring in your duty-free allotment: 1L of spirits and 1L of wine (or 2L of wine), plus 2L of beer. European (EEA)/non-European residents may also import 200/400 cigarettes duty-free.

MONEY

Currency

One Norwegian krone equals 100 øre. There are 50-øre and one-, five-, 10- and 20-kroner coins, while bills come in denominations of 50, 100, 200, 500 and 1000 kroner.

Exchange Rates

The following exchange rates prevailed at the time of printing:

country	unit		kroner
Australia	A$1	=	Nkr4.20
Canada	C$1	=	Nkr4.80
Eurozone	€1	=	Nkr7.40
Iceland	Ikr100	=	Nkr0.08
New Zealand	NZ$1	=	Nkr3.70
Sweden	Skr1	=	Nkr0.81
UK	UK£1	=	Nkr11.70
USA	US$1	=	Nkr7.50

Exchanging Money

Some post offices and all banks will exchange major foreign currencies and accept all travellers cheques, which command a better exchange rate than cash by about 2%. Post offices charge a service fee of Nkr10 per travellers cheque (minimum Nkr20, maximum Nkr100) and Nkr30 for any size cash transaction. Some banks, including Nordea and Den Norske Bank, have slightly higher fees but similar exchange rates.

ATMs are widespread; most accept major credit cards and Cirrus and Plus bank cards.

Visa, Eurocard, MasterCard, American Express and Diners Club cards are widely accepted throughout Norway. Credit cards can be used to buy train tickets but are not accepted on domestic ferries (apart from Hurtigruten).

Costs

Norway can be very expensive. If you only stay in camping grounds and prepare your own meals you might squeak by for Nkr180 a day. If you plan to stay at hostels, breakfast at a bakery, lunch at an inexpensive restaurant and shop at a grocery store for dinner, you should be able to get by for Nkr300 a day. Day trips, entertainment, alcohol, even a couple of soft drinks are going to cost extra.

Once your daily needs are met, you'll need to add transport costs. If you've got a rail pass these costs will be low. Trying to cover the whole country by bus and ferry can be quite expensive, as the distances are great.

Tipping & Bargaining

Service charges and tips are included in restaurant bills and taxi fares, with no additional tip expected. Bargaining (and bargains) are rare.

Taxes & Refunds

The 24% MVA (equivalent of Value-Added Tax in many countries or sales tax in the USA), locally known as MOMS, is normally included in marked prices. In shops marked 'Tax Free for Tourists', goods exceeding Nkr308 are eligible for an MVA refund.

POST & COMMUNICATIONS

Mail can be received c/o poste restante at almost all post offices in Norway.

Norway has no telephone area codes; when making any domestic call all eight digits must be dialled. Card phones, which can be convenient if you have a lot of calls to make, are generally found adjacent to coin phones. Cards can be purchased at post offices and the ubiquitous Narvesen and MIX kiosks. Credit cards can also be used in many card phones.

The country code for Norway is ☎ 47. To make an international call from Norway, dial ☎ 00, then the appropriate country code, area code and number you're calling.

Many public libraries have free online computers, but access for travellers may be restricted. Internet cafés are in the larger cities.

DIGITAL RESOURCES

General and tourism-related information about Norway can be accessed on the Internet at **W** www.visitnorway.com. The most useful tourist-oriented website for western Norway is **W** www.fjordnorway.com. For tours, attractions and accommodation throughout the country, check out **W** www.touristguide.no.

BOOKS

For extensive travel in the country, the best all-round travel guide is Lonely Planet's *Norway* guidebook. To help with communication, pick up LP's *Scandinavian phrasebook*, which includes a section on Norwegian.

An amusing cultural direction is offered in *Culture Shock! Norway: A Guide to Customs & Etiquette* by Elizabeth Su-Dale.

WOMEN TRAVELLERS

Norway is a relatively safe country for women travellers. The main Norwegian feminist organisation is **Kvinnefronten** *(☎ 22 37 60 54; e kvinnefronten@online.no; Holsts gate 1, N-0473 Oslo)*. Women who have been attacked or abused can call the **Krisesenter** *(Oslo ☎ 22 37 47 00, nationwide ☎ 112)*.

GAY & LESBIAN TRAVELLERS

Public displays of affection are not common practice. Gay and lesbian travellers can find gay entertainment spots in the larger cities. For gay issues and activities, contact **Landsforeningen for Lesbisk og Homofil frigjøring** *(LLH; ☎ 22 36 19 48; e llh@c2i.net; St Olavs plass 2, N-0165 Oslo)*.

DISABLED TRAVELLERS

Norway can be a challenging place for disabled travellers; those with special needs should plan ahead. The Norwegian Tourist Board's main accommodation brochure and the hostel association's handbook both list nationwide accommodation that is wheelchair accessible. Most, though not all, trains have coaches that are designed for wheelchair users. **Norges Handikapforbund** *(☎ 22 17 02 55; W www.nhf.no; Schweigaards gate 12, Postboks 9217 Grønland, N-0134 Oslo)* publishes an English brochure with further information.

SENIOR TRAVELLERS

Seniors aged 60 to 67 are often entitled to discounts on museum admissions, air tickets and other transport.

Emergencies

In Norway, dial the following numbers for emergency assistance: ☎ 110 (fire), ☎ 112 (police), ☎ 113 (ambulance) and ☎ 81 00 05 05 (NAF breakdown recovery assistance, 24-hour service).

DANGERS & ANNOYANCES

Sadly, Norway is no longer as safe as it was and robbery is becoming more common; watch your wallet at all times, especially at night.

BUSINESS HOURS

Business hours are generally 9am or 10am to 4pm or 5pm Monday to Friday and 10am to 2pm Saturday, though some shops stay open to around 7pm or 8pm on Thursday.

You should be aware that many museums have short hours (11am to 3pm is quite common), which can make things tight for sightseeing. On Sunday, most shops – including bakeries, supermarkets and some restaurants – are closed.

PUBLIC HOLIDAYS & SPECIAL EVENTS

The following public holidays are observed in Norway: New Year's Day (1 January), Maundy Thursday (Thursday before Easter), Good Friday and Easter Monday (March/April), Labour Day (1 May), Constitution Day (17 May), Ascension Day (40th day after Easter), Whit Monday (eighth Monday after Easter), Christmas Day (25 December) and Boxing Day (26 December).

Constitution Day is Norway's biggest holiday, with events throughout the country and many Norwegians taking to the street in traditional folk costumes. The biggest celebration is in Oslo, where marching bands and thousands of schoolchildren parade down Karl Johans gate to the Royal Palace to be greeted by the royal family.

Midsummer's Eve, which is celebrated by bonfires on the beach, is generally observed on 23 June, St Hans day. The Sami (Lapps) hold their most colourful celebrations at Easter in Karasjok and Kautokeino, with reindeer races, *joik* (traditional chanting) concerts and other festivities.

On 13 December, Christian children celebrate the feast of Santa Lucia by dressing in white and holding a candlelit procession.

ACTIVITIES

Hiking

Norway has some of northern Europe's best hiking, ranging from easy trails in the forests around the cities to long treks through the mountains. Due to deep winter snows, hiking in many areas is seasonal; in the highlands, it's often limited to the period of late June to September. The most popular wilderness hiking areas are Jotunheimen, Rondane and Hardangervidda, but many other areas are just as attractive (or better). For more information on hiking and climbing, contact the Norwegian Mountain Touring Association, **Den Norske Turistforening** *(DNT; ☎ 22 82 28 22; W www.turistforeningen.no; Postboks 7 Sentrum, N-0101 Oslo)*.

Skiing

'Ski' is a Norwegian word, and Norwegians make a credible claim to having invented the sport. You're seldom far from a ski run. Norway has thousands of kilometres of maintained cross-country ski trails and scores of resorts with excellent downhill runs. The Holmenkollen area near Oslo, Geilo on the Oslo–Bergen railway line, and Lillehammer and the surrounding Gudbrandsdalen region are just a few of the more popular spots.

Rafting

Norway's wild and scenic rivers are ideal for rafting, and rafting trips range from short, Class II doddles to Class III and IV adventures and rollicking Class V punishment. **Norges Padleforbund** *(☎ 21 02 98 35; W www.padling.no; Service boks 1, Ullevål stadion, N-0840 Oslo)* provides a comprehensive list of rafting operators.

Fishing

Norway's salmon runs are legendary – in June and July, you can't beat the rivers of Finnmark. No licence is required for saltwater fishing. In fresh water, a national licence (available from post offices for Nkr90 to Nkr180) is mandatory and often a local licence (available from tourist offices, sports shops, hotels and camping grounds for Nkr50 to Nkr300 per day) will also be required.

WORK

Norway has low unemployment, so foreigners can sometimes land a job, particularly in the poorly paid service industry – but a command of Norwegian is generally required and preference is given to Scandinavians.

Norway grants citizens of other EEA countries (essentially EU and Scandinavian countries) the right to look for work for three months without obtaining a permit. Those who find work may remain in Norway for the duration of their employment.

Other foreigners must apply for a work permit through the Norwegian embassy or consulate in their home country before entering Norway.

ACCOMMODATION

Camping & Cabins

Norway has around 1000 camping grounds. Tent space costs from Nkr50 at the most basic sites to Nkr180 in Oslo and Bergen, and many camping grounds also rent simple cabins from about Nkr250 a day. The cabins often have basic cooking facilities, though linen and blankets are rarely provided, so you'll need your own sleeping bag. **Reiselivsbedriftenes Landsforening** *(☎ 23 08 86 20; ⓔ britt.larsen@rbl.no; Postboks 5465 Majorstua, N-0305 Oslo)* publishes a free annual camping guide that lists many camping grounds.

Norway has an 'everyman's right' rule *(allemannsretten)* dating back 1000 years. This allows you to pitch a tent anywhere in the wilderness for two nights, as long as you camp at least 150m from the nearest house or cottage and leave no trace of your stay. From 15 April to 15 September lighting a fire in the proximity of woodlands is strictly forbidden.

The Norwegian Mountain Touring Association, **Den Norske Turistforening** *(DNT; ☎ 22 82 28 22; ⓦ www.turistforeningen.no; Postboks 7 Sentrum, N-0101 Oslo)*, maintains an extensive network of mountain huts a day's hike apart in much of Norway's mountain country. These range from unstaffed huts with just a few beds to large staffed lodges with more than 100 beds and generally superb service. At unstaffed huts, the keys must be picked up in advance at DNT offices in nearby towns; at staffed huts hikers simply show up – no-one is sent away, even if there's only floor space left. Nightly fees for DNT members/ nonmembers in a room with one to three beds are Nkr170/220, but cheaper options may also be available. Basic membership for one calendar year will set you back adult/concession Nkr365/175.

Hostels

Norway has 72 *vandrerhjem* (hostels) affiliated with Hostelling International (HI). Some are quite comfortable lodge-style facilities open year-round, while others operate out of school dorms in summer only. The cost for a dorm bed varies from Nkr90 to Nkr250 per person, with breakfast generally included at the higher-priced hostels. Most hostels also have single, double and family rooms at higher prices. Guests must bring their own sleeping sheets and pillowcases, although most hostels hire sleeping sheets for Nkr40 to Nkr60. From May to September it's best to call ahead and make reservations.

Prices given throughout the Norway chapter are for hostel members with an HI card; nonmembers pay Nkr25 extra per night.

Hostels that don't provide breakfast in their rate usually offer a buffet-style breakfast for an additional Nkr40 to Nkr70. Some also offer dinner for around Nkr70 to Nkr130 and nearly all hostels have kitchens where guests can cook their own meals.

You can pick up a brochure in English listing all hostels from tourist offices, or get the detailed 52-page *Opplev Norge med Norske Vandrerhjem* free at hostels.

The Norwegian Hostelling Association is **Norske Vandrerhjem** *(☎ 23 13 93 00, fax 23 13 93 50; ⓦ www.vandrerhjem.no; Torggata 1, N-0181 Oslo)*. You can book hostels via the website.

Private Rooms & Pensions

Private rooms, usually bookable through tourist offices, average Nkr225/350 for singles/ doubles and breakfast isn't normally included. Many towns also have pensions and guesthouses with singles in the Nkr270 to Nkr400 range, but linen and/or breakfast will only be included at the higher-priced places. A couple of useful listings on the Internet are ⓦ www.bbnorway.com and ⓦ www.bedandbreakfast.no.

Along highways, you may see *Rom* signs, which indicate informal accommodation for around Nkr100 to Nkr250 (without breakfast).

Hotels

Although normal hotel prices are high, most hotels substantially reduce their rates on weekends and in the summer season, which are slow periods for business travel. Nationwide chains like Rainbow Hotels and Rica offer particularly good summer and weekend deals. With Rainbow, you'll get the lowest rates by buying a Scan+ Hotel Pass (sold at hotels for Nkr90) – it usually pays for itself on the first night; doubles start at Nkr295 per person.

One important consideration in this land of sky-high food prices is that hotels usually include an all-you-can-eat buffet breakfast, while most pensions do not.

FOOD & DRINK

Norwegian specialities include grilled or smoked *laks* (salmon), *gravat laks* (marinated salmon), *reker* (boiled shrimp), *torsk* (cod) and other seafood. Expect to see *geitost*, a sweet brown goat cheese (*Gudbrandsdalsost* is a popular brand) and *sild* (pickled herring) alongside the breads and cereals included in breakfast buffets at hostels and hotels. One of the finest Norwegian desserts is *moltebær syltetøy* (warm cloudberry jam) with ice cream – it's fantastic!

If Norway has a national drink, it's coffee (taken black and strong). Beer can be purchased in supermarkets or at a *ølutsalg* (beer outlet), but wine and spirits are only available at government liquor stores (Vinmonopolet).

ENTERTAINMENT

Although Norway isn't known for having a riveting entertainment scene, you can find reasonable nightlife in the bigger cities. Expect to dig deep into your pockets – cover charges for nightclubs average Nkr70.

Getting There & Away

AIR

SAS, British Airways, KLM, Air France, Lufthansa, Swiss International Air Line, Alitalia, Finnair and Icelandair link Oslo's Gardermoen airport with major European and North American cities. The budget airline Ryanair flies from both London Stansted and Glasgow Prestwick to Oslo Torp.

LAND

The E6 Ekspressen bus from Copenhagen to Oslo (Dkr245/345, 9¼ hours, twice daily) runs via Malmö in Sweden; the lower fare is valid Monday to Thursday. Trains from Copenhagen to Oslo (from Dkr330, from 8¾ hours, twice daily) require changing in Gothenburg; lowest fares require booking at least seven days in advance.

In summer, regular bus services are run by the Finnish company **Eskelisen Lapin Linjat** *(Finland ☎ 016-342 2160; w www.eskelisen-lapinlinjat.com)* serve all routes to Finland.

Russia has a short border with northern Norway, and buses run three times weekly between Kirkenes and Murmansk.

For Sweden, **Nor-Way Bussekspress** *(Norway ☎ 815 44 444; w www.nor-way.no)* runs express buses between Oslo, Gothenburg (Skr175/255, 4¼ hours, six daily) and Malmö (Skr280/400, 8½ hours, five daily). Three or four daily buses run between Stockholm and Oslo (Skr300/425, eight hours). The lower fares are valid Monday to Thursday. There are also buses between Skellefteå and Bodø (Skr480, 8¾ hours, once daily except Saturday), and between Umeå and Mo i Rana (Skr244, 7½ to 8¾ hours, once daily).

Daily trains run from Stockholm (from Skr340, seven hours), Gothenburg (from Skr190, four hours) and Malmö (from Skr450, 8¼ hours) to Oslo; cheapest tickets must be booked at least seven days in advance. Journeys from Östersund to Trondheim via Storlien require changing trains at the border. **Tågkompaniet** *(Sweden ☎ 08-629 5050; e info@connex.se)* trains run between Stockholm and Narvik (Skr1307, 18¾ hours, once daily).

SEA

Denmark

DFDS Seaways *(Denmark ☎ 33 42 30 00, Norway ☎ 22 41 90 90; w www.dfdsseaways.com)* runs daily overnight ferries between Copenhagen and Oslo, with the cheapest cabin fare ranging from Dkr525 to Dkr885; cheapest fares are Sunday to Thursday from 4 November to 31 January. With a student card, cabin fares are discounted by 25%. You can take advantage of an excellent dinner buffet en route.

Color Line *(Denmark ☎ 99 56 19 77, Norway ☎ 22 94 44 00; w www.colorline.no)* runs ferries between Hirtshals and Kristiansand, the route with the shortest connection (from 4½ hours) and the most frequent service (two to five sailings daily) between Norway and Denmark. Color Line also operates once or twice daily between Frederikshavn and Larvik (from 6¼ hours) and once daily between Hirtshals and Oslo (eight hours). Passenger fares range from Dkr170 to Dkr360.

NORWAY

Fjord Line *(Denmark 97 96 30 00, Norway ☎ 55 54 88 00 or ☎ 815 33 500; W www.fjord line.com)* sails from Hanstholm to Egersund (from 6¾ hours), once or twice daily through most of the year. Some sailings continue to Bergen. Hanstholm–Egersund fares range from Dkr260 (on some days from October to April) to Dkr550 (all weekends in July). Cabins start at Dkr100 per person (reclining chairs are from Dkr50).

Stena Line *(Denmark ☎ 96 20 02 00, Norway ☎ 23 17 91 00 or ☎ 02010; W www.stena line.com)* operates ferries between Frederikshavn and Oslo daily (except Monday from 2 September to 10 June), taking 12 hours. Cabin fares start at Dkr90 throughout the year.

Germany

Color Line *(Germany ☎ 0431-7300 300, Norway ☎ 22 94 44 00; W www.colorline.no)* operates a daily ferry between Kiel and Oslo. Departures are at 2pm from Kiel and 1.30pm from Oslo; the trip takes from 19½ hours. From 14 June to 18 August (high season), reclining chairs start at €88. The cheapest two-person cabin ranges from €84 at midweek in the low season (19 August to 13 June) to €116 on weekends in the high season (14 June to 18 August).

Iceland & the Faroe Islands

Smyril Line *(Iceland ☎ 587 1919, Faroes ☎ 345900, Norway ☎ 55 32 09 70; W www.smyril-line.com)* runs once weekly from 18 May to 7 September between Bergen and Seyðisfjörður (Iceland), via Lerwick (Shetland) and the Faroe Islands. One-way low/high-season fares to Bergen begin at Dkr630/870 from Tórshavn in the Faroes and cost Ikr15,990/22,790 from Seyðisfjörður. High season is mid-June to 31 July, plus some sailings in August. The boat arrives at/departs Bergen at noon/3pm on Tuesday. It takes 23 to 26½ hours from Tórshavn and 43 hours to five days to/from Seyðisfjörður.

Sweden

DFDS Seaways *(Sweden ☎ 042-266000, Norway ☎ 22 41 90 90; W www.dfdsseaways.com)* runs daily overnight ferries between Helsingborg and Oslo, with fares ranging from Skr575 to Skr975. The trip takes 14 hours, with the boat leaving Helsingborg at 7pm northbound and Oslo at 5pm southbound.

DFDS Seaways also sails between Gothenburg and Kristiansand three days weekly year-round. Passenger/car fares start at Skr150/240 and the journey takes from seven hours.

Two to six times daily, **Color Line** *(Sweden ☎ 0526-62000; W www.colorline.no)* does the 2½-hour run between Strömstad (Sweden) and Sandefjord (Norway). From 28 June to 11 August, passengers/cars pay Skr188/206 and, at other times, Skr153/159.

UK

Fjord Line *(UK ☎ 0191-296 1313, Norway ☎ 815 33 500; W www.fjordline.com)* sails from Newcastle to Bergen, via Haugesund and Stavanger, at least twice weekly. The trip from Newcastle to Bergen takes from 20½ hours. Passenger fares range from UK£50 in winter to UK£110 on summer weekends. Pleasant cabins are available with extra charges starting at UK£10; reclining seats (available 21 March to 20 September only) are included in the fare. Car/motorcycle fares start at UK£60/30.

Smyril Line *(UK ☎ 01595-690845; W www.smyril-line.com)* sails between Lerwick (Shetland) and Bergen, from 20 May to 2 September, taking from 11½ hours. Couchette fares in low/high season are UK£42/59 and cars up to 5m long cost UK£34/50. See also the earlier Iceland & the Faroe Islands section.

DFDS Seaways *(UK ☎ 08705 333000, Norway ☎ 38 17 17 60; W www.dfdsseaways.com)* sails year-round between Newcastle and Kristiansand and takes from 16½ hours. Return fares start at UK£104 for foot passengers and UK£359 for four people in a car.

Getting Around

Public transport in Norway is efficient, with trains, buses and ferries timed to link effectively. The handy *NSB Togruter*, available free at train stations, has rail schedules and information on connecting buses. Boat and bus departures vary with the season and the day, so pick up the latest *ruteplan* (timetables) from regional tourist offices. The Norwegian Tourist Board also publishes a free annual national transport timetable.

AIR

Norway has nearly 50 airports with scheduled commercial flights, from Ny Ålesund (Svalbard) in the north to Kristiansand in the south. Air travel is worth considering, even by budget travellers, due to the great distances involved in overland travel.

Norway's three main domestic airlines are SAS (W www.scandinavian.net), Braathens (W www.braathens.no) and Widerøe (W www.wideroe.no).

BUS

Norway has an extensive bus network, and long-distance buses are quite comfortable. Fares are based on distance, averaging Nkr140 for the first 100km. Many bus companies offer child, student, senior, group and family discounts of 25% to 50% – always ask.

The dominant company, **Nor-Way Bussekspress** *(☎ 815 44 444; W www.nor-way.no)*, operates a far-reaching network of modern express buses, with routes connecting every main city from Mandal in the south to Alta in the north. Nor-Way Bussekspress offers a bus pass covering travel on all its routes for 21 consecutive days at a cost of Nkr2300.

In Nordland, several Togbuss (train–bus) routes offer half price to Eurail, InterRail and ScanRail pass holders. They run between Fauske and Bodø, Narvik, Tromsø, Svolvær and Harstad. To/from the western fjords, between Oslo and Åndalsnes, Ålesund, Molde, Måløy, and various other routes in southern Norway, InterRail and ScanRail passes get half-price bus tickets.

TRAIN

Norway has an excellent, though somewhat limited, national rail system. Almost all railway lines are operated by **NSB** *(Norges Statsbaner or Norwegian State Railways; ☎ 815 00 888; W www.nsb.no)*. The main lines connect Oslo with Stavanger, Bergen, Åndalsnes and Bodø; there are also lines between Sweden and Oslo, Trondheim and Narvik.

The Norway Rail Pass, which allows unlimited train travel within the country, can be purchased either before or after you arrive in Norway. Prices for 2nd-class travel are US$146/146/202 for three/four/five days travel within one month.

CAR & MOTORCYCLE

The **Road User Information Centre** *(☎ 175)* can tell you about the latest road conditions throughout the country.

For a full list of ferry schedules, fares and reservation phone numbers, grab the latest copy of *Rutebok for Norge* (Nkr210), available in larger bookshops and Narvesen kiosks. For more motoring information, contact the national automobile club, **Norges Automobil-Forbund** *(NAF; main office ☎ 22 34 14 00; Storgata 2, N-0105 Oslo)*.

Major car-rental companies, such as Hertz, Avis and Europcar, have offices at airports and in city centres. The walk-in rate for a compact car with 200km free is about Nkr1050 a day, including MVA and insurance.

BICYCLE

Given its great distances, hilly terrain and narrow roads, Norway is not ideally suited for extensive touring by bicycle. The *Sykkelguide* series of booklets have maps and English text; they're available from larger tourist offices for Nkr120 each.

HITCHING

Hitching isn't terribly common. One approach is to ask for rides from truck drivers at ferry terminals and petrol stations.

BOAT

An extensive network of ferries and express boats links Norway's offshore islands, coastal towns and fjord districts. For more than a century, Norway's legendary coastal steamer, *Hurtigruten* *(☎ 810 30 000; e booking@ovds.no)*, has been the lifeline linking the fishing villages and towns scattered along the western and northern coasts.

LOCAL TRANSPORT

Cities and towns in Norway are served by public buses and local ferries.

Taxis are readily available at train stations; daytime fares are Nkr26.80 flag fall and Nkr12 per kilometre. Rates are 21% to 45% higher at night, on weekends and on holidays.

Oslo

pop 508,726

It may be a European capital, but Oslo remains low-key, casual and manageable, exuding a laid-back tranquillity that's suitable for the home of the Nobel Peace Prize. This pacific city dominates the head of the Oslofjord, an inlet of the Skagerrak. Just outside its array of good museums, parks and statues lies Nordmarka, an extensive forest crisscrossed by hiking and skiing trails.

Founded by Harald Hardråda in 1048, Oslo is the oldest of Scandinavia's capitals. Levelled by fire in 1624, the city was rebuilt in brick and stone by King Christian IV, who modestly renamed it Christiania. It Oslo-fied again in 1925 and has flourished as Norway's capital.

Orientation

Oslo's central train station (Oslo Sentralstasjon, or 'Oslo S') is at the eastern end of the city centre. From there the main street, Karl Johans gate, leads through the heart of the city to the Royal Palace. The brick-built Rådhus (City Hall) is located between Karl Johans gate and the harbour.

Most central city sights, including the harbourfront and Akershus Fortress, are within a 15-minute walk of Karl Johans gate, as are the majority of Oslo's hotels and pensions.

Information

Tourist Offices Near the harbour and west of Rådhus, **Oslo Promotion** *(☎ 23 11 78 80, fax 22 83 81 50; W www.visitoslo.com; Brynjulf Bulls plass 1; open Mon-Fri Oct-Mar, Mon-Sat Apr, May & Sept, daily June & Aug)* has tourist information for Oslo. It also maintains a **tourist information window** *(Oslo S; open Mon-Sat, daily May-Sept)* at the central train station.

The staff at **Use-It** *(☎ 22 41 51 32; W www.unginfo.oslo.no; Møllergata 3; open Mon-Fri)*, the youth information office, can give you the lowdown on what's happening in and around Oslo and provide advice on everything.

Money You can change money at the **airport bank** *(Gardermoen airport departure hall; open 5.30am-8pm Mon-Fri, 5.30am-6pm Sat, 6.30am-8pm Sun)*, the **post office** *(street level, Oslo S; open 7am-6pm Mon-Fri, 9am-3pm Sat)*, **Forex** *(Oslo S; open 9am-6pm Mon-Fri)* and **Nordea bank** *(Oslo S; open 7am-7pm Mon-Fri, 8am-5pm Sat & Sun)*, near the airport train platform. ATMs abound.

If you're changing a small amount, you'll usually get the best deal from **American Express** *(Fridtjof Nansens plass 6; open 9am-4.30pm Mon-Fri Jan-Dec, 10am-3pm Sat Jan-Dec, 11am-3pm Sun July & early Aug)*, north of the Rådhus.

Post & Communications The **main post office** *(Dronningens gate 15; open 9am-5pm Mon-Fri)* handles all postal requirements. To receive mail, have it sent to Poste Restante, Oslo Sentrum Postkontor, Dronningens gate 15, N-0107 Oslo.

Check your email at **Coffee & Juice Netcafe** *(Nedre Slotts gate 12; open 10am-1am Mon-Sat, noon-midnight Sun)* or **Studenten Nett-Café** *(Karl Johans gate 45; open noon-8pm Tues-Sat, noon-10pm Sun & Mon)*; both charge Nkr30/55 per 30/60 minutes.

Travel Agencies Others can make arrangements for you, but **Kilroy Travels** *(☎ 02633; Nedre Slottsgate 23)* specialises in student and youth travel. You'll find a handful of travel agencies near the Rådhus, including the American Express office.

Medical & Emergency Services Dial ☎ 112 for police and ☎ 113 for ambulance. Jernbanetorget Apotek, opposite Oslo S, is a 24-hour pharmacy. The medical clinic **Oslo Kommunale Legevakten** *(☎ 22 11 80 80; Storgata 40)* provides 24-hour emergency services.

City Centre

Oslo's twin-towered red-brick **Rådhus** *(City Hall; ☎ 22 46 16 00; Fridtjof Nansens plass; adult/child Nkr30/15, free Sept-May; open 9am-5pm daily May-Aug, 9am-4pm daily Sept-Apr)* features wooden reliefs depicting scenes from Norse mythology.

Nasjonalgalleriet *(National Gallery; ☎ 22 20 04 04; Universitetsgata 13; admission free; open 10am-6pm Mon, Wed & Fri, 10am-8pm Thur, 10am-4pm Sat, 11am-4pm Sun year-round)* houses the nation's largest collection of Norwegian art. Some of Munch's best-known works are on display, including *The Scream*, which created a stir when it was brazenly stolen (and later recovered) in 1994. There's also a respectable collection of other European art, including works by Gauguin, Cézanne, Picasso and Monet.

The highly recommended **Historisk Museet** *(Historical Museum; ☎ 22 85 99 12; Frederiks gate 2; admission free; open 10am-4pm Tues-Sun mid-May–mid-Sept, 11am-4pm Tues-Sun mid-Sept–mid-May)* consists of three museums under a single roof. On the ground floor, the National Antiquities Collection has exceptional displays of Viking-era

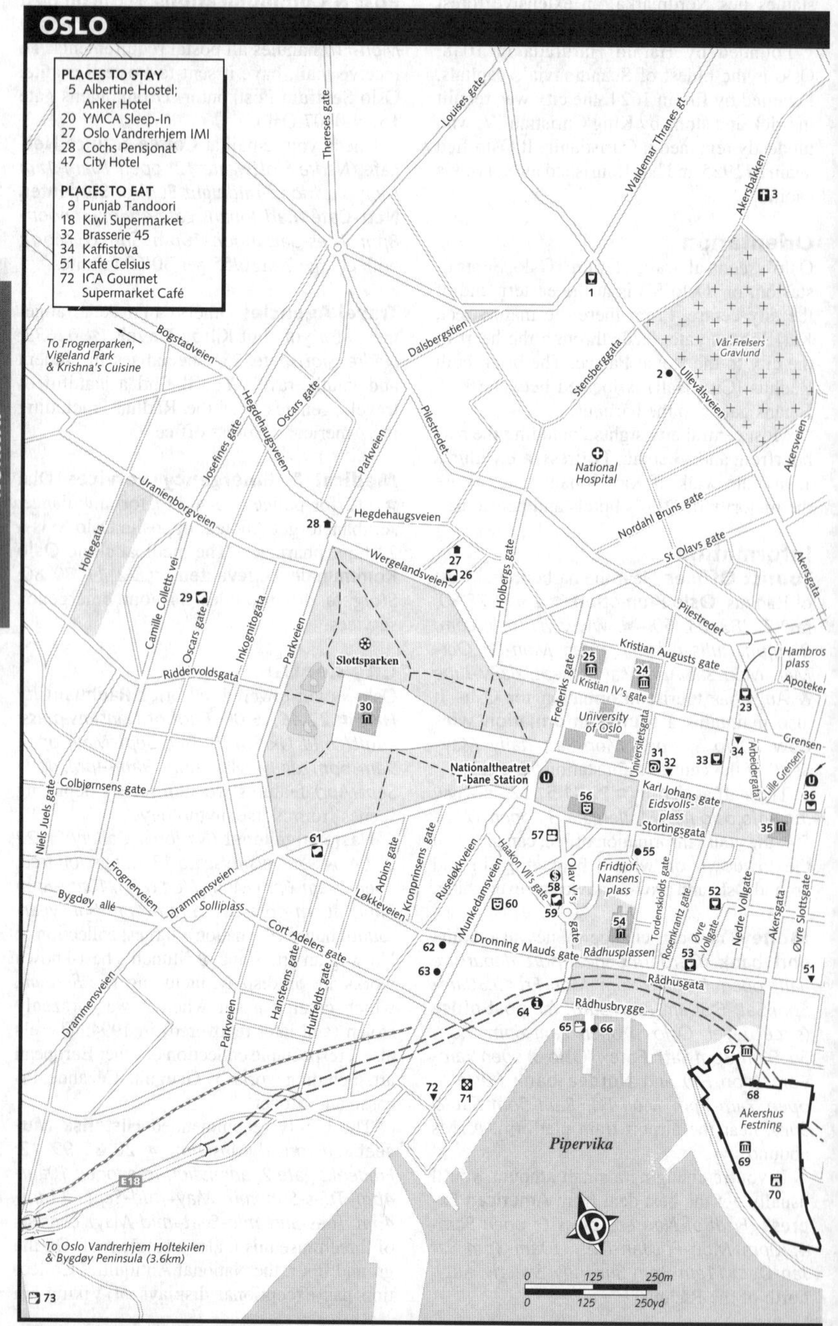

OSLO
PLACES TO STAY
5 Albertine Hostel; Anker Hotel
20 YMCA Sleep-In
27 Oslo Vandrerhjem IMI
28 Cochs Pensjonat
47 City Hotel
PLACES TO EAT
9 Punjab Tandoori
18 Kiwi Supermarket
32 Brasserie 45
34 Kaffistova
51 Kafé Celsius
72 ICA Gourmet Supermarket Café
To Frognerparken, Vigeland Park & Krishna's Cuisine
To Oslo Vandrerhjem Holtekilen & Bygdøy Peninsula (3.6km)
Thereses gate
Louises gate
Waldemar Thranes gt
Akersbakken
Dalsbergstien
Stensberggata
Ullevålsveien
Vår Frelsers Gravlund
Akersveien
National Hospital
Nordahl Bruns gate
St Olavs gate
Akersgata
Pilestredet
Bogstadveien
Hegdehaugsveien
Oscars gate
Josefines gate
Parkveien
Uranienborgveien
Holtegata
Camille Colletts vei
Inkognitogata
Wergelandsveien
Holbergs gate
Slottsparken
Ridderyoldsgata
Frederiks gate
Kristian Augusts gate
Kristian IV's gate
CJ Hambros plass
Apoteker
University of Oslo
Universitetsgata
Grensen
Arbeidergata
Lille Grensen
Nationaltheatret T-bane Station
Karl Johans gate
Eidsvolls-plass
Stortingsgata
Colbjørnsens gate
Niels Juels gate
Frognerveien
Bygdøy allé
Drammensveien
Solliplass
Arbins gate
Kronprinsens gate
Ruseløkkveien
Løkkeveien
Munkedamsveien
Haakon VII's gate
Olav V's gate
Fridtjof Nansens plass
Tordenskiolds gate
Rosenkrantz gate
Øvre Vollgate
Nedre Vollgate
Akersgata
Øvre Slottsgate
Cort Adelers gate
Hansteens gate
Huitfeldts gate
Dronning Mauds gate
Rådhusplassen
Rådhusgata
Rådhusbrygge
Akershus Festning
Pipervika
E18
0 125 250m
0 125 250yd

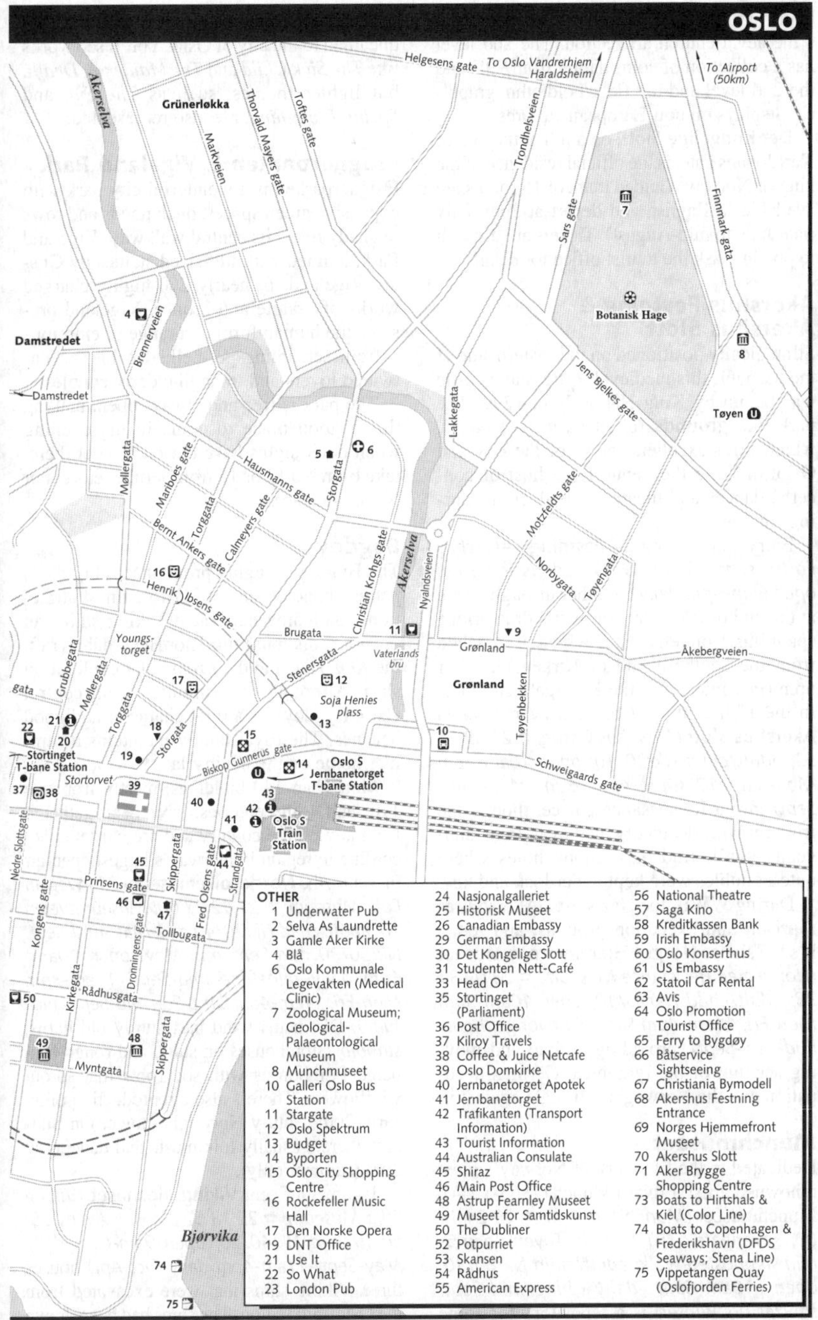
OSLO
Helgesens gate
To Oslo Vandrerhjem Haraldsheim
To Airport (50km)
Akerselva
Grünerløkka
Thorvald Meyers gate
Toftes gate
Markveien
Trondheimsveien
Sars gate
Finnmark gata
Botanisk Hage
Damstredet
Brenneriveien
Damstredet
Jens Bjelkes gate
Tøyen
Lakkegata
Møllergata
Mariboes gate
Hausmanns gate
Storgata
Torggata
Calmeyers gate
Bernt Ankers gate
Motzfeldts gate
Christian Krohgs gate
Akerselva
Nyalndsveien
Norbygata
Tøyengata
Henrik Ibsens gate
Youngs-torget
Brugata
Grønland
Åkebergveien
Vaterlands bru
Stenersgata
Grubbegata
Møllergata
gata
Torggata
Soja Henies plass
Grønland
Tøyenbekken
Storgata
Stortinget T-bane Station
Biskop Gunnerus gate
Oslo S
Jernbanetorget T-bane Station
Schweigaards gate
Stortorvet
Oslo S Train Station
Nedre Slottsgate
Skippergata
Fred Olsens gate
Strandgata
Prinsens gate
Kongens gate
Dronningens gate
Tollbugata
Kirkegata
Rådhusgata
Skippergata
Myntgata
Bjørvika
OTHER
1 Underwater Pub
2 Selva As Laundrette
3 Gamle Aker Kirke
4 Blå
6 Oslo Kommunale Legevakten (Medical Clinic)
7 Zoological Museum; Geological-Palaeontological Museum
8 Munchmuseet
10 Galleri Oslo Bus Station
11 Stargate
12 Oslo Spektrum
13 Budget
14 Byporten
15 Oslo City Shopping Centre
16 Rockefeller Music Hall
17 Den Norske Opera
19 DNT Office
21 Use It
22 So What
23 London Pub
24 Nasjonalgalleriet
25 Historisk Museet
26 Canadian Embassy
29 German Embassy
30 Det Kongelige Slott
31 Studenten Nett-Café
33 Head On
35 Stortinget (Parliament)
36 Post Office
37 Kilroy Travels
38 Coffee & Juice Netcafe
39 Oslo Domkirke
40 Jernbanetorget Apotek
41 Jernbanetorget
42 Trafikanten (Transport Information)
43 Tourist Information
44 Australian Consulate
45 Shiraz
46 Main Post Office
48 Astrup Fearnley Museet
49 Museet for Samtidskunst
50 The Dubliner
52 Potpurriet
53 Skansen
54 Rådhus
55 American Express
56 National Theatre
57 Saga Kino
58 Kreditkassen Bank
59 Irish Embassy
60 Oslo Konserthus
61 US Embassy
62 Statoil Car Rental
63 Avis
64 Oslo Promotion Tourist Office
65 Ferry to Bygdøy
66 Båtservice Sightseeing
67 Christiania Bymodell
68 Akershus Festning Entrance
69 Norges Hjemmefront Museet
70 Akershus Slott
71 Aker Brygge Shopping Centre
73 Boats to Hirtshals & Kiel (Color Line)
74 Boats to Copenhagen & Frederikshavn (DFDS Seaways; Stena Line)
75 Vippetangen Quay (Oslofjorden Ferries)

coins, gold treasure, jewellery, weapons, and a medieval church art section. The 2nd level has a collection of coins dating from 995, and the 2nd level and top floor hold ethnographical displays on non-European cultures.

Det Kongelige Slott, on a hill at the end of Karl Johans gate, is the official residence of the king of Norway. Guided tours of 15 rooms are available in English and depart at 2pm daily (late June to mid-August). Tickets are difficult to obtain – ask the tourist office for details.

Akershus Festning & Akershus Slott

Strategically positioned on the eastern side of the harbour, this medieval fortress and castle was begun by King Håkon V in 1299. The park-like **grounds** *(open 6am-9pm daily)*, which offer excellent views of the city and Oslofjord, are the venue for a host of concerts, dances and theatrical productions during summer.

Entry into **Akershus Festning** *(Akershus Fortress; ☎ 23 09 39 17; admission free; open 6am-9pm daily)* is either through a gate at the end of Akersgata or over a drawbridge spanning Kongens gate, which is reached from the southern end of Kirkegata. After 6pm (in winter), use the Kirkegata entrance. In the 17th century, Christian IV renovated **Akershus Slott** *(Akershus Castle; ☎ 23 09 35 53; adult/child Nkr30/10; open 10am-4pm Mon-Sat, 12.30pm-4pm Sun May–mid-Sept)* into a Renaissance palace, though the front remains decidedly medieval. In its dungeons you'll find dark cubby holes where outcast nobles were kept under lock and key.

During WWII, the Nazis used Akershus as a prison and execution grounds, and today it's the site of **Norges Hjemmefront Museet** *(Norwegian Resistance Museum; ☎ 23 09 31 38; adult/child Nkr25/10; open 10am-3pm Mon-Fri, 11am-4pm Sat & Sun, longer hours mid-Apr–Sept)*, providing a vivid and moving account of the tyrannical German occupation and the Norwegian struggle against it.

Munchmuseet

Dedicated to the life work of Norway's most renowned artist, Edvard Munch (1863-1944), Munchmuseet *(Munch Museum; ☎ 23 24 14 00; Tøyengata 53; T-bane to Tøyen, then 5-min signposted walk; adult/child Nkr60/30; open 10am-6pm daily June–mid-Sept, shorter hrs winter)* is a repository for some 5000 drawings and paintings that Munch bequeathed to the city of Oslo. You'll see works like *The Sick Child* and *The Maiden & Death*, but lighter themes, such as *The Sun* and *Spring Ploughing*, are also represented.

Frognerparken & Vigeland Park

Frognerparken is a wonderful city park with expansive green spaces, duck ponds and rows of shady trees. Its central walkway, Vigeland Park, is lined with life-sized statues by Gustav Vigeland. In nearly 200 highly charged works of granite and bronze, Vigeland presents the human form in a range of emotions – from screaming pot-bellied babies to entwined lovers and tranquil elderly couples.

The park is free and always open, making this a good place to come in the evening when other sights have closed. To get there, take tram No 12 or 15 from Jernbanetorget or Nationaltheatret.

Bygdøy

The Bygdøy (roughly pronounced 'big day') peninsula holds some of Oslo's finest attractions, including excavated Viking ships, an open-air folk museum, Thor Heyerdahl's raft, the *Kon-Tiki*, and the *Fram* polar exploration ship. Although only minutes from central Oslo, Bygdøy has a rural character and good beaches. The royal family maintains a summer home on the peninsula.

More than 140 buildings, mostly from the 17th and 18th centuries, have been gathered from around the country and are clustered according to region in Norway's largest open-air museum, the **Norsk Folkemuseum** *(Norwegian Folk Museum; ☎ 22 12 37 00; Museumsveien 10; adult/child Nkr70/40 mid-May–mid-Sept, Nkr50/30 mid-Sept–mid-May; open 10am-6pm daily mid-June–mid-Sept, 11am-3pm Mon-Fri, 11am-4pm Sat & Sun mid-Sept–mid-June)*. Dirt paths wind past sturdy old barns, *stabbur* (storehouses on stilts) and rough-timbered farmhouses with sod roofs that sprout wildflowers. There's also a reproduction of an early 20th-century Norwegian town. On Sunday, there's usually folk music and dancing at 2pm (summer only).

The magnificent **Vikingskipshuset** *(Viking Ship Museum; ☎ 22 13 52 80; Huk Aveny 35; adult/child Nkr40/20; open 9am-6pm daily May-Sept, 11am-4pm daily Oct-Apr)* houses three Viking ships that were excavated from the Oslofjord region. The ships had been drawn ashore and used as tombs for nobility, who were buried with all they expected to need in the hereafter, including jewels, furniture, food and servants. Built of oak in the 9th century, these Viking ships were buried in blue clay, which preserved two of them amazingly well.

Ferries depart from the pier just north of Akershus Festning from 12 April to 6 October. They make the 15-minute run to Bygdøy (Nkr22) every 20 to 40 minutes, starting at 7.45am (9.05am on weekends). The last crossing returns from Bygdøy at 9.25pm from 25 May to 18 August (otherwise 5.25pm).

Islands & Beaches

Ferries to half a dozen islands in the Oslofjord leave from Vippetangen quay, southeast of Akershus Fortress. **Hovedøya**, the closest island, has a rocky coastline, but its southwestern side is a popular sunbathing area. Boats to Hovedøya leave from Vippetangen once or twice hourly between 6.17am and midnight daily from late May to mid-August, with fewer runs the rest of the year.

Farther south, the undeveloped island of **Langøyene** offers far better swimming. Boats to Langøyene depart 9.35am to 8.25pm daily 26 May to 19 August.

The Bygdøy Peninsula also has two popular beaches, **Huk** and **Paradisbukta**, which can be reached by taking bus No 30 from Jernbanetorget to its last stop.

Activities

A network of hiking trails leads into Nordmarka from Frognerseteren, northwest of the city at the end of T-bane line 1. One fairly strenuous walk is from Frognerseteren over to Lake Sognsvann, where you can take T-bane line 5 back to the city. If you're interested in wilderness hiking, contact the **DNT office** *(☎ 22 82 28 22; Storgata 3)*.

Contact the tourist office for the latest information on bicycle hire. For cycling information contact the local club, **Syklistenes Landsforening** *(☎ 22 47 30 30)*.

Oslo's ski season is roughly December to March. **Tomm Murstad Skiservice** *(☎ 22 13 95 00; W www.skiservice.no; Tryvannsveien 2)*, at Voksenkollen T-bane station, one T-bane stop before Frognerseteren, hires out snowboards and nordic skis. A set of skis, boots and poles costs Nkr140/180 for one/two days. **Skiforeningen** *(Ski Society; ☎ 22 92 32 00; Kongeveien 5)* can provide more information on skiing, or check out W www.holmenkollen.com.

Special Events

Oslo's most festive annual event is the 17 May Constitution Day celebration, when city residents descend on the Royal Palace dressed in traditional outfits.

In March, the Holmenkollen ski festival attracts nordic skiers and ski jumpers from around the world. During the last weekend in July there's the Summer Parade (dominated by techno music), an indoor and outdoor music and dance festival. August sees the Oslo International Jazz Festival and October, the Scandinavia-oriented Ultima Contemporary Music Festival.

Places to Stay

Hostels The Oslo area has four HI-affiliated hostels.

The newly extended **Oslo Vandrerhjem Haraldsheim** *(☎ 22 22 29 65, fax 22 22 10 25; e oslo.haraldsheim.hostel@vandrerhjem.no; Haraldsheimveien 4; tram Nos 12, 13 or 17 from city centre; dorm beds with/without bath Nkr170/190, singles Nkr360/290, doubles Nkr480/400; open year-round)* is a busy place 4km from the city centre. The hostel has kitchen and laundry facilities, 270 beds (mostly in four-bed rooms) and breakfast included.

Oslo Vandrerhjem IMI *(☎ 22 98 62 00; Staffelsgata 4, enter from Linstowsgata; dorm beds Nkr170-190, singles/doubles from Nkr275/430; open 4 June–19 Aug)* is a 46-bed summer hostel in a boarding school conveniently just north of the Royal Palace. There's a kitchen, but prices include breakfast. Tram Nos 10, 11 and 17 stop nearby.

Oslo Vandrerhjem Holtekilen *(☎ 67 51 80 40, fax 67 59 12 30; e oslo.holtekilen.hostel@lvandrerhjem.no; Michelets vei 55, Stabekk; bus Nos 151, 153, 161, 162, 251, 252 or 261; dorm beds Nkr180, singles/doubles Nkr280/460; open year-round)*, 8km southwest of Oslo, has 195 beds and rates include breakfast.

Oslo Vandrerhjem Ekeberg *(☎ 22 74 18 90, fax 22 74 75 05; Kongsveien 82; dorm beds Nkr175, singles/doubles Nkr280/440; open 1 June–27 Aug)*, 4km southeast of Oslo, offers 68 beds in an atmospheric old house. Rates include breakfast. Take tram No 18 or 19 towards Ljabru and get off at Holtet; from there, it's about 100m along Kongsveien.

The bright and airy **Albertine Hostel** *(☎ 22 99 72 10, fax 22 99 72 20; ⓔ albertine@anker.oslo.no; Storgata 55; beds in 4/6-bed rooms with private bath Nkr155/135, 1 or 2-person private room Nkr400; open 6 June–24 Aug)*, used as a student residence except over summer, is a convenient non-HI option located at the rear of the Anker Hotel. Breakfast costs Nkr55 extra; linen and towels also costs Nkr55.

YMCA Sleep-In *(☎ 22 20 83 97; Grubbegata 4; dorm mattresses Nkr130; open 3 July–12 Aug)* has a great position only 10 minutes' walk from Oslo S and fills up quickly. There's no bedding so you'll need a sleeping bag; mattresses are on the floor. Basic shower and kitchen facilities are available.

NORWAY

Private Rooms & Pensions For help getting a double room in a private home, see **Use-It** *(☎ 22 41 51 32; Møllergata 3)*. Rooms range from Nkr300 to Nkr350 (excluding breakfast) and there's no minimum stay or booking fee. If you'll be arriving on a weekend, call ahead and they'll give you phone numbers and/or email addresses of places you can call on your own.

The Oslo S **tourist office window** also books rooms in private homes; these cost Nkr225/350 singles/doubles (excluding breakfast), plus a Nkr35 booking fee. Also worth checking out ⓦ www.bbnorway.com, which lists around a dozen B&Bs in the city.

Cochs Pensjonat *(☎ 23 33 24 00, fax 23 33 24 10; Parkveien 25; singles/doubles from Nkr350/500)*, a bit pricier but closer to the centre, is located just north of the Royal Palace. Most of the 65 rooms are rather spartan, but some are en suite with kitchenette.

Hotels Relatively budget **City Hotel** *(☎ 22 41 36 10; ⓔ booking@cityhotel.no; Skippergata 19; singles Nkr475-635, doubles Nkr595-835)* has a historical ambience but the rooms are mostly fairly basic, with shared bath. The courtyard rooms get less traffic noise. A modern no-frills alternative with very clean en suite rooms is the **Anker Hotel** *(☎ 22 99 75 10, fax 22 99 75 20; ⓔ booking@anker.oslo.no; Storgata 55; singles Nkr450-750, doubles Nkr600-900)*.

Places to Eat

Eating can be an expensive proposition in Oslo. One way to save money is to frequent bakeries, many of which sell reasonably priced sandwiches as well as pastries and hearty wholegrain breads. The **Baker Hansen** chain has numerous shops around Oslo. Among grocery stores, you'll find some of the best prices at **Kiwi**, with branches throughout the city. Around Oslo S, fast food and shopping-mall fare is the way to go.

Grønland, a neighbourhood of Asian and Middle Eastern immigrants, a few minutes' walk northeast of the bus station, has good, affordable ethnic eating places. It's also opening up as the in-place for eating, drinking and dancing among the 20 to 30 crowd. Recommended is **Punjab Tandoori** *(Grønlandsleiret 24; mains around Nkr55)*, which serves things like chicken tandoori, rice and naan bread.

Aker Brygge, the former shipyard turned shopping complex along the western side of the harbour, has a food court with various eating options. Behind Aker Brygge, the **ICA Gourmet supermarket café** sells filled baguettes (Nkr45), wok dishes (Nkr59) and salads (Nkr59).

Brasserie 45 *(Karl Johans gate 45; mains from Nkr63)* features good food at honest prices, including salmon, lasagne, grilled catfish and fried chicken. The friendly **Kaffistova** *(Rosenkrantz gate 8; mains Nkr82-92)* cafeteria serves traditional Norwegian food, including reindeer or elk carbonades (meat cakes), meatballs, pork chops and fish cakes; salad is always included.

An outstanding herbivore option is **Krishna's Cuisine**, *(Kirkeveien 59B; all-you-can-eat meal Nkr90; food available noon- 8pm Mon-Fri)*, near the Majorstuen T-bane station, which serves up soup, salad, vegies and a hot dish.

Local art students hang out at **Kafé Celsius** *(Rådhusgata 19; mains Nkr94-198; open 11am-midnight Mon-Sat, 1pm-10pm Sun)*, a low-key café with a pleasant courtyard beer garden where salads and pastas are served.

Entertainment

The tourist office's monthly *What's on in Oslo* brochure lists concerts, theatre and special events, but the best publication for night owls is the free *Streetwise*. Many nightspots have an unwritten anti-scruffiness dress code.

The Dubliner *(☎ 22 33 70 05; Rådhusgata 28; cover charge Nkr60)* is a friendly and authentic Irish pub that features live Irish folk bands several times weekly. If you prefer a down-to-earth drinking-den atmosphere, try

Stargate *(Grønlandsleiret 2)*, which offers the best-value beer in town; 500mL of draught costs only Nkr24 to Nkr29. The weirdly named and appropriately (if oddly) decorated **Underwater Pub** *(Dalsbergstien 4)* is notable on Tuesday and Thursday, when students of the State School of Opera lubricate their vocal chords and treat patrons to their favourite arias.

Head On *(Rosenkrantz gate 11B)* features funk and house with international DJs; it's currently the hottest place for clubbers.

Skansen *(Rådhusgata 25)*, inside a former public toilet, is one of the city's hottest dance clubs and resounds to the beats of house, funk, jazz and techno. For a laudable attempt at salsa, visit **Shiraz** *(Dronningens gate 17)*. **So What** *(Grensen 9)* is a café and club with alternative music and a young crowd. At **Blå** *(Brenneriveien 9C)*, reputedly the best modern jazz spot in Oslo, you can catch new artistes and bands before they hit the big time.

The main club hang-out for gay men is the **London Pub** *(CJ Hambros plass 5)*, with a good mix of chart sounds. Lesbians favour **Potpurriet** *(Øvre Vollgate 13)*, with its emphasis on techno, Latin and salsa music.

Of the city's largest concert halls, **Oslo Spektrum** *(Sonja Henies plass 2)* features contemporary music, **Oslo Konserthus** *(Munkedamsveien 14)* has an emphasis on jazz and classical, and the **Rockefeller Music Hall** *(Torggata 16)* attracts big-name international contemporary musicians. Each month except July, Oslo's opera company stages opera, ballet and classical concerts at **Den Norske Opera** *(☎ 815 44 488; Storgata 23; tickets from Nkr300, 50% student discount)*.

Getting There & Away

Air Most flights land at Oslo's main international airport in Gardermoen, 50km north of the city.

SAS *(☎ 815 20 400)* and **Braathens** *(☎ 815 20 000)* airlines have ticket offices in the basement at Oslo S. **Ryanair** *(☎ 820 61 100)* flies from London Stansted and Glasgow Prestwick to Oslo Torp, 112km south of the city.

Bus Long-distance buses arrive and depart from the Galleri Oslo terminal, about a 10-minute walk east from Oslo S.

Train All trains arrive and depart from Oslo S in the city centre. The reservation desks are open 6.30am to 11pm daily. There's also an **information desk** *(☎ 815 00 888)* where you will find details on travel schedules throughout Norway.

Car & Motorcycle All major car-rental companies have booths at Gardermoen airport. The following also have offices in the city centre:

Avis (☎ 23 23 92 00) Munkedamsveien 27
Budget (☎ 23 16 32 40) Oslo Spektrum, near Oslo S
Statoil (☎ 22 83 35 35) Dronning Mauds gate 10B

Boat Sea travel to and from Copenhagen, operated by **DFDS Seaways** *(☎ 33 42 30 00)*, and Frederikshavn (Denmark), operated by **Stena Line** *(☎ 23 17 91 00)*, use the docks off Skippergata, near Vippetangen. Bus No 60 brings you to within a couple of minutes' walk of the terminal.

Boats from Hirtshals (Denmark) and Kiel (Germany), run by **Color Line** *(☎ 22 94 44 00)*, dock at Hjortneskaia, west of the central harbour. Connecting buses run to Oslo S, or take tram Nos 10 or 13.

Getting Around

Oslo has an efficient public-transport system. A one-way ticket on any service costs Nkr22 and includes one transfer within an hour of purchase; buy tickets from staff on ferries, from bus or tram drivers, and from service desks or automatic machines in T-bane stations. An unlimited *dagskort* (day ticket) costs Nkr50, but can't be used between 1am and 4am.

Trafikanten *(☎ 815 00 176; open 7am-8pm Mon-Fri, 8am-6pm Sat & Sun)*, below the Oslo S tower on Jernbanetorget, provides free schedules and a handy public transport map, *Sporveiskart Oslo*.

To/From the Airport High-speed trains run every 10 minutes between Oslo S and Oslo International airport in Gardermoen, cost Nkr130 and take 24 minutes. Alternatively, you can take a local train (Nkr70, from 26 minutes, hourly but fewer on Saturday) or an express airport bus (Nkr90, 40 minutes, three or four hourly).

Bus & Tram Bus and tram lines crisscross the city and extend to the suburbs. Most buses and trams converge at Jernbanetorget in front of Oslo S. Most westbound buses, including those to Bygdøy and Vigeland Park, also stop on the southern side of the National Theatre.

The service frequency drops dramatically at night but, on weekends only, *Nattlinjer* night buses No 200 to 218 follow the tram routes until 4am or later (tickets Nkr50; passes not valid).

T-Bane The five-line T-bane metro train network, which goes underground in the city centre, is faster and goes farther outside the city centre than most bus lines. All lines pass through the Nationaltheatret, Stortinget and Jernbanetorget stations.

Taxi Flag fall is up to Nkr91.50 and from Nkr10 to Nkr16 per kilometre thereafter. There are taxi stands at Oslo S, shopping centres and city squares. Any taxi with a lit sign is available for hire. If you must, phone **Taxi2** *(☎ 02202)*, **Norgestaxi** *(☎ 08000)* or **Oslo Taxi** *(☎ 02323)* – but be aware that meters start running at the point of dispatch. Fares are ludicrously high. Oslo taxis accept major credit cards; make sure your credit limit is up to snuff.

Boat Ferries to Bygdøy leave from Rådhusbrygge every 20 to 40 minutes, while ferries to the islands in the Oslofjord leave from Vippetangen.

Southern Norway

Sørlandet, the curving south coast, is magnetic for Norwegians when the weather turns warm. The attraction is generally not as great for foreign travellers, the majority of whom have just arrived from places with warmer water and better beaches.

The Sørland train line, which runs 586km from Stavanger to Oslo via Kristiansand, stays inland most of the way, but buses meet the trains and link the rail line with most south-coast towns.

STAVANGER & AROUND

pop 106,000

Stavanger, Norway's fourth largest city, was once a bustling fishing centre and, in its heyday, had more than 70 sardine canneries. By the 1960s, depletion of fish stocks had brought an end to the industry, but the discovery of North Sea oil spared Stavanger from hard times. The city now holds the title 'Oil Capital of Norway', bringing prosperity (along with tons of Brits and Yanks) to the city.

The adjacent bus and train stations are a 10-minute walk from the harbour. Ask the **tourist office** *(☎ 51 85 92 00; ⓔ info@visitstavanger.com; Rosenkildetorget 1; open Mon-Sat, daily June-Aug)* for details of the 12 annual festivals in Stavanger.

Things to See & Do

The area's most popular outing is the two-hour hike to the top of the incredible **Preikestolen** (Pulpit Rock), 25km east of Stavanger. You can inch up to the edge of its flat top and peer 600m straight down to the Lysefjord. From Stavanger take the 8.20am ferry to Tau (Nkr30, 40 minutes), from where a connecting bus (Nkr45) takes you to the trailhead (mid-June to August only), then returns at 4.15pm.

A fun quarter for strolling about is **Gamle Stavanger**, on the west side of the harbour, where cobblestone walkways lead through rows of well-preserved early 18th-century whitewashed wooden houses.

Stavanger Domkirke *(Haakon VIIs gate; open 11am-6pm Mon & Tues, 10am-6pm Wed-Sat, 1pm-6pm Sun mid-May–mid-Sept, shorter hrs mid-Sept–mid-May)* is an impressive medieval stone cathedral dating from around 1125. An atmospheric time to visit is during the organ recital at 11.15am on Thursday.

The unusual and interesting **Norsk Oljemuseum** *(Norwegian Petroleum Museum; ☎ 51 93 93 00; Kjeringholmen; adult/child Nkr75/35; open 10am-7pm daily June-Aug, 10am-4pm Mon-Sat & 10am-6pm Sun Sept-May)* traces the history of oil formation and exploration in the North Sea.

Places to Stay

The lakeside HI hostel **Stavanger Vandrerhjem Mosvangen** *(☎ 51 87 29 00; ⓔ stavanger.mosvangen.hostel@vandrerhjem.no; Henrik Ibsens gate 21; dorm beds/doubles Nkr145/290; open June-Aug, Sept-May with advance booking)* is 3km from the city centre (bus No 78 or 79). The turf-roofed HI hostel **Preikestolen** *(☎ 97 16 55 51; ⓔ preikestolen.hostel@vandrerhjem.no; dorm beds/doubles from Nkr140/375; open June-Aug)* is within walking distance of Pulpit Rock.

Contact the tourist office to book **B&Bs**, with singles/doubles around Nkr250/420 (plus an Nkr25 booking fee). An evening buffet, and breakfast, is included at the aptly named **Comfort Hotel Grand** *(☎ 51 20 14 00; ⓔ booking.stavanger@comfort.choicehotels.no; Klubbgata 3; singles/doubles from Nkr495/596).*

Places to Eat

Rustic **Dickens** *(Skagenkaien 6; mains Nkr59-176)* has a varied menu and a decent pizza buffet for Nkr76. The Chinese/Japanese-oriented **Mikado** *(Østervåg 9; lunch Nkr48-79, most dinner mains Nkr83-150)* serves a good range of East Asian dishes.

There's a moderately priced **Caroline Café** at the train station and a **fast-food eatery** and **Rema 1000** supermarket at the bus station. In the centre, opposite the Kulturhus, **Finns Konditori** has good pastries and bread.

Entertainment

There's good jazz at the **Bryggeriet Pub** *(Skagen 28)* on weekends. Stavanger's Irish pub, **The Irishman** *(Høleberggata 9)* features live folk music five nights weekly. There's also live music several times weekly at **Hansen Hjørnet** *(Skagenkaien 18; no cover charge).* On weekends, **New York** *(Skagenkaien 24)* has fun and dancing for the young and funky.

Getting There & Away

The Nor-Way Bussekspress bus to Oslo (Nkr620, 10¼ hours) leaves Stavanger at 8.30am daily. Buses from Bergen to Stavanger (Nkr370, 5¾ hours) run roughly every two hours. Stavanger's only railway line runs to Oslo (Nkr700, 7¾ hours, one to three daily) via Kristiansand (Nkr336, three hours, four to seven daily). Daily except Saturday, there's an overnight train, which leaves Stavanger at 10.45pm.

The **HSD Flaggruten** *(☎ 51 86 87 80)* express passenger catamaran goes to Bergen (Nkr620, 4¼ hours) and Haugesund two or three times daily. Eurail, Norway Rail and ScanRail pass-holders get 50% discounts.

KRISTIANSAND

pop 57,039

Busy Kristiansand, the capital of Sørlandet and the fifth largest city in Norway, is Norway's closest port to Denmark and offers the first glimpse of the country for many ferry travellers from the south. Kristiansand has a grid pattern, or *kvadraturen*, of wide streets laid out by King Christian IV, who founded the city in 1641. It's a busy seaside holiday resort for Norwegians, but foreign visitors generally pile off the ferries and onto the first train.

The train, bus and ferry terminals are together on the west side of the city centre. Ask the **tourist office** *(☎ 38 12 13 14; ⓔ destinasjon@sorlandet.com; Vestre Strandgate 32)* for details about tours, including boat trips and elk safaris. Banks are numerous, but the **post office** *(Markens gate 19)* has longer hours and lower exchange fees.

Built between 1662 and 1672, **Christiansholm Fortress** *(admission free; open 9am-9pm daily mid-May–mid-Sept)* is the most prominent feature along Strandepromenaden.

The HI hostel, **Kristiansand Vandrerhjem Tangen** *(☎ 38 02 83 10; ⓔ kristiansand.hostel@vandrerhjem.no; Skansen 8; dorm beds Nkr190, singles/doubles Nkr380/420; open mid-Jan–mid-Dec)*, is a modern place about a 10-minute walk east of the fortress; prices include breakfast. Cosy **Sjøgløtt Hotel** *(☎/fax 38 02 21 20; ⓔ sjoglott@sjoglott.no; Østre Strandgate 25; singles/doubles Nkr350/630, with en suite Nkr590/780)* has 10 rooms.

The **Mega Cafeteria**, in the supermarket opposite the train station, has cheap eats. For a great meal deal, follow the locals to **Snadderkiosken** *(Østre Strand gate 78A; dishes Nkr13-79)*, which offers a relatively vast and great-value menu, including meatballs or cod with mashed potato.

Express buses head north once or twice daily to Haukeligrend, with connections to Bergen (from Kristiansand: Nkr580, 12 hours). Trains run to Stavanger (Nkr336, three hours, four to seven daily) and Oslo (Nkr462, 4¾ hours, three to six daily), as well as express buses.

Regional buses depart hourly for towns along the south coast, including Arendal (Nkr93, 1½ hours) and Mandal (Nkr52, 45 minutes). For Risør (Nkr160, 2¾ hours), Nor-Way Bussekspress allows you to get off the Oslo express, departing Kristiansand at 2pm daily.

Bergen & the Western Fjords

The formidable, sea-drowned glacial valleys of the western fjords, flanked by almost impossibly rugged terrain, haven't deterred Norwegians from settling and farming their slopes and heights for thousands of years. The much-visited region presents some of the most breathtaking scenery in all of Europe. Information on the entire region is available from **Fjord Norge** (*☎ 55 30 26 40; W www.fjordnorway.com; Postboks 4108 Dreggen, N-5835 Bergen*).

OSLO TO BERGEN

The Oslo–Bergen railway line is Norway's most scenic, a seven-hour journey past forests and alpine villages, and across the starkly beautiful **Hardangervidda** plateau.

Midway between Oslo and Bergen is **Geilo**, a ski centre where you can practically walk off the train and onto a lift. From 1 July to mid-September, **Geilo Aktiv** (*☎ 32 09 59 30*) runs rafting tours (Nkr650 to Nkr750).

From Geilo the train climbs 600m through a tundra-like landscape of high lakes and snow-capped mountains to the tiny village of **Finse**, near the glacier **Hardangerjøkulen**. Finse has year-round skiing and is in the midst of a network of summer hiking trails. One of Norway's most frequently trodden trails winds from the Finse train station down to the fjord town of **Aurland**, a four-day trek. **Geilo Aktiv** (*☎ 32 09 59 30*) offers glacier trekking on Hardangerjøkulen (Nkr520) on Monday, Wednesday and Friday from 1 July to 15 September.

Myrdal, further west along the railway line, is the connecting point for the spectacularly steep Flåm railway, which twists and turns its way down 20 splendid kilometres to **Flåm** (see that section later).

NORWAY

BERGEN

pop 230,829

Once Norway's capital (during the 12th and 13th centuries), Bergen also had the distinction of being Scandinavia's largest city in the early 17th century, with a population of 15,000. Bergen's history is closely tied to the sea. It became one of the central ports of the influential Hanseatic League of merchants. The Hanseatic influence is still visible in the sharply gabled row of buildings that lines Bergen's picturesque harbourfront.

Even though it's Norway's second-largest city, Bergen has a pleasant, slow pace. A university town and cultural centre of western Norway, it has theatres, good museums and a noted philharmonic orchestra. And don't be deterred by the 275 annual days of rain – they keep the place clean, green and flowery, lending it a sense of cheeriness on even the dullest of days.

Bergen is the main jumping-off point for journeys to the western fjords; numerous buses, trains, passenger ferries and express boats set off daily.

Orientation & Information

The bus and train stations lie only a block apart on Strømgaten, just a 10-minute walk from the Express Boats (ferry terminals). Most of the restaurants, hotels, museums, tourist sites and picturesque streets and passages cluster around Vågen, which is the inner harbour.

The helpful **tourist office** (*☎ 55 55 20 00; W www.visitbergen.com; Vågsallmenningen 1; open Mon-Sat, daily May-Sept*), opposite the inner harbour, has brochures on destinations throughout Norway. You can change money at **Nordea bank** (*Allehelgensgate 2*) or the nearby main post office. The tourist office changes money commission-free at 3% less than bank rates. Visit the **main post office** (*Småstrandgaten; open 8am-6pm Mon-Fri, 9am-3pm Sat*) for assistance with postal requirements. You can check email for Nkr40 per hour at **Cyberhouse** (*Vetrlidsalmenning 13; open 24 hrs*), or free at the **public library** (*Strømgaten 6*).

Kilroy Travels (*☎ 02633; Vaskerelven 16*) specialises in student tickets, but also handles regular bookings.

In a medical emergency, contact the **medical clinic** (*☎ 55 32 11 20; Vestre Stromkaien 19; open 24 hrs for emergencies*) or head for the **pharmacy** (*open to midnight daily*) at the bus station.

Things to See

Bryggen, site of the old medieval quarter on the eastern side of Vågen, is an eminently explorable and fascinating area. The street side of Bryggen's long timber buildings is home to museums, restaurants and shops, while the alleys that run along their less-restored sides offer an intriguing look at the stacked-stone foundations and rough-plank construction of centuries past.

The fascinating **Hanseatic Museum** (*☎ 55 31 41 89; Finnegårdsgaten 1A; adult/child Nkr40/free; open 9am-5pm daily June-Aug, 11am-2pm daily Sept-May*), in a rough-timber building dating from 1704, retains its period character and furnishings and gives a glimpse of the austere working and living conditions of Hanseatic merchants.

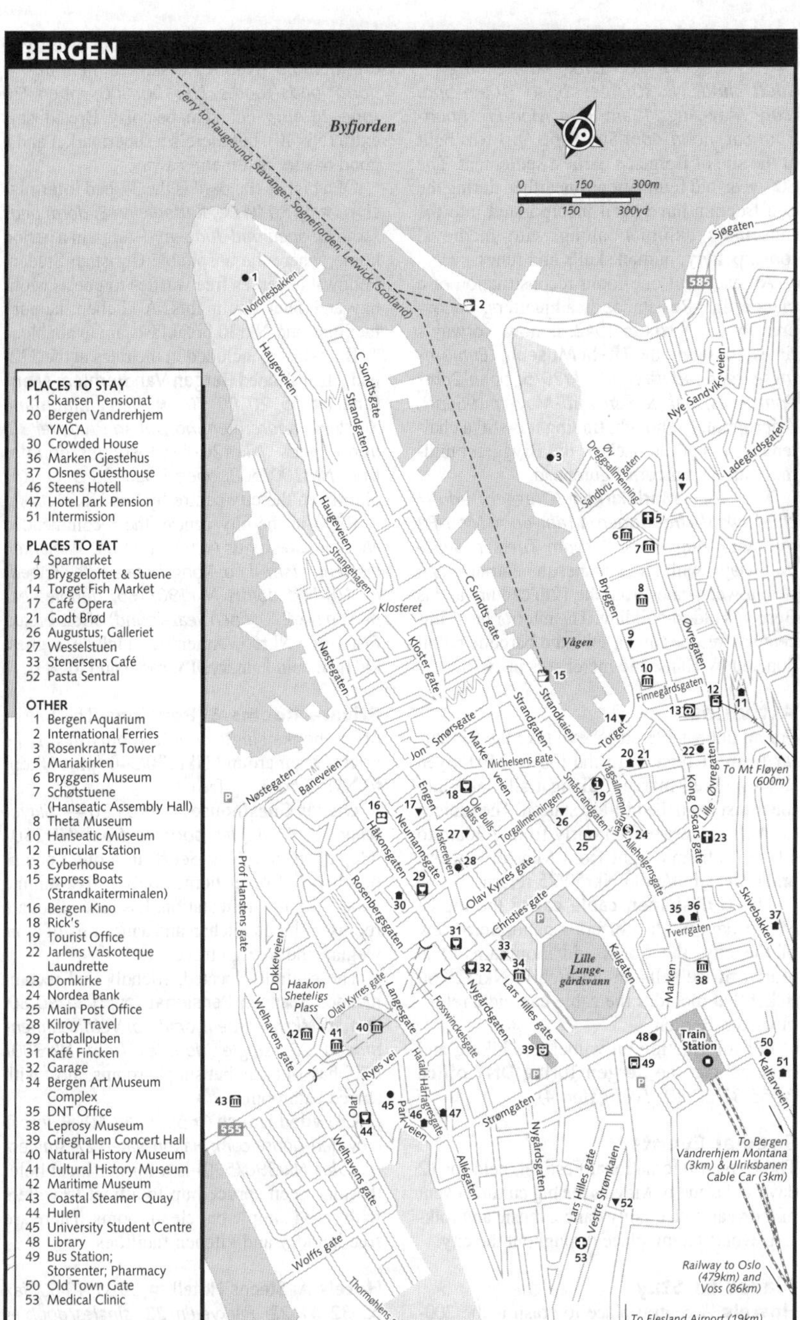
BERGEN
Byfjorden
Vågen
Klosteret
Lille Lungegårdsvann
Train Station
To Mt Fløyen (600m)
To Bergen Vandrerhjem Montana (3km) & Ulriksbanen Cable Car (3km)
Railway to Oslo (479km) and Voss (86km)
To Flesland Airport (19km)
Ferry to Haugesund, Stavanger, Sognefjorden; Lerwick (Scotland)
PLACES TO STAY
11 Skansen Pensionat
20 Bergen Vandrerhjem YMCA
30 Crowded House
36 Marken Gjestehus
37 Olsnes Guesthouse
46 Steens Hotell
47 Hotel Park Pension
51 Intermission
PLACES TO EAT
4 Sparmarket
9 Bryggeloftet & Stuene
14 Torget Fish Market
17 Café Opera
21 Godt Brød
26 Augustus; Galleriet
27 Wesselstuen
33 Stenersens Café
52 Pasta Sentral
OTHER
1 Bergen Aquarium
2 International Ferries
3 Rosenkrantz Tower
5 Mariakirken
6 Bryggens Museum
7 Schøtstuene (Hanseatic Assembly Hall)
8 Theta Museum
10 Hanseatic Museum
12 Funicular Station
13 Cyberhouse
15 Express Boats (Strandkaiterminalen)
16 Bergen Kino
18 Rick's
19 Tourist Office
22 Jarlens Vaskoteque Laundrette
23 Domkirke
24 Nordea Bank
25 Main Post Office
28 Kilroy Travel
29 Fotballpuben
31 Kafé Fincken
32 Garage
34 Bergen Art Museum Complex
35 DNT Office
38 Leprosy Museum
39 Grieghallen Concert Hall
40 Natural History Museum
41 Cultural History Museum
42 Maritime Museum
43 Coastal Steamer Quay
44 Hulen
45 University Student Centre
48 Library
49 Bus Station; Storsenter; Pharmacy
50 Old Town Gate
53 Medical Clinic

The archaeological **Bryggens Museum** *(☎ 55 58 80 10; Dreggsallmenning 3; adult/child Nkr30/free; open 10am-5pm daily May-Aug, 11am-3pm Mon-Fri, noon-3pm Sat, noon-4pm Sun Sept-Apr)* was built at the site of Bergen's earliest settlement. The 800-year-old foundations unearthed during the construction have been incorporated into the museum's exhibits, along with medieval tools, pottery, human skulls and runes.

An excellent one-room reconstruction of a clandestine Resistance headquarters, uncovered by the Nazis in 1942, is now Norway's tiniest museum: the **Theta Museum** *(Enhjørningsgården; adult/child Nkr20/5; open 2pm-4pm Tues, Sat & Sun mid-May–mid-Sept)*. Appropriately enough, finding it is still a challenge – it's at the back of the Bryggen building with the unicorn figurehead.

The stone **Mariakirken** *(Dreggen; adult/child Nkr10/free; open 11am-4pm Mon-Fri mid-May–Aug, noon-1.30pm Tues-Fri Sept–mid-May)*, with its Romanesque entrance and twin towers, dates from the 12th century and is Bergen's oldest building. The interior has 15th-century frescoes and a splendid baroque pulpit donated by Hanseatic merchants in 1676.

NORWAY

Activities

For an unbeatable city view, take the **funicular** from Øvregaten to the top of Mt Fløyen (320m). Well-marked hiking trails lead into the forest from the hill-top station. The funicular runs at least twice hourly from 7.30am to 11pm (until midnight from May to August) and costs adult/child Nkr50/25 return.

The **Ulriksbanen cable car** to the top of Mt Ulriken (642m) offers a panoramic view of the city, the fjords and mountains. The tourist office sells an adult/child Nkr120/60 ticket that includes the cable car and a return bus from Bergen.

For information on wilderness hiking and huts, contact the **Bergen Turlag DNT office** *(☎ 55 32 22 30; Tverrgaten 4)*.

Special Events

The Bergen International Festival, held for 12 days at the end of May, is the big cultural event of the year with quality dance, music and folklore events taking place throughout the city.

Places to Stay

Hostels A central place to crash is the 200-bed HI-affiliated **Bergen Vandrerhjem YMCA** *(☎ 55 31 35 52; e bergen.ymca.hostel@vandrerhjem.no; Nedre Korskirkealmenning 4; dorm beds/rooms Nkr100/600; open 20 June–20 Aug)*, but it can be noisy. Breakfast is extra (Nkr40), but there's a supermarket and a good bakery just metres away.

Of a higher standard is the 37-bed **Intermission** *(☎ 55 30 04 00; Kalfarveien 8; dorm beds Nkr100; open mid-June–mid-Aug)*, in a period home, where the hospitable Christian Student Fellowship serves free waffles to guests Monday and Thursday nights. A kitchen, laundry facilities and Nkr30 breakfasts are available.

Breakfast is included in the rates at the 332-bed, HI-affiliated **Bergen Vandrerhjem Montana** *(☎ 55 20 80 70; e bergen.montana.hostel@vandrerhjem.no; Johan Blyttsvei 30; dorm beds Nkr120-185, singles/doubles from Nkr300/500; open 3 Jan–20 Dec)*. It is 5km from the city centre by bus No 31.

Right in the city centre, the recommended **Marken Gjestehus** *(☎ 55 31 44 04; e markengjestehus@smisi.no; Kong Oscars gate 45; beds in 4/6-bed dorms Nkr190/165; doubles per person Nkr220; open year-round)* offers breakfast from Nkr55. Amenities include a guest kitchen, coin laundry, TV room and lockers.

Private Rooms & Pensions The tourist office books single/double rooms in private homes from around Nkr230/340 (plus Nkr30 to Nkr50 booking fee).

Olsnes Guesthouse *(☎ 55 31 20 44; Skivebakken 24; singles/doubles from Nkr230/340; open mid-May–Sept)*, in a quiet neighbourhood of older homes only a five-minute walk from the train station, has nine adequate rooms, a shared kitchen and a nice mix of Norwegian and foreign travellers.

The centrally located, friendly and recommended **Skansen Pensionat** *(☎ 55 31 90 80; e mail@skansen-pensjonat.no; Vetrlidsalmenningen 29; singles/doubles from Nkr300/550)* has 14 clean but simple rooms, most with shared bathroom.

Crowded House *(☎ 55 23 13 10; e info@crowded-house.com; Håkonsgaten 27; singles/doubles Nkr390/590)* is a former local hotel that has been spruced up to attract travellers with its 34 simple but clean rooms. There are free laundry and kitchen facilities.

Hotels At **Steens Hotell** *(☎ 55 31 40 50, fax 55 32 61 22; Parkveien 22; singles/doubles from Nkr510/750)*, a relatively inexpensive

19th-century-style choice, the en suite rooms all have phone and TV. For a decent family-owned hotel with 19th-century atmosphere and lots of antiques, try **Hotel Park Pension** *(☎ 55 54 44 00; ⓔ booking@parkhotel.no; Harald Hårfagresgate 35; singles/doubles from kr580/830)*.

Places to Eat

In the middle of the historic district, the two-storey **Bryggeloftet & Stuene** *(☎ 55 31 06 30; Bryggen 11; specials Nkr89, mains Nkr95-275)* serves traditional Norwegian fare, including reindeer, venison, *torsk*, catfish and whale in a pleasant atmosphere.

Trendy **Café Opera** *(Engen 18; dishes Nkr56-128)*, popular with artists and students, serves good, reasonably priced food, including ciabatta sandwiches, salads and smoked salmon. The recommended **Augustus** *(Galleriet Shopping Centre, Torgallmenningen 8; specials Nkr99, mains Nkr79-135)* serves modern international dishes.

The unassuming **Pasta Sentral** *(Vestre Strømkaien 6; dishes Nkr59-87)*, which isn't all that central, has great pizza, pasta, and desserts, with a good range of vegetarian choices.

For a cultural treat there's Stenersens Café, on the ground floor of the **Bergen Art Museum** *(Rasmus Meyers Allé)*, which has good pastries, baguette sandwiches and light meals at reasonable prices.

The **Sparmarket** *(Nye Sandviksveien)* has an astonishing takeaway deli with whole grilled chickens for only Nkr30.

A great place for a snack is the bustling **Godt Brød** *(Nedre Korskirkealmenningen 12; open 7.15am-6pm Mon-Fri, 7.15am-3.30pm Sat)*, which offers delicious organic breads and pastries and café tables.

In the **fish market** at Torget you'll find a choice of fresh fruit and seafood snacks, including tasty open-faced salmon rolls for Nkr15; or pick up 500g of boiled crab legs or shrimp for Nkr35 to Nkr75 and munch away at the harbour.

Entertainment

For details and schedules of entertainment events, including classical concerts, contact the tourist office (or see ⓦ www.visitbergen.com). Atop Mt Fløyen, classical concerts are held nightly at 8pm from mid-June to mid-August (Nkr160).

Among Norway's best-value beer venues is the sports bar **Fotballpuben** *(Vestre Torggate 9)*, where 500mL of lager will set you back only Nkr31.

Rick's *(Veiten 3)*, just off Ole Bulls plass, is one of the city's most popular entertainment venues, with live music, a disco, bar and pub. Bergen's top rock music venue, **Garage** *(Christies gate 14)*, attracts students, as does the cave-like **Hulen** *(Olaf Ryes vei 47)* behind the student centre. **Kafé Fincken** *(Nygårdsgaten 2A)* is the main gay and lesbian venue in town.

Getting There & Away

Bus There are daily express buses running to Odda in Hardanger (Nkr233, 3½ hours) and to the western fjord region. From Bergen it costs Nkr395 (6½ hours) to Stryn, Nkr588 (9½ to 10 hours) to Ålesund and Nkr755 (14¼ hours) to Trondheim. There's a bus from Bergen to Stavanger (Nkr370, 5¾ hours) roughly every two hours.

Train There are trains to Oslo (Nkr593, 6½ to 7¾ hours) departing four or five times daily; seat reservations are required. In addition, local trains run between Bergen and Voss (Nkr134, 1¼ hours) every hour or two. Lockers at the train station cost Nkr15 to Nkr40.

Boat Daily Sognefjorden express boats to Balestrand and Flåm, plus northbound express boats to Måløy and southbound express boats to Stavanger, leave from Strandkaiterminalen (ferry terminal) on the western side of Vågen.

The coastal steamer *Hurtigruten* leaves from the quay south of the university at 8pm daily in summer (April to September) and 10.30pm in winter. Details are in the introductory Getting Around section of this chapter.

International ferries to Newcastle, Lerwick (Shetland) and Denmark dock north of Rosenkrantz Tower.

Getting Around

City buses cost Nkr17, while fares beyond the centre are based on the distance travelled. Route information is available on ☎ 177. Free bus No 100 runs between the main post office and the bus terminal.

SOGNEFJORDEN

Sognefjorden, Norway's longest (204km) and deepest (1308m) fjord, cuts a deep slash across the map of western Norway. In some places sheer lofty walls rise more than 1000m above the water, while in others there is a far gentler shoreline with farms, orchards and small towns.

The broad main waterway is impressive, but by cruising into the fjord's narrower arms, such as the deep and lovely Nærøyfjorden to Gudvangen, you'll have idyllic views of sheer cliff faces and cascading waterfalls.

If you need it, tourist information is available at **Sognefjorden** (☎ *57 67 30 83; Postboks 222, N-6852 Sogndal)*.

Getting There & Away

Fylkesbaatane (☎ *55 90 70 70;* 🅦 *www.fylkesbaatane.no)* operates a daily year-round express boat between Bergen and Sogndal, stopping at 10 small towns along the way. Students and InterRail pass holders get a 50% discount. From mid-May to mid-September, Fylkesbaatane runs a second express boat along the same route, except that it terminates in Flåm instead of Sogndal.

There are numerous local ferries linking the fjord towns and an extensive (though not always frequent) network of buses.

Flåm

pop 400

A tiny village scenically set at the head of Aurlandsfjorden, Flåm is a jumping-off spot for travellers taking the Gudvangen ferry or the Sognefjorden express boat. It's also the only place on Sognefjorden with rail connections. The **tourist office** (☎ *57 63 21 06)*, at the train station, rents out bikes. The docks are just beyond the train station.

The pleasant **Flåm Camping & Hostel** (☎ *57 63 21 21;* 🅔 *flaam.hostel@vandrerhjem.no; dorm beds Nkr115, singles/doubles Nkr185/320; open May-Sept)* has just 31 beds – book early. **Heimly Pensjonat** (☎ *57 63 23 00;* 🅔 *post@heimly.no; singles/doubles from Nkr350/690)* has straightforward rooms with great fjord views; breakfast is included.

The Flåm railway runs between Myrdal and Flåm (Nkr125) numerous times daily, in sync with the Oslo–Bergen service. At Flåm, buses and boats head out to towns around the Sognefjord. All ferry tickets and the ferry-bus combination from Flåm to Voss (Nkr230) are sold at the tourist office.

Balestrand

pop 1000

Balestrand, the main Sognefjorden resort destination, enjoys a mountain backdrop and a genteel but low-key atmosphere. The **tourist office** (☎ *57 69 12 55)*, located at the dock, rents out bikes.

The road that runs south along the fjord has little traffic and is a pleasant place to stroll. It's lined with apple orchards, ornate older homes and gardens, a 19th-century English church and Viking burial mounds. One mound is topped by a statue of the legendary King Bele, erected by Germany's Kaiser Wilhelm II who spent his holidays here regularly until WWI.

Balestrand HI Hostel (☎ *57 69 13 03;* 🅔 *balestrand.hostel@vandrerhjem.no; dorm beds/doubles Nkr180/520; open late June–mid-Aug)* is a pleasant lodge-style place; breakfast is included. **Midtnes Pensjonat** (☎ *57 69 11 33;* 🅔 *booking@midtnes.no; singles/doubles from Nkr500/660)*, next to the English church, is popular with returning British holiday-makers. Rates include breakfast. There's a supermarket and a fast-food café opposite the dock, and the hostel restaurant serves dinner for Nkr110.

In addition to the Sognefjorden express boat, local boats run daily to Hella (from Dragsvik, 10km by road north from Balestrand) and Fjærland. Buses go to Sogndal (Nkr83, 1¼ hours) and Bergen (Nkr220, 3½ hours). The latter departs from Vik, reached by boat (Nkr48, 15 minutes), departing Balestrand 7.55am Monday to Friday. This is cheaper than the express boat, and more scenic.

Fjærland

pop 300

Fjærland is a farming village at the head of the beautiful Fjærlandsfjorden and near two arms of the **Jostedalsbreen** ice cap, making it one of Norway's most inviting destinations.

Balestrand tourist office sells a package ticket (Nkr345) that includes the morning ferry to Fjærland, a connecting sightseeing bus and the afternoon return ferry. The tour includes the **Norwegian Glacier Museum**, which has extensive displays on Jostedalsbreen, and visits two arms of the glacier: the **Supphellebreen**, where you can walk up to the glacier's edge and touch the ice, and the creaking, blue-iced **Bøyabreen**, where you might witness ice breaks plunging into the lake beneath the glacier tongue.

Ferries run twice daily from 25 May to 9 September between Fjærland and Balestrand (Nkr130, 1¼ hours). Buses connect Fjærland

and Sogndal (Nkr78, 45 minutes, three to seven daily) and Stryn (Nkr175, two hours).

Sogndal & Around

pop 3000

Sogndal, a modern regional centre, is a starting point for day trips in the area. Of most interest is the **Nigardsbreen glacier** 70km to the north, followed by Norway's oldest **stave church** (c. 1150) in Urnes across the Lustrafjord, and the **Sogn Folkmuseum** near Kaupanger, 11km east of Sogndal. The **tourist office** *(☎ 57 67 30 83; Kulturhus, Gravensteinsgaten)* is about 500m east of Sogndal bus station.

The tourist office books rooms in private homes from Nkr150 per person. There's an **HI Hostel** *(☎ 57 67 20 33; dorm beds Nkr100, singles/doubles Nkr165/230; open mid-June–mid-Aug)* only 15 minutes' east of the bus station.

Buses run from Sogndal to Kaupanger (Nkr23, 10 minutes, hourly) and Balestrand (Nkr98, 1¼ hours, six to nine daily). Twice daily buses (17 June to 26 August) head northeast past Jotunheimen National Park to Lom (Nkr185, 3½ hours) and on to Otta (Nkr255, 4½ hours), on the Oslo–Trondheim railway line.

ÅNDALSNES

pop 3500

Åndalsnes, by the Romsdalsfjord, is the northern gateway to the western fjords. Most travellers arrive on the train from Dombås, a scenic route that descends through a deeply cut valley with dramatic waterfalls. Just before reaching Åndalsnes, the train passes **Trollveggen**, a sheer 1500m-high rock face whose jagged and often cloud-shrouded summit is considered the ultimate challenge among Norwegian climbers.

The town itself is nondescript, but the scenery is top notch. The **tourist office** *(☎ 71 22 16 22)* is at the train station. The mountains and valleys surrounding Åndalsnes offer excellent **hiking**.

A truly outstanding place to stay is the turf-roofed HI **Åndalsnes Vandrerhjem Setnes** *(☎ 71 22 13 82; ⓔ aandalsnes.hostel@vandrerhjem.no; dorm beds Nkr180, singles/doubles Nkr280/450; open 20 May–10 Sept, advance booking other times)*, 2km from the train station on highway E136 towards Ålesund. This wonderfully rustic HI hostel has pleasant rooms with wonderful views and rates include a splendid breakfast. If you don't want to walk, catch the Ålesund bus, which meets the train.

The pleasant and modernised **Alpe Hotel** *(☎ 71 22 21 00; ⓔ alpehotel@sensewave.com; dorm beds Nkr200, singles/doubles Nkr395/495; open year-round)* is just 50m from the train station. The **shop** at the train station sells basic snacks; just 50m away is **Måndalen Bakeri** *(Havnegate 5)*, with good pastries and bread.

The train from Dombås runs to Åndalsnes three or four times daily (Nkr171, 1¼ hours), in sync with Oslo–Trondheim trains. Buses to Ålesund (Nkr162, 2¼ hours) meet the trains. Buses to Geiranger (Nkr137, three hours), via the Trollstigen road, operate from mid-June to late August, leaving Åndalsnes at 8.30am and 5.30pm.

ÅLESUND

pop 24,323

The lovely coastal town of Ålesund, crowded onto a narrow fishhook-shaped peninsula in the sea, is considered by many to be even more beautiful than Bergen – and it's far less touristy. The central streets are lined with handsome Art Nouveau buildings. The **tourist office** *(☎ 70 15 76 00; ⓦ www.visitalesund.com)*, in the town hall, runs guided walks. The most popular thing to do is to walk the 418 steps up **Aksla** for a splendid view of Ålesund and the surrounding islands.

The recommended aquarium **Atlanterhavsparken** *(☎ 70 10 70 60; Tueneset; adult/child Nkr85/55; open 10am-7pm Sun-Fri & 10am-4pm Sat mid-June–mid-Aug, shorter hrs mid-Aug–mid-June)*, 3km from the centre at the western extreme of the fishhook peninsula, introduces visitors to the astonishing marine life around Norway's coast.

The tourist office keeps lists of **private rooms** that start at around Nkr200 per person. At the centrally located **Ålesund HI Hostel** *(☎ 70 11 58 30; ⓔ aalesund.hostel@vandrerhjem.no; Parkgata 14; dorm beds Nkr180, singles/doubles Nkr370/470; open May-Sept)* breakfast is included.

Buses run to Stryn (Nkr203, 3½ hours, one to four daily) via Hellesylt and to other major coastal and fjord towns. *Hurtigruten* coastal steamers arrive/depart at 8.45am/6.45pm northbound and at 11.45pm/12.45am southbound; on its northbound run, there's a popular detour via Geiranger (hence the large gap in arrival and departure times).

Northern Norway

The counties of Sør Trøndelag, Nord Trøndelag, Nordland, Troms and Finnmark comprise a vast and varied area stretching over 1500km, mostly north of the Arctic Circle. The terrain ranges from majestic coastal mountains, which rise above tiny fishing villages and scattered farms, to the barren, treeless, Arctic plateau.

Trains run as far north as Bodø; for destinations further north, there are buses and boats. Bus travel costs can pile up, though Inter-Rail and ScanRail pass-holders can obtain a 50% discount. The *Hurtigruten* coastal steamer passes some of the best coastal scenery in Scandinavia.

RØROS

pop 2592

Røros is a wonderful old copper-mining town with a well-preserved historic district. The first mine opened in 1644, but in 1977, after 333 years of operation, the company went bankrupt. The town makes for some delightful strolling. The **tourist office** *(☎ 72 41 11 65; Peder Hiortsgata 2)* can advise on cycling trips, canoeing, fishing and hiking.

Røros' main attractions are turf-roofed **miners' cottages** and other centuries-old timber buildings, a prominent 1784 **church** *(Kjerkgata; tours adult/child Nkr25/free; open 10am-5pm Mon-Sat, 2pm-4pm Sun 21 June–15 Aug; tours 2pm daily)* with an excellent baroque interior, **slag heaps**, and the old smelting works, now a **mining museum** *(☎ 72 40 61 70; Malmplassen; adult/child Nkr60/30; open 10am-7pm daily mid-June–mid-Aug, shorter hrs mid-Aug–mid-June)*.

Idrettsparken HI Hostel *(☎ 72 41 10 89; Øra 25; camp sites Nkr60, dorm beds Nkr190, cabins Nkr380-600, singles/doubles from Nkr340/400; open year-round)*, at the edge of a sports stadium, offers a wide range of options with good standards. Prices include breakfast. Perhaps the best-value choice is **Vertshuset Røros** *(☎ 72 41 24 11; Kjerkgata 34; singles/doubles from Nkr685/850, 2-person apartments per person from Nkr395)*, which has 24 inviting rooms (breakfast included) and self-catering apartments.

The informal **Kafestuggu cafeteria** *(Bergmannsgata 18; light meals Nkr49-55, mains Nkr70-150; open to 8pm or 10pm daily)* has fascinating decor and offers a good range of coffee, pastries, cold snacks and light meals.

Røros is 46km west of the Swedish border. It's also a stop on the eastern railway line between Oslo (Nkr510, five hours) and Trondheim (Nkr204, 2½ hours). Overnight buses run daily except Saturday to Trondheim (Nkr205, three hours) and Oslo (Nkr450, six hours).

TRONDHEIM

pop 135,879

Trondheim, Norway's third-largest city and its original capital, is a lively university town with a rich medieval history. It was founded at the estuary of the winding Nidelva River in 997 by the Viking king Olav Tryggvason. After a fire razed most of the city in 1681, Trondheim was redesigned, with wide streets and a Renaissance flair, by General Caspar de Cicignon. The steeple of the medieval Nidaros Cathedral is still the highest point in the city centre.

The train station and coastal steamer quay are across the canal, a few minutes' north of the centre. The **tourist office** *(☎ 73 80 76 60; W www.visit-trondheim.com; Torvet; open daily)* helps with inquiries. The **main post office** *(Dronningens gate 10)* handles postal requirements.

Things to See

The grand **Nidaros Domkirke** *(☎ 73 53 91 60; Kongsgårdsgata; adult/child Nkr35/20; open 9am-3pm Mon-Fri, 9am-2pm Sat, 1pm-4pm Sun mid-May–mid-Sept, longer hrs summer, shorter hrs winter)* is the city's most dominant landmark and Scandinavia's largest medieval building. The first church on this site was built in 1070 over the grave of St Olav, the Viking king who replaced the worship of Nordic gods with Christianity. The cathedral, site of Norwegian coronations, displays the crown jewels from 9am to 12.30pm Monday to Thursday and Saturday, 1pm to 4pm on Sunday (1 June to 20 August only) and noon to 2pm on Friday only from 20 August to 31 May.

Completed in 1778, Scandinavia's largest wooden palace, the late baroque **Stiftsgården** *(☎ 73 84 28 80; Munkegata; adult/child Nkr40/20; open 10am-5pm Mon-Sat, noon-5pm Sun, June–mid-Aug, shorter hrs mid-Aug–May)* is now the official royal residence in Trondheim. Admission is by tour only (on the hour).

The **Ringve Museum** *(☎ 73 92 24 11; Lade Allé 60; adult/child Nkr70/25; open 11am-3pm or 5pm daily mid-May–mid Sept, 11am-4pm Sun mid-Sept–mid-May)*, 3km northeast of the city centre, is a fascinating music-history museum in an 18th-century estate. Music students from the university give tours, demonstrating the antique instruments on display. Tours in English are available from April to October. Take bus No 3 or 4 from Munkegaten (Nkr22).

The excellent **Trøndelag Folk Museum** *(☎ 73 89 01 00; Sverresborg Allé; adult/child Nkr75/25; open 11am-6pm daily June-Aug, 11am-3pm Mon-Fri, noon-4pm Sat & Sun Sept-May)* has good hill-top views of the city and over 60 period buildings including a small, 12th-century stave church. It's a 10-minute ride on bus No 8 or 9 from Dronningens gate (Nkr22).

The excavated **ruins of early medieval churches** can be viewed free in the basement of the bank **SpareBank1 Midt-Norge** *(Søndre gate 4)*, and inside the entrance of the nearby **public library** (where there's also a display of two human skeletons discovered during the library's construction).

Places to Stay

From late June to mid-August, university students operate an informal crash pad called **Trondheim InterRail Centre** *(☎ 73 89 95 38; e tirc@stud.ntnu.no; Elgesetergate 1; dorm beds Nkr115)*, a five-minute walk south of the cathedral. Breakfast is included. This friendly operation is free of curfews and has a café with Nkr45 dinners, inexpensive beer and free Internet access.

The impressive **Trondheim HI Hostel** *(☎ 73 87 44 50; e trondheim.hostel@vandrerhjem.no; Weidemannsvei 41; bus No 63; dorm beds Nkr198, singles/doubles Nkr400/530; open 3 Jan–18 Dec)*, 2km east of the train station, includes breakfast in its rates.

At the **Singsaker Sommerhotel** *(☎ 73 89 31 00, fax 73 89 32 00; Rogertsgata 1; dorm beds Nkr125-155, singles/doubles Nkr345/550; open early June–mid-Aug)*, 200m south of Kristiansten Fort, breakfast is also included in the price.

The tourist office books rooms in private homes, mostly in the city outskirts, averaging Nkr250/400 for singles/doubles, plus a Nkr20 booking fee.

Quirky, but personal, **Chesterfield Hotel** *(☎ 73 50 37 50; e hotel@online.no; Søndre gate 26; singles/doubles from Nkr600/775)* has commodious en suite rooms and free Internet facilities for guests. Rooms on the 7th floor have huge skylights and city views. ScanRail pass holders get discounts.

Places to Eat

Zia Teresa *(Vår Frue strete 4; mains Nkr75-185)* is a cosy bistro with authentic Italian food, including pasta dishes averaging Nkr90. The stylish bar and café **Scapa** *(Brattørgata 12B; light meals Nkr55-99, dinner mains Nkr145-188)* serves great food at reasonable prices.

For a more traditional experience, visit **Vertshuset** *(☎ 73 87 80 70; Sverresborg Allé 11; mains Nkr99-235)*, a historic (1739) spot with rotating specials of traditional Norwegian fare, or just coffee and waffles.

Kafé Gjest Baardsen *(Kongens gate; light meals Nkr42-89)*, in the library, is a gathering place for international students and has inexpensive cakes, salads and sandwiches. **Rema 1000** *(Torvet)* has good prices on groceries and bakery items – or munch out on inexpensive fish cakes from the **Ravnkloa fish market**.

Entertainment

Ask the tourist office for the lowdown on pubs and clubs. The English pub **King's Cross** *(Nordre gata; no cover charge)* features live music some weekends, imported beer on tap, wide-screen UK football and bar meals for around Nkr90.

Studentersamfundet *(Elgesetergate 1)*, the university student centre, has a pub, a cinema and some good alternative music. **Rio** *(Nordregate 23)* is currently the flesh-to-flesh dance club for those aged 20 to 25.

Olavshallen *(Kjøpmannsgata 44)*, at the Olavskvartalet cultural centre, is Trondheim's main concert hall, hosting performers ranging from the Trondheim Symphony Orchestra to international rock and jazz musicians.

Getting There & Away

From the airport in Værnes, 32km east of Trondheim, SAS and Braathens fly to major Norwegian cities. SAS also flies daily to Copenhagen.

Nor-Way Bussekspress services run to/from Ålesund (Nkr477, 7¼ hours), Bergen (Nkr755, 14½ hours) and Oslo (Nkr590 to Nkr620, nine to 9½ hours, not Saturday), the latter via either Røros or Lillehammer.

There are four or five trains to Oslo daily (Nkr667, 6½ hours) and two or three trains to Bodø (Nkr773, 10 hours). If you're in a hurry to get north, consider taking the overnight train

Go to Hell

It's easy. Take the train or bus north from Trondheim for about an hour. Say a cheery hell-o to the inhabitants. We hear they're nice.

(If you have time, write us a letter and tell us what the road there is paved with.)

from Oslo and spending the day exploring Trondheim before continuing on an overnight train to Bodø – which goes through Hell just after 10.50pm. There are also trains or buses travelling from Trondheim to Storlien in Sweden (Nkr153, 1¾ hours) at 11.57am and 3.10pm (weekdays only) or 4.20pm (weekends only), with onward connections to Stockholm.

On its northbound journey, the *Hurtigruten* arrives in Trondheim at 8.15am (6am October to May) and departs at noon; southbound, it arrives at 6.30am and departs at 10am.

Getting Around

Airport buses (Nkr54) leave from the train station, the Britannia Hotel and the Radisson SAS Royal Garden Hotel (Kjøpmannsgata 73) in conjunction with SAS and Braathens flights.

The central transit point for all city buses is the intersection of Munkegata and Dronningens gate. The bus fare is Nkr22, or you can buy a 24-hour ticket for Nkr55 to Nkr70, both paid to the driver, exact change only.

About 30 stands spread around the city centre have free bicycles that can be borrowed by inserting a Nkr20 coin in the lock.

BODØ

pop 33,020

In addition to being the terminus for the northern railway line, Bodø is Nordland's largest town and a jumping-off point for Lofoten. Because the town was flattened during WWII air raids and completely rebuilt in the 1950s, Bodø is really quite ordinary in appearance – but it does have a lovely mountain backdrop.

The **tourist office** (*☎ 75 54 80 00; Ⓦ www.bodoe.com; Sjøgata 3*) is near the waterfront. The excellent **aviation museum** (*☎ 75 50 78 50; Olav V gata; adult/child Nkr70/40; open 10am-7pm Sun-Fri, 10am-5pm Sat mid-June–mid-Aug, shorter hrs off-season*), 2km southeast of town, includes some scary simulations of jet-fighter flying.

The 60-bed **Bodø HI Hostel** (*☎ 75 52 11 22; Ⓔ bodo.hostel@vandrerhjem.no; Sjøgata 55; dorm beds Nkr150, singles/doubles Nkr250/330; open May-Sept*) is conveniently located upstairs at the train station. The tourist office books **private rooms** from Nkr150 per person.

Norrøna Hotel (*☎ 75 52 55 50; Ⓔ norrona.hotell@radissonsas.com; Storgata 4B; singles/doubles from Nkr400/500*), opposite the bus station, has comfortable rooms with private bath and affordable summer (July and August) prices.

The historic quayside cafeteria **Løvold's** (*Tollbugata 9; dishes Nkr23-115*) offers sandwiches, grills and hearty Norwegian fare. For inexpensive food, head to the **docks** for fresh shrimp, or **Glasshuset**, which has a supermarket and several quick-service choices.

Trondheim trains arrive in Bodø at 9.10am, 6.30pm and 12.25am. If you're continuing north by bus, be sure to get off 40 minutes before Bodø at Fauske, where the two daily express buses to Narvik (Nkr313, five hours) connect with the train. Southbound trains leave Bodø at 11.35am and 9pm daily.

The northbound coastal steamer arrives in Bodø at 12.30pm and departs at 3pm; southbound, it's in port from 1.30am to 4am.

LOFOTEN

The spectacular glacier-carved mountains of Lofoten, separated from the mainland by Vestfjorden, soar straight out of the sea. From a distance they appear as an unbroken line known as the Lofoten Wall.

Lofoten is Norway's prime winter-fishing ground. The warming effects of the Gulf Stream draw spawning Arctic cod from the Barents Sea south to the Lofoten waters each winter, followed by migrating north-coast farmer-fishermen.

The main islands of Austvågøy, Vestvågøy, Flakstadøy and Moskenesøy are all ruggedly beautiful. Artists are drawn, moth-like, to Austvågøy's light; art galleries proliferate in Svolvær, Kabelvåg and the busy fishing village of Henningsvær.

The four main islands are all linked by bridge or tunnel. Ask **Nordtraffik Buss Lofoten** (*☎ 76 06 40 40*), the regional transport company, if there are currently any discount offers on group travel (two or more people) and return tickets. Bus fares between Bodø and Svolvær are half-price for holders of InterRail and ScanRail passes. Tourist information is available at Ⓦ www.lofoten-tourist.no and Ⓦ www.lofoten-info.no.

Svolvær

pop 4140

By Lofoten standards, the main port town of Svolvær on the island of Austvågøy is busy and modern. On the square facing the harbour, you'll find a couple of banks, a taxi stand and the helpful regional tourist office, **Destination Lofoten** *(☎ 76 07 30 00; e tourist@lofoten-tourist.no)*.

Daredevil mountaineers like to scale **Svolværgeita** (Svolvær Goat), a distinctive, two-pronged peak visible from the harbour, and jump from one horn to the other. A graveyard at the bottom awaits those who miss. There's also a rough route from the Goat over to the extraordinary **Devil's Gate**. A fun excursion from Svolvær is a boat trip into the **Trollfjord**, a spectacularly steep and narrow fjord.

The down-to-earth **Havna Hotel** *(☎ 76 07 10 55; OJ Kaarbøesgata 5; singles/doubles from Nkr595/795)*, near the tourist office, has comfortable rooms with private bath. A **bakery** inhabits the square, and a **Rimi supermarket** *(Torggata)* lives a block inland.

Buses to/from Vesterålen travel between Svolvær and Sortland (Nkr124, 3¼ hours), crossing the dramatically scenic waters of the Fiskebøl–Melbu ferry (Nkr68, car and driver). Buses to Leknes (Nkr88, two hours) with connections to Å (Nkr163, 3½ hours), depart from Svolvær at least four times per day. The Narvik–Lofoten Ekspressen travels daily between Svolvær and Narvik (Nkr388, eight to 9¼ hours).

Express boats ply the waters between Svolvær and Bodø (Nkr246, 3½ hours) and Narvik (Nkr286, 3½ hours), daily except Saturday (but there's no Monday sailing from Svolvær to Narvik).

Svolvær is a stop for the *Hurtigruten*; it departs at 10pm northbound and 7.30pm southbound.

Stamsund

The traditional fishing village of Stamsund makes a fine destination largely because of its dockside hostel, a magnet for travellers, who sometimes stay for weeks on end. The wonderful old beach house in question is **Justad HI Hostel/Rorbuer** *(☎ 76 08 93 34, fax 76 08 97 39; bunks Nkr90, doubles/cabins from Nkr200/400; open mid-Dec–mid-Oct)*, where rowboat rental is free – catch and cook your own dinner! Bicycle rental and laundry facilities are available.

The coastal steamer stops en route (7.30pm northbound, 9.30pm southbound) between Bodø (Nkr306) and Svolvær (Nkr109). Between 20 August to 24 June, buses from Leknes to Stamsund (Nkr29, 25 minutes) run up to eight times daily (less on weekends) with the last bus departing from Leknes at 8.50pm.

Reine

Voted 'the most scenic place in Norway' (by some mysterious electorate), the delightful village of Reine occupies an almost fairy-tale setting. On the island of Moskenesøy, it's on a calm bay backed by ranks of mountain cliffs and pinnacles. All buses from Leknes to Å stop in Reine, making it easy to make an en route break.

Ferries run from Reine to **Vindstad** (Nkr21, 40 minutes) through the scenic Reinefjord. From Vindstad, it's a one-hour hike over a ridge to the abandoned settlement of **Bunes** on the other side of the island, with a magnificent beach, vast quantities of driftwood and the 610m-high cliff of **Helvetestind**.

NORWAY

Å

Å is a very special place – it's a preserved fishing village, the shoreline lined with red-painted rorbu, cod drying on racks everywhere and picture-postcard scenes at almost every turn.

Many of Å's 19th-century buildings are set aside as the **Norwegian Fishing Village Museum** *(☎ 76 09 14 88; open 10am-5pm daily late June–late Aug, 11am-3pm Mon-Fri rest of year)*, complete with old boats and boathouses, a bakery from 1844, Europe's oldest cod liver oil factory, storehouses and so on. A ticket (adult/child Nkr65/45) also lets you into the **Norwegian Stockfish Museum** *(☎ 76 09 12 11)*.

Picturesque Værøy island, a swirling maelstromon the other side of **Moskenesstraumen**, inspired the fictional tales of, among others, Jules Verne and Edgar Allen Poe.

Å HI Hostel *(☎ 76 09 11 21; e aa.hostel@vandrerhjem.no; dorm beds/doubles Nkr125/250; open year-round)* offers accommodation in some of the museum's historic seaside buildings. You can buy fresh fish from local fishers and pick up other supplies at the **food shop** behind the hostel office.

Daily buses travel from Leknes to Å (Nkr84, 1¾ hours). **Ofotens og Vesteraalens Dampskibsselskab** *(OVDS; ☎ 76 96*

76 00; **w** *www.ovds.no)* runs car ferries from Bodø to Moskenes, 5km north of Å. The trip takes four hours, costs Nkr122 for a passenger, and operates up to five times daily from 28 June to 11 August (otherwise, once or twice daily except Saturday).

TROMSØ

pop 47,103

Tromsø, at latitude 69°40'N, is the world's northernmost university town. In contrast to some of the more sober communities dotting the north coast of Norway, it's a spirited place with street music, cultural happenings and more pubs per capita than any other Norwegian town. A backdrop of snow-topped peaks provides spectacular scenery, excellent hiking in summer and great skiing and dogsledding in December to April.

The **tourist office** *(☎ 77 61 00 00;* **w** *www.destinasjontromso.no; Storgata 61; open Mon-Fri, daily June–mid-Aug)* can help with information. The city centre has many period buildings, including the old cathedral, **Tromsø Domkirke**, one of Norway's largest wooden churches. However, Tromsø's most striking church is the **Arctic Cathedral** *(☎ 77 64 76 11; Hans Nilsensvei 41; adult/child Nkr20/free; open 10am-8pm June-Aug)*, which is on the mainland just over the bridge. It's a modernist building that bears an interesting resemblance to the Sydney Opera House.

Tromsø Museum *(☎ 77 64 50 00; Lars Thøringsvei 10; adult/child Nkr30/15; open 9am-8pm daily June-Aug, shorter hrs Sept-May)*, at the southern end of Tromsøya, is northern Norway's largest museum and has some well-presented displays on Arctic wildlife, Sami culture and regional history. Take bus No 28 from Stortorget, the square just west of the harbour.

Take a stroll through the 2-hectare **botanical garden** *(☎ 77 64 50 00; Breivika; bus No 20 or 32; admission free; open daily Jan-Dec)*, which blooms brightly despite its northern locale.

Places to Stay

The tidy **Tromsø HI Hostel** *(☎ 77 65 76 28;* **e** *tromso.hostel@vandrerhjem.no; Åsgårdveien 9; dorm beds Nkr125, singles/doubles Nkr225/300; open 20 June-18 Aug)*, 1.5km west of the city centre, is a good place to crash; phone for directions. The tourist office books rooms in private homes for around Nkr250/450 single/double.

Up on the hillside just west of the centre, **Hotell Nord** *(☎ 77 68 31 59;* **e** *info@hotellnord.no; Parkgata 4; singles/doubles from Nkr450/590)* feels like an informal guesthouse, but staff are knowledgeable and friendly, and rates include breakfast.

Places to Eat

An excellent pizza option is **Allegro** *(☎ 77 68 80 71; Turistveien 19; dishes Nkr60-240)*, between the Arctic Cathedral and the cable car, which also bakes Italian-style pies in a birch-fired oven.

The pub-like **Amtmandens Datter** *(Grønnegata 81)* has reasonable prices, and patrons may use its newspapers, books, board games and free Internet access.

Tromsø's fast-food scene is led by various **kebab carts**. You can buy fresh boiled shrimp from **fishing boats** at Stortorget harbour.

Entertainment

Tromsø enjoys a thriving nightlife. The bustling, youthful **Blå Rock Café** *(Strandgata 14)* features theme evenings, 75 types of beer, live concerts and disco music on weekends. The waterfront **Skarven** *(Strandtorget 1)* offers fine bar meals and is mainly a hangout for over-25s.

You can try Tromsø's own Mack beer at pubs or at **Ølhallen** *(Storgata 4)*, which is near the brewery.

Getting There & Away

Tromsø is the main airport hub for northern Norway, with direct flights to Oslo, Bergen, Bodø, Trondheim, Alta, Hammerfest, Honningsvåg, Kirkenes and Longyearbyen. Airport buses depart from the Radisson SAS Hotel Tromsø.

There are two or three daily express buses between Tromsø and Narvik (Nkr305, four to five hours). Buses to/from Alta (Nkr345, 6¾ hours) run once daily.

The coastal steamer arrives at 2.30pm and departs at 6.30pm northbound and arrives at 11.45pm and departs at 1.30am southbound. Fares are Nkr946 to Bodø and Nkr650 to Hammerfest.

Getting Around

The airport bus (Nkr35) can be picked up at the Radisson SAS Hotel; a taxi to the airport costs about Nkr80. Rides on city buses cost Nkr20, but a better deal is to buy a 24-hour tourist bus pass for Nkr55.

NORDKAPP

Nordkapp (North Cape), a high rugged coastal plateau at 71°10'21śN, claims to be the northernmost point in Europe and is the main destination for most visitors to the far north. The sun never drops below the horizon from mid-May to the end of July. To many visitors, Nordkapp, with its steep cliffs and stark scenery, emanates a certain spiritual aura – indeed, long before other Europeans took an interest in the area, Nordkapp was considered a power centre by the Sami people.

Nowadays, there's a rip-off Nkr175 entrance fee and a touristy complex with exhibits, eateries, souvenir shops and a post office. If you want to really appreciate Nordkapp, take a walk out along the cliffs.

The continent's real northernmost point, **Knivskjelodden** (latitude 71°11'08ś) is inaccessible to vehicles, but you can hike 18km return (five hours) to this promontory from a marked car park, 9km south of Nordkapp.

From mid-May to the end of August, local buses run at least twice daily at 12.15pm and 9pm between Honningsvåg and Nordkapp (Nkr66, one hour). Between 2 June and 9 August, the last bus departs Nordkapp at 1.10am, allowing views of the midnight sun.

Poland

Travellers to Poland will delight in its heroic past, urban vitality and natural beauty. The enduring character of Poland's cities is displayed in the old-world splendour of regal Kraków, in the modern clamour of ambitious Warsaw and in the resilient spirit of maritime Gdańsk. Outdoor enthusiasts will surely be impressed by the undeveloped coastline and intricate waterways in the north, as well as the rugged mountains in the south.

Poland may not be as cheap as it used to be, but it remains an excellent-value destination with solid tourist facilities. And unlike some countries in Eastern Europe, foreigners are charged the same as locals for everything.

In rural areas, you will certainly still see horse-drawn ploughs and carts, but the cities are as dynamic and cosmopolitan as those found in Western Europe. Over the past decade, Poland has developed into a modern, vibrant and progressive nation, yet it has maintained its traditional culture. The country is finally reasserting itself after centuries of occupation and subversion, and it's a great time to visit.

Poland: the Basics

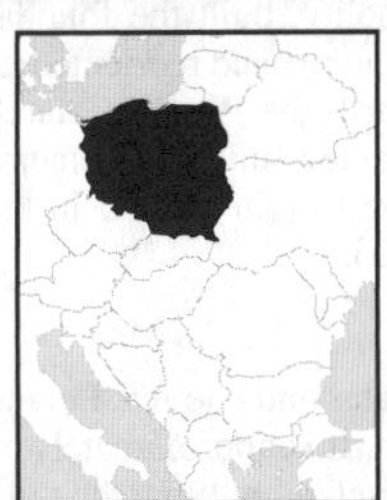

Local name Polska

Capital Warsaw

Population 39 million

Language Polish

Currency złoty (zł) = 100 groszy

Avoid at all costs Making jokes in poor taste

Deflect criticism of your personal appearance by claiming *Jestem z zespołem muzycznym.* (I'm with a band.)

Facts about Poland

HISTORY

During the early Middle Ages, Western Slavs moved into the flatlands between the Vistula and Odra rivers, and became known as Polanians, or 'people of the plains'. In 966 Mieszko I, Duke of the Polanians, adopted Christianity in exchange for official recognition from Rome. While Poland subsequently underwent innumerable territorial reconfigurations, its contemporary borders, drawn by Stalin at the end of WWII, closely resemble those of a millennium ago.

Poland's early success proved short-lived. German encroachment and rapaciousness on the part of nobles divided the realm. The kingdom was finally reconstituted under Kazimierz III Wielki (the Great), who reigned from 1333 to 1370. Scores of new towns sprang up, while Kraków blossomed into one of the leading cultural centres in Europe.

When the daughter of Kazimierz's nephew married the Grand Duke of Lithuania, Jagiełło, Poland and Lithuania were united. The countries flourished during the Renaissance, and in 1569 Poland and Lithuania merged into a single state.

Throughout the 17th century, the regional rivals of Sweden and Russia marched back and forth across Polish territory. In the late 18th century, Russia, Prussia and Austria conspired to carve up the weak Polish state. In a series of three partitions between 1773 and 1795, Poland was removed from the map of Europe.

From the late 18th to the mid-19th century, Poland, now subject to three empires, experienced a nationalist revival. In the early 20th century the empires of Eastern Europe were finally dismembered, and the Versailles Treaty declared Poland a sovereign state.

Hitler used Poland as a headquarters and staging ground for the Nazi offensive against the Soviet Union. When the Red Army's counteroffensive began, Poland became host to a relentlessly grinding campaign of utter devastation. Six million Polish inhabitants (roughly 20% of the population) died during WWII; the country's three million Jews were brutally annihilated in death camps.

After WWII, Poland endured four decades of Soviet-dominated communist rule. Finally, in open elections of 1989, the communists fell from power. In 1990 the communist party disbanded and Solidarity leader Lech Wałęsa became Poland's first democratically elected president.

The postcommunist transition brought radical changes, which induced new social hardships and political crises. But within a decade Poland appeared to have successfully consolidated a democratic polity, built the foundations for a market economy, and reoriented its foreign relations towards the West. In March 1999, Poland was granted full NATO membership and is seeking to join the EU in the next expansion in 2003.

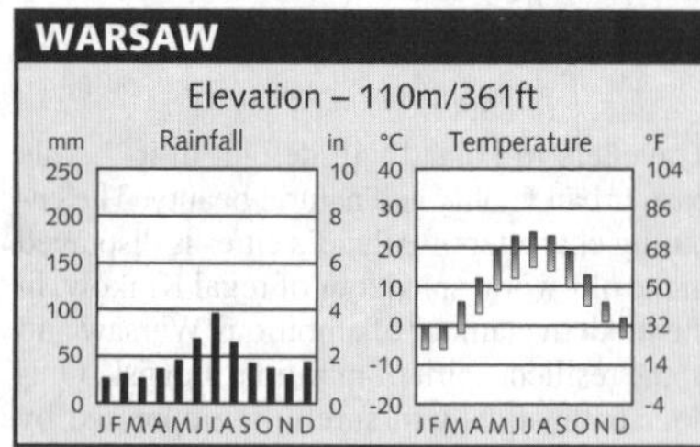

GEOGRAPHY

Bordered by seven states and one sea, Poland covers 312,677 sq km. It is approximately as large as the UK and Ireland put together.

The northern edge of Poland meets the Baltic Sea; the southern border is defined by the Sudeten and Carpathian mountain ranges. The area in between is a vast plain, sectioned by wide north-flowing rivers.

CLIMATE

Poland has a moderate continental climate with considerable maritime influence along the Baltic coast. Summer is usually warm and

POLAND

sunny, with July the hottest month, but it's also the season with the highest rainfall. Spring and autumn are pleasantly warm, but can also be rainy. You can expect snow anywhere in Poland between December and March, lingering until April or even May in the mountains.

GOVERNMENT & POLITICS

The president is directly elected for a five-year term and nominates the prime minister. The parliament consists of two houses: a 460-seat lower house (the Sejm) and a 100-seat upper house (the Senat).

POPULATION & PEOPLE

Because of massacres and forced resettlements after WWII, Poland became an ethnically homogeneous country – about 98% of the population are now Poles.

SOCIETY & CONDUCT

Poles are friendly and polite, but not overly formal. In the countryside a more conservative culture predominates, evidenced by traditional gender roles and strong family ties. In both urban and rural settings, Poles are devoutly religious.

When greeting, Polish men are passionate about shaking hands. Polish women, too, often shake hands with men, but the man should always wait for the woman to extend her hand first.

LANGUAGE

Some older Poles, especially in the west, speak German, while many of the younger set speak English. To polish up your Polish, see the Language chapter at the back of this book.

Facts for the Visitor

HIGHLIGHTS

The beaches of Łeba, perhaps the most inspiring on the coast, are surrounded by miles of unending, desert-like sand dunes. Mikołajki is a charming town that provides access to the Great Masurian Lakes, ideal for biking, sailing and kayaking. Zakopane is the base for hiking and skiing in the Tatras, Poland's most magnificent mountain range.

Poland's rich history is recounted by its imposing medieval castles and charming old town squares. Many of them, such as those in Gdańsk and Wrocław, were lovingly rebuilt after WWII. The royal grandeur of Poland's past is best preserved in Kraków's Old Town.

Auschwitz is the most vivid reminder of the atrocities that occurred during WWII.

PLANNING

The tourist season runs roughly from May to September and peaks in July and August. Many Poles go on holidays during these two months, so transport is crowded and accommodation is often limited. Most theatres and concert halls are also closed at this time.

The best time to visit Poland is either spring (late April to late June) or early autumn (September to mid-October). These periods are pleasantly warm and ideal for general sightseeing and outdoor activities. Many cultural events still take place in both periods.

TOURIST OFFICES

Local Tourist Offices

Almost everywhere of interest in Poland has a regional tourist office. These offices are usually more helpful, and often open longer hours, than offices run by the Polish Tourists Association (PTTK), which are more like organisations of travel agencies offering tours, guides and car hire.

Orbis Travel, the largest travel agency in Poland, is often the best place to buy tickets for domestic and international trains and airlines, and for international ferries.

Tourist Offices Abroad

Polish National Tourist Offices abroad include:

France (☎ 01 47 42 07 42, W www.tourisme.pologne.net) 49 ave de l'Opéra, 75002 Paris
Germany (☎ 030-21 00 92 11, W www.polen-info.de) Marburger Strasse 1, 10789 Berlin
Netherlands (☎ 020-625 35 70) Leidsestraat 64, 1017 PD Amsterdam
UK (☎ 020-7580 8811, W www.pnto.dial.pipex.com) 1st floor, Remo House, 310-312 Regent St, London W1R 5AJ
USA (☎ 212-338 9412, W www.polandtour.org) 275 Madison Ave, Suite 1711, New York, NY 10016

VISAS & DOCUMENTS

Citizens of the European Union, Japan, Switzerland, the UK and the USA can obtain a visa for up to 90 days (Britons up to 180 days) at all major borders, and international airports and sea ports. Citizens of Australia, Canada, New Zealand, South Africa and Israel must obtain a tourist visa before coming to Poland.

Tourist visas from Polish embassies or consulates are issued for up to 180 days. The price varies between countries, but is usually about US$50. You can obtain a 48-hour transit visa (onward visa required) if you need to pass through Poland.

All visas for Poland – whether obtained at an embassy/consulate border, airport or sea port – are only valid for the period specified and normally *cannot* be extended.

EMBASSIES & CONSULATES

Polish Embassies & Consulates

For details about Polish diplomatic missions in other Eastern European countries, refer to the relevant chapters elsewhere in this book.

Australia (☎ 02-6273 1208) 7 Turrana St, Yarralumla, ACT 2600 *Consulate:* Sydney
Canada (☎ 613-789 0468) 443 Daly Ave, Ottawa 2, Ontario K1N 6H3 *Consulates:* Montreal, Toronto and Vancouver
France (☎ 01 43 17 34 22) 5 rue de Talleyrand, 75007 Paris *Consulates:* Lille and Lyons
Germany (☎ 030-22 31 30) Lassenstrasse 19–21, 14193 Berlin *Consulates:* Cologne, Hamburg and Leipzig
Netherlands (☎ 070-360 28 06) Alexanderstraat 25, 2514 JM The Hague
Russia (☎ 095-231 15 00) ul Klimashkina 4, 123447 Moscow *Consulates:* St Petersburg and Kaliningrad
UK (☎ 020-7580 0475) 73 New Cavendish St, London W1N 7RB *Consulate:* Edinburgh
USA (☎ 202-234 3800) 2640 16th St NW, Washington, DC 20009 *Consulates:* New York, Chicago and Los Angeles

Embassies & Consulates in Poland

All diplomatic missions listed are in Warsaw (area code ☎ 022) unless stated otherwise.

Australia (☎ 521 34 44, W www.australia.pl) ul Nowogrodzka 11
Belarus (☎/fax 617 84 11) ul Ateńska 67 *Consulate-General:* (☎/fax 058-341 00 26) ul Jaśkowa Dolina 50, Gdańsk
Canada (☎ 584 31 00, e wsaw@dfait.maeci.gc.ca) Al Jerozolimskie 123
Czech Republic (☎ 628 72 21, e warsaw@embassy.mzv.cz) ul Koszykowa 18
France (☎ 529 30 00, e ambassade@sunik.pagi.pl) ul Puławska 17 *Consulate-General:* (☎ 012-424 53 00) ul Stolarska 15, Kraków
Germany (☎ 617 30 11, W www.ambasadaniemiec.pl) ul Dąbrowiecka 30 *Consulate-General:* (☎ 012-421 84 73, fax 421 76 28) ul Stolarska 7, Kraków *Consulate-General:* (☎ 058-341 43 66) Al Zwycięstwa 23, Gdańsk
Ireland (☎ 849 66 55, W www.irlandia.pl) ul Humańska 10
Lithuania (☎ 625 33 68, e litwa.amb@waw.pdi.net) Al Szucha 5
Netherlands (☎ 849 23 51, fax 849 83 45) ul Chocimska 6
Russia (☎ 621 34 53, fax 625 30 16) ul Belwederska 49 *Consulate:* (☎ 012-422 26 47, fax 422 90 66) ul Biskupia 7, Kraków
Slovakia (☎ 525 81 10, e slovakia@waw.pdi.net) ul Litewska 6
UK (☎ 628 10 01, W www.britishembassy.pl) Al Róż 1
Ukraine (☎ 625 01 27, e emb_pl@mfa.gov.ua) Al Szucha 7 *Consulate:* (☎ 012-429 60 66, fax 429 29 36) ul Krakowska 41, Kraków
USA (☎ 628 30 41, W www.usinfo.pl) Al Ujazdowskie 29/31 *Consulate:* (☎ 012-424 51 00) ul Stolarska 9, Kraków

CUSTOMS

Customs procedures are usually a formality when entering and leaving Poland, and your luggage will probably receive only a cursory glance.

When entering Poland, you're allowed to bring duty-free articles for personal use required for your travel and stay in the country. Note that the export of items manufactured before 9 May 1945 is prohibited.

MONEY

Currency

The official Polish currency is the złoty (pronounced zwo-ti), abbreviated to zł. The złoty is divided into 100 groszy, abbreviated as gr. Denominations of notes are 10, 20, 50, 100 and 200 zł (rare), and coins come in 1, 2, 5, 10, 20 and 50 gr, and 1, 2 and 5 zł.

Exchange Rates

At the time of publication, the approximate rates were:

country	unit		złoty
Australia	A$1	=	2.21zł
Canada	C$1	=	2.60zł
Czech Republic	1 Kč	=	0.12zł
Eurozone	€1	=	3.70zł
Japan	¥100	=	3.15zł
NZ	NZ$1	=	1.89zł
Russia	R1	=	0.11zł
Slovakia	10 Sk	=	0.95zł
UK	UK£1	=	5.85zł
Ukraine	1 hrn	=	0.74zł
USA	US$1	=	4.03zł

Exchanging Money

For maximum flexibility, travellers should bring cash and one or two credit cards. Cash is easy to change and convenient, especially since Poland is a relatively low-crime destination. Private foreign-exchange offices – called *kantors* – are everywhere. The most widely accepted currencies are the US dollar, the euro and the pound sterling (in that order).

Kantors very rarely cash travellers cheques. Not all banks do either and most also charge a commission of 2% to 3%.

ATMs, called *bankomats*, are a convenient way of obtaining local currency. Banks without an ATM may give cash advances over the counter on credit cards, especially Visa. Credit cards are increasingly useful for buying goods and services, although their use is still limited to upmarket establishments.

Costs

Travellers must pay for everything in Poland (except visas and international air fares) in local currency.

If you use camping grounds and/or youth hostels, and self-cater or eat at cheap cafeterias, it's possible to get by on the złoty equivalent of US$15 per person per day. Increase this to $30/25 per person per day travelling as a single/double if you want to stay in decent budget accommodation and eat meals in acceptable restaurants.

Tipping & Bargaining

If a 'service charge' is added to the restaurant bill there is no obligation to tip. In budget-priced restaurants guests rarely leave a tip; in upmarket establishments it is customary to tip 10% of the bill. Tipping taxi drivers is not necessary. Bargaining is rare.

Taxes & Refunds

A Value Added Tax (VAT) of 3% to 22% is added to most goods and services. It is always included in quoted prices. Visitors not from Poland or an EU country are entitled to a refund of VAT paid on goods taken home if they spend more than 200zł in one day at any shop displaying the sign 'Global Refund' (W www.globalrefund.pl).

POST & COMMUNICATIONS

Most cities have a dozen or so post offices. The Poczta Główna (Main Post Office) has the widest range of facilities, including poste restante, fax and sometimes Internet. Poste-restante mail is held for 14 working days.

Major telecommunications facilities are provided by Telekomunikacja Polska (TP), which often provides a telephone centre near or inside the Main Post Office. Most public telephones now use magnetic phonecards, which are available at post offices, kiosks and grocery stores. All numbers throughout Poland have seven digits.

When calling a number from another telephone district within Poland you must add a prefix of 0; then an 'operator code' of 1033, 1044, 1055 or 1066 depending on which telephone operator you choose to use; then the area code (listed in the various sections later); and, eventually, the actual number.

To call Poland from abroad, dial the country code (☎ 48), then the two-digit area code (drop the initial '0' and don't use an operator code), and then the seven-digit local number. The Polish international access code for overseas calls from Poland is ☎ 00. If you need help, try the operators for local numbers (☎ 913), national numbers and codes (☎ 912) and international codes (☎ 908), but don't expect anyone to speak English.

Internet centres can be found all over Poland; smaller towns often have a couple of computers in the Main Post Office, while cities offer a wide choice of trendy cyber-pubs and Internet cafés. Sending/receiving emails and/or surfing the Net usually costs about 10zł per hour.

DIGITAL RESOURCES

Before you travel – or while you're in Poland – you may wish to access one of the following websites:

- W **www.insidepoland.com** – current affairs and reasonable links
- W **www.poland.pl** – an excellent place to start surfing
- W **www.polishpages.com.pl** – best for anything business-related
- W **www.polishworld.com** – directories and travel bookings

BOOKS

Lonely Planet's *Poland* guide covers the country in detail. *Jews in Poland* by Iwo Cyprian Pogonowski provides a comprehensive record of half a millennium of Polish-Jewish relations in Poland. *God's Playground: A History of Poland* by Norman Davies offers an in-depth analysis of Polish history.

WOMEN TRAVELLERS

Travel for women in Poland is hassle-free except for occasional encounters with drunks. Women travellers may wish to contact **International Professional Women of Poland** (*☎/fax 022-606 03 14*) or the **International Women's Group** (*☎ 022-630 72 21*), both based in Warsaw.

GAY & LESBIAN TRAVELLERS

The Polish gay and lesbian movement is less underground than it used to be. Warsaw and Kraków have the most open scene and are the easiest places to make contacts.

The best sources of information in Warsaw are the **Pride Society** (*ⓔ pridesociety@yahoo.com*) and the monthly *Warsaw Insider* magazine, which lists current gay and lesbian clubs in the capital. Otherwise, check out ⓦ www.gej.net.

DISABLED TRAVELLERS

Poland is not well set up for people with disabilities, though there have been significant improvements over recent years. Wheelchair ramps are only available at some upmarket hotels, and public transport will be a real challenge for anyone with mobility problems.

SENIOR TRAVELLERS

Senior visitors (with the appropriate cards) can receive discounts on domestic flights with LOT (20%), buses operated by PKS (30%) from Tuesday to Thursday and, possibly, all of the three international ferry services.

DANGERS & ANNOYANCES

Poland is a relatively safe country, though crime has increased steadily since the fall of communism. Be particularly alert at any time in the Warszawa Centralna (central) train station, the favourite playground for thieves and pickpockets. Smoking is common in all public places, especially on public transport.

BUSINESS HOURS

Most grocery shops are open 7am or 8am to 6pm or 7pm weekdays (Monday to Friday) and until about 2pm on Saturday. Larger stores stay open for a few hours longer. Banks in larger cities are open from about 8am to 5pm weekdays (sometimes until 2pm on Saturday), but have shorter hours in smaller towns. Kantors generally operate from 9am to 6pm on weekdays and until about 2pm on Saturday.

Emergencies

The nationwide, toll-free, 24-hour emergency telephone numbers are ☎ 911 for a pharmacy, ☎ 998 for the fire brigade and ☎ 999 for an ambulance.

For the police dial ☎ 997 – but call ☎ 112 from a mobile (cell) phone.

Roadside assistance is available on ☎ 981.

Don't expect the operators for any of these services to speak English, however.

The opening hours of museums and other tourist attractions vary greatly. They tend to open any time between 9am and 11am and close some time from 3pm to 6pm. Most museums are open on weekends, but many close on Monday and also stay closed on the day following a public holiday.

PUBLIC HOLIDAYS & SPECIAL EVENTS

Poland's official public holidays are New Year's Day (1 January), Easter Monday (March or April), Labour Day (1 May), Constitution Day (3 May), Corpus Christi (a Thursday in May or June), Assumption Day (15 August), All Saints' Day (1 November), Independence Day (11 November) and Christmas (25 and 26 December).

Cultural, musical and religious events are held regularly in Warsaw, Wrocław, Kraków, Częstochowa, Poznań and Gdańsk – refer to the relevant sections later for details.

ACTIVITIES

Hikers can enjoy any of the thousands of kilometres of marked trails across the Tatra and Sudeten mountains and the Great Masurian Lakes district, and at places near Poznań. Hiking trails are easy to follow and detailed maps are available at most larger bookshops. Poland is fairly flat and ideal for cyclists. Zakopane will delight skiers from December to March.

WORK

Travellers hoping to find paid work in Poland will probably be sorely disappointed. The complex paperwork required for a working visa is enough to put most people off the idea. Also, wages are low and you'll probably have to compete for casual work with other Eastern Europeans.

ACCOMMODATION

Camping

Poland has hundreds of camping grounds, many of which offer good-value cabins and bungalows. Theoretically, most grounds are open from May to September, but some really only bother opening their gates between June and August.

Hostels

Youth hostels *(schroniska młodzieżowe)* in Poland are operated by Polskie Towarzystwo Schronisk Młodzieżowych (PTSM), a member of Hostelling International. Currently Poland has about 130 hostels open all year and about 450 open only in July and August. The year-round hostels are more reliable and have more facilities, such as kitchens and dining rooms. Annoyingly, many hostels have no actual names or use ambiguous names.

Youth hostels are now open to all. Curfew is often 10pm, but some hostel staff may be flexible. Most hostels are closed between 10am and 5pm.

A bed in a dormitory costs about 20zł to 25zł per person per night. Single/double rooms, if available, cost about 45/70zł. The youth hostel card gives a 10% to 25% discount on these prices for nationals and, sometimes, for foreigners. Hostels can also provide sheets for about 5zł per person. Given the low prices, hostels are popular and often full. A particularly busy time is early May to mid-June.

In most major cities, a few student dorms open as hostels in summer.

Mountain Refuges

PTTK (see the Tourist Offices section earlier) runs a chain of mountain refuges *(schroniska górskie)* for trekkers. They are usually simple, but the price is right and the atmosphere welcoming. They also serve cheap, hot meals. In the high season even a space on the floor can be hard to find. Refuges are normally open all year, but confirm with the nearest PTTK office.

Hotels

Most cities and towns offer a variety of old and new hotels. Hotel prices often vary according to the season and are usually posted at hotel reception desks. Rates quoted in this chapter include all taxes. If possible, check the room before accepting. Don't be fooled by reception areas.

Two reliable companies can arrange accommodation (sometimes with substantial discounts) over the Internet through **W** www.poland4u.com and **W** www.hotelspoland.com.

Private Rooms

Some cities and tourist-oriented towns have agencies – usually called a *biuro zakwaterowania* or *biuro kwater prywatnych* – that arrange accommodation in private homes. Rooms cost around 55/90zł singles/doubles depending on the season, amenities provided and distance from the city centre. The most important factor to consider is location.

During the high season, home owners directly approach tourists. Prices are often lower than through an agency (and open to bargaining), but you're more likely to be offered somewhere out in the sticks. Also, private homes in smaller resorts and villages often have signs outside their gates or doors offering a *pokoje* (room) or *noclegi* (lodging).

FOOD & DRINKS

Polish food is hearty and filling, abundant in potatoes and dumplings, and rich in meat but not in vegetables. Poland's most famous dishes are *bigos* (sauerkraut with a variety of meats), *pierogi* (ravioli-like dumplings stuffed with cottage cheese, minced meat or cabbage and wild mushrooms) and *barszcz* (red beetroot soup originating from Russian *borshch*).

Hearty soups such as *żurek* (sour soup with sausage and hard-boiled eggs) are a highlight of Polish cuisine. *Placki ziemniaczane* (potato pancakes) and *naleśniki* (crepes) are popular snacks.

Wódka (vodka) is the national drink, which the Poles claim was invented in their country. The most famous variety is *żubrówka* (bison vodka), flavoured with grass from the Białowieża Forest and often drunk with apple juice. Other notable spirits include *krupnik* (honey liqueur), *śliwowica* (plum brandy) and *winiak* (grape brandy). Poles also appreciate the taste of a *zimne piwo* (cold beer).

ENTERTAINMENT

Polish theatre continues to impress foreign audiences. Theatre buffs may want to visit some of the better theatres just to watch the acting. Get rid of the jeans and sneakers for the evening.

Some of the largest cities have opera houses, and those in Warsaw and Łódź offer the best productions. For classical music, the Filharmonia Narodowa (National Philharmonic) usually holds concerts Friday and Saturday night in most major cities.

Warsaw and Kraków have lively jazz scenes. Clubs are popular and usually open from 9pm to late on Thursday, Friday and Saturday. And there's no shortage of places for a drink at any time of the day or night.

Getting There & Away

AIR

The national carrier, **LOT** (*w www.lot.com*), flies to all major European cities. Warsaw is also serviced by most major European carriers, such as Air France, Alitalia, British Airways, KLM-Royal Dutch Airlines and Lufthansa Airlines. Other regional airlines with flights to/from Warsaw include Aeroflot, Aerosvit, Czech Airlines, Malév-Hungarian Airlines, Tarom (from Romania) and Turkish Airlines.

From the USA, LOT offers frequent direct flights to Warsaw from Chicago and New York, and has a code-share agreement with American Airlines for other US cities.

LAND

Border Crossings

Below is a list of major border crossings by road that accept foreigners. These crossings are open 24 hours.

Belarus (south to north) Terespol and Kuźnica Białostocka

Czech Republic (west to east) Porajów, Zawidów, Jakuszyce, Lubawka, Kudowa-Słone, Boboszów, Głuchołazy, Pietrowice, Chałupki and Cieszyn

Germany (north to south) Lubieszyn, Kołbaskowo, Krajnik Dolny, Osinów Dolny, Kostrzyn, Słubice, Şwiecko, Gubin, Olszyna, Łéknica, Zgorzelec and Sieniawka

Lithuania (east to west) Ogrodniki and Budzisko

Russia (east to west) Bezledy and Gronowo

Slovakia (west to east) Chyżne, Chochołów, Łysa Polana, Niedzica, Piwniczna, Konieczna and Barwinek

Ukraine (south to north) Medyka, Hrebenne, Dorohusk and Zosin

Train

Every day, dozens of trains link Poland with neighbouring countries. International train travel is not cheap, especially for longer routes. Domestic trains are significantly cheaper, so you'll save money if you buy a ticket to the first Polish city you arrive at and then take a local train. You can obtain information and buy tickets for some services from w www.wars.pl.

Some international trains to/from Poland have recently become notorious for theft. Some Poles are now too afraid to take any overnight train to/from Poland. Stay alert and keep a grip on your bags, particularly on the Berlin–Warsaw, Prague–Warsaw and Prague–Kraków overnight trains, and on *any* train travelling to/from Gdańsk. Several readers reportedly have been gassed while in their compartments and have had everything stolen while they 'slept'. If possible, sleep in a compartment with others.

Several trains service the Warsaw–Berlin route (via Frankfurt/Oder and Poznań) a day, including three EuroCity express trains that take 6½ hours and cost only €33 in 2nd class. There are also numerous connections between Warsaw and Cologne, Dresden, Frankfurt-am-Main and Leipzig; between Kraków and Berlin, via Wrocław; and between Gdańsk and Berlin, via Szczecin. Four trains a day travel between Prague and Warsaw (10 to 12 hours) via either Wrocław or Katowice. Every day, four trains also travel between Prague and Wrocław (seven hours) and one plies the route between Prague and Kraków (nine hours). Two trains a day travel between Vienna and Warsaw (about 10 hours) and one goes between Vienna and Kraków (seven hours).

Two trains travel daily between Budapest and Warsaw (12 hours), via Bratislava. These trains are routed through a short stretch of the Czech Republic, so get a Czech visa if necessary. The daily train between Budapest and Kraków (11 hours) follows a different route through Košice in eastern Slovakia.

Warsaw has direct train links with Kyiv (Ukraine), Minsk (Belarus), Vilnius (Lithuania), and Moscow and St Petersburg (these trains only have sleeping cars). There are also daily trains between Gdańsk and Kaliningrad (five hours) in Russia.

Remember that you may need to get transit visas for the countries you'll be passing through en route.

Bus

International bus services throughout Western and Eastern Europe are offered by dozens of

Polish and international companies. Prices for international buses are generally cheaper than for trains, but you will undoubtedly find it more comfortable, and probably quicker, to travel to/from Poland by train.

One of the major bus operators is Eurolines, a consortium of affiliated European bus companies including the Polish national bus company **PKS** *(W www.pekaesbus.com.pl)*. PKS operates dozens of buses each week to all major cities in Germany, as well as to Copenhagen on Sunday, from the Dworzec Zachodnia (Western Bus Station) in Warsaw.

Three or four days a week (and daily in summer), **Eurolines** *(☎ 0990-808 080; W www.gobycoach.com)* has services from London (Victoria) to Zamość, via Poznań, Łódź, Warsaw (Zachodnia) and Lublin; and from London to Kraków, via Wrocław and Częstochowa.

Three times a week, Eurolines has bus services from Paris (place de la Concorde) to Białystok, via Poznań and Warsaw; from Paris to Kraków, via Wrocław and Częstochowa; and from Paris to Gdynia, via Poznań, Toruń and Gdańsk. Book at **Polka Service** *(☎ 01 49 72 51 51, 28 ave du Général de Gaulle, Bagnolet)*.

Eurolines also offers regular bus sevices from Hamburg to Częstochowa, via Wrocław; and from Cologne to Warsaw, via Poznań and Łódź.

PKS has regular bus services from Warsaw to Rīga (Friday), to Minsk (Tuesday, Friday and Sunday), to Kyiv (Tuesday, Thursday and Saturday) and Vilnius (daily). These routes should not normally take more than 12 to 15 hours each.

Also, PKS buses run six times a day between Przemyśl and Lviv (three hours), weekly between Suwałki and Vilnius (five hours), regularly between Zakopane and Budapest (nine hours), and twice a day between Gdańsk and Kaliningrad (five hours).

To Kraków, a few buses a week depart from Budapest (10 hours), and one a week makes the long haul from St Petersburg, via Minsk, Warsaw (Dworzec Zachodnia) and Częstochowa.

Car & Motorcycle

To drive a car into Poland you will need your driving licence from home. Also required are vehicle registration papers and liability insurance ('green card'; see Car & Motocycle in the introductory Getting Around chapter).

SEA

Three companies operate passenger and car ferries all year.

Polferries (W www.polferries.pl) offers services between Gdańsk and Nynäshamn (19 hours) in Sweden every day in summer (three times a week in the off season). It also has services from Świnoujście to Ystad (9½ hours) in Sweden, to Rønne (five hours) in Denmark, and to Copenhagen (10½ hours).

Stena Line (W www.stenaline.com) operates between Gdynia and Karlskrona (11 hours) in Sweden.

Unity Line runs ferries between Świnoujście and Ystad (eight hours).

Any travel agency in Scandinavia will sell tickets for these services. In Poland, inquire at any Orbis Travel office. Orbis can also book tickets for other European ferries, eg, between Italy and Greece.

In summer, passenger boats ply the Baltic coast from Świnoujście to Ahlbeck, Heringsdorf, Bansin and Sassnitz in Germany.

Getting Around

BUS & MINIBUS

If you can, avoid using buses because they can be frustratingly slow and indirect.

Most buses are operated by the state bus company, PKS, which has bus terminals *(dworzec autobusowy PKS)* in all cities and towns. PKS provides two kinds of services: ordinary buses, which cover mostly regional routes, and fast buses, which cover mainly long-distance routes. The largest private bus operator is Polski Express.

Tickets for PKS buses must be bought at the terminal. Tickets for Polski Express buses can be bought up to 14 days in advance at the terminals or stops.

For shorter trips, minibuses usually provide a better alternative to PKS buses. Minibuses always travel faster than buses, usually leave more frequently and stop *far* less often. The cost of travelling on a minibus is almost the same as on a bus.

TRAIN

Trains will be your main means of transport, especially for long distances. They are cheap, fairly reliable and rarely overcrowded.

Express trains *(pociąg ekspresowy)* are a faster but more expensive way to travel, while fast trains *(pociąg pospieszny)* are a bit slower and may be more crowded. Slow passenger trains *(pociąg osobowy)* should be used only for short trips.

InterCity trains operate on some major routes out of Warsaw, including Gdańsk, Kraków, Poznań and Szczecin. They only stop at major cities and are faster than express trains (averaging about 100km/h).

Almost all trains offer two classes: 2nd class *(druga klasa)* and 1st class *(pierwsza klasa)*, which is 50% more expensive.

Tickets, Fares & Passes

Be at the station at least half an hour before departure time and make sure you're queueing at the right ticket window *(kasa)*. Better still, buy a ticket up to 30 days in advance from the train station or from any larger Orbis Travel office.

It's important to note that if you do not make a seat reservation, you can travel on *any* train (of the type requested, ie, passenger, fast or express) to the destination indicated on your ticket and on the date specified. If you get on a train without a ticket, you can buy one directly from the conductor for a small supplement – but do it right away.

Tickets for fast trains are 50% to 60% more expensive than those for passenger trains, and tickets for express trains are 33% to 50% more than for fast trains. Only 2nd-class fares are listed in this book.

A Polrail Pass provides unlimited travel on trains throughout Poland. It is valid for all domestic passenger, fast and express trains, but you'll have to pay a surcharge to use the InterCity and EuroCity services. Passes come in durations of eight days (€108) to one month (€182). Persons aged under 26 on the first day can buy a 'Junior' pass for 25% to 30% less.

The pass is available from North American travel agencies through Rail Europe and travel agencies in Western Europe. It can also be bought at the **Wasteels** office *(☎ 022-620 21 49)* in the underground mezzanine level at the Warszawa Centralna train station in the capital, and at **Orbis Travel** *(☎ 022-827 72 65, fax 827 76 05; ul Bracka 16, Warsaw)*.

CAR & MOTORCYCLE

Most major international car-rental companies, such as **Avis** *(W www.avis.pl)* and **Europcar** *(W www.europcar.com.pl)*, are represented in larger cities and have smaller offices at the airports. Prices are comparable to full-price rental in Western Europe. An increasing number of local operators, such as **Payless Car Rental** *(W www.paylesscarrental.pl)*, provide a reliable and more affordable alternative.

Car theft is a problem in Poland.

BICYCLE

Cycling is not great for getting around the cities, but is often a perfect way to travel between villages. Major roads are busy but generally flat, while minor roads can be bumpy.

HITCHING

Car drivers rarely stop to pick up hitchhikers, and large commercial vehicles expect to be paid the equivalent of a bus fare.

LOCAL TRANSPORT

Most cities have buses *(autobus)* and trams *(tramwaj)*, and some also have trolleybuses *(trolejbus)*. Public transport throughout Poland operates from around 5am to 11pm daily, and may become crowded during rush hours. Larger cities also have night-time services on buses and trams.

Taxis in Poland are easily available and not too expensive by Western standards. Legitimate taxis are usually recognisable by large boards on the roof with the company's name and telephone number. By law, these taxis must display a sign on the window with their fares.

Legitimate taxis can be waved down in the street or hired from a taxi stand *(postój taksówek)*. Your hotel will happily order a taxi for you at no extra charge.

Warsaw (Warszawa)

☎ 022 • pop 1.75 million

Warsaw is the geographical, political and economic heart of Poland. It's a large, cosmopolitan and modern city, mostly rebuilt after WWII, and boasts enough museums and other attractions to keep the majority of visitors happy for several days.

When Poland and Lithuania were unified, the capital was transferred here from Kraków. Paradoxically, the 18th century – a period of catastrophic decline for the Polish state – witnessed Warsaw's greatest prosperity. A wealth of splendid churches, palaces and parks were

POLAND

built, and cultural and artistic life flourished. During WWII, however, 700,000 residents perished (over half of the city's population) and 85% of its buildings were destroyed. No other city in Eastern Europe suffered such immense loss of life or devastation.

Immediately after the war the gigantic task of restoration began, and Warsaw re-emerged, phoenix-like. Parts of the historic city, most notably the Old Town, have been meticulously restored to their previous condition.

Information

Tourist Offices The official **tourist organisation** *(☎ 9431; ⓔ info@warsawtour.pl)* has several branches, all open daily: opposite the Royal Castle at Plac Zamkowy, in the arrivals hall of the airport, next to the ticket office at the Dworzec Zachodnia (Western Bus Station) and in the main hall of the Warszawa Centralna train station. Each can provide free city maps of Warsaw, sell maps of other Polish cities, and help you book a hotel room.

Another state-run tourist office, **Warsaw Tourist & Cultural Information** *(☎ 656 68 54; Plac Defilad; open daily)* is on the ground floor of the Palace of Culture & Science building.

These official tourist offices should not be confused with the numerous private offices signposted 'Warsaw Center of Tourist Information'.

Money Foreign-exchange offices, known as *kantors*, and ATMs are easy to find around the city centre. **Bank Pekao** has a dozen branches in the city, including one along ul Krakowskie Przedmieście, next to the Church of the Holy Cross. Also, useful is the **PBK Bank** *(ground floor, Palace of Culture & Science bldg)* and the **PKO Bank** *(Plac Bankowy 2)*. These banks cash major travellers cheques, offer cash advances on Visa and MasterCard, and have ATMs that take just about every known credit card. Another place to cash major travellers cheques is **American Express** *(Marriott Hotel, Al Jerozolimskie 65/79)*.

Post & Communications The best place to send and receive letters and faxes is the **main post office** *(ul Świętokrzyska 31/33; open 24hr)*. Poste restante is at window No 12. Letters should be addressed to Poste Restante, Poczta Główna, ul Świętokrzyska 31/33, 00-001 Warszawa 1.

For telephone calls, use a phonecard at any of the plethora of telephone booths around the city or inside the Main Post Office.

Internet centres and cafés are springing up all over Warsaw. The most atmospheric places to visit are **Casablanca** *(ul Krakowskie Przedmieście 4/6)* and **Studio.tpi** *(ul Świętokrzyska 3)*. Several convenient but dingy **Internet centres** are also located along the underground mezzanine level of the Warszawa Centralna train station.

Medical Services Some of the many pharmacies throughout the city stay open all night, including one in the Warszawa Centralna train station.

The **Hospital of the Ministry of Internal Affairs & Administration** *(☎ 602 15 78; ul Wołoska 137)* is a private hospital that is preferred by important government officials and diplomats.

Things to See & Do

Old Town The main gateway to the Old Town is **Plac Zamkowy** (Castle Square). Amazingly, all of the 17th- and 18th-century buildings around this square were completely rebuilt from their foundations after WWII. In the centre of the square is the **Monument to Sigismund III Vasa**, who moved the capital from Kraków to Warsaw.

The square is dominated by the massive 13th-century **Royal Castle** *(admission free to the courtyards; open 10am-4pm Mon-Sat, 11am-4pm Sun, closed Mon Oct–mid-Apr)*. The castle developed over the centuries as successive Polish kings added wings and redecorated the interior, but it was nothing more than a pile of rubble in 1945. It was completely rebuilt between 1971 and 1984.

From the castle head down ul Świętojańska to the 15th-century Gothic **St John's Cathedral** *(ul Świętojańska 8; admission free; open 10am-1pm & 3pm-5.30pm Mon-Sat)*, the oldest church in Warsaw. This road continues to the magnificent **Rynek Starego Miasta** (Old Town Square).

Alongside this square is the **Warsaw Historical Museum** *(Rynek Starego Miasta 42; admission 5zł, free Sun; open 11am-6pm Tues & Thur, 10.30am-4pm Wed, Fri, Sat & Sun)*. Make sure you're there at noon to see the English-language film (included in the admission fee) that unforgettably depicts the wartime destruction of the city.

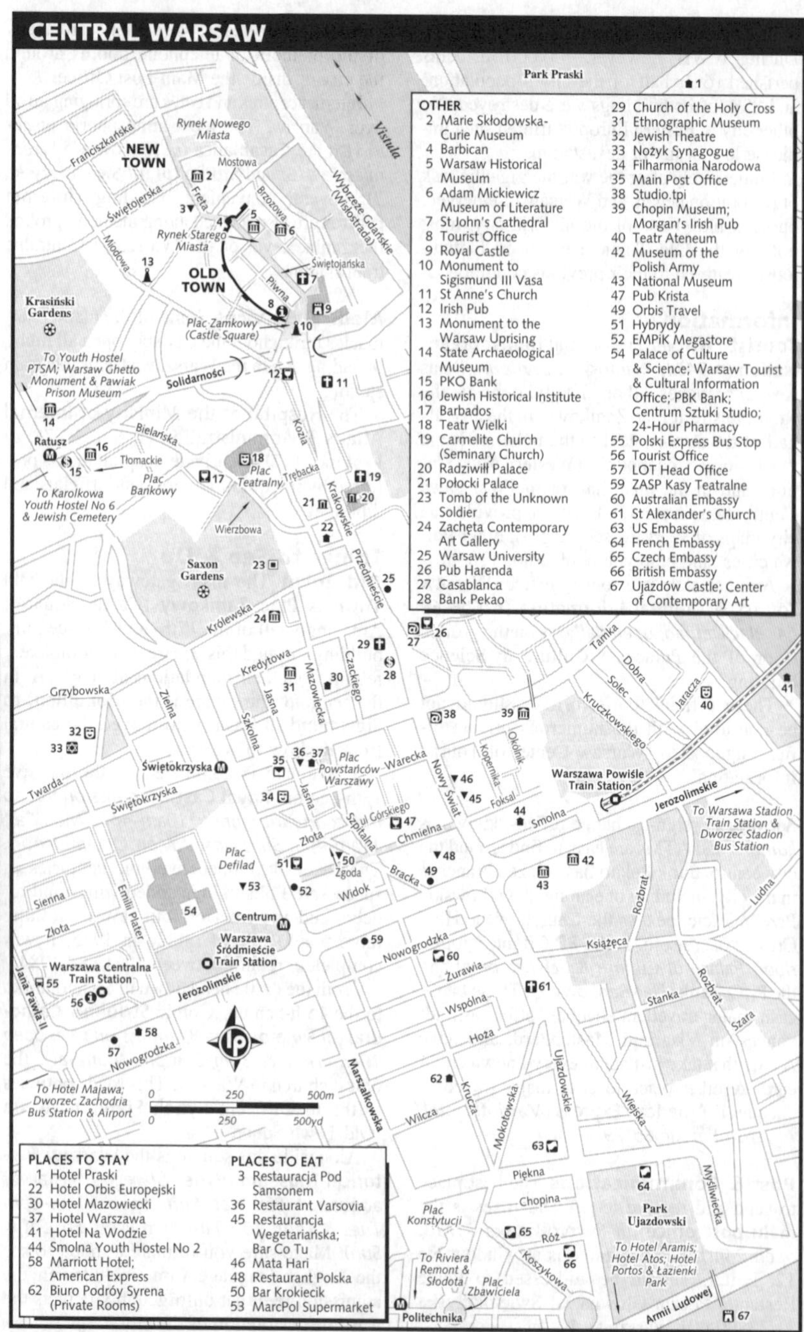

CENTRAL WARSAW
OTHER
2 Marie Skłodowska-Curie Museum
4 Barbican
5 Warsaw Historical Museum
6 Adam Mickiewicz Museum of Literature
7 St John's Cathedral
8 Tourist Office
9 Royal Castle
10 Monument to Sigismund III Vasa
11 St Anne's Church
12 Irish Pub
13 Monument to the Warsaw Uprising
14 State Archaeological Museum
15 PKO Bank
16 Jewish Historical Institute
17 Barbados
18 Teatr Wielki
19 Carmelite Church (Seminary Church)
20 Radziwiłł Palace
21 Połocki Palace
23 Tomb of the Unknown Soldier
24 Zachęta Contemporary Art Gallery
25 Warsaw University
26 Pub Harenda
27 Casablanca
28 Bank Pekao
29 Church of the Holy Cross
31 Ethnographic Museum
32 Jewish Theatre
33 Nożyk Synagogue
34 Filharmonia Narodowa
35 Main Post Office
38 Studio.tpi
39 Chopin Museum; Morgan's Irish Pub
40 Teatr Ateneum
42 Museum of the Polish Army
43 National Museum
47 Pub Krista
49 Orbis Travel
51 Hybrydy
52 EMPiK Megastore
54 Palace of Culture & Science; Warsaw Tourist & Cultural Information Office; PBK Bank; Centrum Sztuki Studio; 24-Hour Pharmacy
55 Polski Express Bus Stop
56 Tourist Office
57 LOT Head Office
59 ZASP Kasy Teatralne
60 Australian Embassy
61 St Alexander's Church
63 US Embassy
64 French Embassy
65 Czech Embassy
66 British Embassy
67 Ujazdów Castle; Center of Contemporary Art
PLACES TO STAY
1 Hotel Praski
22 Hotel Orbis Europejski
30 Hotel Mazowiecki
37 Hiotel Warszawa
41 Hotel Na Wodzie
44 Smolna Youth Hostel No 2
58 Marriott Hotel; American Express
62 Biuro Podróy Syrena (Private Rooms)
PLACES TO EAT
3 Restauracja Pod Samsonem
36 Restaurant Varsovia
45 Restaurancja Wegetariańska; Bar Co Tu
46 Mata Hari
48 Restaurant Polska
50 Bar Krokiecik
53 MarcPol Supermarket
Park Praski
Vistula
Wybrzeże Gdańskie (Wisłostrada)
Rynek Nowego Miasta
NEW TOWN
Franciszkańska
Mostowa
Freta
Świętojerska
Brzozowa
Rynek Starego Miasta
Miodowa
OLD TOWN
Świętojańska
Piwna
Krasiński Gardens
Plac Zamkowy (Castle Square)
To Youth Hostel PTSM; Warsaw Ghetto Monument & Pawiak Prison Museum
Solidarności
Kozia
Bielańska
Ratusz
Tłomackie
Plac Bankowy
Plac Teatralny
Trębacka
Krakowskie
To Karolkowa Youth Hostel No 6 & Jewish Cemetery
Wierzbowa
Przedmieście
Saxon Gardens
Królewska
Kredytowa
Mazowiecka
Czackiego
Tamka
Dobra
Solec
Jaracza
Grzybowska
Zielna
Jasna
Szkolna
Kruczkowskiego
Okólnik
Kopernika
Świętokrzyska
Plac Powstańców Warszawy
Warecka
Nowy Świat
Foksal
Warszawa Powiśle Train Station
Twarda
Świętokrzyska
ul Górskiego
Smolna
Jerozolimskie
To Warsaw Stadion Train Station & Dworzec Stadion Bus Station
Złota
Szpitalna
Chmielna
Plac Defilad
Zgoda
Bracka
Widok
Ludna
Sienna
Rozbrat
Złota
Emilii Plater
Centrum
Warszawa Śródmieście Train Station
Nowogrodzka
Książęca
Warszawa Centralna Train Station
Jana Pawła II
Jerozolimskie
Żurawia
Rozbrat
Stanka
Wspólna
Szara
Nowogrodzka
Hoża
Ujazdowskie
Marszałkowska
To Hotel Majawa; Dworzec Zachodria Bus Station & Airport
0 250 500m
0 250 500yd
Krucza
Wiejska
Wilcza
Mokotowska
Piękna
Mysliwiecka
Chopina
Plac Konstytucji
Park Ujazdowski
Róż
To Riviera Remont & Słodota
Koszykowa
To Hotel Aramis; Hotel Atos; Hotel Portos & Łazienki Park
Plac Zbawiciela
Politechnika
Armii Ludowej
POLAND

Walk west for one block to the **Barbican**, part of a medieval wall that encircled Warsaw and was built on a bridge over a moat.

The Royal Way (Szlak Królewski) This 4km route links the Royal Castle with Łazienki Park via ul Krakowskie Przedmieście, ul Nowy Świat and Al Ujazdowskie. If you want to save time and energy, jump on and off bus No 180, which stops at most places along this route.

Just south of the Royal Castle is the 15th-century **St Anne's Church** *(ul Krakowskie Przedmieście 68; admission free; open daylight hours)*, one of the most ornate churches in the city. You can climb up the **tower** *(admission 3.50zł; open 10am-6pm Tues-Sun)* for views of Plac Zamkowy and the castle. About 300m further south is the former **Carmelite Church** *(ul Krakowskie Przedmieście 52/54; admission free; open daylight hours)*, also known as the Seminary Church. Nearby, the **Radziwiłł Palace** (not open to the public) is occupied by the Polish president.

To the west of the neoclassical Hotel Orbis Europejski are the **Saxon Gardens** *(admission free; permanently open)*. At the entrance is the small but poignant **Tomb of the Unknown Soldier** *(admission free; permanently open)*, which occupies a fragment of an 18th-century royal palace destroyed in WWII.

South of the tomb, the **Zachęta Contemporary Art Gallery** *(ul Królewska; admission 10zł, free Fri; open 10am-6pm Tues-Sun)* features modern painting, sculpture and photography, and many excellent special exhibits. About 200m further south is the **Ethnographic Museum** *(ul Kredytowa 1; admission 5zł; open 9am-4pm Tues, Thur & Fri, 11am-7pm Wed, 10am-5pm Sat & Sun)*. This large building displays various traditional Polish costumes, crafts and folk art.

Back along the Royal Way is the 17th-century **Church of the Holy Cross** *(ul Krakowskie Przedmieście 3; admission free; open most afternoons)*. Here, Chopin's heart is preserved (in the second pillar on the left-hand side of the main nave). It was brought from Paris, where Chopin died of tuberculosis aged only 39. If you want to know more, head along ul Tamka towards the river to the small **Chopin Museum** *(ul Okólnik 1; admission 7zł; open about 10am-4pm Mon-Sat)*. It features, among other things, the great man's last piano and a collection of his manuscripts.

A Curie for Cancer

Many Polish streets are named after the great scientist Marie Curie, but here she has been given the Polish-French name of Marie Skłodowska-Curie. The **Marie Skłodowska-Curie Museum** *(ul Freta 16; admission 5zł; open 10am-4pm Tues-Sat, 10am-2pm Sun)* features modest displays about the woman in the house where she was born.

Marie Curie laid the foundations for radiography, nuclear physics and cancer therapy. She was born in Warsaw, then part of Russia, in 1867. Curie lived in Poland for 24 years before being forced (under Russian law) to leave Poland (because she was a woman) to further her studies.

In Paris, she and her French husband Pierre Curie discovered two new radioactive chemical elements: radium and polonium (named after her homeland). She won numerous awards and distinctions, including two Nobel Prizes. Tragically, she died at the age of 67 from leukemia caused by prolonged exposure to radiation.

Return to the Royal Way and head south along ul Nowy Świat to the roundabout at the junction of Al Jerozolimskie. On the way to the river is the enormous **National Museum** *(Al Jerozolimskie 3; admission to museum 11zł, to temporary exhibitions 15zł, museum only free Sat; open 10am-4pm Tues, Wed & Fri, noon-5pm Thur, 10am-5pm Sat & Sun)*. It houses a magnificent collection of Polish sculptures and art from the medieval period to the present.

Jewish Historical Sites The vast suburbs northwest of the Palace of Culture & Science were once predominantly inhabited by Polish Jews. During WWII the Nazis established a Jewish ghetto in the area, but razed it after crushing the Warsaw Ghetto Uprising in April 1943. This tragic event is immortalised by the **Monument to the Warsaw Uprising** *(cnr ul Długa & ul Miodowa)*.

The **Warsaw Ghetto Monument** *(cnr ul Anielewicza & ul Zamenhofa)* uses pictorial plaques to commemorate victims. The nearby **Pawiak Prison Museum** *(ul Dzielna 24/26; admission free; open about 10am-4pm Wed-Sun)* occupies the former building used as a Gestapo prison during the Nazi occupation.

Moving exhibits include letters and other personal items.

Arguably the most dramatic remnant of the Jewish legacy is the vast **Jewish Cemetery** *(ul Okopowa 49/51; admission free; open 9am-4pm Sun-Fri May-Sept, 9am-3pm Oct-Apr)*. Founded in 1806, it still has over 100,000 gravestones and is the largest collection of its kind in Europe. Visitors must wear a head covering to enter the cemetery, which is accessible from the Old Town on tram Nos 22, 27 and 29.

The **Jewish Historical Institute** *(ul Tłomackie 3/5; admission 10zł; open 9am-4pm Mon-Wed & Fri, 11am-6pm Thur)* features permanent exhibits about the Warsaw Ghetto, as well as art and photos relating to local Jewish history. Tucked away behind the **Jewish Theatre** is the neo-Romanesque **Nożyk Synagogue** *(ul Twarda; admission 3.50zł; open 10am-8pm Sun-Thur, 10am-4pm Fri)*. Warsaw's only synagogue that managed to survive WWII, albeit in a sorry state.

Special Events

Warsaw's major annual events include the International Book Fair (May), the Warsaw Summer Jazz Days (late June/early July), the Mozart Festival (June/July), 'Art of the Street' International Festival (July) and the 'Warsaw Autumn' Festival of Contemporary Music (September).

Places to Stay

Warsaw is the most expensive city in Poland for accommodation. Trying to find anywhere cheap within 30 minutes of the city centre by tram is increasingly difficult. The official tourist offices will help.

Hostels & Private Rooms Each hostel listed below closes between at least 10am and 4pm each day.

Smolna Youth Hostel No 2 *(☎/fax 827 89 52; ul Smolna 30; dorm beds 33zł, singles/doubles with TV & shared bathroom 60/110zł; open year-round)* is the best and most central. For singles or doubles, book in advance and book dorm beds in summer. The three-night maximum is often waived when it's not so busy.

Karolkowa Youth Hostel No 6 *(☎/fax 632 97 46; ul Karolkowa 53a; dorm beds from 35zł; open year-round)* is in the suburb of Wola and accessible by tram No 12, 22 or 24 from the Warszawa Centralna train station. This well-established and friendly place has laundry and Internet facilities.

Youth Hostel PTSM *(☎ 831 17 66; ul Międzyparkowa 4/6; dorm beds 35zł; open Apr-Oct)* is among parkland in the northern suburbs. Rates are cheaper, but the standards are far lower than the other two hostels, and there are no single or double rooms. Take bus No 175 from the central train station or airport.

Private rooms in local homes can be arranged through **Biuro Podróży Syrena** *(☎/fax 629 49 78; ⓔ office@syrena-pl.com; ul Krucza 17)*. Singles/doubles with shared bathroom in the city centre cost 79/110zł for one or two nights, and as little as 68/96zł for three or more nights.

Hotels The best value in the capital is offered by **Hotel Majawa** *(☎/fax 823 37 48; ⓔ camp123@friko6.onet.pl; ul Warszawskiej 1920r 15/17; singles/doubles in hotel with shared bathroom 80/109zł, double bungalows with/without bathroom from 109/79zł)*. The bungalows at this camping ground are private and clean, while the hotel rooms are quiet, spotless and bright.

Hotel Na Wodzie *(☎/fax 628 58 83; ul Wybrzeże Kościuszkowskie; single/double cabins with shared bathroom 65/85zł; open Apr-Nov)* is actually in two boats – the *Aldona* and *Anita* – both anchored along the Vistula River between the railway and Poniatowski bridges. The living quarters are adequate, but the location leaves something to be desired.

The best choice of budget accommodation is along ul Mangalia, where three one-star hotels are located virtually next door to each other. Information is available at ⓦ www.felix.com.pl. Singles/doubles with bathroom at all three costs 120/150zł, and they are accessible by bus Nos 118, 403, 503 and 513 along ul Sobieskiego. **Hotel Aramis** *(☎ 842 09 74; ⓔ aramis@felix.com.pl; ul Mangalia 3b)* is the largest and best set up. **Hotel Atos** *(☎ 841 43 95; ⓔ atos@felix.com.pl; ul Mangalia 1)* only has nine rooms, but is cosy. **Hotel Portos** *(☎ 842 68 51; ⓔ portos@felix.com.pl; ul Mangalia 3a)* is also fairly good value for the price.

Hotel Praski *(☎/fax 818 49 89; ⓦ www.praski.pl; Al Solidarności 61; singles/doubles with shared bathroom & breakfast from 150/200zł)* is on the other side of the river, but little more than 1km from the Old Town.

It has been renovated in recent years and is one of the best two-star places in the capital.

Places to Eat

Warsaw has witnessed a virtual explosion of modern bistros, pizzerias, snack bars and international fast-food chains, yet a number of genuine **milk bars** still provide the cheapest food in town.

Restaurant Polska *(ul Nowy Świat 21; mains from 35zł)* is a favourite spot situated in an elegant basement. The Polish dishes are mouth-watering. Enter gate No 21 and walk straight ahead for 100m. **Restaurant Varsovia** *(ul Świętokrzyska 15; meals about 15zł)* is a reasonably classy place with a range of Polish and Western meals listed on a menu in English. It's just around the corner from the Hotel Warszawa. **Bar Krokiecik** *(ul Zgoda 1; meals 8-10zł)* is a central option for more affordable Polish meals.

Mata Hari *(ul Nowy Świat 52; soups 5zł, mains 7-12zł)* offers delicious and cheap Indian food and is a wonderful option for adventurous vegetarians. **Restauracja Wegetariańska** *(off Nowy Świat; soups & salads from 5zł)* is another enticing place for healthy, meat-free food.

Bar Co Tu *(off ul Nowy Świat; most meals under 10zł)* is a small but popular eatery offering a large array of tasty Chinese meals and a menu in English. It's not far down (south) from Restauracja Wegetariańska.

Restauracja Pod Samsonem *(ul Freta 3/5; mains 19-27zł)*, which is opposite the Marie Skłodowska-Curie Museum, is frequented by locals for inexpensive and tasty meals with a combined Polish and Jewish flavour. Daily specials are listed in crayon on the side of the wooden door.

The most convenient places to shop for groceries are the **MarcPol Supermarket**, in front of the Palace of Culture & Science building, and the downstairs **grocery shop** on the corner of ul Świętokrzyska and ul Marszałkowska.

Entertainment

For more information about what to do, check out *The Buzz* section of *The Warsaw Voice* and the informative *Warszawa: What, Where, When*.

Pubs & Bars Warsaw is flooded with all sorts of pubs and bars. The most charming places for a drink are around Rynek Starego Miasta in the Old Town, but prices are high. Two authentic Irish pubs are great places to enjoy a Guinness (or three): **Irish Pub** *(ul 3 Miodowa)* offers live music most nights, while **Morgan's Irish Pub** *(ul Tamka 40)*, under the Chopin Museum, is well frequented.

Pub Harenda *(ul Krakowskie Przedmieście 4/6)*, at the back of Hotel Harenda, is often crowded. It provides an appealing beer garden and equally appealing happy hours. Live jazz music is performed here during the week and there's dance music on weekends. **Pub Krista** *(ul Górskiego 8)*, along the extension of ul Złota, has been recommended by some readers for its fine ales and cellar atmosphere.

Clubs The following two student clubs are popular and cheap, but open only from June to September. **Riviera Remont** *(ul Waryńskiego 12)* has live music (often jazz) on Thursday and Saturday nights. **Słodoła** *(ul Batorego 10)* is another popular student club, which pulsates with techno music most nights.

Hybrydy *(ul Złota 7/9)* has been going for some 45 years and is still trendy. It features all sorts of taped and live music most nights. **Barbados** *(ul Wierzbowa 9; open Wed-Sat)*, over the road from the Teatr Wielki, is where the 'beautiful people' of Warsaw come.

Theatre, Opera & Ballet Advance tickets for most events at most theatres can be bought at **ZASP Kasy Teatralne** *(Al Jerozolimskie 25; open 11am-6pm Mon-Fri, 11am-2pm Sat)* or at the **EMPiK Megastore** *(ul Marszałkowska 116/122)*. Otherwise, same-day tickets may be available at the relevant box offices. Remember: most theatres close in July and August.

Centrum Sztuki Studio *(Palace of Culture & Science bldg)* and **Teatr Ateneum** *(ul Jaracza 2)* lean towards contemporary Polish-language productions. **Teatr Wielki** *(Grand Theatre; Plac Teatralny 1)* is the main venue for opera and ballet. **Filharmonia Narodowa** *(ul Jasna 5)* has a concert hall and chamber hall.

In **Łazienki Park**, piano recitals are held every Sunday from May to September and chamber concerts are staged there in summer at the **Old Orangery**.

Getting There & Away

Air Frederic Chopin Airport is more commonly called Okęcie Airport, after the suburb, 10km southwest of the city centre, where it's based. Domestic and international flights on LOT can be booked at the **LOT head office** *(☎ 657 80 11; Al Jerozolimskie 65/79)* in the Marriott Hotel complex or from any travel agency, including the ubiquitous Orbis Travel. Other airline offices are listed in the *Warszawa: What, Where, When* and *Welcome to Warsaw* magazines.

Bus Warsaw has two major bus terminals for PKS buses. **Dworzec Zachodnia** *(Western Bus Station; Al Jerozolimskie 144)* handles all domestic buses heading south, north and west of the capital, including Częstochowa (31zł), Gdańsk (55zł), Kazimierz Dolny (17zł), Kraków (36zł), Olsztyn (30zł), Toruń (31zł), Wrocław (41zł) and Zakopane (49zł). This complex is southwest of the city centre and adjoins the Warszawa Zachodnia train station. Take the commuter train from Warszawa Śródmieście station.

Dworzec Stadion *(Stadium Bus Station; ul Sokola 1)* adjoins the Warszawa Stadion train station. It is also easily accessible by commuter train from Warszawa Śródmieście. Dworzec Stadion handles a few domestic buses to the east and southeast, such as Lublin (24zł), Białystok (20zł) and Zamość (35zł), as well as Kazimierz Dolny.

Polski Express *(☎ 620 03 26)* operates coaches from the airport, but passengers can get on or off and buy tickets at the stall along Al Jana Pawła II, next to the Warszawa Centralna train station. Polski Express buses travel daily to Białystok (30zł); Częstochowa (34zł); Gdynia, via Sopot and Gdańsk (53zł); Kraków (54zł); Lublin (31zł); Toruń (35zł); and Wrocław (35zł).

International buses depart from/arrive at Dworzec Zachodnia or, occasionally, outside the Warszawa Centralna train station. Tickets for international buses are available from the bus offices at Dworzec Zachodnia, from agencies at Warszawa Centralna or from major travel agencies, such as Almatur.

Train Warsaw has several train stations, but the one that most travellers will use almost exclusively is **Warszawa Centralna** *(Warsaw Central; Al Jerozolimskie 54)*; it handles the overwhelming majority of domestic trains and all international services.

Remember: Warszawa Centralna is often *not* where domestic and international trains start or finish, so make sure you get on or off the train at this station in the few minutes allotted. And watch your belongings closely at all times, because pickpocketing and theft is an increasing problem.

Some domestic trains also stop at **Warszawa Śródmieście** station, 300m east of Warszawa Centralna, and at **Warszawa Zachodnia**, next to the Dworzec Zachodnia bus station.

Getting Around

To/From the Airport The cheapest way of getting from the airport to the city centre (and vice versa) is on bus No 175. This bus leaves every 10 to 15 minutes for the Old Town, via ul Nowy Świat and the Warszawa Centralna train station. If you arrive in the wee hours, night bus No 611 links the airport with Warszawa Centralna every 30 minutes.

The taxi fare between the airport and the city centre should be around 25zł. Illicit 'Mafia' cabs operate at the airport and charge astronomical rates.

Public Transport Warsaw's public transport is frequent and cheap; it operates from 5am to 11pm daily. The fare (2.40zł) is a flat rate for a bus, tram, trolleybus or metro train travelling anywhere in the city, ie, one 2.40zł fare is valid for one ride on one form of transport. Warsaw is the only place in Poland where ISIC cards get a public-transport discount (50%).

Tickets (valid on all forms of public transport) for 60/90 minutes cost a reasonable 3.60/4.50zł, and passes (for all public transport) are available for one day (7.20zł), three days (12zł), one week (26zł) and one month (66zł). Daily tickets are actually valid for 24 hours and start from the time you first use them. Tickets should be purchased from kiosks (including those marked RUCH) before boarding and punched in one of the small machines on board.

One very useful bus is the 'sightseeing route' No 180, which links Powązki Cemetery with Wilanów Park.

Taxi A quick and easy way to get around is by taxi – as long as you use official taxis and the drivers use their meters. Beware of 'Mafia' taxis parked in front of top-end hotels, at the airport, outside the Warszawa Centralna train station and in the vicinity of most tourist sights.

Małopolska

Małopolska (literally 'little Poland') encompasses the whole of southeastern Poland, from the Lublin Uplands in the north down to the Carpathian Mountains along the borders with Slovakia and Ukraine. Kraków became the royal capital of Małopolska in 1038 and remained so for over 500 years. Visitors to the region can admire the royal dignity of Kraków, explore the rugged beauty of the Tatra Mountains and witness the tragic remnants of the Jewish heritage.

KRAKÓW

☎ 012 • pop 770,000

Kraków is Poland's third-largest city and one of its oldest, dating from the 7th century. The city was founded by Prince Krak, who, according to legend, secured its prime location overlooking the Vistula River after outwitting the resident dragon.

At this crossing of trade routes from Western Europe to Byzantium and from southern Europe to the Baltic Sea, a large medieval city developed. More recently, Kraków became the only large Polish city whose old architecture survived WWII intact. In January 1945 a sudden encircling manoeuvre by the Soviet Red Army forced the Germans to evacuate the city, so Kraków was saved from destruction.

No other city in Poland better captures its intriguing history: the Old Town harbours towering Gothic churches and the splendid Wawel Castle, while Kazimierz, the now-silent Jewish quarter, recounts a more tragic story.

Information

Tourist Offices The array of tourist offices is confusing. The **Municipal Tourism Information Centre** *(Rynek Główny 1/3; ☎ 428 36 00; open daily)* is the major office. There is also a smaller and less busy **tourist office** *(☎ 432 01 10; ⓔ it-krakow@wp.pl; open daily)* along the path between ul Szpitalna and the main train station. Another **tourist counter** *(☎ 421 50 31; ⓔ ap2info@interia.pl; open daily)* is at the far end of the main train station.

The **Tourist Office** *(☎ 432 08 40; ⓔ biuro@kazimierzbiuro.kraknet.pl; ul Józefa 7; open Mon-Fri)* in Kazimierz provides information about Jewish heritage in that area. The **Culture Information Centre** *(☎ 421 77 87; ⓦ www.karnet.krakow2000.pl; ul Św Jana 2; open Mon-Sat)* is the best place to get information about (and tickets for) the plethora of cultural events in the city.

Two free monthly magazines, *Welcome to Craców & Małopolska* and *Kraków: What, Where, When* (the latter also in German), are available at the tourist offices and some travel agencies and upmarket hotels. The *Kraków Insider* booklet (6.50zł) is also very useful.

Money Kantors and ATMs can be found all over the city centre. It's worth noting, however, that most kantors close on Sunday and areas near Rynek Główny square and around the main train station offer terrible exchange rates. For travellers cheques, try **Bank Pekao** *(Rynek Główny 31)*, which also provides cash advances on MasterCard and Visa.

Post & Communications The **Main Post Office** *(ul Westerplatte 20; open 8am-8pm Mon-Fri, 8am-2pm Sat, 9am-noon Sun)* offers poste restante. Mail addressed to Poste Restante, Poczta Główna, ul Westerplatte 20, 31-045 Kraków 1, Poland, can be collected at window No 1. Telephone calls can be made at the **Telephone Centre** *(ul Wielopole; open 24hr)*, next to the Main Post Office, or from the **post & telephone office** *(ul Lubicz 4; open 24hr)*, conveniently opposite the main train station building.

The most atmospheric place to check your emails is the downstairs **Cyber Café U Luisa** *(Rynek Główny 13)*. Otherwise, try **Centrum Internetowe** *(Rynek Główny 9)*, where views of the square from the window are so exceptional that it's hard to concentrate on the computer screen.

Things to See & Do

Old Town The magnificent **Rynek Główny** is the largest (roughly 800m wide and 1200m long) medieval town square in Europe. Dominating the square is the 16th-century Renaissance **Cloth Hall** (Sukiennice). On the ground floor is a large craft market and upstairs is the **Gallery of 19th-Century Polish Painting** *(admission 5zł, free Sun; open 10am-3.30pm Tues, Wed & Fri-Sun, 10am-6pm Thur)*, which includes several famous works by Jan Matejko.

Ostentatious 14th-century **St Mary's Church** *(Rynek Główny 4; admission 2.50zł; open noon-6pm Mon-Sat)* fills the northeastern corner of the square. The huge main altarpiece by Wit Stwosz (Veit Stoss) of Nuremberg is the finest Gothic sculpture in Poland.

A Rough Cut

Every hour a *hejnał* (bugle call) is played from the highest tower of St Mary's Church. The five-note melody was played in medieval times as a warning call. It breaks off abruptly to symbolise the moment when, according to legend, the throat of a 13th-century trumpeter was pierced by a Tatar arrow.

To the west of the Cloth Hall is the 15th-century **Town Hall Tower** *(admission 3zł; open 10am-5pm Wed-Fri, 10am-4pm Sat & Sun)*. The **Historical Museum of Kraków** *(Rynek Główny 35; admission 5zł; open 9am-3.30pm Tues, Wed & Fri, 11am-6pm Thur)* is also worth a visit.

From St Mary's Church, you can walk up (northeast) ul Floriańska to the 14th-century **Florian Gate**, the only one remaining of the original eight gates. Behind the gate is the **Barbican** *(admission 5zł; open 9am-5pm daily May-Sept)*, a defensive bastion that was built in 1498. Nearby, the **Czartoryski Museum** *(ul Św Jana 19; admission 5zł; open around 10am-3.30pm Tues-Sun)* features an impressive collection of European art, including some works by Leonardo da Vinci and Rembrandt.

South of Rynek Główny, along ul Grodzka, is the early-17th-century Jesuit **Church of SS Peter & Paul** *(ul Grodzka 64; admission free; open dawn-dusk daily)*, the first baroque church in Poland. The 11th-century Romanesque **St Andrew's Church** *(ul Grodzka 56; admission free; open 9am-6pm Mon-Fri)* was the only building in Kraków to withstand the Tatar attack of 1241.

POLAND

Wawel Hill South of the Old Town is the dominant Wawel Hill *(admission to grounds free; open 6am-8pm daily May-Sept, 6am-5pm Oct-Apr)*. This hill is topped with a castle and cathedral, both of which are the very symbols of Poland and the guardians of its national history.

Inside the extensive grounds are several worthwhile attractions; all are open 9.30am to 3pm Tuesday to Friday and 10am to 3pm Saturday and Sunday. Each place has different opening hours on Monday (as indicated below). Currently, entry to the Treasury & Armoury and Lost Wawel is free on Monday, but this may change.

As soon as you arrive, stop at the *kasa* (ticket office) in the grounds; entry to most attractions is limited and only available by ticket (even when admission is free).

Inside the magnificent **Wawel Castle**, the largest and most popular exhibits are the **Royal Chambers** *(admission 15zł; closed Mon)* and the **Royal Private Apartments** *(admission 15zł; closed Mon)*. Entry to the latter is only allowed on a guided tour (included in the admission fee); if you want a guide who speaks English, French or German contact the **guides office** *(☎ 422 09 04)* along the laneway up to the hill.

Dominating the hill is the 14th-century **Wawel Cathedral** *(admission to cathedral free, combined admission to tombs & bell tower 6zł; open 9am-5pm Mon)*. For four centuries it was the coronation and burial place of Polish royalty, as evidenced by the **Royal Tombs**, where 100 kings and queens have been buried. The golden-domed **Sigismund Chapel** (1539), on the southern side of the cathedral, is considered to be the finest Renaissance construction in Poland, and the **bell tower** houses the country's largest bell (11 tonnes).

Kazimierz Founded by King Kazimierz the Great in 1335, Kazimierz was an independent town with its own municipal charter and laws until the 1820s. In the 15th century, Jews were expelled from Kraków and forced to resettle in a small prescribed area in Kazimierz, separated by a wall from the larger Christian quarter. The Jewish quarter later became home to Jews fleeing persecution from all corners of Europe.

By the outbreak of WWII there were 65,000 Jews in Kraków (about 30% of the city's population), and most lived in Kazimierz. During the war the Nazis relocated Jews to a walled ghetto in Podgórze, just south of the Vistula River. They were exterminated in the nearby **Płaszów Concentration Camp**, as portrayed in Steven Spielberg's film *Schindler's List*. The current Jewish population in Kraków is about 100.

These days Kazimierz is undergoing a renaissance as citizens of all creeds and religions realise the benefit of living in such a charming place so close to the city centre.

The eastern Jewish quarter is dotted with synagogues, many of which miraculously survived the war. The most important is the 15th-century **Old Synagogue**, which is the

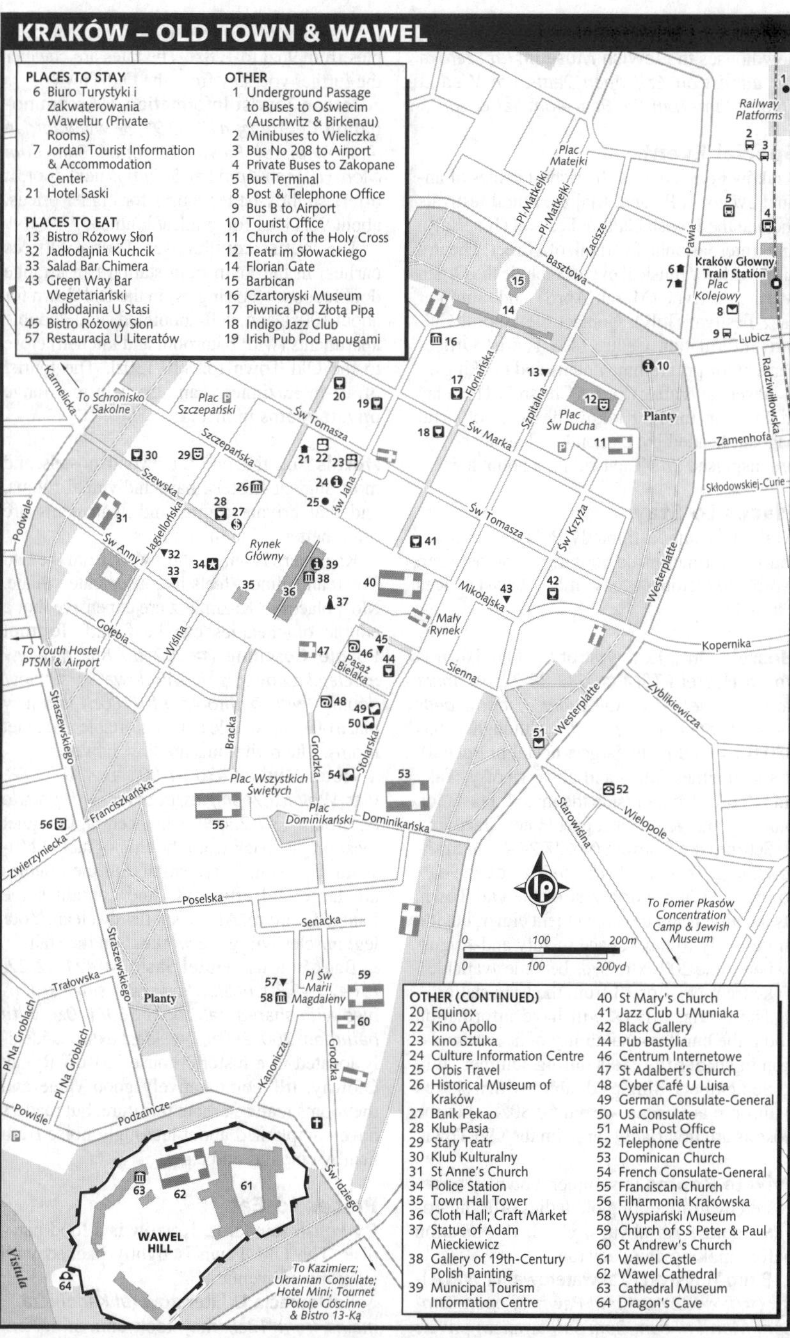
KRAKÓW – OLD TOWN & WAWEL
PLACES TO STAY
6 Biuro Turystyki i Zakwaterowania Waweltur (Private Rooms)
7 Jordan Tourist Information & Accommodation Center
21 Hotel Saski
PLACES TO EAT
13 Bistro Różowy Słoń
32 Jadłodajnia Kuchcik
33 Salad Bar Chimera
43 Green Way Bar Wegetariański Jadłodajnia U Stasi
45 Bistro Różowy Słon
57 Restauracja U Literatów
OTHER
1 Underground Passage to Buses to Oświecim (Auschwitz & Birkenau)
2 Minibuses to Wieliczka
3 Bus No 208 to Airport
4 Private Buses to Zakopane
5 Bus Terminal
8 Post & Telephone Office
9 Bus B to Airport
10 Tourist Office
11 Church of the Holy Cross
12 Teatr im Słowackiego
14 Florian Gate
15 Barbican
16 Czartoryski Museum
17 Piwnica Pod Złotą Pipą
18 Indigo Jazz Club
19 Irish Pub Pod Papugami
OTHER (CONTINUED)
20 Equinox
22 Kino Apollo
23 Kino Sztuka
24 Culture Information Centre
25 Orbis Travel
26 Historical Museum of Kraków
27 Bank Pekao
28 Klub Pasja
29 Stary Teatr
30 Klub Kulturalny
31 St Anne's Church
34 Police Station
35 Town Hall Tower
36 Cloth Hall; Craft Market
37 Statue of Adam Mieckiewicz
38 Gallery of 19th-Century Polish Painting
39 Municipal Tourism Information Centre
40 St Mary's Church
41 Jazz Club U Muniaka
42 Black Gallery
44 Pub Bastylia
46 Centrum Internetowe
47 St Adalbert's Church
48 Cyber Café U Luisa
49 German Consulate-General
50 US Consulate
51 Main Post Office
52 Telephone Centre
53 Dominican Church
54 French Consulate-General
55 Franciscan Church
56 Filharmonia Krakówska
58 Wyspiański Museum
59 Church of SS Peter & Paul
60 St Andrew's Church
61 Wawel Castle
62 Wawel Cathedral
63 Cathedral Museum
64 Dragon's Cave
Railway Platforms
Kraków Głowny Train Station
Plac Kolejowy
Plac Matejki
Pl Matkejki
Basztowa
Zacisze
Pawia
Lubicz
Radziwiłłowska
Zamenhofa
Skłodowskiej-Curie
Planty
Plac Św Ducha
Floriańska
Szpitalna
Św Marka
Św Tomasza
Św Krzyża
Westerplatte
Mikołajska
Mały Rynek
Sienna
Kopernika
Zyblikiewicza
Wielopole
Starowiślna
To Schronisko Sakolne
Plac Szczepański
Szczepańska
Karmelicka
Szewska
Jagiellońska
Podwale
Św Anny
Rynek Główny
Św Jana
Gołębia
Wiślna
To Youth Hostel PTSM & Airport
Pasaż Bielaka
Straszewskiego
Bracka
Grodzka
Stolarska
Plac Wszystkich Świętych
Plac Dominikański
Dominikańska
Franciszkańska
Zwierzyniecka
Poselska
Senacka
Pl Św Marii Magdaleny
Trałowska
Pl Na Groblach
Kanonicza
Powiśle
Podzamcze
Św Idziego
WAWEL HILL
Vistula
To Kazimierz; Ukrainian Consulate; Hotel Mini; Tournet Pokoje Gościnne & Bistro 13-Ką
To Fomer Pkasów Concentration Camp & Jewish Museum
0 100 200m
0 100 200yd
POLAND

oldest Jewish religious building in Poland. It now houses the **Jewish Museum** *(ul Szeroka 24; admission 6zł; open 9am-3pm Wed & Thur, 11am-7pm Fri, 9am-4pm Sat & Sun)*.

Special Events

Kraków boasts one of the richest cycles of annual events in Poland. Major cultural festivals include the Jewish Culture Festival (June/July) and International Festival of Street Theatre (July). Major musical events include the Organ Music Festival (March/April) and Summer Jazz Festival (July). Contact the helpful Culture Information Centre (see Tourist Offices earlier) for programme details and bookings.

Seven days after Corpus Christi (a Thursday in May or June), Kraków hosts a colourful pageant headed by Lajkonik, a legendary figure disguised as a Tatar riding a hobbyhorse.

Places to Stay

Kraków is unquestionably Poland's premier tourist destination, so booking ahead between April and October is essential. Tourist offices can help.

Hostels Only 1km west of the Old Town is **Youth Hostel PTSM** *(☎ 633 88 22; e smkra kow.pro.onet.pl; ul Oleandry 4; dorm beds 14-24zł; open year-round)*. Although it has 380 beds (and is the largest hostel in Poland), it's sometimes full – and always noisy. Take tram No 15 from outside the main train station building and get off just past Hotel Cracovia.

Schronisko Szkolne *(☎ 637 24 41; ul Szablowskiego 1c; dorm beds 15-25zł; open year-round)* is 3.5km northwest of the Old Town. Its location is not too convenient either, but it's more likely to have space in July and August (when some 200 extra beds become available). Take tram No 4 or 13 from the train station.

The tourist offices will have information about the current availability of accommodation in **student hostels** during summer (July to September). Singles/doubles with a shared bathroom are cheap – from 60/80zł – but the hostels are invariably far from the Old Town.

Private Rooms In summer, you may be accosted by intimidating old ladies offering private rooms. As always, check the location before making any decision.

Biuro Turystyki i Zakwaterowania Waweltur *(☎/fax 422 16 40; ul Pawia 8; open 8am-8pm Mon-Fri, 8am-2pm Sat)* arranges private rooms. Singles cost from 64zł to 75zł and doubles from 96zł to 128zł. The rates are cheaper the further you stay from the Old Town.

Jordan Tourist Information & Accommodation Centre *(☎ 422 60 91; w www.jordan.krakow.pl; ul Pawia 12; open 8am-6pm Mon-Fri, 9am-1pm Sat & Sun)* is next door. It offers slightly better rooms for higher prices: about 90/110zł for singles/doubles.

The **tourist counter** (see Tourist Offices earlier) in the main train station can arrange double rooms (no singles) in the Old Town for about 100zł, and well-appointed single/double apartments (with bathroom and kitchen) close to the Old Town for 110/130zł. The tourist office in Kazimierz can also help to arrange **private rooms** in that area.

Hotels Note that one of the youth hostels, and most student hostels, have individual rooms, and that private rooms and apartments are often better value than hotels.

Kazimierz is only a short walk from the Old Town and almost feels like a separate village. Most places in Kazimierz are expensive, but a couple of cheapies can be found. **Tournet Pokoje Gościnne** *(☎ 292 00 88; w www.nocleg.krakow.pl; ul Miodowa 7; singles/doubles with bathroom 140/180zł)* is a new place offering simple but comfortable and quiet rooms. The bathrooms are tiny, however.

Hotel Mini *(☎ 430 61 00, fax 430 59 88; Plac Wolnica 7; singles/doubles with private bathroom 130/220zł)* is in a central but quiet location just back from the Ethnographic Museum. The singles are small, but the doubles are large and attic-style and contain some lounge furniture. All are spotlessly clean. Your leg muscles will get a workout on the stairs.

Back in town, **Hotel Saski** *(☎ 421 42 22, fax 421 48 30; ul Sławkowska 3; singles/doubles with shared bathroom 160/170zł, with bathroom 200/260zł, breakfast extra)* is ideally located in a historic house just off Rynek Główny. It's comparatively good value and the rooms feature ornate furniture, but readers have complained about late-night noise from nearby cinemas and cafés.

Places to Eat

By Polish standards, Kraków is a food paradise. The Old Town is tightly packed with gastronomic venues.

Restauracja U Literatów *(ul Kanonicza 7; mains from 12zł)* may look uninviting, but it's actually a tiny oasis of greenery with a courtyard setting (hidden from the main street). **Jadłodajnia Kuchcik** *(ul Jagiellońska 12; mains 8-15zł)* offers large portions of home-cooked Polish food in unpretentious surroundings. **Bistro Pod 13-ką** *(ul Miodowa 13; mains 10-15zł)* is arguably the best place in Kazimierz to try tasty, authentic Polish cooking at affordable prices.

Salad Bar Chimera *(ul Św Anny 3; salads from 5zł)* is in an attractive cellar along an arcade. It offers some of the best salads in Kraków – all listed alphabetically (in Polish) from 'A to Z'. **Green Way Bar Wegetariański** *(ul Mikołajska 16; snacks from 6zł, mains from 10zł)* has outlets in several Polish cities. It rarely fails to satisfy anyone looking for something healthy and/or meat-free.

Bistro Różowy Słoń *(ul Sienna • ul Szpitalna 38; meals about 6zł)* offers, among other tasty treats, a huge selection of pancakes (about 20 types!) and a salad bar, all at remarkably low prices.

Jadłodajnia U Stasi *(ul Mikołajska 16; mains 6-12zł)*, near the Green Way Bar Wegetariański, is one of the oldest and best-known eateries. This unpretentious place is very popular for its *pierogi* (stuffed dumplings), but it's only open at lunchtime.

There are no supermarkets or major grocery shops in the Old Town; the best place for self-catering is one of the **delikatessy** found along the streets.

Entertainment

The comprehensive (free) English-language booklet, *Karnet*, published by the Culture Information Centre, lists almost every event taking place in the city.

Pubs & Bars There are more than 100 pubs and bars in the Old Town alone. Many are housed in ancient vaulted cellars, but non-smokers beware: all have poor ventilation, and most patrons seem to delight in chain smoking. Some of the best places for a relaxing drink are the places around Rynek Główny, but prices are high.

Irish Pub Pod Papugami *(ul Św Jana 18)* was recently refurbished and is now a charming underground watering hole decorated with old motorcycles (among other strange items). **Klub Kulturalny** *(ul Szewska 25)* is set in a labyrinthine array of beautiful medieval brick vaults.

Piwnica Pod Złotą Pipą *(ul Floriańska 30)* is more suited to conversation than listening to music. **Pub Bastylia** *(ul Stolarska 3)* is a bizarre place on five levels with some floors decorated like a French jail!

Clubs For foot-tapping jazz head to **Jazz Club U Muniaka** *(ul Floriańska 3)* or the **Indigo Jazz Club** *(ul Floriańska 26)*.

Black Gallery *(ul Mikołajska 24)* is a crowded underground pub-cum-nightclub that only gets going after midnight and stays open *really* late. **Klub Pasja** *(ul Szewska 5)* occupies vast brick cellars. It is trendy, attractive and popular with foreigners.

Equinox *(ul Sławkowska 13/15)* has long been one of the most popular haunts in the Old Town. Discos are held most nights.

Theatre & Classical Music The best-known venue, **Stary Teatr** *(ul Jagiellońska 1)*, consistently offers quality productions. **Teatr im Słowackiego** *(Plac Św Ducha 1)*, built in 1893, focuses on Polish classics and large-scale productions. It was totally renovated in 1991 and its interior is spectacular. **Filharmonia Krakówska** *(ul Zwierzyniecka 1)* boasts one of the best orchestras in the country; concerts are usually held on Friday and Saturday.

Getting There & Away

The main **bus terminal** *(Plac Kolejowy)* is conveniently opposite the main train station building and only minutes on foot from the Old Town. Polski Express buses to Warsaw depart from a spot opposite the bus terminal.

The lovely old **Kraków Główny** train station on the northeastern outskirts of the Old Town, handles all international trains and almost all domestic rail services. Each day from Kraków, five InterCity trains speed to Warsaw (2¾ hours) and about four express (46zł in 2nd class) and five fast trains also travel to the capital. Every day from Kraków there are also three trains to Wrocław, two to Poznań, two to Lublin and six to Gdynia, via Gdańsk.

OŚWIĘCIM (AUSCHWITZ) & BIRKENAU

☎ 033 • pop 48,000

The Polish name Oświęcim (osh-FYEN-cheem) may be unfamiliar to outsiders, but the German name, Auschwitz, is not. About 60km west of Kraków, this was the scene of the most extensive experiment in genocide in human history. The area makes for a moving day trip from Kraków.

The Auschwitz camp was established in April 1940 on the outskirts of Oświęcim. Originally intended to hold Polish political prisoners, the camp eventually developed into the largest centre for the murder of European Jews. Towards this end, two additional camps were subsequently established: the much larger Birkenau (Brzezinka) and Monowitz (Monowice). These death factories killed 1.5 to two million people of 27 nationalities – about 90% of whom were Jews.

Auschwitz was only partially destroyed by the fleeing Nazis, so many of the original buildings remain. A dozen of the 30 surviving prison blocks house sections of the **State Museum Auschwitz-Birkenau** *(admission free; open 8am daily, closes 7pm June-Aug, 6pm May & Sept, 5pm Apr & Oct, 4pm March & Nov–mid-Dec, 3pm mid-Dec–Mar)*.

About every half-hour, the cinema in the **Visitors' Centre** at the entrance to Auschwitz shows a 15-minute documentary film (2zł) about the liberation of the camp by Soviet troops on 27 January 1945.

Some basic explanations in Polish, English and Hebrew are provided onsite, but you'll understand more if you buy the *Auschwitz Birkenau Guide Book* (translated into about 15 languages) from the bookshops at the Visitors' Centre. English-language tours (25zł per person, 3½ hours) of Auschwitz and Birkenau leave daily at 11.30am, while another starts at 1pm if there's enough demand.

It was at **Birkenau** *(admission free; same opening hours)* where the extermination of huge numbers of Jews took place. This vast (175 hectares), efficient camp had over 300 prison barracks and four huge gas chambers complete with crematoria. Although much of the camp was destroyed by retreating Nazis, the size of the place, fenced off with barbed wire stretching almost as far as the eye can see, provides some idea of the scale of this heinous crime. In some ways, Birkenau is even more shocking than Auschwitz.

Getting There & Away

From Kraków, most convenient are the 12 buses (10zł, 90 minutes) per day to Oświęcim that depart from the small bus stop on ul Bosacka; the stop is at the end of the underpass below the railway platforms. Get off at the final stop (outside the PKS bus maintenance building), only 200m from the entrance to Auschwitz.

Every hour on the hour from 11am to 4pm (inclusive) between 15 April and 31 October buses shuttle passengers between the visitors' centres at Auschwitz and Birkenau. Otherwise, follow the signs for an easy walk (3km) between both places.

CZĘSTOCHOWA

☎ 034 • pop 260,000

Found 114km northwest of Kraków, Częstochowa (chen-sto-HO-vah), is the spiritual heart of Poland. This likeable town owes its fame to the miraculous Black Madonna kept in the Jasna Góra monastery, founded in 1382 by the Paulites of Hungary. In 1430 the icon was stolen by the Hussites, who slashed the Madonna's face. The wounds began to bleed, so the thieves abandoned the icon and ran off. The monks who found the panel wanted to clean it, and a spring miraculously bubbled from the ground. The spring exists to this day, and St Barbara's Church was founded on the site.

From the train station, and adjacent bus terminal, turn right (north) up Al Wolności – along which there are several Internet centres – to the main thoroughfare, Al Najświętszej Marii Panny (Al NMP). At the western end of this broad avenue is the monastery and at the eastern end is Plac Daszyńskiego. Between both is the **tourist office** *(☎/fax 368 22 60; Al NMP 65; open Mon-Sat)*, and several banks, kantors and travel agencies.

The **Paulite Monastery on Jasna Góra** *(admission free; open dawn-dusk daily)* retains the appearance of a hilltop fortress. The **tower** *(open 8am-4pm daily Apr-Nov)* is the tallest (106m) historic church tower in Poland. The **baroque church** is beautifully decorated. The image of the **Black Madonna** on the high altar of the adjacent chapel is hard to see, so a copy is on display in the **Knights' Hall** *(Sala Rycerska)* in the monastery.

The major Marian feasts at Jasna Góra are 3 May, 16 July, 15 August (especially), 26 August, 8 September, 12 September and 8 December. On these days the monastery is *packed* with pilgrims.

The **youth hostel** *(☎ 324 31 21; ul Jasnogórska 84/90; dorm beds about 18zł; open July-Aug)*, two blocks north of the tourist office, has modest facilities. **Dom Pielgrzyma** *(☎ 324 70 11; ul Wyszyńskiego 1/31; singles/doubles with bathroom from 70/90zł)* is a

POLAND

huge place behind the monastery. It offers numerous quiet and comfortable rooms, and is remarkably good value. Plenty of **eateries** can be found near the Dom Pielgrzyma.

Every day from the **bus terminal** *(Al Wolności 45)* three buses travel to Kraków, three go to Wrocław, one heads for Zakopane and three speed off to Warsaw. International buses also often pass through Częstochowa – see the Getting There & Away section earlier in this chapter. From the impressive **train station** *(Al Wolności 21)*, 11 trains a day go to Warsaw (51zł on 2nd-class express). There are also four to five daily trains to Gdynia, via Gdańsk, Łódź, Olsztyn and Zakopane; six to Kraków; and nine to Wrocław.

ZAKOPANE

☎ 018 • pop 30,000

Nestled at the foot of the Tatra Mountains, Zakopane is the most famous resort in Poland and the major winter sports capital. Although essentially a base for skiing and hiking, Zakopane itself has an enjoyable, laid-back atmosphere, even if it is overbuilt, overpriced and commercialised.

The **Tourist Information Centre** *(☎ 201 22 11; ul Kościuszki 17; open daily)* is extremely helpful. Dozens of **kantors** inhabit the main streets. Several banks along the pedestrian mall, such as **PKO Bank** *(ul Krupówki 19)*, handle foreign exchange. The combined **Main Post Office** and **Telephone Centre** *(ul Krupówki)* is along the mall. **GraNet Internet Café** *(ul Krupówki 2)* is a convenient place to surf the Net.

Centrum Przewodnictwa Tatrzańskiego *(Tatra Guide Centre; ☎ 206 37 99; ul Chałubińskiego 42/44)* and the **Biuro Usług Turystycznych PTTK** *(☎ 201 58 48; ul Krupówki 12)* is able to arrange English- and German-speaking mountain guides. **Orbis Travel** *(☎ 201 48 12; ul Krupówki 22)* provides the usual services.

Mt Gubałówka (1120m) has great views over the Tatras and is a favourite destination for tourists who don't feel like *too* much exercise. The **funicular** (8/14zł one way/return) covers the 1388m-long route in less than five minutes and climbs 300m from the funicular station just north of ul Krupówki. It operates from 9am to 9pm from 1 May to 30 September, but at other times only runs on weekends. An all-day pass for skiers costs 70zł; a one-day pass at other times is 50zł for 10 rides.

Places to Stay

Like all seasonal resorts, accommodation prices fluctuate between the low season and high season (December to February and July to August). Book in advance at peak times. Rates for the high seasons are listed below.

Hostels Along a noisy road about a 10-minute walk from the town centre is **Youth Hostel Szarotka** *(☎ 206 62 03; ul Nowotarska 45; dorm beds 35-50zł, doubles with bathroom 140zł; open year-round)*. This friendly and homely place does get packed (and untidy and sometimes dirty) in the high season, and it's not great value in the low season.

Schronisko Młodzieżowe Żak *(☎ 201 57 06; ul Marusarzówny 15; dorm beds about 20zł, doubles per person from 35zł; open all year)* is in a quiet area to the south. The place is well run and friendly.

Private Rooms & Guesthouses Most travel agencies in Zakopane can arrange **private rooms**, but in the peak season they may not want to offer you anything for fewer than three nights. Expect a double room (singles are rarely offered) to cost about 50zł in the peak season for anywhere in the town centre. Locals offering private rooms may also approach you at the bus or train stations; or just look for signs posted outside private homes. Another place to start looking is the tourist office.

Few travellers stay in hotels. The tourist office usually knows of great bargains for **guesthouses**: from 40zł per double with TV and bathroom.

Places to Eat

The central pedestrian mall, ul Krupówki, is lined with all sorts of eateries. **Bar Mleczny** *(ul Krupówki 1; mains from 6zł)* is about the only milk bar in town these days. **Restaurant Sabala** *(ul Krupówki 11)* has been recommended by readers for its decor, service, meals and friendly, traditionally dressed staff.

Getting There & Away

From the **bus terminal** *(ul Chramcówki)*, fast PKS buses run to Kraków every 45 to 60 minutes (9zł, 2½ hours). Two private companies – Trans Frej and Szwagropol – also operate comfortable buses (10zł) at the same frequency. These private buses leave from a stop along ul Kościuszki in Zakopane, and from a stop opposite the bus terminal in Kraków.

Buy tickets for private buses from counters outside the departure points in Zakopane.

From the **train station** *(ul Chramcówki)*, trains for Kraków (42zł in 2nd-class express, 3½ hours) leave every two hours or so. Per day between one and three trains go to Częstochowa, Gdynia via Gdańsk, Lublin, Łódź and Poznań, and five head to Warsaw.

THE TATRA MOUNTAINS

☎ 018

The Tatras, 100km south of Kraków, are the highest range of the Carpathian Mountains. Approximately 60km long and 15km wide, this mountain range stretches across the Polish–Slovak border. A quarter is in Poland and is now mostly part of the Tatra National Park (about 212 sq km).

Almost every Polish tourist has made the **Mt Kasprowy Wierch cable-car trip** (return 28zł; open daily 7.30am to 8pm in summer, 7.30am to 4pm in winter) from Kuźnice (3km south of central Zakopane) to the summit of Mt Kasprowy Wierch (1985m). At the end of the trip, you can get off and stand with one foot in Poland and the other in Slovakia. Another incredibly popular park destination is the emerald-green **Lake Morskie Oko** (Eye of the Sea), among the loveliest in the Tatras.

If you're doing any hiking in the Tatras, get a copy of the *Tatrzański Park Narodowy* map (1:25,000), which shows all hiking trails in the area.

Zakopane boasts four major ski areas (and several smaller ones) with over 50 ski lifts. **Mt Kasprowy Wierch** and **Mt Gubałówka** offer the best conditions and most challenging slopes in the area, with the ski season extending until early May.

Tourists are not allowed to take their own cars into the park; you must walk in, take the cable car or use an official vehicle owned by the park or a hotel/hostel.

Camping is also not allowed, but eight PTTK mountain refuges/hostels provide simple accommodation. Check availability at the Dom Turysty PTTK in Zakopane or the regional **PTTK headquarters** *(☎/fax 018-438 610)* in Nowy Sącz.

LUBLIN

☎ **081 • pop 360,000**

Throughout its history, Lublin has experienced repeated invasions by Swedes, Austrians, Russians and Germans. During WWII the Nazis established a death camp at nearby Majdanek. The city didn't experience significant wartime damage, so the Old Town has retained much of its historic architectural fabric.

The **LOIT Tourist Information Centre** *(☎ 532 44 12; ⓔ loit@inetia.pl; ul Jezuicka 1/3; open daily)* has helpful English-speaking staff. The **PTTK office** *(☎ 532 96 54; ul Krakowskie Przedmieście 78; open Mon-Fri)* can help with guides, car rental and organised tours. **Bank Pekao** *(ul Królewska 1 • ul Krakowskie Przedmieście 64)* cashes travellers cheques and gives cash advances on Visa and MasterCard. ATMs can be found along ul Krakowskie Przedmieście, but most kantors seem to congregate along ul Peowiaków.

The **main post office** *(ul Krakowskie Przedmieście 50)* is easy to find, but the adjacent **telephone centre** is just back from the main road. For cyber communication, try **Klub Internetowy** *(ul Swietoduska 16)* at the back of a small laneway off ul Wodopojna.

Things to See

Old Town The compact historic quarter is centred on the **Rynek**, the irregularly shaped main square surrounding the oversized neoclassical **Old Town Hall** (1781). The enticing **Historical Museum of Lublin** *(Plac Łokietka 3; admission 3zł; open 9am-4pm Wed-Sat, 9am-5pm Sun)* is inside the 14th-century **Kraków Gate**, the only significant remnant of the medieval fortifications.

For an expansive **view** of the Old Town, climb to the top of the **Trinitarian Tower** (1819), which houses the **Religious Art Museum** *(Plac Kathedralny; admission 8zł; open 10am-5pm daily Apr-Oct)*. According to legend, the metal rooster on top of the tower will crow when a virgin walks past! Next to the tower is the 16th-century **cathedral** *(Plac Kathedralny; admission free; open dawn-dusk daily)* with impressive baroque frescoes.

Castle Built on a hill northeast of the Old Town is a magnificent 14th-century castle *(admission free; open dawn-dusk daily)*. What remains was actually rebuilt as a prison in the 1820s and remained as such until 1944. During the Nazi occupation, over 100,000 people passed through this prison before being deported to the death camps. Most of the edifice is now occupied by the **Lublin Museum** *(ⓦ www.zamek-lublin.pl; admission 6zł; open 9am-4pm Wed-Sat, 9am-5pm Sun)*.

At the eastern end of the castle – but only accessible through the museum entrance – is the exquisite 14th-century **Chapel of the Holy Trinity** *(admission 10zł; open 9am-4pm Mon-Sat, 9am-5pm Sun)*. Its interior is entirely covered with amazing Russo-Byzantine frescoes painted in 1418 – possibly the finest medieval wall paintings in Poland. Tickets must be bought in advance at the museum entrance.

Majdanek About 4km southeast of the Old Town is the **State Museum of Majdanek** *(w www.majdanek.pl; admission free; open daily 8am-6pm May-Sept, 8am-3pm Oct-Apr)*. It commemorates one of the largest death camps in Europe, and was the first such memorial in the world. About 235,000 people, representing 51 nationalities from 26 countries (including over 100,000 Jews), were massacred here. Barracks, guard towers and barbed wire fences remain as they were more than 50 years ago; even more chilling are the crematorium and gas chambers.

Note that children under 14 years old are *not* permitted anywhere in the camp. Trolleybus No 156 from near the Bank Pekao along ul Królewska goes to the entrance of Majdanek.

Places to Stay

The **Youth Hostel** *(☎/fax 533 06 28; ul Długosza 6; dorm beds 20-32zł; open year-round)* is modest but well run. It's 50m up a lane off ul Długosza and in the heart of the university district.

Wojewódzki Ośrodek Metodyczny *(☎ 532 92 41, fax 534 46 34; ul Dominikańska 5; dorm beds about 40zł)* is good value and often busy, so book ahead. Look for the sign 'Wojewódzki Ośrodek Doskonalenia Nauczycieli' outside.

Diecezjalny Dom Rekolekcyjny *(☎ 532 41 38; ul Podwale 15; dorm beds about 30zł)* is a Catholic institution, so behave appropriately. Curfew is 10pm.

Hotel Piast *(☎ 532 16 46; ul Pocztowa 2; dorm beds 25zł, singles/doubles with shared bathroom 50/75zł)*, opposite the train station, is ideal for a late-night arrival or early morning departure. However, it's a long way from anywhere else and not in a pleasant part of town.

Lubelski Dom Nauczyciela *(☎ 533 82 85, fax 533 03 66; ul Akademicka 4; singles/doubles with shared bathroom from 80/83zł, doubles with private bathroom 150zł)* is a teachers' hostel. Most of the rooms are tiny, but clean and perfectly acceptable, while the renovated rooms have a bathroom.

Places to Eat

Bar Uniwersalny Ludowy *(ul Krakowskie Przedmieście 60; mains 8-12zł)* is a long-established milk bar patronised by city workers and university students. **Bar Pod Basztą** *(ul Królewska 6; meals from 8zł)* is a clean and modern place, ideal for a budget lunch of hamburgers or *pierogi ruskie*.

Restauracja Ulice Miasta *(Plac Łokietka 2; mains from 12zł)* has a great position adjoining the Kraków Gate. Enjoy one of their daily three-course specials (about 20zł) or just relax with a drink after traipsing around the Old Town.

Vegetarian Bar *(ul Narutowicza 3)* is downstairs along a courtyard off the main road. It's a popular place with young locals who want cheap, meatless food. There is a **supermarket** and **market** near the bus terminal.

Entertainment

The main venue for drama is **Teatr im Osterwy** *(ul Narutowicza 17)*, which features mostly classical plays with some emphasis on national drama. **Klub Hades** *(ul Hempla)* features live music (including rock and jazz) most nights and a disco on Friday.

Getting There & Away

The **bus terminal** *(Al Tysiąclecia)*, opposite the castle, handles most of the traffic. At least one bus a day heads to Białystok, Kraków, Łódź, Olsztyn, Toruń and Zakopane. Each day, six buses also go to Przemyśl, nine head to Zamość and 12 to 15 travel to Warsaw (three hours). From the same terminal, Polski Express offers eight daily buses to Warsaw.

The **Lublin Główny** train station *(Plac Dworcowy)* is 1.2km south of the Old Town and accessible by trolleybus No 160. At least six trains go daily to Warsaw (45zł for 2nd-class express, 2½ hours) and two fast trains travel to Kraków (four hours).

ZAMOŚĆ

☎ 084 • pop 65,000

Zamość (ZAH-moshch) was founded in 1580 by Jan Zamoyski, chancellor and commander-in-chief of Renaissance Poland, who intended to create an impregnable barrier against Cossack and Tatar raids. During WWII, Polish inhabitants were expelled from the town and its environs, and most of the Jewish population was exterminated.

The helpful **Tourist Information Centre** (*☎ 639 22 93; ⓔ zoit@zamosc.um.gov.pl; Rynek Wielki 13; open daily May-Sept, Mon-Fri Oct-Apr*) is in the town hall. **Bank Pekao** (*ul Grodzka 2*) has an ATM, cashes travellers cheques and gives advances on Visa and MasterCard. The **foreign-exchange counter** inside Hotel Zamojski is open 24 hours. The quaint **Main Post Office** (*ul Kościuszki*) is near the cathedral. If you find an Internet centre in the Old Town, send us an email!

Things to See

Rynek Wielki is an impressive Renaissance square (exactly 100m by 100m) dominated by the lofty **Town Hall** and surrounded by arcaded burghers' houses. Many of these houses have preserved the fancy stucco design on their interiors and exteriors. The **Museum of Zamość** (*admission 5.50zł; open 9am-2pm Mon-Fri*) is based in two of the loveliest buildings at Rynek Nos 24 and 26.

Southwest of the square is the mighty 16th-century **cathedral** (*ul Kolegiacka; admission free; open dawn-dusk daily*), which holds the tomb of Zamoyski in the chapel to the right of the high altar.

Before WWII, Jews accounted for 45% of the town's population (of 12,000) and most lived in the area north and east of the palace. The most significant Jewish architectural relic is the Renaissance **synagogue** (*cnr ul Zamenhofa & ul Bazyliańska*), built in the 1610s.

On the eastern edge of the Old Town is the antiquated **Market Hall**. Behind it is the best surviving **bastion** from the original wall that encircled Zamość.

POLAND

Places to Stay & Eat

The **Youth Hostel** (*☎ 627 91 25; ul Zamoyskiego 4; dorm beds 22-30zł; open July & Aug*) is in a school about 1.5km east of the Old Town and not far from the bus terminal. It's basic but adequate.

Dom Turysty (*☎ 639 26 39; ul Zamenhofa 11; doubles with shared bathroom 45zł*) can't quite decide which of several names to use. The rooms are unexceptional, but the price and location are attractive.

Hotel Arkadia (*☎ 638 65 07; Rynek Wielki 9; doubles with bathroom & breakfast 100zł*) has just six rooms, two of which overlook the main square. It's a grand old place with much charm, but has seen better days.

Bar Asia (*ul Staszica 10; mains from 8zł*) is a popular cafeteria-style place serving cheap and tasty food, though none of the dishes is particularly Asian. **Restauracja-Kawiarnia Ratuszowa** (*Rynek Wielki 13; meals 9-10zł*) in the town hall also offers reasonable food at low prices. Posters on the wall indicate which meals are available (and the cost).

Getting There & Away

Buses are more convenient and quicker than trains. The **bus terminal** (*ul Hrubieszowska*) is 2km east of the Old Town and linked by frequent city buses. Every day, two fast buses go to Kraków, four or five head to Warsaw (five hours) and nine travel to Lublin (two hours).

Far quicker, and surprisingly cheaper, are the minibuses that travel every 30 minutes between Lublin and Zamość. They leave from the minibus stand across the road from the bus terminal in Zamość.

From the **train station**, about 1km southwest of the Old Town, several slow trains head to Lublin (about four hours) every day and three slow trains plod along to Warsaw (six hours).

Silesia

Silesia, in southwestern Poland, includes Upper Silesia, the industrial heart of the country; Lower Silesia, a fertile farming region with a cultural and economic centre in Wrocław; and the Sudeten Mountains, which is a forested range running for over 250km along the Czech border. Silesia has spent much of its history under Austrian and Prussian rule, so the large Polish minority was often subject to Germanisation.

WROCŁAW

☎ 071 • pop 675,000

Wrocław (VROTS-wahf) was originally founded on the island of Ostrów Tumski on the Odra River. About 1000 years ago, Wrocław was chosen as one of the Piast dynasty's three bishoprics (along with Kraków and Kołobrzeg), and it subsequently developed to become a prosperous trading and cultural centre.

Wrocław returned to Poland in a sorry state: during the final phase of WWII, 70% of the city was destroyed. However, the old market square and many churches and other fine buildings have been beautifully restored.

Information

The **Tourist Information Centre** *(☎ 344 11 11; Ⓦ www.wroclaw.pl; Rynek 14; open Mon-Sat)* is very helpful. A **tourist information counter** *(☎ 369 54 97)* is in the Wrocław Główny train station.

Bank Pekao *(ul Oławska 2)* cashes travellers cheques and gives advances on Visa and MasterCard. There are kantors *all* over the city centre and several in the bus and train stations. ATMs are also plentiful.

The **Main Post Office** *(Rynek)* conveniently overlooks the main square. The **Cyber & Tea Tavern** *(ul Kuźnicza 29)* offers visitors the chance to surf the Net while indulging in a drink or two.

Things to See

The **Rynek** is Poland's second-largest old market square (after Kraków) and one of the largest (3.7 hectares) in Europe. The **Town Hall** (built 1327–1504) on the southern side is certainly one of the most beautiful in Poland. Inside, the **Museum of Burgher Art** *(admission 4zł; open about 10am-4pm Tues-Sun)* shows off its splendid period interiors.

In the northwestern corner of the Rynek are two small houses called **Jaś i Małgosia** *(ul Św Mikołaja; not open to the public)* linked by a baroque gate. Just behind them is the monumental 14th-century **St Elizabeth's Church** *(ul Elżbiety 1; admission free; open about 8am-6pm daily)* with its 83m-high tower, which you can climb for city **views**.

One block east of the Rynek is the Gothic **St Mary Magdalene's Church** *(ul Łaciarska; admission free; open 9am-4pm Mon-Sat)* with a Romanesque portal from 1280 incorporated into its southern external wall.

The university quarter is north of the Rynek along the river bank. Further around is **The Arsenal**, the most significant remnant of the town's 15th-century fortifications.

The **Panorama of Racławicka** *(ul Purkyniego 11; admission 19zł; open 9am-4pm Tues-Sun)* is a massive 360-degree painting of the Battle of Racławice (1794). In this battle near Kraków, the Polish peasant army, led by Tadeusz Kościuszko, defeated Russian forces intent on partitioning Poland. Created by Jan Styka and Wojciech Kossak for the centenary of the battle in 1894, the painting is an overwhelming 114m long and 15m high. Obligatory tours (in English, French or German) run every 30 minutes between 9.30am and 3.30pm (inclusive). The entrance ticket also allows you to visit the National Museum on the same day.

The **National Museum** *(Plac Powstańców Warszawy 5; admission 10zł, free Sat; open about 10am-4pm Tues-Sun)* contains exhibits of Silesian medieval art and one of the country's finest collections of modern Polish painting. Entry is free with a ticket to the Panorama.

Special Events

Wrocław's major annual events include the Musica Polonica Nova Festival (February), the Jazz on the Odra International Festival (May) and the Wratislavia Cantans Oratorio and Cantata Festival (September).

Places to Stay

Probably because there are so many transient students, there is no agency that arranges rooms in private homes.

Hostels Not far from the train station, **MDK Youth Hostel** *(☎ 343 88 56; ⓔ mdk.kopernik.wp.pl; ul Kołłątaja 20; dorm beds around 25zł)* is located in a grand (but poorly sign posted) mustard-coloured building. It's almost always full, so book ahead.

Hotel Tumski Youth Hostel *(☎ 322 60 99; Ⓦ www.hotel-tumski.com.pl; ul Słodowy 10; dorm beds from 25zł)* is convenient and staff are friendly. It's good value, but some rooms are cramped.

Bursa Nauczycielska *(☎ 344 37 81; ul Kotlarska 42; singles/doubles with shared bathroom 55/90zł)* is a teachers' hostel ideally located just one block northeast of the Rynek. Rooms are clean and well kept.

Hotels Those listed here offer rooms with a bathroom and TV, and rates include breakfast. Many places offer substantial discounts for Saturday and Sunday nights, and some may offer discounts Friday night if requested.

Hotel Podróżnik *(☎ 373 28 45; ul Sucha 1; singles/doubles 90/130zł)* is on the 1st floor of the bus terminal. It's obviously convenient and noisy, yet surprisingly pleasant.

Hotel Savoy *(☎/fax 372 53 79; Plac Kościuszki 19; singles/doubles around 110/130zł, Sat & Sun around 90/110zł)* offers an excellent location midway between the train station and The Old Town. It's a good-value place, especially on weekends. Breakfast costs an extra 10zł.

Hotel Monopol (*☎ 343 70 41; ⓔ monopol@orbis.pl; ul Modrzejewskiej 2; singles/doubles with shared bathroom from 115/150zł, with private bathroom from 180/260zł*) is beside the Opera House. It's particularly good value and guests can have the dubious honour of staying in the same hotel once frequented by an evil German dictator.

Places to Eat

Bar Mleczny Wzorcowy (*ul Piłsudskiego 86; mains from 8zł*) is a typical milk bar with a long menu (in Polish) and hearty, hot dishes at cheap prices. **Bar Mleczny Miś** (*ul Kużnicza 45-47; mains 8-12zł*), in the university area, is basic but popular with frugal university students.

Bar Wegetariański Vega (*Rynek 1/2; snacks from 5zł, meals about 12zł*) is in the centre of the Rynek and offers the best value in the Old Town. It doesn't have any outdoor tables, but the vegie treats on offer are excellent value.

Entertainment

Wrocław is an important cultural centre, so there's always something going on somewhere. Check out the (free) bimonthly *Wrocław Cultural Guide* for what's on and where (available from tourist offices).

The Irish Pub (*Plac Solny 5*) is one of the more authentic Celtic-style drinking establishments in Poland, but like most places around the Rynek it's expensive. There's live music most nights.

Kalogródek (*ul Kużnicza 29*) is a poky beer garden in a concrete jungle, but popular among students. The surrounding streets are packed with other cheap and friendly haunts.

Teatr Polski (*ul Zapolskiej 3*) is the major mainstream city venue and stages classic Polish and foreign drama. **Teatr Współczesny** (*ul Rzeźnicza 12*) tends more towards contemporary productions.

Filharmonia (*ul Piłsudskiego 19*) hosts concerts of classical music, mostly on Friday and Saturday night.

Getting There & Away

If you're travelling to/from Wrocław on Friday, Saturday or Sunday, book your bus or train ticket as early as possible because of the number of students coming and going over weekends.

The **bus terminal** (*ul Sucha 11*) is just south of the main train station. Several PKS buses a day go to Poznań, Białystok, Częstochowa and Warsaw (seven hours). Polski Express also offers several buses a day to Warsaw.

The **Wrocław Główny** station (*ul Piłsudskiego 105*) was built in 1856 and is an historical monument in itself. Every day, fast trains to Kraków depart every one or two hours, and several InterCity and express trains (62zł for 2nd class) go to Warsaw (six hours), usually via Łódź. Wrocław is also regularly linked by train to Poznań, Częstochowa, Szczecin and Lublin.

Wielkopolska

Wielkopolska (Great Poland) is the cradle of the Polish nation. In the 6th and 7th centuries, Slavic tribes settled the flatlands in this region. Despite the royal seat moving to Kraków in 1038, Wielkopolska remained Poland's most important province until the second partition in 1793, when it was annexed to Prussia. The region then passed back and forth between Polish and German hands several times, culminating in the battles of 1945, which devastated the area.

POZNAŃ

☎ 061 • pop 610,000

Poznań, midway between Berlin and Warsaw, is the focal point of early Polish history. In the 9th century Polanian tribes built a wooden fort on the island of Ostrów Tumski, and from 968 to 1038 Poznań was the de facto capital of Poland. By the 15th century Poznań was already a trading centre and famous for its fairs – reinstituted in 1925 and held to this day.

The **tourist information centre** (*☎/fax 855 33 79; Stary Rynek 59/60; open Mon-Sat*) is helpful. The **City Information Centre** (*☎ 851 96 45; ul Ratajczaka 44; open daily*) handles bookings for cultural events. **Bank Pekao** (*ul Św Marcin 52/56 • ul 23 Lutego*) is probably the best place for travellers cheques and credit cards. For old-fashioned communication visit the **main post office** (*ul Kościuszki 77*) or the **telephone centre** (*Stary Rynek*). Otherwise, check your emails at the **Internet Café** (*Plac Wolności 8*).

Things to See

Stary Rynek (Old Market Square) has been beautifully restored to its historic shape. The focal point is the Renaissance **Town Hall** (built 1550–60). In accordance with a strange custom, at noon two metal goats high above the clock butt their horns together 12 times. Inside the building, the **Poznań Historical Museum** *(admission 5.50zł, free Sat; open about 10am-4pm Mon, Tues, Fri & Sun, noon-6pm Wed)* reveals the city's past through splendid period interiors.

The square also features the unique **Museum of Musical Instruments** *(Stary Rynek 45/47; admission 5.50zł; open 11am-5pm Tues-Sun)*. The **Archaeological Museum** *(ul Wodna 27; admission 3zł; open about 10am-4pm Tues-Sun)* contains displays on the ancient history of the region, as well as some Egyptian artefacts.

The 17th-century **Franciscan Church** *(ul Franciszkańska 2; admission free; open about 8am-8pm daily)*, one block west of the Rynek, has an ornate baroque interior complete with wall paintings and rich stucco work. The **National Museum: Paintings & Sculpture Gallery** *(Al Marcinkowskiego 9; admission 10zł, free Sat; open about 10am-5pm Tues-Sun)*, nearby, holds a typical collection of art, including medieval church woodcarving and Polish paintings.

Located about 1.3km north of the Old Town is the 19th-century Prussian **Poznań Citadel**, where 20,000 German troops held out for a month in February 1945.

The massive 1956 strike by the city's industrial workers was the first major popular upheaval in communist Poland. The strike was cruelly crushed by tanks, leaving 76 dead and over 600 wounded. In a park in the new city centre, the moving **Monument to the Victims of June 1956** commemorates the event.

Special Events

Poznań's trade fairs are its pride. The largest take place in January, June, September and October. A dozen additional smaller fairs also occur throughout the year. Major cultural events include the St John's Fair (June) and the Malta International Theatre Festival (late June).

Places to Stay

During trade fairs, the rates of Poznań's hotels and private rooms tend to increase (and in some cases double). The hard part is knowing when a fair is taking place. The tourist office will help you find a room.

Youth Hostel No 1 *(☎/fax 866 40 40; ul Berwińskiego 2/3; dorm beds 16zł; open all year)* is a 15-minute walk southwest of the train station along ul Głogowska and adjacent to Park Wilsona. It's small and basic, but fills up fast.

Youth Hostel TPD *(☎/fax 848 58 36; ul Drzymały 3; dorm beds 16-28zł; open all year)* is newer and more comfortable. It's 3km north of the train station (take tram No 11), and 3km northwest of the Old Town (tram No 9).

The tourist office should know which **student hostels** and **worker hostels** are open, but most of these are in the outer suburbs.

Glob-Tour *(☎/fax 866 06 67)*, in the main hall of the train station, offers cheap singles from 40zł to 50zł and doubles from 50zł to 60zł. The agency is open 24 hours, but private rooms can only be arranged between 7am and 10pm daily.

Biuro Zakwaterowania Przemysław *(☎ 866 35 60; W www.przemyslaw.com.pl; ul Głogowska 16; open 8am-6pm Mon-Fri, 10am-2pm Sat)* is not far from the train station. Singles/doubles normally cost from 55/75zł.

The rates for the hotels listed below include breakfast. Many places offer substantial discounts on weekends, but not during trade fairs.

Dom Turysty *(☎/fax 852 88 93; W www.domturysty-hotel.com.pl; Stary Rynek 91; dorm beds about 60zł, singles/doubles with bathroom 190/310zł, without bathroom 125/182zł)* is set in an 18th-century former palace. It's a bit musty and old-fashioned, but boasts the best location in Poznań. The breakfast is hardly worth getting up for, however.

Hotel Wielkopolska *(☎ 852 76 31, fax 851 54 92; ul Św Marcin 67; singles/doubles with shared bathroom 130/170zł, with private bathroom & TV 180/230zł)* is better value. The rooms are overdue for some renovation, but it's quiet and comfortable.

Places to Eat

Bar Caritas *(Plac Wolności 1; mains 8-12zł)* is a cheap and convenient milk bar, where you can point at what you want. **Bar Pasibruzch** *(ul Wrocławska 23; lunch specials 8zł)* is another cafeteria with plenty of tasty, hot food waiting to be dolloped onto your plate. It's near **Bar Wegetariański** *(ul Wrocławska 21; meals from 10zł)*, a funky vegetarian place in a cellar off the main road.

Pizzeria di Luigi *(ul Woźna; pizza 10zł, pasta 10-12zł)* serves some of the tastiest pasta northeast of Italy. The owners may not be Italian, but the food is authentic and the setting is cosy.

Entertainment

O'Morgan's Irish Pub *(ul Wielka 7)* is *the* place to go for a beer or two, but beware: any establishment around or near the Rynek is way overpriced. **Déjà Vu** *(ul Woźna 21)* is a very small but cosy bar, popular with students who take advantage of discounted drinks.

Galaxy Klub *(Stary Rynek 85)* is a well-frequented place to let your hair down. **El Otro Muchos Patatos** *(Stary Rynek 92, entrance opposite Dom Turysty)* features taped and live Latin music (sometimes performed by the Polish owners!) most nights.

Teatr Polski *(ul 27 Grudnia 8/10)* is the major centre for plays and dances, while **Teatr Wielki** *(ul Fredry 9)* is where opera and ballet are likely to be held. **Filharmonia** *(ul Św Marcin 81)* offers classical concerts at least every Friday night.

Getting There & Away

The **bus terminal** *(ul Towarowa 17)* is a 10-minute walk east of the train station. The busy **train station** *(ul Dworcowa 1)* is well set up. Every day, it offers nine trains to Kraków (74zł for 2nd-class express, 6½ hours), a dozen to Szczecin, seven to Gdańsk, four to Toruń and seven to Wrocław. About 15 trains a day also head to Warsaw (46zł for 2nd-class express, five hours), including several InterCity services (three hours).

Pomerania (Pomorze)

Pomerania stretches along the Baltic coast from the German frontier to the lower Vistula valley in the east. The region rests on two large urban pillars: Szczecin at its western end and Gdańsk to the east. Between them stretches the sandy coastline dotted with beach resorts. Farther inland is a wide belt of rugged, forested lakeland sprinkled with medieval castles and towns, and the charming city of Toruń.

TORUŃ

☎ 056 • pop 208,000

Toruń is a historic city characterised by its narrow streets, burgher mansions and mighty Gothic churches. The compact Old Town was built on the slopes of the wide Vistula River and is one of the most appealing in central Poland. Toruń is famous as the birthplace of astronomer Nicolaus Copernicus, who spent his youth here. These days, Toruń remains the best-preserved Gothic town in Poland.

The **Tourist Office** *(☎ 621 09 31; W www.it.torun.com.pl; Rynek Staromiejski 1; open daily)* is certainly worth a visit. There's also a **tourist information counter** inside the main train station. **Bank Pekao** *(ul Wielkie Garbary 11)* and **PKO Bank** *(ul Szeroka)* cash travellers cheques and give cash advances on Visa and MasterCard. There's no shortage of ATMs along ul Różana and ul Szeroka.

The **Main Post Office** *(Rynek Staromiejski)* overlooks the main square, **Klub Internetowy Jeremi** *(Rynek Staromiejski 33)*, above the Irish Pub, has Internet-access.

Things to See

Rynek Staromiejski is the focal point of the Old Town. The massive 14th-century brick **Old Town Hall** now shelters the **Regional Museum** *(admission 8.50zł; open 10am-4pm Tues-Sun)*. It features some historical exhibits and regional artwork, and you can climb to the top of the 40m-high **tower** (from May to September only) for fine views.

Just off the northwestern corner of the square is the late 13th-century **St Mary's Church** *(ul Panny Marii; admission free; open dawn-dusk daily)*, a Gothic building with magnificent 15th-century stalls.

In 1473, Copernicus was born in the brick Gothic house that now contains the disappointing **Museum of Copernicus** *(ul Kopernika 15/17; admission 9zł, free Sun; open 10am-4pm Tues-Sun)*.

One block east of the museum is the **Cathedral of SS John the Baptist & John the Evangelist** *(ul Żeglarska; admission free; open 8am-6pm daily)*, started around 1260 but not completed until over 200 years later. Its massive **tower** houses Poland's second-largest bell (after the Wawel Cathedral in Kraków).

Special Events

Toruń breaks out of its comparative slumber during the Probaltica Music & Art Festival of

Baltic States (May), the Contact International Theatre Festival (May/June) and the Music and Architecture International Summer Festival (July & August).

Places to Stay

The **Youth Hostel** *(☎ 654 45 80; ul Św Józefa 22/24; dorm beds 15-25zł; open all year)* is 2km northwest of the Rynek. It's accessible on bus No 11 from the main train station and Old Town.

Schronisko Turystyczne Fort IV *(☎ 655 82 36, fax 655 81 34; ul Chrobrego; dorm beds from 20zł; open all year)* is charmingly located in an old Prussian fort. Although not convenient, it's easy to reach on bus No 14 from the bus terminal and main train station.

All hotels listed (except the Polonia) are charming, old-fashioned pensions, which are both convenient and quiet. Unless stated otherwise, each offers rooms with a bathroom and TV, and rates include breakfast.

Hotel Polonia *(☎ 622 30 28; Plac Teatralny 5; singles/doubles 150/180zł)* has been recently renovated (at last!), but is no longer a bargain. It is, however, still a good mid-range option.

Hotel Trzy Korony *(☎/fax 622 60 31; Rynek Staromiejski 21; singles/doubles with shared bathroom 90/110zł, with private bathroom 150/190zł)* is not quite as nice as the outside would suggest. It does boast a superb location, however, overlooking the main square so ask for a room with a view.

Hotel Pod Orłem *(☎/fax 622 50 24; W www.hotel.torun.pl; ul Mostowa 17; singles/doubles 110/140zł, breakfast 15zł per person)* is good value. The rooms are smallish and have squeaky wooden floors, and some contain poky bathrooms, but the service is good and the scrumptious breakfast will take your mind off its other (minor) faults.

Places to Eat

Bar Mleczny Małgośka *(ul Szczytna 10/12; meals from 7zł)* is a clean and convenient milk bar that also offers passable hamburgers and pizzas.

Restaurant u Sołtysa *(ul Mostowa; mains from 15zł)* serves traditional Polish food.

Piwnica Ratusz *(Rynek Staromiejski; mains about 12zł)* is probably the best-value eatery around the main square. Look out for the daily specials (5zł to 8zł).

Restaurant-Kafeteria Artus *(Rynek Staromiejski 6; soups 5zł, mains 9-12zł)*, inside Dwór Artusa (Artus Court), is the most charming place in Toruń, set up inside an elegant indoor courtyard. Prices are not as high as the setting would suggest.

Entertainment

Piwnica Artystyczna Pod Aniołem *(Rynek Staromiejski 1)*, set in a splendid spacious cellar in the Old Town Hall, offers live music some nights. Other great places for a drink include the quasi-Irish **Dublin Pub** *(ul Mostowa)* and **Piwnica Ratusz** (see Places to Eat), which offers a few outdoor tables in the square and a huge cavernous area downstairs.

Teatr im Horzycy *(Plac Teatralny 1)* is the main stage for theatre performances, while **Dwór Artusa** *(Artus Court; Rynek Staromiejski 6)* often presents classical music.

Getting There & Away

The **bus terminal** *(ul Dąbrowskiego)* is a 10-minute walk north of the Old Town. **Polski Express** *(Al Solidarności)* offers hourly services to Warsaw (four hours) and two a day to Szczecin.

The main **Toruń Główny** train station *(Al Podgórska)* is on the opposite side of the Vistula River and linked to the Old Town by bus Nos 22 and 27. Some trains stop and finish at the more convenient **Toruń Miasto** train station, about 500m east of the New Town.

From the Toruń Główny station, there are daily services to Poznań (three a day), Gdańsk (six), Kraków (three), Łódź (seven), Olsztyn (nine), Szczecin (one) and Wrocław (two). Five trains a day head to Warsaw (51zł for 2nd-class express, four hours).

GDAŃSK

☎ 058 • pop 475,000

Gdańsk came to the fore after the Teutonic Knights seized it in 1308. Within half a century it became a thriving medieval town known as Danzig. In 1454, many inhabitants staged an armed protest against economic restrictions imposed by their rulers and subsequently destroyed the Teutonic Knights' castle and pledged loyalty to the Polish monarch.

Today, Gdańsk is most famous as the birthplace (in 1980) of the Solidarity trade union, which was the catalyst for the fall of communism in Europe.

Information

The **PTTK Office** *(☎/fax 301 13 43; ⓔ pttkgda@gdansk.com.pl; ul Długa 45; open daily)* is conveniently placed opposite the Main Town Hall. **Bank Pekao** *(ul Garncarska 23)* will provide cash advances on Visa and MasterCard. The city centre has plenty of ATMs.

For snail mail, go to the **Main Post Office** *(ul Długa 22)*. Retrieve poste restante from the entrance through the back door, from ul Pocztowa. Mail should be addressed to: Your Name, Poste Restante, ul Długa 22/28, 80-801 Gdańsk 50, Poland. Next to the main entrance of the post office is the **Telephone Centre** *(ul Długa 26)*.

The most convenient place to check your email account is **Rudy Kot** *(ul Garncarska 18/20)*. Otherwise, you can also try **Jazz 'n' Java** *(ul Tkacka)*, which offers music as well.

Almatur *(☎ 301 24 24; Długi Targ 11)* and **Orbis Travel** *(☎ 301 45 44; ul Podwale Staromiejskie 96/97)* provide the usual services to travellers.

Things to See

Main Town The richest architecture and most thorough restoration are in this historic quarter. Ul Długa (Long Street) and Długi Targ (Long Market) form its main thoroughfare, and are both now pedestrian malls. They are known collectively as the **Royal Way**, along which Polish kings traditionally paraded during their periodic visits. They entered the Main Town through the **Upland Gate** (built in the 1770s on a 15th-century gate), passed through the **Golden Gate** (1614) and proceeded east to the Renaissance **Green Gate** (1568).

POLAND

Near the Gothic town hall is **Neptune's Fountain** (1615), behind which stands the **Artus Court Museum** *(ul Długi Targ 43/44; admission 5zł, free Wed; open 10am-4pm Tues-Sat, 11am-4pm Sun)*, where local merchants used to congregate. The adjacent **Golden House** (1618) has perhaps the richest facade in town.

Two blocks north of Green Gate along the waterfront is the 14th-century **St Mary's Gate**. Through this gate, the most picturesque street in Gdańsk – **ul Mariacka** (St Mary's St) – is lined with 17th-century burgher houses.

At the end of ul Mariacka is the gigantic 14th-century **St Mary's Church** *(admission free; open about 8am-8pm daily)*, possibly the largest old brick church in the world. Inside, the 14m-high astronomical clock is certainly unique: its maker's eyes were gouged out to prevent him from creating a rival. The fabulous **panorama** from the 82m-high tower is well worth the climb (405 steps).

Old Town The Old Town, almost totally destroyed in 1945, was never completely rebuilt apart from a handful of churches. The largest and most remarkable of these is **St Catherine's Church** *(ul Wielke Młyny; admission free; open about 8am-6pm Mon-Sat)*, Gdańsk's oldest church (begun in the 1220s). Opposite, the **Great Mill** *(ul Wielke Młyny)* was built by the Teutonic Knights in around 1350. It used to produce 200 tonnes of flour per day and continued to operate until 1945.

Old Suburb This section of Gdańsk was also reduced to rubble in 1945. Little of the urban fabric has been reconstructed, except for the former Franciscan monastery that houses the **National Museum** *(ul Toruńska 1; admission 12zł, free Sat; open 10am-5pm Tues-Sun)*. The museum is famous for its Dutch and Flemish paintings, especially Hans Memling's 15th-century *Last Judgement*. If the museum looks deserted, open the gate yourself; a staff member will soon find you and demand a ticket.

Special Events

The Dominican Fair (first two weeks in August) is an annual shopping fair dating back to 1260. Organ recitals are held at the Oliwa Cathedral twice a week (mid-June to late Aug) as part of the International Organ Music Festival. St Nicholas' and St Bridget's churches also host organ recitals. St Mary's Church is the stage for the International Organ, Choir & Chamber Music Festival (every Friday in July and August). Also popular is the International Street & Open-Air Theatre Festival (July).

Places to Stay

The PTTK Office will be happy to ring a few hotels and hostels (for no charge).

Hostels & Private Rooms The main **youth hostel** *(☎/fax 301 23 13; ul Wałowa 21; dorm beds 15zł, singles/doubles with shared bathroom from 25/50zł; open all year)* is only five minutes' walk northeast of the main train station. It's in a quiet, old building back from the road. It's often full, particularly in summer, so book ahead. The noticeboard next to the reception is a mine of local information.

GDAŃSK

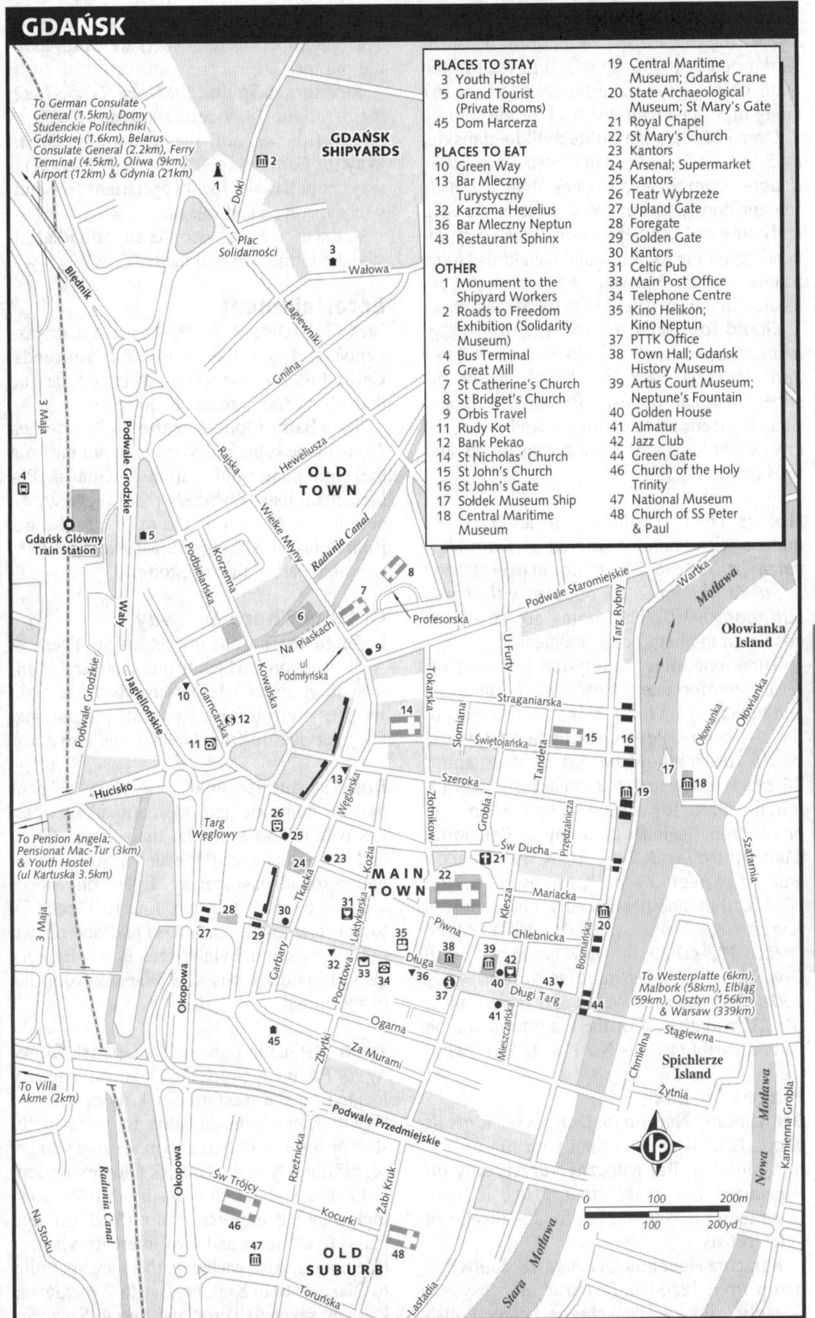
PLACES TO STAY
3 Youth Hostel
5 Grand Tourist (Private Rooms)
45 Dom Harcerza
PLACES TO EAT
10 Green Way
13 Bar Mleczny Turystyczny
32 Karzcma Hevelius
36 Bar Mleczny Neptun
43 Restaurant Sphinx
OTHER
1 Monument to the Shipyard Workers
2 Roads to Freedom Exhibition (Solidarity Museum)
4 Bus Terminal
6 Great Mill
7 St Catherine's Church
8 St Bridget's Church
9 Orbis Travel
11 Rudy Kot
12 Bank Pekao
14 St Nicholas' Church
15 St John's Church
16 St John's Gate
17 Sołdek Museum Ship
18 Central Maritime Museum
19 Central Maritime Museum; Gdańsk Crane
20 State Archaeological Museum; St Mary's Gate
21 Royal Chapel
22 St Mary's Church
23 Kantors
24 Arsenal; Supermarket
25 Kantors
26 Teatr Wybrzeże
27 Upland Gate
28 Foregate
29 Golden Gate
30 Kantors
31 Celtic Pub
33 Main Post Office
34 Telephone Centre
35 Kino Helikon; Kino Neptun
37 PTTK Office
38 Town Hall; Gdańsk History Museum
39 Artus Court Museum; Neptune's Fountain
40 Golden House
41 Almatur
42 Jazz Club
44 Green Gate
46 Church of the Holy Trinity
47 National Museum
48 Church of SS Peter & Paul
To German Consulate General (1.5km), Domy Studenckie Politechniki Gdańskiej (1.6km), Belarus Consulate General (2.2km), Ferry Terminal (4.5km), Oliwa (9km), Airport (12km) & Gdynia (21km)
GDAŃSK SHIPYARDS
Plac Solidarności
OLD TOWN
MAIN TOWN
OLD SUBURB
Gdańsk Główny Train Station
Ołowianka Island
Spichlerze Island
To Pension Angela; Pensionat Mac-Tur (3km) & Youth Hostel (ul Kartuska 3.5km)
To Villa Akme (2km)
To Westerplatte (6km), Malbork (58km), Elbląg (59km), Olsztyn (156km) & Warsaw (339km)
Radunia Canal
Motława
Stara Motława
Nowa Motława
Targ Węglowy
ul Podmłyńska
Profesorska
Podwale Staromiejskie
Podwale Przedmiejskie
Podwale Grodzkie
Wały Jagiellońskie
Długa
Długi Targ
Hucisko
Okopowa
Toruńska
Lastadia
0 100 200m
0 100 200yd

Another **Youth Hostel** *(☎ 302 60 44, fax 302 41 87; ul Kartuska 245b; dorm beds 17-33zł; open year-round)* is 3.5km west of the main train station; take bus No 161 or 167 along ul 3 Maja from the back of the station.

Domy Studenckie Politechniki Gdańskiej *(☎ 347 25 47; ul Wyspiańskiego 7a; singles/doubles from 30/48zł)* opens about 10 of its student dorms as travellers' hostels between early July and late September. Prices vary depending on the facilities and standards (some rooms even have private bathrooms). All are located in the suburb of Gdańsk Wrzeszcz.

Grand Tourist *(☎ 301 26 34; ⓔ tourist@gt.com.pl; ul Podwale Grodzkie 8; open 8am-7pm Mon-Fri, 8am-2pm Sat)* is below the street level and opposite the main train station. It offers private singles/doubles in the city centre for 55/90zł and rooms in the suburbs from 43/75zł.

Hotels The best value and location for any budget-priced hotel is offered by **Dom Harcerza** *(☎ 301 36 21; ⓔ domharcerza@go2.pl; ul Za Murami 2/10; doubles with shared bathroom 60zł)*. The rooms are small but cosy, and the bathrooms are clean.

Three charming, family-run pensions offering comfortable rooms with a bathroom and breakfast are located 3km or less west of the city centre. **Pension Angela** *(☎/fax 302 23 15; ul Beethowena 12; doubles about 100zł)* is cosy and the breakfasts are admirably large. It's accessible by bus Nos 130 or 184 from the main train station. **Pensionat Mac-Tur** *(☎/fax 302 41 70; ⓦ www.mactur.gda.pl; ul Beethowena 8; rooms per person 70-120zł)* is another friendly place, only a few metres from Angela's. **Villa Akme** *(☎/fax 302 40 21; ⓦ www.akme.gda.pl; ul Drwęcka 1; singles/doubles around 110/150zł)* has been renovated and is very nice. It's 2km southwest of the main train station and accessible by bus No 118, 155 or 208.

POLAND

Places to Eat

Bar Mleczny Neptun *(ul Długa 33/34; meals about 12zł)* is classier than your run-of-the-mill milk bar. **Bar Mleczny Turystyczny** *(ul Węglarska 1/4; meals about 10zł)* is more basic than the Neptun, but food is displayed cafeteria-style.

Karzcma Hevelius *(ul Długa 18; soups 5zł, mains from 12zł)* is a favourite; it's cosy and friendly, and you can choose hearty Polish food from a menu in German and English. The lunch specials (from 8zł) are worth looking out for.

Restaurant Sphinx *(ul Długi Targ 31/32; mains about 14zł)* serves pizza, as well as large grills with all the trimmings. **Green Way** *(ul Garncarska 4/6; meals 7-10zł)* is always popular with local vegetarians for sandwiches, crepes and salads.

For self-catering, visit the **supermarket** inside the former Arsenal facing Targ Węglowy.

Entertainment

Jazz Club *(Długi Targ 39/40)* is the main jazz venue and has live music on weekends. **Celtic Pub** *(ul Lektykarska 3)* is popular and doesn't try too hard to be too Irish.

State Baltic Opera Theatre *(Al Zwycięstwa 15)* is in the suburb of Wrzeszcz, not far from the commuter train station at Gdańsk Politechnika. **Teatr Wybrzeże** *(Targ Węglowy 1)*, next to the Arsenal, is the main city theatre. Both Polish and foreign classics (all in Polish) are often part of the repertoire.

Getting There & Away

Refer to the introductory Getting There & Away section earlier in this chapter for information about international bus and train services to/from Gdańsk, and international ferry services to/from Gdańsk and Gdynia.

Bus The **bus terminal** *(ul 3 Maja 12)* handles all domestic and international services. It's behind (west of) the main train station and connected to ul Podwale Grodzkie by an underground passageway. Every day, there are four buses to Olsztyn, four to Toruń, six to Warsaw (50zł, six hours) and one or two to Białystok and Świnoujście. Polski Express also offers daily buses to Warsaw from this bus terminal.

Train The main train station, **Gdańsk Główny** *(ul Podwale Grodzkie 1)*, is conveniently located on the western outskirts of the Old Town. Most long-distance trains actually start or finish at Gdynia, so make sure you get on/off quickly at the Gdańsk Główny station.

Each day about 18 trains head to Warsaw, including 10 express trains (59zł for 2nd class, five hours) and five InterCity services (3½ hours). Also each day, there are six trains to Olsztyn, 10 to Kraków, five to Wrocław via Poznań, seven to Toruń and four to Szczecin.

Trains also head to Białystok and Lublin once or twice a day.

Getting Around

The local commuter train, known as the SKM, runs every 15 minutes almost all day and night between the Gdańsk Główny and Gdynia Główna Osobowa train stations, via the Sopot and Gdańsk Oliwa stations. (Note: the line to Gdańsk Nowy Port, via Gdańsk Brzeżno, is a separate branch line that leaves less regularly from Gdańsk Główny.) Buy tickets at any station and validate them in the machines at the platform entrance.

Warmia & Masuria

THE GREAT MASURIAN LAKES

The Great Masurian Lakes district east of Olsztyn is a verdant land of rolling hills interspersed with glacial lakes, peaceful farms and dense forests. The district has over 2000 lakes, the largest of which is **Lake Śniardwy** (110 sq km), Poland's largest lake. Around 200km of canals connect these lakes, so the area is a prime destination for yachties and canoeists, as well as those who prefer to hike, fish and mountain-bike.

The detailed *Wielkie Jeziora Mazurskie* map (1:100,000) is essential if exploring the region by boat, canoe, bike, car or foot. The *Warmia i Mazury* map (1:300,000), published by Vicon and available at regional tourist offices, is perfect for those using private or public transport, and has explanations in English.

Mikołajki is a picturesque village and is probably the best base for exploring the lakes. The **tourist office** *(☎/fax 421 68 50; Plac Wolności 3)* is in the town centre. There are several kantors, but nowhere to cash travellers cheques or get cash advances.

The bus terminal and the train station are on the southern edge of the town near the lake. Four buses go to Olsztyn each morning. Several buses also go daily to Giżycko and two or three depart in summer for Warsaw. From the sleepy train station, a few slow trains shuttle along daily to Olsztyn and two fast trains head to Gdańsk and Białystok.

Hitler's wartime headquarters, called the **Wolf's Lair** (Wolfsschanze in German), was about 30km west of Giżycko. Hitler stayed here from 1941 to 1944 and survived an assassination attempt by his own officers. Booklets allowing a self-guided walking tour of the remains at this eerie site are available in English and German at the kiosk in the car park.

Portugal

Spirited yet unassuming, Portugal retains a dusty patina of faded grandeur, the quiet remains of a far-flung colonialist realm. Even as it flows towards the economic mainstream of the EU it seems to gaze nostalgically over its shoulder and out to sea.

For visitors, this far side of Europe offers more than just beaches and port wine. Beyond the crowded Algarve, one finds wide appeal: a simple, hearty cuisine based on seafood and lingering conversation, an enticing architectural blend wandering from the Moorish to Manueline to surrealist styles, and a changing landscape that occasionally lapses into impressionism. *Emigrantes* (economically inspired Portuguese who eventually find their way back to their roots) and *estrangeiros* (foreigners) who have tasted the real Portugal can be expected to return.

Portugal: the Basics

Capital
Lisbon

Population
10 million

Language
Portuguese

Currency
euro (€) = 100 centimes

Avoid at all costs Insane Portuguese drivers

Start a debate by saying *Quem é que achas que vai ganhar o Campeonato da Europa?* (Who do you think will win the European Championships?)

Facts about Portugal

HISTORY

Early settlers and invaders of the Iberian Peninsula included the Celts, Phoenicians, Greeks, Romans and Visigoths. In the 8th century the Moors commenced a long occupation that introduced Islamic culture, architecture and agricultural techniques. They were ejected in the 12th century by powerful Christian forces in the north of the country aided by European Crusaders.

In the 15th century Portugal entered a phase of conquest and discovery inspired by Prince Henry the Navigator. Explorers such as Vasco da Gama, Ferdinand Magellan and Bartolomeu Diaz discovered new trade routes and helped create an empire that extended to Africa, Brazil, India and the Far East. This golden age ended in 1580, when Spain occupied the Portuguese throne. The Portuguese regained it within 90 years, but their imperial momentum had been lost.

A period of civil war and political mayhem in the 19th century culminated in the abolition of the monarchy in 1910 and the founding of a democratic republic. A 1926 military coup set the stage for the dictatorship of António de Oliveira Salazar, who clung to power until his death in 1968. Dissatisfaction with his regime and a ruinous colonial war in Africa led to the so-called Revolution of the Carnations, a peaceful military coup on 25 April 1974.

The granting of independence to Portugal's African colonies in 1974–75 produced a flood of nearly a million refugees into the country. The 1970s and early 1980s saw extreme swings between political right and left, and strikes over state versus private ownership.

Portugal's entry into the EU in 1986 and its acceptance as a member of the European Monetary System in 1992 secured a measure of stability, although the 1990s were troubled by recession, rising unemployment and continuing backwardness in agriculture and education.

Expo '98 triggered vast infrastructure projects and launched Portugal into a new era of economic success, furthered by Porto's status as a European Capital of Culture in 2001 and by Portugal's role as host of the Euro2004 European football championships.

GEOGRAPHY

Portugal is about twice the size of Switzerland, just 560km from north to south and 220km from east to west. The northern and central coastal regions are densely populated. The northern interior is characterised by lush vegetation and mountains; the highest range, the Serra da Estrela, peaks at Torre (1993m).

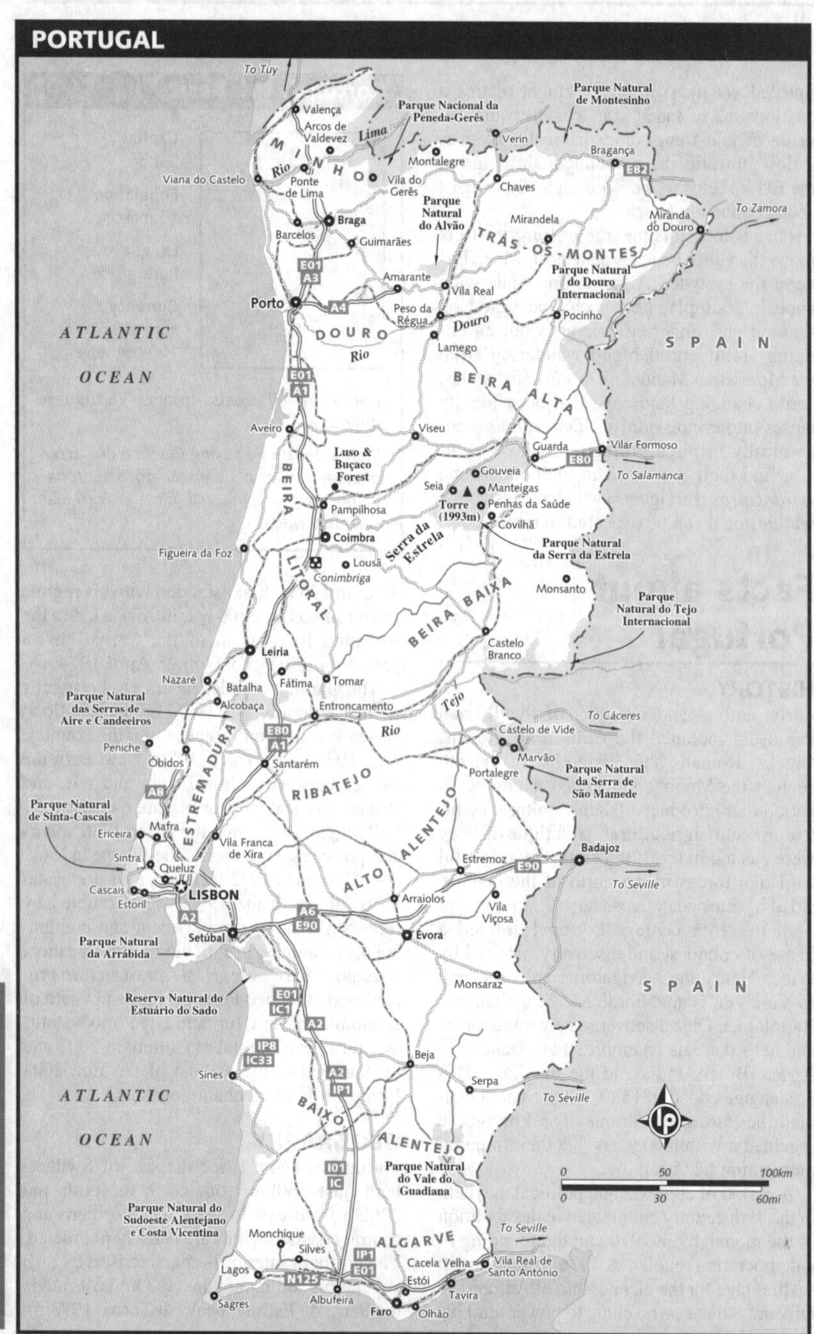
PORTUGAL
To Tuy
Valença
Arcos de Valdevez
Rio Lima
MINHO
Parque Nacional da Peneda-Gerês
Verin
Parque Natural de Montesinho
Montalegre
Bragança
E82
Viana do Castelo
Ponte de Lima
Vila do Gerês
Chaves
Parque Natural do Alvão
Braga
Barcelos
Guimarães
Mirandela
TRÁS-OS-MONTES
Miranda do Douro
To Zamora
E01
A3
Amarante
Vila Real
Parque Natural do Douro Internacional
Porto
A4
Peso da Régua
Douro
Pocinho
DOURO
Rio
Lamego
ATLANTIC OCEAN
SPAIN
E01
A1
BEIRA ALTA
Aveiro
Viseu
Guarda
Vilar Formoso
E80
To Salamanca
Luso & Buçaco Forest
BEIRA
Gouveia
Seia
Manteigas
Torre (1993m)
Penhas da Saúde
Pampilhosa
Covilhã
Coimbra
Serra da Estrela
Parque Natural da Serra da Estrela
Figueira da Foz
Lousã
Conimbriga
LITORAL
Monsanto
BEIRA BAIXA
Parque Natural do Tejo Internacional
Castelo Branco
Leiria
Nazaré
Fátima
Tomar
Batalha
Parque Natural das Serras de Aire e Candeeiros
Alcobaça
Entroncamento
Tejo
Rio
To Cáceres
Castelo de Vide
E80
A1
Marvão
Peniche
Óbidos
Santarém
Portalegre
Parque Natural da Serra de São Mamede
A8
ESTREMADURA
RIBATEJO
Parque Natural de Sinta-Cascais
Ericeira
Mafra
Vila Franca de Xira
ALTO ALENTEJO
Badajoz
Sintra
Queluz
Estremoz
E90
To Seville
Cascais
Estoril
LISBON
Arraiolos
Vila Viçosa
A2
A6
E90
Setúbal
Évora
Parque Natural da Arrábida
Monsaraz
SPAIN
Reserva Natural do Estuário do Sado
E01
IC1
A2
IP8
IC33
Beja
Sines
A2
IP1
Serpa
To Seville
ATLANTIC OCEAN
BAIXO ALENTEJO
I01
IC
Parque Natural do Vale do Guadiana
0
50
100km
0
30
60mi
Parque Natural do Sudoeste Alentejano e Costa Vicentina
To Seville
Monchique
ALGARVE
Silves
IP1
E01
Cacela Velha
Vila Real de Santo António
Lagos
N125
Estói
Tavira
Sagres
Albufeira
Faro
Olhão
lp

PORTUGAL

The south is more sparse and, apart from the mountainous backdrop of the Algarve, flatter and drier.

CLIMATE

Midsummer heat is searing in the Algarve and Alentejo and in the upper Douro Valley, but tolerable elsewhere. The north is rainy and chilly in winter. Snowfall is common in the Serra da Estrela.

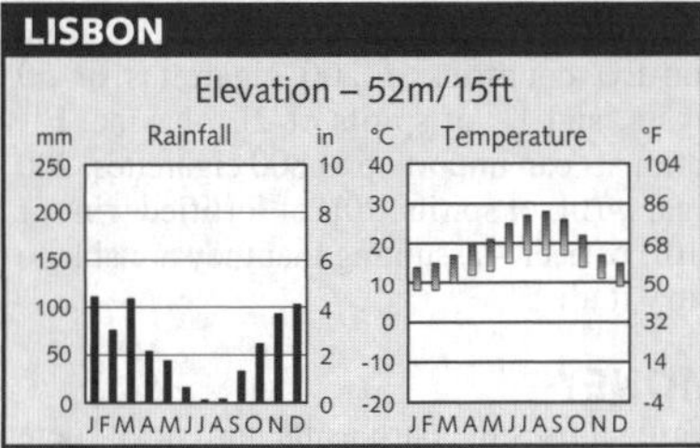

GOVERNMENT & POLITICS

Portugal's Assembleiada República is a single-chamber parliament with an elected president. The right Socialist Party (Partido Socialista; PS) and the Social Democratic Party (Partido Social Democrata; PSD) are the two main parties.

POPULATION & PEOPLE

Portugal's population of 10 million does not include the estimated three million Portuguese living abroad as migrant workers.

SOCIETY & CONDUCT

The Portuguese tend to be very friendly but socially conservative. Win their hearts by dressing modestly outside of the beach resorts (especially in churches) and by greeting and thanking them in Portuguese.

LANGUAGE

Portuguese is spoken by over 10 million people in Portugal and 130 million in Brazil, and is the official language of five African nations. Nearly all *turismo* (tourist-office) staff speak English. In Lisbon, Porto and the Algarve it's easy to find English-speakers, but they are rare in the countryside and among older folk.

See the Language chapter at the back of the book for pronunciation guidelines and useful words and phrases. For more, pick up Lonely Planet's *Portuguese phrasebook*.

Facts for the Visitor

HIGHLIGHTS

Mountain landscapes of the Serra da Estrela and Parque Nacional da Peneda-Gerês are the tops for scenery. Architecture buffs should visit the monasteries at Belém and Batalha, and the palaces of Pena (in Sintra) and Buçaco. Combining the best of both worlds are Portugal's old walled towns such as Évora and Marvão. In Lisbon, don't miss the Museu Calouste Gulbenkian and Europe's largest Oceanarium.

PLANNING

Peak tourist season is June to early September. Travelling earlier (late March or April) or later (late September to early October) offers fewer crowds, milder temperatures, spectacular foliage, and seasonal discounts. The Algarve tourist season is February to November.

TOURIST OFFICES

Called *postos de turismo* or just *turismos*, local tourist offices are found throughout Portugal and offer information, maps and varying degrees of assistance.

Portuguese tourist offices operating abroad under the administrative umbrella of ICEP (Investimentos Comércio e Turismo de Portugal) include the following:

Canada Portuguese Trade & Tourism Commission (☎ 416-921 7376, fax 921 1353, ⓔ iceptor@ idirect.com) 60 Bloor St West, Suite 1005, Toronto, Ontario M4W 3B8
Spain Oficina de Turismo de Portugal (☎ 91 761 7230, fax 570 2270, ⓔ turismo-portugal@ icep.net) Paseo de la Castellana 141-17D, 28046 Madrid
UK Portuguese Trade & Tourism Office (☎ 020-7494 1441, fax 7494 1868, ⓔ iceplondt@aol .com) 22–25a Sackville St, London W1X 1DE
USA Portuguese National Tourist Office (☎ 212-354 4403, fax 764 6137, ⓔ tourism@portugal .org) 590 Fifth Ave, 4th floor, New York, NY 10036-4704

VISAS

No visa is required by EU nationals. Those from Canada, Israel, Australia, New Zealand and the USA can stay up to 60 days without a visa. Others need visas (and should get them in advance) unless they're spouses or children of EU citizens.

Portugal is a Schengen member, but unless you're a citizen of the UK, Ireland or a Schengen country, you should check regulations with the consulate of each Schengen country you plan to visit. You must apply in your country of residence.

Outside Portugal, visa information is supplied by Portuguese consulates. In Portugal, contact the **Foreigners Registration Service** *(Serviço de Estrangeiros e Fronteiras; ☎ 213 585 545; Rua São Sebastião da Pedreira 15, Lisbon; open 9am-noon & 2pm-4pm Mon-Fri)* for information.

EMBASSIES & CONSULATES

Portuguese Embassies & Consulates

Portuguese embassies abroad include:

Australia (☎ 02-6290 1733) 23 Culgoa Circuit, O'Malley, ACT 2606
Canada (☎ 613-729 0883) 645 Island Park Drive, Ottawa, Ont K1Y 0B8
France (☎ 01 47 27 35 29) 3 Rue de Noisiel, 75116 Paris
Ireland (☎ 01-289 4416) Knocksinna House, Foxrock, Dublin 18
Spain (☎ 91 561 78 00) Calle Castello 128, 28006 Madrid
UK (☎ 020-7235 5331) 11 Belgrave Square, London SW1X 8PP
USA (☎ 202-328 8610) 2125 Kalorama Rd NW, Washington, DC 20008

Embassies & Consulates in Portugal

Foreign embassies in Portugal include:

Australia *Embassy:* (☎ 213 101 500) Avenida da Liberdade 200, Lisbon
Canada *Embassy & Consulate:* (☎ 213 164 600) Avenida da Liberdade 196, Lisbon *Consulate:* (☎ 289 803 757) Rua Frei Lourenço de Santa Maria 1, Faro
France *Embassy:* (☎ 213 939 100) Santos o Velho 5, Lisbon *Consulate:* (☎ 226 094 805) Rua Eugénio de Castro 352, Porto
Ireland *Embassy:* (☎ 213 929 440) Rua da Imprensa à Estrela 1, Lisbon
Spain *Embassy:* (☎ 213 472 381) Rua do Salitre 1, Lisbon *Consulate:* (☎ 225 101 685) Rua de Dom João IV 341, Porto *Consulate:* (☎ 251 822 122) Avenida de Espanha, Valença do Minho *Consulate:* (☎ 281 544 888) Avenida Ministro Duarte Pacheco, Vila Real de Santo António
UK *Embassy:* (☎ 213 924 000) Rua de São Bernardo 33, Lisbon *Consulate:* (☎ 226 184 789) Avenida da Boavista 3072, Porto *Consulate:* (☎ 282 417 800) Largo Francisco A Maurício 7, Portimão
USA *Embassy:* (☎ 217 273 300) Avenida das Forças Armadas, Lisbon

New Zealand has an honorary **consul** *(☎ 213 509 690; open 9am-1pm Mon-Fri)* in Lisbon; the nearest **embassy** *(☎ 39-6-441 71 71)* is in Rome.

CUSTOMS

The duty-free allowance for travellers from non-EU countries is 200 cigarettes or 50 cigars, and 1L of spirits or 2L of wine. EU nationals can import up to 800 cigarettes, 200 cigars, 10L of spirits, 20L of fortified wine or 110L of beer – assuming that they are able to carry it all.

MONEY

Portugal uses the euro as its currency. There is no limit on the importation of currency. If you leave Portugal with more than €12,470 you must prove that you brought in at least this much.

Portuguese banks can change most foreign cash and travellers cheques but charge a commission of around €12.50. Better deals are at private exchange bureaus in Lisbon, Porto and tourist resorts.

A handier option is the 24-hour Multibanco ATMs at most banks. Exchange rates are reasonable. Major credit cards – especially Visa and MasterCard – are widely accepted by shops, hotels and a growing number of guesthouses and restaurants.

Portugal remains one of the cheapest places in Europe. On a rock-bottom budget you can squeeze by on US$20 to US$25 a day. With bottom-end accommodation and cheap restaurant meals, figure around US$30. Outside major tourist areas, and in low season, prices dip appreciably. Concessions are often available on admission fees etc if you're over 65, under 26 or have a student card.

A reasonable restaurant tip is 10%. For a snack, a bit of loose change is sufficient. Taxi drivers appreciate 10%, and petrol station attendants €0.50 to €1.

Good-humoured bargaining is acceptable in markets (or with accommodation off season), but you'll find the Portuguese tough opponents!

IVA is a sales tax levied on a wide range of goods and services; in most shops it's

17%. Tourists from non-EU countries can claim a refund on goods from shops belonging to the Global Refund network. The minimum purchase is €60 in any one shop. Ask for a cheque. When you leave Portugal you present the goods, cheque and your passport at customs for a cash, postal-note or credit-card refund. This service is available at Lisbon, Porto and Faro airports. If you're leaving overland, contact customs at your final EU border point, or call **Global Refund** *(☎ 218 463 025; Lisbon)*.

POST & COMMUNICATIONS

Post

Postcards and letters up to 20g cost €0.28 within Portugal, €0.46 to Spain, €0.54 to European destinations and €0.70 worldwide. For delivery to North America or Australasia allow eight to 10 days; to Europe four to six.

Most major towns have a post office with *posta restante* service. Addresses are written with the street name first, followed by the building address and often a floor number with a symbol, eg, 15-3. An alphabetical tag on the address, eg, 2-A, indicates an adjoining entrance or building. R/C *(rés do chão)* means ground floor.

Telephone & Fax

Most domestic numbers have nine digits, all of which must be dialled from any location.

Coin telephones are often broken and will eat your cash. It's easier to buy a PT (Portugal Telecom) phonecard or a discount card, such as the onicard, offering the option of dialling from any fixed-line phone. Both are available from newsagents, tobacconists, post or telephone offices.

Domestic charges drop by 50% from 9pm to 9am on weekdays, and all day Saturday and Sunday. International charges drop by around 10% to 25% from 9pm to 9am, and 20% to 50% during the weekend.

Call Portugal from abroad by dialling the international access code, then Portugal's country code (☎ 351) and the number. From Portugal, the international access code is ☎ 00; for operator help or to make a reverse-charge (collect) call, dial ☎ 171. For domestic inquiries, dial ☎ 118; for numbers abroad, dial ☎ 177. Multilingual operators are available.

Post offices operate a domestic and international service called Corfax, costing €2.70 for the first page sent within Portugal and €4.25 for international destinations. Some private shops offer much cheaper services.

Email & Internet Access

Many towns have a branch of the Instituto Português da Juventude (IPJ), a state-funded youth-centre network. Most of these offer free Internet access during certain hours. Some municipal libraries also have free access. Some newer youth hostels have access for around €2.50 per hour. Internet cafés in bigger towns charge €1.50 to €4 per hour.

DIGITAL RESOURCES

Three useful websites about Portugal are **A Collection of Home Pages about Portugal** *(W www.well.com/user/ideamen/portugal.html)*, **Portugal.com** *(W www.portugal.com)* and **Portugal Info** *(W www.portugal-info.net)*.

BOOKS

Lonely Planet's *Portugal* is the definitive guide to the country. Walkers and car tourers should pack the *Landscapes of Portugal* series, by Brian & Aileen Anderson, including books on the Algarve, Sintra/Estoril and the Costa Verde. More detailed is *Walking in Portugal*, by Bethan Davies and Ben Cole.

WOMEN TRAVELLERS

Outside Lisbon and Porto, an unaccompanied foreign woman is an oddity, and older people may fuss over you as if you were in need of protection. Women travelling on their own or in small groups report few hassles, although in Lisbon and Porto, women should be cautious after dark. Hitching is not recommended for solo women anywhere in Portugal.

GAY & LESBIAN TRAVELLERS

There is little understanding or acceptance of homosexuality. But Lisbon has a flourishing gay scene, with an annual Gay Pride Festival (around 28 June) and a **Gay & Lesbian Community Center** *(Centro Comunitário Gay e Lésbico de Lisboa; ☎ 218 873 918; Rua de São Lazaro 88; open 5pm-9pm daily)*. Check W www.ilga-portugal.org and W www.portugalgay.pt for information on gay-friendly bars, restaurants and clubs in Lisbon and Porto.

DISABLED TRAVELLERS

The **Secretariado Nacional de Rehabilitação** *(☎ 217 936 517, fax 217 965 182; Avenida*

Conde de Valbom 63, Lisbon) publishes the Portuguese-language *Guia de Turismo* with sections on barrier-free accommodation, transport, shops, restaurants and sights in Portugal. It's available at its offices or at Turintegra.

Turintegra, part of the **Cooperativa Nacional Apoio Deficientes** *(CNAD; ☎/fax 218 595 332; Praça Dr Fernando Amado, Lote 566-E, 1900 Lisbon)* keeps a keener eye on developments and arranges holidays and transport for disabled travellers.

SENIOR TRAVELLERS

Travellers aged 60 and over receive various discounts at attractions and on transportation.

DANGERS & ANNOYANCES

The most widespread crime against foreigners is theft from rental cars, followed by pickpocketing, and pilfering from camping grounds. On the increase are armed robberies, mostly in the Algarve, Estoril Coast, parts of Lisbon and a few other cities.

Avoid swimming on beaches that are not marked as safe: Atlantic currents are notoriously dangerous (and badly polluted near major cities).

Emergencies

The national emergency number for police, fire and ambulance is ☎ 112.

BUSINESS HOURS

Most banks are open between 8.30am to 3pm weekdays. Most museums and other tourist attractions are open 10am to 5pm weekdays but are often closed at lunchtime and all day Monday. Shopping hours generally extend from 9am to 7pm on weekdays, 9am to 1pm on Saturday. Lunch is given serious and lingering attention between noon and 3pm.

PUBLIC HOLIDAYS & SPECIAL EVENTS

Public holidays in Portugal include:

New Year's Day (1 January), Carnival (Shrove Tuesday; February/March), Good Friday & the following Saturday (March/April), Liberty Day (25 April), May Day (May), Corpus Christi (May/June) National Day (10 June), Feast of the Assumption (15 August), Republic Day (5 October), All Saints' Day (1 November), Independence Day (1 December), Feast of the Immaculate Conception (8 December) and Christmas Day (25 December).

Portugal's most interesting cultural events include:

Holy Week Festival Easter week in Braga features colourful processions including Ecce Homo, with barefoot penitents carrying torches.

Festas das Cruzes Held in Barcelos in May, the Festival of the Crosses is known for processions, folk music and dance, and regional handicrafts.

Feira Nacional da Agricultura In June, Santarém hosts the National Agricultural Fair, with bullfighting, folk singing and dancing.

Festa do Santo António The Festival of Saint Anthony fills the streets of Lisbon on 13 June.

Festas de São João Porto's big street bash is the St John's Festival, from 16 to 24 June.

Festas da Nossa Senhora da Agonia Viana do Castelo's Our Lady of Suffering Festival, for three days nearest to 20 August, is famed for folk arts, parades and fireworks.

ACTIVITIES

Off-road cycling (BTT; *bicyclete tudo terrano*, all-terrain bicycle) is booming in Portugal, with bike trips on offer at many tourist destinations (see Tavira, Setúbal, Évora and Peneda-Gerês National Park).

Despite some fine rambling country, walking is not a Portuguese passion. Some parks are establishing trails, though, and some adventure travel agencies offer walking tours (see Lisbon, Serra da Estrela, Porto and Parque Nacional da Peneda-Gerês later in this chapter).

Popular water sports include surfing, windsurfing, canoeing, white-water rafting and water-skiing (see Lagos, Sagres, Tavira, Coimbra and Parque Nacional da Peneda-Gerês later in this chapter for local specialists).

Alpine skiing is possible at Torre in the Serra da Estrela from January through March.

The Instituto Português da Juventude (see Lisbon for more on the IPJ) offers holiday programmes for 16- to 30-year-olds (visitors too), including BTT, canoeing and rock climbing. Private organisations offering various activities are listed under Porto and Parque Nacional da Peneda-Gerês.

ACCOMMODATION

Most tourist offices have lists of accommodation to suit a range of budgets and can help you find and book somewhere to stay.

Camping

Camping is popular, and easily the cheapest option. The multilingual, annually updated *Roteiro Campista* (€4.90), sold in larger bookshops, contains details of nearly all Portugal's camping grounds. Depending on facilities and the season, most prices per night run to about €1 to €3 per adult, €1.50 to €3 for a small tent and €1 to €3 per car. Many camping grounds close in low season.

Hostels & Hotels

Portugal has 41 HI-affiliated *pousadas da juventude* (youth hostels). Low rates are offset by segregated dorms, midnight curfews and partial daytime exclusion at most (but not all) of them.

In high season, dorm beds cost €9.50 to €15, and most hostels also offer basic doubles with a shared bathroom for €23 to €30 or with a private bathroom for €26.50 to €42. Bed linen and breakfast are included. Many hostels have kitchens, TV rooms and social areas.

Advance reservations are essential in summer. Most hostels will call ahead to your next stop at no charge, or you can pay €1.50 per set of bookings (with three days' notice) through the country's central HI reservations office, **Movijovem** (*☎ 213 524 072, fax 213 596 001; ⓔ reservas@movijovem.pt; Avenida Duque d'Ávila 137, Lisbon*).

If you don't already have a card from your national hostel association, you can pay a €2 supplement per night (and have a one- or six-night, or a year-long 'guest card').

The government grades hotels with one to five stars. For a high-season double, figure on at least €55. *Estalagem* and *albergaria* refer to upmarket inns. Prices drop spectacularly in low season. Breakfast is usually included.

Private Rooms & Guesthouses

Another option is a *quarto particular* (private room), usually in a private house, with shared facilities. Home-owners may approach you at the bus or train station; otherwise watch for 'quartos' signs or ask at tourist offices. Rooms are usually clean, cheap (€25 to €50 for a double in summer) and free from hostel-style restrictions. A variant is a *dormida* (rooming house), where doubles are about €25. You may be able to bargain in the low season.

The most common types of guesthouse, the Portuguese equivalent of B&Bs, are the *residencial* and the *pensão*. Both are graded from one to three stars, and the best are often cheaper and better run than some hotels. High-season *pensão* rates for a double start from around €30; a *residencial*, where breakfast is normally included, is a bit more expensive. Many have cheaper rooms with shared bathrooms.

FOOD & DRINKS

Eating and drinking get serious attention in Portugal. The *prato do dia* (dish of the day) is often a bargain at around €4.50; the *ementa turística* (tourist menu) rarely is. A *dose* (full portion) is ample for two decent appetites; a *meia dose* (half-portion) is a quarter to a third cheaper. The *couvert* – bread, cheese, butter, olives and other titbits at the start of a meal – costs extra.

Common snacks are *pastéis de bacalhau* (codfish cakes), *prego em pão* (meat and egg in a roll) and *tosta mista* (toasted cheese-and-ham sandwich). Seafood offers exceptional value, especially *linguado grelhado* (grilled sole), *bife de atum* (tuna steak) and the omnipresent *bacalhau* (dried cod), cooked in dozens of ways. Meat is hit-or-miss, but worth sampling are local *presunto* (ham), *borrego* (roast lamb) and *cabrito* (kid). Cafés and *pastelarias* (pastry shops) offer splendid desserts and cakes – try a delicious *pastel de nata* (custard tart).

Coffee is a hallowed institution. In Lisbon a small black espresso is a *bica*, elsewhere simply a *café*. Half-and-half coffee and milk is *café com leite*. For coffee with lots of milk at breakfast, ask for a *galão*. *Chá* (tea) comes *com limão* (with lemon) or *com leite* (with milk). *água mineral* (mineral water) is *com gás* (carbonated) or *sem gás* (still).

Local *cerveja* (beers) include Sagres in the south and Super Bock in the north. A 200mL draught is called *um imperial*; *uma garrafa* is a bottle. Portuguese *vinho* (wine) offers great value in all varieties: *tinto* (red), *branco* (white) and *vinho verde* (semi-sparkling young), which is usually white. Port, synonymous with Portugal, is produced in the Douro Valley east of Porto and drunk in three forms: ruby, tawny and white.

ENTERTAINMENT

Conventional bars, pubs and clubs abound in Lisbon, Porto and the Algarve. Some bigger towns sponsor summer cultural programmes, especially music (rock, jazz and classical) and dance.

SPECTATOR SPORTS

Football (soccer) dominates the sporting scene. Bullfighting remains popular; Portuguese rules prohibit a public kill, though bulls are often dispatched in private afterwards.

Getting There & Away

AIR

BA and TAP Air Portugal have daily direct flights from London to Lisbon; they also go to Porto and Faro. On most days there are direct links to Lisbon and Porto from Paris, Frankfurt, Amsterdam, Brussels and Madrid.

From the UK, high-season London-Faro return fares start at about UK£110 with no-frills carrier **Go** *(☎ 0870 607 6543)*. London-Porto via a third-country carrier can be as low as UK£150, and charter fares to Lisbon or Faro start at about UK£180. **TAP** *(☎ 0845-601 0932)* offers youth/student fares for year-long trips. France has frequent Portugal connections at reasonable prices.

LAND

Bus

Portugal's main Eurolines agents are **Internorte** *(☎ 226 052 420; Porto)*, **Intercentro** *(☎ 213 571 745; Lisbon)* and **Intersul** *(☎ 289 899 770; Faro)*, serving north, central and southern Portugal, respectively. **Busabout** (see the Getting Around chapter earlier) stops in Lisbon and Lagos.

Spanish **Eurolines** *(☎ 915 063 360; Madrid)* connections go at least three times weekly to Madrid-Lisbon (€35.45), Madrid-Porto (€34.25), Seville-Lisbon (€31.25) and Barcelona-Lisbon (€71.92). Spanish operators running to Portugal include **ALSA** *(☎ 902 42 22 42; Madrid)*, with twice-daily Madrid-Lisbon services, and **Damas** *(☎ 959 25 69 00; Huelva)*, running twice daily from Seville to Faro via Huelva, jointly with the Algarve line EVA. Three times weekly, **Transportes Agobe** *(☎ 958 63 52 74)* runs from Granada via Seville and the Algarve to Lisbon, Coimbra and Porto.

Eurolines *(☎ 08705-143219, UK; ☎ 083 669 52 52, France)* runs a variety of services from London via the Channel ferry, with a 7½-hour stopover and change of coach in Paris. These include at least four weekly coaches to Porto (40 hours); and five to Lisbon (42 hours), both UK£82/€134 one way from London/Paris. The independent line **IASA** *(☎ 01 43 53 90 82, Paris; ☎ 225 373 205, Porto; ☎ 213 143 979, Lisbon)* runs three coaches weekly on four routes: Paris–Viana do Castelo; Paris–Braga; Paris–Porto; and Paris– Coimbra–Lisbon. A one-way/return fare to Lisbon is €84/152.

Train

The main rail route from Spain is Madrid-Lisbon on the *Talgo Lusitânia* via Valência de Alcántara. The nightly express takes 9½ hours, and a 2nd-class reserved seat costs €46.28; for a sleeper berth €65.51. Badajoz-Elvas-Lisbon is tedious (one regional service daily), but the scenery is grand. There are no direct southern trains: from Seville you can ride to Huelva (three daily), catch a bus ride to Ayamonte, change bus to cross the border to Vila Real de Santo António then catch one of the frequent trains to Faro and Lagos. The daily Paris–Lisbon train goes via Salamanca, Valladolid, Burgos, Vitória and San Sebastian.

All services from London to Portugal go via Paris, where you change trains (and stations) for the *TGV Atlantique* to Irún in Spain (change trains again). From Irún there are two standard routes: the *Sud-Expresso* across Spain to Coimbra in Portugal, where you can continue to Lisbon or change for Porto; and an express service to Madrid, changing there to the overnight *Lusitânia* to Lisbon. Change at Lisbon for the south of Portugal.

Buying a one-way, 2nd-class, adult/youth London–Lisbon ticket (seat only) for the cheapest route, via the channel ferry, costs UK£102/87; allow at least 30 hours. Tickets are available from bigger train stations or from **Trains Europe** *(☎ 020-8699 3654)* in London. The Eurostar service to Paris via the Channel Tunnel cuts several hours off the trip but bumps up the cost. Ring **Rail Europe** *(☎ 08705-848 848)* for details.

Car & Motorcycle

The quickest routes from the UK are by ferry via northern Spain: from Portsmouth to Bilbao with **P&O Stena Line** *(☎ 08706-003300)*, or, between March and November, with **Brittany Ferries** *(☎ 08705-360360)* from Plymouth to Santander .

DEPARTURE TAX

Airport taxes for return flights between Portugal and other European countries range from about €17 for Spain to UK£22/€34 for the UK.

Getting Around

BUS

A welter of regional bus companies together operate a network of comfortable, direct intercity *expressos,* fast regional *rápidas*, and *carreiras*, which stop at every crossroad. Local weekend services can thin out to nothing, especially up north and when school is out. There is a Lisbon-Porto express (€12.50; 3½ hours), and Lisbon-Faro (€14; under five hours). A youth card gets you discounts of about 20%.

TRAIN

Caminhos de Ferro Portugueses (CP), the state railway company, operates three main services: *rápido* or *intercidade* (IC on timetables), *inter-regional* (IR) and *regional* (R). Intercidade and interregional tickets cost at least twice the price of regional services, with reservations either mandatory or recommended. A special fast IC service called Alfa links Lisbon, Coimbra and Porto. Regional services are somewhat slower and cheaper than buses. Sample 2nd-class IC/Alpha fares include €14.10/19 for Lisbon-Porto. The IC fare for Lisbon-Faro is €11.30 and for Lisbon-Coimbra it's €10.30.

Children aged four to 11 and adults over 65 travel for half-price. Youth-card holders get 30% off R and IR services (except on weekends). One/two/three-week *bilhetes turísticos* (tourist tickets) at €100/170/250 are good for 1st-class travel, but worthwhile only if you're practically living on trains. Frequent train travellers may want to buy the *Guia Horário Oficial* (€1.75), with all domestic and international timetables, from ticket windows at most stations.

CAR & MOTORCYCLE

ACP *(Automóvel Clube de Portugal;* ☎ *213 180 100, fax 213 180 227; Rua Rosa Araújo 24, Lisbon; emergency help numbers for southern Portugal:* ☎ *219 429 103 • northern Portugal:* ☎ *228 340 001)*, Portugal's representative for various foreign car, motorcycle and touring clubs, provides medical, legal and breakdown assistance for members. **ACP Insurance** *(*☎ *217 991 200)* can advise members on car and motorcycle insurance. Petrol is pricey.

Lisbon Lunatics

If you are insane enough to try driving in Portugal, at least make sure that you're marginally more mentally stable than the average highway warrior. Many Portuguese drivers navigate twisting, mountainous terrain with all but suicidal confidence. Blind curves are taken at high speeds and passing is performed cavalierly – to all appearances, the Portuguese believe in the existence of an invisible 'middle lane' in which accidents cannot occur. But they can: Portugal sports Europe's highest road fatality rate. Be very, very careful.

Portugal has dozens of local car-rental firms, many offering lower daily rates than international firms. To rent a small car for a week in high season, figure on about UK£200 from the UK or at least €225 from Portugal (with tax, insurance and unlimited mileage). Fly-drive packages from international firms or TAP Air Portugal can be good value. You must be aged at least 25 and have held your licence for over a year (some companies allow younger drivers at higher rates).

BICYCLE

A growing number of towns have bike rental outfits (€7.50 to €17.50 a day). If you're bringing your own machine, pack plenty of spares. Bikes can no longer be taken with you on trains, though most bus lines will accept them as accompanied baggage.

LOCAL TRANSPORT

Except in Lisbon or Porto there's little reason to take a municipal bus. Lisbon's underground system is handy for getting around the city centre and out to Parque das Nações, the former Expo site (see the Lisbon section for details). Porto is building its own underground system.

Taxis are good value over short distances, especially for two or more people, and are plentiful in towns. Flagfall is €1.50, plus €1.75 for luggage, the fare increases at around €0.35 per kilometre. Fares increase by around 20% at night, at weekends and if you leave the city limits.

Enthusiasts for stately progress shouldn't miss the trams, an endangered species, in Lisbon and Porto and the *elevadores* (funiculars and elevators) of Lisbon, Bom Jesus (in

Braga) and Nazaré. Commuter ferries cross the Rio Tejo all day to/from Lisbon.

Lisbon (Lisboa)

pop 720,000

Although Lisbon has the crowds, noise and traffic of a capital city, its low skyline and breezy position beside the Rio Tejo (Tagus River) lends it a small, manageable feel. Its blend of architectural styles and diverse attractions are underscored by an unpretentious atmosphere, giving it a wide appeal among travellers. As one of Western Europe's most economical towns, Lisbon is growing in popularity among independent voyagers.

Orientation

Activity centres on the Baixa district, focus at Praça Dom Pedro IV (the Rossio). Just north is Praça dos Restauradores, at the bottom of Avenida da Liberdade, Lisbon's park-like 'main street'. West of the Rossio it's a steep climb to the Bairro Alto district, the traditional centre of Lisbon's nightlife. East of the Rossio, it's another climb to the Castelo de São Jorge and the adjacent labyrinthine Alfama district. Several kilometres west is Belém, with a cluster of attractions. Parque das Nações, the former Expo '98 site, lies on the revamped northeastern waterfront.

Information

Tourist Offices Turismo de Lisboa's new main office, **Lisboa Welcome Center** *(☎ 210 312 810, fax 210 312 899; Praça do Comércio; open daily)*, deals specifically with Lisbon inquiries. A **tourist office** *(☎ 213 463 314, fax 213 468 772; Palácio Foz on Praça dos Restauradores; open daily)* run by ICEP deals only with national inquiries.

There are several **Ask Me Lisboa kiosks** *(☎ 213 259 13; Rua Augusta • ☎ 213 463 314; Palácio Foz • ☎ 213 225 128; Mercado da Ribeira • ☎ 218 821 604; Santa Apolónia train station • ☎ 213 658 435; Belém • ☎ 218 450 660; airport; all open daily)*. All of the kiosks have free maps and the bimonthly *Follow me Lisboa,* which lists sights and current events; all sell the Lisboa Card, good for unlimited travel on nearly all city transport and free or discounted admission to many museums and monuments. A 24/48/72-hour card costs €11.25/18.50/23.50.

Money Banks with 24-hour cash-exchange machines are at the airport, Santa Apolónia train station and Rua Augusta 24. A better deal is the exchange bureau **Cota Câmbios** *(Rossio 41; open 8.30am-10pm daily)*. Nearly every bank has an ATM.

Top Tours *(☎ 213 108 800; Avenida Duque de Loulé 108; open Mon-Fri)* offers American Express (AmEx) card or travellers-cheque holders commission-free currency exchange, help with lost cards or cheques and a holding and forwarding service for mail and faxes.

Post & Communications The **central post office & telephone centre** *(Praça dos Restauradores; open 10am-10pm Mon-Fri, 10am-6pm Sat & Sun)* receives Posta Restante addressed to Central Correios, Terreira do Paço, 1100 Lisboa. For telecommunications, there's a **telephone office** *(Rossio 68; open to 11pm daily)*, and another **post and telephone office** in *(Praça do Comércio)*, open weekdays only.

Internet access is available at **Lisboa Welcome Center** *(☎ 210 312 810; Praça do Comércio, 2nd floor; open 9am-8pm daily)* for €2.50 per half-hour. **Portugal Telecom's Hiper Net** *(☎ 213 582 841; Avenida Fontes Pereira de Melo 38; open 9am-9pm Mon-Fri)* offers access at €1 per half-hour; 30 minutes at **Espaço Ágora** *(☎ 213 940 170; Rua Cintura, Armazém 1; open 2pm-1am daily)*, behind Santos train station, costs €1.50. It's €2.50 per half-hour at the relaxed **Web Café bar** *(☎ 213 421 181; Rua do Diário de Notícias 126; open 4pm-2am daily)*.

Travel Agencies Trusty youth-travel agencies are **Tagus** *(☎ 213 525 986, fax 213 532 715; Rua Camilo Castelo Branco 20)* and **Wasteels** *(☎ 218 869 793, fax 218 869 797; Rua dos Caminhos do Ferro 90)*, by Santa Apolónia train station. The **Instituto Português da Juventude** *(IPJ; ☎ 218 920 800, fax 218 920 808; ⓔ ipj.infor@mail.telepac.pt; Via de Moscavide)* is a youth network that offers a range of information resources, courses and holiday programmes for 16- to 30-year-olds.

Medical & Emergency Services The **British Hospital** *(☎ 213 955 067, 213 976 329; Rua Saraiva de Carvalho 49)* has English-speaking staff.

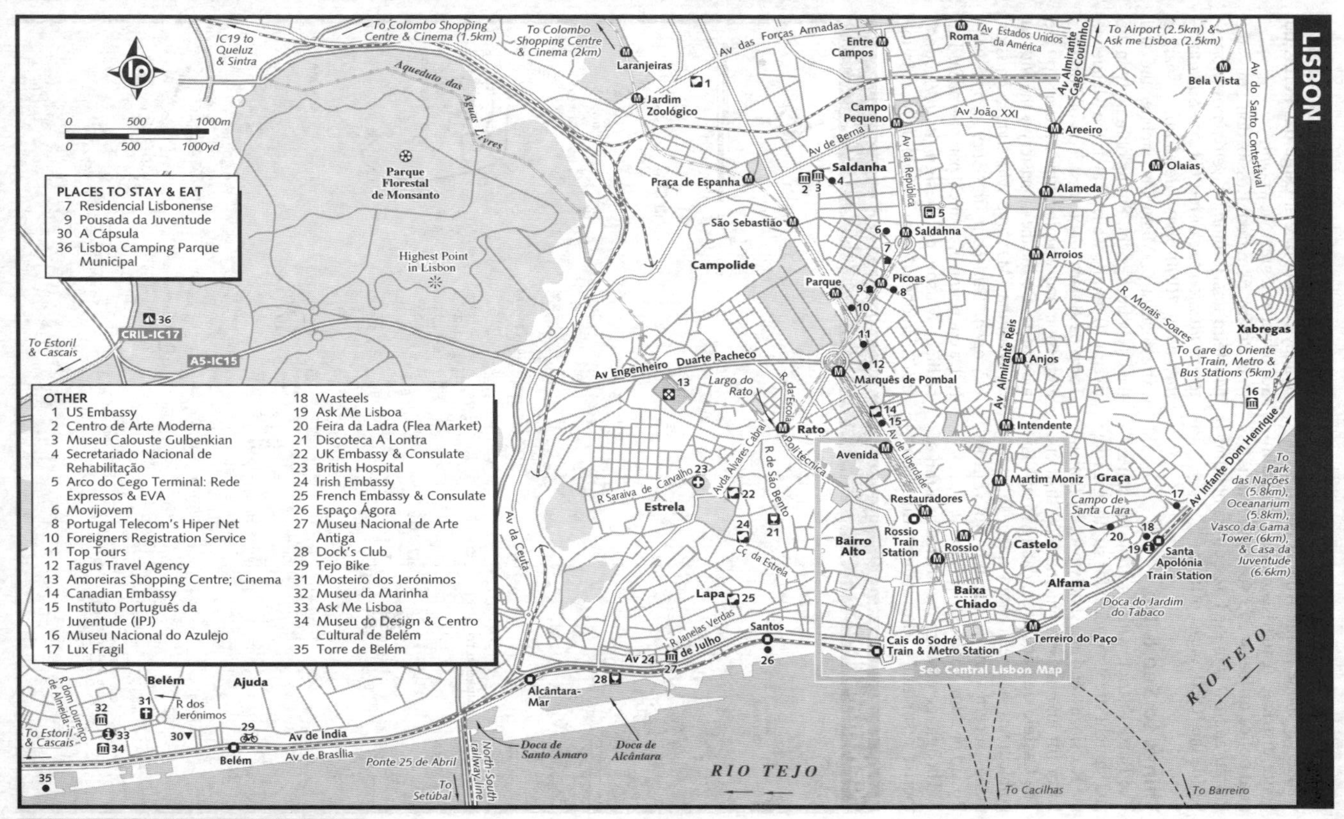
LISBON
PLACES TO STAY & EAT
7 Residencial Lisbonense
9 Pousada da Juventude
30 A Cápsula
36 Lisboa Camping Parque Municipal
OTHER
1 US Embassy
2 Centro de Arte Moderna
3 Museu Calouste Gulbenkian
4 Secretariado Nacional de Rehabilitação
5 Arco do Cego Terminal: Rede Expressos & EVA
6 Movijovem
8 Portugal Telecom's Hiper Net
10 Foreigners Registration Service
11 Top Tours
12 Tagus Travel Agency
13 Amoreiras Shopping Centre; Cinema
14 Canadian Embassy
15 Instituto Português da Juventude (IPJ)
16 Museu Nacional do Azulejo
17 Lux Fragil
18 Wasteels
19 Ask Me Lisboa
20 Feira da Ladra (Flea Market)
21 Discoteca A Lontra
22 UK Embassy & Consulate
23 British Hospital
24 Irish Embassy
25 French Embassy & Consulate
26 Espaço Ágora
27 Museu Nacional de Arte Antiga
28 Dock's Club
29 Tejo Bike
31 Mosteiro dos Jerónimos
32 Museu da Marinha
33 Ask Me Lisboa
34 Museu do Design & Centro Cultural de Belém
35 Torre de Belém
0 500 1000m
0 500 1000yd
To Colombo Shopping Centre & Cinema (1.5km)
IC19 to Queluz & Sintra
To Colombo Shopping Centre & Cinema (2km)
To Airport (2.5km) & Ask me Lisboa (2.5km)
Aqueduto das Águas Livres
Parque Florestal de Monsanto
Highest Point in Lisbon
To Estoril & Cascais
CRIL-IC17
A5-IC15
Av das Forças Armadas
Av Estados Unidos da América
Av Almirante Gago Coutinho
Av do Santo Contestável
Av João XXI
Av de Berna
Av da República
Av Engenheiro Duarte Pacheco
Av Almirante Reis
R Morais Soares
Av Infante Dom Henrique
Av de Liberdade
R da Escola Politécnica
Avda Alvares Cabral
R de São Bento
R Saraiva de Carvalho
Cç da Estrela
R Janelas Verdas
Av 24 de Julho
Av da Ceuta
Av de India
Av de Brasília
R dos Jerónimos
R dom Lourenço de Almeida
Ponte 25 de Abril
North-South railway line
Laranjeiras
Jardim Zoológico
Praça de Espanha
São Sebastião
Campolide
Parque
Entre Campos
Roma
Campo Pequeno
Saldanha
Picoas
Marquês de Pombal
Largo do Rato
Rato
Areeiro
Bela Vista
Olaias
Alameda
Arroios
Anjos
Intendente
Xabregas
To Gare do Oriente Train, Metro & Bus Stations (5km)
Avenida
Martim Moniz
Graça
Restauradores
Rossio Train Station
Rossio
Bairro Alto
Castelo
Campo de Santa Clara
Santa Apolónia Train Station
To Park das Nações (5.8km), Oceanarium (5.8km), Vasco da Gama Tower (6km), & Casa da Juventude (6.6km)
Alfama
Baixa
Chiado
Doca do Jardim do Tabaco
Terreiro do Paço
Cais do Sodré Train & Metro Station
See Central Lisbon Map
Estrela
Lapa
Santos
Alcântara-Mar
Belém
Ajuda
Doca de Santo Amaro
Doca de Alcântara
RIO TEJO
To Setúbal
To Cacilhas
To Barreiro

Dangers & Annoyances At night avoid wandering alone in the Alfama and Cais do Sodré districts. A tourist-oriented, **multilingual police office** *(☎ 213 466 802; Praça dos Restauradores)* is in the Foz Cultura building beside the ICEP tourist office.

Things to See & Do

The Baixa district, with its imposing squares and straight streets, is ideal for strolling. From the Rossio, ascend at a stately pace by funicular or lift into the surrounding hilly districts. The **Castelo de São Jorge**, dating from Visigothic times, has been tarted up but still commands superb views. Take bus No 37 from Rossio or tram No 28.

Though increasingly gentrified and full of tourist restaurants, the ancient district of **Alfama**, below the castle, is a fascinating maze of alleys. The terrace at **Largo das Portas do Sol** provides a great viewpoint.

In **Belém**, 6km from Rossio, don't miss the **Mosteiro dos Jerónimos** *(Jerónimos Monastery; admission to cloisters €3, free Sun morning; open 10am-5pm Tues-Sun)*, a soaring extravaganza of Manueline architecture and the city's finest sight. Sitting obligingly in the river a 10-minute walk away is the Manueline **Torre de Belém**, *the* tourist icon of Portugal; admission and opening times are as for the monastery. Beside the monastery is the **Museu da Marinha** *(Maritime Museum; admission €3; open 10am-6pm Tues-Sun, to 5pm winter)*, a collection of nautical paraphernalia. The brilliant **Museu do Design** *(adult/student €3/1.50; open 11am-7.15pm daily)* is in the

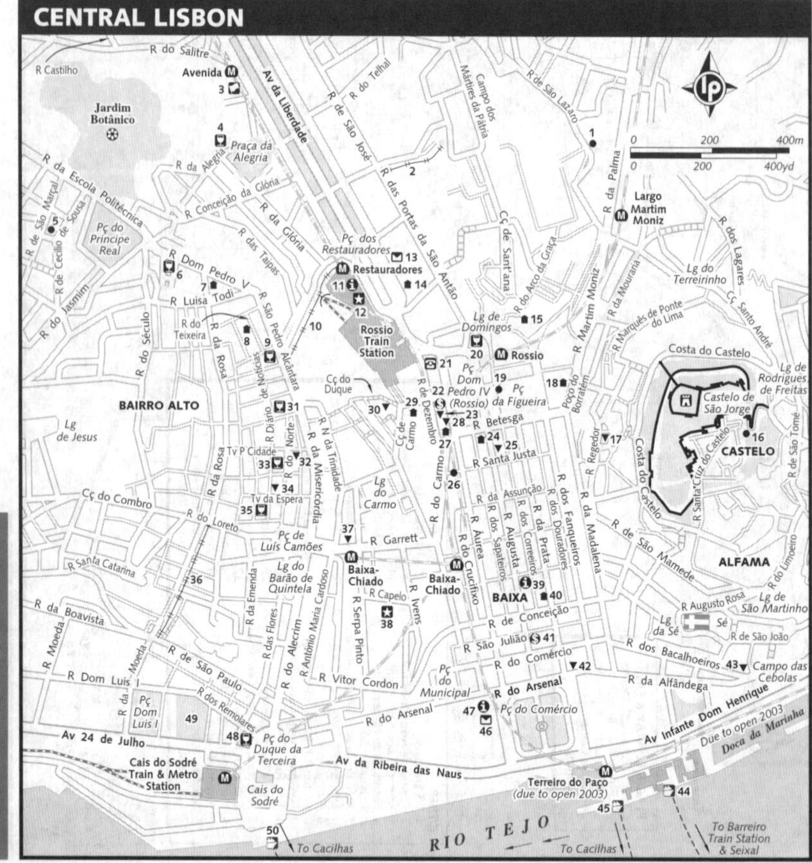

Centro Cultural de Belém, opposite. To reach Belém, take the train (or bus No 43) from Cais do Sodré or tram No 15 from Praça da Figueira.

Lisbon boasts a host of fine museums. The following are open 10am to 6pm (from 2pm Tuesday; closed Monday). The **Museu Calouste Gulbenkian** *(☎ 217 823 000; Avenida de Berna 45A)* is considered Portugal's finest museum. Allow several hours to view its treasures, including paintings, sculptures and jewellery. The adjacent **Centro de Arte Moderna** *(Avenida de Berna 45A)* exhibits a cross section of modern Portuguese art. Admission to each costs €3 (free Sundays). The handiest metro station is São Sebastião.

One of Lisbon's most attractive museums is the **Museu Nacional do Azulejo** *(☎ 218 147 747; Rua da Madre de Deus 4; bus No 40 from Praça do Comércio or No 49 from Rossio; admission €2.50)*, in the former convent of Nossa Senhora da Madre de Deus. The **Museu Nacional de Arte Antiga** *(Antique Art Museum; Rua das Janelas Verdes; bus No 40 or 60 or tram No 15 from Praça da Figueira; adult/student €3/1.50, admission free Sun morning)* houses the national collection of works by Portuguese painters.

Places to Stay

Lisboa Camping Parque Municipal *(☎ 217 623 100; Parque Florestal de Monsanto; bus No 43 from Cais do Sodré)* is 6km northwest of Rossio.

The **pousada da juventude** *(☎ 213 532 696; Rua Andrade Corvo 46; open 24hr)* is central. The closest metro station is Picoas, or take bus No 46 from Santa Apolónia station or Rossio. The newer **casa da juventude** *(☎ 218 920 890; Via de Moscavide)* is 1km north of Gare do Oriente. Take bus No 44 from Praça dos Restauradores or Gare do Oriente to the Avenida da Boa Esperança roundabout. Reservations are essential at both hostels.

In high season – and for central hotels at any time – advance bookings are imperative. In the Baixa and Restauradores area, there are adequate doubles at **Pensão Santo Tirso** *(☎ 213 470 428; Praça Dom Pedro IV 18, 3rd floor; doubles around €40)*, as is the case at **Pensão Prata** *(☎ 213 468 908; Rua da Prata 71, 3rd floor; doubles with/without bath €30/25)* and **Pensão Arco da Bandeira** *(☎ 213 423 478; Rua dos Sapateiros 226, 4th floor)*. More salubrious, with doubles around €35 to €40, are **Pensão Imperial** *(☎ 213 420 166; Praça dos Restauradores 78, 4th floor)* and friendly **Hospedaria Bons Dias** *(☎ 213 471 918; Calçada do Carmo 25, 5th floor)*. Old-fashioned **Pensão Residencial Alcobia** *(☎ 218 865 171, fax 218 865 174; Poço do Borratém 15; doubles with/without bath €45/38)* is a good option. Brighter **Pensão Residencial Gerês** *(☎ 218 810 497, fax 218 882 006; Calçada do Garcia 6; rooms €45)* offers rates without breakfast.

CENTRAL LISBON

PLACES TO STAY
7 Pensão Londres
8 Pensão Globo
14 Pensão Imperial
15 Pensão Residencial Gerês
18 Pensão Residencial Alcobia
24 Pensão Arco da Bandeira
27 Pensão Santo Tirso
29 Hospedaria Bons Dias
40 Pensão Prata

PLACES TO EAT
17 São Cristóvão
23 Pingo Doce Supermarket
25 Nilo
28 Café Nicola
30 Restaurante O Sol
32 Restaurante Sinal Vermelho
34 Restaurante A Primavera
37 Café A Brasileira
42 Solar do Vez
43 Martinho da Arcada

OTHER
1 Gay & Lesbian Community Centre
2 Elevador de Lavra
3 Spanish Embassy
4 Hot Clube de Portugal
5 British Council
6 Pavilhão Chinês
9 Solar do Vinho do Porto
10 Elevador da Glória
11 ICEP Tourist Office
12 Tourist Police
13 Central Post & Telephone Office
16 Largo das Portas do Sol
19 Carris Kiosk
20 A Ginjinha
21 Telephone Office
22 Cota Câmbios
26 Elevador de Santa Justa
31 Web Café Bar
33 Adega Machado (Casa de Fado)
35 Adega do Ribatejo (Casa de Fado)
36 Elevador da Bica
38 Police Sation
39 Ask Me Lisboa
41 24-Hour Cash Exchange Machine
44 Terreiro do Paço Ferry Terminal
45 Cais da Alfândega Ferry Terminal
46 Post and Telephone Office
47 Lisboa Welcome Center
48 Ó Gilíns Irish Pub
49 Mercado da Ribeira; Ask Me Lisboa
50 Cais do Sodré Car Ferry Terminal

Near the Elevador da Glória is pleasant **Pensão Globo** *(☎ 213 462 279; Rua do Teixeira 37; doubles from €30)*. **Pensão Londres** *(☎ 213 462 203, fax 213 465 682; Rua Dom Pedro V 53; doubles from €40)* has spacious rooms, the upper ones with great views. Over in Marquês de Pombal, **Residencial Lisbonense** *(☎ 213 544 628; Rua Pinheiro Chagas 1; doubles with bath €40)* offers bright doubles with breakfast.

Places to Eat

There are dozens of restaurants and cafés in the Baixa (which is the best area for lunchtime bargains) and Bairro Alto (which has pricier evening venues). A trendier restaurant and bar zone is riverside **Doca de Santo Amaro**, near Alcântara-Mar station. The main market, **Mercado da Ribeira**, is near Cais do Sodré station, and the most centrally located supermarket is **Pingo Doce** just off the Rossio on Rua de Dezembro.

In Baixa, minimalist **Nilo** *(☎ 213 467 014; Rua dos Correeiros 217)* is one of many reasonably priced places along Rua dos Correeiros. **Restaurante O Sol** *(☎ 213 471 944; Calçada do Duque 23; set meals around €5)* serves vegetarian cuisine in a great location. Among several restaurants with outdoor seating in lower Alfama, **Solar do Vez** *(☎ 218 870 794; Campo das Cebolas 48; mains €6-8)* features appealing simplicity. **São Cristóvão** *(☎ 218 885 578; Rua de São Cristóvão 30; mains €4-5)* serves up aromatic dishes from Cape Verdean. For coffee or a meal, try Art Deco **Café Nicola** *(☎ 213 460 579; Rossio 24)* or 18th-century **Martinho da Arcada** *(☎ 218 879 259; Praça do Comércio 3)*. The literary pedigree of Art Nouveau **Café A Brasileira** *(☎ 213 469 547; Rua Garrett 120)* is symbolised by the bronze figure of Fernando Pessoa outside.

Over in Bairro Alto and Saldanha, tiny **Restaurante A Primavera** *(☎ 213 420 477; Travessa da Espera 34; mains €7-10)* has a family ambience. **Restaurante Sinal Vermelho** *(☎ 213 461 252; Rua das Gáveas 89; mains €8.50-11.50)* is one of Lisbon's best (great desserts).

A row of attractive restaurants in Belém with outdoor seating includes **A Cápsula** *(☎ 213 648 768; Rua Vieira Portuense 72)*, serving classics like pork Alentejana (€7.50).

Soul Songs

Peculiar to Portugal is *fado*, the melancholy, nostalgic songs that the Portuguese consider their very soul. The name derives from the Latin *fatum* (fate). Singers and guitarists dress in black and lament unrequited love, times gone by and death. No-one seems clear as to *fado's* exact roots. Some say it started with the yearnings of 16th-century sailors. Others believe it came along with the arrival of Brazilian slaves. Lisbonites believe it originated with the Moors.

Lisbon, Porto and Coimbra all have their share of *casas de fado*, adorned with the customary black shawl and guitar – key symbols in this form of music. But be warned: many *fado* houses are little more than money-making schemes to part tourists from their cash with overpriced but obligatory dinners.

So important is *fado* to the national psyche of Portugal that in many record shops you'll be hard pushed to find anything else. A great introduction to the genre is works by Amália Rodrigues, the superstar of her day (she died in 1999), or albums by current diva Dulce Pontes.

Entertainment

For listings, pick up the free bimonthly *Follow me Lisboa* or quarterly *Lisboa Step By Step* from the tourist office, or *Público* from a newsstand.

Many *casas de fado* (which are also restaurants) show pricey, inferior *fado* and have a minimum charge of around €16. In the Bairro Alto, try professional **Adega Machado** *(☎ 213 224 640; Rua do Norte 91)* or simpler **Adega do Ribatejo** *(☎ 213 468 343; Rua Diário de Notícias 23)*.

Hot Clube de Portugal *(☎ 213 467 369; Praça da Alegria 39; open 10pm-2am Tues-Sat)* is part of a thriving live-jazz scene. Live music is on offer on Friday and Saturday nights at **Ó Gilíns Irish Pub** *(☎ 213 421 899; Rua dos Remolares 8-10; open 11am-2am)*

Clubs come and go. Stalwart **Lux Fragil** *(☎ 218 820 890; Avenida Infante Dom Henrique, Cais da Pedra à Santa Apolónia; open midnight-5am)* remains. Riverside options include **Dock's Club** *(☎ 213 950 856; Rua da Cintura do Porto de Lisboa 226; open to 6am Tues-Sat)*.

The African music scene (predominantly Cape Verdean) centres on Rua de São Bento, just west of Central Lisbon; **Discoteca A Lontra** *(☎ 213 691 083; Rua de São Bento 155; open to 4am Tues-Sun)* is popular.

For a taste of real – though hardly undiscovered – Lisbon, sip a sticky glass of *ginjinha* (cherry liqueur) outside **A Ginjinha** *(Largo de Domingos; open 9am-10.30pm)*, by the Rossio. For cocktails in quirky surrounds, ring the bell at **Pavilhão Chinês** *(☎ 213 424 729; Rua Dom Pedro V 89; open 6pm-2am, from 9pm Sunday)*.

Getting There & Away

Lisbon is connected by daily flights to Porto, Faro and many European centres (see the introductory Getting There & Away and Getting Around sections of this chapter). For arrival and departure information call ☎ 218 413 700.

A dozen different bus companies, including **Renex** *(☎ 222 003 395)*, operate from Gare do Oriente. The **Arco do Cego terminal** is the base for **Rede Expressos** *(☎ 707 223 344)* and **EVA** *(☎ 213 147 710)*, whose networks cover the whole country.

Santa Apolónia station (☎ *218 816 121)* is the rail terminus for northern and central Portugal, and for all international services (trains also stop en route at the better-connected Gare do Oriente). Cais do Sodré station is for Belém, Cascais and Estoril. Rossio station serves Sintra. Barreiro station, across the river, is the terminus for southern Portugal; connecting ferries leave frequently from the pier at Terréiro do Paço. The north-south railway line, over the Ponte de 25 Abril, goes to suburban areas and will eventually carry on farther to southern Portugal.

Cais da Alfândega is the terminal for several ferries including to Cacilhas (€0.55), a transfer point for some buses to Setúbal. A car ferry (for bikes too) runs from Cais do Sodré terminal.

Getting Around

The AeroBus runs every 20 minutes from 7.45am to 8.45pm, taking 30 to 45 minutes between the airport and Cais do Sodré, including a stop by the ICEP tourist office. A €2.30/5.50 ticket is good for one/three days on all buses, trams and funiculars. Local bus Nos 44, 45 and 83 also run near the ICEP tourist office; No 44 links the airport with Gare do Oriente too. A taxi into town is about €10.

Two-journey bus and tram tickets are €0.93 from Carris kiosks, most conveniently at Praça da Figueira and the Santa Justa elevador, or €0.90 per ride from the driver. A one/four/seven-day Passe Turístico, valid for trams, buses and the metro, costs €2.55/9.25/13.10. Buses and trams run from 6am to 1am, with some night services. Wheelchair users can call the **Cooperativa Nacional Apoio Deficientes** *(☎ 218 595 332)* for assistance to hire adapted transport. The clattering, antediluvian trams *(eléctricos)* are an endearing component of Lisbon; try No 28 to Alfama from Largo Martim Moniz. The metro is useful for hops across town and to the Parque das Nações. Individual tickets cost €0.55; a *caderneta* of 10 tickets is €4.5. A *bilhete diário* (day ticket) is €1.40. The metro operates from 6.30am to 1am. Beware of rush-hour pickpockets.

Lisbon's plentiful taxis are best hired from taxi ranks. Some at the airport are less than scrupulous. From the Rossio to Belém is around €5, to the castle about €3.50.

Car-rental companies in Lisbon include **Avis** *(☎ 800 201 002)*, **Europcar** *(☎ 218 410 163)* and the cheaper **Rupauto** *(☎ 217 933 258, fax 217 931 768)*. **Tejo Bike** *(☎ 218 871 976)*, 300m east of Belém, rents bikes for €4 an hour to ride along the waterfront.

Around Lisbon

SINTRA

pop 20,000

If you take only one trip from Lisbon, make it Sintra. Beloved by Portuguese royalty and English nobility, its thick forests and startling architecture provide a complete change from Lisbon. The **tourist office** *(☎ 219 231 157, fax 219 235 176; Praça da República 23)*, in the historic centre, sells day passes (€7). On weekends and during the annual July music festival, expect droves of visitors.

The **Palácio Nacional de Sintra** *(☎ 219 106 840; adult/student €3/1.50; open 10am-5pm Thur-Tues)*, Manueline and Gothic, with Moorish origins, dominates the town with its twin chimneys. One of Sintra's best museums is the **Museu do Brinquedo** *(☎ 219 242 172; Rua Visconde de Monserrate; adult/concession €3/1.50; open 10am-6pm Tues-Sun)*, with 20,000 toys from around the world.

An easy 3km climb from the centre leads to ruined **Castelo dos Mouros** *(open 9am-6pm daily)*, providing fine views. Twenty minutes of the climb is on the exuberantly romantic **Palácio da Pena** (☎ *219 105 340; open 10am-4pm Tues-Sun)*, built in 1839. Cars are prohibited; Stagecoach bus No 434 (€3) runs regularly from the station via the tourist office. Rambling **Monserrate Gardens** *(☎ 219 237 300; open 10am-5pm daily)* are 4km from town. A ticket for all three attractions costs adult/concession €5/3.50. En route to the gardens is an extraordinary, mystical mansion, **Quinta da Regaleira** *(☎ 219 106 650; adult/concession €9.98/4.99; open 10am-6pm daily, to 3.30pm winter)*. Visits must be prearranged.

Places to Stay & Eat

Book ahead in high season. The best camping ground is **Camping Praia Grande** *(☎ 219 290 581)*, on the coast 11km from Sintra and easily linked by frequent buses. A **pousada da juventude** *(☎ 219 241 210)* is at Santa Eufémia, 4km from the centre; reservations are essential all year.

Residencial Adelaide *(☎ 219 230 873; Rua Guilherme Gomes Fernandes 11; doubles from €25)*, a 10-minute walk from the station, has reasonable doubles. The tourist office has a list of private rooms at a similar price. Across the tracks is friendly **Piela's** *(☎ 219 241 691; Rua João de Deus 70; doubles €25-50)*, which is due to move in 2003 to Avenida Desiderio Cambournac 1–3.

For good eating, stay close to the tourist office and check out **Tulhas** *(☎ 219 232 378; Rua Gil Vicente 4-6)*, whose hits include bacalhau with cream €6.75. Simple **A Tasca do Manel** *(☎ 219 230 215; Largo Dr Vergílio Horta 5; mains around €6)* serves standards. **Restaurante Parreirinha** *(☎ 219 231 207; Rua João de Deus 41; mains €6-7)* serves up great grilled fish. Cavernous, classy **Xentra** *(☎ 219 240 759; Rua Consiglieri Pedroso 2-A; snacks €2-3, mains around €8)* has a similarly elegant bar (until 2am).

Getting There & Around

The Lisbon-Sintra railway terminates in Estefânia, 1.5km northeast of the historic centre. Sintra's bus station, and another train station, are a farther 1km east in the new-town district of Portela de Sintra. Frequent shuttle buses run to the historic centre from the bus terminal. Trains run every 15 minutes from Lisbon's Rossio station. Buses run regularly from Sintra to Estoril and Cascais.

A taxi to Pena or Monserrate costs around €10 return. Horse-drawn carriages are a romantic alternative: figure on €55 to Monserrate and back. Old trams run from Ribeira de Sintra (1.5km from the centre) to Praia das Maças, 12km to the west.

CASCAIS

pop 30,000

Cascais, *the* beach resort west of Lisbon, is packed in summer. The **tourist office** *(☎ 214 868 204; Rua Visconde de Luz 14)* has accommodation lists and bus timetables; there's also a **tourist police post** *(☎ 214 863 929)*. **Ciber Forum** *(☎ 214 868 311; Rua da Bela Vista 126; open to 8pm daily, to 11pm Fri & Sat)* has Internet access at €2.50 per half-hour and a courtyard café.

Two kilometres east of Cascais, **Estoril** is an old-fashioned resort with Europe's biggest **casino** *(open 3pm-3am daily)*. Praia Tamariz (beside the train station) features an ocean swimming pool.

The sea roars into the coast at **Boca do Inferno** (Hell's Mouth), 2km west of Cascais. Spectacular **Cabo da Roca**, Europe's westernmost point, is 16km from Cascais and Sintra (served by buses from both towns). Wild **Guincho** beach, 3km from Cascais, is a popular surfing venue.

Transrent *(☎ 214 864 566; Centro Commercial Cisne, Avenida Marginal)* rents out bicycles, cars and motorcycles.

Camping Orbitur do Guincho *(☎ 214 871 014, fax 214 872 167)* is 7km from Cascais near Guincho beach. **Residencial Avenida** *(☎ 214 864 417; Rua da Palmeira 14; doubles €30)* is another option. The tourist office can recommend private rooms from around €30.

A Económica *(☎ 214 833 524; Rua Sebastião J C Melo 35; mains €5-7)* serves standards. Try octopus rice (€5.50) at **A Tasca** *(Rua Afonso Sanches 61)*.

Trains run frequently to Estoril and Cascais from Cais do Sodré station in Lisbon.

SETÚBAL

pop 110,000

This refreshingly untouristy city, an easy 50km south of Lisbon, has fine beaches and seafood restaurants and is a good base for exploring nearby **Parque Natural da Arrábida** and **Reserva Natural do Estuário do Sado**. The **tourist office** *(☎/fax 265 534 402; Praça do Quebedo)* is a five-minute walk east from the

bus terminal *(Avenida 5 de Outubro)*. There's also a **regional tourist office** *(☎ 265 539 130, fax 265 539 127; Travessa Frei Gaspar 10)*.

The **Instituto Português da Juventude** *(IPJ; ☎ 265 534 431; Largo José Afonso)* offers free Internet access for limited periods on weekdays. **Sobecome** *(☎ 265 521 150; Avenida Luisa Todi 333, 1st floor; open 10am-2am daily)* charges €2.50 for 30 minutes.

The town's main cultural attraction is the 15th-century **Igreja de Jesus** *(Praça Miguel Bombarda)*, with early Manueline decoration inside. The **Galeria da Pintura Quinhentista** *(admission free; open 9am-noon & 2pm-5pm Tues-Sat)*, around the corner, displays a renowned collection of 16th-century paintings.

Good **beaches** west of town include Praia da Figuerinha (accessible by bus in summer). Across the estuary at Tróia is a more developed beach, plus the ruins of a Roman settlement. On the ferry trip across you may see some of the estuary's 30 or so bottlenosed dolphins.

SAL *(☎ 265 227 685)* organises walks from €5 per person. For jeep safaris, hiking and biking in the Serra da Arrábida, or canoe trips through the Reserva Natural do Estuário do Sado, contact **Planeta Terra** *(☎ 919 471 871; Praça General Luís Domingues 9)*. **Vertigem Azul** *(☎ 265 238 000; Avenida Luísa Todi 375)* offers dolphin-spotting and canoeing trips.

A municipal **camping ground** *(☎ 265 522 475)* is 1.5km west of town. Another option is the **pousada da juventude** *(☎ 265 534 431; Largo José Afonso; dorm beds €9.50, doubles with bath €26.50)*. Crumbling **Residencial Todi** *(☎ 265 220 592; Avenida Luísa Todi 244; doubles with/without bath €20/15)* is basic. **Pensão Bom Regresso** *(☎ 265 229 812; Praça de Bocage 48; doubles €25)* overlooks the square.

Cheap restaurants, east of the regional tourist office, include **Triângulo** *(☎ 265 233 927; Rua Arronches Junqueiro 72)*. Seafood places line the western end of Avenida Luísa Todi; friendly **Casa do Chico** *(☎ 265 239 502)* at No 490 is less touristy than most. **Restaurante Antóniu's** *(☎ 265 523 706; Rua Trabalhadores do Mar 31)* is also popular.

Buses leave frequently from Lisbon's Gare do Oriente and from Cacilhas, a short ferry ride from Lisbon's Cais de Alfândega. Ferries shuttle across the estuary to Tróia regularly; the tourist office has the latest timetable.

The Algarve

Boisterous and full of foreigners, the Algarve is about as far from traditional Portugal as one can get. The focus is on Albufeira and Lagos, with sun, sand and golf (and surfing along the west coast) as the main drawcard, but there are other attractions, including the fortified village of Silves and windswept, historic Sagres. The district capital and largest town is Faro.

Theft is a problem in the Algarve. Don't leave anything valuable in your vehicle, tent or on the beach. Swimmers should be aware of dangerous currents, especially on the west coast. Beaches are marked by coloured flags: red means no bathing, yellow means wading but no swimming, green means anything goes.

Rede Expressos and EVA together run an efficient network of bus services throughout the Algarve. The IP1/EO1 superhighway, to run the length of the coast, is nearly complete. Bicycles, scooters and motorcycles can be rented in most places; see town listings.

FARO

pop 45,000

Pleasantly low-key Faro is the Algarve's main transport hub and commercial centre. The **tourist office** *(☎ 289 803 604; Rua da Misericórdia)* has leaflets on just about every Algarve community.

Pleasant cafés line the palm-clad **waterfront** around Praça de Dom Francisco Gomes. Faro's beach, **Praia de Faro** *(Ilha de Faro)* is 6km southwest of the city; take bus No 16 from opposite the bus station. Less crowded is the unspoilt **Ilha Desserta**, in the nature park **Parque Natural da Ria Formosa** *(☎ 917 811 856)* where lagoon tours are available. Access is by ferry from June to mid-September from Cais da Porta Nova.

At Estói, 12km north of Faro, the romantically ruined **Estói Palace** has a surreal garden of statues, balustrades and azulejos; take the Faro to São Brás de Alportel bus, which goes via Estói.

The **municipal camping ground** *(☎ 289 817 876; Praia de Faro)* is big and cheap. The **pousada da juventude** *(☎ 289 826 521; Rua da Polícia de Segurança Pública 1)* offers dorm beds and rooms. **Residencial Adelaide** *(☎ 289 802 383, fax 289 826 870; Rua Cruz dos Mestres 7; doubles from €45)* is a friendly budget pensão. Aptly named, friendly **Pensão Residencial Centro** *(☎ 289 807 291;*

Largo Terreiro do Bispo 10; doubles €40) is spotless.

For the hungry, lively **Sol e Jardim** *(☎ 289 820 030; Praça Ferreira de Almeida 22)* serves good grilled squid (€7.49). **A Velha Casa** *(☎ 289 824 719; Rua do Pé da Cruz 33; mains €6-7)* has solid charcoaled meat and fish.

From the bus station, just west of the centre, there are at least six daily express coaches to Lisbon (about four hours) and frequent buses to other coastal towns. The train station is a few minutes' walk west of the bus station. Four trains run daily to Lisbon (Barreiro), and about a dozen to Albufeira and 10 to Portimão.

TAVIRA

pop 12,000

Tavira is one of the Algarve's oldest and handsomest towns. The **tourist office** *(☎ 281 322 511; Rua da Galeria 9)* dispenses information. **Cyber Café**, opposite the bus station, *(☎ 281 325 375; Rua dos Pelames 1)* has Internet access for €2 per half-hour.

Bicycles and scooters can be rented from **Loris Rent** *(☎ 964 079 233)* next door. For walking or biking, call **Exploratio** *(☎ 919 338 226)*. Those interested in sailing should contact **Clube Náutico** *(☎ 281 326 858)*. Jose Salvador Rocha organises diving trips *(☎ 939 017 329)*.

In the Old Town, the **Igreja da Misericórdia** features a striking Renaissance doorway and interior azulejos. From there, it's a short climb to the **castle**, which dominates the town. **Ilha da Tavira**, 2km from Tavira, is an island beach connected to the mainland by ferry. Walk 2km along the river to the ferry terminal at Quatro Águas or take the (summer only) bus from the bus station. For a look at the old Algarve, take a bus to nearby **Cacela Velha**, an unspoilt hamlet 8km from Tavira. Another worthwhile day trip is to the fishing centre of **Olhão**, 22km west of Tavira.

Ilha da Tavira has a **camping ground** *(☎ 281 324 455)*, open July to September when ferries operate (times vary). Characterful **Pensão Residencial Lagoas** *(☎ 281 322 252; Rua Almirante Cândido dos Reis 24; doubles €38)* has a pretty roof terrace. **Residencial Imperial** *(☎ 281 322 234; Rua José Pires Padinha 24; doubles €40)* is central.

Budget restaurants on riverside Rua Dr José Pires Padinha include **A Barquinha** *(☎ 281 322 843)* at No 142. **Cantinho do Emigrante** *(☎ 281 323 696; Praça Dr Padinha 27)* also has good-value fare. **Restaurante Bica** *(☎ 281 332 483)* below Residencial Lagoas has delicious specials like sole with orange for €10. Good seafood lunches are up for grabs in Olhão, in the many restaurants that line Rua 5 de Outubro.

Some 15 trains and at least six express buses run daily between Faro and Tavira (30 to 50 minutes).

LAGOS

pop 20,000

This tourist resort offers some of the Algarve's finest beaches. Of the two **tourist offices**, the new municipal **Posto de Informação** *(☎ 282 764 111; Largo Marquês de Pombal; open Mon-Sat)* is the more convenient; the other *(☎ 282 763 031; open Mon-Fri)* is 1km northeast of the centre, at the Situo São João roundabout. The **pousada da juventude** (see later) has Internet access at €1.50 per half-hour.

In the Old Town, the **municipal museum** houses an assortment of exhibits from archaeological finds to ecclesiastical treasures. The adjacent **Igreja de Santo António** has some intricate baroque woodwork. The beach scene includes **Meia Praia**, a vast strip to the east; and to the west **Praia da Luz** and the more secluded **Praia do Pinhão**.

Blue Ocean *(☎ 282 782 718)* organises diving, kayaking and snorkelling safaris. On the seaside promenade, local fishermen offer motorboat jaunts to the nearby grottoes. For horse riding in the Algarve interior, ring **Tiffany's** *(☎ 282 697 395)*.

The camping ground is **Trindade** *(☎ 282 763 893)*, 200m south of the town walls. The **pousada da juventude** *(☎ 282 761 970; Rua Lançarote de Freitas 50)* is another choice. **Residencial Marazul** *(☎ 289 769 749; Rua 25 de Abril 13; doubles from around €55)* has smart rooms. **Private rooms** are plentiful and easy to find (just look for the signs or check with the tourist office) are available for around €35 to €50.

Unassuming **A Gamba** *(☎ 282 760 453; Rua Conselheiro Joaquim Machado 5)* serves good traditional fare for around €5 to €7. A local favourite is **Restaurante Bar Barros** *(☎ 282 762 276; Rua Portas de Portugal 83)*, where creamy grilled scabbard fish is €6.73. **Mullens** *(☎ 282 761 281; Rua Cândido dos Reis 86)* is a wood-panelled pub with good food.

Bus and train services depart frequently for other Algarve towns and around a six times daily to Lisbon; by train, change at Tunes for Lisbon. You can rent bicycles, mopeds and motorcycles from **Motoride** *(☎ 289 761 720; Rua José Afonso 23)*, or agents in town. Figure about €5 a day for a mountain bike or €30 for a motorbike.

SILVES

pop 10,500

Silves was the capital of Moorish Algarve, rivalling Lisbon for influence. Times are far quieter now, but the huge castle is well worth a visit. The **tourist office** *(☎ 289 442 255; Rua 25 de Abril; open Mon-Fri & Sat morning)* is closed during low season. For accommodation, try **Residencial Sousa** *(☎ 282 442 502; Rua Samoura Barros 17; doubles €30)* or **Residencial Ponte Romana** *(☎ 282 443 275; doubles €30)* beside the old bridge. **Restaurante Rui** *(☎ 282 442 682; Rua C Vilarinho 27)*, Silves' best fish restaurant, serves a memorable *arroz de marisco* (shellfish rice €23.50 for two). For cheaper meals, try the **riverfront restaurants** opposite the old bridge.

Silves train station is 2km from town; trains from Lagos (35 minutes) stop nine times daily (from Faro, change at Tunes), to be met by local buses. Six buses run daily to Silves from Albufeira (40 minutes).

SAGRES

pop 2500

Sagres is a small, windy fishing port perched on dramatic cliffs in Portugal's southwestern corner. The **tourist office** *(☎ 282 624 873; Rua Comandante Matoso; open Mon-Fri, & Sat morning)* is just beyond Praça da República. **Turinfo** *(☎ 282 620 003; Praça da República; open daily)* rents cars and bikes, books hotels and arranges jeep and fishing trips.

In the **fort**, on a wide windy promontory, Henry the Navigator established his school of navigation and trained the explorers who later founded the Portuguese empire. You can hire sailboards at sand-dune fringed **Praia do Martinhal**; another option is the beach at the village of **Salema**, 17km east. No Sagres visit would be complete without a trip to **Cabo de São Vicente** (Cape St Vincent), 6km to the west. A solitary lighthouse stands on this barren cape, Europe's southwesternmost point.

Parque de Campismo Sagres *(☎ 282 624 351)* is 2km from town, off the Vila do Bispo road. Many Sagres folk rent rooms for around €25 a double. Good-value traditional dishes can be had at **Restaurante A Sagres** at the roundabout before the village, and at **cafés** in Praça da República.

Frequent buses run daily to Sagres from Lagos (45 to 65 minutes), fewer on Sunday. Three continue out to Cabo de São Vicente on weekdays.

Central Portugal

Central Portugal, good for weeks of desultory rambling, deserves more attention than it receives. From the beaches of the Costa de Prata to the lofty Serra da Estrela and the sprawling Alentejo plains, it is a landscape of extremes.

Some of Portugal's finest wines come from the Dão region, while farther south, the hills and plains are studded with cork oaks. The mountainous centre is dotted with fortresses and walled cities with cobbled streets, clean air and grand panoramas.

ÉVORA

pop 50,000

One of Portugal's architectural gems, the walled town of Évora is the capital of Alentejo province, a vast landscape of olive groves, vineyards and wheat fields. The town's charm lies in the narrow streets of the well-preserved inner town. The focal point is Praça do Giraldo, from where you can wander through backstreets until you meet the city walls. An annotated map is available from the **tourist office** *(☎ 266 702 671; Praça do Giraldo 73)*. For other guides and maps go to **Nazareth bookshop** *(Praça do Giraldo 46)*. Outside the tourist office is an automatic cash-exchange machine. **Oficin@ bar** *(☎ 266 707 312; Rua da Moeda 27)* has Internet access for €1.50 per half-hour.

The **Sé** *(Largo do Marquês de Marialva; admission to cloisters & museum €3; both open Tues-Sun)*, Évora's cathedral, contains cloisters and a museum of ecclesiastical treasures. The **Museu de Évora** *(admission €1.50)* features fantastic 16th-century Portuguese and Flemish paintings. Opposite is the Roman-era **Temple of Diana**, subject of Évora's top-selling postcard.

South of Praça do Giraldo The **Igreja de São Francisco** *(adult/concession €1/0.50)* includes the ghoulish Capela dos Ossos (Chapel of Bones), constructed with the bones and skulls of several thousand people.

Places to Stay & Eat

Accommodation gets tight in summer, so book ahead. There's an **Orbitur camping ground** *(☎ 266 705 190)* 2km south of town (buses to Alcaçovas stop there), and a **pousada da juventude** *(☎ 266 744 848; Rua Miguel Bombarda 40)*. **Residencial O Alentejo** *(☎ 266 702 903; Rua Serpa Pinto 74; doubles €40)* and charismatic **Pensão Policarpo** *(☎/fax 266 702 424; Rua da Freiria de Baixo 16; doubles €43)* are recommended.

O Portão *(☎ 266 703 325; Rua do Cano 27; mains €4.25-6.25)*, by the aqueduct, is a popular budget eatery. Pretty **Café Restaurant O Cruz** *(☎ 266 747 228; Praça 1 de Maio 20)* has traditional fare like sausage-and-bean stew (€5). **Pane & Vino** *(☎ 266 746 960; Páteo do Salema 22)* has great pasta and pizzas. **O Jovem** *(☎ 266 701 180)*, at No 9, has half-portions of pork Alentejana (from the Alentejo region), with clams, for €5.

Entertainment

Student hang-outs include several bars northwest of the centre: **Club Dezasseis** *(☎ 266 706 559; Rua do Escrivão da Cámara 16)*; **Diplomata Pub** *(☎ 266 705 675; Rua do Apóstolo 4)*, with frequent live music; and characterful **Pub O Trovador** *(☎ 266 707 370; Rua da Mostardeira 4)*. **Côdeas** *(☎ 266 709 343; Rua do Cano 11)* has live jazz Wednesday, Friday and Saturday.

ÉVORA

Getting There & Around

Évora has six weekday express coach connections to Lisbon (1¾ hours) and two to Faro (four hours), departing from the terminal off Avenida Túlio Espanca (700m southwest of the centre). Fast trains run from Lisbon (2½ hours, three daily).

Bike Lab *(☎ 266 735 500)* rents bikes for €10 per day. **Policarpo** *(☎ 266 746 970, fax 266 746 984; e viagenspolicarpo@ip.pt; Alcárcova de Baixo 43)* organises city tours and jaunts to megaliths and other attractions.

MONSARAZ

pop 100

Monsaraz, a walled village high above the plain, is well worth the trip for its medieval atmosphere, clear light and magnificent views. Of architectural interest is the **Museu de Arte Sacra**, probably a former tribunal, with a rare 15th-century fresco. The **castle's** parapets have the best views.

Several places along the main Rua Direita offer doubles for around €30-50. The **tourist office** *(☎ 266 557 136)* on the main square has details of Turihab and other elegant places. There are several tourist-geared restaurants, but eat before 8pm: the town goes to bed early.

On weekdays only, buses run to and from Reguengos de Monsaraz (35 minutes, two to four daily), which is connected to Évora (one hour, six daily). The last one back from Monsaraz leaves at 5.30pm.

CASTELO DE VIDE & MARVÃO

pop 4000

From Portalegre it's just a short hop to Castelo de Vide, noted for its picturesque houses clustered below a castle. Highlights are the **Judiaria** (Old Jewish Quarter), in a well-preserved network of medieval backstreets, and the view from the castle. Try to spend a night here or in Marvão (population 190), a mountaintop medieval walled village 12km from Castelo de Vide, with grand views across Spain and Portugal. The **tourist offices** *(☎ 245 901 361, fax 245 901 827; Rua de Bartolomeu Álvares da Santa 81, Castelo de Vide; ☎ 245 993 886, fax 245 993 526; Largo de Santa Maria, Marvão)* can help with accommodation.

On weekdays only, three buses run from Portalegre to Castelo de Vide (20 minutes) and two to Marvão (45 minutes). One daily bus links the two villages (with a change at Portagem, a junction 5km from Marvão).

NAZARÉ

pop 16,000

This once-peaceful 17th-century fishing village was 'discovered' by tourism in the 1970s. Fishing skills and distinctive local dress have gone overboard, and in high season it's a tourist circus, but the beautiful coastline and fine seafood still make it worthwhile. The **tourist office** *(☎ 262 561 194; open daily high season)* is at the end of Avenida da República.

Lower Nazaré's beachfront retains a core of narrow streets now catering to tourists. O Sítio, on the clifftop, offers superb views. You can reach it by a vintage funicular railway. The beaches attract huge summer crowds. Beware of dangerous currents.

Two of Portugal's architectural masterpieces are within easy reach of Nazaré. The huge **Mosteiro de Santa Maria de Alcobaça** *(☎ 262 505 120; adult/concession €3/1.50, church admission free; open 9am-7pm daily, to 5pm winter)*, at Alcobaça, dates from 1178. Batalha's colossal Gothic **Mosteiro de Santa Maria de Vitória** *(☎ 244 765 497; adult/concession Cloisters & Unfinished Chapels €3/1.50; open 9am-6pm daily, to 5pm in winter)*, dating from 1388, is home to Henry the Navigator's tomb.

Two good camping grounds are the well-equipped **Vale Paraíso** *(☎ 262 561 800)*, off the Leiria road, and an **Orbitur** *(☎ 262 561 111)* off the Alcobaça road, both 2.5km from Nazaré. Many townspeople rent out **rooms**; doubles start from €35. Seafront **Pensão Beira Mar** *(☎ 262 561 358; Avenida da República 40; doubles from €50)* has great showers.

Seafront restaurants are expensive. For cheaper fare in simple surroundings, try **Casa Marques** *(☎ 262 551 680; Rua Gil Vicente 37)*. Friendly **A Tasquinha** *(☎ 262 551 945; Rua Adrião Batalha 54)* does good grilled squid (€7). Family run **Casa Bizarro** *(☎ 262 552 981; Rua António Carvalho Laranjo 25)* has an impressive *arroz do marisco* (seafood rice) for under €10.

The nearest train station, which is 6km away at Valado, is connected to Nazaré by frequent bus services. Numerous buses run to the following destinations: Lisbon, Alcobaça, Óbidos and Coimbra.

ÓBIDOS

pop 600

This charming walled village is one of the prettiest (and most touristy) in Portugal. Highlights include the **Igreja de Santa Maria**, with fine *azulejos*, and views from the walls. The **tourist office** *(☎ 262 959 231; Rua Direita)* is near the town gate.

Private rooms are available for around €35 a double. **Pastelaria da Moura** *(☎ 262 959 151; Rua Josefa de Óbidos; doubles from €40)* has good rooms just inside the walls.

Café-Restaurante 1 de Dezembro *(☎ 262 959 298)*, next to the Igreja de São Pedro, has pleasant outdoor seating. Gorgeous **O Barco** *(☎ 262 950 925; Largo Dr João Lourenço; mains €10-15)* offers classy modern Portuguese fare and is a readers' favourite. There's a small **grocery shop** just inside the town gate.

There are regular buses from Lisbon, directly (two hours) or via Caldas da Rainha, 10 minutes away. From the train station, down the hill outside the walls, five services run daily to Lisbon (four with a change at Cacém).

TOMAR

pop 17,000

Home to the outstanding **Convento de Cristo**, the former headquarters of the Knights Templar, Tomar is a gem. Cradling the convent's southern walls is the impressive 17th-century **Aqueduto de Pegões**, beyond which extends the **Mata Nacional dos Sete Montes** (Seven Hills National Forest). The **tourist office** *(☎ 249 322 427; Avenida Dr Cândido Madureira)* helps with accommodation and provide town and forest maps.

Local camping grounds include **Camping Redondo** *(☎/fax 249 376 421; e hansromme@hotmail.com; Poço Redondo)*, with a swimming pool. **Pensão Residencial União** *(☎ 249 323 161; Rua Serpa Pinto 94; doubles with bath & breakfast from €32.50)* is central.

Ivy-clad **Casinha d'Avó Bia** *(☎ 249 323 828; Rua Dr Joaquim Jacinto 16; mains €6.50-10)* makes delicious seafood *açorda* (bread stew). **Snack Bar dos Moinhos** *(Rua dos Moinhos 81; mains €4-6.50)* has good-value Portuguese standards.

There are at least four express buses daily to Lisbon and three to Nazaré. There are eight to 16 trains to/from Lisbon daily.

COIMBRA

pop 150,000

Coimbra is famed for its 13th-century university, and for its role as a centre of culture and art, complemented in recent times by industrial development.

The **regional tourist office** *(☎ 239 855 930, fax 239 825 576; Largo da Portagem)* has pamphlets and cultural-events information, but a **municipal tourist office** *(☎ 239 832 591; Praça Dom Dinis)* and another **tourist office** *(☎ 239 833 202; Praça da República)* are more useful. **Esp@ço Internet** *(Praça 8 de Maio; open 10am-8pm Mon-Fri, to 10pm weekends)* offers free Internet access for 30 minutes.

Coimbra's annual highlight is Queima das Fitas is a boozy week of *fado* and revelry. The celebration begins on the first Thursday in May when students celebrate the end of their academic year.

Things to See & Do

Lower Coimbra's main attraction is the **Mosteiro de Santa Cruz** *(☎ 239 822 941; Rua Visconde da Luz)*, with its ornate pulpit and medieval royal tombs. The new **elevator** *(operates daily; tickets from booth or kiosks; single €1.15)* by the market eases the sweltering summer climb to the Upper Town. At the top, visit the **old university** with its baroque library and Manueline chapel, and the **Machado de Castro Museum** *(☎ 239 823 727; Largo Dr José Rodrigues)*, with a fine collection of sculpture and paintings. The lively back alleys of the university quarter are filled with student hang-outs.

At **Conimbriga** *(ruins open 10am-8pm daily summer, 10am-6pm daily winter)*, 16km south of Coimbra, are the well-preserved ruins of a Roman town, including mosaic floors, baths and fountains. There's a good **site museum** *(adult/concession €3/1.50; open 10am-1pm & 2pm-6pm Tues-Sun)* with a restaurant. Frequent buses run to Condeixa, 2km from the site; direct buses depart at 9.05am or 9.35am (only 9.35am at weekends) from the **AVIC terminal** *(Rua João de Ruão 18)* returning at 1pm and 6pm (only 6pm at weekends).

O Pioneiro do Mondego *(☎ 239 478 385; open 8am-10am, 1pm-3pm & 8pm-10pm daily Apr-Oct)* rents kayaks at €15 for paddling the Rio Mondego. A free minibus takes you to Penacova for the 25km river journey.

Places to Stay

For Coimbra's **pousada da juventude** *(☎ 239 822 955; Rua António Henriques Seco 12–14)*, take bus No 7 from outside the Astoria hotel on Avenida Emídio Navarro 50m south of Coimbra A train station.

Pensão Lorvanense *(☎ 239 823 481; Rua da Sota 27; doubles €25)* is near Coimbra A. **Pensão Santa Cruz** *(☎ 239 826 197; Praça 8 de Maio; doubles €25)* is opposite the Mosteiro. **Pensão Residencial Larbelo** *(☎ 239 829 092, fax 239 829 094; Largo da Portagem 33; doubles with breakfast €33)* is very central.

Friendly **Pensão Flôr de Coimbra** *(☎ 239 823 865, fax 239 821 545; Rua do Poço 5; doubles with shower €30)* has a small daily (except Sunday) vegetarian menu.

Breakfast is included in the room rates at the **Residência Coimbra** *(☎ 239 837 996, fax 239 838 124; Rua das Azeiteiras 55; doubles with bath €40)*.

Near the university, Dutch-run **Casa Pombal Guesthouse** *(☎ 239 835 175, fax 239 821 548; Rua das Flores 18; doubles with/without bath €44/38)* has more expensive rooms with a bird's-eye view, and rates include a huge breakfast.

Places to Eat

Head to the lanes west of Praça do Comércio, especially Rua das Azeiteiras, for cheap eats, or try central **O Cantinho das Escadas** *(☎ 239 820 578; Rua do Gato 29)*, by the steps, whose traditional dishes of the day are €4. **Restaurante Democrática** *(☎ 239 823 784; Travessa da Rua Nova; half-portions around €4)* has Portuguese standards.

Self-service **Restaurante Jardim da Manga** *(☎ 239 829 156; meals from €4.25; open Sun-Fri)* is behind the fountains at the back of the Mosteiro de Santa Cruz. **Zé Manel** *(☎ 239 823 790; Beco do Forno 12; half-portions from €6.25; open Mon-Fri, Sat lunch)* has crazy decor and huge servings; arrive before 8pm to beat the crowds.

East of the university, **Bar-Restaurante ACM** *(☎ 239 823 633; Rua Alexandre Herculano 21A; meals from €4; open Sun-Fri)* serves up plain fare. Downstairs behind the **Centro de Juventude** *(Rua Pedro Monteiro 73; mains around €5)* is a clean canteen with lots of salads. Vaulted **Café Santa Cruz** beside the Mosteiro de Santa Cruz is great for coffee breaks.

Entertainment

Bar Diligência *(☎ 239 827 667; Rua Nova 30)* and **Boémia Bar** *(☎ 239 834 547; Rua do Cabido 6)* are popular *casas de fado*. **Café-Galeria Almedina** *(☎ 239 836 192; Arco de Almedina)* offers *fado* and other live sounds. A good dance bar is **Aqui Há Rato** *(Largo da Sé Velha 20)*. Two fashionable discos are **Vinyl** *(☎ 239 404 047; Avenida Afonso Henriques 43)* and **Via Latina** *(☎ 239 833 034; Rua Almeida Garrett 1)*.

Getting There & Away

At least a dozen buses and as many trains run daily from Lisbon and Porto, plus frequent express buses from Faro and Évora, via Lisbon. The main long-distance train stations are central Coimbra A (on timetables this is called just 'Coimbra') and Coimbra B, 2km northwest of the centre. Most long-distance trains call at both. Other useful connections are to Figueira da Foz and to Luso/Buçaco (from Coimbra A).

LUSO & THE BUÇACO FOREST

pop 2000

A walkers' paradise, the Buçaco Forest was chosen as a retreat by 16th-century monks and has remained relatively untouched ever since. It begins about 1km from the spa resort of Luso, where the **tourist office** *(☎/fax 231 939 133; Avenida Emídio Navarro)* has good maps and leaflets about trails and the forest's 700-plus tree and shrub species. It also offers lists of private rooms for around €20.

Prices at the nearby **Astória** *(☎ 231 939 182; Avenida Emídio Navarro; doubles €32.50)* include breakfast. Hearty meals are available at **Restaurante O Cesteiro** *(☎ 231 939 360)*, on the N234, 500m north of the tourist office.

Four buses daily go to Luso/Buçaco from Coimbra and Viseu (two at weekends). Just one train, departing around 10.30am from Coimbra B, provides enough time for a day trip.

PARQUE NATURAL SERRA DA ESTRELA

The forested Parque Natural Serra da Estrela is Portugal's highest mainland mountain range (1993m), and the core of a designated *parque natural* (national park). With its outlying ranges it almost stretches across Portugal, and it offers some of the country's best hiking.

The best place for information is the **main park office** *(☎ 275 980 060, fax 275 980 069;*

Manteigas); other offices are at Seia, Gouveia and Guarda. Other good sources for regional information are the **tourist offices** *(☎ 271 205 530, Guarda; ☎ 275 319 560, Covilhã)*. The park administration publishes *À Descoberta da Estrela,* a walking guide with maps and narratives. Park offices and some tourist offices sell an English edition (€4.25), plus a detailed topographic map of the park (€5.50).

The **pousada da juventude** *(☎ 275 335 375, fax 275 335 109; Penhas da Saúde)*, 10km above Covilhã, offers meals (or you can cook your own), dorms and a few functional doubles. Buses come from Covilhã twice daily in August only, and hitching is fairly safe and easy. The only other options are your feet, or bicycle, or a taxi (about €8). This makes a good base for excursions. Guarda also has a **pousada da juventude** *(☎/fax 271 224 482)*, and Seia, Gouveia, Guarda and Covilhã have some modestly priced **guesthouses**. Central Manteigas tends to be pricey.

Several buses run each day from Coimbra, along the park's perimeter to Seia, Gouveia, Guarda or Covilhã, plus others from Porto and Lisbon to Guarda and Covilhã. Twice-daily IC trains link Lisbon and Coimbra to Guarda, and two daily IC trains run from Lisbon to Covilhã on the Lisbon–Paris line.

No buses cross the park, though you can go around it: Seia–Covilhã takes two hours via Guarda. At least one or two buses link Seia, Gouveia and Guarda every day, and considerably more run between Guarda and Covilhã.

The North

Many visitors are surprised to discover Portugal's northern tier, with its wine country, forests, mountainous Parque Nacional da Peneda-Gerês and a strand of undeveloped beaches. The urban scene focuses on Porto, with its medieval centre by the Rio Douro. Within easy reach are three historical cities: Braga, the country's religious heart; well-situated Viana do Castelo; and Guimarães, self-proclaimed birthplace of Portugal.

PORTO

pop 300,000

Porto is Portugal's second-largest city and the centre of the port-wine trade. Its reputation as an industrial centre belies considerable charm. The city clings to the northern bank of the Rio Douro, spanned by five bridges. On the far bank is Vila Nova de Gaia, home to the port-wine lodges, and a major attraction.

Central Porto's axis is Avenida dos Aliados. Major shopping areas are eastward around the Bolhão Market and Rua Santa Catarina, home to the glassy shopping complex Via Catarina, and westward along Rua dos Clérigos. At the southern end of Avenida dos Aliados, Praça da Liberdade and São Bento train station are major local bus hubs. Another is Jardim da Cordoaria (called Jardim de João Chagas on some maps), about 400m westward. The picturesque Ribeira district lies along the waterfront, in the shadow of the great Ponte de Dom Luís I bridge.

Information

The main **municipal tourist office** *(☎ 223 393 470, fax 223 323 303; Rua Clube dos Fenianos 25; open daily)* is next door to the **tourist police** office. There's also a smaller **tourist office** *(☎ 222 009 770; Rua Infante Dom Henriques 63; open Mon-Fri)*, as well as a national **ICEP tourist office** *(☎ 222 057 514, fax 222 053 212; Praça Dom João I 43; open daily)*.

Banks with ATMs and exchange desks are everywhere. Better rates for travellers cheques are at the exchange bureaus **Portocâmbios** *(Rua Rodrigues Sampaio 193)*, and **Intercontinental** *(Rua de Ramalho Ortigão 8)*. **Top Tours** *(☎ 222 074 020, fax 222 074 039; Rua Alferes Malheiro 96)* is Porto's American Express representative.

The **main post office** (the place for posta restante) is across Praça General Humberto Delgado from the main tourist office. There's also a **telephone office** *(Praça da Liberdade 62; open 10am-10pm daily)*. Faxes can be sent from the post office. At well-equipped **Portweb** *(☎ 222 005 922; Praça General Humberto Delgado 291)*, Internet access costs a bargain €0.50 per hour from 9am to 4pm daily, and a still reasonable €1.20 from 4pm to 2am.

Youth-oriented travel agencies include **Tagus** *(☎ 226 094 146, fax 226 094 141; Rua Campo Alegre 261)* and **Wasteels** *(☎ 225 194 230, fax 225 194 239; Rua Pinto Bessa 27/29)* near Campanhã station. Local adventure-tour operators with experience in northern Portugal include **Trilhos** *(☎ 225 020 740, fax 225 504 604)* for canyoning and hydrospeed (you're given a body-board and

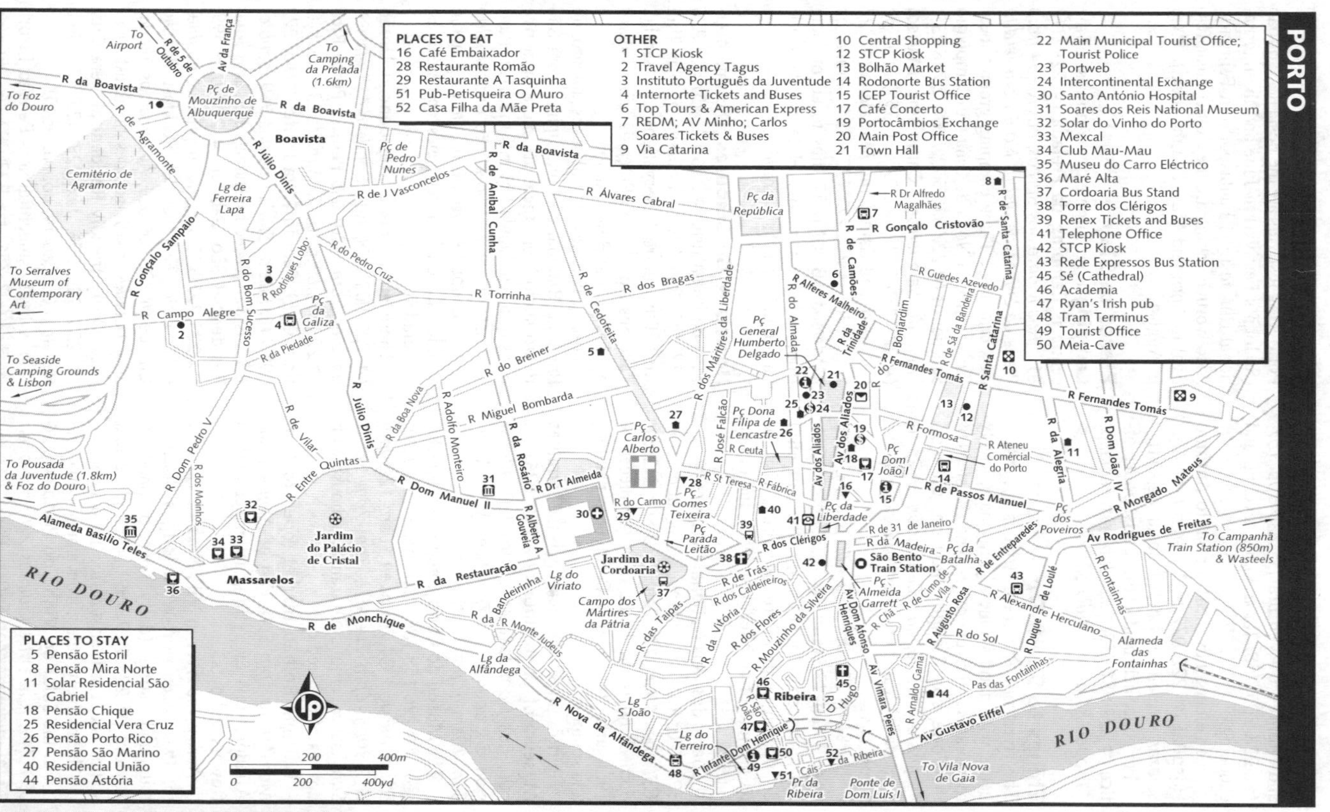
PORTO
PLACES TO EAT
16 Café Embaixador
28 Restaurante Romão
29 Restaurante A Tasquinha
51 Pub-Petisqueira O Muro
52 Casa Filha da Mãe Preta
OTHER
1 STCP Kiosk
2 Travel Agency Tagus
3 Instituto Português da Juventude
4 Internorte Tickets and Buses
6 Top Tours & American Express
7 REDM; AV Minho; Carlos Soares Tickets & Buses
9 Via Catarina
10 Central Shopping
12 STCP Kiosk
13 Bolhão Market
14 Rodonorte Bus Station
15 ICEP Tourist Office
17 Café Concerto
19 Portocâmbios Exchange
20 Main Post Office
21 Town Hall
22 Main Municipal Tourist Office; Tourist Police
23 Portweb
24 Intercontinental Exchange
30 Santo António Hospital
31 Soares dos Reis National Museum
32 Solar do Vinho do Porto
33 Mexcal
34 Club Mau-Mau
35 Museu do Carro Eléctrico
36 Maré Alta
37 Cordoaria Bus Stand
38 Torre dos Clérigos
39 Renex Tickets and Buses
41 Telephone Office
42 STCP Kiosk
43 Rede Expressos Bus Station
45 Sé (Cathedral)
46 Academia
47 Ryan's Irish pub
48 Tram Terminus
49 Tourist Office
50 Meia-Cave
PLACES TO STAY
5 Pensão Estoril
8 Pensão Mira Norte
11 Solar Residencial São Gabriel
18 Pensão Chique
25 Residencial Vera Cruz
26 Pensão Porto Rico
27 Pensão São Marino
40 Residencial União
44 Pensão Astória
0 200 400m
0 200 400yd

you glide down a river through white water) and **Montes d'Aventura** *(☎ 228 305 157, fax 228 305 158)* for trekking, cycling and canoeing.

In an emergency, head for **Santo António Hospital** *(☎ 222 077 500; Largo Prof Abel Salazar)*, which has English-speaking staff.

For police help contact the **tourist police office** *(☎ 222 081 833; Rua Clube dos Fenianos 11; open 8am-2am daily)*.

Things to See & Do

The riverfront **Ribeira** district is the city's heart, with narrow lanes, grimy bars, lovely restaurants and river cruises. The 225 steps of the **Torre dos Clérigos** *(Rua dos Clérigos; admission €1; open 10am-noon & 2pm-5pm daily)* lead to the best panorama of the whole city.

The **Sé** *(☎ 222 059 028; admission €1.25; open 9am-12.30pm & 2.30pm-5.15pm daily, closed Sun morning)*, the cathedral dominating central Porto, is worth a visit for its mixture of architectural styles and ornate interior.

Soares dos Reis National Museum *(☎ 223 393 770; Rua Dom Manuel II 44; admission €3; open 10am-12.30pm Wed-Sun & 2pm-6pm daily)* is the home of masterpieces of 19th- and 20th-century Portuguese painting and sculpture.

Porto's finest new museum is the **Serralves Museum of Contemporary Art** *(☎ 226 156 500; Rua Dom João de Castro 210; admission €4; open 10am-7pm Tues, Wed & Fri-Sun, 10am-10pm Thur)*.

The **Museu do Carro Eléctrico** *(Tram Museum; ☎ 226 158 185; Alameda Basílio Teles 51; admission €1.75; open 10am-12.30pm & 2.30pm-6pm Tues-Fri, 3pm-7pm Sat & Sun)* is a cavernous old tram warehouse with dozens of restored cars.

Bustling **Bolhão market** *(open to 5pm Mon-Fri, to 1pm Sat)*, east of Avenida dos Aliados, sells everything from seafood to flowers and pots.

Across the river in Vila Nova de Gaia, of the two dozen **port-wine lodges** offering tours and tastings (daily, fewer on Sunday), **Taylors** *(☎ 223 719 999)* is the place that stands out. The tourist office has details.

Alternatively, select from a huge port-wine list at the **Solar do Vinho do Porto** *(☎ 226 094 749; Rua Entre Quintas 220; bar open 11am-midnight Mon-Sat)*, in Porto.

PORTUGAL

Special Events

Porto's big festivals are the Festa de São João (St John's Festival) in June and the international film festival Fantasporto in February. Also worth catching are the Celtic music festival in April and May, and the rock festival in August.

Places to Stay

Camping Four kilometres northwest of the centre is **Camping da Prelada** *(☎ 228 312 616; Rua Monte dos Burgos; bus No 54 from Praça de Liberdade or bus No 6 from Jardim da Cordoaria)*. Three camping grounds near the sea in Vila Nova de Gaia are **Campismo Salgueiros** *(☎ 227 810 500, fax 227 718 239; Praia de Salgueiros)*, **Campismo Marisol** *(☎ 227 135 942, fax 227 126 351; Praia de Canidelo)* and **Campismo Madalena** *(☎ 227 122 520, fax 227 122 534; Praia da Madalena)*. Bus No 57 runs to all of them from São Bento station. (Note that the sea is far too polluted for swimming.)

Hostels & Guesthouses The fine **pousada da juventude** *(☎ 226 177 257, fax 226 177 247; Rua Paulo da Gama 551)* is 4km west of the centre. Reservations are essential. Take bus No 35 from Praça da Liberdade or No 1 from São Bento station.

Porto's cheapest guesthouses are around Praça da Batalha, east and uphill from São Bento station, but there are more attractive parts of town. Down towards the river, **Pensão Astória** *(☎ 222 008 175; Rua Arnaldo Gama 56; doubles from €30)* has elegant old doubles, some with river views, and breakfast is included.

There are rooms at **Residencial União** *(☎ 222 003 078; Rua Conde de Vizela 62; doubles from €30)* and **Pensão Porto Rico** *(☎ 223 394 690; Rua do Almada 237; doubles from €25)*. **Pensão Mira Norte** *(☎/fax 222 001 118; Rua de Santa Catarina 969; doubles €30)* is well placed for shopaholics, as is **Solar Residencial São Gabriel** *(☎ 222 005 499, fax 223 323 957; Rua da Alegria 98; doubles €44)*, which also includes breakfast. **Pensão Chique** *(☎ 222 009 011; Avenida dos Aliados 206; doubles €40)* includes breakfast in its rates. Or try friendly **Residencial Vera Cruz** *(☎ 223 323 396, fax 223 323 421; Rua Ramalho Ortigão 14; doubles €45)*.

In a lively student area is **Pensão Estoril** *(☎ 222 002 751, fax 222 082 468; Rua de*

Cedofeita 193) and the better-value **Pensão São Marino** *(☎ 223 325 499; Praça Carlos Alberto 59; doubles with shower from €38)* including breakfast.

Places to Eat

The self-service mezzanine at central **Café Embaixador** *(☎ 222 054 182; Rua Sampaio Bruno 5; open 7am-10pm Mon-Fri, from 8am Sat & Sun)* has good-value grills and salads. There's a handy **supermarket** in Via Caterina on Rua Santa Catarina.

Popular with students is cosy **Restaurante A Tasquinha** *(☎ 223 322 145; Rua do Carmo 23)* which has mastered regional dishes – try the *rojões* (€7.50), a Minho speciality pork dish. Casual **Restaurante Romão** *(☎ 222 005 639; Praça Carlos Alberto 100; half-portions €5-6)* has northern specialities like tripe and roast kid. A lively student haunt at lunchtime is **Café Ancôra Douro** *(☎ 222 003 749; Praça de Parada Leitão 49; mains €2.50-6)*.

An exception to the Ribeira's many overpriced, touristy eateries is **Pub-Petisqueira O Muro** *(☎ 222 083 426; Muro dos Bacalhoeiros 88; open noon-2am daily)*, with decor from dried bacalhau to Che Guevara, and good *feijoado de marisco* (a rich bean and seafood stew) for €4.50. **Casa Filha da Mãe Preta** *(☎ 222 055 515; Cais da Ribeira 40; most mains under €10)* has Douro views.

Entertainment

Lively pubs in the Ribeira include **Academia** *(☎ 222 005 737; Rua São João 80)*, **Ryan's Irish Pub** *(☎ 222 005 366; Rua Infante Dom Henrique 18)* and **Meia-Cave** *(☎ 223 323 214; Praça da Ribeira 6)*. A useful central bar is **Café Concerto** *(☎ 223 392 208; Praça Dom João I)* atop Teatro Rivoli.

A newer generation of clubs in the riverfront area called Massarelos, 2km west of the Ribeira, includes **Mexcal** *(☎ 226 009 188; Rua da Restauração)*, **Club Mau-Mau** *(☎ 226 076 660; Rua da Restauração)* and **Maré Alta** *(☎ 226 162 540; Alameda Basílio Teles)*. All are on the No 1 bus line from São Bento station.

Getting There & Away

Porto is connected by daily flights from Lisbon and London, and almost-daily direct links from other European centres (see the introductory Getting There & Away and Getting Around sections of this chapter). For flight information call ☎ 229 413 260.

Renex *(☎ 222 003 395; Rua das Carmelitas 32; open 24hr)* is the bus choice for Lisbon and the Algarve. From a terminal at Rua Alexandre Herculano 370, **Rede Expressos** *(☎ 222 052 459)* has buses that go all over Portugal. From or near Praceto Régulo Magauanha, off Rua Dr Alfredo Magalhães, **REDM** *(☎ 222 003 152)* goes to Braga, **AV Minho** *(☎ 222 006 121)* to Viana do Castelo, and **Carlos Soares** *(☎ 222 051 383)* to Guimarães. **Rodonorte** *(☎ 222 004 398)* departs from its own terminal *(Rua Ateneu Comércial do Porto 19)*, mainly to Vila Real and Bragança. Northern Portugal's main international bus carrier is **Internorte** (see the Getting There & Away section), whose coaches depart from the **booking office** *(☎ 226 093 220, fax 226 099 570; Praça da Galiza 96)*.

Porto, a northern Portugal rail hub, has three train stations. Most international trains, and all intercidade links, start at Campanhã, 2km east of the centre. Interregional and regional services depart from either Campanhã or the central **São Bento station** *(☎ 225 364 141; open 8am-11pm daily)* – bus Nos 34 and 35 run frequently between these two. At São Bento you can book tickets for services to any destination from any Porto station.

Getting Around

The **AeroBus** *(☎ 808 200 166)* runs between Avenida dos Aliados and the airport via Boavista every half-hour from 7am to 6.30pm. The €2.50 ticket, purchased on the bus, also serves as a free bus pass until midnight of the day you buy it. City bus Nos 56 and 87 run about every half-hour until 8.30pm to/from Jardim da Cordoaria, and until about 12.30am to/from Praça da Liberdade. A taxi costs around €13.

Central hubs of Porto's extensive bus system include Jardim da Cordoaria, Praça da Liberdade and São Bento station (Praça Almeida Garrett). Tickets are cheapest from **STCP kiosks** (eg, opposite São Bento station, beside Bolhão market, and at Boavista) and many newsagents and tobacconists: €0.50 for a short hop, €0.70 to outlying areas or €1.70 for an airport return trip. Tickets bought on the bus are always €1. Also available is a €2 day pass.

Porto has one remaining tram, the No 1E, trundling daily from the Ribeira to the coast at Foz do Douro. Work has begun on Porto's own 'underground', a combination of upgraded and new track that will reach Campanhã, Vila Nova de Gaia and several coastal resorts to the north.

To cross town by taxi, figure on about €4. An additional charge is made to leave the city limits, including across the Ponte Dom Luís I to Vila Nova de Gaia.

ALONG THE RIO DOURO

The Douro Valley is one of Portugal's scenic highlights, with 200km of expansive panoramas from Porto to the Spanish border. In the upper reaches, there are port-wine vineyards that wrap around every hillside.

The river, tamed by eight dams and locks since the late 1980s, is navigable right across Portugal. Highly recommended is the train journey from Porto to Peso da Régua (2½ hours, about a dozen trains daily), the last 50km clinging to the river's edge; four trains continue daily to Pocinho (4½ hours). **Douro Azul** *(☎ 223 402 500, fax 223 402 510; Rua de Saõ Francisco 4, Porto)* and other operators run one and two-day river cruises, mostly from March to October. Cyclists and drivers can choose river-hugging roads along either bank, though they're crowded at weekends. The elegant, detailed colour map *Rio Douro* (€3) is available from Porto bookshops.

VIANA DO CASTELO

pop 18,000

This attractive port at the mouth of the Rio Lima is renowned for its historic Old Town and its folk traditions. The **tourist office** *(☎ 258 822 620, fax 258 827 873; Rua Hospital Velho)* has information on festivals and the region in general. In August, Viana hosts the Festas de Nossa Senhora da Agonia (see the Facts for the Visitor section earlier).

The town's focal point is Praça da República, with its delicate fountain and elegant buildings, including the 16th-century **Misericórdia**. Atop Santa Luzia Hill, the **Templo do Sagrado Coração de Jesus** offers a grand panorama across the river. A funicular railway climbs the hill from 9am to 6pm (hourly in the morning, half-hourly in the afternoon) from behind the train station.

Viana's **pousada da juventude** *(☎ 258 800 260, fax 258 820 870; Rua da Argaçosa)* is about 1km east of the town centre. **Pensão Vianense** *(☎ 258 823 118; Avenida Conde da Carreira 79; doubles from €25)* and **Casa de Hóspedes Guerreiro** *(☎ 258 822 099; Rua Grande 14; doubles from €25)* have plain doubles with shared facilities. **Pensão Dolce Vita** *(☎ 258 824 860; Rua do Poço 44; doubles €30)* is central. Or try **Pensão-Restaurant Alambique** *(☎ 258 823 894; Rua Manuel Espregueira 88; doubles with bath & breakfast €35)*. The tourist office has listings of **private rooms**.

Most pensões have good-value restaurants, open to nonguests too. **A Gruta Snack Bar** *(☎ 258 820 214; Rua Grande 87)* offers lunchtime salads for under €5. **Adega do Padrinho** *(☎ 258 826 954; Rua Gago Coutinho 162; half-portions around €7.50)* serves up traditional dishes like octopus rice. Seafood is pricey, but try the *cervejaria* part of **Os Três Arcos** *(☎ 258 824 014; Largo João Tomás da Costa 25; half-portions from €3.50)*. **Viana's Restaurante** *(☎ 258 824 797; Rua Frei Bartolomeu dos Mártires 179; half-portions €5-9)*, near the fish market, specialises in *bacalhau* in all its forms.

Half a dozen express coaches go to Braga and to Porto every day (fewer at weekends), with daily express services on to Coimbra and Lisbon. Daily train services run north to Spain and south to Porto and Lisbon.

BRAGA

pop 80,000

Crammed with churches, Braga is considered Portugal's religious capital. During Easter week, huge crowds attend its Holy Week Festival. The **tourist office** *(☎ 253 262 550; Praça da República)* can help with accommodation and maps.

In the centre of Braga is the **Sé** *(admission to treasury museum & several tomb chapels €2)*, an elegant cathedral complex. At Bom Jesus do Monte, a hill-top pilgrimage site 5km from Braga, is an extraordinary stairway – the **Escadaria do Bom Jesus**, with allegorical fountains, chapels and a superb view. Buses run frequently from Braga to the site, where you can climb the steps or ascend by funicular.

It's an easy day trip to **Guimarães**, considered the cradle of the Portuguese nation, with a medieval town centre and a palace of the dukes of Bragança.

The **pousada da juventude** *(☎ 253 616 163; Rua de Santa Margarida 6)* is a 10-minute walk from the city centre. A bargain in the centre is **Hotel Francfort** *(☎ 253 262 648; Avenida Central 7; doubles from €25)*, with well-kept old rooms. **Grande Residência Avenida** *(☎ 253 609 020, fax 253 609 028; Avenida da Liberdade 738; doubles with/without bath €37/30)* offers good value.

Lareira do Conde *(☎ 253 611 340; Praça Conde de Agrolongo 56)* specialises in inexpensive grills, including ox (€8.75). Around the corner from the bus station, **Retiro da Primavera** *(☎ 253 272 482; Rua Gabriel de Castro 100; half-portions under €4)* has good fare. Rustic **Taberna do Felix** *(☎ 253 617 701; Praça Velha 17; dishes from €6.75)* has tasty *arroz de pato* (duck rice). For people-watching over coffee or beer, settle down at **Café Vianna** *(Praça da República)*.

The motorway from Porto puts Braga within easy day-trip reach. Intercidade trains arrive twice daily from Lisbon, Coimbra and Porto, and there are daily connections north to Viana do Castelo and Spain. Daily bus services link Braga to Porto and Lisbon.

PARQUE NACIONAL DA PENEDA-GERÊS

This wilderness park along the Spanish border boasts spectacular scenery and a wide variety of fauna and flora. Portuguese day-trippers and holiday-makers tend to stick to the main villages and camping areas, leaving the rest of the park to hikers. The park's main centre is **Vila do Gerês** (or Caldas do Gerês, or just Gerês), a sleepy, hot-spring village.

Gerês' **tourist office** *(☎ 253 391 133, fax 253 391 282)* is in the colonnade at the upper end of the village. For park information, go around the corner to the **park office** *(☎ 253 390 110; head office ☎ 253 203 480, fax 253 613 169; Avenida António Macedo, Braga)*. Other park offices are at Arcos de Valdevez, Montalegre. All have park maps (€2.64) with some roads and tracks (but not trails), and a free English-language booklet on the park's features.

Activities

A long-distance footpath is being developed, mostly following traditional roads or tracks between villages where you can stop for the night. Park offices sell map information (€0.50) about accessible hiking routes.

Day **hikes** around Gerês are popular. At weekends and all summer the Miradouro walk at **Parque do Merendas** is crowded. A more strenuous option is the old Roman road from Mata do Albergaria (10km up-valley from Gerês by taxi or hitching), past the **Vilarinho das Furnas** reservoir to Campo do Gerês. More distant destinations include **Ermida** and **Cabril**, both with simple accommodation and cafés. Guided walks are organised by **PlanAlto** *(☎/fax 253 351 005)* at Cerdeira camping ground in Campo do Gerês, and **Trote-Gerês** *(☎/fax 253 659 860)* at Cabril.

Mountain **bikes** can be hired from **Água Montanha Lazer** *(☎ 253 391 779, fax 253 391 598; e aguamontanha@mail.telepac.pt)* in Rio Caldo, **Pensão Carvalho Araújo** *(☎ 253 391 185)* in Gerês, or Plan Alto.

The national park operates **horse riding facilities** *(☎ 253 390 110)* from beside its Vidoeiro camping ground, near Gerês. Trote-Gerês also has horses for hire.

Rio Caldo, 8km south of Gerês, is the base for water sports on the Caniçada reservoir. Água Montanha Lazer rents canoes and other boats. For paddling the Salamonde reservoir, Trote-Gerês rents canoes from its camping ground at Cabril. Gerês' **Parque das Termas** *(admission €1)* has a swimming pool, open on weekdays/weekends for €3.50/5.

Organised Tours

Agência no Gerês *(☎ 253 391 141)*, at Hotel Universal in Gerês, runs two- to 5½-hour minibus trips around the park in summer, for around €5.50 per person.

Places to Stay & Eat

At Campo do Gerês the **pousada da juventude** *(☎/fax 253 351 339)* and **Cerdeira Camping Ground** *(☎/fax 253 351 005)* make good hiking bases. Trote-Gerês runs its own **Parque de Campismo Outeiro Alto** *(☎/fax 253 659 860)* at Cabril. The park runs a **camping ground** *(☎ 253 391 289)*, 1km north of Gerês at Vidoeiro, and others at Lamas de Mouro and Entre-Ambos-os-Rios.

Gerês has plenty of pensões, though many are block-booked by spa patients in the summer. Try **Pensão da Ponte** *(☎ 253 391 121; doubles with/without bath from €25/40)* beside the river. **Pensão Adelaide** *(☎ 253 390 020, fax 253 390 029; doubles with bath from €35)* is at the top of the hill. Trote-Gerês runs the comfortable **Pousadinha de Paradela** *(☎ 276 566 165; doubles from €25)*, in Paradela.

Most Gerês pensões serve hearty meals, to guests and nonguests. For picnic provisions there are several **restaurants** and shops in the main street. The **Cerdeira Camping Ground** at Campo do Gerês has a good restaurant.

Getting There & Away

From Braga, at least six coaches daily run to Rio Caldo and Gerês, and seven to Campo do Gerês (fewer at weekends). Coming from Lisbon or Porto, change at Braga.

Romania

A country where mass tourism means you, a horse and cart and a handful of farmers, Romania is the Wild West of Eastern Europe. Straddling the rugged Carpathian Mountains, with rich green valleys and farms spread throughout the countryside, it offers an extraordinary kaleidoscope of cultures and sights. Transylvania's colourful old cities are straight out of medieval Hungary or Germany, while Roman and Turkish influences colour Constanţa. Bucharest – seen by travellers as everything from 'the Paris of the East' to 'Hell on Earth' – has a Franco-Romanian charm all of its own.

The secret to exploring this surprise package of delights – declared by many readers as Eastern Europe's most exciting, best-value destination for adventurous travellers – is balance. Romania's historical cities are fascinating, but explore the countryside too. Your most memorable times could be spent atop a horse and cart.

Romania: the Basics

Capital Bucharest

Population 22.4 million

Language Romanian

Currency leu = 100 bani

Avoid at all costs Stray dogs

Avoid pneumonia in taxis by requesting *Va rog inchide fereastra. Din cauza curentului voi fi bolnav citeva zile.* (Please wind the window up. The draft will make me sick for days.)

Facts about Romania

HISTORY

In the 2nd century AD, Romans mixed with the indigenous Thracian (Dacian) tribes to form a Daco-Roman people who spoke Latin. By the 13th century all of Transylvania was under the Hungarian crown. Prince Vlad, ruler of Wallachia in 1456–62 and 1476–77, gained the name Ţepeş (Impaler) after the primary form of capital punishment he used against enemies – driving a wooden stake through the victim's backbone without touching any vital nerve, ensuring at least 48 hours of suffering before death. He was called 'Dracula', meaning 'son of the dragon', after his father, Vlad Dracul.

Transylvania became a vassal of the Ottoman Empire in the 16th century, then fell under Habsburg rule. After the Russian defeat in the Crimean War (1853–56), Romanian nationalism grew and in 1859 Alexandru Ioan Cuza was elected to the thrones of Moldavia and Wallachia, creating a national state, which took the name Romania in 1862. Romania declared independence from the Ottoman Empire in 1877.

In 1916 Romania entered WWI on the Allied side with the objective of taking Transylvania from Austria-Hungary. With the defeat of Austria-Hungary in 1918, the unification of Romania was complete.

As Romania began losing land in WWII, General Ion Antonescu imposed a fascist dictatorship and joined Hitler, sending 400,000 Romanian Jews and 36,000 Roma (Gypsies) to grisly deaths at Auschwitz and other camps. But in 1944 Romania suddenly changed sides, declaring war on Nazi Germany. In 1947 the monarchy was abolished and the Romanian People's Republic was proclaimed.

By the 1960s, Nicolae Ceauşescu had assumed a de facto role as dictator. Ceauşescu's domestic policy was chaotic and megalomaniac. He spent millions of dollars on pet projects and imprisoned people at whim. His great blunder was exporting food to finance his schemes. In the winter of 1988–89 the country suffered its worst food shortages in decades.

On 15 December 1989 Father Lászlo Tökés publicly condemned the dictator, prompting the Reformed Church of Romania to remove him from his post. Police attempts to arrest demonstrating parishioners failed, and civil unrest quickly spread. Ceauşescu dispatched troops to crush the rebellion. On 21 December in Bucharest, an address by Ceauşescu was cut short by booing demonstrators, who were crushed by police gunfire and armoured

ROMANIA

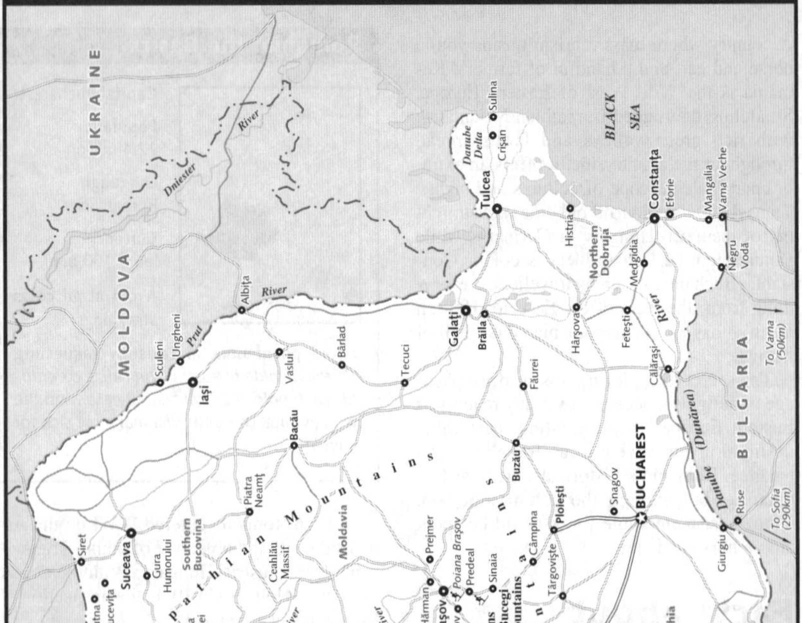

UKRAINE
MOLDOVA
HUNGARY
YUGOSLAVIA
BULGARIA
BLACK SEA
Dniester River
Prut River
Danube Delta
Sulina
Crişan
Tulcea
Histria
Northern Dobruja
Constanţa
Eforie
Mangalia
Vama Veche
Negru Vodă
Medgidia
Hârşova
Feteşti
Călăraşi
Brăila
Galaţi
Albiţa
Ungheni
Sculeni
Iaşi
Vaslui
Bârlad
Tecuci
Făurei
Buzău
Bacău
Piatra Neamţ
Suceava
Siret
Gura Humorului
Southern Bucovina
Putna
Suceviţa
Vatra Dornei
Carpathian Mountains
Ceahlău Massif
Moldavia
Mureş River
Prislop Pass (1416m)
Borşa
Moisei
Bistriţa
Sighetu Marmaţiei
Baia Mare
Satu Mare
Petea
Maramureş
Dej
Cluj-Napoca
Turda
Târgu Mureş
Sighişoara
Mediaş
Transylvania
Făgăraş
Olt
Hărman
Prejmer
Braşov
Râşnov
Bran
Poiana Braşov
Predeal
Sinaia
Câmpina
Bucegi Mountains
Făgăraş Mountains
Mt Moldoveanu (2544m)
Câmpulung
Târgovişte
Ploieşti
Snagov
BUCHAREST
Ruse
Giurgiu
Danube (Dunărea)
To Varna (50km)
To Sofia (290km)
Wallachia
Olt River
Piteşti
Râmnicu Vâlcea
Scorniceşti
Horezu
Sibiu
Sebeş
Alba Iulia
Apuseni Mountains
Şureanu Mountains
Jiu
Târgu Jiu
Craiova
Calafat
Jiu River
Retezat Mountains
Retezat National Park
Deva
Hunedoara
Drobeta-Turnu Severin
Iron Gate
Băile Herculane
Orşova
Caransebeş
Moldova Veche
Moraviţa
Naidăş
Banat
Timişoara
Jimbolia
Arad
Nădlac
Vărşand
Mureş River
Crişana
Beiuş
Crişul Repede
Oradea
Borş
BELGRADE
To Budapest (225km)
0 50 100km
0 30 60mi

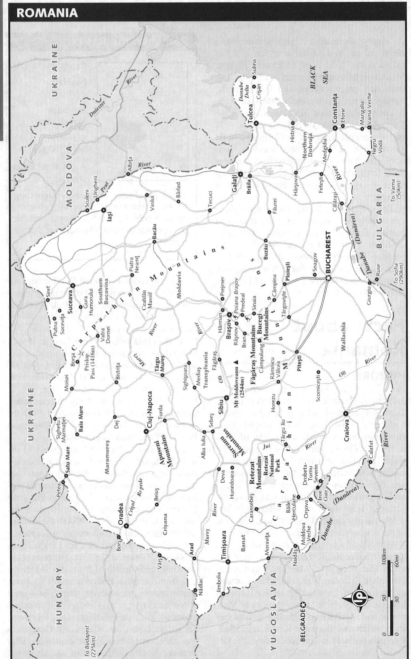

cars. The following morning, thousands more demonstrators took to the streets. By the next day, Ceauşescu and his wife were arrested. On 25 December they were executed by firing squad.

In 1990, Romania held its first democratic elections. Since then, economic reform has been hampered by internal bickering. Romania hoped to be admitted to NATO by 2002 and is negotiating to join the EU by 2007. Meanwhile, the country's politics have been plagued by scandal and corruption.

GEOGRAPHY

Covering 237,500 sq km, Romania is larger than Hungary and Bulgaria combined. The Danube River drains the entire country (except the Black Sea coast) and completes its 2850km course in Romania's Danube Delta.

Central and northern Romania is taken up by the U-shaped Carpathian Mountains. The Transylvanian Plain, a plateau with hills and valleys, occupies the centre of the U, while the Moldavian plateau lies to the east.

CLIMATE

The average annual temperature is 11°C in the south and on the coast, but only 2°C in the mountains. Romanian winters can be cold and foggy with lots of snow from mid-December to mid-April. In summer there's usually hot, sunny weather on the Black Sea coast.

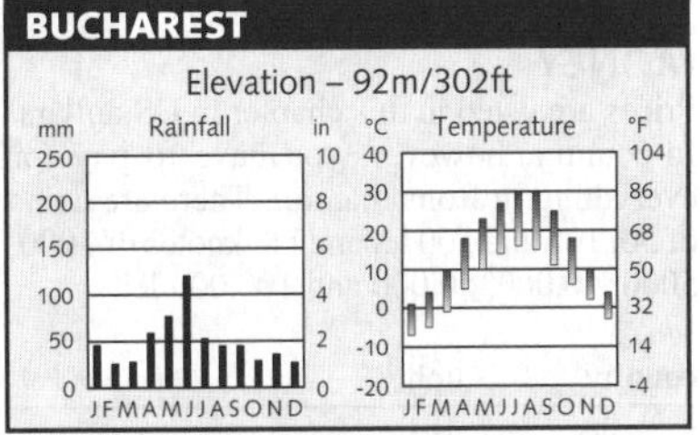

GOVERNMENT & POLITICS

Romania is a constitutional republic with a multiparty parliamentary system. The president is elected by the people. The current president is Ion Iliescu and the prime minister is Adrian Natase. Both belong to the Party of Social Democracy (PDSR).

POPULATION & PEOPLE

Ethnic Romanians comprise 89.5% of the population. Major minority groups include Hungarians and Roma. While the government estimates that 400,000 Roma live in Romania, a more accurate figure would be two million, making it the world's largest Roma community.

SOCIETY & CONDUCT

Romanians are typically strong-minded and stubbornly proud. They take great pride in their country's rich natural heritage and folk culture.

Men and women greet each other with a kiss. Romanians welcome you with open arms into their homes, feed you until you burst, and expect *nothing* in return except friendship. Don't rebuff it.

LANGUAGE

Romanian is closer to classical Latin than other Romance languages. English and French are the first foreign languages taught in schools; German is useful in Transylvania. Russian won't get you very far.

See the Language chapter for pronunciation guidelines and useful words and phrases.

Facts for the Visitor

HIGHLIGHTS

The classic 'must-see' list includes Bucharest's Palace of Parliament and Village Museum; Bran Castle near Braşov; Peleş Castle in Sinaia; the painted monasteries of Southern Bucovina; and the well-preserved medieval towns of Cluj-Napoca, Braşov and Sighişoara.

PLANNING

May and June are the best months to visit, followed by September and early October. Spring in Romania is a pastiche of wildflowers, melodious birdsong and rivers flowing with melted snow. Along the Black Sea coast, resorts start filling up in June and stay packed until the end of August. Romania is famous for its harsh winters.

TOURIST OFFICES

Romania has no national tourist office, engendering a handful of privately run tourist offices and dozens of travel agencies. Services and information range from superb to useless.

However, Romania runs a string of efficient tourist offices abroad, coordinated by Romania's **National Authority for Tourism**

(☎ 021-410 12 62; W www.turism.ro; Str Apolodor 17, RO-70663 Bucharest).

France (☎ 01 40 20 99 33, fax 01 40 20 99 43, e roumanie@office-tourisme-roumanie.com) 12 rue des Pyramides, F-75001 Paris

UK (☎ 020-7224 3692, fax 7935 6435, e uktourff@romania.freeserve.co.uk) 22 New Cavendish Street, London W1M 7LH

USA (☎ 212-545 84 84, fax 251 04 29) 14 East 38th St, 12th Floor, New York, NY 10016

VISAS & DOCUMENTS

Citizens from the EU, Canada, Japan and Switzerland can travel in Romania visa free for up to 90 days. Turkish citizens can stay visa free for 60 days and American citizens for 30 days. All other Western visitors, including Israelis, require a visa, which must be purchased from a Romanian consulate outside Romania.

You can extend your stay by reporting to a passport office, such as the **Visa Extensions Office** *(☎ 012-650 30 50; Str Luigi Cazzavillian 11; open 9am-1pm Mon-Fri, closed Wed)* in Bucharest. A visa extension costs US$30.

EMBASSIES & CONSULATES

Romanian Embassies & Consulates

Romanian embassies and consulates worldwide include:

Australia (☎ 02-6286 2343, fax 6286 2433, e roembcbr@cyberone.com.au) 4 Dalman Crescent, O'Malley, ACT 2606

Canada (☎ 613-789 5345, fax 789 4365, e romania@cyberus.ca) 655 Rideau St, Ottawa, Ontario K1N 6A3

France (☎ 01 40 62 22 02/4, fax 01 45 56 97 47, e ambparis.roumanie@francophonie.org) 3–5 rue de l'Exposition, F-75007 Paris

Germany (☎ 030-803 30 18/19, fax 803 16 84, e ro.amb.berlin@t-online.de) Matterhornstrasse 79, D14129 Berlin

Netherlands (☎ 070-354 37 96, fax 354 15 87, e ambrom@tip.nl) Catsheuvel 55, NL-2517 KA, The Hague

UK (☎ 020-7937 9666, fax 7937 8069, ☎/fax 7937 4675, e romania@roemb.demon.co.uk) 4 Palace Green, London W8 4QD

USA (☎ 202-387 6902, 332 4846, fax 232 4748, e consular@roembus.org) 1607 23rd Street NW, Washington DC 20008
Consulate: (☎ 212-682 9120, fax 972 8463, e mail@romconsny.org) 200 East 38th Street, New York, NY 10016 *Consulate*: (☎ 310-444 0043, fax 445 0043, e consulat.la@roconla.org) 11766 Wilshire Blvd, Suite 560, Los Angeles, CA 90025

Embassies & Consulates in Romania

The following embassies and consulates are in Bucharest (area code ☎ 021):

Australia (☎ 320 98 26, W www.romaniaaustralia.ro) Blvd Unirii 74

Bulgaria (☎ 230 21 50, e bulebassy@pcnet.ro) Str Vasile Lascăr 32

Canada (☎ 307 50 00, W www.dfait-maeci.gc.ca/bucharest) Str Nicolae Iorga 36

France (☎ 312 02 17) Str Biserica Amzei 13–15

Germany (☎ 230 25 80, e germanembassy-bucharest@ines.ro) Str Rabat 21

Hungary *Embassy*: (☎ 312 00 73, e hunembro@ines.ro) Str Jean Louis Calderon 63–65
Consulate: (☎ 312 04 68), Str Henri Coandă 5

Moldova (☎ 230 04 74, e moldova@customers.digiro.net) Aleea Alexandru 40
Consulate: (☎ 410 98 27) Blvd Eroilor 8

UK (☎ 312 03 03, W www.britain.ro) Str Jules Michelet 24

Ukraine (☎ 211 69 86, e emb-ukr@itcnet.ro) Calea Dorobanţilor 16
Consulate: (☎ 223 27 02) Str Tuberozelor 5

USA (☎ 210 40 42, W www.usembassy.ro) Str Nicolae Filipescu 26

Yugoslavia (☎ 211 98 71) Calea Dorobanţilor 34

CUSTOMS

Gifts worth up to a total of US$100 may be imported duty free. For foreigners, duty-free allowances are 4L of wine, 1L of spirits and 200 cigarettes. Valuable goods and foreign currency over US$1000 should be declared upon arrival.

MONEY

Prices are listed in this chapter in US dollars. In-country, however, you have to pay for everything in Romanian *lei*. There are coins of 50, 100 and 500 lei and banknotes of 1000, 5000, 10,000, 50,000 and 100,000 lei.

country	unit		lei
Australia	A$1	=	17,622 lei
Canada	C$1	=	20,610 lei
Eurozone	€1	=	32,205 lei
Japan	¥100	=	27,312 lei
New Zealand	NZ$1	=	15,382 lei
UK	UK£1	=	50,091 lei
USA	US$1	=	31,838 lei

Currency exchanges dot almost every street corner in major cities. By contrast, changing currency in the countryside can present huge challenges. You can cash travellers cheques (into US dollars or lei) and get MasterCard and Visa cash advances (in lei only) for a 3% to 5% commission at most branches of Banca Comercială Română and Banca Ion Ţiriac. American Express (AmEx) has a representative in Bucharest.

ATM machines that give 24-hour advances (Cirrus, Plus, Visa, MasterCard, Eurocard) have mushroomed in recent years, particularly in the capital and major cities. There's a couple of ATMs at Otopeni airport and Gara de Nord in Bucharest.

Whether you change money at a bank or currency exchange, you need your passport. It is illegal for foreigners to change lei back into foreign currencies; however, this law is rarely enforced.

Changing money on the street is illegal and a sure way to get ripped off by professional thieves.

Romania is a relatively inexpensive country for foreigners. On average you'll pay US$20 to US$35 per night for budget accommodation and less than US$10 per day for meals and drinks.

In flashier restaurants in Bucharest, waiters will not hesitate to ask where their tip is if you fail to leave one. Elsewhere, tipping remains a rarity – and often undeserved. 'Tips' should not be offered to officials, including train conductors. Countrywide, taxi drivers drive the hardest bargain. *Always* haggle.

POST & COMMUNICATIONS

Timbre (stamps) are sold at post offices. Post-restante mail (c/o Poste Restante, Poştă Romană Oficiul Bucureşti 1, Str Matei Millo 10, RO-70700 Bucureşti, ROMANIA) can be collected at the main post office in Bucharest at Str Matei Millo 10; it's held for one month.

Romania's telephone system is – in cities and towns at least – pretty reliable. In the countryside, a telephone can be something of a luxury. In towns and cities, making a local, regional or international call from one of the many orange cardphones is simple. You can purchase a *cartela telefonică* (phonecard) at the telephone building in Bucharest or any telex-fax office or post office. Only phonecards worth 50,000 lei (US$1.60) and 100,000 lei (US$3.10) are available.

Romania's international operator is reached by dialling ☎ 971.

To call other cities in Romania, dial the area code, followed by the recipient's number. To call Romania from abroad dial the international access code, Romania's country code (☎ 40), the area code (minus the first 0) and the number.

In Bucharest there are literally dozens of Internet cafés and places that have public Internet access, a couple of which are open 24 hours. You should count on paying around US$1 per hour in the capital. Outside the capital, there are Internet cafés in every city and most smaller towns.

DIGITAL RESOURCES

Among the many online Romanian information resources, find breaking news, views and local press digests at **W** www.centraleurope.com/romaniatoday. A more hands-on approach is taken by locally published city guide *Bucharest In Your Pocket* at **W** www.inyourpocket.com. The Romania Travel Guide at **W** www.rotravel.com is another useful site.

BOOKS

A History of Romania, edited by Kurt Treptow, is the most comprehensive history book around. Lonely Planet's *Romania & Moldova* provides in-depth coverage.

WOMEN TRAVELLERS

Do not wander alone late at night and avoid sitting in empty compartments on long-distance and overnight trains etc. If you should encounter offensive behaviour, a few strong words – such as shouting *poliţia!* – is usually sufficient to ward off trouble.

GAY & LESBIAN TRAVELLERS

In late 2001, homosexual relations were decriminalised. Showing affection in public, however, remains a criminal offence for gays and lesbians, who can still be thrown in jail for five years for so much as holding hands. The Orthodox Church considers homosexuality a sin, and a large number of young Romanians feel that gay and lesbian relationships are 'unnatural'. Hotel managers might turn away openly gay couples.

Bucharest is the only city in Romania that has an active gay and lesbian community, represented by **ACCEPT** *(☎ 021-252 16 37, fax 252 56 20;* **W** *www.accept-romania.ro; CP 34-56, Bucharest)*. In Cluj-Napoca you can find **Association Attitude** *(**e** attitude@rdslink.ro)* for the gay and lesbian community in Transylvania.

Emergencies

For nationwide emergency assistance call ☎ 055 for police and ☎ 061 for ambulance.

DISABLED TRAVELLERS

Disabled travellers will find it difficult to conquer Romania alone. Facilities are woeful.

DANGERS & ANNOYANCES

Bucharest has a stray-dog problem. Bitches with puppies can be snappy; keep well clear.

Other annoyances include heavy pollen, year-round pollution in larger cities and swarms of mosquitoes in summer. Beware of theft.

BUSINESS HOURS

Banking hours are weekdays from 9am to 2pm or 3pm. Most shops and markets close on Sunday. Many museums close on Monday. Theatrical performances and concerts usually begin at 7pm, except on Monday and in summer when most theatres are closed.

PUBLIC HOLIDAYS & SPECIAL EVENTS

Public holidays are New Year (1 and 2 January), Easter Monday (March/April), National Unity Day (1 December) and Christmas (25 and 26 December).

Many festivals take place in summer, including the three-day Bucharest carnival in June and the Golden Stag international pop music festival in Braşov in July. Folklore festivals include the International Festival of Danubian Folklore in Tulcea in August.

In October there's Cluj-Napoca's Musical Autumn. In December the Days of Bihor Culture takes place in Oradea, and Sighetu Marmaţiei celebrates its Christmas festival.

ACTIVITIES

Romania's ski resorts are all in the Carpathian Mountains between Bucharest and Braşov. They offer a variety of slopes suitable for skiers and snowboarders of all abilities. The ski season runs from December to mid-March.

Romania's Carpathian Mountains offer endless opportunities for hikers; the most popular areas are the Bucegi and Făgăraş ranges, south and west of Braşov. Other Carpathian hiking zones include the Retezat National Park, northwest of Târgu Jiu; the Şureanu Mountains, between Alba Iulia and Târgu Jiu; the Apuseni Mountains, southwest of Cluj-Napoca; and the Ceahlău Massif, between Braşov and Suceava.

ACCOMMODATION

Camping

There are dozens of camping grounds around Romania. Sites vary enormously, many are without toilets and/or showers. Most grounds open from around May to September.

Wild camping is prohibited in cities and in the Danube Delta, but not necessarily elsewhere. On the coast it's fairly common.

Mountain Huts

In most mountain areas there's a network of cabins or *cabana* (chalets) with restaurants and dormitories. These are substantially cheaper than hotels. No reservations are required, but

Street Scams

Enterprising Romanians have devised many a scam to part you from your money. Keep your wits about you and don't fall for the following scams.

Tourist Police

A man stops you in the street and asks if you want to change money. You refuse. Seconds later, another man appears, arrests the first man and demands to see your passport, explaining that he is from the tourist police. Simply walk away, even if he flashes an ID badge. As a last resort, insist on being accompanied to the nearest police station – on foot. Stay out of a taxi.

Stupid Tourist

A man stops you on the street, explains that he is from a foreign country, proclaims that he has never seen a 100,000 lei banknote before, and asks you to show him one. If you pull out your wallet, it – and the stupid tourist – will be gone in a flash.

Fake Taxi Driver

A man greets you as you get off the train at Gara de Nord station, explains that he is from Villa Helga hostel, and offers to drive you there. Yeah, whatever. Staff *never* meet guests at the station. Insist on making your own way there. The same scenario has also been used for the new Elvis' Villa Bucharest.

arrive early if the cabana is in a popular location. Count on good companionship rather than cleanliness or comfort.

Hostels

In the last couple of years a number of hostels have sprouted up around the country. Hostels charge around US$10 a night for a bed in a two- to 10-bed room, most including breakfast. Check out Romania's **Youth Hostel Association** *(☎/fax 064-186 616; Ⓦ www.dntcj.ro/yhr; headquarters: Str Clăbucet 2/69, RO-3400 Cluj-Napoca)*. Some of its accredited hostels are, in fact, hotels or cabanas, which also tout dorm beds.

Hotels

Rooms in a good, modern hotel only cost about US$10 more than you'd pay for a flea-pit. So, it may be better value in the long run to take a room with a private bathroom.

All accommodation prices in this chapter are listed in US dollars (US$), calculated at the official rate. Payment is required in Romanian lei in cash in budget hotels, by credit card or cash in better hotels.

Romanian hotels are rated by the government on a star system. Zero- and one-star hotels, while generally clean, almost always have a shared bathroom and toilet. They charge from US$12 to US$25. Most two-star hotels are good value with clean rooms with TV and private bath for between US$20 and US$40. At some hotels *mic dejun* (breakfast) is included in the price.

Private Rooms

Homestays are abundant in most major towns and cities where, chances are, you will be approached by someone offering you a *cameră* (room) the moment you step off the train. Always verify the exact location of the room on a map and insist on seeing it before parting with any cash. Count on paying between US$10 and US$25 per person.

Agrotourism (B&B in the countryside) is popular in many rural areas. The leading organisations in this field are **ANTREC** *(Asociaţia Natională de Turism Rural, Ecologi şi Cultural; head office: ☎/fax 021-223 70 24; Ⓦ www.antrec.ro; Str Maica Alexandra 7, Bucharest)*, which has properties throughout the country, and **Fundaţia OVR Agro-Tur-Art** *(Opération Villages Roumains; ☎/fax 330 171; Ⓦ www.vaduizei.ovr.ro; house No 161, Vadu Izei)*, which works with families in Maramureş and Moldavia.

Count on paying between US$15 and US$30 for a double room, plus US$5 per person for each meal. An excellent independent website is Ⓦ www.ruraltourism.ro, which provides contact details, prices and even pictures of many of the rural homes throughout the country.

FOOD & DRINKS

Romanian favourites include *ciorbă* (soup), *ghiveci* (vegetable stew) and *tocană* (onion and meat stew). Restaurants and beer gardens often offer *mititei* or *mici* (grilled meatballs). Other common dishes are *muşchi de vacă/porc/miel* (cutlet of beef/pork/lamb), *ficat* (liver), *piept de pui* (chicken breast) and *cabanos prăjit* (fried sausages). Vegetarians should opt for a non-meaty *caşcaval pane* (breaded fried cheese) or *castraveţi* (tomatoes and cucumber salad). Folk dishes are harder to find but they're delicious.

Romania is noted for its excellent wine, while the beer is notable mostly for its low price (about US$0.75 for a half-litre). Red wines are called *negru* and *roşu*, while white wine is *vin alb*. *Must* is a fresh unfermented wine available during the wine harvest. *Ţuică* (plum brandy) is a strong liqueur drunk at the start of a meal.

Beware of *Ness*, an awful instant coffee made from vegetable extracts. Unless you ask for it, coffee and *ceai* (tea) are almost never served *cu lapte* (with milk). *Apă minerală* (mineral water) is cheap and widely available.

ENTERTAINMENT

Ask about local events at the main theatre and concert hall and visit any theatre ticket offices you can find. Opera companies exist in Bucharest, Timişoara and Cluj-Napoca. In large towns buy the local paper and try to decipher the entertainment listings.

Bucharest is loaded with hip bars and hot clubs. Most other larger towns are graced with at least one groovy joint.

Getting There & Away

AIR

Romania's state carrier, **Tarom** *(Ⓦ www.tarom.digiro.net)* has weekly flights between Bucharest's Otopeni airport and most European capitals, as well as New York and Tel Aviv.

Numerous other airlines fly to/from Romania, including Air France, Air Ukraine, Alitalia, Austrian Airlines, British Airways, Czech Airlines, KLM, LOT, Lufthansa, Malév Hungarian Airlines, Olympic Airways, Swiss International Air Lines and Turkish Airlines.

LAND

Train

In Romania, international train tickets are sold at Căile Ferate Române (CFR) offices. Most international trains require advance seat reservations (US$2 to US$4), even if you're travelling on an Inter-Rail pass. (Seat reservations are automatically included in tickets purchased in Romania.) If you already have a ticket, you may be able to make reservations at the station an hour before departure, but at least one day in advance is preferable.

There are some six trains daily between Bucharest's Gara de Nord and Budapest-Keleti (2nd-class one way/return US$30/58, 12 hours, 873km). The *Pannonia Expres* arrives from Munich, via Vienna, Prague, Bratislava and Budapest; and the *Dacia Expres* comes from Vienna via Budapest to Bucharest. A cheaper alternative is to hop aboard one of the two daily local Hungarian trains that shuttle between Oradea and Budapest-Nyugati (US$20, five hours). Seat reservations aren't required.

Local trains also depart from Békéscsaba, Hungary, for Oradea (90km) three times daily. The *Carpaţi* makes its way from Warsaw via Kraków, Sibiu and Braşov to Bucharest (2nd-class one way/return US$58/117, 27 hours, 1645km). The *Bulgaria Expres* travels from Bucharest to Moscow (42 hours), stopping in Kyiv (2nd-class one way US$26, 28 hours, 806km), and the *Pretenia* travels to Chişinău (2nd-class one way/return, US$13/25, 13 hours, 637km) in Moldova.

The daily *Bucureşti* train shuttles from Bucharest's Gara de Nord to Belgrade-Dunav (2nd-class one way US$15 plus US$10/15 for a couchette/sleeper, 13 hours, 693km), stopping in Drobeta-Turnu Severin and Timişoara en route.

Trains between Romania and Bulgaria are slow and crowded. Between Sofia and Bucharest (1st-/2nd-class one way seat US$30/21, bed US$38/26, 12 hours) there are two trains, both of which stop in Ruse. The overnight Bucharest–İstanbul *Bosor* express travels through eastern Bulgaria (2nd-class one way/return US$21/42, 17 hours, 803km) and stops in Ruse en route.

Bus

There's little reason to go to Romania by bus with such good train services available. Romania's public bus system is terrible and private bus companies are expensive. The exception is the bus to İstanbul (US$27/51 one way/return, 11 to 14 hours), which is substantially faster than the train.

Numerous private bus companies operate daily buses between Germany and Romania.

Car & Motorcycle

Drivers need vehicle registration papers, liability insurance and a driving licence. Car rental is expensive.

When crossing the border by car, expect long queues at Romanian checkpoints, particularly on weekends. Don't even consider trying to bribe an official.

Walking

You can walk in or out of Romania at most of its border crossings, except those with Moldova and Ukraine. Some travellers hitch instead. Pedestrians are not allowed to use the so-called 'Friendship Bridge' to/from Ruse, Bulgaria.

Getting Around

TRAIN

Căile Ferate Române *(CFR; Romanian State Railways;* W *www.cfr.ro)* runs trains over 11,106km of track across Romania. The national *mersul trenurilor* (train timetable) is published each May and sold for US$1.60 in CFR offices.

There are four types of trains: *personal* (slow) and *inter-city* (IC), *accelerat* and *rapid* (all speedier). Irrespective of class, fares are low: it costs about US$0.85 to travel 100km in 1st class on a local train and US$2.95 to travel in 2nd class on an express.

If possible, buy tickets for express trains a day in advance at a CFR office; remember most are closed on Sunday. CFR offices do not sell tickets for express trains leaving the same day; you must buy a ticket at the station *no more than one hour* before departure.

If you have an international ticket through Romania, you're allowed to make stops along the route but must purchase a reservation ticket each time you reboard an *accelerat* or *rapid* train.

Vagons de dormit (sleepers) are available between large cities and are a good way to cut accommodation expenses. Book these well in advance at a CFR office in town.

Inter-Rail passes (sold to European residents only) and Balkan Flexipasses (available to everyone) are accepted, but Eurail passes are not.

BUS

Buses are less reliable and more crowded than trains. Posted schedules are often out of date, so always check at the ticket window. Purchase your ticket at an *autogară* (bus station) before boarding. If the bus is the only way to get to/from somewhere, try to reserve a seat by buying a ticket the day before.

CAR & MOTORCYCLE

Members of foreign automobile clubs (such as AA and AAA) are covered by Romania's **Automobil Clubul Român** *(ACR; 24hr emergencies: ☎ 927)*. Of course, you must still pay: emergency road service costs upwards of US$10 to US$13, and towing is US$0.57 per kilometre.

Avis, Budget, Hertz and Europcar have offices in most cities. Car rental is expensive (from US$47 per day). If coming from abroad, it is often cheaper to book (and pay) for a car in advance through overseas offices.

HITCHING

Hitching is never entirely safe, and we don't recommend it. Hitchhiking in Romania is variable. Small cars are usually full and there isn't much traffic on secondary roads. It's common practice to pay the equivalent of the bus fare to the driver.

LOCAL TRANSPORT

Public transport is good but overcrowded. Tram, bus and trolleybus services usually run from 5am to 11pm or midnight. Purchase tickets at kiosks marked *bilete* or *casă de bilete* before boarding, and validate them once aboard. Tickets cost less than US$0.20.

Taxi drivers can be shockingly corrupt or surprisingly honest. In Bucharest, Braşov and other larger cities, taxis tout meters which work. Count on paying around US$0.45 per kilometre. If there's no meter, bargain beforehand. It's always cheaper to phone for a taxi.

Bucharest (Bucureşti)

☎ 021 • pop 2.2 million

Tree-lined boulevards, park-girdled lakes and pompous public monuments give Bucharest a smooth Parisian flavour. Founded by a legendary shepherd named Bucur on the plains between the Carpathian foothills and the Danube River, Bucharest became the capital of Wallachia in 1459, during the reign of Vlad Ţepeş (Dracula). The national capital since 1862, it is contemporary Romania's largest and wealthiest metropolis.

During the 1980s the city was transformed by Ceauşescu's attempt to recast Bucharest as a grandiloquent socialist capital, with the behemoth House of the People as its centrepiece. Reminders of the Ceauşescu era remain – from ugly bloc-style apartments to neglected buildings and stray dogs. But Bucharest's greatest and grandest old edifices have been restored, and fashionable new shops, restaurants and nightspots abound. The city is at its best in spring and summer, when relaxed crowds fill the beer gardens and parks.

Orientation

Bucharest's main train station, Gara de Nord, is a few kilometres northwest of central Bucharest. The station is connected by metro to the centre at Piaţa Victoriei on the northern side or to Piaţa Unirii to the south. Bus Nos 79, 86 and 133 will take you mid-centre to Piaţa Romană. The main boulevard runs between Piaţa Victoriei, Piaţa Romană, Piaţa Universităţii and Piaţa Unirii.

Information

Tourist Offices Thanks to Elvis' Villa Bucharest (see Places to Stay), Bucharest finally has an official **Tourist Information Office** *(end of Line 2, Gara de Nord; open daily)*. The staff, who speak English, Italian and Japanese, can make hotel reservations, call taxis and provide detailed information on the city and surrounding sights.

Money Currency exchanges are dotted all over the city, including along Blvd General Magheru and Blvd Nicolae Bălcescu. **Alliance Exchange** *(Blvd Nicolae Bălcescu 30)* and **OK Exchange Nonstop** *(Str George*

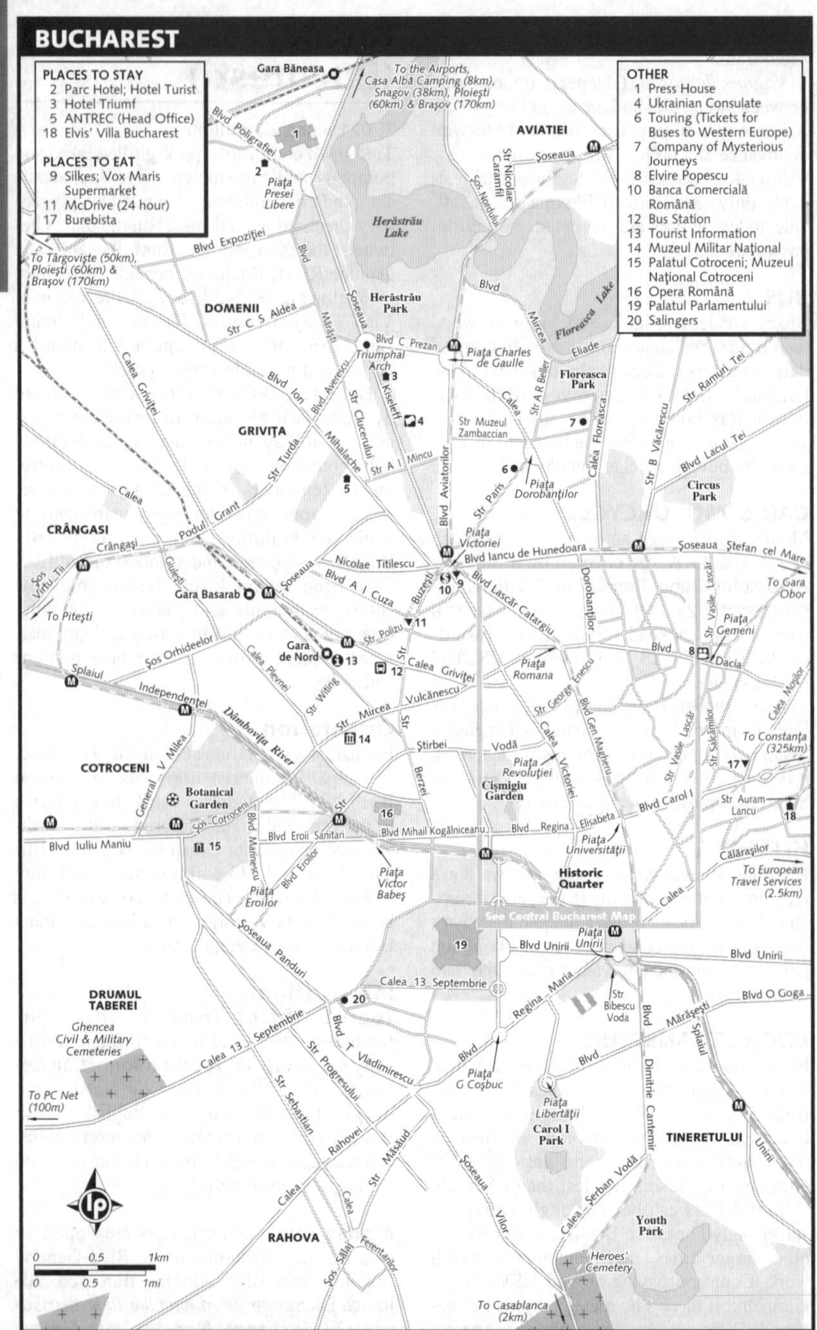
BUCHAREST
PLACES TO STAY
2 Parc Hotel; Hotel Turist
3 Hotel Triumf
5 ANTREC (Head Office)
18 Elvis' Villa Bucharest
PLACES TO EAT
9 Silkes; Vox Maris Supermarket
11 McDrive (24 hour)
17 Burebista
OTHER
1 Press House
4 Ukrainian Consulate
6 Touring (Tickets for Buses to Western Europe)
7 Company of Mysterious Journeys
8 Elvire Popescu
10 Banca Comercială Română
12 Bus Station
13 Tourist Information
14 Muzeul Militar Naţional
15 Palatul Cotroceni; Muzeul Naţional Cotroceni
16 Opera Română
19 Palatul Parlamentului
20 Salingers
Gara Băneasa
To the Airports, Casa Albă Camping (8km), Snagov (38km), Ploieşti (60km) & Braşov (170km)
AVIATIEI
Herăstrău Lake
Herăstrău Park
Floreasca Lake
Floreasca Park
Circus Park
Piaţa Presei Libere
To Târgovişte (50km), Ploieşti (60km) & Braşov (170km)
DOMENII
GRIVIŢA
CRÂNGASI
Triumphal Arch
Piaţa Charles de Gaulle
Piaţa Dorobanţilor
Piaţa Victoriei
Gara Basarab
Gara de Nord
To Piteşti
Piaţa Romana
Piaţa Gemeni
To Gara Obor
To Constanţa (325km)
COTROCENI
Botanical Garden
Dâmboviţa River
Piaţa Revoluţiei
Cişmigiu Garden
Piaţa Universităţii
Historic Quarter
See Central Bucharest Map
Piaţa Victor Babeş
Piaţa Eroilor
To European Travel Services (2.5km)
Piaţa Unirii
DRUMUL TABEREI
Ghencea Civil & Military Cemeteries
To PC Net (100m)
Piaţa G Coşbuc
Piaţa Libertăţii
Carol I Park
TINERETULUI
RAHOVA
Youth Park
Heroes' Cemetery
To Casablanca (2km)
0 0.5 1km
0 0.5 1mi

Enescu), around the corner from McDonald's, are both open 24 hours.

There are numerous ATMs around town accepting Visa and MasterCard, including at Otopeni airport and next to the **IDM Exchange** *(open 5.30am-11pm daily)* at Gara de Nord.

The **Banca Comercială Română** *(Blvd Regina Elisabeta 5; open 9am-5.30pm Mon-Fri, 9am-12.30pm Sat)*, opposite Bucharest University, can cash travellers cheques and gives cash advances on credit cards. It has two ATMs outside, as does its **branch office** *(Calea Victoriei 155)*.

Lost American Express cards/cheques can be replaced at the AmEx representative, **Marshal Turism** *(☎ 223 12 04, fax 223 12 03; w www.marshal.ro; Blvd General Magheru 43; open 9am-7pm Mon-Fri, 9am-1pm Sat)*.

Post & Communications The **Poştă Română Oficiul Bucureşti 1** *(central post office; Str Matei Millo 10; open 7.30am-8pm Mon-Fri, 8am-2pm Sat)* is just off Calea Victoriei. Card-operated public phones are abundant on the streets and in hotel lobbies.

Logging-on is no problem in Bucharest. **PC-Net Internet Café** *(☎ 650 42 14; Calea Victoriei 136 • Blvd Carol I 25)* sports a genuine café as well as several computers. The second branch is just off Piaţa Rosetti. Both are open 24 hours and charge around US$1.25 an hour.

Travel Agencies Bucharest offers numerous travel agencies that take bookings for hotels, run city tours and arrange trips into the countryside.

Nova Tours *(☎ 315 13 57/8, fax 312 10 41; e nova.tour@snmail.softnet.ro; Blvd Nicolae Bălcescu 21)* organises sightseeing tours of Bucharest and fishing trips into the Danube Delta.

ZIP International *(☎/fax 212 35 22; w www.ziptravel.ro; Str A Phillippide 9)* is the local STA Travel representative, catering mostly to students.

There's also the **Company of Mysterious Journeys** *(☎/fax 231 40 22, ☎ 092-599 099; e cdt@art.ro; Str George Călinescu 20)*, which is the official operator for the Transylvanian Society of Dracula's spooky tours.

Medical & Emergency Services A good private clinic with English-speaking staff and 24-hour emergency service is **Medicover** *(☎ 310 44 10; emergencies ☎ 310 40 40; Calea Plevnei 96)*. For emergencies go to the **Emergency Hospital** *(Spitalul de Urgenţă; ☎ 230 01 06; Calea Floreasca 8; open 24hr)*. There is a **24-hour pharmacy** on the corner of Calea Victoriei and Str Stravropoleos.

Call an ambulance on ☎ 961, the police on ☎ 955 and the fire brigade on ☎ 981.

Things to See & Do

Central Bucharest In the Old City lie the ruins of Vlad Ţepeş' **Old Princely Court** *(Str Franceză)* built in 1462. On Str Poştei is the **Biserica Stavropoleos** (Stavropoleos Church), a Unesco-protected building built by a Greek monk in 1724.

To the west is one of Bucharest's most important museums, the **Muzeul Naţional de Istorie** *(National History Museum; ☎ 315 70 56; admission US$0.45; open 10am-6pm Wed-Sun)*, in the former Post Office Palace (1899). Its 41 rooms and 600,000 exhibits tell the story of the country from prehistoric times to WWI. The highlight is its fabulous basement treasury.

North on Calea Victoriei is Piaţa Revoluţiei and **Biserica Creţulescu** (Creţulescu Church), a red-brick structure built in 1722 but badly damaged in the 1989 revolution. To its north, dominating the entire western side of the square, is the massive **Palatul Regal** (Royal Palace), an official royal residence from 1834. The palace displays an extensive collection of Romanian and European art in the four-storey **Muzeul Naţional de Artă** *(National Art Museum; ☎ 313 30 30; e national.art@art.museum.ro; Calea Victoriei 49-53; admission US$1.25; open 10am-6pm Wed-Sun)*.

Ceauşescu made his last speech from the balcony of the former **Central Committee of the Communist Party** building, the white-stone edifice opposite Biserica Creţulescu. Just north is the magnificent neoclassical **Ateneul Român** *(Romanian Athenaeum; ☎ 315 87 98; Str Franklin 1)*, the city's main concert hall, built by French architect Albert Galleron in 1888. Check the box office here for performance schedules.

North again is the excellent **Muzeul Colecţiilor de Artă** *(Art Collection Museum; ☎ 659 66 93; Calea Victoriei 111; adult/concession US$0.95/0.30; open 10am-6pm Wed-Sun)*. Note the many fine works by the 19th-century painter Nicolae Grigorescu that are displayed here.

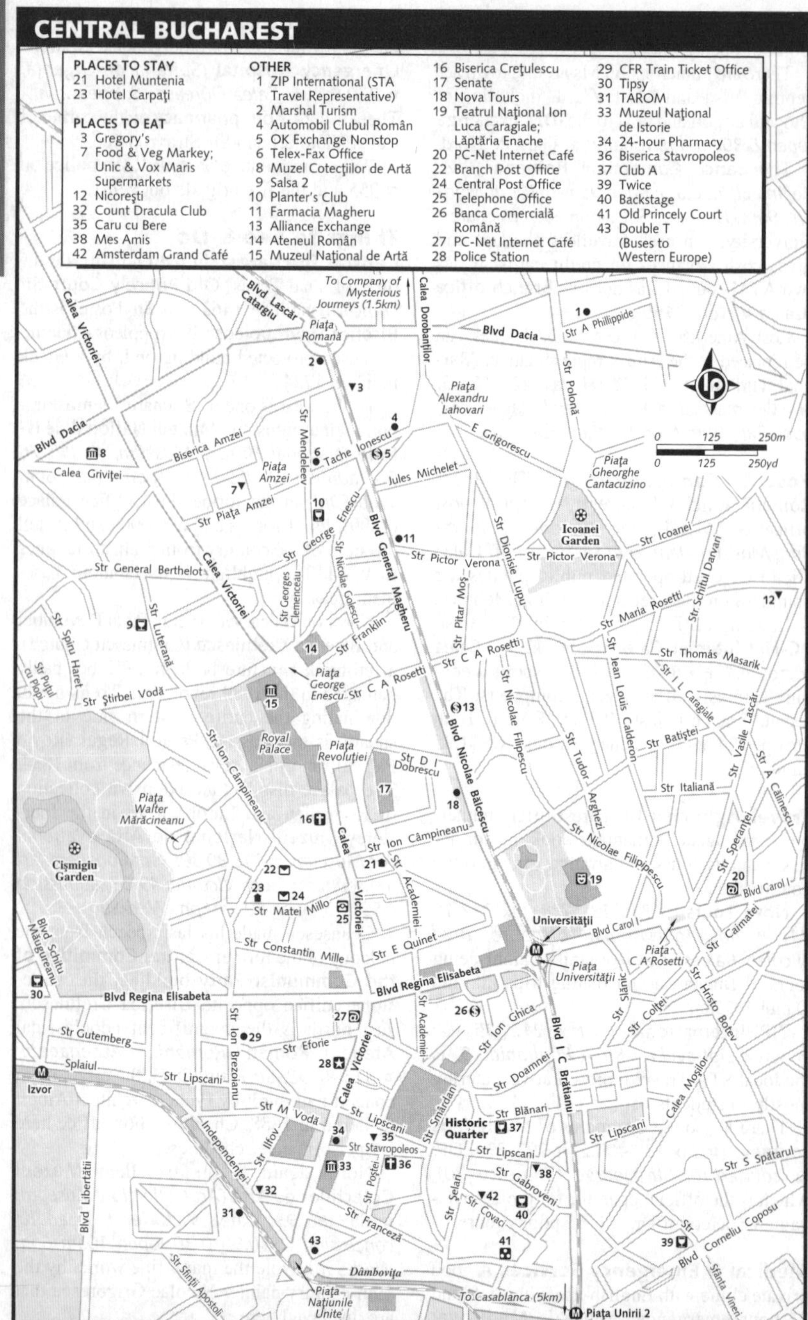
CENTRAL BUCHAREST
PLACES TO STAY
21 Hotel Muntenia
23 Hotel Carpaţi
PLACES TO EAT
3 Gregory's
7 Food & Veg Markey; Unic & Vox Maris Supermarkets
12 Nicoreşti
32 Count Dracula Club
35 Caru cu Bere
38 Mes Amis
42 Amsterdam Grand Café
OTHER
1 ZIP International (STA Travel Representative)
2 Marshal Turism
4 Automobil Clubul Român
5 OK Exchange Nonstop
6 Telex-Fax Office
8 Muzel Cotecţiilor de Artă
9 Salsa 2
10 Planter's Club
11 Farmacia Magheru
13 Alliance Exchange
14 Ateneul Român
15 Muzeul Naţional de Artă
16 Biserica Creţulescu
17 Senate
18 Nova Tours
19 Teatrul Naţional Ion Luca Caragiale; Lăptăria Enache
20 PC-Net Internet Café
22 Branch Post Office
24 Central Post Office
25 Telephone Office
26 Banca Comercială Română
27 PC-Net Internet Café
28 Police Station
29 CFR Train Ticket Office
30 Tipsy
31 TAROM
33 Muzeul Naţional de Istorie
34 24-hour Pharmacy
36 Biserica Stavropoleos
37 Club A
39 Twice
40 Backstage
41 Old Princely Court
43 Double T (Buses to Western Europe)
To Company of Mysterious Journeys (1.5km)
Blvd Lascăr Catargiu
Calea Victoriei
Calea Dorobanţilor
Piaţa Romană
Blvd Dacia
Str A Phillippide
Str Polonă
Piaţa Alexandru Lahovari
E Grigorescu
0 125 250m
0 125 250yd
Piaţa Gheorghe Cantacuzino
Biserica Amzei
Str Mendeleev
Tache Ionescu
Piaţa Amzei
Calea Griviţei
Jules Michelet
Str Piaţa Amzei
Str George Enescu
Blvd General Magheru
Str Dionisie Lupu
Icoanei Garden
Str Icoanei
Str Pictor Verona
Str General Berthelot
Str Nicolae Golescu
Str Georges Clemenceau
Str Pitar Moş
Str Schitul Darvari
Str Maria Rosetti
Str Luterană
Str Spiru Haret
Str Puţul cu Plopi
Str Franklin
Str C A Rosetti
Str Thomás Masarik
Str I L Caragiale
Piaţa George Enescu
Str Ştirbei Vodă
Str Jean Louis Calderon
Str Nicolae Filipescu
Str Vasile Lascăr
Blvd Nicolae Bălcescu
Royal Palace
Piaţa Revoluţiei
Str D I Dobrescu
Str Ion Câmpineanu
Str Tudor Arghezi
Str Batiştei
Str Italiană
Str A Călinescu
Piaţa Walter Mărăcineanu
Cişmigiu Garden
Str Academiei
Str Speranţei
Blvd Carol I
Str Matei Millo
Universităţii
Str Constantin Mille
Str E Quinet
Piaţa Universităţii
Piaţa C A Rosetti
Str Caimatei
Blvd Schitu Măgureanu
Blvd Regina Elisabeta
Str Ion Brezoianu
Str Ion Ghica
Blvd I C Brătianu
Str Slănic
Str Colţei
Str Hristo Botev
Str Gutemberg
Str Eforie
Splaiul
Izvor
Str Lipscani
Str Doamnei
Calea Moşilor
Str M Vodă
Str Smârdan
Str Blănari
Historic Quarter
Independenţei
Str Ilfov
Str Stavropoleos
Str Poştei
Str Gabroveni
Str S Spătarul
Blvd Libertăţii
Str Şelari
Str Covaci
Str Franceză
Blvd Corneliu Coposu
Str Sfânta Vineri
Dâmboviţa
Str Sfinţii Apostoli
Piaţa Naţiunile Unite
To Casablanca (5km)
Piaţa Unirii 2

Southern Bucharest In the last years of the Ceauşescus' reign, the southern section of Bucharest around **Piaţa Unirii** was redesigned to create the new civic centre. Walk southwest, across Blvd Unirii and up Blvd Regina Maria to the **Catedrala Patriarhala** (Patriarchal Cathedral), built in 1658, and **Palatul Patriarhei** (Patriarch's Palace) dating from 1875. To the west, Blvd Unirii runs directly towards the enormous **Palatul Parlamentului** *(Palace of Parliament; ☎ 311 36 11; ⓔ cic@camera.ro; Calea 13 Septembrie 1; admission US$1.90; open 10am-4pm daily)*, Ceauşescu's House of the People. It's an incredible Stalinist structure that was still unfinished when Ceauşescu was overthrown in 1989. Three shifts of 20,000 workers and 700 architects toiled for more than five years on this massive palace, using almost exclusively Romanian materials. At 330,000 sq metres, it is the second-largest building in the world after the US Pentagon.

Northern Bucharest Exiting Piaţa Victoriei metro station, you see the **Muzeul Ţăranului Român** *(Museum of the Romanian Peasant; ☎ 650 53 60; ⓔ muztar@rnc.ro; ⓦ www.itc.ro/mtr/tar–e.htm; Şoseaua Kiseleff 3; adult/concession US$0.60/0.15, guide US$1.55 per hour; open 10am-6pm Tues-Sun)*, a fantastic museum displaying Romania's largest collection of folklore treasures. From here, walk up to the **Arcul de Triumf** (Triumphal Arch), built in 1936 to commemorate the reunification of Romania in 1918. Guess which Parisian building it resembles.

A short walk north is one of Bucharest's best sights, the **Muzeul Satului** *(Village Museum; ☎ 222 91 10; adult/student US$1.25/0.45, plus camera/video US$1.55/9.40; open 9am-6pm Tues-Sun, 9am-5pm Mon)* which has full-scale displays of nearly 300 churches, wooden houses and farm buildings, first assembled here in 1936. To get here by bus, take No 131 or 331 from Blvd General Magheru or Piaţa Romană to the 'Muzeul Satului' stop.

Places to Stay

Hostels Elvis is alive in Bucharest! The King can be found at **Elvis' Villa Bucharest** *(☎ 312 16 53; ⓦ www.elvisvilla.ro; Str Avram Iancu 5; dorm beds from US$8)*, close to the centre, just off Piaţa Pache Protopopescu. It offers free breakfast, laundry service, Romanian cigarettes, beer and one hour of Internet use every day. Take trolleybus No 85 from Gara de Nord to Calea Morşilor; or No 783 from Otopeni airport to Piaţa Universităţii, then any trolleybus three stops east to Calea Morşilor.

Villa Helga *(☎/fax 610 22 14; ⓦ www.rotravel.com/hotels/helga; Str Salcâmilor 2; dorm beds US$9.90)* provides a dorm bed, breakfast, kitchen facilities, free laundry and locally produced Carpaţi cigarettes. It's conveniently close to the centre, east of Piaţa Romană, past Piaţa Gemeni.

Hotels Bucharest features plenty of grotty one- and two-star hotels, clustered around the train station and in the city centre. **Hotel Marna** *(☎ 212 83 66, fax 312 94 55; ⓔ marna@xnet.ro; Str Buzeşti 3; singles/doubles/triples with shared bathroom US$12/20/30)* is perhaps the best of the station bunch, with a welcoming reception and renovated rooms. **Hotel Bucegi** *(☎ 212 71 54, fax 212 66 41; Str Witing 2; singles/doubles/triples/quads with shared bathroom US$16/25/30/40)*, 30m from the train station, is a noisy but surprisingly clean hotel with cramped rooms.

Bucharest's most aesthetically pleasing budget option is **Hotel Carpaţi** *(☎ 315 01 40, fax 312 18 57; Str Matei Millo 16; singles/doubles with shared bathroom US$12/28)*. A sparkling reception area leads to pleasant singles with shared bathroom. Doubles with private shower *or* toilet are more expensive. **Hotel Muntenia** *(☎ 314 60 10, fax 313 68 19; ⓦ muntenia.kappa.ro; Str Academiei 19-21; singles/doubles/triples with shared bathroom US$16/25/33, suite US$50)* is large and noisy but has a great location near the university.

Places to Eat

Bucharest is plastered with fast-food outlets and 24-hour kiosks selling hot dogs, burgers, popcorn, *covrigi* (rings of hard bread speckled with salt crystals) and other munch-while-you-walk snacks.

Restaurants With a rash of flashy restaurants serving expensive international cuisine, dining out can be expensive. However, it is still easy to track down traditional Romanian dishes in cheap and cheerful restaurants.

La Mama *(☎ 212 40 86; Str Barbu Văcărescu 3; mains around US$2.50)*, a convivial contemporary spot a little north of the centre, dishes up hearty portions of munch-worthy Romanian cuisine for a delicious price. Reservations are essential.

Nicoreşti *(☎ 211 24 80; Str Maria Rosetti 40; mains US$1.50-4)* is a popular place with good-sized portions.

Count Dracula Club *(☎ 312 13 53; e romantic@fx.ro; Splaiul Independenţei 8a; mains US$1.70-5)* is a ghoulish restaurant where human skulls, pickled bats and blood-dripping walls enliven the dining experience. For the full house-of-horror effect, eat in the coffin-clad chapel.

Caru cu Bere *(☎ 313 75 60; Str Stavropoleos 3; dishes around US$3.50)*, a beer hall dating from 1875, is worth a visit for its lavish, Gothic-style decor. Traditional Romanian dishes appear dirt-cheap – until you realise prices are listed per 100g.

Cafés Bucharest is riddled with *cofetărias* specialising in Turkish coffee and freshly made cakes, pastries and other sweet-tooth temptations. **Café Einstein** *(☎ 230 43 84; Str Beller 1)*, overlooking Piaţa Dorobanţilor, is connected to Brutăria Deutschland, a German-style bakery producing the best bread in town.

Amsterdam Grand Café *(☎ 313 75 80; Str Covaci 6)*, one block north of the Old Princely Court, is Bucharest's hot new spot to unwind over a frothy cappuccino. With comfy leather chairs, a well-stocked bar, scrumptious snacks and a soon-to-be-opened upstairs restaurant, its longevity is assured.

Self Catering Three **open-air markets** have fresh fruit and vegies: one at Piaţa Amzei between Calea Victoriei and Blvd General Magheru; another on Piaţa Gemeni; and a third east of Piaţa Unirii.

Unic and **Vox Maris** *(open 24hr)* supermarkets have branches on Piaţa Amzei; Vox Maris has a second branch on Piaţa Victoriei. For tasty nutty German breads, try **Brutăria Deutschland** *(Str Edgar Quinet 5, Piaţa Dorobanţilor)*.

Entertainment

For a weekly what's-on listing, pick up a copy of *Şapte Seri* (Seven Evenings), a free entertainment magazine widely distributed across town.

Bars & Clubs Painted a vivid orange, **Bar Fly** *(☎ 252 02 93; Blvd Ferdinand I 3)* is a genial cellar bar playing a thoroughly eclectic mix of music covering everything from the Beatles to Christmas carols – even in April.

The Harp *(☎ 335 65 08; Str Bibescu Voda 1)* is the quintessential Irish pub abroad, with plenty of Guinness and hearty pub grub. **Planter's Club** *(☎ 659 76 06; Str Mendeleev 35)* is one of Bucharest's most popular drinking holes, crammed with an English-speaking crowd most nights until 5am.

Tipsy *(Blvd Schitu Măugureanu 13)* is a simple but soulful bar, which markets itself as the capital's only 'plub' (pub-club). Its outside terrace buzzes until 4am in summer.

Backstage *(☎ 312 39 45; Str Gabroveni 14)* is the top joint for live bands. There's also trendy **Lăptăria Enache** *(w www.laptaria.totalnet.ro; Blvd Nicolae Bălcescu 2)*, a rooftop bar on the 4th floor of the National Theatre (enter via the unmarked entrance on the theatre's northern side).

Club A *(☎ 315 68 53; Str Blănari 4)*, run by university students from the architecture faculty, teems with students seeking cheap drinks most weekends. **Salsa 2** *(Str Luterană)*, a large nightclub behind Hotel Bucureşti, is filled with bongos, steel drums and body-beat dancers.

Twice *(Str Sf Vineri)*, a hot new spot in the centre, pumps nightly to techno (downstairs) and grooves to trashy '80s and '90s disco tunes (upstairs).

The best gay-friendly club in Bucharest is **Casablanca** *(☎ 330 12 06; Sala Polivalentă)*, in Parcul Tineretului.

Classical Music & Theatre Attending a performance at the **Ateneul Român** *(☎ 315 87 98; box office: ☎ 315 68 75; Str Benjamin Franklin 1; tickets US$1.25-3; box office open noon-7pm)*, home to the George Enescu philharmonic orchestra, is a must. Performances start at 6.30pm or 7pm.

Bucharest has countless theatres, offering a lively mix of comedy, farce, satire and straight contemporary plays. Tickets cost about US$3. Theatres close in July and August.

The most sought-after tickets are those for performances at the **Teatrul Naţional Ion Luca Caragiale** *(Ion Luca Caragiale National Theatre; ☎ 614 71 71, 615 47 46; Blvd Nicolae Bălcescu 2)*, opposite Hotel Inter-Continental. The box office is on the southern side of the building facing Blvd Carol I.

Getting There & Away

Air International flights use **Otopeni airport** *(☎ 230 16 02)*, located 17km north of Bucharest. Numerous airlines have offices in the city on Blvd Nicolae Bălcescu or Blvd General Magheru.

Train Most express trains and many local trains use **Gara de Nord** *(☎ 223 08 80; Blvd Gării de Nord 2)*. Some trains to/from Snagov and Tulcea depart from **Gara Obor** *(☎ 252 02 04; Blvd Gării Obor)* and some to Constanţa use **Gara Băneasa** *(☎ 222 48 56; Piaţa Gării)*.

At Gara de Nord, tickets for international destinations are sold in the 1st-class ticket hall. Express train tickets are sold at the station one hour before departure.

Wasteels *(☎ 222 78 44; w www.wasteels travel.ro)*, which sells discounted tickets to Western Europe for under-26s, is on the right as you enter the main building. Advance ticket purchases can be made from a **CFR office** *(main office: Str Domniţa Anastasia 10-14)*.

International trains going to/from Bucharest include services to Belgrade, Bratislava, Budapest, İstanbul, Kyiv, Kraków, Moscow, Munich, Prague, Sofia, Vienna and Warsaw.

Bus Bucharest's central bus station – more a bus stop, really – is outside Hotel Ibis on Calea Griviţei. Domestic services are poor and everchanging timetables are stuck on lamp posts; drivers sell tickets.

Several private bus companies around Piaţa Gara de Nord, such as **Ortadoğu Tur** *(☎ 312 24 23, 637 67 78; Piaţa Gara de Nord 1)*, operate daily buses to İstanbul (US$27/51 one way/return). Tickets for buses to Chişinău (US$10/20 one way/return) in Moldova are sold at **Autotrans** *(☎ 312 22 11, 335 32 90)* next door.

Tickets for daily buses to Germany are sold by **Double T** *(☎ 313 36 42; e doublet@fx.ro; Calea Victoriei 2)* or **Touring** *(☎ 230 36 61; e touring.rez@eurolines.ro; Str Sofia 26)*.

Getting Around

To/From the Airport Going to the city centre from Otopeni, catch bus No 783 outside the main terminal; buy a ticket (double-journey tickets only, US$0.90) at the kiosk or from the bus driver. Avoid using taxi drivers at the airport.

Public Transport For buses, trams and trolleybuses, buy tickets (US$0.17) at streetside RATB kiosks marked *casă de bilete* or *bilete*. Validate your ticket on board or risk a US$5 fine. One-day/weekly passes (US$0.60/2.10) entitle you to unlimited travel on buses, trams and trolleybuses.

The metro has three lines, handy for getting around the centre. You can buy a magnetic-stripped card for two/10 rides (US$0.30/1.50) at a subterranean kiosk.

Taxi Opt for a cab with a meter and honest driver: **Cristaxi** *(☎ 9461/6)* and **Meridian** *(☎ 9444)* are reputable. Flag one down on the street or call one. The fixed metered rate usually works out at US$0.45 per kilometre.

Most taxi drivers that hang around the airports and Gara de Nord are unscrupulous.

Transylvania

To most people, the name 'Transylvania' conjures images of haunted castles, werewolves and vampires. Certainly the 14th-century castles at Râşnov and Bran appear ready-made for a Dracula movie.

The charms of Transylvania are far more diverse – mountain scenery, some of Romania's best hiking and skiing, and rural villages that haven't changed much since the 18th century. For lovers of medieval art and history, it's an unparalleled chance to see an overlooked corner of the old Austro-Hungarian empire.

SINAIA

☎ 0244

OK, strictly speaking Sinaia is in Wallachia – but it's conveniently close to Transylvania (although it's also an easy day trip from Bucharest). This popular ski resort snuggles at an altitude of 800m to 930m in the narrow Prahova Valley, at the foot of the Bucegi Mountains.

Although its monastery has existed since the 17th century, Sinaia developed into a major resort only after King Carol I decided to build his summer residence, the magnificent Peleş Castle, there in 1870. A railway line from Bucharest followed in 1879 and the local elite soon arrived en masse. Until 1920 the Hungarian-Romanian border ran along Predeal Pass just north of Sinaia.

Orientation & Information

The train station is directly below the centre of town. From the station climb up the stairway across the street to busy Blvd Carol I. The Hotel Montana and cable car are to the left, the monastery and palace are uphill to the right.

Surmont Sports *(Str Cuza Vodă)*, at the base of the cable-car station, sells hiking maps, skis, tents and imported outdoor gear.

There are currency exchanges inside Hotels International and Montana along Blvd Carol I. **Banca Comercială Română** *(open 8am-5.30pm Mon-Fri, 8.30am-12.30pm Sat)*, just past the Hotel Montana, gives cash advances on Visa/MasterCard; it also has an ATM.

Things to See & Do

The major sight is **Mănăstirea Sinaia** (Sinaia Monastery), named after Mt Sinai. The large Orthodox church dates from 1846, and an older church (1695) with its original frescoes is in the compound to the left.

Just past the monastery is the road to **Peleş Castle** *(admission US$3)*, the former royal palace, dating from 1883. It is one of Romania's finest castles, built in the German-Renaissance style. The queue can be long on weekends, but it's worth waiting. A few hundred metres uphill from the main palace is the smaller **Pelişor Palace** *(admission US$2)*, in mock-medieval style. Tours for both are given between 9.15am and 3.15pm Wednesday to Sunday.

Sinaia is a great base for **hiking** in the Bucegi Mountains. Nonhikers should take the **cable car** *(☎ 311 674; Str Telecabinei; open 8am-4pm Tues-Sun)* from Hotel Montana to Cota 2000.

Sinaia's big attraction is **skiing**. It has 10 downhill tracts, three cross-country trails, three sleigh slopes and a bobsled slope. The **snow ski school and gear shop** *(☎ 311 198; Str Cuza Vodă 2a)*, at the foot of the cable-car station behind Hotel Montana, rents complete snowboard and ski equipment for US$7 a day.

Places to Stay & Eat

Hang around at the train station for a few minutes and you'll be offered a private room. The going rate is US$8 to US$10 per person.

By the cable-car station is **Hotel Alpin** *(☎ 312 351; Cota 1400)*. Just below it is **Cabana Brădet** *(☎ 311 551; beds in shared rooms year-round US$6)*. There are similar prices for shared rooms at **Cabana Valea cu Brazi** *(☎ 313 635)* above the cable car at 1500m; a path leads up from Hotel Alpin.

The cheapest real hotel option is **Pensiunea Parc** *(☎ 314 821; Blvd Carol I; doubles US$10)*. It has 12 doubles with shared bathroom. **Hotel Sinaia** *(☎ 311 551; w www.mmc.ro/sinaia; Blvd Carol I 8; 2-star singles/doubles US$20/30, 3-star US$27/42)*, across from Pensiunea Parc, has pleasant well-priced rooms. **Hotel Montana** *(☎ 312 751; Blvd Carol I 24; singles/doubles US$25/40)*, near the cable car, is also another affordable option.

Taverna Sârbului *(☎ 314 400; Calea Codrului I; dishes US$1-4)* is a new traditional Romanian restaurant, considered by some to be the region's best. **Brutăria Deutschland** *(☎ 312 552; Blvd Carol I 8; snacks US$0.50-3, dishes US$1-4)* is a good, cheap place to fill up on doughnuts, coffee and beer between ski runs. It also doubles as a German restaurant.

Getting There & Away

Sinaia is on the Bucharest–Braşov train line.

BRAŞOV (BRASSÓ)

☎ 0268 • pop 319,908

Braşov is one of Romania's most visited cities – and for good reason. Piaţa Sfatului, the central square, is the finest in the country, lined with baroque facades and pleasant outdoor cafés. Within easy reach are ski resorts, the castles of Bran and Râşnov, and trails into the dramatic Bucegi Mountains.

The Gara (train station) is a long way from the city centre. Take bus No 4 (buy tickets at a kiosk) to Parcul Central or Str Mureşenilor. Strada Republicii, Braşov's pedestrian-only promenade, is crowded with shops and cafés from Parcul Central to Piaţa Sfatului.

Braşov has two main bus stations: Autogara 1, next to the train station, and Autogara 2, west of the train station near the Stadion Tineretului stop (local bus Nos 12 and 22 go to/from the centre).

Information

At long last Braşov has an official **Tourist Information Office** *(main hall at the train station; open daily)*, which can book accommodation and provide detailed information on Braşov and the surrounding areas.

Numerous currency exchange outlets are scattered throughout the city. **Banca Comercială Română** *(BCR; Piaţa Sfatului 14; open 8.30am-5pm Mon-Fri, 8.30am-noon Sat)* cashes travellers cheques, gives cash advances on Visa/MasterCard and has an ATM, as does **Banca Comercial Ion Ţiriac** *(BCIT;*

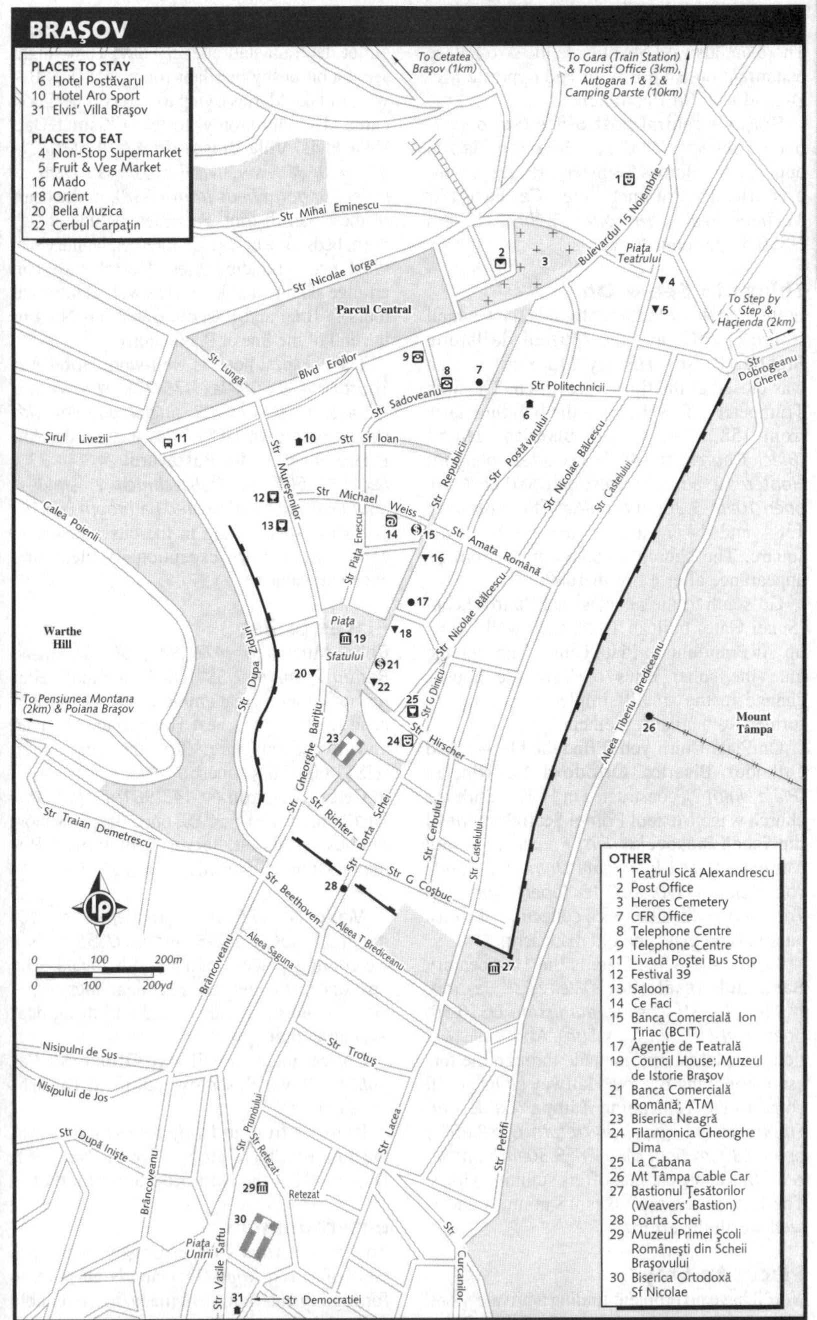
BRAŞOV
PLACES TO STAY
6 Hotel Postăvarul
10 Hotel Aro Sport
31 Elvis' Villa Braşov
PLACES TO EAT
4 Non-Stop Supermarket
5 Fruit & Veg Market
16 Mado
18 Orient
20 Bella Muzica
22 Cerbul Carpaţin
OTHER
1 Teatrul Sică Alexandrescu
2 Post Office
3 Heroes Cemetery
7 CFR Office
8 Telephone Centre
9 Telephone Centre
11 Livada Poştei Bus Stop
12 Festival 39
13 Saloon
14 Ce Faci
15 Banca Comercială Ion Ţiriac (BCIT)
17 Agenţie de Teatrală
19 Council House; Muzeul de Istorie Braşov
21 Banca Comercială Română; ATM
23 Biserica Neagră
24 Filarmonica Gheorghe Dima
25 La Cabana
26 Mt Tâmpa Cable Car
27 Bastionul Ţesătorilor (Weavers' Bastion)
28 Poarta Schei
29 Muzeul Primei Şcoli Româneşti din Scheii Braşovului
30 Biserica Ortodoxă Sf Nicolae
To Cetatea Braşov (1km)
To Gara (Train Station) & Tourist Office (3km), Autogara 1 & 2 & Camping Darste (10km)
To Step by Step & Haçienda (2km)
To Pensiunea Montana (2km) & Poiana Braşov
Str Mihai Eminescu
Str Nicolae Iorga
Bulevardul 15 Noiembrie
Piaţa Teatrului
Parcul Central
Blvd Eroilor
Str Lungă
Str Sadoveanu
Str Politechnicii
Şirul Livezii
Str Sf Ioan
Str Mureşenilor
Str Republicii
Str Poştă varului
Str Nicolae Bălcescu
Str Castelului
Str Dobrogeanu Gherea
Str Michael Weiss
Str Amata Română
Str Piaţa Enescu
Calea Poienii
Piaţa Sfatului
Warthe Hill
Str Dupa Ziduri
Str Gheorghe Baritiu
Str G Dinicu
Str Hirscher
Aleea Tiberiu Brediceanu
Mount Tâmpa
Str Traian Demetrescu
Str Richter
Str Porta Schei
Str Cerbului
Str G Coşbuc
Str Beethoven
Aleea T Brediceanu
Aleea Saguna
Brâncoveanu
Str Trotuş
Nisipulni de Sus
Nisipului de Jos
Str După Inişte
Str Prundului
Str Retezat
Retezat
Str Lacea
Str Petőfi
Str Curcanilor
Piaţa Unirii
Str Vasile Saftu
Str Democratiei
0 100 200m
0 100 200yd

Str Michael Weiss 20; open 9am-3.30pm). There are also ATMs outside the Aro Palace restaurant on Blvd Eroilor and opposite McDonald's on Str Republicii.

Braşov's **central post office** *(Str Iorga 1; open 7am-8pm Mon-Fri, 8am-1pm Sat)* is opposite the Heroes Cemetery. Braşov's most user-friendly Internet café, **Ce Faci** *(Str Michael Weiss 18; open 24hr)*, charges US$0.50 per hour for access.

Things to See & Do

In the middle of Piaţa Sfatului is the Council House (1420), now the **Muzeul de Istorie Braşov** (Braşov History Museum), which was closed at the time of research. The 58m Trumpeter's Tower above the building dates from 1582. The Gothic **Biserica Neagră** *(Black Church; ☎ 144 143; Curtea Johannes Honterus 2; adult/concession US$0.65/0.30; open 10am-3.30pm Mon-Sat)*, built between 1384 and 1477, looms just south of the square. The church's name comes from its appearance after a fire in 1689.

Go south to the neoclassical **Poarta Schei** (Schei Gate) built in 1828, then walk 500m up Str Prundului to Piaţa Unirii. Through the gate the sober rows of Teutonic houses change to the small, simpler houses of the former Romanian settlement.

On Piaţa Unirii you'll find the black-spired Orthodox **Biserica Ortodoxă Sf. Nicolae** *(Piaţa Unirii 2)*, constructed in 1595. Beside the church is the **Muzeul Primei Şcoli Româneşti din Scheii Braşovului** *(First Romanian School Museum; ☎ 143 879; Piaţa Unirii 2-3; adult/concession US$0.30/0.15; open 9am-5pm Tues-Sun)*, which houses a collection of icons, paintings on glass and old manuscripts.

Just before Schei Gate is the 16th-century **Bastionul Ţesătorilor** *(Weavers' Bastion; ☎ 310 919; Str Coşbuc; admission US$0.30; open 9am-5.30pm Tues-Sun)*. Above the bastion is a pleasant promenade through the forest overlooking Braşov. Halfway along you'll come to the **Telecabina Tâmpa** *(Cable Car; Str Brediceanu; one way/return US$0.65/1; open 9.30am-5pm Mon-Fri, 9.30am-6pm Sat & Sun)*, a cable car that offers stunning views. The hike to the top takes 45 minutes and is well worth the effort.

Places to Stay

You'll have no problem finding a private room. The infamous **Maria and Grig Bolea** *(☎ 311 962; rooms per person US$7-10)* hang out at the train station every day. They might seem a bit pushy but their rooms are fine. Beware of fake Marias trying to trade off her good name. The city's only hostel is **Kismet Dao Villa/Elvis' Villa Braşov** *(☎ 478 930, 0721-844 940; W www.elvisvilla.com; Str Democratiei 2B; dorm beds from US$8)*, in the heart of the Schei district. Facilities include comfy dorm beds, free breakfast, Internet, laundry service, beer and cigarettes. Hostel staff can arrange ski hire and lessons as well as informal tours to Bran and Râşnov. Catch bus No 4 to the end of the line at Piaţa Unirii.

The cheapest hotel is well-worn **Hotel Aro Sport** *(☎ 478 800, fax 475 228; W www.aro-palace.ro; Str Sf Ioan 3; singles/doubles with shared bathroom US$11/14)*, behind the Aro Palace Hotel. **Hotel Postăvarul** *(☎ 144 330, fax 141 505; Str Politechnicii 2; singles/doubles/triples with shared bathroom US$14/20/30)* is smack-bang in the city's medieval centre. Rooms are exceptionally clean and excellent value.

Places to Eat

Bella Muzica *(☎ 476 946; Str Gheorghe Baritiu 2; mains US$1.50-4)*, a small cellar restaurant with great ambience, is the place to head for the city's best Hungarian, Mexican and Romanian fare. Try the bean soup (US$1.60) – it's superb!

Cerbul Carpaţin *(☎ 143 981; Piaţa Sfatului 12; mains US$1.50-5)*, once Braşov's most famous restaurant, serves your typical Romanian fare. Some nights there's live folk music.

Mado *(☎ 475 385; Str Republicii 10; menu specials US$2-3, mains US$2-5)* is a welcoming place, popular with locals. The upstairs restaurant has excellent menu specials including a main, salad and drink deal available until 8pm.

Coffee lingerers will love **Orient** *(Str Republicii 2)*, which serves traditional Turkish-style coffee.

Braşov's **fruit and vegetable market** is at the northern end of Str N Bălcescu. Nearby in Duplex '91 is the **Non-Stop Supermarket**.

Entertainment

To find out what's on in Braşov, pick up a copy of *Zile şi Nopţi* (Day and Night), a free fortnightly entertainment magazine, available throughout town.

The three hippest bars in Braşov are **Saloon** *(☎ 141 611; Str Mureşenilor 11-13)*, a pub with a cellar bar; **La Cabana** *(Str Hirsher 1)*, a traditional dimly lit, smoke-filled bar; and the trendy **Festival 39** *(☎ 0754-415 991; Str Mureşenilor 23)*, with cosy decor and delightful staff. **Haçienda** *(☎ 413 971; Str Carpaţilor 17)* is a large disco in an old factory east of the centre.

The **Teatrul Sică Alexandrescu** *(☎ 418 850; Piaţa Teatrului 1)* has plays, recitals and opera throughout the year, or catch performances at the **Filarmonica Gheorghe Dima** *(☎ 143 113; Str Hirscher 10)*. Get information about both at the **Agenţie de Teatrală** *(Str Republicii 4)*, just off Piaţa Sfatului.

Getting There & Around

Train Advance tickets are sold at the **CFR office** *(☎ 142 912; Str Republicii 53; open 8am-7pm Mon-Fri, 9am-1pm Sat)*. International tickets can also be purchased in advance from **Wasteels** *(☎ 424 313)* in the train station hall.

Braşov is well connected to Sighişoara (128km), Cluj-Napoca (331km) and Oradea (484km) by fast trains. Local trains to/from Sinaia (45km) run frequently. Local trains from Braşov to Sibiu (223km) drop off hikers heading for the Făgăraş Mountains. The international trains *Dacia*, *Traianus* and *Ister* go to Budapest (707km). The *Pannonia Expres* runs to Budapest (707km), Bratislava (922km) and Prague (1323km). The *Carpati* goes to Warsaw (1499km) and Kraków.

Bus Braşov has two main bus stations. **Autogara 1** is next to the train station; international buses arrive/depart from here, as do buses to other Romanian towns. Every Thursday there's a 7am bus to Budapest (US$13, 17 hours). Local travel agencies have information on private buses to Germany, Hungary, Poland and Bulgaria.

Autogara 2 *(Str Avram Iancu 114)*, west of the train station, has buses to Bran/Râşnov every half hour (US$0.50, pay the driver). Daily buses also leave here for Făgăraş. Take local bus No 12 or 22 from the centre to the **Stadion Tineretului stop** on Str Stadionului.

BRAN & RÂŞNOV

☎ 0268

It's difficult to visit Romania without seeing **Bran Castle** *(☎ 238 332; Str Principală 498; adult/concession US$2/0.65, camera/video US$1.70/4.70)*, dating from 1378, in travel brochures or on postcards. Though this fairytale 'Dracula' castle is impressive, the real Vlad Ţepeş probably never set foot here. Râşnov offers the ruins of 13th-century **Râşnov Castle** *(☎ 230 255; adult/concession US$0.80/0.50; open Tues-Sun)*, more dramatic and much less touristy than the castle at Bran.

A good lodging option is **Hanul Bran** *(☎ 236 404; Str Principală 363; doubles/triples US$8/12)*, a rustic old inn near the castle. **ANTREC** *(☎/fax 236 884; Str Lucian Bologa 10)* arranges inexpensive accommodation in 250 private homes in Bran and the surrounding villages.

Popasul Reginei *(☎ 236 834; Str Aurel Stoian 398; doubles/triples US$12.50/15.50)* is a clean, modern motel with pleasant rooms and a restaurant. **Vila Bran** *(☎ 236 886; Str Principală 271; doubles/triples with shared bathroom US$16/24)* is superbly positioned in a picturesque orchard.

In Râşnov, **Hotel Cetate** *(☎ 230 266; doubles/triples US$16/22)* is directly below the castle on the road to Poiana Braşov.

Buses to Bran and Râşnov (US$0.50) leave every half-hour from Braşov's Autogara 2. It's best to visit Bran first and then stop at Râşnov on the way back. Return buses leave Bran every hour between 5.30am and 7.30pm.

SIGHIŞOARA

☎ 0265

Sighişoara (Schässburg in German, Segesvár in Hungarian), birthplace of Vlad Ţepeş, is a perfectly preserved medieval town in beautiful hilly countryside. Eleven towers stand along Sighişoara's intact city walls, inside which are sloping cobblestone streets lined with 16th-century burgher houses and untouched churches. All trains between Bucharest and Budapest pass through here, as do several trains a day from Braşov.

Information

Elvis' Villa Sighişoara (see Places to Stay) operates a **Tourist Information Booth** *(open daily)* at the train station. **Steaua Agenţie de Turism** *(☎ 771 932; Str 1 Decembrie 10; open Mon-Sat)* arranges private rooms and has information on weekly buses to Hungary and Germany.

You can cash travellers cheques and get Visa/MasterCard cash advances at **Banca**

Raising the Stakes

The Romanian government plans to breathe life into the country's ailing tourism industry by promoting its notorious son, Vlad Ţepeş (Dracula). Government officials plan to attract one million tourists a year to its new Dracula theme park, being built above Sighişoara. The government hopes the park, expected to open in 2003, will create 3000 much-needed new jobs and generate US$20 million in revenue per year.

Critics fear the park, which has been labelled 'sinful' by a group of Lutheran clergymen, will 'suck the life' out of Sighişoara's charming medieval town. Prince Charles, who visited Romania in May 2000, said the project would 'destroy the city's character' and 'be a tragic loss for the local inhabitants and for Europe as a whole'. Greenpeace has argued that the project not only threatens Sighişoara's Unesco-protected medieval citadel but could lead to the destruction of the nearby ancient oak forests.

Meanwhile, the Romanian government, undeterred, has started construction, determined that the Dracula Park will 'slay 'em'.

Comerciala Română *(Str 1 Mai 12; open 8.30am-noon Mon-Fri)*; or at **Banca Românа Pentru Dezvoltare** *(Piaţa Hermann Oberth; open 8am-2pm Mon-Fri)*. Both have ATMs.

The **telephone centre** *(open 7am-9pm Mon-Fri, 8am-1pm & 5pm-8pm Sat)* is in the **main post office** *(Piaţa Hermann Oberth 17)*. **Net Café** *(Str Nicolae Iorga; open 10am-11pm daily)* charges US$0.50 per hour for Internet access.

Things to See

The first tower above Piaţa Hermann Oberth is the massive **Turnul cu Ceas** *(clock tower; Piaţa Muzeului)*. The 14th-century tower is now the **Muzeul de Istorie**, with a good collection of WWI-era photographs, a scale model of the town and a superb view from the walkway on top. Under the tower is the **Camera de Tortură** (Torture Room Museum). On the western side of the clock tower is a small house that contains a **Muzeul** with antique firearms and a small Dracula exhibition. All three museums are open daily, and the US$1.25 admission price covers all three. Across Piaţa Muzeului is **Casa Vlad Dracul**, where Vlad the Impaler was born in 1431.

Places to Stay

Hostels The third Elvis hostel is friendly **Elvis' Villa Sighişoara** *(☎ 772 546; W www.elvisvilla.com; Str Libertăţii 10; dorm beds from US$8)*. As well as the standard free breakfast, laundry service, Internet, beer and cigarettes, your host Nathan will introduce you to local hiking trails.

Sighişoara Hostel *(☎/fax 772 234; e youthhostel@ibz.org.ro; Bastionul 46; dorm beds US$6.50)*, in the citadel, boasts Internet access, laundry facilities, kitchen and a bar. Breakfast is not included.

Hotels The best deal is the small, clean **Hotel Chic** *(☎ 775 901; Str Libertăţii 44; doubles with shared bathroom US$10)*, directly opposite the train station. This place is rough – lone females should be wary.

Hotel Steaua *(☎ 771 594, fax 771 932; Str 1 Decembrie 12; singles/doubles US$10/14, with bathroom US$14/18)* is a dreary place with dark, musty rooms. **Hotel Rex** *(☎ 777 615; Str Dumbravel 18; doubles US$25)*, 1km east of the old town, is a nicer option. It has clean, modern double rooms with bath and cable TV, and rates include breakfast.

Places to Eat

Restaurant Rustic *(☎ 0723-805 355; Str Hermann Oberth 5; mains US$2-3.50)* serves hearty portions of traditional Romanian dishes.

Casa Vlad Dracul *(☎ 518 108; Str Cositorarilor 5; mains US$2.40-3.70)*, in Vlad's former house, is a must for Dracula freaks.

Scrumptious **Ristorante Pizzeria 4 Amici** *(☎ 772 652; Str Octavian Goga 12; pizzas US$1.20-1.55, pasta US$1-2.45)* has outside tables.

The daily **market** off Str Tîrnavei has a good selection of fruit, vegetables and cheeses. **L&M Alimentara** *(Str Ilarie Chendi)* is a well-stocked supermarket.

Entertainment

Two popular drinking holes in the citadel are **Culture Pub** *(Str Bastionul)*, serving cheap snacks and cold beers, and **Dracula's Club B** *(southern side of the Primăria)*, with pool tables and dart boards. Both have Internet access. **No Limits** *(☎ 0722-593 791; Str Turnului 1; open 10pm-4am)* is a chic disco, on the right of the arched entry into the citadel.

Getting There & Away

The **CFR office** *(☎ 771 820; Str 1 Decembrie 2; open 7.30am-7.30pm Mon-Fri)* sells domestic and international train tickets. All trains between Bucharest (via Braşov) and Cluj-Napoca stop at Sighişoara.

Buses from the **autogara** *(☎ 771 260)*, adjacent to the train station, include one to Făgăraş (US$1.90, 86km).

CLUJ-NAPOCA

☎ 0264 • pop 332,297

Cut in two by the Someşul Mic River, Cluj (Klausenburg to Germans, Kolozsvár to Hungarians) is as Hungarian as it is Romanian. The old Roman name of Napoca was added to the city's official title to emphasise its Daco-Roman origin. Because Cluj is a major university town it has a relaxed, inviting atmosphere, fine architecture and several good museums. Nearby Turda Gorge is also worth a look.

Information

Cash travellers cheques and get Visa/MasterCard cash advances at **Banca Comercială Română** *(Str George Barţiu 10-12; open 8am-12.30pm Mon-Fri)*. **Banca Română Pentru Dezvoltare** *(Piaţa Unirii 7; open 8.30am-1pm & 2pm-4pm Mon-Fri)* gives cash advances on Visa and has an ATM. The **Prima Exchange office** *(Str Bolyai János 2-4)* is open 24 hours.

The **telephone centre** *(open 7.30am-8pm Mon-Fri, 8am-1pm Sat)* is behind the **post office** *(Str Regele Ferdinand 33; open 7am-8pm Mon-Fri, 7am-1pm Sat)*. **Supernet DNT** *(☎ 430 425; e setsala@supernet.dntcj.ro; Str Iuliu Maniu 1; open 24hr)* charges US$0.80 per hour for Internet access.

The **Continental Agenţie de Turism** *(☎ 195 405, fax 193 977; e conticj@codec.ro; Str Napoca 1; open 9am-5pm Mon-Fri)*, at the Continental Hotel, books hotel rooms. **Pan Travel** *(☎/fax 420 516; w www.pantravel.ro; Str Grozavescu 13)* provides top-notch travellers advice, has a variety of regional tours and arranges private accommodation.

Things to See & Do

Biserica Sfântul Mihail (St Michael's Church), a 15th-century Gothic hall church with a neo-Gothic tower (1859), stands impressively above Piaţa Unirii. On the eastern side of the square is the excellent **Muzeul Naţional de Artă** *(National Art Museum; ☎ 196 953; Piaţa Unirii 30; admission US$0.50; open 10am-4.30pm Wed-Sun)*.

To the west on the Piaţa Muzeului is the interesting **Muzeul Naţional de Istorie a Transilvaniei** *(History Museum of Transylvania; ☎ 191 718; admission US$0.25; open Tues-Sun)*, open since 1859.

Cluj is a major centre for mountain biking, hiking and caving enthusiasts. For details on caves and hiking routes contact the **Transylvanian Ecological Club** *(☎/fax 431 626; w www.greenagenda.org/cet; Apt 6, Str Sindicatelor 3; open 11am-5pm Mon-Fri)*. In the apartment next door you'll find the **Napoca Cycloturism Club** *(☎ 450 013; w www.ccn.ro; Apt 8, Str Sindicatelor 3)*.

Places to Stay

Rooms in private houses can be booked through **ANTREC** *(☎ 198 135, 424 536; Piaţa Avram Iancu 15; rooms per person from US$5)*. For hostel accommodation, contact **Youth Hostels România** *(☎/fax 186 616; w www.dntcj.ro/yhr)*. The new **Retro Hostel** *(☎/fax 450 452; w www.retro.ro; Str Potaissa 13; dorm beds US$9, doubles or triples per person US$13)* has opened near the old city wall.

Opposite the train station, **Hotel Pax** *(☎/fax 433 729; e hotelpax@yahoo.com; Piaţa Gării 2; singles/doubles/triples with shared bathroom US$13/17/22)* is noisy but clean.

Spotless, good-value **Hotel Vlădeasa** *(☎ 194 429; Str Regele Ferdinand 20; singles/doubles/triples US$14/22/29)* is the cheapest option in the centre. **Hotel Central-Melody** *(☎ 197 465, fax 197 468; e melody@codec.ro; Piaţa Unirii 29; singles/doubles from US$23/27)*, overlooking the square, has modest rooms at OK prices.

Places to Eat

Restaurant Privighetoarea *(☎ 193 480; Str Regele Ferdinand 16; dishes US$1-3)*, near Hotel Vlădeasu, doles out hearty portions of meat, potatoes and soups, spicy meatballs and breaded cheese.

Escorial *(☎ 196 909; Piaţa Unirii 23; mains US$2-3, side dishes US$1-2)*, an upmarket cellar restaurant and club with a distinct old-worldly air, serves traditional Hungarian cuisine.

Roata *(☎ 192 022; Str Alexandru Ciura 6a; dishes US$1.25-3)* offers good filling

Romanian dishes such as the *Taci şi înghite mămăligă* for US$1.50.

Gente Senior *(☎ 432 807; Str Horea 5; pizzas & pasta US$1.50-2.50)*, with its refreshingly green interior, serves the largest and most delicious pizzas in Cluj by far.

For fresh produce, the **central market** is behind McDonald's on Piaţa Mihai Viteazul. For self-caterers, there's a small **grocery** *(cnr Str Memorandumului & Str David Ferenc; open 24hr)*.

Entertainment

The ever-popular **Music Pub** *(☎ 432 517; Str Horea 5)* hosts live folk, jazz and rock bands on weekends. **Diesel Club** *(☎ 198 441; Piaţa Unirii 17)* and **Flash Bar** *(Piaţa Unirii 10)* attract a more stylish, young crowd. **The King Club** *(☎ 408 392; Str Roosevelt 2; open 24hr)* is a fun bar with a nightly disco. The club draws its large student following with its infamous 'Beer Belly' nights (Wednesday), where for US$2.20 you can drink as much as your 'belly' can stomach.

The neobaroque **Teatrul Naţional & Opera Română** *(National Theatre & Opera House; ☎ 191 799; Piaţa Ştefan cel Mare 24)* was designed by the famous Viennese architects Fellner and Hellmer. Look out for performances at the **Teatrul de Pşi Puck** *(Puck Puppet Theatre; ☎ 195 992; Str Ion IC Brătianu)*. The **Agenţie de Teatrală** *(☎ 195 363; Blvd Eroilor 36)* sells tickets for most events.

Getting There & Away

The **gara** is 1.5km north of the city centre. Advance train tickets are sold at the **CFR office** *(☎ 432 001; Piaţa Mihai Viteazul 20; open 7am-7pm Mon-Fri)*. There are express trains from Cluj to Oradea (2½ hours, 153km), Sighişoara (three hours, 203km), Braşov (five hours, 331km) and Bucharest (eight hours, 497km). Sleepers are available to Bucharest.

A bus to Budapest (US$6.50, 399km, once a week) leaves from the bus station, across the bridge from the train station.

Crişana & Banat

The plains of Crişana and Banat, divided by the Mureş River, merge into Yugoslavia's Vojvodina and Hungary's Great Plain. From the late 9th century until the Ottoman conquest in 1552, the territory was under Hungarian rule.

Crişana and Banat are the door to Romania, and all trains from Hungary and Yugoslavia pass through one of the gateway cities: Timişoara, Arad and Oradea.

ORADEA

☎ 0259 • pop 223,680

Of the cities of the old Austro-Hungarian empire, Oradea (Nagyvárad in Hungarian, Grosswardein in German) is probably the one that has best retained its 19th-century elegance. When Oradea was ceded to Romania in 1920, this example of Habsburg majesty became the backwater it is today – a time capsule for romantics in search of a simpler world.

The gara is a few kilometres north of town; tram Nos 1 and 4 run south from Piaţa Bucureşti (across from the station) to Piaţa Unirii. The main square north of the river is Piaţa Regele Ferdinand.

At the southern end of Piaţa Independenţei **Banca Comercială Română** *(open 8.30am-1pm Mon-Fri)* cashes travellers cheques, gives cash advances on Visa/MasterCard and has an ATM. The bank's Calea Republicii office also has an ATM. The **post office** *(Str Roman Ciorogariu; open 7am-8.30pm Mon-Fri, 8am-1pm Sat)* can help with postal requirements. **Game Star Internet Café** *(Str Mihai Eminescu 4; open 24hr)*, next to the Taverna Bar & Restaurant, charges US$0.50 per hour for access.

Things to See

Oradea's most imposing sights are on Piaţas Unirii and Regele Ferdinand. The Orthodox church on the piaţa is known as the **Biserica cu Lună** (Moon Church), for a 3m sphere that shows the phases of the moon. It was built in 1784. Listen for the trumpet tune playing from the **Primăria Municipiului** (Town Hall) every hour.

Across the bridge from Piaţa Unirii, the green neoclassical **Teatrul de Stat** (State Theatre), designed by Viennese architects Fellner and Hellmer and built in 1900, dominates Piaţa Regele Ferdinand. To its right begins the long, pedestrianised Calea Republicii, lined with bookshops and cafés.

Oradea's other worthy buildings are in a park a block southwest of the train station. Across the road is **Şirul Canonicilor** (Canon's Corridor), a series of archways that date back to the 18th century. The **Catedrala Romano-Catolică** (Catholic Cathedral) built in 1780 is the largest in Romania.

The **Palatul Episcopia Ortodoxă** (Episcopal Palace), with 100 fresco-adorned rooms and 365 windows, was built in 1770 and modelled after Belvedere Palace in Vienna. Now it's the **Muzeul Ţării Crişului** *(Museum of the Land of the Criş Rivers; open Tues-Sun)*, with some of the best history and art exhibits in Romania.

Places to Stay

New **Pension Gobe** *(☎/fax 414 845; Str Dobrogeanu Gherea 26; beds per person from US$10-12)*, on the eastern side of the citadel, is the best budget option. It offers beds in cosy three- or four-bed rooms. There is also a small restaurant and bar, and kitchen facilities are available. Breakfast is included.

The 1908 Art Nouveau **Hotel Vulturul Negru** *(☎ 135 417; Str Independenţei 1; singles/doubles US$7/14, doubles with bathroom US$17)* is musty and worn but otherwise OK. **Hotel Astoria** *(☎ 130 508; Str Teatrului 1; singles/doubles without bathroom US$9/14, doubles with shower US$18)* has more appealing two-star rooms and breakfast is included. Its singles are cramped.

Places to Eat

Restaurant Oradea & Grădina de Vară *(Piaţa Republicii 5-7; dishes US$2-5)* draws a crowd with its lovely outdoor terrace and occasional live music.

Restaurant Olivery *(☎ 432 959; Str Moscovei 12; meals US$3-5)* is an unpretentious cellar restaurant with quality food at reasonable prices.

Calea Republicii is lined with inexpensive cafés and eateries. Stock up on fresh fruit and vegetables at the **Citadel Market** *(Piaţa Independenţei)*.

Getting There & Away

For train inquiries, contact the **CFR office** *(☎ 130 578; Calea Republicii 2; open 7am-7pm Mon-Fri)*. International tickets must be purchased here in advance.

Express trains run east to Cluj-Napoca daily (2½ hours, 153km). Four trains run each day from Oradea to Budapest-Nyugati station (four hours).

From Oradea bus station there are daily services to Deva and Satu Mare, three to Beiuş. A daily bus to Budapest (US$6/10 one way/return, 10 hours) departs from outside the train station at 7.30am. Most of the travel agencies can arrange buses to Budapest, Kraków and cities throughout Austria and Germany.

TIMIŞOARA

☎ 0256 • pop 332,277

Timişoara (Temesvár in Hungarian, Temeschburg in German) was the centre of protests in December 1989, igniting the countrywide uproar that eventually toppled Ceauşescu. Blessed with a beautiful central plaza and some Habsburg-era buildings, it makes for a pleasant stopover on your way into or out of Romania.

Timişoara Nord train station is just west of the city centre. The friendly **Agenţie de Turism Banatul** *(☎ 198 862, fax 191 913; www.turismbanatul.ro; Str 1 Mai 2)* sells town maps. The **Yugoslav consulate** *(☎ 190 334, fax 190 425; Str Remus 4; open 9am-noon Mon-Thur)* is two blocks west of the Technical University.

Cash travellers cheques and get Visa/MasterCard cash advances at **Banca Comercială Română** *(Str 9 Mai; open 8.30am-12.30pm Mon-Fri)*, just off Piaţa Libertăţii. Just off Piaţa Victoriei **Banc Post** *(Blvd Mihai Eminescu; open 8.30am-2.30pm Mon-Fri)* also has an ATM.

Timişoara's most reasonably priced city-centre hotel is **Hotel Banatul** *(☎/fax 191 903; Str Vincenţiu Babes; singles/doubles US$16/22)*. Don't be put off by the grim facade; its newly renovated rooms are spotlessly clean. Breakfast is included.

Hotel Central *(☎ 190 091, fax 190 096; central@online.ro; Str Lenau 6; doubles US$28)*, next door to Cinema Studio, has doubles with bath, TV and breakfast.

Timişoreana Club XXI *(☎ 122 822; Piaţa Victoriei 2; mains US$1-2.85, side dishes US$0.30-0.70)* is a contemporary, 'traditional' Romanian restaurant, complete with loud techno music. Its large outdoor terrace, right in the middle of the Piaţa, is the perfect place to quaff down a local brew of – what else? – Timişoreana Club XXI.

Direct express trains link Timişoara to Iaşi via Cluj-Napoca and Suceava. The service to Bucharest (eight hours) is fairly frequent via Băile Herculane, Drobeta-Turnu Severin and Craiova; sleepers are available to/from

Bucharest. Timişoara is connected with Belgrade by one daily express train, the *Bucureşti* (8 hours, 175km). Advance reservations are required. International tickets must be purchased at the **CFR office** *(☎ 191 889; Piaţa Victoriei 2; open 8am-8pm Mon-Fri)*.

Twice weekly buses connect Timişoara to Békéscsaba (138km) and Szeged (257km). There's a weekly service to Budapest (US$9, eight hours). The international ticket window is open 9am to 5pm weekdays, otherwise you can usually pay the driver.

Southern Bucovina

The painted churches of Southern Bucovina are among the greatest artistic monuments of Europe – in 1993 they were collectively designated a World Heritage Site by Unesco. Erected at a time when northern Moldavia was threatened by Turkish invaders, the monasteries were surrounded by strong defensive walls. Great popular armies would gather inside these fortifications, waiting to do battle. To educate the illiterate peasants who were unable to understand the liturgy, biblical stories were portrayed on the church walls in colourful pictures. The exteriors of many of the churches are completely covered with these magnificent 16th-century frescoes. Remarkably, most of the intense colours have been preserved despite five centuries of rain and wind.

Bucovina's monasteries are generally open 9am to 5pm or 6pm daily. Admission is around US$0.70. The monasteries of Voroneţ, Humor and Moldoviţa, all accessible by bus and train, provide a representative sample of what Bucovina has to offer. The gateway to the painted churches is **Suceava**, erstwhile capital of Moldavia. **Gura Humorului**, a small logging town 37km west of Suceava, is an ideal base for visiting the monasteries.

Slovakia

Vivid folklore, rich architecture and a splendid arts tradition are hallmarks of Slovakia. However, as most tourists don't make it past lively Bratislava, they often miss out on the country's more sublime attractions – the rugged High Tatra mountains, the gentler natural beauty of the Malá Fatra hills, and the canyons of the Slovenský Raj. Meanwhile, East Slovakia boasts a treasury of unspoiled medieval towns, complete with its own mind-boggling array of castles.

Best of all, the majority of Slovaks are warm and friendly people prepared to go out of their way to help you enjoy their country. Even without their help, it's a fantastic destination; with it, you may not want to leave.

Slovakia: the Basics

Local name Slovensko

Capital Bratislava

Population 5.4 million

Languages Slovak, Hungarian

Currency Slovak crown (Sk) = 100 hellers

Avoid at all costs Slovak coffee

Get the most out of rural nightlife by asking *Dá sa tu niekde íst'počúvat' l'udovú hudbu?* (Is there anywhere you can listen to folk music?)

Facts about Slovakia

HISTORY

Slavic tribes first occupied what is now Slovakia in the 5th century AD. When the Turks overran Hungary in the early 16th century, the capital moved to Bratislava. A policy of enforced Magyarisation (Hungarian assimilation) was instituted. As a reaction, Slovak intellectuals cultivated ties with the Czechs. After WWI, Slovakia, Ruthenia, Bohemia and Moravia were united as Czechoslovakia.

But the centralising tendencies of the sophisticated Czechs alienated many Slovaks. The day before Hitler's troops invaded Czech territory in March 1939, a fascist puppet state was set up and Slovakia became a German ally. In August 1944 Slovak partisans instigated the Slovak National Uprising (*Slovenské Národné Povstanie*, or SNP), an event that is now a source of national pride.

After the communist takeover in 1948, power was again centralised in Prague. Many of those who resisted the new communist dictatorship were ruthlessly eliminated by execution, torture or starvation in labour camps. In August 1968, Soviet troops quashed democratic reform.

The Velvet Revolution of 1989 toppled the communist regime. The 1992 elections brought to power the nationalist Movement for a Democratic Slovakia (HZDS), headed by Vladimír Mečiar. In July the Slovak parliament voted to declare sovereignty, and the federation dissolved peacefully on 1 January 1993.

Mečiar's reign saw a proliferation of antidemocratic laws and mistreatment of Slovakia's Hungarian and Roma minorities. It ended when Mikulaš Džurinda, leader of the right-leaning Slovak Democratic Coalition (SDK), was elected prime minister in 1998. Yet Slovak society remains deeply polarised, with continued strong support for Mečiar.

Under Džurinda, Slovakia has moved closer to the West; it is one of 10 countries hoping to enter the EU in 2004, and one of five expected to join NATO by 2003. These plans could go awry if Mečiar regains power.

GEOGRAPHY & CLIMATE

Slovakia sits in the heart of Europe, straddling the northwestern end of the Carpathian

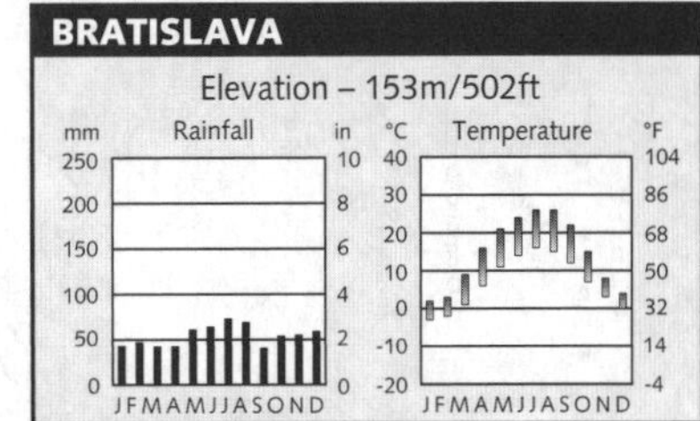

SLOVAKIA

SLOVAKIA

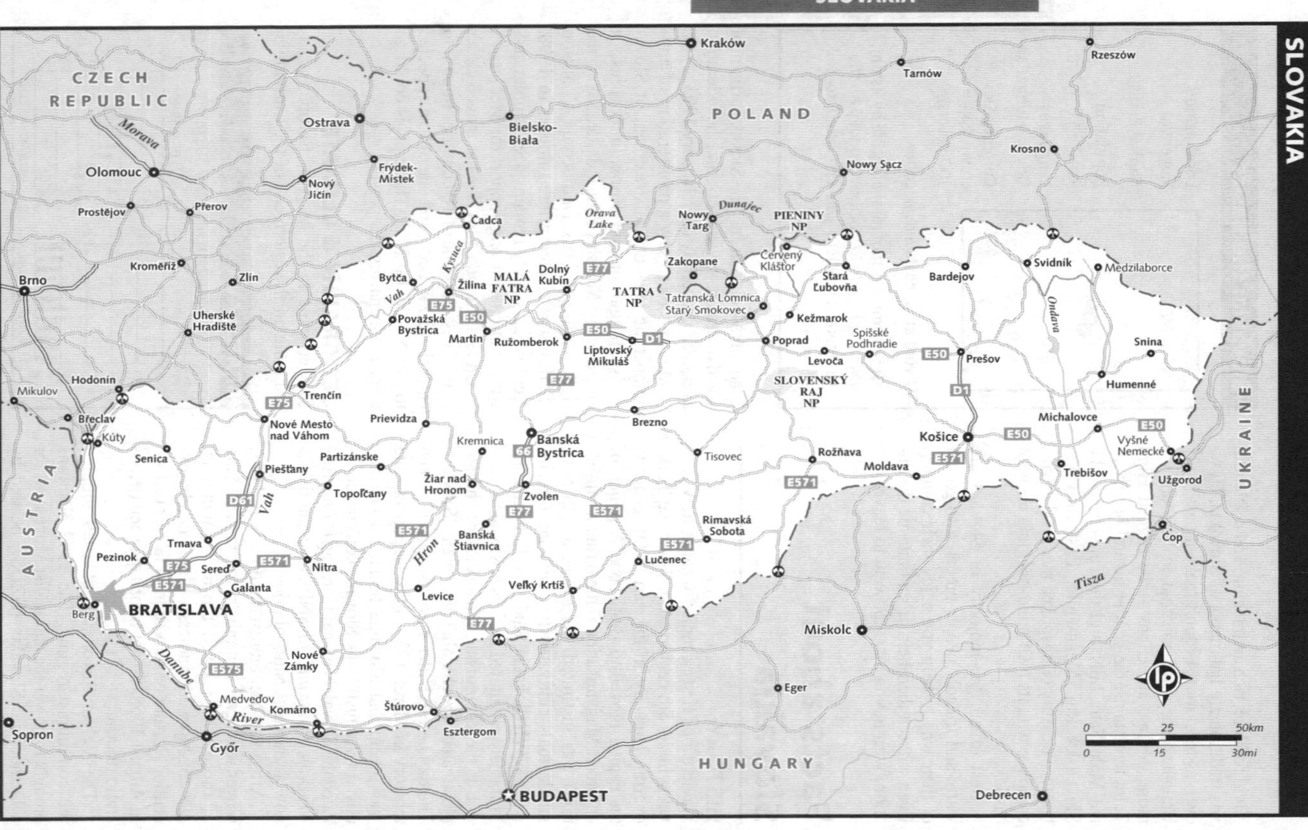

CZECH REPUBLIC
POLAND
UKRAINE
HUNGARY
AUSTRIA
Kraków
Rzeszów
Tarnów
Krosno
Nowy Sącz
Ostrava
Bielsko-Biała
Frýdek-Místek
Nový Jičín
Olomouc
Prostějov
Přerov
Kroměříž
Zlín
Brno
Uherské Hradiště
Hodonín
Mikulov
Břeclav
Kúty
Senica
Čadca
Bytča
Kysuca
Žilina
Považská Bystrica
MALÁ FATRA NP
Martin
Ružomberok
Dolný Kubín
Orava Lake
TATRA NP
Liptovský Mikuláš
Nowy Targ
Dunajec
Zakopane
PIENINY NP
Červený Kláštor
Tatranská Lomnica
Starý Smokovec
Stará Ľubovňa
Kežmarok
Poprad
Spišské Podhradie
Levoča
SLOVENSKÝ RAJ NP
Bardejov
Svidník
Medzilaborce
Ondava
Prešov
Snina
Humenné
Michalovce
Vyšné Nemecké
Užgorod
Trebišov
Čop
Košice
Moldava
Rožňava
Tisovec
Brezno
Trenčín
Nové Mesto nad Váhom
Prievidza
Kremnica
Banská Bystrica
Partizánske
Piešťany
Topoľčany
Žiar nad Hronom
Zvolen
Banská Štiavnica
Rimavská Sobota
Lučenec
Veľký Krtíš
Hron
Váh
Trnava
Pezinok
Sereď
Nitra
Galanta
Levice
Berg
BRATISLAVA
Danube
Nové Zámky
Medveďov
Komárno
River
Štúrovo
Esztergom
Sopron
Győr
BUDAPEST
Miskolc
Eger
Tisza
Debrecen
D1
D61
E50
E571
E77
E75
E575
66
0
25
50km
0
15
30mi

Mountains. Central Slovakia is dominated by the Vysoké Tatry (High Tatra) mountains along the Polish border. The country generally experiences hot summers and cold winters.

GOVERNMENT & POLITICS

Slovakia is a parliamentary republic headed by the president. The cabinet is headed by the prime minister.

POPULATION & PEOPLE

Slovakia's population is 86% Slovak, 10% Hungarian and 1% Czech. Official census figures from 1999 put the Roma population at just 1.7% (90,000), but the true figure is thought to be between 200,000 and 400,000.

SOCIETY & CONDUCT

Slovaks are generally friendly and hospitable. It is customary to say *dobrý den* (good day) when you enter a shop, hotel or restaurant, and *do videnia* (goodbye) when you leave.

If you are invited to someone's home, bring your hosts flowers (an odd number; even numbers are for funerals). If your hosts remove their shoes you should do the same. When attending a classical concert or theatre, dress formally. Casual dress is fine in contemporary venues, such as theatre or rock/jazz concerts.

LANGUAGE

In rural Slovakia very few people speak anything other than Slovak. German is probably the most useful non-Slavic language. See the Language chapter at the back of this book for useful words and phrases.

Facts for the Visitor

HIGHLIGHTS

Bratislava's old town and castle are worth exploring, as are the picturesque, historic towns of Bardejov, Levoča and Košice. Spišský hrad, towering above Spišské Podhradie, is the largest castle in the country.

The rocky peaks of the Vysoké Tatry offer excellent hiking and mountaineering, while the Malá Fatra has good hiking and skiing.

PLANNING

Locals take their holidays in July and August, when mountain areas are at their most crowded, but cities like Bratislava have lower hotel prices and cheap student beds available.

Slow-vakia

Slovakians occasionally seem to harbour a slight inferiority complex with regard to their neighbours and former compatriots, the Czechs. While the inhabitants of the Czech Republic certainly have a more sophisticated reputation than their Slovakian counterparts, boasting larger cities and artistic geniuses such as Kafka and Dvorak, Slovaks actually hit the artistic fast lane before their northern comrades.

Specifically, Slovak folk music is one of the oldest artistic traditions in Europe, tracing its history back to pre-Slavonic days. The melodies and rhythms of the Slovak folk tradition heavily influenced musical development in Eastern Europe, and at festivals (and, occasionally, in pubs) you can hear these sounds much as they developed hundreds of years ago. The musical ethos persists today, evident in the outstanding quality of Slovak orchestras.

So when a Czech brags about living life in the fast lane, you might point out that it might be because the Czechs have so much catching up to do.

Accommodation in mountain resorts is cheapest from May to June and September to October.

TOURIST OFFICES

There is an extensive network of **municipal information centres** *(Mestské informačné centrum; ☎ 16 186)* belonging to the Association of Information Centres of Slovakia (AiCES). The staff speak English, can organise sightseeing tours and guides, and can assist with accommodation. Branches of the commercial agency Satur can also help with accommodation, and ISIC, Euro<26 and IYTC cards are available from some major offices.

The **Slovak Tourist Board** *(☎/fax 224 94 60 82; Purkyňova 4)* has an office in central Prague, but there's no representation in other countries.

VISAS & DOCUMENTS

Nationals of Canada, New Zealand and most European countries do not need a visa for tourist visits of up to 90 days (UK citizens up to 180 days; USA, Italian and South African citizens up to 30 days). At the time of writing, Australians *do* need a visa.

EMBASSIES & CONSULATES

Slovak Embassies

Slovak embassies abroad include:

Australia (☎ 02-6290 1516) 47 Culgoa Circuit, O'Malley, ACT 2606
Austria (☎ 01-318 90 55211) Armbrustergasse 24, 1-1190 Wien
Canada (☎ 613-749 4442) 50 Rideau Terrace, Ottawa, Ontario K1M 2A1
Czech Republic (☎ 233 32 54 43) Pod Hradbami 1, 160 00 Praha 6
France (☎ 01 45 20 78 75) 125 rue de Ranelagh, 75016 Paris
Germany (☎ 030-889 26 20) Pariser Strasse 44, Berlin 107 07 Berlin
Hungary (☎ 01-273 35 00) Stefania ut 22–24, H-1143 Budapest XIV
Netherlands (☎ 070-416 7773) Parkweg 1, 2585 JG The Hague
Poland (☎ 022-525 81 10) Litevska 6, 00-581 Warszawa
UK (☎ 020-7313 6490) 25 Kensington Palace Gardens, London W8 4QY
Ukraine (☎ 044-229 79 22) Jaroslavov val 34, 252 034 Kyiv
USA (☎ 202-237 1054) 3523 International Court NW, Washington, DC 20008

Embassies & Consulates in Slovakia

Australia and New Zealand do not have embassies in Slovakia; the nearest are in Vienna and Berlin respectively. The following are all in Bratislava (area code ☎ 02).

Austria (☎ 54 43 29 85) Ventúrska 10
Czech Republic (☎ 59 20 33 03) Hviezdoslavovo 8
France (☎ 59 34 71 11) Hlavné nám 7
Germany (☎ 54 41 96 40) Hviezdoslavovo nám 10
Hungary (☎ 54 43 05 41) Sedlárska 3
Poland (☎ 54 41 31 96) Hummelova 4
UK (☎ 54 41 96 32) Panská 16
Ukraine (☎ 59 20 28 16) Radvanská 35
USA (☎ 54 43 08 61) Hviezdoslavovo nám 4

CUSTOMS

You can bring in 2L of wine, 1L of spirits and 250 cigarettes, along with a reasonable amount of personal effects and up to 3000 Sk worth of gifts and other noncommercial goods.

You cannot export genuine antiques. If you have any doubts about what you plan to take out of the country, talk to the curatorial staff at the National Museum in Bratislava.

MONEY

Slovakia's currency is the Slovak crown, or Slovenská koruna (Sk), containing 100 *halier* (hellers). There are coins of 10, 20 and 50 hellers, and one, two, five and 10 crowns (Sk). Banknotes come in denominations of 20, 50, 100, 200, 500, 1000 and 5000 crowns.

country	unit		koruna
Australia	A$1	=	24.55 Sk
Canada	C$1	=	28.86 Sk
Eurozone	€1	=	44.52 Sk
Japan	¥100	=	37.91 Sk
NZ	NZ$1	=	21.31 Sk
UK	UK£1	=	70.93 Sk
USA	US$1	=	45.38 Sk

The easiest place to change cash and travellers cheques is at a branch of the Všeobecná úverová banka (VÚB; General Credit Bank), Slovenská sporiteľňa (Slovak Savings Bank) or the Investičná banka (Investment Bank), where you'll be charged a standard 1% commission. Satur offices and post office exchange windows charge 2% commission.

Credit cards (Visa, MasterCard, Eurocard and AmEx mainly) can be used in most major hotels, restaurants and shops. Some of the larger branches of major banks give cash advances on credit cards. ATMs *(bankomat)* are easily found in most towns, and most accept Visa, MasterCard, Eurocard, Plus and Cirrus.

You'll find food, admissions and transport cheap and accommodation manageable, except in Bratislava. If you camp or stay in hostels, eat in local pubs and take local transport, expect to spend about US$15 to US$20 a day.

POST & COMMUNICATIONS

Poste restante mail can be sent to major post offices in larger cities and will be kept for one month; it should be addressed to Poste Restante, Pošta 1.

Old telephone codes (beginning with ☎ 07 to 09) no longer work, but still appear on some signs and publicity materials. For directory inquiries phone ☎ 120 (for the local region) or ☎ 121 (for numbers elsewhere in Slovakia). For international inquiries call ☎ 0149.

International calls can be made at post offices and telephone centres, and from most public phones on the street. Most public telephones now accept cards only, though there are still a few coin phones around. Phonecards *(telefónna karta)* costing 60, 100, 140, 180, or 350 Sk are available from post offices and any shop displaying the phonecard logo.

To call Slovakia from abroad, dial the international access code, ☎ 421 (the country code for Slovakia), the area code (minus the initial zero) and the number. The international access code in Slovakia is ☎ 00.

There are Internet cafés in most large towns and tourist centres.

DIGITAL RESOURCES

The **Slovakia Document Store** *(W slovakia.eunet.sk)* contains links to a wealth of information on Slovakia. Check *The Slovak Spectator* newspaper's site at W www.slovakspectator.sk/default.asp, and W www.slovakia.org for up-to-date news and current affairs.

BOOKS

For a readable history try Stanislav J Kirschbaum's *A History of Slovakia – The Struggle for Survival*. Lonely Planet's *Czech & Slovak Republics* by Richard Nebeský & Neil Wilson gives extensive information on the nuts and bolts of travelling in Slovakia.

GAY & LESBIAN TRAVELLERS

The age of consent is 16, but gay or lesbian partners do not have the same legal status as heterosexual partners. There is a gay organisation called **Ganymedes** *(☎ 02-52 49 57 96; PO Box 4, 830 00 Bratislava)*. The lesbian organisation is **Museion** *(E vamo@ba.psg.sk; Saratovská 3, 841 02 Bratislava for postal inquiries only)*.

DISABLED TRAVELLERS

Transport is a problem as buses and trams have no wheelchair access. For more information contact the **Alliance of Organisations of Disabled People in Slovakia** *(Asociácia organizácií zdravotne postihnutých občanov SR; ☎ 02-52 44 41 19; W www.zutom.sk/aozpo; Žabotova 2, 811 04 Bratislava)*.

DANGERS & ANNOYANCES

Crime is low compared with the West. Some taxi drivers and waiters have been known to overcharge foreigners. Another problem is the increasing number of robberies on international trains.

Recent years have seen a rise in violent racist attacks by skinhead gangs on Roma people, and also on dark-skinned tourists.

BUSINESS HOURS

On weekdays, shops open around 8am or 9am and close at 5pm or 6pm. Many small shops, particularly those in country areas, close for lunch between noon and 2pm, and almost everything closes on Saturday afternoon and all day Sunday.

Most museums and castles are closed on Monday and the day following a public holiday. Many tourist attractions are closed from November to March and open on weekends only in April and October. The main town museums stay open all year.

PUBLIC HOLIDAYS & SPECIAL EVENTS

Public holidays are New Year's & Independence Day (1 January), Three Kings Day (6 January), Good Friday and Easter Monday (March/April), Labour Day (1 May), Cyril and Methodius Day (5 July), SNP Day (29 August), Constitution Day (1 September), Our Lady of Sorrows Day (15 September), All Saints' Day (1 November) and Christmas (24 to 26 December).

During late June or early July folk dancers from all over Slovakia meet at the Východná Folklore Festival, 32km west of Poprad. There are folk festivals in June in Červený Kláštor and Kežmarok, and in many other towns from June to August. The two-week Bratislava Music Festival is held in late September to early October, and the Bratislava Jazz Days weekend is in late October.

ACTIVITIES

Slovakia is one of Eastern Europe's best areas for hiking (see the Malá Fatra, Vysoké Tatry and Slovenský Raj sections for details). There is excellent rock climbing and mountaineering in the Vysoké Tatry, and paragliding is also becoming popular. Contact the **Mountain Guide** *(Horský Vodca; ☎ 052-442 22 60)* office in Starý Smokovec for more information.

Slovakia also offers some of the best cycling terrain in Central Europe, with uncrowded roads and beautiful scenery. East Slovakia,

Emergencies

In the event of an emergency call the following nationwide numbers: ☎ 158 for state police; ☎ 150 for fire, ☎ 155 for ambulance; ☎ 154 for car breakdown assistance.

especially, is prime cycling territory. Mountain biking in the Vysoké Tatry and Slovenský Raj is excellent. **Tatrasport** *(☎ 055-442 52 41)* has branches in Starý Smokovec, Štrbské Pleso and Tatranská Lomnica and rents out mountain bikes for 299 Sk a day.

The country has some of Europe's cheapest ski resorts, but the skiable areas are small and few lifts are linked. The season runs from December to April in the Vysoké Tatry, Nízke Tatry and Malá Fatra. There is good downhill and cross-country skiing in the Vysoké Tatry and the Malá Fatra.

Some of Slovakia's major rivers such as the Váh, Hron and Nitra offer good canoeing and kayaking. **T-Ski** *(☎ 055-442 32 00)* in Starý Smokovec can arrange rafting trips (from 580 Sk per person).

WORK

There are not many job opportunities for non-Slovakian speakers. Your best bet is to find a job teaching English. The **British Council** *(☎ 02-54 43 17 93, Panská 17, Bratislava)* has a teaching centre in Bratislava, or try the **Berlitz Language Centre** *(☎ 02-54 43 37 96; Na vŕšku 6, Bratislava)*.

ACCOMMODATION

Foreigners often pay 30% to 100% more for accommodation than Slovaks. Prices quoted in this chapter are for high season.

Camping

There are several hundred camping grounds, usually open May to September. They're often accessible on public transport, but there's usually no hot water. Most have a small snack bar and many have small cabins for rent that are cheaper than a hotel room. Camping wild in national parks is prohibited.

Hostels

The HI handbook lists an impressive network of hostels, but they're mostly open in July and August only. During this time many student dormitories become temporary hostels. Satur and municipal information offices usually have information on hostels and can make advance bookings for you.

Turistické ubytovňy (tourist hostels) that provide very basic and cheap dormitory accommodation are not connected to the HI network. You can ask about them at information offices.

Private Rooms, Pensions & Hotels

Private rooms (look for signs reading 'privát' or 'Zimmer frei') are usually available in tourist areas (from 200 Sk per person). AiCES tourist information offices and travel agencies like Satur can book them. Some have a three-night minimum-stay requirement.

Many small pensions (often just glorified private rooms) exist in tourist regions, and these usually offer more personalised service and cheaper rates than hotels.

Hotels in Bratislava are considerably more expensive than in the rest of the country. There are five categories, from one star (budget) to five star (luxury). Two-star rooms are typically US$15/20.

FOOD & DRINKS

The cheapest eateries are the self-service restaurants called *jedáleň* or *bistro*, which sometimes have tasty dishes like barbecued chicken or hot German-style sausage.

Soups include *cesnaková polievka* (garlic soup), a treat that is not to be missed. Slovakia's traditional dish is *bryndžové halušky* (dumplings baked with sheep's-milk cheese and bits of bacon). Goulash or *segedín* (also known as *koložárska kapusta* – a beef goulash with sauerkraut in cream sauce) comes with *knedle* (dumplings). *Kapor* (carp) or *pstruh* (trout) can be fried or baked. *Ovocné knedle* or *gulky* (fruit dumplings) come with cottage cheese or crushed poppy seeds as well as melted butter.

Vegetarians are catered for at a small but increasing number of restaurants and health food shops, although in small towns you might be restricted to salads and *vysmážaný syr* (deep-fried cheese). Innocent-looking vegetable-based soups may use a ham or beef stock, and dishes advertised as 'vegetarian' *(bezmasa)* may contain meat.

Slovak wine is good and cheap; the *pivo* (beer) is as good as its Czech equivalents.

Getting There & Away

AIR

Bratislava's MR Štefanik Airport receives only a small number of flights from continental Europe. Vienna's Schwechat airport is just 60km from Bratislava, and is served by a vast range of much cheaper international flights.

LAND

Seven buses a day (four at weekends) link Bratislava to Vienna's Schwechat airport (€7.20, one hour) and central Mitte Busbahnhof (€10.90, 1½ hours). See also Getting There & Away in the Bratislava section.

There are trains from Bratislava to Vienna (Südbahnhof) five times a day (one hour). Bratislava is linked to Budapest (three hours) by several express trains daily. There are daily sleeper services from Bratislava to Kyiv, Ukraine, changing at Košice (30 hours, 1443km), and to Moscow, changing at Warsaw (33 hours, 1991km).

Three daily expresses run between Košice and Muszyna (1¼ hours) in Poland; from Muszyna trains run to Nowy Sącz and (less frequently) to Kraków. There's also a daily train from Košice to Bucharest (15½ hours).

RIVER

An interesting way to enter or leave Slovakia is on the hydrofoils that ply the Danube between Bratislava and Vienna once a day Wednesday to Sunday from mid-April to October (twice daily on Friday and Saturday May to September, and also on Thursday in July and August). Trips cost €19 one way (1¾ hours), €29 return. Buy tickets at Bratislava's **hydrofoil terminal** *(Fajnorovo nábrežie 2)*.

There is also a daily (twice-daily in August) hydrofoil service between Bratislava and Budapest from mid-April to October. The trip downstream to Budapest takes four hours (40 minutes longer upstream to Bratislava), and costs €59/83 one way/return.

Getting Around

BUS

Intercity bus travel, operated by the various branches of Slovenská autobusová doprava (SAD), is generally slower and less comfortable than the train. One-way bus tickets cost around 24/46/96/190 Sk for 25/50/100/200km.

When trying to decipher bus schedules beware of departure times bearing footnotes you don't completely understand. It is helpful to know that *premáva* means 'it operates' and *nepremáva* means 'it doesn't operate'.

TRAIN

Slovak Republic Railways *(Železnice Slovenskej republiky or ŽSR)* provides a cheap and efficient service. One-way fares (2nd class) are 24/48/98/196 Sk for 25/50/100/200km; the surcharge for express services is around 20 Sk to 70 Sk. Most of the places covered in this chapter are on or near the main railway line between Bratislava and Košice.

By express train from Bratislava it's 1¾ hours to Trenčín, almost three hours to Žilina, five hours to Poprad, 5½ hours to Spišská Nová Ves, and 6½ hours to Košice.

Check W www.vlak-bus.cz for Slovakia's national railway and bus timetables.

CAR & MOTORCYCLE

You can drive in Slovakia using your own licence. In order to use Slovakia's motorways (denoted by green signs) all vehicles must have a motorway sticker *(nálepka)*, which should be displayed in the windscreen. You can buy stickers at border crossings, petrol stations or Satur offices (100 Sk for 15 days, 600 Sk for a year, for vehicles up to 1.5 tonnes).

Avis has offices in Bratislava and Košice. Its cheapest cars cost around 1650 Sk a day including unlimited kilometres and collision damage waiver. There are much cheaper local companies (see the Bratislava Getting Around section).

BICYCLE

Roads are often narrow and potholed, and in towns, cobblestones and tram tracks can be a dangerous combination. Theft is a problem in cities, so a good chain and lock are a must.

The cost of transporting a bicycle by rail is usually 10% of the train ticket.

LOCAL TRANSPORT

City buses and trams operate from around 4.30am to 11.30pm daily. Tickets are sold at public transport offices, from ticket machines and newsstands and must be validated once you're aboard.

Bratislava

☎ 02 • pop 441,500

Slovakia's capital marks the point where the Carpathian Mountains, which stretch 1200km from the Iron Gate of Romania, finally slope down towards the Danube River. The Austrian border is almost within sight of the city, and Hungary is just 16km away.

Bratislava became Hungary's capital in 1526 (the Turks captured Buda in 1541) and remained so until 1784. The city flourished during the reign of Maria Teresa of Austria (1740–80), and in 1918 it was included in the newly formed Republic of Czechoslovakia.

Many beautiful monuments survive in the old town to tell of its past under Hungarian rule, and Bratislava's numerous museums are surprisingly rich. The opera productions of the Slovak National Theatre rival anything in Europe. Despite these draws, Bratislava remains relatively unswamped by Western tourism.

Orientation

Hviezdoslavovo nám is a convenient reference point, with the old town to the north, the Danube to the south, the Slovak National Theatre to the east and Bratislava Castle to the west.

Bratislava's main train station, Hlavná stanica, is located several kilometres north of the centre. Tram No 1 runs from the station to nám L Štúra, just south of Hviezdoslavova nám. Bratislava-Petržalka station is south of the river.

The main bus station *(autobusová stanica)* is on Mlynské nivy, a little over 1km east of the old town. Bus No 210 shuttles between the main bus station and the main train station.

Information

Tourist Offices General information about the city is supplied by the **Bratislava Information Service** *(BIS; ☎ 54 43 37 15; Ⓦ www.bratislava.sk/bis; Klobučnícka 2; open Mon-Sat)*. *Kam v Bratislave* (Where in Bratislava), available at BIS, provides detailed information about what's on. There is a second, smaller **BIS** *(☎ 52 49 59 06; open 9am-6pm Mon-Fri)* at the main train station.

BIS runs guided tours of the city at 300 Sk per person. They also sell a 100 Sk ticket that gives admission to all municipal museums and galleries.

Visa Extensions Visa or passport inquiries should be directed to the **Oddelenie cudzineckej polície** *(☎ 61 01 11 11; Sasinkova 23; open 7.30am-noon Mon, Wed & Fri, 1pm-3pm Mon, 1pm-5.30pm Wed)*, on the 1st floor to the left. To get there take tram No 4, 6, 7 or 11 from Špitalská and get off at Americké nám.

Money There's an **exchange office** *(open 7.30am-6pm daily)* and ATM at the main train station near the BIS desk. **Všeobecná úverová bank** *(cnr Poštová & Obchodná; open 9am-4pm Mon-Fri)* changes travellers cheques and gives cash advances on Visa and MasterCard. There's an **American Express office** *(☎ 54 41 40 01; Kuzmányho 8; open 8am-5pm Mon-Fri)* also.

Post & Communications Mail addressed c/o poste restante, 81000 Bratislava 1, can be collected at the **main post office** *(nám SNP 34; open 7am-8pm Mon-Fri, 7am-6pm Sat, 9am-2pm Sun)*. The **telephone centre** *(open 8am-7pm Mon-Fri, 9am-1pm Sat)* is at Kolárska 12.

There are plenty of Internet cafés. **Internet Centrum** *(cnr Michalská & Sedlárska; open 9am-midnight daily)* charges 1 Sk to 2 Sk per minute depending on time used. **Netcafe** *(open 10am-10pm daily)*, along a passage at Obchodná 53, charges 1.50 Sk a minute.

Travel Agencies Both **Satur** *(☎ 55 41 01 28; Jesenského 5-9)* and **Tatratour** *(☎ 52 92 78 88; Mickiewiczova 2)* can arrange air tickets, accommodation and tours in Slovakia, as well as international air, train and bus tickets.

Medical & Emergency Services For medical emergencies call ☎ 155. The main outpatient clinic is at the **hospital** *(Mýtna 5)*. There's a 24-hour pharmacy *(lekáreň)* at nám SNP 20. The main police station *(polícia)* is at Sasinkova 23.

Things to See

Unless otherwise noted, all of Bratislava's galleries and museums are open 10am to 5pm Tuesday to Sunday, and admission is typically around 20 Sk to 40 Sk.

You could begin your exploring at the **Slovak National Museum** *(adult/child 20/10 Sk, admission free last Sun of each month; open 9am-5pm Tues-Sun)*, opposite the hydrofoil terminal on the river. The museum features anthropology, archaeology, natural history and geology exhibits. Farther west along the riverfront is the overhanging facade of the **Slovak National Gallery** *(Rázusovo nábrežie 2; adult/child 80/40 Sk; open 10am-6pm Tues-Sun)*, housing Bratislava's major art collection. The controversial modern building daringly incorporates an 18th-century palace.

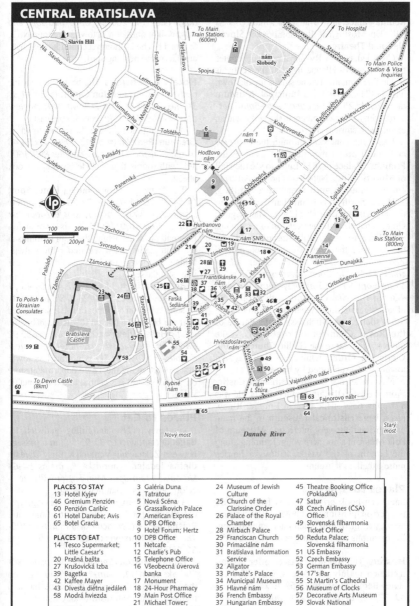

CENTRAL BRATISLAVA

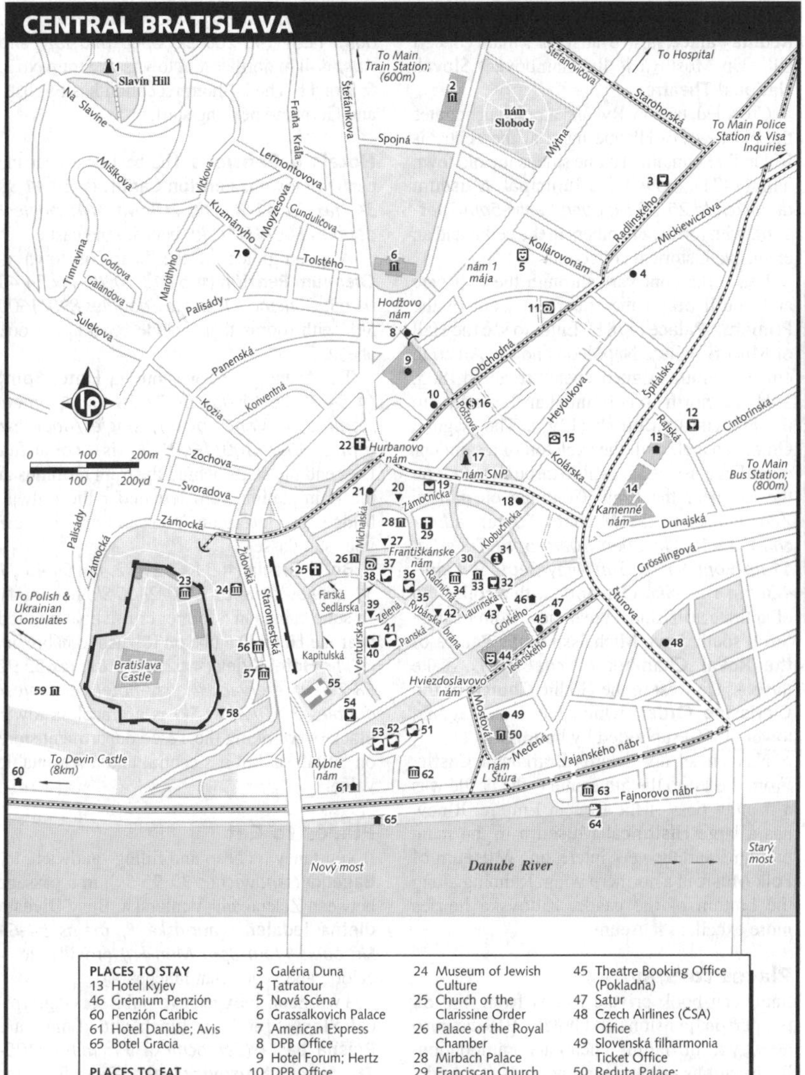

PLACES TO STAY
13 Hotel Kyjev
46 Gremium Penzión
60 Penzión Caribic
61 Hotel Danube; Avis
65 Botel Gracia

PLACES TO EAT
14 Tesco Supermarket; Little Caesar's
20 Prašná bašta
27 Krušovická Izba
39 Bagetka
42 Kaffee Mayer
43 Divesta diétna jedáleň
58 Modrá hviezda

OTHER
1 Slavín War Memorial
2 Archbishop's Summer Palace
3 Galéria Duna
4 Tatratour
5 Nová Scéna
6 Grassalkovich Palace
7 American Express
8 DPB Office
9 Hotel Forum; Hertz
10 DPB Office
11 Netcafe
12 Charlie's Pub
15 Telephone Office
16 Všeobecná úverová banka
17 Monument
18 24-Hour Pharmacy
19 Main Post Office
21 Michael Tower; Montana's Grizzly Bar
22 Church of the Holy Trinity
23 Museum of Folk Music
24 Museum of Jewish Culture
25 Church of the Clarissine Order
26 Palace of the Royal Chamber
28 Mirbach Palace
29 Franciscan Church
30 Primaciálne nám
31 Bratislava Information Service
32 Aligator
33 Primate's Palace
34 Municipal Museum
35 Hlavné nám
36 French Embassy
37 Hungarian Embassy
38 Internet Centrum
40 Austrian Embassy
41 UK Embassy
44 Slovak National Theatre
45 Theatre Booking Office (Pokladňa)
47 Satur
48 Czech Airlines (ČSA) Office
49 Slovenská filharmonia Ticket Office
50 Reduta Palace; Slovenská filharmonia
51 US Embassy
52 Czech Embassy
53 German Embassy
54 17's Bar
55 St Martin's Cathedral
56 Museum of Clocks
57 Decorative Arts Museum
59 Slovak National Parliament
62 Slovak National Gallery
63 Slovak National Museum
64 Hydrofoil Terminal

On nám L Štúra you'll find the neobaroque **Reduta Palace**, now Bratislava's main concert hall. Up Mostová is the flamboyant **Slovak National Theatre**.

Crowded, narrow Rybárska brána penetrates the old town to Hlavné nám; at the centre is Roland's Fountain. To one side is the old town hall (1421), now the **Municipal Museum** *(adult/child 25/25 Sk; open 10am-5pm Tues-Sun)*, with torture chambers in the cellar and an extensive historical collection.

Leave the courtyard through the east gate and you'll be on the square in front of the **Primate's Palace** (1781). Enter to see the Hall of Mirrors, where Napoleon and the Austrian emperor Franz I signed a peace treaty in 1805.

Head north on Františkánske nám to the **Franciscan Church** (1297). The original Gothic chapel, with the skeleton of a saint enclosed in glass, is accessible through a door on the left near the front. Continue on narrow Zámočnícka to the **Michael Tower** *(adult/child 20/10 Sk; open 10am-5pm Tues-Fri, 11am-6pm Sat & Sun May-Sept, 9.30am-4.30pm Tues-Sun Oct-Apr)*, with a collection of antique arms and a great view from the top. Stroll south down Michalská to the **Palace of the Royal Chamber** *(Michalská 1)*. Take the passage west to the Gothic **Church of the Clarissine Order**, which has a pentagonal tower (1360) supported by buttresses.

Next, head up towards **Bratislava Castle**. From the 1st to the 5th century, the castle was a frontier post of the Roman Empire. It now has a large **Historical Museum** in the main building, and the very interesting **Museum of Folk Music** in a northern wing. Running along the bottom of the castle, Židovská houses more excellent museums.

Places to Stay

Satur can book private rooms from 400 Sk per person, pensions and hotels. BIS can also assist you in finding cheap accommodation. Reservations are recommended year-round.

Hostels The following places offer accommodation in July and August only. The 12-storey **Bernolák Hostel** *(☎ 52 49 71 84, fax 52 49 77 24; Bernolákova 1; dorm beds per person from 130 Sk)*, about five blocks east of the main train station, is closest to the centre. There's a swimming pool and disco (audible throughout the building). **Študentský domov Mladá Garda** *(☎ 44 25 30 20, fax 44 45 96 90; ⓔ ubytovacie@garda.sk; Račianska 103; dorm beds 140-200 Sk; open mid-July–end Aug)* is 4km northeast of town; take tram No 3, 5, 7 or 11. The 24-hour reception has English- and German-speaking staff.

Hotels & Pensions The best deal near the centre of town is **Penzión Caribic** *(☎ 54 41 83 34, fax 54 41 83 33; Žižkova 1/A; singles/doubles 800/1500 Sk)*, beneath the castle.

A good place in the heart of town is **Gremium Penzión** *(☎ 54 13 10 26, fax 54 43 06 53; Gorkého 11; singles/doubles 890/1600 Sk)*, with rooms that include breakfast. Book ahead.

The friendly and welcoming **Hotel Spirit** *(☎ 54 77 75 61, fax 54 77 78 17; ⓔ univ@stonline.sk; Vančurova 1; singles/doubles/triples 900/1300/1600 Sk)* is...colourful. Descend the steps behind the tram terminus at the train station, turn left under the railway bridge, then left again. You can't miss it; wear your sunglasses.

Botel Gracia *(☎ 54 43 21 32, fax 54 43 21 31; singles/doubles 1750/2400 Sk)* has comfy en suite cabins in a former cruise boat moored near the Hotel Danube on Rázusovo nábrežie.

The **Hotel Kyjev** *(☎ 52 96 10 82, fax 52 92 68 20; ⓔ rezervacia@kyjev-hotel.sk; singles/doubles 2200/2400 Sk)* is a graceless tower block overlooking the Tesco department store on Špitálska, but it's central and a reasonable value.

Places to Eat

If you fancy a cheap and filling sandwich, try **Bagetka** *(sandwiches 30-95 Sk)*, in a passage between Zelená and Venturská. Busy **Divesta diétna jedáleň** *(Laurinská 8; mains 54-64 Sk; open 11am-3pm Mon-Fri)* provides low-calorie and vegetarian lunches.

Two good inexpensive pubs serving typical Slovak food for lunch and dinner are **Prašná bašta** *(Zámočnicka 11; mains 105-185 Sk)* and **Krušovická Izba** *(Biela 5; mains 80-130 Sk)*.

Modrá hviezda *(Beblavého 14; mains 80-150 Sk; open 11.30am-11pm Mon-Sat)*, on the way up to the castle, is a wine bar and restaurant that features Slovak cuisine.

The streets of central Bratislava have been taken over by countless cafés in the last few years. Classy **Kaffee Mayer** *(Hlavné nám 4)* has excellent but pricey coffee, cakes and light meals.

Entertainment

Live Performance Outstanding opera and ballet are presented at the **Slovak National Theatre** *(Hviezdoslavovo nám)*, except during August. Tickets are sold at the **booking office** *(pokladňa; cnr Jesenského & Komenského; open 8am-5.30pm Mon-Fri, 9am-noon Sat)* behind the theatre.

Nová scéna *(Kollárovo nám 20)* presents operettas, musicals and drama (the latter in Slovak). The ticket office is open 12.30pm to 7pm weekdays.

The **Slovenská filharmonia** *(cnr nám L. Štúra & Medená)* is based in the Reduta Palace, across the park from the National Theatre. The **ticket office** *(Palackého 2; open 1pm-7pm Mon, Tues, Thur & Fri, 8am-2pm Wed)* is inside the building.

Bars & Clubs For loud music and a young crowd, try **Charlie's Pub** *(Špitálska 4)*, one of the city's most popular drinking places. **Montana's Grizzly Bar** *(Michalská 19)*, at the foot of the Michael Tower, is a meeting place for English-speaking expats.

Two bars that have live jazz several times a week are **17's Bar** *(Hviezdoslavovo nám 17)* and **Aligator** *(Laurinská 7; open Mon-Sat)*. **Galéria Duna** *(Radlinského 11)* is a club that hosts rock bands, dance music or whatever the alternative scene has to offer.

Getting There & Away

Air There are daily flights from Bratislava to Prague with **ČSA** *(Czech Airlines; ☎ 52 96 13 25; Štúrova 13)* and to Košice with **Slovak Airlines** *(☎ 44 45 00 96; Trnavská cesta 56)*. The best prices out of Bratislava are available by booking online with the no-frills **Sky Europe Airlines** *(☎ 48 50 48 50; w www.skyeurope.com)*, which flies to Prague (from 1525 Sk one way), Košice (740 Sk) and Split (2525 Sk) in Croatia.

Bus At Bratislava's main **bus station** *(SAD/Eurolines information ☎ 0984-222 222; international lines ☎ 55 56 73 49; Mlynské nivy)*, east of the city centre, buy your ticket from the ticket windows. Reservations for the buses marked 'R' on the posted timetable can be purchased from the AMS counter.

Seven buses a day connect Bratislava to Vienna (Mitte Busbahnhof; €10.90, 1½ hours). Ten express buses a day run to Prague (4¾ hours). Other buses leaving Bratislava daily include nine to Košice (334 Sk, seven hours), three to Bardejov (468 Sk, 9½ hours) and one to Starý Smokovec (336 Sk, 7¾ hours). There's a weekly bus to Győr (200 Sk, 2½ hours), Hungary.

Eurolines buses to Bratislava include five a week from Brussels (€122 one way, 16 hours) via Vienna, one daily from Zürich (65 Sfr, 13 hours) and three a week (five in summer) from London (UK£78, 22 hours). The Zürich bus continues to Košice twice a week (94 Sfr; 21 hours).

There are also buses from Bratislava to Belgrade (9½ hours), on Monday and Friday, to Budapest (four hours, daily), and Kraków (eight hours, weekly). Tickets can be purchased at the international ticket window in the bus station or at the adjacent Eurolines office. If your bus goes through the Czech Republic, make sure you have an appropriate visa.

Train All express trains between Budapest (380 Sk, 2¾ hours) and Prague (528 Sk, 4½ hours) call at Bratislava. There are frequent trains from Bratislava to Košice (414 Sk, six hours) via Trenčín, Žilina and Poprad.

There are hourly trains between Vienna (Südbahnhof) and Bratislava's main train station (1½ hours). One nightly train departs for Moscow (33 hours).

Getting Around

To/From the Airport Bratislava's airport (Letisko MR Štefánika) is 7km northeast of the city centre. Get there on city bus No 61 from the train station or by taxi (around 280 Sk).

Tram & Bus Bratislava's public transport (Dopravný podnik Bratislava, or DPB) is based on an extensive tram network complemented by bus and trolleybus. You can buy tickets (12/14/20 Sk for 10/30/60 minutes) at DPB offices and from machines at main tram and bus stops; validate the ticket in the little red machines on the bus or tram when you board.

Tourist tickets *(turistické cestovné lístky)* valid for one/two/three/seven days (75/140/170/255 Sk) are sold at DPB offices at the train and bus stations, in the underground passageway below Hodžovo nám and on Obchodná near the Hotel Forum. One- and two-day tickets can also be bought from ticket machines. Bags larger than 30cm x 40cm x 60cm need a half-fare ticket.

Taxi Bratislava's taxis all have meters. Call **Fun Taxi** *(☎ 16 777)* or **Otto Taxi** *(☎ 16 322)*.

Car There are several inexpensive local car-rental companies such as **Favorit Car** *(☎ 44 88 41 52; Pri vinohradoch 275)*, which rents out a Škoda Felicie for around 580 Sk per day plus 3 Sk per kilometre. **Avis** *(☎ 53 41 61 11)* has a desk in the Hotel Danube, while **Hertz** *(☎ 43 63 66 62)* has a desk in the lobby of the Hotel Forum.

SLOVAKIA

West Slovakia

TRENČÍN

☎ 032 • pop 57,000

For centuries Trenčín Castle guarded one of the main trade routes from the Danube to the Baltic Sea. Laugaricio, a Roman military post, was established here in the 2nd century; a rock inscription dated AD 179 mentions the Roman 2nd Legion and its victory over the Germanic Kvad tribes. The present castle dates from the 15th century.

From the bus and train stations walk west through the city park and under the highway to the Tatra Hotel, where a street bears left uphill to Mierové nám, the main square. The well-informed staff at the **AiCES information centre** *(☎ 743 35 05; Štúrovo nám 10; open Mon-Sat)* can help you find accommodation. The **Všeobecná úverová banka** *(Mierové nám 48)* changes travellers cheques, and there's an ATM at another VÚB branch across the street at No 37. The telephone centre is in the **main post office** *(Mierové nám)*. Check your email at **Internet Klub Modra Linka** *(open 10am-10pm daily)* for 1 Sk a minute.

At the western end of Mierové nám are the baroque **Piarist Church** and 16th-century **town gate**. A covered stairway from the corner of the square opposite Piarist Church leads to the entrance to **Trenčín Castle** *(admission 80 Sk; open 9am-5pm daily Apr-Sept)*. The highlight of the tour is the view from the top of the tower. At night the castle is illuminated with fairy-tale green and purple lights.

The famous **Roman inscription** of AD 179 is on the cliff behind the Hotel Tatra and can only be seen through a viewing window on the hotel's staircase – ask at reception for permission to see it. The translation reads: 'To the victory of the emperor and the army which, numbering 855 soldiers, resided at Laugaricio. By order of Maximianus, legate of the 2nd auxiliary legion.'

In the town centre the only cheap accommodation is the nonsmoking **Penzión Svorad** *(☎/fax 743 03 22; ⓔ svorad@host.sk; Palackého 4; singles/doubles 500/750 Sk)*. Comfortable **Penzión Royal** *(☎ 640 06 60, fax 640 06 61; Vladimíra Roya 19; singles/doubles/triples 900/1200/1500 Sk)* is a 10-minute walk away across the river. **Gastrocentrum** *(mains 35-65 Sk; open 7am-5pm Mon-Fri)* is a self-service cafeteria serving filling hot meals.

All express trains on the main railway line from Bratislava (142 Sk, 1¾ hours) to Košice via Žilina stop here. There are six buses a day to Bratislava, Žilina and Košice, and several to Brno in the Czech Republic.

Central Slovakia

ŽILINA

☎ 041 • pop 84,000

Žilina, midway between Bratislava and Košice at the junction of the Váh and Kysuca Rivers, is the gateway to the Malá Fatra mountains. Since its founding in the 13th century, Žilina has been an important transportation hub – a status that was confirmed with the arrival of railways from Košice in 1871 and Bratislava in 1883. It's a pleasant, untouristy town with an attractive main square.

The adjacent bus and train stations are near the Váh River on the northeastern side of town, a 10-minute walk along Národná from Mariánské nám, Žilina's old town square. The travel agency **CK Selinan** *(☎ 562 07 89; Burianova medzierka 4; open Mon-Fri)*, in a lane off the western side of Mariánské nám, is part of the AiCES network and can provide information about Žilina and the Malá Fatra. The **Všeobecná úverová banka** *(Na bráne 1; open 7.30am-4.30pm Mon-Wed & Fri, 7.30am-noon Thur)*, two blocks south of Mariánské nám, changes travellers cheques and has an ATM. The **post office** *(Sladkovičova 1)* is three blocks north of Mariánské nám. There's an **Internet Klub** *(open 10am-10pm daily)* in the south end of the Dom Kultúry on Šturovo nám. It charges 1 Sk a minute.

Apart from the renovated old town square, with its picturesque church and covered arcade, the only sight worth seeking out is the collection of naive art figures made of metal and wire at the dilapidated **Regional Museum** *(admission 30 Sk; open 8am-4pm Tues-Sun)*, in the Renaissance castle across the river in Budatín, a 15-minute walk northwest from the train station.

Places to Stay & Eat

Pension GMK Centrum *(☎ 562 21 36; Mariánské nám 3; singles/doubles from 790/1290 Sk)* has smallish rooms, and is tucked away in an upstairs passage off the square. **Penzión Majovey** *(☎ 562 41 52, fax 562 52 39; Jána Milca 3; singles/doubles 700/900 Sk)* is nicer.

If these places are full, you can always resort to the comfortable if slightly run down **Hotel Polom** *(☎ 562 11 51; Hviezdoslavova 22; singles/doubles 820/1050 Sk)* opposite the train station. Older rooms with no frills cost 390/530 Sk.

The **Bageteria** *(Jána Milca 1)* on the corner of Národná is good for hefty sandwiches and inexpensive buffet food. **Radničná vináreň** *(Mariánské nám 28; mains 100-140 Sk; open 10am-midnight Mon-Sat, noon-midnight Sun)* has outdoor tables and a cellar restaurant serving good, inexpensive Slovak dishes.

Getting There & Away

Žilina is on the main railway line from Bratislava to Košice via Trenčín and Poprad. Most trains between Prague and Košice also stop at Žilina. Express trains from Žilina go to Prague (6¼ hours), Trenčín (92 Sk, 1¼ hours), Bratislava (212 Sk, 2¾ hours), Poprad (158 Sk, two hours) and Košice (250 Sk, three hours).

There are also daily direct trains to Kraków in Poland. You can avoid Czech territory by going via Poprad and the Javorina/Łysa Polana border crossing to Zakopane.

There are several buses a day to Brno (134km) and Prague.

MALÁ FATRA

☎ 041

The Malá Fatra (Little Fatra) mountain range stretches 50km across northwestern Slovakia; Veľký Kriváň (1709m) is the highest peak. Two hundred square kilometres of this scenic range, north of the Váh River and east of Žilina, are included in Malá Fatra National Park. At the heart of the park is the Vrátna dolina, a beautiful mountain valley with forested slopes on all sides.

Noted for its rich flora, Vrátna dolina has something for everyone. There are possibilities for hiking, ranging from easy tourist tracks through the forest to scenic ridge walks, and in winter there is downhill and cross-country skiing and snowboarding. The valley is an easy day trip from Žilina.

For information on hiking, skiing and snowboarding, ask at the **Mountain Rescue Service** *(Horská služba; ☎ 569 52 32)*, on the access road to Hotel Boboty. There's an **AiCES Information Centre** *(☎ 599 31 00; ⓔ ztt@terchova.sk; open daily)* in the Obecni úrad (regional offices) in Terchova. The **Slovenská sporiteľňa** bank next door has an exchange counter and an ATM. The **post office** is 100m further east on the main road.

There are lots of *privaty* (private rooms) in Terchova from 200 Sk per person. Friendly **Hotel Terchova** *(☎ 569 56 25, fax 569 56 30; ⓔ vratna@hotel-terchova.sk; singles/doubles 720/1440 Sk)*, at the Vratná road junction in Terchova, is new and comfortable. **Chata Vrátna** *(☎ 569 57 39, fax 569 57 31; ⓔ chatavratna@icos.sk; dorm beds 150 Sk, doubles/triples/quads 460/590/690 Sk)*, a large wooden chalet at the head of the valley, is usually full of hikers in summer and skiers in winter. There are regular hotel rooms as well as dorm beds.

In Štefanová, friendly **Chata vo Vyhnana** *(☎/fax 569 51 24; ⓔ chatavyhnana@stonline.sk; half/full board per person 160/300 Sk)* has good dorm accommodation. There are also several *privaty* around the village – look for the 'Zimmer frei' signs.

The bus from Žilina to Chata Vrátna (one hour, 32km) leaves from platform No 10 at Žilina bus station nine times a day. If you come on a day trip, check the times of return trips at the information counter at Žilina bus station before setting out.

You can hire bicycles in Terchova – ask at the information centre for details.

East Slovakia

East Slovakia is one of the most attractive touring areas in Central Europe. In one compact region you can enjoy superb hiking in the Vysoké Tatry (High Tatra) mountains, rafting on the Dunajec River, historic towns such as Levoča and Bardejov, the great medieval castle at Spišské Podhradie, the charming spa of Bardejovské Kúpele and city life in Košice.

VYSOKÉ TATRY

☎ 0969

The Vysoké Tatry (High Tatras) are the only truly alpine mountains in Central Europe. This 27km-long granite massif covers 260 sq km, forming the northernmost portion of the Carpathian Mountains. At 2654m, Gerlachovský štít (Mt Gerlach) is the highest mountain in the entire 1200km Carpathian range, and several other peaks exceed 2500m. Enhancing the natural beauty packed into this relatively small area are clear mountain lakes, thundering waterfalls and dazzling snowfields.

Since 1949, most of the Slovak portion of this jagged range has been included in the Tatra National Park (Tanap), the first national park to be created in former Czechoslovakia, complementing a similar park in Poland. A 600km network of hiking trails reaches all the alpine valleys and many peaks. Park regulations require you to keep to the marked trails and to refrain from picking flowers.

The region offers an incredible array of hiking possibilities, as well as the chance to ride cable cars over peaks. Mountain climbing is popular, as are skiing and snowboarding in winter. Check at the information centres listed for details on activities.

Keep in mind that the higher trails are officially closed from November to mid-June, to protect the delicate environment. There's snow from November until May or even June. July and August are the warmest (and most crowded) months, while August and September are the best for high-altitude hiking. The **TANAP Mountain Rescue Service office** next to Satur in Starý Smokovec can give you a weather report for the next day.

Starý Smokovec, an early-20th-century resort that is well connected to the rest of the country by road and rail, makes a pleasant base camp. The main **AiCES Tatra information centre** *(☎ 442 34 40; ⓔ tik.vysoketatry@sinet.sk; open Mon-Sat Apr-Nov, daily Dec–mid-April)* in the Dom služieb shopping centre, northwest of Starý Smokovec train station, has plenty of information but doesn't book accommodation. The helpful **Satur office** *(☎ 442 24 97; ⓔ smokovec@satur.sk; open Mon-Fri)*, just above the train station at Starý Smokovec, provides general advice, mountain guides and tours, and can book beds in local hotels, pensions and mountain huts. The Tatra National Park website at ⓦ www.tanap.sk is packed with useful information on accommodation, mountain guides, equipment rental and trail conditions.

Places to Stay

No wild camping is permitted within the Tatra National Park. **Camping Jupela** *(☎ 446 74 93; tent 80 Sk plus per person 90 Sk; open May-Sept)* is 10 minutes' walk downhill from Stará Lesná train station.

Up on the hiking trails are nine mountain chalets *(chaty)*, but they may all be full in midsummer. Many close for maintenance in November and May. Although food is available, you should bring some of your own supplies. All this said, a stay in a *chata* is one of the best mountain experiences the Tatras have to offer.

Satur in Starý Smokovec can reserve beds at most of the chalets. High-season prices are around 300 Sk to 500 Sk per person.

The following are the main chalets on the upper trails, from west to east:

Chata pod Soliskom (1800m) At the top of the chairlift; small and very busy

Chata pri Popradskom plese (1500m; ☎ 449 21 77) Eight-bed, six-bed and double rooms with a restaurant

Sliezský dom (1670m; ☎ 442 52 02; ⓔ gotravel@neta.sk) Large mountain hotel with restaurant and cafeteria

Zbojnícka chata (1960m; ☎ 0903-619 000) Alpine bunks and restaurant

Téryho chata (2015m; ☎ 442 52 45) Alpine bunks and restaurant

Zamkovského chata (1475m; ☎ 442 26 30) Alpine bunks and restaurant

Bilíkova chata (1220m; ☎ 442 24 39) Attractive wooden chalet with double rooms

Chata pri Zelenom plese (1540m; ☎ 446 74 20) Dorm accommodation and restaurant

Satur can help out with private rooms (250 Sk to 500 Sk per person) and apartments. You can also check out ⓦ www.tanap.sk/homes.html.

Hotel prices almost double in the high seasons (mid-December to February and mid-June to September). Most prices quoted in this section are high season.

Starý Smokovec & Around One of the best deals you'll find at Starý Smokovec is the friendly, family-run **Pension Vesna** *(☎ 442 27 74, fax 442 31 09; ⓔ vesna@sinet.sk; per person 700 Sk)*, behind the large sanatorium below Nový Smokovec train station. Spacious three-bed apartments with private bath are available.

Hotel Smokovec *(☎ 442 51 91, fax 442 51 94; ⓔ smokovec@tatry.net; doubles/quads 1980/3560 Sk)*, immediately above Starý Smokovec train station, has spacious rooms including a bath and TV; breakfast is 130 Sk extra. It also has a swimming pool.

The cheapest place to stay if you have a HI or ISIC card is **Hotel Junior** *(☎ 442 26 61, fax 442 24 93; singles/doubles/triples/quads 350/680/840/1010 Sk)*, which is just below the Horný Smokovec train station.

Tatranská Lomnica The best value in town is the **Penzión Bělín** *(☎/fax 446 77 78; ⓔ belin@tatry.sk; per person 240 Sk)*, on the main road, is just a few minutes' walk north of the train station.

The squat, monolithic **Hotel Slovan** *(☎ 446 78 51, fax 446 76 27; ⓔ slovan@tatry.sk; singles/doubles 950/1420 Sk)* is five minutes uphill behind Hotel Slovakia. It lacks character, but is not bad value for rooms with private bath and satellite TV.

Štrbské Pleso The **Hotel Panoráma** *(☎ 449 21 11, fax 449 28 10; ⓔ hotel@hotelpanorama.sk; singles/doubles with bath 985/1770 Sk)* is the 11-storey pyramidal eyesore next to the shopping centre above the Štrbské Pleso train station. The rooms are good, though, and the view is much nicer looking out.

You'll find some cheaper options down the hill in Tatranská Štrba, including **Hotel Junior Rysy** *(☎ 4484 845, fax 448 42 96; ⓔ hotel.rysy@ke.telecom.sk; singles/doubles 700/900 Sk)*, a few minutes' walk from the Tatranská Lieskovec stop on the rack-railway between Tatranská Štrba and Štrbské Pleso.

Places to Eat

Almost all the hotels and chalets in this region have their own restaurants. The self-service **bistro** in Hotel Smokovec is good. For typical Slovak food with a Roma band, head for midrange **Restaurant Koliba**, southwest of the train station. There's a good self-service place in the **Obchodný dom Toliar** *(open 8am-7pm daily)* next to Štrbské Pleso train station.

Getting There & Away

Bus There are regular express buses from Bratislava to Starý Smokovec (seven hours) and Tatranská Lomnica.

From Starý Smokovec there are eight buses a day to -ysa Polana; six to Levoča; two to Bardejov; four to Žilina (125 Sk, 3¼ hours); three to Trenčín; and one to Brno and Prague (11 hours) in the Czech Republic.

The Hungarian Volánbusz bus from Budapest to Tatranská Lomnica runs twice a week (seven hours).

Train To reach Vysoké Tatry, catch any one of the express trains running between Prague, Bratislava and Košice, and change at Poprad. There are frequent narrow-gauge electric trains between Poprad and Starý Smokovec.

Alternatively, get off the express at Tatranská Štrba, a main-line station west of Poprad, and take the rack-railway up to Štrbské Pleso.

The booking offices in Starý Smokovec and Tatranská Lomnica train stations can reserve sleepers and couchettes from Poprad to Bratislava and to Prague, Karlovy Vary and Brno in the Czech Republic.

Walking into Poland For anyone interested in walking between Slovakia and Poland, there's a highway border crossing near Javorina, an hour from Starý Smokovec by bus (46 Sk). The bus stop is 100m from the border (bus times posted).

The rate offered at the border is about 10% worse than in Zakopane. Southbound travellers should buy a few dollars worth of Slovak crowns at an exchange office in Poland to pay the onward bus fare to Starý Smokovec or Poprad.

A bus direct from Poprad to Zakopane, Poland, leaves Starý Smokovec bus station on Thursday and Saturday at 6.15am (two hours). Also ask Satur about its excursion buses to Zakopane and Kraków.

Getting Around

Electric trains run from Poprad to Starý Smokovec (16 Sk, 30 minutes) and Štrbské Pleso (26 Sk, one hour) about every half-hour, and from Starý Smokovec to Tatranská Lomnica (11 Sk, 15 minutes) every 30 to 60 minutes. These trains make frequent stops along their routes; when there isn't a ticket window, go immediately to the conductor on boarding to buy your ticket. A rack-railway connects Štrba (on the main Žilina–Poprad road and railway line) with Štrbské Pleso (22 Sk, 5km). A two/six-day ticket giving unlimited travel on the Tatra trains costs 136/262 Sk.

You can hire **mountain bikes** from Tatrasport in Starý Smokovec for 299 Sk a day.

POPRAD

☎ 052 • pop 53,000

Poprad is an important transportation hub. The electric railway from here to Starý Smokovec was built in 1908 and extended to Štrbské Pleso in 1912. There are buses to almost everywhere in Slovakia from the large bus station next to the train station, including Bratislava (336 Sk, four hours), Košice (158 Sk, two hours), Červený Kláštor (62 Sk, 1¾ hours), Levoča (26km), Spišské Podhradie (41km) and Bardejov (125km).

Express trains run to Žilina (two hours) and Košice (1½ hours) every couple of hours. Electric trains climb 13km to Starý Smokovec, the main Vysoké Tatry resort, every hour or so. A branch line runs northeast to Plaveč (two hours by local train), where you can get a connection to Muszyna, Poland, five times a day.

LEVOČA

☎ 053 • pop 13,000

Levoča, 26km east of Poprad, is one of Slovakia's finest walled towns, with a main square full of beautiful Renaissance buildings. To this day its medieval walls, street plan and central square have survived unspoiled by modern development. The town is an easy stop on the way from Poprad to Košice.

The train and bus stations are 1km south of town. The most convenient bus stop is at nám Štefana Kluberta, outside the Košice Gate. The **AiCES information centre** *(☎ 451 37 63; nám Majstra Pavla 58; open Mon-Sat)* is at the top of the square. **Slovenská sporiteľňa** *(nám Majstra Pavla 56; open 8am-3pm Mon-Fri, 8am-4pm Wed)* changes travellers cheques and has an ATM.

The **telephone centre** is in the **post office** *(nám Majstra Pavla 42; open 8am-noon & 1pm-4.30pm Mon-Fri, 8am-11.30am Sat)*. You can check email at **System House** *(Košická 3; open 8am-11.30am & 12.30pm-4.30pm Mon-Fri)*. It charges 1.50 Sk a minute.

Nám Majstra Pavla, Levoča's central square, is full of superb Gothic and Renaissance buildings. The 15th-century **St James' Church** *(admission 40 Sk; open daily June-Sept, Tues-Sat rest of year)* contains a towering Gothic altar (1517) by Majster Pavol of Levoča. Buy tickets in the Municipal Weights House opposite the north door.

Next to St James' is the Gothic **town hall**, enlivened by Renaissance arcades and murals of the civic virtues. Beside the town hall is a 16th-century **cage of shame** where prisoners were once exhibited.

Places to Stay & Eat

AiCES can book accommodation, including **private rooms** from 250 Sk per person. Most are outside the old town; those inside are more expensive, around 300 Sk to 400 Sk.

The slightly run-down, 25-room **Hotel Faix** *(☎ 451 23 35; Probstnerova cesta 22; doubles 700 Sk)*, between the train station and the old town, has basic doubles with shower/toilet. **Penzión Pri Košickej Bráne** *(☎ 451 28 79; Košická 16; per person 450 Sk)* is just inside the Košice Gate.

The best place for a meal is the homely and inexpensive **Reštaurácia Slovenká** *(nám Majstra Pavla 62; mains 70-110 Sk)*. The popular **Vegetarián** *(Uhoľná 137; mains 30-70 Sk; open 10am-3.15pm Mon-Fri)* is off the northwest corner of the main square. For a beer, try the Slovenká or the lively **Mestský hostinec** *(nám Majstra Pavla 11)*.

Getting There & Away

Levoča is connected by hourly local trains to Spišská Nová Ves (15 Sk, 20 minutes), 13km south on the main line from Bratislava to Košice. Bus travel is more practical as there are frequent services to Poprad (30 minutes) and Spišské Podhradie (20 minutes) and eight daily to Košice (two hours). All buses stop at nám Š Kluberta and some local buses also stop at the train station at the southern end of town.

SPIŠSKÉ PODHRADIE

☎ 053

Considering its nearness to the tourist magnet of Spišský hrad (Spiš Castle), the small town of Spišské Podhradie, 15km east of Levoča, is surprisingly dismal and run-down. There's no reason to linger in the town itself, but nearby Spišský hrad and Spišská Kapitula are sights of prime importance.

If you're arriving by bus from Levoča, ask the driver to drop you at **Spišská Kapitula**, on a ridge 1km west of Spišské Podhradie. This 13th-century ecclesiastical settlement is completely encircled by a 16th-century wall, and the single street running between the two medi-eval gates is lined with picturesque Gothic houses. At the upper end is the magnificent **St Martin's Cathedral** *(admission 30 Sk; open 10am-5pm Mon-Sat, 11am-4pm Sun May-Oct, 1pm-3pm Mon-Fri Nov-Apr)*, built in 1273, with twin Romanesque towers and a Gothic sanctuary. Inside are three folding Gothic altars (1499) and, near the door, a Romanesque white lion. On either side of the cathedral are the seminary and the Renaissance bishop's palace (1652).

Crowning a ridge on the far side of Spišské Podhradie is the 180m-long **Spišský hrad** *(admission 50 Sk; open 9am-6pm daily May-Sept, 9am-3pm Nov-Apr)*, the largest castle in Slovakia. Cross at the tracks near the train station and follow the yellow markers up to the castle. The castle was founded in 1209 and reconstructed in the 15th century. The highest castle enclosure contains a round Gothic tower, a cistern, a chapel and a rectangular Romanesque palace perched over the abyss. Weapons and instruments of torture are exhibited in the dungeon.

The only place to stay in town is at **Penzión Podzámok** *(☎/fax 454 17 55; ⓔ sykora@sn.psg.sk; Podzámková 28; dorm beds per person 350 Sk)*, whihc has a friendly, English-speaking owner. To get there, turn left after the bridge just south of Mariánské nám.

A branch railway line connects Spišské Podhradie to Spišské Vlachy (9km), a station on the main line from Poprad to Košice. Departures are scheduled to connect with the Košice trains. There are frequent buses from Košice (1½ hours), Levoča (15km), Spišská Nová Ves (25km) and Poprad (45 minutes).

KOŠICE

☎ 055 • pop 235,000

Košice is the second-largest city in Slovakia and capital of its eastern part. Before WWI Košice had a Hungarian majority, and the historic and ethnic influence of nearby Hungary remains strong. The town became part of Czechoslovakia in 1918 but was again occupied by Hungary from 1938 to 1945. From 21 February to 21 April 1945, Košice served as the capital of liberated Czechoslovakia.

Although it's now a major steel-making city, there is much in the revamped old town that is of interest to visitors. The city is also a good base for excursions to other East Slovakian towns.

Orientation & Information

The adjacent bus and train stations are just east of the old town. A five-minute walk along Mlynská will bring you into Hlavná (Main Street). The **AiCES information centre** *(☎ 16 168; ⓔ mic@pangea.sk; open 8am-5pm Mon-Fri, 9am-1pm Sat)* in the Dargov department store opposite Hotel Slovan sells maps, guidebooks and concert tickets, and provides accommodation information, as does the **municipal information centre** *(☎ 625 88 88; Hlavná 59; open Mon-Sat)* in the town hall.

The **police and passport office** *(trieda Slovenského Národného Povstania; open 10am-noon & 12.30pm-6pm Mon & Wed, 7am-noon Tues, Thur & Fri)*, across the street from the huge Košice/Mestský municipal administration building, is the place to apply for visa extensions, complete police registration or report a lost visa. Take bus No 19 west from Štúrova.

Všeobecná úverová banka *(Hlavná 112; open 8am-5pm Mon-Wed & Fri, 8am-noon Thur)* changes travellers cheques and has an ATM. There's a telephone centre in the **main post office** *(Poštová 2; open 7am-7pm Mon-Fri, 7am-2pm Sat)*. Check email at **NetClub** *(Hlavná 9; open 9am-10pm daily)* for 50 Sk per hour (minimum of 10 Sk payable).

You can buy international train and bus tickets at **Satur** *(☎ 622 31 22; Hlavná 1)*, next to Hotel Slovan.

Things to See

Unless noted otherwise, admission to museums and galleries is 20 Sk.

Košice's top sight is the recently renovated **Cathedral of St Elizabeth** (1345–1508), a magnificent late-Gothic edifice. In a crypt on the left side of the nave is the tomb of Duke Ferenc Rákóczi, who was exiled to Turkey after the failed 18th-century Hungarian revolt against Austria. On the south side of the cathedral is the 14th-century **St Michael's Chapel**, and to the north is the **Urban Tower**.

Most of Košice's other historic sites are north along Hlavná. In the centre of the square is the ornate **State Theatre** (1899). Facing it at Hlavná 59 is the rococo former **town hall** (1780).

The **East Slovak Museum** *(nám Maratónu mieru; open 9am-5pm Tues-Sat, 9am-1pm Sun)*, at the northern end of Hlavná, is dedicated to regional culture, history and archaeology. Don't miss the Košice Gold Treasure in the basement, a hoard of almost 3000 gold coins dating from the 15th to the 18th centuries and discovered by chance in 1935.

Walk back along Hlavná towards the State Theatre and turn left on narrow Univerzitná to the **Mikluš Prison**. This pair of 16th-century houses once served as a prison equipped with medieval torture chambers and cells.

Ask at the municipal information office about guided tours of the **Lower Gate**, the archaeological remnants of the old city walls that lie beneath nám Slobody south of the cathedral.

Places to Stay & Eat

Dilapidated **Domov mládeže** *(☎ 642 90 52; Medická 2; dorm beds per person 150 Sk)* has beds in two- and three-bed rooms. It's a 15-minute hike west of the centre along Poštova and Vojenská. **TJ Metropol turistická ubytovňa** *(☎ 625 59 48, fax 76 31 10; Štúrova 32; rooms per person 300 Sk)* is an attractive sports complex with bright but basic rooms.

There's a handful of pensions within the old town, including attractive **Penzión Platz** *(☎/fax 622 34 50; Dominikánske nám 23; doubles 1200 Sk)*. Recently renovated **Hotel Alessandria** *(☎ 622 59 03, fax 622 59 18; Jiskrova 3; singles/doubles 1150/1790 Sk)* is hidden away on a quiet back street, and has four-star facilities with a quaint, 1970s feel to it.

A popular restaurant on the main square is inexpensive **Bakchus** *(Hlavná 8; mains 55-90 Sk)*, with an international menu and an open courtyard for summer dining. **Reštaurácia Ajvega/Ajmexica** *(Orlia 10; mains 90-135 Sk)* combines a tasty vegetarian menu with carnivorous Mexican fare. You can get cheap baguette sandwiches at **Bagetéria** *(Hlavná 74)*.

Entertainment

The renovated **State Theatre** *(Hlavné nám)* stages regular performances. The Thália Hungarian Theatre and the State Philharmonic in Dom umenia are in the southwest corner of the old town; performances are held once or twice a week. Recitals are sometimes given at the **Konzervatórium** *(Hlavná 89)*.

The cellar bar **Bomba klub** *(Hlavná 5)* is popular with locals and English-speaking visitors. **Jazz Klub** *(Kováčska 39)* has live jazz twice a week.

Getting There & Away

Train A sleeper train leaves Košice daily at 7.10am for Kyiv (22 hours, 998km). Overnight trains with sleepers and couchettes are also available between Košice and Bratislava (seven hours, 445km) and Prague (11 hours, 708km), Brno (493km), Karlovy Vary (897km) and Plzeň (896km) in the Czech Republic. Daytime express trains connect Košice to Poprad (122 Sk, two hours), Žilina (250 Sk, three hours), Bratislava and Prague.

The daily *Cracovia* express train between Budapest (four hours) and Kraków (five hours) passes through Košice (reservations required). Northbound, the *Cracovia* departs Košice at 1.05am, and southbound at 5.38am.

Bus For shorter trips to Levoča (two hours), Bardejov (1½ hours) and Spišské Podhradie (1½ hours), you're better off taking a bus. A bus to Užgorod, Ukraine (2½ hours), leaves Košice every afternoon. There's also a daily bus to Prague (12 hours).

Heading for Poland, there's a bus from Košice to Nowy Targ (four hours) at 5.45am every Thursday and Saturday, and to Krosno every Wednesday, Friday and Saturday. In both cases the fare is paid to the driver.

There's a bus from Košice to Miskolc (Hungary) at 6.30am on Wednesday, Friday and Saturday (two hours), and at 5.40pm Monday to Thursday. You should book your ticket the day before at window No 1 in the bus station. On Wednesday this bus continues to Budapest (five hours).

Slovenia

Slovenia is one of Europe's overlooked gems. The wealthiest former Yugoslav republic, it has much more in common with its Central-European neighbours than with the Balkans. The nation's relative affluence and orderliness is immediately apparent. Many of its cities and towns bear the imprint of the Habsburg Empire and the Venetian Republic, while the Julian Alps are reminiscent of Switzerland.

Slovenia is less about dirt-cheapness and more about great value. The country offers the same dramatic scenery and thrills as its Western European neighbours at a fraction of the cost. The amazing variety renders Slovenia something of a 'Europe in miniature'. An added bonus is that Slovenia is a nation of friendly, helpful polyglots, ensuring that communication is never difficult.

Slovenia: the Basics

Local name Slovenija

Capital Ljubljana

Population 1.97 million

Language Slovene

Currency 1 tolar (SIT) = 100 stotinov

Avoid at all costs Competing with a Slovenian skier

Endear yourself by saying *Ali je bil tvoj otrok rojen s smučmi na nogah?* (Was your child born with skis on her feet?)

Facts about Slovenia

HISTORY

The Austro-German monarchy ruled the area from the 14th century up to the end of WWI (except for Napoleon's brief reign). Over those centuries, the upper classes became Germanised, though the peasantry retained their Slovenian identity. After WWI, Slovenia was included in the Kingdom of Serbs, Croats and Slovenes. During WWII Slovenian partisans fought courageously against Axis invaders, and Slovenia joined Yugoslavia in 1945.

By the late 1980s, being part of Yugoslavia had not only become an economic burden on Slovenia but also a political threat, as Serbia moved to dominate the region. In the spring of 1990, Slovenia became the first Yugoslav republic to hold free elections and shed communist rule. On 25 June 1991, Slovenia pulled out of the Yugoslav Federation, precipitating a 10-day war with Yugoslavia. Peace was brokered by the European Community (EC), which in 1992 formally recognised Slovenia. The country is expected to become part of the EU in January 2004.

GEOGRAPHY

At just 20,256 sq km, Slovenia is Eastern Europe's smallest country. Much of the country is mountainous, culminating in the northwest with the Julian Alps and the nation's highest peak, Mt Triglav (2864m). Below the limestone plateau of the Karst region between Ljubljana and Koper is Europe's most extensive network of 'karst' caverns.

CLIMATE

Slovenia's topography creates three individual climates: Alpine in the northwest, Mediterranean on the coast and in western Slovenia, and continental in the east. Most of the rain falls in March and April and again in October and November. January is the coldest month with an average temperature of -2°C and July the warmest (21°C).

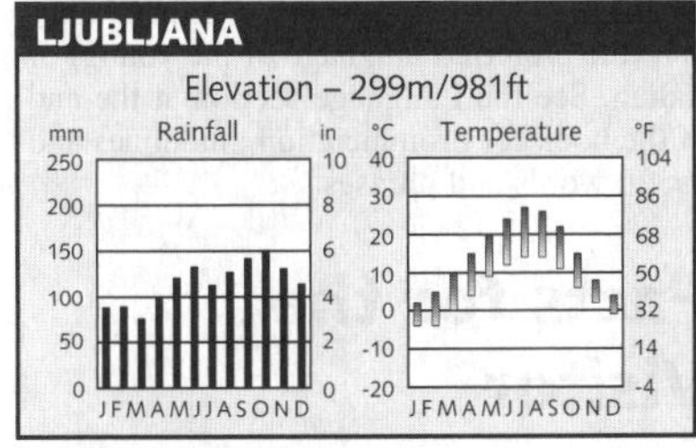

GOVERNMENT & POLITICS

Slovenia enjoys a parliamentary system of government. Executive power is vested in the prime minister and the 15-member cabinet.

POPULATION & PEOPLE

Slovenia is the most homogeneous of all the Yugoslav republics; about 88% of the population (estimated at 1,967,143 in 2001) are Slovenes. Minorities here include Croats, Serbians, Bosnians, Italians and Hungarians.

LANGUAGE

Slovene is written in the Roman alphabet and closely related to Croatian and Serbian. Virtually everyone speaks at least one other language: Croatian, Serbian, German, English (the preferred language of the young) or Italian. See the Language section at the end of the book for pronunciation guidelines and useful words and phrases.

Facts for the Visitor

HIGHLIGHTS

Ljubljana is the most happening town and, along with Piran and Koper, it boasts outstanding architecture. The hill-top castles at both Bled and Ljubljana are impressive. The Škocjan and Postojna Caves are among the foremost underground wonders of the world, and the Soča Valley is indescribably beautiful in spring. Finally, the frescoed Church of St John the Baptist is itself worth the trip to Lake Bohinj.

PLANNING

May and June are great in the lowlands and valleys, when everything is fresh and in blossom. In July and August, hotel rates go up and tourists abound, especially on the coast, but all the hostels are open. In September, the days are long and the weather still warm – it's the best time for hiking and climbing. October and November can be rainy, and winter (December to March) is for skiers.

TOURIST OFFICES

Local Tourist Offices

The **Slovenian Tourist Board** *(STO; ☎ 01-589 1840, fax 189 1841; Ⓦ www.slovenia-tourism.si; Dunajska cesta 156, Ljubljana)* is the umbrella organisation for Slovenian tourist offices. The best office for face-to-face information is the **Ljubljana Tourist Information Centre** (TIC).

Tourist Offices Abroad

The Slovenian Tourist Board maintains tourist offices in the following countries:

Austria (☎ 01-715 4010, fax 713 8177, e slowenien.info@xpoint.at) Hilton Center, Landstrasser Hauptstrasse 2, 1030 Vienna
Croatia (☎ 01-457 2118, fax 457 7921, e kompas-zagreb@zg.tel.hr) Hotel Esplanade, Mihanovičeva 1, 10000 Zagreb
Germany (☎ 089-2916 1202, fax 2916 1273, e slowenien.fva@t-online.de) Maximillians-platz 12a, 80333 Munich
Hungary (☎ 1-269 6879, fax 268 1454, e tourism.and.travel@kompas.hu) Rakoczi ut 14, 1072 Budapest
Italy (☎ 02-29 51 11 87, fax 29 51 40 71, e slovenia@tin.it) Galeria Buenos Aires 1, 20124 Milan
Netherlands (☎ 010-465 3003, fax 465 7514, e kompasnl@euronet.nl) Benthuizerstraat 29, 3036 CB Rotterdam
Switzerland (☎ 01-212 6394, fax 212 5266, e adria.slo@bluewin.ch) Löwenstrasse 54, 8001 Zürich
UK (☎ 020-7287 7133, fax 7287 5476, e slovenia@cpts.fsbusiness.co.uk) 49 Conduit St, London W1S 2YS
USA (☎ 212-358 9686, fax 358 9025, e slotouristboard@sloveniatravel.com) 345 East 12th St, New York, NY 10003

VISAS & DOCUMENTS

Passport-holders from Australia, Canada, Israel, Japan, New Zealand, Switzerland, the USA and EU countries do not require visas for stays up to 90 days; those from the EU and Switzerland can also enter on a national identity card for a stay of up to 30 days. Citizens of countries requiring visas can get them at any Slovenian embassy or consulate. They cost the equivalent of €20 for a single entry and €40 for multiple entries.

EMBASSIES & CONSULATES

Slovenian Embassies

The following are only a selection. For more listings see w www.gov.si/mzz/eng.

Australia (☎ 02-6243 4830) Level 6, Advance Bank Centre, 60 Marcus Clark St, Canberra, ACT 2601
Austria (☎ 01-586 1309) Nibelungengasse 13, 1010 Vienna
Canada (☎ 613-565 5781) Suite 2101, 150 Metcalfe St, Ottawa, Ontario K2P 1P1
Croatia (☎ 01-631 1000) Savska cesta 41/IX, 10000 Zagreb
Germany (☎ 030-206 1450) Hausvogteiplatz 3-4, 10117 Berlin
Hungary (☎ 1-438 5600) Cseppkő ut 68, 1025 Budapest
Italy (☎ 06-80 91 43 10) Via Leonardo Pisano 10, 00197 Rome
UK (☎ 020-7495 7775) Suite 1, Cavendish Crt, 11–15 Wigmore St, London WH1 9LA
USA (☎ 202-667 5363) 1525 New Hampshire Ave NW, Washington, DC 20036

Embassies in Slovenia

Citizens of countries not listed here should contact their embassies in Vienna or Budapest. The following are all based in Ljubljana.

Australia (☎ 01-425 4252) Trg Republike 3/XII
Austria (☎ 01-479 0700) Prešernova cesta 23
Bosnia-Hercegovina (☎ 01-432 4042) Kolarjeva 26
Canada (☎ 01-430 3570) Miklošičeva cesta 19
Croatia (☎ 01-425 6220) Gruberjevo nab 6
France (☎ 01-426 4525) Barjanska 1
Germany (☎ 01-251 6166) Prešernova cesta 27
Hungary (☎ 01-512 1882) ul Konrada Babnika 5
Romania (☎ 01-505 8294) Podlimbarskega 43
UK (☎ 01-200 3910) Trg Republike 3/IV
USA (☎ 01-200 5500) Prešernova cesta 31

CUSTOMS

Travellers can bring in the usual personal effects, a couple of cameras and electronic goods for their own use, 200 cigarettes, a generous 4L of spirits and 1L of wine.

MONEY

Slovenia's currency is the tolar (SIT). Some lodging establishments use the euro. There are coins of one, two, five and 10 tolars and banknotes of 10, 20, 50, 100, 200, 500, 1000, 5000 and 10,000 tolars.

Exchange Rates

country	unit		tolars
Australia	A$1	=	135.70 SIT
Canada	C$1	=	155.20 SIT
Eurozone	€1	=	228.90 SIT
Japan	¥100	=	192.10 SIT
NZ	NZ$1	=	116.80 SIT
UK	UK£1	=	355.40 SIT
USA	US$1	=	237.10 SIT

It's simple to change cash at banks, travel agencies, any *menjalnica* (private exchange bureau) and certain post offices. Slovenia recently had a problem with travellers-cheque fraud, so they are difficult to exchange, but restaurants and hotels will still accept them. Watch for high commission rates.

Visa, MasterCard/Eurocard and American Express (AmEx) cards are widely accepted. ATMs linked to Cirrus or Plus blanket Slovenia. Visa Card-holders can get cash advances in tolars from any A Banka branch; MasterCard and Eurocard holders from any branch of Nova Ljubljanska Banka; and AmEx customers from Atlas Express.

Slovenia remains much cheaper than the neighbouring countries of Italy and Austria, but don't expect the prices you'd see in Eastern European countries such as Hungary or Bulgaria. You could get by for under US$30 a day. Tipping isn't customary, but no one will complain if you leave your change at the table in a restaurant.

A 'circulation tax' *(prometni davek)* applies to the purchase of most goods and services. Visitors can claim refunds on purchases of 15,000 SIT or more (certain tobacco products and spirits are exempt) through Kompas MTS, which has offices at Brnik airport and some two dozen border crossings. Ask for a DDV-VP form at the time of purchase. Most towns and cities levy a 'tourist tax' on overnight visitors of between 150 SIT and 300 SIT per person per night (less at camping grounds), which is included in the prices listed here.

POST & COMMUNICATIONS

Poste restante is generally sent to the main post office (in the capital, it goes to the branch at Slovenska cesta 32, 1101 Ljubljana). AmEx card-holders can have their mail addressed c/o Atlas Express, Trubarjeva cesta 50, 1000 Ljubljana.

The easiest place to make long-distance calls is from a post office or telephone centre; the one at Trg Osvobodilne Fronte (Trg OF) near the train and bus stations in Ljubljana is open 24 hours. Public telephones require a phonecard *(telefonska kartica)*, available at all post offices and some newsstands. The international access code in Slovenia is ☎ 00; dial ☎ 115 for an international operator. To call Slovenia, dial the country code (☎ 386), the area code (without the initial zero) and the number.

There is now an Internet café in almost every town. If you can't find one, try the local university or library.

DIGITAL RESOURCES

The official tourist information website is Ⓦ www.slovenia-tourism.si. The site Ⓦ www.matkurja.com is a comprehensive overview of Slovenian websites, with many sites in English. You can find comprehensive sites on most towns by typing in the city name, such as Ⓦ www.ljubljana.si.

BOOKS

Lonely Planet's *Slovenia* is a complete English-language guide to the country. *Discover Slovenia*, published annually by the Cankarjeva Založba bookshop in Ljubljana (3500 SIT), is a colourful and easy introduction.

WOMEN TRAVELLERS

Women are unlikely to encounter problems: Crime is low and harassment rare. In emergencies, contact the **women's crisis helpline** *(☎ 080 1155)*.

GAY & LESBIAN TRAVELLERS

Slovenia is generally tolerant. The gay association **Roza Klub** *(☎ 01-430 4740; Kersnikova ul 4, Ljubljana)* organises a disco every Sunday night at Ljubljana's Klub K4. The club is made up of gay and lesbian branches of the ŠKUC (Student Cultural Centre).

The **GALfon** *(☎ 01-432 4089; open 7pm-10pm)* is a hotline and source of general information for gays and lesbians. The **Slovenian Queer Resources Directory** *(Ⓦ www.ljudmila.org/siqrd)* leaves no stone unturned.

DISABLED TRAVELLERS

Slovenia's government is currently working on making public spaces more accessible, but it's still a tough going. A good resource is **Zveza Paraplegikov Republike Slovenije** *(ZPRS; ☎ 01-432 7138; Štihova ul 14, Ljubljana)*

SENIOR TRAVELLERS

Senior citizens may be entitled to discounts in Slovenia, provided they show proof of age.

DANGERS & ANNOYANCES

Slovenia is hardly a violent or dangerous place. Police say that 90% of all crimes reported involve theft. Bicycle theft is fairly common in Ljubljana.

BUSINESS HOURS

Shops, groceries and department stores are open 7.30am or 8am to 7pm weekdays and to 1pm Saturday. Bank hours are generally 8am to 4.30pm or 5pm weekdays (often with a lunchtime break) and till noon Saturday. The

Emergencies

Emergency numbers include: police ☎ 113; fire, first aid or ambulance ☎ 112; AMZS automobile assistance ☎ 530 5300 (information); and road emergency & towing service ☎ 1987.

main post office is open 7am to 8pm weekdays, till 1pm Saturday and occasionally 9am to 11am Sunday.

PUBLIC HOLIDAYS & SPECIAL EVENTS

Public holidays include two days at New Year (1 and 2 January), National Culture Day (8 February), Easter Sunday and Monday (March/April), Insurrection Day (27 April), two days for Labour Day (1 and 2 May), National Day (25 June), Assumption Day (15 August), Reformation Day (31 October), All Saints' Day (1 November), Christmas (25 December) and Independence Day (26 December).

Though cultural events are scheduled year-round, the highlights of Slovenia's summer season (July and August) are the International Summer Festival in Ljubljana; the Piran Musical Evenings; the Primorska Summer Festival at Piran, Koper, Izola and Portorož; and Summer in the Old Town in Ljubljana, with three or four cultural events a week taking place.

ACTIVITIES

Skiing is by far the most popular sport. The country has many well-equipped resorts in the Julian Alps, especially Vogel (skiing up to 1840m) above Lake Bohinj, Kranjska Gora (1600m), Kanin (2300m) above Bovec, and Krvavec (1970m), northeast of Kranj. **Hiking** is almost as popular, and there are approximately 7000km of marked trails and 165 mountain huts.

The best white-water **rafting** is on the unspoiled Soča. The best rivers for **angling** are the Soča, the Krka, the Kolpa and the Sava Bohinjka near Bohinj. Lake fishing is good at Bled and Bohinj.

Mountain **bikes** are available for hire at Bled and Bohinj. You can also rent bicycles on the coast and in Ljubljana.

ACCOMMODATION

In summer, camping is the cheapest way to go, and good camping grounds abound. It is forbidden to camp 'rough' in Slovenia.

Slovenia has only a handful of 'official' hostels, including two in Ljubljana and excellent ones in Bled and Piran, but many others aren't open year-round. Some college dormitories accept travellers in summer. Private rooms arranged by tourist offices and travel agencies can be inexpensive, but a surcharge of up to 50% is often levied on stays of fewer than three nights. You can bargain for rooms by going directly to any house with a sign reading *sobe* (rooms). A small guesthouse (a *penzion* or *gostišče*) can be a good value.

The agricultural cooperatives of Slovenia have organised a unique programme to accommodate visitors on working farms. Prices average about 3500 SIT per night for bed and breakfast (30% more if less than a two-night stay) to about 5000 SIT per night with full board during high season (July, August and around Christmas). Contact the **Association of Tourist Farms of Slovenia** *(☎ 03-491 6480; ⓔ ztks@siol.net)*. Bookings can be made through **ABC Farm & Countryside Holidays** *(☎ 01-507 6127, fax 519 9876; Ul Jožeta Jame 16, Ljubljana)*.

Hotel rates vary according to the time of year, with July and August the peak season and May/June and September/October the shoulder seasons. In Ljubljana, prices are constant all year. Practically every hotel price includes breakfast.

FOOD & DRINKS

Slovenian food is heavily influenced by neighbouring cuisines. From Austria, there's *klobasa* (sausage), *zavitek* (strudel) and *Dunajski zrezek* (Wiener schnitzel). *Njoki* (potato dumplings), *rižota* (risotto) and the ravioli-like *žlikrofi* are Italian, and Hungary has contributed *golaž* (goulash), *paprikaš* (beef or chicken 'stew') and *palačinke* (thin pancakes filled with jam or nuts and topped with chocolate). And then there's that old Balkan stand-by, *burek*, a greasy, layered cheese, meat or even apple pie.

No Slovenian meal can be considered complete without soup, be it the simple *goveja juha z rezanci* (beef broth with egg noodles), *zelenjavna juha* (vegetable soup) or *gobova juha* (mushroom soup). There are many types of Slovenian cheese dumplings called *štruklji*. Also try the baked delicacies, including *potica* (walnut roll) and *gibanica* (pastry filled with poppy seeds, walnuts, apple and/or sultanas and cottage cheese and topped with cream).

The wine-growing regions of Slovenia are Podravje in the east, noted for white wines; Posavje in the southeast; and Primorska around the coast. *Žganje*is a strong brandy or *eau de vie* distilled from a variety of fruits but most commonly plums. The finest brandy is Pleterska Hruška, made from pears.

Getting There & Away

AIR

Slovenia's national airline, **Adria Airways** (*☎ 01-231 3312 Ljubljana • ☎ 04-202 5111 Brnik airport; W www.adria.si)* has nonstop flights between Ljubljana and Amsterdam, Brussels, Copenhagen, Frankfurt, İstanbul, London, Moscow, Munich, Ohrid, Paris, Sarajevo, Skopje, Split, Tirana, Vienna and Zürich. From May to October, Adria flies to Dublin, Manchester and Tel Aviv. Lufthansa flies in from Frankfurt and Munich, and Swiss Airlines Ltd from Zürich.

A departure tax of 2700 SIT is almost always included in your airline ticket price.

LAND

Bus

Buses from Ljubljana serve a number of international destinations, including Belgrade (7100 to 7400 SIT, three daily), Frankfurt (17,550 SIT, 7.30pm daily), Munich (7900 SIT, 7.30pm daily), Rijeka (2880 SIT, 7.40pm daily), Split (7140 SIT, 7.40pm daily), Trieste (2110 SIT, 6.25am daily) and Zagreb (2570 SIT, three daily).

Nova Gorica is the easiest departure point from Slovenia to Italy. Take one of 17 daily buses (2020 SIT). Koper also has good connections with Trieste. There's also a daily bus from Trieste to Ljubljana (2110 SIT, 6.25am daily).

There is no direct bus linking Ljubljana to Budapest. Instead, take one of up to five daily buses to Lendava; the Hungarian border is 5km further to the north. The first Hungarian train station, Rédics, is only 2km beyond the border.

Train

The main train routes into Slovenia from Austria are Vienna/Graz to Maribor and Ljubljana and Salzburg to Jesenice. Tickets cost 8000 SIT from Ljubljana to Salzburg (four hours) and 11,558 SIT to Vienna (six hours). But it's cheaper to take a local train to Maribor (1380 SIT) and buy your ticket on to Vienna from there. Similarly, from Austria you should only buy a ticket as far as Jesenice or Maribor.

There are three trains a day between Munich and Ljubljana (12,806 SIT, seven hours). Take either the EuroCity *Mimara* via Salzburg, or the *Lisinski* express, which leaves at 11.30pm (sleeping carriage available). A supplement of 1000 SIT is payable on the *Mimara*. Seat reservations (600 SIT) are available on both.

Two trains a day run from Trieste to Ljubljana (4400 SIT, three hours) via the towns of Divača and Sežana. From Croatia it's Zagreb to Ljubljana (2500 SIT, 2½ hours) via Zidani Most, or Rijeka to Ljubljana (2099 SIT, 2½ hours) via Pivka. The InterCity *Drava* and *Venezia Express* trains link Ljubljana with Budapest (9900 SIT, eight hours, two daily) via northwestern Croatia and Zagreb respectively. Three trains a day go to Belgrade (8000 SIT).

Border Crossings

Slovenia maintains some 150 border crossings with Italy, Austria, Hungary and Croatia, but only 26 are considered international crossings. The rest are only open to citizens of Slovenia or others with special permits.

Getting Around

BUS

Except for long journeys, the bus is preferable to the train. Departures are frequent. In Ljubljana you can buy your ticket with seat reservation (600 SIT) the day before, but many people simply pay the driver on boarding. You might need a reservation on Friday afternoons, though. There is a 220 SIT charge for each bag placed underneath the bus.

Footnotes you might see on schedules include: *vozi vsak dan* (runs daily); *vozi ob delavnikih* (runs working days – Monday to Friday); *vozi ob sobotah* (runs Saturday); and *vozi ob nedeljah in praznikih* (runs Sunday and holidays).

TRAIN

Slovenske Železnice *(SŽ; Slovenian Railways)* operates on just over 1200km of track.

The country's most scenic rail routes run along the Soča River from Jesenice to Nova Gorica via Bled (Bled Jezero station) and Bohinjska Bistrica (89km) and from Ljubljana to Zagreb (160km) along the Sava River.

On posted timetables in Slovenia, *odhod* or *odhodi vlakov* means 'departures' and *prihod* (or *prihodi vlakov*) is 'arrivals'. If you don't have time to buy a ticket, the conductor will sell you one for 200 SIT extra.

CAR & MOTORCYCLE

Tolls are not terribly expensive, and fuel remains relatively cheap. Slovenia's automobile club is the **Avto Moto Zveza Slovenije** *(AMZS; ☎ 01-530 5300)*.

Car rentals vary widely in price, but expect to pay from about 14,750/73,920 SIT plus 20% tax a day/week with unlimited mileage, collision damage waiver, theft protection and personal-accident insurance. Three international car-rental chains are **Kompas Hertz** *(☎ 01-231 1241; Miklošičeva cesta)*, **National** *(☎ 01-588 4450; Baragova ul 5)* and **Avis** *(☎ 01-430 8010; Čufarjeva ul 2)*, all in Ljubljana. They also have counters at the airport. Two excellent smaller agencies are **ABC Rent a Car** *(☎ 04-236 7990; open 24 hrs)*, at Brnik airport, and **Avtoimpex** *(☎ 519 7297; Celovška cesta 252)*.

HITCHING

Hitchhiking is legal except on motorways and some major highways; even young women do it. It's never a totally safe way of getting around, and we don't recommend it.

Ljubljana

☎ 01 • pop 280,000

One letter away from 'beloved' *(ljubljena)* in Slovene, Ljubljana (Laibach in German) is by far Slovenia's largest and most populous city. However, the city feels a lot less like an industrious municipality than a pleasant, self-contented town. The most beautiful parts are the Old Town below the castle and the embankments designed by Plečnik along the narrow Ljubljanica River.

Evidence of Ljubljana's beginnings as the Roman town of Emona is manifest throughout the city, and the Habsburgs built many of the pale churches and mansions that earned the city the nickname 'White Ljubljana'. But despite the patina of imperial Austria, contemporary Ljubljana has a vibrant Slavic air all its own. It's like a little Prague, without the hordes of tourists but with all the facilities. Almost 50,000 students attend Ljubljana University's 20 faculties and three art academies, so the city always feels young.

Orientation

The tiny bus station and renovated train station are opposite each other on Trg Osvobodilne Fronte (known as Trg OF), at the northern end of the town centre (called Center).

Information

Tourist Offices The **Tourist Information Centre** *(TIC; ☎ 306 1215, fax 306 1204; e pcl.tic-lj@ljubljana.si; Stritarjeva ul 2; open daily)* is southeast of Triple Bridge. There is a **branch office** *(☎/fax 433 9475; open daily June-Sept, Mon-Fri Oct-May)* at the train station. The office is worth visiting to grab free maps and brochures, organise sightseeing trips or inquire about accommodation. The main office of the **Alpine Association of Slovenia** *(☎ 231 2553; w www.pzs.si; Dvoržakova ul 9)* can help plan trekking or hiking trips.

Money There are over 50 ATMs in Ljubljana. Many are in the Center, including an **A Banka** *(Trg Osvobodilne Fronte 2)* opposite the train station and another at Slovenska 58. There are branches of **Banka Koper** outside the Globtour agency in the Maximarket passageway connecting Trg Republike with Plečnikov trg and at Cigaletova ul 4.

You can get cash advances on MasterCard at **Nova Ljubljanska Banka** *(Trg Republike 2; open 8am-5pm Mon-Fri, 9am-noon Sat)* and **Atlas Express** *(☎ 433 2024; Kolodvorska ul 20)*. Next to the SKB Banka on Trg Ajdovščina is a **currency exchange machine** that changes the banknotes of 18 countries into tolar at a good rate. **Hida exchange bureau** *(Pogarčarjev trg 1; open 7am-7pm Mon-Fri, 7am-2pm Sat)* is in the Seminary building near the open-air market.

Post & Communications Poste restante is held for 30 days at the **post office** *(☎ 426 4668; Slovenska cesta 32; postal code 1101; open 7am-8pm Mon-Fri, 7am-1pm Sat)*. You can make international telephone calls and send faxes from here or the **main post office** *(Pražakova ul 3; open 7am-8pm Mon-Fri,*

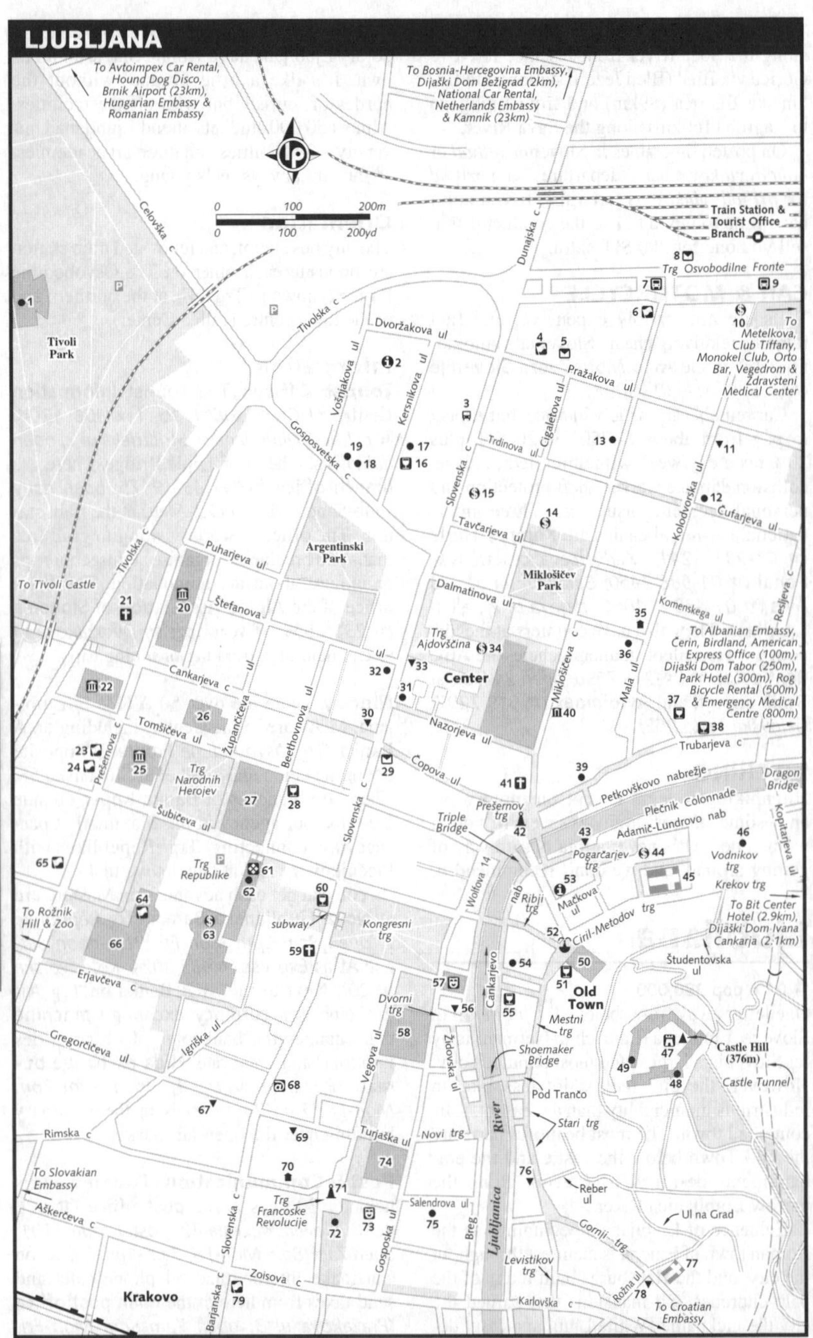
LJUBLJANA
To Avtoimpex Car Rental, Hound Dog Disco, Brnik Airport (23km), Hungarian Embassy & Romanian Embassy
To Bosnia-Hercegovina Embassy, Dijaški Dom Bežigrad (2km), National Car Rental, Netherlands Embassy & Kamnik (23km)
Train Station & Tourist Office Branch
Trg Osvobodilne Fronte
To Metelkova, Club Tiffany, Monokel Club, Orto Bar, Vegedrom & Zdravsteni Medical Center
Tivoli Park
Argentinski Park
Miklošičev Park
To Tivoli Castle
Center
To Albanian Embassy, Čerin, Birdland, American Express Office (100m), Dijaški Dom Tabor (250m), Park Hotel (300m), Rog Bicycle Rental (500m) & Emergency Medical Centre (800m)
Trg Narodnih Herojev
Trg Republike
Prešernov trg
Triple Bridge
Dragon Bridge
Plečnik Colonnade
Pogarčarjev trg
Vodnikov trg
Krekov trg
To Bit Center Hotel (2.9km), Dijaški Dom Ivana Cankarja (2.1km)
To Rožnik Hill & Zoo
Kongresni trg
Old Town
Mestni trg
Castle Hill (376m)
Castle Tunnel
Shoemaker Bridge
Pod Trančo
Stari trg
Dvorni trg
To Slovakian Embassy
Trg Francoske Revolucije
Reber ul
Ul na Grad
Levstikov trg
Krakovo
To Croatian Embassy
Ljubljanica River
Celovška c
Dunajska c
Tivolska c
Dvoržakova ul
Pražakova ul
Gosposvetska c
Trdinova ul
Tavčarjeva ul
Dalmatinova ul
Komenskega ul
Puharjeva ul
Štefanova ul
Cankarjeva c
Tomšičeva ul
Šubičeva ul
Nazorjeva ul
Čopova ul
Petkovškovo nabrežje
Adamič-Lundrovo nab
Ciril-Metodov trg
Študentovska ul
Erjavčeva c
Gregorčičeva ul
Rimska c
Aškerčeva c
Zoisova c
Karlovška c
Salendrova ul
Gornji trg
Rožna ul
Trubarjeva c
Resljeva c
Kopitarjeva ul
Kolodvorska ul
Čufarjeva ul
Mala ul
Miklošičeva c
Cigaletova ul
Slovenska c
Kersnikova ul
Vošnjakova ul
Župančičeva ul
Beethovnova ul
Prešernova c
Igriška ul
Vegova ul
Gosposka ul
Židovska ul
Cankarjevo nab
Wolfova 14
Ribji trg
Mačkova ul
Turjaška ul
Novi trg
Breg
Barjanska c
subway
SLOVENIA

LJUBLJANA

PLACES TO STAY
35 Klub Central
70 Pri Mraku

PLACES TO EAT
11 Burek Stand
30 Quick
33 Šestica
43 Ribca
56 Ljubljanski Dvor
67 Prema
69 Foculus
76 Najboljski Gyros
78 Špajza

OTHER
1 Tivoli Recreation Centre & Zlati Klub
2 Alpine Association of Slovenia
3 City Bus Ticket Kiosks
4 South African Honorary Consulate
5 Main Post Office
6 Canadian Consulate
7 City Airport Buses
8 Post Office (Customs) & Telephone Centre
9 Bus Station
10 A Banka
12 Avis
13 Kompas Hertz
14 Banka Koper
15 A Banka
16 Club K4 Café; Roza Klub
17 ZMT Infopoint
18 Lufthansa Ticket Office
19 Adria Airways
20 National Gallery
21 Church of Sts Cyril & Methodius
22 Museum of Modern Art
23 US Embassy
24 German Embassy
25 National Museum
26 Opera House
27 Parliament Building
28 Jazz Club Gajo
29 Post Office (Poste Restante)
31 Cankarjeva Založba Bookshop
32 Kompas Travel Agency; Holidays' Pub
34 SKB Banka
36 Tour As
37 Patrick's Irish Pub
38 Salon
39 Erazem Travel Office
40 Art Nouveau Bank Buildings
41 Franciscan Church
42 Prešeren Monument
44 Hida Exchange Bureau; Seminary
45 Cathedral of St Nicholas
46 Open-Air Produce Market
47 Ljubljana Castle
48 Pentagonal Tower
49 Castle Tower
50 Town Hall
51 Vinoteka Movia
52 Robba Fountain
53 Tourist Information Centre (TIC)
54 Bicycle Rentals
55 Maček
57 Filharmonija
58 Ljubljana University
59 Ursuline Church of the Holy Trinity
60 Brewery Pub
61 Maximarket Department Store & Supermarket; Banka Koper
62 Globtour Agency
63 Nova Ljubljanska Banka
64 UK Embassy; Australian Consulate
65 Austrian Embassy
66 Cankarjev Dom
68 Cyber Cafe
71 Ilirija Column
72 Križanke Booking Office
73 Križanke Theatre
74 National & University Library
75 Mladi Turist
77 Church of St Florian
79 French Embassy

7am-1pm Sat). To mail a parcel, take it unsealed to the **special customs post office** *(Trg OF 5; open 24 hrs)* opposite the bus station. The maximum weight is about 15kg.

Internet access is free at **Klub K4 Café** *(☎ 431 7010; Kersnikova ul 4)*. **Cyber Café** *(Slovenska cesta 10)* charges 600/400/200 SIT for 60/30/15 minutes, has five terminals and also sells drinks. Students pay half price. **Kavarna Čerin** *(☎ 232 0990; Trubarjeva 52)* is a full-service café with Internet access with the price of a drink.

Travel Agencies Backpackers and students should head to **ZMT Infopoint** *(☎ 438 0312; Kersnikova ul 6)*, which sells ISIC cards; **Mladi Turist** *(☎ 425 9260; Salendrova ul 4)*, the office of the Slovenian Youth Hostel Association; or **Erazem Travel Office** *(☎ 433 1076; Trubarjeva cesta 7)*. There is also an **American Express** representative *(☎ 431 9020; Trubarjeva 50)* in the city.

Medical Services In a medical emergency, dial ☎ 112 or go to the **emergency medical centre** *(☎ 232 3060; Bohoričeva 9)*. To see a doctor, try the **Zdravstveni dom Center** *(☎ 472 3700; Metelkova 9)*.

Things to See

Old Ljubljana's most picturesque sights are along the banks of the Ljubljanica, a tributary of the Sava. Opposite the TIC is the celebrated **Triple Bridge**. In 1931, Jože Plečnik added the side bridges to the original central span dating from 1842. On the northern side of the bridge is Prešernov trg, with its pink **Franciscan church** (1660), a **statue** (1905) of poet France Prešeren and some fine Art Nouveau buildings.

On the south side of the bridge in Mestni trg, the baroque **Robba Fountain** stands before the Gothic **Town Hall** (Magistrat; 1718). To the south is lively **Stari trg**. Northeast are the twin towers of the **Cathedral of St Nicholas** (1708), which contains impressive frescoes.

Ljubljana Castle has been renovated, so you can climb the 19th-century **Castle Tower,** and view the exhibits in the Gothic chapel, and **Pentagonal Tower** *(open Tues-Sun)*. Walk or take the tram, which leaves Prešernov trg (next to the Triple Bridge) hourly (500/350 SIT for adults/children and students).

On Gosposka ul are the 1941 **National & University Library** *(Gosposka ul 14)*, designed by Plečnik, and the main building (1902) of **Ljubljana University** *(Kongresni trg 12)*, formerly the regional parliament. The elegant **Filharmonija** *(Philharmonic Hall; Kongresni Trg)*, on the southeastern corner of the square, is home to the Slovenian Philharmonic Orchestra. The **Ursuline Church of the Holy Trinity** (1726), with an altar by Robba, faces Kongresni trg to the west.

The **National Museum** *(Muzejska ul 1; adult/child 500/300 SIT; open 10am-6pm Tues-Sun)* has prehistory and natural history collections. The highlight is a Celtic *situla*, a kind of pail, from the 6th century BC.

The **National Gallery** *(Prešernova cesta 24; adult/child 700/500 SIT, free Sat afternoon; open 10am-6pm Tues-Sun)* displays European portraits and landscapes from the 17th to 19th centuries, as well as copies of medieval frescoes. The Serbian Orthodox **Church of Sts Cyril & Methodius** *(open 3pm-6pm Tues-Sat)*, opposite the Museum of Modern Art, is worth visiting to see the beautiful modern frescoes.

SLOVENIA

Organised Tours

Guided tours (adults €5.50, students, pensioners and children €2.75) are available in English from in front of the **Town Hall** *(Mestni trg 1)*. Tours leave at 11am and 5pm on Friday, Saturday and Sunday from June to September; in July and August they are at 11am every day. In the low season, there is a tour at 11am on Sunday.

Places to Stay

The TIC has about 40 **private rooms** on its list, but just a handful are in Center. Singles/doubles start at 3500/5000 SIT. If you need an apartment, try **Tour As** *(☎ 434 2660; ⓔ info@apartmaji.si; Mala ul 8)*.

There are three student dormitories *(dijaški dom)* open to foreign travellers in July and August. The most central by far is HI-affiliated **Dijaški Dom Tabor** *(☎ 234 8840; ⓔ ssljddta1s@guest.arnes.si; Vidovdanska ul 7; singles 4000 SIT, doubles or triples per bed members/nonmembers 2900/3400 SIT)*, opposite Park Hotel. Breakfast is included in the price.

Dijaški Dom Bežigrad *(☎ 534 2867; ⓔ dd.lj-bezigrad@guest.arnes.si; Kardeljeva pl 28; bus No 6; singles/shared per person 3800/3300 SIT, breakfast 460 SIT)*, another HI member, is in the Bežigrad district 2km north of the train and bus stations. The Bežigrad has 50 rooms available in July and August.

Dijaška Dom Ivana Cankarja *(☎ 474 8600; ⓔ dd.lj-ic@guest.arnes.si; Polanski cesta 26; per person €10-14, with breakfast €12-15)* is just east of the town centre (10% less for students).

The best hotel for location and quality is the **Pri Mraku** *(☎ 433 4049; ⓔ mrak@daj-dam.si; Rimska cesta 4; singles/doubles/quads 13,950/19,200/33,800 SIT)*. It also has an excellent restaurant.

The 122-room **Park Hotel** *(☎ 433 1306, fax 433 0546; ⓔ hotel.park@siol.net; Tabor 9; singles/doubles from €37/50)* is where most people usually end up as it's the only large budget hotel close to Center. It's pretty depressing, but the price is right. Students with cards get a 20% discount.

Bit Center Hotel *(☎ 548 0055, fax 548 0056; ⓦ www.bit-center.net; Litijska 57; bus No 9 from the railway station; singles/doubles or triples 5490/8190 SIT, breakfast 800 SIT)*, one small step up from a hostel, is also a possibility. Hotel guests get a 50% discount on sauna and health-club services, available in the same building.

Places to Eat

The **supermarket** *(Trg Republike; open 9am-8pm Mon-Fri, to 3pm Sat & Sun)* in the basement of the Maximarket shopping arcade has about the largest selection in town. For healthy snacks and vegetarian food, try **Prema** *(Gregorčičeva 9)*.

Quick *(Cankarjeva cesta 12; open 6.30am-11pm Mon-Sat, 4pm-10pm Sun)* sells fast food such as hamburgers and takeaway coffee.

Ribca *(Pogarčarjev trg)*, a seafood bar below the Plečnik Colonnade, is good for a quick and tasty lunch. **Najboljski Gyros** *(Stari trg 19; open 9am-1am Mon-Thur, noon-1am Fri & Sat)* sells gyros, pizzas and crepes, all under 1000 SIT. There is also a **burek stand** *(Kolodvorska ul 20; open 24 hrs)* if you want a quick bite.

Several excellent restaurants are relatively good values. One is **Šestica** *(Slovenska cesta 40; lunch menus 1000-1400 SIT, mains 1100-2000 SIT)*, a 200-year-old stand-by with a pleasant courtyard. The capital abounds in Italian restaurants and pizzerias. Among the best in town are **Ljubljanski Dvor** *(Dvorni trg 1)*, on the west bank of the Ljubljanica, and **Foculus** *(Gregorčičeva ul 3; small/large pizzas 800/1100 SIT, salad bar available)*, next to the Glej Theatre. **Špajza** *(Gornji trg 28)* is popular with locals. The delicious vegetarian restaurant *(☎ 459 1750, Maistrova 10)* serves Indian cuisine such as *samosas* and *palak paneer*.

Entertainment

Ask the TIC for its monthly programme of events in the English-language *Where to? in Ljubljana* or check out *Ljubljana Life*, the English monthly available at the TIC and in hotels and restaurants.

A fun place to try Slovenian wine is **Vinoteka Movia** *(Mestni trg 2)*, a wine bar next to the Town Hall. Pleasant and congenial places for a *pivo* or glass of *vino* include **Salon** *(Trubarjeva cesta 23)*, **Patrick's Irish Pub** *(Prečna ul 6)* and **Holidays' Pub** *(Slovenska cesta 36)*. Along the river, the most popular bar is **Maček** *(Cankarjevo nab 19)*.

Two of the most popular conventional dance clubs are **Klub Central** *(Dalmatinova ul 15)*, next to the Turist Hotel, and **Hound Dog** *(Trg Prekomorskih Brigad 4)*, in the Hotel M, both populated by a young crowd. The student hang-out **K4** *(Kersnikova ul 4)* has a disco every night, open until the wee hours on Friday and Saturday nights and until around midnight on other nights. A popular spot for both gays and lesbians on Sunday night is **Roza Klub** *(open 10pm-4am)* at K4.

A popular place is **Metelkova mesto** (along Metelkova cesta near Maistrova ul), where squatters have turned former Yugoslav army barracks into the hippest spot in town, with several nightclubs and bars. There's a café/pub for gays called **Club Tiffany,** which also houses **Monokel Club** *(open Thur-Mon)*, a popular spot for lesbians.

Ljubljana has a number of excellent rock clubs with canned or live music, including **Orto Bar** *(Grablovičeva ul 1)* and the **Brewery Pub** *(Plečnikov trg 1)*. For jazz, you can't beat the **Jazz Club Gajo** *(Beethovnova ul 8)* near the Parliament building. **Birdland** *(Trubarjeva cesta 50)* has Wednesday night jam sessions on and occasional jazz concerts on the weekend.

The capital is home to two orchestras. Concerts are held in various locations all over town, but the main venue – with up to 700 cultural events a year – is **Cankarjev Dom** *(Trg Republike)*. The **ticket office** *(☎ 241 7100; tickets 1500-3000 SIT; open 10am-2pm & 4.30pm-8pm Mon-Fri, 10am-1pm Sat & 1hr before performances)* is in the basement of the nearby Maximarket mall. Also check for concerts at the beautiful **Filharmonija** *(Kongresni trg 10)*. The ticket office of the **Opera House** *(☎ 425 4840; Župančičeva ul 1; open 2pm-5pm Mon-Fri, 6pm-7pm Sat & 1hr before performances)* also sells ballet tickets.

For tickets to the Ljubljana Summer Festival and anything else staged at the **Križanke**, go to the attached **booking office** *(☎ 252 6544; Trg Francoske Revolucije 1–2; open 10am-2pm & 4.30pm-8pm Mon-Fri, 10am-1pm Sat & 1hr before performances)*, behind the Ilirija Column.

Getting There & Away

You can get virtually anywhere in the country by bus from the capital. The timetable in the shed-like **bus station** *(☎ 090 4230; Trg OF)* lists all routes and times. Some destinations are Bled (1220 SIT, hourly), Bohinj (1730 SIT, hourly), Koper (2200 SIT, eight a day), Piran (3370 SIT, seven a day) and Postojna (1120 SIT, 25 a day).

All domestic and international trains arrive at and depart from the **station** *(☎ 291 3332; Trg OF 6)*. Local trains leave Ljubljana regularly for Bled (680 SIT, 51km), Koper (1380 SIT, 153km) and Maribor (1380 SIT, 156km). There's a 260 SIT surcharge on domestic InterCity train tickets. For details on international trains, see the Getting There & Away section at the beginning of this chapter.

Getting Around

The city bus from lane No 28 leaves every hour for Brnik airport (680 SIT, 45 minutes), 23km to the northwest, 10 minutes past the hour Monday to Friday and weekends on odd hours. There's also an **airport shuttle** *(☎ 040-887 766)* for about 2500 SIT. A taxi will cost between 5000 SIT and 6500 SIT.

Ljubljana's bus system *(☎ 582 2460)* is excellent and user-friendly. There are 22 lines; five (Nos 1, 2, 3, 6 and 11) are considered 'main lines' (running 3.15am to midnight), while the rest operate from 5am to 10.30pm. You can pay on board (230 SIT) or use tiny yellow plastic tokens (170 SIT) available at the bus station, newsstands, tobacconists, post offices and the two kiosks in front of Slovenska cesta 55. All-day tickets are available for 660 SIT. You can call a taxi on one of 10 numbers: ☎ 9700 to 9709.

Visitors can rent bicycles at **Rog** *(☎ 520 0310; open 8am-7pm Mon-Fri, 8am-noon Sat)*, next to Rozmanova ul 1. From June to the end of September, you can also rent bikes near **Maček** *(☎ 041-696 515)*, on Cankarjevo nab.

Julian Alps

Slovenia shares the dramatic Julian Alps with Italy. Tri-peaked Mt Triglav (2864m), the country's highest summit, is climbed regularly by thousands of weekend warriors, but there are countless less ambitious hikes in the region. Lakes Bled and Bohinj make ideal starting points. Most of this spectacular area falls within the boundaries of the Triglav National Park, established in 1924.

BLED

☎ 04 • pop 5400

A fashionable resort at just over 500m, Bled is set on an idyllic, emerald-green lake with a little island and church in the centre and a dramatic castle towering overhead. Trout and carp proliferate in the clear water, which is surprisingly warm and a pleasure for swimming or boating. To the northeast, the highest peaks of the Karavanke Range form a natural boundary with Austria, and the Julian Alps lie to the west. All in all, it is beautiful – but it can get very crowded and pricey in season.

SLOVENIA

Information

The **tourist office** *(☎ 574 1122, fax 574 1555; w www.bled.si; Cesta Svobode 15; open daily)* offers the useful booklet *Bled Tourist Information* (300 SIT), which is reproduced on the town's useful website. **Kompas** *(☎ 574 1515; Ljubljanska cesta 4)*, in the Triglav shopping centre, sells good hiking maps. The **Triglav National Park office** *(☎ 578 0200; Kidričeva cesta 2; open 7am-3pm Mon-Fri)* is on the lake's northern shore.

The **post office** *(Ljubljanska cesta 10; open 7am-7pm Mon-Fri, 7am-noon Sat)* is in the centre of town. Internet access is available at **Bledec Hostel** at 500 SIT for 30 minutes. In town, **Apropos** *(Ljubljanska cesta 4; open 8am-midnight Mon-Sat)* costs 1000 SIT for one hour, 500 SIT for 30 minutes.

Gorenjska Banka *(Cesta Svobode 15; open 9am-11.30am & 2pm-5pm Mon-Fri, 8am-11am Sat)*, in the Park Hotel shopping complex, has an ATM for MasterCard/Cirrus. The **SKB Banka ATM** *(Ljubljanska cesta 4; open 8.30am-noon & 2pm-5pm Mon-Fri)* accepts all cards. Kompas and the tourist office change money.

Things to See & Do

There are several trails up to **Bled Castle** *(adult/child 700/400 SIT; open 9am-8pm daily May-Sept; open 9am-5pm daily rest of year)*, the easiest being the one going south from behind Bledec Hostel at Grajska cesta 17. The castle was the seat of the Bishops of Brixen (South Tirol) for over 800 years. The **museum** allows a peep into a small 16th-century chapel.

An excellent half-day hike from Bled features a visit to impressive **Vintgar Gorge** *(adult/child 500/300 SIT; open daily May-Oct)*, 4.5km to the northwest. The trek takes in **Šum Waterfall** and the ancient pilgrimage **Church of St Catherine**. Ask at the tourist office for details.

Places to Stay

At the western end of the lake, **Camping Bled** *(☎ 575 2000; adult/child low season 1250/875 SIT, high season 1840/1290 SIT; open Apr–mid-Oct)* is in a quiet valley about 2.5km from the bus station. Facilities include a good location, a beach, tennis courts, a

Ringing in the Good Times

What's that noise constantly echoing off the mountains? It sounds like it might be coming from that tiny little scrap of land over on the western end of the lake, right? Indeed it is – what you're hearing is the famous 'bell of wishes' tolling on li'l ol' **Bled Island** *(Blejski Otok)*. The bell's sonorous peals emit from the island church's tall white belfry, constructed in 1534. Legend has it that everyone who rings the bell shall have their wish granted. Naturally, everyone and their Slavic grandmother rings the thing incessantly.

Underneath the baroque church are the foundations of a pre-Romanesque chapel, unique in Slovenia. You can see it all by taking a *pletna* (a local version of the gondola) or renting your own rowboat.

large restaurant and a supermarket – but it fills up very quickly in summer.

Bledec Hostel *(☎ 574 5250; Grajska cesta 17; beds low/high season with ISIC/IYHF card €14/15, without card €17/19)* has 55 beds available. Breakfast is included.

Finding a private room is easy. The travel agencies have extensive lists, and there are lots of houses around the lake with *'sobe'* or *'Zimmer frei'* signs. **Kompas** *(☎ 574 1515; e kompas.bled@siol.net; Ljubljanska cesta 4; singles €14-21, doubles €18-34; 2-person apartments €24-38)* is a good place to start. Rooms and apartments are also available through the tourist office or at **Globtour Bled** *(☎ 574 4186, fax 574 4185; Ljubljanska cesta 7)*, at Hotel Krim.

Most of Bled's hotels are pretty expensive affairs. Among the cheapest is the 212-bed **Hotel Krim** *(☎ 579 7000, fax 574 3729; e hotelkrim@hotel-krim.si; Ljubljanska cesta 7; singles/doubles high season €48/68)*, in the town centre.

Places to Eat

Bled's best choice for an affordable meal is homy **Gostilna Pri Planincu** *(Grajska cesta 8; meals from 2000 SIT)*, just a stone's throw from the bus station. The menu includes excellent dishes such as mushroom soup and grilled chicken. **Okarina** *(☎ 574 1458; Riklijeva cesta 9)* has first-rate vegetarian Indian cuisine as well as Slovenian specialities. There's a **supermarket** in the Triglav shopping centre.

A few miles out of town in charming Radovljica is **Gostilna Lectar** *(☎ 537 4800; Linhartov trg 2; open Wed-Sun)*. This traditional restaurant is one of the most famous in Slovenia. Take the main highway towards Ljubljana and you'll see signs for Radovljica.

Getting There & Around

If you're coming from Ljubljana, take the bus. Buses run to Ljubljana (hourly) and Bohinj (hourly starting at 7.20am). One bus a day from July to mid-September goes to Bovec via Kranjska Gora and the heart-stopping Vršič Pass.

Lesce-Bled train station handles up to 20 trains a day from Ljubljana (55 minutes). About eight cross the Austrian border and contine on to Germany.

Kompas *(☎ 574 1515; Ljubljanska cesta)* rents out bicycles and mountain bikes for 4700/1500/2200 SIT per hour/half-day/day.

BOHINJ

☎ 04

Exceedingly beautiful Bohinj is a larger and much less-developed glacial lake 26km southwest of Bled. Mountains loom directly from the basin-shaped valley, secluded beaches lie off the trail along the northern shore, and the hiking possibilities include an ascent of Mt Triglav. 'Bohinj' refers to the valley, its settlements and the lake. The largest town is Bohinjska Bistrica, 6km east of the lake. The main settlement on the lake is Ribčev Laz. Here, just up from the bus stop, you'll find the post office, tourist office and the Alpinum travel agency.

About 1km north across the Sava Bohinjka River and at the mouth of the Mostnica Canyon sits the town of Stara Fužina. The Zlatorog Hotel is at Ukanc, at the western end of the lake near the camping ground and the cable car, which takes visitors up to Mt Vogel (1922m).

The helpful and efficient **tourist office** *(☎ 572 3370, fax 572 3330; w www.bohinj.si; Ribčev Laz 48; open daily)* operates a useful website and can change money with a 3% commission. There's an ATM at the post office next door. **Gorenjska Banka** *(Trg Svobode 2b)* has another branch in Bohinjska Bistrica.

The **post office** *(Ribčev Laz 47; open 8am-6pm Mon-Fri, 8am-noon Sat)* takes a couple of half-hour breaks during the day. **Alpinum travel agency** *(☎ 572 3441; Ribčev Laz 50)* organises sporting activities in Bohinj and rents rooms.

Things to See & Do

Don't miss the **Church of St John the Baptist**, on the north side of the Sava Bohinjka across the stone bridge from Ribčev Laz. With exquisite 15th-century frescoes, it can lay claim to being the most beautiful and evocative church in Slovenia.

Sporting equipment is available from **Alpinsport kiosk** *(☎ 572 3486; Ribčev Laz 53)*, just before the stone bridge to the church. Canoes and kayaks cost from 800/3100 SIT per hour/day. It also organises guided tours in the mountains and canoe trips on the Sava.

The **Vogel cable car** *(adult/child return 1000/700 SIT)*, above the camping ground at the western end of Lake Bohinj about 5km from Ribčev Laz, will whisk you 1000m up into the mountains. It runs every half-hour year round except in November. From the upper station (1540m) you can scale **Mt Vogel** for a sweeping view.

Contact the **Alpine Association of Slovenia** *(☎ 231 2553; Ⓦ www.pzs.si; Dvoržakova ul 9)* for information on hiking Mt Trigalv.

Places to Stay & Eat

Autocamp Zlatorog *(☎ 572 3482, fax 572 3483; camp sites per person 1100-2100 SIT; open year-round)* caters mostly to camper vans, but its location on the lake near Zlatorog Hotel can't be beaten.

The tourist office can arrange **private rooms** *(singles/doubles with shower low season 1920/3200 SIT, July & August to 2400/4000 SIT)* in neighbouring villages. There's usually a 30% surcharge for stays of fewer than three days.

Pizza Center *(Ribčev Laz 50)*, next to Alpinum travel agency, is very popular. For a truly different lunch, try **Planšar** *(Stara Fužina 179)*, opposite the Alpine Dairy Museum; it offers home-made dairy specialities for about 700 SIT. A **Mercator supermarket** *(Ribčev Laz 49; open 7am-7pm Mon-Fri, 7am-5pm Sat)* satiates self-caterers.

Getting There & Around

Hourly buses run between Ribčev Laz and Ljubljana via Bled, Radovljica, Kranj and Bohinjska Bistrica. About six local buses a day run to Bohinjska Bistrica. All stop near the post office on Triglavska cesta in Bohinjska Bistrica and in Ribčev Laz (500m from the TIC towards Pension Kristal) before carrying on to Zlatorog Hotel in Ukanc. The closest train station is at Bohinjska Bistrica on the Jesenice-Nova Gorica line.

Mountain bikes and helmets can be rented from **Alpinsport kiosk** *(☎ 572 3486; Ribčev Laz 53)* for 800/3100 SIT per hour/day.

SLOVENIA

Soča Valley

The Soča Valley, defined by the bluer-than-blue Soča River, is one of the most beautiful and peaceful spots in Slovenia. It wasn't always that way. During much of WWI, this was the site of the infamous Soča (or Isonzo) Front, which claimed the lives of an estimated one million people. Hemingway made the region famous in his *Farewell to Arms*.

Although getting here is difficult, it's worth the trip for its amazing beauty. In Kobarid, the **tourist office** is in the Kobarid Museum and, in Bovec, the **Avrigo Tours agency** *(☎ 05-388 6022; Trg Golobarskih Žrtev 47)*, next to the Alp hotel, can organise **private rooms** from 2500 SIT per person for a double. There are four camping grounds in Bovec, the closest is **Polovnik** *(☎ 05-388 6069)*, and there is one in Kobarid – **Koren** *(☎ 05-388 5312)*.

There are up to six daily buses between Kobarid and Bovec. Two to five buses run daily to Ljubljana. In July and August there's a daily bus to Ljubljana via the Vršič Pass and Kranjska Gora. From Bled there are three trains a day to Most na Soći (55 minutes), from which there are regular buses to Kobarid and Bovec (45 minutes).

Karst Region

POSTOJNA & AROUND

☎ 05 • pop 8200

Vying with Bled as Slovenia's top tourist spot, **Postojna Cave** *(adult/student & child 2400/1200 SIT)* attracts the hordes. Get directions to the cave from the **tourist office** *(☎ 726 5183; Jamska cesta 9; Ⓔ td.tic.postojna@siol.net; open Mon-Sat)* in the shopping centre beneath Hotel Jama. Visitors get to see about 5.7km of the cave (which runs for more than 20km) on a 1½-hour tour. About 4km are covered by an electric train that will shuttle you through colourfully lit karst formations along the Old Passage; the remaining 1700m is on foot. The tour ends with a viewing of a tank full of *Proteus anguinus*, the 'human fish' inhabiting Slovenia's karst caves. Dress warmly as the cave is a constant 9.5°C (with 95% humidity) all year. At least two cave tours leave daily (in summer, there are up to eight).

If you have a vehicle, consider visiting the **Škocjan Caves** *(adult/student/child 1700/1000/800 SIT)*, in more natural surroundings than Postojna Cave. They're 4km southeast of Divača (between Postojna and Koper).

Postojna is a day trip from Ljubljana, or a stopover on the way to/from the coast or Croatian Istria; almost all buses between the capital and the coast stop there.

The Coast

KOPER

☎ 05 • pop 24,000

Only 21km south of Trieste, Koper is an industrial port town with a quaint city centre.

Lodging here is expensive, and most travellers treat the town as a transit point. The bus and train stations are in a modern structure about a kilometre southeast of the Old Town.

The **tourist office** *(☎/fax 627 3791; Ukmarjev trg 7; open daily June-Sept, Mon-Sat Oct-May)* is opposite the marina. Inquire here about private rooms (2700 to 3100 SIT per person). The **Nova Ljubljanska Banka** *(Pristaniška ul 45; open 8.30am-noon & 3.30pm-6pm Mon-Fri)* has an ATM. There are also a couple of private exchange offices on Pristaniška ul. The **post office** *(Muzejski trg 3; open 8am-7pm Mon-Fri, 8am-noon Sat)*, with an ATM, is near the **Koper Regional Museum** *(Kidričeva ul 19; adult/student & child 350/250 SIT; open 8am-3pm Mon-Fri, 8am-1pm Sat year-round, also 6pm-8pm Mon-Fri summer)*, which is in the Belgramoni-Tacco Palace. It contains old maps and photos of the port and coast, a 16th- to 18th-century Italianate sculpture garden and paintings and copies of medieval frescoes.

In July and August **Dijaški Dom Koper** *(☎ 627 3252; Cankarjeva ul 5; beds per person 3500 SIT)*, an official hostel in the Old Town east of Trg Brolo, rents out 380 beds in triples. One of the most colourful places for a meal is **Istrska Klet** *(Župančičeva ul 39; mains around 1200 SIT)*, in an old palace. This is a good place to try Teran wine.

There are buses almost every 20 minutes on weekdays to Piran (17km) and Portorož via Izola, and every 40 minutes on weekends. Buses also leave every hour or 90 minutes for Ljubljana (2400 SIT, 2¼ hours) via Divača and Postojna. You can also take the train to Ljubljana (1700 SIT, 2¼ hours), which is much more comfortable.

Up to 17 buses a day depart for Trieste (600 SIT) during the week. Destinations in Croatia include Buzet (three or four daily), Poreč (three or four daily), Pula (one or two daily), Rijeka (10.10am daily), Rovinj (3.55pm daily) and Zagreb (two daily).

PIRAN

☎ 05 • pop 4400

Picturesque Piran (Pirano in Italian) is everyone's favourite Slovenian coastal town. It's a gem of Venetian Gothic architecture, but it can be mobbed at the height of summer. The name derives from the Greek *pyr* (fire), referring to the ones lit at Punta to guide ships to port.

Buses stop just south of Piran Harbour and next to the court house on Tartinijev trg, which is the heart of Piran's Old Town. **Maona travel agency** *(☎ 673 1291; e maona@siol.net; Cankarjevo nab 7; open Apr-Oct)* can organise accommodation and an endless string of activities. **Banka Koper** *(Tartinijev trg 12; open 8.30am-noon & 3pm-5pm Mon-Fri, 8.30am-noon Sat)* changes cash and has an ATM. There's a **post office** *(Cankarjevo nab 5; open 8am-7pm Mon-Fri, 8am-noon Sat)* on the harbourfront.

The **Maritime Museum** *(Cankarjevo nab 3; adult/student 500/400 SIT; open 9am-noon & 3pm-6pm Tues-Sun)*, in a 17th-century harbourside palace, focuses on Piran's three 'S's: sea, sailing and salt-making. The antique model ships are first-rate. The **Town Hall** and **Court House** stand on Tartinijev trg, in the centre of which is a **statue** of local violinist and composer Giuseppe Tartini (1692–1770). Piran is dominated by the tall tower of the **Church of St George** *(Adamičeva ul 2)*, a Renaissance and baroque structure on a ridge above the sea north of Tartinijev trg. It's wonderfully decorated with frescoes and features a statue of George slaying the dragon. The octagonal 17th-century **Baptistry** contains a Roman sarcophagus from the 2nd century.

Places to Stay & Eat

The **tourist offices** in Piran and Portorož *(☎ 674 7015; w www.portoroz.si)* and **Maona travel agency** *(☎ 674 6423; e maona@siol.net)* can arrange **private rooms** and **apartments**. Singles/doubles/triples start at 3100/4600/5800 SIT.

A very central, relatively cheap place is **Val Hostel** *(☎ 673 2555, fax 673 2556; e yhostel.val@siol.net; Gregorčičeva ul 38a; beds €16-18; open year-round)* at Vegova ul. Though not in Piran itself, one of the nicest places on the coast is **Fiesa** *(☎ 671 2200, fax 671 2223; e hotel.fiesa@amis.net; singles/doubles from €35/52)*, overlooking the sea. Back in town, right on the water is **Piran Hotel** *(☎ 676 2100, fax 676 2522; e recepcija.piran@hoteli-piran.si; Kidričevo nab 4; singles/doubles low season from €41/66, high season €58/98)*, with recently refurbished rooms.

Cafe Teater, just south of Piran Hotel, offers six different beers on tap. There are several pizzerias along Prešernovo nab near the Punta lighthouse, including **Flora** and **Punta**.

PIRAN

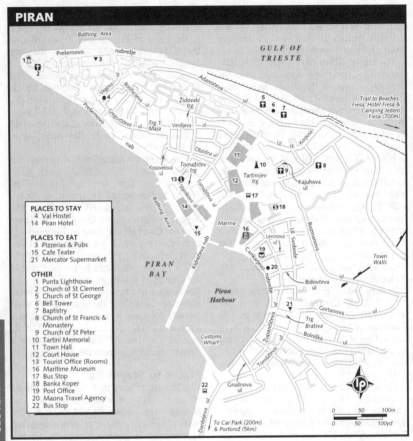

PLACES TO STAY
4 Val Hostel
14 Piran Hotel

PLACES TO EAT
3 Pizzerias & Pubs
15 Cafe Teater
21 Mercator Supermarket

OTHER
1 Punta Lighthouse
2 Church of St Clement
5 Church of St George
6 Bell Tower
7 Baptistry
8 Church of St Francis & Monastery
9 Church of St Peter
10 Tartini Memorial
11 Town Hall
12 Court House
13 Tourist Office (Rooms)
16 Maritime Museum
17 Bus Stop
18 Banka Koper
19 Post Office
20 Maona Travel Agency
22 Bus Stop

Trail to Beaches, Fiesa, Hotel Fiesa & Camping Jezero Fiesa (700m)

To Car Park (200m) & Portorož (5km)

The **Mercator supermarket** *(open 7am-8pm Mon-Fri, 7am-1pm Sat, 7am-11am Sun)* is opposite Trg Bratsva 8.

Getting There & Away

Local bus company I&I links Piran with Portorož and Lucija (bus No 1); with Portorož and Fiesa (No 2; mid-June to August only); with Strunjan and Portorož (No 3); and with Portorož, Sečovlje and Padna (No 4). Schedules vary, but bus No 1 runs about every 10 to 15 minutes. The fare is 210 SIT.

Other destinations include Trieste, Zagreb, and Ljubljana via Divača and Postojna.

Spain

A land of majesty and madness is Spain, where ghosts of a legendary past stalk the earth and seemingly every day is devoted to a frenzied, unrelenting quest for bliss. The clashes and combinations that shaped Spain's history have given rise to a culture painted in the brightest of colours and steeped in the most vivacious of traditions. Spaniards approach life with such exuberance that visitors have to stop and stare. In almost every city, the Spaniards will outlast the foreigners when it comes to the nightlife. And just when the bewildered traveller appears to have come to terms with the pace, she or he is surrounded by the beating drums of a fiesta, with day and night turning into a blur of dancing, laughing, eating and drinking.

Long a meeting point (and battleground) for civilisations, the country brims over with remnants of a chaotic, glorious past – from prehistoric displays at Teruel and Madrid, to Roman ruins in Segovia and Zaragoza, and to the Moorish south. The nation's devotion to the arts is evident in its abundance of world-class museums. And Spain's cultural pluralism is mirrored in its very geography, among the most diverse in Europe.

All these facets render Spain one of Europe's most sublime, inspiring destinations. It doesn't matter how high your expectations are for the country: they will be surpassed.

Spain: the Basics

Local name España

Capital Madrid

Population 40 million

Languages Castilian Spanish, Catalan, Galician, Basque

Currency euro (€) = 100 centimes

Avoid at all costs Going to bed before midnight

Bring on blank stares by asking *No hay ninguna comida sin jamón?* (Do you have any food *without* ham in it?)

Facts about Spain

HISTORY

From around 8000 to 3000 BC, North African pioneers known as the Iberians crossed the Strait of Gibraltar. They were followed by Celts, Phoenicians, Greeks, Carthaginians and Romans. In AD 409 Roman Hispania was overrun by Germanic tribes; 300 years later, the Moors – Muslim Berbers and Arabs from North Africa – took over the region. The arts and sciences prospered in Islamic Spain (known as *al-Andalus*) and new crops and agricultural techniques were introduced.

The 8th century saw the beginning of the Christian Reconquista. By the mid-13th century, the Christians had taken most of the peninsula. In 1469 the kingdoms of Castile and Aragón were united by the marriage of Isabel, princess of Castile, and Fernando, heir to Aragón's throne. Known as the Catholic Monarchs, they united Spain and laid the foundations for the Spanish golden age. They also revived the notorious Inquisition, which expelled and executed thousands of Jews and other non-Christians. In 1492 the last Muslim ruler of Granada surrendered to them, thus marking the completion of the Reconquista.

Also in 1492, Columbus stumbled on the Bahamas and claimed the Americas for Spain. This sparked a period of exploration and exploitation that yielded Spain enormous wealth while destroying the ancient American empires. Spain's downfall began in 1588, when Francis Drake's English fleet annihilated the mighty Spanish Armada. The 1805 Battle of Trafalgar ended Spanish sea power. The disastrous Spanish-American War of 1898 marked the end of the Spanish empire.

During the Spanish Civil War (1936–39), the Nationalists, led by General Francisco Franco, received heavy military support from Nazi Germany and fascist Italy, while the elected Republican government received support only from Russia and, to a lesser degree, from the International Brigades, made up of foreign leftists. By 1939 Franco had won and an estimated 350,000 Spaniards had died. Franco's 35-year dictatorship began with Spain isolated and crippled by recession. It wasn't until the 1950s and 1960s that the

SPAIN

country began to recover. By the 1970s Spain had the fastest-growing economy in Europe.

Franco died in 1975, having named Juan Carlos his successor. King Juan Carlos is widely credited with having overseen Spain's transition from dictatorship to democracy. The first elections were held in 1977 and a new constitution drafted in 1978. Spain joined the European Community in 1986 and, in 1992, celebrated its return to the world stage in style by hosting Expo '92 at Seville and the Olympic Games at Barcelona.

In 1997 Spain became fully integrated into NATO, and in 1999 it met the criteria for launching the euro. Spain assumed the rotating presidency of the EU moments before 1 January 2002, thus presiding over the Eurozone's official transition to the new cash currency.

GEOGRAPHY

Spain is probably Europe's most geographically diverse country, with landscapes ranging from the near-deserts of Almería to the green, Wales-like countryside and deep coastal inlets of Galicia, and from the sunbaked plains of Castilla-La Mancha to the rugged mountains of the Pyrenees. The country covers 84% of the Iberian Peninsula and spreads over nearly 505,000 sq km, more than half of which is *meseta* (high tableland).

CLIMATE

The *meseta* and Ebro basin have a continental climate: scorching in summer, cold in winter, and always dry. The Guadalquivir basin in Andalucía is only a little wetter and positively broils in high summer.

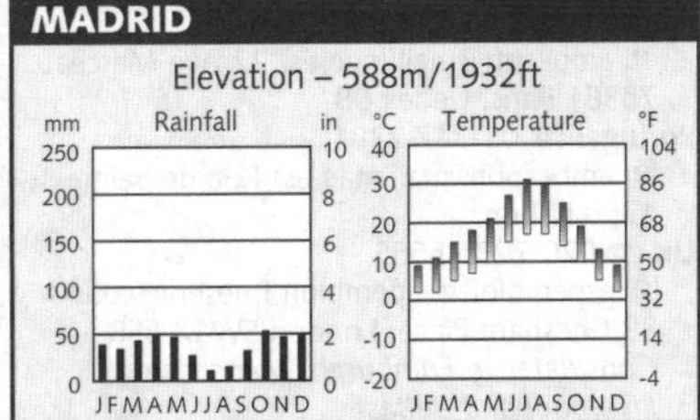

The Pyrenees and the Cordillera Cantábrica bear the brunt of cold northern and northwestern airstreams. Even in high summer you never know when you might get a shower. The Mediterranean coast and Balearic Islands get a little more rain than Madrid, and the southern coast can be even hotter in summer. The Mediterranean provides Spain's warmest waters.

In general you can rely on pleasant or hot temperatures just about everywhere from about April to early November. Snowfalls in the mountains start as early as October, and some snow cover lasts all year on the highest peaks.

GOVERNMENT & POLITICS

Spain is a constitutional monarchy. The 1978 constitution, which followed the death of Franco, restored parliamentary government.

Spain's government has long been embroiled in a campaign against the Basque separatist movement of ETA (see under País Vasco later in this chapter). Although ETA's support and funding has dried up somewhat in recent years, it has pressed on with its agenda, most recently detonating two car bombs in Madrid on 1 May 2002.

POPULATION & PEOPLE

Spain's population of 40 million is descended from the many peoples who have settled here over the millennia, among them Iberians, Celts, Romans, Jews, Visigoths, Berbers and Arabs. Each region proudly preserves its own unique culture, and some – Catalunya and the País Vasco in particular – display a fiercely independent spirit.

SOCIETY & CONDUCT

The Spanish are generally gregarious people who are tolerant and easy-going towards foreigners. However, disrespectful behaviour, including excessively casual dress in churches, is not well received. Contrary to popular belief, the *siesta* is not nap time – it's generally devoted to a long, leisurely lunch and lingering conversation. Then again, if you've stayed out until 5am...

LANGUAGE

Spanish, or Castilian *(castellano)*, as it is often and more precisely called, is spoken by just about all Spaniards, but there are also three widely spoken regional languages. Catalan is spoken by about two-thirds of people in Catalunya and the Balearic Islands and half the people in the Valencia region; Galician is spoken by many in the northwest; and Basque is spoken by a minority in the País Vasco and Navarra. See the Language chapter at the back of this book for pronunciation guidelines and useful words and phrases.

Facts for the Visitor

HIGHLIGHTS

For possibly the best nightlife in the world, don't miss Madrid (although Barcelona will try to win your affections, too). Mallorca and Ibiza are also world-famous party spots.

Cabo Favàtrix in Menorca and some of the secluded coves on Andalucía's Cabo de Gata are gems of beaches, as are secluded spots on the Costa de la Luz, between Tarifa and Cádiz. The Galician coasts boast literally hundreds of fine beaches.

Spain is home to some of the world's finest art galleries. The Madrid's Prado has few rivals, and there are outstanding art museums in Bilbao, Seville, Barcelona, Valencia and Córdoba. Don't miss Andalucía's Muslim-era architecture – Granada's Alhambra, Seville's alcázar and also Córdoba's Mezquita – and Barcelona's extraordinary Sagrada Família. The fairy-tale alcázar in Segovia has to be seen to be believed.

PLANNING

The ideal months to visit Spain are May, June and September (plus April and October in the south). At these times you can rely on good weather, yet avoid the extreme heat and crush of Spanish and foreign tourists.

Winter brings unceasing rains (except when it snows) to the north. At these times Andalucía is the place to be, with temperatures reaching the mid-teens in most places and good skiing in the Sierra Nevada.

TOURIST OFFICES

Most towns and large villages of any interest have an *oficina de turismo* (tourist office). These will supply you with a map and brochures with basic information on local sights, attractions, accommodation, history etc. Staff are generally helpful and often speak some English. A **nationwide phone line** *(☎ 901 30 06 00; open 9am-6pm daily)* offers information in English. Spain has tourist information centres in 29 countries including:

Canada (☎ 416-961 3131, ⓔ toronto@tourspain.es) 2 Bloor St W, 34th floor, Toronto, Ontario M4W 3E2
France (☎ 01 45 03 82 57, ⓔ paris@tourspain.es) 43 Rue Decamps, 75784 Paris, Cedex 16
Portugal (☎ 01-21 354 1992, ⓔ lisboa@tourspain.es) Avenida Sidónio Pais 28 3 Dto, 1050-215 Lisbon
UK (☎ 020-7486 8077, 090-6364 0630, ⓔ londres@tourspain.es) 22–23 Manchester Square, London W1M 5AP
USA (☎ 212-265 8822; ⓔ oetny@tourspain.es) 666 Fifth Ave, 35th floor, New York, NY 10103

VISAS & DOCUMENTS

Citizens of EU countries can enter Spain with their national identity card or passport. UK citizens must have a full passport. Non-EU nationals must take their passport.

EU, Norway and Iceland citizens require no visa. Nationals of Australia, Canada, Israel, Japan, New Zealand, Switzerland and the USA need no visa for stays of up to 90 days in the EU. South Africans do need a visa.

It's best to obtain the visa in your country of residence. Multiple-entry visas save a lot of time and trouble if you plan to leave Spain (say to Gibraltar or Morocco), then re-enter it.

Spain is one of the Schengen Area countries (see Visas in the Facts for the Visitor chapter earlier in this book).

EMBASSIES & CONSULATES

Spanish Embassies & Consulates

Spanish embassies include:

Australia (☎ 02-6273 3555, ⓔ embespau@mail.mae.es) 15 Arkana St, Yarralumba, Canberra, ACT 2600
Consulates in Brisbane, Melbourne, Perth and Sydney
Canada (☎ 613-747 2252, ⓔ spain@DocuWeb.ca) 74 Stanley Ave, Ottawa, Ontario K1M 1P4
Consulates in Toronto (☎ 416-977 1661) *and Montreal* (☎ 514-935 5235)
France (☎ 01 44 43 18 00, ⓔ ambespfr@mail.mae.es) 22 Ave Marceau, 75381 Paris, Cedex 08
Portugal (☎ 01-347 2381, ⓔ embesppt@mail.mae.es) Rua do Salitre 1, 1250 Lisbon
UK (☎ 020-7235 5555, ⓔ espemblon@espemblon.freeserve.co.uk) 39 Chesham Place, London SW1X 8SB
Consulates in Edinburgh, Manchester, Liverpool and Belfast
USA (☎ 202-452 0100) 2375 Pennsylvania Ave NW, Washington, DC 20037
Consulates in Boston, Chicago, Houston, Miami, Los Angeles, New Orleans, New York, San Francisco, Cincinnati, Kansas City, St Louis, Honolulu, Seattle, Albuquerque, Corpus Christi, Dallas, El Paso, San Antonio, San Diego, Atlanta and Baltimore

Embassies & Consulates in Spain

Some 70 countries have embassies in Madrid, including:

Australia (☎ 91 441 93 00) Plaza del Descubridor Diego de Ordás 3-28003, Edificio Santa Engrácia 120
Canada (☎ 91 431 43 00) Calle de Núñez de Balboa 35
France (☎ 91 423 89 00) Calle de Salustiano Olózaga 9
Germany (☎ 91 557 90 00) Calle de Fortuny 8
Ireland (☎ 91 576 35 00) Paseo de la Castellana 36
Japan (☎ 91 590 76 00) Calle de Serrano 109
Morocco (☎ 91 563 10 90) Calle de Serrano 179
Consulate (☎ 91 561 21 45) Calle de Leizaran 31
New Zealand (☎ 91 523 02 26) Plaza de la Lealtad 3
Portugal (☎ 91 561 78 00) Calle de Pinar 1
Consulate (☎ 91 445 46 00) Calle Martínez Campos 11
UK (☎ 91 700 82 00) Calle de Fernando el Santo *16*
Consulate (☎ 91 308 52 01) Edificio Colón, Calle del Marqués Ensenada 16
USA (☎ 91 587 22 00) Calle de Serrano 75

CUSTOMS

From outside the EU you may bring in one bottle of spirits, one bottle of wine, 50mL of perfume and 200 cigarettes. From within the EU you can bring 2L of wine *and* 1L of spirits, with the same limits on the rest.

MONEY

Spain uses the euro. Banks mostly open from 8.30am to 2pm Monday to Friday, and from 8.30am to 1pm Saturday and tend to give better exchange rates than currency-exchange offices. Travellers cheques attract a slightly better rate than cash. ATMs accepting a wide variety of cards are common.

Costs

Spain is one of Western Europe's more affordable countries. It's possible to scrape by on €20 to €30 a day. This would involve staying in the cheapest possible accommodation, avoiding eating in restaurants or going to museums or bars, and not moving around too much. Places such as Madrid, Barcelona, Seville and San Sebastián will place a greater strain on your moneybelt. A more reasonable budget would be €50 a day. Remember that students (and sometimes seniors) are entitled to discounts of up to 50% on admission fees and about 30% on transportation.

In restaurants, prices include a service charge, and tipping is a matter of personal choice – most people leave some small change, and 5% is plenty. It's common to leave small change in bars and cafés.

Taxes

In Spain, VAT (value-added tax) is known as *impuesto sobre el valor añadido* (IVA). On accommodation and restaurant prices, there's a flat IVA of 7%. Ask if the price is 'con IVA' (with VAT). Visitors are entitled to a refund of IVA on any item costing more than €90 that they are taking out of the EU. Ask the shop for a Europe Tax-Free Shopping Cheque when you buy, then present the goods and cheque to customs when you leave. If they can't offer a cheque, at least get an official receipt with the business's address and a description of the item purchased.

POST & COMMUNICATIONS

Main post offices in provincial capitals are usually open from about 8.30am to 8.30pm Monday to Friday and on Saturday morning. Stamps are also sold at *estancos* (tobacco shops with the 'Tabacos' sign in yellow letters on a maroon background) as well as post offices.

Mail within Europe normally takes up to a week, and to North America, Australia or New Zealand around 10 days, but there may be some long delays. Poste-restante mail can be addressed to you at either *poste restante* or *lista de correos* at the city in question.

All phone numbers are nine digits long, without area codes. Blue public pay phones are common and easy to use. They accept coins, *tarjetas telefónicas* (phonecards) and, in some cases, credit cards. Phonecards come in €5 to €20 denominations and are available at main post offices and *estancos*. International reverse-charge (collect) calls are easy to make: from a pay phone or private phone, dial ☎ 900 99 00 followed by 61 for Australia, 44 for the UK, 64 for New Zealand, 15 for Canada, and for the USA 11 (AT&T) or 14 (MCI).

Internet-access points have sprouted up everywhere in major Spanish cities and towns. Larger cities even sport 24-hour cybercafés. Charges for an hour online range anywhere from €0.50 to €4.

DIGITAL RESOURCES

There are thousands of websites devoted to travelling in Spain. Spain's official tourist site is at Ⓦ www.tourspain.es. The British embassy maintains an excellent Web page at Ⓦ www.britishembassy.org.uy/dslc/Websites.htm, with links to Spanish press and cultural sites. For cultural and practical information on the country (for example, lists of festivals, accommodation), check out Ⓦ www.okspain.org.

BOOKS

For a readable and thorough, but not over-long, survey of Spanish history, pick up *The Story of Spain*, by Mark Williams. Of foreign literature set in Spain, Ernest Hemingway's civil war novel *For Whom the Bell Tolls* is a must. *The Sun Also Rises* is partly set in Pamplona.

If you're planning in-depth travels in Spain, get hold of Lonely Planet's *Spain*.

WOMEN TRAVELLERS

Spain has one of the lowest incidences of reported rape in the developed world, and physical harassment is relatively infrequent.

The **Asociación de Asistencia a Mujeres Violadas** (*☎ 91 574 01 10; Calle de O'Donnell 42 bajo, Madrid; open 10am-2pm & 4pm-7pm Mon-Fri*) offers advice and help to rape victims and can provide details of similar centres in other cities, though only limited English is spoken.

GAY & LESBIAN TRAVELLERS

Attitudes to gays and lesbians are pretty tolerant, especially in the cities. Madrid, Barcelona, Sitges, Ibiza and Cádiz all have active gay and lesbian scenes. A good source of information is **Coordinadora Gai-Lesbiana** (*☎ 93 298 00 29, fax 93 298 06 18; Ⓦ www.cogailes.org; Carrer de Finlandia 45, E08014 Barcelona*). In

Madrid, the equivalent is **Cogam** (*☎/fax 91 522 45 17, toll-free throughout Spain ☎ 900 601 601; open 6pm-10pm daily; Calle del Fuencarral 37, 28004 Madrid*).

DISABLED TRAVELLERS

Spain is an increasingly wheelchair-friendly country to visit. Spanish tourist offices in other countries can provide a basic information sheet with some useful addresses, and give information on accessible accommodation in specific places. **INSERSO** (*☎ 91 347 88 88; Calle de Ginzo de Limea 58, 28029 Madrid*) is the government department for the disabled, with branches in all of Spain's 50 provinces.

You'll find some wheelchair-accessible accommodation in main centres, but many budget establishments lack elevators and ramps. Most HI-affliated youth hostels are suitable for wheelchair users.

SENIOR TRAVELLERS

Veterans of life will find Spain a welcoming and accessible destination. There are reduced prices for people aged over 60, 63 or 65 (depending on the place) at some attractions and occasionally on transport.

DANGERS & ANNOYANCES

Always beware of pickpockets and bag-snatchers. Muggings have been on the rise recently in Barcelona, so take extra care in that city. Leave nothing in parked cars. In youth hostels, don't leave belongings unattended.

Emergencies

In a general emergency, call the all-purpose number ☎ 112, which covers police, medical and fire.

BUSINESS HOURS

Generally, people work Monday to Friday from 9am to 2pm and from 4.30pm or 5pm for another three hours. Shops and travel agencies are usually open these hours on Saturday too, though some may skip the evening session. Museums all have their own unique opening hours; major ones tend to open for something like normal business hours (with or without the afternoon break), but often have their weekly closing day on Monday, not Sunday.

PUBLIC HOLIDAYS & SPECIAL EVENTS

Spain has at least 14 official holidays a year, some observed nationwide, some very local. When a holiday falls close to a weekend, Spaniards like to make a *puente* (bridge), taking the intervening day off too.

These holidays are observed nearly everywhere throughout Spain: New Year's Day (1 January); Epiphany or Three Kings' Day (6 January), when children receive presents; Good Friday; Labour Day (1 May); Feast of the Assumption (15 August); National Day (12 October); All Saints' Day (1 November); Feast of the Immaculate Conception (8 December); and Christmas (25 December).

The two main periods when Spaniards go on holiday are Semana Santa (the week leading up to Easter Sunday) and the month of August. At these times accommodation in resorts can be scarce and transport heavily booked, but other cities are often half-empty.

Fiestas & Festivals

Spaniards indulge their love of colour, noise, crowds and partying at innumerable local fiestas and *ferias* (fairs); even small villages will have at least one, probably several, during the year. Local tourist offices can supply detailed information.

Among festivals to look out for are La Tamborada in San Sebastián (20 January), when the whole town dresses up and goes berserk; *carnaval*, a time of fancy-dress parades and merrymaking celebrated around the country about seven weeks before Easter (the wildest celebrations are in Cádiz and Sitges); Valencia's week-long mid-March party, Las Fallas, with all-night dancing and drinking, first-class fireworks and processions; Semana Santa, with its parades of holy images and huge crowds, notably in Seville; Feria de Abril, Seville's week-long party in late April; Sanfermines, with the running of the bulls, in Pamplona in July; Semana Grande, another week of heavy drinking and hangovers, all along the north coast during the first half of August; and Barcelona's week-long party, the Festes de la Mercè, around 24 September.

ACTIVITIES

The País Vasco has good surf spots, including San Sebastián, Zarauz and Mundaca, among others. Tarifa, Spain's southernmost point, is a windsurfer's heaven.

Skiing is cheap, and facilities and conditions are good. The season runs from December to May. The most accessible resorts are in the Sierra Nevada (very close to Granada), the Pyrenees (north of Barcelona) and in the ranges north of Madrid. Affordable day trips can be booked through travel agents.

Bicycle touring isn't as common as in other parts of Europe; it's a more viable option on the Balearic Islands than on much of the mainland. Mountain biking is increasingly popular, and areas such as Andalucía and Catalunya have many good tracks.

Spain is a trekker's paradise, so much so that Lonely Planet has published a guide to some of the best treks in the country, *Walking in Spain*. If you fancy a really long walk, there's the Camino de Santiago. This route, which has been followed by Christian pilgrims for centuries, can be commenced at various places in France. It then crosses the Pyrenees and runs via Pamplona, Logroño and León all the way to the cathedral in Santiago de Compostela.

ACCOMMODATION

Camping

Spain has more than 800 camping grounds. Facilities and settings vary enormously, and grounds are officially rated from 1st to 3rd class. Expect to pay about €4 each per person, car and tent. Many are open year-round, though quite some close from October to Easter. With certain exceptions (such as many beaches and environmentally protected areas), it is legal to camp outside camping grounds. You'll need permission to camp on private land.

Hostels

Spain's *albergues juveniles* (youth hostels) are often the cheapest place for lone travellers, but two people can usually get a double room elsewhere for a similar price. With some exceptions, hostels are only moderate value. Many have curfews or are closed during the day, or they lack cooking facilities. Most are members of the country's Hostelling International (HI) organisation, **Red Española de Albergues Juveniles** *(REAJ; ☎ 91 347 77 00, fax 91 401 81 60; Calle de José Ortega y Gasset 71, 28006 Madrid)*.

Prices often depend on the season or whether you're aged under 26. Some hostels require HI membership; others may charge more if you're not a member. You can buy HI cards for €15 at most hostels.

Pensiones, Hostales & Hotels

Officially, all the establishments are either hotels (from one to five stars), *hostales* (one to three stars) or *pensiones*. In practice, there are all sorts of overlapping categories. In broad terms, the cheapest are usually *fondas* and *casas de huéspedes*, followed by *pensiones*. All normally have shared bathrooms and singles from €10 to €20, doubles from €15 to €25. Some *hostales* and *hostal-residencias* come in the same price range, but others have rooms with bathrooms costing anywhere up to €65 or so.

Room rates vary by season. Prices listed here include the 7% IVA.

FOOD & DRINKS

Most Spaniards start the day with a *desayuno* (light breakfast), perhaps coffee with a *tostada* (piece of buttered toast) or *pastel* (pastry). *Churros con chocolate* (long, deep-fried doughnuts with thick hot chocolate) are a delicious start to the day. *Almuerzo* or *comida* (lunch) is usually the main meal. The *cena* (evening meal) is lighter and may be eaten as late as 10pm or 11pm. It's common to go to a bar or café for a snack around 11am and again around 7pm or 8pm.

Spain has a huge variety of local cuisines. Seafood and meat are prominent almost everywhere. One of the most characteristic dishes is *paella* – rice, seafood, the odd vegetable and often chicken or meat, all simmered up together, and traditionally coloured yellow with saffron. Another dish, of Andalucían origin, is *gazpacho* – a soup made from tomatoes, breadcrumbs, cucumber and/or green peppers – which is eaten cold. *Tortillas* (omelettes) are an inexpensive stand-by and come in many varieties. *Jamón serrano* (cured ham) is a treat for meat-eaters.

You'll be spending plenty of time in cafés and bars, almost all of which offer a range of *tapas*. These saucer-sized mini-snacks come in infinite varieties, from calamari rings to potato salad to spinach with chickpeas to a small serving of tripe. A *ración* is a meal-sized serving; a *media ración* is a half-ración. The other popular snacks are *bocadillos*, long filled white bread rolls. A good vegetarian snack is a *bocadillo vegetal*, a sandwich that has a filling of salad and, often, fried egg (*sin huevo* means 'without egg').

Coffee in Spain is strong. *Café con leche* is about 50% coffee, 50% hot milk; *café solo* is a short black; *café cortado* is a short black with a little milk. The most common way to order a *cerveza* (beer) is to ask for a *caña*, a small draught beer. *Corto* and, in the País Vasco, *zurrito* are other names for this. A larger beer (about 300mL) is often called a *tubo*, or (in Catalunya) a *jarra*. All these words apply to *cerveza de barril* (draught beer) – if you just ask for a cerveza you're likely to get bottled beer.

Vino (wine) comes *blanco* (white), *tinto* (red) or *rosado* (rosé). There are many regional grape specialities such as *jerez* (sherry) in Jerez de la Frontera and *cava* (sparkling wine) in Catalunya. *Sangría*, a sweet punch made of red wine, fruit and spirits, is very refreshing and popular with tourists.

To specify tap water (which is safe to drink almost everywhere), just ask for *agua del grifo*.

ENTERTAINMENT

Spain has some of the best nightlife in Europe; wild and *very* late nights, especially on Friday and Saturday, are an integral part of the Spain experience. Many young Spaniards don't even think about going out until midnight or so. Bars, which come in all shapes, sizes and themes, are the main attractions until around 2am or 3am. Some play great music that will get you hopping before you move on to a disco till 5am or 6am. Discos are generally expensive (think covers of €15 to €30), but not to be missed if you can manage to splurge.

The live-music scene is less exciting. Spanish rock and pop tends to be imitative, though the bigger cities usually offer a reasonable choice of bands.

SPAIN

Getting There & Away

AIR

Spain has many international airports but in general, the best thing to do is to fly to London, Paris, Frankfurt or Rome, then make your way overland. Alternatively, some deals to these centres include a couple of short-haul flights within Europe, and Madrid and Barcelona are usually acceptable destinations for these. Some round-the-world (RTW) fares include stops in Spain.

LAND

Bus

There are buses to Spain from all major centres in Europe, including Lisbon, London and Paris. In London, **Eurolines** (*☎ 0870-514 3219*) has at least three weekly services to Barcelona (UK£90 one way, 23 to 25 hours), Madrid (UK£80 one way, at least 27 hours) and Málaga (UK£80 one way, 34 hours). Tickets are sold by major travel agencies, and people aged under 26, and senior citizens, get a 10% discount. There are also bus services to Morocco from some Spanish cities.

Train

Reaching Spain by train is more expensive than bus unless you have a rail pass, although fares for those under 26 come close to the bus price. Normal one-way fares from London (using the ferry, not Eurostar) to Madrid (via Paris) are under UK£110. For more details, contact the **Rail Europe Travel Centre** (*☎ 08705-848 848*) in London or a travel agent.

Car & Motorcycle

If you're driving or riding to Spain from England, you'll have to choose between going through France (check visa requirements) or taking a direct ferry from England to Spain (see following). The cheapest way is one of the shorter ferries from England to France, then a quick drive down through France.

SEA

The UK

There are two direct ferry services.

Brittany Ferries (*☎ 0870 536 0360 in Britain*) runs Plymouth-Santander ferries twice weekly from about mid-March to mid-November (24 hours), and a Portsmouth-Santander service (30 hours), usually once a week, in other months.

P&O European Ferries (*☎ 08702 424 999 in Britain*) runs Portsmouth-Bilbao ferries on Monday and Thursday, almost all year (35 hours). Prices on all services are similar: one-way passenger fares range from about UK£50 in winter to UK£90 in summer (cabins are extra); a car and driver costs from UK£160 to UK£275, or you can take a vehicle and several passengers for UK£250 to UK£400.

Morocco

Ferry services between Spain and Morocco include Algeciras–Tangier, Algeciras–Ceuta,

Gibraltar–Tangier, Málaga–Melilla, Almería–Melilla and Almería–Nador. Those to and from Algeciras are the fastest, cheapest and most frequent, with over 20 ferries a day to Ceuta (€12.80, 1½ hours) and 14 to Tangier (€13.80, 2½ hours). Hydrofoils make the same trip in half the time for about 75% more. Taking a car costs €60/70 to Ceuta/Tangier.

You can buy tickets at Algeciras' harbour, but it's more convenient to go to one of the many agencies on the waterfront. The price doesn't vary, so just look for the place with the shortest queue.

Buy Moroccan currency when you reach Morocco; you'll get ripped off in Algeciras.

Getting Around

Students and seniors are eligible for discounts of 30% to 50% on almost all types of transportation within Spain.

BUS

Spain's bus network is operated by dozens of independent companies and serves remote towns and villages as well as major routes. Buses to/from Madrid are often cheaper than (or barely different from) cross-country routes. For instance, Seville to Madrid costs €15, while the shorter Seville–Granada trip is €15.50.

Many towns and cities have one main bus station, and these usually have an information desk giving information on all services.

TRAIN

RENFE *(w www.renfe.es)*, the national railway company, runs numerous types of train, and travel times can vary a lot on the same route, as can fares. RENFE's website is an excellent resource for schedule and fare information.

Regionale is an all-stops train (cheap and slow). *Cercanías* provides regular services from major cities to the surrounding suburbs and hinterland, sometimes crossing regional boundaries. Among *largo recorrido* (long-distance) trains, the standard daytime train is the *diurno* (its night-time equivalent is the *estrella*). Quicker is the InterCity (mainly because it makes fewer stops), while the *Talgo* is fastest and dearest.

Best of all is the AVE high-speed service that links Madrid and Seville in just 2½ hours. The *Talgo 200* uses part of this line to speed down to Málaga from Madrid. The *Euromed* is an AVE-style train that speeds south from Barcelona to Valencia and Alicante. A *Tren Hotel* is a 1st-class sleeper-only express.

Ticket clerks are usually happy to go through a few options with you. The cheapest sleeper option is usually a *litera*, a bunk in a six-berth 2nd-class compartment.

You can buy tickets and make reservations at stations, RENFE offices in many city centres, and travel agencies that display the RENFE logo.

Train Passes

Rail passes are valid for all RENFE trains, but Inter-Rail users have to pay €9.50 supplements on Talgo and InterCity services, and on the high-speed AVE service between Madrid and Seville. Pass-holders making reservations for long-distance trains pay a fee of about €5.

RENFE's Tarjeta Turística (also known as the Spain Flexipass) is a rail pass for non-Europeans, valid for three to 10 days travel in a two-month period. In 2nd class, three days costs US$155, and 10 days is US$365. The pass can be purchased from agents outside Europe, or a few main train stations and RENFE offices in Spain.

CAR & MOTORCYCLE

The Spanish automobile club, **Real Automovil Club de España** *(RACE; head office ☎ 91 434 11 22; e inforace@race.es; Avenida Ciudad de Barcelona 132, Madrid)*, has a 24-hour, nationwide, on-road emergency service (toll free ☎ 900 11 22 22).

Rental rates vary widely from place to place. The best deals tend to be in major tourist areas, including at the airports. At Málaga airport you can rent a small car for under €120 a week. More generally, you're looking at up to €50 a day with unlimited kilometres, plus insurance, damage waiver and taxes. Local companies often have better rates than the big firms.

HITCHING

Women should avoid hitching alone. Hitching is illegal on *autopistas* (multilane freeway) and difficult on major highways. Your chances are better on minor roads, although the going can still be painfully slow.

BOAT

For information on ferries to/from the Balearic Islands, see that section later in this chapter.

LOCAL TRANSPORT

Most towns have an effective local bus system. Tourist offices can tell you which buses you need. Barcelona and Madrid both have efficient underground systems that are faster and easier to use than the bus systems.

Taxis are pretty cheap. Rates vary slightly from city to city: in Barcelona, they cost €1.30 flag fall, plus about €1 per kilometre; in Madrid they're a bit more expensive (€1.35 flag fall). There are supplements for luggage and airport trips.

Madrid

pop 3 million

Despite being the country's capital, Madrid has a friendly neighbourhood feel. Right in the city centre lie quaint family-owned shops, and bars packed with locals, and there is an overall lack of stress on the street. While the daytime offers plenty to do and see, including a remarkable collection of museums and galleries, and beautiful parks and gardens, Madrid really gets going at night. Indeed, *madrileños* claim that their town sports more bars per square metre than any other city in Europe. Arguably no other city in the world provides the nightlife frenzy of Spain's largest city.

ORIENTATION

The most interesting part of Madrid lies between Parque del Retiro in the east and Campo del Moro in the west. These two parks are more or less connected by Calle de Alcalá and Calle Mayor, which meet in the middle at Puerta del Sol. Calle Mayor passes the historic main square, Plaza Mayor, on its way from Puerta del Sol to the Palacio Real in front of Campo del Moro.

The main north–south thoroughfare is Paseo de la Castellana, which runs (changing names to Paseo de los Recoletos and finally Paseo del Prado) all the way from Chamartín train station in the north to Madrid's other big station, Atocha.

INFORMATION

Tourist Offices

The **Oficina Municipal de Turismo** *(☎ 91 588 16 36, fax 91 366 54 77; e munemadrid@infoturismo.es; Plaza Mayor 3; metro Sol; open daily)* is conveniently situated in the city's emblematic main square. Additional offices include those at **Chamartín train station** *(☎ 91 315 99 76; open daily)*, **Barajas airport** *(☎ 91 305 86 56; open daily)*, and **Mercado Puerta de Toledo** *(☎ 91 364 18 76; Ronda de Toledo 1; open daily)*. There is a multilingual local information hotline on ☎ 010.

Money

Large banks like Caja de Madrid usually have the best rates, but check commissions first. **American Express** *(☎ 91 527 03 03, 900 99 44 26 for replacing lost travellers cheques; Plaza de las Cortes 2; metro Banco de España; open 9am-5.30pm Mon-Fri, 9am-noon Sat)* is reasonably priced.

If you're desperate, there are plenty of exchange bureaus around Puerta del Sol and Plaza Mayor that have predictably rip-off rates but are often open until midnight.

Post & Communications

The **main post office** *(☎ 91 521 6500; Plaza de la Cibeles; metro Banco de España)* is in the huge Palacio de Comunicaciones. **Poste restante** *(Lista de Correos; open 8am-9.30pm Mon-Fri, 8.30am-2pm Sat)* is at windows 17 to 20. Don't forget your passport.

Telefónica *(☎ 91 522 39 14; Gran Vía 30; metro Gran Vía; open 10am-10pm daily)* has phone books for the whole country and cabins where you can make calls in relative peace.

Internet connection is offered by dozens of cafés, as well as such Net centres as **Navegaweb**, part of the Telefónica centre, which charges €1.80 per hour, **WEC** *(☎ 91429 16 90; Atocha 45; metro Antón Martín; open 10am-10pm daily)*, charging €2.40 an hour, and **ONO** *(☎ 91 547 47 71; Gran Vía 59; metro Gran Vía; open 24hr)* offers varying rates depending on the time.

Travel Agencies

For cheap travel tickets try **Viajes Zeppelin** *(☎ 91 542 51 54; Plaza de Santo Domingo 2; metro Santo Domingo)*. If you are under 25 or a student check out **TIVE** *(☎ 91 543 74 12; Calle de Fernando el Católico 88; metro Moncloa; open 9am-1pm Mon-Fri)* or the **Instituto de la Juventud** *(☎ 91 347 77 00; Calle de José Ortega y Gasset 71; metro Lista; open 9am-1pm Mon-Fri)*.

Medical Services

There are several 24-hour pharmacies, including **Farmacia del Globo** *(☎ 91 369 20*

SPAIN

00; Plaza de Antón Martín 46; metro Ant'n Martín). For more serious problems, head for the nearest emergency health centre **Casa de Socorro** *(Calle Navas de Tolosa 10; ☎ 91 588 96 60; metro Callao)*; it's the most convenient if you are in the centre. You can also get help at the **Anglo-American Medical Unit** *(☎ 91 435 18 23; Calle del Conde de Aranda 1; metro Retiro)*. For an ambulance, call ☎ 061, or Cruz Roja on ☎ 91 522 22 22.

THINGS TO SEE & DO

Museums

Of Madrid's three big-ticket museums, the **Museo del Prado** *(☎ 91 330 29 00; Paseo del Prado s/n; adult/student €3/1.50, admission free 2.30pm-7pm Sat & all day Sun; open 9am-7pm Tues-Sat, 9am-2pm Sun & holidays)* is the best-known and largest. The main emphasis is on Spanish, Flemish and Italian art from the 15th to 19th centuries. Generous coverage is given to certain individual geniuses, such as three of the Spanish greats, Velázquez (people flock to his *Las Meninas*), El Greco and Goya. Other well-represented artists include the Flemish masters Hieronymus Bosch and Peter Paul Rubens, and the Italians Tintoretto, Titian and Raphael. Entry is free on selected national holidays.

Opposite Atocha station, the **Centro de Arte Reina Sofia** *(☎ 91 467 50 62; Calle Santa Isabel 52; adult/student €3/1.50, admission free 2.30pm-7pm Sat & Sun; open 10am-9pm Mon & Wed-Sat, 10am-2.30pm Sun)* houses a superb collection of predominantly Spanish modern art. The exhibition focuses on the period 1900–40 and includes, in room seven, Picasso's famous *Guernica*. The museum also contains further works by Picasso, while room nine is devoted to Salvador Dalí's surrealist work and room 13 contains a collection of Joan Miró's late works.

The **Museo Thyssen-Bornemisza** *(☎ 91 420 39 44; Paseo del Prado 8; adult/student €4.80/3; open 10am-7pm Tues-Sun)* is almost opposite the Prado. Purchased by Spain in 1993 for something over US$300 million (a snip), this extraordinary collection of 800 paintings was formerly the private collection of the German-Hungarian family of magnates, the Thyssen-Bornemiszas. Starting with medieval religious art, it moves on through Titian, El Greco and Rubens to Cézanne, Monet and Van Gogh, then from Miró, Picasso and Gris to Pollock, Dalí and Lichtenstein. It provides one of the best, and definitely the most comprehensive, art-history lessons that you're ever likely to have.

Palacio Real & Campo del Moro

Madrid's 18th-century Palacio Real *(☎ 91 542 00 59; Plaza de Oriente; metro Opera; adult/student €6/3, admission free Wed for EU citizens; open 9.30am-6pm Mon-Sat, 9am-2.30pm Sun & holidays May-Sept; 9.30am-5pm Mon-Sat, 9am-2pm Sun & holidays Oct-Apr)* is a lesson in what can happen if you give your interior decorators a free hand. You'll see some of the most elaborately decorated walls and ceilings imaginable, including the sublime Throne Room (and other rooms of more dubious merit). This over-the-top palace is only used for official receptions and, of course, tourism.

Directly behind the Palacio Real is the stately **Campo del Moro**, an elegant garden. The palace is visible through the trees from just about all points. A couple of fountains and statues, a thatch-roofed pagoda and a carriage museum provide artificial diversions, but nature is the real attraction.

Monasterio de las Descalzas Reales

This monastery *(Convent of the Barefoot Royals; ☎ 91 542 00 59; Plaza de las Descalzas; adult/student €4.80/3.91, admission free Wed for EU citizens; open 10.30am-12.45pm & 4pm-5.30pm Tues-Thur & Sat, 10.30am-12.45pm Fri, 11am-1.45pm Sun & holidays)* was founded in 1559 by Juana of Austria, daughter of the Spanish King Carlos I, and became one of Spain's richest religious houses thanks to gifts from noblewomen. Much of the wealth came in the form of art; on the obligatory guided tour you'll be confronted by a number of tapestries based on works by Rubens and a wonderful painting entitled *The Voyage of the 11,000 Virgins*.

Panteón de Goya

This little church *(☎ 91 542 07 22; Glorieta de San Antonio de la Florida 5; metro Príncipe Pío; adult/student €1.80/0.90, admission free Wed & Sun; open 10am-2pm Tues-Sun July & Aug; 4pm-8pm Tues-Fri, 10am-2pm Sat & Sun Sept-June)* contains not only Goya's tomb, directly in front of the altar, but also one of his greatest works – the entire ceiling and dome – beautifully painted

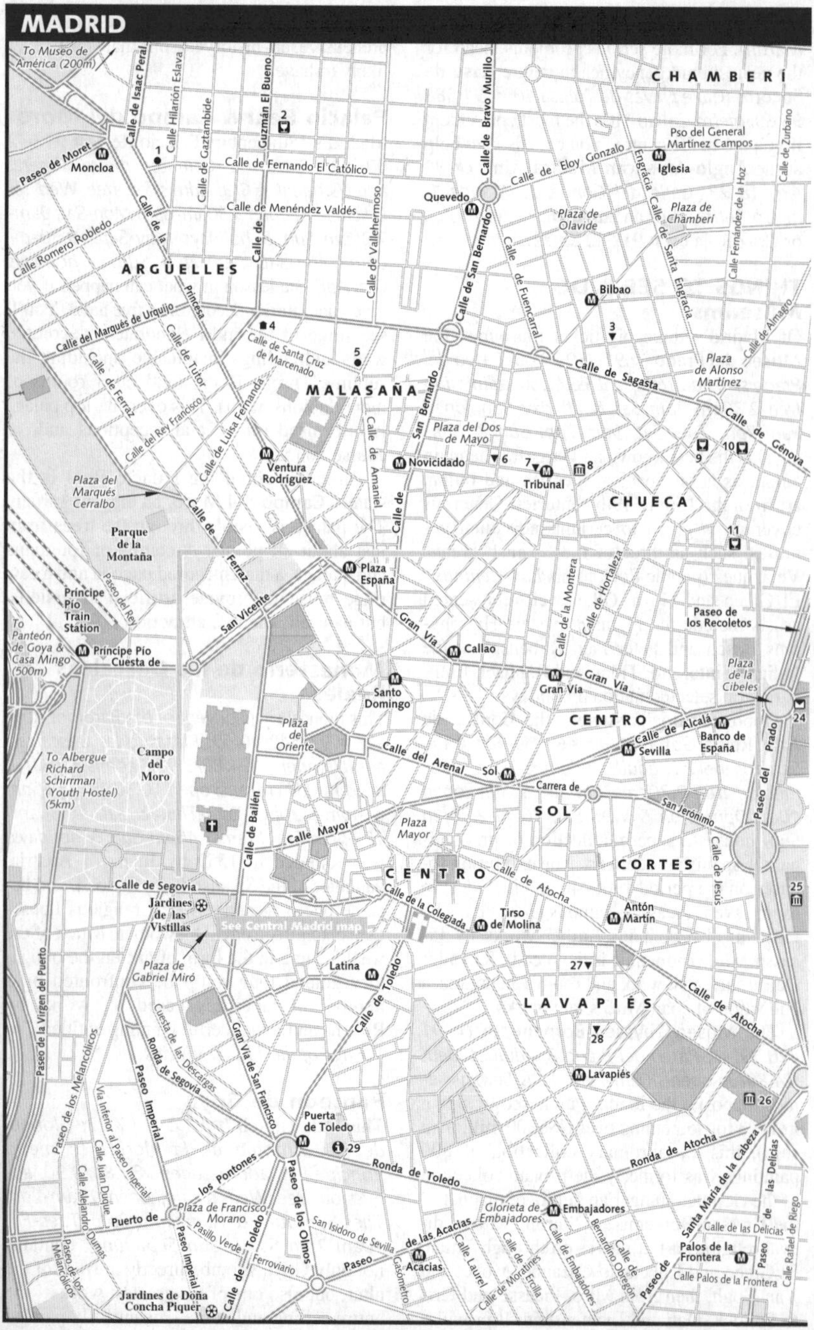

MADRID

To Museo de América (200m)
CHAMBERÍ
Calle de Isaac Peral
Calle Hilarión Eslava
Calle de Gaztambide
Guzmán El Bueno
Calle de Bravo Murillo
Pso del General Martínez Campos
Calle de Zurbano
Paseo de Moret
Moncloa
Calle de Fernando El Católico
Calle de Eloy Gonzalo
Iglesia
Quevedo
Calle de Menéndez Valdés
Calle de Vallehermoso
Engracia
Calle de Santa Engracia
Plaza de Chamberí
Plaza de Olavide
Calle Fernández de la Hoz
Calle Romero Robledo
Calle de la Princesa
ARGÜELLES
Calle de San Bernardo
Calle de Fuencarral
Bilbao
Calle del Marqués de Urquijo
Calle de Tutor
Calle de Ferraz
Calle de Santa Cruz de Marcenado
Calle de Almagro
Plaza de Alonso Martínez
Calle de Sagasta
MALASAÑA
Calle del Rey Francisco
Calle de Luisa Fernanda
San Bernardo
Plaza del Dos de Mayo
Calle de Génova
Ventura Rodríguez
Calle de Amaniel
Novicidado
Tribunal
Plaza del Marqués Cerralbo
CHUECA
Parque de la Montaña
Calle de Ferraz
Paseo del Rey
Principe Pio Train Station
Plaza España
San Vicente
Gran Vía
Calle de la Montera
Calle de Hortaleza
Paseo de los Recoletos
To Panteón de Goya & Casa Mingo (500m)
Principe Pío
Cuesta de
Callao
Gran Vía
Plaza de la Cibeles
Santo Domingo
Plaza de Oriente
CENTRO
Calle de Alcalá
Banco de España
Sevilla
To Albergue Richard Schirrman (Youth Hostel) (5km)
Campo del Moro
Calle del Arenal
Sol
Carrera de
SOL
San Jerónimo
Paseo del Prado
Calle de Bailén
Calle Mayor
Plaza Mayor
Calle de Jesús
CENTRO
Calle de Atocha
CORTES
Calle de Segovia
Jardines de las Vistillas
Calle de la Colegiada
Tirso de Molina
Antón Martín
See Central Madrid map
Plaza de Gabriel Miró
Latina
Calle de Toledo
LAVAPIÉS
Calle de Atocha
Paseo de la Virgen del Puerto
Cuesta de las Descargas
Gran Vía de San Francisco
Ronda de Segovia
Paseo Imperial
Paseo de los Melancólicos
Via Inferior al Paseo Imperial
Lavapiés
Puerta de Toledo
Calle Juan Duque
Calle Alejandro Dumas
los Pontones
Paseo de los Olmos
Ronda de Toledo
Ronda de Atocha
Calle de Santa María de la Cabeza
Paseo de las Delicias
Puerto de
Plaza de Francisco Morano
Pasillo Verde
Paseo Imperial
San Isidoro de Sevilla
Ferroviario
Paseo de las Acacias
Acacias
Gasómetro
Glorieta de Embajadores
Embajadores
Calle Laurel
Calle de Moratines
Calle de Ercilla
Calle de Embajadores
Calle de Bernardino Obregón
Paseo de
Calle de las Delicias
Palos de la Frontera
Calle Palos de la Frontera
Calle Rafael de Riego
Paseo de los Melancólicos
Jardines de Doña Concha Piquer
Calle de Toledo

SPAIN

MADRID

PLACES TO STAY & EAT
3 La Musa
4 Albergue Santa Cruz de Marcenado
6 Pizzeria Mastropiero
7 Cafe Manuela
27 Nuevo Cafe Barbieri
28 Elqui

BARS
9 Cervecería Santa Bárbara
10 El Son
11 Finnegan's

OTHER
1 TIVE
2 Soul Kitchen
5 Moto Alquiler
8 Museo Municipal
12 Museo Arqueológico
13 Biblioteca Nacional
14 Monumento de Colón
15 Airport Bus Terminal
16 Institud de la Juventud
17 TIVE
18 Plaza de Toros Monumental de Las Ventas
19 Museo de la Moneda
20 Anglo-American Medical Unit
21 Palacio de Cristal
22 La Rosaleda
23 El Ángel Caído
24 Palacio de Comunicaciones; Main Post Office
25 Museo del Prado
26 Centro de Arte Reina Sofía
29 Tourist Office

To Museo de la Ciudad (600m) & Auditorio Nacional de la Música (700m)
Avenida de América
0 200 400m
0 200 400yd
Paseo de Castellana
Calle de Serrano
Calle de Diego de León
Calle de Francisco Silvela
Calle de Ardemans
Calle de Cartagena
Paseo Eduardo Data
Rubén Darío
Calle de Juan Bravo
Diego de Leon
Avenida de los Toreros
Ventas
To Airport
SALAMANCA
Plaza del Marqués de Salamanca
Calle de Vergara
Calle de José Ortega y Gasset
Núñez de Balboa
Lista
Calle de Don Ramón de la Cruz
Calle de Alcalá
Plaza de Manuel Becerra
Manuel Becerra
Paseo de la Castellana
Calle de Lagasca
Calle del Príncipe
Calle Conde de Peñalver
Calle de Alcántara
Calle de Ayala
Calle de Hermosilla
Goya
Calle Fuente del Berro
Plaza de Colón
Serrano
Velázquez
Calle de Goya
GOYA
Calle del Doctor Esquerdo
Calle de Velázquez
Príncipe de Vergara
Calle de Vilanuava
Calle del Duque de Sesto
O'Donnell
Calle Columela
Retiro
Calle de O'Donnell
Calle de Alcalá
Plaza de la Independencia
Plaza Maestro Villa
Av Méjico
Avenida de Menéndez Pelayo
Calle de Narváez
Ibiza
Calle de Montalbán
Paseo Salón del Estanque
Estanque
PARQUE DEL RETIRO
Paseo de Venezuela
Paseo del Duque de Fernán Núñez
Calle de Alfonso XII
C de Alfonso XI
Paseo San Pablo
Paseo del Ecuador
Jardín Botánico
Paseo del Urguay
Paseo del Durque
Atocha
Avenidade la Ciudadde Barcelona
Paseo de la Reina Cristina
Plaza de Mariano de Cavia
Conde de Casal
Plaza del Conde de Casal
Atocha Train Station
Calle de Gutenberg
Calle Juan de Urbieta
Calle de Cavanilles
Calle de Valderribas
Menéndez Pelayo
Calle de Méndez Álvaro
Avenida de la Ciudad de Barcelona
Calle Granada Andalucia
Calle del Doctor Esquerdo
Calle de Adelfas
Calle de Pajaritos
Avenida de la Paz
Calle de Téllez
To Estación Sur de Autobuses (1km)
Pacífico

with religious scenes. The images on the dome depict the miracle of St Anthony.

Museo Arqueológico

This museum *(☎ 91 577 79 12; Calle de Serrano; adult/student €3/1.50, admission free Sun & 2.30pm-8.30pm Sat; open 9.30am-8.30pm Tues-Sat, 9.30am-2pm Sun)* traces the history of the peninsula from the earliest prehistoric cave paintings to the Iberian, Roman, Carthaginian, Greek, Visigothic, Moorish and Christian eras. Exhibits include mosaics, pottery, fossilised bones and a partial reconstruction of the prehistoric Altamira cave paintings.

Other Museums

Madrid is museum mad. Examples include the **Museo Municipal**, with assorted art including some Goyas, and some beautiful old maps, scale models, silver, porcelain and period furniture; the **Museo de la Moneda**, which follows the history of coinage in great detail and contains a mind-boggling collection of coins and paper money; the **Museo de América** with stuff brought from the Americas between the 16th and 20th centuries; and even the **Museo de la Ciudad**, perfectly described by one traveller as 'a must for infrastructure buffs!' Check the tourist office's *Madrid* brochure for details.

Parque del Retiro

This is a great place to bench-sit or stroll. Time it right and you may catch a puppet show during the summer.

Walk along **Paseo de las Estatuas**, a path that's lined with statues originally from the Palacio Real. It ends at a lake overlooked by a **statue of Alfonso XII**. There are rowing boats for rent at the northern end when the weather is good.

Perhaps the most important, and certainly the most controversial, of the park's other monuments is *El Ángel Caído* (The Fallen Angel). First-prize winner at an international exhibition in Paris in 1878, it is said to be the first statue in the world dedicated to the devil.

You should also visit some of the park's gardens, such as the exquisite **La Rosaleda** (rose garden), and the **Chinese Garden** located on a tiny island near the Fallen Angel. The all-glass **Palacio de Cristal** in the middle of the park frequently stages modern-art exhibitions.

El Rastro

If you get up early on a Sunday morning, you'll find the city almost deserted, until you get to **El Rastro** *(metro Latina)*. The market spreads along and between Calle de Ribera de Curtidores and Calle de los Embajadores. It is one of the biggest flea markets you're ever see, where you'll find almost anything, from hippy threads to the kitchen sink. It's also said to be the place to go if you want to buy your car stereo back. Watch your pockets and bags.

SPECIAL EVENTS

Madrid's major fiesta celebrates its patron saint, San Isidro Labrador, throughout the third week of May. There are free music performances around the city and one of the country's top bullfight seasons at the Plaza Monumental de las Ventas. The Malasaña district, already busy enough, has its biggest party on 2 May, and the Fiesta de San Juan is held in the Parque del Retiro for the seven days leading up to 24 June. The city sashays through the hottest months, and there are plenty of people around to enjoy the consecutive festivals of La Paloma, San Cayetano and San Lorenzo in August. The last week of September is Chamartín's Fiesta de Otoño (Autumn Festival), the only time you would go to Chamartín other than to catch a train.

PLACES TO STAY

Finding a place in Madrid is never really a problem. However, it is wise to book ahead.

Hostels

There are two HI youth hostels in Madrid. **Albergue Richard Schirrman** *(☎ 91 463 56 99; metro El Lago, bus No 33 from Plaza Ópera; dorm beds under/over 26 €8/12)* is in the Casa de Campo park. B&B is available. This is a seedy area at night, so time your arrival during the day.

Albergue Santa Cruz de Marcenado *(☎ 91 547 45 32; Calle de Santa Cruz de Marcenado 28; dorm beds under/over 26 €8/12)*, has rooms for four, six and eight people. B&B costs the same as in the Richard Schirrman. This is one of the few Spanish hostels in HI's International Booking Network.

Hostales & Hotels

There is an excellent range of accommodation in Madrid. At the budget end, *hostales* and *pensiones* tend to cluster in three or four parts of the city and the price-to-quality ratio is fairly standard. In August you may get a better deal because of the heat, although the city doesn't empty as it once did, due to the influx of visitors and air-conditioning systems.

Around Plaza de Santa Ana Santa Ana is cleaned up and humming, so budget places are starting to disappear. Close to Sol and within walking distance of the Prado and Atocha train station, there are countless bars, cafés and restaurants attracting every class of clientele.

Just off the square **Hostal Rodriguez** *(☎ 91 522 44 31; 3rd floor, Nuñez de Arce 9; doubles €37, with bathroom €40)* has clean and comfortable rooms.

There are small but cute rooms at **Hostal El Pilar** *(☎ 91 531 26 26; Calle de Carretas 13; doubles from €44)*; try for one overlooking the church.

In the same mid-range price bracket, the **Hostal Gonzalo** *(☎ 91 429 27 14, fax 91 420 20 07; Calle de Cervantes 34; singles/doubles with bathroom €35/43)* is in sparkling nick. Rooms have a TV and the staff will take a few euros off the bill if you stay at least three days. Across the road, **Hostal Dulcinea** *(☎ 91 429 93 09, fax 91 369 25 69; e donato@teleline.es; Calle de Cervantes 19; singles/doubles €36/42)* has well-maintained if simply furnished rooms.

Around Puerta del Sol & Plaza Mayor You can't get more central than Plaza Puerta del Sol. This and Plaza Mayor, Madrid's true heart, are not major budget accommodation areas but, if you're euro-economising, there are a few good options tucked away among the cafés, bars and souvenir shops.

The pick of the cheaper bunch is **Hostal Comercial** *(☎ 91 522 66 30; Calle Esparteros 12; singles/doubles €30/35)*, which has rooms with a bathroom, TV and balcony. Right on the square, **Hostal Riesco** *(☎ 91 522 26 92; Calle de Correo 2, 3rd floor; singles/doubles €33/41)* is a natty little place but may require earplugs on a Saturday night. **Hostal Santa Cruz** *(☎ 91 522 24 41; Plaza de Santa Cruz 6; singles/doubles from €24/36)* is bright and smart, in a prime location.

There's a cosy overstuffed-sofa feel at **Hotel Santander** *(☎ 91 429 95 51, fax 91 369 10 78; Echegaray 1; doubles with bath €60)* and this buzzing street has bar choices aplenty. **Hostal Centro Sol** *(☎ 91 522 15 82, fax 91 522 57 78; Carrera de San Jerónimo 5; singles/doubles €46/54)* offers smallish rooms but with all the extras, like TV, phone, heating, air-con, minibar, and even hair-dryer.

Around Gran Vía The *hostales* on and around Gran Vía tend to be a little more expensive, so it's worth shopping around.

A good budget choice is **Hostal El Pinar** *(☎ 91 547 32 82; Calle de Isabel la Católica 19; singles/doubles from €19/31)*, which has a certain old-fashioned charm. **Hostal Residencia Buenos Aires** *(☎ 91 542 01 02, fax 91 542 24 66; Gran Vía 61; doubles from €48)* is shiny smart with mod cons, plus a cafeteria.

Calle de Fuencarral is similarly choked with *hostales* and *pensiones*, especially at the Gran Vía end. **Hostal Ginebra** *(☎ 91 532 10 35; Calle de Fuencarral 17; singles/doubles with bath €32/40)* is a reliable choice not far from Gran Vía. All rooms have TV and phone, and some have private balcony.

Around Ópera The tiny **Hostal Paz** *(☎ 91 547 30 47; Calle Flora 4; singles/doubles €20/30)* looks pretty grim from the outside but the cheap rooms inside are reasonable, if a little cramped. Quietly tucked away **Hostal Mairu** *(☎ 91 547 30 88; Calle del Espejo 2; singles/doubles with bath from €22/33)* is well priced and some rooms include a small fridge. **Hostal Oriente** *(☎/fax 91 548 03 14; Calle Arenal 23; singles/doubles from €33/51)* is a pleasant mid-range choice.

PLACES TO EAT

Madrid throbs with an infinite number of bars and restaurants, ranging from intimate tapas bars shoe-horned into tiny spaces to cavernous old *mesones* (taverns) with smoke-blackened walls, antique furniture and lip-smacking traditional food. Just about anywhere in central Madrid, you can find cheap restaurants with reasonable, filling food.

Restaurants

One of the best seafood restaurants is **Maceira** *(☎ 91 429 42 93; Calle de Jesús 7; open lunch)* tucked away from the main tourist hubbub. Splash (or slurp) your *pulpo a la gallega* (octopus in paprika and oil) down with a crisp white Ribeiro.

Duck in to **Las Bravas** *(☎ 91 532 26 20; Callejón de Álvarez Gato; metro Sol)* for a *caña* (draught beer) and the best *patatas*

CENTRAL MADRID

MALASAÑA
CENTRO
SOL
CORTES
CENTRO

Paseo del Prado
Plaza de Neptuno
Calle del Duque de Medinaceli
C de Jesús
Calle de Alcalá
Banco de España
Calle del Barquillo
Calle de Colmenares
Valgame Dios
Calle de la Libertad
Chueca
Plaza de Chueca
Calle de Pelayo
Campoamor
Calle de Augusto Figueroa
Calle San Bartolomé
Calle de las Infantas
Victor Hugo
Plaza de Vázquez
Calle de la Reina
Gran Vía
C de Pérez Galdós
Calle de Hortaleza
Fuencarral
Calle de Valverde
Calle del Barco
San Pablo
Corredera Baja de San Roque
Calle de la Luna
Calle de la Estrella
Calle del Marqués de Legamés
Calle de San Bernardo
C de Isabel la Católica
Plaza España
Calle Leganitos
Calle del Fomento
Calle de Torija
Calle del Reloj
Palacio del Senado
Plaza de la Marina Española
Cuesta de San Vicente
Calle de Ferraz
Parque de la Montaña
Calle de Irún
Jardines de Sabatini
Calle de Bailén
San Quintín
Jardines Cabo Noval
Plaza de Oriente
Felipe V
Carlos III
Plaza de Isabel II
Ópera
Calle de Arrieta
Cuesta de Santo Domingo
Calle de la Bola
Plaza de Santo Domingo
Santo Domingo
Calle de Preciados
Callao
Plaza del Callao
Calle del Carmen
C de las Navas de Tolosa
Plaza de San Martín
Calle de la Priora Flora
Plaza de las Descalzas
Calle de Tetuán
Calle del Arenal
Plaza del Carmen
Calle de la Salud
Commercio
Calle de los Jardines
Calle Aduana
Calle de la Montera
Sevilla
Calle de los Madrazo
Calle de Zorrilla
Carrera de San Jerónimo
Plaza de las Cortes
Calle de Arlabán
Plaza de Canalejas
Calle de Ventura de la Vega
Calle del Prado
C del Príncipe
Calle Echegaray
Calle de Cervantes
Calle de Lope de Vega
Calle de las Huertas
Calle de León
Antón Martín
Plaza de Santa Ana
Núñez de Arce
Calle de la Cruz
Plaza del Ángel
Calle de Atocha
Calle de Cañizares
Sol
Puerta del Sol
Calle de Carretas
Calle del Correo
Calle de Espateros
Calle de la Bolsa
Plaza de Jacinto Benavente
Tirso de Molina
C Zaragoza
Plaza de Santa Cruz
Calle Mayor
Plaza Mayor
C de los Cuchilleros
Cava de San Miguel
Costanilla Santiago
C de las Fuentes
Calle de la Amnistía
Plaza de la Villa
Plaza Conde de Barajas
Calle de Segovia
Calle del Sacramento
Calle de San Nicolás
Lepanto
Calle de la Colegiata
Calle del Nuncio
Plaza de la Paja
Plaza de Gabriel Miró
Jardines de las Vistillas

0 – 75 – 150m
0 – 75 – 150yd

1, 2, 3, 4, 5, 6, 7, 8, 9, 10, 11, 12, 13, 14, 15, 16, 17, 18, 19, 20, 21, 22, 23, 24, 25, 26, 27, 28, 29, 30, 31, 32, 33, 34, 35, 36, 37, 38, 39, 40, 41, 42, 43, 44, 45, 46, 47, 48, 49, 50, 51, 52, 53, 54, 55, 56, 57, 58, 59, 60, 61

CENTRAL MADRID

PLACES TO STAY
1 Hostal Residencia Buenos Aires
2 Hostal El Pinar
5 Hostal Ginebra
10 Hotel Centro Sol
11 Hostal Centro Sol
16 Hostal Paz
21 Hostal Oriente
22 Hostal Mairu
23 Hostal La Macarena
25 Hostal Santa Cruz
26 Hostal Comercial
27 Hostal Riesco
28 Hostal El Pilar
32 Hotel Asturias
38 Hotel Santander
45 Hostal Rodriguez
49 Hostal Persal
55 Hostal Dulcinea
56 Hostal Gonzalo

PLACES TO EAT
13 Comme Bio
20 Café del Real
31 Museo del Jamón
33 La Finca de Susana
43 La Trucha
47 La Trucha
48 Las Bravas
53 El Salón de Prado
54 Cervecería La Cañita
58 Maceira
59 Café Populart
61 Casa Patas

BARS & CLUBS
4 Morocco Disco
6 Cruising
7 Rimmel
8 Bar Cock
29 Torero
30 Alhambra
39 O'Neills
40 Carbones
41 Los Gabrieles
42 Viva Madrid
46 Suristán
51 Café Central
52 Cervecería Alemana
57 Los Gatos

OTHER
3 ONO
9 Telefónica/ Internet Centre
12 Police Station
14 Monasterio de las Descalzas Reales
15 Casa de Socorro (Emergency Health Centre)
17 Teatro Real
18 Palacio Real
19 Catedral de Nuestra Señora de la Almudena
24 Tourist Office
34 Police Station
35 RENFE Train Booking Office
36 American Express
37 Museo Thyssen-Bornemisza
44 Teatro de la Comedia
50 Teatro Calderón
60 WEC

bravas (fried potatoes with spicy tomato sauce) in town.

La Trucha *(☎ 91 532 08 90; Calle de Núñez de Arce 6; open Tues-Sat)* is one of Madrid's great bars for tapas. It's just off Plaza de Santa Ana, and there's another branch *(Calle de Manuel Fernández y González 3)* nearby. You can eat at the bar or in the restaurant.

To see old men in flat caps, check out the all-time **Cervecería La Cañita** *(☎ 91 429 04 61; Calle Echegaray 20)*, which serves tasty tapas from €2. Something of an institution is the **Museo del Jamón**, a Miss Piggy nightmare with hundreds of hams swinging from the ceiling. There are 10 branches in town, including one at Carrera de San Jerónimo 6.

La Finca de Susana *(☎ 91 369 35 57; Calle de Arlabán 4; dishes around €12)* hums with young couples and atmosphere, and dishes up Spanish-with-a-twist fare for around €12.

Madrid offers a few safe ports of call for vegetarians. **Elqui** *(☎ 91 468 04 62; Calle de Buenavista 18; open lunch-4pm Tues-Sun, dinner Fri & Sat)* is a self-service buffet-style restaurant where you can pile up your plate.

Comme Bio *(☎ 91 354 63 00; Calle Mayor 30)* is excellent and inexpensive, with a health-food shop out front where you can stock up on muesli bars to go.

You know you're getting close to Plaza Mayor when you see signs in English saying 'Typical Spanish Restaurant' and 'Hemingway Never Ate Here'. Nevertheless, when the sun's shining, there's no finer place than one of the outdoor cafés in the plaza. Calle de la Cava San Miguel and Calle de Cuchilleros are packed with *mesones* that are fun for tapas-hopping, if you don't mind paying a little more.

Casa Mingo *(☎ 91 547 79 18; Paseo de la Florida 34; metro Príncipe Pío)*, near the Panteón de Goya, is a bustling place for chicken and cider. A full roast bird, salad and bottle of cider – enough for two – is about €12.

For mainstream fare, head for **Pizzeria Mastropiero** *(Calle de San Vicente Ferrer 34)* on the corner of Calle del Dos de Mayo. This is a justifiably popular Argentine-run joint where you can get pizza by the slice.

Cafés

Madrid has many fine places for a coffee and light bite, ranging from sumptuously elegant with chandeliers and palms, to small and smoky refuges for writing that epic love letter. Historic, elegant **El Salón del Prado** *(☎ 91 429 33 61; Calle del Prado 4; metro Antón Martín)* also has chamber music concerts on Thursday night. There's a crumbling romantic feel about **Nuevo Cafe Barbieri** *(☎ 91 527 36 58; Calle del Ave María 45; metro Lavapiés)*, with its Art Deco light fixtures and red velvet decor. Local artists exhibit at **Cafe**

Manuela *(☎ 91 531 70 37; San Vicente Ferrer 11; metro Tribunal)*, which also has a piano, board games and Belle Époque detailing. **Cafe del Real** *(Plaza de Isabel II; metro Ópera)* has a cosy touch of faded elegance – good for breakfast and busy at night, too.

ENTERTAINMENT

A copy of the weekly *Guía del Ocio* (€1 at newsstands) will give you a good rundown of what's on in Madrid. Its comprehensive listings include music gigs, art exhibitions, cinema, TV and theatre. It's very handy even if you can't read Spanish.

Bars

The epicentres of Madrid's nightlife are the Santa Ana-Calle de las Huertas area and the Malasaña-Chueca zone north of Gran Vía. The latter can be a bit druggy late at night.

The bars on Plaza de Santa Ana are where *todo el mundo* (absolutely everyone) seems to start his or her evening out. Low-key **Cervercería Alemana** *(☎ 91 429 70 33; Plaza de Santa Ana 6)* appeals to travellers, with its beer served in steins. There's not much elbowroom at **Viva Madrid** *(☎ 91 429 36 40; Calle de Manuel Fernández y González 7)* at weekends, but take a look at its tiles and heavy wooden ceilings. On the same street, **Carbones** *(open until 4am)* is a busy place with good mainstream music on the jukebox. **Los Gabrieles** *(☎ 91 429 62 61; Calle Echegaray 17)* is a dazzling tiled bar with a huge history, most famously serving as a meeting point for the beautiful people of Spain's *movida* (an area of town where lively bars and maybe discos are clustered).

Cafe Populart *(☎ 91 429 84 07; Calle de las Huertas 22)* often has music, generally jazz or blues. For more jazz with your drinks, **Cafe Central** *(☎ 91 369 41 43; Plaza del Ángel 10)* is another good choice. Just at the bottom of Huertas is the amiable **Los Gatos** *(☎ 91 429 30 67; Calle de Jesús 2)*, a lively local haunt.

In Malasaña, **Cervecería Santa Bárbara** *(Plaza de Santa Bárbara 8)* is a classic Madrid drinking house and a good place to kick-off a night out. If you fancy some salsa with your cerveza head for **El Son** *(☎ 91 308 04 29; Calle Fernando V1 21)*, a Latino music bar.

Irish pubs are very popular in Madrid: two good ones are **O'Neill's** *(☎ 91 521 20 30; Calle del Principe 12)*, and **Finnegan's** *(☎ 91 310 05 21; Plaza de las Salesas 9)*.

Calle de Pelayo Campoamor is lined with an assortment of bars, graduating from hi-octane rock bars at the northern end to the gay bar centre at the southern Chueca area. **Rimmel** *(Calle de Luis de Góngora 4)* and **Cruising** *(91 521 51 43; Calle de Pérez Galdós 5)* are among the more popular gay haunts. The latter has a dark room and puts on occasional shows.

Raising many a schoolgirl titter, the quaintly named **Bar Cock** *(☎ 91 532 67 37; Calle de la Reina 16)* once served as a discreet salon for high-class prostitution. The ladies in question have gone but this popular bar is still plush and atmospheric.

Live Music & Clubs

If you like the skirt-swirling Spanish sound, head for **Alhambra** *(☎ 91 521 07 08; Calle Victoria 9)*, in Santa Ana, which gathers speed at around 11pm. **Morocco** *(☎ 91 531 31 77; Calle del Marqués de Leganés 7)*, in Malasaña, is still a popular stop on the Madrid disco circuit. It gets going about 1am.

Near Plaza de Santa Ana, Calle de la Cruz has a couple of good dance spaces; try to pick up fliers for them before you go – they may save you queueing. **Suristán** *(Calle de la Cruz 7)* is a buzzing nightclub dedicated to world music with a colourful, multiethnic clientele and modest cover charge. **Torero** *(Calle de la Cruz 26)* has Latin music upstairs and disco house downstairs.

Soul Kitchen *(Calle Fernandez de los Rios 67)* has recently re-opened and is bigger and badder than ever with the latest hip-hop, reggae and house tracks.

Madrid's not the best where authentic flamenco is concerned, although **Casa Patas** *(☎ 91 369 04 96; Calle de Cañizares 10)* hosts recognised masters of flamenco song, guitar and dance. Bigger flamenco names also play some of Madrid's theatres – check listings.

Classical Music, Theatre & Opera

There's plenty happening, except in the height of summer. The city's grandest stage **Teatro Real** *(☎ 91 516 06 06; Plaza de Isabel 11)* is the scene for opera. If you can't get into the Teatro Real, the **Teatro Calderón** *(☎ 91 369 14 34; Calle de Atocha 18)* plays second fiddle. The beautiful old **Teatro de la Comedia** *(☎ 91 521 49 31; Calle del Príncipe 14)*, home to the Compañía Nacional de Teatro Clásico, stages gems of classic Spanish and European theatre. The **Centro Cultural de la Villa** *(☎ 91*

575 60 80), under the waterfall at Plaza de Colón, stages everything from classical concerts to comic theatre, opera and even classy flamenco. Also important for classical music is the **Auditorio Nacional de Música**, *(☎ 91 337 01 40; Avenida del Príncipe de Vergara 146; metro Cruz del Rayo)*.

SPECTATOR SPORTS

Bullfights take place most Sundays between March and October – more often during the festival of San Isidro Labrador in May – and in the height of summer. Madrid has Spain's largest bullring, the **Plaza de Toros Monumental de Las Ventas** *(☎ 91 726 48 00; metro Ventas)*. Tickets are best bought in advance, from agencies or at the rings, and cost up to €12.

GETTING THERE & AWAY

Air

Scheduled and charter flights from all over the world arrive at **Barajas airport** *(☎ 902 35 35 70)*. Airline offices in Madrid include:

Air France (☎ 91 330 04 12, bookings ☎ 90 111 22 66) Torre de Madrid, Plaza de España 18
American Airlines (☎ 91 453 14 00) Calle de Orense 4
British Airways (☎ 91 387 43 00, 902 11 13 33) Calle de Serrano 60
Iberia (☎ 91 587 75 36, bookings ☎ 902 40 05 00) Calle de Velázquez 130
Lufthansa (☎ 902 22 01 01) Calle del Cardenal Marcelo Spinola 2

Bus

There are eight bus stations dotted around Madrid, serving different bus companies. Tourist offices can tell you which one you need for your destination. **Estación Sur de Autobuses** *(☎ 91 468 42 00; Calle de Méndez Álvaro; metro Méndez Álvaro)* services most buses to the south, and some to other places (including a number of international services).

Train

Atocha station, south of the centre, is used by most trains to/from southern Spain and many destinations around Madrid. Some trains from the north also terminate here, passing through Chamartín, the other main station (in the north of the city), on the way. You can reserve ticket's at **RENFE's main booking office** *(☎ 91 328 90 20; Calle de Alcalá 44; open 9.30am-8pm Mon-Fri)*.

Car & Motorcycle

Car-rental companies in Madrid include **Avis** *(☎ 91 547 20 48)*, **Atesa** *(☎ 902 10 01 01)*, **Europcar** *(☎ 91 541 88 92)* and **Hertz** *(☎ 91 542 58 03)*. All have offices at the airport, in the city centre, and often at the main train stations. Highway robbery on hire-cars leaving the airport is a problem, so be careful.

You can rent motorbikes from **Moto Alquiler** *(☎ 91 542 06 57; Calle del Conde Duque 13)*, but it's pricey, starting at €35 per day for a 50cc Vespa. Rental is available 8am to 8pm, and you have to leave a refundable deposit of around €300 on your credit card.

GETTING AROUND

To/From the Airport

The metro runs right into town from the airport, at the upper level of the T2 terminal. Alternatively, an airport bus service runs to/from an underground terminal in Plaza de Colón every 12 to 15 minutes. The trip takes 30 minutes in average traffic and costs €2.46. A taxi between the airport and city centre should cost no more than €20.

Bus & Metro

In general, the underground (metro) is faster and easier than city buses for getting around central Madrid. You can pick up a bus route map from tourist offices. A single ride costs €0.95. A 10-ride *Metrobus* ticket (€5) can be used on buses and metro. Nightowls may find the 20 bus lines, running from midnight to 6am, useful. They run from Puerta del Sol and Plaza de la Cibeles.

Madrid has a very efficient, safe and simple underground system. Trains run from 6.30am to 1.30am and the fares are the same as on buses.

Taxi

Madrid's taxis are inexpensive by European standards. They're handy late at night, although in peak hours it's quicker to walk or get the metro. Flag fall is €1.35, after which you are charged according to time, so avoid rush-hour traffic.

Car & Motorcycle

There's little point subjecting yourself to Madrid's traffic just to move from one part of the city to another, especially at peak hours. There are plenty of car parks across the city, costing about €1.75 an hour.

AROUND MADRID

El Escorial

The extraordinary 16th-century monastery-palace complex of **San Lorenzo de El Escorial** *(adult/student €6/3, guided tour extra €1; open 10am-6pm Tues-Sun Apr-Sept, 10am-5pm Tues-Sun Oct-Mar)* lies one hour northwest of Madrid, just outside the town of the same name.

El Escorial was built by Felipe II, king of Spain, Naples, Sicily, Milan, the Netherlands and large parts of the Americas. It was built to commemorate his victory over the French in the battle of St Quentin (1557) and as a mausoleum for his father Carlos I, the first of Spain's Habsburg monarchs. El Escorial's austere style is loved by some, hated by others. Either way, it's a quintessential monument of Spain's golden age.

Almost all visitors to El Escorial make it a day trip from Madrid. You can get information on El Escorial from tourist offices in Madrid, or from the local **tourist office** *(☎ 91 890 53 13; Calle de Floridablanca 10; open Mon-Sat)*, close to the monastery.

Things to See

Above the monastery's main gateway, on its western side, stands a **statue of San Lorenzo**, holding a symbolic gridiron (he was roasted alive on one). Inside, across the Patio de los Reyes, stands the restrained **basílica**, a cavernous church with a beautiful white-marble crucifixion by Benvenuto Cellini, sculpted in 1576. At either side of the altar stands bronze statues of Carlos I and his family (to the left), and Felipe II with three of his four wives and his eldest son (on the right).

The route you have to follow leads first to the **Museo de Arquitectura**, detailing in Spanish how El Escorial was constructed, and the **Museo de Pintura**, with 16th- and 17th-century Spanish, Italian and Flemish fine art. You then head upstairs to the richly decorated **Palacio de Felipe II**, in one room of which the monarch died in 1598. Next you descend to the **Panteón de los Reyes**, where almost all Spain's monarchs since Carlos I, and their spouses, lie in gilded marble coffins. Three empty sarcophagi await future arrivals. Backtracking a little, you find yourself in the **Panteón de los Infantes**, a larger series of chambers and tunnels housing the tombs of princes, princesses and other lesser royalty.

Finally, the **Salas Capitulares** in the southeast of the monastery house a minor treasure trove of El Grecos, Titians, Tintorettos and other old masters.

When you emerge, it's worth heading back to the entrance, where you can gain access to the **biblioteca** (library), once one of Europe's finest and still a haven for some 40,000 historical and valuable books.

Getting There & Away

The Herranz bus company runs a service every 10 minutes from 10am to 11pm from No 3 bus stop at the Moncloa metro station in Madrid to San Lorenzo de El Escorial (€2.65 one way). Only about 10 run on Sunday and during holidays.

Up to 20 sluggish *cercanías* trains (line C-8a) serve El Escorial from Atocha station (via Chamartín) in Madrid (€2.70). Seven of these go on to Ávila. Local buses will take you the 2km from the train station up to the monastery.

Castilla y León

The one-time centre of the mighty Christian kingdom of Castile, Castilla y León abounds in romantic mist-enshrouded ruins, convoluted medieval districts and delightful hamlets. Both Segovia and Ávila provide impressive reminders of antiquity, León sports a magnificent cathedral, and Salamanca boasts an intellectual, artsy vibe and vivacious nightlife.

SEGOVIA

pop 54,040

Segovia's diminutive ridge-top Old Town and awe-inspiring Roman aqueduct make for a worthwhile day trip from Madrid or a useful launching pad for explorations further into the region. Originally a Celtic settlement, the town was conquered by the Romans around 80 BC.

Both the **main tourist office** *(☎ 921 46 03 34; Plaza Mayor)* and the **branch office** *(☎ 921 46 29 14; Plaza del Azuguejo)*, beside the aqueduct, are open daily. The first thing you'll notice is the 1st-century AD **aqueduct** stretching over 800m away from the Old Town's east end. Its 163 arches reach up to 29m high, all without the aid of a drop of mortar.

At the heart of the Old Town is the 16th-century Gothic **cathedral** *(admission €2)*, on the pretty Plaza Mayor. Its sombre interior is anchored by an imposing choir and enlivened by about 20 chapels. The Capilla del Cristo del Consuelo houses a remarkable Romanesque doorway preserved from the original church.

Rapunzel towers, turrets topped with slate witch's hats and a deep, dark moat render the **Alcázar** *(admission €3.10)* a most memorable monument. A 15th-century fairy-tale castle, perched on a craggy cliff top at the Old Town's west end, it was virtually destroyed by fire in 1862 and reconstructed. Don't leave without climbing the Torre de Juan II.

Places to Stay & Eat

About 2km along the road to La Granja is **Camping Acueducto** *(☎ 921 42 50 00; admission per person or car €4; open Apr-Sept)*.

Pensión Aragón *(☎ 921 46 09 14; Plaza Mayor 4; singles/doubles/quads €13/24/26)* is small, clean and characterless but the cheapest accommodation in town. Far more pleasant (but still small) is **Hostal Plaza** *(☎ 921 46 03 03, fax 921 46 03 05; Calle del Cronista Lecea 11; singles/doubles €34/40)*. Also central is **Hostal Juan Bravo** *(☎ 921 43 55 21; Calle de Juan Bravo 12)*, with similar prices. Outside the Old Town, but close to the aqueduct, is the spic-and-span **Hostal Don Jaime** *(☎ 921 44 47 87; Calle de Ochoa Ondategui 8; singles/doubles €25/41)*, where the doubles also have TV.

The simple **Bar Ratos** *(Calle de los Escuderos; bocadillos €3)* makes generously stuffed sandwiches. **Cueva de San Esteban** *(Calle de Valdeláguila 15; set lunch €6)* has delicious lunch *menús*. A good place to sample Segovia's speciality *cochinillo asado* (roast suckling pig; *ración* €5.50) is the timber-laden dining room of **Mesón José María** *(Calle del Cronista Lecea 11)*, a favourite among Segovians. For meatless fare, try **La Almuzara** *(Marqués del Arco 3; vegie plato combinado €7; open for lunch Wed-Sun, dinner Tues-Sun)*, which has a warm, arty ambience.

Getting There & Around

Up to 30 buses daily run to Madrid (€5, 1½ hours); others serve Ávila and Salamanca. The bus station is 500m south of the aqueduct, just off Paseo Ezequiel González. Trains to Madrid leave every two hours (€4.50, 1¾ hours). The station is southeast of town; take bus No 2 to the centre.

ÁVILA

pop 47,970

Impressive Ávila is one of the world's best-preserved walled cities. Constructed during the 11th and 12th centuries, its imposing *muralla* (rampart) consists of no fewer than eight monumental gates and 88 towers.

At 1130m, Ávila is also Spain's highest city – and the birthplace of St Teresa of Ávila, a 16th-century mystical writer and reformer of the Carmelite order. Less known is that Tomás de Torquemada orchestrated the most brutal phase of the Spanish Inquisition here, sending off 2000 people to be burnt at the stake in the late 15th century.

The folks at the **tourist office** *(☎ 920 21 13 87; Plaza de la Catedral 4; open daily)* are far more friendly than those at Torquemada.

Things to See & Do

Of Ávila's many convents, museums and monuments, the **cathedral** *(admission €2.50; open daily)* is perhaps the most interesting. Not merely a house of worship, it was also an ingenious fortress: its stout granite apse forms the central bulwark in the eastern wall of the town, which was the most open to attack and hence the most heavily fortified. Around the western side, the main facade conceals the Romanesque origins of what is essentially the earliest Gothic church in Spain. You can peek inside for free, but proceeding to the inner sanctum – plus the cloister, sacristy and small museum – requires the entrance fee.

Just outside the walls, the Romanesque **Basílica de San Vicente** *(admission €1.20; open daily)* is striking. Gothic modifications in granite clash with the warm sandstone of the 11th-century Romanesque original.

About 500m east of the Old Town, the **Monasterio de Santo Tomás** *(admission €1; open daily)*, is thought to be Torquemada's burial place. Built hastily in 1482 as a royal residence, it is formed by three interconnecting cloisters and the church.

The **Convento de Santa Teresa** *(admission free; open daily)* was built in 1636, over the saint's birthplace. The room where she was purportedly born is now a gold-smothered chapel. The souvenir shop next door gives access to a small room crammed with Teresa relics, including her ring finger (complete with ring).

Los Cuatro Postes, a lookout point around 1km west of the city gates on the Salamanca road, has the best view of the city and its perfectly preserved walls.

Places to Stay

The well-maintained rooms at **Hostal Jardín** *(☎ 920 21 10 74; Calle de San Segundo 38; singles/doubles from €24/34)* come with TV and shared bathroom. **Hostal El Rastro** *(☎ 920 21 12 18; Plaza del Rastro 1; singles/doubles €27/34)* boasts harshly lit quarters and a good restaurant. More comfortable is **Hostal San Juan** *(☎ 920 25 14 75; Calle de los Comuneros de Castilla 3; singles/doubles €26/34)*, where rooms are sparkly clean and happily orange.

Places to Eat

Pleasant **Posada de la Fruta** *(Plaza de Pedro Dávila 8; bar dishes €3-6, meals €10-13)* serves cheap and informal meals in its cafeteria/bar and more substantial fare in its traditional dining room. **Siglo Doce**, just inside Puerta de los Leales, has good bocadillos for €3. **El Rincón de Jabugo** *(Calle de San Segundo 30; salads or pasta €5)* offers solid Italian fare.

Cafe del Adarve *(Calle de San Segundo 50)* is a hip hang-out and good place for a drink, as is the wine and tapas bar **Bodeguita de San Segundo**, across the street.

Restaurante Los Leales *(Plaza de Italia 4; set menu €8)* offers a filling *menú*.

Getting There & Away

Buses to Madrid leave up to eight times on weekdays, three on weekends (€5.50, 1½ hours), while Salamanca is served four times on weekdays (€4.50, 1½ hours) and Segovia up to seven times (€5, one hour). There are up to 30 trains a day to Madrid (€5.50, 1½ hours); trains to Salamanca cost the same.

The bus and train stations are, respectively, 700m and 1.5km east of the Old Town. Bus No 1 links the train station with the Old Town.

SALAMANCA

pop 158,520

Storied Salamanca presents fairy-tale sights by day and hopping action at night. It's one of Spain's most inspiring cities, both in the beauty of its architecture and its modern, laid-back lifestyle. Year-round, its numerous bars, cafés and restaurants are jam-packed with students and young visitors from around the world.

The **municipal tourist office** *(☎ 923 21 83 42; Plaza Mayor; open daily)* concentrates on city information. A second branch of the **tourist office** *(☎ 923 26 85 71; Casa de las Conchas; open Mon-Sat)* focuses on the wider region. Send mail from the **post office** *(Gran Vía 25)*. For Internet access try **Campus Cibermático** *(Plaza Mayor 10)*.

Things to See

One of the joys of Salamanca is simply wandering the streets. At the heart of the old centre is the harmonious **Plaza Mayor** (1755), designed by José Churriguera and ringed by medallions of sundry famous figures.

Salamanca's **University** was founded in 1218. Its main facade on Calle de los Libreros is a tapestry in sandstone, bursting with images of mythical and historical figures, including a famously elusive frog. Join the throngs trying to find the little creature.

Brace yourself for the **Catedral Nueva** (New Cathedral). This incredible Gothic structure, completed in 1733, took 220 years to build. With its intricate carvings and detailed relief, it's a wonder they did it so fast. From inside you can enter the **Catedral Vieja** *(Old Cathedral; admission €2.40)*.

The 15th-century **Casa de las Conchas** *(admission free; open daily)*, named for the scallop shells that cling to its facade, is a symbol of Salamanca.

Places to Stay & Eat

Salamanca is always in season, so book ahead. The central HI **Albergue Juvenil** *(☎ 923 26 91 41, fax 923 21 42 27; e esterra@mmteam.disbumad.es; Calle Escoto 13-15; dorm beds €12)* has standard bunks. Rates include linen and breakfast.

Hotel Los Ángeles *(☎ 923 21 81 66; Plaza Mayor 10; singles/doubles €13/27)* has low-frills rooms with washbasins and shared bathrooms. A favourite of young travellers is tiny, hospitable **Pensión Las Vegas** *(☎ 923 21 87 49; e lasvegas@iponet.es; Calle de Meléndez 13; singles/doubles €12/18)*. Rooms at **Pensión Feli** *(☎ 923 21 60 10; Calle de los Libreros 58; singles/doubles €12/24)*, near the university, are homey and lively. For more comfort, try **Le Petit Hotel** *(☎ 923 60 07 73; Ronda de Sancti-Spíritus 39; singles/doubles €35/43)*, whose small but tidy rooms have a phone, TV and bathroom.

For good, filling breakfasts, hit **Café Unamuno** *(Calle Zamora 55; breakfast €2.50)*. **MusicArte Café** *(Plaza del Corrillo 22; sand-*

wiches €2, pizzas €8) is a hip hang-out. **El Patio Chico** *(Calle de Meléndez 13; tapas €3, set menu €10)* is a lively place for beers and filling tapas. At **Café El Ave** *(Calle de los Libreros 24; meals €5)* you can fill up at budget prices. Sample the paella at bustling **El Bardo** *(Calle de la Compañía 8; paella €7)*. **El Grillo Azul** *(Calle Grillo 1; set menu €8)* offers inexpensive all-vegie fare in an elegant setting.

Entertainment

Salamanca, with its myriad bars, is the perfect after-dark playground. A drink at **Tío Vivo** *(Calle de Clavel 3)* is a must, if only to experience the whimsical decor. A long-time favourite is **El Gran Café Moderno** *(Gran Vía 75)*, made to resemble an early-20th-century Parisian street. **El Corrillo** *(Calle de Meléndez 8)* is great for a beer and (sometimes) live jazz. **O'Neill's** *(Calle de Zamora 14)* and **The Irish Rover**, by the Casa de las Conchas, are Salamanca's popular Irish pubs.

Capitán Haddock is a surprisingly romantic haunt with a muted nautical theme, in a courtyard off Calle Consejo. A popular bar is **Gatsby** *(Calle de Bordadores 18)*.

Great discos include **Camelot** *(Calle de la Compañía)*, inside an actual convent, and **Posada de las Almas** *(Plaza de San Boal)*, a fantasy world inhabited by lifesize papier-mâché figures and doll houses.

Getting There & Around

Salamanca's bus station is at Avenida de Filiberto Villalobos 85, about 1km northwest of Plaza Mayor. AutoRes has frequent express

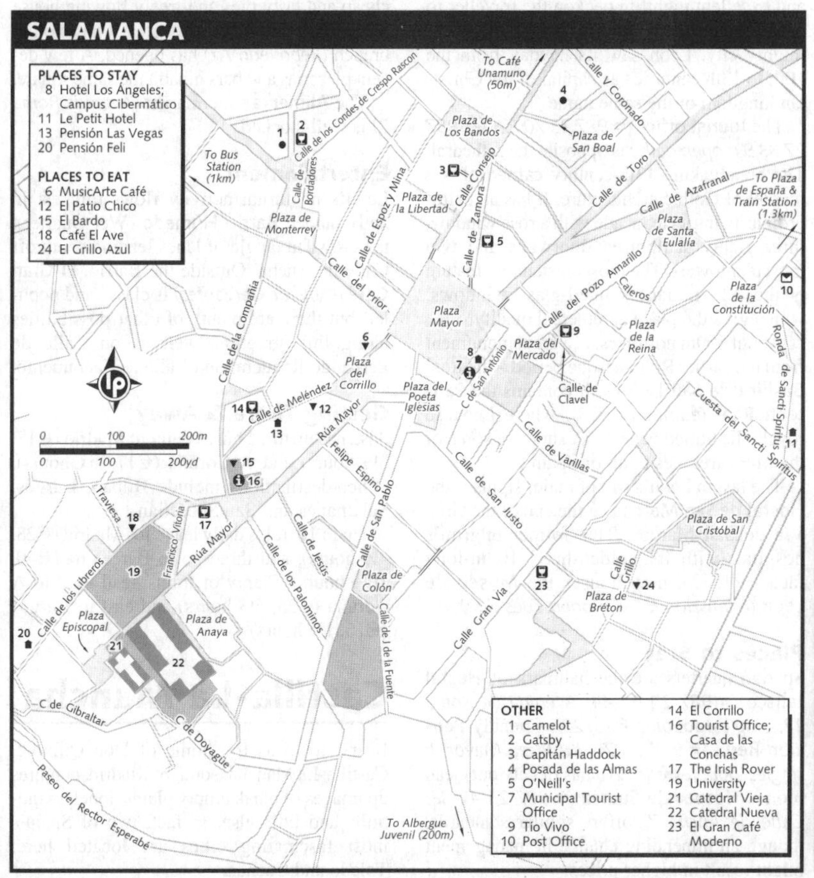

service to Madrid (€15, 2½ hours), as well as a few nonexpress buses. Other destinations served regularly include Santiago de Compostela, Cáceres, Ávila, Segovia, León and Valladolid. Four trains leave daily for Madrid (€13, 2½ hours) via Ávila (€6, 1¾ hours). A train for Lisbon leaves at 4.40am.

Bus No 4 runs past the bus station and around the Old Town perimeter to Gran Vía. From the train station, the best bet is bus No 1, which heads down Calle de Azafranal. Going the other way, pick it up along Gran Vía.

LEÓN

pop 137,380

Oft-ignored León offers more than just another cathedral (although its version is simply a masterpiece). Long boulevards, open squares and excellent nightlife beckon the traveller to pause a day or two and reflect on the once-mighty city. León saw its heyday from the 10th to 13th centuries as capital of the Christian kingdom of the same name.

The **tourist office** *(☎ 987 23 70 82, fax 987 27 33 91; open daily)* is opposite the cathedral. The breathtaking 13th-century **cathedral** is a marvel of Gothic architecture. It has an extraordinarily intricate facade with a rose window, three richly sculptured doorways and two muscular towers. The most outstanding feature is the 128 radiant stained-glass windows, which give the place an ethereal quality.

About 500m northwest is a great monument from the earlier Romanesque period – the **Real Basílica de San Isidoro**. It contains the **Panteón Real** *(admission €3)*, where Leonese royalty lie buried beneath a canopy of some of the finest frescoes in all of Spain.

The last in León's trio of major sights is the **Hostal de San Marcos**, at the end of the Gran Vía de San Marcos. This former pilgrim's hospital, with its golden-hued 100m-long facade (1513), now houses the **Museo de León** *(admission €1.25; open Tues-Sun)*.

Places to Stay

Spartan quarters are the hallmark of **Hostal Jalisco** *(☎ 987 22 64 44; Avenida de Roma 18; singles/doubles €13/20)*. Friendly **Pensión Berta** *(☎ 987 25 70 39; Plaza Mayor 8; singles/doubles €15/20)* has rickety but clean rooms. **Hospedaje Suárez** *(☎ 987 25 42 88; Calle de Ancha 7)* offers similar standards, though an impending change in management might result in higher prices.

Hotel Residencia Reina *(☎ 987 20 52 12; Calle de Puerta de la Reina 2; singles/doubles with washbasin from €15/24)* offers small, basic rooms. **Hostal Orejas** *(☎/fax 987 25 29 09; Calle de Villafranca 6; singles/doubles with washbasin €27/34, with bath €34/47)* has bright but almost creepily quiet rooms.

Places to Eat

Restaurante Honoré *(Calle de los Serradores 4; set menu €7)* offers a belly-expanding good *menú*. **Palomo** *(Calle de la Escalerilla; meals €10-20)*, on a tiny street, offers typical Castilian fare. Next door is popular **Vivaldi** *(meals €10-20)*, where you can wash down your meal with a cider from Asturias.

Pizzeria La Competencia *(Calle Mulhacín; pizzas €5-8)*, wedged into a tight street, offers cheap and tasty pies and freely flowing house wine. Its popularity is so great that another branch *(Rebolledo Az)* has opened. A few decent pizzerias and bars inhabit the same square.

The **Alimerka** supermarket *(Avenida Roma 2)* is well-stocked.

Entertainment

León's nocturnal activity flows thickest in aptly named **Barrio Húmedo** (Wet Quarter), the crowded tangle of lanes leading south off Calle de Ancha. Outside the Barrio, **El Gran Café** *(Calle de Cervantes)* is classy and popular, but there are plenty of other possibilities along this street as well as on Calle de Fernando Regueral and Calle de Sacramento.

Getting There & Away

Alsa has up to 12 buses daily to Madrid (€17, 3½ hours) and A Coruña (€17, six hours). Other destinations include Bilbao, Burgos, Salamanca and San Sebástian.

Up to 10 trains daily leave for Madrid (€28, 4½ hours), and three go to Barcelona (€40, 10½ hours). Plenty of trains head west to A Coruña (€25, 6½ hours) and east to Burgos (€16, 1½ hours).

Castilla-La Mancha

Best known as the home of Don Quixote, Castilla-La Mancha, south of Madrid, conjures up images of bleak empty plains, lonely windmills and little else. In fact, two of Spain's most fascinating cities are located here: Toledo and Cuenca.

TOLEDO

pop 69,450

The narrow, winding streets of Toledo, perched on a small hill above the Río Tajo, are crammed with museums, churches and other monumental reminders of a splendid and turbulent past. As the main city of Muslim central Spain, Toledo was the peninsula's leading centre of learning and the arts in the 11th century. Until 1492, Christians, Jews and Muslims coexisted peaceably here, for which Toledo still bears the label 'Ciudad de las Tres Culturas' (City of the Three Cultures). El Greco lived here from 1577 to 1614, and many of his works can still be seen in the city.

Toledo is packed with tourists during the day. Try to stay here overnight, after the coach tours have left, and when you can really appreciate the spark and soul of the city.

Information

The **main tourist office** *(☎ 925 22 08 43, fax 925 25 26 48)* is just outside Toledo's main gate, the Puerta Nueva de Bisagra, at the northern end of town. A smaller information office is open in the *ayuntamiento* (town hall), across from the cathedral. You can connect to the Internet at **Scorpions** *(☎ 925 21 25 56; Calle Matías Moreno 10; open 12.30pm-2am daily)*, located close to the San Juan de los Reyes monastery. It charges €2.20 per hour.

Things to See

As well as historical sights, Toledo's tourist shops are fun, many reflecting the city's swashbuckling past with suits of armour and swords for sale. Toledo is also famous for its marzipan; try **Santo Tomé** *(Calle Santo Tomé 5)*.

The **cathedral** *(Cardenal Cisneros; open 10.30am-6.30pm daily)*, in the heart of the Old City, is stunning. You could easily spend an afternoon here, admiring the glorious stone architecture, stained-glass windows, tombs of kings in the Capilla Mayor and art by the likes of El Greco, Velázquez and Goya. You have to buy a ticket (€4.80) to enter four areas – the **Coro**, **Sacristía**, **Capilla de la Torre** and **Sala Capitular**, which contain some of the finest art and artisanship.

The **alcázar** *(Calle Cuesta de Carlos V, 2; admission €2, free Wed; open 9.30am-2pm Tues-Sun)*, Toledo's main landmark, was fought over repeatedly from the Middle Ages through to the Spanish Civil War, when it was besieged by Republican troops. Today it's a military museum, created by the Nationalist victors of the Civil War.

The **Museo de Santa Cruz** *(Calle de Cervantes 3; admission €1.20; open 10am-6.30pm Tues-Sat, 10am-2pm Sun)* contains a large collection of furniture, faded tapestries, military and religious paraphernalia, and paintings. Upstairs is an impressive collection of El Grecos, including the masterpiece *La Asunción* (Assumption of the Virgin).

In the southwest of the Old City, the queues outside an unremarkable church, the **Iglesia de Santo Tomé** *(Plaza del Conde; admission €1.20; open 10am-6pm daily)* indicate there must be something special inside. That something is El Greco's masterpiece *El Entierro del Conde de Orgaz*. The painting depicts the burial of the Count of Orgaz in 1322 by San

The Windmills of his Mind

Don't lie. You haven't read *Don Quixote de La Mancha*, have you? Of course not. No-one has. And yet you get the feeling that you should know all about it, right?

Here's what you need to know to impress your newfound *amigos*. Miguel de Cervantes (1547–1616) wrote the book, widely considered the greatest work in the Spanish language. A country gentleman-scholar, Alonso Quejana, becomes so obsessed with tales of chivalry that he goes nuts, dons his grandfather's suit of armour (plus a cardboard helmet), mounts his trusty steed (a dilapidated old nag) and roams the country in search of adventure as the knight Don Quixote. Famous encounters include his persuading of Sancho Panza, a village farmer, to join him as a squire and ride on a donkey; the courtship of a peasant girl, whom Don Quixote names Dulcinea del Toboso; and attacks on 'giants' (windmills), an 'army of enemies' (sheep) and 'devils' (funeral pallbearers). In the end, the villagers of La Mancha imprison Quejana and cure him of his madness, and on his deathbed he renounces his insanity.

Although Cervantes probably wrote the tale as a slapstick parody of chivalric novels, it has come to be viewed as a nostalgic tale of human imagination and fantasy pitted against the cold cynicism of reality. Both Quixote and Panza are eminently likable characters, and one can't help but regret the loss of Quejana's 'madness' as the death of idealism in his world.

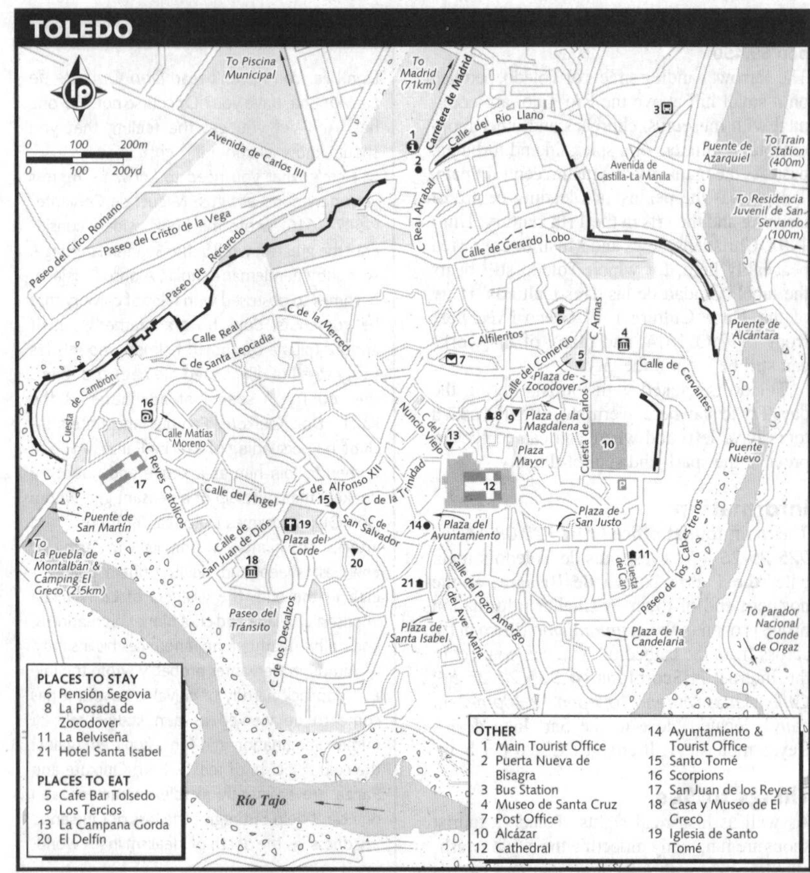

Esteban (St Stephen) and San Agustín (St Augustine), observed by a heavenly entourage, including Christ, the Virgin, John the Baptist and Noah. The church is open later in summer.

The so-called **Casa y Museo de El Greco** *(Calle de Samuel Leví; admission €1.20; open 10am-2pm & 4pm-6pm Mon-Sat, 10am-2pm Sun)*, in Toledo's former Jewish quarter, contains the artist's famous *Vista y Plano de Toledo*, plus about 20 of his minor works.

To the north is one of the city's most visible sights, **San Juan de los Reyes**, the Franciscan monastery and church founded by Fernando and Isabel. The prevalent late Flemish-Gothic style is tarted up with lavish Isabelline ornament and counterbalanced by *Mudéjar* (Islamic-inspired architecture style) decoration. Outside are the chains of Christian prisoners freed after the fall of Granada in 1492.

Places to Stay

Toledo's HI hostel, **Residencia Juvenil de San Servando** *(☎ 925 22 45 54, fax 925 21 39 54; beds under/over 26 €10/13)*, is beautifully located in the Castillo de San Servando. Rates include breakfast. Cheap accommodation in the city is hard to come by, especially from Easter to September. **La Belviseña** *(☎ 925 22 00 67; Cuesta del Can 5; rooms per person €10)* is basic but among the best value. Pleasant **Pensión Segovia** *(☎ 925 21 11 24; Calle de los Recoletos 2; singles/doubles €14.42/19.43)* has simple clean rooms.

Appealing **La Posada de Zocodover** *(☎ 925 22 15 71; Calle Condonerias 6; doubles with* *bath €37.30)* has just seven exquisite rooms that get snapped-up fast. Comfortable and chic, **Hotel Santa Isabel** *(☎/fax 925 25 31 36; Calle de Santa Isabel 24; singles/doubles €28/42)* is well placed near the cathedral, yet away from the tourist hordes.

Places to Eat

Among the cheap lunch spots, **El Delfín** *(☎ 925 21 38 14; Calle Taller del Moro 1; set menu €6)* is acceptable, if unexciting. Similarly priced with spaghetti and macaroni on the menu is **Los Tercios** *(☎ 925 22 05 50; Plaza Solarejo 2)*, on a shady plaza.

If you want to drink and people-gaze, **Cafe Bar Tolsedo** *(Plaza de Zocodover)* has tables on the bustling square and serves good tapas, such as spicy *patatas bravas*. Unpretentious tavern-style, **La Campana Gorda** *(☎ 925 21 01 46; Calle Hombre de Palo 13)* specialises in roast meats and fish, and football on the TV.

Getting There & Around

To reach most major destinations from Toledo, you need to backtrack to Madrid (or at least Aranjuez). Toledo's **bus station** *(☎ 925 22 36 41; Avenida de Castilla-La Mancha)* has buses for €3.66 every half-hour from about 6am to 10pm to/from Madrid (Estación Sur). The Aisa line has a service from Toledo to Cuenca at 5.30pm, Monday to Friday.

Trains from Madrid (Atocha) are more pleasant than the bus, but there are only nine of them daily. The first from Madrid departs at 7.05am, the last from Toledo at 8.58pm (€4.81 one way). Toledo's train station is 400m east of the Puente de Azarquiel on the Calle Paseo de la Rosa *(☎ 902 24 02 02)*.

Bus No 5 links the train and bus stations with Plaza de Zocodover.

CUENCA

pop 46,490

Cuenca's setting is hard to believe. The high Old Town is cut off from the rest of the city by the Júcar and Huécar Rivers, sitting at the top of a deep gorge. Most of its famous monuments appear to teeter on the edge – a photographer's delight.

The **tourist office** *(☎/fax 902 10 01 31; ⓔ ofi.turismo@aytocuenca.org; Plaza Mayor 1)*, just before the arches of the main square, is especially helpful. **Big Play** *(☎ 969 23 69 28; Avenida Castillo de la Mancha 14)* provides Internet access for €2 an hour.

Things to See & Do

Cuenca's **Casas Colgadas** (Hanging Houses), built in the 15th century, are precariously positioned on a cliff top, their balconies projecting out over the gorge. Within one is the **Museo de Arte Abstracto Español** *(☎ 969 21 29 83; admission €1.50; open 11am-2pm & 4pm-6pm Tues-Fri, 11am-2pm & 4pm-8pm Sat, 11am-2.30pm Sun)*. This exciting collection includes works by Fernando Zobel, Sempere, Millares and Chillida. Nearby is the **Museo Diocesano** *(☎ 969 22 42 10; Calle del Obispo Valero 2; admission €1)*. Of the religious art and artefacts inside, the 14th-century Byzantine diptych is the jewel in the crown. Hours are the same as the Museo de Arte Abstracto Español.

South of Plaza Mayor in a former convent is the **Museo de Las Ciencias** *(Science Museum; ☎ 969 24 03 20; admission free; open 10am-2pm & 4pm-7pm Tues-Sat, morning Sun)*. Displays range from a time machine to the study of the resources of Castilla-La Mancha.

On Plaza Mayor you'll find Cuenca's strange **cathedral**. The lines of the unfinished facade are Norman-Gothic and reminiscent of French cathedrals, but the stained-glass windows look like they'd be more at home in the abstract art museum.

As you wander the Old Town's beautiful streets, check out the **Torre de Mangana**, the remains of a Moorish fortress in a square west of Calle de Alfonso VIII, overlooking the plain below.

Places to Stay & Eat

At the top of the *casco* (Old Town) is the budget **Pensión La Tabanqueta** *(☎ 969 21 12 90; Calle de Trabuco 13; doubles from €30)*. Ask for a room with views of the Júcar gorge and check out the lively bar downstairs.

At the edge of the gorge with drop-dead views, the tastefully converted 17th-century former convent **Posada de San José** *(☎ 969 21 13 00, fax 923 03 65; ⓔ info@posadasanjose.com; Calle Julián Romero 4; doubles from €60)* makes for an evocative romantic retreat with every room different but very tastefully done.

Most restaurants and cafés around Plaza Mayor are better for a drink and people-watching than for good-value eating, although **Taberna el Botijo** is of a higher standard. A decent establishment for solid La Manchan food is the **Restaurante Los Arcos 11** *(☎ 969*

21 38 06; Calle Severo Catalina 1; dishes from €5) with some interesting dishes. For superb cheeses and local wines to take away, **La Alacena** delicatessen *(Alfonso VIII 32)* is worth seeking out.

Getting There & Around

There are up to nine buses a day to Madrid (€8.40 to €10, 2½ hours), and daily buses to Barcelona, Teruel and Valencia. There are five trains a day direct to Madrid (Atocha), taking 2½ hours and costing €8.41 one way. There are also four trains a day to Valencia.

Bus No 1 or 2 from near the bus and train stations will take you up to Plaza Mayor in the Old Town.

Catalunya

Many Catalans bristle at the idea of being lumped together with 'ordinary' Spaniards, maintaining that their corner of the universe is a little closer to heaven. And with its soaring peaks, tranquil coastal resorts, sleepy small towns and exuberant capital, Catalunya (Cataluña in Catalan) may well lay claim to being its own world.

BARCELONA

pop 1.5 million

The 1992 Olympic Games served as the coming-out party for Barcelona, stylishly introducing this first-class city to the world. Today, folks come from all over to marvel at Barcelona's transcendent modernist architecture, to visit its top-shelf museums, and to roam the streets of its Old City.

No-one should miss the visionary creations of Antoni Gaudí, including the Sagrada Família and Parc Güell. Visitors can further indulge their souls by spending entire days admiring the works of Pablo Picasso and Joan Miró and spending entire nights in a debauched frenzy, winding their way through the city's myriad bars and clubs. Whether it's midday or midnight, Barcelona's famed street, La Rambla, presents a never-ending stream of hawkers, musicians, beggars, backpackers and villains – nonstop entertainment for everyone.

SPAIN

Orientation

Plaça de Catalunya is a good place to get your bearings. La Rambla extends southwards from the plaza, separating Barri Gòtic (the medieval quarter) and Barri Xinès. Most travellers base themselves in Barcelona's Old City (Ciutat Vella), the area bordered by the harbour Port Vell (south), Plaça de Catalunya (north), Ronda de Sant Pau (west) and Parc de la Ciutadella (east). North of the Old City is L'Eixample, where you'll find the best of Barcelona's modernist architecture. A useful map is Lonely Planet's very own *Barcelona.*

Information

Tourist Offices The main tourist office is the **Centre d'Informació Turisme de Barcelona** *(☎ 906 30 12 82; w www.barcelonaturisme.com; Plaça de Catalunya 17-S; open daily).* Ask here for city maps, lists of attractions and useful discount cards (such as the Barcelona Card and ArTicket) that let you into select locations for reduced admission fees.

Handy offices are at Estació Sants, the main train station, and the EU passengers arrivals hall at the airport; both are open daily.

Money Banks usually have the best rates. The **American Express offices** *(Passeig de Gràcia 101 • La Rambla dels Capuxtins 74; open 9.30am-6pm Mon-Fri, 10am-noon Sat)* offer reasonable rates. For after-hours emergencies, exchange booths throng La Rambla.

Post & Communications The **main post office** *(Plaça d'Antoni López; open 8am-9.30pm Mon-Sat)* has poste restante. For Internet access, both **EasyEverything** *(La Rambla)*, charging €0.50 to €2 per hour, and **Conéct@te** *(Carrer d'Aragó 283)*, charging €1.50 per hour, are open 24 hours, although you might not want to wander too close to unshowered Internet users at 4am.

Travel Agencies Youth and student air, train and bus tickets are sold by **Usit Unlimited** *(☎ 93 412 01 04; Ronda de l'Universitat 16).* There's a branch in the **Turisme Juvenil de Catalunya office** *(Carrer de Rocafort 116-122).* **Halcón Viatges** *(☎ 902-30 06 00; Carrer de Pau Claris 108)* is a reliable chain of travel agents.

Medical & Emergency Services The **Guàrdia Urbana** *(City Police; ☎ 092; La Rambla 43)* has a station opposite Plaça Reial. For an ambulance or emergency medical help call ☎ 061. **Hospital Creu Roja** *(☎ 93 300 20 20; Carrer del Dos de Maig 301)* has an emergency room. For 24-hour tourist assistance in English, call ☎ 93 344 13 00. There are 24-hour pharmacies at Carrer d'Aribau 62, Passeig de Gràcia 26 and La Rambla 98.

Dangers & Annoyances Watch your pockets, bags and cameras on the train to and from the airport, on La Rambla, in Barri Gòtic south of Plaça Reial and in Barri Xinès. In addition, be wary when walking in deserted areas, even strolling in parks during the daytime, as violent muggings of foreigners have been on the rise recently.

La Rambla

The best way to introduce yourself to Barcelona is by taking a leisurely stroll from Plaça de Catalunya down La Rambla. This long strip, shaded by leafy trees and varied buildings, is an ever-changing blur of activity, lined with newsstands, bird and flower stalls, and cafés. It's populated by artists, buskers, human statues, shoe-shine merchants, beggars, and a constant stream of people promenading and just enjoying the sights.

Just off La Rambla, **Plaça Reial** used to be a seedy square, but it's now quite pleasant, with numerous cafés and bars and a couple of music clubs. Just off the other side of La Rambla is Gaudí's moody **Palau Güell** *(Carrer Nou de la Rambla 3-5; admission €3; open 10am-6.30pm Mon-Sat)*. Down at the end of La Rambla stands the **Monument a Colom** *(Columbus Monument; admission €1.80)*.

Barri Gòtic

The Gothic Quarter's centrepiece is its serene **cathedral** *(open 8.30am-1.30pm & 4pm-7.30pm Mon-Fri, 8.30am-1.30pm & 5pm-7.30pm Sat & Sun)*. Be sure to visit the lovely, verdant cloister. Each Sunday at noon, crowds gather here to dance the Catalan national dance, the *sardana*. Just east is the fascinating **Museu d'Història de la Ciutat** *(City History Museum; admission €3.50; open 10am-2pm & 4pm-8pm Tues-Sat, 10am-2pm Sun Oct-May; 10am-8pm Tues-Sat, 10am-2pm Sun June-Sept)*, composed of several buildings around **Plaça del Rei**, the palace courtyard of the medieval monarchs of Aragón. From the royal chapel, climb the multitiered Mirador del Rei Martí for good views. The museum also includes a remarkable subterranean walk through excavated portions of Roman and Visigothic Barcelona.

A few minutes' walk west of the cathedral, **Plaça de Sant Josep Oriol** is a sometimes hang-out for bohemian musicians and buskers.

Waterfront

For a look at the modern face of Barcelona, take a stroll along the once-seedy waterfront. From the bottom of La Rambla you can cross the Rambla de Mar footbridge to the **Moll d'Espanya**, a former wharf in the middle of the old harbour, Port Vell. There you'll find **L'Aquàrium** *(admission €11; open 9.30am-9pm or later daily)*, one of Europe's best aquariums. Northeast of Port Vell, on the far side of the fishing-oriented La Barceloneta area, the city **beaches** begin. After 1.25km you'll reach the touristy **Vila Olímpica**, site of the 1992 Olympic village. Don't come here to hobnob with locals.

La Sagrada Família

Gaudí's life masterpiece *(cnr Carrer de Sardenya & Carrer de Mallorca; metro Sagrada Família; admission €6, with tour €9; open 9am-8pm daily Apr-Sept, 9am-6pm daily Oct-Mar)* has the potential to stir the soul. Construction began in 1882 and is proceeding at a suitably otherworldy pace. Today there are eight towers, all over 100m high, with 10 more to come – the total representing the 12 Apostles, four Evangelists and the mother of God, plus the tallest tower (170m) standing for her son. Although La Sagrada Família is a construction site, the awesome dimensions and extravagant yet careful sculpting make it Barcelona's greatest highlight. The northeast Nativity Facade was done under Gaudí's own supervision; the very different northwest Passion Facade has been built since the 1950s.

Passeig de Gràcia

Many of Barcelona's finest modernist buildings are along the aptly named Passeig de Gràcia in L'Eixample. Gaudí's beautifully coloured **Casa Batlló** *(Passeig de Gràcia 43)* beckons onlookers from afar, while his greystone **La Pedrera** *(Passeig de Gràcia 92; admission €6; open 10am-8pm daily)* ripples around the corner of Carrer de Provença. Don't miss its surreal roof. There are guided tours at 6pm Monday to Friday and at 11am Saturday and Sunday.

Next door to Casa Batlló is **Casa Amatller** *(Passeig de Gràcia 41)*, by another leading modernist architect, Josep Puig i Cadafalch.

BARCELONA

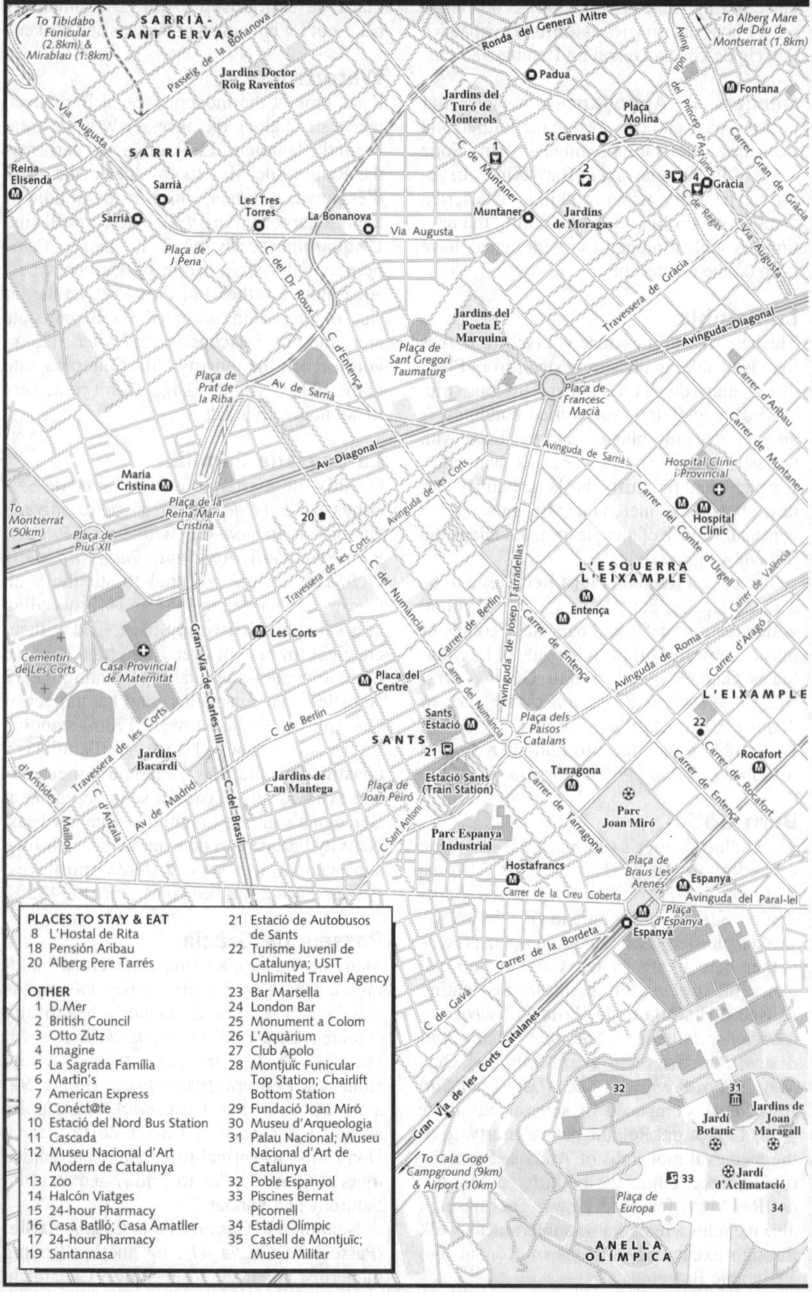

PLACES TO STAY & EAT

8 L'Hostal de Rita
18 Pensión Aribau
20 Alberg Pere Tarrés

OTHER

1 D.Mer
2 British Council
3 Otto Zutz
4 Imagine
5 La Sagrada Família
6 Martin's
7 American Express
9 Conéct@te
10 Estació del Nord Bus Station
11 Cascada
12 Museu Nacional d'Art Modern de Catalunya
13 Zoo
14 Halcón Viatges
15 24-hour Pharmacy
16 Casa Batlló; Casa Amatller
17 24-hour Pharmacy
19 Santannasa
21 Estació d'Autobusos de Sants
22 Turisme Juvenil de Catalunya; USIT Unlimited Travel Agency
23 Bar Marsella
24 London Bar
25 Monument a Colom
26 L'Aquàrium
27 Club Apolo
28 Montjuïc Funicular Top Station; Chairlift Bottom Station
29 Fundació Joan Miró
30 Museu d'Arqueologia
31 Palau Nacional; Museu Nacional d'Art de Catalunya
32 Poble Espanyol
33 Piscines Bernat Picornell
34 Estadi Olímpic
35 Castell de Montjuïc; Museu Militar

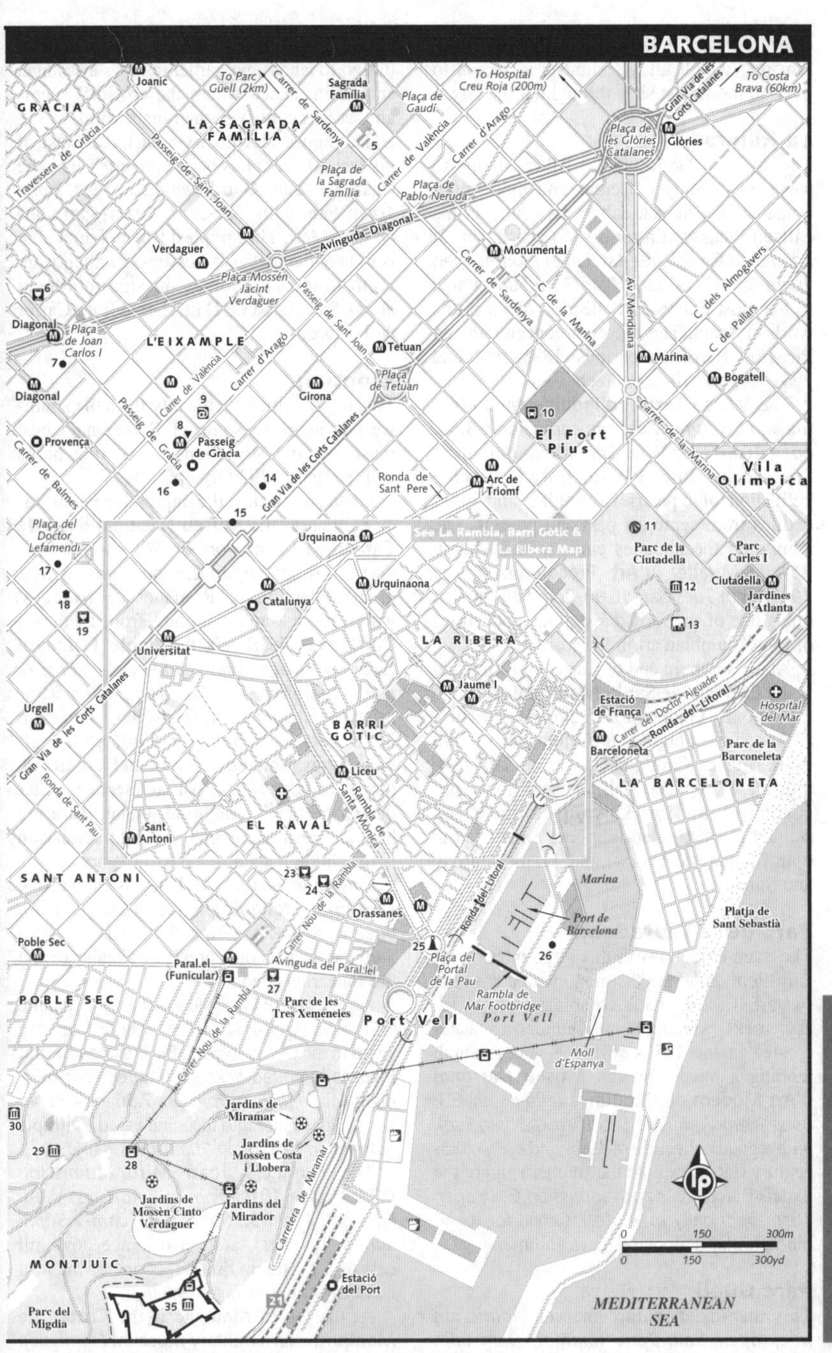
BARCELONA
GRÀCIA
LA SAGRADA FAMÍLIA
L'EIXAMPLE
El Fort Pius
Vila Olímpica
LA RIBERA
BARRI GÒTIC
EL RAVAL
SANT ANTONI
POBLE SEC
LA BARCELONETA
Port Vell
MONTJUÏC
To Parc Güell (2km)
To Hospital Creu Roja (200m)
To Costa Brava (60km)
See La Rambla, Barri Gòtic & La Ribera Map
Plaça de les Glòries Catalanes
Avinguda Diagonal
Gran Via de les Corts Catalanes
Passeig de Gràcia
Passeig de Sant Joan
Carrer de Sardenya
Carrer de València
Carrer d'Aragó
Carrer de Balmes
Travessera de Gràcia
C de la Marina
Carrer de la Marina
Av Meridiana
C dels Almogàvers
C de Pallars
Ronda de Sant Pere
Ronda de Sant Pau
Ronda del Litoral
Carrer del Doctor Aiguader
Rambla de Santa Mònica
Carrer Nou de la Rambla
Avinguda del Paral.lel
Carretera de Miramar
Joanic
Sagrada Família
Verdaguer
Diagonal
Girona
Tetuan
Monumental
Marina
Bogatell
Glòries
Provença
Passeig de Gràcia
Arc de Triomf
Urquinaona
Catalunya
Universitat
Urgell
Jaume I
Liceu
Sant Antoni
Drassanes
Poble Sec
Paral.lel (Funicular)
Ciutadella
Barceloneta
Plaça de Gaudí
Plaça de la Sagrada Família
Plaça de Pablo Neruda
Plaça Mossèn Jacint Verdaguer
Plaça de Joan Carlos I
Plaça de Tetuan
Plaça del Doctor Letamendi
Plaça del Portal de la Pau
Parc de la Ciutadella
Parc Carles I
Jardines d'Atlanta
Estació de França
Hospital del Mar
Parc de la Barceloneta
Marina
Port de Barcelona
Platja de Sant Sebastià
Parc de les Tres Xemeneies
Rambla de Mar Footbridge
Port Vell
Moll d'Espanya
Jardins de Miramar
Jardins de Mossèn Costa i Llobera
Jardins de Mossèn Cinto Verdaguer
Jardins del Mirador
Estació del Port
Parc del Migdia
MEDITERRANEAN SEA
0 150 300m
0 150 300yd

SPAIN

Check here for tickets to the Ruta del Modernisme, which allows sightseers access to over 50 modernist sites throughout the city.

La Ribera

East of Barri Gòtic lies La Ribera, home to some outstanding museums and more modernist works. Smack-dab in its centre is the **Museu Picasso** *(Carrer de Montcada 15-19; admission €4.80, free 1st Sun of month; open 10am-8pm Tues-Sat, 10am-3pm Sun)*, home to the most important collection of Picasso's work in Spain. The museum concentrates on Picasso's Barcelona periods (1895–1900 and 1901–04) early in his career.

The **Museu Textil i d'Indumentària** *(Textile and Costume Museum; admission €3.50; open 10am-8pm Tues-Sat, 10am-3pm Sun)*, opposite the Museu Picasso, has a fascinating collection of tapestries, clothing and other textiles from centuries past and present. The admission fee includes entry to the **Museu Barbier-Mueller d'Art Precolombí** *(open 10am-8pm Tues-Sat, 10am-3pm Sun)*, which holds one of the most prestigious collections of pre-Columbian art in the world.

At the southern end of Carrer de Montcada is the **Església de Santa Maria del Mar**, the most stonily Gothic of Barcelona's churches.

A modernist highpoint is Montaner's **Palau de la Música Catalana** *(Carrer de Sant Pere més alt 11)* concert hall, a marvellous concoction of tile, brick, sculpted stone and stained glass. Guided tours are conducted at 6pm Monday to Friday, and 11am Saturday and Sunday.

Parc de la Ciutadella

The main attractions in this large **park** *(open 8am-9pm daily)* are the monumental **cascada** (waterfall), a dramatic combination of statuary, rocks, greenery and thundering water created in the 1870s with the young Gaudí lending a hand, and the **Museu Nacional d'Art Modern de Catalunya** *(admission €3; open 10am-7pm Tues-Sat, 10am-2.30pm Sun)*, with a good collection of 19th- and early-20th-century Catalan art. At the southern end of the park is Barcelona's **zoo** *(admission €10; open 10am-5pm daily in winter)*, famed for its albino gorilla. It's open later in summer.

Parc Güell

This man-meets-nature marvel *(admission free; open 9am-9pm summer, 9am-6pm winter)* in the north of the city is where Gaudí turned to landscape gardening. It's a strange, enchanting place where the artificial seems almost less contrived than the natural.

The house in which Gaudí lived most of his last 20 years has been converted into the **Casa-Museum Gaudí** *(admission €3; open 10am-8pm daily Apr-Sept, 10am-6pm Sun-Fri Oct-Mar)*. The simplest way to Parc Güell is to take the metro to Lesseps and then walk 10 to 15 minutes; follow the signs northeast along Travessera de Dalt, then left up Carrer de Larrard.

Montjuïc

This hill overlooking the city from the southwest is home to some of Barcelona's best museums and attractions, some fine parks and the main 1992 Olympic sites.

On the north side, the impressive Palau Nacional houses the **Museu Nacional d'Art de Catalunya** *(admission €4.80; open 10am-7pm Tues-Sat, 10am-2.30pm Sun)*, with a great collection of Romanesque frescoes, woodcarvings and sculpture from medieval Catalunya. Nearby is the **Poble Espanyol** *(Spanish Village; adult/child or student €7/3.60, free after 9pm Sun-Thur; open 9am-8pm Mon, 9am-2am Tues-Thur, 9am-4am Fri & Sat, 9am-midnight Sun)*, with craft workshops, souvenir shops and creditable copies of famous Spanish architecture. After dark it becomes a nightlife jungle, featuring bars and restaurants galore. Child admission is for children aged seven to 14 years.

Downhill, east of the Palau Nacional, the **Museu d'Arqueologia** *(admission €2.40; open 9.30am-7pm Tues-Sat, 10am-2.30pm Sun)* has a good collection from Catalunya and the Balearic Islands.

Above the Palau Nacional is the Anella Olímpica (Olympic Ring), where you can swim in the Olympic pool, the **Piscines Bernat Picornell** *(limited tickets €8; open 7am-midnight Mon-Fri, 7am-9pm Sat, 7.30am-4.30pm Sun)*, and wander into the main **Estadi Olímpic** *(admission free; open 10am-6pm daily)*.

The **Fundació Joan Miró** *(admission €7.20; open 10am-7pm or 8pm Tues, Wed, Fri & Sat, 10am-9.30pm Thur, 10am-2.30pm Sun & holidays)*, a short distance downhill east of the Estadi Olímpic, is one of the best modern-art museums in Spain.

At the top of Montjuïc is the **Castell de Montjuïc**, with a **military museum** *(admission*

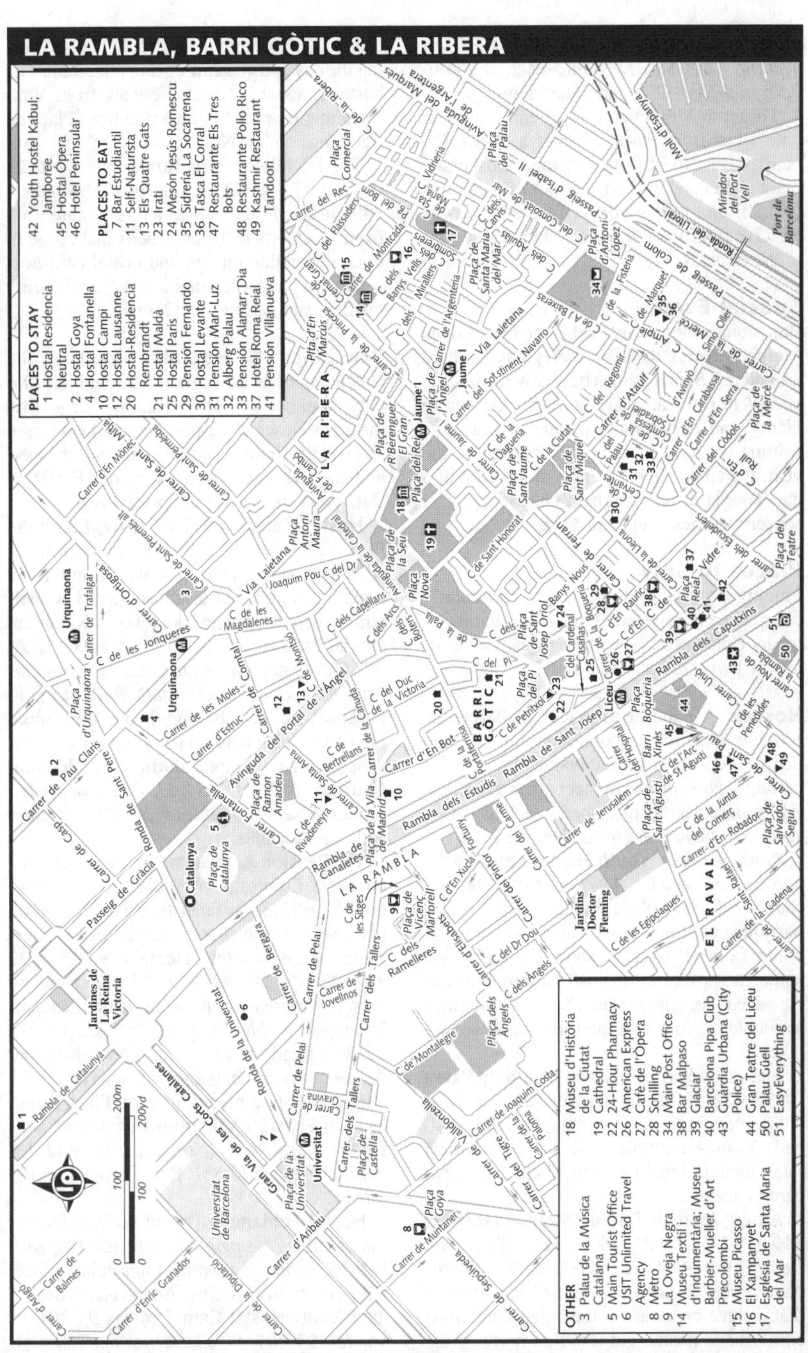
LA RAMBLA, BARRI GÒTIC & LA RIBERA
PLACES TO STAY
1 Hostal Residencia Neutral
2 Hostal Goya
4 Hostal Fontanella
10 Hostal Campi
12 Hostal Lausanne
20 Hostal-Residencia Rembrandt
21 Hostal Maldà
25 Hostal Paris
29 Pensión Fernando
30 Hostal Levante
31 Pensión Mari-Luz
32 Alberg Palau
33 Pensión Alamar; Dia
37 Hotel Roma Reial
41 Pensión Villanueva
42 Youth Hostel Kabul; Jamboree
45 Hostal Òpera
46 Hotel Peninsular
PLACES TO EAT
7 Bar Estudiantil
11 Self-Naturista
13 Els Quatre Gats
23 Irati
24 Mesón Jesús Romescu
35 Sidrería La Socarrena
36 Tasca El Corral
47 Restaurante Els Tres Bots
48 Restaurante Pollo Rico
49 Kashmir Restaurant Tandoori
OTHER
3 Palau de la Música Catalana
5 Main Tourist Office
6 USIT Unlimited Travel Agency
8 Metro
9 La Oveja Negra
14 Museu Textil i d'Indumentària; Museu Barbier-Mueller d'Art Precolombi
15 Museu Picasso
16 El Xampanyet
17 Església de Santa Maria del Mar
18 Museu d'Història de la Ciutat
19 Cathedral
22 24-Hour Pharmacy
26 American Express
27 Cafè de l'Òpera
28 Schilling
34 Main Post Office
38 Bar Malpaso
39 Glaciar
40 Barcelona Pipa Club
43 Guàrdia Urbana (City Police)
44 Gran Teatre del Liceu
50 Palau Güell
51 EasyEverything
Port de Barcelona
SPAIN

museum & castle €2.50; open 9.30am-4.30pm Tues-Sun Nov–mid-Mar, 9.30am-7pm mid-Mar–Oct) and great views.

To get to Montjuïc you can either walk or take a bus from Plaça d'Espanya (metro Espanya). Bus No 61 from here links most of the main sights and ends at the foot of a chairlift (€3.20) up to the castle. A funicular railway (€1.70) from Paral.lel metro station also runs to the chairlift.

Special Events

Barcelona's biggest festival is the Festes de la Mercè, several days of merrymaking held around 24 September. The festival includes *castellers* (human-castle builders), dances of giants, and *correfocs* (a parade of firework-spitting dragons and devils). Throughout the year, the city is apt to go nuts at the drop of a hat. Tourist offices can help but can't predict soccer victories over Real Madrid.

Places to Stay

Finding a place to sleep is not particularly cheap or easy between Semana Santa and October. Unless you're willing to canvass hostels, it's wise to book ahead.

Hostels A handful of places in Barcelona provide dormitory accommodation. For two people they're not great value, but they're certainly good places to meet other travellers. All require you to rent sheets (€1 to €3) if you don't have them (or a sleeping bag).

Grungy, happy **Youth Hostel Kabul** *(☎ 93 318 51 90; Plaça Reial 17; beds €12-18)* is a rough-and-ready place with no curfew and a party-hearty atmosphere. This is where youth come from all over Western Europe to get some…exposure to Spanish culture. No card is needed. Security is slack, but there are safes available for your valuables. Bookings are not taken.

Not as loud or social is the HI **Alberg Palau** *(☎ 93 412 50 80; Carrer del Palau 6; beds €13; open 7am-midnight daily)*, with just 40 beds. Rooms resemble university dormitories; rates include breakfast and kitchen use. No card is needed.

Alberg Mare de Déu de Montserrat *(☎ 93 210 51 51, fax 93 210 07 98; Passeig Mare de Déu del Coll 41-51; beds ISIC or IYTC member or under 25/all others €15/20)*, with rates that include breakfast, is the biggest and most comfortable hostel, but it's 4km north of the centre. A hostel card is needed. It's closed during the day and you can't get in after 3am. The hostel is about a 10-minute walk from Vallcarca metro or a 20-minute ride from Plaça de Catalunya on bus No 28.

The HI **Alberg Pere Tarrés** *(☎ 93 410 23 09, fax 93 419 62 68; Carrer de Numància 149; beds €14-16)*, about a five-minute walk from Les Corts metro, has beds that range in price depending on age and hostel-card possession. It has a kitchen, but it's closed during the day, and curfew is at 2am.

Pensiones & Hostales Most of the cheaper options are scattered through the Old City on either side of La Rambla. Generally, the areas closer to the port and on the western side of La Rambla are seedier and cheaper, and as you move north towards Plaça de Catalunya standards (and prices) rise.

Hostal Maldà *(☎ 93 317 30 02; Carrer del Pi 5; singles/doubles €9/18)*, upstairs in an arcade, is about as cheap as you'll find. It's a rambling family-run establishment that shelters cosy rooms and an adorable cat. Rambling **Hostal Paris** *(☎ 93 301 37 85, fax 93 412 70 96; Carrer del Cardenal Casañas 4; singles from €22, doubles with bath €40)* caters to backpackers. It can be slightly dingy and more than a bit unfriendly, but it's central and reasonable. The simple dorm-style **Pensión Mari-Luz** *(☎ 93 317 34 63; Carrer del Palau 4; beds €12-15, doubles €36-40)* is brighter and more sociable.

The **Pensión Alamar** *(☎ 93 302 50 12; Carrer de la Comtessa de Sobradiel 1; singles/doubles €18/36)* is fantastic value. It's a good place for lone travellers to meet other wanderers in a tranquil setting. **Hostal Levante** *(☎ 93 317 95 65, fax 93 317 05 26; W www.hostallevante.com; Baixada de Sant Miquel 2; singles/doubles €24/46, with bath €27/52)* is a family-run place in a quiet location. Ask about apartments for longer stays.

If you want a nice double on Plaça Reial, head to **Pensión Villanueva** *(☎/fax 91 301 50 84; Plaça Reial 2; singles from €12-18, doubles from €20-35)*. Rates depend on the season.

Hostal Fontanella *(☎/fax 93 317 59 43; Via Laietana 71; singles/doubles €26/41, with bath €32/55)* is a warm, immaculate place, with 10 smallish rooms. An excellent deal is the friendly **Hostal Campi** *(☎/fax 93 301 35 45, fax 93 301 41 33; E hcampi@terra.es;*

SPAIN

Carrer de la Canuda 4; singles/doubles €20/38, doubles with bath €45), with big doubles.

Up near Plaça de Catalunya is the solid **Hostal Lausanne** *(☎ 93 302 11 39; 1st floor, Avinguda Portal de l'Àngel 24; singles/doubles from €22/42)*, with good security and slightly dingy rooms (the doubles are spiffier). **Hostal-Residencia Rembrandt** *(☎/fax 93 318 10 11; Carrer de la Portaferrissa 23; singles/doubles €25/42, doubles with bath €42)* offers rooms ranging from acceptable to stylish. Reservations are accepted only for stays of longer than three nights.

Busy **Hostal Ópera** *(☎ 93 318 82 01; Carrer de Sant Pau 20; singles/doubles €31/50)* offers spotless, bright rooms with bathrooms. **Pensión Fernando** *(☎/fax 93 301 79 93; Carrer de Ferran 4; dorm beds €15, doubles €36, doubles with bath €51)* is a friendly place with a sunny rooftop terrace.

A few cheapies are spread across L'Eixample, north of Plaça de Catalunya. **Hostal Goya** *(☎ 93 302 25 65, fax 93 412 04 35; ⓔ goya@cconline.es; Carrer de Pau Claris 74; singles/doubles €27/45, with bath €32/55)* has several beautifully renovated rooms. **Pensión Aribau** *(☎ 93 453 11 06; Carrer d'Aribau 37; singles/doubles €28/42, doubles with bath €50)* offers reasonable rooms. The singles come with TV, while many doubles have shower, toilet, TV and even a fridge.

A leafier location is **Hotel Residencia Neutral** *(☎/fax 93 487 68 48; Rambla de Catalunya 42; doubles with bath €45)*, a happy, bustling place with friendly management.

Hotels Once-grand **Hotel Peninsular** *(☎ 93 302 31 38, fax 93 412 36 99; Carrer de Sant Pau 34; singles/doubles €45/65)* offers bare rooms that don't quite live up to the impressive foyer and atrium. Higher up the scale, but good value, is **Hotel Roma Reial** *(☎ 93 302 03 66; Plaça Reial 11; singles/doubles €50/65)*, which offers mod cons but tiny rooms.

Places to Eat

They don't want you to find them, but supermarkets do exist in Barcelona's Old City. A convenient one is **Dia**, right next to Pensión Alamar (see Places to Stay).

The greatest concentration of cheap restaurants is within walking distance of La Rambla. There are a few good-value ones on Carrer de Sant Pau, west off La Rambla. **Kashmir Restaurant Tandoori** *(Carrer de Sant Pau 39; dishes €5)* does tasty curries and biryanis. **Restaurante Pollo Rico** *(Carrer de Sant Pau 31; chicken or omelette €5)* serves tasty mains with chips, bread and wine. **Restaurante Els Tres Bots** *(Carrer de Sant Pau 42; set menu €6)* is grungy but cheap, with a good selection of Spanish staples.

There are lots more places in Barri Gòtic. **Self-Naturista** *(Carrer de Santa Anna 13; set menu €6.50)*, a bright self-service vegetarian restaurant, does tasty, fresh dishes. **Mesón Jesús Romescu** *(Carrer dels Cecs de la Boqueria 4; set menu €11)* is a cosy, homey place that serves piping-hot Spanish dishes.

Carrer de la Mercè, running roughly west from the main post office, is a good place to find little northern Spanish cider houses. **Tasca El Corral** *(Carrer de la Mercè 19)* and **Sidrería La Socarrena** *(Carrer de la Mercè 21)* are both worth checking out. A Basque favourite is **Irati** *(Carrer del Cardenal Cassanyes 17; tapas around €4)*. Enjoy a range of mouthwatering tapas and a *zurrito* of beer or six.

Carrer dels Escudellers, Plaça Reial and La Rambla itself also have a couple of good night-time takeaway felafel joints; it's around €2.50 a serving.

A famous institution is **Els Quatre Gats** *(Carrer Montsió 3)*, Picasso's former hangout. The standard café fare costs about 50% more than it should, but it's worth it for the bohemian ambience.

L'Eixample has a few good restaurants. **Bar Estudiantil** *(Plaça de la Universitat)* does economical *plats combinats* (combination plates; eg, chicken, chips and eggplant) for €4. It's open until late into the night and is a

Cool Cats

Way back in the day when Picasso and his artsy friends frequented Barcelona's neighbourhoods, one of the gang decided to open up a bohemian-style café right in the centre of the Gothic Quarter. Folks scoffed at the notion, and to express their opinion about who would visit such an establishment, they used an old Catalan saying in which 'four cats' means 'just about nobody' (as in, 'Who came to the party? Four cats'). Picasso was on board with the idea, however, and he and his chums named the soon-to-be highly successful joint 'The Four Cats' (Els Quatre Gats in Catalan) to mock their critics.

genuine student hangout. **L'Hostal de Rita** *(Carrer d'Aragó 279; mains €5-8, set menu €6.50)*, a block east of Passeig de Gràcia, is an excellent, ultra-popular mid-range restaurant with a four-course lunch *menú* and also à-la-carte mains available.

Entertainment

Barcelona's entertainment bible is the weekly *Guía del Ocio* (€1 at newsstands). Its excellent listings (in Spanish) include films, music, theatre and art exhibitions. Gay and lesbian options have their own special section, labelled 'El Ambiente'.

The tourist office provides information on current festivals, concerts and performances.

Bars Barcelona's multifarious bars are at their busiest from about 11pm to 2am or 3am, especially Thursday to Saturday.

Cafè de l'Òpera *(La Rambla 74)*, opposite the Liceu opera house, is the liveliest place on a very lively street. **Glaciar** *(Plaça Reial 3)* is busy with a young crowd of foreigners and locals. Tiny **Bar Malpaso** *(Carrer d'En Rauric 20)*, just off Plaça Reial, plays great Latin and African music. Another hip low-lit place with a more varied (including gay) clientele is the relaxed **Schilling** *(Carrer de Ferran 23)*.

El Xampanyet *(Carrer de Montcada 22)*, near the Museu Picasso, is a small place specialising in *cava* (Catalan sparkling wine) and good tapas.

West of La Rambla, **La Oveja Negra** *(Carrer de les Sitges 5)* is a noisy, barn-like tavern with a young crowd. Hidden away on a side street is **Bar Marsella** *(Carrer de Sant Pau 65)*, specialising in absinthe (*absenta* in Catalan).

If by 2.30am you still need a drink, your best bet is **London Bar** *(Carrer Nou de la Rambla 36; open until about 5am Mon-Sat)*, which sometimes has live music.

Lesbian bars cluster in Sarrià, north of the city centre. Try the friendly, intimate **D.Mer** *(Carrer de Plató 13)* or the more girly **Imagine** *(Carrer de Marià Cubí 4)*. Gay men can bring friends to **Santannasa** *(Carrer de Aribau 27)*, which sports a cute dance floor.

Live Music & Discos Many music places have dance space, and some discos have bands around midnight or so, to pull in some clientele before the real action starts about 3am. If you go for the band, you can normally stay for the disco at no extra cost. Count on €2 to €6 for a beer in any of these places. Cover charges can range from zero to €25.

Barcelona Pipa Club *(Plaça Reial 3; admission €7)* has jazz Thursday to Saturday around midnight (ring the bell to get in). **Jamboree** *(Plaça Reial 17; admission €9)* has jazz and funk, and a disco later, from about 1.30am. **Club Apolo** *(Carrer Nou de la Rambla 113; admission around €15)* has live world music several nights a week, followed by live salsa or a varied disco. Manhattanites might feel comfortable at chic **Otto Zutz** *(Carrer de Lincoln 15)*. Wear your bestest, blackest outfit.

Mirablau *(Plaça Dr Andrau; open until 5am)*, at the foot of the Tibidabo funicular, is a bar with great views and a small disco floor.

The two top gay discos are **Metro** *(Carrer de Sepúlveda 185)* and **Martin's** *(Passeig de Gràcia 130)*. Metro attracts some lesbians and straights as well as gay men; Martin's is strictly boys only.

Classical Music & Opera The **Gran Teatre del Liceu** *(☎ 93 485 99 00; Ⓦ www.liceubarcelona.com; La Rambla 51-59)* opera house, gutted by fire in 1994, is still being rebuilt but is open for business. Call or check the website for information on opera, dance and concerts.

There are other fine theatres, among them lovely **Palau de la Música Catalana** *(☎ 93 295 72 00; Ⓦ www.palaumusica.org; Carrer de Sant Pere més alt)*, the city's chief concert hall.

Getting There & Away

Bus The terminal for virtually all domestic and international buses is the **Estació del Nord** *(☎ 93 265 65 08; Carrer d'Alí Bei 80; metro Arc de Triomf; information desk open 7am-9pm daily)*. A few international buses leave from Estació d'Autobuses de Sants, beside Estació Sants train station. Several buses a day go to most main Spanish cities, including Madrid (€22, seven to eight hours), Zaragoza (€10, 4½ hours), Valencia (€24, 4½ hours) and Granada (€54, 13 to 15 hours). Buses run several times a week to London, Paris (€80) and other European cities.

Train Virtually all trains travelling to and from destinations within Spain stop at **Estació Sants** *(metro Sants-Estació)*; many international trains use **Estació de França** *(metro Barceloneta)*. For some international destinations you have to change trains at

Montpellier or the French border. There are direct trains daily to Paris, Zürich and Milan.

Daily trains run to most major cities in Spain. There are seven trains a day to Madrid (€42, 6½ to 9½ hours), two to San Sebastián (€31, eight to 10 hours), 10 to Valencia (€32, as little as three hours on high-speed Euromed train) and trains also run to Granada (€46, eight hours).

Tickets and information are available at the stations or from the RENFE office in **Passeig de Gràcia metro/train station** *(Passeig de Gràcia; open 7am-10pm Mon-Sat, 7am-9pm Sun)*.

Getting Around

Trains link the airport to Estació Sants and Catalunya station on Plaça de Catalunya every half-hour. They take 15 to 20 minutes and a ticket is €2. The A1 Aerobús does the 40-minute run between Plaça de Catalunya and the airport every 15 minutes, or every half-hour at weekends. The fare is €3.50. A taxi from the airport to Plaça de Catalunya is around €15 to €20.

Barcelona's metro system spreads its tentacles around the city in such a way that most places of interest are within a 10-minute walk of a station. Buses and suburban trains are needed only for a few destinations. A single metro, bus or suburban train ride costs €1, but a T-1 ticket, valid for 10 rides, costs only €5.60, while a T-DIA ticket gives unlimited city travel in one day for €4.20.

Barcelona's black-and-yellow taxis are plentiful, reasonably priced and especially handy for late-night transport. Flag fall is €1.30, after which it's about €1 per kilometre.

MONESTIR DE MONTSERRAT

Unless you are on a pilgrimage, the prime attraction of Montserrat, 50km northwest of Barcelona, is its incredible setting. The Benedictine monastery sits high on the side of a mountain (1236m) comprised of truly weird rocky peaks, and it's best reached by cable car. Pilgrims come from all over Christendom to pay homage to the Black Virgin (La Moreneta), a 12th-century wooden sculpture of Mary, regarded as Catalunya's patroness.

Montserrat's **information centre** *(☎ 93 877 77 77; open daily)* is to the left along the road from the top cable-car station. It has a couple of good free leaflets and maps on the mountain and monastery.

Two-part **Museu de Montserrat** *(admission €4; open 10am-6pm Mon-Fri, 9.30am-6.30pm Sat & Sun)*, on the plaza in front of the monastery's basilica, has an excellent collection ranging from an Egyptian mummy to art by El Greco, Monet and Picasso.

Opening times when you can file past the image of the Black Virgin, high above the main altar of the 16th-century **basílica**, vary according to season. The Montserrat Boys' Choir (Escolania) sings in the basilica Monday to Sunday at 1pm and 7pm, except in July. The church fills up quickly, so try to arrive early.

There are several accommodation options at the monastery – call ☎ 93 877 77 01. The cheapest rooms are in the **Cel.les Abat Olibia** *(double apartments high season €23-25)*, blocks of simple apartments, with showers, for up to 10 people. Restaurant options are bland and uninspiring. Snack bars and cafeterias line the road-approach to the monastery, and a few shops by the basilica offer cheap snacks.

Trains run from Plaça d'Espanya station in Barcelona to Aeri de Montserrat up to 18 times a day (most often on summer weekdays); it's a 1½-hour ride. Return tickets (€20) include the cable car between Aeri de Montserrat and the monastery. There's also a daily bus to the monastery from Estació d'Autobuses de Sants in Barcelona at 9am (plus 8am in July and August) for €10 return. It returns at 5pm.

COSTA BRAVA

The Costa Brava (Rugged Coast) ranks with Spain's Costa Blanca and Costa del Sol among Europe's most popular holiday spots. It stands alone, however, in its spectacular rugged scenery and proximity to northern Europe, both of which have sent prices skyrocketing.

The main jumping-off points for the Costa Brava are the inland towns of Girona ('Gerona' in Castilian) and Figueres (Figueras). Along the coast, the most appealing resorts are (from north to south) Cadaqués, L'Escala (La Escala), Tamariu, Llafranc, Calella de Palafrugell and Tossa de Mar. **Tourist offices** *(☎ 972 22 65 75; Girona • ☎ 972 50 31 55; Figueres • ☎ 972 30 02 28; Palafrugell • ☎ 972 25 83 15; Cadaqués)*, with branches along the coast, are very helpful with information on accommodation, transport etc.

Coastal Resorts & Islands

The Costa Brava is about picturesque inlets and coves. Beaches are small and scattered.

Cadaqués, about one hour's drive east of Figueres at the end of an agonising series of hairpin bends, is perhaps the most picturesque of all Spanish resorts. It's haunted by the memory of former resident Salvador Dalí, whose name adorns several establishments. Cadaqués is short on beaches, so people spend a lot of time sitting at waterfront cafés or wandering along the beautiful coast.

Further down the coast, past L'Escala and L'Estartit, is Palafrugell, near three gorgeous beach towns that have to be seen to be believed. The most northerly, **Tamariu,** is also the smallest, least crowded and most exclusive. **Llafranc** is the biggest and busiest, and has the longest beach. **Calella de Palafrugell**, with its truly picture-postcard setting, is never overcrowded and always relaxed. If you're driving down this coast, it's worth stopping at some of these towns, particularly out of season.

Among the most exciting attractions on the Costa Brava are the **Illes Medes**, off the coast from the package resort of L'Estartit. These seven islets and their surrounding coral reefs, with a total land area of only 21.5 hectares, have been declared a natural park to protect their extraordinarily diverse flora and fauna. Almost 1500 different life forms have been identified on and around the islands. You can arrange glass-bottom boat trips and diving from L'Estartit.

Museums & Historical Attractions

When you have had enough beach for a while, make sure you put the **Teatre-Museu Dalí** *(Plaça Gala i Salvador Dalí; admission €9; open 9am-7.15pm daily July-Sept, 10.30am-5.15pm daily June, 10.30am-5.15pm Tues-Sun Oct-May)*, in Figueres, at the top of your list. This 19th-century theatre was converted by Dalí and houses a huge and fascinating collection of his strange creations.

Girona sports a lovely, although tiny, Medieval Quarter centred on a Gothic cathedral. For a stroll through antiquity, check out the ruins of the Greek and Roman town of **Empúries**, 2km from L'Escala.

Places to Stay & Eat

Most visitors to the Costa Brava rent apartments. If you are interested in renting your own pad for a week or so, contact local tourist offices in advance for information. Seaside restaurants in the coastal towns provide dramatic settings but often high prices.

Figueres Reasonable rooms are offered at **Pensión Isabel II** *(☎ 972 50 47 35; Carrer de Isabel II 16; singles/doubles with bath €22/26)*. A little grungier but still solid is **Pensión Mallol** *(☎ 972 50 22 83; Carrer de Pep Ventura 9; singles/doubles €15/25)*. Avoid Figueres' Parc Municipal – people have been attacked here at night.

Restaurant Versalles *(Carrer de la Jonquera; platos combinados €5)* is at a sociable location away from the noise and high prices of the main plaza.

Girona Standard HI fare is offered at **Alberg de Joventut** *(☎ 972 21 80 03; Carrer de Ciutadans 9; dorm beds €12)*. **Pensión Viladomat** *(☎ 972 20 31 76; Carrer dels Ciutadans 5; doubles €31)* has comfortable rooms.

Dine on Girona's own Rambla for good people-watching. **Arts Cafe** *(La Rambla 23)* offers a mellow atmosphere and a good range of cheap snacks.

Cadaqués For fresh, bright rooms, try **Hostal Marina** *(☎ 972 25 81 99; Carrer de Riera 3; singles/doubles high season €25/49, rest of year €19/36)*. If you can't find a good beachfront restaurant in Cadaqués, consider getting a dog to help find your way around.

Around Palafrugell Hotel and pensión rooms are relatively thin here, as many people come on package deals and stay in apartments. In Calella de Palafrugell, the friendly **Hostería del Plancton** *(☎ 972 61 50 81; singles €15; open June-Sept)* is one of the best deals on the Costa Brava. In Tamariu, **Hotel Sol d'Or** *(☎ 972 62 01 72; Carrer de la Riera 18; doubles with bath €45)* is near the beach. Numerous food stalls and cafés cluster in Tamariu, Llafranc and Calella de Palafrugell.

Getting There & Around

A few buses run daily from Barcelona to Tossa del Mar, L'Estartit and Cadaqués for a couple of euros, but for the small resorts near Palafrugell you need to get to Girona first. Girona and Figueres are both on the railway connecting Barcelona to France. The dozen or so trains daily from Barcelona to Portbou at the border all stop in Girona, and most in Figueres. The fare from Barcelona to Girona is €5, to Figueres €6.

There are two or three buses a day from Figueres to Cadaqués and three or four to L'Escala. Figueres' bus station is across the road from the train station. Several buses daily run to Palafrugell from Girona (where the bus station is behind the train station), and there are buses from Palafrugell to Calella de Palafrugell, Llafranc and Tamariu. Most other coastal towns (south of Cadaqués) can be reached by bus from Girona.

TARRAGONA

pop 115,150

Tarragona's relaxed, backwards-gazing nature makes a perfect contrast to the frenetic, modern city-life of Barcelona. Founded in 218 BC, the town was for a long time the capital of much of Roman Spain, and Roman structures figure among its most important attractions. Tarragona's archaeological museum is one of the most interesting in Spain. For those who don't want to be too *tranquilo*, Tarragona's large student population and constant stream of travellers ensures a lively beach scene.

Tarragona's main street is Rambla Nova, which runs approximately northwest from a cliff top overlooking the Mediterranean. A couple of blocks east, parallel to Rambla Nova, is Rambla Vella, which marks the beginning of the Old Town.

The **main tourist office** (*☎ 977 25 07 95; Carrer Major 39; open Mon-Sat, morning Sun*) and **regional tourist office** (*Carrer de Fortuny 4; open Mon-Sat*) offers maps and lists of accommodation.

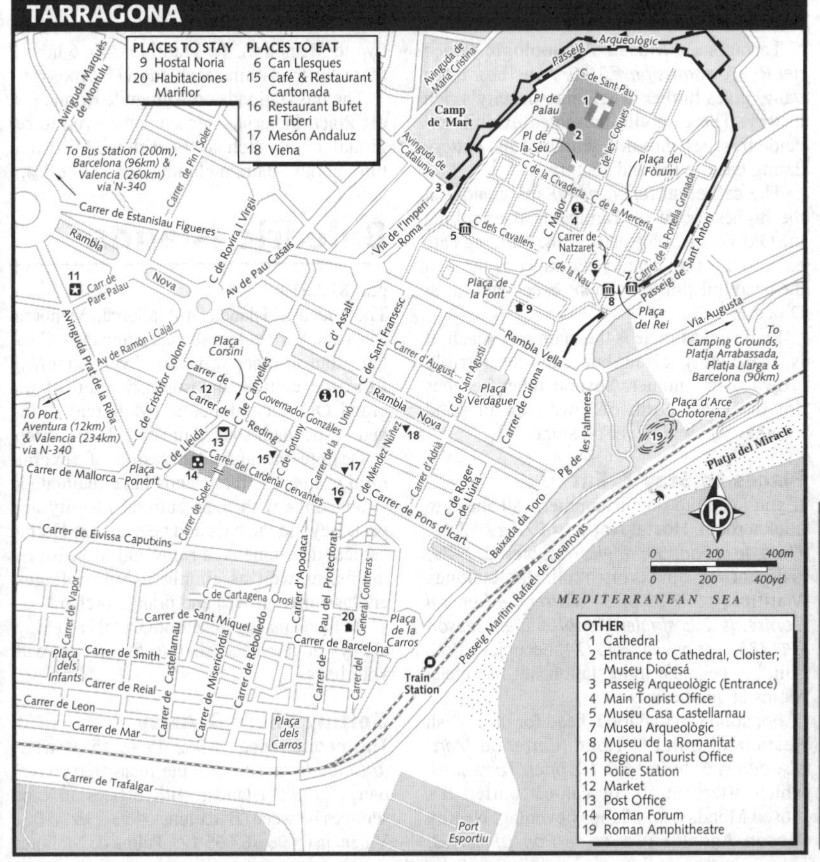

Things to See & Do

The **Museu d'Història de Tarragona** *(admission per site €1.90; open 9am-8pm Tues-Sat, 10am-2pm Sun)* comprises four separate Roman sites around the city, plus the 14th-century noble mansion now serving as the **Museu Casa Castellarnau** *(Carrer dels Cavallers 14)*. A good place to start is the **Museu de la Romanitat** *(Plaça del Rei)*, which includes part of the vaults of the Roman circus, where chariot races were held. Nearby and close to the beach is the well-preserved **Roman amphitheatre**, where gladiators battled each other (or unlucky souls were thrown to wild animals) to the death. On Carrer de Lleida, a few blocks west of Rambla Nova, are the remains of a **Roman forum**. The **Passeig Arqueològic** *(open until midnight)* is a peaceful walkway along a stretch of the Old City walls, which are a combination of Roman, Iberian and 17th-century British efforts.

Tarragona's **Museu Arqueològic** *(Plaça del Rei 5; admission €2.40, free Tues; open daily)* gives further insight into the city's rich history. The carefully presented exhibits include frescoes, mosaics, sculpture and pottery dating back to the 2nd century BC.

The **cathedral** *(open daily)* sits grandly at the highest point of Tarragona, overlooking the Old Town. Some parts of the building date back to the 12th century. Entrance is through the beautiful cloister with the excellent Museu Diocesà.

Platja del Miracle is the main city beach. It is reasonably clean but can get terribly crowded in summer. Several other beaches dot the coast north of town, but in good weather you will never be alone.

Places to Stay & Eat

If you intend to stay in summer, call ahead to book a room. **Hostal Noria** *(☎ 977 23 87 17; Plaça de la Font 53; singles/doubles €17/29)* is decent value but is often full. **Habitaciones Mariflor** *(☎ 977 23 82 31; Carrer del General Contreras 29; singles/doubles high season €17/33, rest of year €13/24)* occupies a drab building near the train station but has clean rooms at good prices.

For solid Catalan food, head for the stylish **Restaurant Bufet El Tiberi** *(Carrer de Martí d'Ardenya 5; buffet €9-10; open Tues-Sun)*, which offers an all-you-can-eat buffet. It's closed Monday, and Sunday evening. Nearby **Mesón Andaluz** *(Carrer de Pons d'Icart 3; set menu €9)* is a backstreet local favourite with a good three-course *menú*.

If cheese is your thing, try a *taula de formatges* (cheeseplatter; €7 to €8) at **Can Llesques** *(Carrer de Natzaret 6)*, a pleasant spot looking onto Plaça del Rei.

Café Cantonada *(Carrer de Fortuny 23)* is a popular place for tapas; next door, **Restaurant Cantonada** *(dishes from €5)* has pizzas and pasta. Rambla Nova has several good places, either for a snack or a meal. **Viena** *(Rambla Nova 50; sandwiches from €0.90)* has good croissants and a vast range of *entrepans* (sandwiches).

Getting There & Away

The train station is southwest of the Old Town, on the coast. Over 20 regional trains a day run from Barcelona to Tarragona (€4.15, one to 1½ hours). There are about 12 trains daily from Tarragona to Valencia (€11.40, two to 3½ hours). To Madrid (€40, 6 hours) there are four trains each day via Zaragoza.

The bus station is on Avinguda Roma, just off Plaça Imperial Tarraco. Buses run to regional cities such as Barcelona (€3) and throughout Spain, including Madrid (€23).

Balearic Islands

pop 878,630

The Balearic Islands of Mallorca, Menorca, Ibiza and Formentera share a language – Catalan – but in other ways are diverse, ranging from the culture and sophistication of the grand Old City of Palma (Mallorca) to the hedonistic foam-soaked fun of an Ibizan disco.

Despite the annual invasion of several-million tourists, the islands have maintained strong links with their cultural identity and past. Beyond the bars and beaches are Gothic cathedrals, Stone Age ruins and Moorish remains, as well as simple fishing villages, endless olive groves and orange orchards.

As many places close from October to May, always double-check before turning up with your bags.

Getting There & Away

Trasmediterránea *(☎ 902 45 46 45; W www.trasmediterranea.es)* is the major ferry company for the islands, with offices in (and services between) Barcelona *(☎ 93 295 90 00)*, Valencia *(☎ 96 367 65 12)*, Palma de Mallorca

(☎ 971 40 50 14), Maó *(☎ 971 36 60 50)* and Ibiza City *(☎ 971 31 51 00)*.

Duration time varies dramatically, depending on the type of ferry. The maximum time is given here, but always check whether there is a faster ferry available. Scheduled services run between Palma and Barcelona (eight hours, up to 13 services weekly), Maó (four hours, two weekly), Valencia (eight hours, seven weekly) and Ibiza (five hours, two weekly). Prices quoted here are the one-way fares during summer; low- and mid-season fares are considerably cheaper.

Fares from the mainland to any of the islands are €45.43 for a *Butaca Turista* (standard seat) and €63 for the same class on a catamaran; a berth in a cabin ranges from €80 (four-share) to €161.70 (single cabin) per person. Taking a small car costs €126.25, or there are economy packages *(Paquete Ahorro)* available.

Inter-island services (Palma–Ibiza City and Palma–Maó) both cost €24.80 for a Butaca Turista, and €69.20 for a small car. Ask, too, about economy packages.

Another company, **Balearia** *(☎ 902 16 01 80; W www.balearia.com)* operates three daily ferries from Dénia (on the coast between Valencia and Alicante) to Ibiza (from €44 one way, three hours). There are also services between Valencia and Palma (from €46 one way, six hours) and between Ibiza and Palma (€35, two hours).

Iscomar *(☎ 902 11 91 28)* has from one to four daily car ferries (depending on the season) between Ciutadella on Menorca and Port d'Alcúdia on Mallorca, as well as between Palma and Dénia and Ibiza and Dénia. **Cape Balear** *(☎ 902 10 04 44)* operates up to three daily fast ferries to Ciutadella from Cala Ratjada (Mallorca) in summer for around €48 return. The crossing takes 75 minutes.

MALLORCA

Most of its five million annual visitors to Mallorca, the largest of the Balearic Islands, are here for the three 's' words: sun, sand and sea. There is, however, far more to see, including the capital city Palma, with its medina-like backstreets, flanked by sun-baked ochre buildings and the fanciful Gaudí/Gothic cathedral. West of the city, the shoreline bubbles up into low, rocky hills, while at Cala Major grand old mansions and Miró's house are a world away from the thumping nightlife of the chip-butty Brit resorts.

Orientation & Information

Palma de Mallorca is on the southern side of the island, on a bay famous for its brilliant sunsets. The Serra de Tramuntana mountain range, which runs parallel with the northwest coastline, is trekker heaven. Mallorca's best beaches are along the north and east coasts, along with most of the big tourist resorts.

All major resorts have at least one tourist office. Palma has four, including the **main office** *(☎ 971 71 22 16, fax 971 72 12 51; W www.balearia.com; Plaça de la Reina)*. Other locations include Plaça d'Espanya *(☎ 971 75 43 29)*, Carrer Sant Domingo 11 *(☎ 971 72 40 90)*, and the airport. Palma has several Internet centres, including the **Big Byte** *(☎ 971 71 17 54; Carrer Apuntadores 6; open 10am-midnight daily)*, charging €2.50 an hour.

Things to See & Do

Overlooking Palma and its port, like a grand old dame, is the enormous **cathedral** *(Plaça Almoina; admission €3.50)*. Some of the interior features were designed by Gaudí.

In front of the cathedral is the **Palau Almudaina** *(admission €3.20)*, the one-time residence of Mallorcan monarchs. Unless you're really into tapestries, visit the rich and varied **Museu de Mallorca** *(Carrer Portella 5; admission €1.80; open 10am-2pm & 5pm-7pm Tues-Sat, morning Sun)* instead.

Also near the cathedral are the interesting **Museu Diocesáno**, and **Banys Árabs** *(Arab baths; Carrer Can Sera 7; open 9.30am-8pm daily)*, the only remaining monument to the Muslim domination of the island. Also worth visiting is the collection of the **Fundació Joan Miró** *(Carrer Joan de Saridakis 29; open 10am-6pm Tues-Sat, morning Sun)*, housed in the artist's one-time home and studio, 2km west of the centre in Cala Major.

Mallorca's northwest coast is a world away from the high-rise tourism on the other side of the island. Dominated by the Serra de Tramuntana mountains, it's a beautiful region of olive groves, pine forests and small villages with stone buildings; it also has a rugged and rocky coastline.

There are a couple of highlights for drivers: the hair-raising road down to the small port of **Sa Calobra** and the amazing trip along the peninsula leading to the island's northern tip, **Cap Formentor**.

If you don't have your own wheels, take the Palma to Sóller train (see Getting Around later in this section). It's one of the most popular and spectacular excursions on the island. Sóller is also the best place to base yourself for trekking. It is a relatively easy three-hour return walk from here to the beautiful village of **Deiá** where Robert Graves, poet and author of *I Claudius*, lived most of his life. The tourist office's *Hiking Excursions* brochure covers 20 of the island's better walks. For more detailed information check out a copy of Lonely Planet's *Walking in Spain*.

Most of Mallorca's best beaches have been consumed by tourist developments but there are exceptions. The lovely **Cala Mondragó** on the southeast coast is backed by a couple of *hostales*, while, farther south, the attractive port town of **Cala Figuera** and nearby **Cala Santanyi** beach, have both escaped many of the ravages of mass tourism. There are also some good quiet beaches near the popular German resort of **Colonia San Jordi**, particularly **Ses Arenes** and **Es Trenc**, both a few kilometres back up the coast towards Palma.

Places to Stay

Palma The cluttered 19th-century charm of **Hostal Pons** *(☎ 971 72 26 58; Carrer Vi 8; singles/doubles €16/32)* overcomes its limitations (spongy beds, only one bathroom). **Hostal Apuntadores** *(☎ 971 71 34 91; ⓔ apuntadores@ctv.es; Carrer Apuntadores 8; dorm beds €14, singles/doubles €21/33, doubles with bath €37)* has a 7th-floor terrace with a view of the city, and a lively downstairs bar/restaurant where you can buy cheap meals and meet other travellers. Next door, **Hostal Ritzi** *(☎ 971 71 46 10; doubles from €23)* needs a lick of paint, but it's very central, with good security and satellite TV in the communal sitting-room.

Hostal Terramar *(☎ 971 739 931; Plaza Mediterraneo 8; singles/doubles €25/30)* is the only hostal in Palma with cooking and laundry facilities.

Other Areas After Palma, head for the hills. In Deiá, **Hostal Miramar** *(☎ 971 63 90 84; singles/doubles €29/57)*, overlooking the town, is a very good value, and rates include breakfast. Beside the train station in Sóller, the down-to-earth **Hotel El Guía** *(☎ 971 63 02 27; singles/doubles €44/65)* has pleasant rooms, and rates include breakfast.

If you want to stay on the southeast coast, the large **Hostal Playa Mondragó** *(☎ 971 65 77 52; Cala Mondragó; rooms per person €11)* has B&B rates. At Cala Figuera, the **Hostal Cán Jordi** *(☎ 971 64 50 35; singles/doubles from €24/33)* is justifiably popular.

You can also sleep cheaply at several quirky old monasteries around the island with prices typically under €18 per person. The tourist offices have a list.

Places to Eat

For Palma's best range of eateries, wander through the maze of streets between Plaça de la Reina and the port. Carrer Apuntadores is lined with restaurants, including seafood and Italian, and an inexpensive takeaway **Bar Dia** *(☎ 971 71 62 64; Carrer Apuntadores 18)*. Around the corner is the incredible **Abaco** *(☎ 971 71 59 11; Carrer Sant Joan 1)*, the bar from your wildest dreams (with the drinks bill from your darkest nightmares).

For the cost-conscious, **Cafeteria Verona** *(☎ 971 71 28 34; Carrer Convento de Santa Magdalena; set menu €6; open lunch)* is a check-cloth, bistro-style place serving inexpensive local and international food. Up the road, **Bar Bosch** *(☎ 971 72 11 31; Plaça Rei Joan Carlos)*, in a prime people-watching spot, is good for sandwiches and snacks.

Rumbling tummies should head for **Restaurant Celler Sa Premsa** *(☎ 971 72 35 29; Plaça del Bisbe Berenguer de Palou 8; set menu €8.90)*, a cavernous atmospheric place with enormous portions of stolid local fare. For vegetarian food, try **Sa Pastanga** *(☎ 971 71 44 47; Carrer Sant Elies 6; set menu €9)*, which serves simple, delicious dishes.

Getting Around

Most parts of the island are accessible by bus from Palma. Buses generally depart from or near the bus station at Plaça Espanya – the tourist office has details. Mallorca's two train lines also start from Plaça Espanya. One goes to the inland town of Inca and the other goes to Sóller (€2.50 one way).

The best way to get around the island is by car – it's worth renting one just for the drive along the northwest coast. There are about 30 rental agencies in Palma and, for those who want to compare prices, many have harbourside offices along Passeig Marítim.

IBIZA (EIVISSA)

Once a hippy hideaway, now more mainstream 'hip', Ibiza is best known for its vibrant clubbing scene. The flip side is very different, particularly in the rural villages to the south. Here the countrywomen still wear long black skirts and wide straw hats and – forget the nudist beaches – the only traffic stoppers are the goatherds.

Orientation & Information

The capital, Ibiza City, is on the southeastern side of the island. This is where most travellers arrive (by ferry or air; the airport is to the south) and it's also the best base. The next largest towns are Santa Eulària des Riu on the east coast and Sant Antoni de Portmany on the west coast – the latter is for those seriously into discos and getting drunk. Other big resorts are scattered around the island.

In Ibiza City, the **tourist office** *(☎ 971 30 19 00, fax 971 30 15 62; ⓔ promocio@cief .es)* is opposite the Estación Marítima. There are numerous cafés with Internet access.

Things to See & Do

Shopping is a major pastime in Ibiza City. The port area of **Sa Penya** is crammed with funky and trashy clothes boutiques and arty-crafty market stalls. From here you can wander up into **D'Alt Vila**, the atmospheric old walled town, with its upmarket restaurants, galleries and the **Museu d'Art Contemporani**. There are fine views from the walls and from the **cathedral** at the top, and, next door, the **Museu Arqueològic** is worth a visit.

The heavily developed **Platja de ses Figueretes** beach is a 20-minute walk south of Sa Penya – you'd be better off taking the half-hour bus ride (€1.50) south to the beaches at **Ses Salines**.

Away from the coach tours, Ibiza has numerous unspoiled and relatively undeveloped beaches. On the northeast coast, **Cala de Boix** is the only black-sand beach on the islands, while further north are the lovely beaches of **S'Aigua Blanca**. On the north coast near Portinatx is **Cala Xarraca**, in a picturesque, secluded bay and, near Port de Sant Miquel, is the attractive **Cala Benirras**. On the southwest coast, **Cala d'Hort** has a spectacular setting overlooking two rugged rock-islets, Es Verda and Es Verdranell.

Places to Stay

Ibiza City There are several *hostales* in the streets around the port, although in midsummer cheap beds are very scarce. On the waterfront, **Hostal-Restaurante La Marina** *(☎ 971 31 01 72, fax 971 31 48 94; Carrer Barcelona 7; singles/doubles €55/75)* has sunny doubles with harbour views.

One of the best choices is **Casa de Huéspedes La Peña** *(☎ 971 19 02 40; Carrer de la Virgen 76; doubles around €30; open June-Oct)* at the far end of Sa Penya. There are 13 simple and tidy doubles with shared bathrooms. **Hostal Parque** *(☎ 971 30 13 58; Plaça del Parque 4; singles/doubles with bath €48/72)* has a revamped new look, but is on one of the liveliest squares so it can be noisy.

Other Areas One of the best of Ibiza's half-dozen camping grounds is **Camping Cala Nova** *(☎ 971 33 17 74)*, 500m north of the resort town of Cala Nova and close to a good beach.

For sand between the toes, **Pensión Sa Plana** *(☎ 971 33 50 73; doubles from €45)* is near the S'Aigua Blanca beaches and has a pool; rates include breakfast. Or you could stay by the black-sand beach at Cala Boix, at the cliff-top **Hostal Cala Boix** *(☎ 971 33 52 24; rooms per person €17.10)*, with breakfast included in the rates.

Places to Eat

Start your evening out with a drink at one of the bars lining the lively Plaça del Parque. **Herry's Bar** does a great tomato and olive-oil *tostada*. For something more substantial, **L'Absinthe**, across the way, is woody and rustic with some innovative salads and pasta dishes. Carnivorous folk may prefer the meaty menu and €3 tapas at **Viejo Almacen** *(☎ 971 31 44 32; Azara 5)*. Hang out with the local fishermen at no-frills **La Estrella** *(Plaça San Antonio Riquer; snacks from €2.50)*, or eat Andalucian-style fare at **La Oliva** *(☎ 971 30 57 52; Calle Santa Cruz)*, which has a pretty patio and excellent fish soup. A hip place for a coffee and *coñac* is **Cafe Libro Azul** *(☎ 971 39 23 80; Calle Cayetano Soler)*, which doubles as a bookshop and plays suitably laid-back jazz.

Entertainment

Ibiza's summer nightlife is renowned. At night, wander the fashion-catwalk of cobbled streets. Here designer-chic couples and seriously studded swingers dodge the outrageous PR performers hired by the discos to attract dusk-to-dawn clubbers. Dozens of bars keep Ibiza City's port area jumping until the early hours – particularly on Carrer de Barcelona and Carrer de Garijo Cipriano. After they wind down, you can continue on to one of the island's world-famous discos – if you can afford the €30 entry, that is. There's a handy 'Discobus' service that operates nightly from midnight until 6am doing circuits between the major discos, bars and hotels in Ibiza City, Platja d'en Bossa, San Rafael and San Antonio. The big names are **Pacha**, on the north side of Ibiza City's port; **Privilege** and **Amnesia**, both 6km out on the road to Sant Antoni; **El Divino**, across the water from the town centre (hop on one of its boats); and **Space**, south of Ibiza City in Platja d'En Bossa.

Getting Around

Buses run between the airport and Ibiza City hourly (€1.50); a taxi costs around €12. Buses to other parts of the island leave from the series of bus stops along Avenida d'Isidoro Macabich. Pick up a copy of the timetable from the tourist office.

If you want to get to some of the more secluded beaches you will need to rent wheels. In Ibiza City, **Autos Isla Blanca** *(☎ 971 31 54 07; Carrer de Felipe II)* will hire out a Renault Twingo for €103 for three days all-inclusive, or a scooter for around €28 a day.

FORMENTERA

A short boat-ride south of Ibiza, Formentera is the smallest and least-developed of the four main Balearic Islands. The island is attracting an increasing amount of package tourists, so it lacks the tranquillity that made it such a hippy haven some 30 years ago. There are excellent short walking and cycling trails, however, and most of the time it is still possible to spread a towel on the beach without kicking sand over your neighbour.

Orientation & Information

Ferries arrive at La Savina on the northwest coast; the **tourist office** *(☎ 971 32 20 57, fax 971 32 38 25; Ⓦ www.illadeformentera.com)* is behind the rental agencies you'll see when you disembark. Three kilometres south is the island's pretty capital, Sant Francesc Xavier, where you'll find a pharmacy, several banks and a good-sized supermarket. From here, the main road runs along the middle of the island before climbing to the highest point (192m). At the eastern end of the island is the Sa Mola lighthouse. Es Pujols, 3km east of La Savina, is the main tourist resort where most of the *hostales* are located (and the only place with any nightlife to speak of).

Things to See & Do

Some of the island's best and most popular beaches are the beautiful white strips of sand along the narrow promontory stretching north towards Ibiza. A 2km walking trail leads from the La Savina–Es Pujols road to the end of the promontory, from where you can wade across a narrow strait to **S'Espalmador**, a privately owned uninhabited islet with beautiful, quiet beaches. If you don't fancy the paddle, there are regular boat rides. Along Formentera's south coast, **Platja de Migjorn** is made up of numerous coves and beaches. Tracks lead down to these off the main road. On the west coast is the lovely **Cala Saona** beach.

The tourist office's *Green Tours* brochure outlines 19 excellent walking and cycling trails in five languages that take you through some of the island's most scenic areas.

Places to Stay & Eat

Camping is not allowed and coastal accommodation caters mainly to package-tourists. In Es Pujols you could try **Hostal Tahiti** *(☎ 971 32 81 22; singles/doubles €58/72; open May-Sept)*, with B&B available. One of the few hotels open year-round, **Hostal Bellavista** *(☎ 971 32 70 16; singles/doubles €54/66)* has sea views and a handy terrace bar. If you prefer peace and quiet, you're better off in Es Caló. **Fonda Rafalet** *(☎ 971 32 70 16; singles/doubles Aug €39/58; open Apr-Oct)* has good rooms on the waterfront or, across the road, there is the tiny and simple **Casa de Huéspedes Miramar** *(☎ 971 32 70 60; rooms per person €30; open May-Sept)*.

Perhaps the best budget bet is to base yourself in one of the small inland towns and bike to the beaches. In Sant Ferrán de ses Roques (1.6km south of Es Pujols) is popular **Hostal Pepe** *(☎ 971 32 80 33; singles/doubles with bath €24/37)*, with rates including breakfast.

There are some excellent seafood restaurants on the island. Many of the *hostales* also have bars/restaurants typically serving fairly uninspired but cheap meals. In Es Pujols, **S'Avaradero** on the seafront *(☎ 971 32 90 43; Avenida Miramar 32-36)* serves great seafood and Argentinean-style meat dishes. Also on the beach, **Bar Restaurant Flipper** *(☎ 971 18 75 96; Playa Mitjorn, Arenals)* is good for fresh fish and typical island dishes. Try the *arroz a la marinera* (rice with seafood) for a real taste of Formentera. Wind up the evening with a blast of good music at the **Blue Bar** *(☎ 971 18 70 11; Playa Mitjorn Km8; open until 4am)*. For tapas and wine, **Bar Sa Barraca** *(☎ 971 32 80 27; Avenida Miramar, Es Pujols)* is good while, among the plethora of pizzerias, **El Gatto E La Volpe** *(☎ 971 32 91 00; Carretera Punta Prima, Es Pujols)* is better than most.

Getting There & Around

There are 20 to 25 ferries daily between Ibiza City and Formentera. The trip takes around half an hour and prices between the various companies are fiercely competitive, but cost around €10 one way.

A string of rental agencies lines the harbour in La Savina. Bicycles start at €5 a day (€6 for a mountain bike). Scooters start at €17 and head up to €25 for more powerful motorbikes. A regular bus service connects all the main towns.

MENORCA

Although Menorca is the second-largest Balearic island, it's the least overrun. In 1993, the island was declared a Biosphere Reserve, with the aim of preserving important environmental areas such as the Albufera d'es Grau wetlands and its unique collection of archaeological sites.

The capital, Maó (Mahón in Castilian), is at the eastern end of the island. Its busy port is the arrival point for most ferries. The main road runs down the middle of the island to Ciutadella, Menorca's second-largest town, with secondary roads leading north and south to the resorts and beaches.

The **main tourist office** *(☎ 971 36 37 90, fax 971 35 45 30; Ⓦ www.caib.es; Plaça de S'Esplanada 40)* is in Maó. There is a second **tourist office** *(☎ 971 38 26 93; Plaça la Catedral)* in Ciutadella. During the summer there is an additional office at the airport. There is a **post office** in Maó *(Carrer del Bon Aire)* and also one in Ciutadella *(Pio V1 4)* .

Things to See & Do

Maó and Ciutadella are both harbour towns, and from either place you'll have to commute to the beaches. Maó absorbs most of the tourist traffic. While you're here, you can sample the local gin at the **Xoriguer distillery** *(open 8.30am-7pm Mon-Fri, 9am-1pm Sat)*. Ciutadella, with its smaller harbour and historic buildings, has a more distinctively Spanish feel about it. Follow the shopping baskets to the colourful market on Plaça Llibertat, surrounded by lively tapas bars.

In the centre, 357m-high **Monte Toro** has great views of the whole island and, on a clear day, you can see as far as Mallorca.

With your own transport and a bit of footwork, you'll be able to discover some of Menorca's more remote beaches. North of Maó, a drive across a lunar landscape leads to the lighthouse at **Cap de Favàritx**. If you park just before the gate to the lighthouse and climb up the rocks behind you, you'll see a couple of the eight beaches just waiting for scramblers like yourself to grace their sands.

On the north coast, picturesque **Fornells** is on a large bay popular with windsurfers. Further west, at the beach of Binimella, you can continue to unspoilt **Cala Pregonda**, which is a good 20-minute walk from the nearest parking spot.

North of Ciutadella is **La Vall** *(admission per car €4.50)*, another stretch of untouched beach backed by a private nature park. On the south coast are two good beaches either side of the Santa Galdana resort – Cala Mitjana to the east and Macarella to the west. The interior of the island is liberally sprinkled with reminders of its rich and ancient heritage. Pick up a copy of *Archaeological Guide to Menorca from* the tourist office.

Places to Stay & Eat

Menorca's two **camping grounds** *(open summer)* are near the resorts of **Santa Galdana** *(☎ 971 37 30 95)*, about 8km south of Ferreries, and **Son Bou** *(☎ 971 37 26 05)*, south of Alaior.

Maó and Ciutadella both have a handful of good budget options. In Maó, **Hostal Orsi** *(☎ 971 36 47 51; Carrer de la Infanta 19; singles/doubles with bath €21/42)* is run by an informative Glaswegian and American. It's bright, clean and well located.

In Ciutadella, **Hostal Oasis** *(☎ 971 38 21 97; Carrer Sant Isidre 33; doubles €42)* has homey rooms around a central courtyard and restaurant. It has lots of atmosphere, but can be noisy at night.

Ciutadella's port is also lined with restaurants. **Cappuccino Menorca** *(☎ 971 35 66 20; Moll de Llevant)* is a classy place for a light meal, cocktail or coffee. After dinner, check out **Jazzbah**, a hip little music bar. In Maó port, **Latitud 40** *(☎ 971 36 41 76; Moll de Llevant 265)* is a popular bar/restaurant with the boating fraternity (socialise here if you're looking for a job scrubbing decks). **Casanova** *(☎ 971 35 41 69; Puerto de Mahon 15)* is a good pizza place.

Getting Around

TMSA *(☎ 971 36 03 61)* runs six buses a day between Maó and Ciutadella (€3.40), with connections to the major resorts on the south coast. In summer there are also daily bus services to most of the coastal towns from both Maó and Ciutadella.

Car-rental rates vary seasonally from around €24 to €48 a day; during the summer, minimum hire periods sometimes apply. In Maó, try **Autos Valls** *(☎ 971 36 84 65; Plaça d'Espanya 13)* and **Autos Isla** *(☎ 971 36 65 69; Avinguda de Josep Maria Quadrado 28)*. **Just Bicicletas** *(☎ 971 36 47 51; Andén de Llevant 35-36)* hires out mountain bikes (€6 per day). At **Motos Gelabert** *(☎ 971 36 06 14; José Anselmo Clavé)* you can rent a scooter from €15 a day.

Valencia

Best known for the package resorts of the Costa Blanca, this region also includes Spain's lively third city, Valencia, and some rare undiscovered secrets if you penetrate inland.

VALENCIA (VALÈNCIA)

pop 746,610

Valencia is a vibrant city, its Old Quarter brimming with gracious baroque-fronted houses and its streets buzzing with life until the early hours – especially during the country's wildest party: Las Fallas (mid-March), an exuberant blend of fireworks, music, all-night partying and over 350 giant sculptures that all go up in flames on the final night.

The action part of the city is oval, bounded by the old course of the Turia River and the sickle-shaped inner-ring roads of Calles Colón, Játiva and Guillem de Castro. These trace the walls of the Old Quarter, demolished in 1865 as – believe it or not – a job-creation project that dismantled one of the major monuments on the Mediterranean coastline.

Within the oval are three major squares: Plaza del Ayuntamiento, Plaza de la Reina (also known as Plaza de Zaragoza) and Plaza de la Virgen. There is a **main tourist office** *(☎ 963 98 64 22, fax 963 98 64 21; e touristinfo.valencia@turisme.m400.gva.es; Calle Paz 48; open Mon-Sat)* in the centre. Three smaller tourist offices are at the train station, town hall and Teatro Principal.

Among several Internet cafés in town is **Jump** *(☎ 963 80 50 34; CalleAlbacete 8)* just south of the Plaza del Ayuntamiento; it charges €1.50 an hour.

Things to See & Do

Located in the dried-up bed of the River Turia, the ultramodern, aesthetically stunning **Ciudad de las Artes y las Ciencias** *(☎ 902 100 031)* includes a planetarium, IMAX cinema and laser show, interactive science museum, aquarium and open-air auditorium.

The **Museo de Bellas Artes** *(Fine Arts Museum; admission free; open 10am-2.15pm & 4pm-7.30pm Tues-Sat, 10am-7.30pm Sun)* ranks among Spain's best, with works by El Greco, Goya, Velázquez, Ribera, and Ribalta.

Beside Puente de las Artes, the **Instituto Valenciano de Arte Moderno** *(IVAM; admission €2.10, free Sun)* houses an impressive permanent collection of 20th-century Spanish art. Valencia's **cathedral** boasts three magnificent portals – one Romanesque, one Gothic and one baroque.

The baroque **Palacio del Marqués de Dos Aguas** *(Calle del Poeta Querol)* is fronted by an extravagantly sculpted facade. It houses the **Museo de Cerámica** *(admission €2.40; open 10am-2pm & 4pm-8pm Tues-Sat, 10am-2pm Sun)*, which has a superb selection of local and international ceramics.

Special Events

Las Fallas de San José in mid-March is an exuberant, anarchic swirl of fireworks, music, festive bonfires and all-night partying. If you're in Spain then, head for Valencia, but don't plan on sleeping – accommodation is booked up months in advance.

Places to Stay

Albergue Las Arenas *(☎/fax 963 56 42 88; Calle Eugenia Viñes 24; open year-round)* is within squinting view of Malvarrosa beach and offers Internet connection; take bus No 32 from Plaza del Ayuntamiento.

Central and near the covered market, **Hostal El Cid** *(☎ 963 92 23 23; Calle Cerra-*

jeros 13; singles/doubles €12/24, doubles with bath €32) is a steep stair climb but excellent value with satellite TV and air-con.

Near Plaza del Ayuntamiento, **Hotel Alkazar** *(☎ 963 51 55 51; Calle Mosén Femades 11; singles/doubles with bath €48/52.29)* is pleasant and comfortable. **Hostal Antigua Morellana** *(☎/fax 963 91 57 73; Calle en Bou 2; doubles with bath €42)*, in a renovated 18th-century building, has cosy rooms.

Places to Eat

Choose anything from a simple tapas to a full-blown meal at **Cervecería-Restaurante Pema** *(☎ 963 56 22 14; Calle Mosén Femades 3; lunch menu €6.50)*. **La Vita é Bella** *(☎ 963 52 21 31; Calle En Llop 4)* is an outstanding Italian restaurant with crisp pizza crust and to-die-for *tiramisù*.

For authentic paella, head for Las Arenas, north of the port, where a long line of restaurants serves up the real stuff. Chocoholics are pandered to at **Valor** *(Plaza de la Reina 20)* where chocolate is served in cups, thick and delicious. And everyone can have fun browsing around the bustling **Mercado Central**, Valencia's *modernista* covered market.

Entertainment

Valencia's nightlife is legendary, as is its gay community – the third largest in Spain, after Madrid and Barcelona.

Much of the action centres around Barrio del Carmen, which has everything from hip designer bars to gloomy heavy-metal hang-outs. For real sophistication, check out **Cafe de las Horas** *(Calle Conde de Almodóvar 1)*, north of Plaza de la Virgen, with its plush baroque interior, or the programme of the Teatro Principal *(☎ 963 51 00 51; Calle Barcas 15)*.

Younger groovers head for the university 2km east (€3.50 by taxi from the centre). Along Avenida Blasco Ibáñez and particularly around Plaza de Xuquer are scores of dusk-to-dawn bars and discos. **Finnegan's** *(Plaza de la Reina)*, an Irish pub, draws mostly English speakers.

Getting There & Away

The **bus station** *(☎ 963 49 72 22; Avenida de Menéndez Pidal)* is beside the old riverbed. Bus No 8 goes to Plaza del Ayuntamiento. Major destinations include Madrid (€17.80 to €20, up to 12 daily), Barcelona (€18, up to 12 daily) and Alicante (€12.20, 2¼ hours).

Express trains run from **Estación del Norte** *(☎ 963 52 02 02, 902 24 02 02)* to/from Madrid (€36.66, 3½ hours, up to 10 daily), Barcelona (€29.16 to €32.16, three to four hours, 12 daily) and Alicante (€8.82, two hours, up to eight daily).

Trasmediterránea *(reservations ☎ 902 45 46 45)* operates regular car and passenger ferries to Mallorca, Ibiza and, less frequently, to Menorca.

Getting Around

EMT *(☎ 963 52 83 99)* buses run until about 10pm with night services continuing on seven routes until around 1am.

The smart high-speed tram is a pleasant way to get to the beach, the paella restaurants of Las Arenas and the port. Metro lines primarily serve the outer suburbs.

ALICANTE (ALACANT)

pop 283,240

Alicante is an underrated city with most tourists heading straight for the Costa Blanca beaches. Yet there's an appealing faded grandeur about the place, particularly around the Old Quarter, overlooked by the majestic limestone cathedral. The nightlife is also equal to that of any self-respecting Andalusian city, particularly during the Fiesta de Sant Joan, 24 June, when Alicante stages its own version of Las Fallas.

Of Alicante's five tourist offices, the most central is the **main tourist office** *(☎ 965 20 00 00; ⓔ turismo@alicante-ayto.es; Rambla de Méndez Núñez 23; open Mon-Sat)*. You can connect to the Internet at **Up Internet** *(☎ 965 20 05 77; Angel Lozano 10; open 10am-2am daily)* for €1.50 an hour.

Things to See & Do

The **Castillo de Santa Bárbara** *(admission free)*, a 16th-century fortress, overlooks the city. Take the lift (€2.40 return), reached by a footbridge opposite Playa del Postiguet, or walk via Avenida Jaime II or Parque de la Ereta.

The **Museo de la Asegurada** *(Plaza Santa María; admission free; open 10am-2pm & 5pm-9pm Tues-Sat, 10am-2pm Sun & Mon)* houses an excellent collection of modern art, including works by Dalí, Miró and Picasso.

The **Museo Arqueológico** *(Plaza Gómez Ulla; adults/students €6/3; open 10am-2pm & 5pm-9pm Tues-Sat, 10am-2pm Sun & Mon)* houses an excellent collection of Roman and medieval antiquities. The emphasis is on local painters at the **Museo de Bellas Artes** *(Calle Gravina; admission free; open 10am-2pm & 5pm-9pm Tues-Sat, 10am-2pm Sun & Mon)*, which has recently moved to this suitably eye-catching 18th-century mansion. All of these three museums are open longer hours in summer.

The closest beach is **Playa del Postiguet**. Larger and less crowded beaches are at **Playa de San Juan**, easily reached by bus Nos 21 and 22.

Most days, **Kontiki** *(☎ 965 21 63 96)* runs boat trips (€13.22 return) to the popular **Isla de Tabarca**, an island where there's good snorkelling and scuba diving from quiet beaches.

Places to Stay & Eat

Alicante's youth hostel, **La Florida** *(☎ 965 11 30 44; Avenida de Orihuela 59)* is 2km west of the centre. Rooms are excellent value at the outstanding **Pensión Les Monges Palace** *(☎ 965 21 50 46, fax 965 14 71 89; Calle de Monges 2; rooms from €22)*.

Pensión La Milagrosa *(☎ 965 21 69 18; Calle de Villavieja 8; rooms per person €15)* has clean, basic rooms and a small guest kitchen. **Hotel San Remo** *(☎ 965 20 95 00; Calle Navas; singles/doubles with bath €39.50/54)* is on a busy shopping street and has pleasant rooms.

Hostal Benamar *(☎ 91 308 00 92; Calle San Mateo 20; rooms per person €18)*, in the heart of the buzzing Chueca and Malasaña areas, is popular with backpackers, with clean, light and airy rooms. **Hostal Riviera** *(☎ 91 527 37 17; Paseo de Santa María de la Cabeza 2; rooms per person €22)* is a handy traditional hostal in an old building near the main train station.

Restaurante Rincón Gallego *(☎ 965 14 00 14; Plaza del Ayuntamiento 7; daily menu €11.45)* is popular with locals and has a vast choice of traditional Galícian *raciónes*. Nearby, **Restaurante Mixto Vegetariano** *(Plaza de Santa María 2; set menu €6)* is a simple hole-in-the-wall place with vegetarian *menús*. **Rincón Huertano** *(☎ 965 14 04 57; Plaza Portal de Elche 4)* serves old-style traditional cuisine such as rice and snails.

Entertainment

Alicante's nightlife zone clusters around the cathedral, where there is a good choice of early evening bars. Later on, look out for **Celestial Copas**, **La Naya**, **Nazca** and **Zoo** discos. In summer, the disco scene at Playa de San Juan is thumping. There are also hundreds of discos in the coastal resorts between Alicante and Denia.

Getting There & Away

There are daily services from the bus station on Calle de Portugal to Almería (€16.07, 4½ hours), Valencia (€12, 2¼ hours), Barcelona (€28, eight hours), Madrid (€31.55, 4¼ hours) and towns along the Costa Blanca.

From the train station on Avenida de Salamanca, there's a frequent service to Madrid (€28, four hours), Valencia (€8.40 to €19, two hours) and Barcelona (€39, around five hours).

From Estación de la Marina, the Ferrocarriles de la Generalitat Valenciana (FGV) station at the northeastern end of Playa del Postiguet, a narrow-gauge line follows an attractive coastal route northwards as far as Denia (€6) via Playa de San Juan (€1), Benidorm (€2.75) and Calpe (€4.20).

COSTA BLANCA

The Costa Blanca, one of Europe's most popular tourist regions, has its share of concrete jungles, particularly around Benidorm. But if you're looking for a rollicking nightlife, good beaches and a suntan, you won't be disappointed. Accommodation is almost impossible to find during the coach-tour circuit months of July and August.

Xàbia (Jávea)

pop 24,650

In contrast to the comparatively Spanish resort of Denia, 10km northwest, over two-thirds of annual visitors to Xàbia are foreigners, so it's not the greatest place to brush up on your Spanish. This laid-back resort is in three parts: the Old Town (3km inland), the port and the beach zone of El Arenal, lined with pleasant bar/restaurants.

The port area is nice and has some reasonably priced *pensiones*. In the Old Town, **Hostal Levante** *(☎ 965 79 15 91; Calle Maestro Alonso 5; singles/doubles €15/30, singles/doubles with shower/bath €28/36)* has basic rooms.

Calpe (Calp)

Calpe, 22km northeast of Benidorm, is dominated by the Gibraltaresque **Peñon de Ilfach**

(332m), a giant molar protruding from the sea. The climb to the summit is popular – while you're up there, enjoy the seascape and decide which of Calpe's two long sandy beaches you want to laze on.

Pensión Céntrica *(☎ 965 83 55 28; Plaza de Ilfach; doubles €22)*, just off Avenida Gabriel Miró, is squeaky clean.

Benidorm

pop 57,230

Benidorm succumbed to cheap package tourism several decades ago. About the only things going for it these days are the 5km of (crowded) white beaches and a high-spirited nightlife with more karaoke bars per square metre than anywhere else in Spain.

There's no truly budget accommodation. **Hostal Santa Faz** *(☎ 965 85 40 63; Calle Sant Faz 18; singles/doubles €42/60)* has attractive rooms with bathrooms.

Andalucía

The stronghold of the Muslims in Spain for nearly eight centuries, Andalucía is an incomparably beautiful province, peppered with Moorish reminders of the past: the magnificent Alhambra in Granada, the timeless elegance of Córdoba's Mezquita and the whitewashed villages nestling in ochre hills. The regional capital, Seville, is one of Spain's most exciting towns.

Away from the cities and resorts, Andalucía is relatively untainted by tourists. Its scenery ranges from semi-deserts to lush river valleys to gorge-ridden mountains. Its long coastline stretches from the remote beaches of Cabo de Gata, past the crowds of the Costa del Sol, comes within 14km of Africa at Tarifa and opens into the Atlantic Ocean with the long sandy beaches of the Costa de la Luz.

SEVILLE

pop 702,520

If you want to inhale some authentic *olé* essence, this is the place. Seville is a Spanish cliche of flamenco, tapas bars, strolling guitarists and bullfighting combined with the marvellous exuberance of its people. Seville's air of contentment is well-founded. An important and prosperous centre in Muslim times and later in the 16th and 17th centuries, the city took the world stage more recently when it hosted its Expo in 1992.

Seville is quite an expensive place, so it's worth planning your visit carefully. In July and August, the city is stiflingly hot and it's a two-hour drive to the nearest beach. The best time to come is during the unforgettable Easter week and April *feria*, although rooms then (if you can get one) almost double in price.

Information

There is a **main tourist office** *(☎ 954 22 14 04, fax 954 22 97 53; ⓔ otsevilla@turismo-andaluz.com; Avenida de la Constitución 21; open daily)*. It's always extremely busy, so you might try the other **tourist offices** *(☎ 954 23 44 65; Paseo de las Delicias 9; open Mon-Fri • ☎ 954 50 56 00; Calle de Arjona 28; open daily)*. Monthly freebie *The Tourist* is worth picking up.

Seville has heaps of public Internet services. A typical rate is €2.50 an hour. One reasonably central place is **Cibercenter** *(☎ 954 22 88 99; Calle Julio César 9; open 10am-10pm Mon-Sat, 4pm-10pm Sun)*.

Things to See & Do

Cathedral & Giralda Seville's massive cathedral *(Calle Alemanes; adult/student or pensioner €6/1.50, admission free Sun; open 11am-5pm Mon-Sat, 2.30pm-6pm Sun)*, one of the biggest in the world, was built on the site of Muslim Seville's main mosque between 1401 and 1507. The structure is primarily Gothic, although most of the internal decoration is in later styles. The adjoining tower, La Giralda, was the mosque's minaret and dates from the 12th century. The puff-you-out climb to the top is worth it for the stunning panoramic views. One highlight of the cathedral's lavish interior is Christopher Columbus' supposed tomb inside the south door. The entrance to the cathedral and La Giralda is the Puerta del Perdón on Calle Alemanes.

Alcázar Seville's alcázar *(adult/student or pensioner €5/free; open 9.30am-5pm Tues-Sat, 9.30am-1.30pm Sun & holidays)*, a residence of Muslim and Christian royalty for many centuries, was founded in AD 913 as a Muslim fortress. It has been adapted by Seville's rulers in almost every century since, which makes it a mishmash of styles but adds to its fascination. The highlights are the **Palacio de Don Pedro**, exquisitely decorated by

SEVILLE

To La Imperdible & Almacén
To El Corto Malte's (200m) & Teleria Platea (200m)
To Compartecoche (100m)
To Camping Sevilla (6km)
Puente de la Cartuja
Río Guadalquivir
Pza San Lorenzo
C Pascual de Gayangos
C Juan Rabadán
Alameda de Hércules
C González Cuadrado
Calle Castellar
C Viriato
Calle del Torneo
Calle de Baños
Calle Golos
C Trajano
Calle Amor de Dios
Calle Tarifa
Calle Alfonso XII
Plaza del Museo
Martí Villa Laraña
Plaza Ponce de León
Plaza San Pedro
C A Apodaca
To Train Station (Estación de Santa Justa) (1.5km)
Plaza Doña Carmen
Calle Marqués de Paradas
Calle San Eloy
San P Matír
Av del Cristo de la Expiación
Calle Canalejas
El Centro
C Velázquez
Calle Sierpes
C Pérez Galdós
C Boteros
Plaza Salvador
Plaza de la Alfalfa
Calle de Arjona
Calle Julio César
C Zaragoza
Calle Tetuán
Plaza Nueva
C Madrid
Álvarez Quintero
Calle Reyes Católicos
Calle Pastor y Landero
Mercado del Arenal
Calle de Castelar
Calle Levíes
Santa María la Blanca
Avenida de la Constitución
Calle de Adriano
Calle García Viñuesa
C Alemanes
Calle Farnesio
Calle Mateos Gago
Plaza de Toros
Puente de Triana (Puente de Isabel II)
C Ximenez Enciso
Barrio de Santa Cruz
C San Jorge
Plaza del Altozano
Paseo de Cristobal Colón
Calle Dos de Mayo
Plaza de Santa Cruz
Avenida Menéndez Pelayo
Los Remedios
Río Guadalquivir
Calle del Betis
Calle Pages del Corro
Alcázar Gardens
Puerta de Jerez
Calle San Fernando
Plaza San Sebastián
Plaza de Cuba
Puente de San Telmo
Av de Roma
University
Avenida de Carlos V
Calle Palos de la Frontera
Avenida del Cid
Prado de San Sebastián
Paseo de las Delicias
Avenida de Portugal
C La Rábida
Av de María Luisa
Avenida de Isabel la Católica
Plaza de España
Puente del Generalísimo
Parque de María Luisa
To Albergue Juvenil Sevilla
0 250 500m
0 250 500yd

PLACES TO STAY
2 Hostal Unión
5 Hotel Londres
6 Hostal Paris
7 Hostal Zahira
17 Hotel San Francisco
19 Hostal Buen Dormir
20 Hostal Córdoba
22 Hostal Goya
25 Hostal Toledo

PLACES TO EAT
8 Patio San Eloy
9 Habanita
14 Jamón Real
15 Mercado del Arenal
23 Pizzería San Marco
26 Agua y Vida
27 Corral del Agua
18 La Carbonería
21 Bar Casa Fernando
24 Casa de la Memoria de Al-Andaluz

OTHER
1 Fun Club
3 Museo de Bellas Artes
4 Plaza de Armas Bus Station
10 La Antigua Bodeguita
11 Bestiario
12 Cibercenter
13 Tourist Office
16 Flaherty Irish Pub
28 Alcázar
29 Archivo de las Indias
30 Cathedral
31 Giralda
32 Main Post Office
33 Sala Boss; Rejones; Lo Nuestro
34 Torre del Oro
35 Main Tourist Office
36 Airport Bus Stop
37 Prado de San Sebastián Bus Station
38 Tourist Office

Muslim artisans for Castilian King Pedro the Cruel in the 1360s, and the large, immaculately tended **gardens**, the perfect place to ease your body and brain after some sightseeing.

Walks & Parks To fully appreciate **Barrio de Santa Cruz**, the old Jewish quarter immediately east of the cathedral, you need to head for the tangle of narrow streets and plazas east of the main Calle Mateus Gago artery. There's no better place to get lost. A more straightforward walk is along the **riverbank**, where the 13th-century **Torre del Oro** contains a small, crowded maritime museum. Nearby, Seville's famous bullring, the **Plaza de Toros de la Real Maestranza** is one of the oldest in Spain (begun in 1758). Interesting tours (€3) tours are given in English and Spanish about every 20 minutes from 9.30am to 2pm, and 3pm to 6pm or 7pm daily (10am to 3pm on bullfight days).

South of the centre is **Parque de María Luisa**, with its maze of paths, tall trees, flowers, fountains and shaded lawns. Be sure to seek out the magnificent **Plaza de Espana** with its fountains, canal and a dazzling semicircle of buildings that are clad in *azuelejo* (ceramic tiles).

Museums The **Archivo de las Indias** *(admission free; open 10am-1pm Mon-Fri)*, beside the cathedral, houses over 40 million documents dating from 1492 through to the decolonisation of the Americas. The **Museo de Bellas Artes** *(Plaza del Museo; adult/student €1.50/1, EU citizen free; open Tues-Sun)* has an outstanding, beautifully housed collection of Spanish art, focusing on Seville artists such as Murillo and Zurbarán.

Special Events

The first of Seville's two great festivals is Semana Santa, the week leading up to Easter Sunday. Throughout the week, long processions of religious brotherhoods, dressed in strange penitents' garb with tall, pointed hoods, accompany sacred images through the city, watched by huge crowds. The Feria de Abril, a week in late April, is a welcome release after the solemnity of Semana Santa. The festivities involve six days of music, dancing, horse-riding and traditional dress on a site in the Los Remedios area west of the river, plus daily bullfights and a general city-wide party.

Places to Stay

Summer prices given here can decrease substantially from October to March.

Seville's hostel, **Albergue Juvenil Sevilla** *(☎ 955 05 65 00; Calle Isaac Peral 2; bus No 34; dorm bed under/over 26 €8.50/11.50)*, with breakfast, has 277 places, all in twins or triples. It's about 10 minutes south by bus No 34, which leaves from opposite the main tourist office. Rates include breakfast. Accommodation in Barrio de Santa Cruz includes the basic, no-frills **Hostal Toledo** *(☎ 954 21 53 35; Calle Santa Teresa 15; doubles from €26)* and the more spacious, central and more costly **Hostal Goya** *(☎ 954 21 11 70; Calle Mateos Gago 31; singles/doubles from €37/47)*.

Freshly refurbished with light wood and a lick of paint, **Hostal Córdoba** *(☎ 954 22 74 98; Calle Farnesio 12; singles/doubles €30/60)* is well-priced. Bright and cheery **Hotel San Francisco** *(☎ 954 50 15 41; Alvarez Quintero 38; singles/doubles from €55/68)* is close to the cathedral.

The area to the north of Plaza Nueva is well-situated for shops as well as sights. No-frills **Hostal Unión** *(☎ 954 22 92 94; Calle Tarifa 4; singles/doubles €27/36)* has nine good clean rooms. **Hotel Londres** *(☎ 954 50 27 45; San Pedro Martir 1; singles/doubles €38/48)* is in a gracious old house with a tiled lobby and pleasant rooms. A few doors down, **Hostal Paris** *(☎ 954 22 98 61, fax 95 421 96 45; singles/doubles €38/51.69)* has a light, cheery interior. Located bang in the centre of one of the city's most attractive pedestrian streets **Hotel Zahira** *(☎ 954 22 10 61, fax 954 21 30 48; Calle San Eloy 43; singles/doubles €32/45)* is sparkling-clean and comfortable.

In the heart of Barrio de Santa Cruz, **Hostal Buen Dormir** *(☎ 95 421 74 92; Farnesio 8; singles/doubles from €18/36)* is quite old-fashioned with an aviary in a central patio.

Places to Eat

Barrio de Santa Cruz provides a wonderful setting for restaurants. The cool courtyard at **Corral del Agua** *(☎ 954 22 48 42; Callejodel Agua 6)* is an ideal summer spot for enjoying excellent fish dishes in the €9 range. On the corner, **Agua y Vida** *(☎ 954 56 04 71; Callejón del Agua 8)* has a good choice of tapas for €1.5, including spinach and chickpeas as a rare vegan option. In the same area, **Pizzería San Marco** *(☎ 954 56 43 90; Calle Mesón del Moro 6; open Tues-Sun)* was once a Moorish bathhouse and does highly popular pizzas and pastas for around €5. Calle Santa María La Blanca has several places with outdoor tables. At **Casa Fernando** *(☎ 954 42 26 60; Calle Santa María la Blanca)* there's plenty of sandwich choices for under €1.40.

West of Avenida de la Constitución, **Jamón Real** *(☎ 954 56 39 98; Calle Pastor y Landero)* specialises in Extremadura cuisine, like *migas* (fried breadcrumbs) with pork and ham for €4.80. Further north, bright, busy **Patio San Eloy** *(☎ 954 22 11 48; Calle de San Eloy 9; tapas €1.50)* is known for its *fino* (sherry) bar and *montaditos* (mutitiered sandwiches). Cuban and vegetarian cuisine is the deal at **Habanita** *(☎ 606 71 64 56; Calle Golfo 3)* in the buzzing Alfalfa district due north.

Mercado del Arenal *(Calle Pastor y Landero)* is the main food market in the centre and also has stalls selling bread and drinks for one-stop picnic planning.

Entertainment

Seville's nightlife is among the liveliest in Spain. On fine nights throngs of people block the streets outside popular bars. As in most places in Spain, the real action begins around midnight on Friday and Saturday.

Bars & Clubs Until about 1am, Plaza Salvador has several popular watering-holes, including **La Antigua Bodeguita** at No 6, with outside barrel tables for checking out the crowd.

There are some hugely popular bars around the cathedral, including **Flaherty Irish Pub** *(Calle Alemanes 7)*, with regular live Celtic music. The crowds from about midnight around Calle de Adriano, west of Avenida de la Constitución, have to be seen to be believed. Busy music bars around here include **Bestiario** *(Calle Zaragoza s/n)*, which is more spacious and modern than some.

Plaza de la Alfalfa is another good area; there are some great tapas bars east along Calle Alfalfa and at least five throbbing music bars north on Calle Pérez Galdós. The **Fun Club** *(Alameda de Hércules 86; open Thur-Sun)* is a small, busy dance warehouse – live bands play some nights. Several good pub-like bars line the same street a little further north. **El Corto Maltés** is a more laid-back drinking den, while **Tetería Platea**, at No 87, is a Moroccan-style teahouse with lots of kick-back space and Arabic music.

In summer there's a lively scene along the eastern bank of the Río Guadalquivir, which is dotted with temporary bars. On the western bank, **Sala Boss**, **Rejones** and **Lo Nuestro**, side by side on Calle del Betis, all play good music year-round, attracting an interesting mix of students and travellers.

Flamenco Seville is arguably Spain's flamenco capital, and you're most likely to catch a spontaneous atmosphere (of unpredictable quality) in one of the bars staging regular nights of flamenco with no entry charge. These include the sprawling **La Carbonería** *(Calle Levíes 18)*, thronged nearly every night from about 11pm to 4am. More touristy with classes available for the intrepid is **Casa de la Memoria de Al-Andaluz** *(☎ 954 56 06 70; Calle Ximenez de Enciso 28)*, with flamenco at 9pm costing €11.

Spectator Sports

The bullfight season runs from Easter to October, with fights most Sundays about 6.30pm, and every day during the Feria de Abril and the preceding week. The bullring is on Paseo de Cristóbal Colón. Tickets start at around €9 or €18, depending on who's fighting.

Getting There & Away

Bus There are buses, which leave from the **Plaza de Armas bus station** *(☎ 954 90 80 40)* to Extremadura, Madrid, Portugal and Andalucía west of Seville. Numerous daily buses run to/from Madrid (€15, six hours) and there are eight weekly buses that go direct to/from Lisbon (€30, eight hours). Daily buses run to/from places on the Algarve such as Faro, Albufeira and Lagos.

Buses to other parts of Andalucía and eastern Spain use **Prado de San Sebastián bus station** *(☎ 954 41 71 11)*. Daily services include nine or more each to Córdoba (€8.90, 1¾ hours), Granada (€15.50, three hours) and Málaga (€13.50, 2½ hours).

Train Seville's Santa Justa train station is 1.5km northeast of the centre on Avenida Kansas City. To/from Madrid, there are 18 superfast AVE trains each day, covering the 471km in just 2½ hours and costing €62.32 in the cheapest class *turista*; a few other trains take 3¼ to 3¾ hours for €52. Other daily trains include about 20 to Córdoba (€6.75 to €9, 45 minutes with AVE, to 1¼ hours) and three or more each to Granada (€17, three hours) and Málaga (€13.21, 2½ hours). For Lisbon (€99, 16 hours) you must change at Madrid.

Getting Around

Amarillos Tour *(☎ 902 21 03 17)* runs buses to/from Puerta de Jerez in the city at least nine times daily (€2.10). Bus No C1, in front of Santa Justa train station, takes a clockwise circuit via Avenida de Carlos V, close to Prado de San Sebastián bus station and the city centre; No C2 does the same route anticlockwise. No C4, south down Calle de Arjona from Plaza de Armas bus station, goes to Puerta de Jerez; take No C3 on your return.

CÓRDOBA

pop 314,030

Roman Córdoba was the capital of Baetica province, covering most of Andalucía. Following the Muslim invasion in AD 711 it soon became the effective Islamic capital on the peninsula. Muslim Córdoba at its peak was the most splendid city in Europe, and its Mezquita (Mosque) is one of the most magnificent of all Islamic buildings. From the 11th century Córdoba was overshadowed by Seville and in the 13th century both cities fell to the Christians in the Reconquista.

Córdoba's Moorish legacy lives on in the winding alleys, archways and flower-filled patios of the Old Quarter. The best time to visit is from about mid-April to mid-June, when the weather is warm and the city stages most of its annual festivals.

Orientation & Information

Immediately north of the Río Guadalquivir is the Old Quarter, a warren of narrow streets surrounding the Mezquita. Around 500m north of here is Plaza de las Tendillas, the main square of the modern city. The helpful **regional tourist office** *(☎ 957 47 12 35; Calle de Torrijos 10; open daily)* faces the Mezquita. The **municipal tourist office** *(☎ 957 20 05 22; Plaza de Judá Leví)* is a block west of the Mezquita.

Connect to the Internet at **Ch@t Is** *(☎ 957 48 50 24; Calle Claudio Marcelo 15; open 10am-10pm)*, near the Plaza de las Tendillas, charging €1.80 per hour.

Things to See & Do

The inside of the famous **Mezquita** *(admission €6.50; open 10am-7.30pm Mon-Sat, 2pm-7.30pm Sun & holidays Apr-Sept; 10am-5.30pm Mon-Sat, 2pm-5.30pm Sun & holidays Oct-Mar)*, begun by emir Abd ar-Rahman I in AD 785 and enlarged by later generations, is a mesmerising sequence of two-tiered arches amid a thicket of columns. From 1236 the mosque was used as a church; in the 16th century a cathedral was built in its centre.

The Judería, Córdoba's medieval Jewish quarter northwest of the Mezquita, is an intriguing maze of narrow streets and small plazas. Don't miss the beautiful little **Sinagoga** *(Calle Judíos; admission €0.30, EU citizens free; open 10am-7pm Tues-Sun)*, one of Spain's few surviving medieval synagogues. Nearby are **Casa Andalusí** *(Calle Judíos 12; admission €2.40; open 10.30am-8pm Mon-Sat)*, a commercialised 12th-century house with exhibits on Córdoba's medieval Muslim culture, and the **Museo Taurino** *(Bullfighting Museum; Plaza de Maimónides; admission €2.95; open 10am-2pm & 5.30pm-7.30pm Tues-Sat)*, celebrating Córdoba's legendary matadors such as El Cordobés and Manolete.

Southwest of the Mezquita stands the **Alcázar de los Reyes Cristianos** *(Castle of the Christian Monarchs; admission €1.87; open 10am-2pm & 5.30pm-7.30pm Tues-Sat)*, with large and lovely gardens.

The **Museo Arqueológico** *(Plaza de Jerónimo Páez 7; admission €1.50, EU citizens free; open 3pm-8pm Tues, 9am-8pm Wed-Sat)*, is also worth a visit. On the south side of the river, across the **Puente Romano**, is the **Torre de la Calahorra** *(admission €3.60; open 10am-2pm & 4.30pm-8.30pm daily)*, with a museum highlighting the intellectual achievements of Islamic Córdoba.

Places to Stay

Córdoba's excellent youth hostel, **Albergue Juvenil Córdoba** *(☎ 957 29 01 66; Plaza de Judá Leví; bed under/over 26 €10/13.20)* is perfectly positioned, has no curfew and includes breakfast in the rates.

Many Córdoba lodgings are built around charming patios. One such place is friendly and central **Hostal Deanes** *(☎ 957 29 37 44, fax 957 42 17 23; Calle Deanes 6; singles/doubles €24/31)*, which has the added plus of a tapas bar styled for the locals.

There are some good places to the east, away from the tourist masses. **Hostal La Fuente** *(☎ 957 48 78 27, fax 957 48 78 27; e terra.es; Calle de San Fernando 51; singles/*

CÓRDOBA

PLACES TO STAY
9 Hostal La Fuente
11 Hostal Los Arcos
12 Hotel Maestre
14 Hostal Osio
16 Hostal Séneca
17 Hostal Deanes
22 Albergue Juvenil Córdoba

PLACES TO EAT
4 Casa El Pisto
7 Market
8 Supermarket
10 Taberna Plateros
15 Taberna Aldaba
19 Casa Rubio
24 Restaurante Bandolero
27 Bodegas Mezquita

OTHER
1 Main Post Office
2 Milenium
3 Soul
5 Magister
6 Ch@t Is
13 Museo Arqueológico
18 Casa Andalusí
20 Sinagoga
21 Museo Taurino
23 Municipal Tourist Office
25 Regional Tourist Office
26 Mezquita
28 Alcázar de los Reyes Cristianos
29 Torre de la Calahorra

To Train Station (250m) & Bus Station (400m)
Ave de América
Avenida de Cervantes
Jardines de la Agricultura
Calle la Bodega
Ave Ronda de los Tejares
Calle José Cruz Conde
C del Caño
Calle del Osario
Alfaros
Calle Juan Rufo
C Carbonell y Morand
Calle Santa Marta
C Conde de Arenales
Calle Alonso de Burgos
Calle Córdova de Veracruz
Avenida del Gran Capitán
Plaza San Miguel
C Robledo
Calle de San Pablo
Villalones
Jardines Diego de Rivas
Avenida de la República Argentina
Calle Góngora
Calle de Alfonso XIII
Calle
Calle Morería
Plaza de las Tendillas
Calle Tundidores
Calle Claudio Marcelo
Calle Pedro López
Calle Concepción
C Conde de Gondomar
C Conde Cárdenas
R Marín
Calle Ambrosio Morales
Diario de Córdoba
Plaza de la Corredera
Jardines de la Victoria
Paseo de la Victoria
San Felipe
C Jesús María
C R Sánchez
Pompeyos
C Cruz Prenza
C Juan Valera
Calle Maese Luis
C Tornillo
Calle de San Fernando
C Lope de Hoces
Calle Barroso
Calle Marqués del Villar
Plaza de Jerónimo Páez
Plaza del Potro
Calle de San Francisco
To Los Negaos (via Calle Antonio Maura) (75m)
Plaza Angel Torres
Calle Blanco Belmonte
Calle de Rey Heredia
R Barros
Calle de Lineros
C Buen Pastor
C Conde y Luque
C Velázquez Bosco
C Encarnación
C Cabezas
C de Lucano
Calle E R Torres
Fernández
C Almanzor
C Céspedes
C M Rücker
Calle Osio
Paseo de la Rivera
To N-IV (East)
Puerta de Almodóvar
C Judíos
Calle Romero
Deanes
C Cardenal Herrero
C Magistral G Francés
Judería
Plaza de Maimónides
Patio de los Naranjos
Luis de la Cerda
C Medina y Corrella
C Luna
Plaza de Judá Leví
C de Torrijos
Calle Corregidor
Calle de Cairuan
Avenida Doctor Fleming
Avenida Conde de Vallellano
Calle Doctor Barraquer
C Amador de los Ríos
Ronda de Isasa
Río Guadalquivir
Acera Mira al Río
Puente Romano
Calle San Basilio
Jardines del Alcázar
Calle del Santo Cristo
To Granada (168km), & Seville (150km)
0 100 200m
0 100 200yd
Plaza Santa Teresa

SPAIN

doubles €24/42) has compact rooms around a large patio. Pretty **Hostal Osio** *(☎/fax 957 48 51 65; e hostalosio@iespana.es; Calle Osio 6; singles/doubles €20/40)* has two patios, pine furnishings and good views. **Hostal Los Arcos** *(☎ 957 48 56 43, 957 486 011; Calle Romero Barros 14; singles/doubles with bath €20/31)* has rooms similarly set around a pretty patio. **Hotel Maestre** *(☎ 957 47 24 10, fax 957 47 53 95; Calle Romero Barros 4; singles/doubles €29/48.15)* is a small bright hotel with a dash of Spanish chic.

Just north of the Mezquita, charming **Hostal Séneca** *(☎/fax 957 47 32 34; Calle Conde y Luque 7; singles/doubles €25/32, with bath €31/39)* has rooms with rates that include breakfast. It's advisable to phone ahead.

Places to Eat

Taberna Aldaba *(☎ 957 48 60 06; Velázquez Bosco 8)*, near the Mezquita, has good tapas deals, such as four plates plus a *cerveza* for €7. **Restaurante Bandolero** *(Calle de Torrijos 6; media raciónes €2.40-4.80)*, across from the great mosque, provides *media raciónes*. **Casa Rubio** *(☎ 957 42 08 53; Puerta de Almodóvar 5; mains around €5)*, in the Judería, serves tasty tapas, such as fried aubergine slices with honey, and good main dishes.

Taberna Plateros *(☎ 957 47 00 42; Calle de San Francisco 6; raciónes €3)* is a large patio tavern and restaurant serving solid homestyle Córdoban fare. There's a general food **market** on Calle de San Fernando. For gourmet products and olive-oil and *fino* tasting, head for **Bodegas Mezquita** *(Corregidor Luis de la Cerda 13)*. **Casa El Pisto** *(Taberna San Miguel; Plaza San Miguel 1; media raciónes €2.50-5; open Mon-Sat)*, is a particularly atmospheric old watering-hole with a good range of tapas, *media raciónes* and *raciónes*.

Entertainment

Córdoba's livelier bars are scattered around the north and west of town. **Casa El Pisto** (see Places to Eat) is one. **Soul** *(Calle Alfonso XIII 3; open until 3am daily)* attracts a studenty/arty crowd, and **Milenium** *(Calle Alfaros 33)* may have live bands a couple of nights a week. **Magister** *(Calle Morería)* brews its own tasty beer (around €1.50 a glass). Just beyond the Jardines de la Victoria, **Los Negaos** *(Calle Magistral Seco de Herrara 6)* has weekly concerts; look for the flyers around town.

Getting There & Away

The train station on Avenida de América, and the **bus station** *(☎ 957 40 40 40; Plaza de las Tres Culturas)* behind it, are about 1km northwest of Plaza de las Tendillas. At least 10 buses a day run to/from Seville (€7.80) and five or more to/from Granada (€9.40), Madrid (€10.20) and Málaga (€9.60), among many other destinations.

About 20 trains a day run to/from Seville (€6.55 to €13, 45 and 75 minutes). Options to/from Madrid range from several AVEs (€36.66 to €43.25, 1¾ hours) to a middle-of-the-night Estrella (€22.80, 6¼ hours).

GRANADA

pop 243,340

From the 13th to 15th centuries, Granada was capital of the last Muslim kingdom in Spain and the finest city on the peninsula. Today it has the greatest Muslim legacy in the country and one of the most magnificent buildings on the continent – the Alhambra. Southeast of the city, the Sierra Nevada (mainland Spain's highest range and the location of Europe's most southerly ski slopes), and the Alpujarras valleys, with their picturesque, mysterious villages, are well-worth exploring.

Information

Granada has a **main tourist office** *(☎ 958 24 71 28; Plaza de Mariana Pineda 10; open Mon-Sat)*. The more central **regional tourist office** *(☎ 958 22 10 22; Corral de Carbón, Calle Libreras 2; open Mon-Sat)* opens the same hours but is tiny and usually crowded.

Navegaweb *(Calle Reyes Católicos 55; open 10am-11pm daily)* offers Internet access for a reasonable €1.05 an hour.

Things to See

Alhambra One of the greatest accomplishments of Islamic art and architecture, the Alhambra *(adult/EU citizen €7/5; open 8.30am-8pm daily Mar-Apr, 8.30am-6pm daily Nov-Feb)* is simply breathtaking. Much has been written about its fortress, palace, patios and gardens, but nothing can really prepare you for what you will see. It is becoming increasingly essential to book in advance, whatever the time of year. You can reserve via any branch of the **Banco Bilbao Viscaya** *(BBV; Plaza Isabel la Católica, Granada)* or by calling ☎ 902 22 44 60 from within Spain and paying by credit card. Alternatively,

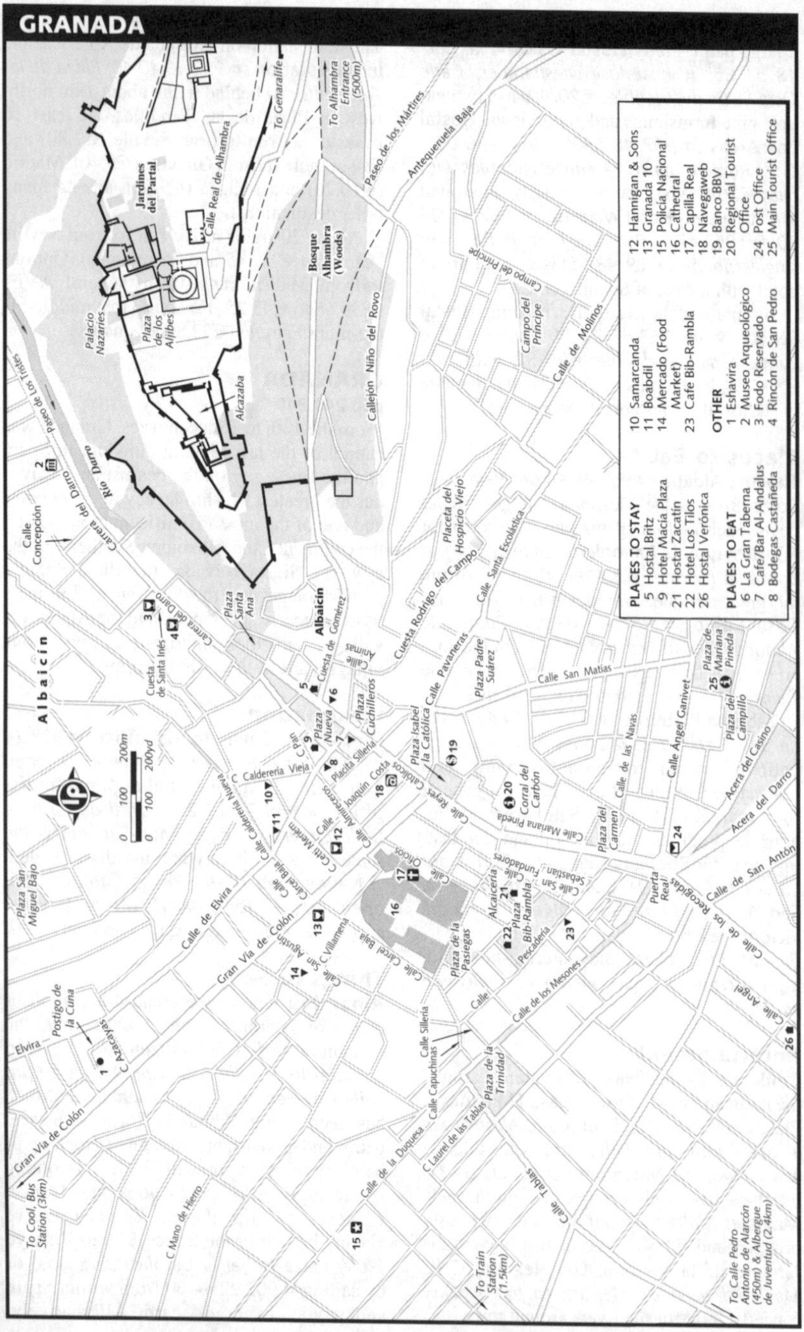
GRANADA
PLACES TO STAY
5 Hostal Britz
9 Hotel Macía Plaza
21 Hostal Zacatín
22 Hotel Los Tilos
26 Hostal Verónica
PLACES TO EAT
6 La Gran Taberna
7 Cafe/Bar Al-Andalus
8 Bodegas Castañeda
10 Samarcanda
11 Boabdil
14 Mercado (Food Market)
23 Cafe Bib-Rambla
OTHER
1 Eshavira
2 Museo Arqueológico
3 Fodo Reservado
4 Rincón de San Pedro
12 Hannigan & Sons
13 Granada 10
15 Policía Nacional
16 Cathedral
17 Capilla Real
18 Navegaweb
19 Banco BBV
20 Regional Tourist Office
24 Post Office
25 Main Tourist Office
Albaicín
Palacio Nazaríes
Plaza de los Aljibes
Jardines del Partal
Calle Real de Alhambra
To Generalife
To Alhambra Entrance (500m)
Bosque Alhambra (Woods)
Alcazaba
Paseo de los Mártires
Antequeruela Baja
Campo del Príncipe
Calle de Molinos
Callejón Niño del Rovo
Placeta del Hospicio Viejo
Cuesta Rodrigo del Campo
Calle Santa Escolástica
Paseo de Los Tristes
Río Darro
Carrera del Darro
Calle Concepción
Plaza Santa Ana
Cuesta de Gomérez
Calle Ánimas
Cuesta de Santa Inés
Plaza Nueva
Plaza Cuchilleros
Placita Sillería
Plaza Isabel la Católica
Calle Pavaneras
Plaza Padre Suárez
Calle San Matías
Calle Reyes Católicos
Corral del Carbón
Calle Mariana Pineda
Calle de las Navas
Calle Ángel Ganivet
Plaza de Mariana Pineda
Plaza del Campillo
Plaza del Carmen
Acera del Casino
Acera del Darro
Puerta Real
Calle de San Antón
Calle de los Recogidas
Calle Ángel
C Caldereria Vieja
C Pan
Calle Caldereria Nueva
Calle Joaquín Costa
Calle Almireceros
C Cetti Meriem
Calle Cárcel Baja
Calle Oficios
Calle de Elvira
Gran Vía de Colón
Calle San Agustín
C Villamena
Plaza de la Pasiegas
Alcaicería
Plaza Bib-Rambla
Calle Fundadores
Calle San Sebastián
Pescadería
Calle de los Mesones
Calle Sillería
Calle Capuchinas
Plaza de la Trinidad
C Laurel de las Tablas
Calle de la Duquesa
Tablas
C Mano de Hierro
Plaza San Miguel Bajo
Postigo de la Cuna
C Azacayas
Elvira
To Cool, Bus Station (3km)
To Train Station (1.5km)
To Calle Pedro Antonio de Alarcón (450m) & Albergue de Juventud (2.4km)
0 100 200m
0 100 200yd

at www.alhambra-patronato.es you can choose the time and day you wish to visit.

The **Alcazaba** is the Alhambra's fortress, dating from the 11th to the 13th centuries. There are spectacular heady views from the tops of the towers. The **Palacio Nazaries** (Nasrid Palace), built for Granada's Muslim rulers in their 13th- to 15th-century heyday, is the centrepiece of the Alhambra. The beauty of its patios and intricacy of its stucco and woodwork are stunning. Don't miss the **Generalife**, the soul-soothing palace gardens.

Other Attractions Explore the narrow, hilly streets of the **Albaicín**, the old Moorish quarter across the river from the Alhambra and head for the **Mirador de San Nicolas** – a steep climb, but worth it for the views. On your way, stop by the **Museo Arqueológico** *(Archaeological Museum; Carrera del Darro)* at the foot of the Albaicín. Another enjoyable area for strolling is **Plaza de Bib-Rambla**, looking in at the **Capilla Real** *(Royal Chapel; Calle Oficios)*, in which Fernando and Isabel are buried. Next door is Granada's **cathedral**, which dates in part from the early 16th century.

Places to Stay

Granada's modern youth hostel, **Albergue de Juventud** *(☎ 958 27 26 38, 958 00 29 00; Calle Ramón y Cajal 2; dorm beds under/over 26 €12.90/17.25)* is 1.7km west of the centre and 600m southwest of the train station.

Right on the bustling Plaza Nueva (well placed for the Alhambra and Albaicín), **Hostal Britz** *(☎/fax 958 22 36 52; Cuesta de Gomérez 1; singles/doubles €17/26.50, doubles with bath €37)* provides bright comfortable rooms, some with balconies. Across the square, tastefully renovated **Hotel Macía Plaza** *(☎ 958 22 75 36, fax 958 28 55 91; e maciaplaza@maciahoteles.com; singles/doubles €41.47/62.51)* has very pleasant rooms.

The Plaza Bib-Rambla area is another with plenty of choice. Good value, no-frills **Hotel Los Tilos** *(☎ 958 26 67 12; Plaza Bib-Rambla; singles/doubles with bath €41/62)* overlooks a daily flower market and has superb views from a fourth-floor terrace. Rates include breakfast. **Hostal Zacatín** *(☎ 958 22 11 55; Calle Ermita 11; singles/doubles €20/28.85)* is a hospitable, simple place. South of the cathedral, **Hostal Verónica** *(☎ 958 25 81 45; Calle Angel 17; singles/doubles €19.30/35.30)* is small and friendly.

Places to Eat

Popular **Bodegas Castañeda** *(☎ 958 22 32 22; Calle Almireceros 1)* is an unpretentious local bar/restaurant serving classic tapas and interesting quasi-international fare. Nearby, **Cafe/Bar Al Andalus** *(☎ 958 22 67 30; Calle Elivira; meat mains around €6)* has good cheap Arabic food. **La Gran Taberna** *(☎ 958 22 88 46; Plaza Nueva 12)* is a traditional-style bodega with untraditional, inexpensive tapas such as trout with cottage cheese.

Samarcanda *(☎ 958 21 00 14; Calle Calderería Vieja 3)* has tasty Lebanese dishes. **Cafe Bib-Rambla** *(Plaza Bib-Rambla)* is great for a breakfast of chocolate and *churros* (spiral-shaped doughnuts). **Boabdil** *(☎ 958 22 81 36; Hospital de Peregrines 2; meals from €5)* is a kitchen sink–informal restaurant with good basic food.

For fresh fruit and vegies, there is the large covered ***mercado*** *(market; Calle San Agustín)*.

Entertainment

Nightlife in the Albaicín centres on Carrera del Darro, with several bars and clubs within a few doors of each other, including **Rincón de San Pedro** *(Carrera del Darro 12)* and **Fodo Reservado** *(Santa Inés 4)*, just around the corner.

For foot-tapping live jazz, head for **Eshavira** *(Postigo de la Cuna 2)*, which features the occasional impromptu flamenco evening. Those suffering from Guinness deprivation should check out **Hannigan & Sons** *(Cetti Meriém 1)*. With a tad more sophistication than most, **Granada 10** *(Calle Cárcel Baja)* attracts a smarter set, while **Cool** *(Calle Dr Guirao)* is the city's largest disco, with three massive dance floors.

Getting There & Away

Granada's **bus station** *(☎ 958 18 54 80; Carretera de Jáen s/n)* is 3km northwest of the centre. Catch a No 3 bus to reach the centre. At least nine daily buses serve Madrid (€12, five to six hours), and others run to Barcelona, Valencia and destinations across Andalucía.

The **train station** *(☎ 958 27 12 72; Avenida de Andaluces)* is about 1.5km west of the centre. Of the two trains daily to Madrid, one takes 9½ hours overnight (€22), the other six hours (€23). To Seville, there are three trains a day (from €15, three hours). For Málaga and Córdoba, you will need to change trains in Bobadilla. There's one train daily to Valencia and Barcelona.

COSTA DE ALMERÍA

The coast east of Almería city in eastern Andalucía is perhaps the last section of Spain's Mediterranean coast where you can have a beach to yourself (not in high summer, admittedly). This is Spain's sunniest region – even in late March it can be warm enough to strip off and take in the rays.

The most useful **tourist offices** are in Almería *(☎ 950 62 11 17)*, San José *(☎ 950 38 02 99)* and Mojácar *(☎ 950 47 51 62)*.

Things to See & Do

The **alcazaba**, an enormous 10th-century Muslim fortress, is the highlight of Almería city. In its heyday the city was more important than Granada.

The best thing about the region is the wonderful coastline and semi-desert scenery of the **Cabo de Gata** promontory. All along the 50km coast from El Cabo de Gata village to Agua Amarga, some of the most beautiful and empty beaches on the Mediterranean alternate with precipitous cliffs and scattered villages. Roads or paths run along or close to this whole coastline. The main village is laid-back **San José**, with excellent beaches such as **Playa de los Genoveses** and **Playa de Mónsul** within 7km southwest. **Mojácar**, 30km north of Agua Amarga, is a white town of Muslim origin, with cube-shaped houses perched on a hill 2km from the coast. Although a long resort strip, Mojácar Playa is still a pretty place and beckons to those who fancy a livelier summer beach scene than Cabo de Gata offers.

Places to Stay & Eat

The oldest hotel in Almería, and still family-run, **La Perla** *(☎ 950 23 88 77, fax 950 27 58 16; Plaza del Carmen 7; doubles from €48)* exudes a certain old-world charm.

In high summer it's a good idea to ring ahead about accommodation in Cabo de Gata, as some places fill up. In San José is the friendly non-HI youth hostel **Albergue Juvenil de San José** *(☎ 950 38 03 53; Calle Montemar s/n; bunk beds €8.40; open Apr-Sept)*. **Hostal Bahía** *(☎ 950 38 03 07; Calle Correo; singles/doubles with bath €35/42)* has attractive rooms. **Restaurante El Emigrante** *(mains €6-9)*, across the road, does good fish and meat mains.

The better-value places in Mojácar are mostly found up in the Old Town. **Hostal La Esquinica** *(☎ 950 47 50 09; Calle Cano 1; singles/doubles €20/24)* is cheap and cheerful. **Hotel Simon** *(☎ 950 47 87 69, fax 950 47 87 69; e hotelsimon@interbook.net; Cruce de la Fuente; doubles with bath from €40)* offers a slick, high standard of rooms. **Restaurante El Viento del Desierto** *(Plaza del Frontón; mains €5-6)* serves the best steamed mussels in town. **Tito's Beach Bar** *(☎ 950 61 50 30; Paseo del Mediterráneo 2)* has good music and an excellent Mexican restaurant with a garden Margarita Bar right next door.

Getting There & Away

Almería is accessible by bus and train from Madrid, Granada and Seville, and by bus from Málaga, Valencia and Barcelona. Buses run from Almería bus station to El Cabo de Gata village and (except non-summer Sundays) to San José. Mojácar can be reached by bus from Almeriá, Murcia, Granada and Madrid.

MÁLAGA

pop 534,200

Although Málaga is still largely ignored by the sun and sand seekers who head straight for the Costa del Sol, the city is well worth a visit. There's plenty to see and savour, ranging from Moorish monuments to arguably the best fried fish in Spain.

The **main tourist office** *(☎ 952 21 34 45; Pasaje Chinitas 4; open Mon-Sat)* is in one of the city's most historic areas. The **municipal tourist office** is near the park *(☎ 952 60 44 10; Avenida de Cervantes 1)*. There are additional information kiosks near the train station and in the centre. **Ciber Málaga Cafe** *(Avenida de Andalucía 11; open 10am-late)* offers Internet access for €2.50 an hour.

Things to See & Do

The historic core of the city lies around the cathedral; a web of narrow cobbled streets lined with faded ochre-coloured buildings, interspersed with small squares, tapas bars, cafés and old-fashioned shops.

A **Roman ampitheatre** is currently under excavation but can be plainly viewed near the Alcazaba's main entrance on Calle Alcazabilla. The **Alcazaba** fortress and palace *(☎ 952 21 60 05; admission free; open 9am-8pm Tues-Sun summer, 9am-7pm Tues-Sun rest of year)* dates from the 8th century and has recently undergone extensive restoration. The cherry on the cake is the hill-top **Castillo Gibralfaro** *(admission free; open 9am-7pm daily)*. The **cathedral** *(admission €1.80; open 10am-6.45pm Mon-Sat)* has a peculiar lopsided look, with one unfinished tower. Check it out from one of the pavement cafés across the way. The long-awaited **Picasso Museum** is scheduled to open in October 2003. Meanwhile, art buffs can make do with the **Casa Natal** *(☎ 952 06 02 15; Plaza de la Merced 15; open 11am-2pm & 5pm-8pm Mon-Sat, morning Sun)*, where Pablo Picasso was born.

Places to Stay & Eat

Málaga is short on accommodation, so book ahead. A cheap option is **Pensión Córdoba** *(☎ 952 21 44 69; Calle Bolsa 9; singles/doubles €18/28)*, a humble friendly place. **Hotel Carlos V** *(☎ 952 21 51 20; Calle Císter 10; singles/doubles €24/46)*, close to the cathedral, has recently been refurbished.

For affordable eats, head for the tapas bars. A good place to start is the spit 'n' sawdust **Antigua Casa de Guardia** *(☎ 952 21 46 80; Alameda Principal 18)*, the oldest bar in town; try the fresh prawns. The nearby **Restaurante El Compá** *(☎ 952 06 07 10; Calle La Bolsa 7)* is fronted by an excellent tapas bar, while the restaurant specialises in rice and fish dishes. Málaga's most famous tapas bar is the tiny **Bar Logueno** *(Marín García s/n; tapas from €1.50)*; there are 75-plus varieties to choose from.

Entertainment

Serious party time starts late around Calle Granada and Plaza de la Merced. **ZZ Pub** *(Calle Tejón y Rodriguez)* has live music on Monday and Thursday. **Warner Bar** *(Plaza de los Martínez)* is good for a little frenetic air punching, while **Doctor Funk** *(Calle José Denis Belgrano 19)*, just off Calle Granada, is a heaving reggae club shoe-horned into a small smoky space. There are several *teterias* (Moroccan-style teahouses) in town, including **Barrakis** *(Calle Horno)*, housed in a former 14th-century Arab bakery.

Getting There & Away

Málaga is linked by train and bus to all major Spanish centres. The bus and train stations are around the corner from each other, 1km west of the city centre.

RONDA

pop 34,210

One of the prettiest and most historic towns in Andalucía, Ronda is a world apart from the nearby Costa del Sol. The town straddles the savagely deep El Tajo gorge, at the heart of some lovely hill country dotted with white villages. The **regional tourist office** *(☎ 952 87 12 72; Plaza de España 1)* has lots of interesting info on the area.

Ronda is a pleasure to wander around, but during the day you'll have to contend with busloads of day-trippers from the coast. The **Plaza de Toros** (1785) is considered the home of bullfighting and is a mecca for aficionados; inside is the small but fascinating **Museo Taurino** *(admission €2.50)*. Vertiginous cliff-top views open out from the nearby Alameda del Tajo park.

The **Puente Nuevo** (New Bridge), built in the 18th-century, is an amazing feat of engineering, crossing the gorge to the originally Muslim Old Town (La Ciudad), littered with ancient churches, monuments and palaces. At **Casa del Rey Moro** *(Calle Santo Domingo 17; admission €4; open daily)*, you can climb down a Muslim-era stairway cut inside the rock right to the bottom of the gorge. Don't miss the **Iglesia de Santa María la Mayor**, a church whose tower was once the minaret of a mosque; the **Museo del Bandolero** *(Calle Armiñán 29)*, dedicated to the banditry for which central Andalucía was once renowned; or the beautiful **Baños Arabes** *(Arab Baths; open Wed-Sun)*.

Places to Stay & Eat

Pleasant **Hotel Morales** *(☎/fax 952 87 15 38; Calle Sevilla 51; singles/doubles €21/39)* has attractive rooms with bath and friendly, informative owners. **Alavera de los Baños** *(☎/fax 952 87 91 43; ⓔ alavera@ctv.es; singles/doubles €42/58)* is a small German-run hotel next to 13th-century Arab baths. Rates include breakfast.

There are some excellent old-style tapas bars among the nondescript international restaurants, including **Marisquería Paco** *(Plaza del Socorro)* – good for seafood – and **Bodega La Giralda** *(Calle Nueva 19)*, a great spot for wine downed with olives, cheese and *chorizo* (red sausage) tapas.

Getting There & Away

Several buses run daily to Seville (€7.80, 2½ hours), Málaga (€6.65, two hours) and Cádiz.

One goes to Algeciras (€6) Monday to Friday. The bus station is on Plaza Concepción García Redondo.

A few direct trains go to Granada (€10.80, 2¼ hours), Málaga (€7.20, two hours), Algeciras, Córdoba and Madrid. For Seville, and further trains to/from the above destinations, change at Bobadilla or Antequera. The station is on Avenida de Andalucía.

ALGECIRAS

pop 105,070

Algeciras, an unattractive industrial and fishing town between Tarifa and Gibraltar, is the major port linking Spain with Morocco. Keep your wits about you, and ignore offers from the legions of moneychangers, drug-pushers and ticket-hawkers.

If you need a room, there's loads of budget accommodation in the streets behind Avenida de la Marina. Friendly **Hostal González** *(☎ 956 65 28 43; Calle José Santacana 7; singles/doubles €15/24)* has good, clean rooms with bathrooms.

Comes *(Calle San Bernardo)*, 400m inland from the port, runs frequent buses to/from La Línea, and several daily to/from Tarifa, Cádiz and Seville. **Portillo** *(Avenida Virgen del Carmen 15)*, 200m north of the port, runs to/from Málaga, the Costa del Sol and Granada. **Bacoma**, inside the port, runs to/from Valencia, Barcelona, France, Germany and Holland.

Direct daily trains run to/from Madrid and Granada, passing through Ronda and through Bobadilla, where you can change for Málaga, Córdoba and Seville.

Trasmediterránea *(☎ 902 45 46 45)*, **EuroFerrys** *(☎ 956 65 11 78)* and other companies operate frequent ferries to/from Tangier in Morocco, and Ceuta, the Spanish enclave on the Moroccan coast. Usually at least 20 daily go to Tangier and 40 or more to Ceuta. From late June to September there are ferries almost around the clock. Buy your ticket in the port or at agencies on Avenida de la Marina – prices are the same. To Tangier, adults pay €13.80 one way (2½ hours). To Ceuta, it's €12.80 by ferry (90 minutes). Cars cost €69. **Buquebus** *(☎ 902 41 42 42)* crosses to Ceuta in 30 minutes for €17.50 (cars €58.51).

SPAIN

CÁDIZ, TARIFA & THE COSTA DE LA LUZ

The historic port of Cádiz has a well-aged atmosphere, with backstreets flanked by magnificent 18th-century buildings interspersed with elegant squares. The best time to visit is during the February **Carnaval**, close to Rio in terms of outrageous exuberance. Ninety kilometres to Cádiz' southeast is windy Tarifa, perched at continental Europe's most southerly point and with a lively windsurfing scene. Stretching between the two places are the long, sandy beaches of the Costa de la Luz (Coast of Light), sheltering stuck-in-a-time-warp villages such as Los Caños de Meca, Zahara de los Atunes and Bolonia.

Things to See & Do

Cádiz The **Museo de Cádiz** *(open 2.30pm-8pm Tues, 9am-2pm Wed-Sat, 9.30am-2.30pm Sun)* has a magnificent collection of archaeological remains, as well as a fine art collection. The **Castillo de Santa Catalina** *(open daily)* dates from 1598, and the large 18th-century **cathedral** *(admission €1.50; open 2.30pm-8pm Tues, 9am-8pm Wed-Sat, 9.30am-2.30pm Sun)* is the city's most striking landmark. The city's lively central market is on Plaza de las Flores, the former site of a Phoenician temple. From Cádiz you can easily visit the historic sherry-making towns of El Puerto de Santa María and Jerez de la Frontera by bus or train (or boat, to El Puerto).

Tarifa A 10km-long beach beloved of windsurfers, **Playa de los Lances** stretches northwest from Tarifa. For **windsurf rental** and classes try places along here such as **Club Mistral** at the Hurricane Hotel or **Spin Out Surf Base**, which charges €48 for 2 hours tuition, in front of Camping Torre de la Peña II. In Tarifa town, enjoy exploring the winding old streets and visit the castle, **Castillo de Guzmán**, dating from the 10th century.

Places to Stay & Eat

Cádiz's excellent independent youth hostel **Quo Qádiz** *(☎/fax 956 22 19 39; Calle Diego Arias 1; dorm beds from €6)* has rates that include breakfast. Plaza de San Juan de Dios and the Plaza de Mina areas are full of varied places to eat.

In Tarifa, a good accommodation choice is the bright and central **Hostal Alborada** *(☎ 956 68 11 40; Calle San José 52; doubles with bath €37.50)*. There are plenty of eating options on and near the central Calle Sancho IV El Bravo.

Getting There & Away

Cádiz' main bus station is on Plaza de Hispanidad, near Plaza de España. There are regular buses to/from Algeciras (€7.90, 2¾ hours), Seville (€8.85, 1½ hours), Córdoba (€15, 4½ hours), Málaga (€14.50, 5 hours), and Ronda and Tarifa. Up to 15 daily trains chuff to/from Seville (€8.20, two hours), with others heading for Córdoba and beyond.

Gibraltar

pop 27,030

The British colony of Gibraltar occupies a huge lump of limestone, almost 5km long and over 1km wide, near the mouth of the Mediterranean. Gibraltar was the bridgehead for the Muslim invasion of Spain in AD 711, and Castile didn't wrest it from the Muslims until 1462. In 1704 an Anglo-Dutch fleet captured Gibraltar. After 300 years of concentrated Britishness, Britain and Spain are now talking about joint Anglo-Spanish sovereignty – to the ire of the Gibraltarians.

Gibraltar is like 1960s Britain on a sunny day. It's old-fashioned and safe, attracting coachloads of day-trippers from the Costa del Sol who come to be reassured by the helmet-wearing policemen, double-decker buses, bangers and mash, and Marks & Spencer.

Information

To enter Gibraltar you need a passport or EU national identity card. EU, US, Canada, Australia, New Zealand, Israel, South Africa and Singapore passport-holders do *not* need visitor's visas for Gibraltar, but anyone who needs a visa for Spain should have at least a double-entry Spanish visa if they intend to return to Spain from Gibraltar.

Gibraltar has a helpful **tourist office** at the border. There is a **main office** *(☎ 45000; Duke of Kent House, Cathedral Square; open Mon-Fri)* and another office at Casemates *(☎ 74982; open daily)*.

The currency is the Gibraltar pound or pound sterling. Change any unspent Gibraltar pounds before you leave. You can always use euros. At the time of writing, the exchange rate is €1 to £0.63.

To phone Gibraltar from Spain, the telephone code is ☎ 9567; from other countries dial the international access code, ☎ 350, and the local number.

Things to See & Do

Central Gibraltar is nothing special – you could almost be in Bletchley or Bradford – but the **Gibraltar Museum** *(Bomb House Lane; admission £2; open 10am-6pm Mon-Fri, 10am-2pm Sat)* has an interesting historical, architectural and military collection, and includes a Muslim-era bathhouse.

The large **Upper Rock Nature Reserve** *(admission per adult £7, per vehicle £1.50; open 9.30am-7pm daily)*, covering most of the upper rock, has spectacular views and several interesting spots to visit.

The rock's most famous inhabitants are its colony of **Barbary macaques**, the only wild primates (apart from *Homo sapien* soccer supporters) in Europe. Some of these hangout around the **Apes' Den** near the middle cable-car station, others can often be seen at the top station or Great Siege Tunnels.

Other attractions include **St Michael's Cave**, a large natural grotto renowned for its stalagmites and stalactites and the **Great Siege Tunnels**, a series of galleries hewn from the rock by the British during the Great Siege to provide new gun emplacements.

From about April to September, several boats make daily **dolphin-watching trips** of about two hours (£12 to £15 per person) from Watergardens Quay or adjacent Marina Bay.

Places to Stay & Eat

Emile Youth Hostel *(☎ 51106; Montagu Bastion, Line Wall Rd; dorm beds £12)* has 43 places in two- to eight-person rooms. **Queen's Hotel** *(☎ 74000; 1 Boyd St; singles/doubles with bath £39/46)* offers a 20% student discount. All rates include an English breakfast.

Most pubs do British pub meals. The **Star Bar** *(Parliament Lane)* has a traditional Sunday roast for £4.95. At **The Market Tavern** *(1 Waterport Market Place)* you can have a choice of four different breakfasts (including Scottish and vegetarian). The Indian food at **Maharajah** *(5 Tuckey's Lane)* is both spicy and good.

Getting There & Around

There are no regular buses to Gibraltar, but La Línea bus station is only a five-minute walk from the border. Buses Nos 3, 9 and 10 run frequently, direct from the border into the town. All of Gibraltar can be easlily covered on foot.

Extremadura

A sparsely populated tableland bordering Portugal, Extremadura is far enough from the most beaten tourist trails to give you a genuine sense of exploration – something that *extremeños* themselves have a flair for. Many epic 16th-century *conquistadores* including Francisco Pizarro (who conquered the Incas) and Hernán Cortés (who did the same to the Aztecs) sprang from this land.

Trujillo and Cáceres are the two not-to-be-missed Old Towns, and Mérida has Spain's biggest collection of Roman ruins. A spot of hiking, or just relaxing, in the valleys of Northeast Extremadura makes the perfect change from urban life.

TRUJILLO

pop 9260

Trujillo can't be much bigger now than in 1529, when Francisco Pizarro set off with his three brothers and a few local buddies for an expedition that culminated in the bloody conquest of the Inca empire three years later. The town is blessed with a broad and fine Plaza Mayor, from which rises its remarkably preserved Old Town. The **tourist office** *(☎ 927 32 26 77; Plaza Mayor)* is right there. You can connect to the Internet at **Ciberalia** *(Calle Tiendas 18)* for €2 an hour.

Things to See

A **statue of Pizarro**, by American Charles Rumsey, dominates the Plaza Mayor. On the plaza's south side, the **Palacio de la Conquista** sports the carved images of Francisco Pizarro and the Inca princess Inés Yupanqui. Two noble mansions you *can* visit are the 16th-century **Palacio de los Duques de San Carlos** *(Plaza Mayor; admission €1.20)*, and **Palacio de Juan-Pizarro de Orellana**, through the alley in the plaza's southwest corner.

Up the hill, the **Iglesia de Santa María la Mayor** *(admission €1.25)* is an interesting hotchpotch of 13th- to 16th-century styles, with some fine paintings by Fernando Gallego of the Flemish school. Higher up, the **Casa-Museo de Pizarro** *(admission €1.25)* has informative displays (in Spanish) on the lives and adventures of the Pizarro family. At the top of the hill, Trujillo's **castillo** is an impressive structure, primarily of Moorish origin with a **hermitage** *(admission €1.25)* within.

Places to Stay & Eat

Plaza Mayor Pension *(☎ 619 54 46 56; Plaza Mayor 6; doubles with bath €30)* has bright tile and pale-wood decor, with rooms overlooking the square. **Pension Roque** *(☎ 927 32 23 13; Calle Domingo de Ramos 30; doubles €21)* is quiet and pleasant with lots of communal space. **Hostal La Cadena** *(☎ 927 32 14 63; Plaza Mayor 8; doubles from €37)* is in a tastefully restored 16th-century building with a handy tapas bar and restaurant downstairs.

Don't miss **Restaurante La Troya** *(☎ 927 23 13 64; Plaza Mayor 10; set menu €15)* if you're a meat-eater. The food isn't cheap, but portions are gigantic and it will save you from eating much else for the next few days. **Cafetería Nuria** *(Plaza Mayor; dishes from €5)* has various dishes. At **La Victoria** *(Plaza Mayor 20)* you can have a dozen frogs' legs for €9.62, or choose from more conventional, inexpensive dishes. **Cafe/Bar Escudo** *(Plaza de Santiago)* serves good tapas from €1.80. After dinner, check out stylish **La Albadia** club *(Calle Garcia)*, which seems surprisingly hip for this neck of the woods.

Getting There & Away

The **bus station** *(☎ 927 32 12 02; Carretera de Mérida)* is 500m south of Plaza Mayor. At least six buses run daily to/from Cáceres (€2.40, 45 minutes), Badajoz (€7.54, 2½ hours) and Madrid (€12.62, four hours), and four or more to/from Mérida (€5.89, 1¼ hours).

CÁCERES

pop 82,030

Cáceres is larger than Trujillo and has an even bigger Old Town, so perfectly preserved that it can seem lifeless at times. The Old Town is worth a visit at night to soak up the atmosphere of accumulated ages.

On Plaza Mayor is the **tourist office** *(☎ 927 24 63 47; open daily)*. **Ciberjust** *(Calle Diego Maria Crehuet 7)* is a good Internet café. The Old Town is still surrounded by walls and towers raised by the Almohads in the 12th century. Entering from Plaza Mayor, you'll see ahead the fine 15th-century **Iglesia de Santa María**, Cáceres' cathedral.

Many of the Old Town's churches and imposing medieval mansions can only be admired from outside, but you *can* enter the good **Museo de Cáceres** *(Plaza de Veletas; admission €2, EU citizens free; open 9.30am-2.30pm Tues-Sat, 10.15am-2.30pm Sun)*,

SPAIN

housed in a 16th-century mansion built over a 12th-century Moorish cistern. Also worth a look is the **Casa-Museo Árabe Yussuf Al-Borch** *(Cuesta del Marqués 4; admission €2; open 10.30am-2pm & 6pm-8pm daily)*, a private house decked out with Oriental and Islamic trappings. The **Arco del Cristo** at the bottom of this street is a Roman gate.

The best area to stay is around recently pedestrianised Plaza Mayor, although it gets noisy at weekends. **Pensión Márquez** *(☎ 927 24 49 60; Calle de Gabriel y Galán 2; doubles €20)*, just off the low end of the plaza, is a friendly place with clean rooms. **Residencia Zurbarán** *(☎ 927 21 04 52; Calle Roso de Luna 11; doubles €30)*, is comfortable and bright.

Cafetería El Puchero *(Plaza Mayor 33)* is a popular hang-out with a huge variety of eating options, from good *bocadillos* (around €2.80) and *raciónes* to à la carte fare. **Sabor a Mistura** *(☎ 927 24 52 31; Calle Pintores 32)*, on the main shopping street, is good for light lunches, while **Corregidor** *(☎ 927 24 48 78; Calle Moret 7)* dishes up tasty local cuisine and is a good breakfast spot.

Minimum daily services from the **bus station** *(☎ 927 23 25 50)* include at least six to Trujillo (€3) and Madrid (€11.50, 3½ hours), five each to Mérida (€4.20, 1¼ hours) and Plasencia, three each to Salamanca (€10.50, three to four hours) and Seville via Zafra (€10.75, four hours), and two to Badajoz.

Three to five trains a day run to/from Madrid (from €14.45, 3½ to five hours) and Mérida (one hour) and two or three each to/from Plasencia (1¼ hours), Badajoz (two hours) and Barcelona. The single daily train to Lisbon (from €27.95, six hours) leaves in the middle of the night.

MÉRIDA

pop 51,060

Once the biggest city in Roman Spain, Mérida is home to more ruins of that age than anywhere else in the country. The **tourist office** *(☎ 924 31 53 53; Avenida de José Álvarez Saenz de Buruaga)* is by the gates to the Roman theatre. **MGK** *(☎ 924 30 40 72; Calle José Ramon; open 10.30am-2pm & 5pm-9pm daily)* is a funky Internet café that charges €1.50 an hour.

For €7.20 (€3.60 for students and over 65s) you can buy a ticket that gives you admission to the **Teatro Romano**, **Anfiteatro**, the **Casa del Anfiteatro**, the **Casa Romana del Mithraeo**, the **Alcazaba**, **Iglesia de Santa Eulalia** and the **Arqueológica de Moreria**. The theatre was built in 15 BC, and the gladiators' ring, or Anfiteatro, seven years later. Combined they could hold 20,000 spectators. Various other reminders of imperial days are scattered about town, including the **Puente Romano**, at 792m one of the longest bridges the Romans ever built.

Pensión El Arco *(☎ 924 31 83 21; Calle de Miguel de Cervantes 16; singles/doubles €12.25/21.60)* is great value and deservedly popular with backpackers. Another option is **Hostal Nueva España** *(☎ 924 31 33 56; Avenida de Extramadura 6; doubles €36)*, which is in a pleasant old house with all mod cons, a short walk from the centre.

Casa Benito *(Calle de San Francisco)* is a great old-style wood-panelled bar and restaurant, decked with bullfighting memorabilia, serving local fare at reasonable prices – try the grilled mushrooms with garlic and parsley. **Restaurante Rafael** *(☎ 924 31 87 52; Santa Eulalia 13; set menu €7.75)*, with tables on a pedestrian street, does a good *montado de lomo* (pork loin) and other traditional dishes.

From the **bus station** *(☎ 924 37 14 04)* at least seven daily buses run to Badajoz (€4.15), Seville (€9.55 to €9.65) and Madrid (from €16.50), and at least four to Cáceres (€4) and Trujillo (€5).

At least four trains run a day to Badajoz, and two or more to Cáceres, Ciudad Real, and Madrid (€18, five to six hours).

Galicia, Asturias & Cantabria

Verdant Galicia has been spared the mass tourism that crowds other parts of Spain. Its often wild coast is indented with a series of majestic estuaries that hide some of Spain's prettiest and least-known beaches and coves. Inland are rolling green hills dotted with bucolic farmhouses. In winter, Galicia can be freezing, but in summer it boasts one of Europe's most agreeable climates (although with every visit a little rain will probably fall).

The coasts of the still greener and even more inspiring Asturias and Cantabria regions, east of Galicia, are dotted with fine sandy beaches and some agreeable villages and towns. Inland are the beautiful Picos de Europa, which provide some of Spain's best walking areas.

SANTIAGO DE COMPOSTELA

pop 93,380

This hauntingly beautiful small city marks the end of the Camino de Santiago, a name given to several major medieval pilgrim routes from as far away as France. Today, avid walkers and bikers join the faithful in crossing the country to attend mass at Santiago's cathedral. Thanks to its university, Santiago is a lively city almost anytime, but it's at its most festive around 25 July, the Feast of Santiago. The **regional tourist office** *(☎ 981 58 40 81; Rúa do Vilar 43; open daily)* can provide a good map, and accommodation advice. Get your Internet fix at **Cyber Nova 50** *(50 Rúa Nova)* for €1.20 per hour.

Things to See & Do

The goal of the Camino de Santiago is the **cathedral** on magnificent **Praza do Obradoiro**. Under the main altar lies the supposed tomb of Santiago Apóstol (St James the Apostle), believed to have been buried here in the 1st century AD. The cathedral is a superb Romanesque creation of the 11th to 13th centuries, with later decorative flourishes, and its *pièce de résistance* is the Pórtico de la Gloria inside the west facade.

Santiago's compact Old Town is a work of art, and a walk around the cathedral will take you through some of its most inviting squares. Also take a stroll in the beautifully landscaped **Carballeira de Santa Susana** park southwest of the cathedral. Just northeast of the Old Town, off Porta do Camino, an impressive old convent houses the **Museo do Pobo Galego** *(admission free; open Mon-Sat)*, covering Galician life from fishing through music and crafts to traditional costume.

Places to Stay & Eat

Santiago is jammed with cheap *pensiones*, but many are full of students. Attractive **Hostal Pazo e Agra** *(☎ 981 58 90 45; Rúa da Caldería 37; singles/doubles €17/26)* may lack amenities, but offers warm, inviting rooms in a spotless old house. Inquire at **Restaurante Zingara** *(Rúa de Cardenal Payá 16)*. Popular little **Hostal Suso** *(☎ 981 58 66 11; Rúa do Vilar 65; doubles €30)* has comfortable modern rooms with bath. **Hotel Real** *(☎ 981 56 92 90; Rúa da Caldereria 49; singles/doubles €43/58)* has diminutive but comfortable and well-laid-out quarters with all the trimmings.

A couple of medium-priced places that shelter some of Santiago's best cuisine are **Restaurante Entre Rúas** and **Restaurante A Tulla**, hidden away in the tiny square on the lane Entrerúas. You should get away with spending under €10.

Highly popular **La Bodeguilla de San Roque** *(Rúa de San Roque 13)* offers excellent, eclectic and moderately priced fare, including enormous salads and good *revolto* (scrambled-egg) concoctions for €5.

Entertainment

For traditional Celtic music, Galician-style (sometimes live), head for **Café das Crechas** *(Via Sacra 3)*. **Paraíso Perdido**, on the tiny square of Entrealtares, is one of Santiago's oldest bars. **Bar-Tolo** *(Rúa de Abril Ares 8)* is a popular new joint. The local drinking and dancing scene is centred in the new town, especially around Praza Roxa (about 800m southwest of the cathedral). Head down there via Rúa de Franco, which offers many bars to prep you up for the disco scene. **Black** *(Avenida de Rosalía de Castro s/n)* is a popular disco. For more of a Latin American touch, look in at **Guayaba** *(Rúa de Frei Rodendo Salvado 16)*.

Getting There & Away

Santiago's bus station is just over 1km northeast of the cathedral, on Rúa de Rodriguez Viguri (connected by city bus No 10 to Praza de Galicia, on the south edge of the Old Town). Castromil runs regular services to A Coruña and Vigo via Pontevedra. Dainco runs two buses to Salamanca and one to Cádiz. Alsa has one or more bus to Madrid (nine hours).

The train station is 600m south of the Old Town at the end of Rúa do Horreo (city bus Nos 6 and 9 from near the station go to Praza de Galicia). Up to four trains a day run to Madrid (€36, eight to 11 hours), and frequent trains head to A Coruña (€3.50, one hour), Pontevedra (€3.50, one hour) and Vigo (€4, two hours).

RÍAS BAJAS

The grandest of Galicia's estuaries are the four Rías Bajas, on its west-facing coast. From north to south these are the Ría de

Muros, Ría de Arousa, Ría de Pontevedra and Ría de Vigo. All are dotted with low-key resorts, fishing villages and good beaches.

There are regional tourist offices in **Pontevedra** *(☎ 986 85 08 14; Calle del General Mola 3)*; **Cambados** *(☎ 986 52 07 86)*, a block from the bus station; and **Vigo** *(☎ 986 43 05 77)*, by the Estación Marítima (port).

Things to See & Do

On Ría de Arousa, **Isla de Arousa** is connected to the mainland by a long bridge. Some of the beaches facing the mainland are very pleasant and protected, with comparatively warm water. **Cambados**, a little further south, is a peaceful seaside town with a magnificent plaza surrounded by easily walkable little streets.

The small city of **Pontevedra** has managed to preserve a classic medieval centre edging Río Lérez. Tranquil beaches fringe the villages of **Aldán** and **Hío**, near the southwest end of the Ría de Pontevedra. **Vigo**, Galicia's biggest city, is a disappointment given its wonderful setting.

The Rías Bajas' best beaches are on the **Islas Cíes**, off the end of the Ría de Vigo. Isla del Faro and Isla de Monte Agudo are linked by a white sandy crescent, together forming a 9km breakwater in the Atlantic. You can visit the islands only from Easter to mid-September, and numbers are strictly limited. Boats from Vigo cost €13.25 return. From mid-June they go daily; before that, only at weekends.

Places to Stay & Eat

The only option to stay on the Islas Cíes is **camping** *(per person & tent €6)*. You must book at the office in Vigo's Estación Marítima. You can then organise a return boat ticket for the days you require.

In Cambados, **Hostal Pazos Feijoo** *(☎ 986 54 28 10; Calle de Curros Enríquez 1B; doubles with bath €32)*, near the waterfront in the newer part of town (one street from the bus station), offers agreeable rooms.

In old Pontevedra you'll find **Casa Alicia** *(☎ 986 83 70 79; Avenida de Santa María 5; doubles €18)*. **Casa Maruja** *(☎ 986 85 49 01; Avenida de Santa María 12; singles/doubles from €15/25)*, around the corner, sports spotless, inviting, fresh-smelling rooms. You can eat cheaply at **O' Merlo** *(Avenida de Santa María 4; set menu €6)*, with a cheap menu and an excellent variety of dishes.

For a bit more seclusion, try **Hostal Stop** *(☎ 986 32 94 75; singles/doubles €20/30 in summer)*, in tiny Hío.

In Vigo, **Hotel Pantón** *(☎ 986 22 42 70; Rúa de Lepanto 18; singles/doubles €25/37 in summer)* has rooms with bath and TV. The Praza de Fefiñáns swarms with **restaurants** serving good local Albariño wine (and decent food).

Old Vigo is laced with tapas bars and eateries of all descriptions. **Restaurante Fay-Bistes** *(Rúa Real 7; set lunch €7.20)* offers delicious Galician snacks.

Getting There & Away

Pontevedra and Vigo are the area's transport hubs. Both are well served by buses and trains from Santiago de Compostela and A Coruña, and Vigo offers service to such distance spots as Madrid and Barcelona. Iberia also flies from Vigo to domestic destinations. Two trains a day run from Vigo to Porto in Portugal (3½ hours).

A CORUÑA (LA CORUÑA)

pop 239,430

A Coruña is an attractive port city with decent beaches and a wonderful seafront promenade, the Paseo Marítimo. A tourist information kiosk, on the waterfront where the Paseo Marítimo meets Avenida de la Marina, dispenses information. The **Ciudad Vieja** (Old Town) is huddled on the headland north of the port, while the most famous attraction, the **Torre de Hércules** *(Tower of Hercules; admission €3; open daily)*, built by the Romans, caps the headland's northern end. The northwest side of the isthmus joining the headland to the mainland is lined with sandy **beaches**.

Calle de Riego de Agua, a block back from Avenida de la Marina on the southern side of the isthmus, is a good spot to find lodgings. **Pensión La Alianza** *(☎ 981 22 81 14; Calle de Riego de Agua 8; singles/doubles €16/39)* has basic rooms but super-friendly management. A step up is **Hostal La Provinciana** *(☎ 981 22 04 00, fax 981 22 04 40; Rúa Nueva 9; singles/doubles €24/32)*, down the street and around a corner, with absolutely enormous rooms and bathrooms.

Calle de la Franja, a block inland from Riego de Agua, has several good places to eat such as **Casa Santiso** *(Calle de la Franja 26; set lunch €7.50)*.

Daily trains and buses run to Santiago de Compostela, Vigo, Santander, León, Madrid and Barcelona.

RÍAS ALTAS

Northeast of A Coruña stretches the alternately pretty and awesome coast of the Rías Altas. The region boasts some of the most dramatic scenery in Spain and beaches that in good weather are every bit as inviting as those on the better-known Rías Bajas. Spots to head for include the medieval towns of **Betanzos**, **Pontedeume** and **Viveiro** (all with budget accommodation), the tremendous cliffs of **Cabo Ortegal** and the **beaches** between there and Viveiro. Buses from A Coruña and Santiago de Compostela will get you into the area. After that you'll need local buses and the occasional walk or lift.

PICOS DE EUROPA

This small region that straddles Asturias, Cantabria and Castilla y León comprises possibly the finest walking country in Spain. The spectacular mountain and gorge scenery ensures a continual flow of visitors from all over Europe and beyond. The Picos begin only 20km from the coast and are little more than 40km long and 25km wide. They comprise three limestone massifs: the eastern Macizo Ándara, with a summit of 2444m, the western Macizo El Cornión, rising to 2596m, and the central Macizo Los Urrieles, reaching 2648m.

The Picos constitute a national park, with a **main information office** *(☎ 985 84 86 14; Casa Dago, Avenida de Covadonga 43)* in Cangas de Onís. Plenty of information on walks is available here and at several other tourist and information offices around the Picos. Trekkers will find Lonely Planet's *Walking in Spain* useful.

The main access towns for the Picos are Cangas de Onís, Arenas de Cabrales and Potes. A good starting point for walks is **Lago Enol**, a lake 7km up from Covadonga, above Cangas de Onís in the northwest Picos. Another, though without public transport, is **Sotres** in the northeast.

SPAIN

Places to Stay & Eat

You can camp free near Lago de Enol. In Sotres, **Pensión La Perdiz** *(☎ 985 94 50 11; singles/doubles with bath €25/30)* offers comfortable rooms. **Casa Cipriano** *(☎ 985 94 50 24)*, across the road, is a little more expensive but also has a good restaurant. The good clean **Albergue Peña Castil** *(☎ 985 94 50 70; dorm beds €9-12)* offers bunks and a decent restaurant.

In Espinama (for a southern approach), the attractive **Hostal Puente Deva** *(☎ 942 73 66 58; singles/doubles €25/40)* has rooms that are well decked out and offers food at its typical Spanish restaurant.

Cangas de Onís, Arenas de Cabrales and Potes all have a wide range of accommodation.

Getting There & Away

From the roads encircling the Picos, three main routes lead into the heart of the mountains: from Cangas de Onís to Covadonga and Lago Enol, from Arenas de Cabrales to Poncebos and Sotres, and from Potes to Espinama and Fuente Dé.

A few buses from Santander, Oviedo and León serve the three main access towns. Buses also run from Cangas de Onís to Covadonga, from Covadonga to Lago de Enol (July and August only), and from Potes to Espinama and Fuente Dé (late June to mid-September).

SANTANDER

pop 185,230

Santander, capital of Cantabria, is a modern, cosmopolitan city with wide waterfront boulevards, leafy parks and crowded beaches. The city gears up to party hard during late July's Semana Grande fiesta. Book accommodation in advance all along the north coast in the second half of July and August. The **city tourist office** *(☎ 942 20 30 00)* is in the harbourside Jardines de Pereda, and the **regional office** *(☎ 942 31 07 08; Plaza Porticada 5)* is nearby. Santander's main attractions are its beaches and bars.

Many lodging rates quoted here rise by 50% to 100% in midsummer. **Pensión La Porticada** *(☎ 942 22 78 17; Calle Méndez Núñez 6; singles/doubles high season €34/45, rest of year €25/32)*, near the train and bus stations and ferry dock, has reasonable rooms, some with bay views. **Pensión La Corza** *(☎ 942 21 29 50; Calle Hernán Cortés 25; singles/doubles from €18/33)* is nicely located on a pleasant square, Plaza de Pombo. Just behind Playa del Sardinero, a splendid choice is **Hostal Carlos III** *(☎/fax 942 27 16 16; Avenida de la Reina Victoria 135; singles/doubles high season €48/63, rest of year €31/44)*, with bright, spacious rooms and all the mod cons.

The older part of town has lots of highly atmospheric old *mesones,* which here refers to traditional wine bars also serving food. **Mesón Goya** *(Calle Daóiz y Velarde 25; meals €6)* is typical and one of the more economical. Near El Sardinero, **La Cañia** *(Calle Joaquin Costa 45; set menu €9.40)* serves up an excellent lunch.

In the Old Town, Calle Río de la Pila – and to a marginally lesser extent Plaza de Cañadio – teems with bars of all descriptions. In summer, there's quite a good scene along the main drag by El Sardinero.

Santander is one of the major entry points to Spain, due to its ferry link with Plymouth, England. The ferry terminal and train and bus stations are all in the centre of Santander, within 300m of each other. Several daily buses head east to Bilbao, San Sebastián (€11, two hours) and Irún, and west to Oviedo (€11) and Gijón. Some stop at smaller places along the coast. Six a day go to Madrid (€21) via Burgos. Others run to Pamplona, Zaragoza, Barcelona, Salamanca and elsewhere.

Trains to Bilbao (€5.80, 2½ hours) and Oviedo are run by **FEVE**, a private line that does not accept rail passes. From Oviedo FEVE continues into northeast Galicia. Trains to Madrid, Castilla y León and the rest of Galicia are run by RENFE, so rail passes are valid. To Madrid there are three trains most days (from €31, 5½ to nine hours), via Ávila.

SANTILLANA DEL MAR

pop 3930

Among the good, sandy beaches and appealing villages along the Cantabrian and Asturian coasts, the least missable destination in the region is the marvellously preserved medieval village of Santillana del Mar, 30km west of Santander. The Romanesque carvings in the cloister of the **Colegiata de Santa Julia** *(admission €2.50; open Tues-Sun)* are Santillana's finest works of art. There's also a **Museo de la Inquisición** *(Inquisition Museum; admission €3.60)* with an alarming collection of instruments of torture and death.

Two kilometres southwest of Santillana are the world-famous **Cuevas de Altamira**, full of wonderful 14,000-year-old Stone Age animal paintings. For those who don't want to wait years to get in, the new **Museo de la Cuevas** *(admission €2.40; open Tues-Sat)* offers a full-scale replica of the caves and the art within.

Santillana has heaps of accommodation but few places are great value. An excellent choice is **Hospedaje Octavio** *(☎ 942 81 81 99; Plaza Las Arenas 4; singles/doubles €24/36)*, where charming rooms have timber-beam ceilings and private baths. **Casa Cossío** *(set menu €8)*, about the nearest restaurant to the Colegiata, serves a wide range of fare.

Several daily buses call in at Santillana en route between Santander and San Vicente de la Barquera, further west.

País Vasco (Euskadi), Navarra & Aragón

The Basque people have lived in Spain's País Vasco (Basque Country), Navarra and the adjoining Pays Basque in southwestern France for thousands of years. They have their own ancient language (Euskara), a distinct physical appearance, a rich culture and a proud history.

The País Vasco shelters a spectacular coastline, a green and mountainous interior and the elegance of San Sebastián and Bilbao's Guggenheim museum. Another great reason to visit is to sample the delights of

Basque ETAmology

Along with a strong sense of regional identity has come, among a significant percentage of Basques in Spain, a desire for Independence. The Basque nationalist movement was born in the 19th century. During the Franco years the Basque people were brutally repressed, and Euskadi ta Askatasuna (ETA; Basque Homeland and Freedom), a separatist movement, began its activities. With Spain's changeover to democracy in the late 1970s, the País Vasco was granted a large degree of autonomy, but ETA has pursued its violent campaign. ETA has recently been declared a terrorist organisation by the EU, and efforts to eliminate its sources of funding and political support are under way. Supporters of the movement see ETA as a freedom-fighting organisation that has been forced to resort to the only effective means of garnering international attention for its cause.

Basque cuisine, considered by most non-Catalanes to be the best in Spain.

Southeast of País Vasco, Navarra and Aragón reach down from the Pyrenees into the drier southern lands. Navarra also has a high Basque population, and you're likely to hear Basque spoken in the streets of its capital, Pamplona – home of the famous Sanfermines festival, with its running of the bulls. The Aragón Pyrenees offer the best walking and skiing on the Spanish side of these mountains.

SAN SEBASTIÁN (DONOSTIA)

pop 181,060

San Sebastián is a stunning city. Long famed as a ritzy resort for wealthy Spaniards, it has also been a stronghold of Basque nationalist feeling since well before Franco. A proud Basque community takes fierce care of its town, making sure that the streets are clean, drugless and prostitute-free. Those who live here consider themselves the luckiest people in Spain, and after spending a few days on the perfect crescent-shaped beaches in preparation for the wild evenings, you may begin to understand why.

Information

The **municipal tourist office** *(☎ 943 48 11 66; Blvd Reina Regente 3; open Mon-Sat, morning Sun)* can point you to accommodation and sightseeing options. Look for the **main post office** *(Calle de Urdaneta)* behind the cathedral. **Donosti-Net** *(Calle de Embeltrán 2)*, in the Parte Vieja (Old Town), is a good Internet café.

Things to See & Do

The **Playa de la Concha** and **Playa de Ondarreta** are among the most beautiful city beaches in Spain. You can reach **Isla de Santa Clara**, in the middle of the bay, by boat from the harbour. In summer, you can also swim out to rafts anchored in the bay. The Playa de la Zurriola (also known as 'Playa de Gros'), east of the Río Urumea, is less crowded and popular with both swimmers and surfers.

San Sebástian's **Aquarium** *(admission €8; open 10am-10pm daily summer, 10am-8pm daily winter)* has 10 large tanks teeming with tropical fish, morays, sharks and other finned creatures. There are also exhibits on pirates, Basque explorers and related themes. The **Museo de San Telmo** *(Plaza de Zuloaga; admission free; open 10.30am-1.30pm & 4pm-8pm Tues-Sat, 10.30am-1.30pm Sun)*, in a 16th-century monastery, has a varied collection with a heavy emphasis on Basque paintings. A highlight is the chapel – its lavish wall frescoes chronicle Basque history.

Overlooking Bahía de la Concha from the east is **Monte Urgull**, topped with a statue of Christ that enjoys sweeping views. It takes 30 minutes to walk up – a stairway starts from Plaza de Zuloaga in the Old Town. The views from the summit of Monte Igueldo are better still.

Places to Stay

Rooms are hard to find in July and August, when prices double, so book ahead. Be aware of huge seasonal price differences.

The HI **Albergue La Sirena** *(☎ 943 31 02 68, fax 943 21 40 90; W www.paisvasco.com/albergues; Paseo de Igueldo 25; dorm beds €13; open to midnight Mon-Fri, to 2am Sat & Sun)* offers standard bunks and rates include breakfast.

In the lively Parte Vieja, consider yourself lucky to score a room at the super-friendly **Pensión San Lorenzo** *(☎ 943 42 55 16; Calle de San Lorenzo 2; singles/doubles with bath €24/48)*, which offers recently renovated, nicely decorated rooms. Internet access is available. Also good and gleaming is **Pensión Loinaz** *(☎ 943 42 67 14; Calle de San Lorenzo 17; rooms per person €12-15)*.

Pensión Aussie *(☎ 943 42 28 74; Calle San Jerónimo 23; dorm beds €15)* works much like a hostel. Two- to four-bed rooms house backpackers from the world over. The affable owner is a good source of information on the town. **Pensión San Vicente** *(☎ 943 42 29 77; Calle San Vicente 7; singles/doubles €18/24)* offers rather bare-bone rooms. A kitchen is available for use off-season.

The area near the cathedral is more peaceful than the Parte Vieja. **Pensión La Perla** *(☎ 943 42 81 23; Calle de Loyola 10; singles/doubles with bath €24/29, rooms €40 in high season)* has excellent rooms with bathrooms; some overlook the cathedral. Also recommended is **Pensión Añorga** *(☎ 943 46 79 45; Calle de Easo 12; singles/doubles €24/30)*, with plain, clean rooms that share bathrooms.

Places to Eat

Bar *pintxos* (tapas) are excellent. Fill up on lunch *menús* during the day, then snack your way through the night.

Many bars cluster in the Parte Vieja, where **Bar Txepetxa** *(Calle Pescadería 5)* and **Borda Berri** *(Calle Fermín Calbetrón 12)* are recommended. Also here is **Juantxo Taberna** *(Calle de Embeltrán 6; bocadillos €2)*, famous for its cheap, super-sized sandwiches. Tiny **Koskol** *(Calle de Iñigo 5; set menu €6.50)* has a delicious, generous *menú*.

A young crowd flocks to **Caravanserai** *(sandwiches or snacks €3)*, next to the cathedral, a trendy bistro with an extensive menu that runs the gamut from burgers to pasta to sandwiches. Several vegetarian options are available.

Entertainment

San Sebastián's nightlife is superb. The Spanish habit of bar-hopping has been perfected in the Parte Vieja, and you might encounter over 30 bars within a two-block radius.

Typical drinks are a *zurrito* (beer in a small glass) and *txacolí* (a tart Basque wine). If you'd like to have a swig of Basque *sidra* (cider), head for **Sagardotegia Itxaropena** *(Calle de Embeltran 16)*.

When the Parte Vieja quietens down around 1am or 2am, the crowd heads to Calle de los Reyes Católicos, behind the cathedral.

Getting There & Away

The **bus station** *(Plaza de Pío XII)* is a 20-minute walk south of the Parte Vieja; ticket offices are along the streets north of the station. Buses leave for destinations all over Spain. PESA has half-hourly express service to Bilbao (€7.50, one hour), while La Roncalesa goes to Pamplona up to 10 times daily (€4.50, two hours). Continental buses to Madrid (€25) run nine times daily.

The **RENFE station** *(Paseo de Francia)* is across the river. There are daily trains to Madrid (€30, eight hours) and Barcelona (€31, 8½ hours). Several trains run to Paris (€77) via Hendaye, France. Other destinations include Salamanca and Lisbon. Eusko Tren is a private company (international passes not valid) that runs trains to Hendaye (€2) and Bilbao (€5.80, 2¾ hours) departing from **Amara station** *(Calle de Easo)*.

COSTA VASCA

Spain's ruggedly beautiful Costa Vasca (Basque Coast) is one of its least touristy coastal regions. A combination of rainy weather, chilly seas and regional violence tends to put some people off. Between the French border and San Sebastián, **Fuenterrabia** ('Hondarribia' in Basque) is a very picturesque fishing town with good beaches, while **Pasajes de San Juan** (Pasaia Donibane) has a pretty old section and some mouthwatering fish restaurants.

The coastal stretch between San Sebastián and Bilbao to the west is considered to be some of the finest **surfing** territory in Europe. **Zarauz** (Zarautz), about 15km west of San Sebastián, stages a round of the World Surfing Championship each September. **Mundaca** (Mundaka), about 12km north of **Guernica** (Gernika – the town Picasso made famous in his poignant painting), is a surfing town.

If you don't have your own transport, take a bus from San Sebastián to Zarauz and Guetaria, or from Bilbao to Guernica. From Guernica you can take a bus to Bermeo that will drop you in Mundaca. Eusko Tren also serves a few coastal towns from Bilbao and San Sebástian.

BILBAO (BILBO)

pop 353,940

Once the ugly industrial heart of the north, Bilbao has spruced itself up and now boasts a prettified downtown area. The friendly denizens of the **main tourist office** *(☎ 94 479 57 60; Paseo Arenal 1)* will be pleased to point out the city's attractions. There's also an **information kiosk** *(open Tues-Sun)* by the Guggenheim. For Internet access, go to **Láser Bilbao** *(Calle de Sendeja 5)* for €3 per hour in the Old Quarter.

In 1997 Bilbao created for itself a tourist gold mine – the US$100 million **Museo Guggenheim de Arte Contemporáneo** *(admission €7; open 10am-8pm Tues-Sun Sept-June, 10am-8pm daily July & Aug)*. Designed by US architect Frank Gehry, this fantastical, swirling structure was inspired in part by the anatomy of a fish and the hull of a boat – both allusions to Bilbao's past and present economy. The permanent exhibit includes works by the likes of Picasso, Mondrian and Kandinsky. Arrive early and ask about free guided English-language tours.

Some 300m up the street is the excellent **Museo de Bellas Artes** *(admission €4.50; open Tues-Sun)*, which boasts works by El Greco, Velázquez and Goya, as well as 20th-century masters such as Gauguin. Basque artists are shown as well.

Places to Stay & Eat

Albergue Bilbao Aterpetxea *(☎ 944 27 00 54, fax 944 27 54 79; Ⓦ www.albergue.bilbao.net; Carretera Basurto-Kastrexana Errep 70; bus No 58; dorm beds €11-13)* is a 10-minute direct bus ride away from the centre. Rooms are bright, bland and boring; rates include breakfast. Bring your hostel card. **Pensión Méndez** *(☎ 944 16 03 64; Calle de Santa María 13; singles/doubles €36/48)* is central and comfy but can be a bit noisy.

Las Siete Calles (Seven Streets), the nucleus of Bilbao's Old Town, brims with tapas bars and restaurants. **Rio-Oja** *(Calle de Perro 6; raciónes €5)* is among the many places for cheap food and drink. **Cafe Boulevard** *(Calle de Arenal 3; breakfasts €2, meals €6)*, Bilbao's oldest coffeehouse (1871), nearby, has full meals and tapas at wallet-friendly prices. The gorgeously decked-out **Café Iruña** *(Calle de Colón Larreátegui; set menu €8)* is Bilbao's most celebrated café, with ornate artwork and a rich history.

Getting There & Away

Buses to Madrid (€22) and Barcelona (€24) depart from the huge **Termibus** *(metro San Mamés)* lot in the southwest corner of town. Cities throughout the region and country are served from here.

Four daily trains to Madrid (€28, 6¼ hours) and two to Barcelona (€31, nine hours) leave from RENFE's central **Abando station**. FEVE runs trains from here to towns in Asturias, Cantabria and Galicia. The Eusko Tren station with regional services picks up passengers from the metro station off Plaza Nueva.

P&O ferries leave for Portsmouth from Santurtzi, about 14km northwest of Bilbao's city centre. The voyage takes about 35 hours from England and 29 hours the other way.

PAMPLONA (IRUÑA)

pop 186,250

The madcap festivities of Sanfermines in Pamplona run from 6 to 14 July. They are characterised by nonstop partying and, of course, the running of the bulls. The bulls are let out at 8am, but if you want to get a good vantage point you will have to be there before the sun rises. If you visit at any other time of year, you'll find a pleasant and modern city, with lovely parks and gardens.

Don't expect the overworked **tourist office** *(☎ 948 20 65 40; Plaza San Francisco; open Mon-Sat, morning Sun)* to be of much help during Sanfermines. Internet access is available at **Kura.net** *(Calle de Curia 15)* for €3 per hour.

During Sanfermines you need to book accommodation months in advance (and pay as much as triple the regular rates). During the festival, beds are also available in *casas particulares* (private houses) – haggle with the locals waiting for you at the bus and train stations. Otherwise, join the many who sleep in one of the parks, plazas or shopping malls.

Pamplona's Old Town is filled with cheap *pensiones* renting basic singles/doubles for around €15/30. Contenders include **Fonda Aragonesa** *(☎ 948 22 34 28; Calle San Nicolás 32)*, **Habitaciones Otano** *(☎ 948 22 50 95; Calle San Nicolás 5)*, and the slightly superior **Camas Escaray Lozano** *(☎ 948 22 78 25; Calle Nueva 24)*, near the tourist office.

Two excellent tapas bars are **Baserri** *(Calle San Nicolás 32)* and **Otano**, across the street. Nearby is the vegetarian **Restaurante Sarasate** *(Calle San Nicolás 19)*, with some inventive lunch options. **Bar Anaitasuna** *(Calle de San Gregorio 58; platos combinados €6, set lunch €8.50)* has uncluttered, modern decor and is busy from breakfast to midnight. The fare is typical and cheap, if not terribly inspired.

The **bus station** *(Avenida de Yangüas y Miranda)* is a five-minute walk south of the Old Town. There are 10 buses daily to San Sebastián (€5.25) and eight to Bilbao (€10). Four daily head for Madrid (€21) and two to Barcelona (€28).

Pamplona is on the San Sebastián–Zaragoza railway line, but the station is awkwardly situated northwest of town. If you arrive this way, catch bus No 9 to the centre.

ZARAGOZA

pop 610,980

Zaragoza, proud capital of once-mighty Aragón and home to half its 1.3 million people, is often said to be the most Spanish city of all. Once the important Roman city of Caesaraugusta, it still shelters a lively and interesting old heart on the southern side of the Río Ebro. The **city tourist office** *(☎ 976 39 35 37; Plaza del Pilar; open daily)* is housed in a surreal-looking glass cube.

Things to See

Zaragoza's focal point is the riverside **Plaza de Nuestra Señora del Pilar** (Plaza del Pilar for short), stretching for 500m. Dominating the north side is the **Basílica de Nuestra Señora del Pilar**, a 17th-century church of epic proportions. At the plaza's southeast end is **La Seo** *(admission €1.50)*, Zaragoza's brooding 12th- to 16th-century cathedral. Its northwest facade is a Mudéjar masterpiece.

The odd trapezoid structure in front of La Seo is the outside of a remarkable museum housing the **Foro de Caesaraugusta** *(admission €1.80; open 10am-2pm & 5pm-8pm Tues-Sat, 10am-2pm Sun)*. About 70m below modern ground level you can visit the remains of shops, porticos and a great sewage system, which are all brought to life by an audiovisual show.

A little over 1km west of the plaza, the **Palacio de la Aljafería** *(admission €1.80; open 10am-2pm & 4pm-6pm Tues, Wed & Sat, 10am-2pm Thur, Fri & Sun)*, housing Aragón's *cortes* (parliament), is Spain's greatest Muslim building outside Andalucía. It was built as the palace of the Muslim rulers who held the city from 714 to 1118.

Zaragoza has some good museums. Three of them, the **Museo Camón Aznar** *(Calle de Espoz y Mina 23; admission €0.60; open Tues-Sat)*, **Museo de Zaragoza** *(Plaza de los Sitios; admission free; open Tues-Sat)* and **Patio de la Infanta** *(admission free; open daily)*, which is closed Sunday afternoon, have good collections of work by Francisco Goya.

Places to Stay & Eat

Zaragoza's HI hostel is the **Albergue Juvenil Baltasar Gracián** *(☎ 976 30 66 90; Calle Franco y López 4; dorm beds €9-12; open Sept-July)*. Rates include breakfast. The cheapest rooms elsewhere are in El Tubo, the maze of lanes and alleys south of Plaza del Pilar. A basic choice is **Pensión La Peña** *(☎ 976 29 90 89; Calle Cinegio 3; singles/doubles €10/20)*. Another cheapie is **Pensión Manifestación** *(☎ 976 29 58 21; Calle Manifestación 36; singles/doubles €15/24)*. Bright **Hostal El Descanso** *(☎ 976 29 17 41; Calle de San Lorenzo 2; singles/doubles €12/22)* is great value.

Cafetería Pizolo *(Calle Prudencio; platos combinados from €5; open until 1am or 2am daily)* serves decent *platos combinados*. Cheery **La Milagrosa** *(Calle Don Jaime I 43; set menu €7)* serves *raciónes* and inexpensive breakfasts. The small plazas and narrow streets southwest of La Seo host some brilliant tapas bars, among them the inexpensive seafood spot **Casa Amadico** *(Calle Jordán de Urries 3)*, **Cervecería Marpy** *(Plaza Santa Marta 8)*, **La Calzorras** *(Plaza de San Pedro Nolasco)* and **Casa Juanico** *(Calle Santa Cruz 21)*.

Entertainment

There's no shortage of bars in and around El Tubo. At **Bar Corto Maltés** *(Calle del Temple 23)* all the barmen sport *corto maltés* (sideburns). **Café El Prior** *(Calle Santa Cruz)* is a good place for a little dancing in the earlier stages of a night out. Much of the late-night action takes place about 1km further southwest, on and around Calle Doctor Cerrada. A good place to start is the Irish bar **Morrissey** *(Gran Vía 33)*, which often has live bands Thursday to Saturday.

Getting There & Away

Bus stations are scattered all over town; tourist offices can tell you what goes where from where. The Agreda company runs to most major Spanish cities from Paseo de María Agustín 7. Trips to Madrid and Barcelona cost €11 each. Oscense buses head towards the Pyrenees from the Agreda station, too.

Up to 15 trains daily run from El Portillo station to both Madrid (€28, three to 4½ hours) and Barcelona (€28, 3½ to 5½ hours). Some Barcelona trains go via Tarragona. Trains also run to Valencia via Teruel, and to San Sebastián via Pamplona.

TERUEL

pop 30,790

Teruel has a flavour all its own thanks to four centuries of Muslim domination in the Middle Ages and some remarkable Mudéjar architecture dating from after its capture by the Christians in 1171. Get the low-down at the **tourist office** *(☎ 978 60 22 79; Calle Tomás Nogués 1)*.

Teruel has four magnificent Mudéjar towers: on the cathedral of **Santa María** (12th to 13th centuries) and the churches of **San Salvador** (13th century), **San Martín** and **San Pedro** (both 14th century). These, and the painted ceiling inside Santa María, are among Spain's best *Mudéjar* architecture and artisanry. The **Museo Provincial de Teruel** *(Plaza Padre Polanco; admission free; open 10am-2pm & 4pm-9pm Tues-Fri, 10am-2pm Sat & Sun)* is well worth a visit, mainly for its fascinating archaeological section.

Places to Stay & Eat

Fonda del Tozal *(☎ 978 60 10 22; Calle del Rincón 5; singles/doubles €10/20)* inhabits an amazing rickety old house run by a friendly family. Most of the rooms have cast-iron beds, enamelled chamber pots and exposed ceiling beams. In winter, you might prefer **Hostal Aragón** *(☎ 978 60 13 87; Calle de Santa María 4; singles/doubles €15/22, with bath €24/35)*, which is also charming but offers luxuries such as heating.

Teruel is famed for its ham. If you can't fit a whole leg in your backpack, at least sample a *tostada con jamón* with tomato and olive oil. One of the best places for hamming it up is **La Taberna de Rokelin** *(Calle de Tozal 33)*, a narrow bar with a beautiful rack of smoked pig hocks.

Getting There & Away

The **bus station** *(Ronda de Ambeles)*, just north of the Old Town, has daily buses heading to Barcelona (6½ hours), Cuenca (2¾ hours), Valencia (two hours) and Madrid (€15, 4½ hours).

By rail, Teruel is about midway between Valencia and Zaragoza, with three trains a day to both places. The **RENFE station** *(Calle de la Estación)* is on the southeast corner of the Old Town.

Sweden

Who wouldn't want to live up to the image Sweden has cultivated? A nation of tall, blonde, attractive types, famously open-minded. A country full of athletic folk, living at the cutting edge of technology and well cared for by the state, spending their long summer days eating meatballs and listening to ABBA (OK, maybe that last bit is taking it too far...).

Well, not only are the cliches mostly spot on, but if you dig below the glossy surface you'll find even more to be impressed by. Sweden boasts masses of historical sights, including burial mounds, rune stones, churches and fortresses galore, in addition to thousands of nature reserves, 28 national parks and more than 10,000km of trekking and bicycle paths – not to mention 10 royal castles in the Stockholm area and hundreds of superb museums. And then there are the vast forested and lake-studded landscapes.

Get the picture? The only obstacle to your thoroughly enjoying Sweden might be the state of your wallet, as the Swedish welfare state is costly to maintain. In the end, you get what you pay for. Although Sweden may pack a punch to your pursestrings, its myriad delights will knock you out even more effectively.

Sweden: the Basics

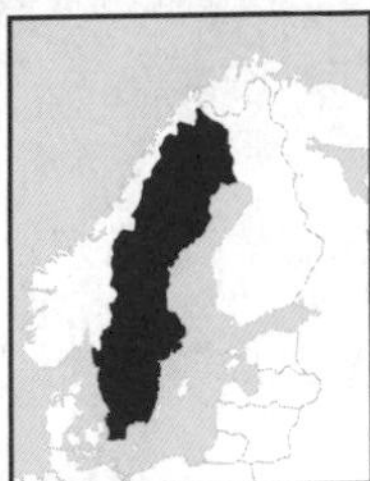

Capital Stockholm

Population 8.9 million

Area 449,964 sq km

Language Swedish

Currency krona (Skr) = 100 öre

Avoid at all costs Going out without mosquito repellent

Procure said repellent by asking *Är det någon som har myggmedel?* (Does anyone have some mosquito repellent?)

Facts about Sweden

HISTORY

Early cultural life is eloquently expressed by the *hällristningar* (rock paintings) that survive in many parts of Sweden. By the 9th century AD Swedish adventurers had explored as far as Russia, Byzantium and Arabia. The wealth and power of the Svea, who inhabited the Mälaren Valley, overwhelmed the southern Gauts (Götar) before the 11th century. Sweden avoided feudalism, but a privileged aristocracy owed its allegiance to the king.

Danish monarchs held the Swedish throne for a while, tolerating a national assembly. The regent, Sten Sture, loosened the Danish hold in 1471. Young nobleman Gustaf Vasa was crowned Gustaf I in 1523 and introduced a powerful, centralised nation-state.

The year 1809 saw the loss of Finland to Russia as well as the introduction of a constitution that divided legislative powers between king and Riksdag (Parliament). Sweden also negotiated with Denmark to exchange Swedish Pomerania for Norway. The enforcement of the 1814 union with Norway was Sweden's last military action.

By 1900 almost one in four Swedes lived in cities, and the level of industry was increasing. In this environment, the working class was radicalised. Sweden declared itself neutral at the outbreak of WWI, but a British economic blockade caused food shortages and civil unrest. The Social Democrats introduced a welfare state after the war.

Serious current-account problems in the early 1990s provoked frenzied speculation against the Swedish krona, forcing a massive devaluation of the currency. With both their economy and national confidence severely shaken, Swedes voted in favour of joining the European Union (EU), effective in 1995. Since then, Sweden's welfare state has undergone major reforms and the economy has improved considerably. The country has remained outside the Eurozone, and a referendum is still to be held on the issue.

GEOGRAPHY

Sweden's maximum north–south extent is 1574km. The dominant characteristics of the

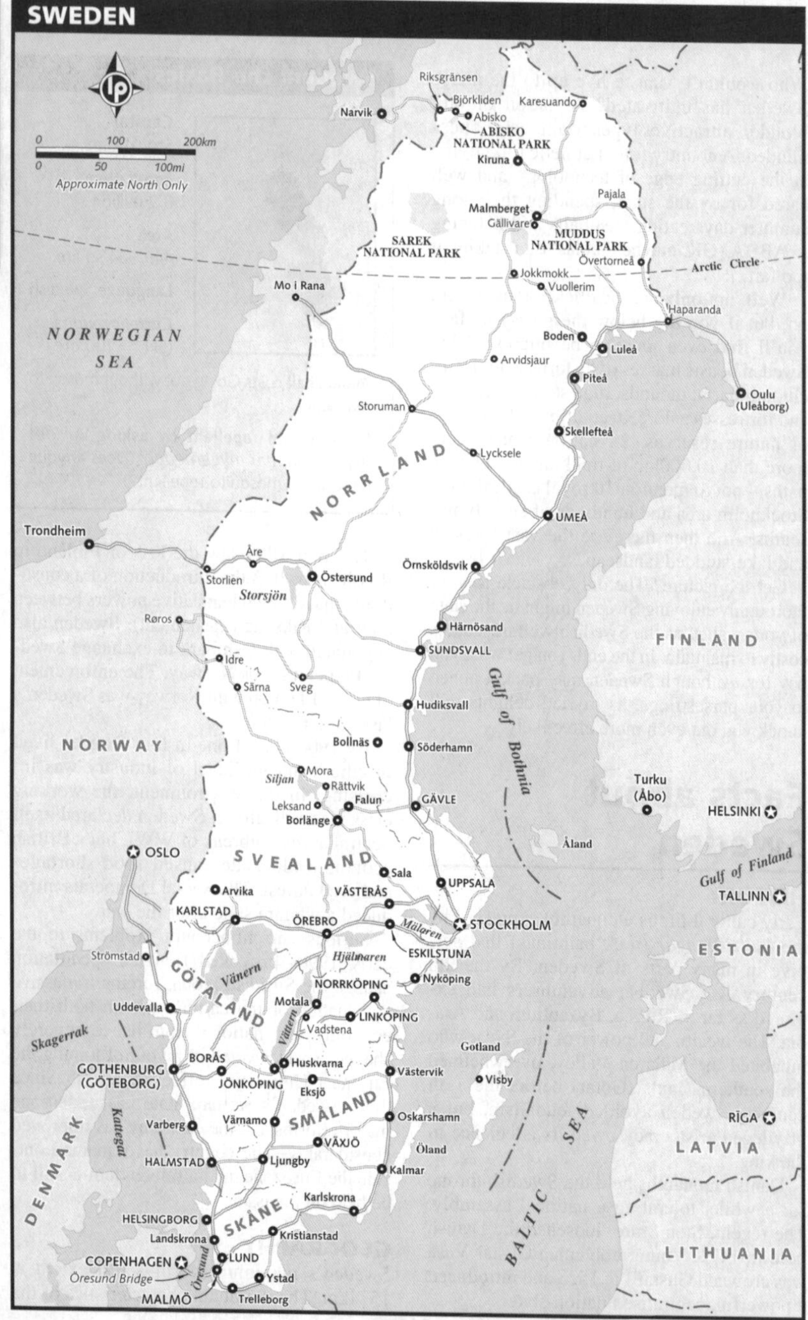
SWEDEN
0 100 200km
0 50 100mi
Approximate North Only
Riksgränsen
Björkliden
Abisko
Narvik
Karesuando
ABISKO NATIONAL PARK
Kiruna
Pajala
Malmberget
Gällivare
SAREK NATIONAL PARK
MUDDUS NATIONAL PARK
Övertorneå
Arctic Circle
Jokkmokk
Vuollerim
Mo i Rana
Haparanda
NORWEGIAN SEA
Boden
Luleå
Arvidsjaur
Piteå
Oulu (Uleåborg)
Storuman
Skellefteå
NORRLAND
Lycksele
UMEÅ
Trondheim
Åre
Storlien
Örnsköldsvik
Östersund
Storsjön
Röros
Härnösand
SUNDSVALL
FINLAND
Idre
Särna
Sveg
Hudiksvall
Gulf of Bothnia
NORWAY
Bollnäs
Söderhamn
Mora
Siljan
Rättvik
Leksand
Falun
GÄVLE
Borlänge
Turku (Åbo)
HELSINKI
Åland
OSLO
SVEALAND
Sala
UPPSALA
Gulf of Finland
Arvika
VÄSTERÅS
TALLINN
KARLSTAD
ÖREBRO
Mälaren
STOCKHOLM
Strömstad
Hjälmaren
ESKILSTUNA
ESTONIA
GÖTALAND
Vänern
Nyköping
NORRKÖPING
Uddevalla
Motala
LINKÖPING
Vättern
Vadstena
Skagerrak
Gotland
BORÅS
Huskvarna
GOTHENBURG (GÖTEBORG)
Västervik
JÖNKÖPING
Visby
Eksjö
Kattegat
SMÅLAND
Varberg
Värnamo
Oskarshamn
RĪGA
VÄXJÖ
SEA
LATVIA
Öland
HALMSTAD
Ljungby
Kalmar
DENMARK
Karlskrona
BALTIC
HELSINGBORG
SKÅNE
Kristianstad
Landskrona
LITHUANIA
COPENHAGEN
LUND
Öresund Bridge
Öresund
Ystad
MALMÖ
Trelleborg

landscape go back to the time of the last glaciation.

The rocky west coast is most notable for its fjords and skerries, although they scarcely compare with the barrage of rocky islets that shield Stockholm. The islands of Öland and Gotland consist of flat limestone and sandstone. There are approximately 100,000 lakes in Sweden.

CLIMATE

Most of Sweden has a cool temperate climate, with precipitation in all seasons, but the southern quarter of the country has a warm temperate climate.

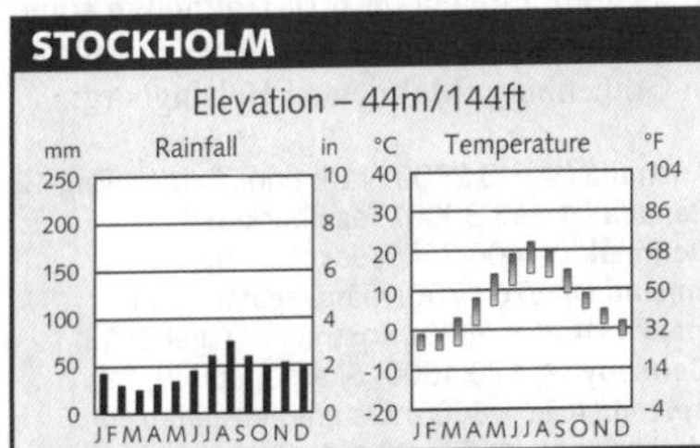

GOVERNMENT & POLITICS

Sweden has maintained its monarch as head of state, but the statsminister is chosen by a majority of the Riksdag.

POPULATION & PEOPLE

Sweden is the most populous Scandinavian country. Low birth and mortality rates have made Swedes among the oldest population on earth, with 17% of the population aged over 65. Over 500,000 are foreign nationals, and an extraordinary 20% of the population is either foreign-born or has at least one non-Swedish parent.

There are two native minorities in Sweden: the 15,000 Sami (formerly called Lapps), who live in the far north, and about 30,000 Finns who live in the northeast near the Finnish border.

SOCIETY & CONDUCT

Swedes are generally decent, law-abiding and serious, and proud of their country's history. Sweden regulates taxes and subsidises every step from cradle to grave. Even queuing is infallibly ordered: press a button for your own numbered ticket, then wait until it comes up on a digital display!

LANGUAGE

Most Swedes speak English as a second language. If you learn common phrases, your attempts will be greatly appreciated. Sami dialects are ancestrally related to Finnish, not Swedish.

See the Language chapter at the back of the book for pronunciation guidelines and useful words and phrases.

Facts for the Visitor

HIGHLIGHTS

The best place to hike and admire the mountains is in vast Sarek, in Lappland.

The Baltic islands of Gotland and Öland are big summer tourist centres. Some 24,000 islands off Stockholm and many more around the long Swedish coastline provide endless opportunities for exploration.

Skansen Museum in Stockholm combines historical buildings, folk-life, wildlife and livestock. Kulturen in Lund and Jamtli in Östersund are among the best locations to taste old-time Sweden. Don't miss Malmöhus Castle in Malmö or the Vasamuseet in Stockholm. Skåne has some very fine Danish castles. Fine examples of cathedral *(domkyrka)* styles include Lund (Romanesque), Uppsala (Gothic) and Kalmar (baroque).

PLANNING

If you want the best chance of getting sunshine, visit between late May and late July, bearing in mind that August can be wet.

There are quite a number of hostels, camping grounds and attractions which only open from late June to mid-August. Summer can be hot, sunny and beautiful, but also busy with holidaying Swedes. Travel in winter is somewhat restricted.

TOURIST OFFICES

Sweden has about 350 local tourist information offices. Most are open long hours in summer and short hours (or not at all) during winter, and a few exhibit nomadic tendencies. Offices in big towns stock brochures from all around Sweden. The website **w** www.turism.se claims to list all of Sweden's tourist information offices and their contact details.

The following overseas-based offices can assist with inquiries and provide tourist promotional material. In countries without a designated tourist office, a good starting point is the Swedish embassy.

France (☎ 01 53 43 26 27, ⓔ servinfo@suede-tourisme.fr) Office Suédois du Tourisme et des Voyages, 18 boulevarde Malesherbes, F-75008 Paris
Germany (☎ 040-32 55 13 55, ⓔ info@swetourism.de) Schweden-Werbung für Reisen und Touristik, Lilienstrasse 19, DE-20095 Hamburg
UK (☎ 020-7870 5600, 00800-3080 3080, ⓔ info@swetourism.org.uk) Swedish Travel & Tourism Council, 5 Upper Montagu St, London W1H 2AG
USA (☎ 212-885 9700, ⓔ info@gosweden.org) Swedish Travel & Tourism Council, PO Box 4649, Grand Central Station, New York NY 10163-4649

VISAS & DOCUMENTS

Citizens of the EU, Norway and Iceland can enter with a passport or a national identification card. Nationals of Nordic countries can stay and work indefinitely.

Passport-holders from Australia, New Zealand, Canada and the US can enter and stay in Sweden without a visa for up to three months. Citizens of South Africa and many other African, Asian and some Eastern European countries require tourist visas.

Migrationsverket *(☎ 011-156000; ⓦ www.migrationsverket.se)* handles all applications for visas and work or residency permits.

EMBASSIES

Swedish Embassies & Consulates

A complete list of Swedish missions abroad is available in English at ⓦ www.utrikes.regeringen.se.

Australia (☎ 02-6270 2700, ⓦ www.embassyofsweden.org.au) 5 Turrana St, Yarralumla ACT 2600
Canada (☎ 613-241 8553, ⓦ www.swedishembassy.ca) 377 Dalhousie St, Ottawa K1N 9N8
Denmark (☎ 33 36 03 70, ⓦ www.sverigesambassad.dk) Sankt Annæ Plads 15A, DK-1250 Copenhagen K
Finland (☎ 09-6877 660, ⓦ www.sverige.fi) Pohjoisesplanadi 7B, 00170 Helsinki
France (☎ 01 44 18 88 00, ⓦ www.amb-suede.fr) 17 rue Barbet-de-Jouy, F-75007 Paris
Germany (☎ 030-505 060, ⓦ www.schweden.org) Rauchstrasse 1, 107 87 Berlin
Ireland (☎ 01-671 5822, ⓦ www.swedishembassy.ie) 13-17 Dawson St, Dublin 2
Netherlands (☎ 070-412 0200, ⓦ www.swedenembnl.org) Burg Van Karnebeeklaan 6A, 2508 Den Haag
New Zealand (☎ 04-499 9895) Vogel Building, 13th Floor, Aitken St, Wellington
Norway (☎ 24 11 42 00, ⓦ www.sverigesambassad.no) Nobelsgate 16, NO-0244 Oslo
UK (☎ 020-7917 6400, ⓦ www.swedish-embassy.org.uk) 11 Montagu Place, London W1H 2AL
USA (☎ 202-467 2600, ⓦ www.swedish-embassy.org) Suite 900, 1501 M St NW, Washington DC 20005-1702

Embassies & Consulates in Sweden

The diplomatic missions listed here are in Stockholm (area code ☎ 08), although some neighbouring countries also have consulates in Gothenburg, Malmö and Helsingborg:

Australia (☎ 613 2900) 11th floor, Sergels Torg 12
Canada (☎ 453 3000) Tegelbacken 4
Denmark (☎ 406 7500) Jakobs Torg 1
Finland (☎ 676 6700) Gärdesgatan 9-11
France (☎ 459 5300) Kommendörsgatan 13
Germany (☎ 670 1500) Skarpögatan 9
Ireland (☎ 661 8005) Östermalmsgatan 97
Netherlands (☎ 556 93300) Götgatan 16A
New Zealand (☎ 660 0460) Nybrogatan 34
Norway (☎ 665 6340) Skarpögatan 4
UK (☎ 671 9000) Skarpögatan 6-8
USA (☎ 783 5300) Dag Hammarskjöldsväg 31

CUSTOMS

Going through customs rarely involves any hassles, but rules on illegal drugs are strictly enforced. Duty-free allowances for travellers from outside the EU are: 1L of spirits or 2L of fortified wine; 2L of wine; and 32L of strong beer. The limits on goods brought into Sweden from another EU country are more generous: 2L of spirits or 6L of fortified wine, 26L of wine and 32L of strong beer.

MONEY

You should encounter few problems if you carry cash in any convertible currency or international travellers cheques. Although not all machines are fully connected, the national Minuten and Bankomat ATM networks provided by Swedish banks accept international Visa, Plus, EC, Eurocard, Cirrus or MasterCard ATM cards.

Forex, found in the biggest cities and most airports and ferry terminals, is one of the cheapest and easiest places to exchange money and charges Skr15 per cheque. Banks charge up to Skr60 per cheque. You can buy foreign notes (no fee) at Forex. The X-Change centres also offer good deals, but have fewer branches.

Currency

The Swedish krona (plural: *kronor*), usually called 'crown' in English, is denoted Skr and divided into 100 *öre* (prices are rounded to the nearest 50 öre). Coins are 50 öre and one, five and 10 kronor, and notes are 20, 50, 100, 500 and 1000 kronor.

Exchange Rates

The following exchange rates prevailed at the time of printing:

country	unit		kronor
Australia	A$1	=	Skr5.15
Canada	C$1	=	Skr6.00
Denmark	Dkr1	=	Skr1.25
Eurozone	€1	=	Skr9.25
New Zealand	NZ$1	=	Skr4.40
Norway	Nkr1	=	Skr1.25
UK	UK£1	=	Skr14.85
USA	US$1	=	Skr9.50

Costs

Prices are high. With a tent you can sleep freely in forests. Bring sheets and a Hostel International (HI) membership card, and you pay Skr80 to Skr200 per night in each of the 300-plus STF hostels. Students with an ISIC card (and often seniors) are eligible for discounts in museums, theatres and cinemas.

Stuff yourself at breakfast buffets for about Skr45 (included in the price at most hotels), or choose a lunch special (the *dagens rätt*, usually around Skr50) instead of dining à la carte in the evening. Takeaway pizzas and kebabs are more inexpensive options, and good kitchen facilities at hostels and camping grounds make self-catering easy.

To save money on transport, ask about daily or weekly passes. Get a rail pass and explore towns and regions by foot or on bicycle.

Tipping & Bargaining

Service charges are usually included in restaurant bills and taxi fares, but there's no problem if you want to reward good service with a tip (or round up the taxi fare).

Bargaining isn't customary.

Taxes & Refunds

The main additional cost for the traveller is *mervärdeskatt* or *moms*, the value-added tax (VAT) on goods and services, included in the marked price. This may be as much as 25%.

At shops that display the sign 'Tax Free Shopping', non-EU citizens making single purchases of goods exceeding Skr200 (including *moms*) are eligible for a VAT refund of 15% to 18% of the purchase price.

POST & COMMUNICATIONS

Service outlets of Posten (the Swedish postal service) are opening in some 3000 new venues and will be open long hours. These outlets will offer stamps *(frimärken)* and a letter *(brev)* and package *(paket)* service. You can also buy stamps from many tourist offices, convenience stores, tobacconists and newsagents. For poste restante, the person sending you mail will need to specify which outlet you'll be collecting from, with a specific address and postal code.

Almost all public telephones in Sweden take Telia phonecards. Many Telia booths also accept credit cards, but there are virtually no coin phones in public areas (although some hostels, camping grounds and restaurants may have them). For directory assistance dial ☎ 118118 (for numbers within Sweden) or ☎ 118119 (international), but note that these services aren't free.

For international calls dial ☎ 00 followed by the country code and the local area code. Calls to Sweden from abroad require the country code (☎ 46) followed by the area code (omitting the initial zero) and telephone number.

Internet cafés typically charge around Skr1 per online minute, or Skr50 per hour. However, facilities to log on can be frustratingly rare outside big cities. Many tourist offices now offer a computer terminal for visitor use (sometimes for free). Nearly all public libraries offer free Internet access.

DIGITAL RESOURCES

Most Swedish organisations have their own websites, and many of these have pages in English. The official website for the Swedish Travel and Tourism Council is at W www.visit-sweden.com. Other good sites for tourist information are W www.sweden.se and W www.sverigeturism.se.

BOOKS

Lonely Planet produces a comprehensive *Sweden* guidebook, which is a good place to start for a more in-depth look at the country.

Lonely Planet also produces a *Stockholm* city guide.

To get a handle on the country, try *A History of Sweden* by Lars O Lagerqvist or *A Journey Through Swedish History* by Herman Lindqvist.

WOMEN TRAVELLERS

Solo female travellers are unlikely to face the sort of harassment received in parts of southern Europe. Some hostels have segregated dorms, and you can ask for a women-only compartment if you don't want male company in a 2nd-class rail sleeping compartment. Some Stockholm taxi firms offer discounts for women at night.

GAY & LESBIAN TRAVELLERS

Sweden is famous for its liberal attitudes, and its laws allowing same-sex 'registered partnerships', which grant most marriage rights. The organisation concerned with equality for lesbians and gays is **Riksförbundet för Sexuellt Likaberättigande** *(RFSL; ☎ 08-736 0213; Sveavägen 59, Stockholm)*.

One of the capital's biggest parties is the annual **Stockholm Pride** *(W www.stockholmpride.org)*, a five-day festival celebrating gay culture, held in late July or early August.

A good source of information for gay travellers is the free, monthly magazine *QX*, giving gay and lesbian information and listings (again, only in Swedish). You can pick it up at many clubs, stores and restaurants, mainly in Stockholm, Gothenburg, Malmö and Copenhagen. Its website (W www.qx.se) has some excellent information and recommendations in English.

DISABLED TRAVELLERS

Sweden is perhaps one of the easiest countries to travel around in a wheelchair. For information about facilities, contact the national organisation for people with disabilities, **De Handikappades Riksförbund** *(☎ 08-685 8000; W www.dhr.se; Katrinebergsvägen 6 (Box 47305), SE-10074 Stockholm)*.

DANGERS & ANNOYANCES

Crimes perpetrated against travellers (such as pickpocketing) are on the increase; take particular care in museums and transport terminals in Stockholm. Drug-related crime and a few trouble spots in big cities are also of some concern.

Emergencies

The toll-free general emergency number is ☎ 112.

BUSINESS HOURS

Businesses and government offices are open 8.30am or 9am to 5pm Monday to Friday, although they can close at 3pm in summer. Banks usually open at 9.30am and close at 3pm, but some city branches open 9am to 5pm or 6pm. Most museums have short opening hours and many tourist offices are closed at weekends from mid-August to mid-June.

Normal shopping hours are 9am to 6pm weekdays and 9am to between 1pm and 4pm on Saturday, but department stores are open longer and sometimes also on Sunday. Some supermarkets in large towns will open until 7pm or 9pm. In restaurants, lunch often begins at 11.30am and is over by 2pm. Stockholm has convenience stores such as 7-Eleven, which are open 24 hours.

Frustratingly, many hostels, especially those belonging to the STF network, are closed between 10am and 5pm. See Hostels in the Accommodation section later in this chapter for information.

PUBLIC HOLIDAYS & SPECIAL EVENTS

There's a concentration of public holidays in spring and early summer, and Midsummer in particular brings life almost to a halt for three days. Transport and other services are reduced, so read your timetables carefully, and plan ahead: some food stores are open and many tourist offices (usually with reduced hours), but not all attractions. Some hotels are closed from Christmas to New Year and it's not uncommon for restaurants in larger cities to close during July and early August (when their owners join the holidaying throngs in beach or lakeside areas).

The following public holidays are observed in Sweden: New Year's Day (1 January), Epiphany (6 January); Good Friday to Easter Monday (March/April); Labour Day (1 May); Ascension Day (May/June); Whit Monday (late May or early June); Midsummer's Day (first Saturday after 21 June); All Saints' Day (a Saturday in late October or early November); Christmas Day (25 December) and Boxing Day (26 December).

Note that some businesses will close early the day before and all day after public holidays. Christmas Eve, New Year's Eve and Midsummer's Eve are not official holidays, but are generally nonworking days for most of the population.

New Year's Eve is a fairly big event. Walpurgis Night (Valborgsmässoafton) on 30 April is popular with students, who are easy to spot in Uppsala and Lund.

May Day (1 May) is observed by marches and other labour movement events that stop the traffic. Flag Day, the national day, is 6 June – but it's not a public holiday.

Midsummer is *the* festival of the year. Maypole dancing is a traditional activity on Midsummer's Eve and most people head for the countryside.

Since 1927, the Lucia festival on 13 December has become very popular. Christmas Eve is the main day of celebration during this season; it's the night of the *smörgåsbord* and the arrival of *jultomten*, the Christmas gnome carrying a sack of gifts.

ACTIVITIES

Outdoor pastimes are popular with Swedes, who are active on bicycles, forest jogging tracks, rivers and lakes, mountain trails and the snow and ice. By law, you're allowed to walk, boat, ski or swim anywhere outside private property. You're allowed to camp in forests, and you may pick berries and mushrooms. You may not leave any rubbish nor take living plants. Fires may be set where safe (not on bare rocks) with fallen wood. Cars may not be driven across open land or on private roads.

Skating

Wherever and whenever the ice is thick enough (usually between December and March), Stockholm's lake and canal system is exploited by skating enthusiasts seeking the longest possible 'run'.

Skiing

Cross-country (nordic) skiing opportunities vary depending on the snow and temperatures, but the northwest usually has plenty of snow from December to April (although not a lot of daylight in December and January). Practically all town areas (except in the far south) have marked skiing tracks, often illuminated. There are large ski resorts catering mainly for downhill skiing in the mountainous areas of the west – Åre is the biggest. The websites **W** www.goski.com and **W** www.thealps.com have good pages reviewing the Swedish ski fields.

Hiking

Popular everywhere, the challenge of hiking in the mountains of the northern national parks is especially compelling. However, these parks are rarely snow-free and the jewel, Sarek, is only for experienced hikers. Good equipment is vital.

Easy walking trails are common. The best time for hiking is between late June and mid-September, but conditions are much better after early August, when all the mosquitoes have gone.

For information on organised group walks and the STF mountain huts, which are placed at intervals averaging about 20km along popular trails such as Kungsleden, contact STF (see Accommodation later in this chapter).

Canoeing & Kayaking

Sweden's superb wilderness lakes and white-water rivers are a real paradise for canoeists and kayakers. The national canoeing body is **Svenska Kanotförbundet** *(☎ 08-605 6000; **W** www.kanot.com; Idrottens Hus, SE-12387 Farsta)*. It provides general advice and produces *Kanotvåg*, an annual brochure listing the 75 approved canoe centres that hire canoes (from Skr140/500 per day/week) throughout the country. Canoeists may paddle or moor virtually anywhere provided they respect the basic privacy of dwellings and avoid sensitive nesting areas within nature reserves. More good information is available on the Internet at **W** www.kanotguiden.com.

WORK

Non-EU citizens need to apply for a work permit and residence permit (for stays over three months), enclosing confirmation of the job offer, a completed form (available from Swedish diplomatic posts), a passport photo and copy of your passport. EU citizens must apply for a residence permit within three months of arrival if they find work; then they can remain in Sweden for the duration of their employment (up to five years). Australians and New Zealanders aged 18 to 30 years can now qualify for a one-year working holiday visa. Full details of all permits and how you can apply are available online at **w** www.migrationsverket.se (the Swedish migration board's site).

Helpful information is available on the Internet at **w** www.ams.se (Swedish National Labour Market Administration or AMV).

ACCOMMODATION

Camping

Sweden has hundreds of camping grounds. The best time for camping is from May to August. Prices vary with facilities, from Skr70 for a basic site to Skr200 for the highest standards. Most camping grounds have kitchens and laundry facilities, and many are extremely popular family holiday spots with the works – swimming pool, minigolf, bicycle and canoe rental, restaurant, store etc. If you're a solo hiker or cyclist, you should be able to get a cheap site (around Skr80); otherwise you'll pay the full rate.

The Camping Card Scandinavia/Svenskt Campingkort is required if to stay at camping grounds in Sweden. Apply, at least a month before your journey, to **Sveriges Campingvärdars Riksförbund** *(fax 0522-642430;* **e** *adm@scr.se; Box 255, SE-45117 Uddevalla)*. If this isn't possible, you'll be given a temporary card on arrival. The card is free, but to be valid you need an annual stamp on your card that costs Skr90 and is obtainable at the first camping ground you visit. Visit **w** www.camping.se for lots of useful information.

See also the Activities section for advice on free camping in Sweden.

Hostels

Sweden has well over 450 hostels (*vandrarhem*); some 320 are 'official' hostels affiliated with **Svenska Turistföreningen** *(STF;* ☎ *08-463 2100;* **e** *info@stfturist.se; Box 25, SE-10120 Stockholm)*, part of HI. All hostel details are on the website **w** www.meravsverige.nu. Holders of HI cards stay at STF hostels for between Skr80 and Skr200. Nonmembers can pay Skr45 extra per night or join up at hostels (membership costs Skr275 for adults, Skr100 for those aged 16 to 25, free for children). In this chapter we have listed prices for members.

Around 150 hostels belong to the 'rival' **Sveriges Vandrarhem i Förening** *(SVIF;* ☎ *0413-553 450;* **e** *info@svif.se; Box 9, SE-45043 Smögen)*. No membership is required and rates are similar to those of the STF. Pick up the free guide at tourist offices or SVIF hostels. Also look out for other hostels that are not affiliated with either STF or SVIF.

Hostels in Sweden are hard to get into outside reception opening times. The secret is to phone and make a reservation during the (usually short) reception hours; they'll provide you with an entry code. Written reservations are recommended, but cancellation is only accepted up to 6pm the previous day, otherwise you'll be charged for one overnight stay. Breakfast is often available (Skr40 to Skr55), but normally has to be arranged the night before.

Many mountain huts and lodges are run by STF and also charge overnight fees.

Cabins & Chalets

Daily rates for cabins and chalets at camping grounds offer good value for small groups and families and range in both facilities and price (Skr200 to Skr800). Some cabins are simple, with bunk beds and little else (you share the bathroom and kitchen facilities with campers); others are fully quipped with their own kitchen, bathroom and even living room. Local and regional tourist offices have listings of cabins and cottages that may be rented by the week and are very popular with Swedes in summer.

Hotels

There are few cheap hotels in Sweden. Budget travellers may find weekend and summer (mid-June to mid-August) rates reasonable, often below Skr700 for a luxurious double with en suite. Stockholm, Gothenburg and Malmö offer cut-price 'packages' that include a hotel room, free entry to the major attractions of the city and free local transport – plus an optional discounted return train ticket. Tourist offices and travel agents can usually give details.

FOOD & DRINKS

Husmanskost specials are solid, meat-based, cafeteria-style meals such as *köttbullar och potatis* (meatballs and potatoes), *lövbiff & strips* (thinly sliced fried meat and chips), *pytt i panna* (Swedish hash) and *black & white* (steak with mashed potato). Other traditional dishes include: *kroppkakor* (boiled balls of potato containing pre-fried pork, found mainly in the south), sausages and *surströmming* (fermented herring – definitely an acquired taste). Meat, game and poultry dishes are the mainstay of Swedish menus. There's usually at least one lamb and one chicken dish on a restaurant menu.

Coffee is Sweden's unofficial national drink, but tea is also available. *Saft* (concentrated fruit juice) is commonly made from lingonberries and blueberries and *Festis* is a pleasant noncarbonated fruit drink.

You're advised to bring your duty-free allowance into Sweden because alcohol is fairly expensive in the country. Beers are ranked by alcohol content, and include *lättöl* (less than 2.25%), *folköl* (2.25% to 3.5%) *mellanöl* (3.5% to 4.5%) and *starköl* (over 4.5%). Sweden produces its own spirit, *brännvin, snaps* or *aquavit* (vodka), which is a fiery drink, usually distilled from potatoes.

ENTERTAINMENT

Discos and nightclubs usually admit no-one aged under 20, although the minimum age limit for men may be 23 and sometimes 25. Drinking at these places is an expensive option. Cover charges range from Skr60 to Skr150 and cloakrooms charge around Skr20. Pubs and restaurants charge around Skr40 to Skr50 for the standard 500mL *storstark* (strong beer), although the cheaper 300mL bottle is common.

Prices of theatre tickets cost from Skr100 to Skr500.

Getting There & Away

AIR

There are plenty of European companies that sell inexpensive flights to Stockholm via their hub. Note that Copenhagen airport is just 25-odd minutes by train from Malmö, so check whether cheaper flights to Copenhagen are available.

Although **SAS** *(w www.scandinavian.net)* is based in Copenhagen, it has plenty of direct international flights to Stockholm. The discount carrier **Ryanair** *(w www.ryanair.com)* flies between London Stansted and Gothenburg, Malmö, and two airports about an hour from Stockholm (Skavsta in Nyköping, and Västerås) from only UK£45 return (plus taxes). **Good Jet** *(w www.goodjet.com)* is a new Swedish budget airline that offers cheap flights from Stockholm, Gothenburg and Malmö to Paris, Nice and Alicante.

LAND

Direct access to Sweden by land is possible from Norway, Finland and Denmark. Train and bus journeys are also possible from the Continent – these vehicles go directly on to ferries and if you sleep, you won't even notice the sea journey!

The new Öresund toll bridge linking Copenhagen with Malmö was officially opened in July 2000, creating a major direct rail/road link with Denmark.

Eurolines *(☎ 020-987377; w www.eurolines.se)*, the long-distance bus operator, is represented in Stockholm by Busstop in Cityterminalen. Tickets can also be purchased from the head office in Gothenburg (Kyrkogatan 40).

The Continent

Eurolines' bus services run between several European cities, including Stockholm and London (from Skr1624/2524 one way/return, 30 hours) via Amsterdam and Hamburg, with one to four services per week. Gothenburg–Berlin costs from Skr549 one way (13 to 16 hours, daily), while Stockholm–Berlin costs from Skr818 (18 to 20 hours, three weekly).

Direct overnight trains run daily between Berlin and Malmö via Trelleborg and Sassnitz. See w www.berlin-night-express.com for details.

Eurolines runs buses five days per week between Stockholm and Copenhagen (Skr433/482 low/high season, nine hours) and daily between Gothenburg and Copenhagen (Skr180/260, 4½ hours). **Säfflebussen** *(☎ 020-160 0600; w www.safflebussen.se)* buses also regularly connect the same cities for much the same prices (slightly cheaper on the daily Stockholm–Copenhagen route).

Trains run every 20 minutes between Copenhagen and Malmö (Skr70, 35 minutes), and connect with many towns in Skåne. Trains usually stop at Copenhagen airport. Around 10 daily X2000 trains run between Copenhagen and Stockholm, via Norrköping, Linköping, Lund and Malmö. A further five or six X2000 services operate between Copenhagen and Gothenburg via Halmstad, Helsingborg, Lund and Malmö. There are trains every hour or two connecting Copenhagen, Kristianstad and Karlskrona.

Finland

There are seven crossing points along the river border – see the Finland chapter for details. Bus services from Luleå to Haparanda, Övertorneå and Pajala on the Swedish side are run by **Länstrafiken i Norrbotten** (☎ *020-470 047*). **Tapanis Buss** (☎ *0922-12955*) runs express coaches from Stockholm to Tornio via Haparanda twice a week (Skr450, 15 hours).

Train passengers can only reach Boden or Luleå in northern Sweden – from there it's necessary to continue by bus.

Norway

There are more than 20 border crossing points and formalities range from the nonexistent to hardly noticeable.

Säfflebussen (☎ *020-160 0600*) runs five times daily between Stockholm and Oslo (from Skr250, 7½ hours), and six times daily between Gothenburg and Oslo (from Skr150, four hours). **Swebus Express** (☎ *0200-218218*; **w** *www.swebusexpress.se*) runs three times daily on the Stockholm–Oslo route and six times daily between Gothenburg and Oslo, charging very similar prices.

Once-daily buses from Umeå to Mo i Rana (Skr210, 8½ hours) and from Skellefteå to Bodø (Skr400, nine hours) are run by **Länstrafiken Västerbotten** (☎ *020-910019*) and **Länstrafiken i Norrbotten** (☎ *020-470047*), respectively. In a number of counties, *länstrafiken* runs buses to within a few kilometres of the Norwegian border.

The main rail links run from Stockholm to Oslo, from Gothenburg to Oslo, from Stockholm to Östersund and Storlien (Norwegian trains continue to Trondheim), and from Luleå to Kiruna and Narvik.

SEA

See the Getting Around chapter for contact details of all the international ferry companies listed here.

Denmark

There are numerous ferries between Denmark and Sweden, although all boats between Malmö and Copenhagen ceased operation in 2002. The quickest and most frequent services are between Helsingør and Helsingborg (Skr18 to Skr22); passenger cars can do the journey with five passengers for Skr245.

There are also services between Jutland and Sweden. **Stena Line** cruises between Gothenburg and Frederikshavn five to seven times daily and takes three hours (Skr100 to Skr170), although their fast ferry covers the journey in only two hours (Skr140 to Skr195). Stena Line also sails numerous times daily between Grenå and Varberg (Skr100 to Skr140, four hours).

Bornholm Ferries sails daily from Ystad to Rønne. There are both conventional (2½ hours) and fast (80 minutes) services, two to nine times daily. Passenger fares are from Skr182 to Skr234.

Finland

Daily services throughout the year are available on Stockholm–Turku and Stockholm–Helsinki routes all via the Åland islands. There are inexpensive connections to Åland from Kapellskär and Grisslehamn, both accessible via Norrtälje, north of Stockholm. Further north, there's a connection from Umeå to Vaasa. See towns sections and the Finland chapter for further details. Note that Helsinki is called Helsingfors in Swedish, and Turku is known as Åbo.

Norway

There are plenty of bus and train services between the two countries, but if you get stuck in Strömstad, there are frequent ferries to Sandefjord.

DFDS Seaways runs daily overnight ferries between Copenhagen and Oslo, via Helsingborg. Fares between Helsingborg and Oslo (14 hours) vary according to the season and day of the week, and range from Skr625 to Skr1025. DFDS Seaways also sails from Gothenburg to Kristiansand (Skr150 to Skr400, seven hours, three per week).

Germany

Trelleborg is the main gateway with more than a dozen ferry services daily. **TT-Line** sails between Trelleborg and both Travemünde and Rostock (prices for both from Skr270); **Scandlines** is cheaper and sails to/from Rostock and Sassnitz (Skr70 to Skr195).

Stena Line cruises between Gothenburg and Kiel daily (Skr310/370/610 low/mid/high season, 13½ hours).

Poland

There are daily summer services (less frequent in winter) between Świnoujście and Ystad (Skr450/520 low/high season, nine hours), provided by **Unity Line**; Gdynia and Karlskrona (Skr335/395, 10½ to 12 hours), operated by **Stena Line**, and Gdańsk and Nynäshamn (Skr470/540, 19 hours), run by **Polferries**.

Baltic Countries

Tallink sails daily between Sweden and Estonia on two routes: Stockholm–Tallinn (from Skr300, 16 hours), and Kapellskär–Paldiski (from Skr175, 10 to 11 hours). **V-V Line** *(W www.vvline.com)* connects Paldiski and Västervik a few times a week (tickets are much more expensive than Tallink at Skr1000). V-V Line also connects Nynäshamn and Ventspils in Latvia daily except Monday (Skr800, 10 hours)

Lisco Line sails on weekdays between Klaipėda in Lithuania and Karlshamn (from Skr570, 18 hours). **Riga Sea Line** sails between Nynäshamn and Riga in Latvia every second day (from Skr672, eight hours).

The UK

DFDS Seaways has two crossings per week from Gothenburg to Newcastle via Kristiansand (Norway), taking 25 hours. Single fares start at Skr550/1175 in the low/high season.

Getting Around

Public transport is well organised using 24 different, heavily subsidised regional networks. Confusion is alleviated by the Tågplus system, where one ticket is valid on trains and *länstrafik* buses. Handy local timetables are available free or at nominal cost from tourist offices or the operators. National air and train networks have discount schemes available.

The helpful site W www.tagplus.se has timetables for all trains, boats and buses in Sweden.

AIR

Sweden's half-dozen domestic airlines mostly use Stockholm Arlanda as a hub. **SAS** *(☎ 020-727000; W www.scandinavian.net)* has daily domestic flights that serve the country from Malmö to Kiruna, but **Skyways** *(☎ 020-959500; W www.skyways.se)* runs a larger network. **Malmö Aviation** *(☎ 020-550010; W www.malmoaviation.se)* also flies between major cities.

Flying is quite expensive, but substantial discounts are available, such as return tickets booked at least seven days in advance or low-price tickets for accompanying family members and seniors.

BUS

You can travel by bus in Sweden either on national long-distance routes, or using any of the regional *länstrafik* networks.

Regional Traffic

Länstrafik is usually complemented by the regional train system, and one ticket is valid on any bus, local or regional. Transfers are usually free within one to four hours. Most counties are divided into zones; travel within one zone will cost from Skr13 to Skr17. Every time you enter a new zone, the price increases.

Timetables explain the various discount schemes. There are usually good-value daily or weekly passes. The *värdekort* (value card), which you can 'top up' at any time, is also good: you pay, say, Skr200 for over Skr250 worth of travelling. Always ask how the regional discount pass works: you may have to run the ticket through a machine, press buttons, tell the driver where you want to go, get your ticket stamped or something else.

Express Buses

Swebus Express *(☎ 0200-218218; W www.swebusexpress.se)* has the largest 'national network' of express buses, but services run only as far north as Mora. Fares for 'long' journeys (over 100km) are 30% cheaper if you travel between Monday and Thursday. **Svenska Buss** *(☎ 0771-676767; W www.svenskabuss.se)* and cheaper **Säfflebussen** *(☎ 020-160 0600; W www.safflebussen.se)* also connect many southern towns and cities with Stockholm. North of Gävle, good connections with Stockholm are provided by **Ybuss** *(☎ 0200-334444; W www.ybuss.se)* from Sundsvall, Östersund and Umeå.

If you're a student or senior, it's worth asking for a discount. Only Swebus Express doesn't require advance seat reservations – it always guarantees a seat.

TRAIN

Using trains is certainly the fastest way to get around. The national network **Sveriges Järnväg** *(SJ; ☎ 0771-757575; W www.sj.se)* covers most main lines, especially in the south.

Its flag carriers are the X2000 fast trains running at speeds of up to 200km/h, with services from Stockholm to major destinations. **Tågkompaniet** (☎ *020-444111*; Ⓦ *www.tagkompaniet.se*) operates train services in the far north, and several counties run small regional train networks.

Full-price 2nd-class tickets are expensive, but there are discounts, especially for booking a week or so in advance. Students (with a Swedish CSN or SFS student card if aged over 26) and people under 26 get a 30% discount. All SJ ticket prices are reduced in summer, from late June to mid-August. X2000 tickets include a seat reservation. SJ trains won't carry bicycles.

In summer, almost 25 different tourist trains offer special rail experiences. The most notable is **Inlandsbanan** (☎ *063-194409*; Ⓦ *www.inlandsbanan.se*), a 1067km route from Mora to Gällivare and one of the great rail journeys in Scandinavia. Travel on this line is slow (the train travels at a speed of 50km/h) and it takes seven hours from Mora to Östersund (Skr240) and 15 hours from Östersund to Gällivare (Skr485). A special card allows 14 days' unlimited travel on the route for Skr950.

Train Passes

The Sweden Rail Pass, Eurodomino tickets and Inter-Rail, Eurail and ScanRail passes are accepted on SJ services and most other operators, such as regional trains. Exceptions are the local SL *pendeltåg* trains around Stockholm, and Inlandsbanan (which only gives ScanRail card-holders a 25% discount on the Skr950, 14-day ticket; Inter-Rail pass-holders aged under 26 can ride the Inlandsbanan for free).

X2000 trains require all rail pass–holders to pay a supplement of Skr50. The reservation supplements for non-X2000 (ie, InterCity) trains (Skr50) aren't obligatory, and there are no supplements for regional *länstrafik* trains.

Obtaining rail passes in Sweden isn't very convenient, but they can be arranged in advance through **Sweden Booking** (☎ *0498-203380*; Ⓦ *www.swedenbooking.com*) for a Skr115 fee.

CAR & MOTORCYCLE

You usually need only a recognised full driving licence, even for car rental. If bringing your own car, take your vehicle registration documents. In case of breakdown, call the **Larmtjänst 24-hour towing service** (☎ *020-910040*).

The Swedish national motoring association is **Motormännens Riksförbund** (☎ *020-211111, 08-690 3800; Sveavägen 159, SE-10435 Stockholm*).

International rental chains are expensive, starting at around Skr600 per day for smaller models. Fly-drive packages can bring some savings, and discount weekend or summer packages may also be offered. All the major firms (eg, Avis, Hertz, Europcar) have desks at Stockholm's Arlanda airport and offices in most major cities. **Mabi Hyrbilar** (☎ *020-110 1000*; Ⓦ *www.mabirent.se*) is a good national company with branches in many major cities and competitive rates.

Cars can be hired from petrol stations at better rates, but must be returned to the hiring point.

BICYCLE

Skåne and Gotland are ideal for cycling. The best season is May to September in the south, and July and August in the north.

One-gear bike hire is free in some towns, but multi-gear bikes can cost up to Skr200/800 per day/week. If you want to buy secondhand, try bicycle workshops in university towns first.

Some country areas, towns and cities have special cycle routes – check with local tourist offices for information and maps.

HITCHING

Hitchhiking isn't popular. However, the main highways (E4, E6, E10 and E22) aren't too bad and very long lifts are possible. You can't hitch on motorways.

BOAT

The national road authority, Vägverket, operates dozens of car ferries, but many are being replaced with bridges. They're part of the road network and are free.

An extensive boat network opens up the attractive Stockholm archipelago, and boat services on Lake Mälaren, west of Stockholm, are busy in summer. Gotland is served by regular ferries from Nynäshamn and Oskarshamn, and summer services run to many other small islands off the coast.

Boat passes, valid for 16 days (Skr385), are available for the Stockholm archipelago.

The canals provide cross-country routes linking the main lakes.

LOCAL TRANSPORT

In Sweden, local transport is always linked with the regional *länstrafik* – rules and prices for city buses may differ slightly from long-distance transport, but a regional pass is valid both in the city and on the rural routes. There's usually a flat fare of around Skr15 in towns.

Stockholm has an extensive underground metro system, and Gothenburg runs a good tram network. Gothenburg also has a city ferry service. Taxis are expensive. Beware of getting ripped off by taxi drivers – don't get in one without agreeing on the fare first.

Stockholm

☎ 08 • pop 755,000

Stockholm is undoubtedly one of the world's most beautiful national capitals, and right now it's an extremely hip destination. True, the city's fringe is an industrial mess and some suburbs seem inspired by Kafkaesque or Stalinist baroque – but Gamla Stan (the Old Town) is particularly lovely, and most travellers won't see the unlovely bits.

Stockholm is a royal capital that has always been ideally situated for trade and maritime connections. The 24,000 islands of the *skärgård* (archipelago) protect the urban islands from the open seas. More than 15% of Greater Stockholm's 1.8 million residents are immigrants, which makes for a lively, international atmosphere.

The city is best seen from the water, but you'll also enjoy seeing the parklands of Djurgården or the alleys of Gamla Stan on foot. Stockholm also has the widest selection of budget accommodation in Scandinavia and, although it isn't really cheap, it's certainly clean and comfortable.

Orientation

Stockholm is built on islands, except for the modern centre (Norrmalm), which is focused on the ugly square known as Sergels Torg. This business and shopping hub is linked by a network of subways to Centralstationen (the central train station); these subways also link with the *tunnelbana* (metro; or T) stations. The large, busy tourist office is in the eastern part of Norrmalm; the popular garden, Kungsträdgården, is almost next door.

Information

Tourist Offices Stockholm's main tourist office is at **Sweden House** *(Sverigehuset; ☎ 789 2490; e info@stoinfo.se; Hamngatan 27; open daily)*, by Kungsträdgården. It has lots of good brochures and can book hotel rooms, theatre and concert tickets, and packages such as boat trips to the archipelago. More convenient for arriving travellers is the busy **Hotellcentralen** *(☎ 789 2490; Centralstationen; open daily)*, inside the main train station. Both offices sell the Stockholm Card (which covers transportation and many attractions), Stockholm Package (which includes the Stockholm Card and a hotel room) and SL Tourist Card.

Money The exchange company **Forex** has about a dozen branches here; all charge Skr15 per travellers cheque. Handy locations are at Arlanda airport; inside Centralstationen (open 7am to 9pm daily) and also opposite it at Vasagatan 14; and inside Sweden House.

There are ATMs all over town, including a few at Centralstationen, usually with long queues. There are banks around Sergels Torg and along Hamngatan.

Post & Communications The longest hours are offered by the always-busy Centralstationen **post office** *(open 7am-10pm Mon-Fri, 10am-7pm Sat & Sun)*. You can now send letters from a number of city locations, including newsagents and some supermarkets.

Café Access *(Sergels Torg; open Tues-Sun)*, downstairs in Kulturhuset, is a central cybercafé where 30 minutes online costs Skr20. On the northern side of town, **Nine** *(Odengatan 44; open to midnight or 1am daily)* charges roughly Skr45 for an hour – and there's a good café here too. **Ice** *(Vasagatan 42; open to midnight)*, close to Centralstationen, charges Skr30/50 for 30/60 minutes online.

At the main city library, **Stadsbiblioteket** *(Sveavägen 73)*, free 'drop-in' computers are available 10am to 7pm daily (maximum 15 minutes online; email is accessible).

Travel Agencies For companies that specialise in discount youth and student flights, try **STA** *(☎ 545 26666; Kungsgatan 30)* and the nearby **Kilroy Travels** *(☎ 0771-545769; Kungsgatan 4)*.

STOCKHOLM

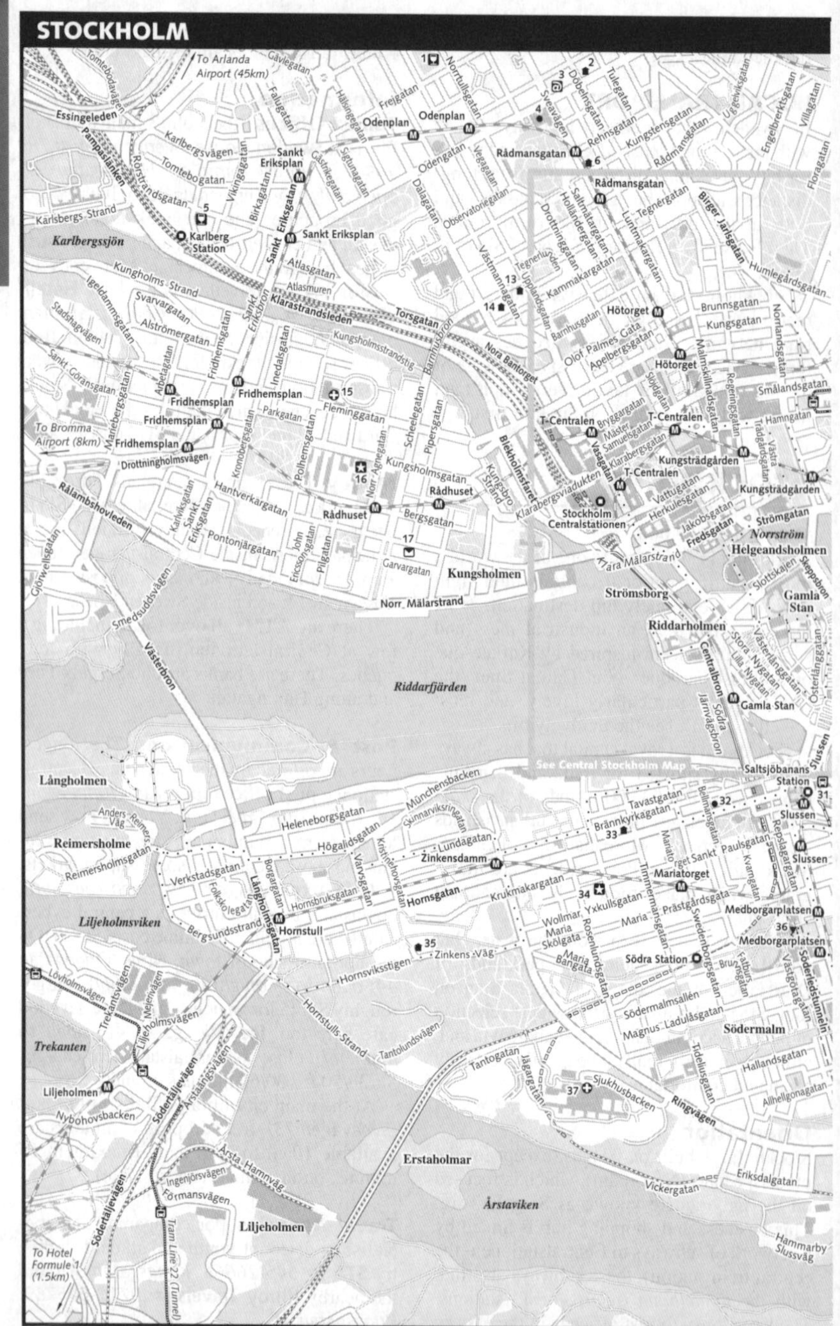
To Arlanda Airport (45km)
To Bromma Airport (8km)
To Hotel Formule 1 (1.5km)
Tram Line 22 (Tunnel)
See Central Stockholm Map
Karlbergssjön
Riddarfjärden
Norrström
Liljeholmsviken
Årstaviken
Kungsholmen
Helgeandsholmen
Gamla Stan
Strömsborg
Riddarholmen
Långholmen
Reimersholme
Trekanten
Erstaholmar
Liljeholmen
Södermalm
Odenplan
Sankt Eriksplan
Rådmansgatan
Hötorget
Fridhemsplan
Rådhuset
T-Centralen
Kungsträdgården
Stockholm Centralstationen
Karlberg Station
Gamla Stan
Slussen
Saltsjöbanans Station
Mariatorget
Medborgarplatsen
Zinkensdamm
Hornstull
Södra Station
Liljeholmen

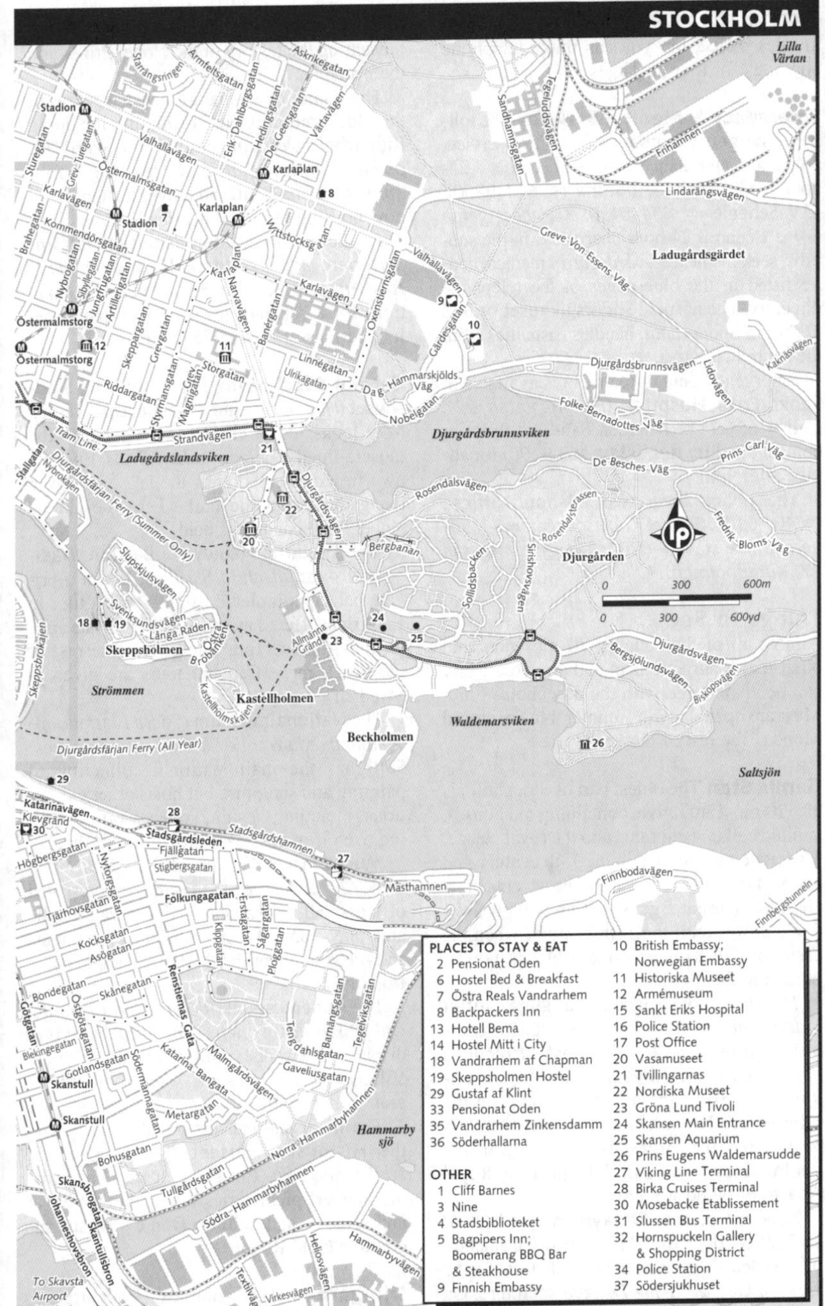
STOCKHOLM
PLACES TO STAY & EAT
2 Pensionat Oden
6 Hostel Bed & Breakfast
7 Östra Reals Vandrarhem
8 Backpackers Inn
13 Hotell Bema
14 Hostel Mitt i City
18 Vandrarhem af Chapman
19 Skeppsholmen Hostel
29 Gustaf af Klint
33 Pensionat Oden
35 Vandrarhem Zinkensdamm
36 Söderhallarna
OTHER
1 Cliff Barnes
3 Nine
4 Stadsbiblioteket
5 Bagpipers Inn; Boomerang BBQ Bar & Steakhouse
9 Finnish Embassy
10 British Embassy; Norwegian Embassy
11 Historiska Museet
12 Armémuseum
15 Sankt Eriks Hospital
16 Police Station
17 Post Office
20 Vasamuseet
21 Tvillingarnas
22 Nordiska Museet
23 Gröna Lund Tivoli
24 Skansen Main Entrance
25 Skansen Aquarium
26 Prins Eugens Waldemarsudde
27 Viking Line Terminal
28 Birka Cruises Terminal
30 Mosebacke Etablissement
31 Slussen Bus Terminal
32 Hornspuckeln Gallery & Shopping District
34 Police Station
37 Södersjukhuset
0 300 600m
0 300 600yd
Lilla Värtan
Stadion
Karlaplan
Östermalmstorg
Skanstull
Ladugårdsgärdet
Djurgårdsbrunnsviken
Ladugårdslandsviken
Djurgården
Skeppsholmen
Kastellholmen
Strömmen
Beckholmen
Waldemarsviken
Saltsjön
Hammarby sjö
Tram Line 7
Djurgårdsfärjan Ferry (Summer Only)
Djurgårdsfärjan Ferry (All Year)
Strandvägen
Valhallavägen
Karlavägen
Narvavägen
Djurgårdsvägen
Rosendalsvägen
Lindarängsvägen
Frihamnen
Greve Von Essens Väg
Djurgårdsbrunnsvägen
Folke Bernadottes Väg
De Besches Väg
Prins Carl Väg
Stadsgårdsleden
Stadsgårdshamnen
Masthamnen
Folkungagatan
Renstiernas Gata
Götgatan
Norra Hammarbyhamnen
Södra Hammarbyhamnen
Finnbodavägen
To Skavsta Airport (100km)

STF *(☎ 020-292929)* doesn't have a drop-in sales office, but you can make telephone bookings for tour packages.

Emergency & Medical Services The toll-free **emergency number** for the fire service, police and ambulance is ☎ 112. There's a 24-hour medical advice **hotline** *(☎ 644 9200)*. **CW Scheele** *(☎ 454 8130; Klarabergsgatan 64)* is a central 24-hour pharmacy. In the suburbs, seek the nearest *vårdcentral* medical centre listed in the blue pages of the telephone directory. The hospital **Södersjukhuset** *(☎ 616 1000)*, in Södermalm, handles casualties from the central city area.

Emergency dental treatment is available at **Sankt Eriks Hospital**, *(Fleminggatan 22)*. Call ☎ 654 1117 between 8am and 9pm, or contact the **duty dentist** *(☎ 463 9100)* for advice after 9pm.

The police have two **24-hour offices** *(☎ 401 0100; Torkel Knutssonsgatan 20, Södermalm • ☎ 401 0200; Kungsholmsgatan 37, Kungsholmen)*.

Things to See

Almost all of the roughly 70 museums and other major attractions in and around the city can be visited free with the Stockholm Card. Most are open daily in summer, but are closed Monday the rest of the year.

Gamla Stan The oldest part of Stockholm is also its most attractive, containing old houses, vaulted cellar restaurants and the royal palace. The city emerged here in the 13th century and adopted the trade and, partly, the accents of its German Hanseatic guests. It grew with Sweden's power until the 17th century, when the castle of Tre Kronor, symbol of that power, burned to the ground.

The 'new' royal palace, **Kungliga Slottet** *(adult/child each attraction Skr70/35, combined ticket Skr110/65; most attractions open 10am-4pm daily mid-May–Aug, noon-3pm Tues-Sun Sept–mid-May)*, built on the ruins of Tre Kronor, is a highlight; with 608 rooms, it's the largest royal palace in the world. Many visitors find the princely **Royal Apartments** most interesting.

Near the palace, **Storkyrkan** *(adult/child Skr20/free; open daily)* is the Royal Cathedral of Sweden. The most notable feature is the 1494 *St George & the Dragon* sculpture. On neaby Stortorget is the excellent new **Nobelmuseet** *(adult/child Skr50/20; open daily)*, presenting the history of the Nobel Prizes and their recipients.

The island of Riddarholmen has some of the oldest buildings in Stockholm, including **Riddarholmskyrkan** *(adult/child Skr20/10; open 10am-4pm daily mid-May–Aug, noon-3pm Sat & Sun Sept)*, no longer a church, but now housing the royal necropolis.

At the site of **Medeltidsmuseet** *(Strömparterren; adult/child Skr40/5; open daily July-Aug, closed Mon rest of year)*, excavations for a car park revealed well-preserved foundations of the medieval town.

Central Stockholm The Town Hall, **Stadshuset** *(Hantverkargatan 1; adult/child Skr50/free)* looks like a church but it features the mosaic-lined *Gyllene salen*, Prins Eugen's own fresco re-creation of the lake view from the gallery, and the hall where the annual Nobel Prize banquet is held.

The delightful **Hallwyl Collection** *(Hamngatan 4; adult/child Skr65/30)* is in a private palace completed in 1898 and a tour in English is offered at 1pm daily from late June to mid-August (1pm Sunday for the rest of the year); more frequent tours are given in Swedish.

The **Nationalmuseum** *(Södra Blasieholmshamnen; adult/child Skr75/free; open Tues-Sun)* has the main national collection of painting and sculpture but hosts other exhibitions, including design, so it's worth checking even if mainstream art isn't your thing.

Musikmuseet *(Sibyllegatan 2; adult/child Skr40/20; open Tues-Sun)* is the best presented of the small collections, and you can handle and play some of the musical instruments and see genuine original ABBA paraphernalia from the 1970s.

The **Armémuseum** *(Riddargatan 13; adult/child Skr60/30; open Tues-Sun)* has vivid displays of Swedish military history from the Vikings to the present, with some rather graphic depictions.

The main national historical collection at the **Historiska Museet** *(Narvavägen 13; adult/child Skr60/free; open daily in summer)* covers prehistoric, Viking and medieval archaeology and culture. Don't miss the incredible Gold Room.

Djurgården This complex is a must-see. Take bus No 47 from Centralstationen or the

Djurgården ferry services from Nybroplan or Slussen (frequent in summer).

Skansen *(adult Skr30-60, child Skr20-30 depending on time of year; park open 10am-8pm May, 10am-10pm June-Aug, 10am-5pm Sept, 10am-4pm Oct-Apr)* was the world's first open-air museum (it opened in 1891); over 150 traditional houses and other exhibits from all over Sweden occupy this attractive hill top. You could spend all day here.

Nordiska Museet *(Djurgårdsvägen 6-16; adult/child Skr60/free; open 10am-5pm daily late June-Aug, closed Mon rest of year)*, founded by Artur Hazelius (who also started Skansen), is housed in an enormous Renaissance-style castle, with notable temporary exhibitions and vast Swedish collections.

The award-winning **Vasamuseet** *(adult/child Skr70/10; open 9.30am-7pm daily June-Aug, 10am-5pm daily rest of year)*, behind Nordiska Museet and on the western shore of Djurgården, allows you simultaneously to look into the lives of 17th-century sailors and appreciate a brilliant achievement in marine archaeology. The crowded **Gröna Lund Tivoli** *(admission Skr50; open May–mid-Sept; noon-11pm or midnight most days mid-June–mid-Aug)* fun park has dozens of amusements.

Prins Eugens Waldemarsudde *(Prins Eugens Väg 6; adult/child Skr70/free; open 11am-5pm Tues-Sun)* was the private palace of a painter-prince who preferred art to royal pleasures. The art galleries, buildings and the old windmill are surrounded by picturesque gardens.

Activities

In summer, many people head for the coast and the islands of the archipelago. The outdoor bar-restaurant **Sjöcafé** *(☎ 660 5757)*, by the bridge leading to Djurgården, rents bicycles, inline skates, kayaks, canoes and rowing boats (costs are from Skr60/200 per hour/day).

Special Events

There are many festivals, concerts and other events at Sergels Torg and Kungsträdgården throughout the summer, and major museums show temporary exhibitions on a grand scale. *What's on Stockholm* lists events.

Places to Stay

Camping A cheap and central option that's open to campers only from late June to mid-August is **Östermalms Citycamping** *(☎ 102 903; Östermalms Idrottsplats, Fiskartorpsvägen 2; tent or campervan site per person Skr60)*. Take the T-bana to Stadion then walk 600m, or take bus No 55.

Hostels Stockholm features four boat hostels, one hostel in an old prison and some central options; two hostels are open in summer only and accommodation is in school classrooms! Most hostels fill up during the late afternoon in summer so arrive early or book in advance. May is also a very busy time. For a Skr20 fee, tourist offices in the city centre can assist in getting a bed – or buy a phonecard and start dialling.

Most travellers head first to Skeppsholmen (take bus No 65 from Centralstationen). The popular STF boat hostel **Vandrarhem af Chapman** *(☎ 463 2266; ⓔ info@chapman.stfturist.se; dorm beds Skr120-150)* has done plenty of travelling of its own. Bunks are below decks; breakfast is Skr55. On dry land next door, with the same reception and prices, is the larger **Skeppsholmen Hostel**, with kitchen and laundry facilities. From August 2004, af Chapman will be closed for an estimated nine months for renovations. The land-based hostel will remain open.

Also part of the STF network, **Backpackers Inn** *(☎ 660 7515; ⓔ backpackersinn@telia.com; Banérgatan 56; metro T-Karlaplan; beds Skr110-150; open late June–mid-Aug)* has 300 beds in a school building (no kitchen facilities, but breakfast is available for Skr50). Nearby, the SVIF **Östra Reals Vandrarhem** *(☎ 664 1114; Karlavägen 79; dorm beds Skr125-150; open mid-June–mid-Aug)* is also in an old school; there are kitchen facilities here (and no bunks!).

Nearer to Centralstationen, **City Backpackers** *(☎ 206920; ⓔ info@citybackpackers.se; Upplandsgatan 2A; dorm beds Skr170-200)* is a clean, friendly and well-equipped hostel. It has a kitchen, sauna, laundry and Internet access. In the same area, a bit north, **Hostel Mitt i City** *(☎ 217630; ⓔ reservations@stockholm.mail.telia.com; Västmannagatan 13; dorm beds from Skr175)* occupies a few floors of an old apartment building. Rates here include breakfast. Also north of the centre, near T-Rådmansgatan, is **Hostel Bed & Breakfast** *(☎ 152 838; ⓔ hostelbedandbreakfast@chello.se; Rehnsgatan 21; dorm beds Skr150-175)* a pleasant, informal basement hostel with

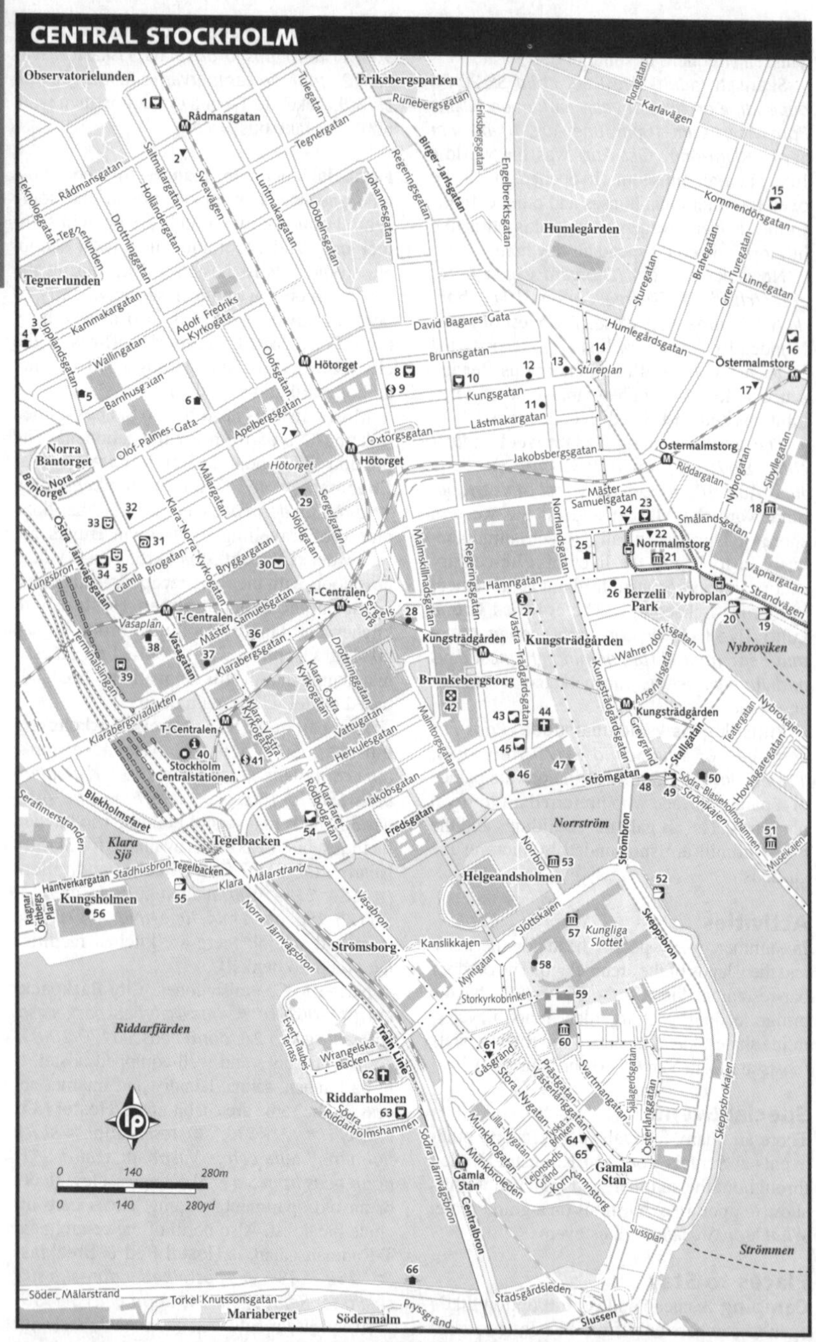
CENTRAL STOCKHOLM
Observatorielunden
Eriksbergsparken
Rådmansgatan
Humlegården
Tegnerlunden
Hötorget
Östermalmstorg
Stureplan
Norra Bantorget
T-Centralen
Norrmalmstorg
Berzelii Park
Nybroplan
Nybroviken
Kungsträdgården
Brunkebergstorg
Stockholm Centralstationen
Klara Sjö
Tegelbacken
Norrström
Helgeandsholmen
Kungsholmen
Strömsborg
Kungliga Slottet
Riddarfjärden
Riddarholmen
Gamla Stan
Strömmen
Slussen
Mariaberget
Södermalm
Train Line
0 140 280m
0 140 280yd

a kitchen and laundry, plus cheap breakfast (Skr25). There's a large summer annex here filled with beds for Skr100, but it's not for those who like their privacy!

There are a fair number of hostels around Södermalm, a good 15-minute walk from the Viking Line boats and Centralstationen. The ship hostel **Gustaf af Klint** *(☎ 640 4077; Stadsgårdskajen 153; dorm beds Skr120-150)* has beds in pretty down-at-heel rooms. West of the railway lines, the red-painted **Mälaren den Röda Båten** *(☎ 644 4385; ⓔ info@icts.se; Söder Malärstrand, Kajplats 6; dorm beds Skr185)* is probably the cosiest of Stockholm's floating hostels and has a good summer restaurant.

In the west end of Södermalm near T-Zinkensdamm, the well-equipped STF **Vandrarhem Zinkensdamm** *(☎ 616 8100; ⓔ mail@zinkensdamm.com; Zinkens väg 20; dorm beds Skr155)* is a large, welcoming complex in a quiet location near a park. Off the northwestern corner of Södermalm, the small island of Långholmen is home to STF **Vandrarhem Långholmen** *(☎ 668 0510; ⓔ vandrarhem@langholmen.com; dorm beds from Skr175)*, formerly a prison. There are dorm beds in former cells (booking is essential) and slightly roomier hotel-standard quarters, with heavily reduced rates on weekends and in the summer season.

Private Rooms A number of agencies, including **Bed & Breakfast Service** *(☎ 660 6654; ⓔ info@bedbreakfast.a.se; ⓦ www.bedbreakfast.a.se)* and **Bed & Breakfast Agency** *(☎ 643 8028; ⓔ info@bba.nu; ⓦ www.bba.nu)*, can arrange good-value apartment accommodation or B&B from around Skr200 per person per night.

Hotels At Centralstationen, **Hotellcentralen** (see Tourist Offices earlier) can usually find you suitable accommodation for a fee of Skr50. The handy booklet *Hotels and Youth Hostels in Stockholm* (free from tourist offices) lists most hotels and rates.

Most Stockholm hotels offer discount rates on weekends (Friday, Saturday and often Sunday night) and in the summer (mid- or late June to mid-August). Discounts can be up to 50% off the normal price. Almost all prices include breakfast.

Hotel Formule 1 *(☎ 744 2044; Mikrofonvägen 30; rooms Skr290)* offers perhaps the best value in Stockholm, with very cheap rooms

CENTRAL STOCKHOLM

PLACES TO STAY
- 4 Oden Pensionat
- 5 City Backpackers
- 6 Queen's Hotel
- 25 Hotel Stockholm; Finnair
- 38 Nordic Sea Hotel; Ice Bar
- 50 Grand Hētel Stockholm
- 66 Mälaren Den Röda Båten

PLACES TO EAT
- 2 Souperb
- 3 Carinas Pizzeria
- 7 Kungshallen
- 17 Östermalms Market Hall; Örtagården
- 22 Restaurant KB
- 24 Birger Jarlspassagen Cafes
- 29 Hötorgshallen
- 32 Kebab House
- 36 Hemköp Supermarket
- 47 Operakällaren; Café Opera
- 61 Hermitage
- 64 Café Art
- 65 Michelangelo

OTHER
- 1 Tip Top; RFSL
- 8 Glenn Miller Café
- 9 X-Change; STA Travel
- 10 The Loft
- 11 American Express
- 12 Kilroy Travels
- 13 Silja Line
- 14 SAS; Skyways; Luftansa; Austrian Airlines; Air Baltic
- 15 French Embassy
- 16 New Zealand Embassy
- 18 Musikmuseet
- 19 Strömma Kanalbolaget Boats
- 20 Stockholm Sightseeing; Djurgården Boats
- 21 Hallwyl Collection
- 23 Dubliner
- 26 British Airways
- 27 Sweden House; Sweden Bookshop; Forex
- 28 Kulturhuset; Access IT; Café Access
- 30 Central Post Office
- 31 Ice
- 33 Vasateatern
- 34 Jazzclub Fasching
- 35 Oscars Teatern
- 37 CW Scheele
- 39 Cityterminalen (Bus Station, Airport Buses)
- 40 Hotellcentralen; Forex; Post Office
- 41 Forex
- 42 Gallerian Shopping Complex
- 43 Finnish Embassy
- 44 Sankt Jakobs Kyrka
- 45 Danish Embassy
- 46 City Sightseeing (Tour Departures)
- 48 Stockholm Sightseeing Office
- 49 Waxholmsbolaget Office & Ferry Terminal
- 51 Nationalmuseum
- 52 Svea Viking (Boat Tour Departures)
- 53 Medeltidsmuseet
- 54 Canadian Embassy
- 55 Lake Mälaren Boats
- 56 Stadshuset
- 57 Museum Tre Kronor
- 58 Royal Apartments Entrance
- 59 Storkyrkan
- 60 Nobelmuseet
- 62 Riddarholmskyrkan
- 63 Stargayte

that can accommodate up to three people for one flat rate (breakfast not included). Rooms are hardly inspiring, facilities are shared, and you're actually 4km southwest of town, but who can argue at that price? Take the T-bana to Telefonplan.

In the middle of town is pleasant **Queen's Hotel** *(☎ 249460; e queenshotel@queenshotel.se; Drottninggatan 71A; singles/doubles from Skr650/750)*, offering comfortable rooms with either shared or private facilities. Just north of the centre is clean and friendly **Hotell Bema** *(☎ 232675; Upplandsgatan 13; singles/doubles Skr820/890, discounted to Skr590/690)*, with modern, good-value rooms.

The people behind welcoming **Oden Pensionat** *(☎ 796 9600; e info@pensionat.nu • Odengatan 38, Södermalm • Hornsgatan 66, Södermalm • Kammakargatan 62)* must be doing well – the third 'branch' of this affordable pension has just opened to the north of Centralstationen. Prices vary at different locations, but generally start at Skr680/750 for smaller rooms with shared facilities, rising to around Skr930/1025 for larger rooms with bathroom. Reasonable summer discounts apply.

Places to Eat

Stockholm has thousands of restaurants, including inexpensive lunch cafeterias and some of the finest dining halls in Scandinavia. The cheapest snacks are found at the numerous **gatukök** outlets, which serve burgers, hot dogs and sausages. There are countless places serving cheap pizzas and kebabs.

The handiest central supermarket is **Hemköp** *(Klarabergsgatan 50)*, and there's a **Systembolaget** *(Klarabergsgatan 62)* nearby for buying alcohol. The colourful market halls are excellent places to sample both local and exotic treats. **Hötorgshallen** *(Hötorget)* has many Mediterranean food stalls and good specialist shops. **Östermalms Saluhall** *(Östermalmstorg)* has some fine restaurants and upstairs you'll find **Örtagården**, which serves great vegetarian food. **Söderhallarna** *(Medborgarplatsen)* is a more modern food centre, and **Kungshallen** *(Hötorget)* has an enormous selection of international-food stalls.

Tourists, not surprisingly, love Gamla Stan, and many dine along Västerlånggatan in places such as **Michelangelo** (pasta from Skr60) or drink their coffee in the stylish vaults of **Café Art**. Check out restaurants on nearby Stora Nygatan, including the vegetarian **Hermitage** at No 11 (*dagens rätt* for Skr60 and dinner for Skr70).

Downtown, a small store with a clever name, **Souperb** *(Sveavägen 92)*, serves up great soups for around Skr55, including bread. Perfect for night owls and close to Centralstationen, **Kebab House** *(cnr Vasagatan & Kungsgatan)* offers kebabs and burgers until 5am nightly. **Carinas Pizzeria** *(Upplandsgatan 9B; pizza Skr35-55)* has a cheap lunch special – pizza for just Skr29.

Next to the Dubliner pub on Smålandsgatan you'll find the entrance to **Birger Jarlspassagen**, a great little arcade full of cool cafés. **Vetekatten** *(Klara Norra Kyrkogatan 26)* is one of the city's most traditional cafés.

Trendy places at the back of the Opera House, facing Kungsträdgården, are the late-19th-century, super-posh **Operakällaren** and lively **Café Opera**, more a nightclub than a café.

Entertainment

Pubs & Clubs Stockholm nightlife centres on neighbourhoods that offer pubs and bars within walking distance. In Södermalm, check the Götgatan, Östgötagatan and Skånegatan area. In Kungsholmen, go to Scheelegatan and Fridhemsplan, and in the northern centre (Vasastaden) try the Tegnérgatan and Rörstrandsgatan areas. For the fashionable late-night bars and nightclubs frequented by the city's hip and beautiful, head to Stureplan.

In the city centre, lively **Dubliner** *(Smålandsgatan 8)* has typical pub food. **The Loft** *(Regeringsgatan 66)* is another great Irish pub with restaurant-quality food. Around Rörstrandsgatan are a few pubs, including the **Bagpiper's Inn** (Scottish) and **Boomerang BBQ & Steakhouse** (Australian). The very popular **Cliff Barnes** *(Nortullsgatan 45)* is a great place named after the loser from *Dallas*. On Gamla Stan, check out **Wirströms Irish Pub** *(Stora Nygatan 13)*. On a balmy summer evening, try the restaurant-bars on either side of the bridge leading across to Djurgården, **Tvillingarnas** and **Sjöcafé**.

Jazz is extremely popular. The small, intimate **Glenn Miller Café** *(Brunnsgatan 21)* has live jazz a few nights a week, and the larger **Jazzclub Fasching** *(Kungsgatan 63)* is one of Stockholm's main jazz venues. **Mosebacke Etablissement** *(Mosebacketorg 3)*, in Söderhalm, is an excellent bar, nightclub and concert venue that features featuring all sorts of music and performers. The outdoor bar offers a great view of the city. Summer sees a lot of outdoor concerts at places such as **Gröna Lund Tivoli**.

Head to the unique **Ice Bar** *(Vasaplan)* inside the Nordic Sea Hotel for a taste of life at the Ice Hotel. For an entry charge of Skr125 you get to play inside a bar filled with ice sculptures and select a drink to imbibe from a glass made of ice.

Sweden's famous open-mindedness means that non-heteros are welcome in all bars and clubs. **Mandus** *(Österlånggatan 7)* is a very popular gay restaurant-bar in Gamla Stan; other hot spots include **Tip Top** *(Sveavägen 57)*, by the RFSL headquarters, and **Stargayte** *(Södra Riddarholmshamnen 19)*.

Theatre Stockholm is a theatre city, with outstanding dance, opera and music performances – for an overview, pick up the free *Teater Guide* from tourist offices. Tickets aren't cheap and are often sold out, especially for Saturday. **Operan** *(☎ 248240; Gustav Adolfs Torg)* is the the place for opera and ballet. The classic **Oscars Teatern** *(☎ 205000; Kungsgatan 64)* runs 'Broadway' musicals, and the small **Vasateatern** *(☎ 102363; Vasagatan 19)*, around the corner, sometimes stages plays in English.

Getting There & Away

Air Stockholm's main airport, **Arlanda** *(☎ 797 6000)*, is 45km north of the city centre. **Skyways** *(☎ 797 7639)* and **SAS** *(☎ 020-727000)* have comprehensive networks of domestic flights.

Bromma airport *(☎ 797 6874)* is 8km west of Stockholm and is used for some domestic flights. **Skavsta airport** *(☎ 0155-280400)*, 100km south of Stockholm, is also used for domestic flights and also by some low-cost carriers, including Ryanair.

Bus Long-distance buses use Cityterminalen, next to Centralstationen. Here you'll find the **Busstop ticket office** *(☎ 440 8570)*, which represents the big concerns such as Eurolines, Svenska Buss and Y-Bussen, along with many of the direct buses to the north. **Swebus Express** *(☎ 0200-218218)* has a ticket office on the second level.

Train Stockholm is the hub for SJ's national services. Direct trains to/from Copenhagen, Oslo, Storlien (for Trondheim) and Narvik arrive and depart from Centralstationen (Stockholm C), as do the SL *pendeltåg*, commuter services that run to/from Nynäshamn, Södertälje and Märsta.

Boat There are **Silja Line** *(☎ 222140; Ⓦ www.silja.com)* ferries departing for Helsinki (from Skr333, including breakfast and cabin) and Turku (from Skr160) from Värtahamnen – walk from T-Gärdet or take bus No 76 from T-Ropsten.

Viking Line *(☎ 452 4000; Ⓦ www.vikingline.fi)* ferries sail daily to Turku (from Skr130) and Helsinki (from Skr270) from the terminal at Tegelvikshamn (bus from Cityterminalen, or walk 1.5km from T-Slussen).

Tallink ferries to Tallinn (Estonia) sail from Tallinnterminalen at Frihamnen (take a connecting bus from Cityterminalen, Skr20). See Getting There & Away, earlier in this chapter.

Getting Around

Storstockholms Lokaltrafik *(SL; Ⓦ www.sl.se)* runs all *tunnelbana* (T or T-bana) metro trains, local trains and buses within the entire Stockholm county. At T-Centralen there are SL information offices in the basement of the station hall (open until 11.15pm daily) and at the Sergels Torg entrance. Both offices issue timetables and sell SL Tourist Cards and the Stockholm Card. You can also call ☎ 600 1000 for schedule and travel information.

The Stockholm Card covers travel on all SL trains and buses in greater Stockholm. The 24-hour (Skr80) and 72-hour (Skr150) SL Tourist Cards are much cheaper alternatives if you just want transport.

On Stockholm's public transport system the minimum fare costs two coupons, and each additional zone costs another coupon. A 10-/20-coupon discount ticket costs Skr60/110. International rail passes aren't valid on SL trains.

To/From the Airport The **Arlanda Express** train from Centralstationen takes only 20 minutes to reach Arlanda; trains run every 15 minutes from about 5am to midnight and cost Skr160. The same trip in a taxi costs from Skr350 to Skr450, but agree on your fare first and use only taxis with contact telephone numbers displayed.

The cheaper option is the **Flygbuss** service between Arlanda airport and Cityterminalen.

Buses leave every 10 or 15 minutes (Skr80, 40 minutes). To Bromma airport, the bus from Cityterminalen costs Skr60 and takes 20 minutes; to Skavsta it costs Skr100 and takes 80 minutes. Call ☎ 600 1000 for bus departure times to/from all airports.

Bus Check where the regional bus hub is for different outlying areas. Islands of the Ekerö municipality (including Drottningholm palace) are served by bus Nos 301 to 323 from T-Brommaplan. Buses to Vaxholm (No 670) and the Åland ferries (No 637 to Grisslehamn and Nos 640/631 to Kapellskär) depart from T-Tekniska Högskolan.

Train Local *pendeltåg* trains are useful for connections to Nynäshamn (for ferries to Gotland), to Märsta (for buses to Sigtuna and Arlanda airport) and Södertälje. There are also services to Nockeby (from T-Alvik), to Lidingö (from T-Ropsten), to Kårsta, Österskär and Näsbypark (from T-Tekniska Högskolan) and to Saltsjöbaden (from T-Slussen).

Tram The historical tram No 7 runs between Norrmalmstorg and Skansen, passing most attractions on Djurgården. Separate fees apply for Stockholm Card–holders, but the SL Tourist Card is valid.

Metro The most useful mode of transport in Stockholm is the *tunnelbana* (T), converging on T-Centralen, connected by an underground walkway to Centralstationen. There are three main through lines with branches.

Taxi There's usually no problem finding a taxi, but they're expensive (about Skr35 flag fall, then around Skr7 per km). At night, women should ask about *tjejtaxa*, a discount rate offered by some operators. Reputable firms are **Taxi Stockholm** *(☎ 150000)*, **Taxi 020** *(☎ 020-939393)* and **Taxi Kurir** *(☎ 300000)*.

Bicycle Stockholm has an extensive network of bicycle paths. Top day trips include Djurgården; a loop going from Gamla Stan to Södermalm, Långholmen and Kungsholmen (on lakeside paths); Drottningholm (return by steamer); Haga Park; and the adjoining Ulriksdal Park.

Sjöcafe *(☎ 660 5757)*, by the bridge across to Djurgården, rents bicycles for Skr60/250 per hour/day (with options for longer rentals).

Boat Djurgårdsfärjan city ferry services connect Gröna Lund Tivoli on Djurgården with Nybroplan and Slussen as frequently as every 10 minutes in summer (considerably less frequently in the low season); a single trip costs Skr20 (free with the SL Tourist Card).

Around Stockholm

You can explore the county of greater Stockholm with the SL Tourist Card or monthly passes that allow unlimited travel on all buses and local trains – pick up timetables from SL centres.

STOCKHOLM ARCHIPELAGO

☎ 08

Depending on which source you read, the archipelago around Stockholm has anything between 14,000 and 100,000 islands, although the common consensus is 24,000. Whatever the number, a summer visit to one is highly recommended. Summer cottages on the rocky islets are popular among the wealthier Stockholmites, and regular boats offer options for outings.

The biggest operator is **Waxholmsbolaget** *(☎ 679 5830; ⓦ www.waxholmsbolaget.se)*; timetables and information are available from offices outside the Grand Hotel on Strömkajen in Stockholm, and at the harbour in Vaxholm.

Each island has its own character. **Sandhamn** is popular among wealthy sailors and best on a day trip. **Finnhamn** is quieter, but book in advance to stay at the **STF hostel** *(☎ 542 46212; ⓔ info@finnhamn.nu; dorm beds Skr180; open year-round)*. **Utö** is popular among cyclists; the **STF hostel** *(☎ 504 20315; dorm beds Skr200; open Apr-Sept)* has its reception at the nearby Utö Värdshus.

EKERÖ DISTRICT

☎ 08 • pop 22,600

Surprisingly rural, Ekerö, 20km west of Stockholm, consists of several large islands on Lake Mälaren, a couple of Unesco World Heritage–listed sites and a dozen medieval churches. Bus Nos 311 and 312 run from T-Brommaplan metro station in Stockholm.

It certainly can be an expensive day out if you wish to see everything at the royal residence and parks of **Drottningholm** *(☎ 402 6280; open daily May-Sept, Sat & Sun Oct-Apr)* on Lovön – it's a good idea to use the

Stockholm Card. The main Renaissance-inspired **palace** *(guided/self-guided tour Skr60/30)*, with geometric baroque gardens, was built about the same time as Versailles. The most pleasant way to get to Drottningholm is by boat. **Strömma Kanalbolaget** *(☎ 587 14000; Ⓦ www.strommakanalbolaget.com)* has boats departing from Stadshusbron in Stockholm daily from May to mid-September (Skr100 return).

Across the road from **Adelsö's** medieval church is **Hovgården**, site of burial mounds associated with nearby Birka. SL bus No 312 runs to Adelsö church from T-Brommaplan metro station via the medieval Ekerö and Munsö churches and the free Adelsö ferry.

At the Viking trading centre of **Birka** *(☎ 5605 1445, open daily May-Sept)*, on Björkö in Lake Mälaren, archaeologists have excavated the town's cemetery, harbour and fortress. Cruises to Birka run from early May to late September; the return trip on Strömma Kanalbolaget's *Victoria* from Stadshusbron in Stockholm, is a full day's outing (Skr220). A visit to the small **museum** and a guided tour in English of the settlement's burial mounds and fortifications are included in the price. Phone ☎ 587 14000 for details. From May to September there are also daily boats from Adelsö (Hovgården) to Birka (Skr70, including museum entry).

Svealand

Svealand is where Sweden was born. Viking rune stones and forts are reminders of the time when Lake Mälaren offered safe harbours and links to the Baltic Sea and Russia. The kingdom of the Svea became synonymous with the entire country.

Further northwest, amid some picturesque lake and forest scenery, lies Dalarna (sometimes called 'Dalecarlia' in English), a county of rich folk culture and beautiful landscapes.

UPPSALA

☎ 018 • pop 191,100

Uppsala is one of Sweden's oldest cities. Gamla (Old) Uppsala flourished as early as the 6th century. The cathedral was consecrated in 1435 after 175 years of building and the castle was first built in the 1540s. The city depends on the sprawling university, Scandinavia's oldest.

The main **tourist office** *(☎ 274800; Ⓦ www.uppsalatourism.se; Fyristorg 8; open Mon-Sat, daily in summer)* is central and helpful. Ask about the **Uppsala Card** (Skr75). The **public library** *(cnr Sankt Olofsgatan & Svartbäcksgatan)* offers free Internet access. The **cybercafé** *(cnr Fyristorget & Drottninggatan)* inside the *Upsala Nya Tidning* newspaper office, right by the tourist office, charges Skr10 for 15 minutes online.

Gamla Uppsala

Uppsala began at the three great **grave mounds** at Gamla Uppsala, 4km north of the modern city *(direct bus No 2 from Stora Torget; admission free; open at all times)*. The mounds, said to be the tombs of legendary pre-Viking kings, lie in a cemetery that includes about 300 smaller mounds and the site of a great temple. A new, modern **historical centre** *(☎ 239300; adult/child Skr50/30; open 11am-5pm daily May-Aug, noon-3pm Sun only Sept-Apr)* has museum-style exhibits of ancient artefacts excavated from Gamla Uppsala and the nearby archaeological sites.

Christianity came in the 11th century and with it the bishops; from 1164 the archbishop had his seat in a cathedral on the site of the present **church**, which, by the 15th century, was enlarged and painted with frescoes.

Uppsala Slott

Constructed by Gustav Vasa, this castle *(open daily June-Aug)* features the state hall where kings were enthroned and a queen abdicated. It's accessible by guided tour only (in English at 1pm and 3pm; Skr60/15). The **Vasa Vignettes** *(adult/child Skr40/15; open noon-4pm Mon-Fri, 11am-5pm Sat & Sun May-Aug)* 'waxworks' museum in the death-stained dungeons illustrates the past intrigues of the castle. **Uppsala Konstmuseum** *(adult/child Skr30/free; open Wed-Sun)*, whose works of art span five centuries, is also housed in southern wing of Uppsala Slott also houses.

Other Attractions

The Gothic **cathedral** dominates the city. Inside, visit the **treasury** *(adult/child Skr30/free; open daily May-Sept, closed Mon rest of year)* in the north tower.

Gustavianum Museum *(Akademigatan 3; adult/child Skr40/free; open 11am-4pm Tues-Sun)* has an excellent antiquities collection and features an old 'anatomical theatre'.

Upplands Museum *(Sankt Eriks Torg 10; adult/child Skr30/free; open noon-5pm Tues-Sun)*, in the old mill, houses county collections from the Middle Ages.

Carolina Rediviva *(Dag Hammarskjöldsväg 1; adult/child Skr20/free; open daily in summer)*, the old university library, has a display hall with maps and historical and scientific literature, the pride of which is the surviving half of the 6th-century Codex Argentus, written on purple vellum in the extinct Gothic language.

The excellent **Botanic Gardens**, including the **Linnaeum Orangery** and a tropical greenhouse, are below the castle hill.

Places to Stay

The pleasant STF hostel **Sunnersta Herrgård** *(☎ 324220; Sunnerstavägen 24; bus No 20 or 50; dorm beds Skr180; open year-round)* is in a manor house some 6km south of the centre. There is a second, summer STF hostel **Vandraren** *(☎ 104300; ⓔ info@vandraren.com; Vattholmavägen; bus No 2, 20, 24, 54; dorm beds Skr165, singles/doubles Skr190/370; open mid-June–mid-Aug)*, 2km north of town. Facilities, including a bathroom for each room, are excellent.

Uppsala Room Agency *(☎ 109533; ⓔ uppsala.rumsformedling@swipnet.se; singles/doubles Skr250/350)* will book private rooms in town. Central **Basic Hotel** *(☎ 480 5000; ⓔ reception@basichotel.com; Kungsgatan 27; singles/doubles from Skr690/790, both discount ed to Skr600)* has excellent rooms with their own self-catering facilties. This is a good place for families or small groups: four-bed rooms cost Skr760 year-round.

Places to Eat

There are several eateries on the pedestrian mall and Stora Torget. When it comes to fast food, **Saffet's** *(Stora Torget)* has the works, all for Skr50 or less. **Ofvandahl's** *(Sysslomansgatan 3-5)* is a classy café full of old-world charm. Some of the best coffee in town and Italian-style food such as pasta and panini (Skr40 to Skr65) can be found at funky **Eko Caféet** *(Drottninggatan 5)*.

If you're self-catering, there's a central **Hemköp supermarket** *(Stora Torget)*. The indoor produce market, **Saluhallen** *(open Mon-Sat)*, is between the cathedral and the river at Sankt Eriks torg.

Svenssons Krog *(Sysslomansgatan 15)* is very popular, as is the sister venue **Svenssons Åkanten**, an outdoor, riverside restaurant and bar by Saluhallen. **William's** *(Övre Slottsgatan 7)*, in the university quarter, is an English pub with an Indian restaurant (lunch buffet Skr50) next door. **O'Connor's** *(Stora Torget 1)*, upstairs from Saffet's, is a friendly Irish pub and restaurant (good pub meals from Skr50). There's also regular live music, and a selection of over 85 beers. **Fredmans** *(Drottninggatran 12)* also has pub food and live music; next door is **Escobar**, a popular bar and nightclub.

Getting There & Around

The bus station is outside the train station. Bus No 801 departs at least twice an hour for nearby Arlanda airport (Skr80). Swebus Express runs regularly to Örebro, Stockholm, Gävle and Västerås. Frequent SJ trains run from Stockholm; all SJ services to/from Gävle, Östersund and Mora stop in Uppsala. SL coupons or passes take you only as far as Märsta from Stockholm.

A local bus ticket costs from Skr20 and gives unlimited travel for two hours – just enough for a visit to Gamla Uppsala. Catch a city bus from Stora Torget or outside Scandic Hotel Uplandia. The **Upplands Lokaltrafik** *(☎ 020-114 1414)* operates regional traffic within the county; if you're staying long in the area, ask about rebate cards and the various passes available.

ÖREBRO

☎ 019 • pop 125,000

The most photogenic castle in Sweden stands by the river in the centre of attractive Örebro. The **tourist office** *(☎ 212121; ⓦ www.orebro.se/turism; open 9am-7pm Mon-Fri, 10am-5pm Sat & Sun June-Aug; 9am-5pm Mon-Fri, 11am-3pm Sat & Sun Sept-May)* is inside the castle.

Admission to the once powerful **Slottet** *(adult/child Skr45/free; open daily year-round)*, now restored, includes a castle tour (in English at noon and 2pm daily in summer). Outside the castle is **Länsmuseum & Konsthall** *(Engelbrektsgatan 3; adult/child Skr20/free; open 11am-5pm daily)*, the combined regional and art museums.

The very good **STF hostel** *(☎ 310240; ⓔ vandrarhem@hepa.se; Fanjunkarevägen 5; dorm beds from Skr120)* is quite well hidden, some 1.6km northeast of the train station (take bus No 16 or 31). Hostel management also has a new complex of well-equipped apartments next door: **Livin' Lägenhetshotell** *(☎ 310240; ⓔ vandrarhem@hepa.se; apartments Skr500)*.

From here, Swebus Express has connections in all directions: to Jönköping, Linköping and Norrköping; Karlstad and Oslo; Mariestad and Gothenburg; Västerås and Uppsala; and Eskilstuna and Stockholm. Train connections are similarly good.

KARLSTAD

☎ 054 • pop 80,800

The port of Karlstad is on Vänern, Sweden's largest lake, and it's the gateway to outdoor experiences in the county of Värmland. **Karlstad Turistbyrå** *(☎ 222140; ⓦ www.karlstad.se; Tage Erlandergatan 10E; open daily June-Aug, closed Sat & Sun rest of year)* has details on town and county activities.

The **STF hostel** *(☎ 566840; ⓔ karlstadvandrarhem@swipnet.se; dorm beds Skr130)* is off the E18 at Ulleberg, 3km southwest of Karlstad's centre (take bus No 11 or 32). There are a number of central hotels opposite the train station, including pleasant **Hotell Freden** *(☎ 216582; ⓔ info@fredenhotel.com; Fredsgatan 1; singles/doubles Skr480/580, discounted to Skr380/480)*.

Swebus Express has daily services running along the Gothenburg–Karlstad–Falun–Gävle and Stockholm–Örebro–Karlstad–Oslo routes. Buses leave from the terminal on Drottninggatan. Trains between Stockholm and Oslo pass through Karlstad and several daily services also run from Gothenburg. **Värmlandstrafik** *(☎ 020-225580)* runs regional buses.

LAKE SILJAN REGION

This pretty, traditional area in the county of Dalarna is a popular summer tourist destination for boths Swedes and foreigners, with numerous festivals and reasonable-sized towns that offer good facilities and attractions. **Siljansleden** extends for more than 300km around Lake Siljan and has excellent walking and cycling paths. Another way to enjoy the lake is by boat: in summer, MS *Gustaf Wasa* has a complex schedule of lunch, dinner and sightseeing cruises from the main towns of Mora, Rättvik and Leksand. Inquire at any of the area's tourist offices for a schedule. Check out the Siljan area website (ⓦ www.siljan.se).

Rättvik is a popular town on Lake Siljan, with sandy beaches in summer and ski slopes in winter. The **tourist office** *(☎ 797210; ⓦ www.rattvik.se; open daily mid-June–mid-Aug, closed Sat & Sun rest of year)* is at the train station. The other hub in the region is **Mora**, whose **tourist office** *(☎ 592020; ⓦ www.mora.se; open same hours as Rättvik)* is also, shockingly, at the train station.

Skåne

The county of Skåne, sometimes anglicised as 'Scania', was Danish until the mid-17th century – still easily detected in the strong dialect and architecture. Its gently rolling landscape is dotted with attractions and more hostels than any other region of Sweden. For information about the Skåne region, contact the **Skåne Tourist Board** *(☎ 046-350570; ⓦ www.skanetur.se)*.

MALMÖ

☎ 040 • pop 262,400

Malmö is a lively and friendly city, perhaps due to the influence of Copenhagen across Öresund. The new 16km Öresund bridge and tunnel link, which includes Europe's longest bridge (7.8km), has brought the two cities even closer.

The **tourist office** *(☎ 300150; ⓦ www.malmo.se; open daily May-Sept; closed Sun Oct-Apr)* is inside Centralstationen. Its free official booklet *Malmö* is a very useful, general guide. The discount card Malmökortet (Skr120/150/180 for one/two/three days) means free bus transport, entry to several museums and discounts at other attractions.

A **Forex** exchange counter can be found inside the tourist office within the train station. The **central post office** *(Skeppsbron 1)* is not far from here. **Cyberspace C@fé** *(Engelbrektsgatan 13)* offers Internet access at Skr22 for 30 minutes.

Things to See

The main museums of Malmö are based around **Malmöhus Castle** *(Malmöhusvägen)*; you can walk through the **royal apartments** with their interiors and portrait collections and see the **Stadsmuseum**, with its Malmö collection, and the galleries of **Konstmuseum**. Especially interesting are the **aquarium** and the **Naturmuseum**. Also included in the ticket (Skr40/10 per adult/child) is admission to the old **Kommendanthuset** arsenal, just opposite the castle, and **Teknikens och Sjöfartens Hus**, a short way to the west, a well-presented technology and maritime museum. The museums are open 10am to 4pm daily June to August (noon to 4pm the rest of the year).

Sankt Petri kyrka *(Göran Olsgatan)* is characteristic of 14th-century Baltic Gothic style, although it has been mostly rebuilt. There's a magnificent altarpiece dating from 1611.

Places to Stay

STF Vandrarhem Malmö *(☎ 82220; e info@malmohostel.se; Backavägen 18; dorm beds from Skr130; open year-round)* is 3.5km south of the city centre. The hostel is big, bright and well equipped, offering breakfast for Skr50 (take bus No 21 from Centralplan in front of Centralstationen).

Bosses Gästvåningar *(☎ 326250; Södra Förstadsgatan 110B; singles/doubles from Skr275/325)* is a central SVIF hostel, close to Möllevangstorget.

Rooms or apartments from about Skr250 per person are available through **City Room** *(☎ 79594; e cityroom@telia.com)*. Otherwise, contact the tourist office.

Hotel Pallas *(☎ 611 5077; Norra Vallgatan 74; singles/doubles from Skr355/395)* is a recommended cheapish hotel near the train station; breakfast is an extra Skr30.

Places to Eat

The central squares become quite a scene on summer evenings, with well over a dozen restaurants offering alfresco dining and drinking. Lilla Torget is a picturesque cobbled square lined by restaurant-bars and often heaving with people. Your best bet is to head

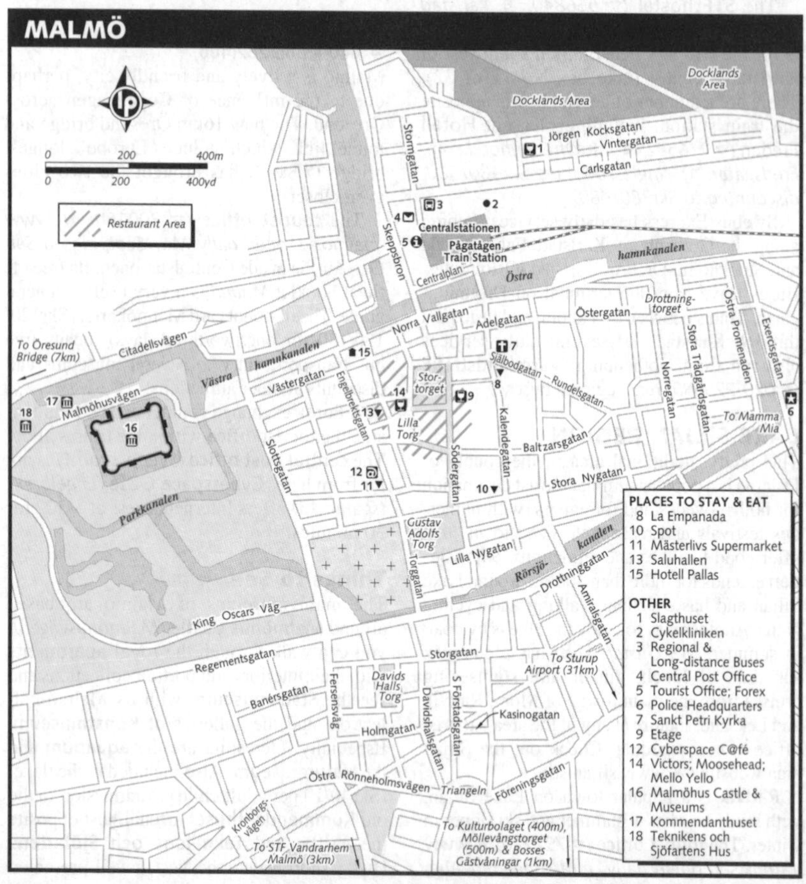

to **Saluhallen** *(Lilla Torget)* here, which has an excellent range of food stalls.

Cheap, cheerful **La Empanada** *(Själbodgatan 10)* is highly recommended for budget travellers. It has an extensive menu of mainly Mexican dishes served cafeteria-style; tacos, enchiladas and burritos cost Skr30 to Skr40.

For excellent Italian sandwiches and salads, visit the stylish **Spot** *(Stora Nygatan 33)*; daily pasta and risotto dishes cost from Skr60.

Entertainment

For evening diversions, head to Lilla Torget or Möllevångstorget and take your pick of bars. On Lilla Torget, **Victors**, **Moosehead** and **Mello Yello** stand side by side and compete for customers. On Möllevångstorget, **Nyhavn** is the drinking spot of choice, but there are numerous places in the vicinity.

Kulturbolaget *(Bergsgatan 18)* has regular live music or DJs; among popular large clubs are **Etage** *(Stortorget)* and **Slagthuset** *(Jörgen Kocksgatan 7A)*.

Getting There & Away

An integrated Öresundregionen transport system incorporates trains from Helsingborg via Malmö and Copenhagen to Helsingør. Malmö to Copenhagen (Skr80) takes 35 minutes, trains leave every 20 minutes. The Öresund Runt card (Skr199) gives two days' free travel on ferries and local trains. The cards can be bought at the Pågatågen train station in Malmo.

SJ trains runs regularly to/from Helsingborg and Gothenburg via Lund. Direct trains run between Stockholm and Malmö, including X2000 services.

Skånetrafiken *(☎ 020-567567; Ⓦ www.skanetrafiken.skane.se)* operates local buses and trains in the Skåne region. It sells a variety of cards and passes, including a useful summer pass costing Skr395, valid for 25 days of travel throughout the county. Pågatågen local trains run to Helsingborg, Lund, Ystad and other destinations in Skåne. International rail passes are accepted.

Regional and long-distance buses depart from Stormgatan, opposite the post office (behind the station). Swebus Express runs daily to Stockholm, Gothenburg and Oslo. Trains are best for trips across the Öresund bridge.

In 2002 all ferry services between Copenhagen and Malmo ceased

Getting Around

The regular Flygbuss runs from Centralstationen to Sturup airport (Skr80); a taxi should cost no more than Sk350.

Malmö Lokaltrafik offices are at Gustav Adolfs torg and Värnhemstorget. Local tickets cost Skr14 for one hour's travel. Bus hubs are Centralplan (in front of Centralstationen), Gustav Adolfs Torg, Värnhemstorget and Triangeln. The Malmökortet includes city bus travel.

Bicycles can be rented for Skr120/600 per day/week from **Cykelkliniken** *(☎ 611 6666)*, behind Centralstationen.

LUND

☎ 046 • pop 99,600

The second-oldest town in Sweden, Lund was founded by the Danes around 1000. Construction of the cathedral began about 1100 and Lund became the largest archbishopric in Europe. Much of the medieval town can still be seen. The university was founded in 1666, after Sweden took over Skåne. Today, Lund retains its quiet yet airy feel and has a youthful population.

The **tourist office** *(☎ 355040; Ⓦ www.lund.se; Kyrkogatan 11; open daily June-Aug, Mon-Sat May & Sept, Mon-Fri Oct-Apr)* is opposite the cathedral. The **public library** *(St Petri kyrkogatan 6)* has free Internet access, but there's also an Internet café nearby, **Studio 9** *(Lilla Gråbrödersgatan)*.

The excellent **Kulturen** *(Tegnerplatsen; adult/child Skr50/free; open 11am-5pm daily mid-Apr–mid-Sept, noon-4pm Tues-Sun Oct–mid-Apr)* claims to be the world's second-oldest open-air museum (it opened in 1892). Its impressive collection of about 40 buildings fills two blocks and includes period homes from the 17th century and countless displays.

The magnificence of Lund's Romanesque **cathedral** *(open daily)* is well known, but for a real surprise visit at noon or 3pm (1pm and 3pm on Sunday and holidays) when the astronomical clock strikes up *In Dulci Jubilo* and the figures of the three kings begin their journey to the child Jesus. Close by, you can find out about the cathedral at **Domkyrkomuseet**, and the attached **Historiska Museet** has pre-Viking finds. Both museums are open 11am to 4pm Tuesday to Friday (combined entry Skr20/free).

Drottens kyrkoruin *(Kattesund 6)* are 11th-century church ruins and the underground **museum** *(adult/child Skr10/free;*

open 9am-4pm Tues-Fri, noon-4pm Sat & Sun) here has models and exhibits that fill in the details of Lund's past.

Places to Stay & Eat

You could easily make Lund a base and take trains to nearby towns if you stay at STF Vandrarhem **Tåget** *(☎ 142820; e trainhostel@ebrevet.nu; beds Skr120)*, behind the station. You sleep in railway carriages set in parkland, with three bunks to a room – quiet yet tiny and perhaps too familiar to weary train travellers.

Private rooms can be booked at the tourist office from Skr200 per person plus a Skr50 fee. Book early for tiny **Gräddhyllan Café & Hotell** *(☎ 157230; e graddhyllans@swipnet.se; Bytaregatan 14; singles/doubles Skr495/795, discounted to Skr400/600)*, a lovely place offering all of four rooms above a café.

Lund has plenty of eating possibilities, ranging from fast-food eateries and library cafés to popular evening hang-outs. **Saluhallen** *(Mårtenstorget)* is a good place for reasonably priced food, from pasta through to hamburgers and kebabs.

Habanero *(Kyrkogatan 21)* is good for an el cheapo Tex-Mex fill (lunch is Skr59). **Govindas** *(Bredgatan 28)* has a lunchtime vegetarian deal for Skr55.

Getting There & Away

It's just 15 minutes from Lund to Malmö by train and there are frequent SJ and Pågatågen departures (Skr34); some trains continue to Copenhagen. All long-distance trains between Stockholm and Malmö stop in Lund. Buses leave from outside the train station.

YSTAD

☎ 0411 • pop 26,200

Rambling cobbled streets and half-timbered houses remain in this agreeable medieval town, which is visited by daily ferries from Bornholm and Poland. The friendly **tourist office** *(☎ 577681; w www.visitystad.com; open daily mid-June–mid-Aug, Mon-Fri rest of year)* is opposite the train station. Next door is the large **Konstmuseum** *(adult/child Skr20/free; open Tues-Sun)*. Don't miss the medieval **Sankta Maria kyrka** *(Stortorget)* or historical **Ystads Stadsmuseum** *(adult/child Skr20/free; open daily)* in the old monastery church of Gråbrödraklostret.

On the Baltic coast, 19km east of Ystad, is **Ales Stenar** *(admission free; open year-round)*, a mysterious pre-Viking stone formation, in the shape of an oval, 67m along its long axis (bus No 322 from Ystad, summer only).

Those with their own wheels can choose B&B or cabin options along the scenic coastal roads. The central **SVIF hostel** *(☎ 577995; e ystad.stationen@home.se; dorm beds Skr 180)* is handily located in a renovated railway building at Ystad's train station. The **STF hostel** *(☎ 66566; dorm beds Skr135)* is 2km east of Ystad in a pleasant beachside recreation area (take bus No 572). **Hotell Bäckagården** *(☎ 19848; Dammgatan 36; singles/doubles from Skr450/650)* is a cosy guesthouse in a 17th-century home behind the tourist office.

Most budget eating places are on Stora Östergatan, the main pedestrian street.

Buses depart from outside the train station. To get to Trelleborg by bus, first take bus No 303 to Skateholm then transfer to bus No 183. Pågatågen trains run roughly hourly to/from Malmö (Skr70).

Unity Line *(☎ 556900)* ferries sail daily between Ystad and Świnoujście in Poland. In Ystad, the ferry terminal is within walking distance of the train station. Frequent ferries also operate between Ystad and the Danish island of Bornholm (see Bornholm in the Denmark chapter).

HELSINGBORG

☎ 042 • pop 118,500

The busy port of Helsingborg is perched on the Öresund coastline. There's a summer boulevard atmosphere in Stortorget, and the older buildings in the winding streets blend well with the newer shops. The seaside character is enhanced by an architectural pastiche of high beachfront houses. Denmark is only 25 minutes away by ferry.

The well-organised Helsingborg **tourist office** *(☎ 104350; w www.visit.helsingborg.se; Stortorget; open 9am-8pm Mon-Fri, 9am-5pm Sat & Sun June-Aug; 9am-6pm Mon-Fri, 10am-2pm Sat Sept-May, also 10am-2pm Sun in May)* can help with visitor inquiries. Most other travel-related needs are met inside the vast Knutpunkten complex at the seafront.

The eye-catching new **Dunkers Kulturhus** *(Kungsgaten 11; admission free; open 11am-6pm daily, to 10pm Tues & Thur)*, in the area just north of the transport terminals, houses the very good **town museum** and **art museum** *(adult/child Skr60/free for both)*, plus concert hall, restaurant and café. The square medieval tower and museum **Kärnan** *(adult/child Skr15/5; open to 7pm daily summer)*, the remains of a 14th-century castle, look over Öresund to the Danish heartland. The site can be accessed from steps near the tourist office.

Places to Stay & Eat

The SVIF hostel **Villa Thalassa** *(☎ 380660; Dag Hammarskjöldsväg; dorm beds from Skr160, singles/doubles from Skr275/400; open year-round)*, 3km north of the city centre, is reached by walking 500m along a path from the bus stop at Pålsjöbaden (bus No 219). The **STF hostel** *(☎ 131130; ⓔ boka@stfvandrarhem.helsingborg.nu; Planteringsvägen 69-71; beds from Skr160)*, 4km south of town, offers high-quality accommodation in a newly fitted and stylishly decorated hostel. Take bus No 1. The most central hostel is **Helsingborgs Vandrarhem** *(☎ 145850; ⓔ info@hbgturist.com; Järnvägsgatan 39; dorm beds from Skr165)*, an excellent place in a nondescript office building about 200m from Knutpunkten.

The quickest snacks and a good variety of restaurants are found upstairs in the **Knutpunkten complex**. **Fahlmans Café** *(Stortorget)* is the most traditional of the city's cafés, serving sandwiches and pastries. Unique **Ebbas Fik** *(Bruksgatan 20)* is styled in 1950s retro with superb results; there's an extensive café menu here, too.

Getting There & Away

The main transport centre is Knutpunkten; the underground platforms serve both the SJ and Pågatågen/Kustpilen trains departing for Stockholm, Gothenburg, Copenhagen, Oslo and nearby towns. At ground level and a bit south, but still inside the same complex, is the bus terminal where regional Skånetrafiken buses dominate, but daily long-distance services run to various destinations, including Gothenburg and Oslo.

Knutpunkten is the terminal for frequent **Scandlines** *(☎ 186300)* car ferries to Helsingør (Skr22, free with rail passes). Across the inner harbour, **Sundsbussarna** *(☎ 216060)* has a terminal with passenger-only ferries to Helsingør every 15 to 20 minutes in summer (Skr20, rail passes valid). The frequent **HH-Ferries** *(☎ 198000)* service to Helsingør is the cheapest, both for cars (from Skr245, including up to five passengers) and individual passengers (from Skr9, rail passes not valid).

DFDS Seaways *(☎ 241000; ⓦ www.dfdsseaways.com)* runs ferries every evening to Oslo (from Skr675/975 low/high season) from the Sunds terminal.

Götaland

The medieval kingdom of Götaland joined Svealand and Norrland to become Sweden 1000 years ago, but remained strongly influenced by Denmark. Soon after Gothenburg was founded by Gustav II Adolf in 1621, Sweden conquered the rest of the region.

Pricey but unforgettable is the long journey along the Göta Canal – from the rolling country of Östergötland, north of Linköping, into the great Lake Vättern, before continuing into the county of Västergötland on the other side and farther to Gothenburg.

GOTHENBURG (GÖTEBORG)

☎ 031 • pop 471,300

Gothenburg, Sweden's second-largest city, is wedded to its port and has a more Continental outlook than Stockholm. There's a lot more to Gothenburg than the showpiece Kungsportsavenyn boulevard and Konstmuseet, not least its heavy industries and heritage as a port. The Liseberg fun park, with its prominent 'space tower', is statistically Sweden's top attraction.

From the centre of the city, Kungsportsavenyn crosses the canal and leads up to Götaplatsen. 'Avenyn' is the heart of the city with boutiques, restaurants, theatres, galleries and street cafés.

Information

The main **tourist office** *(☎ 612500; ⓦ www.goteborg.com; Kungsportsplatsen 2; open 9am-6pm daily June-Aug; 9am-6pm Mon-Fri, 10am-2pm Sat Sept-May, also 10am-2pm Sun in May)* is central and busy. There is also a **branch office** at Nordstan shopping complex *(open daily)*. The Göteborg Pass (Skr175/95 adult/child for 24 hours) is a discount card giving free entry to Liseberg, free city tours and entry to a number of city attractions, as well as free travel by municipal public transport.

Forex offices are at Centralstationen, inside the Nordstan shopping complex, opposite the tourist office on Kungsportsplatsen, and at Kungsportsavenyn 22. Banks with ATMs can be found all over. The **post office** inside the Nordstan complex has long hours.

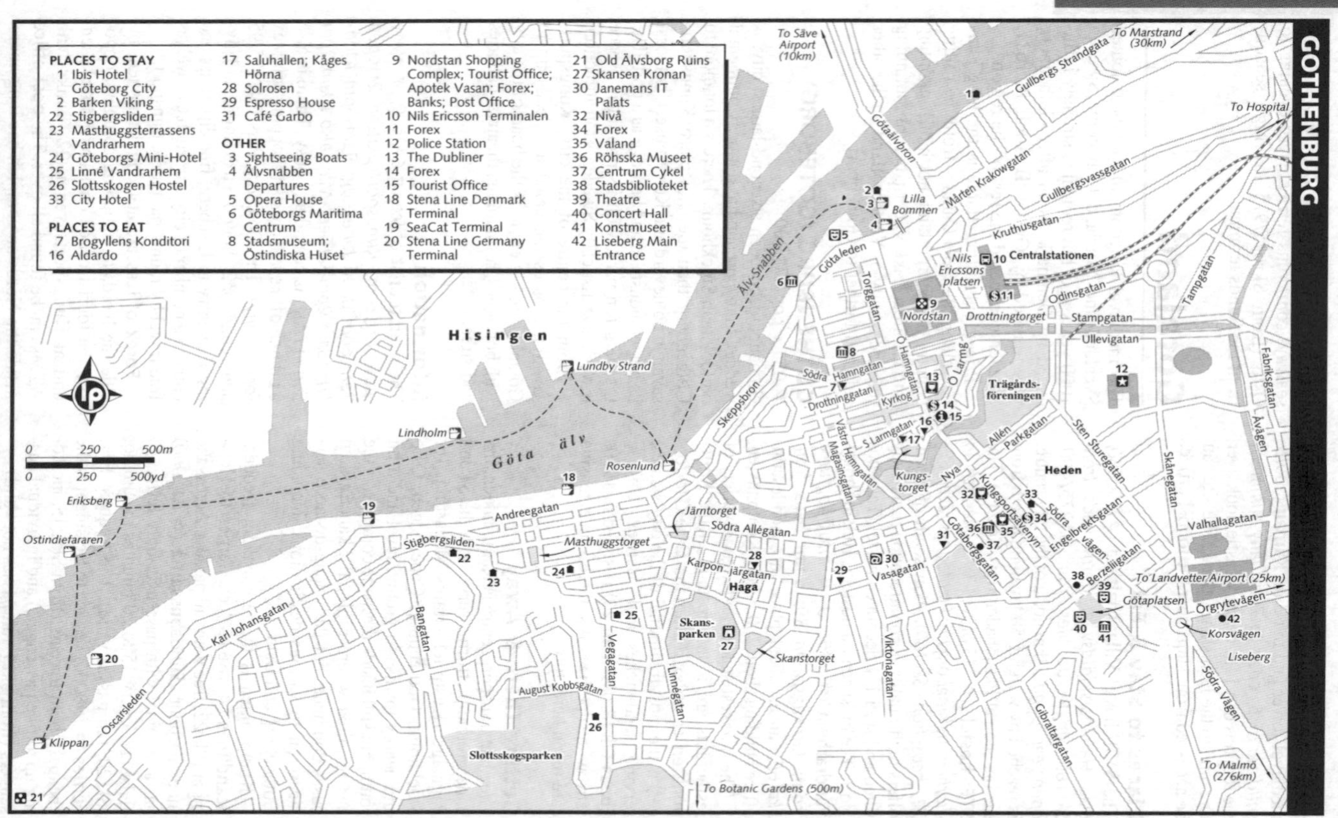
GOTHENBURG
PLACES TO STAY
1 Ibis Hotel Göteborg City
2 Barken Viking
22 Stigbergsliden
23 Masthuggsterrassens Vandrarhem
24 Göteborgs Mini-Hotel
25 Linné Vandrarhem
26 Slottsskogen Hostel
33 City Hotel
PLACES TO EAT
7 Brogyllens Konditori
16 Aldardo
17 Saluhallen; Kåges Hörna
28 Solrosen
29 Espresso House
31 Café Garbo
OTHER
3 Sightseeing Boats
4 Älvsnabben Departures
5 Opera House
6 Göteborgs Maritima Centrum
8 Stadsmuseum; Östindiska Huset
9 Nordstan Shopping Complex; Tourist Office; Apotek Vasan; Forex; Banks; Post Office
10 Nils Ericsson Terminalen
11 Forex
12 Police Station
13 The Dubliner
14 Forex
15 Tourist Office
18 Stena Line Denmark Terminal
19 SeaCat Terminal
20 Stena Line Germany Terminal
21 Old Älvsborg Ruins
27 Skansen Kronan
30 Janemans IT Palats
32 Nivå
34 Forex
35 Valand
36 Röhsska Museet
37 Centrum Cykel
38 Stadsbiblioteket
39 Theatre
40 Concert Hall
41 Konstmuseet
42 Liseberg Main Entrance
To Säve Airport (10km)
To Marstrand (30km)
To Hospital
Gullbergs Strandgata
Götaälvbron
Mårten Krakowgatan
Gullbergsvassgatan
Kruthusgatan
Lilla Bommen
Älv-Snabben
Göta leden
Torggatan
Nils Ericssons platsen
Centralstationen
Odinsgatan
Tampgatan
Nordstan
Drottningtorget
Stampgatan
Ullevigatan
Fabriksgatan
Åvägen
Hisingen
Lundby Strand
Södra Hamngatan
Ö Hamngatan
Ö Larmg
Trägårds-föreningen
Drottninggatan
Kyrkog
Skeppsbron
S Larmgatan
Västra Hamngatan
Magasinsgatan
Kungs-torget
Nya Allén
Parkgatan
Sten Sturegatan
Skånegatan
Heden
Lindholm
Göta älv
Rosenlund
Eriksberg
Andreegatan
Järntorget
Södra Allégatan
Kungsportsavenyn
Södra vägen
Engelbrektsgatan
Götabergsgatan
Valhallagatan
Ostindiefararen
Stigbergsliden
Masthuggstorget
Karpon-järgatan
Vasagatan
Berzeliigatan
To Landvetter Airport (25km)
Götaplatsen
Örgrytevägen
Haga
Korsvägen
Liseberg
Karl Johansgatan
Bangatan
Skans-parken
Skanstorget
Vegagatan
Linnégatan
Viktoriagatan
August Kobbsgatan
Gibraltargatan
Södra Vägen
Oscarsleden
Klippan
Slottsskogsparken
To Malmö (276km)
To Botanic Gardens (500m)
0 250 500m
0 250 500yd

Janemans IT Palats *(Viktoriagatan 14)* is an Internet café charging Sk50 per hour.

Liseberg

The fun park at Liseberg *(☎ 400100; tram No 4, 5, 6 or 8 from Brunnsparken; adult/child under 7 Skr50/free, with Göteborg Card free; open to 10pm or 11pm most days May-Aug)* is dominated by its futuristic spaceport-like tower. The ride up to the top, some 83m above the ground, climaxes in a spinning dance and a breathtaking view of the city. For admission and exact opening hours, check W www.liseberg.se.

Museums

After Liseberg the museums are the strongest attractions. The **Stadsmuseum** *(Norra Hamngatan; adult/child Skr40/10; open 10am-5pm daily May-Aug, closed Mon rest of year)*, in Östindiska huset, has archaeological, local and historical collections, including Sweden's only genuine Viking ship.

The main art collections are at **Konstmuseet** *(Götaplatsen; adult/child Skr40/10; open 11am-6pm Tues-Thur, 11am-5pm Fri-Sun)*. This museum has some impressive collections of Nordic and European masters and is notable for works by Rubens, Van Gogh, Rembrandt and Picasso. The excellent **Röhsska Museet** *(Vasagatan 37; adult/child Skr40/10; open noon-5pm Tues-Sun)* covers modern Scandinavian design and decorative arts. **Göteborgs Maritima Centrum** *(Packhuskajen; adult/child Skr60/30; open daily Mar-Nov)* claims to be the largest floating ship museum in the world and usually displays 13 historical ships, including the submarine *Nordkaparen*.

Places to Stay

Gothenburg has several good hostels near the city centre, with quite reasonable prices compared to other Swedish cities. The tourist office can arrange **private rooms** from Skr175/225 a single/double plus a Skr60 fee.

Hostels There are a number of good hostels, most in the central southwest area, in apartment buildings that sometimes inspire little confidence from the outside, but inside are of a very high standard and are open year-round.

Well-run **Masthuggsterrassens Vandrarhem** *(☎ 424820; e masthuggsterrassen.vandrarhem@telia.com; Masthuggsterrassen 8; dorm beds from Skr150)* is clean, quiet and close to the ferries to Denmark. Take tram No 3, 4 or 9 to Masthuggstorget and follow the signs. Nearby is the STF hostel **Stigbergsliden** *(☎ 241620; e vandrarhem.stigbergsliden@swipnet.se; Stigbergsliden 10; tram No 3, 4 or 9 to Stigbergstorget; dorm beds Skr115)*, in a renovated 18th-century seaman's house. Breakfast is Skr40, and there's a good kitchen, laundry, TV room and garden.

STF's **Slottsskogen** *(☎ 426520; e mail@slottsskogenvh.se; Vegagatan 21; tram No 1 or 2 to Olivedalsgatan; dorm beds from Skr100)* is a friendly, appealing place with excellent facilties. Down the road is another good option, the SVIF hostel **Linné Vandrarhem** *(☎ 121060; Vegagatan 22; beds from Skr160)*. Clean and inviting **Göteborgs Mini-Hotel** *(☎ 241023; e info@minihotel.se; Tredje Långgatan; beds from Skr130)* is in the same area.

Hotels The large floating hotel, **Ibis Hotel Göteborg City** *(☎ 802560; Gullbergskajen 217; rooms Skr525-650)* has comfortable, well-priced rooms. The down side is that it is in quite an isolated part of town. Better located is another large boat hotel, **Barken Viking** *(☎ 635800; Gullbergskajen; singles/doubles 'crew quarters' with shared facilties Skr600/800)*, near Lilla Bommen.

City Hotel *(☎ 708 4000; e receptionen@cityhotelgbg.se; Lorensbergsgatan 6; singles/doubles with shared facilities Skr395/495)* is in a fine location behind Kungsportsavenyn.

Places to Eat

Kungsportsavenyn, the Champs Élysées of Gothenburg, is lined with all kinds of restaurants. Vasagata and Linnégatan are similar, with quite a few popular places.

Right by the tourist office, busy **Aldardo** *(Kungstorget 12)* is a great spot to pick up authentic Italian fast food – home-made pizza *al taglio* (by the slice) costs around Skr25, and pasta is from Skr35. In the middle of neighbouring Saluhällen, full of excellent budget eateries and food stalls, **Kåges Hörna** serves some of the best cheap food around – chicken salad, lasagne and the pasta special all cost about Skr35.

Cafés are numerous and invariably of high quality. **Café Garbo** *(Vasagatan 40)* and the very trendy **Espresso House** *(Vasagatan 22)* are two of several excellent places along the leafy Vasagatan boulevard. **Brogyllens Konditori** *(Västra Hamngatan 2)* is a lovely traditional place selling great breads and pastries. Vegetarians should head for **Solrosen** *(Karponjärgatan 4)*, a slightly grungy place with great buffets and dishes from Skr60.

Entertainment

You'll find some good pubs and bars along the main thoroughfares. **The Dubliner** *(Östra Hamngatan 50B)* is as authentic an Irish pub as you'll ever find on the Continent and has live music nightly in summer.

Kungsportavenyn, often referred to simply as 'Avenyn' (the avenue) is the place to go for nightlife. Take a wander among the restaurant-bars and take your pick. **Nivå** at No 9 and **Valand**, on the corner with Vasagatan, are popular nightclubs.

Facing each other near Konstmuseet are the city **Theatre** and **Concert Hall**, often with interesting performances. The **Opera House** *(Christina Nilssons gata)* is also worth a visit.

Getting There & Away

Bus The modern bus station, Nils Ericsson Terminalen, is next to the train station. There's a Tidpunkten office here giving information and selling tickets for all city and regional public transport within the Gothenburg, Bohuslän and Västergötland region.

Eurolines *(☎ 020-987377; open 9am-5.30pm Mon-Fri)* main Swedish office is at Kyrkogatan 40. **Swebus Express** has an office at the bus terminal and operates frequent buses to most major towns (up to 10 daily to Stockholm, from Skr285). Cheaper **Säfflebussen** *(☎ 020-160 0600)* runs to Copenhagen (from Skr180, six daily), Oslo (from Skr150, six daily) and Stockholm (from Skr240, once or twice daily).

Train Centralstationen serves SJ and regional trains, with direct trains to Malmö, Copenhagen, Oslo and Stockholm. Tågkompaniet night trains run to the far north. Direct trains to Stockholm depart approximately hourly, with X2000 trains every one or two hours.

Boat Gothenburg is a major entry point for ferries. Nearest the city centre, the **Stena Line** *(☎ 704 0000)* Denmark terminal near Masthuggstorget (tram No 3, 4 or 9) has up to 11 daily departures for Frederikshavn in summer, with 50% discount for rail pass-holders. Faster and dearer **SeaCat** *(☎ 720 0800)* catamarans to Frederikshavn depart up to three times daily in summer from near Sjöfartsmuseet. Take tram No 3 or 9 to Stigbergstorget. Farther west is the **Stena Line** *(☎ 031-858000)* terminal for the daily car ferry to Kiel (in Germany). Take tram No 3 or 9 to Chapmans Torg.

DFDS Seaways *(☎ 650650)* sails twice weekly to Newcastle from Skandiahamnen on Hisingen (buses leave 1½ hours earlier from Nils Ericsson Terminalen; Skr50).

Getting Around

Buses, trams and ferries run by **Västtrafik** *(☎ 0771-414300)* make up the city public transport system; there are Tidpunkten information booths inside Nils Ericson Terminalen, at Brunnsparken and on Drottningtorget. An individual ticket costs Skr16. Cheaper and easy-to-use 'value cards' cost Skr100 and reduce the cost considerably. A 24-hour *Dagkort* (day pass) for the whole city area costs Skr50. Holders of the Göteborg Card travel free.

The easiest way to cover lengthy distances in Gothenburg is by tram. Also convenient and fun are the Älvsnabben ferries, which run between Lilla Bommen and Klippan every 30 minutes or so.

Centrum Cykel *(Chalmersgatan 19)* offers bicycle rental for Skr100 per day.

LINKÖPING

☎ 013 • pop 134,000

Known for its medieval cathedral and aeroplane industries, Linköping is both a modern city and a preserver of traditions in its numerous museums. The **tourist office** *(☎ 206835; W www.linkoping.se; Klostergatan 68)* is inside Quality Hotel Ekoxen. The striking city **library**, near the cathedral, has been rebuilt after a fire and offers Internet access. There's also an **Internet café** *(Bantorget 1)* not far from the long-distance bus station.

Things to See & Do

The enormous **cathedral**, with its 107m spire, is Linköping's landmark and one of Sweden's oldest and largest churches. There are numerous gravestones and medieval treasures. The nearby castle houses the **Castle & Cathedral Museum** *(adult/child Skr40/free; open Tues-Sun)*.

Just north of the cathedral, **Östergötlands Länsmuseum** *(adult/child Skr20/10; open Tues-Sun)* houses an extensive collection by a variety of European painters, including Cranach's view of Eden, *Original Sin*, and

Swedish art reaching back to the Middle Ages. The concrete floor of **Sankt Lars kyrka** *(Storgatan; open Mon-Sat)* was built above a medieval church crypt. Downstairs, you can see 11th-century gravestones and skeletons.

Some 2km west of the city is **Gamla Linköping** *(bus Nos 202 or 214; admission free; village & most museums open daily year-round)*, one of the biggest living-museum villages in Sweden. Among the 90 quaint houses are about a dozen theme museums, many shops and a small chocolate factory.

Places to Stay & Eat

The excellent, central STF **Vandrarhem Linköping** *(☎ 149090; e lkpgvandrarhem@swipnet.se; Klostergatan 52A; dorm beds from Skr180, singles/doubles Skr595/680, discounted weekends to Skr455/550; open year-round)* has dorm beds and a few hotel-style rooms, most with kitchenette. In the centre of Valla Fritidsområde is **Mjellerumsgårdens Vandrarhem** *(☎ 122730; dorm beds Skr160; open year-round)*, which doesn't have a kitchen.

Not far from the train station is **Hotell Östergyllen** *(☎ 102075; Hamngatan 2B; singles/doubles with shared facilties from Skr350/500)*, a reasonable mid-range choice.

Most places to eat are on the main square or nearby streets, especially along buzzing Ågatan. **Gula Huset** *(Ågatan)* offers lunch for Skr60 and evening dishes from Skr78. Around Stora Torget, **Linds** has a Skr59 lunch buffet, à-la-carte meals from Skr45 (including nachos and pasta) and a courtyard area.

Getting There & Away

Regional and local buses have terminals adjacent to the train station. Long-distance buses leave from 500m north of the train station. Linköping is on the main north–south railway line and SJ trains stop roughly every hour.

Regional (and local) traffic is run by **ÖstgötaTrafiken** *(☎ 0771-211010)*; there is an information office at the station.

VADSTENA

☎ 0143 • pop 7600

Beautiful Vadstena on Lake Vättern is a legacy of both church and state power. The dominant historical figure was St Birgitta, who established her order of nuns here in 1370. The atmosphere in the old town (and also by the lake) makes Vadstena one of the most pleasant spots in Sweden. The **tourist office** *(☎ 31570; open daily in summer)* is inside the Renaissance **Vadstena slott** *(adult/child Skr50/10; open daily May-Sept)*, which looks straight over the harbour and lake beyond. The superb 15th-century **klosterkyrkan** *(abbey church; admission free; open daily May-Sept)* has a combination of Gothic and some Renaissance features. Inside are the accumulated relics of St Birgitta and medieval sculpture.

A series of ancient legends is connected with **Rökstenen**, Sweden's most impressive and famous rune stone, by the church at Rök, just off the E4 on the road to Heda and Alvastra.

It's essential to book at he central **STF hostel** *(☎ 10302; Skänningegatan 20; dorm beds Skr145; open year-round)* from late August to early June. A more appealing option is the lakeside **STF hostel** *(☎ 20368, e svandrarhem.nu; beds Skr135)*, a friendly place in a lovely, quiet setting 15km southwest of Vadstena. Take bus No 610, and it's about a 750m walk from the stop at Borghamn.

For filled baguettes (from Skr40) and other light meals, visit the open-air café **Hampaviljongen**, in the park in front of the castle. **Vadstena Klosterhotel**, in the abbey area, serves a fine buffet lunch for Skr85.

Only buses run to Vadstena: bus No 661 regularly links the town with Mjölby (where you can catch trains to Linköping and Stockholm). Swebus Express bus No 840 runs once daily from Jönköping to Örebro via Vadstena.

Småland

The forested county of Småland is famous for glass production; you can visit many of its numerous factories. It was the homeland of many 19th-century emigrants to the USA.

GLASRIKET

☎ 0481

With dense forests and quaint red houses, Glasriket (w www.glasriket.net) is popular among tourists – it's the most visited area in Sweden outside Stockholm and Gothenburg. The 'Kingdom of Crystal' has roots that go way back: Kosta village was founded in 1742, and by the end of the 19th century 10 factories were in full swing.

This area is expensive and not particularly easy to explore without your own transport.

Bicycle tours are excellent if you follow the minor roads; there are plenty of hostels and you can camp throughout the countryside.

Of the two glass factories in the eastern part of Glasriket, traditional **Pukeberg** is a worthwhile stop for its quaint setting and higher quality. The **tourist office** *(☎ 45085; ⓦ www.nybro.se; Stadshusplan)* is inside the town hall. **Nybro Lågprishotell & Vandrarhem** *(☎ 10932; Vasagatan 22; dorm beds Skr130, beds in smaller rooms with en suite Skr170)*, south of the centre near Pukeberg, is the local STF hostel; you can rent bicycles here. SJ trains between Alvesta and Kalmar stop here every hour or two. Regional bus No 131 runs to/from Kalmar.

The three small Småland villages of Kosta, Boda and Orrefors are home to the three biggest names in Swedish glass production. **Kosta** is where Glasriket started in 1742. **Boda** is a quaint little village with a large factory outlet and several other shops. **Orrefors** *(ⓦ www.orrefors.se)* was founded in 1898. The factory complex is impressive, and there's a good hostel nearby – the friendly, well-equipped **STF hostel** *(☎ 30020; dorm beds Skr110-150; open May-Aug)*.

KALMAR

☎ 0480 • pop 59,800

The port of Kalmar was long the key to Baltic power, and the short-lived Scandinavian union agreement of 1397 was signed at its grand castle. Kalmar was vital to Swedish interests until the 17th century and its streets and impressive edifices retain a strong historical flavour. Visit the **tourist office** *(☎ 15350; ⓦ www.kalmar.se/turism; Larmgatan 6; open daily in summer)* for information.

The once-powerful Renaissance castle **Kalmar Slott** *(adult/child Skr70/20; open daily Apr-Sept)*, by the sea south of the railway, was the key to Sweden before lands to the south were claimed from Denmark. The panelled King Erik chamber is the highlight of the interior, while another exhibits punishment methods used on women in crueller times.

Vandrarhem Svanen *(☎ 12928; ⓔ info@hotellsvanen.se; Rappegatan 1; dorm beds Skr160)* is a well-equipped STF hostel attached to **Kalmar Lågprishotell** *(☎ 25560; singles/doubles Skr465/595)*, on the adjacent island of Ängö (take bus No 402). **Söderportshotellet** *(☎ 12501; Slottsvägen 1; singles/doubles Skr350/530; open mid-June–mid-Aug)* is right by the castle and offers good summertime accommodation in student digs. **Ströget arcade** *(Storgatan 24)* houses a small food hall, with a good selection of places.

All regional traffic is run by **Kalmar Länstrafik** *(☎ 0491-761200; open daily mid-June–mid-Aug, closed Mon rest of year)*, including the Rasken long-distance services and buses to Öland. A one-way ticket costs Skr16 to Skr117 within the county; a Sommarkort is valid from mid-June to mid-August on all buses and trains within the county and costs around Skr850. All regional and long-distance buses depart from the train station; local town buses have their own terminal on Östra Sjögatan.

SJ trains run every hour or two between Kalmar and Alvesta (with connections to the main north–south line) and to Gothenburg.

ÖLAND

☎ 0485 • pop 25,000

More windmills than Holland? There are 400 on Öland today, but there were once around 2000. Most are the characteristic wooden huts on a rotating base. Also prominent are the lighthouses at the northern and southern tips of the island.

Because Öland is a popular summer destination, budget accommodation options abound. The island is reached from Kalmar via the 6km Ölandsbron (bridge), once the longest in Europe. Buses connect all main towns from Kalmar (bus Nos 101-106 all cross the bridge to Färjestaden; No 101 and 106 go to Borgholm).

Borgholm

The 'capital' of Öland is a pleasant small town with shops, cafés and an enormous ruined castle. The **tourist office** *(☎ 89000; open daily in summer)* is at the bus station.

The town is dominated from the hill just to the south by **Borgholm Slottsruin** *(adult/child Skr50/20; open daily Apr-Sept)*. This castle was finally burned and abandoned early in the 18th century after being used as a dye works. The museum within is excellent. Sweden's most famous 'summer house', **Solliden Palace** *(adult/child Skr50/free; open daily in summer)*, 2.5km south of the town centre, is used by the royal family. It has beautiful parks and pavilion exhibitions.

Coastal **Grönhags Camping** *(☎ 72116; tent sites low/high season Skr100/150)* is one of a half-dozen large, neighbouring camping grounds in Köping (about 4km north of Borgholm). Most camping grounds are open late April to mid-September, and prices are increased in peak summer season (from midsummer to mid-August).

Just outside the centre of town is the **STF hostel** *(☎ 10756; dorm beds Skr110-160; open mid-May–Aug)*, in Rosenfors Manor, set in a pretty garden. **Olssons rumsuthyrning** *(☎ 77939; Tullgatan 12A; doubles winter/summer from Skr400/600)* has some simple double rooms; prices exclude breakfast; but there is a kitchen guests can use.

The main square in town has the usual collection of fast-food stalls and ice-cream kiosks. **Pubben** *(Storgatan 18)* is a classic English-style pub serving up snacks and light meals from Skr40.

Around Öland

Sandvik, on the west coast of Öland 30km north of Borgholm, has the familiar 'Dutch'-type **windmill** *(adult/child Skr15/7; open daily in summer)*. In summer, climb the eight storeys for a great view back to the mainland. The remains of the medieval fortified church **Källa ödekyrka**, at a little harbour, 36km northeast of Borgholm off road 136, are fascinating, as it and other churches actually supplanted the mighty stone fortresses as defensive works. **Grankullavik**, in the far north, has sandy beaches and dense summer crowds, but the natural attractions in the nearby **Trollskogen** nature reserve are worth a visit. Northern Öland has plenty of camping grounds, and the SVIF **Grankullavik Vandrarhem** *(☎ 24040; dorm beds from Skr175; open May-Sept)* has a kitchen, restaurant and bakery. The **STF hostel** *(☎ 22038; dorm beds Skr100-165; open May-Aug)* is in Böda. Bus No 106 goes north.

The long bridge from Kalmar lands you on the island just north of **Färjestaden** ('ferry town' – the pre-bridge name), where there's a **tourist office** *(☎ 560600; Ⓦ www.olandsturist.se; open daily in summer)* at the Träffpunkt Öland centre beside the road. The tourist office will book rooms (free of charge) or cabin accommodation (Skr50 fee) throughout the island. In the middle of the east coast at Långlöt, **Himmelsberga** *(open daily May-Aug)* is a farm village from a bygone age. The quaint cottages have been repainted and fully furnished as a **museum** *(adult/child Skr50/free; open daily in summer)*. The vast **Ismantorp fortress**, with house remains and nine mysterious gates, is 5km west of the museum.

The southern half of the island is chiefly a haven for nature and the relics of humankind's settlements and conflicts, attested to by the Iron Age fortresses and graveyards of all periods. The big ring forts, **Eketorp** *(open daily May-Aug)*, 6km northeast of Grönhögen, has been reconstructed to show what these villages must have been like in early medieval times.

Gotland

☎ 0498 • pop 57,400

Gotland, largest of the Baltic islands, is also one of Sweden's most historical regions. Attractions include more than 100 medieval churches, an untold number of prehistoric sites and the odd *raukar* limestone formations (remains of 400 million-year-old coral reefs).

Gotland is probably the top budget travel destination in Sweden; bicycle travel is by far the best option, free camping in forests is easy and legal, most attractions are free and there are more than 30 hostels around the island. The island is jam-packed, however, with holidaying Swedes in July and August, and is *the* summer party spot for young Swedes, who come for beaches and booze.

Keep an eye out for information boards along roads; they mark prehistoric sites (such as stone ship-settings, burial mounds and hilltop fortresses), which can be visited freely at any time. Nowhere else in northern Europe are there so many medieval churches in such a small area – 92 outside Visby, over 70 of which have medieval frescoes or very rare medieval stained glass.

Skyways flies regularly between Visby and three mainland airports: Stockholm Arlanda, Stockholm Bromma and Norrköping. The cheaper local airline is **Gotlands Flyg** *(☎ 222222; Ⓦ www.gotlandsflyg.se)*. The island's **airport** *(☎ 263100)* is 4km northeast of Visby and is served by buses.

Destination Gotland *(☎ 201020; Ⓦ www.destinationgotland.se)* operates car ferries year-round to/from Visby out of Nynäshamn and Oskarshamn. Departures from the former are from one to five times daily (five hours, or three by high-speed catamaran). From Oskarshamn, there are one or two daily departures (except Saturday, from early November until mid-March) in either direction (four to five hours). Regular one-way adult tickets cost Skr174/276 for the ferry/catamaran, but from mid-June to mid-August there is a more complicated fare system, with prices ranging from Skr152 to Skr258 for the ferry trip, Skr236 to Skr474 for the catamaran sailing (some overnight, evening and early-morning sailings mid-week have the cheaper fares).

Kollektiv Trafiken *(☎ 214112)* runs buses via most villages to all corners of the island. A one-way ticket will not cost more than Skr59 (taking a bicycle on board will cost an additional Skr40), but enthusiasts will find a monthly ticket good value at Skr590.

VISBY

☎ 0498 • pop 21,400

The narrow cobbled streets and impressive town walls of the medieval port of Visby, a living relic with more than 40 proud towers and the ruins of great churches, attest to the town's former Hanseatic glories. Today it leaves no tourist disappointed. From mid-May to mid-August cars are banned in the old town, and the highlight is the costumes and re-enactments of **Medieval Week** *(ⓦ www.medeltidsveckan.com)* during the first week of August. Book accommodation well in advance. The **tourist office** *(☎ 201700; ⓦ www.gotland.com; Hamngatan 4; open daily May-Sept)* can help with visitor information. The public **library** *(Cramérgatan)* is good for free Internet access.

The town is a noble sight, with its 3.5km-long **wall** of 40 towers breached in only two places. The ruins of 10 **medieval churches** within the town walls contrast with the old but sound **Cathedral of St Maria**. Ask at the tourist office about walking tours of the town (Skr80, two hours).

Gotlands Fornsal *(Strandgatan 14; adult/child Skr50/free; open daily in summer, closed Mon rest of year)* is one of the largest and best regional museums in Sweden. Extraordinary 8th-century pre-Viking picture stones, human skeletons, silver treasures and medieval wooden sculptures are highlights.

Places to Stay

The closest camping ground is **Norderstrands Camping** *(☎ 212157; tent sites low/high season Skr85/145; cabins from Skr350/550; open late Apr–mid-Sept)*, by the sea 800m north of Visby's ring wall.

Gotlands Resor *(☎ 201260; ⓔ info@gotlandsresor.se)* is a travel agency that can book private rooms in Visby – singles/doubles cost around Skr285/425 inside the town walls, or Skr240/380 outside.

The **STF hostel** *(☎ 269842; ⓔ carl.tholin@tjelvar.org; dorm beds from Skr115; open mid-June–mid-Aug)* is southeast of the town centre off Lännavägen, in a school residence and open only in peak season. The **Fängelse Vandrarhem** *(☎ 206050; Skeppsbron 1; dorm beds from Skr150; open year-round)* offers beds in the cells of an old jail. You have to call ahead to book a bed at **Jernvägshotellet** *(☎ 271707; ⓔ staff@visbyjernvagshotell.com; Adelsgatan 9; beds from Skr170; open year-round)*, a small, central hostel.

Hamnhotellet *(☎ 201250; Färjeleden 3; singles/doubles low season Skr560/600, high season Skr640/760)* is not far from the ferry terminal and offers uninspiring but cheap (for Visby) hotel rooms.

Places to Eat

Most restaurants and bars are around the Old Town squares, on Adelsgatan or at the harbour. There are a few cheap fast-food places on Adelsgatan. **Nya Effes**, just off Adelsgatan, is an eerie bar built into the town wall and is a good place for a meal or beer; there's regular live music here in summer.

Good places around buzzing Stora Torget include **Restaurang Rosengården**, with weekday lunches for Skr62; **Nunnan**, with a menu featuring Greek dishes; and the cellar restaurant-bars **Gutekällaren** and **Munkkälleren**, both home to nightclubs popular with the summer crowd.

Getting Around

Bicycles can be hired from Skr60/300 per day/week from behind Saluhall on the harbour or at Österport. **Gotlands Cykeluthyrning** *(☎ 214133)*, behind Saluhall, also rents tents for Skr75/250 per day/week.

Norrland

The northern half of Sweden has always been considered a world apart. It's closely associated with the pioneers' struggle to produce the timber and iron ore necessary for the construction of the railways that opened up the region. The Arctic wilderness attracts walkers, skiers and canoeists.

Inlandsbanan, the railway from Mora to Gällivare via Östersund, Storuman, Arvidsjaur and Jokkmokk, offers a great way to see the north. Infrequent express buses follow most main highways.

GÄVLE

☎ 026 • pop 91,200

Gävle, the gateway to Norrland, is probably the most pleasant of the northern cities to walk in because of its architecture and parks; note the contrast between the wooden residences of Villastaden and Gamla Gefle. The helpful **tourist office** *(☎ 147430; W www.gavle.se/turism; Drottninggatan 37; open daily in summer)* is not far from the train station.

The wooden old town of **Gamla Gefle**, south of the city centre, shows what Gävle was like before it was virtually destroyed by fire in 1869. The regional **Länsmuseum** *(Södra Strandgatan 20; adult/child Skr30/free; open Tues-Sun)* has an excellent art collection and interesting historical exhibitions. The oldest of the churches in Gävle is **Heliga Trefaldighets kyrka** at the western end of Drottninggatan, which has an 11th-century **rune stone** inside.

The centrally located **STF hostel** *(☎ 621 745; e stf.vandrarhem@telia.com; Södra Rådmansgatan 1; beds from Skr120)* is clean and quiet and set around a pleasant courtyard. **Nya Järnvägshotellet** *(☎ 120990; singles/doubles Skr395/525, discounted to Skr300/450)*, opposite the train station, is the cheapest hotel in town.

Fashionable **Brända Bocken** *(Stortorget; meals from Skr64)* is right in the heart of the action on the main square, with lots of outdoor seating. Excellent, tiny **Söders Deli** *(Södra Kungsgatan 11)* serves good coffee and authentic Italian *ciabatta* or pasta (Skr40 to Skr75).

There are numerous long-distance bus services to choose from: Y-buss runs daily to Umeå (Skr280) and Östersund (Skr210). **SGS Bussen** *(☎ 133030)* operates two to four daily services to Stockholm (Skr110). Swebus Express runs to Uppsala (Skr125) and Stockholm (Skr165) once or twice daily.

SJ trains run to Stockholm via Uppsala, and northwards to Sundsvall and beyond; there are up to six X2000 services and several slower trains daily. Other useful direct trains include Gävle to Falun and Örebro.

ÖSTERSUND

☎ 063 • pop 58,400

This pleasant, formerly Norwegian town by Lake Storsjön, in whose chill waters lurks a rarely sighted monster, attracts travellers with its outstanding budget accommodation. The **tourist office** *(☎ 144001; W www.ostersund.se/turist; Rådhusgatan 44; open daily in summer)* is opposite the town hall. The large **public library**, opposite the bus station, offers free Internet access.

Don't miss **Jamtli** *(adult/child summer Skr90/free, rest of year Skr60/free; open daily June-Aug, closed Mon at other times)*, 1km north of the town centre. This museum is the highlight of Östersund, combining the lively exhibitions of the regional museum with a large museum village with staff wearing period clothing.

You can live within the museum: the quaint STF **Vandrarhemmet Jamtli** *(☎ 122060; beds Skr140-160; open year-round)* is inside the precinct. **Östersunds Vandrarhem** *(☎ 101027; Postgränd 4; dorm beds Skr145)* is located in the town centre, and **Vandrarhemmet Rallaren** *(☎ 132232; Bangårdsgatan 6; dorm beds Skr140)* is conveniently next to the train station. **Pensionat Svea** *(☎ 512901; e pensionatsvea@spray.se; Storgatan 49; singles/doubles Skr440/540)* is a cosy place close to the heart of town; prices include breakfast.

Kebab City *(Storgatan 31; meals around Skr50)* serves burger, kebab and falafel meals. Most restaurants are on Prästgatan, the main pedestrian street.

The train station is a short walk south from the town centre, but the main regional bus station is central on Gustav III Torg; local buses usually run to both. Local buses Nos 1, 3, 4, 5 and 9 go to Frösön. Bus No 45 runs south to Mora twice a day. Bus No 156 runs west to Åre; bus 63 runs twice daily northeast to Umea.

Direct trains run from Stockholm via Gävle, and some continue to Storlien (from where you can catch trains to Norway). You can also catch a train east to Sundsvall. In summer the Inlandsbanan train runs once daily, to Gällivare (Skr485) or Mora (Skr240).

ÅRE & AROUND

☎ 0647 • pop 9600

Arguably Sweden's top mountain sports destination, the Åre area (W www.skistar.com/are) has 45 ski lifts that serve some 100 pistes and 1000 vertical metres of skiable slopes, including a superb 6.5km downhill run (day pass Skr270). The skiing season is from November to mid-May, but conditions are best from February. A whole range of winter activities, as well as countless opportunities for summer outdoor recreation, are available. Åre's **tourist office** *(☎ 17720; open daily in summer & winter)*, in the train station, can help you out. In winter it's best to book accommodation and skiing packages through **Åre Resor** *(☎ 17700; ⓔ reservations@areresort.se)*.

Åre Camping *(☎ 50054; tent sites from Skr130)* is a good summer option. **Park Villan** *(☎ 17733; Parkvägen 6; beds Skr170)*, the yellow house in the park opposite the train station, offers good backpacker accommodation outside of the ski season. The **STF hostel** *(☎ 30138; ⓔ brattlandsgarden@user.bip.net; dorm beds Skr120)* is 8km east of Åre. Not all hotels stay open in summer, but those that do offer great bargains. **Åre Fjällby** *(☎ 13600; ⓔ reception@arefjallby.com; self-contained apartments in summer from Skr520)*, for example, offers a three-nights-for-the-price-of-two package.

Like the hotels, the majority of restaurants are closed in summer, but there are still some very good choices, primarily centred on the main square. Typical Swedish fast food is available at **Åre Kiosk & Grill**, but nearby **Liten Krog** and **Werséns** (both with dishes from around Skr70) have more style.

Regional bus No 156 runs from Östersund and connects Åre to the nearby winter-sports centre of **Duved** (much quieter and more family-oriented than Åre). Regular trains between Stockholm and Storlien, via Östersund, stop at Åre. Storlien is the terminus for SJ trains; change here for Norwegian trains to Hell and Trondheim.

UMEÅ

☎ 090 • pop 105,000

The port and university city of Umeå is among Sweden's fastest-growing towns. The **tourist office** *(☎ 161616; ⓦ www.umea.se/turism; Renmarkstorget 15; open daily in summer)* can organise outdoor activities. **Spixel** *(Skolgatan 44)* is an Internet café not far from the hostel.

Gammlia, 1km east of the town centre, has several museums and shouldn't be missed. It includes the regional **Västerbottens Museum** *(adult/child Skr20/free)*, the modern art museum **Bildmuseet** and the **Maritime Museum**. The **Friluftsmuseet**, with old houses and staff wearing period clothes is also worth a visit. The museums are open daily in summer (closed Monday in winter).

The well-run **STF hostel** *(☎ 771650; ⓔ info@vandrarhemmet.se; Västra Esplanaden 10; beds from Skr115)* is clean and central.

Umeå is the main centre for **Länstrafiken Västerbotten** *(☎ 020-910019)*, the regional bus network. Direct buses to Mo i Rana in Norway run daily; other daily destinations include Östersund, Skellefteå and Luleå. Tågkompaniet trains leave daily from Umeå to connect with the north–south trains between Stockholm and Luleå.

There are two companies operating ferries between Umeå and Vaasa in Finland. **RG Line** *(☎ 090-185200; ⓦ www.rgline.com)* is more passenger-friendly. **Botnia Link** *(☎ 0611-550555, ⓦ www.botnialink.se)* is primarily used by freight trucks.

KIRUNA

☎ 0980 • pop 23,900

Kiruna is the northernmost municipality in Sweden. The area includes Sweden's highest peak, Kebnekaise (2117m), and several fine national parks and trekking routes. It's worth making the effort to get up here! This far north, the midnight sun lasts from 31 May to 14 July, and there's a bluish darkness throughout December and New Year. The helpful and efficient **tourist office** *(☎ 18880; ⓦ www.kiruna.se; Lars Janssonsgatan 17; open daily in summer)* is next to the Scandic Hotel. Another excellent website is ⓦ www.lapland.se.

The highlight is a visit to the fabulous **Ice Hotel** *(ⓦ www.icehotel.com)*. Every winter at Jukkasjärvi, 18km east of Kiruna (take bus No 501, Skr23), an amazing structure is built from hundreds of tonnes of ice. This 'igloo' has a chapel, bar and exhibitions of ice sculpture by international artists. It also has 50 'hotel rooms' where guests can stay, on beds covered with reindeer skins, and inside sleeping bags. All this can be quite pricey for a budget traveller, but anyone can visit the hotel on a day visit (adult/child Skr100/50).

In summer, after the Ice Hotel has melted away, visitors can still experience a little of the magic. Inside a giant freezer warehouse, called the **Ice Hotel Art Center** *(adult/child Skr 100/50)* are a few of the Ice Hotel features: a bar, ice sculptures, and even small igloos.

The central **STF hostel** *(☎ 17195; Bergmästaregatan 7; beds Skr130-155; open* *year-round)* has excellent facilities, as does the SVIF **Yellow House** *(☎ 13750; ⓔ yellow house@mbox301.swipnet.se; Hantverkaregatan 25; dorm beds Skr120, singles/doubles Skr300/400)*. **Kiruna Rumsservice** *(☎ 19560; ⓔ krs@kiruna.se; Hjalmar Lundbohmsvägen 53; doubles from Skr350)* is a good option, especially for small groups. It offers rooms and apartments with a varying number of beds. Breakfast is extra (Skr45). Or try **Hotell Kebne** *(☎ 68180; ⓔ info@hotelkebne; Konduktörsgatan 7; singles/doubles Skr945/1125, discounted to Skr595)*, with good summer rates.

Central **Kupolgrillen** *(Vänortsgatan 2)* has decent burgers and kebabs. **Restaurang Winter City** is at the STF hostel, offering lunch for Skr65 (Chinese and other Asian dishes).

The small airport, about 7km east of the town, has nonstop flights to/from Stockholm with SAS (daily). Regional buses to/from the bus station, on Hjalmar Lundbohmsvägen opposite the Stadshus (town hall), serve all major settlements around Norrbotten. To reach Karesuando (Skr46), Sweden's northernmost settlement, take bus No 50 (no service Saturday). Bus No 91 runs two or three times daily to Riksgränsen (Skr110) via Abisko (SKr87). Regular trains connect Kiruna with Luleå, Stockholm and Narvik (Norway).

Switzerland

Chocolate, cheese and clocks...strait-laced bankers and big business – the cliches paint only a limited picture. Broader brushstrokes might add elegant cities buzzing with nightlife, a taste for eclectic culture, and some of Europe's most exquisite natural beauty. Goethe's description of Switzerland (Schweiz, Suisse, Svizzera) as a combination of 'the colossal and the well-ordered' still fits, typified by its awe-inspiring Alps set against tidy, efficient towns and cities.

Budgets will take a beating in Switzerland, but the payoff is a super-slick infrastructure giving easy access to everything the country has to offer. Switzerland's distinct regional personalities are united by a sophisticated sensibility and financial savvy. Add an independent streak born of an obsession with getting along with the neighbours, and it's clear why Switzerland remains an oasis of stability.

Switzerland: the Basics

Capital
Bern

Population
7.3 million

Languages
German, French & Italian

Currency
1 Swiss franc (Sfr) = 100 centimes

Avoid at all costs Paying for a taxi

Hit on someone by saying *Isch das ä Toblerone i dine Hose, oder bisch de eifach froh mii gseh?* (Is that a Toblerone in your pocket or are you just glad to see me?)

Facts about Switzerland

HISTORY

The first inhabitants of the region were a Celtic tribe, the Helvetii. The Romans arrived in 107 BC but were gradually driven back. The territory was united under the Holy Roman Empire but central control was never tight. In 1291, the forest communities of Uri, Schwyz and Nidwalden formed an alliance that is seen as the origin of the Swiss Confederation. The Swiss began seizing more land, but finally over-reached themselves. Defeated by a superior force of French and Venetians, they declared neutrality. Swiss mercenaries continued to serve in other armies for centuries, earning an unrivalled reputation for skill and courage.

The French invaded in 1798, but following Napoleon's defeat at Waterloo, Switzerland gained full Independence. In 1848 the Swiss agreed upon a new federal constitution. Having achieved political stability, Switzerland could concentrate on economic and social matters.

The Swiss carefully guarded their neutrality during the World Wars and emerged with an expanded (and expanding) commercial, financial and industrial base. Zürich developed as an international banking centre, and many international bodies based their headquarters in Geneva.

In a March 2002 referendum the Swiss voted in favour of UN membership, but continued to reject the EU. Meanwhile, an independent commission of historians confirmed that tens of thousands of Jewish refugees were turned back from Switzerland's border and left to face their fate in Nazi Germany. Swiss banks were also accused of banking Nazi plunder and holocaust victims' accounts during WWII.

GEOGRAPHY

Mountains make up 70% of Switzerland's 41,290 sq km. Not a square inch of land is wasted in this compact country, with 30% meadow and pasture, 32% forest, 10% arable and 28% put to other use. The Alps occupy the central and southern regions of the country.

CLIMATE

Ticino has a hot, Mediterranean climate, and Valais is dry. Elsewhere the temperature is typically from 20° to 25°C in summer and 2° to 6°C in winter. Be prepared for a range of temperatures depending on altitude.

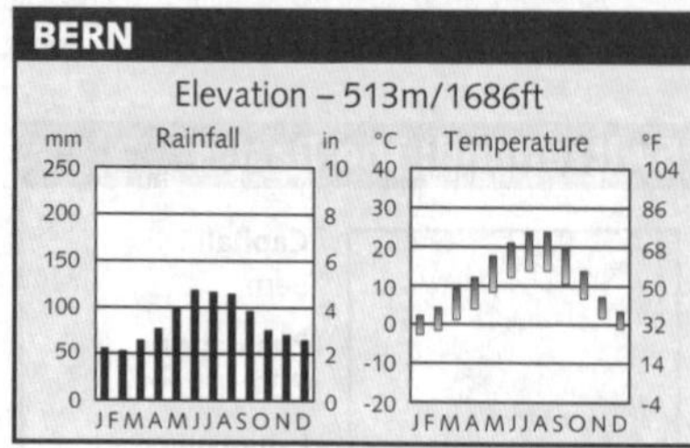

GOVERNMENT & POLITICS

The Swiss Confederation is made up of 23 cantons; three are subdivided, bringing the total to 26. National power is in the hands of the bicameral Federal Assembly, headed by a president. Under the 1874 constitution, Swiss citizens enjoy direct democracy.

POPULATION & PEOPLE

With a population of 7.28 million, Switzerland averages 174 people per sq km. Around 20% of people living in the country are not Swiss citizens.

SOCIETY & CONDUCT

Living quietly is a national obsession (eg, no baths or flushing toilets after 10pm – tourist accommodation excepted). Politeness is the cornerstone of all social intercourse. Always shake hands when being introduced. Don't forget to greet shopkeepers when entering shops. Remember to say *'Grüezi'* before launching into your question or request.

LANGUAGE

Switzerland has three official languages: Swiss German (spoken by 64% of the population), French (19%) and Italian (8%). A fourth language, Rhaeto-Romanic, or Romansch, is spoken by less than 1% of the population, mainly in Graubünden.

English speakers will have few problems in the German- or French-speaking parts. Italian Switzerland is where you will have the greatest difficulty. See the Language chapter at the back of the book for German, French and Italian pronunciation guidelines and useful words and phrases.

Toast Before Tipple...or Else

When drinking with the Swiss, always wait until everyone has their drink and toast each of your companions, looking them in the eye and clinking glasses. Drinking before the toast is unforgivable and will lead to seven years of bad sex. Don't say you weren't warned.

Facts for the Visitor

HIGHLIGHTS

The Jungfrau region offers unforgettable mountain vistas. Challenging hikes and some dazzling views mark the peaks above Lake Lucerne and at Zermatt, in the Matterhorn's shadow. Catch a steamer on Lake Geneva to Château de Chillon, the most famous castle in Switzerland. For buzzing nightlife and medieval town centres creaking with history, head for Bern and Zürich. Culture buffs will find plenty of interest in Basel and Geneva.

PLANNING

Visit Switzerland from December to April for winter sports, and May to October for general sightseeing and hiking. Alpine resorts all but close down in late April, May and November.

TOURIST OFFICES

Local Tourist Offices

Verkehrsbüro or *Tourismus* (tourist offices) are extremely helpful. The staff invariably speak English. Offices will often book hotel rooms and organise excursions. Switzerland Tourism sells the handy **Swiss Museum Passport** (*w www.museums.ch; adult/student Sfr30/25*), which will save big bucks if you plan to visit several museums.

Tourist Offices Abroad

Switzerland Tourism has a free-phone number for Europe (*☎ 00800 100 200 30*) and the USA/Canada (*☎ 011800 100 200 30*). Offices can be found in:

UK (☎ 020-7734 1921, fax 7437 4577; e info.uk@switzerland.com) 10th Floor, Swiss Centre, 10 Wardour St, London W1D 6QF
USA (☎ 1-877-794-8037; e info.usa@switzerlandtourism.ch) 608 Fifth Ave, New York, NY 10020

VISAS & DOCUMENTS

Visas are not required for passport holders of the UK, USA, Canada, Australia, New Zealand or South Africa. A maximum three-month stay applies.

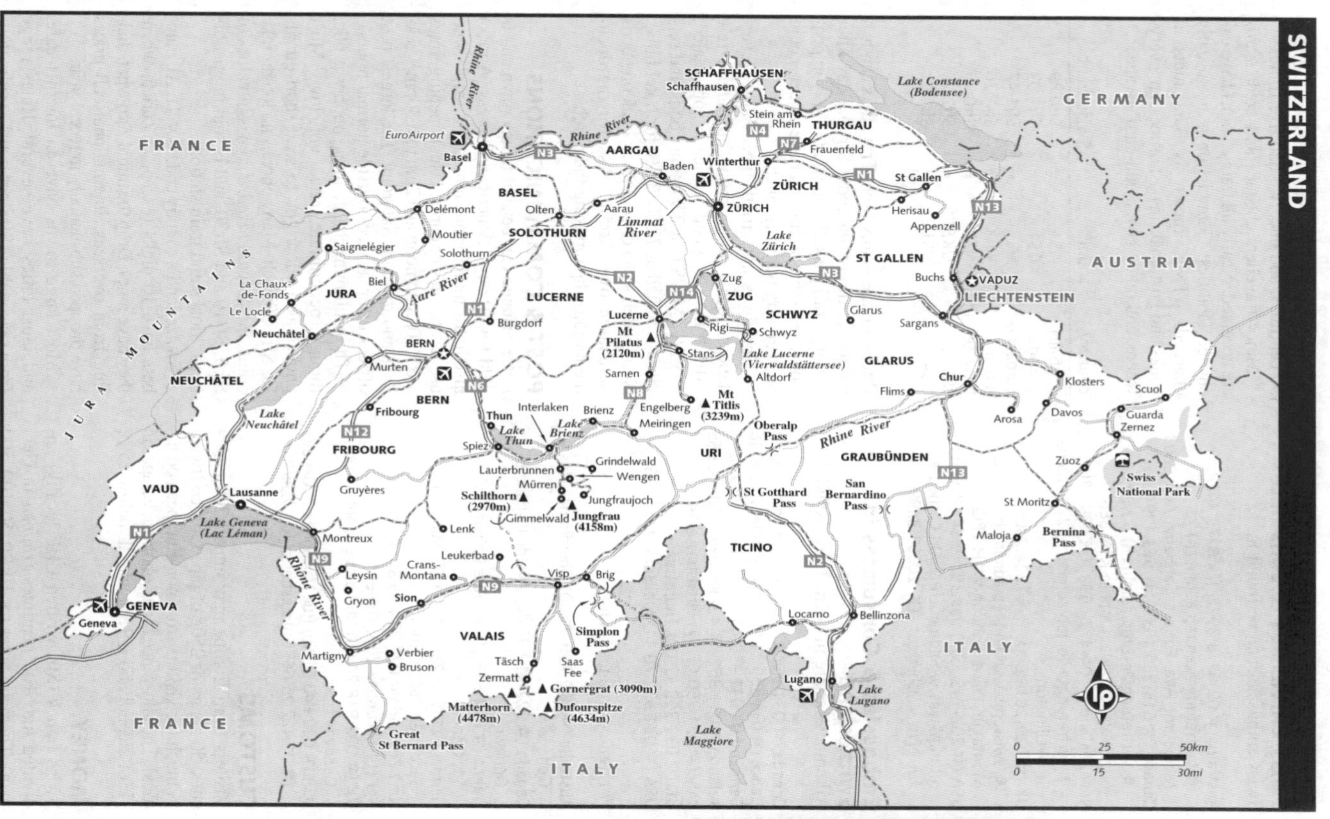

SWITZERLAND

EMBASSIES & CONSULATES

Swiss Embassies & Consulates

Swiss embassies can be found in:

Australia (☎ 02-6273 3977, fax 6273 3428, ⓔ vertretung@can.rep.admin.ch) 7 Melbourne Ave, Forrest, Canberra, ACT 2603
Canada (☎ 613-235 1837, fax 563 1394, ⓔ vertretung@ott.rep.admin.ch) 5 Marlborough Ave, Ottawa, Ontario K1N 8E6
New Zealand (☎ 04-472 1593, fax 499 6302, ⓔ vertretung@wel.rep.admin.ch) 22 Panama St, Wellington
UK (☎ 020-7616 6000, fax 7724 7001, ⓔ swissembassy@lon.rep.admin.ch) 16–18 Montague Place, London W1H 2BQ
USA (☎ 202-745 7900, fax 387 2564, ⓔ vertretung@was.rep.admin.ch) 2900 Cathedral Ave NW, Washington, DC 20008-3499

Embassies & Consulates in Switzerland

All embassies are in Bern. They include:

Canada (☎ 031 357 32 00) Kirchenfeldstrasse 88
France (☎ 031 359 21 11) Schosshaldenstrasse 46
Germany (☎ 031 359 41 11) Willadingweg 83
Ireland (☎ 031 352 14 42) Kirchenfeldstrasse 68
Italy (☎ 031 350 07 77) Elfenstrasse 14
UK (☎ 031 359 77 00) Thunstrasse 50
USA (☎ 031 357 70 11) Jubiläumsstrasse 93

Foreign consulates include:

Australia (☎ 022 799 91 00) Chemin des Fins 2, Geneva
Canada (☎ 022 919 92 00) Ave de l'Ariana 5, Geneva
France (☎ 022 319 00 00) Rue Imbert Galloix 11, Geneva
Germany (☎ 022 730 11 11) Chemin du Petit-Saconnex 28C, Geneva
New Zealand (☎ 022 734 95 30) Chemin du Petit-Saconnex 28A, Geneva
UK (☎ 022 918 24 00) Rue de Vermont 37–39, Geneva
USA (☎ 022 840 51 60) Rue Versonnex 7, Geneva (☎ 01 422 25 66) Dufourstrasse 101, Zürich

CUSTOMS

Visitors from Europe may import 200 cigarettes, 50 cigars or 250g of pipe tobacco (twice as much for visitors from non-European countries). The allowance for alcoholic beverages is 1L of alcohol above 15% and 2L below 15%.

MONEY

Swiss francs (Sfr, written CHF locally) are divided into 100 centimes (*rappen* in German). There are notes for 10, 20, 50, 100, 500 and 1000 francs, and coins for five, 10, 20 and 50 centimes, and one, two and five francs.

Major travellers cheques and credit cards are accepted. Nearly all train stations have exchange facilities. Commission is not usually charged. ATMs, known as Bancomats in banks and Postomats in post offices, are everywhere, and many give credit-card advances.

country	unit		Swiss franc
Australia	A$1	=	Sfr0.89
Canada	C$1	=	Sfr1.03
Eurozone	€1	=	Sfr1.47
Japan	¥100	=	Sfr1.26
New Zealand	NZ$1	=	Sfr0.75
UK	UK£1	=	Sfr2.29
USA	US$1	=	Sfr1.57

Prices are inevitably high. Travellers can just barely scrimp by on about Sfr60 a day after buying a rail pass. If you want to stay in pensions, see some sights and have a beer, count on spending twice as much.

Tipping is not strictly necessary. Nevertheless, locals often 'round up', and a few extra francs for good service is appreciated.

VAT (MWST or TVA) on goods and services is levied at 7.5% (3.5% for hotel bills). Nonresidents can claim the tax back on goods purchased over Sfr500. Ask for the documentation when making the purchase.

POST & COMMUNICATIONS

Poste restante can be sent to any town and is held for 30 days. American Express (AmEx) also holds mail for one month for people who use its cheques or cards. Usual opening times are 7.30am to noon and 2pm to 6.30pm weekdays and to 11am Saturday. The largest post offices offer services outside normal hours.

The minimum charge in payphones is 60c, though per-minute rates are low. Most phones also allow you to send short emails for Sfr1.50 each. Many phones no longer take coins; the prepaid *taxcard* comes in values of Sfr5, Sfr10 and Sfr20, and is sold in post offices, kiosks and train stations.

Switzerland's country code is ☎ 41. All numbers have 10 digits (except in Zürich, where they have nine). Drop the initial zero when dialling from overseas. International call prices have dropped substantially in recent years.

Most large towns have an Internet café, and most cities have several. Rates range from reasonable (Sfr8 per hour) to ridiculous

(Sfr24 per hour!!). Youth hostels are often the best places to do a quick email check.

DIGITAL RESOURCES

A good place is **Switzerland Tourism** (*W www.myswitzerland.com*), with many useful links. For current news, try W www.sri.ch, and for coverage of major cities, check out W www.swisstownguide.ch.

BOOKS

See Lonely Planet's *Switzerland* and *Walking in Switzerland* for detailed information. *Living and Working in Switzerland* by David Hampshire is an excellent practical guide. Paul Bilton's *The Xenophobe's Guide to the Swiss* is informative and amusing.

GAY & LESBIAN TRAVELLERS

Attitudes are reasonably tolerant, and the age of consent is 16. Zürich has a lively gay scene and hosts the Christopher Street Day march in late June. It's also home to *Cruiser* (*☎ 01 388 41 54; W www.cruiser.ch*), a magazine that lists gay and lesbian organisations and has extensive listings of Swiss bars and events; *Cruiser* costs Sfr4.50. For more insight, check out **Pink Cross** (*W www.pinkcross.ch*).

DISABLED TRAVELLERS

Many hotels have disabled access and most train stations have a mobile lift. For information, contact Switzerland Tourism or the **Swiss Invalid Association** (*Schweizerischer Invalidenverband; ☎ 062 206 88 88, fax 062 206 88 89; Froburgstrasse 4, Olten CH-4601*).

DANGERS & ANNOYANCES

Take special care in the mountains as helicopter rescue (☎ 1414) is expensive. Make sure your travel insurance covers alpine sports.

BUSINESS HOURS

Most shops are open 8am to 6.30pm weekdays, with a 90-minute or two-hour break for lunch at noon. In towns there's often a late shopping day till 9pm, typically Thursday or Friday. Saturday closing is usually 4pm or 5pm. Banks are generally open 8.30am to 4.30pm weekdays.

PUBLIC HOLIDAYS & SPECIAL EVENTS

National holidays are 1 January, Good Friday, Easter Monday, Ascension Day, Whit Monday, National Day (1 August), and the 25 and 26 December. Some cantons observe 2 January, Labour Day (1 May), Corpus Christi and All Saints' Day (1 November). Many local events take place throughout the year (check with the local tourist office). This is a brief selection:

Fasnacht In February, a lively spring carnival of wild parties and parades is celebrated country wide, but with particular enthusiasm in Basel and Lucerne.

Combats de Reines From March to October, the lower Valais stages traditional cow fights.

Montreux Jazz Festival Big-name rock/jazz acts hit town in July for this famous festival.

National Day On 1 August, celebrations and fireworks mark the country's National Day.

Street Parade In early August, Zürich lets its hair down with a huge techno parade with 30 lovemobiles and more than half-a-million ravers.

Vintage Festivals In October, down a couple in wine-growing regions such as Neuchâtel and Lugano.

Onion Market In late November, Bern takes on a carnival atmosphere for a unique market day.

Escalade Festival This historical festival in Geneva celebrates deliverance from would-be conquerors.

Emergencies

Emergency telephone numbers are: police ☎ 117 and fire ☎ 118 and ambulance (most areas) ☎ 144. The national 24-hour number for roadside assistance in the event of breakdown is ☎ 140.

ACTIVITIES

There are many ski resorts throughout the Alps, the pre-Alps and the Jura, with some 200 ski schools. Equipment hire is available at resorts, and passes allow unlimited use of mountain transport.

There are 50,000km of designated **walking paths**. Signs make it difficult to get lost. More strenuous mountain paths have white-red markers. The **Schweizer Alpen-Club** (*SAC; ☎ 031 370 1818, fax 031 370 18 00; W www.sac-cas.ch; Monbijoustrasse 61, Bern*) maintains huts and can help with information. Lonely Planet's *Walking in Switzerland* contains notes for walking in the countryside.

You can **water-ski**, **sail** and **windsurf** on most lakes. There are over 350 lake beaches. **Anglers** should contact the local tourist office for a permit. **Rafting** is possible on many Alpine rivers.

Bungee-jumping, paragliding, canyoning and other high-adrenalin sports are widely available, especially in the Interlaken area.

WORK

Switzerland's agreement with the EU has eased regulations for EU citizens. Non-citizens officially need special skills, but people still manage to find work in ski resorts. Hotel work has the advantage of including meals and accommodation. In theory, jobs and work permits should be sorted out before arrival, but if you find a job there the employer may well have unallocated work permits.

ACCOMMODATION

Camping

There are about 450 camping grounds. Nightly charges are around Sfr7 per person plus Sfr5 to Sfr10 for a tent, and around Sfr5 for a car. Many sites offer a discount if you have a Camping Carnet. Free camping is discouraged. Contact the **Schweizerischer Camping und Caravanning-Verband** *(Swiss Camping & Caravanning Federation; ☎ 041 210 48 22; Habsburgerstrasse 35, Lucerne CH-6004)* for more information.

Hostels

There are 63 official, HI-affiliated Swiss Youth Hostels *(Jugendherberge, auberge de jeunesse, alloggio per giovani)*. Nearly all hostels include breakfast and sheets in their rates. Average high-season prices are Sfr30/50/80 for dorm beds/singles/doubles. Most hostels charge a few francs less during the low season (this chapter quotes prices for the high season). Many places have double or family rooms available (with single or bunk beds), and around half have kitchen facilities. Reception desks are often closed during the day, with check-in usually available from mid- to late afternoon.

Membership cards must be shown. Non-members pay a Sfr6 'guest fee'; six of these add up to a full international membership card. Buying membership before you leave home is usually cheaper.

It's wise to book ahead by phone, by email or via **W** www.youthhostel.ch. You can also ask your hostel to reserve ahead for your next one. A hostel map is available free from hostels and some tourist offices. For more information contact the **Schweizer Jugendherbergen** *(Swiss Youth Hostel Association or SYHA; ☎ 01 360 14 14;* **e** *marketing@youthhostel.ch; Schaffhauserstrasse 14, Zürich CH-8042)*.

Some of the best budget accommodation you'll find is in independent 'backpacker hostels' – they're listed in *Swiss Backpacker News*, free from hostels and some tourist offices, and on **W** www.backpacker.ch. Prices are similar to SYHA hostels and membership is not required. The Schweizer Alpen-Club maintains around 150 dormitory-style mountain huts at higher altitudes.

Hotels & Private Homes

Even budget rooms are fairly comfortable (and pricey). The high-season prices quoted could be reduced by 10% (towns) to 40% (alpine resorts) during low season. Prices start at around Sfr50/90 for a basic single/double. 'Hotel Garni' means a B&B establishment without a restaurant. For more about options available, contact the **Schweizer Hotelier-Verein** *(Swiss Hotel Association; ☎ 031 370 41 11;* **W** *www.swisshotels.ch; Monbijoustrasse 130, Bern CH-3001)*.

Private houses in rural areas sometimes offer inexpensive rooms; look for signs saying *Zimmer frei*. Some farms also take paying guests. Self-catering accommodation is available in holiday chalets, apartments or bungalows. Local tourist offices have lists of everything on offer.

FOOD & DRINKS

Lactose intolerants will struggle in this dairy-obsessed country. The best-known dish is fondue, in which melted Emmental and Gruyére are combined with white wine, served in a large pot and eaten with bread cubes. Another popular artery-hardener is *raclette* – melted cheese, served with potatoes. *Rösti* (fried, buttery shredded potatoes) is German Switzerland's national dish.

Veal is highly rated in the country. *Bündnerfleisch* is dried beef, smoked and thinly sliced. Like their northern neighbours, the Swiss munch on a variety of *Wurst* (sausage).

Rivella is a refreshing soft drink made from whey. Lager comes in 0.5L or 0.3L bottles, or on draught *(vom Fass* or *à la pression)*, from 0.2L to 0.5L. Cardinal is a popular local brand. Wine is an essential accompaniment to lunch and dinner. The main growing regions are the Italian- and French-speaking areas, particularly in Valais and by lakes Neuchâtel and Geneva.

Finally, Switzerland makes some of the world's most delectable chocolate – don't miss it!

ENTERTAINMENT

In cities, nightlife centres on a thriving café culture and an ever-changing wave of hip bars and clubs. Check free newspapers or city listing guides for the latest hotspots. Many places stay open all day, transforming into bars/clubs at night. There's a robust alternative scene, with old factories and warehouses being converted into clubs, restaurants, art spaces and live music venues.

Getting There & Away

AIR

The busiest airports are Zürich and Geneva, each with several nonstop flights a day to major transport hubs such as London, Paris and Frankfurt. Budget airline **Easyjet** (*www.easyjet.com*) offers regular services from London to Zürich and Geneva.

Swiss International Air Lines (Swiss) is the national airline. Swiss luggage check-in facilities are at major train stations around the country. For reservations throughout Switzerland, call ☎ 0848-85 2000.

LAND

Busabout (*www.busabout.com*) stops in Geneva, Interlaken, Lucerne and Lauterbrunnen. Geneva has bus connections to Barcelona, and Zürich has various services to Eastern Europe.

Switzerland is a hub for train connections. Zürich is the busiest international terminus, with two direct day trains and one night train to Vienna (nine hours). There are several trains daily to Geneva and Lausanne from Paris (three to four hours by superfast TGV). Paris to Bern takes 4½ hours by TGV. Most connections from Germany pass though Zürich or Basel. Nearly all connections from Italy pass through Milan before branching off to Zürich, Lucerne, Bern or Lausanne. Reservations on international trains are subject to a surcharge of Sfr5 to Sfr30.

Upon entering Switzerland, drivers who wish to use motorways must purchase a *vignette* (Sfr40). The sticker is valid for a year.

SEA

Switzerland can be reached by lake steamers: from Germany via Lake Constance (Bodensee); from Italy via Lake Maggiore; and from France via Lake Geneva (Lac Léman).

Getting Around

Swiss public transport is an efficient, fully integrated and comprehensive system incorporating trains, buses, boats and funiculars. Convenient discount passes make the system even more appealing.

The Swiss Pass is the best deal for people planning to travel extensively, offering unlimited travel on Swiss Federal Railways, boats, most Alpine postbuses, and trams and buses in 35 towns. Reductions of 25% apply to funiculars and mountain railways. These passes are available for periods from four days (Sfr240) to one month (Sfr525). The Swiss Flexi Pass allows free, unlimited trips for three to eight days within a month and costs Sfr230 to Sfr420 (2nd class). With either, two people travelling together get 15% off.

The Swiss Card allows a free return journey from your arrival point to any destination in Switzerland; 50% off rail, boat and bus excursions; and reductions on mountain railways. It costs Sfr165 (2nd class) and is valid for a month. The Half-Fare Card (Sfr99) is a similar deal minus the free return trip. Except for the Half-Fare Card, these passes are best purchased before arrival in Switzerland from Switzerland Tourism or a travel agent. Regional passes provide free travel on certain days and half-price travel on other days within a seven- or 15-day period.

All the larger lakes are serviced by steamers, for which rail passes are usually valid.

BUS

Yellow postbuses are a supplement to the rail network, following postal routes and linking towns to more inaccessible regions. Departures tie in with train arrivals. Postbus stations are next to train stations.

TRAIN

The Swiss rail network is a combination of state-run and private lines. Prices are high, though passes will cut costs. All fares quoted are for 2nd class. In general, Eurail passes are not valid for private lines and Inter-Rail pass holders get a 50% discount. Services stop from around midnight to 6am.

Train stations offer luggage storage, either at a counter (usually Sfr5 per piece) or in 24-hour lockers (Sfr2 to Sfr7). Schedules are revised yearly, so double-check details before travelling. For information, consult the excellent **SBB** *(☎ 0900-300 300 Sfr1.19/min; W www.sbb.ch)*.

CAR & MOTORCYCLE

You need a *vignette* to use motorways and semi-motorways (see Getting There & Away earlier). For information, check with tourist offices or motoring organisations such as **The Swiss Touring Club** *(TCS; ☎ 022 417 27 27)*. Ring ☎ 140 for the national 24-hour breakdown service.

BICYCLE

Despite the hilly countryside, many Swiss choose to get around on two wheels. You can hire bikes from most train stations (adult/child Sfr30/25 per day) and return to any station with a rental office, though this incurs a Sfr6 surcharge. Bikes can be transported on most trains; SBB rentals travel free (maximum five bikes per train). If you have your own wheels you'll need a bike pass (one day Sfr15, with Swiss travel pass Sfr10). Look for the *Cycling in Switzerland* booklet (Sfr37.80) in bookshops, which covers nine routes and 3300km of bike paths. Basel, Geneva and Zürich offer free bike loans.

HITCHING

Lonely Planet does not recommend hitchhiking. Most hitchers will be picked up by foreigners. Hitching is illegal on motorways.

LOCAL TRANSPORT

All city transport is linked together on the same ticketing system, and you must buy tickets before boarding. One-day passes are usually available and are much better value than paying per trip. There are regular checks for fare dodgers. Taxis are always metered and expensive.

Vertigo sufferers will be challenged by the main modes of transport used in steep Alpine regions. A funicular *(Standseilbahn, funiculaire)* is a pair of counterbalancing cars on rails, drawn by cables. A cable car *(Luftseilbahn, téléphérique)* is dramatically suspended from a cable high over a valley. A gondola *(Gondelbahn, télécabine)* is a smaller version of a cable car. A cable chair *(Sesselbahn, télésiège)* is likewise hitched on to a cable but not enclosed.

Bern (Berne)

pop 122,000

Bern, the nation's capital, retains a relaxed, small-town charm. Surrounded on three sides by the deep-green Aare River, its medieval Old Town features 6km of covered arcades and countless historic fountains and monuments. Founded in 1191 by Berchtold V, Bern was named for the unfortunate bear *(Bärn)* who was Berchtold's first hunting victim.

Information

Bern Tourismus *(☎ 031 328 12 28; e info-res@bernetourism.ch; open daily)*, in the train station, offers a free booklet with plenty of useful information. The online **Bern Youth Guide** *(W www.youthguide.ch)* has some excellent tips and links. There's another tourist office by the bear pits. The **SBB exchange office** *(open 6.30am-9pm daily)* is in the lower level of the train station.

The **main post office** *(Schanzenstrasse; open 7.30am-6.30pm Mon-Fri, 8am-noon Sat)* has convenient automatic stamp machines. **ispace** *(☎ 031 327 76 77; e info@comperio .ch; Zeughausgasse 14; open 9am-5.30pm Mon-Fri)*, in the basement of Medienhaus, is a good place for a quick email check (free/Sfr4/6 for 10/30/45 minutes). **Bycom Internet Pub** *(☎ 031 313 81 91; Aarbergergasse 46; open 6am-11.30pm Mon-Thur & Sun, 6am-3am Fri, 9am-3am Sat)* is a two-level lounge bar/cybercafé with 50 terminals and a groovy atmosphere at Sfr5 per hour.

STA Travel *(☎ 031 302 03 12; Falkenplatz 9 • ☎ 031 312 07 24; Zeughausgasse 18; both open 9.30am-6pm Mon-Fri, 10am-1pm Sat)* can help with travel advice.

To be healed, visit the **university hospital** *(☎ 031 632 21 11; Freiburgstrasse)*. For help in locating a doctor or dentist, call ☎ 0900 57 67 47.

Things to See & Do

Walk down Marktgasse and Kramgasse, with their covered arcades, colourful fountains, and hidden shops, bars and theatres. Check out the ogre fountain in Kornhausplatz, depicting a giant enjoying a meal of wriggling children.

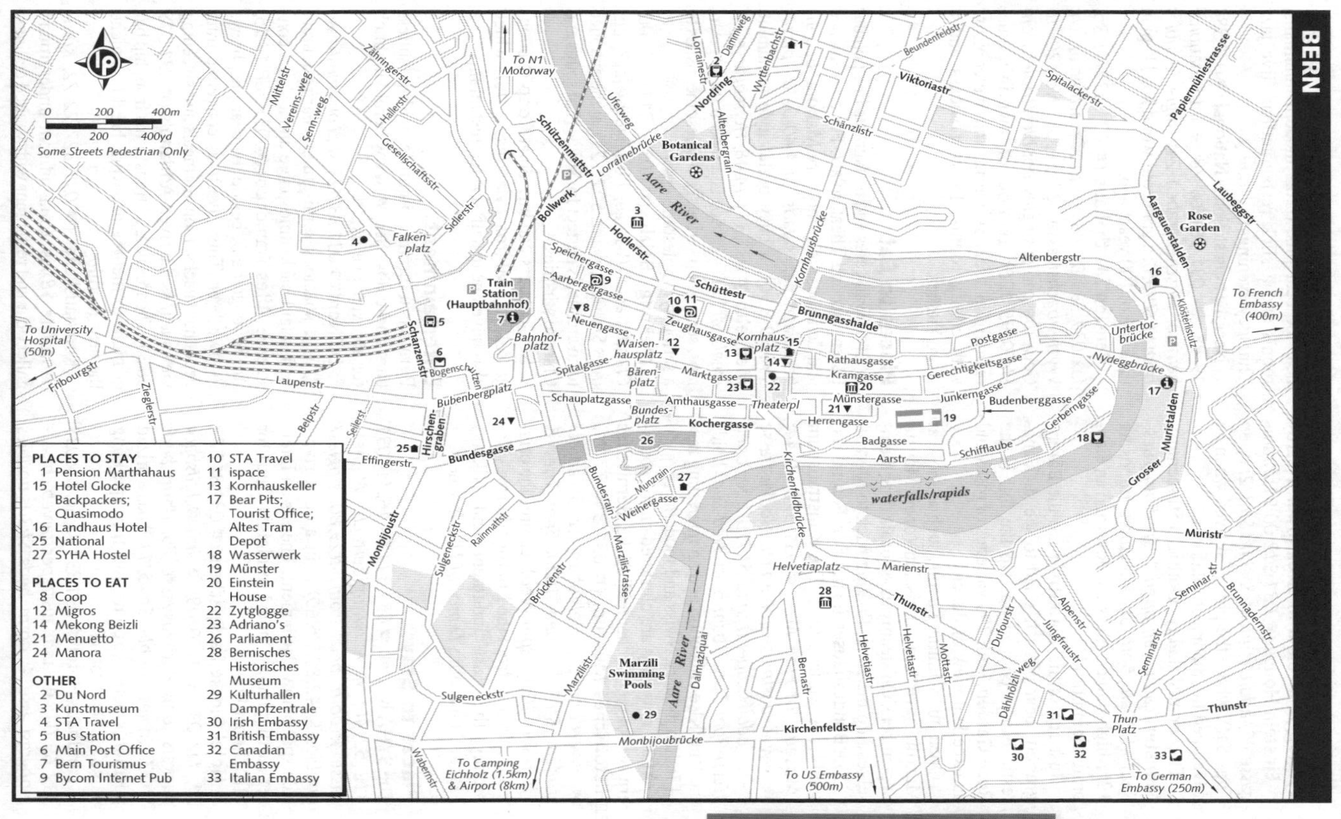
BERN
To N1 Motorway
To University Hospital (50m)
To French Embassy (400m)
To Camping Eichholz (1.5km) & Airport (8km)
To US Embassy (500m)
To German Embassy (250m)
0 200 400m
0 200 400yd
Some Streets Pedestrian Only
Train Station (Hauptbahnhof)
Botanical Gardens
Rose Garden
Aare River
waterfalls/rapids
Marzili Swimming Pools
PLACES TO STAY
1 Pension Marthahaus
15 Hotel Glocke Backpackers; Quasimodo
16 Landhaus Hotel
25 National
27 SYHA Hostel
PLACES TO EAT
8 Coop
12 Migros
14 Mekong Beizli
21 Menuetto
24 Manora
OTHER
2 Du Nord
3 Kunstmuseum
4 STA Travel
5 Bus Station
6 Main Post Office
7 Bern Tourismus
9 Bycom Internet Pub
10 STA Travel
11 ispace
13 Kornhauskeller
17 Bear Pits; Tourist Office; Altes Tram Depot
18 Wasserwerk
19 Münster
20 Einstein House
22 Zytglogge
23 Adriano's
26 Parliament
28 Bernisches Historisches Museum
29 Kulturhallen Dampfzentrale
30 Irish Embassy
31 British Embassy
32 Canadian Embassy
33 Italian Embassy
SWITZERLAND

Dividing Marktgasse and Kramgasse is the **Zytglogge**, a colourful clock tower. Nearby is **Einstein House** *(☎ 031 312 00 91; Kramgasse 49; adult/student & child Sfr3/2; open Tues-Sat)*, where the physicist lived when he developed his theory of relativity.

The unmistakably Gothic 15th-century **Münster** *(cathedral; open 10am-5pm Tues-Sat, 11.30am-5pm Sun)* features imposing 12m-high stained-glass windows and an elaborate main portal.

Just across the Aare River are the **Bärengraben** (bear pits). It's sad to see such majestic beasts cooped up. Up the hill is the **Rose Garden**, with 200 varieties of roses and an excellent view of the city.

Open-air swimming pools, such as those at Marzili, have free admission (open May to September). On steamy days locals fling themselves into the Aare, floating back to Marzili.

The **Bundeshäuser**, home of the Federal Assembly, is worth a look. The **Kunstmuseum** *(Museum of Fine Arts; ☎ 031 328 09 44; W www.kunstmuseumbern.ch; Hodlerstrasse 8–12; adult/student/child Sfr7/5/free; open 10am-9pm Tues, 10am-5pm Wed-Sun)* holds the Paul Klee collection and an interesting mix of Italian masters, Swiss and modern art.

Many museums are clustered on the southern side of the Kirchenfeldbrücke. **Bernisches Historisches Museum** *(☎ 031 350 77 11; W www.bhm.ch; Helvetiaplatz 5; adult/student Sfr5/3; open 10am-5pm Tues & Thur-Sun, 10am-8pm Wed)* features the original sculptures from the Münster doorway depicting the Last Judgment and Niklaus Manuel's macabre *Dance of Death* panels.

Places to Stay

The **SYHA hostel** *(☎ 031 311 63 16, fax 031 312 52 40; W www.jugibern.ch; Weihergasse 4; dorm beds from Sfr29.80, singles/doubles Sfr42.80/75.60)* is in a quiet riverside spot below Parliament. There's an Internet surfing happy 'hour' (midnight-7am) for Sfr2.50 per hour.

Hotel Glocke Backpackers *(☎ 031 311 37 71, fax 031 311 10 08; e info@chilisbackpackers.com; Rathausgasse 75; dorm beds Sfr27, singles/doubles Sfr75/110)* has a prized position, spotless rooms and tiny sparkling white hall bathrooms.

Landhaus Hotel *(☎ 031 331 41 66, fax 031 332 69 04; e landhaus@spectraweb.ch; Altenbergstrasse 4; dorm beds Sfr30, doubles without/with bathroom from Sfr110/140)*, near the bear pits, offers modern minimalist rooms and a slick restaurant/bar (live jazz Thursday evenings).

Near the train station is **National** *(☎ 031 381 19 88, fax 031 381 68 78; e info@nationalbern.ch; Hirschengraben 24; singles/doubles from Sfr60/95)*, a grand old-world hotel kept in the style of 100 years ago.

Pension Marthahaus *(☎ 031 332 41 35, fax 031 333 33 86; e info@marthahaus.ch; Wyttenbachstrasse 22a; bus No 20 to Gewerbeschule; singles/doubles/triples from Sfr60/95/120)*, 1km out of town in a quiet residential area, is warm and welcoming, with comfy rooms, Internet access and a share kitchen.

Places to Eat

Wall-to-wall cafés and restaurants line popular Bärenplatz and Theaterplatz. For convenience and delicious fresh food, try **Manora** *(Bubenbergplatz 5a; salads Sfr4.40-9.40, pizzas Sfr6.90-8.90)*, a busy buffet-style restaurant. **Menuetto** *(☎ 031 311 14 48; Herrengasse 22; meals Sfr13.80-23.50)* is a mecca for vegetarians, serving up seriously wholesome dishes to a seriously wholesome crowd.

MeKong Beizli *(☎ 031 311 26 00; Chindlifrässer-Passage, Kornhausplatz 7; entrees Sfr10.50, mains Sfr21-29)*, at the entrance to an arcade, is perfect for spicy Thai soups and Chinese stir-fries.

Self-caterers can buy up at **Coop** *(Neuengasse)* and **Migros** *(Marktgasse 46)*, which also have cheap self-service restaurants.

Entertainment

Bern has a thriving nightlife, with countless bars and clubs. See W www.bernbynight.ch for an extensive list.

Du Nord *(☎ 031 332 23 38; Lorrainestrasse 2)* is a spacious semi-grungy bar/restaurant with a laid-back atmosphere and a social conscience. **Altes Tramdepot** *(☎ 031 368 14 15; Am Bärengraben)*, beside the bear pits, brews its own beer. This cavernous converted tram depot has snacks, monster meals and sweeping views across the river. **Adriano's** *(☎ 031 318 88 31; Theaterplatz 2)* transforms from hip bar at night to mellow pre-work breakfast niche the next morning.

Kornhauskeller *(☎ 031 327 72 72; Kornhausplatz 18)* is a magnificent underground gallery bar and restaurant with vaulted ceilings, frescoes and comfy sofas overlooking diners below. Drinks are dear, but it's worth sipping slowly to soak up the atmosphere.

Wasserwerk *(☎ 031 312 12 31; Ⓦ www.wasserwerk.ch; Wasserwerkgasse 5; gigs free-Sfr30)*, inside a converted riverside warehouse, is a favourite hangout for local pool-players and clubbers, with international DJs and regular special events.

Quasimodo *(☎ 031 311 13 81; Rathausgasse 75; admission free; open Mon-Sat)*, underneath Hotel Glocke, is a dimly-lit techno bar/club pumping out a hard electronic pulse.

There's almost always something interesting on at **Kulturhallen Dampfzentrale** *(☎ 031 311 63 37; Ⓦ www.dampfzentrale.ch; Marzilistrasse 47; bus No 30 to Marzili)*, with an eclectic mix of acts from jazz and flamenco to classical and club DJs. The late-night Moonlinerbus shuttles from Dampfzentrale to the station on weekends.

Getting There & Away

There are daily flights to European cities from Bern-Belp airport. Postbuses depart from the western side of the train station. There are at least hourly train connections to most Swiss cities, including Geneva (Sfr50, 1¾ hours), Basel (Sfr37, 70 minutes), Interlaken (Sfr25, 50 minutes) and Zürich (Sfr48, 70 minutes).

Getting Around

A bus links the airport to the train station (Sfr14, 30 minutes).

Bus and tram tickets cost Sfr1.60 (maximum six stops) or Sfr2.50. A day pass for the city and regional network is Sfr8. A 24/48/72-hour pass costs Sfr6.50/10.50/14.50. Buy single-journey tickets at stops and passes from the tourist office or the BernMobil office at Bubenbergplatz 5. Taxis charge Sfr6.80 plus Sfr3.10 per kilometre (Sfr3.40 after 8pm daily and on Sunday).

From May to October there are free daily loans of city bikes outside the train station. ID and Sfr20 deposit are required.

Around Bern

NEUCHÂTEL

The town of Neuchâtel lies on the northwest shore of the large lake that shares its name. This laid-back resort, surrounded by vineyards, has a cruisey café culture and an inviting medieval Old Town. The train station (Gare CFF) has money exchange and bicycle rental. The central pedestrian zone and Place Pury (the hub for local buses) are about 1km away down the hill on Ave de la Gare. The **tourist office** *(☎ 032 889 68 90; ⓔ tourisme.neuchatelois@ne.ch; Place du Port; open Mon-Sat)* is in the main post office by the lake.

The Old Town's centrepiece is the 12th-century **Chateau de Neuchâtel** *(tours daily Apr-Sept)*, now housing cantonal offices, and the adjoining **Collegiate Church**. Nearby, the **Prison Tower** *(admission Sfr1; open Apr-Aug)* offers broad views of the town and lake. Visit the **Musée d'Art et d'Histoire** *(Museum of Art & History; ☎ 032 717 79 20; Esplanade Léopold-Robert 1; adult/student Sfr7/4, Wed free; open 10am-6pm Tues-Sun)*, on the waterfront, to see its beloved 18th-century clockwork figures.

Places to Stay & Eat

Hôtel Marché *(☎ 032 723 23 30, fax 032 723 23 33; ⓔ info@hoteldumarche.ch; Place des Halles 4; singles/doubles/triples Sfr70/100/125)* offers basic rooms right in the thick of it.

Bach et Buck Creperie *(☎ 032 725 63 53; Ave du 1er-Mars 22; crepes Sfr6-10.50)* has a menu of 130 crepes and good vegie options. Night-owls should keep an eye out for Neuchâtel's *restaurants de nuit*, all-night eateries throughout town that are usually open from 9pm to 6am. Self-caterers can stock up on local wines and cheeses at **Coop** *(Rue de la Treille 4)* and **Aux Gourmets** *(cnr Rue de Seyon & Rue de L'Ancien Hôtel-de-Ville)*, both near Place Pury.

Entertainment

Chauffage Compris *(☎ 032 721 43 96; Rue des Moulins 37)* is a funky café/bar with quality coffee, a range of spirits and beers and a daily lunch menu. Grab a board game from the bar and settle in for a few hours. **Café du Cerf** *(☎ 032 724 27 44; Rue de L'Ancien Hôtel-de-Ville 4)* is a friendly, popular beer-lover's paradise (150 choices) with Cambodian specialities from the linked restaurant Le Lotus upstairs.

Getting There & Around

There are hourly fast trains to Geneva (Sfr42, 70 minutes) and Bern (Sfr17.20, 35 minutes). Postbuses heading to the Jura leave from the station. Local buses cost Sfr1.60 to Sfr2.60 per trip, or Sfr7 for a 24-hour pass.

SWITZERLAND

Geneva (Genève, Genf, Ginevra)

pop 176,000

Switzerland's third-largest city sits comfortably on the shore of Lake Geneva (Lac Léman). The canton is surrounded by France on three sides, and Gallic influence is everywhere. Birthplace of the Red Cross, once League of Nations headquarters and now European home of the UN, Geneva belongs not so much to Switzerland as to the world. This city of bankers, diplomats and transients has a truly international flavour. Despite the city's affluence and impressive lakeside position, a short step into the back blocks reveals a scruffier, seedier side.

The Rhône River runs through the city, dividing it into *rive droite* (north) and *rive gauche* (south). On the northern side is the main train station, Gare de Cornavin; south of the river lies the Old Town.

Information

For advice, head to **Genéve Tourisme** *(☎ 022 909 70 00; ⓔ info@geneve-tourism.ch; Rue du Mont-Blanc 18; open Mon-Sat, daily summer)*. There's also the **city information office** *(☎ 022 311 98 27; Pont de la Machine; open Mon-Sat)* and **Centre d'Accueil et de Renseignements** *(CAR; ☎ 022 731 46 47; open daily mid-June–mid-Sept)*, with youth-oriented information dispensed from a bus parked at the station end of Rue du Mont-Blanc.

An **exchange office** *(open 6.45am-9.30pm daily summer, shorter hours rest of year)* is in Gare de Cornavin. Not far from the station is the **main post office** *(Rue du Mont-Blanc 18; open 7.30am-6pm Mon-Fri, 8.30am-noon Sat)*. Near the tourist office you'll find excellent Internet rates (Sfr1/3/4 for 10/30/60 minutes) at **Video Club** *(☎ 022 731 47 48; Rue des Alpes 19; open to midnight daily)*.

American Express *(☎ 022 731 76 00; Rue du Mont-Blanc 7; open 8.30am-5.45pm Mon-Fri, plus 9am-noon Sat & Sun summer)* is among a string of travel agencies and airline offices. On the other side of town is **STA Travel** *(☎ 022 329 97 33; Rue Vignier 3; open 9.15am-6pm Mon-Fri, 9am-noon Sat)*.

For medical services there's the **Cantonal Hospital** *(☎ 022 372 33 11; Rue Micheli-du-Crest 24)* or a private 24-hour clinic, **Permanence Médico Chirurgicale** *(☎ 022 731 21 20; Rue de Chantepoulet 1–3)*.

Things to See & Do

Start a walk through the Old Town at **Île Rousseau**, which is home to a statue in honour of the Enlightenment philosopher Jean-Jacques Rousseau. Turn right (west) along the Rhône's southern side until you reach 13th-century **Tour de L'Île**, once part of the medieval city fortifications. Off Grand-Rue is the part-Romanesque, part-Gothic **Cathédrale St Pierre**, where John Calvin preached. The location has been a place of worship since the 4th century, and you can see evidence of this in the **archaeological site** *(adult/student Sfr5/3; open Tues-Sun)*. Grand-Rue terminates at **Place du Bourg-de-Four**, site of a medieval marketplace.

On the lakeside is the **Jet d'Eau**. Calling this a fountain is an understatement: in summer the water shoots up with incredible force to create a 140m-high plume.

The European arm of the UN is the Art Deco **Palais des Nations** *(☎ 022 907 48 96; Ave de la Paix 9–14; tour adult/student Sfr8.50/6.50; open 10am-5pm daily July-Aug; 10am-noon & 2pm-4pm daily Apr-June & Sept-Oct; 10am-noon & 2pm-4pm Mon-Fri Nov-Mar)*. You can see where decisions about world affairs are made on the hour-long tour (bring your passport). The **International Red Cross & Red Crescent Museum** *(☎ 022 748 95 25; Ave de la Paix 17; Bus No 5 or 8; adult/student Sfr10/5; open 10am-5pm Wed-Mon)*, next to the UN, proudly tells the story of the world's first humanitarian organisation.

Musée d'Art et d'Histoire *(Museum of Art and History; ☎ 022 418 26 00; Rue Charles-Galland 2; admission free; open 10am-5pm Tues-Sun)* has an enormous collection of paintings, sculpture, weapons and archaeological displays.

Maison Tavel *(☎ 022 418 37 00; 6 Rue du Puits Saint Pierre; admission free; open 10am-5pm Tues-Sun)* focuses on the history of urban life in Geneva.

Geneva has more parkland than any other Swiss city, much of it along the lakefront. There's the **Jardin Anglais**, near the jet, featuring a large flower clock; and the impressive **Jardin Botanique** *(admission free; open 9.30am-5pm daily winter, 8am-7.30pm daily rest of year)* with exotic plants and an aviary. South of Grand-Rue is **Promenade des Bastions**, containing a massive monument to the Reformation.

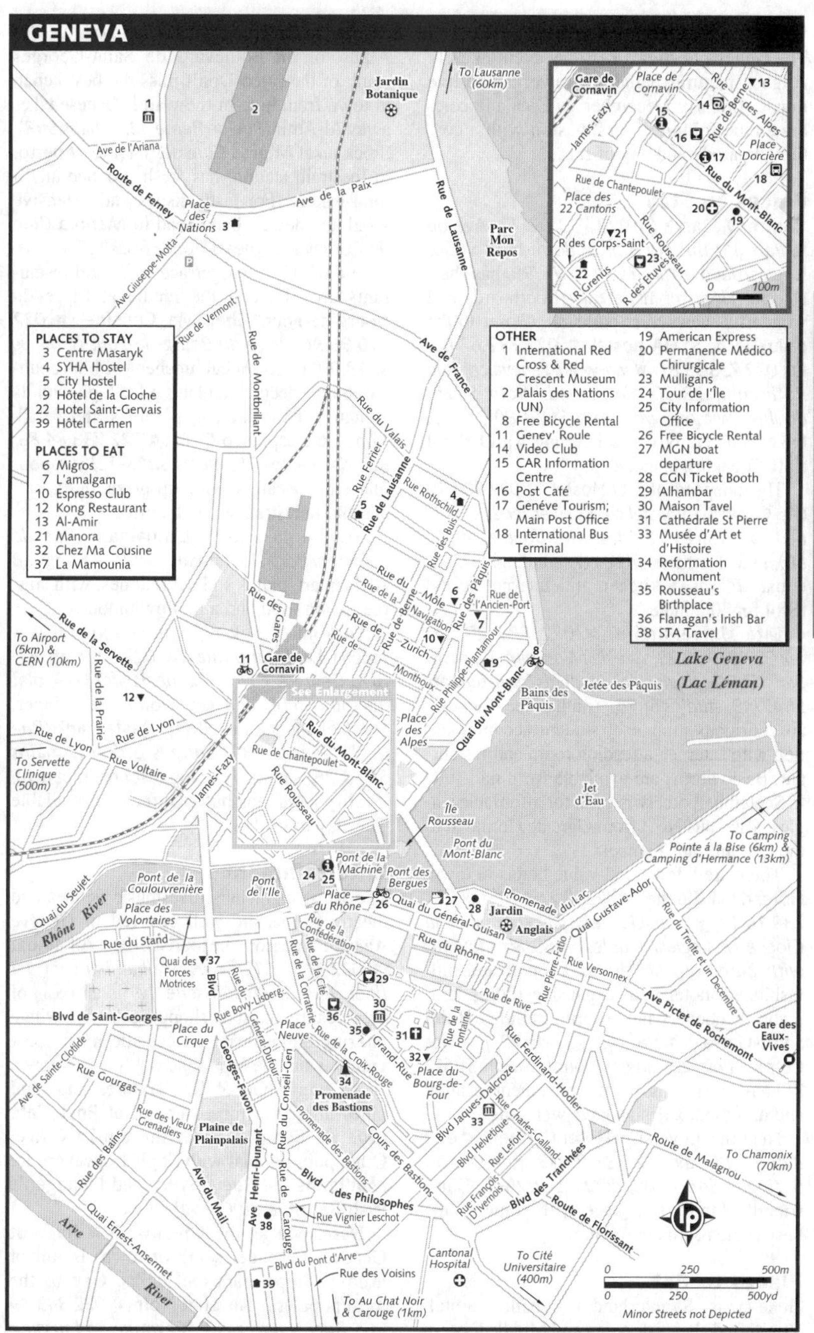
GENEVA
PLACES TO STAY
3 Centre Masaryk
4 SYHA Hostel
5 City Hostel
9 Hôtel de la Cloche
22 Hotel Saint-Gervais
39 Hôtel Carmen
PLACES TO EAT
6 Migros
7 L'amalgam
10 Espresso Club
12 Kong Restaurant
13 Al-Amir
21 Manora
32 Chez Ma Cousine
37 La Mamounia
OTHER
1 International Red Cross & Red Crescent Museum
2 Palais des Nations (UN)
8 Free Bicycle Rental
11 Genev' Roule
14 Video Club
15 CAR Information Centre
16 Post Café
17 Genéve Tourism; Main Post Office
18 International Bus Terminal
19 American Express
20 Permanence Médico Chirurgicale
23 Mulligans
24 Tour de l'Île
25 City Information Office
26 Free Bicycle Rental
27 MGN boat departure
28 CGN Ticket Booth
29 Alhambar
30 Maison Tavel
31 Cathédrale St Pierre
33 Musée d'Art et d'Histoire
34 Reformation Monument
35 Rousseau's Birthplace
36 Flanagan's Irish Bar
38 STA Travel
Jardin Botanique
To Lausanne (60km)
Parc Mon Repos
Lake Geneva (Lac Léman)
To Airport (5km) & CERN (10km)
To Servette Clinique (500m)
Gare de Cornavin
See Enlargement
Bains des Pâquis
Jetée des Pâquis
Jet d'Eau
Île Rousseau
Pont du Mont-Blanc
To Camping Pointe á la Bise (6km) & Camping d'Hermance (13km)
Jardin Anglais
Rhône River
Arve River
Plaine de Plainpalais
Promenade des Bastions
Place du Bourg-de-Four
Gare des Eaux-Vives
To Chamonix (70km)
Cantonal Hospital
To Cité Universitaire (400m)
To Au Chat Noir & Carouge (1km)
0 250 500m
0 250 500yd
Minor Streets not Depicted
SWITZERLAND

Special Events

The Geneva Festival, a 10-day event in early August, features parades, fireworks and live music. In early December, L'Escalade celebrates the foiling of an invasion with a costumed parade and day of races.

Places to Stay

Centre Masaryk *(☎ 022 733 07 72; Ave de la Paix 11; Bus No 5 or 8; dorm beds Sfr30, singles/doubles/triples Sfr40/76/99)* has characterful large rooms, creaky floorboards and wonderful views over parkland. Closer to the centre is the **SYHA hostel** *(☎ 022 732 62 60, fax 022 738 39 87; W www.yh-geneva.ch; Rue Rothschild 28-30; dorm beds from Sfr25, doubles without/with bath Sfr70/80)*, a big, busy, concrete box of a building with helpful staff. Breakfast is included.

The independent **City Hostel** *(☎ 022 901 15 00; e info@cityhostel.ch; Rue Ferrier 2; 4/3/2-bed dorms Sfr25/28/31, singles/doubles Sfr55/80)*, in a charmless '70s-style building, has adequate rooms, a kitchen and Internet access (Sfr4 for 30 minutes).

Cité Universitaire *(☎ 022 839 22 22, fax 022 839 22 23; Ave de Miremont 46; dorm beds Sfr20, singles for students/nonstudents Sfr42/49, studios Sfr75)*, south of the Rhône, is an enormous jumble of student accommodation with Internet, a reading room and restaurant. Basic dorms are available from mid-June to September; otherwise, ask for affordable singles. Take bus No 3 from Gare de Cornavin to the terminus at Champel.

There are a few good-value hotels in town. **Hôtel de la Cloche** *(☎ 022 732 94 81, fax 022 738 16 12; e hotelcloche@span.ch; Rue de la Cloche 6; singles/doubles Sfr60/85, doubles with bathroom Sfr120)* is a small and old-fashioned, hotel with expansive rooms, dramatic chandeliers and towering ceilings. **Hotel Saint-Gervais** *(☎/fax 022 732 45 72; Rue des Corps-Saints 20; singles/doubles from Sfr62/78)* has tiny rooms, but its convenient location and unorthodox design have won fans.

Near the university, **Hôtel Carmen** *(☎ 022 329 11 11, fax 022 781 59 33; Rue Dancet 5; singles Sfr55-100, doubles Sfr75-126)* is a friendly family-run place with some of the best value rooms in town.

Places to Eat

Geneva is Switzerland's cuisine capital. You'll find cheapish Asian and Middle Eastern eateries in the seedy streets north of Rue des Alpes, or on Boulevard de Saint-Georges south of the river. Don't miss the best kebab in town from hole-in-the-wall Lebanese takeaway **Al-Amir** *(Rue de Berne 22; kebabs Sfr8)*. Stock up at **Migros** *(Rue des Pâquis)*. **Aperto**, in the train station, has fresh produce and a mini-bakery. For tasty dishes and extensive salad and dessert bars, head to **Manora** *(Rue de Cornavin 4; meals from Sfr6.90)*.

In the Old Town, terrace cafés and restaurants crowd along the medieval Place du Bourg-de-Four. **Chez Ma Cousine** *(☎ 022 310 96 96; Place du Bourg-de-Four 6; meals Sfr13.90)* entices local lunchers with its country cottage decor and plates piled high with its signature half-chicken, potatoes and salad. Minuscule **Espresso Club** *(☎ 022 738 84 88; Rue des Paquis 25; meals Sfr13-22)* is a popular cruisey café serving up pizza, pasta, salads and industrial-strength coffee.

Around the corner, **L'amalgam** *(Rue de l'Ancien-Port 13; meals Sfr16-18)* is all African art, palms and ochre tones, with simple fusion food and a mellow mood.

Tuck into the plentiful *plat du jour* at Moroccan **La Mamounia** *(☎ 022 329 55 61; Blvd Georges-Favon 10; meals Sfr23-29, plat du jour Sfr16)* and you won't need dinner. West of the station, **Kong Restaurant** *(Rue de la Servette 31; entrees Sfr7-14, mains Sfr10-26)* satisfies the biggest appetites with its all-you-can-eat buffet (Sfr17.50; available Tuesday to Friday).

Entertainment

The latest nightclubs, live-music venues and theatre events are well covered in *Genéve Agenda*, free from the tourist office. **Alhambar** *(☎ 022 312 13 13; W www.alhambar.com; 1st floor, Rue de la Rôtisserie 10)* is an oasis of theatricality in a staid shopping district, with a buzzing atmosphere, an eclectic music programme and the best Sunday brunch in town.

An odd blend of Brit fixtures and loud blues attracts a mixed crowd at **Post Café** *(Rue de Berne 7)*, near the tourist office. Other pubs popular with English speakers are **Mulligans** *(14 Rue Grenus)* and **Flanagan's Irish Bar** *(Rue du Cheval-Blanc)*.

Described as the Greenwich Village of Geneva, Carouge (south of town) is full of groovy shops, bars and clubs. One of the most popular is **Au Chat Noir** *(☎ 022 343 49 98; Rue Vautier 13, Carouge; admission*

Sfr15), serving up funk, African beats, jazz and DJs well into the wee hours.

Getting There & Away

Geneva airport has frequent connections to every major European city.

International buses depart from **Place Dorcière** *(☎ 022 732 02 30)*, off Rue des Alpes. There are several buses a week to London (Sfr145, 17 hours) and Barcelona (Sfr100, 10 hours).

There are more-or-less hourly rail connections to most Swiss towns; the Zürich trip takes three hours (Sfr76), as does Interlaken (Sfr63), both via Bern. There are regular international trains to Paris (Sfr95 by TGV, 3½ hours), Hamburg (Sfr280, 10 hours), Milan (Sfr81, four hours) and Barcelona (Sfr100, nine hours). **Gare des Eaux-Vives** is the best station for Annecy and Chamonix. To get there from Gare de Cornavin, take tram No 16.

Next to Jardin Anglais is a ticket booth for **Compagnie Générale de Navigation** *(CGN; ☎ 022 312 52 23; ⓦ www.cgn.ch)*, which operates a steamer service to all towns and major villages bordering Lake Geneva, including those in France. Destinations include Lausanne (Sfr34.80, 3½ hours) and Montreux (Sfr40.80, 4½ hours). Eurail and Swiss passes are valid on CGN boats, or there are CGN boat day passes for Sfr55 and circular excursions.

Smaller boat companies operate excursions on the lake between April and October (no passes valid). Ticket offices and departures are along Quai du Mont-Blanc and next to the Jardin Anglais. Trips range from 45 minutes (Sfr8) to two hours (Sfr20).

Getting Around

Getting from the airport is easy, with regular trains into Gare de Cornavin (Sfr5.20, six minutes). Bus No 10 (Sfr2.20) does the same 5km trip.

Local-transport ticket dispensers are found at all stops. Tickets cost Sfr1.80 (within one zone, 30 minutes) and Sfr2.20 (two zones, 60 minutes). A day pass costs Sfr6 for the city or Sfr12 for the whole canton. Tickets and passes are also valid for MGN boats that travel along the city shoreline. Taxis are Sfr6.30 flag fall plus Sfr2.90 per kilometre (Sfr3.50 from 8.30pm to 6.30am).

You can rent bikes from **Genev' Roule** *(☎/fax 022 740 13 43; Place de Montbrillant 17; Sfr10/42 per day/week)*, right next to the station. From May to October, Genev' Roule has bikes *free of charge*, available here and at Bains des Pâquis, Place du Rhône and Plaine de Plainpalais. Some ID and Sfr50 deposit is required.

Lake Geneva Region

LAUSANNE

pop 115,500

Lausanne is a beautiful hillside city overlooking Lake Geneva, with several distinct personalities. There's the former fishing village, Ouchy, with its summer beach resort feel; Place St-Francois, with stylish cobblestone shopping streets; and Flon, a warehouse district of bars, galleries and boutiques.

The **main tourist office** *(☎ 021 613 73 21; ⓔ information@lausanne-tourisme.ch; open daily)* is in the Ouchy metro station. The train station also has a **tourist office** *(open daily)*, as well as bicycle rental and money exchange. The **main post office** *(open 7.30am-6.30pm Mon-Fri, 8am-noon Sat)* is by the train station. Across the road is **Quanta** *(open 9am-midnight daily)*, offering Internet access at Sfr4/8 for 30/60 minutes.

Things to See & Do

Worth the hill climb is the glorious Gothic **Cathedrale de Lausanne** *(open 7am-7pm Mon-Fri, 8am-7pm Sat-Sun Apr-Sept; closes 5.30pm Oct-Mar)*, built in the 12th and 13th centuries. Highlights include the stunningly detailed carved portal, vaulted ceilings and archways, and carefully restored stained-glass windows.

Musée de l'Art Brut *(☎ 021 647 54 35; Ave de Bergiéres 11; ⓦ www.artbrut.ch; adult/student Sfr6/4; open 11am-1pm & 2pm-6pm Tues-Fri, 11am-6pm Sat-Sun)* is a fascinating amalgam of 15,000 works of art created by untrained artists. Biographies and explanations are in English.

Sports fans can immerse themselves at the information-packed **Musée Olympique** *(☎ 021 621 65 11; ⓦ www.olympic.org; Quai d'Ouchy 1; adult/student/child Sfr14/9/7; open 9am-6pm Mon-Wed & Fri-Sun, 9am-8pm Thur May-Sept; closed Mon Oct-Apr)* – after all, Lausanne *is* home of International Olympic Committee (IOC) headquarters.

For a range of museum subjects under one roof, the **Palais de Rumine** *(Place de la Riponne 6; most museums open 11am-5pm Tues-Sun)* is a one-stop shop covering fine arts, natural history, geology and zoology.

Musee de l'Elysee *(☎ 021 316 99 11; W www.elysee.ch; Ave de L'Elysée 18; adult/student/child Sfr8/4/free; open 11am-6pm daily)* exhibits thought-provoking classical and contemporary works of photography.

For hiking, the tourist office can provide lists of area vineyards, as well as walking and cycling maps.

SWITZERLAND

Places to Stay

Lakeside camping is available at **Camping de Vidy** *(☎ 021 622 50 00; e info@camping lausannevidy.ch; Chemin du Camping 3; bus No 1; adult/child/tent/car-park Sfr7.70/5/8/3, 2/4-person bungalow Sfr55.30/87.30; open year-round)*.

Lausanne Guesthouse & Backpacker *(☎ 021 601 80 00, fax 021 601 80 01; e info@lausanne-guesthouse.ch; Chemin des Epinettes 4; dorm beds Sfr29-34, singles Sfr80-88, doubles Sfr86-98)*, in an elegant, tastefully renovated 1894 townhouse, is high on the hill near the train station. It offers stunning views, sparkling bathrooms and a nonsmoking environment.

The **SYHA hostel** *(☎ 021 626 02 22, fax 021 626 02 26; e lausanne@youth hostel.ch; Chemin du Bois-de-Vaux 36; bus No 2; dorm beds from Sfr28, singles/doubles from Sfr53/80)* provides no-frills accommodation by the lake.

Hôtel Le Chalet *(☎ 021 616 52 06; Ave d'Ouchy 49; metro to Jordils; singles/doubles from Sfr50/90)* is a welcoming old-world family hotel whose owner has an infectious *joie de vivre*.

Places to Eat

The **Manora** *(Place St François 17; meals from Sfr10.40)* is the place for delicious fresh food, with particularly tempting salad and dessert buffets.

Dig into North African sausages, spiced rice and couscous at **Au Couscous** *(☎ 021 321 38 40; 1st floor, Rue Enning 2; meals Sfr19-34, banquets Sfr29-51)*, a Tunisian and macrobiotic specialist.

La Pizzeria Chez Mario *(☎ 021 323 74 01; 1st floor, Rue de Bourg 28; pizzas Sfr13-20, pasta Sfr15.50-20.50)* serves up delicious pizzas in a graffiti-plastered den. Follow the scrawl to find the entrance.

Entertainment

Le Bleu Lézard *(☎ 021 321 38 35; Rue Enning 10)* offers snacks by day, and a cave-like basement bar for concerts, jam sessions and DJs by night. **La Bavaria** *(☎ 021 323 39 13; Petit-Chêne 10)* serves up big beers in dark-wood Bavarian surrounds. Other popular watering holes are **Le Capitaine Cook** *(Rue Enning 2)*, under Au Couscous; or mellow **MGM Café** *(Rue du Lac 14)* on the waterfront.

With its large student population, Lausanne has a thriving club scene, particularly in the Flon district. Check out **MAD** *(☎ 021 312 11 22; W www.mad.ch; Rue de Genéve)* or **Loft Electroclub** *(☎ 021 311 64 00; W www.loft club.ch; Place Bel Air 1)*. Both are closed Monday and Tuesday.

Getting There & Away

There are trains to/from Geneva (Sfr18.80, 50 minutes, three hourly), Bern (Sfr30, 70 minutes, one or two hourly) and Interlaken Ost (Sfr52, two hours, two hourly). For boat services, see the Geneva section.

MONTREUX

pop 22,300

Centrepiece of the 'Swiss Riviera', Montreux is an affluent lakeside town with stunning views of the French Alps, excellent lakeside walks and the ever-popular Château de Chillon. The **train station** and **main post office** are on Ave des Alpes, with the town centre to the left (south). The **tourist office** *(☎ 021 962 84 36; e tourism@montreuxtourism.ch; open daily)* is in the pavilion on the lakeshore.

Things to See & Do

Château de Chillon *(☎ 021 966 89 10; W www.chillon.ch; adult/student/child Sfr8.50/6.50/4; open 9am-7pm daily Apr-Sept, 9.30am-5pm Mar & Oct, 10am-4pm Nov-Feb)* deservedly receives more visitors than any other historical building in Switzerland. The 11th-century fortress caught the public imagination when Lord Byron wrote The Prisoner of Chillon about Bonivard, a prior chained in the dungeons for almost four years. You can easily spend a couple of hours touring the tower, courtyards, dungeons and staterooms.

Montreux's idyllic location has attracted writers, musicians and artists for hundreds of years. To learn more about the likes of Noel Coward, Vladimir Nabokov and Charlie Chaplin, ask for the **Hemingway Trail** map from the tourist office. Montreux also has many famous music links (it's the subject of Deep Purple's famous *Smoke on the Water*). Freddy Mercury was a regular visitor. And then there's the annual **Jazz Festival** *(☎ 021 963 82 82; Ⓦ www.montreuxjazz.com)* every July.

Places to Stay & Eat

The modern **SYHA hostel** *(☎ 021 963 49 34, fax 021 963 27 29; Passage de l'Auberge 8, Territet; bus No 1; dorm beds Sfr30, doubles without/with bathroom Sfr76/84; open mid-Feb–mid-Nov)*, a 30-minute walk from the centre, is on the waterfront just 15 minutes from Chateau Chillon.

Hôtel Wilhelm *(☎ 021 963 14 31, fax 021 963 32 85; Ⓔ hotel.wilhelm@span.ch; Rue de Marché 13-15; singles/doubles Sfr60/100, with bathroom Sfr70/120)* is a traditional family-run hotel, just near the train station.

Hotel Elite *(☎ 021 966 03 03; Ave du Casino 25; singles/doubles with breakfast from Sfr70/130)* is a small, quiet alternative with friendly staff and spacious renovated rooms.

Paradise *(☎ 021 963 19 35; Grand-Rue 58; meals from Sfr8)* has a sprawling salad buffet with 40 dishes and flavoursome kebabs and souvlakis.

Getting There & Away

There are trains to/from Geneva (Sfr26, 70 minutes, hourly) and Lausanne (Sfr9.80, 25 minutes, three hourly). Make the scenic journey to Interlaken via the GoldenPass Panoramic, with changeovers at Zweisimmen and Spiez (Sfr54, rail passes valid, three hours). For boat services, see the Geneva section.

Valais (Wallis)

The dramatic Alpine scenery of Valais once made it one of the most inaccessible regions of Switzerland. Today, the mountains and valleys have been opened up for keen skiers and hikers by an efficient network of roads, railways and cable cars.

ZERMATT

pop 5340

This skiing, mountaineering and hiking mecca bathes in the reflected glory of the most famous peak in the Alps, the Matterhorn (4478m). The town is small and easy to navigate, and it's car-free except for tiny electric taxis and vans. **Zermatt Tourismus** *(☎/fax 027 966 81 00; Ⓔ zermatt@wallis.ch; open Mon-Sat, daily in high season)* is beside the train station. Next door is **Zermatt Tour**, a travel agency that also changes money. **Alpin Center** *(☎ 027 966 24 60; open 8am-11.30am & 4pm-6.30pm daily)*, on Bahnofstrasse near the post office, is a one-stop shop for all adventure needs.

Activities

Zermatt is arguably the country's best ski resort, with plenty of demanding slopes and panoramic views at every turn. February to April is peak time, but high-altitude ski fields make skiing possible through summer.

A highlight of the area is the cog-wheel railway to Gornergrat (3090m; Sfr63 return; departures every 20 minutes). Topped by the highest cable station in Europe (3820m), the Klein Matterhorn provides access to summer skiing slopes, as well as the ski route down to Cervinia in Italy (don't forget your passport). A day pass for all lifts, excluding Cervinia, is Sfr64. For one day, equipment-hire prices are Sfr28 for skis and stocks and Sfr15 for boots.

In summer, Zermatt becomes a hub for hikers, attracted by 400km of trails through high-Alpine scenery with views of Europe's highest mountains.

Places to Stay & Eat

The tourist office can help with a list of chalets and apartments. Many hotels and restaurants close between seasons.

The **SYHA hostel** *(☎ 027 967 23 20, fax 027 967 53 06; Ⓔ zermatt@youthhostel.ch; dorm beds with half-board from Sfr48; closed mid-Apr–June)*, a 20-minute walk from the station, is a five-storey chalet high on the hill with excellent views of the Matterhorn.

Matterhorn Hostel *(☎ 027 968 19 19, fax 027 968 19 15; Ⓦ www.matterhornhostel.com; Schluhmattstrasse 32; dorm beds Sfr29, doubles Sfr78; open year-round)*, a short walk from the station, is the independent option, with Internet access (Sfr2 for 10 minutes) and its own restaurant.

Directly opposite the station is **Hotel Bahnhof** *(☎ 027 967 24 06, fax 027 967 72 16; Ⓔ welcome@hotelbahnhof.com; dorm beds Sfr30; singles/doubles Sfr56/86, with*

SWITZERLAND

Battling Bovines

Spain is famous for its bullfighting, but in Switzerland it's the cows who lock horns. After a long period of being kept in a barn, it's no wonder the cows are so full of beans when they're let loose in the spring. In Valais villages, cow fights are waged to determine the best beast to lead the herd to summer pastures. Far from a blood sport, the battles consist of cows butting heads and throwing their weight around – most beasts come away without a scratch. The owner of the 'Queen' cow wins great kudos, but the unfortunate beast is rewarded with an enormous bell to lug around. Fights are held on selected Sundays from late March to October; see the Valais Tourism website (W www.matterhornstate.com).

SWITZERLAND

shower Sfr68/96), which has an impressive industrial-size kitchen, ski storage room in the basement, large dorms, and twins with balconies facing the Matterhorn.

Squeezed between old mountain huts on cobblestoned streets, the **Hotel Gabelhorn** *(☎ 027 967 22 35; singles/doubles from Sfr40/80; closed May, June & Oct)*, in the Hinter Dorf area of the village, is a traditional family-run pension. It's full of character but a little cramped.

A favourite hangout for resort workers is the **Brown Cow** *(Hotel de la Poste; ☎ 027 967 19 32; snacks Sfr6-14)*, with great music, hearty food and cow-hide decor. Within the same complex is the **Old Spaghetti Factory** and **Broken's Pizza Factory**. For Valais specialities, there's **Walliserkanne** *(☎ 027 966 46 10; Bahnhofstrasse; meals from Sfr15)*, by the post office.

Head to the **North Wall Bar** *(☎ 027 967 28 63)* for cheap beer, inspirational ski videos and 'the best pizza in town' (from Sfr12).

Getting There & Away

Hourly trains depart from Brig, calling at Visp. The steep, scenic journey takes 80 minutes and costs Sfr35/69 one way/return. Swiss Passes are valid and Inter-Rail passes give 50% off for those aged under 26 years. The only way out is to backtrack. The popular scenic *Glacier Express* travels to/from St Moritz from Zermatt (see under Getting There & Away in the St Moritz section later in this chapter for details).

Ticino (Tessin)

South of the Alps, Ticino enjoys a Mediterranean climate and has an unmistakable Italian flavour. Cuisine, architecture and plant life mirrors that of its southern neighbour, and Italian is the official language. The region boasts spectacular scenery, with dramatic gorges in the north and languid, lakeside towns in the south. Free open-air music festivals include Bellinzona's Piazza Blues (late June), and Lugano's Estival Jazz (early July) and Blues to Bop Festival (late August).

LOCARNO

pop 14,600

Locarno, at the northern end of Lake Maggiore, has a quaint Old Town with Italianate townhouses, piazzas and arcades, and a laid-back summer-resort atmosphere. Piazza Grande is the centre of town and location of the **main post office**. In the nearby casino complex is the **tourist office** *(☎ 091 751 03 33, fax 091 751 90 70; e locarno@ticino.com; open daily)*. A five-minute walk east is the train station, where there's an Aperto supermarket, money exchange and bike rental. You can gulp shots and smoke Cubans while checking your email (Sfr4 for 20 minutes) at **Pardo Bar** *(☎ 091 752 21 23; Via della Motta 3; open 11am-1am Mon-Sat, 4pm-1am Sun)*.

Don't miss the formidable **Madonna del Sasso**, up on the hill with panoramic views of the lake and town. The sanctuary was built after the Virgin appeared in a vision in 1480. It features a church with 15th-century paintings, a small museum and several distinctive statues. In the Old Town are a couple of churches worth visiting, including the 17th-century **Chiesa Nuova** *(Via Cittadella)*. **Giardini Jean Arp** is a small lakeside park off Lungolago Motta, dotted with sculptures by the surrealist.

In August, over 150,000 film buffs hit town for the Locarno International Film Festival. For information see W www.pardo.ch.

Places to Stay & Eat

Delta Camping *(☎ 091 751 60 81; camp sites low/high season Sfr21/47, plus Sfr11/18 per person; open Mar-Oct)* is family-friendly and pricey. There are plenty of cheaper options on Lake Maggiore outside Locarno.

The **SYHA hostel** *(☎ 091 756 15 00, fax 091 756 15 01; e locarno@youthhostel.ch; Via Varenna 18; dorm beds/doubles from Sfr32/*

72), 500m west of Piazza Grande, is in the charmless *Palagiovani* (Palace of Youth).

At **Pensione Cittá Vecchia** *(☎/fax 091 751 45 54; ⓔ cittavecchia@datacomm.ch; Via Toretta 13; dorm beds Sfr28-35, singles/doubles Sfr37/74; open Mar-Nov)*, a non-smoking hostel with basic dorms (breakfast included), the staff are all smiles .

Convenient to the station and lake is the clean, if clinical, **Garni Montaldi** *(☎ 091 743 02 22, fax 091 743 54 06; Piazza Stazione; singles/doubles from Sfr58/110)*. Rates include continental breakfast. The reception is also here for **Stazione** *(singles/doubles from Sfr44/88; open Apr-Oct)*, an older building to the rear with spacious, rudimentary rooms.

By the train station **Manora** *(Via Stazione 1; small/large meals from Sfr6.90/8.90)* has excellent self-service meals.

Lungolago *(Lungolago Motta; pizza from Sfr12.50)*, a popular haunt for snackers and beer-guzzlers, is perfect for steamy summer evenings. On Piazza Grande there's a **Coop** supermarket, and a **Migros De Gustibus** snack bar opposite.

Getting There & Away

There are trains every one to two hours from Brig, passing through Italy en route (Sfr50, 2½ hours). You change trains at Domodóssola across the border, so take your passport. One-day travel passes for boats on Lake Maggiore cost Sfr12 to Sfr21, depending on the coverage. For more information, contact **Navigazione Lago Maggiore** *(NLM; ☎ 091 751 18 65)*.

LUGANO

pop 25,900

Switzerland's southernmost tourist town is a sophisticated slice of Italian life, with colourful markets, upmarket shops, pedestrian-only piazzas and lakeside parks. It's also a great base for lake trips, water sports and hillside hikes.

The train station has money exchange, bike rental and an Aperto supermarket. The Old Town is a 10-minute walk down the hill to the east. On the lake side of the Municipio building is the **tourist office** *(☎ 091 913 32 32, fax 091 922 76 53; ⓔ info@lugano-tourism.ch; Riva Albertolli; open daily, Mon-Fri winter)*. The **main post office** *(Via della Posta 7)* is in the centre of the Old Town. There are four Internet terminals (Sfr5 for 30 minutes) on the 3rd floor of the **Manor** *(Piazza Dante)* department store.

Things to See & Do

At the end of Via Nassa, pop into **Santa Maria degli Angioli Church** *(Piazza Luini)*, featuring a vivid 1529 fresco of the Crucifixion by Bernardino Luini.

Art-lovers can get their fix of 19th- and 20th-century works at the **Museo Cantonale d'Arte** *(☎ 091 910 47 80; ⓦ www.museo-cantonale-arte.ch; Via Canova 10; adult/student Sfr7/5; open 2pm-5pm Tues, 10am-5pm Wed-Sun)*. The café set can pay homage at the **Coffee Museum** in Balerna or **Alpenrose Chocolate Museum** in Caslano.

Take a boat trip to one of the many photogenic villages hugging the shoreline of Lake Lugano. One of the most popular is car-free Gandria, with historic homes and shops and narrow winding alleyways. You can see how the smugglers plied their trade at the **Swiss Customs Museum** *(☎ 091 910 48 11; admission free; open 1.30pm-5.30pm daily Apr–mid-Oct)*, across the water.

There are excellent hikes and views from **Monte San Salvatore** and **Monte Bré**. The **funicular** *(one-way/return ticket Sfr12/18)* from Paradiso up Monte San Salvatore operates from mid-March to mid-November. To ascend Monte Bré, take the year-round **funicular** *(one-way/return Sfr13/19)* from Cassarate.

Places to Stay

An excellent budget option close to the station is **Hotel Montarina** *(☎ 091 966 72 72, fax 091 966 00 17; ⓔ info@montarina.ch; Via Montarina 1; dorm beds Sfr25, singles/doubles from Sfr70/100; open mid-Mar–Oct)*. This lovingly renovated 19th-century villa is heaven in summer, with a swimming pool, large dorms and a garden with palm trees.

The **SYHA hostel** *(☎ 091 966 27 28, fax 091 968 23 63; Via Cantonale 13; dorm beds/doubles Sfr31/72; open mid-Mar–Nov)* is a hard 20-minute walk uphill from the train station. You can cool off in the swimming pool. Closer to the Old Town is **Albergo Ristorante Pestalozzi** *(☎ 091 921 46 46, fax 091 922 20 45; ⓔ pestalo@bluewin.ch; Piazza Indipendenza 9; singles/doubles from Sfr60/100)*, an inviting Art Nouveau hotel with a variety of renovated rooms.

Places to Eat

Head to the pedestrian-only piazzas to tempt the tastebuds with panini (Sfr5) and gelati (Sfr3) from street stalls, or larger meals in the pizzerias and cafés. Self-caterers can stock up at the large **Migros** *(Via Pretorio)*.

Make your own pizzettes at the sprawling **Manora** *(meals from Sfr8.90)*, with a wide range of self-service food. **Panino Gusto** *(☎ 091 922 51 51; Via Motta 7a; panini Sfr9-19)* offers panini overflowing with smoked meats, salmon and cheeses.

Ristorante Pestalozzi *(☎ 091 921 46 46; Piazza Indipendenza 9; meals from Sfr11)* has a changing daily menu with plenty of vegie options in a large alcohol-free dining room.

The critically acclaimed **La Tinéra** *(Via dei Gorini; dishes Sfr11-27)*, off Piazza della Riforma, is a tiny cellar restaurant serving local specialities to a jam-packed crowd.

Getting There & Away

Lugano is on the same road and rail route as Bellinzona. Two postbuses run to St Moritz daily in summer and cut back to one during winter (only on Friday, Saturday and Sunday during some weeks). It costs Sfr50 (plus Sfr12 reservation fee) and takes 4½ hours. Reserve your seat the day before at the bus station or train information office, or by phoning ☎ 091 807 85 20. Buses leave from the station on Via Serafino Balestra, though the St Moritz bus also calls at the train station.

Graubünden

Graubünden (Grisons, Grigioni, Grishun) has some of the most developed winter sports centres in the world. Away from the international resorts, it's a relatively unspoiled region of rural villages, alpine lakes and hill-top castles. The largest town and regional gateway is Chur, which offers a **local tourist office** *(☎ 081 252 18 18; Grabenstrasse 5; open Mon-Sat)* and a **regional tourist office** *(☎ 081 254 24 24; e contact@graubuenden.ch; Alexanderstrasse 24; open Mon-Fri)*. Chur is only 90 minutes by fast train from Zürich (Sfr35), and two hours from St Moritz (Sfr38).

ST MORITZ

pop 5600

St Moritz has built its reputation as the playground of the international jet-set for more than a century, but the curative properties of its waters have been known for 3000 years. In winter, superb ski fields are the main drawcard; in summer, visitors come for the hiking, windsurfing, kitesurfing and inline skating. The plush main town, St Moritz Dorf, lounges on the slopes overlooking Lake St Moritz. To the southwest, 2km around the lake lies the more downmarket St Moritz Bad.

The **train station** near the lake rents out bikes in summer and changes money. Up the hill on Via Serlas is the post office, and five minutes further is the **tourist office** *(☎ 081 837 33 33, fax 081 837 33 77; e information@stmoritz.ch; Via Maistra 12; open Mon-Sat, daily in high season)*, with friendly, helpful staff. You can check your favourite websites (at Sfr2 for 10 minutes) at **Bobby's Pub** *(☎ 081 834 42 83; Via dal Bagn 50a; open 9am-1.30am Mon-Sat, 2pm-1.30am Sun)*.

There are 350km of downhill runs around St Moritz. A day pass costs Sfr63, and ski and boot rental is about Sfr43 per day. There are also 160km of cross-country trails (equipment rental Sfr20) and 120km of marked hiking paths. Sporting activities abound both in winter and summer. You can try golf (play on the frozen lake in winter), tennis, inline skating, fishing, horse riding, sailing, windsurfing and river rafting, to mention a few. The tourist office has a list of prices and contacts.

Places to Stay & Eat

Naturally, cheaper digs are in the 'Bad' part of town. The **SYHA hostel** *(☎ 081 833 39 69, fax 081 833 80 46; Via Surpunt 60; w www.youthhostel.ch/st.moritz; dorm beds with half-board Sfr45.50; doubles without/with bathroom Sfr117/140)* offers excellent modern facilities. There's mountain-bike rental, compulsory half-board, a ski room and Internet access (Sfr4 for 15 minutes).

If the hostel is full, head next door to **Hotel Stille** *(☎ 081 833 69 48, fax 081 833 07 08; e hotel.stille@bluewin.ch; singles/twins summer Sfr57/114, winter Sfr72/144)*, which attracts a young, sporty crowd.

You'll get basic budget rooms in a convenient lakeside location at **Bellaval** *(☎ 081 833 32 45, fax 081 833 04 06; e hotel-bellaval@bluewin.ch; Via Grevas 55; singles/doubles from Sfr55/110, with bathroom from Sfr80/140)*. Prices include breakfast.

Heading into St Moritz Bad, there's a clutch of good-value pizzerias and Italian restaurants, including **La Fontana** *(☎ 081 833 12 66; Via dal Bagn 16; mains Sfr12-28)*, a cosy rustic restaurant with candle lighting;

and **Pizzeria La Botte** *(☎ 081 833 39 88; Via dal Bagn 15; mains Sfr16-24)*, with rich, buttery Italian dishes.

Getting There & Away

The *Glacier Express* is one of Switzerland's most famous scenic train routes, connecting St Moritz to Zermatt via the 2033m Oberalp Pass. It takes 7½ hours to cover 290 scenic kilometres and cross 291 bridges (Sfr138). Two postbuses run to/from Lugano daily in summer – in winter, there's a daily bus on Friday, Saturday and Sunday. You must reserve a seat the day before on ☎ 081 837 67 64. Nine daily trains travel south to Tirano in Italy with connections to Milan.

Zürich

pop 339,300

Switzerland's most populous city offers an ambience of affluence, style and culture. Banks and art galleries greet you at every turn in a marriage of finance and aesthetics, and at night, the pin-stripe brigade yields the streets to bar-hoppers and clubbers.

Orientation & Information

Zürich is at the northern end of Lake Zürich (Zürichsee), with the centre split by the Limmat River. The main train station (Hauptbahnhof) is on the western bank of the river, close to the old centre.

The **Zürich Tourist Service** *(☎ 01 215 40 00, fax 01 215 40 44; ⓔ information@zurichtourism.ch; open daily)* is in the train station's main hall.

Banks are open 8.15am to 4.30pm Monday to Friday (until 6pm Thursday).

The main post office is **Sihlpost** *(☎ 01 296 21 11; Kasernenstrasse 95-97; open 7.30am-8pm Mon-Fri, 8am-4pm Sat)*, but there's a more convenient one at the main train station. Several tables of Internet terminals (at Sfr10 per hour) vie for space in **Quanta Virtual Fun Space** *(cnr Niederdorfstrasse & Mülegasse)*.

STA Travel *(☎ 01 261 97 57; Leonhardstrasse 10; open 10am-6pm Mon-Wed & Fri, 10am-8pm Thur, 10am-1pm Sat)* offers budget fares.

For medical and dental help, ring ☎ 01 269 69 69. There's a 24-hour chemist at **Bellevue Apotheke** *(☎ 01 252 56 00; Theaterstrasse 14)*.

Things to See

The cobblestoned pedestrian streets of the Old Town offer surprises at every turn – 16th- and 17th-century houses and guildhalls, tiny boutiques and cafés, courtyards and fountains. Elegant **Bahnhofstrasse** is perfect for window-shopping and affluent-Zürcher-watching. Vaults beneath the street are said to be crammed with gold and silver.

The 13th-century tower of **St Peterskirche** *(St Peter's Church)* is hard to miss, with the largest clock face in Europe (8.7m in diameter). The part-Romanesque, part-Gothic **Fraumünster** features *The Heavenly Paradise* window by Augusto Giacometti and magnificent stained-glass works by surrealist Marc Chagall. Across the river, the dual-towered **Grossmünster** looms. Highlights are the choir windows designed by Augusto Giacometti (1933) and an imposing statue of Charlemagne (1107) in the crypt.

Kunsthaus *(Museum of Fine Arts; ☎ 01 253 84 84; ⓦ www.kunsthaus.ch; Heimplatz 1; adult/student/child Sfr10/6/free, Wed free; open 10am-9pm Tues-Thur, 10am-5pm Fri-Sun)* has one of the best collections in the country, with works by Dalí, Man Ray, Hockney, Renoir, Monet and Marc Chagall.

The **Lindt & Sprüngli chocolate factory** *(☎ 01 716 22 33; Seestrasse 204; bus No 165 from Bürkliplatz to Schooren; admission free; open 10am-noon & 1pm-4pm Wed-Fri)* has a small exhibit and corny documentary. Free chocolate samples abound.

Special Events

On the third Monday in April, Zürich celebrates the arrival of warmer weather with Sechseläuten. Guild members parade the streets in historical costume, playing music. A fireworks-filled 'snowman' (the Böögg) is ignited at 6pm. Zürich lets its hair down in August with the techno Street Parade, attracting well over half-a-million ravers. In February, just after Ash Wednesday, the city celebrates Fasnacht, with parades and festive costumes. Zürcher Festspiele, from mid-June to mid-July, offers a programme of music, dance and theatre.

Places to Stay

Accommodation can be hard to find, particularly from August to October. Book ahead, or use the information board and free phone in the train station. The tourist office can sometimes get lower rates.

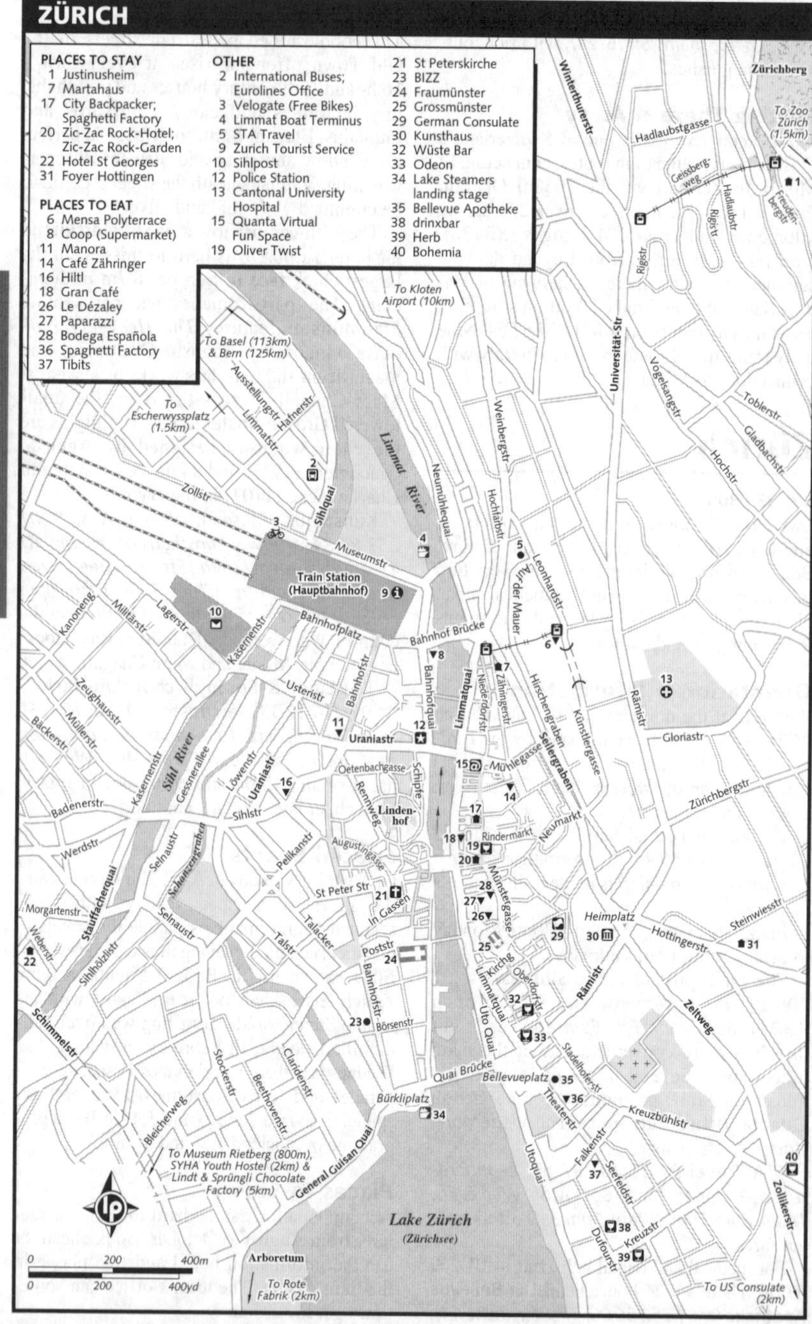
ZÜRICH
PLACES TO STAY
1 Justinusheim
7 Martahaus
17 City Backpacker; Spaghetti Factory
20 Zic-Zac Rock-Hotel; Zic-Zac Rock-Garden
22 Hotel St Georges
31 Foyer Hottingen
PLACES TO EAT
6 Mensa Polyterrace
8 Coop (Supermarket)
11 Manora
14 Café Zähringer
16 Hiltl
18 Gran Café
26 Le Dézaley
27 Paparazzi
28 Bodega Española
36 Spaghetti Factory
37 Tibits
OTHER
2 International Buses; Eurolines Office
3 Velogate (Free Bikes)
4 Limmat Boat Terminus
5 STA Travel
9 Zurich Tourist Service
10 Sihlpost
12 Police Station
13 Cantonal University Hospital
15 Quanta Virtual Fun Space
19 Oliver Twist
21 St Peterskirche
23 BIZZ
24 Fraumünster
25 Grossmünster
29 German Consulate
30 Kunsthaus
32 Wüste Bar
33 Odeon
34 Lake Steamers landing stage
35 Bellevue Apotheke
38 drinxbar
39 Herb
40 Bohemia
To Kloten Airport (10km)
To Basel (113km) & Bern (125km)
To Escherwyssplatz (1.5km)
To Zoo Zürich (1.5km)
Zürichberg
Train Station (Hauptbahnhof)
Limmat River
Sihl River
Lindenhof
Lake Zürich (Zürichsee)
Arboretum
To Rote Fabrik (2km)
To Museum Rietberg (800m), SYHA Youth Hostel (2km) & Lindt & Sprüngli Chocolate Factory (5km)
To US Consulate (2km)
Heimplatz
Bellevueplatz
Bürkliplatz
0 200 400m
0 200 400yd
SWITZERLAND

Hostels The **SYHA hostel** *(☎ 01 482 35 44, fax 01 480 17 27; ⓔ zurich@youthhostel.ch; Mutschellenstrasse 114, Wollishofen; dorm beds/singles/doubles from Sfr32/69/90)* is large and modern with 24-hour service and excellent facilities. Take tram No 6 or 7 to Morgental, or S-Bahn 8 to Wollishofen.

Bar-hoppers will feel more at home at **City Backpacker** *(☎ 01 251 90 15, fax 01 251 90 24; ⓔ backpacker@access.ch; Niederdorfstrasse 5; dorm beds without/with sheets Sfr29/32, singles/doubles/triples/quads Sfr66/92/126/164)*, in the heart of busy Niederdorfstrasse. Facilities include Internet access (Sfr5 for 25 mins) and a rooftop area.

Removed from the busy city streets is the tranquil student home **Justinusheim** *(☎ 01 361 38 06, fax 01 362 29 82; Freudenbergstrasse 146; singles/doubles/triples from Sfr50/80/120)*. Overlooking carefully tended gardens, spartan, spacious rooms are available during student holidays (particularly mid-July to mid-October), though there are vacancies during term time too. Take tram No 10 from the train station to Rigiblik, then the frequent Seilbahn (every 6 mins) to the top station.

Foyer Hottingen *(☎ 01 256 19 19, fax 01 256 19 00; ⓔ info@foyer-hottingen.ch; Hottingerstrasse 31; dorm beds Sfr35, singles/doubles/triples from Sfr70/110/140)* has sparkling white minimalist rooms and a peaceful pace well away from the hubbub. Dorm beds are women-only.

Hotels The **Hotel St Georges** *(☎ 01 241 11 44, fax 01 241 11 42; ⓔ st-georges@bluewin.ch; Weberstrasse 11; singles/doubles from Sfr78/102)*, on the western bank of the Sihl River, is a bit of a hike, but it's quiet and comfortable, and includes continental breakfast.

A more convenient option is the recently renovated **Martahaus** *(☎ 01 251 45 50, fax 01 251 45 40; ⓔ info@martahaus.ch; Zähringer strasse 36; dorm beds Sfr37, singles/doubles/triples from Sfr75/98/129)*, just five minutes' walk from the station. Privacy prevails with individual cubicles fashioned from partitions and curtains. Book ahead.

Zic-Zac Rock-Hotel *(☎ 01 261 21 81, fax 01 261 21 75; ⓔ rockhotel.ch@bluewin.ch; Marktgasse 17; singles from Sfr75, doubles without/with bathroom Sfr120/160)*, with a bold paint job, rock-star room names and gold discs, is a bit of a novelty, but its cramped conditions make it a no-go for claustrophobes.

Places to Eat

Zürich has a thriving café culture and hundreds of restaurants serving a huge variety of cuisines. A good place is Niederdorfstrasse and the backstreets nearby. Cheap eats abound around the train station, especially in the underground Shopville, which has a **Migros**. Above ground by the station, there's a large **Coop** supermarket. Niederdorfstrasse has a string of snack bars offering pretzels, bratwurst, kebabs and Asian food.

Cafés The enourmous **Mensa Polyterrace** *(Leonhardstrasse 34; meals around Sfr10.50)* is a bustling university cafeteria next to the Polybahn (funicular) top station.

Pile your plate high with tasty fresh food at the buffet-style **Manora** *(5th floor, Manor department store, Bahnofstrasse; salads Sfr4.40-9.40, meals from Sfr8.90; open Mon-Sat)*.

Creative vegetarian options are a highlight at **Tibits** *(☎ 01 260 32 22; Seefeldstrasse 2)*, a sprawling modern vegie restaurant with purple walls and comfy lounges. Run by a collective, **Café Zähringer** *(☎ 01 252 05 00; Zähringerplatz 11; snacks Sfr5.50-7.50, meals Sfr10.50-22)* provides mellow music, a relaxed atmosphere and scrumptious low-fat soups and snacks.

Paparazzi *(☎ 01 250 55 88; Nägelihof 1, Limmatquai; snacks Sfr5-14)* is a fun place to hang out among old movie posters, cameras and early paparazzi snaps.

Old photos of famous folk also adorn the **Gran Café** *(☎ 01 252 31 19; Limmatquai 66)*, by the river, with bargain all-you-can-eat spaghetti for Sfr10.90 (from 6pm).

Restaurants With 22 choices, **Spaghetti Factory** *(☎ 01 251 94 00; Niederdorfstrasse 5; pasta Sfr13.50- 22)* has a fun, buzzing atmosphere and big steaming bowls of its namesake dish. Night owls with the munchies can fill up at a second **branch** *(Theaterstrasse 10; open all night Fri & Sat)*.

For melt-in-your mouth garlic mushrooms and other delicious tapas, head to the ground-level café section of **Bodega Española** *(☎ 01 251 23 10; Münstergasse 15; tapas Sfr4.80)*.

Hiltl *(☎ 01 227 70 00; Sihlstrasse 28; mains Sfr20-25)* is an institution, serving tasty vegie meals to Zürchers since 1898 (when vegetarians were thought of as crackpots). Try the Indian buffet (Sfr4.60 per 100g, Sfr42 all-you-can-eat; from 5pm nightly).

In the shadow of Grossmünster is stylish **Le Dézaley** *(☎ 01 251 61 29; Römergasse 7; dishes from Sfr22)*, the locals' choice for fondue and Vaudois specialities.

Entertainment

Like most big cities, Zürich has a fickle, ever-changing entertainment scene. Pick up the free *Züritipp* from the tourist office or check daily listings at W www.zueritipp.ch. Tickets for many events are available from **Billettzentrale** *(BIZZ; ☎ 01 221 22 83; Bahnhofstrasse 9; open 10am-6.30pm Mon-Fri, 10am-2pm Sat)*.

Late-night pubs, clubs and discos clutter Niederdorfstrasse and adjoining streets. English speakers gravitate towards **Oliver Twist** *(Rindermarkt 6)* and the constantly crowded **Zic-Zac Rock-Garden** *(Marktgasse 17)*.

Lenin and James Joyce once downed drinks at the **Odeon** *(☎ 01 251 16 50; Am Bellevue)*, a swish smoky bar packed with an arty crowd. More laid-back is **Bohemia** *(☎ 01 383 70 60; am Kreuzplatz)*, a spacious, Cuban-themed café/bar. **Wüste Bar** *(☎ 01 251 22 07; Oberdorfstrasse 7)*, underneath the Otter Hotel, is small and groovy with plush red seats and a cowhide bar.

You'll pay around Sfr15 entrance fee for most clubs; however, a couple of small, central establishments have no cover. Try **Herb** *(Kreuzstrasse 24)* and **drinxbar** *(Dufourstrasse 24)*.

Rote Fabrik *(☎ 01 481 9143; W www.rotefabrik.ch; Seestrasse 395; bus No 161 or 165 from Bürkliplatz)*, once a cutting-edge centre for alternative arts, is more mainstream these days. It offers a range of music, original-language films, theatre and dance, as well as a bar/restaurant.

Factories in the industrial quarter, west of the train station, are gradually being taken over by a wave of hip bars, clubs and restaurants. Head to Escherwyssplatz (tram No 4 or 13) and follow your ears. The **Peugeot Bar** *(☎ 01 273 11 25; Pfingstweidstrasse 6)* draws big crowds with its unpretentious atmosphere and produce-market setting. Nearby, **Moods Jazz Club** *(☎ 01 276 80 00; Schiffbaustrasse 6)* is in a former ship-building factory.

Getting There & Away

Kloten airport, 10km north of the centre, has several daily flights. **Swiss** *(☎ 0848 85 2000)* has an office in the main train station.

Various buses head east to Budapest, Belgrade, Dubrovnik and elsewhere. The Eurolines office behind the train station is open daily, but intermittently. For information call ☎ 01 272 40 42, or ask at the tourist office.

There are direct trains to Stuttgart (Sfr62, three hours), Munich (Sfr89, 4½ hours), Innsbruck (Sfr69, four hours), Milan (Sfr75, four hours) and many other international destinations. There are also at least hourly departures to most Swiss towns including Lucerne (Sfr22, 50 minutes), Bern (Sfr48, 70 minutes) and Basel (Sfr32, 65 minutes).

Getting Around

Regular trains make the 10-minute trip from the airport to the main train station (Sfr5.40).

There's a comprehensive unified bus, tram and S-Bahn service in the city that includes boats plying the Limmat River. All tickets must be bought in advance from dispensers. Short trips under five stops are Sfr2.30. A one-/24-hour pass for the city costs Sfr3.60/7.20, while a 24-hour pass including travel to/from the airport is Sfr10.80.

Lake steamers depart from Bürkliplatz between early April and late October (Swiss Pass and Eurail are valid, Inter-Rail 50% discount). A popular option is the two-hour journey to Rapperswill (round-trip Sfr20). Contact **Zürichsee-Schifffahrtsgesellschaft** *(ZSG; ☎ 01 487 13 33; W www.zsg.ch)* for more information.

Use of city bikes is free of charge from **Velogate** *(platform 18, main train station; open 7.30am-9.30pm year-round)*. Bring photo ID and Sfr20 deposit.

Central Switzerland

This is what many visitors consider the 'true' Switzerland. Rich in mountains, lakes, tinkling cowbells and alpine villages, it's also where Switzerland began as a nation. The original pact of 1291, signed by the communities of Uri, Schwyz and Nidwalden, can be viewed in Schwyz's Bundesbriefarchiv hall.

LUCERNE (LUZERN)

pop 57,100

Ideally situated in the historic and scenic heart of Switzerland, Lucerne is an excellent base for mountain excursions, with easy access to the towering peaks of Mt Pilatus and Mt Rigi.

The mostly pedestrian-only Old Town is on the northern bank of the Reuss River. The train station is centrally located on the southern bank. Beside platform three is **Luzern Tourismus** *(☎ 041 227 17 17; ⓔ luzern@luzern.org; Zentralstrasse 5; open daily)*. In front of the train station is the boat landing stage and across the road is the **main post office** *(open 7.30am-6.30pm Mon-Fri, 8am-noon Sat)*. For cheap Internet (Sfr2 for 30 minutes) head to the **Stadtbibliothek** *(Library; Löwenplatz 10; open 1.30pm-6.30pm Mon, 10am-6.30pm Tues-Wed & Fri, 10am-9pm Thur, 10am-4pm Sat)*. **American Express** *(☎ 041 410 00 77; Schweizerhofquai 4; open 8.30am-5pm Mon-Fri, plus 8.30am-noon Sat in summer)* has an ATM and money exchange.

Things to See

Your first stop should be the medieval Old Town, with ancient rampart walls and towers, 15th-century buildings with painted facades and the two much-photographed covered bridges. **Kapellbrücke** *(Chapel Bridge)*, dating from 1333, is Lucerne's best-known landmark, famous for its distinctive water tower and the spectacular 1993 fire that nearly destroyed it. In better condition, but rather dark and dour, are the *Dance of Death* panels under the roofline of **Spreuerbrücke** *(Spreuer Bridge)*.

Set aside a few hours for the fascinating **Gletschergarten** *(Glacier Garden; ☎ 041 410 43 40; Denkmalstrasse 4; ⓦ www.gletschergarten.ch; adult/student/child Sfr9/7/5.50; open 9am-6pm daily Apr-Oct, 10am-5pm daily Nov-Mar)*, where you can peer into the giant glacial potholes that prove Lucerne's prehistory as a subtropical palm beach.

Nearby is the poignant **Lion Monument**, which is dedicated to the Swiss soldiers who died during the French Revolution. Another moving historical exhibit is the **Bourbaki Panorama** *(☎ 041 412 30 30; Löwenplatz 11; ⓦ www.panorama-luzern.ch; adult/student/child Sfr7/6/5; open 9am-6pm daily)*, an 1100-sq-metre circular painting with commentary depicting the first Red Cross efforts during the Franco-Prussian War.

From mid-August to mid-September, Lucerne hosts the annual **Internationale Musikfestwochen** *(International Festival of Music; ☎ 041 226 44 00; ⓦ www.lucernemusic.ch)*.

Places to Stay

Backpackers Lucerne *(☎ 041 360 04 20, fax 041 360 04 42; Alpenquai 42; dorm beds from Sfr24)*, a 12-minute walk southeast of the station, is a cheerful independent with sprawling parkland frontage and a scrap of lakefront beach.

The **SYHA hostel** *(☎ 041 420 88 00, fax 041 420 56 16; ⓔ luzern@youthhostel.ch; Sedelstrasse 12; bus No 18 from Bahnhofplatz; dorm beds from Sfr31.50; singles/doubles from Sfr64/78)*, around 1km north of the city walls, is a large, modern, reliable option.

Good for novelty value is **Hotel Löwengraben** *(☎ 041 417 12 12, fax 041 417 12 11; ⓔ hotel@loewengraben.ch; Löwengraben 18; dorm beds from Sfr30, singles/twins/doubles with breakfast Sfr120/165/190, suites Sfr250-300)*, a converted prison with basic, whitewashed, 'cell-like' rooms and some fancier suites (albeit with bars on the windows). Its transformation comes complete with a stylish restaurant, trendy bar and nightclub, and Internet access.

Simple but centrally located is **Hotel Linde** *(☎ 041 410 31 93; Metzgerrainle 3; singles/doubles Sfr44/88; open Apr-Oct)*, off Weinmarkt in the Old Town, offers six cheap and cheerful rooms with crisp white linen. Check-in is through the ground-floor Italian restaurant.

Hotel Schiff *(☎ 041 418 52 52; fax 041 418 52 55; ⓔ contact@hotel-schiff-luzern.ch; Unter der Egg 8; singles/doubles from Sfr80/120, with bathroom from Sfr150/190)*, overlooking the Reuss River, has mostly spacious, renovated rooms. Rates include breakfast.

Places to Eat

Good eating is easy to find, particularly along the Reuss River, around Kornmarkt or in the winding maze of streets in the Old Town. A reliable cheapie is the buffet-style **Manora** *(5th floor, Weggisgasse 5; salads Sfr4.40-9.40)*.

For speedy service, try **Pizzeria al Forno** *(1st floor, Hotel zum Weissen Kreuz; pizza/pasta from Sfr14/13)*, with 34 varieties of mouth-watering wood-fired pizza. Wander in and smell the coffee at **La Barca Vincafé**, hidden away under the Hotel Schiff, an antipasto bar serving up super-strong Italian blends.

Self-caterers should head to Hertensteinstrasse, where cheap eats abound. There's also a Coop restaurant, two Migros restaurants and a supermarket.

Entertainment

Jazzkantine *(☎ 041 410 73 73; W www.jsl.ch; Grabengasse 8)* is a groovy hangout frequented by the young, creative types from the adjoining jazz school. More laid-back is **Cafe Parterre** *(☎ 041 210 40 93; Mythenstrasse 7; W www.parterre.ch)*, south of the train station. Bar-hoppers can take their pick from **Rathaus Brauerei** *(Unter der Egg 2)*, serving big home brews on the waterfront; **Nix** *(Mühlenplatz 4)*, a low-key wine bar; or **Mr Pickwick Pub** *(Rathausquai 6)*, for Brit beer, food and footy.

Behind Lake Rotsee near the youth hostel is **Sedel** *(☎ 041 420 63 10; W www.sedel.ch)*, a former women's prison with rock concerts and DJs at the weekend.

Getting There & Around

Hourly trains connect Lucerne with Zürich (Sfr11, 50 minutes), Bern (Sfr32, 1½ hours), Interlaken (Sfr29, two hours), Lugano (Sfr58, 2½ hours) and Geneva (Sfr70, 3¼ hours). The N2/E9 motorway connecting Basel and Lugano passes by Lucerne, and the N14 provides the road link to Zürich.

INTERLAKEN

pop 15,000

Interlaken, flanked by stunning Lakes Thun and Brienz and within yodelling distance of the mighty Jungfrau peaks Mönch and Eiger, is a popular base for exploring the delights of the Jungfrau region.

Lovers of kitsch will have a field day in the town itself. Interlaken is also a mecca for thrillseekers, with a flourishing adventure-sports industry.

Orientation & Information

Most of Interlaken lies between its two train stations, Interlaken Ost and West. Each offers bike rental, money-exchange facilities and a landing for boat services.

Near Interlaken West is the **main post office** *(cnr Marktgasse & Höheweg)* and **Interlaken Tourismus** *(☎ 033 826 53 00; e mail@interlakentourism.ch; Höheweg 37; open daily)*. There's a hotel board and free phones outside the tourist office and at both train stations. Backpackers Villa (see Places to Stay later) has cheap Internet access.

Things to See & Do

Interlaken bursts with options for **hiking, rafting, bungee-jumping, heli-skiing, skydiving** and **paragliding**. Local operators include **Alpin Raft** *(☎ 033 823 41 00; W www.alpinraft.ch)* and **Alpin Center** *(☎ 033 823 55 23; W www.alpincenter.ch)*.

Hiking trails dot the surrounding area. Find time to get out on a lake if possible. **Lake Thun** has the greater number of resorts and medieval villages, including Spiez (Sfr13/8.60 by steamer/train) and Thun (Sfr19.20/13.60). **Lake Brienz** has a more rugged shoreline and fewer resorts than its neighbour.

Places to Stay

The Guest Card (available from accommodation places) provides useful discounts.

There are a dozen camping grounds in and around Interlaken (see W www.campinginterlaken.ch). Most convenient is **Sackgut** *(☎ 033 822 44 34; e sackgut@swisscamps.ch; Brienzstrasse; adult/child/tent from Sfr8.20/5.20/6.50; open Apr-Oct)*, behind Interlaken Ost station.

The **SYHA hostel** *(☎ 033 822 43 53, fax 033 823 20 58; e boenigen@youthhostel.ch; Aareweg 21, am See, Bönigen; bus No 1; dorm beds from Sfr28, singles/doubles Sfr41/81; open mid-Dec–Oct)*, a 20-minute walk around Lake Brienz from Interlaken Ost, has large dorms. What it lacks in elegance it makes up for with fantastic views.

For 50 years, young Americans have flocked to **Balmer's Herberge** *(☎ 033 822 19 61, fax 033 823 32 61; e balmers@tcnet.ch; Hauptstrasse 23–25; dorm beds Sfr24-26, singles/doubles/triples/quads Sfr40/68/90/120)*. It has excellent facilities (games rooms, kitchen, bar and restaurant) and a raucous summer-camp feel.

For a similarly rambunctious but Australasian flavour, head to **Funny Farm** *(☎ 079-652 61 27; e james@funny-farm.ch; dorm beds from Sfr25)*, a converted farmhouse behind the Mattenhof Hotel. This free-and-easy place has basic, colourful rooms, didgeridoo workshops, a swimming pool, bar and party atmosphere.

If you'd prefer some shut-eye, try the **Backpackers Villa** *(☎ 033 826 71 71, fax 033 826 71 72; e backpackers@villa.ch; Alpenstrasse 16; dorm beds Sfr32, doubles Sfr88)*, an ordered hostel with spacious, renovated rooms.

The aptly named **Happy Inn Lodge** *(☎ 033 822 32 25, fax 033 822 32 68; ⓔ info@happy-inn.com; Rosenstrasse 17; dorms Sfr19-30, singles/doubles per person from Sfr30/60)* has a merry bartender/owner serving drinks in the pub below and basic rooms.

Places to Eat

Self-caterers can pick up supplies at **Migros** *(cnr Rugenparkstrasse & General Guisan-Strasse)* and **Coop**, with branches on Bahnhofstrasse, and opposite Interlaken Ost.

Brasserie 17, underneath the Happy Inn Lodge, is a fun local hangout serving up chicken wings, spare ribs and live music on Thursday night.

The ravenous can fill up with tasty thin-crust pizzas and plentiful pasta plates at **Pizzeria Mercato** *(☎ 033 827 87 71; Postgasse 1; pizzas from Sfr14)*. Exotic options include **Spice of India** *(Postgasse 6)*, serving delicious dishes with a kick; or **El Azteca** *(Jungfraustrasse 30)*, with friendly waitresses and passable Mexican food.

Entertainment

Sip on a cocktail and enjoy sweeping mountain views from **Top o'Met** *(18th floor, Höheweg 37)*. Other popular watering holes include English-style **Buddy's Pub** *(Höheweg 33)*; the larger, rowdier **Café-Bar Hüsi** *(Postgasse 3)*; and grungy **Postiv Einfach** *(Centralstrasse)*, with DJs, live music and a black-clad crowd.

Getting There & Away

Trains to Lucerne (Sfr30, two hours) depart hourly from Interlaken Ost. Trains to Brig and Montreux (via Bern or Zweisimmen) depart from Interlaken West or Ost. Main roads head east to Lucerne and west to Bern, but the only way south for vehicles, without a major detour around the mountains, is to take the car-carrying train from Kandersteg, south of Spiez.

JUNGFRAU REGION

This region's most popular peak is the Schilthorn, but you can also enjoy marvellous vistas and hikes from Schynige Platte, Männlichen and Kleine Scheidegg. In winter, the Jungfrau is a magnet for skiers and snowboarders, with 200km of pistes. Ski passes cost Sfr52/95 for one/two days (discounts for seniors and teens).

Grindelwald

Once a simple farming village, Grindelwald is now the Jungfrau's largest ski resort. In the First region are 90km of hiking trails above 1200m, with 48km open year-round. The First is the main skiing area in winter. You can catch the longest cable car in Europe from Grindelwald-Grund to Männlichen, where there are more extraordinary views and hikes (one-way/return Sfr29/46).

Grindelwald Tourism *(☎ 033 854 12 12; ⓔ touristcenter@grindelwald.ch; open Mon-Sat, daily in season)* is in the centre at the Sportzentrum, 200m up from the train station. Ask here for a list of camping grounds and countless holiday apartments and chalets.

Above the town the **SYHA hostel** *(☎ 033 853 10 09, fax 033 853 50 29; ⓔ grindelwald@youthhostel.ch; Terrassenweg; dorm beds from Sfr29.50)*, a hillside wooden chalet, has magnificent views. Avoid the tough climb from the station by taking the Terrassenweg-bound bus to the Gaggi Säge stop. If the hostel's full, try the nearby **Naturfreundehaus** *(☎ 033 853 13 33, fax 033 853 43 33; ⓔ nfhostel@grindelwald.ch; Terrassenweg; dorm beds from Sfr27)*. Both hostels are closed between seasons.

Modern **Mountain Hostel** *(☎ 033 853 39 00; ⓔ mhostel@grindel wald.ch; dorm beds/doubles with breakfast from Sfr34/88)*, near the Mälichen cable-car station is a good base for ski-junkies eager to get to the slopes.

Onkel Tom's Hütte *(☎ 033 853 52 39; pizza from Sfr10)*, on the way out of town, is a cosy California-style barn with cheap tucker and an excellent wine list. Self-caterers can stock up at the **Coop** supermarket opposite the tourist office.

Grindelwald is only 40 minutes by train from Interlaken Ost (Sfr9.40 each way), and is easily reachable by road.

Lauterbrunnen Valley

The Lauterbrunnen Valley branches out from Interlaken with sheer rockfaces and towering mountains on either side, attracting an army of hikers and mountain bikers. The first village reached by car or rail is **Lauterbrunnen**, known mainly for the trickling **Staubbach Falls** and the much more impressive **Trümmelbach Falls** *(admission Sfr10; open Apr-Oct)*, 4km out of town. Find out more from the **tourist office** *(☎ 033 855 19 55; ⓔ info@lauterbrunnen.tourismus.ch)*, on the main street.

Above the village (via funicular) is Grütschalp, where you switch to the train to **Mürren**, a skiing and hiking resort. Mürren's efficient **tourist office** *(☎ 033 856 86 86; ⓔ info@muerren.ch)* is in the sports centre. A pleasant 40-minute walk downhill is tiny **Gimmelwald**, a minute rural village. Gimmelwald and Mürren can also be reached from the valley floor by the Stechelberg cable car.

Gimmelwald and Lauterbrunnen have some of the cheapest accommodation in the region. Another base with plenty of appeal is Wengen, a hiking and skiing centre clinging to the eastern side of the valley. Here, reader-recommended hostel **Hot Chili Peppers** *(☎ 033 855 50 20; ⓔ chilis@wengen.com; dorm beds/doubles Sfr26/99)* features chatty staff and a popular ground-floor bar.

In Lauterbrunnen, you won't get much cheaper than **Matratzenlager Stocki** *(☎ 033 855 17 54; dorm beds Sfr13; closed Nov & Dec)*, a cosy mountain cabin with a homely feel and extremely close quarters. Another excellent option is the newish **Valley Hostel** *(☎/fax 033 855 20 08; ⓔ valleyhostel@bluewin.ch; dorm beds/doubles from Sfr22/52)*, with comfy rooms. Cheap eats are harder to track down. Stock up in the **Coop** near the tourist office, or try one of the hotel restaurants.

In Gimmelwald, the **Mountain Hostel** *(☎ 033 855 17 04, fax 033 855 26 88; ⓔ mountainhostel@tcnet.ch; dorm beds Sfr18)*, close to the cable-car station, has jaw-dropping views, Internet access and a pool table. If you don't mind the occasional roll in the hay, **Esther's Guesthouse** *(☎ 033 855 54 88; ⓔ evallmen@bluewin.ch)* offers beds of straw in a big, old barn (Sfr20, including a generous breakfast). **Restaurant-Pension Gimmelwald** *(☎/fax 033 855 17 30; ⓔ pension gimmelwald@tcnet.ch; meals from Sfr14)* has hearty home cooking.

Northern Switzerland

This region is important for industry and commerce, yet by no means lacks tourist attractions. Take time to explore the tiny rural towns set among green rolling hills, and Lake Constance (Bodensee) and the Rhine on the German border.

BASEL (BÂLE)

pop 163,800

Basel is an affluent city squeezed into the top left corner of the country. Although a major hub of commerce and industry, it has an idyllic Old Town and many enticing museums. The tomb of famous Renaissance humanist Erasmus rests in the cathedral. The pedestrian-only Old Town is on the river's southern bank in Grossbasel (Greater Basel).

Basel Tourismus *(☎ 061 268 68 68; ⓔ office@baseltourismus.ch; Schifflände 5; open Mon-Sat)* is by the Mittlere Brücke. There's also a hole-in-the-wall tourist office in the main SBB train station, which also has bike rental and money exchange. The **main post office** *(Freie Strasse; open 7.30am-6.30pm Mon-Wed & Fri, 7.30am-10pm Thur, 8am-noon Sat)* is in the city centre, and there's another by the train station. You can check your emails in quiet, modern comfort (Sfr5/8 for 30/60 minutes) at the **Tiscali Internet Center** *(☎ 0844 89 19 91; ⓔ info@tiscalinet.ch; Steinentorstrasse 11; open 9am-10pm Mon-Thur, 9am-8pm Fri, 9am-5pm Sat)*.

Things to See & Do

Walk through the Old Town, with its cobbled streets, colourful fountains, and Middle Age churches and stately buildings. The 12th-century **Münster** (cathedral) is a highlight. Theaterplatz sports a curious **fountain** designed by Swiss sculptor Jean Tinguely.

The **Kunstmuseum** *(Art Museum; ☎ 061 206 62 62; ⓦ www.kunstmuseumbasel.ch; St Albangraben 16; adult/student/child Sfr10/8/free, first Sun of month free; open 10am-5pm Tues-Sun)* features religious and local art, a cubism collection including a palette of Picassos, and a copper etchings gallery. Admission also grants entry to the **Museum für Gegenwartskunst** *(☎ 061 272 81 83; St Alban-Rheinweg 60; same opening hours as Kunstmuseum)*, exhibiting works by Andy Warhol and Joseph Beuys.

If you're lucky enough to be in town on the Monday after Ash Wednesday you'll be treated to Fasnacht, a three-day spectacle of parades, masks, music and costumes, all starting at 4am.

Places to Stay

Hotels are often full, so book ahead. Don't forget to ask your accommodation for the Mobility Card, which gives free local transport.

The **SYHA hostel** *(☎ 061 272 05 72, fax 061 272 08 33; St Alban Kirchrain 10; dorm beds Sfr30-32, singles/doubles Sfr80/100)*, 10 minutes from the centre, is in St Alban, a quiet, leafy old-money part of town. It has small spick-and-span rooms and Internet access (Sfr5 for 20 minutes).

Hotel Stadthof *(☎ 061 261 87 11, fax 061 261 25 84; e info@stadthof.ch; Gerbergasse 84; singles/doubles from Sfr70/120)* offers rudimentary rooms with shared hall shower. Tucked in the corner of buzzing Barfüsserplatz, its bar and restaurant do a roaring trade.

Places to Eat

For a quick, cheap bite on the run, the daily market on Marktplatz has tasty bratwurst (Sfr5) and delicious breads (Sfr3 to Sfr7). Alternatively, there's the pedestrian-only Steinenvorstadt, with countless fast-food outlets, cafés and restaurants.

Cafe Zum Roten Engel *(☎ 061 261 20 08; Andreasplatz 15; meals Sfr9-14)*, hidden away in a quiet leafy courtyard, is a busy student hangout serving delicious vegie snacks and gigantic mugs of coffee.

For Basel specialities and a traditional atmosphere, try **Weinstube Gifthüttli** *(☎ 061 261 16 56; Schneidergasse 11; mains Sfr25-38)*, where prices on the daily lunch menu are Sfr17 to Sfr20.

The local **Migros** *(Sternengasse 17; open 7.30am-6.30pm Mon-Wed & Fri, 7.30am-10pm Thur, 7.30am-5pm Sat)* is handy for self-caterers.

Entertainment

There's a bar/café/restaurant to suit every taste in Steinenvorstadt. **Paddy Reilly's Irish Pub** *(☎ 061 281 33 36; Steinentorstrasse 45; bar meals Sfr5-12.50)* entices ex-pats with Brit beers and big-screen TV. For everything from house to pop, soul and R&B, there's **Atlantis** *(☎ 061 228 96 96; w www.atlan-tis.ch; Klosterberg 13)*. In Kleinbasel, the grungier **Hirscheneck** *(☎ 061 692 73 33; w www.hirscheneck.ch; Lindenberg 23; admission Sfr8-15)* is a melting pot of nonconservatives, with DJs and thrashy live music on weekends and occasional weekdays. For smoother grooves, try the **Bird's Eye Jazz Club** *(☎ 061 263 33 41; w www.birdseye.ch; Kohlenberg 20; admission from Sfr10; open Tues-Sun)*.

Getting There & Around

Basel is a major European rail hub. Trains to France leave from the SNCF section of SBB station; there are seven daily to Paris (Sfr69, five hours). Germany-bound trains stop at Badischer Bahnhof (BBF) on the northern bank; fast EC services stop at SBB, too.

Main destinations are Amsterdam (Sfr180, eight hours), Frankfurt (Sfr80, three hours) and Hamburg (Sfr198, 6½ hours). Services within Switzerland leave from SBB: there are two fast trains hourly to both Geneva (Sfr71, three hours; via Bern or Biel/Bienne) and Zürich (Sfr30, 70 minutes).

City buses and trams run every six to 10 minutes (Sfr1.80 for four or fewer stops, Sfr2.80 for central zone, and Sfr8 for day pass). By the SBB station is a hut offering free bike loans in summer.

SCHAFFHAUSEN

pop 32,900

Schaffhausen is a quaint medieval town on the northern bank of the Rhine surrounded by German territory. Beautiful oriel windows, painted facades and ornamental fountains crowd the streets of the Old Town. For the best views, climb to the 16th-century hill-top **Munot fortress**. **Rhine Falls** is a 40-minute stroll westward along the river, or take bus No 1 to Neuhausen. The waterfall is considered the largest in Europe, with an extraordinary amount of water thundering over it. The 45km of the Rhine from Schaffhausen to Constance is one of the river's most stunning stretches, passing by meadows, castles and ancient villages, including **Stein am Rhein**, 20km to the east.

Hourly trains run to Zürich (Sfr17.20, 50 minutes). Constance and Basel can be reached by cheaper German trains. **Untersee Und Rhein** *(☎ 052 634 08 88; e info@urh.ch)* runs steamers to/from Constance (Sfr38; four hours, four daily May to October).

ST GALLEN

pop 70,300

In AD 612, an Irish monk called Gallus fell into a briar. He interpreted it as a sign from God and decided to build a hermitage. From this inauspicious beginning St Gallen evolved and developed into an important medieval cultural centre.

The **main post office** is located opposite the train station. Just two minutes away is **St**

Gallen-Bodensee Tourismus *(☎ 071 227 37 37; ⓔ info@stgallen-bodensee.ch; Bahnhofplatz 1a; open Mon-Sat).*

Many buildings in St Gallen's Old Town have distinctive oriel windows, with the best to be found on Gallusplatz, Spisergasse and Kugelgasse. Be sure not to miss the twin-tower **Kathedrale**, with an ostentatious interior. Bookworms will treasure the nearby **Stiftsbibliothek** *(Abbey Library; ☎ 071 227 34 16; adult/student Sfr7/5)*, one of the oldest libraries of the Western world.

The modern **SYHA hostel** *(☎ 071 245 47 77, fax 071 245 49 83; Jüchstrasse 25; dorm beds Sfr26, singles/doubles Sfr46.50/72; open Mar–mid-Dec)* is a signposted 15-minute walk east of the Old Town. Fast-food stalls proliferate around the Old Town, selling St Gallen sausage and bread for around Sfr6.

St Gallen is a short train ride from Lake Constance (Bodensee), upon which boats sail to Bregenz in Austria, and to Constance and Lindau in Germany (not in winter). There are also regular trains to Constance and Zürich.

SWITZERLAND

Turkey

Turkey is Asia's foothold in Europe, bridging the vast physical and cultural gap to the Middle East. For centuries Ottoman sultans ruled a realm from the Balkans to Iran, and Turkish influence remains in all the countries once controlled by İstanbul. Turks have since looked to Europe and North America for political inspiration, establishing a democracy and joining NATO – yet their culture is proudly steeped in Islam, maintaining an exotic allure for visitors from the West.

Boasting over 4000km of magnificent Mediterranean coastline, Turkey has long attracted pleasure seekers from around the world – giving rise to an efficient tourism industry and introducing rock music and topless beaches to the nation. However, travellers who seek out less-popular destinations will immediately discover that Turkey is far more than a Muslim extension of Europe. With famously hospitable people, hundreds of spectacular historic ruins, varied countryside and excellent food, Turkey is sure to captivate you.

Turkey: the Basics

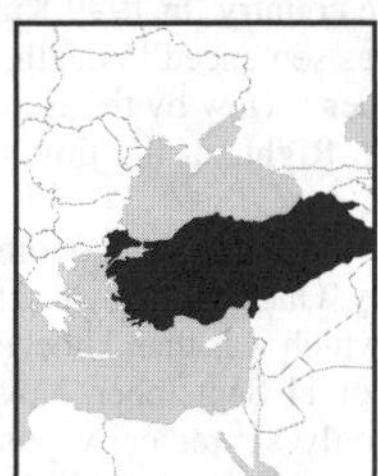

Local name Türkiye

Capital Ankara

Population 68 million

Language Turkish

Currency Turkish lira (TL)

Avoid at all costs Half-built coastal resorts

Make instant friends by saying *Türkiye öteki takımdan çok daha iyi!* (Turkey is much better than the other soccer team!)

Facts about Turkey

HISTORY

By 7000 BC, a Neolithic city, one of the oldest ever recorded, was already established at Çatal Höyük, near Konya. The greatest early Anatolian civilisation was the Hittites, a force to be reckoned with from 2000 to 1200 BC. After the collapse of the Hittite empire, parts of the country were not reunited until the Graeco-Roman period. Later, the area was Christianised by Paul of Tarsus.

In AD 330 the Roman emperor Constantine founded an imperial city at Byzantium. Renamed Constantinople, it became the capital of the Eastern Roman Empire and was the centre of the Byzantine Empire for 1000 years, enduring through the Middle Ages. However, invasion by the Seljuk Turks drastically reduced the empire's territory. The Byzantines endeavoured to protect Constantinople and reclaim Anatolia, but the Fourth Crusade (1202–04) proved disastrous for them when a Crusader force took and plundered Constantinople. The Byzantines eventually regained the ravaged city in 1261.

In 1453 Constantinople fell to Ottoman Turk Sultan Mehmet II (the Conqueror) and became known as İstanbul. A century later, under Süleyman the Magnificent, the Ottoman Empire reached the peak of its power, spreading deep into Europe, Asia and North Africa.

By the 19th century, European nationalism led to the independence of Greece, Serbia, Romania and Bulgaria, and in 1913 the Ottomans lost Albania and Macedonia. The Turks emerged from WWI stripped of their last non-Turkish provinces – Syria, Palestine, Mesopotamia (Iraq) and Arabia. Most of Anatolia itself was parcelled out to the victorious Europeans, leaving the Turks virtually nothing.

At this low point, Mustafa Kemal, the father of modern Turkey, took over. Atatürk, as he was later called, repelled the Anzacs at Gallipoli and deposed the last Ottoman ruler. Under him, the Turks won their War of Independence by pushing the invading Greeks into the sea at Smyrna (İzmir).

After renegotiation of the WWI treaties a new Turkish republic, reduced to Anatolia and part of Thrace, was born. Atatürk embarked on a rapid modernisation programme, establishing a secular democracy, introducing Latin script and European dress, and adopting (in theory) equal rights for women.

Since Atatürk's death, Turkey has experienced three military coups and considerable political turbulence. During the 1980s and '90s it was wracked by the conflict with the

PKK (Kurdistan Workers Party), which wanted the creation of a Kurdish state in Turkey's southeast corner. This conflict led to an estimated 35,000 deaths and huge population shifts inside the country. In 1999 Kurdish leader Öcalan was sentenced to death, a sentence which is under review by the European Court of Human Rights at the time of writing.

In February 2001 the Turkish economy collapsed spectacularly. One of the few bright sectors was tourism, which was then knocked for six by the events of 11 September. However, Turkey is not only strategically positioned but also the only Muslim member of NATO, so by late 2001 the IMF was pumping in funds to refloat the economy. It remains to be seen how quickly tourism can recover.

GEOGRAPHY

The Dardanelles, Sea of Marmara and Bosphorus strait divide Turkey between Asia and Europe, but Eastern Thrace (European Turkey) makes up only 3% of the 788,695 sq km land area. The remaining 97% is Anatolia, a vast plateau rising eastward towards the Caucasus Mountains. Large parts of Turkey's 6000km-long coastline are given over to tourism.

CLIMATE

The Aegean and Mediterranean coasts have mild, rainy winters and hot, dry summers. In İstanbul, summer temperatures average around 28°C to 30°C; the winters are chilly but usually above freezing. The Anatolian plateau can be boiling hot in summer and freezing in

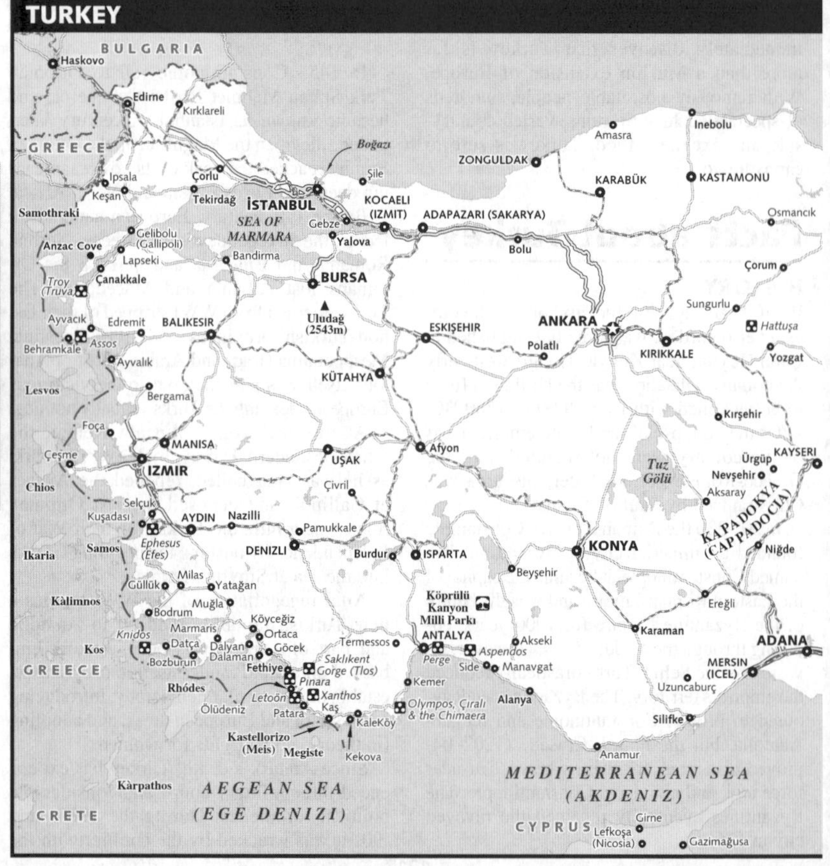

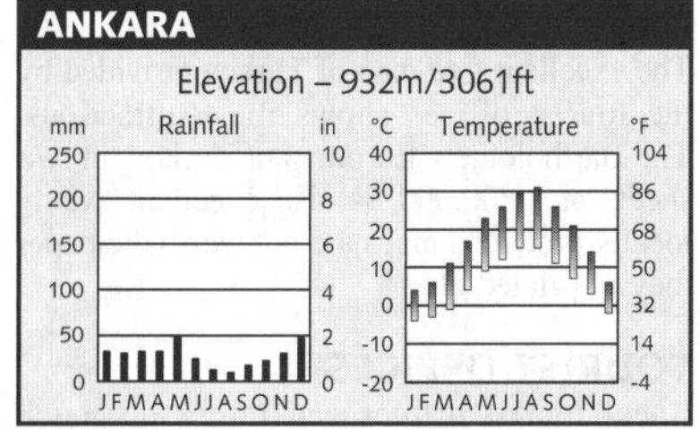

winter. The Black Sea coast is mild and humid in summer, chilly and wet in winter.

Mountainous eastern Turkey is icy cold and snowy in winter, and only pleasantly warm during high summer. The southeastern parts are dry and mild in winter and baking hot during summer.

GOVERNMENT & POLITICS

In theory Turkey is a multiparty democracy, although it has proved to be more of a semi-democracy, with the military wielding considerable power behind the scenes. In 2002 the coalition government was struggling in the face of the EU's demands for greater freedom of speech and abolition of the death penalty.

POPULATION & PEOPLE

Turkey's roughly 68 million people are predominantly Turks, with a large Kurdish minority (perhaps 12 million) and much smaller groups of Laz, Hemsin, Arabs, Jews, Greeks and Armenians. Arab influence is strongest in the Hatay area abutting Syria. Southeastern Turkey is solidly Kurdish.

TURKEY

SOCIETY & CONDUCT

Republican Turkey has largely adopted a Westernised lifestyle, at least on the surface. In smaller towns and villages, however, you may find people more conservative. A small but growing group of 'born again' Muslims may make travellers uncomfortable about alcohol, skimpy clothing and anything pertaining to religion.

Women should keep their legs, upper arms and neckline covered except on the beach. When going into a mosque, women should cover their heads and shoulders, while men and women should cover their legs and remove their shoes.

LANGUAGE

Turkish is the official language and almost everyone understands it. In big cities and tourist areas, many locals will speak passable English, French, German or Japanese. See the Language chapter at the back of this book for pronunciation guidelines and useful words and phrases.

Facts for the Visitor

HIGHLIGHTS

Check out İstanbul's must-see sights: Topkapı Palace, Aya Sofya (Hagia Sofia), the Blue Mosque, the Turkish and Islamic Arts Museum, the Basilica Cistern and the Chora Church.

Heading down the Aegean from İstanbul, don't miss Çanakkale for the Gallipoli battlefields and the ruins of Troy, or Selçuk for excursions to the ruins at Ephesus, Priene, Miletus and Didyma. Along the Mediterranean coast, particularly inviting small resorts include Dalyan, Kaş and Olympos, which are perfect bases for exploring archaeological sites.

Turkey's best beaches are at Pamucak (near Ephesus), Ölüdeniz, Bodrum, Patara, Antalya, Side and Alanya. Inland, Turkey's premier attraction is the spectacular landscape of Cappadocia, where the village of Göreme makes a popular base.

PLANNING

When to Go

In general, spring (April to May) and autumn (September to October) have the most pleasant weather. The heat and crowds of July and August can be pretty intense, especially in İstanbul.

Maps

The excellent free map of Turkey provided by the tourist offices shows most attractions. The Bartholomew Euromap of Turkey, in two sheets at 1:800,000, is also excellent. Many locally produced maps are not worth the paper they're printed on.

TOURIST OFFICES

Local tourist offices can rarely do much more than hand out glossy brochures and sketch maps. Turkey has tourist offices in the following countries:

Australia (☎ 02-9223 3055; ⓔ turkish@ozemail.com.au) Room 17, Level 3, 428 George St, Sydney NSW 2000
Canada (☎ 613-230 8654) Suite 801, Constitution Square, 360 Albert St, Ottawa, Ontario K1R 7X7
UK (☎ 020-7629 7771; ⓔ TTO@cityscape.co.uk) 1st floor, 170–173 Piccadilly, London W1V 9DD
USA (☎ 212-687 2194; ⓔ tourny@idt.net) 821 UN Plaza, New York, NY 10017

VISAS & DOCUMENTS

Nationals of the following countries don't need a visa to visit Turkey for up to three months: Belgium, Denmark, Finland, France, Germany, Japan, The Netherlands, New Zealand, Norway, Sweden and Switzerland. Although nationals of Australia, Austria, Canada, Greece, Ireland, Israel, Italy, Portugal, Spain, the UK and the USA need a visa, this is just a sticker you buy on arrival; join the queue before immigration. British citizens pay UK£10, Australians US$20 and Canadians and Americans a hefty US$45. You *must* pay cash in hard currency. The standard visa is valid for three months and usually allows for multiple entry into the country.

EMBASSIES & CONSULATES

Turkish Embassies Abroad

Turkey has diplomatic representation in the following countries:

Australia (☎ 02-6295 0227) 60 Mugga Way, Red Hill ACT 2603
Canada (☎ 613-789 4044) 197 Wurtemburg St, Ottawa, Ontario KIN 8L9
France (☎ 01 53 92 71) 16 Ave de Lamballe, 75016 Paris
Germany (☎ 49-228 95 38 30) Utestr 47, 53179 Bonn 2
Ireland (☎ 1-668 5240) 11 Clyde Rd, Ballsbridge, Dublin 4

TURKEY

Netherlands (☎ 70-360 4912) Jan Evenstraat 2514 BS, The Hague
New Zealand (☎ 4-472 1290) 15–17 Murphy St, Level 8, Wellington
UK (☎ 020-7393 0202) 43 Belgrave Square, London SW1X 8PA
USA (☎ 202-659 8200) 1714 Massachusetts Ave, NW Washington, DC 20036

Foreign Consulates in Turkey

Most embassies are in Ankara. Countries with consulates in İstanbul (code ☎ 0212) include:

Australia (☎ 257 7050) Tepecik Yolu 58, Etiler, İstanbul
France (☎ 293 2460) İstiklal Caddesi 8, Taksim, İstanbul
Germany (☎ 334 6100) İnönü Caddesi 16–18, Taksim, İstanbul
Greece (☎ 245 0596) Ağahamam Turnacıbaşı Sokak 32, Beyoğlu, İstanbul
Ireland (☎ 246 6025) Cumhuriyet Caddesi 26/A, Harbiye, İstanbul
Netherlands (☎ 251 5030) İstiklal Caddesi 393, Beyoğlu, İstanbul
New Zealand (☎ 327 2211) Yeşilgimen Sokak 75, Ihlamur, Beşiktaş, İstanbul
UK (☎ 293 7546) Meşrutiyet Caddesi 34, Beyoğlu, İstanbul
USA (☎ 229 0075) Şehit Halil İbrahim Caddesi 23, İstiniye, İstanbul

CUSTOMS

Two hundred cigarettes, 50 cigars or 200g of tobacco, 1L of liquor and 4L of wine can be imported duty-free. Duty-free items can be bought both on arrival and departure from Turkey's international airports. It's strictly illegal to buy, sell or export antiquities.

MONEY

The Turkish lira (TL) comes in coins of 25,000, 50,000, 100,000 and 250,000 lira, and notes (bills) of 100,000, 250,000, 500,000, one million, five million, 10 million and 20 million lira. Prices in this chapter are quoted in more stable, and less unwieldy, US dollars.

Exchanging Money

During 2001 the Turkish lira devalued steadily. Check exchange rates shortly before your visit and be prepared for fluctuations.

country	unit		Turkish lira
Australia	A$1	=	TL908,146
Canada	C$1	=	TL1,050,843
Eurozone	€1	=	TL1,648,156
Japan	¥100	=	TL13,598
New Zealand	NZ$1	=	TL792,832
UK	UK£1	=	TL2,621,733
USA	US$1	=	TL1,670,000

It's easy to change major currencies in most exchange offices, post offices (PTTs), shops and hotels. Cashing travellers cheques is harder (try post offices in tourist areas), and the exchange rate is usually worse. Places that don't charge a commission usually offer a poor exchange rate.

Major foreign currencies are accepted in shops, hotels and restaurants in the main tourist areas. Visa and MasterCard/Access are widely accepted. Widespread ATMs dispense cash for cards on the Visa, MasterCard, Cirrus, Maestro and Eurocard networks.

Costs

Turkey is still relatively cheap, especially away from İstanbul and the coast. You can travel on as little as US$15 to US$20 per person per day if you use buses or trains, stay in pensions and eat only one restaurant meal a day. By spending between US$20 and US$35 per day you can upgrade to one- and two-star hotels, eat most meals in restaurants and manage some of the heftier monument admission fees.

Tipping & Bargaining

Leave waiters and bath attendants around 10% of the bill and a hotel porter US$0.50 to US$1. You might round up your taxi fare but there's no need to tip *dolmuş* (minibus) drivers. It's wise to bargain for souvenirs, even if prices are 'fixed'.

Taxes & Refunds

Value-added tax (VAT) is included in the price of most items and services: look for signs saying *KDV dahil* (VAT included). If you buy an expensive item, ask the shopkeeper for a *KDV iade özel fatura* (special VAT-refund receipt). Get it stamped as you clear customs, then try and get a refund at a bank in the airport departure lounge.

POST & COMMUNICATIONS

The Turkish postal service is known as the PTT. Turkish *postanes* (post offices) are indicated by black-on-yellow 'PTT' signs. If you have mail addressed to you care of poste restante in a major city, the address should include 'Merkez Postane' (central post office), or the name of the local post office where you wish to retrieve it.

Phoning home from Turkey is surprisingly expensive, mainly because of taxes. The cheapest rates are at night and on Sunday. Wherever possible, try to make collect (reverse charge) calls. To call from one Turkish town to the next, dial the area code including the initial '0'. Note that İstanbul has two codes: 0212 for the European side and 0216 for the Asian side. When calling from outside Turkey, dial the international access code□ then the country code ☎ 90, followed by the area code (minus the zero) and the seven-digit subscriber number.

These days almost all Türk Telekom's public telephones require telephone cards, which can be bought at telephone centres or at some shops. If you're only going to make one call, it's easier to look for a booth with a sign saying 'köntörlü telefon', where the cost of your call will be metered.

Turkish post offices offer Internet access, but you're better off using one of the ubiquitous Internet cafés. Many pensions will also let you use their Internet for a small fee.

DIGITAL RESOURCES

The **Turkey Home Page** (W *www.turkey.org/*) has news, arts and cultural features, upcoming events and links to dozens of Turkey-related websites. The *Turkish Daily News* site, at W www.turkishdailynews.com, is also useful. For public transport information (but no fare listings), try W www.neredennereye.com.

BOOKS

Lonely Planet's *Turkey* offers details about the entire country. LP also publishes a *Turkish phrasebook* and a *World Food Turkey* guide. Jeremy Seal's *A Fez of the Heart* and Tim Kelsey's *Dervish* are very readable accounts of recent travels in Turkey.

WOMEN TRAVELLERS

Turkish society is still basically sexually segregated, especially once you get away from the big cities and resorts. Foreign women may still find themselves being hassled. Mostly it's just silliness, but serious assaults do occasionally occur. Travelling with companions usually improves matters.

Turkish women ignore men who speak to them in the street. Wearing a headscarf, a skirt that falls below the knees, a wedding ring and sunglasses makes you less conspicuous. Away from beach resorts you should certainly avoid skimpy tops and brief shorts.

GAY & LESBIAN TRAVELLERS

Overt homosexuality is not socially acceptable except in a few small pockets of İstanbul and some resorts. Laws prohibiting 'lewd behaviour' can be turned against homosexuals, so be discreet. Some *hammams* (Turkish baths) are known to be gay meeting places.

For more information, contact Turkey's own gay and lesbian support group, **Lambda İstanbul** (e *lambda@lambdaistanbul.org*).

DANGERS & ANNOYANCES

Although Turkey is one of the safest countries in the region, the number of ne'er-do-wells seems to be increasing. Wear a moneybelt under your clothing and be wary of pickpockets in buses, markets and other crowded places. Keep an eye out for anyone suspicious lurking near ATM machines.

In İstanbul, single men are sometimes lured to a bar (often near İstiklal Caddesi) by new Turkish 'friends', then made to pay an outrageous bill. Drugging is also becoming a serious problem. Be a tad wary who you befriend, especially when you're new to the country.

BUSINESS HOURS

Most banks, museums and offices are open 8.30am to noon and 1.30pm to 5pm Monday to Friday. In tourist areas food and souvenir shops are often open virtually around the clock.

PUBLIC HOLIDAYS & SPECIAL EVENTS

Public holidays in Turkey include New Year's Day (1 January), Children's Day (23 April), Youth & Sports Day (19 May), Victory Day (30 August), Republic Day (29 October) and Atatürk's Death (10 November).

Emergencies

In case of emergency please call the following nationwide numbers: ambulance ☎ 112, doctor (after hours) ☎ 141, fire ☎ 110, Jandarma (Gendarmerie) ☎ 156 and police ☎ 155. You're likely to be connected to only Turkish-speaking operators if you ring any of these numbers, so your best bet is to find an English-speaking local, such as hotel staff, to act as an intermediary.

Turkey also celebrates all major Islamic festivals and holidays, of which the most important are Şeker Bayramı, which comes at the end of the month-long Ramazan, and, two months later, Kurban Bayramı.

On Anzac Day (25 April) huge crowds descend on Çanakkale to attend the dawn services in memory of the failed Anzac landings of WWI. In June crowds assemble to watch oil-covered men wrestling in a field at Kırkpınar near Edirne. The International İstanbul Music Festival in late June/early July takes place in a variety of atmospheric venues around town. Then from 10 to 17 December dervishes whirl at the Mevlâna Festival in Konya.

ACTIVITIES

Popular activities include hiking and trekking in national parks. With the opening of the 500km Lycian Way from Fethiye to Antalya, Turkey also has its first waymarked national trail.

All sorts of water sports, including diving, water-skiing, rafting and kayaking, are available in the Aegean and Mediterranean resorts. Skiing is becoming more popular, with the best facilities at Uludağ, near Bursa, and on Mt Erciyes, near Kayseri. Those of a lazier disposition may want to take a *gûlet* (yacht) trip along the coast and stop off along the way to swim in the bays.

The laziest 'activity' of all consists of paying a visit to a *hammam*, where you can get yourself scrubbed and massaged for a fraction of what it would cost in most Western countries. Sexes are still segregated inland, but along the coast, mixed bathing has become the norm.

ACCOMMODATION

Camping facilities are dotted around Turkey, although not perhaps as frequently as you might hope. Some hotels and pensions will also let you camp on their grounds and use their facilities for a small fee (US$2 to US$4). A few resorts boast well-equipped European-style sites.

Tourist areas usually boast lots of small family-run pensions, some of them offering self-catering facilities, most offering services such as tours and book exchanges. Given that pensions are so inexpensive, Turkey has no real hostel network.

There are plenty of cheap hotels, although the very cheapest will be too basic for many tastes and not really suitable for lone women. The price of most hotels is fixed by local authorities and should be on display in the reception; often you'll be offered a cheaper price (it should *never* be more). One- and two-star hotels (US$15 to US$40 for a double) offer reasonable comfort and private bathrooms at excellent prices.

FOOD & DRINKS

Turkish cuisine is one of the world's greatest. No-one need fear going hungry here. The *kebap* (kebab) is, of course, the mainstay of restaurant meals, and you'll find *lokantas* (basic restaurants) selling a wide range of kebaps everywhere you go. Try the ubiquitous *durum döner kebap* – sliced lamb rolled up in *pide* bread. The calorie-packed *İskender kebap* consists of lamb slices and yogurt that's drizzled with tomato puree and melted butter.

For a quick, cheap fill, grab a freshly cooked *pide* (Turkish pizza) topped with cheese or meat. For vegetarians, a meal of *mezes* (hors d'oeuvres) can be an excellent way to ensure a varied diet. Most restaurants will be able to rustle up at least *beyaz peynir* (white sheep's milk cheese), *börek* (flaky pastry stuffed with white cheese and parsley), *kuru fasulye* (dried beans) and *patlıcan tava* (fried aubergine).

The Turkish liquor of choice is *rakı*, a fiery aniseed drink; cut it by half with water. Turkish wine is worth the occasional splurge. Not a day will pass without your being offered a glass of *çay* (tea). Turkish tea is grown on the eastern Black Sea coast and served in tiny tulip-shaped glasses with copious quantities of sugar. If it's too strong for you, ask for the milder but wholly chemical *elma çay* (apple tea). If offered a tiny cup of traditional Turkish *kahve* (coffee), order it *sade* (no sugar), *orta* (medium-sweet) or *çok şekerli* (very sweet).

For more information on Turkish cuisine, look for Lonely Planet's *World Food Turkey* guide.

ENTERTAINMENT

İstanbul, Ankara and İzmir have opera, symphony, ballet and theatre, and most Turkish towns have at least one cinema, often showing films in their original language. In summer, resorts such as Bodrum throb to the sound of innumerable clubs and discos.

Getting There & Away

You can get in and out of Turkey by air, sea, train and bus, across the borders of eight countries.

AIR

The cheapest fares are almost always to İstanbul. Turkish Airlines and European carriers fly to İstanbul from all the European capitals. It's usually advisable to buy an excursion ticket (from London starting at US$300) even if you don't plan to use the return portion. If you're planning a two- or three-week stay, it's also worth inquiring about cheaper charter flights.

Turkish Airlines offers flights to İstanbul from New York for about US$625/649 for a single/return. From Los Angeles fares start at US$757/740 single/return.

The cheapest flights to İstanbul from Sydney or Melbourne are on Egyptair via Singapore and Cairo; single/return flights start at A$985/1695. Japanese Airlines, Malaysian Airlines and Singapore Airlines also offer fairly competitive fares. Fares to İstanbul from Auckland in New Zealand start from NZ$1440/2400 single/return on Air New Zealand.

Turkish Airlines offers daily nonstop flights to İstanbul from Athens and Tel Aviv, as well as to Bangkok, Karachi, Singapore, Tokyo and many Middle Eastern cities.

LAND

No direct trains run between Western Europe and Turkey. Instead, one train a day heads from İstanbul to Bucharest (17 hours) and then onto Budapest (31 hours), with connections to elsewhere in Europe. There have been reports of long delays and hassle, especially of women, at the Bulgarian border.

Getting to Turkey overland is usually cheaper and faster by bus. Several Turkish lines, including Ulusoy, Varan and Bosfor, offer reliable, comfortable services between İstanbul and major European cities such as Frankfurt, Munich and Vienna for around US$70 one way. These services travel via Greece and the ferry to Italy, thereby avoiding any hassle at the Bulgarian border.

If you're planning to travel from mainland Greece, note that the daily Thessaloniki to İstanbul passenger train takes 16 to 18 hours, with a change of train (and a delay) at the border. The bus covers the distance in greater comfort in about 10 hours.

SEA

Turkish Maritime Lines *(TML; ☎ 464 8864)* runs car ferries from İzmir to Venice weekly from May to mid-October. Fares start at US$160 one way with reclining seat.

Private ferries link Turkey's Aegean coast and the Greek Islands, which are in turn connected by air or boat to Athens. Services are usually daily in summer, several times a week in spring and autumn and perhaps once a week in winter. In summer expect daily boats connecting Lesvos–Ayvalık, Chios–Çeşme, Samos–Kuşadası, Kos–Bodrum, Rhodes–Marmaris, Rhodes–Bodrum, Rhodes–Fethiye and Kastellorizo–Kaş. The cheapest and most-frequent ferries are Samos–Kuşadası and Rhodes–Marmaris; the most expensive and most hassle is the Lesbos–Ayvalık ferry.

There are daily services to Turkish Cyprus from Taşucu (near Silifke), and less-frequent services from Alanya.

Getting Around

BUS

Turkish buses go just about everywhere; they do so cheaply, comfortably and free of smoke. Kamil Koç, Metro, Ulusoy and Varan are the premium companies, offering greater speed and comfort for slightly higher fares. They have a better safety record than most companies – an important consideration in a country where traffic accidents claim hundreds of lives every year.

A town's *otogar* (bus terminal) is often on the outskirts, but the bigger bus companies usually offer *servis* (free minibuses) to the centre. Most *otogars* have an *emanet* (left-luggage room) with a small charge. Don't leave valuables in unlocked luggage.

Local routes are usually operated by midibuses or *dolmuşes*, minibuses that sometimes run to a timetable but more often set off when they're full.

Fez Bus *(☎ 516 9024; W www.feztravel.com; Aybıyık Caddesi, Sultanahmet, İstanbul)* is a hop-on, hop-off bus service linking the main resorts of the Aegean and the Mediterranean with İstanbul and Cappadocia. Fez Bus also offers the Turkish Delight

TURKEY

pass (İstanbul–Gallipoli–Bergama–Selçuk–Köceğiz–Fethiye–Olympos–Cappadocia–İstanbul), which costs from US$174.

TRAIN

Turkish State Railways (TCDD) has a hard time competing with the long-distance buses for speed and comfort, although trains are usually a bit cheaper than buses. Only special express trains, such as the *Fatih* and *Başkent*, are faster than the bus.

Ekspres and *mototren* services often have only one class. These trains are a little slower than buses, but you can get up and move around. On *yolcu* and *posta* trains you could grow old and die before ever reaching your destination.

Sleeping-car trains linking İstanbul, İzmir and Ankara are good value; the cheaper *örtülü kuşetli* carriages have four simple beds per compartment.

CAR & MOTORCYCLE

Türkiye Turing ve Otomobil Kurumu *(TTOK, Turkish Touring & Automobile Association; ☎ 0212-282 8140; Oto Sanayı Sitesi Yanı, Seyrantepe, 4 Levent, İstanbul)* can help with questions and problems. An International Driving Permit may be handy. In the major cities plan to park your car and use public transport.

All the main car-rental companies are represented in İstanbul, Ankara and İzmir, but car hire in Turkey is pricey (around US$35 a day) and driving is hazardous.

BICYCLE

The countryside is varied and beautiful, and road surfaces acceptable if a bit rough. Turkish drivers regard cyclists as a curiosity and/or a nuisance.

HITCHING

Hitching is not common in Turkey. Women should never hitchhike, especially alone.

BOAT

Turkish Maritime Lines *(TML; ☎ 0212-249 9222; information ☎ 244 0207; Rıhtım Caddesi, Karaköy, İstanbul)* operates a year-round car-ferry service between İstanbul and İzmir, departing İstanbul every Friday afternoon and departing İzmir every Sunday afternoon. Fares start at US$17 for a reclining seat; a car costs US$28.

İstanbul

☎ 0212 (European side)
☎ 0216 (Asian side) • pop 12 million

With 3000 years of colourful history, İstanbul, formerly Constantinople, has plenty to show for itself. This city can take you back through the Crusades to the Romans and beyond, yet it's more than a step back in time. An effervescent cultural scene manifests itself in fascinating theatres and galleries, while after dark a plethora of bars and fine restaurants will sate the most energetic of souls. As the gateway to the East, İstanbul combines the magic of the Orient with the blistering pace of the West.

HISTORY

Late in the 2nd century AD, the Roman Empire conquered the small city-state of Byzantium, which was renamed Constantinople in AD 330 after Emperor Constantine moved his capital there. The city walls kept out barbarians for centuries while the western part of the Roman Empire collapsed. When Constantinople fell for the first time, it was to the misguided Fourth Crusade in 1204. Bent on pillage, the Crusaders ravaged Constantinople's churches, shipping out the art and melting down the silver and gold. By the time the Byzantines regained the city in 1261 it was a mere shadow of its former glory.

The Ottoman Turks first attacked in 1314. Finally, in 1453, after a long and bitter siege, the walls were breached just north of Topkapı Gate on the western side of the city. Mehmet II, the Conqueror, marched to Aya Sofya (Hagia Sofia) and converted the church into a mosque.

As capital of the Ottoman Empire the city experienced a new golden age. During the glittering reign of Süleyman the Magnificent (1520–66), the city was graced with many beautiful new buildings. Later, even during the empire's long decline, the capital retained much of its charm. Occupied by Allied forces after WWI, it came to be thought of as the decadent capital of the sultans; meanwhile Atatürk's armies were shaping a new republican state.

When the Turkish Republic was proclaimed in 1923, Ankara became the new capital. Nevertheless, İstanbul remains the centre for business, finance, journalism and the arts.

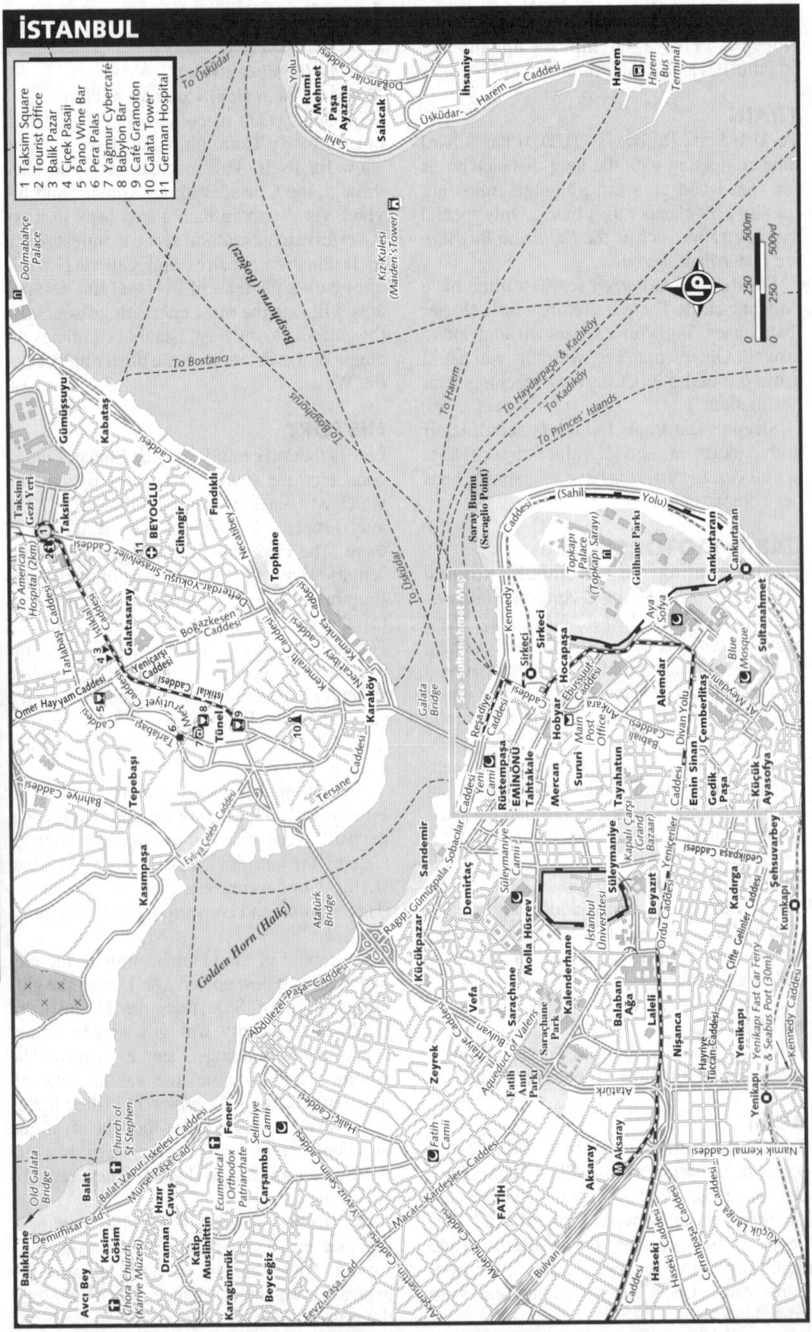
İSTANBUL
1 Taksim Square
2 Tourist Office
3 Balik Pazar
4 Çiçek Pasaji
5 Pano Wine Bar
6 Pera Palas
7 Yağmur Cybercafé
8 Babylon Bar
9 Café Gramofon
10 Galata Tower
11 German Hospital
Bosphorus (Boğaziçi)
Golden Horn (Haliç)
Kız Kulesi (Maiden's Tower)
Dolmabahçe Palace
To Üsküdar
To Bostancı
To Bosphorus
To Harem
To Haydarpaşa & Kadıköy
To Kadıköy
To Princes' Islands
Saray Burnu (Seraglio Point)
Topkapı Palace (Topkapı Sarayı)
Gülhane Parkı
See Sultanahmet Map
Aya Sofya
Blue Mosque
Sultanahmet
Cankurtaran
Galata Bridge
Atatürk Bridge
Old Galata Bridge
Taksim
Taksim Gezi Yeri
To American Hospital (2km)
Gümüşsuyu
Kabataş
BEYOĞLU
Cihangir
Fındıklı
Tophane
Galatasaray
Tünel
Karaköy
Tepebaşı
Kasımpaşa
Sirkeci
EMİNÖNÜ
Rüstempaşa
Tahtakale
Hocapaşa
Hobyar
Mercan
Sururi
Tayahatun
Alemdar
Çemberlitaş
Emin Sinan
Gedik Paşa
Küçük Ayasofya
Süleymaniye
Süleymaniye Camii
Kapalı Çarşı (Grand Bazaar)
İstanbul Üniversitesi
Beyazıt
Kadırga
Şehsuvarbey
Kumkapı
Demirtaş
Sandemir
Molla Hüsrev
Kalenderhane
Küçükpazar
Vefa
Saraçhane
Saraçhane Park
Fatih Anıtı Parkı
Aqueduct of Valens
Balaban Ağa
Laleli
Nişanca
Yenikapı
Yenikapı Fast Car Ferry & Seabus Port (30m)
Aksaray
Zeyrek
FATİH
Fatih Camii
Haseki
Balıkhane
Balat
Avcı Bey
Kasim Gösim
Hızır Çavuş
Draman
Katip Muslihittin
Karagümrük
Beyceğiz
Çarşamba
Fener
Church of St Stephen
Chora Church (Kariye Müzesi)
Ecumenical Orthodox Patriarchate
Selimiye Camii
Üsküdar
Harem
Harem Bus Terminal
İhsaniye
Salacak
Rumi Mehmet Paşa Ayazma
İstiklal Caddesi
Kennedy Caddesi
Ordu Caddesi
Divan Yolu
At Meydanı
Namık Kemal Caddesi
0 250 500m
0 250 500yd

ORIENTATION

The Bosphorus strait, between the Black and Marmara Seas, divides Europe from Asia. European İstanbul is divided by the Haliç (Golden Horn) estuary into the 'newer' quarter of Beyoğlu in the north and Old İstanbul in the south; the Galata Bridge spans the two.

Sultanahmet, the heart of Old İstanbul, has many tourist sites, cheap hotels and restaurants. Divan Yolu runs west through Sultanahmet, past the *Kapalı Çarşı* (Grand Bazaar) and İstanbul University to Aksaray, a major traffic intersection.

Eminönü, north of Sultanahmet at the southern end of Galata Bridge, is the terminus of a tram line as well as many bus lines and ferries. Sirkeci train station, the terminus for the European train line, is 100m east of Eminönü.

Karaköy, at the northern end of Galata Bridge, is another ferry terminus. Up the hill from Karaköy is the southern end of Beyoğlu's pedestrian mall, İstiklal Caddesi. At the northern end of the street is Taksim Square, heart of 'modern' İstanbul, with many fancy hotels and airline offices. İstanbul's otogar is at Esenler, about 10km west of the city.

Lonely Planet publishes an *İstanbul City Map*. Tourist offices also supply an excellent free map of the city showing all the important attractions.

INFORMATION

Tourist Offices

There are tourist offices in the international arrivals hall at Atatürk airport *(☎ 573 4136)*; at Sirkeci station *(☎ 511 5888)* and in Sultanahmet *(☎ 518 8754)*.

Money

Ubiquitous ATMs spit out Turkish liras upon insertion of your credit or ATM card; **Yapı Kredi** seems best, while **İş Bankası** is the least good because it lets you withdraw so little at a time. Exchange offices are cheapest outside the Grand Bazaar, but are also plentiful in Sultanahmet, Sirkeci and Taksim. Most are open 9am to 9pm.

Post & Communications

For poste restante go to the **Merkez Postane** *(Main Post Office; Sehinşah Pehlevi Sokak; tram: Sirkeci)*, just west of Sirkeci station. For much of the year a small PTT booth also opens in Sultanahmet Meydanı.

All phone numbers in this section use the 0212 area code unless indicated otherwise.

You can check your email at several hostels and cafés in Cankurtaran and Sultanahmet, including the Orient Youth Hostel and Mavi Guesthouse (see Places to Stay, later); and at **Yağmur Cybercafe** *(☎ 292 3020; Şeyh Bender Sokak 18/2, Asmalımescit, Tünel; tram: Tünel)*. Expect to pay around US$1 an hour for Internet services.

Travel Agencies

Divan Yolu in Sultanahmet boasts several travel agencies that sell cheap air and bus tickets, but you will need to shop around for the best deals. **Marco Polo** *(☎ 519 2804; e marco_polo@superonline.com; Divan Yolu 54)* can make airline reservations while you wait, while others such as **Backpackers Travel** *(☎ 638 6343; w www.backpackers travel.net; Yeni Akbıyık Caddesi 22)* will have to use an intermediary.

Medical Services

In an emergency the **American Hospital** *(☎ 311 2000; Güzelbahçe Sokak 20, Nişantaşı; bus: Nişantaşı)*, 2km northwest of Taksim Square, or the **German Hospital** *(Alman Hastanesi; ☎ 293 2150; Sıraselviler Caddesi 119; bus: Taksim)*, near Taksim Square, are both very well regarded.

Emergency

Head straight for the **tourist police** *(☎ 527 4503; Yerebatan Caddesi 6, Sultanahmet)* across the street from the Basilica Cistern.

OLD İSTANBUL

Make a beeline for Sultanahmet; all the major sights are arranged around the Hippodrome.

Aya Sofya (Church of Holy Wisdom)

When the Emperor Justinian ordered work to start on Aya Sofya *(Hagia Sofia or Sancta Sophia; ☎ 522 0989; Aya Sofya Meydanı; tram: Sultanahmet; admission US$10; open 9am-4.30pm Tues-Sun)* in 532 AD, he meant to create the grandest church in the world. For 1000 years it was certainly Christendom's largest temple, and despite the scaffolding that seems to have become a permanent feature, the interior is still magnificent. It must have been truly overwhelming centuries ago, when it was covered in gilded mosaics.

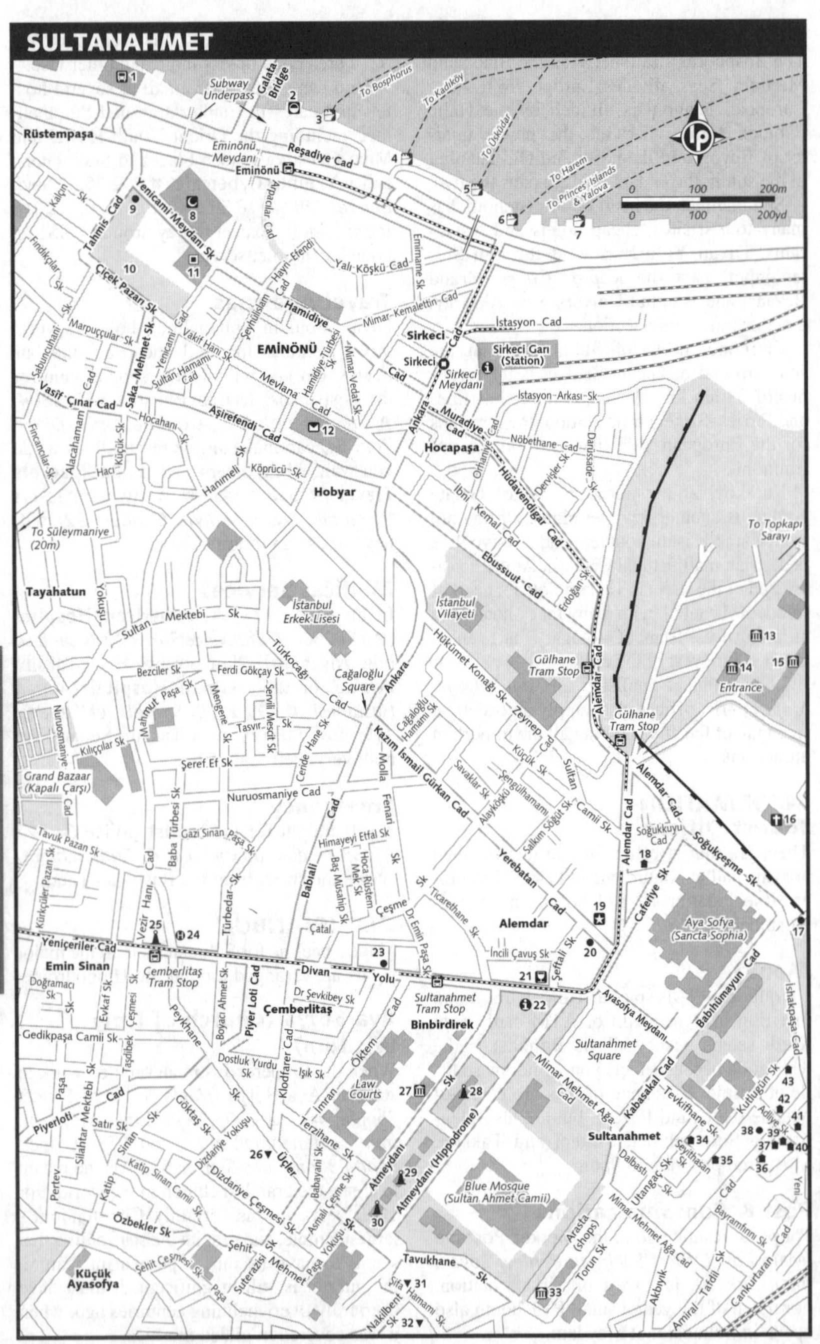
SULTANAHMET
Subway Underpass
Galata Bridge
To Bosphorus
To Kadıköy
To Üsküdar
To Harem
To Princes' Islands & Yalova
0 100 200m
0 100 200yd
Rüstempaşa
Eminönü Meydanı
Reşadiye Cad
Eminönü
Yenicami Meydanı Sk
Tahmis Cad
Kalçın Sk
Fındıkçılar Sk
Çiçek Pazarı Sk
Arpacılar Cad
Hayrı Efendi Cad
Yalı Köşkü Cad
Eminame Sk
Hamidiye Cad
Mimar Kemalettin Cad
İstasyon Cad
Sirkeci
Sirkeci Garı (Station)
Sirkeci Meydanı
Ankara Cad
EMİNÖNÜ
Marpuççular Sk
Şabuncuhani Sk
Saka Mehmet Sk
Yenicami Cad
Vakıf Hanı Sk
Sultan Hamamı Cad
Hamidiye Türbesi Sk
Mimar Vedat Sk
Mevlana Cad
Vasıf Çınar Cad
Aşirefendi Cad
Hocahanı Sk
Küçük Sk
Fincancılar Sk
Alacahamam Cad
Hacı
Hanımeli Sk
Köprücü Sk
Hobyar
İstasyon Arkası Sk
Muradiye Cad
Hocapaşa
Nöbethane Cad
Orhaniye Cad
Dervişler Sk
Darüssade Sk
Hüdavendigar Cad
İbni Kemal Cad
Ebussuut Cad
Erdoğan Sk
To Süleymaniye (20m)
To Topkapı Sarayı
Tayahatun
Yokuşu
Sultan Mektebi Sk
İstanbul Erkek Lisesi
İstanbul Vilayeti
Hükümet Konağı Sk
Gülhane Tram Stop
Alemdar Cad
Entrance
Bezciler Sk
Ferdi Gökçay Sk
Türkocağı Cad
Cağaloğlu Square
Ankara Cad
Zeynep Sultan Camii Sk
Mahmut Paşa Sk
Mengene Sk
Servili Mescit Sk
Tasvır Sk
Nuruosmaniye Sk
Kılıççılar Sk
Şeref Ef Sk
Ceride Hane Sk
Cağaloğlu Hamamı Sk
Kazım İsmail Gürkan Cad
Molla Fenari Sk
Savaklar Sk
Şengülhamamı Sk
Küçük Sk
Alayköşkü Cad
Salkım Söğüt Sk
Grand Bazaar (Kapalı Çarşı)
Nuruosmaniye Cad
Gazi Sinan Paşa Sk
Baba Türbesi Sk
Tavuk Pazarı Sk
Kürkçüler Pazarı Sk
Vezir Hanı Cad
Türbedar Sk
Babıali Cad
Himayeyi Etfal Sk
Hoca Rüstem Mek Sk
Baş Müsahip Sk
Çeşme Sk
Dr Emin Paşa Sk
Ticarethane Sk
Yerebatan Cad
Soğukkuyu Cad
Soğukçeşme Sk
Caferiye Sk
Aya Sofya (Sancta Sophia)
Alemdar
Çatal
İncili Çavuş Sk
Şeftali Sk
Yeniçeriler Cad
Emin Sinan
Çemberlitaş Tram Stop
Divan Yolu
Sultanahmet Tram Stop
Doğramacı Sk
Evkaf Sk
Çeşmesi Sk
Boyacı Ahmet Sk
Piyer Loti Cad
Çemberlitaş
Dr Şevkibey Sk
Binbirdirek
Ayasofya Meydanı
Babıhümayun Cad
İshakpaşa Cad
Gedikpaşa Camii Sk
Peykhane
Taşdibek Çeşmesi Sk
Dostluk Yurdu Sk
Işık Sk
Klodfarer Cad
Öktem Sk
Law Courts
Sultanahmet Square
Mimar Mehmet Ağa Cad
Kabasakal Cad
Tevkifhane Sk
Kutlugün Sk
Adliye Sk
Paşa Cad
Piyerloti Cad
Silahtar Mektebi Sk
Satır Sk
Sinan Sk
Göktaş Sk
Dizdariye Yokuşu
Üçler Sk
İmran Sk
Terzihane Sk
Atmeydanı Sk
Atmeydanı (Hippodrome)
Sultanahmet
Seyithasan Sk
Utangaç Sk
Dalbastı Sk
Pertev
Katip Sinan Camii Sk
Dizdariye Çeşmesi Sk
Babayani Sk
Asmalı Çeşme Sk
Blue Mosque (Sultan Ahmet Camii)
Arasta (shops)
Mimar Mehmet Ağa Cad
Bayramfırını Sk
Cankurtaran Cad
Özbekler Sk
Şehit Mehmet Paşa Yokuşu
Suterazisi Sk
Tavukhane Sk
Torun Sk
Akbıyık
Amiral Tafdil Sk
Yeni
Küçük Ayasofya
Şehit Çeşmesi Sk
Şifa Hamamı Sk
Nakilbent Sk

SULTANAHMET

PLACES TO STAY
- 18 Yücelt Interyouth Hostel & Hobby Laundry
- 34 Side Hotel & Pension
- 35 Istanbul Hostel
- 36 Sultan Hostel
- 37 Orient Youth Hostel
- 39 Hanedan Guest House
- 40 Şebnem Hotel
- 41 Alp Guest House
- 42 Hotel Empress Zoe
- 43 Mavi Guesthouse

PLACES TO EAT
- 26 Yeni Birlik Lokantasi
- 31 Buhara 93
- 32 Doy Doy

OTHER
- 1 City Buses
- 2 Seabus
- 3 Boğaz Ferry; Bosphorus Tour
- 4 Eminönü Ferry Port
- 5 Sirkeci Ferry Port
- 6 Harem (Car Ferry)
- 7 Yalova, Çınarcîk & Adalar (Princes' Islands) Ferry
- 8 Yeni Cami
- 9 Main Entrance to Egyptian Bazaar & Pandeli Restaurant
- 10 Egyptian Bazaar (Mısır Çarsisi)
- 11 Tomb of Valide Sultan Turhan Hatice
- 12 Central Post Office
- 13 Tiled Pavilion (Çinili Kösk)
- 14 Museum of the Ancient Orient
- 15 Istanbul Archaeology Museum
- 16 Aya Irini Church of Divine Peace
- 17 Imperial Gate, Topkapı Palace
- 19 Tourist Police
- 20 Basilica Cistern (Yerebatan Sarniçi)
- 21 Sultan Pub
- 22 Tourist Office
- 23 Marco Polo
- 24 Çemberlitaş Hamamı
- 25 Çemberlitaş
- 27 Turkish & Islamic Arts Museum
- 28 Obelisk of Theodosius
- 29 Spiral Column
- 30 Obelisk of Constantine
- 33 Great Palace Mosaic Museum
- 38 Backpackers Travel

Climb up to the **gallery** *(US$10; closed 11.30am-1pm)* to see the splendid surviving mosaics. After the Turkish conquest and the subsequent conversion of Aya Sofya to a mosque (hence the minarets), the mosaics were actually covered over, as Islam prohibits images. They were not revealed until the 1930s, when Atatürk declared Aya Sofya a museum.

Blue Mosque

The Blue Mosque *(Mosque of Sultan Ahmet I; Hippodrome)* is just south of Aya Sofya. Built between 1609 and 1619, it's light and delicate compared with its squat ancient neighbour. The exterior is notable for its six slender minarets and a cascade of domes and half-domes, but inside is where you'll find the luminous blue impression created by the tiled walls and painted dome. Make a small donation and leave your shoes outside.

Rents from the Arasta carpet shops to the east provide support for the Blue Mosque's upkeep. Near the Arasta is the entrance to the **Great Palace Mosaic Museum** *(Büyüksaray Mozaik Müzesi; admission US$2; open 9am-4.30pm Tues-Sun)*, a spectacular stretch of ancient Byzantine pavement featuring hunting scenes.

Hippodrome

In front of the Blue Mosque is the *Atmeydanı* (Hippodrome), erstwhile scene of chariot races and the Byzantine riots.

The **Obelisk of Theodosius** is an Egyptian column from the temple of Karnak, resting on a Byzantine base and with 3500-year-old hieroglyphics. The 10m-high **Obelisk of Constantine Porphyrogenitus** was once covered in bronze plates (which were later stolen by the Crusaders). The base rests at the former level of the Hippodrome, several metres below the ground. Between these two monuments are the remains of a spiral column of intertwined snakes which were originally erected by the Greeks at Delphi to celebrate their victory over the Persians.

Turkish & Islamic Arts Museum

On the western side of the Hippodrome, the Turkish and Islamic Arts Museum *(Türk ve İslam Eserleri Müzesi; ☎ 518 1805; Hippodrome; tram: Sultanahmet; admission US$2; open 9.30am-5.30pm Tues-Sun)* is housed in the former palace of İbrahim Paşa, grand vizier and son-in-law of Süleyman the Magnificent. Inside, the most spectacular exhibits are the wonderful floor-to-ceiling Turkish carpets, but don't miss the fascinating ethnographic collection downstairs either.

Basilica Cistern

Across the tram lines from Aya Sofya is the entrance to the Basilica Cistern *(Yerebatan Sarnıçı; ☎ 522 1259; Yerebatan Caddesi 13; tram: Sultanahmet; admission US$2.75; open 9am-4.30pm daily)*, which was built by Constantine and enlarged by Justinian. This vast, atmospheric cistern filled with columns held water not only for regular summer use but also for times of siege.

Topkapı Palace

Just northeast of Aya Sofya is the sprawling Topkapı Palace *(Topkapı Sarayı; ☎ 512 0480; Soğukçeşme Sokak; tram: Sultanahmet; admission US$10 plus US$10 for treasury & US$10 for harem; palace open 9.30am-5pm Wed-Mon, harem open 9.30am-noon & 1pm-3.30pm)* the opulent palace of the sultans from 1462 until they moved to Dolmabahçe Palace in the 19th century. Topkapı is not just a palace but a collection of courtyards, houses and libraries, with an intriguing 400-room harem.

In the vast First Court is the **Aya İrini** (Church of Divine Peace), dating from around AD 540. Buy your ticket at the Middle Gate (Orta Kapı) leading to the Second Court.

Within the Second Court are exhibits of priceless porcelain, silverware and crystal, arms, and calligraphy. Right beside the Imperial Council Chamber (Kubbealtı) is the entrance to the **harem**, a succession of sumptuously decorated rooms that served as the sultan's family quarters.

On show in the Third Court are the sultan's ceremonial robes and the **Imperial Treasury**, with its incredible wealth of gold and gems. The **Sacred Safekeeping Rooms** hold a solid-gold casket containing the Prophet Mohammed's cloak and other Islamic relics.

In the Fourth Court, beautiful tiled kiosks offer fine views of the city.

İstanbul Archaeology Museum

Down the hill from the outer courtyard to the west of Topkapı Palace is the İstanbul Archaeology Museum (İstanbul Arkeoloji Müzesi; ☎ 520 7740; Osman Hamdi Bey Yokuşu; tram: Gülhane; admission US$3.40; open 9.30am-5pm Tues-Sun). The main building houses an outstanding collection of Greek and Roman statuary, including the magnificent sarcophagi from the royal necropolis at Sidon in Lebanon, while, in a separate building on the same site, the **Museum of the Ancient Orient** houses Hittite and other older archaeological finds. Also on the grounds is the graceful Tiled Pavilion (Çinili Köşk), built on the orders of Sultan Mehmet II the Conqueror in 1472 and one of İstanbul's oldest Turkish buildings. Although it houses a museum of Turkish tile work, you'll be lucky to find it open.

Grand Bazaar

Just north of Divan Yolu, near İstanbul University, is the Grand Bazaar, or Covered Market *(Kapalı Çarşı; W www.mygrandbazaar.net; tram: Universite; open 8.30am-6.30pm Mon-Sat)*, a labyrinthine medieval shopping mall of 4500 shops. It's a fun place to wander around and get lost – which you certainly will!

Chora Church

To the west, near Edirnekapı, is the marvellous **Chora Church** *(Kariye Müzesi; ☎ 523 3009; Kariye Camii Sokak; admission US$10; open 9am-4.30pm Thur-Tues)*, a Byzantine building with the best 14th-century mosaics east of Ravenna as well as some glorious frescoes. Built in the 11th century, it was restored and converted to a mosque and is now a museum. To get there, take an Edirnekapı bus along Fevzi Paşa Caddesi.

Eminönü

Near Galata Bridge's southern end looms the large **Yeni Cami** (New Mosque), built between 1597 and 1663. Beside it, the **Egyptian Bazaar** (Mısır Çarşısı), full of spice and food vendors, is worth a wander.

DOLMABAHÇE PALACE

Cross the Galata Bridge and follow Necatibey Caddesi along the Bosphorus from Karaköy eastwards and you'll come to the grandiose Dolmabahçe Palace *(☎ 236 9000; Dolmabahçe Caddesi; bus: Kabataş; admission Selamlik US$4, Haremlik US$4, combined ticket US$7; open 9am-3pm Tues-Wed & Fri-Sun)*, right on the waterfront. The palace was built between 1843 and 1856 as home for some of the last Ottoman sultans, but was guaranteed its place in the history books when Atatürk died there on 10 November 1938.

Visitors are taken on guided tours of the two main buildings: the Selamlik (or men's apartments) and Haremlik (or family apartments). Both are stuffed to the gills with over-elaborate furniture and fittings, and as the tour is also very rushed not everyone will want to put aside the two hours required to see both parts. If you must choose, go for the Haremlik.

Any bus heading out of Karaköy along the Bosphorus shore road will take you to Dolmabahçe.

BEYOĞLU

The heart of Beyoğlu is İstiklal Caddesi, a pedestrian street served by a picturesque restored tram (US$0.30). The famed **Pera Palas Oteli**, patronised by the likes of Agatha Christie and Atatürk, is off to the west. Near the big Galatasaray Lisesi (high school) are the colourful **Balık Pazar** (Fish Market) and **Çiçek Pasajı** (Flower Passage), an assortment of fish-and-beer restaurants where a fun night out is guaranteed.

Taksim Square, with its huge hotels, is the hub of modern İstanbul.

THE BOSPHORUS

The shores of the Bosphorus north of İstanbul are home to some beautiful old Ottoman buildings, including **Rumeli Hisarı** *(Rumeli Castle; admission US$2; open 9.30am-5pm Thur-Tues)*, the huge castle built by Mehmet the Conqueror on the European side to complete his stranglehold on Constantinople. To get there, take any bus or dolmuş going north along the European shore of the Bosphorus to Bebek, Emirgan, Yeniköy or Sarıyer.

In summer a ferry ride up the Bosphorus is *de rigueur* for visitors and is more than likely to prove a highlight. Organised excursion ferries depart from Eminönü daily at 10.35am, 12.35pm and 2.10pm Monday to Friday, stopping at Beşik-taş, Kanlıca, Yeniköy, Sarıyer, Rumeli Kava-ğı and Anadolu Kavağı (1¾ hours). Extra trips are added on Sunday and holidays.

The weekday return fare is US$5, half price on Saturday and Sunday. Hold on to your ticket as you need it to re-board the boat for the return trip.

PLACES TO STAY

The best place to head for accommodation to suit all budgets is the Sultanahmet/Cankurtaran district. Camping in İstanbul is hardly convenient and costs about as much as staying in a cheap hotel, on top of which you must pay fares in and out of the centre. **Ataköy Mokamp** *(☎ 559 6000; Ataköy Sahil Yolu, Bakırköy; camp sites US$11)*, near the airport, has camping facilities.

İstanbul's hostels charge around US$8 for a bed in summer, less in winter. In high summer even the hostels fill up (with the inevitable problems of noise and overstretched facilities), and roof space becomes available for around US$5.

Yücelt Interyouth Hostel *(☎ 513 6150; Caferiye Sokak 6/1, Sultanahmet)*, a little way from the other hostels, is a big, brash place with lots of facilities including a mini-gym and laundry.

İstanbul Hostel *(☎ 516 9380; W www.istanbul-hostel.com; Kutlugün Sokak)*, in Cankurtaran, is immaculately clean, and shows movies in its basement bar.

Mavi Guesthouse *(☎ 516 5878; W www.maviguesthouse.com; Kutlugün Sokak 3)* is small and welcoming. Rates include breakfast, and the cosy ground-floor lounge is a plus.

One block over is Akbıyık Caddesi, with lots of places to stay, eat and drink.

Orient Youth Hostel *(☎ 518 0789; W www.hostels.com/orienthostel; Akbıyık Caddesi 13)* is a popular place with some newly decorated rooms, a top-floor café that has marvellous Bosphorus views and a basement bar that features belly dancers and water-pipes. **Sultan Hostel** *(☎ 516 9260; W www.sultanhostel.com; Terbıyık Sokak 3)*, just around the corner, is used as a base by Fez Bus. It also boasts Marmara views from its roof.

Many Cankurtaran pensions are gradually upgrading into classy, small hotels. **Side Hotel & Pension** *(☎/fax 517 6590; W www.sidehotel.com; Utangaç Sokak 20; singles/doubles from US$20/35)* is one of those places where you arrive knowing no-one and leave with a whole bunch of new friends. To find it, head down from Aya Sofya and you'll come to Utangaç Sokak on the right. Breakfast is included.

Three small places in Adliye Sokak, a turn-off from Akbïyïk Caddesi, are likely to be quieter than those right on it. **Hanedan Guest House** *(☎ 516 4869; singles/doubles with shower US$25/35)* is simplest but has a small roof-top café. **Alp Guest House** *(☎ 517 9570; Adliye Sokak 4; singles/doubles with shower US$35/50)* has pleasingly decorated rooms. Smartest of them all is **Sebnem Hotel** *(☎ 517 6623; W www.sebnemhotel.com; singles/doubles with shower from US$45/55)*, across the road, which has comfortable and colour-coordinated rooms.

PLACES TO EAT

Every Wednesday you can pick up what you need at the Akbıyık Caddesi street market. The Egyptian Bazaar and surrounding streets sell dried fruit, pulses, fish and more.

Yeni Birlik Lokantası *(Uçler Sokak 46; meals US$3-5; open 8am-3pm)* is favoured by lawyers and a good place to find a choice of stews at lunchtime. From the far end of the Hippodrome, walk up Uçler Sokak one block.

Doy Doy *(Şifa Hamamı Sokak 13; meals US$3.50)* is a long-time favourite, downhill from the southeastern end of the Hippodrome. Offering cheap, simple Turkish staples, it's usually busy with locals and travellers. Across the road, **Buhara 93** *(Nakilbent Sokak 15/A)* has similarly cheap and appetising meals.

Although there's a reasonable selection of places to eat in Sultanahmet, for a bigger choice head across town to Beyoğlu. Hop on a bus to Taksim Square (T4 from the Hippodrome) and start walking along İstiklal Caddesi and you'll be spoilt for choice, from the takeaway *döner* places right at the start of the street to the flashier, Westernised bar/cafés at the Tünel end.

Konak *(İstiklal Caddesi 259)*, near the big Galatasaray Lisesi (high school), is a great place to tuck into an İskender kebap beneath plaster ceilings and chandeliers that hint at the area's past glory. A meal with cold drink will cost around US$4, a pide even less.

ENTERTAINMENT

İstanbul's most interesting historical *hammams* are pretty touristy, with prices to reflect their non-Turkish clientele. The best for first-timers is the beautiful **Çemberlitaş Hamamı** *(Vezirhan Caddesi 8; tram: Çemberlitaş; admission US$18; open 6am-midnight daily)*, just off Divan Yolu beside the Çemberlitaş monument.

TURKEY

Near the Basilica Cistern are a group of bars. Bunker-style **Bodrum** really fires up, and **Gila** attracts *some* locals and has awesome views of Aya Sofya, but **The Sultan Pub** is better for a quiet drink (and good for women travellers). The Orient and Yücelt hostels also have popular, smoky bars.

Cross to Beyoğlu to party with İstanbul's wealthier youth. Ritzy **Café Gramofon**, at the southern end of İstiklal Caddesi, has live jazz (and a comfortable environment for women). **Pano** wine bar, opposite the British consulate, is so popular you may have to queue.

At **Babylon** *(☎ 292 7368; Şehbender Sokak 3, Beyoğlu; tram: Tünel)* big-name bands occasionally play to rapturous audiences.

Beyoğlu can be seedy. Ignore touts who try to encourage you onto their turf – it'll only end in tears.

GETTING THERE & AWAY

Air

Most people fly into İstanbul's Atatürk International Airport, Turkey's flight hub. Most foreign airlines have their offices near Taksim, or north of it, along Cumhuriyet Caddesi.

Bus

İstanbul Otogar *(Uluslararası İstanbul Otogarı; ☎ 658 0036)*, at Esenler, is a monster of a place, with 168 ticket offices and buses leaving for all parts of Turkey and beyond. To get to it from Sultanahmet take the tram to Aksaray, switch to the metro and get out at Otogar.

Buses depart for Ankara (US$12 to US$24, six hours) roughly every 15 minutes, day and night; buses for most other cities depart at least every hour. Heading east to Anatolia, you might want to board at the smaller **Harem Otogar** *(☎ 0216-333 3763)*, north of Haydarpaşa on the Asian shore, which is accessible via ferry from Karaköy, but the choice of service there is more limited.

Train

Sirkeci *(☎ 520 6575)* is the station for services to Edirne, Greece and Eastern Europe. From Sirkeci there are three express trains a day to Edirne (US$3, 6½ hours). The nightly *Bosfor Expresi* goes to Bucharest (US$26, 18 hours) and Budapest (US$95, 32 hours).

Haydarpaşa *(☎ 0216-336 4470)*, on the Asian shore, is the terminus for trains to Anatolia, Syria and İran. From Haydarpaşa there are seven express trains a day to Ankara (US$10 to US$28, seven to 10 hours), the fastest being sleeper only.

Boat

For information on car ferries to İzmir, see the introductory Getting Around section in this chapter. Yenikapı, south of Aksaray Square, is the dock for *hızlı feribot* (fast car-ferries) across the Sea of Marmara. Heading for Bursa, take a Yalova ferry or catamaran, which will get you to Yalova in less than an hour for US$35 (car and driver). The voyage to Bandırma takes less than two hours and costs US$70 (car and driver) or US$12 (per passenger).

GETTING AROUND

To/From the Airport

The fastest way into town from the airport is by taxi. During the *gündüz* (day) it costs US$10 to Sultanahmet (20 minutes), US$12 to Taksim (30 minutes) and US$8 to the otogar (20 minutes), although fares are higher at *gece* (night).

A cheaper but slower alternative is the Havaş airport bus (US$2, 30 to 60 minutes), which goes to Taksim Square via Aksaray. Buses leave every 30 minutes from 5am to 11.30pm.

Many Divan Yolu travel agencies and Sultanahmet hostels book minibus transport from the hotels to the airport for about US$4 a head. Unfortunately, this option only works going from town to the airport, not vice versa.

Bus

City buses are crowded but useful. Destinations and intermediate stops are indicated at the front and side of the bus. On most routes you must have a ticket (US$0.50) before boarding; stock up on tickets in advance from the white booths near major stops, or nearby shops.

Train

To get to Sirkeci station, take the *tramvay* (tram) from Aksaray or Sultanahmet, or any bus for Eminönü. Haydarpaşa station is connected by ferry to Karaköy (US$0.60, at least every 30 minutes).

Every 20 minutes suburban trains from Sirkeci (US$0.40) run along the southern walls of Old İstanbul and west along the Marmara shore. There's a handy station in Cankurtaran for Sultanahmet.

Underground

The Tünel, İstanbul's ancient underground train, mounts the hill from Karaköy to Tünel Square and İstiklal Caddesi (US$0.50, every 10 or 15 minutes from 7am to 9pm).

Tram

The useful *hızlı tramvay* (fast tram) network has three lines. The first runs between Eminönü and Aksaray via Divan Yolu and Sultanahmet; the second runs west from Aksaray to the otogar. A third line runs from Taksim to 4 Levent. Another restored tram trundles along İstiklal Caddesi to Taksim. All tram tickets cost US$0.50.

Taxi

İstanbul has 60,000 yellow taxis, all of them with meters (although not every driver wants to run them). A trip from Sultanahmet to Taksim costs around US$5; to the otogar around US$10.

Boat

The cheapest and nicest way to travel any distance in İstanbul is by ferry. Short ferry hops cost US$0.60, longer ones US$1.20. The main ferry docks are located at the mouth of the Golden Horn (Eminönü, Sirkeci and Karaköy) and at Kabataş, just before Dolmabahçe Palace.

Around İstanbul

Since İstanbul is such a vast city, few places are within easy day-trip reach. However, if you make an early start it's possible to see the sites of Edirne in Thrace (Trakya), the only bit of Turkey that is geographically within Europe. The fast ferry link means that you can also just about make Bursa and back in a day, although it's much better to plan on an overnight stay.

EDİRNE

☎ 284 • pop 115,000

Edirne is a surprisingly pleasant, under-visited town with several fine old mosques. If you're passing through, have a look at the **Üçşerefeli Cami**, the **Eski Cami** and especially the **Selimiye Camii**, the finest work of Süleyman the Magnificent's master architect Sinan. The impressive **Beyazit II Camii** complex is on the outskirts. There are several good, cheap hotels a few blocks from the **tourist office** *(☎/fax 225 1518; Hürriyet Meydanı 17)* in the town centre.

Buses from İstanbul run every 20 minutes (US$5, three hours, 235km).

BURSA

☎ 224 • pop 1 million

Sprawling at the base of Uludağ, Turkey's biggest winter sports centre, Bursa was the Ottoman capital before İstanbul. It retains several fine mosques and pretty neighbourhoods from early Ottoman times, but its biggest attractions are the thermal springs in the village-like suburb of Çekirge. Bursa's wonderful covered market should also delight anyone who finds İstanbul's version too touristy.

The city centre is along Atatürk Caddesi between the Ulu Cami (Grand Mosque) to the west and the main square, Cumhuriyet Alanı (commonly called Heykel) to the east. The PTT is on the southern side of Atatürk

Caddesi, opposite the Ulu Cami. Çekirge, with its hot springs, is about 6km west of Heykel. The otogar is located an inconvenient 10km north of the centre on the Yalova road.

The **tourist office** *(☎ 251 1834; Orhangazi Altgeçidi subway, Ulu Cami Parkı)* is opposite the Koza Han (Silk Market).

Things to See & Do

The largest of Bursa's beautiful mosques is the 20-domed **Ulu Cami** *(Grand Mosque; Atatürk Caddesi)*, built in 1399. Northeast of Ulu Cami is the **bedesten** (covered bazaar), where you'll find the **Karagöz shop** *(☎ 221 8727)* which details on puppet shows. The **Koza Han** is worth a wander, too.

Northwest of Ulu Cami is the **Muradiye Complex**, which has decorated tombs dating from the 14th and 15th centuries. Continue onto the **mineral baths** in the suburb of Çekirge. Rejuvenation at **Eski Kaplıca**, beside the Kervansaray Termal Hotel, will set you back US$5, and it's another US$5 for a scrub or a limp-wristed massage.

About 1km east of Heykel you'll find the early Ottoman **Yeşil Cami** (Green Mosque), built in 1424, and its beautifully tiled **Yeşil Türbe** *(Green Tomb; admission free; open 8.30am-5.30pm)*. Nearby is the **Turkish & Islamic Arts Museum** *(admission US$0.75; open 8.30am-noon & 1pm-5pm Tues-Sun)*.

On a clear day it's worth going up **Uludağ**. From Heykel take bus 3/B or 3/C, or a dolmuş east to the *teleferik* (cable car) up the mountain (US$3 return).

Places to Stay

The centre of town has a motley bunch of places to stay. You're better off forking over a bit more and staying in Çekirge, where you'll also get free mineral baths. **Öz Yeşilyayla Termal Otel** *(☎ 239 6496; Selvi Sokak 6; singles/doubles US$15/20)* is straight from the 1950s – everything creaks as you walk across the floor. There's free use of the basement mineral baths.

Boyugüzel Termal Otel *(☎/fax 233 9999; Selvi Sokak; singles/doubles with shower US$20/30)*, right next door, is smart and modern and throws 30 minutes in the mineral bath downstairs in with the room price.

In the centre, **Otel Güneş** *(☎ 222 1404; İnebey Caddesi 75; singles/doubles US$5/8)*, in an old wooden building, is clean and simple, if somewhat cramped. **Hotel Çeşmeli** *(☎ 224 1511; Gümüşçeken Caddesi 6; singles/doubles with shower US$19/30)*, just north of Atatürk Caddesi, is better – friendly, fairly quiet and very clean.

Places to Eat

Bursa was the birthplace of the *İskender kebap* although these days the quality of kebaps seems to be going downhill.

Kebapçi İskender *(Ünlü Caddesi 7; full meals US$6)*, just east of Heykel, dates back to 1867 and is beginning to show its age, although the İskender kebap is still tasty. **Adanur Hacibey**, opposite, costs the same but is less fancy.

Çiçek Izgara near the half-timbered Belediye in the flower market, *(Belediye Caddesi 15; full meals US$2.50; open 11am-3.30pm & 5.30pm-9pm daily)*, is bright, modern, super-popular and good for lone women.

Çınar Izgara *(Atatürk Caddesi, Ulucami Yani; full meals US$4)* is housed in what was the old toilet block of the Ulu Cami and has pictures of old Bursa on the walls. Service is attentive, the food tasty.

For a jolly evening of seafood and drinks, head straight for Sakarya Caddesi, off Altıparmak Caddesi. **Arap Şükrü** *(☎ 221 1453; Sakarya Caddesi 6; meals US$10)* is usually reliable. Enjoy the calamari (US$2) or grilled mackerel (US$3.50).

Getting There & Around

The fastest way to get to İstanbul is to take the hourly bus to Yalova (US$2, one hour), then a catamaran or fast car-ferry to İstanbul's Yenikapı docks (US$5, one hour, at least seven a day). Get a bus that departs at least 1½ hours before the scheduled boat departure.

Buses that are designated *karayolu ile* (via road) take four hours to İstanbul and drag you around the Bay of İzmit. Those designated *feribot ile* (via ferry) take you to Topçular, east of Yalova, and then travel by car ferry to Eskihisar, which is a much more pleasant way to go.

There are no *servis* buses to the otogar, so you must take a bus (US$0.30, 45 minutes, 10km) between the otogar and the city centre. City buses (BOİ; US$0.30) have stops marked on the front. The best place to pick them up is on Atatük Caddesi just before Heykel. Many dolmuşes wait in front of Ulu Cami Parkı, although the Çekirge dolmuş waits at the northeast end of Feraizcizade Sokak.

The Aegean Coast

While the coastal scenery of the Aegean coast is not as spectacular as that of the Mediterranean, the area makes up for it with some fantastic historic sites, including the ruins of Troy, Ephesus and Pergamum. This is also home of the moving battlefield sites at Gallipoli (Gelıbolu).

ÇANAKKALE

☎ 286 • pop 60,000

Çanakkale makes a good base for visiting Troy and Gallipoli, across the other side of the Dardanelles. During WWI, Kemal Atatürk led his troops to a Turkish victory over Anzac (Australian and New Zealand) forces on 18 March 1916, now a big local holiday. But even more people flock to town on 25 April for Anzac Day, when a dawn service commemorates the anniversary of the Allied landings on the peninsula in 1915.

The **tourist office** *(☎ 217 1187)*, all the cheap hotels and a range of restaurants are close to the ferry pier, near the town's landmark clock tower. Built by Sultan Mehmet the Conqueror in 1452, the **Ottoman castle** now houses an **Army Museum** *(admission US$0.75; open 9am-noon & 1.30pm-5pm Fri-Sun & Tues-Wed)*. Just over 2km south of the ferry pier on the road to Troy, the **Archaeological Museum** *(admission US$0.75; open 9am-5pm daily)* holds artefacts found at Troy and Assos.

Places to Stay & Eat

Except on Anzac Day, Çanakkale has plenty of accommodation. Unfortunately the stresses and strains of 25 April result in more complaints from readers about Çanakkale hotels than just about anywhere else in the country. Do yourself a favour and check prices carefully before settling in.

In summer camping is available at **Mocamp Trova** *(☎ 232 8025; Güzelyalı Beach)*, 15km south of Çanakkale, off the road to Troy.

Anzac House *(☎ 213 5969; ⓔ www.anzachouse.com; Cumhuriyet Bulvarı; dorm beds US$5, singles/doubles US$9/14)* provides clean, simple budget accommodation, although some of the rooms are windowless boxes.

Hotel Efes *(☎ 217 3256; Aralık Sokak 5; dorm beds US$5, singles/doubles with shower US$10/14)*, behind the clock tower, is bright, cheerful and female-run.

Hotel Kervansaray *(☎ 217 8192; Fetvane Sokak 13; singles/doubles US$5/9)* is in a quaint old pasha's house. The rooms are very basic, but there's an inviting courtyard garden.

Yellow Rose Pension *(☎/fax 217 3343; Yeni Sokak 5; dorm beds US$4, singles/doubles US$6/12)*, 50m southeast of the clock tower, offers simple rooms in an attractive house on a quiet side street.

Trakya Restaurant *(Cumhuriyet Meydanı; meals US$5)*, across the road from Anzac House, can fill you up with pide and other staples 24 hours a day.

Gülen *(Cumhuriyet Meydanı; meals US$5)* has cheerier decor and does a decent İskender kebap, as well as a range of pides.

Getting There & Away

There are hourly buses to Çanakkale from İstanbul (US$11, six hours, 340km), with equally frequent onward buses to İzmir (US$8, five hours, 340km).

GALLIPOLI (GELİBOLU)

Always the first line of defence for İstanbul, the Dardanelles proved their worth in WWI. Atop the narrow, hilly peninsula, Mustafa Kemal Atatürk and his troops fought off a better equipped but badly commanded force of Anzac and British troops. After nine months of horrendous casualties, the Allied forces withdrew. For most people a visit to the battlefields and war graves of Gallipoli (now a national park) is a poignant experience.

If time is tight, the easiest way to see the sights is on a minibus tour from Çanakkale with **Troyanzac Tours** *(☎ 217 5849)* or **Hassle Free Tours** *(☎ 213 5969)* for about US$20 per person. **Down Under Travel** *(☎ 814 2431; Eceabat)* garners lots of praise from readers.

With time on your hands, it's cheaper to take a ferry from Çanakkale to Eceabat and a dolmuş to Kabatepe, then follow the heritage trail described in a booklet sold at the visitors centre there.

Most people use Çanakkale as base for exploring Gallipoli, but you could also stay at Eceabat, on the Thracian (European) side of the strait. **TJs Hostel** *(☎ 814 2940; ⓔ tjs_tours@mail.excite.com; Cumhuriyet Caddesi 5; beds with shower US$5)* gets particularly fond reviews from its guests.

Hourly car ferries cross the strait from Çanakkale to Eceabat and from Lapseki to Gallipoli (US$0.50). More-frequent private ferries (US$0.30) cross to Kilitbahir from in front of Çanakkale's Hotel Bakır.

TROY

According to Homer, Paris abducted the beautiful Helen from her husband Menelaus, King of Sparta. He whisked her off to Troy, precipitating the Trojan War. After 10 years of carnage, Odysseus came up with the idea of filling a wooden horse with soldiers and leaving it outside the west gate for the Trojans to wheel inside the walls.

The story is a lot more exciting than modern Troy *(Truva; admission US$7; open 8.30am-5pm daily Nov-May, 8am-7.30pm daily June-Oct)*, as there's little left to see. And you probably won't be thrilled with the tacky imitation 'Trojan Horse'. It's estimated that nine successive cities have been built on this site: Troy I goes right back to the Bronze Age; legendary Troy is thought to be Troy VI; and most of the ruins you see are Roman ones from Troy IX. You may want to take one of the tours offered in Çanakkale to get more out of Troy.

In summer, frequent dolmuşes run from Çanakkale (US$1.50, 30km). Walk straight inland from the ferry pier to Atatürk Caddesi, and turn right towards Troy; the dolmuş stop is at the bridge.

BEHRAMKALE (ASSOS)

☎ 286

Behramkale, 19km southwest of Ayvacık, consists of a beautiful hill-top village, with the ruins of a **Temple of Athena** *(admission US$0.75; open 8am-5pm Tues-Sun)* looking across the water to Lesvos in Greece; and a small *iskele* (port), 2km further on. Both get overcrowded in summer, especially at weekends, so visit in low season if possible

Çakır Camping *(☎ 721 7048; camp sites US$5)* is right on the beach, but there are other possibilities in the olive groves nearby. In Behramkale itself **Dolunay Pansiyon** *(☎ 721 7271)* and other pensions can put you up for around US$12.50 a head.

Get to Behramkale by infrequent dolmuş (US$1.50) from Ayvacık (not to be confused with nearby Ayvalık). Ayvacık is linked by bus to Çanakkale and Ayvalık.

AYVALIK

☎ 266 • pop 30,000

Inhabited by Ottoman Greeks until 1923, this small fishing port and beach resort is the point of departure for ferries to Lesvos. The otogar is 1.5km north of the town centre, the **tourist office** *(☎/fax 312 2122)* 1km south, opposite the marina. Offshore is **Alibey Island** (Cunda), lined with open-air fish restaurants and linked by ferries and a causeway to the mainland.

Places to Stay & Eat

Taksiyarhis Pansiyon *(☎ 312 1494; Mareşal Çakmak Caddesi 71; beds US$7)*, a renovated Ottoman house, is the most interesting place to stay. It's five minutes' walk east of the PTT behind the former Taxiarkhis church and is often full in summer. Breakfast is US$2.50.

Bonjour Pansiyon *(☎ 312 8085; Fevzi Çakmak Caddesi, Çeşme Sokak 5; singles/doubles with shower US$12/20; open May-Sept)* is in the fine, restored house of a French ambassador to the sultan.

Chez Beliz Pansiyon *(☎ 312 4897; Mareşal Çakmak Caddesi 28; beds from US$10; open May-Nov)* boasts a gorgeous garden, an exuberant hostess and excellent food.

Hüsnü Baba'nin Yeri *(Tenekeciler Sokağı 16; meals US$4)*, just off İnönü Caddesi in a shady alley, doesn't look like much but offers excellent mezes to wash down with rakı. Anyone for sea urchins? In season only, of course.

15 Kardeşler *(Talatpaşa Caddesi; meals US$4.50)*, in the street behind the waterfront, offers cheap soup and kebap suppers.

Getting There & Away

There are frequent direct buses from İzmir to Ayvalık (US$3.50, three hours, 240km). Coming from Çanakkale (US$5, 3½ hours, 200km) the buses will probably drop you off on the main highway to hitch to the centre. Daily boats operate to Lesvos from late May to September (US$40/50 one way/return); there's at least one boat a week even in winter.

BERGAMA

☎ 232 • pop 46,900

From the 3rd century BC to the 1st century AD, Bergama (formerly Pergamum) was a powerful and cultured kingdom. A line of rulers beginning with one of Alexander the Great's generals reigned over this small but wealthy kingdom, famous now for its extensive ruins. The **tourist office** *(☎ 633 1862; İzmir Caddesi 57)* is midway between the otogar and the market.

The **Asclepion** *(Temple of Asclepios; admission US$4; open 8.30am-5.30pm daily)*,

3.5km from the city centre, became a famous medical school with a library that rivalled that of Alexandria in Egypt. The **Acropolis** *(admission US$4; open 8.30am-5.30pm daily)*, a hill-top site 6km from the city centre, has a spectacular sloping theatre. You can follow the pretty path marked by dots down through the ruins to get back to town. The excellent **Archaeology & Ethnography Museum** *(admission US$2; open 8.30am-5.30pm daily)* contains finds from both these sites.

Pension Athena *(☎ 633 3420; İmam Çıkmazı 5; beds US$5, with shower US$7)*, in an old Ottoman house, is run by natural-born host Aydın Şengül. A feast of a breakfast is US$2 extra. It's at the Acropolis end of town. **Böblingen Pension** *(☎ 633 2153; Asklepion Caddesi 2; singles/doubles with shower US$10/20)*, spotless and family-run, is at the start of the road to the Asclepion. Breakfast is included.

Meydan Restaurant *(İstiklal Meydanı; meals US$5)*, near the Basilica (Red Hall) on the main street, serves meals on a vine-shaded terrace. **Sağlam 3 Restaurant** *(Cumhuriyet Meydanı 29; meals US$4)* serves a range of kebap, while **Sağlam 2** *(İstiklal Meydanı 3; meals US$3)* has cheaper soups and pides, with live music upstairs to round off the evening.

There are buses that shuttle between Bergama and İzmir every half-hour in summer (US$3, two hours, 100km). Fairly frequent buses also connect Bergama with Ayvalık (US$2.50, 1¾ hours, 60km).

İZMİR

☎ 232 • pop 2.5 million

Although it's the birthplace of Homer (around 700 BC) and the main transport hub for the Aegean coast, Turkey's third-largest city, İzmir (once Smyrna), is a good place to skip on a short trip. It's spread out and baffling to find your way around, its sites are relatively minor and its hotels are overpriced.

You'll go mad without a map – the **tourist office** *(☎ 484 2147; Gaziosmanpaşa Bulvarı 1/C, Cumhuriyet Meydanı)* supplies a good free one.

Since most of old İzmir was destroyed by fire there's little to see. You can check out the remains of an extensive 2nd-century AD **Roman agora** *(admission US$1.40; open 8.30am-noon & 1pm-5pm daily)*, on the eastern edge of the sprawling, atmospheric bazaar. It's also worth taking a bus to the hilltop **Kadifekale** fortress, where women still weave kilims (rugs) on horizontal looms.

Places to Stay & Eat

Decent mid-range places are scarce and İzmir has more than its fair share of seedy dives. For the cheapest places to stay, walk out of the front of Basmane train station, turn left, cross the main road and walk up shady Anafartalar Caddesi towards the bazaar area.

Otel Hikmet *(☎ 484 2672; 945 Sokak No 26; singles/doubles US$3.50/5.50)*, near Hatuniye Camii, is clean and dirt-cheap but the owner seems unsure if he really wants guests.

Otel Antik Han *(☎ 489 2750; Anafartalar Caddesi 600; singles/doubles with shower US$20/30)*, in a restored house in the bazaar, is a good choice. Rooms have TVs, ceiling fans and plenty of character but can be noisy because of nearby music-halls.

For bargain basement meals, head into the bazaar and take your pick. **Gönlibel** *(Anafartalar Caddesi 878; full meals US$4)* does a delicious *kiremitte tavuk* (chicken baked on a tile) for just US$2. **Dört Mevsim Et Lokantası** *(1369 Sokak 51/A; meals US$5-6)* is an excellent place with an open *ocakbaşı* (grill), a range of kebaps and welcoming service.

Getting There & Around

Many bus companies have ticket offices around Dokuz Eylül Meydanı, near Basmane station. They usually provide a *servis* (free minibus) to the otogar. From İzmir there are frequent buses to Selçuk (US$1.75, one hour, 80km), Çanakkale (US$8, five hours, 340km) and Pamukkale (US$4, four hours, 260km).

The evening *Mavi Tren* (US$10, 14 hours) hauls sleeping cars from Basmane station to Ankara; or you can take the *İzmir Express* for US$8. For İstanbul, take the *Marmara Express* to Bandırma (US$2), then a fast ferry.

For details of summer-only ferry services from Venice, see the Getting There & Away section earlier in this chapter. For details of the ferry service linking İstanbul and İzmir, see the Getting Around section.

Local bus tickets cost US$0.40; you must buy before boarding. Bus No 33 goes to Kadifekale, Nos 601, 603 and 605 to the otogar.

SELÇUK & EPHESUS

☎ 232

Selçuk is an easy one-hour bus trip south of İzmir. Almost everybody comes here to visit the splendid Roman ruins of Ephesus. In its heyday only Athens was more magnificent; Ephesus was once Rome's capital in Asia.

Although touristy, Selçuk is a backwater compared with coastal playpens such as Kuşadası. Most of the pensions are on the quieter western side of the highway (Atatürk Caddesi) behind the museum; others are on the eastern side along with the otogar, restaurants and train station. The **tourist office** *(☎/fax 892 1328)* is in the park across from the otogar.

Ephesus is a 3km, 35-minute walk west from Selçuk's otogar along a shady road – turn left (south) at the Tusan Motel. Frequent dolmuşes to Pamucak and Kuşadası pass the Ephesus turn-off (US$0.50, five minutes).

Things to See

Ephesus *(admission US$10; open 8am-5pm daily, 8am-7pm in summer)* first flourished as a centre for worship of the Anatolian goddess later identified with Diana/Artemis. The Arcadian Way through Ephesus was the main street to the port, which has long been silted up. The immense Great Theatre holds 24,000 people. The Temple of Hadrian, Celsus Library, Marble Way (where the rich lived), **Terraced Houses** *(Yamaç Evleri; admission US$20)* and Fountain of Trajan are still in amazingly good shape (or under painstaking restoration).

Selçuk's main attraction is the excellent **Ephesus Museum** *(admission US$2; open 8.30am-noon & 12.30pm-4.30pm)*, with its priceless collection of artefacts from the Roman period. Above Selçuk, visit the **Basilica of St John** *(admission US$2; open 8am-6pm)*, said to be built over his tomb. Between Ephesus and Selçuk, the foundations of the **Temple of Artemis** are all that remain of one of the Seven Wonders of the Ancient World.

Places to Stay

Selçuk has almost 100 small pensions, mostly charging US$7 per person with perhaps another US$2 for breakfast. They're modest, friendly places, and sometimes it's possible to sleep on the roof or camp in the garden for US$2 to US$3 per person.

Garden Motel & Camping *(☎ 892 1163; camp sites for two US$7)* is west of Ayasuluk Hill, with camp sites in an idyllic location amid fruit orchards.

Homeros Pension *(☎ 892 3995; Asmali Sokak 17)* offers the option of some simple pension rooms, across the road from a set of beautiful, individually decorated rooms. You can hang out on the roof terrace, too.

Australia & New Zealand Pension *(☎ 892 1050; W www.anzturkishguesthouse.com; Profesör Mitler Sokak 17)* has a dormitory and comfortable rooms with showers set round a courtyard. Excellent meals are served on its roof terrace.

Artemis Guest House *(Jimmy's Place; ☎ 892 6191; W www.artemisguesthouse.com; 1012 Sokak 2)*, in the newer part of town, offers a multitude of services for travellers, including a library of information that puts official tourist offices to shame.

Kiwi Pension *(Alison's Place; ☎ 891 4892; W www.kiwipensioncom; Kubilay Caddesi 8)* is a spotless place just south of the centre. Its lovely swimming pool is 1km away in an orange orchard.

Places to Eat

Artemis Pide Salonu *(Cengiz Topel Caddesi; meals US$1.50-2.50)*, a half-block south of the tea garden, is a great place for hit-and-run meals. On the next block, **Firuze** and **Bizim** are a bit simpler, with slightly lower prices. Also popular is **Tat** *(meal with wine about US$6)*.

In a lovely location opposite the İsa Bey Camii, **Karameşe Anadolu Köy Sofraları** *(☎ 892 0466; meals US$5)* serves average kebaps amid picturesque water and greenery.

Getting There & Away

Selçuk's hassley otogar is opposite the tourist office. Buses from İzmir (US$1.75, one hour, 80km) usually drop you on the main highway nearby. Frequent minibuses head for Kuşadası (US$0.90, 30 minutes, 20km) and the beach at Pamucak (US$0.75, 10 minutes, 7km).

KUŞADASI

☎ 256 • pop 37,100

Kuşadası is a shameless tourist trap, and you'll probably want to whip through to catch a boat out to Samos (Greece). The nightlife is raging, though. The **tourist office** *(☎ 614 1103)* is beside the pier, near the ferry offices. Apart from the 16th-century **castle** in the harbour, Kuşadası is short on sights, although it does make a good base for visits to the ancient cities of **Priene**, **Miletus** and **Didyma** to the south; admission to all three cities is US$1 each.

From the harbour, walk up Barbaros Hayrettin Caddesi, turn right towards the Akdeniz Apartotel, and take either Yıldırım Caddesi (the road to the left of the Akdeniz) or Aslanlar Caddesi (the road to the right) to reach most of the pensions and cheap hotels. Get to **Düsseldorf Pansiyon** *(☎ 613 1272; rooms per person US$6)*, an excellent choice with spotless rooms, by walking up steep Yıldırım Caddesi. **Pension Golden Bed** *(☎ 614 8708)*, just off Aslanlar Caddesi, is friendly and peaceful and might suit solo women.

Sezgin Hotel *(☎/fax 514 4225; W hotelsezgin.freeyellow.com; Aslanlar Caddesi 68; doubles with shower US$13, with air-con US$17)* offers a swimming pool and garden.

Kuşadası is fish and chips and 'full English breakfast' country. For something more Turkish, cut into the Kaleiçi district behind the harbour and try **Avlu** *(Cephane Sokak; meals US$3)*, with indoor and outdoor tables and tasty soups and stews.

Kuşadası's otogar is 1.5km southeast of the centre on the bypass at the southern end of Kahramanlar Caddesi. Direct buses depart for far-flung parts, or you can transfer at İzmir (US$2.50, every 30 minutes) or Söke. In summer there are frequent buses to Bodrum (US$4, two hours, 151km) and Denizli (for Pamukkale; US$6, three hours, 220km). For Selçuk (US$0.90, 30 minutes, 20km) pick up a minibus on Adnan Menderes Bulvarı.

In summer three boats daily sail to Samos (US$30 one way). In winter there may be only one or two boats a week.

PAMUKKALE

☎ 258

Way inland east of Selçuk, Pamukkale is renowned for the brilliant white ledges with pools (travertines) that flow over the plateau edge. Sadly, in recent years the water supply has dried up and you can only swim in odd corners here and there. But behind this natural wonder lie the extensive ruins of a Roman Hierapolis, an ancient spa town.

Travertines & Hierapolis Ruins

Climbing the hill above Pamukkale village, you pay to enter the **travertines and Hierapolis** *(admission US$3; open ticket valid from 9am-9am next day)*. The Hierapolis ruins, including a theatre, colonnaded street with public toilet and vast necropolis, are very spread out; at least half a day will do them justice.

Afterwards, swim amid sunken Roman columns at **Pamukkale Termal** *(US$3)*, on top of the ridge, and visit **Hierapolis Archaeology Museum** *(admission US$0.75; open 9am-noon & 1pm-5pm Tues-Sun)*, which contains some spectacular sarcophagi and friezes from Hierapolis and nearby Afrodisias.

Places to Stay & Eat

Over 60 pensions and hotels lurk below the travertines in Pamukkale village. For cheerful service and decent rooms, good bargains are **Kervansaray Pension** *(☎ 272 2209; e kervansaray2@superonline.com; singles/doubles with shower US$12/18)* and the nearby **Aspawa** *(☎ 272 2094; e aspawa@mail.koc.net.tr; singles/doubles US$8/12)*. Breakfast is included at both places. **Weisse Burg Pension** *(☎ 272 2064; singles/doubles US$6/12)* is recommended by readers. An excellent breakfast costs US$2, dinners are US$5.

Meltem Motel *(☎ 272 2413; e meltemmotel@superonline.com; dorm beds US$4, singles/doubles US$5/8)* is big and popular with backpackers. Guests can enjoy the pool and rooftop terrace.

Eating in your pension or hotel is usually the best idea. Of Pamukkale's restaurants, **Gürsoy** *(meals US$4-6)*, opposite the Yörük Motel, has the nicest terrace, but **Han** *(meals US$4-6)*, around the corner, offers best value for money.

Getting There & Away

Frequent buses run from İzmir to Denizli (US$4, four hours, 260km). There are also regular buses from Denizli to Konya (US$10, seven hours, 440km). Municipal buses and dolmuşes make the half-hour trip between Denizli and Pamukkale every 30 minutes or so (US$0.50).

BODRUM

☎ 252 • pop 30,000

Bodrum (formerly Halicarnassus) is the site of the Mausoleum, the monumental tomb of King Mausolus and another of the Seven Wonders of the Ancient World. By some miracle Bodrum has managed to avoid the urban sprawl that has so damaged Kuşadası and Marmaris. In spring and autumn it's still a delightful place to stay.

The otogar is 500m inland along Cevat Sakir Caddesi from the Adliye Camii, a small mosque that marks the town centre. The PTT as well as several banks are on Cevat Sakir. The **tourist office** *(☎ 316 1091)* is beside the Castle of St Peter.

Things to See

There's little left of the **Mausoleum** *(admission US$2; open 8am-noon & 12.30pm-5pm Tues-Sun)*, although the **Castle of St Peter**, built in 1402 and rebuilt in 1522 by the Crusaders using stones from the tomb, makes up for its shortcomings. The castle houses the **Museum of Underwater Archaeology** *(admission US$7; open 8am-noon & 1pm-5pm Tues-Sun)*, containing finds from the oldest Mediterranean shipwreck ever discovered and a model of a Carian princess' tomb.

West past the marina and over the hill, the beach at Gümbet is solid package-holiday territory. You may prefer less-developed **Ortakent**. **Gümüşlük**, to the west of the Bodrum peninsula, is the least spoilt of the many smaller villages nearby. Hourly dolmuşes (US$1) run there.

Places to Stay

The narrow streets north of Bodrum's western harbour have pleasant family-run pensions, generally charging around US$18 to US$25 for a double in high season. Those behind the western bay tend to be quieter than those on the eastern bay because they're further from the famously noisy Halikarnas Disco. Few places stay open in winter.

Two quiet, modern places are tucked away down a narrow alley that begins between Neyzen Tevfik 84 and 86: **Yenilmez** *(☎ 316 2520; Menekşe Çıkmazı 30; doubles with shower US$18)* and **Menekşe** *(☎ 316 5890; Menekşe Çıkmazı 34; doubles with shower US$18)*. **Emiko Pension** *(☎/fax 316 5560; Atatürk Caddesi, Uslu Sokak 11; beds with shower US$5)* is spotless and quiet. You can practice your Japanese with the owner.

Türkkuyusu Sokak starts just north of the Adliye Camii and cuts up past several good, cheap pensions with shaded courtyards. **Şenlik Pansiyon** *(☎ 316 6382; Türkkuyusu Sokak 115; beds with showers from US$6)*, right on the street, could do with new mattresses but stays open late. **Sedan** *(☎ 316 0355; Türkkuyusu Sokak 121; doubles US$16, with shower US$24)*, just behind it, is a family-run place with some newer rooms.

Places to Eat

The small streets east of the Adliye Camii harbour several cheap eateries where you can grab a döner kebap for less than US$2 at a streetside buffet. Otherwise, continue eastward to Kilise Meydanı, a plaza filled with open-air restaurants. At either **Nazilli** or **Karadeniz** a pide topped with meat or cheese should cost only US$3. **Vida** *(meals US$5)*, just round from Karadeniz, does an excellent tomato soup for US$0.75.

In warm weather, check out Meyhaneler Sokak (Taverna St), off İskele Caddesi. Wall-to-wall tavernas serve food, drink and live music to appreciative crowds for US$10 to US$15; **İbo** seems particularly good and offers mezes such as stuffed vine leaves and octopus salad.

Getting There & Away

There are frequent bus services from Bodrum to Antalya (US$10, 11 hours, 640km), Fethiye (US$6, 4½ hours, 265km), İzmir (US$10, four hours, 250km), Kuşadası and Selçuk (US$4, three hours) and Marmaris (US$5, three hours, 165km).

In summer daily hydrofoils and boats link Bodrum with Kos (from US$14 one way, US$18 day return); in winter services shrink to three times weekly. In summer there are also boats to Datça, Knidos, Marmaris and Rhodes; check with the ferry offices near the castle.

The Mediterranean Coast

Turkey's Mediterranean coastline winds eastward for more than 1200km from Marmaris to Antakya near the Syrian border. From Marmaris to Fethiye the gorgeous 'Turquoise Coast' is perfect for boat excursions, with many secluded coves for swimming. The rugged peninsula east of Fethiye to Antalya and the Taurus Mountains east of Antalya are wild and beautiful. Further east you pass through fewer resorts and more workaday cities. The entire coast is liberally sprinkled with impressive ruins.

MARMARİS

☎ 252 • pop 22,700

Like Bodrum, Marmaris sits on a beautiful bay at the edge of a hilly peninsula. Unlike Bodrum, however, Marmaris has succumbed to unplanned, haphazard development, which has robbed it of much of its charm – although you may still want to drop by to sample the nightlife and to hop a boat to Rhodes.

TURKEY

İskele Meydanı (the main square) and the **tourist office** *(☎ 412 1035)* are by the ferry pier northeast of the castle. The **PTT** *(Fevzipaşa Caddesi)* is in the bazaar, which is mostly a pedestrian precinct. Haci Mustafa Sokak, also known as Bar St, runs inland from the bazaar; action here keeps going until the early hours. The otogar is 2km north of town, off the road to Bodrum.

Boat Excursions

Wooden boats along the waterfront offer tours of outlying beaches and islands. Before picking your boat, check carefully what the excursion costs, where it goes, whether lunch is included and, if so, what's on the menu. A day's outing usually costs around US$16 to US$20 per person.

The most popular excursions are to **Dalyan** and **Kaunos** or to the bays around Marmaris, but you can also take longer, more serious boat trips to Datça and the ruins at Knidos. It's also worth asking about boats heading for **Cleopatra's Island**, which offers silky-soft sand and water as warm as a Jacuzzi.

Places to Stay & Eat

Unlike Kuşadası and Bodrum, Marmaris lacks a network of small, welcoming pensions. Almost all the cheaper places have been squeezed out by the relentless growth of hotels for package holiday-makers. The cheapies that remain are fairly central but are often noisy and uninspiring. There are several moderately priced hotels a short walk from İskele Meydanı.

The **Interyouth Hostel** *(☎/fax 412 7823; Tepe Mahallesi, 42 Sokak 45)* is deep in the bazaar. In season it's a good travellers' hangout with lots of services and atmosphere. Out of season, it charges more for grim rooms without shower than some of the cheaper hotels.

Otherwise, to find the cheapest accommodation stroll along the waterfront to Abdi İpekçi Park and turn inland just past the park, then left at the first street and right into 64 Sokak. **Maltepe Pension** *(☎ 412 1629; rooms with shower US$20)*, across a wooden footbridge, is serviceable. **Özcan Pension** *(☎ 412 7761; Çam Sokak 3)*, next door, is bigger but similarly priced. **Hotel Aylin** *(☎ 412 8283; 1 Sokak 4; singles/doubles with shower from US$5/9)* offers reasonably comfortable rooms even at times of year when most places close.

Marmaris has literally hundreds of restaurants. For the cheapest fare, head towards the PTT in the bazaar. Just inland are several good, cheap restaurants including **Sofra** *(36. Sokak 23; meals US$3.50)* and **Liman Restaurant** *(40. Sokak 32; meals US$5)*. Both places heave with happy diners at lunchtime.

Cut inland from the Atatürk statue along Ulusal Egemenlik Bulvarı and turn right opposite the Tansaş shopping centre to find **Kırçiçeği Pide-Pizza Çorba ve Kebap Salonu** *(Yeni Yol Caddesi 15; meals US$3)*, which is always crowded with locals tucking into soups and filling pides.

Getting There & Away

Marmaris' otogar has frequent buses and minibuses to Antalya (US$9.50, seven hours, 590km), Bodrum (US$4, three hours, 165km), Dalyan (via Ortaca; US$2, two hours), Datça (US$3, 1¾ hours, 75km) and Fethiye (US$4, three hours, 170km). Car ferries run to Rhodes daily in summer and less frequently in winter. They cost US$32 one way and US$50 return.

DATÇA

☎ 0252 • pop 6100

Marmaris not your scene? Then take a spectacular bus ride west to Datça, a smaller, quieter reminder of what Marmaris might have been in its heyday. In summer, take boat trips to Knidos or the Greek islands of Rhodes and Symi. For the utmost in tranquillity, visit Old Datça, a picturesque hamlet of cobbled streets and old stone houses on the eastern outskirts.

Chill out in the clean, comfortable rooms of **Tuna Pansiyon** *(☎ 712 3931; İskele Caddesi; singles/doubles with shower US$10/13)*; some sport sea-facing balconies. **Huzur Pansiyon** *(☎ 712 3364; Yat Liman Mevii; singles/doubles with shower US$13/20)* is similar but much closer to the harbour with its bars and restaurants.

Regular buses shuttle between Marmaris and Datça (US$3, 1¾ hours). Minibuses from Datça to Karaköy pass the junction to Old Datça regularly (US$0.30).

KÖYCEĞİZ

☎ 252 • pop 7,600

In early spring Köyceğiz smells sweetly of orange blossom, a reminder that this quiet town on the edge of a placid lake still has a farming life beyond tourism. It makes a pleasant alternative to Dalyan if you want to visit Kaunos, wallow in the mud baths and laze on İztuzu beach.

Tango Pansiyon *(☎ 262 2501; W www.tangopension.com; Alihsan Kalmaz Caddesi; dorm beds US$5, singles/doubles with shower US$10/12)* has clean, pleasant rooms and activities ranging from moonlight cruises to short treks. The same people run **Samba Pension**.

Hotel Kaunos *(☎ 262 4288; singles/doubles with shower US$5/10)* has a decent waterfront location but rather faded rooms. **Hotel Alila** *(☎/fax 262 1150; Emeksiz Caddesi; singles/doubles with shower US$14/24)* is newer and altogether more cheerful, with a fine pool and an inviting dining room.

Çiçek Restaurant *(meals US$5)*, on the main square, is good for people-watching while you eat standard fare, but **Colıba** *(Emeksiz Caddesi; meals US$5)* has more flair in its menu and decor alike.

Hourly dolmuşes to Köyceğiz run from Ortaca (US$0.75, 25 minutes, 20km) and Muğla (US$1.50, one hour, 57km).

DALYAN

☎ 252

Set on the banks of a placid river and backed by a cliff face cut with elegant Lycian tombs, Dalyan was always too good to remain undiscovered by the tour operators, and some people feel it is now a bit too touristy. Still, **İztuzu beach**, a short boat hop along the river, is a gorgeous place to sun yourself (as well as being one of the few remaining nesting grounds of the *carretta carretta* (sea turtle). The same boat trips (US$5.50) usually take in a visit to the ruined city of **Kaunos** *(admission US$2; open 8.30am-5.30pm daily)* and the **Sultaniye hot springs** *(admission US$0.75)* on the shores of Köyceğiz Lake.

Dalyan Camping *(camp sites US$4)* is 500m southwest of the dolmuş stand. There's a cluster of places in Yalı Sokak, northwest of Maraş Caddesi past the school. **Hotel Caria** *(☎ 284 2075; doubles with shower US$20)* has comfortable rooms with balconies and a gorgeous, river-facing roof terrace. **Hotel Dönmez** *(☎ 284 2107; doubles with shower US$17)*, nearby, has a swimming pool.

Most Dalyan restaurants serve a predictable menu of mezes, kebaps and fish, but **Metin Pide & Pizza Restaurant** *(Sulungur Sokak; meals US$2)* rustles up excellent Italian-style pizzas.

From Marmaris, take a bus to Ortaca and change for a minibus to Dalyan (US$0.50, 30 minutes).

TURKEY

FETHİYE

☎ 252 • pop 48,200

Despite its picture-postcard harbour backdrop, Fethiye still has much more of the feel of a living town than big resorts like Kuşadası and Marmaris. It can be very hot and crowded in summer but is still worth a visit and makes a good base for visiting the beautiful **Saklıkent Gorge** and the ruins at **Tlos** and **Pınara**. The hotel-backed beach at **Calış**, 5km northeast of the centre, is many kilometres long.

Fethiye's otogar is 2km east of the centre. Karagözler dolmuşes ply the main street, taking you past government buildings (and PTT) and several banks, before skirting the bazaar district, curving round the bay past the **tourist office** *(☎/fax 614 1527)*, and cutting up by the marina on the western side of the town.

Things to See & Do

Of ancient Telmessos, little more remains than the ruins of a theatre and several Lycian sarcophagi dating from about 400 BC. The picturesque rock-cut **Tomb of Amyntas** *(admission US$2; open 8am-7pm)* makes a perfect vantage point for watching the sun set over the harbour.

Most people succumb to, and enjoy, the **12 Island boat tour**, which mixes swimming, cruising and sightseeing; prices start at around US$8 per person. Don't miss the **hammam** *(open 7am-midnight)* in the bazaar either. Dolmuşes run to the nearby evocative Ottoman Greek 'ghost town' of **Kaya Köy** *(admission US$2)*, abandoned after the population exchange of 1923.

Places to Stay & Eat

İdeal Pension *(☎ 614 1981; Zafer Caddesi 1; singles/doubles with shower US$5/10)*, one street back from the harbour road, has superb views from its terrace and a full range of backpacker services: laundry, Internet access, book exchange etc.

Ferah Pension *(Monica's Place; ☎ 614 2816; 2 Karagözler Mahallesi, Ordu Caddesi 2; dorm beds US$5, doubles US$10, with shower US$12)* has nicer rooms but is a little further from the centre; dinners are said to be impressive. Breakfast is US$2 extra. **Cennet Pansiyon** *(☎ 614 2230; 2 Karagözler Mahallesi; doubles with shower US$7)* has a pleasant waterside location. An on-site restaurant makes up for the rather remote position. Most of the nicer pensions are uphill from the yacht marina along Fevzi Çakmak Caddesi; take a Karagözler dolmuş along the harbour road to reach them.

Side by side on Tütün Sokak are two local favourites – **Sedir Restaurant** and **Şamdan Restaurant**. Both serve excellent pizza for around US$3.50. In Eski Cami Geçidi Likya Sokak look out for the popular **Meğri** *(meals US$5)* with a wide range of piping hot meals. Right opposite the post office, **Birlik Lokantası** *(Atatürk Caddesi; meals US$4)* serves up big portions of İskender kebap. Near the hammam, **Café Oley** *(Eski Meğri Sokak 4; meals US$5)* offers such unexpected delights as smoked salmon sandwiches if you're kebaped out.

Getting There & Away

If you're heading for Antalya, note that the *yayla* (inland) route is shorter and cheaper (US$6) than the *sahil* (coastal) route (US$8). The coastal route also serves Patara, Kınık (for Xanthos; US$2) and Kaş (US$3). Minibuses to local destinations leave from behind the big white Yeni Cami in the town centre.

A summer hydrofoil service links Rhodes (Greece) and Fethiye on Tuesday and Thursday (US$50, one way).

ÖLÜDENİZ

☎ 252

Over the mountains to the south of Fethiye, lovely **Ölüdeniz** (Dead Sea) has proved a bit too beautiful for its own good and now has far too many hotels catering for the package-holiday market backed up behind the sands. Still, the **lagoon** *(admission US$0.50; open 8am-8pm)* remains tranquillity incarnate and along its banks you'll find moderately priced bungalows and camping areas.

A popular budget choice is **Ölüdeniz Camping** *(☎ 617 0048; treehouse beds US$1.75, tents US$3, bungalows from US$8)*. There are several similar camping grounds further around the lagoon, near the Hotel Meri. When it comes to eating, you may feel disinclined to venture further than the cafés attached to the camping grounds.

Frequent dolmuşes to Ölüdeniz (US$1, 30 minutes, 17km) run from behind Fethiye's Yeni Cami.

PATARA

☎ 0242

Patara's main claim to fame is its superb 20km-long beach, one of Turkey's best. A secondary attraction are the extensive **ruins** *(admission US$7; open 7.30am-7pm daily May-Oct, 8am-5.30pm Nov-Mar)*. Nearby are two Unesco World Heritage Sites: the **Letoön** *(admission US$2)*, with excellent mosaics and a sacred pool, and impressive **Xanthos** *(admission US$2)*, which boasts a Roman theatre and Lycian pillar tombs.

Most places to stay and eat are in Gelemiş village, 1.5km inland from the beach. The following offer beds for US$7. **Flower Pension** *(☎ 843 5164)* is one of the furthest inland but has a particularly welcoming host. **St Nicholas Pension** *(☎ 843 5024)* is a bit more central and offers services such as a terrace restaurant and canoe hire. **Golden Pension** *(☎ 843 5162)*, opposite, also boasts a restaurant.

Midibuses plying the Fethiye-Antalya main road will drop you 2km from Gelemiş (3.5km from the beach, signposted 'Patara').

KAŞ

☎ 242 • pop 8,000

Kaş is another of those places which seems to have everything: a picturesque quayside, pleasant restaurants, excellent shops, a scattering of Lycian tombs and a big Sunday market. Even the **tourist office** *(☎ 836 1238)*, on the main square, is better informed than most. Midibuses connect Kaş with places nearby.

Apart from enjoying the town's ambience and few small pebble beaches, you can also walk west a few hundred metres to the well-preserved **theatre**. Lycian **sarcophagi** are dotted about the streets, and tombs cut into the cliffs above the town.

The most-popular boat trip sails round **Kekova island** and out to beautiful **Kaleköy** (Simena), passing over Lycian ruins beneath the sea. You'll pay around US$10 per person in a glass-bottomed boat. Other excursions take in Patara, Xanthos and the wonderful 18km **Saklıkent Gorge**, where you can eat trout on platforms over an ice-cold river.

Places to Stay & Eat

Kaş Camping *(☎ 836 1050; camp sites US$5)* is in an olive grove just west of town.

Kaş' quietest places to stay are all on the western side of town and rise in price (and quality) the nearer they are to the sea. Yenicami Caddesi, just south of the otogar, has lots of small, family-run pensions, such as **Orion Hotel** *(☎/fax 836 1286)*; **Anıl Motel** *(☎ 836 1791)*; **Hilal** *(☎ 836 1207)*; and **Santosa**

(☎ *836 1714)*. In high season a bed with shower costs US$10, including breakfast.

Hotel Korsan Karakedi *(☎ 836 1887; Yeni Cami Sokak 7; singles/doubles with shower US$10/23)*, up the hill, offers a warm welcome to compensate for lumpy bedding.

Ateş Pension *(☎ 836 1393; e atespension@superonline.com; doubles with shower US$10)*, one more street back, rambles across two buildings but has a good rooftop terrace.

Corner Café, near the PTT on İbrahim Serin Caddesi, serves juices or vegetable omelettes for US$1 and yogurt with fruit and honey for US$1.75. **Café Merhaba**, across the street, is good for cakes, coffee and newspapers.

Sympathy Restaurant *(☎ 836 2418, Uzunçarşı Gürsöy Sokak 11; meals about US$8)* offers excellent cooking, including a fine spread of mezes, in a cosy atmosphere. For cheaper eats, cut up Atatürk Bulvarı and try **2000 Restaurant** or **Kervan Restaurant**, both busiest at lunchtime.

OLYMPOS & ÇIRALI

☎ 0242

Further east, after climbing into the mountains, the switchback coast road reaches a turn-off for Olympos. From here it's about 8km down a winding unpaved road to the village and a further 3.5km along an ever-worsening road to **ancient Olympos** *(admission US$7)*, a wild, abandoned place where ruins peek out from forest copses, rock outcrops and riverbanks. You have to pay the admission fee here to reach the beach, although your ticket should be valid for a week. Most come here to stay in the treehouses lining the road from the beach. If that's not your thing, there are normal pensions and hotels at neighbouring Çıralı.

TURKEY

According to legend, the nearby **Chimaera** (Yanartaş), a natural eternal flame, was the hot breath of a subterranean monster. Easily sighted by mariners in ancient times, it is now a mere glimmer of its former fiery self but no less exotic. To find the Chimaera, follow the signs 3km east down a neighbouring valley. A half-hour climb leads to the flames.

Places To Stay & Eat

Lining the road to the ruins are assorted treehouse-cabin-bar complexes where prices of around US$5 per person in a treehouse or US$7 in a cabin include breakfast and dinner.

Kadir's *(☎ 892 1250)*, the grandaddy of them all and still the most visually inviting, offers rustic, ramshackle charm with Internet connections, but is furthest from the beach.

Bayram's *(☎ 892 1243; w www.bayrams.com)* doesn't look quite so pretty but is the sort of place where you arrive for a day and find yourself staying a week.

A separate turn from the Fethiye-Antalya highway, less than 1km east of the Olympos one, leads to the more conventional pensions and hotels at Çıralı. You can also get there by walking 1km along the beach from Olympos. **Sima Peace Pension** *(☎ 825 7245; singles/doubles with shower US$10/15)* is a pleasing group of wooden chalets set round a garden.

For some good eatin' in Olympos, **Türkmen** *(☎ 892 1249)* is popular with holidaying Turkish families, while both **Orange** *(☎ 892 1242)* and **Şaban** *(☎ 892 1265)* get rave reviews.

Getting There & Away

Buses and midibuses playing the Fethiye-Antalya road will drop you at the Olympos or Çıralı turn-offs. In summer dolmuşes wait to run you down to Olympos (US$0.50); if you don't want to walk the 7km to Çıralı you may need to ring a pension to collect you or take a taxi.

The nicest way to get between Olympos and Fethiye is on a three- or four-day 'blue cruise' on a *gûlet* (wooden yacht), calling in at bays along the way. Prices for three-day cruises start from around US$100.

ANTALYA

☎ 242 • pop 509,000

A bustling, modern town of around half a million people, Antalya has more than just its lovely harbour setting. As a result, it avoids that soullessness that comes over resorts that live only for tourism. It's fun to kick around in Kaleiçi, the old restored Ottoman town that spreads back from a beautiful marina and the sea-facing Karaalioğlu Parkı. Pebbly Konyaaltı beach spreads out to the west of town, sandy Lara beach to the east. Both are solidly backed with package-holiday hotels – you'd do best to wait until Olympos for a swim.

Orientation & Information

The otogar is 4km north of the centre on the D650 highway to Burdur. The city centre is at Kalekapısı, a major intersection marked by a landmark clock tower.

The **tourist office** *(☎/fax 241 1747; Cumhuriyet Caddesi 91)* is located 600m west of Kalekapısı in the Özel İdare Çarşısı building. The PTT is around the corner in Güllük Caddesi. The **Owl Bookshop** *(☎ 243 5718; Akarçeşme Sokak 21)* sells second-hand books.

Things to See

Antalya Museum *(Cumhuriyet Caddesi; tram: Müze; admission US$7; open 9am-6pm Tues-Sun)* houses spectacular finds from nearby Perge, Aspendos and Side as well as a wonderful ethnographical collection. Get there on the *tramvay* (tram; US$0.30) from Kalekapısı.

To get into **Kaleiçi**, head south down the hill from the clock tower. You'll pass the **Yivli Minare** (Grooved Minaret), which rises above an old mosque. Further into Kaleiçi the **Kesik Minare** (Truncated Minaret) is built on the site of a ruined Roman temple. Just off Atatürk Caddesi, the monumental **Hadriyanüs Kapısı** (Hadrian's Gate) was built for the Roman emperor's visit in AD 130. The **Suna & İnan Kıraç Kaleiçi Museum** *(☎ 243 4274; Kocatepe Sokak; admission US$0.75; open 9am-noon & 1pm-6pm Thur-Tues Oct-May, 9am-noon & 2pm-7.30pm June-Sept)* houses a fine collection of pottery together with rooms set up to show important events in Ottoman family life.

Places to Stay

Kaleiçi is full of pensions, and more seem to open (and close) every year.

Pansiyon White Garden *(☎ 241 9115; Hesapçı Geçidi 9; doubles with shower US$15, with air con US$18)* is a spotless family-run place with a pleasant courtyard bar/restaurant.

Senem Family Pension *(☎ 247 1752; Zeytingeçidi Sokak 9; singles/doubles with shower & air con US$15-18)*, near the Hıdırlık Kulesi, offers clean, simple rooms and an inviting roof terrace.

Sabah Pension *(☎ 247 5345, Hesapçı Sokak 60/A; singles/doubles with shower US$10/16)*, a popular backpacker's place, offers tours, car hire and decent evening meals.

Hadrianüs Pansiyon *(☎ 244 0030; Zeytin Sokak 4/A-B; singles/doubles with shower US$10/20)* is a series of old, mostly unrestored buildings around a large walled garden.

Antique Pension *(☎ 242 4615; ⓔ antique@ixir.com; Paşa Camii Sokak 28; singles/doubles with shower US$10/17)* is equally as old but has had the necessary makeover.

Places to Eat

Eski Sebzeciler İçi Sokak, an alley close to the junction of Cumhuriyet and Atatürk Caddesis, is lined with open-air restaurants, where a *tandır kebap* (mutton cooked in earthenware), salad and drink can cost as little as US$4.

At **Parlak Restaurant** *(meals US$5-10)*, a block up Kazım Özalp/Sarampol Caddesi on the left, skewered chicken and lamb kebaps sizzle in the courtyard as patrons down rakı and beer.

Mermerli Restaurant *(meals US$7-10)* is perched above the eastern end of the harbour and can't be beaten for its sunset views over the bay. Prices are lower than at most harbour restaurants.

Gül Restaurant & Cafe *(Kocatepe Sokak 1; meals US$5-10; closed Sunday lunch)* is a cosy place offering a plate of appetisers big enough for three for US$2.50.

Getting There & Away

From the otogar, buses head for Alanya (US$3, 2½ hours, 115km), Göreme (US$12, 10 hours, 485km), Konya (US$12, six hours, 349km), Olympos (US$2, 1½ hours, 79km) and to Manavgat/Side (US$2, 1¾ hours, 65km).

SİDE

☎ 242 • pop 18,000

Because of its fine sandy beaches, Side, 4km south of Manavgat, has been overrun by tourists and is now a tawdry, overcrowded caricature of its former self. Impressive ancient structures include a Roman bath, the old city walls, a huge amphitheatre, and seaside temples to Apollo and Athena. The village is packed with pensions and hotels.

Frequent minibuses connect Side with Manavgat otogar (US$0.30) where there are onward buses to Antalya (US$2, 1¾ hours, 65km) and Alanya (US$2, one hour, 63km).

ALANYA

☎ 242 • pop 110,100

Alanya is as close as Turkey gets to a no-go zone for independent travellers. Most hotels are firmly closed in winter and block-booked to package-holiday companies in summer. The one reason to visit is to take in the ruins of a magnificent **Seljuk castle** *(admission US$10; open 8am-7pm daily)* perched high on a hill above town. It's also worth visiting the **Kızıl Kule** *(Red Tower; admission US$2;*

open 8am-noon & 1.30pm-5.30pm Tues-Sun), down by the harbour which was also built in 1226.

There are frequent buses to Alanya from Antalya (US$3, 2¾ hours) and Manavgat (US$2, one hour). The otogar is 3km west of the centre; to get there take a bus from the road leading to the sea (US$0.20), outside the otogar, and get off by the Küyülarönü Camii.

Central Anatolia

İstanbul may be exotic and intriguing, the coasts pretty and relaxing, but the Anatolian plateau is Turkey's true heartland.

ANKARA

☎ 312 • pop 4 million

Despite being the capital of Turkey, Ankara is far from thrilling. Nevertheless, due to its central location, there's a good chance you'll at least pass through. If so, see its fine museum.

Ankara's *hisar* (citadel) crowns a hill 1km east of Ulus Meydanı (Ulus Square), the heart of Old Ankara, which has several medium-priced hotels. Nearby Opera Meydanı (Opera Square) has lots of cheap hotels. Modern Ankara lies further south, around Kızılay Meydanı (Kızılay Square) and Kavaklıdere.

Atatürk Bulvarı is the city's main north–south axis. Ankara's mammoth otogar is 6.5km southwest of Ulus Meydanı and 6km west of Kızılay Meydanı. The Havaş bus terminal is next to Ankara Garı (train station), 1.4km southwest of Ulus Meydanı.

The **tourist office** *(☎/fax 231 5572; Gazi Mustafa Kemal Bulvarı 121)* is opposite Maltepe Ankaray station. The **main post office** *(Atatürk Bulvarı)* is just south of Ulus Meydanı, although there's a handy branch beside Ankara Garı. There are branches of the main banks with ATMs in Ulus.

Things to See

The **Anatolian Civilisations Museum** *(Anadolu Medeniyetleri Müzesi; ☎ 329 3160; Hisarparkı Caddesi; admission US$5.50 Tues-Sun, US$8 Mon; open 8.30am-5pm daily)* is Ankara's most worthwhile attraction. With the world's richest collection of Hittite artefacts, it's an essential supplement to visiting central Turkey's Hittite sites. The Phyrgian collection is equally spectacular. It's uphill from Ulus Meydanı, next to the citadel.

North of Ulus Meydanı, on the eastern side of Çankırı Caddesi (the continuation of Atatürk Bulvarı), are some Roman ruins including the **Column of Julian**, erected in AD 363 and the **Temple of Augustus & Rome**. On the western side of Çankırı Caddesi are remains of the **Roman Baths** *(admission US$0.75; open 8.30am-noon & 1pm-5pm)*.

The **Anıt Kabir** *(Mausoleum of Atatürk; admission free; open 9am-5pm daily)*, 2km west of Kızılay Meydanı, is the monumental tomb of modern Turkey's founder.

Places to Stay

Ulus has numerous budget hotels. Along the eastern side of Opera Meydanı, on the corner of Sanayı Caddesi and Tavus Sokak, are a row of small, cheap hotels.

Otel Mithat *(☎ 311 5410; Tavus Sokak 2; singles/doubles with shower US$9/14)* is probably most comfortable, despite its minimalist decor. Breakfast costs US$1.50 extra.

Ferah Oteli *(☎ 309 1174; Denizciler Caddesi 58; singles/doubles with shower US$6/12)*, one street back, is a quieter choice. Some of the back rooms have fine city views.

Hotel Spor *(☎ 324 2165; Rüzgarlı Plevne Sokak 6; singles/doubles with shower US$18/25)*, north of Ulus, is spotless and welcoming, and it's a good choice for women travelling in the area.

Places to Eat

Kebabistan *(Atatürk Bulvarı 3; meals US$3-5)*, at the southeastern corner of Ulus above the courtyard of a block of offices and shops, offers a full range of kebap lunches and dinners. **Akman Boza ve Pasta Salonu**, underneath, does the dessert and coffee afterwards.

Uğrak Lokantası *(Çankırı Caddesi, Ulus; meals US$4-5)* has a mouth-watering array of desserts such as stuffed quince (US$1) to round off a tasty soup-and-stew meal.

For more choice, head straight for Kızılay to find lots of stalls selling delicious food such as stuffed baked potatoes. **Kösk** *(Tuna Caddesi, İnkılap Sokak 2; meals US$4-5)* offers excellent İskender kebap (US$3) and *İnegöl köfte* (meatballs, US$2.50) in bright, cheerful surroundings.

Zenger Paşa Konağı *(☎ 311 7070; Doyran Sokak 13; meals US$6-12)*, an old house in the citadel with wonderful ethnographic displays, is a memorable place for a very reasonably priced dinner.

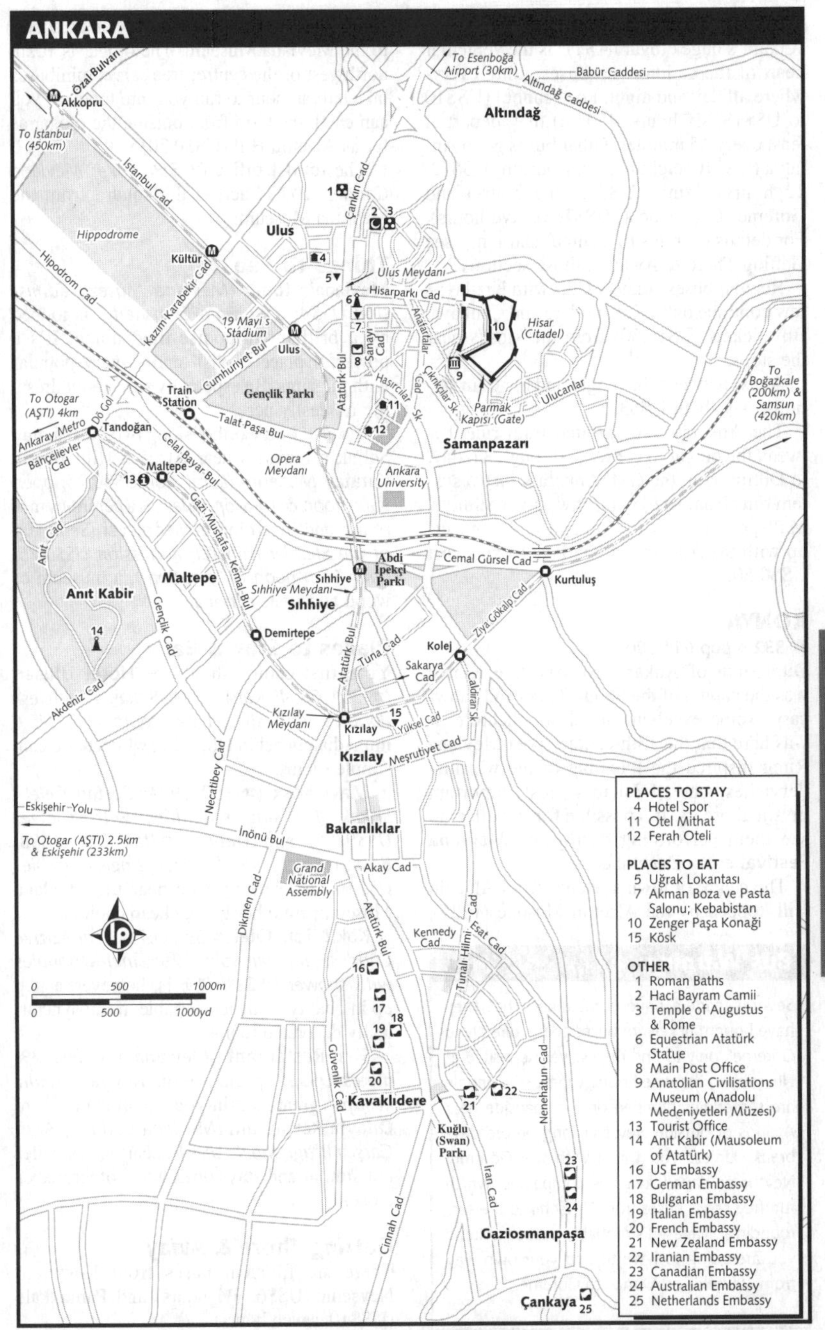
ANKARA
To Esenboğa Airport (30km)
Babür Caddesi
Altındağ Caddesi
Altındağ
Özal Bulvarı
Akkopru
To İstanbul (450km)
İstanbul Cad
Çankırı Cad
Hippodrome
Ulus
Kültür
Hipodrom Cad
Kazım Karabekir Cad
Ulus Meydanı
Hisarparkı Cad
19 Mayıs Stadium
Ulus
Cumhuriyet Bul
Sanayi Cad
Anafartalar Cad
Çıkrıkçılar Sk
Hisar (Citadel)
Hasırcılar Sk
Atatürk Bul
Gençlik Parkı
Train Station
To Otogar (AŞTİ) 4km
Dö Gol
Ankaray Metro
Tandoğan
Talat Paşa Bul
Parmak Kapısı (Gate)
Ulucanlar
To Boğazkale (200km) & Samsun (420km)
Samanpazarı
Bahçelievler Cad
Celal Bayar Bul
Maltepe
Opera Meydanı
Ankara University
Gazi Mustafa Kemal Bul
Anıt Cad
Abdi İpekçi Parkı
Cemal Gürsel Cad
Kurtuluş
Maltepe
Sıhhiye
Sıhhiye Meydanı
Sıhhiye
Anıt Kabir
Gençlik Cad
Demirtepe
Ziya Gökalp Cad
Tuna Cad
Kolej
Sakarya Cad
Akdeniz Cad
Kızılay Meydanı
Kızılay
Yüksel Cad
Çaldıran Sk
Kızılay
Meşrutiyet Cad
Necatibey Cad
Eskişehir Yolu
İnönü Bul
Bakanlıklar
To Otogar (AŞTİ) 2.5km & Eskişehir (233km)
Grand National Assembly
Akay Cad
Dikmen Cad
Atatürk Bul
Kennedy Cad
Tunalı Hilmi Cad
Esat Cad
0 500 1000m
0 500 1000yd
Güvenlik Cad
Kavaklıdere
Kuğlu (Swan) Parkı
Nenehatun Cad
İran Cad
Cinnah Cad
Gaziosmanpaşa
Çankaya
PLACES TO STAY
4 Hotel Spor
11 Otel Mithat
12 Ferah Oteli
PLACES TO EAT
5 Uğrak Lokantası
7 Akman Boza ve Pasta Salonu; Kebabistan
10 Zenger Paşa Konaği
15 Kösk
OTHER
1 Roman Baths
2 Haci Bayram Camii
3 Temple of Augustus & Rome
6 Equestrian Atatürk Statue
8 Main Post Office
9 Anatolian Civilisations Museum (Anadolu Medeniyetleri Müzesi)
13 Tourist Office
14 Anıt Kabir (Mausoleum of Atatürk)
16 US Embassy
17 German Embassy
18 Bulgarian Embassy
19 Italian Embassy
20 French Embassy
21 New Zealand Embassy
22 Iranian Embassy
23 Canadian Embassy
24 Australian Embassy
25 Netherlands Embassy
TURKEY

Getting There & Around

Ankara's huge otogar (AŞTİ) is the vehicular heart of the nation, with buses going everywhere all day and night. For İstanbul (US$10 to US$18, six hours, 450km) they depart at least every 15 minutes. Other buses go to Antalya (US$10, eight hours), Bodrum (US$12, 12 hours), İzmir (US$9, nine hours) and Göreme (Cappadocia, US$7.50, five hours). For details of trains to İstanbul and İzmir see Getting There & Away in those sections.

Regular buses connect Ulus with Kızılay; a few continue on to Kavaklıdere and Çankaya. Buy tickets (US$0.50) from the kiosks near the stops.

A taxi between the otogar and the train station costs about US$3.

The Ankaray underground train runs between the otogar in the west, through Kızılay, to Dikimevi in the east. Ankara's metro system runs from Kızılay northwest via Sıhhiye, Maltepe and Ulus to Batıkent and connects up with the Ankaray at Kızılay. Tickets cost US$0.50.

KONYA

☎ 332 • pop 611,000

Due south of Ankara, conservative Konya was the capital of the Seljuk Turks and showcases some excellent Seljuk architecture. It was here that the 13th-century poet Mevlana Rumi inspired the founding of the whirling dervishes, one of Islam's most important mystical orders. It's possible for travellers to see them performing during the **Mevlana Festival** every December.

The centre of town stretches from Alaettin Hill, topped by the Alaettin Mosque (1221), along Alaettin Caddesi and Mevlana Caddesi to the Mevlana Museum. The otogar is 10km northwest of the centre; free *servis* minibuses take half an hour to run you into town, or you can catch the tram from outside the otogar as far as Alaettin Hill (US$0.30).

The **tourist office** *(☎ 351 1074; Mevlana Caddesi 21)* is across the square from the Mevlana Museum.

Bus Warning

Several readers have complained that they have bought tickets for buses going 'directly to Göreme', only to find themselves deposited at Nevşehir in the wee hours. Worse still, people are sometimes dumped on the roadside near Avanos or outside Nevşehir long before daybreak. Unless you travel with the Göreme, Nevtur or Kapadokya bus companies, which run free *servis* buses from Nevşehir to the surrounding villages, it's probably best to assume you are going to have to find your own way from Nevşehir or Avanos to Göreme.

Things to See

Mevlana's **tomb** *(Mevlana Müsezi; admission US$4; open 9am-5pm daily)* is topped by a brilliant turquoise-tiled dome. It's a powerful place to visit and is very popular with pilgrims. Be especially sure about dressing modestly here.

It's also well worth visiting two outstanding Seljuk seminaries near Alaettin Hill: **Büyük Karatay Museum** *(admission US$0.75; open 9am-noon & 1pm-5pm daily)*, a ceramics museum; and **İnceminare Medresesi** *(Seminary of the Slender Minaret; admission US$0.75; open 9am-noon & 1pm-5pm)*, a museum of wood and stone carving.

Places to Stay & Eat

Your first choice should be **Hotel Ulusan** *(☎ 351 5004; Kurşuncular Sokak 2; singles/doubles with shared bathroom US$6/12)*, immediately behind the PTT, which has clean, simple rooms.

Mavi Köşk *(☎ 350 1904; Bostan Çelebi Sokak 13; singles/doubles with shower US$9/11)* and **Derviş** *(☎/fax 351 1688; Bostan Çelebi Sokak 11/D; singles/doubles US$10/15)*, side by side near the Mevlana Museum, are other good, cheap choices.

Kök & Esra Otel *(☎ 352 0671; Yeni Aziziye Caddesi, Kadılar Sokak 28; singles/doubles with shower USS$10/15)* is, however, a step up in quality, with comfortable, if idiosyncratically decorated rooms.

Sifa Restaurant *(Mevlana Caddesi 29; meals US$6)* specialises in Konya's *tandir kebap*, a great melt-in-your-mouth lamb dish. **Dilayla Restaurant** *(Mevlana Caddesi, Altın Çarşışı Bitiği, meals US$4)*, nearby, is smaller but similar and stays open when other places close.

Getting There & Away

There are frequent buses from Konya to Nevşehir (US$6, 3½ hours) and Pamukkale (US$10, seven hours).

Cappadocia

Cappadocia, the region between Ankara and Malatya, and between Aksaray and Kayseri, is famous for its fantastic natural rock formations. Over the centuries people have carved houses, churches, fortresses, even complete underground cities, into the soft, eerily eroded volcanic stone. Attractions include the Göreme valleys; the pretty Ihlara Gorge with a stream flowing through it; and the huge underground cities at **Kaymaklı** and **Derinkuyu** *(admission US$7; open 8am-5pm daily)*.

INFORMATION

Ürgüp, Avanos and Uçhisar have plenty of hotels and pensions, but Göreme is most attractive to budget travellers. Good daily tours (around US$30) of local highlights, eg Ihlara Gorge are offered by **Ötuken Voyage** *(☎ 271 2757)*, **Neşe Tour** *(☎ 271 2525)* and **Zemi Tour** *(☎ 271 2576)* in Göreme. **Kirkit Voyage** *(☎ 511 3259; Avanos; W www.kirkit.com/)* and **Argeus** *(☎ 341 4688; Ürgüp; W www.argeus.com.tr)* are experienced, professional travel agencies with more varied programmes including horse riding and cycling tours.

GÖREME

☎ 0384 • pop 2000

The Göreme landscape is one of Turkey's most amazing sights. Over the centuries a thick layer of volcanic tufa has been eroded into fantastic, eerie shapes, dubbed 'fairy chimneys' by the locals. Into the chimneys early Christians carved chambers and vaults for use as churches, stables and homes.

Gape at medieval frescoes in the rock-hewn monastery, nunnery and cave churches of the **Göreme Open Air Museum** *(admission US$7, with Karanlık Kilisesi US$10; open 8am-5.30pm daily May-Oct, 8am-4.30pm Nov-Apr)*. Some date from the 8th century, although the best are from the 10th to 13th centuries. The churches are tiny, so try and visit when the adjacent bus parking is not looking too full. Don't miss the **Tokalı church**, across the road from the main entrance, which has some of the best frescoes.

Places to Stay

You can camp at the **Dilek** or **Berlin camping grounds** *(camp sites US$6)*, side by side amid wonderful rock formations on the road leading to the open-air museum.

Göreme has some of Turkey's best-value pensions, many offering the chance to try out the troglodyte lifestyle. In most, a dorm bed costs US$3.50, a bed in a room US$5 (with shower US$7).

Köse Pension *(☎ 271 2294; W www.kosepension.com)*, near the PTT, is a very popular choice, with a gorgeous swimming pool, a book exchange and good home-cooked food for vegetarians and meat-eaters alike.

Kelebek *(☎ 271 2531; W www.kelebekhotel.com)*, right up in the old village, boasts spectacular views, great food and a wide range of rooms, including a cave honeymoon suite complete with Jacuzzi (US$60). **Paradise** *(☎ 271 2248)*, tucked amid fairy chimneys just off the open-air museum road, is also popular with backpackers.

Flintstones *(☎ 271 2555)*, along the road leading to the Pigeon Valley, is quiet and secluded with a pleasant swimming pool.

Shoestring Cave Pension *(☎ 271 2450)* has simple cave rooms set round a pleasant courtyard. Its meals get good reports.

Tuna Caves *(☎ 271 2236)*, off the road leading up to the old village, are used by Fez Bus.

Ottoman House *(☎ 271 2616; doubles with shower US$15)* boasts of offering luxury at affordable prices in a modern building.

Places to Eat

Best of Göreme's restaurants is **Orient** *(meals from US$5)*, up the hill towards Uçhisar; the steaks (US$4) are especially well regarded. Also popular is **Local**, handily placed on the corner of the road leading up to the open-air museum and offering very tasty 'Ottoman' specials. Along the main road to Avanos, **Sedef** and **Sultan** offer a wide choice of mezes, while **Tardelli** majors in pizzas and pides. **Mercan** and **SOS** tend to have the lowest prices.

Getting There & Away

Although you can fly from İstanbul to Kayseri and then travel down to Göreme, most arrive on the overnight bus from İstanbul (US$15, 11 hours, 725km) or Antalya (US$13, 10 hours, 485km). Half-hourly dolmuşes connect Göreme with Nevşehir via Uçhisar (US$0.50). There are also buses to Avanos and Ürgüp.

ÜRGÜP

☎ 0384 • pop 13,500

Despite being a bigger town, Ürgüp still has plenty of appeal, with old sandstone buildings, cobbled streets and a stone hill shot through with rooms and passages. It also boasts Cappadocia's best wineries. The helpful **tourist office** *(☎/fax 341 4059; Kayseri Caddesi)* is downhill in the park.

Hotel Elvan *(☎ 341 4191; Dutlu Cami Mahallesi, Barbaros Hayrettin Sokak 11; doubles with shower US$15-25)* has homely rooms around a courtyard. **Asia Minor Hotel** *(☎ 341 4645; İstiklal Caddesi; doubles with shower US$40)* has stylish rooms and a pleasant garden. **Hitit Hotel** *(☎ 341 4481; İstiklal Caddesi)* is marginally cheaper, with an equally inviting garden but more mundane rooms.

Sömine Restaurant *(meals US$8-14)* is the town's most prominent eatery. It's right on the main square, with indoor and outdoor tables. Ürgüp-style kebaps baked on tiles are a speciality. **Ocakbaşı** *(meals US$15)*, beside the otogar, offers better food – especially grills and mezes – if in a less immediately inviting setting.

Hourly buses run to Ürgüp from Nevşehir and every two hours from Göreme (US$0.75).

IHLARA GORGE

☎ 0382

A once remote, beautiful canyon full of rock-cut churches dating back to Byzantine times, Ihlara is now a mainstay of all the day-trip excursions run out of Cappadocia. With time on your hands, you're better off staying and walking the entire 16km length of the gorge.

Ihlara village is 40km southeast of Aksaray. **Anatolia Pansiyon** *(☎ 453 7440; camping per person US$3, doubles with shower US$16)* offers comfortable rooms on the road that runs along the top of the gorge. **Akar Pansiyon** *(☎ 453 7018; doubles with shower US$16)*, on the road towards Aksaray, has a handy shop close by. There are more inviting camp sites and simple restaurants in the gorge itself, near the village of Belisırma.

Several daily buses connect Ihlara with Aksaray (US$0.75).

KAYSERİ

☎ 352 • pop 425,000

In the shadow of Mt Erciyes, Kayseri, a conservative but fast-modernising town, was once the capital of Cappadocia and boasts many ancient buildings tucked away behind the ugly high-rises.

Near the **tourist office** *(☎ 222 3903)* is the beautiful **Hunat Hatun mosque, tomb and seminary**. Opposite, behind the massive 6th-century city walls, is the **Ulu Cami** (Great Mosque), begun by the Seljuks in 1136. Also inside the walls is the ancient **Vezirhanı**, once a caravanserai. Don't miss the beautifully decorated **Güpgüpoğlu Konağı** *(admission US$0.75; open 8am-5pm Tues-Sun)*, an 18th-century mansion.

The cheapest accommodation is friendly **Hunat Oteli** *(☎ 232 4319; Zengin Sokak 5; beds without shower US$7)*, behind the Hunat Mosque. **Hotel Turan** *(☎ 222 5537; Turan Caddesi 8; singles/doubles with shower US$18/28)* is right in the heart of the shopping centre with some sizeable rooms.

Beyaz Saray *(Millet Caddesi 8)* boasts a mouth-watering İskender kebap (US$3), as does **İskender Kebap Salonu** opposite.

A dolmuş to Kayseri from Ürgüp costs US$2; a bus from Göreme US$3.

Black Sea Coast

Turkey's Black Sea coast is steep and craggy, damp and lush, and isolated behind the Pontic Mountains along most of its length. The quantities of nuts grown here make Turkey the world's biggest hazelnut exporter. The tea you drink in İstanbul probably comes from east of Trabzon; the cigarette smoke probably comes from tobacco grown west of Samsun.

Partly because of heavy industry around Zonguldak, the coast west from Sinop to the Bosphorus is little visited, although the fishing port of **Amasra**, with its Roman and Byzantine ruins and small, cheap hotels, is worth a look. **Sinop**, three hours northwest of Samsun, is a fine little backwater, with beaches on both sides of the peninsula.

There's little of interest for tourists, but **Samsun** makes a good starting point for coastal travel as it's the first port of call for the İstanbul ferry. Atatürk landed here on 19 May 1919 to begin the Turkish War of Independence.

There are excellent beaches around the cheerful resort town of **Ünye**, on a wide bay 85km east of Samsun. Beaches are the only reason to stop in the glum town of **Ordu**, 80km further to the east.

Europe's first cherry trees came from **Giresun** courtesy of Lucullus, the Roman general and famous epicure, and the town is still surrounded by cherry orchards.

TRABZON

☎ 0462

Trabzon is by far the most interesting place along the Black Sea coast, with lots of old Byzantine buildings and the amazing Sumela Monastery right on its doorstep. It held out against the Seljuks and Mongols and was the last town to fall to the Ottoman Turks. Today it still feels very different from other Turkish towns, not least because its trading focus is on Russia and the Caucasus.

Modern Trabzon is centred on Atatürk Square, on a steep hill above the harbour. The **tourist office** *(☎/fax 321 4659)* is off the square's southern side, near Hotel Nur. Minibuses plying the coastal highway wait at the foot of a hill; to reach Atatürk Square, just take the steepest climb up. About 3km to the east is the otogar for long-distance buses.

Things to See

A 20-minute walk west of Atatürk Square are the dark walls of the Byzantine city. The **old town**, with its timber houses and stone bridges, still looks medieval.

In Trabzon itself the main attraction is the 13th-century **Aya Sofya** *(admission US$0.75; open 8am-5pm Tues-Sun)*, reachable by dolmuş from Atatürk Square. The **Atatürk Köşkü** *(Atatürk Villa; admission US$0.75; open 9am-5pm daily)* is a beautiful 19th-century house set high above the town.

Many travellers come to Trabzon just to visit **Sumela Monastery** *(admission US$3; open 9am-6pm, shorter hours in winter)*, built into a cliff face like a swallow's nest and dating back to Byzantine times. Newly restored, it boasts fine murals (damaged by vandals) and amazing views. Ulusoy buses (US$6, 45 minutes, 46km) depart for Sumela from a small terminal on Taksim Caddesi, across the street and uphill a few steps from Atatürk Square. You can also visit on a tour from Trabzon (US$6) or by taking a shared taxi (around US$30).

Places to Stay & Eat

Sadly, traders and prostitutes from former Soviet states often fill the cheapest hotels, so you may have trouble finding somewhere affordable and tolerable. The cheapest rooms are east of Atatürk Square on Güzelhisar Caddesi and surrounding streets.

Hotel Anıl *(☎ 326 7282; Güzelhisar Caddesi 10; singles/doubles US$12/18)* has a flashy lobby and fairly clean rooms.

Hotel Benli *(☎ 321 1022; Cami Çıkmazı 5; singles/doubles with sink US$5/10, with shower US$7/12)* is uphill behind the Belediye. Small, old and drab, it has clean-enough rooms. Facing it is the newly renovated **Hotel Nur** *(☎ 323 0445; Cami Sokak 4; singles/doubles with shower US$12/20)*, a good bet for single women.

Sankta Maria Katolik Kilisesi *(☎ 321 2192; Sümer Sokak 26)*, a few blocks downhill from Atatürk Square, has a hostel (with spotless rooms and hot showers) which welcomes travellers. Don't forget to leave a (realistic) donation.

Lots of cheap food is available right around Atatürk Square. Try **Derya** and **Volkan 2** near the cheap hotels for *sulu yemek* (fast food). **Murat Balık Salonu**, on the northern side of the square, fries up mackerel (US$3) and *hamsi* (anchovy), a Black Sea delicacy when in season. **Güloğlu** serves a wide range of meals (and baklava to follow) in cheerful surroundings.

Getting There & Around

West-bound dolmuşes run to Ordu from the minibus yard on the highway below the bazaar. East-bound dolmuşes to Rize and minibuses to Maçka and Sumela go from the yard east of Atatürk Square near the ferry terminal. From the otogar, minibuses leave for Rize, Hopa and Artvin every 30 minutes. A dozen buses a day head for Erzurum (US$8, five hours, 325km), a beautiful ride via Gümüşhane.

See the Getting Around section at the beginning of this chapter for details on car ferries to İstanbul.

Dolmuşes connect the otogar with Atatürk Square (US$0.30).

Eastern Turkey

The east is probably the most exciting (and toughest) part of Turkey to travel in, and certainly the part that feels least affected by mass tourism. The weather can be bitterly cold and snowy in winter – only well equipped masochists travel this region from January through to April.

Turkey's southeastern corner was once Upper Mesopotamia, a historic area drained by the Tigris (Dicle) and Euphrates (Fırat) Rivers. They are also some of the most exotic-feeling places you'll visit in Turkey, with the influence of neighbouring Syria and Iraq plain to see.

Since the capture of PKK leader Abdullah Öcalan in 1999, the security situation in southeastern Turkey has improved considerably. See the boxed text 'Southeast Turkey & the Kurds' for information on travelling in that area.

ERZURUM

☎ 0442

Erzurum is a big town famous for its harsh climate but it has some striking Seljuk buildings that justify a stay of a day or so. Both the **tourist office** *(☎ 218 5697, fax 218 5443; Cemal Gürsel Caddesi)* and otogar are inconveniently located; the tourist office far out on the main street, west of Havuzbaşı, the otogar 3km from the centre on the airport road. Luckily the centre itself is compact with all the main sites within walking distance of each other.

The **Iranian consulate** *(☎ 218 3876, fax 316 1182)*, just off Atatürk Bulvarı, likes to say yes to visa requests from all but American and British travellers.

Things to See

The well-preserved walls of the 5th-century **citadel** loom over a maze of narrow streets, offering good views of the town's layout and the bleak surrounding plains.

The beautifully symmetrical **Çifte Minareli Medrese** (1253) is a famous example of Seljuk architecture. Its classic carved portal is flanked by twin minarets, which, in turn, frame a conical dome behind.

Next door is the oldest mosque, **Ulu Cami** (1179). Further west along Cumhuriyet Caddesi is a square with an Ottoman mosque and, at the western corner, another seminary, the Yakutiye Medresesi, built by the local Mongol emir in 1310 and now a **museum** *(admission US$0.75; open 8.30am-5pm Tues-Sun)*.

Places to Stay & Eat

The area around Kazım Karabekir Caddesi has lots of cheapies, although some are dismal. **Hitit Otel** *(☎ 218 1204; Kazım Karabekir Caddesi 27; singles/doubles with shower US$9/12)* and the similarly priced **Örnek Otel** *(☎ 218 1203; Kazım Karabekir Caddesi 8)* look bashed about but will do for an overnight stay.

Yeni Otel Çınar *(☎ 212 1050; Ayazpaşa Caddesi 18; doubles with shower US$10)* is friendly and popular, with cleaner, more comfortable rooms. To find it, look for the Gürpınar Cinema in the bazaar. The street opposite leads to the Çınar.

Otel Polat *(☎ 218 1623; Kazım Karabekir Caddesi 4; singles/doubles with shower US$13/21)* is a step up in quality, with decent bathrooms and double-glazed windows.

There are several reasonable restaurants along Cumhuriyet Caddesi near the Yakutiye Medresesi. **Güzelyurt Restorant** is cheap, good and long-lived; try the *mantarlı güveç* (lamb and mushroom casserole), with drinks, for less than US$10. **Salon Çağın** and **Salon Asya**, a block away, are reliable student hangouts where a kebap meal rarely tops US$4.

Getting There & Around

Erzurum is an important transport hub, with frequent buses to most big towns in eastern Turkey, including Doğubayazıt (US$6, four hours, 285km) and Sivas (US$10, six hours, 485km). The train station is at the northern end of İstasyon Caddesi, within walking distance of most hotels. The *Yeni Doğu Ekspresi* offers good rail connections with İstanbul and Ankara via Kayseri and Sivas.

Bus No 2 will run you into town from the otogar (US$0.30); a taxi costs about US$2.50. Buses for the town centre depart from outside the train station every 30 minutes.

KARS

☎ 0474

About 260km northeast of Erzurum, Kars is not the most inviting town at first sight, although if you roam the back streets you soon discover its massive fortress, innumerable *hammams* and fine old Russian houses.

Most people come to Kars to visit the dramatic, romantic ruins of **Ani** *(admission US$3.50; open 8.30am-5pm)*, 45km east of town. Formerly the capital of the Urartian and Armenian kingdoms, Ani was completely deserted in 1239 after a Mongol invasion. Fronted by a hefty wall, the ghost city now lies in fields overlooking the Arpaçay River, which forms the border with Armenia.

In a piece of nonsense left over from Cold War days, to get permission to visit Ani you must first visit the **tourist office** *(☎ 223 2300, fax 223 8452; 1st floor, Milli Eğitim Müd, Hizmet Binası, Atatürk Caddesi)*, then visit the Emniyet Müdürlüğü (Security Directorate) at Faik Bey Caddesi to get your permit stamped, then buy a ticket at the **Kars Museum** *(Cumhuriyet Caddesi; open 8.30am-5.30pm daily)*. Only then can you set off for Ani itself.

Southeast Turkey & the Kurds

For most of the 1980s and 1990s, southeast Turkey was torn apart by the struggle between the Kurdistan Workers Party (PKK) and the Turkish army, rendering the area unsafe for travellers. Turkey has a large minority population of ethnic Kurds, many of whom, while not necessarily supporting the PKK's early demands for a separate state, want to be able to read newspapers and watch television in their own language. Unfortunately, the Kurds were not one of the groups (like the Christians, Jews and Armenians) guaranteed certain rights under the terms of the Treaty of Lausanne, which effectively created modern Turkey. Indeed, until recently the Turkish government refused to even recognise the existence of the Kurds, insisting they be called 'mountain Turks'.

After almost 20 years of fighting and the deaths of around 30,000 people, the long civil war in southeastern Turkey may at last be over. Perhaps the best hope lies in Turkey's eagerness to join the European Union, which champions the rights of minorities. For travellers, this means that southeastern Turkey is beginning to return to normal. However, there are still a few hot spots, such as Tunceli, Hakkarı and Şirnak.

It remains wise to read your embassy's advice before venturing east. Contacts include the **British Foreign Office** *(☎ 020-7238 4503; W www.fco.gov.uk/travel/countryadvice.asp)*, the **Australian Department of Foreign Affairs & Trade** *(☎ 1300-555 135)*, and the **US Department of State** *(☎ 202-647 5225)*.

Places To Stay & Eat

Otel Kervansaray *(☎ 223 1990; Faik Bey Caddesi 124)* and neighbouring **Hotel Nur Saray** *(☎ 223 1364)* are as basic as they come. Both offer singles/doubles with shower for US$5/11.

Güngören Oteli *(☎ 212 5630; Halit Paşa Caddesi, Millet Sokak 4; singles/doubles with shower US$15/25)*, with its own *hammam* and *ocakbaşı* restaurant, offers the best value for money in Kars.

Several shops near the Temel and Güngören hotels sell Kars honey as well as tasty local cheeses – perfect picnic ingredients.

Şirin Anadolu Mutfağı *(Karadağ Caddesi 55; meals US$5)* has a bright, cheerful dining room with an upstairs café, and is deservedly popular with local students of both sexes.

Cafe Kristal *(Atatürk Caddesi; meals US$3)* serves a wide range of ready meals, including *piti*, a local meat and chickpea stew (US$1.75).

Getting There & Away

Kars is not well served by transport, although there are a few daily minibuses to Erzurum (US$5, 3½ hours, 205km) and a few buses to Doğubayazıt (US$4, three hours, 240km).

Taxi drivers usually charge US$40 to ferry people round Kars getting their permit and ticket and then to take them to Ani, with around 2½ hours waiting time thrown in – a lot if you're alone. The tourist office may be able to help assemble a group, but don't bank on it.

DOĞUBAYAZIT

☎ 0472

This drab little town is Turkey's last outpost on the road to Iran. It's dramatically sited at the far side of a sweeping grass plain that runs to the foot of Mt Ararat. Everything is within a five-minute stroll of the centre.

Snowcapped **Mt Ararat**, a dormant volcano alongside the main road between Erzurum and the Iranian border, makes an impressive sight rising sheer from the surrounding plain. When the biblical 40 days and 40 nights finally ended, Noah and his flock are said to have landed on Mt Ararat – a story that innumerable mountaineers have failed to confirm. It is once again possible to climb the mountain and check for yourself, although you need to pick your dates carefully and come equipped with suitable gear. For more information, inquire at local travel agencies.

Otherwise, most people come here to visit **İshak Paşa Palace** *(İshak Paşa Sarayı; admission US$4; open 8am-5.30pm daily)*, perched romantically among rocky crags 5km east of town. Built between 1685 and 1784, this palace-fortress brings together elements of Seljuk, Ottoman, Georgian, Persian and Armenian architecture.

If you want to camp, **Murat Camping** *(camp sites US$1)*, on the road to the İshak Paşa Sarayı, is very popular. **Hotel Erzurum** *(☎ 312 5080; Belediye Caddesi; doubles without shower US$7)* is one of the best of

Doğubayazı's many cheap and spartan hotels. **Ararat Hotel** *(☎ 312 8889; singles/doubles with shower US$12/20)*, near the otogar, gets consistently good reviews from readers and boasts fine views of Ararat from some rooms.

Bus services to Doğubayazıt are fairly limited and usually go via Erzurum (US$4, four hours, 285km) or Iğdır (US1.50, 45 minutes, 51km). Minibuses to Gürbülak for Iran cost US$1; if your visa is in order the crossing should only take about 20 minutes. A shared taxi on to Maku will cost around US$0.35.

MT NEMRUT

Mt Nemrut (Nemrut Dağı) is one of the great must-see attractions of eastern Turkey. Two thousand years ago, an obscure Commagene king chose to erect his **memorial sanctuary** right on top of the mountain and pretty much in the middle of nowhere. The fallen heads of the gigantic decorative statues of gods and kings, toppled by earthquakes, form one of Turkey's most enduring images.

There are several possible bases for visiting Mt Nemrut. To the north is fast modernising Malatya, where the **tourist office** *(☎ 323 3025, fax 324 2514)* organises daily minibus tours (US$30; April to mid-October) that take in a sunset visit to the heads, a night at a hotel near the summit and a second visit at dawn. Alternatively you can visit the mountain from the south via the oil-prospecting town of Kahta.

Because of the transport difficulties, many people prefer to take a three-day tour from Göreme in Cappadocia. For only US$150 per person these take in other places in the east, too, making them particularly good value. You can also arrange a tour from Şanliurfa.

In Malatya, **Otel Tahran** *(☎ 0422-324 3615; PTT Caddesi; singles/doubles US$5/9)* is as basic as they come. **Otel Kantar** *(☎ 0422-321 1510; Atatürk Caddesi 21; singles/doubles with shower US$7/12)* would make a better choice, with clean, if simple, rooms.

In high summer the nicest places to stay, especially with your own transport, are on the slopes of the mountain near Kahta. **Karadut Pension** *(☎ 0416-737 2169; beds US$7)* is very basic but makes up for its primitive facilities with views to die for.

In Kahta itself, **Anatolia Pension** *(☎ 0416-725 6483; singles/doubles US$5/9)* is too basic for most people. **Pension Kommagene** *(☎ 0416-725 5548; singles/doubles with shower US$12/18)*, at the start of the Nemrut road, is a better choice. **Hotel Mezopotamya** *(☎ 0416-725 5112; singles/doubles with shower & air-con US$9/18)* gets good reports.

VAN

☎ 0432

On the southeastern shore of vast Lake Van, Van boasts the 3000-year-old **Rock of Van citadel** *(admission US$0.75)* and an interesting **museum** *(admission US$0.75; open 9am-6pm daily)*. The 10th-century church on **Akdamar Island** in the lake is a fascinating piece of Armenian architecture in a beautiful setting, with biblical frescoes and reliefs. To get there you need to take a dolmuş from Beş Yol in Van to the harbour or at least to Gevaş (US$1) and then pick up a ferry from the harbour. An inclusive ticket for the crossing and admission should cost no more than US$4.50.

Accommodation in the bazaar to the west of Cumhuriyet Caddesi tends to be cheapest, to the east it's slightly more expensive but also cleaner and more comfortable. Several hotels in the bazaar charge US$4.50 per person in rooms with sink and/or private shower. **Aslan Oteli** *(☎ 216 2469; beds US$5)* is one of the better choices.

Büyük Asur Oteli *(☎ 216 8792; Cumhuriyet Caddesi, Turizm Sokak 5; singles/doubles with shower US$18/25)* is an excellent choice with a helpful manager who speaks English. **Hotel Bayram** *(☎ 216 1136; Cumhuriyet Caddesi 1/A; singles/doubles with shower US$15/20)* is another good choice, with clean, modern rooms.

There are several buses a day to Diyarbakır (US$7.50, seven hours) and several dolmuşes to Doğubayazıt (US$3, 2½ hours).

The Van Monster

An enduring Van myth tells of the Van Gölü Canavarı (Lake Van Monster). Rumours of this Nessie lookalike surfaced in the 1960s, when a newspaper article referred to a 2m-long otter-like animal spotted swimming in the lake. Since then the stories have gotten wilder. Sometimes the monster is said to resemble a horse; at other times it's more like a dinosaur. All attempts to track the beastie to its lair have been unsuccessful thus far. Meanwhile, Van's inhabitants have been capitalising on the story, selling Canavar Salam (Monster Salami) and backing a team known as the Canavarlar (Monsters).

Yugoslavia

A re-invigorated Yugoslavia is inventing itself anew and gradually returning to our world. As the dust settles, after years of turmoil, travellers are beginning to rediscover this country's cosmopolitan cities, eventful history and awe-inspiring landscapes.

The Federal Republic of Yugoslavia consists of Serbia and Montenegro. At the heart of the Balkans, it straddles major routes between Western Europe and Asia Minor. The southern province of Kosovo has been a UN-NATO protectorate since June 1999.

Yugoslavia: the Basics

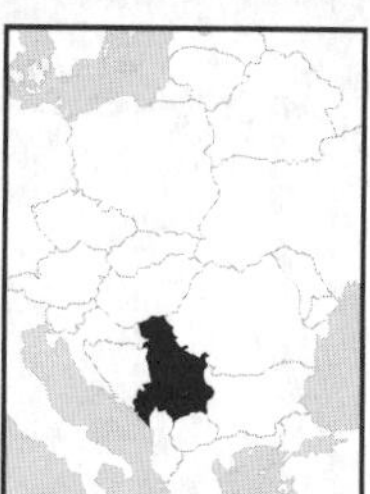

Local name Југославија

Capital Belgrade

Population 10.7 million

Language Serbian, Albanian in Kosovo

Currency dinar (DIN), euro (€)

Avoid at all costs Unventilated cafés

Get used to saying *Zašto su vam čaršavi manji od kreveta?* (Why are your sheets smaller than the bed?)

Facts about Yugoslavia

HISTORY

The region's original inhabitants were the Illyrians, followed by the Celts. The conquering Romans arrived in the 3rd century BC. In AD 395 what is now Serbia passed to the Byzantine Empire, while Croatia remained part of the western Roman Empire. Serbia won independence in 1217. At the Battle of Kosovo in 1389 the Ottomans defeated Serbia, ushering in almost 500 years of Turkish rule. An 1815 revolt led to de facto Serbian independence from the Turks.

In 1914 Austria-Hungary invaded Serbia, sparking WWI. After the war, Croatia, Slovenia, Vojvodina, Serbia, Montenegro and Macedonia formed what became Yugoslavia. In 1941 the Yugoslavs revolted against a Nazi alliance, prompting invasion by Hitler and partition among Germany, Italy, Hungary and Bulgaria.

The Communist Party, under Josip Broz Tito, declared an armed uprising and proclaimed Yugoslavia a federal republic. Serbia's size was reduced, with Bosnia-Hercegovina, Montenegro and Macedonia being granted republic status – a privilege not granted the Kosovar Albanians or Vojvodina Hungarians. Tito broke with Stalin in 1948 and was rewarded with US$2 billion in aid from the US and UK between 1950 and 1960.

In 1986, new Communist Party leader Slobodan Miloševic espoused a 'Greater Serbia' that horrified Slovenia and Croatia. On 25 June 1991, these countries declared their independence, sparking a federal Yugoslavian invasion of Slovenia. In response the European Community (EC) imposed a weapons embargo on Yugoslavia and recognised Croatia and Slovenia as independent. Macedonia and Bosnia-Hercegovina demanded recognition as well, and in 1992 a third Yugoslav federation was declared by Serbia and Montenegro. The new constitution made no mention of 'autonomous provinces', infuriating Albanians in Kosovo, long brutally repressed by Serbia. Violence in Kosovo erupted in January 1998, mostly provoked by the Yugoslavian federal army and police, while the West stood by. In March 1999, Serbia rejected a US-brokered peace plan and began 'cleansing' the country of its Albanian population. Hundreds of thousands fleeing into Macedonia and Albania finally galvanised NATO into action. Bombarded by NATO air strikes, Serbian forces withdrew from Kosovo.

In the September 2000 federal presidential elections, opposition candidate Vojislav Koštunica claimed victory, but Miloševic refused to accede. The constitutional court annulled the election. On 5 October opposition supporters occupied parliament and the state TV station. The next day Russia recognised Koštunica's presidency, effectively ousting Miloševic.

Yugoslavia restored ties with Europe, acknowledged atrocities in Kosovo and rejoined the UN. In December, Miloševic's party was

YUGOSLAVIA

HUNGARY
Szeged
Baja
Horgoš
Pécs
Subotica
0 50 100km
0 30 60mi
Srpska Crnja
Timişoara
E75
Tisa River
Danube River
Novi Sad
CROATIA
Vatin
Vojvodina
Vršac
Sava River
E70
ROMANIA
Bijeljina
BELGRADE
Golubac
Drina River
Smederevo
Kladovo
Sandžak
Zvornik
Danube River
Negotin
SERBIA
BOSNIA-HERCEGOVINA
Manasija
Vidin
Morava River
Zaječar
Čačak
Užice
Ćuprija
Požega
Guča
Zlatibor
Kraljevo
Ušće
Kruševac
Studenica
Tara River
Brus
Ibar River
E75
Pljevlja
Kapaonik (2017m)
Niš
Raška
Žabljak
Đurđevića Tara
Durmitor National Park
Novi Pazar
Bijelo Polje
Leskovac
Dimitrovgrad
MONTENEGRO
Mojkovac
Mitrovicë (Mitrovica)
Berane
Kolašin
Rožaje
Nikšić
Prekaz
Klisura
Peja (Peć)
Klinë (Klina)
Prishtina (Priština)
Herceg Novi
BULGARIA
Bijela
Kotor
Deçani (Dečani)
Gadimë (Gadimlje)
Cetinje
Fushë Kosovë (Kosovo Polje)
Tivat
Podgorica
KOSOVO
Virpazar
Božaj
Budva
Bay of Kotor
Sveti Stefan
Lake Skadar
Hani Elezit (Đeneral Janković)
Preševo
Prizren
Sutomore
Shkodra
Kumanovo
To Ancona, Italy
Bar
Brezovica
ALBANIA
Šar Planina
Kukës
SKOPJE
To Bari, Italy
Ulcinj
ADRIATIC SEA
MACEDONIA

Note: At the time of publication the railway network in Kosovo was not operating

soundly defeated in parliamentary elections, and in April 2001 Miloševic was arrested for misappropriating state funds and abusing his position. In June he was extradited to the Netherlands to stand trial at the international war crimes tribunal.

In April 2002 Serbia and Montenegro agreed to replace the Yugoslavian federation with a union of 'Serbia & Montenegro'. The constitutional detail still has to be written, wrangled over and ratified by parliament. Until then, the name Yugoslavia lives on.

GEOGRAPHY

Mountains and plateaus account for the lower half of this 102,350-sq-km federation. Serbia covers 77,651 sq km, Montenegro 13,812 sq km, and Kosovo 10,887 sq km. Most rivers flow north into the Danube. Yugoslavia's only coast is the scenically superb 150km Montenegrin coast. The Bay of Kotor is southern Europe's only real fjord.

CLIMATE

The north has a continental climate with cold winters and hot, humid summers. The coastal region has hot, dry summers and relatively cold winters with heavy snowfall occurring inland.

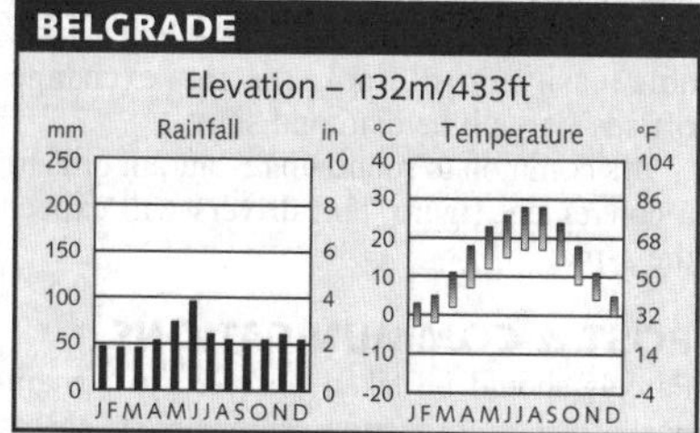

GOVERNMENT & POLITICS

Under arrangements in the new union, Serbia and Montenegro will be semi-independent states with foreign affairs, customs and defence controlled federally.

POPULATION & PEOPLE

The last published figures came from the 1991 census. Estimated population (2002) is 11 million, made up of Serbs (62%), Albanians (17%), Montenegrins (5%), Hungarians (3%), Slavic Muslims (3%) and other groups. War has altered those figures. About 23% of Vojvodina's population is Hungarian. There are large Slavic Muslim and Albanian minorities in Montenegro and southern Serbia; Belgrade has an estimated population of 10,000 Muslims.

> **Watch this space**
>
> By the time you read this chapter it could be in the wrong part of the book, it should be under 'S' for Serbia and Montenegro. There's still a lot of wrangling and politicking to be done before the parliaments of Serbia and Montenegro agree to dump the name (and constitution) of Yugoslavia. So to be safe, and accurate, we've decided to wait until it's official.

SOCIETY & CONDUCT

All nationalities are very hospitable to visitors. Respect should be shown for religious establishments and customs. Dressing appropriately and learning a few basic words of the language will open doors and prompt smiles.

RELIGION

Serbs and Montenegrins are predominantly Orthodox, Hungarians are Roman Catholic and Albanians are predominantly Muslim.

LANGUAGE

Serbian is the common language, with Albanian spoken in Kosovo. Many Yugoslavs know German, English and French. Hungarians use the Latin alphabet, Montenegrins and Serbians use both Latin and Cyrillic. See the language section at the back of this book for useful phrases.

Facts for the Visitor

HIGHLIGHTS

Castles include the magnificent baroque Petrovaradin Citadel at Novi Sad and Belgrade's Kalemegdan Citadel. Kosovo's Turkish architecture and street cafés are impressive, while Cetinje will please romantics. Of the beach resorts, Budva is chic but Kotor more impressive. Montenegro's Tara Canyon and Durmitor National Park stack up to any natural wonders in the world.

PLANNING

When to Go

Avoid the Montenegrin coast during July and August, when accommodation becomes both expensive and scarce. The ski season is generally December to March.

Maps

The Freytag & Berndt map *Yugoslavia, Slovenia, Croatia* shows former Yugoslavia with the new countries. The *Savezna Republika Jugoslavija Autokarta*, available from the Tourist Organisation of Belgrade, shows new borders and has some town maps.

TOURIST OFFICES

There are tourist offices in Belgrade, Novi Sad, Prishtina and Prizren. Elsewhere, travel agencies may help with information.

VISAS & DOCUMENTS

A visa is required for Serbia, but not for Montenegro or Kosovo. You need an initial hotel booking to accompany your application. The **Ministry of Foreign Affairs** (w *www.mfa.gov.yu*) provides details.

Serbia has been granting 30-day visas at Belgrade airport and border posts; this situation may become permanent. Crossings between Serbia and Kosovo or Montenegro are not through border posts.

EMBASSIES

Yugoslav Embassies

Yugoslavia has embassies in the following countries:

Australia (☎ 02-6290 2630, fax 6290 2631; e yuembau@ozemail.com.au) 4 Bulwarra Close, O'Malley, Canberra, ACT 2606

Canada (☎ 613-233 6289, fax 233 7850; w www.yuemb.ca) 17 Blackburn Ave, Ottawa, Ontario, K1A 8A2

France (☎ 01 40 72 24 24, fax 01 40 72 24 11; e pariz@compuserve.com) 54 rue Faisanderie, 75116 Paris

UK (☎ 207-235 9049, fax 235 7092; w www.yugoslavembassy.org.uk) 28 Belgrave Square, London, SW1X 8QB

USA (☎ 202-332 0333, fax 332 3933; w www.yuembusa.org) 2134 Kalorama Rd NW, Washington DC, 20008

Embassies in Yugoslavia

Countries with embassies in Belgrade include:

Albania (☎ 646 864) Kneza Miloša 56
Australia (☎ 624 655) Cika Ljubina 13
Bulgaria (☎ 3613 980) Birčaninova 26
Canada (☎ 644 666) Kneza Miloša 75
France (☎ 636 555) Pariska 11
Germany (☎ 3614 255) Kneza Miloša 74–76
Hungary (☎ 4440 472) Krunska (Proleterskih Brigada) 72
Romania (☎ 646 071) Kneza Miloša 70
UK (☎ 645 087) Resavska (Generala Ždanova) 46
USA (☎ 645 655) Kneza Miloša 50

MONEY

Currency

Montenegro and Kosovo have adopted the euro and the dinar is no longer accepted there. Serbia however retains the dinar, which is used for most transactions, but the euro is readily accepted. Some international train journeys may require part payment in dinar and part in euro.

Exchange Rates

country	unit		dinar
Australia	A$1	=	37.80 DIN
Canada	C$1	=	44.20 DIN
Eurozone	€1	=	62.40 DIN
Japan	¥100	=	54.40 DIN
NZ	NZ$1	=	32.00 DIN
UK	UK£1	=	98.70 DIN
USA	US$1	=	67.80 DIN

Until global banking agreements are made, few banks deal with travellers cheques or credit cards, so come with easily exchangeable cash euros. Look for the exchange offices' large blue diamond signs.

It's common to round up restaurant bills to a convenient figure; taxi drivers will expect the same.

POST & COMMUNICATIONS

Parcels should be taken unsealed to a main post office for inspection. Allow time to check packing and complete the transaction. You can receive poste restante mail in all towns for a small charge.

The international access code for outgoing calls is ☎ 99. To call Yugoslavia, dial the country code (☎ 381), area code (without the initial zero) and the number.

In Serbia you can use a phone card (100, 300 or 500 DIN) to make an international call from a public phone. In Montenegro and Kosovo, the highest-value phone card (€1.70) doesn't allow enough time, so use the post office. Faxes can be sent from post offices, which in Serbia charge 172/236/236 DIN per page to Europe/Australia/North America.

Internet cafés are widespread.

DIGITAL RESOURCES

If you are looking for tourism information **W** www.serbia-tourism.org, **W** www.beograd.org.yu and **W** www.visit-montenegro.com are very useful sites.

WOMEN TRAVELLERS

Travel in Yugoslavia is generally easy and hassle-free. Dress conservatively in Muslim areas of Kosovo.

GAY & LESBIAN TRAVELLERS

Homosexuality has been legal in Yugoslavia since 1932. For more information, contact **Arkadia** *(Brace Baruh 11, 11000 Belgrade)* or **W** www.gay-serbia.com.

DISABLED TRAVELLERS

There are very few facilities in the region for those with disabilities. Wheelchair access may be problematic in Belgrade with its numerous inclines, however most hotels will have lifts.

DANGERS & ANNOYANCES

Travel in Yugoslavia is generally safe, but avoid southeastern Serbia and Mitrovica in Kosovo, where there is still Serb-Albanian tension. There are still landmines in Kosovo, so look out for warnings. If you're going off the beaten track check with United Nations Interim Administration Mission (UNMIK) or Kosovo Force (KFOR)

'No smoking' signs are routinely ignored. Check with police before taking photographs of any official building they're guarding.

Emergencies

In an emergency dial ☎ 92 for police, ☎ 93 for the fire service and ☎ 94 for the ambulance.

For motoring assistance in Belgrade phone ☎ 987 and in Serbia and Montenegro (ie, outside Belgrade) the motoring assistance number is ☎ 011 9800.

BUSINESS HOURS

Banks keep long hours, often 7am to 7pm weekdays and 7am to noon Saturday. On weekdays many shops open from 7am, close from noon to 4pm, then reopen until 8pm. Department stores, supermarkets and some restaurants stay open all day. Most government offices are closed on Saturday; many other businesses stay open until 2pm.

PUBLIC HOLIDAYS & SPECIAL EVENTS

Public holidays in Serbia and Montenegro include New Year (1 and 2 January), Orthodox Christmas (6 and 7 January), Serbia Constitution Day (28 March), Constitution Day of Federal Republic of Yugoslavia (27 April), International Labour Days (1 and 2 May), Victory Day (9 May) and Montenegro Uprising Day (13 July). Orthodox churches celebrate Easter between one and five weeks later than other churches.

In Kosovo, 28 November is Flag Day and Easter Monday is a public holiday.

Belgrade hosts a film festival (FEST) in February, a jazz festival in August, an international theatre festival (BITEF) in mid-September and a festival of classical music in October. Every July or August, Novi Sad hosts the Exit music festival (see the boxed text 'A Graceful Exit' later in this chapter), which attracts bands from all over Europe. There is an annual festival of brass band music at Guča near Čačak in the last week of August. Budva puts on a summer festival in July and August.

ACTIVITIES

Serbia's main skiing resorts are Zlatibor and Kopaonik, while Montenegro's is Žabljak. Kosovo's resort at Brezovica has now reopened. Ski season is from December to March; in summer, resorts become popular hiking areas. The Tara River in Montenegro's Durmitor National Park provides the best rafting.

ACCOMMODATION

For hostel accommodation contact Ferijalni Savez Beograd (see Places to Stay in Belgrade for details). Hostels exist in Belgrade, Palić (Subotica), Kladovo (eastern Serbia), Kopaonik (southern Serbia) and Sutomore and Bijela (southern Montenegro).

The prices of Belgrade hotels are fairly reasonable for a capital city; Montenegrin hotels outside the coast and Žabljak are iniquitously expensive; and in Kosovo accommodation is scarce and pricey. Private rooms (to be found along the coast, but seldom inland and not in Belgrade) that are organised through travel agencies, are your best option. In summer you can camp along the Montenegrin coast at a few organised camping grounds.

A Raw Deal

If your Serbian (or Croatian, or Bosnian) language skills aren't absolutely up to scratch, then you're going to be paying about twice what native Yugoslavians are charged for accommodation. Don't get angry, and don't take it personally – foreigners are (often justifiably) viewed as excellent sources for boosting the Yugoslav economy, and all are treated pretty much similarly in this respect.

Should the unjustness of it all really get to you, you can always try asking:

Kad mi več naplaćujete duplo smeštaj jer sam stranac, mogu li onda dobiti i dva doručka ujutro? (Since you're charging me double because I'm a foreigner, can I get two breakfasts in the morning?)

Delivered properly, this may elicit at least a laugh.

FOOD & DRINKS

The region is a delight for meat eaters but a trial for vegetarians. The cheapest snack is *burek*, a greasy pie made with cheese, meat, potato or mushrooms. A good midday meal of soup or kebabs should cost about 120 DIN/€2.

Yugoslavia's regional cuisines range from spicy Hungarian goulash to Turkish kebab. A Vojvodina speciality is *alaska čorba* (fiery riverfish stew). In Montenegro, try *kajmak* (salted cheese). Serbia is famous for grilled meats such as *ćevapčići* (spiced kebabs), *pljeskavica* (hamburger steak) and *ražnjići* (pork or veal shish kebab with onions and peppers). *Duveć* is grilled pork cutlets with spiced stewed peppers, zucchini and tomatoes in rice cooked in an oven – delicious. Other popular dishes are *musaka* (aubergine and potato layered with minced meat), *sarma* (cabbage stuffed with minced meat and rice), *kapama* (stewed lamb, onions and spinach with yogurt) and *punjena tikvica* (zucchini stuffed with minced meat and rice).

For vegetarians there's pizza or a Serbian salad *Srpska salata* of raw peppers, onions and tomatoes, seasoned with oil, vinegar and maybe chilli. Also ask for *gibanica* (cheese pie), *zeljanica* (cheese pie with spinach) or *pasulj prebranac*, a dish of cooked and spiced beans. *Šopska salata* consists of chopped tomatoes, cucumber and onion, topped with grated soft white cheese.

Pivo (beer) is universally available. *Nikšičko pivo*, brewed at Nikšić, is transcendent. Yugoslav *vinjak* (cognac), plum brandy and red wine provide good tipples.

Coffee is usually served Turkish-style – 'black as hell, strong as death and sweet as love'. Superb espresso and cappuccino are available in cafés.

Getting There & Away

You must fill out a currency declaration form on arrival and show it on departure. Visitors entering from Kosovo can legally enter Serbia only via Macedonia, as there are no immigration facilities between Kosovo and Serbia or Montenegro (there'll be no entry stamp in your passport).

AIR

JAT (Yugoslav Airlines) has regional services throughout Europe. Lufthansa and Aeroflot fly to Belgrade, while Austrian Airlines, Swiss Air, Adria Airlines, British Airways, Turkish Airlines fly into Prishtina. Departure tax is 600 DIN.

LAND

Train

International trains from Belgrade call at Novi Sad and Subotica for destinations north and west, and Niš for those going east. No trains run in Kosovo, and Montenegro has no international services. Bookings are recommended and a student card will get you a reduction on some trains. Eurail and Inter-Rail passes are accepted and sold at Belgrade train station. Sample services from Belgrade are as follows:

destination	frequency	journey time (hrs)	cost DIN
Bucharest	daily	14	1799
Budapest	daily	7	2311
Istanbul	daily	26	5787
Lubljana	daily	10	1731
Moscow	daily	50	6423
Munich	daily	17	4940
Sofia	daily	11	1250
Thessaloniki	daily	16	1933
Vienna	daily	11	3518
Zagreb	daily	7	1110

YUGOSLAVIA

Car & Motorcycle

An International Drivers Permit is a good idea. Vehicles need third-party insurance recognised in Yugoslavia plus insurance bought at the border. For more details contact **Auto-Moto Savez Jugoslavije** *(Yugoslav Automotive Association; ☎ 011-9800; Ⓦ www.amsj.co.yu; Ruzveltova 18, Belgrade)*.

Sea

A ferry service operates between Bar and Italy (see the Bar section).

Getting Around

Buses are necessary for travel in Kosovo and to Rožaje (Montenegro) and Novi Pazar (Serbia), both gateways to Kosovo. You'll also need buses for the Montenegrin coast and getting to Žabljak.

Jugoslovenske Železnice (JŽ) provides adequate railway services from Belgrade serving Novi Sad, Subotica and the highly scenic line down to Bar. There are four classes of train: *ekspresni* (express), *poslovni* (rapid), *brzi* (fast) and *putnicki* (slow), so make sure you have the right ticket.

VIP, Hertz, Europcar and Net Rent a Car all have offices at Belgrade's airport. Typical price for a small car is €55 a day.

Serbia Србија

The dominant role of Serbia (Srbija) in Yugoslavia was underlined by its control of two formerly autonomous provinces, Vojvodina and Kosovo, and the location of the federal capital.

BELGRADE БЕОГРАД

☎ 011 • pop 2 million (est. 2002)

Belgrade (Beograd) is strategically situated on the southern edge of the Carpathian Basin where the Sava River joins the Danube. Destroyed and rebuilt 40 times in its 2300-year history, today it's a lively, vibrant city with fine restaurants, shops, bars and street cafés, and chic crowds.

Orientation & Information

The train station and the two adjacent bus stations are on the south side of the city. From the train station, travel east along Milovana Milovanovića and up Balkanska to Terazije, the heart of modern Belgrade. Kneza Mihaila, Belgrade's lively pedestrian boulevard, runs northwest through the old town from Terazije to the Kalemegdan citadel that overlooks the Sava and Danube Rivers.

The friendly, helpful **Tourist Organisation of Belgrade** *(☎ 635 622, fax 635 343; Terazije Passage; open 9am-8pm Mon-Fri, 9am-4pm Sat)* is in the underpass near Kneza Mihaila (note the public toilets here). There is a **tourist office** *(☎ 601 555; open 8am-8pm daily)* at Belgrade airport.

Most travellers cheques can be cashed at **Atlas Bank** *(☎ 302 4000; Emilijana Josimovića 4)* or the **Astral Banka** *(cnr Maršala Birjuzova & Pop Lukina)*. Private exchange offices abound. The only ATM is in the **Hotel InterContinental** *(Vladimira Popovića 10)*. Also here, **Delta Banka** *(open 6.30am-10pm daily)* cashes travellers cheques.

To make phone calls, try the **central post office** *(Zmaj Jovina 17; open 7am-8pm daily)* or **telephone centre** *(Takovska; open 7am-midnight Mon-Fri, 7am-10pm Sat & Sun)* in the large post office by Sveti Marko church. For Internet access, **IPS** *(Makedonska 4; open 24 hours)* charges 80 DIN an hour, while **Plato Cyber Club** *(Akademski plato 1; open 24 hours)* charges 35 DIN an hour.

Putnik *(☎ 323 2911, fax 323 4461; Ⓦ www.putnik.co.yu/; Terazije 27)* offers a wide range of domestic and international transport and tour services. **Turist Biro Lasta** *(☎ 641 251, fax 642 473; Milovana Milovanovića 1)*, **Bas Turist** *(☎ 638 555, fax 784 859; BAS bus station)* and **Putnik Travel Agency** *(Milovana Milovanovića; Ⓦ www.putnik.co.yu; open 7am-7pm)* sell bus tickets. **KRS Beograd Tours** *(☎ 641 258, fax 687 447; Milovana Milovanovića 5; open Mon-Sat)* has train information and tickets at station prices.

Two handy 24-hour pharmacies are the **Prvi Maj** *(☎ 324 0533; Srpskih Vladara 9)* and **Sveti Sava** *(☎ 643 170; Nemanjina 2)*. For emergencies, try the **Boris Kidrič Hospital Diplomatic Section** *(☎ 643 839; Pasterova 1; open 7am-7pm Mon-Fri)* or the clinics in **Klinički Centar** *(Pasterova; open 24 hrs)*.

Things to See

Kalemegdan Citadel *(tram No 1, 2 or 13)* has been fortified since Celtic times, with the Roman settlement of Singidunum on the flood plain below. Much of what is seen

CENTRAL BELGRADE

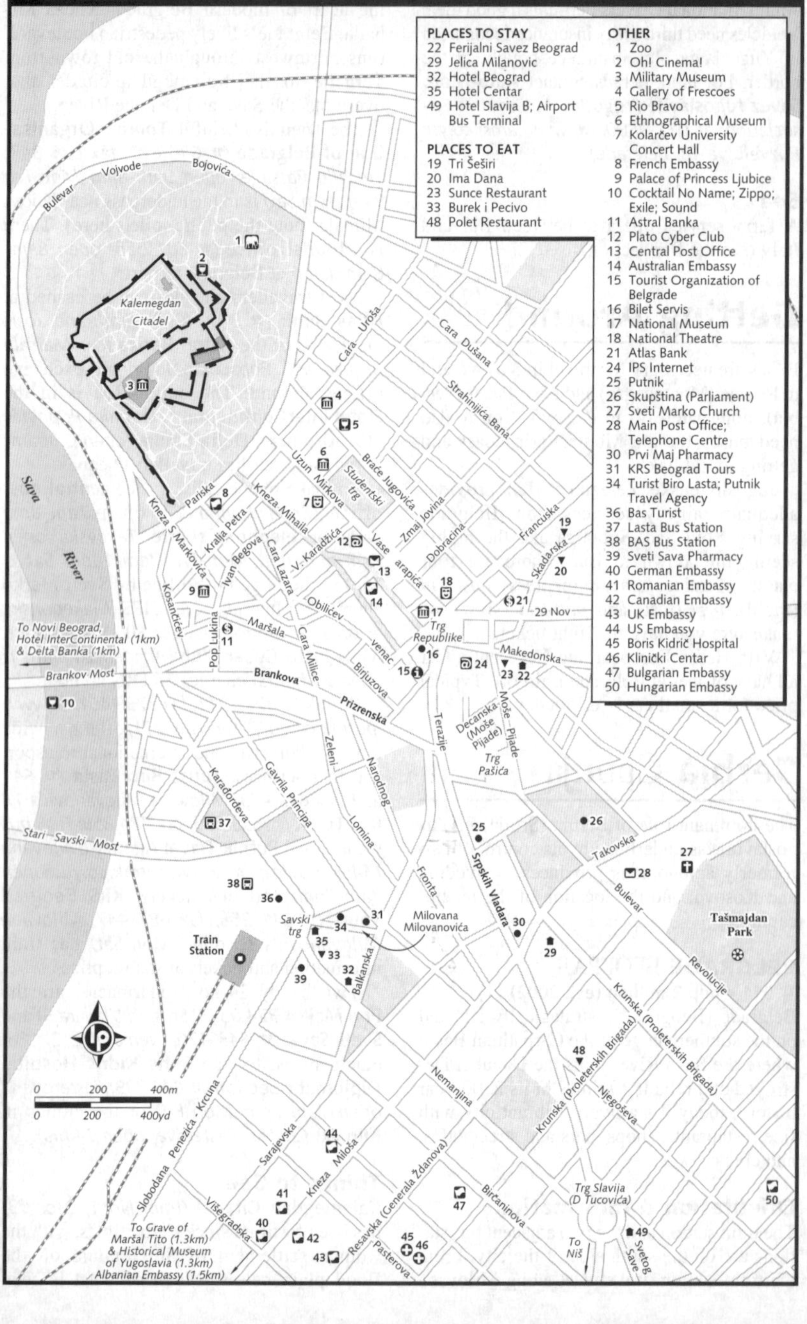

PLACES TO STAY

22 Ferijalni Savez Beograd
29 Jelica Milanovic
32 Hotel Beograd
35 Hotel Centar
49 Hotel Slavija B; Airport Bus Terminal

PLACES TO EAT

19 Tri Šeširi
20 Ima Dana
23 Sunce Restaurant
33 Burek i Pecivo
48 Polet Restaurant

OTHER

1 Zoo
2 Oh! Cinema!
3 Military Museum
4 Gallery of Frescoes
5 Rio Bravo
6 Ethnographical Museum
7 Kolarčev University Concert Hall
8 French Embassy
9 Palace of Princess Ljubice
10 Cocktail No Name; Zippo; Exile; Sound
11 Astral Banka
12 Plato Cyber Club
13 Central Post Office
14 Australian Embassy
15 Tourist Organization of Belgrade
16 Bilet Servis
17 National Museum
18 National Theatre
21 Atlas Bank
24 IPS Internet
25 Putnik
26 Skupština (Parliament)
27 Sveti Marko Church
28 Main Post Office; Telephone Centre
30 Prvi Maj Pharmacy
31 KRS Beograd Tours
34 Turist Biro Lasta; Putnik Travel Agency
36 Bas Turist
37 Lasta Bus Station
38 BAS Bus Station
39 Sveti Sava Pharmacy
40 German Embassy
41 Romanian Embassy
42 Canadian Embassy
43 UK Embassy
44 US Embassy
45 Boris Kidrič Hospital
46 Klinički Centar
47 Bulgarian Embassy
50 Hungarian Embassy

To Novi Beograd, Hotel InterContinental (1km) & Delta Banka (1km)

To Grave of Maršal Tito (1.3km) & Historical Museum of Yugoslavia (1.3km) Albanian Embassy (1.5km)

To Niš

today dates from the 17th century, but there are also medieval gates, Orthodox churches, Muslim tombs and Turkish baths.

The large **Military Museum** *(☎ 360 4149; Kalemegdan; admission 20 DIN; 10am-5pm daily)* presents a complete military history of Yugoslavia. Proudly displayed are captured Kosovo Liberation Army weapons and bits of a downed American stealth fighter. Nearby is Stari Grad, the oldest part of Belgrade. Here you'll find the **National Museum** *(☎ 624 322; Trg Republike; admission 50 DIN, Sun free; open 10am-5pm Tues, Wed, Fri & Sat, noon-8pm Thurs, 10am-2pm Sun)*, the third-floor gallery of which displays a fraction of an enormous national collection of European art, including works by Picasso and Monet. Nadežeta Petrović (1873–1915), one of Serbia's first women artists, is well represented. A few blocks away is the **Ethnographical Museum** *(☎ 328 1888; Studentski Trg 13; admission 40 DIN; open 10am-5pm Tues-Fri, 9am-5pm Sat, 9am-1pm Sun)*, with a comprehensive collection of Serbian costumes and folk art. Nearby is the **Gallery of Frescoes** *(☎ 621 491; Cara Uroša 20; admission 50 DIN; 10am-5pm Mon-Wed, Fri & Sat, noon-8pm Thurs, 10am-2pm Sun)* with full-size replicas (and some originals) of paintings from churches and monasteries.

Behind the main post office is **Sveti Marko Serbian Orthodox Church**, containing the grave of the Emperor Dušan (1308–55). Don't miss **Maršal Tito's grave** *(Bulevar Mira; admission free; trolleybus No 40 or 41; open 9am-2pm Tues-Sat)*. Next door is the **Historical Museum of Yugoslavia** *(admission free; 10am-5pm Tues-Sun)*.

At the airport is the exceptional **Yugoslav Aeronautical Museum** *(☎ 670 992; Belgrade International Airport; admission 300 DIN; open 8.30am-2.30pm Tues-Fri, 11am-3.30pm Sat & Sun)* – particularly wonderful if you're an aircraft buff.

Places to Stay

For youth-hostel bookings, contact helpful **Ferijalni Savez Beograd** *(☎ 324 8550, fax 322 0762; W www.hostels.org.yu; Makedonska 22, 2nd floor)*. You need HI membership (300 DIN to join) and an international student card.

Belgrade has two hostels. **Hotel Slavija B** *(☎ 450 842; Svetog Save 1–9; rooms per person including breakfast US$11.50)* offers singles and doubles with bath to budget travellers. This special price is only available through Ferijalni Savez Beograd. **Jelica Milanovic** *(☎ 323 1268; Krunska 8; open July & Aug; rooms per person from €7.50)* offers college accommodation but only during holiday time.

There's plenty of state-owned B-category hotels, which provide breakfast. **Hotel Centar** *(☎ 644 055, fax 657 838; Savski trg 7; singles/doubles 680/1360 DIN)*, opposite the train station, has spartan accommodation in a rear annexe. **Hotel Beograd** *(☎ 645 199, fax 643 746; Nemanjina 6; singles/doubles 1522/2044 DIN)*, visible from the train station, has time-worn rooms with bathrooms.

Places to Eat

Kiosks and cafés offer *burek*, *čevapčići*, pastries, hot dogs and some inventive pizzas. Those around trg Republika are open 24 hours. You can fill yourself up for under 100 DIN.

A great place for a breakfast *burek* near the train station is the **Burek i Pecivo** *(Nemanjina 5; open 5am-1pm Mon-Fri, 5am-11am Sat)*, near the Hotel Beograd. Sip Belgrade's best cappuccino at **City Garden Cafe** *(Vuka Karadžića)*.

Sunce Restaurant *(☎ 324 8474; Dečanska 1; buffet 249 DIN; open 9am-9pm Mon-Sat)* is a rare vegetarian restaurant – with an all-you-can-eat buffet to boot! For inexpensive seafood try the **Polet Restaurant** *(Njegoševa; meals 140-300 DIN; open 11am-11pm daily)* and their spicy fish soup *corba* for 60 DIN. Portions are large and the service is attentive.

For local colour visit the atmospheric cobbled street of Skadarska, with evening open-air performances in summer. The **Tri Šeširi** *(Three Hats; ☎ 324 7501; Skadarska 29; dishes 300-460 DIN; open for lunch & dinner daily)* offers meat dishes plus a nightly folk band. The **Ima Dana** *(☎ 323 4422; Skadarska 38; meals 250-350 DIN; open 11am-5pm, 7pm-1am daily)* does a lovely pike dish. They also have a resident band performing the Skadarska songs composed in the 19th century, when this area was the Bohemian part of the Balkans.

Entertainment

Party life revolves around the many barges and boats moored on the Sava and Danube Rivers. Along Kej Oslobođenja, adjacent to Hotel Yugoslavia, is a kilometre-long strip of some 20 barges. Bus Nos 15, 84, 706 and 84 will get you here from central Belgrade. At

Bibis *(open 10am-2am daily)*, popular in winter, the beer comes in large pottery mugs decorated with a green kangaroo.

On the west bank of the Sava River is another 1½km strip of floating bars, restaurants and discos. Here you'll find **Cocktail No Name** playing pop and '80s music, **Zippo** for Serbian folk music, **Exile** pounding out techno and nearby **Sound** playing house and disco. Get there by walking over the Brankov Most or catching trams 7, 9 or 11.

Back on land there's the interesting **Oh! Cinema!** *(☎ 328 4000; Kalemegdan Citadel)* café/bar overlooking the Danube and zoo. It's a favourite place to hang out through summer nights with live music, probably causing insomnia for the tigers below. **Rio Bravo** *(ul Kralja Petra 54; open 11am-2am Mon-Fri, 5pm-2am Sat & Sun)* has live bands on weekends and recorded music other nights. This is the place for jazz and 1920s Chicago music. For club hopping, the best place to wander is down Strahinjića Bana, four bocks northeast of Studentski trg.

As for live performances, **The Bilet Servis** *(☎ 625 365; Trg Republike 5; open 9am-8pm Mon-Fri, 9am-3pm Sat)* has a ticket counter and the English-speaking staff will happily search for something for you. In winter there's opera at the elegant **National Theatre** *(☎ 620 946; Trg Republike; box office 10am-2pm Tues-Sun, 10am-3pm performance days)*. **Belgrade Philharmonia** concerts usually take place in the **Kolarčev University Concert Hall** *(☎ 630 550; Studentski trg 5; box office 10am-noon & 6pm-8pm daily)* every Wednesday and Friday except in July and August. In October it hosts a festival of classical music.

Getting There & Away

Both the BAS and Lasts bus stations have frequent departures to domestic destinations (which are posted in Cyrillic only). It's easier to buy your ticket from a ticket agency. Sample services are Budva (900 DIN, 12 hours) and Novi Pazar (275 DIN, three hours), for connections to Kosovo.

Overnight trains with couchettes or sleepers run from Belgrade to Bar (1100 DIN, nine to 11 hours); a sleeper supplement costs 2000 DIN. There are four trains a day to Novi Sad (120 DIN, two hours) and two to Subotica (155 DIN, 3½ hours). All trains to Subotica call at Novi Sad, and international trains also call at both places. International tickets are sold at Belgrade station at counters 11 and 12, regular tickets at 7 to 20. Sleeper and couchette reservations are made at counters 19 and 20 and information is at 23 and 24. Timetables are in the Latin alphabet.

Getting Around

Surcin airport is 18km west of Belgrade. Ignore taxi drivers in the airport; instead go outside and look for a fare from 450 to 600 DIN. The best transport to the airport is the **JAT bus** *(30 DIN; airport-town hourly from 5am-9pm, town-airport hourly from 7am-8pm)* which departs from the Hotel Slavija B and runs via the train station.

Private and state-owned buses, trams and trolleybuses charge 10 DIN for any journey. Belgrade's taxis are plentiful; flag fall is 40 DIN. Check that the taxi meter is running.

VOJVODINA ВОЈВОДИНА

Vojvodina (21,506 sq km) was an autonomous province until annexed by Serbia in 1990. The region was under Turkish rule from the 16th century until the Habsburgs cleared them out in the late 17th century. Vojvodina remained a part of Hungary until 1918. These days, this fertile plain provides much of Yugoslavia's wheat, corn and crude oil.

Novi Sad Нови Сад

☎ 021 • pop 270,000

Vojvodina's capital is a modern city situated at a strategic bend on the Danube. Novi Sad developed in the 18th century as a Habsburg fortress. Its attractions these days include wandering the pedestrian streets and visiting the Petrovaradin Citadel. In July or August, the town hosts the popular Exit music festival (see the boxed text).

The **tourist office** *(☎ 421 811; Dunavska 27)* is in a quaint old part of town. The **telephone centre** *(open 24 hrs)* is next to the main post office.

The main museum in Novi Sad, **Muzej Vojvodine** *(☎ 26 555; Dunavska 35 & 37; admission 20 DIN; open 9am-7pm Tues-Fri, 9am-2pm Sat & Sun)* is in two buildings. No 35 covers Vojvodina history from Palaeolithic times to the late 19th century, and No 37 takes the story to 1945 with an emphasis on WWI and WWII. Across the river is the majestic **Petrovaradin Citadel**, the 'Gibraltar of the Danube', built from 1699 to 1780 and designed by French architect Vauban. Stairs beside the

A Graceful Exit

Every August, musicians from all over Europe invade Novi Sad for the Exit music festival. While a raucous, rollicking time is generally had by all, Exit is not just about rocking out. Organised by student and youth organizations from around southeastern Europe – especially the former Yugoslav republics – these days Exit has adopted a mission of cultural harmony as well. Workshops and lectures contribute to the educational aspect of the festival, and the emphasis is on building understanding and friendship among recently bitter Balkan enemies.

For more information on upcoming dates and schedules for the festival, contact the Novi Sad tourist office.

large church lead up to the fortress. The clock tower's hour hand is the longer one, rendering it easy to read from the river.

On the Danube, the large **autocamp** *(☎ 368 400, fax 366 801; Ribarsko Ostrvo; bungalows per double/triple 1400/1745 DIN)* has some basic well-used bungalow accommodation, with two restaurants on site. Take bus No 4 from the train station or city centre to Liman and then walk towards the river or take a 80 DIN taxi ride.

Alla Lanterna *(☎ 622 002; Dunavska 27; meals 240-290 DIN; open 8am-midnight)* is a pizza/pasta place with bags of atmosphere (maybe it has to do with the pebble-heavy wall decorations). **Pizzeria La Forza** *(Katolicka Porta 6; pasta dishes 150-180 DIN; open 8am-11pm Mon-Sat, 3pm-11pm Sun)* is a bright and cheery spot for some filling pasta. The **Red Cow** *(cnr Dunavska & Zmaj Jovina)* is a trendy Irish pub that's just the place for a refreshing Guinness or draught Nikšić.

Novi Sad is served by frequent local trains to Belgrade (120 DIN, two hours) and Subotica (112 DIN, 1½ hours) plus international trains. It's easier to buy train tickets from **KRS Beograd Tours** *(☎ 27 445, fax 27 423; Svetozara Miletića 4)* than at the train station.

Subotica Суботица

☎ 024 • pop 150,000 (est 2002)

Ten kilometres from the border at Kelebija, Subotica is a useful transit point to Hungary. The train station, with a left-luggage office and exchange office, is just a short walk from the town centre. **Micro Finance Bank** *(Lenjina Park 8)* cashes travellers cheques, and there's a **currency exchange office** *(open 8am-7pm Mon-Fri, 8am-1pm Sat)* in the old town hall.

The imposing Art Nouveau town hall (1910) contains an excellent **historical museum** *(open 9am-2pm Tues-Sat)*. Check whether the exquisitely decorated council chambers are open. An equally superb piece of architecture is the amazing art nouveau **Modern Art Gallery** *(trg Lenina 5; open 7am-1pm Mon-Fri, to 6pm Tues & Thurs, 9am-noon Sat)*.

At **Hotel Patria** *(☎ 554 500, fax 551 762; Đure Đakovica; singles/doubles 1800/2800 DIN)*, rooms come with bath and breakfast. Youth hostel **Zorka** *(☎ 754 418; Palić; per person €6, full board €12)*, by the lake at Palić, offers budget accommodation.

Pizza Vento *(Borisa Kidriča 2; pizzas 160-200 DIN; open 7am-midnight)* is a relaxing spot for a pizza and beer. Go to **Lipa** *(Đure Đakovica 13; burek 60 DIN; open 24hr daily)*, a bakery and burek shop, for excellent cheese-and-mushroom burek and yogurt for breakfast.

There are two local trains a day to/from Szeged, Hungary (155 DIN, 1¾ hours), plus international trains. Trains to Belgrade (155 DIN, 3½ hours) also call at Novi Sad.

Montenegro
Црна Гора

Only tiny Montenegro (Crna Gora) kept its head above the Turkish tide that engulfed the Balkans. The republic has been in the Yugoslav federation through its many incarnations, but recently an independence movement has flourished. Under the proposed new union with Serbia, President Milo Đukanović has put any independence moves on hold.

From an interior with Alpine-type scenery to giddy-deep canyons, coastal fjords, and a sparsely vegetated and highly folded limestone mountain range that plummets down to an azure Adriatic sea, the 13,812-sq-km republic has got the works. North of Podgorica, both railway and road run through the Moraca Canyon, while 40km west of Mojkovac is the 1.3km-deep Tara Canyon. Other striking features are the winding Bay of Kotor, the largest fjord in southern Europe, and the vast, beautiful Lake Skadar. Of historical interest are the old towns of Budva, Cetinje and Kotor.

Montenegro is a very popular holiday spot; June to September is the high season peaking in July and August. Quoted accommodation prices are for the high season.

You can enter Montenegro by road from Croatia, Serbia, Kosovo and Albania or by ship from Italy. The only international rail connections are through Serbia. A main rail line runs from Belgrade to Bar, where ferries connect with Italy.

BAR БАР

☎ 085

Backed by a precipitous coastal range, wannabe-modern Bar is Yugoslavia's only port and a convenient transport centre. The best bet for information is **Montenegro Tourist** *(☎ 311 133; Obala 13 Jula)*, by the ferry terminal.

Visitors with time or their own transport will be able to choose from a whole range of accommodation, with 'sobe', 'zimmer' or 'private room' signs all along the coast. Places to eat are limited. **Pizeria Bell** *(Vladimira Rolovic, Podkovica C; pizza €3, pasta €4-5; open 7am-11pm daily)* just up the street from the ferry terminal is a small cosy pizza/pasta joint that's open year-round.

Four trains a day travel to/from Belgrade (€8, nine hours). The overnight train provides cheap accommodation. There are two daily buses to Ulcinj (€1.80, 1½ hours) and frequent buses to Budva (€2, 45 minutes) and Kotor (€3.20, three hours).

Montenegro Lines *(☎ 312 336; Obala 13 Jula)* sail 10pm on Tuesday, Thursday and Saturday to Bari (Italy). In summer it's a daily service. Deck passage (10 hours) costs €40 and a bunk from €13. For ferries to Ancona (Italy), contact **Mercur** *(☎ 313 617, fax 313 618; ⓔ mercur@Eunet.yu; Obala 13 Jula)*. The Thursday service takes 16 hours and costs €46 for a deck seat.

ULCINJ УЛЦИЊ

☎ 085

Ulcinj gained notoriety as a North African pirate base and slave market between 1571 and 1878. The Turks held the area for over 300 years, and today the town shelters many Muslim Albanians. Many Kosovars fled here as refugees in 1999.

In July and August, Ulcinj bulges with several thousand extra people. Mala Plaža (Small Beach) is below the old town at the end of 26 Novembar. Velika Plaža (Great Beach), Ulcinj's famous 12km stretch of unbroken sand, begins about 5km southeast of town (take the Ada bus or minibus).

Tomi camping ground *(open May-Sept)* is east of Milena, adjacent to Velika Plaža. Farther on is **HTP Velika Plaža** *(☎ 413 145; Ada road)*, with a variety of accommodation. Inappropriately named houses (€3 per person) have two beds with just enough walk-around space; bungalows (€5 per person) take three people and have more space, and **pavilions** (€8 per person) are larger still and also take three people. Off-season prices are 20% cheaper. Breakfast/lunch/dinner costs €3/6/4. You can book private rooms and apartments through a travel agency such as **Real Estate Tourist Agency** *(☎ 421 609, fax 421 612; ⓦ www.realestate.cg.yu; ul 26 Novembar)*.

Numerous inexpensive cafés around town offer *ćevapčići*. **Gallo Nero** *(☎ 315 245; ul 26 Novembar; dishes €5-12; open 10am-late daily)* matches the best food in Ulcinj with excellent service.

Buses to Bar (€1.60, 45 minutes) run every couple of hours in season. Many minibuses and buses ply the road to Ada (and Velika Plaža) from the market place or main post office for €1.50 in season.

BUDVA БУДВА

☎ 086

Budva is Yugoslavia's top beach resort. A series of fine beaches punctuates the coastline all the way to Sveti Stefan, with high barren coastal mountains forming a magnificent backdrop.

Budva's big tourist-puller is its old **walled town**. Levelled by two earthquakes in 1979, it has since been completely rebuilt as a tourist attraction, so picturesque it seems almost contrived. **Mogren Beach**, to the north of town, is a decent strip.

If you have a tent, try **Autocamp Avala** *(☎ 451 205; open June-Sept)* at Boreti, 2km on the road to Bar. There's a whole string of private rooms along this coastal strip; just look out for *sobe, zimmer* or 'rooms' signs. The helpful **Globtour** *(☎ 451 020, fax 452 827; ⓔ globtourbd@cg.yu; Mediteranska 23)* can arrange private rooms.

Probably the best restaurant is **Restaurant Jadran** *(☎ 451 028; Slovenska obala 10; dishes €5-10; open 8am-late daily)*, with some very appetising fish dishes.

There are frequent buses to Kotor (€1.70, 30 minutes) and Bar (€2, one hour). Eight buses run daily to Belgrade (€15, 12 hours), one to Žabljak (€8, four hours).

KOTOR КОТОР

☎ 082

Shhh! Kotor is a big secret. Not only is the town at the head of southern Europe's deepest fjord, but it also boasts a Unesco-listed walled medieval city. Don't tell anyone.

Four kilometres of walls encircle the old town. Within is an entanglement of small lanes linking squares housing mansions of the main aristocratic families. Of the six 12th- and 13th-century Romanesque churches, St Tripun's Cathedral (1166) is the most important. Also significant is a 6th-century clock tower. Slog up the steep path up to the fortifications on the mountainside above Kotor, where you'll be rewarded with stunning views of Kotor fjord. Vistas are also spectacular around the fjord and on the road to Cetinje.

For **private rooms** *(from €8 per person)* contact the information booth outside the main entrance or try a travel agency. **Mercur Intours** *(☎ 325 113, fax 325 137; Stari Grad)*, opposite the main entrance, and **Meridian Travel Agency** *(☎ 11 188, fax 11 226; ⓔ travel@cg.yu; Stari Grad)* both have helpful English-speaking staff.

Pizzeria Giardino *(Stari Grad; meals €3.50-5; open 9am-late)* is probably the best-value restaurant within the old town. Their pizza marinara is among Montenegro's best.

Frequent buses ply to/from Budva (€1.50, 30 minutes).

CETINJE ЦЕТИЊЕ

☎ 086

Perched on a high plateau above Budva, Cetinje is Montenegro's old capital, subject of songs and epic poems. Much remains of old Cetinje, from museums to palaces, mansions to monasteries. All the large states of Europe used to have embassies here.

The most imposing building in Cetinje is the former parliament, now the **National Museum of Montenegro** *(Novice Cerovic; admission €1.50; open 9am-2.30pm Mon-Fri off season & 9am-5pm daily in season)*. On display are many old books, some copies of frescoes, 44 captured Turkish flags and the coat (three bullet holes in the back) of Duke Danlo, the last prince-bishop, killed in 1860.

Founded in 1484, **Cetinje Monastery** *(admission €0.50; 8am-7pm daily May-Oct, groups only rest of year)* contains a copy of the *Oktoih* or *Octoechos* (Book of the Eight Voices), printed near here in 1494 – one of the oldest collections of Slavic liturgical songs. The monastery also boasts a portion of the true cross and the mummified right hand of St John the Baptist.

Twenty kilometres away on the summit of **Mount Lovcen** (1749m), the 'Black Mountain' that gave Montenegro its name, is the mausoleum of Petar II Petrovic Njegoš, a revered poet and ruler. Take a taxi there and then climb 461 steps to the mausoleum, with its sweeping view of the Bay of Kotor, coast, mountains, and (on a clear morning) Italy.

For a **private room** *(€5 per person)* ask at **Alliance Tours** *(☎ 31 157; ⓔ alliance@cg.yu; Njegoševa 32; closed Sat)* next to the post office; it also has tourist information. **Petar Martinovic** *(☎ 31 809; Bajova Pivljanina 19; beds €7.50-10)* offers comfortable rooms.

Restoran Korzo *(Njegoša; mains €3-5; open 8am-11pm daily)*, next to the post office, offers a big, popular mixed-grill speciality. **Gradska Kafana** *(dishes €4-6; open 7am-11pm daily)*, next to the Royal Court, has an expansive courtyard for al fresco dining.

With a frequent bus services from Kotor (€2, 45 minutes) and Budva (€2, 35 minutes), Cetinje can be an easy day trip.

DURMITOR NATIONAL PARK

☎ 0872

Durmitor National Park is a popular hiking and mountaineering area just west of the ski resort **Žabljak**, the highest town in Yugoslavia (1450m). Some 18 mountain lakes dot the Durmitor Range, and you can walk around the largest, **Crno jezero** (Black Lake), 3km from Žabljak, in an hour or two and take a swim in summer. The rounded mass of Meded (2287m) rises directly behind the lake surrounded by a backdrop of other peaks, including Savin kuk (2313m). The 1.3km-deep **Tara Canyon**, which cuts dramatically into the earth for about 80km, is best seen from a rock promontory at Curevac.

The **Durmitor National Park office** *(☎ 61 474, fax 61 346; next to Hotel Durmitor; open 7am-2pm Mon-Fri)* sells good park maps. In the town centre are a taxi stand, a bus stop and the **Tourist Information Centre** *(☎ 61 659; open 8am-8pm daily in season, to*

3pm out of season), with maps and some fine books. The staff can help arrange accommodation but don't speak English. For more information go to **Sveti Đordije** *(☎/fax 61 367; ul Njegoševa)*, just opposite the turn-off to Hotel Jezera. The English-speaking manager here can also arrange private rooms (from €6.50 per person).

Winter activities include skiing, snowboarding and sledding. In summer rafting trips are possible down the steep forested Tara Gorge and over countless foaming rapids. There's also horse riding, hiking, cycling, mountaineering and paragliding. The Tourist Information Centre can point you in the right direction.

On a hill top five minutes' walk beyond the national park office is **Autocamp Ivando**, which is just a fenced-off field. People here rent out **private rooms** *(€6 per person)* but bring your own sleeping bag.

National Restaurant *(☎ 61 337; behind city council offices; dishes €5-8.50; open 8am-late daily)* is a new restaurant/bar. Its *kačamak* with sour milk (like yogurt) takes the place of three meals.

There are 4.30am and 4pm buses to Belgrade (€12.25, 10 hours), Nikšić (€5, 2½ hours) and Mojkovac (€3.5, 3½ hours). At Mojkovac you can connect with Bar to Belgrade trains. There is one daily direct bus from Belgrade to Žabljak (750 DIN, 10 hours).

Kosovo

Although Kosovo is populated mainly by Kosovar Muslims, the area holds a special place in Serbian history as the site of fateful battles against the Turks. In modern times, Kosovo has lived up to its battle-ridden past, raging with war between the independence-seeking Kosovo Liberation Army and Yugoslavia at the end of the 20th century.

Since June 1999, Kosovo has been administered as a UN-NATO protectorate. Before Serb-instigated 'ethnic cleansing', some two million people occupied Kosovo's 10,887 sq km, making it a densely populated region. The province is now ethnically divided between Albanian Muslims and Serbs.

Four direct buses run between Prishtina and Novi Pazar in Serbia (€4.50, three hours) with frequent connections to Belgrade (370 DIN, six hours). From Peja there's an 8am bus to Rožaje (€5, two hours). Alternatively there are minibuses (€ 5) or taxis (€ 20) outside the bus station. A 9am daily service from Prizren (€14, 11½ hours) calls in at Peja (€11, 9½ hours). A direct bus runs from Prishtina to Ulcinj (€36, 10 hours). Many international bus services are run by a variety of companies and travel agencies, serving much of Europe.

Excellent bus services link all the main towns and villages. Frequent services link Prishtina and Prizren (€3.00, 1½ hours).

PRISHTINA (PRIŠTINA)

☎ 038 • pop 160,000

Kosovo's capital, with all the beauty and grace that Soviet-style concrete can bestow, is little more than a jumping-off point to the more interesting Prizren.

Confusion still reigns as street names have yet to be settled; most people navigate by landmarks. The main streets are Mother Theresa and Ramiz Sadiku Sts, which run from the south to converge near the National Theatre. UNMIK headquarters are off Mother Theresa, by the Grand Hotel. Maps can be difficult to find; ask at kiosks or bookshops along Mother Theresa.

A useful information source is the **Humanitarian Community Information Centre** *(HCIC; ☎ 549 168, fax 549 169; W www.reliefweb.int/hcic; UNHCR Bldg)*; it has a useful atlas on Kosovo, books and press releases. **Turist Kosova** *(☎ 243 688; Nënë Tereza 36)* can provide travel information and book international buses.

Micro Enterprise Bank *(☎ 548 052, fax 549 625; Rr Skenderbeu; open 9am-4pm Mon-Fri)*, off Mother Theresa, will cash travellers cheques. **PTK** *(Post Telephone Kosova; open 8am-9pm Mon-Fri, 8am-3pm Sat)* is in the stylish copper-roofed building next to the National Theatre. Alternatively, **Premium Internet Cafe** *(opposite UNMIK; open 24 hrs)* charges €1 a minute for a call anywhere in the world. Internet access is €2.50 an hour, and you can quaff a beer while you surf.

Numbered Kombis (minibuses) roam the streets. Bus Nos 1 and 2 go down Kral Petri St, from where it's a short walk through a housing estate to the bus station. The fare is €0.50.

Places to Stay & Eat

The **Iliria** *(☎ 24 042; Mother Theresa; singles/doubles €30/60)* is the cheapest place in town and comes with very helpful staff.

Many places to eat lie along Mother Theresa and Ramiz Sadiku Sts. Side-street cafés abound, selling burek and hamburgers for €1 to €1.50. Pasta and pizza cafés charge up to €2.50. With a cosy ambience, **A&A Pizza Restaurant** *(☎ 044 161 713; Rr Rexhep Mala 39; dishes €2-6; open 11am-11pm daily)* is as good as any Italian restaurant could offer.

One of the most prominent bars serving the large expat population is **John's Kukri Bar** *(north of UNMIK; open 7am-midnight daily)*, offering big breakfasts, snacks and booze throughout the day and evening. There's live music most weekends. **Boom Boom Room** *(west of UNMIK; open 10am-late)* is a large single room pub that's again popular with the expat crowd and young Kosovars.

Around Prishtina

Gadimë Cave Thirty five kilometres south of Prishtina **Gadimë Cave** *(Marble Cave; admission €2.50; open 9am-6pm daily; 30-minute tour)*, the only show cave in Kosovo, is worth a plunge underground. It's renowned for its helictites (thin stalactites growing at strange angles). Your imagination will get a tour, as the guide proudly points out various formations as the map of Kosovo or the eagle of Albania. Despite what everyone else does, don't touch the formations.

There are two buses (11am and 2 pm) from Prishtina. As it's the end of the line you can ask the driver to wait for you to return from the cave tour.

PRIZREN

☎ 029

Although Prizren was the medieval capital of 'Old Serbia', the architectural influence is Turkish. The place seems like a party town, as people throng the bars and cafés along the river and in Shadrvan. On Sunday evenings groups and families promenade through the area.

One of the delights in visiting Prizren is wandering through the old streets looking at the old architecture. There's far more here than in Prishtina. At the time of writing KFOR was experimenting with having no curfew, but check when you get there to see if it's been reinstated. The town revolves around the river and Shadrvan, a cobblestone plaza with a fountain. Crossing the river just west of the main bridge is a 'new' medieval bridge built to replace the old one destroyed by floods in 1979. The bus station is on the Peja road about 2km from the centre.

The **Tourist Association of Prizren** *(☎ 32 843; Sheshi Lidhjës se Prizrenit; open 8am-7.30pm Mon-Sat)* has information and **Micro Entreprise Bank** *(☎ 42 550, fax 44 338; Rr. Shadërvani)* cashes travellers cheques. The **main post office** *(next to Theranda Hotel; open 8am-9pm daily)* also has telephones.

Private travel agencies in the town also run international buses. **Dardania Tours** *(☎ 22 358; Lidhja Prizrenit)* have buses going to İstanbul and Tirana, as do **Gold Tours** *(☎/fax 23 149; ⓔ goldtours2@hotmail.com; Rr Remzi Ademi 31)*. **Big Ben Internet Caffe** *(Seshi i Lidhjës; open 24hr daily)* behind Theranda Hotel has a satellite connection and charges €2 an hour.

The soldiers guarding the Orthodox **Church of Bogorodica Ljeviška** (1307) and **Sveti Georgi** (1856) might let you in for a look, if you're lucky. Out of bounds are the **Sveti Spas** church above the town and the fine castle atop the hill.

The **Sinan Pasha Mosque** (1561), beside the river, dominates the centre. You can actually go in and gape at its finely decorated high-dome ceiling. Up the road from the Theranda Hotel are the newly restored **Gazi Mehmed Pasha Baths** (1563). Check at the tourist office for a visit.

Places to Stay & Eat

Accommodation is limited. The faded and ill-maintained **Theranda Hotel** *(☎ 22 292; singles/doubles/triples €25/35/45)* in the town centre has rooms with bathrooms and carpet to trip over. **Hotel Prizren** *(☎ 30 106, fax 41 552; Rr Bajram Curri; singles/doubles/triples €25/35/45)*, a kilometre northwest, offers more switched-on management. It also features wheelchair access.

An abundance of cafés, bars and restaurants clusters around the river and Shadrvan. **Holiday** *(Sheshi Shadrvan; open 8am-midnight daily; dishes €2.50-5.50, fish €5.50-13)*, down by the 'new' medieval bridge, enjoys a good reputation among local families. **MCM Liridona restaurant** *(dishes €1.50-4; open 8am-midnight daily)* is an excellent, filling Turkish restaurant down near the river. Have a refreshing glass of *ajran* (yogurt drink).

Appendix – Telephones

Dial Direct

You can dial directly from public telephone boxes from almost anywhere in Europe to almost anywhere in the world. This is usually cheaper than going through the operator. In much of Europe, public telephones accepting phonecards are becoming the norm and in some countries coin-operated phones are difficult to find.

To call abroad simply dial the international access code (IAC) for the country you are calling from (most commonly ☎ 00 in Europe but see the following table), the country code (CC) for the country you are calling, the local area code (usually dropping the leading zero if there is one) and then the number. If, for example, you are in Italy (international access code ☎ 00) and want to make a call to the USA (country code ☎ 1), San Francisco (area code ☎ 415), number ☎ 123 4567, then you dial ☎ 00-1-415-123 4567. To call from the UK (☎ 00) to Australia (☎ 61), Sydney (☎ 02), number ☎ 1234 5678, you dial the following: ☎ 00-61-2-1234 5678.

Home Direct

If you would rather have somebody else pay for the call, you can, from many countries, dial directly to your home country operator and then reverse charges; you can also charge the call to a phone company credit card. To do this, simply dial the relevant 'home direct' or 'country direct' number to be connected to your own operator. For the USA there's a choice of AT&T, MCI or Sprint Global One home direct services. Home direct numbers vary from country to country – check with your telephone company before you leave, or with the international operator in the country you're ringing from. From phone boxes in some countries you may need a coin or local phonecard to be connected with the relevant home direct operator.

In some places (particularly airports), you may find dedicated home direct phones where you simply press the button labelled USA, Australia, Hong Kong or whatever for direct connection to the operator. Note that the home direct service does not operate to and from all countries, and that the call could be charged at operator rates, which makes it expensive for the person paying. Placing a call on your phone credit card is more expensive than paying the local tariff.

Dialling Tones

In some countries, after you have dialled the international access code, you have to wait for a second dial tone before dialling the code for your target country and the number. Often the same applies when you ring from one city to another within these countries: wait for a dialling tone after you've dialled the area code for your target city. If you're not sure what to do, simply wait three or four seconds after dialling a code – if nothing happens, you can probably keep dialling.

Phonecards

In major locations phones may accept credit cards: simply swipe your card through the slot and the call is charged to the card, though rates can be very high. Phone-company credit cards can be used to charge calls via your home country operator.

Stored-value phonecards are now almost standard all over Europe. You usually buy a card from a post office, telephone centre, newsstand or retail outlet and simply insert the card into the phone each time you make a call. The card solves the problem of finding the correct coins for calls (or lots of correct coins for international calls) and generally gives you a small discount.

Call Costs

The cost of international calls varies widely from one country to another: a US$1.20 call from Britain could cost you US$6 from Turkey. The countries shown in the 'Telephone Codes & Costs' table that follows are rated from * (cheap) to *** (expensive), but rates can vary depending on which country you are calling to (for example, from Italy it's relatively cheap to call North America, but more expensive to call Australia). Reduced rates are available at certain times, usually from mid-evening to early morning, though it varies from country to country – check the local phone book or ask the operator for more details. Calling from hotel rooms can be very expensive.

Telephone Codes & Costs

	CC	cost (see text)	IAC	IO
Albania	355	***	00	12
Andorra	376	**	00	821111
Austria	43	*	00	09
Belgium	32	**	00	1224 (private phone) 1223 (public phone)
Bosnia-Hercegovina	387	**	00	900/901/902
Bulgaria	359	**	00	0123 (calls) 0124 (inquiries)
Croatia	385	**	00	901
Cyprus	357	***	00	
Cyprus (Turkish)	90+392		00	
Czech Republic	420	*	00	1181/0149
Denmark	45	**	00	141
Estonia	372	***	000	165
Finland	358	**	00, 990, 994, 999	020 208
France	33	*	00(w)	12
Germany	49	*	00	11834
Gibraltar	350	***	00	100
Greece	30	*	00	161
Hungary	36	*	00(w)	199
Iceland	354	***	00	5335010
Ireland	353	*	00	114
Northern Ireland	44+28	*	00	155
Italy	39	**	00	15 (Europe) 176 (other countries)
Latvia	371	***	00	115
Liechtenstein	423	***	00	114
Lithuania	370	***	00	194/195
Luxembourg	352	**	00	0010
Macedonia	389	***	99	901
Malta	356	**	00	1154
Morocco	212	***	00(w)	12
Netherlands	31	**	00	0800-0410
Norway	47	**	00	181
Poland	48	**	00	908
Portugal	351	*	00	177
Romania	40	***	00	971
Russia	7	**	8(w)10	
Slovakia	421	**	00	0149
Slovenia	386	**	00	115
Spain	34	**	00(w)	025
Sweden	46	**	00	118119
Switzerland	41	**	00	114
Turkey	90	***	00	115
UK	44	*	00	155
Ukraine	380	**	810	079/073
Yugoslavia	381	***	99	901

CC – Country Code (to call into that country)
IAC – International Access Code (to call abroad from that country)
IO – International Operator (to make inquiries)
(w) – wait for dialling tone

Other country codes include: Australia ☎ 61, Canada ☎ 1, Hong Kong ☎ 852, India ☎ 91, Indonesia ☎ 62, Israel ☎ 972, Japan ☎ 81, Macau ☎ 853, Malaysia ☎ 60, New Zealand ☎ 64, Singapore ☎ 65, South Africa ☎ 27, Thailand ☎ 66, USA ☎ 1

Language

This Language chapter contains pronunciation guidelines and basic vocabulary to help you get around Eastern Europe. For background information about the languages, see the Language sections under Facts for the Visitor in the relevant country chapters.

Some of the languages in this chapter use polite and informal modes of address (indicated by the abbreviations 'pol' and 'inf' respectively). Use the polite form when addressing older people, officials or service staff. For more detailed coverage of all the languages included in this chapter, check out Lonely Planet's extensive series of phrasebooks.

Albanian

Pronunciation

Written Albanian is phonetically consistent and pronunciation shouldn't pose too many problems for English speakers. The Albanian **rr** is trilled and each vowel in a diphthong is pronounced. However, Albanian possesses certain letters that are present in English but rendered differently. These include:

ë	often silent; at the beginning of a word it's like the 'a' in 'ago'
c	as the'ts' in 'bits'
ç	as the 'ch' in 'church'
dh	as the 'th' in 'this'
gj	as the 'gy' in 'hogyard'
j	as the 'y' in 'yellow'
q	between 'ch' and 'ky', similar to the 'cu' in 'cure'
th	as in 'thistle'
x	as the 'dz' in 'adze'
xh	as the 'j' in 'jewel'

Basics

Hello.	*Tungjatjeta/Allo.*
Goodbye.	*Lamtumirë.*
	Mirupafshim. (inf)
Yes.	*Po.*
No.	*Jo.*
Please.	*Ju lutem.*
Thank you.	*Ju falem nderit.*
That's fine.	*Eshtë e mirë.*
You're welcome.	*S'ka përse.*
Excuse me.	*Me falni.*
Sorry. (excuse me, forgive me)	*Më vjen keq* or *Më falni, ju lutem.*

Signs – Albanian

Hyrje	**Entrance**
Dalje	**Exit**
Informim	**Information**
Hapur	**Open**
Mbyllur	**Closed**
E Ndaluar	**Prohibited**
Policia	**Police**
Stacioni I Policisë	**Police Station**
Nevojtorja	**Toilets**
Burra	**Men**
Gra	**Women**

Do you speak English?	*A flisni anglisht?*
How much is it?	*Sa kushton?*
What's your name?	*Si quheni ju lutem?*
My name is ...	*Unë quhem ...* or *Mua më quajnë ...*

Getting Around

What time does the ... leave/arrive?	*Në ç'orë niset/ arrin ...?*
boat	*barka/lundra*
bus	*autobusi*
tram	*tramvaji*
train	*treni*
I'd like ...	*Dëshiroj ...*
a one-way ticket	*një biletë vajtje*
a return ticket	*një biletë kthimi*
1st/2nd class	*klas i parë/i dytë*
timetable	*orar*
bus stop	*stacion autobusi*
Where is ...?	*Ku është ...?*
Go straight ahead.	*Shko drejt.*
Turn left.	*Kthehu majtas.*
Turn right.	*Kthehu djathtas.*
near/far	*afër/larg*

Around Town

a bank	*një bankë*
chemist/pharmacy	*farmaci*
the ... embassy	*... ambasadën*
my hotel	*hotelin tim*
the market	*pazarin*
newsagency	*agjensia e lajmeve*
the post office	*postën*
the telephone centre	*centralin telefonik*

Emergencies – Albanian

Help!	*Ndihmë!*
Call a doctor!	*Thirrni doktorin!*
Call the police!	*Thirrni policinë!*
Go away!	*Zhduku!/Largohuni!*
I'm lost.	*Kam humbur rrugë.*

the tourist office	*zyrën e informimeve turistike*
What time does it open/close?	*Në ç'ore hapet/ mbyllet?*

Accommodation

hotel	*hotel*
camping ground	*kamp pushimi*
Do you have any rooms available?	*A keni ndonjë dhomë të lirë?*
a single room	*një dhomë më një krevat*
a double room	*një dhomë më dy krevat*
How much is it per night/per person?	*Sa kushton për një natë/ për një njeri?*
Does it include breakfast?	*A e përfshin edhe mëngjesin?*

Time, Days & Numbers

What time is it?	*Sa është ora?*
today	*sot*
tomorrow	*nesër*
yesterday	*dje*
in the morning	*në mëngjes*
in the afternoon	*pas dreke*
Monday	*e hënë*
Tuesday	*e martë*
Wednesday	*e mërkurë*
Thursday	*e ënjte*
Friday	*e premte*
Saturday	*e shtunë*
Sunday	*e diel*

1	*një*
2	*dy*
3	*tre*
4	*katër*
5	*pesë*
6	*gjashtë*
7	*shtatë*
8	*tetë*
9	*nëntë*
10	*dhjetë*
100	*njëqind*
1000	*njëmijë*
one million	*një milion*

Bulgarian

Alphabet

Bulgarian uses the Cyrillic alphabet (see The Cyrillic Alphabet boxed text in the Russian section of this chapter.)

Basics

Hello.	*zdraveyte* *zdrasti* (inf)
Goodbye.	*dovizhdane* *chao* (inf)
Yes.	*da*
No.	*ne*
Please.	*molya*
Thank you.	*blagodarya* *mersi* (inf)
I'm sorry. (forgive me)	*sâzhalyavam (prostete)*
Excuse me.	*izvinete me*
I don't understand.	*az ne razbiram*
What's it called?	*kak se kazva tova?*
How much is it?	*kolko struva?*

Getting Around

What time does the ... leave/arrive?
v kolko chasa zaminava/pristiga ...?

city bus	*gradskiyat avtobus*
intercity bus	*mezhdugradskiyat avtobus*
plane	*samolehtât*
train	*vlakât*
tram	*tramvayat*
arrival	*pristigane*
departure	*zaminavane*
timetable	*razpisanie*

Where is the bus stop?
kâde e avtobusnata spirka?

Signs – Bulgarian

Вход	**Entrance**
Изход	**Exit**
Информация	**Information**
Отворено	**Open**
Затворено	**Closed**
Забранено	**Prohibited**
Полицейско Управление	**Police Station**
Тоалетни	**Toilets**
Мъже	**Men**
Жени	**Women**

Emergencies – Bulgarian

Help!	*pomosh!*
Call a doctor!	*povikayte lekar!*
Call the police!	*povikayte politsiya!*
Go away!	*mahayte se!*
I'm lost.	*zagubih se.*

Where is the train station?
kâde e zhelezopâtnata gara?
Where is the left-luggage room?
kâde e garderobât?
Please show me on the map.
molya pokazhete mi na kartata

straight ahead	*napravo*
left	*lyavo*
right	*dyasno*

Around Town

the bank	*bankata*
the hospital	*bolnitsata*
the market	*pazara*
the museum	*muzeya*
the post office	*poshtata*

the tourist office
byuroto za turisticheska informatsiya

Accommodation

Do you have any rooms available?
imateh li svobodni stai?
How much is it?
kolko struva?
Does it include breakfast?
zakuskata vklyuchena li e?

camping ground	*kâmpinguvane*
youth hostel	*obshtezhitie*
guesthouse	*pansion*
hotel	*khotel*
private room	*stoya v chastna kvartira*
single room	*edinichna staya*
double room	*dvoyna staya*

Time, Days & Numbers

What time is it?	*kolko e chasât?*
today	*dnes*
tonight	*dovechera*
tomorrow	*utre*
yesterday	*vchera*
in the morning	*sutrinta*
in the evening	*vecherta*

Monday	*ponedelnik*
Tuesday	*vtornik*
Wednesday	*sryada*
Thursday	*chetvârtâk*
Friday	*petâk*
Saturday	*sâbota*
Sunday	*nedelya*

1	*edno*	7	*sedem*
2	*dve*	8	*osem*
3	*tri*	9	*devet*
4	*chetiri*	10	*deset*
5	*pet*	100	*sto*
6	*shest*	1000	*hilyada*

one million	*edin milion*

Croatian & Serbian

Serbian uses the Cyrillic alphabet and it's worth familiarising yourself with it (see The Cyrillic Alphabet boxed text in the Russian section of this chapter). Croatian uses a Roman alphabet and many letters are pronounced as in English. Note the following exceptions:

c	as the 'ts' in 'cats'
ć	as the 'tch' sound in 'future'
č	as the 'ch' in 'chop'
đ	as the 'dy' sound in 'verdure'
dž	as the 'j' in 'just'
j	as the 'y' in 'young'
lj	as the 'lli' in 'million'
nj	as the 'ny' in 'canyon'
š	as the 'sh' in 'hush'
ž	as the 's' in 'pleasure'

In the following phrase list, variations in vocabulary between Croatian and Serbian are indicated by 'C' and 'S' respectively.

Basics

Hello.	*Zdravo.*
Goodbye.	*Doviđenja.*
Yes.	*Da.*
No.	*Ne.*
Please.	*Molim.*
Thank you.	*Hvala.*
That's fine/ You're welcome.	*U redu je/ Nema na čemu.*
Excuse me.	*Oprostite.*
Sorry. (excuse me, forgive me)	*Pardon.*
Do you speak English?	*Govorite li engleski?*
How much is it ...?	*Koliko košta ...?*

Getting Around

What time does the ... leave/arrive?
Kada ... polazi/dolazi?

boat — *brod*
city bus — *autobusgradski*
intercity bus — *autobus međugradski*
train — *voz* (S)/*vlak* (C)
tram — *tramvaj*

one-way ticket — *kartu u jednom pravcu*
return ticket — *povratnu kartu*
1st class — *prvu klasu*
2nd class — *drugu klasu*

Where is the bus/tram stop?
Gde je autobuska/tramvajska stanica? (S)
Gdje je autobuska/tramvajska postaja? (C)
Can you show me (on the map)?
Možete li mi pokazati (na karti)?
Go straight ahead.
Idite pravo napred (S)/*naprijed.* (C)
Turn left.
Skrenite lijevo (C)/*levo.* (S)
Turn right.
Skrenite desno.
near/far
blizu/daleko

Around Town

I'm looking for ... — *Tražim ...*
a bank — *banku*
the ... embassy — *... ambasadu*
my hotel — *moj hotel*
the market — *pijacu*
the post office — *poštu*

Signs – Croatian & Serbian

Entrance/Exit
Улаз/Излаз
Ulaz/Izlaz
Open/Closed
Отворено/Затворено
Otvoreno/Zatvoreno
Information
Информације
Informacije
Police
Милиција
Milicija **(S)/*****Policija*** **(C)**
Police Station
Станица Милиције
Stanica Milicije **(S)/*****Policija*** **(C)**
Prohibited
Забрањено
Zabranjeno
Toilets
Тоалети
Toaleti **(S)/*****Zahodi*** **(C)**

Emergencies – Croatian/Serbian

Help! — *Upomoć!*
Call a doctor! — *Pozovite lekara!* (S)
Pozovite liječnika! (C)
Call the police! — *Pozovite miliciju!* (S)
Pozovite policiju! (C)
Go away! — *Idite!*
I'm lost. — *Izgubio/Izgubila sam se.* (m/f) (S)
Izgubljen/Izgubljena sam. (m/f) (C)

the telephone centre — *telefonsku centralu*
the tourist office — *turistički biro*

Accommodation

hotel — *hotel*
guesthouse — *privatno prenoćište*
youth hostel — *omladinsko prenoćište*
camping ground — *kamping*

Do you have any rooms available?
Imate li slobodne sobe?
How much is it per night/per person?
Koliko košta za jednu noć/po osobi?
I'd like a (single/double) room. — *Želim sobu sa (jednim/duplim) krevetom.*

Time, Days & Numbers

What time is it? — *Koliko je sati?*
today — *danas*
tomorrow — *sutra*
yesterday — *juče* (S)/*jučer* (C)
in the morning — *ujutro*
in the afternoon — *popodne*

Monday — *ponedeljak*
Tuesday — *utorak*
Wednesday — *sreda* (S)/*srijeda* (C)
Thursday — *četvrtak*
Friday — *petak*
Saturday — *subota*
Sunday — *nedelja* (S)/*nedjelja* (C)

1	*jedan*	7	*sedam*
2	*dva*	8	*osam*
3	*tri*	9	*devet*
4	*četiri*	10	*deset*
5	*pet*	100	*sto*
6	*šest*	1000	*hiljada* (S)/ *tisuću* (C)

one million — *jedan milion* (S)/ *jedan milijun* (C)

Czech

Pronunciation

Many Czech letters are pronounced as per their English counterparts. An accent lengthens a vowel and the stress is always on the first syllable. Words are pronounced as written, so if you follow the guidelines below you should have no trouble being understood. When consulting indexes on Czech maps, be aware that **ch** comes after **h**. An accent over a vowel indicates that it is lengthened.

c	as the 'ts' in 'bits'
č	as the 'ch' in 'church'
ch	as in Scottish *loch*
d'	as the 'd' in 'duty'
ě	as the 'ye' in 'yet'
j	as the 'y' in 'you'
ň	as the 'ni' in 'onion'
ř	as the sound 'rzh'
š	as the 'sh' in 'ship'
t'	as the 'te' in 'stew'
ž	as the 's' in 'pleasure'

Basics

Hello/Good day.	*Dobrý den.* (pol)
Hi.	*Ahoj.* (inf)
Goodbye.	*Na shledanou.*
Yes.	*Ano.*
No.	*Ne.*
Please.	*Prosím.*
Thank you.	*Dekuji.*
That's fine/You're welcome.	*Není zač/Prosím.*
Sorry. (forgive me)	*Promiňte.*
I don't understand.	*Nerozumím.*
How much is it?	*Kolik to stojí?*

Getting Around

What time does the ... leave/arrive?	*Kdy odjíždí/přijíždí ...?*
boat	*loď*
city bus	*městský autobus*
intercity bus	*meziměstský autobus*
train	*vlak*
tram	*tramvaj*
arrival	*příjezdy*
departure	*odjezdy*
timetable	*jízdní řád*
Where is the ...?	*Kde je ...?*
bus stop	*autobusová zastávka*
station	*nádraží*
left-luggage room	*úschovna zavazadel*
Please show me on the map.	*Prosím, ukažte mi to na mapě.*
left/right	*vlevo/vpravo*
straight ahead	*rovně*

Signs – Czech

Vchod	**Entrance**
Východ	**Exit**
Informace	**Information**
Otevřeno	**Open**
Zavřeno	**Closed**
Zakázáno	**Prohibited**
Policie	**Police Station**
Telefon	**Telephone**
Záchody/WC/ Toalety	**Toilets**

Around Town

Where is it?	*Kde je to?*
the bank	*banka*
the chemist	*lékárna*
the market	*trh*
the museum	*muzeum*
the post office	*pošta*
the tourist office	*turistické informační centrum (středisko)*

Accommodation

hotel	*hotel*
guesthouse	*penzión*
youth hostel	*ubytovna*
camping ground	*kemping*
private room	*privát*
single room	*jednolůžkový pokoj*
double room	*dvoulůžkový pokoj*
Do you have any rooms available?	*Máte volné pokoje?*
How much is it?	*Kolik to je?*

Time, Days & Numbers

What time is it?	*Kolik je hodin?*
today	*dnes*
tonight	*dnes večer*
tomorrow	*zítra*
yesterday	*včera*
in the morning	*ráno*
in the evening	*večer*
Monday	*pondělí*
Tuesday	*úterý*
Wednesday	*středa*

Emergencies – Czech

Help!	*Pomoc!*
Call a doctor/ ambulance/police!	*Zavolejte doktora/ sanitku/policii!*
Go away!	*Běžte pryč!*
I'm lost.	*Zabloudil jsem.* (m) *Zabloudila jsem.* (f)

Thursday	*čtvrtek*
Friday	*pátek*
Saturday	*sobota*
Sunday	*neděle*

1	*jeden*	7	*sedm*
2	*dva*	8	*osm*
3	*tři*	9	*devět*
4	*čtyři*	10	*deset*
5	*pět*	100	*sto*
6	*šest*	1000	*tisíc*

one million	*jeden milión*

Danish

Pronunciation

a	as in 'father'
a, æ	as in 'act'
o, å, u(n)	a long rounded 'a' as in 'walk
e(g)	as in 'eye'
e, i	as the 'e' in 'bet'
i	as the 'e' in 'theme'
ø	as the 'er' in 'fern'
o, u	as the 'oo' in 'cool'
o	as in 'pot'
o(v)	as the 'ou' in 'out'
o(r)	as the 'or' in for' with less emphasis on the 'r'
u	as in 'pull'
y	say 'ee' while pursing your lips
sj	as in 'ship'
c	as in 'cell'
(o)d	a flat 'dh' sound, like the 'th' in 'these'
r	a rolling 'r' abruptly cut short
j	as the 'y' in 'yet'

Basics

Hello.	*Hallo.* *Hej.* (informal)
Goodbye.	*Farvel.*
Yes.	*Ja.*
No.	*Nej.*
Please.	*Må jeg bede/Værsgo.*
Thank you.	*Tak.*
That's fine/ You're welcome.	*Det er i orden/ Selv tak.*
Excuse me. (sorry)	*Undskyld.*
Do you speak English?	*Taler De engelsk?*
How much is it?	*Hvor meget koster det?*

Getting Around

What time does ... leave/arrive?	*Hvornår går/ ankommer ...?*
the boat	*båden*
the bus (city)	*bussen*
the bus (intercity)	*rutebilen*
the tram	*sporvognen*
the train	*toget*

I'd like ...	*Jeg vil gerne have ...*
a one-way ticket	*en enkeltbillet*
a return ticket	*en tur-retur billet*
1st/2nd class	*første/anden klasse*

left luggage office	*reisegodsoppbevaringen*
timetable	*køreplan*
bus stop	*bus holdeplads*
tram stop	*sporvogn holdeplads*
train station	*jernbanestation (banegård)*

Where can I hire a car/bicycle?	*Hvor kan jeg leje en bil/cykel?*
Where is ...?	*Hvor er ...?*
Go straight ahead.	*Gå ligefrem.*
Turn left/right.	*Drej til venstre/højre.*
near/far	*nær/fjern*

Around Town

a bank	*en bank*
a chemist/pharmacy	*et apotek*
the ... embassy	*den ... ambassade*
the market	*ma rkedet*
a newsagent	*en aviskiosk*

Signs – Danish

Indgang	**Entrance**
Udgang	**Exit**
Information	**Information**
Åben	**Open**
Lukket	**Closed**
Forbudt	**Prohibited**
Politistation	**Police Station**
Toiletter	**Toilets**
Herrer	**Men**
Damer	**Women**

Emergencies – Danish

Help!	*Hjælp!*
Call a doctor!	*Ring efter en læge!*
Call the police!	*Ring efter politiet!*
Go away!	*Forsvind!*
I'm lost.	*Jeg har gået vild.*

the post office	*postkontoret*
the tourist office	*turistinformationen*
What time does it open/close?	*Hvornår åbner/ lukker det?*

Accommodation

hotel	*hotel*
guesthouse	*gæstgiveri*
hostel	*vandrerhjem*
camping ground	*campingplads*
Do you have any rooms available?	*Har I ledige værelser?*
How much is it per night/ per person?	*Hvor meget koster det per nat/ per person?*
one day/two days	*en nat/to nætter*
I'd like ...	*Jeg ønsker ...*
a single room	*et enkeltværelse*
a double room	*et dobbeltværelse*

Time, Days & Numbers

What time is it?	*Hvad er klokken?*
today	*i dag*
tomorrow	*i morgen*
yesterday	*i går*
morning	*morgenen*
afternoon	*eftermiddagen*
Monday	*mandag*
Tuesday	*tirsdag*
Wednesday	*onsdag*
Thursday	*torsdag*
Friday	*fredag*
Saturday	*lørdag*
Sunday	*søndag*

0	*nul*	7	*syv*
1	*en*	8	*otte*
2	*to*	9	*ni*
3	*tre*	10	*ti*
4	*fire*	11	*elve*
5	*fem*	100	*hundrede*
6	*seks*	1000	*tusind*

one million	*en million*

Dutch

Pronunciation

au, ou	pronounced somewhere between the 'ow' in 'how' and the 'ow' in 'glow'
eu	a tricky one; try saying 'eh' with rounded lips and the tongue forward, then slide the tongue back and down to make an 'oo' sound; it's similar to the 'eu' in French *couleur*
i, ie	long, as the 'ee' in 'meet'
ij	as the 'ey' in 'they'
oe	as the 'oo' in 'zoo'
ui	a very tricky one; pronounced somewhere between **au/ou** and **eu**; it's similar to the 'eui' in French *fauteuil*, without the slide to the 'i'
ch, g	in the north, a hard 'kh' sound as in the Scottish *loch*; in the south, a softer, lisping sound
j	as the 'y' in 'yes'; also as the 'j' in 'jam' or 'zh' 'pleasure'
r	in the south, a trilled sound; in the north it varies, often guttural

Basics

Hello.	*Dag/Hallo.*
Goodbye.	*Dag.*
Yes.	*Ja.*
No.	*Nee.*
Please.	*Alstublieft/Alsjeblieft.*
Thank you.	*Dank U/je (wel).*
You're welcome.	*Geen dank.*
Excuse me.	*Pardon.*
Sorry.	*Sorry.*
Do you speak English?	*Spreekt U/spreek je Engels?*
How much is it?	*Hoeveel kost het?*

Getting Around

What time does the ... leave/arrive?	*Hoe laat vertrekt/ arriveert de ...?*
(next)	*(volgende)*
boat	*boot*
bus	*bus*
train	*trein*
tram	*tram*
I'd like to hire a car/bicycle.	*Ik wil graag een auto/fiets huren.*
I'd like a one-way/ return ticket.	*Ik wil graag een enkele reis/een retour.*
1st/2nd class	*eerste/tweede klas*
left luggage locker	*bagagekluis*
bus/tram stop	*bushalte/tramhalte*
train station/ ferry terminal	*treinstation/ veerhaven*

Where is the ...?	*Waar is de ...?*
Go straight ahead.	*Ga rechtdoor.*
Turn left/right.	*Ga linksaf/rechtsaf.*
far/near	*ver/dichtbij*

Around Town

a bank	*een bank*
the ... embassy	*de ... ambassade*
the market	*de markt*
the pharmacy	*de drogist*
the newsagent/stationer	*de krantenwinkel/kantoorboekhandel*
the post office	*het postkantoor*
the tourist office	*de VVV/het toeristenbureau*
What time does it open/close?	*Hoe laat opent/sluit het?*

Accommodation

hotel	*hotel*
guesthouse	*pension*
youth hostel	*jeugdherberg*
camping ground	*camping*
Do you have any rooms available?	*Heeft U kamers vrij?*
single/double room	*eenpersoons/tweepersoons kamer*
one/two nights	*één nacht/twee nachten*
How much is it per night/per person?	*Hoeveel is het per nacht/per persoon?*

Time, Days & Numbers

What time is it?	*Hoe laat is het?*
today	*vandaag*
tomorrow	*morgen*
in the morning	*'s-morgens*
in the afternoon	*'s-middags*

Signs – Dutch

Ingang	**Entrance**
Uitgang	**Exit**
Informatie/Inlichtingen	**Information**
Open/Gesloten	**Open/Closed**
Verboden	**Prohibited**
Politiebureau	**Police Station**
WC/Toiletten	**Toilets**
Heren	**Men**
Dames	**Women**

Emergencies – Dutch

Help!	*Help!*
Call a doctor!	*Haal een dokter!*
Call the police!	*Haal de politie!*
Go away!	*Ga weg!*
I'm lost.	*Ik ben de weg kwijt.*

Monday	*maandag*
Tuesday	*dinsdag*
Wednesday	*woensdag*
Thursday	*donderdag*
Friday	*vrijdag*
Saturday	*zaterdag*
Sunday	*zondag*

0	*nul*	7	*zeven*
1	*één*	8	*acht*
2	*twee*	9	*negen*
3	*drie*	10	*tien*
4	*vier*	11	*elf*
5	*vijf*	100	*honderd*
6	*zes*	1000	*duizend*

one million	*één miljoen*

Estonian

Alphabet & Pronunciation

The letters of the Estonian alphabet are: **a b d e f g h i j k l m n o p r s š z ž t u v õ ä ö ü**.

a	as the 'u' in 'cut'
b	similar to English 'p'
g	similar to English 'k'
j	as the 'y' in 'yes'
š	as 'sh'
ž	as the 's' in 'pleasure'
õ	somewhere between the 'e' in 'bed' and the 'u' in 'fur'
ä	as the 'a' in 'cat'
ö	as the 'u' in 'fur' but with rounded lips
ü	as a short 'you'
ai	as the 'i' in 'pine'
ei	as in 'vein'
oo	as the 'a' in 'water'
uu	as the 'oo' in 'boot'
öö	as the'u' in 'fur'

Greetings & Civilities

Hello.	*Tere.*
Goodbye.	*Head aega* or *Nägemiseni.*
Yes.	*Jah.*
No.	*Ei.*
Excuse me.	*Vabandage.*

Please.	*Palun.*
Thank you.	*Tänan* or *Aitäh.* (thanks)
Do you speak English?	*Kas te räägite inglise keelt?*

Getting Around

airport	*lennujaam*
bus station	*bussijaam*
port	*sadam*
stop (eg, bus stop)	*peatus*
train station	*raudteejaam*
bus	*buss*
taxi	*takso*
train	*rong*
tram	*tramm*
trolleybus	*trollibuss*
ticket	*pilet*
ticket office	*piletikassa/kassa*
soft class/deluxe	*luksus*
sleeping carriage	*magamisvagun*
compartment (class)	*kupee*

Around Town

bank	*pank*
chemist	*apteek*
currency exchange	*valuutavahetus*
market	*turg*
toilet	*tualett*
Where?	*Kus?*
How much?	*Kui palju?*

Time, Days & Numbers

today	*täna*
tomorrow	*homme*
yesterday	*eile*
Monday	*esmaspäev*
Tuesday	*teisipäev*
Wednesday	*kolmapäev*
Thursday	*neljapäev*
Friday	*reede*
Saturday	*laupäev*
Sunday	*pühapäev*

Signs – Estonian

Sissepääs	**Entrance**
Väljapääs	**Exit**
Avatud/Lahti	**Open**
Suletud/Kinni	**Closed**
Mitte Suitsetada	**No Smoking**
WC	**Public Toilet**
Meestele	**Women**
Naistele	**Men**

Emergencies – Estonian

Help!	*Appi!*
I'm ill.	*Ma olen haige.*
I'm lost.	*Ma olen eksinud.*
Go away!	*Minge ära!*
Call ...!	*Kutsuge ...!*
a doctor	*arst*
the police	*politsei*

1	*üks*	7	*seitse*
2	*kaks*	8	*kaheksa*
3	*kolm*	9	*üheksa*
4	*neli*	10	*kümme*
5	*viis*	100	*sada*
6	*kuus*	1000	*tuhat*

Finnish

Pronunciation

The final letters of the alphabet are **å**, **ä** and **ö** (important to know when looking for something in a telephone directory).

y	as the 'u' in 'pull' but with the lips stretched back (like the German 'ü')
å	as the 'oo' in 'poor'
ä	as the 'a' in 'act'
ö	as the 'e' in 'summer'
z	pronounced (and sometimes written) as 'ts'
v/w	as the 'v' in 'vain'
h	a weak sound, except at the end of a syllable, when it is almost as strong as 'ch' in German *ich*
j	as the 'y' in 'yellow'
r	a rolled 'r'

Basics

Hello.	*Hei/Terve.* *Moi.* (informal)
Goodbye.	*Näkemiin.* *Moi.* (informal)
Yes.	*Kyllä/Joo.*
No.	*Ei.* (pronounced 'ay')
Please.	*Kiitos.*
Thank you.	*Kiitos.*
That's fine/You're welcome.	*Ole hyvä.* or *Eipä kestä.* (informal)
Excuse me. (sorry)	*Anteeksi.*
Do you speak English?	*Puhutko englantia?*
How much is it?	*Paljonko se makasaa?*

Getting Around

What time does ... leave/arrive?	*Mihin aikaan ... lähtee/saapuu?*
the boat	*laiva*
the bus (city)	*bussi*
the bus (intercity)	*bussi/linja-auto*
the train	*juna*
the tram	*raitiovaunu/raitikka*

I'd like a one-way/ return ticket.	*Saanko menolipun/ menopaluulipun.*
Where can I hire a car?	*Mistä mina voisin vuokrata auton?*
Where can I hire a bicycle?	*Mistä mina voin vuokrata polkupyörän?*

1st class	*ensimmäinen luokka*
2nd class	*toinen luokka*
left luggage	*säilytys*
timetable	*aikataulu*
bus/tram stop	*pysäkki*
train station	*rautatieasema*
ferry terminal	*satamaterminaali*

Where is ...?	*Missä on ...?*
Go straight ahead.	*Kulje suoraan.*
Turn left.	*Käänny vasempaan.*
Turn right.	*Käänny oikeaan.*
near/far	*lähellä/kaukana*

Around Town

bank	*pankkia*
chemist/pharmacy	*apteekki*
... embassy	*... -n suurlähetystöä*
market	*toria*
newsagent	*lehtikioski*
post office	*postia*
tourist office	*matkailutoimistoa/ matkailutoimisto*

What time does it open/close?	*Milloin se aukeaan/ sul jetaan?*

Signs – Finnish

Sisään	**Entrance**
Ulos	**Exit**
Opastus	**Information**
Avoinna	**Open**
Suljettu	**Closed**
Kiellety	**Prohibited**
Poliisiasema	**Police Station**
WC	**Toilets**
Miehet	**Men**
Naiset	**Women**

Emergencies – Finnish

Help!	*Apua!*
Call a doctor!	*Kutsukaa lääkäri!*
Call the police!	*Soittakaa poliisi!*
Go away!	*Mene pois! (Häivy!)*
I'm lost.	*Minä olen eksynyt.*

Accommodation

hotel	*hotelli*
guesthouse	*matkustajakoti*
youth hostel	*retkeilymaja*
campground	*leirintäalue*

Do you have any rooms available?	*Onko teillä vapaata huonetta?*

How much is it ...?	*Paljonko se on ...?*
per night	*yöltä*
per person	*hengeltä*

I'd like ...	*Haluaisin ...*
a single room	*yhden hengen huoneen*
a double room	*kahden hengen huoneen*

one day	*yhden päivän*
two days	*kaksi päivää*

Time, Days & Numbers

What time is it?	*Paljonko kello on?*
today	*tänään*
tomorrow	*huomenna*
yesterday	*eilen*
morning	*aamulla*
afternoon	*iltapäivällä*

Monday	*maanantai*
Tuesday	*tiistai*
Wednesday	*keskiviikko*
Thursday	*torstai*
Friday	*perjantai*
Saturday	*lauantai*
Sunday	*sunnuntai*

0	*nolla*	7	*seitsemän*
1	*yksi*	8	*kahdeksan*
2	*kaksi*	9	*yhdeksän*
3	*kolme*	10	*kymmenen*
4	*neljä*	11	*yksitoista*
5	*viisi*	100	*sata*
6	*kuusi*	1000	*tuhat*

one million	*miljoona*

French

Basics

Hello.	*Bonjour.*
Goodbye.	*Au revoir.*
Yes.	*Oui.*
No.	*Non.*
Please.	*S'il vous plaît.*
Thank you.	*Merci.*
That's fine, you're welcome.	*Je vous en prie.*
Excuse me.	*Excusez-moi*
Sorry. (apology)	*Pardon*
Do you speak English?	*Parlez-vous anglais?*
How much is it?	*C'est combien?*

Getting Around

When does the next ... leave/arrive?	*À quelle heure part/ arrive le prochain ...?*
boat	*bateau*
bus (city)	*bus*
bus (intercity)	*car*
train	*train*
tram	*tramway*

left luggage (office)	*consigne*
timetable	*horaire*
bus stop	*arrêt d'autobus*
tram stop	*arrêt de tramway*
train station	*gare*
ferry terminal	*gare maritime*

I'd like a ... ticket.	*Je voudrais un billet ...*
one-way	*aller simple*
return	*aller retour*
1st class	*de première classe*
2nd class	*de deuxième classe*

I'd like to hire a car/bicycle.	*Je voudrais louer une voiture/un vélo.*

Signs – French

Entrée	**Entrance**
Sortie	**Exit**
Renseignements	**Information**
Ouvert/Fermée	**Open/Closed**
Interdit	**Prohibited**
(Commissariat de) Police	**Police Station**
Toilettes, WC	**Toilets**
Hommes	**Men**
Femmes	**Women**

Emergencies – French

Help!	*Au secours!*
Call a doctor!	*Appelez un médecin!*
Call the police!	*Appelez la police!*
Leave me alone!	*Fichez-moi la paix!*
I'm lost.	*Je me suis égaré/e*

Where is ...?	*Où est ...?*
Go straight ahead.	*Continuez tout droit.*
Turn left.	*Tournez à gauche.*
Turn right.	*Tournez à droite.*
far/near	*loin/proche*

Around Town

a bank	*une banque*
chemist/pharmacy	*la pharmacie*
the ... embassy	*l'ambassade de ...*
market	*le marché*
newsagent	*l'agence de presse*
post office	*le bureau de poste*
the tourist office	*l'office de tourisme/le syndicat d'initiative*

What time does it open/close?	*Quelle est l' heure de ouverture/fermeture?*

Accommodation

the hotel	*l'hôtel*
the youth hostel	*l'auberge de jeunesse*
the camping ground	*le camping*

Do you have any rooms available?	*Est-ce que vous avez des chambres libres?*
for one person	*pour une personne*
for two people	*deux personnes*

How much is it ...?	*Quel est le prix ...?*
per night	*par nuit*
per person	*par personne*

Time, Days & Numbers

What time is it?	*Quelle heure est-il?*
today	*aujourd'hui*
tomorrow	*demain*
yesterday	*hier*
morning	*matin*
afternoon	*après-midi*

Monday	*lundi*
Tuesday	*mardi*
Wednesday	*mercredi*
Thursday	*jeudi*
Friday	*vendredi*
Saturday	*samedi*
Sunday	*dimanche*

1	*un*	7	*sept*
2	*deux*	8	*huit*
3	*trois*	9	*neuf*
4	*quatre*	10	*dix*
5	*cinq*	100	*cent*
6	*six*	1000	*mille*

one million	*un million*

German

Pronunciation

Vowels

As a rule, German vowels are long before one consonant and short before two consonants, eg, the **o** is long in the word *Dom* (cathedral), but short in the word *doch* (after all).

au	as the 'ow' in 'vow'
ä	short, as in 'cat' or long, as in 'care'
äu	as the 'oy' in 'boy'
ei	as the 'ai' in 'aisle'
eu	as the 'oy' in 'boy'
ie	as the 'brief'
ö	as the 'er' in 'fern'
ü	similar to the 'u' in 'pull' but with lips stretched back

Consonants

The consonants **b**, **d** and **g** sound like 'p', 't' and 'k', respectively, when word-final.

ch	as in Scottish *loch*
j	as the 'y' in 'yet'
qu	as 'k' plus 'v'
r	can be trilled or guttural, depending on the region
s	as in 'sun'; as the 'z' in 'zoo' when followed by a vowel
sch	as the 'sh' in 'ship'
sp, st	as 'shp' and 'sht' when word-initial
tion	the 't' is pronounced as the 'ts' in 'its'
v	as the 'f' in 'fan'
w	as the 'v' in 'van'
z	as the 'ts' in 'its'

Basics

Good day.	*Guten Tag.*
Hello. (in Bavaria and Austria)	*Grüss Gott.*
Goodbye.	*Auf Wiedersehen.*
Bye.	*Tschüss.* (informal)
Yes.	*Ja.*
No.	*Nein.*
Please.	*Bitte.*
Thank you.	*Danke.*
You're welcome.	*Bitte sehr.*
Sorry. (excuse me, forgive me)	*Entschuldigung.*
What's your name?	*Wie heissen Sie?*
My name is ...	*Ich heisse ...*
Do you speak English?	*Sprechen Sie Englisch?*
How much is it?	*Wieviel kostet es?*

Getting Around

What time does ... leave/arrive?	*Wann (fährt ... ab/ kommt ... an)?*
the boat	*das Boot*
the city bus	*der Bus*
the intercity bus	*der überland Bus*
the train	*der Zug*
the tram	*die Strassenbahn*

I'd like to hire a car/bicycle.	*Ich möchte ein Auto/ Fahrrad mieten.*
I'd like a one-way/ return ticket.	*Ich möchte eine Einzel-karte/Rückfahrkarte.*

1st/2nd class	*erste/zweite Klasse*
left luggage lockers	*Schliessfächer*
timetable	*Fahrplan*
bus stop	*Bushaltestelle*
tram stop	*Strassenbahnhaltestelle*
train station	*Bahnhof (Bf)*
ferry terminal	*Fährhafen*

Where is the ...?	*Wo ist die ...?*
Go straight ahead.	*Gehen Sie geradeaus.*
Turn left.	*Biegen Sie links ab.*
Turn right.	*Biegen Sie rechts ab.*
near/far	*nahe/weit*

Around Town

I'm looking for ...	*Ich suche ...*
a bank	*eine Bank*
the ... embassy	*die ... Botschaft*
my hotel	*mein Hotel*
the market	*der Markt*
the newsagency	*der Zeitungshändler*
the pharmacy	*die Apotheke*

Signs – German

Eingang	**Entrance**
Ausgang	**Exit**
Zimmer Frei	**Rooms Available**
Auskunft	**Information**
Offen	**Open**
Geschlossen	**Closed**
Polizeiwache	**Police Station**
Toiletten (WC)	**Toilets**
Herren	**Men**
Damen	**Women**

Emergencies – German

Help!	*Hilfe!*
Call a doctor!	*Holen Sie einen Arzt!*
Call the police!	*Rufen Sie die Polizei!*
Go away!	*Gehen Sie weg!*
I'm lost.	*Ich habe mich verirrt.*

the post office	*das Postamt*
the stationers	*der Schreibwaren-geschäft*
the tourist office	*das Verkehrsamt*
What time does it open/close?	*Um wieviel Uhr macht es auf/zu?*

Accommodation

hotel	*Hotel*
guesthouse	*Pension, Gästehaus*
youth hostel	*Jugendherberge*
camping ground	*Campingplatz*
Do you have any rooms available?	*Haben Sie noch freie Zimmer?*
a single room	*ein Einzelzimmer*
a double room	*ein Doppelzimmer*
How much is it ...?	*Wieviel kostet es ...?*
per night	*pro Nacht*
per person	*pro Person*

Time, Days & Numbers

What time is it?	*Wie spät ist es?*
today	*heute*
tomorrow	*morgen*
yesterday	*gestern*
in the morning	*morgens*
in the afternoon	*nachmittags*
Monday	*Montag*
Tuesday	*Dienstag*
Wednesday	*Mittwoch*
Thursday	*Donnerstag*
Friday	*Freitag*
Saturday	*Samstag/Sonnabend*
Sunday	*Sonntag*

0	*null*	8	*acht*
1	*eins*	9	*neun*
2	*zwei/zwo*	10	*zehn*
3	*drei*	11	*elf*
4	*vier*	12	*zwölf*
5	*fünf*	13	*dreizehn*
6	*sechs*	100	*hundert*
7	*sieben*	1000	*tausend*

one million	*eine Million*

Greek

Basics

Hello.	*yasu* (informal) *yasas* (polite/plural)
Goodbye.	*andio*
Yes.	*ne*
No.	*okhi*
Please.	*sas parakalo*
Thank you.	*sas efharisto*
That's fine/ You're welcome.	*ine endaksi/parakalo*
Excuse me. (forgive me)	*signomi*
Do you speak English?	*milate anglika?*
How much is it?	*poso kani?*

Getting Around

What time does the ... leave/arrive?	*ti ora fevyi/apo horito ...?*
boat	*to plio*
bus (city/intercity)	*to leoforio (ya tin boli/ya ta proastia)*
train	*to treno*
tram	*to tram*
I'd like a ... ticket.	*tha ithela isitirio ...*
one-way	*horis epistrofi*
return	*met epistrois*
1st class	*proti thesi*
2nd class	*dhefteri thesi*
left luggage	*horos aspokevon*
timetable	*dhromologhio*
bus stop	*i stasi tu leoforiu*
Go straight ahead.	*pighenete efthia*
Turn left.	*stripste aristera*
Turn right.	*stripste dheksya*

Signs – Greek

ΕΙΣΟΔΟΣ	**Entrance**
ΕΞΟΔΟΣ	**Exit**
ΠΛΗΡΟΦΟΡΙΕΣ	**Information**
ΑΝΟΙΚΤΟ	**Open**
ΚΛΕΙΣΤΟ	**Closed**
ΑΣΤΥΝΟΜΙΚΟΣ ΣΤΑΘΜΟΣ	**Police Station**
ΑΠΑΓΟΡΕΥΕΤΑΙ	**Prohibited**
ΤΟΥΑΛΕΤΕΣ	**Toilets**
ΑΝΔΡΩΝ	**Men**
ΓΥΝΑΙΚΩΝ	**Women**

Emergencies – Greek

Help!	*voithia!*
Call a doctor!	*fona kste ena yatro!*
Call the police!	*tilefoniste stin astinomia!*
Go away!	*fighe/dhromo!*
I'm lost.	*eho hathi*

Around Town

a bank	*mia trapeza*
the ... embassy	*i ... presvia*
the market	*i aghora*
newsagent	*efimeridhon*
pharmacy	*farmakio*
the post office	*to takhidhromio*
the tourist office	*to ghrafio turistikon pliroforion*
What time does it open/close?	*ti ora aniyi/klini?*

Accommodation

a hotel	*ena xenothohio*
a youth hostel	*enas xenonas neoitos*
a camping ground	*ena kamping*
I'd like a ... room.	*thelo ena dhomatio ...*
single	*ya ena atomo*
double	*ya dhio atoma*
How much is it ...?	*poso kostizi ...?*
per night/person	*ya ena vradhi/atomo*

Time, Days & Numbers

What time is it?	*ti ora ine?*
today	*simera*
tomorrow	*avrio*
yesterday	*hthes*
in the morning	*to proi*
in the afternoon	*to apoyevma*
Monday	*dheftera*
Tuesday	*triti*
Wednesday	*tetarti*
Thursday	*pempti*
Friday	*paraskevi*
Saturday	*savato*
Sunday	*kiryaki*

1	*ena*	7	*epta*
2	*dhio*	8	*okhto*
3	*tria*	9	*enea*
4	*tesera*	10	*dheka*
5	*pende*	100	*ekato*
6	*eksi*	1000	*khilya*

one million	*ena ekatomirio*

Hungarian

Pronunciation

The letters **cs**, **zs**, **gy** and **sz** (consonant clusters) are separate letters in Hungarian and appear that way in telephone books and other alphabetical listings, eg, *cukor* (sugar) appears in the dictionary before *csak* (only).

c	as the 'ts' in 'hats'
cs	as the 'ch' in 'church'
gy	as the 'j' in 'jury'
j	as the 'y' in 'yes'
ly	as the 'y' in 'yes'
ny	as the 'ni' in 'onion'
r	like a slightly trilled Scottish 'r'
s	as the 'sh' in 'ship'
sz	as the 's' in 'set'
ty	as the 'tu' in British English 'tube'
w	as 'v' (found in foreign words only)
zs	as the 's' in 'pleasure'

The meaning of words with **a**, **e** or **o** with and without an accent mark is great. For example, *hát* means 'back' while *hat* means 'six'.

a	as the 'o' in hot
á	as in 'father'
e	a short 'e' as in 'set'
é	as the 'e' in 'they' with no 'y' sound
i	as in 'hit' but shorter
í	as the 'i' in 'police'
o	as in 'open'
ó	a longer version of o above
ö	as the 'o' in 'worse' with no 'r' sound
ő	a longer version of ö above
u	as in 'pull'
ú	as the 'ue' in 'blue'
ü	similar to the 'u' in 'flute'; purse your lips tightly and say 'ee'
ű	a longer, breathier version of ü above

Basics

Hello.	*Jó napot kívánok.* (pol)
	Szia/Szervusz. (inf)
Goodbye.	*Viszontlátásra.* (pol)
	Szia/Szervusz. (inf)
Yes.	*Igen.*
No.	*Nem.*
Please.	*Kérem.*
Thank you.	*Köszönöm.*
Sorry. (forgive me)	*Sajnálom/Elnézést.*
Excuse me.	*Bocsánat.*
What's your name?	*Hogy hívják?* (pol)
	Mi a neved? (inf)
My name is ...	*A nevem ...*

I don't understand.	*Nem értem.*
Do you speak English?	*Beszél angolul?*
How much is it?	*Mennyibe kerül?*

Getting Around

What time does the ... leave/arrive?	*Mikor indul/érkezik a ...?*
boat/ferry	*hajó/komp*
city bus	*helyi autóbusz*
intercity bus	*távolsági autóbusz*
plane	*repülőgép*
train	*vonat*
tram	*villamos*
arrival	*érkezés*
departure	*indulás*
timetable	*menetrend*
Where is ...?	*Hol van ...?*
the bus stop	*az autóbuszmegálló*
the station	*a pályaudvar*
the left-luggage room	*a csomagmegőrző*
(Turn) left.	*(Forduljon) balra.*
(Turn) right.	*(Forduljon) jobbra.*
(Go) straight ahead	*(Menyen) egyenesen elore.*
near/far	*közel/messze*

Around Town

Where is ...?	*Hol van ...?*
a bank	*bank*
a chemist	*gyógyszertár*
the market	*a piac*
the museum	*a múzeum*
the post office	*a posta*
a tourist office	*idegenforgalmi iroda*
What time does it open?	*Mikor nyit ki?*

Signs – Hungarian

Bejárat	**Entrance**
Kijárat	**Exit**
Információ	**Information**
Nyitva	**Open**
Zárva	**Closed**
Tilos	**Prohibited**
Rendőrőr-Kapitányság	**Police Station**
Toalett/WC	**Toilets**
Férfiak	**Men**
Nők	**Women**

Emergencies – Hungarian

Help!	*Segítség!*
Call a doctor!	*Hívjon egy orvost!*
Call an ambulance!	*Hívja a mentőket!*
Call the police!	*Hívja a rendőrséget!*
Go away!	*Menjen el!*
I'm lost.	*Eltévedtem.*

What time does it close?	*Mikor zár be?*

Accommodation

hotel	*szálloda*
guesthouse	*fogadót*
youth hostel	*ifjúsági szálló*
camping ground	*kemping*
private room	*fizetővendég szoba*
Do you have rooms available?	*Van szabad szobájuk?*
How much is it ...?	*Mennyibe kerül ...?*
per night	*éjszakánként*
per person	*személyenként*
single room	*egyágyas szoba*
double room	*kétágyas szoba*

Time, Days & Numbers

What time is it?	*Hány óra?*
today	*ma*
tonight	*ma este*
tomorrow	*holnap*
yesterday	*tegnap*
in the morning	*reggel*
in the evening	*este*
Monday	*hétfő*
Tuesday	*kedd*
Wednesday	*szerda*
Thursday	*csütörtök*
Friday	*péntek*
Saturday	*szombat*
Sunday	*vasárnap*

1	*egy*	7	*hét*
2	*kettő*	8	*nyolc*
3	*három*	9	*kilenc*
4	*négy*	10	*tíz*
5	*öt*	100	*száz*
6	*hat*	1000	*ezer*

one million	*millió*

Icelandic

Pronunciation

i, y	as the 'e' in 'pretty'
í, ý	as the 'e' in 'evil'
ú	as the 'o' in 'moon', or as the 'o' in 'woman'
ö	as the 'er' in 'fern', but without a trace of 'r'
á	as the 'ou' in 'out'
ei, ey	as the 'ay' in 'day'
ó	as the word 'owe'
æ	as the word 'eye'
au	as 'er' + 'ee' (as in French *oeil*)
é	as the 'y' in 'yet'
ð	as the 'th' in 'lather'
j	as the 'y' in 'yellow'
þ	as the 'th' in 'thin' or 'three'

Basics

Hello.	*Halló.*
Goodbye.	*Bless.*
Yes.	*Já.*
No.	*Nei.*
Please.	*Gjörðu svo vel.*
Thank you.	*Takk fyrir.*
That's fine/ You're welcome.	*Allt í lagi/ Ekkert að þakka.*
Excuse me. (Sorry)	*Afsakið.*
Do you speak English?	*Talar þú ensku?*
How much is it?	*Hvað kostar tað*

Getting Around

What time does ... leave/arrive?	*Hvenær fer/kemur ...?*
the boat	*báturinn*
the bus (city)	*vagninn*
the tram	*sporvagninn*

I'd like ...	*Gæti ég fengid ...*
a one-way ticket	*miða/aðra leiðina*
a return ticket	*miða/báðar leiðir*
1st-class	*fyrsta farrými*
2nd-class	*annað farrými*

timetable	*tímaáætlun*
bus stop	*biðstöð*
ferry terminal	*ferjuhöfn*
I'd like to hire a car/bicycle.	*Ég vil leigia bíl/reiðhjól.*
Where is ...?	*Hvar er ...?*
Go straight ahead.	*Farðu beint af áfram.*
Turn left.	*Beygðu til vinstri.*
Turn right.	*Beygðu til hægri.*
near/far	*nálægt/langt í burtu*

Around Town

bank	*banka*
chemist/pharmacy	*apótek*
... embassy	*... sendiráðinu*
market	*markaðnum*
newsagent/ stationer	*blaðasala/bókabúð*
post office	*pósthúsinu*
tourist office	*upplýsingaþjónustu fyrir ferðafólk*

Accommodation

hotel	*hótel*
guesthouse	*gistiheimili*
youth hostel	*farfuglaheimili*
camping ground	*tjaldsvæði*

Do you have any rooms available?	*Eru herbergi laus?*
How much is it per night/per person?	*Hvað kostar nóttin fyrir manninn?*
one day	*einn dag*
two days	*tvo daga*

I'd like ...	*Gæti ég fengið ...*
a single room	*einstaklingsherbergi*
a double room	*tveggjamanna-herbergi*

Time, Days & Numbers

What time is it?	*Hvað er klukkan?*
today	*í dag*
tomorrow	*á morgun*
yesterday	*í gær*
in the morning	*að morgni*
in the afternoon	*eftir hádegi*

Monday	*mánudagur*
Tuesday	*þriðjudagur*
Wednesday	*miðvikudagur*
Thursday	*fimmtudagur*
Friday	*föstudagur*
Saturday	*laugardagur*
Sunday	*sunnudagur*

Signs – Icelandic

Inngangur/Inn	**Entrance**
Útgangur/Út	**Exit**
Upplýsingar	**Information**
Opið	**Open**
Lokað	**Closed**
Bannað	**Prohibited**
Lögreglustöð	**Police Station**
Snyrting	**Toilets**
Karlar	**Men**
Konur	**Women**

Emergencies – Icelandic

Help!	*Hjálp!*
Call a doctor!	*Náið í lækni!*
Call the police!	*Náið í lögregluna!*
Go away!	*Farðu!*
I'm lost	*Ég er villtur/villt.* (m/f)

0	*núll*	7	*sjö*
1	*einn*	8	*átta*
2	*tveir*	9	*níu*
3	*þrír*	10	*tíu*
4	*fjórir*	20	*tuttugu*
5	*fimm*	100	*eitt hundrað*
6	*sex*	1000	*eitt þúsund*

one million *ein milljón*

Italian

Many older Italians expect to be addressed in the second person formal – *Lei* instead of *tu*. It isn't polite to use *ciao* when addressing strangers, unless they use it first; use *buongiorno* and *arrivederci*.

Pronunciation

c	as 'k' before **a**, **o** and **u**; as the 'ch' in 'choose' before **e** and **i**
ch	a hard 'k' sound
g	as in 'get' before **a**, **o** and **u**; as in 'gem' before **e** and **i**
gh	as in 'get'
gli	as the 'lli' in 'million'
gn	as the 'ny' in 'canyon'
h	always silent
r	a rolled 'rrr' sound
sc	as the 'sh' in 'sheep' before **e** and **i**; a hard sound as in 'school' before **h**, **a**, **o** and **u**
z	as the 'ts' in 'lights' or the 'ds' in 'beds'

Signs – Italian

Ingresso/Entrata	**Entrance**
Uscita	**Exit**
Informazione	**Information**
Aperto	**Open**
Chiuso	**Closed**
Proibito/Vietato	**Prohibited**
Polizia/Carabinieri	**Police**
Questura	**Police Station**
Gabinetti/Bagni	**Toilets**
Uomini	**Men**
Donne	**Women**

Basics

Hello.	*Buongiorno.* (polite) *Ciao.* (informal)
Goodbye.	*Arrivederci.* (polite) *Ciao.* (informal)
Yes.	*Sì.*
No.	*No.*
Please.	*Per favore/Per piacere.*
Thank you.	*Grazie.*
That's fine/ You're welcome.	*Prego.*
Excuse me.	*Mi scusi.*
Sorry.	*Mi scusi/Mi perdoni.*
Do you speak English?	*Parla inglese?*
How much is it?	*Quanto costa?*

Getting Around

When does the ... leave/arrive?	*A che ora parte/ arriva ...?*
boat	*la barca*
bus	*l'autobus*
ferry	*il traghetto*
train	*il treno*
bus stop	*fermata dell'autobus*
train station	*stazione*
ferry terminal	*stazione marittima*
1st/2nd class	*prima/seconda classe*
left luggage	*deposito bagagli*
timetable	*orario*
I'd like a one-way/ return ticket.	*Vorrei un biglietto di solo andata/ di andata e ritorno.*
I'd like to hire a car/bicycle.	*Vorrei noleggiare una macchina/bicicletta.*
Where is ...?	*Dov'è ...?*
Go straight ahead.	*Si va sempre diritto.*
Turn left/right.	*Giri a sinistra/destra.*
far/near	*lontano/vicino*

Around Town

a bank	*una banca*
chemist/pharmacy	*la farmacia*
the market	*il mercato*
newsagent	*l'edicola*
post office	*la posta*
the tourist office	*l'ufficio di turismo*
What time does it open/close?	*A che ora (si) apre/chiude?*

Accommodation

hotel	*albergo*
guesthouse	*pensione*

Emergencies – Italian

Help!	*Aiuto!*
Call a doctor!	*Chiama un medico!*
Call the police!	*Chiama la polizia!*
Go away!	*Vai via!*
I'm lost.	*Mi sono persoa. (m/f)*

youth hostel	*ostello per la gioventù*
camping ground	*campeggio*
Do you have any rooms available?	*Ha delle camere libere/ C'è una camera libera?*
How much is it per (night/person)?	*Quanto costa per (la notte/ciascuno)?*
a single room	*una camera singola*
a twin room	*una camera doppia*
a double-bed room	*una camera matrimoniale*
for one night	*per una notte*
for two nights	*per due notti*

Time, Days & Numbers

What time is it?	*Che (ora è?/ore sono)?*
today	*oggi*
tomorrow	*domani*
yesterday	*ieri*
morning	*mattina*
afternoon	*pomeriggio*
Monday	*lunedì*
Tuesday	*martedì*
Wednesday	*mercoledì*
Thursday	*giovedì*
Friday	*venerdì*
Saturday	*sabato*
Sunday	*domenica*

1	*uno*	7	*sette*
2	*due*	8	*otto*
3	*tre*	9	*nove*
4	*quattro*	10	*dieci*
5	*cinque*	100	*cento*
6	*sei*	1000	*mille*

one million *un milione*

Latvian

Alphabet & Pronunciation

The letters of the Latvian alphabet are: **a b c č d e f g ģ (Ģ) h i j k ķ l ļ m n ņ o p r s š t u v z ž**.

c	as the 'ts' in 'bits'
č	as the 'ch' in 'church'
ģ	as the 'j' in 'jet'
j	as the 'y' in 'yes'
ķ	as 'tu' in 'tune'
ļ	as the 'lli' in 'billiards'
ņ	as the 'ni' in 'onion'
o	as the 'a' in 'water'
š	as the 'sh' in 'ship'
ž	as the 's' in 'pleasure'
ai	as the the 'i' in 'pine'
ei	as in 'vein'
ie	as in 'pier'
ā	as the 'a' in 'barn'
ē	as the 'e' in 'where'
ī	as the 'i' in 'marine'
ū	as the 'oo' in 'boot'

Greetings & Civilities

Hello.	*Labdien* or *Sveiki.*
Goodbye.	*Uz redzēšanos* or *Atā.*
Yes.	*Jā.*
No.	*Nē.*
Excuse me.	*Atvainojiet.*
Please.	*Lūdzu.*
Thank you.	*Paldies.*
Do you speak English?	*Vai jūs runājat angliski?*

Getting Around

airport	*lidosta*
train station	*dzelzceļa stacija*
train	*vilciens*
bus station	*autoosta*
bus	*autobuss*
port	*osta*
taxi	*taksometrs*
tram	*tramvajs*
stop (eg, bus stop)	*pietura*
departure time	*atiešanas laiks*
arrival time	*pienākšanas laiks*
ticket	*biļete*
ticket office	*kase*

Signs – Latvian

Ieeja	**Entrance**
Izeja	**Exit**
Informācija	**Information**
Atvērts	**Open**
Slēgts	**Closed**
Smēķet Aizliegts	**No Smoking**
Policijas Iecirknis	**Police Station**
Maksas Tualetes	**Public Toilets**
Sieviešu	**Women**
Vīriešu	**Men**

Emergencies – Latvian

Help!	*Palīgā!*
Call a doctor!	*Izsauciet ārstu!*
Call the police!	*Izsauciet policiju!*
I'm ill.	*Es esmu slims/ slima.* (m/f)
I'm lost.	*Es esmu apmaldījies/ apmaldījusies.* (m/f)
Go away!	*Ejiet projam!*

Around Town

bank	*banka*
chemist	*aptieka*
currency exchange	*valūtas maiņa*
hotel	*viesnīca*
market	*tirgus*
post office	*pasts*
toilet	*tualete*
Where?	*Kur?*
How much?	*Cik?*

Time, Days & Numbers

today	*šodien*
yesterday	*vakar*
tomorrow	*rīt*
Sunday	*svētdiena*
Monday	*pirmdiena*
Tuesday	*otrdiena*
Wednesday	*trešdiena*
Thursday	*ceturtdiena*
Friday	*piektdiena*
Saturday	*sestdiena*

1	*viens*	7	*septiņi*
2	*divi*	8	*astoņi*
3	*trīs*	9	*deviņi*
4	*četri*	10	*desmit*
5	*pieci*	100	*simts*
6	*seši*	1000	*tūkstots*

Lithuanian

Alphabet & Pronunciation

The letters of the Lithuanian alphabet are: **a b c č d e f g h i/y j k l m n o p r s š t u v z ž**. The **i** and **y** are partly interchangeable.

c	as 'ts'
č	as 'ch'
y	between the 'i' in 'tin' and the 'ee' in 'feet'
j	as the 'y' in 'yes'
š	as 'sh'
ž	as the 's' in 'pleasure'
ei	as the 'ai' in 'pain'
ie	as the 'ye' in 'yet'
ui	as the 'wi' in 'win'

Accent marks above and below vowels (eg, **ā**, **ė** and **į**) all have the general effect of lengthening the vowel:

ā	as the 'a' in 'father'
ę	as the 'ai' in 'air'
į	as the 'ee' in 'feet'
ų	as the 'oo' in 'boot'
ū	as the 'oo' in 'boot'
ė	as the 'a' in 'late'

Greetings & Civilities

Hello.	*Labas/Sveikas.*
Goodbye.	*Sudie* or *Viso gero.*
Yes.	*Taip.*
No.	*Ne.*
Excuse me.	*Atsiprašau.*
Please.	*Prašau.*
Thank you.	*Ačiū.*
Do you speak English?	*Ar kalbate angliškai?*

Getting Around

airport	*oro uostas*
bus station	*autobusų stotis*
port	*uostas*
train station	*geležinkelio stotis*
stop (eg, bus stop)	*stotelė*
bus	*autobusas*
taxi	*taksi*
train	*traukinys*
tram	*tramvajus*
departure time	*išvykimo laikas*
arrival time	*atvykimo laikas*
ticket	*bilietas*
ticket office	*kasa*

Around Town

bank	*bankas*
chemist	*vaistinė*
currency exchange	*valiutos keitykla*

Signs – Lithuanian

Įėjimas	**Entrance**
Išėjimas	**Exit**
Informacija	**Information**
Atidara	**Open**
Uždara	**Closed**
Nerūkoma	**No Smoking**
Patogumai	**Public Toilets**

Emergencies – Lithuanian

Help!	*Gelėbkite!*
Call the police!	*Iššaukite policiją!*
Call a doctor!	*Iššaukite gydytoją!*
I'm ill.	*Aš sergu.*
I'm lost.	*Aš paklydęs/ paklydusi.* (m/f)
Go away!	*Eik šalin!*

hotel	*viešbutis*
market	*turgus*
post office	*paštas*
toilet	*tualetas*
Where?	*Kur?*
How much?	*Kiek?*

Times, Days & Numbers

today	*šiandien*
tomorrow	*rytoj*
yesterday	*vakar*
Monday	*pirmadienis*
Tuesday	*antradienis*
Wednesday	*trečiadienis*
Thursday	*ketvirtadienis*
Friday	*penktadienis*
Saturday	*šeštadienis*
Sunday	*sekmadienis*

1	*vienas*	7	*septyni*
2	*du*	8	*aštuoni*
3	*trys*	9	*devyni*
4	*keturi*	10	*dešimt*
5	*penki*	100	*šimtas*
6	*šeši*	1000	*tūkstantis*

Macedonian

Pronunciation

There are 31 letters in the Macedonian Cyrillic alphabet (see The Cyrillic Alphabet boxed text).

Basics

Hello.	*zdravo*
Goodbye.	*priatno*
Yes.	*da*
No.	*ne*
Please.	*molam*
Thank you.	*blagodaram*
You're welcome.	*nema zoshto/milo mi e*
Excuse me.	*izvinete*
Sorry. (forgive me)	*oprostete ve molam*
Do you speak English?	*zboruvate li angliski?*
What's your name?	*kako se vikate?*
My name is ...	*jas se vikam ...*
How much is it?	*kolku chini toa?*

Getting Around

What time does the next ... leave/arrive?	*koga doagja/zaminuva idniot ...?*
boat	*brod*
city bus	*avtobus gradski*
intercity bus	*avtobus megjugradski*
train	*voz*
tram	*tramvaj*
I'd like ...	*sakam ...*
a one-way ticket	*bilet vo eden pravec*
a return ticket	*povraten bilet*
1st class	*prva klasa*
2nd class	*vtora klasa*
timetable	*vozen red*
bus stop	*avtobuska stanica*
train station	*zheleznichka stanica*
Where is ...?	*kade je ...?*
Go straight ahead.	*odete pravo napred*
Turn left/right	*svrtete levo/desno*
near/far	*blisku/daleku*
I'd like to hire a car/bicycle.	*sakam da iznajmam kola/tochak*

Around Town

bank	*banka*
chemist/pharmacy	*apteka*
my hotel	*mojot hotel*
the market	*pazarot*
newsagent	*kiosk za vesnici*
the post office	*poshtata*
the tourist office	*turistichkoto biro*

Signs – Macedonian

Entrance	**Влез**
Exit	**Излез**
Open	**Отворено**
Closed	**Затворено**
Information	**Информации**
Police	**Полиција**
Police Station	**Полициска Станица**
Prohibited	**Забрането**
Toilets	**Клозети**
Men	**Машки**
Women	**Женски**

Emergencies – Macedonian

Help!	*pomosh!*
Call a doctor!	*povikajte lekar!*
Call the police!	*viknete policija!*
Go away!	*odete si!*
I'm lost.	*jas zaginav*

What time does it open/close?	*koga se otvora/ zatvora?*

Accommodation

hotel	*hotel*
guesthouse	*privatno smetuvanje*
youth hostel	*mladinsko prenocjishte*
camping ground	*kamping*
Do you have any rooms available?	*dali imate slobodni sobi?*
How much is it per night/per person?	*koja e cenata po nocj/po osoba?*
a single room	*soba so eden krevet*
a double room	*soba so brachen krevet*
for one/two nights	*za edna/dva vecheri*

Time, Days & Numbers

What time is it?	*kolku e chasot?*
today	*denes*
tomorrow	*utre*
yesterday	*vchera*
morning	*utro*
afternoon	*popladne*
Monday	*ponedelnik*
Tuesday	*vtornik*
Wednesday	*sreda*
Thursday	*chetvrtok*
Friday	*petok*
Saturday	*sabota*
Sunday	*nedela*

1	*eden*	7	*sedum*
2	*dva*	8	*osum*
3	*tri*	9	*devet*
4	*chetiri*	10	*deset*
5	*pet*	100	*sto*
6	*shest*	1000	*hiljada*

one million *eden milion*

Maltese

Pronunciation

ċ	as the 'ch' in child
g	as in good
ġ	as the 'j' in job
għ	silent; lengthens the preceding or following vowel
h	silent, as in 'hour'
ħ	as the 'h' in 'hand'
j	as the 'y' in 'yellow'
ij	as the 'igh' in 'high'
ej	as the 'ay' in 'day'
q	a glottal stop; like the missing 't' between the two syllables in 'bottle'
x	as the 'sh' in shop
z	as the 'ts' in `bits'
ż	soft as in `buzz'

Basics

Hello.	*Merħba*
Good morning/ Good day.	*Bonġu.*
Goodbye.	*Saħħa.*
Yes.	*Iva.*
No.	*Le.*
Please.	*Jekk jogħoġbok.*
Thank you.	*Grazzi.*
Excuse me.	*Skużani.*
Do you speak English?	*Titkellem bl-ingliż?* (informal)
How much is it?	*Kemm?*

Getting Around

When does the boat leave/arrive?	*Meta jitlaq/jasal il-vapur?*
When does the bus leave/arrive?	*Meta titlaq/jasal il-karozza?*
I'd like a ... ticket.	*Nixtieq biljett ...*
one-way/return	*'one-way/return'*
1st-/2nd-class	*'1st/2nd class'*
left luggage	*hallejt il-bagalji*
bus/trolleybus stop	*xarabank/coach*
I'd like to hire a car/bicycle.	*Nixtieq nikri karozza/rota.*
Where is a/the ...?	*Fejn hu ....?*
Go straight ahead.	*Mur dritt.*

Signs – Maltese

Dhul	**Entrance**
Hrug	**Exit**
Informazjoni	**Information**
Miftuh	**Open**
Maghluq	**Closed**
Tidholx	**No Entry**
Pulizija	**Police**
Toilets	**Toilets**
Rgiel	**Men**
Nisa	**Women**

Emergencies – Maltese

Help!	*Ajjut!*
Call a doctor!	*Qibgħad ghat-tabib!*
Police!	*Pulizija!*
I'm lost.	*Ninsab mitluf.*
hospital	*sptar*

Turn left.	*Dur fuq il-lemin.*
Turn right.	*Dur fuq ix-xellug.*
near/far	*il-viċin/-bogħod*

Around Town

the bank	*il-bank*
chemist/pharmacy	*l-ispiżerija*
the ... embassy	*l'ambaxxata ...*
the market	*is-suq*
the post office	*il-posta*
shop	*ħanut*
What time does it open/close?	*Fix'ħin jiftaħ/jagħlaq?*

Accommodation

Do you have a room available?	*Ghandek kamra jekk jogħoġbok?*
Do you have a room for one person/ two people?	*Ghandek kamra għal wieħed/ tnejn?*
Do you have a room for one/two nights?	*Ghandek kamra ghal lejl/zewgt iljieli?*

Time, Days & Numbers

What's the time?	*X'ħin hu?*
today	*illum*
tomorrow	*għada*
yesterday	*il-bieraħ*
morning	*fil-għodu*
afternoon	*nofs in-nhar*

Monday	*it-tnejn*
Tuesday	*it-tlieta*
Wednesday	*l-erbgħa*
Thursday	*il-ħamis*
Friday	*il-gimgħa*
Saturday	*is-sibt*
Sunday	*il-ħadd*

0	*xejn*	7	*sebgħa*
1	*wieħed*	8	*tmienja*
2	*tnejn*	9	*disgħa*
3	*tlieta*	10	*għaxra*
4	*erbgħa*	11	*ħdax*
5	*ħamsa*	100	*mija*
6	*sitta*	1000	*elf*

one million *miljun*

Moroccan Arabic

Pronunciation

A stroke over a vowel ('macron') gives it a long sound.

a	as in 'had' (sometimes very short)
e	as in 'bet' (sometimes very short)
i	as in 'hit'
o	as in 'hot'
u	as the 'oo' in 'book'
aw	as the 'ow' in 'how'
ai	as the 'i' in 'high'
ei, ay	as the 'a' in 'cake'
j	more or less as the 'j' in 'John'
H	a strongly whispered 'h', almost like a sigh of relief
q	a strong guttural 'k' sound
kh	a slightly gurgling sound, like the 'ch' in Scottish 'loch'
sh	as in 'she'
z	as the 's' in pleasure
gh	called 'ghayn', similar to the French 'r', but more guttural

Glottal Stop (')

The glottal stop is the sound you hear between the vowels in the expression 'oh oh!'. In Arabic it can occur anywhere in a word – at the beginning, middle or end. When the (') occurs before a vowel (eg, 'ayn), the vowel is 'growled' from the back of the throat. If it's before a consonant or at the end of a word, it sounds like a glottal stop.

Basics

Hello.	*as-salām 'alaykum*
Goodbye.	*ma' as-salāma*
Yes.	*īyeh*
No.	*la*
Please.	*'afak*
Thank you (very much).	*shukran (jazilan)*
You're welcome.	*la shukran, 'ala wajib*
Excuse me.	*smeH līya*
Do you speak English?	*wash kat'ref neglīzīya?*
I understand.	*fhemt*
I don't understand.	*mafhemtsh*
How much (is it)?	*bish-hal?*

Getting Around

What time does the ... leave/arrive?	*emta qiyam/wusūl ...*
boat	*al-babūr*
bus (city)	*al-otobīs*
bus (intercity)	*al-kar*
train	*al-mashīna*

Emergencies – Arabic

Help!	*'teqnī!*
Call a doctor!	*'eyyet at-tabīb!*
Call the police!	*'eyyet al-bolīs!*
Go away!	*sīr fHalek!*
I'm lost.	*tweddert*

1st class	*ddarazha llūla*
2nd class	*ddarazha ttanīya*
train station	*maHattat al-mashīna/ al-qitar*
bus stop	*mawqif al-otobis*
Where can I hire a car/bicycle?	*fein yimkin ana akra tomobīl/beshklīta?*
Where is (the) ...?	*fein ...?*
Go straight ahead.	*sīr nīshan*
Turn right.	*dor 'al līmen*
Turn left.	*dor 'al līser*

Around Town

the bank	*al-banka*
the embassy	*as-sifāra*
the market	*as-sūq*
the police station	*al-bolīs*
the post office	*al-būsta, maktab al-barīd*
a toilet	*bayt al-ma, mirHad*

Accommodation

hotel	*al-otēl*
youth hostel	*dar shabbab*
camp site	*mukhaym*
Is there a room available?	*wash kayn shī bīt xawīya?*
How much is this room per night?	*bshaHal al-bayt liyal?*

Time, Dates & Numbers

What time is it?	*shHal fessa'a?*
today	*al-yūm*
tomorrow	*ghaddan*
yesterday	*al-bareh*
in the morning	*fis-sabaH*
in the evening	*fil-masa'*
Monday	*(nhar) al-itnēn*
Tuesday	*(nhar) at-talata*
Wednesday	*(nhar) al-arba'*
Thursday	*(nhar) al-khamīs*
Friday	*(nhar) al-juma'*
Saturday	*(nhar) as-sabt*
Sunday	*(nhar) al-ahad*

1	*wāHid*	7	*saba'a*
2	*jūj* or *itnīn*	8	*tamanya*
3	*talata*	9	*tissa'*
4	*arba'a*	10	*'ashara*
5	*khamsa*	100	*miyya*
6	*sitta*	1000	*alf*

one million *melyūn*

Norwegian

Pronunciation

å	as the 'aw' in 'paw'
æ	as the 'a' in 'act'
ø	long, as the 'er' in 'fern'; short, as the 'a' in 'ago'
u, y	say 'ee' while pursing your lips
ai	as the word 'eye'
ei	as the 'ay' in 'day'
au	as the 'o' in 'note'
øy	as the 'oy' in 'toy'
d	at the end of a word, or between two vowels, it's often silent
g	as the 'g' in 'get'; as the 'y' in 'yard' before **ei, i, j, øy, y**
j	as the 'y' in 'yard'
k	as in 'kin'; as the 'ch' in 'chin' before **ei, i, j, øy,** and **y**
r	a trilled 'r'. The combination **rs** is pronounced as the 'sh' in 'fish'.
s	as in 'so' (never as in 'treasure'); as the 'sh' in 'ship' before **ei, i, j, øy** and **y**

Basics

Hello.	*Goddag.*
Goodbye.	*Ha det.*
Yes.	*Ja.*
No.	*Nei.*
Please.	*Vær så snill.*
Thank you.	*Takk.*
That's fine/You're welcome.	*Ingen årsak.*
Excuse me. (sorry)	*Unnskyld.*
Do you speak English?	*Snakker du engelsk?*
How much is it?	*Hvor mye koster det?*

Getting Around

What time does ... leave/arrive?	*Når går/kommer ...?*
the boat	*båten*
the (city) bus	*(by)bussen*
the intercity bus	*linjebussen*
the tram	*trikken*
the train	*toget*

I'd like ...	*Jeg vil gjerne ha ...*
a one-way ticket	*enkeltbillett*
a return ticket	*tur-retur*
1st class	*første klasse*
2nd class	*annen klasse*

left luggage	*reisegods*
timetable	*ruteplan*
bus stop	*bussholdeplass*
tram stop	*trikkholdeplass*
train station	*jernbanestasjon*
ferry terminal	*ferjeleiet*

Where can I rent a car/bicycle?	*Hvor kan jeg leie en bil/sykkel?*
Where is ...?	*Hvor er ...?*
Go straight ahead.	*Det er rett fram.*
Turn left.	*Ta til venstre.*
Turn right.	*Ta til høyre.*
near/far	*nær/langt*

Around Town

bank	*banken*
chemist/pharmacy	*apotek*
... embassy	*... ambassade*
market	*torget*
newsagent	*kiosk*
post office	*postkontoret*
telephone centre	*televerket*
tourist office	*turistinformasjon*

Accommodation

hotel	*hotell*
guesthouse	*gjestgiveri/pensionat*
youth hostel	*vandrerhjem*
camping ground	*kamping/leirplass*

Do you have any rooms available?	*Har du ledige rom?*
How much is it per night/ per person?	*Hvor mye er det pr dag/ pr person?*
one day/two days	*en dag/to dager*

Signs – Norwegian

Inngang	**Entrance**
Utgang	**Exit**
Opplysninger	**Information**
Åpen	**Open**
Stengt	**Closed**
Forbudt	**Prohibited**
Politistasjon	**Police Station**
Toaletter	**Toilets**
Herrer	**Men**
Damer	**Women**

Emergencies – Norwegian

Help!	*Hjelp!*
Call a doctor!	*Ring en lege!*
Call the police!	*Ring politiet!*
Go away!	*Forsvinn!*
I'm lost.	*Jeg har gått meg vill.*

I'd like ...	*Jeg vil gjerne ha ...*
a single room	*et enkeltrom*
a double room	*et dobbeltrom*

Time, Days & Numbers

What time is it?	*Hva er klokka?*
today	*i dag*
tomorrow	*i morgen*
yesterday	*i går*
in the morning	*om formiddagen*
in the afternoon	*om ettermiddagen*

Monday	*mandag*
Tuesday	*tirsdag*
Wednesday	*onsdag*
Thursday	*torsdag*
Friday	*fredag*
Saturday	*lørdag*
Sunday	*søndag*

0	*null*	7	*sju*
1	*en*	8	*åtte*
2	*to*	9	*ni*
3	*tre*	10	*ti*
4	*fire*	11	*elleve*
5	*fem*	100	*hundre*
6	*seks*	1000	*tusen*

one million	*en million*

Polish

Pronunciation

Written Polish is phonetically consistent, which means that the pronunciation of letters or clusters of letters doesn't vary from word to word. The stress almost always goes on the second-last syllable.

Vowels

a	as the 'u' in 'cut'
e	as in 'ten'
i	similar to the 'ee' in 'feet' but shorter
o	as in 'lot'
u	a bit shorter than the 'oo' in 'book'
y	similar to the 'i' in 'bit'

There are three vowels unique to Polish:

ą a nasal vowel sound like the French *un*, similar to 'own' in 'sown'
ę also nasalised, like the French *un*, but pronounced as 'e' when word-final
ó similar to Polish **u**

Consonants

In Polish, the consonants **b**, **d**, **f**, **k**, **l**, **m**, **n**, **p**, **t**, **v** and **z** are pronounced more or less as they are in English. The following consonants and clusters of consonants sound distinctly different to their English counterparts:

c as the 'ts' in 'its'
ch similar to the 'ch' in the Scottish *loch*
cz as the 'ch' in 'church'
ć much softer than Polish **c** (as 'tsi' before vowels)
dz similar to the 'ds' in 'suds' but shorter
dź as **dz** but softer (as 'dzi' before vowels)
dż as the 'j' in 'jam'
g as in 'get'
h as **ch**
j as the 'y' in 'yet'
ł as the 'w' in 'wine'
ń as the 'ny' in 'canyon' (as 'ni' before vowels)
r always trilled
rz as the 's' in 'pleasure'
s as in 'set'
sz as the 'sh' in 'show'
ś as **s** but softer (as 'si' before vowels)
w as the 'v' in 'van'
ź softer version of **z** (as 'zi' before vowels)
ż as **rz**

Basics

Hello. (inf)	*Cześć.*
Hello/ Good morning.	*Dzień dobry.*
Goodbye.	*Do widzenia.*

Signs – Polish

Wejście	**Entrance**
Wyjście	**Exit**
Informacja	**Information**
Otwarte	**Open**
Zamknięte	**Closed**
Wzbroniony	**Prohibited**
Posterunek Policji	**Police Station**
Toalety	**Toilets**
Panowie	**Men**
Panie	**Women**

Emergencies – Polish

Help!	*Pomocy!/Ratunku!*
Call a doctor!	*Proszę wezwać lekarza!*
Call the police!	*Proszę wezwać policję!*
I'm lost.	*Zgubiłem się.* (m) *Zgubiłam się.* (f)

Yes/No.	*Tak/Nie.*
Please.	*Proszę.*
Thank you.	*Dziękuję.*
Excuse me/ Forgive me.	*Przepraszam.*
I don't understand.	*Nie rozumiem.*
What is it called?	*Jak to się nazywa?*
How much is it?	*Ile to kosztuje?*

Getting Around

What time does the ... leave/arrive?	*O której godzinie przychodzi/odchodzi ...?*
plane	*samolot*
boat	*statek*
bus	*autobus*
train	*pociąg*
tram	*tramwaj*
arrival	*przyjazd*
departure	*odjazd*
timetable	*rozkład jazdy*
Where is the bus stop?	*Gdzie jest przystanek autobusowy?*
Where is the station?	*Gdzie jest stacja kolejowa?*
Where is the left-luggage room?	*Gdzie jest przechowalnia bagażu?*
Please show me on the map.	*Proszę pokazać mi to na mapie.*
straight ahead	*prosto*
left	*lewo*
right	*prawo*

Around Town

the bank	*bank*
the chemist	*apteka*
the church	*kościół*
the city centre	*centrum miasta*
the market	*targ/bazar*
the museum	*muzeum*
the post office	*poczta*
the tourist office	*informacja turystyczna*
What time does it open/close?	*O której otwierają/ zamykają?*

Accommodation

hotel	*hotel*
youth hostel	*schronisko młodzieżowe*
camping ground	*kemping*
private room	*kwatera prywatna*
Do you have any rooms available?	*Czy są wolne pokoje?*
How much is it?	*Ile to kosztuje?*
Does it include breakfast?	*Czy śniadanie jest wliczone?*
single room	*pokój jednoosobowy*
double room	*pokój dwuosobowy*

Time, Days & Numbers

What time is it?	*Która jest godzina?*
today	*dzisiaj*
tonight	*dzisiaj wieczorem*
tomorrow	*jutro*
yesterday	*wczoraj*
in the morning	*rano*
in the evening	*wieczorem*
Monday	*poniedziałek*
Tuesday	*wtorek*
Wednesday	*środa*
Thursday	*czwartek*
Friday	*piątek*
Saturday	*sobota*
Sunday	*niedziela*

1	*jeden*	7	*siedem*
2	*dwa*	8	*osiem*
3	*trzy*	9	*dziewięć*
4	*cztery*	10	*dziesięć*
5	*pięć*	100	*sto*
6	*sześć*	1000	*tysiąc*

one million	*milion*

Portuguese

Note that Portugese uses masculine and feminine word endings, usually `-o' and `-a' respectively – to say `thank you', a man will therefore use *obrigado*, a woman, *obrigada*.

Nasal Vowels Nasalisation is represented by an 'n' or an 'm' after the vowel, or by a tilde over it, eg, **ã**. The nasal 'i' exists in English as the 'ing' in 'sing'.

ão	nasal 'ow' (owng)
ãe	nasal 'ay' (eing)
õe	nasal 'oy' (oing)
ui	similar to the 'uing' in 'ensuing'
é	short, as in 'bet'
ê	long, as the 'a' in 'gate'
ô	long, as in 'note'
c	as in 'cat' before **a**, **o** or **u**; as the 's' in 'sin' before **e** or **i**
ç	as the 'c' in 'celery'
g	as in 'go' before **a**, **o** or **u**; as the `s' in 'treasure' before **e** or **i**
h	never pronounced when word-initial
nh	as the 'ni' in 'onion'
lh	as the 'lli' in 'million'
j	as the 's' in 'treasure'
m	not pronounced when word-final – it simply nasalises the previous vowel, eg, *um* (oong), *bom* (bõ)
x	as the 'sh' in 'ship', as the 'z' in 'zeal', or as the `x' in 'taxi'
z	as the 's' in 'treasure' before a consonant or at the end of a word

Basics

Hello.	*Olá.*
Goodbye.	*Adeus/Ciao.* (informal)
Yes.	*Sim.*
No.	*Não.*
Please.	*Se faz favor.*
Thank you.	*Obrigado/a.* (m/f)
You're welcome.	*De nada.*
Excuse me.	*Com licença.*
Sorry. (forgive me)	*Desculpe.*
Do you speak English?	*Fala Inglês?*
How much is it?	*Quanto custa?*

Getting Around

What time does the ... leave/arrive?	*A que horas parte/chega ...?*
boat	*o barco*
bus (city)	*o autocarro*
bus (intercity)	*a camioneta*
tram	*o eléctrico*
train	*o combóio*

Signs – Portuguese

Entrada	**Entrance**
Saída	**Exit**
Informações	**Information**
Aberto	**Open**
Fechado	**Closed**
Proibido	**Prohibited**
Posto Da Polícia	**Police Station**
Lavabos/WC	**Toilets**
Homens (h)	**Men**
Senhoras (s)	**Women**

Emergencies – Portuguese

Help!	*Socorro!*
Call a doctor!	*Chame um médico!*
Call the police!	*Chame a polícia!*
Go away!	*Deixe-me em paz!/ Vai-te embora! (inf)*
I'm lost.	*Estou perdido/a. (m/f)*

bus stop — *paragem de autocarro*
train station — *estação ferroviária*
timetable — *horário*

I'd like a ... ticket. — *Queria um bilhete ...*
one-way — *simples/de ida*
return — *de ida e volta*
1st class — *de primeira classe*
2nd class — *de segunda classe*

I'd like to hire ... — *Queria alugar ...*
a car — *um carro*
a bicycle — *uma bicicleta*

Where is ...? — *Onde é ...?*
Go straight ahead. — *Siga sempre a direito/ Siga sempre em frente.*
Turn left. — *Vire à esquerda.*
Turn right. — *Vire à direita.*
near/far — *perto/longe*

Around Town

a bank — *um banco*
the chemist/pharmacy — *a farmácia*
the ... embassy — *a embaixada de ...*
the market — *o mercado*
the newsagent — *a papelaria*
the post office — *os correios*
the tourist office — *o (posto de) turismo*

What time does it open/close? — *A que horas abre/ fecha?*

Accommodation

hotel — *hotel*
guesthouse — *pensão*
youth hostel — *pousada da juventude*
camping ground — *parque de campismo*
Do you have any rooms available? — *Tem quartos livres?*
How much is it per night/per person? — *Quanto é por noite/ por pessoa?*

a single room — *um quarto individual*
a twin room — *um quarto duplo*
a double bed room — *um quarto de casal*
for one night — *para uma noite*
for two nights — *para duas noites*

Time, Days & Numbers

What time is it? — *Que horas são?*
today — *hoje*
tomorrow — *amanhã*
yesterday — *ontem*
morning — *manhã*
afternoon — *tarde*

Monday — *segunda-feira*
Tuesday — *terça-feira*
Wednesday — *quarta-feira*
Thursday — *quinta-feira*
Friday — *sexta-feira*
Saturday — *sábado*
Sunday — *domingo*

0	*zero*	7	*sete*
1	*um/uma*	8	*oito*
2	*dois/duas*	9	*nove*
3	*três*	10	*dez*
4	*quatro*	11	*onze*
5	*cinco*	100	*cem*
6	*seis*	1000	*mil*

one million — *um milhão*

Romanian

Pronunciation

Until the mid-19th century, Romanian was written in the Cyrillic script. Today Romanian employs 28 Latin letters, some of which bear accents. At the beginning of a word, **e** and **i** are pronounced 'ye' and 'yi', while at the end of a word **i** is almost silent. At the end of a word **ii** is pronounced 'ee'. The stress is usually on the penultimate syllable.

ă	as the 'er' in 'brother'
î	as the 'i' in 'river'
c	as 'k', except before **e** and **i**, when it's as the 'ch' in 'chip'
ch	always as the 'k' in 'king'
g	as in 'go', except before **e** and **i**, when it's as in 'gentle'
gh	always as the 'g' in 'get'
ş	as 'sh'
ţ	as the 'tz'in 'tzar'

Basics

Hello. — *Bună.*
Goodbye. — *La revedere.*

Yes.	*Da.*
No.	*Nu.*
Please.	*Vă rog.*
Thank you.	*Mulţumesc.*
Sorry. (forgive me)	*Iertaţi-mă.*
Excuse me.	*Scuzaţi-mă.*
I don't understand.	*Nu înţeleg.*
What is it called?	*Cum se cheamă?*
How much is it?	*Cît costă?*

Getting Around

What time does the ... leave/arrive?	*La ce oră pleacă/soseşte ...?*
boat	*vaporul*
bus	*autobusul*
train	*trenul*
tram	*tramvaiul*
plane	*avionul*

arrival	*sosire*
departure	*plecare*
timetable	*mersul/orar*

Where is the bus stop?	*Unde este staţia de autobuz?*
Where is the station?	*Unde este gară?*
Where is the left-luggage room?	*Unde este biroul pentru bagaje de mînă?*
Please show me on the map.	*Vă rog arătaţi-mi pe hartă.*

straight ahead	*drept înainte*
left	*stînga*
right	*dreapta*

Around Town

the bank	*banca*
the chemist	*farmacistul*
the church	*biserica*
the city centre	*centrum oraşului*
the ... embassy	*ambasada ...*
the market	*piaţa*
the museum	*muzeu*
the post office	*poşta*
the tourist office	*birou de informatii turistice*

Signs – Romanian

Intrare	**Entrance**
Ieşire	**Exit**
Informaţii	**Information**
Deschis	**Open**
Inchis	**Closed**
Nu Intraţi	**No Entry**
Staţie de Poliţie	**Police Station**
Toaleta	**Toilets**

Emergencies – Romanian

Help!	*Ajutor!*
Call a doctor!	*Chemaţi un doctor!*
Call the police!	*Chemaţi poliţia!*
Go away!	*Du-te!/Pleacă!*
I'm lost.	*Sînt pierdut.*

Accommodation

hotel	*hotel*
guesthouse	*casa de oaspeţi*
youth hostel	*camin studentesc*
camping ground	*camping*
private room	*cameră particulară*
single room	*o cameră pentru o persoană*
double room	*o cameră pentru două persoane*

Do you have any rooms available?	*Aveţi camere libere?*
How much is it?	*Cît costă?*
Does it include breakfast?	*Include micul dejun?*

Time, Days & Numbers

What time is it?	*Ce oră este?*
today	*azi*
tonight	*deseară*
tomorrow	*mîine*
yesterday	*ieri*
in the morning	*dimineaţa*
in the evening	*seară*

Monday	*luni*
Tuesday	*marţi*
Wednesday	*miercuri*
Thursday	*joi*
Friday	*vineri*
Saturday	*sîmbătă*
Sunday	*duminică*

1	*unu*	7	*şapte*
2	*doi*	8	*opt*
3	*trei*	9	*nouă*
4	*patru*	10	*zece*
5	*cinci*	100	*o sută*
6	*şase*	1000	*o mie*

one million	*milion*

Russian

Russian uses the Cyrillic alphabet, which resembles Greek with some extra characters. (See the Cyrillic Alphabet boxed text on p????.)

Basics

Hello.	*zdrastvuyte*
Good morning.	*dobraye utra*
Good afternoon.	*dobryy den'*
Good evening.	*dobryy vecher*
Goodbye.	*da svidaniya*
Bye! (inf)	*paka!*
How are you?	*kak dila?*
Yes.	*dat*
No.	*net*
Please.	*pazhalsta*
Thank you (very much).	*(bal'shoye) spasiba*
Pardon me.	*prastite/pazhalsta*
No problem/ Never mind.	*nichevo* (literally, 'nothing')
Do you speak English?	*vy gavarite pa angliyski?*
What's your name?	*kak vas zavut?*
My name is ...	*minya zavut ...*
How much is it?	*skol'ka stoit?*

Getting Around

What time does the ... leave?
f katoram chasu pribyvaet ...?
What time does the ... arrive?
f katoram chasu atpravlyaetsa ...?

bus	*aftobus*
fixed-route minibus	*marshrutnaye taksi*
steamship	*parakhot*
train	*poyezt*

Signs – Russian

Вход	**Entrance**
Выход	**Exit**
Открыто	**Open**
Закрыто	**Closed**
Справки	**Information**
Касса	**Ticket Office**
Больница	**Hospital**
Милиция	**Police**
Туалет	**Toilets**
Мужской (М)	**Men**
Женский (Ж)	**Women**

Ukrainian

Because of Ukraine's history of domination by outside powers, the language was often considered inferior or subservient to the dominant languages of the time – Russian in the east, Polish in the west. Today, the Ukrainian language is slowly being revived, and in 1990 it was adopted as the official language. Russian is understood everywhere by everyone, so although it may be diplomatic and polite to speak Ukrainian (especially in the west), you'll have no problem being understood if you speak Russian.

tram	*tramvay*
trolleybus	*traleybus*
pier/quay	*prichal/pristan'*
train station	*zhilezna darozhnyy vagzal*
stop (bus/trolleybus/tram)	*astanofka*
one-way ticket	*bilet v adin kanets*
return ticket	*bilet v oba kantsa*
two tickets	*dva bilety*
soft or 1st-class (compartment)	*myahkiy*
hard or 2nd-class (compartment)	*kupeyny*
3rd-class (carriage)	*platskartny*

Where is ...?	*gde ...?*
to (on) the left	*naleva*
to (on) the right	*naprava*
straight on	*pryama*

Around Town

bank	*bank*
market	*rynak*
pharmacy	*apteka*
post office	*pochta*
telephone booth	*tilifonnaya budka*
open	*otkryta*
closed	*zakryta*

Accommodation

hotel	*gastinitsa*
room	*nomer*
breakfast	*zaftrak*
How much is a room?	*skol'ka stoit nomer?*

Time, Date & Numbers

What time is it?	*katoryy chas*
today	*sivodnya*

Emergencies – Russian

Help!	*na pomashch'!/ pamagite!*
I'm sick.	*ya bolen* (m)
	ya bal'na (f)
I need a doctor.	*mne nuzhin vrach*
hospital	*bal'nitsa*
police	*militsiya*
I'm lost.	*ya zabludilsya* (m)
	ya zabludilas' (f)

yesterday	*vchira*
tomorrow	*zaftra*
am/in the morning	*utra*
pm/in the afternoon	*dnya*
in the evening	*vechira*

Monday	*panidel'nik*
Tuesday	*ftornik*
Wednesday	*srida*
Thursday	*chitverk*
Friday	*pyatnitsa*
Saturday	*subota*
Sunday	*vaskrisen'e*

0	*nol'*	7	*sem'*
1	*adin*	8	*vosim'*
2	*dva*	9	*devit'*
3	*tri*	10	*desit'*
4	*chityri*	11	*adinatsat'*
5	*pyat'*	100	*sto*
6	*shest'*	1000	*tysyacha*

one million *(adin) milion*

The Cyrillic Alphabet

Cyrillic	Roman	Pronunciation
А а	a	as in 'father'; also as in 'ago' when unstressed in Russian
Б б	b	as in 'but'
В в	v	as in 'van'
Г г	g	as in 'go'
Ѓ ѓ (Macedonian only)	gj	as the 'gu' in 'legume'
Д д	d	as the 'd' in 'dog'
Е е	ye	as in 'yet' when stressed; as in 'year' when unstressed (Russian)
	e	as in 'bet' (Bulgarian); as in 'there' (Macedonian)
Ё ё (Russian only)	yo	as in 'yore'
Ж ж	zh	as the 's' in 'measure'
З з	z	as in 'zoo'
Ѕ ѕ (Macedonian only)	zj	as the 'ds' in 'suds'
И и	i	as the 'ee' in 'meet'
Й й	y	as in 'boy'
Ј ј (Macedonian only)	j	as the 'y' in 'young'
К к	k	as in 'kind'
Ќ ќ (Macedonian only)	kj	as the 'cu' in 'cure'
Л л	l	as in 'lamp'
Љ љ (Macedonian only)	lj	as the 'lli' in 'million'
М м	m	as in 'mat'
Н н	n	as in 'not'
Њ њ (Macedonian only)	nj	as the 'ny' in 'canyon'
О о	o	as in 'more' when stressed; as the 'a' in 'ago' when unstressed (Russian)
		as in 'hot' (Bulgarian & Macedonian)
П п	p	as in 'pick'
Р р	r	as in 'rub' (but rolled)
С с	s	as in 'sing'
Т т	t	as in 'ten'
У у	u	as in 'rule'
Ф ф	f	as in 'fan'
Х х	kh	as the 'ch' in 'Bach' (Russian & Bulgarian)
	h	as in 'hot' (Macedonian)
Ц ц	ts	as in 'bits'
Џ џ (Macedonian only)	dz	as the 'j' in 'judge'
Ч ч	ch	as in 'chat'
Ш ш	sh	as in 'shop'
Щ щ	shch	as 'shch' in 'fresh chips' (Russian)
	sht	as the '-shed' in pushed' (Bulgarian)
Ъ ъ (Bulgarian only)	â	as the 'a' in 'ago'
ъ		'hard' sign (Russian)
Ы ы (Russian only)	y	as the 'i' in 'ill'
ь (Russian only)		'soft' sign
Э э (Russian only)	e	as in 'end'
Ю ю	yu	as the word 'you'
Я я	ya	as in 'yard'

Slovak

Pronunciation

In words of three syllables or less the stress falls on the first syllable. Longer words generally also have a secondary accent on the third or fifth syllable. There are thirteen vowels (**a, á, ä, e, é, i, í, o, ó, u, ú, y, ý**), three semi-vowels (**l, l', r**) and five diphthongs (**ia, ie, iu, ou, ô**).

c	as the 'ts' in 'its'
č	as the 'ch' in 'church'
dz	as the 'ds' in 'suds'
dž	as the 'j' in 'judge'
ia	as the 'yo' in 'yonder'
ie	as the 'ye' in 'yes'
iu	as the word 'you'
j	as the 'y' in 'yet'
ň	as the 'ni' in 'onion'
ô	as the 'wo' in 'won't'
ou	as the 'ow' in 'know'
š	as the 'sh' in 'show'
y	as the 'i' in 'machine'
ž	as the 'z' in 'azure'

Basics

Hello.	*Ahoj.*
Goodbye.	*Dovidenia.*
Yes.	*Áno.*
No.	*Nie.*
Please.	*Prosím.*
Thank you.	*D'akujem.*
Excuse me/ Forgive me.	*Prepáčte mi/ Odpuste mi.*
I'm sorry.	*Ospravedlňujem sa.*
I don't understand.	*Nerozumiem.*
What is it called?	*Ako sa do volá?*
How much is it?	*Koľko to stojí?*

Getting Around

What time does the ... leave/arrive?	*Kedy odchádza/ prichádza ...?*
boat	*loč*
city bus	*mestský autobus*
intercity bus	*medzimestský autobus*
plane	*lietadlo*
train	*vlak*
tram	*električka*

arrival	*príchod*
departure	*odchod*
timetable	*cestovný poriadok*

Where is the bus stop?	*Kde je autobusová zastávka?*
Where is the station?	*Kde je vlaková stanica?*
Where is the left-luggage room?	*Kde je úschovňa batožín?*
Please show me on the map.	*Prosím, ukážte mi to na mape.*
left	*vľavo*
right	*vpravo*
straight ahead	*rovno*

Signs – Slovak

Vchod	**Entrance**
Východ	**Exit**
Informácie	**Information**
Otvorené	**Open**
Zatvorené	**Closed**
Zakázané	**Prohibited**
Polícia	**Police Station**
Telefón	**Telephone**
Záchody/WC/ Toalety	**Toilets**

Emergencies – Slovak

Help!	*Pomoc!*
Call a doctor!	*Zavolajte doktora/ lekára!*
Call the police!	*Zavolajte políciu!*
Go away!	*Choď preč!* (sg)/ *Choďte preč!* (pl)
I'm lost.	*Nevyznám sa tu.*

Around Town

the bank	*banka*
the chemist	*lekárnik*
the market	*trh*
the post office	*pošta*
the telephone centre	*telefónnu centrálu*
the tourist office	*turistické informačné centrum*

Accommodation

hotel	*hotel*
guesthouse	*penzion*
youth hostel	*mládežnícka ubytovňa*
camping ground	*kemping*
private room	*privat*

Do you have any rooms available?	*Máte voľné izby?*
How much is it?	*Koľko to stojí?*
Does it include breakfast?	*Sú raňajky zahrnuté v cene?*

single room	*jednolôžková izba*
double room	*dvojlôžková izba*

Time, Days & Numbers

What time is it?	*Koľko je hodín?*
today	*dnes*
tonight	*dnes večer*
tomorrow	*zajtra*
yesterday	*včera*
in the morning	*ráno*
in the evening	*večer*

Monday	*pondelok*
Tuesday	*utorok*
Wednesday	*streda*
Thursday	*štvrtok*
Friday	*piatok*
Saturday	*sobota*
Sunday	*nedeľa*

1	*jeden*	7	*sedem*
2	*dva*	8	*osem*
3	*tri*	9	*deväť*
4	*štyri*	10	*desať*
5	*päť*	100	*sto*
6	*šesť*	1000	*tisíc*

one million *milión*

Slovene

Pronunciation

The letters **l** and **v** are both pronounced like the English 'w' when they occur at the end of syllables and before vowels. Though words like *trn* (thorn) look unpronounceable, most Slovenes (depending on dialect) add a short vowel like an 'a' or the German 'ö' in front of the 'r' to give a Scot's pronunciation of 'tern' or 'tarn'.

c	as the 'ts' in 'its'
č	as the 'ch' in 'church'
ê	as the 'a' in 'apple'
e	as the 'a' in 'ago' (when unstressed)
é	as the 'ay' in 'day'
j	as the 'y' in 'yellow'
ó	as the 'o' in 'more'
ò	as the 'o' in 'soft'
r	a rolled 'r' sound
š	as the 'sh' in 'ship'
u	as the 'oo' in 'good'
ž	as the 's' in 'treasure'

Basics

Hello.	*Pozdravljeni.* (pol) *Zdravo/Živivo.* (inf)
Good day.	*Dober dan!*
Goodbye.	*Nasvidenje!*
Yes.	*Da* or *Ja.* (inf)
No.	*Ne.*
Please.	*Prosim.*
Thank you (very much).	*Hvala (lepa).*
You're welcome.	*Prosim/Ni za kaj!*
Excuse me.	*Oprostite.*
What's your name?	*Kako vam je ime?*
My name is ...	*Jaz sem ...*

Getting Around

What time does ... leave/arrive?	*Kdaj odpelje/ pripelje ...?*
boat/ferry	*ladja/trajekt*
bus	*avtobus*
train	*vlak*

one-way (ticket)	*enosmerna (vozovnica)*
return (ticket)	*povratna (vozovnica)*

Around Town

Where is the/a ...?	*Kje je ...?*
bank/exchange	*banka/menjalnica*
post office	*pošta*
telephone centre	*telefonska centrala*
tourist office	*turistični informacijski urad*

Accommodation

hotel	*hotel*
guesthouse	*gostišče*
camping ground	*kamping*

Do you have a ...?	*Ali imate prosto ...?*
bed	*posteljo*
cheap room	*poceni sobo*
single room	*enoposteljno sobo*
double room	*dvoposteljno sobo*

How much is it per night?	*Koliko stane za eno noč?*
How much is it per person?	*Koliko stane za eno osebo?*
for one/two nights	*za eno noč/za dve noči*
Is breakfast included?	*Ali je zajtrk vključen?*

Signs – Slovene

Vhod	**Entrance**
Izhod	**Exit**
Informacije	**Information**
Odprto	**Open**
Zaprto	**Closed**
Prepovedano	**Prohibited**
Stranišče	**Toilets**

Emergencies – Slovene

Help!	*Na pomoč!*
Call a doctor!	*Pokličite zdravnika!*
Call the police!	*Pokličite policijo!*
Go away!	*Pojdite stran!*

Time, Days & Numbers

today	*danes*
tonight	*nocoj*
tomorrow	*jutri*
in the morning	*zjutraj*
in the evening	*zvečer*

Monday	*ponedeljek*
Tuesday	*torek*
Wednesday	*sreda*
Thursday	*četrtek*
Friday	*petek*
Saturday	*sobota*
Sunday	*nedelja*

1	*ena*	7	*sedem*
2	*dve*	8	*osem*
3	*tri*	9	*devet*
4	*štiri*	10	*deset*
5	*pet*	100	*sto*
6	*šest*	1000	*tisoč*

one million *milijon*

Spanish

Basics

Hello/Goodbye.	*¡Hola!/¡Adiós!*
Yes.	*Sí.*
No.	*No.*
Please.	*Por favor.*
Thank you.	*Gracias.*
You're welcome.	*De nada.*
I'm sorry. (forgive me)	*Lo siento/Discúlpeme.*
Excuse me.	*Perdón/Perdoneme.*
Do you speak English?	*¿Habla inglés?*
How much is it?	*¿Cuánto cuesta?/ ¿Cuánto vale?*

Getting Around

What time does the next ... leave/arrive?	*¿A qué hora sale/ llega el próximo ...?*
boat	*barco*
bus (city)	*autobús, bus*
bus (intercity)	*autocar*
train	*tranvía*

I'd like a :... ticket.	*Quisiera un billete ...*
one-way	*sencillo/de sólo ida*
return	*de ida y vuelta*
1st class	*de primera clase*
2nd class	*de segunda clase*

left luggage	*consigna*
timetable	*horario*
bus stop	*parada de autobus*
train station	*estación de ferrocarril*

I'd like to hire ...	*Quisiera alquilar ...*
a car	*un coche*
a bicycle	*una bicicleta*

Where is ...?	*¿Dónde está ...?*
Go straight ahead.	*Siga/Vaya todo derecho.*
Turn left.	*Gire a la izquierda.*
Turn right.	*Gire a la derecha/recto.*
near/far	*cerca/lejos*

Around Town

a bank	*un banco*
the chemist	*la farmacia*
the ... embassy	*la embajada ...*
the market	*el mercado*
newsagent/ stationer	*papelería*
the post office	*los correos*
the tourist office	*la oficina de turismo*

What time does it open/close?	*¿A qué hora abren/ cierran?*

Accommodation

hotel	*hotel*
guesthouse	*pensión/casa de huéspedes*
youth hostel	*albergue juvenil*
camping ground	*camping*

Do you have any rooms available?	*¿Tiene habitaciones libres?*

Signs – Spanish

Entrada	**Entrance**
Salida	**Exit**
Información	**Information**
Abierto	**Open**
Cerrado	**Closed**
Prohibido	**Prohibited**
Comisaría	**Police Station**
Servicios/Aseos	**Toilets**
Hombres	**Men**
Mujeres	**Women**

Emergencies – Spanish

Help!	*¡Socorro!/¡Auxilio!*
Call a doctor!	*¡Llame a un doctor!*
Call the police!	*¡Llame a la policía!*
Go away!	*¡Váyase!*
I'm lost.	*Estoy perdido/a.* (m/f)

How much is it per night/per person? — *¿Cuánto cuesta por noche/por persona?*

a single room — *una habitación individual*
a double room — *una habitación doble*
a room with a double bed — *una habitación con cama de matrimonio*
for one night — *para una noche*
for two nights — *para dos noches*

Time, Days & Numbers

What time is it? — *¿Qué hora es?*
today — *hoy*
tomorrow — *mañana*
yesterday — *ayer*
morning — *mañana*
afternoon — *tarde*

Monday — *lunes*
Tuesday — *martes*
Wednesday — *miércoles*
Thursday — *jueves*
Friday — *viernes*
Saturday — *sábado*
Sunday — *domingo*

1	*uno/una*	10	*diez*
2	*dos*	11	*once*
3	*tres*	12	*doce*
4	*cuatro*	13	*trece*
5	*cinco*	14	*catorce*
6	*seis*	15	*quince*
7	*siete*	16	*dieciéis*
8	*ocho*	100	*cien/ciento*
9	*nueve*	1000	*mil*

one million — *un millón*

Swedish

Pronunciation

å long, as the word 'awe'; short as the 'o' in 'pot'
ä as the 'a' in 'act'
ö as the 'er' in 'fern', but without the 'r' sound
y try saying 'ee' while pursing your lips
c as the 's' in 'sit'
ck as a double 'k'; shortens the preceding vowel
tj, rs as the 'sh' in 'ship'
sj, ch similar to the 'ch' in Scottish *loch*
g as in 'get'; sometimes as the 'y' in 'yet'
lj as the 'y' in 'yet'

Basics

Hello. — *Hej.*
Goodbye. — *Adjö/Hej då.*
Yes. — *Ja.*
No. — *Nej.*
Please. — *Snälla/Vänligen.*
Thank you. — *Tack.*
That's fine/You're welcome. — *Det är bra/Varsågod.*
Excuse me. (sorry) — *Ursäkta mig/Förlåt.*
Do you speak English? — *Talar du engelska?*
How much is it? — *Hur mycket kostar den?*

Getting Around

What time does ... leave/arrive? — *När avgår/kommer ...?*
 the boat — *båten*
 the city bus — *stadsbussen*
 the intercity bus — *landsortsbussen*
 the tram — *spårvagnen*
 the train — *tåget*

I'd like ... — *Jag skulle vilja ha ...*
 a one-way ticket — *en enkelbiljett*
 a return ticket — *en returbiljett*
 1st class — *första klass*
 2nd class — *andra klass*

left luggage — *effektförvaring*
timetable — *tidtabell*
bus stop — *busshållplats*
train station — *tågstation*

Where can I hire a car/bicycle? — *Var kan jag hyra en bil/cykel?*

Signs – Swedish

Ingång	**Entrance**
Utgång	**Exit**
Information	**Information**
Öppet	**Open**
Stängt	**Closed**
Förbjudet	**Prohibited**
Polisstation	**Police Station**
Toalett	**Toilets**
Herrar	**Men**
Damer	**Women**

Emergencies – Swedish

Help!	*Hjälp!*
Call a doctor!	*Ring efter en doktor!*
Call the police!	*Ring polisen!*
Go away!	*Försvinn!*
I'm lost.	*Jag har gått vilse.*

Where is ...?	*Var är ...?*
Go straight ahead.	*Gå rakt fram.*
Turn left.	*Sväng till vänster.*
Turn right.	*Sväng till höger.*
near/far	*nära/långt*

Around Town

bank	*bank*
chemist/pharmacy	*apotek*
... embassy	*... ambassaden*
market	*marknaden*
newsagent/ stationer	*nyhetsbyrå/ pappers handel*
post office	*postkontoret*
tourist office	*turistinformation*

What time does it open/close?	*När öppnar/ stänger de?*

Accommodation

hotel	*hotell*
guesthouse	*gästhus*
youth hostel	*vandrarhem*
camping ground	*campingplats*

Do you have any rooms available?	*Finns det några lediga rum?*
How much is it per night/ per person?	*Hur mycket kostar det per natt/ per person?*
for one night	*i en natt*
for two nights	*i två nätter*

I'd like ...	*Jag skulle vilja ha ...*
a single room	*ett enkelrum*
a double room	*ett dubbelrum*

Time, Days & Numbers

What time is it?	*Vad är klockan?*
today	*idag*
tomorrow	*imorgon*
yesterday	*igår*
morning	*morgonen*
afternoon	*efter middagen*

Monday	*måndag*
Tuesday	*tisdag*
Wednesday	*onsdag*
Thursday	*torsdag*
Friday	*fredag*
Saturday	*lördag*
Sunday	*söndag*

0	*noll*	7	*sju*
1	*ett*	8	*åtta*
2	*två*	9	*nio*
3	*tre*	10	*tio*
4	*fyra*	11	*elva*
5	*fem*	100	*ett hundra*
6	*sex*	1000	*ett tusen*

one million	*en miljon*

Turkish

Pronunciation

A, a	as the 'ar' in 'art' or 'bar'
E, e	as in 'fell'
İ, i	as 'ee'
I, ı	as 'uh'
O, o	as in 'hot'
U, u	as the 'oo' in 'moo'
Ö, ö	as the 'ur' in 'fur'
Ü, ü	as the 'ew' in 'few'

Note that both **ö** and **ü** are pronounced with pursed lips.

Ç, ç	as the 'ch' in 'church'
C, c	as English 'j'
Ğ, ğ	not pronounced; draws out the preceding vowel a bit – ignore it!
J, j	as the 's' in 'treasure'
S, s	hard, as in 'stress'
Ş, ş	as the 'sh' in 'shoe'
V, v	as the 'w' in 'weather'

Basics

Hello.	*Merhaba.*
Goodbye.	*Allahaısmarladık/ Güle güle.*

Yes.	*Evet.*
No.	*Hayır.*
Please.	*Lütfen.*
Thank you.	*Teşekkür ederim.*
That's fine/You're welcome.	*Bir şey değil.*
Excuse me.	*Affedersiniz.*
Sorry/Pardon.	*Pardon.*
Do you speak English?	*ºngilizce biliyor musunuz?*
How much is it?	*Ne kadar?*

Getting Around

What time does the next ... leave/arrive?	*Gelecek ... ne zaman kalkar/gelir?*
ferry/boat	*feribot/vapur*
bus (city)	*şehir otobüsü*
bus (intercity)	*otobüs*
tram	*tramvay*
train	*tren*
I'd like ...	*... istiyorum*
a one-way ticket	*gidiş bileti*
a return ticket	*gidiş-dönüş bileti*
1st/2nd class	*birinci/ikinci mevkii*
left luggage	*emanetçi*
timetable	*tarife*
bus/tram stop	*otobüs/tramvay durağı*
train station	*gar/istasyon*
boat/ship dock	*iskele*
I'd like to hire a car/bicycle.	*Araba/bisiklet kirala mak istiyorum.*
Where is a/the ...?	*... nerede?*
Go straight ahead.	*Doğru gidin.*
Turn left.	*Sola dönün.*
Turn right.	*Sağa dönün.*
near/far	*yakın/uzak*

Around Town

a bank	*bir banka*
a chemist/pharmacy	*bir eczane*
the ... embassy	*... büyükelçiliği*
the post office	*postane*
the market	*çarşı*
the tourist office	*turizm danışma bürosu*
What time does it open/close?	*Ne zamam açılır/kapanır?*

Signs – Turkish

Giriş	**Entrance**
Çikiş	**Exit**
Danişma	**Information**
Açik/Kapali	**Open/Closed**
Yasak(tir)	**Prohibited**
Polis Karakolu/ Emniyet Müdürlüğü	**Police Station**
Tuvalet	**Toilets**

Emergencies – Turkish

Help!/Emergency!	*İmdat!*
Call a doctor!	*Doktor çağırın!*
Call the police!	*Polis çağırın!*
Go away!	*Gidin/Git!/Defol!*
I'm lost.	*Kayboldum.*

Accommodation

hotel	*otel(i)*
guesthouse	*pansiyon*
student hostel	*öğrenci yurdu*
camping ground	*kampink*
Do you have any rooms available?	*Boş oda var mı?*
How much is it per night/per person?	*Bir gecelik/Kişibaşına kaç para?*
a single room	*tek kişilik oda*
a double room	*iki kişilik oda*

Time, Days & Numbers

What time is it?	*Saat kaç?*
today	*bugün*
tomorrow	*yarın*
yesterday	*dün*
morning	*sabah*
afternoon	*öğleden sonra*
Monday	*Pazartesi*
Tuesday	*Salı*
Wednesday	*Çarşamba*
Thursday	*Perşembe*
Friday	*Cuma*
Saturday	*Cumartesi*
Sunday	*Pazar*

1	*bir*	8	*sekiz*
2	*iki*	9	*dokuz*
3	*üç*	10	*on*
4	*dört*	11	*on bir*
5	*beş*	12	*on iki*
6	*altı*	100	*yüz*
7	*yedi*	1000	*bin*

one million	*bir milyon*

Thanks

Many thanks to the travellers who used the last edition and wrote to us with helpful hints, useful advice and interesting anecdotes:

Palmer Acheson, Alwyn Adams, Jodi Adams, Nick Adlam, Sabine Agena, Christine M Agnitti, Helen Ahern, Husain Akbar, Amie Albrecht, Brooke Aldrich, Rene Allen, Jane Alston, Unal Altinyay, Pedro Alvarez, Sheila Aly, Bashar Amso, Kasper Anderson, Lainie & Craig Anderson, Ryan Anderson, Phil & Hilary Andre, Alan Andrews, Lee Andrews, Cynthia Ang, Carrie Appleton, Mike Appleyard, J M Aranaz, Josee Archambault, Daniel Arenas, Tanya Arnoldi, Elizabeth Arnstein, Elena Arriero, Gary Artim, Karin Arver, Saara Arvo, Hiroyuki Asakuno, Hilmir Ásgeirsson, Glenn Ashenden, Becky Askew, Kyle Austen, Andrei Avram, Kris Ayre, Jerry Azevedo, PL Baas, Ivan Babiuk, Brendon Bailey, Monika Bailey, Ali Baldwin, Rebecca Balsamo, Anne Kisi Bancroft, Renee Banky, Christine Barbour, Gord Barentsen, Ann Barker, Leah Barnett, Steve Barnett, Michael Barr, Andrew Barton, Georgina Barton, Montse Baste-Kraan, Dobromir Batinkov, Ken Baxter, Kate Bayne, Andrew Baynham, Wes Beard, Gregory Becker, John Bedford, Matt Beks, C B Belcher, Jacqui Belgrave, Adam Bell, Keith & Bronwen Bell, Roy Bell, Tony Bellette, Barb Bellinger, Tony Benfield, Koos Berkhout, Annika Bernascone, Jeff Berry, Mark Bersten, Christian Bertell, David Bertolotti, Ann Best, Heather Beswick, Gordon Bettenay, Michelle Beveridge, Luisa Bezzola, Ami Bhatt, Alisa Bieber, Sylvain Biemont, Alexandre Billette, Maurizio Bilotta, Jackie Binger, Jane & Steve Bland, Louise & Brad Bland, Ezster Blaskovics, Cindy & Maggie Blick, Misty Bliss, Mandi Booth, Christopher Borgmann, Dirk Borowski, Bela Borsos, Andre Bosmans, Ren Bostelaar, Carmen Boudreau-Kiviaho, Julie Bowden, Melissa Bowtell, Joanna & Don Box, Belinda Boyd, Mahmut Boynudelik, Jean-Claude Branch, A Breet, Ben Brehmer, Jeanne Brei, Paul Brians, Claire Briggs, Evan Brinder, Micheal Britton, George Aaron Broadwell, Thessa Brongers, Abe Brouwer, Carol Brown, Edmund Brown, Kevin Brown, Marl Allen Brown, Miriam Brown, Dylan Browne, Hanna Bruin, Ang Bryans, Craig Bryant, Rod George Bryant, Renay Buchanan, Martin Buekers, David Bugden, Jan Bullerdieck, Simon Bunt, Cameron Bush, Michelle Bush, Rob Butler, Emanuel Buttigieg, Armando Cabrera, Doris Calhoun, Tui Cameron, Cory Camilleri, Samantha Campbell, Simone Candido, John Cappelletti, Drew Caputo, Jennifer Carlson, Clare Carmody, Fred Carreon, Steven Carrick, Julie Carroll, Kent Carter, Michael Cassidy, Terry Casstevens, Carolyn Castiglia, Scott Caufield, Luigi Ceccarini, Sandy Ceniseros, Celia Cerbon, Andrew Cerchez, Matt Chaffe, Bradley Chait, Myriam Champagne, Greg Chandler, Rebekka Chaplin, Anthi Charalambous, Dr C W Chen, Stanley Cheng, Farid Chetouani, Alison Cheung, Anna Chilton, Terrie Chin, Ian Chivas, Kah Chong, Sutapa Choudhury, K M Chow, Alfred Choy, Hanno Christ, Mark Christian, Leigh Churchill, Mollie Churchill, Niko Cimbur, Lisa Cipelli, Chrissy & Malcolm Clark, Darren Clarke, Erica Clarke, Joe Clavan, Charles & Anne Clayton, Stephen Coast, Ian Coggin, Robyn Cohen, Peter Collins, Edward Congdon, Elizabeth Connolly, Martha W Connor, Paul Conway, Mrs Cook, Karen Cooper, W B Cooper, Andrew Cork, Ed Cornfield, Ursula Cornu, Catalin Coroama, Paolo Criscione, Alma Cristina, Stuart Cruickshank, Sarok Csaba, Ricardo Cuan, Phil Cubbin, Desmond Cumiskey, Dennis & Anne Cumming, Carrie Cunningham, Madi Dale, Paul Dalton, Robert K Daly, Jane d'Arcy, Neil Datta, Harry Davidson, Shaun Davidson, J Davies, James Davis, Robert Davison, Susan & Stewart Davison, Jeannie & Keith de Jong, Shane de Malmanche, Johan de Vetti, Sander de Vries, Hayley Dean, Susan Del Gobbo, Phill Dellow, Michel Delporte, Carine Delvaux, RJ Dempsey, Philippe Dennler, Colleen Densmore, Carine Derch, Walter Derks, Luc Desy, Chris Detmar, Sante D'ettorre, David Deutscher, Stelios N Deverakis, Robin Deweerdt, Nathan Dhillon, Kathleen Diamond, Carlos Diaz, Floris Dirks, Jan Ditheridge, Rachel Dodds, Sarah Dodson, Elizabeth Doggett, Birge Dohmann, Mathew Dolenac, Matjaz Dolenc, Steffi Domagk, Nicola Doran, Alexander Doric, Lana Dorset, Ryan Dougherty, Majorie Douglass, Andrea Doukas, Sasa Drach, Jason Dressler, Ravit & Sagi Dror, Pattie Dubaere, Liesbeth Dubois, Nick Duke, Laurent-Jan Dullaart, Anne Dupuis, Loretta Dupuis, Kim Duva, Sonya Dykstra, John Dynan,

Ben Earl, Jason Earle, Mary-Anne Easton, Matt Eaton, Jutta Eberlin, Ben Edmunds, Bronwyn Edwards, Dr Alison Edwards, Jack Egerton, Bernie Eglinton, Katie Elder, Robin Elliott, Caghan Elsiz,

Kim Elton, Andrew Embick, Ruth Emblin, Vincent-Frechette Emmanuel Andre, Jennifer Emmert, Marvin Engel, Reinhard Enne, Marleen Enschede, Gennevene Ensor, Ket Ericson, Nikita Eriksen-Hamel, Kelly Eskridge, Andrea Evans, Lucy Evans, Louisa Fagan, Martin Fagerer, Eva Fairnell, Michael Falk, Victor Falzon, Teresa Fanning, Bernard Farjounel, Eli Feiman, Christina J Felker, Anne Fenerty, Armando Ferra, Wendy Finch-Turner, Deborah Fink, Philippa Fleetwood, Anders Flensborg, Amy Fletcher, Tyler Flood, Kristine Flora, Mark Forrest, Dell Forrester, Richard Forsaith, Carmen Luisa Forsberg, Jordi Fortia-Huguet, Liz Foulis, Joao Fraga, Nicky Francis, Viola Franke, Sia Frederick, Gemma French, Marvin Ross Friedman, Ludek Frybort, Louise Fryer, Reyes Moran Fuertes, Werner Furrer, Helene Gabriel, Ricardo Gama, Angel Gambrel, Reshma Ganpat, Elizabeth Garber, Sally Gardner, Matthew Garfein, Alissa Garner, Dorin Garofeanu, Martin Garvey, Felicity Gatchell, Gaelen Gates, Ryan Gawel, Terry Geisecke, Sarit Gelbart, Tom Genway, Simon & Georgie, Alan Gibbons, Claire Gibbons, Jill & Ian Gibson, Serge Gielkens, Bart Giepmans, Monique Gijsbrechts, Linda Gillespie, Tim Gilley, Paul W Gioffi, Ewan Girvan, Ian Glennon, Arno Gloeckner, Matthew Goadby, Gerard Godbaz, Genevieve Godbout, Alan Godfrey, David Godfrey, Carla Goldchmit, Jane Golding, Jemma Golding, Irene Gomez, Miguel Alvim Gonzalez, Antonio Gonzalez-Avila, Samantha Gordon, Neale Gover, Paul Graalman, Meahan Grande, Elena Grant, Gordon Grant, Phyllis Grant, Luca Grassi, Deborah Gravrock, Beth Gray, Ed Graystone, Duncan Greaves, Louise Greaves, Justin K Green, Nicole Grima, Frederik Grufman, Patricia Grumberg, Karen Grunow, Gabriel Gruss, Dorry Grzinic, Kreso Gudelj, Ben Guezentsvey, Efe Gulagaci, Cher Guldemond, Rene Gulden, Kumar Gupta, Lars Gyllenhaal, Brian Aslak Gylte, Stefan Haberl, Joanne Hackett, Claudia Hackh, Erja Haenninen, Pamela Hagedorn, Sally Hagen, Paul Hagman, Warren Halliday, Roy F Halvorsen, Andrew Hamilton, Roswitha Hammer, Mikael Hanas, John Hanks, Cedric Hannedouche, Maria Hannon, Lars Folmer Hansen, Luc & Anja Hansenne-Geril, Peter Harris, Stephen & Akkelin Harris, Sue Harrison, Richard Harvey, Joseph Harwell, Chloe Harwood, Donald Hatch, Jan Havranek, Shona Hawkes, Tony Hayman, Esther Hecht, Edgar Hee, Scott Hegerty, K G Hellyen, James Hemingway, Mark Henderson, Barry Hennessy, Lisa Herb, Alison Herbst, Irene Herrera, Peter Hertrampf, Margaret Heuen, Heather J Hevey, Peter Hicks, Coleman Higgins, Alyson & David Hilbourne, Nick Hind, Kym Hirst, Jan & Mirjam Hissink, Simon Ho, Michelle Hodge, Marrianne Hoeyland, Belinda Hogan, Jim Hogue, Ville Holmberg, Josinda Holst, Tomas Homann, Clarie Hood, Erik Hoogcarspel, Chong Hoong Yin, Matt Hoover, Bruce Hope, Alex Hopkins, Fran Hopkins, Cherrie Hosken, Kim Houghton, Brent Hourd, Sue Houston, Karen Howat, Matt Howes, Petr Hruska, Michael Huber, Keven, Marianne & Alexander Huckel, Fra Huges, Laura Hughes, John Hulme, Stephen Humphrey, Mary Hunt, Mark Huntsman, Aline Huppi, Darcy Hurford, Joanne Hutchinson, Steuart Hutchinson, Josephine Hutton, Steve Hutton, Howard Huxter, Nobi Hyakutake, Bruce & Kay Ikawa, Christian Ilcus, Molnar Ildiko, Ahmet Incesu, Dancea Ioana, Victor & Agnes Isaacs, Katherine Iwankiw,

Jade Jackson, Trygve Jackson, Jessica Jacobson, Melissa Jacobson, Jani Jaderholm, Zsolt Jakab, Diana James, Jennifer Jansma, Daniel Jaramillo, Rok Jarc, Graham S Jarvis, Marie Javins, Prashant Jayaprakash, Janaka Jayasingha, Hayley Jenkins, Joyce Jenkins, Ida Johansson, David John, Ludmila Johnsen, Nicky Johnson, Patrick Johnson, Sally Jo Johnson, Miles Johnston, Andrew Jones, Chris Jones, Hywel Jones, Jenny Jones, Peter D Jones, Scott L Jones, W Jules, Roman Kaczaj, Benno Kaestli, Judith Kahan, Alexandra Kainz, Niki Kalogiratou, Lili Kalp, Teemu Kankaanpaa, Aziz Kara, Cynthia Karena, Joakim Karlsson, Ayla Karmali, Karles Karwin, Richard Katz, Jim Kellogg, Abby Kennedy, Matthew Kenny, Thecle Kentfield, Svensson Kerstin, Christoph Kessel, John Killick, Ronald Kim, Seamus King, Rob Kingston, Kathleen Kirby, Susan Kirinich, Dean & John Klinkenberg, Teja Klobucar, Wim Klumpenhouwer, David Klur, Timo Knaebe, Geof Knight, J E Knowles, Paul Knudsen, Barbara Kocot, George Koenig, Heike Koenig, Melanie Koppes, Nathan Korpela, Igor Korsic, Minette Korterink, Juraj Kosticky, Mihaly Kovacs, Sari Kreitzer, Sharon Kristoff, Nicole Kroon, Donna Krupa, Carlo Krusich, Petra Kubalcik, James Kueh, Cintia Kurimoto, Erki Kurrikoff, Kurtis Kurt, Karen Lamorey, Francesca Lanaro, Fernando Landro, Arnoud Langelaar, Espen Lauritzen, San Lauw, Annette Lawrence, Ron Leach, Lee Leatham, Antonio Lee, Denise Lee, Naomi Lee, Marc Lees, Sabine Legrand, Dr P A Lekhi, Desmond Leow, Matthew Lerner, Birgitte Lerno, Franck Lesage, Bert Leunis, Phil Lewis, George Liangas, John Libby, Ralf Liebau, Daniel Lieberfeld, Marge Lilane, Rich Lillywhite, Kimmo Linkama, Jeroen Lintjens, Chris Little, Harriet Little, Jean Regis Llewellyn-Bonnin,

Loepoldo Llorente, Anna Lochmann, Kristi Lockyer, Sabine Loebbe, Lisa Long, Simon Looi, Barbara Lopes-Cardozo, Hanne Lorimer, Serena Love, Michael Low, Christina Lowe, Allan Lucas, Nick Lux, Andrew Lyons, Oliver Lyttelton, P A MaCaitlem, Lachlan MacArthur, Deirdre MacBean, Debbie MacDonald, Frank MacDonald, Alex MacKenzie, Lachlan MacQuarrie, Kevin Madden, Kjell J Madsen, Diana Maestre, Mike Maglalang, Dee Mahan, Louise Mair, Jonna Makkonen, Kim Malcom, Veronique Manapeau, Roberto Manfredi, Rebecca Manvell, Lia Marcote, Eric Markowitz, John Marquis, Carolyn Marr, Jillian Marshall, Cathy & Kevin Marston, Christine Martens, Alberto Martin, Antoinette & Gerald Martin, Paul Martin, Steve Martin, Maile Martinez, Dave Mason, Alina Matei, Stefano Materassi, Peta Mathias, Phillip Matthews, Olivier Mauron, Kirstyn Mawdsley, Eileen Mazur, Glenn McAllister, Florence & Michael McBride, Mark McCabe, Jeff McCartney, Tania McCauley, Melvin McClanahan, Nora McComiskey, Damian McCormack, Edmund McCosh, Jennifer & Bruce McCoy, Charlene McDonald, Kathryn McDonnell, Tom McElderry, Ian McElmoyle, Sarah McElwain, Andrea McEneaney, Grainne McEvoy, David McGowan, Jamie McGraw, Delia McInerney, John McIntyre, Kevin McIntyre, Malcolm Mckay, John McKellar, John McKenzie, Emily McKenzie-Kay, Paul McKernan, Ralph McLean, Ian McLoughlin, Paul McLoughlin, Kenneth McLuskey, David McMahon, Sonja McShane, Janet Mead, Lucas Meijknecht, Heather Meldrom, Lori Mendel, Gunnar Merbach, Majda Mesic, Muhamed Mesic, Nedim Mesic, Gina Messenger, Constance Messer, Pierre Messier, Bas Metolli, Julian Mettler, Patrice Meunier, Tale Meyer, Robin Meyerhoff, Stefano Micchia, Vicky Michels, Karen Mickle, Lucia Miele, Aubree Miller, John Miller, Rachel Miller, Valerie Miller, Eric Milsom, Ming Ming Teh, Haleema Mini, Andre Minor, Basit Mirza, Martin Mischkulnig, Claire Missing, Kenny Mitchell, Sarah Moffat, Lee Gerard Molloy, Shane Monks, Jesse Monsour, J J Monte, Gary Moon, Matt Moore, Rebekah Moore, Geraldine Moran, Rich Moser, Hakon Mosseby, Inge Mossige, Jason Mote, Jean Mounter, Katie Mountford, Marcus Muhlethaler, K Mulzer, Veronica Munguia, Dave Munn, Simon Munt, Franklin Murillo, Jasper & Vincent Murphy, Sally Murphy, Terry Murphy, Tracey Murphy, Kate Murray, Roberta Murray, Kathryn Murtagh, Karen Myhill-Jones, Tatu Myohanen, Petra Naavalinna, Dan Nadel, Ludwig Naf, Jonas Nahm, Monica Naish, Karen Nalbandyan, MaryAnne Nelson, Ross Nelson, T Nelson, Jan Nesnidal, Steve Newcomer, Kate Nicholson, Anna Nicolaou, Mairi Nicolsen, Jen Noble, Bjorn Norheim, Jamie Norris, Klara Novakova, Rudy Nuytten,

Davor Obradovic, Debbie O'Bray, Erin K O'Brien, Judith O'Brien, Con O'Conaill, Jacqui O'-Connell, Christine Louise Oddy, Robin O'-Donoghue, Kevin O'Donovan, Carrie Oelberger, Mick Ogrizek, Ricardo Olaeta, Lars Olberg, Matt Oliver, Elka Olsen, Jacquie Olsen, Dana Olson, Ryan & Peter Olwagen, Andre Oord, Gustavo Orlando-Zon, Carlos Ortiz, Rikke Ortved, Michaela Osborne, Julie & Sener Otrugman, Kate Overheu, Vivien Ow, Anders Paalzow, Megan Packer, J Padget, Manuel Padilla, Sandra Pagano, Darja Pahic, Rolf Palmberg, Craig Palmer, John Papageorgiou, Lars Pardo, James Parkhurst, Thea Parkin, Keith Parsons, R F Parsons, Tanya Pashkuleva, S Patel, Baz Pattison, Stuart Pattullo, Steve Paul, James Payne, Justin Peach, Roger Peake, Jill Pearson, Carol Peddie, Jerry Peek, Valentina M Pennazio, Jan M Pennington, Steve Penny, Claus Penz, Richard Perillo, Andrew Perry, Elaine Perry, Jane Perry, Richard Perry, Sam Perry, Piergiorgio Pescali, Rick Petkovsek, Bill Petrovic, Elena Peytcheva, Suzanne Pfouts, Eric Philpott, Stacey Piesner, Tero Pikala, Michael Pike, John Pilgrim, Michel Pinton, John Pirra, David Pitchford, Zoli Pitman, David John Pitts, Sean Plamondon, Paul Plaza, Scott Plimpton, Dimitris Ploumides, Krys Pogoda, Robertas Pogorelis, Graham Pointon, Magdalena Polan, Elizabeth Poole, Tony & Jill Porco, Kieth Porteous Wood, Shari Posey, Janice Potten, Heidi Potts, Pirasri Povatong, Beth Powell, Cristina Pratas, Paul Proulx, Scott Prysi, Anna Ptaszynska, Marc Purnal, Steve Pyle, Roy Pyne, Ramu Pyreddy, Gayle Quagliata, SB Rader, Matine Rahmani, Kat Rainford, Maria Ralph, Francesco Randisi, Bernt Rane, Andrea Rausch, Suzanne Ravenhall, Kurt Rebry, Paul Reed, Bard Reian, Volker Reichhardt, Melinda Reidinger, Vera Reifenberg, Gretchen Reinhart, Patrick Reinquin, Hanneke Renes, Catherine Rentz, Grant Reynolds, Claire Rhodes, Charlie Rich, Reuben Rich, Helen Richards, Tony Richmond, Benjamin Richter, Kornelia Ring, Jan Doeke Rinzema, Roberto Riofrio, Judith Ripoli, Dan Robinson, Melina Rodde, Jason Rodrigues, Nicola Romeo, Bjorn Ronnekliev, Paul Roos, Brenda Roscoe, Clare Rose, Nicolas Rosenbaum, Miga Rossetti, Matthew Rothschild, Vicki Roubicek, John Rowe, Alison Rowlands, Stephen Rowlands, Justin Rubinstein, Jaroslaw Rudnik, Maike Rudolph, Esa Ruotsalainen, Melissa Russel, Wouter Rutten,

David Rutter, Heather Ryan, Kym Ryan, Patti Ryan, Krysztof Rybak, Marcin Sadurski, Carmen Salazar, Mike Sampson, Rachel Samsonowitz, Stefan Samuelsson, Claudio Sandroni, Wendy Scaife, Dietmar Schaeper, Judith Schaniel, Karl Scharbert, Jacco Scheffer, Vincent Scheib, Carola Schellack, Frede Scheye, Asya Schigol, Joe Schill, Sabine Schmitz, Matthias Schmoll, Inga Schonning, Bram Schout, Elan Schultz, Larry Schwarz, Eric Schwenter, Paola Sconzo, Suzy Scorer, Donna Scriven, Allan Sealy, Oliver Selwyn, Elizabeth Sercombe, Rick Seymour, Brett Shackelford, Nadeem Shah, Eyal Shaham, Gwen & Norm Shannon, Robert & Ruth Shannon, Tal Shany, Joshua Sharkey, Mark & Stephanie Shattuck, Mary Sheargold, Barbara Sheerman-Chase, Jessica Sherwood, Bilal Sidani, Bogdan Siewierski, Dragon Simic, Carol & Ron Simmons, Lia Singer, Anneke Sips, Alec Sirken, Alan Sirulnikoff, Frank Sitchler, P Skinner, Peter Slade, Kara Slaughter, J M Haw Smalley, Kerry Smallman, Marc Smeehuijzen, Ella Smit, Alex Smith, Jonathon Smith, Owen Smith, K Smith-Jones, Carolyn Snell, Anthony Snieckus, Ann Snyder, Raewyn Somerville, Ana Eloisa Soto Canino, Tina Souvlis, Eduardo Spaccasassi, David Spiers, John Spilos, Steven Stahl, Maarten Stam, Kevin Stanes, Joesph T Stanik, Donna Stark, Marshall Stark, David Staunton Lambert, Georgeta Stefan, Steven Stefanovic, Julie Stenberg, Kim Stewart, Franco Stibiel, Elena Stocco, Ivan Stockley, Irina Stojanovic, Kathryn Stokes, Derek Stone, Bill & Ann Stoughton, Samo Stritof, Stuart Suckling, Errin Sucur, Paul Sullivan, Timothy Sullivan, Deanie Sultana, Tarren Summers, Jerker Svantesson, Matthew Swadener, Rita Swiecilo, Clare Szilagyi, Amanda Fay Szumutku,

Lamija M Tabak-Didic, Zara Tai, Alan Tan, Andrew Tan, Patricia Tandy, Kenneth Tangnes, Chester Tapley, Eric Telfer, Anke Temmink, Vera ten Hacken, Ivo Tence, Mara Tenis, Ravindran Thanikaimoni, Kate Thomas, Katrin Thomas, Bruce Thompson, Kelly Thompson, Silje Figenschou Thoresen, Fred Thornett, Daz Thornton, Anouchka-Virginie Thouvenot, Kristien Thys, Diane Tider, Petr Tieftrunk, Robert Tissing, Marie Tjosevik, Brian Tlongan, Paul Tod, Clark Toes, Sylvia Tomlinson-Hoehndorf, Stefano Tona, Martin Torres, J Toth, Abi Tovarloza, Nick Townsend, Anna Travali, Brian Travers, Michael Travis, O G Trawt, Geoffrey Trotter, Metaxia Tsoukatos, Riikka Tuomisto, Kim Tuorila, Dean Turner, Emily Turner-Graham, Ann Tuxford, Helen Twitt, Micheal Unwin, Dave Upton, Boaz Ur, Yusuf Usul, Cagri Uyarer, Teune van der Wildt, Marco van de Sande, Hanny van den Bergh, Caroliena van den Bos, Marlies van den Nieuwendijk, Chris van der Starre, Corne van Dyk, Erwin van Engelen, Nootje & Marcel van Gorp, Jacqueline van Klaveren, Frank van Rijn, Dirk van Rooy, Aletta & Ruud van Uden, Mathieu Vandermissen, Stefan Vanwildemeersch, Kim Vaughan, Holly Venable, Kirsty Venning, Walter Verdonk, Maarten Vermeulen, Florens Versteegh, Lea Vesine, Matthew Vincent, Susan Viner, Manfred Von Carstein, R Vos, Fons Vrouenraths, Michelle Vujovic, Petar Vujovic, Benedict Wabunoha, Jost Wagner, Henrik Waldenstrom, Leslie Waldorf, James Walker, John Walker, Nick Walmsley, Karen Walsh, Louise Walters, Damian Wampler, Michelle Warburton, Julian & Steve Warner, Jim Warren, Dennis Waterman, Jo Watkins-Wade, A Watson, Julie Webb, Demaris Wehr, Jan Wergeland, David Westland, Caroline White, John White, Valda White, Stephen Whittaker, Ruben Wickenhauser, Kate Wierciak, Froy Lode Wiig, Brita Wilfling, Hanna Wilhelm, Veryan Wilkie-Jones, Ian Wilkinson, Paddy Willems, Aled Williams, Alwyn Williams, Ernst Williams, Aaron Wilmarth, Helen Wilms, Fiona Wilson, Roxanne Winkler, Alex & Rhonda Wittmann, Kori Wolfard, Justin Wong, John Wood, Peta Woodland, Natalie Wray, Dion & Donna Wright, Kate Wrigley, Raymond Wu, Roger Wu, John Yates, Pazu Yau, Whui Mei Yeo, Yoram Yom-Tov, David Young, Jim Young, D Yudhope, Imran Yusuf, R A Zambardino, Karla Zimmerman, Holger zimmermann, Paul Zoglin, Anne Zouridakis, Will Zucker

Guides by Region

Lonely Planet is known worldwide for publishing practical, reliable and no-nonsense travel information in our guides and on our Web site. The Lonely Planet list covers just about every accessible part of the world. Currently there are 16 series: Travel guides, Shoestring guides, Condensed guides, Phrasebooks, Read This First, Healthy Travel, Walking guides, Cycling guides, Watching Wildlife guides, Pisces Diving & Snorkeling guides, City Maps, Road Atlases, Out to Eat, World Food, Journeys travel literature and Pictorials.

AFRICA Africa on a shoestring • Botswana • Cairo • Cairo City Map • Cape Town • Cape Town City Map • East Africa • Egypt • Egyptian Arabic phrasebook • Ethiopia, Eritrea & Djibouti • Ethiopian Amharic phrasebook • The Gambia & Senegal • Healthy Travel Africa • Kenya • Malawi • Morocco • Moroccan Arabic phrasebook • Mozambique • Namibia • Read This First: Africa • South Africa, Lesotho & Swaziland • Southern Africa • Southern Africa Road Atlas • Swahili phrasebook • Tanzania, Zanzibar & Pemba • Trekking in East Africa • Tunisia • Watching Wildlife East Africa • Watching Wildlife Southern Africa • West Africa • World Food Morocco • Zambia • Zimbabwe, Botswana & Namibia
Travel Literature: Mali Blues: Traveling to an African Beat • The Rainbird: A Central African Journey • Songs to an African Sunset: A Zimbabwean Story

AUSTRALIA & THE PACIFIC Aboriginal Australia & the Torres Strait Islands •Auckland • Australia • Australian phrasebook • Australia Road Atlas • Cycling Australia • Cycling New Zealand • Fiji • Fijian phrasebook • Healthy Travel Australia, NZ & the Pacific • Islands of Australia's Great Barrier Reef • Melbourne • Melbourne City Map • Micronesia • New Caledonia • New South Wales • New Zealand • Northern Territory • Outback Australia • Out to Eat – Melbourne • Out to Eat – Sydney • Papua New Guinea • Pidgin phrasebook • Queensland • Rarotonga & the Cook Islands • Samoa • Solomon Islands • South Australia • South Pacific • South Pacific phrasebook • Sydney • Sydney City Map • Sydney Condensed • Tahiti & French Polynesia • Tasmania • Tonga • Tramping in New Zealand • Vanuatu • Victoria • Walking in Australia • Watching Wildlife Australia • Western Australia
Travel Literature: Islands in the Clouds: Travels in the Highlands of New Guinea • Kiwi Tracks: A New Zealand Journey • Sean & David's Long Drive

CENTRAL AMERICA & THE CARIBBEAN Bahamas, Turks & Caicos • Baja California • Belize, Guatemala & Yucatán • Bermuda • Central America on a shoestring • Costa Rica • Costa Rica Spanish phrasebook • Cuba • Cycling Cuba • Dominican Republic & Haiti • Eastern Caribbean • Guatemala • Havana • Healthy Travel Central & South America • Jamaica • Mexico • Mexico City • Panama • Puerto Rico • Read This First: Central & South America • Virgin Islands • World Food Caribbean • World Food Mexico • Yucatán
Travel Literature: Green Dreams: Travels in Central America

EUROPE Amsterdam • Amsterdam City Map • Amsterdam Condensed • Andalucia • Athens • Austria • Baltic States phrasebook • Barcelona • Barcelona City Map • Belgium & Luxembourg • Berlin • Berlin City Map • Britain • British phrasebook • Brussels, Bruges & Antwerp • Brussels City Map • Budapest • Budapest City Map • Canary Islands • Catalunya & the Costa Brava • Central Europe • Central Europe phrasebook • Copenhagen • Corfu & the Ionians • Corsica • Crete • Crete Condensed • Croatia • Cycling Britain • Cycling France • Cyprus • Czech & Slovak Republics • Czech phrasebook • Denmark • Dublin • Dublin City Map • Dublin Condensed • Eastern Europe • Eastern Europe phrasebook • Edinburgh • Edinburgh City Map • England • Estonia, Latvia & Lithuania • Europe on a shoestring • Europe phrasebook • Finland • Florence • Florence City Map • France • Frankfurt City Map • Frankfurt Condensed • French phrasebook • Georgia, Armenia & Azerbaijan • Germany • German phrasebook • Greece • Greek Islands • Greek phrasebook • Hungary • Iceland, Greenland & the Faroe Islands • Ireland • Italian phrasebook • Italy • Kraków • Lisbon • The Loire • London • London City Map • London Condensed • Madrid • Madrid City Map • Malta • Mediterranean Europe • Milan, Turin & Genoa • Moscow • Munich • Netherlands • Normandy • Norway • Out to Eat – London • Out to Eat – Paris • Paris • Paris City Map • Paris Condensed • Poland • Polish phrasebook • Portugal • Portuguese phrasebook • Prague • Prague City Map • Provence & the Côte d'Azur • Read This First: Europe • Rhodes & the Dodecanese • Romania & Moldova • Rome • Rome City Map • Rome Condensed • Russia, Ukraine & Belarus • Russian phrasebook • Scandinavian & Baltic Europe • Scandinavian phrasebook • Scotland • Sicily • Slovenia • South-West France • Spain • Spanish phrasebook • Stockholm • St Petersburg • St Petersburg City Map • Sweden • Switzerland • Tuscany • Ukrainian phrasebook • Venice • Vienna • Wales • Walking in Britain • Walking in France • Walking in Ireland • Walking in Italy • Walking in Scotland • Walking in Spain • Walking in Switzerland • Western Europe • World Food France • World Food Greece • World Food Ireland • World Food Italy • World Food Spain **Travel Literature:** After Yugoslavia • Love and War in the Apennines • The Olive Grove: Travels in Greece • On the Shores of the Mediterranean • Round Ireland in Low Gear • A Small Place in Italy

LONELY PLANET

Mail Order

Lonely Planet products are distributed worldwide. They are also available by mail order from Lonely Planet, so if you have difficulty finding a title please write to us. North and South American residents should write to 150 Linden St, Oakland, CA 94607, USA; European and African residents should write to 10a Spring Place, London NW5 3BH, UK; and residents of other countries to Locked Bag 1, Footscray, Victoria 3011, Australia.

INDIAN SUBCONTINENT & THE INDIAN OCEAN Bangladesh • Bengali phrasebook • Bhutan • Delhi • Goa • Healthy Travel Asia & India • Hindi & Urdu phrasebook • India • India & Bangladesh City Map • Indian Himalaya • Karakoram Highway • Kathmandu City Map • Kerala • Madagascar • Maldives • Mauritius, Réunion & Seychelles • Mumbai (Bombay) • Nepal • Nepali phrasebook • North India • Pakistan • Rajasthan • Read This First: Asia & India • South India • Sri Lanka • Sri Lanka phrasebook • Tibet • Tibetan phrasebook • Trekking in the Indian Himalaya • Trekking in the Karakoram & Hindukush • Trekking in the Nepal Himalaya • World Food India **Travel Literature**: The Age of Kali: Indian Travels and Encounters • Hello Goodnight: A Life of Goa • In Rajasthan • Maverick in Madagascar • A Season in Heaven: True Tales from the Road to Kathmandu • Shopping for Buddhas • A Short Walk in the Hindu Kush • Slowly Down the Ganges

MIDDLE EAST & CENTRAL ASIA Bahrain, Kuwait & Qatar • Central Asia • Central Asia phrasebook • Dubai • Farsi (Persian) phrasebook • Hebrew phrasebook • Iran • Israel & the Palestinian Territories • Istanbul • Istanbul City Map • Istanbul to Cairo • Istanbul to Kathmandu • Jerusalem • Jerusalem City Map • Jordan • Lebanon • Middle East • Oman & the United Arab Emirates • Syria • Turkey • Turkish phrasebook • World Food Turkey • Yemen **Travel Literature:** Black on Black: Iran Revisited • Breaking Ranks: Turbulent Travels in the Promised Land • The Gates of Damascus • Kingdom of the Film Stars: Journey into Jordan

NORTH AMERICA Alaska • Boston • Boston City Map • Boston Condensed • British Columbia • California & Nevada • California Condensed • Canada • Chicago • Chicago City Map • Chicago Condensed • Florida • Georgia & the Carolinas • Great Lakes • Hawaii • Hiking in Alaska • Hiking in the USA • Honolulu & Oahu City Map • Las Vegas • Los Angeles • Los Angeles City Map • Louisiana & the Deep South • Miami • Miami City Map • Montreal • New England • New Orleans • New Orleans City Map • New York City • New York City City Map • New York City Condensed • New York, New Jersey & Pennsylvania • Oahu • Out to Eat – San Francisco • Pacific Northwest • Rocky Mountains • San Diego & Tijuana • San Francisco • San Francisco City Map • Seattle • Seattle City Map • Southwest • Texas • Toronto • USA • USA phrasebook • Vancouver • Vancouver City Map • Virginia & the Capital Region • Washington, DC • Washington, DC City Map • World Food New Orleans **Travel Literature**: Caught Inside: A Surfer's Year on the California Coast • Drive Thru America

NORTH-EAST ASIA Beijing • Beijing City Map • Cantonese phrasebook • China • Hiking in Japan • Hong Kong & Macau • Hong Kong City Map • Hong Kong Condensed • Japan • Japanese phrasebook • Korea • Korean phrasebook • Kyoto • Mandarin phrasebook • Mongolia • Mongolian phrasebook • Seoul • Shanghai • South-West China • Taiwan • Tokyo • Tokyo Condensed • World Food Hong Kong • World Food Japan **Travel Literature**: In Xanadu: A Quest • Lost Japan

SOUTH AMERICA Argentina, Uruguay & Paraguay • Bolivia • Brazil • Brazilian phrasebook • Buenos Aires • Buenos Aires City Map • Chile & Easter Island • Colombia • Ecuador & the Galapagos Islands • Healthy Travel Central & South America • Latin American Spanish phrasebook • Peru • Quechua phrasebook • Read This First: Central & South America • Rio de Janeiro • Rio de Janeiro City Map • Santiago de Chile • South America on a shoestring • Trekking in the Patagonian Andes • Venezuela **Travel Literature**: Full Circle: A South American Journey

SOUTH-EAST ASIA Bali & Lombok • Bangkok • Bangkok City Map • Burmese phrasebook • Cambodia • Cycling Vietnam, Laos & Cambodia • East Timor phrasebook • Hanoi • Healthy Travel Asia & India • Hill Tribes phrasebook • Ho Chi Minh City (Saigon) • Indonesia • Indonesian phrasebook • Indonesia's Eastern Islands • Java • Lao phrasebook • Laos • Malay phrasebook • Malaysia, Singapore & Brunei • Myanmar (Burma) • Philippines • Pilipino (Tagalog) phrasebook • Read This First: Asia & India • Singapore • Singapore City Map • South-East Asia on a shoestring • South-East Asia phrasebook • Thailand • Thailand's Islands & Beaches • Thailand, Vietnam, Laos & Cambodia Road Atlas • Thai phrasebook • Vietnam • Vietnamese phrasebook • World Food Indonesia • World Food Thailand • World Food Vietnam

ALSO AVAILABLE: Antarctica • The Arctic • The Blue Man: Tales of Travel, Love and Coffee • Brief Encounters: Stories of Love, Sex & Travel • Buddhist Stupas in Asia: The Shape of Perfection • Chasing Rickshaws • The Last Grain Race • Lonely Planet ... On the Edge: Adventurous Escapades from Around the World • Lonely Planet Unpacked • Lonely Planet Unpacked Again • Not the Only Planet: Science Fiction Travel Stories • Ports of Call: A Journey by Sea • Sacred India • Travel Photography: A Guide to Taking Better Pictures • Travel with Children • Tuvalu: Portrait of an Island Nation

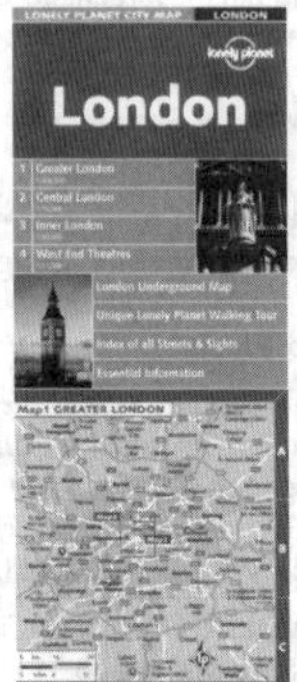
LONELY PLANET CITY MAP
LONDON
lonely planet
London

lonely planet
AMSTERDAM
CONDENSED

lonely planet
EUROPE
PHRASEBOOK

lonely planet
Spain

lonely planet
Paris

lonely planet
Walking in
ITALY

Index

Abbreviations

A – Austria
AL – Albania
AND – Andorra
B – Belgium
BG – Bulgaria
BIH – Bosnia-Hercegovina
CH – Switzerland
CY – Cyprus
CZ – Czech Republic
D – Germany
DK – Denmark
E – Spain
EST – Estonia
F – France
FIN – Finland
GB – Britain
GR – Greece
H – Hungary
HR – Croatia
I – Italy
IRL – Ireland
IS – Iceland
L – Luxembourg
LI – Liechtenstein
LT – Lithuania
LV – Latvia
M – Malta
MA – Morocco
MK – Macedonia
N – Norway
NL – Netherlands
P – Portugal
PL – Poland
RO – Romania
RUS – Russia
S – Sweden
SK – Slovakia
SLO – Slovenia
TR – Turkey
YU – Yugoslavia

Text

Bold indicates maps.

Bold indicates maps.

N

O

P

Bold indicates maps.

T

Bold indicates maps.

Boxed Text

MAP LEGEND

CITY ROUTES

Freeway	Freeway		Unsealed Road
Highway	Primary Road		One Way Street
Road	Secondary Road		Pedestrian Street
Street	Street		Stepped Street
Lane	Lane		Tunnel
	On/Off Ramp		Footbridge

REGIONAL ROUTES

- Tollway, Freeway
- Primary Road
- Secondary Road
- Minor Road

BOUNDARIES

- International
- State
- Disputed
- Fortified Wall

TRANSPORT ROUTES & STATIONS

- Train
- Ferry
- Underground Train
- Walking Trail
- Metro
- Walking Tour
- Tramway
- Path
- Funicular Railway
- Pier or Jetty

HYDROGRAPHY

- River, Creek
- Dry Lake; Salt Lake
- Canal
- Spring; Rapids
- Lake
- Waterfalls

AREA FEATURES

- Building
- Market
- Beach
- Forest
- Park, Gardens
- Sports Ground
- Cemetery
- Plaza

POPULATION SYMBOLS

CAPITAL	National Capital
CAPITAL	State Capital
CITY	City
Town	Town
Village	Village
	Urban Area

MAP SYMBOLS

- Place to Stay
- Place to Eat
- Point of Interest

- Airport
- Bank
- Border Crossing
- Bus Station
- Cable Car, Funicular
- Castle, Chateau
- Cathedral, Church
- Cinema
- Embassy, Consulate
- Fountain
- Hospital
- Internet Cafe
- Mounment
- Museum
- Police Station
- Post Office
- Pub or Bar
- Pub or Bar (Ire)
- Ruins
- Shopping Centre
- Ski Field
- Swimming Pool
- Synagogue
- Taxi Rank
- Telephone
- Theatre
- Tourist Information
- Zoo

Note: not all symbols displayed above appear in this book

LONELY PLANET OFFICES

Australia
Locked Bag 1, Footscray, Victoria 3011
☎ 03 8379 8000 fax 03 8379 8111
email: talk2us@lonelyplanet.com.au

UK
10a Spring Place, London NW5 3BH
☎ 020 7428 4800 fax 020 7428 4828
email: go@lonelyplanet.co.uk

USA
150 Linden St, Oakland, CA 94607
☎ 510 893 8555 TOLL FREE: 800 275 8555
fax 510 893 8572
email: info@lonelyplanet.com

France
1 rue du Dahomey, 75011 Paris
☎ 01 55 25 33 00 fax 01 55 25 33 01
email: bip@lonelyplanet.fr
www.lonelyplanet.fr

World Wide Web: www.lonelyplanet.com *or* AOL keyword: lp
Lonely Planet Images: lpi@lonelyplanet.com.au